shakespearean criticism

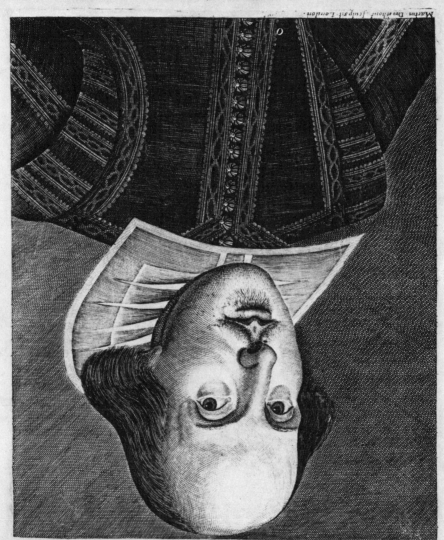

Frontispiece to the First Folio (1623). By permission of the Folger Shakespeare Library.

ISSN 0883-9123

Volume 3

shakespearean criticism

Excerpts from the Criticism of
William Shakespeare's Plays and Poetry,
from the First Published Appraisals
to Current Evaluations

Laurie Lanzen Harris
Mark W. Scott

Editors

Gale Research Company
Book Tower
Detroit, Michigan 48226

89

STAFF

Laurie Lanzen Harris, Mark W. Scott, *Editors*

Michael S. Corey, Mark Koch, Daniel J. Montgomery, Sandra L. Williamson, *Assistant Editors*

Phyllis Carmel Mendelson, *Contributing Editor*

Lizbeth A. Purdy, *Production Supervisor*
Denise Michlewicz Broderick, *Production Coordinator*
Eric Berger, *Assistant Production Coordinator*
Robin DuBlanc, Sheila J. Nasea, *Editorial Assistants*

Victoria B. Cariappa, *Research Coordinator*
Jeannine Schiffman Davidson, *Assistant Research Coordinator*
Vincenza G. DiNoto, Daniel Kurt Gilbert, Maureen Richards, Filomena Sgambati,
Valerie J. Webster, *Research Assistants*

Linda Marcella Pugliese, *Manuscript Coordinator*
Donna Craft, *Assistant Manuscript Coordinator*
Maureen A. Puhl, Rosetta Irene Simms, *Manuscript Assistants*

Jeanne A. Gough, *Permissions Supervisor*
Janice M. Mach, *Permissions Coordinator, Text*
Patricia A. Seefelt, *Permissions Coordinator, Illustrations*
Susan D. Battista, *Assistant Permissions Coordinator*
Margaret A. Chamberlain, Sandra C. Davis, Mary M. Matuz, *Senior Permissions Assistants*
Colleen M. Crane, Kathleen J. Grell, Josephine M. Keene, Mabel C. Schoening, *Permissions Assistants*
Margaret A. Carson, H. Diane Cooper, Dorothy J. Fowler, Anita Williams, *Permissions Clerks*

Frederick G. Ruffner, *Publisher*
Dedria Bryfonski, *Editorial Director*
Christine Nasso, *Director, Literature Division*
Laurie Lanzen Harris, *Senior Editor, Literary Criticism Series*
Dennis Poupard, *Managing Editor, Literary Criticism Series*

Library of Congress Cataloging-in-Publication Data

Main entry under title:

Shakespearean criticism.

Includes bibliographies and index.
1. Shakespeare, William, 1564-1616—Criticism and
interpretation—History. 2. Shakespeare, William, 1564-
1616—Criticism and interpretation—Addresses, essays,
lectures. 3. Shakespeare, William, 1564-1616—
Bibliography. I. Harris, Laurie Lanzen. II. Scott,
Mark W. III. Gale Research Company.
PR2965.S43   1984   822.3'3   84-4010
ISBN 0-8103-6125-6 (v. 1)
ISBN 0-8103-6127-2 (v. 3)

ISSN 0883-9123

Computerized photocomposition by
Typographics, Incorporated
Kansas City, Missouri

Printed in the United States

Contents

Preface

The works of William Shakespeare have delighted audiences and inspired scholars for nearly four hundred years. Shakespeare's appeal is universal, for in its depth and breadth his work evokes a timeless insight into the human condition.

The vast amount of Shakespearean criticism is a testament to his enduring popularity. Critics of each epoch have contributed to this critical legacy, responding to the comments of their forebears, bringing the moral and intellectual atmosphere of their own era to the works, and suggesting interpretations which continue to inspire critics of today. Thus, to chart the history of criticism on Shakespeare is to note the changing aesthetic philosophies of the past four centuries.

The Scope of the Work

The success of Gale's four existing literary series, *Contemporary Literary Criticism (CLC), Twentieth-Century Literary Criticism (TCLC), Nineteenth-Century Literature Criticism (NCLC),* and *Children's Literature Review (CLR),* suggested an equivalent need among students and teachers of Shakespeare. Moreover, since the criticism of Shakespeare's works spans four centuries and is larger in size and scope than that of any author, a prodigious amount of critical material confronts the student.

Shakespearean Criticism (SC) presents significant passages from published criticism on the works of Shakespeare. Eight volumes of the series will be devoted to aesthetic criticism of the plays. Performance criticism will be treated in separate special volumes. Other special volumes will be devoted to such topics as Shakespeare's poetry, the authorship controversy and the apocrypha, stage history of the plays, and other general subjects, such as Shakespeare's language, religious and philosophical thought, and characterization. The first eight volumes will each contain criticism on four to six plays, with an equal balance of genres and an equal balance of plays based on their critical importance. Thus, Volume 3 contains criticism on one major tragedy *(Macbeth),* one major comedy *(A Midsummer Night's Dream),* one minor comedy *(Troilus and Cressida),* and three histories *(Henry VI, Parts 1, 2,* and *3),* which because a great many critics have treated them together are handled as one entry.

The length of each entry is intended to represent the play's critical reception in English, including those works which have been translated into English. The editors have tried to identify only the major critics and lines of inquiry for each play. Each entry represents a historical overview of the critical response to the play: early criticism is presented to indicate initial responses and later selections represent significant trends in the history of criticism on the play. We have also attempted to identify and include excerpts from the seminal essays on each play by the most important Shakespearean critics. We have directed our series to students in late high school and early college who are beginning their study of Shakespeare. Thus, ours is not a work for the specialist, but is rather an introduction for the researcher newly acquainted with the works of Shakespeare.

The Organization of the Book

Each entry consists of the following elements: play heading, an introduction, excerpts of criticism (each followed by a bibliographical citation), and an additional bibliography for further reading.

The *introduction* begins with a discussion of the date, text, and sources of the play. This section is followed by a critical history which outlines the major critical trends and identifies the prominent commentators on the play.

Criticism is arranged chronologically within each play entry to provide a perspective on the changes in critical evaluation over the years. For purposes of easier identification, the critic's name and the date of the essay are given at the beginning of each piece. For an anonymous essay later attributed to a critic, the critic's name appears in brackets at the beginning of the excerpt and in the bibliographical citation.

Within the text, all act, scene, and line designations have been changed to conform to *The Riverside Shakespeare,* published by Houghton Mifflin Company, which is a standard text used in many high school and college English classes. Most of the individual essays are prefaced with *explanatory notes* as an additional aid to students using *SC.* The explanatory notes provide several types of useful information, including: the importance of the critics in literary history, the critical schools with which they are identified, if any, and the importance of their comments on Shakespeare and the play discussed. The explanatory notes also identify the main issues in the commentary on each play and include cross references to related criticism in the entry. In addition, the notes provide previous publication information such as original title and date for foreign language publications.

A complete *bibliographical citation* designed to facilitate the location of the original essay or book follows each piece of criticism.

Within each play entry are *illustrations,* such as facsimiles of title pages taken from the quarto and First Folio editions of the plays as well as pictures drawn from such sources as early editions of the collected works and artists' renderings of some of the famous scenes and characters of Shakespeare's plays. The captions following each illustration indicate act, scene, characters, and the artist and date, if known. The illustrations are arranged chronologically and, as a complement to the criticism, provide a historical perspective on Shakespeare throughout the centuries.

The *additional bibliography* appearing at the end of each play entry suggests further reading on the play. This section includes references to the major discussions of the date, the text, and the sources of each play.

Each volume of *SC* includes a cumulative index to plays that provides the volume number in which the plays appear. *SC* also includes a cumulative index to critics; under each critic's name are listed the plays on which the critic has written and the volume and page where the criticism appears.

As an additional aid to students, beginning with volume 3 *SC* will provide a glossary of terms relating to date, text, and source information frequently mentioned by critics and used throughout the introductions to the plays. The glossed terms and source names are identified by small capital letters when they first appear in the introductions.

An appendix is also included that lists the sources from which the material in the volume is reprinted. It does not, however, list every book or periodical consulted for the volume.

Acknowledgments

No work of this scope can be accomplished without the cooperation of many people. The editors wish to thank the copyright holders of the excerpts included in this volume, the permissions managers of the book and magazine publishing companies for assisting us in securing reprint rights, and the staffs of the Detroit Public Library, the University of Michigan libraries, and the Wayne State University Library for making their resources available to us. We would especially like to thank the staff of the Rare Book Room of the University of Michigan Library for their research assistance and the Folger Shakespeare Library for their help in picture research. We would also like to thank Jeri Yaryan and Anthony J. Bogucki for assistance with copyright research.

Suggestions Are Welcome

The editors welcome the comments and suggestions of readers to expand the coverage and enhance the usefulness of the series.

shakespearean criticism

Henry VI, Parts 1, 2, and 3

DATE: There is general agreement among critics that *1, 2,* and *3 Henry VI* are among Shakespeare's earliest works, if not the earliest, written between 1589 and 1592. The exact chronology, along with the authorship of the plays, has been a matter of dispute from the very beginning: many scholars believe that Shakespeare wrote *2* and *3 Henry VI* first and added *1 Henry VI* later; other commentators, most notably the editor of the Arden edition of the trilogy, Andrew S. Cairncross, have maintained that the three plays were written consecutively, beginning with Part 1 in 1589 and ending with Part 3 in late 1591 or early 1592. The earliest known reference to any of the plays comes from the theatrical diary of Philip Henslowe, who on March 3, 1592, referred to a very successful "ne[w]" play called "Harey the vj" performed by the acting company of Lord Strange. Although Henslowe did not identify the dramatist of this play, critics have traditionally assumed that "Harey the vj" is actually *1 Henry VI* and that Shakespeare was the author of the work. However, a number of scholars, including the noted textual authority Peter Alexander, have opposed this assumption, maintaining that Henslowe's reference is to an older play written by someone other than Shakespeare. Alexander and others based their conclusion on the fact that no records exist placing the dramatist in the employment of Strange's company in 1592 or before; indeed, what records do exist, they declared, suggest that Shakespeare at this point in his career was connected with the company of Lord Pembroke, a rival of Strange's men. Further evidence often used to determine the composition date of *1 Henry VI* includes the comment by the Elizabethan playwright Thomas Nashe in his *Pierce Penniless,* entered in the STATIONERS' REGISTER on August 8, 1592, on the current popularity of a play featuring "brave Talbot." Although most commentators have accepted Nashe's remarks as referring to *1 Henry VI,* once again a sizeable number have argued that the allusion is to an older play, now lost, written by one of Shakespeare's predecessors. No additional evidence exists to help scholars determine a definitive composition date for *1 Henry VI,* or even resolve the question of the order in which the plays were written. As such, commentators have generally acknowledged that Henslowe's and Nashe's remarks refer to *Henry VI;* textual authorities have also tentatively agreed upon late 1591 as the period when Shakespeare composed *1 Henry VI,* and early 1592 as the date of its first performance.

There is a consensus among most scholars that *2* and *3 Henry VI* were written sometime between 1590 and 1592, although the earlier date, again, remains a matter of dispute. Shortly before his death in September 1592, the Elizabethan dramatist Robert Greene wrote a pamphlet containing a satiric allusion to a line from *3 Henry VI;* critics have generally cited this reference to support a theory that Shakespeare composed *2* and *3 Henry VI* consecutively and that Part 3 must have been in performance by at least June of 1592—when all London theaters were first closed for a period of almost two years because of an outbreak of the plague—for Greene to have satirized Shakespeare through a parody of his verse. John Dover Wilson postulated that *2* and *3 Henry VI* were written, at the latest, by 1591 and that *1 Henry VI* was composed the following year. There is no record of performances of *2* and *3 Henry VI* before 1660, although Greene's comment suggests that Part 3, perhaps

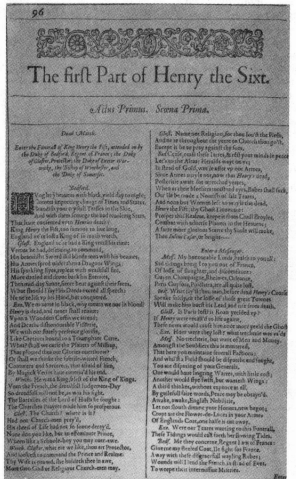

Title page of 1 Henry VI taken from the First Folio (1623).

in conjunction with Part 2, was staged sometime between 1591 and 1592.

No QUARTO edition of *1 Henry VI* exists; it initially appeared in print in the FIRST FOLIO of 1623, along with *The Second Part of Henry the Sixt with the death of the Good Duke Humfrey* and *The Third Part of Henry the Sixt with the death of the Duke of Yorke.* A quarto version of *2 Henry VI,* entitled *The First Part of the Contention betwixt the two famous Houses of Yorke and Lancaster,* appeared in 1594, and a quarto version of *3 Henry VI,* entitled *The true Tragedie of Richard Duke of Yorke . . . with the whole contention between the two Houses Lancaster and Yorke,* was issued in 1595. These quarto plays were later reprinted in 1600 and again in 1619.

TEXT: The only authoritative text of *1 Henry VI* is that of the First Folio. It was entered in the Stationers' Register on November 8, 1623, as ". . . The thirde part of Henry ye Sixt . . . ," quite possibly under this title because the quarto versions of *2* and *3 Henry VI* had been registered almost thirty years earlier. The irregularities, contradictions, and inconsistencies in *1 Henry VI* have led critics to form diverse conclusions about the authenticity of the text. Some have attributed these irregularities to Shakespeare's use of multiple sources or to stage adapters' annotations on the original manuscript, while other critics have regarded them as evidence that more than one author worked on the play.

The reliability of the First Folio texts of *2* and *3 Henry VI* has been challenged on the basis of the earlier (1594 and 1595) printed quarto versions known as *The Contention* and *The True Tragedy*. In 1787 Edmond Malone provided the first critical comparison of the texts of the quarto and Folio plays. He judged the versification of *2* and *3 Henry VI* to be not only stylistically inferior, but wholly unlike that of those plays which were undisputably Shakespearean. He concluded that *2* and *3 Henry VI* were revisions of the quarto plays, which were themselves the work of another playwright, and that other dramatists had participated with Shakespeare in the revision process. His arguments were widely accepted until the first part of the twentieth century. Other revisionist critics variously ascribed parts of the *Henry VI* trilogy to Christopher Marlowe, Robert Greene, Thomas Nashe, and George Peele.

In the late 1920s, Peter Alexander and Madeleine Doran each offered proof that *The Contention* and *The True Tragedy* were abridged versions of *2* and *3 Henry VI*. They demonstrated that actors had reconstructed Shakespeare's plays from memory (see MEMORIAL RECONSTRUCTION in *Glossary*), either consciously or unconsciously altering and deleting portions of the original texts. The work of Alexander and Doran is considered influential in establishing Shakespeare's authorship of *1, 2,* and *3 Henry VI*, as well as confirming the authenticity of the Folio texts of those plays. However, a small number of scholars, including Dover Wilson, have continued to debate Shakespeare's contribution to the trilogy, often suggesting Greene or Nashe as the principal authors.

SOURCES: Shakespeare's chief source for the historical events and characters of *1, 2,* and *3 Henry VI* was EDWARD HALL's *The Union of the Two Noble and Illustre Families of Lancaster and York* (1548). Hall's account of sixteenth-century England exemplifies the view that history is determined in accordance with a divine moral purpose; as such, the historian interpreted the disastrous reign of Henry VI and the civil dissension in England during that time as the result of divine retribution for Henry IV's "original sin" of usurping the throne from Richard II. A major critical concern in both nineteenth- and twentieth-century commentary on *Henry VI* has been the question of Shakespeare's acceptance of this historical process. Opinion has been divided on whether Hall's providential view is evident in Shakespeare's treatment of his source material or whether the dramatist intended to demonstrate that the course of fifteenth-century English history was determined by the actions of powerful and ambitious individuals at war with each other. Shakespeare also relied on RAPHAEL HOLINSHED's *The Chronicles of Englande, Scotlande, and Irelande* (second edition, 1587) as a supplementary source in his composition of *Henry VI*, particularly for an account of the Peasants' Revolt of 1381, elements of which he incorporated into the Cade scenes of *2 Henry VI*. The spurious miracle scene involving Simpcox, also in *2 Henry VI*, does not appear in either Hall or Holinshed. It is likely that for this incident Shakespeare used either Richard Grafton's *A Chronicle at Large* (1569) or John Foxe's *Actes and Monuments of Martyrs* (third edition, 1583), which both treat the matter straightforwardly and without humor. Whether Shakespeare was influenced by *THE MIRROR FOR MAGISTRATES* (1559) is not certain, but it is the only Elizabethan work to allege that King Henry was murdered by Richard of Gloucester: it was

also the most popular account of the rising and falling fortunes of historical figures, a pattern—known as the wheel of fortune motif in literature—which certain critics have identified in *Henry VI*.

For dramatic purposes, Shakespeare inverted historical order, transferred events and characters, and compressed and expanded the material he found in his sources. Critics have pointed out that he altered the way in which some characters are presented in the chronicles, noting especially the defamation of Joan of Arc's reputation and the elaboration of sinister elements in the figures of York and Richard of Gloucester; for example, there is no factual basis for Shakespeare's depiction of Richard abusing the corpse of Somerset after the Battle of Saint Albans, since in reality Richard was only three years old and living in France at the time of that battle. Scholars have also identified scenes, particularly in *1 Henry VI*, that have no historical basis in the chronicles and which, they argued, Shakespeare must have invented, such as the Temple Garden scene, the episode between Talbot and the Countess of Auvergne, and the introduction of Sir William Lucy in the French campaign. Further, the chronicles only describe Suffolk as a favorite courtier of Margaret and do not provide a foundation for the love affair Shakespeare developed between these dramatic characters.

CRITICAL HISTORY: Until the second quarter of the twentieth century, the dominant question in criticism of *1, 2,* and *3 Henry VI* was whether these plays could be attributed solely to Shakespeare. Basing their analyses on a variety of approaches, including textual or bibliographical study, verse tests, and historical research, many commentators argued that little in the trilogy supported Shakespeare's authorship. Others maintained that Shakespeare merely acted as a reviser of the so-called quarto plays, either alone or in collaboration with one or more contemporaries. And there were those critics, primarily in the nineteenth century, who regarded *Henry VI* as Shakespeare's work throughout, if for no other reason than the lack of definitive evidence to the contrary. It was not until Madeleine Doran and Peter Alexander issued their studies in the twentieth century that commentators seemed willing to accept Shakespeare as the sole author of *1, 2,* and *3 Henry VI*. A second important issue in *Henry VI* criticism has been Shakespeare's view of the historical process as presented in the plays. Whether divine retribution is shown to be behind the ordering and outcome of events or whether Shakespeare demonstrates that men and women are ultimately responsible for their own destinies has been a central dispute of critics since the nineteenth century. In conjunction with this issue, commentators have debated the various views of kingship and governance depicted in the plays. Questions of dramatic structure and unity and the importance of Shakespeare's language and characterization have also drawn critical attention.

Available evidence suggests that few critics seriously considered *Henry VI* in the sixteenth and seventeenth centuries. As mentioned above, the first known reference to any of the plays, and one of the earliest known references to Shakespeare, was Robert Greene's venomous attack in 1592. Greene alluded to Shakespeare, in a parody of York's description of Queen Margaret in *3 Henry VI* (I. iv. 137), as "an upstart Crow, beautified with our feathers . . . , with his *Tygers heart wrapt in a Players hide.*" Although most critics interpreted this remark as a reference to Shakespeare's career as an actor, some—those who maintained that *Henry VI* is largely the work of other dramatists—understood Greene's words as a charge of plagiarism against Shakespeare. Other references to *Henry VI* during this period include Thomas Nashe's favorable allusion to the play of "brave Talbot" in 1592, also noted above, and John Crowne's preface to his version of Part 1 of *Henry VI*, in which he commends his work over Shakespeare's. But it was not until the end of the seventeenth century that anyone subjected the plays to serious evaluation. At that time, the theater critic Gerard Langbaine noted that the trilogy violates the Neoclassical precept that a drama should take place in less than twenty-four hours, but he nevertheless generally admired the plays.

Henry VI enjoyed its first critical popularity during the eighteenth century, when scholars began to debate over its authenticity and to judge its merits in light of Neoclassical standards. Nicholas Rowe was one of the first to defend the plays against allegations that they violated principles of unity, time, and setting. Instead, he argued that although Shakespeare lacked the necessary knowledge of classical composition, his natural genius, evidenced in *Henry VI*, more than compensated for this shortcoming. Later critics, however, including Charles Gildon, Lewis Theobald, Charlotte Lennox, and Francis Gentleman, reapplied the age's demand for classical composition and argued that *Henry VI* violates both the probability of nature and the facts of history and disrupts the moral sympathies of its audience. On the issue of Shakespeare's authorship, Theobald was among the first to venture the possibility of collaboration or revision, claiming that incidents and characterizations in *1 Henry VI*, especially that of Joan of Arc, were too crude for Shakespeare's pen. Samuel Johnson countered this assertion and contended that although the *Henry VI* trilogy may be judged "inferior" to Shakespeare's later works, there exists no real evidence of "spuriousness" in the plays. Johnson was also the first critic to assert that the quarto versions of *2* and *3 Henry VI* were not the work of Shakespeare, but, instead, were copies made by an auditor while attending performances of the plays—a possibility that was not addressed again until Doran and Alexander did so in the twentieth century. Edward Capell also examined the authenticity of *Henry VI* and, like Johnson, concluded that the work was strictly Shakespeare's, noting the presence of certain "beauties" and "grandeurs" in the plays "of which no other author was capable." However, near the end of the eighteenth century, Edmond Malone leveled the most convincing refutation of the sole authorship theory written thus far. In his *Dissertation* on the trilogy, Malone postulated that *1 Henry VI* was the work of "some ancient dramatist," and that in *2* and *3 Henry VI* Shakespeare merely revised two plays, *The First Part of the Contention* and *The True Tragedy*, which had been printed earlier in quarto form and were themselves the work of another playwright. Analyzing the dramatic styles of the plays, Malone concluded initially that they were written by Greene, but later changed his mind and credited Marlowe with their composition.

During the nineteenth and early twentieth centuries, the question of authorship remained a dominant issue in the commentaries on *Henry VI*. However, as Romantic sentiments supplanted Neoclassical standards critics turned to other issues. Despite the popularity of Malone's conclusions, some nineteenth-century German and American critics continued to support Shakespeare's authorship of the trilogy. August Wilhelm Schlegel linked *Henry VI* with Shakespeare's other history plays, regarding all ten works as comprising a sweeping epic cycle of English history. Similarly, another influential German scholar, Hermann Ulrici, viewed Shakespeare's historical dramas as interrelated, noting that *1, 2,* and *3 Henry VI* and *Richard III* may be regarded as a single tetralogy. Ulrici was also one of the earliest critics to argue that the *Henry VI-Richard III* te-

trilogy is based on the providential view of English history advanced by the sixteenth-century chronicler Edward Hall. Thus, the critic maintained that in *Henry VI* Shakespeare intended to dramatize divine retribution against England for Henry IV's usurpation of the crown. This concept has often recurred in the criticism of *Henry VI*. A late nineteenth-century American critic, Denton J. Snider, also argued that divine retribution against England is a fundamental theme of both the *Henry VI* trilogy and *Richard III*, although he regarded England's invasion of France, and not Henry IV's usurpation of the crown, as the crime which must be punished. Snider, like Schlegel and Ulrici, also viewed these plays as linked together in the form of a tetralogy. In the twentieth century, E. M. W. Tillyard and others revived these interpretations, rediscovering in *1, 2,* and *3 Henry VI* a sense of continuity with the other histories and evidence of Shakespeare's belief in the Elizabethan providential worldview underlying the chaotic events of Henry VI's and Richard III's reigns. Another nineteenth-century American scholar, Henry Norman Hudson, disputed Malone's assessment of the authorship of the plays, maintaining that their diction and versification are closer to the method of Shakespeare's early dramas than they are to the works of such contemporaries as Greene and Peele. On the other hand, G. G. Gervinus, a prominent German critic, agreed with Malone that Shakespeare had little share in *1 Henry VI*, and that in *2* and *3 Henry VI* he merely revised the earlier quarto plays. Gervinus contended that the structural unity of the trilogy is entirely borrowed from the chronicle sources and that the plays evidence "no poetic plan" of composition. In addition, as with many critics before and after, Gervinus examined the characterization in *Henry VI*, especially that of King Henry, which he claimed is more satisfying in Shakespeare's plays than in the original quarto versions.

Like their German and American counterparts, nineteenth-century English commentators on *Henry VI* were principally concerned with the question of authorship. Most of their arguments were based on examinations of such internal evidence as the style and verse structure of the plays. Charles Knight took issue with Malone's theory that *1 Henry VI* could not be Shakespeare's, since it is obviously based on Hall's chronicles and Hall, said Malone, was not "Shakespeare's historian." Knight considered such evidence specious and contended instead that it is very likely that Shakespeare would have borrowed from one of the principal authorities on the subject of his plays. However, other critics, often referred to as "disintegrationists," still perceived the work of other dramatists in the trilogy. Anna Brownell Jameson, an Irish critic, judged these plays stylistically inferior to Shakespeare's other works. She further disparaged the recurring bloodshed and violence, the absence of unity in the dramatic action, and the characterization of Margaret, which she said lacked even "an atom of poetry"; thus, Jameson concluded that Shakespeare's contribution to the trilogy was minimal. Samuel Taylor Coleridge went further than Malone, asserting that the language in *Henry VI* was so inferior to Shakespeare's usual style that it could not possibly be his.

Toward the end of the nineteenth century, textual scholars applied close comparisons of the texts of the quarto plays with those of *2* and *3 Henry VI* in an attempt to resolve the authorship controversy. On the basis of such a comparison, Jane Lee concluded that Marlowe and Greene originally wrote the quarto plays and that Shakespeare simply revised them into *2* and *3 Henry VI,* possibly with Marlowe's assistance. Edward Dowden also postulated that Shakespeare and Marlowe had collaborated on the composition of the trilogy. One of the most extreme disintegrationist views was that of F. G. Fleay, who argued that Shakespeare's only contribution to the *Henry VI* trilogy was the Temple Garden scene in *1 Henry VI.* Applying what he called a "qualitative test" to the metrics of the trilogy, Fleay ascribed all but this one scene in the plays to Peele, Greene, and Marlowe. Thus, one hundred years after the publication of Malone's *Dissertation,* Shakespeare's authorship of *1, 2,* and *3 Henry VI* had become almost totally denied.

In the second quarter of the twentieth century, the judgment of Malone and his successors was reversed and the authenticity of *1, 2,* and *3 Henry VI* was gradually established. Alexander and Doran each successfully argued that *The Contention* and *The True Tragedy* were not the works of earlier dramatists which Shakespeare merely revised, but were in fact memorial reconstructions of the original *2* and *3 Henry VI.* Alexander and Doran demonstrated that certain actors who had performed in these original dramas had produced the quarto versions from their own memories and, perhaps, from fragments of their players' parts. Some critics, however, continued to question Shakespeare's contribution to the trilogy. Dover Wilson endorsed Alexander's and Doran's theory of memorial reconstruction to explain the quarto versions, but he continued to maintain that Greene, Peele, and Nashe originally wrote the trilogy and that Shakespeare only added or revised certain scenes. In a similar manner, Charles Tyler Prouty argued that *2 Henry VI* is essentially Shakespeare's close revision of its quarto counterpart. Generally, however, the studies of Alexander and Doran have been accepted as accurately representing the relationship between the quarto and Folio plays, and Shakespeare's authorship of *1, 2,* and *3 Henry VI* has since ceased to be a controversial issue.

One of the first formal elements to be analyzed closely was the language of the plays. At the beginning of the twentieth century, Adolphus William Ward demonstrated that Shakespeare's language formed an integral element of the trilogy and that the poetry of *2* and *3 Henry VI* reflected a "greater maturity of style" than the bombast, alliteration, and tautological diction apparent in Part 1. While critics from Malone onward had viewed the poetry of the trilogy as un-Shakespearean, leading them to discount or severely reduce Shakespeare's contribution to the dramas, critics in the 1930s interpreted the language as very similar to Shakespeare's early dramatic style. The poetic use of images and symbols to enhance the atmosphere of disorder in *1, 2,* and *3 Henry VI* was studied by G. Wilson Knight. Knight particularly noted the relation of sea/tempest imagery to the battles and struggles of *3 Henry VI.* Other twentieth-century critics—including Caroline F. E. Spurgeon, Alvin B. Kernan, and Carol McGinnis Kay—also emphasized the importance of sea and storm symbols in *Henry VI.* One of the leading scholars of Shakespeare's poetic language, Wolfgang H. Clemen, analyzed the imagery of the trilogy in terms of its organic relation to other dramatic elements and concluded that it is less direct and more ornamental than in Shakespeare's more mature work.

One important trend in evaluating the language of *1, 2,* and *3 Henry VI* was to examine Shakespeare's poetic antecedents and the stylistic traditions of the Renaissance that influenced his work. In light of this assessment, commentators argued that a modern audience must appreciate the importance of the formal

rhetorical tradition in order to understand the stylized verse employed in the trilogy. Muriel C. Bradbrook, David Riggs, and Robert Y. Turner all demonstrated the effect of formal rhetorical devices to move and persuade, to enhance themes, and to direct an audience's attention to moral views presented in the plays. Gladys Dodge Willcock analyzed Shakespeare's use of the devices of amplification and variation to extend the metaphor of a shipwreck into an allegory symbolizing political upheaval. Riggs asserted that the "oratorical forms of praise, lament, and self-assertion," together with motifs of "personal worth," are all used by Shakespeare to underscore the theme of the progressive deterioration of heroic idealism—an idea also discussed by Robert B. Pierce and Leslie A. Fiedler. Turner indicated how Shakespeare's copious restatement, speeches of emotion and persuasion, and dialogue as debate all heighten the plays' emphasis on the moral significance of historical events.

Related to the idea of Shakespeare's use of the rhetorical tradition was his introduction into *Henry VI* of elements from medieval drama. Turner noted this relationship in the static method of characterization in the trilogy, which he claimed Shakespeare borrowed from medieval morality plays. Other critics who traced elements from the medieval dramatic tradition in *Henry VI* include Ernest William Talbert, Muriel C. Bradbrook, S. L. Bethell, John D. Cox, and Irving Ribner. Talbert argued that Shakespeare incorporated into the structure of *Henry VI* the motif of repetition and cyclical movement from both miracle and morality plays, and Bradbrook commented on the relationship between the "molehill" speech and mirror scene of *3 Henry VI* and Shakespeare's use of allegorical and symbolic modes of expression apparent in medieval literature. Bethell viewed Richard of Gloucester as a descendant of the comic villain in morality drama, whereas Cox pointed out that Shakespeare's use of analogies from the mystery plays—specifically, references to Lucifer and Christ—creates an ambivalent attitude toward certain of his characters. In addition to demonstrating how the traditions of miracle and morality plays influenced the form of *Henry VI,* Irving Ribner showed that elements of the *de casibus* tragedy and of Senecan drama are also evident in the trilogy.

Even more important to twentieth-century critics than analyses of Shakespeare's skills as a craftsman has been the investigation into his themes and worldview. The dominant question has been whether Shakespeare was, indeed, advancing a moral viewpoint in *1, 2,* and *3 Henry VI.* One popular argument centered on the so-called "Tudor myth," which identified Henry IV's usurpation of the crown as the source of the English civil wars during the reign of his grandson Henry VI. E. M. W. Tillyard maintained that Shakespeare based the *Henry VI* trilogy on this view, representing divine providence as directing the course of history so that England would atone for that crime. Tillyard's thesis received much attention and was endorsed by such later critics as Irving Ribner and M. M. Reese. But less than twenty years after his essay first appeared, commentators began disputing his notion that Shakespeare consistently endorsed the Tudor interpretation of history in his English dramas. The judgment of the past twenty-five years has been that Shakespeare's *Henry VI* trilogy emphasizes a more humanistic view of history—one in which men and women control their own destinies. Reese agreed with Tillyard that the history plays essentially endorse the Tudor social and political attitude in their emphasis on order and degree, but he argued that Shakespeare combined a belief in divine retribution with a conviction that through their actions individuals shape the course of events.

Moving further away from "the Tudor myth" were such critics as A. C. Hamilton, S. C. Sen Gupta, James Winny, and A. L. French. They all argued that *1, 2,* and *3 Henry VI* demonstrate that passion, ambition, and human weakness—not divine retribution for earlier sins—were responsible for the War of the Roses. Recent critics addressing Tillyard's thesis have also rejected it. Henry Ansgar Kelly, David Riggs, John C. Bromley, Robert Ornstein, and David L. Frey basically concurred that there is no evidence of the operation of divine providence in the *Henry VI* trilogy, maintaining instead that the plays express a humanistic rather than deterministic outlook on life.

Many of these same critics have studied the trilogy to determine Shakespeare's view of political authority and governance in a monarchical system, concluding that the theme of legitimacy and inheritance is central to *1, 2,* and *3 Henry VI.* Ronald S. Berman focused on the importance of the transmission of both political and moral virtues, and he noted that neither Yorkists nor Lancastrians sufficiently possessed these virtues to substantiate their claims to the crown. For Berman, the central theme of *Henry VI* is the relationship between fathers and sons—a relationship which has been so corrupted by the dynastic struggles of the aristocracy that spiritual evil is transmitted from one generation to the next together with the claims of birthright. Robert B. Pierce pointed out that the principle of royal succession in the trilogy depends on the belief that virtue and social responsibility must be inherited along with the transmission of authority itself; otherwise, Pierce concluded, authority loses its effectiveness and integrity, thus leading to the dissolution of familial and political ideals. Marilyn French also discerned legitimacy and inheritance from fathers to sons at the center of these plays, noting, in addition, that the female characters are drawn by Shakespeare as subversive agents who threaten that legitimacy. French maintained that the dramatist regarded women, by virtue of their gender, as incapable of legitimately possessing political power, and he thus depicted the overreaching females of the trilogy as outlaw figures who undermine the proper order of nature and society. French is one of many critics, beginning with Charlotte Lennox in the eighteenth century and including Leslie A. Fiedler and others in the twentieth, who have discussed Shakespeare's depiction of women in *Henry VI.* H. M. Richmond and Michael Manheim contended that the *Henry VI* trilogy dramatizes the conflict between moral and political values. They both emphasized that in the world of these plays the authoritative use of power, regardless of how it is attained and retained, is central to national governance. Manheim also focused on the character of Henry VI, asserting, as did Harold C. Goddard earlier, that previous critics erred in blaming the king for the horrors of his reign. Goddard and Manheim viewed Henry as a sympathetic figure, in Goddard's words, "a morally courageous and genuinely religious man" whose goodness was rendered ineffective by the greed and ambition of his court.

Other twentieth-century critics have addressed these same thematic issues not to discover Shakespeare's political and historical beliefs, but to determine the dramatic unity or structure of the *Henry VI* trilogy. Using this approach, many commentators have moved away from the concept proposed by Schlegel and amplified by Tillyard that *1, 2,* and *3 Henry VI* represent one division of Shakespeare's epic cycle of English history. In a highly praised essay on the construction of *1 Henry VI,* Hereward T. Price altered this traditional view of defining the play's structural unity solely on the basis of plot, action, or the depiction of historical events; instead, seeking a thematic continuity, Price argued that the responsibility of those who govern is the "controlling moral idea" of the play, and he added that Shakespeare used this concept—what Price termed as "the specialty of rule"—to construct and order the dramatic material of *1 Henry VI.* David M. Bevington and Don M. Ricks posited the theme of dissension and division as a unifying element in the trilogy. Ricks maintained that Elizabethans regarded themselves as living from one political crisis to another and that Shakespeare had a didactic purpose in dramatizing in the trilogy "the terrible nature of civil dissension"; he further argued that this theme lends structural coherence to these three disparately designed plays. Bevington's analysis of those scenes in *Henry VI* which feature attempts by "domineering" females to gain control over their male counterparts led him to conclude that these episodes echo "the larger theme of discord and division" in the plays, as well as dramatize the major subtheme of masculine reason threatened by feminine sensuality. John W. Blanpied and Larry S. Champion identified other elements that both emphasized and unified Shakespeare's themes. Blanpied argued that Shakespeare's use of irony in *1 Henry VI* was designed to "undermine the authority of the monumental past"; according to the critic, Shakespeare deliberately styled the speeches of Talbot and other members of the old aristocracy to parody the formalized conventions of medieval and earlier Elizabethan dramatic language and thus represent these figures as anachronistic and almost comical. Champion focused on the conflicting perspectives presented in the plays, maintaining that these ambivalent angles of vision are a dramatically effective means of presenting the complexities of Shakespeare's historical theme and of reinforcing the importance of historical events over individual characterization.

Critical appreciation of the *Henry VI* trilogy has increased steadily in the fifty or so years since Peter Alexander and Madeleine Doran issued their respective studies and, in the opinion of most critics, firmly established Shakespeare as the sole author of the work. Whereas scholars before Alexander and Doran, especially those of the nineteenth century, were admittedly more concerned with dissociating the trilogy from Shakespeare's canon than with analyzing its content, later critics have been willing to forsake the question of authorship for a closer examination of its structure, thematics, imagery, characterization, and literary antecedents. Such notable commentators as Muriel C. Bradbrook, David Riggs, and Robert Y. Turner have all demonstrated how the poetics of *Henry VI* was influenced by the formal rhetorical tradition pervasive throughout sixteenth-century English literature. Others, including E. M. W. Tillyard, Irving Ribner, Robert Ornstein, and John D. Cox, have focused on the elements of morality and medieval tradition in the plays. Still others, such as Caroline F. E. Spurgeon, Wolfgang H. Clemen, Alvin B. Kernan, James L. Calderwood, and Carol McGinnis Kay, have studied Shakespeare's language and image-patterns in an attempt to identify the trilogy's central themes and illustrate each play's inherent structure. In the past twenty-five years, critics have also generally abandoned the providential interpretation of *Henry VI,* first suggested in the nineteenth century by Hermann Ulrici and later amplified by Denton J. Snider and Tillyard, for the acceptance of a more individual, dynamic, and creative construction on Shakespeare's part. Such critics as A. C. Hamilton, S. C. Sen Gupta, James Winny, Riggs, and Ornstein have all argued that the plays present a humanistic rather than a providential view of history during Henry VI's reign. This has further led some commentators to conclude that the trilogy exhibits, above all else, the proper means of governing and Shakespeare's own attitude toward political authority—an issue he was to return to repeatedly in the subsequent histories. In fact, many of these postmodern critics have maintained that *Henry VI* deals not only with the dangers of disorder and personal ambition, or the consequences of a weak king, but reflects the complexities of legitimacy and inheritance that plagued England throughout its political history, particularly during Shakespeare's lifetime. What thus becomes evident upon reviewing *Henry VI* criticism of the past fifty years is that the plays demonstrate a cohesiveness and thematic integrity far more complex than previous centuries recognized; what is also apparent is that the trilogy, despite its obvious shortcomings and artistic lapses, includes important elements, themes, motifs, and formal characteristics that echo similar concerns or techniques developed more successfully in Shakespeare's later works, and, in this respect, shed valuable light on the dramatist's early career.

ROBERT GREENE (essay date 1592)

[*Between 1588 and 1592, Greene authored numerous pamphlets, romances, and dramas, including the popular romantic comedy,* Friar Bacon and Friar Bungay *(1592). The excerpt below is taken from an autobiographical pamphlet,* Green's Groatsworth of Wit bought with a million of Repentence *(1592), in which he renounces poetry and regrets having devoted his life to dramatic literature. The savage tone has been attributed to the fact that Greene was financially destitute and mortally ill at the time he composed it. The tract concludes with an "Address" to his fellow playwrights (who have generally been identified as Christopher Marlowe, Thomas Nashe, and George Peele), urging them to pursue "more profitable courses" than composing dramas which will be distorted by actors' performances. The italicized line has been regarded as a parody of York's excoriation of Margaret: "O tiger's heart wrapp'd in a woman's hide!" (*3 Henry VI *, 1. iv. 137). This earliest known reference to Shakespeare has been interpreted variously in the almost four centuries since its publication, and it has been used frequently by scholars in their attempts to fix the date and authorship of the* Henry VI *trilogy. Some critics, such as Edmond Malone (1787), interpreted the "beautified with our feathers" phrase to mean that Shakespeare plagiarized the works of his contemporaries, while others read the passage as a reference to Shakespeare's career as an actor as well as a dramatist (see the essay by Peter Alexander cited in the Additional Bibliography). Many textual critics, including Jane Lee (1876), ascribed portions of the* Henry VI *trilogy to Greene himself. For more on the subject of Greene's possible authorship of parts of the trilogy, refer to the essays by George Brandes, F. G. Fleay, and John Dover Wilson listed in the Additional Bibliography.*]

Base minded men al three of you, if by my miserie ye be not warned: for unto none of you (like me) sought those burres to cleave: those Puppits (I meane) that speake from our mouths, those Anticks garnisht in our colours. Is it not strange that I, to whom they al have beene beholding: is it not like that you, to whome they all have beene beholding, shall (were ye in that case that I am now) be both at once of them forsaken? Yes, trust them not: for there is an upstart Crow, beautified with our feathers, that with his *Tygers heart wrapt in a Players hide,* supposes he is as well able to bumbast out a blanke verse as the best of you: and being an absolute *Johannes fac totum,* is in his owne conceit the onely Shake-scene in a countrie. O that I might intreate your rare wits to be imployed in more profitable courses: & let these Apes imitate your past excellence, and never more acquaint them with your admired inventions. (p. 2)

Robert Greene, in an extract from The Shakspere Allusion-Book: A Collection of Allusions to Shakspere from 1591 to 1700, Vol. I, *edited by John Munro, revised edition, 1932. Reprint by Books for Libraries Press, 1970; distributed by Arno Press, Inc., pp. 2-3.*

THOMAS NASH[E] (essay date 1592)

[*Nashe was an English dramatist who also wrote religious tracts and prose satires. Along with Marlowe, Greene, and Peele, he is often identified as one of the "university wits"—dramatists with formal academic educations who wrote primarily during the final years of the sixteenth century. The following excerpt is from his* Pierce Penniless, His Supplication to the Divell *(1592), a discourse on the vices of the Elizabethan age written in the form of a comic complaint. Critics generally agree that the reference to "brave Talbot" is an allusion to the character of the same name in* 1 Henry VI. *Nashe's assertion that "ten thousand spectators . . . (at severall times)" wept at the portrayal of Talbot may not be an exaggeration; contemporary theater records from the late sixteenth century indicate that* 1 Henry VI *was an extremely popular play. The following comment, along with that of Robert Greene (1592), has been regarded as a significant piece of evidence in scholars' attempts to date the* Henry VI *plays.*]

How would it have joyed brave *Talbot* (the terror of the French) to thinke that after he had lyne two hundred yeares in his Tombe, hee should triumphe againe on the Stage, and have his bones newe embalmed with the teares of ten thousand spectators at least, (at severall times) who, in the Tragedian that represents his person, imagine they behold him fresh bleeding! (p. 5)

Thomas Nash[e], in an extract from The Shakspere Allusion-Book: A Collection of Allusions to Shakspere from 1591 to 1700, Vol. I, *edited by John Munro, revised edition, 1932. Reprint by Books for Libraries Press, 1970; distributed by Arno Press, Inc., p. 5.*

JOHN CROWNE (essay date 1681)

[*Crowne was a Restoration dramatist whose best-known work is his popular comedy,* Sir Courtly Nice *(1685). For his plays* Henry the Sixth, The First Part. With the Murder of Humphrey Duke of Glocester *and* Henry the Sixth, The Second Part; or, The Misery of Civil War, *Crowne borrowed heavily from Shakespeare's* 2 *and* 3 Henry VI, *adopting entire sections and plots, and distorting Shakespeare's verse and characterization in order to promote the royalist cause which he supported. In an epistle dedicatory prefacing the printed version of* Henry the Sixth, The First Part *(1681), from which the following excerpt is taken, Crowne maintains that his play not only owes little to Shakespeare's, but actually improves the earlier work by presenting on stage the murder of Duke Humphrey.*]

I called [*Henry the Sixth, The First Part*] in the Prologue *Shakespear's* Play, though he has no Title to the 40th part of it. The Text I took out of his Second Part of *Henry* the Sixth, but as most Texts are serv'd, I left it as soon as I could. For though *Shakespear* be generally very delightful, he is not so always. His Volumn is all up-hill and down; *Paradise* was never more pleasant than some parts of it, nor *Ireland* and *Greenland* colder, and more uninhabitable than others. And I have undertaken to cultivate one of the most barren Places in it. The Trees are all shrubs, and the Men Pigmies, nothing has any Spirit or shape; the Cardinal is duller then ever Priest was. And he has hudled up the Murder of Duke *Humphry,* as if he had been guilty of himself, and was afraid to shew how it was done: But I haue been more bold, to the great displeasure of some, who are it seems ashamed of their own mysteries. (pp. 278-79)

> *John Crowne, in an extract from* The Shakspere Al-
> lusion-Book: A Collection of Allusions to Shakspere
> from 1591-1700, Vol. II, *edited by John Munro,
> revised edition, 1932. Reprint by Books for Libraries
> Press, 1970; distributed by Arno Press, Inc., pp.
> 278-79.*

GERARD LANGBAINE   (essay date 1691)

[Langbaine is credited with being the first historian of the English theater. In his An Account of the English Dramatick Poets *(1691), from which the following excerpt is taken, Langbaine provides biographies of the dramatists, together with a catalogue of plays ascribed to them and their sources. The "strict rules" to which he alludes in his discussion of the* Henry VI *trilogy are those of English Neoclassicism, which held that dramas should have a single setting, take place in less than twenty-four hours, and have a causally connected plot. Langbaine was the first critic to apply these Neoclassical standards to the trilogy. Other commentators who did so include Nicholas Rowe (1709), who argued that the application of strict precepts would have hampered Shakespeare's natural ability, and Charles Gildon (1710), who asserted that Shakespeare's soliloquies violated the rules of probability. Several critics, including Lewis Theobald (1733), Charlotte Lennox (1754), and Francis Gentleman (1774), also charged that Shakespeare distorted actual historical chronology in his presentation of events in* Henry VI.]

These three Plays [*1, 2,* and *3 Henry VI*] contain the whole length of this Kings Reign, *viz.* Thirty eight Years, six Weeks, and four Days. Altho' this be contrary to the strict Rules of *Dramatick Poetry;* yet it must be own'd, even by Mr. *Dryden* himself, That this Picture in *Miniature,* has many Features, which excell even several of his more exact Strokes of Symmetry, and Proportion. (p. 420)

> *Gerard Langbaine, in an extract from* Shakespeare,
> the Critical Heritage: 1623-1692, Vol. 1, *edited by
> Brian Vickers, Routledge & Kegan Paul, 1974, pp.
> 417-23.*

N[ICHOLAS] ROWE   (essay date 1709)

[Rowe was the editor of the first critical edition of Shakespeare's plays (1709) and the author of the first authoritative Shakespeare biography. Rowe believed that Shakespeare had not read classical Greek and Roman playwrights and was thus unaware of classical rules of dramaturgy. Contrary to Charles Gildon (1710) and other early eighteenth-century critics, Rowe postulated that had Shakespeare been constrained by Neoclassical standards, his plays might not have embodied "that Fire, Impetuosity, and even beautiful Extravagance which we admire in Shakespeare." In the excerpt below, taken from the preface to his 1709 edition of Shakespeare's works, Rowe argues that the untutored dramatist was able to achieve the effects classical dramatists aimed for, and he points to the Henry VI *plays as examples of this success. For additional commentary on Shakespeare's violation of Neoclassical principles in* Henry VI, *see the excerpts by Gerard Langbaine (1691), Charles Gildon (1710), Lewis Theobald (1733), and Charlotte Lennox (1754).]*

If one undertook to examine the greatest part of these by those Rules which are establish'd by *Aristotle,* and taken from the Model of the *Grecian* Stage, it would be no very hard Task to find a great many Faults: But as *Shakespear* liv'd under a kind

of mere Light of Nature, and had never been made acquainted with the Regularity of those written Precepts, so it would be hard to judge him by a Law he knew nothing of. We are to consider him as a Man that liv'd in a State of almost universal License and Ignorance: There was no establish'd Judge, but every one took the liberty to Write according to the Dictates of his own Fancy. When one considers, that there is not one Play before him of a Reputation good enough to entitle it to an Appearance on the present Stage, it cannot but be a Matter of great Wonder that he should advance Dramatick Poetry so far as he did. The Fable is what is generally plac'd the first, among those that are reckon'd the constituent Parts of a Tragick or Heroick Poem; not, perhaps, as it is the most Difficult or Beautiful, but as it is the first properly to be thought of in the Contrivance and Course of the whole; and with the Fable ought to be considered, the fit Disposition, Order and Conduct of its several Parts. As it is not in this Province of the *Drama* that the Strength and Mastery of *Shakespear* lay, so I shall not undertake the tedious and ill-natur'd Trouble to point out the several Faults he was guilty of in it. . . . But in Recompence for his Carelessness in this Point, when he comes to another Part of the *Drama, The Manners of his Characters, in Acting or Speaking what is proper for them, and fit to be shown by the Poet,* he may be generally justify'd. and in very many places greatly commended. For those Plays which he has taken from the *English* or *Roman* History, let any Man compare 'em, and he will find the Character as exact in the Poet and the Historian. . . . What can be more agreeable to the Idea our Historians give of *Henry* the Sixth, than the Picture *Shakespear* has drawn of him! His Manners are every where exactly the same with the Story; one finds him still describ'd with Simplicity, passive Sanctity, want of Courage, weakness of Mind, and easie Submission to the Governance of an imperious Wife, or prevailing Faction: Tho' at the same time the Poet do's Justice to his good Qualities, and moves the Pity of his Audience for him, by showing him Pious, Disinterested, a Contemner of the Things of this World, and wholly resign'd to the severest Dispensations of God's Providence. There is a short Scene [III. iii.] in the Second Part of *Henry* VI. which I cannot but think admirable in its Kind. Cardinal *Beaufort,* who had murder'd the Duke of *Gloucester,* is shewn in the last Agonies on his Death-Bed, with the good King praying over him. There is so much Terror in one, so much Tenderness and moving Piety in the other, as must touch any one who is capable either of Fear or Pity. (pp. xxvi-xxix)

> *N[icholas] Rowe, "Some Account of the Life, &c. of
> Mr. William Shakespear," in* The Works of Mr. Wil-
> liam Shakespear, Vol. I *by William Shakespeare,
> edited by Nicholas Rowe, 1709. Reprint by AMS Press,
> Inc., 1967, pp. iii-xl.*

[CHARLES GILDON]   (essay date 1710)

[Gildon was the first critic to write an extended commentary on Shakespeare's plays. Like many other Neoclassicists, Gildon regarded Shakespeare as an imaginative playwright who lacked knowledge of the dramatic "rules" necessary for correct writing. In the following excerpt, Gildon argues that Richard of Glouces-ter's lengthy soliloquy in 3 Henry VI *is unnatural and therefore "not at all according to Art." In short, Gildon questions the propriety of the soliloquy in light of the Neoclassical emphasis on literature's adherence to nature. For further commentary on Shakespeare's violation of such Neoclassical rules in* Henry VI, *see the excerpts by Gerard Langbaine (1691), Nicholas Rowe (1709), Lewis Theobald (1733), and Charlotte Lennox (1754).]*

The long Soliloquy of *Richard* [in *3 Henry VI*, III. ii. 124-95] is highly unnatural; for as the Duke of *Buckingham* justly has observ'd they ought to be few, and short. Nor wou'd this, which is so frequent in our Poet be born from the best Hand, that cou'd now arise; but there is always by the Many biggotted Deference paid to our Predecessors; and Years add Authority to a Name. Our young Poets, shou'd never imitate our *Shakespear* in this; for tho' a Man may be suppos'd to speak a few Words to himself in the Vehemence of a Passion, as it do's happen in Nature, of which the Drama is in all its Parts an Imitation; yet to have near fourscore Lines of calm Reflections, nay Narrations to my self, by which the Hearer shou'd discover my Thoughts and my Person, as here, and before when *Henry* VI. is discover'd and taken, is unpardonable, because against Nature, and by Consequence not at all according to Art. There are several good Lines in this Speech of *Richard* but ill brought in. The Instances which *Shakespear* makes him give of *Nestor, Ulysses,* and *Sinon* are a Proof still of his Knowledge at least in *Ovid,* and some other of the Latin *Classics.* . . . (pp. 352-53)

> [*Charles Gildon*], "*Remarks on the Plays of Shake-spear,*" *in* The Works of Mr. William Shakespear, *Vol. 7 by William Shakespear, 1710. Reprint by AMS Press, Inc., 1967, pp. 257-444.*

LEWIS THEOBALD   (essay date 1733)

[*Theobald, a dramatist and classical scholar, was also one of the most important editors of Shakespeare's plays in the first half of the eighteenth century. Although his reputation as a Shakespearean editor declined after his death and opinion of the value of his work remains divided today, he nonetheless contributed significant emendations which have been adopted by modern editors. However, his adaptation of Shakespeare's plays, revised to adhere to Neoclassical dramatic rules, have been less well received. In the following excerpt, he points out Shakespeare's alteration of the actual sequence of historical events in the* Henry VI *trilogy, which in his assessment violates the Neoclassical concept of the "Order of Time." Also, in questioning whether the* Henry VI *plays were written by someone other than Shakespeare, Theobald ventures a speculation about multiple authorship that received support from numerous later critics, beginning with Edmond Malone (1787) and continuing in the studies by G. G. Gervinus (1849-50), Jane Lee (1876), Edward Dowden (1881), and John Dover Wilson (see the Additional Bibliography).*]

The Historical Transactions, contain'd in [*1 Henry VI*], take in the Compass of above 30 Years. I must observe, however, that our Author, in the three Parts of K. *Henry* VI. has not been very precise to the Date and Disposition of his Facts; but shuffled them, backwards and forwards, out of Time. For Instance; The Lord *Talbot* is kill'd at the End of the 4th Act of this Play, who in reality did not fall till the 13th of *July* 1453: and the 2d Part of *Henry* VI. opens with the Marriage of the King, which was solemniz'd 8 Years before *Talbot*'s Death, in the Year 1445. Again, in the 2d Part, Dame *Eleanor Cobbam* is introduc'd to insult *Q. Margaret;* though her Penance and Banishment for Sorcery happen'd three Years before that Princess came over to *England.* I could point out many other Transgressions against History, as far as the Order of Time is concern'd. Indeed, tho there are several Master-Strokes in these three Plays, which incontestibly betray the Workmanship of *Shakespeare;* yet I am almost doubtful, whether they were entirely of his Writing. And unless they were wrote by him very early, I shou'd rather imagine them to have been brought to him as a Director of the *Stage;* and so to have receiv'd some finishing Beauties at his hand. An accurate Observer will easily

see, the *Diction* of them is more *obsolete*, and the *Numbers* more *mean* and *prosaical*, than in the Generality of his genuine Compositions. (pp. 109-10)

> *Lewis Theobald, in notes to* "*King Henry VI,*" *Parts I, II, and III, in* The Works of Shakespeare, Vol. 4 *by William Shakespeare, edited by Lewis Theobald, 1733. Reprint by AMS Press, 1968, pp. 109-395.*

[CHARLOTTE LENNOX]   (essay date 1754)

[*Lennox was an American-born novelist and Shakespearean scholar who compiled a three-volume edition of translated texts of the sources used by Shakespeare in twenty-two of his plays, together with some analyses of the ways in which he used these sources. In her discussion of* Henry VI, *Lennox is principally concerned with Shakespeare's deviations from the chronicles, contending that his depictions of incidents and characters are frequently inaccurate and inconsistent. She judges the portrayal of the relationship between Margaret and Suffolk, as well as the queen's cruel execution of Richard of York following the Battle of Wakefield, to be coarse and unfair. Lennox further charges that Shakespeare distorted the justice of Margaret's struggle to regain the throne for her husband and her son. For additional discussion of Shakespeare's alterations of his historical sources in* Henry VI, *see the excerpts by Lewis Theobald (1733) and Francis Gentleman (1774).*]

The historical Transactions contained in this Play [*1 Henry VI*], take in the Compass of about thirty Years; they are all extracted from *Holingshed*'s Chronicle: But *Shakespear*, in this, as well as in the two following Parts of this King's Reign, has not been very exact to the Date and Disposition of the Facts, shuffling them backwards and forwards, out of the Order of Time in which they happened, as it best suited his Purpose. The Characters are almost all faithfully copied from the Historian; but the Poet has exaggerated the Affection of Queen *Margaret* for the Duke of *Suffolk*, representing that Princess as engaged in a criminal Amour with the Duke, for which there is no Foundation in History.

The Loves of the Queen and Duke of *Suffolk*, which make the Subject of several Scenes in the Play, not being mentioned either by *Hall* or *Holinshed*, 'tis probable that *Shakespear* saw some little Novel of the Lives of these two great Persons, from whence he copied such Incidents as he thought proper for the Embellishment of his Play; but, by introducing the Queen in the second Part, weeping and lamenting over the Head of her murdered Lover, which lyes on her Bosom, in the Presence of the King her Husband, and several Noblemen, he has either very injudiciously copied, or very coarsly invented. For the absurdity of such a Behaviour must give disgust to the meanest and least intelligent Reader or Spectator.

But if *Shakespear* has been misled by Romance, or oral Tradition, to give such improper Manners to a Queen, and in a Historical Play, contradict the known Facts on which it is founded, he has, on the other Hand, worked up the simple Relation of the Deaths of a Father and Son, in the History, into one of the most beautiful and affecting Episodes imaginable.

Holingshed after a circumstantial Detail of all the great Actions of the warlike *Talbot*, Earl of *Shrewsbury*, proceeds to give an Account of his Death and that of his Son's as they were endeavouring to raise the Siege of *Chastillon* in *France*. (pp. 143-44)

On this Incident [scenes v, vi, and vii in Act IV of *1 Henry VI*] are founded, in which the Poet has given us the finest Pictures imaginable, of true Heroism, paternal Tenderness, and filial Love. (p. 146)

Shakespear has copied *Holingshed* pretty closely throughout [*2 Henry VI*], except in his Relation of the Duke of *Suffolk's* Death. The Chronicle tells us, that King *Henry,* to satisfy the Nobility and People, who hated this Favourite, condemned him to Banishment during the Space of five Years. In his Passage to *France* he was taken by a Ship of War belonging to the Duke of *Exeter,* Constable of the *Tower;* the Captain of which Ship carried him into *Dover* Road, and there struck off his Head on the Side of a Cock-boat.

In *Shakespear,* he is taken by *English* Pyrates on the Coast of *Kent,* who, notwithstanding the large Ransom he offers them, resolve to murder him: One of them in the Course of his Conversation with the Duke, tells him, that his Name is *Walter Whitmore;* and observing him start, asks him, if he is frightened at Death, to which *Suffolk* replied.

> Thy Name affrights me, in whose Sound is
>   Death,
> A cunning Man did calculate my Birth,
> And told me that by *Walter* I should die.
>   [*2 Henry VI*, IV. i. 33-5]

This Circumstance is not to be found, either in *Hall* or *Holingshed;* and as it has greatly the Air of Fiction, *Shakespear* probably borrowed it from the same Tale that furnished him with the Loves of *Suffolk* and the Queen, on which several passionate Scenes in this Play, as well as the former, are Built.

The Scene of [*3 Henry VI*] opens just after the Battle of *St. Albans,* wherein the *York* Faction was Victorious, and closes with the Murder of King *Henry* the sixth and the Birth of Prince *Edward,* afterwards King *Edward* the fifth; so that this History takes in the space of sixteen Years. The Facts are all extracted from *Holingshed,* and most of the Incidents very closely copied. The struggle between the two Houses of *York* and *Lancaster* for the Crown being the Subject pursued in this Drama, every Scene almost presents us with a new Battle, a flying Army, or the Carnage of a bloody Field; where the inhuman Conquerors unsated with the Slaughters of the Fight, sacrifice their defenceless Enemies to the Fury of their Revenge, and exult over them, when dying, with a Cruelty truly diabolical.

Shakespear has given the same inconsistent and improper Manners to all the chief Persons in this Play; the brave old Duke of *York,* the gallant *Edward* his Son, afterwards King, the heroic *Warwick,* whom the Poet so often styles the Maker and Subduer of Kings, are all Murderers; at once the Heroes and the Villains of the Scene, equally exciting our Praise and Detestation. The Poet, in order to display this predominant Passion, Cruelty, in Characters where it is lest expected to be found, the Heroe and the Prince, has not scrupled to violate sometimes the Truth of History.

The Chronicles say, that the Duke of *York,* who pretended to the Crown, was killed in the Battle of *Wakefield,* and being found dead in the Field by the Lord *Clifford,* he cut off his Head and presented it to the Queen of *Henry* the sixth, who was in Person at this Battle. *Shakespear* makes him to be taken Prisoner by the Earls of *Northumberland* and *Clifford,* who

bring him to the Queen and ask what she would have done to him: To which she replies,

> QUEEN
> Brave Warriors, *Clifford* and *Northumberland*
> Come, make him stand upon this Mole-hill
>   here,
> That raught at Mountains with out-stretched
>   Arms,
> Yet parted but the Shadow with his Hand:
> What, was it you, that would be *England*'s
>   King?
> Was't you, that revell'd in our Parliament,
> And made a Preachment of your high Descent? . . .
> *York* cannot speak unless he wear a Crown.
> A Crown for *York*——And, Lords, bow low
>   to him;
> Hold you his Hands, while I do set it on.
>   [*putting a Paper Crown on his Head.*]
> Ay, marry Sir, now looks he like a King:
> Ay, this is he, that took King *Henry*'s Chair;
> And this is he, was his adopted Heir.
> But how is it that great *Plantaganet*
> Is crown'd so soon, and broke his solemn Oath
> As I bethink me, you should not be King
> Till our King *Henry* had shook Hands with
>   Death.
> And will you pale your Head in *Henry*'s Glory
> And rob his Temples of the Diadem,
> Now in his Life, against your holy Oath?
> Oh, 'tis a Fault too too unpardonable.
> Off with the Crown, and with the Crown his
>   Head;
> And whilst we breathe, take Time to do him
>   dead,
>   [*3 Henry VI*, I. iv. 66-108]

With this more than fiendlike Cruelty, has *Shakespear* represented a Queen, whose Motives for taking Arms were far from being unjust; the recovery of her Husband's Liberty and Crown, and the restoring her Son to the Rights and Privileges of his Birth. And for the Sake of this shocking Absurdity in the Manners of a Female Character, in so high a Rank, he contradicts a known Fact in History, and makes one of the greatest Captains of the Age die by the cowardly Stabs of a Woman, and a Ruffian, who, according to the Chronicles fell in the Field of Battle, covered with Wounds and Glory. (pp. 153-58)

For many of the Murders which the Followers of each Party commit on those of the other in this Play, *Shakespear* had no Foundation in the History; but that of the young Earl of *Rutland* by *Clifford,* is copied with all its Circumstances from *Holingshed.* The Character of King *Henry* the Sixth, whose unfortunate Reign makes the Subject of these three Plays, is drawn by *Shakespear* exactly conformable to that given him by the Historians. As to the Manner of his Death, several different Opinions prevailed; but the Poet, by making the Duke of *Gloucester* murder him in the *Tower,* has followed that which was most probable and most generally believed. (p. 161)

[*Charlotte Lennox*], *in remarks on "King Henry the Sixth," Parts I, II, and III, in her* Shakespear Illustrated; or, The Novels and Histories, on Which the Plays of Shakespear Are Founded, *Vol. III, 1754. Reprint by AMS Press Inc., 1973, pp. 143-61.*

SAMUEL JOHNSON   (essay date 1765)

[Johnson has long held an important place in the history of Shakespearean criticism. He is considered the foremost representative

of moderate English Neoclassicism and is credited by some literary historians with freeing Shakespeare from the principles of the three unities valued by strict Neoclassicists: that dramas should have a single setting, take place in less than twenty-four hours, and have a causally connected plot. More recent scholars portray him as a critic who was able to synthesize existing critical theory rather than as an innovative theoretician. Johnson was a master of Augustan prose style and a personality who dominated the literary world of his epoch. The following excerpt is from his observations printed at the end of 3 Henry VI *in his 1765 edition of* The Plays of William Shakespeare. *Commenting on the "inferiority" of the* Henry VI *trilogy, Johnson points out that among an artist's work not every effort will be superior. Addressing the question of authorship initiated by Lewis Theobald (1733), he finds no "marks of spuriousness" and judges that the "diction, the versification, and the figures" are all undoubtedly Shakespeare's. He regards the inclusion of these three plays in the First Folio and the reference to them in the epilogue to Shakespeare's* Henry V *to be convincing evidence of their authenticity.*]

The three parts of *Henry VI.* are suspected, by Mr. Theobald [see excerpt above, 1733], of being supposititious, and are declared, by Dr. Warburton, to be "certainly not Shakespeare's." Mr. Theobald's suspicion arises from some obsolete words; but the phraseology is like the rest of our authour's stile, and single words, of which however I do not observe more than two, can conclude little.

Dr. Warburton gives no reason, but I suppose him to judge upon deeper principles and more comprehensive views, and to draw his opinion from the general effect and spirit of the composition, which he thinks inferior to the other historical plays.

From mere inferiority nothing can be inferred; in the productions of wit there will be inequality. Sometimes judgment well err, and sometimes the matter itself will defeat the artist. Of every authour's works one will be the best, and one will be the worst. The colours are not equally pleasing, nor the attitudes equally graceful, in all the pictures of Titian or Reynolds.

Dissimilitude of stile and heterogeneousness of sentiment, may sufficiently show that a work does not really belong to the reputed authour. But in these plays no such marks of spuriousness are found. The diction, the versification, and the figures, are Shakespeare's. These plays, considered, without regard to characters and incidents, merely as narratives in verse, are more happily conceived and more accurately finished than those of *King John, Richard II*, or the tragick scenes of *Henry IV.* and *V.* If we take these plays from Shakespeare, to whom shall they be given? What authour of that age had the same easiness of expression and fluency of numbers?

Having considered the evidence given by the plays themselves, and found it in their favour, let us now enquire what corroboration can be gained from other testimony. They are ascribed to Shakespeare by the first editors, whose attestation may be received in questions of fact, however unskilfully they superintended their edition. They seem to be declared genuine by the voice of Shakespeare himself, who refers to the second play in his epilogue to *Henry V.* and apparently connects the first act of *Richard III.* with the last of the third part of *Henry VI.* If it be objected that the plays were popular, and therefore he alluded to them as well known; it may be answered, with equal probability, that the natural passions of a poet would have disposed him to separate his own works from those of an inferior hand. And indeed if an authour's own testimony is to be overthrown by speculative criticism, no man can be any longer secure of literary reputation.

Of these three plays I think the second the best. The truth is, that they have not sufficient variety of action, for the incidents are too often of the same kind; yet many of the characters are well discriminated. King Henry, and his queen, King Edward, the Duke of Gloucester, and the Earl of Warwick, are very strongly and distinctly painted. (pp. 611-12)

> *Samuel Johnson, "Notes on Shakespeare's Plays: '3 Henry VI'," in his* The Yale Edition of the Works of Samuel Johnson: Johnson on Shakespeare, Vol. VIII, *edited by Arthur Sherbo, Yale University Press, 1968, pp. 597-612.*

EDWARD CAPELL (essay date 1768)

[*Capell was one of the first editors of Shakespeare to collate First Folio and quarto editions of the plays. His 1768 edition of the works of Shakespeare, from which the excerpt below is taken, was based on a careful comparison of all extant versions of the plays. Like Samuel Johnson (1765), Capell is convinced that the* Henry VI *trilogy is the work of Shakespeare, though not only on the basis of textual evidence that supports this finding. Responding to charges that the style of the plays is unworthy of Shakespeare and thus they should not be attributed to him—an assessment first presented by Lewis Theobald (1733)—Capell commends certain "beauties" and "grandeurs" found in them "of which no other author was capable." He also praises Shakespeare's characterization throughout the trilogy, an assessment countering Charlotte Lennox (1754), who argued that many of Shakespeare's characters are inaccurately and crudely represented.*]

[*1, 2,* and *3 Henry VI*] have been inconceivably mangl'd either in the copy or the press, or perhaps both. Yet this may be discover'd in them, that the alterations made afterwards by the Author are nothing near so considerable as those in some other plays, the incidents, the characters, every principal out-line in short being the same in both draughts; so that what we shall have occasion to say of the second [part] may in some degree, and without much violence, be apply'd also to the first. And this we presume to say of it; that, low as it must be set in comparison with his other plays, it has beauties in it and grandeurs, of which no other author was capable but Shakespeare only. That extreamly-affecting scene of the death of young *Rutland*, that of his father which comes next it, and of *Clifford* the murtherer of them both; *Beaufort*'s dreadful exit, the exit of king *Henry*, and a scene of wondrous simplicity and wondrous tenderness united, in which that *Henry* is made a speaker while his last decisive battle is fighting,—are as so many stamps upon these plays by which his property is mark'd, and himself declar'd the owner of them, beyond controversy as we think. And though we have selected these passages only, and recommended them to observation, it had been easy to name abundance of others which bear his mark as strongly; and one circumstance there is that runs through all the three plays by which he is as surely to be known as by any other that can be thought of, and that is, the preservation of character. All the personages in them are distinctly and truly delineated, and the character given them sustain'd uniformly throughout. The enormous *Richard*'s, particularly, which in the third of these plays is seen rising towards it's zenith; and who sees not the future monster, and acknowledges at the same time the pen that drew it in these two lines only, spoken over a king who lies stab'd before him:

> What, will the aspiring blood of *Lancaster*
> Sink in the ground? I thought, it would have mounted
>
> [*3 Henry VI*, V. vi. 61-2]

let him never pretend discernment hereafter in any case of this nature. (pp. 316-17)

> *Edward Capell, in an extract from* Shakespeare, the Critical Heritage: 1765-1774, Vol. 5, *edited by Brian Vickers, Routledge & Kegan Paul, 1979, pp. 303-27.*

[FRANCIS GENTLEMAN]   (essay date 1774)

[*Gentleman was an actor as well as a playwright, and he was especially concerned with how Shakespeare's plays should be performed in the theater. In the following excerpt on* Henry VI, *he considers Shakespeare's presentation of historical figures "faithful and adequate," an opinion also voiced by Edward Capell (1768) but opposed by Charlotte Lennox (1754). Yet Gentleman faults the trilogy for a "sameness of incidents," a lack of sympathetic material, and a confused ordering of events which, in his assessment, make it unworthy of production.*]

However commendable our Author might be in his desire of furnishing a Dramatic commemoration of such incidents and characters as are materially connected with the history of this island, yet we think him particularly unhappy in tracing the troubles and imbecilities of *Henry* the Sixth; for though he is very faithful and adequate in delineating personages, and correct in regard to facts, yet there is such an unavoidable sameness of incidents, such a want of matter in general to touch the tender passions, such a repetition of unentertaining, nay sometimes vulgar squabbles, amongst elevated characters, such repeated slaughters, and such a confused precipitancy of events, that these pieces cannot, with any great hope of success, be produced in action. In several places, it is true, the *"Muse of fire"* evidently breaks forth; and it is most certain no other author could have brought so much historical matter into the same compass, to so much and so great advantage.

> [*Francis Gentleman*], *in an introduction to "King Henry VI, Part III," in* Bell's Edition of Shakespeare's Plays, Vol. VII *by William Shakespeare, John Bell, 1774, p. 275.*

EDMOND MALONE   (essay date 1787)

[*An eighteenth-century Irish literary scholar and editor, Malone was the first critic to establish a chronology of Shakespeare's plays. He was also the first scholar to prepare a critical edition of Shakespeare's sonnets and the first to write a comprehensive history of the English stage based on extensive research into original sources. As the major Shakespearean editor of the eighteenth century, Malone collaborated with George Steevens on Steevens's second and third editions of Shakespeare's plays, and issued his own edition in 1790. The following excerpt is taken from Malone's "A Dissertation of the Three Parts of 'King Henry VI'" (1787). Although Lewis Theobald (1733) and other critics had doubted the authenticity of the* Henry VI *trilogy earlier in the eighteenth century, Malone was the first to present a detailed challenge to Shakespeare's authorship of these plays. Malone hypothesizes that* 1 Henry VI *was the work of "some ancient dramatist," and that in* 2 *and* 3 Henry VI *Shakespeare merely revised two earlier plays,* The First Part of the Contention *and* The True Tragedy of Richard Duke of Yorke, *which had been printed in quarto form. He relies on some external evidence to support his theory—for instance, that the quartos were printed anonymously and that these plays appear to rely on Hall as a source (Hall was not "Shakespeare's historian," according to Malone). But Malone's proof rests principally on his examination of the versification in the plays, which he compares with the poetry in Shakespeare's undisputed dramas. He concludes that the versification in* 1 Henry VI *is not only unlike that in* 2 *and* 3 Henry*

VI, but is unlike that in any other Shakespearean play. He finds that the quarto plays show no evidence of the peculiarly Shakespearean "inaccuracies and phraseology" found in* 2 *and* 3 Henry VI. *Malone's view of the authorship of the trilogy influenced such later critics as G. G. Gervinus (1849-50), Jane Lee (1876), George Brandes, and F. G. Fleay (see Additional Bibliography) in their treatments of the authorship controversy. One exception to this critical trend in the nineteenth century was Henry Norman Hudson (1851), who attributed all three plays to Shakespeare. It was not until the works of Peter Alexander and Madeleine Doran (see Additional Bibliography) were published in the late 1920s that Malone's theory was generally rejected by Shakespeare critics. One notable scholar who was not persuaded by Alexander and Doran was John Dover Wilson (see Additional Bibliography), who maintained that in the* Henry VI *plays Shakespeare either collaborated with or revised the work of other dramatists.*]

Several passages in *The* Second *and* Third *Part of King Henry VI.* appearing evidently to be of the hand of Shakspeare, I was long of opinion that the *three* historical dramas which are the subject of the present disquisition, were properly ascribed to him; not then doubting that the whole of these plays was the production of the same person. But a more minute investigation of the subject, into which I have been led by the present revision of all our author's works, has convinced me, that, though the premises were true, my conclusion was too hastily drawn; for though the hand of Shakspeare is unquestionably found in the two latter of these plays, it does not therefore necessarily follow, that they were *originally* and *entirely* composed by him. (p. 381)

What at present I have chiefly in view is, to account for the visible *inequality* in these pieces; many traits of Shakspeare being clearly discernible in them, while the inferior parts are not merely unequal to the rest, (from which no certain conclusion can be drawn,) but of quite a different complexion from the inferior parts of our author's undoubted performances.

My hypothesis then is, that *The* First *Part of K. Henry VI.* as it now appears, (of which no quarto copy is extant,) was the entire or nearly the entire production of some ancient dramatist; that *The Whole Contention of the two Houses of York and Lancaster,* &c. written probably before the year 1590, and printed in quarto, in 1600, was also the composition of some writer who preceded Shakspeare; and that from this piece, which is in two parts, (the former of which is entitled, *The first Part of the Contention of the two famous Houses of Yorke and Lancaster, with the death of the good duke Humphrey,* &c. and the latter, *The true Tragedie of Richard duke of Yorke, and the death of good King Henrie the Sixt,*) our poet formed the two plays, entitled *The* Second *and* Third *Parts of King Henry VI.* as they appear in the first folio edition of his works.

Mr. [John] Upton has asked, "How does the painter distinguish copies from originals but by manner and style? And have not authors their peculiar style and manner, from which a true critick can form as unerring a judgment as a painter?" Dr. Johnson [see excerpt above, 1765], though he has shewn, with his usual acuteness, that "this illustration of the critick's science will not prove what is desired," acknowledges in a preceding note, that "dissimilitude of style and heterogeneousness of sentiment may sufficiently shew that a work does not really belong to the reputed author. But in these plays (he adds) no such marks of spuriousness are found. The diction, the versification, and the figures, are Shakspeare's."—By these criterions then let us examine *The* First *Part of K. Henry VI.* (for I choose to consider that piece separately;) and if the diction, the figures, or rather the allusions, and the versification of that play, (for these are our surest guides) shall appear to be different from the other two parts, *as they are exhibited in the folio,* and from our author's other plays, we may fairly conclude that he was not the writer of it.

With respect to the diction and the allusions, which I shall consider under the same head, it is very observable that in *The* First *Part of King Henry VI.* there are more allusions to mythology, to classical authors, and to ancient and modern history, than, I believe, can be found in any one piece of our author's written on an English story; and that these allusions are introduced very much in the same manner as they are introduced in the plays of Greene, Peele, Lodge, and other dramatists who preceded Shakspeare; that is, they do not naturally arise out of the subject, but seem to be inserted merely to shew the writer's learning. (pp. 381-83)

Of particular expressions there are many in this play, that seem to me more likely to have been used by the authors [mentioned above], than by Shakspeare; but I confess, with Dr. Johnson, that single words can conclude little. (p. 384)

The versification of this play appears to me clearly of a different colour from that of all our author's genuine dramas, while at the same time it resembles that of many of the plays produced before the time of Shakspeare.

Part I. Act I. Scene vi. Reignier, Joan de Pucelle, the Dolphin, and Soldiers. Frontispiece to the Rowe edition (1709). By permission of the Folger Shakespeare Library.

In all the tragedies written before his time, or just when he commenced author, a certain stately march of versification is very observable. The sense concludes or pauses almost uniformly at the end of every line; and the verse has scarcely ever a redundant syllable. (pp. 384-85)

The tragedies [by T. Lodge, R. Greene, and T. Kyd] . . . will all furnish examples of a similar versification; a versification so exactly corresponding with that of *The first Part of King Henry VI.* and *The Whole Contention of the two Houses of Yorke and Lancaster,* &c. as it originally appeared, that I have no doubt these plays were the production of some one or other of [these] authors. . . .

A passage in a pamphlet written by Thomas Nashe [see excerpt above, 1592], an intimate friend of Greene, Peele, &c. shews that The *first* part of *King Henry VI.* had been on the stage before 1592; and his favourable mention of this piece inclines me to believe that it was written by a friend of his. (p. 390)

This passage was several years ago pointed out by my friend Dr. [Richard] Farmer, as a proof of the hypothesis which I am now endeavouring to establish. That it related to the old play of *K. Henry VI.* or, as it is now called, *The* first *Part of King Henry VI.* cannot, I think, be doubted. *Talbot* appears in the *first* part, and not in the *second* or *third* part; and is expressly spoken of in the play, (as well as in Hall's Chronicle) as "the terror of the French." Holinshed, who was Shakspeare's guide, omits the passage in Hall, in which Talbot is thus described; and this is an additional proof that this play was not our author's. (pp. 390-91)

The first *part of King Henry VI.* (as it is now called) furnishes us with other *internal* proofs also of its not being the work of Shakspeare.

The author of that play, whoever he was, does not seem to have known precisely how old Henry the Sixth was at the time of his father's death. He opens his play indeed with the funeral of Henry the Fifth, but no where mentions expressly the young king's age. It is clear, however, from one passage, that he supposed him to have passed the state of infancy before he lost his father, and even to have remembered some of his sayings. . . . But Shakspeare, as appears from two passages, one in the *second* [IV. ix. 3-4], and the other in the *third* part of *King Henry VI.* [I. i. 112], knew that that king could not possibly remember any thing his father had said; and therefore Shakspeare could not have been the author of the *first* part. (p. 391)

A second internal proof that Shakspeare was not the author of the *first* part of these three plays, is furnished by that scene [II. iv. 90-9], in which it is said, that the earl of Cambridge *raised an army* against his sovereign. But Shakspeare in his play of *K. Henry V.* has represented the matter truly as it was; the earl being in the second act of that historical piece condemned at Southampton for conspiring to *assassinate* Henry.

I may likewise add, that the author of The *first* part of *K. Henry VI.* knew the true pronunciation of the word *Hecate,* and has used it as it is used by the Roman writers:

> I speak not to that railing *Heca-té.*
>
> [III. i. 64]

But Shakspeare in his *Macbeth* always uses *Hecate* as a dissyllable; and therefore could not have been the author of the other piece. (p. 392)

Before I quit this part of the subject, it may be proper to mention one other circumstance that renders it very improbable that Shakspeare should have been the author of The *First* Part of *K. Henry VI.* In this play, though one scene is entirely in rhyme, there are very few rhymes dispersed through the piece, and no alternate rhymes; both of which abound in our author's undisputed *early* plays. This observation indeed may likewise be extended to the *second* and *third* part of these historical dramas; and perhaps it may be urged, that if this argument has any weight, it will prove that he had no hand in the composition of those plays. But there being no alternate rhymes in those two plays may be accounted for, by recollecting that in 1591, Shakspeare had not written his *Venus and Adonis,* or his *Rape of Lucrece;* the measures of which perhaps insensibly led him to employ a similar kind of metre occasionally in the dramas that he wrote shortly after he had composed those poems. The paucity of regular rhymes must be accounted for differently. My solution is, that working up the materials which were furnished by a preceding writer, he naturally followed his mode: and in the original plays from which these two were formed very few rhymes are found. Nearly the same argument will apply to the *first* part; for its date also, were that piece Shakspeare's, would account for the want of alternate rhymes. The paucity of regular rhymes indeed cannot be accounted for by saying that here too our author was following the track of another poet; but the solution is unnecessary; for from the beginning to the end of that play, except perhaps in some scenes of the fourth act, there is not a single print of the footsteps of Shakspeare. (pp. 394-95)

It has long been a received opinion that the two quarto plays, one of which was published under the title of *The First Part of the Contention of the two Houses of Yorke and Lancaster,* &c. and the other under the title of *The true Tragedie of Richarde duke of Yorke,* &c. were spurious and imperfect copies of Shakspeare's *Second* and *Third Part of King Henry VI.;* and many passages have been quoted in the notes to the late editions of Shakspeare, as containing merely the various readings of the quartos and the folio; the passages being supposed to be in substance the same, only variously exhibited in different copies. The variations have been accounted for, by supposing that the imperfect and spurious quarto copies (as they were called) were taken down either by an unskilful short-hand writer, or by some auditor who picked up "during the representation what the time would permit, then filled up some of his omissions at a second or third hearing, and when he had by this method formed something like a play, sent it to the printer." To this opinion, I with others for a long time subscribed: two of Heywood's pieces furnishing indubitable proofs that plays in the time of our author were sometimes imperfectly copied during the representation, by the ear, or by short-hand writers. But a minute examination of the two pieces in question, and a careful comparison of them with Shakspeare's *Second* and *Third Part of King Henry VI.* have convinced me that this could not have been the case with respect to them. No fraudulent copyist or short-hand writer would invent circumstances *totally different* from those which appear in Shakspeare's new-molded draughts as exhibited in the first folio; or insert *whole speeches,* of which scarcely a trace is found in that edition. (pp. 406-07)

The supposition of imperfect or spurious copies cannot account for such numerous variations in the *circumstances* of these pieces; (not to insist at present on the *language* in which they are clothed;) so that we are compelled (as I have already observed) to maintain, either that Shakespeare wrote *two* plays

on the story which forms his *Second Part of King Henry VI.* a hasty sketch, and an entirely distinct and more finished performance; or else we must acknowledge that he formed that piece on a foundation laid by another writer, that is, upon the quarto copy of *The First Part of the Contention of the Houses of Yorke and Lancaster,* &c.—And the same argument precisely applies to *The Third Part of King Henry VI.* which is founded on *The true Tragedie of Richard duke of Yorke,* &c. (p. 412)

Let us now advert to the *Resemblances* that are found in these pieces as exhibited in the folio, to passages in our author's undisputed plays; and also to the *Inconsistencies* that may be traced between them; and, if I do not deceive myself, both the one and the other will add considerable support to the foregoing observations.

In our author's genuine plays, he frequently borrows from himself, the same thoughts being found in nearly the same expressions in different pieces. In *The* Second *and* Third *Part of King Henry VI.* as in his other dramas, these coincidencies with his other works may be found; and this was one of the circumstances that once weighed much in my mind, and convinced me of their authenticity. But a collation of these plays with the old pieces on which they are founded, has shewn me the fallacy by which I was deceived; for the passages of these two parts of *K. Henry VI.* which correspond with others in our author's undisputed plays, exist *only* in the *folio* copy, and not in the *quarto;* in other words, in those parts of these new-modelled pieces, which were of Shakspeare's writing, and not in the originals by another hand, on which he worked. (pp. 412-13)

[It] is undoubtedly a very striking circumstance that *almost* all the passages in The *Second* and *Third Part of King Henry VI.* which resemble others in Shakspeare's undisputed plays, are not found in the original pieces in quarto, but in his *Rifacimento* ["refashioning"] published in folio. As these Resemblances to his other plays, and a peculiar Shakspearian phraseology, ascertain a *considerable portion* of these disputed dramas to be the production of Shakspeare, so on the other hand certain passages which are *discordant* (in matters of fact) from his other plays, are proved by this *Discordancy,* not to have been composed by him; and these discordant passages, being found in the original quarto plays, prove that those pieces were composed by another writer. (pp. 414-15)

One point only remains. It may be asked, if *The First Part of King Henry VI.* was not written by Shakspeare, why did Heminge and Condell print it with the rest of his works? The only way that I can account for their having done so, is by supposing, either that their memory at the end of thirty years was not accurate concerning our author's pieces, (as appears indeed evidently from their omitting *Troilus and Cressida,* which was not recollected by them, till the whole of the first folio, and even the table of contents, (which is always the last work of the press,) had been printed; or, that they imagined the insertion of this historical drama was necessary to understanding the two pieces that follow it; or lastly, that, Shakspeare, for the advantage of his own theatre, having written a few lines in *The* First *Part of King Henry VI.* after his own *Second* and *Third* Part had been played, they conceived this a sufficient warrant for attributing it, along with the others, to him, in the general collection of his works. If Shakspeare was the author of any part of this play, perhaps the second and the following scenes of the fourth act were his; which are for the most part written in rhyme, and appear to me somewhat of a different complexion from the rest of the play. (p. 424)

Shakspeare's referring in the Epilogue to *K. Henry V.* which was produced in 1599, to these three parts of *King Henry VI.* of which the first, by whom soever it was written, appears from the testimony of a contemporary to have been exhibited with great applause; and the two latter, having been, as I conceive, eight years before new-modelled and almost re-written by our author, we may be confident were performed with the most brilliant success; his supplicating the favour of the audience to his new play of *King Henry V.* *"for the sake"* of these old and *popular* dramas, which were so closely connected with it, and in the composition of which, as they had for many years been exhibited, he had so considerable a share; the connexion between the last scene of *King Henry VI.* and the first scene of *K. Richard III.;* the Shakspearian diction, versification, and figures, by which the *Second* and *Third Part of King Henry VI.* are distinguished; "the easiness of expression and the fluency of numbers," which, it is acknowledged, are found here, and were possessed by no other author of that age; all these circumstances are accounted for by the theory now stated, and all the objections that have been founded upon them, in my apprehension, vanish away.

On the other hand, the entry on the Stationers' books of the old play, entitled *The first part of the Contention of the two houses of Yorke and Lancaster,* &c. without the name of the author; that piece, and *The true Tragedie of Richarde duke of Yorke,* &c. being printed in 1600, anonymously; their being founded on the Chronicle of *Hall,* who was not Shakspeare's historian, and represented by the servants of Lord Pembroke, by whom none of his uncontested dramas were represented; the colour, diction, and versification of these old plays; the various circumstances, lines, and speeches, that are found in them, and not in our author's new-modification of them, as published in folio by his original editors; the resemblances that have been noticed between his other works and such parts of these dramas as are *only* exhibited in their folio edition; the discordances (in matters of fact) between certain parts of the old plays printed in quarto and Shakspeare's undoubted performances; the transpositions that he has made in these pieces; the repetitions, and the peculiar Shakspearian inaccuracies, and phraseology, which may be traced in the folio, and not in the old quarto plays; these and other circumstances, which have been stated in the foregoing pages, form, when united, such a body of argument and proofs, in support of my hypothesis, as appears to me, (though I will not venture to assert that "the probation bears no hinge nor loop to hang a doubt on,) to lead directly to the door of *truth.*" (pp. 425-26)

Edmond Malone, *"A Dissertation of the Three Parts of 'King Henry VI',"* in The Plays and Poems of William Shakspeare, Vol. 6 *by William Shakespeare, edited by Edmond Malone, AMS Press, 1968, pp. 381-429.*

AUGUST WILHELM SCHLEGEL   (lecture date 1808)

[Schlegel holds a key place in the history of Shakespeare's reputation in European criticism. His translations of thirteen of the plays are still considered the best German editions of Shakespeare. Schlegel was also a leading spokesman for the Romantic movement which permanently overthrew the Neoclassical contention that Shakespeare was a child of nature whose plays lacked artistic form. As evidenced in the following excerpt, Schlegel was one of the first critics to view the Henry VI *trilogy as part of a*

larger Shakespearean epic comprising the ten English history plays, a point later developed by E. M. W. Tillyard (1944). Schlegel praises Shakespeare's ability to move his audience through characterization and depiction of emotion, and he describes Cardinal Beauford's death-bed scene as "sublime beyond all praise." His view of the Margaret-Suffolk relationship as "invested with tragical dignity" is in sharp contrast with that of Charlotte Lennox (1754), Anna Brownell Jameson (1833), and Marilyn French (1981), all of whom condemned Shakespeare's depiction of the affair. Schlegel's essay was originally delivered as a lecture in 1808 and first published in 1811 in his Über dramatische Kunst und Literatur.]

The dramas derived from the English history, ten in number, form one of the most valuable of Shakspeare's works, and partly the fruit of his maturest age. I say advisedly *one* of his works, for the poet evidently intended them to form one great whole. It is, as it were, an historical heroic poem in the dramatic form, of which the separate plays constitute the rhapsodies. The principal features of the events are exhibited with such fidelity; their causes, and even their secret springs, are placed in such a clear light, that we may attain from them a knowledge of history in all its truth, while the living picture makes an impression on the imagination which can never be effaced. (p. 419)

The three parts of *Henry the Sixth* . . . were composed much earlier than [*1* and *2 Henry IV* and *Henry V*]. Shakspeare's choice fell first on this period of English history, so full of misery and horrors of every kind, because the pathetic is naturally more suitable than the characteristic to a young poet's mind. We do not yet find here the whole maturity of his genius, yet certainly its whole strength. Careless as to the apparent unconnectedness of contemporary events, he bestows little attention on preparation and development: all the figures follow in rapid succession, and announce themselves emphatically for what we ought to take them; from scenes where the effect is sufficiently agitating to form the catastrophe of a less extensive plan, the poet perpetually hurries us on to catastrophes still more dreadful. The first Part contains only the first forming of the parties of the White and Red Rose, under which blooming ensigns such bloody deeds were afterwards perpetrated; the varying results of the war in France principally fill the stage. The wonderful saviour of her country, Joan of Arc, is portrayed by Shakspeare with an Englishman's prejudices: yet he at first leaves it doubtful whether she has not in reality a heavenly mission; she appears in the pure glory of virgin heroism; by her supernatural eloquence (and this circumstance is of the poet's invention) she wins over the Duke of Burgundy to the French cause; afterwards, corrupted by vanity and luxury, she has recourse to hellish fiends, and comes to a miserable end. To her is opposed Talbot, a rough iron warrior, who moves us the more powerfully, as, in the moment when he is threatened with inevitable death, all his care is tenderly directed to save his son, who performs his first deeds of arms under his eye. After Talbot has in vain sacrificed himself, and the Maid of Orleans has fallen into the hands of the English, the French provinces are completely lost by an impolitic marriage; and with this the piece ends. The conversation between the aged Mortimer in prison, and Richard Plantagenet, afterwards Duke of York, contains an exposition of the claims of the latter to the throne: considered by itself it is a beautiful tragic elegy.

In the Second Part, the events more particularly prominent are the murder of the honest Protector, Gloster, and its consequences; the death of Cardinal Beaufort; the parting of the Queen from her favourite Suffolk, and his death by the hands of savage pirates; then the insurrection of Jack Cade under an assumed name, and at the instigation of the Duke of York. The short scene where Cardinal Beaufort, who is tormented by his conscience on account of the murder of Gloster, is visited on his death-bed by Henry VI. is sublime beyond all praise. Can any other poet be named who has drawn aside the curtain of eternity at the close of this life with such overpowering and awful effect? And yet it is not mere horror with which the mind is filled, but solemn emotion; a blessing and a curse stand side by side; the pious King is an image of the heavenly mercy which, even in the sinner's last moments, labours to enter into his soul. The adulterous passion of Queen Margaret and Suffolk is invested with tragical dignity and all low and ignoble ideas carefully kept out of sight. Without attempting to gloss over the crime of which both are guilty, without seeking to remove our disapprobation of this criminal love, he still, by the magic force of expression, contrives to excite in us a sympathy with their sorrow. In the insurrection of Cade he has delineated the conduct of a popular demagogue, the fearful ludicrousness of the anarchical tumult of the people, with such convincing truth, that one would believe he was an eye-witness of many of the events of our age, which, from ignorance of history, have been considered as without example.

The civil war only begins in the Second Part; in the Third it is unfolded in its full destructive fury. The picture becomes gloomier and gloomier; and seems at last to be painted rather with blood than with colours. With horror we behold fury giving birth to fury, vengeance to vengeance, and see that when all the bonds of human society are violently torn asunder, even noble matrons became hardened to cruelty. The most bitter contempt is the portion of the unfortunate; no one affords to his enemy that pity which he will himself shortly stand in need of. With all party is family, country, and religion, the only spring of action. As York, whose ambition is coupled with noble qualities, prematurely perishes, the object of the whole contest is now either to support an imbecile king, or to place on the throne a luxurious monarch, who shortens the dear-bought possession by the gratification of an insatiable voluptuousness. For this the celebrated and magnanimous Warwick spends his chivalrous life; Clifford revenges the death of his father with blood-thirsty filial love; and Richard, for the elevation of his brother, practises those dark deeds by which he is soon after to pave the way to his own greatness. In the midst of the general misery, of which he has been the innocent cause, King Henry appears like the powerless image of a saint, in whose wonder-working influence no man any longer believes: he can but sigh and weep over the enormities which he witnesses. In his simplicity, however, the gift of prophecy is lent to this pious king: in the moment of his death, at the close of this great tragedy, he prophesies a still more dreadful tragedy with which futurity is pregnant, as much distinguished for the poisonous wiles of cold-blooded wickedness as the former for deeds of savage fury. (pp. 432-35)

August Wilhelm Schlegel, "Criticisms on Shakspeare's Historical Dramas," in his A Course of Lectures on Dramatic Art and Literature, *edited by Rev. A.J.W. Morrison, translated by John Black, revised edition, 1846. Reprint by AMS Press, Inc., 1965, pp. 414-45.*

WILLIAM HAZLITT (essay date 1817)

[*Hazlitt is considered a leading Shakespearean critic of the English Romantic movement. A prolific essayist and critic on a wide range of subjects, Hazlitt remarked in the preface to his* Characters of Shakespear's Plays, *first published in 1817, that he was inspired by the German critic August Wilhelm Schlegel and was determined to supplant what he considered the pernicious influence of Samuel Johnson's Shakespearean criticism. Hazlitt's criticism is typically Romantic in his emphasis on character studies. Also, his experience as a drama critic played an important role in shaping his descriptive, as opposed to analytical, interpretations of Shakespeare. In the following excerpt from the work mentioned above, Hazlitt expresses the view that the* Henry VI *trilogy is stylistically inferior to Shakespeare's other history plays. However, he approves Shakespeare's depiction of characters, especially the two deposed kings, Henry VI and Richard II. Hazlitt views Henry VI as good-natured and indolent, fearful of misusing his power, whereas he regards Richard II as "proud, revengeful," and thoughtless in his political ambitions. Other critics who have examined the characterization of Henry VI include Edward Dowden (1881), Harold C. Goddard (1951), M. M. Reese (1961), Michael Manheim (1973), and John D. Cox (1978).*]

During the time of the civil wars of York and Lancaster, England was a perfect bear-garden, and Shakespear has given us a very lively picture of the scene. The three parts of *Henry VI.* convey a picture of very little else; and are inferior to the other historical plays. They have brilliant passages; but the general ground-work is comparatively poor and meagre, the style "flat and unraised." There are few lines like the following:—

> Glory is like a circle in the water;
> Which never ceaseth to enlarge itself,
> Till by broad spreading it disperse to nought.
> *[1 Henry VI, I. ii. 133-35]*

The first part relates to the wars in France after the death of Henry V. and the story of the Maid of Orleans. She is here almost as scurvily treated as in Voltaire's Pucelle. Talbot is a very magnificent sketch: there is something as formidable in this portrait of him, as there would be in a monumental figure of him or in the sight of the armour which he wore. The scene in which he visits the Countess Auvergne, who seeks to entrap him, is a very spirited one, and his description of his own treatment while a prisoner to the French not less remarkable. (pp. 133-34)

The second part relates chiefly to the contests between the nobles during the minority of Henry, and the death of Gloucester, the good Duke Humphrey. The character of Cardinal Beaufort is the most prominent in the group: the account of his death is one of our author's master-pieces. So is the speech of Gloucester to the nobles on the loss of the provinces of France by the King's marriage with Margaret of Anjou. The pretensions and growing ambition of the Duke of York, the father of Richard III. are also very ably developed. Among the episodes, the tragi-comedy of Jack Cade, and the detection of the impostor Simcox are truly edifying.

The third part describes Henry's loss of his crown: his death takes place in the last act, which is usually thrust into the common acting play of *Richard III.* The character of Gloucester, afterwards King Richard, is here very powerfully commenced, and his dangerous designs and long-reaching ambition are fully described in his soliloquy in the third act, beginning, "Aye, Edward will use women honourably" [*3 Henry VI*, III. ii. 124]. Henry VI. is drawn as distinctly as his high-spirited Queen, and notwithstanding the very mean figure which Henry makes as a King, we still feel more respect for him than for his wife. (pp. 134-35)

The characters and situations of [Richard II. and Henry VI.] were so nearly alike, that they would have been completely confounded by a common-place poet. Yet they are kept quite distinct in Shakespear. Both were kings, and both unfortunate. Both lost their crowns owing to their mismanagement and imbecility; the one from a thoughtless, wilful abuse of power, the other from an indifference to it. The manner in which they bear their misfortunes corresponds exactly to the causes which led to them. The one is always lamenting the loss of his power which he has not the spirit to regain; the other seems only to regret that he had ever been king, and is glad to be rid of the power, with the trouble; the effeminacy of the one is that of a voluptuary, proud, revengeful, impatient of contradiction, and inconsolable in his misfortunes; the effeminacy of the other is that of an indolent, good-natured mind, naturally averse to the turmoils of ambition and the cares of greatness, and who wishes to pass his time in monkish indolence and contemplation.—Richard bewails the loss of the kingly power only as it was the means of gratifying his pride and luxury; Henry regards it only as a means of doing right, and is less desirous of the advantages to be derived from possessing it than afraid of exercising it wrong. (pp. 135-36)

> William Hazlitt, *"Characters of Shakespear's Plays: 'Henry VI', in Three Parts," in his* Characters of Shakespear's Plays & Lectures on the English Poets, *Macmillan and Co. Limited, 1903, pp. 133-40.*

MRS. [ANNA BROWNELL] JAMESON   (essay date 1833)

[*Jameson was a well-known nineteenth-century essayist. Her essays and criticism span the end of the Romantic age and the beginning of Victorian realism, reflecting elements of both periods. She is best remembered for her study* Shakspeare's Heroines *(1833), which was originally published in a slightly different form in 1832 as* Characteristics of Women: Moral, Poetical, and Historical. *This work demonstrates both her historical interests and her sympathetic appreciation of Shakespeare's female characters. In an unexcerpted portion of her essay on Margaret of Anjou, Jameson addresses the question raised by Edmond Malone (1787) on the authenticity of the* Henry VI *trilogy. In the excerpt below, she argues that, despite unmistakable signs of Shakespeare's authorship in 2 and 3* Henry VI, *the style of the trilogy is generally inferior to the rest of his works. Jameson's thesis is that the character of Margaret is a strong argument against the authenticity of the plays. She describes Margaret as "a heroine without a touch of heroism," lacking "a single personal quality which would excite our interest in her bravely-endured misfortunes." Even though Jameson suggests that Shakespeare may have written some of her more poetical speeches, such as the scene where Margaret and Suffolk part in 2* Henry VI, *she contends that some other dramatist conceived the character of Margaret herself. For further discussion of the character of Margaret, as well as the other women in the* Henry VI *plays, see the excerpts by Charlotte Lennox (1754), Henry Norman Hudson (1851), J. A. R. Marriott (1918), David M. Bevington (1966), H. M. Richmond (1967), Leslie A. Fiedler (1972), and Marilyn French (1981).*]

To me it appears that the three parts of "Henry VI." have less of poetry and passion and more of unnecessary verbosity and inflated language than the rest of Shakespeare's works, that the continual exhibition of treachery, bloodshed, and violence is revolting, and the want of unity of action and of a pervading interest oppressive and fatiguing; but also that there are splendid passages in the Second and Third Parts such as Shakspeare alone could have written. And this in not denied by the most sceptical [of critics].

Among the arguments against the authenticity of these plays, the character of Margaret of Anjou has not been adduced, and yet to those who have studied Shakspeare in his own spirit it

will appear the most conclusive of all. When we compare her with his other female characters, we are struck at once by the want of family likeness: Shakspeare was not always equal, but he had not two *manners,* as they say of painters. I discern his hand in particular parts, but I cannot recognise his spirit in the conception of the whole. He may have laid on some of the colours, but the original design has a certain hardness and heaviness very unlike his usual style. Margaret of Anjou, as exhibited in these tragedies, is a dramatic portrait of considerable truth and vigour and consistency, but she is not one of Shakspeare's women. He, who knew so well in what true greatness of spirit consisted, who could excite our respect and sympathy even for a Lady Macbeth, would never have given us a heroine without a touch of heroism; he would not have portrayed a high-hearted woman struggling unsubdued against the strangest vicissitudes of fortune, meeting reverses and disasters, such as would have broken the most masculine spirit, with unshaken constancy, yet left her without a single personal quality which would excite our interest in her bravely-endured misfortunes; and this, too, in the very face of history. He would not have given us, in lieu of the magnanimous queen, the subtle and accomplished Frenchwoman, a mere "Amazonian trull," with every coarser feature of depravity and ferocity; he would have redeemed her from unmingled detestation; he would have breathed into her some of his own sweet spirit; he would have given the woman a soul. (pp. 280-82)

Margaret is portrayed with all the exterior graces of her sex: as bold and artful, with spirit to dare, resolution to act, and fortitude to endure, but treacherous, haughty, dissembling, vindictive, and fierce. The bloody struggle for power in which she was engaged, and the companionship of the ruthless iron men around her, seem to have left her nothing of womanhood but the heart of a mother—that last stronghold of our feminine nature! So far, the character is consistently drawn; it has something of the power, but none of the flowing ease of Shakspeare's manner. There are fine materials not well applied, there is poetry in some of the scenes and speeches, the situations are often exceedingly poetical, but in the character of Margaret herself there is not an atom of poetry. In her artificial dignity, her plausible wit, and her endless volubility, she would remind us of some of the most admired heroines of French tragedy but for that unlucky box on the ear which she gives the Duchess of Glo'ster—a violation of tragic decorum which, of course, destroys all parallel.

Having said thus much, I shall point out some of the finest and most characteristic scenes in which Margaret appears. The speech in which she expresses her scorn of her meek husband, and her impatience of the power exercised by those fierce, overbearing barons, York, Salisbury, Warwick, Buckingham, is very fine, and conveys as faithful an idea of those feudal times as of the woman who speaks. (pp. 282-83)

Her intriguing spirit, the facility with which she enters into the murderous confederacy against the good Duke Humphrey, the artful plausibility with which she endeavours to turn suspicion from herself, confounding her gentle consort by mere dint of words, are exceedingly characteristic, but not the less revolting.

Her criminal love for Suffolk (which is a dramatic incident, not an historic fact), gives rise to the beautiful parting scene in the third act, a scene which it is impossible to read without a thrill of emotion, hurried away by that power and pathos which forces us to sympathise with the eloquence of grief, yet excites not a momentary interest either for Margaret or her lover. The ungoverned fury of Margaret in the first instance, the manner in which she calls on Suffolk to curse his enemies, and then shrinks back overcome by the violence of the spirit she had herself evoked, and terrified by the vehemence of his imprecations, the transition in her mind from the extremity of rage to tears and melting fondness, have been pronounced, and justly, to be in Shakspeare's own manner. . . . (pp. 283-84)

In the third part of "Henry VI.", Margaret, engaged in the terrible struggle for her husband's throne, appears to rather more advantage. The indignation against Henry, who had pitifully yielded his son's birthright, for the privilege of reigning unmolested during his own life, is worthy of her, and gives rise to a beautiful speech. We are here inclined to sympathise with her; but soon after follows the murder of the Duke of York; and the base revengful spirit and atrocious cruelty with which she insults over him, unarmed and a prisoner—the bitterness of her mockery, and the unwomanly malignity with which she presents him with the napkin stained with the blood of his youngest son and "bids the father wipe his eyes withal" [*3 Henry VI*, I. iv. 139], turn all our sympathy into aversion and horror. (pp. 284-85)

> Mrs. [Anna Brownell] Jameson, "Margaret of Anjou," in her Shakspeare's Heroines: Characteristics of Women, Moral, Poetical, & Historical, *George Newnes, Limited, 1897, pp. 280-87.*

SAMUEL TAYLOR COLERIDGE   (essay date 1834?)

[*Coleridge's lectures and writings on Shakespeare form a major chapter in the history of English Shakespearean criticism. As the channel for the critical ideas of the German Romantics and as an original interpreter of Shakespeare in the new spirit of Romanticism, Coleridge played a strategic role in overthrowing the last remains of the Neoclassical approach to Shakespeare and in establishing the modern view of the dramatist as a conscious artist and masterful portrayer of human character. Coleridge's remarks on Shakespeare come down to posterity largely as fragmentary notes, marginalia, and reports by auditors on the lectures, rather than in polished essays. The excerpt below was reproduced by the Coleridge editor T. M. Raysor from marginalia found in Coleridge's hand in a one-volume edition of Shakespeare's works. This volume was owned by Ann and James Gillman, with whom Coleridge resided from 1816 until his death in 1834 and during which time he penned the marginalia from which the following is taken. Coleridge's brief comments on the opening lines of* 1 Henry VI *constitute an unequivocal claim that Shakespeare could not have written them, a suggestion more fully developed, with respect to the entire play, by Edmond Malone (1787), G. G. Gervinus (1849-50), Jane Lee (1876), and John Dover Wilson (see Additional Bibliography).*]

> Hung be the heavens with black, yield day to night!
> Comets, importing change of times and states,
> Brandish your crystal tresses in the sky;
> And with them scourge the bad revolting stars
> That have consented unto Henry's death!
> Henry the Fifth, too famous to live long!
> England ne'er lost a king of so much worth.
>   [*1 Henry VI*, I. i. 1-7]

Read aloud any two or three passages in blank verse even from Shakespeare's earliest dramas, as *Love's Labor['s] Lost* and *Romeo and Juliet;* and then read in the same way the introductory speech of *Henry VI*, [Part] I, with especial attention to the *metre;* and if you do not feel the impossibility of the latter having been written by Shakespeare, all I dare suggest is, that you may have ears, for so have asses! But *an ear* you can not have, *judice* ["in my judgment"].

> Samuel Taylor Coleridge, "Notes on the History Plays of Shakespeare: 'Henry VI, Part I'," in his Shakespearean Criticism, Vol. 1, *edited by Thomas Middleton Raysor, second edition, Dutton, 1960, p. 127.*

HERMANN ULRICI   (essay date 1839)

[*A German scholar, Ulrici was a professor of philosophy and the author of works on Greek poetry and Shakespeare. The following excerpt is from an English translation of his* Über Shakespeares dramatische Kunst, und sein Verhältniss zu Calderon und Göthe, *a work first published in 1839. This study exemplifies the "philosophical criticism" developed in Germany during the nineteenth century. The immediate sources for Ulrici's critical approach appear to be August Wilhelm Schlegel's conception of the play as an organic, interconnected whole and Georg Wilhelm Friedrich Hegel's view of drama as an embodiment of the conflict of historical forces and ideas. Unlike his fellow German Shakespearean critic G. G. Gervinus, Ulrici sought to develop a specifically Christian aesthetics, but one which, as he carefully points out in the introduction to the work mentioned above, in no way intrudes on "that unity of idea, which preeminently constitutes a work of art a living creation in the world of beauty." In an unexcerpted portion of his essay on Shakespeare's entire historical "cycle," Ulrici established himself as one of the earliest critics to consider* Henry IV's *usurpation of the throne from* Richard II *the original cause of England's civil dissension under* Henry VI *and* Richard III. *In the excerpt below, Ulrici traces the inevitable course of "the general corruption" begun by Henry IV's evil deed. Pointing out that no individual within the nation is exempt, he perceives divine purpose behind the civil war and the "purification" of defeat. Thus, the Christian concepts of original sin and divine retribution are the key themes that Ulrici uncovers in Shakespeare's trilogy. Critics who shared Ulrici's view that retribution is a central element in* Henry VI *include Denton J. Snider (1890), E. M. W. Tillyard (1944), and Irving Ribner (1965). Later twentieth-century commentators have generally opposed the idea that the trilogy reflects the operation of divine will behind historical events; for discussions supporting this point of view, see the excerpts by A. C. Hamilton (1961-62), S. C. Sen Gupta (1964), H. M. Richmond (1967), James Winny (1968), and Robert Ornstein (1972).*]

[No piece] exhibits the two opposite aspects of the Christian view of things in the mutual interpenetration in which they occur in the historic drama, more distinctly that "Henry the Sixth," and its continuation, "Richard the Third." In these plays evil is made to find its own corrective and destruction in evil and moral weakness and perversity; vice and folly mutually frustrate each other as in Comedy. The good obtains, no doubt, by God's grace, the final victory, but not within the immediate limits of the represented time and action; it passes beyond the acting personages of the piece into the wide futurity of history. For the present the tragical rules uncontrolled, not merely annihilating evil, but also destroying whatsoever is great, noble, and beautiful in humanity. For amid the *general* decay of an age and nation, the virtue and good intentions of individuals can never preserve themselves entirely spotless, inasmuch as the individual does not stand isolated and alone, but is an *organic* member of society—the child of his nation, and the creature of his age. The universal sinfulness must seize upon him also in the same way that one foul spot infects the whole fruit, and as, conversely, it is the corruption of the whole that originates the foulness of the particular spot.

This saddening thought, which is identical in principle with the christian dogma of original sin, forms the ground idea of this great trilogy. With various modifications it is carried through each of the three parts, as being indeed necessarily implied in the historical import of *civil war*. But the same reference of all history to the divine grace, which, in its delineation of the great national war, [''Henry the Fifth''] had conveyed by representing war as an immediate judgment of God, is here again repeated; the civil war being regarded as an antidote and restorative of the general corruption and suffering, and defeat as tending to the purification and refinement of human goodness and nobility. This is the other—the soothing and consolatory aspect of the poem. The life and fortunes of Henry the Sixth reflect both aspects in the most immediate and clearest manner. His personal history forms, indeed, the foundation of the whole, and the link which connects together the several parts. Henry, indeed, takes no share in the action; all he does is to pray and to suffer, and yet all that happens falls upon his devoted head, and his doing nothing is even the principal cause of all that is done and happens. Accordingly in this piece the interest is greatly divided. The chief part of it is no doubt claimed by the King and his family, but they have to share it in the first part with Talbot and his son, in their noble struggle against France, with the defeat of Gloster, and the victory of York in the second; and in the third, the end of York, and the conduct of Edward, arrest our attention. And yet the true unity is manifestly preserved by the oneness of the interest of the story, and of the ground idea which animates it. To establish this point it will be necessary to enter upon a close examination of each of the three parts.

To begin with *the first,* which forms the proper conclusion of ''Henry the Fifth, '' since the national war which is there exhibited now first attains to a real end. It concludes to the advantage of France, even because the intrinsic moral right has gone over to her side. For although the nobles and commonality of France are not much better as yet, and are at best but more prudent and sharpened by experience, they have nevertheless abandoned their haughty self-confidence and groundless vanity, and a growing esteem for their adversary has laid the first step to victory. And, what is more important still, England, on the other hand, has lost her moral superiority. We are conscious at once of this loss in the introductory scenes, amid the selfish intrigues and quarrels of the nobles, in whose wake the people blindly follow, and that the people and army are no longer animated by the same spirit which gave the victory to Henry the Fifth, is proved, among other incidents of the campaign, by the disgraceful and cowardly flight of Fastolfe. Accordingly, the piece opens well with the funeral of Henry, as with the entombment of the victories and conquests of England. (pp. 386-88)

But the divine interposition has its outward manifestation in the ''Maid of Orleans.'' Though Shakspeare from the very first makes her to be in league with the evil one, he is nevertheless far from wishing to have it thought that her appearance on the scene is without the divine permission, and does not exercise an important influence in the fortunes of the campaign. For in a certain sense the interference of supernatural agency in human affairs must be mediately divine, inasmuch as the evil one cannot operate on them without the permission of God. The more sentimental critics, indeed, are disposed to recognise in Shakspeare's ''Joan of Arc'' a pure and spotless maiden, at first acting under the immediate inspiration of heaven, but subsequently losing her moral purity under the corrupting influence of success. The error of this view is, however, obvious and at once refuted by the boldness with which this modest damsel mixes with the French warriors, and receives their adoration. In his conception of the character of ''Joan of Arc,'' Shakspeare followed the national opinion of his countrymen,

which was indeed the general belief of her contemporaries. No doubt it was untrue in all essential points; yet the truth could not and ought not to have been established in the present piece. For the *historical* drama ought to exhibit its subject matter as it *existed,* and to paint with the utmost truth the feelings and characters *of its age.* (p. 389)

[Joan's death] appears as the organic contrast to the fall of Salisbury and of the Talbots. The elder Talbot is decidedly the noblest character of the piece. Patriotism, knightly honour, and bravery, are the guiding principles of his whole life; of any higher idea he is wholly unconscious; he can win a battle, but is unable to command an army; he is an excellent officer, but no general, full of courage, and not without prudence and foresight, (as proved by his encounter with the Duchess of Auvergne) but yet without a prompt and creative presence of mind, and a wide forecasting circumspection. This defect, and the rough sternness of his virtue, which has much of the race of the lion in it, is the failing which leads to his death. His character was little suited for the crooked and complicated relations of the age in which he lived; under the iron rod of correction, he was likewise stern and iron-like—untempered, and without grace to submit. In such times an honourable death is to the noble a blessing from God; to die is victory and pleasure, but to live is to be subject to the cruel empire of necessity and crime. The living cannot escape entirely the contagion of the universal sinfulness; while the victorious pleasure of death which emancipates the dying from the general misery is at once exalting and incorruptible. This reflection constitutes the particular modification which the ground idea of the whole receives in the first part, and which all its several parts are designed to elucidate. (pp. 390)

In *the second part,* the hidden disease has broken out in all its force. We have here the wide and complicated tissue of factions, with their quarrels and intrigues, vices and atrocities, in which the domestic policy of England became entangled after the loss of France, and the end of the foreign war. The germs of these troubles were alone present in the first part; they have now grown up into a wide-spreading and vigorous tree. . . . Death and crime reap an ample harvest; the great and the little, the wicked and the good, are alike mown down. For in such times of wide and general corruption, good ceases to be good; in the universal sinfulness, the boundary lines between vice and virtue are lost and disappear. Virtue is no longer virtue, when, as in the case of Gloster, Buckingham, Clifford, and others, it is associated with such passionate heat and party rage; evil gains a seeming sanction when the good itself comes forward in such disguise. In such times the death of the noble is but an unsuccessful effort at life, and vice alone maintains its ground, because it only is consistent with itself. This is the dreadful truth which is conveyed to us by this drama, as well as by its mistress, History herself. History, as we have frequently observed, requires above all things active consistent energy; if good has associated itself with this quality it will invariably maintain outwardly the pre-eminence which belongs to it intrinsically; if, on the contrary, evil possesses the energy which consistency lends, the good must succumb, as forfeiting, by the loss of it, its own essential property. Evil must, and indeed ought, to prevail, in order that it may work its own destruction, which the good by its own imperfection is unable to accomplish. The victory of evil is, in short, its own annihilation.

Viewed in this light, under which the general idea of the whole exhibits itself in this second part, every thread of the complicated web appears to be judiciously arranged. The sorceries of the Pucelle have their counterpart in the incantation scene, which is the ruin of the noble-hearted Duchess of Gloster, and the first stain on the honour of the Protector; and with the flattering Peter and his master, the rascally Simcox, and the episode of Jack Cade and his rascally rabble, are full of deep significance, and at the same time indispensable, as shewing that in such periods the noblest minds even are liable to the strangest aberrations, and that the weakest men are most irretrievably the victims of the darkest powers of hell. . . . These inferior parties, like Falstaff and his motley fellows in [''Henry the Fourth''], furnish also in their peculiar comic colouring a parody on the subject-matter of the proper historic action, while they exhibit evil in its true light, as irrational, ridiculous, and absurd.

Sentimental critics, like F. Horn and others, have blamed the poet for his conception of the character of the Queen, which the second part develops in detail. She is, they say, made unnecessarily revolting, a perfect fury; and, above all, it is offensive to our feelings, for the good but unfortunate king to be represented as so manifestly henpecked. No doubt the same sounds of the horrible which in ''Titus Andronicus'' strike the ear in full accord, are heard in dying echoes in the character of Margaret; a fact which proves with some degree of certainty that the two latter parts of ''Henry the Sixth'' must be classed among the earliest productions of Shakspeare's pen. No doubt the guilt of the Queen is deep enough, without the imaginary addition of adultery: yet without this poetical but significant touch, it is clear that the picture would have been incomplete. A mind so perfectly unfeminine, so energetic, so passionate, violent, and fiery, must have felt itself ill matched with the cool and unimpassioned Henry. . . . Moreover, such terrific energy and enormity, such undisguised shamelessness of sin, as is here exhibited in the character of a woman, is doubtless more poetical and more dramatic, and, indeed, in a poem more moral, than any darkly crawling and secret sins, or the mere hint of their existence, when the spectator could not fail to suspect them. Besides, such completeness of crime, a character in short in which all the immorality of the age might seem to have centered itself, was absolutely necessary for the poet's purpose of exhibiting the true nature of *such* times, and of perspicuously elucidating the ground-idea of the whole. The devilish Richard stands worthily by the side of the fury— Margaret; the two characters mutually complete each other; they learn of, and form themselves by, one another, in order to become the mighty instruments of the divine retribution which visited England, and the members of the royal family especially, at the close of Henry's long but unhappy reign. Lastly, the unmanly and womanish king required the organic contrast of his malignant and masculine consort. Henry, indeed, willingly risked his own dishonour, when, with a disposition like his, *he* allowed himself to be persuaded into taking *such* a woman for a wife. This his first and only sin of *commission*— all his later faults were but sins of omission—required to be thrown out in a strong light, in order to show how in the rank soil of such a period the smallest seed of crime bears an infinite crop of deadly effects and consequences. The queen governs in the king's place, and of bad, makes worse. Thrust into the back-ground by her inordinate love of power, and confirmed in his weak inactive meditation, he becomes more and more a sovereign in name only; the open infidelity of his queen is insufficient to rouse him. His calm, humble, and resigned frame of mind, in other circumstances deserving of the highest commendation, acquires in his case day by day a more sinful character of weakness and indecision. The re-

lation subsisting between Henry and Margaret does but reflect the leading idea of the second part under a peculiar modification, which at the same time perfectly justifies in a poetic light the character of the queen, as Shakspeare has here drawn it. (pp. 391-94)

[In the third part of ''Henry the Sixth,'' England's] best and noblest sons have fallen, and none remain to supply their places; the wicked abound more and more, and every where gain ascendancy. In such periods of convulsion, the sons are usually more evil and corrupt than their sires. This truth is fully confirmed by the children of Henry and York, and by the younger Clifford and Buckingham. Darker clouds gather around the horizon, while Henry, driven at first to flight, and then in prison, resigns himself to prayer and meditation. And what is the subject of his thoughts? He calls himself ''A *man* at least, for less he should not be,'' a king—''whose crown is called content'' [*3 Henry VI*, III. i. 57, 64]. He is ready to do, and humbly yields himself to, whatever God wills; he sees into the future with a prophet's eye, and dies asking forgiveness for himself and his murderer. In death the storm which had spent itself on his troubled life clears off. His last moments bespeak a mind strong in its victory over self, and the renunciation of all earthly interests to which by the sufferings of life he had attained.

It is this profound Christian truth that the third part of this trilogy unfolds before our eye. In times like those which are here depicted no one is the complete master of his own movements, while the soil totters beneath his feet. He cannot escape the contagion which infects the whole community. In a period of such disorder, it is only some mighty and heaven-sent spirit that can restore peace; while the heavenly deliverer is absent, the evil must rage until it has exhausted or destroyed itself. Having brought ruin upon himself chiefly by his own weakness and inactivity, he becomes, by the way in which he meets his fate, a pattern of noble resignation. In such trials and emergencies, the man who does not feel a divine commission inciting him to action, does better to *suffer* than to act; he *must* receive the times as a divine visitation, and dispose himself in humble hope to suffering and to patience. By means of them he is to raise himself above all that is earthly—by submitting to affliction, as a just visitation on his *inability* to act with moral firmness, amid the general corruption which has mixed together right and wrong, good and evil, in indistinguishable confusion. (pp. 395-96)

Thus, in all the several parts of this drama, we have the same idea reflected—the same law, that is, the same view of history, which, in this third part, forms the modification of the ground-idea of the whole trilogy; around this centre all adjusts itself into an organic whole. At the same time, at its close, Richard comes forward conspicuously into the foreground. He, the fearfully consistent villain—that has neither pity, love, nor fear— ordained to be an executioner, nature's abortion—stands forth in full vigour and freshness—the dregs of the antidote of the poisoned period, in order to close the last act of the grand tragedy. (p. 397)

Hermann Ulrici, ''Criticisms of Shakspeare's Dramas: 'Henry VI','' in his Shakspeare's Dramatic Art: And His Relation to Calderon and Goethe, *translated by A. J. W. Morrison, Chapman, Brothers, 1846, pp. 385-97.*

CHARLES KNIGHT (essay date 1842)

[*Knight, an English educator and publisher, wrote numerous books and periodicals intended to better educate the Victorian working*

Part I. Act II. Scene iv. Warwick, Vernon, Richard Plan-
tagenet, Lawyer, Somerset, and Suffolk. Frontispiece to the
Hanmer edition by H. Gravelot (1744). By permission of
the Folger Shakespeare Library.

class. Among these were his highly popular illustrated edition of
Shakespeare's plays and a complementary illustrated biography
of Shakespeare. In addition, Knight also produced a book of
critical commentary on the plays, Studies in Shakspere *(1849),*
and was a founder of the first Shakespeare Society. In his dis-
cussion of 1 Henry VI, *first published in his 1842 edition of*
Shakespeare's works, he agrees with Edmond Malone (1787) that
Hall's chronicle was a central source for the play. But whereas
Malone used this as a basis for claiming that Shakespeare could
not have written 1 Henry VI, *because Hall was not "Shake-*
speare's historian," Knight argues that the claim is specious.
There is no proof that Shakespeare never consulted Hall, contends
Knight, and it is highly likely that he would have reviewed one
of the principal authorities on the subject of his plays. For a
further examination of Shakespeare's use of his sources, see the
excerpt by J. A. R. Marriott (1918). Also, see the essay on Henry
VI *by Geoffrey Bullough listed in the Additional Bibliography.]*

If we were in the habit . . . of taking upon trust what the
previous editors of Shakspere have authoritatively held, we
should either reject ['The First Part of Henry VI'] altogether,
or, if we printed it, we should inform our readers that "the
hand of Shakspere is nowhere visible throughout" [see excerpt
above by Edmond Malone, 1787]. We cannot consent to follow
either of these courses; and, even at the risk of being held
presumptuously to open a question which has been long considered to be finally disposed of, we print the play, and we do
not tell the reader that Shakspere never touched it.

Malone's 'Dissertation of the Three Parts of King Henry VI.,
tending to show that those plays were not written originally
by Shakspeare,' is the most careful and elaborate of his productions, and that upon which his reputation as a critic was
mainly built. (pp. 435-36)

[However, it] appears to us that he has left many important
points untouched, and has dwelt somewhat too much upon
minute distinctions. The question is not one merely of verbal
criticism. It is connected with some of the most interesting
inquiries as to the history of the English drama and the early
life of Shakspere. It is a subject, therefore, that we cannot take
up and dismiss in a hasty or fragmentary manner, or in a spirit
of tame acquiescence in prevailing opinions of the one hand,
or of inconsiderate controversy on the other. (pp. 436-37)

It is a favourite theory with all the commentators upon Shakspere, since the time of Dr. [Richard] Farmer, that the acquired
knowledge of the poet was of the most limited character. According to these critics, he was not only unable to read any
language but his own, but his power even of reading in English
books was limited in a degree that would indicate him to have
been the most idle or the most incurious of mankind. Malone's
favourite opinion is, that Shakspere consulted but *one* historical
writer for the materials of his Histories. In a note upon the
passage in the first act of 'Henry V.' in which the King of
France is erroneously called "king Louis the tenth," Malone
says that Holinshed led Shakspere into the mistake, and that
Hall calls the King correctly Charles the ninth; and he adds,—
"Here, therefore, we have a decisive proof that our author's
guide in *all* his historical plays was Holinshed, and not Hall."
In a note upon the second act of 'The First Part of Henry VI.,'
where an English soldier enters, crying "A Talbot, a Talbot!"
the same critic says, "I have quoted a passage from Hall's
Chronicle, which probably furnished the author of this play
with this circumstance. It is not mentioned by Holinshed (*Shak-*
spere's historian), and is one of the numerous proofs that
have convinced me that this play was not the production of
our author." Without entering into a discussion in this place
as to the value of Malone's argument that Shakspere was not
the author of 'The First Part of Henry VI.,' because the author
of that play had evidently consulted Hall's Chronicle, we must
express a decided opinion of the worthlessness of this point. . . .
We believe that the question whether Shakspere was the author
of 'The First Part of Henry VI.' is not in the slightest degree
affected by the circumstance that the author of this play appears
to have been familiar with the narrative of Hall, in which the
circumstances of this period of history are given more in detail
than by Holinshed. It was perfectly impossible that any writer
who undertook to produce four dramas upon the subject of the
wars of York and Lancaster should not have gone to Hall's
Chronicle as an authority; for that book is expressly on the
subject of these wars. . . . If it could be proved that Shakspere
had not consulted a book the entire subject of which he has
dramatised, devoting to that subject nine out of his ten historical
plays, we should consider it the most marvellous circumstance
in literary history, and totally inexplicable upon any other theory than that of the grossest ignorance on the part of the author.
The phrase of Malone, "Shakspeare's historian," assumes that
Shakspere could only read in one book. It was perfectly natural
that he, for the most part, should follow Holinshed's account,
which is a compilation from all the English historians; but, as
Holinshed constantly refers to his authorities, and in the period
of the civil wars particularly to Hall, it is manifest that for
some of his details he would go to the book especially devoted

to the subject, in which they were treated more fully than in the abridgment which he generally consulted. (pp. 463-64)

Malone did some injustice to Shakspere in maintaining that he could not have been the author of 'The First Part of Henry VI.,' because the author consulted Hall; for, as it is manifest that the author consulted both chroniclers, Malone gives to his unknown author the merit of doing what he affirms Shakspere did not do—consult two writers on one subject. To have been consistent in his argument, he ought to have shown that the unknown author did not consult Holinshed. (pp. 465-66)

> *Charles Knight, "Introductory Notice: 'King Henry VI—Part I'" and "Historical Illustration," in The Comedies, Histories, Tragedies, and Poems of William Shakspere, Vol. V, by William Shakespeare, edited by Charles Knight, second edition, 1842. Reprint by AMS Press, 1968, pp. 435-41, 463-68.*

G. G. GERVINUS (essay date 1849-50)

[*One of the most widely read Shakespearean critics of the latter half of the nineteenth century, the German critic Gervinus was praised by such eminent contemporaries as Edward Dowden, F. J. Furnivall, and James Russell Lowell; however, he is little known in the English-speaking world today. Like his predecessor Hermann Ulrici, Gervinus wrote in the tradition of the "philosophical criticism" developed in Germany in the mid-nineteenth century. Under the influence of August Wilhelm Schlegel's literary theory and Georg Wilhelm Friedrich Hegel's philosophy, German critics like Gervinus tended to focus their analyses around a search for the literary work's organic unity and ethical import. Gervinus believed that Shakespeare's works contained a rational ethical system independent of any religion—in contrast to Ulrici, for whom Shakespeare's morality was basically Christian. In the excerpt below, taken from his* Shakespeare *(1849-50), Gervinus sides with Edmond Malone (1787) on the issue of the authorship of the* Henry VI *trilogy, contending that Shakespeare had little share in* 1 Henry VI, *and that in* 2 *and* 3 Henry VI *he merely revised the earlier quarto plays,* The Contention *and* The True Tragedy, *which Gervinus maintains were written by another dramatist. With regard to the topic of dramatic construction, and in an attempt to bring greater coherence to* 1 Henry VI, *Gervinus would excise from it the scenes which he contends were added by Shakspere. He also argues that any degree of structural unity in* 2 *and* 3 Henry VI *is to be found entirely in the chronicle sources, from which Shakespeare borrowed heavily, and he concludes that the "whole catastrophe" depicted in the trilogy "is only history," to which Shakespeare added little in terms of poetic or dramatic construction. John Bell Henneman (1900) agreed with Gervinus on the lack of unity in* 1 Henry VI, *but Hereward T. Price (1951) and A. C. Hamilton (1961-62) each contended that the* Henry VI *trilogy is bound together by a superior construction. Robert Ornstein (1972) also treated the question of structure in the trilogy, maintaining that the plays show strong evidence of imaginative plotting. Lastly, Gervinus argues that Shakespeare's artistry is most apparent in the characterization of* 2 *and* 3 Henry VI, *which he compares with that in* The Contention *and* The True Tragedy. *He notes that the figure of Henry VI is a "cypher" in the older plays, whereas in* 2 *and* 3 Henry VI *"he is the source of all the misdeeds which disorder the kingdom," an opinion also reached by Edward Dowden (1881) and M. M. Reese (1961). Those critics who view Shakespeare's depiction of the king as more sympathetic than censorious include William Hazlitt (1817), H. V. D. Dyson (1950), Harold C. Goddard (1951), and Michael Manheim (1973).*]

The two last parts of *Henry VI.* are worked up by Shakespeare from an existing original, which may have early suggested to our poet the idea, not alone of appropriating them with additions to his stage, but also of appending to them the whole series of his histories, and this not only as regards the facts,

but even the leading idea. For the First Part, on the contrary, we possess no sources; in its purport it is but very slightly united with the two last parts, and this union did not originally exist in the piece. The latter parts afford the counterpart to Shakespeare's *Richard II.* and *Henry IV.;* as the former treat of the elevation of the House of Lancaster, the latter refer to the retribution of the House of York; the First Part, on the other hand, in its original form treated only of the French wars under Henry VI. and the civil discord which occasioned the losses in France. The satirist Thomas Nash, in his 'Pierce Penniless' Supplication to the Devil,' [see excerpt above, 1592], alludes to a piece in which the 'brave Talbot,' the dread of the French, is raised from the tomb 'to triumph again on the stage.' Whether this allusion refers to our drama or to another *Henry VI.,* which, as we know, was acted in 1592, by Henslowe's company, it is evident that this is indeed the essential subject of our play; all that relates to the rising York and his political plans was without doubt added by Shakespeare, in order to unite the play with the two others. It may almost with certainty be denied that Shakespeare had any farther share in the piece than this. From Malone's ample dissertation upon the three parts of *Henry VI.* [see excerpt above, 1787] until [Alexander] Dyce, our poet has generally been refused in England all share in the authorship of this first part. The extraordinary ostentation of manifold learning in the play is not like Shakespeare, nor is the style of composition. . . . If the subject induced the poet to appropriate the piece as a supplement to the completion of the two following parts, without question his share in it is a very small one. That he himself, after the custom of the time, originally composed the piece in company with other poets, is not credible, because a man of Shakespeare's self-reliance must have early felt the unnaturalness of his habit. It is, on the other hand, probable that the piece which he elaborated occupied various hands at the same time, because the marks of them are plainly to be discerned.

No piece is more adapted to the explanation of the manner in which Shakespeare, as soon as he was himself, did *not write* his dramatic works. His historical plays follow for the most part the historical facts of the well-known chronicle of Holinshed, and adhere rigorously to succession and order, rejecting all fable. *The First Part of Henry VI.,* on the contrary, follows another historical narrative (Hall), and adds single events from Holinshed and other partly unknown sources; great historical errors, a medley of persons, a remarkable confusion in the computation of time, and a series of non-historical additions, characterise the treatment of this history—faults of which Shakespeare has never been guilty. (pp. 113-14)

If we take the piece purely in a dramatic point of view, and consider it as a work for the stage, it affords, as we before said, an excellent lesson, in its contrast to Shakespeare's general mode of proceeding. There is here no unity of action, indeed not even, as in *Pericles,* a unity of person. If we look strictly into the single scenes, they are so loosely united, that whole series may be expunged without injuring the piece, indeed perhaps not without improving it—an attempt which even in *Pericles* could not be carried far. We need only superficially perceive this, in order to feel how far removed the dramatic works of art previous to Shakespeare were from that strong and systematic inner structure, which admits of no dismemberment without distortion. (p. 115)

If we separate all the scenes [in the *First Part of Henry VI.*] between York and Somerset, Mortimer and York, Margaret and Suffolk, and read them by themselves, we feel that we are looking upon a series of scenes which exhibit Shakespeare's style in his historical plays just in the manner in which we should have expected him to have written at the commencement of his career. We see the skilful and witty turn of speech and the germ of his figurative language; we perceive already the fine clever repartees and the more choice form of expression; in Mortimer's death scene and in the lessons of his deeply-dissembled silent policy, which while dying he transmits to York, we see . . . all the genuine feeling and knowledge of human nature which belongs to Shakespeare in similar pathetic or political scenes in his other dramas; all, not in that abundance and masterly power which he subsequently manifested, but certainly in the germ which prefigures future perfection. These scenes contrast decidedly with the trivial, tedious war scenes and the alternate bombastic and dull disputes between Gloster and Winchester; they adhere to the common highway of historical poetry, though they have sufficient of the freshness of youthful art to furnish Schiller in his 'Maid of Orleans' with many beautiful traits, and indeed with the principal idea of his drama. If we consider it as settled that Shakespeare inserted all these scenes, we can fully explain for what reason he did so. They unite this First Part most closely with the Second and Third, while before it had been totally unconnected with them. York, the principal hero of the two last parts, here appears with his claims at the commencement of his career; Margaret, who next to him forms the most prominent figure, is here rising into note; the last scene of the First Part is intentionally placed in the closest connection with the first scene of the Second Part. The later work of *Richard II.*, standing as it does in historical contrast to these parts of *Henry VI.*, is accordingly treated by Shakespeare in evident dramatic relation to this same supplemented scene. As in *Richard II.* the dangerous rise of the house of Lancaster issues from the single combat of Norfolk and Henry, so in *Henry VI.* the strife of the two roses arises from the challenge between Vernon and Basset; as in the one the weak Richard at first disregards and threatens Henry Bolingbroke, and then spares and by sparing promotes him, so in the other the weak young Henry VI. emancipates the injured and dishonoured York to his own destruction. Thus by the addition of these scenes Shakespeare has made the *First Part of Henry VI.*, regarded as a separate piece, still more disconnected than it originally was; but, on the other hand, he has so united the three parts that they afford a perfect picture of the rule of Henry VI., and, at the same time, in depicting the rise of York, a complete counterpart to that of the house of Lancaster, the description of which he had probably already planned during the elaboration of these three parts of *Henry VI.*

We may consider the two last parts of *Henry VI.* as a single play; that is, as a dramatic chronicle in ten acts; neither in outer form nor in inner idea are the two pieces otherwise than mechanically divided. The events in France, which formed the principal subject in the First Part, are here removed to the farthest background; the reader scarcely observes the short passages in which we learn that Somerset is sent to France, and that this valuable possession is completely lost to England. The subject of the two last parts is the contest of the houses of York and Lancaster, the decline of England's power under the weak and saintly Henry VI., and the rise of York, the father of the terrible Richard III. (pp. 116-18)

We have already said that Shakespeare, in the two last parts of *Henry VI.*, only revised two plays ['The First Part of the Contention betwixt the two famous Houses of York and Lancaster,' and 'The True Tragedy of Richard, Duke of York']. . . .

To compare these works, which by a plausible conjecture are attributed to Robert Greene, with Shakespeare's elaborations, is to take a glance into the innermost workshop of his youthful poetic genius. (p. 118)

The general reader is not acquainted with these two plays, and cannot therefore compare them with Shakespeare's elaboration of them; but it is necessary to speak of them as they are in their original form, in order to show what help they afforded to Shakespeare, how far they were suggestive for his historical dramas, and what he added in his *own Henry VI*.

When [Ludwig] Tieck says that nothing of Shakespeare's—not even his noblest and best works—can be compared in plan with the historical tragedy of *Henry VI.*, and that the mind of the poet grows with his subject, and when Ulrici states the composition to be truly Shakespeare-like, both these critics betray that they do not distinguish between matter and form, and that they have not compared the chronicles which these dramas follow with the poetical version. There cannot be much question of plan and composition in a piece which simply follows, with few exceptions and errors, the course of the chronicle; which like the chronicle unfolds in succession the various strata of matter, and brings forward a series of scenes, such as the anecdote of the armourer and the lame simpcox, standing in but very slight connection with the great course of the whole. Whoever reads the narrations of Hall and Holinshed by the side of *Henry VI.*, whether Greene's version or Shakespeare's, will perceive the most accurate transcript of the text of the narrative, even in passages where he would have least supposed it. The whole insurrection of Cade, in the Second Part, full as it is of popular humour, proceeds so entirely from the historical sources, that even the speeches of the rough rebels, which appeared more than anything else to be the property of the poet, are found partly verbatim in the chronicle of St. Albans, from which Stowe quotes them in his account of the insurrection of Wat Tyler and Jack Straw. Single highly-poetical passages, such as the prophecy of Henry VI. concerning Richmond, the bold answer of the captive Prince of Wales, the assassination of the young Rutland, and others, are not only borrowed from the chronicle, but the last scene makes in Holinshed also an affecting and poetical impression. When, according to Tieck's expression, the poetical power in these plays increases with the subject, it is because this is the case with the matter of the chronicle also; in reading the Second Part, we need only follow the corresponding passages in Holinshed, and we find after Gloster's assassination that the history becomes richer and more attractive, just as the drama itself does. It is the subject that forms the grandeur and attraction of these pieces, and this even in the plainest historical structure. The drama of this great avalanche of ruin which overwhelms all the powers in the native state; this dissolution of all bonds, this chaos in which misdeed succeeds misdeed, crime rises above crime, and an inexorable Nemesis follows close at the heels of the offending man; all this bears in itself a powerful interest, which rather carries away the poet than that the poet himself creates it. . . . We see foremost, in the Second Part, the Protector of the kingdom perishing through his own weakness, and his queen through her criminal pride. They fall by the cabals of the hostile nobility, who are leagued together for evil; of that nobility who had produced nothing but mischief to the country ever since the days of Richard II. Again, the fall of Suffolk and the rebellion of Cade are entirely represented as a retributive judgment upon the aristocracy, as a rising of the suffering lower classes against the oppression, unscrupulousness, and severity of the rule of the nobles. This democracy we see in its turn quickly perishing in its own fury and folly; and on the ruins of the aristocracy and the incited people, the tools of a crafty ambition, York raises himself to the dignity of a new Protector, relying upon popular favour and upon his warlike deeds and merits. Having attained his object, he allows himself to be tempted to perjury, and vengeance follows his footsteps. Rutland, one of his sons, shares his terrible fall. The king himself, who stands in inactive weakness and contemplative devotion, scarcely accountable amidst the ruin of all things, is now on his side tempted by the queen to become a perjurer, and falls into the power and under the sword of his enemies. From the blood of Rutland and of the Prince of Wales springs a new harvest of avenging destinies. Clifford, the murderer of the former, falls; Edward, who was present at the assassination of the prince, totters on his throne; the valiant Warwick, who at last from personal indignation was unfaithful to his old party, perishes. Through all these disasters and retributions Queen Margaret passes unscathed, like some embodiment of fate, pursued by the most refined vengeance of the Nemesis: raised as a captive to the English throne, as 'a beggar mounted,' she had, according to the adage, 'run the horse to death,' and, surviving to her own torment, she sees all her glory buried; the source as she is of all these sufferings, she is to drink them even to the dregs. Yet this whole catastrophe, we see plainly, is only history, and no poetic plan and composition; this administration of justice, which appears so systematic and poetic, is simply taken from the chronicle. (pp. 119-21)

This important historical subject was intelligently apprehended by Robert Greene, in his two plays (if they are rightly his), though it was dramatised in a very different manner. He directed his attention entirely to the importance of the material, and to the details in the historical sources which lay before him—a sufficient proof that artistic form but little interfered. And here lies the great difference between this and the Shakespeare histories: that in the latter, when they even follow the chronicle with as much fidelity as Greene's 'Henry VI.,' the poet generally appears greatest just where the chronicle leaves him. In the Second Part of Greene's 'Henry VI.', the third act exhibits able and powerful arrangement; the popular scenes of Cade's insurrection are full of happy humorous life. In the first act of the Third Part, the fall of York, a high pathos is preserved, without the usual exaggerations of the older dramatic school; in the words of York and Margaret, Shakespeare could learn the genuine language of great passion, and he found here no inducement to add much of his own. In the second act, where York's sons are aroused, an excellent warlike spirit prevails throughout; and here also Shakespeare, with the most correct feeling, has restrained his improving hand. But from the third act, and especially in the fourth and fifth, where the history of Henry VI. is almost reflected in miniature in the weak voluptuous Edward and his beggar queen, there begins a series of political scenes with little pathetic emotion; quickly and mechanically these scenes follow each other without exciting any attractive interest; they are scanty even in Shakespeare's version, though he nevertheless took pains to make something out of the still more scanty and skeleton-like scenes of Greene, to lengthen their contents, and to subdue the strange hurry with which Greene pressed on to the end. Even in Shakespeare's version the reader may observe these naïve deficiencies. In the eighth scene of the fourth act Warwick goes to Coventry, and at the same moment Edward is aware of it, as if they had just met on the stairs. In [*3 Henry VI*] the Prince of Wales is murdered; in the succeeding scene the father already knows it. The hurry to the end is so great that it plainly betrays

itself in repeated phrases. The questions, 'What now remains?' 'And now what rests?' 'What then?' are repeated several times in the two last acts. The inequality observable in the dramatisation of the historical matter is also evident in the delineation of the characters. Whatever in the history struck the poet's mind as strongly delineated, he treated with intelligence and generally with success. Warwick, the darling of the people; 'the setter-up and puller-down of kings' [*3 Henry VI,* III. iii. 157], the 'coal-black haired' [*3 Henry VI,* V. i. 54], the stuttering and noisy favourite and strengthener of the Yorkists, was one of these characters which was written and acted *con amore* ["with passion"]—a most grateful part to those 'robustious periwig-pated fellows' [*Hamlet,* III. ii. 9] whom Hamlet ridiculed. The Cardinal of Winchester, full of ambition and priestly arts, with his 'red sparkling eyes' [*2 Henry VI,* III. i. 154], blabbing the malice of his heart, which breaks at last in the pangs of conscience; the defying insolent aristocrat Suffolk, unworthy in prosperity, proudly defiant in danger, and meeting death with the dignity and remembrance of the great men of old, who in similar manner fell by vile hands—these were the forms of character to which poets like Greene or Marlowe were equal. York also, and the female characters, to which we shall revert, are excellently maintained. The more deeply designed nature of a Humphrey, on the contrary, is only sketched for the most part; and the tender saintly figure of Henry VI. was left entirely in the silent background, and first acquired life and soul from Shakespeare. Unequal, therefore, are the characters, unequal is the organisation of single parts, and unequal is the poetic diction. While single passages are not without great and natural feeling, the plays on the whole are poor and dry; nowhere so clumsy that Shakespeare could have found much that required to be rejected, but in very few passages sufficiently full and elaborated for him to have added nothing. As in the personal characteristics, so in the diction there occurs many a strong and successful stroke, but the colours are not blended or worked up. The poet is not devoid of assonance, and he plays skilfully upon words and rhymes. Many a proverbial passage of universal truth and many an excellent poetic image glances forth from his versified prose; and it is a peculiarity of these images and similes that they are taken from the chase, from animals and their properties, and that they abound, as it were, in physiological conceits, in which (in the coarse taste of *Titus Andronicus*) the human organs, lips, mouth and eyes, are endowed with life, and are frequently exhibited in most revolting positions.

Such were the dramas to which Shakespeare turned to appropriate them to his stage by manufacturing them afresh. That he did so with the reverence of a scholar is betrayed in his reluctance to erase; that he did so with the skill of future mastery is betrayed in the ardent desire for improvement, which suffered him to leave scarcely a single line intact. Much of the coarseness of the taste of the age was still left even in his improved work; nay, his own additions were sometimes of a similar character. Delight in deeds of horror and blood is not only seen in that lament of Margaret over Suffolk's head, and in Warwick's description of the corpse of the murdered Humphery, which Shakespeare found in Greene's text, but in those words also which Edward addresses to Warwick [*3 Henry VI,* V. i. 54-6], and which proceed from Shakespeare himself:

> This hand, fast wound about thy coal-black hair,
> Shall, whiles thy head is warm, and new cut-off,
> Write in the dust this sentence with thy blood, &c.

Much of that hyperbolic poetry of the Italian style, to which Shakespeare does homage in his narratives, is also to be found here; it displays itself chiefly in description, in the accumulation of artificial epithets, and in false affectation of the ancients in mythological images and learned quotations. The bombast in those passages where he speaks of tearful eyes adding water to the sea, and of the lion's 'devouring paws,' has been often censured; the far-fetched exaggerated expressions of the passion of Queen Margaret [*3 Henry VI,* I. iv. 67-108] remind us perfectly of the style of *Lucrece.* But in general the natural and simply historical material has extricated the poet from this unnatural and artificial mode of diction. His inclination to unusual and choice language, his abundance of metaphor, and the soaring of his poetic fancy, have never on the whole led him to extravagance of style, but have only served to give flesh and blood to the dry skeleton of his predecessors. The natural train of thought, the richness of feeling, the order in which passion is developed and expressed—all that reveals the true power of the poet—places him, if we compare the two texts, in the rank of a master at the side of Greene. If we read the original at almost any exciting passage, we shall find it, if not bad and faulty, almost throughout poor and defective; that which we vaguely miss and want is brought by the true poet from the depths of the soul, and is added with unique tact and natural feeling. The stem is firm around which he clings, but only through the influence of his warm poetical embrace does it shoot forth in leaves and blossoms. He who can compare the originals of Greene with Shakespeare's revision should read, in the Second Part, the scene between Gloster and his wife [II. i], and see how desultorily in the one the thoughts suddenly and unnaturally change in the words of the duchess, while in the other Shakespeare has filled up the gaps with the links required. He should read, in the plot for the overthrow of Humphrey [*2 Henry VI,* I. i], how the queen awkwardly and unexpectedly breaks in with the council, while on the other hand Shakespeare smoothes and prepares the way for her accusations. After Humphrey is murdered [*2 Henry VI,* III. ii. 65-71], the queen only coldly deliberates: 'I stood badly with Gloster, they will believe I killed him.' But Shakespeare makes her unfold the arts of female dissimulation; and while she conceals the agitation of her breast by self-accusation, what resources he bestows upon her of falsehood, deception, and hypocrisy! He should follow the poet from thence, especially to the soliloquies of the crafty York. In his first monologue (in the old play) he states his political plans with cold calculation; he relates, as dryly as the chronicle, the actual state of things; there is no emotion of feeling, no lively picture of the situation. All this is animated by Shakespeare with poetic ornament, with traits of character, with richness of language, and with descriptive detail; we do not only learn that York has seduced the popular leader Cade 'to make commotion,' but also who Cade is, and why he is thought fit for this bold part. Just so, in another soliloquy in Greene's original, York clings to the simple account of facts and the consideration suggested by them: 'I require troops: you give me them, I shall use them.' Shakespeare's addition to this just gives the feeling and passion required; he portrays the promptings of a mind deeply agitated by ambition and the restless activity of a brain through which the aspiring thoughts chase each other with their dreams of dignity; it is the picture of the man as he stands alone, conversing with himself, and not the cold enumeration of deeds which lie in the future, the motives to which alone belong to this his solitary present. In the one we receive the impression of the icy calculator sketching out his ambitious views as systematically as he planned his deeds, whilst in the other we see at work the innate powers within him, mastering his mind, brooding over the hindrances and promotions of his projects,

and lightly sketching the actions to which it spurs and incites the energy and will.

From what we have said it is evident that it is especially in the development of character that Shakespeare's talent strikes us in this comparison of the two works. Several of the characters of the play afforded him little interest. It is worthy of observation—and it points out Shakespeare's natural inclination to shun all trivialities—that foremost among the personages indifferent to him stands the grateful and heroic character of Warwick. This character, the popular hero and darling, the warrior stammering in his impetuosity and vain-glorious in his self-reliance, was afterwards depicted by Shakespeare in Percy; and this illustrious counterpart ought to be compared with Warwick by the panegyrists of the plays of *Henry VI.*, if they would accurately determine their relation to the works of the matured poet. The Cardinal of Winchester and the Duke of Suffolk were finished by Shakespeare according to the outline designed, without any great sympathy with these characters, though not without certain masterly touches which would have betrayed his hand if we did not know him as the elaborator. In that passage in the old piece, where Suffolk asks the murderers of Humphrey whether they have despatched him, Shakespeare characterises the man by the cutting heartless question: 'Now, sirs, have you despatched *this thing?*' [*2 Henry VI,* III. ii. 6]. The excellent contrast of the two masculine women, Eleanor and Margaret, Shakespeare found already before him; Greene had worked at both these characters with the greatest success and industry. The jealousy and hatred between the rich, proud, ambitious duchess, with her unconquerable mind, and the upstart portionless woman, with her fierce malicious nature, are excellently portrayed. The vindictive, furious, and unrestrained character of the queen, whose face, 'visor-like, unchanging' [*3 Henry VI,* I. iv. 116], expresses the frigidity of her nature, is depicted, in glaring but striking touches, in the scene of York's death, where in cruel wantonness she trifles as the cat with the mouse. To atone in some degree for this flinty heart, Greene has imputed to her a true, perhaps too tender feeling for Suffolk, the origin of her doubtful good fortune. Shakespeare has here added but little; still that little is perfectly in the spirit of the plot. Let us only compare attentively in the scene of the farewell between Eleanor and her husband the trait he has interwoven: how, after her fall, the most fearful thing to the ambitious woman is that the 'giddy multitude do point' at her [*2 Henry VI,* II. iv. 21], and how her unbridled worldly ambition is suddenly changed into a longing for death. Characters of finer mould, which demanded Shakespeare's finer nature, are Gloster and the king. Duke Humphrey of Gloster, who appears in the second part totally different to the Gloster of the first, is invested with the great qualities of consummate mildness and benevolence, with a Solomon-like wisdom, with freedom from all ambition, and with severe Brutus-like justice towards everyone, even towards his wife, in whose last dishonour he notwithstanding shares as a private character. The greatness of his self-command, which is contrasted with the unbridled passion of his wife, has been rendered prominent by Shakespeare in one of his happy touches. In the passionate scene [*2 Henry VI,* II. iii], preparatory to his own fall and that of his duchess, he goes out and returns without reason; Shakespeare explains this as an intentional movement, with which the loyal man endeavoured to suppress his excitement and choler. There is too much noble and quiet grandeur in Humphrey for us not to be grieved at his fall, which appears merely an exemplification of the fable of the lamb that had troubled the wolf's water. It is Shakespeare's addition that he entwined in the garland of his virtues that foolish reliance upon his innocence which leads him to destruction, and which renders him careless amid the persecutions of his enemies, although he knew that York's 'overweening arm was reaching at the moon' [*2 Henry VI*, III. i. 159]. At the moment of his fall, he too late becomes keen-sighted, and predicts his own ruin and that of his king. That weakness is a crime is indicated by Shakespeare in this character, and is more closely worked out in Henry VI. This character, indeed, is entirely due to him; Greene placed the king as a cypher silently into the background, but Shakespeare drew him forth and delineated his nothingness. A saint, 'whose bookish rule had pulled fair England down' [*2 Henry VI*, I. i. 259], formed rather for a pope than a king, more fit for heaven than earth—a king, as Shakespeare adds, who longed and wished to be a subject more than any subject longed to be a king—he is in his inaction the source of all the misdeeds which disorder the kingdom. 'Weakness makes robbers bold;' in these words the weakness of the king is condemned, and Shakespeare exhibits this distinctly in his relations to individuals and to the country generally. He defends (all this is Shakespeare's addition) the persecuted Protector [*2 Henry VI*, III. i. 66-73, 201-22] with eloquence, and afterwards suffers him to fall: this distinctly places his impotence in relief. When Humphrey is arrested, the older play places in the king's mouth two meagre lines, while Shakespeare in fuller language displays in a masterly manner the picture of weakness, the powerless man comparing himself to the dam who can do naught but low after her calf, which the butcher bears to the slaughter-house. When afterwards [*2 Henry VI*, III. ii.] they go to look after the murdered duke, the older play has again only two bald lines for Henry while Shakespeare puts into his mouth an agitated prayer [*2 Henry VI*, III. i. 136-48], and by so doing prepares the way for that state of mind in which the king, supported by the valiant Warwick, is afterwards induced to an act of severity against Suffolk. Just as the pious king here leaves unperformed the commonest acts of gratitude and attachment towards his beloved protector, so the saint forgets the most sacred duties towards his kingdom; from weakness he becomes a perjurer, from weakness he disinherits his son, thus acting as even 'unreasonable creatures' do not with their young. After he has persuaded himself that he is to expiate the sins of the house of Lancaster, he exposes himself with fatalistic equanimity to blind destiny; and whilst the civil war is raging (in a soliloquy entirely inserted by Shakespeare [*3 Henry VI*, II. v. 1-54]), he wishes himself a 'homely swain' in the repose of contemplation and in the simple discharge of duty. Those abstract pictures of the civil war in which the son has slain the father and the father the son, the scenes which so powerfully touch our own Schiller, appear but in scanty outline in the older play; Shakespeare's touch first gave expression to them, and by connecting them with that idyllic soliloquy of the king he first gave them their depth; for, thus introduced, they remind the king of the higher duties of his position, which he had forgotten in his selfish desire for repose.

If we may call the character of Henry VI. Shakespeare's own creation, that of Richard of Gloster, on the contrary, was wholly prepared for his use in the Third Part. The aspiring spirit inherited from his father; the glance of the eagle at the sun; the great ambition, the indifference to the means for an object; the valour, the superstition which represents in him the voice of conscience; the subtle art of dissimulation; the histrionic talent of a 'Roscius,' the faithless policy of a Cataline; these had been already assigned to him by Greene in this piece. But how excellent even here have been Shakespeare's after-touches is evinced in the soliloquy [*3 Henry VI*, III. ii. 124-95], where the ambitious projects of the duke hold counsel as it were with

his means of realizing them; it is the counterpart to the similar soliloquy of his father York [*2 Henry VI*, III. i. 331-83], and permits us to anticipate how far the son will surpass the father. The principal figure of the two plays, Richard of York, is almost throughout delineated as if the nature of his more fearful son was prefigured in him. Far-fetched policy and the cunning and dissimulation of a prudent and determined man are blended in him—not in the same degree but in the same apparent contradiction as in Richard—with firmness, with a hatred of flattery, with inability to cringe, and with bitter and genuine discontent. With the same assurance and superiority as Richard the son, he is at one time ready to decide at the point of the sword, and at another to shuffle the cards silently and wait 'till time do serve' [*2 Henry VI*, I. i. 248]; both alike are animated by the same aspirations and ambitions. Had he been endowed with the same favour of nature as his father, Richard would have developed the same good qualities which the father possessed in addition to his dangerous gifts. Ugly, misshapen, and despised, without a right to the throne and without any near prospect of satisfying his royal projects, his devouring ambition was poisoned; in his father, called as he was the flower of the chivalry of Europe, convinced of his rights and proud of his merits, the aspiring disposition was moderated into a more legitimate form. At the death of his son Rutland his better nature bursts forth forcibly to light. He is honest enough, upon the pretended disgrace of his enemy Somerset, to dismiss his 'powers' and to give his sons as pledges; had he not been led away by his sons he is moderate enough, and is even ready to suspend his claims to the throne until Henry's death, whom, in the course of nature, he was not likely to survive; he laboured for his house, and not as his son, for himself. His claims and those of his house, which he asserts in opposition to the helpless and inactive Henry, he grounds not upon the malicious consciousness of personal superiority, as his son Richard does subsequently; but upon a good right, upon his favour with the people, upon his services in France and Ireland. Contrasted with Henry, he feels himself more kingly in birth, nature, and disposition. When he exercises his retaliation on the Lancastrians, he utters those words which Bolingbroke had before more cunningly applied to Richard II.: 'Let them obey, that know not how to rule' [*2 Henry VI*, v. i. 6]. This contrast of York to Henry VI. is the soul of both pieces. The claims of the hereditary right of an incapable king who is ruining the country, in comparison with those of the personal merit which saves the country from destruction, is the thought that involuntarily arises from the history of the reign of Henry VI.; the poet of the older plays has uncertainly siezed it; Shakespeare conceived it more fully, and carried it out. In the elaboration of these two plays this is not strikingly apparent. Shakespeare has too mechanically and timidly followed the arrangement of the whole history; we are obliged to confess that the drama, adhering to the history, creates the idea far more than that the idea, as ought to be the case, pervades the drama, and thus really animates and creates it. (pp. 122-30)

> *G. G. Gervinus, "Shakespeare's First Dramatic Attempts: 'Henry VI'," in his* Shakespeare Commentaries, *translated by F. E. Bunnètt, revised edition, Smith, Elder, & Co., 1877, pp. 113-32.*

HENRY NORMAN HUDSON   (essay date 1851)

[*Hudson was a nineteenth-century American clergyman and literary scholar whose Harvard edition of Shakespeare's works, published in twenty volumes between 1880 and 1881, contributed substantially to the growth of Shakespeare's popularity in Amer-*

ica. He also produced an eleven-volume edition of Shakespeare's plays between 1851 and 1856 and issued two critical works on Shakespeare, one a collection of lectures, the other—and the more successful—a biographical and critical study entitled Shakespeare, His Life, Art, and Characters (1872). In an unexcerpted portion of his introduction to the three Henry VI plays, published in 1851, Hudson asserts his conviction that Shakespeare authored the entire trilogy and that Edmond Malone (1787) was in error in ascribing them to other dramatists. Although in the following excerpt Hudson admits that these plays are not equal to Shakespeare's mature writings, he sees in them many elements of "Shakespeare's ripened power," especially the humor in the Cade scenes in 2 Henry VI, the skill with which the dramatist depicts the growing discord, and the selection of historical events from the chronicles to convey the essential truth of history. Other critics who have held that Shakespeare presented an accurate and fair account of historical events and characters in the Henry VI trilogy include Adolphus William Ward (1907), J. A. R. Marriott (1918), and S. C. Sen Gupta (1964). Hudson also considers Shakespeare's characterizations of Margaret and Suffolk a strong rebuttal to the view that the dramatist adopted a pro-Lancastrian bias in the trilogy.]

It must be owned, indeed, that *The First Part of Henry VI,* granting it to be Shakespeare's, can add nothing to his reputation. But it may throw not a little light on his mental history, showing, along with several other plays, that his hand waxed cunning and mighty by long labor and discipline; that in forming him for the office of universal teacher art had perhaps as great a share as nature; and that Ben Jonson knew what he was about, when saying with reference to him,—"For a good poet's made, as well as born." Moreover, the play yields acceptable testimony that Shakespeare, following the fashion of his time, had at first an excess of classical allusion; that even his genius was not in the outset proof against the then besetting vice of learned pedantry; thus guiding us to the reasonable conclusion, that his later freedom from such excess and pedantry was the result of judgment, not of ignorance. (p. xxxi)

In comparison, however, of the Poet's other histories, it must be confessed that the arrangement of this play is inartificial and clumsy, the characterization loose and sketchy, and the action inconsequential; there being many changes of scene which involve no real progress, and often no reason appearing in the thing itself but that the order might just as well have been quite other than it is: all which, to be sure, is but an argument that the author had not then acquired the power of moulding the stiff materials of history to the laws of art and the conditions of dramatic effect. Yet, though, as a whole, the piece be somewhat rambling and unknit, several of the parts are replete with poetic animation, many of the characters are firmly outlined, and in some of them, especially Beaufort and Talbot, the coloring is strong and well-laid; through, perhaps, in regard to the former, the conception has more of dramatic vigor than of historic truth.

In the character of the heroic maiden [Joan of Arc] we seem to have an apt instance of struggle between the genius of the poet and the prejudices of the Englishman. For it is observable that many of the noblest thoughts and images in the drama come from her; and in her interview with Burgundy the Poet could scarce have put into her mouth a higher strain of patriotic eloquence, had she been regarded as the patron saint of his father-land. But to have represented her throughout as a heaven-sent deliverer, besides being repugnant to the hereditary sentiment of the author, had been sure to offend the prepossessions of his audience. It is to this cause, probably, that we should attribute whatsoever of discrepancy there may be in the rep-

resentation. . . . What a subject she would have been for Shakespeare's hand, could he have done, what no good man has been able to do, namely, viewed her in the pure light of universal humanity, free from the colorings and refractings of national prepossession!

Amidst the general comparative tameness of the drama in hand, several scenes and parts of scenes may be specified as holding out something more than a promise of Shakespeare's ripened power. Such are the maiden's description of herself in [I. ii. 72-92], beginning,—"Dauphin, I am by birth a shepherd's daughter;"—and Talbot's account of his entertainment by the French while their prisoner, in sc. 4 of the same Act, where the story relishes at every turn of the teller's character, and the words seem thoroughly steeped in his individuality. Not less admirable, perhaps, in its way, is the pungent and pithy dialogue between Winchester and Gloster, Warwick, and Somerset, at the opening of Act iii., where the words strike fire all round, and where the persons, because they dare not speak, therefore out of their pent-up wrath speak all the more spitefully. Again, of whole scenes, the third in Act ii., between old Talbot and the countess of Auvergne, is in the conception and the execution a genuine stroke of Shakespearian art, full of dramatic spirit, and making a strong point of stage-effect in the most justifiable sense. And in the Temple Garden scene, which is the fourth of the same Act, we have a concentration of true dramatic life issuing in a series of forcible and characteristic flashes, where every word tells with singular effect both as a development of present temper and a germ of many tragic events. And, on the higher principles of art, how fitting it was that this outburst of smothered rage, this distant ominous grumbling of the tempest, should be followed by the subdued and plaintive tones that issue from the prison of the aged Mortimer, where we have the very spring and cause of the gathering storm discoursed in a strain of melancholy music, and a virtual sermon of revenge and slaughter breathed from dying lips. And of the fifth, sixth, and seventh scenes in Act iv., also, we may well say with Dr. Johnson, "If we take these *scenes* from Shakespeare, to whom shall they be given?" [see excerpt above, 1765]. (pp. xxxiii-xxxv)

• • • • •

[The] proceedings of the *Second Part* for the most part grow forth naturally and in course from the principles of the *First,* the two plays being as closely interwoven as any two acts of either. The criminal passion of Margaret and Suffolk, which was there presented in the bud, here blossoms and goes to seed, setting him near the throne, and thereby at once feeding his pride and chafing the pride of his enemies; while the losses in France, before represented, are ever and anon recurring as matter of continual twittings and jerks, the rust of former miscarriages thus at the same time keeping the old wounds from healing, and causing the new ones to fester and rankle. As the amiable imbecility of the king invites and smooths the way for the arrogance and over weening of the queen and her favorites, this naturally sets the aspiring and far-reaching York upon the policy of hewing away one after another the main supports of the rival house, that so at last he may heave it to the ground, and out of its ruins build up his own. The fall of Gloster is the first practicable breach, though, in making York a secret plotter and instigator of the conspiracy against him, it may be questionable whether the interest of the drama be not served too much at the expense of history. Then, in strict accordance with the suspicions of the time, York is represented as scheming afar off the insurrection of Cade, as a sort of feeler of the public pulse, and then taking advantage of it to push his designs. That insurrection comes in aptly as the first outbreak of the great social schism, the elements of which had been long working in secret, and growing to a head. The passages of humor, interspersed through the scenes of Cade and his followers, being mostly the same in the original form of the play, yield strong evidence in the question of authorship. It seems hard to believe that any one but Shakespeare could have written them, no instances in that line at all approaching these having been elsewhere given by any other writer of that time. For in poetry merely, Shakespeare, though immeasurably above any or all of his senior contemporaries, differs from them but in degree; but in the article of humor he shows a difference from them in kind. (pp. xxviii-xxix)

The Second Part of Henry VI is manifestly a great advance upon the *First,* and that in nearly all the particulars of dramatic excellence. The several members are well knit together; the characterization is bold, but, in the main, firm and steady; the action clear, free, and generally carried on in that consecutiveness that every later part seems the natural growth and issue of what had gone before. Much of this superiority, no doubt, was owing to the nature of the materials, which, besides yielding a greater variety of interest, were of themselves more limber and pliant to the shaping of art, and presented less to distract and baffle the powers of dramatic assortment and composition. The losses in France having been despatched in the former play, nothing of them remained for the Poet's use, but the domestic irritations they had engendered; which irritations were as so many eggs of discord in the nest of English life, and Queen Margaret the hot-breasted fury that hatched them into effect. The hatching process is the main subject of this play, and to that end the representation is ordered with considerable skill. (p. xxx)

· · · · ·

The Third Part of King Henry the Sixth resumes the course of history just where it paused at the close of the preceding play, and carries it on from the first battle of St. Albans, May, 1455, till the death of King Henry, which took place in May, 1471. And the connection of this play with the foregoing is much the same as that between the *First Part* and the *Second,* there being no apparent reason why the *Third* should begin where it does, but that the *Second* ended there. The parliamentary doings, which resulted in a compromise of the two factions, are here set in immediate juxtaposition with the first battle of St. Albans, whereas in fact they were separated by an interval of more than five years. Nevertheless, the arrangement is a very judicious one; for that interval was marked by little else than similar scenes of slaughter, which had no decisive effect of the relative condition of parties; so that the representing of them would but have encumbered the drama with details without helping on the purpose of the work. Not so, however, with the battle of Wakefield, which followed hard upon those doings in parliament; for this battle, besides that it yielded matter of peculiar dramatic interest in itself, had the effect of kindling that inexpressible rage and fury of madness, which it took such rivers of blood to slake. For historians note that from this time forward the war was conducted with the fiercest rancor and exasperation, each faction seeming more intent to butcher than to subdue the other. The cause of this demoniacal enthusiasm could not well be better presented than it is in the wanton and remorseless savagery displayed at the battle in question. And the effect is answerably told in the next battle represented, where the varying fortune and long-doubtful issue served but to multiply and deepen the horrors of the tragedy. (pp. vii-viii)

Thus in these two points of the drama the spirit and temper of the whole war is concentrated. Nor is it easy to see how the materials could have been better selected and disposed, so as to give out their proper significance, without bruising the feelings or distracting the thoughts of the spectator. (p. viii)

By a little attention to the dates it will be seen that throughout this play the Poet keeps to the actual order of events. And a more careful observation will readily perceive, that out of a large mass of materials Shakespeare judiciously selected such portions, and arranged them in such fashion, as might well convey in dramatic form the true historical scope and import of the whole. As the period brought forth little that was memorable save battles, all of which were marked by much the same bloodthirstiness of spirit, it was scarce possible to avoid an unusual degree of sameness in the action of the play; and the Poet seems to have made the most of whatever means were at hand for giving variety to the scenes. Such are the angry bickerings in parliament at the beginning; the cruel slaughter of young Rutland, and the fiendish mockeries heaped upon York, at Wakefield; the lyrical unbosomings of Henry when chidden from the field by Clifford, and when taken prisoner by the huntsmen; the wooing of lady Elizabeth by Edward, and the biting taunts and sarcasms which his brothers vent upon him touching his marriage; and especially the passages between Lewis, Margaret, Oxford, and Warwick, at the French court; in some of which the Poet seems rather to have overworked his matter of purpose to relieve and diversify the representation. Yet this play is by no means equal to the Second Part in variety of interest; and, but for the pungent seasoning sprinkled in here and there from the bad heart and busy brain of the precocious

Part I. Act I. Scene ii. The Dolphin, Reignier, and Joan de Pucelle. By F. Pecht (n.d.). The Department of Rare Books and Special Collections, The University of Michigan Library.

Richard, would be in some danger of perishing by its own monotony. (pp. x-xi)

Much has been said by one critic and another about the Poet's Lancastrian prejudices as manifested in these plays. One may well be curious to know whether those prejudices are to be held responsible for the portrait of Queen Margaret, wherein we have, so to speak, an abbreviature and sum-total of nearly all the worst vices of her time. The character, however lifelike and striking its effect, is colored much beyond what sober history warrants: though some of the main features are not without a basis of fact, still the composition and expression as a whole has hardly enough of historical truth to render it a caricature. Bold, ferocious, and tempestuous, void alike of delicacy, of dignity, and of discretion, all the bad passions, out of which might be engendered the madness of civil war, seem to flock and hover about her footsteps. Her speech and action, however, impart a wonderful vigor and lustihood to the movement of the drama; and perhaps it was only by exaggerating her or some other of the persons into a sort of representative character, that the springs and processes of that long national bear-fight could be developed in a poetical and dramatic form. Her penetrating intellect and unrestrainable volubility discourse forth the motives and principles of the combatant factions; while in her remorseless impiety and revengeful ferocity is impersonated, as it were, the very genius and spirit of the terrible conflict. So that we may regard her as, in some sort, an ideal concentration of that murderous ecstasy which seized upon the nation. (p. xiv)

Much might be said by way of explaining how, in the drama, the union of Henry and Margaret has the effect of making them both more and more what they ought not to be; his doing too little evermore stimulating her activity, and her doing too much as constantly opiating his. And by their endeavoring thus to repair each other's excess, that excess is not only heightened in itself, but rendered on both sides more mischievous in its effects, forasmuch as it practically inverts the relation between them: her energy cannot make up for his imbecility, because in either case the quality does not fit the person. For in seeking to make his place good she only displaces both herself and him, and, of course, the more she does out of her place, the more she undoes her cause. All which shows that in such matters it is often of less consequence what is done, than by whom, and how; for the simple reason that the issue depends not so much on the form of the act, as on the manner in which it is viewed by those to whom it refers. Finally, if any one think that Margaret's ferocity is strained up to a pitch incompatible with her sex, and unnecessary for the occasion; perhaps it will be deemed a sufficient answer, that the spirit of such a war could scarce be dramatically conveyed without the presence of a fury, and that the Furies have always been represented as females.

Warwick and Clifford are appropriate specimens of the old English feudal baronage in the height of its power and splendor; a class of men brave, haughty, turbulent, and rough, accustomed to wield the most despotic authority on their estates, and therefore spurning at legal restraint in their public capacity; and individually able, sometimes, to overawe and browbeat both king and parliament. In the play, however, we see little of their personal traits, these being, for the most part, lost in the common habits and sentiments of their order; not to mention that, in the collision of such steel-clad champions, individual features are apt to be kept out of sight, and all distinctive tones are naturally drowned in the clash of arms. It is mainly what

they stand for in the public action, that the drama concerns itself about, not those characteristic issues which are the proper elements of a personal acquaintance. Yet they are somewhat discriminated: Clifford is more fierce and special in his revenge, because more tender and warm in his affections; while Warwick is more free from particular hate, because his mind is more at ease in the magnitude of his power, and the feeling of his consequence. (pp. xv-xvi)

The representation of Suffolk in the *Second Part* might also be cited in disproof of Shakespeare's alleged bias to the Lancastrian side. Ambitious, unprincipled, impatient of every one's pride and purpose but his own, a thorough-paced scoundrelism is depicted in him without mitigation or remorse. Yet if his dramatic character be compared with the worst that history has alleged concerning him, the portrait will probably appear to have rather the overcoloring of a young author aiming at effect, than the temperance and moderation of conscious strength. Generally, however, the *Second Part* and the *Third* are in effect a pretty fair revivification of history, in that they set before us an overgrown nobility, a giant race of iron-bound warriors, who being choked off from foreign conquest, and unused to the arts of peace, their high-strung energies got corrupted into fierce hatreds and revengeful passions; and they had no refuge from the gnawings of pride and ambition, but to struggle and fight at home for that distinction which they had been bred to anticipate by fighting abroad.

In the *Second* and *Third Parts of Henry VI* the character of Richard is set forth in the processes of development and formation; whereas in *King Richard III* we have little else than the working-out of his character as already formed. In Shakespeare's time the prevailing idea of Richard was derived from the *History of his Life and Reign,* put forth by Sir Thomas More. . . . (p. xvii)

It is evident that this furnished the matter and form of the Poet's conception; his character of Richard being little other than the historian's descriptive analysis reduced to dramatic life and expression. In accordance with Shakespeare's usual method, at our first meeting with Richard, in the *Second Part,* act v. sc. 1, is suggested the first principle and prolific germ out of which his action is mainly evolved. He is called "foul stigmatic," because the stigma set on his person is both to others the handiest theme of reproach, and to himself the most annoying; like a huge boil on a man's face, which, because of its unsightliness, is the point that his enemies see most, and, because of its soreness, strike first. And his personal deformity is regarded not only as the proper outshaping and physiognomy of a certain original malignity of soul, but as yielding the prime motive of his malignant dealing, in so far as this dealing proceeds from motive as distinguished from impulse; his shape having grown ugly because his spirit was bad, and his spirit growing worse because of his ugly shape. For his ill-looks invite reproach, and reproach quickens and heightens his malice; and because men hate to look on him, he therefore cares all the more to be looked on; and as his aspect repels admiration, he has no way to win it but by power, that so fear may compel what inclination denies. Thus experience generates in him a most inordinate lust of power; and the circumstantial impossibility of coming at this, save by crime, puts him upon such a course of intellectual training and practice as may enable him to commit crimes, and still avoid the consequences, thus reversing the natural proportion between success and desert. (pp. xviii-xix)

It should be remarked that Richard, steeped as he is in essential villainy, is actuated by no such "motiveless malignity" as distinguishes Iago. Cruel and unrelenting in pursuit of his end, yet there is no wanton and gratuitous cruelty in him: in all his crimes he has a purpose beyond the act itself. Nor does he seem properly to hate those whom he kills: they stand between him and his ruling passion. . . . And he has a certain redundant, impulsive, restless activity of nature, that he never can hold still; in virtue of which, as his thought seizes with amazing quickness and sureness where, and when, and how to cut, so he is equally sudden and sure of hand: the purpose flashes upon him, and he instantly darts to the crisis of performance, the thought setting his whole being a-stir with executive transport. It is as if such an excess of life and energy had been rammed into his little body, as to strain and bulge it out of shape. (pp. xx-xxi)

> *Henry Norman Hudson, in introductions to "King Henry VI, Parts I, II, and III," in* The Works of Shakespeare, Vol. I, *Robt. Rivière & Son, Ltd., 1937, pp. xix-xxxvi, vii-xxxi, vii-xxi.*

JANE LEE   (lecture date 1876)

[*Acknowledging her debt to Edmond Malone (1787), Lee compares textual details of* The Contention *and* The True Tragedy *with* 2 *and* 3 Henry VI. *She concludes that Marlowe and Greene wrote the former two plays, and that Shakespeare merely reworked and improved them in writing* 2 *and* 3 Henry VI, *perhaps with the assistance of Marlowe. The possibility of Marlowe's hand in the composition of* 2 *and* 3 Henry VI *was also posited by Edward Dowden (1881). Another extensive comparison between the so-called quarto plays and* 2 *and* 3 Henry VI *was presented by G. G. Gervinus (1849-50), who similarly concluded that the earlier works were written by Greene and the Folio versions adapted by Shakespeare. For further commentary on the authorship of the* Henry VI *trilogy, see the essays by Peter Alexander, W. J. Courthope, Madeleine Doran, F. G. Fleay, and Allison Gaw listed in the Additional Bibliography. Lee's essay was originally delivered as a lecture before the New Shakspere Society on October 13, 1876.*]

Many questions are summed up in the one question: "Who wrote the *Henry VI* plays?" We have to decide not only whether Shakspere was their author, but also whether he worked single-handed, or with fellow-workers?—when the plays were written?—whether they are original, or founded on certain older plays?—and, if this be so, who was the author, or who were the authors of those older plays, as well as at what time were they written? (pp. 219-20)

The first part of the *Henry VI* plays does not stand on the same footing as the two latter parts. We possess no early sketch, or imperfect transcript of it (if such ever existed); and whilst it is abundantly evident that Parts 2 and 3 were written by the same men, it is by no means so evident that they were written by the same men as composed Part 1. The first Part of *Henry VI*, therefore, cannot be considered in connection with the second and third Parts.

In entering on the question of the authorship of Parts 2 and 3 I think our first point should be to decide whether they are copies—enlarged and improved—of the *Contention* and *True Tragedy;* or whether they are themselves original works of which the *Contention* and *True Tragedy* are imperfect transcripts. The last of the writers who have maintained this view is Mr Fleay, in an interesting paper in *Macmillan's Magazine* for Nov. 1875 [see Additional Bibliography]. His reasons for holding this opinion are as follows: 1st, he finds, in the *Con-*

tention and *True Tragedy* words omitted which are needful to the sense; 2nd, words misplaced; 3rd, wrong metrical arrangement; 4th, gaps filled up with inferior matter. The first three reasons do not, I think, prove much either way. Every editor of our early plays tells the same tale: he finds only too often words omitted, words misplaced, and the metre wrongly arranged. It is because of these very omissions, displacements, and misarrangements that we are still perplexed as to the sense of many passages in our old dramatists. The 4th reason presents the divergence of opinion in the clearest light. . . . Those who differ from Mr. Fleay say: 'Here is inferior matter; but it is to us one among many proofs that the *Contention* and *True Tragedy* are older and weaker plays. This inferior matter was weighed in the balance and found wanting by that later writer or those later writers who constructed out of them the fuller and more sustained dramas which we know as *Henry VI*, Parts 2 and 3.'

On this disputed question I am on the side of those who hold that the *Contention* and *True Tragedy* are the older plays. I will give my reasons presently for thinking this; but lest it should seem to some that I linger unnecessarily over the question, let me say that I do so because I myself hesitated long, and because it was not until I had gone patiently through the arguments which I have here brought together, that I convinced myself that the *Contention* and *True Tragedy* are older plays on which *Henry VI*, Parts 2 and 3, are founded. (pp. 220-21)

The first consideration which leads to the belief that the *Contention* and *True Tragedy* are older plays than *Henry VI*, Parts 2 and 3, is the nature of their versification and general metrical arrangement. This resembles the versification of the dramatists anterior to Shakspere's time far more than that of Shakspere and his immediate contemporaries. The general want of regularity and equality—the monotonous sing-song rhythm of some scenes, the irregular and careless metre of others—which characterized the versification of our earlier dramatic writers, is in great measure characteristic of the versification of the *Contention* and *True Tragedy*. Such plays as *Locrine*, and *The Famous Victories*, and some parts of the *True Tragedy of Richard III* will afford examples of what I mean. Now, in the *Henry VI* plays, though there is much that is monotonous and tame, yet the many careless, meagre, and irregular lines which disfigure the *Contention* and *True Tragedy* are absent; so that the want of balance and equality in the various passages and scenes never jars on our ears. And thus there is fair ground for concluding that *Henry VI*, Parts 2 and 3, belong to a later time than the *Contention* and *True Tragedy*. One can hardly suppose that any possible transcriber of the *Henry VI* plays could have, as it were, mentally dropped back into the metrical style of an earlier period of dramatic poetry. (p. 222)

Several particulars are related in the *Contention* and *True Tragedy* of which there is no mention made in *Henry VI*, Parts 2 and 3. It is reasonable to suppose that the author of *Henry VI* might have rejected these particulars as superfluous or trivial: but it is scarcely probable that any copyist would have invented and inserted them. (p. 224)

It is [also] noticeable that in the midst of scenes where there are many and considerable differences between the *Contention* and *True Tragedy,* and *Henry VI*, Parts 2 and 3, where many lines are partly, and many lines are wholly, different,—we suddenly come upon a group of lines quite the same; lines often spoken by the less important characters of the plays. One can hardly imagine that a copyist would preserve intact the unimportant words spoken by minor personages, while he gave only garbled and imperfect versions of the speeches assigned to the chief characters. (pp. 225-26)

I have said that the additional particulars found in the *Contention* and *True Tragedy* are an argument against their being spurious copies of the *Henry VI* plays. The omission from them of some of the finest passages is an even stronger argument.

Turn to York's speech with which 2 *Henry VI*, I. i. closes. Of the first half there is no trace whatever in the *Contention*, while the last half is exactly the same in both. Are we to suppose that the transcriber deliberately passed by these first 20 lines (lines which are full of life and power) while he copied the remainder with conscientious care? (p. 226)

To me it seems that the differences between the *Contention* and *True Tragedy* and *Henry VI*, Parts 2 and 3, are so many and so important, that if we allow the former to be imperfect transcripts of the latter, we must suppose that some dramatist took his stolen copies or his short-hand notes and regularly re-wrote them. We must suppose that he newly versified the plays; that he introduced fresh circumstances; that he added much new and poor matter; and that he left out the greatest and most thoughtful passages. On no other supposition can the *Contention* and *True Tragedy* be imperfect copies of *Henry VI*, Parts 2 and 3. A play printed from short-hand notes or from a stage copy would (perhaps necessarily) be inferior to the original, but it could not, I maintain, exhibit the radical differences from it which I have shown to be contained in the *Contention* and *True Tragedy* as compared with 2 and 3 *Henry VI*. (p. 229)

It remains for me to show that there is good ground, that there is, indeed, every reason, for believing that it was Shakspere who out of the *Contention* and *True Tragedy* created the 2nd and 3rd parts of *Henry VI*. The amount of rime in Shakspere's early plays—even in his historical play of *Richard II*—might be an argument against the Shaksperian authorship of *Henry VI*, Parts 2 and 3, did we not believe that they were founded on older plays in which but little rime appears. Even were there no other evidence, the unity of design and of character between Shakspere's *Richard III* and the *Henry VI* plays would suggest that they must have preceeded from one and the same mind. General tradition declares the plays to be by Shakspere; the open and clamorous charges made by his rivals suggest that they are his; and internal evidence, as I am now about to show, goes far to prove the same result:—The great verses which sum up the character of Richard are identical in the *True Tragedy* and in *3 Henry VI*. . . .

> I have no brothers; I am like no brothers.
> And this word love, which grey beards term divine,
> Be resident in men like one another,
> And not in me: I am myself alone.
>   [*3 Henry VI*, V. vi. 80-3]
>   (p. 263)

Another, no less sure, mark of Shakspere's hand, we find in the words spoken by the Duchess of Gloster, when—her penance performed—Stanley is conducting her to her place of banishment:

> Go, lead the way—I long to see my prison.
>   [*2 Henry VI*, II. iv. 110]

The impatience of a proud spirit wishful to know the worst. (p. 264)

Many of the epithets, verbal expressions and phrases, which occur in the *Henry VI* plays are akin to or identical with those of Shakspere's undoubted works. In *Venus and Adonis* occurs the epithet 'ill-nurtured':

> Ill-nurtured, crooked, churlish, harsh in voice.
>   [*Venus and Adonis*, 134]

It is found also in *2 Henry VI:*

> Presumptuous dame, ill-nurtured Eleanor.
>   [*2 Henry VI*, I. ii. 42]

Compare with the words in *Coriolanus:*

> The man I speak of cannot in this world
> Be singly counterpoised.
>   [*Coriolanus*, II. ii. 86-7]

the lines in *2 Henry VI:*

> The lives of those which we have lost in fight
> Be counterpoised with such a petty sum.
>   [*2 Henry VI*, IV. i. 21-2]
>   (p. 265)

Throughout his writings, Shakspere often uses an adjective in the place of a substantive. In *Venus and Adonis* we have: "A Sudden *pale* usurps her cheek" [589-91]. In the *Tempest*, "The *vast* of night" [I. ii. 32]. In *Julius Caesar*, "The *deep* of night" [IV. iii. 226]. So in [*2 Henry VI*, I. iv. 16]: "Deep night, dark night, the *silent* of the night;" while in the *Contention* the corresponding line has: "The silence of the night." (p. 266)

Internal evidence thus points to the hand of Shakspere. Moreover Shakspere himself claims the plays as his own. For, what other inference than that Shakspere claimed for himself the authorship of *Henry VI*, Parts 2 and 3, can be drawn from the fact that they are found in the first printed collection of his undoubted plays—a collection which was made by his intimate friends Heminge and Condell. (p. 268)

I should like to go through the *Henry VI* plays scene by scene, and point to the added lines and passages in each which I instinctively feel to be Shakspere's; but space would fail, and I must content myself with pointing to a few instances which may serve to illustrate the rest.

Take Gloster's spirited speech in [*2 Henry VI*, I. i. 77], describing the "common grief of all the land"—where Shakspere's patriotism and public spirit shine clearly forth. How different is it from the unanimated, unimpassioned language of the Gloster of the *Contention!* Or, take Margaret's speech—*2 Henry VI*, I. iii.—where Shakspere's unequalled power of delineating and discriminating character is forcibly manifested. . . . With what skill, then, does Shakspere re-mould and develop a conception which was not originally his own! Surely it is Shakspere who here sets before us with a few strokes of his pen the pitiable weakness of the saintly King, and the lovelessness of the wife who thus laughs to scorn the failings of her husband. . . . (pp. 268-69)

Turn now to the additions made to the latter part of sc. iii., Act I., of *2 Henry VI*. Suffolk, Cardinal Beaufort, Somerset, Buckingham, the Queen, hurl accusations against Gloster: He is Protector, and therefore the Dauphin has prevailed beyond the seas; the peers have been made subject to his sovereignty; the commons have been racked; the clergy's bags are lean and lank; his sumptuous buildings and his wife's attire have cost a mass of public treasure; his sale of offices and towns in France, were they known, would quickly make him lose his head.

At these charges Gloster as ever "bears him like a noble gentleman" [2 Henry VI, I. i. 183-84]. He will not answer hastily: he goes out, and then returns and speaks with calmness:

> Now, lords, my choler being overblown
> With walking once about the quadrangle,
> I come to talk of commonwealth affairs.
> As for your spiteful false objections,
> Prove them, and I lie open to the law:
> But God in mercy so deal with my soul,
> As I in duty love my king and country!
> But to the matter that we have in hand:—
> I say, my sovereign, York is meetest man
> To be your regent in the realm of France.
> [2 Henry VI, I. iii. 152-61]

Listen to the deep pathos of the words spoken by the Duchess of Gloster when she is parted from her husband and hurried into ignominious banishment:

> Duchess. Art thou gone too? All comfort go with
>   thee!
>   For none abides with me: my joy is
>   death;
>   Death at whose name I oft have been
>   afeared:—
>   Because I wished this world's
>   eternity. . . .
> Stanley. Madam, your penance done, throw off
>   this sheet,
>   And go we to attire you for your journey.
> Duchess   My shame will not be shifted with my
>   sheet;
>   No, it will hang upon my richest robes,
>   And shew itself attire me how I can.
>   Go, lead the way: I long to see my
>   prison.
>   [2 Henry VI, II. iv. 87-90, 101-10]

We seem to see these scenes as vividly, and to hear the voices as distinctly, as if we ourselves were carried back to the fifteenth century—into the midst of the jealous nobles, or as spectators of the departure of the Duchess in her misery. No other writer ever possessed in an equal degree the power of giving form to the thoughts which his imagination had pictured—of calling up scenes, of summoning characters before the very eyes of his hearers. The few instances here given of the vivid power of characterization, peculiar to Shakspere, displayed in the Henry VI plays, have all been taken from the early scenes of the second part; but any one acquainted with the plays will readily recall many more and equally striking examples.

In every respect the 2nd and 3rd parts of Henry VI are finer and more perfectly developed dramas than their originals. The whole form and spirit of the plays is altered. Careless, slipshod lines are cut out; trivial, unnecessary details are omitted; gross, historical blunders are swept away; the rhythm of the lines is more musical; the diction more elevated; the action more fully matured: above all, the characters in every instance stand out more distinctly. Every scene has been more or less changed; and every change made is a change for the better. Shakspere has gathered the wheat into his garner, and has cast the chaff away.

I have said that I consider Marlowe to have been, at this period, a greater poet than Shakspere, and in here attributing to Shakspere the special excellencies of the Henry VI plays I have

endeavoured carefully to discriminate between the qualities in which Marlowe seems to me to have excelled, and the qualities in which, in common with all the world, I hold Shakspere to have been (even in early life) preëminent.

But did Shakspere work alone, or is it admissible to believe that in his work of revision and re-formation Marlowe was his fellow-worker? Certain it is that Marlowe's peculiar style appears as distinctly in the reformed as in the unreformed plays. . . . The savage words spoken by Iden when he slays Cade and gloats over the death of "a poor famished man" [2 Henry VI, IV. x. 44] are more like the author of Tamburlaine than 'gentle' Shakspere. (pp. 269-71)

There is nothing inherently improbable in the supposition that Shakspere and Marlowe re-wrote the plays together. To suppose it, removes from Shakspere the unjust reproach of plagiarism which Greene and others have flung in his teeth [see excerpt above, 1592]; and which Mr Knight holds (somewhat unnecessarily) would attach to him if he were not the author of the plays in their original state. Shakspere was in many points Marlowe's faithful disciple. (p. 273)

Careful study has convinced me that the Henry VI plays, in their reformed and revised state, were not written by Shakspere unaided and alone. It is not, indeed, possible for us to do more than conjecture who his fellow-worker may have been. The foregoing remarks show that there is, at least, nothing unreasonable, or even improbable, in supposing his fellow-worker to have been Marlowe. I have not proved this; nor can it, in my opinion, be proved with our present knowledge. But could Marlowe's share in the work be demonstrated, it would, I think, go far to remove the mystery which hangs round the authorship of the Henry VI plays.

I began this paper by putting to myself the several questions which are included in the one question, "Who wrote Henry VI?" I will end it by gathering together in a few words the several answers which I have offered. I believe that Shakspere was the author of Henry VI, Parts 2 and 3, and that there is some ground for concluding that Marlowe was his fellow worker: that Henry VI, Parts 2 and 3, were written about the year 1590: that they were not original plays, but were founded on certain older plays known as the Contention and True Tragedy: and that Marlowe and Greene, and possibly Peele, were the writers of these older plays, which were written some time, perhaps some years, before the 2nd and 3rd Parts of Henry VI. (p. 275)

Jane Lee, "On the Authorship of the Second and Third Parts of 'Henry VI', and Their Originals," in The New Shakspere Society's Transactions, No. 4, 1875-76, pp. 219-79.

EDWARD DOWDEN (essay date 1881)

[Dowden was an Irish critic and biographer whose Shakspere: A Critical Study of His Mind and Art (rev. ed. 1881) was the leading example of the biographical criticism popular in the English-speaking world near the end of the nineteenth century. Biographical critics sought in the plays and poems a record of Shakespeare's personal development. As that approach gave way in the twentieth century to aesthetic theories with greater emphasis on the constructed, technical nature of literary works, Dowden and other biographical critics came to be considered limited. In his preface to the work mentioned above, Dowden lists 1 Henry VI as only "Touched by Shakspere" and 2 and 3 Henry VI as belonging to the "Marlowe-Shakspere Group," thus establishing himself in agreement with such other critics of the period as G. G. Gervinus (1849-50) and Jane Lee (1876), both of whom regarded

the Henry VI *trilogy as the work of more than one dramatist. In the excerpt below, Dowden examines the character of Henry VI, arguing that although Shakespeare "is as favorably disposed to him as is possible," Henry's weakness, his passivity, and his self-centered abandonment of his responsibilities adversely influence the audience's perception of his character. For further discussion of the character of Henry VI, see the excerpts by William Hazlitt (1817), Harold C. Goddard (1951), M. M. Reese (1961), Michael Manheim (1973), and John D. Cox (1978). Also see the essays by David L. Frey and Mattie Swayne listed in the Additional Bibliography.]*

Whether any portions of the first part of *Henry VI.* be from the hand of Shakspere, and, if there be, what those portions are, need not be here investigated. The play belongs, in the main, to the pre-Shaksperian school. Shakspere finds his own genius for the dramatic rendering of history for the first time distinctly in the second and third parts of *Henry VI.* The writer of the first part does not stand above the characters which he creates; he is violently prejudiced against some, and he feels a lyrical delight in singing the praises of others. But in the treatment of the characters of the King, of Gloster, of York, of Richard, in the later parts of the trilogy the Shaksperian impartiality and irony are clearly discernible. Shakspere does not hate King Henry; he is as favorably disposed to him as is possible; but he says, with the same clear and definite expression in which the historical fact uttered itself, that this saint of a feeble type upon the throne of England was a curse to the land and to the time only less than a royal criminal as weak as Henry would have been.

The heroic days of the fifth Henry, when the play opens, belong to the past; but their memory survives in the hearts and in the vigorous muscles of the great Lords and earls who surround the King. He only, who most should have treasured and augmented his inheritance of glory and of power, is insensible to the large responsibilities and privileges of his place. He is cold in great affairs; his supreme concern is to remain blameless. Free from all greeds and ambitions, he yet is possessed by egoism, the egoism of timid saintliness. His virtue is negative, because there is no vigorous basis of manhood within him out of which heroic saintliness might develop itself. For fear of what is wrong, he shrinks from what is right. This is not the virtue ascribed to the nearest followers of "the Faithful and True" who in his righteousness doth judge and make war. Henry is passive in the presence of evil, and weeps. He would keep his garments clean; but the garments of God's soldier-saints, who do not fear the soils of struggle, gleam with a higher, intenser purity.... These soldiers in heaven have their representatives in earth, and Henry was not one of these. Zeal must come before charity, and then when charity comes it will appear as a self-denial. But Henry knows nothing of zeal; and he is amiable, not charitable.

There is something of irony in the scene with which the second part of *Henry VI.* opens. Suffolk, the Lancelot of this tragedy, has brought from France the Princess Margaret, and the joy of the blameless King, upon receiving, at the cost of two hard-won provinces, this terrible wife, who will "dandle him like a baby" [*2 Henry VI,* I. iii. 145], has in it something pitiable, something pathetic, and something ludicrous. The relations of the King to Margaret throughout the play are delicately and profoundly conceived. He clings to her as to something stronger than himself; he dreads her as a boy might dread some formidable master:

> *Exeter.* Here comes the Queen, whose looks betray her
>   anger: I'll steal away.
> *Henry.* And so will I.
>   [*3 Henry VI,* I. i. 211-13]

Yet through his own freedom from passion he derives a sense of superiority to his wife; and after she has dashed him all over with the spray of her violent anger and her scorn, Henry may be seen mildly wiping away the drops, insufferably placable, offering excuses for the vituperation and the insults which he has received:

> Poor Queen, how love to me and to her son
> Hath made her break out into terms of rage!
>   [*3 Henry VI,* I. i. 264-65]
>   (pp. 153-55)

[The] morbid scrupulosity of conscience which characterizes Henry while he neglects the high duties of his position sets him speculating uneasily about the validity of his title to the throne—a title which has descended through the great victor of Agincourt from Henry's grandfather. He turns from York to Warwick, from Warwick to Northumberland, uncertain what he ought to think. Clifford boldly cuts the knot; and Henry's courage revives:

> King Henry, be thy title right or wrong,
> Lord Clifford vows to fight in thy defense.
>   [*3 Henry VI,* I. i. 159-60]

But the King, in the presence of armed force, cannot maintain his resolution, and ends by a compromise, which, upon condition of the forfeiture of his son's rights, will secure peace in *his* days. We sympathize with the indignant Margaret. Yet in Henry's conduct there has been no active selfishness; he has only accepted peace at the price required. (pp. 157-58)

In prison Henry, at last, is really happy; now he is responsible for nothing; he enjoys, for the first time, tranquil solitude; he is a bird who sings in his cage. His latter days he will spend, to the rebuke of sin and the praise of his Creator, in devotion. Henry's equanimity is not of the highest kind; he is incapable of commotion. His peace is not that which underlies wholesome agitation, a peace which passes understanding.... If Henry had known the nobleness of true kingship, his content in prison might be admirable; as it is, the beauty of that content does not strike us as of a rich or vivid kind. But the end is come, and that is a gain. Henry has yielded to the House of York, and the evil time is growing shorter. The words of the great Duke of York are confirmed by our sense of fact and right:

> King did I call thee? nay, thou art not king....
> Give place; by heaven, thou shalt rule no more
> O'er him whom heaven created for thy ruler!
>   [*2 Henry VI,* V. i. 93, 104-05]
>   (pp. 159-60)

Edward Dowden, "The English Historical Plays," in his Shakspere: A Critical Study of His Mind and Art, *third edition, Harper & Brothers Publishers, 1881, pp. 144-97.*

DENTON J. SNIDER (essay date 1890)

[Snider was an American scholar, philosopher, and poet who followed closely the precepts of the German philosopher Georg Wilhelm Friedrich Hegel and contributed greatly to the dissemination of his dialectical philosophy in America. Snider's critical writings include studies on Homer, Dante, and Goethe, as well as Shakespeare. Like Hermann Ulrici and G. G. Gervinus, Snider sought the dramatic unity and ethicality in Shakespeare's plays, but he presented a more rigorous Hegelian interpretation than those two German philosophical critics. In the introduction to his three-volume work The Shakespearian Drama: A Commentary*

(1887-90), Snider states that Shakespeare's plays present various ethical principles which, in their differences, come into "Dramatic Collision," but are ultimately resolved and brought into harmony. He claims that these collisions can be traced in the plays' various "Dramatic Threads" of action and thought, which together form a "Dramatic Movement," and that the analysis of these threads and movements—"the structural elements of the drama"—reveal the organic unity of Shakespearean drama. In the excerpt below, Snider contends that the fundamental theme of the Henry VI and Richard III tetralogy is "national retribution," for the plays demonstrate the idea that England must atone for its unlawful conquest of France. He traces in the structure of the Henry VI trilogy Shakespeare's development of this theme. Many critics have addressed the question of whether there is a purposeful, providential order operating in the Henry VI trilogy or whether events are the inevitable outcome of the conflict between careless and overly ambitious individuals. Among those who see the operation of God or divine providence in the plays is Hermann Ulrici (1839), E. M. W. Tillyard (1944), Irving Ribner (1965), and M. M. Reese (1961); those critics who share the nonprovidential or humanistic view include A. C. Hamilton (1961-62), S. C. Sen Gupta (1964), H. M. Richmond (1967), James Winny (1968), David Riggs (1971), Robert B. Pierce (1971), and Robert Ornstein (1972). For further discussion of this issue, see the essays by Edward I. Berry, David L. Frey, and Henry Ansgar Kelly listed in the Additional Bibliography.]

The First Part of *Henry the Sixth* is not a great play; even that Shakespeare was its author is denied by many good judges of the Poet's writings. But let this question of authenticity be dropped at once. The organization is rather loose, yet might be worse; the action is not controlled by a strong inner thought, but moves through a series of pictorial scenes in an external fashion; liveliness it has, though only playing over the surface. That deep, central flame which fuses all the materials of the drama into oneness—of which the events are merely the fiery outbursts—is wanting here, though there is much activity and struggle. The play, however, has one general purpose to which it seeks to give utterance; this purpose . . . is to show the loss of the French territory through English dissension.

The clearest and best point in the structure of the present work is its division into two threads, which may be called the external conflict and the internal conflict. The scene of the first thread lies in France; it portrays the struggle between the French and the English. The former are fighting for national independence, the latter for the subjugation of their neighbors. This is a contest in which England must lose, and ought to lose, for she is really violating her own deepest principle, namely, nationality. The second thread will show the means—internal strife will paralyze her efforts; the hatred of parties will turn from the enemy abroad to the opponents within. The reader, for his own advantage, may note the inherent relation between these two threads—war upon your neighbor seems ultimately to mean war upon yourself.

The movements, which the reader may possibly inquire after next, are not very distinctly marked; the turning-point may be considered to be where Burgundy goes over to the French, and thus unites his nation against the invader. Yet the whole action only exhibits occurrence after occurrence sweeping away the English conquests. The two threads, however, proceed with perfect distinctness through the entire play. (pp. 432-34)

The first thread, as it shows a conflict, is divided into two sides—the French and the English. The French are striving with success to redeem their country from a foreign yoke; town after town, and province after province, are falling into their hands. They have in these wars their heroic character—the

supreme representative of the struggling nation. But it is not the King, not a nobleman, not even a man; it is a poor shepherd's daughter named Joan of Arc, now far more famous than the greatest monarch of that age. Truly she is a remarkable appearance—in the history of the world a glowing point of light which darts up and illumines an epoch. (p. 434)

Shakespeare, or the author of the First Part of *Henry the Sixth*, has not taken much advantage of the imposing figure of Joan of Arc; he has rather left her character and her mission in a state of perplexing doubt. . . . [The] character fluctuates; it has no unity in its development, but sways from one side to the other, finally resting under an English cloud of suspicion. Still the main fact cannot be obscured—a woman of humble station rises to be a national heroine, heroic above all men of that age; the champion of the Family has become the champion of the State.

We now turn to the side of the English, in order to see what offset they have to the wonderful Maid of Orleans. A national hero appears also among them, but of quite a different kind. It is Talbot, a man trained to the use of arms, of great experience in war, and of noble rank. He is mainly the courageous soldier, whose very name puts the French to flight. There is in his actions a wild daring which magnetizes the troops under him into huge masses of fiery valor; this wild daring, coupled with a chivalrous, open-hearted devotion to his country, is his characteristic trait. The Soldier meets the Maid; there is much fluctuation in the conflict, but the English poet cannot disguise the fact that the result is general defeat.

But the crowning glory of Talbot's career is the manner of his death. He is a sacrifice to the hatred between two party-leaders, who were also generals in this unfortunate time—York and Somerset; neither will send aid to Talbot in his perilous situation at Bordeaux. He perishes; the English national hero becomes the victim of English dissension—an ominous emblem of England herself. But to his patriotic devotion is now added a new trait of character—parental love. His young son, John Talbot, has just come to France in order to receive under his father's eye a military training; when destruction lowers from every quarter of the sky, the parent beseeches his boy to escape—from out the rugged breast of the soldier is seen to leap the pure fire of domestic affection. But the son is a Talbot; he will not fly from the enemy; his father is going to stay and die—so will he if he be truly a son. (pp. 434-36)

Such is by all means the most powerful portion of the play; it is an incident which is worthy of the highest inspiration. There is portrayed in the hardy bosom of Talbot a conflict between the parent and the soldier, right in the midst of the battle raging around—a truly tragic theme in the best sense of the word. (p. 437)

We pass now to the second thread, portraying the internal conflict of England, which runs parallel with the external conflict given in the first thread. There are two sets of partisans, with very different objects in view. The one set is struggling for the control of the weak-minded Monarch. Henry is a cipher in the government; two great lords, Gloster and Winchester, are fighting for the substance of regal authority. . . . Both men seem to be animated merely by a vulgar desire of power; neither stands as the advocate of any great national principle. Winchester is a churchman, and pleads the rights and immunities of his organization; hence Gloster is made to appear as the enemy of the Church—indeed, of religion itself. Still, there is little depth to Winchester's piety or to Gloster's skepticism; a pretext was needed by both to cloak their ambition—this is what determined their religious attitude.

But in these disputes the utter incompetency of Henry stands out in the strongest light; he can not unify his counselors at home—much less is he able to lead his army abroad. He has but to go back to the time of his grandfather when he will find a legitimate King—Richard the Second—deposed mainly on account of incapacity. His own dynasty, the Lancastrian, has no title to the throne except the ability to rule; what then must happen in his case? (pp. 437-38)

We now see that the national spirit engendered by the Lancastrians is lost, and with it has perished every reasonable ground for the continuance of their dynasty. France, the great foreign conquest, is gone from their grasp; the crown, unsupported by a strong ruler, must fall back into the hand of the true heir, who is here on the spot ready to assert his right. The play, therefore, leaves us with this new conflict ready to burst forth. (p. 439)

In the Second Part of *Henry the Sixth* the struggle is wholly internal; France has been lost to the English, and, hence, there is no French thread required to show the foreign war. The strife which England brought upon a neighboring people has turned back into herself; from her own hands she receives the punishment for the wrong done by her to another country, whose right of existence was as good as her own. National retribution is the fundamental principle of this whole Lancastrian Tetralogy—one party is swept off by a second, which, in its turn, is destroyed by a third; thus they rise and fall; every class of men seems to be infected with a corruption whose sole cure is death. The present play shows the transition from the loss of France to the first opening of the great dynastic quarrel—the Wars of the Roses. English dissension, which previously had defeated the English armies abroad, now raises its hand against England herself upon her own soil.

There are two movements, which are very plainly marked, and which present distinct phases of the conflict. The first is the struggle among the Lancastrians themselves—between those who agree in supporting the throne of King Henry the Sixth, but who, in other respects, are the bitterest enemies. Here there are naturally two main threads, made up of the opposing parties, the one side being headed by Humphrey, Duke of Gloster, the other by Queen Margaret. The result is that Gloster's party is annihilated, but the Duke of York, who has all along been waiting for his opportunity, at once springs up with a new and far more dangerous party. This is the second general movement of the play; the struggle is no longer among the Lancastrians themselves, but between the Lancastrians and Yorkists; the conflict has deepened into a fight against the supremacy of the reigning house. The present government means foreign defeat and civil dissension—it is, indeed, no government; hence its title, which rests upon the capacity of the ruler, is called in question by the true heir. The threads are now the two Roses—the parties of York and of Lancaster.

Beginning at once with the first movement, we notice that the one party at court is grouped around the brother of the late King, the protector of the realm—Humphrey, Duke of Gloster. His power is evidently declining; the marriage of King Henry with Margaret, and, above all, the concessions made in consequence of that event, were contrary to his policy, and meet with his strongest disapprobation. Gloster represents the old national spirit of England; he cannot be brought to yield the English claim to France by any measure. This marriage, cou-

pled with the surrender of Anjou and Maine, he looks upon as the disgrace of his country. He manifests, in this drama at least, the feeling of true patriotism; he will do nothing against the King; he cannot be seduced into ambitious thoughts, though he is next in succession to the throne. In general, he, amid a crowd of depraved self-seekers, upholds the principle of nationality. His character here will be noticed to be different from, though not inconsistent with, what it was represented to be in the First Part of *Henry the Sixth,* as love of power, which seems to be his leading trait there, may exist along with patriotic devotion.

At his side is placed his wife, the Duchess Eleanor, a haughty, indiscreet woman, whose strongest passion is ambition. She is a germ of Lady Macbeth. She tries to excite the thought of revolt in her husband, but he puts her down with an emphatic reproof. But that which gives her most prominence is the fact that she is the special object of Queen Margaret's hatred. The wife of the Protector and the wife of the Monarch thus manifest mutually the strongest jealousy; the two women fill the court with strife, for both are seeking the same thing—authority. (pp. 440-42)

The Yorkists also lean to the side of the Duke of Gloster in this first movement, though not without much ambiguous deal-

Part I. Act I. Scene i. Funeral of Henry V in Westminster Abbey. By G. F. Sargent (1841). The Department of Rare Books and Special Collections, The University of Michigan Library.

ing. Richard, the Duke of York, is, indeed, playing for the crown; his general scheme is to let the Lancastrians eat one another up, when he will step in and seize the prey. At first he proposes to "make a show of love to proud Duke Humphrey" [2 Henry VI, I. i. 241]; then he goes to the aid of the other side. Full of treachery and deep dissimulation is his character. It is hard to see wherein he is any better than the ruling powers; in some respects he is clearly worse. No improvement in the affairs of England can come through him; the same moral and political rottenness will continue, and the fiery process of war must go on till both sides be exterminated. Nor need the further reflection be withheld here—his whole generation, if they inherit his character, can never remain long in possession of the throne. His children will destroy one another till his line be extinct; then there may be some hope for peace to England.

But other Yorkists are different. The Nevills—Salisbury and Warwick—cling to the Duke of Gloster, and are ready to punish his murderers. They are also strongly national, and have been deeply chagrined at the policy toward France. But the main event of their history now is their conversion to the House of York. (pp. 443-44)

Passing now to the side hostile to the Duke of Gloster, which is the second thread of the first movement, we observe that its leader is no longer Cardinal Beaufort, but Margaret, the English Queen. This woman remains henceforward the central figure of her party; France has not only reconquered her provinces from England, but the latter is now subjected to the domination of a French Princess, whose domestic rule will be far more fatal than foreign defeat. Margaret is essentially a will-character; her intelligence, though of a high order, is not her supreme trait; that in which she is chiefly deficient is a moral nature. She is not faithful to the Family—she loves another man than her husband; like so many royal women, domestic instincts are swallowed up in political ambition. As ruler of the State, her career is still less commendable than as wife; she is going to control affairs even at the cost of the existence of the country. No great national purpose is seen in her conduct, or in that of her advisers; to have matters her own way is quite the sum total of her policy. The weak King, her husband, she despises. But she is determined to govern; this brings her at once into conflict with the "good Duke Humphrey," the Protector of the realm; the result is that Humphrey is deposed from his office, arraigned for high treason, and finally murdered in the most treacherous manner. With him was destroyed the peace of England, and, indeed, the Lancastrian tenure of the throne; the last man of that House worthy of rule has been butchered by his own kindred; the Lancastrian Family is rapidly putting an end to its own existence.

The group of men around Queen Margaret are animated with her principle; they are pursuing a selfish ambition to the detriment of their country. No spark of nationality illumines, even faintly, a single action of theirs; the fact is, they are united against the national man, Humphrey, but they would all desert and betray one another with the same readiness for the sake of personal advantage. The faithless cannot be faithful, even to their kind. (pp. 444-45)

King Henry, the helpless puppet around which all these crimes and intrigues are spinning, is the express contrast to his Queen. He absolutely possesses no power of will. His intellect, however, is not by any means so defective; he often shows insight into the true condition of affairs; he tries also to soften the rancor of parties—not by decisive action, but by amiable exhortation. His moral instinct is pure and true; he cannot be brought to believe in the guilt of his uncle Gloster. Of his religious nature, Margaret and others even make fun, coupling it with his utter weakness of resolution. King Henry is, therefore, supremely contemptible; he is not a man, since he lacks the will of a man, while his wife, as if to set him off more prominently, possesses a masculine energy of character.

The party of Margaret is, therefore, triumphant; her chief enemies are dead or banished; peace would now seem possible. But behold there arises a new conflict—deeper, more intense, more terrific than before. The Queen has really undermined the Lancastrian dynasty; its national purpose has perished with Gloster. With the might of destiny there comes up the rival claim of York, and finds many supporters. For the Lancastrians are legally usurpers; their sole title was their fidelity to the spirit of the nation, which accordingly supported their House. But this title has perished in an imbecile ruler, in foreign defeat, and in domestic strife; the same reasons which brought them to the throne can now be urged to drive them from the throne.

The second movement of the play has for its theme this struggle between York and Lancaster. (pp. 446-47)

In [2 Henry VI] the conflict between the Houses of York and Lancaster opened, but nothing was decided. The two parties are still quite equal; both are willing to compromise their extreme claims. The Third Part of Henry the Sixth shows, in general, the transition from this condition of balanced chances to the overthrow and annihilation of the Lancastrians; the crown passes to the Yorkists. The change is one of the bloodiest scenes in History, to which characteristic the play is true in the fullest measure. It is war and bustle from beginning to end—a carnival of barbaric butchery; every character seems to delight in smearing himself with gore; even the language bears often a furious and sanguinary aspect. A red, volcanic fire breaks fiercely from all sides; one towering form after another is swept down and burnt up in that molten stream of vindictive passion. But these outbursts are, in the main, confused, irregular, uncertain; the Titanic forces of Nature are manifestly at work here; the result is not a well-ordered work of Art—not a work of beautiful, though colossal, proportion, but a mass made up of immense fragmentary boulders. In other words, the elements of the grandest poem are here, but these elements are not fused into a harmonious unity. There is often the mighty Shakespearian expression; often the mighty Shakespearian conception of character; but the whole gives the appearance of terrific struggle—of chaos trying to organize itself, and, in spite of all effort, remaining, to a great extent, formless.

Of course the structure of such a drama cannot be of a high order. There are merely the two hostile parties, which constitute the two threads running through the action; these join in battle, then separate to give utterance to their feelings and opinions, after which they begin the conflict anew. The play is thus a series of battle-pieces, with short intervening pauses; fortune fluctuates from one side to the other, evidently working to destroy both sides. (pp. 449-50)

After the defeat of the Lancastrians, recounted at the end of the previous play, Richard, Duke of York, and King Henry make a treaty settling the disputed succession. But no peace is possible; the extremists in both parties control; their death is the only peace. Margaret on the one side, the sons of Richard on the other, force the violation of the compact. A French Fury is thus the guiding spirit of the Lancastrians; she is driving them rapidly into the jaws of Fate. Note also the sons of Richard; they are the future rulers of England; this whole war is made in their interest; can any hope of national regeneracy be seen in them? More vindictive, worse in every respect, they are than their father, who is bad enough. Fate cries out—they, too, must be got out of the way before peace can return to distracted England. Let the mills of the gods now begin grinding.

Another battle takes place; Richard, the father, is slain—slain by butcher Clifford, whose father had previously been slain. Blind Nemesis is smiting right and left in the field, gigantic, vigorous, having much work yet to do. Blind she is, verily, for she crops the innocent, sweet youth Rutland—the innocent son of York, not the guilty ones. A piteous spectacle it is— an offenseless child ground to death with the wicked. The last time defeat had overwhelmed the Lancastrians; this time the Yorkists experience disaster. It is well; both races must be deracinated from the soil of England.

Edward—guilty, licentious son of York—succeeds to the leadership; still, much work for retributive Nemesis, presiding Goddess of this Lower World. Another battle; now it is the turn of the Lancastrians to be defeated—indeed, already a second time their turn has come; defeated they are. . . . Edward is now crowned a king; the House of York has vindicated its title; the usurping, wicked, effete line is driven away. Cannot a little peace be now granted to this land? No; Nemesis must finish her work.

Poor King Henry has, therefore, lost his throne, which it is his curse to have possessed. His regal dignity he would gladly put aside: "Methinks it were a happy life to be no better than a homely swain" [*3 Henry VI*, II. v. 21-2]. In a tempest, tied to the rudder, which he cannot move, but which always moves him, he well may be weary of the place of Governor. A most amiable, deeply religious man, yet without will—how can he control the raging elements? An angelic nature, indeed, is his, by destiny allotted to rule over demons; he stands out in spotless white raiment mid the soot and flames of Tartarus. Yet he possesses intelligence; he knows the result of this strife going on around him; he sees that the present wretchedness comes from past wrong:—

> I'll leave my son my virtuous deeds behind,
> And would my father had left me no more.
> [*3 Henry VI*, II. ii. 49-50]

Also, he possesses a prophetic insight—he foretells to the Yorkists the destruction of their House through its own members, and he beholds in young Richmond the future redeemer of England. A person of a quiet, contemplative nature, born perhaps to be a holy prophet—but, alas, he is King—King of the infernal regions, with countless fiends to be tamed or strangled. Why does he not fly off and leave the Stygian pool? A domestic bond holds him; his other half—or, rather, his whole— his Stygian queen, and clutches him fast to subserve her purposes. A hapless sight is that—an Angel linked to a Fury. The Fury, too, has a will—has all the will; white, angelic Henry is dragged through murky Pandemonium, and to his honor comes out unstained. Still, the act of a man who cannot act is not likely to be ever very wicked.

The House of York is next seen disintegrating within, for it contains elements which can never be harmonized. The marriage of King Edward it was chiefly which caused a double disaffection—that of the brothers and that of Warwick. . . . Warwick is really the embodiment of disorganization; he overturned the Lancastrians, now he overturns the Yorkists. A great colossal character he is, the natural outgrowth of the age; in

him the spirit of insubordination and rebellion is manifested in its gigantic dimensions. But the mighty figure must be cast down; let his own principle be applied to himself; he once destroyed the supporters of the worthless Lancastrians—destroyed just what he now is himself. Nemesis will bring his deed back to him, swooping from above on speediest wing. (pp. 450-54)

But why should these Lancastrians be permitted continually to fight their lost battles over again? Let them be annihilated; then the contest can be brought to an end. King Henry is assassinated in prison by Gloster; his son also is cruelly butchered in cold blood. All the branches of the House of Lancaster are now lopped off except one frail, distant twig; for them Nemesis had done her work. So the drama ends with Edward of York once more upon the throne; incapacity of the monarch has again brought revolution; the Red Rose is plucked, and its petals scattered in the earth.

But, amid all these scenes of savagery one man has shown himself to be the supreme savage—Richard, Duke of Gloster, brother of the King. His body is as misshapen as his soul; ominous breathings he has given out in the course of the play; demoniac rage impels him to the most cruel deeds. But ambition also has filled his thoughts; he wishes to be King—King he will be. Several of his nearest relatives stand between him and the throne; he will have to get them out of the way. Nemesis is again at work; she is here preparing a dire instrument for some terrible purpose of hers. The House of York, too, must be smitten to earth; Gloster is to be the scourge of his family, which now is destroyed from within. (pp. 454-55)

Denton J. Snider, "'King Henry VI'," in his The Shakespearian Drama, a Commentary: The Histories, *Sigma Publishing Co., 1890, pp. 431-55.*

JOHN BELL HENNEMAN   (essay date 1900)

[*On the basis of internal evidence alone, Henneman postulates that an earlier Talbot play preceded* 1 Henry VI *and that Shakespeare used this work as a basis for his drama. Henneman states that Shakespeare's combination of the older, probably condensed Talbot parts with scenes that feature episodes from Henry VI's reign may well account for the episodic quality of* 1 Henry VI, *as well as for "the confusion of dates, chronological disorders, and more than one bewildering repetition of the same event." Further discussion of Shakespeare's possible sources for* 1 Henry VI *can be found in the essays by J. M. Brockbank and Geoffrey Bullough cited in the Additional Bibliography.*]

An analysis of *I. Henry VI.* shows not the close fusion of parts into a spiritual whole as in a later play like *Much Ado* or *King Lear,* or even in a comparatively early play like the *Merchant of Venice* or *A Midsummer Night's Dream.* There are not a few passages of no mean rhetorical power, more, indeed, than is generally supposed, but the play as a whole is structurally weak. There is little elaboration of character or development of plot. The play is characterized by the loose putting together of parts; each part being but the result of a succession or stringing together of scenes or episodes. (p. 293)

[In] the structure of *I. Henry VI.* there are two leading parts into which the play falls. These two parts may be generally designated as the Talbot or French portion and the Henry or English portion.

As the Folio edition gives the play there are twenty-seven scenes. By separating the episodes of the wooing of Margaret by Suffolk from the Joan episode that immediately precedes, as independent by its very content, there will be twenty-eight. Of these twenty-eight scenes at least sixteen belong to the Talbot part, eight to the Henry part, and the remaining four serve to connect and weld these together. Of these four one is about, and two others intimately concerned with, the Talbot wars; the fourth is the scene of the wooing of Margaret. Also two of the eight Henry scenes transfer the English king to France, and may be treated as connecting scenes; certainly, as will be shown, they bear a peculiar relation one to the other.

The French War or Talbot portion, into which the Joan of Arc scenes naturally fall, is thus apparently the original basis of the play. It is more closely related to the chronicles of Holinshed and Hall, and apart from specific exceptions presently to be noted, is the more archaic in manner and principle. Upon this Talbot part as ground stock is grafted the Henry part—the scenes comprising the quarrels of the nobles. The general jealousy between Gloucester and Winchester—at the Abbey, at the Tower, in the Parliament and in the Palace of the King—passes over into the specific enmity between Plantagenet and Somerset in the Temple Garden, followed at once by the death of Mortimer and bringing in its train all the horrors the factions of the Red and White Roses entail. These are hardly one-half so many as the Talbot scenes, but they are among the longest and most independently developed scenes in the play.

Also the four connecting or welding scenes, which bring the Talbot episodes into connection with the others, are largely independent and free in development. For instance, the long opening scene of the First Act is an introduction to the general situation. The accounts of the three messengers arriving in succession interrupt the quarrels of the nobles and tell of Talbot's distress. By the simple device of the messengers, taken from the old Senecan tragedy to serve as chorus, the English and the French parts are brought together at the opening of the play. Again, into the midst of the Fourth Act, where the death of Talbot is developed out of all due proportion, but in a distinctly elevated strain, by a poet who shows at once both lyric and dramatic power, two other connecting scenes are thrust. Scenes 3 and 4 of this Act are absolutely parallel in construction: Sir William Lucy appeals to both York and Somerset for succor in vain, and the death of Talbot is ascribed not to the French and to Joan, but to the jealousies and quarrels of the parties of the Red and the White Rose. And in the last Act occurs the final connecting scene: the wooing of Margaret by Suffolk. It is an episode of the battlefield; yet it is at the same time but another element of discord among the nobles: Suffolk becomes an influence in moving the King's choice in opposition to Gloucester. But this episode has a deeper significance than helping to connect the Talbot and Henry portions of the drama: it prepares intimately for Parts II. and III. of *Henry VI.*, wherein Margaret and her guilty love fill so large a part. Suffolk's speech:

> Thus Suffolk hath prevailed; and thus he goes. . . .
> Margaret shall now be queen, and rule the king;
> But I will rule both her, the king, and realm—
>   [*1 Henry VI*, V. v. 103, 107-08]

are the last words of Part I., and a sombre note is struck as the curtain falls. If ever there was intentional preparation for matter to come, it is surely here. . . . It is the figure of Margaret, amid the jarring contentions of parties, that moves sombrely through the four plays and binds the first tetralogy into a single whole—one ultimate consistent conception, though of unequal execution. (pp. 293-96)

Not that the whole plan was seen from the beginning. It gradually grew out of the material at hand. Part I. prepared for Parts II. and III.; Parts II. and III. are intimately connected; and *Richard III.* completed Part III. Or there may have been a different order of writing. So specifically does I. prepare for II. and III. in certain particulars that it is conceivable that I. was written after II. and that III. had been already planned. . . . Part I., therefore, could be made to serve as introduction. The Talbot material already well-known and existing in chronicle form, even if not, as is probable, as an old play, could be compressed, altered, and added to, and other non-chronicle parts introduced. The Henry, and particularly the Margaret, episodes became emphasized to accord with the two plays, the early forms of *II.* and *III Henry VI.*, already existing. Finally, *Richard III.* served as conclusion, after II. and III. had been put into final form. Such would be a conceivable hypothesis as to the relation of Part I. to Parts II. and III. (p. 296)

[Whatever] may be the precise order and dates of these several plays brought in question, the method and spirit of the writing of *I. Henry VI.* hardly admits of doubt. To work up or rewrite the Talbot portions of the Chronicles, probably, though not necessarily, already crystallized into an old play on the triumph of "brave Talbot" over the French, which possessed the hated Joan of Arc scenes and all; to intensify the figure and character of Talbot; to work over or add scenes like those touching Talbot's death; to connect him with the deplorable struggles of the nobles; to invent, by a happy poetical thought, the origin of the factions of the Red and White Roses in the Temple Garden; to sound at once the note of weakness in the king continued in the succeeding Parts, and thus convert the old Talbot material effectually into a Henry VI. drama; and to close with the wooing of Margaret as specific introduction to Part II.,—something like this seems the task that the dramatist set himself to perform.

Such a process as this mingling of themes in *I. Henry VI.* best accounts for obvious difficulties: the confusion of dates, chronological disorders, and more than one bewildering repetition of the same event. The portrayal of the death of Talbot before the marriage of the king to Margaret is historically an anomaly, but dramatically easily understood. Also the return of the Duke of Burgundy to the French occurred historically after the death of Joan and was in no wise caused by her; but there seems to have been some traditional or chronicle authority for the episode, apart from the freshness and spirit of the dramatic conception of the passage. Certain obscurities of reference may likewise be the result of the condensation of the old Talbot parts, just as in *King John* some of the deeds and words of the Bastard Faulconbridge are to be referred to the older play for proper understanding. Such may be a possible explanation of a vagueness in the presentation of the figures of the Master Gunner and his Boy, and of certain peculiarities in the structure of the Joan episodes as well as in the conception of the character of Joan herself. (pp. 296-97)

There is suggested at once that some of the contradictions and repetitions in the play can hardly be due to anything else than to the writing over existing dramatic material in new forms and keeping some parts of the old side by side. The strongest internal evidence of the probable existence of an older Talbot play seems to rest here; although one must be careful in drawing too rigid conclusions from the structure of a play that admittedly belongs to a formative period and nowhere applies very closely the laws of sequence and consistency. (p. 298)

[But] if there be an original Talbot portion, based either on an older play or directly upon the chronicles, adapted and strengthened by dramatic emphasis upon Talbot's character and Talbot's death, and expanded into a Henry VI. drama, and thus given a place in a larger tetralogy;—the person ordering this material and effecting these changes, in other words, the real creator of the play as it stands, could well be Shakespeare near the beginning of his art. At least one principle is clear. By a study of the earliest plays attributed to Shakespeare, for themselves and in their historic and comparative relations, there will be found to be more and more points in common with the Shakespeare of the later plays;—not yet in the fulness of his power, but at any rate with suggestions of the method, structure, habit of thought, characterization, and art of the master to be. (p. 320)

> *John Bell Henneman, "The Episodes in Shakespeare's 'I Henry VI'," in PMLA, 15, Vol. XV, No. 3, 1900, pp. 290-320.*

RICHARD G. MOULTON   (essay date 1903)

[*Moulton's works include* Shakespeare as a Dramatic Artist *(1885) and* The Moral System of Shakespeare *(1903). In the excerpt below, taken from the latter work, he traces the development of Richard of Gloucester in* 2 *and* 3 Henry VI *and finds in the character much that is appealing, as long as he stems his ambition. Moulton views Richard's long soliloquy (*3 Henry VI, III. ii. 124ff.*) as the turning point in the evolution of his persona; he also regards "the crowning incident" at the close of the trilogy, when Gloucester confronts Henry in the Tower, as "the graduation exercise of Richard's education in villainy." The character of Richard of Gloucester in the* Henry VI *plays has interested several critics: Mark Van Doren (1939) argued that he is the first individualized figure in Shakespearean drama and H.V.D. Dyson (1950) regarded Richard's isolation as a central aspect of his character. Also, Michael Manheim (1973) related the characterization of Richard to traditions of medieval drama and politics.*]

[Whatever] may be the precise facts as to the authorship of the three parts of *Henry the Sixth,* it is felt by many readers that they do not make a continuous and consistent scheme like that of the other trilogy. The contents of the plays are crude history, with elementary passions and melodramatic incident: for the most part scenes of factious turbulence, and civil wars in which father kills son, and son father. The heroes are such as butcher Clifford, thundering blood and death; or his son, in cruelty seeking out his fame; or wind-changing Warwick, setter up and setter down of kings; or the "tiger's heart wrapp'd in a woman's hide" [*3 Henry VI,* I. iv. 137] of Margaret, antipodal to all that is good. Amongst these are plunged from their earliest youth the "forward sons of York": Richard is the most forward of them all. There is that which marks him off from all the rest of his handsome family. He is a "valiant crook-back prodigy" [*2 Henry VI,* V. i. 157], a "heap of wrath, foul indigested lump" [*3 Henry VI,* I. iv. 75], the language is the bitter satire of enemies, but Richard's own soliloquies are enough to show that his physique is either an outward symbol of a distorted soul, or else an accident that contributes its share to the prince's predisposition towards evil. In the earlier pictures of Richard we can see, with much that is merely boyish, suggestions of the strength and the moral distortion that are to combine later into consummate villany. In warlike deeds he is early pronounced by his father to have deserved best of the sons. In council we have him struggling to be beforehand with his elders, and he leaves them far behind in audacity of moral perversion.

York.	I took an oath that he should quietly reign.
Edward.	But for a kingdom any oath may be broken: I would break a thousand oaths to reign one year.
Richard.	No; God forbid your grace should be forsworn.
York.	I shall be, if I claim by open war.
Richard.	I'll prove the contrary, if you'll hear me speak.
York.	Thou canst not, son; it is impossible.
Richard.	An oath is of no moment, being not took Before a true and lawful magistrate, That hath authority over him that swears: Henry had none, but did usurp the place; Then, seeing 'twas he that made you to depose, Your oath, my lord, is vain and frivolous.

[*3 Henry VI,* I. ii. 15-27]

It is just here that we get our first glimpse of the master passion beneath this boy's vigorous personality.

> And, father, do but think
> How sweet a thing it is to wear a crown;
> Within whose circuit is Elysium
> And all that poets feign of bliss and joy.
> [*3 Henry VI,* I. ii. 28-31]

Richard is dominated by ambition; but at present it is within the bounds of vehement partisanship, sympathy with the ambition of his father. And in the earlier scenes Richard seems not devoid of natural feelings; though side by side with these are also suggestions of what will be the demonic levity of the fully developed villain. He has freshness of soul enough to become enthusiastic about a brilliant sunrise; but when the natural sun turns into the miraculous omen of three suns, and his elder brother exclaims—

> Whate'er it bodes, henceforward I will bear
> Upon my target three fair-shining suns—
> [*3 Henry VI,* II. i. 39-40]

Richard instantly comes out with a pun at Edward's expense—

> Nay, bear three daughters: by your leave I speak it,
> You love the breeder better than the male.
> [II. i. 41-2]

There is room for bitter taunts as the brothers stand over the fallen body of their father's torturer and their brother's murderer, but with Richard the taunt can become a gibe:

> What, not an oath? nay, then the world goes hard
> When Clifford cannot spare his friends an oath.
> [*3 Henry VI,* II. vi. 77-8]

Richard seems to be sincere—though we cannot be sure—in his hero-worship of Warwick and Northumberland, and when he deems it prize enough to be his valiant father's son. Nay, there even seems to be a point at which he is open to the touch of popular superstition, and in the moment of being ennobled shrinks from the 'ominous' dukedom of Gloucester.

The turning-point in the movement of the third play is found where King Edward succumbs to the charms of Lady Grey, and by a mésalliance alienates his strong supporters, and causes the current of events to flow backward. This is a turning-point also for Richard: a long soliloquy reveals the changing character, the constituent elements precipitating into a unity of unscrupulous ambition. The new suggestion of royal offspring brings out, with a shock, the personal hopes that had been silently forming in the breast of the remoter heir.

> Would he were wasted, marrow, bones and all,
> That from his loins no hopeful branch may spring,
> To cross me from the golden time I look for!
> *[3 Henry VI,* III. ii. 125-27]

This thought yields to the natural reflection on the number of personages who already—without waiting for possibilities—stand between Richard and his soul's desire; until sovereignty seems but a dream:

> Like one that stands upon a promontory
> And spies a far-off shore where he would tread,
> Wishing his foot were equal with his eye,
> And chides the sea that sunders him from thence.
> [III. ii. 135-38]

With empty impatience he says to himself in reference to these obstacles to his rise—

> I'll cut the causes off,
> Flattering me with impossibilities.
> [III. ii. 142-43]

He turns to other alternatives: but the bitter thought of his deformity comes to check aspirations after a life of pleasure.

> I'll make my heaven to dream upon the crown,
> And, while I live, to account this world but hell,
> Until my mis-shaped trunk that bears this head
> Be round impaled with a glorious crown.
> [III. ii. 168-71]

But again Richard is plunged in despair at the many lives that ''stand between me and home'' [III. ii. 173]. He struggles out of the tormenting perplexity by a review of his resources—resources of his own personal qualities. . . .

> Why, I can smile, and murder whiles I smile,
> And cry 'Content' to that which grieves my heart,
> And wet my cheeks with artificial tears,
> And frame my face to all occasions.
> I'll drown more sailors than the mermaid shall;
> I'll slay more gazers than the basilisk;
> I'll play the orator as well as Nestor,
> Deceive more slily than Ulysses could,
> And like a Sinon take another Troy.
> I can add colours to the chameleon,
> Change shapes with Proteus for advantages,
> And set the murderous Machiavel to school.
> Can I do this, and cannot get a crown?
> [III. ii. 182-94]

Here then a clear stage in his development has been completely attained by Richard: he is a man of one idea and one ambition, consciously emancipated from all moral scruples.

In the latter half of the play, if there is a note of ambiguity in Richard's action, it is the ambiguity of the part he has set himself to play: he is hostile to the King, faithful to the crown, with the faithfulness of the butcher to the sheep he means to eat. Richard seconds, or even leads, in the discontent at the royal marriage, until Clarence has reached the point of threatening open rupture, when Richard draws back:

> I hear, yet say not much, but think the more.
> *[3 Henry VI,* IV. i. 83]

The fruit of this ill-fated marriage becomes manifest in the revolt of Warwick, Clarence deserting to him. Richard remains with the King, ''not for the love of Edward, but the crown'']*3 Henry VI,* IV. i. 126]. In the rapidly changing events that succeed, Richard is the follower who pushes his leader forward from point to point. In the tragedy of young Prince Edward's assassination Richard has no greater share than his brothers; the difference is that these brothers have exhausted their souls by this horror, Richard has but whetted his appetite.

> *Q. Margaret.*　O, kill me too!
> *Gloucester.*　　Marry, and shall.
> *[Offers to kill her.]*
> *[3 Henry VI,* V. v. 41-2]

Held back by main force from this atrocity, the resources of Gloucester have found him another.

> *Gloucester.*　Clarence, excuse me to the king
>   my brother;
>   I'll hence to London on a serious matter.
> *[3 Henry VI,* V. v. 46-7]

They all understand, but none dares follow to the assassination of a king.

We thus reach the crowning incident of the trilogy, as it were the graduating exercise of Richard's education in villany. He has long been a man of one ambition; but, so far as the path of his ambition is concerned, the single quick stab in which Richard has had so much practice would be all that is required. Wherefore then the long protracted scene? The peaceful Henry is no bad reader of men, and he catches exactly the spirit of the incident with his question—

> What scene of death hath Roscius now to act?
> *[3 Henry VI,* V. vi. 10]

There is now artistic appreciation of the villany, as well as ambitious purpose to indicate the crime. With Mephistophelean restraint of passion the murderer gravely mocks his victim from point to point; when the helpless Henry in his outpouring has passed from bitter taunts and descriptions of hideous deformity to enumeration of the evils the monster is ordained to bring on his country, the point has been reached for the dramatic coup:

> *Gloucester.*　I'll hear no more: die, prophet,
>   in thy speech:　*[Stabs him.]*
>   For this, amongst the rest, was I
>   ordain'd.
> *[3 Henry VI,* V. vi. 56-7]

Richard mocks the aspiring blood of Lancaster sinking into the earth, and then with a superfluous stab starts a summary of the whole situation.

> Down, down to hell; and say I sent thee thither:
> I, that have neither pity, love, nor fear.
> Indeed, 'tis true that Henry told me of;
> For I have often heard my mother say
> I came into the world with my legs forward:
> Had I not reason, think ye, to make haste,
> And seek their ruin that usurp'd our right?
> The midwife wonder'd and the women cried
> 'O, Jesus bless us, he is born with teeth!'

And so I was: which plainly signified
That I should snarl and bite and play the dog.
Then, since the heavens have shaped my body so,
Let hell make crook'd my mind to answer it.
I have no brother, I am like no brother;
And this word 'love,' which greybeards call divine,
Be resident in men like one another
And not in me: I am myself alone.

[3 Henry VI, V. vi. 67-83]

It is natural to place this soliloquy side by side with that of the third act. In the one, Richard devoted himself to ambition, at whatever cost of villanous action; in the other, the villany is embraced. In the third act there was enumeration, in the nature of a claim, of qualities suitable to evil deeds; in the fifth act the claim has been vouched for by the dripping sword and murdered King. In the third act Richard aspired: in the fifth act Richard has attained. (pp. 33-9)

> Richard G. Moulton, "Wrong and Retribution: The Second Four Histories," in his The Moral System of Shakespeare: A Popular Illustration of Fiction as the Experimental Side of Philosophy, The Macmillan Company, 1903, pp. 33-45.

ADOLPHUS WILLIAM WARD (essay date 1907)

[The following excerpts are taken from Ward's introductions to 1, 2, and 3 Henry VI, part of a 1907 edition of the works of Shakespeare edited by Sidney Lee. The introductions are principally concerned with Shakespeare's "treatment of historical proof," and they provide extensive comparisons of the Henry VI trilogy with the chronicles and other accounts of sixteenth-century England, as well as with The Contention and The True Tragedy. In the excerpt below, Ward discusses the language of the Henry VI trilogy, noting that in 1 Henry VI the style is often bombastic, heavily alliterative, and replete with tautological diction. He finds evidence of more care and method in the style of 2 and 3 Henry VI, remarking on the modified use of alliteration and decreased repetition of words and sounds. Ward's is one of the earliest critical examinations of Shakespeare's language in Henry VI; for a fuller treatment of the issue of language in the plays, particularly how those characteristics disparaged by Ward are related to Shakespeare's use of the formal rhetorical tradition, see the excerpt by David Riggs (1971). Other critics who have examined the language, style, and imagery of Henry VI include Caroline F. E. Spurgeon (1935), John Middleton Murry (1936), Mark Van Doren (1939), John Dover Wilson (1951), S. L. Bethell (1951), Wolfgang H. Clemen (1951), Alvin B. Kernan (1954), Charles R. Forker (1965), James L. Calderwood (1967), and Carol McGinnis Kay (1972).]

From the point of view of style and diction, the most striking characteristic of the "First Part of Henry VI" is beyond a doubt the large element of bombast contained in it—bombast at times quite unintentionally comic; at other times, whether intentionally or not, devoid of meaning. Ancient Pistol [2 Henry IV] could hardly have outdone "old Talbot," when . . . he comforts Salisbury, one of whose eyes a shot has just "struck off," by the following simile:

> One eye thou hast to look to heaven for grace:
> The sun with one eye vieweth all the world.

[I. iv. 83-4]

And from what anthology of lovers' nonsense could Suffolk have culled a figure so unintelligible as the following . . . :

> As plays the sun upon the glassy streams,
> Twinkling another counterfeited beam,
> So seems this gorgeous beauty to mine eyes.

[V. iii. 62-4]

The alliteration in which the play abounds, and which may generally be described as explosive rather than melodious, seems to be part of its bombast. It is mostly reserved for the use of great nobles—especially for Talbot, for Mortimer, and (though in a less ample measure) for Warwick; and it seems on the whole to be more frequently employed in the first three acts than in the last two. Rime is not largely introduced, except in scenes iii and v-vii of Act IV, where both the Talbots discourse almost entirely in rime, and where it is noticeable that alliteration almost entirely disappears. In other scenes rime concludes a few speeches; elsewhere it is employed occasionally, but without any obvious purpose. More peculiar is what may be described as a constant repetition of words—sometimes of sounds—to which some ears may possibly be more sensitive than others, but which to mine (certain Greek analogies notwithstanding) conveys a certain impression of awkward energy—like the speech of a pedantic and unpolished schoolmaster. To be sure, some emphasis is gained, even though it is not always the emphasis of antithesis; and the attention of the audience is thus more certainly arrested; but this is at the expense of euphony, and of a pleasing flow of style.

In the diction of this play there is observable a tendency to tautology of expression, which seems to be distinctive of it as compared with Parts II and III. Such combinations as "replete with mirth and joy" [I. vii. 15], "black and swart" [I. ii. 84], recur in several later scenes. They may be regarded as exemplifications of a certain carelessness of style or perhaps of a kind of indolence which resorts to the means most readily at hand for making up a line. Careless phraseology is also here and there to be noticed. On the other hand, we find, not only a very large number of classical similes and allusions, which Part I affects like the two other Parts, but also some out-of-the-way words, coined or imported, and not recurring in either of these. The omission of the definite article in such phrases as "to sun's parching heat" [I. ii. 77], "if Dauphin and the rest" [III. iii. 8], "the sound of drum" [III. iii. 29], and the insertion of it, not, I think, to be met with elsewhere in Shakespeare, before proper names such as "the Talbot" [II. ii. 37; II. iii. 16; and III. iii. 20], and "the Burgundy" [III. iii. 37], may be due to carelessness, or, more probably, to a desire for peculiarity. (pp. li-liii)

* * * * *

With "Part II of Henry VI," to which Part III is in organic union, we enter into a new dramatic atmosphere. This fact, which has always been more or less accepted by the readers of these plays, seems to have impressed itself with fresh force on those who have enjoyed an opportunity of seeing them acted in immediate sequence to Part I. While in Part I there is much to interest the spectator, and while some of its scenes are in themselves decidedly striking, the impression produced by the play as a whole is that of crowding, clamour, and confusion. Part II affects the reader, and seems to have affected the theatrical audience, very differently. It conveys throughout a sense of perfect clearness in the conception and in the management of the dramatic action, which is carried on by groups of personages kept perfectly distinct from one another. In the long First Act in particular, where several groups or characters are, as it were, each in its turn eliminated, the ground is cleared by a thoroughly perspicuous, if in its method very simple, process. And, as the action proceeds, the spectator is overtaken by no sense of crowding or confusion, as in Part I, and oppressed only by an ever-present consciousness of the lurking hatreds which, like underground fire, lie at the bottom of the tragedy, and ever and again flare up with appalling fury. Withal, incidents of the most startling and direct force—*horrors,* in a word—succeed each other with extraordinary rapidity; and both in this Part and in its successor, which carries on the action almost without a break, the contrasts are so frequent and so vivid as to overpower even a strong capacity for mental assimilation and digestion.

The differences in style between Part I and the two "later" Parts are not less marked. From the first, the ear seems conscious of a roll—unceasing, like that of the sea upon the shore. The rhetoric, though vehement and at times excessive, is very rarely meaningless or absurd. Alliteration is indeed still employed; but it is used with more care and method than it was in Part I; it points the sententious speeches of the King and some of Gloucester's caustic observations, rather than overcharges them. Rime, too, is more sparingly employed; and, though the trick of repeating words or sounds, which was noted in Part I, also occurs in Part II, less frequent resort is on the whole here had to it; a trying play on words (a pun) is, however, on more than one occasion introduced. Classical allusions are as plentiful as ever; and it is as if only when the attention is strung up to the highest pitch, as in the scene of Cardinal Beaufort's death, all tricks of style were left aside. (pp. ix-xi)

* * * * *

[The] "Third Part of Henry VI," which carries on the action without a break from that of the Second part, follows the "True Tragedie of Richard Duke of Yorke, and the Death of Good King Henrie the Sixt," so closely that the alterations contained in the later play may be said to consist only of details, and of the insertion of additional speeches or parts of speeches. (p. xi)

As to style and diction, there seems little to distinguish the "Third Part of Henry VI" from the "Second" in those characteristics which were noted in it above. Alliteration is much employed in Part III, but in that modified form which was found to prevail in the earlier Part,—being most largely used by personages whose utterances have manifestly been elaborated with special care, such as King Henry and Clifford; and this again tallies with the greater apparent frequency of alliteration in Part I than in either. Part III has more rime than Part II; that in Part III is largely but by no means entirely taken over from the "True Tragedie," and is nearly always to be found at the end of speeches. The peculiar feature of a repetition of words or sounds, which was noticed above as observable in both Parts I and II, is also to be found in Part III, where it appears in instances reproduced from the "True Tragedie," but with augmentation. Finally, the classical allusions in Part III are for the most part, but not entirely, taken over from the same play. The mannerism of the omitted definite article also occasionally recurs. Of more significance, as indicating greater maturity of style, is a certain conscious irony. The phrase (subsequently repeated) "Thou setter up and plucker down of kings," descriptive in [II. iii. 37] (as in the "True Tragedie") of the power of the Almighty, is in [III. iii. 157] savagely applied by Queen Margaret to Warwick (this is not in the "True Tragedie"), and again calmly by Warwick to himself [V. i. 26] (this is substantially in the "True Tragedy"). The sneers in scriptural parlance of Richard of Gloucester [I. i. 18 and IV. i. 21-3] are not in the older play.

Altogether the Third Part, towards its close, suggests a very explicable determination on the part of the author or authors to wind up the action of the play; their adherence to the "True Tragedie" becomes, if possible, more marked than it was be-

fore; and there is about the progress towards the end an unmistakable air of business—a desire, not to treat things perfunctorily, but to spend no unnecessary time over them. And yet (this should by no means be overlooked) the reader or spectator is left with a sense of *more to come* beyond the framework of the play; no doubt is left as to the personage to whom the future will appeal—to whom perhaps that future may belong. This personage is not the "sportful" King Edward IV, in whose concluding hope of "lasting joy" [V. vii. 46] little interest can be felt, nor the shifting Clarence—but the prince who seals the bargain of national peace and fraternal concord with a Judas kiss. (pp. xii-xiv)

> *Adolphus William Ward, in introductions to "King Henry VI, Parts I, II, and III," in* The Complete Works of William Shakespeare, *Vols. XVII, XVIII, and XIX by William Shakespeare, edited by Sidney Lee, George D. Sproul, 1907, pp. ix-lix; ix-xxv; ix-xxxviii.*

J. A. R. MARRIOTT (essay date 1918)

[*An English historian and member of Parliament, Marriott approached the chronicle plays as a student of history and politics. In an unexcerpted section of his* English History in Shakespeare *(1918), he judges that "national unity was to Shakespeare the one supreme condition of national greatness." In support of this point, Marriott finds evidence in the* Henry VI *trilogy that Shakespeare presented Henry IV's usurpation of the throne from Richard II as a Lancastrian crime which nemesis must avenge. Other critics who have seen the operation of divine retribution in the* Henry VI *trilogy include Hermann Ulrici (1839), Denton J. Snider (1890), E. M. W. Tillyard (1944), M. M. Reese (1961), and Irving Ribner (1965). Marriott notes that whereas a modern historian would regard history in terms of social, economic, and political movements, Shakespeare viewed it "primarily in the play of personal forces . . . [as] a record of the deeds good and bad of eminent individuals." In the excerpt below, Marriott argues that Shakespeare has made Margaret of Anjou the "political pivot" of* 2 *and* 3 Henry VI *and drawn her with historical accuracy. See the excerpted essays by Charlotte Lennox (1754), Anna Brownell Jameson (1833), Henry Norman Hudson (1851), and Marilyn French (1981) for further discussions of Shakespeare's characterization of Margaret.*]

[Shakespeare has given a] dramatic turn [in Parts II and III of *Henry VI*] to the historical feuds between Yorkist and Lancastrian by connecting them with the personal rivalry of two ambitious women: Henry's Queen, Margaret of Anjou, and Eleanor Cobham, the second wife of Humphrey of Gloucester. . . . In his account of the gradual formation of the cabal against Duke Humphrey, Shakspeare has closely followed Holinshed, but Queen Margaret had no part whatever in the prosecution of Eleanor Cobham. The arrest of the Duchess took place in 1441; Margaret of Anjou did not arrive in England until four years afterwards—in 1445. Nevertheless, here as always, despite what dryasdust would describe as historical inaccuracy, Shakspeare shows himself true to the essential verities of the historical situation. He wanted to exhibit Henry's French Queen as a high-spirited, proud and courageous woman, but yet as the evil genius of the Lancastrian House. That is the exact historical truth. Mrs. Jameson [see excerpt above, 1833] is too jealous for her sex to allow her to admit the accuracy of the portrait; or rather, she is more concerned to repudiate the artist. "Margaret of Anjou as exhibited in these tragedies is a dramatic portrait of considerable truth, vigour and consistency," she writes, "but she is not one of Shakspeare's women

Part I, Act II, Scene iv. Somerset, Suffolk, Warwick, Richard Plantagenet, Vernon, and a Lawyer. By John Boydell (n.d.).

... The character ... has something of the power, but none of the flowing ease of Shakspeare's manner." (pp. 183-84)

[Margaret] is the woman whom Shakspeare selects, and with ample historical warrant, as the political pivot of Parts II and III of *Henry VI.* So far, therefore, from repudiating, with Mrs. Jameson, the Shaksperian authorship, I take it as a very characteristic illustration of his dramatic insight and of his historical acumen that he should have thus, from the outset of the drama, have concentrated attention upon the character of the Queen. The workmanship, I allow, is immature, the colours are crude, the delineation lacks subtlety and *chiaroscuro,* but the outlines are typically bold and clear. The portrait of Queen Margaret seems to me to be not only true, reasonably true, to history, but Shaksperean to the finger tips. (pp. 184-85)

J. A. R. Marriott, "The House Divided: Lancaster and York—Henry the Sixth and Edward the Fourth—The Wars of the Roses," in his *English History in Shakespeare,* E. P. Dutton & Company, 1918, pp. 167-205.

CAROLINE F. E. SPURGEON (essay date 1935)

[Spurgeon's Shakespeare's Imagery *(1935) inaugurated the ''image-pattern analysis'' method of studying Shakespeare's plays, one of the most widely used techniques of the mid-twentieth century. In this work, she interpreted the thematic structure of the plays through an examination of patterns in the imagery. Spurgeon also sought to learn about Shakespeare's personality from a study of his images, a course which few of her disciples followed. In the excerpt below, Spurgeon focuses solely on the prevalence of specific symbolic language in* Henry VI: *she does not connect imagery to other aspects of the plays, nor does she discuss the impact of certain metaphors and similes on the meaning of the text itself. She classifies the metaphor of growth as the central image in the Henry VI trilogy and identifies several ''subsidiary running images.''—for instance, celestial bodies in 1 Henry VI, butchery and slaughter-house analogies in 2 and 3 Henry VI, and the imagery of sea and ships in 3 Henry VI. Alvin B. Kernan (1954) has also noted the prevalence of marine imagery in 3 Henry VI, whereas Carol McGinnis Kay (1972) has focused on the use of garden and slaughter-house symbols, as well as images of trapping-enclosures and the sea. For more on the use of symbolic language in the Henry VI trilogy, see the excerpts by Wolfgang H. Clemen (1951) and James L. Calderwood (1967); also, see the essays by G. Wilson Knight cited in the Additional Bibliography.]*

[An] undertone of running symbolic imagery is to be found to some extent in almost every one of Shakespeare's plays, contributing in various ways to the richness and meaning of the play, and, in some cases, profoundly influencing its effect upon us. Its function and importance vary greatly according to the type of play, and the profundity of thought or imaginative vision which informs it. In the histories as a whole, such continuous symbolism as we find is of a very elementary and obvious nature. There is a simple but persistent running image through all the early histories from the first part of *Henry VI* (where there are touches of it only), culminating in *Richard II*. (p. 215)

The most constant running metaphor and picture in Shakespeare's mind in the early historical plays as a whole (from 1 *Henry VI* to *Richard II* inclusive) is that of growth as seen in a garden and orchard, with the deterioration, decay and destruction brought about by ignorance and carelessness on the part of the gardener, as shown by untended weeds, pests, lack of pruning and manuring, or on the other hand by the rash and untimely cutting or lopping of fine trees.

We find it first in the scene in the Temple Gardens in 1 *Henry VI* [II. iv], with its continuous play, in true Shakespearian style, on white and red roses, thorns, blossoms, canker, plucking, cropping, rooting, withering, growing and ripening, which is carried over into the following scene, where we have the vivid picture of Mortimer as a withered vine, pithless and strengthless, drooping 'his sapless branches to the ground', detained during his 'flowering youth' in a loathsome dungeon, in consequence of an attempt to 'plant' him as the rightful heir; while Richard Plantagenet is described as 'sweet stem from York's great stock' [1 *Henry VI*, II. v. 12, 56, 41].

The metaphor—which probably takes its rise very simply from the badges of York and Lancaster, together with the meaning of the name Plantagenet—clearly pleases Shakespeare, and, having started it in the first part of *Henry VI*, he carries it on in the second and third parts, developing it considerably in *Richard III*, and making it finally the central theme of *Richard II*. Thus, in a scene undoubtedly written by him [2 *Henry VI*, III. i], Queen Margaret, warning the king against the good Duke Humphrey, and urging his removal, uses for the first time the metaphor of the untended garden:

> Now 'tis the spring, and weeds are shallow-rooted;
> Suffer them now, and they'll o'ergrow the garden,
> And choke the herbs for want of husbandry.
> [2 *Henry VI*, III. i. 31-3]

Later the king ironically thanks his nobles, who are eagerly supporting the queen and doing their utmost to blacken the character of the duke, for the care they take

> To mow down thorns that would annoy our foot;
> [2 *Henry VI*, III. i. 67]

and York carries on the picture when, on hearing the bad news from France, he mutters,

> Thus are my blossoms blasted in the bud,
> And caterpillars eat my leaves away.
> [2 *Henry VI*, III. i. 89-90]

The idea of the royal house as a tree or branches or slips of a tree is also present in this second part of the play, as when Warwick describes York's two sons as 'fair slips of such a stock' [2 *Henry VI*, II. ii. 58], or Suffolk accuses Warwick of being 'graft with crab-tree slip' [2 *Henry VI*, III. ii. 214], and pictures Duke Humphrey as a lofty pine, who droops 'and hangs his sprays' [2 *Henry VI*, II. iii. 45].

In 3 *Henry VI* the metaphor becomes more definite. Warwick vows he will 'plant Plantagenet, root him up who dares' [3 *Henry VI*, I. i. 48]; and in dying he cries,

> Thus yields the cedar to the axe's edge.
> [3 *Henry VI*, V. ii. 11]

Clifford declares that until he *roots* [3 *Henry VI*, I. iii. 32] out the accursed line of York, he lives in hell; Clarence tells Queen Margaret they have *set the axe* to her *usurping root*, and will not leave till they have hewn her down [3 *Henry VI*, II. ii. 163-68]; Richard reminds Edward that Clifford was

> not contented that he lopp'd the branch
> In hewing Rutland when his leaves put forth,
> But set his murdering knife unto the root
> From whence that tender spray did sweetly spring.
> [3 *Henry VI*, II. vi. 47-50]

When Prince Edward shows signs of being troublesome, the king (Edward IV) says, 'What! Can so young a thorn begin to prick?' [3 *Henry VI*, V. v. 13] and, when a few minutes later he is stabbed to death by his cousins, his mother cries, 'How sweet a plant have you untimely cropp'd!' [3 *Henry VI*, V. v. 62].

Gloucester, when born, was an

> indigested and deformed lump,
> Not like the fruit of such a goodly tree;
> [3 *Henry VI*, V. vi. 51-2]

he describes his shrunken arm as a 'wither'd shrub' [3 *Henry VI*, III. ii. 156], he trusts no 'hopeful branch' [3 *Henry VI*, III. ii. 126] may spring from Edward, and at the end he mockingly greets his infant nephew, saying,

> And, that I love the tree from whence thou sprang'st,
> Witness the loving kiss I give the fruit.
> [3 *Henry VI*, V. vii. 31-2]
> (pp. 216-18)

Apart from this image of the fruit and flower garden in which these five early historical plays share, there are other subsidiary running images to be found in individual plays.

It seems to me that, even in 1 *Henry VI*, some indications of this peculiar habit of Shakespeare's can intermittently be traced.

Thus, in the first scene—the funeral of Henry V in Westminster Abbey—we are at once struck by the effect produced upon us by the contrast of a blaze of dazzling light—comets, planets, sun and stars—against a background of black and mourning, typifying the brilliance and glory of the dead king and the heavy gloom of his loss. The first line strikes the note of mourning:

> Hung be the heavens with black, yield day to night;
> [1 *Henry VI*, I. i. 1]

and this is followed by the rapidly moving pictures of comets brandishing their crystal tresses and scourging the stars who have consented to Henry's death, of his flashing sword blinding men with its beams, his arms spread wider than a dragon's wings, and his sparkling eyes shooting fire, which

> More dazzled and drove back his enemies
> Than mid-day sun fierce bent against their faces.
> [1 *Henry VI*, I. i. 13-14]

The mourning note is then revived, with the colour red added:

> We mourn in black: why mourn we not in blood?
> [1 *Henry VI*, I. i. 17]

and the sense of contrast and conflicting emotions is maintained by the picture of the mourners following the wooden coffin

Like captives bound to a triumphant car.
[*1 Henry VI*, I. i. 22]

The loss of Henry is so great that it is natural it should be the concern of the heavenly bodies themselves, and Exeter asks,

What! shall we curse the planets of mishap
That plotted thus our glory's overthrow?
[*1 Henry VI*, I. i. 23]

Bedford follows by bidding the gold-coated heralds to attend them to the altar draped in mourning, where, instead of gold, they offer up their arms, and he ends by invoking the dead king's spirit, begging him to prosper his realm, and to combat on its behalf with adverse planets in the heavens.

And the last picture he gives us of the great king is in keeping with the whole scene:

A far more glorious star thy soul will make
Than Julius Caesar or bright——
[*1 Henry VI*, I. i. 55-6]

a cry which is rudely interrupted and the mourners brought with a shattering blow from heaven to earth by the succession of messengers rushing in with ill tidings of the loss, with 'slaughter and discomfiture' [*1 Henry VI*, I. i. 59] of the greater part of Henry's brilliant and hard-won conquests in France.

The imagery of the heavenly bodies is carried over into scene 2, which opens with the picture of the planet Mars and his uncertain or eccentric orbit, shining sometimes on the English, sometimes on the French side, and ends with Charles' apostrophe to Joan as

Bright star of Venus, fall'n down on the earth.
[*1 Henry VI*, I. ii. 144]
(pp. 225-26)

In 2 and 3 *Henry VI*, outside the symbol of the fruit and flower garden, already noticed, there is the even more obvious one of the butcher and slaughter-house, slightly carried on in *Richard III*.

This figure is first used by Henry, when, in a long simile, he pictures the helplessness both of himself and of the chief victim in the play, in the hands of their enemies, and sees Duke Humphrey as a calf taken away by the butcher, bound, beaten, and borne to 'the bloody slaughter-house' [*2 Henry VI*, III. i. 210-12], while he, Henry,

As the dam runs lowing up and down,
Looking the way her harmless young one went.
[*2 Henry VI*, III. i. 214-15]

The same image comes naturally to Warwick, when, after the duke's murder, the queen asks him does he suspect Suffolk, and he answers caustically, if you find a 'heifer dead and bleeding fresh', and see 'fast by a butcher with an axe', you will suspect ''twas he that made the slaughter' [*2 Henry VI*, III. ii. 188-90]. York also touches it again at the end, when in his anger he declares he could spend his fury on sheep and oxen [*2 Henry VI*, V. i. 27]. The image naturally recurs with Dick the butcher in Cade's rebellion, who is to strike down sin like an ox, and cut iniquity's throat like a calf [*2 Henry VI*, IV. ii. 26-7], and who is commended by his leader because his enemies fell before him 'like sheep and oxen', and he behaved himself as if he had been in his own slaughter-house [*2 Henry VI*, IV. iii. 3-5].

In 3 *Henry VI*, Clifford, Edward and Clarence are all called 'butchers', Richard is 'that devil's butcher' [*3 Henry VI*, V. v. 77], parliament is thought of as a 'shambles' [*3 Henry VI*, I. i. 71] and the realm as a 'slaughter-house' [*3 Henry VI*, V. iv. 78], Gloucester sees himself hewing his way to the crown with a bloody axe, and Henry, when Gloucester comes to kill him, pictures himself very aptly as a sheep yielding his throat unto the butcher's knife. (pp. 227-28)

Henry's enemies are also thought of occasionally as wild beasts, ravening wolves, beating away the shepherd (Duke Humphrey) from the lamb so that they may devour it, and in 3 *Henry VI*, lions, tigers, wolves and bears completely take the place of the serpents in symbolising the enemies or claimants to the crown.

Queen Margaret sees the king as a 'trembling lamb environed with wolves' [*3 Henry VI*, I. i. 242], and when he is finally taken prisoner, she calls Edward 'the wolf that makes this spoil' [*3 Henry VI*, V. iv. 80]. Henry also, when Gloucester comes to kill him, and dismisses his guard, sees himself as a 'harmless sheep' [*3 Henry VI*, V. vi. 7] deserted by the shepherd when the wolf appears, and elsewhere pictures the civil wars as the 'bloody times',

Whiles lions war and battle for their dens,
Poor harmless lambs abide their enmity.
[*3 Henry VI*, II. v. 74-6]

Young Rutland, shrinking with shut eyes from Clifford's murderous stab when forced to face his murderer, cries,

So looks the pent-up lion o'er the wretch
That trembles under his devouring paws;
[*3 Henry VI*, I. iii. 12-13]

and Richard, when pursuing Clifford in battle, tells Warwick to

single out some other chase;
For I myself will hunt this wolf to death.
[*3 Henry VI*, II. iv. 12-13]
(pp. 229-30)

There is also in 3 *Henry VI* an unusually large number of pictures of the sea and ships, more than in any other play. Thus King Henry, in a fine passage already referred to, describes the battle of Towton swaying like a mighty sea

Forced by the tide to combat with the wind.
[*3 Henry VI*, II. v. 5]

Gloucester, in a very vivid simile, dreaming of his desire for the crown, sees himself standing on a promontory gazing at a far-off shore 'where he would tread' [*3 Henry VI*, III. ii. 136], and chiding

the sea that sunders him from thence,
Saying, he'll lade it dry to have his way,
[*3 Henry VI*, III. ii. 138-39]

the sea in this instance symbolising the king and all his kinsmen who stand between Gloucester and the throne.

The picture of the wrecked ship is in King Henry's mind, when, on entering York, the queen, pointing to the head of the Duke of York set upon the gates, asks, 'Doth not the object cheer your heart, my lord?' and he answers, 'Ay, as the rocks cheer them that fear their wreck' [*3 Henry VI*, II. ii. 4-5]. It is rather a peculiarity of this play that the various characters are repeatedly thought of as ships fighting the waves or borne before the wind. There are two touches of the figure in 2 *Henry VI* [III. ii. 411, IV. ix. 31-3], but it is in the third part that it becomes noticeable. Thus York describes his beaten soldiers as flying 'like ships before the wind' [3 *Henry VI*, I. iv. 4], Edward pictures 'calm Henry' being led into battle by the bloody-minded queen

> As doth a sail, fill'd with a fretting gust,
> Command an argosy to stem the waves.
>
> [*3 Henry VI*, II. vi. 35-6]

Margaret herself, in a moment of unwonted humility, tells Lewis of France that she

> Must strike her sail and learn a while to serve
> Where kings command;
>
> [*3 Henry VI*, III. iii. 5-6]

and when urged by Gloucester to kneel to Edward as king, Warwick declares he would rather chop one hand off and with the other fling it in Gloucester's face

> Than bear so low a sail, to strike to thee;
>
> [*3 Henry VI*, V. i. 52]

to which Edward answers,

> Sail how thou canst, have wind and tide thy friend,
>
> [*3 Henry VI*, V. i. 53]

but when your head is newly cut off, this sentence shall be written in the dust with your blood,

> Wind-changing Warwick now can change no more.
>
> [*3 Henry VI*, V. i. 57]

The culmination of this figure occurs in an unusually elaborate simile, thirty-four lines in length, in which, after Henry has been carried off to the Tower, Queen Margaret compares the condition of the king's army to a ship in distress, near rocks and quicksands, her mast blown overboard, her cable broken, her holding-anchor lost, half her crew drowned, but with the young prince, her pilot, still alive. Warwick she calls the anchor, Montague the topmast, 'our slaughter'd friends the tackles' [3 *Henry VI*, V. iv. 15]; these, she says, can be replaced, and she and the prince will keep their course

> From shelves and rocks that threaten us with wreck.
>
> [*3 Henry VI*, V. iv. 23]

Edward is the ruthless sea (to which indeed he has already likened himself in [3 *Henry VI*, IV. viii. 55]), Clarence a quicksand of deceit ('false, fleeting, perjured Clarence'), Richard a 'ragged fatal rock' [3 *Henry VI*, V. iv. 27], and there is no mercy to be hoped for from any of the three brothers

> More than with ruthless waves, with sands and rocks.
>
> [*3 Henry VI*, V. iv. 36]
>
> (pp. 230-32)

Caroline F. E. Spurgeon, "Leading Motives in the Histories," in her Shakespeare's Imagery and What It Tells Us, *1935. Reprint by Cambridge at the University Press, 1971, pp. 213-58.*

JOHN MIDDLETON MURRY   (essay date 1936)

[*A twentieth-century English editor and critic, Murry has been called the most "level-headed" of Shakespeare's major biographical critics. Unlike other biographical scholars, such as Frank Harris and Edward Dowden, Murry refused to attribute to Shakespeare a definite personality or creative neurosis which deter-*

mined all his work, but regarded the poet as a man of powerful insights rather than character, an individual possessing Keats's negative capability, in the sense that he was able to withstand "uncertainties, mysteries, doubts, without any irritable reaching after fact and reason." What Murry identified as Shakespeare's greatest gift was his ability to uncover the true spirit of Elizabethan England, to fuse "not merely the poet and dramatist in himself," but to establish a "unique creative relation between himself, his dramatic material, his audience, and his actors." In the following excerpt, Murry maintains that he can discover no real evidence, either internal or external, for the claim that Shakespeare did not substantially compose the Henry VI *trilogy. Although he doubts that the authenticity of the plays can be indisputably determined by an examination of their verse styles, he proceeds to offer one anyway, isolating those passages which clearly bear Shakespeare's stamp and which, Murry theorizes, could be used as a guide in determining the authorship of other early works attributed to Shakespeare. Murry focuses on these passages as evidence of what he calls Shakespeare's "process of formation," identifying their two principal characteristics as: "a formal patterning employed to bring variety into the blank-verse on every appropriate occasion" and "a simple and lovely periodic* flow *of verse." The style and language of the* Henry VI *trilogy has also been examined by Adolphus William Ward (1907) and Mark Van Doren (1939). In addition, David Riggs (1971) has related the language of the trilogy to the formal rhetorical tradition prevalent during Shakespeare's lifetime. For more on this subject, see the essays by B. Ifor Evans and Gladys D. Willcock listed in the Additional Bibliography.*]

I can discover no real ground, external or internal, for denying that Shakespeare was substantially the writer of all three parts of *Henry VI*, of *Titus Andronicus*, and *The Taming of the Shrew.* Yet at one time or another all these plays have been repudiated by intelligent critics on grounds of substance or of style; and at one time or another in his life the careful student of Shakespeare feels the same impulse to repudiate them. He feels that they are unworthy of Shakespeare. But when he pauses to take a more advised aim, and questions the grounds of his impulse, he finds that the Shakespeare of whom he judged the plays unworthy is Shakespeare the master. Since, on any showing, the plays which he has the impulse to repudiate are the work of the apprentice Shakespeare, a feeling that they are unworthy of Shakespeare the master is no criterion whatever of their authenticity.

Further, it is plain that no convincing case against any of these plays can be made on the ground of their substance. (pp. 66-7)

[Yet, there] remains the possibility of a case against them on the ground of style. Such a case must rest on a demonstration (which can, in the nature of things, never be compulsive, but at best persuasive) that the style of the early plays is in contradiction with itself. Such a demonstration is not, perhaps, theoretically impossible; but when we consider that Shakespeare's style was in process of formation, that the process by which it was formed was largely a process of imitation, and that he must have done a great deal of re-writing of other men's work, such a demonstration is in fact inconceivable. In order to undertake it, a critic would need to have established, not merely to his own satisfaction, but to that of other competent critics, the nature and peculiarities of Shakespeare's early style; and he would need to assume and to persuade other critics to assume, that Shakespeare's style was highly individualized from the beginning—a fantastic assumption.

Still, let us suppose that a critic did undertake this task. How could such an inquiry be conducted? At what point would it begin? Could he fix on any passage in the earliest plays that is vouched as Shakespeare's by other warrant than the evidence of the Folio, or his own instinct? There is only one such passage: the speech of York to Margaret in *Henry VI,* Part III. . . .

> YORK. She-wolf of France, but worse than wolves of
>   France,
>   Whose tongue more poisons than the adder's tooth!
>   How ill-beseeming is it in thy sex
>   To triumph, like an Amazonian trull,
>   Upon their woes whom fortune captivates? . . .
>   O tiger's heart wrapped in a woman's hide!
>   How could'st thou drain the life-blood of the child,
>   To bid the father wipe his eyes withal,
>   And yet be seen to wear a woman's face?
>   Women are soft, mild, pitiful and flexible;
>   Thou stern, obdurate, flinty, rough, remorseless.
>   Bid'st thou me rage? Why, now thou hast thy wish:
>   Wouldst have me weep? Why, now thou hast thy
>   will:
>   For raging wind blows up incessant showers,
>   And when the rage allays, the rain begins.
>   These tears are my sweet Rutland's obsequies:
>   And every drop cries vengeance for his death,
>   'Gainst thee, fell Clifford, and thee, false
>   Frenchwoman.
>
>   [*3 Henry VI,* I. iv. 111-49]

There is little sign of an individualized style so far. If the passage belonged to an anonymous play, no one would dream of attributing the play to Shakespeare on the strength of it— nor to anybody else. For the truth is, there is only one marked style in the English drama about 1590: and that is Marlowe's, and Marlowe . . . was getting rid of it. So far, the passage is in anybody's style, or rather in no style at all. But the lines immediately following begin to show traces of a nascent individuality.

> NORTHUMBERLAND. Beshrew me, but his passion
>   moves me so
>   That hardly can I check my eyes from tears.
> YORK. That face of his the hungry cannibals
>   Would not have touch'd, would not have stain'd
>   with blood.
>   But you are more inhuman, more inexorable,
>   O, ten times more, than tigers of Hyrcania.
>   See, ruthless queen, a hapless father's tears:
>   This cloth thou dipp'dst in blood of my sweet boy,
>   And I with tears do wash the blood away. . . .
> NORTH. Had he been slaughter-man to all my kin,
>   I should not for my life but weep with him
>   To see how inly sorrow gripes his soul.
> Q. MAR. What, weeping-ripe, my Lord Northumber-
>   land?
>   Think but upon the wrong he did us all
>   And that will quickly dry thy melting tears.
>
>   [*3 Henry VI,* I. iv. 150-73]

There is a simple, limpid movement in these lines which is unlike that of any contemporary blank-verse known to me. It is quite imperceptible and indistinguishable if we come to it from the rich music of Shakespeare's prime; but when we are steeped in the language of these early plays, we can catch the silvery accent. This is Shakespeare's style at the earliest moment of formation at which I can distinguish it. There are, besides, characteristic early Shakespearian touches in the diction: 'Weeping-ripe', 'inly sorrow'. (pp. 67-72)

[The passage] is, I think, a miniature example of Shakespeare's experimental attitude at this moment, round about 1590. He is

feeling his way into a style, groping for his own mode of utterance, and he is half-way towards achieving it. If we take that passage as a whole, and set it against a comparable passage of the work of the greatest of Shakespeare's contemporaries [Marlowe] at about the same moment, we can enter more nearly into the nature of this early style of Shakespeare's. (p. 72)

Compared with the Shakespeare, Marlowe's verse is curiously monotonous. . . . The total effect is that of an accumulation of self-contained lines, of exactly the same rhythmical pattern, gasped out one after the other. . . . (pp. 73-4)

In the [passage by] Shakespeare, however, there is a constant variation of verse-melody. The devices by which it is produced are indeed crude compared with those he was later to employ; but they are effective. (And one is not a device at all: it was pure instinct which led Shakespeare to avoid letting the speech accent and the metrical accent coincide for long.) There are six-foot lines, there is a sudden sequence of sense-couplets, ('Tis beauty . . . abominable), followed by a sense triplet, a single line, a triplet, a couplet—one six-foot line, one with a weak ending—then an internal variation:

> Bid'st thou me rage? Why, now thou hast thy wish:
> Would'st have me weep? Why, now thou hast thy
>   will.

The rhythmical variations are incessant, although the verse itself is almost as rigidly end-stopped as Marlowe's; and the variations are achieved in the main by the constant introduction of semi-formal elements—balanced groups of lines.

If we take another passage in the same play (*Henry VI,* Part III) we can see the technique more plainly:

> Q. MAR. Great lords, wise men ne'er sit and wail their
>   loss,
>   But cheerly seek how to redress their harms.
>   What though the mast be now blown overboard,
>   The cable broke, the holding anchor lost,
>   And half our sailors swallow'd in the flood?
>   Yet lives our pilot still. Is't meet that he
>   Should leave the helm and like a fearful lad
>   With tearful eyes add water to the sea
>   And give more strength to that which hath too
>   much,
>   Whiles, in his moan, the ship splits on the rock,
>   Which industry and courage might have saved?
>   Ah, what a shame! ah, what a fault were this!
>   Say Warwick was our anchor; what of that?
>   And Montague our topmast: what of him?
>   Our slaughter'd friends the tackles: what of these?
>   Why, is not Oxford here another anchor?
>   And Somerset another goodly mast?
>   The friends of France our shrouds and tackelings? . . .
>   This speak I, lords, to let you understand,
>   In case some one of you would fly from us,
>   That there's no hoped-for mercy with the brothers
>   More than with ruthless waves, with sands and rocks.
>   Why, courage then! what cannot be avoided
>   'Twere childish weakness to lament or fear.
>
>   [*3 Henry VI,* V. iv. 1-38]

Here the limpid and melodious movement of the opening lines contrasts effectively with the formal antiphonies beginning: 'Say Warwick was our anchor . . .' These are the most marked elements in Shakespeare's early style. I do not believe that it is possible to say which came first; I think that they were parallel developments. . . . In yet another speech of this same play (*Henry VI*, Part III)—a speech which even the most ruthless repudiator would, we suppose, admit to be genuine early Shakespeare, we have another example of the method:

> KING. This battle fares like to the morning's war,
> When dying clouds contend with growing light,
> What time the shepherd, blowing of his nails,
> Can neither call it perfect day or night. . . .
> O God, methinks it were a happy life
> To be no better than a homely swain;
> To sit upon a hill, as I do now,
> To carve out dials quaintly, point by point,
> Thereby to see the minutes how they run,
> How many make the hour full complete;
> How many hours bring about the day;
> How many days will finish up the year;
> How many years a mortal man may live.
> When this is known, then to divide the times:
> So many hours must I tend my flock;
> So many hours must I take my rest;
> So many hours must I contemplate;
> So many hours must I sport myself;
> So many days my ewes have been with young;
> So many weeks ere the poor fools will ean;
> So many years ere I shall shear the fleece:
> So minutes, hours, days, months and years,
> Pass'd over to the end they were created,
> Would bring white hairs unto a quiet grave.
> Ah, what a life were this! how sweet! how lovely!
> Gives not the hawthorn-bush a sweeter shade
> To shepherds looking on their silly sheep
> Than doth a rich embroider'd canopy
> To kings that fear their subjects' treachery?
> O, yes, it doth; a thousand-fold it doth.
> And to conclude, the shepherd's homely curds,
> His cold thin drink out of his leather bottle,
> His wonted sleep under a fresh tree's shade,
> All which secure and sweetly he enjoys,
> Is far beyond a prince's delicates,
> His viands sparkling in a golden cup,
> His body couched in a curious bed
> When care, mistrust, and treason waits on him.
>   [*3 Henry VI*, II. v. 1-54]

This is, undeniably, the most beautiful of the passages we have chosen from the play; it was an opportunity for the lyrical 'wood-note wild' which was never far from the lips of Shakespeare: but, as verse, it is of the same kind as the other passages. The same elaborate formalism is used to vary the melody. The weak ending is more exquisitely managed than in the other passages: even the mature Shakespeare never used it more perfectly than in the two lines:

> Pass'd over to the end they were created. . .
> His cold thin drink out of his leather bottle. . . .

And the speech as a whole gives a more definite hint of the consummate verse artist to be than anything else in the play; but it seems impossible to deny that it is the natural product of the hand which wrote York's speech and Margaret's; and that the difference in quality between them is due to the opportunity of a more congenial theme. (pp. 74-9)

It would obviously be wrongheaded to use this early individual style of Shakespeare's which we have tried to distinguish at its emergence, as a touchstone to try the authenticity of the earliest plays, for the early plays are the apprentice-work by and out of which this individual style was developed. At some time Shakespeare had to begin; and he began under the compulsions of the playhouse, not in the freedom of the study. We cannot tell how much of already existing material he was required to use in constructing his plays of 'York and Lancaster's long jars.'. . . (pp. 83-4)

All that we can say is that in the early histories we can trace an individual verse-style emerging, and that there are two main elements in it; one, the more striking, a formal patterning employed to bring variety into the blank-verse on every appropriate occasion; the other a simple and lovely periodic *flow* of verse, liquid and almost naive. To my sense this is the blank-verse of a poet who has learned to write blank-verse by speaking it, who therefore, in composing, speaks it rather than writes it, and who is always instinctively striving to reconcile a larger and freer breath with clarity. (p. 84)

> *John Middleton Murry, "The Pupil Age," in his* Shakespeare, *Jonathan Cape, 1936, pp. 57-90.*

MARK VAN DOREN (essay date 1939)

[*Van Doren was a Pulitzer prize-winning American poet, educator, editor, and novelist. In the introduction to his* Shakespeare *(1939), he states that he "ignored the biography of Shakespeare, the history and character of his time, the conventions of his theater, the works of his contemporaries" to concentrate instead on the interest generated by the plays themselves. In the excerpt below, Van Doren argues that both the language and the characterization in* Henry VI *are unsubtle and indistinct. He judges that the "prevailing style of the verse is stiff," delivered in "undifferentiated voices" by generally indistinguishable characters. However, he finds one exception in Richard of Gloucester, whom he identifies as Shakespeare's first individualized character. The question of style and language in the* Henry VI *plays has also been addressed by Adolphus William Ward (1907), John Middleton Murry (1936), Charles R. Forker (1965), and David Riggs (1971). In addition, the characterization of Richard of Gloucester has been analyzed by Henry Norman Hudson (1851), Richard G. Moulton (1903), H. V. D. Dyson (1950), and Michael Manheim (1973).*]

The three parts of "Henry VI" taken together are a massive and masculine performance. They are built with blocks, as befits the youth of their author. Shakespeare—assuming, as it is still permissible to assume, that he was substantially the sole author—must have learned invaluable lessons from the experience of writing so busy a work, with so many people in it, so many individual and group actions, so many documents from Holinshed to study and trim, so much sheer weight to move. One lesson he had already learned, for "Henry VI" is continuously interesting, not to say exciting. He was to know more, however, about the concealment of machinery and the manipulation of motives.

Here all is explicit. The spring of every action is exposed; each person tells the audience at the top of his voice both what he privately intends and what he means publicly to be understood as intending. Enmities are confessed and clear. Conflicts are obvious, as of large bodies moved up to each other and palpably colliding on an open field. There is no mystery or ambiguity of purpose, there are no uninterpretable acts. The fifteenth century is for Shakespeare a time filled solidly with faction; parties split, feuds rage, and oversized heroes growl at one another's tough throats. Hatred is elementary and theatrical, whether it is the hatred of Gloucester for Winchester, Talbot for Joan of Arc, Margaret for the Duchess of Gloucester and the house of York, Suffolk for Gloucester, York for Clifford, Somerset for York, Warwick for Edward IV, Jack Cade for the nobility, Vernon for Basset, or Red for White. No sounder apprenticeship could have been served by a playwright whose destiny it was to be subtle. Subtlety counts most in one who is capable of plainness. Shakespeare was to have had his plainness, as indeed he was to keep a necessary portion of it to the end. He could have traveled toward his later plays from no better direction than "Henry VI." Toward, for example, "Othello," where the theme of witchcraft taints a whole play from sources somehow hidden, and is not, as here in the persons of Joan and the Duchess of Gloucester, merely an aspect of intrigue or an excuse for calling names.

"Henry VI" assaults both the eye with tableaux and the ear with choral effects. Color is recklessly splashed—Blue versus Tawny, Red versus White. The son who has killed his father and the father who has killed his son [*3 Henry VI*, II. v] rush on the stage and declare the grossest irony. Mortimer dying in gaol [*1 Henry VI*, II. v] and York baited like a bear at the stake [*3 Henry VI*, I. iv] are lugubrious and horrible spectacles. The first part begins with a dead march and the bells of Westminster Abbey tolling for Henry V.

> Hung be the heavens with black, yield day to night!
> Comets, importing change of times and states,
> Brandish your crystal tresses in the sky. . . .
> England ne'er lost a king of so much worth.
> England ne'er had a king until his time. . . .
> He was a king bless'd of the King of kings.
>   [*1 Henry VI*, I. i. 1-28]

And the tolling of the verse is interrupted only by three messengers from France who enter one after the other with news that runs from bad to worse to worst. The three plays everywhere are plangent. Talbot and his son [*1 Henry VI*, IV, V, VI, VII] rant to each other in high rhyme, their oaths and their boasts falling antiphonally on our ears until their deaths soon after; when the French take up the chant in their praise. . . . King Henry wanders over the battlefields singing endlessly of the shepherd's life which he envies:

> Would I were dead! if God's good will were so;
> For what is in this world but grief and woe?
> O God! methinks it were a happy life,
> To be no better than a homely swain;
> To sit upon a hill, as I do now,
> To carve out dials quaintly, point by point,
> Thereby to see the minutes how they run,
> How many makes the hour full complete,
> How many hours bring about the day,
> How many days will finish up the year,
> How many years a mortal man may live.
>   [*3 Henry VI*, II. v. 19-29]

Henry's long woe sounds forward to the exquisite elegies of Richard II, but it is not so exquisite, or so nicely adjusted to dramatic necessity. And the stichomythia of the wooing scene between Edward IV and Lady Grey [*3 Henry VI*, III. ii] is permitted to become monotonous as never again in Shakespeare.

The prevailing style of the verse is stiff, in harmony with the "antient, unlettered, martial nobility," says Dr. Johnson [see excerpt above, 1765], who deliver it with undifferentiated voices. The unit of utterance is regularly the line; each of the lines stands sturdily like a tree, a falls as stolidly. Breath is taken

at measured intervals; the drums never tire of beating; and the poet seldom hesitates to pad for the sake of rhythm, which means that most of his dialogue is undistinguished:

> One drop of blood drawn from thy country's bosom
> Should grieve thee more than streams of foreign gore.
> Return thee therefore with a flood of tears,
> And wash away thy country's stained spots.
>   [*1 Henry VI*, III. iii. 54-7]

> Speak, Winchester, for boiling choler chokes
> The hollow passage of my poison'd voice.
>   [*1 Henry VI*, V. iv. 120-21]

> Hast thou not worldly pleasure at command,
> Above the reach or compass of thy thought?
> And wilt thou still be hammering treachery,
> To tumble down thy husband and thyself
> From top of honour to disgrace's feet?
>   [*2 Henry VI*, I. ii. 45-9]

> What louring star now envies thy estate,
> That these great lords and Margaret our queen
> Do seek subversion of thy harmless life?. . .
>   [*2 Henry VI*, III. i. 206-08]

"Come, 'the croaking raven doth bellow for revenge'" [*Hamlet*, III. ii. 254], cried Hamlet to the player ten years later. Hamlet had outgrown this stuffed verse, these labored lines that drag their way so wearisomely up a stubborn hill. But the personages of "Henry VI" insist on speaking so, and there is a certain grandeur in their will, even though their accents are all alike and sincerity can never be distinguished from insincerity. Henry means his rhetoric over the death of Gloucester, and Margaret does not mean hers [*2 Henry VI*, III. ii], but the verse of neither would tell us this, just as the epithets which the style of the play makes so inevitable—"Thou ominous and fearful owl of death" [*1 Henry VI*, IV. ii. 15], "Obscure and lousy swain" [*2 Henry VI*, IV. i. 50], "Rebellious hinds, the filth and scum of Kent" [*2 Henry VI*, IV. ii. 122], "Outcast of Naples, England's bloody scourge" [*2 Henry VI*, V. i. 118]—fail to identify their speakers in the way that Othello, Lear, Timon, and Coriolanus are identified by theirs. (pp. 17-21)

[Richard of Gloucester's] brilliant emergence as a character from this crowd of persons who are so appallingly alike is the most interesting thing about the second and third parts of "Henry VI." He has the power to make them prologues to his own play, so that the trilogy proper is "Henry VI 2-3" and "Richard III." At his first appearance he is struck at like a snake:

> Hence, heap of wrath, foul indigested lump,
> As crooked in thy manners as thy shape!
>   [*2 Henry VI*, V. i. 157-58]

He is the first character in Shakespeare to achieve his own form, to have sinuous and purposeful movement controlled from within. His being hunch-backed and a "foul stigmatic" makes success relatively easy. Yet the success is real. Richard's force is felt from the first as something mysteriously and malignly different from that of the stuffed heroes who stand so erect around him. He is picturesque:

> For you shall sup with Jesu Christ tonight.
>   [*2 Henry VI*, V. i. 214]

He is melodramatic with a vengeance, as when he brings Somerset's head into Parliament [*3 Henry VI*, I. i] and waits for the most effective moment to give it in evidence of his prowess during the recent battle. His eloquence, unlike that of the other heroes, has an intellectual edge; he can prove the impossible [3 Henry VI, I. ii. 20-1], and there is always something in his speech that can revive the spirits of his family; he can make anybody believe anything. His epithets may not roar, but they really cut. Margaret has art enough to call him "a foul mis-shapen stigmatic," a "toad," and a "lizard" [3 Henry VI, II. ii. 136-38]. He has the deadlier art to call her "Iron of Naples hid with English gilt" [3 Henry VI, II. ii. 139]. He can crouch and lie with the smoothest smile of irony on his face. We know what he thinks of Edward's marriage to Lady Grey and how he intends to use it for his own advancement; yet when Edward asks him in public whether he is offended he puts his brother off with misleading mockery:

Not I.
No, God forbid that I should wish them sever'd
Whom God hath join'd together; ay, and 't were pity
To sunder them that yoke so well together.
                        [3 Henry VI, IV. i. 20-3]

His hatred is brilliant, his guile diabolical; and his next move is never apparent to those who watch him. "He's sudden, if a thing comes in his head," says Edward [3 Henry VI, V. v. 86] when Richard has disappeared to make his bloody supper of old Henry in the Tower.

Richard is of course a roaring devil in an old play. He has his set speeches in which he assures the audience of his villainy; he will "set the murderous Machiavel to school" [3 Henry VI, III. ii. 193] and frame his face to all occasions; he has neither pity, love, nor fear; because he was born with teeth he will snarl and bite and play the dog. "Why, I can smile, and murder whiles I smile" [3 Henry VI, II. ii. 182]. "I have no brother, I am like no brother" [3 Henry VI, V. vi. 80]. "I am myself alone" [3 Henry VI, V. vi. 83]. He is as much of the stage as Aaron the Moor [Titus Andronicus], and on another level as Iago. But it is not his set speeches that measure his force. It is his suddenness when things come in his head, it is his serpentlike appearances and disappearances, it is his way of moving. With him wriggling under his hand Shakespeare is ready to write the youthful masterpiece of "Richard III." (pp. 25-7)

Mark Van Doren, " 'Henry VI'," in his Shakespeare, *Henry Holt and Company, 1939, pp. 17-27.*

E. M. W. TILLYARD (essay date 1944)

[*Tillyard's* Shakespeare's History Plays *(1944), one of the most influential twentieth-century works in Shakespearean studies, is regarded by many scholars as the leading example of historical criticism. Tillyard's thesis, which is shared, with variations, by other historical critics, posits the existence of a systematic world view in Shakespeare's plays—and one common to educated Elizabethans—in which reality is understood to be structured in a hierarchical Great Chain of Being. On a social level such a philosophy valued order, hierarchy, and civil peace as the chief political goals. Further, Tillyard noted a basic acceptance in Shakespeare's histories of "the Tudor myth," the critic's term for an interpretation of English history from Richard II to Henry VIII. According to this "myth," Henry IV was a usurper, and his usurpation set into motion the disastrous chain of events which culminated in the War of the Roses between 1455 and 1485. In the excerpt below, Tillyard maintains that in the* Henry VI *trilogy there is no hero; instead, the protagonist is "England, or in Morality [play] terms, Respublica." God must punish England, Tillyard argues, for Henry IV's crime of usurpation, but He also pities her and will ultimately permit the "suppressed good in her" to emerge and restore the country to health. Tillyard traces the disintegration of the principles of order and degree throughout*

the action of 1, 2, and 3 Henry VI—*from the defeat of Talbot, to the spread of disorder among the commoners, to the multiple catastrophes of the last play in the trilogy. Among later critics who addressed the question of whether Shakespeare was promoting the Tudor myth in* Henry VI, *M. M. Reese (1961) and Irving Ribner (1965) have generally agreed with Tillyard that he was, while S. C. Sen Gupta (1964) denied the idea that Shakespeare was a Tudor propagandist. In interpretations similar to Tillyard's, Hermann Ulrici (1839), Denton J. Snider (1890), and J. A. R. Marriott (1918) all asserted that divine providence operates in a retributive way in the* Henry VI *plays, whereas A. C. Hamilton (1961-62), H. M. Richmond (1967), James Winny (1968), and Robert Ornstein (1972) denied any evidence of providential retribution in the trilogy.*]

[The *Henry VI-Richard III*] tetralogy to an equal extent with the later tetralogy and more powerfully than the most civilised of the Chronicle Plays shows Shakespeare aware of order or degree. Behind all the confusion of civil war, and the more precious and emphatic because of the confusion, is the belief that the world is a part of the eternal law and that earthly mutability, as in Spenser's last cantos, is itself a part of a greater and permanent pattern. Further, human events as well as being subject to the eternal law are part of an elaborate system of correspondences and hence the more firmly woven into the total web of things. (p. 150)

[Shakespeare's] most effective statement of the principle of order occurs in the passage which largely by accident is the most famous of all three Henry VI plays, Henry's pathetic soliloquy where he regrets that he was born a king and not a shepherd.

O God! methinks it were a happy life
To be no better than a homely swain;
To sit upon a hill, as I do now,
To carve out dials quaintly, point by point,
Thereby to see the minutes how they run,
How many make the hour full complete;
How many hours bring about the day;
How many days will finish up the year;
How many years a mortal man may live.
When this is known, then to divide the times:
So many hours must I tend my flock;
So many hours must I take my rest;
So many hours must I contemplate;
So many hours must I sport myself;
So many days my ewes have been with young;
So many weeks ere the poor fools will ean;
So many years ere I shall shear the fleece:
So minutes hours days months and years,
Pass'd over to the end they were created,
Would bring white hairs unto a quiet grave.
Ah, what a life were this, how sweet, how lovely!
                        [3 Henry VI, II. v. 21-41]
                                        (p. 152)

The context is the Battle of Towton, where the Lancastrians suffered their bloodiest defeat and which Shakespeare selects from all the battles as most emphatically illustrating the full horrors of civil war. Henry has been "chidden from the field" by his terrible queen and the fierce Clifford, because he brings bad luck; but immediately after his soliloquy he witnesses two spectacles of the utmost horror, first a son discovering that he has killed his father and then a father discovering that he has killed his son. Henry's speech must be judged before this background of chaos. It signifies not, as naturally thought of out of its context, a little bit of lyrical escapism but Henry's yearning for an ordered life. This ordered life of the shepherd is a pitifully small thing compared with the majestic order he as a king should have been able to impose. Yet it stands for the great principle of degree, while bringing out Henry's personal tragedy: his admirable intentions and his utter inability to carry them out.

Another most explicit version of the same thing is the contrast between the lawlessness of Jack Cade and the impeccable moderation and discipline of the Kentish squire Iden, in *2 Henry VI*. Cade openly boasts, ''But then we are in order when we are most out of order'' [*2 Henry VI*, IV. ii. 189-90]. All degree is to be levelled away:

> There shall be in England seven halfpenny loaves
> sold for a penny; the three-hooped pot shall
> have ten hoops; and I will make it a felony to
> drink small beer: all the realm shall be in com-
> mon; and in Cheapside shall my palfry go to
> grass . . . there shall be no money; all shall eat
> and drink on my score; and I will apparel them
> all in one livery that they may agree like broth-
> ers and worship me their lord.
> [*2 Henry VI*, IV. ii. 65-75]

Iden, who catches the fugitive Jack Cade in his garden and kills him, is a flat symbolic character, beautifully contrasted with the realism of the rebels. He is entirely content with his own station in the social hierarchy, as smug as any eighteenth century moralist over the virtues of the middle station of life. He introduces himself to us by this soliloquy in his garden:

> Lord, who would live turmoiled in the court,
> Who may enjoy such quiet walks as these?
> This small inheritance my father left me
> Contenteth me, and worth a monarchy.
> I seek not to wax great by others' waning;
> Or gather wealth I care not, with what envy:
> Sufficeth that I have maintains my state
> And sends the poor well pleased from my gate.
> [*2 Henry VI*, IV. x. 16-23]

This speech for all its smugness is perfectly serious in giving the norm of order, upset by Cade.

As powerful as the theme of order in the tetralogy is the continual insistence on cause and effect in the unfolding of history. Shakespeare adopts the whole teaching of Hall and of the *Mirror for Magistrates*. . . . [Again] and again, at any great happening, Shakespeare seeks to bring out the concatenation of events. Thus in *2 Henry VI* Gloucester, about to be murdered, sees his death the cause of great misery to the land and of ruin to his king. (pp. 152-54)

Again Margaret of Anjou is not merely a strong-minded and troublesome woman who prolongs the civil wars by her tenacity and fulfils the dramatic part of avenging fury; she has her precise place in the chain of events. Her marriage with Henry VI was from the first a disaster and brought to a head the troubles between Lancaster and York which otherwise would have lain quiet. (p. 154)

It is in the last two plays of the tetralogy that the prevalent high theme of the *Mirror for Magistrates*, the fall of an eminent and erring statesman, is most evident. In the first two plays Talbot and Humphrey of Gloucester are too individual and too virtuous to fit into the norm of that poem. But in the third play the tragedy of Richard Duke of York is solemnly enacted, and

in *Richard III* the motive of the *Mirror* occurs with great power. (p. 156)

So much for Shakespeare's use in his tetralogy of the conceptions of world order and the process of history: the ideas that appear so little in the Chronicle Plays and seems to have been the property of a select and educated class. . . . His use of them illustrates the academic side of himself that was so prominent in his early years. It is to his History Plays what the Plautine form is to the *Comedy of Errors* and the Senecan and Ovidian elements and conventions to *Titus Andronicus*.

But Shakespeare was not only academic in his first historical tetralogy: he was a popular dramatist too. Not that the populace would have objected to his superior opinions on history; they would have been willing to be impressed if they also got the things they expected: which they most certainly did. And first, for this popular material, there is what I have called sometimes Higden and sometimes Holinshed: the mediation of sheer fact. For though Shakespeare did see history in an intelligible pattern he compressed into a popular and lively form an astonishing quantity of sheer historical fact. He can indeed be nearly as informative as the author of the *True Tragedy of Richard III*. . . . This, for instance, is how York begins the genealogical statement on which he claims his title to the throne in *2 Henry VI*:

> Edward the Third, my lords, had seven sons:
> The first, Edward the Black Prince,
>   Prince of Wales;
> The second, William of Hatfield, and the third,
> Lionel Duke of Clarence; next to whom
> Was John of Gaunt, the Duke of Lancaster;
> The fifth was Edmund Langley, Duke of York;
> The sixth was Thomas of Woodstock,
>   Duke of Gloucester;
> William of Windsor was the seventh and last.
> [*2 Henry VI*, II. ii. 10-17]

There seems to have been a genuine popular demand for this sheer information. And beyond presenting this unmitigated fact Shakespeare succeeded conspicuously in making palatable to his public a greater bulk of chronicle material than other dramatists were able to do.

Shakespeare also satisfied the popular taste in setting forth the great popular political theme, the horror of civil war, and in giving his plays the required chauvinist tone. Joan of Arc is a bad enough woman, Margaret of Anjou an intriguing enough queen; an Englishman is worth a sufficient number of Frenchman; Frenchmen are sufficiently boastful and fickle, to satisfy every popular requirement.

Finally, Shakespeare occasionally satisfies the taste for the startling but irrelevant anecdote; the pieces of sensation that pleased the people but could be spared from the play. There is for example the scene in *I Henry VI* [II. iii] where the Countess of Auvergne plots Talbot's death by inviting him to her house and he prevents her by summoning his men by a blast from his horn; and the scene in *2 Henry VI* [I. iv] where Bolingbroke the conjurer calls up spirits at the command of the Duchess of Gloucester.

In sum Shakespeare in his effort could beat the writers of Chronicle Plays on their own ground.

Among the strains found in Tudor history was that akin to [Thomas] Froissart and shown in the work of [Thomas] More and [William] Cavendish: a dramatic liveliness and a closeness to the event. This strain appears in Shakespeare's first historical tetralogy; but how much he owed to [Thomas] Berners's Froissart and to the lives of Richard III and Wolsey, and how much to his own dramatic inclinations, it is impossible to assess. However, it matters little whence he got the strain, but much more that it should be there. It is of course precisely this strain that the disintegrators have been after whenever they have wished to fish out any fragments of true Shakespeare from the general wreckage; and they have found it, for instance, in the first declaration of the feud between red and white rose in *I Henry VI* and in the Jack Cade scenes in *2 Henry VI*. There is nothing wrong in praising these scenes and calling them typical of Shakespeare. But is is very wrong indeed to emphasise them and to make them the norm by which to judge the whole tetralogy. They enrich the tetralogy but on a balance they are exceptional to it.

To redress this wrong emphasis we must think of yet another strain in this tetralogy: that of formalism and stylisation. It is something archaic, inherited from the Morality Play. But it is the very feature through which the essential life of the poetry is expressed. When we encounter an unnatural and stylised balance of incident or an artificial patttern of speech we must not think that here is merely an archaic survival: we must accept them as things having contemporary vitality and must make them the norm of the play. We must in fact be good Aristotelians, for the moment, and believe that the soul of the play is in plot rather than in character. The realism of the Jack Cade scenes is not their main point but a subsidiary enrichment. Their main point is to make half a pattern, the other half being implied by the blameless orderliness of Iden. We are apt to praise the Cade scenes for being realistic and jeer at Iden for being a dummy, when we should merge praise and blame into the appreciation of a piece of stylisation which includes the whole. Similarly Henry VI's pathetic piece of nostalgia as he sits on the molehill watching the Battle of Towton has been isolated into a piece of poetic and "human" writing in a boring and inhuman context. Actually it loses most of its virtue apart from the context; apart from the terrible scene of the father killing his son and the son killing his father. That scene embodies a traditional motive; for these acts had been chosen by the authors of the Homilies, by Hall, and by the authors of the *Mirror for Magistrates* as the clearest symbol of the horrors of civil war. Shakespeare's fathers and sons here are as flat characters as Iden; and they have no business to be anything else. They stand as great traditional types, in whom realism would be impious. They enact a tableau; though they speak they are not far off a dumb-show: and their flatness adds enormous point to the ineffective humanity of the weak king. (pp. 157-59)

But if the Morality Play prompted the formality of Shakespeare's first tetralogy it also supplied a single pervasive theme; one which overrides but in no way interferes with the theme he derived from Hall. In none of the plays is there a hero: and one of the reasons is that there is an unnamed protagonist dominating all four. It is England, or in Morality terms Respublica. . . . England, though she is now quite excluded as a character, is the true hero of Shakespeare's first tetralogy. She is brought near ruin through not being true to herself; yielding to French witchcraft and being divided in mind. But God, though he punishes her, pities her and in the end through his grace allows the suppressed good in her to assert itself and restore her to health. . . .

Finally Shakespeare reinforces the structural unity which the themes of the Morality and of Hall create, by sowing in one play the seeds that are to germinate in the next and by constant references back from a later play to an earlier. (p. 160)

For all the inequality of execution, the vast crowding in of historical incident (some of it inorganic), Shakespeare planned his first historical tetralogy greatly, reminding one of [Thomas] Hardy in the *Dynasts*. When we consider how deficient his fellow-dramatists were in the architectonic power, we can only conclude that this was one of the things with which he was conspicuously endowed by nature. Far from being the untidy genius, Shakespeare was in one respect a born classicist. (pp. 160-61)

The *First Part of Henry VI* is the work of an ambitious and reflective young man who has the power to plan but not worthily to execute something great. His style of writing lags behind the powerful imagination that arranged the inchoate mass of historical material into a highly significant order. The characters are well thought out and consistent but they are the correct pieces in a game moved by an external hand rather than self-moving. Yet they come to life now and then and, in promise, are quite up to what we have any right to expect from Shakespeare in his youth.

If this play had been called the *Tragedy of Talbot* it would stand a much better chance of being heeded by a public which very naturally finds it hard to remember which part of *Henry VI* is which, and where Joan of Arc or Jack Cade, or Margaret crowning York with a paper crown, occur. And if we want something by which to distinguish the play, let us by all means give it that title. It is one that contains much truth, but not all. The whole truth in this matter is that though the action revolves round Talbot, though he stands pre-eminently for loyalty and order in a world threatened by chaos, he is not the hero. For there is no regular hero either in this or in any of the other three plays; its true hero being England or Respublica after the fashion of the Morality Play. . . . It is therefore truer to the nature of the separate plays that they should be given colourless regal titles than that they should be named after the seemingly most important characters or events.

Along with the Morality hero goes the assumption of divine interference. The theme of the play is the testing of England, already guilty and under a sort of curse, by French witchcraft. England is championed by a great and pious soldier, Talbot, and the witchcraft is directed principally at him. If the other chief men of England had all been like him, he could have resisted and saved England. But they are divided against each other, and through this division Talbot dies and the first stage in England's ruin and of the fulfilment of the curse is accomplished. Respublica has suffered the first terrible wound.

As so often happens in literature the things which initially are the most troublesome prove to be the most enlightening. The Joan episodes, unpleasant and hence denied Shakespeare, are the clue to the whole plot. They are hinted at right in the front of the play. In the first scene Exeter, commenting on the funeral of Henry V, says:

> What! shall we curse the planets of mishap
> That plotted thus our glory's overthrow?
> Or shall we think the subtle-witted French
> Conjurers and sorcerers, that afraid of him
> By magic verses have contriv'd his end?
>
> [*1 Henry VI,* I. i. 23-7]

One cannot understand the bearing of these lines on the play without remembering how the influence of the stars and witchcraft fitted into the total Elizabethan conception of the universe. Though these two things were thought to be powerful in their effects and were dreaded, they did not work undirected. God was ultimately in control, and the divine part of man, his reason and the freedom of his will, need not yield to them. Further, God used both stars and evil spirits to forward his own ends. Joan, then, is not a mere piece of fortuitous witchcraft, not a mere freakish emissary of Satan, but a tool of the Almighty, as she herself (though unconsciously) declares in her words to Charles after her first appearance,

> Assign'd am I to be the English scourge.
> [*1 Henry VI*, I. ii. 129]

Who but God has assigned her this duty? True, if this line were unsupported, we might hesitate to make this full inference. But combined with the various cosmic references and the piety of Talbot, it is certain. For not only the first scene of the play, but the second scene (where Joan first appears) begins with a reference to the heavens. The first passage was quoted above; the Dauphin Charles begins the second scene:

> Mars his true moving, even as in the heavens
> So in the earth, to this day is not known:
> Late did he shine upon the English side;
> Now we are the victors; upon us he smiles.
> [*1 Henry VI*, I. ii. 1-4]

Not only do these words contrast significantly with Bedford's opening speech about the "bad revolted stars" [*1 Henry VI*, I. i. 4]; they combine with it in presenting the whole world order with God, the unmoved mover, directing it. And the full context of witchcraft is implied when Talbot before Orleans, already harassed by Joan's supernatural power, exclaims of the French:

> Well, let them practise and converse with spirits:
> God is our fortress, in whose conquering name
> Let us resolve to scale their flinty bulwarks.
> [*1 Henry VI*, II. i. 25-7]

A modern, who needs much working up to pay any real heed to witchcraft, is apt not to notice such a passage and to pass on faintly disgusted with Talbot for being not only a butcher but a prig: an Elizabethan, granted a generally serious context, would find Talbot's defiance apt and noble. (pp. 163-65)

In the second part [of *Henry VI*] the dissensions, which in the first part had been the background, are developed at home as the main theme, with the Duke of York the emergent figure. They cause Duke Humphrey's fall and at the end bring the country to the edge of chaos. The play pictures the second stage in the country's ruin, in the working out of the inherited curse.

In many ways the second part is contrasted with the first. The plot-pattern is the main thing in the first part, and with this emphasis goes a pageantlike, stylised execution. One happening is contrasted ironically with another, the irony being more important than the richness of either happening. Characters may have much abstract meaning but as persons have little depth. Talbot is a grand symbol of loyalty and order; his touch of coarse humour goes a little way and only a little way towards making him interesting. The second part is very well plotted, yet with another emphasis. Events, as befits the domestic setting, matter more in themselves. They are richly and elaborately developed. And they concern a wider section of the community. We are shown dissension affecting not only the prime movers of it, the nobles, but the common people and

the middle classes. The whole frame of Respublica is beginning to suffer. Thus it is that the scenes of Horner the armourer and his man Peter, of the pirates who capture Suffolk, and of Jack Cade and Iden, at first sight episodic, are greatly to the point. Lastly there is a vastly heightened interest in personality. Shakespeare is wonderfully alive to the fascination of the mere force of character. The main English nobles are bad and they ruin the country, but they are all positive characters, characters who start trains of events, who are at the centre of living. Gloucester's description of the men who are plotting against him brings out to perfection this side of the play:

> I know their complot is to have my life,
> And if my death might make this island happy
> And prove the period of their tyranny,
> I would expend it with all willingness.
> But mine is made the prologue to their play;
> For thousands more, that yet suspect no peril,
> Will not conclude their plotted tragedy.
> Beaufort's red sparkling eyes blab his heart's malice,
> And Suffolk's cloudy brow his stormy hate;
> Sharp Buckingham unburthens with his tongue
> The envious load that lies upon his heart;
> And dogged York, that reaches at the moon,
> Whose overweening arm I have pluck'd back,
> By false accuse doth level at my life;
> And you, my sovereign lady, with the rest
> Causeless have laid disgraces on my head
> And with your best endeavour have stirr'd up
> My liefest liege to be mine enemy.
> [*2 Henry VI*, III. i. 147-64]
> (pp. 173-74)

The central theme then is political intrigue, which of itself dictates that greater stress on events and smaller emphasis on symbol and principle, already noted. Shakespeare may have made this change for the sake of variety, but it also corresponds to his growing power; for in this play he shows to the full, as he hardly did in the first part, his wonderful faculty of animating a heavy mass of material: a repetition, on the serious historical side, of his masterly manipulation of a complicated comic situation in the *Comedy of Errors*. Reviewing the opening scenes of *1 and 2 Henry VI*, which both get through a great deal of business and succeed in setting forth the whole situation, one must contrast the staccato presentation of events in the first part with the melting of one event into another of the second part; and wherever there is a large, exciting, and quickly moving political theme, as the events round Gloucester's murder and the final alignment of Yorkists against Lancastrians before the battle of St. Albans, Shakespeare is no longer the compiler but the controller of his material.

It has not been the practice to consider *2 Henry VI* as a whole. But it is pre-eminently as such, as a fine piece of construction, that it is to be enjoyed. (pp. 175-76)

[Although in *2 Henry VI*] Shakespeare has extended the range of his characters and gone farther towards making them lifelike and in entering their minds, the problem of character to which he applies himself most steadily is that of the right kind of king. In fact this is the first play in which he set forth a problem that was to maintain its interest for him all through his working career. There are three regal figures: Henry the actual king, Gloucester the regent, and York the claimant of the throne. In their joint characters they possess the requirements for a good king, and in ther relations they make a set of character-patterns that gives coherence to the play. Of the three York is the dominant character and he is contrasted with Gloucester at the beginning and with Henry at the end of the play. York has eminent kingly qualities: he is strong both in character and in his title to the throne. He speaks the truth when he says of himself:

> I am far better born than is the king,
> More like a king, more kingly in my thoughts.
>
> [2 Henry VI, V. i. 28-9]

He is also an excellent diplomat. In fact he combines the two great qualities of lion and fox. He would have been a great king if he had reigned; and his repeated assurances that he would win back France if he had the chance are not hollow. But Shakespeare did not think that lion and fox alone made a good king. A third quality, disinterestedness, the attribute of the pelican, was needed: and this York did not possess. Gloucester had the qualities of lion and pelican but not of fox. Henry had those of the pelican alone. That is the formal pattern of the three regal characters. (pp. 185-86)

Though not the best play of the tetralogy, 2 Henry VI is perhaps the most harmonious. Shakespeare was able to concentrate on the business in hand. He was interested in what he was doing, for he had acquired new powers and was able to occupy them fully in coping with the sort of material that previously had been rather too much for him. He achieved a happy adjustment of material and means of expression that was to be upset in his next play, better though that play was in some ways to be. (p. 188)

In the third part [of Henry VI] Shakespeare shows us chaos itself, the full prevalence of civil war, the perpetration of one horrible deed after another. In the second part there had remained some chivalric feeling. At the battle of St. Albans York says to Clifford,

> With thy brave bearing should I be in love,
> But that thou art so fast mine enemy.
>
> [2 Henry VI, V. ii. 20-1]

And Clifford answers,

> Nor should thy prowess want praise and esteem,
> But that 'tis shown ignobly and in treason.
>
> [2 Henry VI, V. ii. 22-3]

But in the third part all the decencies of chivalric warfare are abandoned. Young Clifford kills the twelve-year-old Rutland at Wakefield. The three sons of York successively stab Prince Edward, son of Henry VI, taken prisoner at Tewkesbury. At Towton is displayed the supreme and traditional picture of chaos, the denial of all chivalric pieties, a father killing and robbing a son and a son killing and robbing a father. Here is the culminating expression of the horrors and wickedness of civil war.

In such a welter of crime the part of heaven is mainly to avenge. And Shakespeare is extremely punctilious in furnishing a crime to justify every disaster. Indeed his lavishness tends to monotony. Edward IV, for instance, commits three major crimes, any one of which was enough to imperil himself and his posterity. He encouraged his father, York, to go back on his oath of loyalty to Henry VI in return for the reversion of the crown; he promised the Mayor of York that he had returned to England to claim his dukedom and not the crown; and he stabbed his prisoner the young prince Edward. There is, however, sufficient reference to the positive principles of order for us not to forget the less immediate and more beneficent workings of

heaven. It is Henry VI who is the chief instrument of their expression. Whereas in the second part he was conspicuous for his weakness, he is now more conspicuous by his high principles and his humanity. At Towton, as described above, he set up the miniature order of the shepherd's life against the major chaos of battle. In front of York he protests against the brutality of the head of his dead enemy York being set up on the walls. And it is he and no one else who blesses the boy Richmond and, as if divinely inspired, prophesies a rescue through him from the present ills:

> Come hither, England's hope. If secret powers
> Suggest but truth to my divining thoughts,
> This pretty lad will prove our country's bliss.
> His looks are full of peaceful majesty,
> His head by nature fram'd to wear a crown,
> His hand to wield a sceptre, and himself
> Likely in time to bless a regal throne.
> Make much of him, my lords, for this is he
> Must help you more than you are hurt by me.
>
> [3 Henry VI, IV. vi. 68-76]
>
> (pp. 188-89)

With chaos as his theme it was not likely that Shakespeare would wish to cast this play into the clear patterns of the first and second parts. Indeed, formlessness of a sort was as necessary to his purposes here as the wide scattered geography of Antony and Cleopatra was to the imperial setting of that play. But unfortunately with the relaxation of form goes a decline of vitality. Shakespeare had a great mass of chronicle matter to deal with and he failed to control it; or rather in paring it to manageable length he fails to make it significant. The third part of Henry VI is Shakespeare's nearest approach to the Chronicle Play. There are indeed splendid things in it, but they are rather islands sticking out of a sea of mediocrity than hills arising from the valleys or undulations of an organic landscape. In the intermediate passages Shakespeare is either tired or bored: or perhaps both. He may have been tired because he had already sustained his theme of civil dissension so long; he may have been bored because he was even then absorbed in the character of Richard and anxious to write the play to which he gave his name. He may too have disliked repeating himself; yet felt too much committed to a certain kind of play to be able to fashion something quite new. Thus he entirely omits one of his masterthemes in the previous play: the character of the good king. But he cannot escape giving more examples of fierce noblemen exchanging high words. And in plotting out cause and effect, in consonance with his loyalty to Hall and the Mirror for Magistrates, whereas in the other two plays he worked freely and with enthusiasm, he now repeats from a sense of duty. (p. 190)

Shakespeare wanted to give his picture of civil chaos and to prepare for his next play. But he was committed, as a dramatic chronicler of history, to including a very big body of material. In his two first plays, not having included more matter than suited him, he was able to organise it into two well-proportioned wholes. But he paid for it by being left with a large and scarcely manageable residue. He spent himself on two great scenes of civil war, the battles of Wakefield and Towton, and on building up the character of Richard in the second half of his play. Into the gaps he fitted the bulk of his stuff as best he could. It is possible, however, that he tried to give some vague shape to the play through a hierarchy in the characters. Though the pirated version named the play after the Duke of York, he is not the chief character, for he is killed in the first act; nor

are his sons, Edward and Richard, though all necessary preparations are made for Richard to become so in the next play.
The chief characters are the instigators of the two kings who
figure in the play, Margaret wife of Henry VI and Warwick
on whose backing the sons of York rely. Such plot as there is
(mere chronicling apart) consists in the emergence of these two
as the truly dominant persons in the civil war, their opposition
and varying fortunes, their unexpected reconciliation, and their
final defeat largely through the expanding genius of Richard
Duke of Gloucester. If these two characters were sufficiently
emphasised, the play as a whole might not act too badly. (pp.
191-92)

E. M. W. Tillyard, "The First Tetralogy," in his
Shakespeare's History Plays, *Chatto & Windus, 1944,*
pp. 147-214.

H. V. D. DYSON   (essay date 1950)

[*Although Dyson regards the early Shakespeare as primarily con-*
cerned with dramatizing events, not delineating character, he
postulates that there are elements in Shakespeare's first plays
which foreshadow the major tragedies. In the following excerpt,
he proposes that there are three types of "tragic solitary" figures
in Shakespearean drama: the egotistical villain, the man who is
trapped in his own interior world, and the "noble figure who . . .
begins in full communion with his fellows" but is "forced into
isolation by the movement of the tragedy." Dyson includes Rich-
ard of Gloucester in the first category, along with Iago and Ed-
mund; he places Henry VI—"who has no place" in the cunning
and violent world of the Henry VI *trilogy—in the second category,*
along with Hamlet and Richard II; and he counts Humphrey of
Gloucester in the third division, in company with Othello, Lear,
and Macbeth. Shakespeare's characterization of Richard of
Gloucester has also been examined by Henry Norman Hudson
(1851), Richard G. Moulton (1903), and Mark Van Doren (1939).
For further discussion of Shakespeare's depiction of Henry VI,
see the essays by William Hazlitt (1817), Edward Dowden (1881),
Harold C. Goddard (1951), M. M. Reese (1961), Michael Man-
heim (1973), and John D. Cox (1978).]

In [Shakespeare's] early histories, where tragic plot and character were first outlined, kings are the most powerful and the
most vulnerable of men. Shakespeare had not yet developed
love as a characteristic tragic *motif*. Kings, having most, had
most to lose; it was they and their competing rivals who could
most affect the lives of others and to whom most could happen.
As Hamlet is most vulnerable in his sonship, Othello as husband, Lear in his fatherhood, so Henry VI and Richard II and
John expose their royalty to treason, self-betrayal, and mischance. (p. 84)

Kings served Shakespeare well. He learned to be a tragic poet
while dramatizing the royalty of England. In a sense all his
tragedies are history, and the earlier histories are tragic, if not
greatly tragic. In them we find ineptitude and wickedness alike
leading to disaster, to the deaths of the leading characters, to
the rending of England. Kings offered splendid raw material,
they were tragedy ready-made. They were a special race of
men owing their position to chance of birth, deriving their
sanctions from the fact that they were consecrated beings. Representing in worldly affairs the authority of God, they seemed
also His personal representatives on earth. Their sufferings
recalled the sufferings of God incarnate. Between a king's
divinity and his mortality was a relationship which involved a
tragic contradiction. Death kept his bare court about their crowned
and anointed temples, and imbecility, incompetence, or treason
could waste or ravish the divinity that hedged a king. It was

a divinity that could not only be lost, it could be stolen by a
cutpurse of empire. The royal sanctity could be usurped and a
successful crowned usurper offered again a mass of tragic possibilities.

Is it to consider too curiously to recognize as early as *Henry*
VI some of the interests, somewhat obscurely foreshadowed it
may be, which engaged Shakespeare in his prime? Certainly
the crowned baby, King Henry, seems a long way from the
crowned babyhood of Lear, and his youthful innocence remote
from the aged innocence of Duncan, whose murder, yet but
fantastical in Macbeth's mind, called up the image of pity as
a naked new-born babe.

At least two types of character, which, greatly developed, are
conspicuous in the later plays, already appear. The abdicator,
recognizing his own inadequacy in the stress of the situation
with which he is confronted, and the aggressor, the bold opportunist, eager to exploit the very situation which daunts the
other.

Solitude, severance from one's fellows and at times from oneself, is the fate of heroes in tragedy. We may here distinguish
two kinds of solitude. That of a villain, isolated in his self-
esteem, loveless and efficient:

> Then, since this earth affords no joy to me
> But to command, to check, to o'erbear such
> As are of better person than myself,
> I'll make my heaven to dream upon the crown,
> And, whiles I live, to account this world but hell,
> Until my mis-shaped trunk that bears this head
> Be round impaled with a glorious crown.
>
> [*3 Henry VI,* III. ii. 165-71]

Gloucester, emerging from the bitterness and chaos of the Wars
of the Roses, is in his solitude the forerunner of such great
tragic solitaries and masters of aggression as Iago and Edmund,
who avenge themselves on the world for their own disabilities
by turning it into a desert, by infecting others with their own
poison.

Richard II and Hamlet represent another type. The man who
is unable or unwilling to break from his own interior world
which is in part at least satisfying and pleasing. Richard cannot
wake from his royal dreams, those musical alternations of grandeur and cold despair, to exercise the function to which his
genuine royalty was born. Hamlet, complex and contradictory,
is reluctant to break from the too-satisfying nutshell in which
he could contentedly be bound and count himself a king of
infinite space. Lover, prince, avenger, son, Denmark's heir,
observer and commentator, these are for him but actions that
a man might play; like Richard he finds acting easier than
action.

And this eternal questioning, this unequal poise of will and
circumstance, we find as early as in Henry VI himself. Not,
indeed, from any great complexity of character, or depth of
speculation, but simply that he has never found his place among
events. King too young, mated with a worldling, holy amidst
a ravening pack of royal and baronial brigands, peace-loving
in a world torn by war, he longs for a cloister or a sheepfold.
His tragic dilemma is apparent, even if his character is but
rawly conceived. His situation is heavy with tragic possibilities
that will be fully realized in later plays. In a world of fierce
endeavour, of cunning and violence, he has no place; yet he
was born to set things right. Already we are shown a man
inhabiting two worlds simultaneously, at home in neither. In

Part I. Act II. Scene iii. Soldiers, Talbot, Countess of Auvergne, and Porter. By John Opie (n.d.).

his reign the order and tradition for which he was responsible and which are embodied in his person collapse and the adventurous aggressors creep through the cracks; Beaufort, Suffolk, York, finally the full-fledged emergent from the world's confusion, Richard of Gloucester, in turn contend for mastery. In a troubled world any adventurer might hope to wear the crown or to wield its authority, and so through weakness and greed the splendid empire of Henry V falls apart. Shakespeare's first great theme was the dividing and diminishing of a kingdom. France falls off from England, whom Burgundy has betrayed. Talbot is deserted through the rivalry of Somerset and York; Lancaster falls apart, the royal House of England itself does sliver and disbranch. Beaufort against Humphrey of Gloucester, Suffolk and the queen against the king, Humphrey, alone amongst the great men loyal and true, is isolated and killed. Beaufort and Suffolk perish and York, of the rival branch of the royal House, makes a push for power. But here, too, are the seeds of self-destruction, and Richard, the ill spirit of that unquiet time, having disposed alike of inconvenient Lancastrians and Yorkists, rules for a time over a tired and frightened land.

Duke Humphrey is the only representation in the early plays of a third kind of tragic solitary; the noble figure, who, like Othello, Lear, and Macbeth, begins in full communion with his fellows, filling an honourable position, and who as the play proceeds is forced into isolation by the movement of the trag-

edy. But Humphrey is in a tragic situation only, he has not range or intensity enough to engage our minds as a genuine tragic character. By a reach of fantasy, Eleanor his wife may be seen to anticipate some of the ambition of Lady Macbeth and some of the habits of the witches.

In these early histories neither time nor troubles reveal characters or promote development. Virtually Shakespeare is still simply the entertainer. He is experimenting here as in the earliest comedies, in the business of stage entertainment, in devices to catch and to hold an audience. His problems are to dramatize whatever he found in his sources, chronicle, tradition, or play, to present a mass of English history suitably organized for presentation on the stage. He begins and ends where he can. He does not, as in the tragedies, choose deliberately the closing period of a man's life and show how events, in part his own fault, in part that of others, in part mere chance happenings, concur in his destruction. We learn much of the possibilities of drama, little of those of human life. Although the turncoats Burgundy and Clarence and Warwick change sides, their changing of allegiance marks no change in their characters. We watch and are excited by the turn of events but do not ourselves turn with them. (pp. 84-7)

H. V. D. Dyson, "The Emergence of Shakespeare's Tragedy," in Proceedings of the British Academy, *Vol. XXXVI, 1950, pp. 69-93.*

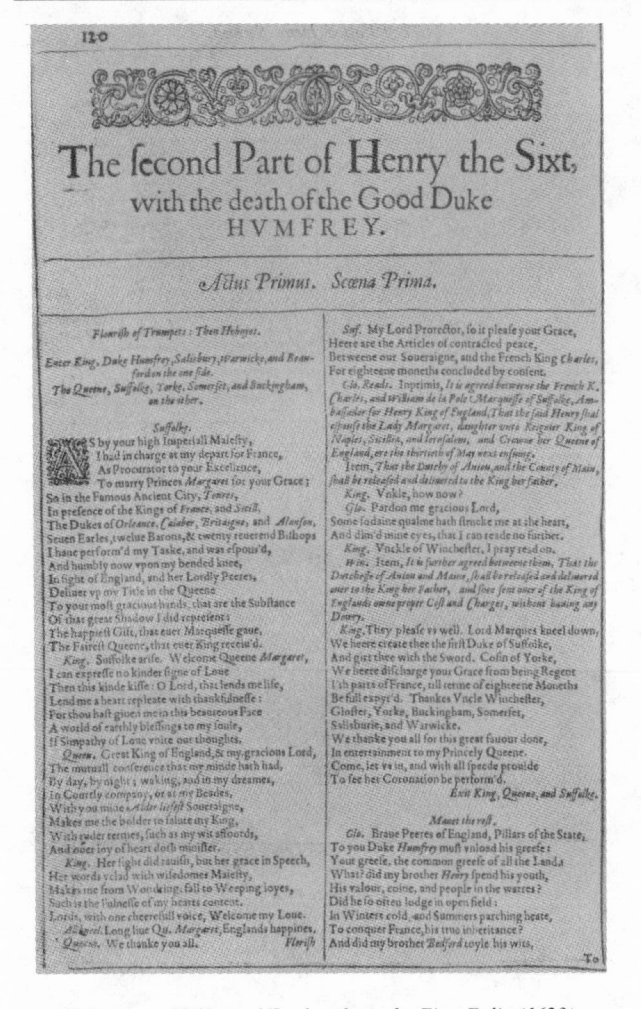

Title page of 2 Henry VI *taken from the First Folio (1623).*

JOHN DOVER WILSON (essay date 1951)

[*Dover Wilson was a highly regarded Shakespearean scholar who was involved in several aspects of Shakespeare studies. As an editor of the* New Cambridge Shakespeare, *he made numerous contributions to twentieth-century textual criticism of Shakespeare, making use of the scientific bibliography developed by W. W. Greg and Charlton Hinman. As a critic, Dover Wilson combined several contemporary approaches and does not fit easily into any one critical "school." He was concerned with character analysis in the tradition of A. C. Bradley; he studied Elizabethan culture like the historical critics, but without their usual emphasis on hierarchy and the Great Chain of Being; and his interest in visualizing possible dramatic performances of the plays linked him with his contemporary Harley Granville-Barker. In his introductions to the* New Cambridge editons *of* 1, 2, *and* 3 Henry VI, *Dover Wilson established himself as one of the few modern scholars to dispute the conclusions of Peter Alexander and Madeleine Doran (see Additional Bibliography) that Shakespeare was the sole author of the trilogy. Instead, he ascribed major portions of the plays to other dramatists, including Robert Greene, Thomas Nashe, and possibly George Peele, and maintained that Shakespeare only added a few scenes of his own and revised others. Earlier critics who doubted the authenticity of the* Henry VI *plays include Edmond Malone (1787), G. G. Gervinus (1849-50), Jane Lee (1876), George Brandes, and F. G. Fleay (see Additional Bibliography). In the excerpt below, taken from his introduction to* 2 *and* 3 Henry VI *written in 1951, Dover Wilson argues that the Temple Garden scene of* 1 Henry VI *is "thoroughly char-*

acteristic of Shakespeare's early dramatic manner," especially in its extensive use of metaphor and the easy flow of the verse. He also regards the imagery in this scene as integrally related to the context of the dramatic situation, noting that however much Shakespeare drew on Elizabethan literary conventions for effect, he always exhibited "the poet's tongue, the poet's ear, and the poet's eye." For an opposing judgment of the organic quality of the imagery in Shakespeare's early plays, specifically Henry VI, *see the excerpt by Wolfgang H. Clemen (1951). Also, see the excerpts by John Middleton Murry (1936), Mark Van Doren (1939), and David Riggs (1971) for explications of Shakespeare's early dramatic style. For other essays by Dover Wilson, refer to the Additional Bibliography.*]

Probably the most indisputably Shakespearian scene in *Henry VI* is the Temple Garden scene of Part I, 2. 4. A brief examination of that will therefore form a suitable, not to say a safe, introduction to the question of Shakespeare's early dramatic style. And it is perhaps significant of his general attitude towards the chronicles that no authority has yet been discovered in them for this incident of the plucking of the Roses which he makes the opening chapter of the Wars of the Roses. Almost without doubt the scene is entirely of his own invention. Certainly his hand is evident from the outset and there is not a hint anywhere that he is revising a previous draft. And how quickly he gets off the mark! Dramatic situation and *mise en scène* ["setting"] are alike evoked in the first half-dozen lines, which immediately transform six players entering a bare Elizabethan stage, or the still barer stage of the reader's mind, into a knot of hot-headed nobles who, having fallen out, we are told in the third line, on a point of law in Temple Hall, are now withdrawn into the garden to quarrel in privacy together. Characteristic of him, too, is the metaphorical use of words like 'wrangling' and 'truant' to suggest a disputation of law-students and so add a touch to the inns-of-court atmosphere. Moreover, the scene thus set, what follows bears all the marks of the early Shakespeare. Suffolk, for instance, illustrates the pleasure his creator takes at this date in a curvetting Pegasus, when, after confessing to a neglect of the study of law, he remarks haughtily:

> And never yet could frame my will to it;
> And therefore frame the law unto my will;
> [*I Henry VI*, II. iv. 8-9]

while word-play becomes word-fence as Plantagenet protests:

> The truth appears so naked on my side
> That any purblind eye may find it out,
> [II. iv. 20-1]

and Somerset catches him up with:

> And on my side it is so well *apparelled*,
> So clear, so shining, and so evident,
> That it will glimmer though a *blind* man's eye.
> [II. iv. 22-4]
> (pp. vii-viii)

The first twenty-five lines of *I Henry VI*, 2. 4 are therefore as indisputably Shakespeare's as any passage of like length in the canon. And that the rest are equally Shakespearian is proved by the many parallels they show with other plays of his; by the ease, flow, and pregnancy of the verse; and by the frequent resort to metaphor of a character which he alone employed at this period. (p. ix)

As to the verse, the dialogue, consisting as it does of short speeches, gives little scope for enjambement and none for paragraphing, both characteristic of Shakespeare from the outset of his dramatic career. Yet, though most of the lines are end-stopped, the voice of the speaker sweeps on so naturally that we never notice the ticking of the metrical clock. Nor is our attention diverted from the sense by any of those forced constructions or tautological devices dictated by the blank verse frame, which are plentifully illustrated in other scenes of *Henry VI,* and commonly deface the verse of Kyd, Peele and Greene, and even at times of Marlowe. Furthermore, not a line, not a word, is wasted; and every line is full of meaning, even if the meaning be a quibble or a conceit that seems a little trivial to the modern sense. I stress this wealth of matter in particular, since it is here that Shakespeare most markedly shows his superiority to his early contemporaries. Marlowe himself is empty beside him. And what especially enriches Shakespeare's verse is his use of metaphor.

Many books of recent years have been published on Shakespeare's imagery and Elizabethan poetic imagery in general. I cannot profess to have read most of them; but as far as my reading goes they are mainly concerned with subject-matter and function, and seldom if ever touch upon the different modes of expressing such images and the tendency of dramatists to adopt one mode or the other. It is therefore worth while pointing out here that Shakespeare is more prone to metaphor, as distinct from simile or comparison, than any of the 'university wits', and that his metaphor, although in his early plays a little obtrusive, is never like theirs merely ornamental. On the contrary, it almost always springs directly from the dramatic situation or is suggested by some word natural or essential to the context: the metaphor 'apparelled' in Somerset's retort above quoted is, for example, suggested by Plantagenet's reference to the 'naked' truth. In other words, with Shakespeare imagery and verbal ambiguity are so near allied as often to be barely distinguishable, though the earlier the play the easier it is to see the connexion between them. The distinction is visible enough, for instance, in the scene before us, which largely consists of a chain of quibbles, and images begotten of quibbles, as Shakespeare plays his variations on the twin theme of roses red and roses white; variations which are as a two-finger exercise on the spinet compared with the fugue-like imagery of *Macbeth* and *Antony and Cleopatra.* Yet elementary and obvious though it be in 1592, it is found in Shakespeare and Shakespeare alone. (pp. x-xi)

Of action in the Temple Garden scene there is little enough. The principals pick their roses; and, as the rest follow suit and tempers wax angrier and angrier, the dramatist tosses the white and red roses to and fro in quibble and word-play and metaphor, exactly as, a few months later, he amuses himself for four stanzas with a 'silent war of lilies and roses' which false Tarquin observes in the face of chaste Lucrece [*The Rape of Lucrece*]. Nor from first to last are we told the 'point of law' which leads to the quarrel. Greene or Peele would never have omitted a piece of information of that kind. But they were Masters of Art, who had to keep up appearances by displaying knowledge even when they lacked it, whereas the unlearned man from Stratford was an adept at concealing ignorance. For what spectator, or reader either for that matter, ever stops to wonder what the legal point may have been? Did even the students from the inns-of-court who formed part of the original audience, and for whose benefit, we may guess, the whole scene was invented? They sat enchanted by the representation of men like themselves, quarrelling like themselves, in the garden they re-created at once from memory. The enchanter was not going to risk destroying the illusion by wading out of his depth into legal terminology.

The scene, then, full of life and without a wooden line, a tawdry image, or a false note of any kind, though freely proliferating into quibble and conceits, is thoroughly characteristic of Shakespeare's early dramatic manner; the manner of a writer brimming over with energy and self-confidence, the manner above all of a poet. I would insist upon this last in reply to critics who are prepared to saddle him with any verse, however feeble or empty, provided they find it within the cover of the First Folio. It is, indeed, my simple faith, a faith which has inspired me from the beginning of this edition in 1918, only to be strengthened with every fresh play taken up since, that Shakespeare was a born poet, as Mozart was a born musician. In other words, however much he may have 'played the sedulous ape' [Robert Louis Stevenson in *Memories and Portraits*] at the outset, or yielded himself to succeeding poetic fashions as time went on (and I believe he did neither of these things as much as is generally supposed); however often he showed himself the child of his age in a tendency to bombast, or in his later plays allowed his 'rapidity of imagination' to 'hurry him to a second thought before he had fully explained the first' [Samuel Johnson]; in brief, however many or great were his faults, faults due to working under pressure, to the literary conventions of his day, or to sheer bad taste (as it may appear to us), three things he had by nature and could no more dispense with than he could dispense with breath or heart-beat: I mean the poet's tongue, the poet's ear, and the poet's eye. True, as Ben Jonson (thinking of himself) said of him, 'a good poet's made as well as born'. True, he acquired such a wealth of language, by experience in the use of it, that in the end there was nothing he could not do with it. Yet the words he needed never at any period refused to come at command; were indeed always present below the threshold of consciousness, ready to pass into the thought-stream like the blood in his veins, so that word and thought were in fact born at an instant. Thus, any note of hesitancy, any hint of verbal penury, above all any sign of effort in the filling-out of the verse line are to me certain indications of foreign matter when they occur in the plays of the canon, whether it be matter untouched, or merely touched up, by him. (pp. xiii-xv)

> *John Dover Wilson, "Introduction to 'Henry VI',*
> *Parts II and III (Continued)," in* The Third Part of
> King Henry VI *by William Shakespeare, edited by*
> *John Dover Wilson, Cambridge at the University*
> *Press, 1952, pp. vii-xxxviii.*

S. L. BETHELL   (lecture date 1951)

[In an unexcerpted portion of his "The Comic Element in Shakespeare's Histories," a paper read at the Shakespeare Conference at Stratford-on-Avon in 1951, Bethell contends that the elements of comedy in the history plays are intended to support the moral and metaphysical designs of those works. He maintains that all of the comic scenes in 1, 2, and 3 Henry VI were taken from the sources and were not Shakespeare's inventions, although he admits that some scenes, such as the spurious miracle at St. Albans, were treated seriously in the chronicles. In the excerpt below, Bethell identifies three main types of comedy in the early Shakespearean histories: that of the common people, including the Simpcox scene, the Horner-apprentice duel, and the Cade scenes, all in 2 Henry VI; that of the comic villain, derived from medieval dramatic tradition, exemplified by Richard of Gloucester in 2 and 3 Henry VI; and the "use of wit in dialogue to express comically a serious theme." It is in the last mode, Bethell argues, that Shakespeare is "unique among writers of history plays." Bethell demonstrates how, in the Cade scenes of 2 Henry VI, Shakespeare inverted logic and rhetoric in order to emphasize the general

theme of disorder and confusion. Waldo F. McNeir, listed in the Additional Bibliography, discusses comic elements in the Henry VI *trilogy and disagrees with Bethell on several points. Also in the Additional Bibliography, see the essay by John W. Blanpied for a discussion of Shakespeare's use of ironic language in* I Henry VI.]

There are three main types [of comedy in Shakespeare's early histories]: (i) We have the comedy of the common people. This is to be found throughout the Elizabethan histories. One aspect of it is that vulgar humour which can have free play only in a class untrammelled by social delicacies; but there is the more thematically significant humour of pretentious ignorance, in a rebellious mob or a jack-in-office. It comes of the Elizabethan sense of social hierarchy and the social superiority of the writer (? and the majority of the audience). The bourgeois—citizen—plays have the same sort of thing, except that substantial citizens are exempt from criticism, whereas Shakespeare's tone is aristocratic, the Lord Mayor is gulled by Richard between his two bishops [*Richard III,* III. vii], and the merchant class is little represented. Of course, in Shakespeare, criticism goes hand in hand with sympathetic understanding of the common people. Of this type of comedy we have the clashes between the serving-men of the Duke of Gloucester and the Bishop of Winchester in *I Henry VI,* I. iii and III. i: the Lord Mayor is unheroic:

> Good God, these nobles should such stomachs bear!
> I myself fight not once in forty year.
> [*I Henry VI,* I. iii. 90-1]

In *2 Henry VI* there are the feigned miracle at St. Albans; the combat between Peter and Thomas Horner (treated comically although a man dies as a result of it); and the Cade scenes, which I shall take up later. A general function of such material, as has been commonly recognized, is to give a fuller picture of the background of English life. It is notable that Iden, the yeoman contented with his place, is treated with great seriousness: it is, as we have said, false pretensions which are castigated.

(ii) There is, again, the typically Elizabethan humour of the comic villain, derived, no doubt, from the comic devils of the miracles and the Vice of the moralities, combined with the new Machiavel. In the early histories the example is Richard III. . . . People can't—or a popular audience can't—be serious all the time. Comic angels would be indecorous and so we must have comic devils. I cannot believe that an Elizabethan audience would have much sympathy for the opponents of universal order. Shakespeare, in the histories, accepting the traditional association of comedy with disorder, uses it, as we shall see, to reinforce his dramatic statement, but never primarily to evoke sympathy. With a character like Richard III the levity is a part of the psychology of the person, and, from the point of view of the audience, it serves at the same time to sharpen the horror intellectually, by contrast, and yet, physically, to provide some relief from its tension.

(iii) It is the third mode of comedy that I want to dwell on: that in which I believe Shakespeare to be unique among writers of history plays. It consists in the use of wit in the dialogue to express comically a leading serious theme. It occurs in the histories in the treatment of the fundamental theme of disorder, and in the early histories is to be found only in the Cade scenes of *2 Henry VI.* In these scenes the rebels are presented as desiring the overthrow of law, learning and the political hierarchy. Shakespeare treats the rebellion as comedy. This may not be entirely new and is certainly not unique. There is a

clown among the rebels in [the anonymous] *The Life and Death of Jack Straw* and the (later) [Thomas] Heywood play of *Edward IV* has a good deal of comedy in the Falconbridge rebellion scenes. But in *Jack Straw* the comedy is incidental and largely irrelevant, and in *Edward IV* only the matter of the comic dialogue is concerned with the rebellion. In the Cade scenes, however, Shakespeare employs the very form of the dialogue to demonstrate the perversity and illogicality of political revolution and its foundation in moral and metaphysical confusion. What he does is to use the techniques of logic and rhetoric, so well understood by the Elizabethans, to bring out the notion of complete inversion, topsyturvydom. The rhetoric is deliberately defective partly through false logic, partly through other technical faults. Almost at the beginning of the first Cade scene we have a figure which for the audience may carry a different evaluation from that obviously put upon it by the speaker: "I tell thee, Jack Cade the clothier means to dress the commonwealth, and turn it, and set a new nap upon it" [IV. ii. 6]—here at once is inversion. The old clothes metaphor for the commonwealth is meiosis which the speaker might intend, but the "turning" does not sound reassuring—turned clothes do not even look as good as new, and so much can go wrong in the process! "The nobility think scorn to go in leather aprons" [IV. ii. 12-13]: what is, at least by Elizabethan theory, natural is treated as unnatural. Moreover, "it is said, labour in thy vocation; which is as much to say as, let the magistrates be labouring men; and therefore should we be magistrates" [IV. ii. 16-18]: "Labour" is taken as meaning "manual labour"; which is only part of what it truly signifies. This is accompanied by a false conversion, since it does not follow that, because magistrates should be labouring men, therefore all labouring men should be magistrates. Cade when he first appears uses a false derivation of his own name, clearly intending to derive it from *cadere* ["fall"]: "For our enemies shall fall before us"; though Dick's suggestion might be preferred: that it comes of his "stealing a cade of herrings" [IV. ii. 33-4]. His successive boasts, all involving ambiguity, are wittily turned by his followers (inversion again): "Valiant I am"; "A' must needs; for beggary is valiant" [IV ii. 44-6], etc. (It is dramatically curious to find the followers of Cade so without illusions: presumably it is "episodic intensification", though perhaps it suggests their lack of scruple and mere malcontent spirit—they don't really believe in the cause they espouse.) Then we have Cade's promises: "There shall be in England seven halfpenny loaves sold for a penny: the three-hooped pot shall have ten hoops" [IV. ii. 65-7]. These statements are self-contradictory, for if seven loaves are sold for a penny, they are not halfpenny loaves, and a pot with ten hoops cannot be a three-hooped pot. The modern audience, slovenly about speech, might miss these points; their natural reaction would be: "We know what he means." But an audience trained to logic and rhetoric and the precise expression of exactly what is meant would surely respond smartly to this display of what is, quite strictly, nonsense and its implication of chaos. It paves the way for a deeper contradiction: "all the realm shall be in common", but "all shall eat and drink on my score; and I will apparel them all in one livery, that they may agree like brothers and worship me their lord" [IV. ii. 68, 73-5]. Thus the obverse of communism is tyranny and these twin evils may be expected to arise from "democracy" in the Tudor sense of "mob-rule". Tyranny means the overthrow of law, and this is the next theme to arise:

> *Dick.* The first thing we do, let's kill all the
> lawyers.

Cade. Nay, that I mean to do. Is not this a lamentable thing, that of the skin of an innocent lamb should be made parchment? that parchment, being scribbled o'er, should undo a man? [Material for efficient cause.] Some say the bee stings: but I say, 'tis the bee's wax; for I did but seal once to a thing, and I was never mine own man since. [False transition from literal to tropological significance of "sting".]

[IV. ii. 76-83]

So it continues. The Clerk of Chatham—clerk = *clericus*, churchman, and his name is Emmanuel—"has a book in his pocket with red letters in't", presumably a missal or breviary with rubrics; "Nay, then, he is a conjuror" [IV. ii. 90-2]—and God's servant is transformed into a servant of the devil in the eyes of the ignorant mob. He is hanged chiefly, however, for the crime of being literate. Immediately after comes the climax of inverted nonsense when Cade kneels down and knights himself, as if authority inhered in the individual rather than the body politic. Then, faced with Sir Humphrey Stafford, Cade asserts his claim to be the son of Edmund Mortimer's elder son, who, he says, was stolen away and became a bricklayer. Smith the weaver adds proof: "Sir, he made a chimney in my father's house, and the bricks are alive at this day to testify it; therefore deny it not" [IV. ii. 148-50]. I think we can dispense with technical analysis here.

Cade next accuses Lord Say of being a traitor because he can speak French, and "can he that speaks with the tongue of an enemy be a good counsellor, or no?" [IV. ii. 170-72]—confusing two metaphorical senses of "tongue": (a) "language", (b) "with the tongue of an enemy" = "with the mind of an enemy". The scene ends with an unequivocal statement—depersonalised—which sums up the significance of the whole, and indeed defines this characteristic use of wit in the histories:

Dick. They are all in order and march toward us.
Cade. But then are we in order when we are most out of order.

[IV. ii. 188-90]

The theme of disorder, confusion, inversion, topsyturvydom, is expressed through a deliberate and witty use of logical and rhetorical fallacy. The proper attitude to rebellion is thus established in the first scene in which Cade appears; the other rebellion scenes are more concerned with action and there is little of this sort of wit in them. Characteristically, Cade is given a touch of nobility as he sees his followers desert him, but he remains essentially a comic character, even in Iden's garden: "come thou and thy five men, and if I do not leave you all as dead as a doornail, I pray God I may never eat grass more" [IV. x. 39-41]. (pp. 87-92)

S. L. Bethell, "The Comic Element in Shakespeare's Histories," in Anglia, *Vol. LXXI, No. 1, 1952-53, pp. 82-101.*

HEREWARD T. PRICE (essay date 1951)

[*Price's perception of the construction of* 1 Henry VI *significantly altered the way in which later critics viewed the artistry of the* Henry VI *trilogy. In the following excerpt, he asserts that Shakespeare, "already a master of construction," "imposed upon a body of historical data a controlling idea . . . that constructs the play." That central theme concerns the responsibility of those who govern. Price also points out that Shakespeare adapted from*
Marlowe the structural principle of multiplicity which permits the dramatist to present his material from more than a single angle of vision. In 1 Henry VI *there are many scenes in which several characters offer divergent points of view; Price maintains that this clash of characters' perceptions results in a masterful irony. Larry S. Champion (1979) has also commented on the multiple angles of vision in* 3 Henry VI. *Price's assessment of the careful structuring of the* Henry VI *trilogy is shared by A. C. Hamilton (1961-62). Other critics who have discussed the structure of* Henry VI *include Robert Ornstein (1972), Ralph Berry (1981), and Faye L. Kelly (see Additional Bibliography).*]

Marlowe created the form of the Elizabethan drama. His example determined that it should be multiple. He invented a drama characterized by a long series of many actions or events, by multiple changes of time and place, and by a multitude of actors. He worked out each scene carefully and with some nicety of detail, both fitting it into the general construction of the play and giving it a value of its own. The successive scenes he unified by centering them round the hero, who completely dominated the play. His unity was not merely mechanical. The ethical problem of the hero gives a meaning to all the actions that make up the action as a whole. It is not right to break the play up into two, but one might perhaps say there is an inner intellectual development rising with the development of the outer plot. We may say this if we never forget that inner and outer are inseparable.

Shakespeare knew his Marlowe well. He often imitated Marlowe, but he enjoyed making fun of him, and, by implication at least, he endeavored to debunk Marlowe's puffed-up heroes. He was a successor rather than a follower of Marlowe, not servile, but detached and independent. He took over Marlowe's structure, that is to say, he based his work on the principle of multiplicity, on the long sequence of many scenes, some of which he so elaborately finished with a beginning, a middle, and an end as to make them little plays in their own right. (pp. 18-19)

Shakespeare's play or Shakespeare's form, like Marlowe's, consists of a series of scenes pyramiding to a climax. The scenes vary in function: some . . . are intensely dramatic; some retard, others speed the action; some are purely narrative, like a chapter from a novel; others hold up the action in order to comment upon it.

Construction is the ordering of these parts, placing them into relationship with one another—though let me say again we must not forget this relationship of part to part is not so important as the relationship of all the parts to a central idea. Shakespeare's advance upon Marlowe is shown in the immense variety of relationships that he uses to symbolize his idea, in the complexity that he gives to form.

But construction of individual scenes is not enough; we must take a whole play. Let us start at the beginning of Shakespeare's work, with *1 Henry VI*. And let us begin with [W. Somerset] Maugham's maxim: ". . . in a story as in a play, you must make up your mind what your point is and stick to it like grim death. That is just another way of saying that it must have form." Let us also remember the essence of all pattern, namely, the repetition of likeness with difference. Now scholars and critics usually dismiss *1 Henry VI* with contempt as something artless, chaotic, or merely discursive. I hope to show that the design or pattern is so severely controlled that it is almost as schematic as the black and white squares of a chessboard. (p. 24)

The responsibility of those that govern, especially the effects arising from the strength or weakness, competence or incompetence of the King—here is the main subject of *Henry VI* and of all the Histories. (p. 25)

In *I Henry VI* [this] specialty of rule is neglected. Shakespeare shows us a king whose title to the crown is so flawed that, in those turbulent times, only a strong ruler could maintain it against attack. But Henry is too weak to enforce his will or, indeed, to direct the affairs of the kingdom at all. As a result, the great feudal nobles of royal descent begin to aim at the throne, becoming more eager to fight one another than the French. In the end the disunion and treachery resulting from the weakness of the King cause the loss of France. The play was no doubt topical. Shakespeare was voicing the fears that many Elizabethans felt about what might happen if the Queen grew infirm with old age or died suddenly without leaving the succession provided for. Like his fellow dramatists, Shakespeare was warning his generation against the wounds of civil war. In the other plays that form the tetralogy he passes from foreign to civil war, in which the rude son strikes his father dead, and all the evils Ulysses predicts [in *Troilus and Cressida*] come true. (pp. 25-6)

In reality, then, Shakespeare is imposing upon a body of historical data a controlling idea, an idea that constructs the play. He does the same thing in all his historical plays, English or Roman. Critics who cannot follow Shakespeare's intentions pick holes in the construction of these plays. Looking for plot, they ignore design. It never occurs to them that Shakespeare was daringly original, that his mastery of design was just as superb as his mastery of language, and that his conception of design opens for modern times a new era in drama. (p. 26)

Part 1 of *Henry VI* opens as imposingly as Shakespeare knows how. Drums that beat a dead march usher in a solemn procession of great nobles attending the coffin of Henry V. This funeral pomp was such a success on the stage that Shakespeare used it again to start *Titus Andronicus*. The nobles then celebrate Henry V in the interlaced images of the *laudatio* ["eulogy"]. . . , lamenting that the planets have turned against them. But even during so grave a ceremony Gloucester and Winchester fall to reviling one another, and the *laudatio* itself is broken off in the middle of a figure by a succession of messages announcing disasters in France. The bad news culminates in the defeat and capture of the great Talbot through the treachery of Fastolf. The lords separate quickly, each going his own way, apparently leaving Henry unburied. One noble goes to prosecute the war, another to protect the person of the King, and the last noble, Winchester, proclaims his ambition to steal the King, and "sit at chiefest stern of public weal" [*1 Henry VI*, I. i. 177].

The scene appears to be simple, and it certainly has none of the profundity which Shakespeare was able to put into a play later on. But it does everything a first scene should do, it gives the situation: Henry V is dead, Henry VI is a baby; the nobles are ready to fly at one another's throats, and each does what is right in his own eyes; Talbot is introduced, and his importance stressed; the treachery that is to strike him down and to cause the loss of France is foreshadowed. Notice the last speech. Shakespeare gives it to Winchester to express his treachery. It is part of Shakespeare's construction to lead along to the last speech and make that sum up to the scene and fix the impression he wants to leave in our minds. That impression of course is treachery at home, in the very court. Here is a scene full of matter and incident, condensed, swift, and clear, imposing as

a stage spectacle, presenting the principal characters on the English side and introducing the principal motifs of the play, leading up to an important climax that suggests what the whole play is to be about—here Shakespeare shows that he is already a master of construction.

We have noticed that Shakespeare breaks off the *laudatio* and leaves Henry unburied. This motif of the interrupted ceremony Shakespeare gives us three times. At Act III, scene i, the proceedings in the Parliament House are stifled by the dispute of Winchester and Gloucester, and at Act IV, scene i, the coronation ends in hopeless wrangling. . . . The spacing of the three occasions of frustrated splendor shows how carefully Shakespeare planned the whole. He was not careless or haphazard. He looked before and after. And while these scenes are significant, while they carry Shakespeare's design, they are extremely effective as so much "theater."

Scene ii offers us the contrast of the French court. It was a normal part of Shakespeare's construction to establish two points of contrast, as, for instance, Belmont and Venice [in *The Merchant of Venice*], Egypt and Rome [in *Antony and Cleopatra*], court and country, and, by regularly switching from one to the other, to enforce his idea. In *1 Henry VI* the rhythm of the play consists in the alternation between England and France. The French are introduced not by a dead march but by a flourish and martial music. Bedford had opened for the English by saying the planets were now hostile to them. For the French Charles starts off by saying the planet Mars has deserted the English and now smiles on the French. This is a clear case of scenes interlinked by figure. Full of confidence, the French try to raise the siege of Orleans. They are beaten back with great loss, but at this moment the Bastard of Orleans introduces Joan. They gather round her, she unites them by the trust she inspires in them all, and they at once march off to battle again. Here Shakespeare gives us the pattern of French action which he is to use repeatedly in the play. They have a leader who unites them and in whom they never lose confidence. Even after defeat their belief in their cause is unshakable. Notice, too, how Shakespeare strengthens the scene by leading up the rich imagery at the end. . . . As yet he has been niggardly of figure, but at this point he puts forth all his power in order to emphasize a great moment. No one else in the 1590's was so careful in placing his figures as Shakespeare or could approach his skill in using them as part of his construction.

Scene iii switches back to London, and now Shakespeare shows us the blue coats of Gloucester fighting the tawny coats of Winchester. Notice how this tragic dissension is emphasized by the symbolism of color. You never hear of color against color with the French. This time the quarrel is young—a mere civilian, the Lord Mayor, is able to put an end to the fighting. Again Shakespeare leads this scene along to a most effective last speech, in which he makes the Lord Mayor comment on the action. Notice also that the action carries forward the idea of division among the English, while at the same time the street fighting between the great nobles is good theater. Shakespeare continues to make the inner and the outer help one another.

Then Shakespeare switches to France and to the greatest of his sensations. It is the siege of Orleans again. Talbot is with Salisbury and other nobles high up on some turret, when a French gunner shoots off a gun [from the platform of the stage] and kills Salisbury. It is a real *coup de théâtre*. And then to heighten the effect Shakespeare gives us thunder and lightning, a tumult in the heavens [I. iv. 98], and Talbot drives off the French, but Joan returns to drive off Talbot. The act ends with

Joan and the French nobles in Orleans advancing their "waving colours on the walls" (a new theatrical effect of color), while the French King celebrates her in the stateliest figures Shakespeare can invent. Here you see Shakespeare's design. By a series of rapidly shifting contrasts he shows the English breaking down, while the French, closing their ranks round a revered leader, increase their strength. All of this he makes as concrete as possible by appeals to the eye and to the ear, to color and to sound, and by designing action for theatrical effect. He keeps a close eye on the correspondence between speech and action, reinforcing the important moments of action by appropriate elevation of style. The scenes are also united to one another by a thread of allusions to some hostility in the heavens and the planets towards the English. Although there is multiplicity of event and the stage is always crowded with people, there is no confusion. The action is quite clear, and it moves with an imposing sweep to a great culmination. Shakespeare was to invent greater first acts, but nobody else in the Elizabethan period wrote a first act that showed any comparable mastery of all the elements of design. (pp. 26-30)

The middle of the play repeats . . . the motifs of the beginning. Act III, scene i, corresponds to Act I, scene i, in which the nobles are assembled for the funeral of Henry V. In Act III, scene i, Shakespeare invents a full meeting of all the great nobles in the Parliament House. Henry VI has grown up, but he is still just as helpless as a child. With the exception of Bedford, the same nobles appear as in Act I, scene i, and—ominous addition—Shakespeare brings in York and Somerset as well. The fatal difference between the two scenes is that England is now more hopelessly divided than ever. Gloucester is about to propose a bill, but Winchester snatches it from his hand and tears it to pieces. The other lords immediately take sides for the one party or the other. Then Shakespeare repeats Act I, scene iii, with bitter intensification. The Lord Mayor enters complaining that he cannot keep Winchester's and Gloucester's men from knocking one another's brains out—in Act I, scene i, he had found it easy to pacify them. The retainers burst in with bloody pates. That they should fight in the very presence of the King and his council is a scandal without precedent. The quarrel is far more bitter and dangerous than in Act I. Henry forces a hollow reconciliation between the great nobles, whereby Shakespeare represents the Churchman as being inveterately malignant. Shakespeare is showing how hopelessly corrupt is the state where the Church is consumed by political ambition. Now there is no source of health left. Exeter's closing soliloquy makes clear the coming disaster. (pp. 31-2)

[In the following scenes] Shakespeare shows the French gaining more and more cohesion as the English forces fall more and more apart. Then [in Act III, scene iv] Shakespeare shifts to the English, to Paris, where Henry is crowned King of France—a splendid scene but that, like the other splendid scenes on the English side, it ends in quarreling. Henry thinks to quiet the nobles by putting on the red rose of Somerset; naturally, he only enrages York the more. Here we have an almost too schematic repetition of what happens in the first part of the play, but this time more terrible, giving ominous indication of catastrophe. Shakespeare has stuck to his point like grim death and so created form.

And now he reaches the climax. Talbot is hard beset by the French. York and Somerset with their separate armies are not far off. Either could save him; combined they could crush the French. Jealous of one another, they refuse to move, and they abandon Talbot to the enemy.

Shakespeare has made every incident in the play lead to this disaster. It is the summing up of all he has had to say about weak leadership resulting in disunion, faction, and treachery among the English, and about the unbreakable unity of the French under their great leader, Joan of Arc.

Talbot does not die alone. Shakespeare shows us Talbot, the great warrior, ordering his young son home, away from certain death in the coming battle, and the son's insistence on fighting by his father's side. Amid all the treachery of the play the utter loyalty of the son stands out resplendent. The deep love of father and son for one another, their magnificent courage, the sight of old Talbot dying with the body of his son in his arms, make defeat at once glorious and tragic. The tragedy is revealed in the waste of greatness, in the needless destruction of the finest souls in the play. (p. 33)

In Act V the threads of the French war are knotted. Ironically, the English unite when it is too late. They capture and execute Joan, but are obliged to conclude a rotten peace with France. Then Shakespeare introduces new disloyalty. Suffolk woos Margaret, ostensibly to be Henry's wife, really for himself. He buys her by abandoning Anjou and Maine to her father, an inveterate enemy of England, who, as the play shows, has fought for the French side all through the war. Suffolk, to gain his nefarious ends, cajoles Henry VI into breaking off an engagement to a princess that would have brought him land, wealth, and influence in France. Thus Act V concludes with frivolous abandonment of English territories, disloyalty at court, weak and imbecile leadership, dishonourable breach of the pledged word. Shakespeare of course left *I Henry VI* unfinished; he meant it "to be continued in our next." But he has stuck to his point to the bitter end: Act V is about the same subject as all the other acts—treachery in high places encouraged or supported by the weakness of the King and ending in disaster. (pp. 34-5)

In *I Henry VI* [Shakespeare] has endeavored to free his drama from the conventional plot or fable and to design it entire as the exponent of an idea. We have seen that Shakespeare, like Marlowe, makes multiplicity the basis of all his art, but this principle he carries further. Shakespeare's art is polyphonic, or it would, perhaps, be better to say prismatic; he decomposes his truth into many shades of color. Each of his numerous characters reflects the idea in his own special way. Marlowe's plays are centered round a hero and his problem, and they all have the excitement of plot. *Henry VI,* on the other hand, is not about the fate of one man but about two nations, and its scope is as wide as all England and all France. Shakespeare was always daringly original. The young man who designed *Henry VI* showed superb courage. The easy thing was to do what Marlowe was doing. But Shakespeare threw away all the props and aids that "plot" could give him and devised an entirely new kind of drama, the drama of severely controlled design, the control being apparent in every speech and every scene. (p. 36)

> *Hereward T. Price, in his* Construction in Shakespeare, *The University of Michigan Press, 1951, pp. 18-33.*

WOLFGANG H. CLEMEN (essay date 1951)

[*A German Shakespearean scholar, Clemen was among the first critics to consider Shakespeare's imagery an integral part of the development of his dramatic art. J. Dover Wilson described Clemen's method as focusing on "the form and significance of partic-*

ular images or groups of images in their context of the passages, speech or play in which they occur." This approach was quite different from that of the other leading image-pattern analyst, Caroline F. E. Spurgeon, whose work was more statistical in method and partly biographical in aim. In his discussion of the Henry VI *trilogy, Clemen states that he can find no organic relation of the plays' imagery to the characters, situations, or the drama as a whole. Instead, he contends that the imagery in these three plays serves decorative rather than expressive purposes. He also notes that the poetic style of the* Henry VI *trilogy relies heavily on the amplification of figures of speech; according to Clemen, this "detailed elaboration" of similes and metaphors conveys an impression of superfluity and a sense that the images offer little more than "mere padding." Clemen also finds that the imagery in the plays' soliloquies is more direct and expressive than in other passages—a fact which he attributes to the "retarding quality of the monologue," which "leaves more time for the elaboration of images" than in the faster-paced dialogues. For additional discussions of the imagery in the* Henry VI *trilogy, see the excerpts by Caroline F. E. Spurgeon (1935), John Dover Wilson (1951), Alvin B. Kernan (1954), James L. Calderwood (1967), and Carol McGinnis Kay (1972).]*

"Amplification" was the most important feature of poetics in the Middle Ages; the tendency to amplify, adorn and expand accounts for most of the devices and figures found in "rhetorical" poetry of the Middle Ages and the Renaissance. Indeed, "amplification" is, too, a main feature of Shakespeare's early style. In Shakespeare's early plays the rhetorical style discloses itself not only in artificial and formal patterning, in the frequent use of symmetry, parallelism, antiphony, but also in the taste for digressions and in the endeavour to weave into the tissue of the play at every opportunity some sort of decorative device.

All this explains, too, why most of the images in *Henry VI* are not organically related to their context. They often seem superfluous, mere "padding". There is good evidence for this in the fact that to one image or comparison a second, expressing the same thing, is added, linked with the first by the particle *or*. One image would have been quite sufficient, but this accumulation of images shows that the pleasure of finding nice comparisons is [Shakespeare's] chief motive.

One type of imagery, frequent in *Henry VI*, is particularly characteristic:

> And such high vaunts of his nobility,
> Did instigate the bedlam brain-sick duchess
> By wicked means to frame our sovereign's fall.
> Smooth runs the water where the brook is deep;
> And in his simple show he harbours treason.
> The fox barks not when he would steal the lamb.
> No, no, my sovereign; Gloucester is a man
> Unsounded yet and full of deep deceit.
>   [*2 Henry VI*, III. i. 50-7]

These two proverb-like images are rather loosely inserted into Suffolk's speech. Suffolk, in introducing these commonplace remarks wants to strengthen his argument and to adorn his speech. These images are rhetorical devices which Shakespeare introduces into speeches of this kind in order to make them more persuasive, more emphatic. In *Henry VI*, whenever the lords meet in solemn and pompous assembly we find these argumentative and formal speeches in which the lords or the king himself utter loud and grandiose protestations. And here we find, too, the same type of imagery. Thus there becomes apparent a relationship between a certain type of imagery and a certain type of situation. Such scenes are modelled on the

same pattern, a pattern which determines the structure of the speeches and also the use of imagery.

And so the question arises: In what soil does imagery flourish best? Is there, among the dramatic forms of speech (dialogue, monologue) one which more than the others nourishes imagery? If we peruse the early histories we find that it is above all the monologue that breeds imagery. The retarding quality of the monologue leaves more time for the elaboration of images than the usually quicker speed of the dialogue. The stream of action flows more slowly in the monologue, which is often like a pause in the course of action. The reflective, often introspective mood prevailing in the monologue quite naturally chooses imagery as the most adequate form of expression.

Images occurring in Shakespeare's early monologues appear to be more direct, more "expressive" than the often superfluous and merely decorative imagery in other passages. If we consider, for instance, this passage from Gloucester's monologue in the third part of *Henry VI*:

> Like one that stands upon a promontory,
> And spies a far-off shore where he would tread,
> Wishing his foot were equal with his eye,
> And chides the sea that sunders him from thence,
> Saying, he'll lade it dry to have his way:
> So do I wish the crown, being so far off.
>   [*3 Henry VI*, III. ii. 135-40]

This image is called forth by Gloucester's overpowering desire to gain the crown. It is not casual or ornamental, for the central motive of the play is embodied in this image. Plain language was unable to give vent to this passionate wish of Gloucester's. Only the wide imaginative space of the scenery of which Gloucester is dreaming could express it. (pp. 40-3)

Are there particular events which more than other occasions call forth imagery? We find that in the presence of death Shakespeare's characters always use metaphorical language. The incomprehensible mystery of death, transcending the compass of human understanding, demands language different from the common and direct speech of every day. Thus the younger Clifford, on finding his father dead on the battlefield, bursts out:

> O, let the vile world end,
> And the premised flames of the last day
> Knit earth and heaven together!
>   [*2 Henry VI*, V. ii. 40-2]

This image is neither ornament nor rhetorical prolixity but simply the most direct expression of the extremity of grief Clifford is feeling at the sight of his dead father.

But this spontaneous and expressive sort of imagery foreshadowed by the outburst of the young Clifford is not yet characteristic of *Henry VI*. Even on the occasion of death the language is often artificial. Henry VI, with a premonition of imminent death, elaborates a simile in which he rather learnedly assigns mythological names to himself, his son and to other persons involved in his tragic end.

> I, Daedalus; my poor boy, Icarus;
> Thy father, Minos, that denied our course;
> The sun that sear'd the wings of my sweet boy
> Thy brother Edward, and thyself the sea
> Whose envious gulf did swallow up his life.
>   [*3 Henry VI*, V. iv. 21-5]

This method of inventing a suitable simile for a certain situation by means of which a detailed survey of the state of affairs is given is typical of Shakespeare's early manner. Its best example is the long speech of Queen Margaret towards the close of *Henry VI*, where she compares her distressing situation with a shipwreck. As in allegorical poetry, the simile is first developed and then applied to the situation of the moment:

> What though the mast be now blown overboard,
> The cable broke, the holding anchor lost,
> And half our sailors swallow'd in the flood?
> Yet lives our pilot still. . . .
>
> [*3 Henry VI*, V. iv. 3-6]

After ten lines Queen Margaret's words become more concrete and she likens the persons around her to the details of the shipwreck.

> Say Warwick was our anchor; what of that?
> And Montague our topmast; what of him?
> Our slaughter'd friends the tackles; what of these?
> Why is not Oxford here another anchor? . . .
> And what is Edward but a ruthless sea?
> What Clarence but a quicksand of deceit?
> And Richard but a ragged fatal rock?
> All these the enemies to our poor bark.
>
> [*3 Henry VI*, V. iv. 13-28]

It may well be said that this pseudo-allegorical interpretation of the situation by means of a detailed or extended simile constitutes one of the formal devices which wandered from medieval poetry into Elizabethan literature. The fullness and explicitness with which such images are treated in Shakespeare's early work result no doubt from the young dramatist's eagerness to explain as fully as possible what is going on, what is imminent, and what has just been happening. Later, Shakespeare's dramatic technique rids itself entirely of these rather obtrusive expositions. In fact, at every stage of the drama we know precisely what is happening, although it is not expressly told us. In a quite unobtrusive and subtle manner Shakespeare intersperses occasional hints throwing light upon the historical, political or personal issues involved in the situation. Unconsciously we become informed about all the circumstances. But in Shakespeare's early plays information is usually given all at once, in one piece, and the imagery bears testimony to it.

Thus, besides detailed elaboration, obtrusiveness may be counted among the characteristic features of Shakespeare's early imagery. Whenever imagery is used we cannot but notice it, it strikes us as something exceptional—while in later plays it often escapes our attention that images are being employed at all. The images protrude themselves as unexpected surprises. One example only: Suffolk, wooing Margaret, says when she is about to depart:

> My hand would free her, but my heart says no.
> As plays the sun upon the glassy streams,
> Twinkling another counterfeited beam,
> So seems this gorgeous beauty to mine eyes.
> Fain would I woo her, yet I dare not speak:
>
> [*1 Henry VI*, V. iii. 61-5]

This is in Shakespeare's earliest and most conventional manner, somewhat playful and artificial. But in other passages, too, the superimposed nature of imagery is striking. This impression is confirmed by the fact that most of the images (as in the last passage cited) are loosely linked with their context by "as", "like", "even as", or "thus".

In later plays it becomes an important function of imagery to create the atmosphere of nature. But in *Henry VI* this is seldom found. Take, for instance, this passage which is to create a background of nature for the murder of Suffolk that is to come:

> The gaudy, blabbing and remorseful day
> Is crept into the bosom of the sea;
> And now loud-howling wolves arouse the jades
> That drag the tragic melancholy night;
> Who, with their drowsy, slow and flagging wings,
> Clip dead men's graves and from their misty jaws
> Breathe foul contagious darkness in the air.
> Therefore bring forth the soldiers of our prize;
>
> [*2 Henry VI*, IV. i. 1-8]

This little "introduction" is rather transparently put at the beginning of the scene. Again, we find all that is said about nature in this scene in one compact piece, all at once. Whereas in Shakespeare's more mature plays (in fact, as early as *Romeo and Juliet*) the phrases that create a background of nature grow naturally and necessarily from the subject matter, this passage has no special relation to the speaker. The captain who utters these words is only the vehicle whereby Shakespeare introduces this nature-background. The words are put into his mouth, but any other character could just as well have spoken them. (pp. 43-6)

Wolfgang H. Clemen, "Henry VI," in his The Development of Shakespeare's Imagery, *Cambridge, Mass.: Harvard University Press, 1951, pp. 40-6.*

HAROLD C. GODDARD (essay date 1951)

[*In his essay on the* Henry VI *trilogy, Goddard offers the first solid defense of Henry's kingship as presented in these plays. He attributes the violence and civil dissension depicted in the trilogy not to the failure of Henry to exercise his authority—as suggested by such later critics as Irving Ribner (1965), H. M. Richmond (1967), James Winny (1968), and Robert Ornstein (1972)—but to the English nobles. Goddard describes Henry as "a morally courageous and genuinely religious man and king," who might have ruled successfully had it not been for the violent, selfish, and deceitful behavior of his courtiers. This idea was more fully developed in the essay by Michael Manheim (1973).*]

[In] the reign of Henry VI [Shakespeare] came face to face, probably for the first time, with a subject that continued to enthral him to the end of his days. That subject was nothing other than *chaos*. In the political turmoil of the fifteenth century he encountered chaos itself. Later, in his other Histories and in his Tragedies, he went on to inquire into its causes and effects. Each of the protagonists of his greatest plays, Brutus, Hamlet, Othello, Macbeth, King Lear, Antony, Cleopatra, Coriolanus, confronts chaos in one form or another. In the brawling factions of *Henry VI* and the Wars of the Roses there is already a clear forecast of the "universal wolf" of Ulysses in *Troilus and Cressida*, and at least an intimation of the ominous words of Albany in *King Lear:*

> Humanity must perforce prey on itself,
> Like monsters of the deep.
>
> [*King Lear*, IV. ii. 49-50]

The political chaos of *Henry VI* is the embryo of the cosmic chaos of *King Lear*. It would be folly to try to subsume Shakespeare's works under one head, but, if we were forced to do so, one of the least unsatisfactory ways would be to say that they are an attempt to answer the question: What is the cure for chaos? (pp. 28-9)

Here, in the death of Henry V and the sudden loss of France, was an extreme example of nemesis, of "the fall of princes," or at any rate of the sudden and utter collapse of all that a mighty monarch's life had stood for, the *débâcle* of an imperialistic dream.

Here, writ large, was the truth that chaos in the state is part and parcel of chaos in the minds and souls of individuals, that the political problem is, once and for all, a function of the psychological problem. It is an old truth that he who ruleth himself is better than he who taketh a city. Shakespeare seems to have sensed very early—what the world at large has still to learn—that he who cannot rule himself is not entitled to rule a city, still less a nation.

Here was a demonstration that tyranny and anarchy, force and the lawless resistance to force, are extremes that meet, each so terrible that its opposite seems like a relief—until it comes. And here, therefore, was the inevitable question: Is history doomed to be nothing but a perpetual oscillation between the two?

Already, even in this play, there is a hint of another way out, a possible escape from the fatal circle. It is found in various little touches, but chiefly in the figure of Henry VI himself.

Whatever one thinks of Henry as a man, no one can deny that his role—except perhaps for a few passages that seem inconsistent with the rest—is a remarkable piece of characterization, so remarkable that one is tempted to think that Shakespeare may have revised it at a later date to bring it more into line and to enhance its contrasts with the roles of Henry's father and grandfather. (His speech on the Simple Life, for instance, seems expressly conceived as a companion piece to that of Henry IV on Sleep and that of Henry V on Ceremony.) However that may be, Henry VI has been the most critically neglected of Shakespeare's kings. Pages have been written about the others for every paragraph about him. There are few characters in Shakespeare the conventional picture of whom stands in greater need of revision, not to say reversal.

Henry, in contrast with his illustrious father, is generally dismissed as a weakling. His political inefficiency and practical unfitness for the crown need no demonstration. But to liken him to Richard II, as has been done over and over, is to misunderstand and underrate him utterly. Richard and Henry were alike in that each came to the throne in his minority and each realized himself most fully through the inner life. But there the resemblance ends. Richard was a dupe of his dreams, a sentimentalist, an actor and self-worshiper, and so, though unintentionally, a liar, a coward and a tyrant—in spite of splendid native gifts. Henry was a simple and sincere, a morally courageous and genuinely religious man and king. He is the only one of Shakespeare's kings whose public and private personalities are identical. As he himself reminds us, he was only nine months old when he came to the throne, and the situation in which he found himself later was not of his making. That he was frequently bewildered by the problems thrust upon him and willing to shed political responsibility is true. But he was child-like—not childish, as Richard was. No other king in Shakespeare had the good of his kingdom so at heart or suffered so keenly at the sufferings of his subjects. When he declares that he would give his life to save them, we do not doubt his word for a second. (pp. 29-31)

But the most remarkable thing about this childlike and saintly king is that he nearly succeeded in accomplishing what the astute and "practical" men around him were powerless to

effect: an understanding between the warring factions of Lancaster and York. Had it not been for that Amazon, Margaret of Lancaster, and that fiend in human shape, the younger Richard of York, he would have. As Richard's brother Edward— later Edward IV—says to Margaret as he looks back:

> Hadst thou been meek, our title still had slept;
> And we, in pity of the gentle king,
> Had slipp'd our claim until another age.
>
> [*3 Henry VI*, II. ii. 160-62]

An astounding admission, and the highest tribute to the quiet power of Henry's character. They are possibly the three most significant lines in these plays. (p. 31)

Henry was a shining example of the truth that even in a palace life may be lived well. Of all the deaths with which the History Plays are crowded, Henry's, among the major characters, is far and away the best. His final words of forgiveness to his murderer,

> O, God forgive my sins, and pardon thee!
>
> [*3 Henry VI*, V. vi. 60]

are a plain echo of the dying words of Christ.

Doubtless Henry was better fitted for the role of saint than of king. But as Plato declares that the perfect state will not be attained until philosophers are kings, so Shakespeare may be intimating that in a happier time than the fifteenth century the ideal ruler may have more of the characteristics of the saint than then seemed feasible. Malcolm in *Macbeth*, makes a list of the "king-becoming graces":

> justice, verity, temperance, stableness,
> Bounty, perseverance, mercy, lowliness,
> Devotion, patience, courage, fortitude.
>
> [*Macbeth*, IV. iii. 92-4]

It is a startling thought that Henry VI had every one of these virtues. Is there another king in Shakespeare of whom that may be said? (pp. 31-2)

Henry is the first of a long line of Shakespearean characters who, born to power or having power thrust on them, have a strong distaste for it and a corresponding longing for the simple life. Across Shakespeare's entire dramatic activity Henry VI, the king who longed to be a shepherd, reaches out a hand to Prospero, the Duke who presided over the enchanted isle. Between them are many others of the same type, including the exiled Duke in *As You Like It* and the self-exiled Duke of *Measure for Measure*. Even the misanthropic Timon and the deposed King Lear have bonds of kinship with the rest. The persistence of this type is further testimony to the continuity of Shakespeare's development. This group of characters carries a political implication of especial importance for our day. One of the weakest aspects of democracy as it has so far worked out is that under it the aggressive type that desires power and likes to rule tends to gain power and so does rule—whereas genuine democracy is the art of getting those who are naturally averse to holding power to accept it.

But there is an even subtler truth implicit in Henry's life. He demonstrates—in an almost Chinese fashion—that there is such a thing as being as well as doing, such a thing as doing through being. In this respect Henry is a prophecy, and in a sense a progenitor, of the most saintly character Shakespeare ever created—the divine Desdemona. (p. 32)

Harold C. Goddard, ''The Three Parts of 'Henry VI','' in his The Meaning of Shakespeare, The University of Chicago Press, 1951, pp. 28-32.

M[URIEL] C. BRADBROOK (essay date 1951)

[Bradbrook is an English scholar specializing in the development of Elizabethan drama and poetry. In her Shakespearean criticism, she combines biographical and historical research, paying particular attention to the stage conventions popular during Shakespeare's lifetime. Her Shakespeare and Elizabethan Poetry (1951) is a comprehensive work which relates Shakespeare's poetry to that of George Chapman, Christopher Marlowe, Edmund Spenser, and Philip Sidney, and describes the evolution of Shakespeare's verse. Also in this work, Bradbrook points out the dependence of medieval writers on allegorical and symbolic modes of expression to represent the nature of the universe, and she examines how this tradition continued to influence poets and dramatists of the English Renaissance. In the following excerpt, she identifies one example of this influence in 3 Henry VI, Act II, Scene iii. According to Bradbrook, the so-called ''molehill'' speech of Henry, together with the mirror scene of the father who has slain his son and the son who has slain his father, serves as a symbolic moment where the larger themes of the drama are embodied in a type of play-within-the-play. Bradbrook also directs attention to the ''sensuous qualities of the language'' evoked by the imagery in the concluding lines of Henry's soliloquy and analyzes the manner in which Shakespeare combined elements of the medieval ''lament'' with Elizabethan rhetorical and literary devices. Among other critics who have discussed this scene, Charles R. Forker (1965) related it to the play's pastoral elements, Robert B. Pierce (1971) commented on the way it highlights the relationship of family and political themes, and David M. Bergeron (1977) analyzed its structural function as a play-within-the play. Also, for further commentary on Shakespeare's use of elements from medieval literary tradition, see the excerpts by E. M. W. Tillyard (1944), Irving Ribner (1965), H. M. Richmond (1967), and John D. Cox (1978).]

The 'New Look' in the reading of Shakespeare's histories first appeared in the nineteen-thirties and became general in the nineteen-forties. The moral theme is stressed by Dover Wilson, Tillyard, Miss Lily Campbell, Theodore Spencer, [W. G.] Zeeveld and others. According to this view Shakespeare's histories are designed as moral exempla, illustrating the evils springing from rebellion and disorder. The basic pattern is that set down in Hall's Chronicle with its moral interpretation of history—deriving of course from the medieval view: the ethics are those set forth in the Homilies on obedience: the structure is that of the secular morality play. . . . On this reading, history is seen always as a guide to the present; its lessons are always relevant, and perpetually applicable: Clio holds up to Nature a particularly truthful dial, looking-glass, or mirror, which enables the judicious to plot their future actions in confidence of the outcome. (p. 123)

Henry VI has a great deal of drum and trumpet fighting. Only with the great scenes at the end of the third part does moral history clearly emerge from the hurly-burly; especially in the killing of York, Henry's speech on the miseries of kingship, and the soliloquy of Gloucester.

H. T. Price [see excerpt above, 1951] has given the name of 'Mirror Scenes' to these symbolic moments in which the theme of the play is directly embodied and fully stated, by figures who are often grouped in [a] statuesque manner. . . . Such scenes have something of the quality of an Induction, or a play within the play, and may be written in a heightened style to emphasize their special function. Henry VI's speech on king-

ship, following on the laments of the father who has killed his son and the son who has killed his father in the recent battle, constitute such a scene. At this stage of Shakespeare's development, such a scene called out all his powers. Action is suspended, whilst the king and his subjects mourn alike the 'fatal colours of our striving houses' [3 Henry VI, II. v. 92], horridly depicted in the red blood and pale faces of the dead. The whole theme of contest, disorder, and unnatural division is stated. Henry's description of the chaos of battle in terms of the contests of dark and light at dawn, or of wind and sea in a storm, is the prelude to a full lament in which the natural images of the shepherd's life and the progress of the seasons are contrasted with the unnatural life of the king, surrounded by pomp and treachery. In its formal pattern, and in the beauty of its imagery, this speech stands out from the play, and the theme it sounds is of such permanent significance in Shakespeare's work that Richard II on time, Henry IV on sleeplessness and Henry V on ceremony, all seem to find their germ and origin here.

The lament of a great man was the medieval form of tragic statement, which Shakespeare knew through the Mirror for Magistrates. In [Thomas Sackville's] Induction to the Complaints which make up the body of that work, the atmosphere is set in terms of the scene, the desolate scene with which the poem begins. (pp. 125-26)

The setting makes tragedy as inevitable as the seasons, so that the allegorical figure of Sorrow which presently appears seems a part of the scene:

Her body small, forwithered and forspent
As is the stalk that summer's drought oppressed,

while her tears drop down abundantly like rain.

Sorrow is a figure from a pageant or tapestry: she is fixed in one attitude. She tells the poet that she will show him a true image of his mood, and leads him to the Entrance to Hell, which is filled with allegorical figures. Here appear the Ghosts whose laments form the main body of the poem. The great distance between Sackville and Shakespeare should not obliterate the connexion. Shakespeare broke into history from the tragic lament.

King Henry is fixed in a pose of Sorrow: the father and the son are 'supporters' who uphold the heraldic device. Henry's lament is marked off by the strictness of its rhetorical 'Schemes'— the most elaborate in the trilogy—and by the sympathetic beauty of the images or 'Tropes'. Both are interwoven to form a pattern, the poetic equivalent of the pattern provided by the action and the story.

Henry begins by describing the uncertainty of the issue in highly schematic terms, but suddenly two lines of pure Shakespeare appear:

What time the shepherd, blowing of his nails,
Can neither call it perfect day nor night.
[3 Henry VI, II. v. 2-3]

The shepherd reappears later as the king contrasts his own hard life with that of a swain. The elaborate Scheme used here looks forward to the verse of Richard III in style:

So many hours must I tend my flock;
So many hours must I take my rest;
So many hours must I contemplate;
So many hours must I sport myself;

So many days my ewes have been with young;
So many weeks ere the poor fools will ean;
So many years ere I shall shear the fleece:
So minutes, hours, days, months and years,
Passed over to the end they were created,
Would bring white hairs unto a quiet grave.

                              [*3 Henry VI*, II. v. 31-40]

Such flat use of 'figures of speech', i.e. verbal pattern or Schemes is suddenly modulated into a deeper style evoked by 'figures of thought', i.e. images or Tropes where the depth, associative power and sensuous qualities of the language are called out.

        The shepherds homely curds,
        His cold thin drink out of his leather bottle,
        His wonted sleep under a fresh trees shade,
        All which secure and sweetly he enjoys,
        Is far beyond a prince's delicates,
        His viands sparkling in a golden cup,
        His body couched in a curious bed,
        Where care, mistrust and treason waits on him
                              [*3 Henry VI*, II. v. 47-54]

The variety of sensuous imagery (*cold thin drink*) and of rhythm (*a prince's delicates*) are hardly to be found again in Shakespeare's dramatic poetry for some years. The father and the son are poetically very indifferent, but the visual pattern is highly dramatic and is recalled at the end of *Richard III* in the speech of the triumphant Richmond [V. iv. 36-9]. . . . (pp. 126-28)

The two common soldiers of *Henry VI*, like the gardeners of [*Richard II*], are representative of the humbler undergrowth, the life of the soil. . . . [Their] presence is an ironic reflection upon Henry's praise of the shepherd's life, which is no less disorganized by war than his own. The poor men who lament with him might well be shepherds; they belong to the humble people and represent their plight symbolically. They are no allegorical figures of Wrath or Contention, but as solid as Piers the Plowman. (p. 129)

        M[uriel] C. Bradbrook, "Tragical-Historical: 'Henry
        VI', 'Richard III', 'Richard II'," in her Shakespeare
        and Elizabethan Poetry: A Study of His Earlier Work
        in Relation to the Poetry of the Time, Chatto and
        Windus, 1951, pp. 123-40.

ALVIN B. KERNAN   (essay date 1954)

[*Kernan has written extensively on modern and Renaissance forms of satire and has edited several plays of Shakespeare and Ben Jonson. In the essay from which the following excerpt is taken, Kernan compares the imagery in* 3 Henry VI *with that in* The True Tragedy of Richard Duke of Yorke. *He points out that while metaphoric patterns of garden-fertility, animal brutality, and butchery-slaughter are frequently found in both plays, the sea-wind-tide image, "the most comprehensive symbol in* 3 Henry VI," *is almost entirely absent from* The True Tragedy. *In the excerpt below, Kernan argues that although the sea-wind-tide figure is a conventional one, Shakespeare's handling of it is unconventional. The dramatist associates this image-pattern, Kernan contends, with different characters at various points in the play, but he consistently uses it to emphasize the theme of disordered nature. Although Kernan notes signs of awkwardness in the symbolic language of* 3 Henry VI, *he praises the atmosphere of formlessness prevalent in the play—an atmosphere which emphasizes the idea that civil war itself "has no more proportion or structure than a storm at sea." Other critics who have treated*

image patterns in the Henry VI *trilogy include Caroline F. E. Spurgeon (1935), John Dover Wilson (1951), Wolfgang H. Clemen (1951), James L. Calderwood (1967), and Carol McGinnis Kay (1972).*]

[The] comprehensive symbol in *3 Henry VI* is a sea-wind-tide figure in which the sea is now forced toward the land by the tide and now blown back by the wind—a traditional idea, but the fashion in which it is handled here is not at all conventional. Actually the symbol is very complex and many variations on the basic pattern are introduced during the course of the play. At times the sea alone appears, at others only the storm-wind; sometimes it incorporates objects floating on the sea buffeted by the elements, and at other times it takes the form of some supernatural power which controls both wind and tide. While it cannot be proven finally that this is the dominant symbol, its regular recurrence at crucial points in the action, its appearance in contexts where it is irrelevant without reference to the pattern as a whole, and the fact that it provides the deepest insight we get into the fundamental nature of the subject, all suggest how close it lies to the heart of the play. (p. 433)

The aptness of the sea-wind-tide symbol is evident. It first appears in I, iv, where York, his young son Rutland murdered by Clifford, his army beaten and dispersed in the Battle of Wakefield, laments his unfortunate position.

        The Army of the Queene hath got the field:
        My Unckles both are slaine, in rescuing me;
        And all my followers, to the eager foe
        Turne back, and flye, like ships before the Winde.
                              [*3 Henry VI*, I. iv. 1-4]

And a few lines later on he says that his army has charged,

            As I have seene a Swan
        With bootlesse labour swime against the Tyde,
        And spend her strength with over-matching Waves.
                              [I. iv. 19-21]

Taken by themselves, of course, these two images provide little hint of their relationship to the major theme, but in the following act in the scene in which King Henry bemoans the carnage of the Battle of Towton and civil war in general, the figure is picked up again and appears with its full significance. Speaking of the battle, he says,

        Now swayes it this way, like a Mighty Sea,
        Forc'd by the Tide, to combat with the Winde:
        Now swayes it that way, like the selfe-same Sea,
        Forc'd to retyre by furie of the Winde.
        Sometime, the Flood prevailes; and then the Winde.
                              [II. v. 5-9]

Here we get our first glimpse into the meaning of the play. The disorder-in-nature theme which is a typical Shakespearean device for paralleling the chaotic and unnatural in the affairs of men, the elemental and relentless character of the storm at sea, the weariness which such a spectacle evokes, and the equal strength of the two factions which can only result in an endless, meaningless deadlock, all ask how anything can be made of the internecine war it mirrors, so violent and yet so empty of any moral value.

The symbol next appears in II, vi, where young Edward, now Duke of York and soon to be Edward IV, refers to Margaret as

            . . . the bloody-minded Queene,
        That led calme *Henry*, though he were a King,
        As doth a Saile, fill'd with a fretting Gust,
        Command an Argosie to stemme the Waves.
                              [II. vi. 33-6]

After the coronation of Edward and the flight of Henry to Scotland while Margaret goes to France, Richard turns his thoughts to his own ambition, utilizing the sea symbol to play off his despair against his determination to get the crown.

> Why then I doe but dreame on Soveraigntie,
> Like one that stands upon a Promontorie,
> And spyes a farre-off shore, where hee would tread,
> Wishing his foot were equall with his eye,
> And chides the Sea, that sunders him from thence,
> Saying hee'le lade it dry, to have his way.
>
> [III. ii. 134-39]

This passage when read in conjunction with those already quoted illustrates both the logical vagueness and emotional richness typical of the Shakespearean pattern of imagery. It is noticeable that where the wind and the tide appear they are not identified with one faction or another exclusively; the wind at one time will represent the Lancastrians, at another time the Yorkists, or it may be applied to them both. Nor is the sea confined to a single meaning in the play. In the speech of Richard just quoted it refers immediately to those who stand between Richard and the kingship: Edward and his sons and Clarence. But as a result of its appearance in other contexts, the sea begins to take on a number of emotionally related overtones. In the speech of Henry, for example, which I have quoted above, it suggests England and Nature, both human and external, agitated and whipped by the forces of civil war; and Richard's description of himself as one who "chides the sea" and who will "lade it dry," identifies him with the now familiar wind and tide which struggle for the sea, underscoring his brutality which is thus seen as a departure from natural order and harmony. Here and elsewhere the symbol continues to reveal new facets, a widening number of attitudes toward the theme which are interlocked through a common denominator of civil war as political chaos. (pp. 433-35)

In [V, iv] Margaret encourages her army with a long and elaborate parallel between the perilous state of the Lancastrian hopes and a battered ship in stormy and treacherous waters.

> What though the Mast be now blowne over-boord,
> The Cable broke, the holding-Anchor lost,
> And halfe our Saylors swallow'd in the flood?
> Yet lives our Pilot still, Is't meet that hee
> Should leave the Helme and like a fearful Lad,
> With tearefull Eyes adde Water to the Sea,
> And give more strength to that which hath too much,
> Whiles in his moane, the Ship splits on the Rock,
> Which Industrie and Courage might have sav'd?...
> Say you can swim, alas 'tis but a while,
> Tread on the Sand, why there you quickly sinke,
> Bestride the Rock, the Tyde will wash you off,
> Or else you famish, that's a three-fold Death.
> This speake I (Lords) to let you understand,
> If case some one of you would flye from us,
> That there's no hop'd-for Mercy with the Brothers,
> More then with ruthlesse Waves, with Sands
>   and Rocks.
> Why, courage then, what cannot be avoided,
> 'Twere childish weaknesse to lament, or fear.
>
> [V. iv. 3-38]

This is clearly the early style with its parallelisms, repetitions, and self-conscious delight in an extended figure ingeniously worked out: but even in the midst of the rhetorical exercise there are flashes of a less artificial nature than the rest (e.g.,

"though the rough wind say no," "the Tyde will wash you off,"'). And though such a rhetorical *tour de force* ["wondrous feat"] may offend modern readers through its open statement of ideas which we would prefer to remain more implicit, it must be recognized that during the 1580's and early 1590's this style was the sort of thing that every author had to do to show his skill in the trade. (pp. 437-38)

The sea-wind-tide pattern of imagery, then, enriches *3 Henry VI* in a number of ways. It provides a moral commentary on what otherwise is merely formless succession of gory events, what [Ben] Jonson sneeringly referred to as "York and Lancaster's long jars." Indeed, the use of this particular type of imagery suggests that formlessness is the very effect the dramatist is striving for in order to illuminate the nature of civil war which has no more proportion or structure than a storm at sea. But the advantages derived from using imagery rather than direct statement for suggesting meaning are also utilized fully in this case. Nothing connected with the affairs of men, not even civil war, is so simple as to admit flat settlement, and the sea image also contains suggestions of the smashing and destructive power of the men engaged in a struggle for power, the elemental nature of their drives, their vigor and stamina; and while these may not be the virtues to be most admired in civilized man, they have an undeniable attractiveness. To leave this side of the picture out would be to present only a half-truth, and the result could only be a companion piece to [Thomas Norton and Thomas Sackville's] *Gorboduc.* It is interesting to see that even so early in his career Shakespeare was employing imagery in such a skilful fashion, though the actual tropes were still somewhat awkwardly handled. (p. 441)

Alvin B. Kernan, "A Comparison of the Imagery in '3 Henry VI' and 'The True Tragedie of Richard Duke of York'," in Studies in Philology, *Vol. LI, No. 3, July, 1954, pp. 431-42.*

M. M. REESE (essay date 1961)

[*Reese's intention in* The Cease of Majesty *(1961) is to modify the idea that, politically, Shakespeare was a "champion of the Establishment, always cautious and conservative." Reese agrees with E. M. W. Tillyard (1944) that the history plays are essentially didactic and consonant with the Tudor view of society; but he contends that Shakespeare was also attempting to reconcile that Tudor concept with a conviction that through their actions men and women participate in shaping their individual destinies. In a portion of his essay not excerpted below, Reese argues that in the history plays Shakespeare was not only searching for the ideal king, he was also seeking "the ideal social relationship in which king and people were united in a conception of their mutual duty"; according to Reese, the privilege of majesty ceases when this sense of mutual duty has been destroyed. In his comments on the* Henry VI *trilogy, Reese states that "majesty has entirely ceased" and cannot be restored until the Lancastrians' crime of usurpation has been expiated. Other critics who have seen divine retribution operating in the* Henry VI *trilogy include Hermann Ulrici (1839), Denton J. Snider (1890), J. A. R. Marriott (1918), and Irving Ribner (1965). Reese further suggests that it is not until 3* Henry VI *that Shakespeare begins to modify the providential view of history and to humanize his treatment of kingship, primarily through more psychologically complex characterizations. Specifically, the critic compares Henry and Richard of Gloucester in 3* Henry VI *with Shakespeare's delineation of these figures in Part 2, maintaining that the dramatist became tired of his didactic structure and, through most of the action of Part 3, attempted to depict the effect of kingship on the characters in a more realistic, individual manner. For additional discussions of Shakespeare's view of kingship, see the essays by Michael Manheim (1973) and Edward I.*

Berry (Additional Bibliography). Also, see the excerpts by A. C. Hamilton (1961-62), S. C. Sen Gupta (1964), H. M. Richmond (1967), James Winny (1968), and Robert Ornstein (1972) for an opposing stance on the role of providence or divine retribution in Henry VI.]

[In *1, 2* and *3 Henry VI*, Shakespeare] attempts the orthodox reconciliation between a providential view of history and the conviction that man, while not the total author of his fate, does by his own actions co-operate in his destiny, however slightly or obscurely. Thus the unhappy story of fifteenth-century England originated in the dethronement of Richard II, described by Hall as 'the beginning and root of the great discord and division'. . . . After this crime everything was in a sense fore-doomed. France must be lost and England suffer civil war; while within this scheme the fate of individuals would be determined by the ups and downs of Fortune's wheel, with the added implication that Fortune itself was God's agent in demanding the expiation of a crime. But the dramatist's attitude is not wholly fatalistic. Henry himself marvels 'to see how God in all his creatures works' [*2 Henry VI*, II. i. 7], and the suffering in these plays can be traced to direct human action. Personal wickedness is part of the penalty that God inflicts, and so the erring individual is at once an agent of God's purpose and a man aware of his own evil and capable of at any rate an illusion of choice. The plays present an ominous cycle of sin and retribution, with every crime brought terribly home to its author and its consequences made evident in misery to himself and those he loves. It is an arrangement which makes effective characterisation impossible, as all the characters are victims of their own unruly natures and also of the disasters to which the whole country is fated. They are imprisoned in various kinds of anti-social attitude, and in spite of their noise and energy they are men without personal authority. (p. 166)

Shakespeare is not particularly concerned in these plays to study the effects of power or look for kingly types. He is writing of an England where majesty has entirely ceased and kings, prelates, statesmen and people will be unable to restore it until God decides that the Lancastrians' crime has been expiated and sends Henry of Richmond as deliverer. This largely accounts for the strident monotony of *Henry VI*. For the length of three plays the poet has nothing but violence and calamity to write about and it was not until *Richard III* that he found a way to make this sort of catastrophe interesting. So any inferences we care to make about royalty and power are only casual, and at the time they may have been unsuspected by Shakespeare himself. In Part Two he dislikes Henry, and contemptuously dismisses him as the sort of weak, self-centred ruler—a Richard II without the *panache*—under whom states will never prosper. In the third part he comes to value Henry as a man, but he has already decided that in kings it is the public virtues that matter. In the heat of battle Henry sits upon a molehill, satisfied that 'to whom God will, there be the victory' [*3 Henry VI*, II. v. 15]. His fatalism and surrender to despair are tantamount to abdication.

Shakespeare also exposes the essentially destructive ambition of York and the young Richard of Gloucester, but beyond this he has little to say about the specialty of rule. His concerns here are more primitive. *Henry VI* is a prolonged morality, with England as its central character, betrayed by a long line of evil and selfish men. These egotists overwhelm the few faithful servants who point the way to better things, and although the plays get their undoubted momentum from the energy of the sinners, it is Shakespeare's anxiety about his own times that gives them their real significance and interest. . . .

The Tudors had put an end to civil war, but there were conditions in which it might recur. The whole of *Henry VI* is long-drawn demonstration that internal dissension, caused by a factious nobility, is the greatest scourge that a nation can suffer.

> 'Tis much when sceptres are in children's hands;
> But more, when envy breeds unkind division:
> There comes ruin, there begins confusion.
> [*1 Henry VI*, IV. i. 192-94]

The child here is Henry VI, but in the uncertainty of the immediate future even this misfortune might return when Elizabeth died. The three plays therefore embody the standard Tudor warning against rebellion, and Shakespeare insists that, however bad or weak the ruler, he must be obeyed. He must be obeyed even if his title is not impeccable. The genealogical argument, strenuously conducted, is on the side of York against Lancaster, but that does not justify York's rebellion. Nothing justifies the risk of civil war. (pp. 166-68)

[*1 Henry VI*] is primarily a play about the French wars, showing how Talbot, a rugged, selfless warrior, lost the English provinces in France because his [simple] loyalties were powerless against the witchcraft of Joan of Arc and the dissensions of his principal lieutenants. These dissensions, which will grow later into the Wars of the Roses, provide the secondary theme of the play. (p. 168)

1 Henry VI has an earnestness which distinguishes it from most of the rather turgid and meaningless entertainments offered on the public stages at the time of the [Spanish] Armada. It is far from being a rumbustious glorification of England such as the audiences of the early nineties are supposed to have enjoyed, and its purpose, with an unmistakable eye upon contemporary uncertainties, was to underline the evils of disunity. Elizabethan England is here being reminded that disunity was the means which God formerly chose for the terrible fulfilment of the curse brought upon the nation by the usurping House of Lancaster. The stars had revolted and the French were receiving unnatural courage from the aid of sorcery, but the English co-operated in their doom by the sin of disloyalty. Shakespeare divides the responsibility between fate and individual weakness. At times he regarded the quarrelling noblemen as helpless victims of the Lancastrians' curse, which compelled them to act as they did; but he could not think of them as wholly free from blame, and at times he seems to forget the stars and simply lay the guilt upon those evil counsellors of the king who neglected the common weal for their own feuds and ambitions. . . . The play makes the same appeal as *King John*, imploring the English to close their ranks and forsake the divisions through which alone they are vulnerable. (pp. 179-80)

The theme [of *2 Henry VI*] is still to show the wickedness of dissension, the implicit consequence of the Lancastrian usurpation, and it is here embodied in the ambitions of York, whose success is made possible by the weakness of the King and the overthrow of Humphrey of Gloucester, the conventional good counsellor. (p. 180)

2 Henry VI still adopts in the main the structure of the morality, with *Respublica* threatened by the various personifications of Lust, Pride and Ambition; and the special political lesson that Shakespeare wishes to use for the instruction of his contemporaries is that prescriptive right—York has a better claim to the throne than Henry—does not justify an attack on the *de facto* possessor. . . . Shakespeare's handling of York shows his real preoccupations at this time. In discovering the causes of weakness and disunity, the history play was to be a serious instrument of political education, and for this purpose the important thing was to expose the effects of York's egoism on the other people. Shakespeare was much more concerned with this than with the effects on York himself. The rise and fall of a particular individual meant less to him than the disaster he brought to England. (pp. 181-82)

In [2 Henry VI] Henry is drawn with a surprising lack of charity. He can no longer be acquitted with the fatalistic reflection that it is always thus when sceptres are in children's hands. He is a man now, and a responsible king, and the insipid pieties with which he greets misfortune are no substitute for good government; nor, which would have partly redeemed them, do they bear the mark of a truly Christian resignation. His failures are many. Although he weeps for Gloucester's death, he has already abandoned him to his enemies; and he grieves just as much when the wicked Beaufort dies. When his subjects quarrel in his presence, he is just a feather puffed to and fro upon their angry breath. In IV ix, which is only a short scene, he begins by wishing that he were no longer king and ends with a resolve to 'learn to govern better' [2 Henry VI, IV. ix. 48]. After the miltary failure at St. Albans he immediately wants to give up the struggle altogether: 'Can we outrun the heavens?'[2 Henry VI, V. ii. 73]. A man so conscious of his own unfitness and disinclination to rule cannot hope to inspire either loyalty or achievement.

These weaknesses are not lost on York. His picture of Henry 'surfeiting in joys of love' [2 Henry VI, I. i. 251] is just a smear (the Queen's affections are directed elsewhere) but he has two trenchant phrases about Henry's 'church-like honours', unsuitable in the occupant of a throne, and the 'bookish rule' that has 'pull'd fair England down' [2 Henry VI, I. i. 259]. York knows that he would make a better king:

> Let them obey that know not how to rule;
> This hand was made to handle nought but gold.

> I am far better born than is the king,
> More like a king, more kingly in my thoughts.
>   [2 Henry VI, V. i. 6-7, 28-9]

As soon as the crown is his, he will wipe out the disgrace of the long defeats in France. These are not idle boasts, and his ability is not in doubt; for the moment we may even forget his ambition and accept his good intentions. In capacity for leadership Shakespeare deliberately contrasts him with Henry and so foreshadows the theme of Richard II.

But the idea is only casually introduced and we should not make too much of it. In so far as reality intrudes upon the conventional pattern of the play, it is a source of artistic weakness, and anyway it made no difference to Shakespeare's conclusions. Supreme rights were vested in the king de facto ["in reality"] even if his rival had a better claim by inheritance. Shakespeare's dread of civil war was too strong to be qualified by extenuations of any kind, and ultimately his recognition of Henry's failure, or of York's patriotism and political abilities, was less significant to him than his determination to reveal York without sympathy as a monster of ambition. But he has already realised that power is a trust which it is sinful to refuse. If there could be a political crime graver than rebellion, it would be the failure of a king to do his duty. (pp. 182-84)

2 Henry VI is not a good play but it achieves the effect that Shakespeare intended, of a society ravaged by mortal disease. The victims cannot help themselves, and when they speak of the normal human virtues, it is in a sense of something unat-

Part II. Act III. Scene ii. Humphrey and First Murderer. Frontispiece to the Rowe edition (1709). By permission of the Folger Shakespeare Library.

tainable and not perfectly understood. They know themselves to be the victims that they are. The play is remarkable in the Shakespeare canon as the only one that has no single character with a redeeming vision of an uncorrupted society and the possibility of virtue. Gloucester and the Nevilles are better than the rest but there is no depth in them. They are no more than conventional attitudes of goodness, easily deceived, and their very simplicity is a vice. Shakespeare is at pains to show how the contagion of evil has spread to the least of men. Cade and his followers are the gullible architects of anarchy; Horner and his man Peter play out the political feud in miniature; the Duchess of Gloucester's familiars seem to be the twisted fancies of a brain tormented by ambition; and the episode of Simpcox, while it enables Gloucester to prove his superiority to elementary impostures, shows how easily the simple affections of ordinary folk have been corrupted by credulity and deception. Although the King is much to blame, the play pictures a society wholly incapable of virtue. It is a grim illustration of the total cease of majesty. (p. 188)

[3 Henry VI] carries on the story in a gathering crescendo of destruction. The sea and the wind become the most potent images of these final episodes of the trilogy, as if it were only by means of this symbol that Shakespeare could realise the horrors which civil war had brought upon the kingdom. The

Part II. Act III. Scene iii. Warwick, Henry VI, Salisbury, and Cardinal Beauford. Frontispiece to the Hanmer edition by H. Gravelot (1744). By permission of the Folger Shakespeare Library.

images already familiar in the preceding plays, of the axe wantonly laid to the fruitful tree and England become a jungle and a slaughter-house, still have some force but they are now subordinate to the dominant symbol of the destructive, unheeding storm. To emphasise their helplessness, the characters are conceived as ships struggling against the tide or carried inertly before the gale, and the storm thus appears as the arbitrary instrument of the chaos which men's actions have created. Chaos, to Shakespeare, was never a passive condition. It was always a compulsive force, a ravening wolf or universal appetite, devouring and destroying. In *3 Henry VI*, where statecraft is stripped of its modest pretences and even the common decencies of war give place to acts of monstrous cruelty, the winds are fierce with the savagery and capriciousness of Fortune's wheel itself. The tide in men's affairs is no longer one which their own choice and energy will bring on to success. It will throw them on the rocks, try how they may. (p. 193)

The men and women of this trilogy do not inhabit a withdrawn world of hints and shrugs and oblique allusions. The amplification which encumbers their heavier speeches is without nuance or hidden meaning. Even when they are most longwinded, they are deafeningly downright. In Part Three their voices howl more shrilly than elsewhere, as if they were trying to outshriek the competing winds. It often leads them into

absurdities, as when Queen Elizabeth fears that her weeping and 'blood-sucking sighs' [*3 Henry VI*, IV. iv. 22] may blast or drown the infant she carries in her womb, but it expresses their sense of helplessness in a world become infinitely violent and dangerous. Desperation is their only pilot, and each seasick weary bark is destined to founder on the rocks. (pp. 194-95)

[The pattern of Part Three is] largely artificial, and in his insistence upon it Shakespeare was deliberately organising a crude, episodic story to an artistic purpose. As yet his art was self-conscious and over-didactic. He saw certain things more simply then than he was to see them later, and he had no need of ambiguities. Ambition and civil war were unmitigatedly evil. To make others feel the horror of his story as deeply as he felt it himself, he employed the consistent formality of art: a stylised balancing of the plot and a narrative method that had the tidiness of fable.

Thus in the central scene of the play, at Towton, the horror of civil war is taken up into pure symbol. The King's speech in envy of the shepherd's lot is entirely conventional in spirit and content. An imagined rustic bliss was the salve monotonously applied to minds weary of the life of court and city. . . . Henry's soliloquy established a mood that the audience would recognise and would not probe too deeply. It is followed by the parallel episodes in which a Son finds that he has killed his Father, and a Father finds that he has killed his Son. . . . Shakespeare did not invent this particular symbol. It was already familiar from the chronicles and *A Mirror for Magistrates*, where it epitomised the blind wastefulness of civil war, but familiarity does not diminish its effect. The characters stiffen into the rigid attitudes of figures in a stained-glass window as their emblematic language echoes with the horror of those 'erroneous, mutinous and unnatural' days [*3 Henry VI*, II. v. 90].

With this, Shakespeare had virtually said all that he needed to say upon this particular theme. He still had half a play to write and he continued dutifully on his way, but he seems to be losing interest. He is obviously perfunctory in observing the moral law that for every disaster there should be a precedent crime, usually perjury. This oath-breaking, already compelled into service before Wakefield and before Towton, becomes less effective with each repetition, and there are many repetitions. Edward of York throws over a French marriage because he is infatuated with Lady Grey; perjured Clarence change sides twice; and Edward again, after being admitted to the city of York on the understanding that he is only come to claim his dukedom, is urged by Gloucester not to heed 'nice points' and agrees to declare himself king. Overworked to this extent, it is revealed as merely a device to keep the plot moving. Shakespeare seems to have felt it so, for he adds a fresh and individual touch by suggesting that Edward's main offence is not perjury but lust. (pp. 197-98)

[For] almost the first time Shakespeare turns his attention to the personal qualities of a king, something particular to the man himself and distinct from his predestined lot in a disastrous age. We met something of the kind at the end of Part One, where Henry broke his pledge to marry Armagnac's daughter because Suffolk's description of Margaret had stirred him to 'passion of inflaming love' [*1 Henry VI*, V. v. 82]. There it was quite out of character, and it was not seriously suggested that the priggish boy was overwhelmed by desire for a girl he had never seen. Its repercussions are only political. If Henry obtained any sensual satisfactions from his young bride, we are left to imagine them. Whatever his failings, lust is not one of them. But it is otherwise with Edward. His swift passion for Lady Grey is laid bare to the innuendoes of Gloucester and is lightly suggested as an indulgence of which a king should not be guilty. His acts of perjury are sins, but it is Gloucester who makes him commit them and they seem to lie only on the surface of his character. They are just a piece of the story-teller's mechanism. But his sensuality, prompting him to throw over a diplomatic marriage for the sake of a pretty face, belongs to himself, and it tangles his kingliness. Retribution, in War-wick's desertion and the temporary loss of the throne, comes too pat and copy-book to be convincing, but when he is re-stored, with his wife and all her relations about him, a doubt has been raised. His fitness has been called in question, and we can already see ahead to the haunted, ineffectual creature that he becomes in the earlier scenes of *Richard III*.

We must not insist too much on this, for Shakespeare himself is indirect in his handling of it. He is not particularly interested in Edward anyway. But it does point the way to a change of the highest importance. It is clear that as the play proceeds, Shakespeare begins to tire of the chronicle form, with its mech-anical motivation, and to concern himself rather with the human problems of kingship. He never loses sight of his main purpose, which was to teach the same lessons he had already made evident in Part Two, but in the second half of *3 Henry VI* he is feeling his way towards something much more original and striking.

This is his changing conception of the character of the King. In Part Two Henry was not an individual. He was just a symbol of unfitness to be a king, wearing his piety and vacillation like a concealing mask. York, too, was incarnate ambition, not a man. Shakespeare made no attempt to consider either of them as a human being; he was content for them to express an attitude. He seems to have started Part Three in a similar frame of mind, and it is not until he has mastered his material and organised the plot within its conventional framework that he begins to find certain people interesting for what they are. He wants to look behind the mask and examine the fascinating idea that the man who is called to rule is a man as well as a king. He seems to realise that he will presently have to start his examination from the other end: not with the king but with the man.

He begins to discover new potentialities in Henry. There has been an earlier intimation of it in a short scene in Part Two (III iii), when his attitudinising piety seems for a moment to be the expression of an inner strength and conviction. Glouces-ter has just been murdered. Suffolk, one of the contrivers of the act, has been sent into banishment and word is brought that another, the Cardinal Beaufort, is mortally ill. Henry would have been only human if he had watched the Cardinal's last agonies with a certain satisfaction, but in genuine distress he asks for heaven's mercy on his enemy:

> O thou eternal Mover of the heavens!
> Look with a gentle eye upon this wretch;
> O! beat away the busy meddling fiend
> That lays strong siege unto this wretch's soul,
> And from his bosom purge this black despair.
> [*2 Henry VI*, III. iii. 19-23]

When Warwick sanctimoniously suggests that an ugly death is a fit conclusion to an evil life, Henry tells him to 'forbear to judge, for we are sinners all' [*2 Henry VI*, III. iii. 31]. It is to be his verdict on all his enemies. But elsewhere in Part Two his religiosity is too good to be true. Either it is a cover for his irresolution, a series of phrases brought out to disarm re-

buke; or, if it is sincere, it provokes the sort of dislike that certain critics of *Measure for Measure* have felt for Isabella's chastity. In the first half of the following play, he is just as effective. If he had had his wish to be a shepherd, he would certainly have lost his sheep.

The change is first evident after Towton, when Shakespeare seems at last to discover what may be made of him. His mind has achieved a new discipline when the keepers find him wan-dering, a fugitive from Scotland, in the northern forests. Re-flecting on his predicament, he reaches the conclusion—so different from the merely facile self-criticism of earlier scenes—that the king who cannot help himself is powerless to help his subjects, and he welcomes 'sour adversity' as a tonic, 'for wise men say it is the wisest course' [*3 Henry VI*, III. i. 24-5]. When the keepers accost him, he can even speak in riddles:

> More than I seem, and less than I was born to:
> A man at least, for less I should not be;
> And men may talk of kings, and why not I?
> [III. i. 56-8]

His voice has never before carried such a note of maturity and confidence; and to the observation that he is speaking as if he were a king, he makes what is, considering his outward state at the time, a remarkable reply: 'Why, so I am, in mind; and that's enough' [III. i. 60]. His kingdom is in his mind:

> My crown is in my heart, not on my head;
> Not deck'd with diamonds and Indian stones,
> Not to be seen: my crown is called content;
> A crown it is that seldom kings enjoy.
> [III. i. 62-5]

Henry has found himself, and found at the same time the unique place that he occupies in Shakespeare's histories. Outwardly the least fortunate of his kings, he is the only one who is able to say that he is content. Hallowed by suffering and his calm acceptance of it as his worldly lot, no one henceforth can harm him. Self-knowledge has set him free.

A man who is king cannot be otherwise than as he is. Once he has ceased to aspire to the sort of royalty that he could never command, Henry is free to display his true qualities of patience, humility and love. These are what he is and what he has to offer to his troubled age. At other times they might have prevailed, for they are qualities proper to a king. They will not prevail now, but at least Henry can leave them as a gracious memory to times when they will, and it is right that he should be the man chosen to speak prophetically of the young Rich-mond:

> Come hither, England's hope: If secret powers
> Suggest but truth to my divining thoughts,
> This pretty lad will prove our country's bliss.
> His looks are full of peaceful majesty,
> His head by nature fram'd to wear a crown,
> His hand to wield a sceptre, and himself
> Like to bless in time a regal throne.
> Make much of him, my lords; for this is he
> Must help you more than you are hurt by me. . . .
> [*3 Henry VI*, IV. vi. 68-76]

Henry offers a recognisable ideal of kingship at which no one else in the trilogy has even hinted. It is disregarded, since his supporters simply treat him as a factor in the political struggle, useful because the monarchy will always command certain resources of loyalty and prestige. They seem to feel, too, that his sanctity lays on ordinary men a burden heavier than they should be expected to endure: which is an effect that sanctity often produces. But even if the characters on the stage are blinded to it, Henry's ideal of kingship prevails in the promise that the young Richmond shall one day be the sort of king that Henry himself would have liked to be. Henry has taught that he who would be master of a kingdom must first have settled his own estate. The whole trilogy is proof that other qualities are necessary too, but Henry has won the victory that all kings must win, and with it his peace of mind. (pp. 198-202)

The ideal that Henry represents is illuminated by the contrast with the aims of Richard of Gloucester, whose development runs parallel with his own. Even in Part Two Gloucester's sardonic realism has set him apart from the other combatants. He seems to have been born disenchanted, with a ruthless steely intransigence that scorns accommodation. 'Honour, love, obedience, troops of friends' are ethical perquisites in which he is simply not interested. His sword and speech are so readily turned to war that Shakespeare knew what he was about when he brought him to the battlefield at the age of something over two.

> Teeth hadst thou in thy head when thou wast born,
> To signify that thou cam'st to bite the world.
> [*3 Henry VI*, V. vi. 53-4]

At first his very considerable courage is at the service of a much-vaunted clannishness. The young Richard is a good Yorkist, vehement in his father's and his brother's cause. It is he who, playing for the highest prize, urges his father into the fatal perjury that precedes the rout at Wakefield; and in the scene (II i) that follows the battle it is his leadership that cheers his broken party and gives them confidence to change their fortunes. His own grief at his father's death is a spur to action:

> To weep is to make less the depth of grief:
> Tears, then, for babes; blows and revenge for me!
> [*3 Henry VI*, II. i. 85-6]

Warwick, beaten at St. Albans, has to be cajoled and mocked and flattered out of his pessimism at the Yorkists' double defeat:

> 'Tis love I bear thy glories makes me speak.
> But, in this troublous time what's to be done?
> Shall we go throw away our coats of steel,
> And wrap our bodies in black mourning gowns,
> Numb'ring our Ave-Maries with our beads?
> Or shall we on the helmets of our foes
> Tell our devotion with revengeful arms?
> [*3 Henry VI*, II. i. 158-64]

At Towton it is Richard again who rallies his brothers and Warwick when they would leave the field for rest or retreat.

But this clannishness presently proves to have been no more than the instinct which says that it is safer to keep with the pack while the jungle is dangerous. With Edward crowned and Richard himself raised to the dukedom of Gloucester, he reveals himself as the solitary hunter that at heart he has always been. The claws show as he spits out his hatred of Edward:

> Would he were wasted, marrow, bones and all,
> That from his loins no hopeful branch may spring,
> To cross me from the hopeful time I look for!
> [*3 Henry VI*, III. ii. 125-27]

From his earliest appearance he has always been the member of his family that the Lancastrians have hated and feared the most, and the audience will not forget the caressing, seductive words in which he has spoken to his father of the crown:

> And, father, do but think
> How sweet a thing it is to wear a crown,
> Within whose circuit is Elysium,
> And all that poets feign of bliss and joy.
> [*3 Henry VI*, I. ii. 28-31]

So far the practised Machiavel has kept his ambitions hidden, but in the second half of the play, as a complement to the growing importance of the King, the character is given greater room for deployment. A comparison between his long speech at III. ii. 124-95 with the similar speeches of his father in the previous play (I. i. 215-60 and III. i. 331-83) will show how much more skilful Shakespeare has become, and how his interest has shifted from the formal narration of the chronicle story, with its moral embellishments, to the sort of problem indicated in his maturer treatment of Henry VI. The sin of perjury, the seemingly capricious motions of Fortune's wheel, the inescapable doom of the House of Lancaster were all time-honoured mechanisms that helped to unfold the plot at a certain level. More than that, they were the dramatist's means of ensuring that his didactic intention should not be mistaken. But there are signs that Shakespeare was already looking for a more satisfactory explanation of human affairs, and he seems to have found it in moral conceptions rather different from the straight-forward, eye-for-an-eye morality of the chronicles. He found it superficial and inadequate to go on seeking the causes of events in men's outward actions, since their actions are only a consequence of the sort of men they are, their response or resistance to the forces working on them. The real causes are to be found in their minds, for being is as important as doing, and what a man is will in the long run matter more than what he does. Civil war is ultimately the product of disorder in the soul. York's massive declarations of ambition are only mechanical and formal. They have no real significance, as York is not in the least a human being. But it is otherwise with his terrible son, lost in the thorny wood of his bloody imaginings. Where York conventionally absorbs himself in visions of cosmic upheaval, Richard is breezily practical in his revelations. Here is one who will smile and murder while he smiles, and frame his face to all occasions, and add colours to the chameleon.

Thus the play's interest is withdrawn from the lesser men and their predestined doings and is concentrated upon the two who stand at opposite extremes of good and evil. Henry lacks the power of action, but his saintliness and serenity shed their own illumination; Richard, the man of deeds, is sheerly wicked. The play moves to its climax under the shadow of their conflict. In so far as it is still a morality, they have something in common with the Fairy Queen and Demon King who contend in fable for possession of the hero—in this case England. These roles never quite desert them. But there is a very real difference between York and Gloucester, on the one hand, and on the other between the Henry of Part Two, with his church-like humours and bookish rule, and the man whose crown is called content. It is the difference between characters who are merely the embodiment of moral attitudes and characters who are struggling towards individuality and life. Henry's new-found insight gives him a self-contained strength which works upon men who hold him of no account as a political factor. Gloucester, though naïvely theatrical (Shakespeare was not to learn everything at once), is a master of wickedness who may contaminate a nation. (pp. 203-05)

> *M. M. Reese, "Shakespeare's England," in his* The
> Cease of Majesty: A Study of Shakespeare's History

Plays, *Edward Arnold (Publishers) Ltd., 1961, pp. 159-332.*

A. C. HAMILTON (essay date 1961-62)

[*Hamilton's essay on* 1, 2, *and* 3 Henry VI *in his* The Early Shakespeare *(1967) was first delivered in 1961-62 as introductions to portions of the British Broadcasting Corporation's television series, "An Age of Kings." Hamilton emphasizes the superior craftsmanship that he finds apparent even in these early plays, demonstrating that the "dramatic control Shakespeare exercises over events" distinguishes his work from the chronicle plays of other Elizabethan dramatists. Hamilton examines such elements as language, characterization, plot, and theme, finding that all successfully contribute to an overall plan; thus, like Hereward T. Price (1951), the critic praises Shakespeare's masterful construction of the trilogy. Hamilton also disputes the views of E. M. W. Tillyard (1944) on the role of divine intervention in* Henry VI, *contending that although several characters may invoke God's intercession, this is "only for the sake of dramatic irony"; according to Hamilton, God forebears to act on behalf of those on the side of right, for in the world of* 1, 2, *and* 3 Henry VI, *"right does not matter; all that matters is the rule of force and the desire for revenge." Other commentators who have disputed the presence of divine will in* Henry VI *include S. C. Sen Gupta (1964), H. M. Richmond (1967), James Winny (1968), and Robert Ornstein (1972).*]

Unlike comedy and tragedy with their self-contained worlds of fiction, the history play turns outward to historical fact. Yet the antithesis between poetry and history goes back to Plato; it is indicated even in the paradoxical term "history play." Though the writer of tragedy may seek Jonson's "truth of argument" by taking his material from history, he is free, as Aristotle says, . . . to make historical events more philosophical and universal. . . . The illusion of truth, without an allusion to truth, suffices. In the history play, fact limits, or at least controls, the dramatist's invention. . . . [But] even here Shakespeare is free to select, rearrange, and adapt those of his facts that have not settled into conventions, provided only that he keep, in Coleridge's phrase, "the essential truth of history." Such restriction does not apply to form. History gives the content; the play provides the unifying form. To treat a history play in terms of its genre, then, involves seeing the element of "play" in tension with "history," that is, fiction as it counters fact, or what is (the play) in relation to what was (history as recorded in the chronicles). The history play, by satisfying the demands of history, informs and instructs; but it delights an audience by being an imitation of history.

Unfortunately we come to the *Henry VI* plays from Shakespeare's later plays, with critical expectations about language, character, and plot that the early plays do not—and should not—satisfy. It requires some effort of the imagination to approach them as Shakespeare did, as his first endeavors of art. Shakespeare as the dramatist of the *Henry VI* plays is difficult to accept; and, in reading the plays, we find it hard to suppress the regret that they are not the later plays. Being readers rather than spectators, we are deprived of the spectacle—the pageantry, ceremony, and ritual—upon which the early history plays depend. Further, we are cut off from what the first audience brought to the play, the immediate and powerful pressure of a shared and living history. Yet we must accept the plays as they are and, in attempting to do so, recognize that the characteristics that disturb us may suggest what is dramatically significant in the plays.

The term "chronicle play" suggests history in blank verse, a drama that does hardly more than dramatize events recorded in the chronicles. In such a play, language and action are not a function of the inner life of the characters, nor are the characters a function of the plot, and the scenes are episodic rather than shaped into the logic of a plot. On such dramatic grounds *Henry VI Part I* may be regarded as a chronicle play and dismissed. . . . Most critics have agreed to show how it is not worthy, while others offer the apology that it is early Shakespeare. It is worth an effort to see what may be said for the play. Even the grounds for regarding it as a chronicle play may reveal how it escapes that category.

Its language has the anonymity, the facelessness, to be expected in a chronicle play as it opens ceremoniously with the funeral of Henry V. Yet this scene serves to illustrate the special problems of its language. Bedford exclaims:

> Hung be the heavens with black, yield day to night!
> Comets, importing change of times and states,
> Brandish your crystal tresses in the sky
> And with them scourge the bad revolting stars
> That have consented unto Henry's death!
> King Henry the Fifth, too famous to live long!
> England ne'er lost a king of so much worth.
>
> [*I Henry VI,* I. i. 1-7]

The incantation around Henry's corpse continues with Gloucester's chiming response:

> England ne'er had a king until his time.
> Virtue he had, deserving to command;
> His brandish'd sword did blind men with his beams.
>
> [I. i. 8-10]

Though such language becomes extravagant, it serves usefully enough to point up the shattering impact of Henry's death. Yet with Bedford's next speech there occurs a startling image that offends. One reader finds it "revolting to sense and sensibility" to believe that Shakespeare wrote such lines as Bedford's:

> Posterity, await for wretched years,
> When at their mothers' moist'ned eyes babes shall suck,
> Our isle be made a nourish of salt tears,
> And none but women left to wail the dead.
>
> [I. i. 48-51]

Dover Wilson finds the image "repulsive" [see Additional Bibliography]; and Coleridge heaps ridicule upon anyone who would claim the language of the opening scene to be Shakespeare's: ". . . you may have ears,—for so has another animal,—but an ear you cannot have" [see excerpt above, 1816-34]. To my ears Bedford uses a startling image by which to prophesy the disaster that will overwhelm England. Instead of being nourished by milk from their mothers and their mother country, children will suck salt tears from weeping eyes. (pp. 9-13)

This opening scene may be considered again to answer a more serious judgment against the play: that its events are included more for their topicality than for the demands of the plot. With Elizabethan notions of how history offers parallels to contemporary events, a chronicle play would make some local impact upon an audience. Yet topicality can be relevant only to what is in the minds of those spectators who allow their attention to wander from the play. Dover Wilson, quoting from Coningsby's *Journal of the Siege of Rouen* (1591), comments about the scene before Rouen in which Joan thrusts a burning torch from the tower as a signal to the French forces: ". . . any soldier in the theatre recently back from Rouen would recognize an allusion to disturbing 'notices of fyre' given 'out of a high steeple in the towne' to friends beyond the lines of the besiegers.'' In making this connection with his military experience, however, the soldier might well miss its dramatic connection with the opening scene, where Bedford implores the comments to ''scourge the bad revolting stars / That have consented unto Henry's death.'' He prophesies that Henry's soul will reappear as ''A far more glorious star . . . / Than Julius Caesar'' [I. i. 55-6], but the new star that appears is Joan, whom the French worship as ''Bright star of Venus, fall'n down on the earth'' [I. ii. 144]. When she holds up the burning torch, she appears as a comet that prophesies England's ruin:

> See, noble Charles, the beacon of our friend;
> The burning torch in yonder turret stands.
> Now shine it like a comet of revenge,
> A prophet to the fall of all our foes!
>
> [III. ii. 29-32]

As a dramatic symbol, her gesture points forward to her death at the stake. Now at the height of her triumph, she is ''on the top, thrusting out a torch burning'' (stage direction [III. ii. 25]); after her fall, the burning torch is under her. Even though this scene is occasioned by some topical matter, Shakespeare turns it inward for his play's design. (pp. 14-15)

Another adverse judgment upon the play attacks the weakness of the plot as shown in the concluding scenes. The romantic interlude in which Suffolk gains Margaret to be both his mistress and Henry's queen seems tacked onto the tragedy of Talbot in order to introduce 2 *Henry VI*. Hardin Craig writes: ''The Suffolk-Margaret scenes . . . are intruded into the play obviously as a preparation for 2 *Henry VI*. They serve no dramatic purpose within the plot.'' Yet it is difficult to know by what dramatic conventions we may reject the ending. By the conventions of comedy, tragedy lacks a final act to resolve all in happiness; by the conventions of tragedy, comedy adds a final act to escape a tragic resolution; but the conventions of the history play are not known. If the genre is open-ended in the sense that its resolution leads to a continuation, it may still possess a unity of its own.

The importance of the concluding scenes to *1 Henry VI* itself appears if we look at the play's total shape, which, on first impression, seems merely confusing. Victory turns into defeat, then defeat into victory. One never knows when the tide of battle will turn, as Charles says in his opening words:

> Mars his true moving, even as in the heavens
> So in the earth, to this day is not known.
>
> [I. ii. 1-2]

If we stand back from the action, however, a pattern emerges. At first the action moves from England to France and back again; later it centers more on France and shifts to England only to prepare for disaster there. England's victories are marked by the deaths of her heroes. When Henry goes to France to be crowned and receive the gift of France from Talbot, he carries with him the dissension that destroys Talbot. Though at the end England has the victory, by the pattern already set up in the play that victory promises defeat. The first withdrawal from France leaves the dissension that ruins English power in France; the second withdrawal, in the person of Margaret attended by Suffolk, will ruin England herself.

Dissension reaches its climax with the appearance of Margaret. She is the new and greater Joan—one was ''the English scourge'' [I. ii. 129], the other will become ''England's bloody scourge''

[2 *Henry VI* V. i. 118]—and we watch her assume her predecessor's role. At the beginning, Joan enchants Charles, who sees her as the ''Divinest creature'' [I. vi. 4] and to whom he yields, burning with desire; at the end, Margaret enchants Henry, who is astonished even by her description:

> So am I driven by breath of her renown
> Either to suffer shipwreck or arrive
> Where I may have fruition of her love.
>
> [V. v. 7-9]

After the death of Talbot and his English forces, Lucy exclaims that ''from their ashes shall be rear'd / A phoenix that shall make all France afeard'' [IV. vii. 92-3]; instead, Margaret becomes that phoenix who will make all England afraid. The scene of Joan's burning is followed by one in which Margaret infects Henry with ''inflaming love'' [V. v. 82]. Dissension that had been seen in the quarrels between Gloucester and Winchester, and between York and Suffolk, now appears within the king himself through desire for Margaret:

> but this I am assur'd,
> I feel such sharp dissension in my breast,
> Such fierce alarums both of hope and fear,
> As I am sick with working of my thoughts.
>
> [V. v. 83-6]

This last and greatest example of dissension, now in the heart of England, ensures England's fall. For this reason the concluding scenes adopt some comic conventions such as peace and preparation for marriage, but with a certain irony that may make them appear irrelevant.

The deliberate craftsmanship that is shown in the play's language, in the handling of episodes, and in the structure of its plot suggests that it goes beyond the limited artistic purpose of merely dramatizing the chronicles. Analysis of how it treats history reveals how it may best be understood in generic terms as a history play. (pp. 17-19)

The matter of history upon which the play imposes dramatic form comprises, primarily, the historical events recorded in the chronicles. It includes also the interpretation given those events by the chroniclers, both the general themes that they trace in the events and the larger conception that they add to those events. It involves a knowledge not only of what the chroniclers read in history but also what they went there to read. It is important to consider how this matter—the events together with the significances given them—appears in the play, in order to understand how the play becomes an imitation of history.

In the scene in which Mortimer informs York of his claim to the crown, he gives almost straightforward history:

> Henry the Fourth, grandfather to this king,
> Depos'd his nephew Richard, Edward's son,
> The first-begotten and the lawful heir
> Of Edward king, the third of that descent . . .
>
> [II. v. 63-6]

and so he goes on for another thirty lines. That York would be ''ignorant and cannot guess'' [II. v. 60] why his father was executed and Mortimer imprisoned seems a feeble excuse to inform the audience, rather than York, of its past history. Hall records only that in 1425 ''Edmonde Mortimer, the last Erle of Marche of that name (whiche long tyme had been restrained from his liberty, and finally waxed lame) diseased without issue, whose inheritaunce discended to lorde Richarde Plantagenet, sonne and heire to Richard erle of Cambridge, beheded, as you have heard before, at the toune of Southhampton." Being told by the dying Mortimer, these historical facts gain an urgency and confirmation not given by the chronicles; and being told to York, who now realizes his claim to the throne, they become intensely dramatic. In one powerful line Mortimer tells him: "Thou art my heir; the rest I wish thee gather" [II. v. 96], suggesting that York infer what he might say had he the strength, but also enjoining him to claim the crown. Past and future are brought to bear upon the present moment in the contrast between the aged Mortimer who forsakes all past ambition and the young York who now awakens to future ambition. One is "Swift-winged with desire to get a grave" [II. v. 15], the other, to get a crown; thus, in *3 Henry VI* the king will speak of York as one "winged with desire" [I. i. 267] for kingship.

Being thus more than a spokesman for past history, Mortimer becomes a dramatic symbol within the play. Without having seen the play on the stage, one can only imagine how effective his presence must be in relation to the whole play. The "dead march" and the funeral of Henry V that stand as prelude to the action define the world of the play: the actions of men are played in the shadow of sudden, violent death. Then follows dissension in England and fighting in France; and now, at the play's still center, the dying Mortimer, a ghost from England's past, woos death in loving words:

> Yet are these feet, whose strengthless stay is numb,
> Unable to support this lump of clay,
> Swift-winged with desire to get a grave. . . .
> But now the arbitrator of despairs,
> Just Death, kind umpire of men's miseries,
> With sweet enlargement doth dismiss me hence.
>   [II. v. 13-15, 28-30]

At the beginning of the play, Talbot "craved death / Rather than I would be so vile esteem'd" [I. iv. 32-3] as to be cheaply ransomed, and in all his action he braves death. Near the end, he smiles at Death:

> Triumphant death, smear'd with captivity,
> Young Talbot's valour makes me smile at thee.
>   [IV. vii. 3-4]

When Talbot sees his son dead, Death laughs at him; but the same moment brings his triumph over Death:

> Thou antic Death, which laugh'st us here to scorn,
> Anon, from thy insulting tyranny,
> Coupled in bonds of perpetuity,
> Two Talbots, winged through the lither sky,
> In thy despite shall scape mortality.
>   [IV. vii. 18-22]

At the beginning of the play, Henry V's body is borne upon the stage; in the middle the aged Mortimer is brought in a chair; and near the end Old Talbot is led by a servant. Mortimer's words to his jailers, "Direct mine arms I may embrace his neck" [II. v. 37], find an echo in Talbot's words to the servant: "Come, come, and lay him in his father's arms" [IV. vii. 29]. Bedford's dying question, "What is the trust or strength of foolish man?" [III. ii. 112] finds its answer in Mortimer's aged figure:

> These eyes, like lamps whose wasting oil is spent,
> Wax dim, as drawing to their exigent;
> Weak shoulders, overborne with burdening grief,
> And pithless arms, like to a withered vine
> That droops his sapless branches to the ground.
>   [II. v. 8-12]

Mortimer's state prefigures Talbot's when no longer supported by the soldiers who are "his substance, sinews, arms, and strength" [II. iii. 63]. Such relationships are too carefully patterned not to be deliberate. (pp. 21-4)

The dramatic control that Shakespeare exercises over events as he gives them dramatic form extends to the meanings or themes that the chroniclers saw in history. (p. 24)

Hall's major theme, which he hammers with repeated emphasis, is the danger of dissension. . . . The moral lesson fervently upheld in Hall becomes in the play an impassioned exploration of the nature and working of dissension. At the beginning the Messenger relates how the English forces are defeated and Talbot captured because of factions at home. The quarrel between Gloucester and Winchester develops until the Mayor reads the Riot Act and the king pleads with them. Their dissension is resolved, at least by Gloucester, only to be replaced by that conflict between York and Somerset which cannot be resolved. (pp. 24-5)

The moral lesson is here for anyone who wants what modern educational jargon calls "the take-home package." Its dramatic significance, however, is to make the present moment ominous and the future to be dreaded. While Talbot's death soon confirms Exeter's prophecy, the warning against dissension as such figures little in our response. The dissension elaborated in the previous scenes merely renders Talbot's death poignant. Earlier, he triumphs in life; now, in death. (p. 25)

Shakespeare's dramatic control over his matter extends to the larger religious conception into which the chroniclers fit English history. Ribner takes that conception to be Shakespeare's, by arguing that in the *Henry VI* plays the dramatist's purpose is to suggest "that all of this [the chaos of the Wars of the Roses] is God's punishment visited upon England for Henry Bolingbroke's deposition and murder of King Richard II a half-century before" [see excerpt below, 1965]. . . . He believes that Shakespeare presents "a portrait of decades of civil chaos as a reminder to his contemporary Englishmen of what might again return upon the death of the now old and childless Elizabeth, should the succession to the throne be left uncertain and powerful nobles again vie with one another for the crown." . . . Tillyard gives evidence for this purpose in the play: "We are never allowed to forget that, as Hall said in his preface, 'King Henry the Fourth was the beginning and root of the great discord and division'" . . . , and he cites the dying Mortimer's speech:

> Henry the Fourth, grandfather to this king,
> Depos'd his nephew Richard, Edward's son,
> The first-begotten and the lawful heir
> Of Edward king, the third of that descent;
> During whose reign the Percies of the north,
> Finding his usurpation most unjust,
> Endeavour'd my advancement to the throne.
>   [II. v. 63-9]

Yet this is the only place in *1 Henry VI* where we are reminded of Bolingbroke's deposition of Richard, and the lines refer only to Mortimer's ambitions, not to the discord and dissension shown in the play. Tillyard believes further that the play expresses Hall's providential view of history: "Behind all the confusion of civil war . . . is the belief that the world is a part of the eternal law and that earthly mutability . . . is itself a part

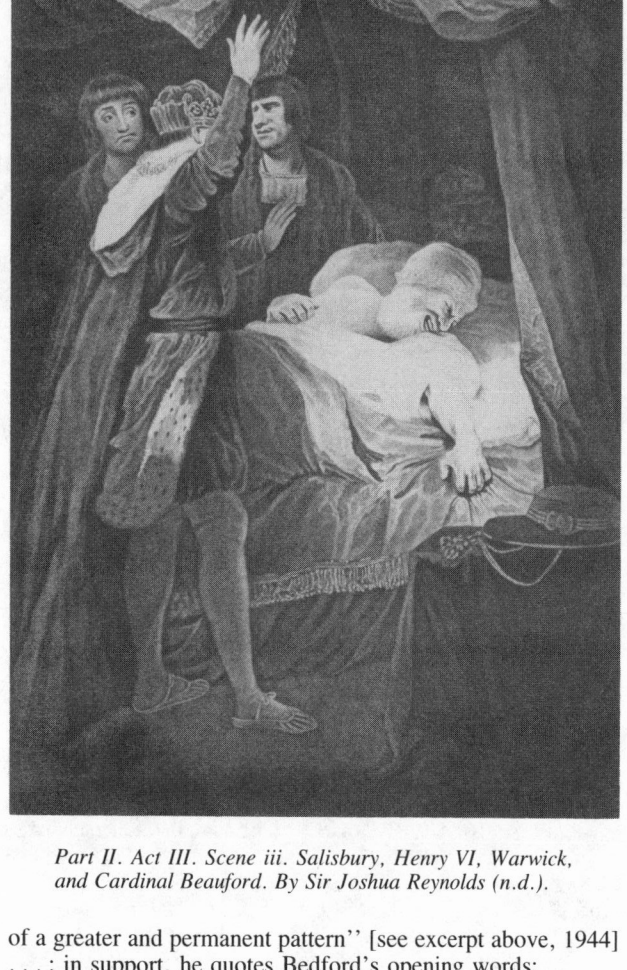

*Part II. Act III. Scene iii. Salisbury, Henry VI, Warwick,
and Cardinal Beauford. By Sir Joshua Reynolds (n.d.).*

of a greater and permanent pattern'' [see excerpt above, 1944]
. . . ; in support, he quotes Bedford's opening words:

> Hung be the heavens with black, yield day to night!
> Comets, importing change of times and states,
> Brandish your crystal tresses in the sky
> And with them scourge the bad revolting stars
> That have consented unto Henry's death!
>
>   [I. i. 1-5]

If a belief in ultimate order is behind these lines, it is far behind.
Immediately and powerfully present is the belief that the "bad
revolting stars" govern events: the phrase significantly links
the present moment with that first fall of Lucifer and his host
from heaven. The power in the comets that Bedford invokes
had been Henry's when his "sparkling eyes, replete with wrathful fire, / . . . drove back his enemies"; only his ghost may
be invoked to "Combat with adverse planets in the heavens"
[I. i. 12-13, 54]. Now the "adverse planets" rule, and that
"star-cross'd" warrior, Talbot, laments at his death, "O malignant and ill-boding stars!" [IV. v. 6].

The providential view of history is expressed only negatively
by its inversion in the play. Death, dissension, defeat, and
despair mark the world revealed in the opening scene. In the
following scene, the opening words that note the ominous disorder in the planet Mars suggest a world governed by mutability
such as we see illustrated in the repeated reversals in the action.
The power of Mars is joined with that of his consort, that
"Bright star of Venus, fall'n down on the earth" [I. ii. 144]

who appears as Joan. Like Spenser's Duessa, she shines in
"borrowed light" (*The Faerie Queene* I. viii. 49). Her heroic
role, which later writers exploit, is controlled throughout the
play by the bawdy reference, most blatantly when Charles
explains how he spent the night "Within her quarter and mine
own precinct / . . . employ'd in passing to and fro," and then
adds lamely, "About relieving of the sentinels" [II. i. 68-70].
She is a witch who can raise "familiar spirits . . . / Out of the
powerful regions under earth" [V. iii. 10-11] and in the air,
as the Folio reference to her as "Joan of Aire" [V. iv. 49]
may indicate. She displays her demonic power when she amazes
Charles, but even more clearly when she enchants Talbot until
he cries out:

> My thoughts are whirled like a potter's wheel;
> I know not where I am nor what I do.
> A witch by fear, not force, like Hannibal,
> Drives back our troops and conquers as she lists.
>
>   [I. v. 19-22]

In the agony of defeat, he cries: "Heavens, can you suffer hell
so to prevail?" [I. v. 9]; the heavens can, and hell prevails.
In this satanic world, human nature is a helpless prey to malignant powers. (pp. 26-9)

The scope of *1 Henry VI* meets the challenge of history as fully
as possible. In the opening scene it extends the historical events
to include almost all of Henry's reign; its subject, the war with
France, would provoke distracting emotions and topical reference; and it begins with the aftermath of Henry V's death,
a disastrous time that invited the official predestinarian interpretation of history. Shakespeare seems deliberately to explore
the potentialities of "play" to control "history." For this reason it becomes possible to separate the two: to see how language
suddenly becomes full of conceits in order to make a dramatic
point, how plot uses character as a dramatic symbol, and how
it includes deliberate fiction to force a certain structure. In
addition, dissension can be isolated as a controlling idea: first
we witness a quarrel among the nobility; then Exeter, like a
choric commentator, prophesies ensuing disaster, and afterwards his prophecy is fulfilled. In reading the play, we become
conscious of the artifice that is used to shape chronicle history.

In *2 Henry VI* "history" and "play" are more closely integrated, and the stress falls upon "play." Shakespeare accepts
his historical matter instead of struggling against it, and the
play's form arises out of the matter rather than being imposed
upon it. (p. 32)

The marriage that brings a dramatic resolution to the dissension
in *1 Henry VI* provides a comic beginning for *2 Henry VI*. At
the end of the former, the king reveals that he is "sick with
working of my thoughts" [V. v. 86] through his passion for
Margaret; now he is, in York's contemptuous phrase, "surfeiting in joys of love" [*2 Henry VI*, I. i. 251]. Margaret greets
him:

> Great King of England, and my gracious lord,
> The mutual conference that my mind hath had,
> by day, by night, waking and in my dreams,
> In courtly company or at my beads,
> With you, mine alder-liefest sovereign,
> Makes me the bolder to salute my king
> With ruder terms, such as my wit affords
> And over-joy of heart doth minister.
>
>   [I. i. 24-31]

He replies:

> Her sight did ravish, but her grace in speech,
> Her words y-clad with wisdom's majesty,
> Makes me from wond'ring fall to weeping joys,
> Such is the fulness of my heart's content.
>
> [I. i. 32-5]

He is very sick indeed, for the greeting that he calls "words y-clad with wisdom's majesty" is only the inflated rhetoric of Margaret's claim that she greets him boldly because she has been thinking of him day and night. The term "alder-liefest" that grates upon the ear—it is Shakespeare's only use of the term—suggests affectation rather than affection, and the archaism "y-clad" belongs to the artificial style mocked in *Love's Labour's Lost*. Margaret's role suggests that of Joan in *1 Henry VI*, before whom the French court yields in lust and astonishment. There is fine irony in having all the English court kneel, praying "Long live Queen Margaret, England's happiness!" [I. i. 37] to one who proves herself to be "England's bloody scourge" [V. i. 118] as she presides over most of their deaths. Gloucester points out the ominous inferences of this opening scene in his outburst of grief to the lords:

> shameful is this league!
> Fatal this marriage, cancelling your fame,
> Blotting your names from books of memory,
> Razing the characters of your renown,
> Defacing monuments of conquer'd France,
> Undoing all, as all had never been!
>
> [I. i. 98-103]

The marriage proves fatal to him and to all the lords to whom he speaks. In contrast to the tragic beginning of *1 Henry VI*, this play opens with marriage, a ritual that in comedy affirms order and final harmony. This marriage, however, ruins Gloucester, who, being Protector of England, alone wields the power to maintain order. With his defeat, order gives way to chaos.

A comparison of the opening scenes, which correspond in their larger outlines, reveals the differences between the plays. Public ceremony with its formal ritual (funeral: marriage) is interrupted by news of English losses in France (the reports of the Messengers: the announcement of the marriage terms), is marred by dissension among the nobility (chiefly between Gloucester and Winchester), and concludes with the nobles determined to serve either the realm or themselves. In *1 Henry VI* this material is organized around a single theme, dissension, in a simple, linear progression. The quarrel between Gloucester and Winchester shows the nature of the theme; its dangers are pointed out when Bedford invokes Henry V's ghost to "Prosper this realm, keep it from civil broils" [*1 Henry VI*, I. i. 53] and then confirmed when the Messenger tells of disasters in France because "here you maintain several factions" [I. i. 71]. *2 Henry VI* handles the working of dissension in a more complex way. In opposing the king's marriage, Gloucester wins the support of Salisbury, Warwick, and York, and apparently the others except Winchester. When he leaves, he is denounced by Winchester, Buckingham, and Somerset. Winchester, when he leaves to get the support of Suffolk, is denounced by Buckingham and Somerset. After they leave, they are denounced by Salisbury, Warwick, and York; and after Salisbury and Warwick leave, York denounces them all. His final lines, threatening that "force perforce I'll make him yield the crown, / Whose bookish rule hath pull'd fair England down" [*2 Henry VI*, I. i. 258-59], turn dissension against the king himself. This sequence displays dissension first in an open quarrel between Gloucester and Winchester, as in *1 Henry VI*, and then as an allegorical pageant, when Salisbury says of the departing Winchester followed by Buckingham and Somerset: "Pride went before, ambition follows him" [I. i. 180]. Finally, it expresses dissension as a conflict within York.

York's long soliloquy [I. i. 214-59] may well be Shakespeare's first effort to create character; it certainly marks a major breakthrough in the imitation of history. York embodies here the allegorical figures of both Pride and Ambition. Pride, his sense of injured merit, leads him to claim England as his flesh:

> Methinks the realms of England, France,
>   and Ireland,
> Bear that proportion to my flesh and blood
> As did the fatal brand Althaea burnt
> Unto the prince's heart of Calydon.
>
> [I.i.232-35]

When Talbot boasts that "his substance, sinews, arms and strength" [*1 Henry VI*, II. iii. 63] are the English forces, he projects an image of himself as composed of many men that is self-effacing and impersonal. He serves England; but York claims England as his own: he speaks of "flesh *and* blood," and of the heart rather than the body. Pride arouses Ambition to seize the crown:

> A day will come when York shall claim his own;
> And therefore I will take the Nevils' parts,
> And make a show of love to proud Duke Humphrey,
> And when I spy advantage, claim the crown,
> For that's the golden mark I seek to hit.
>
> [*2 Henry VI*, I. i. 239-43]

His determination to seize time recalls his claim to Somerset in *1 Henry VI* to prove his worth "Were growing time once ripened to my will" [*1 Henry VI*, II. iv. 99]; now he reaffirms it as he counsels himself: "Then, York, be still awhile, till time do serve" [*2 Henry VI*, I. i. 248]. Up to this point in the two plays, character and event are distinct: Bedford, Salisbury, Talbot, and the rest are victims of the time. History, that "change of times and states" mentioned in the second line of *1 Henry VI*, dominates men's lives. Now there appears one who will shape history according to his own will and desire. Through him, history takes on human form. In contrast to the other historical figures, he is the first *political* character. (pp. 34-7)

In contrast to Gloucester, who sees in his position the virtues he upholds, York with passionate intensity sees himself as the laboring spider that weaves snares to trap his enemies, the starved snake that stings the hearts of those who cherish him, and the madman who destroys:

> I will stir up in England some black storm
> Shall blow ten thousand souls to heaven or hell;
> And this fell tempest shall not cease to rage
> Until the golden circuit on my head,
> Like to the glorious sun's transparent beams,
> Do calm the fury of this mad-bred flaw.
>
> [III. i. 349-54]

Far from being the passive victim of a "plotted tragedy," he will be its creator.

Henry's lament, "O God, seest Thou this, and bearest so long?" [II. i. 151], is the play's epigraph, for the action reveals God's forbearance, not His judgment. In place of God's judgment, we see the commons taking judgment upon themselves and forcing the king to banish Suffolk. The providential view of history is invoked in the play by Winchester, who finds "God's secret judgment" [III. ii. 31] in the murder that he planned. When Henry receives Cade's head, his response, "Great God, how just art Thou!" [V. i. 68], is made in the presence of York, whose fury breaks out in the next moment. The frequent appeals to God only stress the isolation of events from His guidance. When Henry takes the protectorship to himself, he claims that "God shall be my hope / My stay, my guide, and lantern to my feet" [II. iii. 24-5]; but we see Margaret and the others assuming these roles. God's intercession is repeatedly invoked, but only for the sake of dramatic irony. (pp. 38-9)

In *1 Henry VI*, with its emphasis upon the element of "history," the structure is thematic in its straightforward representation of the concept of dissension; and in *2 Henry VI*, with its emphasis upon "play," the structure is cumulative, handling the same theme in a complex manner. *3 Henry VI* uses both structures and shows a mastery of both elements of the history play.

The play's mastery of history may be shown by examining its relation to the chronicles. Surprisingly, it seems to follow them very closely.... [But] analysis of even the first three scenes shows how significantly it departs from them.

The opening scene combines York's victory at the Battle of St. Albans in 1455 with his claim to the crown in the Parliament of 1460. According to the chronicles, Parliament agreed after lengthy debate that Henry should possess the throne during his lifetime, with York as heir apparent. In omitting York's passionate defense of his right to the crown, Shakespeare departs radically and significantly from history. (pp. 47-8)

In the world of the play, right does not matter; all that matters is the rule of force and the desire for revenge. Henry asserts his "right" in terms of force:

> I am the son of Henry the Fifth,
> Who made the Dauphin and the French to stoop,
> And seiz'd upon their towns and provinces.
>
> [*3 Henry VI,* I. i. 107-09]

He cites as proof of his title's soundness that "Henry the Fourth by conquest got the crown" [I. i. 132]; and he is forced to admit, "I know not what to say; my title's weak" [I. i. 134]. Exeter is resurrected from *1 Henry VI*, where he warned against York's dissension, in order now to support the Duke: "His is the right, and therefore pardon me" [I. i. 148]. Clifford supports the king only through desire for revenge:

> King Henry, be thy title right or wrong,
> Lord Clifford vows to fight in thy defence.
> May that ground gape, and swallow me alive,
> Where I shall kneel to him that slew my father!
>
> [I. i. 159-62]

That Henry, rather than Parliament, should yield the succession to York makes a nice ironic point. The wheel has come full circle when Bolingbroke's heir is brought to that position to which he had brought Richard II. (p. 49)

While the opening scene shows Shakespeare's adaptation of historical events for his own dramatic purposes, the second, in which York breaks his oath, shows his control over their thematic significance.... Holinshed writes of York's death: "Manie deemed that this miserable end chanced to the duke

of Yorke, as a due punishment for breaking his oath of allegiance unto his sovereigne lord king Henrie: but others held him discharged thereof, bicause he obteined a dispensation from the pope, by such suggestion as his procurators made unto him, whereby the same oth was adjudged void, as that which was received unadvisedlie, to the prejudice of himself, and disheriting of all his posterie." In the play, Margaret accuses York of breaking his oath, but this only one of many charges, and one of which she is guilty. Henry's selling of his son's birthright precedes York's oath-breaking, as, in *2 Henry VI*, his breaking of his word precipitates York's first claim to the crown.

York's easy oath-breaking—in an anti-Roman touch, he obtains his dispensation from Richard—is only the first of a number of oaths that are broken in this play. "Wind-changing Warwick" [V. i. 57] is perjured when he readily forsakes his oath to support York's claim to the crown [III. iii. 181-98]. Clarence is doubly perjured, to his brothers and to Warwick. Edward is thrice-perjured: he breaks his oath to the Mayor of York that he seeks only his dukedom [IV. vii. 23-4].... In the world of the play, Edward's remark that "for a kingdom any oath may be broken: / I would break a thousand oaths to reign one year" [I. ii. 16-17] guides all men's actions; and Richard's cynical rejoinder, "God forbid your Grace should be forsworn" [I. ii. 18] becomes the norm. (pp. 51-2)

Even more effective in relation to the play's form than such control over thematic significance is the patterning of events in the third scene. Shakespeare simply changes the chronicle order of the deaths of Rutland and York.... By having Rutland slain before York, Shakespeare is free to invent the detail of Margaret's offering the father the napkin stained with his son's blood:

> Look, York: I stain'd this napkin with the blood
> That valiant Clifford with his rapier's point
> Made issue from the bosom of the boy;
> And if thine eyes can water for his death,
> I give thee this to dry thy cheeks withal.
>
> [I. iv. 79-83]

Her mock becomes the focus of his rage against her:

> O tiger's heart wrapp'd in a woman's hide!
> How couldst thou drain the life-blood of the child,
> To bid the father wipe his eyes withal,
> And yet be seen to bear a woman's face?
>
> [I. iv. 137-40]

It also provides the pathos of his death:

> Keep thou the napkin, and go boast of this;
> And if thou tell'st the heavy story right,
> Upon my soul, the hearers will shed tears;
> Yea, even my foes will shed fast-falling tears
> And say "Alas, it was a piteous deed!"
>
> [I. iv. 159-63]

In the chronicles, York's death remains an exemplum that shows the consequences of too much boldness or of the breaking of an oath. In the play, the inversion of the deaths lifts York's to the level of "The True Tragedy of Richard Duke of York," the play's original title. His grief turns back to Talbot's grief for his son and forward, in an ironic reversal, to Margaret's grief for her son. The mirror scene at the Battle of Towton, where the horror of war unfolds in the father's grief for the son whom he has slain, displays such grief emblematically. Besides thus patterning the action, the "heavy story" of Margaret's ''piteous deed'' transforms Richard from a loyal and loving son into that furious avenger who becomes Richard III.

Through such dramatic control over the chronicle matter, *3 Henry VI* incorporates and extends the simple thematic structure of *I Henry VI* and the cumulative structure of *2 Henry VI*. Its action becomes strongly patterned, with the end of each act pointing to Richard. Act I treats the fall of the house of York, and York's death completes the action, except for the presence of his sons, particularly of Richard. At the beginning of Act II, Richard assumes Clifford's role as one who seeks revenge for his father's death, and the action shows the rise of the house of York. In the battle that follows, Warwick, George, and Edward fall exhausted, as did York in the first cycle; but this time Richard rouses them to victory. Act III shows the triumph of the house of York, with Henry's capture and Edward's marriage to Elizabeth. Though Warwick's and Margaret's missions to France leave unfinished business, the cycle of action is complete, again except for the presence of Richard. (pp. 52-4)

Act IV combines the fall and the rise of the house of York. At its center, the queen's lament at Edward's capture completes the action; but then Richard comes to rescue him and they recapture Henry. Act V shows the final triumph of the house of York. . . . Action is so carefully designed that, except for the presence of Richard, the play would break into distinct parts. Acts IV and V, for example, would make a separate play: King Edward's marriage is marred by quarrels with his brothers and by the threatened invasion of Warwick, Prince Edward, and Margaret on behalf of Henry VI. In the central action, Edward is captured, his queen flees, and Henry is restored to the throne. At the end, Henry is captured, and, through the renewed friendship among the brothers, Warwick and Prince Edward are slain, Margaret is exiled, and this ''play'' concludes with ''stately triumphs, [and] mirthful comic shows'' [V. vi. 43], as King Edward with his new heir celebrates his own reinstatement. (p. 54)

In addition to the thematically simple and cumulative structures, the play upholds another, as suggested by the Quarto's extended title: ''The true Tragedie of Richard Duke of Yorke, and the death of good King Henrie the Sixt.'' At first this title seems oddly given: York's death takes place in the first act, and Henry's murder is only a consequence of Edward's final victory, ''a bloody supper'' [V. v. 85] that Richard enoys before he takes part in the final festivities. Yet these two events frame the entire action.

The play opens with the murder of York's son, followed by the father's murder; it ends with the murder of Henry's son, followed by Henry's murder. The first murders provoke Richard to seek revenge: his great love for his father and hatred of ''that cruel child-killer'' [II. ii. 112], Clifford, lead him at the end to slay the son and father. The difference between the beginning and end of the play is Richard. The chronicle of his metamorphosis from the loving son and brother into the murderer of son and father is central to the play. The scope of the action may be defined as the difference between the ritual slaying of York, with its formal pageantry, its parody of the Crucifixion, its elaborate mockery, and its formal laments, and the private murder of Henry, which is intense, personal, and almost comic in intent and execution. The terms ''true tragedy'' and ''death'' suggest this difference. The play moves from a world where death is accompanied with dignity, compassion,

and pathos to a world where death is brutally mocked. (pp. 60-1)

A. C. Hamilton, in his The Early Shakespeare, *The Huntington Library, 1967, 237 p.*

RONALD S. BERMAN (essay date 1962)

[*Berman contends that the relationship between fathers and sons provides a central, unifying theme in 1, 2, and 3 Henry VI. He maintains that, beyond the questions of legitimacy and birthright raised in the plays, Shakespeare focuses on the idea of moral inheritance. With respect to birthright, Berman continues, both Yorkists and Lancastrians have legitimate claims to the throne, but neither side possesses the political and moral virtues required to rule the kingdom. Berman views the sacred relationship of fathers and sons as so corrupt in Henry VI's reign that one generation transmits to the next not only its birthright, but also its blood hatred and spiritual evil. Robert B. Pierce (1971) also regards the idea of moral inheritance as central to the Henry VI trilogy, and Marilyn French (1981) discusses the importance of the concept of legitimacy in the plays.*]

The feeling of critics has been that [Shakespeare] has not disciplined his material [in *Henry VI*] to the point where each play has either a consistent theme or a clear-cut relationship to its companion pieces, yet a reading of these plays may lead us to think otherwise. Our reception of them should depend on our recognition of their historical awareness. What they seem simply enough to state is that history is a painful process in which the individual more often than not acts the part of Pharaoh; continually afflicted by tragedy, he refuses the enlightenment of experience. Although the plays are by Shakespearian standards immature, they share the perceptiveness of Aeschylus and Sophocles, for whom the most significant tragic act was that emanating from guilt of the past, and affecting the family and the state. Thus the vehicle that Shakespeare has selected is the relationship of fathers and sons within a history-making dynasty.

The first play furnishes a dramatic perspective of spiritual decadence. Since the deposition of Richard II there has been an immoral taint on the monarchy. The long-deferred retribution for this ''original sin'' is to be visited on the Plantagenet line. Ironically, the rights of birth, violated in the time of Richard, will be instrumental as the cause of tragedy when asserted now. In this first play the house of Plantagenet has reached a point where neither branch is fitted for its pretentions. The Lancastrians have been denied the political virtues, and the Yorkists the moral virtues of kingship. The rights of inheritance, which delude the protagonists of both houses, are not enough. The tragedy is one not only of the misfortunes of princes, as Professor Tillyard has pointed out [see excerpt above, 1944], but of a realm destined to suffer because none of the aspirants to power has that combination of piety and power necessary to purge England of a hereditary curse. (pp. 487-88)

[*I Henry VI*] does not have the structural coherence of the later history plays. But the themes which are basic to its meaning foliate and become more precise. The famous scene in Temple Garden (II. iv) revolves about the arguments for and against the attainder of Richard Plantagenet, the future Duke of York. While Warwick introduces the consideration of the descent of Plantagenet,

> His grandfather was Lionel Duke of Clarence,
> Third son to the third Edward King of England;
> Spring crestless yoemen from so deep a root?
>
> [*1 Henry VI*, II. iv. 83-5]

Somerset responds that it is not the lineal descent of Plantagenet, but his direct inheritance from his father that marks him as corrupt. The treason of Richard, Earl of Cambridge, father of Plantagenet, has stigmatized him: "His trespass yet lives guilty in thy blood" [II. iv. 94]. York's position between his father and his own son, Richard III, suggests that this judgment may not be wrong. The question of the birthright becomes the great wedge into the solidarity of the state. The association, underscored by Shakespeare, between the rights (and guilt) of kindred, and civil war, indicates that the spiritual chaos of rebellion is not confined to a particular moment of time, but rather that it descends in blood, and affects the lives of the entire nation. This open breach, impelled by the guilt of a father and son, as Warwick prophesies,

> Shall send between the red rose and the white
> A thousand souls to death and deadly night.
>
> [II. iv. 126-27]

The next important theme, contingent both dramatically and morally upon the above, is that of the persecution of kindred, in the scene of Mortimer's death and "benediction". Like Plantagenet's justification of his right to Warwick and Salisbury (*2 Henry VI*, II. ii), Mortimer's emphasizes the rights of blood. His Biblical characterization of Richard II, "the first-begotten and the lawful heir" [II. v. 95], reminds us of the ultimate origins of the Plantagenet tragedy. And his attempt to justify his own birthright ("next by birth and parentage" [II. v. 73]) reveals that the original deposition of the "first-begotten" engendered evil among kindred of the next generation. The play is beginning to come to terms with the realities in the idea of inheritance, which is the superficial pattern of its development. There is more involved, however, than "honour and inheritance". Mortimer has been the heir not only to the inheritance of the throne, but to the fatal hatred and guilt surrounding it. His is not an image of reverent age and guidance, but of the man whose testament is grief,

> Even like a man new haled from the rack,
> So fare my limbs with long imprisonment;
> And these grey locks, the pursuivants of death,
> Nestor-like aged in an age of care . . .
>
> [II. v. 3-6]

and whose benediction ("Thou art my heir"[II. v. 96]) is destruction.

The rights of inheritance are delusive in another sense as well. Legitimacy itself is ambiguous; the abstract "right" of birth alone confers no virtue. We can see that the spiritual decadence of the Plantagenet line transcends legitimacy, that moral bastardy becomes increasingly dominant. The idea of moral bastardy comes to constitute more and more of a mocking counterpoint to the passionate claims made on behalf of the privileges of kinship, and derides the righteousness of the protagonists. The Mortimer interview and the gradual moral hardening of York are meant, I believe, to show that justification of the inheritance really implies the denial of kindred.

The play proceeds with swift interweavings of the blood themes. One important statement is in the scene of the brawl between the servants of Gloucester and those of Winchester. This scene might almost be felt to be gratuitous, yet it does not fail in its way to delineate the loyalties and hatreds of fathers and sons:

> And ere that we will suffer such a prince,
> So kind a father of the commonweal,
> To be disgraced by an inkhorn mate,
> We and our wives and children all will fight
> And have our bodies slaughter'd by thy foes.
>
> [III. i. 97-101]

The conflict is widening from the kindred of the royal line to the "kindred" of the state. Gloucester, the "shepherd", the "father of the commonweal", will be the father for whom the sons of the nation will atone, since he is all that stand between them and anarchy. Exeter, who summarizes the moral direction of the drama, ends this scene with a speech of particular significance:

> As fester'd members rot but by degree,
> Till bones and flesh and sinews fall away,
> So will this base and envious discord breed.
>
> [III. i. 191-93]
> (pp. 488-90)

The tragedy of fathers and sons takes on a new aspect in the second play. Spiritual corruption has disfigured court and kingdom; a web of disunified, conflicting loyalties and interests enmeshes the state. To be loyal to Henry is to be disloyal to the integrity of the realm. Most important, in order to demonstrate devotion and filial piety man must change the moral standards of loyalty to those of the vendetta. Loyalty among kindred disappears; in its place is planted the idea, which is to grow in *3 Henry VI* and ripen in *Richard III*, that blood relationships, the sacred obligations of the past, are inconveniences in the way of ambition. In short, we see the spiritual chaos of rebellion.

This play receives its immediate impetus from Gloucester's passionate denunciation of the "fatal marriage". The inheritance of Henry VI is more than material; it is the symbol of a lifetime's work and of a glorious reign. It comprises "labours" and "honours" which must not die. The extraordinary emotion of both Warwick and York is evidence that the inheritance is part of their own flesh and blood. In renouncing the French inheritance, Henry denies his claim to loyalty. Warwick is prepared for rebellion because his own symbolic fatherhood of the French conquests is denied. He takes care actually to use the language of fatherhood, "and are the cities, that I got with wounds . . ." [*2 Henry VI*, I. i. 121].

The second strain in the theme of loyalty is the rebelliousness of the Duchess of Gloucester. In I. ii, her treason to the blood of her kinsman is like Lady Macbeth's—yet Gloucester keeps true to the argument of conscience, "as I am his kinsman and his subject". The contagion of disloyalty continues to be exhibited in the entirely inferior but nevertheless decisive scene of the combat between Peter and Horner, master and man. (Their own symbolical relationship contains a good deal of that between father and son, considering the economic-social relationships of the time.) From nobleman to plebeian the revolt against the king, the "father" of the realm, begins to emerge. Its next appearance is in the more dangerous resolution of Warwick and Salisbury to disdain Henry and accept York as king. Warwick's speech (II. ii) is pregnant with allusions to the birthright of Richard, and contains the masterful irony of the line on York's sons:

> What plain proceeding is more plain than this?
> Henry doth claim the crown from John of Gaunt
> The fourth son; York claims it from the third.
> Till Lionel's issue fails, his should not reign:
> It fails not yet, but flourishes in thee
> And in thy sons, fair slips of such a stock.
> Then, father Salisbury, kneel we together;
> And in this private plot be we the first
> That shall salute our rightful sovereign
> With honour of his birthright to the crown.
>
> [II. ii. 53-62]

By now we can see that such legalistic logic is a delusion. The real pattern of inheritance is not the transmission of the birthright, but the transmission of spiritual evil. York reveals this plainly in his answering speech, when he couples the idea of inheritance with the great underlying themes of blood-hatred:

> But I am not your king
> Till I be crown'd and that my sword be stain'd
> With heart-blood of the house of Lancaster.
>
> [II. ii. 64-6]
> (pp. 490-91]

The spiritual debasement of the idea of kinship is not, however, complete. The travesty of "blood" in Jack Cade's manifesto (IV. ii) of his birth adds a telling counterpoint to the overt themes of the play. Our experience of Cade, like our experience with the moral bastardy of the various conspiring agents, allows us to look at the pretentions of inheritance in the same sardonic light as Dick and Smith:

> *Cade.* We John Cade, so termed of our
> supposed father,—
> *Dick.* [Aside] Or rather, of stealing a cade of
> herrings.
> *Cade.* For our enemies shall fall before us,
> inspired with the spirit of putting down
> kings and princes,—Command silence.
> *Dick.* Silence!
> *Cade.* My father was a Mortimer,—
> *Dick.* [Aside] He was an honest man, and a
> good bricklayer.
> *Cade.* My mother a Plantagenet,—
> *Dick.* [Aside] I knew her well; she was a
> midwife.
> *Cade.* My wife descended of the Lacies,—
> *Dick.* [Aside] She was indeed, a pedlar's
> daughter, and sold many laces.
> *Smith.* [Aside] But now of late, not able to
> travel with her furred pack, she washes
> bucks here at home.
> *Cade.* Therefore am I of an honorable house.
>
> [IV. ii. 31-49]

In defense of his "honorable house", Cade resorts to the same cunning savagery as does York in defense of his "honorable house". The two are linked not only by conspiracy, but by an identical obsession which brings chaos to the realm. The comedy of Cade turns into a bitter blood-letting, in which the love of kindred is travestied in death. Lord Say and Sir John Cromer, who "loved well when they were alive" [IV. vii. 131], are decapitated, and made to kiss "at every corner" in advance of the mob. The relationship of kindred is corrupted symbolically, if not over-subtly, by the gross, passionate assertiveness of the polity's lowest element. This brutishness will from here on have more and more obvious parallels. (pp. 492-93)

[*2 Henry VI*] ends with the triumph of York, but the particularly bestial tragedy of the succeeding play's events is prophesied by Clifford in his revenge speech. The tragedy will move into its final phase: Political right leads to murder, and the necessities of loyalty to brutal, unnatural cruelty. The juxtaposition of the myths of Aeneas and Medea by Clifford condenses the intermingling of piety and barbarity.

The pattern of *3 Henry VI* is unmistakably that of irony. The spiritual disease is at its greatest heat, and under its influence man reverts to the behavior of a lower form of life. Loyalty leads to revenge, but revenge leads only to futility. There is no moral resolution, only a furious recapitulation of crime, quite unlike the ultimate synthesis of crime and "justice" of some sort even in the denouement of the revenge play. The utter, sodden concentration upon self-interest, and the single-minded "loyalty" to the dead are the last stages of spiritual degradation. The events of the play are far more telling than has been generally realized. The inheritance has been achieved by the house of York, but at the terrible price of its moral right. Finally, and most important, the full flowering of moral evil on both sides has escaped the perception of the protagonists. No tragic catharsis takes place. Instead, the protagonists left alive by the end of *3 Henry VI* are blind, cynical, and embittered, having learned nothing from tragedy except the art of existing without a moral foundation.

The first act—indeed the first scene—takes hold of the revenge obsession, never to relinquish it. Henry reminds Clifford and Northumberland that York has slaughtered their fathers. Warwick fans the flames by his taunts:

> . . . we are those which chased you from the field
> And slew your fathers, and with colours spread
> March'd through the city to the palace gates.
>
> [*3 Henry VI*, I. i. 90-2]

After Henry's sudden negation of his right the father-son relationship focuses on the obligation of a father to a son by the act of bequest. Henry's plea, "let me for this my life-time reign as king" [I. i. 171], evokes many responses, but the first, by Clifford, "what wrong is this unto the prince your son!" [I. i. 176] stands for the fundamental belief of the Lancastrians. The "blessed peacemakers" receive short shrift in the affairs of the world, and, in Westmoreland's pragmatic if obtuse words, Henry is "faint-hearted and degenerate", in whose blood "no spark of honour bides" [I. i. 183-84]. The passionate elemental nature of Margaret reduces the problem simply to the obligations of a father to his son, and even Henry sighs for Edward, "whom I unnaturally shall disinherit" [I. i. 193]. It is worth noting the necessary ambiguities of "blood" in the speech of Margaret, since they are the supreme determinants of her political rationale.

We have in the succeeding scenes of this play very nearly an embarrassment of riches for our theme. In I. ii, the ambitious sons of York overcome his qualms of honor. Richard particularly, by his ingenious sophistry and blithe savagery, reveals the intensified corruption of the house of York in its latest generation:

> An oath is of no moment, being not took
> Before a true and lawful magistrate,
> That hath authority over him that swears:
> Henry had none, but did usurp the place;
> Then, seeing 'twas he that made you to depose,
> Your oath, my lord, is vain and frivolous.
> Therefore, to arms! And, father, do but think
> How sweet a thing it is to wear a crown;
> Within whose circuit is Elysium
> And all that poets feign of bliss and joy.
> Why do we linger thus? I cannot rest
> Until the white rose that I wear be dyed
> Even in the lukewarm blood of Henry's heart.
>
> [I. ii. 22-34]

The following scene, a wonderful tear-jerker for the Elizabethan audience, alternates between rant and perspicacity. In the "best" tradition of the revenge tragedy Clifford has become a spirit of nemesis to the house of his enemies:

> The sight of any of the house of York
> Is as a fury to torment my soul;
> And till I root out their accursed line
> And leave not one alive, I live in hell.
>
> [I. iii. 30-3]

He carries out this declaration, insofar as he is able, and Rutland is dispatched amid a cloud of rhetoric.

I. iv contains one of the focal points of the Henry VI cycle, the tormented death of York. Before his death York enigmatically remarks that his ashes will bring forth "A bird that will revenge upon you all" [I. iv. 36], a warning taken all too lightly by his captors. Margaret, in fact, tempts the fates by her contemptuous dismissal of the house of York, asking, "Where are your mess of sons to back you now?" [I. iv. 73]. Her needless cruelty to York, giving to him the napkin stained with Rutland's blood, is the symbolical counterpart of the feast of Thyestes, a feast of which she too will partake.

In the second scene of Act II we find Clifford's peroration to Henry in which his description of the life of nature relates the themes of the play to the obvious laws of society. To Clifford's simple military mind any values beyond the obvious, as in the relationship of fathers and sons, are illusory:

> Unreasonable creatures feed their young;
> And though man's face be fearful to their eyes,
> Yet, in protection of their tender ones,
> Who hath not seen them, even with those wings
> Which sometime they have used with fearful flight,
> Make war with him that climb'd unto their nest,
> Offering their own lives in their young's defence?
> For shame, my liege, make them your precedent!
> Were it not pity that this goodly boy
> Should lose his birthright by his father's fault,
> And long hereafter say unto his child,
> "What my great-grandfather and grandsire got
> My careless father fondly gave away"?
>
> [II. ii. 26-38]

He and Margaret completely miss the signficance of Henry's response. Henry refuses to blind himself by the righteousness to which every other agent in the plays subscribes, responding in a stoical vein that inheritance implies virtue as well as the privilege of possession. This intensely noble expression is dismissed with typical obtuseness as "soft courage" [II. ii. 57]. The piety of Henry has not been perverted enough to command respect in the world of the play. (pp. 494-96)

The crescendo in the sacred, corrupted theme of fathers and sons comes quite at the end. The fifth act's first scene turns on Clarence's doubly perjured speech:

> Father of Warwick, know you what this
>   means? [Taking his red rose out of his hat].
> Look here, I throw my infamy at thee:
> I will not ruinate my father's house,
> Who gave his blood to lime the stones together.
>
> [V. i. 81-4]

In the great counterpart to the scene of the death of York (V. v), Edward of Lancaster is stabbed, and Margaret's speech,

> What's worse than murderer, that I may name it?
> No, no, my heart will burst, an if I speak:
> And I will speak, that so my heart may burst.
> Butchers and villains! bloody cannibals!
>
> [V. v. 58-61]

is the voice of grief and, for once, morality. We are now at the point where the acuity of grief may be most relevant in defining the madness of the actions. If the phrase "bloody cannibals" does not symbolize the nature of the house of Plantagenet, very little else will. The deepest irony of the cycle comes perhaps in the interchange immediately following:

> K. Edw.   Where's Richard gone?
> Clar.   To London, all in post; and, as I guess,
>   To make a bloody supper in the Tower.
> K. Edw.   He's sudden, if a thing comes in his
>   head,
>   Now march we hence: discharge the
>   common sort
>   With pay and thanks, and let's away to
>   London
>   And see our gentle queen how well she
>   fares:
>   By this, I hope, she hath a son for me.
>
> [V. v. 83-90]

Margaret's preceding speech was a moment of moral truth, and Richard, gone "to make a bloody supper in the Tower", reveals that it is a dramatic truth as well. There is a further irony in Edward's casual dismissal of Richard's purpose, and in the sublimely pointed last line. The sons of York accept their destiny of consuming their own race; the "bloody supper" has been the purpose of their existence. While Richard goes to feed on his own race, Edward thinks of his new generation, the inevitable victim of the cannibalism that he accepts. (pp. 496-97)

> *Ronald S. Berman, "Fathers and Sons in the Henry VI Plays," in* Shakespeare Quarterly, *Vol. XIII, No. 4, Autumn, 1962, pp. 487-97.*

S. C. SEN GUPTA   (essay date 1964)

[*An important Indian critic, Sen Gupta has written extensively on Shakespearean drama, particularly Shakespeare's tragedies and comedies. In his examination of* 1, 2, *and* 3 Henry VI, *he disputes the validity of the historical-political approach to the plays used by E. M. W. Tillyard (1944) and M. M. Reese (1961) because, he argues,* Henry VI *is more concerned with passions and the enigma of human character than with moral or political issues. Although Sen Gupta agrees that the evil of civil dissension is the leading theme of the trilogy, he disagrees with the theory that the plays reflect Shakespeare's acceptance of the so-called Tudor view of history—an interpretation offered not only by Tillyard and Reese, but also by Hermann Ulrici (1839), J. A. R. Marriott (1918), and Irving Ribner (1965), among others. In Sen Gupta's assessment, the plays are dramatic and individual rather than didactic or moralistic, particularly in their representation of history as a continuous flow of events shaped by dominant personalities. In support of his argument, Sen Gupta points out Shakespeare's enlargement of the significance of Jack Cade and Richard of Gloucester from the chronicle sources—an individualized, dramatic treatment which he believes Shakespeare would never have included had he been concerned only with demonstrating a moral thesis. For further discussion of the Cade scenes in* 2 Henry VI, *see the essays by S. L. Bethell (1951) and Waldo F. McNeir (Additional Bibliography). Also, see the excerpts by A. C. Hamilton (1961-62), James Winny (1968), and Robert Ornstein (1972) for additional reaction against the providential reading of the* Henry VI *plays.*]

In *1 Henry VI*, there are two prominent personalities—Joan and Talbot—but it is primarily a chronicle of incidents—true and invented, ranging from the death of Henry V to the marriage of Henry VI and Margaret of Anjou. In the Second Part, the centre of interest is the quarrel between Humphrey, Duke of Gloucester and his enemies, which soon broadens into the mightier conflict of York and Lancaster which occupies the Third Part. In these two plays, greater respect is shown to history than in the First Part, but what is more important dramatically is that the focus of interest definitely shifts from the chronicling of events to the portraiture of dominant personalities. . . . There is in all [Shakespeare's] early plays an increasing tendency to simplify the network of history and to trace historical changes to the unpredictable element in human character. Not that there is any anticipation of the intricacy and depth of the later tragedies, but there can be no doubt about Shakespeare's conception or method. The characters are black and white sketches rather than delicately shaded polychromes, but history is shown as primarily a representation of the movements they initiate. (p. 56)

The First Part of *Henry VI*, which is probably the earliest of these plays, takes so many liberties with the chronicle account of historical incidents that Bullough calls it 'a fantasia on historical themes' rather than a historical drama. It is supposed to begin in 1422 when Henry V is just dead and has yet to be interred, but this single scene lumps together events that are separated by more than a decade. . . . There is scarcely any other scene in a historical drama in which so many liberties have been taken with historical time. Not only is time telescoped and chronology turned topsy-turvy but the account of historical events is mixed with a good deal of invention. We hear of the defeat and imprisonment of Talbot, which did not occur until several years later, and the whole account of Talbot is a curious mixture of fact and fiction. (p. 58)

Yet in spite of the violence done to history, it would be a mistake to regard the play as a mere fantasia. Although the dramatist departs from the historical sequence and lumps together far-fetched events and introduces episodes for which there is no authority, the representation is not unhistorical in substance. First of all, Shakespeare correctly envisages the spirit and atmosphere of the times—the personal heroism and headlong courage of feudal barons, their ambitions and intrigues, the terror inspired by Talbot and the irrepressible nationalism of the French, of which Joan was the symbol. Even the fictitious episode of the Countess of Auvergne correctly reflects the life of the English on foreign soil—the amours of lusty young men with French ladies, the risks such amours involved, and Talbot's resourcefulness and courage for which the French dreaded him so much that mothers would lull their children to sleep, crying, 'A Talbot! A Talbot!' The principal theme of *1 Henry VI* is the loss of the French possessions, ending with the negotiations of marriage between Henry VI and Margaret. (pp. 59-60)

In history as well as in Shakespeare's play, the decline of the English set in after Henry V's death, and Talbot's death meant the end of English adventurism in France; but in the play the story becomes more probable because Suffolk's peaceful diplomacy follows Talbot's exit from the stage. Two landmarks in this downward process were the deaths of Salisbury and Bedford, and Shakespeare, following Hall, gives due prominence to both. A very important factor of French success was Burgundy's defection, but more vital than any other force was resurgent French nationalism, the alacrity with which the French threw off the English yoke and re-asserted their allegiance to the Dauphin. . . . Thus although Shakespeare treats historical details in a bewildering way and the treatment is more episodic

than dramatic, he preserves the essence of history intact, giving us what Bernard Shaw calls 'A true history that never happened', or happened very perfunctorily.

Immature as the play is, critics have found in it a central meaning in the light of which the multifarious incidents may be organized. According to Tillyard, the dominant theme of the tetralogy is order [see excerpt above, 1944]. . . . Tillyard supports his thesis, so far as the first part of *Henry VI* is concerned, by referring to the very first words of the play, in which Bedford speaks of 'bad revolting stars', and then also to the homage paid by Talbot to Henry VI at the time of the French coronation of the English monarch. These, however, are two stray speeches in which the idea of order and pattern is only remotely suggested. Bedford's words are nothing but an extravagant expression of grief as Talbot's speech is just a vassal's homage to his lord. To read a philosophical meaning into either of them would be to ignore their contextual significance, and to make them the repository of Shakespeare's total meaning would be to throw the rest of the play out of focus. . . . Shakespeare's portraiture, which is aesthetic and dramatic, represents every point of view, that of the Lancastrians as well as of the Yorkists, of Henry V as well as of Mortimer, of the English as well as of the French. (pp. 60-2)

[Shakespeare] portrays a world that is not merely large and dazzling but also in continual flux. If the details of history have been re-arranged and facts have been embroidered with fiction, the modifications seem primarily to have been made to bring out this idea of ceaseless movement, of the evolution of one kind of dissension into another. The old feudal order in which kings could claim territories in other countries is succeeded by a new order—equally feudal—in which barons try to rule both the king and his kingdom. Salisbury and Bedford are representatives of the chivalry of an age that is passing away; they are being superseded by men like York and Somerset who have different ambitions and attitudes. The Temple Garden scene, a dramatic invention, marks the onset of new forces, new ambitions and alignments. Talbot's career furnishes another clue to this change. When the play opens he is hefty and vigorous and young enough to receive an assignation from a lady; above all, he is a sturdy fighter for his king. Towards the end of the play he is a worn out old man, the victim of the intrigues of a new generation of barons who think more of their own interests than of the king whom they are expected to serve. In the opening scene *2 Henry VI*, Gloucester protests along with Warwick and York against the surrender of the French heritage of the English king. But their tone— very different from that of the lords in the first scene of *1 Henry VI*—is elegiac and not militant; they only bewail the passing away of a heroic age they are powerless to recall. Gloucester and Suffolk, and York and Somerset will soon be enmeshed in the toils of power politics and Henry V's French victories will be no more than an echo from a buried past. (pp. 62-3)

The heroic Talbot is the most important character in [*1 Henry VI*]. We have the contemporary testimony of Nashe that it was his exploits, occupying about three quarters of the play, which drew large audiences [see excerpt above, 1592], and amongst modern critics Tillyard is inclined to call this part of the tetralogy the *Tragedy of Talbot*. Talbot is a Titan, both on the field and off it, and Shakespeare draws a very grand picture of the intrepid warrior whose name was a terror to the French. But the portrait is too flamboyant to be quite human. The colours are laid on too garishly, and although Shakespeare tries here and there to reveal the man behind the heroic mask, there is neither subtlety nor psychological development. Bernard Shaw complains that Shakespeare's heroes are not 'self-acting'; if there is any leading character in the whole range of Shake-spearian drama who is open to this charge it is Talbot. Even when he urges his son to save his life by flight, it is the English scourge of France more than an anxious father that speaks:

Fly, to revenge my death when I am dead;
The help of one stands me in little stead.
O! too much folly is it, well I wot,
To hazard all our lives in one small boat.
If I to-day die not with Frenchmen's rage,
To-morrow I shall die with mickle age:
By me they nothing gain an if I stay;
'T is but the short'ning of my life one day.
In thee thy mother dies, our household's name,
My death's revenge, thy youth, and England's fame.

[1 Henry VI, IV. vi. 30-9]

Talbot's exploits take up a disproportionately large space when the three parts of *Henry VI* are considered as forming a single unit. It is not improbable that the first draft—whosoever made it—was designed as a play of French warfare with Talbot as the hero. But as the larger theme dawned on Shakespeare, he subordinated Talbot's tragedy to it, although this meant a fla-

grant departure from history. The leading theme of the three plays on *Henry VI* is the catastrophic result of civil strife; it is broached in the opening scene of *1 Henry VI*, it comes suddenly and vividly to life in the Temple Garden scene, and all the other episodes are subsumed under it. Shakespeare displays remarkable constructional skill by trying to re-write history in the interests of drama. Talbot's death in 1453 brought the Hundred Years' War to a close, and in this play too it draws the curtain over the French adventure set on foot by Henry V. The negotiations of Henry VI's marriage with a French Princess come, therefore, appropriately after Talbot's death, and not, as in history, before it. What is equally important is that taking a hint from the chronicle account that Talbot's defeat was due to inferiority in numbers and deficiency in supply, Shakespeare connects this inadequacy with the personal animosities of York and Somerset, and thus the Talbot episode, long as it is, becomes a vital part of the main theme of the tetralogy—the evils of civil dissension. (pp. 65-6)

A. W. Ward says that the First Part of *Henry VI* produces an impression of 'crowding, clamour and confusion'. The Second Part affects us differently. It is as crowded and clamorous as the First, but largely free from confusion. The scenes are all laid in England, and there is a clear line of development from the beginning to the middle and from the middle to the end, with the middle—the murder of the Duke of Gloucester—

Part II, Act I, Scene iv. Margery Jordan, Hume, Southwell, Eleanor, and Bolingbrook. By John Opie (n.d.).

coming half way through in the Third Act. In the First Part, Talbot, who has been acclaimed as the hero by some critics, is only incidentally connected with the plot; his death at Bourdeaux coincides with the end of the long Anglo-French conflict, which, if we confine our attention to the events recorded in the play, has covered a period of about thirty years. His defeat is represented as a symptom of a malady that has atrophied the English war effort, and the disasters in the battlefield are due to the operation and interaction of forces with which Talbot has had nothing to do. There is much greater concentration in the Second Part, in which there are one or two episodes—Jack Cade's rebellion, for example—which are given more importance than is consistent with unity of the plot. The disasters in France are referred to, and they tilt the scales against Suffolk and Somerset, but that is about all there is on the French war. The surrender of Anjou and Maine was part of the marriage contract and belongs really to *1 Henry VI.* As regards the other possessions, Somerset thus quietly announces the 'cold news' of their loss:

> all your interest in those territories
> Is utterly bereft you; all is lost.
>
> [*2 Henry VI,* III. i. 84-8]

It makes clear that the theme of the Second Part is not foreign war, but civil strife; it is a drama primarily of personal ambition and political intrigue.

As has been pointed out, *2 Henry VI* divides itself into two halves, each with its own protagonist—the Duke of Gloucester in the first half and the Duke of York in the second. In the first two acts, all the forces combine against Gloucester, and after his death in the Third Act, all that happens in the play converges on a single point—the growing predominance of York. The other characters are intended to play a subordinate role, though sometimes we feel that their importance is either exaggerated, or not properly stressed if the scramble for power is to be correctly grasped. Jack Cade is the most interesting figure in the play, but the space—almost a whole act—given to his adventures is excessive, if we regard York as the protagonist. . . . A different criticism has to be made of the prominence given to the Duke of Somerset in the Fifth Act of *2 Henry VI.* Till now, although not in the background, he is not one of the major figures in the wranglings portrayed here. But suddenly he becomes the principal target for the Duke of York, who wants to 'heave' him from the Court and the King is anxious to hide him from York. Now Somerset is in the centre of a tense drama, for the Queen clings to him as feverishly as York is determined to throw him out, and it is his head with which the Duke of York's ablest son Richard greets the victorious assembly after the Battle of Saint Alban's, in the opening scene of *3 Henry VI.* Unless we refer back to the chronicles, there is nothing in the play to prepare us for the pivotal role assigned to Somerset in the closing stages of this play.

This brings us to the principal limitation of a drama (or a novel) that claims to be historical. History is primarily a chronicle of events, and that is why in history as well as in works of art based on history character is often subordinated to action or plot, and the inventive power of the artist partly controlled by recorded facts. If in portraying Cade, the dramatist's imagination has gone beyond the chronicle, he has overstepped the limits of historical drama. Of course, if history objects to such liberty, so much the worse for history! Again, when representing the career of the Duke of York, the dramatist must assign to Somerset the importance he had in history, although it might be out of proportion to the drama as originally conceived. Another weakness stemming from this basic limitation is that history spreads the canvas on which the dramatist or novelist paints his portraits. All historical dramatists (and novelists)—and most of all Shakespeare—have, therefore, to effect a simplification of historical forces and issues in order to be able to focus attention on inner motives and impulses, but as they have to lay emphasis on the movement of events and changes in the background they often miss the subtlety and mystery of human character. (pp. 69-71)

Historical drama selects certain incidents which are often telescoped into one another, and as it cannot go into psychological subtleties characters are portrayed in broad outline rather than in minute detail. This simplification is suitable for didactic treatment, and we may be tempted to look upon Elizabethan historical drama as an extension of the methods and principles of the morality play out of which it grew. (p. 71)

The first half of *2 Henry VI* looks, indeed, like a morality play on honest statesmanship set off against unscrupulous ambition. Although Good is sacrificed, Evil does not thrive. The punishment of Winchester and Suffolk is swift—in history there is an interval of three years between Winchester's death and Suffolk's banishment—and that of Margaret is delayed till towards the end of this play and beyond this play to its successor. J. P. Brockbank looks upon *2 Henry VI* as a morality on the sacrifice of Gloucester and the consequent dissolution of law [see Additional Bibliography]; he observes in its central acts 'the confluence of the Senecal dramatic tradition, with its ruthless retributive morality, and the Christian (or Hebraic) cult of *Vindicta Dei*'. Tillyard, who recognizes the firmer dramatic treatment of materials in the Second Part of *Henry VI* as contrasted with the First, stresses what he considers the essentially didactic nature of the play. The large variety of incidents and characters shows that not merely the nobility but the whole frame of *Respublica* is in agony. . . . Wilson Knight [see Additional Bibliography] finds a basic sense of moral law in pious Henry's oft-quoted exclamation:

> What stronger breastplate than a heart untainted!
> Thrice is he arm'd that hath his quarrel just,
> And he but naked, though lock'd up in steel,
> Whose conscience with injustice is corrupted.
>
> [*2 Henry VI,* III. ii. 232-35]

For Reese [see excerpt above, 1961] the central figure is York, and *2 Henry VI* 'adopts in the main the structure of the morality, with *Respublica* threatened by the various personifications of Lust, Pride and Ambition; and the special political lesson that Shakespeare wishes to use for the instruction of his contemporaries is that prescriptive right—York has a better claim to the throne than Henry,—does not justify an attack on the *de facto* possessor'.

If we confine our attention to the play itself, it will be seen that there is little justification for reading it as a morality, for not one of the above theories emerges out of the interaction between plot and character, in which lies the substance of Shakespearian drama. Henry claims that there is no stronger breastplate than a heart untainted and that a man who has a just quarrel is thrice armed, but although Henry has an untainted heart, is his quarrel just? All through this play and also in the other plays in which this question is raised, it is clearly suggested that the Lancastrian title is weak and Henry himself, although somewhat falteringly, recognizes this. But there is not a scrap of evidence to suggest that rebellion, even for a right cause, is unjustified. This problem is raised in *King John,* where different characters approach it in different ways, but not in this play where might fights with might. Indeed, the three parts of *Henry VI* are the nearest approach to perfect amoral history: Henry has an untainted heart and York has a just quarrel, but both come to grief. Nor can we say that Shakespeare juxtaposes different specimens of royalty in order to develop his own view of a perfect king. There is no doubt that Henry is a very pious man and yet unfit to occupy the throne at a time when the king must either rule or be ruled. On the other hand, York's strength and craftiness are never presented as virtues that Henry VI would have done well to imitate. The good Duke Humphrey is outnumbered and out-manoeuvred by unscrupulous adventurers and let down by his wife's guilty ambition. The first half of *2 Henry VI* has the appearance of a morality, but the simple morality structure is complicated by Eleanor Cobham's arrogance and treasonable designs. Departing from history where Eleanor was disgraced long before Margaret's marriage, Shakespeare brings the two ambitious women together and the drama becomes too personal and complex to fit into any narrow pattern. Eleanor's ambition provides Margaret and her accomplices with an excuse for their campaign against Gloucester, who becomes tainted with his wife's criminal folly which he cannot stop and does not expose, and no simple generalization can be made out of this tense drama of intricate personal rivalry. If, as many Tudor moralists have argued, Henry VI suffered for his grandfather's crime, how much more contaminated must Gloucester be by his wife's unlawful ambition? Shakespeare tells the same story we find in his sources and analogues, but while making it more vivid and endowing the wooden figures of history with 'an active life', he does not bring out the moral so facilely drawn by his Elizabethan contemporaries or his modern critics.

In his earliest plays as well as in his latest, Shakespeare takes a total view of life and although the total view includes the moralistic interpretation it also transcends it. Indeed, a proper appreciation of Shakespeare's plays shows how drama emerges out of the narrow structure of the morality, and the most important feature of *2 Henry VI* is that it reveals a large area of life, sweeping forward in continuous movement. In spite of the fact that in this play there is no French scene and all the incidents take place in England, there is much greater variety than in the First Part, for characters are taken from all walks of life. There are noblemen and ordinary men, hardy soldiers as well as hardened sea-dogs, high-born lords and ladies as well as disreputable conjurors and ragamuffins and impostors. Jack Cade and his associates are given more space than their rebellion may rightfully claim in a historical play, and the Simpcox incident violates the canon of unity, because its removal will not 'disjoin and dislocate the whole'. But even the characters that lie on the fringe of the action and the incidents that are loosely connected contribute to the impression of comprehensiveness. It is a large world that has been set in motion by the warring ambitions of the lords and ladies of the Court, in whom there is greater complexity than in the monolithic figures of the First Part. Not that there is, except in Jack Cade, any trace of the intricate artistry we find in Shakespeare's greater dramas, but there are some indications of his later workmanship. Gloucester is a good steward of the realm, but neither his clinging to office nor his wrangling with Winchester is pelican-like. Margaret makes an uneasy compromise between devotion to a lover and fidelity to her husband, and more compelling than either of these traits is her lust for power. York has a passionate sense of the injustice done to his family, but he is also a Machiavellian intriguer and a violent disrupter of public tranquillity. Jack Cade, the most subtly drawn char-

acter in the whole play, is a complex figure who combines a soaring imagination with a hard sense of reality, and wants to establish a commonwealth in which the most uncompromising despotism is compatible with the most broad-based democracy.

This play produces another impression that is dramatically more suggestive. It not only presents a large area of life but presents it as in continuous progress. This is different from the flux presented in the First Part, where the same kind of change—victory followed by defeat—is noticeable from one stage of the action to another. Indeed, there seems to be no adequate reason—in spite of the defeat and death of Talbot, which is followed immediately by the capture of Joan—why the English should be anxious for peace, and the proposal of marriage between King Henry and Margaret of Anjou is more the result of a personal fascination than a military or diplomatic necessity. *2 Henry VI* is dynamic in a different way; here the movement is not wheel-like but wavy and winding. The squabbles which at the beginning were purely personal have now acquired a broader basis, because Winchester, the principal enemy of Gloucester, has been strengthened by the support of the Queen and her paramour Suffolk, and they proceed to throw the Protector out. York is interested in Gloucester's disgrace and death, but he stands aloof, and two of the Yorkists—Salisbury and Warwick—seem to be puzzled. Although adherents of the Yorkist cause, they appreciate the services rendered by Gloucester and are interested in the welfare of the commonwealth:

> Join we together for the public good,
> In what we can to bridle and suppress
> The pride of Suffolk and the cardinal,
> With Somerset's and Buckingham's ambition;
> And, as we may, cherish Duke Humphrey's deeds,
> While they do tend the profit of the land.
> [*2 Henry VI*, I. i. 199-204]

But they can do little to protect the good Duke from his enemies and do not bestir themselves until it is too late. (pp. 73-6)

From yet another point of view there is an impression of progressive movement in this play such as we do not find in the First Part of the trilogy. In *1 Henry VI,* Salisbury and Bedford die old, and Talbot's age is set off against his son's youth, but there is no impression of one generation handing over the torch of life to another. The advent in the Fifth Act of Suffolk and Margaret, who look forward to the future, seems to be an abrupt transition. But it is such transition from the old generation to the new that is strikingly expressed in *2 Henry VI.* York begins taking over in devious ways the reins of power once held by Gloucester, and in spite of the carnage that has been let loose we feel that a hardy warrior and crafty diplomat is supplanting a man of ebbing energy, who, even before he is murdered, has become a back-number. Behind the ageing, though still vigorous York, loom his two sons—Edward, and even more than Edward, Richard, whose words and deeds give unmistakable indication of the sweeping changes that will soon follow. (pp. 77-8)

'The third part of *Henry VI*', says Tillyard, 'is Shakespeare's nearest approach to the Chronicle play'. And the opinion is largely true. In this play, as also in the First Part, he draws on a vast body of chronicle material, but here although he takes liberties, he treats his materials with fidelity, bringing out their 'accidental (and partly chronological) relations'. The thrilling events constituting the plot come in close succession and are grouped round certain characters—Henry and Margaret on the one side and York and Edward on the other. With the exception of Henry VI who contrasts sharply with the society he moves in, all the important figures are governed by lust for power and thirst for vengeance. We seldom see behind the surface into those instincts and elementary inhibitions in which lies the essence of personality; even Richard of Gloucester, the most powerfully drawn figure in the play, seems to hide himself behind a mask. Tillyard holds that while writing this play Shakespeare was 'tired' and 'bored', and he detects a certain falling-off from the standard reached in the Second Part. This, however, does less than justice to the play's dramatic vividness and Shakespeare's capacity for organizing a mass of materials. No episode is given undue prominence here and no episode hangs loosely from the dramatic fabric; from this point of view there is an improvement on rather than a falling-off from Part Two. . . . The various episodes of the plot are so intimately connected that the action progresses in a continuous line without a jolt and without a diversion. There is a central theme—the supersession of the Red Rose by the White—and one episode so smoothly slides into another that there is no break when Edward takes up the Yorkist leadership from his father. Richard, York's youngest son, about whom more will have to be said presently, stands out, without any basis in history, as the most prominent character, but even he is only a part of the crowded stage, and it is not till the end, when we are on the threshold of the next play, that we have the first glimpse of his loneliness.

The impression produced by *3 Henry VI* is of a grand procession rather than of the dramatic interaction of plot and character. Events separated by many years are telescoped, irrelevant details are rejected and new episodes added—all with a view to producing an impression of vivid contrast. The chronicles dwell emphatically on the ever-changing tide of Fortune, and Shakespeare gives a graphic account of this fluctuation through characterization, imagery, and primarily through the organization of plot. (pp. 78-80)

3 Henry VI is a chronicle account rather than a historical play, because both in narration and characterization it follows, with one exception, the lines laid down by Hall and others. That one exception is Richard of Gloucester, the Duke of York's youngest son, whom Shakespeare deliberately gives a prominence that is flatly contradicted by facts. In *2 Henry VI*, he plays an important part in the Battle of Saint Alban's, killing Somerset, but at the time of this battle he was a toddler of three, and he could not have been present at Wakefield, where his father died in an unequal conflict; he was then seven years old and soon away from England. . . . Shakespeare ignores this clear direction of history and gives him a prominence that at this stage did not belong to him. Indeed, it is for his sake that Shakespeare minimizes the importance of his eldest brother who played a leading part in the events dramatized in *3 Henry VI*, and later on he passes quickly over what Hall calls the prosperous reign of Edward IV. Shakespeare must have given excessive importance to Richard designedly, and the design is primarily aesthetic and only incidentally moral. The Wars of the Roses appeared to his Tudor imagination as a clash of rival ambitions which made light of moral scruples. Richard is the latest of the agents in this holocaust, and he is in every sense the greatest of them all. He has all the brutality and greed for power seen in Clifford, Margaret, and Warwick and yet a zestfulness combined with a sardonic humour which sets him above them. In him unprincipled ambition reaches its climax and with him it comes to an appropriate end. Whether Henry VI or the Duke of York had the better title to the throne or whether the rebellion of Bolingbroke in the past or that of the Yorkists later on is justified is a politico-ethical problem which Shakespeare leaves unresolved. But there is no doubt that Richard of Gloucester, the youngest of the Duke of York's sons, had not originally even a shadow of a claim; in Shakespeare's play, however, he is determined, quite early in life, to sweep his way to the throne, because he lives in a world where it is an accepted principle that Providence is on the stronger side, and where none but the impotent Henry VI makes 'weapons' of 'holy saws of sacred writ' [*2 Henry VI*, I. iii. 58]. Indeed, in this 'miserable age', success is the only criterion by which one is to judge whether a thing is good or bad. (pp. 83-4)

Both in theory and practice Richard is an exponent of what later came to be popularly described as Machiavellism; and Henry VI, a man of church-like humours and a bookish rule, enunciates a philosophy of pastoral content, far from the madding barons' ferocious strife. This is why critics with a didactic turn have been tempted to look upon this play as primarily a clash between these two protagonists. According to Reese, 'the play's interest is withdrawn from the lesser men and their predestined doings and is concentrated upon the two who stand at opposite extremes of good and evil. Henry lacks the power of action, but his saintliness and serenity shed their own illumination; Richard, the man of deeds, is sheerly wicked. The play moves to its climax under the shadow of their conflict'. Henry VI does not play any important part in the trilogy of which he is the titular hero, but he is the central character because all the incidents revolve round him, and he is a contrast to the other figures because he is a good man without ambition and they are ferociously ambitious people without goodness. He is a saintly man and yet very much a man. He is open to the charm of beauty, even on hearsay; that is the only explanation for his accepting the bride chosen by Suffolk. Although unfit for the office of a king, he yet clings to the throne and is even ready to disinherit his son if he is allowed to reign during his lifetime. But in his heart of hearts he loves the Glad Poverty held forth as an ideal by [Giovanni] Boccaccio and [John] Lydgate, whereas the powerful people about him are imbued with the Renaissance lust for power. In a sense he stands severely alone, but in his holiness and helplessness he is a refreshing contrast to his sordid environment. This contrast, suggested all through the play, reaches its climax in the last scene but one where the pious man, sitting at his book, is set upon and stabbed to death by his most brutal enemy. (pp. 85-6)

S. C. Sen Gupta, in his Shakespeare's Historical Plays, *Oxford University Press, London, 1964, 172 p.*

CHARLES R. FORKER (essay date 1965)

[*Forker contends that Shakespeare adapted for his history plays several features of the pastoral tradition of English literature. He postulates that the playwright's juxtaposition of epic and pastoral elements in 1, 2, and 3* Henry VI *allowed him to dramatize more effectively the conflicts between public and private life, and between chaos and order, which are central concerns of the trilogy. Forker's examples of Shakespeare's use of the contrast between epic and pastoral include Henry's "molehill" speech in 3* Henry VI, *Act II, Scene v, the murder of Henry by Richard of Gloucester, the Jack Cade episode, and the Temple Garden scene in 1* Henry VI. *For further explications of the "molehill" scene in 3* Henry VI, *see the excerpts by Muriel C. Bradbrook (1951), Robert B. Pierce (1971), and David M. Bergeron (1977). Also, for additional commentary on the importance of garden and enclosure images in the* Henry VI *trilogy, see the excerpts by Caroline F. E. Spurgeon (1935) and Carol McGinnis Kay (1972).*]

The subtle and complex dramatic form which the greatest Elizabethan plays exemplify is based not on unity of action (in the Aristotelian sense) but on multiple actions related to each other, as musical themes are related, by repetition and variation—by a system of ironic contrasts and parallels. This principle of organization, though of course Shakespeare uses it elsewhere, was perhaps especially significant to him in the history plays because of the special problems of ordering in dramatic compass the epic sweep and multitudinousness of the chronicle source material.

What I propose to argue in this essay is that Shakespeare often found it convenient to organize his system of contrasts and parallels in the histories with reference to another traditional literary dichotomy—one exploited almost contemporaneously by Tasso in *Jerusalem Delivered,* Spenser in *The Faerie Queene,* and Sidney in *The Arcadia*—that between epic and pastoral. I must warn readers at the outset that I am using the term "pastoral" very elastically, for to the formal pastoral drama of Tasso and Guarini, the drama that Jonson and Fletcher were later to imitate in England, Shakespeare owed comparatively little. His tradition was rather the rustic, spontaneous, and popular pastoralism of his native country—the tradition to which the medieval nativity plays, the popular romances, the Robin Hood ballads, and other folklore contributed much, and in which the word "shepherd" could suggest a various world of lovers, poets, holiday humor, nobles disguised as peasants, and Christian simplicity. The familiar Renaissance contrasts of court vs. country and art vs. nature, for instance, lie very close to its heart. My central point is that by drawing upon this pastoral tradition directly and also indirectly by making the audience aware of nature and the natural world through language, character, action, and setting, Shakespeare was able to dramatize more effectively some of the ironic contrasts between public and private life and between order and chaos that give the history plays their special richness.

Shakespeare introduces the pastoral tradition most schematically in the earliest plays—those that make up the *Henry VI* trilogy. Probably the most obvious and familiar example occurs in the third part where "Holy Harry of Lancaster" (as he was sometimes called in the sixteenth century) contemplates the advantages of the shepherd's life as the battle of Towton rages around him [II. v.]. He sits upon a molehill which reminds us ironically of another molehill earlier in the play upon which the ambitious York aspirant to the crown, Richard Plantagenet, has been ritually mocked, crowned with paper, and murdered. As the king sits, meditative and withdrawn, wishing he had only sheep to tend instead of warring subjects, he watches an emblematic little morality play on the unnaturalness of civil war in which a son kills his father unwittingly and a father kills his son. . . . Shakespeare is dramatizing several ideas in this scene. Henry represents the timorous warrior and incompetent king who retreats from the harsh realities of his reign into an imaginary, golden world where "the lion fawns upon the lamb" [*3 Henry VI,* IV. viii. 49]. But the king's pastoral daydream characterizes him also as a kind of Holy Idiot (like Dostoevsky's Prince Myshkin). The molehill is an emblem of his humility (just as the contrasting molehill was a bitter mock of his Yorkist rival's reaching at mountains). His meditation throws the unnatural savagery of the civil war into vivid relief, and Shakespeare forges a symbolic link between the golden world of pastoral and the eternal world of Henry's religious commitment. A few scenes later, King Henry, now unsuccessfully disguised, becomes a deer in his own deer-park and is taken prisoner by two of his own gamekeepers to be delivered over to the new York claimant, Edward IV. He is only too willing to make a spiritual kingdom of his cell, where he may be a king, as he says, "in mind":

> My crown is in my heart, not on my head;
> Not deck'd with diamonds and Indian stones,
> Nor to be seen. My crown is call'd content;
> A crown it is that seldom kings enjoy.
> [*3 Henry VI,* III. i. 62-5]

The pastoral motif here betokens Shakespeare's concern with the conflict between private and public values and their relation to order in the universe, the state, and the individual soul. Henry's golden world, his "crown of content," contrasts finely with Richard of Gloucester's idea of a golden world. For him, as for Tamburlaine, the perfect bliss and sole felicity is the sweet fruition of an *earthly* crown ("the golden time I look for") and, like one "lost in a thorny wood," he will hew his way to it "with a bloody axe" [*3 Henry VI,* III. ii. 127-81]. In the penultimate scene of *3 Henry VI* the worlds of force and spirit are effectively juxtaposed through metaphor: Richard murders Henry in the Tower of London, and Shakespeare transforms the pastoral associations used earlier into ritual sacrifice. The protective jailer, suddenly dismissed from the room, becomes the timorous shepherd driven from his charge, and Henry, "the harmless sheep," "yield[s] his fleece" [V. vi. 8] and "make[s] a bloody supper" [V. v. 85] for the ravenous wolf. Such imagery becomes nearly automatic throughout the early tetralogy. Peace, order, and innocence are repeatedly thought of in terms of the shepherd with his sheep; and the ruthless forces of power that turn the pastoral landscape into a scene of slaughter are imaged in terms of preying wolves and foxes. (pp. 87-9)

Since pastoral values typically suggest some sort of peaceful, civilized social norm, the abandonment or perversion of these values usually signifies anarchy. It is as if Shakespeare were reminding us that particular historical disorders may be rooted in some fundamental crime against Nature herself, in a violation of natural law. Some such purpose seems to lie behind Shakespeare's portrayal of Joan of Arc, whose dark character in Holinshed he manages to blacken further. Although she is "by birth a shepherd's daughter" who "waited on . . . tender lambs" [*1 Henry VI,* I. ii. 72-6], she repudiates the pastoral world that is her lot, and, assisted by hellish powers, helps to turn a peaceful land into a battlefield. Shakespeare makes her into a sort of female Tamburlaine (who was also a shepherd to begin with)—a conqueror, not only of the English, but of her own sovereign. The Dauphin inverts traditional order in one scene by acknowledging her his vanquisher:

> Thou art an Amazon
> And fightest with the sword of Deborah. . . .
> Let me thy servant and not sovereign be.
> [*1 Henry VI,* I. ii. 104-11]

At the end of the play she is revealed to be not only a witch but a lascivious hypocrite arrogant enough to claim that royal blood runs in her veins. Shakespeare makes the moral contrast between order and disorder unmistakable when her own father, a humble shepherd content with his lot, curses Joan as unnatural, and reflects that it would have been better if "some ravenous wolf had eaten thee" "when thou didst keep my lambs afield" [V.iv.30-1].

Jack Cade, "born under a hedge" [*2 Henry VI,* IV. ii. 51], is another of Shakespeare's falsely aspiring and misplaced rustics. His rebellious energies create the very chaos that Henry VI's inept rule has courted and portend the even greater chaos that the rising house of York already threatens. Cade, like Joan, claims royal descent with a bogus tale of mixed-up twins that might come straight out of some pastoral romance. His watchwords are ignorance and brute force, and he sits on London Stone, a kind of surrogate king, and imagines a silly communist utopia where the exercise of reason in any form is a hanging offense and where ''the pissing conduit'' shall ''run nothing but claret wine this first year of our reign'' [IV. vi. 3-4]. The frightening commonwealth that Cade dreams of is a sort of peasant's brave new world, a parody version of the legendary golden world that Gonzalo later imagines in *The Tempest* [II.i.147-56] and that Shakespeare partly derived from the fifteenth book of Ovid's *Metamorphoses* and Montaigne's delightful essay on cannibals. But Cade's imaginary order is really the very opposite of Gonzalo's idyllic primitivism. Cade's idea of the state of nature, because it is uncultivated by art or learning, is savage and unnatural. Dick Butcher cries out in his enthusiasm for reform, ''let's kill all the lawyers'' [*2 Henry VI*, IV. ii. 76-7]; and Cade says to his rabble army, ''then are we in order when we are most out of order'' [IV. ii. 189-90]. (pp. 92-3)

When Shakespeare is not reinforcing the various aspects of the pastoral theme by contrasts in action and characterization, he often seems to do so obliquely by evoking a sense of ideal landscape through imagery and setting. One cannot read the histories consecutively without being struck by the constant prevalence of natural imagery. As early as *Titus Andronicus* Shakespeare had begun ''to warble his native woodnotes wild'' [John Milton] and, indeed, we are never very far from the out-of-doors throughout Shakespeare's poetry. But in the history plays especially, landscape is often symbolic of moral attitude rather than merely decorative or atmospheric. (p. 94)

One of the most illuminating examples of Shakespeare's use of emblematic setting occurs in the famous Temple Garden scene of *1 Henry VI*, where with ingenious wit and ceremonial rhetoric he dramatizes the growing faction between the red rose of Lancaster and the white rose of York. The whole episode is an extended metaphysical conceit in dramatic form. The plucking of the red and white roses with its accompanying verbal quarrel constitutes both a prophecy and a pastoral reduction of the fratricidal war to follow. In this sense it serves as an analogue to the Fall. The garden setting establishes, in fact, a whole complex of interrelated ironies. As in *Richard II*, it is a foil to set off the sickness and chaos in the state against the health and order in nature. Indeed, this contrast becomes the more emphatic because the garden adjoins an ancient school of law. Moreoever, the garden is rich in connotations that go back to medieval literary tradition. We recall the gardens of Chaucer's *Troilus* and *Canterbury Tales* that often mingle the erotic associations of *The Romance of the Rose* with the idea of gardens as types of Eden and therefore allegories of sacred order, divine love, and human charity. The birth of a national blood feud therefore takes place in a setting that normally connotes love, whether secular or religious. In the great chain of being, the rose was traditionally at the top of the floral hierarchy and hence analogous to royalty. . . . The color contrast is symbolic too: Shakespeare exploits its ironic possibilities when he makes the traditional symbolism of white for innocence and red for love prefigure pale fear and gory death:

Rich.	Now, Somerset, where is your argument?
Som.	Here in my scabbard, meditating that Shall dye your white rose in a bloody red.
Rich.	Meantime your cheeks do counterfeit our roses; For pale they look with fear, as witnessing The truth on our side.
Som.	No Plantagenet! 'Tis not for fear, but anger, that thy cheeks Blush for pure shame to counterfeit our rose.

[*1 Henry VI*, II. iv. 59-66]

The plucking of the roses, then, becomes the emblem of natural law violated. It expresses in iconographic form the same sentiment that one of the remorseful murderers in *Richard III* utters:

We smothered
The most replenished sweet work of nature
That from the prime creation e'er she fram'd.
[*Richard III*, IV. iii. 17-18]

King Henry, sitting on his molehill, later notices ''The red rose and the white . . . The fatal colours of our striving houses'' [*3 Henry VI*, II. v. 97-8] on the mangled face of the boy slain by his father.

Gardens, orchards, parks, and forests keep reappearing in the history plays. In her husband's garden the Duchess of Gloucester [*2 Henry VI*, I. iv] dabbles with black magic by involving herself with the notorious witch Margery Jourdain and two sinister priests. There by blasphemous invocations and other occult ceremonies—to the accompaniment of thunder and lightning—they raise ''a spirit'' who, in riddling fashion, foretells the deposition of the king and the deaths of York, Somerset, and Suffolk. Richard Plantagenet allies himself with Warwick the kingmaker in another garden scene [*2 Henry VI*, II. ii]. Strolling together in a ''close walk'' [II. ii. 3], later described as ''this private plot'' [II. ii. 60], they plan to root up the red rose and plant the white, biding their time until their enemies ''have snar'd the shepherd of the flock / That virtuous prince, the good Duke Humphrey'' and the hour be ripe to stain their swords ''With heart-blood of the house of Lancaster'' [II. ii. 66-74]. The walled garden or *hortus conclusus* (as it was called in the Middle Ages) is traditionally the place for quiet contemplation and retirement. Yet here the contemplation runs on political murder—as it does later for Brutus in still another garden [*Julius Caesar*]. The ordered gardens become ironic settings in which to mirror impending chaos, to commune with evil forces, to sow seeds of destruction, to contemplate the annihilation of all that's made with green thoughts in a green shade. (pp. 96-7)

To summarize then, Shakespeare uses the pastoral motif and its extension in details of landscape, imagery, and setting both to mirror and to challenge ideas of order and disorder in the great world of affairs. The green world becomes for Shakespeare what Northrop Frye has called a ''complex variable,'' a kind of archetypal symbol which functions in such a way as to express a continuing tension between the ideal and the actual as it affects both the individual and the state. The ''pastoral'' emphasis shows us, as it were, the underside of epic. It permits points of rest between the excursions and alarums. By allowing for reflection, sometimes choric reflection, upon the action, it helps to evoke what is timeless in the context of speeding time. The contrast partly enables Shakespeare to dramatize history in both long and short perspective at once—and in a way that ultimately humanizes the grand as well as the trivial in the lives of men and nations. (p. 100)

> Charles R. Forker, "Shakespeare's Chronicle Plays As Historical-Pastoral," in Shakespeare Studies: An Annual Gathering of Research, Criticism, and Reviews, Vol. I, 1965, pp. 85-104.

IRVING RIBNER   (essay date 1965)

[*Ribner's critical work includes the new Kittredge edition of the works of Shakespeare and* The English History Play in the Age of Shakespeare *(1957); the excerpt below is taken from a revised edition of the latter book. Ribner identifies and discusses three different literary traditions which he maintains influenced the structure of the* Henry VI *trilogy: the miracle and morality dramas of medieval literature, the de casibus tragedy of the sixteenth century—perhaps derived by Shakespeare from the popular handbook* A Mirror for Magistrates—*and the rhetorical and stylistic literature of Seneca. Ribner demonstrates how Shakespeare combined these different traditions in* Henry VI *to present "a deliberate and consistent philosophy of history." Other critics who have traced Shakespeare's use of medieval dramatic traditions in the* Henry VI *trilogy include S. L. Bethell (1951), Muriel C. Bradbook (1951), and John D. Cox (1978). Ribner further explains that divine providence as a "ruling force in a well-ordered universe" and the doctrine of degree were central to the philosophy of history which Shakespeare dramatized in* Henry VI. *In this respect, his interpretation of the trilogy has much in common with the readings offered by Hermann Ulrici (1839), J. A. R. Marriott (1918), E. M. W. Tillyard (1944), and M. M. Reese (1961).*]

With so wide a scope, so many dramatic purposes to accomplish, it is almost inevitable that all three of the *Henry VI* plays should be episodic in structure; scenes are often poorly related to one another, and what unity the plays possess is that implicit in a theme of general disorder and chaos brought about by treachery and self-seeking on the part of nobles who should instead be devoted entirely to the good of England. Such loyalty is reflected in the Talbots of *Part I* who expose by contrast the shortcomings of the other nobles. The trilogy presents a vast pageant of the chaos of the Wars of the Roses, with loss of the hard-won conquests in France, rebellion and disorder at home, noble turning against noble, and faction destroying faction. England is torn by greed, treachery, and sensuality in high place, and behind it all is the suggestion—never strongly emphasized, however, as it is in Hall—that all of this is God's punishment visited upon England for Henry Bolingbroke's deposition and murder of King Richard II a half-century before. Shakespeare is presenting a portrait of decades of civil chaos as a reminder to his contemporary Englishmen of what might again return upon the death of the now old and childless Elizabeth, should the succession to the throne be left uncertain and powerful nobles again vie with one another for the crown. (pp. 95-6)

In this episodic treatment of a long series of tragic events, the *Henry VI* plays carry on the dramatic tradition of the miracle drama as it had developed through the Digby *Mary Magdalene, Cambises* and *Tamburlaine*. The relation of the plays to *Tamburlaine* is particularly close in *Parts II* and *III*, for just as in Marlowe's play we have the figure of Tamburlaine steadily

expanding through an episodic series of battles, here we have the figure of Richard, Duke of York, steadily expanding in a similar episodic manner. An important difference, however, is that York falls before he reaches the summit of his glory, whereas Tamburlaine is triumphant to the end. There is little in Shakespeare of Marlowe's humanistic philosophy of history. Richard's personal abilities avail him nothing in the face of a hostile fortune which destroys him in retribution for his sins. (p. 96)

Shakespeare wrote in the episodic tradition of the miracle plays and *Tamburlaine* because it was the tradition which best fitted his dramatic requirements and which he found almost prescribed for him by his close following of the chronicles and his attempt to attain something of their epic sweep. But upon this episodic structure he superimposed another dramatic tradition, that of the English morality play. . . . (p. 97)

History for Shakespeare was never mere pageantry. He saw significant meaning in it, and he seized upon morality devices to make its meaning clear, clearer than the factual method of the chronicles themselves could make it. . . . The *Henry VI* plays, in spite of their unintegrated, episodic structure, carry on the dramatic tradition of such political morality plays as *Respublica*. The three plays, with *Richard III*, embody one vast scheme in which England, like a morality hero, brings evil upon herself; she suffers degradation in the Wars of the Roses, loses her conquests in France, and is brought almost to total destruction under the tyranny of Richard III. But God pities England, shows her His grace, and, through the person of Henry of Richmond, allows her to make a proper choice upon which the factions among her nobles can unite. Thus England attains a new and greater felicity to be exemplified in the reign of the Tudors. This scheme of salvation for England is at the heart of the four plays; it is the scheme which Shakespeare found in Edward Hall's chronicle; it embodies a Christian philosophy of history, and it is cast in the pattern of the morality drama, which had itself sprung from characteristically Christian assumptions.

There is thus nothing unusual in the structure of the *Henry VI* plays; they embody the normal devices and traditions of the English drama as it had evolved from the Middle Ages onward. It is significant, however, that the *Henry VI* plays embody another medieval tradition which is of only slight significance in the earlier drama, but which is of great significance in nondramatic treatments of history, and which is to have a profound influence upon history plays later than these of Shakespeare. This is the medieval theme of the fall of kings through the operations of fortune. Man rises to the top of the wheel of fortune and then is suddenly cast down to the very depths, while another rises in his place. (pp. 97-8)

The three *Henry VI* plays, with *Richard III*, may be viewed as virtually a series of successive waves, in each of which one hero falls and another rises to replace him. The most significant of the falls are displayed as divine retribution for sin, but there are some also which seem to illustrate only an arbitrary and capricious fortune. The most significant rise and fall, of course, is that of Richard, Duke of York, from the Temple Garden scene (II, iv) in *Part I* to his murder in the second scene of *Part III*. His destruction is displayed as divine punishment for his ruthless ambition and perhaps chiefly for his sacrifice of Talbot in France. With his death begins the rise of Richard of Gloucester, whose fall is to come in the succeeding play, *Richard III*. The pattern of rise and fall is repeated in lesser instances. The good Duke Humphrey of Gloucester begins his decline at the beginning of *Part I,* and with his death at the end of the play begins the rise of Suffolk, who suffers retribution for his murder of Humphrey and his treachery to Henry VI by his own ignominious end in *Part II.* . . . This medieval pattern of rise and fall lends a certain unifying element to the structure of the trilogy, and it is used to emphasize the moral lessons inherent in the subject matter.

Still another tradition which helped to shape the *Henry VI* plays is that of Senecan tragedy. All of the characteristic marks of Senecan style are present in the plays, although they are less marked in *Part I* than in the other two plays. The long Senecan soliloquy of self-revelation, in which the speaker characterizes himself, describes his motives, and indicates the course of future action, in *Part II* is particularly obvious in the speeches of Richard, Duke of York. . . . (pp. 99-100)

We thus find in the *Henry VI* plays a combination of at least three traditions which had already been used in the dramatic presentation of history, and one, the *de casibus* theme, which had been common in non-dramatic historical writings. These are divergent strands going back to medieval times, but all combine and complement each other as the new dramatic genre, the history play, develops. The episodic structure of the *Henry VI* plays carries on the dramatic tradition of the miracle plays, of *Cambises* and *Tamburlaine,* and at the same time captures some of the variety and scope of the prose chronicles. Superimposed upon this structure we find many of the rhetorical devices of Senecan drama which had long been used . . . in the dramatic treatment of history throughout Europe. Added to this we find, moreover, certain ritual and symbolic elements whose purpose is symbolic commentary rather than graphic depiction of events, and which carry on the morality play tradition. And throughout the trilogy there is the pattern of the rise and fall of statesmen at the hands of fortune, the pattern of medieval *de casibus* tragedy made popular in Shakespeare's England by *A Mirror for Magistrates.* (p. 101)

Implicit in the *Henry VI* plays is a philosophy of history which was medieval in origin, but still much a part of the intellectual life of Elizabethan England. Its keystone is the concept of divine providence as the ruling force in a well-ordered universe, in which each element is designed to serve its proper function. The events of history are never arbitrary or capricious; they are always in accordance with God's beneficent and harmonious plan. Virtue is rewarded and sins are punished in accordance with a heavenly plan of justice which it is the duty of the historian to elucidate. (p. 103)

The doctrine of degree is an inherent part of this world view. Each man must keep his allotted station in life and desire no more; to aspire above one's station is to violate the divinely ordained order of the universe, and such violation, particularly if it manifests itself in rebellion against God's agent on earth, the king, must inevitably be punished by God. The proper attitude for a Tudor gentleman is well expressed by Shakespeare in *2 Henry VI* in the speech of Iden:

> Lord, who would live turmoiled in the court,
> And may enjoy such quiet walks as these?
> This small inheritance my father left me
> Contenteth me, and worth a monarchy.
> I seek not to wax great by others' waning,
> Or gather wealth, I care not, with what envy:
> Sufficeth that I have maintains my state
> And sends the poor well pleased from my gate.
>
> [*2 Henry VI,* IV. x. 16-23]

Iden's acceptance of order is contrasted to the violent disruption of it envisioned by Jack Cade and his followers:

> There shall be in England seven halfpenny loaves sold for a penny: the three-hooped pot shall have ten hoops; and I will make it felony to drink small beer: all the realm shall be in common; and in Cheapside shall my palfry go to grass.
>
> [*2 Henry VI,* IV. ii. 65-9]

The order which Iden accepts and which Cade would destroy is what God's providence has designed for man, and the lesson of history as Hall and Shakespeare see it is that when such order is destroyed, God's curse will plague England until it is restored. This lesson the *Henry VI* plays graphically illustrate.

The providential view of history is, of course, an old and commonplace one. Hall's interpretation of the Wars of the Roses in the light of it, however, belongs particularly to the age in which he wrote and to the particular political prejudices to which he catered. For Hall perpetuated what Tillyard . . . has called 'the Tudor Myth', and this myth Shakespeare incorporated into his *Henry VI* plays. (pp. 103-04)

That Shakespeare accepted this providential view of history and that he saw the period with which he was dealing within the terms of the 'Tudor Myth' have, I believe, been amply demonstrated by Tillyard. In the *Henry VI* plays Shakespeare shows us the Wars of the Roses in which England suffers for her sins, and although he does not emphasize the deposition and murder of Richard II, that initial crime is nevertheless in the background. The violations of divine harmony and order—the sins for which England must suffer—which Shakespeare does emphasize are those committed within the *Henry VI* plays themselves: the sacrifice of Talbot to the personal ambition and rivalry of York and Somerset, the murder of Duke Humphrey, the treason and lechery of Suffolk, the murder of young Rutland, the perfidy of Clarence. The catalogue is a long one, and in each instance the sinner suffers retribution for his crime in accordance with the historical order of cause and effect. (p. 105)

It is in part because Shakespeare emphasizes the sins committed during the reign of Henry VI rather than the initial crime against Richard II that I cannot share Tillyard's view that the *Henry VI* plays and *Richard III* form one vast epic unit with the second tetralogy he was to begin some five or six years later to cover the years from Richard II to Henry V. . . . Shakespeare, like Hall, saw the events of Henry VI's reign within the general pattern which began with Richard II's deposition, but there is no evidence that when he wrote the *Henry VI* plays he was much concerned with the earlier events. (pp. 105-06)

The political doctrine of the *Henry VI* plays is simple and obvious; most of it has already been pointed out by Tillyard and others. Shakespeare's primary purpose, as I have already indicated, is to present a vivid picture of the horrors of internal dissension and civil war as a reminder of the chaos from which England was liberated by the Tudors and as a warning of what England might again experience should Elizabeth die with the succession to the throne still in dispute. This horror of civil war is portrayed throughout the three plays, but perhaps most forcefully in Act II, Scene v of *3 Henry VI,* when King Henry, having been driven from the Battle of Towton by Queen Margaret and the Earl of Warwick who fear the bad luck he brings, sits upon a molehill and, while lamenting the cares of kingship and longing for the simple shepherd's life, sees a son bear in the body of a father he has killed and then a father bear in the body of a son he has killed. Henry, father, and son chorally lament the tragedy of civil war. To the son Henry says:

> O piteous spectacle! O bloody times!
> While lions war and battle for their dens,
> Poor harmless lambs abide their enmity.
> Weep, wretched man, I'll aid thee tear for tear;
> And let our hearts and eyes, like civil war,
> Be blind with tears, and break o'ercharged with grief.
> [*3 Henry VI*, II. v. 73-8]

And to the mourning father:

> Woe above woe! grief more than common grief!
> O that my death would stay these ruthful deeds!
> O, pity, pity, gentle heaven, pity!
> [II. v. 94-6]

The scene, of course, is artificial and stylized, but as an allegorical symbol of the horror and pathos of civil war it is nevertheless very effective.

Allied with this purpose is Shakespeare's desire to show the seeds of civil war: faction among the nobles, with rule in dispute, and—worst of all evils that may befall a kingdom— a child king. King Henry in *1 Henry VI* points to the evil which the dissension between Winchester and Gloucester must breed:

> O, what a scandal is it to our crown,
> That two such noble peers as ye should jar!
> Believe me, lords, my tender years can tell
> Civil dissension is a viperous worm
> That gnaws the bowels of the commonwealth.
> [*1 Henry VI*, III. i. 69-73]

And the Duke of Exeter, left behind at the end of the scene to speak a soliloquy, emphasizes the moral for the audience:

> This late dissension grown betwixt the peers
> Burns under feigned ashes of forged love
> And will at last break out into a flame:
> As fester'd members rot but by degree,
> Till bones and flesh and sinews fall away,
> So will this base and envious discord breed.
> [III. i. 188-93]

And in a later scene Exeter, who throughout *I Henry VI* serves as a kind of chorus, in a soliloquy again emphasizes the moral lesson:

> But howsoe'er, no simple man that sees.
> This jarring discord of nobility,
> This shouldering of each other in the court,
> This factious bandying of their favourites,
> But that it doth presage some ill event.
> 'Tis much when sceptres are in children's hands;
> But more when envy breeds unkind division;
> There comes the ruin, there begins confusion.
> [IV. i. 187-94]

Shakespeare's deliberate didacticism is obvious.

Shakespeare indicates in all three plays that Henry VI is by nature not fit for kingship. It is obvious that Richard of York, if crowned, would make a better monarch. York's title, moreover, is a better one; Shakespeare is careful to give his genealogy in great detail [*1 Henry VI*, II. v. 63-92, and *2 Henry VI*, II. ii. 10-24 and 34-52], and Henry VI himself admits in an aside [*3 Henry VI*, I. i. 134] that his own title is weak. In spite of this, however, Shakespeare censures rebellion against

the *de facto* ["actual"] ruler, and an important purpose of the play is to teach the sinfulness of such rebellion. This may be, in part, an answer to those Englishmen, particularly Catholics, who throughout her reign pointed to the weakness of Elizabeth's claim to the throne.

The principal rebel, of course, is Richard of York, but to display the horrors of rebellion Shakespeare uses chiefly Jack Cade and his followers, who are suborned by York to rebel against Henry. The Cade scenes in *2 Henry VI* are a skilful attempt to present a portrait of disorder, the very antithesis of God's plan, and to show the effects of such disorder in the commonwealth. Cade himself says that he and his men are 'in order when we are most out of order' [IV. ii. 189-90]. The clerk of Chatham is slain because 'he can write and read and cast accompt' [IV. ii. 85-6]. Particularly cruel and sacrilegious is the execution by Cade of Lord Say, who is carefully portrayed as one who has always been a friend to the commonwealth. The culminating indignity comes when Cade places the heads of Lord Say and Sir James Cromer on poles so that the two heads may kiss [IV. vii. 130-36]. The rule of Cade is carefully portrayed as a perversion of all that Elizabethans held sacred.

These are commonplace political purposes; they are largely in Shakespeare's sources as well, although the theory of divine right is emphasized in neither Hall nor Holinshed, Hall having borrowed from writers who wrote before the formulation of the doctrine by Tudor divines, and Holinshed being largely unconcerned with the matter. These notions Shakespeare developed far beyond anything in his known sources. In the *Henry VI* plays he further introduced several other ideas which are not necessarily in his sources, and which he was to develop much further in his second historical tetralogy. They obviously were matters of particular interest to him. The first of these is the large question of what constitutes a good king. In his condemnation of York's rebellion Shakespeare enunciates a principle which is to dominate the later *Henry IV* plays; that a *de facto* title is a primary requisite. No matter how superior to the king a claimant to a throne may be, both in legitimacy of birth and in personal attributes, the rule of the *de facto* king must not be challenged, for the worst of all evils is civil war, and even a bad king is preferable to that.

Throughout the plays, and particularly in *2 Henry VI*, Shakespeare presents us with contrasting examples of kingship, a device he is to repeat on a larger scale in his second tetralogy, where Richard II, Henry IV, and Henry V are offered in contrast. In *2 Henry VI* Shakespeare gives us King Henry, Humphrey of Gloucester, and Richard of York for comparison. York has kingly qualities and a good title to the throne; he is brave and he is crafty, combining the qualities of the lion and the fox. He lacks, however, the qualities of the pelican: unselfishness and a disinterested devotion to his country. Humphrey of Gloucester is brave and unselfishly devoted to his country; he combines the qualities of the lion and the pelican, but he lacks the craftiness of the fox. King Henry, the actual king, has only the qualities of the pelican. Thus each of the three is lacking in at least one essential requirement for successful kingship. The king, as Shakespeare sees it, must be strong, crafty, and unselfishly devoted to his people. All three men combined might have constituted one perfect king, but any one of them alone was insufficient and doomed to failure.

Shakespeare in the *Henry VI* plays is absorbed with the relation between the public and the private virtues—those qualities which make for the good private man, as contrasted with those which make for the efficient king—a problem with which he was to be concerned throughout his career as a dramatist. . . . That Henry VI is a good man is emphasized over and over throughout the trilogy. Of his personal piety there can be no question. He is kind, loving, sympathetic; the tears he weeps for the woes of his country are sincere. But in spite of those qualities which might endear him to an audience as a man, and which win for him a large measure of sympathy in his misfortune, he is unsuccessful as a king. He is wanting in the public virtues, and it is England that primarily pays the penalty for this shortcoming in its king. No matter how rich in personal virtue a man may be, if he does not have the public virtue which makes him a good ruler, his country will suffer. Shakespeare makes this very clear in 3 Henry VI in the death speech of Clifford:

> And, Henry, hadst thou sway'd as kings should do,
> Or as thy father and his father did,
> Giving no ground unto the house of York,
> They never then had sprung like summer flies;
> I and ten thousand in this luckless realm
> Had left no mourning widows for our death;
> And thou this day hadst kept the chair in peace.
>
> [3 Henry VI, II. vi. 14-20]

This theme of the insufficiency of private virtue in the conduct of a state, Shakespeare is to develop at length in Richard II and with it he will develop the corollary principle of the inadequacy of the public virtues by themselves. The ability to rule is to him always a prime requisite of kingship, but this ability must be combined with personal goodness, for public virtue can only rest upon a sound foundation of private morality. This is the great political principle which all of Shakespeare's histories, English and Roman, together affirm. (pp. 106-11)

> Irving Ribner, "The Early Shakespeare," in his The English History Play in the Age of Shakespeare, revised edition, Methuen & Co. Ltd., 1965, pp. 92-122.

DAVID M. BEVINGTON (essay date 1966)

[Bevington contributes further evidence to the contention of such critics as Hereward T. Price (1951) and A. C. Hamilton (1961-62) that 1 Henry VI is more structurally integrated than had been recognized by earlier critics. In the following excerpt, Bevington argues that the manner in which Joan of Arc, the Countess of Auvergne, and Margaret of Anjou seek to gain mastery over the male characters "echoes the larger theme of discord and division" in 1 Henry VI. The behavior of these three characters also comprises what he calls the "main subtheme" of masculine reason subjugated by feminine sensuality. Bevington analyzes several scenes featuring these "domineering" women—scenes which have often been regarded as unrelated to the rest of the play—and demonstrates their relation to each other and the manner in which they reinforce Shakespeare's theme of civil dissension. For a further discussion of the role of women in the Henry VI trilogy, see the excerpts by H. M. Richmond (1967), Leslie A. Fiedler (1972), and Marilyn French (1981).]

1 Henry VI, long condescended to as the ugly duckling of Shakespeare's earliest dramatic offspring, is at last being grudgingly allowed a certain severe beauty of its own. The play may even live down the charge implicitly levelled at all ugly ducklings, of having resulted from questionable or promiscuous fathering. Now generally accepted as Shakespeare's own, 1 Henry VI has surprised us all by its promise of thematic unity and its integral relationship to Shakespeare's first historical tetralogy. My purpose is to bolster appreciation of structural integrity, by tropological analysis of a Renaissance commonplace: the relationship of men and women. The three women in 1 Henry VI—Joan of Arc, the Countess of Auvergne, and Margaret of Anjou—resemble one another in their desire for mastery over the male and in the enchanting spells they use to ensnare the intended victim. The theme of feminine supremacy echoes the larger theme of discord and division throughout 1 Henry VI and the tetralogy. Several scenes of temptation that are often thought to be structurally intrusive, added belatedly to provide comic digression or to link 1 Henry VI with succeeding plays, take on new relevance when compared with one another. Such a comparison also unifies the considerable wealth of iconographical allusions used to portray the women. The theme of the domineering female brings to bear a number of medieval and Renaissance truisms concerning antifeminism, rational soul versus fleshly sense, and literary interpretations of such myths as Mars and Venus, the Garden of Adonis, and Circe.

These supposedly intrusive scenes, furthermore, are not all derived from the chronicles of Holinshed and Hall, so that we cannot simply attribute consistent handling of women to the play's sources. Satirical treatment of Joan is to be found in the chronicles: her ignoble birth, her sorcery, her desperate and fallacious confession of pregnancy to avoid execution. Yet her relationship to the Dauphin in the chronicles is uncertain, with the merest hint in Holinshed of sexual attraction. Hall, on the other hand, makes a point of Joan's chastity. Shakespeare has invented and greatly elaborated the theme of sexual domineering. The episode of Talbot with the Countess of Auvergne is entirely fictional. So too is Suffolk's capture of Margaret of Anjou. A considerable proportion of the episodes in 1 Henry VI for which there is no chronicle basis, in fact, concerns these domineering women. Lack of historical sanction has no doubt contributed to the charge of irrelevancy. Yet the very presence of a unifying theme in these invented scenes reveals a focus in Shakespeare's altering of historical fact, even in his earliest contribution to the genre.

In the meeting of the Dauphin and Joan of Arc (I. ii), Shakespeare clearly lampoons the right relation of men and women in a dazzling array of epic and Biblical allusions. One myth familiar for his purposes was that of Mars and Venus, who in their right relationship display the qualities of rationality, honor, and action in hierarchical supremacy to subservient fleshly pleasure. When reason is pandered to sense, however, the masculine principle becomes debased and emasculated. Bestial man wallows in Circean excess. The woman domineers, becoming progressively masculine. Accordingly, when Joan overcomes the Dauphin in a test of physical strength, he apostrophizes her as

> Bright star of Venus, fall'n down on the earth,
> How may I reverently worship thee enough?
>
> [1 Henry VI, I. ii. 144-45]

Yet earlier, in his first speech, the Dauphin had identified his fortunes with those of Mars: "Now we are victors; upon us he smiles" [I. ii. 4]. Even in their first conjunction, the soldier and the lady have assumed unnatural roles of enervated warrior and seductress, signifying disorder in the cosmos and in the state as well.

Other allusions reinforce the theme of sexual inversion and blasphemous parody. The allusions are complexly ironic, sometimes contrasting Joan with positive ideals of divine harmony and sometimes likening her to infamously wanton women.

Her diabolical powers of prophecy, for instance, bear only a perverted resemblance to the prophetic spirit of "the nine sibyls of old Rome" [I. ii. 56], or of St. Philip the Evangelist's daughters who were prophesying virgins, or of Constantine's mother Helen who reputedly discovered the true cross. Serving as object of the Dauphin's veneration, Joan displaces true respect for the divine wisdom of Homer's *Iliad*, encased in Darius' rich-jewelled casket. She is the Dauphin's Saint, and will intercede for him in place of the traditional Saint of Paris, St. Denis. Beneath the anti-Catholic jesting on saint-worship are darker suggestions of pagan idolatry and conversation with evil spirits.

As a blasphemous type of incarnation, Joan competes even more impudently with otherworldly visitors of divine inspiration, both Christian and classical. Her chief identification is with the Virgin Mary, yet Joan is herself a strumpet. Her claim of pregnancy to avoid execution (V. iv.) is an outrageous travesty of the Virgin birth. As her English captors, York and Warwick, wrily comment, "Now, heaven forfend, the holy maid with child!" "The greatest miracle that e'er ye wrought" [V. iv. 65-6]. Like Mohammed, who claimed to partake directly of the secrets of God by means of a dove, Joan boasts of visitations from the Holy Ghost. After her first and greatest victory at Orleans (I. vi) she is likened to Astraea's daughter [I. vi. 4], embodiment of justice in a mythic golden age, and now descended to earth once more in a type of incarnation. Comparison with the genius of the garden of Adonis [I. vi. 6] calls up, to Joan's manifest discredit, an image of pervasive harmony transcending worldly mutability. (pp. 51-2)

Joan's method of seduction, in an ageless antifeminist tradition, is a hypocritical combination of modesty and availability. She is not interested in sex for its own sake; she yields her body for power. This discrepancy between appearance and intention is treated by Shakespeare as a comic discrepancy, and produces an emphasis on salacious double entendres throughout her conversations. The pun is not simply an undignified form of wit intended to provoke coarse laughter, but a thematic device. In virtually every instance, the point is that sexual war is replacing military war. When Joan proposes to the Dauphin that she become his "warlike mate" [I. ii. 92], she suggests not only sexual companionship but that sex become their battlefield, usurping the English war. The Dauphin responds in kind, proposing that "in single combat thou shalt buckle with me" [I. ii. 95]. And so the metaphor continues through the Dauphin's surrender and request for mercy, to Joan's hinting at a ransom.

Of course their union at first produces success against the English as well as in bed, but the inversion of masculinity can ultimately lead only to the Dauphin's enervation as a soldier. Dallying results in a neglecting of the guard and English recapture of Orleans. The Dauphin's watchfulness has been shamefully nonmilitary:

> And for myself, most part of all this night
> Within her quarter and mine own precinct
> I was employed in passing to and fro.
>
>   [II. i. 67-9]

As a witch desiring mastery over men, Joan is not content with the Dauphin alone. Effortlessly she adds the Duke of Burgundy to her menagerie, wooing him to the French side with rhetoric and with witchcraft: "enchant him with thy words" [III. iii. 40], "she hath bewitched me with her words" [III. iii. 58], "I am vanquished" [III. iii. 78]. Having overcome, she contemptuously dismisses her victim with "Done like a French-

man—turn and turn again" [III. iii. 85]. The line is in character for a "foul fiend" and "hag of all despite" [III. ii. 52] who uses rousing jingoistic speech only as a veneer to deceive her victims. Similarly she employs her military authority over the French to seduce Reignier, Alençon, and other of the Dauphin's courtiers. Finally she turns to sexual practices with spirits as well as men.

Three men whom Joan cannot seduce, however, are Lord Talbot, his son John, and his successor as conqueror of the French, the Duke of York. Her attempts to win these champions to her lust are explicit, as York observes in capturing her:

> Unchain your spirits now with spelling charms
> And try if they can gain your liberty.
> A goodly prize, fit for the devil's grace!
> See how the ugly witch doth bend her brows
> As if, with Circe, she would change my shape.
>
>   [V. iii. 31-5]

The allusion to Circe, one of two actual citations of her name in Shakespeare, emphasizes the ugliness of temptation when viewed by the temperate man. York, despite his less attractive qualities of political ambition, is at least indifferent to feminine allure. It is Talbot, however, who most valiantly withstands Joan's power in repeated encounters. In so rejecting temptation he accomplishes what the effete French Dauphin failed to do. The structural comparison between the two as Joan's "wooers" is emphasized once again by the language of double entendre. Just as the Dauphin offers to "buckle" with Joan, Talbot vows to "have a bout with thee" [I. v. 4, III. ii. 56]. She taunts him in the same metaphor with "Are ye so hot, sir?" [III. ii. 58]. She challenges young Talbot, "Thou maiden youth, be vanquished by a maid" [IV. vii. 38]. (pp. 53-4)

Talbot is by no means lacking in Biblical and other allusions to match those of Joan. A type both of folk and Scriptural hero, he suggests echoes of Robin Hood and Alexander the Great. Particularly in his relations with the opposite sex he is reminiscent of Samson with Delilah and Solomon with the Queen of Sheba. He is in each case, however, a transcending figure: a Samson unshorn of his locks, a wise Solomon who is never uxorious. This correctness of attitude, evident in his conduct with Joan, is even more dominant in his relations with the Countess of Auvergne.

Ordinarily dismissed as "both clumsily and unnecessarily introduced" [see essay by John Bell Henneman in the Additional Bibliography], the Auvergne episode is a narrative digression from the French wars but is thematically central. It is once again the type of episode of "the soldier and the lady." The Countess bears important similarities to Joan of Arc. She is a temptress, and an Amazon:

> I shall as famous be by this exploit
> As Scythian Tomyris by Cyrus' death.
>
>   [II. iii. 5-6]

Like the Queen of Scythia who overcame the seemingly unconquerable Cyrus the Great and threw his severed head into a wineskin of human blood, the Countess longs to overcome this second Cyrus, this "bloodthirsty lord" [II. iii. 34]. She wishes to be, like Joan of Arc or Deborah, the feminine savior of her country. The Countess and Joan are both Frenchwomen, both are concerned with their fame, both move with the ruthless certainty of one who has received a divine command. Both desire mastery over men. In perhaps the most significant parallel, the Countess boasts magical powers of attraction:

> And for that cause I trained thee to my house.
> Long time thy shadow hath been thrall to me.
> For in my gallery thy picture hangs;
> But now thy substance shall endure the like.
>   [II. iii. 35-8]
>   (pp. 54-5)

If the Countess is like Joan in thematic ways, the parallel is ultimately intended to convey contrasts. The Countess is, after all, a "virtuous lady" of "modesty" who puts forth a "gentle spirit" in her invitation to Talbot [II. ii. 38-47]. Her identification with the Queen of Sheba is in her favor; the Queen of Sheba is a glorious lady, rich, not profligate, and virtuously impressed with the wisdom of Solomon (II *Chron*.ix. 1-9.) The Countess is of unquestioned high birth. Although the overtones of feminine desire and mastery are not to be denied, they are not erotic; this is a battle between the sexes, but not for bestial pleasure. Even her penchant for witchcraft is alluded to ambiguously. Her motives are unquestionably patriotic, her desire for fame ennobled. Hers is a temptation that Talbot relishes and finds worth even a pause in his military efforts. Talbot finds in the Countess an admiring, rational woman who is ready to be persuaded by firm argument, courage, and a sense of humor. She gladly submits to his mastery, apologizes for her inhospitable behavior, and responds to his gallantry with the courteous entertainment of a feast. Although Talbot triumphs by his foresighted military pragmatism, he also prevails by his courtesy, making peace with a worthy enemy. France must be subservient, but also must be respected. Even if Talbot later falls victim to disorder in the state, he has nobly exemplified the natural order of the right relation between Mars and Venus. The Countess is a credit to her nation and her sex, a rare atonement in this play for an almost universal Gallic depravity.

The third and in a sense the most ominous Frenchwoman in *1 Henry VI* is Margaret of Anjou. Even if she is less openly evil than Joan of Arc, her baleful influence is to be felt as participant, prophetess, and chorus of doom throughout all the tetralogy. Because she makes no appearance in this first play until V. iii, her nascent love affair with the Duke of Suffolk has struck many critics as an unrelated new episode, perhaps a revision added (with the advantage of hindsight) as a narrative link to Part II. A comparison of Margaret with Joan and the Countess reveals, however, that Margaret belongs as much to Part I as to the ensuing cycle. Her subjugation of Suffolk and especially of young Henry VI is fitting climax—or anticlimax—for a play of disorder in which a main subtheme is the subjugation of reason by the flesh.

Margaret is explicitly the successor to Joan as *femme fatale*. Her appearance as Suffolk's captive coincides, though not by coincidence, with York's capture of Joan. Whereas Joan's capture leads to her just trial and execution, Margaret's capture leads by a turning of the tables to her enslaving of the English king. A French woman is to rule an English monarch. This fateful reversal, brought about by Henry's corrupted will, signifies national as well as familial inversion of authority. The enemy in Henry's affections is more dangerous than the devil abroad. (pp. 55-6)

Her powers of enchantment are like those of Joan and the Countess, especially the former. Chief strength is to be found in her eyes and her physical beauty. Her appeal magically

confounds and muddles the senses of those who behold, producing in turn an inability to move, to speak, to exercise self-control [V. iii. 61-71]. (pp. 56-7)

Resemblances to the episode of the Countess of Auvergne are manifest. We find once again the configuration of the soldier and the lady. In this instance (V. iii) it is the lady who as captive turns the tables. Like the Countess, Margaret is of noble blood and bearing. Yet her father's royal title is merely titular and his treasury depleted. Margaret is a courtly lady but slightly disreputable and on the make, heartless and conniving, crafty like the Countess but with none of the Countess' patriotic motive.

She is the perfect mate for Suffolk, who similarly throws away all national concern in his quest for stolen pleasure. Suffolk has never exhibited much sense of public duty; in his very first appearance he has boasted of his intention to "frame the law unto my will" [II. iv. 9]. Such a person is no better than the Dauphin, and like him exchanges the war of military conquest for the war of amorous glances. His hope to rule Margaret and hence the king [V. v. 108] is not self-willed machination but the blind striving of an enslaved appetite.

The final seduction or attempted seduction by an Amazonian woman in *1 Henry VI* is that practised upon Henry himself. This spectacle is the most saddening because it is anticlimactically easy. The lady is not even present. Henry is overcome by words and images appealing to his fatuous inexperience. It is saddening too because it sums up so much of what has been wrong with the corrupted English in the present play and because of its premonitions of future ill. The scene is at once a completion and an opening. The significance of this final fall of man is heightened by the alarmingly representative nature of the protagonist: Henry, the King, who for all his weakness is the central figure and epitome of England's decline. (p. 57)

Here begins the self-indulgent withdrawal of which Henry is so blameworthy in *2 Henry VI*, although it has not been characteristic of him until now. Cultivation of whimsical mood must now precede state affairs. Henry's surrender of reason to flesh is central and gravely serious. As a structural and thematic device, the surrender culminates earlier temptation scenes involving Margaret's predecessors and counterparts, Joan and the Countess of Auvergne. (pp. 57-8)

> *David M. Bevington, "The Domineering Female in '1 Henry VI'," in Shakespeare Studies: An Annual Gathering of Research, Criticism, and Reviews, Vol. II, 1966, pp. 51-8.*

JAMES L. CALDERWOOD   (essay date 1967)

[Calderwood is best known for his examinations of what he calls Shakespeare's "metadrama," published in two studies, Shakespearean Metadrama *(1971) and* Metadrama in Shakespeare's "Henriad" *(1979). In his essay on* 2 Henry VI *excerpted below, Calderwood, like Wolfgang H. Clemen (1951), concludes that much of the imagery in that play is "ornamental and local," rather than integral to the dramatic action. However, Calderwood argues that there are four important patterns of imagery in* 2 Henry VI *that do contribute to the structure of the play, and these he identifies as the patterns of "trapping, sight, elevation, and hands." Of these, he regards the recurring image of sight as the most pervasive and fundamental, particularly in its association with the intrigue against Humphrey of Gloucester. Other critics who have discussed the imagery in* 2 Henry VI *include Caroline F. E. Spurgeon (1935) and Carol McGinnis Kay (1972).]*

Shakespeare's imagery, at least so far as the histories are concerned, begins in [2 Henry VI] to break its ties with the set rhetorical speech and acquire a linear development of its own, begins to move from the static and ornamental toward the active and functional. In fact, some of the imagery in 2 Henry VI, in addition to creating 'atmosphere' and embroidering sentiment, is used in ways that suggest that subtle, inner collusion between word and both deed and character which distinguishes Shakespearean drama at its best. (p. 481)

Four patterns of imagery are especially noteworthy, those having to do with trapping, sight, elevation, and hands. Though these patterns have significance with respect to most of the characters in the play, they are most relevant to Shakespeare's exploration of the kingly character, not in terms of King Henry alone but in terms of the two other regal figures as well—Gloucester the regent and York the claimant.

We might look first at the simplest pattern of imagery, that of trapping. This image first appears when Suffolk, responding to Margaret's expression of hatred for Humphrey's wife Eleanor, says:

> Madam, myself have lim'd a bush for her,
> And placed a choir of such enticing birds
> That she will light to listen to the lays,
> And never mount to trouble you again.
>   [2 Henry VI, I. iii. 88-91]

Suffolk refers to his having lured Eleanor into consorting with necromancers in hopes of finding prophetic support for her ambitions. The lure works, and the trap springs in I. iv when Eleanor is arrested by York and Buckingham at the conjuring session. The ultimate effect, and the intended aim, of this is the partial dishonoring of Duke Humphrey, a sullying of his family 'name' [II. i. 195] if not his personal honor. But the conspirators are after more than just Humphrey's honor: York advises Salisbury and Warwick to put up with Suffolk, Beaufort, Somerset, and Buckingham,

> Till they have snar'd the shepherd of the flock,
> That virtuous prince, the good Duke Humphrey.
>   [II. ii. 73-4]

During Eleanor's scene of humiliation (II. iv) she too employs the trapping image when she sarcastically berates Humphrey for not countering craft with craft: Suffolk, York, and Beaufort, she says,

> Have all lim'd bushes to betray thy wings,
> And fly thou how thou canst' they'll tangle thee.
> But fear not thou, until thy foot be snar'd
> Nor never seek prevention of thy foes.
>   [II. iv. 54-7]

And in III. i, the conspirators having chosen murder as the best means of eliminating Humphrey, Suffolk says:

> And do not stand on quillets how to slay him;
> Be it by gins, by snares, by subtlety,
> Sleeping or waking, 'tis no matter how,
> So he be dead.
>   [III. i. 261-64]

In the following scene, Humphrey is done away with in his sleep by hired murderers.

Operating at this relatively simple level, the trapping imagery does not accomplish a great deal. That the trappers are identified as such by this imagery merely reinforces an already clear characterization of them as dealers in duplicity; and that Humphrey must be trapped merely reinforces the already obvious fact of his guiltlessness. The division of characters into the trappers and the trapped by images of fixed significance, which neither develop nor alter in expression, is at best a rudimentary means of distinguishing Humphrey from the nobles, and one which fails entirely to distinguish the individual nobles from one another. (pp. 483-84)

But for one exception, the trapping imagery ends with Humphrey's death. In III. iii, Cardinal Beaufort, Humphrey's old enemy, dies in wretched conscience. But before he dies he is preyed upon by hallucinations in which he sees the dead Humphrey alive again, and he cries out:

> Comb down his hair; look, look! it stands upright,
> Like lime-twigs set to catch my winged soul.
>   [III. iii. 15-16]

This represents the only attempt to break the trapping imagery out of its rigid mold. At the spiritual level, traps appear as instruments too crude and gross to snare the innocent soul of Humphrey; but the Cardinal has apparently discovered that the lure of luring leads the would-be worldly trapper into a greater trap, the nets of which are woven exceedingly fine.

If none of the trappers in the play sees well enough to discern the spiritual implications of trapping, they all display a great deal of visual acuity nevertheless. The most pervasive kind of recurrent image in 2 Henry VI is that having to do with sight, and although Shakespeare employs this image with much less skill than he does later on, yet he makes it considerably more serviceable than the trapping image. How and what men see is of course highly indicative of what they are and wish to become. There are no neat divisions consistently maintained here, but in general we can distinguish at least two major ways of seeing: in Henry, innocence of vision, and in the conspirators, malignity of vision. In accord with their major mode of operation, duplicity, the conspirators are adept in the manipulation of appearances, controllers of both their own and others' seeing. York, for instance, advises Salisbury and Warwick to adopt a form of selective blindness:

> Do you as I do in these dangerous days;
> Wink at the Duke of Suffolk's insolence,
> At Beaufort's pride, at Somerset's ambition,
> At Buckingham and all the crew of them,
> Till they have snar'd the shepherd of the flock,
> That virtuous prince, the good Duke Humphrey.
>   [II. ii. 69-74]

Watchfulness, keenness of sight, a predilection for seeing into or through: these are characteristics of the conspirators in general. (pp. 484-85)

In [the] latter half of the opening scene of the play we [are] given, one by one, the various kinds of seeing employed by the major characters. The Cardinal is watching Humphrey; Buckingham and Somerset are watching the Cardinal; and York is watching everybody. The conspirators are almost literally 'all eyes'. At this point, however, their mode of seeing is essentially passive, mere watchfulness. Until they are ready to make their moves, they simply register all that goes on, waiting to 'spy advantage' [I. i. 242]. When they do spy advantage, this passive kind of vision is transformed into an active kind which we might call discernment or visual penetration.

The major attack upon Humphrey, the failure of which precipitates the shift to violence, appears in III. i and is dramatized as a matter of seeing. The conspirators are no longer waiting and watching but acting and discerning, seeing into and through. Their task here is to make Henry see both as and what they see. The fact that Humphrey has not 'shown up' yet at the Abbey offers Margaret her opening: 'Can you not see', she asks Henry, 'or will ye not observe / The strangeness of [Humphrey's] alter'd countenance?' [III. i. 4-5]. In a speech too long to quote, she displays for Henry's sight various images of Humphrey's supposed maleficence: formerly 'if we did but glance a far-off look, / Immediately he was upon his knee' [III. i. 10-11], but now 'He knits his brow and shows an angry eye' [III. i. 15]. Concluding, she appeals to the others and is quickly seconded by Suffolk: 'Well hath your Highness seen into this duke'—

> Smooth runs the water where the brook is deep;
> And in his simple show he harbours treason.
> [III. i. 42, 53-4]

Cardinal Beaufort and York chime in with accusations against Humphrey, after which Bolingbroke reaches the heights of optical speciousness in his claim that, contrary to William of Occam, supposedly visible entities should be multiplied by invisible ones: 'Tut, these are petty faults to faults unknown / Which time will bring to light in smooth Duke Humphrey' [III. i. 64-5]. This is the culmination of the sight imagery so far as it concerns the plot against Humphrey. The conspirators' case rests finally upon 'faults unknown' within a Humphrey whose corruption can be seen only by eyes gifted with special powers of discernment.

Unfortunately for the conspirators, however, Henry lacks this kind of ocular penetration. . . . With some notable exceptions, Henry's sight is limited throughout the play. His inability to see deeply, which precludes a proper assessment of Suffolk or Margaret, or indeed any of the plotters, may be the vice of innocence; however, when there is simply nothing to see into or through, that vice becomes a cardinal virtue. 'Can you not see, or will ye not observe', Margaret demands, with the vexation of the keen-eyed for the myopic, but Henry can neither see nor observe as she would have him. Though he permits, or at least does nothing to prevent, the arrest and imprisonment of Humphrey, he can no more see Humphrey's 'faults unknown' than his supposedly visible faults. . . . [One] effect of the scene in which Humphrey discredits the supposedly blind man (II. i) is to distinguish Humphrey's perception from Henry's comparative sightlessness. Humphrey reveals not only that those who claim blindness may actually see but also that those who claim sight may actually be blind. Unfortunately, the lesson does not take. Henry's reaction is, as usual, pious, but it also, as usual, shifts the responsibilities of seeing and doing elsewhere: 'O God, seest Thou this, and bearest so long?' [II. i. 151]

If while Humphrey is alive he cannot enable Henry to see for himself, his death nevertheless provides Henry considerable illumination. No sooner does Suffolk announce Humphrey's death than Henry faints. Margaret calls out, 'O Henry, ope thine eyes' [III. ii. 35] and so he does, to behold Suffolk in his true light:

> Thou baleful messenger, out of my sight!
> Upon thy eye-balls murderous tyranny
> Sits in grim majesty, to fright the world.
> Look not upon me, for thine eyes are wounding.
> Yet do not go away. Come, basilisk,
> And kill the innocent gazer with thy sight.
> [III. ii. 48-53]

Innocence acquires its first genuine view of evil, and sums up in the figure of the basilisk that penetrative form of vision which we have called discernment. Humphrey's life, it seems, is the price paid for Henry's vision of Suffolk and, to a certain extent, of himself. (pp. 486-88)

The sight imagery, then, is employed by most of the characters and is especially relevant as an accompaniment of the intrigue plot which culminates in Humphrey's death. After that, as the manipulation of appearances gives way to the wielding of arms, first with Cade's rebellion, then with York's, the hand and the arm become prominent as symbols of power and aspiration. Before focusing upon this imagery, however, let us turn to what I have called imagery of elevation, although what we're dealing with here, even if it has some resemblance to imagery, is less a matter of images than of perspectives. In I. ii, for instance, Humphrey and Eleanor are characterized largely in terms of their angles of vision with respect to the ground. Eleanor asks:

> Why are thine eyes fix'd to the sullen earth,
> Gazing on that which seems to dim thy sight?
> What seest thou there? King Henry's diadem,
> Enchas'd with all the honours of the world?
> If so, gaze on, and grovel on thy face,
> Until thy head be circled with the same.
> Put forth thy hand, reach at the glorious gold,
> What, is't too short? I'll lengthen it with mine;
> And, having both together heav'd it up,
> We'll both together lift our heads to heaven
> And never more abase our sight so low
> As to vouchsafe one glance unto the ground.
> [I. ii. 5-16]

Humphrey looks upon 'the sullen earth'; Eleanor is willing to do so only if 'King Henry's diadem' lies there, in which case she even advocates groveling, though afterwards she will 'never more abase' her sight by glancing at the ground. Humphrey's willingness to look upon the earth becomes symbolic of his humility, and suggests that the up-down perspectives can be associated with metaphors of social elevation—part of Humphrey's power, and therefore danger to the plotters, is his popularity with the commons [I. i. 158-59, III. i. 240]. In Eleanor's inverted scale of values, highmindedness—Humphrey's refusal to countenance her ambitions—signifies a 'base and humble mind' [I. ii. 62]. She, on the other hand, has the true climbing spirit; her gaze is upward, disdaining the world though not the worldly: 'Hast thou not worldly pleasure at command / Above the reach or compass of thy thought?' Humphrey asks her [I. ii. 45-6]. To help confirm her aspirations upward, however, she is not above calling upon the underworld; the necromancers, as Hume tells her, have promised 'to show your Highness / A spirit rais'd from depth of underground' [I. ii. 78-9]. Ironically, her reliance upon the depths to aid her to 'Highness' brings her low, to the point where, under the contemptuous gaze of the multitude as she walks the flinty ground barefoot, she can ask, 'Trow'st thou that e'er I'll look upon the world, / Or count them happy that enjoys the sun?' [II. iv. 38-9].

Humphrey's humility of vision—his willingness not only to look down but even to be looked down upon by social inferiors . . . —has for its complement an elevation of mind and spirit. At the opening of II. i., Suffolk glibly remarks upon the superiority of Humphrey's falcons:

> No marvel, an it like your Majesty,
> My Lord Protector's hawks do tower so well.

Part II. Act II. Scene ii. Warwick, Salisbury, and York. By William Hamilton (n.d.).

They know their master loves to be aloft
And bears his thoughts above his falcon's pitch.

[II. i. 9-12]

Humphrey replies: 'My lord, 'tis but a base ignoble mind / That mounts no higher than a bird can soar' [II. i. 13-14]. Humphrey's downcast sight and his elevation of mind appear to represent a dual perspective the coexistence of which is essential to genuine honor and moral rectitude. (pp. 489-90)

Although this by no means exhausts the imagery or perspectives of elevation, the basic pattern has been suggested. Let us now return to the hand-arm imagery, which is most significant with respect to Henry and, especially, York, though there are of course other instances of it. In the opening lines of the play, Suffolk, having acted as Henry's proxy in marriage, delivers up his 'title in the Queen' to Henry's 'most gracious hand' [I. i. 12-13]. Graced though they may be, Henry's hands are ineffectual instruments of power, more suited to telling beads than to wielding either sceptres or swords: as York says near the end of the scene, Henry holds the sceptre in a 'childish fist' [I. i. 245]. In Cardinal Beaufort's speech against Humphrey, the latter's popularity with the commons is illustrated by the fact that they call him

> 'the good Duke of Gloucester',
> Clapping their hands, and crying with loud voice,
> 'Jesus maintain your royal Excellence!'

[I. i. 159-61]

To these benign sorts and uses of hands is added a suggestion of malign employments when Buckingham assures the Cardinal and Somerset that by united action they will 'quickly hoise Duke Humphrey from his seat' [I. i. 169]. Later on, Suffolk, who is an inveterate parodist of the symbolic gestures of honor, pledges to the Cardinal his aid in the strangling of Humphrey: 'Here is my hand, the deed is worthy doing' [III. i. 278]. Thus, after Humphrey's murder, it is fitting that Henry's enlightened view of Suffolk be expressed as a recognition of the deadliness not only of Suffolk's vision but also of his hands: 'Lay not thy hands upon me; forbear, I say! / Their touch affrights me as a serpent's sting' [III. ii. 46-7].

However, it is chiefly York of whom the hand becomes an emblem. Uncharacteristically, his first mention of hands stresses his helplessness: at the end of I. i he likens his dismay at the loss of French lands to that of an owner of goods that have been stolen and given away by 'pirates'; all he can do is weep over his losses and wring 'his helpless hands . . . while all is shar'd and all is borne away, / Ready to starve and dare not touch his own' [I. i. 226-29]. This is the York who is compelled to wait until his hands have been supplied with weapons sufficiently powerful to justify bringing his dormant revolt into the open. 'Then', as he says in an image suggesting the flower within the mailed fist, 'will I raise aloft the milk-white rose' [I. i. 254]. In the next scene in which he appears, York bursts in upon the Duchess and the necromancers with the words, 'Lay hands upon these traitors and their trash', adding with the self-satisfaction of the keen-eyed, 'Beldam, I think we watch'd you at an inch' [I. iv. 41-2]. In III. i, where the plotters make their major public attack upon him, Humphrey says of York:

> And dogged York, that reaches at the moon,
> Whose overweening arm I have pluck'd back,
> By false accuse doth level at my life.

[III. i. 158-60]

At the close of this scene, York deftly maneuvers the other plotters into giving him command of an army, the importance of which he afterwards soliloquizes about:

> 'Twas men I lack'd and you will give them me.
> I take it kindly; yet be well assur'd
> You put sharp weapons in a madman's hands.

[III. i. 345-47]

When York next reappears, at the opening of V. i, he says:

> Ah! *sancta majestas*, who would not buy thee dear?
> Let them obey that knows not how to rule;
> This hand was made to handle nought but gold,
> I cannot give due action to my words
> Except a sword or sceptre balance it.

[V. i. 5-9]

And finally, when Henry's failure to keep Somerset imprisoned (whether Margaret released Somerset with or without Henry's knowledge is not clear) is revealed, York 'braves' Henry to his face with the claim, 'Thy hand is made to grasp a palmer's staff / And not to grace an awful princely sceptre', whereas 'Here is a hand to hold a sceptre up / And with the same to act controlling laws' [V. i. 97-103].

Throughout the play, then, the hand that is either raised up in assertion ('Then will I raise aloft the milk-white rose') or reached up to seize ('And dogged York, that reaches at the moon') symbolizes York's regal aspirations and the strength and tenacity which undergird them. In itself, the hand image is an

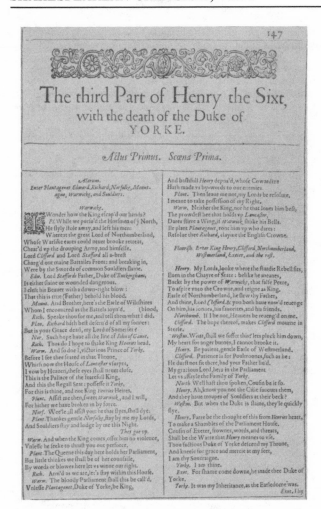

Title page of 3 Henry VI *from the First Folio (1623).*

especially appropriate symbol for the man of action that York is: however, the symbolic meanings are compounded. Used by himself (e.g., 'I cannot give due action to my words / Except a sword or sceptre balance [my hand]'), the image implies York's fragmentary existence and uncompleted nature: in his own view of himself, he is a part seeking its whole, a hand without the body which only kingship can give it. At the same time, the hand imagery suggests a radical limitation of York's character, especially of his character as potential king, and in this respect it reinforces the imagery of sight and of perspective; for York's limited kinds of vision and his inverted kinds of perspective argue according to the symbolic logic of the play his inappropriateness for kingship. The hand imagery, however, not only reinforces the fact of York's regal deficiencies but also helps clarify their nature. In disputing Henry's right to the crown [V. i. 97-8] and in proclaiming his own kingly virtues [V. i. 102-3], York finds the hand and its functions inordinately relevant. It seems clear that he regards kingship less as a position which imposes responsibilities than as one which licenses power. If his nature cannot acquire perfect freedom of expression until his hand is joined to a sceptre, he thinks of this freedom primarily as enabling his hand to turn the sceptre into a club. Granted that Henry's reign has brought England to the point where strength and vigor of command are cardinal requisites for any program of national reconstruction, still York's preoccupation with power as such, rather than with

responsible power, morally invalidates his claims upon the crown. In fact, once York does acquire military power, his willingness to subordinate England's welfare to his own ambitions is exemplified by his irresponsible loosing of Cade's forces upon England and, later, by his initiating the civil wars. To give York power, whether it be swords to subdue the Irish or a sceptre to rule the English, is clearly, in his words, to 'put sharp weapons in a madman's hands'. The sceptre, of course, never comes into York's hand, though a paper crown goes onto his head in *3 Henry VI*. In time, however, his namesake son acquires both sword and sceptre, and in his 'madman's hands' the two become indistinguishable. (pp. 490-93)

[We] do not find at this stage of Shakespeare's development the sort of constant imagistic relevance we find in, say, *King Lear* or *Macbeth,* where virtually every image of a particular kind is significantly related to others of its kind as well as to larger issues of plot, character, and theme. At this stage, in short, much remains ornamental and local. But if the patterns we have traced are patterns within a larger nebula of imagery, still they are patterns; they reveal correspondences and interrelationships rather than merely haphazard recurrences, and thus they create a dimension to the drama that deserves exploring. The rewards of exploring are, at this early transitional phase of Shakespeare's development, less impressive than they are at a later point; but the germs of the later successes are here—if they were not, what comes later might not have come at all. (p. 493)

> *James L. Calderwood, "Shakespeare's Evolving Imagery: '2 Henry VI'," in* English Studies, *Vol. XLVIII, No. 6, December, 1967, pp. 481-93.*

H. M. RICHMOND   (essay date 1967)

[*Richmond regards Shakespeare's historical cycle as an extensive study of the complex origins of political authority. Unlike Hermann Ulrici (1839), E. M. W. Tillyard (1944), M. M. Reese (1961), and Irving Ribner (1965), Richmond does not view the* Henry VI *trilogy as propagating the Tudor interpretation of English history, or even as endorsing the idea of providential retribution; instead, like A. C. Hamilton (1961-62) and S. C. Sen Gupta (1964), he argues that the trilogy presents a dramatic, complex investigation of "the nature and hazards of political and moral judgment." Also, like Hereward T. Price (1951), Richmond perceives a subtle thematic unity in each of the* Henry VI *plays which is based on the conflict between the ethical and political perceptions of the various characters. Particularly in 2 and 3* Henry VI, *Richmond contends, this conflict centers around those characters—primarily Shakespeare's women, but also Jack Cade and Richard of Gloucester—who possess the ability to manipulate reality through language and rhetoric, and those characters— like Henry, Suffolk, and, to a certain degree, Duke Humphrey— who either naively accept appearances or who, as with Suffolk, base their perception of reality on a facile, romantic system of language and thought. The dominance of Shakespeare's women in* Henry VI *has also been discussed by David M. Bevington (1966), Leslie A. Fiedler (1972), and Marilyn French (1981). Other critics who disagree with either the Tudor or the providential interpretation of the trilogy include James Winny (1968) and Michael Manheim (1973).*]

In *Henry VI,* despite the appearance of King Henry in all three parts, there are no central personal relationships of the kind that define other tragic drama. The focus shifts freely from Gloucester to Talbot, to Joan, to the King and so on, in a seemingly endless series of juxtapositions. The work thereby defies Aristotelian aesthetics of the kind that is so characteristic of post-medieval European writing, in which overt structure and consistency are highly prized. Modern drama, for example, affords almost no parallels to the *Henry VI* series, whose norms belong rather to a literary tradition that was nearing its end when this series was written. This is the medieval tradition of the multiple narrative, which is best compared—if to any classical genre—to that of the Hesiodic epic. (p. 19)

[It] is not enough to dismiss the plays as so confused as to be necessarily the work of an ill-assorted team of co-authors, even if there are some grounds for linking them (at least for their sources or models) with Greene, Marlowe, and Peele, as well as with Shakespeare. Nor can we deal with the plays in terms of the problems involved in a naive chronicle of national history: the tone is too harsh to suit local patriotism. While the plays often appear to be made up of arbitrarily chosen episodes from the fifty-year reign of Henry VI, one can still strongly sense the unique cumulative effect that these scenes have in reading, not to speak of performance. The critic's real need is to determine whether this effect is of a memorable and significant kind; for the result of such complex literary and social combinations is not necessarily fragmentary, even if its genesis does defy neat explanation. It may display that unity, larger than the perspective of a single author or principle, which is sometimes seen in Homer. (pp. 20-1)

As for the memorableness of the first part, of that there can be no doubt. The play contains a galaxy of brilliant scenes, beginning with the elegiac opening, through which the death of Henry V dominates the characters and plot. This stroke of literary strategy definitively establishes the gloomy medieval rhythm of the wheel of fortune which destroys both the English hero Talbot and his enemy Joan of Arc, and governs all the plots of the tetralogy. This first disastrous setback to English leadership in the wars with France leads naturally to the discussion of various aspects of the nature of military and political efficiency in the state. The theme provides us with a first glimpse of the implicit statement about the instability of public life of which the action of the plays is the correlative.

It is the essence of the history play (as opposed to narrative history) to present by epitome—to intensify confrontations and polarize issues. In *Henry VI, Part 1*, this process is typified by the brilliantly improvised scene in the Temple Garden (II. iv.). Here the factionalism that progressively undermines Henry V's achievement of a unified and aggressive England is heraldically epitomized through the plucking of red and white roses by the factions of York and Lancaster—a scene for which there was no precedent in history. The abuse of humane reason in this vivid confrontation is carefully stressed. After agreeing to a trial by vote of the issue (itself so incidental as never to be established), both factions fail to maintain decorum. The outcome of the reasonable idea of a vote thus merely intensifies the acerbity of the quarrel.

In the previous scene, by profoundly appropriate juxtaposition, there had also appeared in the conduct of the representative of the best among the English, the elder Talbot, a seemingly no less gross surrendering of his faculties of judgment to facile emotion, aroused by the charms of a French patriot, the seductive Countess of Auvergne. She, like St. Joan, anticipates that fatal energy that so many of Shakespeare's tragic women display. But while Talbot's instincts in the presence of the seductive French Countess also appear to be submerging his reasoning powers, the conclusion of the scene achieves a dramatic reversal, in which he reveals that he has anticipated and neutralized the Countess' emotional strategy. The irony lies in the contrast within each of these two scenes—Talbot appears

naive, yet proves discreet, and even ultimately gallant; the factions affect polite and rational debate, yet proceed rapidly to insults and physical threats.

From this particular sequence, it is easy to move out into the larger patterns of the play. The sexual axis of Talbot and the Countess is of the greatest relevance to the recurring rhythms both of this play and of the tetralogy that it introduces. We later find Talbot, for example, confronted by another female representative of the subtle, even diabolical wiles of the French—deceits that Shakespeare characteristically associates with women (even the best of them, such as Viola, Rosalind, and Portia, exploit disguise extravagantly and often quite sadistically). Joan appears to epitomize such traits in this play—she captures Rouen through a disguise that so offends Talbot's sense of decorum that he calls it "treason." Of course, the play takes here, as generally, an anti-French view of Joan. It seems naive, however, to be indignant now over the harshness of the portrait. To expect any Protestant Elizabethan to show a French Catholic heroine as advised not by devils but by angels, so soon after the massacre of St. Bartholomew's day, would be the equivalent of showing in our own post-war years that, say, Bismarck had been similarly well-advised. Furthermore, the play passes a far less contemptuous judgment on Joan's actions than it does on most of the failings of the English representatives—as, for example, on the cowardice of Fastolfe (historically, a mistaken accusation), or the factious dilatoriness of Somerset and York:

> The fraud of England, not the force of France
> Hath now entrapp'd the noble-minded Talbot.
> [*1 Henry VI*, IV. iv. 36-7]

Yet even this contrast provides an inadequate conclusion about the status of Joan. The play is "against" Joan in much the same way as Aeschylus is against the Persians or Clytemnestra. Just as the Greek author had censured Clytemnestra while still making her a dominating and even heroic figure in the *Oresteia,* so Shakespeare's figure of Joan displays heroic power—even something of the magnetism that the real Joan undoubtedly possessed—and Talbot is made to recognize his weakness in confronting such a figure:

> My thoughts are whirled like a potter's wheel.
> I know not where I am, nor what I do:
> A witch, by fear, not force, like Hannibal,
> Drives back our troops and conquers as she lists.
> [I. v. 19-22]

No audience can be insensitive to the energy and passion of this Joan, nor to her subtlety and finesse, which a nominal shift in perspective could readily convert into saintly insight. Her speech to the wavering Burgundy is masterly in its emphasis and emotional strategy:

> Look on thy country, look on fertile France,
> And see the cities and the towns defaced
> By wasting ruin of the cruel foe.
> As looks the mother on her lowly babe
> When death doth close his tender dying eyes,
> See, see the pining malady of France;
> Behold the wounds, the most unnatural wounds,
> Which thou thyself hast given her woeful breast.
> O, turn thy edged sword another way;
> Strike those that hurt, and hurt not those that help.
> [III. iii. 44-53]

Joan can strike as true a chord as this—and her power to do so is as much explained as degraded by her final acid comment on the reversed allegiance of the vacillating Burgundy in *Henry VI:* ''Done like a Frenchman: turn, and turn again!'' [III. iii. 85]. (pp. 21-4)

This element in the portrait of Joan has, of course, no foundations in the Joan of history and the records of her trial, but that incredible person defies literary imagination and has only the authority of fact to support her. As Aristotle observed, drama should be more concerned with what is probable than with that which is merely possible. Joan as she appears in *Henry VI* is frightening rather than noble, but her superhuman effectiveness is very plausible and altogether memorable. Her savage resolution as her army fails [V. ii. 1-29] is as monumental as Lady Macbeth's when faced with the risk of her husband's failure. Joan's confrontation with her father after her capture and her shifts and turns to escape execution are full of an intense energy and love of life that display that potency of Shakespeare's women from which, in part, [George Bernard] Shaw developed his theory of the alliance between women and the life force.

One feels indeed the emergence of a plausible interpretation of that almost irresistible determination which had enabled Joan of Arc to transform the military situation in France. The play needs no apology as drama for having substituted near-Machiavellian insight (a far more plausible resource) for the naive faith that, almost incredibly, carried the historical St. Joan so far. And the play does give Joan the last word—one that resonates down to the horrible deaths of York and his family in *Part 3* and beyond. York's dismissal of Joan to death provokes her dying curse, which has the prophetic authority that Shakespeare always gives to those who are soon to die:

> Then lead me hence; with whom I leave my curse:
> May never glorious sun reflex his beams
> Upon the country where you make abode;
> But darkness and the gloomy shade of death
> Environ you, till mischief and despair
> Drive you to break your necks or hang yourselves!
>   [V. vi. 86-91]
>   (pp. 24-5)

At the heart of the failure of the English to achieve [Joan's] ruthless efficiency stands Henry VI himself. His character and situation are the key to the whole tetralogy—and the play may seem to go almost extravagantly out of its way in order to clarify the dynastic situation, if we do not remember that, no matter how insignificant Henry may seem at first, he is the pivot on which the action turns. This is the reason for the long expository scene in the Tower between Mortimer and his gaolers, and later with Richard Plantagenet (II. v.). The scene establishes a fascinating contrast between the two branches of the Plantagenet family—the usurping Lancastrians, and the Yorkists who claim the right of true succession to the throne. The Lancastrians begin as brilliant and calculating opportunists who are vindicated by their very success. . . . But Henry VI is of a different temper from his father and grandfather, as his surrender to Suffolk's romanticism at the end of the play makes clear in a different respect. While his title to the throne is not unquestionable, yet no one would dare to challenge his grip on the sceptre—as long as it is a firm one. It is not. (pp. 32-3)

Just as the very innocence of Othello's mind exposes him all the more fully to the rationalized promptings of evil, in the form of Iago, so it is Henry's impulsive desire to resolve [political issues] by a consistent and appealing emotional attitude that is ultimately fatal to the stability and well-being of En-

gland. In the very scene after that in which Mortimer and Richard had both analyzed their claims to Henry's throne, Henry innocently restores to Richard the high title of Duke of York, suppressed on the execution of Richard's father for treason. Worse, he gives substance to this ominous title that his father Henry V had firmly kept vacant, by adding,

> . . . all the whole inheritance I give
> That doth belong unto the house of York.
>   [III. i. 163-64]

Thus we are confronted with a king who takes satisfaction in making the gestures of royalty, but remains unaware of the substructure of political mastery which must underlie the grand act, if it is to achieve anything of permanent value. (p. 34)

[*Henry VI, Part 1*] has a genuine thematic unity. But it is a subtle and substantial one, based on a complex interaction of ethics and politics, and not merely a formal aesthetic organization. Joan embodies all those dangerous resources and that virile energy that the effeminate Henry lacks; in this, she is paradoxically closer to the practical character of the true saint than is the amiable and mystical Henry whom she opposes. The French are conscious masters of those elusive manipulations that dominate circumstance, while still playing deceptively on the rhetoric of emotion that Henry mistakes for political reality. And just as the English lose their mastery in France because, with the exception of Talbot, they lack this sleight of mind, so at home their country drifts into ruin as these devices are used increasingly there—not to buttress, but to subvert established authority.

The strength of the play lies almost entirely in the plot's vigorous exposition of these political issues, for its style rarely rises to memorable heights, even in the speeches of Joan, who is appropriately its most dynamic character. At its best, the style shows a sure-footed exploitation of conventional resources, as in Suffolk's speeches to and about Margaret. The literary finesse of the author appears far more clearly in his choice of events—even his creation of them—to epitomize phases of the political situation, and the juxtaposition of these events in subtle counterpoint. The best scenes are those that are marked by acute value conflicts—as when Joan meets and repudiates her father, or seeks desperate subterfuges to avoid execution by her English captors (a scene memorable enough to provide a model for Webster's scene of Cariola's death in *The Duchess of Malfi*). The tone of the play does not seem at once to contrast with the patriotic concern of the earlier chronicle plays (one of which may have dealt with Talbot's career); their anti-French, anti-Catholic moralizing reappears in many scenes, and sententious choric speeches still abound. Nevertheless, unlike Hall's *Chronicles* (in which this moralizing, patriotic norm is well revealed) the play often also seems to show less fully defined yet exciting reservations about the simple themes of Protestant nationalism.

The very choice of the weak Henry VI rather than the dashing Talbot as the play's pivot is curious. Despite elements in each vein, this is no simple story of triumphant heroism, like that of Henry V, nor of supposed patriotic issues, like that of King John; it is not a piece of useful political propaganda for the Tudors, like the conventional treatment of Richard III. Henry tries to say all the right things, yet somehow even the best sentiments in the play always have a faint false echo; and the most suspect figures, like the three French women, show hypnotic qualities that are absent from the others. Suffolk anticipates the conventional ecstasies of Romeo, but in infinitely more compromising circumstances, which even call into question any simple uncritical delight in the romanticism of the later play. Such an effect typifies the earlier play's alertness to the potential paradoxes that are inherent in those values which, for the most part, it conscientiously pursues on the surface. It may be that these curious dissonances do reflect merely a patched-up piece of work, designed to act as a sort of prelude to *Part 2,* yet their presence in all the best scenes suggests that the author already has that fascination with reversals and paradoxes that is characteristic of the work of the mature Shakespeare. The dramatic irony of the scene between Talbot and the Countess neatly epitomizes this aspect. Talbot reduces her to bewilderment at the very instant when she is preparing to shackle him, by mocking her desire to imprison a mere shadow. She exclaims:

> This is a riddling merchant for the nonce;
> He will be here, and yet he is not here:
> How can these contraries agree?
>
> [II. iii. 57-9]

Only then does Talbot cut through the ambiguities of meaning to call up his real strength in the form of his concealed army. The realities of power and the contrasting ambiguities of language and appearance are perfectly expressed in this scene. (pp. 36-8)

The society of the first part of *Henry VI* is on the verge of disintegration, but it is still recognizably an ordered society. The innocence of its ruler still allows power only in France to those deadly forces that are grouped around the French women, and more particularly around Joan of Arc (where they appear to take the form of devils). In the second part of *Henry VI,* these forces have invaded English society, largely through the agency of Margaret. Under her impact, that society begins to disintegrate; a kind of blight spreads from her every contact, fostering such monstrosities as the witchcraft that results from the envy of the termagant Duchess of Gloucester. As the play progresses, there is an almost total disintegration of political and moral order within the state. Few elements of the play are more morbidly hypnotic than the painful erosion of the position and personality of the well-meaning Lord Protector, Humphrey Duke of Gloucester, regent during Henry's minority. One watches with fascination the almost tangible currents of evil thus undercutting the foundations of the state. Indeed, the destruction of the state proves to be a mental process, for one perceives that it is essentially semantic (as George Orwell has observed in his famous essay on politics and the English language). Aided skillfully by the no less ambitious Cardinal Beaufort, Bishop of Winchester, Margaret pursues the attainment of dominion over the king by heightening the latent schism between what is said and what is meant and done, thus destroying the possibility of rational judgment and action.

Again certain scenes epitomize this central concern of the play: the nature and hazards of political and moral judgment. The theme is particularly important to the long, complex scene at the start of Act II. Ironically, it is the doomed Gloucester himself who here shows how to distinguish the true from the false, rather as the equally doomed Talbot had mastered the deceit of the Countess of Auvergne in the previous play. He deftly demonstrates the feigned character of the "miracle" that has deceived king and court, and accomplishes a further "miracle" himself by frightening the supposed cripple out of his invalid chair, thereby revealing the deception to the scandalized king, who exclaims, horrified by the trickery he has now discovered:

O God, seest Thou this, and bearest so long?

[*2 Henry VI,* II. i. 151]

Nevertheless, the moral of the episode escapes the king: that truth is rarely palatable and almost never in harmony with one's hopes—that it is to be attained only by a relentless investigation which requires rigorous, even brutal methods. Yet if Gloucester, at least, has the wit to perceive the truth on this occasion, his uncertain authority as regent prevents him from exercising his insight effectively in the interests of the state.

The susceptibility of the king to Suffolk's blend of sentimentality and covert ambition is shown by his acceptance of the marriage to Margaret that makes her queen. This has already begun the play on an ominous note of courtly affectation triumphing over political incompetence, which is further stressed when Gloucester discovers that the terms of the marriage contract negotiated by Suffolk have in fact cost England the two major parts of her possessions in France, and thereby the security of all the rest. His stupefaction, distress, and final anger are promptly and willfully misinterpreted by the Cardinal as symptoms of haughty pride and ambition, an accusation that is beautifully capped by the soliloquy of York with which the scene ends—in which York proves to be in fact possessed of the very motives and character of which Gloucester has been falsely accused. . . . Here is another of those ironic juxtapositions that are the hallmark of Shakespearean plot structure, which depends for its impact on the reversal of the expectations of conventional judgment. The man who appears to behave immoderately is in fact virtuous, while the true source of danger lies concealed under the mask of decorum. (pp. 39-41)

The nature of the moral order of the universe in its relation to political and judicial acts becomes the central concern of the play through this kind of counterpoint of fact and interpretation; the scenes of Gloucester's fall show the secularization of the drama, in that Henry's faith in the realization of God's justice on earth has been proven to be shockingly at odds with the truth of particular situations. The issue is further intensified by the scene of separation, in which the exiled Duchess grimly warns her husband that mere innocence will be no security against his subtle enemies; but with strenuous conviction Humphrey refuses, like the king, to believe in the powers of evil:

> Ah, Nell, forbear! thou aimest all awry;
> I must offend before I be attainted;
> And had I twenty times so many foes,
> And each of them had twenty times their power,
> All these could not procure me any scathe,
> So long as I am loyal, true and crimeless.
>
> [II. v. 58-63]

The two following scenes, which demonstrate the folly both of Gloucester's self-assurance and of the king's faith in the triumph of virtue, are made painful and often intensely dramatic by such skillful alternations as that of the accusations against Gloucester and York's second soliloquy, in which he avows the very treason of which Gloucester is wrongfully accused. Neither Gloucester nor the king can cope with the relentless misrepresentations of the queen, who is aided and abetted by the Cardinal. Where evil is so strenuous, virtue tends to be defensive; or sometimes it becomes guilty of no less stridency, to its own disadvantage.

The murder of Gloucester alone can shock Henry into effective action in banishing the transparently guilty Suffolk. And here begins the countermovement of the play. Gloucester's murder is a pivotal event in the tetralogy, an action so monstrous as to set on foot forces that demonstrate that the characters still exist in an ultimately ordered universe—although one by no means as wholly subject to Providence as Henry imagines, or as the old morality plays had shown. Virtue may be destroyed often in the world of *Henry VI*, but Nemesis always overtakes the guilty. The Duchess of Gloucester's diabolism meets its deserts, as does the comparable guilt of the queen and Suffolk. In fact, the audience cannot but be struck by the duplication of the Gloucesters' scene of separation in the later one at Act III, Scene ii; only now it is Suffolk who is exiled from England and, along with him, his mistress the queen laments their resulting separation.

Even in the midst of Suffolk's romantic exclamations comes a more dreadful, yet equally justified stroke of fate. We have already been told by the second murderer of the full innocence of Gloucester's death: "O that it were to do! What have we done? Didst ever hear a man so penitent?" [III. ii. 3-4]. Now we hear about the state of the dying Cardinal, who had taken the initiative in proposing that murder. Like Lady Macbeth's, his mind has disintegrated under the stress of his own villainy. Vaux reports

> That Cardinal Beaufort is at point of death;
> For suddenly a grievous sickness took him,
> That makes him gasp and stare and catch the air,
> Blaspheming God and cursing men on earth.
> [III. ii. 369-72]

It is with this sinister association in mind that we hear the characteristic sentimentality of romantic love from Suffolk's lips after the queen has warned him of the approach of the king, with death as the penalty of discovery:

> If I depart from thee I cannot live;
> And in thy sight to die, what were it else
> But like a pleasant slumber in thy lap?
> Here could I breathe my soul into the air. . . .
> [III. ii. 388-91]

His farewell is similarly redolent with affectation, yet it is brutally loaded with unconscious prophecy: "This way fall I to death" [III. ii. 412].

It might be thought that, with the hysterical death of the Cardinal, and the calculated humiliation of Suffolk's assassination on the Kentish coast, the action has established the scope of retributive fate. But Shakespeare takes a far more tragic view of the working out of the movements initiated by these victims. Suffolk is, after all, only a type of the anarchistic self-interest and egotistical sentimentality of the English upper classes. The supercilious behavior of Suffolk on the verge of death sets essentially aristocratic viciousness in contrast to lower-class indignation at such traitorous depravity. Suffolk's extravagant words to his assassins again remind us of the allegorical absolutism of characters in the morality plays:

> Obscure and lowly swain, King Henry's blood,
> The honorable blood of Lancaster,
> Must not be shed by such a jaded groom.
> Hast thou not kissed thy hand and held my stirrup? . . .
> It is impossible that I should die
> By such a lowly vassal as thyself.
> [IV. i. 50-3, 110-11]

Suffolk's rodomontade is answered by the crude realism of his captors:

> Convey him hence and on our longboat's side
> Strike off his head.
> [IV. i. 68-9]

His vanity is judged as

> . . . kennel, puddle, sink; whose filth and dirt
> Troubles the silver spring where England drinks.
> [IV. i. 71-2]

The revolutionary overtones of this encounter are not incidental; they are part of the vast convulsion set afoot by Henry's innocent incompetence and the aristocracy's resulting egotistical irresponsibility. York has been shipped off to Ireland by the queen and Suffolk, who think to cut him off from political influence, but before he leaves he sets the fuse to a disastrous explosive: the resentment of the lower classes, from which the feudal aristocracy will never recover, either in the tetralogy or in historic fact:

> You put sharp weapons in a madman's hands.
> Whiles I in Ireland nourish a mighty band,
> I will stir up in England some black storm
> Shall blow ten thousand souls to heaven or hell;
> And this fell tempest shall not cease to rage
> Until the golden circuit on my head, . . .
> Do calm the fury of this mad-bred flaw.
> And for the minister of my intent,
> I have seduced a headstrong Kentishman,
> John Cade of Ashford, . . .
> This devil here shall be my substitute.
> [III. i. 347-52, 354-57, 371]

Again one sees the imagery turning history into allegory—the "devil" Cade functions as a kind of abstract of the indignant responses of the lower class (such as we see at the execution of Suffolk). Though he too is corrupt and cynical, he has (like Joan) the insight of the politically gifted—and when he declaims to a horrified aristocrat, "I am the besom that must sweep the court clean of such filth as thou art" [IV. vii. 31-2], one feels the ring of an authority like Joan's. The scenes in which Cade and his sympathizers terrorize the upper classes do have a kind of macabre humor, but this should not conceal their basically serious intent. We may laugh when Dick suggests as the first act of revolution, "Let's kill all the lawyers" [IV. ii. 76-7], or when Cade declares to Lord Say: "It will be proved to thy face that thou hast men about thee that usually talk of a noun and a verb, and such abominable words as no Christian can endure or hear" [IV. vii. 37-40]. Again, a wretched clerk is hung for confessing he can sign his name, just as the Roman mob in *Julius Caesar* murders Cinna the poet "for his bad verses" [*Julius Caesar*, III. iii. 31-2]. But what is involved here is no mere vulgar hatred of learning; it is rather the commonsense suspicion of courtly and academic affectation, of the kind favored by Suffolk and the king, which has already reduced the country to its present state of anarchy. (pp. 45-9)

It is clear that Suffolk and King Henry VI are two of these affected aristocrats, whose gallantry and academicism have strayed from the world of comedy into that of political history, with tragic results. Just as in *Love's Labour's Lost* the lower classes are finally driven to harsh and authoritative denunciation of their superiors: "This is not generous, not gentle, not humble" [*Love's Labour's Lost*, V. ii. 629], so figures like the sea captain or Cade carry conviction in their pitiless pursuit of the intelligentsia and the aristocracy, whose wits have been devoted to the corruption and betrayal of their country. The point is perceptive, and the play functions on a moral level superior to that of the old political morality plays and patriotic histories, which scarcely reflected any such refinement of values and division of sympathies.

The precarious balance of values and sympathies that emerges in these last scenes illustrates Shakespeare's characteristic strength as moralist, dramatist, and political historian. To see the Joan of *Part 1* as merely a monstrous caricature of a noble young woman is not to do justice to the strength and political finesse of her portrait. Similarly, Cade in *Part 2* is a curious mixture of viciousness and insight, which marks out this character as superior to most of the others in the play. Although he appears in York's soliloquy as a monster, he is moved by Lord Say's desperate plea of innocence. There is a fascinating ambivalence in his response:

> I feel remorse in myself with his words; but
> I'll bridle it: he shall die, an it be for pleading
> so well for his life. Away with him! he has a
> familiar under his tongue; he speaks not o' God's
> name. Go, take him away, I say, and strike off
> his head presently.
>
> [IV. vii. 105-10]

One must admire, if not the historical probability of the character, at least the virtuosity of mind of its creator, who will devote this kind of finesse to the development of another, far more interesting character, who appears a few scenes later— the younger son of York, who is finally to become Richard III. Like Richard, Cade is under no illusions about his followers: "Was ever feather so lightly blown to and fro as this multitude?" [IV. viii. 55-6], and when they betray him, he cuts his way through them like chaff. However, Shakespeare's sense of irony metes out justice on Cade himself, who accurately anticipates his own fall in this ominous self-analysis:

> Fie on ambition! fie on myself, that have a
> sword, and yet am ready to famish! These five
> days I have hid me in these woods and durst
> not peep out, for all the country is laid for me.
>
> [IV. x. 1-4]

Yet Cade is too symbolic of lower class resentment and primitive vitality to meet his death at the hands of the effete aristocracy. There is a profound symbolism in his destruction at the hands of Iden, the rural squire who delights in his avoidance of the corruptions of the court, and the fickleness of fortune:

> Lord, who would live turmoiled in the court,
> And may enjoy such quiet walks as these?
> This small inheritance my father left me
> Contenteth me, and worth a monarchy.
> I seek not to wax great by others' waning,
> Or gather wealth, I care not, with what envy:
> Sufficeth that I have maintains my state
> And sends the poor well pleased from my gate.
>
> [IV. x. 16-23]

Here is a man who has escaped the Wheel of Fortune, and he alone can justly hope to confront and destroy Cade, the other pole of those resentments that Iden's more rational and temperate outlook has already addressed against the aristocracy. (pp. 50-2)

The two earlier parts of *Henry VI* make serious claims upon our critical attention, despite their failure to conform to some aesthetic norms through their diffusion of interest over a wide variety of actions and personalities. They are not lacking in deliberate progressions, whose political and moral implications are subtle and dexterously evoked. The counterpoint of personality and issue is complex and epic in its range; it creates a sense of an actual rather than a theoretical study of a social

organism, in which English history in all its vivid variety is unfolded to the audience. The success of the plays in both Elizabethan and modern times shows that an audience as attuned to political debate and sociological tensions as Shakespeare's audience has been in both ages cannot but be fascinated by the diversity of incident and the deftness of juxtaposition. In their vividness and variety, as well as in their purpose, these two history plays mark a distinctive achievement in the long evolution of the form from the morality plays through the chronicles to the more truly literate Elizabethan theater.

Yet, if the plays have many excellences, they also have some conspicuous defects. There are frequent lapses of taste, of the kind to which popular art is prone—such as the crude caricatures of the French that diminish the power of the first part. More serious, from the point of view of drama, is the proliferation of overlong, pedantically sententious speeches, in which historical trivia and platitude deaden interest. Sometimes, too, the academic conventions of Latin drama along Senecan lines overload exchanges of even the most bitter enemies with clumsy formality and rhetorical cadences.

The third part of *Henry VI* is heavily burdened with all these limitations, so that is seems a more immature work than the preceding plays in the series. If anything, its defects predominate, as if the author, in trying to write more seriously and solemnly, had failed to sustain the coarser energies and sharp contrasts of the other plays. The long, flat, fatuous speech of Henry on the battlefield is indefensible in many respects, and the crude parallelisms of this speech are matched by the symmetrically conceived situations (a son who has killed his father, and a father who has killed his son) that are presented immediately afterwards. In general, Henry's part now shows the defects of his character, without any compensating artistic excellence in the execution of this portrait. While some episodes, such as his quite artificial forecast of the great future of Henry Tudor, are somewhat implausibly handled, his death at the hand of Richard of Gloucester suggests that Richard is almost justified in getting rid of such a bore. Indeed, his son had earlier been avowedly murdered for tactlessly irritating Richard and the other victorious Yorkists.

However, if the part of Henry must put great strain on any director's ingenuity, the part of Richard is a considerable compensation. While Henry's sententiousness is stilted, Richard's extraordinary "aria" at the end of Act III, Scene ii represents a real artistic breakthrough in the series (suggesting perhaps the mature revision of a text that had preceded the first two parts in date of composition). (pp. 56-7)

Throughout *Part 3*, Richard usurps that pivotal, initiatory role that had been played by the women of the earlier plays—Joan, Eleanor and Margaret. England's corruption is no longer the product of a facile and deceptive rhetoric, but of a relentless, utterly amoral lust for power. This savage outlook has no room for anything but the shadow of Joan's nationalism, Henry's idealism, or Suffolk's sentimental passion; it regularly achieves monstrosities of the order of the casual assassinations of the innocent Henry and his young son. These acts are so brutal and callous as to transform even Queen Margaret from a viciously ambitious woman into something like that quintessence of outraged motherhood and wifehood that Aeschylus makes of his Furies in the Agamemnon trilogy. Yet, appropriately, it is she who first lends an edge to Richard's savagery, providing it with a model by her merciless treatment of the captured Duke of York before his death. This scene is one of the most gruesome in Shakespeare, and clearly aims at Senecan horror, with such details as the offer of a napkin to York steeped in his own son's blood. Yet the scene has resonances of a curious and memorable kind.

It has been commonly observed that the Duke is forced to undergo sufferings comparable to Christ's; Northumberland even observes:

> Beshrew me, but his passion moves me so
> That hardly can I check my eyes from tears.
> [*3 Henry VI*, I. iv. 150-51]

And if the blood-soaked cloth is grotesquely analogous to the one offered by St. Veronica to Christ, Richard also has his mock crown, from the hands of Margaret:

> Thou wouldst be fee'd, I see, to make me sport:
> York cannot speak, unless he wear a crown.
> A crown for York! and, lords, bow low to him:
> Hold you his hands, whilst I do set it on.
> [*Putting a paper crown on his head.*]
> Ay, marry, sir, now looks he like a king!
> Ay, this is he that took King Henry's chair,
> And this is he was his adopted heir.
> [I. iv. 92-8]

Yet many commentators fail to see that all these analogies to Christ's passion are savagely ironic—the scene is in fact as double-edged as Shakespeare's greatest (for example, the banishment of Falstaff). Far from being an innocently suffering Christ, York is a brutally ambitious man who is now meeting his just deserts for having broken his oath to King Henry.

York may finally die religiously:

> Open Thy gate of mercy, gracious God!
> My soul flies through these wounds to seek out Thee.
> [I. iv. 77-8]

but his life has been evil in the highest degree, and every clashing analogy to the death of Christ drives home that fact. Margaret is consciously the agent of just retribution visited upon a man who has broken a twice-taken oath—although Shakespeare refuses, appropriately, to allow Margaret unequivocal authority in the role of agent of retribution. For the fact is that she proves even more callous and brutal than York at this point, so that he in turn, at the moment of merited destruction, achieves a moral advantage over her, who will shortly suffer as exquisitely as he:

> How could thou drain the life-blood of the child,
> To bid the father wipe his eyes withal,
> And yet be seen to bear a woman's face?
> Women are soft, mild, pitiful and flexible;
> Thou stern, obdurate, flinty, rough, remorseless.
> [I. iv. 138-42]

Margaret's loss of both son and husband will alone suffice to return her to a feminine role in the last play of the tetralogy. Only there does she achieve a truly monumental status, through suffering. (pp. 60-2)

> *H. M. Richmond, in his* Shakespeare's Political Plays, *Random House, 1967, 241 p.*

JAMES WINNY (essay date 1968)

[*Winny disputes the thesis of such earlier critics as Hermann Ulrici (1839), E. M. W. Tillyard (1944), M. M. Reese (1961), and Irving Ribner (1965) that Shakespeare's* Henry VI *was de-*

Part III. Act III. Scene ii. Serving Woman, Edward IV, Lady Grey, Gloucester, and Clarence. Frontispiece to the Rowe edition (1709). By permission of the Folger Shakespeare Library.

signed to depict the evil consequences of Henry IV's usurpation of the throne from Richard II. Winny argues that in the Henry VI *trilogy the deposition of Richard II is referred to only as a political event, not as "a crime for which England continues to suffer." Instead, he contends that Shakespeare attributes the disordered state of the kingdom to the weakness of Henry himself, who possesses the ideals of majesty but lacks the personal qualities necessary to fulfill the role of king, and to the attempts of certain powerful individuals to subvert moral and social responsibility in order to satisfy their selfish ambitions. Critics who similarly deny the role of retribution in the* Henry VI *trilogy include A. C. Hamilton (1961-62), S. C. Sen Gupta (1964), H. M. Richmond (1967), and Robert Ornstein (1972). A number of recent commentators, including Harold C. Goddard (1951) and Michael Manheim (1973), have attempted to exonerate Henry VI himself from responsibility for the violence and chaos of his reign, maintaining that Shakespeare regarded the king as a morally courageous and religious man who might have ruled successfully had it not been for the contentious, ambitious, and deceitful behavior of his English nobles.*]

However it may have developed later, Shakespeare's early interest in history was not activated by a sense of moral retribution working itself out through political disorder and bloodshed. Upheaval and disquiet form a leading theme of the Histories because these conditions match Shakespeare's awareness of the driving energies impelling growth and change, in political affairs as in the world of natural life. In its concern with the decisive events of human destiny, and the thrusting ambitions and passions that brought them about, history gave Shakespeare the only matter that could absorb his giant energies at the beginning of his career.

An imaginative view of life does not necessarily exclude moral awareness, but homiletic commentary on the events of history is alien to Shakespeare's creative purpose. So far as it is valid to speak of his moral outlook, its conditions are those formed by the action and interests of the play, and not added to it from outside. . . . Although *Macbeth* enacts the moral truth that man is harmed by the evil he commits, this finding is meaningful only within the context which makes it imaginatively true; that is, the play. The same applies to the moral outlook of the Histories.

Belief that the history-plays act out the moral argument of the Homilies has encouraged an assumption that eight of the plays form tetralogies, to be read as a continuous work showing the evil consequences of deposing Richard II, which were to trouble England for the next eighty years. This view of the Histories is open to several objections. The most obvious is that their order of composition suggests no such purpose. Had Shakespeare intended from the outset to make the crime of deposing a lawful king responsible for all the disorder and havoc which the two tetralogies depict, he would hardly have chosen to begin his series with *Henry VI,* historically the midpoint of the whole timespan which his plays cover. If the moral theme entered his purposes when he began to write the so-called second tetralogy, *Henry VI* and *Richard III* cannot be claimed as part of an extended moral commentary. The first four Histories have their own imaginative *raison d'être* ["reason for existence"], and are unlikely to share a common purpose with a group of plays written at a later point of Shakespeare's development. It is more reasonable to suppose that if the Histories contain some collective meaning, it is compatible with their order of composition. (pp. 17-19)

Objection to the moral interpretation of the Histories does not rest on general arguments alone. We are entitled to ask what indications of Shakespeare's moral purpose are to be found in the earlier tetralogy; especially in backward references to the crime committed by Bolingbroke, from which 'disorder, horror, fear and mutiny' [*Richard II,* IV. i. 142] were to spring. *Henry VI,* with its endless turmoil and carnage, could be held to represent the fulfilling of Carlisle's prophecy. But, setting aside the fact that all Shakespeare's history-plays are concerned with political disorder, there is no evidence in *Henry VI* that at that time Shakespeare recognised any special significance in Bolingbroke's crime. Throughout this first history-play the deposition of Richard is spoken of simply as a political event, whose importance lies in its bearing upon the claims and counterclaims of the Yorkist struggle. Bolingbroke's interruption of the royal line deprived Richard's chosen heir of his inheritance, and gave the crown to a house whose authority was to be questioned by repeated uprisings against the Lancastrian kings. Richard is mentioned only as the starting-point of this interminable conflict. The circumstances of his deposition are related as plain historical facts, without overtones of moral condemnation. Mortimer, as Richard's intended successor hardly an impartial witness, recalls the usurpation simply as an event of past history:

> Henry the Fourth, grandfather to this king,
> Deposed his nephew Richard, Edward's son,

The first begotten and the lawful heir
Of Edward King, the third of that descent.
> [*1 Henry VI,* II. v. 63-6]

When York repeats the story in order to win Salisbury and Warwick to his cause, he shows more sense of the injustice of Bolingbroke's proceeding; but like Mortimer he makes no appeal to moral indignation, and does not suggest that the deposition was a crime for which England continues to suffer. 'The eldest son and heir of John of Gaunt,' he reminds his audience,

> Seized on the realm, deposed the rightful king,
> Sent his poor queen to France, from whence she came,
> And him to Pomfret; where, as all you know,
> Harmless Richard was murdered traitorously.
> [*2 Henry VI,* II. ii. 22-6]

York, it might be observed, is hardly the character to protest at Bolingbroke's contempt for the sanctity of the king. If his own cause is to prosper, he too must depose an anointed sovereign, breaking his oath of fealty and bringing bloodshed upon the kingdom. But we are concerned with Shakespeare's purposes, not with the motives he imputes to York. Had it been ironically presented, York's speech could have admitted the moral implications of the crime he intends to re-enact, with the same disregard of established law. The device is not used, and York's summary of past history offers no hint of a sacrilegious wrong committed two generations earlier. No character of *Henry VI* attempts to attribute the confusion and misery of civil war to the sin perpetrated by Bolingbroke. The disordered state of the kingdom derives chiefly from the failure of a weak-willed King to enforce his authority. The situation is accountable by circumstances which the action makes plain, and Shakespeare does not look towards the reading of historical events outlined by Carlisle in a play not yet written, and with which *Henry VI* would bear very little imaginative relationship. (pp. 19-21)

The moral awareness of *Henry VI* lies elsewhere. The charge that the usurping house of Lancaster has no title to the crown is not treated seriously by either side, mere legality counting for nothing among men who settle disputed issues by main force. York has a more effective argument in the innate authority which he enjoys and Henry lacks. 'Thou art not king,' he tells his sovereign,

> Not fit to govern and rule multitudes,
> Which darest not, no, nor canst not rule
> a traitor . . .
> Here is a hand to hold a sceptre up,
> And with the same to act controlling laws.
> Give place: by heaven, thou shalt rule no more
> O'er him whom heaven created for thy ruler.
> [*2 Henry VI,* V. i. 93-105]

His claim involves moral contradictions which, although unobserved by York, have a place in Shakespeare's purposes. The speaker sees himself as king by natural right, yet to prove Henry's impotence he admits himself a traitor whom his appointed sovereign cannot put down. The heaven which created York to be a ruler is not the power acknowledged by Henry, 'whose far unworthy deputy I am' [*2 Henry VI,* III. ii. 286], but a savage natural impulse which drives him to satisfy a craving for personal magnificence, at whatever cost. The King himself is a figure of paradox, a possessor of the crown whose perverse ambition is to become a commoner:

> Was never subject longed to be a king
> As I do long and wish to be a subject.
> [*2 Henry VI,* IV. ix. 5-6]

The paradox is inverted in a succession of subjects burning with impatience to be king, for whom life can only justify itself when it is linked with supreme power. 'Steel thy fearful thoughts' [2 *Henry VI*, III. i. 331], York encourages himself,

> Be that thou hop'st to be, or what thou art
> Resign to death; it is not worth th'enjoying.
> [2 *Henry VI*, III. i. 333-34]

His assertion that he deserves the crown by virtue of his soaring pride and energy would be accepted even by some of Henry's supporters, who are exasperated by the King's unmanly tameness. When Queen Margaret voices her incredulous feelings,

> Enforced thee? Art thou king, and wilt be forced?
> [3 *Henry VI*, I. i. 230]

she reveals a conception of kingly majesty which only Henry himself does not respect. The King should prove his title not by wise government, personal sanctity or concern for his people, but by a display of unchallenged power. Henry, who begins by abjectly surrendering France, who disinherits his son in favour of an impudent rebel, who allows himself to be silenced and driven from the battlefield by his own supporters, cannot claim to personate this figure. York shows a more appropriate respect for the awesome power of kingship:

> That gold must round engirt these brows of mine,
> Whose smile and frown, like to Achilles' spear,
> Is able with the change to kill and cure.
> [2 *Henry VI*, V. i. 99-101]

Like the claim through ancestral right, this conception of royal authority is supported by an irresistible urge towards personal power, which uses the forms of moral law only to disguise its true nature. In common with other aspirants to supreme power, York is driven by a consuming and unreasoning passion which cares nothing for the legal arguments in his favour. They follow, and do not motivate his attempt to seize the crown. From the beginning he is dazzled by a prospect which makes him contemptuous of restraint and caution, and regardless of moral law. Some part of his mind seems to recognise that he is possessed by a frenzy that will destroy him; for he comments that the nobles who provide him with troops for his Irish campaign have 'put sharp weapons in a madman's hands' [2 *Henry VI*, III. i. 347]; but the ironic truth of the comparison escapes him. He sees himself as a man infuriated by the frustration of personal energies which can only fulfil themselves in kingship:

> This fell tempest shall not cease to rage
> Until the golden circuit on my head,
> Like to the glorious sun's transparent beams,
> Do calm the fury of this mad-bred flaw.
> [2 *Henry VI*, III. i. 351-54]

His ambition is a madness that blinds him to hazards, that induces him to gamble life, honour and possessions on the outcome of a reckless throw, and which will eventually destroy him. His insane venture ends in an insulting parody of the magnificence which he thought to possess. Helplessly pinioned, invested with a makeshift crown and ceremoniously mocked by his murderous captors, he discovers the emptiness of the kingly illusion for which he has ruined himself. His sons are not warned by this tragic example. Unlike his father, Clarence recognises that the lure of kingly power and majesty maddens its victims with a self-destructive fury; but he refuses to be deterred by the suicidal risks of continuing the struggle.

'We set the axe to thy usurping root,' he tells Queen Margaret before the battle of York,

> And though the edge hath something hit ourselves,
> Yet know thou, since we have begun to strike,
> We'll never leave till we have hewn thee down,
> Or bathed thy growing with our heated bloods.
> [3 *Henry VI*, II. ii. 165-69]

His brother Richard, obsessed by the same senseless ambition, is twisted out of shape by a compulsion that destroys all peace of mind and drains him of human sympathies. Like York, he is tormented by a frustrated appetite for absolute power, feeling himself in hell

> Until my misshaped trunk that bears this head
> Be round impaled with a glorious crown.
> [3 *Henry VI*, III. ii. 170-71]

He knows what hurt he must inflict upon himelf in forcing a path through lacerating obstacles towards his goal; and accepts the hazards like a man drugged or brutalised into insensibility. His soliloquy, one of the earliest passages of imaginative self-disclosure in the plays, reveals Richard's helpless inability to control his lust for power, and the frenzy of mind which drives him towards the satisfaction of a tormenting desire:

> Like one lost in a thorny wood,
> That rents the thorns, and is rent with the thorns;
> Seeking a way, and straying from the way,
> Not knowing how to find the open air,
> But toiling desperately to find it out,
> Torment myself to catch the English crown.
> [3 *Henry VI*, III. ii. 174-79]

His cruelty to others reflects the inward anguish of a nature wrenched out of true by a compulsion too overwhelming to be mastered. As he struggles to break out of the restraints that thwart his will to power, gashing and impaling himself upon the disregarded curbs which goad him forward, he becomes increasingly benighted. When, at the end of this soliloquy, he recalls himself from bewilderment in a sudden outburst of resolution,

> And from that torment I will free myself,
> Or hew my way out with a bloody axe
> [3 *Henry VI*, III. ii. 180-81]

he admits his helplessness to act except through the violence which must destroy his own being. The thorny wood in which he is lost is the nightmarish world of his own monstrously distorted and protesting humanity.

Richard's soliloquy, and the related speeches of York and Clarence, help to resolve the moral viewpoint from which Shakespeare presents the behaviour of these allied figures. Each of them is torn between an instinctive drive towards self-fulfilment in political power and an awareness of obligations to moral law which cannot be crushed without fatally injuring man's implanted nature. Shakespeare's awareness of the driving energies which moral respect should contain is obviously very keen. His imaginative concern with the sheerly brutish impulses which impel man to repudiate the restraints of moral law is unmistakably declared in [*The Rape of Lucrece*], and becomes a persistent motif of Shakespearean history. In *Henry VI* York rejects the restraints of loyalty and subordination which safeguard society, claiming allegiance for himself in contempt of established order. His insanely selfish ambition throws the kingdom into confusion; but this triumph of private will over reason and moral conscience has consequences for York that are no less disastrous. Like his son Richard, whose misshapen body and wolfish isolation characterise the ugly impulses which moral law should subdue, York inflicts fatal injury upon himself by outraging the respects by which humanity is nourished. Man's moral consciousness, Shakespeare implies, cannot be tied off if the individual is to survive. His instinctive desire for society and friendship, and for the deeper satisfactions of true allegiance, faithful service and ordered prerogative, spring from an implanted impulse that is vital to his existence as a man. When he repudiates this impulse, letting private will determine his behaviour, he cuts himself off from rational judgement and self-knowledge, and becomes a madman blundering through the labyrinth of his own passions, more confused at every step.

Such a moral positive is stated early in the trilogy of *Henry VI,* in the only scene of the play to provide a retrospective link with the events of Richard II's reign. Edmund Mortimer, named by the childless Richard as his heir, and subsequently held a lifelong prisoner by three Lancastrian kings, makes his single appearance in the second act of Part I; a blind and broken figure who dies in prison after wishing prosperity to York. He has a dramatic function of some importance. From him the Yorkist cause derives its decisive initial impulse, when Mortimer describes in detail how he and his descendants have been forcibly disinherited by Bolingbroke, and then exhorts his kinsman to recover the title wrongfully held by the usurper's grandson. The upheaval of civil war treated in the two later parts of *Henry VI* and in *Richard III* is seen to draw its original impulse from Mortimer in this scene, where frustrated ambition is passed down to a youthful successor, eager to renew an almost extinguished claim to the crown.

As the tragic relic of an insurrection ruthlessly crushed by Bolingbroke nearly thirty years earlier, Mortimer symbolises the tragic emptiness of the ambition which has wasted the vitality and promise of his own youth. In a play whose action is dominated by a series of attempts to snatch the crown, he is the first representative of the lust for power which impels them all; but Mortimer's attempt is long past, and the figure who communicates the same deadly impulse to York embodies the futility of all such aspirations. Emaciated, sightless and physically impotent after a lifetime of imprisonment, he is blind to his own example, and cannot warn York against the waste of life and substance that his pursuit of the crown has entailed; nor can York appreciate the moral lesson which confronts him. (pp. 24-31)

The brutality, violence and moral obliviousness that typify political ambition in the early-history plays are most fully embodied in the deformed figure of Richard of Gloucester. Ugly, hated, and proud of his moral repulsiveness, he repudiates all claims of kinship and affection which might weaken his determination to hack out a path to the crown. 'I have no brother,' he affirms,

> I am like no brother;
> And this word 'love', which greybeards call divine,
> Be resident in men like one another,
> And not in me: I am myself alone.
>
> [*3 Henry VI,* V. vi. 80-3]

He sees his isolation as a personal triumph over the affections which soften other men; but in fact it represents a perversion of the instinct which makes man a social creature who relies upon the environment of family and society to realise his im-

planted nature. By dissociating himself from human ties Richard displays a monstrousness of character in keeping with his warped and stunted body: he is not more but less than other men. Modern psychology may see his sadistic cruelty and appetite for power as a consequence of the physical deformity which constantly humiliates him. Shakespeare probably intended his ugliness to reflect his misshapen moral nature, as a man whose rapacious animal will has smothered all sense of kindly relationship. It is imaginatively and dramatically appropriate that Richard should strike down the now saintly King, destroying the figure of gentle humanity which stands as a rebuke to his brutishness. The crime has a strongly emblematic quality. It brings together on the stage, alone, characters who personify the warring houses of Lancaster and York; and who also embody the moral polarity between kindliness and ferocity, restraint and lawlessness, which underlies the action of *Henry VI* as a persistent theme of attention. To interpret this scene—whose moral and dramatic issues bear closely upon Shakespeare's imaginative purposes—on simply political lines would be to ignore its poetic significance. The outraging of helpless innocence by blindly passionate will is a major theme of Shakespeare's work, realised in the simplest and most potent terms in *The Rape of Lucrece*. At a much later point of Shakespeare's career the same theme, its basic form unchanged, provides the central event of *Macbeth;* where the murdered King who 'hath borne his faculties so meek' [*Macbeth,* I. vii. 17] bears a suggestive likeness to the pious and gentle-hearted figure butchered by Richard in *Henry VI*. In none of these three works does Shakespeare seem interested in developing the story along moralistic lines, to show the eventual punishment of crime: rather, he is concerned with an insistent imaginative figure whose meaning must be sought in the terms through which it finds expression. (pp. 34-5)

In all of [the Histories] the efforts of a king to impose his authority upon an unruly kingdom, or to resist the challenge of open rebellion, is a matter of first account. The persistence of this subject, from *Henry VI* onwards, has been the main support of interpretations based upon the political morality of the Homilies, and of the argument that the two tetralogies show the consequences of lifting hands against God's deputy. If, instead, we assume that Shakespeare used the matter of the English chronicles for an essentially imaginative purpose, the repeated—and generally unsuccessful—attempts of a king to assert his authority over rebellious subjects take on a very different appearance. It now becomes a point of imaginative significance that none of the six kings in these eight plays enjoys an undisputed title to the crown, and must fight to retain it. The first of Shakespeare's sovereigns, 'in infant bands crowned king' [*Henry V,* Epilogue, 9], is the weakest and least effectual in resisting the challenge to his title and possession; the last the strongest and most assured of his legitimacy. This development running through the Histories, by which the king acquires an increasing force of authority, shows why it must be mistaken to treat the series as though it were intended to begin with the deposition of Richard and to end with the accession of Henry Tudor. The historical order of the six reigns is not relevant to Shakespeare's imaginative purpose: the chronological order of the plays is. The historical matter is treated in a sequence which illustrates that purpose; beginning at the point of greatest political confusion and national weakness, with a king incapable of ruling his insubordinate subjects, and ending after a great victory by the only English monarch whom Shakespeare presents as a national hero.

Throughout the series the king, whether usurper or rightful heir, sits uneasily on this throne; under assault from rivals whose ambition he must contain if he is not to lose his crown. His task is one of personal domination; to prove himself king by mastering the rebellious factions that deny his authority and threaten to unseat him. In Henry VI Shakespeare depicts a king whose gentle nature is appalled by the savagery of political conflict, and who cannot face the necessity of forcing obedience upon the mutinous nobles whom his own weakness has encouraged. Their unruly energy can only be held in balance by an equally resolved force impressing order upon them, but the King evades his obligation in the pious hope that mild persuasion will prove an effective substitute for political mastery. Held in contempt by both sides, he is thrust outside the arena of political decisions, a king only in his own thoughts; having lost all influence upon the government of his disordered kingdom. (pp. 38-9)

King is not merely a title but an identity, and in Henry the two do not coincide. The bare name of king demands to be supported by personal qualities, or its bearer makes a mockery of his great office; yet personal majesty without legal title falls short of what kingship should involve just as badly. Shakespeare's kings are a mixture of legal inheritors without natural title to the crown, and men of kingly ability debarred from true possession of the name they seize. The true inheritor put out of office becomes an anonymous figure, with neither royal title nor the identity of an individual man. When Henry is captured by the foresters after the battle of York he has been deposed by Edward IV, and cannot answer their question who he is:

King	More than I seem, and less than I was born to; A man at least, for less I should not be; And men may talk of kings, and why not I?
2 Keep	Ay, but thou talk'st as if thou wert a king.
King	Why, so am I, in mind, and that's enough.
2 Keep	But if thou be a king, where is thy crown?

[3 Henry VI, III. i. 56-61]

The situation is developed without much subtlety, but Shakespeare is giving notice of an imaginative interest which will be pressed more firmly in plays still to come. In each of the later Histories the King is forced to come to terms with the nature of the royal identity which he has tried to assume, and to recognise a disparity between his ideal of majesty and his personal ability to fill the role assigned to him. The costume is laid out and the part rehearsed, but the performance falls short in respects which both actor and audience acknowledge. The player is not the king. (pp. 45-6)

> James Winny, in an introduction to his The Player King: A Theme of Shakespeare's Histories, Chatto & Windus, 1968, pp. 9-47.

DAVID RIGGS (essay date 1971)

[In an unexcerpted portion of his Shakespeare's Heroical Histories: "Henry VI" and Its Literary Tradition (1971), Riggs argues that the language of 1, 2, and 3 Henry VI is heavily influenced by the formal rhetorical tradition prevalent throughout the sixteenth century in England. He asserts that the "oratorical forms of praise, lament, and self-assertion and the set topoi ('motifs') of personal worth" in the plays are used "to define and express

the attributes of eminent men" and to enhance the theme of the progressive deterioration of heroic idealism. Riggs also contends that in the Henry VI trilogy Shakespeare presents history in humanistic terms, emphasizing the clash of human ideals and political realities rather than the effects of providential retribution. Thus, in the excerpt below, Riggs takes issue with the interpretation of Henry VI as a work based primarily on the Tudor view of English history (see the excerpts above by Hermann Ulrici, 1839; J. A. R. Marriott, 1918; E. M. W. Tillyard, 1944; M. M. Reese, 1961; and Irving Ribner, 1965), claiming instead that the trilogy represents Shakespeare's depiction of the decline of heroic idealism during the Hundred Years' War and the reign of Henry VI. According to Riggs, Shakespeare personifies this aristocratic ideal in such figures as Talbot, Salisbury, Bedford, and Richard of York—all of whom exhibit its qualities of "noble ancestry, strength and beauty, courage and wisdom." But, Riggs continues, Shakespeare contrasts the heroic ideal with characters such as Joan of Arc, the French nobles, and the "fashionable courtiers" in England, who exhibit the opposing qualities: brutality and cunning, viciousness, and the selfish quest for unrestrained power. The critic notes that Part 2 of the trilogy signifies the transposition of the heroic ideal from the battlefield to the political arena, where its corruption is evident in the "courtly posturing" and affectations of Suffolk and other members of the nobility; Part 3, he continues, satisfies the violent expectations established in 2 Henry VI and culminates in "the utter dissolution of all aristocratic values and social obligations." Riggs's commentary on the facile, affected rhetoric of Henry's court echoes an idea presented more fully by H. M. Richmond (1967), and his assessment of 2 Henry VI as a "revenge tragedy" is further developed by Ronald S. Berman (1962). Also, for additional discussion of the Henry VI trilogy as a humanistic rather than a Tudor study of English history, see the excerpts by S. C. Sen Gupta (1964), James Winny (1968), and Robert Ornstein (1972).]

Henry VI is designed to disclose a set of exemplary truths drawn from the playwright's reading of fifteenth-century English history. There is little basis, however, for supposing that these truths will always conform to orthodox Tudor doctrine, and still less to indicate that they point to a stable, didactic allegory of "moral history" underwritten by a providential guidance. One may begin simply by postulating that the trilogy encompasses Shakespeare's presentation of the "agents" that gave the reign of Henry VI its distinctive contours. Like any good humanist historian, he is concerned to produce moral judgments, but these will involve a wide spectrum of ethical standards. . . . More particularly, it should be stressed at the outset that in no one of these plays—to say nothing of the entire trilogy—is there some unifying idea that will enable the reader to place every episode (except the "extraneous" ones) in its proper context.

With this caveat in mind, I shall pursue through all three plays Shakespeare's treatment of one very general theme: the gradual deterioration of heroic idealism between the Hundred Years' War and the Yorkist accession. Not that this interpretation of his chronicle sources was necessarily in Shakespeare's mind from the start; but it does provide the most thorough account of his historical judgments about the reign of Henry VI. (p. 97)

The first part of Henry VI recasts the latter part of the Hundred Years' War as an exercise in "parallel lives." The opening funeral oration indicates that the emphasis will be upon an ideal of heroic conduct, and the ensuing sequence of two council scenes (one English, the other French), three battle scenes, a "triumph," and a second funeral confirms this impression while introducing us to the two principal antagonists, Talbot and Joan la Pucelle. (p. 100)

It must be granted at the outset that the poetic texture of I Henry VI does not encourage one to expect anything very subtle or even clearly defined in the way of characterization, and my own efforts to show Talbot and Joan as two sides of a complex statement about aristocratic values will rely more on an analysis of the rhetorical structure of the play. But even in the transparently bookish similes cited by Malone [see excerpt above, 1787] there may be some basis for a comparison between the two characters in ethical terms. When Shakespeare compares Talbot to Hercules, Hector, and the "desperate sire of Crete" who sought his fame in "the lither sky" [*I Henry VI*, IV. vi. 54; IV. vii. 21], on the one hand, and Joan to Hannibal, the greatest of military strategists, and Mahomet, a "pagan" hero who is recalled as a magician and a religious charlatan [I. ii. 140], on the other, it need not be supposed that the allusions are inserted "merely to shew the writer's learning" [Malone]. In order to appreciate their specific meanings, however, they must be seen within a narrow range of conventions and a special system of values—one that is perhaps most easily introduced by some . . . reference to the profession of arms as it is practiced in *I Henry VI*.

The historical basis for all of the distinctions that I wish to emphasize is treated in such works as Sidney Painter's *French Chivalry* and Arthur Ferguson's *The Indian Summer of English Chivalry*, but the contrasts within *I Henry VI* will be clear enough without any special commentary. A few specific details, taken from the battle scenes, will serve to indicate where Shakespeare's interests lie. While the English, on the one hand, seem scarcely aware that gunpowder has been invented, the French do use artillery, and with devastating effectiveness, on the only occasions when they kill English peers. The mastergunner's boy ambushes Salisbury in the first act, and in his final battle at Bordeaux Talbot finds that "Ten thousand French have ta'en the sacrament / To rive their dangerous artillery / Upon no Christian soul but English Talbot" [IV. ii. 28-30]. By contrast, the English limit themselves to feats of sheer personal strength. It is reported in the first act, for example, that Talbot has "Enacted wonders with his sword and lance" [I. i. 122], and that his French captors held him with a "guard of chosen shot" because they surmised that he could "rend bars of steel / And spurn in pieces posts of adamant" [I. iv. 50-3] with his arms, not to mention his "bare fists" [I. iv. 36] and "horses' heels" [I. iv. 108]. (pp. 101-02)

With regard to military strategy, the French generally seek the security of siege walls, and in two different scenes (III. ii.; IV. ii.) they taunt the English from the upper gallery of the stage. The English never adopt this posture, and Talbot is quite explicit in his opinion of it: "Dare ye come forth and meet us in the field?" he asks; "Will ye, like soldiers, come and fight it out?" [III. ii. 61, 66].

> Base muleteers of France!
> Like peasant foot-boys do they keep the walls,
> And dare not take up arms like gentlemen.
>
> [III. ii. 68-70]

The "muleteers" refuse to behave like *chevaliers*, however, and they never do "take up arms like gentlemen." Talbot's capture, as reported in the opening scene, occurs when "A base Walloon, to win the Dauphin's grace, / Thrust Talbot with a spear into the back" [I. i. 137-38]. . . . Thereafter the Dauphin relies on Joan's "stratagems" and "policy," a mixture of deception and diplomacy by which he "wrongs his fame" [II. i. 16]—but gets results.

By contrast, the English are so much concerned with fighting by the book as to appear, at times, almost oblivious to any ulterior objectives. When Talbot first speaks, he is complaining that the French had offered to exchange him for a "baser man of arms" than "the brave Lord Ponton de Santrailles" [I. iv. 30, 27]. Not only was this offer refused, but Talbot "craved death" in preference to being "so vile esteem'd" [I. iv. 32-3]. Whenever the British do battle, it is specifically in revenge for some breach of martial decorum: the "torments" Talbot endured as a French prisoner, the treacherous ambush of Salisbury and Gargrave, the "hellish mischief" used to capture Rouen, and the "false dissembling guile" of Burgundy. For them, every battle represents the fulfilment of a vow to right some violation of chivalric ideals. Their ostensible cause for fighting, Henry's "right," is mentioned only once in all of those battle scenes, and then in a decidedly offhand manner ("Now, Salisbury, for thee and for the right / Of English Henry" [II. i. 35-6]). . . . (pp. 102-03)

These specific contrasts between two different ways of making war form one basis for Shakespeare's general effort to reformulate Marlowe's heroic ideal in a framework of aristocratic values. In the sixteenth century, as in the fifteenth, the right to bear arms was still an operative definition of a gentleman. And the source of that right continued of course to be gentle birth (technically speaking, armigerous parents). Accordingly, the play includes a parallel set of contrasts juxtaposing characters of base and gentle birth, and these comprise the other important factor in the ideal of aristocratic conduct that emerges. A brief exchange between Talbot and his son, who is being urged to flee from the fatal battle of Bordeaux, will help to illustrate how the Talbots unite both requisites:

> *Tal.* Thou never hadst renown, nor canst not lose it.
> *John.* Yes, your renowned name: shall flight abuse it?
>
> [IV. v. 40-1]

Talbot's "renown," or fame, is the permanent record of his honorable deeds, and it is symbolized by his "name," which recalls those deeds. The soldier who finds that "The cry of 'Talbot' serves me as a sword" [II. i. 79] is simply putting this premise to practical use. The basis of Talbot's readiness to face death and his circumspect valor is the understanding that his "name" is a timeless family possession, to be transmitted to his son, who will in turn be incited to meet that standard. The Talbots construe this doctrine so literally that valor becomes, in effect, a test of legitimacy: "Surely, by all the glory you have won, / And if I fly, I am not Talbot's son" [IV. vi. 50-1], argues Young Talbot. By the same token, the stain of illegitimacy is presumptive evidence of someone's unworthiness to bear arms, as Talbot reminds the Bastard of Orleans:

> I quickly shed
> Some of his bastard blood, and in disgrace
> Bespoke him thus: 'Contaminated, base,
> And misbegotten blood I spill of thine,
> Mean and right poor, for that pure blood of mine
> Which thou didst force from Talbot, my brave boy.'
>
> [IV. vi. 19-24]

If the "Bastard" is a special case here, Joan's career embodies an extended parody of this ideal, in which her unorthodox tactics on the battlefield only serve to expose the baseness of her origins. When she is introduced to the Dauphin's court (appropriately, by the Bastard of Orleans), the French peers are told that she is a "shepherd's daughter" who has been inspired to forsake her "base vocation" and "be the English scourge" [I. ii. 72, 80, 129]. She seeks to establish her claims to nobility by "high terms" and "single combat"; but both her sex and her parentage would disqualify her from bearing arms at all. If her martial career amounts to a shameful assortment of policies and stratagems, her death scene, which can be taken as an ironic counterstatement to those of the Talbots, only brings to light the fact that she lacks any family name to augment and transmit. In a desperate effort to escape death she denies her father (an inoffensive old rustic who materializes to make the fact of her base origins perfectly clear) and claims to be issued from the "progeny of kings" [V. iv. 38]. As this transparent hoax fails to win any mercy from her captors, she claims to be with child herself; but the English will "have no bastards live" [V. iv. 70] and duly proceed to burn her as a witch.

The larger network of comparisons of course extends beyond the special case of Talbot and Joan. If she epitomizes the external forces that threaten the aristocratic ideal of military service and gentle blood, there are signs of internal erosion as well. The most ominous of these come from the professional civil servant Winchester, who is a "bastard" by birth [III. i. 42], and from the contentious, quarrelsome gentlemen of the Inns of Court, one of whom, York, also bears a dishonored family name. "Stand'st thou not attainted, / Corrupted, and exempt from ancient gentry?" [II. iv. 92-3]. (pp. 103-05)

Joan is generically an impostor, created only to exhibit the ornate theatrical façade, as well as the policy and "stratagems," by which aspirant baseness masquerades as nobility. Hence the scenes in which she is exposed and burnt as a witch, like the stripping of Duessa in [Edmund Spenser's] *The Faerie Queene*, serve a formal expository purpose that supersedes any need for a controlled, sequacious plot. A consort of "familiar spirits" [V. iii. 10] arrives to make unmistakably plain the truth that lies behind her claim to be the chosen agent of God. These are followed by the shepherd who underscores the real baseness of her origins with his unvarnished testimony that "She was the first fruit of my bachelorship" [V. iv. 13]. Finally, the reiterated innuendo of sexual misconduct is made utterly explicit in her confession that Charles (or Alençon or Reignier) has left her with the child whom the English will not allow to be born.

Where the rhetoric surrounding Joan uses the conventions of praise to project an image of spurious glamor, the deeds of Talbot and his son, and of Salisbury, Bedford, and their great predecessor Henry V, are for the most part treated through forms of the funeral oration. More than a third of Talbot's three hundred lines would fall into this oratorical genre, and most of what remains either grows directly out of it (as the vow to revenge is a kind of *hortatio* ["encouragement"]) or is distinctly elegiac in tone (for example, the speech in rebuke of Falstaffe at [IV. i. 33-44] beginning "When first this Order was ordain'd, my lords, / Knights of the Garter were of noble birth"). Indeed, Talbot's main function in this play is to solemnize the fall of the great English peers, of whom he is the last representative. While his antagonist defies what is ephemeral and merely glamorous about heroic "bravery,' Talbot finds a context in which to define true heroic virtue and the permanent compensation that it offers in the face of death: the immortality conferred by earthly fame. Fame is introduced as the set topic of *consolatio* ["consolation"] in the extended funeral oration for Henry V that opens the play. (p. 107)

At Talbot's last battle, however, the problem of consolation arises in quite a different context. Talbot and his son must die, and Bordeaux will never be retaken. For Shakespeare, this is to be the last battle of the Hundred Years' War and the last stand of English chivalry. Whatever "victory" Talbot and his son might achieve there will not be commemorated in the actualities of human history. Talbot unwittingly formulates their problem when he commands his son, "Fly, to revenge my death if I be slain" [IV. v. 18]. Young Talbot's answer— "He that flies so will ne'er return again" [IV. v. 19]—serves to expose the insolubility of their dilemma. If Young Talbot flees this battle, he will, as it were, cease to be Talbot's son:

> Is my name Talbot? and am I your son?
> And shall I fly? O, if you love my mother,
> Dishonour not her honourable name,
> To make a bastard and a slave of me!
>
> [IV. v. 12-15]

But if he remains, as the father reminds the son, their "name" will be extinct in another sense: "In thee thy mother dies, our household's name, / My death's revenge, thy youth, and England's fame" [IV. vi. 38-9]. Like Antony and Coriolanus, the Talbots discover that the ideal figured by their heroic "name" is too pure for sublunary existence. It can be ratified only in the very act of death. Talbot's final words, spoken over the body of his dead son, accept and transcend this dilemma by returning to the classical consolation of fame and formulating it in an enlarged context:

> Thou antic Death, which laugh'st us here to scorn,
> Anon, from thy insulting tyranny,
> Coupled in bonds of perpetuity,
> Two Talbots winged through the lither sky,
> In thy despite shall scape mortality.
>
> [IV. vii. 18-22]

Here the humanistic reward of earthly fame (suggested by Icarus and Daedalus) is combined, at least implicitly, with the Christian consolation of resurrection after death. Their "name," and the aspirant quest for fame that motivates the noble life, is not cut off by death, but translated into the permanence of rhetorical *exemplum*. From this last oration Talbot moves surely to the clear-eyed acceptance of his fate that concludes the speech, even as it foreshadows the final lucidity of Shakespeare's later tragic heroes.

> Soldiers, adieu! I have what I would have,
> Now my old arms are young John Talbot's grave.
>
> [IV. vii. 31-2]

The funeral oration that began the play and was interrupted by the "sad tidings" from France here finds its *consolatio*: the "bright star" of Henry's fame has been set within a larger constellation.

The subplot involving Somerset, York, and the quarrel of the roses provides a third set of contrasts: the fields of France shrink to the Inns of Court, the epic warrior gives way to the fashionable courtier, the incentives of ancestral fame are replaced by a contentious aristocratic disdain, and the rites of war are but faintly recalled by adversaries who are careful, as Touchstone would say, to "quarrel in print, by the book, as you have books for good manners" [*As You Like It*, V. iv. 90-1]. Unlike Joan, the young men who quarrel in the Temple Garden have every reason to behave like aristocrats. They stand as Shakespeare's example of natural nobility diverted to trivial ends. If their modish and courtly wit is something of an anachronism in Talbot's world, the anachronism nevertheless helps us to see just where that world was heading. (pp. 109-11)

Part III. Act II. Scene v. Son who has killed his Father,
Henry VI, Father who has killed his Son, and Soldiers.
Frontispiece to the Hanmer edition by H. Gravelot (1744).
By permission of the Folger Shakespeare Library.

The crowning irony of *I Henry VI* is that this essentially trivial sense of honor should prove a greater threat to Talbot's ideals, and indeed to his very existence, than all the base stratagems devised by the French. In the climactic scenes of act four, while Talbot is "ring'd about with bold adversity" [IV. iv. 14], York and Somerset are characteristically quarreling about which of them is to be held responsible for his plight. . . . Talbot is thus sacrificed to a point of courtly etiquette. When this happens, Somerset and York stand judged as "seditious" peers, and in a context that would have seemed especially appropriate to the Elizabethan audience. The courtier has failed to accept his real responsibilities as a social and military leader; and this decay of the aristocracy, which is assailed from without by "upstarts" of ungentle birth like Winchester and Joan, portends a more general decline in national greatness.

Hence the final act can be taken as further commentary on the failure of a courtly aristocracy to provide an adequate image of feudal service and chivalry. Criticism of *I Henry VI* has understandably tended to treat Margaret and Suffolk as an end-link to the next play in the trilogy, but they also serve to bring the general declension from heroic action to courtly posturing to its appropriate conclusion: the pseudo-Petrarchan lover. Suffolk appears as a mannered Elizabethan amorist from his earliest exchanges with Margaret:

> Be not offended, nature's miracle,
> Thou art allotted to be ta'en by me:

So doth the swan her downy cygnets save,
Keeping them prisoner underneath her wings.
Yet, if this servile usage once offend,
Go and be free again as Suffolk's friend.

[V. iii. 54-9]

What is at stake here is the power of these romantic clichés to corrupt still further the integrity of the English court. . . . Suffolk concludes the play by acknowledging his own cynical motives, and foreshadowing, in a final portentous allusion to the Trojan *débacle,* the havoc of *2 Henry VI:*

> Thus Suffolk hath prevail'd; and thus he goes,
> As did the youthful Paris once to Greece;
> With hope to find the like event in love,
> But prosper better than the Trojan did.
> Margaret shall now be Queen, and rule the King;
> But I will rule both her, the King, and realm.

[V. v. 103-08]

Here the tradition of fame serves as an ironic backdrop, a final testimony to the ethical and political confusions of the present. What began as a viable aristocratic ideal of conduct, rooted in social customs and familial bonds, has become a mere precedent for aristocratic misadventure. The Talbots' fame, as it was earned at Bordeaux, embodies the high ethical ideals of the play; and their death effectively removes those ideals from the world of the play. From the moment of their apotheosis in the "lither sky" their name forfeits its slender hold on the actualities of history and achieves the perfection of heroic *exemplum*—a tale to be told in an increasingly harsh world.

The opening acts of *2 Henry VI* transport a reader of the trilogy from the siege walls and battlefields of France to the public halls and inmost recesses of the English court. For a popular history belonging to the early 1590's, the setting is still relatively novel, especially when it is recalled that this play probably preceded *Woodstock* and [Christopher Marlowe's] *Edward II.* The stage directions that the New Arden editor supplies for its first eleven scenes will immediately suggest how foreign its dramatic environment is to the tradition of [Marlowe's] *Tamburlaine:* London, the palace, the Duke of Gloucester's house, Gloucester's garden, Saint Alban's, the Duke of York's garden, a hall of justice, the abbey at Bury St. Edmunds, a room of state, a bedchamber. By introducing a set of Elizabethan courtiers into *I Henry VI,* Shakespeare had begun to engage the political crises of sixteenth-century England within the conventions of popular heroic drama. In *2 Henry VI* the nobility become recognizable as precisely what they were for Shakespeare's audience: "brave halfe paces between a throne and a people," in Fulke Greville's phrase, centered at the court in London. Scenes such as the one where Suffolk discovers some villagers with a petition "Against the Duke of Suffolk, for enclosing the commons of Long Melford" [*2 Henry VI,* I. iii. 20-2] dramatize the social status of that nobility in terms that could hardly be more explicit. Nor is this episode at all unusual. Comparable transactions bring the court aristocracy into conjunction with a disloyal household servant (I. ii), a pair of coney-catching vagabonds (II. i), a treasonous armorer and his loyal apprentice (II. iii), an outraged House of Commons (III. ii), a crew of discontented seaman (IV. i), the rebellious tradesmen of Kent (IV. ii-x), and a representative of the squirearchy named Alexander Iden (V. i). As if to emphasize and complicate the social and political implications of these encounters, Shakespeare makes Henry's court into what is virtually a cross section of sixteenth-century aristocracy: there is the judicious administrator and friend of the commons,

''Good Duke Humphrey'' of Gloucester; the proud, ambitious, and unscrupulous prelate Winchester; the loyal members of the country aristocracy, Salisbury and his son Warwick, who is commended for his ''plainness'' and ''housekeeping'' [I. i. 191]; the courtier Suffolk, an ''Image of Pride'' [I. i. 176] who has exchanged ''two dukedoms for a duke's fair daughter'' [I. i. 119] in France; and the glamorous conqueror-intriguer York, who is already maneuvering for the ''golden mark'' of Henry's crown. (pp. 111-14)

In terms of the continuities that I have set out to trace, the consequences of this changed setting—at least for the first three acts—are clear enough. The two characters who might have presented the strongest appeal to the heroic mood, Suffolk and York, are drastically reduced in stature, while Duke Humphrey suggests a new type of ideal ruler, the Ciceronian governor. . . . The controlling image of Gloucester's judicial rectitude and expertise is established in a series of trial scenes, in which he pronounces variously upon the dispute between Peter and Horner (I. iii), the qualifications of York and Somerset for the French regency (I. iii), the fraudulent ''miracle'' invented by Saunder Simcox and his wife (II. i), the misdemeanors of Dame Eleanor (II. i), and, finally, the accusations that are brought against him at Bury St. Edmunds (III. i). By contrast, throughout the first four acts York's projected rise to eminence is less a matter of his own special abilities than of his systematic effort to subvert the principles thus established. His principal strategies, the alliance with the Nevilles and the manipulation of Jack Cade, exhibit a valor that has ceased to find expression in the open trial of warfare, while it seeks out the privacy of schemes and soliloquies. Similarly, Suffolk's pride in rank and title is exemplified not in the martial deeds that would add to his family name, but rather in his illicit courtship of Queen Margaret, and his contemptuous exchanges with such ''base'' types as the humble petitioners (''Sir knave'' and his ''fellow'') who mistakenly approach him in act one [I. iii. 1-41]. . . . In so far as these contexts tend to deny the would-be hero his normal theater of operations—the battlefield and the tournament—the play as a whole may be said to embody ''historical assessment'' with a vengeance and, indeed, to mark a radical departure from [Shakespeare's] literary antecedents. . . . But there is a marked shift in emphasis within the play itself, one which serves to reopen the entire question of Suffolk's and York's value in a more hospitable setting.

The murder of Gloucester, which comes midway through the play, represents the most severe possible judgment on the ambitious nobles, and particularly Suffolk. At the same time, however, this event removes from the scene the one figure who embodies a thoroughgoing criticism of their personal aspirations. Instead of proceeding directly to their appointed miserable ends, therefore, both York and Suffolk enjoy a renewed vitality in the latter half of the play, as the social commentary, without Gloucester to interpret it, recedes into the background, and impinges less directly on the values of the two aristocrats. In effect, Shakespeare provides each of them with a new idiom and a new vision of nobility. The courtier, at his final parting with Margaret (III. ii), suddenly becomes an idealized and gracious amorist who measures the necessity of death against the permanence of love. York, the scheming Machiavel of the first three acts, reappears in the fifth as a visible embodiment of heroic authority, urging his claim to the throne on that basis. The impact of these scenes depends, of course, on the fact that they are set in an ambience so utterly different from that of I Henry VI. They take place not on a battlefield but in the court, where Suffolk and York already stand judged as instances of

''foul ambition'' [III. i. 143]. As a result, both characters now appear from a double perspective. The social stereotypes (corrupt courtier, rebellious baron) have been assimilated to more sympathetic theatrical roles, and, as the rhetorical elaboration unfolds, those roles enlarge the stereotypes into examples of personal ambition that cannot be adequately judged within a social order that is itself deeply compromised. Neither of these characters, in the hierarchical metaphor, ''knows his place,'' and as a result each becomes a far more interesting and problematic case than such professional caterpillars as Winchester and Buckingham. So Clifford's first response to York in act five is one of puzzled amazement: ''To Bedlam with him! Is the man grown mad!'' [V. i. 131]. The dramatist has discovered, however distantly, a radical form of tragic irony: when heroic and aristocratic values are transferred from the purely martial world of Talbot and Joan into a court where the nobility are ''brave halfe paces between a throne and a people,'' they may appear as inherently anarchic even though they are still admirable in themselves. It is Shakespeare's tentative acknowledgement of this predicament with respect to Suffolk and, more especially, York that makes them truly represent the crisis of the aristocracy in 2 Henry VI.

This transition from a drama of mordant social commentary to a more idealized and sympathetic portrayal of heroic aspiration poses some large problems of interpretation. . . . But it should be quite clear that the critique of Suffolk and York that is sustained by Gloucester never begins to generate a vision of the aristocratic life which convincingly supplants their own. Hence, after Gloucester's death, the reassertion of order and stability, such as it is, can only be accomplished by one of them. That is the crucial difference between 2 Henry VI and Richard II, a play which it closely resembles in many respects. In 2 Henry VI, the analysis of decay in the state is still predicated on the conception of the body politic and the ideal ruler that is common to all heroical-historical drama: the warrior prince leading his feudal ranks in wars of conquest. Richard II also shows what happens when aristocratic caterpillars corrupt the royal court and threaten the anointed body of the king; but in the later play the caterpillars are seen within the whole ''garden'' of the state, a type of Eden that evolves according to its own higher moral laws, while the ''body'' of the king, like the body of Christ, figures the health of the entire commonweal. As long as it remained uninformed by such a sacramental conception of politics and kingship, the social ethos of 2 Henry VI was bound finally to accommodate the same contentious aristocrats whom it set out to criticize. The only real gain (if one can call it that) lay in the dramatist's perception, which was to carry over into 3 Henry VI and Richard III, that the whole humanistic ideal of the hero king necessarily contained the seeds of its own deterioration.

This interdependence between the play's ethical criticism and its heroic themes is firmly established in the opening scene, which seems to me one of the finest in the play. It begins with the ceremonial addresses of Suffolk and Margaret, which usher in the style of courtly posturing and decadent ''magnificence'' that was adumbrated at the close of I Henry VI. . . . As soon as the royal couple and their favorite depart, Gloucester duly measures the ugly substance that this Petrarchan shadow conceals against the great achievements of the era that has just passed:

Brave peers of England, pillars of the state,
To you Duke Humphrey must unload his grief—
Your grief, the common grief of all the land.

What! did my brother Henry spend his youth,
His valour, coin, and people, in the wars?
Did he so often lodge in open field,
In winter's cold, and summer's parching heat,
To conquer France, his true inheritance?
And did my brother Bedford toil his wits,
To keep by policy what Henry got? . . .
O peers of England! shameful is this league,
Fatal this marriage, cancelling your fame,
Blotting your names from books of memory,
Razing the characters of your renown,
Defacing monuments of conquer'd France,
Undoing all, as all had never been!

                                    [I. i. 75-84, 98-103]

Gloucester is a type of the Renaissance governor whom humanists like [Roger] Ascham and [Sir Thomas] Elyot saw as supplanting such medieval *chevaliers* as Talbot, and his tone here is hardly bellicose. It would be impossible to find, among the earlier histories, a more balanced portrayal of the ideal ruler through humanistic topics. The emphasis falls on fortitude ("Did he so often lodge in open field / In winter's cold and summer's parching heat") and prudence ("And did my brother Bedford toil his wits, / To keep by policy what Henry got"). Both these virtues are put in the service of Henry's patrimony, "his true inheritance." By exemplifying them, Henry's peers all achieved an honored place in the registers of fame. Gloucester is ideally suited to witness the decay of this high tradition in the ambience of Henry's court, but, as the survivor, along with Salisbury and Beaufort, of a departed order, he is powerless to do anything about it. In this scene, as elsewhere, he shows his frustration and impotence by abrupt fits of choler and sadness, which are relieved only by unexplained silences and departures.

Hence it is York who, at the conclusion of the scene, ventures to translate Gloucester's themes into action, although he does so in a radically new context. . . . The tone and imagery of this passage [I. i. 214-59], which recall Marlowe's Machiavellian Duke of Guise, could hardly be farther from Gloucester's. This flippant, mercantile appraisal of "his own" inheritance makes it clear that York is alive to the ancestral values of *I Henry VI* only in a very limited way. Nevertheless, it should already be apparent that York is not, finally, going to be the mere villain of the piece, for he is only measuring himself against the humanistic standards that Gloucester has just invoked. Like the Henry of noble memory, York is ready to "grapple" in the field while others surfeit in the joys of love; like Bedford, York will use his wits "To pry into the secrets of the state," and like all the learned Council of the realm he will watch and wake "when others be asleep." If their aim was to secure Henry's true inheritance, York would only "claim his own"; if they erected characters of renown, York will "raise aloft the milk-white rose."

This transition from Gloucester's highminded critique of Henry's court to York's half ironic reassertion of the *topoi* on which he bases that critique foreshadows the basic design of the entire play. As the portrayal of social corruption broadens and unfolds, Margaret, Suffolk, and their new allies continue to beguile Henry with games of courtly makebelieve, and Gloucester continues to expose their foul practices wherever he can. His effectiveness, however, is always limited by his reliance on purely judicial procedures . . . , and he is finally sacrificed to his own faith in legal rectitude.

By the beginning of the fourth act the homiletic moral, "Virtue is chok'd with foul Ambition" [III. i. 143], has virtually been played out: it is concluded by the expulsion of Suffolk and the eschatological horrors of Winchester's demise. It is just at this point that York, who has been mostly in the wings up to now, determines to raise aloft the milk-white rose and purge Henry's court of its corrupted elements. For York alone, of all the decadent aristocrats, has still managed to preserve some semblance of the antique pattern of heroical worth that was established by Henry V. Hence he alone can raise himself from the status of a symptom of courtly viciousness in the earlier acts to that of a judgment on it in the later ones. (pp. 116-22)

York's ambivalent status as both remedy and cause of the decay in Henry's court is epitomized by the connection between his lofty aspirations and the peasants' revolt engineered during his absence in act four. While he is in Ireland, Jack Cade and his followers also weigh the claims of *noblesse de robe* ["nobility of the long robe"] and *noblesse d'épée* ["nobility of the sword"], and reach similar conclusions:

Bev.   O miserable age! Virtue is not regarded in
            handicraftsmen.
Hol.   The nobility think scorn to go in leather
            aprons.
Bev.   Nay, more; the King's Council are no good
            workmen.
Hol.   True; and yet it is said, "Labour in thy
            vocation": which is as much to say as,
            "Let the magistrates be labouring men";
            and therefore should we be magistrates.
Bev.   Thou hast hit it; for there's no better sign
            of a brave mind than a hard hand.

                                              [IV. ii. 10-20]

The relevance of this burlesque to the main plot is assured by its place within York's own strategy. York is Jack Cade's silent partner, and he begins his own campaign only after Cade's revolt is under way. Cade himself ensures that the connection is not forgotten by imitating his patron's claims to royal ancestry [IV. ii. 39-49], his intention to purge Henry's court of "false caterpillars" [IV. iv. 37; see also IV. ii. 65-9; IV. vii. 31-2], his detestation of all things French [IV. ii. 160-72], his admiring recollection of Henry V [IV. ii. 156-59], his distaste for "bookish rule" [IV. ii. 85-110], his insistence on martial eminence as requisite for aristocratic station [IV. vii. 79-80], and his easy association of martial bravery and material prosperity [IV. ii. 64-75]. These details are set, moreover, within a continuous parody of the conventional formulas for heroic self-assertion. As in the comedy of *I Henry VI*, the favorite joke consists in puncturing the would-be hero's set speeches by irreverent asides that specify social realities:

Cade.   My father was a Mortimer,—
But.   [*Aside.*] He was an honest man, and a good
            bricklayer.
Cade.   My mother a Plantagenet,—
But.   [*Aside.*] I knew her well; she was a
            midwife.
Cade.   My wife descended of the Lacies,—
But.   [*Aside.*] She was, indeed, a pedlar's
            daughter, and sold many laces.

                                              [IV. ii. 39-46]

by outlandish attempts at magnificence:

        [*Cade.*] Wither, garden; and be henceforth a
        burying-place to all that do dwell in this house,
        because the unconquer'd soul of Cade is fled.

[IV. x. 63-5]

and by reductive detail:

> *Cade.* Iden, farewell; and be proud of thy victory. Tell Kent from me, she hath lost her best man, and exhort all the world to be cowards. . . .

[IV. x. 72-4]

The vitality of these scenes, as with any exercise in mock-heroic, stems from their bringing widely disparate elements into a momentary comic equilibrium; and it is to Shakespeare's purpose that two of those elements—Richard Plantagenet, lineal heir to the House of York, and Jack Cade, clothier of Kent—are set in the most improbable proximity to one another. When Stafford's brother exclaims ''Jack Cade, the Duke of York hath taught you this'' [IV. ii. 153-54], one may take his words in the broadest sense. York sets Cade an example, or, in theatrical terms, teaches him a part; and Cade plays it to the hilt, not wisely but too well. Measuring Cade's performance in act four against his patron's in act five, one learns to judge York's ideals by their consequences within the social order. The point is not simply that the audience now sees the meaning of the accusation that York is ''treasonable''; it has also been made clear that in a body politic where the speciality of rule is constantly violated, York's claims to sovereignty assume a special validity. When he exclaims

> King did I call thee? No, thou art not king;
> Nor fit to govern and rule multitudes,
> Which dar'st not, no, nor canst not rule a traitor.

[V. i. 93-5]

he stands exposed as both the cause and the remedy of the condition he describes. If the paradox is not a facile one, that is in part because it is rooted in the whole series of ironic parallels and contrasts between York and Cade: York is disruptive and ambitious—but by Cade's standards he is not anarchic; his hereditary claim to the throne is so distant as to make his motives suspect, but it is hardly an outright fraud; he acquiesces in the murder of Humphrey and demands the imprisonment of Margaret's new favorite, Somerset, but he does not advocate the wholesale execution of ''scholars, lawyers, courtiers, gentlemen,'' and other ''false caterpillars'' [IV. iv. 36-7]. In effect he epitomizes the ambiguous place of heroic virtue in a court that is weak and corrupt, has forfeited its claims to authority, but still believes in order. (pp. 123-26)

The very different image of heroic character that is to predominate in *3 Henry VI* is already apparent in the first few lines of the play, which, like the second scene of *Macbeth*, probe the uncertain boundaries that divide acts of war from crimes of blood. York's stirring account of his army's victory over Clifford, Stafford, and the ''great Lord of Northumberland, / Whose war-like ears could never brook retreat'' [*3 Henry VI*, I. i. 4-5] finds its gruesome sequel in the reports of his assembled family. Edward announces that ''Lord Stafford's father, Duke of Buckingham, / Is either slain or wounded dangerous'' and invites his father to ''behold his blood'' [I. i. 10-11, 13]. His brother Falconbridge adds to this ''the Earl of Wiltshire's blood'' [I. i. 14]. Richard rounds off the demonstration by throwing down the Duke of Somerset's head, and concluding ''Thus do I hope to shake King Henry's head'' [I. i. 20]. Such relish of violence and bloodshed places York's struggle to attain his ''right'' in rather a new perspective. His wish to ''raise aloft the milk-white rose'' [*2 Henry VI*, I. i. 254] now appears as an unrelenting compulsion to slaughter all the House of

Lancaster. Hence, one is not surprised to discover later in this scene that the Lancastrians themselves now act from motives of revenge rather than the feudal loyalties displayed in the last act of *2 Henry VI*. There is to be no more talk of ''praise and esteem,'' or of ''justice and true right.'' When Young Clifford meets York, and is himself challenged to personal combat, Northumberland advises him that ''It is war's prize to take all vantages; / And ten to one is no impeach of valor'' [*3 Henry VI*, I. iv. 60]. Not surprisingly, the play's chief oratorical forms are the *vituperatio* [''censure''] and the lament. Within these set speech types the formulaic virtues of a noble ancestry, strength and beauty, courage and wisdom are continually ''reversed,'' in keeping with the regular procedures of rhetorical invective, into their opposites: congenital viciousness, deformity and ugliness, brutality and cunning.

If the play as a whole is to be seen as anything more than a nihilistic bloodbath of tragedy and revenge, it is necessary to keep in mind the vision of aristocratic ideals and public order that makes the implicit contrast to these ''reversals.'' For the transition from *2 Henry VI* to *3 Henry VI* marks the dramatist's continuing discovery of an historical process that followed naturally from the extension of heroic ideals into Tudor politics. An analysis of aristocratic corruption portends the rise of a new ''prince,'' one who still identifies himself with the traditional values of hereditary nobility, strength, and courage, although he presses his claims with an unexampled show of ruthlessness and cunning. He offers the hope of a return to a nobler age; but the very act of violence that brings about his accession foreshadows the utter dissolution of all aristocratic values and social obligations until, finally, the torrent of revenge and civil war gives rise to a new Machiavel, and a last parody of heroic *virtù*. (pp. 128-30)

If *3 Henry VI* does not degenerate into a pseudopolitical revenge tragedy like *The Battle of Alcazar*, is because all of its important characters have, in effect, a double role. Each is conceived both as a member of an aggrieved family and as a participant in a complex political struggle. . . . As in *2 Henry VI*, only on a universal scale, the public status and obligations of these characters are measured against the increasingly dubious claims of their personal ideals. Familial honor, hitherto a counterweight to uncontrolled ambition and reckless personal ideals, now becomes the source of new atrocities. The sundering of honor and politics is nowhere more apparent than in this play, where every attempt to invoke a political compromise is frustrated by the demand for personal revenge, until one finally arrives at the hollow pretense of ''country's peace and brothers' loves'' [V. vii. 36] that concludes the action even as it foreshadows the frauds and fratricides of *Richard III*. (pp. 131-32)

To arrive at a more detailed estimate of the play's politics, one must again turn to its dramatic format and rhetorical designs. As an historical revenge play, *3 Henry VI* finds its operative conceptions of human character in the set topics of rhetorical invective. York's great *vituperatio* of Margaret [I. iv. 111-68], the Lancastrian queen who has learned to play the Amazon, enumerates the significant ''topics'' of revenge drama by reversing all the set commonplaces of demonstrative oratory. The despised ''She-wolf of France'' whose father is ''not so wealthy as an English yeoman'' [I. iv. 111, 123], has exchanged her feminine *bona animi* [''spiritual attributes''], modesty and ''government'' [I. iv. 132], for the impudent ferocity of an ''Amazonian trull'' [I. iv. 114]. Her grotesque display of ''courage'' can only be understood as an inexplicable deviation from nature, a relinquishment of human identity for the unchanging ''vizard'' [I. iv. 116] of the actor.

> 'Tis beauty that doth oft make women proud;
> But God he knows thy share thereof is small.
> 'Tis virtue that does make them most admir'd;
> The contrary doth make thee wonder'd at.
> 'Tis government that makes them seem divine;
> The want thereof makes thee abominable.
> Thou art as opposite to every good
> As the Antipodes are unto us,
> Or as the south to the Septentrion.
>
> [I. iv. 128-36]

The descriptive figures amplify this reversal of the civilized into the barbarous through stock epithets like the ''outdoing'' comparison to ''tigers of Hyrcania'' [I. iv. 155], and the celebrated ''tiger's heart wrapp'd in a woman's hide'' [I. iv. 137]. Elsewhere in the play, these formulas for an unnatural revenge are reproduced in a wide variety of situations, usually in tiny pieces of invective interspersed throughout the dialogue, and occasionally in longer set speeches, but almost always with reference to Clifford or Richard. Local instances would include epithets like ''cruel child-killer,'' ''crook-back,'' and ''foul misshapen stigmatic'' [II. ii. 112, 96, 136], as well as more extended figures such as Rutland's comparison of Clifford to a ''pent-up lion'' [I. iii. 12-15] or Henry's picture of Richard as an ''indigest, deformed lump'' [V. vi. 51], and lengthy pieces of invective such as Margaret's portrayal of Richard and his brothers as ''bloody cannibals,'' ''butchers,'' and ''deathsmen'' [V. v. 61, 63, 67]. All these examples (and more could be cited) point back to the elementary definitions of humanity invoked in York's address to Margaret. Together they present a composite image of the revenging son who determines to reproduce the original ''crime'' by destroying still another family: the playwright has come full circle from the idealistic wish of Old York and Young Talbot simply to ''die in pride.'' His leading characters have become, in effect, the base, unnatural monsters that the Herculean hero originally set out to destroy. (pp. 133-34)

> David Riggs, ''The Hero in History: A Reading of 'Henry VI','' in his Shakespeare's Heroical Histories: ''Henry VI'' and Its Literary Tradition, Cambridge, Mass.: Harvard University Press, 1971, pp. 93-139.

ROBERT B. PIERCE (essay date 1971)

[*Pierce contends that in 1, 2, and 3* Henry VI *the family functions both as a microcosm of the kingdom and as a commentary on the political themes of the plays. He argues that the breakdown or destruction of the family, the often fatal results of marriage, and the corruption of noble inheritance in the trilogy all support and contribute to Shakespeare's larger concentration on chaos and political dissolution. Pierce notes that moral and political inheritance are equally important in* Henry VI, *for the essence of the principle of royal succession is that the heir to the throne ''inherits not only his position but also his virtue and social responsibility.'' Like Ronald S. Berman (1962), Pierce traces Shakespeare's depiction of moral inheritance from* 1 Henry VI *to* 3 Henry VI, *demonstrating its gradual decline from young Talbot's emulation of his father's chivalric behavior to the opposite extreme of Henry's disinheriting his own son. Like David M. Bevington (1966) and H. M. Richmond (1967), among others, Pierce comments on the political superiority of the female characters over the male and on the bastardization of language by such figures as Henry, Suffolk, and Margaret through courtly affectation and facile, ro-*]*

mantic rhetoric. According to Pierce, these elements underscore the general theme of political/social dissolution. And like David Riggs (1971), Pierce views the trilogy as depicting the destruction of the aristocratic ideal and the birth of a more cunning, deceitful, individualistic form of government, epitomized in the figure of Richard of Gloucester. Pierce also alludes to growth imagery in the plays, a topic treated more fully by Caroline F. E. Spurgeon (1935) and Carol McGinnis Kay (1972).]

The family in the Henry VI trilogy has no independent role; it is not a conflicting center of interest that competes with the political theme for attention. Rather it functions almost entirely as a commentary on the causes and consequences of political disorder. . . . What is most real in the plays is historical destiny, to which the personal identities of the characters are subdued.

Reference to the family is often a device to bring their political roles closer to the immediate experience of the audience. We understand Henry as king because we understand him as father and husband. We know what is happening to England because we see what is happening to fathers and sons and husbands and wives. This pattern reflects the doctrine of correspondences. Since what infects the kingdom infects everything in it, marriage becomes just another part of the struggle for power and loved ones are hostages to fortune in a violent world. The very channels that perpetuate order are corrupted to breed disorder. Inheritance, turned to a monstrous thing that demands vengeance rather than noble emulation, finally produces a demon who is the enemy of both family and state.

Shakespeare also uses the family to suggest what political disorder is destroying in the commonwealth. Especially in the first two plays glimpses of a yet-uncorrupted family life contrast ironically with the decline of justice and harmony among the governors. This contrast does not suggest that personal virtue conflicts with political virtue—quite the opposite, though in some degree Henry VI's piety cripples his political realism. Still there may be some hint that his early piety does not run very deep. Certainly his asceticism vanishes quickly at Suffolk's descriptions of Margaret in *1 Henry VI*. And in adversity Henry gains a real political wisdom, while at the same time his piety becomes more convincing. Better than anyone else in *3 Henry VI*, he understands the plight of England, including the threat of Richard, Duke of Gloucester; and he foresees England's redemption by the young Richmond. More serious weaknesses than unworldly piety cripple Henry both as king and as husband and father. The key to his character is that he is a partial man and a partial monarch.

More typical of these plays is the illusory personal loyalty of the York family. It quickly collapses because, in a realm where no strong king commands unexceptionable loyalty, every man is tempted to struggle for himself, even against his brothers. Thus one remarkable achievement of the Henry VI plays is the way they marshal the powerful claims of family loyalty in defense of political order. Above all they show that the family is involved in the destructive impact of disorder. Partly for this reason, they are significant achievements in dramatic craftsmanship. It is no disparagement of Shakespeare's youthful talents to attribute them to his pen. (pp. 35-7)

Birth and inheritance are prominent in the language of [*1 Henry VI*]. The interview between York and his dying uncle, Mortimer, brings out one of the central political issues of the play, the doubtfulness of the king's title. Here and elsewhere the favorite metaphor for orderly succession is growth, especially a flourishing tree or garden. Any interruption of the pattern—depicted as cutting down or transplanting—perverts a natural process. One inherits not only his position but also his virtue and social responsibility. When Joan charges Burgundy with an unnatural betrayal of his country, she goes on to question his "birth and lawful progeny" [lineage or descent] [*1 Henry VI*, III. iii. 61]. When Talbot strips Falstaff of his Garter, he denounces the recreant as a "hedge-born swain" despite his pretensions to good blood [IV. i. 43]. Here the embodiment of virtue and order, whose son shortly demonstrates the proper inheritance of valor, describes his opposite. (pp. 39-40)

Talbot is an earlier and simpler version of the warrior-hero Henry V. Neither of these men makes any pretense to super-humanity like Tamburlaine's. They find their strength where a weakling like Richard II finds despair, in their ordinary human nature. Whether the hero-king woos Katherine in bluff English fashion or wanders incognito through the night to meet his soldiers as one of them, he grounds his royalty in the earth. Nor is Talbot the stock image of a hero; Shakespeare even changes his sources to make the terror of the French physically dwarfish. There are times when he speaks with the stereotyped rant of heroes and behaves with unrealistic bravado. Thus he brags that, while a prisoner, he refused to be exchanged for an unworthy opposite. But his behavior in captivity shows an almost animal ferocity rather than heroic dignity. . . . The extremes of behavior thus crudely juxtaposed are more subtly fused in Henry V, but the Shakespearian impulse to ground the hero in something more solid than epic glory is already present.

Talbot's self-discipline and virtue appear primarily in his military feats, but on two occasions he is measured by more personal values. The first of these is a light interlude in the French wars, the Countess of Auvergne's attempt to trap him by inviting him to an assignation. Talbot reveals a Guyon-like continence when he brings his army along to the dinner. His domestic virtue resists French seductiveness as strongly as his courage resists French arms. The connection of this episode with Talbot's heroic career is tenuous, but for that very reason Shakespeare's intention of measuring the private virtue of a public figure is apparent.

This episode is most important in preparing the way for the more effective scenes in which Talbot and his son fight and die together near Bordeaux (IV. v-vii). Here most clearly Shakespeare uses the values of the family to complete the ideal portrait of Talbot and to provide an ironic contrast with the disorder and disloyalty of the court. This relationship of father and son symbolizes the kind of political order that is dying along with Talbot. When he calls young John "the son of chivalry" [IV. vi. 29], he means "my chivalric son," but the loose Elizabethan grammar allows the phrase to suggest that chivalry is an inherited virtue, a mark of the noble family.

Young Talbot's refusal to abandon his father proves that he has inherited that heroic warrior's zeal for honor. His argument against flight is unanswerable:

> The world will say, he is not Talbot's blood
> That basely fled when noble Talbot stood.
>
> [IV. v. 16-17]

Talbot endorses this traditional doctrine when he reports having taunted the Bastard Orleans:

> Contaminated, base,
> And misbegotten blood I spill of thine,
> Mean and right poor, for that pure blood of mine
> Which thou didst force from Talbot, my brave boy.
>
> [IV. vi. 21-4]

In the dying chivalric order, not only does the father's blood infuse strength and virtue into the veins of his son, but the effect of breeding is reinforced by example, a kind of emulation in courage. Hence Talbot's son inspires him to new deeds of valor, and John demands parity with his father even while affirming their unity:

> No more can I be sever'd from your side
> Than can yourself yourself in twain divide.
>
> [IV. v. 48-9]

The destruction of this family foreshadows the collapse of the state, for at King Henry's court the old order has already degenerated into bastard feudalism, a disorderly society of Machiavellian scheming veiled by remnants of the old ceremony. (pp. 41-4)

Joan is Talbot's "mighty opposite," the epitome of disorder and rebellion just as he is the epitome of order and loyalty. They share a blunt directness of speech that gives them force in this world of empty rhetoric and aimless plotting. Talbot would not be ashamed to choose his sword like Joan, "Out of a great deal of old iron" [I. ii. 101]; after all, he was willing to fight his captors with stones. But he would not have the blasphemous audacity to attribute the choice to divine guidance [I. ii. 98-101]. Like Richard III, Joan arouses her creator's interest, not because of any goodness in her, but because she has a real zest for evil. She is absolutely corrupt from beginning to end, a degeneracy shown in part by her violation of familial sanctions.

Most obvious are the constant references to her sexual libertinism. The innuendos start when she first appears, and later she is openly the Dauphin's paramour. In ironic proximity to Talbot's victory over temptation by the Countess of Auvergne, Burgundy describes having seen "the Dauphin and his trull" in undignified flight together [II. ii. 28]. Her corruption is yet more obvious when she offers her body to fiends, and she becomes ludicrous when she abandons her pose of virgin purity and proclaims herself with child in order to avoid execution. Allowing such a trull to stand boasting over the dead Talbot suggests the triumph of degeneracy. And even her death does not purge the world, because she is soon to be replaced by Queen Margaret, another Frenchwoman and one equally vicious though less contemptible.

Heavily symbolic of Joan's evil is a violation of family duty when at the point of death she repudiates her father. As France rebels against England's rightful dominion, so its champion denies her parentage. The half-comic scene is in a rude, blunt language appropriate to Joan and her father, yet through the coarse irony appears something of Shakespeare's usual compassion for the sufferings of old men. To an Elizabethan the stage picture of a daughter refusing to kneel for her father's blessing goes beyond comedy; it is a terrible image of disorder. (pp. 46-8)

Thus the family is significant in the structure of *1 Henry VI*. Its system of values provides a standard to measure the disorder and moral nihilism that are infecting England and even beginning to corrupt the domestic lives of the rulers. What prevents this dramatic technique from having more than occasional flashes of power is that Shakespeare's exploitation of it lacks immediacy. . . . In the scene between Joan and her father the symbolic action briefly takes on dramatic life, but the scenes of Talbot and his son generate their power as stylized renditions of an idea, as tableaux. Even the Temple Garden episode partakes more of this quality than of the character-centered drama that one associates with the later Shakespeare. (p. 51)

In language and structure [*2 Henry VI*] is far more sophisticated than its predecessor, though at the cost of a certain untidiness. *2 Henry VI* is built on contrasts of character, especially between Henry and two other royal figures, Gloucester and York. . . . The contrast among the three is more elaborate than that between Talbot and Joan in *1 Henry VI,* and they are more fully and vividly developed than any characters in the earlier play. Once again Shakespeare illuminates the personal lives of these political figures through the family. The dramatic technique is much the same, though it displays greater skill and subtlety. (p. 52)

The theme of disorder becomes more and more prominent not only in events but also in the poetry [of *2 Henry VI*]. References and images suggest that the civil strife infecting the commonwealth has spread through its whole body. The ordinary Englishman, who receives more attention in this play, suffers from the conflicts in the court. A group of petitioners to Gloucester have the misfortune to encounter Suffolk and the queen instead. Comic though it is, one man's complaint suggests how disorder is breeding injustice: "Mine is, an 't please your Grace, against John Goodman, my Lord Cardinal's man, for keeping my house, and lands, and wife, and all, from me" [*2 Henry VI,* I. iii. 16-18]. Suffolk and Margaret find the loss of his wife amusing and make no effort to help him. (p. 53)

Like the previous play, *2 Henry VI* emphasizes the theme of inheritance. When the Cardinal demands to be treated with respect as John of Gaunt's son, Gloucester bluntly reminds him of his bastardy [*1 Henry VI,* III. i. 42]. When Warwick accuses Suffolk of Gloucester's murder, the two exchange traditional insults about their mothers' chastity, with Suffolk outdoing the "Blunt-witted lord" in vigor and detail [*2 Henry VI,* III. ii. 210-14, 222-23]. This language of birth and inheritance has a parallel in the characterization of Salisbury and his son Warwick, who illustrate the inheritance of virtue in a noble family. They confront the dilemma of all men of good will in a disordered state, who can find no clear object for their loyalty. They support Gloucester as the main force for order and virtue, but when York presents his claim to the throne, they feel obliged to throw their backing to him. Warwick as yet shows none of his kingmaker's arrogance, though there may be some foreshadowing in his blunt pride. Now, however, he acts as the outspoken voice of simple honesty, like Kent in *King Lear.*

The first scene of the play establishes Salisbury as a choric voice of English wisdom, and he is shown in ideal harmony with his son: "Warwick, my son, the comfort of my age" [*2 Henry VI,* I. i. 190]. When these men reveal that they are supporting York's claim, it is a blow to Henry, and he touches on moral inheritance in his grieved outcry:

> Old Salisbury, shame to thy silver hair,
> Thou mad misleader of thy brain-sick son!
>
> [V. i. 162-63]

Even that fundamental principle, the inheritance of true nobility, seems to be corrupted in this anarchic time. Whether or not Salisbury's choice for York is correct (and the play does not decide that issue), he is a man of good will. His son could become a mighty force for good in an ordered community, another good Duke Humphrey or Talbot, but in the weak reign of Henry VI his immense energy turns into a disruptive force. Warwick's degeneration from Salisbury's noble son to the arrogant, impulsive kingmaker suggests what is happening to the inherited virtue of England, the mighty tradition of Crécy and Agincourt to which these plays so often look back.

Thus the leitmotiv of inheritance is developed in characterization with Salisbury and Warwick. It is also used in the one obviously emblematic scene of this play, in which Alexander Iden kills Jack Cade. Cade's appearance marks the spread of anarchy to all of the commonwealth. Like Joan of Arc he shows the dregs of society making claim to lofty position in a prodigious manifestation of disorder. He too repudiates his actual parentage in order to claim high birth. . . . Also like Joan, he avows libertine naturalism, even substituting it officially for law. (pp. 54-6)

When he staggers into Alexander Iden's garden, the types of order and disorder meet. In the symbolic garden that fascinates Shakespeare's imagination, Cade faces its owner, who has expressed his contentment with rural seclusion in a charming brief soliloquy:

> Lord! who would live turmoiled in the court,
> And may enjoy such quiet walks as these?
> This small inheritance my father left me
> Contenteth me, and worth a monarchy.
>
> [IV. x. 16-19]

Unlike Cade, Iden accepts his inheritance, about which he sounds a note common in Latin poetry, the quiet joy of country retreat. The victory of such a man over Jack Cade suggests that virtue is not lost to England, that it has merely fallen back to its rural fastnesses. Iden's quaintly artificial blank verse sets off Cade's vigorous prose, though the former never lives up to the pretty charm of the opening speech. In fact, Shakespeare seems to be so much fascinated with his tough-minded rebel that he gives him a wryly noble death, even at the expense of the emblematic picture. And at most this scene is a perfunctory expression of the ideal while civil strife dominates the dramatic foreground.

Even more central than inheritance in *2 Henry VI* is marriage, which is of special importance for two of the chief kingly characters, Henry and Gloucester. (pp. 56-7)

Duke Humphrey is a powerful force for good, as the frequent punning references to his title of Protector suggest. His weakness is an innocence that leaves him vulnerable to the plots of other, more ambitious, people. . . . [His wife] takes advantage of this weakness. Like the plotting nobles she is ambitious; she dresses more richly than the queen and even dreams of seizing the crown for her husband. Gloucester's rebuke to her arrogance is imperious; but when she starts to lose her temper, he quickly pacifies her, and she goes right on scheming. The conjuring scene (I. iv) exists largely to please the crowd with displays of magic and to foreshadow later deaths, but it also shows the Lord Protector's wife in the blasphemous act of calling up demons. When her enemies seize on her in this act and humiliate her, the shame of her penance subdues her pride, but by then it is too late to save Gloucester.

The disorder of the kingdom has tempted Eleanor to reach beyond her place in society. As a result, Gloucester is destroyed as a governor, and his marriage crumbles in his hands. . . . [Gloucester] has the simplicity of an older world, the days when a man needed only to be strong and loyal to his king. His wife adapts herself to the current morality of personal ambition, but she is not clever enough to survive against such adversaries as the Cardinal, Margaret, Suffolk, and York. (pp. 58-9)

2 Henry VI opens with a spectacular ceremony to impress the importance of the marriage between Henry and Margaret. In every sense this is an unnatural union. Not only has the king neglected his duty in wedding Margaret at all, but she will assume an unwomanly dominion over him and form an adulterous liaison with Suffolk. When Henry receives her from his "procurator," Suffolk, he echoes the amorous preciosity of the end of *1 Henry VI* along with his usual bland piety:

> I can express no kinder sign of love
> Than this kind kiss. O Lord, that lends me life,
> Lend me a heart replete with thankfulness!
> For thou hast given me in this beauteous face
> A world of earthly blessings to my soul,
> If sympathy of love unite our thoughts.
>
> [I. i. 18-23]

The pun on "kinder" in the first line evokes the standard of nature by which this artificial ceremony is found wanting. Henry fuses Petrarchanism and piety in the tangled figure of a face that represents "earthly blessings" to a soul; the clumsiness of the poetry is in part justified by its suitability to Henry's confusion.

The first scene shows little of Margaret's character, since she makes only conventional speeches, but Gloucester's shock at the marriage contract makes clear the unsuitability of the terms. After the king and new queen go out in state, he delivers an impressive harangue in high oratorical style, one that rises through a series of rhetorical questions to a final impassioned exclamation:

> O peers of England! shameful is this league,
> Fatal this marriage, cancelling your fame,
> Blotting your names from books of memory,
> Razing the characters of your renown,
> Defacing monuments of conquer'd France,
> Undoing all, as all had never been!
>
> [I. i. 98-103]

Henry's marriage has become a weapon destroying the traditional way of life, the noble code of chivalric glory. (pp. 60-1)

Of the two important marriages in the play, Shakespeare gives the greater complexity and depth to that of Henry and Margaret; but its implications extend into *3 Henry VI*, whereas the study of Gloucester and Eleanor is largely within this play. Gloucester can no more control his wife's ambition than he can maintain order and degree in the commonwealth. Her usurpation of manly concerns shows in little what is happening in the kingdom. She and the other ambitious and mannish women of these plays show that in a collapsing social order women cannot fulfill their natural and traditional functions. In Henry's court, love is either a deceit or a weakness. Margaret's love language can have no meaning except as a mask. The strongest man in the play, Richard, Duke of York, is the one least encumbered with traditional emotions and loyalties. Although these characters are more vital than those in *1 Henry VI* (even the same people), none of them is so strong as the impersonal force that dominates events, the historical power that drives England nearer and nearer to chaos. In this least Senecan play of the first tetralogy, what is most like Seneca is this sense of a fatal curse dominating men's actions. Past events and dead men lurk in the background, and in the last two plays their presence will be felt even more.

The disorder reaches its climax in the last of the Henry VI plays, which has neither the mechanical structure of the first

Part III. Act IV. Scene iii. Warwick, Edward IV, and Soldiers. By M. Adamo (n.d.). The Department of Rare Books and Special Collections, The University of Michigan Library.

part nor the balanced characters of the second. Insofar as it achieves a unified effect, it does so by its theme and, ultimately, by its poetic language. Not figures but acts and events are balanced against each other. The characters lose themselves in the welter of words and action—all but one, that is. For Richard, Duke of Gloucester, stands out from the fabric of the play in a way that imperils its dramatic and poetic proportion even while creating a high point of dramatic interest. Nevertheless, what is most impressive about the play is not the emerging Richard, who has freer rein in the next [*Richard III*], but its attainment of poetic unity without entirely sacrificing the remarkable diversity of poetic modes in *2 Henry VI*.

The family is more prominent as emblem and symbol in this part than in the previous two. It is so richly woven through the language that it helps greatly in the unity of effect that this play achieves. (pp. 64-6)

Underlying this pattern in the language is constant emphasis on a few new key ideas, the themes of disorder and corrupted marriage and inheritance. Thus frequent references to disorder in the family suggest the chaos to which civil war has brought England. Since the poles of this disorder are two men, Henry in his weakness and Richard in his evil strength, a reference to the effect of each of them on the family will illustrate the technique. The dying Clifford asserts that if Henry had not been a weak king,

> I, and ten thousand in this luckless realm
> Had left no mourning widows for our death.
> [II. vi. 18-19]

And when Henry is about to die, he prophesies of Richard:

> And many an old man's sigh, and many a widow's,
> And many an orphan's water-standing eye—
> Men for their sons', wives for their husbands',
> Orphans for their parents' timeless death—
> Shall rue the hour that ever thou wast born.
> [V. vi. 39-43]

Both speeches emphasize the sheer number of those who are to suffer rather than the intensity of the individuals' grief. The abstractness of the images is in keeping with the lofty Senecan mode. Most of the references to the family are of this sort, though the most striking examples gain force from their dramatic context.

The themes of marriage and inheritance are also present in this play, but they are more thoroughly woven into complexes of character and action. The language is less a separable element than in *2 Henry VI*, even while it plays a bigger role.

The last of the Henry VI plays has the most impressive of the emblematic scenes, one that helps to enrich the many references to the family. At the battlefield of Towton, Henry soliloquizes on the woes that he has brought to himself and England. Then he overhears and joins in the laments of a father who has killed his son and a son who has killed his father. (pp. 67-8)

One should not so much listen to the speakers' words as respond to the symbolic picture of King Henry sitting on his molehill and the father and son kneeling beside their victims, all mourning. The father and son are nameless because they are England. Even Henry for once transcends his weakness and in his grief becomes the king and father of a suffering land. Thus for a moment the play shifts to a level of powerful abstraction.

It is with grim irony that the action resumes and the normal view of Henry returns. The first speaker after this antiphony is Prince Edward, the son whom Henry has disinherited and whom his weakness will shortly destroy. The king relapses into his normal, blandly conciliating manner and hurries off after being bullied by Margaret and Exeter. In the normal life of this play the only kind of antiphony is parodic, as in the next scene, when the victors mockingly lament over Clifford's body. Their sarcastic echoing of the themes of mercy and father-and-son emphasizes that they are immersed in the violent strife, that ceremony and ritual have no meaning for them:

Rich.	Clifford, ask mercy, and obtain no grace.
Edw.	Clifford, repent in bootless penitence.
War.	Clifford, devise excuses for thy faults.
Geo.	While we devise fell tortures for thy faults.
Rich.	Thou didst love York, and I am son to York.
Edw.	Thou pitied'st Rutland, I will pity thee.
	[*3 Henry VI*, II. vi. 69-74]

Here as elsewhere the perversion of ceremony is a sign of the corruption of all meaningful order. In a play marked by these parodic ceremonies, only the visionary Henry can detach himself from the violence to partake of a genuine ritual, one that evokes the standards of order by which these bloody rivals are finally judged.

The themes of marriage and inheritance are both important in *3 Henry VI*. As visionary, Henry may rise above the others; but as husband and father, he epitomizes the disorder of the commonwealth. His wife's infidelity with Suffolk is not forgotten, for Edward calls her a Helen to Henry's Menelaus [II. ii. 146-49], and York compares her to "an Amazonian trull" [I. iv. 114]. This last insult also suggests what is more prominent in this play, her unnatural assumption of a masculine role, in effect usurping her husband's kingship. It is she who gathers an army to oppose York's enforced settlement after the battle of Saint Albans. She will not allow her husband to speak before the battle of Towton, or to be present at the battle, lest he demoralize the army. But even this inverted marriage is shaken by Henry's weakness. Since *2 Henry VI* began with the formal ceremony of their marriage, the effect is all the more powerful when in the first scene of this play she formally renounces her husband because he has disinherited his son. It is ironic that Margaret should thus appeal to the sanctions of the family. They have a purely verbal currency among these selfish and ambitious conspirators, who flagrantly ignore them in practice. In defeat Margaret will earn our sympathy, yet there is a fierce justice in her being forced to see her son stabbed to death. (pp. 73-5)

The most important family theme in this play is inheritance, of which Clifford gives the orthodox doctrine: "Who should succeed the father but the son?" [II. ii. 94]. The words "father" and "son" occur 137 times, the references centering on the two rival houses. In the first scene their rights of inheritance are disputed at length. Henry's descent from the warrior king Henry V is his main claim to the throne. Even York's supporter Warwick does not attack the dead hero, but he is quick to point out that Henry VI is not his father's moral inheritor. Henry V's virtue has been lost to his country; the suggestion may be that Henry VI's weakness is a delayed effect of the curse on his grandfather's usurpation. Exeter's decision to support York's title emphasizes that the right of inheritance cannot be bartered away by men. In the curiously repetitive structure of *3 Henry VI*, the gist of this discussion is repeated when Warwick debates Margaret and her followers at the French court, where Oxford traces Henry's heroic lineage back to a John of Gaunt unhistorically given Spanish conquests.

Nothing was more sacred in Elizabethan eyes and more firmly established by law than the son's right of inheritance. One of Henry's weakest acts is to disinherit his son in favor of York. Both he and Margaret refer to his deed as unnatural in the first scene, and she renounces their marriage on that ground. Prince Edward completes the destruction of natural order when he too repudiates his father to follow his mother into battle. Curiously enough, however, the young prince more than his father is Henry V's moral heir. At the battle of Tewkesbury his courageous words inspire Oxford to exclaim:

> O brave young Prince! thy famous grandfather
> Doth live again in thee: long may'st thou live
> To bear his image and renew his glories!
> [V. iv. 52-4]
> (pp. 76-7)

In an ordered society the son can by emulation learn his forebears' virtue even while he takes over their social position. But in the chaos of *3 Henry VI* moral order is dissolved; the forces of inheritance are perverted to an unnatural function, the perpetuation of a curse. Not only does this distortion affect the two rival houses, but it encompasses the supporting nobles of each side. One recurrent event includes a son who commits violence in revenge for the death of his father or some other member of his family. . . . [Clifford] is led to commit the most brutal act of a violent play. When he encounters the youngest son of his enemy York, he declares:

> As for the brat of this accursed duke,
> Whose father slew my father, he shall die.
>
> [I. iii. 4-5]

This theme becomes obsessive in the many debates between such opponents as Clifford and York's sons about who is fighting whom in revenge for what butchered relatives.

Much subtler is the treatment of the House of York, to which the center of attention shifts as the Lancastrian power fades. Early in the play the loyalty of York's sons seems a remarkable exception to the destruction of traditional bonds. . . . Is it possible that this family, rightful heirs to the throne, are not infected by the general disorder? . . . Their success applies the critical test, for all three brothers begin to pursue their individual ends when Edward reaches the throne. (pp. 78-9)

Richard, Duke of Gloucester, is the final inheritor of the York cause, and his attitude toward the family most fully expresses the corruption of his house. He reveals himself at length in *Richard III*, but *3 Henry VI* raises an interesting technical question: how can the loyal son of the early acts be reconciled with the ruthless schemer who emerges in the soliloquy of III. ii? (pp. 80-1)

The simplest explanation is that in the puzzling early speeches he is merely a type, an expression of the family loyalty of the Yorks, whereas later he becomes an independent character. In most of his speeches he has a distinctive poetic idiom, but his expressions of concern for his father are conventional and artificially elevated. This early nature could reflect what Samuel Bethell calls depersonalization [see excerpt above, 1951]; Richard loses his identity in order to express a general theme. The family loyalty of the Yorks must be established at first so that its collapse may illustrate the consequences of rebellion. One question about this explanation is why Shakespeare uses the most individual of the three sons to express loyalty to York. Clarence, for example, is a shadowy enough figure that he could have voiced Richard's sentiments in II. i without appearing notably inconsistent, yet he is not even present.

On the other hand, there is a more elaborately psychological explanation. From his first appearance in *2 Henry VI* Richard is a powerful force, one who slices through the cant of those around him in a single-minded pursuit of whatever seems important to him. As the early Warwick illustrates, such a man can be a strong support for order and virtue if something larger than himself attracts his loyalty. York is the only man in *3 Henry VI* whose ambition and strength of will are enough to compel Richard's support. Although his son can teach York something of Machiavellian casuistry [I. ii. 22-34], York's massive violence of nature is worthy of Richard's respect. It is the most powerful force of the early civil wars. Richard never expresses without irony an attachment to anyone but his father. When the strength of his nature is freed from its filial tie, the last remnant of an order into which he can fit, he inevitably becomes a destructive force. (pp. 82-3)

Shakespeare may well have had these ideas about Richard or something like them, but he has not really embodied them in

dramatic action. We do not see Richard becoming a monster; we only see him as son and then as monster. Change in the state and change between generations are important themes in *3 Henry VI*, but change in character has not yet enlisted Shakespeare's full imaginative powers. This is not finally a play of character but of atmosphere, the atmosphere of disorder and chaos.

The corruption of the House of York is apparent in one final irony, the false dawn with which the play ends. When the Yorkists murder Prince Edward before his mother's eyes, she cries out a curse on their children. Only a score of lines later Edward says of his queen, "By this, I hope, she hath a son for me" [V. v. 90]. With pomp and circumstance the last scene of the play reveals the king, the queen, and this new heir to the throne. Edward proclaims the triumph of the York cause in the last lines of the play:

> Sound drums and trumpets! Farewell, sour annoy!
> For here, I hope, begins our lasting joy.
>
> [V. vii. 45-6]

But the image that remains is of the crook-backed Richard kissing his nephew. Order in the family and the state may seem to have been restored, but the appearance is illusory. The chain of guilt is too strong to be broken without still more violence and suffering for England. (pp. 84-5)

> *Robert B. Pierce, "The Henry VI Plays," in his* Shakespeare's History Plays: The Family and the State, *Ohio State University Press, 1971, pp. 35-88.*

CAROL McGINNIS KAY　(essay date 1972)

[*Kay contends that the patterns of imagery in 1, 2, and 3* Henry VI *are closely related to Shakespeare's perception of the historical process as presented in these plays. She demonstrates that the progression of images from the beginning of the* Henry VI *trilogy to the close is from "rational to animal to cosmic"—from images of artificial enclosures, to those of vicious slaughter, and to those of tempests at sea. Kay argues that these patterns of symbolic language reinforce Shakespeare's view that men and women are at least partially responsible for their individual fates, particularly because of their innate ability to effect either order or disorder and thereby secure or destroy the welfare of the state. As such, Kay disputes the importance of the Tudor myth in the trilogy, despite its apparent relevance, maintaining that Shakespeare was more interested in dramatizing the sins and consequences of the actions taken by those directly involved with Henry's court. For a dissenting argument on the organic relationship of the imagery in 1, 2, and 3* Henry VI *and other elements of dramatic structure, see the excerpt by Wolfgang H. Clemen (1951). Also, see the excerpts by Alvin B. Kernan (1954) and James L. Calderwood (1967) for further discussion of the sea/tempest imagery and the trapping/enclosure references in the plays.*]

Initial probes into the imagery of . . . intrigues and deceptions [in *I Henry VI*] uncover a variety of metaphoric vehicles: acting, battle, disease, sex, the Bible, blood, death, sun, star, light versus dark, school-boys, gems, shadow versus substance, music, garden, animals, and the sea. Some images, such as that in Warwick's refusal to take sides in the Temple Garden quarrel between Plantagenet and Somerset (II. iv), are detachable purple passages; they are what Clemen calls "embroidery" inserted deliberately into the text for decorative rather than expressive purpose [see excerpt above, 1951]. Others obviously do serve an organic function; for example, a network of sexual and distasteful images is used to coarsen Joan la Pucelle so that we are prepared for her degrading trial scene.

Such organic use of imagery to create character is, however, not typical of *Part I*'s language. One might expect Lord Talbot to be characterized by military images, but he is not. One might expect Henry VI to be surrounded by a dominant image pattern, but he is not. With the exception of Joan, the characters seldom use or are surrounded by language that is peculiarly theirs. Instead, what seems significant is that out of the wealth of images in *Part I* a pattern begins to emerge, a pattern which offers insight into the play as a whole rather than into any specific character.

This pattern is based upon the more than seventy metaphoric passages in *Part I* involving animals, specifically dragons, bears, wolves, deer, lions, sheep, horses, worms, mules, mice, dogs, rabbits, oxen, bees, and fish. But of the many animal images in *I Henry VI*, the most numerous are those involving birds of various kinds. Some are named: a French general addresses Talbot as an "ominous and fearful owl of death" [*I Henry VI*, IV. ii. 15], combining the Renaissance concept of the owl as a harbinger of doom with Talbot's destructive power as "the Scourge of France" [II. iii. 15]. Sir William Lucy, angry at York's and Somerset's selfish refusals to aid Talbot, mutters against "the vulture of sedition" [IV. iii. 47]. As Lucy carries away the bodies of Talbot and his son for burial, he warns the French that "from their ashes shall be rear'd / A phoenix that shall make all France afeard" [IV. vii. 92-3]. This classical bird with its regenerative qualities is alluded to on several occasions in the trilogy and is singularly appropriate to the three plays in its idea of the destroyed becoming the destroyer, an ironic twist of fate which occurs several times in the trilogy's narrative. Other birds specifically named include those in the Dauphin Charles' praise of Joan, that were "Mahomet inspired with a dove," traditionally associated with gentleness and peace, she must surely be inspired "with an eagle" [I. ii. 140-41], associated in the Elizabethan mind with kingship and power. The birds named in these and similar passages are utilized in a wholly conventional manner; that is, they appear because of the qualities traditionally associated with them—the dove for peace, the eagle for strength, and so on. The images function as embellishments of an idea and are significant only in their immediate context. They form no pattern, enunciate no theme, and after their initial appearance, they are seldom seen again.

What does receive functional emphasis in the bird imagery and what appears to be more important in forming a thematic pattern are certain characteristics common to the entire species. Significantly, those qualities which might be termed the pleasant ones (color, beauty, singing, nest-building, grace, and so forth), make no appearance at all in the animal imagery of the *Henry VI* plays. Instead the aspects which receive repeated emphasis are wings and flying, with attention repeatedly directed to the picture of a bird in flight either to escape a danger or to attack a foe. (pp. 3-4)

Escape is necessary in *I Henry VI* because the animal world—and man's world—are filled with many threats to life and liberty. Animals of prey, eager to devour the weak, offer perils and danger. For example, Talbot upbraids his weary soldiers in Orleans:

> Sheep run not half so treacherous from the wolf,
> Or horse or oxen from the leopard,
> As you fly from your oft-subdued slaves.
> 　　　　　　　　　　　　　　　　[I. v. 30-2]

Talbot later recalls his son's bravery in battle when he "like a hungry lion did commence / Rough deeds of rage and stern

impatience" [IV. vii. 7-8]. Talbot's characterization portrays the beast of prey as motivated by hunger, a partial justification for violence which appears in several other instances. This uniting of beasts of prey images with references to hunger is noticeably present in passages describing Talbot and/or the English army. (p. 5)

While these hungry beasts of prey do prowl the poetic landscape of *Part I*, their presence should not be exaggerated. The threat offered by such creatures is not overwhelming in *Part I* as it will be in *Part II*. The beasts of prey constantly lurk behind the scenes but seldom dominate a scene. The more constant and more emphasized threat to the weaker animals in *Part I* is the endless harassment of traps, snares, chains, cages, and hunts—all sorts of man-made devices of enclosure, used in a deliberate effort, primarily, to curtail liberty, or, secondarily, to destroy life.

Beginning with the third messenger's report in Act I, scene i, that Talbot has been "round encompassed and set upon" and captured [I. i. 114], limitations and restrictions of all kinds encroach from every side in *Part I*. They are not a natural threat; they are man-made artificial barriers which can be controlled at will. Man and animal alike may be victimized by a ruthless manipulator: during his captivity Talbot is led about like the bear in a game of bear-baiting. He later describes his treatment:

> In open market-place produc'd they me
> To be a public spectacle to all;
> Here, said they, is the Terror of the French,
> The scarecrow that affrights our children so.
> Then broke I from the officers that led me, . . .
> My grisly countenance made others fly;
> None durst come near for fear of sudden death.
> 　　　　　　　　　　　　　　　　[I. iv. 40-4, 47-8]

Talbot momentarily escapes captivity when the French exchange him for their English-held leader, Lord Ponton de Santrailles. But he remains the eagerly-sought object of the French chase. Indeed, much of the action and the thematic point of *Part I* lies in this very entrapment of the English leader who embodies the entire system of order. Talbot is more than an effective army commander whose name alone can bring terror to the enemy; he is the manifestation of all the ceremony, rank, degree, and order so rightly observed in the previous age of Henry V's brightness and now so disastrously neglected in Henry VI's dimness. (pp. 6-7)

The stage directions opening Act IV, scene vi, realize the network of trapping images in dramatic terms: "*Alarum: excursions, wherein* TALBOT's *Son is hemmed about, and* TALBOT *rescues him.*" Talbot's son is entrapped by precisely the same predicament that the spectator has seen Talbot's entire army face at Bordeaux, and he is saved by precisely the same kind of help from another that would save Talbot's army. We see Talbot perform on an individual level what York and Somerset should be doing on a national level. Because York and Somerset will not stop their bickering to send support to Talbot in time, this physical manifestation of all that England might be is trapped one final time, and he dies in battle.

The animal traps which catch Talbot, his men and his son in Act IV are not the only enclosing devices in *Part I*. In fact, the first play of the *Henry VI* trilogy is curiously packed with such devices, many obvious, some trivial: city walls, doors, gates, towers, prisons, chains, pyramids, urns, and even jewel-boxes receive both literal and metaphorical attention. It seems throughout the play as if some character is constantly trying to keep another character either *in* or *out* of somewhere. Barriers between men and objects are deliberately erected by one man or a group and then the opponent(s) must decide whether or not to break that barrier. (pp. 9-10)

The play's structure is based on enclosures and their control: four of the six scenes in Act I concern the English siege of Orleans; the first two scenes of Act II continue the Orleans struggles; the second and third scene of Act II form the Countess of Auvergne's attempt to trap Talbot, and in the fifth scene Plantagenet visits his uncle Mortimer imprisoned in the Tower of London; two of the four scenes in Act III concern the battle for Rouen; six of the seven scenes in Act IV involve the entrapment of Talbot, and Act V includes the captures of Joan and Margaret. While a play about an international war may naturally involve city walls, and while the apprentice Shakespeare, still learning his craft, might be careful to have his characters establish the setting with such lines as Joan's "Advance our waving colours on the walls" [I. vi. 1], nonetheless, when two-thirds of the scenes in a play focus on such enclosures, deliberate emphasis on Shakespeare's part may reasonably be assumed. Such an assumption is supported by the observation that none of the play's battles are fought in an open field as one might expect in any war; like the Gloucester-Winchester quarrel at the Tower, they become non-political, non-ethical contests over the control of boundaries. Talbot and Salisbury want into the city of Orleans and Joan wants them kept out. Joan wants into the city of Rouen and Talbot wants her kept out. And so the pattern goes. Even the non-battle scenes repeat the pattern: Mortimer wants out of prison and Henry V has wanted to keep him in; the Countess wants to keep Talbot in her castle and he wants out. Such an emphasis on walls, towers, and restrictions is simply too excessive to be explained away as inherent in a play about war or as setting identification.

The enclosure pattern is subtly reinforced by brief images of all sorts of enclosing devices, pleasant and unpleasant. Happy with Joan's victory during the early stages of the battle for Orleans, the Dauphin wants to rear "A statlier pyramid to her . . . / Than Rhodope's of Memphis ever was" [I. vi. 21-2]. Plantagenet says Somerset's accusations in the Temple Garden "set bars before my tongue" [II. v. 49], and as he leaves his uncle Mortimer, Plantagenet determines to "lock his counsel in my breast" [II. v. 118]. These and similar images join the verbal images of birds' flights, animal traps and snares, and the non-verbal images involving city walls, towers, capture, and imprisonment to create a sometimes subtle, sometimes obvious pattern—the enclosure motif, the distinctive characteristic of *I Henry VI.*

What should be kept in mind is that each of these enclosing devices, whether it is a city wall or an urn for Joan's ashes or a snare for a bird, is a man-made contrivance, constructed deliberately to restrict or contain and used with full consciousness on the user's part. Some degree of rational thinking is required for their construction and destruction alike. Not uncontrollable forces of nature or the turning of Fortune's wheel, these enclosures exist only because a human being thought of them, built them, and uses them. They are part and parcel of the world view which in Henry V's reign observed each thing, each link in the Great Chain of Being, in its proper place. Not all of the enclosures are pleasant, but they are all the result of man's deliberate effort to impose some type of order on the natural landscape; they are the result of man's choice. The

word "choice" is significant: in *Part I* man has a chance to control his fate; he can erect a wall or he can tear one down. He can make the decisions that will govern his future and that of his nation.

Gloucester chooses to enter the Tower; Winchester chooses to seize the kingdom for himself; Suffolk chooses to have Margaret as his mistress and the King's wife; Margaret chooses to join Suffolk; York and Somerset choose not to help Talbot until it is too late, and so the choices continue. Although Henry VI is too young to have much real power when the play opens, by the time we actually see him in Act III, he has matured, and he too has choices. Just as the nobles have the opportunity to bury petty differences for the national good but choose to act on personal ambition instead, so Henry VI has the opportunity to rule his nobles and subjects with firmness and wisdom but chooses instead to do nothing. Foolishly hoping that the wedges in court driven by the Gloucester-Winchester quarrel, the York-Somerset conflict, and the Suffolk-Margaret alliance, will disappear by themselves, Henry decides to take no action himself. These two types of decisions in *Part I*—one for action, the other for inaction—set in motion forces which will later destroy the entire kingdom. In short, man in *Part I* is a rational being who has alternatives of action open to him and who has the freedom to choose the alternative he prefers. But what happens when man makes the *wrong* choice? *II* and *III Henry VI* show us.

The enclosure motif which so characterizes *Part I* gradually disappears in *Part II* as a new type of animal image becomes dominant. Many of the same animals continue to appear—birds, dogs, horses, lions, deer, bees, wolves, and sheep but as the enclosure motif disappears so does the emphasis on birds and animals escaping snares and traps. Animals, and therefore men, are no longer the victims of man-made traps as much as they are the victims of each other's uncontrollable viciousness. The animal world of *Part I* had its threat of captivity, but the animal world of *Part II* becomes a slaughter house, a cruel jungle where killing, blood, and violence reign unchecked. Just as *Part I* was dominated by an enclosure motif, so *Part II* is dominated by slaughter imagery.

Many passages (over 100) of slaughter imagery may be noted, but the most elaborate examples are in the opening scenes of Act III, perhaps the most crucial two scenes of the play. The first scene is long (383 lines) and its action is a turning point in the play and in Henry VI's reign: Humphrey, the Duke of Gloucester, is seized by Suffolk's treacherous cohorts and led away to prison and, unknowingly, to his death, while the meek King simply stands by hoping for Gloucester's deliverance. Up to this point in the play the nobles' quarrels continued from *Part I* have been just that—verbal quarrels, exchanges of insults, court spats—but with the bodily seizure of Gloucester the disunion of Henry's court takes on a deadlier aspect, for Gloucester becomes the Talbot-figure of *Part II.* . . . The nobles have come to the edge of a precipice beyond which lies national destruction; rejecting their opportunities to turn back, they plot the murder of a peer. Afterwards, the swift fall to the rocks of dynastic war below is inevitable. Thus, Act III, scene i is a key scene. (pp. 10-13)

The slaughter imagery around Gloucester in this and the subsequent scene is the primary method of creating the character of "good Duke Humphrey." In this scene he is a protective shepherd, and in the next one he is the innocent lamb butchered by Suffolk and the Cardinal. Prior to Act III Gloucester has seemed just another bickering nobleman, little changed from

Part I and scarcely distinguishable from any other aristocratic squabbler, but in Act III a transformation takes place: here a cluster of slaughter-house images creates the figure of Gloucester as the sole protective innocent left in Henry's court. Although we are somewhat prepared for the change by such scenes as the Simpcox "miracle" of Act II, scene i, when only Gloucester had the ability to realize that Simpcox's claims that his blindness was miraculously cured were false, the change in Gloucester's portrayal in Act III is too sudden and too complete a reversal to be credible. But it is fascinating for a student of language to watch a new character being created in two scenes.

Continuing the slaughter images, Henry VI bemoans Gloucester's fate:

> as the butcher takes away the calf,
> And binds the wretch, and beats it when it strains,
> Bearing it to the bloody slaughter-house;
> Even so, remorseless have they borne him hence;
> And as the dam runs lowing up and down,
> Looking the way her harmless young one went,
> And can do nought but wail her darling's loss;
> Even so myself bewails good Gloucester's case.
>
> [III. i. 210-17]

The royal saint, who thus envisions himself in a helpless feminine role, feels that he can do nothing to aid Gloucester, and, weeping, he leaves the stage without making a single gesture towards saving Gloucester. (pp. 13-14)

Fatal wounds, stinging snakes, poisonous scorpions, blood-stained foxes, dead and bleeding heifers, web-weaving spiders, beaten and slaughtered calves, innocent lambs surrounded by snarling wolves, butchers with knives and axes, shepherds unable to save their flock, headless bodies on piles of dung, the actual and metaphorical world of *II Henry VI* is terrifying. Clearly the enclosure motif of *Part I* has been shattered and those creatures and emotions and ambitions held in confinement in the earlier play have been released to rain havoc on man in this play. The thin veneer of the civilization which built the enclosures has been scratched, and the primitive forces underneath have been let loose. This is not to say that all of *Part II* is without hope for England's salvation; as has been mentioned, up until Gloucester's murder there is hope, for a reversal of the first play's decisions by almost any major figure could return England to the right course, to order and stability. It is the old "if" story—England could be restored to order *if* Henry VI would take action to control his nobles, *if* Queen Margaret would discard her lover and turn her attention from political power to marital harmony, *if* Gloucester would recognize England's danger in time to curb his temper and protect his King, *if* York and Somerset would subordinate selfish aims to the cause of national unity, and so the story goes. Each character is free to change his mind and England's direction until Gloucester's murder. But with this deed of blood the English court is set on a path from which there is no turning back. From this point on man is no longer in control: he slowly falls prey to the animal within himself. Decisions made in *Part I* and maintained in *Part II* have released a ferocity which now runs wild, transforming a formerly ordered nation into a scorpion's nest, a place of vipers and wolves, a slaughter-house. (pp. 16-17)

The prey-thirsty menagerie and axe-wielding butchers who prowled through *Part II* continue their terror into *Part III*. The metaphorical animal populace is much the same: yelping curs, stinging insects, poisonous snakes, buzzing flies, ravenous wolves, lions, foxes, innocent lambs and sheep, birds either attacking or escaping attack, captured and chained bears, and bridled horses. Animal images still emphasize slaughter and beasts of prey, particularly in the scenes of York's murder and Henry VI's murder. In Act I, scene iv, the defeated and exhausted Duke of York is surrounded by Margaret and her followers who taunt him as a feeble woodcock . . . , a struggling cony . . . , and a weak dove pecking "the falcon's piercing talons" [*3 Henry VI*, I. iv. 61, 62, 41]. Like Gloucester in *Part II*, York has done little to win our admiration before this scene, but he strikes a sympathetic chord in this scene as he becomes the hapless victim of Margaret and Clifford's blood-lust. Like Gloucester, York is characterized through the scene's imagery and dramatic situation as the innocent prey of savage butchers. Margaret gloats over a napkin dipped in the blood of York's young son Rutland, brutally murdered in the previous scene, and so relishes tormenting him that York is prompted to call Margaret "a tiger's heart wrapp'd in a woman's hide" [I. iv. 137]. Tired of toying with their mouse, Margaret and Young Clifford move in for the kill and stab York to death. And in Act V, scene vi we find Henry VI also victimized by a creature more beast than man. After the Yorkist victory at Tewkesbury, Richard, Duke of Gloucester, heads immediately for the Tower of London where Henry is imprisoned. As he enters Henry's room he dismisses the guard. Henry watches his retreating jailor and observes:

> So flies the reckless shepherd from the wolf;
> So first the harmless sheep doth yield his fleece,
> And next his throat unto the butcher's knife.
>
> [V. vi. 7-9]

Displaying what for him is unusual understanding, Henry faces his own death bravely (although still picturing himself as a sheep rather than the shepherd), but he bitterly regrets that there will be "much more slaughter after this" [V. vi. 59]. He knows that Richard will be responsible for most of it because he was born with teeth "which plainly signified / That [he] should snarl, and bite and play the dog" [V. vi. 76-7]. Richard fulfills Henry's expectations about his vicious nature as he stops the King's predictions with a sword. He repeatedly stabs Henry and then delights in his sword which appears to weep "purple tears" [V. vi. 64] with the dead King's blood.

Despite such bloody scenes as the murders of York and Henry VI, butchers and beasts of prey do not dominate *Part III* as they did the previous play. Another area of imagery is the major motif of the trilogy's third play—sea imagery, particularly tempests at sea.

Throughout the first two plays sea imagery has increased in length and violence until it becomes a raging storm which inundates England in *Part III*. In *Part I* only twenty passages of sea imagery may be noted and the images generally have little thematic value; *Part II* increases both the number of sea images and the violence of their nature, but by the last play the spectator may be justified in feeling almost drowned himself by the elaborate rhetoric about seas and storms which floods the stage, for no other vehicle in all of the *Henry VI* trilogy enjoys a more lengthy or detailed attention than does sea imagery in *Part III* (over 200 images). Examples abound: Clifford "thunders to his captives blood and death" [II. i. 127], and York complains that his soldiers "Turn back and fly, like ships before the wind" [I. iv. 4]. Some images are brief and casual; many involve the comparison of human emotions to storms, but most of the sea imagery is related to the war/tempest analogy, another common Elizabethan correspondence.

Almost every character in *Part III* makes reference to the Yorkist-Lancastrian strife in terms of a storm. Somerset speaks of the "storms . . . of civil enmity" [IV. vi. 98], and Montgomery leads troops "To help King Edward in his time of storm, / As every loyal subject ought to do" [IV. vii. 43-4]. And Montague regrets the fact that King Edward chose to wed Lady Elizabeth Grey rather than his French fiancee, Lady Bona, because such a marriage "Would more have strengthen'd this our commonwealth / 'Gainst foreign storms than any home-bred marriage" [IV. i. 37-8]. But, as might be expected, it is the play's major figures—the kings Henry VI and Edward IV, Queen Margaret, and Richard, Duke of Gloucester—who have the longest passages of war/tempest rhetoric. (pp. 17-19)

Margaret's speech [in Act I, scene iv] clearly illustrates the relationship between tempests in nature and tempests in human affairs. Wherever the storms appear they are equally destructive and equally uncontrollable. No longer is man a raging animal attacking and mutilating another animal; in *III Henry VI* he is part of an even larger scheme of chaos. When we look back at the steps which led to the development of this national chaos, we find the value of an approach through imagery becoming apparent as we realize that the *Henry VI* trilogy is not just another set of plays about English civil wars but rather three plays about the inevitable changes man undergoes during those wars. Those changes are made clear as we look at the three plays and their dominant modes of expression from the vantage point of *Part III*.

Of course, the enclosure motif of *Part I*, the slaughter images of *Part II*, and the storm images of *Part III* develop a pattern of degeneration which needs exploration, but what may first strike us from this vantage point is the presence of a nondeveloping pattern not yet remarked upon, the garden imagery. This image pattern does not dominate any single play; it remains consistent throughout the trilogy, forming a kind of poetic context for the plays' action.

Since the garden/state analogy was an Elizabethan commonplace, one is scarcely surprised to find Shakespeare using garden images in his first plays, especially plays about politics. Indeed, one might justifiably expect Henry VI, like Richard II, to be characterized as the neglectful gardener who fails to weed and trim his garden/kingdom. Or one might expect some use of flowers for their traditional associations. But these expectations are curiously unfulfilled: Ophelia scattering her rosemary and rue [*Hamlet*, IV. v.] would be out of her element on this stage, and Henry VI receives scant attention for his poor gardening. Instead, Shakespeare emphasizes a more general point of comparison between man and plant; almost every garden image is directed toward that characteristic common to all living things: ultimate death. (p. 23)

Several major facts emerge from [the] volume of garden images except—for roses—which are obviously appropriate—specific plants are seldom named, and therefore traditional associations are minimal: the entire growth process is utilized, with most attention given to the last stages, and as was the case with bird imagery, almost no emphasis is placed on any pleasant aspects of the garden. Most of the images focus on the manifold threats to life. Life is fragile in Henry VI's garden: at best, maturity is slow in coming and quick in leaving; at worst, maturity is never reached because of myriad destructive forces. In either case death and decay are the ultimate rulers. In short, the garden

metaphor's constant emphasis on the life-death struggle within a garden, on the natural frangibility of any living thing, on decay as the final victor, serves as a grim poetic context in which the three plays may unfold.

Yet within this bleak frame of ultimate withering, Shakespeare recognizes man's ability to control or at least to co-operate in determining what his period of maturity will be like. *I Henry VI*, which plants the seeds leading to civil war, is dominated by an enclosure motif: animal images of flight from traps and snares are reinforced by a marked attention to walls, towers, chains, and other man-made devices of restraint. Through this motif, Shakespeare makes clear the rational nature of man, a somewhat ordered, thinking being who is capable of erecting barriers and destroying them, or making decisions and carrying them out. In *Part I* the few sea images are brief and generally non-organic. *Part II*, which nurtures the seedlings of domestic disorder, is dominated by slaughter and butchering imagery in which *Part I*'s concern for confinement gives way to a new appetite for blood, death, and mutilation. At the same time, sea images are becoming more frequent, and quite unpleasantly violent. Again through the play's imagery we learn what happens to the nature of man as those rampant destructive forces he himself unleashed take over: man becomes victim of his own brutalizing essence and is transformed into a raging animal. As *Part III* unfolds, the full scope of mayhem is revealed: slaughter and butchery images continue unchanged in cruelty, while sea images reach their peak in stormy violence, length, and frequency, and destruction becomes universal. As the imagery moves from rational to animal to cosmic, a pattern of human degradation emerges.

Shakespeare makes it clear that the Wars of the Roses sweep England not because Henry IV sinned years ago, but because Henry VI, his queen, and his nobles commit their own sins. Certainly the main tenets of the "Tudor myth" are present: as Henry himself admits, Henry VI's claim to the throne is shaky, and the nemesis pursuing him because of his grandfather's deposition of Richard II is implicitly present throughout the trilogy. It is, however, the actions of the characters actually on the stage which release the anarchy of civil war. Each character by deliberate choice fails to enact his assigned role in the national drama. Henry refuses to act; Suffolk plots for power; Margaret wants to rule England herself and decides to become Suffolk's mistress, and the nobles fall into petty squabbles. England is gradually reduced to chaos because none of her national figures chooses to fulfill his proper role. The decisions of Henry and his court in *Part I* break all bounds of order in England and man falls from the level of rational life where there are choices to the bestial life where there are no choices left. In *Part I* man sells his birthright, *i.e.*, his ability to reason and choose alternatives, and in *Part II* he refuses to reclaim that birthright. He is no longer in control of himself or the non-rational animal forces within him; he becomes subject to the animal within his own nature released by his making the wrong rational choices earlier. With Gloucester's murder in *Part II* the beast can never be caged again, for each violent deed necessitates another until the chaos of *Part III* is inevitable.

In *III Henry VI* man's personal chaos assumes wider proportions and becomes part of a cosmic chaos. The last vestiges of rational control have disappeared and man is the floundering victim of a tide of passions and events over which he can exert no guidance at all. Brother kills brother, subject betrays king, father kills son, king violates vows, wife betrays husband, rebel betrays rebel, queen kills noble, son kills father—all domestic, political, and human bonds disappear. All ties dissolve and man becomes a non-rational non-animal object, just another inanimate entity tossed about by the rhythmical repetitions of a universal storm. Through the trilogy's dramatic imagery this point is clearly made: man has choices for order or disorder, and when man makes the wrong choices, he releases uncontrollable natural forces which can reduce the entire universe to chaos. In the three *Henry VI* plays we watch this inevitable and complete degradation of man at war, of man when he makes the wrong choices. (pp. 24-6)

> Carol McGinnis Kay, *"Traps, Slaughter, and Chaos: A Study of Shakespeare's 'Henry VI' Plays," in* Studies in the Literary Imagination, *Vol. V, No. 1, April, 1972, pp. 1-26.*

ROBERT ORNSTEIN   (essay date 1972)

[*Ornstein is an American critic and scholar. His* A Kingdom for the Stage: The Achievement of Shakespeare's History Plays *(1972) has been called one of the most important contributions to Shakespearean studies in recent years, as well as the most influential study of the history plays since E. M. W. Tillyard's* The Elizabethan World Picture *(1944). The purpose of Ornstein's book was to challenge the popular belief that Shakespeare's histories dramatize not such universal concerns as human nature and the effects of power, but the orthodox view of English history as championed by the Tudor monarchy. Ornstein's attempt to interpret the history plays as drama rather than historical documents contributed to a reappraisal of these works, specifically with regard to their political assumptions, and signified their return to the same standard of evaluation accorded the rest of Shakespeare's canon. In the following excerpt, Ornstein sharply disagrees with the providential interpretation of* Henry VI *offered by such critics as Tillyard, Hermann Ulrici (1839), Irving Ribner (1965), and M. M. Reese (1961). Instead, he states that the trilogy reveals "not the slightest hint that present ills are a retribution for earlier guilts," nor any evidence that the catastrophic civil wars are related to any other agents than the English nobles of King Henry's court. In denying the role of providence in the trilogy, Ornstein expresses a view shared by such earlier critics as A. C. Hamilton (1961-62), S. C. Sen Gupta (1964), H. M. Richmond (1967), James Winny (1968), Robert B. Pierce (1971), and Carol McGinnis Kay (1972). Ornstein also disputes the idea, at least with respect to* 1 Henry VI, *that Shakespeare borrowed heavily from medieval morality drama, maintaining that Talbot, the only typically medieval character, is derived from romance, not morality, literature; the other principal figures all exhibit "more of the psychological substance and individuality of observed life." Ornstein devotes the remainder of his study to an examination of Shakespeare's early artistry, focusing particularly on his subtlety of language, imaginative plotting and staging, and use of soliloquies to increase the dimensions of individual characters. For further discussion of the medieval and morality influence on* Henry VI, *see the excerpts by E. M. W. Tillyard (1944), Muriel C. Bradbrook (1951), Irving Ribner (1965), and John D. Cox (1978).*]

Shakespeare's artistic powers were such that his rudest apprentice work succeeded and survived in the *Henry VI* plays. There is enough that is skillful, lively, and thoughtful in *Part I* for us to say that here is Shakespeare's apprentice craftsmanship, were it not for the presence of the Temple Garden scene (II. iv), which is so superior to all else in the play that it makes all else seem less than "Shakespearean." (p. 36)

A triumph of the dramatic imagination over the inartistic formlessness of Tudor historiography, the Temple Garden scene adumbrates the danger of York and of divisive factionalism before that danger historically existed. In Hall, the early years

of the reign of Henry VI have no particular political character. The tide of battle in France shifts back and forth; sometimes the noble English armies are checked by a lack of supplies and reinforcements, sometimes they are defeated by the treachery of the French. The English court is repeatedly disturbed by Gloucester and Winchester's quarrels, but their feud seems to have no special significance. No great figures dominate the political landscape: Henry is a child, and York, whose role in events is minor, is only a latent threat. It is Shakespeare who brings York to the fore by inventing the quarrel in the Temple Garden scene, and the following one in which York meets with the dying Mortimer. It is Shakespeare who also magnifies the impact of York's quarrel with Somerset by making York, quite unhistorically, a party to the betrayal of Talbot in France. Boldly ignoring chronology and Chronicle "fact," he interweaves the destinies of Talbot, Joan of Arc, and York by making Talbot, Joan's adversary and victim, and York, Joan's nemesis and counterpart. Where she invokes the powers of darkness, he plots a Machiavellian conspiracy that will send ten thousand souls to hell. In this complex moral design, which pits chivalry against policy, England against France, and, most tragically, Englishmen against Englishmen, Talbot plays a major role, but rather than the protagonist of the play, he is the last exemplar of England's vanishing chivalric greatness. First Salisbury falls, then Bedford, and when Talbot and his son die, the plant and seed of English heroism are lost.

A flesh and blood hero, Talbot descends from the epic figures of medieval romance, not from the didactic figures who people *Gorbuduc* and the Tudor political Moralities. His death is a page out of Malory, or, perhaps out of the *Chanson de Roland*, whose hero is similarly betrayed. Like Gawain in another respect, Talbot proves himself in the trials of lust by conquering the treacherous French Countess, who would have kept him in her *daunger*. Immediately afterward, there is a more sardonic remembrance of romance in the Temple Garden scene, which uses the setting and allegory of the *Roman de la Rose* to dramatize deadly enmity. Talbot has the two-dimensional quality of a literary memory and type. Other characters in *Part I* have more of the psychological substance and individuality of observed life. With a strong instinct for human realities, Shakespeare makes no attempt to conceptualize and allegorize virtues and vices in the manner of earlier Moralities. Even with his very limited artistic powers, he seeks to differentiate the emotional drives of the English opportunists—for example, Winchester's gnawing sense of inferiority from Suffolk's urbane cynicism and sensuality. Where Tudor didacticists drive home their Morality Lessons by stark contrasts between good and evil, Shakespeare shades his melodramatic portraits. On the one hand, he allows the diabolical Joan her measure of greatness; on the other, he shows the irascible pride that flawed Gloucester's nobility. And just as the choleric Gloucester profanes the funeral rites of Henry V by pursuing his quarrel with Winchester, the chivalric Bedford has his moment of vainglory in the opening scene. When the news comes of Talbot's capture, Bedford exclaims, "His ransom there is none but I shall pay" [I. i. 148].

Fortune plays its role in *Part I* in such accidents as the untimely death of Henry V, or in the killing of the great Salisbury by a mere boy. But the tragical rhetoric of the play provides a literary atmosphere rather than a philosophical perspective. What happens happens because the characters are what they are and do what they do. If England is "doomed" to calamity, it is because the Englishmen *we see* are careless of their principles and untrue to their traditions. There is not the slightest

Part III. Act I. Scene iii. Soldiers with Tutor, Clifford, and Rutland. By H. Brockenden (1826). The Department of Rare Books and Special Collections, The University of Michigan Library.

hint that present ills are a retribution for earlier guilts, nor is there any intimation that England is cursed because three generations ago its people deposed their king. Only once in the play is the deposition of Richard II mentioned, and then it is by the dying Mortimer, who whispers to York a very partisan view of Bolingbroke's ascent to the throne and of the Percy rebellion that followed. Quite obviously York does not aspire for power because he is convinced that he is a true inheritor. Malcontented before he learns about his link to the throne, he finds the justification for his conspiratorial ambition in Mortimer's account of the Yorkist claim to the succession, a claim that must be whispered fearfully because no others question Henry's title. It is Henry's failure to rule that makes his authority weak, not the flaw in his title that prevents him from ruling effectively. (pp. 36-8)

[Henry] remains for too long a child, weak-willed and indecisive. Innocent and kindhearted, he is a paragon of virtue compared to most of his barons and to the Dauphin of France, but he is unable or unwilling to act the king. Desiring the public good, and seeing clearly enough what that good is, he never exerts his authority to achieve it. When Gloucester and Winchester and their servants quarrel in his presence, he asks them to join their hearts in amity. He pleads when he should demand, and his appeal is to men's sympathies, not to their allegiances.... Against swords and masculine fury, Henry employs a woman's arsenal of sighs and tears, and he is too ready to accept at face value transparently hypocritical pledges of love and friendship. (pp. 38-9)

In portraying Henry's personal decencies and public failings, Shakespeare does not accept Machiavelli's differentiation of individual and political morality. He does not suggest that Henry's decency is politically irrelevant or a hindrance to po-

litical competence, nor does he suggest that Henry would have been more successful had he been more ruthless. Henry is not "too good" to rule; he is unable to translate his goodness into political action. (p. 39)

The popularity of *Henry VI Part I,* which was probably composed about 1590, must have been considerable—or at least considerable enough to encourage Shakespeare to continue his dramatic history of the War of the Roses. The success of *Parts II* and *III,* written not many months later, was extraordinary enough to excite Greene's envy [see excerpt above, 1592]. Now other playwrights hastened to beautify their History Plays with feathers plucked from Shakespeare's poetic wings, and more determined plagiarists exploited his success by publishing pirated and shortened memorial reconstructions of *Parts II* and *III.* In a very brief space, the apprentice Shakespeare had become a teacher of his contemporaries, though he was not yet fully in command of his own artistic purposes.

The first two acts of *Henry VI Part II,* for example, seem diffusely and episodically plotted; they unfold a mosaic of events rather than a unified dramatic action. Some scenes document Henry's naïveté; others suggest that York is secretly publishing his claim to the throne. Casual incidents expose Suffolk's ruthlessness and Margaret's restless urge for power, which is matched by the high-vaulting ambition of Eleanor, Gloucester's wife, who is like Joan in her masculine spirit and faith in witchcraft. (p. 42)

The climax of *Part II,* as of *Part I,* is the betrayal of England's champion by politic noblemen, only Gloucester, whom the Chronicles term "the good Duke Humphrey," plays Talbot's role. In *Part I* Gloucester's patriotism was sullied by his irascible temper and his eagerness to feud with Winchester. In *Part II* Gloucester is not more amiable toward Winchester but takes his duty as Protector to the youthful King more seriously. Though his temper flares again in the first scene, when he learns of the terms Suffolk has compounded with France, he schools his anger and allows only a silent gesture of outrage: he drops the parchment and finds an excuse not to continue reading it. Only when Henry, Margaret, and Suffolk exit, does Gloucester reveal his anger to the other English barons, and when Winchester breaks in to resume their quarrel, Gloucester leaves to avoid their "ancient bickering."

Gloucester is, from the start, a somewhat older and wiser man in *Part II.* Margaret first enters very much like the youthful innocent whom Suffolk encountered in *Part I,* but when she next appears she speaks bitterly to Suffolk of Henry's unmanliness. Restless, disillusioned, and exasperated by her husband's timidity and piety, she wants the power that Henry is reluctant to exercise. Mated to Suffolk in ambition and sensuality, she joins with him and the other conspirators against Gloucester, who protects the realm from their predatory appetites; and even here she demonstrates the fierceness of spirit that will make her equal to the Yorkists in ruthlessness and brutality in *Part III.* Margaret's evolution during the tetralogy from romantic stereotype to pitiless Fury is a remarkable achievement for an apprentice playwright, because the pathological warping of her character is acutely and convincingly portrayed. Not born the she-devil the Chronicles describe, Margaret becomes one as frustration and vindictive rage coarsen her passionate nature.

One doubts that the months between the composition of *Part I* and *Part II* lengthened Shakespeare's psychological perceptions. What did develop was his sense of the possibilities of characterization and his range of dramatic and poetic techniques. With more understanding of his medium and a more flexible blank verse, he no longer has to limit himself in *Part II* to bold strokes of characterization; he need not always extrovert passion or inflate it with hyperboles. He still aims at the bravura in Margaret's operatic speeches and in York's Marlovian soliloquies, but he is also capable of nuance of tone, and he knows how to use figurative language to delineate shadings of emotion. Some of the finest touches in *Part II* appear in what seem at first to be artificial set speeches. Suffolk's farewell to Margaret at the close of Act III, for example, echoes the Petrarchanism of their meeting in *Part I,* with a psychological difference. He does not confess his adulterous passion, but his Petrarchan language and conceits bespeak erotic memories and longings. And though he and Margaret adopt the neoplatonic postures and the pseudo-spiritual vocabulary of Petrarchan devotion, their hunger of the flesh shows through. (pp. 43-4)

To perform *Part II* Shakespeare's company had to learn a subtler language of emotional inflection and gesture. The actors, in turn, schooled his audience in more sensitive responses so that they could distinguish nuances—differentiate between a genuine and an imagined frustration. Unable to protest the shameful treaty with France, York compares his situation to that of a merchant robbed by pirates:

> Pirates may make cheap pennyworths of their pillage,
> And purchase friends, and give to courtesans,
> Still revelling like lords till all be gone,
> While as the silly owner of the goods
> Weeps over them and wrings his hapless hands
> And shakes his head and trembling stands aloof
> While all is shar'd and all is borne away,
> Ready to starve and dare not touch his own,
> So York must sit and fret and bite his tongue
> While his own lands are bargain'd for and sold.
>   [*2 Henry VI,* I. i. 222-31]

Henry expresses a similar helplessness just before he leaves Gloucester, falsely accused, to his fate:

> And as the butcher takes away the calf
> And binds the wretch and beats it when it strays,
> Bearing it to the bloody slaughterhouse,
> Even so remorseless have they borne [Gloucester] hence;
> And as the dam runs lowing up and down,
> Looking the way her harmless young one went,
> And can do naught but wail her darling's loss,
> Even so myself bewails good Gloucester's case
> With sad unhelpful tears, and with dimm'd eyes
> Look after him and cannot do him good,
> So mighty are his vowed enemies.
>   [III. i. 210-20]

York's manner of speech is characteristically practical and unsentimental. His frustration is real in that he can no more revoke the treaty Suffolk has made than a captured merchant can save his goods from the pirates. Henry's vignette of the cow and the calf expresses a more tender heart, but his pathetic analogy is false and his tone self-pitying. Unlike York, Henry is helpless only because he is too weak and too timid to act against Gloucester's "mighty" enemies. He knows that Gloucester is innocent, that his accusers "seek subversion of his harmless life." But though he has the power to save the "good Humphrey" (the calf who will be butchered), he cannot outface his

wife and her fellow conspirators. As so often before, sorrow is Henry's refuge. Imagining himself the helpless dam, he weeps as much for his loss of Gloucester as for Gloucester himself. (pp. 45-6)

[Because] Henry merely wrings his hands, the assault on Gloucester can be brutally direct. The accusations hurled against him are patently false, the slanders gross and incredible. Yet the conspirators bow to no one in their moral earnestness; seeking only the common good, they are determined to strip away Gloucester's disgusting pretense of virtue, for "who cannot steal a shape that means deceit?" . . . And since they cannot find a "color" for Gloucester's death in what he is—Brutus' very predicament—they come to a Brutus-like conclusion: that the guiltless Gloucester must die *before* he can fulfill his murderous nature. . . . Men of judgment and "reasons," they know, like Goneril, it is better to fear too far than trust too far.

Another Elizabethan dramatist would have staged the actual murder of Gloucester as the tragic climax of his action. Shakespeare's plotting is more daring and imaginative. Having foreshadowed the terrible deed in recurrent allusions to snaring, liming, trapping, and slaughtering that verbalize the horror of a court turned into a hunting ground and a shambles, he allows the murder to occur offstage, so that he can make the discovery of the murder his climactic moment. Then one long, superbly fashioned dramatic sequence poses Henry's grief against Margaret's hypocrisy and Suffolk's brazenness against Warwick's accusations, which begin with a vivid description of the death agony etched on Gloucester's face. The scene opens with the stealthy conversation of Gloucester's murderers hastening to tell Suffolk of their deed. It rises to a crescendo of excitement as Suffolk and Warwick duel and the clamor of the offstage mob threatens the palace. The tension subsides when Henry banishes Suffolk, and the scene closes on a quiet note as Suffolk and Margaret, who have found the success of their plot against Gloucester an ironic peripeteia, bid one another farewell. (pp. 47-8)

The banishing of Suffolk is at best a partial and ironic justice. Margaret, Winchester, and York, the other conspirators, are not accused or judged. The Nevils' role of King's Counsels is a sham, and Suffolk's trial is a farcical proceeding, because no witness except Warwick appears against him, and no real evidence of his guilt is brought forth. Cowering before the threat of mob violence, Henry sentences Suffolk, even as later, cringing before the threat of York's armies, he imprisons Somerset. A triumph of policy rather than of justice, Suffolk's banishment brings England one step closer to chaos because it removes the only nobleman strong enough to oppose York. Indeed, there is only a short step from the uproar of the commoners in the palace to the violence and anarchy of the Cade rebellion, when justice will be meted out by lynch mobs to those guilty of knowing how to read.

The scenes of *Part I* tell all we know and need to know about the intrigues of the court. The scenes of *Part II* present only the visible surface of the iceberg of York's intrigues, an economy that allows Shakespeare more scope in his representation of Gloucester's fall. But since York is to emerge as the supreme antagonist of the play, he cannot be too elusive or shadowy a presence; and since the plot demands that York be offstage during half of Act III and all of Act IV, he must tower over the other characters when on stage so that he is not out of mind when out of sight. In short, York needs the special relation with the audience and the extra dimension of personality which his florid soliloquies provide. Sent to lead the army in Ireland, he gloats over this opportunity to realize his politic schemes:

> Now, York, or never, steel thy fearful thoughts
> And change misdoubt to resolution.
> Be that thou hop'st to be; or what thou art
> Resign to death: . . .
> Whiles I in Ireland nourish a mighty band,
> I will stir up in England some black storm
> Shall blow ten thousand souls to heaven or hell;
> And this fell tempest shall not cease to rage
> Until the golden circuit on my head,
> Like to the glorious sun's transparent beams,
> Do calm the fury of this mad-bred flaw.
>
>   [III. i. 331-34, 348-54]

If this hyperbolic rage for destruction does not square with York's sober machinations, it does give him the mythic largeness of the Marlovian superman, and it reinforces the contrast between his temper and Henry's. Where Henry is weak, York is strong. Where Henry is compassionate, York is ruthless. Where Henry is naively credulous, York is a cunning dissembler and manipulator of others. Where York is a man able to keep his own counsel, Henry is a child whose tears flow in the first scene at the sight of Margaret, and who weeps even as he abandons Gloucester to his murderous enemies.

If Henry really were too innocent and child-simple for this world, his case would be merely pitiable. But though he is easily duped, he can tell the very obvious: he knows that the good Gloucester is falsely accused. Nevertheless, he thanks the conspirators for their care and allows Gloucester to be arrested. His conscience tells him that Gloucester's life is threatened by his enemies, but it does not insist that he must protect him from judicial murder. His heart "drown'd with grief," he tells the conspirators, "My lords, what to your wisdoms seemeth best / Do or undo, as if ourself were here" [III. i. 195-96]. (pp. 48-50)

When the King will not defend the right, the people grow muddied, ready to take justice into their own hands or to redress grievances with force. When the King cannot lead, the commoners will follow a Warwick or a Cade or a York. In the Chronicles the English people appear to be a fickle lot who change allegiances easily. Shakespeare sees the commoners more as the victims of disorder than as its many-headed beast and senses that their instinct is for survival, not for giddy change. Although he spares no detail of the atrocities committed by the Cade rebels, he does not make them appear any worse than their aristocratic betters, who more deliberately subvert the law and murder their enemies. Compared to the malevolent impulses and acts of Margaret and York, the mindless violence of the rebels is almost innocent. Shrewd, good-humored, and clear-sighted about their leader, the rebels want excitement, booty, and some revenge on those with money, privilege, and education. Since they are not revolutionaries and they do not want Cade as their king, they quickly return to obedience when Clifford reminds them of the spoils they can win in France:

> To France, to France, and get what you have lost!
> Spare England, for it is your native coast.
>
>   [IV. viii. 48-9]

Here is the first intimation in the History Plays of the virtue of foreign wars which legitimize pillage and ennoble the cutting of throats.

Cade's ramshackle army is the antimasque to York's rebellion even as Cade's claim to royal descent is a parody of York's pretension to the throne. Cade's neighbors joke about his fictitious ancestry and follow him nevertheless. The Nevils, York's allies, take a more serious view of his claim to be the true inheritor. By the indirections of his genealogical arguments in II. ii, they find directions out and declare his claim a "plain proceeding." It is quite clear, however, that the Nevils do not support York because they are legitimists; rather they are "legitimists" because they support York. When Henry asks how they can dishonor their oaths after a lifetime of obedience, they plead a care for their immortal souls:

> It is a great sin to swear unto a sin,
> But greater sin to keep a sinful oath.
>
>   [V, i. 182-83]

As scrupulous as Sir John Falstaff, they will not be damned for any Lancastrian prince in Christendom. There is nothing theoretical in their attachment to York, who promises them power and greatness, just as there is nothing theoretical about York's claim to the throne when he faces Henry in the last act. His argument is that Henry is "not fit to govern and rule multitudes," while his own hand was made "to hold a sceptre up" [V. i. 94, 102].

The battle of St. Albans marks the end of intrigue and conspiracy, and the outbreak of civil war. Now all enmities and ambitions are declared and all conflicts openly waged. The eruption of the impostume of disorder fails, however, to relieve the diseased state, even as the call to arms fails to resurrect England's chivalric greatness. Where Talbot achieved a heroic apotheosis in defeat, Clifford, the Lancastrian champion, rages for destruction after St. Albans and swears to revenge his father's death on York's babes. The age of chivalry is dead, and the time will soon be at hand when political conflict descends to vendetta, when the murder of children will become commonplace, and severed heads will be casually tossed down as trophies of victory. Yet, even while moral restraints threaten to disappear, some kind of moral order asserts itself in the destinies of evil men. Suffolk is exiled and lynched, Winchester dies maddened by the fear of a last judgment, and Cade ends his life a starving fugitive. Shakespeare takes little satisfaction, however, in pointing out that blood will have blood, because he has no taste for the ghastly retributions that fall on innocent children, and he does not believe in the providentiality of barbarous acts. The Chroniclers speak of the divine judgment that fell on Suffolk, who was beheaded by Exeter's soldiers. Shakespeare turns these agents of retribution into freebooters, who parcel out their prisoners as booty and extort ransom by threats of death. Their captain invokes the cause of York and the memory of Richard II in "sentencing" Suffolk, but the trial is a kangaroo proceeding and the executioner a sullen pirate who would slaughter all the prisoners to "revenge" the eye he lost in attacking Suffolk's vessel. However one may moralize it, the murder of Suffolk is, in the play, a "barbarous and bloody spectacle" [IV. i. 144]. More thoughtful about human nature than the Chroniclers, Shakespeare knows that when crime answers crime, morality is debased. The hope of the future does not depend on the tally of horrible "retributions" which Margaret draws up in *Richard III;* it depends upon the capacity of men to forgive their enemies and to forego the promptings of hatred and revenge. (pp. 50-2)

Robert Ornstein, "The 'Henry VI' Plays," in his A Kingdom for a Stage: The Achievement of Shakespeare's History Plays, *Cambridge, Mass.: Harvard University Press, 1972, pp. 33-61.*

LESLIE A. FIEDLER   (essay date 1972)

[*Although Fiedler has been criticized for what some consider eccentric pronouncements on literature, he has also been praised for his adventuresome and eclectic approach. Generally, Fiedler believes that the conventions and values of a society are powerful determinants on the direction taken by its authors' works. In a section of his* The Stranger in Shakespeare *(1972) not excerpted here, he claims that Shakespeare consciously subscribed to the Elizabethan mythic concept of women as alien beings. In the excerpt below, Fiedler notes that the three female characters in* 1 Henry VI *are "all 'black,' all French, and all bent on betraying the male champion of the English," namely, Talbot. He contends that the figure of Joan enrages Shakespeare because "everything about her is a lie, an illusion." Although she first appears to be "a golden girl," by the close of the play she is revealed as "a swarthy hag in disguise, as Shakespeare has all along suspected every woman is in essence." For further discussion of the female characters in* Henry VI *as either dominant or outlaw figures, see the excerpts by David M. Bevington (1966), H. M. Richmond (1967), Robert B. Pierce (1971), and Marilyn French (1981).*]

Obviously, the beginning for Shakespeare is the problem of woman, or, more exactly perhaps, his problem with women. Certainly, in his first plays, members of that sex are likely to be portrayed as utter strangers: creatures so totally alien to men as threaten destruction rather than offer the hope of salvation, much less the possibility of a union in which male and female might become, as the Christian Scriptures seem to promise, one flesh and one soul. Hard enough, Shakespeare apparently felt, for two unique individuals of the same kind, two males, to achieve unity in love; impossible for male and female (i.e., alien beings), each the other's other, to attain such communion. (p. 43)

Generally speaking, play acting, the theater itself, represents always and everywhere an attempt to mitigate, if not bridge, the mythological gap which men feel between themselves and the other, whoever that other may be, by permitting representatives of the reigning group in a culture (at first the sons of the best families, then their paid surrogates or servants) to *play*, that is, mythically to become, the feared and desired other. "Disguising" is another word for the process, a term still used in fact to describe a favorite form of dramatic entertainment at the courts of Henry VII and Henry VIII, and one which reminds us of the link between acting and the child's "dressing up" like his parents, on the one hand, or the gods' mythological changing of shape, on the other. Acting is, in any case, no mere matter of imitating another individual, at least when drama is most alive, but of metamorphosing into another kind.

So, for instance, in the heyday of Greek drama, men played gods or the half-divine children of gods, thus creating possibilities for the kind of dramatic punning practiced by Euripides in *The Bacchae*, in which the god who, inside of the play's fiction, plays he is a man, becomes, once we fall back into our own realm of truth, a man playing he is a god playing he is a man. This can be read, on the final level of myth, as the god in us all (whom we have been ordinarily too obtuse to know) playing he is a man playing he is a god playing he is a man. And so at the climax of his career, Shakespeare, in a final involution of drama's essential device, turned it back onto the nature of acting itself, creating in *The Tempest* that play within a play, which (as Tillyard long ago remarked) "is ex-

ecuted by players pretending to be spirits, pretending to be real actors, pretending to be supposed goddesses and rustics."

Long before this, however, he has brought that same device to bear on the problem of the original stranger, the woman, most spectacularly in *As You Like It*, in which the full meaning of the play is only established by the last turn of the mythological screw, when the boy who has been playing Rosalind playing she is Ganymede playing Rosalind, steps out of his role and stage-sex to speak the Epilogue. And though in his-her wedding dress still, he-she informs the audience that, "If I were a woman I would kiss as many of you as had beards that pleased me, complexions that liked me, and breaths that I defied not" [*As You Like It*, Epilogue, 18-20]. Then he-she curtsies with that strange perfection of grace possible only to a male playing the idea of femininity and sets throbbing—we are free to imagine—more than one male heart in that largely homosexual circle of gallants, which, sitting on stage rather than standing in the pit, must have felt itself sometimes more actor or chorus than audience.

But the Shakespeare who manipulated the four contrasted boy-girls in *As You Like It*—voice against voice, style against style, and complexion against complexion—was immensely more sophisticated and artful than the beginning playwright of *Henry VI, Part I*. He had not yet, of course, discovered how the device of disguising could be used to make his heroines seem as much boys as girls, and therefore less disturbingly alien. Nor could he even manage to differentiate the female parts demanded by his fable, creating over and over the same abstract dark lady. In the first part of *Henry VI*, there are actually three female characters: Joan of Arc, the Countess of Auvergne, and Margaret, who becomes Queen of England; but they never appear on the stage together and could easily have been played by a single actor. Indeed, mythologically speaking, they *are* one, being all "black," all French, and all bent on betraying the male champion of the English.

The Countess of Auvergne, to be sure, though she begins, like Joan, as the enemy of the play's archetypal English male, Talbot, ends with a quick, unconvincing capitulation before his power. "Alas," she cries on first confronting him, "this is a child, a silly dwarf! / It cannot be this weak and writhled shrimp / Should strike such terror to his enemies" [*1 Henry VI*, II. ii. 22-4]. But once he has, like some latter-day Roland, wound "his horn" to call up reinforcements and reveal that he is more than his single self, being all England, all masculine chivalry, the lady concedes, "I find thou art no less than fame hath bruited / And more than may be gathered by thy shape" [II. ii. 68-9]. She attempts vainly, that is, to play Delilah to a "weak and writhled" English Samson, destined by the irrelevant exigencies of history to die at other hands. And she is dismissed in a single scene, having illustrated in baldest allegory that the enemy = France = traitor = woman = the blackness of darkness, which is to say, Hell, but also that in the end, that enemy is powerless against England and Saint George.

Margaret, on the other hand, who also demonstrates the same equation, is permitted to appear on stage in all three of the *Henry VI* plays and in *Richard III*, as well. But she does not enter until the Countess of Auvergne has disappeared into the wings and Joan herself has exited, discomfited and in chains. She seems in fact to be, in some real sense, Joan's successor, a relationship made manifest in the speech with which she introduces herself to the other players and us: "Margaret my name, and daughter to a King, / The King of Naples . . ." [V. iii. 51-2]. But Joan, who reappears once more after Margaret's entrance, is led off to her death asserting (in what may be her last lie or her first truth) that precisely the father of Margaret has also fathered the unborn bastard she claims to be carrying in her belly. "'Twas neither Charles nor yet the Duke I named," she explains, "but Reignier, King of Naples, that prevailed" [V. iv. 77-8].

Reflecting afterward on the line—for the play's quick pace at this point scarcely leaves time for reflection—we realize that given a few more months, another act, Joan might have borne a half sister to Margaret, who succeeds her on stage as "the English scourge." Or, let us rather say that in the nighttime illogic of dream and myth, she *did* bear a "banning hag" [V. iii. 42] quite like herself in Margaret, an archetypal daughter-alter ego.

That daughter-alter ego, at any rate, continues to dominate the scene throughout the rest of Shakespeare's first historical tetralogy, the sole character who survives the bloody events from almost start to almost finish, though transformed step by step from a fatal Aphrodite to a cursing Hecate. She constitutes, in fact, the sole principle of unity in a series of events otherwise rendered in all the formless confusion of the Lancastrian wars themselves. (pp. 46-9)

[The] series of plays begins with a lament for that most phallic of English kings, Henry V, of whom the Duke of Gloucester says, "His brandished sword did blind men with his beams. / His arms spread wider than a dragon's wings" [I. i. 10-11], and who, the Duke of Bedford boasts, was superior to Caesar: "A far more glorious star thy soul will make / Than Julius Caesar . . ." [I. i. 55-6]. But even he, being born of woman, did not possess the mana of Posthumus [*Cymbeline*] or Macduff [*Macbeth*], the sole effective antidote against the female "arts." And consequently, the Duke of Exeter suggests, "the subtle-witted French / Conjurers and sorcerers . . . / By magic verses have contrived his end" [I. i. 25-7].

With his death, at any rate, his country seems on the verge of losing its last claim to the male principle, which is to say, its own identity, since in Shakespeare's mythological geography, England represents masculinity as France does femininity. In the very first scene of *Part I,* the keening wail has gone up: "Our isle be made a nourish of salt tears, / And none but women left to wail the dead" [I. i. 50-1]. *"None but women left":* it is the threat which hangs over a realm ruled by a boy king obviously destined never to become a real man. In all England, so far as the play will permit us to see, there is only a single claimant to the role of male champion, one warrior capable of resisting the incursion of the female from without and creeping feminization from within. And this is Talbot, "English John Talbot," contrasted from the start with the "coward" John Fastolfe, who, his accusers assert, "doth but usurp the sacred name of knight . . ." [IV. i. 40]. Yet he is by an irony no less real for being unintended, destined to be transmogrified into the antihero of *Henry IV,* the craven tub of guts loved by Shakespeare's readers more than any hero, not excepting his own beloved Prince Hal.

Though Talbot speaks sometimes of his wife, it is impossible to imagine him at home; for the battlefield is where alone he becomes himself, joined in mutual loyalty with his fighting men and with that son for whom he feels the deepest affection he can sustain. To be faithful father to son and son to father: this is for Shakespeare, at the moment of writing *Henry VI,* the greatest of all virtues. And the two Talbots enact that faith almost allegorically in the emblematic scenes which portray

the death of both. They begin with a sticomythic exchange, flat and stiff as an engraving on a sepulcher.

> TAL: Shall all thy mother's hopes lie in one tomb?
> JOHN: Aye, rather than I'll shame my mother's womb.
> TAL: Upon my blessing, I command thee go.
> JOHN: To fight I will, but not to fly the foe.
> TAL: Part of thy father may be saved in thee.
> JOHN: No part of him but will be the shame in me.
>
> [IV. v. 34-9]

Then in the very midst of battle, both become less cryptic and more allusive.

> JOHN: Surely, by all the glory you have won,
>   And if I fly, I am not Talbot's son.
>   Then talk no more of flight, it is no boot;
>   If son to Talbot, die at Talbot's foot.
> TAL: Then follow thou thy desperate sire of Crete,
>   Thou Icarus. Thy life to me is sweet.
>   If thou wilt fight, fight by thy father's side,
>   And, commendable proved, let's die in pride.
>
> [IV. vi. 50-7]

It is the beginning of their mutual transformation into their mythological prototypes, Daedalus and Icarus, another father and son lost in the maze of female lechery and dreaming the flight that is to kill them. Toward the end of the play, the Minotaur is mentioned by Suffolk, who, contemplating adultery and treachery, admonishes himself, "But, Suffolk, stay, / Thou mayst not wander in that labyrinth. / There Minotaurs and ugly treasons lurk" [V. iii. 187-89]. In the Talbot scenes, however, the dark female chamber at the center of the maze is not evoked, only the open masculine heavens, where what seems to have been lost in time ("and there died, / My Icarus, my blossom, in his pride" [IV. vii. 15-16]) is preserved in eternity:

> Two Talbots, winged through the lither sky,
> In thy despite shall 'scape mortality.
>
> [IV. vii. 21-2]

But this is not Talbot's final word, for even more than immortality, he seems to have desired the filial-paternal *Liebestod* ["conjunction of love and death"] he celebrates with his last breath.

> Poor boy! He smiles, methinks, as who should say,
> "Had Death been French, then Death,
>   had died today."
> Come, come and lay him in his father's arms.
> My spirit can no longer bear these harms.
> Soldiers, adieu! I have what I would have;
> Now my old arms are young John Talbot's grave.
>
> [*Dies.*]
> [IV. vii. 27-32]
> (pp. 54-6)

Joan, however, is given the last word, allowed to undercut—with a kind of ironic realism not unlike Falstaff's in his famous reflections on honor—the code by which Talbot lived and died.

The exemplar of that code, as well as of the heroic style which sustains it, is Sir William Lucy, who just after Talbot's death, enters the French camp, crying:

> But where's the great Alcides of the field,
> Valiant Lord Talbot, Earl of Shrewsbury,
> Created for his rare success in arms,
> Great Earl of Washford, Waterford, and Valence;

Lord Talbot of Goodrig and Urchinfield,
Lord Strange of Blackmere, Lord Verdun of Alton,
Lord Cromwell of Wingfield, Lord Furnival
  of Sheffield,
The thrice-victorious Lord of Falconbridge;
Knight of the noble order of Saint George,
Worthy Saint Michael and the Golden Fleece;
Great Marshal to Henry the Sixth
Of all his wars within the realm of France?

                                           [IV. vii. 60-71]

After this grandiloquence, the Pucelle answers so quietly and
with such good sense that for one instant the balance of Shakespeare's sympathy (along with ours) tilts in her direction. For
the first time in his career, perhaps, he betrays his ambivalence
about the reigning values of his time, his suspicion, later expressed in certain speeches of Shylock [*Merchant of Venice*]
and Caliban [*The Tempest*], that by virtue of his strangeness
the stranger in our midst can sometimes see the silliness of the
games we play in deadly earnest. And though such perceptions
are not all the truth they are, like Joan's rejoinder, *also* true.

          Here's a silly stately style indeed!
          The Turk, that two and fifty kingdoms hath,
          Writes not so tedious a style as this.
          Him that thou magnifiest with all these titles,
          Stinking and fly-blown lies here at our feet.

                                           [IV. vii. 72-6]

To make matters worse, Shakespeare's ironic strangers often
possess a mythic dimension lacking in the official spokesmen
they challenge. Certainly, this is the case in *Henry VI, Part I;*
for Talbot is a provincial hero and Joan a universal myth, a
figure of inexhaustible archetypal resonance. Even inside the
play, he cannot ever touch her; they exist, as it were, in different dimensions, and she fades from his solidity like a dream.
True, he is permitted to abuse her roundly, calling her "Devil
or Devil's dam," "witch," "high-minded strumpet," "foul
fiend of France," "hag of all despite," and "railing Hecaté"
[I. v. 5, I. v. 21, I. v. 12, III. ii. 52, III. ii. 64]. But it is she
who pronounces his epitaph, not he, hers. (pp. 57-8)

Shakespeare is interested, like the Tudor chroniclers on whom
he drew and those who sat in the ecclesiastical court which
originally condemned the Pucelle to be burned, on making a
case for England, or rather against France. But there is in him,
too, despite what allegiance he may have felt he owed the old
Roman faith of his mother, a Protestant, Puritan, Hebraic,
finally patriarchal distrust of Mariolatry in all its forms, any
attempt to smuggle into Christianity or patriotic piety homage
to the Goddess. For him, in general as well as particular, the
virgin is a whore; which is . . . why he lingers so obscenely
over Joan's desperate attempts to escape the fire by claiming
pregnancy—though by which of her many lovers she finds it
hard to be sure. (p. 60)

It is not merely the fact of Joan's having been a whore that
stirs the fury of English Shakespeare and his English heroes
against her ("Break thou in pieces and consume to ashes, /
Thou foul accursèd minister of Hell!" [V. iv. 92-3]). Even
more it is the fact of her having claimed to be the total opposite,
of having been a liar as well. Like Chaucer, Shakespeare seems
to have felt that the three natural gifts of God to women are
"Deceite, wepyng, spynnyng" (lies, tears, and skill with the
distaff). Unlike Chaucer, however, he could not contain that
belief in ironical acceptance, not even in the *Sonnets,* where
he makes a show of such containment ("I do believe her,

though I know she lies" [Sonnet 138, 2]), and certainly not
in the first part of *Henry VI.* Everything about Joan enrages
Shakespeare, because everything about her is a lie, an illusion.
She enters, for instance, in the guise of a golden girl; but she
is revealed, before all the play is played, a swarthy hag in
disguise, as Shakespeare has all along suspected every woman
is in essence. Joan herself confesses the fact with a kind of
pride on first meeting the Dauphin.

          And, whereas I was black and swart before,
          With those clear rays which she infused on me
          That beauty am I blessed with which you see.

                                           [I. ii. 84-6]

It is the Blessed Virgin herself, "God's Mother. . . . in complete glory" [I. ii. 78-83], supreme symbol in the Christian
world of divine womanhood, whom she claims as the source
of her magical transformation. And, indeed, before that initial
encounter is over, a whole gamut of mythological or semi-
mythological females has been evoked, from classical antiquity
and medieval hagiography as well as the Testaments, Old and
New: Saint Katherine, Deborah, the Amazons, the "mother
of Great Constantine," "Saint Philip's daughter" [I. ii. 142,
143], and at last the goddess of love herself. "Bright star of
Venus, fall'n down on the earth," the Dauphin says toward
the scene's end, "How may I reverently worship thee enough?"
[I. ii. 144-45]. (pp. 61-2)

Until Act V of *Henry VI, Part I,* we are left uncertain as to
whether Joan is, in [a] full sense, a witch, a practicing disciple
of Satan, or only, as it were, a witch by analogy, a lying and
lascivious woman who, in despite of biblical injunctions, has
put on the garments of a man. But the third scene of that act
removes all of our doubts, beginning with Joan's ritual evocation of her infernal accomplices, in a desperate attempt to
turn the tide of war which now runs against her:

          You speedy helpers, that are substitutes
          Under the lordly monarch of the North,
          Appear and aid me in this enterprise.

                                           [V. iii. 5-7]

and reaching a quick climax with their appearance. The "Fiends"
enter, but they do not talk, as if Shakespeare were not yet able
to imagine a voice and a style for such creatures. *"They walk,
and speak not,"* say the stage directions. *"They hang their
heads." "They shake their heads." "They depart."* Yet before
they have left, Joan has betrayed all: her earlier dealings with
them ("I was wont to feed you with my blood. . . ." [V. iii.
14]), as well as her willingness at this point to make the final
sacrilegious offerings to hell ("Then take my soul, my body,
soul and all. . . ." [V. iii. 22]). But nothing helps; for, Shakespeare suggests, in the end hell betrays its most abject servitors.
And as the dark spirits exit, York enters to take her prisoner.
(p. 68)

[Although Joan] names three possible fathers for her perhaps
imaginary child-to-come—the Dauphin and Alençon, as well
as Reignier, King of Naples—on scene she makes love to no
one and betrays no one except her father and herself. She is,
that is to say, a daughter-witch, whom Shakespeare has imagined not as a decrepit hag whose treason to her sex a beard
declares, but as a beautiful young woman who might well be
a beardless boy. And her denial of all that is "soft, mild,
pitiful, and flexible" [*3 Henry VI,* I. iv. 141] in herself is
revealed by the sword she wields with such success. Later in
his career, Shakespeare will learn to make runaway girls in
boy's clothing seem lovable, even when they buckle a man's

weapon to their sides. But he will never let them use that weapon with any skill, much less defeat with it a male champion like Talbot.

But Joan is by definition (which is to say, in patriotic myth) a successful warrior as well as a perfidious Frenchwoman and a witch, so that her battlefield transvestism, unlike, say, Portia's assumption of "the lovely garnish of a boy" [*Merchant of Venice*, II. vi. 45], must be rendered as a final horror rather than a redeeming grace. And, in any case, becoming a warrior, she proves herself a bad daughter, her father's enemy, which constitutes for Shakespeare the worst of treasons. "This argues," York says at one point, speaking of Joan's denial of her origins, "what her kind of life hath been— / Wicked and vile . . ." [V. iv. 15-16]. And one cannot doubt that Shakespeare concurs.

She had begun modestly and piously enough, introducing herself to the court of France with the declaration: "Dauphin, I am by birth a shepherd's daughter" [I. ii. 72]. But just before her death, she gives her English captors a totally different account of her origins, a seeming bald-faced lie. That lie can be read . . . as a higher truth, a ritual affirmation of her faith in the Great Goddess, whose avatar she feels herself to be at the point of sacrifice.

> First, let me tell you whom you have condemned:
> Not me begotten of a shepherd swain,
> But issued from the progeny of kings,
> Virtuous and holy, chosen from above
> By inspiration of celestial grace
> To work exceeding miracles on earth.
>
> [V. iv. 36-41]

And for one moment she sounds like the female Antichrist: a daughter of the Heavenly Mother, even as Jesus was Son to the Heavenly Father.

Her earthly father, however, can read all this only as filial impiety, for when he cries in pity, "Ah, Joan, sweet daughter Joan, I'll die with thee" [V. iv. 6], she screams back at him in rage:

> Decrepit miser! Base ignoble wretch!
> I am descended of a gentler blood.
> Thou art no father nor no friend of mine.
>
> [V. iv. 7-9]

And when he begs, "Deny me not, I prithee, gentle Joan," she answers brusquely, "Peasant, avaunt!" [V. iv. 20-1] Then turning to the English bystanders who plead on his behalf ("Graceless! Wilt thou deny thy parentage?" [V. iv. 14]) she says accusingly, "You have suborned this man / Of purpose to obscure my noble birth" [V. iv. 21-2].

Such actual apostasy to a living sire no theoretical allegiance to a maternal deity can justify, especially in a patriarchal world in which the Goddess's proper names cannot even be spoken. It is to "our Lady gracious," "God's Mother," "Christ's Mother" [I. ii. 74, 78, 106] that Joan, in the beginning, attributes her special powers, using, that is to say, her Christian pseudonyms. And when the Dauphin calls her "Bright star of Venus," she turns away in silence, having already declared, "I must not yield to any rites of love" [I. ii. 113]. In the end, however, no holy name at all is on her cursing tongue, only satanic epithets, "darkness . . . death . . . mischief and despair . . ." [V. iv. 89-90]. We must, therefore, accept as just the judgment York makes after her final exit, "Thou foul accursed minister of Hell!" [V. iv. 93]. (pp. 77-9)

Leslie A. Fiedler, "The Woman as Stranger; or, 'None but Women Left. . . .'," in his The Stranger in Shakespeare, *Stein and Day, Publishers*, 1972, pp. 43-81.

MICHAEL MANHEIM   (essay date 1973)

[*Manheim argues that in 1, 2, and 3* Henry VI *Shakespeare dramatized the growing acceptance among his Elizabethan contemporaries of a modified form of Machiavellianism. Manheim contends that in the world of the trilogy the "chief overriding good is the ability to take, and retain, power," and that deceit and violence are demonstrably the tools for achieving these ends. He contends that Shakespeare deliberately manipulates audience sympathies toward Henry—the only truly Christian figure throughout the trilogy—by showing him to be in turn admirable in his virtues and pitiable in his human weakness. Yet Manheim supports the thesis of Harold C. Goddard (1951) that Henry is a benevolent, charitable, and well-meaning ruler caught in an age of violence, deceit, and self-ambition, and he maintains that the civil dissension of the king's reign was not so much the result of his failure to rule—as suggested by numerous earlier critics, including Hereward T. Price (1951), H. M. Richmond (1967), and James Winny (1968)—but the inevitable outcome of the inhumanity, selfishness, and Machiavellian thirst for power among his aristocracy. Manheim concludes by noting a savage irony at the close of the* Henry VI *trilogy, namely, Shakespeare's depiction of a Christian, benevolent king who is unable to prevail against the Machiavellian politics of his court. Manheim's examination of the conflict between Christian and Machiavellian politics in* Henry VI *recalls the commentary by H. M. Richmond (1967), David Riggs (1971), and Robert B. Pierce (1971) on similar political complexities in the plays.*]

Shakespeare's three parts of *Henry VI*, which are of course among his first plays, stretch to its limits the dilemma over whether an inadequate monarch ought to be deposed. For Henry's inadequacies result in part not from his desire for sensual pleasures but from his love for his fellow man and his desire to do good in the world. He has other failings to be sure—a measure of vindictiveness and a willingness at times docilely to be led by others—but his downfall results as much from his adherence in political life to traditional Christian virtues as it does to those shortcomings. Henry's experience in these plays has suggested to many that adherence to those traditional virtues is probably as much an invitation to political disintegration as excessive desire for sensual pleasures. But there is also more than a suggestion in these early works that given the chance Henry could have been successful, in spite of his ordinary human weaknesses, and that the troubles of his kingdom really result from the nobility's crude but exclusive acceptance of deceit and violence as their political equipment. While it is clear that the king's failure results in part from his Christian nature, it is equally clear that only the virtues associated with that nature could have saved the country from the disaster it experiences in these plays. The political evil in these plays is not so much the king's weakness as the attempts to appear strong on the part of those around him. The dilemma might now read: Should a weak but Christian king be deposed by a seemingly strong but Machiavellian nobility? Although the answer implicit in these plays may appear to be no, neither Henry's personal failings nor the seeming practical ineffectiveness of Christian leadership are glossed over. (pp. 76-7)

In considering the Machiavellian influence in *Henry VI* the ambivalence, or "dualism," which Felix Raab, in *The English Face of Machiavelli*, finds characteristic of response to Machiavelli in the age is extremely important. Political leaders were victims of a kind of double-think whereby they sincerely believed themselves true and devout Christians at the same time that they felt increasingly justified in ignoring Christian precepts in political dealings. What once might have been considered hypocrisy was coming to be thought of as policy. The anti-religious attitudes of *The Prince* might be vehemently rejected, but methods of behavior suggested there eagerly adopted. Men who sought to apply Machiavellian practices in political life, while personally remaining sincere men of faith, dominated government offices of the 1580s and 1590s and as a class were the likeliest models for the majority of characters in the history plays. And while in some of these plays their Machiavellianism might be of minor importance, in *Henry VI* it is of fundamental importance.

Throughout the three parts of *Henry VI* there are the stage Machiavels, of course, whose attitude toward Christian morality, it may fairly be said, is knowingly and basely hypocritical. Aside from Richard, there is Joan la Pucelle and her replacement Margaret of Anjou, as well as Margaret's English allies Suffolk and Beaufort. And of course, Jack Cade. They are villains, and if the world of *Henry VI* were clear of them, it ought to be a better world. Ought to be, but would it be? Leaving aside the minor French figures of Part 1 (they are villains simply because they are French), what of the duke of York and his sons Edward and George; what of Warwick and the Salisbury of Part 2; what of Clifford and Oxford; what of the Somersets and Buckingham; of Vernon, Basset, Northumberland, and Hastings; what of Dame Eleanor (Humphrey's wife)? Which of these is not at some time motivated by the lust for political advancement to employ nearly any form of deceit or violent action to attain it? Yet these figures do not seem Machiavels, as do those mentioned earlier. The more important ones confess their true motives in soliloquy, but for the most part they only occasionally reveal what they are and what they are really after. But when they do, those motives are unmistakable, and the incidents involved give us glimpses, however brief, of just how ruthless a world this is. Early in Part 2, Somerset and Buckingham exchange the following comments on Duke Humphrey:

> *Som.*   Cousin of Buckingham, though Humphrey's pride
> And greatness of his place be grief to us,
> Yet let us watch the haughty Cardinal.
> His insolence is more intolerable
> Than all the princes in the land beside,
> If Gloucester be displaced, he'll be Protector.
>
> *Buck.*   Or thou or I, Somerset, will be Protector,
> Despite Duke Humphrey or the Cardinal.
>   [*2 Henry VI*, I. i. 172-79]

Part III, Act II, Scene v. Father that has killed his Son, Henry VI, Son that has killed his Father, and Soldiers. By John Boydell (n.d.).

Buckingham's ambition is obvious enough, but note Somerset's "let us watch." The key to all Machiavellian design is patience, the knowing when to act. (pp. 80-1)

Out of the lives and actions of the contending nobility in *Henry VI* there emerges something like a perverse moral code. This code is hardly very complete as a working philosophy, but it is the standard by which most of the peers (and some recent critics as well) judge the king's effectiveness. And that it is a Machiavellian code is indicated as follows. The chief overriding good is the ability to take, and retain, power—and only vaguely and at times does this good have anything to do with unifying the nation. To achieve this good, it seems agreed by the contending nobility, one must be patient, alert, swift in action, courageous, physically strong, and ruthless. One must use deceit with great skill, since it is the chief tool at one's disposal, and one must use violence, at the right time, since it is the only type of activity which gets results. Following from this, the bad is indifference to the taking and retaining of power and, of crucial importance as far as Henry is concerned, the absence of deceit and lack of inclination to violent action. One must also be convinced that others are motivated by the same goals and are using the same methods. No man should be trusted, and the prospect of sudden violence from the outside must always be guarded against. Significantly, retaining power one already has (inherited or seized) requires the same skills as taking it. When York says he is better suited to wear the crown than Henry, he means that he would be able to hold it more securely by the means indicated above. He is not referring to the good deeds he would do as king or to the general welfare of his people except insofar as a stable monarchy might improve their lot. That word *stable* is the one usually used today, and it means planted so firmly at the top of the hill that one cannot be pushed off. But opponents will be constantly trying—backhandedly and frontally—and one can hold his position only by being both more devious than his opponents and a warrior of greater prowess. And by such a standard, of course, York is indeed far better suited to the throne than Henry. One of York's sons, though, is still better suited.

By the Machiavellian standards which govern almost everyone else in the play, Henry is surely the most wretched king in "Christendom." Not only does he fail to use the techniques presumed indispensable for retaining power, he also fails to exploit that ancient sense of a divinity that hedges a king. Such divinity is viewed as so much window dressing by the Machiavels, but useful window dressing in creating the illusion of invulnerability which clearly assists in the actual achievement of that invulnerability. Henry is no showman. He simply cannot and will not behave as though he were invulnerable when he is not. At times, he makes a feeble effort to be a real king, but always that effort is both ineffective and short-lived. Were pity allowed, he might be pitied. But pity by others might reveal weakness on the part of the one doing the pitying, and so must be avoided—at least according to the code. All Henry wishes is "a heart untainted" [*2 Henry VI*, III. ii. 232], and this, the plays protest with savage irony, will never do. (pp. 81-3)

Shakespeare's irony in his treatment of the relations between Henry and his nobility has been recognized by surprisingly few commentators. Not that anyone actually admires the contending barons; but most critics reject Henry outright as a political leader, and in terms of the alternatives the play represents, they unwittingly accept the barons' methods when they reject

Henry. No mid-point or compromise, such as is implicit in *King John* and *Henry V*, is suggested anywhere in the *Henry VI* trilogy. If the actions of the king are evaluated by the Machiavellian standard discussed here, then its only successful character is its arch-villain, and it is against young Richard that all other characters should be measured. If we say Henry is "bad" because he is utterly without the ability to govern by force or guile, and the lords have their "weaker moments" because they fail to be sufficiently patient, alert, or self-centered, then we must call Richard, who is all force and guile and who has no weaker moment, "good." (pp. 85-6)

Richard of Gloucester is Shakespeare's first great character, and his portrayal in *Richard III* is brilliantly anticipated in *3 Henry VI*. So great is he that critics tend at times to find the incredible "alacrity of spirit" which makes him the most memorable of stage Machiavels an adequate substitute for morality itself. But even the temptation to do this does great harm to *Henry VI*. Shakespeare the beginning playwright has in these plays no ambivalence toward the new Machiavellianism. The proof that it is detestable resides in the creature that it breeds. It is difficult to imagine Shakespeare's reaction to an attitude which suggests that somehow Richard's evil is so engaging as to make him genuinely attractive. Two recent interpretations do almost approach a kind of Richard-worship rooted in the contempt which he possesses for the slovenly incompetence of most men of affairs [see excerpt above by H. M. Richmond, 1967, and the essay by John Bromley cited in the Additional Bibliography]. But the effort which has gone into the creation of this character has been to suggest the effect of carrying to their logical conclusions the seemingly quite practical aspects of evil represented in a new, tantalizing, man-centered morality, particularly evident in Shakespeare's day in the ambitions of an emerging new governing class. . . . (p. 87)

What Harold C. Goddard said of Henry VI still stands. He is "the most critically neglected of Shakespeare's kings" [see excerpt above, 1951]. . . . Creating "the good" in dramatic terms is a fantastically more difficult problem than creating evil . . . , and if Henry is not so successful a characterization as Richard, the task of creating him is of much greater dimension. Shakespeare did not attempt to come to grips with anything like it until he wrote *King Lear*. Shakespeare must somehow strike a balance between the sententious and the human in Henry, and given this problem, he succeeds, as Goddard seems justified in claiming.

In terms of moral standards, it seems obvious but necessary to state that a traditional Christian view of good government underlies the Henry VI plays. It is not Henry who is out of step, who is inadequate, who is ill-suited to govern—but just about everyone else. Without bitterness, cynicism, or guile (which would be the signs of maturity in Machiavellian terms), he remains childlike throughout the three plays. . . . Those who wish Henry VI to be more effective are wishing for a different character and one impossible in human terms. Henry is quite effective in his love, understanding, and trust. It is the others who need thus to be more effective. He is the only character who sees the full horror of civil disorder, and he sacrifices his family honor to prevent its continuance. He alone believes in justice and the triumph of truth. In his actions and responses, he alone believes in the natural dignity of man. If man has betrayed that dignity, it is insufficient to say that the terms of the betrayal must therefore be the terms by which men are led and governed. (pp. 87-9)

Making the good king a human king results in the same problem associated with the royal personality in *Woodstock, Edward II,* and *Richard II.* I speak now not in terms of the standards by which the Machiavels judge him, but of those by which a Christian humanist, an Erasmus or Thomas More, might judge him. Henry avoids being the stick-figure saint of medieval statuary precisely because he often fails to live up to the image he inherently has of himself. In other words, our sympathy toward him shifts considerably in the course of the three plays—and quite independently of the Machiavellian question. He is not a Machiavel, and in contrast to the contending nobles he is indeed a saint. But set against the ideal image of a Christian king, he falls short. He is a human king and thus, just as much as Edward II and Richard II, a weak king. In his striving to "govern better" [*2 Henry VI,* IV. ix. 48] he is to be praised, perhaps beyond any king in Shakespeare, but because of his inescapable human weaknesses as king, he must fail—and our feelings toward him must vacillate. Henry's perceptions throughout are those Lear comes to only following his agony on the stormy heath, but his actions frequently fail to suit those perceptions. He is the weak king in a more perplexing sense than the others because it is insufficient to call him unsympathetic when he is invulnerable and sympathetic when he is vulnerable. Far more honest about himself and the nature of his royal prerogatives than Richard II, he at times governs very well, even when he is seemingly secure, and at times he falters. Similarly, his reactions when he is under attack sometimes seem highly creditable and sometimes not. The shifts in appeal to our sympathies are more frequent, but their effects are not so final as in the other plays. Over-all, he emerges as a much better king, but still the weak king—weak because he is human, better because he is trying to govern better. (pp. 89-90)

Henry's innocence is the quality for which he is condemned . . . , but his innocence is what makes him Henry. . . . Through it we see how men of authority in a Christian commonwealth ought to behave. Henry possesses no miraculous powers—only trust, gentleness, and honesty. But these are powers by which men and societies may survive and which are deteriorating in a state increasingly entranced by the illusory practicality of Machiavellian methods.

The strength implicit in Henry's innocence is revealed in the fall and murder of Duke Humphrey in Part 2, an episode in which his actions have been roundly condemned by characters and critics alike. In the face of the many accusations made against the protector early in the second play, Henry has two choices. He can either engage in the Machiavellian practices suggested earlier, or he can agree, as he does, to a trial by Humphrey's peers which he is confident will reveal Humphrey's innocence. . . . The conspirators are also confident that a trial will reveal Humphrey's innocence; hence they feel Humphrey must be murdered. Henry is not guilty of inaction. He protests his faith in Humphrey with great emotion, but the appearance that he is weak results from his inability to use Machiavellian tactics. He instead relies on the legal machinery of his state and his own conviction that right will triumph. He receives a rude shock as a result.

That Henry is disillusioned in Part 2 III. 2 by Humphrey's murder is not surprising. What is surprising is that he does not really change. He continues to be uncynical, trusting, and gentle. Revenge never enters his mind when he banishes Suffolk. He is clearly above revenge. But he is extremely angry and terribly sad. And if he does not change, he does learn. While each of the others is engaged in furthering a deception whereby

his or her cause will be advanced by Humphrey's death, Henry, bewildered with grief, is searching for the reality in the situation—and he finds it. (pp. 98-9)

Throughout the long and angry interchange between Suffolk and Warwick that dominates the middle of this scene, Henry says nothing. Then he speaks four lines which seem almost irrelevant to the situation at hand but are in fact most relevant to it and to the entire trilogy:

> What stronger breastplate than a heart untainted!
> Thrice is he armed that hath his quarrel just,
> And he but naked, though locked up in steel,
> Whose conscience with injustice is corrupted.
>   [*2 Henry VI,* III. ii. 232-35]

The lines are apothegmatic, and the success achieved in keeping Henry sounding human results largely from the near total absence of the sententious in his lines. But his few moral pronouncements are important. Henry's lines here are clearly a response to something, but not to anything the contending Suffolk and Warwick have just been saying. His last previous utterance, some eighty lines earlier, was his memorial to the qualities of the dead duke. During the succeeding quarrel, Henry's thoughts, not the quarrel itself, are what prompt the lines quoted above. Those thoughts must have to do with whether or not it is worth trying to lead the kind of life Humphrey led, since the conclusion stated in the lines is that truth and justice are inherently stronger attributes than falsity and injustice—appearances to the contrary. Thus while others may be content with stratagems and threatened force, Henry resolves to defend himself solely with the "breastplate" of "a heart untainted" in the troublesome days that lie ahead. It is a direct ruling out of both force and deceit from all his endeavors, and is most important in judging Henry as he will later appear.

Henry becomes no saint following these rather saintly lines. He appears from time to time uncertain, frightened, and even paltry. Our sympathies continue to vacillate. The lines quoted above represent only what he has learned from the experiences of his life thus far. The question often implied in commentary about Henry is: "When will he ever learn?" But what can he learn from the behavior of those around him other than to be like them, which constitutionally he could not do even if he wanted to? Rather, he learns from Humphrey and the manner of Humphrey's death that he must be faithful only to truth and justice—or try to be. Like the other kings, he is a man. That is to say, he is weak and will make errors which can only make him look terribly weak as king. But here he has the insight that the sole approach to genuine strength is unceasing adherence to the simplest verities. Such adherence, perhaps, looks easy enough in the stone and wood of medieval statuary, or in plays about ideal kings, but it proves almost impossible for Henry, who is in no way more than human. (pp. 100-01)

The most severe test of audience sympathies toward Henry, as it is the most severe test for Henry, is the opening episode of Part 3. The chief difficulty here is that he seems so utterly craven even though he is rationally so utterly right. A few scenes into the play Shakespeare assigns Henry lines which make his responses in Part 3. I. 1 reasonable and plausible; but in the situation itself he seems helpless, almost crushed by his fear. Our sympathies toward Henry in the scene are certainly divided, but the elements that go into the scene must be considered carefully.

In Hall's chronicle, the events of Part 3. I. 1. never take place. There, following York's victory in battle at Northampton, a parliament attended by York, but not by Henry, proclaims that Henry shall reign for the remainder of his days, to be succeeded by York. Henry, in prison, is forced to accede. Shakespeare makes of this affair of state a personal confrontation between the two sides. York, surrounded by his followers, defiantly sits on Henry's throne, while the Lancastrians in the vestibule angrily demand that he be forcefully removed. The Yorkists thus invite a bloody test within the palace walls to assure their hold, and Clifford is ready to fight them, despite the certain outcome provided by the circumstances. Exeter says if they slay York, his troops will "quickly fly" [3 Henry VI, I. i. 69], but when York is later slain, his forces regroup and subsequently triumph. And there is little possibility here that they can even get at the duke.

Henry, who is the first to express his outrage, is also the first to see the realities of the situation: "Ah, know you not the city favors them, / And they have troops of soldiers at their beck?"[3 Henry VI, I. i. 67-8]. And few could fault his determination to avoid bloodshed in this location. Henry seeks to make headway with verbal exchange, but he is no thunderer and anything but a spellbinder. In political negotiations, as in everything else, he stumbles over his old infirmity: absolute respect for the truth. York handles him with consummate Machiavellian skill. Rather than threaten him—Henry is a passive man but hardly the coward he is made out to be by everyone—York again rehearses his hereditary claim. And Henry, faced with irrefutable facts, can only retreat: "I know not what to say, my title's weak" [3 Henry VI, I.i. 134]. No Machiavellian would so hesitate, but Henry is no Machiavellian. His title is weak! If Henry is to wear the "breastplate" of "a heart untainted," this must be admitted. And it is the confusion over commitment to honesty or crown which gives him the appearance of uncertainty and cowardice through the remainder of the scene. Since Henry's position is not a secure one morally, he does not know how to react. As king of England and head of the House of Lancaster, he has a natural desire to retain his throne and is grateful for Clifford's defiant words. But commitment to truth provokes a terrible dilemma, which the changing sides by the long-loyal Exeter greatly intensifies. That York is doing the very thing for which he here condemns the long-dead Bolingbroke makes no difference to Henry. Both York now and Bolingbroke then are Machiavels, but Henry is dedicated to truth and justice. His instinctive loyalty to his crown and his house is thus powerfully challenged by the fact of his tainted title.

What lies behind Henry's divided response is the whole ugly tale of deception and violence that ended the reign of Richard II and prepared the way, not for the legitimacy of York's claim, but for the total absence of an untainted title in Henry's time. The ruthless act of an earlier Machiavel in a previous age produced the state of affairs Henry is faced with, and its renewal can only result in total chaos—a chaos caused exclusively by human irresponsibility, not Divine Providence. In groping for a solution, Henry is not so much concerned for himself as for his country. His confusion and uncertainty are not fear, but his reaction to the shock of realizing that his breastplate of truth is marred by his own birth, that he is willynilly as corrupt as those around him. At the same time he cannot suddenly throw off the inborn conception of himself as rightful king of England.

Henry's decision to "unnaturally disinherit" his own son is not the result of selfishness and cowardice but a fruitless attempt to right the wrong done Richard II so many years before.

This attempt is quite in keeping with his desire in Part 1 to right the wrong done York's father. But abdicating would do another wrong. As legitimate successor to his father and crowned king of England, he is both de facto and de jure monarch, and he would be breaking his own sworn oaths were he to relinquish the crown. Under duress, he seeks a solution honorable for both houses, though such a solution is no longer possible. . . . Hoping for peace and unity, Henry acts selflessly and against instinct in adopting York as his heir. It is of course a useless gesture since it accomplishes none of its ends. Neither peace nor unity results, and Henry feels very bad after it has been done. Again, the Christian king has been victimized by the Machiavellianism of ambitious men, this time including one who lived well before the king was born. The Bolingbroke of old provokes Henry's dilemma here more than York, and Henry's attempt to resolve it fails both in personal and political terms. (pp. 102-04)

[Henry] is not a bad king who happens to be a good man. He would be as good a king as is humanly possible if men would let him. But they would rather have their kings of stratagem and force, regardless of the accompanying bloodshed and hardship, and they pronounce sadly the doom of a king of peace, honesty, and mercy—who is, they say, unfit to rule. As humans, all kings are weak—and our feelings toward them must vacillate. Most kings refuse to acknowledge this and thus normally are unsympathetic until vulnerable. Henry acknowledges it with his every move, and thus while our superficial feelings fluctuate, even sharply, in the long run (and Henry VI is a "long run") he is the one king who has the capacity to rule well—not a wish-fulfillment king, but a flesh-and-blood king. The point at which we realize this is the point at which our basic sympathies toward him shift. But by that time, the game of king-of-the-hill is in full swing—and in that game Henry possesses no ability and, with occasional lapses, wants none. Each dying Machiavel realizes, if not explicitly the wisdom of Henry's way, at least the folly of his own. (pp. 107-08)

Henry's way is perhaps best illustrated in Part 3 III. 1., in which two gamekeepers capture him and take him to the newly crowned King Edward. Henry here is frequently pictured, in dramatic productions as well as criticism, as bewildered and abjectly forlorn, but he conveys a quite different image to me. His key lines are those made in answer to the first keeper's asking where his crown is:

> My crown is in my heart, not on my head;
> Not decked with diamonds, and Indian stones,
> Nor to be seen. My crown is called content,
> A crown it is that seldom kings enjoy.
>   [3 Henry VI, III. i. 62-5]

More than simply the pastoral wisdom of the exiled Duke Senior in As You Like It, these lines are a political comment on the proper humility required of the Christian king. Henry is as intelligent and resourceful in this scence as he is patient and compassionate. His concerns in having lost his crown are in having lost his freedom to enjoy the land of which he has been the incarnate symbol, in having lost the responsibility which he has sworn to fulfill in the eyes of God, and in having lost the ability to help petitioning subjects:

> No, Harry, Harry, 'tis no land of thine.
> Thy place is filled, thy scepter wrung from thee,
> Thy balm washed off wherewith thou wast anointed.
> No bending knee will call thee Caesar now,
> No humble suitors press to speak for right,
> No, not a man comes for redress of thee;
> For how can I help them, and not myself?
>   [3 Henry VI, III. i. 15-21]

Richard II, acknowledging Bolingbroke's ascendancy at Flint Castle, begins with a similar lament, but he significantly omits the last part. Henry's conception of his function as "Caesar" is that of benefactor and judge. Richard lived mostly in the adulation and ease of majesty, little in its responsibilities. Henry cared little for the ease and had the responsibilities, which he welcomed, largely denied him—well before he was deposed.

Henry's essential relationship with his subjects is briefly enacted in the exchange which follows. He does not plead with them, as might at first be supposed. Rather, he instructs them—and then is compassionate toward their limitations, submissive in the face of their ignorant force. He at first resorts to the interrogatory method of the patient teacher, later to example:

Hen.	But did you never swear, and break an oath?
Keep.	No, never such an oath, nor will not now.
Hen.	Where did you dwell when I was King of England?
Keep.	Here in this country where we now remain.
Hen.	I was anointed King at nine months old.
	My father and my grandfather were Kings,
	And you were sworn true subject unto me.
	And tell me, then, have you not broke your oaths?
Keep.	No, For we were subjects but while you were King.
Hen.	Why, am I dead? Do I not breathe a man?
	Ah, simple men, you know not what you swear!
	Look, as I blow this feather from my face,
	And as the air blows it to me again,
	Obeying with my wind when I do blow
	And yielding to another when it blows,
	Commanded always by the greater gust,
	Such is the lightness of you common men.
	But do not break your oaths, for of that sin
	My mild entreaty shall not make you guilty.
	Go where you will, the King shall be commanded;
	And be you kings. Command, and I'll obey.

[*3 Henry VI*, III. i. 72-93]

Henry's paraphrase of Christ on the cross and his concluding charity and forgiveness should indicate, if nothing else does, that he, not the keepers, is in command of the situation. And his final line—"And be you kings"—lights up the whole play. The way of the Machiavel indeed makes the keepers kings, as much as it makes Edward IV king or Richard of Gloucester king (or Henry Richmond king, though Shakespeare did his utmost to muffle that clear resonance).

But Henry is far from a uniformly ideal figure of wisdom and detachment. Perhaps more than ever before, he is pictured late in Part 3 as resentful at the usurpation of his throne. At the beginning of III. 1 he wishes Margaret well in her appeal for aid from France, despite his feelings about her methods; and his joy at Warwick's defection to the Lancastrian side prompts him in IV. 8 to refer to that Machiavel as "my Hector and my Troy's true hope" [*3 Henry VI*, IV. viii. 25]. Again, our admiration based on his patience and Christian submission is shaken by his desire to be victorious in worldly terms and his joy at finding a worldly champion. Again we find Henry weak. Or, better, again we find him human. The king who could put aside entirely his earthly desires, who could maintain indifference to a crown he has held from birth and is more his right than anyone else's, tainted title or no, would not be a human

king but a superhuman one, typical of the plays in which a king can do no wrong. Henry's rapture at Warwick's presence in III. 1 is similar to his rapture at Suffolk's description of Margaret late in Part 1. Warwick here is as devious in his motives as Suffolk was then. Moreover, now in the pattern of the other plays, the king is less admirable when he is less vulnerable and more admirable when he is more vulnerable. At this moment of seeming recovery in Henry's fortunes he is weak by his own Christian standard in flattering Warwick and weaker still in yielding Warwick kingly prerogatives; but when challenging Clifford and instructing the keepers, he is anything but weak.

In Henry's final appearance, he is murdered by Richard, now duke of Gloucester.... The episode represents the murder of "pity, love, and fear" in political life by cold, ruthless pragmatism, but it is Richard who makes this explicit following the murder. (pp. 108-11)

Henry dies asking God's forgiveness for his own sins and pardon for Richard, which may be in character but is surprising nevertheless. Imagine the dying York forgiving Margaret or the dying Clifford and Warwick forgiving Richard. Henry does not speak bitterly and his words betray no irony. They are a mark of benevolence beyond anything else we see in these plays. He forgives one of the worst villains in Shakespeare. No one does as much for Iago, or even the dying Edmund, who so desperately wants to be forgiven. But Richard at the start of his bloody rise is forgiven by the holiest man he kills. (pp. 111-12)

Even the worst of the Machiavels have heretofore paid lip-service to the old Christian morality. But not Richard. He is refreshing to some in killing Henry the way he does, partly because he has put aside even the façade of that old morality; it is this new freedom from pretense that carries him along so much farther than earlier, lesser Machiavels like his father York. After all the pretenses and self-deceptions we have witnessed going all the way back to the Temple Garden scene (*1 Henry VI* II. 4), we are grateful for his underlying honesty, which takes the shape here of undisguised adherence to Machiavellian means. It is his proud assertion that he has successfully suppressed all human feeling which allows his disdain for even the formalities of Christian sentiment and the conventions of honorable behavior.... And it is a long time in *Richard III* before that quality in Richard is finally tested. His father led the way, but the struggle in York's nature with the modicum of honor he possessed kept getting in the way and finally destroyed him. Richard is the first one who seems fully able to deny that Christian (or human) motives need deter him in the least.

There is no doubt that a part of us is with Richard in this scene. A part of us is gratified to see unvarnished evil, so vital and engaging, destroy the good king, who in the final analysis perhaps is something of a bore. But it is that part of us which can temporarily shut out the vivid images of a strangled lord, a slaughtered child, and even the innocent life's blood that spurts out on Richard's dagger in the scene before us. It is that part of us which can temporarily shut out compassion. And the temptation to be with Richard is great because humanity and compassion tend to be a bore, having no guide or means of operation other than seemingly impractical, certainly tedious, moral virtues. Above all, acknowledgement of human response also involves that which we wish to deny most of all—human weakness. Richard offers an escape from the essential burdens of life, as *The Prince* did to a new, spirited

Renaissance youth reacting against the restrictions imposed by a medieval view of man's existence. (pp. 112-13)

The villain in *Henry VI* is not the king's humanity. It is the inhumanity, or the struggle toward inhumanity, of his nobles. And in the presence of that inhumanity Henry's inevitable human weaknesses drag him down. But a Henry VI might also overcome those inevitable human weaknesses. His reign could succeed through his mercy, truth, and justice—but he would have to be supported by subjects equally human and willing to face their limitations honestly. Henry's lords seek other means to deal with their limitations. They reject mercy, truth, and justice in favor of power achieved through force and deceit. By rejecting the Christian virtues in favor of newer, seemingly more practical methods of political behavior, they bring about a state of affairs in which the worst inherent human weaknesses prevail. (p. 114)

Unless we recognize in the behavior of the Machiavels our own political disposition, which is of course quite possible, we are likely to be more frustrated at *3 Henry VI* than at the end of the others. The Machiavellian victory is clear. We are not left in a state of divided sympathies. In retrospect, there is nothing to consider but the whole frightful cacophony all over again. Nothing is likely to occur to us that is not readily apparent while it is happening. There seems nowhere to go from here, and though the plays follow on to a redemption in Henry Richmond, that is a redemption necessarily rooted in Tudor political propaganda. The greatness of *Richard III* hardly lies in its ending. With all Henry VI's virtuous qualities, one cannot construct an image of him reigning successfully in this world. No man has a better chance, perhaps, but that still does not make him plausible as a leader of those who refuse to yield their greed and duplicity. The Christian king cannot win with a Machiavellian nobility, and there is little chance of that nobility changing its ways, as there was little chance of that parallel actual nobility of the 1590s changing its ways.

The Henry VI plays are written in anger at political realities as Shakespeare and his audience knew them. Gradually both would become sufficiently inured to those realities to think that they might serve better ends than they serve here. The plays which follow suggest the sad acknowledgment by late sixteenth-century Englishmen that in one form or another Machiavellianism was there to stay. (p. 115)

Michael Manheim, "The Meek King," in his The Weak King Dilemma in the Shakespearean History Play, *Syracuse University Press, 1973, pp. 76-115.*

DAVID M. BERGERON (essay date 1977)

[Bergeron explores Shakespeare's use of the dramatic device of the play-within-the-play in 3 Henry VI *as a structural or thematic preliminary for later developments in the drama. He identifies four episodes where characters act out roles before an onstage audience—the ritual killing of York, the tableau of the father who has killed his son and the son who has killed his father, Henry's imagined scene of Margaret at the court of Lewis of France, and Edward's wooing of Lady Grey—and maintains that each of these instances of "the play-within" demonstrates Shakespeare's awareness of his artistry, even at this early stage in his career, and further contributes to the thematics of the entire play. Other critics who have focused on the play-within-the-play and additional elements of structure in the* Henry VI *trilogy include Hereward T. Price (1951), Muriel C. Bradbrook (1951), A. C. Hamilton (1961-62), and Charles R. Forker (1965).]*

Critical attention to the common dramatic device of the play-within-the-play has focused on such plays as *The Taming of the Shrew, Love's Labour's Lost, A Midsummer Night's Dream,* and *Hamlet;* seldom is one reminded that the history plays share this device.... And yet, in light of Shakespeare's obvious experimentation in his early plays it would be surprising indeed if there were not some evidence of his use of the play-within-the-play in the histories. I argue that there is such evidence in *3 Henry VI,* one of Shakespeare's earliest plays.

A common denominator through many of the histories is the idea of the "player king," which is but a variation of the play metaphor—the acting out of a role within the historical frame. Prince Hal, Richard II, and Richard III come immediately to mind, as each performs a role that disarms or confuses those around him, though Richard II is less aware and more self-deluded than the others. Who can forget Richard III's stunning performance in the wooing of Anne, a performance so successful that it startles the actor? The epitome may be in III. vii, where Richard aloft between two bishops first refuses the crown and then reluctantly accepts it; in this instance he and Buckingham have stage-managed the whole scene. Perhaps one of the most artistically self-conscious moments in the use of the play metaphor comes in II. iv, of *I Henry IV,* in which Hal and Falstaff assume roles, then exchange them, the whole episode pointing to the relationship of Hal to his father and to Falstaff. Surely this moment qualifies as a play-within-the-play as we benefit from watching the stage audience observe the performance. While no events in *3 Henry VI* closely resemble the ones mentioned here, I believe that at least four episodes partake of some of the traditional qualities of the play-within-the-play. I do not mean to imply some necessary or inevitable evolution from this play to the early comedies, but rather I propose to examine *3 Henry VI* alone in order to explore how the device contributes to the play.

Two of the four scenes deal with death; the other two illustrate the drive toward love and power. The first is I. iv, the ritual killing of York by Queen Margaret and others. (pp. 37-8)

The ritualistic slaying of York is both a parody of a coronation, which he had anticipated, and a parallel to the Crucifixion, an idea hinted at in Holinshed but richly expanded and embellished by the dramatist. Margaret's principal speech [*3 Henry VI,* I. iv. 66-108], is an orgy of accusation, touching all the nerve ends of York's sensitive spirit. She makes him stand on a molehill, while observing that he "raught at mountains with outstretched arms" [I. iv 68]. She chides him for his "preachment of . . . high descent" [I. iv. 72], an echo of accusations against Jesus for his insistence on holy lineage. But the pace quickens when Margaret begins her litany of denigration of York's sons: the "wanton Edward," the "lusty George," and "that valiant crookback prodigy, / Dicky your boy . . ." [I. iv. 74-6]—the same sons whose heroism York had praised in the first part of the scene. Those harsh words of Margaret are as nothing, however, compared to her offering York the napkin dipped in the blood of his son Rutland, earlier killed by Clifford in I. iii. She gives York this bloody napkin "to dry [his] cheeks withal" [I. iv. 83], just as the dying Jesus was offered a sop of vinegar, in each instance the gesture savagely intensifies the pain. Margaret's theatrical bag of tricks includes this most cruel stage prop. But that is not the final insult; she also produces a paper crown, which she puts on York's head: "A crown for York! and, lords, bow low to him" [I. iv. 94]. The mocking and the crown again parallel the Crucifixion, but the paper crown even undercuts the image of the martyr's crown of thorns.

What a falling-off from Richard's earlier comment to his father: "How sweet a thing it is to wear a crown, / within whose circuit is Elysium" [I. ii. 29-30]. Step by step, Margaret strips York of dignity and humiliates him—death is all that remains.

Tortured almost beyond belief, York nevertheless summons the last measure of his strength and lashes at Margaret with the only weapon he has—his tongue. (Obviously the analogy with the Crucifixion no longer holds.) York captures the spirit of drama as he insists: "This cloth thou dipp'dst in blood of my sweet boy, / And I with tears do wash the blood away / Keep thou the napkin . . ." [I. iv. 157-59]. He also returns the crown: "There, take the crown, and with the crown my curse" [I. iv. 164]. Divesting himself of these properties, York claims that even his foes in generations to come will say of the event, "'Alas, it was a piteous deed!'" [I. iv. 163].

On the stage at that moment we get just such a response from Northumberland, who remarks: "Beshrew me but his passion moves me so / That hardly can I check my eyes from tears" [I. iv. 150-51]. And later, "Had he been the slaughterman to all my kin, / I should not for my life but weep with him" [I. iv. 169-70]. These comments are, it seems to me, the inevitable response from an audience and the perspective which we in the theater surely must have. Caught in the vortex between the suffering York and the perverse Clifford and Margaret, Northumberland assumes the spectator role, somewhat detached but emotionally involved. In the theater we become interested in his response to the event. Interestingly, it is Clifford and Margaret who stab York; Northumberland does nothing, though

*Part III. Act I. Scene iii. Clifford, Rutland and his Tutor,
and Soldiers. By James Northcote (n.d.).*

one can easily imagine his turning away, helpless and pained. So do we.

In another episode, King Henry in II. v, functions as audience to the representation of a son who has killed his father and a father who has killed his son. Drained of the immediate theatrical savagery of I. iv, this event nevertheless constitutes a tableau statement on the theme of war and death. Unnecessary to the narrative development of the play, it reinforces the tone of the larger play by throwing into relief another graphic statement of the ravages and ironies of war.

Henry enters alone, escaping the battle, and says, "Here on this molehill will I sit me down" [II. v. 14], perhaps the dramatist's intentional ironic echo of York forced to stand on the molehill in I. iv. In any event, Margaret and Clifford have sent him away from battle, "swearing both / They prosper best of all when I am thence" [II. v. 17-18]. But Henry wishes, "Would I were dead, if God's good will were so, / For what is in this world but grief and woe?" [II. v. 19-20]. What he witnesses shortly thereafter is but another example of the grief and woe of the world, but not before he has waxed enthusiastic about the life of the "homely swain." The illusion of the idyllic life of the shepherd is shattered by the reality of war, as Henry in his soliloquy demonstrates again his inability to reconcile conflicting demands of the world. He would be saint and shepherd, but his office demands that he be king and warrior.

Presumably seated in the center of the stage, Henry's reverie is broken by the appearance of the Son bearing in his arms the body of his father. Thus the play-within-the-play begins. We in the theater are as interested in Henry's reaction as in the tableau itself, for he is not passive audience but instead he responds to what he sees. Job-like himself, he can readily understand and sympathize with the little drama that unfolds. The form and order of the play-within belie the chaos implicit in its subject matter, as in the larger play Shakespeare gives artistic shape to massive disorder. (pp. 39-41)

This tableau, a play-within-the-play, is in a sense a dumb show with words. Its dramatic stasis, symbolic quality, anonymous characters (with the obvious exception of Henry who is spectator), and formal structure suggest some of the characteristic features of dumb shows. This play-within is grounded on a structure of three as the two characters on either side of the stage are joined by the audience (Henry) in the middle. The dramatic movement is also tripartite: discovery, lamentation, and departure. Interestingly, such a structure is found in the total context of the scene as Henry discovers himself alone and reveals his longings, endures the lamentations of the tableau, and finally departs when his son and Margaret arrive and urge him to flee with the enemy hard on their heels [II. v. 125-33]. Therefore, I argue that in this instance the play-within-the-play not only underscores the theme of war and death but also imitates the dramatic structure of the whole scene.

Of a much different order is the moment in III. i that constitutes an imagined play-within-the-play, namely Henry's vision of Warwick and Margaret vying for the support of the French king [III. i. 28-54]. While this may strain the point slightly, Henry clearly has a dramatic sense of the anticipated event, an event that is dramatically realized in the play itself in [III. iii. 1-161]. In III. i, Henry enters disguised and is observed by two "Keepers," who overhear him; thus Henry cannot know that there is a type of audience listening to his soliloquy.

Henry notes in his speech that though Warwick is a "subtle orator" [III. i. 33], one mustn't rule out the possibility that

Margaret may win the King's support: "Her sighs will make a batt'ry in his breast; / Her tears will pierce into a marble heart" [III. i. 37-8]. Henry appreciates the likelihood of dramatic conflict between these antagonists. And in his vision he sets the stage, in an arrangement similar to II. v: "She on his [Lewis'] left side, craving aid for Henry; / He [Warwick] on his right, asking a wife for Edward" [III. i. 43-4]. Henry contrasts their techniques: "She weeps, and says her Henry is deposed; / He smiles, and says his Edward is installed" [III. i. 45-6]. The likely success for Warwick is predicated on Henry's understanding that "she's come to beg; Warwick, to give" [III. i. 42.].

Henry's reverie is interrupted by the Keepers, who finally lead him away. But Henry's imagined scene is correct, as shown in III. iii, except that Warwick's cause is crippled by Edward's own arrangement of marriage; thus Margaret actually wins the support of Lewis and Warwick also. But the little play-within-the-play here demonstrates the intermingling of love and power as forces in shaping events. More strikingly, it clearly anticipates a later dramatic scene that fulfills what is only envisioned here. This corresponds well with Shakespeare's formal structure of the whole play and is another sign of his self-conscious artistry as a scene is first played out on the stage of Henry's mind before it takes shape in the real play world, as if one is the rehearsal for the other.

Robert Ornstein writes: "The play within the play in *Part III* actually begins when Richard and Clarence play audience and comic interlocutors to Edward's wooing of Elizabeth." The episode in III. ii does constitute a play-within-the play; but if what I have argued thus far is valid, then the dramatic device appears much sooner. As is so often the case, the stage audience here is not passive but rather participates in the event, in this instance through witty, sometimes cynical asides. The whole arrangement may remind one of audience response to the Pageant of the Nine Worthies in *Love's Labour's Lost* or to the Pyramus and Thisby interlude in *A Midsummer's Night's Dream*. But here, of course, Richard and Clarence do not drive the "actors," Edward and Elizabeth Grey, out of character.

The thematic issue is again the relationship of love and power. Lady Grey comes seeking to repossess the lands of her slain husband, and Edward finds this a golden opportunity to press the cause of love (or as it seems for a while, lust). (The scene has a number of features to be echoed later in the confrontation of Angelo and Isabella in *Measure for Measure*.) Edward's every move against a naive, then resistant, Elizabeth is commented on by Richard and Clarence, who finally step aside [III. ii. 33-5] and view the scene from the perspective of an audience. Aware of the type of performance he is about to give, Edward says: "Lords, give us leave. I'll try this widow's wit" [III. ii. 33]. Edward's process of temptation, for which he has met his match, provokes such comments from his brothers: Richard, "He plies her hard, and much rain wears the marble" [III. ii. 50]; Clarence, "As red as fire? Nay then, her wax must melt" [III. ii. 51]. Their remarks also underscore the difficulty and resistance that Edward finds: Richard, "The widow likes him not; she knits her brows" [III. ii. 82]; Clarence, "He is the bluntest wooer in Christendom" [III. ii. 83]. The widow Elizabeth is ultimately successful against the force of Edward, vying for her soul and body, and agrees to become his queen (one thinks ahead perhaps to Anne who could not triumph against the persuasion of Richard in *Richard III*). Edward, unaware that spectators have watched and commented on his performance, says to his brothers, "Brothers, you muse

what chat we two have had" [III. ii. 109]. Of course, they do not, having heard and seen everything. They can, however, appreciate the dramatic irony of the situation. The deadly sin of Edward is overcome by the moral virtue of Elizabeth, a process noted by the comic interlocutors who share the perspective of the theater audience.

As the scene closes, we hear Richard's famous, revealing, and terrifying soliloquy [III. ii. 124-95], which sets the stage for all his future actions. In it he deals with his deformity, his lack of love, and the consequent insatiable thirst for power and the crown—his new Jerusalem. He notes also: "Why, I can smile, and murder whiles I smile" [III. ii. 182]; "And wet my cheeks with artificial tears, / And frame my face to all occasions" [III. ii. 184-85]. Richard the perverse actor truly begins to emerge, and most of the remainder of the play will now focus on his actions. One observes that from this moment there are no more plays-within-the-play; there can be none, for Richard has moved to the center of the stage and becomes the highly self-conscious artist. Shakespeare no longer requires the structural or thematic preliminaries of a play-within-the-play. But in a sense, the four episodes discussed here indirectly prepare the way for Richard by calling attention to the manipulative power of drama. Richard—dramatist, stage manager, actor, and even audience—assists Shakespeare's purpose of dramatic structure in the remainder of *3 Henry VI* and certainly in *Richard III*. It seems especially important in a history play, where the parameters are established by historical fact or source, that the dramatist call attention to the power of men to shape events and illustrate also his own artistic craft.

The device of the play-within-the-play emphasizes the dramatist's awareness and control of his artistry as in part it shows the dramatist looking at his own artifice. The plays-within in *3 Henry VI* contribute symbolically and dramatically to the effect of the play. The ritual slaying of York may be a terrifying emblem of the irrationality and inhumanity of war, but it also becomes for York's sons a rallying cry in their attempt to avenge the father's death. It is a justification for what they do to capture the throne; thus ironically Margaret has contributed to the ultimate downfall of Henry and the defeat of her cause. (Surely the scene of York's death is several times remembered in *Richard III*.) The tableau of II. v reinforces the war theme, as it also underscores the importance of family relationships throughout the play (indeed throughout all the histories). Each instance of the play-within-the-play raises yet again the problem of appearance and reality, reflecting this issue in the larger play. Henry's vision in III. i and the reality of III. ii help predict future events as Shakespeare gives us microcosmic dramatizations of what is to come. These plays-within-the-play in *3 Henry VI* reveal more fully than elsewhere in Shakespeare's early plays the serious and even tragic potentiality of such a dramatic device; they provide the other side of the coin of the comic and entertaining interludes of *Taming of the Shrew*, *Love's Labour's Lost*, and *A Midsummer Night's Dream*. (pp. 42-5)

David M. Bergeron, "The Play-within-the-Play in '3 Henry VI'," in Tennessee Studies in Literature, *Vol. XXII, 1977, pp. 37-45.*

JOHN D. COX (essay date 1978)

[*Cox attributes the often-noted ambiguities in* 3 Henry VI *to Shakespeare's dramatic use of certain elements found in medieval mystery plays. Whereas some critics have maintained that Shakespeare borrowed from medieval literature in order to reinforce orthodox doctrines in his* Henry VI *trilogy—such as the concept of the Tudor myth put forth by Hermann Ulrici (1839), E. M. W. Tillyard (1944), and M. M. Reese (1961)—Cox argues that the dramatist uses analogies from the medieval literary tradition, specifically, the medieval mystery or salvation play, in order to create an "ambivalence and uneasiness about his characters." Cox points to those scenes in* 3 Henry VI—Act I, Scene i *and Act I, Scene iv—in which York is presented first as a Lucifer-figure and then as the martyred Christ, and at one moment Henry is paralleled with God and the next is shown as a weak, ineffective king, in order to substantiate his thesis that Shakespeare was concerned less with dramatizing divine or providential will than with portraying the realities of temporal order on earth. Thus, according to Cox, the uncertainty and ambiguity of characterization which Shakespeare presents through a seeming misuse of his Christian archetypes are deliberately designed elements in his effort to dramatize political events in a "human historical context." For further commentary on Shakespeare's use of medieval literature, see the excerpts by S. L. Bethell (1951), Muriel C. Bradbrook (1951), Irving Ribner (1965), and Robert Ornstein (1972).]*

[It] is certainly true, as several critics have noticed, that *3 Henry VI* is a play without heroes—that is, it lacks characters of the stature of Talbot in *1 Henry VI* or Humphrey Duke of Gloucester in the second play, who unambiguously engage our sympathy. Though a few characters successively win our uncertain pity in *3 Henry VI,* no character ever has our wholehearted admiration and approval. It seems possible, therefore, that the play's peculiarity should be attributed to the ambivalence it invokes rather than to the quality of its plotting. If such an attribution can indeed be sustained, it is surely no cause for condemning *3 Henry VI,* given the modern interest in ambiguity, ambivalence, and "the dramatist's manipulation of response" in general. I would suggest that in *3 Henry VI* the ambiguity can pretty certainly be traced to Shakespeare's combining various elements of his dramatic heritage for the purpose of holding the mirror up to history, that is, of revealing the nature of temporal order in human affairs. When *3 Henry VI* is viewed in this way, moreover, it can be seen not as an anomaly but as a paradigm of the Shakespearean history play.

Let us first consider the most traditional aspects of Shakespeare's dramaturgy, for in shaping our attitudes toward his characters he appeals to some remarkably archaic models. In the opening lines of *3 Henry VI* we notice an unambiguous smearing of the Yorkists. Though this is not inconsistent with the attitude we have been invited to take toward Richard Duke of York in the first two plays, the process is carried to unprecedented lengths at this point. The clan gathers in Westminster Hall, the very seat of parliamentary and royal authority, where they have "broken in by force" [*3 Henry VI,* I. i. 29]. Their boldness is heightened by the reason for this gathering: to celebrate their first taste of successful rebellion, the Yorkist victory at St. Albans. They are blackened further by dramatically effective but literally impossible details as they display their fresh battle trophies: dripping swords whose victims are mordantly identified, and the newly severed head of Somerset, gruesomely rolling about the floor while York and his youngest son address it inhumanly:

Richard.	Speak thou for me and tell them what I did.
York.	Richard hath best deserved of all my sons.
	But is your grace dead, my Lord of Somerset?
	[I. i. 16-18]

By means of a few carefully contrived details Shakespeare thus succeeds in winning our wholehearted disapprobation of the Yorkists as the play opens. He adds another dimension to our natural repugnance, moreover, when the action begins to follow the pattern of the opening scene in all the extant mystery cycles: the fall of Lucifer. This happens when the Duke of York mounts the dais of King Henry's empty throne and takes his seat. York's gesture is a symbolic move of immense importance and unimaginable effrontery by any standard, but its dramatic significance in *3 Henry VI* can be better appreciated by its closest stage analogue in Elizabethan England. In the scriptural plays the usurper is Lucifer who boldly occupies the throne of God in his absence. York attaches himself to this paradigm of cosmic rebellion by virtue of the commonplace notion that the king was God's earthly representative and by the dramaturgical parallels between this secular scene and its sacred forebear. (pp. 43-4)

In the Chester cycle Lucifer and Lightborne (who later rebels as well) gracefully hymn God's praises along with the other angels until God leaves to "take my trace / And see this blesse in every tower"; then Lucifer suddenly makes his unexpected move. This kind of dissembling typifies York above all other characters in the first two parts of *Henry VI*: "A day will come when York shall claim his own"; "Then, York, be still awhile, till time do serve" [*2 Henry VI,* I. i. 239, 240]. In the Towneley play Lucifer confidently claims to possess God's throne by both right and might:

> If that ye will behold me right,
> This maistre longys to me.
> Agans my grete might
> May [no]thing stand then be.

York likewise mounts King Henry's throne with the intention "to take possession of my right" [*3 Henry VI,* I. i. 44], and his precaution in concealing soldiers throughout the hall clearly signals his belief that he can make good his right by might. "By words or blows here let us win our right," he urges [I. i. 37]. Still another parallel in the old plays is the debate that occupies the *Boni* and *Mali Angeli* ["Virtuous and Evil Angels"] after Lucifer has taken his wrongful place. The long debate that rages between Yorkists and Lancastrians in the first scene of *3 Henry VI* is a clear analogue to the celestial debate about Lucifer's right to sit in God's throne. In all these respects, then, *3 Henry VI* begins like the cosmic history of salvation; we see a repugnant and hypocritical usurper; he boldly occupies the empty throne of his seemingly rightful superior; he claims his right to do so; he is urged on by his conniving lieutenants; he argues his case at length with those who believe he has acted wrongly. Though Shakespeare took the suggestion for this scene from the chronicles of Hall and Holinshed, it seems unlikely that he would have been unmindful of such a striking dramaturgical tradition as he sought to turn the interminable chronicle narratives into an imposing dramatic confrontation.

Though there is much that demands attention in the opening scene of *3 Henry VI* to qualify the significance of the medieval analogue, it will be helpful first to consider another such analogue that appears at the end of the first act. Importantly this scene again involves the Duke of York, but this time in his defeat rather than his triumph. Again the scriptural allusion serves to emphasize our natural reaction, this time a feeling of surprise at the reversal of fortune in York's pitiable death. The gross inequity of several combatants against one, the deliberate mental torture of taunting him with the news of his young son's murder, the unqueenly cruelty of Margaret, York's pious frame of mind in death—all these factors weigh heavily against the Lancastrians in this incredibly savage scene. If the Yorkists have also earned our disapprobation by taunting a fallen enemy as the play opened, they at least waited until he was dead.

But the archetypal dramatic analogue of York's death contributes more than anything to our feeling that nothing in York's life became him like the leaving it. This analogue is suggested by a passing reference in Holinshed:

> Some write that the duke was taken alive, and in derision caused to stand upon a molehill, on whose head they put a garland in steed of a crowne, which they had fashioned and made of sedges or bulrushes; and having so crowned him with that garland, they kneeled downe afore him (as the Jews did unto Christ) in scorne, saieng to him; Haile king without rule, haile king without heritage, haile duke and prince without people or possessions.

Among several possible versions of how York died, this is the one that Shakespeare chose to dramatize (Hall makes no mention of it), and he could hardly have done so in ignorance of the well-developed medieval tradition depicting the buffeting and scourging of Christ. Like the fall of Lucifer, this event is found in all the extant mystery cycles, and its treatment produced some of the most effective scenes in medieval drama. . . . If our natural sympathy is engaged for York in this incredible ordeal, our sympathy can only be heightened by the play's dramaturgical allusion to the archetypal innocent sufferer.

Whatever else can be said about York's medieval archetypes in 3 Henry VI, it is clear that they pose difficult questions for an orthodox interpretation of the play. Thirty years ago the question of how to deal with the cosmic significance of the first scene would have been answered by the nature of the parallel itself. Assuming that Shakespeare's histories were staged versions of the Tudor homilies or mirrors of Elizabethan policy, older critics naturally tended to emphasize whatever orthodox elements they could find in the plays and to let their interpretation go at that. Indeed, Tillyard's dissatisfaction with 3 Henry VI may have derived from the difficulties it presents for homiletic assumptions. If we assume, for instance, that the cosmic analogue of the first scene is designed to reinforce our disapproval of wilful disobedience and rebellion, we are at a loss to interpret the Christlike death of the Luciferian rebel three scenes later. H. M. Richmond concludes that the scene is "savagely ironic," so that "every clashing analogy to the death of Christ drives home" the lesson that York is being repaid for a life that "has been evil in the highest degree" [see excerpt above, 1967]. This seems an unlikely conclusion for an audience to draw in the theater, however, since the dominant effect of the scene on stage is the pity of human suffering. In light of this effect, the evil of York's life is, if anything, qualified rather than intensified by the allusion to Christ's death.

A similar dilemma is posed by another possible medieval parallel in 3 Henry VI: the slaughter of the innocents. Shortly before York's death we witness the murder of his twelve-year-old son, the Earl of Rutland, whom Shakespeare portrays as an unarmed schoolboy. His murderer, young Clifford, ludicrously claims to be avenging the death of old Clifford, who was killed in fair fight at the battle of St. Albans. This grandiose excuse for attacking a child may owe something to the debased idea of heroism that characterizes Herod's soldiers in the medieval plays. In the Chester cycle, for instance, the *Primus*

Miles ["principal soldier"] initially balks at Herod's command to slay the infants, until he discovers that the order concerns thousands of babies, not just one or two, for this news appeals to his warped sense of epic derring-do. But if the scene in *3 Henry VI* does allude to the slaughter of the innocents, it creates difficulties for orthodox expectations, since the Yorkists later repeat the same crime when they murder Prince Edward (5.5). This time the scene includes a distraught mother, Queen Margaret, who was another feature of the medieval plays, as Shakespeare remembered when he had Henry V threaten the citizens of Harfleur that if they did not surrender they would see their

> naked infants spitted upon pikes,
> Whiles the mad mothers with their howls confused
> Do break the clouds, as did the wives of Jewry
> At Herod's bloody-hunting slaughtermen.
>
> [*Henry V*, III. iii. 38-41]

If Bethlehem innocents appear on both sides of the conflict in *3 Henry VI*, whom are we to execrate as Herod? When the slaughter of the innocents appears again in *Macbeth* Shakespeare brilliantly uses it as part of a theme of outraged innocence that runs throughout the play ("'Macbeth does murder sleep'—the innocent sleep"); but in *3 Henry VI* he creates the equivalent of a child-murdering Macduff as well.

Far from reinforcing orthodox doctrine, then, Shakespeare's use of medieval analogues only has an unsettling effect, creating ambivalence and uneasiness about his characters rather than allowing us to praise or condemn them with confidence. This effect is also achieved naturally, of course, by portraying both sides as equally brutal, but the medieval allusions immeasurably heighten the ambiguity. (pp. 44-8)

If York's bold occupation of King Henry's throne has a Luciferian distinctness about it, the effect is blurred long before York's death: it begins to lose its clarity almost as soon as Henry comes on stage. What God had always done in Henry's situation was to hurl the usurper from the pageant's heaven to its hell mouth by his very reappearance on the scene: this was the true consequence of rebellion in the purity of its sacred archetype. But what Shakespeare gives us is very different: the supposedly godlike King Henry is all too human to handle the situation effectively. He challenges York bravely enough at first, but as soon as his partisans take up the same line Henry suddenly and inexplicably (one is tempted to say perversely) appeals to them to be patient. The impatient Clifford's answer falls just short of insolence as he tellingly contrasts the King with Henry the Fifth: "Patience is for poltroons such as [York]. / He durst not sit there had your father lived" [*3 Henry VI*, I. i. 62-3]. Clifford's manner exposes the King's lack of authority even further, and at the same time his retort introduces an undeniable reality about the dynamics of temporal power. For in his peremptory action against a nascent rebellion inspired by York's father (Richard Earl of Cambridge), Henry V had demonstrated—as he had in his French campaign—that the king's legal right is inextricably bound up with his ability to make it good in fact. This ability is clearly lacking in his unfortunate son.

The effect of crossing audience expectation in the first scene of *3 Henry VI*, then, is not necessarily subversive; rather, the effect is to focus attention on the failure of temporal order to conform to its sacred archetypes where we most expect it to—and want it to. York should be treated like Lucifer but he isn't, because Henry—although he is God's representative on earth—is not God. Though the Elizabethan legal doctrine of the king's two bodies is usually associated with *Richard II,* I would suggest that an imaginative equivalent of the doctrine informed Shakespeare's view of history from the beginning, and that *3 Henry VI* is best understood in light of a contrast between sacred and secular order. If the office of the king is to represent God on earth, it does not follow that every man who is given that office will fulfill it with equal ability. Henry's inability, for example, to establish his right by forceful command of the situation is matched by his ineffectual attempt to defend his legal right.... What follows is the desperate compromise in which Henry disinherits his son in order to retain the throne for his lifetime; this is a move not only ungodlike but politically suicidal, as Queen Margaret incisively points out.... By the end of the first scene Henry has been abandoned by his wife ..., by his son, and by all of his followers except Exeter, who had candidly admitted his disbelief in the King's inheritance. The play's promising start, with its suggestion of a clear-cut moral opposition, has dissolved into the ambiguities and frustrations of power politics—a dissolution Shakespeare effectively creates by inducing our ambivalence and uneasiness about his characters.

A closer look at the ... first scene of *3 Henry VI* thus suggests that whatever skepticism we feel appears to be directed toward humanity's ability to govern itself perfectly. Such a skepticism is not only orthodox (as the doctrine of original sin indicates), it is also consistent with sixteenth-century humanism. More's *Utopia* is a good example, since it is explicitly concerned with the perfect state of a commonwealth. The philosopher Hythlodaeus in More's work is so skeptical about the possibility of good order in real kingdoms that he will have nothing to do with them, preferring to spin yarns about the ideal commonwealths he has discovered on fantastic sea voyages. Hythlodaeus' interlocutor, persona More, is less dubious than his philosophical companion, but only slightly less so; he argues that the philosopher should serve a real prince because "what you cannot turn to good you must make as little bad as you can." This formulation suggests that political order is a process of continual reform—a struggle against inevitable decline rather than the establishment of anything positive. If Shakespeare's Henry VI had a little of More's wisdom he would clearly be a better king, since he does not effectively combat the evil in his kingdom, much less promote anything good. This is not to say that Henry is an evil man himself; on the contrary, he seems unusually good, but his unsympathetic lack of authority continually compromises our inclination to side with him in the face of overweening Yorkist opposition. (pp. 49-52)

If this interpretation of order in a temporal kingdom subverts anything, it is the myth of perfect order in which every move can be exactly weighed and calculated in the balances of God's eternal direction. This kind of order cannot be imposed on the *Henry VI* plays, as several critics have convincingly shown, but to demonstrate the failure of such an order in Shakespeare's depiction of history is not necessarily to prove that he was radically skeptical or Machiavellian: it only suggests that he did not view history as simplistically as a propagandist like John Foxe. (pp. 52-3)

Like the first scene, virtually everything else in *3 Henry VI* is designed to focus attention on the process of decaying order in the kingdom. The opening confrontation between Henry and York is finally settled by an appeal to effective power when York signals his concealed soldiers to show themselves [s.d., I. i. 169]. This way of settling the question exactly parallels Lord Talbot's tactic at the Castle of Auvergne when he con-

cealed his soldiers to prevent a surprise capture [*I Henry VI,* II. iii.]. But this parallel only serves to show how far we have come since *I Henry VI.* Talbot had used the precaution to prove that the substance of his heroic reputation was in his deeds; but York uses it to turn the balance of power in his favor as he challenges the very sovereign whom Talbot had ceremoniously acknowledged with "submissive loyalty of heart" [*I Henry VI,* III. iv. 10]. Whereas Talbot's use of this tactic won our admiration for his soldierly defense of the order established by Henry V, York emblematizes his contribution to the kingdom's disarray with a show of force against Henry V's son in the Parliament House, the seat and symbol of legislative order. This assault on the kingdom's source of authority is possible because, again, the King is not a perfect representative of eternal order but shares the human weakness that makes politics (i.e., maintaining order in a temporal kingdom) the bastard child of the Fall.

Moreover, Henry's chief enemy, the Duke of York, shares the same weakness, as we see not only in his self-seeking ambition but also in his pitiable death where the unexpected archetype is the suffering of Christ. If the King is not God, it follows that his opponents are not devils, but men, and this includes York as well. The pity we feel for him is for a human being under extreme duress, no matter how disruptive he has been. The distant comparison with the human suffering of Christ is therefore appropriate and effective in offsetting a tendency to identify York absolutely with a principle of evil in the play. Evil there is, to be sure—even Henry's weakness has a part in it—but no one has a premium on it, and very few characters are utterly without redeeming human features. This is not to say that York exhibits the kind of saintliness that Henry does in his death, but only to suggest that the human historical context is always emphasized in the play, no matter what may be put forward in the way of archetypes from the drama of salvation history. York would be more convincingly Christlike if he patiently kept quiet throughout his torture; but our engagement with his suffering is qualified by our detachment from his vindictiveness, bitterness, and disappointed ambition when he finally decides to give his assailants a tongue-lashing [*3 Henry VI,* I. iv. 111-68]. If his angry outburst reduces our inclination to see his suffering as transcendent, we are also reminded that the events we witness have their origin and reach their fruition in "this breathing world" [*Richard III,* I. i. 21]. In other words, the ambiguities that surround York's death are in decorum with the kind of play in which he appears: a history play. (pp. 53-5)

John D. Cox, "'3 Henry VI': Dramatic Convention and the Shakespearean History Play," in Comparative Drama, *Vol. 12, No. 1, Spring, 1978, pp. 42-60.*

LARRY S. CHAMPION   (essay date 1979)

[*Champion reconstructs the dramatic development of the* Henry VI *trilogy and argues that* 3 Henry VI *is structurally superior to* 1 *and* 2 Henry VI. *He demonstrates that the multiple plot lines and the numerous soliloquies by different characters in* 3 Henry VI *provide the audience with a variety of angles from which to view the dramatic action, allowing that audience to experience the play both objectively and sympathetically through what he calls Shakespeare's method of "detachment" and "engagement." Champion also notes the ambivalent quality of* 3 Henry VI, *as did John D. Cox (1978), claiming that Shakespeare deliberately confounds our perceptions of the characters in order to increase our sympathy for Henry and to stress "the physical atrocities of war and man's brutality." Other critics who have analyzed the structure of* 1, 2, *and* 3 Henry VI *include Hereward T. Price (1951), A. C. Hamilton (1961-62), and David M. Bergeron (1977).*]

Nowhere [in *Henry VI* is Shakespeare's] development more crucially evident than in the delineation of the title figure. Ancillary to the action in *Part I* and strikingly ambivalent in *Part II,* Henry is emotionally the central figure in *Part III.* In *Part I* he as a character is virtually an irrelevancy..... His role in *Part II,* on the other hand, is significant both physically and emotionally. The play at first glance appears to have a melodramatically simplistic protagonist in Gloucester and villain in York, but Henry cuts a figure of genuine ambiguity and thereby conditions the spectators' response to each. Gloucester, himself blameless, is caught up in a struggle with opponents whose villainy in part is attributable to the King himself; York, in one sense destructively ambitious, in another sense purges the court and addresses the political dangers of the power vacuum created by the king's passivity. Henry's incongruous inactivity, by nourishing the evil natures of various figures, serves as a catalyst for the destructive forces in the play; but, since there is a pious idealism in the man which prompts a sense of respect, the spectators' response hovers between admiration and disdain. In *Part II,* then, Henry is a complex character who provides the ambiguity for the action. The title role is even more significant in *Part III,* in which Henry is the sole figure with whom the spectators can identify emotionally. His total repudiation of both sides in the Lancastrian-Yorkist struggle suggests a kind of wisdom honed in adversity and brings him to the verge of effective tragic development. If the spectators sit in awe of the superhuman Machiavellian determination of Richard, they pity Henry, perceiving him—for all his flaws—as something better than that which surrounds him and sensing in him the universal human condition, a state in which man copes inadequately with the evil in his environment and must suffer the consequent waste and destruction.

In these early plays Shakespeare seems progressively to be striving for a dramatic perspective of sufficient scope to accommodate the movement of national forces through a significant period of time, yet of sufficient detail to provide the interest in character on which drama depends. The broad historical perspective of *1 Henry VI* is created by a combination of structural features. Four separate plot strands are interwoven—the struggle for power between Gloucester the Lord Protector and the Bishop of Winchester, a similar struggle involving York and the Lancastrian Somerset, the battlefield operations of the opposing national stalwarts, Talbot and Joan of Arc, along with the enigmatic support each receives from his colleagues, and the Machiavellian romantic intrigues of the Earl of Suffolk with Margaret, daughter of the Duke of Anjou. Each of these plot strands follows a similar narrative pattern—beginning in seeming harmony, then dissolving into overt, vicious enmity, and in turn moving to a precarious and clearly unstable resolution. Hence, through the several lines of action, a general plot movement develops which is vital to the individual dramatic entity depicting a nation beset with internal political problems that fatally offset the conduct of her foreign wars. At the same time, the plot projects a continued dissension to be resolved far beyond the confines of that particular stage world with the accession of Henry VII and a reasonably permanent resolution of the dilemma of kingship. Countering these multiple lines, a feature which creates breadth but at some obvious expense to the spectator's focus and the intensity of his interest, is Shakespeare's extensive use of the soliloquy, a feature which normally encourages the spectator's emotional

commitment to the character. Admittedly, a number of soliloquies in the early plays are choric and expository rather than psychologically revealing. . . . Even so, an individual character directly addressing the audience, whether struggling internally at a moment of critical decision or merely commenting upon past events and anticipating those to come, provokes a sense of familiarity which at least momentarily narrows the spectators' focus. (pp. 219-21)

The structure of *2 Henry VI* represents a significant advancement over that of *1 Henry VI.* Again the perspective is fragmented; no individual speaks more than twelve percent of the total lines, and no fewer than five deliver between ten and twelve percent. These characters—Henry, Gloucester, York, Suffolk, and Margaret—represent a continuation of three of the four plot strands from *Part I.* And, while there is more extensive use of the soliloquy than in *Part I* . . . , once again Shakespeare scatters the internalization—among eleven characters, only one of whom speaks more than thirteen percent of such lines. Again, also, no character appears in as many as half of the scenes. As in *1 Henry VI,* then, the structural features incorporate elements of both engagement and detachment, and the perspective is distinctly broader than that of Shakespeare's contemporary comedies and tragedies. In this play, however, instead of a unity based on action—parallel thematic movement in four plot strands—Shakespeare through two major dramatic focal points achieves a unity based on character: the fall of Gloucester and the overt rebellion of York. The first is a contained unit of action of dominant significance to the individual play and the limited time span it represents, a telescoping of ten years from Henry's marriage in 1445 to the Battle of St. Albans in 1455. The second again projects beyond the limits of the stage world and suggests the interminable cycle of political struggles which characterizes fifteenth-century British history. Additionally, as we have noted earlier, the figure of King Henry serves to intensify the ambivalence of the situation: on the one hand, he deplores violence and genuinely strives to achieve peace and harmony for his kingdom; on the other, his innocence and idealism hardly conceal his refusal or his inability to act expediently—whether against wife or political foe—and in the final analysis he cannot escape bearing a major part of the blame for permitting the seeds of envy and ambition in those around him to grow to such monstrous proportions. (pp. 221-22)

While Shakespeare's concern for form and perspective and for effective control of the spectators' response is increasingly obvious in these early plays, the structure of *3 Henry VI* is a more notable achievement both in itself and in terms of Shakespearian things to come. The elements of detachment are once more fundamental to the design, with multiple plot lines again serving to fragment the perspective and create the sense of breadth—York's confrontation with the king's forces, Henry's struggle with his own conscience and with members of his own party, Edward's amorous intrigues in defiance of his best political interests, and Richard's private aspirations for power. (p. 223)

If these elements of detachment contribute to the historical focus of the play, it is in the elements of engagement that Shakespeare registers his significant progress as a dramatist. For one thing, *3 Henry VI* represents Shakespeare's first major accumulation of soliloquies and asides for internal focus. . . . For another, as in *Othello* some ten years later, Shakespeare intersects two patterns of internalization—the one character painfully aware of his moral dilemma, the other a cold and calculating schemer devoted entirely to Machiavellian principles. In *Othello* the spectator views the first half of the tragedy primarily through Iago's jaundiced eyes as the opportunist seizes every moment for enlarging his scheme to destroy the Moor; in the last half the spectator experiences privately with the Moor first the agony of jealousy and passion and then the trauma of illumination. In *3 Henry VI* this pattern is reversed as the spectator moves from the morally sensitive mind to that of the amoral schemer. The order is critically significant: emphasis in *Othello* is on the aesthetic resolution of a plot in which—in convenient Aristotelian terms—a potentially noble figure has succumbed to error, in part at least because of his own pride, a figure who by the end of the play has recognized his flaw and achieved a kind of an anagnorisis which bespeaks both the destructive waste and the moral catharsis of tragedy. Conversely, in *3 Henry VI*, the final emphasis is upon the rise to power of an awesomely fascinating figure possessed of a maniacal dedication to seizing the throne, a pattern which imaginatively casts the reader forward in space and time and thus reinforces the double sense of time so vital to Shakespeare's historical perspective—both the moment addressed by the single play and also the events before and after. (pp. 224-25)

3 Henry VI offers in Henry and Richard figures far more compelling dramatically than any Shakespeare has previously depicted. Equally significant, the playwright—through an increasingly intense rotation between the two major value structures in the play—provides an emotional coherence for the multiple plot strands far more effective than the parallel narrative patterns of *Part I*. This rotation does not primarily involve attachment to the two political causes; instead, as the fortunes of battle shift, the spectators' attention is drawn increasingly to the victims of the struggle, whether Lancastrians or Yorkists. Consequently, sympathy becomes increasingly stronger for Henry, who in both moral and physical terms denounces everything for which the war stands.

Fundamentally, six emotional focal points exist in the play, shifting from pro-Lancastrian (I, i), to pro-Yorkist (I, iii—II, ii), to pro-Lancastrian (II, vi—III, i), to pro-Edwardian (III, ii—IV, iv), to pro-Lancastrian (V, v—V, vi), to pro-Edwardian (V, vii). In the first scene, for example, the spectators hear the Yorkists reporting the death of their adversaries, Lord Clifford and Lord Stafford, by the swords of common soldiers, and they are repelled by Edward's grisly boast that his gory sword bears the blood of the Duke of Buckingham. . . . The tone of the initial scene is disturbing, suggesting not merely that the Yorkists are celebrating a military victory but that they revel in the atrocities which it has spawned. And this suggestion is reinforced two scenes later—from the Lancastrian perspective—as Clifford, permitting no moment even for prayer, stabs York's young son Rutland in a mood of frenzied delight. . . . (pp. 231-32)

Shakespeare, then, achieves a measure of artistic ambivalence through a series of scenes forcing the spectator alternately to respond with antipathy to pro-Lancastrian and pro-Yorkist figures. Admittedly, the pattern is purely external, based as it is on repugnance to the physical atrocities of war and man's brutality; but it prefigures a structural principle to be utilized more effectively in *Richard II*. Moreover, this rotating pattern of broken oaths, murders, and betrayals—in conjunction with the general opposition to the internecine warfare voiced by Henry with increasing poignancy and sincerity—produces in the spectators a mounting horror toward the struggle which transcends the concerns or the sympathies of any particular

moment. Such thematic unity, providing coherence for the myriad events following the Battle of St. Albans in 1455 and Edward's accession to the throne and Henry's murder in 1471, brings *3 Henry VI* to a level of artistic achievement unparalleled in the spate of chronicle plays to this date. (p. 233)

Whatever the order of composition, structurally *3 Henry VI* is a significant advancement over *Part I* and *Part II*. In each of the plays Shakespeare seems conscious of the necessity for a breadth of vision which will effectively serve the historical theme. Such a perspective, by forcing the spectators to observe the action from a multiplicity of angles, accommodates a focus larger than the fortunes and misfortunes of any single individual; that is, the political context, itself composed of complex human interactions—far from being merely a background against which an individual's destiny is portrayed—becomes the dominant concern of the play. To this end, *Parts I, II,* and *III* all use multiple plot strands; no single figure is predominant in lines spoken or time spent upon the stage, and the devices of internalization are spread among a wide range of characters. At the same time Shakespeare clearly seems to realize that genuine dramatic involvement is founded on compelling characterization; and, consequently, in the *Henry VI* plays he increasingly seeks the harmonious blend of those elements of detachment and breadth with those of emotional engagement through depth of characterization. In *Part I* the four thematically related plot strands which provide the structural unity tend to call attention to the pattern of action itself, and interest in individual characterization is perforce minimized; even so, the soliloquies spoken by Talbot, Gloucester, and Winchester provide compelling vignettes to which the spectators cannot be unresponsive.

In *Part II* the action tends to center on two individuals—the virtuous Gloucester and the scheming, ruthless York; yet, through the ambivalent characterization of Henry, Shakespeare not only avoids a melodramatic encounter but also directly involves the spectators in the value judgments central to the drama. The king's passivity, though motivated perhaps by a moral sensibility, provokes both Gloucester's murder and York's ambition, and the spectators must sit in final judgment on both the characters and the ambiguous situations prompting their actions. *Part III*, again, centers primarily on two figures, Richard and Henry, both of whom are more complex than the major figures in *Part II*. Richard's steely determination to rule at any cost, expressed privately to the spectators, commands an awesome fascination, even as Henry's tragic role is afforded full development. Yet the shifting emphases provoking increasing attention to the victims of the struggle, reinforced by emblematic scenes spaced throughout the action, establish a theme of political turmoil which transcends interest in any particular individual. Finally, Shakespeare uses specific plot devices—omens, prophecies, pledges of vengeance—to reinforce the theme of moral anarchy and suggestively to foreshadow the events of the plot, thereby establishing a pattern of anticipation which heightens the spectators' tension and response and provides a touch of the architectonic quality to be used so extensively in *Richard III*. Such a structure may indeed be primitive by later standards, but it is a highly sophisticated dramatic design for the early 1590's. . . . In a word, Shakespeare begins to provide history with a genuine human dimension, holding in precarious emotional balance for the spectators the dynamic forces of society—those who would maintain the established order and those who would destroy or rebuild—the omniscient view, in other words, of the paradox that constitutes the human condition. (pp. 236-37)

Larry S. Champion, "Developmental Structure in Shakespeare's Early Histories: The Perspective of '3 Henry VI'," in Studies in Philology, Vol. LXXVI, No. 3, Summer, 1979, pp. 218-38.

MARILYN FRENCH (essay date 1981)

[In a section of her Shakespeare's Division of Experience (1981) not excerpted here, French postulates that human beings have always conceptualized their experience of the world in terms of masculine and feminine principles. She states that her book is an examination of these gender principles in Shakespeare's work and an analysis of "what is properly masculine, what is properly feminine" in his plays. In the excerpt below, French argues that the idea of legitimacy and how it is conferred is the central issue in 1, 2, and 3 Henry VI. She contends that Shakespeare shows that women may never possess power legitimately; thus, whenever female characters seek domination, they become outlaw figures, threatening the masculine principles of courage, loyalty, and honor most fully personified in 1 Henry VI in the figures of Talbot and his son. She concludes that in the Henry VI trilogy, Shakespeare's women are "fundamentally antistructure, fundamentally under-miners of masculine legitimacy." Ronald S. Berman (1962) has also viewed the theme of legitimacy as central to the Henry VI trilogy, and David M. Bevington (1966), H. M. Richmond (1967), Robert B. Pierce (1971), and Leslie A. Fiedler (1972) have all examined Shakespeare's concern with the dominant, manipulative women and their threat to the masculine, heroic code depicted in these plays.]

1 Henry VI opens with a lament. It is on one level a lament for the death of Henry V, who was a great warrior, a king, and a father. But the lament hardly fits a mere mortal, albeit an important one: the language suggests that what has died is legitimacy itself. (The shaky origins of Henry's legitimacy are not touched on in discussion of him, in this play.) The lords who commemorate him are the most powerful men in England, and what they demand is that the cosmos itself recognize the catastrophe this death represents: "Hung be the heavens with black, yield day to night!" [1 Henry VI, I. i. 1]. Bedford demands that the "bad revolting stars" that allowed Henry's death be "scourge[d]" [I. i. 4]. Such references imply analogues: the death of Jesus and the fall of the revolting angel Lucifer from heaven.

More has died than just a man. An age that miraculously combined power with virtue has ended: "England ne'er had a king until his time: / Virtue he had, deserving to command; / . . . He ne'er lift up his hand but conquered" [I. i. 8-9, 16]. The nobles question the reason for this unhappy termination: is it mere mischance, or is it the French who have toppled the giant by "magic verses" recited by "subtile-witted . . . Conjurers and sorcerers" [I. i. 27, 25-6]? This language associates the French with the "revolting stars"—the devil—and with magic. Within twenty-seven lines, the battle lines of value are drawn.

The English represent a moral position in which God, power, prowess, courage, virtue, and legitimacy are identified: the masculine principle. The French undermine, are subtle and devilish, and use magic: outlaw feminine principle. The war is between the two most powerful areas of the gender principles. But there are two wars: one against France, and one within England. The latter is, on a philosophical level, a struggle to define legitimacy.

Within two more speeches, this struggle becomes overt. Winchester, the Bishop, draws an explicit parallel between Henry V and God, and between the French and the forces of ungodliness, and claims the power of the Church empowered Henry.

Gloucester scoffs, claiming that the Church undermined Henry because it likes only "an effeminate prince" [I. i. 35], one it can dominate. Winchester retorts that Gloucester's wife dominates him more than either God or Church. Gloucester attacks, accusing the Bishop of loving "the flesh" [I. i. 41]. Bedford tells them both to cease, lest only weeping women and babies be left in England.

There is considerable mention of women and feminacy in these speeches, more than one imagines there would have been in actuality. But it is part of, and develops, the value structure that will dominate the play. What Gloucester and Winchester are accusing each other of is being under domination of either a woman or the feminine principle. Whenever the feminine principle dominates (has worldly power) in Shakespeare, it is outlaw. Bedford reminds the men of the other aspect, the inlaw, the supposed end of power struggles.

The remainder of scene i brings in wave after wave of news of English defeats, reinforcing Bedford's warning. The way the news is delivered and received makes us feel as if England were in danger from a foreign invader, and were not the invader itself. The English are in dire straits: the ideal father (God) is dead, and with him the supreme power (force and righteousness) of the masculine principle. He has left only an infant son. The two most powerful men in the kingdom, Gloucester and Winchester, are to some degree subject to the feminine principle, and thus lack the legitimacy of a sovereign. The enemy, France, possesses the outlaw power of magic. The next scene, in which Joan introduces herself to the Dauphin, expands the associations.

Shakespeare's handling of Joan is troubling. It is true that the British of the Renaissance saw Joan as an enemy (and most unforgivably, a successful one) and a witch. But this does not fully account for Shakespeare's treatment of the character.

An important way of deducing Shakespeare's intentions in these four plays is to study his departure from his sources. There are many, which is significant since he was writing history plays. Such embroidering on fact was of course not uncommon in the Renaissance; nevertheless, Shakespeare's departures and inventions are not mainly stylistic—that is, compressions or omissions made for the sake of dramatic unity and force. They are, rather, ideological, creating associations he wished to make. (pp. 44-6)

Shakespeare's Joan is coarse and crude in language and sensibility. As soon as she appears, sexual innuendoes begin. She temporizes with the Dauphin's instant desire; Alanson comments, "Doubtless he shrives this woman to her smock" [I. ii. 19]. Although he suspects the Dauphin's sexual intentions, he places the responsibility for them on Joan: "These women are shrewd tempters with their tongues" [I. v. 123]. Talbot no sooner hears her name than he puns on it: "Pucelle or puzzel" [I. iv. 107]. At his first encounter with her, he conjures her as "devil or devil's dam" and as "witch" [I. v. 5-6]. Burgundy calls her a "trull" [II. ii. 28]. The continuing alignment of the French with magic, the British with God and righteousness, could be written off as understandable patriotism, or chauvinism. The British lost their war: some explanation is necessary. But the magical, diabolical means used by the French are also continually associated with women and with sex. (This continues even after Joan is dead.) The sub-surface, "mythic" war waged in this play is a war against women, identified with sexuality: it is a war against the outlaw feminine principle. It is a paradoxical war, as well, for the gender principles, as they are divided, insist that women *cannot* possess physical prowess and courage. The only battle Joan is shown as winning is a duel with the French Dauphin. We are told that Joan vanquishes the English, but we never see her doing it. In her first encounter with Talbot, she flees to help the Dauphin; during the night attack, she and her party flee at the mere mention of Talbot's name. At Rouen, she wins by "policy"; and when Talbot challenges the French to combat after the loss of Rouen, he pointedly excludes Joan from the discussion, refusing to speak with a "railing Hecate" [III. ii. 64]. Joan's persuasion of Burgundy is essentially a verbal seduction which feels to him as if he'd been "bewitch'd" [III. iii. 58]. And although we are told that it is Joan with her magic who has changed the English fortunes, Talbot, when he exhorts himself to action, and lists his enemies, omits Joan's name.

That this handling has a peculiar bias, and certainly clouds historical reality, could also be written off. Humans still write this way. War movies frequently show American enemies in World War II, whether German or Japanese, to be stupid, silly, fanatic, and absurd, to the point where one wonders why it took so long to win that war. But this paradox—the attribution of great power to "feminine" figures, simultaneous with the denial of any worldly power—is the pattern of treatment of all the female figures in the *Henry VI* trilogy. The real enemy is not France, or even dominant women: it is sexuality and "anarchy"—the urge located within the outlaw feminine principle to overthrow all hierarchies, all legitimacy. Thus, it functions organically in a play which seeks to define the grounds of "true" legitimacy.

The allusions surrounding Joan associate her with what is pagan, dark, and female. But her character is most denigrated by two scenes that have nothing to do with witchcraft or whoredom. Both of these scenes are Shakespeare's inventions, and one of them totally reverses the known facts. In actuality, Bedford presided over Joan's trial and her execution by burning. But Shakespeare shows him sitting in a chair, ill and dying, being taunted from the walls of Rouen by a crassly triumphant Joan. The second invented scene is one in which Joan repudiates her father. The father is shown as loving and heartbroken: he offers to die with his daughter. Joan denies his parentage, claiming a "gentler" descent. The father's final curse and consent to her execution place an almost divine seal on the justice of her fate.

One point of both scenes is to stamp England's enemy with every moral obloquy possible. But both scenes involve an identical act: the denial of the authority, legitimacy, and worthiness—lovableness, even—of the father figure. Joan challenges the very notion of legitimacy, like the outlaw feminine principle of which she is a part. (pp. 47-8)

The external war fought in this play, then, is waged by the masculine principle against the feminine. But the nourishing and supportive qualities of the latter principle are essential to human felicity and stability. If women are false, sexual, and aggressive, the compassionate qualities they are supposed to uphold must be taken over by men. Thus the external war is connected to the internal one. For the problem of legitimacy is connected with the relations between men and women. Since Shakespeare's women can never attain legitimacy, they are given to undermine it. In doing so, they betray their inlaw aspect. But both (male) legitimacy and the inlaw feminine principle can be upheld by men operating in a tradition of father to son.

The father-son relation is central in *1 Henry VI*. In this relation is found the core of legitimacy, the passage from one male to another of virtue, courage, and prowess. There is a set of father figures in the play: Salisbury, Bedford, and Talbot, the hero warriors, and Mortimer. Each of them is free from the taint of female domination; each supplies in himself the necessary "feminine" qualities: "A braver soldier never couched lance, / A gentler heart did never sway in court" [III. ii. 134-36], Talbot says of the dead Bedford. Bedford has remained with his men, ill as he is, to hearten them; he suffers silently Joan's mockery. Salisbury's death is mourned in terms as hyperbolic as those used about Henry V; exequies are promised Bedford as well. Each warrior is a "father" to his men, and to the other warriors, who seem to gain strength from each other's heroism.

It is Talbot, however, who is the greatest hero, and who unites the gender principles most fully. Some critics have seen the opposition of Talbot and Joan as the major one of the play. Such a reading is inadequate to support all five acts, but there is no question that the major opposition of the play is between the principles the two represent. Talbot is the central and exemplary figure. He is the standard, the sturdy Briton whose patriotism, courage, control, and implicit sexual purity never waver. His main scenes occur near the center of the play, surrounded by the demise of Henry V, and the foreshadowed ascendency of Margaret. Those scenes are framed by the squabbling of his countrymen (IV, i) and the mockery of the French (IV, vii), and function much as what C. S. Lewis, writing about *The Fairie Queene,* called the "shrine" cantos, emblematic episodes which enrich and illuminate the surrounding material. (pp. 49-50)

This "shrine" section makes explicit one form of true legitimacy, the succession from father to son of courage, honor, and heroic ideals. The relationship is similar to that of God and Jesus; the woman who provides it is, like Mary, a vessel, passing from father to son an identical spirit. If anything other than the identical spirit is passed, the honor of the woman is impeached. John proves his legitimacy—he urges his father not to make a "bastard and a slave" of him by ordering him from the battle—by saving his father, and dying in the act. Both are eventually wounded, and Talbot (like Aeneas carrying his father out of the flames of Troy) carries his son in the womb/tomb of his arms, and dies with him, although not before predicting for himself and his son, transcendence of mortality like that of Daedalus and Icarus. (p. 50)

Another father-son succession is the oblique one of Mortimer and York (who, like other survivors, promises Mortimer proper funerary ceremonies). Mortimer's long recital of his titles and successions emphasizes that York is as legitimate through bloodlines as is Henry VI. The ambiguity of legitimacy is underscored by Shakespeare's placing of the scene between Mortimer and Richard immediately after the disputatious Temple Garden scene.

And the consequences of disputed legitimacy are the loss of clear authority and thus the loss of civil peace. The rebellious outlaw feminine principle is rampant throughout England and France. A resentful, insubordinate sentinel is responsible for the success of Talbot's night attack; at its conclusion, the French nobles bicker about blame. Winchester and Gloucester (as well as their servingmen), York and Somerset, Vernon and Basset all quarrel because when there is no clear authority, every man is his own rabbi. Henry VI, still young in this play, can only "prevail, if prayers might prevail" [III. ii. 67] and offer "sighs and tears" [III. i. 108].

As *1 Henry VI* ends, the hero-fathers are all dead, and a son has attained maturity. But it is already clear that this son is not at all like *his* hero-father.

Although father figures exist in [*2 Henry VI*], something is wrong in their relations with their sons. And it is sons—brothers—who are the focus of *2 Henry VI*. Henry is beginning to function as king, but like his uncles (fathers), he is tainted by subjection to a woman and by his own ''effeminacy,'' his piety. (p. 51)

In this section of the trilogy, the trend begun in the middle of the first part is continued: not only women, but lower-class men rebel against ''authority,'' and peers contest against each other. Although there are two main factions, Henry's and York's, each person is really a faction to himself. Various characters combine and ally, then abandon their allies, announce private purposes. The males bicker among each other in ''masculine'' self-assertion; the women challenge male supremacy; the commoners rebel against the nobles. What is under attack by all of them is either legitimacy itself or the legitimacy of another rather than the self: for most of the characters, the latter is nearer to the point.

The sons in this play are either spurious or unlike their fathers. Henry VI is his father's opposite; despite allusions to God and Christ, Aeneas and Anchises, Cade's claim to a relation to Mortimer is false and ludicrous; and Clifford, whose father was a hero like Talbot, has none of the Talbot delicacy, and vows a cruelty like that of Medea in revenge for his father's death. (Since Medea is female and not noted for preserving members of her family, she seems an inappropriate allusion for Clifford to make. The allusion serves, however, to link Clifford's rage for revenge to the outlaw feminine principle.)

Horner and Peter are another destructive ''father-son'' team, as are Winchester and Gloucester, whose avuncular relation is stressed. Something has gone wrong in the line of transmission.

The action whirls around the still center that is Henry VI. Some readers believe that Shakespeare saw the King as a saintly ideal. It is true that Henry VI is an exemplar of the inlaw feminine principle: he urges harmony, piety, meekness, and is himself often willingly subordinate to others; it is also true that elsewhere Shakespeare upholds as divine this gender principle. But it is impossible that Shakespeare could have intended Henry as an ideal figure. He is weak, easily swayed, mealymouthed, whining, and uses his piety to evade responsibility. Until his final scenes, he lacks totally the authority of a Cordelia, the enduring steadfastness of a Hermione [*The Winter's Tale*]. At the end of the play, he represents a moral ideal, perhaps, but not a political one. (pp. 52-3)

Shakespeare does not paint a respectful portrait of Henry VI (although he omits mention of Henry's mad periods), but he also darkens York's character somewhat. There has been considerable discussion of the playwright's views on kingship, assertions that he found the murder or overthrow of an annointed king a crime of cosmic proportions. Careful analysis of all the plays in which such an act occurs, however, seems to indicate that he slanted his attitude towards such acts according to the central idea of his drama. In this case, it seems, he implies that Henry's overthrow was inevitable. Softening Henry's inadequacies, but making him sound like a dithering idiot, darkening York's character somewhat, but presenting the Duke's claim to the throne without scant or irony, Shakespeare avoids bias. There is truth in York's claim that he would be a better king than Henry. What Shakespeare is working towards

in this tetralogy is a definition of legitimacy that is not limited to, but synthesizes claims based on bloodlines, prowess, or morality. True legitimacy consists in possession of all three. Neither Henry nor York possesses all three: neither does anyone else in the play. (p. 53)

The warring elements of *1 Henry VI* are extended and elaborated in *2 Henry VI*, but they are the same elements. The father figures in this play are less noble, and all of them die—Winchester, Gloucester, and Clifford. In place of the exalted eulogies of *1 Henry VI*, however, there are only Henry's tears for Humphrey, his pieties over the body of the guilt-ridden Winchester, and young Clfford's ugly vow of revenge. Suffolk too is dead, and the civil war in progress: war between ''brothers'' is now physical as well as verbal. The masculine principle is in contest with itself.

At the same time, the feminine principle is in revolt. Women strive for mastery (ominously but unsuccessfully); the lower classes rebel (ominously but unsuccessfully). And the proper leader, Henry, cannot deal with this situation.

The scene in the garden of Alexander Iden is sometimes seen as providing the mean in this play. Sometimes it is Gloucester's, sometimes Henry's beliefs. All three do provide a mean of sorts, but all three are ineffectual. Iden kills the intruder, but his pastoral ideal is fragile, and can be invaded. Males who uphold the inlaw feminine principle in this play, like the females who uphold it (sometimes with male assistance) in later plays, are seen as morally excellent, but politically inadequate. The ''shrine'' scenes are those featuring Jack Cade, who is exemplary in a negative way in *2 Henry VI* as Talbot is exemplary in a positive way in *1 Henry VI*. When clear legitimacy is doubted, when authority is not granted respect, even the worms rebel. In *1 Henry VI*, Shakespeare provided a model for proper grounds for legitimacy in Talbot and his son. In this play, he demonstrates with increasing force, the necessity for such a quality.

An ideal and exemplary father-son tradition, postulated in *1 Henry VI*, gives way in *2 Henry VI* to a contentious rivalry in which the political ''sons''—the lower classes—rebel against the upper classes, which are supposed to be benevolently paternal, like Gloucester, but are not. Father figures die, brothers war on each other. In the final part of the trilogy, not only brothers but even fathers and sons battle against each other. The basic unit of legitimacy has turned murderous. *3 Henry VI* is a play in which, as Tillyard points out, all decencies are abandoned, and even children are murdered [see excerpt above, 1944]. David Riggs demonstrates that there is no longer any talk of justice and rightness (although there is of rights), no more praise for heroism: ''the chief oratorical forms are the *vituperatio* and the lament'' [see excerpt above, 1971].

In fact, Shakespeare shows the characters of the drama as behaving even worse than they actually did. *3 Henry VI* presents a nightmare world so hideous it is capable of breeding a Richard, who will incarnate its values and take it to its full degradation in the last play in the tetralogy.

The first scene is an argument about legitimacy and succession. Henry insists he will retain the crown, but agrees to make York his heir, cutting off his son. (This, although in *2 Henry VI*, Henry has protested he longs to be a subject, not a king.)

This wrong to his son enrages Clifford, Warwick, and Northumberland, who calls the act ''unmanly'' [*3 Henry VI*, I. i. 186]. Henry himself sees it as unnatural, but shrugs it off: ''Be it as it may'' [I. i. 194]. Margaret immediately accuses him of being an unnatural father and divorces herself from him.

Henry's failure to maintain proper succession is immediately followed by a contrast, as York's sons insist that he break his oath and press his claim, and that is followed by Clifford's hideous murder of a child, Rutland, in vengeance for his own father's death. The next scene shows Margaret taunting the captured York with a handkerchief stained with Rutland's blood, and the ugly murder of York. Thus the entire first act, as cruel a set of scenes as can be found in Shakespeare, focuses on parents and children, on succession and lack of it.

Henry continues to act the wimp, wringing his hands over his broken oath while Margaret and Clifford prepare to attack the town of York. But when Clifford urges him to fight for his son's right, Henry answers, for the first time in the trilogy, with dignity and force. He asserts that ill means poison their ends, and that some ends are not worth the means used to achieve them. This is a turning point in his characterization, although not a complete one: Henry goes on being blind and self-absorbed to some degree right until the end of his life. (pp. 56-7)

The shift in the characterization of Henry is pivotal in the play. The first part of the trilogy has a clear standard, the legitimacy of the heroic, masculine line as exemplified by Talbot and John. It is undermined by destructive, underhanded women and by "effeminate" or contentious men. There is clear knowledge of right (and thus, of rights): honor is a greater good than power, but the greatest good is the two combined.

2 Henry VI shows a world unsure of right—and therefore of rights. Authority (Henry) is undermined by evil, destructive women and its own "effeminacy." Henry is virtuous, but cannot handle power; those who can are not virtuous. Humphrey emerges as the most admirable figure in the play, suggesting that a new set of values is being introduced—humanitarianism combined with willingness to hold power. But even he is too naive, too "feminine" to gain control, for he is a man who, like his nephew, can be dominated by a woman.

In *3 Henry VI*, among all the competing claims of legitimacy, in fact only power matters—power as might, force, rather than authority. Thus in the three plays, three different standards for legitimacy are tried—and found inadequate. In the world of might, there is no mercy, no concern with moral right, no thought of "feminine" ends (thus the emphasis on the murder of children).

In the midst of this, Henry takes on a higher stature. He begins to assert real values, rather than utter pious formulas of disengagement, and to maintain them in the face of force. His values are the opposite of those the world around him holds. He is destroyed, but he will remain in memory. His values will combine with Gloucester's humanitarianism and the values of the hero-warriors of *1 Henry VI* to produce the fully legitimate king: Richmond, the first Tudor king.

There are important shifts in the conception of women in this play, also, as shown in the character of Margaret. No longer the shrewish, sexual, intruding busybody she was in *2 Henry VI,* now that Suffolk is dead, she has moved into some authority and control. She openly announces her contempt for Henry and divorces him (verbally). She is concerned now only with the future of her son: she has become a full mother figure. But since she also dares to move into the realm of power-in-the-

world, she is steeped in the evil Shakespeare associated with such behavior. (p. 59)

[Shakespeare alters his success and] removes Margaret from any direct political power or action, although by depicting the actual events, he could have laid responsibility for the war entirely on her. However, that would also show Margaret to be a very powerful woman, able to muster an army on her own, and fight against a union of the most powerful nobles in the land (which she was, and did). Instead, he shows the nobles—Westmoreland, Northumberland, and Clifford—rejecting the compromise. Margaret—and her child (she is seen as mother rather than governor)—enters only afterwards, and Margaret's act is a personal one, the divorcing of herself from her husband. Shakespeare shows the King winning back the lords by writing to them.

He places the words of contempt for a woman general in the mouth of Richard rather than York—he must have already had Richard's intensely misogynistic character firmly in mind. He invented the terrible scene with the pinioned York and the bloody handkerchief: he made Margaret the instigator and Margaret the killer, but not as the general, the warrior. She is aggressive in a vile and insidious and indirect way. The scene also permits him to put into York's mouth words, like those of Talbot to Joan (about her taunting of Bedford), excoriating women who move out of their proper sphere, and defining women's place and function: to be "soft, mild, pitiful, and flexible" [I. iv. 141].

Margaret's gloating over York about the death of the child Rutland is equivalent to Lady Macbeth's avowal that she would dash out an infant's brains had she sworn to do it. It constitutes the final stamp of "unnaturalness" on her, just as Joan's repudiation of her father constitutes hers. York calls Clifford, who actually murdered Rutland, *fell;* he calls Margaret *false.* But there is nothing false about Shakespeare's Margaret: she is openly horrible. Her only "falseness" is that she is female but does not behave as women are supposed to: she is false to her skin. She has a "tiger's heart wrapp'd in a woman's hide" [I. iv. 137]. She is not called *cruel* or *wicked* like the men. Because she has not behaved better than the men, but rather, has acted *like* them, Margaret has become a "she-wolf of France, but worse than wolves of France" [I. iv. 111]: renouncing the inlaw feminine principle, she has inevitably slid into the outlaw aspect, into the subhuman, into the "bestiality" of nature. (pp. 60-1)

Shakespeare alters his source again, in his depiction of Margaret after she hears the news of Warwick's death. She is courageous and valiant and not at all "drouned in sorowe." Her behavior is admirable, but her insistence on carrying on the war makes her responsible in some way for her son's death, which occurs in the next scene. It also prepares for a shift in Margaret's role. In her speech, she claims the aegis of the usurped king, justice, and God's name; she concludes in tears. She has not appeared thus before. Within moments, her son is dead, and she begs the Yorkists to kill her too. With the death of her son, her own life is over.

Like Eleanor in *2 Henry VI,* Margaret has learned too late that her power is not really hers, but resides in the male. Women have only two choices—to undermine that male power, or to support it. All Margaret is capable of now is "to fill the world with words" [V. v. 44]. The death of her son means her death as well, because children, procreation, are the end of the feminine principle Margaret has, throughout this trilogy, repudiated. When she appears again (in *Richard III*), she will be a walking curse, a walking lament, still fierce, but powerless except for her words.

In his alterations of his source, Shakespeare makes explicit some of his attitudes towards women. They are as split as the split in the feminine principle. Women are powerful, capable of sorcery, pride, sexual promiscuity, and atrocity; but they are not powerful in the world, they can fight only in underhanded ways. When women attempt to move into the pole of power, they necessarily attempt to dominate men, which was for Shakespeare at this point in his life, abhorrent. When women connect themselves with power, they can will only evil and their effect is malign, because they cannot extirpate from themselves the outlaw aspect of the feminine principle. Thus, they are fundamentally antistructure, fundamentally underminers of masculine legitimacy.

Characters like Joan and Margaret crop up again in later plays—Goneril, Regan, Lady Macbeth, for instance. But these later versions have more dignity than their predecessors; they are less shrewish, coarse, or unpolished. In terms of moral position Joan's and Margaret's closest relatives in Shakespeare are actually Adriana of *Comedy of Errors* and Kate of *The Taming of the Shrew*, two early comedies. As Shakespeare grows older, he concentrates on a different kind of female character, one who accepts the limitations of her role, and finds ways to assert herself (mildly) within it. These characters are compounded of the inlaw feminine qualities *purified* of the sexual taint that makes the unified feminine principle terrifying and threatening. (pp. 61-2)

Shakespeare will, however, never again treat male legitimacy with quite the same respect and reverence he shows in these plays. He seems to have thought it through in this tetralogy, and decided that legitimacy is not a sacred and sacrosanct gift conferred by God, but an earthly necessity that carries a heavy price. . . .

At the conclusion of *3 Henry VI*, Gloucester departs for London "to make a bloody supper in the Tower" [V. v. 85], and argues with Henry, alluding to the Icarus myth which Talbot had alluded to just before he died. Richard disposes of the myth with his usual mocking humor and in doing so, lays the father-son theme to rest. It will appear in *Richard III* only as a litany, a funeral dirge. Legitimacy requires more than bloodlines, virtue, or force, and the old traditional personal passage of power from father to son is part of a myth as lost as that of Daedalus and Icarus. (p. 63)

> *Marilyn French, "Introduction" and "Power: The First Tetralogy," in her* Shakespeare's Division of Experience, *Summit Books, 1981, pp. 11-18, 43-75.*

ADDITIONAL BIBLIOGRAPHY

Alexander, Peter. *Shakespeare's "Henry VI" and "Richard III."* Cambridge: At the University Press, 1929, 229 p.

    Refutes the view that *2* and *3 Henry VI* were Shakespeare's reworkings of *The First Part of the Contention* and *The True Tragedy*, contending instead that the latter were actors' abridged memorial reconstructions of *Henry VI, Parts 2* and *3*. This work, developed from articles first published in 1924, is considered by most critics to have firmly established Shakespeare's authorship of *1, 2,* and *3 Henry VI*.

Arthos, John. "The *Henry VI* Plays." In his *Shakespeare: The Early Writings*, pp. 174-230. London: Bowes & Bowes, 1972.

    Regards the trilogy as humanistic rather than providential. Arthos emphasizes the scale and energy of the characters, stating that the "largeness of men who honour the claims of blood justifies, even sanctions civil strife."

Berry, Edward I. *Patterns of Decay: Shakespeare's Early Histories*. Charlottesville: University Press of Virginia, 1975, 130 p.

    Traces the disintegration of the ideal of community through the progress of the *Henry VI* trilogy. Berry asserts that theme is more important than character in these plays and that individuality is subordinate to the personification of moral norms as a result of Shakespeare's stylized, emblematic presentation.

Billings, Wayne L. "Ironic Lapses: Plotting in *Henry VI*." *Studies in the Literary Imagination* V, No. 1 (April 1972): 27-49.

    Demonstrates how Shakespeare used conventions of Elizabethan heroic drama to show the deterioration of the "heroic code" in *1, 2,* and *3 Henry VI*. Billings argues that the disparities between opportunities for heroic action and the characters' numerous lapses from heroic conduct enhance Shakespeare's view that a sovereign must combine political virtues with moral ones if he is to rule effectively.

Blanpied, John W. "'Art and Baleful Sorcery': The Counterconsciousness of *Henry VI, Part I*." *Studies in English Literature, 1500-1900* XV, No. 2 (Spring 1975): 213-27.

    Agrees with Hereward T. Price's view that irony informs the structure of *1 Henry VI* (see excerpt above, 1951). Through an analysis of several scenes, Blanpied asserts that Shakespeare deliberately subverted the formalized conventions of Elizabethan theater and language in order to "undermine the authority of the monumental past." According to the Blanpied, Talbot's "deadly conventional style" has become so petrified in his final speeches that it is almost comical.

Boas, Frederick S. "Joan of Arc in Shakespeare, Schiller, and Shaw." *Shakespeare Quarterly* 2 (1951): 35-45.

    Examines the divergent treatment of Joan by three dramatists, noting particularly each author's departure or adherence to historical accounts of her life. Although Boas finds her characterization in *1 Henry VI* dramatically inconsistent, he maintains that Shakespeare's depiction generally corresponds with his sources and with the Elizabethan view of Joan.

Bordinat, Philip. "Shakespeare's Suffolk: An Exercise in Tragic Method." *Philological Papers: West Virginia University* 21, Series 75 (December 1974): 9-16.

    Argues that in depicting both Suffolk's love for Margaret and his "tragic recognition and recovery" before his death, Shakespeare foreshadows in this figure important characteristics that he would later develop in the protagonists of his major tragedies.

Brandes, George. "The '*Henry VI*' Trilogy." in his *William Shakespeare*, pp. 21-6. 1898. Reprint. London: William Heinemann, 1920.

    Comparison of *2 Henry VI* and *3 Henry VI* with *The Contention* and *The True Tragedy*. Brandes affirms that Greene, Marlowe, and Shakespeare jointly authored all four plays.

Brockbank, J. M. "The Frame of Disorder: *Henry VI*." in *Early Shakespeare*, edited by John Russell Brown and Bernard Harris, pp. 73-100. London: Edward Arnold, 1961.

    Claims that while Shakespeare remained faithful to the spirit of Holinshed's chronicle, he also selected and reshaped certain episodes in the source to emphasize the idea that rebellion is evil. Brockbank extols the epitomization of the York-Lancaster struggle in the *Henry VI* trilogy, noting that the theme of anarchy is presented more keenly there than in the chronicle.

Bromley, John C. "The Bitter Road from Agincourt: *1, 2, 3 Henry VI*." In his *The Shakespearean Kings*, pp. 7-28. Boulder: Colorado University Press, 1971.

    Disputes the theory of E. M. W. Tillyard that Shakespeare was promoting Tudor political orthodoxy in the *Henry VI* trilogy (see excerpt above, 1944). Instead, Bromley claims, divine providence is not manifest in the plays, for Shakespeare depicted the decline in English fortunes as the consequence of ''that Lancastrian line which was first murderous, then overreaching, and at last simply inept.''

Bullough, Geoffrey. Introductions to *1, 2, 3 Henry VI*. In *Narrative and Dramatic Sources of Shakespeare, Vol. III*, edited by Geoffrey Bullough, pp. 23-41, 89-100, 157-71. London: Routledge and Kegan Paul, 1960.

Discussion of Shakespeare's sources and his use of them in the *Henry VI* trilogy. Bullough specifies instances of Shakespeare's departures from his sources, stating that *1 Henry VI* is ''not so much a Chronicle play as a fantasia on historical themes.''

Cairncross, Andrew S. Introduction to *The Second Part of King Henry VI*, by William Shakespeare, edited by Andrew S. Cairncross, pp. xi-liv. The Arden Edition of the Works of William Shakespeare, edited by Una Ellis-Fermor and Harold F. Brooks. Cambridge: Harvard University Press, 1957.

Comprehensive review of the controversy over the authorship of *Henry VI*. Cairncross concludes that *The Contention* is not an earlier play which Shakespeare merely revised in *2 Henry VI*, but an actors' memorial reconstruction of the dramatist's original manuscript.

————. Introduction to *The First Part of King Henry VI*, by William Shakespeare, edited by Andrew S. Cairncross, pp. xii-lvii. The Arden Edition of the Works of William Shakespeare, edited by Harold F. Brooks and Harold Jenkins. London: Methuen & Co., 1962.

Endorses the view of Hereward T. Price (see excerpt above, 1951) that *1 Henry VI* shows clear evidence of Shakespeare's careful planning and design. The inconsistencies and irregularities in the text, Cairncross argues, do not by themselves imply composite authorship or revision, but instead may be the result of either Shakespeare's use of multiple sources or the intervention of scribes, prompters, and compositors during the play's production and publication.

————. Introduction to *The Third Part of King Henry VI*, by William Shakespeare, edited by Andrew S. Cairncross, pp. xiii-lxvi. The Arden Edition of the Works of William Shakespeare, edited by Harold F. Brooks and Harold Jenkins. London: Methuen & Co., 1964.

Detailed study of the question of the authenticity of the text of *3 Henry VI*. According to Cairncross, the ''main positive general argument'' for Shakespeare's complete authorship of this play, as well as of *1* and *2 Henry VI*, ''remains that of [its] unity of conception and execution.''

Candido, Joseph. ''Getting Loose in the *Henry VI* Plays.'' *Shakespeare Quarterly* 35, No. 4 (Winter 1984): 392-406.

Contends that the multiple occasions of capture and escape in the dramatic action, together with the use of metaphors of trapping and release, provide the *Henry VI* trilogy with both structural and thematic unity. Candido traces these motifs through the Talbot episodes, the Margaret and Suffolk scenes, the fortunes of York, and the captures of Henry VI and Edward IV, demonstrating that the poetic language of these events intensifies Shakespeare's depiction of the dissolution of heroic idealism into animal primitivism.

Champion, Larry S. ''The Search for Dramatic Form: *1, 2, 3 Henry VI*.'' In his *Perspective in Shakespeare's English Histories*, pp. 12-53. Athens: University of Georgia Press, 1980.

Examines the complex and ambivalent angles of vision in the *Henry VI* trilogy caused by Shakespeare's fragmented points of view. Champion argues that the ambivalence in the plays is intentional and that Shakespeare did not focus on a single protagonist in order to present more effectively the complexities of his historical theme.

Courthope, W. J. ''On the Authenticity of Some of the Early Plays Assigned to Shakespeare, and Their Relationship to the Development of His Dramatic Genius.'' In his *A History of English Poetry, Vol. IV*, pp. 455-76. 1895-1910. Reprint. New York: Russell & Russell, 1962.

Examines the structure and characterization of *The Contention, The True Tragedy*, and the *Henry VI* trilogy, and concludes that Shakespeare was the author of all three works. Courthope's study represents one of the most comprehensive and well-ordered discussions of the authorship controversy in *Henry VI* criticism.

Cutts, John P. ''The Early Histories: *1 Henry VI, 2 Henry VI, 3 Henry VI*.'' In his *The Shattered Glass: A Dramatic Pattern in Shakespeare's Early Plays*, pp. 109-28. Detroit: Wayne State University Press, 1968.

Examines Shakespeare's use of imagery of mirrors, substance and shadow, vision and blindness, and ''fragmentation and synthesis.'' According to Cutts, the symbolic language of the *Henry VI* trilogy emphasizes the disintegration of three kinds of power: political, ecclesiastical, and military.

Dean, Paul. ''Shakespeare's *Henry VI* Trilogy and Elizabethan 'Romance' Histories: The Origins of a Genre.'' *Shakespeare Quarterly* 33, No. 1 (Spring 1982): 34-48.

Contends that in the *Henry VI* trilogy Shakespeare incorporated elements of ''supernaturalism, love-triangles, disguise, and the concept of kingship'' from sixteenth-century English ''romance'' histories. Dean further suggests that Shakespeare employed these devices as a means of making an ironic commentary on the dramatic action of the *Henry VI* plays.

Doran, Madeleine. *Henry VI, Parts II and III*. University of Iowa Humanistic Studies, edited by Franklin H. Potter, vol. IV, no. 2. Iowa City: University of Iowa, 1928, 88 p.

Agrees with Peter Alexander that *The Contention* and *The True Tragedy* are adapted or reported versions of Shakespeare's *2* and *3 Henry VI*. Doran points out that the abridgements and ''occasional patching where cuts have been made'' are similar to the irregularities characteristic of memorial reconstructions.

Evans, B. Ifor. ''The Early Histories.'' In his *The Language of Shakespeare's Plays*, pp. 31-44. London: Methuen & Co., 1952.

A discussion of the linguistic elements other than imagery in the *Henry VI* trilogy. Evans notes that there are many passages in *2* and *3 Henry VI* where the lanuage has a stronger quality than in *1 Henry VI*, and he attributes this to Shakespeare's preoccupation in the first play with ''containing the material within the medium.''

Fleay, F. G. ''Who Wrote *Henry VI*.?'' *MacMillan's Magazine* XXXIII (November 1875): 50-62.

Disintegrationist view that Shakespeare's only contribution to the *Henry VI* trilogy was the Temple Garden scene in *1 Henry VI*. Fleay examines the status of Elizabethan actors' companies, as well as the aesthetics, characterization, and metrics of *Henry VI*, and concludes that Peele, Greene, and Marlowe were the original authors.

French, A. L. ''Joan of Arc and *Henry VI*.'' *English Studies* XLIX, No. 5 (October 1968): 425-29.

Disputes E. M. W. Tillyard's view of Joan as the agent of divine retribution against England for Henry IV's usurpation of the throne from Richard II (see excerpt above, 1944). French points out that the English defeat is more their own contrivance than Joan's, and he questions the operation of vengeance in the trilogy.

————. ''The Mills of God and Shakespeare's Early History Plays.'' *English Studies* LV, No. 4 (August 1974): 313-24.

Discussion of whether the first tetralogy supports the ideas of order, justice, and moral equity. French analyzes the deaths of the principal figures in the *Henry VI-Richard II* plays and concludes that Shakespeare depicted blind forces, not divine justice, governing human life.

Frey, David L. ''*Henry VI* versus the Tudor Myth—The General Challenge.'' In his *The First Tetralogy: Shakespeare's Scrutiny of the Tudor Myth*, pp. 6-71. The Hague: Mouton & Co., 1976.

Contends that the first tetralogy raises fundamental questions about ''divine justice, personal providence, and divine intervention,'' thus casting doubts on the orthodox Tudor view of history. To explicate his theme of undeserved human suffering, Frey argues, Shakespeare departed from his sources to show Henry's progressive despair, "in order that we may subsequently witness the growth of a man."

Gaw, Allison. *The Origin and Development of "1 Henry VI."* University of Southern California Studies, first series, no. 1. Los Angeles: University of Southern California Press, 1926, 180 p.

Supplements the view of F. G. Fleay (see entry above) by claiming that four dramatists coauthored *1 Henry VI*, and that Shakespeare merely revised, interpolated, and added some scenes. Gaw maintains that the multiple authorship theory is the most probable way to explain the "marked inconsistencies in character and incident, the unusual diversity of sources, and the inequalities in treatment of sources and in style" apparent in *1 Henry VI*.

Harbage, Alfred. *As They Liked It: An Essay on Shakespeare and Morality.* New York: Macmillan Co., 1947, 238 p.

Discussion of Shakespeare's plays from the perspective of the dramatist's first audience. Harbage contends that Holinshed's belief in the rectitude of English rule in France is endorsed in the *Henry VI* trilogy, and that Shakespeare's nationalistic bias would have pleased an Elizabethan audience.

Hinchcliffe, Judith. *"King Henry VI, Parts 1, 2, and 3": An Annotated Bibliography.* New York: Garland Publishing, 1984, 368 p.

A comprehensive listing, with descriptive notes, of published commentary on the *Henry VI* trilogy. The entries are organized into sections reflecting different scholarly concerns, including criticism, authorship, textual studies, and sources.

Jenkins, Harold. "Shakespeare's History Plays: 1900-1951." *Shakespeare Survey* 6 (1953): 1-15.

Traces the development of critical commentary on Shakespeare's history plays in the first half of the twentieth century. Jenkins provides an overview of critical efforts during that period to establish Shakespeare's authorship of *1, 2,* and *3 Henry VI*.

Kelly, Faye L. "Oaths in Shakespeare's *Henry VI* Plays." *Shakespeare Quarterly* 24, No. 1 (Winter 1973): 357-71.

Discusses the manner in which oaths and oath-taking in the *Henry VI* trilogy serve to unify the dramatic structure of these plays. Kelly posits that the progressive chaos represented in the trilogy stems from violations of sacred vows which the characters have made to each other.

Kelly, Henry Ansgar. *Divine Providence in the England of Shakespeare's Histories.* Cambridge: Harvard University Press, 1970, 344 p.

Disputes E. M. W. Tillyard's position that divine providence operates in the *Henry VI* trilogy (see excerpt above, 1944). Kelly points out that although the chronicle sources hypothesize that the various disasters of Henry VI's reign were the result of God's judgment on his marriage to Margaret, Shakespeare nowhere alludes to this. With regard to characters' references to the providential outcome of solitary events, Kelly argues that these should be evaluated as only the sentiments of the characters, and not Shakespeare's own view.

Kirschbaum, Leo. "The Authorship of *1 Henry VI*." *PMLA* LXVII (September 1952): 809-22.

Asserts that the editors of the First Folio were acting in good faith when they included *1 Henry VI* in their edition of Shakespeare's plays. Kirschbaum contends that listings of verbal parallels between *1 Henry VI* and plays by other dramatists are not adequate evidence to support claims of revision or collaboration; this is especially true, he concludes, since "dramatists of the early nineties were eternally echoing each other."

Knight, Charles. Introduction to *Henry VI, Parts II and III*. In *The Comedies, Histories, Tragedies, and Poems of William Shakespeare, Vol. 6*, by William Shakespeare, edited by Charles Knight, pp. 3-6, pp. 169-75. 1842. Reprint. New York: AMS Press, 1968.

Discussion of fifteenth-century costume and surviving representations of the actual historical figures dramatized in the *Henry VI* trilogy. Unsure about the relationship between *2* and *3 Henry VI* and *The Contention* and *The True Tragedy*, Knight here reproduces the four works together so readers can compare the texts.

Knight, G. Wilson. "The Histories, Early Tragedies, and Poems." In his *The Shakespearean Tempest*, pp. 20-74. London: Methuen & Co., 1932.

Examines the manner in which the imagery of the *Henry VI* trilogy heightens the atmosphere of disorder in the plays. Knight demonstrates that images of storms, sea-wrecks, and the contention of wind and water are correlated to the battles and struggles of individuals who suffer from the ravages of civil disorder.

——. "Roses at War." In his *The Olive and the Sword*, pp. 4-11. London: Oxford University Press, 1944.

Proposes that images of brutality and savagery predominate in the *Henry VI* trilogy. Knight maintains that Shakespeare's extensive use of feral and ruthless analogies from nature "expand the condemnation" of the civil war depicted in *1, 2,* and *3 Henry VI*.

Leech, Clifford. "The Two-Part Play: Marlow and the Early Shakespeare." *Shakespeare-Jahrbuch* 94 (1958): 90-106.

Argues that *Parts 1* and *2* of Marlowe's *Tamburlaine* served as structural models for Shakespeare's *2* and *3 Henry VI*.

McNeal, Thomas H. "Margaret of Anjou: Romantic Princess and Troubled Queen." *Shakespeare Quarterly* 9 (Winter 1958): 1-10.

Contends that Shakespeare relied on the anonymous chronicle play *King Leir* for his characterization of Margaret. McNeal draws parallels between Cordella in the earlier play and Margaret in *1 Henry VI*, and between Gonorill and Ragan and the characterization of the English queen in *2* and *3 Henry VI*.

McNeir, Waldo F. "Comedy in Shakespeare's Yorkist Tetralogy." *Pacific Coast Philology* IX (April 1974): 48-55.

Disputes S. L. Bethell's conclusion that all of the comic incidents in *Henry VI* are to be found in the chronicles (see excerpt above, 1951) and provides examples of some that were Shakespeare's inventions. According to McNeir, an Elizabethan audience would have found humor in the incompatibility of Margaret and Henry, the cowardice of Sir John Falstaff, and Shakespeare's treatment of Joan.

Pratt, Samuel M. "Shakespeare and Humphrey Duke of Gloucester: A Study in Myth." *Shakespeare Quarterly* 16, No. 2 (Spring 1965): 201-16.

Extended discussion of the historical figure who was the basis for Humphrey's character in *1* and *2 Henry VI*. Pratt points out that in Shakespeare's plays Humphrey is not depicted as a "spotless hero"; rather, his stature increases as the result of other characters' reports of him.

Prior, Moody E. "Ideas of History: *1, 2,* and *3 Henry VI, Richard III*" and "Legitimacy and Sovereign Power: *1, 2,* and *3 Henry VI*." In his *The Drama of Power: Studies in Shakespeare's History Plays*, pp. 34-58, pp. 101-19. Evanston, Ill.: Northwestern University Press, 1973.

Contends that the question of legitimacy and power is the central theme of the *Henry VI* trilogy. Prior views the plays as presenting a political rather than providential view of events, asserting that Henry's "invocations to God's providence and justice" do not furnish a philosophical basis for the trilogy, but instead "establish Henry's simple, passive submissiveness" to the will of God.

Prouty, Charles Tyler. *"The Contention" and Shakespeare's "2 Henry VI."* New Haven, Conn.: Yale University Press, 1954, 157 p.

Claims that Peter Alexander and Madeleine Doran (see entries above) were in error in their belief that *The Contention* is a memorial reconstruction of *2 Henry VI*. Prouty asserts that it was a common practice among Elizabethan dramatists to revise the works of others, and that Shakespeare followed *The Contention* closely when he wrote *2 Henry VI*.

Quinn, Michael. "Providence in Shakespeare's Yorkist Plays." *Shakespeare Quarterly* 10 (1959): 45-52.

Maintains that a limited scepticism is evident in *1, 2,* and *3 Henry VI*. Quinn argues that Shakespeare differentiated between particular and generalized providence, and that while he suggested in his plays that complete trust in God may inhibit intelligence and action, he did not "deny the possibility of miraculous or arbitrary interventions by God."

Ravich, Robert A. "A Psychoanalytic Study of Shakespeare's Early Plays." *Psychoanalytic Quarterly* XXXIII, No. 3 (1964): 388-410.
　　Treats the eleven earliest plays "as if they were the productions of a patient in analysis." Ravich concludes that the *Henry VI* trilogy reveals an obsession with "the destructive power of the phallic woman" and indicates that Shakespeare harbored "the passive dependant man's fear that he will be killed or driven mad."

Ricks, Don M. *Shakespeare's Emergent Form.* Utah State University Monograph Series XV, no. 1. Logan: Utah State University Press, June 1968, 103 p.
　　Disputes E. M. W. Tillyard's view that the *Henry VI* trilogy is part of an epic cycle (see excerpt above, 1944). Analyzing the changes in plotting and structure from *1 Henry VI* to *2* and *3 Henry VI*, Ricks argues that the plays are individually constructed, although they have in common the theme of civil dissension. In his judgment, *2 Henry VI* is much superior to *1* and *3 Henry VI* in terms of structure.

Riddell, James A. "Talbot and the Countess of Auvergne." *Shakespeare Quarterly* 28, No. 1 (Winter 1977): 51-7.
　　Disagrees with critics who regard the scene between Talbot and the Countess as either irrelevant or comic. Riddell points out that the qualities Talbot exhibits in this scene, especially his magnanimous attitude toward the Countess and his indifference to scorn, represent essential aspects of chivalric behavior in battle and, as such, contribute further to our impression of him as a heroic figure.

Simpson, Richard. "The Politics of Shakspere's Historical Plays." *The New Shakspere Society's Transactions,* Series I, No. 1 (1874): 396-411.
　　Postulates that Shakespeare altered historical accounts in his chronicle sources in order to emphasize the mismanagement that led to England's loss of France. Simpson believes that Shakespeare intended to show parallels between the precarious political situations in Elizabethan and fifteenth-century England.

Stauffer, Donald A. "The Country Mouse." In his *Shakespeare's World of Images,* pp. 11-38. New York: W. W. Norton & Co., 1949.
　　Contends that in *1, 2,* and *3 Henry VI* Shakespeare was not presenting a personal, well-developed theory of history, but merely repeating "the platitudes of the chroniclers and the saws of the pulpit."

Stirling, Brents. "The Plays." In his *The Populace in Shakespeare,* pp. 19-63. New York: Columbia University Press, 1949.
　　Proposes that the Cade scenes in *2 Henry VI,* in addition to providing comic relief, serve to emphasize Shakespeare's political viewpoint. Stirling calls attention to Shakespeare's departures from the chronicle sources, noting that the dramatist mixed together accounts of Cade's Rebellion with those of the more violent and outrageous Peasants' Revolt in 1381 to darken his picture of the later events.

Swayne, Mattie. "Shakespeare's King Henry VI as a Pacifist." *College English* III, No. 2 (1941): 143-49.
　　Argues that Shakespeare intended his audience to admire Henry and to view him as triumphant in defeat. Swayne regards the depiction of the king as an expression of Shakespeare's belief that private virtues are necessary, even thought they may incapacitate the individual for his public role.

Talbert, Ernest William. "The Henry VI Trilogy and *Richard III.*" In his *Elizabethan Drama and Shakespeare's Early Plays: An Essay in Historical Criticism,* pp. 161-234. New York: Gordian Press, 1973.
　　Maintains that Shakespeare borrowed structural elements from both miracle and morality plays in composing *1, 2,* and *3 Henry VI.* Talbert contends that the dramatic movement in the trilogy is cyclical and repetitive and that Shakespeare's control of this cycl-

ical process, as well as his creation of theatrically effective climactic scenes, shows a "sure, purposeful . . . [and] precise" technique.

Turner, Robert Y. "Characterization in Shakespeare's Early History Plays." *ELH* 31, No. 3 (September 1964): 241-58.
　　Maintains that in the *Henry VI* trilogy the characterization is static because the behavior of the dramatic figures is intended to represent fixed moral qualities, rather than psychological conflict or change. Turner asserts that Shakespeare borrowed this method of characterization from medieval morality plays.

—————. *Shakespeare's Apprenticeship.* Chicago: University of Chicago Press, 1974, 293 p.
　　Traces Shakespeare's reliance on formal rhetorical devices in *1, 2,* and *3 Henry VI.* Turner demonstrates how the dramatist's moral didacticism is enhanced though the use of copious restatement, speeches of emotion and persuasion, and dialogue in the form of debate. Turner notes that in this nonmimetic style of drama, the moral significance of historical events is more important than the characters' responses to those events.

Willcock, Gladys D. "Language and Poetry in Shakespeare's Early Plays." *Proceedings of the British Academy 1954* XL (1954): 103-18.
　　Examines the language of Margaret of Anjou's "shipwreck" speech in *3 Henry VI,* Act V, Scene iv to demonstrate Shakespeare's knowledge and use of the rhetorical devices of amplification and variation. Willcock notes that through expansion and diversity Shakespeare extends the metaphor of the shipwreck into allegory.

Wilson, F. P. "Marlowe and Shakespeare." In his *Marlowe and the Early Shakespeare,* pp. 104-31. Oxford: At the Clarendon Press, 1953.
　　Asserts that *1, 2,* and *3 Henry VI* were the first popular, as opposed to academic, dramatizations of English history. Wilson's view of the trilogy as emphasizing the importance of order and degree is similar to that of E. M. W. Tillyard (see excerpt above, 1944).

Wilson, J. Dover. "Malone and the Upstart Crow." *Shakespeare Survey* 4 (1951): 56-68.
　　Disputes Peter Alexander's conclusion that Robert Greene's attack on Shakespeare (see excerpt above, 1592) alludes to the latter's career as an actor. Dover Wilson contends that the reference to the crow "beautified with our feathers" would have been understood by Greene's contemporaries as an accusation that Shakespeare plagiarized the works of other writers in composing his early plays.

—————. Introduction to *The First Part of King Henry VI.* In *The Works of Shakespeare,* by William Shakespeare, edited by John Dover Wilson, pp. ix-lv. Cambridge: At the University Press, 1952.
　　An overview of *1 Henry VI* which presents the play as a collaboration among Nashe, Greene, and Shakespeare. Dover Wilson argues that his view of multiple authorship relieves Shakespeare "of all responsibility for the dull, miserably commonplace, and often unmetrical verse" found in several scenes of the play.

Yoder, Audrey. *Animal Analogy in Shakespeare's Character Portrayal.* New York: King's Crown Press, 1947, 150 p.
　　An examination of animal fables and imagery which Shakespeare used to strengthen characterization in the *Henry VI* trilogy. Yoder notes that Shakespeare compared men to animals "most frequently with hostile intent," although he also used the device for satirical purposes and to heighten the tone of certain passages.

Zeeveld, W. Gordon. "The Influence of Hall on Shakespeare's English Historical Plays." *ELH* III, No. 3 (September 1936): 317-53.
　　Evaluation of the characterizations and themes in Hall's chronicles in relation to the *Henry VI* trilogy. Zeeveld asserts that the central motif in Hall's *The Union of the Two Noble and Illustrious Families*—the national peril of domestic sedition—was adopted by Shakespeare as the theme of his trilogy.

Macbeth

DATE: It is generally conceded that Shakespeare wrote *Macbeth* sometime between the accession of King James I in 1603 and the first recorded performance of the play at the GLOBE THEATRE in the spring of 1611. A more specific and the most probable date, scholars concur, is 1606. As early as 1607 there are possible allusions to Shakespeare's *Macbeth* in such contemporary plays as Beaumont and Fletcher's *The Knight of the Burning Pestle*. Also, most critics agree that the comments of the Porter in Act II, Scene iii probably refer to certain events occurring in 1606, particularly the Gunpowder Plot, a Roman Catholic conspiracy to blow up the British Houses of Parliament while King James was in attendance. The Porter's reference to a treasonous equivocator has been linked to the March 1606 trial of Henry Garnet, a Jesuit priest who was implicated in the Gunpowder Plot and, after perjuring himself, pleaded that such equivocation was justifiable if done for a good cause. It has also been suggested that the Porter's mention of a farmer who hanged himself "on the expectation of plenty" (II. iii. 5) may refer to the low wheat prices of 1606. Yet John Dover Wilson proposed that topical references were added to *Macbeth* for a court performance before King James in 1606 and that an earlier version of the play was composed around the time of *Hamlet* in 1601-02. Nonetheless, because the play's subject matter would have been of special interest to James—who was known to be intrigued with witchcraft—most scholars concur that it must have been written after 1603, possibly for a performance before the king in August 1606, while his brother-in-law, King Christian IV of Denmark, was visiting England. This hypothesis has been supported by the play's brevity, which, some scholars maintain, is due to Christian's limited knowledge of English and to James's impatience with longer plays.

TEXT: The FIRST FOLIO of 1623 contains the only authoritative and probably the first published text of *Macbeth*, which was quite likely printed from a PROMPT-BOOK or a transcript of one. Controversy over the authorship of *Macbeth* has centered around two major textual issues, abridgement and interpolation. While earlier editors discerned a number of "un-Shakespearean" scenes, including the Porter scene, most scholars now consider only the whole of Act III, Scene v, and certain lines in Act IV, Scene i, to be the interpolations of another author. All of these spurious lines involve Hecate and the witches and are usually attributed to Thomas Middleton, who, it is thought, was employed to revise Shakespeare's *Macbeth* to make it more operatic by introducing songs which he later incorporated into his *The Witch*. Other critics, however, contend that *Macbeth*'s Hecate is considerably different from the character in *The Witch* and that, despite the presence of Middleton's songs, some anonymous author and not Middleton is the more likely composer of the interpolated lines. The other textual concern about *Macbeth* is the apparent abridgement of the original text. Because *Macbeth* is one of the shortest plays in the Shakespearean canon—2107 lines compared to *Hamlet*'s 3924—and because some critics have suggested that there are gaps in the text, it has been argued that the play was shortened. John Dover Wilson proposed that Shakespeare originally composed a longer *Macbeth* in 1601-02, but that he revised and abridged it in 1606 for a court performance. Kenneth Muir, however, contended that if such an abridgement occurred, the deleted scenes would most likely have been preserved for later performances

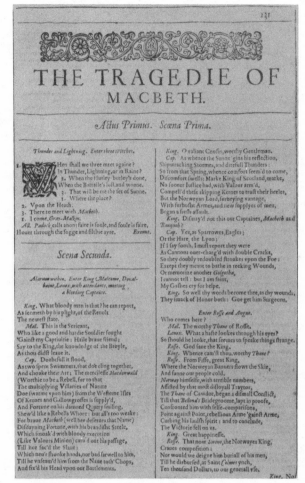

Title page of Macbeth taken from the First Folio (1623).

in the public theater; yet, they are unknown. A number of other critics have argued that *Macbeth* was not shortened and that its brevity is simply the result of its being written for a court performance before King James I, who, as Henry N. Paul has suggested, was known to have a short attention span for drama. However, D. A. Traversi has explained the play's abruptness by contending that what appear to be textual gaps are in fact "demonstrably necessary to the feeling of the tragedy."

SOURCES: Shakespeare's primary source for *Macbeth* was RAPHAEL HOLINSHED's *Chronicles of England, Scotlande and Irelande* (1577). Although Shakespeare used Holinshed's account for the major elements of the plot, he altered the story for his purposes. The battle against the rebels described at the beginning of *Macbeth* is in the *Chronicles* three separate campaigns. Shakespeare also compressed the reign of Macbeth to a short and tyrannous period; according to Holinshed, Macbeth's reign lasted seventeen years, during ten of which he was considered a good ruler. Some of the characters are more virtuous in *Macbeth* than in the play's source: Duncan, in Holinshed's history, was a younger, ineffectual leader, and Banquo and others were accomplices in the murder of Duncan. Macbeth, on the other hand, had a legitimate claim to the throne in the *Chronicles* because Duncan broke the traditional Scottish pattern of kingly succession by naming his son heir. The banquet scene and the appearance of the ghost of Banquo as well as the complex character of Lady Macbeth and the sleepwalking episode were Shakespeare's inventions and are not found in the *Chronicles*. The circumstances surrounding the actual murder of Duncan Shakespeare most likely derived from Holinshed's account of the murder of an earlier monarch, King Duff, by Donwald, who was also urged along by an ambitious wife.

Yet Holinshed's history of Macbeth was itself derived from a line of different sources and it is possible that Shakespeare may have made use of these as well. Holinshed's main source was Hector Boece's *Scotorum Historiae* (c. 1527), a book which was later translated into Scottish by John Bellenden (c. 1536) and may have been known to Shakespeare; as noted by Geoffrey Bullough, Boece's depiction of Lady Macbeth's attitude toward her husband, not developed in Holinshed, is quite close to Shakespeare's. An earlier source for the Macbeth legend was Andrew Wynton's *The Original Chronicle of Scotland* (c. 1424). Wynton's metrical history introduced the prophecy of the Weird Sisters, Macbeth's reliance on them, and his ambitious nature. Before Wynton, John Fordun presented, in his *Chronica Gentis Scotorum* (c. 1384), the Macbeth story, emphasizing the goodness of Duncan and Malcolm's testing of Macduff. In addition, scholars have noted that certain passages in *Macbeth* offer evidence of the influence of Senecan tragedy on Shakespeare.

After Holinshed, George Buchanan published the *Rerum Scoticarum Historia* (1582), which Shakespeare may also have used as a source. Although Buchanan's account differs little from Holinshed's, he developed the idea of the criminal's remorse and hallucinations and described Macbeth's ambitious character in terms similar to Shakespeare's. Another possible source is John Leslie's *De Origine Scotorum* (1578), which presented the Weird Sisters as devils disguised as women and stressed the concept of the royal family tree, possibly reflected in the tree imagery found in *Macbeth*. It is also possible that Shakespeare knew of Matthew Gwinn's pageant *Tres Sibyllaes,* presented before King James I in the summer of 1605. Upon entering the city of Oxford, three youths appeared before the king dressed as sybils, reminded him that they had once promised his ancestor, Banquo, royal descendants, and then saluted him individually, saying: "Hail, thou who rulest Scotland!" "Hail, thou who rulest England!" "Hail, thou who rulest Ireland!"—a ritual reminiscent of Macbeth's first encounter with the witches. Finally, in William Kemp's *Nine Daies Wonder* (1600), a reference to a ballad suggests that there may have been some other dramatic version of the Macbeth story around Shakespeare's time. Kemp ridiculed some "penny Poet whose first making was the miserable stolne story of Macdoel or Macdobeth or Macsomewhat, for I am sure a Mac it was though I neuer had the maw to see it." That the Weird Sisters were included in this "stolne story" is implied by Kemp's advice to its author to "leaue writing these beastly ballets, make not good wenches prophetesses for little or no profit."

CRITICAL HISTORY: *Macbeth,* although it has not received the same kind of critical consideration afforded either *Hamlet* or *King Lear,* is considered one of Shakespeare's greatest works. Like the play itself, the commentary on *Macbeth* appears to be at once simple and complex. Much of the criticism written during the last three hundred years suggests a number of well-defined interpretive issues: the problematic nature of the witches; free will versus fate; Macbeth's essential goodness or evilness;

his motive for murdering Duncan; the role of Lady Macbeth; the relation of the Porter scene to the play's action; Shakespeare's technique for creating an atmosphere of evil and presenting a sympathetic portrayal of the tragic hero. Yet, despite an apparent consensus on the key questions raised by the play, there has been little unanimity on the answers. Often the various interpretations have been antithetical, suggesting that in the realm of *Macbeth* criticism, as with the world that Macbeth perceives, "Nothing is but what is not" (I. iii. 141-42).

Seventeenth- and eighteenth-century critical response to *Macbeth* offered both positive and negative assessments. Samuel Pepys praised it as "one of the best plays for a stage," but John Dryden complained of its bombastic speeches. In the eighteenth century, Charles Gildon protested that Macbeth and Lady Macbeth are "too monstrous for the Stage" and a similar complaint was later made by Francis Gentleman.

Gentleman also condemned Shakespeare for his representation of the witches in *Macbeth,* charging that it inculcates superstitious beliefs and weakens reason and, thus, rather than improving the minds of the audience, becomes detrimental. Yet a number of other eighteenth-century critics, reacting against such censures as Gentleman's, defended Shakespeare's use of witches and the supernatural. Samuel Johnson noted King James's particular interest in the subject of witches and argued that in representing these supernatural elements Shakespeare merely made use of the commonly held beliefs of his time. Elizabeth Montagu remarked that the supernatural in the play is essential in producing a sense of terror that cannot be achieved by "the operation of human agency." An anonymous critic in the *British Magazine,* defending Shakespeare's presentation of the Weird Sisters, argued that ancient literature is infused with similar mythological personages. Arthur Murphy suggested that in *Macbeth* Shakespeare illustrated that ghosts and apparitions are merely the products of a guilty or fearful mind.

Another strong current in eighteenth-century criticism of *Macbeth* was the consideration of the characters of Macbeth and Lady Macbeth. Despite their condemnation by Gildon and Gentleman, other critics discerned in both of these characters genuinely human qualities. Montagu perceived "something feminine" in Lady Macbeth's inability to kill Duncan and attributed to Macbeth "a generous disposition." Johnson stated that the manner in which Lady Macbeth persuades Macbeth to murder Duncan affords "a Proof of *Shakespeare*'s Knowledge of Human Nature." Johnson also laid heavy emphasis on Macbeth's courage, commenting that it preserves some esteem for him, but he also remarked that generally the play "has no nice discriminations of character." The issue of sympathy for Macbeth was also addressed by Thomas Davies, who contended that it is not Macbeth's courage but his initial reluctance to murder Duncan and subsequent guilty conscience that evoke some degree of pity for him.

Towards the end of the eighteenth century, Thomas Whately, in his essay comparing Macbeth to Richard III, provided one of the first fully developed analyses of a Shakespearean character. Whately ascribed to Macbeth several distinct personality features, including gentleness and timidity, and stated that he was a more complicated and highly finished character than Richard. Macbeth, he argued, is induced to kill Duncan by the witches and commits the subsequent murders out of a fearful insecurity. Whately also stated that Macbeth frequently displays both cowardice and irresolution, an observation later discussed by George Steevens and, in the nineteenth century, by John Philip Kemble. Steevens contended that Macbeth initially possesses a "genuine intrepidity," but that he loses this quality as he ceases to be virtuous, and that his bravery is consequently supplanted by timidity and uncertainty. Kemble, however, reacted strongly to Whately's and Steevens's assessments of Macbeth's character. In an effort to refute their notion that Macbeth is cowardly, Kemble cited evidence throughout the play of the protagonist's courage and argued that it is essential to the effect of the tragedy that Macbeth be allowed some esteem for his bravery.

Nineteenth-century critics continued to discuss the central characters in *Macbeth*. Like its protagonist, Lady Macbeth also elicited contradictory assessments. William Hazlitt observed the ambition and masculinity in Lady Macbeth's character and deemed her "a great bad woman, whom we hate, but whom we fear more than we hate." Anna Brownell Jameson and William Maginn, however, offered an alternative view of the character whom many critics considered, in Malcolm's words, a "fiend-like queen." Jameson minimized Lady Macbeth's role in the murder of Duncan, attributed to her several admirable characteristics, and stressed her essential femininity. She also argued that the sleepwalking scene evokes our sympathy for Lady Macbeth. Maginn furthered this interpretation of her character by contending that she did not tempt Macbeth and that her only sin was her unwavering devotion to her husband. Combining many of his predecessors' comments, H. N. Hudson maintained that Lady Macbeth is actually two different characters: a matter-of-fact woman of firm intellect and an individual possessed by a sympathetic conscience.

The critical consideration of the significance of the witches in *Macbeth* also continued throughout the nineteenth century, although the discussion no longer centered on the appropriateness of their representation, but rather on the degree of their influence on Macbeth. Like Whately and Steevens in the eighteenth century, both of whom contended that Macbeth's murderous actions were incited by the Weird Sisters, Charles Lamb asserted that the witches "begin bad impulses to men" and sway Macbeth's destiny. August Wilhelm Schlegel, however, suggested that the Weird Sisters merely "cheat" Macbeth into believing that their prophecies have the solidity of fate. As this issue of free will versus fate became the focal point of nineteenth-century commentary on the witches, many critics contended that Macbeth possesses free will and that the Weird Sisters do not determine his course of action. Franz Horn argued that Macbeth's tragedy is caused not by destiny but by a lack of faith in his own freedom and that the only determinant of his actions "exists in his own heart." G. G. Gervinus similarly stated that the witches are "simply the embodiment of inward temptation" and that they represent fate not as an external force, but "only in the sense in which men carry their own fates within their own bosoms." Also, A. J. F. Mézières agreed that the Weird Sisters have no external influence over Macbeth, but merely impel him to commit a crime towards which he was already inclined, while J. L. F. Flathe charged that Macbeth "pursued the path of evil," for "the devil visits those only who invite him in." Gustav von Rümelin proposed that the witches exert no more control over Macbeth than does the Delphic oracle over Oedipus. A different interpretation of fate was suggested earlier in the century by Hermann Ulrici, who, applying a rigorous Christian aesthetic to the play, maintained that the witches represent, in part, human spirits fallen from original innocence and illustrate "the all-pervading sinfulness of all human and earthly beings."

Several critics of the late nineteenth and early twentieth centuries rejected the notion of the Romantics that Macbeth possesses an absolute free will. Edward Dowden contended that Macbeth is not immune to external forces and that he is "infected" by the influence of the witches. Denton J. Snider and A. C. Bradley, both influenced by the philosophy of Georg Wilhelm Friedrich Hegel, interpreted the witches' power in dialectical terms. They asserted that Macbeth's actions are determined by a synthesis of the dialectic of both internal and external forces. For Snider, the Weird Sisters embodied "the totality of conditions, internal and external, which determine conduct to evil." Bradley similarly argued that they represent "not only the evil slumbering in the hero's soul, but all those obscure influences of the evil around him in the world."

Snider and Bradley also agreed with Flathe on the question of Banquo's innocence. Flathe had challenged the traditional reading of Banquo as an innocent foil to Macbeth's evil and charged that Banquo is in fact guilty of not taking action against Macbeth. Snider and Bradley likewise asserted that Banquo, influenced by the witches' prophecy, yields to evil and chooses a course of inaction in order to serve his own ambition.

The power of Macbeth's imagination was also commented on by both Snider and Bradley. Snider, employing his thesis that Shakespearean tragedy presents a movement from guilt to retribution, observed that quite early in the play Macbeth realizes the necessity of earthly retribution and suffers internal punishment through his imagination. Snider also remarked that Macbeth's imagination, "the center of his spiritual activity," is desiccated at the play's conclusion, and the protagonist becomes "an inward desert." Snider thus designated *Macbeth* the "Tragedy of the Imagination." For Bradley, Macbeth possesses the "imagination of a poet" and because of this he evokes some measure of sympathy. Bradley also stressed the atmosphere of *Macbeth,* pointing out the strong images of darkness, blood, and violence that permeate the play. In addition, he stated that the simplicity of the plot and secondary characters suggests that Shakespeare may have intended the play to have a classical quality.

One of the most famous nineteenth-century interpretations of *Macbeth* was written by the Romantic essayist Thomas De Quincey. De Quincey singled out one event in the play for consideration, the knocking at the gate following Duncan's murder, and explained its profound dramatic effect. When Macbeth kills Duncan, De Quincey argued, the "world of the ordinary life" is suspended and replaced by a "world of darkness." But the knocking at the gate, he proposed, represents a human reaction to this fiendish, dark world and reasserts the operations of an ordinary, mundane reality. De Quincey's friend and fellow Romantic Samuel Taylor Coleridge, however, was less impressed by this episode in the play. Coleridge maintained that the "low Porter soliloquy" was written not by Shakespeare but "for the mob by some other hand." Coleridge was not the first to complain of the Porter scene; in the eighteenth century, Francis Gentleman had called it "an insult upon judgment" and Elizabeth Montagu was most likely referring to the Porter scene when she stated that *Macbeth* contains "one whole scene entirely absurd and improper." Later critics, however, defended the appropriateness of the scene. Gervinus contended that the soliloquy presents an "uncomfortable joviality," providing a contrast which is "very suitable to the circumstances." H. N. Hudson and John W. Hales maintained that the disputed scene is characteristic of Shakespeare's style, and Hales further argued that it is essential to the drama because it affords a necessary comic relief from the surrounding horror.

In the early twentieth century, with the advent of Freudian psychology, several psychoanalytic interpretations of the characters in *Macbeth* appeared. Perhaps the most notable of these readings was presented by Isador H. Coriat, whose essay on Lady Macbeth was one of the first fully developed psychoanalytic treatments of a Shakespearean character. Coriat argued that Lady Macbeth is "a typical case of hysteria," that her ambition to be queen is actually a sublimated desire for a child, and that this is a repressed sexual impulse which occasionally surfaces throughout the play, most fully emerging in the sleepwalking scene. He also stated that Lady Macbeth's compulsive act of washing her hands is "a compromise for self-reproach and repressed experiences" and that because she cannot free herself from her repressed unconscious, she is subjected to a relentless fate. Freud himself also offered a commentary on some of the characters in *Macbeth*. He viewed Lady Macbeth as an example of an individual who falls ill "precisely because" a strongly desired wish is finally fulfilled. Freud proposed that Lady Macbeth cannot enjoy her queenship because she believes her barrenness is related to her crimes. He also noted Shakespeare's frequent references to violations of the relationship of father and child and stated that the childlessness of Macbeth and Lady Macbeth is appropriate retribution for their "crimes against the sanctity of geniture." A few years later, Ludwig Jekels developed some of Freud's suggestions about the father-child references in *Macbeth*. Jekels argued that just as Macbeth acts as a bad "son" by murdering the father figure, Duncan, he is also a bad father to his figurative sons, Macduff and Banquo, and therefore forfeits the hope of fathering heirs to the crown.

In the 1930s, the reaction against character analysis in Shakespearean criticism was evident in several essays on *Macbeth* that focused on the play's imagery and atmosphere. In one such essay, G. Wilson Knight argued that Shakespeare presents an experience of absolute evil in the play by creating an atmosphere of abysmal darkness and uncertainty. The imagery, he stated, evokes a strong sense of fear and is thus analogous to the experience of a nightmare. In another essay on *Macbeth*, Knight examined what he called the "life-themes" represented by the imagery. He maintained that such positive "life forces" as honor, imperial magnificence, sleeping, feasting, creation, and innocence are opposed by forces of evil and death. Like other twentieth-century critics, Knight observed that Macbeth continually upsets the unity of nature and sets destruction against creation, but he also noted that, in the end, the positive forces of nature triumph over Macbeth's evil.

The experience of evil in *Macbeth* was also the focus of L. C. Knights in his famous essay entitled *How Many Children Had Lady Macbeth?*. Knights's commentary was significant because in it he challenged the predominant critical approach to Shakespeare, which emphasized character analysis, and focused instead on the imagery and themes in *Macbeth*. He identified as the play's thematic concerns the reversal of values, unnatural disorder, and deceitful appearances. In particular, he examined the conflict between the images of unnatural chaos and those of supernatural grace, concluding that the natural order is restored by the representatives of supernatural grace, Malcolm and Macduff—an interpretation which later appeared in Christian interpretations of the play.

Caroline F. E. Spurgeon commented on the clothing imagery in *Macbeth*, pointing out the frequent references to Macbeth's borrowed and poorly fitting robes. In a notable essay on the poetic language in *Macbeth*, Cleanth Brooks developed Spur-

geon's suggestion of the clothing motif, particularly in relation to the metaphors of the "naked new-born babe" and the "breech'd" daggers that appear at I. vii. 21 and II. iii. 116. He argued that these images are not overwrought poetic conceits, but are parts of the "great symbols" which "furnish Shakespeare with his most subtle and ironically telling instruments." In his treatment of the baby imagery in *Macbeth*, Brooks explained that the naked babe symbolizes the future that Macbeth attempts to control by killing children and that Macduff, who ultimately destroys Macbeth, is another representative of the naked babe.

The issue of the witches was raised once again by Walter Clyde Curry. Like Samuel Johnson, Curry examined the background of Elizabethan notions of demonic spirits, concluding that the witches in *Macbeth* are the representatives of an objective evil. In addition, Curry proposed that the natural disturbances, Macbeth's hallucinations, and Lady Macbeth's somnambulism are all meant to be products of demonic powers. Other critics suggested that a certain measure of the evil presented in *Macbeth* is linked to the protagonist's attempts to manipulate time. Knight observed the destructive effect of Macbeth's effort to "dislocate time." Stephen Spender developed the suggestion, discussing the "chaos of time" in *Macbeth* and arguing that Macbeth tries to prevent the past and the future from affecting the present. Another interpretation of time in *Macbeth* was later presented by Tom F. Driver. Driver, like Spender, remarked that Macbeth attempts to manipulate time. He also noted that against Macbeth's sense of time is set "Providential time," providing a proper temporal order and historic succession which ultimately triumphs over Macbeth. Driver also compared the view of time presented in *Macbeth* with that of *Oedipus Rex*, concluding that whereas in Sophocles's play the future is preordained and therefore closed, Shakespeare's play, reflecting Judeo-Christian culture rather than Greek, offers the possibility of an "open future."

The language of *Macbeth* became a concern for several twentieth-century commentators on the play. Early in the century, Bradley suggested that Lady Macbeth's language demonstrates that she is more realistic than her husband. Edith Sitwell examined certain vowel sounds in key speeches which, she claimed, suggest discordant dissonance and contribute to the presentation of evil. M. M. Mahood discussed the puns and double entendres in *Macbeth*, stating that while it is less obvious than in other Shakespearean plays, the wordplay serves to link the play's themes together into a unified dramatic poem. Several interpretations of the play focused specifically on Macbeth's use of language. John Arthos stated that the protagonist's speeches at first reflect a vivid imagination and an impulse to personify, but that as his crimes continue his language indicates a concern with lifeless materiality. Arnold Stein proposed that Macbeth invokes a "word-magic," similar to that of the Weird Sisters, which allows him to transform himself into a murdering "werewolf" or to pretend innocence. Stein argued, however, that towards the conclusion of the play Macbeth's confidence in the power of words is shaken and he turns instead to unreasoned and desperate action. More recently, Bertrand Evans asserted that Shakespeare provides Macbeth with language that is deceptively poetic, making him appear better than he is. Evans stated that it is this "witchcraft of poetry" that allows Shakespeare to present Macbeth, a murderer, as a sympathetic tragic hero.

That issue—how Shakespeare manages to retain the audience's sympathy for Macbeth—was broached early in the twentieth century by Arthur Quiller-Couch and became a frequent concern for later Shakespearean critics. Quiller-Couch proposed that Shakespeare preserves sympathy for Macbeth by making the murder of Duncan proceed from a "fatal hallucination." Wayne Booth noted a number of dramatic devices that Shakespeare uses to present a sympathetic portrayal of the hero. He argued that the testimony heard from other characters and Macbeth's reluctance to kill Duncan early in Act I suggest that he is not a naturally evil man. He also pointed out that Duncan's murder is never represented or narrated, that Macbeth has a limited role in the other murders, and that he never commits any act of "wicked violence" on stage. Booth, like Evans, also explained that Macbeth's poetic language affords him further sympathy. Robert Heilman, discussing the playwright's achievement, argued that Shakespeare "so manages the situation that we become Macbeth" and "accept ourselves as murderers." He maintained that Macbeth's anxiety and fear are emotions familiar to us and thus evoke our pity. Even when Macbeth is most likely to be regarded as a monster, Heilman stated, he is also shown as lonely, reflective, and not completely reproachable. Yet, Heilman concluded that while such empathy with a murderer may provide a fuller understanding of humanity, that view too easily overlooks Macbeth's essential deficiency as a tragic hero.

The issue of the Porter scene was also revived by critics considering Shakespeare's dramatic technique in *Macbeth,* and Coleridge's dismissal of the scene has generally been refuted. Kenneth Muir argued that the episode is "an integral part of the play" in both style and content. He emphasized the antithetical quality of the Porter's speech, associating it with the overall subject of equivocation throughout the play. Muir also remarked that the thematic concern with the conflict between desire and action is present in both this scene and the play as a whole. John B. Harcourt stated that the scene "gives every evidence of careful planning" and the Porter's low comedy deflates the "pseudo-heroic illusion" of Macbeth's character. Like Muir, Harcourt also observed that certain themes in the Porter's "little morality-scene" are developed elsewhere in the play.

The dramatic function of the play's personae led a few critics to question the complexity of the characters' personalities and motivations. Leo Kirschbaum opposed previous critics who had accused Banquo of duplicitous guilt, stating that he is intended not as a psychologically realistic character, but rather as a dramatic device, a symbolic foil to Macbeth's evil. Kirschbaum maintained that because Banquo is more an "instrument" than a character, for dramatic purposes, he must be viewed as innocent and in contrast to Macbeth. Irving Ribner similarly argued that the characters in *Macbeth* have specific dramatic functions for the purpose of illustrating the workings of an ethical system. They are, he stated, primarily "dramatic vehicles."

A number of twentieth-century critics have, like Hermann Ulrici before them, examined the Christian implications of *Macbeth.* Roy Walker, noting parallels between *Macbeth* and New Testament scriptures, argued that the murder of Duncan and its consequences are "profoundly impregnated with the central tragedy of the Christian myth"—the betrayal of Christ. He interpreted the knocking at the gate as "a pulse of doom to the guilty souls within the castle" and associated it with the opportunity for Christian salvation. Harcourt proposed that Macduff's knocking at the gate suggests Christ's entrance into the gates of hell to save the souls of the just; the critic thus

perceived Macduff's role as symbolically linked to the apocryphal "Harrower of Hell." Other critics argued for a more comprehensive Christian reading of *Macbeth.* In a scene-by-scene analysis of *Macbeth,* G. R. Elliott emphasized the Renaissance concept of divine grace and, like Ulrici, maintained that the play demonstrates the tragedy of humanity and ambitious evil; he proposed that Macbeth's actions are "essentially very human." Elliott also stated that the play expresses the Christian belief that even the wicked Macbeth could be converted if he allowed grace to supplant his pride and that man alone cannot overcome supernatural evil without the aid of supernatural goodness. Roy W. Battenhouse similarly discussed Macbeth's fall from Christian grace and noted his loss of faith and denial of the afterlife. Battenhouse also asserted that the play contains biblical parallels and compared the temptation of Macbeth and Lady Macbeth to that of Adam and Eve and Macbeth's ambition to Satan's.

Battenhouse was not the first critic to propose the latter analogy. A note in his marginalia suggests that Coleridge had perceived the similarity between Macbeth and Milton's Satan over a century earlier. Later, in the twentieth century, Quiller-Couch also commented on the similarity of these two characters. More recently, Robert Pack and Herbert R. Coursen, Jr., have developed this comparison. Pack remarked that Macbeth, unlike the heroes in Shakespeare's other major tragedies, is his own antagonist and more in control of his fate, and that while Hamlet, Othello, and Lear—provoked by external forces—"sin like Adam," Macbeth's sin, motivated by pride and ambition, is akin to Satan's. Like Satan, Pack argued, Macbeth is fully aware of the consequences of his defiant action and is not a creator but a destroyer. Coursen claimed that *Macbeth* is similar to the myth of Adam in its concern with the protagonist's moral decision, feminine temptation, and his "cosmic retribution." He observed that both Lady Macbeth and Eve are responsible for inciting the latent ambition in their husbands' hearts. Coursen also asserted that the name of Macbeth's armor-bearer, Seyton, suggests Satan and reinforces the theme of damnation.

Another frequent focus in twentieth-century criticism of *Macbeth* has been the opposition of the natural and the unnatural. Besides G. Wilson Knight and L. C. Knights, who made some notice of this conflict in their readings of the play, Theodore Spencer stated that "everything about Macbeth is a violation of nature." Paul N. Siegel, in examining the conflict between Christian humanist and "Machiavellian" views of human nature, concluded that Macbeth is punished for violating laws of nature and humanity. D. A. Traversi commented on a similar opposition, noting that while Duncan's speeches imply a natural and harmonious social order, Macbeth's suggest disorder and anarchy. In his efforts to destroy harmonious life, Traversi stated, Macbeth is defeated by the natural order, represented by Malcolm's "army of deliverance."

Such commentators as J. P. Dyson and Terence Eagleton identified other conflicts as central in *Macbeth.* Dyson posited that the opposition in the play exists between the dark, disruptive, "raven" elements and the lighter, harmonious, "martlet" elements, explaining that Macbeth, a representative of the "raven" world, futilely pretends to the "martlet" world and a hollow kingship. Eagleton identified the conflict as one between individual action and social responsibility. He claimed that Macbeth's service to Duncan is also his source of joy and self-expression; thus, in killing Duncan he destroys himself and is never allowed to enjoy his kingship.

Commentators on *Macbeth* in recent years have suggested that perhaps the conclusion of the play is not so optimistic as previous critics had believed. Jan Kott referred to Macbeth's ability to reach the threshold beyond which all killing is as easy as the "Auschwitz experience" and claimed that the play offers no catharsis, since Macbeth possesses no belief in human dignity and dies taking with him "into nothingness as many living beings as possible." Bernard Mc Elroy, describing *Macbeth* as a tragedy of self-loathing, perceived a tension between the protagonist's evil actions and his conscious abhorrence of those actions. The play's conclusion, stated Mc Elroy, is "retributive but not redemptive." The death of Young Siward was the focus of Karl F. Zender's comments on *Macbeth*. He argued that Siward's reaction to his son's death just prior to the play's conclusion represents an ironic comment on the limits of providential order. This death, Zender maintained, allows Macbeth's "nihilistic vision" a temporary victory and suggests that tragic error can be defeated but cannot be abolished. In examining the idea of manhood in *Macbeth*, a topic previously treated by Eugene M. Waith, Marilyn French declared that Shakespeare demonstrates the subjugation of feminine principles by masculine, "heroic" principles. She claimed that from the outset Macbeth is rewarded for his capacity to kill and that this unbridled masculine course of "purposeless slaughter" remains unchallenged at the conclusion of the play.

Harry Berger, Jr., looked to the early scenes of *Macbeth* for evidence that "there is something rotten in Scotland." Berger contended that rather than showing the social cohesion of Scotland, the reports of Macbeth's actions against the rebels suggest a sense of uncertainty and apprehensiveness, and his courtly exchanges with Duncan reveal an ominous tension between the speakers. The more a king does for his subjects in *Macbeth*'s Scotland, posited Berger, the more his subjects threaten his sovereignty. Finally, Stephen Booth proposed that in *Macbeth* Shakespeare illustrates the "ultimate impossibility" of limits and definition. There are no closed categories: time, place, words, characters—nothing "will stay fixed," Booth maintained. Beginnings in the play are uncertain, while endings lack finality. Thus, he argued, the speech Malcolm makes at the conclusion is analogous to the speech made by Duncan following the rebellion and suggests that "the old cycle is starting over again in the new."

While remarking that Shakespeare presents a limitlessness in *Macbeth*, Booth also noted that he does so within the limitations of an orderly, unified, and coherent work of art. Indeed, perhaps it is the paradox of this simultaneous appearance of unity and limitlessness that is frequently reflected in the antithetical commentary on the play. Critics have noted that *Macbeth* is one of Shakespeare's shortest plays, yet their interpretations indicate it is surprisingly complex. As Schlegel stated early in the nineteenth century: "We can hardly conceive how so very much could ever have been compressed into so narrow a space."

SAMUEL PEPYS   (essay date 1667)

[*A diversified background of travel, intellectual pursuits, and public office gave Pepys the opportunity to be a close observer of his society. His unique* Diary *is an unreserved study of the affairs and customs of his time. His personal revelations create a document of unusual psychological interest as well as providing a history of the Restoration theater. In the following two diary*

entries of 1667, Pepys praises Macbeth *for its variety and deems it "one of the best plays for a stage."*]

[January 7, 1667]

To the Duke's house and saw *Macbeth*, which, though I saw it lately, yet appears a most excellent play in all respects, but especially in divertisement, though it be a deep tragedy; which is a strange perfection in a tragedy, it being most proper here and suitable. (p. 453)

[April 19, 1667]

To the playhouse, where we saw *Macbeth*, which, though I have seen it often, yet is it one of the best plays for a stage, and a variety of dancing and music, that ever I saw. (p. 486)

> *Samuel Pepys, in diary entries of January 7, 1667 and April 19, 1667, in his* The Diary of Samuel Pepys, *Macmillan & Co., 1905, pp. 453, 486.*

JOHN DRYDEN   (essay date 1667)

[*Dryden, the leading poet and playwright of Restoration England, helped formulate the Neoclassical view of Shakespeare as an irregular genius whose native talent overcame his ignorance of the proper "rules" and language for serious drama. He was also instrumental in establishing Shakespeare's reputation as the foremost English dramatist, and his assessment of Shakespeare influenced critics well into the following century. In the following excerpt, drawn from his* A Defence of the Epilogue; or, An Essay on the Dramatique Poetry of the Last Age *(1672), Dryden concurs with Ben Jonson's purported response to the "bombast speeches" in* Macbeth.]

In reading some bombast speeches of *Macbeth*, which are not to be understood, [Ben Jonson] us'd to say that it was horrour, and I am much afraid that this is so. (p. 147)

> *John Dryden, in an extract from* Shakespeare, the Critical Heritage: 1623-1692, Vol. 1, *edited by Brian Vickers, Routledge & Kegan Paul, 1974, pp. 143-52.*

A FARTHER DEFENCE OF DRAMATIC POETRY   (essay date 1698)

[*In the following excerpt drawn from an unsigned pamphlet entitled* A Farther Defence of Dramatic Poetry *(1698), the author discusses the artistic limits imposed on drama by a strict adherence to the classical rules of unity of time and place, charging that Corneille's observation of these rules leads to "narrow Stage-restrictions." In* Macbeth, *the author argues, Shakespeare falsifies history, manipulates both time and place, and, in doing so, conveys the whole story of Macbeth in a manner that allows an audience, "both willing and prepar'd to be deceived," to "pass over a considerable distance both of time and place unheeded and unminded."*]

Here the shortest way to tell you what *will* please an *English* Audience, I think, is to look back and see what *has* pleased them. And here let us first take a view of our best English Tragedies, as our *Hamlet, Macbeth, Julius Caesar, Oedipus, Alexander, Timon of Athens, Moor of Venice*, and all the rest of our most shining Pieces. All these, and the Rest of their Honourable Brethren, are so far from pent up in *Corneille*'s narrower *Unity Rules*—viz. the Business of the Play confined to no longer Time than it takes up in the Playing, or his largest Compass of 24 Hours—that nothing is so ridiculous as to pretend to it. The Subjects of our English *Tragedies* are generally the whole Revolutions of Governments, States or Families, or those great Transactions, that our *Genius* of Stage-poetry can no more reach the Heights that can please our Audience under his Unity Shackles than an Eagle can soar in a Hen-coop. If the *French* can content themselves with the sweets of a single Rose-bed nothing less than the whole Garden, and the Field round it, will satisfie the *English*. Every Man as he likes. *Corneille* may reign Master of his own Revels but he is neither a Rule-maker nor a Play-maker for our Stage. And the Reason is plain. For as Delight is the great End of Playing, and those narrow Stage-restrictions of *Corneille* destroy that Delight by curtailing that Variety that should give it us, every such Rule therefore is Nonsense and Contradiction in its very Foundation. Even an Establish'd *Law,* when it destroys its own *Preamble* and the *Benefits* design'd by it, becomes void and null in it self.

'Tis true, I allow thus far, that it ought to be the chief care of the Poet to confine himself into as narrow a Compass as he can, without any particular stint, in the two First Unities of *Time* and *Place;* for which end he must observe two Things. First, upon occasion (suppose in such a Subject as *Macbeth*) he ought to falsifie even History it self. For the Foundation of that Play in the *Chronicles* was the Action of 25 Years: but in the Play we may suppose it begun and finish'd in one third of so many Months. Young *Malcom* and *Donalbain,* the Sons of *Duncan,* are but Children at the Murder of their Father, and such they return with the Forces from *England* to revenge his Death: whereas in the true Historick Length they must have set out Children and return'd men. Secondly, the length of Time and distance of Place required in the Action ought to be never pointed at, nor hinted in the Play. For example, neither *Malcolm* nor *Donalbain* must tell us how long they have been in *England* to raise those Forces, nor how long those Forces have been Marching into *Scotland;* nor *Macbeth* how far *Scone* and *Dunsinane* lay asunder, &c. By this means the Audience, who come both willing and prepar'd to be deceiv'd . . . and indulge their own Delusion, can pass over a considerable distance both of *Time* and *Place* unheeded and unminded if they are not purposely thrown too openly in their way to stumble at. (pp. 90-2)

An extract from Shakespeare, the Critical Heritage: 1693-1733, Vol. 2, *edited by Brian Vickers, Routledge & Kegan Paul, 1974, pp. 89-92.*

[CHARLES GILDON]   (essay date 1710)

[*Gildon was the first critic to write an extended commentary on Shakespeare's plays. Like many other Neoclassicists, he regarded Shakespeare as an imaginative playwright who nevertheless lacked knowledge of the dramatic "rules" necessary for correct writing. In the excerpt below, Gildon complains that the characters of Macbeth and Lady Macbeth "are too monstruous for the Stage" and that the play is lesser in both length and beauty than most of Shakespeare's dramas.*]

To say much in the Praise of this Play I cannot, for the Plot is a sort of History, and the Character of *Mackbeth* and his Lady are too monstruous for the Stage. But it has obtained, and in too much Esteem with the *Million* for any Man yet to say much against it.

The Topics and Lines of this Play are less in Number and Beauty than most of his. (p. 394)

[*Charles Gildon*], "Remarks on the Plays of Shakespear," *in* The Works of Mr. William Shakespear,

Vol. 7 by William Shakespeare, 1710. Reprint by AMS Press, Inc., 1967, pp. 257-444.

SAMUEL JOHNSON   (essay date 1745)

[*Johnson has long held an important place in the history of Shakespearean criticism. He is considered the foremost representative of moderate English Neoclassicism and is credited by some literary historians with freeing Shakespeare from the strictures of the three unities valued by strict Neoclassicists: that dramas should have a single setting, take place in less than twenty-four hours, and have a causally connected plot. More recent scholars portray him as a critic who was able to synthesize existing critical theory rather than as an innovative theoretician. Johnson was a master of Augustan prose style and a personality who dominated the literary world of his epoch. The following excerpt is taken from Johnson's* Miscellaneous Observations on the Tragedy of "Macbeth" *(1745), much of which he incorporated in his later edition of Shakespeare published in 1765. Like the* British Magazine *(1767), Elizabeth Montagu (1769), and August Wilhelm Schlegel (1808), but unlike Francis Gentleman (1770), Johnson defends Shakespeare's use of witches in the play, arguing that he merely made use of a commonly held belief of his age, a position later developed by Walter Clyde Curry (1933). Johnson also discusses King James's interest in witchcraft and notes that the subject became popular throughout England during James's reign. He considers the character of Lady Macbeth, stating that her challenge to Macbeth's courage is sophistry but that she nonetheless achieves her desired end. For further consideration of the character of Lady Macbeth, see the excerpts by Anna Brownell Jameson (1833), William Maginn (1837), A. C. Bradley (1904), and Isador H. Coriat (1912).*]

In order to make a true Estimate of the Abilities and Merit of a Writer it is always necessary to examine the Genius of his Age, and the Opinions of his Contemporaries. A Poet who should now make the whole Action of his Tragedy depend upon Enchantment, and produce the chief Events by the Assistance of supernatural Agents, would be censured as transgressing the Bounds of Probability. He would be banished from the Theatre to the Nursery, and condemned to write Fairy Tales instead of Tragedies. But a Survey of the Notions that prevailed at the Time when [*Macbeth*] was written will prove that *Shakespeare* was in no Danger of such Censures, since he only turned the System that was then universally admitted to his Advantage, and was far from overburthening the Credulity of his Audience.

The Reality of Witchcraft or Enchantment—which, though not strictly the same, are confounded in this Play—has in all Ages and Countries been credited by the common People, and in most by the Learned themselves. These Phantoms have indeed appeared more frequently, in proportion as the Darkness of Ignorance has been more gross; but it cannot be shown that the brightest Gleams of Knowledge have at any Time been sufficient to drive them out of the World. (pp. 165-66)

In the Time of Queen *Elizabeth* was the remarkable Trial of the Witches of *Warbois,* whose Conviction is still commemorated in an annual Sermon at *Huntingdon.* But in the Reign of King *James,* in which this Tragedy was written, many Circumstances concurred to propagate and confirm this Opinion. The King, who was much celebrated for his Knowledge, had, before his Arrival in *England,* not only examined in Person a Woman accused of Witchcraft but had given a very formal Account of the Practices and Illusions of evil Spirits, the Compacts of Witches, the Ceremonies used by them, the Manner of detecting them, and the Justice of punishing them, in his Dialogues of *Daemonologie,* written in the *Scottish* Dialect and published at *Edinburgh.* This Book was, soon after his Accession, reprinted at *London,* and as the ready way to gain K. *James*'s Favour was to flatter his Speculations the System of *Daemonologie* was immediately adopted by all who desired either to gain Preferment or not to lose it. Thus the Doctrine of Witchcraft was very powerfully inculcated, and as the greatest Part of Mankind have no other Reason for their Opinions than that they are in Fashion, it cannot be doubted but this Persuasion made a rapid Progress, since Vanity and Credulity co-operated in its favour and it had a Tendency to free Cowardice from Reproach. (p. 166)

Upon this general Infatuation *Shakespeare* might be easily allowed to found a Play, especially since he has followed with great Exactness such Histories as were then thought true; nor can it be doubted that the Scenes of Enchantment, however they may now be ridiculed, were both by himself and his Audience thought awful and affecting. (p. 167)

The Arguments by which Lady *Macbeth* persuades her Husband to commit the Murder afford a Proof of *Shakespeare*'s Knowledge of Human Nature. She urges the Excellence and Dignity of Courage, a glittering Idea which has dazzled Mankind from Age to Age, and animated sometimes the Housebreaker and sometimes the Conqueror; but this Sophism *Macbeth* has for ever destroyed by distinguishing true from false Fortitude in a Line and a half, of which it may almost be said that they ought to bestow Immortality on the Author though all his other Productions had been lost.

> I dare do all that may become a Man,
> Who dares do more is none.
>
> [I. vii. 46-7]

This Topic, which has been always employed with too much Success, is used in this Scene with peculiar Propriety, to a Soldier by a Woman. Courage is the distinguishing Virtue of a Soldier, and the Reproach of Cowardice cannot be borne by any Man from a Woman without great Impatience.

She then urges the Oaths by which he had bound himself to murder *Duncan,* another Art of Sophistry by which Men have sometimes deluded their Consciences and persuaded themselves that what would be criminal in others is virtuous in them; this Argument *Shakespeare,* whose Plan obliged him to make *Macbeth* yield, has not confuted, though he might easily have shown that a former Obligation could not be vacated by a latter. (pp. 172-73)

> *Samuel Johnson, in an extract from* Shakespeare, the Critical Heritage: 1733-1752, Vol. 3, *edited by Brian Vickers, Routledge & Kegan Paul, 1975, pp. 165-85.*

[CHARLOTTE LENNOX]   (essay date 1753)

[Lennox was an American-born novelist and Shakespearean scholar who compiled a three-volume edition of translated texts of the sources used by Shakespeare in twenty-two of his plays, including some analyses of the ways in which he used these sources. In the excerpt below, drawn from the first volume of her Shakespear Illustrated *(1753), Lennox compares the characters of Macbeth and Duncan with those in Shakespeare's sources, finding Shakespeare's portrayal of Macbeth to be less "rugged" and more contemplative and his Duncan to be less excessive in his virtues than the man of the chronicles.]*

The Character of *Macbeth* is drawn after the Historians, yet *Shakespear* has softened a little some of the most rugged Features; he shews him doubtful and irresolute about the Murder of the King, spurred on by Ambition to commit it, but re-

strained by his Abhorrence of the Action, and when by the Instigations of his Wife he is prevailed upon to do it, his Mind is afterwards filled with Remorse, and all the uneasy Sensations that attend repentant Guilt.

The Character *Macbeth* gives of *Duncan* in the Play is not inconsistent with that in the History, yet it is not the same; *Macbeth* speaks only of his Virtues, and his Faults were those Virtues carried to Excess. (p. 279)

> *[Charlotte Lennox], "Observations on the Use Shakespear Has Made of the Foregoing History of 'Macbeth'," in her* Shakespear Illustrated; or, The Novels and Histories, on Which the Plays of Shakespear Are Founded, Vol. I, *1753. Reprint by AMS Press Inc., 1973, pp. 269-92.*

ARTHUR MURPHY   (essay date 1754)

[An eighteenth-century dramatist and critic, Murphy was the editor of the Gray's Inn Journal *and is best remembered for his animated, two-act comedies and his often spurious and untrustworthy biographies of Henry Fielding and David Garrick. In the following excerpt, taken from the November 1754 issue of the* Entertainer, *Murphy attributes the perceptions of ghosts and apparitions to "guilt or weakness" and considers* Macbeth *a "finely pictured" illustration of a guilty mind.]*

This nation has in all ages been much more addicted to folly and superstition than any other whatever. The belief of GHOSTS and APPARITIONS is at present as strongly implanted in the minds of the major part of the inhabitants of this kingdom as it was in the days when ignorance and want of knowledge and experience blinded the eyes of men. I have always looked upon this foible as the creation of guilt or weakness. FEAR is the centre of both, and this continually fills our thoughts with unreal objects, full of darkness and horror. (p. 156)

In the tragedy of *Macbeth* the bard has finely pictured the condition of a guilty mind, and the scene when MACBETH goes to murder DUNCAN is one of the strongest proofs that a GHOST or APPARITION proceeds either from GUILT or FEAR, or is a mixture of both. The thoughts of MACBETH are solely engaged by the deed he is going to act. That unhappy prince, we are told, was a virtuous man until, corrupted by his wife and misled by AMBITION, he is prompted to murder the KING, his benefactor. His forsaken virtue fills him with fear, and makes him sensible of his guilt; it presents to his view a DAGGER in the AIR leading him to DUNCAN. . . . (p. 157)

> *Arthur Murphy, in an extract from* Shakespeare, the Critical Heritage: 1753-1765, Vol. 4, *edited by Brian Vickers, Routledge & Kegan Paul, 1976, pp. 156-58.*

SAMUEL JOHNSON   (essay date 1765)

[In his concluding remarks on Macbeth *in his edition of Shakespeare's plays (1765), excerpted below, Johnson discerns a flatness in the play's characters, noting that "the events are too great to admit the influence of particular dispositions." He adds that while Macbeth's courage is somewhat admirable, "yet every reader rejoices at his fall." For further commentary on the issue of Macbeth's courage, see the excerpts by Thomas Whately (1772), George Steevens (1787), and J. P. Kemble (1817).]*

[*Macbeth*] is deservedly celebrated for the propriety of its fictions, and solemnity, grandeur, and variety of its action; but it has no nice discriminations of character, the events are too great to admit the influence of particular dispositions, and the course of the action necessarily determines the conduct of the agents.

The danger of ambition is well described; and I know not whether it may not be said in defence of some parts which now seem improbable, that, in Shakespeare's time, it was necessary to warn credulity against vain and illusive predictions.

The passions are directed to their true end. Lady Macbeth is merely detested; and though the courage of Macbeth preserves some esteem, yet every reader rejoices at his fall. (p. 795)

> Samuel Johnson, "Notes on Shakespeare's Plays: 'Macbeth'," in his The Yale Edition of the Works of Samuel Johnson: Johnson on Shakespeare, Vol. VIII, edited by Arthur Sherbo, Yale University Press, 1968, pp. 752-95.

BRITISH MAGAZINE (essay date 1767)

[The essay from which the following excerpt is drawn first appeared in the British Magazine in October 1767 and was attributed only to "T. W." The author praises Macbeth for its ability to "excite terror and compassion" and for its "natural representation" of the state of mind of a murderer. The reviewer also remarks that the effective portrayal of Lady Macbeth's madness "greatly increases" the play's horror. Like Samuel Johnson (1745), the author defends Shakespeare's use of witches in Macbeth, noting similar mythological personages in ancient literature, and further proposes that the play is superior to Shakespeare's other tragedies "in having no mixture of buffoonery or low humour in it."]

There are no poetical beauties which so powerfully affect the imagination as those to which Longinus has given the appellation of the Terrible Graces. In these Shakespeare has surpassed all other poets; and in the tragedy of Macbeth he has even surpassed himself. If the chief end of tragedy be to excite terror and compassion, that of Macbeth must be allowed to surpass all others, whether antient or modern. Every circumstance preparatory to the murder of Duncan is admirably calculated to raise terror in the minds of the spectators; and their agitation is gradually increased till the perpetration of that execrable deed, by which it is raised to the highest pitch of horror.

In the soliloquy which precedes the murder, the poet with great judgment represents Macbeth so disordered in his imagination as to think he sees a dagger pointing to the apartment of Duncan and directing his foot-steps. There cannot be a more admirable representation of the state of mind of a man who has conceived a design replete with horror, and is meditating upon the means of putting it in execution. Nothing is more common at such a juncture than for the mind to hold a sort of conference with the instruments to be used in effecting the bloody purpose. (p. 288)

There is an admirable contrast between the characters of Macbeth and his wife. Her harden'd insensibility makes his horrors and remorse more striking, and contributes to render the loss of her senses and her raving, upon the murder of Duncan in the last scene, in a particular manner affecting. Shakespeare has, in many of his pieces, represented the raving of a disordered mind with great success; but I think in none so well as in this tragedy. The madness of Ophelia in Hamlet, and the songs which she sings are little suited to the dignity of tragedy; and that of Lear is continued too long, and of consequence in part loses its effect. But the madness of lady Macbeth, occasioned by her stings of conscience, is perfectly in nature and

has in it something shocking, which greatly increases the horror raised by the sanguinary catastrophe of the piece. The circumstance of her constantly rubbing her hand in order to wipe out the stain made by Duncan's murder, is admirably imagined; and her exclamation, 'Who would have thought that there was so much blood in the old man's body!' [V. i. 39-40] is a most natural representation of the state of a mind racked with the consciousness of having committed murder. (p. 289)

The appearance of the witches and Hecate have been censured by many critics as offending against probability; but this, in my opinion, is carrying criticism too far. The persuasion of the vulgar is a sufficient foundation for a poet to introduce marvellous events and imaginary personages; and if this reasoning was admitted it would be sufficient to make us condemn all the poetry of the antients, as their mythology is interwoven with it in such a manner that one cannot subsist without the other. The prophecy of the witches, 'that none of woman born should be able to hurt Macbeth, and that he need fear nothing till Birnam wood should come to Dunsinane,' have, when fulfilled in a sense different from what the words seemed to import, an excellent effect in rendering the fall of the bloody tyrant dreadful and shocking. The scene in which the Ghost of the murdered Banquo appears is an admirable picture; at each subsequent appearance Macbeth's horror and astonishment are increased by the most natural gradation, till at last he can contain no longer but exclaims, upon lady Macbeth's asking him, 'Are you a man?'

> Ay, and a bold one too,
> That dare look on that which might appal the devil.
> [III. iv. 57-9]

There is something sufficient to chill the blood with horror in the following speech, which Macbeth makes to the Ghost:

> Approach thou like the rugged Russian boar. . . .
> [III. iv. 99]

How admirably emphatical are the lines which follow soon after:

> Thy bones are marrowless, thy blood is cold;
> There is no speculation in those eyes
> Which thou dost glare with—
> [III. iv. 93-5]
> (pp. 289-90)

If the tragedy of Macbeth surpasses all the other tragedies of Shakespeare in exciting terror, it is likewise superior to them in having no mixture of buffoonery or low humour in it, and may, of consequence, be justly considered as the master-piece of that great poet. The several attempts made to alter this piece serve only to set the genius of Shakespeare in a stronger light, as they all shew the superiority of the original. (p. 290)

> T. W., in an extract from Shakespeare, the Critical Heritage: 1765-1774, Vol. 5, edited by Brian Vickers, Routledge & Kegan Paul, 1979, pp. 288-90.

[ELIZABETH] MONTAGU (essay date 1769)

[A well-known English writer and wit, Montagu was an original member of the Bluestocking Society, an association of women who pursued their intellectual and literary interests in an era when men dominated the world of letters. Montagu's most important critical work, Essay on the Writings and Genius of Shakespear (1769), was written primarily in response to Voltaire's harsh criticism of Shakespeare for failing to adhere to the ancient rules *and models for drama. Montagu argued that following such rigid strictures is not the concern of a creative genius. She also defended Shakespeare's mixture of comedy and tragedy and praised the dramatist for his depiction of ghosts and other supernatural beings in a manner consistent with the nature of his dramas. In the excerpt below, Montagu, like Samuel Johnson (1745) and the British Magazine (1767), defends Shakespeare's use of supernatural elements in* Macbeth, *remarking that they produce a sense of terror that cannot be achieved by "the operation of human agency." She also discusses the conflicting impulses of good and evil in both Macbeth and Lady Macbeth. Montagu states that Macbeth has "a generous disposition" but that he is also ambitious, and she praises Shakespeare's portrayal of the movement of Macbeth's thoughts. In Lady Macbeth, Montagu perceives "something feminine" in her inability to kill Duncan and comments that her character illustrates "the difference between a mind naturally prone to evil, and a frail one warped by force of temptations." She concludes that, despite "some faulty speeches" and an "entirely absurd and improper" scene, most probably a reference to the Porter scene,* Macbeth *is one of Shakespeare's best compositions. For further commentary on Macbeth's "disposition," see the excerpts by Francis Gentleman (1770), Thomas Whately (1772), Thomas Davies (1784), and George Steevens (1787).]*

[*Macbeth*] is perhaps one of the greatest exertions of the tragic and poetic powers, that any age, or any country has produced. Here are opened new sources of terror, new creations of fancy. The agency of witches and spirits excites a species of terror, that cannot be effected by the operation of human agency, or by any form or disposition of human things. For the known limits of their powers and capacities set certain bounds to our apprehensions; mysterious horrors, undefined terrors, are raised by the intervention of beings whose nature we do not understand, whose actions we cannot control, and whose influence we know not how to escape. Here we feel through all the faculties of the soul, and to the utmost extent of her capacity. The apprehension of the interposition of such agents is the most salutary of all fears. It keeps up in our minds a sense of our connection with awful and invisible spirits, to whom our most secret actions are apparent, and from whose chastisement innocence alone can defend us. From many dangers power will protect; many crimes may be concealed by art and hypocrisy; but when supernatural beings arise, to reveal, and to avenge, guilt blushes through her mask, and trembles behind her bulwarks. (pp. 173-74)

The dexterity is admirable with which the predictions of the witches (as Macbeth observes) prove true to the ear, but false to the hope, according to the general condition of vain oracles. With great judgment the poet has given to Macbeth the very temper to be wrought upon by such suggestions. The bad man is his own tempter. Richard III. had a heart that prompted him to do all that the worst demon could have suggested, so that the witches had been only an idle wonder in his story; nor did he want such a counsellor as Lady Macbeth; a ready instrument like Buckingham, to adopt his projects, and execute his orders, was sufficient. But Macbeth, of a generous disposition, and good propensities, but with vehement passions and aspiring wishes, was a subject liable to be seduced by splendid prospects, and ambitious counsels. This appears from the following character given of him by his wife:

> Yet do I fear thy nature;
> It is too full o'th' milk of human kindness
> To catch the nearest way. Thou wouldst be great;
> Art not without ambition; but without
> The illness should attend it. What thou wouldst highly,

> That wouldst thou holily; wouldst not play false,
> And yet wouldst wrongly win.
>
> [I. v. 16-22]

So much inherent ambition in a character, without other vice, and full of the milk of human kindness, though obnoxious to temptation, yet would have great struggles before it yielded, and as violent fits of subsequent remorse.

If the mind is to be medicated by the operations of pity and terror, surely no means are so well adapted to that end, as a strong and lively representation of the agonizing struggles that precede, and the terrible horrors that follow wicked actions. Other poets thought they had sufficiently attended to the moral purpose of the drama in making the furies pursue the perpetrated crime. Our author waves their bloody daggers in the road to guilt, and demonstrates, that as soon as a man begins to hearken to ill suggestions, terrors environ, and fears distract him. Tenderness and conjugal love combat in the breasts of a Medea and a Herod in their purposed vengeance. Personal affection often weeps on the theatre, while jealousy or revenge whet the bloody knife; but Macbeth's emotions are the struggles of conscience; his agonies are the agonies of remorse. They are lessons of justice, and warnings to innocence. I do not know that any dramatic writer, except Shakespear, has set forth the pangs of guilt separate from the fear of punishment. (pp. 176-78)

Our author has so tempered the constitutional character of Macbeth, by infusing into it the milk of human kindness, and a strong tincture of honour, as to make the most violent perturbation, and pungent remorse, naturally attend on those steps to which he is led by the force of temptation. Here we must commend the poet's judgment, and his invariable attention to consistency of characer; but more amazing is the art with which he exhibits the movement of the human mind, and renders audible the silent march of thought: traces its modes of operation in the course of deliberating, the pauses of hesitation, and the final act of decision: shews how reason checks, and how the passions impel; and displays to us the trepidations that precede, and the horrors that pursue acts of blood. No species of dialogue but that which a man holds with himself could effect this. The soliloquy has been permitted to all dramatic writers; but its true use has been understood only by our author, who alone has attained to a just imitation of nature in this kind of self-conference. (pp. 183-84)

The man of honour pierces through the traitor and the assassin. His mind loses its tranquillity by guilt, but never its fortitude in danger. His crimes presented to him, even in the unreal mockery of a vision, or the harmless form of sleeping innocence, terrify him more than all his foes in arms.—It has been very justly observed by a late commentator [see excerpt above by Samuel Johnson, 1765], that this piece does not abound with those nice discriminations of character, usual in the plays of our author, the events being too great to admit the influence of particular dispositions. It appears to me, that the character of Macbeth was also represented less particular and special, that his example might be of more universal utility. He has therefore placed him on that line on which the major part of mankind may be ranked, just between the extreams of good and bad; a station assailable by various temptations, and which stands in need of the guard of cautionary admonition. The supernatural agents, in some measure, take off our attention from the other characters, especially as they are, throughout the piece, what they have a right to be, predominant in the events. They should not interfere but to weave the fatal web, or to unravel it; they ought ever to be the regents of the fable and artificers of the catastrophe, as the witches are in this piece. To preserve in Macbeth a just consistency of character; to represent that character naturally susceptible of those desires that were to be communicated to it; to render it interesting to the spectator by some amiable qualities; to make it exemplify the dangers of ambition, and the terrors of remorse; was all that could be required of the tragedian and the moralist. (pp. 195-96)

The difference between a mind naturally prone to evil, and a frail one warped by force of temptations, is delicately distinguished in Macbeth and his wife. There are also some touches of the pencil that mark the male and female character. When they deliberate on the murder of the king, the duties of host and subject strongly plead with him against the deed. She passes over these considerations; goes to Duncan's chamber resolved to kill him, but could not do it, because, she says, he resembled her father while he slept. There is something feminine in this, and perfectly agreeable to the nature of the sex; who, even when void of principle, are seldom entirely divested of sentiment; and thus the poet, who, to use his own phrase, had overstepped the modesty of nature in the exaggerated fierceness of her character, returns back to the line and limits of humanity, and that very judiciously, by a sudden impression, which has only an instantaneous effect. Thus she may relapse into her former wickedness, and, from the same susceptibility, by the force of other impressions, be afterwards driven to distraction. As her character was not composed of those gentle elements out of which regular repentance could be formed, it was well judged to throw her mind into the chaos of madness; and, as she had exhibited wickedness in its highest degree of ferocity and atrociousness, she should be an example of the wildest agonies of remorse. As Shakespeare could most exactly delineate the human mind in its regular state of reason, so no one ever so happily caught its varying forms in the wanderings of delirium. (pp. 200-02)

This piece may certainly be deemed one of the best of Shakespear's compositions, and, though it contains some faulty speeches, and one whole scene entirely absurd and improper, [II. iii. 1-41] which art might have corrected or lopped away; yet genius, powerful genius only, (wild nature's vigour working at the root!) could have produced such strong and original beauties, and adapted both to the general temper and taste of the age in which it appeared. (pp. 202-03)

> [*Elizabeth*] *Montagu, "The Tragedy of 'Macbeth',"*
> *in her* An Essay on the Writings and Genius of Shakespear, *1769. Reprint by Augustus M. Kelley Publishers, 1970, pp. 173-203.*

FRANCIS GENTLEMAN   (essay date 1770)

[*Gentleman, an Irish actor and playwright, was the author of* The Dramatic Censor; or Critical Companion *(1770) and contributed the introduction to John Bell's 1774 Edition of Shakespeare's Plays. In the following excerpt from the first work mentioned above, Gentleman declares that Macbeth is "a detestable monster" and does not, as Elizabeth Montagu (1769) argues, possess "a generous disposition." He offers evidence that Macbeth, from the play's beginning, is "composed of the worst materials" and refers to both Macbeth and Lady Macbeth as the kind of "frightful deformities" of nature which "should be excluded from the stage." Gentleman charges that some of Macbeth's language is unfit for a king, that the murder of Macduff's son is too horrid for the stage, and that the off-stage killing of Macbeth deprives "the audience of a most satisfactory circumstance." He also refers to*

the Porter scene as "an insult upon judgement," a position earlier suggested by Elizabeth Montagu and later developed by Samuel Taylor Coleridge (1813-34), but one strongly refuted in the twentieth century by Shakespearean critics, especially by John B. Harcourt (1961), and Kenneth Muir (1962). Gentleman, in opposition to Samuel Johnson (1745), the British Magazine *(1767), and Elizabeth Montagu, considers Shakespeare's use of witches in* Macbeth *inexcusable, stating that it inculcates a belief in the supernatural and weakens reason. He concludes that if a play cannot improve an audience, it should at least leave them "no worse than it finds them, equally avoiding vice and credulity."*]

There are many circumstances and events to bring about the most unthought-of changes in human affairs. Wherefore that man who premeditates the worst means at first must have by nature a deep depravation of heart; and such Macbeth will appear infected with from the whole of that speech which begins 'Two truths are told,' &c [I. iii. 127] notwithstanding somewhat like palliation is offered in two or three lines. Indeed, his conclusion seems to banish what he beautifully stiles *fantastical murther,* but cannot banish from spectators his barbarous ideas so suddenly conceived. We have dwelt upon this circumstance to strengthen our opinion that the author meant to draw him a detestable monster, which some critics have rather disputed, allowing him a generous disposition which we find no instance of; even the conscientious struggles which we shall presently find him engaged with might arise in the most villainous nature. He who does a bad action precipitately, or without knowing it to be such, may stand in some measure excusable. But when a man has scrupulously weighed every relative circumstance in the nicest scale of reflection, and after all determines upon what nature, gratitude, and justice would avoid, he must be composed of the worst materials.

To corroborate the general idea of Macbeth's character which we have here offered . . . , let us view him in the very next scene, where, after a most cordial reception from the king, with unbounded promises of future favours, he is so possessed of his base purpose that, void of even common gratitude, he replies upon Duncan's appointing Malcolm prince of Cumberland,

> The prince of Cumberland! that is a step   [*aside.*
> On which I must fall down, or else o'er leap:
> For in my way it lies—Stars hide your fires,
> Let not night see my black and deep desires;
> The eye wink at the end—yet let that be,
> Which the eye fears, when it is done, to see.
>
> [I. iv. 48-53]

From this passage it appears that, not content with the simple idea of regicide he determines to cut off the whole family; in return for being loaded with honours by royal favour, and at the very instant when this unsuspecting monarch and friend places himself upon his hospitable reception. If this does not prove Macbeth an exception to [Juvenal's] remark, *Nemo repente fuit turpissimus* ["No one reaches the depths of turpitude all at once"], we know not what can.

Lady Macbeth, and her husband's letter, are judiciously introduced. But sure such sympathetic barbarity was never in nature as suddenly, on the instant, breaks out in these words,

> Glamis thou art and Cawdor—and shalt be
> What thou art promised.
>
> [I. v. 15-16]

What follows accuses Macbeth of a milky softness in his nature, of which he does not seem at all possessed, for unsuccessful struggles of conscience cannot justly be called so. However, that he may not have the whole load of aggravated guilt to bear alone, our author has made this matchless lady—we lament so detestable, though a possible picture of the fair sex—exert uncommon talents of temptation. On hearing of the king's visit, with most unrelenting precipitation of thought she dooms the royal visitant. (pp. 385-86)

In such a state of guilty perturbation as Macbeth now appears [I. vii], no mode of expression could be so suitable as that of soliloquy. It were to be wished, however, that our great author, pursuing energy, had not in some sentences bordered upon obscurity, especially if we consider those passages as only repeated on the stage, where the ear must inevitably be too quick for reception. In an alteration of this play which has been often performed, there are some attempts to render the lines we speak of more intelligible; but, like most other paraphrases, they destroy the essential spirit. (p. 387)

Lady Macbeth comes to speak in rather plainer terms. Yet, unless we allow great latitude of expression, what follows evidently admits of objection:

> ——Was the hope drunk
> Wherein you drest yourself? Hath it slept since,
> And wakes it now to look so pale and sickly.
>   [I. vii. 35-7]

Suppose we pass over the literal acceptation of *hope* being drunk, surely we must blame a lady of high rank for descending to such a vulgar and nauseous allusion as the paleness and sickness of an inebriated state; nor is her comparison of the cat in the adage much more the effect of good breeding....

If it should be urged that such characters have been, and may be, we still contend that they are among the frightful deformities and essential concealments of nature, which should be excluded from the stage. (p. 388)

To what end Shakespeare could introduce so incongruous a character as the porter, who is commendably omitted in representation, we believe no mortal can tell. At such an interesting period to turn the most serious feelings into laughter, or rather into distaste, by a string of strained quibbles is an insult upon judgment, and must fill the imagination with chaos of idea. Some more suitable pause might have been made to give Macbeth time for composing his ruffled figure....

The successive entrances and exits of various characters, the real grief of some and the feigned sorrow of others, Macbeth's apology for his political stroke of killing the grooms by an affecting picture of Duncan's situation, and the rapid resolution of enquiring judicially into so unaccountable an event, are all well arranged and happily expressed. But the amazing precipitate flight of Malcolm and Donalbain, without any apology except the paltry one of the instantaneous fear, places these sprigs of royalty in a contemptible light, and for its effect on the stage proves the justice of this remark. For when one says, 'I'll to England,' and the other comically replies, 'To Ireland I' [II. iii. 137-38], nine times out of ten the audience are thrown into a horse-laugh.—We could wish this circumstance was altered, as it easily might be, by giving a few speeches of spirit and dutiful affection to one or both the princes, expressive of their particular determination to discover and revenge their father's death; which might be overruled by Macduff's representation of the danger they stand exposed to, and that for their greater security it would be better to retire till the unavoidable convulsions of state were subdued, or till proper mea-

sures could be taken to establish the legal succession. This, we apprehend, would have carried them off with some grace, whereas in their present disposition they make such a wretched figure that we can scarce forget it when Malcolm appears to assert his right at the head of an army.... (pp. 389-90)

The intelligence of Macduff's flight to England is well thrown in to give spirit and an opening of business; his wife and children being devoted to destruction in consequence, we might reasonably expect from what has been already shewn of Macbeth's jealous, impatient cruelty. The next scene of Macduff's lady and son, where murtherers come and demolish the latter in view of the audience is, if we can be allowed the phrase, farcically horrid; as disgraceful an oddity as ever invaded Shakespeare's muse, and therefore with great justice omitted in representation.... (p. 392)

Macbeth's expressions, at his entrance [V. ii.], most plainly evince a disturbed brain and forced resolution. Flying for safety to the prediction of the witches is a well-timed additional proof of that superstitious weakness which, stimulated by ambition, has hurried him into all his guilt and consequent misfortunes. The expressions he uses to the servant or officer who enters with intelligence of the English army are low and gross, far beneath even a private gentleman; and why Shakespeare should make a monarch run into such vulgarisms is not easy to guess, for the rage or grief of a king should always preserve peculiar dignity, without which the author cannot boast a chaste preservation of character. The following speech [V. ii. 19-29], however, makes full amends for a thousand venial slips. The breaks in the two first lines afford a beautiful variety of action of tones of voice, and countenance—those which succeed are as fine declamatory reflections arising from the consciousness of guilt and general dislike in a sensible man as the severest criticism could relish; nor is it easy to determine which claims preference, the sentiment or versification. (pp. 393-94)

Macduff's encounter with Macbeth raises expectation to the very top of its bent, and justice sits trembling in every humane bosom for so essential a sacrifice to her as the tyrant. The introduction of Macbeth's sole remaining hope, that of being invulnerable to any person born of a woman, shews great judgment, and his feelings on being told the fallacy of his charm are expressed in very apt terms.—Why the author chose to execute so great a culprit behind the scenes, thereby depriving the audience of a most satisfactory circumstance, is not easy to imagine. Death certainly is made in this instance too modest, and the bringing on a head defeats every trace of the author's new-born false delicacy. (pp. 394-95)

It has been already hinted, and may be laid down as an irrefragable maxim, that moral tendency is the first great and indispensible merit of any piece written for the stage. In which light I am afraid the tragedy before us, though a favourite child of genius, will not hold a very distinguished place. Fate, necessity or predestination, has embarrassed the most inquisitive philosophers, the most painful theologists, and still remains matter of much perplexity to those who endeavour to develope it. SHAKESPEARE, therefore, who was no doubt an able moralist, should have declined any subject which glanced an eye that way. Yet we find his *Macbeth* strongly inculcates power of prediction, even in the worst and most contemptible agents; inculcates a supernatural influence of one mortal being over another. It is but a very weak defence to say he only wrote according to the accepted notions of those times from whence he drew his plot.——Admitted, but whatever tends to weaken reason, to mislead the understanding and intimidate the heart, should not be used as a subject for dramatic composition, which adorns fiction with her most persuasive charms. Weak minds are ever more liable to receive prejudicial than advantageous impressions; wherefore any character, incidents, or sentiments which may work the former effect should be industriously avoided. If the stage upon some occasions does not improve, it should at least leave an audience no worse than it finds them, equally avoiding vice and credulity. (pp. 395-96)

Francis Gentleman, in an extract from Shakespeare, the Critical Heritage: 1765-1774, Vol. 5, *edited by Brian Vickers, Routledge & Kegan Paul, 1979, pp. 384-98.*

THOMAS WHATELY   (essay date 1772?)

[*Whately was best known to his contemporaries as the author of* Observations on Modern Gardening *(1770), but he also undertook a study of Shakespearean characters in* Remarks on Some of the Characters of Shakespere, *a book published in 1785, thirteen years after his death. Whately's study was but a portion of an intended longer work, containing only an introduction and an essay on Macbeth and Richard III, but it is important for its illumination of the distinct and complex nature of individual Shakespearean characters. In the excerpt below, Whately compares the characters of Macbeth and Richard III and notes that while their circumstances are similar, their dispositions are quite different. He argues that, unlike Richard, Macbeth possesses elements of a kind, gentle, and timid nature, an observation similar to that of Elizabeth Montagu (1769). Broaching the issue of free will and fate in* Macbeth, *he further asserts that it is the "intervention of a supernatural cause" that accounts for Macbeth's murderous behavior, a position also taken by Charles Lamb (1808) but challenged by a number of later critics, especially Franz Horn (1823), G. G. Gervinus (1849-50), and A. J. F. Mézières (1860). Macbeth, states Whately, had no ambition for the crown until he heard the witches' prophecy, and the murders he commits after Duncan's death are motivated by a fearful insecurity, not, like Richard's murders, by a desire for power. In examining Macbeth's timidity and irresolution, he remarks, "Macbeth is always shaken upon great, and frequently alarmed upon trivial, occasions"—an interpretation in opposition to Samuel Johnson (1765) and J. P. Kemble (1817). Whately concludes that Macbeth is a more complicated and "highly finished" character than Richard, "for it required a greater variety, and a greater delicacy of painting, to express and to blend with consistency all the several properties which are ascribed to him."*]

Every Play of Shakespere abounds with instances of his excellence in distinguishing characters. It would be difficult to determine which is the most striking of all that he drew; but his merit will appear most conspicuously by comparing two opposite characters, who happen to be placed in similar circumstances:—not that on such occasions he marks them more strongly than on others, but because the contrast makes the distinction more apparent; and of these none seem to agree so much in situation, and to differ so much in disposition, as RICHARD THE THIRD and MACBETH. Both are soldiers, both usurpers; both attain the throne by the same means, by treason and murder; and both lose it too in the same manner, in battle against the person claiming it as lawful heir. Perfidy, violence and tyranny are common to both; and those only, their obvious qualites, would have been attributed indiscriminately to both by an ordinary dramatic writer. But Shakespere, in conformity to the truth of history, as far as it led him, and by improving upon the fables which have been blended with it, has ascribed opposite principles and motives to the same designs and actions, and various effects to the operation of the same events

upon different tempers. Richard and Macbeth, as represented by him, agree in nothing but their fortunes.

The periods of history, from which the subjects are taken, are such as at the best can be depended on only for some principal facts; but not for the minute detail, by which characters are unravelled. That of Macbeth is too distant to be particular; that of Richard, too full of discord and animosity to be true: and antiquity has not feigned more circumstances of horror in the one, than party violence has given credit to in the other. Fiction has even gone so far as to introduce supernatural fables into both stories: the usurpation of Macbeth is said to have been foretold by some witches; and the tyranny of Richard by omens attending his birth. From these fables, Shakespere, unrestrained and indeed uninformed by history, seems to have taken the hint of their several characters; and he has adapted their dispositions so as to give to such fictions, in the days he wrote, a show of probability. The first thought of acceding to the throne is suggested, and success in the attempt is promised, to Macbeth by the witches: he is therefore represented as a man, whose natural temper would have deterred him from such a design, if he had not been immediately tempted, and strongly impelled to it. Richard, on the other hand, brought with him into the world the signs of ambition and cruelty: his disposition, therefore, is suited to those symptoms; and he is not discouraged from indulging it by the improbability of succeeding, or by any difficulties and dangers which obstruct his way.

Agreeable to these ideas, Macbeth appears to be a man not destitute of the feelings of humanity. His lady gives him that character.

> ———I fear thy nature;
> It is too full o' the milk of human kindness,
> To catch the nearest way.
>
>   [I. v. 16-18]

Which apprehension was well founded; for his reluctance to commit the murder is owing in a great measure to reflections which arise from sensibility:

> ———He's here in double trust:
> First, as I am his kinsman and his subject;
> Strong both against the deed; then as his host,
> Who should against his murderer shut the door,
> Not bear the knife myself.
>
>   [I. vi. 12-16]

Immediately after he tells Lady Macbeth,—

> We will proceed no further in this business;
> He hath honoured me of late.
>
>   [I. vii. 31-2]

And thus giving way to his natural feelings of kindred, hospitality, and gratitude, he for a while lays aside his purpose. A man of such a disposition will esteem, as they ought to be esteemed, all gentle and amiable qualities in another: and therefore Macbeth is affected by the mild virtues of Duncan; and reveres them in his sovereign when he stifles them in himself. That

> ———This Duncan
> Hath borne his faculties so meekly; hath been
> So clear in his great office,
>
>   [I. vii. 16-18]

is one of his reasons against the murder: and when he is tortured with the thought of Banquo's issue succeeding him in the throne, he aggravates his misery by observing, that,

For them the gracious Duncan have I murder'd;
[III. i. 65]

which epithet of *gracious* would not have occurred to one who
was not struck with the particular merit it expresses.

The frequent references to the prophecy in favour of Banquo's
issue, is another symptom of the same disposition: for it is not
always from fear, but sometimes from envy, that he alludes to
it: and being himself very susceptible of those domestic affections, which raise a desire and love of posterity, he repines at
the succession assured to the family of his rival, and which in
his estimation seems more valuable than his own actual possession. He therefore reproaches the sisters for their partiality,
when

Upon my head they plac'd a fruitless crown,
And put a barren sceptre in my gripe,
Thence to be wrench'd with an unlineal hand,
No son of mine succeeding. If 'tis so,
For Banquo's issue have I 'fil'd my mind. . . .
[III. i. 60-64]
(pp. 27-33)

Thus, in a variety of instances, does the tenderness in his
character shew itself; and one who has these feelings, though
he may have no principles, cannot easily be induced to commit
a murder. The intervention of a supernatural cause accounts
for his acting so contrary to his disposition. But that alone is
not sufficient to prevail entirely over his nature: the instigations
of his wife are also necessary to keep him to his purpose; and
she, knowing his temper, not only stimulates his courage to
the deed, but, sensible that, besides a backwardness in daring,
he had a degree of softness which wanted hardening, endeavours to remove all remains of humanity from his breast, by
the horrid comparison she makes between him and herself [at
I. vii. 54-9]. . . . The argument is, that the strongest and most
natural affections are to be stifled upon so great an occasion:
and such an argument is proper to persuade one who is liable
to be swayed by them; but is no incentive either to his courage
or his ambition.

Richard is in all these particulars the very reverse to Macbeth.
He is totally destitute of every softer feeling:

I that have neither pity, love, nor fear,
[*3 Henry VI*, V. vi. 68]

is the character he gives of himself, and which he preserves
throughout; insensible to his habitudes with a brother, to his
connexion with a wife, to the piety of the king, and the innocence of the babes, whom he murders. (pp. 33-5)

But the characters of Richard and Macbeth are marked not only
by opposite qualities; but even the same qualities in each differ
so much in the cause, the kind, and the degree, that the distinction in them is as evident as in the others. Ambition is
common to both; but in Macbeth it proceeds only from vanity,
which is flattered and satisfied by the splendour of a throne:
in Richard it is founded upon pride; his ruling passion is the
lust of power:

——this earth affords no joy to him,
But to command, to check, and to o'erbear.
[*3 Henry VI*, III. ii. 165-66]
(pp. 48-9)

But the crown is not Macbeth's pursuit through life: he had
never thought of it till it was suggested to him by the witches;
he receives their promise, and the subsequent earnest of the

truth of it, with calmness. But his wife, whose thoughts are
always more aspiring, hears the tidings with rapture, and greets
him with the most extravagant congratulations; she complains
of his moderation; the utmost merit she can allow him is, that
he is

——not without ambition.
[I. v. 19]

But it is cold and faint, for the subject of it is that of a weak
mind; it is only preeminence of place, not dominion. He never
carries his idea beyond the honour of the situation he aims at;
and therefore he considers it as a situation which Lady Macbeth
will partake of equally with him: and in his letter tells her,

This have I thought good to deliver thee, my
dearest partner of greatness, that thou mightest
not lose the dues of rejoicing, by being ignorant
of what greatness is promised thee.
[I. v. 10-13]

But it was his rank alone, not his power, in which she could
share: and that indeed is all which he afterwards seems to think
he had attained by his usurpation. He styles himself,

——high-plac'd Macbeth:
[IV. i. 98]

but in no other light does he ever contemplate his advancement
with satisfaction; and when he finds that it is not attended with
that adulation and respect which he had promised himself, and
which would have soothed his vanity, he sinks under the disappointment, and complains that

——my way of life
Is fallen into the sear, the yellow leaf;
And that which should accompany old age,
As honour, love, obedience, troops of friends,
I must not look to have.
[V. iii. 22-6]

These blessings, so desirable to him, are widely different from
pursuits of Richard. He wishes not to gain the affections, but
to secure the submission of his subjects, and is happy to see
men shrink under his control. But Macbeth, on the contrary,
reckons among the miseries of his condition

——mouth-honour, breath,
Which the poor heart would fain deny, but dare not . . .
[V. iii. 27-8]

and pities the wretch who fears him.

The towering ambition of Richard, and the weakness of that
passion in Macbeth, are further instances wherein Shakespere
has accommodated their characters to the fabulous parts of their
stories. The necessity for the most extraordinary incitements
to stimulate the latter, thereby becomes apparent; and the meaning of the omens, which attended the birth of the former, is
explained. Upon the same principle, a distinction still stronger
is made in the article of courage, though both are possessed
of it even to an eminent degree; but in Richard it is intrepidity,
and in Macbeth no more than resolution: in him it proceeds
from exertion, not from nature; in enterprise he betrays a degree
of fear, though he is able, when occasion requires, to stifle
and subdue it. When he and his wife are concerting the murder,
his doubt,

——If we should fail,
[I. vii. 59]

is a difficulty raised by apprehension; and as soon as that is removed by the contrivance of Lady Macbeth, to make the officers drunk, and lay the crime upon them, he runs with violence into the other extreme of confidence, and cries out, with a rapture unusual to him,

> ——Bring forth men-children only!
> For thy undaunted metal should compose
> Nothing but males. Will it not be receiv'd,
> When we have mark'd with blood these sleepy two
> Of his own chamber, and us'd their very daggers,
> That they have done it?
>
> [I. vii. 72-7]

Which question he puts to her, who but the moment before had suggested the thought of

> His spongy officers, who shall bear the guilt
> Of our great quell.
>
> [I. vii. 71-2]

And his asking it again proceeds from that extravagance, with which a delivery from apprehension and doubt is always accompanied. Then summoning all his fortitude, he says,

> ——I am settled, and bend up
> Each corporal agent to this terrible feat;
>
> [I. vii. 79-80]

and proceeds to the bloody business without any further recoils. But a certain degree of restlessness and anxiety still continues, such as is constantly felt by a man not naturally very bold, worked up to a momentous achievement. His imagination dwells entirely on the circumstances of horror which surround him; the vision of the dagger; the darkness and the stillness of the night; and the terrors and the prayers of the chamberlains. Lady Macbeth, who is cool and undismayed, attends to the business only; considers of the place where she had laid the daggers ready; the impossibility of his missing them; and is afraid of nothing but a disappointment. She is earnest and eager; he is uneasy and impatient, and therefore wishes it over:

> I go, and it is done; the bell invites me.
> Hear it not, Duncan, for it is a knell
> Which summons thee to heaven or to hell.
>
> [II. i. 62-4]

But a resolution, thus forced, cannot hold longer than the immediate occasion for it: the moment after that is accomplished for which it was necessary, his thoughts take the contrary turn, and he cries out in agony and despair,

> Wake, Duncan, with this knocking; would thou could'st!
>
> [II. ii. 71]

That courage, which had supported him while he was *settled and bent up,* forsakes him so immediately after he has performed the *terrible feat* for which it had been exerted, that he forgets the favourite circumstance of laying it on the officers of the bed-chamber; and when reminded of it, he refuses to return and complete his work, acknowledging that

> I am afraid to think what I have done;
> Look on't again I dare not.
>
> [II. ii. 47-8]

His disordered senses deceive him, and his debilitated spirits fail him; he owns that

> ——every noise appals him.
>
> [II. ii. 55]

He listens when nothing stirs; he mistakes the sounds he does hear; he is so confused, as not to distinguish whence the knocking proceeds. (pp. 50-8)

Macbeth indeed commits subsequent murders with less agitation than that of Duncan: but this is no inconsistency in his character; on the contrary, it confirms the principles upon which it is formed; for besides his being hardened to the deeds of death, he is impelled to the perpetration of them by other motives than those which instigated him to assassinate his sovereign. In the one he sought to gratify his ambition; the rest are for his security: and he gets rid of fear by guilt, which, to a mind so constituted, may be the less uneasy sensation of the two. The anxiety which prompts him to the destruction of Banquo, arises entirely from apprehension:

> ——to be thus, is nothing;
> But to be safely thus:—our fears in Banquo
> Stick deep; and in his royalty of nature
> Reigns that which would be fear'd. . . .
>
> [III. i. 47-50]

For though one principal reason of his jealousy was the impression made on Macbeth's mind, by the prophecy of the witches in favour of Banquo's issue; yet here starts forth another, quite consistent with a temper not quite free from timidity. He is afraid of him personally: that fear is founded on the superior courage of the other, and he feels himself under an awe before him; a situation which a dauntless spirit can never get into. (pp. 66-8)

The same motives of personal fear, and those unmixed with any other, impel him to seek the destruction of Macduff. . . . (p. 71)

But all the crimes Richard commits are for his advancement, not for his security: he is not drawn from one into another; but he premeditates several before he begins, and yet can look upon the distant prospect of a long succession of murders with steadiness and composure. . . . The danger of losing the great object of his ambition is that which alone alarms Richard: but Macbeth dreads the danger which threatens his life; and that terror constantly damps all the joys of his crown. When he says,

> ——Duncan is in his grave;
> After life's fretful fever, he sleeps well;
> Treason has done his worst; nor steel, nor poison,
> Malice domestic, foreign levy, nothing
> Can touch him further!
>
> [III. ii. 22-6]

he only enumerates the mischiefs he fears; none of which are ever Richard's concern; those which are present he opposes with spirit, and such as are imaginary never occur to him. (pp. 74-5)

Upon no occasion, however tremendous, and at no moment of his life, however unguarded, does he betray the least symptom of fear; whereas Macbeth is always shaken upon great, and frequently alarmed upon trivial, occasions. Upon the first meeting with the witches, he is agitated much more than Banquo; the one expresses mere curiosity, the other, astonishment: Banquo speaks to them first; and, the moment he sees them, asks them several particular and pertinent questions. . . . But Macbeth, though he has had time to recollect himself, only repeats the same inquiry shortly; and bids them,

Speak, if you can:—What are you?

[I. iii. 47]

Which parts may appear to be injudiciously distributed; Macbeth being the principal personage in the play, and most immediately concerned in this particular scene; and it being to him that the witches first address themselves. But the difference in their characters accounts for such a distribution; Banquo being perfectly calm, and Macbeth a little ruffled by the adventure. The distinction is preserved through the rest of their behaviour; for Banquo treats them with contempt, tells them that he

——neither begs, nor fears,
Their favours, nor their hate;

[I. iii. 60-61]

which defiance seemed so bold to Macbeth, that he long after mentions it as an instance of his dauntless spirit, when he recollects that he

——chid the sisters. . . .

[III. i. 56]

Upon the rising of Banquo's ghost, though that was a spectre which might well terrify him, yet he betrays a consciousness of too much natural timidity, by his peevish reproaches to Lady Macbeth, because she had not been so frightened as himself, when he tells her,

——you make me strange
E'en to the disposition that I owe,
When now I think you can behold such sights,
And keep the natural ruby of your cheeks,
When mine is blanch'd with fear.

[III. iv. 111-15]

Another symptom of the same disposition is his catching the terrors he sees expressed in the countenance of the messenger, who informs him of the numbers of the enemy; and whom, in the most opprobrious language, he reviles for that

——those linen cheeks of thine
Are counsellors to fear:

[V. iii. 16-17]

and immediately, on seeing this affrighted wretch, he himself sinks from the most assured confidence into the lowest despondency. These are all symptoms of timidity, which he confesses to have been natural to him, when he owns that

The time has been, my senses would have cool'd
To hear a night-shriek, and my fell of hair
Would at a dismal treatise rouse and stir,
As life were in it.

[V. v. 10-13]

But still he is able to suppress this natural timidity; he has an acquired, though not a constitutional, courage, which is equal to all ordinary occasions; and if it fails him upon those which are extraordinary, it is however so well formed, as to be easily resumed as soon as the shock is over. But his idea never rises above manliness of character, and he continually asserts his right to that character; which he would not do, if he did not take to himself a merit in supporting it.

I dare do all that may become a man;
Who dares do more, is none,

[I. vi. 46-7]

is his answer to the reproaches of Lady Macbeth, for want of spirit in the execution of his design upon Duncan. (pp. 76-81)

But though Richard has no timidity in his nature which he wishes to conceal, yet he is conscious of other qualities, which it is necessary he should disguise; for if the wickedness of his heart had been fully known, he could not have hoped for success in his views: and he, therefore, from the beginning, covers his malice under an appearance of sanctity. . . . (p. 85)

But Macbeth wants no disguise of his natural disposition, for it is not bad; he does not affect more piety than he has: on the contrary, a part of his distress arises from a real sense of religion; which, in the passages already quoted, makes him regret that he could not join with the chamberlains in prayer for God's blessing; and bewail that he has *given his eternal jewel to the common enemy of man* [III. i. 67-8]. He continually reproaches himself for his deeds; no use can harden him; confidence cannot silence, and even despair cannot stifle the cries of his conscience. (pp. 89-90)

Richard is able to put on a general character, directly the reverse of his disposition; and it is ready to him upon every occasion. But Macbeth cannot effectually conceal his sensations, when it is most necessary to conceal them; nor act a part which does not belong to him with any degree of consistency: and the same weakness of mind, which disqualifies him from maintaining such a force upon his nature, shows itself still further in that hesitation and dulness to dare, which he feels in himself, and allows in others. His whole proceeding in his treason against Duncan is full of it; of which the references already made to his behaviour then are sufficient proofs. Against Banquo he acts with more determination, for the reasons which have been given: and yet he most unnecessarily acquaints the murderers with the reasons of his conduct; and even informs them of the behaviour he proposes to observe afterwards, by saying to them,

——though I could
With barefac'd power sweep him from my sight,
And bid my will avouch it, yet I must not,
For certain friends that are both his and mine,
Whose loves I may not drop; but wail his fate,
Whom I myself struck down:

[III. i. 117-22]

which particularity and explanation to men who did not desire it; the confidence he places in those who could only abuse it; and the very needless caution of secrecy implied in this speech, are so many symptoms of a feeble mind. . . . His sending a third murderer to join the others, just at the moment of action, and without any notice, is a further proof of the same imbecility; and that so glaring as to strike them, who observe upon it, that

He needs not our mistrust, since he delivers
Our offices, and what we have to do,
To the direction just.

[III. iii. 2-4]

Richard, always determined, and taking his determination himself, never waits to be incited, nor ever idly accounts for his conduct; but fixed to his purpose, makes other men only his instruments, not his confidents or advisers. . . . Shakespere, who had such variety of phrase at command, does not repeat the same without a design. An example has already been given of a particular meaning conveyed by the frequent use which Macbeth makes of the same terms, in asserting his pretensions to the character of manliness. Another instance, of the like kind, is the repetition by Richard, of the same words, *off with his head!* upon three or four different occasions. The readiness and the certainty of his resolutions are expressed by them. . . . Macbeth, on the contrary, is irresolute in his counsels, and languid in the execution; he cannot look steadily at his principal object, but dwells upon circumstances, and always does too much or too little. (pp. 94-100)

A mind so framed and so tortured as that of Macbeth, when the hour of extremity presses upon him, can find no refuge but in despair; and the expression of that despair by Shakespere is perhaps one of the finest pictures that ever was exhibited. It is wildness, inconsistency, and disorder, to such a degree, and so apparent, that

> Some say he's mad; others, who lesser hate him,
> Do call it valiant fury: but for certain,
> He cannot buckle his distemper'd cause
> Within the belt of rule.
>
> [V. ii. 13-16]

It is presumption without hope, and confidence without courage: that confidence rests upon his superstition; he buoys himself up with it against all the dangers that threaten him, and yet sinks upon every fresh alarm:

> Bring me no more reports; let them fly all:
> Till Birnam wood remove to Dunsinane,
> I cannot taint with fear. . . .
>
> [V. iii. 1-3]

His faith in these assurances is implicit; he really is persuaded that he may defy the forces of his enemies, and the treachery of his friends; but immediately after, only on seeing a man who, not having the same support, is frightened at the numbers approaching against them, he catches his apprehensions; tells him,

> ——those linen cheeks of thine
> Are counsellors to fear;
>
> [V. iii. 16-17]

and then, though nothing had happened to impeach the credit of those assurances on which he relied, he gives way to the depression of his spirits, and desponds in the midst of security. . . . (pp. 102-04)

Thus, from the beginning of their history to their last moments, are the characters of Macbeth and Richard preserved entire and distinct: and though probably Shakespere, when he was drawing the one, had no attention to the other; yet as he conceived them to be widely different, expressed his conceptions exactly, and copied both from nature, they necessarily became contrasts to each other; and, by seeing them together, that contrast is more apparent, especially where the comparison is not between opposite qualities, but arises from the different degrees, or from a particular display, or total omission, of the same quality. This last must often happen, as the character of Macbeth is much more complicated than that of Richard; and therefore, when they are set in opposition, the judgment of the poet shews itself as much in what he has left out of the latter, as in what he has inserted. The picture of Macbeth is also, for the same reason, much the more highly finished of the two; for it required a greater variety, and a greater delicacy of painting, to express and to blend with consistency all the several properties which are ascribed to him. (pp. 118-20)

Thomas Whately, in his Remarks on Some of the Characters of Shakespere, *edited by Richard Whately,*

third edition, 1839. Reprint by Augustus M. Kelley Publishers, 1970, 128 p.

JOSHUA REYNOLDS   (essay date 1780)

[*Reynolds, an aesthetic theorist and the first president of the Royal Academy of Arts, was the most celebrated portrait painter of eighteenth-century England. Reynolds also associated with such notable literary figures as Samuel Johnson, Edmund Burke, and Oliver Goldsmith and contributed the following commentary on* Macbeth *to the* Supplement to the Edition of Shakespeare's Plays Published in 1778 by Samuel Johnson and George Steevens *(1780). He notes the relaxed naturalness of the conversation between Duncan and Banquo as they approach Macbeth's castle, remarking that it offers a necessary "repose" in the surrounding violence of the play's action.*]

This short dialogue between Duncan and Banquo, whilst they are approaching the gates of Macbeth's castle [I. vi. 1-10], has always appeared to me a striking instance of what in painting is termed *repose*. Their conversation very naturally turns upon the beauty of its situation, and the pleasantness of the air; and Banquo observing the martlet's nests in every recess of the cornice, remarks that where those birds most breed and haunt the air is delicate. The subject of this quiet and easy conversation gives that repose so necessary to the mind after the tumultuous bustle of the preceding scenes, and perfectly contrasts the scene of horror that immediately succeeds. It seems as if Shakespeare asked himself, What is a prince likely to say to his attendants on such an occasion? Whereas the modern writers seem, on the contrary, to be always searching for new thoughts, such as would never occur to men in the situation which is represented.

Sir Joshua Reynolds, in an extract from Shakespeare, the Critical Heritage: 1774-1801, *Vol. 6, edited by Brian Vickers, Routledge & Kegan Paul, 1981, p. 283.*

THOMAS DAVIES   (essay date 1784)

[*Davies, a Scottish bookseller, introduced James Boswell to Samuel Johnson and composed a biography of the actor David Garrick. He also wrote* Dramatic Miscellanies: Consisting of Critical Observations on Several Plays of Shakespeare *(1784), from which the following excerpt is taken. Davies contends against Samuel Johnson (1765) that it is not so much Macbeth's courage, but his initial reluctance to murder Duncan and his subsequent guilty conscience that renders him "not entirely unmeriting our pity." The suggestion that Macbeth's nature evokes some degree of sympathy is also made by Elizabeth Montagu (1769), Thomas Whately (1772), and George Steevens (1787), but is rejected by Francis Gentleman (1770).*]

Dr. Johnson thinks the courage of Macbeth preserves some esteem; but that quality he had in common with Banquo and others. I am of opinion that his extreme reluctance to murder his royal master, his uncommon affliction of mind after he had perpetrated the crime, with the perpetual revolt of his conscience upon the commission of each new act of cruelty, are the qualities which render Macbeth, though not worthy of our esteem, yet an object not entirely unmeriting our pity, in spite of his ambition and cruelty.

Thomas Davies, in an extract from Shakespeare, the Critical Heritage: 1774-1801, *Vol. 6, edited by Brian Vickers, Routledge & Kegan Paul, 1981, p. 376.*

GEORGE STEEVENS   (essay date 1787)

[Steevens was an English scholar who collaborated with Samuel Johnson on a ten-volume edition of Shakespeare's works in 1773. The subsequent revision of this collection, along with Steevens's own edition of 1793, formed the textual basis for the first two Variorum editions of Shakespeare's plays. In the excerpt below, first published in the European Magazine *in April, 1787, Steevens, while agreeing with most of Thomas Whately's observations on the character of Macbeth (see excerpt above, 1772), argues against his assertion that Macbeth is naturally disposed toward timidity. Instead, contends Steevens, Macbeth once possessed "genuine intrepidity," but lost it when "he ceased to be a virtuous character." He states that Macbeth's guilty conscience supplants bravery with timidity and irresolution, and he notes that Richard III, showing no trace of a moral conscience, retains an unfaltering and superior courageousness. For other observations on Macbeth's courage, see the excerpts by Samuel Johnson (1765) and J. P. Kemble (1817). Like Whately, Steevens also blames Macbeth's loss of virtue on "the illusions of witchcraft" and "the suggestions of his wife."]*

The late Mr. Whately's *Remarks on some of the Characters of Shakespeare* have shown with the utmost clearness of distinction and felicity of arrangement, that what in Richard III is fortitude, in Macbeth is no more than resolution. But this judicious critic having imputed the cause of Macbeth's inferiority in courage to his natural disposition, induces me to dissent in one particular from an Essay which otherwise is too comprehensive to need a supplement, and too rational to admit of confutation.

Throughout such parts of this drama as afford opportunities for a display of personal bravery, Macbeth sometimes *screws his courage to the sticking place* [I. vii. 60] but never rises into constitutional heroism. Instead of meditating some decisive stroke on the enemy, his restless and self-accusing mind discharges itself in splenetic effusions and personal invectives on the attendants about his person. His genuine intrepidity had forsaken him when he ceased to be a virtuous character. He would not deceive himself into confidence, and depends on forced alacrity, and artificial valour, to extricate him from his present difficulties. Despondency too deep to be rooted out, and fury too irregular to be successful, have by turns possession of his mind. Though he has been assured of what he certainly credited, that *none of woman born shall hurt him,* he has twice given us reason to suppose he would have *fled,* but that he *cannot,* being *tied to the stake* and compelled to *fight the course.* Suicide also has once entered into his thoughts; though this idea, in a paroxysm of noisy rage, is suppressed. Yet here it must be acknowledged that his apprehensions had betrayed him into a strange inconsistency of belief. As he persisted in supposing he could be destroyed by *none of woman born,* by what means did he think to destroy himself? for he was produced in the common way of nature, and fell not within the description of the only object that could end the being of Macbeth. In short, his efforts are no longer those of courage but of despair excited by self-conviction, infuriated by the menaces of an injured father, and confirmed by a presentiment of inevitable defeat. Thus situated, he very naturally prefers a manly and violent to a shameful and lingering termination of life. (pp. 462-63)

Between the courage of Richard and Macbeth . . . no comparison in favour of the latter can be supported. Richard was so thoroughly designed for a daring, impious, and obdurate character that even his birth was attended by prodigies, and his person armed with ability to do the earliest mischief of which infancy is capable. Macbeth, on the contrary, till de-

ceived by the illusions of witchcraft, and depraved by the suggestions of his wife, was a religious, temperate and blameless character. The vices of the one were originally woven into his heart; those of the other, were only applied to the surface of his disposition. They can scarce be said to have penetrated quite into its substance, for while there was shame there might have been reformation. (p. 464)

The truth is that the mind of Richard, unimpregnated by original morality, and uninfluenced by the laws of Heaven, is harrassed by no subsequent remorse. . . . Even the depression he feels from preternatural objects is speedily taken off. In spite of ominous visions he sallies forth, and seeks his competitor *in the throat of death.* Macbeth, though he had long abandoned the practice of goodness, had not so far forgot its accustomed influence, but that a virtuous adversary whom he had injured is as painful to his sight as the spectre in a former scene, and equally blasts the resolution he was willing to think he had still possessed. His conscience (as Hamlet says of the poison) *overcrows his spirit,* and all his *enterprizes are sicklied over by the pale cast of thought* [*Hamlet,* V. ii. 353, III. i. 84]. . . . Had Richard once been a feeling and conscientious character, when his end drew nigh, he might also have betrayed evidences of timidity—'there sadly summing what he had, and lost;' and if Macbeth originally had been a hardened villain no terrors

Act IV. Scene i. Three Witches, Banquo, Kings, and Macbeth. Frontispiece to the Rowe edition (1709). By permission of the Folger Shakespeare Library.

might have obtruded themselves on his close of life. . . . In short, Macbeth is timid in spite of all his boasting, as long as he thinks timidity can afford resources; nor does he exhibit a specimen of determined intrepidity till the completion of the prophecy, and the challenge of Macduff, have taught him that life is no longer tenable. Five counterfeit Richmonds are slain by Richard, who, before his fall, has *enacted wonders* beyond the common ability of man. The prowess of Macbeth is confined to the single conquest of Siward, a novice in the art of war. Neither are the truly brave ever disgraced by unnecessary deeds of cruelty. The victims of Richard therefore are merely such as obstructed his progress to the crown, or betrayed the confidence he had reposed in their assurances of fidelity. Macbeth, with a savage wantonness that would have dishonoured a Scythian female, cuts off a whole defenceless family, though the father of it was the only reasonable object of his fear.—Can it be a question then which of these two personages would manifest the most determined valour in the field? Shall we hesitate to bestow the palm of courage on the steady unrepenting Yorkist, in whose bosom ideas of hereditary greatness, and confidence resulting from success, had fed the flame of glory, and who dies in combat for a crown which had been the early object of his ambition? and shall we allot the same wreath to the wavering self-convicted Thane, who, educated without hope of royalty, had been suggested into greatness and yet, at last, would forego it all to secure himself by flight, but that flight is become an impossibility?

To conclude, a picture of conscience encroaching on fortitude, of magnanimity once animated by virtue and afterwards extinguished by guilt, was what Shakespeare meant to display in the character and conduct of Macbeth. (pp. 465-66)

> *George Steevens, in an extract from* Shakespeare, the Critical Heritage: 1774-1801, Vol. 6, *edited by Brian Vickers, Routledge & Kegan Paul, 1981, pp. 462-66.*

AUGUST WILHELM SCHLEGEL　(lecture date 1808)

[*A prominent German Romantic critic, Schlegel holds a key place in the history of Shakespeare's reputation in European criticism. His translations of thirteen of the plays are still considered the best German editions of Shakespeare. Schlegel was also a leading spokesman for the Romantic movement, which permanently overthrew the Neoclassical contention that Shakespeare was a child of nature whose plays lacked artistic form. In the excerpt below, first delivered as a lecture in 1808, Schlegel justifies Shakespeare's use of witches in* Macbeth—*as do Samuel Johnson (1745), the* British Magazine *(1767), and Elizabeth Montagu (1769)—noting that their peculiar language forms "the hollow music of a dreary witch-dance." He also states that the weird sisters "cheat" Macbeth by suggesting that "what in reality can only be accomplished by his own deed" is the work of fate, an observation which anticipates later critical debate over the witches and the problem of free will in* Macbeth *by such critics as Franz Horn (1823), G. G. Gervinus (1849-50), A. J. F. Mézières (1860), Denton J. Snider (1887), and A. C. Bradley (1904). Schlegel observes that despite his actions Macbeth evokes compassion and that the struggle of his "brave will" with his "cowardly conscience" is admirable. Schlegel also comments on* Macbeth's *brevity, saying, "we can hardly conceive how so very much could ever have been compressed into so narrow a space."*]

[Who] could exhaust the praises of this sublime work? Since *The Eumenides* of Aeschylus, nothing so grand and terrible has ever been written [as *Macbeth*]. The witches are not, it is true, divine Eumenides, and are not intended to be: they are ignoble and vulgar instruments of hell. . . . Whether the age of Shakspeare still believed in ghosts and witches, is a matter of perfect indifference for the justification of the use which in *Hamlet* and *Macbeth* he has made of pre-existing traditions. No superstition can be widely diffused without having a foundation in human nature: on this the poet builds; he calls up from their hidden abysses that dread of the unknown, that presage of a dark side of nature, and a world of spirits, which philosophy now imagines it has altogether exploded. In this manner he is in some degree both the portrayer and the philosopher of superstition; that is, not the philosopher who denies and turns it into ridicule, but, what is still more difficult, who distinctly exhibits its origin in apparently irrational and yet natural opinions. But when he ventures to make arbitrary changes in these popular traditions, he altogether forfeits his right to them, and merely holds up his own idle fancies to our ridicule. Shakspeare's picture of the witches is truly magical: in the short scenes where they enter, he has created for them a peculiar language, which, although composed of the usual elements, still seems to be a collection of formulae of incantation. The sound of the words, the accumulation of rhymes, and the rhythmus of the verse, form, as it were, the hollow music of a dreary witch-dance. He has been abused for using the names of disgusting objects; but he who fancies the kettle of the witches can be made effective with agreeable aromatics, is as wise as those who desire that hell should sincerely and honestly give good advice. These repulsive things, from which the imagination shrinks, are here emblems of the hostile powers which operate in nature; and the repugnance of our senses is outweighed by the mental horror. With one another the witches discourse like women of the very lowest class; for this was the class to which witches were ordinarily supposed to belong: when, however, they address Macbeth they assume a loftier tone: their predictions, which they either themselves pronounce, or allow their apparitions to deliver, have all the obscure brevity, the majestic solemnity of oracles.

We here see that the witches are merely instruments; they are governed by an invisible spirit, or the operation of such great and dreadful events would be above their sphere. With what intent did Shakspeare assign the same place to them in his play, which they occupy in the history of Macbeth as related in the old chronicles? A monstrous crime is committed: Duncan, a venerable old man, and the best of kings, is, in defenceless sleep, under the hospitable roof, murdered by his subject, whom he has loaded with honours and rewards. Natural motives alone seem inadequate, or the perpetrator must have been portrayed as a hardened villain. Shakspeare wished to exhibit a more sublime picture: an ambitious but noble hero, yielding to a deep-laid hellish temptation; and in whom all the crimes to which, in order to secure the fruits of his first crime, he is impelled by necessity, cannot altogether eradicate the stamp of native heroism. He has, therefore, given a threefold division to the guilt of that crime. The first idea comes from that being whose whole activity is guided by a lust of wickedness. The weird sisters surprise Macbeth in the moment of intoxication of victory, when his love of glory has been gratified; they cheat his eyes by exhibiting to him as the work of fate what in reality can only be accomplished by his own deed, and gain credence for all their words by the immediate fulfilment of the first prediction. The opportunity of murdering the King immediately offers; the wife of Macbeth conjures him not to let it slip; she urges him on with a fiery eloquence, which has at command all those sophisms that serve to throw a false splendour over crime. Little more than the mere execution falls to the share of Macbeth; he is driven into it, as it were, in a tumult of fascination. Repentance immediately follows, nay, even precedes the deed, and the stings of conscience leave him rest neither night nor day. But he is now fairly entangled in the snares of hell; truly frightful is it to behold that same Macbeth, who once as a warrior could spurn at death, now that he dreads the prospect of the life to come, clinging with growing anxiety to his earthly existence the more miserable it becomes, and pitilessly removing out of the way whatever to his dark and suspicious mind seems to threaten danger. However much we may abhor his actions, we cannot altogether refuse to compassionate the state of his mind; we lament the ruin of so many noble qualities, and even in his last defence we are compelled to admire the struggle of a brave will with a cowardly conscience. We might believe that we witness in this tragedy the over-ruling destiny of the ancients represented in perfect accordance with their ideas: the whole originates in a supernatural influence, to which the subsequent events seem inevitably linked. Moreover, we even find here the same ambiguous oracles which, by their literal fulfilment, deceive those who confide in them. Yet it may be easily shown that the poet has, in his work, displayed more enlightened views. He wishes to show that the conflict of good and evil in this world can only take place by the permission of Providence, which converts the curse that individual mortals draw down on their heads into a blessing to others. An accurate scale is followed in the retaliation. Lady Macbeth, who of all the human participators in the king's murder is the most guilty, is thrown by the terrors of her conscience into a state of incurable bodily and mental disease; she dies, unlamented by her husband, with all the symptoms of reprobation. Macbeth is still found worthy to die the death of a hero on the field of battle. The noble Macduff is allowed the satisfaction of saving his country by punishing with his own hand the tyrant who had murdered his wife and children. Banquo, by an early death, atones for the ambitious curiosity which prompted the wish to know his glorious descendants, as he thereby has roused Macbeth's jealousy; but he preserved his mind pure from the evil suggestions of the witches: his name is blessed in his race, destined to enjoy for a long succession of ages that royal dignity which Macbeth could only hold for his own life. In the progress of the action, this piece is altogether the reverse of *Hamlet:* it strides forward with amazing rapidity, from the first catastrophe (for Duncan's murder may be called a catastrophe) to the last. "Thought, and done!" is the general motto; for as Macbeth says,

> The flighty purpose never is o'ertook,
> Unless the deed go with it.
>
> [IV. i. 149, 145-46]

In every feature we see an energetic heroic age, in the hardy North which steels every nerve. The precise duration of the action cannot be ascertained,—years perhaps, according to the story; but we know that to the imagination the most crowded time appears always the shortest. Here we can hardly conceive how so very much could ever have been compressed into so narrow a space; not merely external events,— the very inmost recesses in the minds of the dramatic personages are laid open to us. It is as if the drags were taken from the wheels of time, and they rolled along without interruption in their descent. Nothing can equal this picture in its power to excite terror. We need only allude to the circumstances attending the murder of Duncan, the dagger that hovers before the eyes of Macbeth, the vision of Banquo at the feast, the madness of Lady Macbeth; what can possibly be said on the subject that will not rather weaken the impression they naturally leave? Such scenes stand alone, and are to be found only in this poet; otherwise the tragic

muse might exchange her mask for the *head of Medusa*. (pp. 407-10)

> *August Wilhelm Schlegel, "Criticisms on Shakspeare's Tragedies," in his* A Course of Lectures on Dramatic Art and Literature, *edited by Rev. A. J. W. Morrison, translated by John Black, revised edition, 1846. Reprint by AMS Press, Inc., 1965, pp. 400-13.*

CHARLES LAMB (essay date 1808)

[Lamb is considered one of the leading figures of the Romantic movement and an authority on Elizabethan drama. Although he was, like William Hazlitt, a theatrical critic, Lamb argued that the stage was an improper medium for Shakespeare's plays, mainly because visual dramatizations marred their artistic and lyrical effects. Like Samuel Taylor Coleridge, Lamb reverenced Shakespeare as a poet rather than a playwright. Although many scholars consider his views sentimental and subjective and his interpretations of Shakespeare's characters often extreme, Lamb remains an important contributor to the nineteenth-century's reevaluation of Shakespeare's genius. In the following commentary on Macbeth, presented as a note to Thomas Middleton's The Witch *in 1808, Lamb compares the witches of Middleton with those of Shakespeare in* Macbeth. *The Weird Sisters, asserts Lamb, "begin bad impulses to men" and "have power over the soul." He also states that their meeting with Macbeth "sways his destiny," a suggestion in agreement with the comments of Thomas Whately (1772), but in sharp opposition to Franz Horn (1823), G. G. Gervinus (1849-50), A. J. F. Mézières (1860), and other critics who contend that the witches do not determine Macbeth's fate.]*

Though some resemblance may be traced between the Charms in Macbeth, and the Incantations in [*The Witch*], which is supposed to have preceded it, this coincidence will not detract much from the originality of Shakspeare. His Witches are distinguished from the Witches of Middleton by essential differences. These are creatures to whom man or woman plotting some dire mischief might resort for occasional consultation. Those originate deeds of blood, and begin bad impulses to men. From the moment that their eyes first met with Macbeth's, he is spell-bound. That meeting sways his destiny. He can never break the fascination. These Witches can hurt the body: those have power over the soul.—Hecate in Middleton has a Son, a low buffoon: the hags of Shakspeare have neither child of their own, nor seem to be descended from any parent. They are foul Anomalies, of whom we know not whence they are sprung, nor whether they have beginning or ending. As they are without human passions, so they seem to be without human relations. They come with thunder and lightning, and vanish to airy music. This is all we know of them.—Except Hecate, they have no names; which heightens their mysteriousness. Their names, and some of the properties, which Middleton has given to his hags, excite smiles. The Weird Sisters are serious things. Their presence cannot co-exist with mirth. (pp. 271-72)

> *Charles Lamb, in a note on "The Witch," in his* Specimens of English Dramatic Poets Who Lived about the Time of Shakespeare, Vol. I, *edited by Israel Gollancz, Johnson Reprint Corporation, 1970, pp. 271-72.*

SAMUEL TAYLOR COLERIDGE (essay date 1813-34?)

[Coleridge's lectures and writings on Shakespeare form a major chapter in the history of English Shakespearean criticism. As the channel for the critical ideas of the German Romantics and as an original interpreter of Shakespeare in the new spirit of Romanticism, Coleridge played a strategic role in overthrowing the

last remains of the Neoclassical approach to Shakespeare and in establishing the modern view of the dramatist as a conscious artist and masterful portrayer of human character. Coleridge's remarks on Shakespeare come down to posterity largely as fragmentary notes, marginalia, and reports by auditors on the lectures, rather than in polished essays. The following two excerpts reveal Coleridge's conviction that the Porter scene in Macbeth *was not written by Shakespeare, a position that is later refuted by most Shakespearean scholars, particularly G. G. Gervinus (1849-50), H. N. Hudson (1872), John W. Hales (1874), George Lyman Kittredge (1916), John B. Harcourt (1961), and Kenneth Muir (1962). In the first passage, which appeared only as marginalia in his notes and is hence undated, Coleridge maintains that the Porter's soliloquy was inserted into* Macbeth *"for the mob by some other hand," and that with the exception of one line, "not one syllable" of the rest of the speech "has the ever-present being of Shakespeare." In the second passage, drawn from notes intended for an 1813 lecture at Bristol, he reasserts his position on the Porter scene, argues that* Macbeth *is remarkably free of puns— an observation later challenged by M. M. Mahood (1957)—and notes the "wholly tragic" play's "absence of comedy."]*

[The] low porter soliloquy I believe written for the mob by some other hand, perhaps with Shakespeare's consent—and that finding it take, he with the remaining ink of a pen otherwise employed just interpolated it with the sentence, 'I'll devil-porter it no further' and what follows to 'bonfire' [II. iii. 17-19]. Of the rest not one syllable has the ever-present being of Shakespeare. (p. 67)

• • • • •

Excepting the disgusting passage of the Porter, which I dare pledge myself to demonstrate an interpolation of the actors, I do not remember in *Macbeth* a single pun or play on words. I defer my answer to this thousand times repeated charge against Shakespeare to a more fit opportunity, and merely mention the fact [of Macbeth's freedom from puns] as justifying a candid doubt at least, whether even in these figures of speech and fanciful modifications of language Shakespeare may not have followed rules and principles that merit and stand the test of philosophic examination.

Entire absence of comedy, nay, even of irony and philosophic contemplation in *Macbeth*—because wholly tragic. (pp. 69-70)

Samuel Taylor Coleridge, "Notes on the Tragedies of Shakespeare: 'Macbeth'," in his Shakespearean Criticism, Vol. 1, *edited by Thomas Middleton Raysor, second edition, Dutton, 1960, pp. 60-73.*

WILLIAM HAZLITT   (essay date 1817)

[Hazlitt is considered a leading Shakespearean critic of the English Romantic movement. A prolific essayist and critic on a wide range of subjects, Hazlitt remarked in the preface to his Characters of Shakespear's Plays, *first published in 1817, that he was inspired by the German critic August Wilhelm Schlegel, and was determined to supplant what he considered the pernicious influence of Samuel Johnson's Shakespearean criticism. Hazlitt's criticism is typically Romantic in its emphasis on character studies. His experience as a drama critic was an important factor in shaping his descriptive, as opposed to analytical, interpretations of Shakespeare. In his comments on* Macbeth, *Hazlitt states that the play contains "violent antitheses of style," juxtaposes conflicting and contradictory elements, and follows "every passion" with "its fellow-contrary," an observation that anticipates a number of twentieth-century critics' comments on the play's style, including A. C. Bradley (1904) and Brents Stirling (1953). Hazlitt compares* Macbeth *to "a vessel drifting before a storm," tossed by the "violence of his fate," declaring that he "is not equal to*

the struggle with fate and conscience." In Lady Macbeth he descries a "masculine firmness" and a "strong-nerved ambition." She is, he states, "a great bad woman, whom we hate, but whom we fear more than we hate." Hazlitt also notes that Lady Macbeth and the Weird Sisters are "equally instrumental" in inciting Macbeth's actions.]

Shakespear excelled in the openings of his plays: that of *Macbeth* is the most striking of any. The wildness of the scenery, the sudden shifting of the situations and characters, the bustle, the expectations excited, are equally extraordinary. From the first entrance of the Witches and the description of them when they meet Macbeth,

> ————What are these
> So wither'd and so wild in their attire,
> That look not like the inhabitants of th' earth
> And yet are on't?
>
> [I. iii. 39-42]

the mind is prepared for all that follows.

This tragedy is alike distinguished for the lofty imagination it displays, and for the tumultuous vehemence of the action; and the one is made the moving principle of the other. The overwhelming pressure of preternatural agency urges on the tide of human passion with redoubled force. Macbeth himself appears driven along by the violence of his fate like a vessel drifting before a storm: he reels to and fro like a drunken man; he staggers under the weight of his own purposes and the suggestions of others; he stands at bay with his situation; and from the superstitious awe and breathless suspense into which the communications of the Weïrd Sisters throw him, is hurried on with daring impatience to verify their predictions, and with impious and bloody hand to tear aside the veil which hides the uncertainty of the future. He is not equal to the struggle with fate and conscience. He now "bends up each corporal instrument to the terrible feat" [I. vii. 79-80]; at other times his heart misgives him, and he is cowed and abashed by his success. "The deed, no less than the attempt, confounds him" [II. ii. 10-11]. His mind is assailed by the stings of remorse, and full of "preternatural solicitings" [I. iii. 130]. His speeches and soliloquies are dark riddles on human life, baffling solution, and entangling him in their labyrinths. In thought he is absent and perplexed, sudden and desperate in act, from a distrust of his own resolution. His energy springs from the anxiety and agitation of his mind. His blindly rushing forward on the objects of his ambition and revenge, or his recoiling from them, equally betrays the harassed state of his feelings.— This part of his character is admirably set off by being brought in connection with that of Lady Macbeth, whose obdurate strength of will and masculine firmness give her the ascendancy over her husband's faultering virtue. She at once seizes on the opportunity that offers for the accomplishment of all their wished-for greatness, and never flinches from her object till all is over. The magnitude of her resolution almost covers the magnitude of her guilt. She is a great bad woman, whom we hate, but whom we fear more than we hate. She does not excite our loathing and abhorrence like Regan and Gonerill. She is only wicked to gain a great end; and is perhaps more distinguished by her commanding presence of mind and inexorable self-will, which do not suffer her to be diverted from a bad purpose, when once formed, by weak and womanly regrets, than by the hardness of her heart or want of natural affections. The impression which her lofty determination of character makes on the mind of Macbeth is well described where he exclaims,

> ————Bring forth men children only;
> For thy undaunted mettle should compose
> Nothing but males!
>
> [I. vii. 72-4]

Nor do the pains she is at to "screw his courage to the sticking-place," the reproach to him, not to be "lost so poorly in himself," the assurance that "a little water clears them of this deed," shew any thing but her greater consistency in depravity [I. vii. 60, II. ii. 68-9, 64]. Her strong-nerved ambition furnishes ribs of steel to "the sides of his intent" [I. vii. 26]; and she is herself wound up to the execution of her baneful project with the same unshrinking fortitude in crime, that in other circumstances she would probably have shewn patience in suffering. The deliberate sacrifice of all other considerations to the gaining "for the future days and nights sole sovereign sway and masterdom," by the murder of Duncan, is gorgeously expressed in her invocation on hearing of "his fatal entrance under her battlements.". . . [I. v. 69-70, 39-40] When she first hears that "Duncan comes there to sleep" she is so overcome by the news, which is beyond her utmost expectations, that she answers the messenger, "Thou'rt mad to say it" [I. v. 32]; and on receiving her husband's account of the predictions of the Witches, conscious of his instability of purpose, and that her presence is necessary to goad him on to the consummation of his promised greatness she exclaims—

> Hie thee hither,
> That I may pour my spirits in thine ear,
> And chastise with the valour of my tongue
> All that impedes thee from the golden round,
> Which fate and metaphysical aid doth seem
> To have thee crowned withal.
>
> [I. v. 25-30]

This swelling exultation and keen spirit of triumph, this uncontroulable eagerness of anticipation, which seems to dilate her form and take possession of all her faculties, this solid, substantial flesh and blood display of passion, exhibit a striking contrast to the cold, abstracted, gratuitous, servile malignity of the Witches, who are equally instrumental in urging Macbeth to his fate for the mere love of mischief, and from a disinterested delight in deformity and cruelty. They are hags of mischief, obscene panders to iniquity, malicious from their impotence of enjoyment, enamoured of destruction, because they are themselves unreal, abortive, half-existences—who become sublime from their exemption from all human sympathies and contempt for all human affairs, as Lady Macbeth does by the force of passion! Her fault seems to have been an excess of that strong principle of self-interest and family aggrandisement, not amenable to the common feelings of compassion and justice, which is so marked a feature in barbarous nations and times. A passing reflection of this kind, on the resemblance of the sleeping king to her father, alone prevents her from slaying Duncan with her own hand. (pp. 11-14)

Macbeth (generally speaking) is done upon a stronger and more systematic principle of contrast than any other of Shakespear's plays. It moves upon the verge of an abyss, and is a constant struggle between life and death. The action is desperate and the reaction is dreadful. It is a huddling together of fierce extremes, a war of opposite natures which of them shall destroy the other. There is nothing but what has a violent end or violent beginnings. The lights and shades are laid on with a determined

hand; the transitions from triumph to despair, from the height of terror to the repose of death, are sudden and startling; every passion brings in its fellow-contrary, and the thoughts pitch and jostle against each other as in the dark. The whole play is an unruly chaos of strange and forbidden things, where the ground rocks under our feet. Shakespear's genius here took its full swing, and trod upon the farthest bounds of nature and passion. This circumstance will account for the abruptness and violent antitheses of the style, the throes and labour which run through the expression, and from defects will turn them into beauties. "So fair and foul a day I have not seen," &c. "Such welcome and unwelcome news together." "Men's lives are like the flowers in their caps, dying or ere they sicken." "Look like the innocent flower, but be the serpent under it" [I. iii. 38, IV. iii. 138, IV. iii. 171-73, I. v. 65-6]. The scene before the castle-gate follows the appearance of the Witches on the heath, and is followed by a midnight murder. Duncan is cut off betimes by treason leagued with witchcraft, and Macduff is ripped untimely from his mother's womb to avenge his death. Macbeth, after the death of Banquo, wishes for his presence in extravagant terms, "To him and all we thirst," and when his ghost appears, cries out, "Avaunt and quit my sight," and being gone, he is "himself again" [III. iv. 90, 92, 107]. Macbeth resolves to get rid of Macduff, that "he may sleep in spite of thunder" [IV. i. 86]; and cheers his wife on the doubtful intelligence of Banquo's taking-off with the encouragement— "Then be thou jocund: ere the bat has flown his cloistered flight; ere to black Hecate's summons the shard-born beetle has rung night's yawning peel, there shall be done—a deed of dreadful note" [III. ii. 40-4]. In Lady Macbeth's speech "Had he not resembled my father as he slept, I had done 't" [II. ii. 12-13], there is murder and filial piety together; and in urging him to fulfil his vengeance against the defenceless king, her thoughts spare the blood neither of infants nor old age. The description of the Witches is full of the same contradictory principle; they "rejoice when good kings bleed," they are neither of the earth nor the air, but both; "they should be women, but their beards forbid it" [I. iii. 45-6]; they take all the pains possible to lead Macbeth on to the height of his ambition, only to betray him "in deeper consequence" [I. iii. 126], and after shewing him all the pomp of their art, discover their malignant delight in his disappointed hopes, by that bitter taunt, "Why stands Macbeth thus amazedly?" [IV. i. 125-26]. We might multiply such instances every where. (pp. 15-16)

William Hazlitt, "'Macbeth'," in his Characters of Shakespear's Plays & Lectures on the English Poets, *The Macmillan Company, 1903, pp. 10-20.*

J[OHN] P[HILIP] KEMBLE (essay date 1817)

[Kemble was a theater manager and a prominent actor in England during the reign of George III; he is notable for the use of historically accurate costumes and stage settings in his Shakespearean productions. Kemble also wrote Macbeth, *and* King Richard the Third: An Essay, in Answer to "Remarks on Some of the Characters of Shakspeare" *(1817), an enlarged edition of an essay first published in 1786. In this treatise, excerpted below, Kemble attacks the argument put forth by Thomas Whately (1772) and George Steevens (1787) that Macbeth shows signs of timidity and cowardice. Kemble cites evidence throughout the play in an effort to prove that Macbeth is indeed courageous, that he does not personally fear Banquo or Macduff, and that he is equal to Richard III in intrepidity. He notes that the first description given of Macbeth emphasizes his bravery and that the murders subsequent to Duncan's are motivated by ambition to retain the throne, not by fear as those earlier critics charged. Kemble also asserts that*

Richard, too, is sometimes shaken by a fearful conscience and that while Richard is only intrepid, Macbeth is "intrepid and feeling." He concludes that it is crucial to the tragedy that Macbeth be allowed some esteem for his "virtuous scruples" and personal courage, for if he is not, "it would entirely counteract the salutary effect of the finest tragedy that has ever been written."]

The appeal for judgement on the quality of the courage of Macbeth, does not depend, as questions of criticism often necessarily must, on conjecture and inference; it addresses itself directly to the plain meaning of every passage where Shakspeare touches on this subject. The shortness of the time allotted for the performance of a play, usually makes it impracticable to allow the principal personages space sufficient for their unfolding themselves gradually before the spectator; it is, therefore, a necessary and beautiful artifice with dramatic writers, by an impressive description of their heroes, to bring us in great measure acquainted with them, before they are visibly engaged in action on the stage; where, without this previous delineation, their proceedings might often appear confused, and sometimes perhaps be unintelligible. We are bound, then, to look on the introductory portrait which our author has drawn of Macbeth, as the true resemblance of him; for the mind may not picture to itself a person of the poet's arbitrary invention, under any features, but those by which that invention has thought fit to identify him.—Here is the portrait.

> *Serg.* The merciless Macdonwald. . .
> Show'd like a rebel's whore: But all's too
>   weak;
> For brave Macbeth, (well he deserves that
>   name,)
> Disdaining Fortune, with his brandish'd steel,
> Which smok'd with bloody execution,
> Like Valour's minion,
> Carv'd out his passage, till he fac'd the slave;
> And ne'er shook hands, nor bade farewell to
>   him,
> Till he unseam'd him from the nave to the
>   chaps,
> And fix'd his head upon our battlements.
>   [I. i. 9, 15-23]

Why does Shakspeare appoint Macbeth to the noble hazard of meeting the fierce Macdonwald in single opposition, hand to hand? Why does he call him brave, and emphatically insist on deserving that name? Why does he grace him with the title of Valour's minion; and presently,—styling him Bellona's bridegroom,—deem him worthy to be matched even with the Goddess of War? Could the poet thus labour the description of his hero, and not design to impress a full idea of the loftiness of his intrepidity? Macbeth's great heart pants to meet the barbarous leader of the rebels: his brandished steel, reeking with intermediate slaughter, has hewn out a passage to him; and he maintains the combat, till the death of his antagonist crowns his persevering valour with a glorious victory. (pp. 13-19)

The imagination being now fully prepared to receive him, Macbeth presents himself on the scene. A deputation from his sovereign meets him, with . . . gracious acknowledgements of his important services. . . . (p. 28)

The King congratulates Macbeth on his success; and professes, that the praises due to his personal valour in the first battle with the rebels, are stifled in wonder at the excess of his daring. How unutterable, then, must Duncan's feelings be, when he finds him, the self-same day, not only again engaged, but,

deep in the hostile ranks, fearlessly dealing death in every shape of horror among the squadrons that surrounded him! The King confers on his dauntless warrior the forfeited honours of the traitorous Cawdor, only as an earnest of those higher dignities which, on the applauding testimony of every tongue, his prosperous courage in the kingdom's wonderful defence has justly merited.

Such is the character with which Shakspeare arrays the son of Sinel, while yet the pureness of his heart remains uncontaminated. The bold decision and unshaken persistence of Glamis throughout the stubborn struggles against Macdonwald and Sweno, establish his title to the praise of the sublimest heroism; the feats of his own hand assure to him the renown of hardihood; and the whole tenor of his deportment through the adventure of this perilous day, unequivocally displays a natural alacrity in the discharge of all the parts of a consummate soldier.

With these extracts from the play before his eyes, Mr. Steevens has ventured to say:—"Throughout such parts of this drama as afford opportunity for a display of personal bravery, Macbeth sometimes *screws his courage* to the sticking place, but *never* rises into constitutional heroism" [see excerpt above, 1787].

Had not Mr. Steevens, here and there, prudently provided himself with an escape from the full reproach of this surprizing proposition, it would have been unworthy of serious notice: The evident drift, however, of his dissertation on the character of Macbeth being, to leave his readers in a complete conviction of the truth of all the material part of Mr. Whateley's theory, the best way of refuting him, it was thought, was, at once, to root up the foundation of his system, without spending any time on the guarded intricacy of his arguments. (pp. 29-33)

That Macbeth felt *a personal fear of Banquo on account of his superior courage,* is an opinion founded, perhaps, on an erroneous conception of Shakspeare's meaning in the following lines:—

> ————Our fears in Banquo
>   Stick deep;—

and

> ————There is none, but he,
> Whose being I do fear.
>   [III. i. 48-9, 53-4]

In order that no shadow of doubt may rest on the quality of the fears mentioned in these passages, it will be proper to trace the course of reasoning pursued through the context of the soliloquy from which they are taken. (pp. 64-5)

In this soliloquy, Macbeth considers that, after all the guilt he has waded through in order to ascend the throne, he is still in the perpetual danger of being hurled from it; he weighs the causes of that danger; and determines by the removal of the persons who seem appointed to depose him, to take the only certain means of assuring the crown to himself, and his posterity. I have, he says, possessed myself of the supreme power: But to what avail, since, in an instant, it may be wrested from me? Banquo is impatient to be the father of a king; and there reigns in his very nature a royalty that seems to realize his expectations. . . . (pp. 71-2)

Macbeth, then, does not plunge into fresh crimes, in order *to get rid of* (personal) *fear:* Ambition impelled him to the murder of Duncan; and ambition still,—and no other motive,—urges him to the destruction of Banquo and Fleance; because they threaten to reduce him and his lineage from the splendours of monarchy to the obscurity of vassalage.

A moment's attention must now be bestowed on Macbeth's conduct towards Macduff; in which the *Remarks* find additional proofs of his cowardice:—*The same motives of personal fear, and those unmixed with any other, impel him to seek the destruction of Macduff* (see excerpt above by Thomas Whately, 1772).

Macbeth is not wrought by *personal* fear to destroy Macduff: it is from conviction of the Thane's indisposition to his government, that he wishes to have him within his grasp. . . . (pp. 74-5)

When Macbeth and the Thane of Fife encounter each other in battle, the tyrant does not resort to that power over his life with which he believed himself gifted, as, in the true spirit of a coward, he instantly would have done, had he *personally* feared him; but, yielding to a noble compunction for the inhuman wrongs he has done him, is desirous to avoid the necessity of adding the blood of Macduff himself to that already spilled in the slaughter of his dearest connexions:—

> *Macb.* Of all men else, I have avoided thee:
> But get thee back; my soul is too much
>   charg'd
> With blood of thine already. . . .
>
>   [V. viii. 4-6]

Unmoved by Macduff's taunts and determined assault, Macbeth counsels him to employ his valour where success may attend on it; and generously warns him not to persist in urging an unequal contest with a foe, whom Destiny has pronounced invincible. Here is demonstration that, in the scene with the Witches, Macbeth does not from *personal* fear *revert to his former resolution* against the life of Macduff.

In a word, Macbeth does not determine on the death of Banquo, Fleance, and Macduff, from *personal* fear: he conceives the perpetration of these crimes, evidently because his ambition renders the father and son objects of his envy, and the disobedient Thane, of his hatred.

We come now to consider Macbeth and King Richard the Third, as they are immediately opposed to each other in the *Remarks;* and are to answer the arguments employed to prove, that *Richard is superior to Macbeth in personal courage.* (pp. 82-5)

Macbeth and Richard are now to be compared while their minds are under the influence of visions and superstition. It is true, that the guilty conscience of Macbeth, overpowering his judgement, conjures up before him the accusing ghost of Banquo: but it is equally true, that his constitutional courage enables him resolutely to face this ghastly fantom of his disordered imagination:—

> *Lady M.* Are you a man?
> *Macb.* Ay, and a bold one, that dare look
>   on that,
> Which might appal the devil.
> *Lady Macb.* O proper stuff!
> This is the very painting of your fear. . . .
>
>   [III. iv. 57-60]
>   (pp. 119-20)

Notwithstanding the firmness which Macbeth summons into his defiance of this frightful "painting of his fear," it is not to be supposed, but that he labours with an inward terror while he utters it:—Neither can it be denied, that the intrepid Richard

is shaken with at least equal alarm, when, starting from the dream in which the souls of those whom he had murdered had appeared to him, he cries:—

> Have mercy, Jesu!—Soft!—I did but dream.
> O coward conscience, how dost thou afflict
>   me!—
> The lights burn blue. It is now dead midnight.
> Cold fearful drops stand on my trembling
>   flesh, &c.
>
>   [*Richard III*, V. iii. 178-80]
>   (pp. 121-22)

It is true, that Macbeth is with difficulty wrought to the murder of his gracious King; but it is not true, that he discovers any *hesitation and dulness to dare,* after he has imbrued his hands in the blood of Duncan. When once he enters the path of guilt, he treads it with resolute rapidity:—

> The flighty purpose never is o'ertook,
> Unless the deed go with it:—
>
>   [IV. i. 145-46]

he needs no other instigators to the death of Banquo, Fleance, and Macduff, but the dark and violent passions of his own corrupted heart:—

> Strange things I have in head, that will to
>   hand;
> Which must be acted, ere they may be scann'd.
>
>   [III. iv. 138-39]

If Shakspeare, after the murder of Duncan, meant Macbeth to show *dulness and hesitation* in evil, he has, with the most unlucky forgetfulness, thoroughly defeated his own design. . . . (pp. 138-39)

The *Remarks* would next presume, that Macbeth is clearly convicted of cowardice on his own acknowledgement: Alluding principally to the passages already refuted, they say,—*These are all symptoms of timidity, which he confesses to have been natural to him, when he owns,—*

> The time has been, my senses would have
>   cool'd
> To hear a night-shriek; and my fell of hair
> Would at a dismal treatise rouse, and stir
> As life were in't.
>
>   [V. v. 10-13]

Had the author of the *Remarks* quoted the whole speech on this occasion, instead of giving only an extract from it, he must have flatly contradicted his own assertion. If Macbeth, as the *Remarks* interpret these lines, confesses that he was *formerly* timid; still they must allow that, in the same breath, as it will in a moment be seen, he denies that he has any such weakness in his constitution *at present:* Now, if they take Macbeth's word for the state of his mind in the one instance, they are bound to receive it for truth in the other; and, consequently, Mr. Whateley and Mr. Steevens are no longer justified in charging him with pusillanimity.

The speech, however, relates neither to bravery, nor timidity; and Mr. Whateley has again entirely mistaken the sentiment of the poet. Macbeth hears the shrieks of women, and demands with haughty indifference,—

> What noise is that?—
>
>   [V. v. 7]

but instantly reflecting on his insensibility to cries so piercing, and uttered too by female voices, he is shocked at the total want of common feeling in his bosom, and, "sadly summing what he has lost," vents his self-reproach in this touching effusion of remorse:—

> I have almost forgot the taste of fears:
> The time has been, my senses would have
>   cool'd
> To hear a night-shriek; and my fell of hair
> Would at a dismal treatise rouse and stir
> As life were in't: I have supp'd full with
>   horrors;
> Direness, familiar to my slaught'rous thoughts,
> Cannot once start me.
>
> [V. v. 9-15]

The fears of which Macbeth laments that he has forgotten the taste, are not fears of danger personal to himself;—(of which it would be strange indeed, if he were sorry to be rid;)—the fears of which he regrets the loss, are those tender apprehensions which formerly he instinctively and keenly felt, not only for any fellow-creature in real peril and calamity, but even for the fictitious distresses of tragical romance. In this beautiful passage, the tyrant, whose nature had been "full of the milk of human kindness" [I. v. 17], mournfully contemplates the dismal change produced in his humane (not *timid*) disposition, by the habitual practice of such cruelties, as have finally hardened his temper against any impression of sympathy, against all the charities of our nature.

Mr. Whateley and Mr. Steevens, while they regard these sentiments as proofs of timidity in Macbeth, unaccountably leave unobserved the similar, and stronger, terrors and remorse that harrow up the soul of the intrepid and hardened Richard:—

> *K. Rich.* My conscience hath a thousand
> several tongues,
> And every tongue brings in a several tale,
> And every tale condemns me for a villain. . . .
>
> [*Richard III*, V. iii. 193-95]
(pp. 141-46)

The *Remarks*, to sum up all, would make it a reproach to Macbeth, that, *when the hour of extremity presses upon him, he can find no refuge but in despair.*

What timidity there is in this, it is not easy to perceive. Macbeth finds refuge, where alone the brave man in the hour of extremity can find it, in himself,—in an unyielding spirit, that nobly, though hopelessly, struggles to the last with overpowering adversity:—he rushes to battle, and encounters the only enemy he had to fear; the strange completion of his destiny suddenly suspends the vigour of his powers; but, in a moment, scorning the juggling fiends who have deceived him, he rouses all himself, and boldly trusts his fate to that inborn intrepidity on whhich he knows he can rely:—

> I will not yield,
> To kiss the ground before young Malcolm's
>   feet,
> And to be baited with the rabble's curse.
>
> [V. viii. 27-9]
(pp. 153-55)

The appeals which Macbeth makes to his own conscious valour for support in all his extremities, are another conclusive proof that Shakspeare means him to be esteemed a man of indisputable spirit; in the mouth of one whom we knew to be a braggart, these self-confident expressions would degenerate into mere farce, and provoke only our ridicule and laughter. (p. 161)

In the performance, on the Stage,—the valour of the tyrant, hateful as he is, invariably commands the administration of every spectator of the play, rude or learned: this circumstance alone would be an evident demonstration that the poet never intended we should entertain a doubt of his dauntless intrepidity: And, indeed, were not the horror excited by Macbeth's crimes, qualified by the delight we receive from our esteem for his personal courage, the representation of this tragedy would be insupportable.

Macbeth, unable to bear the reproach of cowardice from a woman,—a woman too who holds the complete sway of his affections and his reason,—in one sentence vindicates to himself the dignity of true courage, and unfolds the whole nature of the character we are to expect in him:—

> I dare do all that may become a man;
> Who dares do more, is none.
>
> [I. vii. 46-7]
(pp. 161-63)

Macbeth and Richard are, both, as intrepid as man can be; yet it may be said of each, without any diminution of that praise, that he is sometimes terror-struck at the recollection of his crimes. The characters that Shakspeare draws, are human creatures; and however their peculiarities may individuate them, yet they are always connected with the general nature of man by some fine link of universal interest, and by some passion to which they are liable in common with their kind. On the eve of the battle that is to decide his doom, Richard acknowledges a conscience: Bold in supernatural assurances of security from all peril, Macbeth sighs for the protection of his former popularity. (pp. 166-67)

The character of Richard is simple; that of Macbeth is mixed: Richard is only intrepid; Macbeth, intrepid and feeling. Richard's crimes are the suggestions of his own disposition, originally bad, and at last confirmed in evil; he knows no "compunctious visitings of nature" [I. v. 45]; alive only to the exigencies of his situation, he is always at full leisure to display his valour. Macbeth is driven into guilt by the instigations of others; his early principles of virtue are not extinct in him; distracted by remorse, he forgets the approach of danger in the contemplation of his crimes; and never recurs to his valour for support, till the presence of the enemy rouses his whole soul, and conscience is repelled by the necessity for exertion.

It is now shown, that Macbeth has a just right to the reputation of intrepidity; that he feels no personal fear of Banquo and Macduff; and that he meets equal, if not superior, trials of fortitude, as calmly as Richard: It may, therefore, be presumed, that no future Critic or Commentator in his observations on Shakspeare, will ascribe either the virtuous scruples of Macbeth, or his remorseful agonies, to so mean a cause as constitutional timidity. If so mistaken a persuasion could prevail, it would entirely counteract the salutary effect of the finest tragedy that has ever been written, and defeat the moral purpose to which, in every age, the Stage has been indebted for the favour and the works of wise and virtuous men, and the protection and support of all good governments. (pp. 169-71)

J[ohn] P[hilip] Kemble, in his Macbeth, and King
Richard the Third: An Essay, in Answer to "Remarks
on Some of the Characters of Shakspeare," *1817.*

Reprint by Augustus M. Kelley Publishers, 1970, 171 p.

FRANZ HORN (essay date 1823)

[*Horn, a German novelist and critic, made his contribution to Shakespearean criticism with his* Shakespeare's Schauspiele erläutert *(1823). In the following excerpt, drawn from a translated portion of that work, Horn develops the issue of free will in* Macbeth, *stating that the course of Macbeth's tragic action is willed not by destiny, but is the result of a lack of faith in his own freedom. He further states that the "necessity" that determines Macbeth's actions "exists in his own heart." Horn's assertion that Macbeth possesses free will runs counter to the comments of Thomas Whateley (1772) and Charles Lamb (1808), but is supported by a number of later critics, including G. G. Gervinus (1849-50) and A. J. F. Mézières (1860).*]

We possess, first of all, in this drama what there is much said about at random, a pure, simple tragedy of Destiny, that is, as concerns Macbeth, the representation of a conflict in which freedom, not yet complete in itself, suffers defeat and becomes the prey of necessity. But this result by no means proves the absolute supremacy of destiny, but only the danger in a certain individual of an ill-secured and imperfect freedom which, as such, must necessarily yield to destiny. The Poet shows throughout that Macbeth was not *forced* to act because destiny *willed* it, but that he fell because he put no faith in his freedom; but he could not trust that, because he understood not how to render it complete. . . .

In the life of every human being of any force of character there are everywhere abysses, whence ascends a bewildering perfume as from blooming valleys; but may he who yields to this intoxication lay the blame upon Destiny? Everywhere dazzling colors and alluring voices entice us, and we can follow them or not; accordingly the true Poet knows no one-sided necessity, but only a freedom that has become a beautiful necessity, or a necessity exalted into freedom.

The necessity which Macbeth obeys, because he is not free, exists in his own heart, whose weakness the dark powers make use of to prepare him for his fall. He is of sufficient importance to stir up all hell against him; a prey, such as he is, is quite worth the trouble, and Hell *as* Hell is perfectly right when it busies itself so eagerly about him. (pp. 458-59)

> *Franz Horn, in an extract translated by Horace Howard Furness, in* A New Variorum Edition of Shakespeare: "Macbeth," *Vol. II by William Shakespeare, edited by Horace Howard Furness, J. B. Lippincott Company, 1873, pp. 458-62.*

THOMAS DE QUINCEY (essay date 1823)

[*De Quincey, a Romantic essayist, critic, and author of* Confessions of an English Opium Eater, *contributed to Shakespearean criticism with his famous essay "On the Knocking at the Gate in* Macbeth," *first published in 1823. In the excerpt below, De Quincey explains the profound effect of the knocking heard in* Macbeth *following Duncan's murder. He notes that the killing of Duncan suspends "the world of the ordinary life" and allows the "entrance of the fiendish Heart" and a "world of darkness." The knocking, De Quincey proposes, represents a reaction to this dark world and indicates that "the human has made its reflux on the fiendish." Finally, he states that it reestablishes the workings of an ordinary world and "makes us profoundly sensible of the awful parenthesis that had suspended them." For a response to De Quincey, see the essay by John Webster Spargo listed in the*

Additional Bibliography. Also, for additional commentary on the knocking at the gate, see the excerpts by John W. Hales (1874) and John B. Harcourt (1961).]

From my boyish days I had always felt a great perplexity on one point in *Macbeth.* It was this:—The knocking at the gate which succeeds to the murder of Duncan produced to my feelings an effect for which I never could account. The effect was that it reflected back upon the murderer a peculiar awfulness and a depth of solemnity; yet, however obstinately I endeavoured with my understanding to comprehend this, for many years I never could see *why* it should produce such an effect. (p. 389)

My understanding could furnish no reason why the knocking at the gate in Macbeth should produce any effect, direct or reflected. In fact, my understanding said positively that it could *not* produce any effect. But I knew better; I felt that it did; and I waited and clung to the problem until further knowledge should enable me to solve it. . . . At length I solved it to my own satisfaction; and my solution is this:—Murder, in ordinary cases, where the sympathy is wholly directed to the case of the murdered person, is an incident of coarse and vulgar horror; and for this reason,—that it flings the interest exclusively upon the natural but ignoble instinct by which we cleave to life: an instinct which, as being indispensable to the primal law of self-preservation, is the same in kind (though different in degree) amongst all living creatures. This instinct, therefore, because it annihilates all distinctions, and degrades the greatest of men to the level of "the poor beetle that we tread on," exhibits human nature in its most abject and humiliating attitude. Such an attitude would little suit the purposes of the poet. What then must he do? He must throw the interest on the murderer. Our sympathy must be with *him* (of course I mean a sympathy of comprehension, a sympathy by which we enter into his feelings, and are made to understand them,—not a sympathy of pity or approbation). In the murdered person, all strife of thought, all flux and reflux of passion and of purpose, are crushed by one overwhelming panic; the fear of instant death smites him "with its petrific mace." But in the murderer, such a murderer as a poet will condescend to, there must be raging some great storm of passion,—jealousy, ambition, vengeance, hatred,—which will create a hell within him; and into this hell we are to look.

In *Macbeth,* for the sake of gratifying his own enormous and teeming faculty of creation, Shakspere has introduced two murderers: and, as usual in his hands, they are remarkably discriminated: but,—though in Macbeth the strife of mind is greater than in his wife, the tiger spirit not so awake, and his feelings caught chiefly by contagion from her,—yet, as both were finally involved in the guilt of murder, the murderous mind of necessity is finally to be presumed in both. This was to be expressed; and, on its own account, as well as to make it a more proportionable antagonist to the unoffending nature of their victim, "the gracious Duncan," and adequately to expound "the deep damnation of his taking off," this was to be expressed with peculiar energy. We were to be made to feel that the human nature,—*i.e.* the divine nature of love and mercy, spread through the hearts of all creatures, and seldom utterly withdrawn from man,—was gone, vanished, extinct, and that the fiendish nature had taken its place. And, as this effect is marvellously accomplished in the *dialogues* and *soliloquies* themselves, so it is finally consummated by the expedient under consideration; and it is to this that I know solicit the reader's attention. If the reader has ever witnessed a wife, daughter, or sister in a fainting fit, he may chance to have observed that the most affecting moment in such a spectacle is *that* in which a sigh and a stirring announce the recommencement of suspended life. Or, if the reader has ever been present in a vast metropolis on the day when some great national idol was carried in funeral pomp to his grave, and, chancing to walk near the course through which it passed, has felt powerfully, in the silence and desertion of the streets, and in the stagnation of ordinary business, the deep interest which at that moment was possessing the heart of man,—if all at once he should hear the death-like stillness broken up by the sound of wheels rattling away from the scene, and making known that the transitory vision was dissolved, he will be aware that at no moment was his sense of the complete suspension and pause in ordinary human concerns so full and affecting as at that moment when the suspension ceases, and the goings-on of human life are suddenly resumed. All action in any direction is best expounded, measured, and made apprehensible, by reaction. Now, apply this to the case in *Macbeth*. Here, as I have said, the retiring of the human heart and the entrance of the fiendish heart was to be expressed and made sensible. Another world has stept in; and the murderers are taken out of the region of human things, human purposes, human desires. They are transfigured: Lady Macbeth is "unsexed"; Macbeth has forgot that he was born of woman; both are conformed to the image of devils; and the world of devils is suddenly revealed. But how shall this be conveyed and made palpable? In order that a new world may step in, this world must for a time disappear. The murderers and the murder must be insulated—cut off by an immeasurable gulf from the ordinary tide and succession of human affairs—locked up and sequestered in some deep recess; we must be made sensible that the world of ordinary life is suddenly arrested, laid asleep, tranced, racked into a dread armistice; time must be annihilated, relation to things without abolished; and all must pass self-withdrawn into a deep syncope and suspension of earthly passion. Hence it is that, when the deed is done, when the work of darkness is perfect, then the world of darkness passes away like a pageantry in the clouds: the knocking at the gate is heard, and it makes known audibly that the reaction has commenced; the human has made its reflux upon the fiendish; the pulses of life are beginning to beat again; and the re-establishment of the goings-on of the world in which we live first makes us profoundly sensible of the awful parenthesis that had suspended them. (pp. 390-93)

Thomas De Quincey, "On the Knocking at the Gate in 'Macbeth'," in his The Collected Writings of Thomas De Quincey, *edited by David Masson, A. & C. Black, 1897, pp. 389-94.*

[ANNA BROWNELL] JAMESON (essay date 1833)

[*Jameson was a well-known nineteenth-century essayist. Her essays and criticism span the end of the Romantic age and the beginning of Victorian realism, reflecting elements from both periods. She is best remembered for her study* Shakspeare's Heroines *(1833), which was originally published in a slightly different form in 1832 as* Characteristics of Women: Moral, Poetical, and Historical. *This work demonstrates both her historical interests and her sympathetic appreciation of Shakespeare's female characters. In the excerpt below, Jameson presents the first full interpretation of Lady Macbeth, a character later analyzed by William Maginn (1837), H. N. Hudson (1872), and Isador H. Coriat (1912). While Jameson admits that Lady Macbeth is "a terrible impersonation of evil passions," she contends that her character is "never so far removed from our own nature as to be cast beyond the pale of our sympathies." In defense of Lady Macbeth, Jameson points out that the idea to murder Duncan occurs first to Macbeth and*

that Lady Macbeth does not incite Macbeth to commit the subsequent "gratuitous murders." Jameson also attributes to Lady Macbeth an "amazing power of intellect," a "superhuman strength of nerve," but also a "touch of womanhood." She further observes that at those moments when Lady Macbeth appears most savage, her speeches are so worded as to "place the woman before us in all her dearest attributes, at once softening and refining the horror, and rendering it more intense." Of Lady Macbeth's sleepwalking, Jameson states that it evokes sympathy and "we rather sigh over the ruin than exult in it." She concludes that Shakespeare never presents evil without "a consciousness of the opposite good which shall balance and relieve it." Although Jameson's relatively positive assessment of Lady Macbeth is supported by Maginn and is a significant break from earlier, more condemnatory views of her nature, such sentimentalizing of the character is challenged by later critics such as A. C. Bradley (1904).]

Generally speaking, the commentators seemed to have considered Lady Macbeth rather with reference to her husband, and as influencing the action of the drama, than as an individual conception of amazing power, poetry, and beauty. . . . (pp. 312-13)

In the mind of Lady Macbeth, ambition is represented as the ruling motive, an intense overmastering passion which is gratified at the expense of every just and generous principle, and every feminine feeling. In the pursuit of her object, she is cruel, treacherous, and daring. She is doubly, trebly, dyed in guilt and blood; for the murder she instigates is rendered more frightful by disloyalty and ingratitude, and by the violation of all the most sacred claims of kindred and hospitality. When her husband's more kindly nature shrinks from the perpetration of the deed of horror, she, like an evil genius, whispers him on to his damnation. The full measure of her wickedness is never disguised, the magnitude and atrocity of her crime is never extenuated, forgotten, or forgiven, in the whole course of the play. Our judgment is not bewildered, nor our moral feeling insulted, by the sentimental jumble of great crimes and dazzling virtues, after the fashion of the German school, and of some admirable writers of our own time. Lady Macbeth's amazing power of intellect, her inexorable determination of purpose, her superhuman strength of nerve, render her as fearful in herself as her deeds are hateful; yet she is not a mere monster of depravity, with whom we have nothing in common, nor a meteor whose destroying path we watch in ignorant affright and amaze. She is a terrible impersonation of evil passions and mighty powers, never so far removed from our own nature as to be cast beyond the pale of our sympathies; for the woman herself remains a woman to the last—still linked with her sex and with humanity.

This impression is produced partly by the essential truth in the conception of the character, and partly by the manner in which it is evolved; by a combination of minute and delicate touches, in some instances by speech, in others by silence: at one time by what is revealed, at another by what we are left to infer. As in real life, we perceive distinctions in character we cannot always explain, and receive impressions for which we cannot always account, without going back to the beginning of an acquaintance and recalling many and trifling circumstances— looks, and tones, and words: thus, to explain that hold which Lady Macbeth, in the midst of all her atrocities, still keeps upon our feelings, it is necessary to trace minutely the action of the play, as far as she is concerned in it, from its very commencement to its close.

We must then bear in mind, that the first idea of murdering Duncan is not suggested by Lady Macbeth to her husband: it springs within *his* mind, and is revealed to us before his first interview with his wife—before she is introduced, or even alluded to. . . . (pp. 314-15)

It will be said, that the same "horrid suggestion" presents itself spontaneously to her on the reception of his letter; or rather, that the letter itself acts upon her mind as the prophecy of the Weird Sisters on the mind of her husband, kindling the latent passion for empire into a quenchless flame. We are prepared to see the train of evil, first lighted by hellish agency, extend itself to *her* through the medium of her husband: but we are spared the more revolting idea that it originated with her. The guilt is thus more equally divided than we should suppose, when we hear people pitying "the noble nature of Macbeth," bewildered and goaded on to crime, solely or chiefly by the instigation of his wife.

It is true that she afterwards appears the more active agent of the two; but it is less through her pre-eminence in wickedness than through her superiority of intellect. The eloquence—the fierce, fervid eloquence, with which she bears down the re-lenting and reluctant spirit of her husband, the dexterous so-phistry with which she wards off his objections, her artful and affected doubts of his courage, the sarcastic manner in which she lets fall the word coward—a word which no man can endure from another, still less from a woman, and least of all from the woman he loves—and the bold address with which she removes all obstacles, silences all arguments, overpowers all scruples, and marshals the way before him, absolutely make us shrink before the commanding intellect of the woman with a terror in which interest and admiration are strangely mingled. (pp. 315-16)

Again, in the murdering scene, the obdurate inflexibility of purpose with which she drives on Macbeth to the execution of their project, and her masculine indifference to blood and death, would inspire unmitigated disgust and horror, but for the in-voluntary consciousness that it is produced rather by the ex-ertion of a strong power over herself than by absolute depravity of disposition and ferocity of temper. This impression of her character is brought home at once to our very hearts within us, the most subtle mastery over their various operations, and a feeling of dramatic effect not less wonderful. The very passages in which Lady Macbeth displays the most savage and relentless determination are so worded as to fill the mind with the idea of sex, and place the *woman* before us in all her dearest attri-butes, at once softening and refining the horror, and rendering it more intense. Thus, when she reproaches her husband for his weakness—

> From this time,
> Such I account thy love!
> [I. vii. 38-9]

Again—

> Come to my woman's breasts,
> And take my milk for gall, ye murd'ring ministers.
> [I. iv. 47-8]

>   *   *   *   *   *

> That no compunctious visitings of nature
> Shake my fell purpose, &c.
> [I. v. 45-6]

> I have given suck, and know
> How tender 'tis to love the babe that milks me, &c.
> [I. vii. 54-5]

And lastly, in the moment of extremest horror comes that unexpected touch of feeling, so startling, yet so wonderfully true to nature—

> Had he not resembled
> My father as he slept, I had done it!
> [II. ii. 12-13]

Thus, in one of Weber's or Beethoven's grand symphonies, some unexpected soft minor chord or passage will steal on the ear, heard amid the magnificent crash of harmony, making the blood pause, and filling the eye with unbidden tears.

It is particularly observable that in Lady Macbeth's concen-trated, strong-nerved ambition, the ruling passion of her mind, there is yet a touch of womanhood; she is ambitious less for herself than for her husband. It is fair to think this, because we have no reason to draw any other inference either from her words or actions. In her famous soliloquy, after reading her husband's letter, she does not once refer to herself. It is of him she thinks: she wishes to see her husband on the throne, and to place the sceptre within *his* grasp. The strength of her af-fections adds strength to her ambition. Although in the old story of Boethius we are told that the wife of Macbeth "burned with unquenchable desire to bear the name of queen," yet, in the aspect under which Shakspeare has represented the char-acter to us, the selfish part of this ambition is kept out of sight. We must remark also, that in Lady Macbeth's reflections on her husband's character, and on that milkiness of nature which she fears "may impede him from the golden round" [I. v. 28], there is no indication of female scorn: there is exceeding pride, but no egotism in the sentiment or the expression; no want of wifely and womanly respect and love for *him,* but, on the contrary, a sort of unconsciousness of her own mental supe-riority, which she betrays rather than asserts, as interesting in itself as it is most admirably conceived and delineated. (pp. 317-19)

Nor is there anything vulgar in her ambition: as the strength of her affections lends to it something profound and concen-trated, so her splendid imagination invests the object of her desire with its own radiance. We cannot trace in her grand and capacious mind that it is the mere baubles and trappings of royalty which dazzle and allure her: hers is the sin of the "star-bright apostate," and she plunges with her husband into the abyss of guilt, to procure for "all their days and nights sole sovereign sway and masterdom" [I. v. 69-70]. She revels, she luxuriates in her dream of power. She reaches at the golden diadem which is to sear her brain; she perils life and soul for its attainment, with an enthusiasm as perfect, a faith as settled, as that of the martyr, who sees at the stake heaven and its crowns of glory opening upon him. . . . (pp. 319-20)

Lady Macbeth having proposed the object to herself, and ar-rayed it with an ideal glory, fixes her eye steadily upon it, soars far above all womanish feelings and scruples to attain it, and stoops upon her victim with the strength and velocity of a vulture; but having committed unflinchingly the crime nec-essary for the attainment of her purpose, she stops there. After the murder of Duncan, we see Lady Macbeth, during the rest of the play, occupied in supporting the nervous weakness and sustaining the fortitude of her husband. . . . But she is nowhere represented as urging him on to new crimes; so far from it, that when Macbeth darkly hints his purposed assassination of Banquo, and she inquires his meaning, he replies—

> Be innocent of the knowledge, dearest chuck,
> Till thou applaud the deed.
> [III. ii. 45-6]

The same may be said of the destruction of Macduff's family. Every one must perceive how our detestation of the woman had been increased, if she had been placed before us as suggesting and abetting those additional cruelties into which Macbeth is hurried by his mental cowardice.

If my feeling of Lady Macbeth's character be just to the conception of the poet, then she is one who could steel herself to the commission of a crime from necessity and expediency, and be daringly wicked for a great end, but not likely to perpetrate gratuitous murders from any vague or selfish fears. I do not mean to say that the perfect confidence existing between herself and Macbeth could possibly leave her in ignorance of his actions or designs: that heart-broken and shuddering allusion to the murder of Lady Macduff (in the sleeping scene) proves the contrary—

The thane of Fife had a wife: where is she now?
[V. i. 42-3]

But she is nowhere brought before us in immediate connection with these horrors, and we are spared any flagrant proof of her participation in them. This may not strike us at first, but most undoubtedly has an effect on the general bearing of the character, considered as a whole. (pp. 320-22)

Lastly, it is clear that in a mind constituted like that of Lady Macbeth, and not utterly depraved and hardened by the habit of crime, conscience must wake some time or other, and bring with it remorse closed by despair, and despair by death. This great moral retribution was to be displayed to us—but how? Lady Macbeth is not a woman to start at shadows: she mocks at air-drawn daggers: she sees no imagined spectres rise from the tomb to appal or accuse her. The towering bravery of *her* mind disdains the visionary terrors which haunt her weaker husband. We know, or rather we feel, that she who could give a voice to the most direful intent, and call on the spirits that wait on mortal thoughts to "unsex her," and "stop up all access and passage of remorse" [I. v. 44]—to that remorse would have given nor tongue nor sound; and that rather than have uttered a complaint, she would have held her breath and died. To have given her a confidant, though in the partner of her guilt, would have been a degrading resource, and have disappointed and enfeebled all our previous impressions of her character; yet justice is to be done, and we are to be made acquainted with that which the woman herself would have suffered a thousand deaths of torture rather than have betrayed. In the sleeping scene we have a glimpse into the depths of that inward hell: the seared brain and broken heart are laid bare before us in the helplessness of slumber. By a judgment the most sublime ever imagined, yet the most unforced, natural, and inevitable, the sleep of her who murdered sleep is no longer repose, but a condensation of resistless horrors which the prostrate intellect and the powerless will can neither baffle nor repel. We shudder and are satisfied; yet our human sympathies are again touched: we rather sigh over the ruin than exult in it; and after watching her through this wonderful scene with a sort of fascination, we dismiss the unconscious, helpless, despair-stricken murderess, with a feeling which Lady Macbeth, in her waking strength, with all her awe-commanding powers about her, could never have excited.

It is here especially we perceive that sweetness of nature which in Shakspeare went hand in hand with his astonishing powers. He never confounds that line of demarcation which eternally separates good from evil, yet he never places evil before us without exciting in some way a consciousness of the opposite good which shall balance and relieve it. (pp. 323-25)

> *Mrs. [Anna Brownell] Jameson, "Lady Macbeth," in her* Shakspeare's Heroines: Characteristics of Women, Moral, Poetical, & Historical, *George Newnes, Limited, 1897, pp. 309-31.*

WILLIAM MAGINN (essay date 1837)

[*In the excerpt below, Maginn, an Irish essayist, calls* Macbeth *"the gloomiest" of Shakespeare's plays and examines the blood imagery that runs throughout the drama. Like Anna Brownell Jameson (1833), Maginn defends the character of Lady Macbeth. He argues that her "guiding passion" is her love for her husband and that her participation in Duncan's murder is motivated by her concern for him. Maginn further states that Lady Macbeth is "not the tempter of Macbeth," and that her only sin is her energetic devotion "to minister to his hopes and aspirations." He concludes that "it is [a] pity that such a woman should have been united to such a man" and encourages "a kindly construing" for her motives. Such kind "construing" of Lady Macbeth's motives is later challenged by A. C. Bradley (1904), and further discussion of her character is presented by H. N. Hudson (1872) and Isador H. Coriat (1912). Maginn's essay was first published in* Bentley's Miscellany *in 1837.*]

Macbeth is the gloomiest of the plays. Well may its hero say that he has supped full of horrors. It opens with the incantations of spiteful witches, and concludes with a series of savage combats, stimulated by quenchless hate on one side, and by the desperation inspired by the consciousness of unpardonable crime on the other. In every act we have blood in torrents. The first man who appears on the stage is the *bleeding* captain. The first word uttered by earthly lips is, "What *bloody* man is that ?" [I. ii. 1] The tale which the captain relates is full of fearful gashes, reeking wounds, and *bloody* execution. The murder of Duncan, in the second act, stains the hands of Macbeth so deeply as to render them fit to incarnadine the multitudinous seas, and make the green—one red. His lady imbrues herself in the crimson stream, and gilds the faces of the sleeping grooms with gore. . . . Gloom, ruin, murder, horrible doubts, unnatural suspicions, portents of dread in earth and heaven, surround us on all sides. In the third act, desperate assassins, incensed by the blows and buffets of the world, weary with disasters, tugged with fortune, willing to wreak their hatred on all mankind, and persuaded that Banquo has been their enemy, set upon and slay him, without remorse and without a word. The prayer of their master to Night, that she would, with

> *Bloody* and invisible hand,
> Cancel and tear to pieces that great bond
> [III. ii. 47-8]

which kept him in perpetual terror, is in part accomplished; and he who was his enemy in, as he says—

> Such *bloody* distance,
> That every minute of his being thrusts
> Against my life   [III. i. 115-17]

lies breathless in the dust. The murderers bring the witness of their deed to the very banquet-chamber of the expecting king. They come with *blood* upon the face. (pp. 187-89)

The sanguine stain dyes the fourth act as deeply. A head severed from the body, and a bloody child, are the first apparitions that rise before the king at the bidding of the weird sisters. The blood-boltered Banquo is the last to linger upon the stage, and sear the eyes of the amazed tyrant. The sword of the assassin is soon at work in the castle of Macduff; and his wife and children fly from the deadly blow, shrieking "murder"— in vain. And the fifth act—from its appalling commencement, when the sleeping lady plies her hopeless task of nightly washing the blood-stained hand, through the continual clangor of trumpets calling, as clamorous harbingers, to blood and death, to its conclusion, when Macduff, with dripping sword, brings in the freshly hewn-off head of the "dead butcher," to lay it at the feet of the victorious Malcolm—exhibits a sequence of scenes in which deeds and thoughts of horror and violence are perpetually, and almost physically, forced upon the attention of the spectator. In short, the play is one clot of blood from beginning to end. (pp. 190-91)

Of such a gory poem, Macbeth is the centre, the moving spirit. From the beginning, before treason has entered his mind, he appears as a man delighting in blood. . . . The witches had told him he was to be king: they had not said a word about the means. He instantly supplies them:

> Why do I yield to that suggestion
> Whose horrid image doth unfix my hair,
> And make my seated heart knock at my ribs
> Against the use of nature?   [I. iii. 134-37]

The dreaded word itself soon comes:

> My thought, whose MURDER yet is but fantastical,
> Shakes so my single state of man, that function
> Is smothered in surmise.
>
>   [I. iii. 139-41

To a mind so disposed, temptation is unnecessary. The thing was done. Duncan was marked out for murder before the letter was written to Lady Macbeth, and she only followed the thought of her husband.

Love for him is in fact her guiding passion. She sees that he covets the throne—that his happiness is wrapped up in the hope of being a king—and her part is accordingly taken without hesitation. With the blindness of affection, she persuades herself that he is full of the milk of human kindness, and that he would reject false and unholy ways of attaining the object of his desire. She deems it, therefore, her duty to spirit him to the task. Fate and metaphysical aid, she argues, have destined him for the golden round of Scotland. Shall she not lend her assistance? She does not ask the question twice. She will. Her sex, her woman's breasts, her very nature, oppose the task she has prescribed to herself; but she prays to the ministers of murder—to the spirits that tend on mortal thoughts—to make thick her blood, and stop up the access and passage of remorse; and she succeeds in mustering the desperate courage which bears her through. Her instigation was not, in reality, wanted. (pp. 193-95)

[Macbeth's] wife has not to suggest murder, for that has been already resolved upon; but to represent the weakness of drawing back, after a resolution has once been formed. She well knows that the momentary qualm will pass off—that Duncan is to be slain, perhaps when time and place will not so well adhere. Now, she argues—now it can be done with safety. . . . She therefore rouses him to do at once that from which she knows nothing but fear of detection deters him; and, feeling that there are no conscientious scruples to overcome, applies herself to show that the present is the most favorable instant. It is for him she thinks—for him she is unsexed—for his ambition she works—for his safety she provides. (p. 196)

Lady Macbeth is stigmatized as the fiend-like queen. Except her share in the murder of Duncan—which is, however, quite sufficient to justify the epithet in the mouth of his son—she does nothing in the play to deserve the title; and for her crime she has been sufficiently punished by a life of disaster and remorse. She is not the tempter of Macbeth. It does not require much philosophy to pronounce that there were no such beings as the weird sisters; or that the voice that told the Thane of Glamis that he was to be King of Scotland, was that of his own ambition. In his own bosom was brewed the hell-broth, potent to call up visions counselling tyranny and blood; and its ingredients were his own evil passions and criminal hopes. Macbeth himself only believes as much of the prediction of the witches as he desires. The same prophets who foretold his elevation to the throne, foretold also that the progeny of Banquo would reign; and yet, after the completion of the prophecy so far as he is himself concerned, he endeavors to mar the other part by the murder of Fleance. The weird sisters are, to him, no more than the Evil Spirit which, in Faust, tortures Margaret at her prayers. They are but the personified suggestions of his mind. She, the wife of his bosom, knows the direction of his thoughts; and, bound to him in love, exerts every energy, and sacrifices every feeling, to minister to his hopes and aspirations. This is her sin, and no more. He retains, in all his guilt and crime, a fond feeling for his wife. Even when meditating slaughter, and dreaming of blood, he addresses soft words of conjugal endearment; he calls her "dearest chuck," while devising assassinations, with the fore-knowledge of which he is unwilling to sully her mind. Selfish in ambition, selfish in fear, his character presents no point of attraction but this one merit. Shakespeare gives us no hint as to her personal charms, except when he makes her describe her hand as "little." We may be sure that there were few "more thorough-bred or fairer fingers," in the land of Scotland, than those of its queen, whose bearing in public toward Duncan, Banquo, and the nobles, is marked by elegance and majesty; and, in private, by affectionate anxiety for her sanguinary lord. He duly appreciated her feelings, but it is pity that such a woman should have been united to such a man. If she had been less strong of purpose, less worthy of confidence, he would not have disclosed to her his ambitious designs; less resolute and prompt of thought and action, she would not have been called on to share his guilt; less sensitive or more hardened, she would not have suffered it to prey for ever like a vulture upon her heart. She affords, as I consider it, only another instance of what women will be brought to, by a love which listens to no considerations, which disregards all else besides, when the interests, the wishes, the happiness, the honor, or even the passions, caprices, and failings of the beloved object, are concerned; and if the world, in a compassionate mood, will gently scan the softer errors of sister-woman, may we not claim a kindly construing for the motives which plunged into the Aceldama of this blood-washed tragedy the sorely-urged and broken-hearted Lady Macbeth? (pp. 204-08)

William Maginn, "Lady Macbeth," in his The Shakespeare Papers of the Late William Maginn, LL.D., *edited by Shelton Mackenzie, Redfield, 1856, pp. 171-208.*

HERMANN ULRICI (essay date 1839)

[*A German scholar, Ulrici was a professor of philosophy and the author of works on Greek poetry and Shakespeare. The following excerpt is from an English translation of his* Über Shakespeares dramatische Kunst, und sein Verhältniss zu Calderon und Göthe, *a work first published in 1839. This study exemplifies the "philosophical criticism" developed in Germany during the nineteenth century. The immediate sources for Ulrici's critical approach appear to be August Wilhelm Schlegel's conception of the play as an organic, interconnected whole and Georg Wilhelm Friedrich Hegel's view of drama as an embodiment of the conflict of historical forces and ideas. Unlike his fellow German Shakespearean critic G. G. Gervinus, Ulrici sought to develop a specifically Christian aesthetics, but one which, as he carefully points out in the introduction to the work mentioned above, in no way intrudes on "that unity of idea, which preeminently constitutes a work of art a living creation in the world of beauty." This Christian interpretation is prominent in Ulrici's comments on* Macbeth. *He describes the play as the tragedy, "above all others," in which Shakespeare maintained his "genuine Christian sentiments, and a truly Christian view of the system of things." Ulrici explains the witches in* Macbeth *as "partly rulers of nature" and "partly human spirits, fallen from their original innocence, and deeply sunk in evil." The witches, he argues, illustrate Shakespeare's general concern in* Macbeth, *"which is nothing less than that of the all-pervading sinfulness of all human and earthly beings." He goes on to assert that all of the characters are guilty of sinful wilfullness and that all are met with "sure but varying degrees of retribution," a point also suggested by Denton J. Snider (1887) and G. Wilson Knight (1930). Ulrici concludes that Macbeth's death produces a "purifying and instructive result" and that the sufferings he has caused allow the other characters to atone for their faults and weaknesses. For other considerations of the Christian implications in* Macbeth, *see the excerpts by Roy Walker (1949), Roy W. Battenhouse (1952), G. R. Elliott (1958), and John B. Harcourt (1961).*]

[In "Macbeth"] we have, as the principal motive of the tragic development, the *will* with its forecasting—the manly act, with all the deep, hidden springs of its first conception, and the deliberate purpose of its final accomplishment. The poet has abandoned the simple, primary, and natural relations of life, and entered upon a different and more complicated stage of human civilization. He places before us, the *state*, whose real foundation is in the first instance justice, and the morality of external *works*, and whose ruling principle, consequently, is not the youthful immediateness of feeling and passion, but the manly will, as manifested in the deliberate act. On this stage of civilization has the poet taken his stand in "Macbeth," in order to sketch his tragic, poetic picture of history, and to describe the grandeur and sublimity of an heroic energy of purpose and action, and its final fall and ruin. The particular modification of the general tragic view which thence results is here . . . further limited, and made to take its shape, from the peculiar characters and fortunes of the leading personages, as well as from the circumstances of the age and nation in which the scene is laid.

The tragedy opens with the marvellous appearance of the three witches, who flit across the scene, and vanish, after an obscure intimation of their designs upon Macbeth. This opening, and indeed the whole matter of the witches, has been blamed by some as belonging to the old rubbish of a degrading superstition, and by others as unpoetical, and inconsistent with the very essence of tragedy. The former objection owes its origin to the arrogated wisdom of a shallow Rationalism, with its morbid wish, now happily dying away, to account for everything, or to reject what it cannot explain. The latter is absolutely unintelligible, and rests in part on an erroneous view of the nature of tragedy, and in part on a superficial knowledge of the censured drama. If lofty energy of will and action be the particular field on which the force of the tragic principle is here to manifest itself, then opening scene, with the invention of the witches, is particularly well calculated to place at once

in the clearest light the tragic basis on which the whole fable is to be raised. . . . His witches are a hybrid progeny: partly rulers of nature, and belonging to the nocturnal half of this earthly creation; partly human spirits, fallen from their original innocence, and deeply sunk in evil. They are the fearful echo which the natural and spiritual world gives back to the evil, which sounds forth from within the human breast itself, eliciting it, helping it to unfold and mature itself into the evil purpose and the wicked deed.

After the appearance of the witches has served to indicate the general point of view for which Shakspeare had sketched the entire fable, which is nothing less than that of the all-pervading sinfulness of all human and earthly beings, the heralds of Macbeth's glory and valour are introduced. (pp. 205-07)

The real criminal, who, as his actions shew, has no will but for his own interest, is by his very nature solitary. Consequently, Macbeth, with his wife, stands alone on one side, while on the other are collected together against him the nobles of his kingdom, the whole state and people, and all the human race, in short. Accordingly, the moral of the *action* lies partly in this unavoidable and gradually deepening estrangement of the guilty one from God, and all his fellows, and partly in the fearful rapidity with which the criminality of Macbeth swells and grows up from moment to moment by an intrinsic necessity, until it reaches its inevitable goal of retribution and death. . . . The organic unity and intrinsic necessity with which the whole action of "Macbeth" is gradually evolved out of the given characters and incidents, constitute, as in all other Shakspeare's dramas, the beauty and perfection of the *composition*, which are reflected again with twofold splendour in the conclusion. As the universal sinfulness of man is made from the very beginning the groundwork of the whole fable, so, in the conclusion, the power of sin is carried to its highest pitch, as it reveals itself objectively in the utter disorganization and helplessness of the whole nation, and subjectively in Lady Macbeth's aberration of intellect, and the moral blindness of her husband, equally bordering on madness, and passing at last into the mental weakness of despair. The terrible and horrible, and, to speak generally, the unpoetical element, which is involved in the description of such mental states, has its justification in the present case, as in Lear, not only in psychological reasons, but also in aesthetic considerations, and in the fundamental idea of the piece. Although evil is thus made its own avenger, still, wherever it has struck so deep a root, true help and restoration can only come from the redeeming grace and love of God. This truth is embodied in the person of the pious, holy, and divinely gifted King of England, who, by his miraculous touch, diffuses the blessing of health, and who is here called in to rescue a neighbouring kingdom from tyranny and ruin. As, however, his holy arm and healing hand cannot consistently wield the sword of vengeance, he is represented by the noble, pious, and magnanimous Siward, whose son falls a sacrifice for the delivery of Scotland. By the aid of England, Malcolm and Donaldbain, with the Scottish nobles, succeed in destroying this monster of tyranny, and in restoring order and justice to their oppressed country.

But it may be asked, where, in all the course of this tragic development, are we to look for any consolatory and elevating counteraction? Where is the necessity for the immolation of so many innocent victims, who, apparently at least, have no share in the represented guilt? Our answer must primarily be directed to the second objection. The Tragic poet is not required to imitate history in all its length and breadth, but to condense its general features within a particular and limited space. Accordingly, he must be at liberty to set up as many subordinate figures as may appear necessary, and to employ them as such agreeably to the purpose he had in view in creating them. If, therefore, he introduces any personages merely as the passive objects of the actions and influences of others, and not as independent agents, it will be sufficient if he exhibit their fortunes and sufferings objectively only, while, from their subjective basis in their individual characters and pursuits, from which alone the true reason of their destiny is to be discovered, he does not attempt to account for it, except by a few slight hints and allusions. Of the latter, however, sufficient is furnished us by Shakspeare in the present piece. Thus the gracious Duncan does not seem to have fallen altogether blameless. This we are led to infer from the numerous revolts against his authority, which Macbeth successively suppressed. Whether they were the result of an arbitrary rule or injustice, or (as the Chronicles assert, from which Shakspeare drew his materials) of an unkingly weakness and cowardice, at any rate he is open to the reproach of unfitness for the duties of his office and state. His sons, again, expose themselves to the suspicion of having slain their own father, by their precipitate, and though prudent, yet most unmanly and cowardly flight. Banquo, too, evidently broods with arrogant complacency on the promised honours of his posterity, and so brings destruction on his own head. Lastly, the wife and children of Macduff suffer for the selfishness of their natural protector, who, forgetful of his duty as a husband and father, has left them, to secure his own personal safety. Accordingly, he is punished by the loss of all his little ones, while the fate which falls upon Lady Macduff is not altogether unmerited by the unamiable asperity with which she rails at her husband for his desertion of her. All, in short, both nobles and commons, are guilty. With a mean and selfish cowardice, and a sinful compliance, they overlook the lawful successor to the throne, and submit to the usurped authority of Macbeth. He who weakly complies with evil involves himself in its guilt and fearful consequences. In such matter there reigns an intrinsic necessity, and the more imperceptible its threads are, the more inextricably do they seize upon and wind themselves around us. The fundamental idea of the piece is not merely illustrated in the characters and fortunes of Macbeth and his wife, but all the subordinate personages and incidents reflect it in a great variety of light and shade. Throughout we meet with the same sinful wilfulness and conduct under various modifications, and equally visited with sure but varying degrees of retribution.

An answer to the second of the previous objections satisfies at the same time the first also in some measure. The tragical is not confined exclusively to the fate and fortune of Macbeth, which form at most but one portion of it. The death of Macbeth awakens no other sensation than a painful conviction of the frailty of all human grandeur; certainly it suggests, in the immediate instance, no soothing or elevating thought, and does but breathe of eternal ruin and death. Mediately, however, it does give rise to higher and calmer feelings; this purifying and instructive result, however, is the other element of the tragical in this drama, which at the same time is closely and influentially connected with the first. Something, no doubt, is lost of force and effect by this division of the tragic interest; nevertheless, together, the two parts make it complete. By the sufferings which the crime of Macbeth brings upon all the other characters, their own faults and weaknesses are atoned for, their virtue and resolution confirmed, and their minds purified, until at last they rise great and powerful, and throw off the unworthy yoke which they had been in such a criminal haste to accept.

In the suicidal consequences of evil, as here exhibited, we may read the comfortable and instructive lesson, that ultimately victory is ever with the good. (pp. 208-11)

The tyranny of Macbeth plunges a whole people in misery, and his crimes have set two great nations in hostile array against each other. There could not be a more pregnant and impressive illustration of the solemn truth, that the evil influence of crime, like a poisonous serpent coiled within the fairest flowers, spreads over the whole circle of human existence, not only working the doom of the criminal himself, but scattering far and wide the seeds of destruction; but that, nevertheless, the deadly might of evil is overcome by the love and justice of God, and good at last is enthroned as the conqueror of the world. Lastly, ''Macbeth'' is the tragedy in which, above all others, Shakspeare has distinctly maintained his own genuine Christian sentiments, and a truly Christian view of the system of things. (p. 212)

> Hermann Ulrici, ''Criticisms of Shakspeare's Dramas: 'Macbeth','' in his Shakspeare's Dramatic Art: And His Relation to Calderon and Goethe, *translated by A. J. W. Morrison, Chapman, Brothers, 1846, pp. 204-12.*

G. G. GERVINUS   (essay date 1849-50)

[*One of the most widely read Shakespearean critics of the latter half of the nineteenth century, the German critic Gervinus was praised by such eminent contemporaries as Edward Dowden, F. J. Furnivall, and James Russell Lowell; however, he is little known in the English-speaking world today. Like his predecessor Hermann Ulrici, Gervinus wrote in the tradition of the ''philosophical criticism'' developed in Germany in the mid-nineteenth century. Under the influence of August Wilhelm Schlegel's literary theory and Georg Wilhelm Friedrich Hegel's philosophy, German critics like Gervinus tended to focus their analyses around a search for the literary work's organic unity and ethical import. Gervinus believed that Shakespeare's works contained a rational ethical system independent of any religion—in contrast to Ulrici, for whom Shakespeare's morality was basically Christian. In the following commentary, first published in his Shakespeare (1849-50), Gervinus compares the characters of Hamlet and Macbeth. He states that while Hamlet shows ''an excess of weakness'' and resembles a civilized man in a world of ''rough manners,'' Macbeth strains ''human might and manly audacity to the utmost,'' living ''like a man belonging to the wilder past'' in a society that aims ''at milder Christian manners.'' Gervinus also remarks that Macbeth, in opposition to Hamlet, is characterized as a man of action and ambition. Yet he notes that both characters, at the outset, possess ''tender sentiments'' and fanciful imaginations. However, Macbeth's ''excitable imagination,'' he continues, ''does not rest in doubts and soliloquies, but impels to action.'' Gervinus further states that the witches do not determine Macbeth's fate, but merely tempt him with prophesies which ''leave ample scope for freedom,'' a point earlier suggested by August Wilhelm Schlegel (1808) and Franz Horn (1823). Gervinus also contends against Samuel Taylor Coleridge (1813-34) regarding the authenticity of the Porter scene, stating that it is ''very suitable to the circumstances,'' a position later argued by H. N. Hudson (1872), John W. Hales (1874), and, in the twentieth century, John B. Harcourt (1961) and Kenneth Muir (1962).*]

The ancients depicted as tragic characters those especially who broke out into violent opposition to the divine law and justice, through excess of courage and strength, and through an overestimate of human will and human freedom; but in Hamlet an excess of weakness is tragically depicted, and he is punished for tardiness of action. In Macbeth, on the other hand, this is reversed. He is the direct opposite to Hamlet, a tragic character in the full sense of the ancients, straining human might and manly audacity to the utmost, whilst he rashly dares fate to enter the lists against him. In that just medium in which Prince Henry is represented, accomplishments, mind, youth, and piety restrain him not from action, and ambition, power, happiness, and opportunity seduce him not to deeds of insolence and injustice; to this medium Hamlet and Macbeth stand in opposite extremes, and perish through their own excess. In both, as it says in *Macbeth*, 'a good and virtuous nature recoils in an imperial charge' [IV. iii. 19-20], but in each in a manner wholly different; the tragic reaction is in both equally terrible, but the palsied effort of the one stands in strong contrast to the spasmodic action of the other. The external character of both plays is in perfect accordance with this inner and fundamental difference. The slow advance of the action in *Hamlet* affords a striking contrast to the rapid march of the catastrophe in *Macbeth*, the dimness of the former to the strong light and glowing colouring in the latter, the creeping fever of passion in the one to the hasty movement in the other, where the passions, as in *Lear*, are carried to the utmost bounds of nature, and that of the strongest human kind. The character of the uncertain, fluctuating, wavering Hamlet imparts to the action in the one play the image of standing stagnant water, stirred only in places by whirlpools, while in this play a mighty dangerous rushing stream roars past, in which the boldest swimmer loses power and mastery. (p. 586)

[We perceive] in *Hamlet* an intention on the part of the poet to depict, as it were, a double-sided period, a turning point in civilisation and development in the relation of the hero to his fellow-men; a man of a civilised period standing in the centre of an heroic age of rough manners and physical daring. Here it is reversed, and this appears to us to prove that the contrast was intended; a man possessed with the old energy of the heroic age stands on a similar boundary line, at which the age and society are aiming at milder Christian manners, whilst Macbeth stands like a man belonging to the wilder past, not exactly by nature, but by his deed and its effects; just as, on the other hand, it seemed the task of Hamlet to maintain the usages of the olden time by the exercise of his revenge. (pp. 586-87)

The essential difference in the natures of Hamlet and Macbeth is the heroic physical strength which Goethe found lacking in the one, and which the other so fully possesses. When Macbeth appears at the beginning of the play, he is, in all eyes, an admired general; during the fight he had coolly manifested all the qualities of a perfect soldier, 'valour's minion,' 'Bellona's bridegroom.' As a man of action exclusively, he is deficient in the intellectual culture which was Hamlet's pride. Not that he, like Percy, resisted and strove against it; it never even approached him; nothing of the kind is ever alluded to, not even as a contrast to those around him. At the most, Macbeth's disinclination to all refined cultivation shows itself in . . . [his] contempt of 'the English epicures' [V. iii. 8]. It belongs to this simple soldier nature that he does not possess a trace of that histrionic art and dissimulation which necessarily resulted from Hamlet's turn of mind. Even where these qualities would have been helpful to him in forwarding his aims or in defending him against danger, he knew not how to adopt them, in spite of his willingness, and in spite of his wife's good example, instructions, and impressive warnings. At the very first prediction of the weird sisters, he betrays his emotion to Banquo. He meets his wife with a pre-occupied countenance, which she immediately enjoins him to change for one of concealment. In deep thought he quits the table where the king is his guest. Garrick played this part so as to show that, when once excited,

he could not conceal the emotions of his soul, even before Duncan, least of all in the moment of the promotion of the Prince of Cumberland. The quality which further distinctly distinguishes Macbeth from Hamlet, and which is in close connection with his innate thirst for action, is his ambition. This displays itself when he is newly excited by the Northern Fates, in the letter to his wife, the 'dearest partner of his greatness' [I. v. 11]. Macbeth's whole communication with her leads us to infer long-cherished projects of ambition, for his soaring aims lodge deeper in his wife's bosom than even in his own. For a great object, for a certain gain in this life, Macbeth is ready (and this is the boldest expression of the passion in him) to 'jump the life to come' [I. vii. 7], which filled Hamlet with fear and doubts. And when once this ambition is set in violent motion by all the combining circumstances of fortune and opportunity, we see Macbeth, the vassal, unlawfully and bloodily taking possession of the throne of his king and benefactor; whilst Hamlet, the true heir, feels neither courage nor inclination to reclaim by a lawful act the throne that is his by right.

However criminal and violent this passion may appear to us thus developed in Macbeth, it is not in him from the outset; the strongest temptations were necessary to bring it into this rapid flow. As long as his ambition yet untempted slumbered within him, we look upon a better nature in Macbeth, which even in his extremest decline never suffers him to sink quite below himself, nor to lose all his dignity. Before the fatal resolve of the king's murder is fully ripened in his mind, good and evil are weighed in equal balance within him. When his mind is first overtaken with the temptation, he hesitates whether to wait till the way may open to him of itself, or to force the obstruction to yield; before the good nature in the one scale is overburdened by the pressure of his wife's ambition on the other, the equal balance of his nature is strikingly indicated by the characterisation of Macbeth in the lips of this very wife. Macbeth appears to us here exactly at the point where this double nature separates, just as Hamlet does in his first soliloquy, when he stands suspended between his high resolves and the downward pressure of his sluggish temperament. 'Thou would'st be great,' says Lady Macbeth,—

Art not without ambition; but without
The illness should attend it. What thou would'st highly,
That would'st thou holily; would'st not play false,
And yet would'st strongly win: thoud'st have, great
    Glamis,
That which cries *Thus thou must do, if thou have it:
And that which rather thou dost fear to do,
Than wishest should be undone'*.

[I. v. 18-25]

She calls him 'too full of the milk of human kindness to catch the nearest way' [I. v. 17-18]. This is a description which brings him in his inner undisturbed self in close relation to Hamlet; these words might even be spoken of Hamlet. The poet intends to intimate that he does not find a delicate mental organisation inconsistent with strong physical power. He invests Macbeth at the outset with the tender sentiments of Hamlet; they display themselves in him by the powerful stirrings of his conscience. This voice is in him no less loud, nay, perhaps it is even louder than in Hamlet; only that in the man of business and action it has not the same convenient scope for its extension as in the other. Conscience has not alone in Macbeth, as in the passive Hamlet, to reflect and to doubt, but it has to *do*; it has before the deed to struggle with ambition;

then, victorious in its overthrow, at the very deed itself, it rouses repentance in him to a degree of fearful torture. . . . If Macbeth, in this point, is not unlike Hamlet in the original constitution of his mind, he resembles him still more in the excitability of his fancy. But if Hamlet's irresolution sprang out of his conscientiousness, and his cowardice out of his imagination, there is evidence in Macbeth, on the other hand, that an innate manly power and effort can master the strongest stirrings of conscience, as well as the mightiest workings of the fancy. For as we have said that the voice of conscience was *perhaps* louder in Macbeth than in Hamlet, so the paralysing effect of imagination was without doubt stronger in him than in the other. Anxious presentiments find in him a nature easily alarmed. He says himself that, in ordinary circumstances, his fancy gave rise to fear and excitement. The time had been when a night-shriek would have cooled his senses, and a dismal treatise would rouse his 'fell of hair.' His wife was aware of this his peculiarity, and knew how apt it was to weaken his activity and his resolve; she warns him, therefore, continually not to be alone, nor to indulge in dark thoughts; 'you do unbend your noble strength,' she says to him, 'to think so brain-sickly of things' [II. ii. 42-3]. Nevertheless, in this very quality, which in the energetic man is energetic and therefore indeed of a different nature and effect to that in Hamlet, Macbeth possessed an actual incentive to action, 'Present fears are less' to this man of action than 'horrible imaginings' [I. iii. 137-38]; on the battle-field he maintained a natural cheerfulness; under the power of evil forebodings he becomes weak. The mere conception of the murder makes his 'seated heart knock at his ribs,' and 'shakes his single state of man' so violently, that 'function is smothered in surmises' of the future, and nothing is present to him, 'but what is not' [I. iii. 137, 140-42]. Thus, quite unlike Hamlet, who inactively revels and delights in the appearance of the ghost, and in the torture of his forebodings and fancies, Macbeth gives us the impression of rushing into action to escape the agony of mental struggle and terror. On his way to commit the crime, his heated imagination brings a dagger before him, on which he sees 'gouts of blood' arise; his eyes are here 'the fools o' the other senses' [II. i. 46, 44], as his ear is afterwards, when he fancies he hears the voice cry, 'Glamis hath murdered sleep!' [II. ii. 39]. But this imagination restrains him not from murdering the servants, nor did that first apparition withhold him from the murder of the king. The contrast exists here also, for Macbeth's fancy does not rest in doubts and soliloquies, but impels to action, picturing to him the very weapon for his deed; whereas in Hamlet's case, the admonisher both seen and heard, the ghost of his father, vanishes again from his remembrance like a delusion. That they see ghosts is, with both Hamlet and Macbeth, the strongest proof of the power of the imaginative faculty. We need hardly tell our readers, whom we imagine to be more and more initiated into the mind of our poet, that his spirit-world signifies nothing but the visible embodiment of the images conjured up by a lively fancy, and that their apparition only takes place with those who have this excitable imagination. The cool Gertrude sees not Hamlet's ghost, the cold, sensible Lady Macbeth sees not that of Banquo, the dry, ironical Lenox and his companions see neither this nor the witches; these appear indeed to Banquo, who is neither free from ambitious ideas nor is mastered by them, but the witches address him not till he speaks to them.

In the witches, Shakespeare has made use of the popular belief in evil geniuses and in adverse persecutors of mankind, and has produced a similar but darker race of beings, just as he made use of the belief in fairies in the *Midsummer Night's*

Dream. This creation is less attractive and complete, but not less masterly. . . . The reverse of the ancient Eumenides, these weird sisters are not avengers afer the deed, but tempters to it, the panders to sin. A definite and mechanical power over man is, however, in nowise bestowed on them; and Lamb was utterly wrong in his opinion that they *generated* deeds of blood and *originated* evil impulses in the soul [see excerpt above, 1808]. Thus Schlegel also said that Macbeth yielded to a deep-laid hellish temptation and to supernatural impulses [see excerpt above, 1808], but this gives throughout an opposite idea of Shakespeare's meaning, if we are to understand more by it than that the soaring and ambitious desires of Macbeth himself are of a supernatural and more than ordinary strength. The poet has endowed these creatures with the power to tempt and delude men, to entangle them with oracles of double meaning, with delusion and deception, and even to try them, as Satan in the book of Job, with sorrow and trouble, with storms and sickness; but they have no authority with fatalistic power to do violence to the human will. Their promises and their prophecies leave ample scope for freedom of action; their occupations are 'deeds without a name' [IV. i. 49]. They are simply the embodiment of inward temptation; they come in storm and vanish in air, like corporeal impulses, which, originating in the blood, cast up bubbles of sin and ambition in the soul; they are weird sisters only in the sense in which men carry their own fates within their own bosoms. Macbeth, in meeting them, has to struggle against no external power, but only with his own nature; they bring to light the evil side of his character, which was not to be read in his face; he does not stumble upon the plans of his royal ambition, because the allurement approaches him from without; but this temptation is sensibly awakened in him, because those plans have long been slumbering in his soul. Within himself dwell the spirits of evil which allure him with the delusions of his aspiring mind. (pp. 587-92)

Macbeth has always been a trial piece for the best stages. The directors ought only to be careful in attempting any abridgments and improvements. This play is most closely and connectedly fashioned as a whole, and bears no omissions. Schiller has left out the scene of the murder of Macduff's family. What we have already said shows why this is inadmissible. An instance of the horrors which Macbeth perpetrated must be brought forward; the weighty cause which planted the thirst for vengeance in Macduff's soul is only comprehended when the eye has seen it. . . . Besides this scene of horror, it has also been decided to cut out the comic character of the porter. Coleridge [see excerpt above, 1813-1834?] and [Jeremy] Collier are in favour of this omission, as they consider his soliloquy to be the unauthorised interpolation of an actor. It may be so. Yet at all events it is not inappropriate: there is an uncomfortable joviality, which, by way of contrast, is very suitable to the circumstances, when the drunken warder, whom Duncan's gifts and the festivities of the evening have left in a state of excitement, calls his post 'hell's gate,' in a speech in which every allusion bears a point. (pp. 608-09)

G. G. Gervinus, "Third Period of Shakespeare's Dramatic Poetry: 'Macbeth'," in his Shakespeare Commentaries, *translated by F. E. Bunnètt, revised edition, 1877. Reprint by AMS Press Inc., 1971, pp. 583-610.*

A. [J. F.] MÉZIÈRES   (essay date 1860)

[*In the following excerpt, first published in his* Shakespeare, ses oeuvres et ses critiques *(1860), Mézières discusses the dramatic*

Act V. Scene i. Lady Macbeth, Doctor, and Gentlewoman.
Frontispiece to the Hanmer edition by H. Gravelot (1744).
By permission of the Folger Shakespeare Library.

unity in Macbeth. *He notes that while the action of the play is spread over seventeen years, it is nonetheless unified in the character of Macbeth: "Everything refers to him." Mézières also states that Shakespeare's use of the supernatural in* Macbeth *illustrates his developing genius as a playwright and, like Franz Horn (1823) and G. G. Gervinus (1849-50), argues that the witches have no fatalistic influence on Macbeth's actions.*]

[The historical events chronicled in *Macbeth*], happening within the space of seventeen years, are compressed in Shakespeare's play into the narrow limits of the drama. He represents to us the three successive stages in the life of Macbeth,—his crime, his prosperity, and his punishment. What the Greeks would have developed in a trilogy, as in *Orestes,* for example, to which *Macbeth* has been more than once compared, is here confined to a single drama. We need be in nowise surprised at the multiplicity of events unfolded in this play, knowing the freedom of the English dramatists in this respect. Yet can we find in it no element foreign to the action. Every circumstance contributes towards the *dénoûment;* and we cannot fail to admire the powerful art with which Shakespeare has maintained the unity amid the numberless catastrophes of the piece.

This unity results from the developement of a single character. Macbeth fills the play. Everything refers to him. Present or absent, he never ceases to occupy our attention, and nothing happens that does not bear upon his destiny. When the Scottish lords discuss the unfortunate condition of their country, Macbeth is the subject of their discourse, and it is to him, without naming him, that they attribute all their woes. When the assassins present themselves at the castle of Macduff to murder his children, it is Macbeth who has sent them. When the witches assemble on the heath, it is to breathe their cruel thoughts into the soul of Macbeth. When Hecate appears among them, to hasten the work of crime, it is to lure Macbeth to his destruction. This character binds in one all portions of the drama. If we seek for unity, not in the developement of a single event, but in the complete representation of the feelings and of the actions of one person, we shall find that Shakespeare has observed it in no other play more closely than in this. Wherefore, many critics consider *Macbeth* as his *chef-d'oeuvre.* (pp. 488-89)

We find exemplified in every tragedy of Shakespeare some dominant passion, whose workings the poet depicts, and from which he deduces a moral lesson. Here he has painted Ambition, laying the strongest colors on the canvas. Macbeth is the type of Ambition, just as he has made Othello the type of Jealousy. Had he been better acquainted with the Greeks, or had he needed to imitate any model to express energetic sentiments, we might be tempted to say that this piece was inspired by the strong soul of Aeschylus. Its characters are as rude, its manners as barbarous, its style is as vigorous and full of poetry, as in the old Grecian tragedies. There is no trace of the artificial rhetoric which disfigures *Romeo and Juliet.* In the space of nine years, from 1596 to 1605, the possible date of *Macbeth,* the poet threw aside that false style and rose to the noblest conceptions of art.

The use he makes of the Supernatural is proof of the new force of his genius. Dramatic action must be regarded from a lofty point of view before we can dare mingle with it an epic element rarely found disconnected from mythical subjects. Not to lose sight of this work-a-day world, to keep up, as is the duty of the dramatist, the rôle of observer, and all the while to pierce with the eyes of the imagination the darkness that shrouds the invisible world, to bring into play the most trenchant logic even while accepting all the absurdities of popular fictions; such are the difficulties that encountered Shakespeare, and over which he rose triumphant when he summoned into being the Witches of *Macbeth.* A few years earlier he would have shrunk from the task.

He reconciles dramatic poetry here with epic by connecting the supernatural element with the moral aim of the piece. We have already remarked that the witches are in perfect harmony with the character of Macbeth. They wield no influence over him in opposition to his will; on the contrary, they only flatter his instincts and embody the mental temptation that possesses him. They never exercise the irresistible influence of ancient fatalism, which forces even the innocent to become criminal; they impel to crime him only who is already inclined to it. They never represent a blind fatality, but the fate that we mould for ourselves by our own actions. When Macbeth listens to them, it is the voice, not of strangers, but of his own ambition, which speaks. . . . (pp. 489-90)

> *A. [J. F.] Mézières, in an extract, translated by Horace Howard Furness, in* A New Variorum Edition of Shakespeare: "Macbeth," *Vol. II by William Shakespeare, edited by Horace Howard Furness, J. B. Lippincott Company, 1873, pp. 488-90.*

J. L. F. FLATHE   (essay date 1864)

[*In the excerpt below, drawn from his* Shakespeare in seiner Wirklichkeit (1864), *Flathe rejects the assertion of August Wilhelm*

Schlegel (1808) and other German critics that Banquo remains innocent throughout Macbeth. *Instead, Flathe contends that both Macbeth and Banquo are implicated in Duncan's murder. Macbeth, he argues, chooses a "path of evil" long before the temptings of Lady Macbeth and may have been more corruptive than corrupted. Like Denton J. Snider (1887) and A. C. Bradley (1904), Flathe maintains that Banquo is guilty of dishonest inaction and, because of the witches' promise, he "abstains from working for Duncan or against Macbeth." He also argues that Banquo, like the equivocator mentioned by the Porter, is self-deceived and shelters his "treacheries behind the name of God." For an opposing view of Banquo's actions, see the excerpt by Leo Kirschbaum (1957).*]

Shakespeare's Macbeth at the moment when he first appears in the tragedy thinks of murder and of nothing but murder. . . .

The devil visits those only who invite him in. A fall from grace is the result of man's alienating his heart from the Being to whom his love should belong. Only when man has driven forth from his heart its inborn purity, and wilfully opened the door of his inner world to demons, does evil acquire vitality within him, and find expression in action. These are the actual, oft-repeated thoughts of Shakespeare. He never entertains the idea that the devil can be the lord and master of our existence. On the contrary, it is said in *Macbeth*, as we shall hereafter show, that all the power of hell has been crippled.

Schlegel [see excerpt above, 1808], with great coolness and self-complacency, has copied what he found in Steevens concerning Banquo. Consequently he declares that Banquo preserves all his purity and honesty of purpose, unaffected by the infernal suggestions to which poor, gallant Macbeth succumbs.

But we are constrained to ask, what devil gives the devil such power over this poor devil of a Macbeth, that he is so immediately led astray, while we see, in the case of Banquo, that any man who chooses can easily withstand the devil? . . .

In common with all human-kind, Macbeth was at the first, if not honest, at least not dishonest, for good not evil is original and innate in us. It is true it must be elevated and ennobled by that free will, without which no conflict with evil is possible. Macbeth's position in life was an exalted one. Sordid want and poverty could not so nearly approach him as to lure him from the path of duty and virtue. Power and honor, on the contrary, attracted him to remain true to the Right. Their increase, with promise of calm enjoyment, would be the result of that adherence to it, to which he was still more constrained by his rich and varied mental endowments.

But in spite of every incitement to good, Macbeth gradually pursued the path of evil. He turned aside from the wisdom which is love of the Divine, renounced the morality which consists in a life of intellectual activity, and even abjured conscience in its prime and essential significance, the peculiarly human attribute of humanity. Thus he rendered all his knowledge not only empty and unproductive, but it was a positive torture to him. Macbeth was disposed to sensuality and sensual delights. They did not seek him, they did not thrust themselves upon him, he summoned them to him. (p. 474)

Macbeth had probably long revolved in his own breast thoughts of murder and the ambitious hopes connected with them. But man is a social and sympathetic being. Macbeth needs a human breast in which to confide, that can revel with him in his dreams of future grandeur and magnificence. And to whom could he more prudently turn than to his wedded wife, who was to share with him the crown *he* hoped to *win?* And yet such a confidence even to a wife is a serious, if not a dangerous affair. Macbeth

can only have brought himself to reveal his murderous design to his spouse in the certainty that it would find welcome lodgement with her.

Thus Lady Macbeth makes her appearance as the second tragic figure in the poetic fable. German aesthetic criticism, following the lead given it in England, will have it that Lady Macbeth seduced poor, gallant Macbeth to commit the murder, because she was an evil woman, familiar with crime, in fact more a tiger than a human being. Now, since no human being comes into the world a tiger, certainly German criticism, especially since it lays claim to such immense erudition, ought to declare by whom the Lady has been led astray and transformed to a tiger. But it eludes the trouble of such a revelation, and insists that its assertion that the Lady was a tiger shall be satisfactory. The tragedy itself proves as clearly as daylight that Shakespeare, if he thought of seduction at all, did not dream of it as practised upon Macbeth by his wife. If there were any hint of such arts, born as they are of the slough of pseudo-rationalism, it might far sooner be shown that the lady was seduced by her husband; at least some apparent proofs in support of such an idea might be gleamed from the drama. (pp. 475-76)

If Shakespeare had any idea of a seduction from the path of virtue, surely it must be maintained that both Macbeth and Banquo were the victims of the witches. It is ridiculous for German aesthetic criticism to talk so much of an uncorrupted Banquo.

Banquo believes that, if the prophecy with regard to the royal honors of his posterity be true, Macbeth must first be king—the sceptre must fall into his hands for a while. At least the witches point to such a course and sequence of events. Therefore he abstains from working for Duncan or against Macbeth. He will do nothing that may interfere with the future greatness of his line. If worldly affairs run smoothly, men do not greatly trouble themselves as to whether or not they are adulterated by something of the devilish element.

In the legend, Banquo's sympathy with, nay, complicity in, the murder of Duncan is made perfectly clear. This it was the poet's task to do away with. He transforms Banquo's crime into one which consists in remaining silent, in refusing to act—and thus to a degree veils it. . . .

When Macbeth says: 'Speak, if you can.—What are you?' [I. iii. 47] it must not be inferred that he has just met these evil beings for the first time. Witches can take upon themselves a variety of material forms. Macbeth may not have seen them before in their present shapes. By his question he wishes to ascertain if these apparitions belong to the class of evil spirits with which he is familiar. In this very scene there is proof that Macbeth is well acquainted with witches and their kind. . . .

This warning: 'oftentimes to win us to our harm' [I. iii. 123], &c., comes oddly enough from the lips of a man who has just questioned the witches himself with such haste and eagerness. Here we have the first glimpse of the deceit and falsehood practised by Banquo upon himself. . . .

Banquo would so gladly esteem himself an honourable man; therefore he warns Macbeth, although as briefly as possible, against the devil. He knows that a mere warning will avail nothing, but he ignores this, wishing to be able to say to himself, when Macbeth has attained his end, 'I am guiltless, I warned him against the devil.' Had Banquo been really true, how differently he would have borne himself! . . .

When Macbeth says, 'Come what come may, Time and hour run through the roughest day' [I. iii. 146-47], he for the first time resolves to murder Duncan. His second resolution starts into life when the King announces the Prince of Cumberland as his successor. . . .

One word of caution from Banquo [when the King was lavishing honors upon Macbeth] would have sufficed to establish measures that would have made it impossible for assassination to find a way at night through unclosed doors. But Banquo takes good care to speak no such word. A villain at heart, he does nothing to impede the fulfilment of crime. . . .

Almost every line of the tragedy shows the falseness of the German aesthetic criticism which prates smoothly on about the evil seed first sown by the witches, and developed to murder in the Castle of Macbeth. On the contrary, every line goes to prove that evil has been long contemplated there, and has only awaited a favorable opportunity. . . .

Banquo enters [II, i] with his son Fleance, who holds a torch. Will not the man do something at last for his king, take some measures to prevent a cruel crime? Everything combines to enjoin the most careful watchfulness upon him, if duty and honour are yet quick within his breast; and here we come to a speech of Banquo's to his son to which we must pay special heed, since upon it the earlier English commentators, Steevens among them, have based their ridiculous theory that in this tragedy Banquo, in contrast to Macbeth, who is led astray, represents the man unseduced by evil. Steevens says that this passage shows that Banquo too is tempted by the witches in his dreams to do something in aid of the fulfilment of his hopes, and that in his waking hours he holds himself aloof from all such suggestions, and hence his prayer to be spared the 'cursed thoughts that nature gives way to in repose' [II. i. 8-9].

A stranger or more forced explanation of this passage can hardly be imagined. It is true that somewhat later in the scene, after the entrance of Macbeth, Banquo speaks of having dreamed of the witches, but that has not the faintest connection with these expressions. He is neither alluding to the witches nor to a former dream, nor to dreaming at all, but he is thinking of the sleep that awaits him and the thoughts that may visit him in it. A merely superficial reading of his words declares decidedly against Steevens's interpretation of them; and their whole meaning and connection are still more opposed to it. It is impossible that Banquo should be incited, either waking or dreaming, by the witches to action in aid of the fulfilment of his hopes. What direction could such action take?

Banquo's hopes for his lineage can only be furthered by the removal of Duncan and by Macbeth's accession to the throne. In the existing state of affairs nothing is necessary to effect both these ends, upon Banquo's part, but that he should do nothing for Duncan or against Macbeth. And he has faithfully remained inactive; he has exactly obeyed the unspoken injunction of the witches to pay no heed to the voice of truth, of duty, nor of honour. Therefore it is clearly impossible that the witches should come to the sleeping Banquo to require anything more of him than what he is already doing. He opposes no obstacle to the murder. What more can the witches require of him?

The passage in question, therefore, must be elucidated more naturally, and more in harmony with the whole. As he has already done, Banquo here [II, i] endeavours as far as possible to assert his own innocence to himself, while, for the sake of his future advantage, he intends to oppose no obstacle to the

sweep of Macbeth's sword. It is, therefore, necessary that he should pretend to himself that here in Macbeth's castle no danger can threaten Duncan nor any one else. Therefore his sword need not rest by his side this night, and he gives it to his son. He must be able to say to himself, in the event of any fearful catastrophe, 'I never thought of, or imagined, any danger, and so I laid aside my arms.'

And yet, try as he may, he cannot away with the stifling sensation of a tempest in the air, a storm-cloud destined to burst over Duncan's head this very night. He cannot but acknowledge to himself that a certain restless anxiety in his brain is urging him, in spite of his weariness, to remain awake during the remaining hours of the night. But this mood, these sensation, must not last, or it might seem a sacred duty either to hasten to the chamber of King Duncan or to watch it closely, that its occupant may be shielded from murderous wiles. To avoid this, Banquo denounces the thoughts of Macbeth that arise in his mind as 'cursed thoughts.' So detestably false are they that a merciful Power must be entreated to restrain them during sleep, when the mind is not to be completely controlled.

With every change in the aspect of affairs Banquo's self-deceit appears in some new form. Banquo here banishes his thoughts from his mind, or rather maintains to himself that he has banished them, or that he must banish them because they do injustice to noble Macbeth, whom, nevertheless, he has thought it necessary to warn against the devil. . . .

The rôle that the porter, in his tipsy mood, assigns himself, and the speeches that he makes in character, stand in significant connection with the whole tragedy. Awakened by the knocking at the castle gate, he imagines himself porter at the entrance of hell. And this brings us to the central point of the drama, wherein is revealed to us the deepest fall made by man into the abyss of evil. For those who, like Macbeth, plunge into it, voluntarily and knowingly, the other world can unclose no garden of delights; an allegorical hell awaits them.

Therefore it is of hell that the porter speaks: and therefore it is that the poet makes him speak thus. But Macbeth is not the only one who goes this way; men press hither in crowds, and often take the greatest pains and trouble not to avoid the entrance to this place of punishment. And so the porter grumbles that there is such a constant knocking at the gate of hell, and that crowds of all conditions stand without, who have journeyed along the primrose way to the everlasting bonfire. As he enumerates the various kinds of guests at this gate, he mentions equivocators, traitors who juggle with the Highest, who swear by this to-day, by that to-morrow, pursuing their wiles beneath God's protection and invoking his aid.

Some of the earlier English critics most oddly opine that the poet here intended an allusion to the Jesuits. How could so great and ingenious a poet dream of interpolating in his work so foreign a subject? The porter's speech evidently hints at Banquo. As if by chance, the man imagines waiting for admission at the infernal gate just such another as Banquo; one who, like him, would fain shelter his treacheries behind the name of God taken in vain. Banquo did that, when, in gross self-deception, he implored the 'merciful powers' to restrain in him his perfectly just thoughts of Macbeth, which he would fain persuade himself are 'cursed.' . . . (pp. 476-79)

And Banquo . . . can declare firm, unalterable fealty to the very man whom to himself he has just accused, almost in so many words, of attaining the throne by the assassination of his royal master! Such a declaration could only have been made by one whose own heart is closely allied to evil. The emotion excited in Banquo's breast against Macbeth must become stronger. He feels obliged to invent fair words to conceal his secret. The hypocrite Macbeth is served with hypocrisy. . . .

It is not without significance that in this scene [III, vi] there is frequent mention of most pious men and holy angels. Such mention is meant to remind us that there is a moral force always present in the world, ready to come forth victorious in its time and place. . . .

Macbeth enters [IV, i] and bears unmistakeable testimony to the fact that he has been familiar with this company long before the beginning of the tragedy. He needs not to inquire the way leading hither, he knows it already. (pp. 479-80)

> *J. L. F. Flathe, in an extract, translated by Mrs. A. L. Wister, in* A New Variorum Edition of Shakespeare: "Macbeth," *Vol. II by Shakespeare, edited by Horace Howard Furness, J. B. Lippincott Company, 1873, pp. 474-80.*

[GUSTAV VON] RÜMELIN (essay date 1866)

[*In the commentary below, first published in his* Shakespeare-studien *(1866), Rümelin considers the problem of free will and fate in* Macbeth, *an issue previously noted by August Wilhelm Schlegel (1808) and Franz Horn (1823). Rümelin states that the Weird Sisters' prophecies determine Macbeth's destiny no more than "the oracles of the Delphic god debarred Oedipus from being a free agent." Rümelin also perceives inconsistencies in the characters of Macbeth and Lady Macbeth. In Macbeth, he states, Shakespeare "exaggerates the contrast" between Macbeth's former "noble nature" and his criminal evil. In Lady Macbeth, he perceives an inconsistency between her "ice-cold reasoning" in support of Duncan's murder and her later tormented conscience. Nonetheless, Rümelin concludes,* Macbeth *is "the mightiest and most powerful of all tragedies."*]

The dramatic treatment in *Macbeth* offers but small scope for realistic criticism, since from beginning to end the drama is enacted in the mythological region of hoary eld, and supernatural powers are employed, against which there can be no pragmatic criticism. This freedom the poet had of course the same right to use as had the old tragedians, or Goethe in his 'Iphigenia,' when they transported us to the land of the old gods and legendary demigods. If, however, the weird sisters are not to be considered as real, as the majority of Shakespeare critics would fain persuade us, but only as the hero's visions, like the Ghosts in Richard III, merely external manifestations of mental experiences, desires and torments, then indeed the critic from the realistic point of view would have to assert himself with redoubled power, and the action of the tragedy would be utterly inconceivable. But this conception rests upon the weakest of arguments, and is opposed to every natural interpretation.

One essential point is clear—namely, that the witches foretell the future, and with an accuracy that does not fail in the very smallest particular. Of all their prophecies, only one, that he should be king, has any previous lodgement in Macbeth's breast; that the crown should descend to Banquo's children, of whom the last two should bear two-fold balls and treble sceptres, that Macduff should slay Macbeth, that Birnam's wood should come to Dunsinane, and the like, are not for a moment to be conceived of if we adopt that interpretation. These weird sisters had, in sooth, no control over Macbeth; their prophecies no more annihilated his free-will than the oracles of the Delphic god debarred Oedipus from being a free agent. That Banquo

stood in a different relation to these prophecies from Macbeth, whereon this interpretation lays so much stress, does not in the least change the state of the case. Moreover, the tenor of the prophecy which referred to him was not of such a nature as called for any action on his part. It was readily conceivable, since he himself belonged to the royal family, that his descendants should wear the crown: as far as he was concerned he could neither aid nor hinder it. Clearly enough, indeed, does the poet depict his witches not as divine, creative beings, bearing sway over man, but as devilish ones, leading him into temptation and delighting in evil. That the poet must have conceived of them as creatures real and supernatural, and prescient of the future, no unprejudiced reader will have the least doubt. . . . A poet has an undisputed right to choose for himself the scene of his dramatic action. If he transport us to a world of pure or only partial fantasy, we must follow him thither and give due credit to all the imaginary conditions which he devises for us; but if he transport us to real and historic ground, then he himself must respect the laws which they there bear sway, and must submit himself to the criticism which they sanction. Thus alone shall we be able to understand Shakespeare's *Macbeth* in all its magnificent beauty; but not if we resolve the forms, to which his imagination imparts in the realm of poetry a real existence, into vague, mongrel things of vision and convenience. Under such conditions there is little to be said against the action in *Macbeth*. There are, perchance, a few trifling gaps in the action; for instance, the instantaneous flight of the two Princes after Duncan's death is noticeable and not sufficiently accounted for. Also, the incentive to the murder of Banquo is not wholly satisfactory. Since Macbeth is childless, and Banquo belongs to the royal race, the thought that Banquo's descendants should be kings could convey nothing shocking nor intolerable to Macbeth; moreover, he must take the prophecy of the witches as whole, without being permitted to bring to naught any particular item of it that he pleased. We must have recourse to the excuse that in the soliloquy where he resolves upon the murder, Macbeth contemplates the possibility of his having sons, or else, which is more likely, that the poet, who in this place also may have written from scene to scene, forgot in this passage what elsewhere he has expressly stated, that Macbeth was a childless father.

More serious difficulties occur in the character of Lady Macbeth. Her demeanor before the deed and after it appears to violate that psychological law of essential unity and consistency of character to which Shakespeare in general, although with some exceptions, adheres. The workings of conscience in her case are magical and demonical, and not psychologically conceivable. Whether or not we conceive of conscience as an innate, or as an inculcated, belief in the absolute obligation of certain rules in human life, there still remains a something in the consciousness, a quality or a force, which can work only in harmony with the law of all forces. Whenever, then, we find that the memory of a criminal act, however successful and enduring in its issues it may have been, awakens a repentance and moral detestation so consuming that for no single instant is it absent from the mind of the criminal, and that self-abhorrence leads to insanity and suicide, then we may properly assume for such a character a susceptibility to moral emotions of no common strength. Furthermore, it is conceivable that with such a susceptibility there may coexist a proneness to the blackest of crimes; for in the same breast passions and desires of a different and far more violent nature may be harboured; but in this case it appears to us to follow of necessity that we must be made to see how, in the moment of a lawless deed, the voice of conscience is drowned, thrust down into a corner of the heart, overwhelmed by the tempest of stormy passion. But that ice-cold reasoning with which Lady Macbeth enkindles her husband to the most horrible of crimes, and sneers at the promptings of his conscience as though they were despicable, womanish weakness; the barbarous roughness with which she speaks of plucking her nipple from the boneless gums of the babe smiling in her face, and dashing its brains out; the wild strength with which, after the deed, she encourages Macbeth and spurs him on,—all this appears to us unreconcileable with what we have laid down. It is not till late that the Eumenides enter into her, and like Demons from without, whereas the poet ought to have shown us how all along they were lurking in ambush at the bottom of her heart, and how the violence of their onslaught can be calculated by the long and powerful pressure to which the nobler emotions were subjected.

In the character of Macbeth, wonderfully and strikingly as he is depicted, we miss something also. Before he falls into temptation he is represented by the poet as of a noble nature, as we gather not only from his own deportment, but more clearly from the esteem in which he is held by the king and others. We have a right to expect that this better nature would reappear; after his glowing ambition had attained its end he ought to have made at least one attempt, or manifested the desire, to wear his ill-gotten crown with glory, to expiate or extenuate his crime by sovereign virtues. We could then be made to see that it by no means follows that evil must breed evil, and that Macbeth must wade on in blood in order not to fall. But from the very first meeting with the witches Macbeth appears like one possessed of all the devils of Hell, and rushes so like a madman from one crime to another, that the nobler impulses of former days never for one moment influence him. Here too, as frequently elsewhere, Shakespeare exaggerates the contrast, and the effect, at the expense of psychological truth; for, to completely subvert the fundamental basis of a character assuredly partakes, always and everywhere, of the nature of untruth. Without the idea of consistency we can conceive of no development either in nature or man. . . .

And yet all such criticisms cannot keep from pronouncing Shakespeare's *Macbeth* the mightiest and most powerful of all tragedies. (pp. 481-82)

> [*Gustav von*] *Rümelin, in an extract, translated by Horace Howard Furness, in* A New Variorum Edition of Shakespeare: "Macbeth," Vol. II *by William Shakespeare, edited by Horace Howard Furness, J. B. Lippincott Company, 1873, pp. 480-82.*

REV. H. N. HUDSON (essay date 1872)

[*Hudson was a nineteenth-century American clergyman and literary scholar whose Harvard edition of Shakespeare's works, published in twenty volumes between 1880 and 1881, contributed substantially to the growth of Shakespeare's popularity in America. Hudson also published two critical works on Shakespeare, one a collection of lectures, the other—and the more successful— a biographical and critical study entitled* Shakespeare, His Life, Art, and Characters *(1872). Like Anna Brownell Jameson (1833), William Maginn (1837), and Isador H. Coriat (1912), Hudson discusses the character of Lady Macbeth, noting how her firm intellect and reliance on "nothing but facts" contrasts with Macbeth's superstition. Yet Hudson also remarks that Lady Macbeth is actually composed of two different characters and that this ferocious "matter-of-factness" is foreign to her true character. Her true character, states Hudson, is revealed in the sleepwalking scene in which her senses are "dominated by the conscience." He also observes that this scene, "which is more intensely tragic* *than any other scene in Shakespeare," is written in prose because it is "too sublime, too austerely grand, to admit of anything so artificial as the measured language of verse." The Porter scene, which is regarded as spurious by Samuel Taylor Coleridge (1813-34), is, Hudson contends, in the "true spirit" of Shakespeare's method, for by introducing humor in the midst of "a congregation of terrors" it "deepens their effect." For other commentary on the effect of the Porter scene, see excerpts by Thomas De Quincey (1823), G. G. Gervinus (1849-50), John W. Hales (1874), John B. Harcourt (1961), and Kenneth Muir (1962).]*

In the structure and working of her mind and moral frame, Lady Macbeth is the opposite of her husband, and therefore all the fitter to countervail his infirmity of purpose; that is, she differs from him in just the right way to supplement him. Of a firm, sharp, wiry, matter-of-fact intellect, doubly charged with energy of will, she has little in common with him save a red-hot ambition: hence, while the Weird disclosures act on her will just as on his, and she jumps forthwith into the same purpose, the effect on her mind is wholly different. Without his irritability of understanding and imagination, she is therefore subject to no such involuntary transports of thought. Accordingly she never loses herself in any raptures of meditation; no illusions born of guilty fear get the mastery of her; at least, not when her will is in exercise: in her waking moments, her senses are always so thoroughly in her keeping, that she hears and sees things just as they are. As conscience draws no visions before her eyes, and shapes no voices in her hearing; so, while he is shaken and quite unmanned with fantastical terrors, she remains externally calm, collected, and cool. Her presence of mind indeed seems firmest when his trances of illusion run highest; so that, instead of being at all infected with his agitations, her forces then move in the aptest order to recover him from them. Which shows that her sympathy with his ambition, intense as it is, has no power to make her sympathize with his mental workings. It may almost be said indeed that what stimulates his imagination stifles hers.

Almost any other dramatist would have brought the Weird Sisters to act immediately on Lady Macbeth, and on her husband through her, as thinking her more open to superstitious allurements and charms. Shakespeare seems to have judged that aptness of mind for them to work upon would have disqualified her for working upon her husband in aid of them. Enough of such influence has already been brought to bear: what is needed further, is quite another sort of influence, such as could only come from a mind not much accessible to the Weird Sisters.

There was strong dramatic reason, therefore, why Lady Macbeth should have such a mind and temper as to be moved and impressed, when awake, by nothing but facts. She ought to be, as indeed she is, so constituted, that the evil which has struck its roots so deep within never comes back to her in the elements and aspects of Nature, either to mature the guilty purpose or to obstruct the guilty act. It is remarkable that she does not once recur to the Weird Sisters, nor make any use of their salutations: they seem to have no weight with her, but for the impression they have wrought on her husband. That this impression may grow to the desired effect, she refrains from meddling with it, and seeks only to fortify it with impressions of another sort. And what could better approve her shrewdness and tact than that, instead of overstraining this one motive, and so weakening it, she thus lets it alone, and labours to strengthen it by mixing others with it. For, in truth, the Weird Sisters represent, in most appalling sort, the wickedness of the purpose they suggest: so that Macbeth's fears as well as his hopes are stimulated, and his fears even more than his hopes, by the recollection of their greetings: the instant he reverts to them, his imagination springs into action,—an organ of which ambition works the bellows indeed, but conscience still governs the stops and keys. The very thought of them indeed seems to put him at once under a fascination of terror. All this does not escape his wife; who therefore judges it best rather to draw his thoughts off from that matter, and fix them on other inducements. He had thought of the murder, when as yet he could see no opportunities for doing it. When those opportunities come, *they* are the arguments that tell with her; and she therefore makes it her business to urge them upon him, invoking his former manhood withal, to redintegrate and shame him out of his present weakness. . . . That the King has cast himself unreservedly on their loyalty and hospitality, this she puts forth as the strongest argument for murdering him! An awful stroke of character indeed, and therefore awful, because natural. By thus anticipating his greatest drawbacks, and urging them as the chief incentives, she forecloses all debate. Which is just what she wants; for she knows full well that the thing will not stand the tests of reason a moment: it must be done first, and discussed afterwards. And throughout this wrestling-match she surveys the whole ground, and darts upon the strongest points with the quickness and sureness of instinct; the sharpness of the exigency being to her a sort of practical inspiration. The finishing stroke in this part of the work is when, her husband's resolution being all in a totter, she boldly cuts the sinews of retreat, casting the thing into a personal controversy, and making it a theme of domestic war:

> *Lady M*.   Art thou afeard
> To be the same in thine own act and valour
> As thou art in desire? . . .
>
>   [I. vii. 39-41]

After this, it is hardly possible they should live together, unless he do the deed. The virtues and affections of the husband are now drawn up against the conscience of the man. For, to be scorned and baited as a coward by the woman he loves, and by whom he is loved, is the last thing a soldier can bear: death is nothing to it! Macbeth, accordingly, goes about the deed, and goes through it, with an assumed ferocity caught from his wife.

Nor is that ferocity native to her own breast: surely, on her part too, it is assumed; for, though in her intense overheat of expectant passion it is temporarily fused into her character, it is disengaged and thrown off as soon as that heat passes away; as men, in the ardour of successful effort, sometimes pass for a while into a character which they undertake to play. Lady Macbeth begins with acting a part which is really foreign to her; but which, notwithstanding, such is her energy of will, she braves out to issues so overwhelming, that her husband and many others believe it to be her own. (pp. 338-42)

Lady Macbeth is indeed a great bad woman whom we fear and pity; but neither so great nor so bad, I am apt to think, as is commonly supposed. She has closely studied her husband, and penetrated far into the heart of his mystery: yet she knows him rather as he is to her than as he is to himself; hence in describing his character she interprets her own. She has indeed the ambition to wish herself unsexed, but not the power to unsex herself except in words. For, though she invokes the "murdering ministers" to "come to her woman's breasts, and take her milk for gall" [I. v. 47-8], still she cannot make then come; and her milk, in spite of her invocation, continues to be milk. (p. 342)

Two characters, however, may easily be made out for Lady Macbeth, according as we lay the chief stress on what she says or what she does. For, surely, no one can fail to remark that the anticipation raised by her earlier speeches is by no means sustained in her subsequent acts. When she looks upon the face of the sleeping King, and sees the murderous thought passing, as it were, into a *fact* before her, a gush of womanly feeling or of native tenderness suddenly stays her hand: "Had he not resembled my father as he slept, I had done't" [II. ii. 12-13]. That such a real or fancied resemblance should thus rise up and unsinew her purpose in the moment of action, is a rare touch of nature indeed; and shows that conscience works even more effectually through the feelings in her case than through the imagination in that of her husband. And the difference of imagination and feeling in this point is, that the one acts most at a distance, the other on the spot. This sharp contradiction between her tongue and her hand has often reminded me of a line which Schiller puts into the mouth of Wallenstein: "Bold were my words, because my deeds were *not*." And it seems to me that the towering audacity of her earlier speeches arises, at least in part, from an overstrained endeavour to school herself into a firmness and fierceness of which she feels the want.

Her whole after-course, I think, favours this view. For instance, when she hears from Macbeth how he has murdered the two grooms also, she sinks down at the tale. For I can by no means regard that as a counterfeit swoon. The thing takes her by surprise, and her iron-ribbed self-control for once gives way. The announcement of the King's murder had no such effect upon her, for she was prepared for that. And that was when she would have counterfeited fainting, if at all. So bold of tongue, she could indeed say, "the sleeping and the dead are but as pictures; 'tis the eye of childhood, that fears a painted devil" [II. ii. 50-2]; but the sequel proves her to have been better than she was aware. In truth, she has undertaken too much: in her efforts to screw her own and her husband's courage to the sticking-place, there was exerted a force of will which answered the end indeed, but at the same time flawed the core of her being. She has quite as much of conscience as her husband; but no such sensitive redundancy of imagination, as that her conscience should be in her senses, causing the howlings of the storm to syllable the notes of remorse. Here, again, we see her characteristic matter-of-factness. It is deeds, not thoughts, that kindle the furies in her soul. And because the workings of guilt do not pass out of her, as it were, and take on the form of spectral illusions, therefore they just eat back and consume all the more fatally within: had she an organ to project and shape them outwardly in fantastical terrors, their action would be tempered more equally to her powers of endurance. With her prodigious force of will, she may indeed keep them hidden from others, but she can neither repress nor assuage them. And for the same cause she is free alike from the terrible apprehensions which make her husband flinch from the first crime, and from the maddening and merciless suspicions that sting him on to other crimes.

Accordingly she give no waking sign of the dreadful work that is doing within; the unmitigable corrodings of her rooted sorrow, even when busiest in destruction, do not once betray her, except when her self-rule is dissolved in sleep. But the truth comes out with an awful mingling of pathos and terror, in the scene where her conscience, sleepless amidst the sleep of nature, nay, most restless even then when all others' cares are at rest, drives her forth, open-eyed yet sightless, to sigh and groan over spots on her hands that are visible to none but herself, nor even to herself save when she is blind to every

thing else: a living automaton worked by the agonies of remorse! How perfectly her senses are then dominated by the
conscience, is shown with supreme effect in "Here's the smell
of blood still" [V. i. 50]; which has been aptly noted as the
only instance in modern times where the sense of smell has
been successfully employed in high tragic expression. An awful
mystery, too, hangs over her death. We know not, the Poet
himself seems not to know, whether the gnawings of the un-
dying worm drive her to suicidal violence, or themselves cut
asunder the cords of her life: all we know is, that the death of
her body springs somehow from the inextinguishable life and
the immedicable wound of her soul. What a history of her
woman's heart is written in her thus sinking, sinking away
where imagination shrinks from following her, under the violence of an invisible yet unmistakable disease, which still
sharpens its inflictions and at the same time quickens her sensibilities!

Lady Macbeth dies before her husband. This is one of the most
judicious points of the drama. Her death touches Macbeth in
the only spot where he seems to retain the feelings of a man,
and draws from him some deeply-solemn, soothing, elegiac
tones; so that one rises from the contemplation of his history
"a sadder and a wiser man".... (pp. 342-45)

The style of this mighty drama is pitched in the same high
tragic key as the action. Throughout, we have an explosion,
as of purpose into act, so also of thought into speech, both
literally kindling with their own swiftness. No sooner thought
than said, no sooner said than done, is the law of the piece.
Therewithal thoughts and images come crowding and jostling
each other in such quick succession as to prevent a full utterance; a second leaping upon the tongue before the first is fairly
off. I should say the Poet here specially endeavoured how much
of meaning could be conveyed in how little of expression; with
the least touching of the ear to send vibrations through all the
chambers of the mind. Hence the large, manifold suggestiveness which lurks in the words: they seem instinct with something which the speakers cannot stay to unfold. And between
these invitations to linger and the continual drawings onward
the reader's mind is kindled to an almost preternatural activity.
All which might at length grow wearisome, but that the play
is, moreover, throughout, a conflict of antagonist elements and
opposite extremes, which are so managed as to brace up the
interest on every side: so that the effect of the whole is to
refresh, not exhaust the powers; the mind being sustained in
its long and lofty flight by the wings that grow forth as of their
own accord from its superadded life. The lyrical element, instead of being interspersed here and there in the form of musical
lulls and pauses, is thoroughly interfused with the dramatic;
while the ethical sense underlies them both, and is forced up
through them by their own pressure. The whole drama indeed
may be described as a tempest set to music. (pp. 346-47)

It has often struck me as a highly-significant fact, that the
sleep-walking scene, which is more intensely tragic than any
other scene in Shakespeare, is all, except the closing speech,
written in prose. Why is this? The question is at least not a
little curious. The diction is of the very plainest and simplest
texture; yet what an impression of sublimity it carries! In fact,
I suspect the matter is too sublime, too austerely grand, to
admit of any thing so artifical as the measured language of
verse, even though the verse were Shakespeare's; and that the
Poet, as from an instinct of genius, saw or felt that any attempt
to heighten the effect by any such arts or charms of delivery
would unbrace and impair it. And I think that the very diction

of the closing speech, poetical as it is, must be felt by every
competent reader as a letting-down to a lower intellectual plane.
Is prose, then, after all, a higher form of speech than verse?

Diverse critics have spoken strongly against the Porter-scene:
Coleridge denounces it as unquestionably none of Shakespeare's work [see excerpt above, 1813-1834]. Which makes
me almost afraid to trust my own judgment concerning it; yet
I always feel it to be in the true spirit of the Poet's method.
This strain of droll broad humour, oozing out amid such a
congregation of terrors, to my mind deepens their effect, the
strange but momentary diversion causing them to return with
the greater force. Of the murder-scene, the banquet-scene, the
sleep-walking-scene, with their dagger of the mind, and Banquo of the mind, and blood-spots of the mind, it were vain to
speak. Yet over these sublimely-terrific passages there everywhere hovers a magic light of poetry, at once disclosing the
horrors of the scene and annealing them into matter of delight.
(pp. 348-49)

Rev. H. N. Hudson, "'Macbeth'," in his Shakespeare: His Life, Art, and Characters, Vol. II, *revised
edition, Ginn & Company, 1872, pp. 313-49.*

JOHN W. HALES (lecture date 1874)

[*In the excerpt below, from an essay originally given as a lecture
in 1874, Hales challenges the position, held by Samuel Taylor
Coleridge (1813-34), that Shakespeare did not write the Porter
scene in* Macbeth. *Like Thomas De Quincey (1823), Hales argues
that the knocking at the gate in Act II, Scene iii is crucial to the
play's dramatic effect and further states that the Porter himself
is "an integral part" of this effect. He maintains, as do G. G.
Gervinus (1849-50), H. N. Hudson (1872), John B. Harcourt
(1961), and Kenneth Muir (1962), that the Porter scene is appropriate to the play, noting the necessity of introducing humor
to "relieve the surrounding horror."*]

I propose in this paper to consider whether the Porter is not
after all a genuine offspring of Shakespeare's art. It is possible
to show beyond controversy, that he is an integral part of the
original play; and therefore we must conclude, if he is not the
creation of Shakespeare, that the play was originally the fruit
of a joint authorship, and not merely amended by some reviser.
But if, in addition to this, it can be shown that his appearance
is in accordance with the artistic system by which Shakespeare
worked, that it relieves the awful intensity of the action, and
permits the spectator to draw breath,—further, that he satisifies
that law of contrast which rules, not unfrequently in a manner
that perplexes and astonishes, the undoubted compositions of
Shakespeare—that his speech has a certain dramatic pertinence,
and is by no means an idle outflow of irrelevant buffoonery;—
if such theses can be maintained, then certainly the Porter is
the result of Shakespeare's direct dictation, if not his own
manufacture. Lastly, if his particular style and language prove
to be Shakespearian, it must surely be a confirmed hypersceptic
that persists in believing that he is not of the family of Shakespeare, but begotten by some skilful mimic. Certainly these
are the five points which should be thoroughly considered before any final verdict is pronounced. On each one of them I
shall try to offer a few suggestions. For the sake of clearness
I recapitulate them:—

(i.) That a Porter's speech is an integral part of the play.

(ii.) That it is necessary as a relief to the surrounding horror.

(iii.) That it is necessary according to the law of contrast elsewhere obeyed.

(iv.) That the speech we have is dramatically relevant.

(v.) That its style and language are Shakespearian.

(i.) *That a Porter's speech is an integral part of the play.*

This is a very simple matter. No one will deny that the knocking scene is an integral part of the play. In the whole Shakespearian theatre there is perhaps no other instance where such an awful effect is produced by so slight a means, as when, the deed of blood accomplished, in the frightful silence that the presence of death under any circumstances ever imposes on all around it, when the nerves of Macbeth are strained to the uttermost, and without any external provocation he hears an unearthly voice crying "Sleep no more"—

> Still it cried, 'Sleep no more' to all the house:
> Glamis hath murder'd sleep, and therefore Cawdor
> Shall sleep no more; Macbeth shall sleep no more—
> [II. ii. 38-40]

At this ghastly moment there is a knocking heard. The spiritual and the material seem merged; and one half fancies that it is Conscience herself that has taken a bodily form, and is beating on the gate, or that Vengeance has already arisen and is clamorous for its victim.

> 'Whence is that knocking?' cries Macbeth.
> 'How is't with me, when every noise appals me?'
> [II. ii. 54-5]

It comes again, and his wife now hears it, and recognizes it as made at the south entry. To her with her marvellous self-command it is intelligible enough; but even for her how terrible, and, as in due time appears, how burnt in on the memory this first arrival of the outer world, now that the old conditions of her life are all deranged and convulsed.

>   I hear a knocking
> At the South entry; retire we to our chamber;
> A little water clears us of this deed;
> How easy is it then! your constancy
> Hath left you unattended.   [*Knocking within*]
>   Hark! more knocking.
> Get on your night-gown, lest occasion call us,
> And show us to be watchers. Be not lost
> So poorly in your thoughts.
>   *Macbeth.* To know my deed, 'twere best not know
> myself.   [*Knocking within*]
>   Wake Duncan with thy knocking! I would thou
> couldst!   [II. ii. 62-72]

And then, as he leaves the stage, "Enter a Porter," the knocking continuing with slight intermissions; and at last, when the door is opened, Macduff interrogates the opener as to his lying so late. And when Macbeth appears, after whom he is at the moment inquiring, he says,

> *Our knocking* has awaked him; here he comes.
> [II. iii. 43]

Later on in the play, when Lady Macbeth's overtasked physique gives way under the pressure of vast and truceless anxieties, and reason dethroned, we see something of the impressions which, in spite of herself, have been stamped and branded upon her mind; we learn how that knocking thrilled and pierced her too. "To bed, to bed!" she exclaims, in the awful scene of the delirium; "there's *knocking at the gate;* come, come, come, give me your hand" [V. ii. 66-7].

The knocking scene, then, is of no trivial importance. But with the knocking the Porter is inseparably associated. If we retain it, we must retain him. And if we retain him, he must surely make a speech of some sort; or are we to picture to ourselves a profoundly dumb functionary? Are we to conceive him as crossing the stage, thinking a great deal but saying nothing?— nodding perhaps with all the amazing volubility of Sheridan's Lord Burleigh, or brandishing his keys with a mysterious cunning, or perhaps rushing headlong to his post as if his life was at stake, but with his tongue fast tied and bound? There is probably no student of Shakespeare who is prepared to accept such a phenomenon. Clearly, then, the Porter speaks, to whatever effect.

(ii.) *That some speech of a lighter kind is necessary to relieve the surrounding horror.* In the scene that includes the enactment of Duncan's murder, the latter part of which has already been discussed and quoted, the intensity of the Tragedy reaches the highest possible point of endurance. Such is the mighty power of the dramatist, that we find ourselves transported into the midst of the scenes he portrays. They are not images for us, but realities. We verily see Macbeth pass into the King's chamber, and share his frightful excitement. "The owls scream, and the crickets cry" [II. ii. 15]. And we hear one "laugh in 's sleep," and one cry "Murder" [II. ii. 20]. And the wild weird fancies that overcome him are vivid with us too, and the air is filled with ominous visions and ghastly voices, and the shadows of horror encompass us round as with a cloak. We reach the *ne plus ultra* of dramatic terror. Nature can bear no more. We cannot breathe in so direful an atmosphere. The darkness is crushing us like a weight. (pp. 274-78)

Now if ever in the plays of Shakespeare some relaxation is needed for the nerves tense and strained to the utmost, if ever some respite and repose are due to prevent the high mysterious delight which it is the province of the artist to kindle within us, corrupting into a morbid panic, if ever, as we read or listen, one's heart threatens to suspend its beating, and a very palsy seems imminent, should the awful suspense be protracted, it is so in the terrible scene now before us. . . . A monotony of horror cannot be sustained. In that appalling night scene the very air seems poisoned; and any disturbance of it is infinitely welcome. The sound of a fresh voice, after we have listened so long to that guilty conference, is a very cordial. If it would be going too far to say, with an important alteration of the poet's words, that

> We must laugh or we must die,

one may fairly maintain that the terror must be drawn out no further, or our sensibilities will be either numbed and stupified, or roused into a wild fever of excitation. (pp. 279-80)

(iii.) *Some lighter speech is necessary according to the law of contrast elsewhere observed by Shakespeare.* Perhaps there is no characteristic of the Romantic drama more striking than the frequent or rather the habitual, juxta-position of opposites. It delights in the meeting of extremes. The Tragi-Comedy, or Comi-Tragedy, was a form of its own peculiar invention. The Masque had its Antimasque. This law of contrast may seem at first sight identical with the law of relief just discussed. But it is not so. It springs not from the practical restraints of the drama in its demands upon human endurance, as does that law of relief, but from far wider considerations. It springs from the grand ambition of Teutonic art to embrace in its representation life in all its length and breadth. This art is not content with a mere excerpt from life, a mere fragment, a single side of life, as the phrase is. It yearns to comprehend life in its totality. . . . [The true humorist] does not trouble himself about the labels that are placed by conventional persons on the various departments of existence. He laughs everywhere, and he cries everywhere. It is all infinitely sad, and infinitely comic. Heraclitus and Democritus meet in him. As you look at him you cannot say whether his eyes are filled with tears or with smiles. The beauty of summer and the bleakness of winter, the gaiety of youth and the torpor of age, the gladness of life and the dulness of death;—these are omnipresent with him. And so to him there is nothing shocking or abhorrent in the inter-proximities of things apparently alien to each other. For him the very jaws of death are capable of laughter.

And so in the Shakespearian drama we find strange neighbourhoods. Jesters and jestings in the midst of that stupendous storm in *King Lear*. In *Hamlet* the gravedigger is one with the clown! In *Othello*, amidst all its bitter earnest, there are foolings and railleries. In fact, *Macbeth* would be unique amongst the tragedies of Shakespeare if the comic element were utterly absent from it. (pp. 281-83)

(iv.) *The Speech of the Porter is dramatically relevant.* In order to justify this speech as it stands, it is not enough to point out, as I have tried to do, the general laws of relief and contrast by which Shakespeare works. For in his modes of providing relief and contrast he does not proceed recklessly. He does not ignore harmony when he aims at securing variety. There is a real concord in the seeming discord. All things work together to one general effect. Amidst apparent confusion and chaos there is absolute subordination and symmetry. (p. 283)

"Yet, at all events," says Gervinus of this soliloquy, after mentioning, as we have seen above, the theory of those who would excise it, "it is not inappropriate; there is an uncomfortable joviality which by way of contrast is very suitable to the circumstances, when the drunken warder, whom Duncan's gifts or festivities of the evening have left in a state of excitement, calls his post 'hell-gate,' in a speech in which every allusion bears point" [see excerpt above, 1849-50].

Surely what these two comments put forward must have occurred to every thoughtful reader. The whole speech of the Porter is in fact a piece of powerful irony, "If a man were porter of hell-gate" [II. iii. 1-2]. But is this man not so? What then is hell? and where are its gates? and what is there within them? What of the "scorpions," of which Macbeth's mind is presently full? Knowing what we know of the hideous doings that night has witnessed in his castle, may we not well say: "How dreadful is this place! This is none other but the house of the devil, and this is the gate of hell?" (p. 284)

(v.) *Are the style and language of the Porter's speech Shakespearian?*

Surely the fancy, which is the main part of the Porter's speech, must be allowed to be eminently after the manner of Shakespeare. He was well acquainted with the older stage, as his direct references to it show . . . and this conception of an infernal janitor is just such a piece of antique realism as he would delight in. He has it elsewhere; see *Othello*, where Othello cries out to Emilia:

> You, mistress,
> That have the office opposite to St. Peter,
> And keep the gate of hell.
>
> [IV. ii. 90-92]

The manner in which Macduff "draws out" the Porter is exactly like that of Shakespeare in similar circumstances elsewhere. "What three things does drink especially provoke?" says Macduff [II. iii. 27]; and then the Porter delivers himself of his foolery, which is coarse enough, and to our taste highly offensive, it must be allowed. Compare the way in which Orlando is made to elicit the wit of Rosalind in *As You Like It*. . . . If this likeness of manner has no great positive, yet it has some negative value. We see that the manner is not un-Shakespearian, if it cannot be pronounced definitely Shakespearian; and we need not go to Middleton's plays for an illustration of it.

The passage is written in the rhythmic, or "numerous," prose, that is so favourite a form with Shakespeare. Compare it in this respect, for instance, with Mrs. Quickly's account of Falstaff's end [*Henry V,* II. iii. 9-28].

And so for the language, there is certainly nothing in it un-Shakespearian. (pp. 287-88)

I have not been careful to allude in this Paper to what is commonly said as to the disputed passage by those who allow it to be by Shakespeare, that it was inserted for the sake of the groundlings, or the gods, as we should say, because I am not inclined to think that Shakespeare would have made any undue sacrifice to that part of his audience. They were certainly to be considered by a theatrical writer, and certainly Shakespeare did not forget them. But to suppose that he would have glaringly disfigured—if the passage is to be regarded a disfigurement—one of the greatest passages of his art from any such consideration, is surely audacious and extravagant. Moreover, is it so certain that such an interruption of the terror would have gratified the "groundling?" Would not the genuine animal—and individuals of his species were and are to be found in other parts of the theatre besides that from which he derives his name—have rather had

> On horror's head horror accumulate?
>
> [*Othello,* III. iii. 370]

the darkness deepened, his blood yet more severely chilled his every hair made to stand on end? The thorough-bred sensationalist would surely vote the Porter to be an obnoxious intrusion. He would long for a draught of raw terror, and it is from such a potation that the Porter debars him. (pp. 288-89)

> *John W. Hales, "The Porter in 'Macbeth',"* in his
> Notes and Essays on Shakespeare, *George Bell and
> Sons, 1884, pp. 273-90.*

EDWARD DOWDEN (essay date 1881)

[*Dowden was an Irish critic and biographer whose* Shakspere: A Critical Study of His Mind and Art (rev. ed. 1881) was the leading example of the biographical criticism popular in the English-speaking world near the end of the nineteenth century. Biographical critics sought in the plays and poems a record of Shakespeare's personal development. As that approach gave way in the twentieth century to aesthetic theories with greater emphasis on the constructed, objective nature of literary works, the biographical analysis of Dowden and other critics came to be regarded as limited and often misleading. In the excerpt below, Dowden comments on the tone of* Macbeth, *stating: "It is the tragedy of the twilight and the setting-in of thick darkness upon a human soul." He also discusses the problem of free will in the play. Unlike Franz Horn (1823), G. G. Gervinus (1849-50), and A. J. F. Mézières (1860), Dowden does not believe that Macbeth possesses an absolute free will or that the witches are merely tempters.*

Rather, he states that Macbeth is "infected" by the influence of the witches and not immune to external forces—a position similar to that of Denton J. Snider (1887) and A. C. Bradley (1904). Dowden further contends that the notion that humans exist independent of the influence of external forces is "the dream of an idealist."]

There is a line in the play of *Macbeth*, uttered as the evening shadows begin to gather on the day of Banquo's murder, which we may repeat to ourselves as a motto of the entire tragedy, "Good things of day begin to droop and drowse" [III. iii. 52]. It is the tragedy of the twilight and the setting-in of thick darkness upon a human soul. We assist at the spectacle of a terrible sunset in folded clouds of blood. To the last, however, one thin hand's-breadth of melancholy light remains—the sadness of the day without its strength. Macbeth is the prey of a profound world-weariness. And while a hugh *ennui* pursues crime, the criminal is not yet in utter blackness of night. When the play opens, the sun is already dropping below the verge. And as at sunset strange winds arise and gather the clouds to westward with mysterious pause and stir, so the play of *Macbeth* opens with movement of mysterious, spiritual powers, which are auxiliary of that awful shadow which first creeps and then strides across the moral horizon. (pp. 217-18)

The weird sisters, says Gervinus, "are simply the embodiment of inward temptation" [see excerpt above, 1849-50]. They are surely much more than this. If we must regard the entire universe as a manifestation of an unknown somewhat which lies behind it, we are compelled to admit that there is an apocalypse of power auxiliary to vice, as really as there is a manifestation of virtuous energy. All venerable mythologies admit this fact. The Mephistopheles of Goethe remains as the testimony of our scientific nineteenth century upon the matter. The history of the race, and the social medium in which we live and breathe, have created forces of good and evil which are independent of the will of each individual man and woman. The sins of past centuries taint the atmosphere of to-day. We move through the world subject to accumulated forces of evil and of good outside ourselves. We are caught up at times upon a stream of virtuous force, a beneficent current which bears us onward towards an abiding-place of joy, of purity, and of sacrifice; or a counter-current drifts us towards darkness and cold and death. And therefore no great realist in art has hesitated to admit the existence of what theologians name divine grace, and of what theologians name Satanic temptation. There is, in truth, no such thing as "naked manhood." The attempt to divorce ourselves from the large impersonal life of the world, and to erect ourselves into independent wills, is the dream of the idealist. And between the evil within and the evil without subsists a terrible sympathy and reciprocity. There is in the atmosphere a zymotic poison of sin; and the constitution which is morally enfeebled supplies appropriate nutriment for the germs of disease; while the hardy moral nature repels the same germs. Macbeth is infected; Banquo passes free. Let us, then, not inquire after the names of these fatal sisters. Nameless they are, and sexless. It is enough to know that such powers auxiliary to vice do exist outside ourselves, and that Shakspere was scientifically accurate in his statement of the fact. (pp. 219-21)

*Edward Dowden, "'Othello', 'Macbeth', 'Lear',"
in his* Shakspere: A Critical Study of His Mind and
Art, *third edition, Harper & Brothers Publishers,
1881, pp. 198-244.*

DENTON J. SNIDER   (essay date 1887)

[*Snider was an American scholar, philosopher, and poet who followed closely the precepts of the German philosopher Georg*

Wilhelm Friedrich Hegel and contributed greatly to the dissemination of his dialectical philosophy in America. Snider's critical writings include studies on Homer, Dante, and Goethe, as well as Shakespeare. Like Hermann Ulrici and G. G. Gervinus, Snider sought for the dramatic unity and ethical import in Shakespeare's plays, but he presented a more rigorous Hegelian interpretation than those two German philosophical critics. In the introduction to his three-volume work The Shakespearian Drama: A Commentary (1887-90), *Snider states that Shakespeare's plays present various ethical principles which, in their differences, come into "Dramatic Collision," but are ultimately resolved and brought into harmony. He claims that these collisions can be traced in the plays' various "Dramatic Threads" of action and thought, which together form a "Dramatic Movement," and that the analysis of these threads and movements—"the structural elements of the drama"—reveal the organic unity of Shakespeare's art. Snider observes two basic movements in the tragedies—guilt and retribution—and three in the comedies—separation, mediation, and return. In his commentary on* Macbeth, *excerpted below, Snider argues that throughout the play's first movement, during which the criminal guilt unfolds, Macbeth demonstates a strong belief in earthly retribution for "the wicked deed," and that he already begins to experience "inner retribution through the imagination." The play's second movement, he continues, externalizes this retribution, in Malcolm's avenging forces, and "brings home to the guilty man the true equivalent of his deeds." Snider divides* Macbeth's *characters into those of the Supernatural World and those of the Natural World, but notes that Macbeth, Lady Macbeth, and Banquo are fused with the Supernatural World as well as the Natural World, because of the Weird Sisters' influence on them. Like J. L. F. Flathe (1864) and A. C. Bradley (1904), Snider remarks that Banquo is "paralyzed in his action" by the prophecy of the Weird Sisters and that while he is not tempted to do evil, he is tempted to do no good and refrains from acting against Macbeth. For Snider, the witches "represent the totality of conditions, internal and external, which determine conduct to evil." They are, he asserts in concurrence with Bradley, neither completely subjective nor completely objective; "the Weird Sisters are both outside and inside the man." In discussing the Supernatural World, Snider emphasizes the mythic nature of* Macbeth, *stating that mythology is an effort of the human soul "to utter its greatest and profoundest problems" and that it "seeks to show a providential world-order and man therein." Commenting on Lady Macbeth, Snider points out her affinity with the witches when she calls for evil spirits to unsex her. He also observes that, in the first movement of* Macbeth, *Lady Macbeth suppresses her imagination while Macbeth yields to his, but that this is reversed in the play's second movement. He further notes that when Macbeth's imagination, "the center of his spiritual activity," dies, he becomes "an inward desert." Snider concludes that the psychological interest is central to the play and he designates it the "Tragedy of the Imagination."*]

[*Macbeth*] is not an historical play, though the chief personages that appear in it have a place in history. On the contrary, its soul is mythical, and it belongs to an age of fable as thoroughly as Oedipus. Even in Holinshed, the chronicler from whom the poet derived almost wholly the outer body of his drama, the narrative is mythical, changing suddenly from dry fact into a Marvelous Tale, as we often behold in Herodotus, the Father of History. . . . But Shakespeare has taken these mythical outlines, and filled them with human motives and actions; moreover he has organized the whole into the structure of his drama, though in the chronicle also the narration often falls of itself into a dramatic form, and seems to be calling for the poet. He must, indeed, have the Mythus, yet the Mythus must have him also, to reach its true completion and fulfilment. (pp. 210-11)

Let us seek to take in the entire orbit of Macbeth's career at a glance. The poet shows in him a man, who, having saved the State, becomes the Hero, greater and more powerful than the King, and who then wheels about at the very point of supreme greatness, and turns faithless to the State and Ruler that he has saved, a traitor to his own heroic action. The drama will show such a man, meted, condemned and executed by his own standard; as he put down rebellion, so he a rebel, will be put down, by the law of his own deed. What he measured out to others in strict justice, is in strict justice measured out to him, with Providence holding the scales, as the World's Justiciary. (pp. 212-13)

Macbeth then, has done the great action, which is also good; but just out of this great and good action is conjured the demon who is to destroy him. For the Great Deed, however worthy, has in it the Great Temptation, or rather it has the Tempter himself ensconced, secretly coiled up in its very excellence. (pp. 212-13)

The Dramatic Structure at once reveals the fundamental fact of the play in its external form, as well as hints its inner meaning. The first thing we notice here is that there are two worlds, the natural and supernatural, which run through the entire action, and which, therefore, we shall call its Threads. These two worlds are respectively portrayed in two sets of characters, in which they are wholly distinct, then in one set of characters, in which they come together.

The Supernatural World is that of the Weird Sisters, who seem to enter the action from the outside, and to direct its course; yet they also belong inside and work from thence. They appear in their own independent realm in two scenes, and then they are shown, in two other scenes, connecting with Macbeth, who thus has the two great turning-points in his career marked in the drama; the first time he is incited to Guilt, the second time he is led to Retribution. Moreover, the first time the Weird Sisters alone appear, who are subordinates in this realm; but the second time, Hecate, the queen of the witch-world, comes forth also, who is not only tempter, but punisher as well. Their two appearances thus divide the Tragedy into its two Movements, the one of which unfolds the crime, the other its punishment.

The Natural World, which is the Second Thread of the play, separates easily into two well-defined groups, each of which must be looked at by itself, and then taken in conjunction with the other. The first group contains the three capital personages of the drama, those in whom the Natural and Supernatural Worlds fuse together; they are the three whom the Weird Sisters influence—Banquo, Macbeth, and, less directly and less strongly, Lady Macbeth. They manifest a regular gradation in their attitude toward this magical power: Banquo resists its temptations; Lady Macbeth follows them, or, rather, she brings to their aid her own strength of will; Macbeth fluctuates—entertaining them at first, then resisting, but finally yielding. These three characters unite in the point of showing the influence of imagination; they all have that double element above mentioned, they are impelled both by external shapes and internal motives. This imagination of which we are speaking, is essentially the poetic, the maker of images for the spirit's activities; Macbeth, Lady Macbeth, and Banquo, though not intending to make a poem, are great poets; their language is full of white-hot conception and mighty figurative energy; their poetizing, however, is not a pretty play of fancy, but the rush of the life-blood of their very existenc.

There remains the second group of the Natural World, which embraces Duncan, the King, and those around him, the representatives of the established institutions, against whom the

Weird Sisters are driving the previous group. These people do not come in contact with the Weird Sisters, nor are they directly influenced by the prophetic utterances of the same; still, they are made to feel the supernatural impulse through the previous set of characters, with whom they are brought into collision, except in the case of Banquo, who resists the demonic influence, and hence, himself conflicts with Macbeth, the instrument of that influence. But this second group, which we may name the institutional group, after being overwhelmed and driven out of Scotland, will, in the second part of the play, return as the supporters of a grand reaction, will punish the usurper, and restore the rightful King. Thus Scotland is brought back to order, not through herself, but through England, which country is shown by her poet to be the great bearer of the institutional world, and this has been and still is largely her function in History. (pp. 216-19)

Two grand Movements we notice in the play, each being strongly marked by the appearance of the Weird Powers; also we observe two well-defined Threads running through the entire dramatic Action. (p. 219)

The First Movement starts with the first appearance of the Weird Sisters, and extends to the intervention of Hecate; it gives the subtle inter-action as well as the mighty crash between the Supernatural and Natural Worlds, in which all the individuals of that Scottish life are, more or less directly caught, being driven step by step, some to the guilty deed, others to flight or death. Society is disrupted, institutions are violated, in fact the whole ethical world is toppling to ruin under the blows of a demonic power.

The First Thread is this demonic power, the Weird Sisters, who dwell in a realm of their own, distinct and complete. (pp. 219-20)

They represent the totality of conditions, internal and external, which determine conduct to evil; impart to that totality a voice, and you have the prophetic [third] Weird Sister. Given all the circumstances, the occurence must take place; if then, all these circumstances can find utterance, that utterance must be an announcement of the event which is to happen. The powers which control and impel the individual are united together, and endowed with speech and personality in the case of the Weird Sister. When she gives expression to her own essence, it is a prophecy. (p. 222)

So the Weird Sister is the prophetic voice of the environment, and her own prophecy is itself an active part of this environment; a personification, we may call her, of the influences which impel the individual to evil; yet this individual must have her shape within him also, to see her and to hear her voice. Now let us search the environment and try if we can find these influences. We have not far to look, for immediately after the first scene, which shows the witch-world, comes the second scene, which shows the actual world in emphatic contrast yet harmony. We see the spiritual hurlyburly into which society is whelmed—a great rebellion, then two victorious generals, also a weak King, who owes his kingdom to their ability and valor, who could not resist their power, were they to turn against him. What situation would be more likely to stir up ambitious thoughts concerning the throne? And it is toward the throne that the prediction of the Weird Sister mounts and ends. (pp. 223-24)

At this point we must grasp the very heart of the poet's conception: the Weird Sisters are both outside and inside the man. They are twofold, yet this twofoldness must be seen at last in unity, as the double manifestation of the same ultimate spiritual fact. So all mythology must be grasped: the deities of Homer are shown both as internal and external in relation to the acting person. So too Religion teaches: God is in the world, is its ruler, but He is also in the heart of man; still in both He is one and the same. In like manner is the evil principle to be conceived, be it the Devil or the Weird Sister. We must not then say that the Weird Sister is simply an embodiment of an inner temptation; she is such, but is far more, she has reality and is not to be evaporated into a mere subjective condition. On the other hand we must not say that she is only an external spectacular scare-crow or stage-trick, gotten up to produce an effect, or to cater to the superstitions of the people; thus we lose her soul and our own too. Such is the grand mythical procedure of the poet, itself two-sided, and requiring the reader to be two-sided; he must have two eyes, and both open, yet one vision.

To lay stress upon the reality of the Weird Sisters, the poet has introduced two men beholding them at the same time, so that we cannot well assert the appearances to be a mere subjective delusion, as we might, if only one man saw them. (pp. 224-25)

[The] Weird Sisters are beheld by Macbeth and Banquo alone, and it must be considered as the strong distinctive phase of their spiritual being that they behold the appearances. Both have the same temptation; both are endowed with a strong imagination; both being in the same environment, witness the same apparition; in other words, the external influences which impel to evil, to ambitious thoughts, to future kingship are the same for both, and, in their excited minds, these influences take the form of the Weird Sisters. Such is the design of the poet; he shows us the soul-form of these characters, the tendency to cast the great spiritual facts of existence into the shapes of the imagination, which seem actual beings, and mislead men into following their fantastic suggestions.

That is, these two characters have in them the mythical spirit, their ways of thinking are mythical, evil and temptation take the mythical form; for them the world, indeed, has a tendency to become a Mythus. Their age, too, is a mythical one, also their nation in particular; hence Mythology is their final utterance, and this Mythology will be that of their age and nation. The prosaic Understanding is not their gift, rather the poetic Imagination, which figures realities. To our age, indeed, this mythical spirit is lost, is hardly comprehensible; the Weird Sisters are not real to us, as shapes, but their ethical meaning is as valid for us to-day, as it was for Macbeth and Banquo. Two different soul-forms of the same eternal fact, are ours and theirs; an unreal shape of a reality is what we call their vision of the Weird Sisters—the untrue appearance of a truth. (pp. 226-27)

[The] poet has scrupulously guarded the reality of the Weird Sisters; whenever they appear they are treated as positive objective existences, in spite of Banquo's doubts. Mark the fact—that two persons behold them at the same time, address them and are addressed by them. Now, if they were seen by one person only, or by each person at different times, there would be no mystery, everybody would at once declare it to be a subjective phantom. Such is the case when the ghost of Banquo appears to Macbeth, but is seen by nobody else, though a number of guests with Lady Macbeth are present. The poet, then, is specially careful to preserve the air of reality in these shapes. For such a procedure he has a most excellent reason, one that lies at the very basis of Tragedy. He wishes to place

his audience under the same influences as his hero, and involve them in the same doubts and conflicts. We, too, must look upon the Weird Sisters with the eyes of Macbeth and Banquo; we may not believe in them, or we may be able to explain them, still the great dramatic object is to portray characters which do behold them and believe in them, and for a time, to lend us the eyes and faith of such people. The audience must feel the same problem in all its depth and earnestness, and must be required to face the enigma of these appearances, for a character can be truly tragic to the spectators only when they are assailed by its difficulties and involved in its collision. (pp. 227-28)

Both Banquo and Macbeth question the spectral appearances, when the later prophesy the future of the two warriors; especially the third Sister is prophetic, like the third Norse Valkyr, and hails him: "Macbeth that shalt be King hereafter" [I. iii. 50]. It strikes home to his secret thought, for he starts and seems "to fear things that do sound so fair" [I. iii. 51-2]; well he may, as they have also their "foul" side for him. Banquo doubts: "Are ye fantastical, or that indeed which ye outwardly show?" [I. iii. 53-4]. Are ye in me or outside of me? No, they speak not to such a doubter; yet they will, if he rise to stronger demand and faith. "Speak, then, to me, who neither beg nor fear your favors nor your hate" [I. iii. 60-1]. Rather a defiant mood toward the temptresses; so they give him a very ambiguous prophecy compared to the definiteness of the answer to Macbeth; Loxias could not frame a more doubtful oracle: "Lesser and greater than Macbeth;" "not so happy, yet much happier" [I. iii. 65-6]. But the third Valkyr will hit him; "Thou shalt get Kings, though thou be none" [I. iii. 67]. It would seem that such an answer would paralyze personal ambition for the throne; it does, and just therein reflects Banquo, and, moreover, laps him in the coils of destiny. He is, paralyzed in his action, and thus is caught in the sweep of the man who is not paralyzed in action.

Manifestly the fate of the two heroes is mysteriously wrapped up in these oracles, which in part foreshadow, and in part cause what they foreshadow. In the case of Macbeth, it is plain that the Weird Sister mirrors his inner thought back to him in a sudden startling sentence; kingship is that thought. But in the case of Banquo does she the same? Not so plainly, but none the less certainly; her first words to him, "greater and lesser" cancel each other, and so give his spiritual portrait. She paralyzes him, the moral man, though she cannot seduce him to the wicked act, as she can Macbeth; she says, can only say to him: "thou shalt be no King." Still she can tempt him with a little hope beyond: "thou shalt get Kings," wherein the thought of that son Fleance seems remotely to play. Success cannot mislead his moral nature, but may hamstring it, and prevent it from activity against the wrongful deed. Banquo has yielded just enough to the Weird Sister to palsy his arm from smiting Macbeth, who has yielded entirely. He does not the bad act, but he does not the good act, he the hero, the doer of great deeds; that is his fate, he is untrue to his heroic nature, for he is the successor of Macbeth, when the latter has fallen from duty. So the Great Deed, though it could not tempt him to do the wrong, could tempt him into not doing the right, and thus whirl him into the torrent of a tragic destiny.

It will be noticed that the moment the Weird Sisters are asked concerning their nature and origin, they vanish; such a response they cannot give, or, rather, their response to it is their disappearance. They are not to be investigated too closely, and Banquo still doubts in his way; yet a drop of their poison is in him and will remain. (pp. 234-36)

At this point in the career of Macbeth, his wife is introduced. She, too, is connected with the Weird Sisters, a fact which must not be forgotten; the first sentence of the letter which she is reading, and her own first sentence start from them. Their promises are just what she desired, and we at once hear their connection with her will in the strong resolve: "Thou shalt be what thou are promised" [I. v. 15-16]. . . . [Lady Macbeth] makes herself the instrument of the Weird Sisters, yet of herself also; they are both outside of her, and in her too. She does not see them, like Banquo and Macbeth, but she feels them and addresses them. She is, indeed, the Weird Sister realized, not of the Supernatural, but of the Natural World. But this high strung condition is not her normal one, she forces herself into it by an act of will. When the servant announces the approach of the King toward her castle, she is momentarily thrown off her bent by the sudden emergency, and exclaims "Thou'rt mad to say it" [I. v. 31]; but she soon recovers herself. To be the instrument of the powers of evil, has required in her a prodigious effort of resolution; but she is ready, she will even abjure womanhood. She invokes the "spirits that tend on mortal thoughts" [I. v. 40-1] to unsex her; she will become herself a Weird Sister, a sexless woman, a monstrosity in nature and in soul. Such she has not been hitherto, manifestly. She will be all cruelty—no conscience, no pity; she is will wrought up to frenzy. Again she addresses the supernatural powers in the "murdering ministers" who are to transform her womanly attributes into those of the demon. She, too, is gifted with imagination, and is grandly poetic in these passages, being on this side also allied to Banquo and Macbeth. (pp. 237-39)

Again in the beginning of the [second] Act the poet touches his first chord—the similarity and the difference in the characters of Macbeth and Banquo. Both have the same strong imagination; both the same temptation. Banquo is disturbed during the day by bad fancies; but particularly he is worried by wicked dreams during the night, when he cannot control the fantastic play of his mind. He wishes not to sleep, and prays to be kept free from "the cursed thoughts that nature gives way to in repose" [II. i. 8-9]. The moral restraint continues in him; still he cannot keep from telling Macbeth: "I dreamt last night of the three Weird Sisters" [II. i. 20]; surely their virus is working within him in spite of himself. "To you they have showed some truth" [II. i. 21]—and why not to me, the mind adds. That son Fleance at his side falls within the prophecy, if he himself does not; truly his dearest object, his very love, has in it the danger of temptation. But Macbeth is already beyond that first stage of the Weird Sisters: "I think not of them" [II. i. 22]; he hints some dark plan or conspiracy to Banquo, which "shall make honor for you" [II. i. 26]. But listen to Banquo's answer:

> So I lose none
> In seeking to augument it, but still keep
> My bosom franchised and my allegiance clear,
> I shall be counselled.
>
> [II. i. 26-9]

Which again marks strongly the contrast between the two men, and seems to hint the suspicion of Banquo.

But now we are to see Macbeth alone and hear what he is thinking about. He beholds the image of a dagger hovering in the air and marshalling "me the way that I was going" [II. i. 42], when he has resolved upon the murder. So real is this dagger that he clutches for it, and wonders that it is not as "sensible to feeling as to sight" [II. i. 37]. He even draws his own dagger from his side and compares the two: "I see thee

yet, in form as palpable as this which now I draw" [II. i. 40-1]. Surely the poet tells us here that Macbeth is not fully able to distinguish the images of his fancy from real things. The dagger even changes before his eyes: "On thy blade and dudgeon gouts of blood, which was not so before" [II. i. 46-7]. A terrible image of Temptation, employing the very instrument of murder, lures him on; it is as if the Weird Sister held that dagger toward his hand and marshalled him forward. (pp. 243-45)

The deed is done, the King is murdered. What now? This same imagination rise up in tenfold power and becomes the instrument of punishment—the mighty weapon of his own soul. We have seen all along how Macbeth believed in retribution; now it appears in those fearful voices which he hears from the sleepers, because he is murdering sleep, "the innocent sleep;" religious fear, too, plays in, he cannot say "amen" to the cry "God bless us." But the culmination is the very voice of retribution, crying

> Glamis hath murdered sleep and therefore Cawdor
> Shall sleep no more, Macbeth shall sleep no more.
>
> [II. ii. 39-40]

He has slain repose in the sleeping Duncan. The prophecy of that voice will be fulfiled to the letter. (pp. 245-46)

Thus that castle has been turned into a Hell with fiends in it; here enters the porter who imagines himself to be the porter of Hell-gate. He too, has imagination in accord with the spirit of the whole play, and he has all to himself a small Last Judgment for sinners of the time. It is an humble comic reflection of the monstrous deed within and of the judgment coming, its most external manifestation just at the gate of the castle, which lets in the outer world. But here is that outer world, knocking, knocking, with its fearful echo through the halls, reaching to the very hearts of the guilty master and mistress; it cannot be kept out, it must come upon murder and collide with it. This, then, is the second strand of the Natural World which the poet now interweaves into the action. (pp. 247-48)

[In the third act], Banquo is again touched upon, he is deeply aroused by the fulfilment of the prophecy in the case of Macbeth, though he suspects "thou play'dst most foully for it" [III. i. 3]. More strong than ever is that fatal paralysis of his, the temptation stays his hand from taking part against guilt, he prefers to think of his posterity as Kings. . . . (p. 250)

As in both the previous crises, we see Macbeth again turning over the new state of things in a soliloquy. We have noticed how the fear of retribution was generated even out of his good deed, the suppression of treason, to such a degree that he feared to kill the King; so now the fear of retribution in a new shape is generated out of his bad deed, the murder of Duncan. He has himself taught the "bloody instructions which return to plague the inventor" [I. vii. 9-10]; he must believe that he will be punished. But by whom? Banquo is the man; was he not the first to swear to fight against "treasonous malice?" But still further, he, with the same environment and the same imagination as Macbeth, has not turned traitor, has resisted all the attempts which have been made to draw him into conspiracy. No wonder, then, that "our fears in Banquo stick deep;" no wonder that "under him my Genius is rebuked" [III. i. 48-9, 54-5]; for Banquo is a perpetual picture held up before Macbeth's guilty conscience, a continual reminder of that which he ought to have done, a rebuke to his character. Banquo rightly refrained then from doing, but now such refraining is his doom. (p. 251)

After the death of Banquo, imagination will again punish Macbeth as it punished him after the death of Duncan, only with greater intensity. Then he heard the imagined voice of retribution, now the murdered man appears in person with "gory locks," and with "twenty mortal murders" on his crown [III. iv. 50, 80], and takes his seat at the table of the guests. Imagination now has all the force of reality; it controls Macbeth, even in the presence of company, and makes him reveal the dreadful secret. (pp. 254-55)

The ethical world has been thrown into confusion by the guilt of Macbeth; now the movement sets in toward the restoration of its harmony. He who put down the traitor has himself become the successful traitor, and has secured his position by removing Banquo, who was next to him in greatness and in prospective power. But his own action is to be brought back to him; as he served traitors, so will he be served himself, and the circle of his deed will be made complete. The State and the social system which he has perverted by crime are to be purified; the ethical order of the world is to be vindicated; the man who introduces disturbance into it is to be eliminated. The process of this elimination will be shown in the Second Movement.

The turning point of the drama is emphatically marked by the second appearance of the Weird Sisters. Temptation has culminated, now retribution sets in strongly, not however so much the inner retribution through the imagination, which has been already portrayed, but the external retribution, which brings home to the guilty man the true equivalent of his deeds, and at the same time cleanses the institutional world, which the great criminal has polluted at its very fountain head. (pp. 259-60)

[We] pick up at this point our first Thread again—the Supernatural World. We catch a new hint of its organization; it has a queen, Hecate, taken from Classic Mythology, and placed over Teutonic witches, in the true spirit of the Renascence. Her function is particularly marked, she is to change the previous course of the poem. Hence she reproves the Weird Sisters for the favors to Macbeth, who is "but a wayward son," and selfish; manifestly a case of Satan reproving sin. Her authority has not been recognized, now she will show what it means, both for the witches and for Macbeth.

Well, what does it mean? Hecate is, indeed, a phase of this diabolic process; she is evil, but that evil which punishes evil. That is, the wicked act has now reached the point at which it becomes self-destructive. The first witches led into crime, they were the temptresses; the second and supreme one, Hecate, is the punisher, mainly; hence she undoes the work of the first, and thus brings forth the good. In the universal order evil is a self-canceling process, it turns upon itself and wipes itself out. Accordingly, if the first witchery was temptation, the second is retribution; and if the first witches were subjects, the second witch is a queen, rules, and over-rules the first. (pp. 262-63)

[The Supernatural World] is shown in three phases: Hecate, the queen, who deludes into security; the Witches, who cook the diabolic gruel for Macbeth; the Apparitions, who, while showing him the very process of his death, flatter him into a defiance of it. All have one thing in common: they lead him swiftly toward the penalty by having him suppress the fear of it; they are the voices of Destiny bringing on punishment through a disbelief in punishment.

But thus the witch-world has destroyed itself; we remember that it sprang from the fear of retribution; when that fear is quenched, it is quenched. Macbeth will still cling to the two ambiguous prophecies, but the terror which called up in so much vigor the imaginary world, is gone; the specters have, as far as he is concerned, ended themselves. (pp. 269-70)

In the case of Lady Macbeth, as well as in the case of her husband, we behold the internal retribution accomplished through the imagination. But her it destroys; she cannot withstand its attacks, nor avoid them by outward activity. We must consider her to have been left alone some length of time—"since his majesty went into the field." She thus was handed over to her own thoughts—no doubt her most terrible enemies. She began with unsexing herself, in which step is contained the germ of her fate; for to unsex the woman is to destroy the woman as woman. Abjuring her emotional nature she proceded to cruelty and crime. At last we see her in the process of being eaten up by the Furies of her own creation. The exact manner of her death is not given, nor need it be. The motive, however, is most ample; imagination, with its "thick-coming fancies," is her executioner.

The somewhat prevalent notion of making love the mainspring of Lady Macbeth's actions, and of seeing in her the tender, devoted wife, who committed the most horrible crimes merely out of affection for her husband, is ridiculous, and is, one may well assert, contradicted by the whole tenor of the play. The very point emphasized in her characterization at the beginning is that she abjured womanhood, with its tenderness and love, and prayed to be filled, "from the crown to the toe, top full of direst cruelty," and her woman's breasts to be milked for gall! [I. v. 42-3, 48]. To be the wife is clearly not her highest ambition—that she is already; but it is to be the queen. There is no consistency or unity in her character if love be its leading principle. To this passion the husband may justly lay some claim, but not the wife, who suppresses her emotional nature. (pp. 275-76)

The main fact now to be noticed in the character of Macbeth is that he is no longer swayed by his imagination. This change was indicated at the end of his interview with the Weird Sisters; he is now able to dismiss such "sights" altogether. His outward activity must help to absorb his mind, for his foes are marching against him; the reality before him is quite as terrible as any image can be. (p. 278)

Familiarity with crime has hardened his thoughts; repetition of guilt has seared his conscience. Hence no retributive ghosts appear after the murder of Macduff's family. But his whole mind is seared too—it is a desolation; "life is but a walking shadow;" "I have lived long enough;" "life is fall'n into the sear, the yellow leaf;" "I 'gin to be a-weary of the sun," etc. [V. iv. 24, V. iii. 22, V. iii. 22-3, V. iv. 48]. That is, since the cessation of his imagination his spirit is dead—an inward desert—because his imagination was the center of his spiritual activity. There, is, however, one object to which he still shows attachment—it is his wife. She dies—the victim of "thick-coming fancies;" there remains only his dependence upon the two prophecies; these also break down, for, though their reality is carefully maintained, they are merely symbols of his external reliance upon his imagined destiny, to the disregard of all ethical conduct. He tries to believe that he will not perish, no matter what he does. Hence the prophecies are a delusion—in fact, his own delusion. It will thus be seen that both Macbeth and his wife have their common psychological principle in the imagination, though its development in each is just the opposite. In the first Movement of the drama Lady Macbeth suppresses her imagination, while Macbeth yields to his; in the second the reverse takes place. (pp. 279-80)

One of the peculiarities of the present drama is the fate that overtakes a series of characters, whose sole guilt is the refusal to act at the providential moment—the sin of omission. These are especially Duncan, Banquo, and Lady Macduff, but their trait seems common at the time to all Scotland. They are not shown committing any ethical violation worthy of death; they appear innocent beings overwhelmed in a catastrophe from the outside; and this treatment is deeply consistent with the form and movement of the play, which exhibits Destiny. The Weird Sisters, instruments of Destiny, give to Macbeth his impulse; he is driven upon these victims, apparently guiltless, who fall because they stand in the way of a mighty force. Still, in their case, also, Destiny is internal as well as external; it is their refusal to act when the call comes—that dire paralysis of duty. In this drama, inaction is Fate, quite as much as bad action.

We must notice, too, that the ethical elements, which are usually the most prominent matter, and are given in their native form in other plays, are here somewhat withdrawn into the background, and are clothed in an alien mythical shape. To be sure the ethical world is the main thing, and cannot be absent; it has been pointed out in the career of Macbeth. But the psychological interest equals, possibly surpasses, the ethical; the activities of mind, as well as the world's moral forces, appear to spring at once into independent forms of the imagination. Life with its inner and outer influences is sporting in the mask of fantasy. Macbeth knows abstractly of his own ambition, but his chief temptation seems to be held out to him by the phantoms of the air; and, though an external punishment

Act V. Scene i. Lady Macbeth, Doctor, and Gentlewoman. By William Kaulbach (n.d.). The Department of Rare Books and Special Collections, The University of Michigan Library.

is brought home to him, still his inner retribution, as well as that of his wife, is mainly found in the fantastic workings of the brain. Judging by its treatment, its theme, its language, and its characters, we may call this play, distinctively, the Tragedy of the Imagination. (pp. 283-84)

> *Denton J. Snider, "'Macbeth'," in his* The Shakespearian Drama, a Commentary: The Tragedies, *Sigma Publishing Co., 1887, pp. 210-85.*

A. C. BRADLEY (essay date 1904)

[*Bradley was a major Shakespearean critic whose work culminated the method of character analysis initiated in the Romantic era. He is best known for his* Shakespearean Tragedy *(1904), a close analysis of* Hamlet, Othello, King Lear, *and* Macbeth. *Bradley concentrated on Shakespeare as a dramatist, and particularly on his characters, excluding not only the biographical questions so prominent in the works of his immediate predecessors but also the questions of poetic structure, symbolism, and thematics which became prominent in later criticism. He thus may be seen as a pivotal figure in the transition in Shakespearean studies from the nineteenth to the twentieth century. He has been a major target for critics reacting against Romantic criticism, but he has continued to be widely read to the present day. In his treatment of* Macbeth, *excerpted below, Bradley begins by briefly comparing* Macbeth *with the other tragedies named above. He then discusses the images of darkness, blood, and violence and their effect on the atmosphere of the play. Considering the witches, he contends that they neither determine Macbeth's action, nor merely symbolize his unconscious guilt. Instead, Bradley contends, like Denton J. Snider (1887), that Macbeth's actions are determined by forces both inside and outside of him: "the inward powers of the soul answer in their essence to vaster powers without, which support them and assure the effect of their exertion." In his analysis of the play's characters, Bradley states that Macbeth displays "the imagination of a poet" and suggests that it is this imagination that allows him a degree of sympathy. Lady Macbeth, he asserts, is neither the "fiend-like queen" that critics like Samuel Johnson (1765), Francis Gentleman (1770), and William Hazlitt (1817) argued she is, nor is she the feminine and sentimentalized character suggested by Anna Brownell Jameson (1833) and William Maginn (1837). Rather, claims Bradley, while Lady Macbeth would "have given the world to undo what she had done," she was "too great to repent." In his assessment of Banquo, Bradley agrees with J. L. F. Flathe (1864) and Denton J. Snider (1887), stating that Banquo is influenced by the Weird Sisters "much more truly than Macbeth," a point later challenged by Leo Kirschbaum (1957). Bradley concludes by noting the simplicity of the plot and secondary characters, suggesting that Shakespeare may have "meant to give to his play a certain classical tinge."*]

Macbeth, it is probable, was the last-written of the four great tragedies, and immediately preceded *Antony and Cleopatra*. In that play Shakespeare's final style appears for the first time completely formed, and the transition to this style is much more decidedly visible in *Macbeth* than in *King Lear*. Yet in certain respects *Macbeth* recalls *Hamlet* rather than *Othello* or *King Lear*. In the heroes of both plays the passage from thought to a critical resolution and action is difficult, and excites the keenest interest. In neither play, as in *Othello* and *King Lear*, is painful pathos one of the main effects. Evil, again, though it shows in *Macbeth* a prodigious energy, is not the icy or stony inhumanity of Iago or Goneril; and, as in *Hamlet*, it is pursued by remorse. Finally, Shakespeare no longer restricts the action to purely human agencies, as in the two preceding tragedies; portents once more fill the heavens, ghosts rise from their graves, an unearthly light flickers about the head of the doomed man. The special popularity of *Hamlet* and *Macbeth* is due in part to some of these common characteristics, notably to the fascination of the supernatural, the absence of the spectacle of extreme undeserved suffering, the absence of characters which horrify and repel and yet are destitute of grandeur. The reader who looks unwillingly at Iago gazes at Lady Macbeth in awe, because though she is dreadful she is also sublime. The whole tragedy is sublime.

In this, however, and in other respects, *Macbeth* makes an impression quite different from that of *Hamlet.* The dimensions of the principal characters, the rate of movement in the action, the supernatural effect, the style, the versification, are all changed; and they are all changed in much the same manner. In many parts of *Macbeth* there is in the language a peculiar compression, pregnancy, energy, even violence; the harmonious grace and even flow, often conspicious in *Hamlet,* have almost disappeared. The chief characters, built on a scale at least as large as that of *Othello,* seem to attain at times an almost superhuman stature. The diction has in places a huge and rugged grandeur, which degenerates here and there into tumidity. The solemn majesty of the royal Ghost in *Hamlet,* appearing in armour and standing silent in the moonlight, is exchanged for shapes of horror, dimly seen in the murky air or revealed by the glare of the caldron fire in a dark cavern, or for the ghastly face of Banquo badged with blood and staring with blank eyes. The other three tragedies all open with conversations which lead into the action: here the action bursts into wild life amidst the sounds of a thunderstorm and the echoes of a distant battle. It hurries through seven very brief scenes of mounting suspense to a terrible crisis, which is reached, in the murder of Duncan, at the beginning of the Second Act. Pausing a moment and changing its shape, it hastes again with scarcely diminished speed to fresh horrors. And even when the speed of the outward action is slackened, the same effect is continued in another form: we are shown a soul tortured by an agony which admits not a moment's repose, and rushing in frenzy towards its doom. *Macbeth* is very much shorter than the other three tragedies, but our experience in traversing it is so crowded and intense that it leaves an impression not of brevity but of speed. It is the most vehement, the most concentrated, perhaps we may say the most tremendous, of the tragedies. (pp. 331-33)

Darkness, we may even say blackness, broods over this tragedy. It is remarkable that almost all the scenes which at once recur to memory take place either at night or in some dark spot. The vision of the dagger, the murder of Duncan, the murder of Banquo, the sleep-walking of Lady Macbeth, all come in night-scenes. The Witches dance in the thick air of a storm, or, 'black and midnight hags' [IV. i. 48], receive Macbeth in a cavern. The blackness of night is to the hero a thing of fear, even of horror; and that which he feels becomes the spirit of the play. The faint glimmerings of the western sky at twilight are here menacing: it is the hour when the traveller hastens to reach safety in his inn, and when Banquo rides homeward to meet his assassins; the hour when 'light thickens,' when 'night's black agents to their prey do rouse' [III. ii. 50, 52], when the wolf begins to howl, and the owl to scream, and withered murder steals forth to his work. Macbeth bids the stars hide their fires that his 'black' desires may be concealed; Lady Macbeth calls on thick night to come, palled in the dunnest smoke of hell. The moon is down and no stars shine when Banquo, dreading the dreams of the coming night, goes unwillingly to bed, and leaves Macbeth to wait for the summons of the little bell. When the next day should dawn, its light is 'strangled,' and 'darkness does the face of earth

entomb' [II. iv. 9]. In the whole drama the sun seems to shine only twice: first, in the beautiful but ironical passage where Duncan sees the swallows flitting round the castle of death; and, afterwards, when at the close the avenging army gathers to rid the earth of its shame. (pp. 333-34)

The atmosphere of *Macbeth,* however, is not that of unrelieved blackness. On the contrary, as compared with *King Lear* and its cold dim gloom, *Macbeth* leaves a decided impression of colour; it is really the impression of a black night broken by flashes of light and colour, sometimes vivid and even glaring. They are the lights and colours of the thunder-storm in the first scene; of the dagger hanging before Macbeth's eyes and glittering alone in the midnight air; of the torch borne by the servant when he and his lord come upon Banquo crossing the castle-court to his room; of the torch, again, which Fleance carried to light his father to death, and which was dashed out by one of the murderers; of the torches that flared in the hall on the face of the Ghost and the blanched cheeks of Macbeth; of the flames beneath the boiling caldron from which the apparitions in the cavern rose; of the taper which showed to the Doctor and Gentlewoman the wasted face and blank eyes of Lady Macbeth. And, above all, the colour is the colour of blood. It cannot be an accident that the image of blood is forced upon us continually, not merely by the events themselves, but by full descriptions, and even by reiteration of the word in unlikely parts of the dialogue. (pp. 334-35)

Let us observe another point. The vividness, magnitude, and violence of the imagery in some of these passages are characteristic of *Macbeth* almost throughout; and their influence contributes to form its atmosphere. Images like those of the babe torn smiling from the breast and dashed to death; of pouring the sweet milk of concord into hell; of the earth shaking in fever; of the frame of things disjointed; of sorrows striking heaven on the face, so that it resounds and yells out like syllables of dolour; of the mind lying in restless ecstasy on a rack; of the mind full of scorpions; of the tale told by an idiot, full of sound and fury;—all keep the imagination moving on a 'wild and violent sea' [IV. ii. 21] while it is scarcely for a moment permitted to dwell on thoughts of peace and beauty. In its language, as in its action, the drama is full of tumult and storm. (p. 336)

Now all these agencies—darkness, the lights and colours that illuminate it, the storm that rushes throught it, the violent and gigantic images—conspire with the appearances of the Witches and the Ghost to awaken horror, and in some degree also a supernatural dread. And to this effect other influences contribute. The pictures called up by the mere words of the Witches stir the same feelings. . . . In Nature, again, something is felt to be at work, sympathetic with human guilt and supernatural malice. She labours with portents.

> Lamentings heard in the air, strange screams of death,
> And prophesying with accents terrible,
>
> [II. iii. 56-7]

burst from her. The owl clamours all through the night; Duncan's horses devour each other in frenzy; the dawn comes, but no light with it. Common sights and sounds, the crying of crickets, the croak of the raven, the light thickening after sunset, the home-coming of the rooks, are all ominous. Then, as if to deepen these impressions, Shakespeare has concentrated attention on the obscurer regions of man's being, on phenomena which make it seem that he is in the power of secret forces lurking below, and independent of his consciousness and will:

such as the relapse of Macbeth from conversation into a reverie, during which he gazes fascinated at the image of murder drawing closer and closer; the writing on the face of strange things he never meant to show; the pressure of imagination heightening into illusion, like the vision of a dagger in the air, at first bright, then suddenly splashed with blood, or the sound of a voice that cried 'Sleep no more' [II. ii. 38] and would not be silenced. To these are added other, and constant, allusions to sleep, man's strange half-conscious life; to the misery of its withholding; to the terrible dreams of remorse; to the cursed thoughts from which Banquo is free by day, but which tempt him in his sleep: and again to abnormal disturbances of sleep; in the two men, of whom one during the murder of Duncan laughed in his sleep, and the other raised a cry of murder; and in Lady Macbeth, who rises to re-enact in somnambulism those scenes the memory of which is pushing her on to madness or suicide. All this has one effect, to excite supernatural alarm and, even more, a dread of the presence of evil not only in its recognised seat but all through and around our mysterious nature. Perhaps there is no other work equal to *Macbeth* in the production of this effect. (pp. 337-38)

It would be almost an impertinence to attempt to describe anew the influence of the Witch-scenes on the imagination of the reader. Nor do I believe that among different readers this influence differs greatly except in degree. But when critics begin to analyse the imaginative effect, and still more when, going behind it, they try to determine the truth which lay for Shakespeare or lies for us in these creations, they too often offer us results which, either through perversion or through inadequacy, fail to correspond with that effect. This happens in opposite ways. On the one hand the Witches, whose contribution to the 'atmosphere' of *Macbeth* can hardly be exaggerated, are credited with far to great an influence upon the action; sometimes they are described as goddesses, or even fates, whom Macbeth is powerless to resist. And this is perversion. On the other hand, we are told that, great as is their influence on the action, it is so because they are merely symbolic representations of the unconscious or half-conscious guilt in Macbeth himself. And this is inadequate. (pp. 340-41)

[While] the influence of the Witches' prophecies on Macbeth is very great, it is quite clearly shown to be an influence and nothing more. There is no sign whatever in the play that Shakespeare meant the actions of Macbeth to be forced on him by an external power, whether that of the Witches, or of their 'masters,' or of Hecate. It is needless therefore to insist that such a conception would be in contradiction with his whole tragic practice. The prophecies of the Witches are presented simply as dangerous circumstances with which Macbeth has to deal: they are dramatically on the same level as the story of the Ghost in *Hamlet,* or the falsehoods told by Iago to Othello. (p. 343)

Macbeth himself nowhere betrays a suspicion that his action is, or has been, thrust on him by an external power. He curses the Witches for deceiving him, but he never attempts to shift to them the burden of his guilt. Neither has Shakespeare placed in the mouth of any other character in this play such fatalistic expressions as may be found in *King Lear* and occasionally elsewhere. He appears actually to have taken pains to make the natural psychological genesis of Macbeth's crimes perfectly clear, and it was a most unfortunate notion of Schlegel's that the Witches were required because natural agencies would have seemed too weak to drive such a man as Macbeth to his first murder [see excerpt above, 1808].

'Still,' it may be said, 'the Witches did foreknow Macbeth's future; and what is foreknown is fixed; and how can a man be responsible when his future is fixed?' With this question, as a speculative one, we have no concern here; but, in so far as it relates to the play, I answer, first, that not one of the things foreknown is an action. This is just as true of the later prophecies as of the first. That Macbeth will be harmed by none of woman born, and will never be vanquished till Birnam Wood shall come against him, involves (so far as we are informed) no action of his. It may be doubted, indeed, whether Shakespeare would have introduced prophecies of Macbeth's deeds, even if it had been convenient to do so; he would probably have felt that to do so would interfere with the interest of the inward struggle and suffering. And, in the second place, *Macbeth* was not written for students of metaphysics or theology, but for people at large. . . . This whole difficulty is undramatic; and I may add that Shakespeare nowhere shows, like Chaucer, any interest in speculative problems concerning foreknowledge, predestination and freedom.

We may deal more briefly with the opposite interpretation. According to it the Witches and their prophecies are to be taken merely as symbolical representations of thoughts and desires which have slumbered in Macbeth's breast and now rise into consciousness and confront him. With this idea, which springs from the wish to get rid of a mere external supernaturalism, and to find a psychological and spiritual meaning in that which the groundlings probably received as hard facts, one may feel sympathy. But it is evident that it is rather a 'philosophy' of the Witches than an immediate dramatic apprehension of them; and even so it will be found both incomplete and, in other respects, inadequate.

It is incomplete because it cannot possibly be applied to all the facts. Let us grant that it will apply to the most important prophecy, that of the crown; and that the later warning which Macbeth receives, to beware of Macduff, also answers to something in his own breast and 'harps his fear aright' [IV. i. 74]. But there we have to stop. Macbeth had evidently no suspicion of that treachery in Cawdor through which he himself became Thane; and who will suggest that he had any idea, however subconscious, about Birnam Wood or the man not born of woman? It may be held—and rightly, I think—that the prophecies which answer to nothing inward, the prophecies which are merely supernatural, produce, now at any rate, much less imaginative effect than the others,—even that they are in *Macbeth* an element which was of an age and not for all time; but still they are there, and they are essential to the plot. And as the theory under consideration will not apply to them at all, it is not likely that it gives an adequate account even of those prophecies to which it can in some measure be applied.

It is inadequate here chiefly because it is much too narrow. The Witches and their prophecies, if they are to be rationalised or taken symbolically, must represent not only the evil slumbering in the hero's soul, but all those obscurer influences of the evil around him in the world which aid his own ambition and the incitements of his wife. Such influences, even if we put aside all belief in evil 'spirits,' are as certain, momentous, and terrifying facts as the presence of inchoate evil in the soul itself; and if we exclude all reference to these facts from our idea of the Witches, it will be greatly impoverished and will certainly fail to correspond with the imaginative effect. The union of the outward and inward here may be compared with something of the same kind in Greek poetry. [Bradley cites here Athene's appearance and it's influence on Achilles in the

Iliad, Book One]. . . . [The] inward powers of the soul answer in their essence to vaster powers without, which support them and assure the effect of their exertion. So it is in *Macbeth*. The words of the Witches are fatal to the hero only because there is in him something which leaps into light at the sound of them; but they are at the same time the witness of forces which never cease to work in the world around him, and, on the instant of his surrender to them, entangle him inextricably in the web of Fate. If the inward connection is once realised (and Shakespeare has left us no excuse for missing it), we need not fear, and indeed shall scarcely be able, to exaggerate the effect of the Witch-scenes in heightening and deepening the sense of fear, horror, and mystery which pervades the atmosphere of the tragedy. (pp. 345-49)

[There] is in Macbeth one marked peculiarity, the true apprehension of which is the key to Shakespeare's conception. This bold ambitious man of action has, within certain limits, the imagination of a poet,—an imagination on the one hand extremely sensitive to impressions of a certain kind, and, on the other, productive of violent disturbance both of mind and body. Through it he is kept in contact with supernatural impressions and is liable to supernatural fears. And through it, especially, come to him the intimations of conscience and honour. Macbeth's better nature—to put the matter for clearness' sake too broadly—instead of speaking to him in the overt language of moral ideas, commands, and prohibitions, incorporates itself in images which alarm and horrify. His imagination is thus the best of him, something usually deeper and higher than his conscious thoughts; and if he had obeyed it he would have been safe. But his wife quite misunderstands it, and he himself understands it only in part. The terrifying images which deter him from crime and follow its commission, and which are really the protest of his deepest self, seem to his wife the creations of mere nervous fear, and are sometimes referred by himself to the dread of vengeance or the restlessness of insecurity. His conscious or reflective mind, that is, moves chiefly among considerations of outward success and failure, while his inner being is convulsed by conscience. And his inability to understand himself is repeated and exaggerated in the interpretations of actors and critics, who represent him as a coward, coldblooded, calculating, and pitiless, who shrinks from crime simply because it is dangerous, and suffers afterwards simply because he is not safe. (pp. 352-53)

So long as Macbeth's imagination is active, we watch him fascinated; we feel suspense, horror, awe; in which are latent, also, admiration and sympathy. But so soon as it is quiescent these feelings vanish. He is no longer 'infirm of purpose' [II. ii. 49]: he becomes domineering, even brutal, or he becomes a cool pitiless hypocrite. He is generally said to be a very bad actor, but this is not wholly true. Whenever his imagination stirs, he acts badly. It so possesses him, and is so much stronger than his reason, that his face betrays him, and his voice utters the most improbable untruths or the most artificial rhetoric. But when it is asleep he is firm, self-controlled and practical, as in the conversation where he skilfully elicits from Banquo that information about his movements which is required for the successful arrangement of his murder. Here he is hateful; and so he is in the conversation with the murderers, who are not professional cut-throats but old soldiers, and whom, without a vestige of remorse, he beguiles with calumnies against Banquo and with such appeals as his wife had used to him. On the other hand, we feel much pity as well as anxiety in the scene (I. vii.) where she overcomes his opposition to the murder; and we feel it (though his imagination is not specially active) because this scene shows us how little he understands himself. This is his great misfortune here. Not that he fails to realise in reflection the baseness of the deed (the soliloquy with which the scene opens shows that he does not). But he has never, to put it pedantically, accepted as the principle of his conduct the morality which takes shape in his imaginative fears. (pp. 356-57)

To the end he never totally loses our sympathy; we never feel towards him as we do to those who appear the born children of darkness. There remains something sublime in the defiance with which, even when cheated of his last hope, he faces earth and hell and heaven. Nor would any soul to whom evil was congenial be capable of that heart-sickness which overcomes him when he thinks of the 'honour, love, obedience, troops of friends' which 'he must not look to have' (and which Iago would never have cared to have), and contrasts with them

> Curses, not loud but deep, mouth-honour, breath,
> Which the poor heart would fain deny, and dare not,
>
> [V. ii. 25-8]

(and which Iago would have accepted with indifference). Neither can I agree with those who find in his reception of the news of his wife's death proof of alienation or utter carelessness. There is no proof of these in the words,

> She should have died hereafter;
> There would have been a time for such a word,
>
> [V. iv. 17-18]

spoken as they are by a man already in some measure prepared for such news, and now transported by the frenzy of his last fight for life. He has no time now to feel. Only, as he thinks of the morrow when time to feel will come—if anything comes, the vanity of all hopes and forward-lookings sinks deep into his soul with an infinite weariness, and he murmurs,

> To-morrow, and to-morrow, and to-morrow,
> Creeps in this petty pace from day to day
> To the last syllable of recorded time,
> And all our yesterdays have lighted fools
> The way to dusty death.
>
> [V. iv. 19-23]

In the very depths a gleam of his native love of goodness, and with it a touch of tragic grandeur, rests upon him. The evil he has desperately embraced continues to madden or to wither his inmost heart. No experience in the world could bring him to glory in it or make his peace with it, or to forget what he once was and Iago and Goneril never were. (pp. 364-65)

The greatness of Lady Macbeth lies almost wholly in courage and force of will. It is an error to regard her as remarkable on the intellectual side. In acting a part she shows immense self-control, but not much skill. Whatever may be thought of the plan of attributing the murder of Duncan to the chamberlains, to lay their bloody daggers on their pillows, as if they were determined to advertise their guilt, was a mistake which can be accounted for only by the excitement of the moment. But the limitations of her mind appear most in the point where she is most strongly contrasted with Macbeth,—in her comparative dulness of imagination. I say 'comparative,' for she sometimes uses highly poetic language, as indeed does everyone in Shakespeare who has any greatness of soul. Nor is she perhaps less imaginative than the majority of his heroines. But as compared with her husband she has little imagination. It is not *simply* that she suppresses what she has. To her, things remain at the most terrible moment precisely what were at the calmest, plain facts which stand in a given relation to a certain deed, not visions which tremble and flicker in the light of other worlds. The probability that the old king will sleep soundly after his long journey to Inverness is to her simply a fortunate circumstance; but one can fancy the shoot of horror across Macbeth's face as she mentions it. She uses familiar and prosaic illustrations, like

> Letting 'I dare not' wait upon 'I would,'
> Like the poor cat i' the adage,
>
> [I. vii. 44-5]

either that they may gain such power as to ruin the scheme, or that, while they mean present weakness, they mean also perception of the future. At one point in the murder scene the force of his imagination impresses her, and for a moment she is startled; a light threatens to break on her:

> These deeds must not be thought
> After these ways: so, it will make us mad,
>
> [II. ii. 30-31]

she says, with a sudden and great seriousness. And when he goes panting on, 'Methought I heard a voice cry, "Sleep no more," ' . . . she breaks in, 'What do you mean?' half-doubting whether this was not a real voice that he heard. Then, almost directly, she recovers herself, convinced of the vanity of his fancy. Nor does she understand herself any better than him. She never suspects that these deeds *must* be thought after these ways; that her facile realism,

> A little water clears us of this deed,
>
> [II. ii. 64]

will one day be answered by herself, 'Will these hands ne'er be clean?' or that the fatal commonplace, 'What's done is done,' will make way for her last despairing sentence, 'What's done cannot be undone' [V. i. 43, III. ii. 12, V. i. 68].

Hence the development of her character—perhaps it would be more strictly accurate to say, the change in her state of mind—is both inevitable, and the opposite of the development we traced in Macbeth. When the murder has been done, the discovery of its hideousness, first reflected in the faces of her guests, comes to Lady Macbeth with the shock of a sudden disclosure, and at once her nature begins to sink. The first intimation of the change is given when, in the scene of the discovery, she faints. When next we see her, Queen of Scotland, the glory of her dream has faded. She enters, disillusioned, and weary with want of sleep: she has thrown away everything and gained nothing:

> Nought's had, all's spent,
> Where our desire is got without content:
> 'Tis safer to be that which we destroy
> Than by destruction dwell in doubtful joy.
>
> [III. ii. 4-7]

Henceforth she has no initiative: the stem of her being seems to be cut through. (pp. 371-75)

'Lady Macbeth,' says Dr. Johnson, 'is merely detested' [see excerpt above, 1765]; and for a long time critics generally spoke of her as though she were Malcolm's 'fiend-like queen.' In natural reaction we tend to insist, as I have been doing, on the other and less obvious side; and in the criticism of the last century there is even a tendency to sentimentalise the character. But it can hardly be doubted that Shakespeare meant the predominant impression to be one of awe, grandeur, and horror, and that he never meant this impression to be lost, however it

might be modified, as Lady Macbeth's activity diminishes and her misery increases. I cannot believe that, when she said of Banquo and Fleance,

> But in them nature's copy's not eterne,
>
> [III. ii. 38]

she meant only that they would some day die; or that she felt any surprise when Macbeth replied,

> There's comfort yet: they are assailable;
>
> [III. ii. 39]

though I am sure no light came into her eyes when he added those dreadful words, 'Then be thou jocund' [III. ii. 40]. She was listless. She herself would not have moved a finger against Banquo. But she thought his death, and his son's death, might ease her husband's mind, and she suggested the murders indifferently and without remorse. The sleep-walking scene, again, inspires pity, but its main effect is one of awe. There is great horror in the references to blood, but it cannot be said that there is more than horror. . . . Doubtless she would have given the world to undo what she had done; and the thought of it killed her; but, regarding her from the tragic point of view, we may truly say she was too great to repent.

The main interest of the character of Banquo arises from the changes that take place in him, and from the influence of the Witches upon him. And it is curious that Shakespeare's intention here is so frequently missed. Banquo being at first strongly contrasted with Macbeth, as an innocent man with a guilty, it seems to be supposed that this contrast must be continued to his death; while, in reality, though it is never removed, it is gradually diminished. Banquo in fact may be described much more truly than Macbeth as the victim of the Witches. (pp. 377-79)

At the opening of the Second Act we see him with Fleance crossing the court of the castle on his way to bed. The blackness of the moonless, starless night seems to oppress him. And he is oppressed by something else.

> A heavy summons lies like lead upon me,
> And yet I would not sleep: merciful powers,
> Restrain in me the cursed thoughts that nature
> Gives way to in repose!
>
> [II. i. 6-9]

On Macbeth's entrance we know what Banquo means: he says to Macbeth—and it is the first time he refers to the subject unprovoked,

> I dreamt last night of the three weird sisters.
>
> [II. i. 20]

His will is still untouched: he would repel the 'cursed thoughts'; and they are mere thoughts, not intentions. But still they are 'thoughts,' something more, probably, than mere recollections; and they bring with them an undefined sense of guilt. The poison has begun to work.

The passage that follows Banquo's words to Macbeth is difficult to interpret:

> I dreamt last night of the three weird sisters:
> To you they have show'd some truth.
>   *Macb.*   I think not of them:
> Yet, when we can entreat an hour to serve,
> We would spend it in some words upon that business,
> If you would grant the time,

Ban.   At your kind'st leisure.
Macb. If you shall cleave to my consent, when 'tis,
It shall make honour for you.
Ban.   So I lose none
In seeking to augment it, but still keep
My bosom franchised and allegiance clear,
I shall be counsell'd.
Macb.   Good repose the while!
Ban. Thanks, sir: the like to you!

                                    [II. i. 20-30]

Macbeth's first idea is, apparently, simply to free himself from any suspicion which the discovery of the murder might suggest, by showing himself, just before it, quite indifferent to the predictions, and merely looking forward to a conversation about them at some future time. But why does he go on, 'If you shall cleave,' etc.? Perhaps he forsees that, on the discovery, Banquo cannot fail to suspect him, and thinks it safest to prepare the way at once for an understanding with him (in the original story he makes Banquo his accomplice *before* the murder). Banquo's answer shows three things,—that he fears a treasonable proposal, that he has no idea of accepting it, and that he has no fear of Macbeth to restrain him from showing what is in his mind.

Duncan is murdered. In the scene of discovery Banquo of course appears, and his behaviour is significant. . . . He is watching Macbeth and listening as he tells how he put the chamberlains to death in a frenzy of loyal rage. At last Banquo appears to have made up his mind. On Lady Macbeth's fainting he proposes that they shall all retire, and that they shall afterwards meet,

And question this most bloody piece of work
To know it further. Fears and scruples shake us:
In the great hand of God I stand, and thence
Against the undivulged pretence I fight
Of treasonous malice.

                                    [II. iii. 128-32]

His solemn language here reminds us of his grave words about 'the instruments of darkness,' and of his later prayer to the 'merciful powers' [I. iii. 124, II. i. 7]. He is profoundly shocked, full of indignation, and determined to play the part of a brave and honest man.

But he plays no such part. When next we see him, on the last day of his life, we find that he has yielded to evil. The Witches and his own ambition have conquered him. He alone of the lords knew of the prophecies, but he has said nothing of them. He has acquiesced in Macbeth's accession, and in the official theory that Duncan's sons had suborned the chamberlains to murder him. Doubtless, unlike Macduff, he was present at Scone to see the new king invested. He has, not formally but in effect, 'cloven to' Macbeth's 'consent'; he is knit to him by 'a most indissoluble tie' [III. i. 17]; his advice in council has been 'most grave and prosperous' [III. i. 21]; he is to be the 'chief guest' [III. i. 11] at that night's supper. (pp. 382-85)

His punishment comes swiftly, much more swiftly than Macbeth's, and saves him from any further fall. He is a very fearless man, and still so far honourable that he has no thought of *acting* to bring about the fulfilment of the prophecy which has beguiled him. And therefore he has no fear of Macbeth. But he little understands him. To Macbeth's tormented mind Banquo's conduct appears highly suspicious. . . . So he kills Banquo. But the Banquo he kills is not the innocent soldier who

met the Witches and daffed their prophecies aside, nor the man who prayed to be delivered from the temptation of his dreams.

Macbeth leaves on most readers a profound impression of the misery of a guilty conscience and the retribution of crime. And the strength of this impression is one of the reasons why the tragedy is admired by readers who shrink from *Othello* and are made unhappy by *Lear.* But what Shakespeare perhaps felt even more deeply, when he wrote this play, was the *incalculability* of evil,—that in meddling with it human beings do they know not what. The soul, he seems to feel, is a thing of such inconceivable depth, complexity, and delicacy, that when you introduce into it, or suffer to develop in it, any change, and particularly the change called evil, you can form only the vaguest idea of the reaction you will provoke. All you can be sure of is that it will not be what you expected, and that you cannot possibly escape it. Banquo's story, if truly apprehended, produces this impression quite as strongly as the more terrific stories of the chief characters, and perhaps even more clearly, inasmuch as he is nearer to average human nature, has obviously at first a quiet conscience, and uses with evident sincerity the language of religion.

Apart from his story Banquo's character is not very interesting, nor is it, I think, perfectly individual. And this holds good of the rest of the minor characters. They are sketched lightly, and are seldom developed further than the strict purposes of the action required. From this point of view they are inferior to several of the less important figures in each of the other three tragedies. The scene in which Lady Macduff and her child appear, and the passage where their slaughter is reported to Macduff, have much dramatic value, but in neither case is the effect due to any great extent to the special characters of the persons concerned. Neither they, nor Duncan, nor Malcolm, nor even Banquo himself, have been imagined intensely, and therefore they do not produce that sense of unique personality which Shakespeare could convey in a much smaller number of lines than he gives to most of them. (pp. 385-87)

Is it possible to guess the reason of this characteristic of *Macbeth*?. . . *Macbeth* is distinguished by its simplicity,—by grandeur in simplicity, no doubt, but still by simplicity. The two great figures indeed can hardly be called simple, except in comparison with such characters as Hamlet and Iago; but in almost every other respect the tragedy has this quality. Its plot is quite plain. It has very little intermixture of humour. It has little pathos except of the sternest kind. The style, for Shakespeare, has not much variety, being generally kept at a higher pitch than in the other three tragedies; and there is much less than usual of the interchange of verse and prose. All this makes for simplicity of effect. And, this being so, is it not possible that Shakespeare instinctively felt, or consciously feared, that to give much individuality or attraction to the subordinate figures would diminish this effect, and so, like a good artist, sacrificed a part to the whole? And was he wrong? He has certainly avoided the overloading which distresses us in *King Lear,* and has produced a tragedy utterly unlike it, not much less great as a dramatic poem, and as a drama superior.

I would add, though without much confidence, another suggestion. The simplicity of *Macbeth* is one of the reasons why many readers feel that, in spite of its being intensely 'romantic,' it is less unlike a classical tragedy than *Hamlet* or *Othello* or *King Lear.* And it is possible that this effect is, in a sense, the result of design. . . . [If] we suppose that Shakespeare meant to give to his play a certain classical tinge, he might naturally carry out this idea in respect to the characters, as well as in other respects, by concentrating almost the whole interest on the important figures and leaving the others comparatively shadowy. (pp. 388-89)

A. C. Bradley, "Lecture IX: 'Macbeth' " and "Lecture X: 'Macbeth'," in his Shakespearean Tragedy: Lectures on "Hamlet," "Othello," "King Lear," "Macbeth," Macmillan and Co., Limited, 1904, pp. 331-65, 366-400.

ISADOR H. CORIAT (essay date 1912)

[In the excerpt below, Coriat, an American psychoanalyst, presents one of the first fully developed psychoanalytic treatments of a Shakespearean character. Lady Macbeth, he argues, suffers from "a typical case of hysteria," presented by Shakespeare with "remarkable insight" and culminating in the sleepwalking scene. Coriat states that Lady Macbeth's ambition to be queen, for which she helps murder Duncan, is but a sublimation of her true desire for a child. She thus represses her natural cowardice from her consciousness, he continues, but after the regicide her repressed emotions begin to "break through in dreams" and surface most fully in the sleep-walking scene. Coriat further asserts that, in her somnambulistic state, Lady Macbeth reveals a "condensed panorama" of her repressed crimes and that the compulsive act of washing her hands is "a compromise for self-reproach and repressed experiences." Lady Macbeth, he concludes, is subject to a relentless fate because she cannot free herself from the complexes of her repressed unconscious. Coriat further adds that the witches instigate "the unconscious wishes of the chief characters." For other examinations of the character of Lady Macbeth, see the excerpts by Anna Brownell Jameson (1833) and William Maginn (1837); for other psychoanalytic approaches to Macbeth, see the comments of Sigmund Freud (1915) and Ludwig Jekels (1917).]

When we approach the problem of the somnambulism of Lady Macbeth, it must be remembered that the sleep-walking scene does not stand isolated and alone in the tragedy, but that it is the definite and logical evolution of Lady Macbeth's previous emotional experiences and complexes. In other words, she is not a criminal type or an ambitious woman, but the victim of a pathological mental dissociation arising upon an unstable, day-dreaming basis, and is due to the emotional shocks of her past experiences. Lady Macbeth is a typical case of hysteria; her ambition is merely a sublimation of a repressed sexual impulse, the desire for a child based upon the memory of a child long since dead.

In fact, an analysis of the sleep-walking scene demonstrates that it is neither genuine sleep nor the prickings of a guilty conscience, but a clear case of pathological somnambulism, a genuine disintegration of the personality. As such, it offers as wonderful and as complex a problem as Hamlet—probably more so, for Lady Macbeth's disease is clearly defined and admits of easier clinical demonstration. An analysis of the repressed emotional complexes in Lady Macbeth must of necessity illuminate the motives of the entire tragedy, such as the mental disease of Macbeth, his hallucinations and the symbolism represented by the three weird sisters. (pp. 28-9)

Lady Macbeth first appears in the fifth scene of the first act, reading her husband's letter, which briefly described his meeting with the three weird sisters. Therefore, any ideas which might enter into the mind of Lady Macbeth, were due to hints contained in the letter betraying her husband's wishes, and were elaborated in a soliloquy which revealed the very rapture of ambition. This first soliloquy is remarkable, it is her first daydream of ambition, so strong and dominating, that she be-

lieves she possesses what she really does not possess—namely, bravery. It is this imaginary wish fulfillment to be queen which later causes the hysterical dissociation. As can be demonstrated later in the sleep-walking episode, this daydream of bravery was merely assumed, a mask for the realization of the sudden uprush of her ambition. The genuine underlying cowardice was suppressed.

But the suppressed complex of ambition has become dominating and will now stop at nothing to accomplish its ends. At first consciously prodded on, it soon becomes automatic, beyond her control, she becomes dominated by the fixed idea which causes her disease and which later is responsible for the somnambulism. When the messenger arrives with the news that "the King comes here tonight" [I. v. 31], the suppressed complex of the desire to be queen and the means to be employed to accomplish the desire, breaks through for the first time. Like slips of the tongue in everyday life, which modern psychopathology have shown are not accidental, but are predetermined by antecedent complexes, so the immediate answer is not the usual one of welcome, but one tinged and distorted by her dreams of ambition and the first vague glimmering of homicide. Here the disturbing thought is caused or conditioned by the repressed complex and she replies

> Thou'rt mad to say it.
>
> [I. v. 31]

Then she suddenly feels that she has disclosed herself and her innermost thoughts and in order to disarm suspicion, the remainder of the reply becomes commonplace.

The modern theory of the bursting of suppressed complexes into speech, indicates a sudden removal of the censorship and an uprushing of the subconscious ideas. This alternate play of free speech and of repression forms one of the most characteristic features of Lady Macbeth's mental disorder. In the presence of the messenger, after the revealing of the complex, a compromise with the unconscious takes place, she again becomes the calm Lady Macbeth and attempts to assume an indifferent attitude by pretending that it is lack of preparation for the sudden visit of the King which led to this emotional outburst.

> Is not thy master with him? who, were't so,
> Would have inform'd for preparation.
>
> [I. v. 32-3]

When the messenger leaves, the suppressed complex again breaks forth into a daydream of ambition, of a burning desire and wish to be queen. She imagines, but immediately represses it, at least so far as can be determined by her words, that the opportune moment has arrived and the King will walk into the trap she has prepared for him. In order to brace herself for the ordeal and for the rapidly forming plans of the "taking off" of Duncan, she again deceives herself into thinking that she possesses bravery for a deed which is clearly present in the background of her mind. This, I take it, is the most logical interpretation of the remainder of that remarkable soliloquy which follows. . . . (pp. 39-43)

Then, in the first appearance of Macbeth before his wife, the conversation clearly reveals the working of Lady Macbeth's mind. It is only in her waking condition that she is master of the situation, influences her husband, and maintains herself in a logical relation to her surroundings. This is not spontaneous, however, but is the effect of a suppression brought about through a colossal effort of the will. In the somnambulistic personality, she loses this mastery, becomes a coward and the subject of a depression which finally terminates in suicide. (p. 44)

Lady Macbeth is next brought face to face with the King and in response to his greetings, there follows a reply, which is the very quintessence of hypocrisy, and which may be interpreted as a substitution or a compensation for the gradually dominating but repressed complex.

> All our service
> In every point twice done, and then done double,
> Were poor and single business to contend
> Against those honors deep and broad wherewith
> Your majesty loads our house: for those of old,
> And the late dignities heap'd up to them,
> We rest your hermits.
>
> [I. vi. 14-20]

Then, when the time for the great deed approaches, and Macbeth wavers, she goads him on and in the words

> I have given suck, and know
> How tender 'tis to love the babe that milks me:
> I would, while it was smiling in my face,
> Have pluck'd my nipple from his boneless gums,
> And dash'd the brains out, had I so sworn as you
> Have done to this.
>
> [I. vii. 54-9]

Here is an example of a substitution, or what is termed in modern psychopathology as a sublimation or transformation of a sexual complex into ambition, a mechanism which is frequently found in hysteria. The theme of childlessness is here revealed for the first time. In fact, so complete does the transformation sometimes become, that the hysterics fail to recognize the sexual thoughts underlying their symptoms and they can be revealed only through the technical devices of psychoanalysis. In both Lady Macbeth and Macbeth, the sexual energy is transformed—in the former it leads to an ambition complex, in the latter to criminality. In this remarkable dialogue between Lady Macbeth and her husband, we see how constant reiteration gradually fixes the complex into consciousness, an identical mechanism found in one of the scenes between Iago and his dupe Roderigo in the constant reiteration of "Put money in thy purse" [*Othello*, I. iii. 39ff].

As the final moment approaches for the murder, the so-called courage which Lady Macbeth had deluded herself that she possessed, has not remained in the "sticking place," but she weakens perceptibly and is compelled to have recourse to alcohol in order to make her brave. She is not brave naturally, but is a coward at heart, as is particularly shown in the lines:

> That which hath made them drunk hath made me
> bold;
> What hath quench'd them hath given me fire.
>
> [II. ii. 1-2]

This cowardice is again later seen in the words uttered after the first cry of Macbeth heard from the King's chamber—when she becomes afraid that perhaps the possets have not been sufficiently drugged and the grooms or perhaps the King himself has awakened. The words uttered are an artful excuse, a substitution for her cowardice, and not, as one critic has stated, because some fancied resemblance to her father had arisen to stay her uplifted arm and thus worked on her conscience. Here the motive is far deeper—a symptomatic, unconscious substi-

tution for her cowardice and not due to any prickings of conscience in the relation of child to parent. Thus the words

> I laid their daggers ready;
> He could not miss 'em. Had he not resembled
> My father as he slept, I had done't.
>
> [II. ii. 11-13]

acquire a new significance in the light of modern psychopathology. (pp. 48-52)

But after the deed is done, there arises the first premonition of the impending mental dissociation and suicide. So terrible has become her fear and horror, the repression has become so intense, that she shrinks from the guilty secret, and here enters the first element of the mechanism which leads to the hysterical dissociation. She chooses repression and not free expression, thus erroneously feeling that the former will neutralize the emotional shock. Thus her warning to Macbeth

> These deeds must not be thought
> After these ways; so, it will make us mad,
>
> [II. ii. 30-1]

shows an attitude which is characteristic of an impending mental disintegration.

Later in the scene, her words:

> The sleeping and the dead
> Are but as pictures,
>
> [II. ii. 50-1]

indicate the beginning of a dissociation of the personality, in an attempt to cut off or repress the thoughts of the tragedy from the rest of her experience.

That Shakespeare was fully aware that repression of the emotions was not only painful but dangerous, is shown in the words of Malcolm to Macduff, after the latter has been informed of the murder of his wife and children.

> What, man! ne'er pull your hat upon your brows;
> Give sorrow words: the grief that does not speak
> Whispers the o'erfraught heart, and bids it break.
>
> [IV. iii. 208-10]
> (pp. 53-4)

The knocking at the gate furnishes a distinct emotional contrast to the terror of this scene and is a bursting of reality upon the unreality of things which Lady Macbeth feels creeping upon her. The silence and the whispering, the hallucinatory phenomena which Macbeth relates to his wife, the tenseness of Lady Macbeth, these all are suddenly broken into by the stern realism of the knocking. It is easy to conceive, under these circumstances, how this knocking could act as a psychic traumatism upon the tense emotions of Lady Macbeth, how it transformed her assumed bravery into terrorizing fear and how these elements alone, if necessary, could act as efficient causes for the development of the hysterical disturbance. The repression of the secret of the murder, the imaginary wish to be the mother to a line of Kings, here coincides in consciousness with terror and excitement. The repressed emotions have thus been injured and out of this injured repression, the hysteria arose.

Thus two complexes were already at work in the consciousness of Lady Macbeth and it is these complexes or rather the repression of these complexes which led to the mental dissociation. The ambition complex is based upon daydreams of ambition, not so much for herself as for her husband. It is a substitute for her childlessness or rather for the children which she has lost and it may be termed a sublimated sexual complex. (pp. 55-7)

In the third act, the words of the muttering soliloquy

> 'Tis safer to be that which we destroy
> Than by destruction dwell in doubtful joy,
>
> [III. ii. 6-7]

marks the preparation for the sleepwalking scene and for her later suicide.

The preparations for Banquo's murder have been completed and both husband and wife are in a state of terror and mental anguish. Even in sleep the repressed complexes continue to break through in dreams, perhaps literal, perhaps symbolic.

> Ere we will eat our meal in fear, and sleep
> In the affliction of these terrible dreams
> That shake us nightly: better be with the dead,
> Whom we, to gain our peace, have sent to peace,
> Than on the torture of the mind to lie
> In restless ecstasy.
>
> [III. ii. 17-22]

These words show that Lady Macbeth likewise suffered from terrible dreams, and that both related these dreams to each other. Now it is well known that during the waking state, complexes may be kept repressed by a constant censorship of consciousness. In sleep, this censorship becomes relaxed and the repressed experiences appear either as literal or symbolic dreams. Thus dreams are not chance phantasmagoria of thought disturbing sleep, but are really the logical result of stored-up but repressed experiences. (pp. 60-1)

In the sleep-walking scene, Shakespeare reached the summit of his art in creating an abnormal mental state. While some of the episodes in Hamlet may have caused more discussion and a greater literature, yet much of Hamlet is problematical, while in Lady Macbeth, there can be but one interpretation of this scene, namely, a case of hysterical somnambulism, and conforming to all the known laws of the psychological phenomena of somnambulistic mental states. The entire scene furnishes a splendid illustration of Shakespeare's remarkable insight into mental mechanisms, particularly into abnormal states of consciousness.

This somnambulistic scene is predetermined by the existing, suppressed complexes. It is a subconscious automatism. Lady Macbeth during this scene is not in a state of unconsciousness or even sleep, for in fact her consciousness is very active, but she is rather in a condition of special consciousness. In such a mental condition very complicated but natural acts may be performed.

These somnambulistic phenomena, on account of the close linking of the association of ideas are machine-like and automatic in their repetition. As the mental state in which they occur excludes any voluntary action of the will, when once started they inevitably follow the same order. Now this is precisely what occurred to Lady Macbeth. As an analysis of the mental mechanism of her particular somnambulistic state will distinctly show, the entire episode closely corresponds to the form of the condition termed monoideic somnambulism.

I must fully agree with Coleridge that Lady Macbeth is essentially of the daydreaming type. It is interesting to note that in all carefully analyzed cases of hysteria, this daydreaming will be found to be a prominent characteristic. The daydreams were partly those of ambition and partly sexual—both were imagi-

nary wish fulfillments to be queen and to have a son as a compensation for her childlessness and thus have some one inherit the throne, since the witches hailed Macbeth as father to a line of Kings. These daydreams of Lady Macbeth furnish the key to the later night dreams and the somnambulism. Daydreams may express themselves in various hysterical symptoms and attacks, such as somnambulism, sudden losses of consciousness and amnesia, all of which are found in Lady Macbeth. This is particularly liable to occur when the daydreams and complexes are intentionally forgotten and merge into the unconscious by repression, a mental mechanism which is a prominent characteristic of Lady Macbeth. It is this mental mechanism of repression which finally developed into the somnambulism.

The sleep-walking scene is not mentioned in Holinshed and it must therefore be looked upon as an original effort of Shakespeare's creative imagination. Lady Macbeth had none of the usual phenomena of sleep, but she did show with a startling degree of accuracy all the symptoms of hysterical somnambulism. Somnambulism is not sleep, but a special mental state arising out of sleep through a definite mechanism. The sleep-walking scene is a perfectly logical outcome of the previous mental state. From the very mechanism of this mental state, such a development was inevitable. She is not the victim of a blind fate or destiny or punished by a moral law, but affected by a mental disease.

It is evident from the first words uttered by the Doctor in the sleep-walking scene, that Lady Macbeth had had several previous somnambulistic attacks. That we are dealing with a genuine somnambulism is shown by the description of the eyes being open and not shut. Now several complexes or groups of suppressed ideas of an emotional nature enter into this scene and are responsible for it. The acting out of these complexes themselves are based upon reminiscences of her past repressed experiences.

The first complex relates to the murder of Duncan as demonstrated in the continual washing of the hands, an act not seen earlier and here clearly brought out in the sleep-walking scene. This automatic act is a reminiscence of her earlier remark after the murder of Duncan, "A little water clears us of this deed" [II. ii. 64].

The second complex refers to the murder of Banquo, clearly shown in the words, "I tell you yet again, Banquo's buried; he cannot come out of his grave" [V. i. 63-4], thus demonstrating that she is no longer ignorant of this particular crime of her husband.

The third complex entering into the sleep-walking scene distinctly refers to the murder of Macduff's wife and children—"The Thane of Fife had a wife, where is she now?" [V. i. 42]. Various other fragmentary reminiscences enter into this scene, such as Macbeth's terror at the banquet in the words, "You mar all with this starting" [V. i. 44-5], the striking of the clock before the murder of King Duncan, and the reading of the first letter from Macbeth announcing the witches' prophecy. Thus a vivid and condensed panorama of all her crimes passes before her. Like all reported cases of hysterical somnambulism, the episode is made up, not of one, but of all the abnormal fixed ideas and repressed complexes of the subject. The smell and sight of blood which she experiences, is one of those cases in which hallucinations developed out of subconscious fixed ideas which had acquired a certain intensity, as in Macbeth's hallucination of the dagger. Since blood was the dominating note of the tragedy, it was evidence of Shakespeare's remarkable insight that the dominating hallucination of this scene should refer to blood. The analysis of this particular scene also discloses other important mental mechanisms.

There is a form of nervous disease known as a compulsion neurosis in which the subject has an almost continuous impulsion to either wash the hands or to repeat other actions almost indefinitely. As a rule, this compulsion appears meaningless and even foolish to the outside observer and it is only by an analysis of the condition, that we can understand its nature and true significance. The compulsion may arise from the idea that the hands are soiled or contaminated or there may be a genuine phobia of infection or contamination. As an example, I had the opportunity to observe the case of a young girl who would wash her hands a number of times during the day. She could give no explanation for this impulsion. A psychoanalysis, however, disclosed the fact that the washing of the hands was due to ideas of religious absolution from certain imaginary sins and arose as an act of defense against imaginary contamination. Now a similar group of symptoms is found in Lady Macbeth. In the sleep-walking scene the following dialogue occurs—

> *Doctor.* What is it she does now? Look, how she rubs her hands.
> *Gentlewoman.* It is an accustomed action with her, to seem thus washing her hands: I have known her continue in this a quarter of an hour.
>
> [V. i. 26-30]

Then later in the scene, Lady Macbeth speaks as follows, disclosing the complex which leads to this apparently meaningless action. "What, will these hands ne'er be clean? . . . Here's the smell of the blood still: All the perfumes of Arabia will not sweeten this little hand" [V. i. 43-51].

Here the symptom develops through Lady Macbeth transferring an unpleasant group of memories or complexes, which have a strong personal and emotional significance, to an indifferent act or symptom. The act of washing the hands is a compromise for self-reproach and repressed experiences. The mechanism here is the same as in the compulsion neuroses, a proof of Shakespeare's remarkable insight into the workings of the human mind. When the doctor later states, "This disease is beyond my practise" [V. i. 59], he expressed the attitude of the medical profession towards these psychoneurotic symptoms until the advent of modern psychopathology.

In the words, "Out damned spot—Out I say" [V. i. 35], the mechanism is that of an unconscious and automatic outburst. It is very doubtful if Lady Macbeth would have used these words if she were in her normal, waking condition. Thus the difference between the personality of Lady Macbeth in her somnambulistic and in the normal mental state, is a proof of the wide gap existing between these two types of consciousness.

Lady Macbeth may therefore be looked upon as possessing two personalities, which appear and disappear according to the oscillations of her mental level. In her normal, waking state, repression and an assumed bravery are marked. In the sleeping or somnambulistic state, the repression gives way to free expression and her innate cowardice becomes dominant. In her waking condition, she shows no fear of blood, but shrinks from it when in a state of somnambulism. Her counsel to her husband while awake is that of an emotionless cruelty, while in som-

nambulism she shows pity and remorse. If one could believe in the womanliness of Lady Macbeth, then her sleeping personality must be interpreted as the true one, because removed from the inhibition and the censorship of voluntary repression.

Thus Shakespeare, with most remarkable insight, has made the sleep-walking scene exactly conform to all the characteristics of a pathological somnambulism—that is—the subject sees and hears everything, there is a regularity of development, as the subject repeats the same words and gestures as in the original experience and finally, on a return to the normal personality after the attack is over, there is no memory for the attack, in other words, amnesia has taken place. Lady Macbeth's actions during the sleep-walking scene are very complicated, show a clear memory of her past repressed experiences, in fact, they are an exact reproduction and rehearsal of these experiences. Finally, she shows an amount of reasoning and association which would be impossible during the annihilation of consciousness during sleep and which only could have taken place when consciousness was very active. (pp. 66-77)

After the sleep-walking episode comes the last scene of all— the final picture of the catastrophe—the only possible solution of Lady Macbeth's mental disease—namely her suicide. We are left completely in the dark as to the method of suicide— here both drama and chronicle are silent. The impulse to suicide has occasionally followed an hysterical somnambulistic delirium and likewise has occurred in the course of the attack. (pp. 87-8)

The relentless fate of Greek tragedy, of Hamlet, King Lear, Othello, Rosmersholm, also dominates the tragedy of Macbeth. In Lady Macbeth there is a constant battle between free will and determination. Determinism is triumphant, because Lady Macbeth cannot emancipate herself from the suppressed complexes which inevitably led to her mental disorder. She thinks she chooses her actions whereas in reality they are chosen for her by the unconscious complexes. Macbeth is likewise the victim of the same mental mechanism.

This ethical relentlessness of the tragedy is due to the hysteria of Lady Macbeth, with its strong, deterministic factors. Because Lady Macbeth in her somnambulistic state was different from Lady Macbeth in her waking condition, she suffered from a disintegration or a dissociation of the personality. . . . Lady Macbeth's personality was doubled, normal and abnormal, alternating, but at the same time co-conscious. The dissociation resulted from repressed, unconscious motives and conflicts, due, not to a sudden emotional shock, but to a series of repressed complexes.

Thus in the tragedy of Macbeth we move in a kind of symbolized world. The Macbeth legend is a symbol and it conceals within itself the theme of childlessness in the same manner that a dream may symbolize underlying strong, personal motives and interests. This is the reality behind the symbolism. *Macbeth* is primitive, myth-like and it is now well recognized that the formation of myths and legends has the same mechanism as the formation of dreams. In *Macbeth* as in dreams, we move in a world of supernatural activities—witches and ghosts, exaggerated and heroic deeds, even at times emotionless murders—a mechanism identical with dreaming. The witches are primitive myth creations, sexless, yet old women, emotionless yet exciting to ambition, motiveless, yet furnishing the main motive of the tragedy. They are thoroughly Shakespearean and in them we see how the creative imagination of the poet is related to the primitive myth maker. They wield their power over Macbeth (and secondarily over Lady Macbeth) because they stimulate his half-formed unconscious and repressed wish to be King. The witches are thus the instigators of the entire tragedy and of the unconscious wishes of the chief characters. They set its machinery in motion in the same way that a dream may be instigated by the events of the day. Thus their meaning becomes clear in the light of psycho-analysis. They are erotic symbols, representing, although sexless, the emblems of the generative power in nature. In the "hell broth" are condensed heterogeneous materials in which even on superficial analysis one can discern the sexual significance. If it be asked, why this particular symbolism? it is because they bring to maturity Macbeth's "embryo wishes and half formed thoughts." When Macbeth shrinks, it is not from the horrors involved in their prophecies, but from his own imaginary wish fulfillment and mental conflicts. The shrinking is overcome, however, by their constant harping and the unconscious wish becomes an obsession. This is the mental mechanism of Macbeth, which, by a kind of mental contagion he transfers to his wife and which finally develops in her, into a typical case of hysteria. (pp. 89-92)

> *Isador H. Coriat, in his* The Hysteria of Lady Macbeth, *Moffat, Yard and Company, 1912, 94 p.*

SIGMUND FREUD   (essay date 1915-16)

[An Austrian neurologist and the father of psychoanalysis, Freud is considered one of the most influential thinkers of the twentieth century. Although he was often harshly criticized for his innovative theories, especially for such ideas as infantile sexuality and the Oedipus and Electra complexes, he was for the most part greatly respected as a thinker and teacher. In addition, Freudian thought has had significant influence on various schools of philosophy, religious and political ideas, and such artistic endeavors as surrealism in art, atonal music, and stream of consciousness in literature. In the excerpt below, from an essay first published in Imago *in 1915-16, Freud employs* Macbeth *to illustrate his ideas about the effects of conscience in producing illness that sometimes arises in people when "a deeply-rooted and long-cherished wish has come to fulfilment." Lady Macbeth, he argues, is an example of this kind of person "who collapses on attaining her aim." Despite his admission that a final explanation is impossible, Freud conjectures that Lady Macbeth cannot enjoy her queenship because of her barrenness. It would be, he states, "a perfect example of poetic justice" to have Macbeth and Lady Macbeth punished with childlessness for their "crimes against the sanctity of geniture," noting the play's frequent references to violations of "the father-and-children relation." Freud also points out the parallels between the concern with childlessness and the barrenness of Queen Elizabeth, adding that the accession of James I "was like a demonstration of the curse of unfruitfulness and the blessings reserved for those who carry on the race." Isador H. Coriat (1912) and Ludwig Jekels (1917) also present pyschoanalytic interpretations of* Macbeth.]

Psycho-analytic work has furnished us with the rule that people fall ill of a neurosis as a result of *frustration*. The frustration meant is that of satisfaction for their libidinal desires and a long circumlocution is necessary before the law becomes comprehensible. That is to say, for a neurosis to break out there must be a conflict between the libidinal desires of a person and that part of his being which we call his ego, the expression of his instinct of self preservation, which also contains his ideals of his own character. A pathogenic conflict of this kind takes place only when the libido is desirous of pursuing paths and aims which the ego has long overcome and despised, and has therefore henceforth proscribed; and this the libido never does

until it is deprived of the possibility of an ideal satisfaction consistent with the ego. Hence privation, frustration of a real satisfaction, is the first condition for the outbreak of a neurosis, although, indeed, it is far from being the only one.

So much the more surprising, indeed bewildering, must it appear when as a physician one makes the discovery that people occasionally fall ill precisely because a deeply-rooted and long-cherished wish has come to fulfilment. It seems then as though they could not endure their bliss, for of the causative connection between this fulfilment and the falling-ill there can be no question. (pp. 323-24)

Analytic work soon shows us that it is forces of conscience which forbid the person to gain the long-hoped-for enjoyment from the fortunate change in reality. It is a difficult task, however, to discover the essence and origin of these censuring and punishing tendencies, which so often surprise us by their presence where we do not expect to find them. What we know or conjecture on the point I shall discuss, for the usual reasons, in relation not to cases of clinical observation, but to figure which great writers have created from the wealth of their knowledge of the soul.

A person who collapses on attaining her aim, after striving for it with single-minded energy, is Shakespeare's Lady Macbeth. In the beginning there is no hesitation, no sign of any inner conflict in her, no endeavour but that of overcoming the scruples of her ambitious and yet gentle-hearted husband. She is ready to sacrifice even her womanliness to her murderous intention, without reflecting on the decisive part which this womanliness must play when the question arises of preserving the aim of her ambition, which has been attained through a crime.

> Come, you spirits
> That tend on mortal thoughts, unsex me here
> . . . Come to my woman's breasts,
> And take my milk for gall, you murdering ministers!
> [I. v. 40-48]

> . . . I have given suck, and know
> How tender 'tis to love the babe that milks me:
> I would, while it was smiling in my face,
> Have pluck'd my nipple from his boneless gums,
> And dashed the brains out, had I so sworn as you
> Have done to this.
> [I. vii. 54-9]

One solitary stirring of unwillingness comes over her before the deed:

> . . . Had he not resembled
> My father as he slept, I had done it. . . .
> [II. ii. 12-13]

Then, when she has become Queen by the murder of Duncan, she betrays for a moment something like disillusion, like satiety. We know not why.

> . . . Nought's had, all's spent,
> Where our desire is got without content:
> 'Tis safer to be that which we destroy,
> Than by destruction dwell in doubtful joy.
> [III. ii. 4-7]

Nevertheless, she holds out. In the banquet-scene which follows on these words, she alone keeps her head, cloaks her husband's distraction, and finds a pretext for dismissing the guests. And then we see her no more; until (in the first scene of the fifth act) we again behold her as a sleep-walker, with the impressions of that night of murder fixed on her mind. Again, as then, she seeks to put heart into her husband:

> Fie, my lord, fie! a soldier, and afeard? What
> need we fear who knows it, when none can call
> our power to account?
>
> [V. i. 36-9]

She hears the knocking at the door, which terrified her husband after the deed. Next, she strives to 'undo the deed which cannot be undone' [V. i. 68]. She washes her hands, which are blood-stained and smell of blood, and is conscious of the futility of the attempt. Remorse seems to have borne her down—she who had seemed so remorseless. When she dies, Macbeth, who meanwhile has become as inexorable as she had been in the beginning, can find only a brief epitaph for her:

> She should have died hereafter;
> There would have been a time for such a word.
>
> [V. v. 17-18]

And now we ask ourselves what it was that broke this character which had seemed forged from the most perdurable metal? Is it only disillusion, the different aspect shown by the accomplished deed, and are we to infer that even in Lady Macbeth an originally gentle and womanly nature had been worked up to a concentration and high tension which could not long endure, or ought we to seek for such signs of a deeper motivation as will make this collapse more humanly intelligible to us?

It seems to me impossible to come to any decision. Shakespeare's *Macbeth* is a *pièce d'occasion,* written for the accession of James, who had hitherto been King of Scotland. The plot was ready-made, and had been handled by other contemporary writers, whose work Shakespeare probably made use of in his customary manner. It offered remarkable analogies to the actual situation. The 'virginal' Elizabeth, of whom it was rumoured that she had never been capable of childbearing and who had once described herself as 'a barren stock', in an anguished outcry at the news of James's birth, was obliged by this very childlessness of hers to let the Scottish king become her successor. And he was the son of that Mary Stuart whose execution she, though reluctantly, had decreed, and who, despite the clouding of their relations by political concerns, was yet of her blood and might be called her guest.

The accession of James I. was like a demonstration of the curse of unfruitfulness and the blessings reserved for those who carry on the race. And Shakespeare's *Macbeth* develops on the theme of this same contrast. The three Fates, the 'weird sisters', have assured him that he shall indeed be king, but to Banquo they promise that *his* children shall obtain possession of the crown. Macbeth is incensed by this decree of destiny; he is not content with the satisfaction of his own ambition, he desires to found a dynasty and not to have murdered for the benefit of strangers. This point is overlooked when Shakespeare's play is regarded only as a tragedy of ambition. It is clear that Macbeth cannot live for ever, and thus there is but one way for him to disprove that part of the prophecy which opposes his wishes—namely, to have children himself, children who can succeed him. And he seems to expect them from his vigorous wife:

> Bring forth men-children only!
> For thy undaunted mettle should compose
> Nothing but males. . . .
>
> [I. vii. 72-4]

And equally it is clear that if he is deceived in this expectation he must submit to destiny; otherwise his actions lose all purpose

and are transformed into the blind fury of one doomed to destruction, who is resolved to destroy beforehand all that he can reach. We watch Macbeth undergo this development, and at the height of the tragedy we hear that shattering cry from Macduff, which has often ere now been recognized to have many meanings and possibly to contain the key to the change in Macbeth:

> He has no children!
>
> [IV. iii. 216]

Undoubtedly that signifies 'Only because he is himself childless could he murder my children'; but more may be implied in it, and above all it might be said to lay bare the essential motive which not only forces Macbeth to go far beyond his own true nature, but also assails the hard character of his wife at its only weak place. If one looks back upon *Macbeth* from the culmination reached in these words of Macduff's, one sees that the whole play is sown with references to the father-and-children relation. The murder of the kindly Duncan is little else than parricide; in Banquo's case, Macbeth kills the father while the son escapes him; and he kills Macduff's children because the father has fled from him. A bloody child, and then a crowned one, are shown him by the witches in the conjuration-scene; the armed head seen previously is doubtless Macbeth's own. But in the background arises the sinister form of the avenger, Macduff, who is himself an exception to the laws of generation, since he was not born of his mother but ripp'd from her womb.

It would be a perfect example of poetic justice in the manner of the talion if the childlessness of Macbeth and the barrenness of his Lady were the punishment for their crimes against the sanctity of geniture—if Macbeth could not become a father because he had robbed children of their father and a father of his children, and if Lady Macbeth had suffered the unsexing she had demanded of the spirits of murder. I believe one could without more ado explain the illness of Lady Macbeth, the transformation of her callousness into penitence, as a reaction to her childlessness, by which she is convinced of her impotence against the decrees of nature, and at the same time admonished that she has only herself to blame if her crime has been barren of the better part of its desired results.

In the *Chronicle* of Holinshed (1577), whence Shakespeare took the plot of *Macbeth,* Lady Macbeth is only once mentioned as the ambitious wife who instigates her husband to murder that she may herself be queen. Of her subsequent fate and of the development of her character there is no word at all. On the other hand, it would seem that there the change in Macbeth to a sanguinary tyrant is motivated just in the way we have suggested. For in Holinshed ten years pass between the murder of Duncan, whereby Macbeth becomes king, and his further misdeeds; and in these ten years he is shown as a stern but righteous ruler. It is not until after this period that the change begins in him, under the influence of the tormenting apprehension that the prophecy to Banquo will be fulfilled as was that of his own destiny. Then only does he contrive the murder of Banquo, and, as in Shakespeare, is driven from one crime to another. Holinshed does not expressly say that it was his childlessness which urged him to these courses, but there is warrant enough—both time and occasion—for this probable motivation. Not so in Shakespeare. Events crowd breathlessly on one another in the tragedy, so that to judge by the statements made by the persons in the play about one week represents the duration of time assigned to it. This acceleration takes the ground from under our attempts at reconstructing the motives for the change in the characters of Macbeth and his wife. There is no time for a long-drawn disappointment of their hopes of offspring to enervate the woman and drive the man to an insane defiance; and it remains impossible to resolve the contradiction that so many subtle inter-relations in the plot, and between it and its occasion, point to a common origin of them in the motive of childlessness, and that yet the period of time in the tragedy expressly precludes a development of character from any but a motive contained in the play.

What, however, these motives can have been which in so short a space of time could turn the hesitating, ambitious man into an unbridled tyrant, and his steely-hearted instigator into a sick woman gnawed by remorse, it is, in my view, impossible to divine. I think we must renounce the hope of penetrating the triple obscurity of the bad preservation of the text, the unknown intention of the dramatist, and the hidden purport of the legend. But I should not admit that such investigations are idle in view of the powerful effect which the tragedy has upon the spectator. The dramatist can indeed, during the representation, overwhelm us by his art and paralyse our powers of reflection; but he cannot prevent us from subsequently attempting to grasp the psychological mechanism of that effect. And the contention that the dramatist is at liberty to shorten at will the natural time and duration of the events he brings before us, if by the sacrifice of common probability he can enhance the dramatic effect, seems to me irrelevant in this instance. For such a sacrifice is justified only when it merely affronts probability, and not when it breaks the causal connection; besides, the dramatic effect would hardly have suffered if the time-duration had been left in uncertainty, instead of being expressly limited to some few days. (pp. 326-32)

> *Sigmund Freud, "Some Character-Types Met with in Psycho-Analytic Work," translated by E. Colburn Mayne, in his* Collected Papers: Papers on Meta-psychology, Papers on Applied Psycho-Analysis, Vol. IV, *authorized translation under the supervision of Joan Riviere, The Hogarth Press and The Institute of Psycho-Analysis, 1925, pp. 318-44.*

GEORGE LYMAN KITTREDGE (lecture date 1916)

[*Kittredge was an American scholar and a renowned lecturer and professor at Harvard University from 1888 to 1936. Although he never wrote a full-length study of Shakespeare's work, Kittredge exerted considerable influence on Shakespearean studies through his numerous lectures on and annotations of the plays, many of which were later edited and published. In the following commentary, first delivered as a lecture in April 1916, Kittredge attacks the Romantic criticism of Shakespeare, stating that "it opened the door to the deadliest kind of obvious moralizing." Kittredge singles out the treatment of the Porter scene in* Macbeth *by such Romantics as Samuel Taylor Coleridge (1813-34) and the German poet J. C. Friedrich von Schiller. For Kittredge, the Porter scene functions as "comic relief" and offers "no mystery at all, nor much chance for moralizing, provided the play is looked upon as a play." Coleridge, he charges, allows the scene not "a hint of the place" it occupies in the dramatic structure, while, "worse" yet, Schiller refined and transformed the character of the "rough porter" into a "lyric personage" in his adaptation of* Macbeth. *For other comments on the Porter scene, see the excerpts by G. G. Gervinus (1849-50), H. N. Hudson (1872), John W. Hales (1874), John B. Harcourt (1961), and Kenneth Muir (1962).*]

To the Romantic writers Shakspere appeared as a liberator. He was the archrebel who had triumphed, the Prometheus whom no tyrant Zeus could bind. Therefore they worshipped him as a kind of deity, creating him anew in their own image. (p. 26)

The criticism of this period busied itself extensively with the great tragic characters or, when turning aside to comedy, it treated the more intellectually significant among the comedy group with a touch of seriousness which too often robbed them of their lighthearted irresponsibility. Laughter was not the gift of the Romanticist. This tendency to what may be called the portentous happened to fit the Anglo-Saxon temper, ever propense to revel in seriousness and plunge into debauches of the dismal. It suited our idiosyncrasy also in another way: it opened the door to the deadliest kind of obvious moralizing. (p. 27)

Take the soliloquy of the drunken porter in *Macbeth*. Here there is no mystery at all, nor much chance for moralizing, provided the play is looked upon as a play. Shakspere needed a short scene to fill an interval between the exit of Macbeth and his wife immediately after the murder, and Macbeth's re-entrance with the blood washed off his hands, and the air of one called up from bed by an early knock at the portal. Obviously he could not utilize any of the principal characters for the purpose. Obviously, too, the scene could not be allowed to advance the action. Obviously, again, the spectators needed relief. Their emotions had just been strung to the highest tension. Yet another moment was soon to come of tension equally terrific, when the deed should be discovered, and the murderers should have to face their crime. For Shakspere—profoundly and practically versed in stagecraft, and intimately acquainted with the audience from the actor's point of view—there was but one method of filling such a gap: by comic relief. And the comedy had to be low, so that the laughter might be full-throated. A drunken porter, philosophizing on human society as he rubbed the sleep from his eyes—cataloguing the stock of traditional sinners when he ought to have been opening the door—and coming at last to be broad awake, as his body realized that the place was "too cold for hell" and his mind reasserted itself sufficiently to ask for his tip ("I pray you remember the porter" [II. iii. 20-1])! What lay readier at hand, particularly since the whole thing would be a realistic touch? For there was a porter, of course, and of course he had been carousing with his fellows until the second cock. For had not the gracious Duncan sent forth great largess to the servants? A simple passage, assuredly! safe, one might suppose, in its strict conformity to method, its manifest adaptation to the emergencies of the curtainless Elizabethan stage!

But how was it dealt with? Why, variously, variously— on the *quot homines* principle ["so many men, so many minds"]. Some demanded its excision. Away with it! it is mere foolery, and not good foolery either. Argal, it is spurious and out it should go. This dictum was, after all, but an idolatrous variant of the eighteenth-century manner. Instead of censuring Shakspere for mixing drollery with tragedy (a stricture which, be it right or wrong, was at least intelligible and regular), this idolatrous variant, though condemning the passage equally and on much the same grounds, absolved the author by assuming an interpolation. Yet, after all, one phrase was too Shaksperean to reject: "the primrose way to the everlasting bonfire." That could not be the coinage of any clownish player, or jog-trot fabricator of counterfeit speeches. What then? Why, we must save that phrase and delete the residue. The passage, we are told, was "written for the mob by some other hand, perhaps with Shakspere's consent; and, finding it take, he, with the remaining ink of a pen otherwise employed, just interpolated the words" in question. "Of the rest, not one syllable has the ever-present being of Shakspere" [see excerpt above by Samuel Taylor Coleridge, 1813-34]. Now this subjective and impressionistic tinkering with the text is not, as one might fancy, the toilsome trifling of some academic pedant, one of those humble scholiasts whose lives are spent in piling up junkheaps for a Variorum to sort and sift. By no means. It is the handiwork of a noble poet and a profound, if somewhat misty, thinker—of no less a man than Coleridge. Yet what could be more futile? Not a word of the real pertinency of the passage! Not a hint of the place it occupies in the structural economy of the drama as a drama—as a play to be performed, that is, on an actual stage, by human beings, who have their exits and their entrances, for which it is the business of the playwright to provide in a workmanlike manner.

Still, a worse thing was possible; and of course it was duly perpetrated—this time by a constructive reviser. Schiller transforms the character of the rough porter completely. Under his refining hand he becomes a lyric personage, who might be singing an aubade to Romeo:—"The gloomy night has departed; the lark is carolling; the day awakes; the sun is rising in splendor; he shines alike on the palace and the cottage. Praise be to God, who watches over this house!" O most gentle pulpiter! what a tedious homily have you wearied your parishioners withal, and never cried "Have patience, good people!" (pp. 28-33)

George Lyman Kittredge, in his Shakspere: An Address, *Cambridge, Mass.: Harvard University Press, 1916, 54 p.*

LUDWIG JEKELS (essay date 1917)

[*In the following excerpt, from an essay published in* Imago *in 1917, Jekels develops the psychoanalytic interpretation of* Macbeth *suggested by Sigmund Freud (1915-16). Like Freud, Jekels considers Duncan's murder a parricide and emphasizes the play's concern with the father-son relationship. In his relation to Duncan, states Jekels, Macbeth acts as a bad, "wayward" son. Consequently, he argues, Macbeth is also a bad father to his figurative sons, Macduff and Banquo, and he therefore "forfeits the blessing of continuous descent." Jekels further notes that Macduff is similarly left childless and he concludes by suggesting that the circumstances of Macduff's "unfatherly" flight from Scotland and the murder of his son parallel Shakespeare's own departure from Stratford and the death of his son Hamnet. For another pyschoanalytic consideration of the play, see the excerpt by Isador H. Coriat (1912).*]

The psychological structure of [*Macbeth*], which seems so bewildering at first, becomes clearer if we conceive the king as a father-symbol—a conception revealed and confirmed again and again by psychoanalysis.

We should then conclude that Macbeth's psychic function is twofold. First, like Banquo and Macduff, he is son to the father (King), Duncan. Secondly, however, when he himself has become King, he is father to Banquo and Macduff: these two come to be seen as his sons, just as they are originally conceived as Duncan's sons. Macbeth's first phase thus concerns the relationship of son to father; his second phase involves the opposite relationship, that of father to son.

In order to facilitate orientation, let us first investigate the son-father relationship. Needless to say, the murder of Duncan cannot be classified, analytically, as other than parricide.

As a son, Macbeth is therefore parricidal, or—to put it less strongly—hostile, rebellious; Hecate calls him the "wayward son" [III. v. 11].

The motive of the parricide, the reason for the hostility against the father, is personified in Lady Macbeth. She is the "demon-woman," who creates the abyss between father and son. We can prove the correctness of this interpretation by a number of instances. To begin with, Lady Macbeth is accomplice only to the crime Macbeth commits as son, i.e., before he had become King (father). From the moment he obtains the throne, she has no part at all in his criminal deeds: apparently she is not in on his murderous plans against either Banquo or Macduff.

Shakespearean scholars seem scarcely to have been startled by this fact. Supported by psychoanalytic insight, however, we gain the most important corroboration of our conception of Lady Macbeth from the following dialogue. (In the great seventh scene of the first act, in which she finally induces the still reluctant Macbeth to murder, the Lady refers to the past):

> What beast was't then
> That made you break this enterprise to me?
> . . . Nor time nor place
> Did then adhere, and yet you would make both. . . .
> [I. vii. 47-52]

[The] words quoted point to abysmal psychic depths. Lady Macbeth, the "demon-woman," refers Macbeth to the past—indeed, "woman," in the guise of the three witches, had already stepped between him and the father.

"Macbeth" by Lestudier Lacour (n.d.). The Department of Rare Books and Special Collections, The University of Michigan Library.

A good deal has been written and argued about the witches in *Macbeth*. . . . (pp. 367-69)

Schiller is doubtless right in concluding that the three witches represent the three Fatal Sisters, the Norns of the Edda, the Parcae of the Romans, the Moires of the Greeks. According to an essay by *Freud,* the same is true of Lear's three daughters, Cordelia, Regan, and Goneril, and of the three caskets in *The Merchant of Venice*.

To the same engrossing essay by *Freud,* we owe the insight that the motif of the three sisters, which is customarily conceived as an allegory of the past, the present, and the future, also means "the three inevitable relations man has with woman," the three forms into which the image of the mother is cast for man in the course of his life: "the mother herself, the beloved who is chosen after her pattern, and finally the Mother Earth . . .". Lady Macbeth's vague allusion to the past refers in reality to the mother as the origin and the deepest source of hostility against the father.

That is why the poet has the three witches meet the hero on a "blasted heath" with the prophecy that he will become Thane of Cawdor. The title of Thane of Cawdor does not mean an elevation in rank; it is rather a symbol of treason. For Ross calls the Thane a "most disloyal traitor" [I. ii. 52], and Angus reports that "treasons capital, confess'd and prov'd, / Have overthrown him" [I. iii. 115-16]. By this detail Shakespeare implies that, through his mother, the son turns traitor to his father: Lady Macbeth, though the image of the mother, symbolizes the abyss separating father and son.

Finally, this conception of Lady Macbeth is corroborated by the character of Banquo. Having no part at all in the murder, he stands for the exact opposite of the bad son, Macbeth, and must represent the good son. (pp. 369-70)

In short, the woman—Lady Macbeth—makes Macbeth turn into a bad son, and thus the woman is the son's doom.

In his second psychic phase, Macbeth is the "father." As such, he has one son, Banquo, murdered, and also seeks the life of his other son, Macduff; consequently, he is the bad father, hostile to his sons and ready to kill them.

The validity of this interpretation is established by the great emphasis with which Macbeth orders the hired assassins not to kill Banquo alone, but also to kill his son, Fleance. When the murderers talk, after Fleance's successful flight, their stress is obviously on "son":

Third Murderer: There's but one down; the son is
                     fled.
Second Murderer: We have lost
                     Best half of our affair.

[III. iii. 19-21]

This problem of hostility against the son becomes even clearer when Macduff's little son is murdered; though we are repeatedly told that Macduff has lost *all his kith and kin,* yet the son is emphatically singled out, it is the fate of the son that Shakespeare puts into the foreground.

What is the motif of this hostility against the son?

Suffice it that we hint at the famous vision of Banquo's ghost—often interpreted and as often misunderstood—whom Macbeth sees taking his, the father's, seat, just as formerly he himself had dislodged Duncan from his seat. And let us recall Macbeth's word at this moment:

Ay, and a bold one, that dare look on that
Which might appal the devil.

[III. iv. 58-9]

Here the poet dramatizes, with wonderful clarity, the fear of the son, now a father, upon confronting, in his own son, the same hostility he had himself harbored against his father—a motif Rank has also disclosed in Hamlet.

This *fear of requital,* a fear nourished and maintained by consciousness of the wrong committed against the father, explains Macbeth's desperate outcry at the news that although Banquo is dead, his son, Fleance, has succeeded in escaping:

Then comes my fit again. I had else been perfect;
Whole as the marble, founded as the rock,
As broad and general as the casing air.
But now I am cabin'd, cribb'd, confin'd, bound in
To saucy doubts and fears.

[III. iv. 20-24]

It is the father within Macbeth, the never-silenced memories of hatred against his father and of the injury inflicted on that father in his thoughts, that nourishes suspicions of the very same feelings in the son; it is the father surviving within him that demands the death of the son. Malcolm, the cautious son, therefore speaks of

. . . wisdom
To offer up a weak, poor, innocent lamb
T'appease an angry God.

[IV. iii. 15-17]

Obviously, the relation to one's son appears to the poet as strictly conditioned by the relation to one's father; one will be, as a father, as one was as a son. *Macbeth demonstrates the fact that a bad son will make a bad father.*

The same close connection of the psychical functions of son and father, is revealed in other characters of the tragedy, especially in Macduff and Banquo. (pp. 371-72)

For Macduff must be called a bad, obstinate son, quite as much as Macbeth. Despite his love for his father (amply demonstrated for Duncan, and hinted at even for Macbeth), Macduff rebels against Macbeth. He does not attend the coronation at Scone; he uses "broad words," according to Lennox [III. vi. 21]; and, unlike the submissive son, Banquo, who accepts unhesitatingly, Macduff refuses the invitation to the banquet offhand.

Why does he act this way?—because Macbeth has murdered Duncan, committed parricide, shown the traditional hostility against the father.

It is Macduff's rebellion against the father, however, which destroys all his kin. Persecuted by the father, he is forced to abandon them to the murderous hand, especially his son, who is stabbed to death before our very eyes. That is why he wails,

Sinful Macduff,
They were all struck for thee! Naught that I am,
Not for their own demerits, but for mine,
Fell slaughter on their souls.

[IV. iii. 224-27]

Here is the same motif as in the story of Macbeth; Macduff, too, demonstrates the fact that a bad son is also a bad father.

This identical content is communicated to us, however, in two distinct dialects. Macduff's fate proclaims in an undisguised, direct manner what the character of Macbeth expresses in a veiled and therefore indirect form; the latter seems to be a symbolic presentation of the former. Analysis of Macbeth should, then, disclose a technique similar to that which is frequently used in dreams. Everyone familiar with *Freud's theory of dreams* knows that they discard nuances and tints and instead adopt a lapidary brevity and a violent imagery. Almost every negative emotional relation is expressed by death, for example. Macbeth's murder of the King thus corresponds to Macduff's mere unconcern about him.

The same insight is even more accurate for the female characters.

Is not Lady Macduff, in her little scene (IV, ii) but reproducing Lady Macbeth's actions in the first two acts? Macduff's wife incites her little son against his father, calling her husband a traitor who swears and does not keep his word, a man who should be hanged. She deeply degrades the child's father before him by saying how easily he could be replaced by another father. Schiller, in his translation, thought this scene so irrelevant that he left it out. But can Lady Macduff's words be symbolized more adequately than by Lady Macbeth's daggers? Hamlet, reproaching his mother with her sins, says, *"I will speaker daggers to* her but use none" [*Hamlet*, III. ii. 396]; even in colloquial language, "words like daggers" is a familiar figure.

What could have led Shakespeare to the double presentation of this motif? We shall not answer this question fully at this stage of our investigation. We may, however, venture the surmise that the character of Macduff, so poorly outlined in the legend, has been endowed so richly by Shakespeare because he saw in it a more concrete, more cleanly cut, more specific formulation of the motif which Macbeth's character expresses in a much more general way. This may explain why he developed the Macduff nucleus of the legend, treated it separately and paralleled it to Macbeth, almost pointing out that in this case Macbeth should be understood as practically identical with Macduff.

Combing these elements, we reach a conclusion essential for the understanding of the tragedy: that *not Macbeth, but Macduff, is the true hero*. Similarly, the further development of the basic idea of the drama—the concatenation of the father function with that of the son—proceeds, not in Macbeth, but in Macduff, who becomes, as it were, the continuation of Macbeth.

Banquo is, so to speak, the positive of the picture of which Macduff is the negative. In saving himself from Macbeth's persecutions, Macduff disregards his son and sacrifices him; when Banquo is attacked by murderers, however, he gives his last thought to his son. "Fly, good Fleance, fly!" are his dying words [III. iii. 17]. His fate therefore symbolizes the idea treated in the play, that one's conduct as father is conditioned by one's attitude as son; here, the meaning is reversed, however, and the implication is that only a good son can become a good father.

Our original interpretation of Banquo as, notwithstanding his inner contradictions, a tractable son, is borne out if we interpret the allegory as meaning that while such a son may fall victim to his father, he will safeguard his own son. Furthermore, the apparition of the infinitely long line of Stuart kings (IV, i) shows that by saving his child a good son may expect further reward, since this action guarantees the undisturbed succession of generations: the House of Stuart originates from that same Fleance.

Applying this insight to Macbeth, *the basic idea is* discovered to be *that a bad son not only sacrifices his son, but, in so doing, also forfeits the blessing of continuous descent.*

This complex, we believe, this worry about the preservation of the clan, bears the main emphasis of the drama. The son is regarded primarily as a means to this end, that is, as the first-born male descendant. Although Banquo is represented in the procession of king, therefore, Fleance is missing.

The historical incident to which the drama can be traced also supports the supposition that the author aims principally at the problem of preservation of the line of descent. When Elizabeth died, and the Tudor dynasty was ended, the transference of the crown to the Stuarts offered an analogy with the contrasting fates of Banquo and Macduff in the tragedy. The same disappointment at the disruption of the line of descent can also be inferred from Macduff's reaction to Ross's report of the murder of

> Wife, children, servants, all
> That could be found.
>
> [IV. iii. 211-12]

In his desperate outcry, what he bemoans is the loss of *all* his children:

> He has no children. All my pretty ones?
> Did you say all? O hell-kite! All?
> What, all my pretty chickens . . .
>
> [IV. iii. 216-18]

This grief is not directed to the children as such, but to their function as links in the chain of generations. Macduff's exclamation, "He has no children," which has so often been reinterpreted, may favor this interpretation. It refers to Macbeth, and, keeping the congruity of the two figures, could be replaced by a resigned, "And so I have no children." That these words, in so general a form, and in the specific situation, can only reflect on the lost prospect of continuous descent, can hardly be denied. What else, moreover, could Macbeth mean when he tells his wife,

> Bring forth men-children only;
> For thy undaunted mettle should compose
> Nothing but males.
>
> [I. vii. 72-4]

Some doubt may be aroused, however, by the unexplained distinction with which Macduff's son, among all his kin, has been treated. The individual treatment of this character's fate has proven very useful for our understanding of the drama: perhaps this son, even more than his counterpart, Fleance, has shown how the tragedy is built around the son problem. The question is why Shakespeare so fully displayed this part of the problem, "the Son," when he wrapped the other part, "the Father," in so foggy a symbolic darkness? What was his purpose, what did he want to express? Holinshed cannot answer; he does not mention Macduff's son. Could the character be elucidated from another viewpoint, from reality? The biographies may answer that question.

Among their meager data, the biographies include the fact that when he was twenty-one, Shakespeare left his hometown, Stratford, his wife and his children, and moved to London. The biographers agree that this serious step, this separation from all that should be dearest to him, was mainly and almost exclusively due to his conflict with the wealthy squire, Sir Thomas Lucy. Caught while poaching, William Shakespeare was punished somewhat severely by Lucy. His revenge was a satiric ballad against Lucy. That, however, had merely the effect that the squire now "redoubled the persecution against him to that degree that he was obliged to leave his business and family . . . and shelter himself in London" [Nicholas Rowe cited in George Brandes's *Shakespeare*]. (pp. 373-76)

And what if we suggested that Shakespeare's relationship to his father might also have been one of the motives prompting his departure? This conjecture gains considerable support from a hint that the conflict between father and son became more marked at this time. Shortly before Shakespeare's departure, the woman, Lady Macbeth, had stepped between father and son. Not quite three years earlier, William, at the age of eighteen, had married a farmer's daughter, much older than himself. She was of socially inferior parentage, and the marriage was contracted under unusual circumstances, without the father's consent, though this, for minors, was indispensable. . . . With these facts before us, do not Lady Macduff's words sound almost like a spontaneous confession of the dramatist? (She reproaches her husband, who has fled before the king's wrath:)

> . . . to leave his wife, to leave his babes,
> His mansion and his titles, in a place
> From whence himself does fly? He loves us not,
> He wants the natural touch.
>
> [IV. ii. 6-9]

The certainty of this supposition is particularly strengthened by another fact. It is not easy to discover why Shakespeare has Macduff's son stabbed *after* the escape of the father instead of *before*. If the stabbing took place first, not only would there be sufficient motivation for that base deed (especially when compared with the causes of Banquo's fate), but there would be much better reasons for Macduff's flight—which otherwise lacks the added incentive of retaliation. As it is, the irrationality of Macduff's action leads his wife to exclaim, "What had he done to make him fly the land?" and "His flight was madness" [IV. ii. 1, 3]. Some commentators seem to agree with her. *Gervinus* actually slights the fact that the sequence of events is reversed in this way, and says that Macduff was not prepared to oppose Macbeth until after the murder of his family [see excerpt above, 1849-50]. And Ulrici calls the flight of Macduff unmanly and unfatherly [see excerpt above, 1839].

This incongruity, however, also disappears once we understand the allegory, and realize that a personal experience of Shakespeare has been transposed into the drama. Exactly as in the tragedy, Shakespeare, while living far from his family and unconcerned about them for several years, lost his eleven-year old son, Hamnet. Surely Macduff embodies this intimate personal experience of the dramatist. (pp. 377-78)

Ludwig Jekels, "The Riddle of Shakespeare's 'Macbeth'," in The Psychoanalytic Review, Vol. XXX, No. 4, October, 1943, pp. 361-85.

SIR ARTHUR QUILLER-COUCH (essay date 1918)

[*Quiller-Couch was editor with J. Dover Wilson of the New Cambridge edition of Shakespeare's works. In his study* Shakespeare's Workmanship, *and in his Cambridge lectures on Shakespeare, Quiller-Couch based his interpretations on the assumption that Shakespeare was mainly a craftsman attempting, with the tools and materials at hand, to solve particular problems central to his plays. In the excerpt below, Quiller-Couch discusses the problem of retaining the sympathy of the audience for an evil hero like Macbeth, an issue also treated by Wayne Booth (1963), Robert B. Heilman (1966), and Bertrand Evans (1979). Quiller-Couch argues that Shakespeare preserves the audience's sympathy for Macbeth because the murder of Duncan proceeds from a "fatal hallucination," a "dreadful mistake." He further states that the vagueness of the witches' influence on Macbeth and of his acceptance of the hallucination contributes to the sympathy he receives. Quiller-Couch also notes a similarity between Shakespeare's Macbeth and Milton's Satan, an observation first suggested by Samuel Taylor Coleridge in a brief note in his marginalia and later made by Roy W. Battenhouse (1952), Robert Pack (1956), and Herbert R. Coursen, Jr. (1967).*]

[The story of Macbeth from] the *Chronicle* has one fatal defect as a theme of tragedy. For tragedy demands some sympathy with the fortunes of its hero: but where is there room for sympathy in the fortunes of a disloyal, self-seeking murderer?

Just there lay Shakespeare's capital difficulty. (p. 28)

Aristotle says this concerning the hero, or protagonist, of tragic drama, and Shakespeare's practice at every point supports him:—

(1) A Tragedy must not be the spectacle of a perfectly good man brought from prosperity to adversity. For this merely shocks us.

(2) Nor, of course, must it be that of a bad man passing from adversity to prosperity: for that is not tragedy at all, but the perversion of tragedy, and revolts the moral sense.

(3) Nor, again, should it exhibit the downfall of an utter villain: since pity is aroused by undeserved misfortunes, terror by misfortunes befalling a man like ourselves.

(4) There remains, then, as the only proper subject for Tragedy, the spectacle of a man not absolutely or eminently good or wise, who is brought to disaster not by sheer depravity but by some error or frailty.

(5) Lastly, this man must be highly renowned and prosperous—an Oedipus, a Thyestes, or some other illustrious person.

Before dealing with others, let us get this last rule out of the way; for, to begin with, it presents no difficulty in *Macbeth*, since in the original—in Holinshed's *Chronicles*—Macbeth is an illustrious warrior who makes himself a king; and moreover the rule is patently a secondary one, of artistic expendiency rather than of artistic right or wrong. It amounts but to this, that the more eminent we make our persons in Tragedy, the more evident we make the disaster—the dizzier the height, the longer way to fall, and the greater shock on our audience's mind. (pp. 30-1)

But, touching the other and more essential rules laid down by Aristotle, let me—very fearfully, knowing how temerarious it is, how imprudent to offer to condense so great and close a thinker—suggest that, after all, they work down into one:—that a hero of Tragic Drama must, whatever else he miss, engage our sympathy; that, however gross his error or grievous his frailty, it must not exclude our feeling that he is a man like ourselves; that, sitting in the audience, we must know in our hearts that what is befalling him might conceivably in the circumstances have befallen us, and say in our hearts, "There, but for the grace of God, go I."

I think, anticipating a little, I can drive this point home by a single illustration. When the ghost of Banquo seats itself at that dreadful supper, who sees it? Not the company. Not even Lady Macbeth. Whom does it accuse? Not the company, and, again, not even Lady Macbeth. Those who see it are Macbeth and you and I. Those into whom it strikes terror are Macbeth and you and I. Those whom it accuses are Macbeth and you and I. And what it accuses is what, of Macbeth, you and I are hiding in our own breasts.

So, if this be granted, I come back upon the capital difficulty that faced Shakespeare as an artist.

(1) It was not to make Macbeth a grandiose or a conspicuous figure. He was already that in the *Chronicle*.

(2) It was not to clothe him in something to illude us with the appearance of real greatness. Shakespeare, with his command of majestic poetical speech, had that in his work-bag surely enough, and knew it. When a writer can make an imaginary person talk like this:—

> She should have died hereafter;
> There would have been a time for such a word.
> To-morrow, and to-morrow, and to-morrow
> Creeps in this petty pace from day to day
> To the last syllable of recorded time;
> And all our yesterdays have lighted fools
> The way to dusty death—
>
> [V. v. 17-23]

I say, when a man knows he can make his Macbeth talk like that, he needs not distrust his power to drape his Macbeth in an illusion of greatness. Moreover, Shakespeare—artist that he was—had other tricks up his sleeve to convince us of Macbeth's greatness. (pp. 32-4)

But (here lies the crux) how could he make us sympathise with him—make us, sitting or standing in the Globe Theatre some time (say) in the year 1610, feel that Macbeth was even such a man as you or I? He was a murderer, and a murderer for his private profit—a combination which does not appeal to most of us, to unlock the flood-gates of sympathy or (I hope) as striking home upon any private and pardonable frailty. The *Chronicles* does, indeed, allow just one loop-hole for pardon. It hints that Duncan, nominating his boy to succeed him, thereby cut off Macbeth from a reasonable hope of the crown, which he thereupon (and not until then) by process of murder usurped, "having," says Holinshed, "a juste quarrell so to do (as he took the mater)."

Did Shakespeare use that one hint, enlarge that loop-hole? He did not.

The more we study Shakespeare as an artist, the more we must worship the splendid audacity of what he did, just here, in this play of *Macbeth*.

Instead of using a paltry chance to condone Macbeth's guilt, he seized on it and plunged it threefold deeper, so that it might verily

> the multitudinous seas incarnadine . . .
>
> [II. ii. 59]

Think of it:—

He made this man, a sworn soldier, murder Duncan, his liege-lord.

He made this man, a host, murder Duncan, a guest within his gates.

He made this man, strong and hale, murder Duncan, old, weak, asleep and defenceless.

He made this man commit murder for nothing but his own advancement.

He made this man murder Duncan, who had steadily advanced him hitherto, who had never been aught but trustful, and who (that no detail of reproach might be wanting) had that very night, as he retired, sent, in most kindly thought, the gift of a diamond to his hostess.

To sum up: instead of extenuating Macbeth's criminality, Shakespeare doubles and redoubles it. Deliberately this magnificent artist locks every door on condonation, plunges the guilt deep as hell, and then—tucks up his sleeves.

There was once another man, called John Milton, a Cambridge man of Christ's College; and, as most of us know, he once thought of rewriting this very story of Macbeth. The evidence that he thought of it—the entry in Milton's handwriting—may be examined in the library of Trinity College, Cambridge.

Milton did not eventually write a play on the story of Macbeth. Eventually he preferred to write an epic upon the Fall of Man, and of that poem critics have been found to say that Satan, "enemy of mankind," is in fact the hero and the personage that most claims our sympathy.

Now (still bearing in mind how the subject of Macbeth attracted Milton) let us open *Paradise Lost* at Book IV. upon the soliloquy of Satan, which between lines 32-113 admittedly holds the *clou* [main point] of the poem:

> O! thou that, with surpassing glory crown'd—

Still thinking of Shakespeare and of Milton—of Satan and of Macbeth—let us ponder every line: but especially these:—

> Lifted up so high,
> I 'sdain'd subjection, and thought one step higher
> Would set me highest, and in a moment quit
> The debt immense of endless gratitude,
> So burdensome, still paying, still to owe:
> Forgetful what from him I still receiv'd;
> And understood not that a grateful mind
> By owing owes not, but still pays at once
> Indebted and discharg'd. . . .

And yet more especially this:—

> Farewell, remorse! All good to me is lost:
> *Evil, be thou my good.*
>
> (pp. 34-6)

How could it lie within the compass even of Shakespeare, master-workman though he was and lord of all noble persuasive language, to make a tragic hero of this Macbeth—traitor to his king, murderer of his sleeping guest, breaker of most sacred trust, ingrate, self-seeker, false kinsman, perjured soldier? Why, it is sin of this quality that in *Hamlet,* for example, outlaws the guilty wretch beyond range of pardon—our pardon, if not God's.

> Upon my secure hour thy uncle stole. . . .
>
> [*Hamlet*, I. v. 61]

Why, so did Macbeth upon Duncan's. . . . How could Shakespeare make his audience feel pity or terror for such a man? Not for the deed, not for Duncan; but for Macbeth, doer of the deed; how make them sympathise, saying inwardly, "There, but for the grace of God, might you go, or I"?

He could, by majesty of diction, make them feel that Macbeth was somehow a great man: and this he did. He could conciliate their sympathy at the start by presenting Macbeth as a brave and victorious soldier: and this he did. He could show him drawn to the deed, against will and conscience, by persuasion of another, a woman: and this—though it is extremely dangerous, since all submission of will forfeits something of manliness, lying apparently on the side of cowardice, and ever so little of cowardice forfeits sympathy—this, too, Shakespeare did. He could trace the desperate act to ambition, "last infirmity of noble minds": and this again he did. All these artifices, and more, Shakespeare used. But yet are they artifices and little more. They do not begin—they do not pretend—to surmount the main difficulty which I have indicated, How of such a criminal to make a hero?

Shakespeare did it: *solutum est agendo* [the explanation is in the plan]. How?

There is (I suppose) only one possible way. It is to make our hero—supposed great, supposed brave, supposed of certain winning natural gifts—proceed to his crime *under some fatal hallucination*. It must not be an hallucination of mere madness: for that merely revolts. . . . No: the hallucination, the dreadful mistake, must be one that can seize on a mind yet powerful and lead it logically to a doom that we, seated in the audience, understand, awfully forebode, yet cannot arrest—unless by breaking through the whole illusion heroically, as did a young woman of my acquaintance who, on her second or third visit to the theatre, arose from her seat in the gallery and shouted to Othello, "Oh, you great black fool! Can't you *see?*"

Further, such an hallucination once established upon a strong mind, the more forcibly that mind reasons the more desperate will be the conclusion of its error; the more powerful is the will, or combination of wills, the more irreparable will be the deed to which it drives, as with the more anguish we shall follow the once-noble soul step by step to its ruin.

Now, of all forms of human error, which is the most fatal? Surely that of exchanging Moral Order, Righteousness, the Will of God (call it what we will) for something directly opposed to it: in other words, of assigning the soul to Satan's terrible resolve, "Evil, be thou my good."

By a great soul such a resolve cannot be taken save under hallucination. But if Shakespeare could fix that hallucination upon Macbeth and plausibly establish him in it, he held the key to unlock his difficulty. I have no doubt at all where he found it, or how he grasped it.

Suppose that Shakespeare as a workman had never improved on what Marlowe taught. Suppose, having to make Macbeth choose evil for good, he had introduced Satan, definite, incarnate, as Marlowe did. Suppose he had made the man assign his soul, by deed or gift, on a piece of parchment and sign it with his blood, as Marlowe made Faustus do. What sort of play would *Macbeth* be?

But we know, and Shakespeare has helped to teach us, that the very soul of horror lies in the vague, the impalpable: that nothing in the world or out of it can so daunt and cow us as the dread of *we know not what*. Of darkness, again—of such darkness as this tragedy is cast in—we know that its menace lies in *suggestion* of the hooded eye watching us, the hand feeling to clutch us by the hair. No; Shakespeare knew what he was about when he left his witches vague. (pp. 50-1)

Let us pause here, on the brink of the deed, and summarise:

(1) Shakespeare, as artificer of this play, meant the Witches, with their suggestions, to be of capital importance.

(2) Shakespeare, as a workman, purposely left vague the extent of their influence; purposely left vague the proportions of their influence and Macbeth's own guilty promptings, his own acceptance of the hallucination, contribute to persuade him; vague as the penumbra about him in which—for he is a man of imagination—he sees that visionary dagger. For (let us remember) it is not on Macbeth alone that this horrible dubiety has to be produced; but on us also, seated in the audience. We see what he does not see, and yearn to warn him; but we also see what he sees—the dagger, Banquo's ghost—and understand why he doubts.

(3) As witchcraft implies a direct reversal of the moral order, so the sight and remembrance of the witches, with the strange fulfilment of the Second Witch's prophecy, constantly impose the hallucination upon him—"Fair is foul, and foul is fair" [I. i. 11]. "Evil, be thou my good." (pp. 52-3)

> *Sir Arthur Quiller-Couch, "'Macbeth': I" and "'Macbeth': II," in his* Shakespeare's Workmanship, *T. Fisher Unwin Ltd., 1918, pp. 17-36, 37-55.*

G. WILSON KNIGHT (essay date 1930)

[*Knight is one of the most influential Shakespearean critics of the twentieth century; he helped shape a new interpretive approach to Shakespeare's work and promoted a greater appreciation of many of the plays. In his studies* The Wheel of Fire (1930) *and* The Shakespearian Tempest (1932), *Knight rejected criticism which emphasizes sources, character analysis, psychology, and ethics and outlined his principles of interpretation which, he claimed, would "replace that chaos by drawing attention to the true Shakespearean unity." Knight argued that this unity lay in Shakespeare's poetic use of images and symbols—particularly in the opposition of "tempests" and "music." He also maintained that a play's spatial aspects, or "atmosphere," should be as closely considered as the temporal elements of the plot if one is "to see the whole play in space as well as time." Knight argues in the following excerpt from* The Wheel of Fire, *that* Macbeth *presents an experience of absolute evil. In his analysis of the play's imagery he observes, as did A. C. Bradley (1904), an abysmal darkness that is nonetheless "shot through and streaked with vivid colour." He also notes that the characters exhibit an overriding sense of doubt and uncertainty and he points out the frequent references to "strange and hideous creatures" and abnormalities of nature. These and other images, argues Knight, combine to suggest a predominant emotion of fear—"Everyone is afraid"—and* Macbeth's *impact is "thus exactly analogous to nightmare." Like Hermann Ulrici (1839) and Denton J. Snider (1887), Knight states that all of the characters are to some extent guilty of yielding to evil and are "paralyzed by fear." He concludes that, as the play draws to a close, Macbeth, no longer in conflict with himself, "faces the world fearless" and allows balance and harmony to replace the disorder of evil.*]

Macbeth is Shakespeare's most profound and mature vision of evil. In the ghost and death themes of *Hamlet* we have something of the same quality; in the Brutus-theme of *Julius Caesar* we have an exactly analogous rhythm of spiritual experience; in *Richard III* we have a parallel history of an individual's crime. In *Macbeth* all this, and the many other isolated poetic units of similar quality throughout Shakespeare, receive a final, perfected form. Therefore analysis of *Macbeth* is of profound value: but it is not easy. Much of *Hamlet*, and the *Troilus-Othello-Lear* succession culminating in *Timon of Athens,* can be regarded as representations of the 'hate-theme'. We are there faced by man's aspiring nature, unsatiated of its desire among the frailties and inconsistencies of its world. They thus point us to good, not evil, and their very gloom of denial is the shadow of a great assertion. They thus lend themselves to interpretation in terms of human thought, and their evil can be regarded as a negation of man's positive longing. In *Macbeth* we find not gloom, but blackness: the evil is not relative, but absolute. In point of imaginative profundity *Macbeth* is comparable alone to *Antony and Cleopatra*. There we have a fiery vision of a paradisal consciousness; here the murk and nightmare torment of a conscious hell. This evil, being absolute and therefore alien to man, is in essence shown as inhuman and supernatural, and is thus most difficult of location in any philosophical scheme. *Macbeth* is fantastical and imaginative beyond other tragedies. Difficulty is increased by that implicit blurring of effects, that palling darkness, that overcasts plot, technique, style. The persons of the play are themselves groping. Yet we are left with an overpowering knowledge of suffocating, conquering evil, and fixed by the basilisk eye of a nameless terror. (p. 140)

Macbeth is a desolate and dark universe where all is befogged, baffled, constricted by the evil. Probably in no play of Shakespeare are so many questions asked. It opens with 'When shall we three meet again?' and 'Where the place?' [I. i. 1, 6]. The second scene starts with, 'What bloody man is that? [I. ii. 1], and throughout it questions are asked of the Sergeant and Ross. This is followed by:

> *First Witch*. Where hast thou been, sister?
> *Second Witch*. Killing swine.
> *First Witch*. Sister, where thou?
>
> [I. iii. 1-3]

And Banquo's first words on entering are: 'How far is't called to Forres? What are these . . .?' [I. iii. 39]. Questions succeed each other quickly throughout this scene. Amazement and mystery are in the play from the start, and are reflected in continual questions—there are those of Duncan to Malcolm in I. iv, and of Lady Macbeth to the Messenger and then to her lord in I. v. They continue throughout the play. In I. vii they are tense and powerful:

> *Macbeth*.   . . . How now! What news?
> *L. Macbeth*. He has almost supp'd: why have you left the chamber?
> *Macbeth*. Hath he asked for me?
> *L. Macbeth*.   Know you not he has?
>
> [I vii. 28-30]

This scene bristles with them. At the climax of the murder they come again, short stabs of fear: 'Didst thou not hear a noise?—Did not you speak?—When?—Now.—As I descended? . . .' [II. ii. 16]. Some of the finest and most heart-rending passages are in the form of questions: 'But wherefore could I not pronounce Amen?' and, 'Will all great Neptune's ocean wash this blood clean from my hand?' [II. ii. 28, 57-8]. The scene of the murder and that of its discovery form a series of questions. To continue the list in detail would be more tedious than difficult. . . .

These questions are threads in the fabric of mystery and doubt which haunts us in *Macbeth*. All the persons are in doubt, baffled. Duncan is baffled at the treachery of a man he trusted [I. iv. 11-14]. Newcomers strike amaze:

> What a haste looks through his eyes! So should he look
> That seems to speak things strange.
>
> [I. ii. 46-7]

Surprise is continual. Macbeth does not understand how he can be Thane of Cawdor [I. iii. 108-109]. Lady Macbeth is startled at the news of Duncan's visit [I. v. 33]; Duncan at the fact of Macbeth's arrival before himself [I. vi. 20-24]. There is the general amazement at the murder; of Lennox, Ross, and the Old Man at the strange happenings in earth and heaven on the night of the murder [II. iii. 54-61, II. iv. 1-20]. Banquo and Fleance are unsure of the hour [II. i. 1-3]. No one is sure of Macduff's mysterious movements. Lady Macbeth is baffled by Macbeth's enigmatic hints as to the 'deed of dreadful note' [III. ii. 44]. The two murderers are not certain as to who has wronged them, Macbeth or Banquo [III. i. 75-8]; they do not understand the advent of the 'third murderer' [III. iii. 1]. Ross and Lady Macduff are at a loss as to Macduff's flight, and warning is brought to Lady Macduff by a mysterious messenger who 'is not to her known' [IV. ii. 65]. Malcolm suspects Macduff, and there is a long dialogue due to his 'doubts' (IV. iii); and in the same Malcolm recognizes Ross as his countryman yet strangely 'knows him not' [IV. iii. 160]. As the atmosphere brightens at the end of the play, the contrast is aptly marked by reference to the stroke of action which will finally dispel the fog of insecurity:

> The time approaches
> That will with due decision make us know
> What we shall say we have and what we owe.
> Thoughts speculative their unsure hopes relate,
> But certain issues strokes must arbitrate.
>
> [V. iv. 16-20]

This blurring and lack of certainty is increased by the heavy proportion of second-hand or vague knowledge reported during the play's progress. . . . The persons of the drama can say truly, with Ross, 'we . . . do not know ourselves' [IV. ii. 19]. We too, who read, are in doubt often. Action here is illogical. Why does Macbeth not know of Cawdor's treachery? Why does Lady Macbeth faint? Why do the King's sons flee to different countries when a whole nation is ready in their support? Why does Macduff move so darkly mysterious in the background and leave his family to certain death? Who is the Third Murderer? And, finally, why does Macbeth murder Duncan? All this builds a strong sense of mystery and irrationality within us. We, too, grope in the stifling dark, and suffer from doubt and insecurity.

Darkness permeates the play. The greater part of the action takes place in the murk of the night. . . . Now this world of doubts and darkness gives birth to strange and hideous creatures. Vivid animal disorder-symbolism is recurrent in the play and the animals mentioned are for the most part fierce, ugly, or ill-omened significance. We hear of 'the Hyrcan tiger' and the 'armed rhinoceros' [III. iv. 100], the 'rugged Russian bear' [III. iv. 99]; the wolf, 'whose howl's his watch' [II. i. 54]; the raven who croaks the entrance of Duncan under Lady Macbeth's battlements [I. v. 39]; the owl, 'fatal bellman who gives the stern'st goodnight' [II. ii. 3]. There are 'maggot-pies and choughs and rooks' [III. iv. 124], and

> . . . hounds and greyhounds, mongrels, spaniels, curs,
> Shoughs, water-rugs, and demi-wolves . . .
>
> [III. i. 92-3]

We have the bat and his 'cloistered fight', the 'shard-borne beetle', the crow making wing to the 'rooky wood'; 'night's black agents' rouse to their preys; Macbeth has 'scotch'd the snake, not killed it'; his mind is full of 'scorpions' [III. ii. 13-53]. All this suggests life threatening, ill-omened, hideous:

and it culminates in the holocaust of filth prepared by the Weird Sisters in the Cauldron scene. But not only are animals of unpleasant suggestion here present: we have animals, like men, irrational and amazing in their acts. A falcon is attacked and killed by a 'mousing owl', and Duncan's horses eat each other [II. iv. 11-18]. There is a prodigious and ghastly tempest, with 'screams of death'; the owl clamoured through the night; the earth itself shook [II. iii. 54-61]. We are thus aware of a hideous abnormality in this world; and again we feel its irrationality and mystery. In proportion as we let ourselves be receptive to the impact of all these suggestions we shall be strongly aware of the essential fearsomeness of this universe.

We are confronted by mystery, darkness, abnormality, hideousness: and therefore by fear. The word 'fear' is ubiquitous. All may be unified as symbols of this emotion. Fear is predominant. Everyone is afraid. There is scarcely a person in the play who does not feel and voice at some time a sickening, nameless terror. The impact of the play is thus exactly analogous to nightmare, to which state there are many references. . . . There is no nearer equivalent, in the experience of a normal mind, to the poetic quality of *Macbeth* than the consciousness of nightmare or delirium. That is why life is here a 'tale told by an idiot' [V. v. 26-7], a 'fitful fever' after which the dead 'sleep well' [III. ii. 23]; why the earth itself is 'feverous' [II. iii. 61]. The Weird Sisters are nightmare actualized; Macbeth's crime nightmare projected into action. Therefore this world is unknowable, hideous, disorderly, and irrational. The very style of the play has a mesmeric, nightmare quality, for in that dream-consciousness, hateful though it be, there is a nervous tension, a vivid sense of profound significance, an exceptionally rich apprehension of reality electrifying the mind: one is in touch with absolute evil, which, being absolute, has a satanic beauty, a hideous, serpent-like grace and attraction, drawing, paralysing. This quality is in the poetic style: the language is tense, nervous, insubstantial, without anything of the visual clarity of *Othello,* or the massive solemnity of *Timon of Athens.* The poetic effect of the whole, though black with an inhuman abysm of darkness, is yet shot through and streaked with vivid colour, with horrors that hold a mesmeric attraction even while they repel; and things of brightness that intensify the enveloping murk. There is constant reference to blood. . . . But though blood-imagery is rich, there is no brilliance in it; rather a sickly smear. Yet there is brilliance in the fire-imagery: the thunder and lightning which accompanies the Weird Sisters; the fire of the cauldron; the green glint of the spectral dagger; the glaring eyes which hold 'no speculation' of Banquo's Ghost, the insubstantial sheen of the three Apparitions, the ghastly pageant of kings unborn.

Macbeth has the poetry of intensity: intense darkness shot with the varied intensity of pure light or pure colour. In the same way the moral darkness is shot with imagery of bright purity and virtue. There is 'the temple-haunting martlet' [I. vi. 4] to contrast with evil creatures. We have the early personation of the sainted Duncan, whose body is 'the Lord's anointed temple' [II. iii. 68], the bright limning of his virtues by Macbeth [I. vii. 16-20], and Macduff [IV .iii. 108-109]; the latter's lovely words on Malcolm's mother who, 'oftener upon her knees than on her feet, died every day she lived' [IV. iii. 110-111]; the prayer of Lennox for 'some holy angel' [III. vi. 45] to fly to England's court for saving help; Macbeth's agonized vision of a starry good, of 'Heaven's cherubim' horsed in air, and Pity like a babe; those who pray that God may bless them in their fevered dream; above all, Malcolm's description of England's holy King [IV. iii.], health-giver and God-elect who, unlike

Macbeth, has power over 'the evil', in whose court Malcolm borrows 'grace' to combat the nightmare evil of his own land. . . . This description is spoken just before Ross enters with the shattering narration of Macbeth's most dastardly and ruinous crime. The contrast at this instant is vivid and pregnant. The King of England is thus full of supernatural 'grace'. In *Macbeth* this supernatural grace is set beside the supernatural evil. Against such grace Macbeth first struck the blow of evil. Duncan was 'gracious' [III. i. 65]; at his death 'renown and grace is dead' [II. iii. 94]. By the grace of Grace' [V. ix. 38] alone Malcolm will restore health to Scotland. The murk, indeed, thins towards the end. Bright daylight dawns and the green leaves of Birnam come against Macbeth. A world climbs out of its darkness, and in the dawn that panorama below is a thing of nightmare delusion. The 'sovereign flower' [V. ii. 30] is bright-dewed in the bright dawn, and the murk melts into the mists of morning: the Child is crowned, the Tree of Life in his hand.

I have indicated something of the imaginative atmosphere of this play. It is a world shaken by 'fears and scruples' [II. iii. 129]. It is a world where 'nothing is but what is not' [I. iii. 141-42], where 'fair is foul and foul is fair' [I. i. 11]. I have emphasized two complementary elements: (i) the doubts, uncertainties, irrationalities; (ii) the horrors, the dark, the abnormalities. These two elements repel respectively the intellect and the heart of man. And, since the contemplating mind is thus powerfully unified in its immediate antagonism, our reaction holds the positive and tense fear that succeeds nightmare, wherein there is an experience of something at once insubstantial and unreal to the understanding and apallingly horrible to the feelings: this is the evil of *Macbeth.* In this equal repulsion of the dual attributes of the mind a state of singleness and harmony is induced in the recipient, and it is in respect of this that *Macbeth* forces us to a conciousness more exquisitely unified and sensitive than any of the great tragedies but its polar opposite, *Antony and Cleopatra.* This is how the *Macbeth* universe presents to us an experience of absolute evil. Now, these two peculiarities of the whole play will be found also in the purely human element. The two main characteristics of Macbeth's temptation are (i) ignorance of his own motive, and (ii) horror of the deed to which he is being driven. Fear is the primary emotion of the *Macbeth* universe: fear is at the root of Macbeth's crime. (pp. 141-50)

Many minor persons are definitely related to evil: the two— or three—Murderers, the traitors, Cawdor and Macdonald, the drunken porter, doing duty at the gate of Hell. But the major ones too, who are conceived partly as contrasts to Macbeth and his wife, nevertheless succumb to the evil downpressing on the *Macbeth* universe. Banquo is early involved. Returning with Macbeth from a bloody war, he meets the three Weird Sisters. We may imagine that the latter are related to the bloodshed of battle, and that they have waited until after 'the hurly-burly's done' [I. i. 3] to instigate a continuance of blood-lust in the two generals. We must observe that the two generals' feats of arms are described as acts of unprecedented ferocity:

> Except they meant to bathe in reeking wounds,
> Or memorize another Golgotha,
> I cannot tell.
>
> [I. ii. 39-41]

This campaign strikes amaze into men. War is here a thing of blood, not romance. Ross addresses Macbeth:

> Nothing afeared of what thyself did make,
> Strange images of death.
>
> [I. iii. 96-7]

Macbeth's sword 'smoked with bloody execution' [I. ii. 18]. The emphasis is important. The late wine of blood-destruction focuses the inward eyes of these two to the reality of the sisters of blood and evil, and they in turn urge Macbeth to add to those 'strange images of death' the 'great doom's image' [II. iii. 78] of a murdered and sainted king. This knowledge of evil implicit in his meeting with the three Weird Sisters Banquo keeps to himself, and it is a bond of evil between him and Macbeth. It is this that troubles him on the night of the murder, planting a nightmare of unrest in his mind: 'the cursed thoughts that nature gives way to in repose.' He feels the typical *Macbeth* guilt: 'a heavy summons lies like lead' upon him [II. i. 6]. He is enmeshed in Macbeth's horror, and, after the coronation, keeps the guilty secret, and lays to his heart a guilty hope. Banquo is thus involved. So also is Macduff. His cruel desertion of his family is emphasized:

> *L. Macduff.* His flight was madness; when our actions do not,
> Our fears do make us traitors.
> *Ross.*   You know not
> Whether it was his wisdom or his fear.
> *L. Macduff.* Wisdom! to leave his wife, to leave his babes,
> His mansion and his titles in a place
> From whence himself does flee?
>
> [IV. ii. 3-8]

For this, or for some nameless reason, Macduff knows he bears some responsibility for his dear ones' death:

>   Sinful Macduff,
> They were all struck for thee! Naught that I am,
> Not for their own demerits, but for mine,
> Fell slaughter on their souls. Heaven rest them now!
>
> [IV. iii. 224-27]

All the persons seem to share some guilt of the down-pressing enveloping evil. Even Malcolm is forced to repeat crimes on himself. He catalogues every possible sin, and accuses himself of all. Whatever be his reasons, his doing so yet remains part of the integral humanism of this play. The pressure of evil is not relaxed till the end. Not that the persons are 'bad characters'. They are not 'characters' at all, in the proper use of the word. They are but vaguely individualized, and more remarkable for similarity than difference. All the persons are primarily just this: men paralysed by fear and a sense of evil in and outside themselves. They lack will-power: that concept finds no place here. Neither we, nor they, know of what exactly they are guilty: yet they feel guilt.

So, too, with Lady Macbeth. She is not merely a woman of strong will: she is a woman possessed—possessed of evil passion. . . . To interpret the figure of Lady Macbeth in terms of 'ambition' and 'will' is, indeed, a futile commentary. The scope and sweep of her evil passion is a thing tremendous, irresistible, ultimate. She is an embodiment—for one mighty hour—of evil absolute and extreme.

The central human theme—the temptation and crime of Macbeth—is, however, more easy of analysis. The crucial speech runs as follows:

> Why do I yield to that suggestion,
> Whose horrid image doth unfix my hair,
> And makes my seated heart knock at my ribs
> Against the use of nature? Present fears
> Are less than horrible imaginings.

> My thought whose murder yet is but fantastical
> Shakes so my single state of man that function
> Is smother'd in surmise, and nothing is
> But what is not.
>
> [I. iii. 134-42]

These lines, spoken when Macbeth first feels the impending evil, expresses again all those elements I have noticed in the mass-effect of the play: questioning doubt, horror, fear of some unknown power; horrible imaginings of the supernatural and 'fantastical'; an abysm of unreality; disorder on the plane of physical life. This speech is a microcosm of the *Macbeth* vision: it contains the germ of the whole. . . . In this speech we have a swift interpenetration of idea with idea, from fear and disorder, through sickly imaginings, to abysmal darkness, nothingness. 'Nothing is but what is not': that is the text of the play. Reality and unreality change places. We must see that Macbeth, like the whole universe of this play, is paralysed, mesmerized, as though in a dream. This is not merely 'ambition'—it is fear, a nameless fear which yet fixes itself to a horrid image. He is helpless as a man in a nightmare: and this helplessness is integral to the conception—the will-concept is absent. Macbeth may struggle, but he cannot fight: he can no more resist than a rabbit resists a weasel's teeth fastened in its neck, or a bird the serpent's transfixing eye. Now this evil in Macbeth propels him to act absolutely evil. (pp. 150-53)

Whilst Macbeth lives in conflict with himself there is misery, evil, fear: when, at the end, he and others have openly identified himself with evil, he faces the world fearless: nor does he appear evil any longer. The worst element of his suffering has been that secrecy and hypocrisy so often referred to throughout the play. . . . Dark secrecy and night are in Shakespeare ever the badges of crime. But at the end Macbeth has no need of secrecy. He is no longer 'cabin'd, cribb'd, confined, bound in to saucy doubts and fears' [III. iv. 23]. He has won through by excessive crime to an harmonious and honest relation with his surroundings. He has successfully symbolized the disorder of his lonely guilt-stricken soul by disorder in the world, and thus restores balance and harmonious contact. The mighty principle of good planted in the nature of things then asserts itself, condemns him openly, brings him peace. Daylight is brought to Macbeth, as to Scotland, by the accusing armies of Malcolm. (p. 156)

> *G. Wilson Knight, " 'Macbeth' and the Metaphysics of Evil," in his* The Wheel of Fire: Interpretations of Shakespearian Tragedy, *Methuen & Co. Ltd., 1949, pp. 140-59.*

G. WILSON KNIGHT   (essay date 1931)

[*In the following commentary on* Macbeth, *from his* The Imperial Theme *(1931), Knight identifies four primary "life-themes" in the play's imagery, including "warrior-honour," "imperial magnificence," "sleep and feasting," and "ideas of creation and nature's innocence." He proposes that these "life forces" are opposed by forces of evil and death and that Macbeth's courageous warrior-honour conflicts with his ignoble fear—particularly his fear of fear. Macbeth's dream of imperial magnificence, continues Knight, is similarly opposed by the insubstantiality of his false kingship. He also asserts that the play's frequent images of sleeping and feasting suggest the "creative, restorative, forces of nature," but that these too turn against Macbeth. The image of socially unifying feasting that Macbeth desecrates in Acts I and II, Knight argues, becomes, with the witches cauldron scene in Act IV, "a parody of banqueting, a death-banquet." He also states that Macbeth disrupts the unity of nature—"destruction is*

set against creation"—but that in the end Macbeth, *"himself*
destruction, is destroyed." Finally, Knight discusses Macbeth's
attempt to "dislocate time" and destroy the present, an issue
later treated by Stephen Spender (1941) and Tom F. Driver (1960).]

The opposition of life and death forces is strong in *Macbeth.*
Here we find the dark and evil negation endued with a positive
strength, successfully opposing things of health and life. Elsewhere I have discussed the evil: here I give a primary attention
to the life-themes it opposes. They are: (i) Warrior-honour, (ii)
Imperial magnificence, (iii) Sleep and Feasting, and (iv) Ideas
of creation and nature's innocence. These are typical Shakespearian themes. In *Hamlet* we find the same opposition. There
it is often baffling. Here life forces are vividly and very clearly
contrasted with evil, with forces of death and ill-omen, darkness and disorder. Especially, creation is opposed by destruction.

Throughout the main action of *Macbeth* we are confronted by
fear. The word occurs ubiquitously. Fear is at the heart of this
play. Now, if we consider the beginning and ending too, we
find a very clear rhythm of courage, fear, and courage. The
play ends on a note of courage. Macbeth is from the first a
courageous soldier. His warrior-honour is emphasized. He is
'brave Macbeth' [I. ii. 16], 'valour's minion' [I. ii. 19], 'Bellona's bridegroom' [I. ii. 54], 'noble Macbeth' [I. ii. 67].

Duncan exclaims:

> O valiant cousin! worthy gentleman!
>
> [I. ii. 24]

He is 'a peerless kinsman' [I. iv. 58]—the Duncan-Macbeth
relationship is always stressed. Courage in war is a thing of
'honour' [I. ii. 44]. So Macbeth is rewarded for his valour by
a title, earnest of an even greater 'honour' [I. iii. 104]. At the
start Macbeth's honourable valour is firmly contrasted with the
traitor's ignoble revolt. There is no honour in absolute courage:
it must be a service, or it is worthless. Macbeth knows this.
Duncan lavishes praises on him and he replies:

> The service and the loyalty I owe,
> In doing it, pays itself. Your highness' part
> Is to receive our duties; and our duties
> Are to your throne and state, children and servants,
> Which do but what they should, by doing everything
> Safe toward your love and honour.
>
> [I. iv. 22-7]

'Honour' again: the word occurs throughout, strongly emphasized. Notice the 'family' suggestion. Throughout thoughts of
the family (especially childhood), clan, or nation are associated
here. All are units of peace, concord, life. All are twined with
'honour'. So the subject is bound to his lord by love and honour.
The value of warriorship may not be dissociated from allegiance: it is one with the ideal of kingship and imperial power.
But against this bond the evil is urging Macbeth. The evil in
him hates to hear Duncan proclaiming princely honours on
Malcolm, despite the promise of more distinctions for such as
himself. . . . Macbeth really gives way all along from fear:
from fear of fear. He has fought for the King, exulting wildly
in absolute courage. Next there is an extreme reaction to absolute fear. Thus the evil finds the only thing he fears: dishonour. He suffers at his first temptation from abstract fear,
which fixes itself to a ghastly act so that it may form some
contact with the real. That act is one of essential dishonour.
He has thus been terrified ever since the evil gripped him, ever
since he muttered 'present fears are less than horrible imaginings' [I. iii. 137-38]. The same contrast is expressed by him

when fronting Banquo's ghost [III. iv. 98-106]. He fears no
hostile actuality, only the unreal evil, the abstract and absolute
fear. This evil he dare not face from the start, so flies from it
to actuality, expresses it there. He lacks spiritual courage to
meet it on its own spiritual terms, and hence projects his disordered soul into action and murders Duncan. Undue horror
and fear of the deed drives him to it: in the same way his fearful
conscience will not let him rest there, and he commits more
murders. He is all the time flying from evil instead of facing
it. But at the end he emerges fearless. And this is not only a
warrior's valour when opposed by Malcolm's army. By his
murderous acts he has at last actually conquered his fear of
evil, that is, his fear of fear:

> I have supp'd full with horrors;
> Direness, familiar to my slaughterous thoughts,
> Cannot once start me.
>
> [V. v. 13-15]

He sees himself a criminal: sees the evil in himself. Not daring
to see his own potential criminality, he became a criminal. But
now, seeing his own evil, he becomes fearless. From the beginning there was no possible antagonist for the supernatural
evil but an equivalently supernatural good. The evil was never
properly actualized: to fight it there must be a good also set
beyond the actual. Hence the birth of our religions; hence, too,
the constant opposition of 'grace' and thoughts of divinity in
Macbeth set against the things of dark and evil. Macbeth at
the last, by self-knowledge, attains grace. (pp. 125-28)

This warrior-theme is closely twined with our next positive
value: imperial magnificence. On the ethical—as opposed to
the metaphysical—plane, Macbeth fails through trying to advance from deserved honour as a noble thane to the higher
kingly honour to which he has no rights. This kingship he
attains, yet never really possesses it. He is never properly king:
his regality is a mockery. Now, through the murk which envelops the action, there are yet glimpses of this sensuous glory
which Macbeth desires but which ever eludes his grasp. Such
suggestions stare out, dully glowing, solid things of world-
power. This sensuous glory is always undermined, blurred, by
the dark, the abysmal negation, the evil. The *Macbeth*-world
is insubstantial, an emptiness, its bottom knocked out of it; a
hideous nightmare falling, like Satan dropping in his flight
through chaos. Solidity, reality, are grasped in vain by the
falling soul. Macbeth and his wife reach out for power and
glory: the sense-forms correspondent are crowns and sceptres.
The glint of these burns grimly and sullenly through the murk.
Their solidity is rendered dubious, is blurred by the evil, the
dark, the insubstantiality. They are things of noble reality dreamed
in hell; unenjoyed by the guilty soul, to whom nightmare is
reality and all sense-splendour an unattainable dream. Outward
royalty is, by itself, a nothing in comparison with nature's
kingliness:

> Our fears in Banquo
> Stick deep; and in his royalty of nature
> Reigns that which would be fear'd.
>
> [III. i. 48-50]

So he fears, envies, hates Banquo who has the reality of honour
whereas he has but a mockery, a ghoulish dream of royalty.
He envies Banquo's posterity their royal destiny won in terms
of nature, not in terms of crime; and is maddened at the insecure
mockery of his own kingship:

> Upon my head they placed a fruitless crown,
> And put a barren sceptre in my gripe . . .
>
> [III. i. 60-1]

He has grasped these gold power-symbols to himself: and they are utterly 'barren' in every sense; barren of joy and content, barren of posterity. So falsely has Macbeth made himself the centre and end of all things: a 'fruitless' philosophy. To this evil has tricked him. He and his wife are without 'content' [III. ii. 5]. . . . Macbeth's agony is not properly understood till we realize his utter failure to receive any positive joy from the imperial magnificence to which he aspired. Hence his violent jealousy when he sees Banquo's crowned and sceptred posterity. He lives a life of death, in darkness, reft of all sense-grandeur and solid joy. He cannot conquer the evil in his soul and rest in the acclamations and honour of his land: rather spreads his own spiritual darkness over Scotland. (pp. 129-32)

So much for Macbeth's insecure tenure of imperial magnificance. Now I pass to the even more fundamental ideas of 'sleep', 'feasting', and 'nature'. Sleep and feasting are important. Peaceful sleep is often disturbed by nightmare; this I have observed elsewhere. Here we may observe how closely 'sleep' is twined with 'feasting'. Both are creative, restorative, forces of nature. So Macbeth and his Queen are reft of both during the play's action. Feasting and sleep are twin life-givers:

> Methought I heard a voice cry, 'Sleep no more!
> Macbeth does murder sleep', the innocent sleep,
> Sleep that knits up the ravell'd sleave of care,
> The death of each day's life, sore labour's bath,
> Balm of hurt minds, great nature's second course,
> Chief nourisher in life's feast—
>
> [II. ii. 32-7]

The retributive suffering is apt. Macbeth murdered Duncan in sleep, after feasting him. It was a blow delivered at 'innocent sleep'; sleep, like death in *Antony and Cleopatra,* the gentle nurse of life. Macbeth does more than murder a living being: he murders life itself. Because he murdered hospitality and sleep, therefore his punishment is a living death, without peaceful sleep or peaceful feeding. The thought is ever—as I have noted above—of a society, or family, built into a unity by mutual respect, place and degree, in which alone 'honour' can exist: so Macbeth's crime is a kind of parricide—hence the suggestions of parricide in II. iv. and III. vi. Such suggestions, untrue to fact, hold yet an imaginative truth. And this society is a life-force blending with 'sleep' and 'feasts'.

Now the evil-feasting opposition is powerful here. Duncan compares his joy in Macbeth's success to a banquet:

> True, worthy Banquo; he is full so valiant;
> And in his commendations I am fed;
> It is a banquet to me.
>
> [I. iv. 54-6]

Macbeth's honourable prowess is a life-bringing food to Duncan, to Scotland. Lady Macbeth's hospitality to Duncan is emphasized: she is his 'honoured hostess' [I. vi. 10], his 'fair and noble hostess' [I. vi. 24]. She and Macbeth entertain him with a fine feast:

> *Hautboys and torches. Enter a Sewer, and divers Servants with dishes and service, and pass over the stage.*
>
> [s.d. I. vii]

Feasting and music: a usual grouping of effects, as in *Timon, Coriolanus,* and *Antony and Cleopatra.* Lady Macbeth plots murder whilst Duncan is feasting:

He has almost supp'd: why have you left the chamber?

> [I. vii. 29]

Duncan, wearied by 'his day's hard journey' [I. vii. 63], goes to his chambers to sleep 'soundly' [I. vii. 63], after having distributed his bounty to his hosts: he is 'in unusual pleasure' and 'shut up in measureless content' [II. i. 13-17], the 'content' that his murderers never achieve [III. ii. 5]. So Lady Macbeth is again called 'most kind hostess' [II. i. 16]. Next 'wine and wassail' [I. vii. 64] is put to the dastardly use of drugging Duncan's grooms. They are made 'the slaves of drink and thralls of sleep' [III. vi. 13]. Lady Macbeth steels herself by the same means [II. ii. 1]. There is the grim irony of the bell which 'invites' Macbeth to the murder:

> Go, bid thy mistress, when my drink is ready
> She strike upon the bell.
>
> [II. i. 31-2]

The domestic and feminine note jars hideously with the horror beneath. 'Drink' is often suggested. There is the porter whose drunken festivities are used to heighten our awareness that hellish evil is stalking the earth: here again, evil conquers the innocent festivity. Through all these effects we see the same opposition: feasting, a life-force, especially the hospitality wherewith the sacred Duncan is greeted by his 'kinsman' and 'subject'; and against this, the hideous murder. It is at once, as Macbeth observes [I. vii. 12-16] a desecration of a 'double trust': hospitality, social order, allegiance, life itself: 'the wine of life' [II. iii. 95] is drawn.

After the murder, feasting is again emphasized. It is shown how

> . . . this even-handed justice
> Commends the ingredients of our poisoned chalice
> To our own lips.
>
> [I. vii. 10-11]

Macbeth finds he has 'put rancours in the vessel of' his 'peace' [III. i. 66]. He may not feast with his lords in peace and harmony. Banquo's ghost breaks into the attempted festivity, disperses it, throws it into disorder. At the start, hospitality, conviviality, 'welcome' and 'degree' are emphasized: the very things Macbeth has so brutally desecrated. . . . The murderer withdraws Macbeth's attention and Lady Macbeth again stresses the thought of welcome:

> *Lady Macbeth.*   My royal lord,
> You do not give the cheer: the feast is sold
> That is not often vouch'd, while 'tis a-making,
> 'Tis given with welcome: to feed were best at home;
> From thence the sauce to meat is ceremony;
> Meeting were bare without it.
> *Macbeth.*   Sweet remembrancer!
> Now, good digestion wait on appetite,
> And health on both!
>
> [III. iv. 31-8]

'Digestion', 'health', 'sauce', 'meat'. Against this life-force of feasting, conviviality, social friendliness and order, comes a death, a ghost, smashing life-forms with phantasms of evil and guilt: an unreality, a 'nothing', like the air-drawn dagger, creating chaos of order and reality, dispersing the social unit. It is the conquest of the real and the life-giving by the unreal and deathly. It corresponds to the murderous deed whose 'hideous trumpet' [II. iii. 82] waked the 'downy sleep' [II. iii. 76] of Macbeth's guests at Inverness, raising them to walk like 'sprites' [II. iii. 79] from death, like Hamlet's father, shattering at that dead hour all natural peace and rest. After the ghost's disappearance Macbeth recovers, again speaks words of 'love', 'health', and friendly communion:

> Come, love and health to all;
> Then I'll sit down. Give me some wine; fill full.
> I drink to the general joy o' the whole table,
> And to our dear friend Banquo, whom we miss;
> Would he were here! to all, and him, we thirst,
> And all to all.
>
> [III. iv. 86-91]

The ghost reappears. It is, like the phantasmal dagger, a 'horrible shadow', an 'unreal mockery' [III. iv. 105-06], and it opposes the natural joys of feasting and 'health', life-forms, life-forces, just as Macbeth's original 'horrible imaginings', the 'horrid-image' of the proposed murder, unfixed his hair and made his heart beat wildly 'against the use of nature', shook his 'state of man' and smothered 'function' in 'surmise' [I. iii. 140-41]. So the evil makes of unity, 'love', feasting and social order a chaos, dispersing and disintegrating the society. The disorder-thought is important, running throughout Shakespeare and vividly apparent here: order is the natural grouping of life-forms, disorder is evil—Macbeth's crime was essentially an act of disorder, a desecration of the ties of hospitality, blood-relationship, and allegiance. (pp. 134-38)

The three outstanding scenes of the middle action all illustrate the evil-feasting opposition. First there is Duncan's murder in sleep and after elaborate feasting by his host, kinsman, and subject: all concepts which stress Macbeth's ruthless desecration of social units of human life. Next, we find Banquo's ghost violently forbidding that Macbeth enjoy that hospitality and feasting which he has desecrated. Our third scene is that with the Weird Sisters in their cavern. The contrast with the banquet scene is vivid. Here we watch a devil's-banqueting, the Weird Women with their cauldron and its holocaust of hideous ingredients. The banquet-idea has been inverted. Instead of suggesting health, this one is brewed to cause 'toil and trouble'. The ingredients are absurd bits of life like those of Othello's ravings [*Othello,* iv. i. 42], now jumbled together to 'boil and bake' in the cauldron: 'eye of newt', 'toe of frog', a dog's tongue, a lizard's leg, and so on. . . . But not only are there animal-pieces: we have a Jew's liver, a Turk's nose, a Tartar's lips, the 'finger of birth-strangled babe' [IV. i. 13]. Though the bodies from which these are torn are often themselves, by association, evil, yet we must note the additional sense of chaos, bodily desecration, and irrationality in the use of these absurd derelict members, things like the 'pilot's thumb' [I. iii. 28] mentioned earlier. The ingredients suggest an absolute indigestibility. It is a parody of banqueting, a death-banquet, a 'hell-broth' [IV .i. 19]. It is all quite meaningless, nameless, negative, utterly black:

> *Macbeth.* How now, you secret, black and midnight hags!
>   What is't you do!
> *The Weird Women.* A deed without a name.
>
> [IV. i. 48-9]

Formerly an 'unreal mockery', a death-phantom, shattered a life-giving banquet. Here, by inversion, a death-banquet produces from its hideous 'gruel' [IV. i. 32] not bodily sustenance, but more phantoms. The one is a life reality disorganized by a spirit suggesting life that is past (Banquo's ghost); the other is a feast of death and essential disorder (because of the disjointed ingredients) giving birth to spirits suggesting life that is to come (the Apparitions and their prophecies). The evil

disorder in the cauldron produces forms of futurity, futurity being essentially a disorder-force until it is bodied into the life-forms of the present. Thus the spirits, whether of life past or life to come, are equally inimical to Macbeth's peace. This hell-broth is a death-food, though it is not meant to be eaten: eating is good, in the cause of life. It brings forth spirits, that is evil, not earthly, things: spirit uninfused in bodies being, in the phraseology of my interpretations, purely evil. Equally evil are the correspondent bodies disorganized (bodies of nature, state, family, or man): for bodies disorganized are formless, and, if formless, soulless, 'soul' and 'form' being naturally equated. Therefore here and elsewhere, all disorder symbols may readily be equated with 'naked spirit'. So here the disordered ingredients produce correlevant spirits, apparitions rise from the deathly cauldron and its chaotic contents. Though in this sense, and in their effect, evil, these spirits yet accomplish their purpose by suggesting life-forces: the Bloody Child and the Child crowned with a Tree in his hand. But to Macbeth they bring evil. On them Macbeth's derelict soul feeds its fill, feeds on death-food—'I have supp'd full with horrors' [V. v. 13]. He drinks down the ghostly future. . . . It is all a death-banquet and its spiritual food, to him, a poison. Hence it at once leads Macbeth to a deed of family destruction. He murders Lady Macduff, her children, Macduff's household, all that 'trace him in his line' [IV. i. 153]; again, a chaotic blow against a life-force, a family unit.

The Cauldron Scene, with its disjected members of animal and human bodies, and also its prophecies relating to 'nature', suggests a yet wider view of the opposition active throughout *Macbeth*. The *Macbeth*-evil attacks honour and imperial magnificence, life-forms of feeding, health, society: it also decisively attacks 'nature'. Nature in its purity is clearly another 'life' theme, only one degree removed from 'feasting'. But nature is seldom apparent here in purity and grace: when it is, that appearance is important. Nature-references blend with human themes, especially in point of procreation and childhood. (pp. 138-41)

Macbeth's crime is a blow against nature's unity and peace, a hideous desecration of all creative, family, and social duties, all union and concord: this is the bond he breaks, the 'great bond' that keeps him 'pale' [III. ii. 49]. Now that 'humane statute' has 'purged the general weal' [III. iv. 75] it is natural to mankind to live in peace and love. But Macbeth breaks all fetters of restraining humanity. He ruthlessly destroys Macduff's family. Lady Macduff thus compares her lord to a parent bird in a passage which closely corresponds to the dialogue just quoted. Macduff, mysteriously conquered by the evil, or, rather, in order to oppose it (both are fundamentally the same) has deserted his family:

> He loves us not;
> He wants the natural touch: for the poor wren,
> The most diminutive of birds, will fight,
> Her young ones in her nest, against the owl.
>
> [IV. ii. 8-11]

She urges that Macduff's flight was dictated by 'fear', not 'love' or 'wisdom'. It is partly true: fear grips everyone whilst the evil rages in Scotland. Macduff is forced to sacrifice the bond of family love—'those precious motives, those strong knots of love' [IV. iii. 27]. He leaves them to their death:

> What, all my pretty chickens and their dam
>   At one fell swoop?
>
> [IV. iii. 218-19]

An unnatural act, necessitated by the unnatural evil. All is chaos, turbulence, disorder—to be contrasted with family or national peace, humanity's natural concord. (pp. 142-43)

Most important of all, we must observe the emergence of child-references. The negation here opposes all values, health, and nature: the creative process. Destruction is set against creation: hence our many references to mother's 'milk', the martlet's and wren's nest and young, to 'chickens', 'lambs', the strange use of 'egg' and 'fry' [IV. iii. 83-4], and the child-themes: the phrase, 'child of integrity' [IV. iii. 115], Lady Macbeth's baby at her breast, the baby-spirit of Pity astride the winds of heaven, the two child apparitions—the Bloody Child, and the Child whose 'baby-brow' is crowned with gold: Banquo's descendants, Malcolm, Donalbain, Fleance, the scene of Macduff's son, his 'babes' [IV. i. 152], crying 'orphans' [IV. iii. 5], the birth-strangled babe [IV. i. 30], young Siward, who 'only lived but till he was a man' [V. ix. 6], and the other 'unrough youths' [V. ii. 10]. Subjects are 'children' [I. iv. 25] of the king, Scotland the 'mother' of its people now turned to a 'grave', a vivid birth-death contrast [IV. iii. 166], Scotland's peace is those people's 'birth-dom' [IV. iii. 4], the throne Malcolm's 'due of birth' [III. vi. 25], the Queen that 'bore' him a saintly mother [IV. iii. 109]. The 'nothing' of death-atmosphere, here active and pervasive, silhouettes these 'birth' and 'child' themes which struggle to assert themselves, struggle to be born from death into life. At the end youth comes armed against Macbeth. Birth opposes death. 'Issue' is an important word. Youth and babyhood oppose our evil. Macbeth murdered aged innocence and purity linked to the 'great office' [I. vii. 18] of kingship. Child innocence with all heaven, all imperial sovereignty, and all nature on its side, tree-sceptred, confronts the murderer:

> What is this
> That rises like the issue of a king,
> And wears upon his baby-brow the round
> And top of sovereignty?
>
> [IV. i. 86-9]

Macbeth, himself destruction, is destroyed: thus he is a symbol of time itself from its death-aspect. In so far as you see time as destruction, you see it itself continually destroyed: in so far as a man becomes destructive, he is himself destroyed. The time-concept is very clearly woven with Macbeth's tale; contrasting with the eternity of *Antony and Cleopatra*. The Weird Women first met Macbeth as voices of the past, present, and future, with their prophecies about Glamis, Cawdor, and Kingship. They suggest absolute time. Macbeth's crime is, however, an attempt to dislocate time, to wrench the future into the present, just as it is a crime against order and degree, a wild vaulting ambition to attain unrightful 'honour'. He wants all time to be his, and so gets none of it. He would 'ravin up' his 'own life's means' [II. iv. 28-9]. He wrongs the majestic and unhurrying pace of time. What is time but a succession of deaths, minute by minute? And yet again it is a succession of births. Macbeth would expedite the death-aspect of time, and so catch the 'future in the instant' [I. v. 58], would destroy the present, Duncan. But in the Cauldron Scene we see time as creation. There is a vivid destruction-birth sequence. The Armed Head, recalling Macdonwald's head 'fixed' on the 'battlements' [I. ii. 23], blends with the 'chaos' and 'disorder' thought throughout, the torn animal and human limbs that constitute the cauldron's ingredients, and moreover suggests both the iron force of evil and also its final destruction. This is followed by the Bloody Child and the 'Child, crowned, with

a Tree in his hand'; observe how the crowned contrasts with the severed head, and how its victory is directly associated with nature. The order is important. Violent destruction, itself to be destroyed; the blood-agony of birth that travails to wrench into existence a force to right the sickening evil; the future birth splendid in crowned and accomplished royalty. It suggests the creative process in all its miraculous strength and power to pursue its purpose. Ironically, these apparitions give to Macbeth, who regards their words whilst remaining blind to themselves, not despair, but hope. He, who has placed his trust in chaos, hopes himself to 'live the lease of nature' [IV. i. 99]. But this joy is short-lived. For we may note again how powerfully our positive, creative essences are next suggested by the 'show of eight Kings'. They are rich in imperial glory. But they are more. They, too, suggest, in a wide sense, the creative process itself, the process Macbeth would annihilate, would cut off at the present root. He too readily grasped his own future to himself: but would annihilate the future of others. He would have time disjointed to serve his ends. But Banquo is to have all the wealth of posterity, all that creative joy in which alone human happiness consists. Too late he learns that to get kings is more blessed than to be king, creation more blessed than possession. For possession divorced from creation melts in the grasping hand: like flowers 'dying or ere they sicken' [IV. iii. 173]. . . . . Macbeth is childless, with a fruitless crown and barren sceptre, as evil is ever childless, unproductive. So he knows the process of life to hold no hope for him. It is merely a cruel catalogue of deaths strung together in time:

> To-morrow, and to-morrow, and to-morrow,
> Creeps in this petty pace from day to day
> To the last syllable of recorded time,
> And all our yesterdays have lighted fools,
> The way to dusty death. Out, out, brief candle!
> Life's but a walking shadow, a poor player
> That struts and frets his hour upon the stage
> And then is heard no more: it is a tale
> Told by an idiot, full of sound and fury,
> Signifying nothing.
>
> [V. v. 19-28]

He sees all life from the death-aspect of time. And he is now himself reconciled to the 'nothing', the negation of evil and death. He finds peace in the profundities of his own nihilistic death-experience: death and 'nothing' are realities: life has no meaning. The evil has worked its way with him, and left him with no hope in life. Even so, there is yet death. Like the earlier Cawdor, he dies well.

The Weird Women, I have said, are not themselves from every aspect opposed to creation and life. They know evil to be futile, they know their own futility. They are unreal, and know it, know their existence and purposes to be self-contradictory. So, of their two main prophecies in the Cauldron Scene, those relating to Birnam Wood and Macduff's birth, the one is fulfilled in terms of natural law, the other in terms of an event itself so abnormal as to be all but unnatural:

> And let the angel whom thou still hast served
> Tell thee, Macduff was from his mother's womb
> Untimely ripp'd.
>
> [V. viii. 14-16]

If, as has been sometimes suggested, Macduff means that his mother died before his birth, the suggestion is pregnant to our interpretation: life born out of death. But, in whatever sense we take its meaning, we see that disorder itself turns on disorder. So, too, the death-concept ever contradicts itself and becomes life to any intense contemplation. Absolute disorder prohibits self-consistency: it helps to slay itself. Death gives birth to life. Not nature alone, but 'both the worlds' [III. ii. 16], natural and unnatural, life and death, come against Macbeth. (pp. 149-53)

In a final judgement the whole play may be writ down as a wrestling of destruction with creation: with sickening shock the phantasmagoria of death and evil are violently loosed on earth, and for a while the agony endures, destructive; there is a wrenching of new birth, itself disorderly and unnatural in this disordered world, and then creation's more firm-set sequent concord replaces chaos. The baby-peace is crowned. (p. 153)

> G. Wilson Knight, "The Milk of Concord: An Essay on Life-themes in 'Macbeth'," in his The Imperial Theme: Further Interpretations of Shakespeare's Tragedies Including the Roman Plays, Oxford University Press, London, 1931, pp. 125-53.

WALTER CLYDE CURRY   (essay date 1933)

[Curry, an American scholar, produced studies on Chaucer and Milton as well as Shakespeare's Philosophical Patterns (1937), which contains two chapters treating the philosophical background of Macbeth. In the first of these chapters, originally published in the journal Studies in Philology in 1933, Curry discusses the witches in Macbeth and the precise nature of the evil they embody, an issue that has been treated variously by Samuel Johnson (1745), Charles Lamb (1808), Franz Horn (1823), G. G. Gervinus (1849-50), Denton J. Snider (1887), and A. C. Bradley (1904). Curry argues that the witches are consistent with Eliza-

Act V. Scene vii. Macbeth and Young Siward. By H. Corbould (1826). The Department of Rare Books and Special Collections, The University of Michigan Library.

bethan notions of demonic spirits and that they are not merely hallucinations, but representatives of an objective evil. The Weird Sisters, he continues, are but one part of the demonic powers that "insinuate themselves into the essence of the natural world"; the natural disturbances, Macbeth's visionary dagger, Banquo's ghost, and Lady Macbeth's "demoniacal somnambulism" are also manifestations of these powers. Shakespeare has dramatized, Curry concludes, "the Christian conception of a metaphysical world of objective evil." In Curry's second chapter on Macbeth, not excerpted here, he examines Macbeth as an individual possessed of free will who, according to the moral philosophy of Shakespeare's age, forsakes good for evil.]

That the Weird Sisters possess . . . perennial and astounding vitality is attested by the whole sweep of Shakespearean criticism. All hands seem to be convinced that they symbolize or represent evil in its most malignant form, though there is to be found little unanimity of opinion regarding the precise nature of that evil, whether it is subjective or objective or both, whether mental or metaphysical. (pp. 55-6)

The single purpose of this study is to examine, as thoroughly as possible, the nature of that evil which the Weird Sisters are said to symbolize or represent, and to reproduce one aspect at least of the metaphysical groundwork of the drama. It presupposes that in Shakespeare's time evil was considered to be both subjective and, so far as the human mind is concerned, a non-subjective reality; that is to say, evil manifested itself subjectively in the spirits of men and objectively in a metaphysical world whose existence depended in no degree upon the activities of the human mind. This objective realm of evil was not governed by mere vague and irrational forces; it was peopled and controlled by the malignant wills of intelligences—evil spirits, devils, demons, Satan—who had the ability to project their power into the workings of nature and to influence the human spirit. Such a system of evil was raised to the dignity of a science and a theology. (p. 58)

Since . . . this belief was so universal at the time, we may reasonably suppose that Shakespeare's Weird Sisters are intended to symbolize or represent the metaphysical world of evil spirits. Whether one considers them as human witches in league with the powers of darkness, or as actual demons in the form of witches, or as merely inanimate symbols, the power which they wield or represent or symbolize is ultimately demonic. Let us, therefore, exercise wisdom in the contemplation of the nature, power, and illusions of unclean spirits.

In the meantime, we may conveniently assume that in essence the Weird Sisters are demons or devils in the form of witches. At least their control over the primary elements of nature . . . would seem to indicate as much. Why, then, should Shakespeare have chosen to present upon his stage these witch-likenesses rather than devils in devil-forms? Two equally valid reasons may be suggested. In the first place, the rather sublime devil and his angels of the earlier drama, opponents of God in the cosmic order and destroyers of men, had degenerated in the hands of later dramatists into mere comic figures; by Shakespeare's time folk conception had apparently so dominated dramatic practice and tradition that cloven hoof, horns, and tail became associated in the popular imagination only with the ludicrous. . . . In the second place, witches had acquired no such comic associations. They were essentially tragic beings who, for the sake of certain abnormal powers, had sold themselves to the devil. As we have seen, everybody believed in them as channels through which the malignity of evil spirits might be visited upon human beings. Here, then, were terrifying figures, created by a contemporary public at the most intense moment of witchcraft delusion, which Shakespeare found ready to his hand. Accordingly he appropriately employed witch-figures as dramatic symbols, but the Weird Sisters are in reality demons, actual representatives of the world of darkness opposed to good. (pp. 59-61)

[The] Weird Sisters take on a dignity, a dark grandeur, and a terror-inspiring aspect which is in no way native to the witch-symbol as such. In the first place, they are clairvoyant in the sense that whatever happens outwardly among men is immediately known to them. In the thunder and lightning of a desert place they look upon the distant battle, in which Macbeth overcomes the King's enemies, and conjecture that it will be lost and won before the day ends. They do not travel to the camp near Forres where Duncan receives news of the battle, but when Macbeth is created Thane of Cawdor they seem to know it instantly. They must be aware that it is Macbeth who murders Duncan, because Hecate berates them for having trafficked with him in affairs of death without her help. All the events of the drama—the murder of Banquo and the escape of Fleance, the striking down of Lady Macduff and her children, Macbeth's accumulating sins and tragic death—must, as they unfold in time, be immediately perceived by these creatures in whom the species of these things are connatural. Moreover, by virtue of their spiritual substance they are acquainted with the causes of things, and, through the application of wisdom gained by long experience, are able to prognosticate future events in relation to Macbeth and Banquo: Macbeth shall be king, none of woman born shall harm him, he shall never be overcome until Birnam wood shall come against him to Dunsinane; Banquo shall be no king, but he shall beget kings. The external causes upon which these predictions are based may to a certain extent be manipulated by these demonic forces: but the internal causes, *i.e.,* the forces which move the will of Macbeth to action, are imperfectly known and only indirectly subject to their influence. They cannot read his inmost thoughts—only God can do that—but from observaton of facial expression and other bodily manifestations, they surmise with comparative accuracy what passions drive him and what dark desires of his await their fostering. Realizing that he desires the kingdom, they prophesy that he shall be king, thus arousing his passions and inflaming his imagination to the extent that nothing is but what is not. This influence gained over him is later augmented when they cause to appear before him evil spirits, who condense the air about them into the shapes of an armed Head, a bloody Child, and a crowned Child. These demonic presences materialize to the sound of thunder and seem to speak to him with human voices, suggesting evil and urging him toward destruction with the pronouncement of half-truths. These are illusions created by demonic powers, objective appearances with a sensible content sufficient to arouse his ocular and auditory senses.

Indeed, the Weird Sisters are always illusions when they appear as such upon the stage; that is to say, their forms clothe the demonic powers which inform them. This is suggested by the facility with which they materialize to human sight and disappear. King James suspects that the Devil is able to render witches invisible when he pleases, but these Weird Sisters seem of their own motion to melt into thin air and vanish like a dream. Instead of disappearing with the swift movement which characterizes demonic transportation of bodies, they simply fade into nothingness. This suggests that their movements from place to place are not continuous necessarily. Though one of them plans to sail to Aleppo in a sieve, we feel that for the most part they appear in one place at one instant and at another place the next instant, or at whatever time pleases them, without being subject to the laws of time and place. I would not, however, force this point. At any rate, all their really important actions in the drama suggest that they are demons in the guise of witches.

But the witch-appearances constitute only a comparatively small part of the demonic manifestations in *Macbeth.* Many of the natural occurrences and all of the supernatural phenomena may be attributed to the activities of the metaphysical world of evil spirits. Whether visible or invisible these malignant substances insinuate themselves into the essence of the natural world and hover about the souls of men and women; they influence and in a measure direct human thought and action by means of illusions, hallucinations, and inward persuasion. For example, since they are able to manipulate nature's germens and control the winds, we may reasonably suppose that the storm which rages over Macbeth's castle and environs in Act II is no ordinary tempest caused by the regular movements of the heavenly bodies, but rather a manifestation of demonic power over the elements of nature. Indeed, natural forces seem to be partly in abeyance; o'er the one half-world nature seems dead. A strange, mephitic atmosphere hangs over and pervades the castle and adjacent country-side; an unnatural darkness, for ages the milieu of evil forces, blots out the stars and in the morning strangles the rising sun. Where Lennox lies—evidently not far distant—the night is so unruly that chimneys are blown down, lamentings and strange screams of death are heard in the air; and the firm-set earth is so sensitized by the all-pervading demonic energy that it is feverous and shakes. Macbeth senses this magnetization, and fears that the very stones will prate of his whereabouts. As the drunken Porter feels, Macbeth's castle is literally the mouth of hell through which evil spirits emerge in this darkness to cause upheavals in nature. Within the span of his seventy years the Old Man has experienced many strange and dreadful things, but they are as trifles in comparison with the occurrences of this rough night. Demonic powers are rampant in nature. (pp. 77-81)

Macbeth's vision of a dagger is an hallucination caused immediately, indeed, by disturbed bodily humours and spirits but ultimately by demonic powers, who have so controlled and manipulated these bodily forces as to produce the effect they desire. And a like explanation may be offered of the mysterious voice which Macbeth seems to hear after the murder, crying exultantly to all the house, 'Sleep no more! Macbeth does murder sleep' [II. ii. 32-3]. (p. 84)

Banquo's ghost is an infernal illusion, created out of air by demonic forces and presented to Macbeth's sight at the banquet in order that the murderer may be confused and utterly confounded. The second appearance of Banquo's ghost, together with the show of eight kings [IV. i. 112], is undoubtedly the result of demonic machinations. Having persuaded and otherwise incited Macbeth to sin and crime, the Devil and his angels now employ illusions which lead to his betrayal and final destruction.

And finally, certain aspects of Lady Macbeth's experience indicate that she is possessed of demons. At least, in preparation for the coming of Duncan under her battlements, she calls upon precisely those metaphysical forces which have seemed to crown Macbeth. The murdering ministers whom she invokes for aid are described as being sightless substances, *i.e.,* not evil thoughts and 'grim imaginings' but objective substantial forms, invisible bad angels, to whose activities may be attributed all the unnatural occurrences of nature. Whatever in the phenomenal world becomes beautiful in the exercise of its normal function is to them foul, and *vice versa;* they wait upon nature's mischief. She recognizes that they infest the filthy atmosphere of this world and the blackness of the lower regions; therefore she welcomes a night palled in the dunnest smoke of hell, so dense that not even heaven may pierce the blanket of the dark and behold her projected deed. Her prayer is apparently answered; with the coming of night her castle is, as we have seen, shrouded in just such a blackness as she desires. (pp. 85-6)

What happens to Lady Macbeth in the course of Act IV is not immediately clear. Apparently there is a steady deterioration of her demon-possessed body until, at the beginning of Act V, the organs of her spirit are impaired to the point of imminent dissolution. Such a great perturbation of nature has seized upon her that she walks night after night in slumbery agitation, with eyes wide open but with the senses shut. There appears a definite cleavage in her personality. Her will, which in conscious moments guards against any revelation of her guilty experiences, is submerged; and her infected mind is forced to discharge its secrets in the presence of alien ears. Her symptoms in these circumstances resemble those of the ordinary somnambulist, but the violence of her reactions indicates that her state is what may be called 'somnambuliform possession' or 'demoniacal somnambulism.' . . . The most outstanding characteristic of this demoniacal somnambulism, which in the course of history has been more common than any other form of possession, is that the normal individuality disappears and seems to be replaced by a second personality, which speaks through the patient's mouth. This strange individuality always confesses wrong-doing, and sometimes relates a sort of life-history consisting frequently of the patient's reminiscences or memories. Now the physician to Lady Macbeth recognizes these symptoms in his patient. Sometimes, to be sure, he has known those who have walked in their sleep who have died holily in their beds. But this disease is beyond his practice; this heart sorely charged with perilous stuff needs the divine more than the physician. The demonic substances she welcomed into her body now employ her bodily functions to disclose her criminal experiences. (pp. 89-90)

Shakespeare's age would undoubtedly have pronounced Lady Macbeth's sleep-walking an instance of demoniacal somnambulism. Practically everybody, so far as may be determined, accepted demonic possession as an established fact. The New Testament affirmed it; the Church Fathers had elaborated and illustrated it; the Catholic Church made of it a firm article of faith and proceeded to exorcise demons by means of recognized rituals involving holy-water and cross, bell, book, and candle; and Protestants could not consistently deny it, or if some of them did, peremptory experience forced them to take a doubtful refuge in the conception of obsession, which produced the effects of possession. . . . Fortunately Shakespeare has spared us, in the case of Lady Macbeth, a representation of the more disgusting physical symptoms of the diabolically possessed, such as astounding contortions of the body and fantastic creations of the delirious mind. He merely suggests these horrors in the report of the Doctor that the Lady is troubled with thick-coming fancies and in the expressed opinion of some that she took her own life by self and violent hands. He is interested primarily in presenting not so much the physical as the spiritual disintegration of this soul-weary creature possessed of devils.

In this manner, it seems to me, Shakespeare has informed *Macbeth* with the Christian conception of a metaphysical world

of objective evil. The whole drama is saturated with the malignant presences of demonic forces; they animate nature and ensnare human souls by means of diabolical persuasion, by hallucination, infernal illusion, and possession. They are, in the strictest sense, one element in that Fate which God in his providence has ordained to rule over the bodies and, it is possible, over the spirits of men. And the essence of this whole metaphysical world of evil intelligences is distilled by Shakespeare's imagination and concentrated in those marvellous dramatic symbols, the Weird Sisters. (pp. 91-3)

Walter Clyde Curry, "The Demonic Metaphysics of Macbeth," in his Shakespeare's Philosophical Patterns, *Louisiana State University Press, 1937, pp. 53-93.*

L. C. KNIGHTS (essay date 1933)

[*A renowned English Shakespearean scholar, Knights followed the precepts of I. A. Richards and F. R. Leavis and sought an underlying pattern in all of Shakespeare's work. His* How Many Children Had Lady Macbeth? *(1933)—a milestone study in the twentieth-century reaction to the Shakespearean criticism of the previous century—disparages the traditional emphasis on "character" as an approach that inhibits the reader's total response to Shakespeare's plays. In the application of the critical approach developed in that essay, Knights calls* Macbeth *"a statement of evil." He argues that the play contains two main themes, "the themes of the reversal of values and of unnatural disorder," and a related third theme involved with "deceitful appearance." Knights examines the references to these concerns throughout the play, noting in particular the conflict between the images of unnatural chaos and those of supernatural grace, an issue later treated by Paul N. Siegel (1957) and D. A. Traversi (1968). Macbeth, Knights asserts, attempts to restore order to the confusion caused by Duncan's murder, but fails tragically because his efforts rely on murder. He further states that the natural order is reestablished by the forces of Malcolm and Macduff, who are associated with supernatural grace.*]

Macbeth is a statement of evil. I use the word "statement" (unsatisfactory as it is) in order to stress those qualities which are "nondramatic," if drama is defined according to the canons of William Archer or Dr. Bradley. It also happens to be poetry, which means that the apprehension of the whole can only be obtained from a lively attention to the parts, whether they have an immediate bearing on the main action or "illustrate character," or not. Two main themes, which can only be separated for the purpose of analysis, are blended in the play,—the themes of the reversal of values and of unnatural disorder. And closely related to each is a third theme, that of the deceitful appearance, and consequent doubt, uncertainty and confusion. All this is obscured by false assumptions about the category "drama"; *Macbeth* has greater affinity with *The Waste Land* than with *The Doll's House.*

Each theme is stated in the first act. The first scene, every word of which will bear the closest scrutiny, strikes one dominant chord:

> Faire is foule, and foule is faire,
> Hover through the fogge and filthie ayre.
>
> [I. i. 11-12]

It is worth remarking that "Hurley-burley" implies more than "the tumult of sedition or insurrection." Both it and "when the Battaile's lost, and wonne"[I. i. 4] suggest the kind of metaphysical pitch-and-toss which is about to be played with good and evil. At the same time we hear the undertone of uncertainty: the scene opens with a question, and the second line suggests a region where the elements are disintegrated as they never are in nature; thunder and lightning are disjoined, and offered as alternatives. We should notice also that the scene expresses the same rhythm as the play as a whole: the general crystallizes into the immediate particular ("Where the place?"— "Upon the Heath."—"There to meet with Macbeth." [I. i. 6-7] and then dissolves again into the general presentment of hideous gloom. All is done with the greatest speed, economy and precision.

The second scene is full of images of confusion. It is a general principle in the work of Shakespeare and many of his contemporaries that when A is made to describe X, a minor character or event, the description is not merely immediately applicable to X, it helps to determine the way in which our whole response shall develop. This is rather crudely recognised when we say that certain lines "create the atmosphere" of the play. Shakespeare's power is seen in the way in which details of this kind develop, check, or provide a commentary upon the main interests which he has aroused. In the present scene the description

> Doubtfull it stood,
> As two spent Swimmers, that doe cling together,
> And choake their Art
>
> [I. ii. 7-9]

applies not only to the battle but to the ambiguity of Macbeth's future fortunes. The impression conveyed is not only one of violence but of unnatural violence ("to bathe in reeking wounds"[I. ii. 39]) and of a kind of nightmare gigantism—

> Where the Norweyan Banners flowt the Skie,
> And fanne our people cold.
>
> [I. ii. 49-50]

(These lines alone should be sufficient answer to those who doubt the authenticity of the scene). When Duncan says, "What he hath lost, Noble *Macbeth* hath wonne" [I. ii. 67], we hear the echo,

> So from that Spring, whence comfort seem'd to
>   come,
> Discomfort swells,
>
> [I. ii. 27-8]

—and this is not the only time the Captain's words can be applied in the course of the play. Nor is it fantastic to suppose that in the account of Macdonwald Shakespeare consciously provided a parallel with the Macbeth of the later acts when "The multiplying Villanies of Nature swarme upon him" [I. ii. 11]. After all, everybody has noticed the later parallel between Macbeth and Cawdor ("He was a Gentleman, on whom I built an absolute Trust" [I. iv. 13-14]).

A poem works by calling into play, directing and integrating certain interests. If we really accept the suggestion, which then becomes revolutionary, that *Macbeth* is a poem, it is clear that the impulses aroused in Act I, Scenes I and II, are part of the whole response, even if they are not all immediately relevant to the fortunes of the protagonist. If these scenes are "the botching work of an interpolator" he botched to pretty good effect.

In Act I, Scene III, confusion is succeeded by uncertainty. . . . The whole force of the uncertainty of the scene is gathered into Macbeth's soliloquy,

> This supernaturall solliciting
> Cannot be ill; cannot be good . . .
>
> [I. iii. 130-31]

which with its sickening see-saw rhythm completes the impression of "a phantasma, or a hideous dream" [*Julius Caesar*, II. i. 65]. Macbeth's echoing of the Witches' "Faire is foule" has often been commented upon.

In contrast to the preceding scenes, Act I, Scene IV suggests the natural order which is shortly to be violated. It stresses: natural relationships—"children," "servants," "sons" and kinsmen"; honourable bonds and the political order—"liege," "thanes," "service," "duty," "loyalty," "throne," "state" and "honour"; and the human "love" is linked to the more purely natural by images of husbandry. Duncan says to Macbeth,

> I have begun to plant thee, and will labour
> To make thee full of growing.
>
> [I. iv. 28-9]

When he holds Banquo to his heart Banquo replies,

> There if I grow,
> The Harvest is your owne.
>
> [I. iv. 32-3]

Duncan's last speech is worth particular notice,

> . . . in his commendations, I am fed:
> It is a Banquet to me.
>
> [I. iv. 55-6]

At this point something should be said of what is meant by "the natural order." In *Macbeth* this comprehends both "wild nature"—birds, beasts and reptiles—and humankind since "humane statute purg'd the gentle Weale" [III. iv. 75]. The specifically human aspect is related to the concept of propriety and degree,—

> communities,
> Degrees in Schooles and Brother-hoods in Cities,
> Peacefull Commerce from dividable shores,
> The primogenitive, and due of byrth,
> Prerogative of Age, Crownes, Scepters, Lawrels.
>
> [*Troilus and Cressida*, I. iii. 103-07]

In short, it represents society in harmony with nature, bound by love and friendship, and ordered by law and duty. It is one of the main axes of reference by which we take our emotional bearings in the play.

In the light of this the scene of Duncan's entry into the castle gains in significance. The critics have often remarked on the irony. What is not so frequently observed is that the key words of the scene are "loved," "wooingly," "bed," "procreant Cradle," "breed, and haunt," all images of love and procreation, supernaturally sanctioned, for the associations of "temple-haunting" colour the whole of the speeches of Banquo and Duncan. We do violence to the play when we ignore Shakespeare's insistence upon the "holy supernatural" as opposed to the "supernaturall solliciting" of the Witches. I shall return to this point. Meanwhile it is pertinent to remember that Duncan himself is "The Lords anoynted Temple" [II. iii. 68].

The murder is explicitly presented as unnatural. After the greeting of Ross and Angus, Macbeth's heart knocks at his ribs "against the use of Nature" [I. iii. 137]. Lady Macbeth fears his "humane kindnesse"; she wishes herself "unsexed," that she may be troubled by "no compunctious visitings of Nature," and invokes the "murth'ring Ministers" who "wait on

Natures Mischiefe'' [I. v. 17-50]. The murder is committed when

> Nature seemes dead, and wicked Dreames abuse
> The Curtain'd sleepe,
>
> [II. i. 50-1]

and it is accompanied by portents "unnaturall, even like the deed that's done" [II. iv. 10-11]. The sun remains obscured, and Duncan's horses "Turn'd wilde in nature" [II. iv. 16]. (pp. 34-41)

"Confusion now hath made his Master-peece" [II. iii. 66], and in the lull that follows the discovery of the murder, Ross and an Old Man as chorus, echo the theme of unnatural disorder. The scene (and the act) ends with a "sentence" by the Old Man which is capable of three interpretations:

> Gods benyson go with you, and with those
> That would make good of bad, and Friends of Foes.
>
> [II. iv. 40-1]

It may refer to Ross who intends to make the best of a bad business, by accepting Macbeth as king. It may refer to Macduff who is destined to "make good of bad" by destroying the evil. More important, in its immediate application it may refer to Macbeth, for the next movement is concerned with his attempt to make good of bad by restoring the natural order; the tragedy lies in his failure.

A key is found in Macbeth's words spoken to the men hired to murder Banquo [III. i. 91-100]. When Dr. Bradley is discussing the possibility that *Macbeth* has been abridged he remarks . . . , "surely, anyone who wanted to cut the play down would have operated, say, on Macbeth's talk with Banquo's murderers, or on Act III, Scene VI, or on the very long dialogue of Malcolm and Macduff, instead of reducing the most exciting part of the drama." No, the speech to the murderers is not very "exciting"—but its function should be obvious to anyone who is not blinded by Dr. Bradley's preconceptions about "drama." By accepted canons it is an irrelevance; actually it stands as a symbol of the order that Macbeth wishes to restore. In the catalogue

> Hounds, and Greyhounds, Mungrels, Spaniels, Curres,
> Showghes, Water-Rugs, and Demy-Wolves
>
> [III. i. 92-3]

are merely "dogs," but Macbeth names each one individually; and

> the valued file
> Distinguishes the swift, the slow, the subtle,
> The House-keeper, the Hunter, every one
> According to the gift, which bounteous Nature
> Hath in him clos'd.
>
> [III. i. 94-8]

It is an image of order, each one in his degree. At the beginning of the scene, we remember, Macbeth had arranged "a feast," "a solemn supper," at which "society" should be "welcome." And when alone he suggests the ancient harmonies by rejecting in idea the symbols of their contraries—"a fruitlesse Crowne," "a barren Scepter," and an "unlineall" succession. But this new "health" is "sickly" whilst Banquo lives, and can only be made "perfect" by his death. In an attempt to recreate an order based on murder, disorder makes fresh inroads. This is made explicit in the next scene (Act III, Scene II). Here the snake, usually represented as the most venomous of creatures, stands for the natural order which Macbeth has

"scotched" but which will "close, and be her selfe" [III. ii. 13-14].

At this point in the play there is a characteristic confusion. At the end of Act III, Scene II, Macbeth says, "Things bad begun, make strong themselves by ill" [III. ii. 55-6], that is, all that he can do is to ensure his physical security by a second crime, although earlier [III. i. 106-07] he had aimed at complete "health" by the death of Banquo and Fleance, and later he says that the murder of Fleance would have made him

> perfect,
> Whole as the Marble, founded as the Rocke.
>
> [III. iv. 20-1]

The two possibilities are only gradually disentangled. (pp. 43-6)

Although the play moves swiftly, it does not move with a simple directness. Its complex subtleties include cross currents, the ebb and flow of opposed thoughts and emotions. The scene in Macduff's castle, made up of doubts, riddles, paradoxes and uncertainties, ends with an affirmation, "Thou ly'st thou shagge-ear'd Villaine." But this is immediately followed, not by the downfall of Macbeth, but by a long scene which takes up once more the theme of mistrust, disorder and evil.

The conversation between Macduff and Malcolm has never been adequately explained. We have already seen Dr. Bradley's opinion of it. The Clarendon editors say, "The poet no doubt felt this scene was needed to supplement the meagre parts assigned to Malcolm and Macduff." If this were all, it might be omitted. Actually the Malcolm-Macduff dialogue has at least three functions. Obviously Macduff's audience with Malcolm and the final determination to invade Scotland help on the story, but this is of subordinate importance. It is clear also that Malcolm's suspicion and the long testing of Macduff emphasize the mistrust which has spread from the central evil of the play. But the main purpose of the scene is obscured unless we realize its function as choric commentary. In alternating speeches the evil which Macbeth has caused is explicitly stated, without extenuation. And it is stated impersonally. . . . With this approach we see the relevance of Malcolm's self-accusation. He has ceased to be a person. His lines repeat and magnify the evils which have already been attributed to Macbeth, acting as a mirror wherein the ills of Scotland are reflected. And the statement of evil is strengthened by contrast with the opposite virtues, "As Justice, Verity, Temp'rance, Stablenesse" [IV. iii. 92].

There is no other way in which the scene can be read. And if dramatic fitness is not sufficient warrant for this approach, we can refer to the pointers which Shakespeare has provided. Macbeth is "luxurious" and "avaricious," and the first sins mentioned by Malcolm in an expanded statement are lust and avarice. When he declares,

> Nay, had I powre, I should
> Poure the sweet Milke of Concord, into Hell,
> Uprore the universall peace, confound
> All unity on earth,
>
> [IV. iii. 97-100]

we remember that this is what Macbeth has done. Indeed Macduff is made to answer,

> These Evils thou repeat'st upon thy selfe,
> Hath banish'd me from Scotland.
>
> [IV. iii. 112-13]

Up to this point at least the impersonal function of the speaker is predominant. And even when Malcolm, once more a person in a play, announces his innocence, it is impossible not to hear the impersonal overtone:

> For even now
> I put my selfe to thy Direction, and
> Unspeake mine owne detraction. Heere abjure
> The taints, and blames I laide upon my selfe,
> For strangers to my Nature.
>
> [IV. iii. 121-25]

He speaks for Scotland, and for the forces of order. The "scotch'd Snake" will "close, and be herselfe."

There are only two alternatives; either Shakespeare was a bad dramatist, or his critics have been badly misled by mistaking the *dramatis personae* for real persons in this scene. Unless of course the ubiquitous Interpolator has been at work upon it.

I have called *Macbeth* a statement of evil; but it is a statement not of philosophy but of ordered emotion. This ordering is of course a continuous process (hence the importance of the scrupulous analysis of each line), it is not merely something that happens in the last act corresponding to the dénouement or unravelling of the plot. All the same the interests aroused are heightened in the last act before they are finally "placed," and we are given a vantage point from which the whole course of the drama may be surveyed in retrospect. There is no formula which will describe this final effect. It is no use saying that we are "quietened," "purged" or "exalted" at the end of *Macbeth* or of any other tragedy. It is no use taking one step nearer the play and saying we are purged, etc., because we see the downfall of a wicked man or because we realize the justice of Macbeth's doom whilst retaining enough sympathy for him or admiration of his potential qualities to be filled with a sense of "waste." It is no use discussing the effect in abstract terms at all; we can only discuss it in terms of the poet's concrete realization of certain emotions and attitudes.

At this point it is necessary to return to what I have [said elsewhere] . . . about the importance of images of grace and of the holy supernatural in the play. . . . [For] the last hundred years or so the critics have not only sentimentalized Macbeth— ignoring the completeness with which Shakespeare shows his final identification with evil—but they have slurred the passages in which the positive good is presented by means of religious symbols. In Act III the banquet scene is immediately followed by a scene in which Lennox and another Lord (both completely impersonal) discuss the situation; the last half of their dialogue is of particular importance. The verse has none of the power of, say, Macbeth's soliloquies, but it would be a mistake to call it undistinguished; it is serenely harmonious, and its tranquillity contrasts with the turbulence of the scenes which immediately precede it and follow it, as its images of grace contrast with their "toile and trouble." Macduff has fled to "the Pious Edward," "the Holy King," who has received Malcolm "with such grace." Lennox prays for the aid of "some holy Angell,"

> that a swift blessing
> May soone returne to this our suffering Country,
> Under a hand accurs'd.
>
> [III. vi. 45-9]

And the "other Lord" answers, "Ile send my Prayers with him" [III. vi. 49]. Many of the phrases are general and abstract—"grace," "the malevolence of Fortune," "his high

respect"—but one passage has an individual particularity that gives it prominence:

> That by the helpe of these (with him above
> To ratifie the Worke) we may againe
> Give to our Tables meate, sleepe to our Nights:
> Free from our Feasts, and Banquets bloody knives;
> Do faithful Homage, and receive free Honors,
> All which we pine for now.
>
> [III. vi. 32-7]

Food and sleep, society and the political order are here, as before, represented as supernaturally sanctioned. I have suggested that this passage is recalled for a moment in Lady Macduff's answer to the Murderer [IV. ii. 81-2], and it is certainly this theme which is taken up when the Doctor enters in Act IV, Scene III; the reference to the King's Evil may be a compliment to King James, but it is not merely that. We have only to remember that the unseen Edward stands for the powers that are to prove "the Med'cine of the sickly Weale" [V. ii. 27] of Scotland to see the double meaning in

> there are a crew of wretched Soules
> That stay his Cure. . . .
>
> [IV. iii. 141-42]

Their disease "is called the Evill" [IV. iii. 146]. The "myraculous worke," the "holy Prayers," "the healing Benediction," Edward's "vertue," the "sundry Blessings . . . that speake him full of Grace" [IV. iii. 147-59] are reminders not only of the evil against which Malcolm is seeking support, but of the positive qualities against which the evil and disorder must be measured. Scattered notes ("Gracious England," "Christendome," "heaven," "gentle Heavens") remind us of the theme until the end of the scene when we know that Macbeth (the "Hell-Kite," "this Fiend of Scotland")

> Is ripe for shaking, and the Powers above
> Put on their Instruments.
>
> [IV. iii. 238-39]

The words quoted are not mere formalities; they have a positive function, and help to determine the way in which we shall respond to the final scenes. (pp. 49-57)

We have already noticed the association of the ideas of disease and of the unnatural in these final scenes—

> unnatural deeds
> Do breed unnatural troubles,
>
> [V. i. 71-2]

and there is propriety in Macbeth's highly charged metaphor,

> My way of life
> Is falne into the Seare, the yellow Leafe.
>
> [V. iii. 22-3]

But the unnatural has now another part to play, in the peculiar "reversal" that takes place at the end of *Macbeth*. Hitherto the agent of the unnatural has been Macbeth. Now it is Malcolm who commands Birnam Wood to move, it is "the good Macduff" who reveals his unnatural birth, and the opponents of Macbeth whose "deere causes" would "excite the mortified man" [V. ii. 5]. Hitherto Macbeth has been the deceiver, "mocking the time with fairest show" [I. vii. 81]; now Malcolm orders,

> Let every Souldier hew him downe a Bough,
> And bear't before him, thereby shall we shadow
> The numbers of our Hoast, and make discovery
> Erre in report of us.
>
> [V. iv. 4-7]

Our first reaction is to make some such remark as "Nature becomes unnatural in order to rid itself of Macbeth." But this is clearly inadequate; we have to translate it and define our impressions in terms of our response to the play at this point. By associating with the opponents of evil the ideas of deceit and of the unnatural, previously associated solely with Macbeth and the embodiments of evil, Shakespeare emphasizes the disorder and at the same time frees our minds from the burden of the horror. After all, the movement of Birnam Wood and Macduff's unnatural birth have a simple enough explanation.

There is a parallel here with the disorder of the last Act. It begins with Lady Macbeth sleepwalking—a "slumbry agitation"—and the remaining scenes are concerned with marches, stratagems, fighting, suicide, and death in battle. If we merely read the play we are liable to overlook the importance of the sights and sounds which are obvious on the stage. The frequent stage directions should be observed—*Drum and Colours, Enter Malcolm . . . and Soldiers Marching, A Cry within of Women*—and there are continuous directions for *Alarums, Flourishes,* and fighting. Macduff orders,

> Make all our Trumpets speak, give them all breath,
> Those clamorous Harbingers of Blood, and Death,
>
> [V. vi. 9-10]

and he traces Macbeth by the noise of fighting:

> That way the noise is: Tyrant shew thy face.
> . . . There thou should'st be,
> By this great clatter, one of the greatest note
> Seemes bruited.
>
> [V. vii. 14-22]

There are other suggestions of disorder throughout the Act. Macbeth

> cannot buckle his distemper'd cause
> Within the belt of Rule.
>
> [V. ii. 15-16]

He orders, "Come, put mine Armour on," and almost in the same breath, "Pull't off I say" [V. iii. 48, 54]. His "Royal Preparation" is a noisy confusion. He wishes "th' estate o' th' world were now undon" [V. v. 49], though the tone is changed now since he bade the Witches answer him,

> Though bladed Corne be lodg'd, and Trees blown
>   downe,
> Though Castles topple on their Warders heads:
> Though Pallaces, and Pyramids do slope
> Their heads to their Foundations.
>
> [IV. i. 55-8]

But all this disorder has now a positive tendency, towards the good which Macbeth had attempted to destroy, and which he names as "Honor, Love, Obedience, Troopes of Friends" [V. iii. 25]. At the beginning of the battle Malcolm says,

> Cosins, I hope the dayes are neere at hand
> That Chambers will be safe,

and Menteith answers, "We doubt it nothing" [V. iv. 1-2]. Siward takes up the theme of certainty as opposed to doubt:

> Thoughts speculative, their unsure hopes relate,
> But certaine issue, stroakes must arbitrate,
> Towards which, advance the warre.
>
> [V. iv. 19-21]

And doubt and illusion are finally dispelled:

> Now neere enough:
> Your leavy Skreenes throw downe,
> And shew like those you are.
>
> [V. vi. 1-3]

By now there should be no danger of our misinterpreting the greatest of Macbeth's final speeches.

> Life's but a walking Shadow, a poore Player,
> That struts and frets his houre upon the Stage,
> And then is heard no more. It is a Tale
> Told by an Ideot, full of sound and fury
> Signifying nothing.
>
> [V. v. 24-28]

The theme of the false appearance is revived—with a difference. It is not only that Macbeth sees life as deceitful, but the poetry is so fine that we are almost bullied into accepting an essential ambiguity in the final statement of the play, as though Shakespeare were expressing his own "philosophy" in the lines. But the speech is "placed" by the tendency of the last Act (order emerging from disorder, truth emerging from behind deceit), culminating in the recognition of the Witches' equivocation ("And be these Jugling Fiends no more believ'd . . ." [V. viii. 19]), the death of Macbeth, and the last words of Siward, Macduff and Malcolm. . . .

This tendency has behind it the whole weight of the positive values which Shakespeare has already established, and which are evoked in Macbeth's speech—

> My way of life
> Is falne into the Seare, the yellow Leafe,
> And that which should accompany Old-Age,
> As Honor, Love, Obedience, Troopes of Friends,
> I must not looke to have: but in their stead,
> Curses, not lowd but deepe, Mouth-honor, breath
> Which the poore heart would faine deny, and dare not.

Dr. Bradley claims, on the strength of this and the "To-morrow, and to-morrow" speech, that Macbeth's "ruin is never complete. To the end he never totally loses our sympathy. . . . In the very depths a gleam of his native love of goodness, and with it a tinge of tragic grandeur, rests upon him" [see excerpt above, 1904]. Dr. Bradley's emotion is out of place; the statement is impersonal. It is the keystone of the system which gives emotional coherence to the play. Certainly the system will remain obscured if we concentrate our attention upon "the two great terrible figures, who dwarf all the remaining characters of the drama," if we ignore the "unexciting" or "undramatic scenes," or if conventional "sympathy for the hero" is allowed to distort the pattern of the whole. (pp. 59-64)

L. C. Knights, in his How Many Children Had Lady Macbeth? An Essay in the Theory and Practice of Shakespeare Criticism, *The Minority Press, 1933, 70 p.*

CAROLINE F. E. SPURGEON   (essay date 1935)

[*Spurgeon's* Shakespeare's Imagery *(1935) inaugurated the "image-pattern analysis" method of studying Shakespeare's plays, one of the most widely used methods of the mid-twentieth century. In this work, she interprets the thematic structure of the plays through an examination of patterns in the imagery. Spurgeon also sought to learn about Shakespeare's personality from a study of his images, a course which few of her disciples followed. Since publication of her book, earlier works on image patterns in Shake-*

speare have been discovered, but none was so important in the history of Shakespearean criticism as Spurgeon's. In the excerpt below, Spurgeon examines the clothing imagery in Macbeth, *noting that there are frequent metaphorical references to Macbeth's wearing borrowed, ill-fitting robes. These images, says Spurgeon, suggest a "picture of a small, ignoble man encumbered and degraded by garments unsuited to him."*]

The imagery in *Macbeth* appears to me to be more rich and varied, more highly imaginative, more unapproachable by any other writer, than that of any other single play. It is particularly so, I think, in the continuous use made of the simplest, humblest, everyday things, drawn from the daily life in a small house, as a vehicle for sublime poetry. (p. 324)

Few simple things—harmless in themselves—have such a curiously humiliating and degrading effect as the spectacle of a notably small man enveloped in a coat far too big for him. Comic actors know this well—Charlie Chaplin, for instance—and it is by means of this homely picture that Shakespeare shows us his imaginative view of the hero, and expresses the fact that the honours for which the murders were committed are, after all, of very little worth to him.

The idea constantly recurs that Macbeth's new honours sit ill upon him, like a loose and badly fitting garment, belonging to someone else. Macbeth himself first expresses it, quite early in the play, when, immediately following the first appearance of the witches and their prophecies, Ross arrives from the king, and greets him as thane of Cawdor, to which Macbeth quickly replies,

> The thane of Cawdor lives: why do you dress me
> In borrow'd robes?
>
> [I. iii. 108-09]

And a few minutes later, when he is rapt in ambitious thoughts suggested by the confirmation of two out of the three 'prophetic greetings', Banquo, watching him, murmurs,

> New honours come upon him,
> Like our strange garments, cleave not to their mould
> But with the aid of use.
>
> [I. iii. 144-46]

When Duncan is safely in the castle, Macbeth's better nature for a moment asserts itself, and, in debate with himself, he revolts from the contemplated deed for a threefold reason: because of its incalculable results, the treachery of such action from one who is both kinsman and host, and Duncan's own virtues and greatness as king.

When his wife joins him, his repugnance to the deed is as great, but it is significant that he gives three quite different reasons for not going ahead with it, reasons which he hopes may appeal to her, for he knows the others would not. So he urges that he has been lately honoured by the king, people think well of him, and therefore he should reap the reward of these things at once, and not upset everything by this murder which they have planned.

There is irony in the fact that to express the position he uses the same metaphor of clothes:

> I have bought
> Golden opinions from all sorts of people,
> Which would be worn now in their newest gloss,
> Not cast aside so soon.
>
> [I. vii. 32-5]

To which Lady Macbeth, quite unmoved, retorts contemptuously:

> Was the hope drunk
> Wherein you dress'd yourself?
>
> [I. vii. 35-6]

After the murder, when Ross says he is going to Scone for Macbeth's coronation, Macduff uses the same simile:

> Well, may you see things well done there: adieu!
> Lest our old robes sit easier than our new!
>
> [II. iv. 37-8]

And, at the end, when the tyrant is at bay at Dunsinane, and the English troops are advancing, the Scottish lords still have this image in their minds. Caithness sees him as a man vainly trying to fasten a large garment on him with too small a belt:

> He cannot buckle his distemper'd cause
> Within the belt of rule;
>
> [V. ii. 15-16]

while Angus, in a similar image, vividly sums up the essence of what they all have been thinking ever since Macbeth's accession to power:

> now does he feel his title
> Hang loose about him, like a giant's robe
> Upon a dwarfish thief.
>
> [V. ii. 20-22]

This imaginative picture of a small, ignoble man encumbered and degraded by garments unsuited to him, should be put against the view emphasised by some critics (notably Coleridge and Bradley) of the likeness between Macbeth and Milton's Satan in grandeur and sublimity.

Undoubtedly Macbeth is built on great lines and in heroic proportions, with great possibilities—there could be no tragedy else. He is great, magnificently great, in courage, in passionate, indomitable ambition, in imagination and capacity to feel. But he could never be put beside, say Hamlet or Othello, in nobility of nature; and there *is* an aspect in which he is but a poor, vain, cruel, treacherous creature, snatching ruthlessly over the dead bodies of kinsman and friend at place and power he is utterly unfitted to possess. It is worth remembering that it is thus that Shakespeare, with his unshrinking clarity of vision, repeatedly *sees* him. (pp. 324-27)

> Caroline F. E. Spurgeon, *"Leading Motives in the Tragedies," in her* Shakespeare's Imagery and What It Tells Us, *Cambridge at the University Press, 1935, pp. 309-55.*

STEPHEN SPENDER   (essay date 1941)

[*Spender, an English poet and critic, was associated as a young man with a group of Oxford Marxists that included W. H. Auden and C. Day Lewis. In the following excerpt, Spender discusses time and the futile efforts of Macbeth and Lady Macbeth to separate past, present, and future. Their happiness, states Spender, relies on their ability to prevent both the anticipated and, later, the remembered murder of Duncan from affecting their present. The "chaos of time" pervades* Macbeth, *he continues, until a proper sense of time is restored by Malcolm. Spender concludes by paralleling the "loss of the sense of time and measure and place" with the modern world. For additional commentary on the issue of time in* Macbeth, *see the excerpts by G. Wilson Knight (1931) and Tom F. Driver (1960).*]

I do not know whether any Shakespearean critic has ever pointed out the significant part played by ideas of time in *Macbeth*.

One often hears quoted:

> Come what may
> Time and the hour runs through the roughest day.
>
> [I. iii. 146-47]

Actually the tragedy of Macbeth is his discovery that this is untrue.

Macbeth and Lady Macbeth are as haunted as James Joyce and Proust by the sense of time. After she has received his letter describing the meeting with the witches, Lady Macbeth's first words to her husband are:

> . . . Thy letters have transported me beyond
> The ignorant present, and I feel now
> The future in the instant.
>
> [I. v. 56-8]

Their trouble is though that the future does not exist in the instant. There is another very unpleasant instant preceding it which has to be acted on—the murder of Duncan.

In the minds of Macbeth and Lady Macbeth there are, after the prophetic meeting with the weird sisters, three kinds of time: the time before the murder, the time of the murder of Duncan, and the enjoyable time afterwards when they reap the fruits of the murder. Their problem is to keep these three times separate and not to allow them to affect each other. If they can prevent their minds showing the sense of the future before the murder, and of the past, after it, they will have achieved happiness. As soon as the murder has been decided on, Lady Macbeth scents the danger:

> Your face, my thane, is as a book where men
> May read strange matters: to beguile the time,
> Look like the time.
>
> [I. v. 62-4]

How little Macbeth succeeds in this, we gather from his soliloquy before the murder:

> If it were done—when 'tis done—then 'twere well
> If it were done quickly: if the assassination
> Could trammel up the consequence, and catch
> With his surcease, success: that but this blow
> Might be the be-all and the end-all here,
> But here upon this bank and shoal of time,
> We'ld jump the life to come. But in these cases
> We still have judgement here; that we but teach
> Bloody instructions, which, being taught, return
> To plague th' inventor.
>
> [I. vii. 1-10]

Macbeth certainly has good reason to fear 'even-handed justice.' But, I think, the second part of this speech is only a rationalization of his real fear, as unconvincing in its way as Hamlet's reasons against self-murder. The real fear is far more terrible: it is a fear of the extension into infinity of the instant in which he commits the murder. 'The bank and shoal of time' is time that has stood still; beyond it lies the abyss of a timeless moment.

He loses his nerve, but Lady Macbeth rallies him:

> When you durst do it, then you were a man;
> And, to be more than what you were you would

Be so much more the man. Nor time nor place
Did then adhere, and yet you would make both:
They have made themselves, and that their fitness now
Does unmake you.

> [I. vii. 49-54]

She forces his mind upon the conjunction of time and place which may never occur again. They never do, indeed, recur. The murder of Banquo is ill-timed, Malcolm escapes, everything is botched, and Macbeth swears that after this he will carry out those crimes which are the 'firstlings of his heart' [IV. i. 147].

The soliloquy in which Macbeth sees the dagger before him is the first of his hallucinations. Yet the delusion is not complete. He is able to dismiss it from his mind, and he does so by fixing down the time and place, in order to restore his mind to sanity.

> There's no such thing:
> It is the bloody season which informs
> Thus to mine eyes. Now o'er the one half world
> Nature seems dead.
>
> [II. i. 47-50]

He reminds himself of the exact time of night, and this calms him. He invokes the hour, and he invokes the place, with a reason: to relegate this moment preceding the murder to the past from which it cannot ever escape into a future. As some people say, 'I will remember this moment for the rest of my life,' Macbeth tries to say, 'I will uproot this moment from my memory.'

> Thou sure and firm-set earth,
> Hear not my steps, which way they walk, for fear
> Thy very stones prate of my whereabout,
> And take the present horror from the time
> Which now suits with it.
>
> [II. i. 56-60]

He is more afraid of the associations of the stones than any evidence they may actually reveal to living witnesses.

Immediately after the murder we are left in no doubt that Macbeth and Lady Macbeth have failed in their main purpose of killing in memory the moment of the murder itself.

Macbeth tells his wife how he could not say 'Amen' to the prayer of the man in his sleep. 'Amen' is the conclusion of prayer, which is inconcludable. 'Methought I heard a voice cry, "Sleep no more! Macbeth does murder sleep"' [II. ii. 32-3].

There is no 'Amen' nor night of sleep which will ever end that moment which opens wider and wider as the play proceeds. Macbeth's speech in the next scene is a naif deception, which happens also to be the truth wrung from his heart:

> Had I but [died] an hour before this chance,
> I had lived a blessed time.
>
> [II. iii. 91-2]

With this he tries to fob off his followers. Meanwhile, one is left in some doubt as to Lady Macbeth's state of mind. The Sleepwalking scene is a shocking revelation which shows that the moment when she smeared the faces of the grooms has died no more for her than has the murder for Macbeth. 'Here's the smell of blood still.' The ailment of indestructible time is revealed by Macbeth to the doctor:

> Canst thou not minister to a mind diseased;
> Pluck from the memory a rooted sorrow;
> Raze out the written troubles of the brain;

And with some sweet oblivious antidote
Cleanse the stuft bosom of the perilous stuff
Which weighs upon the heart?

[V. iii. 40-45]

Thus, after the murder the past comes to life again and asserts itself amid the general disintegration. An old man appears on the stage to compare the horrors of the past with the monstrosities of the present. Ross says:

By the clock 'tis day,
And yet dark night strangles the travelling lamp.

[II. iv. 6-7]

The present disgorges the past. The horror of not being able to live down his deeds is symbolized by the appearance of Banquo's ghost. Macbeth looks back on a time when the past was really past and the present present:

The time has been
That, when the brains were out, the man would die,
And there an end.

[III. iv. 77-9]

There is no end within the control of Macbeth. In the fourth act, we even have a feeling that everything has stopped. The play seems to spread out, burning up and destroying a wider and wider area, without moving forward.

'To-morrow, and to-morrow and to-morrow' [V. iv. 19] is not merely the speech of a disillusioned tyrant destroyed by the horror which he has himself created; it has a profound irony, coming from Macbeth's mouth, because he of all people ought to have been able to make to-morrow different from to-day and yesterday. But all his violence has done is to create a deathly sameness.

This view of *Macbeth* struck me as I was reading it recently. The only doubt in my mind was whether the last speech in the play would bear out my theory that it was time which, even more than in *Hamlet,* had got out of joint in *Macbeth.* This is what Malcolm says to the lords who have rebelled against the tyrant:

We shall not spend a large expense of time
Before we reckon with your several loves
And make us even with you. . . .

What's more to do,
Which would be planted newly with the time . . .

We will perform in measure, time, and place.

[V. ix. 26-39]

The emphasis of Malcolm is on time and measure and place, which he is restoring.

Macbeth is naturally the play of Shakespeare's to which we are most likely to turn if we look for parallels with the present. It is impossible to read the lines beginning 'Our country sinks beneath the yoke; It weeps, it bleeds' [IV. iii. 38-9], without thinking of half a dozen countries under the yoke of a tyrant. It is impossible not to wonder whether modern tyrants are haunted by their Banquos, and surrounded by a sense of gloomy waking nightmare. But the instruments of justice are weaker than in Shakespeare's time; the consciences of men, brought up on an inverted philosophy of materialism, are not so tender, or so superstitious perhaps. The loss of the sense of time and measure and place, the past rising in solemn visions and portents in the midst of the present, the sense of endless waiting

and of time standing still in the midst of the most violent happenings; these provide deeper parallels.

In his book *Pain, Time and Sex,* Gerald Heard claims that man has reached a stage in his evolution in which he has to take a great and decisive step forward which would involve revising not only his social institutions but also his whole conception of the meaning of life. A tyranny, a murder, and a great decision at the end, are the plot of *Macbeth.* The chaos of time, the sense of being haunted by past examples, is connected not only with the tyranny, but also with the decision. The strange scene between Malcolm and Macduff in which Malcolm recites all the vices of past kings and declares that he embodies them; and then contradicts himself and stands forth in his virginity; this is a ranking of all the forces of evil against the forces of the good; and the decision is for the good.

But Malcolm is a restorer, not a revolutionary or an innovator. He takes it for granted that the strange confusion of time that has opened out in *Macbeth* is wrong. It is here that the parallel of our own day with Shakespeare fades. It is even possible that in a sense the stage which we have reached is an advance on Shakespeare. We are living in an age of chaos and confusion, but we cannot go back, we have to go forward. It may be then that the very disorder may show us the way out of our confusion. Our loss of the sense of the continuity of time may give us an entirely new idea of time within which it will be possible to establish a new kind of order. We cannot dismiss the dreams and hallucinations of art in our time as a sign of decadence and of an end. They may be an end; on the other hand, they may be the beginning of something. We only know that we do not exist to restore a past, but to create a future which embodies the greatness of the past. (pp. 120-26)

Stephen Spender, "Books and the War—II," in The Penguin New Writing, *No. 3, February, 1941, pp. 115-26.*

THEODORE SPENCER   (essay date 1942)

[*Spencer, an American literary critic, editor, poet, and educator, is best known for his studies of Elizabethan drama and metaphysical poetry. Concurrently with E. M. W. Tillyard, Spencer elucidated and examined the traditional religious, moral, and social doctrines that he felt informed Elizabethan literature. His most important work,* Shakespeare and the Nature of Man *(1942), explores Shakespeare's dramatic technique and attempts to explain how the playwright resolved the tension between the forces of order and chaos—which Spencer defined as the conflicting attitudes of the Elizabethan world view—in his tragedies. In the excerpt below, Spencer observes the contrasting movements in* Macbeth *and* King Lear: *Lear "opens out," whereas* Macbeth *"closes in"; Lear's sufferings "end in release," while* Macbeth *"becomes trapped by his own crimes"; Lear is purged of his bad qualities, but Macbeth develops them. Spencer also discusses Shakespeare's concern with illusion and reality in the play, concluding the Macbeth is a "tragic victim of appearance" who fights against "the reality of natural and normal good."*]

One of the most remarkable things about Shakespeare is that although he uses the same materials for the achievement of size and universality in his great tragedies, he creates in each a distinctive and particular world. In *Macbeth,* as in *King Lear,* the individual, the state, and external nature are seen as interrelated parts of a single whole, so that a disturbance in one disturbs the others as well—and yet the atmosphere and tone of the two plays are very different; we may say that *Lear* is a play that opens out, whereas *Macbeth* is a play that closes in.

Lear's sufferings end in release, but Macbeth, in the course of his career, becomes trapped by his own crimes, until he sees himself, at the end, as a captured animal:

> They have tied me to a stake; I cannot fly,
> But bear-like I must fight the course.
>
> [V. vii. 1-2]

In *Macbeth* there is nothing like the purgation of King Lear. As the action of *King Lear* progresses the main character *loses* his bad qualities; in the course of *Macbeth,* the main character *develops* them. This is something new. Iago, for example, does not become increasingly evil as the play goes on; he is thoroughly and completely bad from the beginning. But Macbeth *grows* into evil; that is why those critics are right who describe the play as a more intense study of evil than any other. Unlike *King Lear* it portrays, not the whitening, but the blackening of a soul. (p. 153)

The murder is crucial in the development of Macbeth's character. At the beginning of the play he is, like the weather, both fair and foul—neither one nor the other, and with potentialities for either. The witches, the symbols both of external destiny and of his own character, send him toward evil, as does his wife. Brewing their disgusting potions from the filthiest parts of the vilest sort of animals, the witches represent a different degree, though not a different kind, of dramatic orchestration from that in the mad scenes of *King Lear*. They, too, are on a bare heath, like Edgar, Lear and the Fool, but they are completely depersonalized from humanity, being, in spite of their connection with human affairs, supernatural, or subnatural, or both; whereas Edgar, Lear and the Fool, no matter how mad they are or appear to be, are nevertheless human beings. The chorus of weird sisters represents a different kind of abstraction from the abstractions that are developed from the human mind.

From another point of view the weird sisters—sponsors and prophets of chaos and of order, of delusion and reality—may be regarded as a final dramatic realization of the Elizabethan dramatic convention which invariably tended to see individual human experience in relation to some power—God, the stars, or Fortune—larger than itself. An earlier, a more didactic and moralistic dramatist would have made only too obvious what abstraction they were supposed to personify. Shakespeare was wiser. We never know, as we see or read *Macbeth,* whether the weird sisters control Macbeth's fate, or whether their prophecies are a reflection of Macbeth's own character. The problem of predestination and free-will is presented, but is left unanswered. Or, to put it in more Shakespearean terms, the dictation of what seems to be external destiny and the impulses of individual character are seen as parts of the same vision, and, in a technical sense, as parts of the same dramatic whole.

One of the reasons why *Macbeth* is so dark a play is that the striking emphasis on the unnaturalness of both the chief and the subsidiary events is paralleled by a continually expressed uncertainty as to what is real. In his previous plays Shakespeare presents many aspects of the difference between appearance and fact, but never was the subject so ubiquitous as in the murky fog of *Macbeth*. Are the witches only a product of imagination, or have they a true existence? "I' the name of truth," says Banquo,

> Are ye fantastical, or that indeed
> Which outwardly ye show?
>
> [I. iii. 53-4]

Macbeth himself is troubled by a similar confusion in his mind:

> My thought, whose murder yet is but fantastical,
> Shakes so my single state of man that function
> Is smother'd in surmise, and nothing is
> But what is not.
>
> [I. iii. 139-42]

Illusion and reality change places with each other; Macbeth's imaginary dagger is as

> palpable
> As this which now I draw,
>
> [II. i. 40-41]

just as the hand of Lady Macbeth cannot be sweetened from its imaginary smell of blood by all the perfumes of Arabia. The "horrible shadow," the "unreal mockery," of Banquo's ghost is only a stool to Lady Macbeth. The prophecies of the witches about the man not of woman born and about Birnam wood coming to Dunsinane—both, incidentally, *unnatural* circumstances—turn out to be only an appearance, so that Macbeth cries out:

> And be these juggling fiends no more believ'd,
> That palter with us in a double sense;
> That keep the word of promise to our ear,
> And break it to our hope.
>
> [V. viii. 19-22]

At least twice in the play the difference between appearance and reality is made the basis for a very effective dramatic irony. In the first act, Duncan says of the revolted Cawdor:

> There's no art
> To find the mind's construction in the face;
> He was a gentleman on whom I built
> An absolute trust.
>
> [I. iv. 11-14]

And immediately after this comment on the falseness of appearance, Macbeth enters, apparently a loyal general, but with murder already in his heart. Again Duncan's famous description as he enters Macbeth's castle—

> This castle hath a pleasant seat; the air
> Nimbly and sweetly recommends itself
> Unto our gentle senses—
>
> [I. vi. 1-3]

which is taken up by Banquo—

> This guest of summer,
> The temple-haunting martlet, does approve
> By his lov'd masonry that the heaven's breath
> Smells wooingly here—
>
> [I. vi. 3-6]

this description is clearly in ironic contrast to the true nature of Macbeth's habitation and what takes place there:

> The raven himself is hoarse
> That croaks the fatal entrance of Duncan
> Unto our battlements.
>
> [I. v. 38-40]

Macbeth realizes that his situation demands that he and his wife must

> make our faces vizards to our hearts,
> Disguising what they are;
>
> [III. ii. 34-5]

and in fact the progress of both Macbeth and Lady Macbeth throughout the play is an ironic and terrible comment on the difference between what seems and what is. Lady Macbeth believes that "a little water clears us of this deed" [II. ii. 64]; she does not conceive that the deed has left an indelible stain that nothing can remove. Macbeth himself—and this is the final irony—discovers that his crimes lead to nothing, they turn to ashes in his mouth. The crown for which he had "filed" his mind is in reality, like everything else, sterile, empty and meaningless. He too, like Hamlet, comes to a conclusion about life, but his conclusion is not a neo-stoic acceptance of things, nor is it, like Othello's last speech, a momentary recapturing of a lost nobility. Macbeth's final generalization is something much more terrible—a fitting conclusion to a scene of disorder, confusion and disillusionment:

> Out, out, brief candle!
> Life's but a walking shadow, a poor player
> That struts and frets his hour upon the stage,
> And then is heard no more; it is a tale
> Told by an idiot, full of sound and fury,
> Signifying nothing.
>
> [V. v. 23-8]

Yet out of this "great perturbation of nature" [V. i. 9], to use the doctor's words, which is the tragedy of *Macbeth,* naturalness and order eventually emerge. As in *Lear,* there is an upward movement into order as well as a downward movement into chaos; the difference being that in *Lear* the upward movement occurs in the realm of the individual, while in *Macbeth* it occurs in the realm of the state. In the fourth act we have a reversal of the usual situation in the play and instead of the appearance being good and the reality evil, it is the other way around, for the appearance is evil while the reality is good. Malcolm, the prospective king of Scotland, describes himself at length as a mass of lechery and avarice, as the worst possible type of king, as much worse, even, than Macbeth. But in reality he is quite otherwise, he is as chaste as he is generous,

> would not betray
> The devil to his fellow,

and he delights "No less in truth than life" [IV. iii. 128-30]. (pp. 157-61)

Parallel to this, and dramatically more successful, is what happens as Macbeth is finally defeated. For, again in terms of the difference between seeming and fact, what had appeared to be unnatural turns out to be natural after all. Everything about Macbeth is a violation of Nature—the witches, his murder of his king and kinsman, the portents in the external world, and finally, his apparent security against death. He can only be killed by a man not born of a woman, and when Birnam wood comes to Dunsinane. But Birnam wood *does* come to Dunsinane, carried by men, and Macbeth is killed by Macduff, who, though he was untimely ripped from his mother's womb, is obviously a human being. Macbeth, tragic victim of appearance that he is, moved throughout the play by unnatural forces and desires, fights desperately and in vain against the reality of natural and normal good. And he dies at the hands of normal human beings who will restore, in Malcolm's words, "by the grace of Grace" what Macbeth has unnaturally destroyed, and will perform what needful else, "in measure, time, and place," to re-establish the state that has been ruined by the "watchful tyranny"

Of this dead butcher and his fiend-like queen.

(pp. 161-62)

Theodore Spencer, "'Macbeth' and 'Antony and Cleopatra'," in his Shakespeare and the Nature of Man, *The Macmillan Company, 1942, pp. 153-76.*

JOHN ARTHOS (essay date 1947)

[*In the following excerpt, Arthos examines the relationship between Macbeth's imagination and his language. He argues that as Macbeth's criminal actions progress his language, which earlier reflected a vivid imagination and impulse to personify his ideas, becomes more concerned with lifeless materiality. Arthos concludes that because of his contemplation of these lifeless images, "Macbeth was either transformed into the likeness of the death his imagination materialized, or else he recognized them as the prophecy of what he was to become, matter bereft of life." For other interpretations of Macbeth's use of language, see the excerpts by Arnold Stein (1951) and Bertrand Evans (1979).*]

The murder of Duncan was the shock that unmanned Macbeth. But he was a man of magnificent strength and a warrior, and his will to live remained magnificently strong even while he suffered so grievously from the knowledge of the evil he had done. His will to live eventually failed partly because his imagination betrayed his will. The images crowding his mind more and more confused his understanding of the laws of life, the primary distinctions he had otherwise known how to make easily, the difference between what is alive and what is dead, what was useful to him and what was harmful. He made every effort to continue his miserable life, and his resources were great enough to prevent the immediate disintegration either of his mind or his will. But the disintegration was none the less not to be halted, his feeling was to be dulled along with his will, and the images of what once were lively passions would now be represented in terms of the most insensitive matter.

After Macbeth had taken to crime, he became aware of the deep unsettling of his nature. He found himself believing that both his ambition and his regrets were valid, but in assuming responsibility for both he was miserably aware that he was losing his assurance. He fought to preserve it, and he believed he was helped in this struggle by his imagination. In these strange new circumstances he felt he could rely upon that wonderful faculty of his mind that had served him so splendidly in the past in revealing the significance of things. But now the images he was to create needed to do more than provide the means of understanding. They needed to be independent of his inner disturbance, images that, once created, would be independent of his dilemma. As such they would be evidence of a kind of special existence in a world where a special aspect of the truth prevailed. As images of the truth they would have the truth's saving power. They would provide him with an understanding of the war of feeling that distracted him, and by fixing the picture of this war in long clusters of images he must have thought he would rid himself of the pain they described. This was for him, of so sensitive a conscience, a most urgent delusion.

It is only before the murder that Macbeth expresses any doubt of the pictures presented to his mind, and this obviously in the horror the idea of murder raises in him:

> My thought, whose murder yet is but fantastical,
> Shakes so my single state of man that function
> Is smother'd in surmise, and nothing is
> But what is not.
>
> [I. iii. 139-42]

Even when he is confronted with the miraculous appearance and disappearance of the witches, visible to both Banquo and himself, it is clear that mere insubstantialness in no way causes him to doubt their reality,

> . . . what seem'd corporal melted
> As breath into the wind,
>
> [I. iii. 81-2]

and as time proved their prophecies he had no reason to doubt the reality of that vision. By nature, as well as by such circumstances, he was disposed to trust his sight and his visual imaginings.

As he is hurried into planning for the murder he is confronted by the hallucination of the dagger, but this time he realizes that this is a child of his mind, and not real as the witches are. But he immediately understands that the dagger is an image of the truth, it tells him how horrible the thing is he is about to do:

> It is the bloody business which informs
> Thus to mine eyes.
>
> [II. i. 48-9]

He denies the "reality" of the image, but he knows that it expressed the ugly truth of his intent. And he also knows that even as he imagined the dagger, and was reaching for it, he was fascinated by it. The evil it represented had already taken possession of him. He had only strength enough to wrench his mind from the picture of what he was to do, not enough to free himself from the idea.

It is important to observe that before the murder Macbeth pictured the world predominantly in terms of personification.

> If chance will have me King, why, chance
> may crown me.
>
> [I. iii. 143-44]

In the first important soliloquy before the murder, the figures of his speech are crowded with personifications:

> If the assassination
> Could trammel up the consequence, and catch
> With his surcease success. . . .
>   . . . . we but teach
> Bloody instructions, which, being taught, return
> To plague th' inventor. This even-handed justice
> Commends th' ingredients of our poison'd chalice
> To our own lips.
>
> . . . his virtues
> Will plead like angels, trumpet-tongu'd, against
> The deep damnation of his taking-off;
> And pity, like a naked new-born babe
> Striding the blast, or heaven's cherubin hors'd
> Upon the sightless couriers of the air,
> Shall blow the horrid deed in every eye,
> That tears shall drown the wind. I have no spur
> To prick the sides of my intent, but only
> Vaulting ambition, which o'erleaps itself
> And falls on th' other—
>
> [I. vii. 2-28]

After he has seen the dagger it is still pretty much the same (though the appearance of the drops of blood on the dagger has introduced the first intense perception of material detail):

Act III. Scene iv. Banquo's Ghost, Macbeth, and Lady Macbeth. By R. Westall (n.d.).

> Now o'er the one half-world
> Nature seems dead, and wicked dreams abuse
> The curtain'd sleep. Witchcraft celebrates
> Pale Hecate's offerings, and wither'd Murder,
> Alarum'd by his sentinel, the wolf,
> Whose howl's his watch, thus with his stealthy pace,
> With Tarquin's ravishing [strides], towards his design
> Moves like a ghost.
>
> [II. i. 49-6]

And in the same speech his fear leads him to imagine life and speech in the earth and in stones, though there is no doubt that he recognizes this for the fiction it is:

> Thou [sure] and firm set earth,
> Hear not my steps, which [way they] walk, for fear
> The very stones prate of my whereabout
> And take the present horror from the time,
> Which now suits with it.
>
> [II. i. 56-60]

But immediately after the murder, and after the terrible personification—"Macbeth does murder sleep"—there appears a sad transformation in the pictures of his mind:

> —the innocent sleep,
> Sleep that knits up the ravell'd sleave of care,
> The death of each day's life, sore labour's bath,
> Balm of hurt minds, great nature's second course,
> Chief nourisher in life's feast.
>
> [II. ii. 33-7]

Life is falling away into parts, weakly personified, or, at best, dully sensitive. Shortly after, there is the overwhelming thought of the indelible stain of the blood he imagines upon his hand:

> Will all great Neptune's ocean wash this blood
> Clean from my hand? No, this my hand will rather
> The multitudinous seas incarnadine,
> Making the green one red.
>
> [II. ii. 57-60]

The strength of his soul is given over to the conviction once and for all that he has brought inevitable destruction upon himself. The crime has transformed his life, and what remains is a dead life, an indelible stain, something neither under the control of his desires or hopes or even his will. The stain, just as it would change the color of the sea, will overcome the natural order of his life.

And at the end, when he turns from the thought of his dying wife to the state of his own feeling, the lively motions of his life have turned to insensitive matter:

> Canst thou not minister to a mind diseas'd,
> Pluck from the memory a rooted sorrow,
> Raze out the written troubles of the brain,
> And with some sweet oblivious antidote
> Cleanse the stuff'd bosom of the perilous stuff
> Which weighs upon the heart?
>
> [V. iii. 40-5]

Diseas'd, rooted, written, stuff—here Macbeth makes one effort after another to find the word to name his feelings or an aspect of them, and finally he ends with *stuff*, and repeats it as if he knew no other meaningful term for the pain that has all but replaced his other feelings. His mind is now so surely reflecting his disintegrating will that it can provide him only with pictures of something merely material. What was alive is dead.

It would seem that the images of Macbeth's speech are more and more frequently images of matter that is not personified, and that this development keeps pace with the loss of hope and the increase of despair. But this materializing habit, however suddenly it forced itself upon him immediately after the murder, was not in the nature of things complete. Even at the end he thought of tomorrows and yesterdays and life as actors upon a stage, though they turn out to be frail figures compared to his early imagining of the swelling prologue to the imperial theme. And meanwhile it occurs to him to think of his life as a dead leaf, and to think that his mind and heart are full of diseased matter. But Macbeth did not die easily, and the survival in his mind of images with life in them is proof of the brilliance with which he struggled to make up for the terrible defeat he suffered in committing his crimes. His will to live was tremendous, and he meant his imagination to help him live. But his imagination was not under the control of his will.

The images betrayed Macbeth and hastened his deterioration because he clung to them as possessing some instructive reality apart from his conscience. He needed to believe his life could still prosper though he was more and more involved in destroying others' lives. As if to say these lives he was destroying amounted to nothing, trying to believe even life was nothing, his mind was dwelling more and more on mere physical details, conceived in the most vivid strength:

> Here lay Duncan,
> His silver skin lac'd with his golden blood,
> And his gash'd stabs look'd like a breach in nature
> For ruin's wasteful entrance.
>
> [II. iii. 111-14]

> Better be with the dead
> Whom we, to gain our peace, have sent to peace,
> Than on the torture of the mind to lie
> In restless ecstasy.
>
> [III. ii. 19-22]

> Come, seeling night,
> Scarf up the tender eye of pitiful day.
>
> [III. ii. 46-7]

> I had else been perfect,
> Whole as the marble, founded as the rock,
> As broad and general as the casing air.
>
> [III. iv. 20-2]

The materiality of the descriptions became what was most important in them. His greatest fear was that the dead Banquo and Birnam Wood should come to life. To see the world as it was not, a world that did not judge him, gave him its false relief:

> I am in blood
> Stepp'd in so far that, should I wade no more,
> Returning were as tedious as go o'er.
>
> [III. iv. 135-37]

Just as a river might be safely forded, so might a river of blood.

Determined to rid himself of the sense of evil and of retribution, he fed his searching mind with the pictures of physical things he thought there was no harm in, things that, once imagined, would have satisfied his desire to know how things stood, and that by offering no judgment would cease to exist just as right and wrong had. But the pain continued and the images only changed their shape. As more and more presented themselves in the form of material things, they came to represent the incorruptible finality of matter, something that could not speak like angels trumpet-tongued nor prate like stones. Having given his imagination so much of his trust, Macbeth felt that the images had become lastingly part of him, and they had replaced his feelings:

> I have supp'd full with horrors;
> Direness, familiar to my slaughterous thoughts,
> Cannot once start me.
>
> [V. v. 13-15]

Direness—which means, the images of dire things—can no longer offend his sight, and this for him is especially significant, for he seems from the beginning to have been abnormally offended by ugly sights:

> Stars, hide your fires;
> Let not light see my black and deep desires;
> The eye wink at the hand; yet let that be
> Which the eye fears, when it is done, to see.
>
> [I. iv. 50-3]

> Thy crown does sear mine eye-balls....
> Start, eyes!
>
> [IV. i. 113, 116]

The most ominous figure of all was the image of the thickening light:

> Light thickens, and the crow
> Makes wing to th' rooky wood;
> Good things of day begin to droop and drowse,
> Whiles night's black agents to their preys do rouse.
>
> [III. ii. 50-3]

Just as the visual perception of objects depends upon light, so images in the mind are always accompanied by the appearance of light. Aristotle's crude etymology is to the point: "But since vision is pre-eminently sensation, the name [*phantasia*] (imagination) is derived from [*phaos*] (light), because without light it is impossible to see." Light, when congealed to darkness, would conceal from him those sights and images he had to flee: the images would destroy him if he saw them. But as long as he lived he continued to see them, only they were increasingly mere matter, with the life and light gone out of them. And they shared the nature of the serpent in the *Inferno*, who stared at its prey, the soul of Agnello, transfixing it until the soul became that which stared at it. Regarding these lifeless images, Macbeth was either transformed into the likeness of the death his imagination materialized, or else he recognized them as the prophecy of what he was to become, matter bereft of life. (pp. 119-26)

John Arthos, "The Naïve Imagination and the Destruction of Macbeth," in ELH, *Vol. 14, No. 2, June, 1947, pp. 114-26.*

CLEANTH BROOKS   (essay date 1947)

[*Brooks is a prominent proponent of New Criticism, an influential movement in American criticism whose practitioners believe that a work of literature has to be examined as an object in itself through a process of close analysis of symbol, image, and metaphor. For Brooks, metaphor is the primary element of literary art, and his most characteristic essays are detailed studies of metaphoric structure, particularly in poetry. In the following excerpt, Brooks examines two of Shakespeare's metaphoric conceits in* Macbeth. *He begins his discussion, in an unexcerpted portion of this essay, by considering John Donne's "witty" and "self-conscious" conceits as a touchstone for an evaluation of Shakespeare's use of metaphor. The metaphors of the "naked new-born babe" and the "breech'd" daggers in* Macbeth, *Brooks argues, each "contain a central symbol of the plays." The "breech'd" daggers, he contends, contribute to the prevalent clothing imagery in the play, first noted by Caroline F. E. Spurgeon (1935), which suggests masking or cloaking. The "naked new-born babe," states Brooks, can be linked to the play's many references to children and babies—a recurrent image also discussed by Sigmund Freud (1915-16), Ludwig Jekels (1917), G. Wilson Knight (1931), and Paul A. Jorgensen (1971). He asserts that, among other things, the babe symbolizes the future; although Macbeth kills children, he cannot control the future, and Macduff, the baby of the prophecy, destroys him. Brooks concludes that these two "great symbols," the garment and the baby, "furnish Shakespeare with his most subtle and ironically telling instruments."*]

I began by suggesting that our reading of Donne might contribute something to our reading of Shakespeare, though I tried to make plain the fact that I had no design of trying to turn Shakespeare into Donne, or—what I regard as nonsense—of trying to exalt Donne above Shakespeare. I have in mind specifically some such matter as this: that since the *Songs and Sonets* of Donne, no less than *Venus and Adonis*, requires a "perpetual activity of attention . . . on the part of the reader from the rapid flow, the quick change, and the playful nature of the thoughts and images" [Samuel Taylor Coleridge in his *Biographia Literaria*], the discipline gained from reading Donne may allow us to see more clearly the survival of such qualities in the later style of Shakespeare. And, again, I have in mind some such matter as this: that if a reading of Donne has taught us that the "rapid flow, the quick change, and the playful nature of the thoughts and images"—qualities which we are all too prone to associate merely with the fancy—can, on oc-

casion, take on imaginative power, we may, thus taught, better appreciate details in Shakespeare which we shall otherwise dismiss as merely fanciful, or, what is more likely, which we shall simply ignore altogether.

With Donne, of course, the chains of imagery, "always vivid" and "often minute" are perfectly evident. For many readers they are all too evident. The difficulty is not to prove that they exist, but that, on occasion, they may subserve a more imaginative unity. With Shakespeare, the difficulty may well be to prove that the chains exist at all. In general, we may say, Shakespeare has made it relatively easy for his admirers to choose what they like and neglect what they like. What he gives on one or another level is usually so magnificent that the reader finds it easy to ignore other levels.

Yet there are passages not easy to ignore and on which even critics with the conventional interests have been forced to comment. One of these passages occurs in *Macbeth*, Act I, Scene vii, where Macbeth compares the pity for his victim-to-be, Duncan, to

> a naked new-born babe,
> Striding the blast, or heaven's cherubim, hors'd
> Upon the sightless couriers of the air. . .
>
> [I. vii. 21-3]

The comparison is odd, to say the least. Is the babe natural or supernatural—an ordinary, helpless baby, who, as newborn, could not, of course, even toddle, much less stride the blast? Or is it some infant Hercules, quite capable of striding the blast, but, since it is powerful and not helpless, hardly the typical pitiable object?

Shakespeare seems bent upon having it both ways—and, if we read on through the passage—bent upon having the best of both worlds; for he proceeds to give us the option: pity is like the babe "or heaven's cherubim" who quite appropriately, of course, do ride the blast. Yet, even if we waive the question of the legitimacy of the alternative (of which Shakespeare so promptly avails himself), is the cherubim comparison really any more successful than is the babe comparison? Would not one of the great warrior archangels be more appropriate to the scene than the cherub? Does Shakespeare mean for pity or for fear of retribution to be dominant in Macbeth's mind?

Or is it possible that Shakespeare could not make up his own mind? Was he merely writing hastily and loosely, letting the word "pity" suggest the typically pitiable object, the babe naked in the blast, and then, stirred by the vague notion that some threat to Macbeth should be hinted, using "heaven's cherubim"—already suggested by "babe"—to convey the hint? Is the passage vague or precise? Loosely or tightly organized? Comments upon the passage have ranged all the way from one critic's calling it "pure rant, and intended to be so" to another's laudation: "Either like a mortal babe, terrible in helplessness; or like heaven's angel-children, mighty in love and compassion. This magnificent passage . . .".

An even more interesting, and perhaps more disturbing passage in the play is that in which Macbeth describes his discovery of the murder:

> Here lay Duncan,
> His silver skin lac'd with his golden blood;
> And his gash'd stabs, look'd like a breach in nature
> For ruin's wasteful entrance: there, the murderers,

Steep'd in the colours of their trade, their daggers
Unmannerly breech'd with gore. . . .

[II. iii. 111-16]

It is amusing to watch the textual critics, particularly those of the eighteenth century, fight a stubborn rear-guard action against the acceptance of "breech'd." Warburton emended "breech'd" to "reech'd"; Johnson, to "drench'd"; Seward, to "hatch'd." Other critics argued that the *breeches* implied were really the handles of the daggers, and that, accordingly, "breech'd" actually here meant "sheathed." The Variorum page witnesses the desperate character of the defense, but the position has had to be yielded, after all. *The Shakespeare Glossary* defines "breech'd" as meaning "covered as with breeches," and thus leaves the poet committed to a reading which must still shock the average reader as much as it shocked that nineteenth-century critic who pronounced upon it as follows: "A metaphor must not be far-fetched nor dwell upon the details of a disgusting picture, as in these lines. There is little, and that far-fetched, similarity between *gold lace* and *blood,* or between *bloody daggers* and *breech'd legs.* The slightness of the similarity, recalling the greatness of the dissimilarity, disgusts us with the attempted comparison."

The two passages are not of the utmost importance, I dare say, though the speeches (of which each is a part) are put in Macbeth's mouth and come at moments of great dramatic tension in the play. Yet, in neither case is there any warrant for thinking that Shakespeare was not trying to write as well as he could. Moreover, whether we like it or not, the imagery is fairly typical of Shakespeare's mature style. Either passage ought to raise some qualms among those who retreat to Shakespeare's authority when they seek to urge the claims of "noble simplicity." They are hardly simple. Yet it is possible that such passages as these may illustrate another poetic resource, another type of imagery which, even in spite of its apparent violence and complication, Shakespeare could absorb into the total structure of his work.

Shakespeare, I repeat, is not Donne—is a much greater poet than Donne; yet the example of his typical handling of imagery will scarcely render support to the usual attacks on Donne's imagery—for, with regard to the two passages in question, the second one, at any rate, is about as strained as Donne is at his most extreme pitch.

Yet I think that Shakespeare's daggers attired in their bloody breeches can be defended as poetry, and as characteristically Shakespearean poetry. Furthermore, both this passage and that about the newborn babe, it seems to me, are far more than excrescences, mere extravagances of detail: each, it seems to me, contains a central symbol of the play, and symbols which we must understand if we are to understand either the detailed passage or the play as a whole. (pp. 26-30)

I should like to use the passages as convenient points of entry into the larger symbols which dominate the play. They *are* convenient because, even if we judge them to be faulty, they demonstrate how obsessive for Shakespeare the symbols were—they demonstrate how far the conscious (or unconscious) symbolism could take him.

If we see how the passages are related to these symbols, and they to the tragedy as a whole, the main matter is achieved; and having seen this, if we still prefer "to wish the lines away," that, of course, is our privilege. In the meantime, we may have learned something about Shakespeare's methods—not merely of building metaphors—but of encompassing his larger meanings.

One of the most startling things has come out of Miss Spurgeon's book on Shakespeare's imagery is her discovery of the "old clothes" imagery in *Macbeth.* As she points out: "The idea constantly recurs that Macbeth's new honours sit ill upon him, like a loose and badly fitting garment, belonging to someone else" [see excerpt above, 1935]. And she goes on to quote passage after passage in which the idea is expressed. But, though we are all in Miss Spurgeon's debt for having pointed this out, one has to observe that Miss Spurgeon has hardly explored the full implications of her discovery. (p. 30)

[The] series of garment metaphors which run through the play is paralleled by a series of masking or cloaking images which—if we free ourselves of Miss Spurgeon's rather mechanical scheme of classification—show themselves to be merely variants of the garments which hide none too well his disgraceful self. He is consciously hiding that self throughout the play.

"False face must hide what the false heart doth know" [I. vii. 82], he counsels Lady Macbeth before the murder of Duncan; and later, just before the murder of Banquo, he invokes night to "Scarf up the eye of pitiful day" [III. ii. 47].

One of the most powerful of these cloaking images is given to Lady Macbeth in the famous speech in Act I:

> Come, thick night,
> And pall thee in the dunnest smoke of hell,
> That my keen knife see not the wound it makes,
> Nor heaven peep through the blanket of the dark,
> To cry, "Hold, Hold!"

[I. v. 50-4]

I suppose that it is natural to conceive the "keen knife" here as held in her own hand. Lady Macbeth is capable of wielding it. And in this interpretation, the imagery is thoroughly significant. Night is to be doubly black so that not even her knife may see the wound it makes. But I think that there is good warrant for regarding her "keen knife" as Macbeth himself. She has just, a few lines above, given her analysis of Macbeth's character as one who would "not play false, / And yet [would] wrongly win" [I. v. 21-2]. To bring him to the point of action, she will have to "chastise [him] with the valour of [her] tongue" [I. v. 27]. There is good reason, then, for her to invoke night to become blacker still—to pall itself in the "dunnest smoke of hell." For night must not only screen the deed from the eye of heaven—conceal it at least until it is too late for heaven to call out to Macbeth "Hold, Hold!" Lady Macbeth would have night blanket the deed from the hesitant doer. The imagery thus repeats and reinforces the substance of Macbeth's anguished aside uttered in the preceding scene:

> Let not light see my black and deep desires;
> The eye wink at the hand; yet let that be
> Which the eye fears, when it is done, to see.

[I. iv. 51-3]

I do not know whether "blanket" and 'pall" qualify as garment metaphors in Miss Spurgeon's classification: yet one is the clothing of sleep, and the other, the clothing of death—they are the appropriate garments of night; and they carry on an important aspect of the general clothes imagery. It is not necessary to attempt to give here an exhaustive list of instances of the garment metaphor; but one should say a word about the remarkable passage in II, iii.

Here, after the discovery of Duncan's murder, Banquo says

> And when we have our naked frailties hid,
> That suffer in exposure, let us meet,
> And question this most bloody piece of work—
>
> [II. iii. 126-28]

that is, "When we have clothed ourselves against the chill morning air, let us meet to discuss this bloody piece of work." Macbeth answers, as if his subconscious mind were already taking Banquo's innocent phrase, "naked frailties," in a deeper, ironic sense:

> Let's briefly put on manly readiness. . . .
>
> [II. iii. 133]

It is ironic; for the "manly readiness" which he urges the other lords to put on, is, in his own case, a hypocrite's garment: he can only pretend to be the loyal, grief-stricken liege who is almost unstrung by the horror of Duncan's murder.

But the word "manly" carries still a further ironic implication: earlier, Macbeth had told Lady Macbeth that he dared

> do all that may become a man;
> Who dares do more is none.
>
> [I. vii. 46-7]

Under the weight of her reproaches of cowardice, however, he *has* dared do more, and has become less than a man, a beast. He has already laid aside, therefore, one kind of "manly readiness" and has assumed another: he has garbed himself in a sterner composure than that which he counsels to his fellows—the hard and inhuman "manly readiness" of the resolved murderer.

The clothes imagery, used sometimes with emphasis on one aspect of it, sometimes, on another, does pervade the play. And it should be evident that the daggers "breech'd with gore"—though Miss Spurgeon does not include the passage in her examples of clothes imagery—represent one more variant of this general symbol. Consider the passage once more:

> Here lay Duncan,
> His silver skin lac'd with his golden blood;
> And his gash'd stabs look'd like a breach in nature
> For ruin's wasteful entrance: there, the murderers,
> Steep'd in the colours of their trade, their daggers
> Unmannerly breech'd with gore. . . .

The clothes imagery runs throughout the passage; the body of the king is dressed in the most precious of garments, the blood royal itself; and the daggers too are dressed—in the same garment. The daggers, "naked" except for their lower parts which are reddened with blood, are like men in "unmannerly" dress—men, naked except for their red breeches, lying beside the red-handed grooms. The figure, though vivid, is fantastic; granted. But the basis for the comparison is *not* slight and adventitious. The metaphor fits the real situation on the deepest levels. As Macbeth and Lennox burst into the room, they find the daggers wearing, as Macbeth knows all too well, a horrible masquerade. They have been carefully "clothed" to play a part. They are not honest daggers, honorably naked in readiness to guard the king, or, "mannerly" clothed in their own sheaths. Yet the disguise which they wear will enable Macbeth to assume the robes of Duncan—robes to which he is no more entitled than are the daggers to the royal garments which they now wear, grotesquely.

The reader will, of course, make up his own mind as to the value of the passage. But the metaphor in question, in the light of the other garment imagery, cannot be dismissed as merely a strained ingenuity, irrelevant to to the play. And the reader who *does* accept it as poetry will probably be that reader who knows the play best, not the reader who knows it slightly and regards Shakespeare's poetry as a rhetoric more or less loosely draped over the "content" of the play.

And now what can be said of pity, the "naked new-born babe"? Though Miss Spurgeon does not note it . . . , there are, by the way, a great many references to babes in this play—references which occur on a number of levels. The babe appears sometimes as a character, such as Macduff's child; sometimes as a symbol, like the crowned babe and the bloody babe which are raised by the witches on the occasion of Macbeth's visit to them; sometimes, in a metaphor, as in the passage under discussion. The number of such references can hardly be accidental; and the babe turns out to be, as a matter of fact, perhaps the most powerful symbol in the tragedy. (pp. 33-7)

Tempted by the Weird Sisters and urged on by his wife, Macbeth is . . . caught between the irrational and the rational. There is a sense, of course, in which every man is caught between them. Man must try to predict and plan and control his destiny. That is man's fate; and the struggle, if he is to realize himself as a man, cannot be avoided. The question, of course, which has always interested the tragic dramatist involves the terms on which the struggle is accepted and the protagonist's attitude toward fate and toward himself. Macbeth in his general concern for the future is typical—is Every Man. He becomes the typical tragic protagonist when he yields to pride and *hybris*. The occasion for temptation is offered by the prophecy of the Weird Sisters. They offer him knowledge which cannot be arrived at rationally. They offer a key—if only a partial key—to what is otherwise unpredictable. Lady Macbeth, on the other hand, by employing a ruthless clarity of perception, by discounting all emotional claims, offers him the promise of bringing about the course of events which he desires.

Now, in the middle of the play, though he has not lost confidence and though, as he himself says, there can be no turning back, doubts have begun to arise; and he returns to the Weird Sisters to secure unambiguous answers to his fears. But, pathetically and ironically for Macbeth, in returning to the Weird Sisters, he is really trying to impose rationality on what sets itself forth plainly as irrational: that is, Macbeth would force a rigid control on a future which, by definition—by the very fact that the Weird Sisters already know it—stands beyond his manipulation.

It is because of his hopes for his own children and his fears of Banquo's that he has returned to the witches for counsel. It is altogether appropriate, therefore, that two of the apparitions by which their counsel is revealed should be babes, the crowned babe and the bloody babe.

For the babe signifies the future which Macbeth would control and cannot control. (pp. 41-2)

The logic of Macbeth's distraught mind, thus, forces him to make war on children, a war which in itself reflects his desperation and is a confession of weakness. Macbeth's ruffians, for example, break into Macduff's castle and kill his wife and children. The scene in which the innocent child prattles with his mother about his absent father, and then is murdered, is typical Shakespearean "fourth act" pathos. But the pathos is not adventitious; the scene ties into the inner symbolism of the play. For the child, in its helplessness, defies the murderers. Its defiance testifies to the force which threatens Macbeth and which Macbeth cannot destroy.

But we are not, of course, to placard the child as The Future in a rather stiff and mechanical allegory. *Macbeth* is no such allegory. Shakespeare's symbols are richer and more flexible than that. The babe signifies not only the future; it symbolizes all those enlarging purposes which make life meaningful, and it symbolizes, furthermore, all those emotional and—to Lady Macbeth—irrational ties which make man more than a machine—which render him human. It signifies pre-eminently the pity which Macbeth, under Lady Macbeth's tutelage, would wean himself of as something "unmanly." Lady Macbeth's great speeches early in the play become brilliantly ironical when we realize that Shakespeare is using the same symbol for the unpredictable future that he uses for human compassion. Lady Macbeth is willing to go to any length to grasp the future: she would willingly dash out the brains of her own child if it stood in her way to that future. But this is to repudiate the future, for the child is its symbol. (pp. 42-3)

Most fittingly, the last of the prophecies in which Macbeth has placed his confidence, concerns the child: and Macbeth comes to know the final worst when Macduff declares to him that he was not "born of woman" but was from his "mother's womb / Untimely ripp'd" [V. viii. 15-16]. The babe here has defied even the thing which one feels may reasonably be predicted of him—his time of birth. With Macduff's pronouncement, the unpredictable has broken through the last shred of the net of calculation. The future cannot be trammelled up. The naked babe confronts Macbeth to pronounce his doom.

The passage with which we began this essay, then, is an integral part of a larger context, and of a very rich context:

> And pity, like a naked new-born babe,
> Striding the blast, or heaven's cherubim, hors'd
> Upon the sightless couriers of the air,
> Shall blow the horrid deed in every eye,
> That tears shall drown the wind.

Pity is like the naked babe, the most sensitive and helpless thing; yet, almost as soon as the comparison is announced, the symbol of weakness begins to turn into a symbol of strength; for the babe, though newborn, is pictured as "Striding the blast" like an elemental force—like "heaven's cherubim, hors'd / Upon the sightless couriers of the air." We can give an answer to the question put earlier: is Pity like the human and helpless babe, or powerful as the angel that rides the winds? It is both; and it is strong because of its very weakness. The paradox is inherent in the situation itself; and it is the paradox that will destroy the overbrittle rationalism on which Macbeth founds his career.

For what will it avail Macbeth to cover the deed with the blanket of the dark if the elemental forces that ride the winds will blow the horrid deed in every eye? And what will it avail Macbeth to clothe himself in "manliness"—to become bloody, bold, and resolute,—if he is to find himself again and again, viewing his bloody work through the "eye of childhood / That fears a painted devil"? [II. ii. 51-2]. Certainly, the final and climactic appearance of the babe symbol merges all the contradictory elements of the symbol. For, with Macduff's statement about his birth, the naked babe rises before Macbeth as not only the future that eludes calculation but as avenging angel as well.

The clothed daggers and the naked babe—mechanism and life—instrument and end—death and birth—that which should be left bare and clean and that which should be clothed and warmed—these are facets of two of the great symbols which run throughout the play. They are not the only symbols, to be sure; they are not the most obvious symbols: darkness and blood appear more often. But with a flexibility which must amaze the reader, the image of the garment and the image of the babe are so used as to encompass an astonishingly large area of the total situation. And between them—the naked babe, essential humanity, humanity stripped down to the naked thing itself, and yet as various as the future—and the various garbs which humanity assumes, the robes of honor, the hypocrite's disguise, the inhuman "manliness" with which Macbeth endeavors to cover up his essential humanity—between them, they furnish Shakespeare with his most subtle and ironically telling instruments. (pp. 44-6)

Cleanth Brooks, "The Naked Babe and the Cloak of Manliness," in his The Well Wrought Urn: Studies in the Structure of Poetry, *1947. Reprint by Harcourt Brace Jovanovich, 1956?, pp. 21-46.*

EDITH SITWELL (essay date 1948)

[*In the following excerpt, Sitwell, an important English poet, presents a detailed analysis of several speeches in* Macbeth, *emphasizing the effect of their linguistic composition. Lady Macbeth's invocation to the evil spirits in Act I, Scene v, states Sitwell, presents "an untuned and terrible effect" because of the "discordant, dissonantal o's." In Act II, Scene ii, she further asserts, the sense of Macbeth's despair "is brought home to us by the dark, hollow, ever-recurrent echoes of the* ore . . . aw *sounds." Sitwell also argues that the tragic themes of* Macbeth *are concerned with the separation of the man and woman, who, as the play progresses, take different paths of damnation: Macbeth's is of the spirit, Lady Macbeth's is of the earth.*]

The events in the life of a character, as well as the personality, even the appearance of Shakespeare's men and women, are suggested by the texture, the movement of the lines. In *Macbeth*, for instance, we find, over and over again, schemes of tuneless dropping dissonances:

FIRST WITCH

When shall we three meet againe?
In thunder, lightning, or in raine?

SECOND WITCH

When the hurly-burly's done,
When the battle's lost and won.

THIRD WITCH

That will be ere set of Sun.

FIRST WITCH

Where the place?

SECOND WITCH

Upon the heath.

THIRD WITCH

There to meet with Macbeth.

[I. i. 1-7]

'Done' is a dropping dissonance to 'raine', 'heath' to the second syllable of 'Macbeth', and these untuned, dropping dissonances, falling from the mouths of the three Fates degraded into the shapes of filthy hags, have a prophetic and terrible significance.—So do Macbeth and Lady Macbeth, slow step by step, descend into Hell. (p. 24)

In this vast world torn from the universe of night, there are three tragic themes. The first theme is that of the actual guilt, and the separation in damnation of the two characters—the man who, in spite of his guilt, walks the road of the spirit, and who loves the light that has forsaken him—and the woman who, after her invocation to the 'Spirits who tend on mortall thoughts' [I. v. 40-1], walks in the material world, and who does not know that light exists, until she is nearing her end and must seek the comfort of one small taper to illumine all the murkiness of Hell.—That small taper is her soul. (pp. 27-8)

The second tragic theme of the play is the man's love for the woman whose damnation is of the earth, who is unable, until death is near, to conceive of the damnation of the spirit, and who in her blindness therefore strays away from him, leaving him for ever in his lonely hell.

The third tragic theme is the woman's despairing love for the man whose vision she cannot see, and whom she has helped to drive into damnation.

The very voices of these two damned souls have therefore a different sound. His voice is like that of some gigantic being in torment—of a lion with a human soul. In her speech invoking darkness, the actual sound is so murky and thick that the lines seem impervious to light, and, at times, rusty, as though they had lain in the blood that had been spilt, or in some hell-born dew. There is no escape from what we have done. The past will return to confront us. And that is even shown in the verse. In that invocation there are perpetual echoes, sometimes far removed from each other, sometimes placed close together.

For instance, in the line

> And fill me from the Crowne to the Toe, top-full
> > [I. v. 42]

'full' is a darkened dissonance to 'fill'—and these dissonances, put at opposite ends of the line,—together with the particular placing of the alliterative *f*'s of 'fill' and 'full' and the alliterative *t*'s, and the rocking up and down of the dissonantal *o*'s ('Crowne', 'Toe', 'top') show us a mind reeling on the brink of madness, about to topple down into those depths, yet striving to retain its balance.

Let us examine the passage for a moment. The manner in which the stressed assonances are placed is largely responsible for the movement, and the texture is extremely variable—murky always, excepting for those few flares from the fires of Hell, but varying in the thickness of that murk.

> The Raven himselfe is hoarse
> That croakes the fatall entrance of Duncane
> Under my Battlements. Come, you Spirits
> That tend on mortall thoughts! unsex me here,
> And fill me from the Crowne to the Toe, top-full
> Of direst Cruelty! Make thicke my blood;
> Stop up the accesse and passage to Remorse,
> That no compunctious visitings of Nature
> Shake my fell purpose, nor keepe peace betweene
> The effect and it. Come to my Woman's Brests,
> And take my Milke for Gall, you murthering Ministers,
> Where-ever in your sightlesse substances
> You waite on Nature's Mischiefe. Come, thicke Night,

> And pall thee in the dunnest smoake of Hell,
> That my keene knife see not the Wound it makes,
> Nor Heaven peepe through the Blanket of the darke
> To cry Hold, Hold.
> > [I. v. 38-54]

Throughout the whole of this speech, an untuned and terrible effect is produced by these discordant, dissonantal *o*'s, used outwardly and inwardly—'hoarse' echoed by 'croakes' (I am assuming, from the evidence of other words, that the *oa* of 'croakes' was then pronounced as an assonance to the 'oar' of 'hoarse')—these thickening to 'come', darkening again to 'mortall thoughts' and then—supreme example—making the line rock up and down, and finally topple over, in

> And fill me from the Crowne to the Toe, top-full.

'Blood', 'Stop', 'Remorse', 'Come',—each of these dissonantal *o*'s has a different height or depth, a different length or choked shortness. There is a fabric, too, of dull and rusty vowels, thickened *m*'s, and unshaping *s*'s—(these latter are unshaping because they are placed close together, and so deprive the line of form, to some extent, as in

> Stop up the accesse and passage to Remorse,
> That no compunctious visitings of Nature

or

> Where-ever in your sightlesse substances).

Throughout the passage, the consonants are for ever thickening and then thinning again—perhaps as the will hardens and then, momentarily, dissolves. In the lines

> That croakes the fatall entrance of Duncane
> Under my Battlements. Come, you Spirits

'Come' is a thickened, darkened assonance (almost a dissonance) to the 'Dun' of Duncane and of the first syllable of 'under'. And in the line

> That no compunctious visitings of Nature

the first syllable of 'compunctious' is a kind of darkened, thickened reverberation of the word 'Come' (darkened or thickened because what follows throws a shade backward); the second syllable is a thickened echo of the first syllable of 'Duncane'.

As the giant shuttles of Fate weave, closing and opening, so do the lines of this speech seem to close and open, and to change their length. But this change is in appearance only, and not real. By this I mean that there are no extra syllables to the line. The apparent change is due to the lightening and lengthening of the vowel sounds. For though, as I have said already, the words are frequently dull and rusty in this passage, at times they stretch out into a harsh shriek, which sometimes is sustained, sometimes broken,—as with the broken echoes 'Raven', 'fatall'.

There are moments, too, when the line is prolonged for other reasons than that of the changing vowel-lengths:

> And take my Milke for Gall, you murthering Ministers

is an example. Here, in spite of the fact that all the vowels are dulled (with the exception of the high *a* of 'take' and the *a* of 'gall'), the *l*'s prolong the line slightly, the thick, muffled reverberations of the alliterative *m*'s, placed so close together, produce a peculiar effect of dull horror. In

> Stop up the accesse and passage to Remorse

we shall find that instead of the line being slowed (and therefore, in appearance, lengthened) by the s's, the dull assonantal a's, a more powerful factor, when placed close together actually shorten the line, which, again, is thickened by the p's ending words that are placed side by side. The effect produced in a line by p's *ending* a word, and by p's *beginning* a word, is completely different. A p beginning a word does not necessarily thicken the line.

Sometimes the particular placing of the assonances produces a sound like that of a fevered, uneven pulse,—an example is the effect brought about by the drumming of the dull un . . . om sounds in the lines

> . . . Duncane
> Under my Battlements. Come.

This terrible drumming sound is heard over and over again throughout the passage, and is due not only to the placing of the assonances, but also to the particular placing of double-syllabled and—(this has a still stronger effect)—treble-syllabled words and quick-moving, unaccented one-syllabled words. In the line

> And fill me from the Crowne to the Toe, top-full

'to the' gives an example of the effect of those quick-moving, unaccented one-syllabled words:

> That no compunctious visitings of Nature

is an example of the use of three-syllabled words, disturbing, purposely, the movement of the line.

This march towards Hell is slow, and has a thunderous darkened pomp. It is slow, and yet it has but few pauses (for that march is of her own will, she is driven by that will as by a Fury) and these pauses are not long, but deep, like fissures opening down into Hell. There is, however, a stretching pause after the word 'Gall'.

In the Second Scene of Act Two, while the sleeping King is being sent to his death, Lady Macbeth's voice has a different tone:

> That which hath made them drunke hath made me bold,
> What hath quench'd them hath given me fire.
> > Hearke!
> Peace!
> It was the Owle that shriek'd, the fatall Bell-man,
> Which gives the stern'st good-night.
> > [II. ii. 1-4]

Here we actually feel the silence of the night, broken by that long flame of a voice, like a torch held by a Fury before the destruction of a world is begun. That voice, pausing, as it seems, for ever on the long sound of 'Peace' (a word that has the high doom-haunted tone of the owl's shriek), echoes, in a straight line, down all the corridors of the Dead.

The speeches of Macbeth have a different sound. He, at least, would retreat from the path, if only it were possible. But he is a prisoner, bound for ever to his first hell-born deed, and he must go where his deed drags him.

The dark and terrible voice of Macbeth is not covered by a blood-dewed rust, is not like a black and impenetrable smoke from Hell, or the torch of a Fury—as is the voice of the woman who, to him, is Fate. It is hollow like the depths into which he has fallen, it returns ever (though it, too, has discordances)

to one note, dark as the Hell through which he walks with that sleepless soul. The sound is ever 'no more'.

> > Cawdor
> Shall sleepe no more, Macbeth shall sleepe no more.
> > [II. ii. 39-40] . . .

The despair of Macbeth, hearing the voice that cries these words, his sense that there is no escape, is brought home to us by the dark, hollow, ever-recurrent echoes of the *ore* . . . *aw* sounds. That is the keynote of the whole speech.

As with Lady Macbeth's speech quoted above, the magnificence is largely brought about and controlled by the particular places in which the alliterations and assonances are placed (though in the two speeches they are used completely differently, and have an entirely different effect).

MACBETH

> Me thought I heard a voyce cry 'Sleepe no more',
> Macbeth does murder Sleepe, the innocent Sleepe,
> Sleepe that knits up the ravell'd sleave of Care,
> The death of each daye's Life; sore Labour's Bath,
> Balme of hurte mindes, Great Nature's second Course,
> Chiefe Nourisher in Life's Feast—

LADY MACBETH

> > What doe you meane?

MACBETH

> Still it cry'd 'Sleepe no More'! to all the house:
> Glamis hath murder'd Sleepe, and therefore Cawdor
> Shall sleepe no more, Macbeth shall sleepe no more.
> > [II. ii. 32-40]

The hollow vowels are like 'Burrows, and Channels, and Clefts, and Caverns, that never had the comfort of one beam of light since the great fall of the Earth' [Thomas Burnet in his *The Theory of the Earth*].

Twice, a word shudders in that dark voice. The first time, it is the word 'innocent'—that word which must henceforth fly in terror from the voice that uttered it,—but that will yet sound again from those guilty lips, bringing with it a renewed agony of soul.

Sometimes an awe-inspiring, drum-beating sound is heard. Once it is slow, and is caused by placing alliterative b's, with near-assonantal vowel-sounds—'Bath', 'Balme'—(these being pronounced at that time 'Bawth', 'Baulme')—at the end of one line and the beginning of the next. (There is a strong pause between these words.) These dark a's are not an exact assonance, because of the difference in thickness between the th and the 'lme'. Then, for a second time, two a sounds are placed together, 'Great Nature's', and here the beat is less emphatic; there is no pause between the sounds.

But above all, the quickened beat of a terror-stricken heart is heard, in 'therefore Cawdor'—'fore' being a darkened dissonance to 'there', and the two other syllables being as nearly as possible assonances to 'fore', to 'Balme' and to 'Bath', though all have different degrees of darkness.

This is followed by the long, stately, and inexorable march of Doom:

> Shall sleepe no more, Macbeth shall sleepe no more.

It is in this scene that we first become aware of the different paths of damnation,—the path of the spirit that sees not all great Neptune's ocean will wash his hand clear of blood,—and that of the earth-bound Fate who, until she is near her end, dreams that

> A little water cleares us of this deede,
>
> [II. ii. 64]

and who, when the voice cries

> Cawdor
> Shall sleepe no more, Macbeth shall sleepe no more.

hears only the small voice of the cricket—or a dark, but yet human voice:

MACBETH

I have done the deed. Didst thou not heare a noyse?

LADY MACBETH

I heard the Owle screame, and the Crickets cry.
Did not you speake?

MACBETH

When?

LADY MACBETH

Now.

MACBETH

As I descended?

LADY MACBETH

Aye.

MACBETH

Hearke!
Who lyes i' the second chamber?

LADY MACBETH

Donalbaine.
[II. ii. 14-18]

'Did not you speake? . . .' Often, in this drama, Fate takes to herself, and uses, the voice of one of the protagonists. . . . And, as Macbeth must hear the voices of the three Sisters and the Apparitions speaking through the lips of his wife, and her voice through theirs—('Be bloody, bold, and resolute'. Who spoke those words: 'who was it thus that cry'd?' as Lady Macbeth asked)—so, here, in the words 'As I descended', it may be that the descent was into Hell, and that his doom spoke through his unknowing lips.

Doom and he were one.

Macduff, discovering the murder of the King, shouts:

> Banquo and Donalbain! Malcolm! Awake!
> Shake off this downy sleepe, Death's counterfeit,
> And looke on Death itselfe!—up, up, and see
> The great Doome's image!—Malcolm! Banquo!
> As from your graves rise up, and walk like sprights
> To countenance this horror!
>
> [II. iii. 75-80]

These words, that have a strange echoing sound like that of a boulder being thrown into deep water, must have struck the soul of the guilty man with terror. . . .

Malcolm, who must fly, if he would escape his father's fate, Banquo, who must soon die, are called as from their graves,—

and to look on what? The great Doome's image. Duncan? *Or Macbeth*. For so he must have seen himself—as the great Doome. (pp. 28-36)

From now onward, only blood, and the road that he must tread, exist for Macbeth in the tangible world.

> Who lyes i' the second chamber?

. . . Who must be the next to fall under his blood-stained hands, upon that road? . . . But to Lady Macbeth, he is speaking, not of a grave that must be dug, and of a man about to die, but of one sleeping in his bed—Donalbain.

Here, then, in these few lines, the two guilt-stricken souls say farewell, for ever. The immense pause after Lady Macbeth's 'Aye' is a gap in time, like the immense gap betweenn the Ice Age and the Stone Age, wherein, as Science tells us, 'the previously existing inhabitants of the earth were almost wholly destroyed, and a different class of inhabitants created'.—On the other side of that gap in time, Macbeth rises as the new inhabitant of a changed world—and alone in the universe of eternal night, although the voice of Lady Macbeth, his Fate, his loving Fury, still drives him onward. (p. 37)

Though these souls are separated for ever, yet sometimes the appalling necessities arising from their crime leash them together for a moment . . . as in the scene (Act III, Scene I) where, with a sort of crouching, horror-inspiring quietness, like that of a tiger about to lap blood, Macbeth says

> Heere's our chiefe Guest.
>
> [III. i. 11]

And, stretching beyond him, straining even more eagerly towards the doomed Banquo, Lady Macbeth continues:

> If he had beene forgotten,
> It had beene as a gap in our great Feast
> And all-thing unbecomming.
>
> [III. i. 11-13]

—the sound of the word 'forgotten' being like that of a beast lapping. (pp. 38-9)

After [the scene in which Banquo's ghost appears], the gulf separating the two beings is impassable. Not only the change of the world in which they live, but the whole depth of the soul, separates them. They are divided in all but love. . . . She will love him for ever: but he has gone beyond love. . . . Ambition, Avarice, had no stronger root than love in Macbeth. But now there is no room for her in that Hell.

He asks her

> What is the night?

and she replies

> Almost at oddes with morning, which is which.
>
> [III. iv. 125-26]

Here, I think, Macbeth is asking if the night is blacker for this fresh crime. But Lady Macbeth is speaking of the physical universe.

Macbeth then utters these words:

> How sayst thou, that Macduff denies his person
> At our great bidding?
>
> [III. iv. 127-28]

He is speaking to the invisible beings who now, with the past and future victims of his guilt, alone inhabit his world. His wife, surprised by the question, replies:

> Did you send to him, Sir?
>
> [III. iv. 128]

And Macbeth, from his polar solitude, answers this being of another universe, who is separated from him by the whole darkness of her spiritual blindness:

> I heare it by the way: but I will send.
>
> [III. iv. 129]

From that moment, I think that the appearance of Macbeth must have inspired terror. . . . (pp. 43-4)

And Lady Macbeth—how changed is she, in that pitiful scene when she who had cried to 'thicke Night' to envelop the world and her soul, she who had rejected light, seeks the comfort of one little taper,—the small candle-flame of her soul, to light all the murkiness of Hell. Yet still, in the lonely mutterings of one who must walk through Hell alone, save for the phantom of Macbeth, we hear that indomitable will that pushed him to his doom, rising once more in the vain hope that she may shield and guide him.

There is, in these two beings, the faithfulness of the lion and his mate. It is not their fault that never more can she be his companion. (p. 44)

> Edith Sitwell, " 'Macbeth'," in her *A Notebook on William Shakespeare*, *Macmillan & Co. Ltd.*, 1948, pp. 24-46.

ROY WALKER (essay date 1949)

[*In the following excerpt, drawn from his book* The Time Is Free: A Study of "Macbeth", *Walker argues that Duncan's murder and its consequences "are profoundly impregnated with the central tragedy of the Christian myth," an interpretation also suggested by Roy W. Battenhouse (1952), G. R. Elliott (1958), and John B. Harcourt (1961). He notes parallels between passages in* Macbeth *and the New Testament scriptures. Walker also discusses the knocking at the gate in Act II, Scene iii, stating that while the knocking is a reflux of the human upon the fiendish, as Thomas De Quincey (1823) proposed, it is also "a pulse of doom to the guilty souls within the castle." He further associates the knocking with Christian salvation, an observation also made by Harcourt.*]

Like Hamlet, Macbeth knows the 'dread of something after death' [*Hamlet*, III. i. 77]. Unlike Hamlet, he thrusts it aside, reduces murder from sacrilege to crime and meditates upon expediency. If regicide is expedient here and now, he will jump the life to come, leap out of the Christian mystery of eternity into time, an insane succession of meaningless to-morrows. In John's gospel it is during the last supper that Jesus says to Judas *That thou doest, do quickly*. Duncan has almost supped when Macbeth deliberates

> If it were done when 'tis done, then 'twere well
> It were done quickly.
>
> [I. vii. 1-2]

The divine-king at his last supper is stripped of divinity that murder may be judged by worldly standards. But time is not outside eternity, the moral order impinges upon history.

> We still have judgment here; that we but teach
> Bloody instructions, which, being taught, return
> To plague th' inventor: this even-handed justice
> Commends th' ingredients of our poisoned chalice
> To our own lips.
>
> [I. vii. 8-12]

The chalice is the Eucharist-cup. Macbeth is still in the grip of eternity. In Revelation those who have shed the blood of saints are given blood to drink. In Dante, the ninth and last circle of Hell is the place of those who committed murder under cover of hospitality, and those—among them Judas—who were traitors to their lords and benefactors. Macbeth has not jumped the life to come as he argues now:

> He's here in double-trust:
> First, as I am his kinsman and his subject,
> Strong both against the deed; then, as his host,
> Who should against the murderer shut the door,
> Not bear the knife myself.
>
> [I. vii. 12-16]

These are not sentiments proper to a political realist. They are the misgivings of a man who sees his action judged in the light of eternity, and the light of eternity plays now over the figure of his royal victim, investing him with a golden halo of divinity. It might be Judas speaking. Duncan:

> Hath born his faculties so *meek*, hath been
> So clear in his great office, that *his virtues*
> *Will plead like angels, trumpet-tongued, against*
> *The deep damnation* of his taking-off;
> And *pity, like a naked new-born babe*,
> Striding the blast, or *heaven's cherubin*, hors'd
> Upon the sightless couriers of the air,
> Shall blow the horrid deed in every eye,
> That tears shall drown the wind.
>
> [I. vii. 17-25]

Against the murdering ministers in their *sightless* substances ride heaven's cherubin, horsed upon the *sightless* couriers of the air. The babe whose brains the she-devil would dash out is pity, striding the blast of the storm of evil. Drowning the elemental thunder are the voices of angels, pleading trumpet-tongued. This is indeed the life and death struggle of the man who is tempted to memorize another Golgotha—whose crime when consummated raises among men the awful cry:

> Confusion now hath made his masterpiece!
> Most sacrilegious murder hath broke ope
> The Lord's anointed temple, and stole thence
> The life o' the building!
>
> [II. iii. 66-9]

The murder of Duncan and its consequences are profoundly impregnated with the central tragedy of the Christian myth.

'And supper being ended, the devil having now put into the heart of Judas . . . to betray him . . .'. Macbeth has come near to breaking away from temptation and enchantment. The devil must intervene. Lady Macbeth comes from the supper-room, he gazes on her face and his return upwards is for ever lost. She says:

> He has almost supp'd: Why have you left the chamber?
>
> [I. vii. 29]

(pp. 53-5)

De Quincey, in his famous essay on [the knocking at the gate in *Macbeth*], is both right and wrong. The knocking *is* the reflux of the human upon the fiendish, 'the pulses of life are beginning to beat again' but not yet does the world of darkness pass away like 'a pageantry in the clouds' [see excerpt above, 1823]. The pulse of life without is a pulse of doom to the guilty souls within the castle. It awakens a knowledge of the darkness within that intensifies the horror. The sunless dawn is not yet. Macbeth cries out:

> Whence is that knocking?
> How is't with me when every noise appals me?
> What hands are here? Ha! *they pluck out mine eyes!*
>
>   [II. ii. 54-6]

Oedipus scratches out his eyes when he comprehends his own deed. The shock that Macbeth sustains at this sound of the pulse of life is the extreme of the experience that Lady Macbeth underwent when her servant cried, 'The king comes here to-night' [I. v. 31]. For a moment he thinks the knockers have come to proclaim his guilt; his crime is discovered. At once he realises that this is his guilt responding, the sound is natural and commonplace. The natural is now a nightmare to him. His own hands pluck at his eyes. The cause of this further reaction is not obvious. We must turn aside to look for a possible explanation.

In Luke's gospel we read, 'Knock, and it shall be opened unto you.' It is a metaphor of hope. In the same chapter (xi.), 'The light of the body is in the eye: therefore when thine eye is single, thy whole body also is full of light; but when thine eye is evil, thy body also is full of darkness. Take heed therefore that the light that is in thee be not darkness.' The knocking on the door that shall be opened and the evil eye recall a metaphor in Matthew (xviii.) that comprehends both meanings: 'And if thine eye offend thee, pluck it out and cast it from thee: it is better for thee to enter into life with one eye, rather than having two eyes to be cast into hell fire.' It is Luke's single eye that fills the whole body with light.

When Shakespeare wrote *Macbeth* the translators were hard at work on the great Authorized translation of the Bible. The time was one of intense awareness of the Christian scriptures and passionate searching for their meaning. We have seen that the symbolism and phraseology of the Christian scriptures occur frequently and purposefully in *Macbeth*. Golgotha, the chalice, the Amen speeches, most sacrilegious murder that hath broke ope the Lord's anointed temple—one wonders what the critics have been about to ignore so persistently the significant allusions. To find illumination on this particular passage in the gospels may or may not be sound. But to look for it there is not the bias of a piety to which the present writer can in any case advance no claim, but the plain duty of honest literary criticism. If we are willing to admire *Macbeth* only on the understanding that the play must not be made too Christian we shall never know the tragedy that Shakespeare wrote. We should, however, be cautious about reading the Christianity of *Macbeth* back into its author. Shakespeare was a supreme poet, handling the symbols which would be most familiar to his listeners and at the same time most capable of stirring the depths of imagination. He was striving to convey a spiritual ordeal of his own with the aid of universal symbols related to a supreme ordeal not qualitatively unlike his own. In what relationship Shakespeare saw the Christian tragedy and his own guilt-experience we both know and do not know if we read *Macbeth* aright.

On the basis of the texts from Luke and Matthew we can reconstitute Macbeth's reaction to the knocking at the gate in some such fashion as this, bearing in mind that the spontaneity of poetic drama and of the intuitive appreciation of its masterstrokes is not reducible to the pedestrian stages of analysis. Macbeth hears the knocking and is afraid; realises that the sound is natural, the fear is consciousness of his own guilt. He also imagines the knocking at the gate as a symbol of salvation from guilt, raises his own hand as though to knock and sees it stained with the divine-king's blood. For a terrible moment Macbeth faces the truth about himself. Had he not prayed:

> Stars, hide your fires!
> Let not light see my black and deep desires;
> The eye wink at the hand; yet let that be,
> Which the eye fears, when it is done, to see.
>
>   [I. iv. 50-3]

' 'Tis the eye of childhood,' Lady Macbeth sneered, 'That fears a painted devil' [II. ii. 51-2]. Macbeth sees with the eye of childhood, of innocence, and his eye fears. He is not innocent, it is imagination that has lent him childhood's vision with which to see his own guilt. The eye that winked at the hand is evil, his body is full of darkness akin to the darkness that has engulfed the world in which the tragedy is acted. His hands move at once to pluck out the eyes that betrayed vision. His eye has offended; he will pluck it out so that vision may be single and light be returned into his body, his own hand raised to knock— and the door be opened so that he may say 'Amen' when others cry 'God bless us' [II. ii. 26-7]. It is a convulsion of imagination, struggling to re-create cleansed vision. But his murdering reason triumphs. 'Go, get some water' [II. ii. 43], his wife said. He despairs of such advice:

> Will all great Neptune's ocean wash this blood
> Clean from my hand? No, this my hand will rather
> The multitudinous seas incarnadine,
> Making the green one red.
>
>   [II. ii. 57-60]

Lady Macbeth returns, hears the knocking and repeats her advice:

> A little water clears us of this deed:
> How easy is it then!
>
>   [II. ii. 64-5]

It is another Christian symbol of salvation, and the tragic irony of hearing it from her is terrible. She will wash off the blood but not the guilt, and we shall hear her moaning in her own murdered sleep:

> Here's the smell of the blood still: all the perfumes
> of Arabia will not sweeten this little hand. Oh! oh! oh!
>
>   [V. i. 50-1]

The knocking is repeated again and again. They dare not open; they retire. The porter of hell-gate shall open this door in the name of Beelzebub. He is wrong in supposing the place is too cold for hell. In the fourth and last round of the lowest circle of hell Dante saw those who had betrayed their benefactors wholly covered with ice. The porter is not very funny and is not meant to be. His appearance marks the beginning of scene iii. and indicates a slight pause after Macbeth and Lady Macbeth have left the stage. The groundlings may laugh if they choose; it does not matter here. But the porter, as the actor who has the part should know, is needed to bridge the gulf between the world of evil chained down to time, in which

Macbeth is now a prisoner and the free world of nature interfused with supernature which Macduff and Lennox inhabit. The porter himself must be something of an equivocator. His humour and his nature is contaminated with something of the ghoulish quality of the element in which Macbeth's castle is now subdued. (pp. 70-5)

> *Roy Walker, in his* The Time Is Free: A Study of *"Macbeth," Andrew Dakers Limited, 1949, 234 p.*

EUGENE M. WAITH   (essay date 1950)

[*In the excerpt below, Waith examines the idea of manhood in* Macbeth, *an issue later treated by Marilyn French (1975). Macbeth, argues Waith, is divided between a definition of manliness that is based solely on valor and one that considers morality. He asserts that Lady Macbeth encourages Macbeth to choose a "beastly" manhood that stifles his conscience. Waith claims that Macduff embodies a more humane valor than Macbeth, stating that he is "a complete man" who is aware of his moral responsibilities.*]

Plutarch, in the opening sentences of his life of Coriolanus, provides a valuable lead for the interpretation of several of Shakespeare's soldier-heroes:

> Nowe in those dayes, valliantnes was honoured in ROME above all other vertues: which they called *Virtus,* by the name of vertue selfe, as including in that generall name, all other speciall vertues besides. So that *Virtus* in the Latin, was as muche as valliantnes.

The asumption that valor is an all-inclusive virtue, and hence the very emblem of manhood, appears here and there in the literature of all times and leads to the depiction of the courageous soldier as the epitome of the noblest sort of man. Soldiers as different as [Spenser's] Red Cross Knight and [Hemingway's] Robert Jordan are held up for our admiration because their physical prowess is not only admirable in itself but symbolical of spiritual strength. Since bravery in battle is often closely allied to the most unfeeling cruelty, however, the soldier is often a confusing symbol whose ambivalence is suggested by the following comment on war and peace in Thomas Beard's *The French Academy* (1602), translated from the French of Pierre de la Primaudaye:

> For as he is pernitious that mooveth and continueth war onely to subdue his neighbours, to inlarge the borders of his Countrey, and to usurp other mens right, which savoureth more of brutishnesse, than of humanitie: so a long peace bringeth with it many discommodities, making men insolent commonly through too great prosperitie, as also nice, lavish, and effeminate, through aboundance of wealth and idlenes.

Thus, the soldier may avoid the danger of effeminacy only to incur the still greater danger of brutishness. Macbeth, as I shall suggest, makes this very error.

Machiavelli's praise of *virtu,* that uncompromising strength of mind and will essential to the successful prince, is a Renaissance reflection of the Roman attitude noted by Plutarch. To the more conservative contemporaries of Machiavelli such an identification of force and virtue was repugnant, if not actually (along with the rest of his ideas) Satanic. The Machiavellian man, as he was usually conceived in France and England, had so little room in his nature for those virtues which should

complement fortitude that his manhood was fatally reduced. One further illustration of the orthodox view is provided by Thomas Milles in a passage of *The Treasurie of Auncient and Moderne Times* (1613) in which he objects to the popular degeneration of the concept of "manhood or true valour" (as distinguished from "meere and naked valiancy, or valour"):

> There are so many incivilities mingled with our Man-hood, that they simpathize rather with wild Goats, or the heat of Bulles; then with the reall excellencie of humaine Nature, which beeing the Image of the Divinitie, figures unto us another kinde of strength and courage, then that which is proper to brute Beasts onely.

True manhood is a comprehensive ideal, growing out of the familiar Christian concept that man is between the beasts and the angels in the hierarchy of creation. To be worthy of this station a man must show more than the physical valor which characterizes the soldier and traditionally distinguishes the male of the species. (pp. 262-63)

In *Macbeth* . . . there is an explicit contrast between two ideals of manhood. Macbeth is a soldier whose valor we hear praised throughout the play. To the "bleeding Sergeant" he is "brave Macbeth," to Duncan "valiant cousin, worthy gentleman" [I. ii. 24]; Ross calls him "Bellona's bridegroom." To be courageous is to be "manly," as the soldier understands that word, and hence at the end of the play, when Macduff reveals the fatal circumstances of his birth, Macbeth says that the news has "cow'd my better part of man," to which Macduff replies, "Then yield thee, coward" [V. vii. 18, 23]. After the death of the hero physical valor is given final emphasis in a speech of Ross to Siward:

> Your son, my lord, has paid a soldier's debt.
> He only liv'd but till he was a man,
> The which no sooner had his prowess confirm'd
> In the unshrinking station where he fought
> But like a man he died.
>
> [V. ix. 5-9]

In all these comments there is implied one ideal—the soldier's, or as Plutarch says, the Roman's ideal—of what it is to be a man. Lady Macbeth clearly subscribes to it when she urges her husband to "screw his courage to the sticking place." In her speeches she makes explicit the contrast between the sexes which underlies this concept of manhood. To strengthen her resolve she appeals to the spirits to "unsex me here":

> Come to my woman's breasts
> And take my milk for gall. . . .
>
> [I. v. 41, 47-8]

She fears that Macbeth has too much of the "milk of human kindness," and he himself says to her,

> Bring forth men-children only;
> For thy undaunted mettle should compose
> Nothing but males.
>
> [I. vii. 72-4]

Thus not to be a man is to be effeminate.

In this same scene, however, Macbeth introduces another antithesis—that of man and beast. When Lady Macbeth taunts him for his cowardice, he replies,

> I dare do all that may become a man.
> Who dares do more is none.
>
> [I. vii. 46-7]

That Lady Macbeth understands his implication is clear from her scoffing question:

> What beast was't then
> That made you break this enterprise to me?
>
> [I. vii. 47-8]

This important point is that Macbeth's distinction rests, as we can see from his soliloquy at the opening of the scene, upon his awareness of the moral nature of man. His mental torment grows out of the conflict between the narrow concept of man as the courageous male and the more inclusive concept of man as a being whose moral nature distinguishes him from the beasts. The first is that debased ideal of manhood censured by Milles, while the second is the "reall excellencie of humaine Nature" based on "another kinde of strength and courage, then that which is proper to brute Beasts only."

Shakespeare keeps the two concepts before us throughout the play. The pangs of Macbeth's conscience after the murder (note his inability to say "amen") are no more than effeminate or childish fears to Lady Macbeth (II, ii). In urging his hired assassins to the murder of Banquo, Macbeth echos his wife, contrasting patience and piety with the manhood necessary to perform the bloody deed (III, i). When Banquo's ghost brings on Macbeth's "fit," Lady Macbeth asks him, "Are you a man?" [III. iv.]. And then:

> O, these flaws and starts
> (Impostors to true fear) would well become
> A woman's story at a winter's fire. . . .
> What, quite unmann'd in folly?
>
> [III. iv. 62-4, 72]

Macbeth says, "What man dare I dare" [III. iv. 98].

In the puzzling scene (IV, iii) in which Malcolm tests Macduff, Macbeth's formidable antagonist is established as the exact antithesis of the sort of man Lady Macbeth admires. When Malcolm accuses himself of all Macbeth's sins, Macduff demonstrates his "truth and honor" by his horrified rejection of Malcolm, and thus reveals the moral qualifications of "true" manhood. Then, when Ross tells him of the murders of Lady Macduff and of his children, Macduff appears so overwhelmed by grief that Malcolm says to him, "Dispute it like a man" [IV. iii. 220]. His reply is most significant:

> I shall do so;
> But I must also feel it as a man.
> I cannot but remember such things were
> That were most precious to me. Did heaven look on
> And would not take their part? Sinful Macduff,
> They were all struck for thee! Naught that I am,
> Not for their own demerits, but for mine,
> Fell slaughter on their souls.
>
> [IV. iii. 220-27]

Macduff is a complete man: he is a valiant soldier, ready to perform "manly" deeds, but is neither ashamed of "humane" feelings nor unaware of his moral responsibilities. This combination is emphasized in his next speech, where he shows clearly that his admirable sensibility does not make him womanish:

> O, I could play the woman with mine eyes
> And braggart with my tongue! But, gentle heavens,
> Cut short all intermission. Front to front
> Bring thou this fiend of Scotland and myself.

> Within my sword's length set him. If he scape,
> Heaven forgive him too!
>
> [IV. iii. 230-35]

Malcolm's comment is: "This tune goes manly" [IV. iii. 35].

The development of Macbeth's character is a triumph for Lady Macbeth's ideal, for conscience is stifled, and Macbeth, like Hamlet, becomes increasingly "bloody, bold and resolute" [IV. i. 79]. His deliberate decision, against the dictates of his better judgment, to be a "man" in this narrow sense of the word is one of the most important manifestations of the evil which dominates the entire play: to his subjects Macbeth now seems a devil. Shakespeare's insistence upon this narrowing of character is also a commentary on Macbeth's ambition. In "the swelling act of the imperial theme" [I. iii. 129], the hero becomes fatally diminished. The final stage of the development is revealed in Macbeth's speeches at the time of Lady Macbeth's death. Here we are confronted by the supreme irony that when she dies, tortured by the conscience she despised, Macbeth is so perfectly hardened, so completely the soldier that she wanted him to be, that he is neither frightened by the "night-shriek" nor greatly moved by the news of her death. Death has no meaning for him, and life is

> a tale
> Told by an idiot, full of sound and fury,
> Signifying nothing.
>
> [V. v. 26-8]

Though Macduff's announcement that he was "untimely ripp'd" from his mother's womb causes Macbeth to falter, he dies a courageous soldier, and hence, according to that narrower definition, "like a man." It is appropriate that his death is immediately followed by the last statement of the soldierly standard of values in the tribute Ross pays to Siward's son: "Like a man he died" [V. ix. 9]. But on the battlefield is Macduff, who is even more of a man—a soldier who fights only in a good cause, and in whose nature valor is not the sole virtue. (pp. 265-68)

> *Eugene M. Waith, "Manhood and Valor in Two Shakespearean Tragedies," in* ELH, *Vol. 17, No. 4, December, 1950, pp. 262-73.*

ARNOLD STEIN (essay date 1951)

[*In the excerpt below, Stein discusses Macbeth's use of language, an issue also treated by John Arthos (1947) and Bertrand Evans (1979). Stein argues that Macbeth invokes a "word-magic" similar to that of the Weird Sisters. He further states that Macbeth, acknowledging the power of words, creates a "world of witchcraft and murder" and transforms himself into a savage murderer. Stein also notes that Macbeth relies on this style of language when pretending innocence. Yet, he continues, Macbeth begins to show a contempt for language as the power of his word-magic decreases. In the end, Stein concludes, Macbeth renounces words and reason for "the desperate logic of action," but nonetheless clings to the "ruins of his dependence on words, the verbal charms."*]

The sympathetic, and symbolic, relationship between Macbeth and the weird sisters is not confined to their traffic in evil. Macbeth, poet that he is, can address them with perfect decorum—"How now, you secret, black, and midnight hags!" [IV. i. 48]. But the appropriateness of his speech, one feels, is no mere act of will; Macbeth, whether because of a characteristic attitude toward language, or because of an inner kinship to the witches, finds it easy to enter into the spirit and style of supernatural enterprise:

> I conjure you, by that which you profess,
> Howe'er you come to know it, answer me!
> Though you untie the winds and let them fight
> Against the churches; though the yesty waves
> Confound and swallow navagation up;
> Though bladed corn be lodg'd and trees blown down;
> Though castles topple on their warders' heads;
> Though palaces and pyramids do slope
> Their heads to their foundations; though the treasure
> Of nature's germen tumble all together,
> Even till destruction sicken; answer me
> To what I ask you.
>
> [IV. i. 50-61]

Yet this is, however appropriate and easy, self-conscious word-magic. Macbeth is deliberately entering into the spirit of black magic, into the atmosphere of the play that is created by the witches' charms wound up, by their verbal spells and darkly suggestive hints of things done and about to be done.

There is another kind of word-magic, less self-conscious and more personal, that Macbeth customarily reserves for private use, in talking to himself. In the long soliloquy beginning "If it were done when 'tis done" [I. vii. i], we get our first real insight into the workings of Macbeth's mind and into a characteristic way of using words. His evident purpose in this long reflection is to dissuade himself from the temptation that both attracts and repels him. Eloquence here is "discourse of reason," used in traditional moral ways, in alliance with the part of man's divine nature that distinguishes him from the beasts. But the alliance, as the development of the speech seems to indicate, already has an element of desperation in it. The argument of the first section, underneath its magnificence of language, is merely and coldly rational, an expression of practical Renaissance *prudentia* [prudence]: the emphasis is all on "this bank and shoal of time" [I. vii. 6], where violence provides "Bloody instructions" that find their way back to the teacher. From the rational, Macbeth proceeds to the ethical, to his obligations as kinsman, subject, and host, to the reverence that Duncan has earned through his personal and kingly virtues. At this point Macbeth's eloquence transcends both the rational and the ethical. He turns the full force of his word-power against the temptation that is stubbornly expressing itself, however inarticulately, somewhere in his consciousness. The angels pleading "trumpet-tongued" (and the verse trumpeting with indignation against "The deep damnation of his taking-off") give way to the softer image of "pity, like a naked new-born babe" [I. vii. 20-1]; but just before the image comes to a focus it shifts with sudden shock the range of its connotations, and the babe is threateningly "Striding the blast"; and pity may not be "a naked new-born babe" after all, but "heaven's cherubin hors'd" [I. vii. 22]. Macbeth, it seems, is drawing upon both his capacity for fear and his capacity for pity, as earlier he had appealed to—separately—the rational and ethical parts of his nature. In his emotional peroration he appears to be entirely intent upon moving his will, and if his eloquence does not make a simple sense it makes a complicated sense. What the cherubim threaten, after all, is pity—the deed will be blown in every eye, "That tears shall drown the wind" [I. vii. 25]. And then, suddenly, abruptly, Macbeth drops the emotional eloquence and returns to the coldly rational—as if part of his mind had never really left that basis for persuasion. His only actual motive, he acknowledges, is ambition.

There is perhaps another plane of meaning involved here. Macbeth may be groping toward the emotional realization that the rational and the ethical are not really separated at all. To follow ambition wilfully is, for an Elizabethan, to renounce the laws of God and the laws of man. To deny pity is to evoke "even-handed justice." For the tears that drown the wind, that threaten through pity as it were, anticipate Macbeth's ultimate isolation in the symbolic castle that even he, in despair, abandons. It is easy for tyrants to underestimate the potential powers of the gentler human emotions. But Macbeth, with his milk of human kindness, is not at this point a tyrant, and pity is an important value to him. . . . Macbeth is a tragic hero and not a successful villain. Pity, love, and fear are strong forces in his nature, and when he tries to submerge them, they resist and steadily exact their penalty.

From this vantage point it is worth looking back to the scene where Macbeth, just after he has become Thane of Cawdor, reflects on the ethical import of the supernatural soliciting he has experienced. Here we see what is clearer after the speech on pity, a poet using the sensations that are the intuitions of his conscience, and using his verbal command of these sensations, to bolster his moral nature. His verbal command is the voice of "right reason" and his sensations are the prompter of that voice:

> If good, why do I yield to that suggestion
> Whose horrid image doth unfix my hair
> And make my seated heart knock at my ribs,
> Against the use of nature? Present fears
> Are less than horrible imaginings.
> My thought, whose murder yet is but fantastical,
> Shakes so my single state of man that function
> Is smother'd in surmise.
>
> [I. iii. 134-41]

But something happens to this alliance between eloquence and good. The key to the change, it seems possible, lies in the desperate intensity of the speech on pity. Psychologically it is a small step, morally it is a great step from verbal white magic to black. That significant step is taken as he reflects upon the "air-drawn dagger."

"There is no such thing" [II. i. 47] Macbeth says, and then proceeds by incantation to shatter the world of reality in which the dagger is a "false creation," and to remold it—by the power implicit in poetry—closer to his heart's desire:

> Now o'er the one half-world
> Nature seems dead, and wicked dreams abuse
> The curtain'd sleep: witchcraft celebrates
> Pale Hecate's offerings, and wither'd Murder,
> Alarum'd by his sentinel, the wolf,
> Whose howl's his watch, thus with his stealthy pace,
> With Tarquin's ravishing strides, towards his design
> Moves like a ghost.
>
> [II. i. 49-56]

In creating, by words and rhythms and imges, this world of witchcraft and murder, he transforms himself into a murdering creature. It is a sort of savage ceremony in which Macbeth, by pronouncing the right charms, invokes the spirits of Hecate . . . and Tarquin; and by the use of verbal magic turns himself into a kind of werewolf.

We can measure something of the development in Macbeth if, with soliloquy in which he movingly dissuades himself—or seems to—from killing Duncan, we compare the parallel soliloquy in which he persuades himself to have Banquo killed. He begins calmly enough and states his real motive, fear of Banquo and the genuine "royalty" of his nature. From his analysis of the immediate situation, with his clear-eyed objective appraisal and praise of Banquo, he moves to another level. In the soliloquy on Duncan ethical considerations provided him with the starting-place for his final burst of eloquence. And here, moving from Banquo to Banquo's sons, he falls into a kind of false ethical rage by which he projects under camouflage his own deepest fears and frustrations.

> For Banquo's issue have I fil'd my mind;
> For them the gracious Duncan have I murder'd;
> Put rancours in the vessel of my peace
> Only for them; and mine eternal jewel
> Given to the common enemy of man,
> To make them kings, the seeds of Banquo kings!
>
> [III. i. 64-9]

And so through use of the same means by which he once tried to turn himself from a course of action, he now tries to confirm a course of action he has already decided upon. (pp. 271-76)

This, surely, involves some recognition by Macbeth of the power he can evoke by words. The power that was a part of his moral nature; the power he turned to naturally and unconsciously when he was shrinking from the suggestion "Whose horrid image doth unfix my hair" [I. iii. 135]; that he turned to, though perhaps less naturally and unconsciously, when he was struggling to resist by compulsions stronger than those of mere practical rationality or abstract ethics the temptation to kill Duncan: this power he now turns to because it can help him get what he wants.

He weaves his spell of incantation for the death of Banquo, though there is no need now of working himself into a proper mood for murder—his hired assassins do not need magic:

> ere the bat hath flown
> His cloister'd flight, ere to black Hecate's summons
> The shard-borne beetle with his drowsy hums
> Hath rung night's yawning peal, there shall be done
> A deed of dreadful note.
>
> [III. ii. 40-44]

Nor is he really talking to Lady Macbeth, for he refuses to tell her what the deed is. He continues with his verbal ceremony:

> Come, seeling night,
> Scarf up the tender eye of pitiful day,
> And with thy bloody and invisible hand
> Cancel and tear to pieces that great bond
> Which keeps me pale! Light thickens and the crow
> Makes wing to th' rooky wood;
> Good things of day begin to droop and drowse,
> While night's black agents to their preys do rowse.
>
> [III. iii. 46-52]

The private incantation is really an integral part of the dramatic atmosphere of the play, drawing the audience as well as Macbeth into the web of black awe. In a play as tightly woven as *Macbeth* a speech is likely to serve more than one purpose. There are symbolic levels as well as dramatic; sometimes they coincide and sometimes they do not; but they are not separate in their final effect. (pp. 276-77)

Macbeth, it is worth noting, does not seem to use on others the power he has discovered in poetry. The persuasion he applies to the murderers, for instance, is coldly and brutally

rational. But there are two occasions when, addressing others, he falls into the kind of speech we have come to recognize as peculiar to his self-hypnosis. First there is the speech shortly after the murder of Duncan is discovered:

> Had I but died an hour before this chance,
> I had liv'd a blessed time; for, from this instant,
> There's nothing serious in mortality.
> All is but toys; renown and grace is dead;
> The wine of life is drawn, and the mere lees
> Is left this vault to brag of.
>
> [II. iii. 91-6]

Then there is the speech that precedes Lady Macbeth's fainting and follows Macbeth's announcement that he has killed the grooms:

> Here lay Duncan,
> His silver skin lac'd with his golden blood,
> And his gash'd stabs look'd like a breach in nature
> For ruin's wasteful entrance; there, the murderers,
> Steep'd in the colours of their trade, their daggers
> Unmannerly breech'd with gore. Who could refrain,
> That had a heart to love, and in that heart
> Courage to make 's love known?
>
> [II. iii. 111-18]

Why the rising pitch of intensity? Perhaps it is sufficient answer to say that Macbeth is in a difficult position and must work his way out by any means possible. But that does not explain

Act I. Scene iii. The Three Witches. By R. Westall (n.d.).

why he had to speak up at all the first time, and why more than briefly. Of course it is the act of a guilty conscience pretending innocence before it can be accused, and one might let it go at that if it were an isolated occurrence and did not fit into an already established pattern of behavior. . . . His first speech reflects the feelings that we know possessed him right after the act. The second speech passes the bounds of persuasive rhetoric (one need not try to determine the precise reason for Lady Macbeth's collapse). Macbeth puts into the speech more of himself—not the self of fact and reality but the self he mangled and could not kill when he killed Duncan—more of himself than he ought if his controlled purpose is to persuade others. We can recognize the emotional pitch of mood-invoking poetry. Whatever his other intentions are, Macbeth is also trying to talk himself back into his sense of innocence. . . . (pp. 279-81)

So far the attitudes we have been considering seem to begin as unconscious ones, develop into attitudes revealing some consciousness, but still hover between these two poles, as between good and evil. But Macbeth, on one level of his consciousness at least, remains consistently aware of language, and he maintains an attitude that is worth examining. "Whiles I threat he lives" [II. i. 60], he can say *after* he has established the mood for murder of Duncan. "Words," he can say with an air of nonchalant contempt—"Words to the heat of deeds too cold breath gives" [II. i. 61]. Similarly, after he has determined to murder Macduff's family he seems to feel it necessary to express scorn for words, though this time he has not had to use words to initiate or justify an action:

> No boasting like a fool;
> This deed I'll do before this purpose cool.
>
> [IV. i. 153-54]

"Boasting like a fool" seems to refer to his characteristic self-hypnosis but it is hardly an accurate description. Nor can one easily recall what purpose—by implication, verbally induced—he may have let cool.

Why this contempt for language? It is not that Macbeth has Hamlet's sense of shame at unpacking his heart with words. Hamlet, too, it is interesting to note, can fall for a moment into incantation:

> Tis now the very witching time of night
> When churchyards yawn and hell itself breathes out
> Contagion to this world: now could I drink hot blood
> And do such bitter business as the day
> Would quake to look on.
>
> [*Hamlet*, III. ii. 387-92]

But with Hamlet it is the reflection of a passing mood; with Macbeth it is neither a mood nor passing. And yet there is no more incantation after the spell woven for Banquo's death. It is true there is one more example of the power of words, a shocking example that would have cured anyone but Macbeth. Banquo's ghost does not become visible the first time until after Macbeth has expressed some very indiscreet regrets—apparently accepted as invitation—over the absence of "the grac'd person of our Banquo":

> Who may I rather challenge for unkindness
> Than pity for mischance.
>
> [III. iv. 40-42]

And the second appearance is in response to a direct invitation:

> I drink to th' general joy o' the whole table,
> And to our dear friend Banquo, whom we miss;
> Would he were here!
>
> [III. iv. 88-90]

This is enormously successful word-magic, but it is not incantation. Why then the contempt for language and why no more incantation? One mark of development may be the degree of weak cursing that Macbeth falls back upon in his second interview with the witches. There has been a noticeable shrinking up of his capacity to move himself by his sensations (with what that implies). Not even a night-shriek can cool his senses. He no longer has faith in himself, nor in his own magic. But there has been no change in his basic dependence on words. The words are different, it is true; they swim on the lips, too easily; they are verbal formulas, charms to be repeated without hope, but he is without hope in anything else. (pp. 281-83)

If he still has faith in words, then why the contempt? Why the emphasis on deeds, which are contrasted with "boasting like a fool"?—

> The flighty purpose never is o'ertook
> Unless the deed go with it. From this moment
> The very firstlings of my heart shall be
> The firstlings of my hand. And even now,
> To crown my thoughts with acts, be it thought and
>   done.
>
> [IV. i. 145-49]

> Strange things I have in head, that will to hand,
> Which must be acted ere they may be scann'd.
>
> [III. iv. 138-39]

Purpose: deed; heart: hand; thought: acts; head: hand. It is not only language that he wants to eliminate but the intellectual element involved in language. For thought is still potentially "right reason," still part of his conquerable but inextinguishable moral nature. What he is saying, and often enough to convince himself, is the charm, "We are yet but young in deed" [III. iv. 143]. Through action he hopes, following a familiar human pattern, to escape from the thoughts that haunt him, even from the necessity of thinking at all. Action is the illusion, and the "function" that once was able to be "smother'd in surmise" [I. iii. 141] must now be protected against thought: and surmise must instead be smothered in function.

And so we are back where we started, with language as "discourse of reason," in alliance with the part of man's nature that distinguishes him from the beasts and relates him to the angels. Macbeth has misused and perverted his gift of eloquence as he has misused his gift of a moral nature. And he has consequently learned to distrust and fear his words; for words, to the degree that they can still express his intellectual and moral nature, are a threat to the security of an impetus that dares not pause to be questioned. But still he cannot overcome his dependence on words. For action is not enough, the "firstlings" are not enough; and Macbeth needs something at once more tangible and more abstract; something beyond the immediate and self-contained logic of the moment, or even the last-ditch egocentricity of "For mine own good / All causes shall give way" [III. iv. 134-35]; something that can look forward and backward, however superficially, and can promise a security beyond that of his impetus alone.

And so this man in whom evil wars with good, callous desire with moral sensitivity; in whom moral vitality still flickers for a moment at the end of the play when he sees Macduff ("my soul is too much charg'd / With blood of thine already" [V. viii. 5-6])—this man can neither obey nor suppress the verbal power that moves him to good, and must in the end renounce both words and reason while he winds through the desperate logic of action clinging without hope to the distorted and disguised ruins of his dependence on words, the verbal charms. (pp. 283-84)

Arnold Stein, ''Macbeth and Word-Magic,'' in The Sewanee Review, *Vol. LIX, No. 2, Spring, 1951, pp. 271-84.*

FRANCIS FERGUSSON   (essay date 1952)

[*Fergusson is one of the most influential drama critics of the twentieth century. In his seminal study,* The Idea of a Theater *(1949), he claims that the fundamental truths present in all drama are defined exclusively by myth and ritual, and that the purpose of dramatic representation is, in essence, to confirm the ''ritual expectancy'' of the society in which the artist works. Fergusson's method has been described as a combination of the principles of Aristotle's* Poetics *and those of modern myth criticism. As a Shakespearean critic, Fergusson regards many of the plays as dramatizations of the primitive ''scapegoat ritual''; in numerous others, such as the major tragedies, he discerns the mythic pattern of purgation, regeneration, and continuity. In general, Fergusson considers Shakespeare an artist who never deviated from a vision of human life and experience which was immediately accepted and understood by his Elizabethan audience. In the following excerpt, from an essay first published in 1952, Fergusson argues that the action of the play is best summarized by Macbeth's maxim, ''to outrun the pauser, reason.'' He begins by discussing Aristotle's notion of praxis and drama as ''the imitation of an action.'' He then notes that throughout* Macbeth *characters are ''compelled in their action to strive beyond what they can by reason alone,'' which, for Shakespeare, involves a violation of nature and, in Macbeth's case, results in evil. Fergusson further states that the lengthy dialogue between Malcolm and Macduff in Act IV, Scene iii, illustrates a positive instance of action moving beyond reason and marks the play's turning point.*]

I propose to attempt to illustrate the view that *Macbeth* may be understood as ''the imitation of an action,'' in approximately Aristotle's sense of this phrase.

The word ''action''—*praxis*—as Aristotle uses it in the *Poetics*, does not mean outward deeds or events, but something much more like ''purpose'' or ''aim.'' Perhaps our word ''motive'' suggests most of its meaning. (p. 115)

When Aristotle says that a tragedy is the imitation of an action, he is thinking of an action, or motive, which governs the psyche's life for a considerable length of time. Such an action is the quest for Laius's slayer in *Oedipus Rex*, which persists through the changing circumstances of the play. In this period of time, it has a beginning, a middle, and an end, which comes when the slayer is at last identified.

I remarked that action is not outward deeds or events; but on the other hand, there can be no action without resulting deeds. We guess at a man's action by way of what he does, his outward and visible deeds. We are aware that our own action, or motive, produces deeds of some sort as soon as it exists. Now the plot of a play is the arrangement of outward deeds or incidents, and the dramatist uses it, as Aristotle tells us, as the first means of imitating the action. He arranges a set of incidents which point to the action or motive from which they spring. You may say that the action is the spiritual content of the tragedy—the playwright's inspiration—and the plot defines its existence as an intelligible *play*. Thus, you cannot have a play without both plot and action; yet the distinction between plot and action is as fundamental as that between form and matter. The action is the matter; the plot is the ''first form,'' or, as Aristotle puts it, the ''soul,'' of the tragedy.

The dramatist imitates the action he has in mind, first by means of the plot, then in the characters, and finally in the media of language, music, and spectacle. In a well-written play, if we understood it thoroughly, we should perceive that plot, character, and diction, and the rest spring from the same source, or, in other words, realize the same action or motive in the forms appropriate to their various media. (pp. 116-17)

The action of the play as a whole is best expressed in a phrase which Macbeth himself uses in Act II, scene 3, the aftermath of the murder. Macbeth is trying to appear innocent, but everything he says betrays his clear sense of his own evil motivation, or action. Trying to excuse his murder of Duncan's grooms, he says,

> The expedition of my violent love [for Duncan, he means]
> Outran the pauser, reason.
>
> [II. iii. 110-11]

It is the phrase ''to outrun the pauser, reason,'' which seems to me to describe the action, or motive, of the play as a whole. Macbeth, of course, literally means that his love for Duncan was so strong and swift that it got ahead of his reason, which would have counseled a pause. But in the same way we have seen his greed and ambition outrun his reason when he committed the murder; and in the same way all of the characters, in the irrational darkness of Scotland's evil hour, are compelled in their action to strive beyond what they can see by reason alone. Even Malcolm and Macduff, as we shall see, are compelled to go beyond reason in the action which destroys Macbeth and ends the play.

But let me consider the phrase itself for a moment. To ''outrun'' reason suggests an impossible stunt, like lifting oneself by one's own bootstraps. It also suggests a competition or race, like those of nightmare, which cannot be won. As for the word ''reason,'' Shakespeare associates it with nature and nature's order, in the individual soul, in society, and in the cosmos. To outrun reason is thus to violate nature itself, to lose the bearings of common sense and of custom, and to move into a spiritual realm bounded by the irrational darkness of Hell one way, and the superrational grace of faith the other way. As the play develops before us, all the modes of this absurd, or evil, or supernatural, action are attempted, the last being Malcolm's and Macduff's acts of faith.

In the first part of the play Shakespeare, as is his custom, gives us the intimate feel of this paradoxical striving beyond reason in a series of echoing tropes and images. I remind you of some of them, as follows.

From the first Witches' scene:

> When the battle's lost and won. . . .
>
> Fair is foul and foul is fair.
>
> [I. i. 4-10]

From the ''bleeding-sergeant'' scene:

> Doubtful it stood;
> As two spent swimmers that do cling together
> And choke their art. . . .
>
> So from that spring whence comfort seem'd to come
> Discomfort swells. . . .
>
> Confronted him with self-comparisons
> Point against point rebellious, arm 'gainst arm. . . .

What he hath lost noble Macbeth hath won.
                    [I. ii. 7-9, 27-8, 55-6, 67]

From the second Witches' scene:

So fair and foul a day. . . .

Lesser than Macbeth, and greater.

His wonders and his praises do contend
Which should be thine or his. . . .

This supernatural soliciting
Cannot be ill, cannot be good. . . .

                    . . . nothing is
But what is not.
                    [I. iii. 38, 65, 92-3, 130-31, 141-42]

These are only a few of the figures which suggest the desperate and paradoxical struggle. They are, of course, not identical with each other or with outrunning reason, which seems to me the most general of all. But they all point to the "action" I mean, and I present them as examples of the imitation of action by means of the arts of language.

But notice that though these images themselves suggest the action, they also confirm the actions of the characters as these are shown in the story. The bleeding sergeant, for instance, is striving beyond reason and nature in his effort to report the battle—itself a bewildering mixture of victory and defeat—in spite of his wounds. Even the old King Duncan, mild though he is, is caught in the race and sees his relation to Macbeth competitively. "Thou art so far before," he tells Macbeth in the next scene, "That swiftest wing of recompense is slow / To overtake thee" [I. iv. 16-18]. He then races Macbeth to his castle, whither the Messenger has outrun them both; and when he arrives, he is at once involved in a hollow competition with Lady Macbeth, to outdo her in ceremony.

I do not need to remind you of the great scenes preceding the murder, in which Macbeth and his Lady pull themselves together for their desperate effort. If you think over these scenes, you will notice that the Macbeths understand the action which begins here as a competition and a stunt, against reason and nature. Lady Macbeth fears her husband's human nature, as well as her own female nature, and therefore she fears the light of reason and the common daylight world. As for Macbeth, he knows from the first that he is engaged in an irrational stunt: "I have no spur / To prick the sides of my intent, but only / Vaulting ambition, which o'erleaps itself / And falls on the other" [I. vii. 25-8]. In this sequence there is also the theme of outwitting or transcending time, an aspect of nature's order as we know it: catching up the consequences, jumping the life to come, and the like. But this must suffice to remind you of the Macbeths' actions, which they paradoxically understand so well.

The Porter scene has been less thoroughly studied as a variation on the play's main action. But it is, in fact, a farcical and terrible version of "outrunning reason," a witty and very concentrated epitome of this absurd movement of spirit. The Porter first teases the knockers at the gate with a set of paradoxes, all of which present attempts to outrun reason; and he sees them all as ways into Hell. . . . When the Porter has admitted the knockers he ironically offers them lewd physical analogies for outrunning reason: drink as tempting lechery into a hopeless action; himself as wrestling with drink. The relation of the Porter to the knockers is like that of the Witches to Macbeth—he tempts them into Hell with ambiguities. And the inebriation

of drink and lust, lewd and laughable as it is, is closely analogous to the more terrible and spiritual intoxication of the Macbeths.

Thus, in the first part of the play both the imagery and the actions of the various characters indicate or "imitate" the main action. Aristotle says the characters are imitated "with a view to the action"—and the Porter, who has little importance in the story—is presented to reveal the action of the play as a whole in the unexpected light of farcical analogies, contemporary or lewd and physical.

Before I leave this part of the play I wish to point out that the plot itself—"the arrangement or synthesis of the incidents"—also imitates a desperate race. This is partly a matter of the speed with which the main facts are presented, partly the effect of simultaneous movements like those of a race: Lady Macbeth is reading the letter at the same moment that her husband and Duncan are rushing toward her. And the facts in this part of the play are ambiguous in meaning and even as facts. (pp. 117-21)

Macbeth and his Lady are embarked on a race against reason itself; and all Scotland, the "many" whose lives depend upon the monarch, is precipitated into the same darkness and desperate strife. Shakespeare's monarchs do usually color the spiritual life of their realms. And we, who remember Hitlerite Germany, can understand that, I think. Even Hitler's exiles, like the refugees from Russian or Spanish tyranny, brought the shadow to this country with them.

I now wish to consider the action of the play at a later stage, in Act IV, scene 3. This is the . . . beginning of Malcolm's and Macduff's act of faith, which will constitute the final variation on "outrunning reason." The scene is laid in England, whither Malcolm and Macduff have fled, and it immediately follows the murder of Macduff's wife and child. Like the exiles we have known in this country, Macduff and Malcolm, though in England, have brought Scotland's darkness with them. They have lost all faith in reason, human nature, and common sense, and can therefore trust neither themselves nor each other. They are met in the hope of forming an alliance, in order to get rid of Macbeth; and yet under his shadow everything they do seems unreasonable, paradoxical, improbable.

In the first part of the scene, you remember, Malcolm and Macduff fail to find any basis for mutual trust. Malcolm mistrusts Macduff because he has left his wife and child behind; Macduff quickly learns to mistrust Malcolm, because he first protests that he is unworthy of the crown, to test Macduff, and then suddenly reverses himself. The whole exchange is a tissue of falsity and paradox, and it ends in a sort of nightmarish paralysis. (pp. 121-22)

After the Doctor's interlude, Ross joins Malcolm and Macduff, bringing the latest news from Scotland. To greet him, Malcolm clearly states the action, or motive, of the scene as a whole: "Good God, betimes remove / The means that makes us strangers!" [IV. iii. 162-63] he says. Ross's chief news is, of course, Lady Macduff's murder. When he has gradually revealed that, and Macduff and Malcolm have taken it in, accepting some of the guilt, they find that the means that made them strangers has in fact been removed. They recognize themselves and each other once more, in a sober, but not nightmarish, light. And at once they join in faith in their cause and prepare to hazard all upon the ordeal of battle, itself an appeal beyond reason. The scene, which in its opening sections moved very slowly, reflecting the demoralization of Malcolm and Macduff, ends hopefully, with brisk rhythms of speech which prepare the marching scenes to follow.

> This tune goes manly. . . .
> > *Receive what cheer you may:*
> The night is long that never finds the day.
> > > [IV. iii. 235-40]
> > > (pp. 122-23)

Now, one of the reasons I chose this scene to discuss is that it shows, as does the Porter scene, the necessity of distinguishing between plot and action. One cannot understand the function of the scene in the whole plot unless one remembers that the plot itself is there to imitate the action. It is then clear that this scene is the peripeteia, which is brought about by a series of recognitions. It starts with Malcolm and Macduff blind and impotent in Macbeth's shadow and ends when they have gradually learned to recognize themselves and each other even in that situation. "Outrunning reason" looks purely evil in the beginning, and at the end we see how it may be good, an act of faith beyond reason. The scene moves slowly at first because Shakespeare is imitating the action of groping in an atmosphere of the false and unnatural; yet we are aware all the while of continuing speed offstage, where

> > each new morn
> New widows howl, new orphans cry, new sorrows
> Strike heaven on the face. . . .
> > > [IV. iii. 4-6]

The scene is thus (within the rhythmic scheme of the whole play) like a slow eddy on the edge of a swift current. After this turning, or peripeteia, the actions of Malcolm and Macduff join the rush of the main race, to win. I admit that these effects might be hard to achieve in production, but I believe that good actors could do it.

Shakespeare's tragedies usually have a peripeteia in the fourth act, with scenes of suffering and prophetic or symbolic recognitions and epiphanies. In the fourth act of *Macbeth* the Witches' scene reveals the coming end of the action in symbolic shows; and this scene also, in another way, foretells the end. The last act, then, merely presents the literal facts, the windup of the plot, long felt as inevitable in principle. The fifth act of *Macbeth* shows the expected triumph of Malcolm's and Macduff's superrational faith. The wood does move; Macbeth does meet a man unborn of woman; and the paradoxical race against reason reaches its paradoxical end. The nightmare of Macbeth's evil version of the action is dissolved, and we are free to return to the familiar world, where reason, nature, and common sense still have their validity. (pp. 123-24)

> *Francis Fergusson, " 'Macbeth' as the Imitation of an Action," in his* The Human Image in Dramatic Literature: Essays, *Doubleday & Company, Inc., 1957. pp. 115-25.*

ROY W. BATTENHOUSE (essay date 1952)

[*Battenhouse is well known for his studies on religion and literature and for his theory that Shakespeare's works embody a specifically Christian world view. In the following commentary on* Macbeth, *Battenhouse discusses the protagonist's fall from Christian grace, emphasizing his nihilistic loss of faith and denial of "the everlasting life." Arguing that the play contains biblical parallels, he compares Macbeth's ambition to Satan's and his and Lady Macbeth's temptation to that of Adam and Eve—an interpretation also suggested by Arthur Quiller-Couch (1918),*

Robert Pack (1956), and Herbert R. Coursen, Jr. (1967). He also emphasizes Macbeth's anti-Christian role as "high-priest of Night." In addition, Battenhouse makes a comparison between the tyranny in Scotland under Macbeth and Nazi Germany and between Macbeth's nihilism and the mood of modern Europe, particularly as reflected in the "melodrama" of Jean-Paul Sartre. For other Christian interpretations of Macbeth, *see the excerpts by Hermann Ulrici (1839), Roy Walker (1949), and G. R. Elliott (1958).*]

As the tragedy of *Macbeth* draws toward a close, a soldier-hero voices his spiritual bankruptcy. Life is "a tale Told by an idiot, full of sound and fury, Signifying nothing" [V. v. 26-8]. Life offers for him none of the goods he has hoped for, such as "honor, love, obedience, troops of friends" [V. iii. 25]. Instead, there is the restless ecstasy of terrible dreams. He is, he sees, in blood "stept in so far" that "returning were as tedious as go o'er" [III. iv. 136-37]. Utterly weary, he is recklessly willing to let "the frame of things disjoint, both the worlds suffer" [III. ii. 16]. Let the whole estate of the world be "undone" along with himself! For his heroism can boast nothing now but the desperate courage of the trapped: "They have tied me to the stake: I cannot fly, But bear-like, I must fight the course" [V. vii. 1-2]. What is he, then, but a "player," fated to strut and fret his "hour" in a world which is only "stage"—nothing but theatre?

I think we can say that the spirit of nihilism abroad in much of modern Europe today repeats this mood. One can find it in the plays of Sartre. Sartre revels in melodrama; and that is what Macbeth's view of his own life adds up to. So do the stories we occasionally get in our newspapers of European spy trials. The actors in them no longer believe in themselves: they merely rehearse a theatrical role which they accept as fate. Melodrama is thus one of the fashions of our times. Behind it lies a resoluteness emptied of hope. Like Macbeth, the survivors of Blitzkriegs that bring no peace have "supped full of horrors" [V. iv. 13]. To many of these men, new deaths can bring no tears. Life has been hollowed out. Passion is reduced to haunting fear and impulsive recklessness.

Does Shakespeare in *Macbeth* give us any key to the causes? I think he does. He makes plain that such an ending has its beginning in a *Walpurgisnacht*, or witches' holiday. There are times in history when demonic "revelations" arise to tempt a man's soul. The propitious moment is at the end of some bloody war, in which the habit of slaughter, as if to "memorize another Golgotha" [I. ii. 40], has become ingrained even in a noble nature like Macbeth's. He is a warrior "nothing afeared," we are told, to make "strange images of death" [I. iii. 96-7]. The demonic temptation takes advantage of this temporary callousness, this moment of man's elation in his natural powers. It attacks when his horizons are cloudy. A cultural atmosphere of fog brings unexpected prophets, who confuse values with the chanted propaganda: "Fair is foul and foul is fair" [I. i. 11]. Dark prospects of an untasted glory are then suggested. The temptation is heightened if it coincides, as in Macbeth's case, with someone else's being made heir to the coveted crown; for then is aroused envy, the sin which along with pride caused Satan to feed on his own will and dream of making himself into the image of his own hopes.

In such a situation, Macbeth's imagination takes fire from cloudy promises. Christ's cross having faded out of memory, its substitute appears—"A dagger of the mind, a false creation"—and "marshall'st me the way that I was going" [II. i. 38, 42]. Thus man is tempted when he has made himself ripe for temptation: he inherits the dark when he begins to accept it as normal. The imaginations of his heart, "deceitful from his youth'' as Genesis says, overwhelm reason; for now he is feeding on what Banquo calls "the insane root [original sin?] That takes the reason prisoner" [I. iii. 84-5]. Yet where reason is strong, as in Macbeth, it offers protests of conscience in the name of naturally ingrained principles. Where it is weak, as in Lady Macbeth, it capitulates immediately to desire (compare Eve in the Genesis story), letting dream and hunger incite reason into perverse argument, and impatient abuse of all opposition. Lady Macbeth's revolutionary theory of manliness, her interpretation of courage as unscrupulous valor, has had a modern parallel in the propaganda of the Nazis. The Nazis, by appealing to the heroism of brute will, won acceptance in a nation noted for reason and philosophy. Evidently human reason is frail; it cannot withstand the arguments of a willful imagination, once the light of grace is strangled. (pp. 518-20)

One circumstance in the Bible story is here particularly relevant. Adam and Eve fell when they overlooked the divine promise of life in the world to come, trusting instead imagination's promise of freer life here. Macbeth makes the same mistake. He tells us in a speech in which he is considering the step into crime, that as far as "the life to come" is concerned he's quite willing to "jump" it [I. vii. 7], that is, set it aside. All that worries him is the chain of consequences his act will set in motion in this world, on "this bank and shoal of time" [I. vii. 6]. Tyrants in our own era generally start with this same attitude. They persuade themselves and others to forget about other-worldly considerations and focus on this-worldly ones. The equivocal promise, "Thou shalt be king hereafter" [I. iii. 50], means for them, as for Macbeth, not hereafter in Heaven (where, according to Revelation 20, faithful men and women sit on thrones and judge the nations), but hereafter on earth—because that is what their own dark souls wish the prophecy to mean, and they are willing to storm heaven in pursuit of this interpretation. The prophecy in itself is ambiguous: it is they (not the "weird" or fatal sisters) who resolve its meaning in a lower sense. They reduce supernatural riddle to common sense.

No doubt Shakespeare intends to indicate that a willful disregard of eternal life in man's thinking about his destiny is the first step on the downward path to nihilism. In any case it is clear that without the support of belief in the life-to-come Macbeth's reason is not able to curb desire; for although his reason condemns the act of murder on the ground of foreseen consequences in this life, his will at the same time sanctions the drugging of his reason:

> Stars, hide your fires!
> Let not the light see my black and deep desires:
> The eye *wink* at the hand! Yet let that be,
> Which the eye fears, when it is done, to see.
>
> [I. iv. 50-3]

By the prayer of his own will he bids his reason nod.

Shakespeare makes clear that from the moment Macbeth concedes the life to come he has removed the setting, so to speak, which guards his "eternal jewel," the soul. Once this jewel is regarded as not heaven's, he can give it to the witches. There is no returning after that. The crime follows, and Macbeth regrets it; but regret is not the same as repentance. Repentance is possible only when one has faith; and Macbeth no longer has any faith. He can sigh over the consequences of his deed, lament its thorns and increase of labor, but not repent. He knows himself "deep in blood" but not deep in sin. We can see Lady Macbeth's tortures as those of guilt; but her husband

sees them as evidences only of a "mind diseased," which a physician may perhaps cure. Yet the physician who is called in remarks: "More needs she the divine than the physician" [V. i. 74]. The suggestion is not followed. Lady Macbeth is allowed to go on to eventual suicide. At her end there are no priestly rites, prayers, or even a husband's tears. "She should have died hereafter" [V. v. 17], is his cold comment.

But note here what has happened as the result of Macbeth's concern for the time-world only. The present moment, with its real sorrow, seems not to exist for Macbeth. Time has lost meaning for the man who thought that only time had meaning. What's "here" has lost significance for the very man who let himself believe that only the "here" was important. Is that not, indeed, the essence of his tragedy, as for so many modern dreamers; by setting aside the everlasting life, they have abolished the everliving present. For unless the moment can be seen as immediately present to eternal Being, its presentness evaporates. Macbeth, we soon see, lives in his "tomorrows" and his "yesterdays." Anticipation and recall—always these two, the shadow of the present rather than the present moment itself. Notice now the words with which he began his earlier decision to "jump" the life to come: "If it were done—when 'tis done—then 'twere well It were done quickly" [I. vii. 1-2]. This is a world of subjunctives. It has no genuine imperatives as basis for action.

Macbeth's sense of duty, we may say, has become involved in an equivocation. His statement that it were "*well*" it were done quickly" is true—provided *it* (the choice of treason) has been made in the heart. (Cf. John 13: 27, "That thou doest, do quickly.") The killing "would be" a duty—if this man can once put aside the duty to face his whole duty. Macbeth is adventuring in a realm of "if" duty. He is equivocating with heaven by urging ambition's would-be imperative against heaven's imperative that "I . . . as his host . . . should against the murderer shut the door, Not bear the knife myself" [I. vii. 13-16]. And by considering ambition's imperative first he is in fact already opening the door to "o'erleap" heaven's. "O, come in, equivocator," says the drunken porter a few scenes later [II. iii. 11]. For the comic gate-of-hell which this porter imaginatively guards is actually, in symbol, the gate at which Macbeth himself began to knock when he drank of an intoxicating equivocation. . . . Equivocation is illustrated also in Lady Macbeth's, "I would . . . have . . . dash'd the brains out, had I so sworn as you Have done to this." This is a subjunctive statement of duty which hides from the imperative to swear aright. It sacrifices "brains" to the worship of a would-be world to which the will has sworn!

A spurious world (of imagination divorced from grace) has, along with its own god, its own ritual. A black-mass is hinted at in Shakespeare's description of Macbeth's preparations for the murder:

> Go bid thy mistress, when my drink is ready,
> She strike upon the bell. . . .
> Is this the dagger, which I see before me,
> The handle toward my hand? Come, let me clutch thee.
>
> [II. i. 31-4]

Then when the bell strikes, he ministers to his communicants, the grooms, and to himself also, a poisoned challice (consecrated by his prayers, shall we say), and places a dagger (his crucifix) in the hands of each. Now "witchcraft celebrates Pale Hecate's offerings" [II. i. 51-2] says Macbeth, and the description is apt. He is himself in symbol a kind of high-priest of Night, binding his whole household in a covenant of Death. His crowning act is a "Most sacrilegious" murder, which breaks open his true Lord's "anointed temple," stealing thence the "life o' the building," and making "a breach in nature For ruin's wasteful entrance" [II. iii. 68-9, 113-14]. Henceforth "grace is dead" [II. iii. 94].

Grace dead, breach in nature, the entrance of ruin—this is the logic of rebellion against God exactly as Christian theology teaches it. From it follows, as Shakespeare next shows, a gradually expanding sickness which engulfs the life of the state in tyranny. Freedom of speech is throttled, Banquo is "purged," a spy system is set up which reaches into every household, and for every citizen obedience becomes "mouth-honor" which "the poor heart would fain deny, and dare not." The state becomes in symbol a seething cauldron, bubbling with "Double, double toil and trouble" [IV. i. 10]. Parallels to our modern dictatorships are all too obvious.

But the story does not end here. For though the head of the state, Macbeth, may resort to witches who have power to "untie the winds, and let them fight against the churches" [IV. i. 52-3]; though he may be willing, in order to secure *his* peace, that "the treasure Of nature's germen tumble all together" [IV. i. 58-9] (as by some modern atom bomb), he gains from these unholy advisers of his only a greater sense of lurking danger to his own regime. What he must now fear is the intervention of the unbelievable, some miracle in nature: a "man not of woman born" and a moving wood. (The symbols have both a pagan and a Christian hidden meaning. In pagan lore the "man not of woman born" was, historically, the miraculous Caesar; in Christian lore, he is Christ. In Germanic religious legend the moving forest was associated with the Spring festival, when boughs were carried to welcome the May and mark the end of the Winter-Giant's dominion; in Christian lore the "moving wood" is the Cross, by faith in which men move mountains.)

Macbeth has no eye for seeing either of these possibilities; but they have been secretly preparing for some time an "underground" movement which will unseat him. Macduff, a soldier of greater natural genius than Macbeth, and moreover a man of Christian faith, has escaped Macbeth's arm and is in a neighboring country, land of "the pious Edward" [III. vi. 27]. This "holy King" has already received "with such grace" the exiled true king of Scotland, the murdered Duncan's son Malcolm [III. vi. 30, 27]. In this land, where the king's touch has power to cure the (scrofula) Evil of a "crew of wretched souls" [IV. iii. 141], a "med'cine of the sickly weal" [V. ii. 27] of Scotland can be concocted. As Act IV ends we learn that Macbeth

Is ripe for shaking, and the powers above
Put on their instruments. Receive what cheer you may;
The night is long that never finds the day.
[IV. iii. 238-40]

Then when these instruments of "powers above" move against Macbeth, the very woods of his own country rise up against him, carried in part by citizens waiting to aid the invaders. A few moments later we see [Macduff] bringing in the usurper's "cursed head" and uttering the significant words: "The time is free" [V. ix. 21].

The time is free; but ransoming the time has cost. Young Siward, "God's soldier," slain in this his first battle is symbol of one type of cost. More significant is the type presented earlier in Macduff's "wife and babes, Savagely slaughtered"

[IV. iii. 205-06] in retaliation for Macduff's escape. Wholly innocent, kept even from knowledge of his plan, they must pay for his mission of salvation for Scotland. It is agony to Macduff:

Did Heaven look on,
And would not take their part? Sinful Macduff!
They were all struck for thee. Naught that I am,
Not for their own demerits, but for mine,
Fell slaughter on their souls. Heaven rest them now!
[IV. iii. 223-27]

[Macduff's] "demerits," certainly, can not refer to his leave-taking (though his wife has not faith enough to forgive him that); it must point, rather, to the whole complex of Scotland's failure, for which Macduff accepts individual responsibility, and to atone for which failure he, "sinful Macduff," has felt called to leave wife and children under the command of a greater love.

It has been pointed out by Roy Walker [see excerpt above, 1949] that Macduff as hero stands, along with Malcolm, for Scotland's Christian traditions. He comes from Fife, where at the beginning of the play the Norwegians are defeated and required to disburse ten thousand dollars at "Saint Colme's inch" (the island off the coast of Fife once occupied by St. Columba, where stood an abbey dedicated to this saint). Later, when Macbeth is to be crowned at Scone, Macduff absents himself, retiring to this Fife, his home. He is thinking of Duncan, who after his murder was "carried to Colme-Kill, The sacred storehouse of his predecessors" [II. iv. 33-4]—that is, to the chapel of St. Columba on the island of Iona. Finally, in loyalty to what Duncan represents, Macduff dares exile to seek out Malcolm. Together these two leaders bring back to Scotland freedom, and the promise that

                              what needful else
That calls upon us, by the grace of Grace,
We will perform in measure, time, and place.
[V. ix. 38-40]

Words suggestive of a "sin-grace" context, someone has calculated, occur more than 400 times in *Macbeth*. A story which begins with radical sin could have no happy ending without superabundant grace. (pp. 520-25)

Roy W. Battenhouse, "Shakespeare and the Tragedy of Our Time," in Theology Today, *Vol. VIII, No. 4, January, 1952, pp. 518-34.*

BRENTS STIRLING   (essay date 1953)

[*In the excerpt below, Stirling proposes that the poetics and dramatic structure of* Macbeth *are unified by four traditionally Elizabethan themes, "darkness, sleep, raptness, and contradiction—which combine to give the play much of its essential character." He analyses the images of darkness, also noted by A. C. Bradley (1904) and G. Wilson Knight (1930), and the references to sleep throughout the play. Stirling also emphasizes Macbeth's raptness, stating that obsession becomes "a ruling trait of the protagonist." These themes, he argues, are connected with the theme of contradiction, suggesting "chaos and overturned hierarchy." Stirling states that this theme is especially prominent in the speech of the Porter, who is "the perfect embodiment of contradiction" and thus resembles the Fool in* King Lear. *For other considerations of the element of contradiction in* Macbeth, *see the excerpts by William Hazlitt (1817) and A. C. Bradley (1904).*]

Macbeth is a definitive contribution by Shakespeare to the art of unifying poetics of setting and "mood" with dramatic motivation and structure. I hope to show that this achievement is partly based upon four themes—darkness, sleep, raptness, and contradiction—which combine to give the play much of its essential character. Although darkness and sleep have long been recognized as thematic elements in *Macbeth,* neither their extent nor their relationship to other ingredients has been noted. Their familiarity, however, makes it unnecessary to define them, so that preliminary explanation may be confined to the two remaining themes. Raptness (Banquo's word) is a quality of obsessed drift, which varies from simple abstraction to a condition bordering upon hypnosis. Contradiction (the Porter's "equivocation") appears in two forms: there is the outright expression of it in "fair is foul and foul is fair" [I. i. 11], or "nothing is but what is not" [I. iii. 141-42], and there is its appearance simply as inverted nature, exemplified by the beards of the weird sisters or by Duncan's horses which eat each other. In Elizabethan tradition, however, the two categories were one in that they both connoted chaos and overturned hierarchy. All four themes, incidentally, were conventional, and the purpose of this essay is not to "discover" them but to show with what skill they are amplified, varied, and unified to an end.

Not only do these four strands underlie the poetry of *Macbeth;* they all appear in terms of outward drama, and thus become clear and direct with no loss of suggestive quality: darkness is a constant setting for the action; sleep is murdered by Macbeth who then "shall sleep no more" [II. ii. 32]; raptness is rendered dramatically before the murder, during it, and afterward (the sleep-walking scene); and contradiction is a key to the tragic "reversal." The themes as drama, moreover, merge completely with their poetic equivalents.

Such a unity of poetic and dramatic structure would scarcely be challenging if the significance of *Macbeth* could not be stated in terms of the design itself, and I shall attempt the statement: *Macbeth* is based upon a familiar motive of tragedy, that of transgression and self-destruction which are compulsive. Obsession becomes therefore a ruling trait of the protagonist, as well as a continuous note in the play. Parenthetically, the stressing of compulsion does not mean that *Macbeth* is a tragedy of "clinical" neurosis since the import is more moral than psychological. Nor is the play a clear tragedy of fate, for although Macbeth's conduct after his traffic with the witches may be determined, his early submission to them can be viewed as an act of free will. Shakespeare's concern, however, is with obsessive deeds which follow this, so that abstraction under the spell of evil becomes central. Macbeth's tragic course may now be traced in terms of all four themes: Shakespeare presents his surrender to the witches as a surrender to "instruments of darkness" [I. iii. 124] to "secret, black, and midnight hags" [IV. i. 48]. Out of it arises the raptness which Banquo twice observes, a nearly hypnotic state which contains, moreover, the element of contradiction, since from its onset "nothing is but what is not." Contradiction within raptness now becomes pervasive: even a splendid rhetoric of conscience is ironically part of Macbeth's absorption in the murder of sleep. And as obsession under the spell of darkness leads to further violence in the name of peace and sleep, the ultimate contradiction occurs. Macbeth's abstraction gives way to clear awareness of reality, while Lady Macbeth's early command of "reality" advances into the guilty raptness of walking sleep. Such is the formula; we may now turn to the play itself.

The themes of darkness and contradiction are presented in the opening incantation scene. "When shall we three meet again /

In thunder, lightning, or in rain?" are lines which suggest the gloom of storm; they are succeeded by "When the battle's lost and won," an assertion of contradiction, and are reinforced immediately with another connotation of darkness, "That will be ere the set of sun" [I. i. 1-5]. This is followed five lines later with the contradiction of "Fair is foul, and foul is fair," and the last line of the short scene then reverts to cloudiness: "Hover through the fog and filthy air" [I. i. 11-12]. Thus are established in twelve opening lines two of the themes from which the quality of *Macbeth* is derived. And while the ensuing scene of the bleeding messenger is one of mechanical exposition, the effects of darkness and contradiction are not allowed to lapse:

> As whence the sun 'gins his reflection
> Shipwrecking storms and direful thunders break,
> So from that spring whence comfort seem'd to come
> Discomfort swells.
>
> [I. ii. 25-8]

This introduction to the uneasy turn of battle stresses the blackness of storm proceeding from sunlight, and moves from the simile itself into outright statement of the inversion it represents. Darkness and contradiction are combined in one figure.

The second incantation of the witches which opens Scene iii is significant because the curse pronounced upon the sailor, "master o' the tiger," is the fate which Macbeth himself will suffer:

> Sleep shall neither night nor day
> Hang upon his pent-house lid;
> He shall live a man forbid.
> Weary sev'nights nine times nine
> Shall he dwindle, peak, and pine.
> Though his bark cannot be lost,
> Yet it shall be tempest-tost.
>
> [I. iii. 19-25]

This thematic passage introduces the symbol of sleep similar to the "murdered" sleep of later events, and continues the previous design; it maintains the setting of night, and ends in a contradiction image of the loss-threatened bark which can never be lost. Then, as the "charm's wound up," the line, "So foul and fair a day I have not seen" [I. iii. 37-8], echoes the fair-foul contradiction which closed Scene i. This is succeeded and augmented by symbols of inverted nature: unearthly inhabitants of earth and bearded women. Now, as the triple prophecy of Macbeth's fortune is concluded, the raptness theme is introduced by Banquo: "My noble partner / You greet with present grace and great prediction / . . .That he seems rapt withal" [I. iii. 54-7], echoed toward the end of the scene with "Look, how our partner's rapt" [I. iii. 142], and two scenes later with the line from Macbeth's letter, "Whiles I stood rapt in the wonder of it . . ." [I. v. 5-6].

Scene iii is thus one of motivation, for the two moods which will lend character to Macbeth are both presented. His abstracted state which will lead to murder appears through Banquo's lines, and the state of ruined sleep which will follow his act is suggested by the witch's curse upon the sailor. (pp. 385-87)

The opening of I. vii asserts contradiction again in its allusion to that which is done, yet never is to be finished: "If it were done when 'tis done . . ." [I. vii. 1]. The thought is then expanded in a passage which is ultimate, for a turn of phrase, "that but this blow / Might be the be-all and the end-all here

. . ." [I. vii. 4-5], expresses all of Macbeth's struggle for rest in a present which can offer nothing but guilt from the past and fear for the future. It is partly because the tragedy is built around this irony that the pattern of inversion in *Macbeth* is so telling. To say that the whole play is an extended metaphor of contradiction would be to state a kind of truth, but it would lead us into paradox fetishism, as well as into the adage that tragedy involves irony. Not all tragedy, however, involves schematic play upon contradiction in skillful combination with other themes, and it is upon this characteristic of *Macbeth* that my interpretation rests.

"If it were done when 'tis done, then 'twere well / It were done quickly" [I. vii. 1-2]. Done quickly it is; in the speed of the doing Shakespeare shows himself the tested dramatist, for he rests his motivation less upon psychological traits of the protagonist than upon a pervasive quality of the play itself, and thus employs a method suited to concentration. At the basis of this quality which pervades *Macbeth* are the associated themes of raptness, contradiction, troubled sleep, and darkness. (pp. 388-89)

With the opening of Act II movement is accelerated, but Shakespeare intensifies the pattern of themes: "How goes the night . . .?" [II. i. 1]—"The moon is down . . ." [II. i. 2]—"There's husbandry in heaven; / Their candles are all out" [II. i. 5]— "A heavy summons lies like lead upon me, / And yet I would not sleep" [II. i. 6]—"The King's a-bed" [II. i. 12]—"Good repose the while" [II. i. 29]—"Get thee to bed" [II. i. 32]. Then as the symbolic dagger appears, a theme comes physically upon the stage as the vision draws Macbeth in rapt movement toward the murder chamber, to an accompaniment of lines which express this state and blend with it the elements of night and sleep. . . . (pp. 389-90)

We have now come to the murder scene, and it is here that underlying theme and external action meet in climactic unity. As figures of night and darkness preside, the killing of Duncan is made physically the murder of sleep ("Had he not resembled / My father as he slept, I had done 't" [II. ii. 12-13]), a fusion of symbol with action which leads to the great passage ending "Glamis hath murder'd sleep . . . / Macbeth shall sleep no more" [II. ii. 39-40]. And here raptness again becomes action as Macbeth enters bearing abstractedly the incriminating daggers. Summary or quotation cannot convey his "brain-sickly" isolation and Lady Macbeth's attempts to break through the barrier: "Be not lost so poorly in your thoughts" [II. ii. 68-9].

No less prominent is a translation into dramatic terms of the remaining theme. Our drunken porter is no longer viewed as non-Shakespearian, but the arguments for readmitting him to *Macbeth* are whimsically confirmed when we realize that he is the perfect embodiment of contradiction. Not only are the porter's lines dominated by inverted logic; his character itself is symbolic of the quality. Lear's fool is scarcely more appropriate than he as the spokesman of a world in which *non-sequitur* has final relevance because degree and a stable "chain of being" have been destroyed. "Knock, knock"—images of contradiction spill upon the scene: the farmer "that hanged himself on th' expectation of plenty"; the equivocator who "could swear in both scales against either scale . . . ," whose treason for God's sake could not equivocate him into heaven; lechery which drink "provokes and unprovokes. . . . It makes him and it mars him; it sets him on, and it takes him off; it persuades him, and disheartens him; makes him stand to, and not stand to . . ." [II. iii. 4-34]. Truly, nothing is but what is

not. With this *tour de force* the murder scenes are complete in their stressing of previously set themes; darkness has been the setting, Duncan has become the stage of presence of sleep, and Macbeth himself has "enacted" the quality of raptness. Through the porter Shakespeare dramatizes the fourth element of contradiction.

". . . In conclusion, equivocates him in a sleep . . ." [II. iii. 35]—the porter thus ends his speech, and sleep, with night, now strangely prevails in the hectic scene of discovery. Inquiries which precede the disclosure come in ironic terms of this theme: "Is thy Master stirring? / Our knocking has awak'd him."—"Is the King stirring . . .?" [II. iii. 42-5]. The setting of darkness is reestablished: "The night has been unruly. . . . The obscure bird / Clamour'd the livelong night" [II. iii. 54-60]. When mood and suspense are secured in this way, the murder is suddenly revealed in Macduff's passage beginning "Confusion now hath made his masterpiece" [II. iii. 66], and the hue and cry comes in terms of sleep equated with death, and of raptness represented by spirits who rise and walk.

> Malcolm! awake!
> Shake off this downy sleep, death's counterfeit,
> And look on death itself! Up, up, and see . . .
> As from your graves rise up, and walk like sprites,
> To countenance this horror!
>
> [II. iii. 75-80]

The unmasking of murder within the precincts of sleep is finally capped by Lady Macbeth's "What's the business, / That such a hideous trumpet calls to parley / The sleepers of the house?" [II. iii. 81-3]. (pp. 390-91)

Act III continues the course of murder in which "returning were as tedious as go o'er," and the onslaught upon Banquo is accompanied by the same thematic design which gave meaning to Acts I and II. Even such a dramatic commonplace as the tragic irony of Banquo's departure into the trap prepared for him appears in terms of darkness:

> Go not my horse the better,
> I must become a borrower of the night
> For a dark hour or twain,
>
> [III. i. 25-7]

which is strengthened by Macbeth's ironical reply, "Hie you to horse; adieu, / Till you return at night" [III. i. 34-5]. The scene now presents Macbeth and the two murderers, and in the soliloquy which ends it the same theme takes prominence: "for't must be done tonight / . . . . Banquo, thy soul's flight, / If it find heaven, must find it out tonight" [III. i. 130, 140-41]. Should this linkage of Banquo's fate with the symbol of darkness seem incidental, a reference forward to the commentary of Scene vi may be reassuring. There the fate of Banquo is summed up as a direct result of traffic with night:

> The gracious Duncan
> Was pitied of Macbeth; marry, he was dead.
> And the right-valiant Banquo walk'd too late. . . .
>
> [III. vi. 3-5]

And lest the allusion escape as casual, it is immediately repeated:

> Whom [Banquo], you may say, if't please you, Fleance killed,
> For Fleance fled; men must not walk too late.
>
> [III. vi. 6-7]

If after this reference ahead for validation of method, we return to Scene ii, there will be found a major rendering of the night-spell which dooms Banquo. Preceding this, however, the note of contradiction appears in Lady Macbeth's "Naught's had, all's spent, / Where our desire is got without content" [III. ii. 4-5], and the murdered sleep symbol comes in redoubled irony with "Duncan is in his grave; / After life's fitful fever he sleeps well" [III. ii. 22-3]. As before, in close association with these two themes appears that of night. The passage begins:

> Ere the bat hath flown
> His cloister'd flight, ere to black Hecate's summons
> The shard-borne beetle with his drowsy hums
> Hath rung night's yawning peal. . . .
>
> [III. ii. 40-3]

And as the night imagery multiplies it evolves to raptness equalling hypnosis: first made sightless by the invocation to darkness, "pitiful day," the symbol of conscience, begins "to droop and drowse."

> Come seeling night,
> Scarf up the tender eye of pitiful day,
> And with thy bloody and invisible hand
> Cancel and tear to pieces that great bond
> Which keeps me pale! Light thickens and the crow
> Makes wing to the rooky wood;
> Good things of day begin to droop and drowse,
> Whiles night's black agents to their preys do rouse.
> Thou marvell'st at my words.
>
> [III. ii. 46-54]

Nor should it escape us that the sleep-raptness note in this address to night also takes auditory form: "summons," "hums," "yawning," "drowse," "rouse" transmit it in the manner of Spenser's *m, n,* and *z* sounds in the Cave of Morpheus episode.

The prelude to Banquo's murder thus reproduces and intensifies the setting which accompanied the murder of Duncan. All of the previous themes are repeated, and they appear in such concentrated suspension that the burst of action in III. iii occurs as a sudden liberation of evil: in some twenty lines the death of Banquo is accomplished, just as the killing of Duncan was carried out in a quick scene which followed similar dramatic preparation. But in this kinetic release darkness can still accompany the action and, in fact, strike the climax: "The west yet glimmers . . ."—"Give us a light there!"—"A light, a light!" [III. iii. 5, 9, 14]. And as Banquo dies, the Third Murderer: "Who did strike out the light?" [III. iii. 18].

After Banquo's ghost has walked, Macbeth makes his last trial for the certainty, the sleep, which he has lost irrevocably. In IV. i his second visit to the witches will yield the false prophecy of safety, and as the creatures prepare for his coming their incantation draws appreciably upon imagery of darkness: "wool of bat," "owlet's wing," "root of hemlock digg'd i' th' dark," "slips of yew / Sliver'd in the moon's eclipse" [IV. i. 15-28]—all of this provides the setting for Macbeth's entry line, "How now, you secret, black, and midnight hags!" [IV. i. 48] which recalls Banquo's earlier allusion to the witches as "instruments of darkness." With this greeting Macbeth submits himself finally to the world of night and draws from it the tragic afflatus which will collapse when Birnam Wood comes to Dunsinane.

But if Macbeth's drawing of solace from the witches has been his definitive entry into the dark, so has Lady Macbeth's enduring of torment become the last stage of her traffic with night. Hell here is not fiery, but "murky." Primarily, of course,

the sleep-walking scene enacts the raptness or near-hypnosis which has sustained so much of the play. The scene is more, however, than a presentation of this single theme; it offers in some form all of the others—sleep, darkness, contradiction—and thus preserves the unified design. Prior to this scene, raptness has not always been associated with sleep, nor do the two imply each other, but here, from the nature of Lady Macbeth's affliction, they appear in combination. The quality of darkness, of course, is immediately to be linked with somnambulism, but Shakespeare is not content with the obvious association; he specifically introduces fear of night as a motive: "How came she by that light? . . . She has light by her continually; 'tis her command" [V. i. 21-3]. And the line "Hell is murky!" [V. i. 36] suggests more than random combination. Finally, contradiction in its Elizabethan form appears in a description by the Doctor of sleep-walking as "a great perturbation in nature" [V. i. 9]. It is present, however, in a sense far more pervasive than this, for Lady Macbeth's last scene is the terminus of a great inversion which has been shaping itself throughout the play. In the opening action Macbeth was almost the somnambulist, so stricken was he by prophecy that he drifted toward and through the murder scene in rapt isolation; and also in the beginning it was Lady Macbeth who exhibited supremely the hyper-consciousness, the "outside" directive force which controlled the movements of her husband's abstracted state. From thence, however, the major reversal begins; it is Macbeth who becomes the active, conscious force and his wife who lapses into semi-conscious passivity: "Be innocent of the knowledge, dearest chuck, / Till thou applaud the deed" [III. ii. 45-6]—through this stage of the inversion she passes, as her husband's pragmatic awareness grows, until in the sleep-walking scene she assumes his former role of absent, lonely obsession. So at this stage of the play she has herself become a symbol of contradiction; in a world where fair is foul and foul is fair, where the battle's lost and won, where storms issue from sunlight and night falls by day, the watchful puppeteer has turned into the unseeing puppet. And this transformation has been concluded in a setting of darkness, sleep, and raptness which preserves the prevailing context of themes.

"Tomorrow, and tomorrow, and tomorrow" [V. v. 19] marks the stage at which Macbeth's inner defeat becomes final. Save for the missing sleep theme, this episode also is carried by elements which have supplemented one another throughout and which have so unified action, character, and mood. Here, in the drawing by beacon-light of fools into dusty death, is connoted the scene of Macbeth led raptly by the "air-drawn dagger" and, as well, the spectacle of Lady Macbeth with her light amidst the darkness of walking sleep. Life, the "walking shadow," suggests further this abstracted drift. In the strut and fret of the player, emphasis without sense, comes the note of contradiction which is struck again in the idiot's tale, "signifying nothing." Once more the fatal insight, the function-smothering surmise in terms of contradictory being; again "nothing is but what is not." Lastly, the symbol of darkness persists in "Out, out, brief candle" [V. v. 23], and a continuation of the night theme is allowed to end the tragic unfoldment after the soliloquy is finished. Macbeth, no longer responsive even to the "night-shriek," can now say "I gin to be aweary of the sun . . ." [V. v. 48]. (pp. 392-94)

Brents Stirling, "The Unity of 'Macbeth'," in Shakespeare Quarterly, *Vol. IV, No. 4, October, 1953, pp. 385-94.*

ROBERT PACK (essay date 1956)

[*Pack contrasts Macbeth with the protagonists of Shakespeare's other major tragedies. Unlike Hamlet, Othello, and Lear, argues Pack, Macbeth is "more the master of his fate" because he is his own antagonist, but he is the only one of these characters to conclude that life is worthless. Noting Macbeth's affinity with Satan, a point also made by Roy W. Battenhouse (1952) and Herbert R. Coursen, Jr. (1967), Pack states that while Hamlet, Othello, and Lear are provoked by external forces and "sin like Adam," Macbeth sins out of an "inexplicable pride and ambition" and with a full knowledge of the consequences of such defiant action. He also proposes that Macbeth, like Satan, is an "extreme romantic" who is not a creator but a destroyer and anarchist, and that his punishment is "to lose those things which made up his humanity." Pack concludes that Macbeth receives no sympathy because he has "ceased to be human."*]

Macbeth differs from Hamlet, Othello, and Lear in that he is a good man whose intention is to do evil and who succeeds, while the others are all good men whose intentions are to do good and who, for the most part, fail. In compensation for their failure, Hamlet, Othello, and Lear all learn something in the course of their plays, but Macbeth is only confirmed in what he already knew, that "We still have judgment here." To call Macbeth a good man is perhaps merely to call him a man, for Shakespeare's understanding of human nature is that it is essentially moral, and that each man contains within himself his own heaven and hell, with virtue its own reward and evil its own punishment: Macbeth suffers not because he is evil, but because he is a good man doing evil. Why, we then ask, does Macbeth, or any man, if all men are of such a moral nature, commit evil deeds? Is Macbeth's sin simply pride or ambition? Evil is mysterious, beyond prediction or explanation, for it follows no psychological laws which make it inevitable; it is the product of a free will. Shakespeare knows that good may come from evil—indeed, this is the wisdom we learn from all tragedy, but though Shakespeare accepts this paradox, he also embraces the further paradox that, though evil may be necessary in a world of free men, it must be opposed as if this necessity did not exist.

In Shakespeare's plays, the World, the State, and the Individual are interrelated, macrocosm to microcosm. Any influence on one affects the others. A broken law in the affairs of men will be felt throughout the cosmos. The morning after Duncan's murder, Ross says:

> Thou seest, the heavens, as troubled with man's act,
> Threatens his bloody stage: by the clock 'tis day,
> And yet dark night strangles the travelling lamp.
>
> [II. iv. 5-7]

Animals no longer act according to their kind, but become strangely violent: a falcon is killed by a mousing owl, and Duncan's horses, "turn'd wild in nature," attack and eat each other. The world is in turmoil, the state is disrupted with the killing of the king, and, metaphorically, Macbeth has also killed the king within himself.

In the instance of Hamlet this universal moral structure is both accepted and doubted. . . . The world is harsh, but it is, all in all, a good world, one in which Hamlet desires to have his story told. Life for Macbeth seemed in the end, "a tale / Told by an idiot, full of sound and fury, / Signifying nothing" [V. v. 26-8], while for Hamlet, his own tale became the tale of life—man's moral struggle—and Hamlet's ultimate tragic ecstasy was that he came to know that it had *signified everything*. And the play ends with Horatio—like Shakespeare—bent upon

telling this story: "And let me speak to the yet unknowing world / How these things came about" [*Hamlet*, V. ii. 379-80].

Othello also learns that the world is better than he had somehow ever really believed. (pp. 533-35)

Only Macbeth feels in the end that life is worthless and that its story is not worth telling. He fights his last battles, not because he desires to win, not to achieve or to gain something, but out of blind defiance. Even Lear, who undergoes the greatest suffering of the four tragic figures, does not renounce life, but desires it more intensely than ever. (p. 535)

In Shakespeare's plays, all reward, retribution, and punishment take place on earth and within the sphere of mortal life. It is this world that is ordered by moral law and justice. Reward therefore is not reserved for heaven, it is not simply a beatific state, nor is punishment merely something that is imposed upon one like physical torture. The assuming of a burden or a responsibility may be its own reward: the wisdom acquired through suffering, the joy in right action, in fulfilling one's proper role, the elation in a friendship or a love proven true, the ecstatic moment when one sees into the heart of things, the purging of the corrupt, light replacing dark, the upright man in his place, the ordered and harmonious state, the affirmation of moral values. Like reward, punishment may be a state of conscience, of being.

"Macbeth" is a play about a man who violates the moral order, and is punished for it. If we compare "Macbeth" with Dante's "Inferno," we see that no torture is imposed upon Macbeth to fit his crimes, but the blessings of Macbeth's natural humanity fall from him one by one, until he is ultimately deprived of all human ties, even concern for himself. Macbeth's punishment is to lose those things which made up his humanity.

Macbeth is his own antagonist. The entire moral order is reflected within his conscience and suffering as the functioning of his imagination. The conflict of the play is primarily interior. Hamlet is oppposed by Claudius, Othello by Iago, Lear by Regan, Goneril, and Edmund; their fates are partially determined by hostile, external forces. But Macbeth, more than any other tragic hero, can anticipate and calculate the results of his actions, and for this reason is most the master of his fate. He falls, not out of ignorance, foible, or weakness, but like Satan, out of defiance and ambition, willingly embraced. Conscience, with all its vivid imagery of warning, is willfully rejected.

Once Macbeth has killed the king, the entire natural and moral order is disrupted, and in this chaos results can no longer be calculated from causes. Shakespeare describes this disorder by showing us storms, winds, wild seas, thunder, war, and witches, or in subtle dramatic ways as in the banquet scene when everybody enters in proper order (Macbeth says: "You know your own degrees; sit down: at first and last" [III. iv. 1-2]) but exits in confusion (Lady Macbeth says: "You have displac'd the mirth, broke the good meeting, / With most admir'd disorder" [III. iv. 107-08]). . . . The reverberation of sounds echoing over vast regions, filling all of space, suggests the incalculable and boundless effect and spread of evil issuing from a single source. But perhaps the most important of all the play's imagery, as Cleanth Brooks has pointed out [see excerpt above, 1947], is that of the child. The child is the symbol of Macbeth's ambition: to break down the laws of nature and redirect fate, shaping the future according to his own anarchic order. Macbeth's free and proper choice was, in a sense, to stand still, to accept his role, his place in society, the natural order. But in choosing otherwise, Macbeth determines his personal doom, although control of the future, which the child represents, is beyond him. (pp. 536-38)

Before Macbeth began his career in crime, he knew fully—unlike Lady Macbeth—that punishment and judgment must follow. But what he did not realize (and here if anywhere lies his tragic foible) is the means by which this punishment will be carried out. The means are nature's means—nature working through himself as imagination, and by the dissembling signs of the external world. Macbeth ceases to be able to tell the false from the true, the real from the illusory, and is brought to his death as if nature, like the gods in classical mythology, had a personality which was expressed actively and with conscious intent in the affairs of men.

At the play's commencement, Macbeth exhibits a balance of hard and soft virtues: courage, bravery, strength, defiance, pride and ambition; but also kindness and conscience. In the play's unfolding, he loses the soft virtues, and we cease to feel sympathy for him; but he retains, throughout, his hard virtues, and whenever we are in his presence, our awe is without bounds. He is that spectacle of horror from which we cannot take our eyes. Because his strength is admirable, he is doubly dangerous, both for doing evil and for making it secretly appealing. Like Satan, he is a fallen angel and there is something within all of us that is of the devil's party. Shakespeare does not pretend that there is nothing attractive about evil—for why else should so much evil be done—but he wants to show how the human devil is destroyed, not by punishment through authoritative judgment, but through the acting out of his own evil.

Satan, it has been suggested, was the first romantic. His evil was the result of a surplus of energy not being directed as love or for creative purposes, and therefore endangering the moral or social order. The extreme romantic is not the creator, but the destroyer, not the reformer, but the anarchist. Macbeth is such a romantic. Because of an excess of selfish energy, he attempts to exploit even the forbidden possibilities of his life, and tries to shape the order of nature to fit his own demands.

The idea of Macbeth as Satan is suggested within the play in many forms and guises. There is much talk about rebels; there are references to hell and images of hell; and there are many allusions to the devil himself. Lady Macbeth says to her husband before Duncan arrives: ''Look like the innocent flower, / But be the serpent under 't''[I. v. 65-6]. Malcolm, speaking of Macbeth, remarks: ''Angels are bright still, though the brightest fell'' [IV. iii. 22]; and a little later in the conversation, Macduff replies: ''Not in the legions / Of horrid hell can come a devil more damn'd / In evils to top Macbeth'' [IV. iii. 55-7].

Macbeth's evil is primarily self-generated. Hamlet, Othello, and Lear are provoked from without; they are confused, and are trapped by extreme and extenuating circumstances. Out of their ignorance, they are tempted into acting wrongly, or not at all, and they suffer for it. They sin like Adam, who in the course of being tested was still being created, but Macbeth sins like Satan—without any provocation except his own inexplicable pride and ambition; his crime is treason. To think he is seduced into crime by Lady Macbeth when she argues that his reluctance is cowardice and that he is bound to a promise to go through with the deed—a promise Lady Macbeth probably invented—is to underestimate Macbeth's intelligence.

The most important analogy between Satan and Macbeth is that they are both fully aware they are opposing an ultimately indestructible moral order, so that they enter into crime aware of the inevitability of their punishment. Macbeth knows fully,

even before the murder of Duncan, that crime has its consequences, fitting and justly punishing, but nevertheless he proceeds. . . . Macbeth defies the repeated warnings of conscience and of his own knowledge, and suffers a series of punishments all consisting of deprivations, until he has lost what the poorest of men have—that most precious gift of all—his humanity:

He loses the ability to pray.

> *Macbeth:* Listening their fear, I could not say 'Amen,'
>   When they did say 'God bless us!'
> *Lady Macbeth:*   Consider it not so deeply.
> *Macbeth:* But wherefore could I not pronounce 'Amen'?
>   I had most need of blessing, and 'Amen'
>   Stuck in my throat.
>
>   [II. ii. 26-30]

He loses the blessing of sleep.

> *Macbeth:* Methought I heard a voice cry 'Sleep no more!
>   Macbeth does murder sleep,' the innocent sleep, . . .
>   Balm of hurt minds, great nature's second course,
>   Chief nourisher in life's feast—
>
>   [II. ii. 32-7]

He loses his sense of the seriousness of life, making of his own ambition an ironic mockery.

> *Macbeth:* Had I but died an hour before this chance,
>   I had liv'd a blessed time; for, from this instant,
>   There's nothing serious in mortality:
>   All is but toys; renown and grace is dead;
>   The wine of life is drawn, and the mere lees
>   Is left this vault to brag of.
>
>   [II. iii. 91-6]

He loses his trust in even the men who work for him, and sends a third murderer to watch after the first two.

> *Second Murderer:* He needs not our mistrust, since he delivers
>   Our offices and what we have to do
>   To the direction just.
>
>   [III. iii. 2-4]

He loses the power of rational thought, and is trapped within his own fears and emotions.

> *Murderer:*   Most royal sir,
>   Fleance is 'scaped.
> *Macbeth:* Then comes my fit again; I had else been perfect;
>   Whole as the marble, founded as the rock,
>   As broad and general as the casing air:
>   But now I am cabin'd, cribb'd, confin'd, bound in
>   To saucy doubts and fears.
>
>   [III. iv. 19-24]

He loses trust in his senses, and is seized by madness. Like distrust, madness separates men from their society.

> *Lennox:*   What is it that moves your highness?
> *Macbeth:* Which of you have done this?
> *Lords:* What, my good lord?
> *Macbeth:* (To Banquo's ghost who is sitting in Macbeth's chair)
>   Thou canst not say I did it: never shake
>   Thy gory locks at me.
> *Ross:* Gentlemen, rise; his highness is not well.
>
>   [III. iv. 47-51]

He loses all companionship and the comfort of family and society, and falls into complete loneliness and isolation.

> *Macbeth:* I have liv'd long enough: my way of life
> Is fallen into the sear, the yellow leaf;
> And that which should accompany old age,
> As honor, love, obedience, troops of friends,
> I must not look to have.
>
> [V. iii. 21-6]

He loses the power of compassionate feeling, and cannot even grieve at the death of his wife.

> *Seyton:* The queen, my lord, is dead.
> *Macbeth:* She should have died hereafter;
> There would have been a time for such a word.
>
> [V. v. 16-18]

It is this complete loss of pity that leads Macbeth to the nadir of his nihilism, and it is a mistake on our part ever to think that the sentiments within these following words are Shakespeare's as well as Macbeth's. For Macbeth has lost love for everything and can take pleasure in nothing.

> *Macbeth:* Life's but a walking shadow, a poor player
> That struts and frets his hour upon the stage,
> And then is heard no more; it is a tale
> Told by an idiot, full of sound and fury,
> Signifying nothing.
>
> [V. v. 24-8]

Macbeth, stripped of his humanity, is left with only blind animal defiance, fitting to the beast that he has become. (pp. 539-43)

Macbeth has violated Nature's moral order and has thus become estranged from it, so that to him the face of Nature becomes a false one whose smiles are deceit and whose warnings are misleading. As Macbeth has acted falsely to his nature, so Nature equivocates in its appearances, rendering Macbeth's punishment, the deprivation step by step of his humanity, to its culmination by means of Birnam Wood and Macduff's premature birth—whereby Macbeth is defeated in battle and destroyed. Between the blindness of hopeless and loveless defiance and the blindness and hopelessness of death, there is little space.

By the end of the play, we have lost all compassion and sympathy for Macbeth, so that our feelings for him have been completely reversed, and he evokes in us fear and horror. Since Macbeth has, in effect, ceased to be human, the most we can feel is an abstract pity; we are not sorry for *him* because of the fate that he suffers, but we are sorry that in *our* world such corruption may take place, and that such power, of potential good, may release what is terrible and dark in human affairs.

Our pity and sympathy for Hamlet, for Othello, and for Lear increase as the tragedy of their drama directs them to their one, inevitable end. It is the necessity of their suffering, and their humanity which is released through it, that fixes our fascination and makes us love them. For with our knowledge of their loss, we recognize the inevitability of our loss, which tragedy defines as the necessary condition of human life; and since to understand loss, to feel the weight of suffering through it, is also to understand *that which has been lost,* we recognize that through the suffering of loss our love and affirmation of life is expressed and revealed. This is the knowledge by which, at the time of their deaths, Hamlet, Othello, and Lear accept their own fates while affirming the goodness of life, and feel love most strongly out of the depths of their loss.

Macbeth does not make such an affirmation; in dying, he does not affirm the moral order, nor spiritual love, nor any force of life, but the moral world *affirms itself* in the way it has punished and destroyed him. For it is an order in which its opponents are punished by the very fact of their opposition, so that Macbeth suffers commensurately with his power to defy its laws. Out of the same necessity that makes suffering a means to the recognition of the good, comes the reëstablishment of harmony after the hour of evil.

If in the course of the play our feelings for Macbeth move from sympathy and admiration to horror and awe, our feelings for Lady Macbeth move in an opposite way: from horror and revulsion to pity and sympathy. At the beginning, she is unable to understand Macbeth, mistaking conscience for cowardice, and is therefore unable to help him; and in the end, Macbeth, having opposed and rejected his own conscience, can no longer sympathize with his wife or help her when she suffers the extreme recriminations of her conscience. Macbeth knows before he acts that the rhythm which leads from deed to consequence is a rhythm compounded in the stars and not made or changed by man: "If it were done when 'tis done then 'twere well / It were done quickly" [I. vii. 1-2]. But Lady Macbeth does not learn this lesson until temptation is chronicled in action: "What's done cannot be undone" [V. ii. 68]. Shakespeare's repetition of the word "done" and "do" throughout the play teaches of an inevitability and the necessity that leads us toward it.

Macbeth's greatness, let us remember, is opposite and opposed to his goodness. The evil giant is nonetheless a giant, and is able to accomplish feats beyond the powers of ordinary men. Macbeth possesses a greatness of will which enables him to detach himself from his own personality and act against the dictates of his own knowledge and his own conscience. It is a kind of stoicism by which he refuses to be himself, maintaining this position no matter what the outcome, and without self-pity or regret. This is a fantastic feat, one which Lady Macbeth thinks she can execute, but at which she fails miserably. Macbeth, by his success, wins our hatred. Lady Macbeth, by her failure, wins our pity. It is a paradoxical ascent that Lady Macbeth travels, for she is destroyed by the goodness of her moral nature, by her conscience. It is not by a strength of will that she repents; her nature repents for her. (pp. 543-45)

At her death, Lady Macbeth has lost all will to oppose the will of nature as it exists in the society of men and in its manifestation as her guilt and her conscience. She ends in the weakness of utter submission to this greater will, and the doctor who has tended her has no prescription for her but forgiveness:

> *Doctor:*   Unnatural deeds
> Do breed unnatural troubles; infected minds
> To their deaf pillows will discharge their secrets;
> More needs she the divine than the physician.
> God, God forgive us all!
>
> [V. i. 71-5]

That the doctor should ask "all" to be forgiven proves that in some secret way there is something in himself that he identifies in Lady Macbeth, and we too feel this bond, so that Lady Macbeth receives the sympathy that returns her to the fellowship of men and reaffirms her threatened humanity. She rises into the heaven of our affection and acceptance.

Greatness is an attribute of will. Goodness is the natural attribute of heart. Will may either be in opposition to goodness or may embrace it, so that for Shakespeare moral action exists in this freedom of choice: sin is opposition to the natural order, and virtue is acceptance of it. Though greatness in itself is no virtue, it is always fascinating to man, because it is the power by which man is capable of destroying himself. All men are alike in their instinctual goodness; but all men are unique in their greatness. Thus goodness is a social and moral force, while greatness is primarily anarchical, romantic, and individualistic. It is the conflict in men between these two forces, heightened by circumstances, that makes possible the sublime: that mixture of terror and beauty in struggle.

The heroes of tragedy are always romantics, men who first know and desire the order that their singular selves would have shape the world and give it its motion and its laws. Ultimately, their greatness and their goodness are reconciled when they accept the natural order as one imposed by a greater power than their own. Macbeth is Shakespeare's exception; he is egotistically romantic to the end, unwilling to bow himself to an order other than his own. The penalties follow; for him there is not any recovery, no pardon, no tender memory. (pp. 546-47)

Robert Pack, "Macbeth: The Anatomy of Loss," in
The Yale Review, Vol. XLV, No. 4, June, 1956, pp.
533-48.

LEO KIRSCHBAUM   (essay date 1957)

[*In the excerpt below, Kirschbaum challenges the position taken by J. L. F. Flathe (1864), Denton J. Snider (1887), and A. C. Bradley (1904) that Banquo, as well as Macbeth, is influenced by the witches' prophecy. Bradley, charges Kirschbaum, interprets Banquo as "a psychologically valid being," instead of as a symbolic foil to Macbeth's evil. He argues that Banquo is essentially innocent, that he is more "an instrument" than a character, and that for dramatic reasons he "must be maintained as contrast." Kirschbaum concludes that Macbeth's murder of Banquo is an effort to "destroy his own better humanity" because Banquo's virtues epitomize what Macbeth both loves and hates.*]

If we consider Banquo as a dramatic function rather than as a character in the usual sense, we shall be able to avoid Bradley's erroneous and confusing misreading of him as another whom the witches' influence finally debases. . . . Bradley, with his customary approach, tended to consider Banquo as a whole man, a psychologically valid being; he did not see that the playwright has so depicted the character that he will always be a dramaturgic foil to Macbeth.

As Banquo and Macbeth meet the witches in I. 3, Banquo notes that Macbeth 'start[s]' and 'seem[s] to fear' the witches' [I. iii. 51] prophecies, that he 'seems rapt withal'; but by his bold words to them, Banquo indicates that *he* has a free soul, 'who neither beg nor fear / Your favors nor your hate' [II. iii. 60-1]. Again, when Ross calls Macbeth Thane of Cawdor, it is Banquo who once and for all clearly indicates to the audience the true nature of the witches: 'What, can the devil speak true?' [III. iii. 107]. Although Banquo suspects nothing of Macbeth's intentions, he does know the nature of man and of Satan:

> And oftentimes to win us to our harm,
> The instruments of darkness tell us truths,
> Win us with honest trifles, to betray's
> In deepest consequence.
>
> [III. iii. 123-126]

Hence, he already knows what Macbeth does not learn completely until the very end: he has immediately recognized the witches as cunning emissaries of the enemy of mankind. And it is significant that Macbeth immediately wants to win Banquo to his side: 'let us speak / Our free hearts each to other' [III. iii. 154-55]. *Free* means *open* as well as *innocent*. Banquo replies, 'Very gladly.' The ease of the answer indicates once more a truly free heart. So, already, Shakespeare's pattern is emerging; Macbeth, tempted by evil, feels a strong desire to negate the difference which Banquo stands for.

In I. 5, Lady Macbeth prays (I mean this word literally) the 'murth'ring ministers' to unsex her. Begging the devil to deprive her of the ordinary human qualities of pity and remorse, she requests the 'dunnest smoke of hell' [I. v. 51] in which to commit the crime. It is meaningfully to Banquo in I. 6 that Shakespeare gives the lines describing Inverness castle in semi-religious terms—'temple-haunting martlet', 'heaven's breath', 'pendent bed and procreant cradle' [I. vi. 4-8]. We are meant to feel deeply here the contrast between Banquo's vision and the devil-haunted castle of actuality. The next scene, I. 7, shows us a Macbeth who almost seems to have felt the implications of those words of Banquo:

> [Duncan's] virtues
> Will plead like angels, trumpet-tongu'd, against
> The deep damnation of his taking off;
> And pity, like a naked new-born babe,
> Striding the blast, or heaven's cherubin, hors'd
> Upon the sightless couriers of the air,
> Shall blow the horrid deed in every eye,
> That tears shall drown the wind.
>
> [I. vii. 18-25]

But his devil-possessed lady wins him over. And note how tightly Shakespeare has woven his pattern of contrasts: In I. 5 Lady Macbeth prayed to Satan to turn her 'milk' into 'gall'. In I. 6 Banquo referred to the evidence of a godly home, the 'procreant cradle'. In I. 7 Macbeth speaks of 'pity, like a naked new-born babe' [I. vii. 21]. Later in I. 7 Lady Macbeth says that she could snatch the smiling babe from her breast and dash its brains out!

At the beginning of Act II, just before the entrance of Macbeth, who will leave the stage to murder Duncan, Shakespeare once more presents Banquo. In his customary manner, he is aware of the supernatural powers above and below. It is a dark night: 'There's husbandry in heaven; / Their candles are all out' [II. i. 4-5]. ('Stars, hide your fires!' 'Nor heaven peep through the blanket of the dark' [I. iv. 50, I. v. 53]. Apparently, the demonic prayers of Macbeth and his lady have been answered.) But though the night is indeed dark, Banquo's words have, beyond his awareness, a prophetic undertone: if *husbandry* means thrift, it also means wise management. Hence, through Banquo, obliquely, the irresistible justice and omniscience of heaven is being urged. Banquo continues to Fleance, 'A heavy summons lies like lead upon me, / And yet I would not sleep' [II. i. 6-7]. The first line might suggest that the dark powers are working upon him to get him out of the way of the criminals; at any rate, his soul apprehends evil. So, being the kind of man he is, he prays to the instruments of light to fight against the instruments of darkness:

> Merciful powers,
> Restrain in me the cursed thoughts that nature
> Gives way to in repose.
>
> [II. i. 7-9]

Act IV. Scene i. The Three Witches, Macbeth, Hecat, and Apparitions. By Sir Joshua Reynolds (n.d.).

To Bradley, 'the poison [of the witches] has begun to work' [see excerpt above, 1904], but that is not at all the purport of these lines; they are there for comparison. Everyman is constantly being tempted by evil: during waking hours, he is free to expel it from his mind; but while he and his will are asleep, the demons can invade his dreams. (Macbeth a few lines later puts the matter clearly: 'wicked dreams abuse / The curtain'd sleep' [I. ii. 50-1].) Therefore, Banquo prays for grace, for holy power outside himself to repel the demons. In contrast Macbeth and Lady Macbeth have prayed far otherwise.

After Macbeth's entrance, Banquo declares: 'I dreamt last night of the three weird sisters. / To you they have showed some truth' [I. ii. 20-1]. These are the 'cursed thoughts' that Banquo wishes to expunge—and it is as though Banquo, as instrument rather than as character, unwittingly, is testing Macbeth. Macbeth feels this, he wants to get Banquo on his side, he wants to talk to Banquo about the witches.

> *Ban.* At your kind'st leisure.
> *Mac.* If you shall cleave to my consent, when 'tis,
> It shall make honor for you.
> *Ban.*   So I lose none
> In seeking to augment it but still keep
> My bosom franchis'd and allegiance clear,
> I shall be counsel'd.
>
>   [I. ii. 24-9]

Bradley found this Banquo-Macbeth colloquy 'difficult to interpret'. So it is, inspected as realism, but if one regards the two speakers here not so much as people but as morality play figures who have chosen different sides in the struggle between Heaven and Hell, there is little difficulty. Macbeth is the representative of the Tempter, and Banquo refuses the bait, not with polite evasiveness but with formal rejection. For there is a dichotomy both in Macbeth and in Macbeth's world as long as Banquo represents the good; from Macbeth's viewpoint, Banquo must either be absorbed or destroyed if Macbeth is to gain ease.

In 2.3, when Macduff tells Banquo that their king has been murdered, Lady Macbeth cries, 'Woe, alas! / What, in our house?' [II. iii. 87-8]. Banquo's reply is a semi-rebuke that comes automatically to his lips, 'Too cruel anywhere' [II. iii. 88]. He is not hiding anything: there is such correspondence between his mind and his mouth that his three words dismiss his hostess' apparently limited morality and express a universal reaction. But Banquo is not suspicious of any single person, yet; he does not know who or what the enemy is, yet. All he knows is that he is innocent and that a great crime has been committed:

> In the great hand of God I stand, and thence
> Against the undivulg'd pretense I fight
> Of treasonous malice.
>
>   [II. iii. 130-32]

Note how the combatants in the action have been depersonalized by Banquo's words; the war between Good and Evil is
larger than people. (pp. 2-5)

Act III begins with Macbeth king, and Banquo suspecting he
played most foully for it. It is not allowable, dramatically
speaking, to conjecture anything about Banquo between his
last appearance and his present appearance. Furthermore, the
'indissoluble tie' is that between a king and his subject, and
there is nothing evil in it. The 'grave and prosperous' advice
is not criminal aid to the murderer but political counsel to his
sovereign. As to Banquo's character and motives in regard to
the crown, all the soliloquy tells us is that he anticipates great
honour as a founder of a royal line. There is not a hint that he
will play 'most foully' to make the prophecy come true. Primarily, the soliloquy is meant to remind the audience of what
the witches told Banquo two full acts back, for that promise
may be said to guide the action of the play until the blood-
boltered Banquo points at the show of the eight kings—and
even then Macbeth's horror at this truth motivates his slaughter
of Lady Macduff. As usual Shakespeare's purpose with Banquo
here is not similarity but dissimilarity. Dramaturgically, Banquo *must* be maintained as contrast.

That it is not Banquo so much as person but what he still
epitomizes which prompts Macbeth to kill his one-time companion is brought out, I believe, in Macbeth's famous soliloquy:

> To be thus is nothing
> But to be safely thus. Our fears in Banquo
> Stick deep, and in his royalty of nature
> Reigns that which would be fear'd. . . .
>
> [III. 48-51]

What is it that Macbeth fears? Is it really Banquo the man? Or
is it the latter's still unsullied qualities—his natural royalty,
his dauntless temper, his wise valour? Banquo represents what
a part of Macbeth wants and, also, what a part of Macbeth
hates. He is truly, as the witches declared, both happier and
greater than the regicide. Let us put it this way: Macbeth is
jealous of Banquo's virtues, wants them but cannot have them,
feels belittled by them, fears them, and hence must destroy
them. The killing of Banquo may be interpreted as a futile
effort on Macbeth's part to destroy his own better humanity;
it is a ghastly effort to unify Macbeth's inner and outer world,
for Banquo has a daily beauty in his life that makes Macbeth
ugly. The fear of an 'unlineal hand', the belief that Banquo's
issue will immediately succeed him are rationalizations, the
false coinage of an agonized man who has sold his soul to the
devil, who has exchanged his 'eternal jewel' for a poisoned,
tortured mind. It is not really Banquo the person whom Macbeth fears: it is Banquo as symbol, he who stood 'In the great
hand of God'. (pp. 6-8)

> Leo Kirschbaum, "Banquo and Edgar: Character or
> Function?" in Essays in Criticism, Vol. VII, No. 1,
> January, 1957, pp. 1-21.

PAUL N. SIEGEL   (essay date 1957)

[In the excerpt below, Siegel discusses the triumph of nature in
Macbeth. *He examines the conflict between "Christian humanist
and 'Machiavelian'" views of human nature in the play, particularly in the opposition of the "milk of human kindness" and
blood. Macbeth, states Siegel, rejects the milk of humanism for
"the 'Machiavellian' way of blood and guile." Along with G. Wilson
Knight (1931), L. C. Knights (1933), and D. A. Traversi (1968),*

*Siegel asserts that Macbeth is punished for violating the laws of
nature and man, and the natural reasserts itself.*]

In the world of *Macbeth* the masked omnipresence of evil
brings doubt and confusion. With the discovery of the murder
of Duncan consternation and suspicion become rife. Malcolm
and Donalbain suspect everybody, not knowing who or how
many are involved, but fearing most the nobles who are most
closely related to them [II. iii. 140-41]: "There's daggers in
men's smiles: the near in blood, / The nearer bloody." They
flee, putting upon themselves suspicion of the deed. The election thus lights on Macbeth, but Macduff has vague doubts
about him. He does not go to Scone to see Macbeth crowned
and expresses some fear of his accession to the throne [II. iv.
37-8]: "Well, may you see things well done there: adieu! /
Lest our old robes sit easier than our new!" The old man who
discusses the recent events and Macbeth's assumption of the
kingship with him and Ross recognizes with the wisdom and
insight of age the terrible mistake that the Scotch nobility has
made in electing Macbeth king, but he can speak of it only in
soliloquy. Banquo fears that Macbeth has played foully for the
kingship, but he, too, must keep his fear to himself.

Yet murder will out. The ugliness of evil's visage is revealed,
and men of good will, although they must first make sure of
each other, since they are suspicious and fearful of everyone
in the dark world in which they are living, proceed together
against it. For, although evil is present throughout nature, it
is monstrous, unnatural. It comes unbidden into men's thoughts,
but in doing so is immediately and intuitively perceived and
proclaimed by the heart as contrary to nature. "If good," says
Macbeth of the witches' tempting prophecy [I. iii. 134-37],
"why do I yield to that suggestion / Whose horrid image doth
unfix my hair / And make my seated heart knock at my ribs, /
Against the use of natures?"

But Macbeth and Lady Macbeth cast out nature from within
them. "Yet do I fear thy nature," says she of him in her
soliloquy [I. v. 16-18]. "It is too full o' the milk of human
kindness / To catch the nearest way." "Human kindness" here
means both "those qualities peculiar to mankind" and "compassion," compassion being precisely one of those qualities
which human beings absorb with their mother's milk so that
it is a part of their very being. Macbeth has too much of ordinary
human nature in him to resort to crime without external stimulus, although, like ordinary weak human beings, he may think
longingly of the death of the man who stands in his way and
hope that his crime be done for him. Lady Macbeth, however,
teaches him to suppress his natural inclinations. She herself
calls upon the "spirits / That tend on mortal thoughts" [I. v.
40-1], the evil spirits whose business it is to foster thoughts
which are "mortal," deadly, murderous—"mortal," too, because they are all too characteristic of men, frail as they are
in their mortality—she calls upon them to take her milk for
gall so that "no compunctious visitings of nature" [I. v. 45],
no instinctive feelings of pity, may prevent her from fulfilling
her purpose. "Milk" here, as in "milk of human kindness,"
signifies the gentle qualities in human nature, the tender, womanly feelings she describes herself as having had when she says
[I. vii. 54-5], "I have given suck, and know / How tender 'tis
to love the babe that milks me," and "gall" signifies black,
inhuman cruelty, the unnatural feeling that makes it possible
for her, now possessed with the spirit of evil, to go on to say
that she would rather have dashed her infant's brains out than
to have failed to perform a vow to murder.

Although in her invocation to the powers of darkness, where she calls upon evil to be her good, she impliedly recognizes that the social feelings are natural to man, she acts upon a different view of man, a view in which intrepid and conscience-less ambition, ready to dare all and disregard ordinary morality to fulfill itself, replaces these feelings as the highest quality of man. She exhorts Macbeth to practice the Machiavellian virtues of craftiness and courage, to dissimulate, play the part of the welcoming host, "look like the innocent flower, / But be the serpent under 't'" [I. v. 65-6], and to seize boldly his supreme opportunity to gain that "which thou esteem'st the ornament of life" [I. vii. 42], the crown. In this view of man the conventional virtues are reasons for reproach. "Milk of human kindness," as far as Lady Macbeth—if not the audience—is concerned, is a contemptuous phrase alluding to the proverb that milk is a food for infants as against meat for grown men, as in Goneril's scorn for the "milky gentleness" of Albany [*King Lear*, I. iv. 341] and Richard's scorn for the "milksop" Richmond [*Richard III*, V. iii. 325]. For Lady Macbeth "milk of human kindness" is a symbol for the weakness of ordinary men incapable of greatness. "Thou wouldst be great," she goes on,

Art not without ambition, but without
The illness should attend it: what thou wouldst highly,
That wouldst thou holily; would not play false,
And yet wouldst wrongly win.

[I. v. 18-22]

Ambition, and with it the ruthlessness necessary for its achievement, is represented as the supreme virtue; moral scruples standing in its way, the desire to act "holily", like a saint ignorant of practical affairs, is represented as shameful.

The clash between the Christian humanist and the "Machiavellian" views as to what is proper to man forms a kind of running debate in *Macbeth* and is part of its dramatic texture. The Machiavellian villain of Elizabethan drama is distinguished by the fact that he gleefully boasts to the audience of the crimes of which the other characters do not suspect him. Macbeth is not at all this melodramatic stereotype. However, the principles by which he seeks to guide himself are those of the Machiavellian villain, and this would have been recognized by the perceptive members of Shakespeare's audience.

The Machiavellian villain regards himself as a superman and the vast majority of mankind as children, lacking in courage and energy and stupidly beguiled by religious superstitions. . . . "Lac pueris cibus est: sanguine vescor ego" ["As milk is children's food, blood feeds me," (Machiavelli in Gabriel Harvey's "Epigramma in effigiem Machiavelli.")] In its expression of a drive for power and its statement that milk is food for children, unlike the blood on which he feeds, this is echoed by Lady Macbeth's soliloquy. So, too, Machiavelli's "I count religion but a childish toy" in the Prologue to Marlowe's *Jew of Malta* is echoed by her "'Tis the eye of childhood / That fears a painted devil" [II. ii. 51-2]. Her statement that Macbeth is too weak to "catch the nearest way," to proceed by the most direct course regardless of the human lives blocking it, is reminiscent of Richard's speech in which he proclaims that he will "set the murderous Machiavell to school" [*3 Henry VI*, III. ii. 193]—that is, reduce even the progenitor of the superman idea to the level of a schoolboy. He is, he says, as one "lost in a thorny wood" and "seeking a way . . . to catch the English crown" who will "hew [his] way out with a bloody axe" [*3 Henry VI*, III. ii. 174-81]. Blood, the image which pervades *Macbeth*, was associated with the name of

Machiavelli, who had observed at one point in his *Discourses* that Christian forbearance and submission had done away with the valor of the pagans, whose religious ceremonies, unlike the Christian ceremonies, "were sacrificial acts in which there was much shedding of blood and much ferocity. . . ." Macbeth takes the "Machiavellian" way of blood and guile, performing, although in a far different spirit, the actions which Richard boasts he will perform [*3 Henry VI*, III. ii 182-5].

Why, I can smile, and murder whiles I smile,
And cry "Content" to that which grieves my heart,
And wet my cheeks with artificial tears,
And frame my face to all occasions.

But unlike the orthodox Machiavellian villain Macbeth takes this way in a kind of hypnotized fascination that breaks down his will and continues along it with a weary desperation. "I dare do all that may become a man. / Who dares do more is none," he replies to his wife's taunt of cowardice [I. vii. 46-7], affirming that murder is inhuman and that boldness shown in performing it is not a proof of manliness. Lady Macbeth retorts fiercely and with scornful logic that, if this is so, then he must have been ruled by the spirit of a beast when he broached the enterprise to her, rejecting this idea immediately: "When you durst do it, then you were a man" [I. vii. 49]. If he would only do now what he had before resolved to do, he would be still more a man. Instead, the opportunity for which he had longed has only served to "unmake" [I. vii. 54] him, undo his manhood. She prevails over him, and he exclaims in admiration: "Bring forth men-children only; / For thy undaunted mettle should compose / Nothing but males" [I. vii. 72-4]. She is all the more praiseworthy, he thinks, for having the hardiness of a proper man in that she is a woman, who would be expected to have the weakness women ordinarily have, a view of womanliness which stands in contrast to that implied in the dramatically ironic words of Macduff to Lady Macbeth shortly after, when he has discovered the murder of Duncan [II. iii. 83-6]: "O gentle lady, / 'Tis not fit for you to hear what I can speak: / The repetition, in a woman's ear, / Would murder as it fell."

When Macbeth speaks to those who are to murder Banquo, ruined gentlemen turned malcontent, disgusted with life and desperately ready to do anything "to spite the world" [III. i. 110] and advance their fortunes, he urges them, if they are "not i' the worst rank of manhood" [III. i. 102], to revenge themselves on Banquo, to whom he falsely ascribes their broken careers, and incidentally to gain his favor. He thus implies that men can be marshaled according to an order of manliness and that in this order those filled with murderous vengefulness stand in the front ranks. Christian forgiveness and the endurance of worldly misfortune in the reliance on the justice of God he disposes of by implication with the same rhetorical scorn that Lady Macbeth had used in sweeping aside his moral objections:

Do you find
Your patience so predominant in your nature
That you can let this go? Are you so gospell'd
To pray for this good man and for his issue,
Whose heavy hand hath bow'd you to the grave
And beggar'd yours for ever?

[III. i. 85-90]

There is no direct attack on the Christian ethic, but the first question implies: do you have the despicable patience of a saint or the spirit of a true man? In the second question "gospell'd" is used in the general sense of "taught"—is *this* what you have accepted as your guiding principle?—but it recalls that what is being contemptuously rejected is indeed the injunction of the Gospel (Matt. v, 44) to "pray for them which despitefully use you." "We are men, my liege" [III. i. 90], replies the first murderer, speaking for both, accepting the view implied by Macbeth's rhetorical questions that men with the passions of men and not the listlessness of weaklings can respond in but one way: bloody revenge.

When Lady Macbeth seeks to impel Macbeth to conquer his fear of Banquo's ghost so that he may cease betraying himself before the nobles assembled as his guests, it is to his manhood that she appeals [III. iv. 57, 72]: "Are you a man? . . . What, quite unmann'd in folly?" It is folly that unmans him because the visions that he sees she, in her skeptical rationalism, can believe only to be delusions rising from the womanish credulity that accepts old wives' tales: "O, these flaws and starts, / Imposters to true fear, would well become / A woman's story at a winter's fire, / Authorized by her grandam" [III. iv. 62-5]. Macbeth defends his courage in terms similar to those he used before: "What man dare, I dare" [III. iv. 98]. If he tremble before any natural danger, he asserts, "protest me / The baby of a girl" [III. iv. 104-05], the weakling infant of an immature mother, but such supernatural visitations must rob any man of his courage. The vanishing of the ghost, however, brings back the resolution in crime which he thinks of as his manhood: "Why, so: being gone, I am a man again" [III. iv. 106-07]. Further crime, he thinks, will harden him against fear and obliterate the horrible visions which by the end of the scene he has come around to believing are imagined by him: "My strange and self-abuse / Is the initiate fear that wants hard use: / We are yet but young in deed" [III. iv. 142-43]. "We are yet but young in deed"—he will cease to be a fearful novice and will become mature, a man, in crime, ridding himself of the bogeyman terrors of the child. In spite of the evidence to the contrary, he has taken to himself the rationalism of Lady Macbeth, who had said [II. ii. 50-2], "The sleeping and the dead / Are but as pictures: 'tis the eye of childhood / That fears a painted devil." (pp. 145-53)

At the conclusion, when Macduff meets Macbeth, Macbeth, old and weary in crime, has become inured to horror, a man at last, according to the standard he has accepted. The sudden shriek of women does not disturb him [V. v. 14-15]: "Direness, familiar to my slaughterous thoughts, / Cannot once start me." But this indifference to horror is the apathy of one who has been drained of human feeling and for whom life has lost all significance. Informed that the shrieks were caused by the death of his wife, who had once been so close to him, he does not even inquire concerning the manner or the cause, but receives the news with the statement that she had to die sometime or other and that it makes no difference just when, life being meaningless and futile.

But now that he has become dead to all social feeling and that the horror of the invisible and the supernatural holds no terror for him, now that he exists merely in the immediate moment, a thing unto himself, fear of a natural danger, the end of his life in single combat, comes to him. When Macduff tells him that he is a man not born of woman, he exclaims [V. viii. 16-17], "Accursed be that tongue that tells me so, / For it hath cow'd my better part of man!" Nature, the order of God whose creative processes Macbeth has disturbed, revenges itself against him through one who, as if to meet the harsh needs of the time, was "from his mother's womb / Untimely ripp'd" [V.

viii. 15-16], a bloody prodigy of nature in travail. He now momentarily feels fear not in the presence of a supernatural visitation but of a man, for in this man he sees the bloody child of the witches' prophecy who is fated to put an end to him and also that other bloody child, the one he has had slain, no longer pitifully weak but terrifyingly invincible. Daunted, he refuses to fight, but, on learning that he must either do so or yield "to be baited with the rabble's curse" [V. viii. 29] and continue to suffer that wearisome harassment to which, bearlike, he has been subjected, he opposes Macduff with satanic defiance in the face of the inevitable. Terrible in his desperation and in his sense of isolation from humanity, he nevertheless does not, in the courage of his despair (which recalls his former valor while contrasting with it) and in his weary yearning of a few moments ago for "the honour, love, obedience, troops of friends" [V. iii. 25] which he once had had, permit us to see him depart forever without some sense of loss for the extinguished glory of this figure of darkness. (pp. 153-55)

Human nature and nature generally, which have been violated by Macbeth, triumph over him. The youth of Scotland, grown to be men, and the greenery of Burnam Wood rise against him. Before nature violently expels Macbeth from herself, however, he, as part of nature, is caught up in her convulsions. Like the tyrant that he is, he brings an ever-deepening anarchic chaos to his "single state of man" [I. iii. 140], the kingdom of his own being, as well as to the kingdom of Scotland. The unnatural thought of murder unfixes his hair and makes his heart beat against his ribs; his will weakening before this thought, he calls upon his "eye" to "wink at the hand" [I. iv. 52]; his body resists that which his will commands, and he has to "bend up / Each corporal agent to this terrible feat" [I. vii. 79-80]; he cannot say "amen" to the chamberlains' "God bless us," although he desires desperately to do so [II. ii. 26-7]; his bloody hands "pluck out mine eyes" [II. ii. 59]; he cannot keep the "natural ruby" of his cheek at the sight of Banquo's ghost [III. v. 114]. As one of the Scotch lords says of him at the end [V. ii. 22-5], "Who then shall blame / His pester'd senses to recoil and start, / When all that is within him does condemn / Itself for being there?" (pp. 155-56)

For having violated the laws of nature Macbeth suffers the penalty of nature. A usurping tyrant, in seeking peace of mind for himself, he can only devastate his country, which shares the "fitful fever" [III. ii. 23] that life has become for him, a fever in which he continually passes back and forth from the mad frenzy to which he is stimulated by his desperately held belief in his invulnerability to the despairing apathy into which he is sunk by the recognition of the futility of any effort to bring him contentment. Malcolm, the instrument of "the powers above" [IV. iii. 238], is "the medicine of the sickly weal" who will "purge it to a sound and pristine health" by ridding it of the "mind diseased" that rules it [V. ii. 27, V. iii. 52, 40]. Having defeated Macbeth, he stands amid his nobles on the field of battle in a closing tableau, "compass'd," as Macduff says [V. ix. 22], "with thy kingdom's pearl," like the sun surrounded by its planets. He acknowledges his debt of gratitude as Duncan had done after the quelling of the rebellion at the beginning of the play, using the same imagery suggesting nature's bounty [I. iv. 28-9, V. ix. 31], proclaims his thanes and kinsmen earls, the first of that title in Scotland, promises to perform whatever rectifications and reforms are necessary "in measure, time, and place" [V. ix. 39]—observing the propriety and order violated by Macbeth—and announces his forthcoming coronation at Scone. We think back to Duncan's promise that when Malcolm is invested with his title "signs of nobleness, like stars, shall shine / On all deservers'' [I. iv. 41-2]. The promise is fulfilled. Macbeth and Lady Macbeth had in their adjurations . . . given themselves and Scotland over to darkness. Now the stars shine once more.

More than a return to normality, however, is implied. The world of *Macbeth* is one of gloomy castles whose massive strength and outlying walls and fortifications ''laugh a siege to scorn'' [V. v. 3], with boding ravens croaking hoarsely in their battlements, barred gates, and alarum bells to call to arms; of barren heaths and uninhabited spaces where ''spurs the lated traveller apace / To gain the timely inn'' [III. iii. 6-7], and murder takes place unobserved less than a mile from the king's residence; of savage hand-to-hand conflicts in which the brandished steel rips the foe from the jaws to the navel. It is a world of a vaguely suggested early feudalism that has established a social order after the bloody chaos of presocial communism but that is still struggling to maintain it:

> Blood hath been shed ere now, i' the olden time,
> Ere humane statute purged the gentle weal;
> Ay, and since too, murders have been perform'd
> Too terrible for the ear.
>
> [III. iv. 74-7]

In the coronation of Malcolm and the proclamation of thanes and kinsmen as earls is indicated the dawn of a new epoch, with hereditary succession of the monarchy and a more sharply defined and stable social hierarchy.

But while indicating the beginning of a new epoch for Scotland and giving promise, in the pageant seen by Macbeth and in the joining of the English and Scottish forces against him, of the union of Scotland and England, the play would also have brought forcefully before its Elizabethan audience, both that at the court and at the Globe Theatre, before both of which it was probably presented in 1606, the dangers which had only recently threatened the achievements of the past and the prospects of the future. Macbeth's and Lady Macbeth's Machiavellian plotting of Duncan's murder and the enormity of the crime—which includes in itself violation of the family blood tie and of feudal hospitality, ''most sacrilegious murder'' breaking open ''the Lord's anointed temple'' [II. iii. 67-8], and the parricide of one to whom his subjects owe the duties of ''children and servants'' [I. iv. 25]—must have called to their minds the Gunpowder Plot of November 1605, which so terrified the king and excited the people of London. The plot, by which the king, the nobility, Parliament, and part of London were to be wiped out, was regarded as exhibiting to broad daylight the devilish Machiavellianism of the Catholics, which was further illustrated by the confession of the plotter Garnet to the use of equivocation, the swearing to statements made with mental reservations or deceptive ambiguities which Jesuit doctrine permitted before questioners whose authority the Pope did not recognize. ''Faith, here's an equivocator . . . who committed treason enough for God's sake, yet could not equivocate to heaven,'' says the drunken porter [II. iii. 8-11], welcoming him with grim irony to hell and reminding the audience of the Machiavellian wickedness of regicide in the present as in the past. Disguise itself in the habiliments of religion though it might, assume whatever form it would, evil remained evil, and the struggle between it and good went on everlastingly, in their time as before. (pp. 158-60)

> *Paul N. Siegel, '' 'Macbeth','' in his* Shakespearean Tragedy and the Elizabethan Compromise: A Marxist Study, *1957. Reprint by University of America Press, 1983, pp. 142-60.*

M. M. MAHOOD   (essay date 1957)

[*In the excerpt below, Mahood contends that Shakespeare makes frequent use of puns in* Macbeth, *a position opposed to Samuel Taylor Coleridge's assertion that the play contains no puns (see excerpt above, 1813-34). Mahood treats Shakespeare's use of the word ''time'' and its relevance to the play's overriding theme of time, a theme also discussed by G. Wilson Knight (1931), Stephen Spender (1941), and Tom F. Driver (1960). In addition, she analyzes other double entendres, particularly those used by Macbeth and Lady Macbeth. Mahood concludes that while the wordplay in* Macbeth *is less obvious than in other Shakespearean plays, it nonetheless ''welds the themes of the play together into the imaginative unity of a great dramatic poem.''*]

Whereas Coleridge could not recall a single pun or play on words in *Macbeth*, with the exception of the Porter's speeches which he thought to be an interpolation of the actors [see excerpt above, 1813-34], the play's most recent editor [Kenneth Muir] discovers them in almost every scene. Coleridge, of course, was thinking only of deliberate, witty wordplay. Although the play is not devoid of such puns in character, the ambiguities revealed by present-day commentators are rather Shakespeare's own puns, the ironic *double-entendres* we should expect in a tragedy of equivocation. At each turn of the action Shakespeare palters with us not merely in a double but in a treble sense; the irony is often negative as well as positive, since this is a play in which 'nothing is, but what is not' [I. iii. 141-42]. Duncan, for example, bestows Cawdor's title on Macbeth with the words 'What he hath lost, Noble Macbeth hath wonne' [I. ii. 67]; a statement that is true and untrue in ways unsuspected by the king. Cawdor's repentant death is to free him from the opprobrium of treachery which Macbeth is now to assume; on the other hand Cawdor does not lose that manliness which Macbeth, although he possessed it in the battle, relinquishes when he dares do more than may become a man and so 'is none'.

Time and again the play of verbal meanings reinforces such irony. It happens in the tragic anticipation of Macduff after the murder has been discovered:

> Malcolme, Banquo,
> As from your Graues rise vp, and walke like Sprights,
> To *countenance* this horror.
>
> [II. iii. 78-80]

Countenance here means, for Macduff, 'be in keeping with'. It also means for Shakespeare, and ultimately for us the hearers, 'give tacit consent to'. By a time-serving assent to Macbeth's election, Banquo puts himself in a position of danger and finally is murdered—only to walk as a ghost and confront his murderer. On re-readings of *Macbeth*, instances of wordplay such as this fall together with other aspects of the play's language into that pattern of ideas which contributes so much, though often at an unconscious level, to our excitement in the play's action.

A predominant element in this pattern is the theme of time—a theme which is hard to discuss since the most casual speculation about time can plunge us out of our depth in metaphysical deep waters. In discussing Shakespeare's use of the time theme in *Macbeth* I am using as a lifeline the main distinctions of meaning drawn by the *N.E.D.* [*New English Dictionary*]. They are not philosophical, but they represent the universally recognised distinctions which would have, and still have, meaning for Shakespeare's audience. The dictionary, then, gives us three main definitions: a space or extent of time; a point of time, a space of time treated without reference to its duration; and the first and most important of various general meanings, 'indefinite continuous duration'. The relation between the second and third of these meanings is paradoxical. If time is a continuum, it can be argued that there is no such thing as 'a time' but only the flux of events towards and away from a point without extension; we cannot step even once into the same stream. On the other hand, the reality of an action is not lessened or removed by its distancing in time: 'All time is eternally present.' In *Macbeth,* this contradiction between the fixed and the moving aspects of time is in some degree reconciled by the use of the word in the dictionary's first meaning and the supplementary meanings that derive from it. It is tempo, rhythm, measure, the fitness of the natural order—order, that is, seen as a recurrent succession of events, season after season, generation after generation; the revolution of the starry wheels under the law that preserves the stars from wrong. Fundamentally, it is a religious concept of time, in which the change of hour and season, the bow in the heavens, symbolises both the impermanence of things within time and their extra-temporal permanence. In the play it is associated with the powers of good—Duncan, Malcolm, Macduff—whereas the concept of time as the momentous event alone might be said to dominate the thoughts and actions of Lady Macbeth, and the concept of time as duration alone might be said to belong to Macbeth. The confrontation of these notions of time, the religious and the irreligious, is the play's major dramatic conflict. Lady Macbeth tells Macbeth to 'beguile the time', he bids her 'mock the time'; and, when Malcolm depicts himself as a second Macbeth, Macduff tells him that he may 'hood-wink' the time. In each phrase *time* means society, whose rhythm of times and seasons, being divinely appointed, cannot be mocked.

De Quincey's great essay on *Macbeth* presents the murder of Duncan as a parenthesis in time: 'In order that a new world may step in, this world must for a time disappear. The murderers, and the murder, must be insulated—cut off by an immeasurable gulf from the ordinary tide and succession of human affairs—locked up and sequestered in some deep recess; we must be made sensible that the world of ordinary life is suddenly arrested . . . time must be annihilated; relation to things without abolished; and all must pass self-withdrawn into a deep syncope and suspension of earthly passion' [see excerpt above, 1823]. If *time* implies the fit social order, the hour of Duncan's murder and the interval between the crime and Macbeth's election to the throne are timeless; and during these hours in which Scotland is without a king a corresponding disorder in the heavens sets the elements at odds and turns day into night. The two murderers have mocked and beguiled time-as-order with their own distorted and partial concepts of time. For both the deed is a parenthesis, a timeless moment, though each apprehends this timelessness in a different way from the other.

Lady Macbeth contemplates the deed in a mood of clear-sighted exultation; time stands still for 'this Nights great businesse' [I. v. 68]. Already she has proclaimed her master over the natural sequence of time in

> Thy Letters haue transported me beyond
> This ignorant present, and I feele now
> The future in the instant,
>
> [I. v. 56-8]

and in the triumph with which she sets her hand on the wheel of Duncan's days:

> O neuer,
> Shall Sunne that Morrow see.
>
> [I. v. 60-1]

It is one of the greater ironies of the play that the instant of Duncan's murder, which Lady Macbeth feels to be timelessly momentous, should in fact become timeless as it is perpetuated in the recesses of her mind. Time being the condition of human life, the moment out of time must have the nature of heaven or hell. That it can belong to either is suggested in Macbeth's words before the banquet:

> Better be with the dead,
> Whom we, to gayne our peace, haue sent to peace,
> Then on the torture of the Minde to lye
> In restlesse *extasie,*
>
> [III. ii. 19-22]

where *ecstasy* implies, not 'a heavenly rapture' but 'the state of being beside oneself with anxiety or fear'. When Lady Macbeth invokes the powers that 'Stop up th'accesse, and passage to Remorse' [I. v. 44], she creates a hell within the mind, and the sleep-walking scene shows that, by the end of the play, she is never out of it.

Macbeth also conceives the murder as a timeless act, but in the sense that it belongs to time seen as flux and duration, so that the fatal moment is anticipated and recalled but never recognised as the *now.* This way of regarding time allays his revulsion from the deed: 'Time, and the Houre, runs through the roughest Day' [I. iii. 147]. It sets him safely upon the bank and shoal of time—the timeless moment in the river of successive events. Even his last speech before the murder jumps over the deed itself in its sequence of ideas: 'I goe and it is done' [II. i. 62]. But once again time which may not be mocked takes its ironic revenge. Lady Macbeth sees time as the great instant, and that instant persists traumatically in her mind. Macbeth sees it only as flux, and the flux of time brings the children of his victims to maturity and power so that they may avenge their fathers. Before Banquo is killed, Macbeth mocks the time by talk of their future meetings at the evening's banquet and the next day's Council. Time is in his power. He can shorten Banquo's days as easily as he has shortened Duncan's; after dismissing the thanes with the injunction that 'euery man be master of his time, Till seuen at Night' [III. i. 40-1], he calls in Banquo's assassins. But the next scene with Lady Macbeth shows him to be mastered by time, overpowered by fears lest his plans go astray and the succession pass from his line to Banquo's. Because murder has proved so easy, he may as easily be murdered before he has secured the succession to his own heirs.

Several critics have shown that children are a *leitmotiv* of *Macbeth* and that the play abounds in contrasting images of barrenness and fertility. Verbal ambiguities help to buttress the stress and counterstress of these themes. The heath which is *blasted* in a double sense—both barren and accursed—affords the right setting for the asexual witches who belong, in the play's pattern of ideas, with Lady Macbeth's readiness to dash her own child to death, with Macbeth's willingness to see nature's germens tumble altogether 'Euen till destruction sicken' [IV. i. 60], with the avaricious farmer who hanged himself on the expectation of plenty, and with Malcolm's threat, in the disguise of a tyrant, to 'Poure the sweet Milke of Concord, into Hell' [IV. iii. 98]. On the other hand, the association of Duncan, Banquo and the English king Edward with images of health and fertility is helped by such phrases as Duncan's

> My plenteous Ioyes,
> Wanton in *fulnesse,* seeke to hide themselues
> In drops of sorrow,
>
> [I. iv. 33-5]

where *fulness* has the suggestion of 'pregnancy' as well as its more general meaning of 'abundance'; and by the words of Lennox who is ready with the other thanes to shed his blood against tyranny: 'To dew the *Soueraigne* Flower, and drowne the Weeds' [V. ii. 30]. *Sovereign,* by its double meaning of 'royal' and 'healing' recalls the curative powers of the holy Edward, the pattern of kings and the greatest possible contrast to the barren tyrant Macbeth.

Time had once seemed to befriend Macbeth, when its flow had carried him safely past the intolerable moment of Duncan's murder. Now this same movement, by its renewal of a broken social order, makes time Macbeth's greatest enemy. He first comes to feel the antagonism after his second encounter with the witches. As the vision of Banquo's progeny fades, messengers gallop past with the news that Macduff has fled to join Malcolm:

> Time thou anticipat'st my dread exploits:
> The flighty purpose neuer is o're-tooke
> Vnlesse the deed go with it. From this moment,
> The very *firstlings* of my heart shall be
> The *firstlings* of my hand.
>
>   [IV. i. 144-48]

Firstlings can mean 'firstborn young' as well as 'the first results of anything, or first-fruits'. Macbeth has no children but acts of violence against the children of others. Meanwhile the young Malcolm, so seemingly helpless at the time of the murder, is strengthened by the quickening power of the English king and by the 'bloody babe', Macduff, and thus finds 'the time to friend' [IV. iii. 10] and 'the time of help' [IV. iii. 186]. When Macduff swears revenge on the murderer of his children, Malcolm cries 'This time goes manly' [IV. iii. 235]. . . . Time now connotes only barrenness, sterility, 'dusty death' to Macbeth. On the other hand, natural abundance and the seasonal, renewing aspect of time are brought together in the wish of the anonymous Lord that

>   we may againe
> Giue to our Tables meat, sleepe to our Nights
>   [III. vi. 33-4]

—a wish fulfilled when Malcolm and Macduff, who will do all things 'in measure, time and place' declare that 'the time is free' [V. ix. 39, 21]. (pp. 130-36)

A theme in *Macbeth* which is closely linked with that of time, and which is likewise built up largely through a play of meanings, is the theme of darkness. Light measures time; there is no time in the dark, and before the parenthesis-in-time of Duncan's murder a menacing darkness is created in the edgy conversation of Banquo and Fleance as they cross the courtyard on their way to bed. Images of sight and blindness are a constituent part of this darkness theme, and they reveal, as vividly as the time theme, a fundamental difference between Macbeth and Lady Macbeth. Whereas both husband and wife seek to conceal their act from the eyes of men and heaven ('Starres hide your fires'—'Come thick Night' [I. iv. 50, I. v. 50]), Macbeth performs blindly an act that Lady Macbeth is able to contemplate clear-sightedly. She bids him 'Onely looke vp cleare' [I. v. 71]; but he desires the action to be lost in the dark as the moment of its perpetration is lost in the sequence of time. He must compel his eye to wink at his hand in doing the deed, and cannot return to the sight of the murdered Duncan once he has left the chamber. The blood which evokes his horrifying cry—'What Hands are here? hah: they pluck out mine Eyes', is to Lady Macbeth merely 'this filthie Witnesse'

[II. ii. 56, 44] which may give away their complicity to others. The same decisive clarity shows itself in her grim and lucid puns, which are the voluntary wordplay of a totally self-possessed mind:

>   He that's comming,
> Must be prouided for: and you shall put
> This Nights great Businesse into my *dispatch;*
>   [I. v. 66-8]

> But screw your courage to the *sticking place;*
>   [I. vii. 60]

> Ile guild the Faces of the Groomes withall,
> For it must seeme their *Guilt.*
>   [II. ii. 53-4]

As Cleanth Brooks has shown [see excerpt above, 1947], this last pun is deeply expressive; Lady Macbeth sees guilt as something that can be washed off or painted on. The crime's real horror appears to her as a mere image:

>   the sleeping, and the dead,
> Are but as Pictures: 'tis the Eye of Child-hood,
> That feares a painted Deuill,
>   [II. ii. 50-2]

and in the same fashion she dismisses Banquo's ghost, real to Macbeth and the audience although invisible to her, as the 'very painting' of his fear. To Macbeth, on the other hand, mere images such as those that form when the witches drag to the surface his thoughts of murder, have a seemingly tangible reality. The 'horrid Image' which takes shape after Ross has hailed him thane of Cawdor is more real and fearful to him than the 'Strange Images of death' [I. iii. 97] he had himself made in the battle. Whereas Lady Macbeth's *double-entendres* clinch her arguments by their neat riveting of two distinct meanings (and *clinch* was one seventeenth-century name for a pun), Macbeth's wordplay is exploratory and indicates his gropings in the chimera-haunted darkness of his mind. (pp. 141-43)

The moral blindness of Macbeth comes involuntarily upon him as a result of the murder; and the success with which Lady Macbeth has taught him bloody instructions shows itself when he begins to imitate her wordplay. The horror of 'sticking-place' which presents Macbeth, his nerves as taut as lute-strings, stabbing the sleeping king, is rekindled by 'Our feares in Banquo *sticke* deepe' [III. i. 48-9], preparing us for the twenty trenched gashes of the second murder and for Macbeth's callous equivocation: 'But Banquo's *safe*?' [III. iv. 24]. Once again a reversal of Macbeth's and Lady Macbeth's experience has been achieved by the turning wheel of an ironic fate. Lady Macbeth, for whom the real murder seemed a mere picture, comes to accept the images of nightmare as actuality. She begins in the light, acting with decision and clarity, knowing her own mind as Macbeth never knows his; she ends in the dark, open-eyed and carrying a light, but seeing only Duncan's blood on her hands. Macbeth begins in the dark:

>   To know my deed,
> 'Twere best not know my selfe.
>   [II. ii. 70]

He ends in the light, forced into the open by the powers of order whose lighting of the play's darkness begins at 'The Night is long, that neuer findes the Day' [IV. iii. 240]; forced also by the bitterness of experience to see life as a candle that lights folly its way into the dark.

The wordplay of *Macbeth*, less obvious than that of other plays, is some of the most subtle Shakespeare has given us. It welds the themes of the play together into the imaginative unity of a great dramatic poem. At the same time it preserves the play's theatrical vigour by contributing to the interplay of characters as fully realised as any in the major group of Shakespeare's tragedies. (p. 145)

> M. M. Mahood, "'Macbeth'," in her Shakespeare's Wordplay, *Methuen & Co. Ltd., 1957, pp. 130-45.*

G. R. ELLIOTT   (essay date 1958)

[In his book *Dramatic Providence in "Macbeth"* (1958), Elliott presents a scene-by-scene analysis of the play, emphasizing the Renaissance concept of divine Grace. In the introduction to this study, excerpted below, Elliott outlines his thesis and states that Macbeth "bodies forth the essence of the tragedy of mankind." Shakespeare, he argues, demonstrates in the play that "human-kindness" cannot overcome supernatural evil without the aid of supernatural goodness. Elliott further asserts that Shakespeare is also concerned with the Christian belief that "even the most wicked person may at any time be converted if he allows his pride to be overcome by divine Grace." Like D. A. Traversi (1968), Elliott notes the "grace" and virtue of Macbeth's antagonists. He concludes that Macbeth's denial of grace and his "nightmare career is essentially very human." For other discussions of the Christian influence in Macbeth, see the excerpts by Hermann Ulrici (1839), Roy Walker (1949), Roy W. Battenhouse (1952), and John B. Harcourt (1961).]

Evil in [*Macbeth*] is uniquely concentrated, insidious, and powerful; but also it is uniquely fantastic. The more potent it is in action the more abnormal is it seen to be in essence, from the standpoint of Nature and Grace. Accordingly *Macbeth*, Shakespeare's ultimate tragedy, is the precursor of his romances, culminating in *The Tempest*. This visionary, masque-like poem repeats the ethical theme of *Macbeth* but with shifted emphasis: the innate abnormality of evil is stressed while its actual strength in the world is viewed at a divine distance. Significant, then, is the fact that the preposterousness of evil, though elaborately displayed in the romances, is shown more mightily in *Macbeth*. Shakespeare is true to human history (notably to the history of the middle twentieth century) in his conviction that we can realize the strangeness of evil only in proportion as we realize its terrific might in the world: the very fact that a thing so essentially thin and misty as evil, so air-like . . . , can be so powerful is highly fantastical. Hence *Macbeth* is at once greatly dramatic and, because of its fantastic element, extremely theatrical. (pp. 11-12)

According to a general opinion Shakespeare's subtilty, so outstanding in *Hamlet* and *Othello*, is supplanted by passionate forcefulness in *Lear* and *Macbeth*. That is true of *Lear* but not of *Macbeth*. This drama, while violent like *Lear*, resumes the subtilty of the first two main tragedies, though with a radical difference. Here it is fused with classic simplicity of whole design and with extreme tensity of episode. In this respect *Macbeth* is at the opposite pole from *Hamlet*. The opening scene of *Macbeth* says as much in ten lines—conveys as much of the play's whole meaning—as the first scene of *Hamlet* does in a hundred and sixty. The method of *Macbeth*, as in that opening scene, is *dramatic abruption*. In *Hamlet* Shakespeare meditates extensively. In *Macbeth* the net result of all his tragic thinkings is supremely and imaginationally condensed. The play is a series of abruptly shifting but subtly related images; they emerge from, and merge mystically into, a single vision.

But that single vision has two aspects; and the movement of the drama is double. *Macbeth* is a spiritual moving-picture in which close-ups and vistas fade into one another with insensible swiftness. Indeed they do not so much alternate as occur together: their profiles mingle. Close up, the realm of evil, of satanic wickedness abetting "nature's mischief" [I. v. 50], appears hideously strong; but at the same time clear adumbrations are given of the encompassing world of good, of true "Nature" inspired by "Heaven" [I. v. 45, 53], which, seemingly distant at the moment, is supreme in beauty and ever ready, when occasion serves (as in IV. iii), to move close up powerfully, dimming though never obliterating the lurid contours of hell. (pp. 13-14)

[The] atmosphere of fantasticality so notable in the *Tragedy of Macbeth* centers in the hero's amazing imagination; and certainly in this respect he is *not* typical of average persons. He *is* typical in being from first to last a politician. Man is a political animal; and therefore when Shakespeare came to create the fourth and last of his main tragic heroes he made him, not a graduate of Wittenberg, not a Moorish soldier of fortune, not (like Lear) an imprudent old man, but an ambitious politician in the prime of life. But certainly not even the most eloquent politician, let alone the ordinary person who devours the political news in the daily papers, is possessed of the Macbethian imagination. Here Shakespeare employs poetic license, as he does in the case of all his leading dramatis personae, endowing them with a gift beyond common capacity; though Macbeth is especially outstanding because he is more worldly than the others: in real life this type of person does not speak so poetically. But be it noted that all ambitious persons use their modicum of imagination in exactly the same way as he uses his great gift. Everyone of us has one or another ambition which, like Macbeth, we manage to conceal at the first from other persons, excepting our spouses. We strongly desire something we have not, and we may desire it evilly if we let our imagination enhance its value inordinately. Bradley, under the influence of Romanticism, declares that Macbeth's imagination is, in itself, entirely good [see excerpt above, 1904]. But the Renaissance view is more truly human: imagination is a great but neutral power, apt to be employed either for good or for evil ends. For instance, at the beginning of Act II "high heaven" (to adduce the *Measure for Measure* passage [II. ii. 121]) enables Macbeth to have a "phantastique" but crucial vision of a bloody dagger which could forestall his slaughter of Duncan; but his evil will, swaying his evenly balancing imagination, makes that dagger usher him the way he was going. Of course his better imagination—that is, his imagination swayed by his better will—which has antecedently caused him to postpone the crime, brings terrible remorse upon him afterwards. But the remorse is mainly (not utterly) self-centered; and it comforts him falsely by renewing continually his sense of his innate human-kindness. In this respect he evinces strikingly a trait which, recurrent in Shakespeare's characters, is evidently regarded by him as a fateful human proclivity; namely one's ability to distract one's attention from the evil in oneself—thus preparing the way for further evildoing—by occupying his fantasy with the proud assurance that he is, after all, very human.

Along with pride Shakespeare makes use in this drama of three cognate ideas which, though they have not appealed to the modern mind, are deeply rooted in human consciousness and were prominent throughout the Renaissance. First, the supernatural origin of evil, in particular the belief that pride at its worst is devilish. Second, the supernatural origin of goodness, especially of the basic virtue, humility. Third, the possibility that even the most wicked person may at any time be converted if he allows his pride to be overcome by divine Grace. This idea enabled the dramatist, in a manner overlooked by criticism, to intensify greatly the element of suspense in Macbeth's career. (pp. 21-2)

In the first Act, studied as a whole, it is quite evident that Macbeth did declare emphatically to his wife before the opening of the play an intention to destroy the king ... but that this resolve, made by a very moody and human-kindly man, was far from irrevocable. In the first half of Scene iv that resolve is silently revoked by the hero, so entirely is he overpowered for the time being by the presence and gracious goodness of his sovereign. But thereupon, with acute dramatic irony, Duncan, sure of his most powerful thane's loyalty to the regime, appoints his son Malcolm his successor to the throne; with the result that Macbeth's evil design is revived and strengthened far more than it was by the Witches in the preceding scene. Thus Scene iv, with its vivid contrast between the hero's opening and closing moods, prefigures the great Scene vii, ... wherein for the first time Macbeth's evil volition becomes firmly fixed. The dramatist's point here, as so often in his plays, is that a wicked intention must in the end produce wicked action unless it is, not merely revoked by the protagonist's better feelings, but entirely eradicated by his inmost will, aided by divine Grace; which in Act I is mediated to Macbeth through the honesty of Banquo and, supremely, through the gracious generosity and trustfulness of Duncan. Only that view of the matter, I think, brings out the full dramatic quality of the first Act, particularly its suspensefulness.

Shakespeare was very bold in having his hero commit regicide as early as the start of Act II; for thereupon the suspense, hitherto great, collapses abruptly. But it is revived in the ensuing scene (II. ii) for those who, like the Elizabethan spectators, perceive that Macbeth's remorse, here profound, keeps open the possibility of his repentance. He hears a supernatural voice saying he shall sleep no more; he tries to pray to God, confesses that his guilt is ocean-like, and at the end of the scene wishes that his deed could be undone. And in the ensuing ensemble (II. iii) he seems, at first, likely to collapse. But his pride sustains him, as it is apt to do in the presence of others because of his strong, misemployed social sense. And in the climax he utters a lengthy, magnificent speech asseverating his love for the dead Duncan [II. iii. 108-18]. This monologue, in which the dramatist with fine art shows that the speaker is mainly sincere though unveracious, has two effects. It makes Macbeth king of Scotland but also it demonstrates conclusively that his conscience will not let him be happy on Duncan's throne. In the third Act his restless ecstasy brings about, but at the same time is intensified by, his destruction of Banquo. And in the close of the Feast scene (III. iv), alone with his wife, he is confronted definitively with two alternatives: he may repent; or he may harden his will by an orgy of evildoing. He chooses the second course. But he does so in such a vague and general fashion, not yet deciding upon any particular deed, that we are still kept in suspense.

Only in the end of the Cauldron scene (IV. i) does he definitely undertake his third and worst crime. Under the influence of the powers of evil, obeying their final injunction to "Be Lyonmettled, proud" [IV. i. 90]—the reader may recall the Lion in the outset of Dante's *Inferno*—he determines, in revenge for Macduff's flight to England, to slaughter his innocent wife and children. Here, deliberately cruel, Macbeth for the first time in his life chooses evil as evil. His pride in his human-

kindness gives way entirely to his pride in the might of his evil will. But even here our suspense is not ended; for we cannot believe that he will succeed in extinguishing completely the remorsefulness displayed in the first three Acts. To be sure his present gracelessness stands out in vivid contrast with the conduct of Macduff, Malcolm, and Ross at the court of the saintly King Edward the Confessor of England (IV. iii). Here the theme of Grace, hitherto in the background, is brought to the fore. But in the Elizabethan outlook—formally, at least, Christian and certainly very dramatic (unlike modern lyric fatalism)—the fate of Macbeth's soul is still undecided. For the very Grace that can so remarkably animate his foes (who are far from unworldly by nature) may yet manage to lay hold of him too.

And in Act V he is certainly lifted above the subhuman, hellish level to which he sank in the preceding Act. Before he reappears on the stage his final state of mind is carefully foreshadowed by the dramatist in the first two scenes. In the Sleepwalking scene (V. i) the *extent* of Lady Macbeth's remorse is somewhat surprising. We easily imagine that if her husband with his larger conscience were the protagonist here his words would have been still more piercing. Thus Shakespeare, with the dramatic economy so characteristic of this play, disposes of the guilty queen while suggesting her royal husband's greater sense of guilt. Her vain attempt to cleanse her hands recalls inevitably his bloody hand incarnadining the ocean after his first murder [II. ii. 56-60]. And in the ensuing scene (V. ii) the dramatist, speaking through minor personages, tells us that Macbeth, now more than ever, feels his secret murders sticking on his hands, and that all that is within him condemns itself for being there. So that when he reappears in V. iii we know that his accumulated wicked deeds—not now mentioned by him explicitly but luridly recounted in V. i—are the essential cause of his great despair. And this despair, unlike that of Dante's and Milton's allegoric Satan, is entirely and grippingly human. It is touched, at least, with a humility he has not previously shown. Here at long last he knows that his career has been futile. He ceases to be ignorant of his glassy essence, of the glittering and brittle transiency of his earthly being. He sees he has been dressed in a little brief authority. His life is a "breefe Candle"; and, finally, he is "aweary of the Sunne" [V. v. 23, 50]. But, continually alternating with that better attitude, is a very different one, a mood of defiant boastfulness, sustained by the lying predictions of the hellish spirits of the Cauldron scene. He brags: "The minde I sway by, and the heart I beare, / Shall never sagge with doubt, nor shake with feare" [V. iii. 9-10]. And so we are kept in keen suspense, wondering what will be the outcome of the extremely ambivalent, though very human, state of his spirit.

The last scene of all gives a supreme instance of Shakespeare's art of prepared surprise. Macbeth, surrounded by overwhelming forces but still fighting desperately, vaunting his determination to kill all he meets, is confronted suddenly with his greatest foe, Macduff, whom he is still certain of being able to defeat in single combat. Here he has the opportunity to cover himself, before his final exit, with the kind of glory he has always valued highly. He recoils from Macduff, however, and far more abjectly than he did in III. iv from the Ghost of Banquo; he cries out,

> Of all men else I have avoyded thee—
> But get thee backe, my soule is too much charged
> With blood of thine already.
>
> [V. viii. 4-6]

This has been termed Macbeth's sole touch of real remorse; but that view overlooks the distinction, so sharp in the Renaissance mind, between remorse and penitence. Macbeth's remorse, though for the most part self-centered, has been real and great all along. But now he makes an impressive gesture, if nothing more, of penitence; that is, of willingness to sacrifice his lust of fame by way of compensating for the evil he has done. And the passage quoted above returns upon Lady Macbeth's fearful outcry at the heart and center of the Sleepwalking scene: "The Thane of Fife had a wife—where is she now?" [V. i. 42-3]. There the speaker, who had absolutely nothing to do with the massacre of Macduff's family, expresses, as we are now clearly shown, that within Macbeth's "soule" which most condemns itself for being there. And presently, somewhat astonishingly, Macduff offers his great wronger the option of living out his natural life in a state of humiliating captivity—which is precisely the lot that Macbeth must endure if his penitence is to become real repentance. But this final and providential opportunity is rejected, only too naturally, by his resurgent pride; he fights Macduff and is slain. In contrast with the first Thane of Cawdor he does not at the end of his life "set forth a deepe Repentance" [I. iv. 6-7]. He has shown, however, that he has some sense, however slight, of his need of purgatorial contrition. As for his eternal destiny, Shakespeare, unlike many of his modern critics, is characteristically willing to leave that matter to the Almighty. (pp. 23-7)

The question as to the central meaning of this drama turns upon the difference, not commonly recognized by the modern secular mind, between the true charity, which is *justly and righteously kind,* and that inadequate sort of charity which is the *milk* of human-kindness. The word milk, here as elsewhere in Shakespeare's works, is ambiguous: it may denote either nourishment or weakness, chiefly the latter in the case of Macbeth. But he is very typical; his conduct evinces both the potential value and the tragic limitation of that fellow-feeling, that human-kindness, which most people have most of the time. Ordinarily it serves to cement human society; but this cement melts very quickly, and for most persons surprisingly, in the heat of selfish interests. In vivid contrast is the virtuous charity of King Duncan, so carefully shown by the dramatist in the first Act. Unlike Macbeth, Duncan is not proudly conscious of his own kindness; in him it is a subordinate and nourishing constituent of the true charity. This king bears his faculties meekly and is clear in his great office, gentle but firm, mercifully just. He has the manly meekness that inherits the earth in the sense that it alone can transform human society into a real human family. And Shakespeare, with beautiful art, makes the spirit of Duncan persist throughout the play after his death, to become victorious at the close.

While Duncan sleeps well in that eternal peace which appeared in his life on earth, his virtues do indeed plead trumpet-tongued against the deep damnation of his taking-off. Continually the recollection of "the gracious Duncan" [III. i. 65], this "most-Sainted king" [IV. iii. 109], is present to others for reproach or for inspiration. And his sort of charity appears in a number of other personages: in three minor characters, the Old Man in the end of Act II, Ross in Act IV, and the good Doctor in Act V; and in three important persons, Banquo, Macduff, and Malcolm. The character of Malcolm, developed in the last two Acts, reproduces that of his father: he reincarnates the humble benevolence and justness of Duncan. And in the play's final episode Malcolm, now king, is the head of a nation which has become again an organic society. The spirit of Duncan has triumphed, with the aid of "the Powers above" [IV. iii. 238].

In the closing lines of the play the new sovereign speaks of "the Grace of Grace" [V. ix. 38], a striking phrase which seems to echo, at a reverent distance, the declaration in the first chapter of St. John's Gospel regarding the Word of God made flesh: "of his fullness have we all received, grace upon grace". . . . Here the dramatist, speaking through Malcolm, alludes conclusively to a main theme of this play. In each and all of the six dramatis personae mentioned above, climactically in Malcolm, human-kindness is sublimated by divine Grace (as in Duncan) into true charity, humble, merciful, and righteous.

This drama in its whole pattern is the tragedy of human-kindness (or humanity) and ambitious evil—this rather than evil ambition. Macbeth's ambitiousness is not in itself evil. His very strong social sense, worldly but valuable, together with that gift of imaginative expression whereby he far outshines all the others, makes him naturally and rightly desirous of winning "Golden Opinions from all sorts of people" [I. vii. 33] and of standing very high in the realm. But Shakespeare as a political thinker (an aspect of him well brought out by recent critics) shows that this hero, quite apart from his evil doings, is temperamentally unfitted for sovereignty at its best. He is designed by God and nature to be a very excellent second in command under the better balanced personalities of Duncan and Malcolm—the very position that devolves in the end upon the noble but temperamental Macduff, whose modesty and humility enable him to have a right self-esteem. But Macbeth slenderly knows himself, like Lear and Shakespeare's other tragic heroes, and like most persons in real life when blindly driven by one or another sort of ambition. So he yearns for a status higher than he is fitted to have. And as soon as his will is murderously tainted it becomes a vehicle for the ambitious evil of the powers of the air, who, unlike him, aim to reduce human society to chaos. They are symbolized, somewhat melodramatically, by the Witches; more humanly by their successor in the second half of the first Act, the demon-inspired Lady Macbeth; but most effectually by the murky or hellish imagery pervading the play, recurrent and most telling in the speeches of Macbeth himself. This diabolic atmosphere moves us deeply because all of us are aware at times of black desires arising in our consciousness suddenly and shockingly. These, we nowadays believe, derive from the subconscious fund of evil propensities accumulated in mankind during the past million years or so. That belief is comprised, really, in the outlook of Shakespeare though, for dramatic purposes at least, he also accepts the older belief that evil is fundamentally devilish, created by that which Macbeth terms "the common Enemie of Man" [III. i. 68], Satan. For Shakespeare, as for Dante and most of the other great Renaissance writers, evil is both human and hellish. And the pressure of the hellish realm of evil upon Macbeth is so dreadfully heavy that he never completely loses our sympathy. But all of his wicked decisions, as the dramatist is careful to make clear, are ultimately his own: he has our human free will. His nightmare career is essentially very human. We ourselves could easily enter upon a similar "way of life," falling at last "into the Seare, the yellow Leafe" [V. iii. 22-3], if we should let our wills be swayed by the ambitious evil at work in the depths of human nature and, perhaps, of the universe.

In Macbeth Shakespeare has succeeded in creating a person who at his worst embodies the blackest evil but who, nevertheless, has a remarkable whiteness, a native candor. (pp. 27-9)

The whitest feature of Macbeth . . . is that, like his wife and unlike a multitude of other sinners, he does not strive to cloak his wickedness with conventional religiosity. Many a tyrant in pagan and Christian times, including Henry Eighth, has succeeded in conceiving his evil doings as in the main condoned by the gods or God. But Macbeth, with all his imagination, never imagines that. In the close of the play, for the first time in his career, he has to hear himself utterly condemned to his face for his wickedness: two noble gentlemen, Young Siward and Macduff, representing a wide range of human society, tell him plainly and strongly that he has become a servant of hell and the devil. And he does not utter a single word in repudiation of that verdict. So that our sense of uplift at the end of this tragedy is due in no small measure to the fact that Macbeth has at least the grace not to claim for his doings any tinge of Grace. And in this respect he adumbrates a characteristic of Shakespeare himself, who continually in his works shows up the hollowness and black deceptiveness of a merely conventional, egoistic piety.

Of course Shakespeare is nothing of a preacher. With the possible exception of Homer he is the most sheerly artistic of the world's chief poets. His life-aim was merely to achieve the maximum of poetic and dramatic effects. We cannot know to what extent he had a *personal* belief in Renaissance doctrines; I have tried to show only that he used them for the purposes of his dramatic art. The question I have wished to raise is simply: what interpretation of *Macbeth* is truest to its author's aim of producing in this play the utmost of pity and fear, of dramatic suspense, irony, contrast, and surprise? In *Twelfth Night,* the last of his four main comedies, he achieved the utmost *comic* concentration and effect; in *Macbeth,* the last of his four main tragedies, he concentrated upon producing the utmost *tragic* effect. But in so doing he laid hold, consciously or not, of the most tragic feature of human life, man's overweening belief in the capability of his own nature, particularly his human-kindness—a belief all the more tragical just because human sympathy (or empathy) is so essential for us and at its best so lovely. Constantly in his writings Shakespeare shows an eager appreciation of any touch, no matter how slight and transient, of human-kindness. But also, and above all in *Macbeth,* he reveals his sharp awareness that *natural* benevolence cannot withstand the assault of supernatural (or preternatural) evil desire. This can be overcome only by supernatural (or preternatural) goodness; to the influence of which, however, man will not as a rule open his spirit simply and humbly. Instead he seeks a little brief authority for himself as man— proud man. Macbeth is a thoroughly representative human being. And the *Tragedy of Macbeth,* in its whole design, bodies forth the essence of the tragedy of mankind. (pp. 31-2)

G. R. Elliott, "Introduction: On 'Macbeth' as Apex of Shakespearean Tragedy," in his Dramatic Providence in "Macbeth": A Study of Shakespeare's Tragic Theme of Humanity and Grace, *Princeton University Press, 1958, pp. 3-32.*

IRVING RIBNER (essay date 1959)

[*Ribner, author of* The English History Play in the Age of Shakespeare *(1957) and* Patterns in Shakespearian Tragedy *(1960), argues in the following excerpt that the function of the characters in* Macbeth *is essentially symbolic. He maintains that Shakespeare cast Macbeth's role "into a symbolic pattern" to reflect his view of "evil's operation in the world." Ribner, like Denton J. Snider (1887), contends that Shakespeare presents evil in the context of an ethical system and not merely in a poetic "atmosphere," as G. Wilson Knight (1930 and 1931) and other critics have argued. He also challenges critics, such as A. C. Bradley (1904), who view characters in a realistic and psychological manner. Rather, counters Ribner, the characters in* Macbeth *are primarily "dramatic vehicles" and have "choral and symbolic functions." Thus, Ribner, like Leo Kirschbaum (1957), views Banquo as a necessary foil to Macbeth, Macduff as Macbeth's dramatic nemesis, and Lady Macbeth as the embodiment of unnatural evil. Ribner also traces Macbeth's crimes against the ethical order of the state and the family, which, he asserts, isolates Macbeth from humanity. The play's dominant theme, he concludes, illustrates the necessary emergence of good over evil in "a harmonious world order."*]

Macbeth is in many ways Shakespeare's maturest and most daring experiment in tragedy, for in this play he set himself to describe the operation of evil in all its manifestations: to define its very nature, to depict its seduction of man, and to show its effect upon all of the planes of creation once it has been unleashed by one man's sinful moral choice. It is this final aspect which here receives Shakespeare's primary attention and which conditions the sombre mood of the play. Shakespeare anatomizes evil both in intellectual and emotional terms, using all of the devices of poetry, and most notably the images of blood and darkness which so many commentators have described. For his final end of reconciliation, he relied not upon audience identification with his hero, but rather upon an intellectual perception of the total play. In this lay his most original departure.

Macbeth is a closely knit, unified construction, every element of which is designed to support an intellectual statement, to which action, character, and poetry all contribute. The idea which governs the plays is primarily explicit in the action of the central character, Macbeth himself; his role is cast into a symbolic pattern which is a reflection of Shakespeare's view of evil's operation in the world. The other characters serve dramatic functions designed to set off the particular intellectual problems implicit in the action of the central figure. The basic pattern of the play is a simple one, for which Shakespeare returned to an earlier formula he had used in *Richard III.* The hero accepts evil in the third scene of the play. In the second act he commits the deed to which his choice of evil must inevitably lead him, and for the final three acts, as he rises higher in worldly power he sinks deeper and deeper into evil, until at the end of the play he is utterly and finally destroyed.

There is here no pattern of redemption or regeneration for the fallen hero as in *King Lear.* Shakespeare's final statement, however, is not one of despair, for out of the play comes a feeling of reconciliation which does affirm the kind of meaning in the world with which great tragedy must end. In the earlier tragedies this feeling had been created largely through the regeneration of an essentially sympathetic hero. In *Macbeth,* however, there can be little doubt of the final damnation of "this dead butcher and his fiend-like queen" [V. ix. 35]. The audience is made to see, however, that Macbeth is destroyed by counterforces which he himself sets in motion. We may thus, viewing the play in its totality, see good, through divine grace, inevitably emerging from evil and triumphant at the play's end with a promise of rebirth. (pp. 147-48)

Symbolic elements in *Macbeth* have been treated in two well-known essays by G. Wilson Knight [see excerpts above, 1930 and 1931]. He has pointed, like A. C. Bradley before him [see excerpt above, 1904], to the pervading mood of darkness and fear in the play, to the imagery of blood, fire, sleep, and animal nature, and all of the symbols in the play combine for him to convey an imaginative impression of evil. But Knight sees in *Macbeth* merely a poetic recreation of an atmosphere of evil, unrelated to any ethical system. I should like to suggest, on the contrary, that Shakespeare describes evil—and much in the poetic terms which Wilson Knight so well recognizes—not merely for the sake of the imaginative creation, but in terms of a definite ethical system which the play as a whole is designed to embody, that the basic element in a Shakespearian tragedy is ethical idea, and that it is this which informs and shapes plot and character as well as mood.

The action of *Macbeth* falls into two distinct parts, each carefully shaped as part of the greater whole. There is first a choice of evil by the hero, in which Shakespeare defines the nature of evil and explains the process by which man is led to choose it. This occupies roughly the first two acts, although Shakespeare by recurrent image and symbol keeps these dominant ideas before his audience throughout the rest of the play. The last three acts exhibit the manner of evil's operation simultaneously on four levels: that of fallen man himself, that of the family, the state, and the physical universe. As evil operates on each of these planes, however, it generates at the same time forces of good, until at the end of the play we see evil destroyed on each of the four planes of creation and the harmonious order of God restored. The play is an ordered and controlled exploration of evil, in which Shakespeare fulfills the function of the philosophical poet as surely as did Dante in the *Divine Comedy*.

It has been pointed out that Othello and Lear in their falls parallel the fall of Adam, and like Adam they are able to learn in their disasters the nature of evil and thus attain a kind of victory in defeat. The destruction of Macbeth, on the contrary, is cast in the pattern of the fall of Satan himself, and the play is full of analogies between Satan and Macbeth. Like Satan, Macbeth is from the first entirely aware of the evil he embraces, and like Satan he can never renounce his free-willed moral choice, once it has been made. It is thus appropriate that the force of evil in *Macbeth* be symbolized by Satan's own sin of ambition. This sin for Shakespeare, as it had been for Aquinas, was an aspect of pride, the worst of the medieval seven deadly sins. In the neatly ordered and harmonious universe of which Renaissance man conceived, it stood for a rebellion against the will of God and thus against the order of nature. . . . Macbeth, through love of self, sets his own will against that of God, chooses a lesser finite good—kingship and power—rather than a greater infinite one. Shakespeare in Macbeth's moral choice is offering a definition of evil in fairly traditional terms.

The ambitious man will strive to rise higher on the great chain of being than the place which God has ordained for him. To do so he must break the bond which ties him on the one hand to God and on the other to humanity. Immediately before the murder of Banquo, Macbeth utters lines which often have been misinterpreted by commentators:

> Come seeling night,
> Scarf up the tender eye of pitiful day;
> And with thy bloody and invisible hand
> Cancel and tear to pieces the great bond
> Which keeps me pale!
>
> [III. ii. 46-50]

The "great bond" has usually been glossed either as the prophecy of the witches or as Banquo's lease on life, neither of which is very meaningful within the context of the passage. The bond, as Wilson Knight has perceived, can only refer to the link which ties Macbeth to humanity and enjoins him to obey the natural law of God. Macbeth is calling upon the Satanic forces of darkness to break this bond of nature and thus

enable him again to defy the laws of man and God, to murder his friend and guest.

Many critics have pointed out that Macbeth's crime is specifically depicted by Shakespeare as unnatural, as opposed to the harmony of the universe. This statement of the nature of evil is reinforced by "life images", the imagery of planting and husbandry, of feasting and conviviality, by the pleasant evocation of the calmness and beauty of nature as Duncan and Banquo enter the dread castle walls [I. vi. 1-10]. Duncan himself is symbolic of the fruitful aspects of nature; he is the source of the goodness which Macbeth may hope to glean from life:

> I have begun to plant thee, and will labour
> To make thee full of growing.
>
> [I. iv. 28-9]

Macbeth in murdering Duncan thus cuts off the source of his own being, and this idea is echoed in Lady Macbeth's "Had he not resembled / My father as he slept, I had done it" [II. ii. 12-13], for this line is largely choral commentary to emphasize the father symbolism with which Duncan is endowed.

Macbeth's sin, like that of Satan before him, is thus a deliberate repudiation of nature, a defiance of God. (pp. 148-50)

Other examples could be cited of the constant references to Macbeth's crimes as contrary to nature, to the diabolic imagery, the juxtaposition in poetic terms of Macbeth's crime against the source of life which it destroys. Suffice it to emphasize that Shakespeare here is using the dramatic and poetic devices at his command in order to define evil as a corrupting force which destroys the harmonious order of nature and which cuts off at the root the sustenance which makes life possible; that evil operates through deception, appealing to those emotions in man which may cause him to set a lesser good above a greater one. These deliberate intellectual statements condition the content of the play.

The characters of *Macbeth* are not shaped primarily to conform to a psychological verisimilitude, but to make explicit the intellectual statements with which the play is concerned. They have choral and symbolic functions. The illusion of reality with which Shakespeare endows them serves merely to embody their symbolic functions in specific emotional terms. Successful as the illusion may be, Lady Macbeth, Banquo, the witches are not whole figures about whom we can ask such questions as Bradley asked and could only answer by divorcing them from the context of the play. All that we need know about the witches is that they are as Dover Wilson has well put it "the incarnation of evil in the universe, all the more effective dramatically that their nature is never defined" [see Additional Bibliography]. They are no more than convenient dramatic symbols for evil. To question closely the motives of Banquo or Lady Macbeth, with their many and obvious inconsistencies, is equally fruitless, for they function primarily as dramatic vehicles whose action is governed by the demands not of fact or psychology, but of intellectual design.

As symbols of evil, the witches are made contrary to nature. They are women with the beards of men; their incantation is a Black Mass, and the hell broth they stir consists of the disunified parts of men and animals, creation in chaos. They deliberately wait for Macbeth and Banquo, as they wait for all men. They do not, however, suggest evil to man . . . , for the impulse to evil must come from within man himself. They simply suggest an object which may incite the inclination to evil which is always within man because of original sin, and they do this by means of prophecy. Thus the good man, like Banquo, can resist their appeal, for man shares in the grace of God as well as in original sin.

The witches hold forth the promise of worldly good, as all evil must, for if it were not attractive it would offer no temptation to man. What Shakespeare wishes to stress is that its promises are false ones, that seeming truths are half truths, and that, in general, evil works through deception, by posing as the friend of man. Thus Eve had been seduced by Satan, and thus Othello had been seduced by "Honest" Iago. Banquo recognizes the Satanic origin of the witches: "What, can the devil speak true?" and he perceives the manner in which they work:

> And oftentimes, to win us to our harm,
> The instruments of darkness tell us truths,
> Win us with honest trifles, to betray's
> In deepest consequence.
>   [I. iii. 123-126]

To make this statement about the deceptive nature of evil, Shakespeare works into the texture of his play the theme of appearance versus reality which so many critics have noticed. There is always confusion and uncertainty in the appearance of evil, darkness rather than light, never the clear, rational certainty which is in the natural order of the good. This theme is in Macbeth's opening remark: "So foul and fair a day I have not seen" [I. iii. 38]. "There's no art / To find the mind's construction in the face" [I. iv. 11-12] says Duncan, and Lady Macbeth cautions her husband to "look like the innocent flower, / But be the serpent under't" [I. v. 65-6]. Macbeth himself acknowledges that "False face must hide what the false heart doth know" [I. vii. 82]. (pp. 150-52)

Banquo, as Kirchbaum has indicated [see excerpt above, 1957], stands opposed to Macbeth as a kind of morality figure. The witches offer him temptation not unlike what they offer Macbeth, and Banquo is sorely tempted, as any man must be. . . . The difference between the two men is that Banquo is able to resist the temptation to which Macbeth succumbs. Banquo is ordinary man, with his mixture of good and evil, open to evil's soliciting, but able to resist it. It is in such a man, Shakespeare is saying, that the hope for the future lies. This hope is embodied in Fleance, and thus, in terms of the play's total conceptual pattern, it is impossible for Macbeth to kill him. Evil can never destroy the ultimate promise of good.

Banquo, humanly weak and subject to temptation, stands nevertheless, "in the great hand of God" [II. iii. 130]. Symbolically he represents one aspect of Macbeth, the side of ordinary humanity which Macbeth must destroy within himself before he can give his soul entirely to the forces of darkness. For this reason he must murder Banquo, and it is why the dead Banquo returns to him as a reminder that, as a man, he cannot easily extinguish the human force within himself, that the torment of fear, the "terrible dreams / that shake us nightly" [III. ii. 18-19], the scorpions in his mind [III. ii. 36], will continue until his own final destruction. Banquo and his ghost are used to illuminate the basic conflict within the mind of Macbeth.

Macduff and Malcolm serve similar symbolic functions. Macduff, in particular, is a force of nemesis generated by Macbeth's own course of evil. Malcolm, as E.M.W. Tillyard has indicated [see Additional Bibliography], is Shakespeare's portrait of the ideal king, and his function chiefly is to represent a restitution of order in the state. One of the basic spheres of action in this play, of course, is on the level of the state, and *Macbeth* is full of political considerations which come to a head in the crucial scene in which Macduff and Malcolm meet in England. . . . Suffice it to note here that it is designed by Shakespeare to define the nature of tyranny, to delineate the character of the ideal king, and to prepare for the restitution of order in Scotland with the coming of such a king.

Just as Banquo symbolizes that side of Macbeth which would accept nature and reject evil, Lady Macbeth stands for the contrary side. Her function is to second Macbeth in the moral choice which is his alone, to mitigate against those forces within him which are in opposition to evil. Macbeth is thus much in the position of the traditional morality play hero placed between good and evil angels. The side of his wife seduces him, and that of Banquo must be destroyed.

It is for this reason, as has so often been pointed out, that the imagery of her speeches draws upon corruptions of nature and reversal of the normal life impulses. . . . It is fitting that Shakespeare should use a woman for this purpose, for woman is the normal symbol of life and nourishment, and thus the dramatist can emphasize the strangeness and unnaturalness of the very contraries to which Lady Macbeth appeals and for which she stands. She must become unsexed, and her milk must convert to gall. Her very need, moreover, to put aside her feminine nature informs the illusion of reality in her characterization and gives to her emotional appeal as well as intellectual meaning. (pp. 152-54)

Throughout the play Lady Macbeth's femininity is held in constant juxtaposition to the unnatural forces she would call into play. In the murder scene her unnatural aspect is dominant, but her femininity comes through in her inability to kill the king herself. When the body is discovered, she is the first to collapse. This careful juxtaposition of contraries comes to a head when she walks in her sleep in the fifth act. Here the images of blood are mingled with her feminine desire for the "perfumes of Arabia" to "sweeten this little hand" [V. i. 51]. No more than Macbeth can lightly break his bond with humanity, can his wife escape the woman in her which mitigates against the unnatural force of evil which in the thematic structure of the play she represents. In her death by suicide, moreover, there is further emphasis upon the theme which dominates the play; that evil inevitably must breed its own destruction.

All of the characters thus perform symbolic functions within the greater intellectual whole which constitutes the play. They embody specific ideas which are emplicit in action, and taken together they represent the sum of humanity in relation to evil. Humanity in this play, Speaight has written, "is divided into three groups; there is man in a state of damnation—Macbeth and his wife; there is average sinful man—Malcolm, Macduff and Banquo; and there is man in a state of innocence, represented by the two kings Duncan and Edward" [see Additional Bibliography]. We must qualify this, however, by noting that Malcolm and Macduff represent something more than ordinary, sinful man, and that all of the other characters are secondary to Macbeth, whose behavior they are designed to set off and explain. Wilson Knight, in his preoccupation with the mood of evil which dominates the play, sees all of the characters as equally ensnared by it [see excerpt above, 1930]. He thus fails to note the distinction among character functions which is part of the symbolism of the play, and in which its ethical idea is implicit. This may well illustrate the dangers of a concentration upon poetic atmosphere which slights the logic of action and negates the factors of audience participation and sympathy which are indispensable considerations in drama.

The specific act of evil occurs on two planes, that of the state and that of Macbeth's "single state of man" [I. iii. 140]; the crime is both ethical and political, for Macbeth murders not only his kinsman and guest, but his king as well. Once evil is unleashed, however, it corrupts all of the planes of creation, not only those of man and the state, but those of the family and the physical universe as well. Action, character, symbolic ritual and the powerful emotional impact of poetic imagery all combine to further a specific intellectual concept: the all-embracing destructive force of evil which touches every area of God's creation. (pp. 154-55)

On the level of the state Macbeth unleashes the greatest evils of which Shakespeare's audience could conceive, tyranny, civil war, and an invading foreign army. The tyranny of Macbeth's reign, moreover is set off by the initial description of the gentility and justice of Duncan's previous rule. Shakespeare here deliberately alters his source, for Holinshed had stressed Duncan's feeble and slothful administration, and he had, by way of contrast, praised Macbeth for his striving after justice and for the excellence of at least the first ten years of his reign.

The disorder in the state as it works out its course is also the source of its own extinction and the restoration of political harmony. The very tyranny of Macbeth arouses Macduff against him, causes Malcolm to assert the justice of his title, and causes the saint-like English King, Edward the Confessor, to take arms against Macbeth. King Edward's curing of the scrofula (IV. ii), an episode which Dover Wilson [see Additional Bibliography] like so many other critics has regarded as "of slight dramatic relevance", is Shakespeare's means of underscoring that Edward is an instrument of supernatural grace, designed to cleanse the unnatural evil in the state, just as he may remove evil from individual man. It is Macbeth's very tyranny which has made him "ripe for shaking, and the powers above / Put on their instruments" [IV. iii. 238-39].

On the level of the family, the relationship between Macbeth and his wife steadily deteriorates. At the beginning of the play their relationship is one of the closest and most intimate in all literature. She is "my dearest partner in greatness" [I. v. 11], and much as it harrows him himself to think of its implications, he sends her immediate word of the witches' prophecy, so that she may not "lose the dues of rejoicing" [I. v. 11-12]. The very terror of the murder scene only further emphasizes the closeness of the murderers. But as the force of evil severs Macbeth from the rest of humanity, it breaks also the bond which ties him to his wife. He lives more and more closely with his own fears into which she cannot intrude, as the banquet scene well illustrates. She cannot see the ghost which torments her husband.

The gradual separation of man and wife first becomes apparent just before the murder of Banquo. No longer does he confide in her. At the play's beginning they plan the future together; at the end each dies alone, and when the news of her death comes to Macbeth, he shows little concern:

> She should have died hereafter;
> There would have been a time for such a word.
>
> [V. v. 17-18]

This theme of family disintegration is echoed, moreover, in Macduff's desertion of his wife and children to be destroyed by the tyrant whom the father flees.

It is upon the disintegration of Macbeth himself, however, that Shakespeare lavishes his principal attention. He is careful to paint his hero in the opening scenes as a man of great stature, the savior of his country, full of the "milk of human kindness" [I. v. 17], with an infinite potentiality for good. He has natural feelings which link him to his fellow men and make him view with revulsion the crime to which ambition prompts him. Once the crime is committed, however, these feelings are gradually destroyed, until at the end of the play he is a symbol of unnatural man, cut off from his fellow men and from God. As his link with humanity weakens, moreover, so also does his desire to live, until finally he sinks into a total despair, the medieval sin of *acedia,* which is the surest evidence of his damnation.

Macbeth's extraordinary powers of imagination have been amply commented upon. Imagination itself, however, cannot be viewed as a cause of man's destruction within any meaningful moral system. Shakespeare endows Macbeth with this ability to see all of the implications of his act in their most frightening forms even before the act itself is committed as an indication of Macbeth's initial strong moral feelings. . . . Imagination enables Macbeth emotionally to grasp the moral implications of his crime, to participate imaginatively, as does the audience, in the full horror of the deed. Macbeth is entirely aware of God's moral system with its "even-handed justice", which "commends the ingredients of our poison'd chalice / To our own lips" [I. vii. 10-12]. His great soliloquy in contemplation of Duncan's murder [I. vii. 1-28] is designed to underscore Macbeth's initial feelings of kinship with the natural order.

As he prepares to commit the act he dreads, he calls for the suppression of these feelings within him. In a kind of devilish incantation he calls for darkness and the extinction of nature, conjuring the earth itself to look aside while he violates the harmonious order of which he and it are closely related parts. . . . (pp. 156-57)

That Macbeth cannot say "amen" immediately after the murder is the first clear sign of his alienation from God. He will sleep no more, for sleep is an aspect of divine mercy. Steadily Macbeth moves farther and farther from God and his fellow men, and his bond with nature is weakened. He becomes committed entirely to an unnatural course from which he cannot retreat:

> For mine own good,
> All causes shall give way: I am in blood
> Stepp'd in so far that, should I wade no more,
> Returning were as tedious as go o'er.
>
> [III. iv. 134-37]

He has become the center of his own little alien world, for which "all causes shall give way". Now Macbeth is ready to seek the witches out, a commitment to evil as total as that of Marlowe's Faustus in his summoning of Mephistopheles. And the words of the weird sisters lead him to the most horrible excess of all, the wanton murder of the family of Macduff. At the beginning of the play, evil had come to Macbeth unsought, as it does to all men; he had followed its promptings in order to attain definite ends, and not without strong misgivings. Now he seeks evil himself; he embraces it willingly and without fear, for no other end than the evil act itself.

The divided mind and the fear felt by the early Macbeth were not weakness; they were . . . signs of his kinship with man and God. But, by the fifth act:

> I have almost forgot the taste of fears:
> The time has been, my senses would have cool'd
> To hear a night-shriek; and my fell of hair
> Would at a dismal treatise rouse and stir
> As life were in't: I have supp'd full with horrors;

Act I. Scene v. Lady Macbeth. By R. Westall (n.d.).

Direness, familiar to my slaughterous thoughts,
Cannot once start me.

[V. v. 9-15]

With the loss of human fear, Macbeth must forfeit also those human attributes which make life livable: ''that which should accompany old age, / As honour, love, obedience, troops of friends'' [V. iii. 24-25]. There is nothing left for him but the utter despair of his 'To-morrow and to-morrow'' speech [V. v. 19-28]. Even with this unwillingness to live, which is in itself a denial of the mercy of God (as the medieval mind conceived of *acedia*), Shakespeare will not allow to Macbeth the heroic gesture of suicide which he grants to Brutus and Othello. Macbeth will not ''play the Roman fool'' [V. viii. 1]. His spiritual destruction must be reflected in an ignominious physical destruction, and thus the play ends with the gruesome spectacle of the murderer's head held aloft in triumph.

Brents Stirling has called the principle themes of *Macbeth* ''darkness, sleep, raptness and contradiction'' [see excerpt above, 1953]. That these motifs run through the imagery of the play is certain, as do the colors red and black and the names of animals and birds. Too much of recent criticism has been devoted to the isolation of specific poetic themes, with inadequate attention to the governing idea which molds these themes, along with character and plot, into a coherent meaningful whole. I have attempted to show that in *Macbeth* all of the elements of the plays are governed by an intellectual purpose, a specific statement about the nature of evil and its manner of operation in the world. This statement is carried primarily in action, to which all other elements of the play are subsidiary. The action

of *Macbeth* is cast into a meaningful pattern centering about the hero, and the roles of characters are governed not so much by the requirements of psychological consistency as by specific symbolic functions. (pp. 158-59)

If we are to isolate a dominant theme in the play, it must be one of idea: that through the working out of evil in a harmonious world order good must emerge. This idea is embodied in specific action and specific character, and thus by imaginative exploration the dramatist is able to illuminate it more fully than any prose statement ever could. Great tragedy involves a tension between emotion and intellect. The horrors of the action move our emotions as the play progresses, but when the last curtain has fallen and we can reflect upon *Macbeth* in its totality, we see that although one man has been damned, there is an order and meaning in the universe, that good may be reborn out of evil. We may thus experience that feeling of reconciliation which is the ultimate test of tragedy. (p. 159)

Irving Ribner, '''Macbeth': The Pattern of Idea and Action,'' in Shakespeare Quarterly, *Vol. X, No. 2, Spring, 1959, pp. 147-59.*

TOM F. DRIVER   (essay date 1960)

[*In the excerpt below, Driver argues that* Macbeth *and Sophocles's* Oedipus *present two essentially different views of time that reflect the different cultures from which they come.* Macbeth, *he proposes, contains three kinds of time: ''chronological time,'' ''providential time,'' and ''Macbeth's time.'' Driver notes the play's frequent references to chronological time, which, he says, establishes time ''as a meaningful reality.'' Providential time Driver describes as ''an expression of social and universal righteousness,'' and he asserts that it is demonstrated in the temporal order, historical succession, and the ''proper relationship of past and future.'' Opposed to providential time, he continues, is Macbeth's view of time, which futilely attempts to control the future by separating it from the past—an observation also made by Stephen Spender (1941). Yet, Driver argues, the action of* Macbeth *is not dominated by the past, as in* Oedipus, *but contains a Judeo-Christian view of time which ''involves the possibility of the new, the possibility of decision.'' He concludes that these two plays present different views of time—one in which the future is closed, the other in which the future is open—and reflect the variances in the ''fundamental presuppositions'' of the Greek and Christian cultures.*]

Everyone agrees that Sophocles' *Oedipus Tyrannus* and Shakespeare's *Macbeth* are masterpieces of dramatic construction. It seems not to have been noticed, however, that one thing these two plays hold in common as a corollary to their admirable form is an acute awareness of the problem of dramatic time. (p. 143)

In *Macbeth* there are three kinds of time: (1) time measured by clock, calendar, and the movement of sun, moon, and stars, which for the sake of convenience we may call ''chronological time''; (2) an order of time which overarches the action of the entire play and which may be called ''providential time''; and (3) a time scheme, or an understanding of time, belonging to Macbeth, which may be called ''Macbeth's time.'' (pp. 143-44)

The play contains a very large number of references to chronological time; that is, to the day, the night, or the hour. There is no point in citing all of them, but one example may serve to show the deliberateness with which the hour is sometimes established. Act I, scene vii, in which the resolution to commit the murder of Duncan is made firm, takes place at supper time.

The next scene (II. i) must establish that the hour has come for all to be retired, a matter accomplished in four lines:

BAN. How goest the night, boy?
FLE. The moon is down; I have not heard the
      clock.
BAN. And she goes down at twelve.
FLE.   I take 't, 'tis later, sir.
BAN. Hold, take my sword. There's husbandry in
      heaven:
      Their candles are all out.

                                      [II. i. 1-5]
                                        (p. 145)

In addition to such specific references to time (of which there are many) the play contains a very great number of lines which give merely a sense of time, inducing in the spectator a kind of temporal anxiety. For instance, there is such a large number of speeches employing the words "when," "yet," and "until" that the effect is striking. As an example, the opening lines of the play:

1. WITCH. When shall we three meet again
           In thunder, lightning, or in rain?
2. WITCH. When the hurlyburly's done,
           When the battle's lost and won.

                                      [I. i. 1-4]

Throughout the play, adverbs of time are important because the weird sisters, at the beginning, put the future into our minds. In scene iv, Macbeth, having learned that two of the prophecies are true, talks with himself about the third:

               Present fears
    Are less than horrible imaginings.
    My thought, whose murder yet is but fantastical,
    Shakes so my single state of man that function
    Is smother'd in surmise. . . .

                                    [I. iii. 137-41]

At the end of the scene he invites Banquo to speak with him "at more time" regarding what has transpired, and arouses our expectations with the concluding phrase, "Till then, enough" [I. iii. 153, 156]. (p. 146)

In *Macbeth*, Shakespeare, as usual, is careful in his "imitation" of chronological time. He is not slavish to detail, but he strives for an effect in which the feeling of being in a real world of time is extremely important. Shakespeare's adroit compression of time, his use of a fast and slow scheme of double-time, his concrete references to passing time, and the temporal note diffused throughout the speeches, all locate the audience in a temporal world and prepare it to accept time as a meaningful reality upon which rests much of the imaginative structure of the play.

Connected with chronological time in *Macbeth,* but not equated with it, is providential time, which is to say, time as an expression of social and universal righteousness. (p. 148)

How does Shakespeare communicate the idea of a providential time? In the first place, he assumes an objective, temporal order, distinguished on the one hand from mere chronology and on the other hand from anyone's subjectivity. Early in the play, Duncan sets the order of historical succession:

               Sons, kinsmen, thanes,
    And you whose places are the nearest, know
    We will establish our estate upon
    Our eldest, Malcolm, whom we name hereafter
    The Prince of Cumberland; which honor must
    Not unaccompanied invest him only.

But signs of nobleness, like stars, shall shine
On all deservers.

                                    [I. iv. 35-42]

Here is the proper relationship of past and future, the historical succession guaranteeing order a passage through the present into what comes "hereafter." To such historical order, Macbeth is immediately thrown into opposition:

MACB. (*Aside*) The Prince of Cumberland! That is a step
       On which I must fall down, or else o'erleap,
       For in my way it lies.

                                    [I. iv. 48-50]

The prophecies of the weird sisters also contribute to an idea of objective time. They provide a sense of destiny, or an order in future events already set. The objectivity of the time they represent would, of course, evaporate if it were admitted that the weird sisters are primarily a symbol of Macbeth's imagination. That they are not. They appear to the audience before they are seen by Macbeth, so that the spectator naturally takes them to have an existence apart from Macbeth. The sisters therefore stand for a knowledge of the future, and the accuracy of their knowledge is confirmed in the unfolding events of the play. After seeing them, the audience harbors a conception of what is *supposed* to happen, which it continually plays off against what it sees taking place.

The weird sisters' first speeches to Macbeth (I. iii) imply a fulfillment of time. "Glamis," "Cawdor," and "King" are not only names designating rank in the Scottish hierarchy, they are also, in this case, expressions of past, present, and future; Macbeth has been thane of Glamis, he this day becomes thane of Cawdor, and he shall "be King hereafter" [I. iii. 50]. (pp. 149-51)

In Macbeth's second meeting with the weird sisters the temporal note is struck yet more distinctly. Macbeth is given assurance of victory until a certain event ("until / Great Birnam wood to high Dunsinane hill / Shall come against him"—[IV. i. 92-4]. Although he does not know it, the moment of his defeat is set. It is noteworthy that he is not given a certain number of days, but rather he is vouchsafed power until certain things shall come to pass. He is actually given a lease which will expire very shortly, while he confidently interprets it to be "the lease of nature" [IV. i. 99]. In this scene also there is a return to the theme of historical continuity. The time which the weird sisters proclaim is partner to the time which Duncan had represented in establishing the historical succession upon his son. The show of eight kings, which is set before Macbeth upon his own insistence to know the future of Banquo's line, implies a continuation of the historical succession through Banquo's descendants as far as the mind can reach:

    What, will the line stretch out to th' crack of doom?
    Another yet! A seventh! I'll see no more.
    And yet the eighth appears, who bears a glass
    Which shows me many more.

                                    [IV. i. 117-20]

This vision of the ordering of the future, bringing the constituted authority in a straight line to Shakespeare's new monarch, James I, and on to the rim of time, is a step which Macbeth cannot o'erleap. It is a "horrible sight" [IV. i. 122] and because of it Macbeth damns the time in which he stands: "Let this pernicious hour / Stand aye accursed in the calendar!" [IV. i. 133-34]

It is possible to see the full reality of providential time only when Macbeth's time is thrown into relief against it. More than one critic has noticed that a change takes place in Macbeth's understanding and experience of time. (pp. 151-52)

Macbeth opposes a more ultimate time than his own. He would "let the frame of things disjoint" [III. ii. 16]; he would "jump the life to come" [I. vii. 7]; he murders sleep, that daily symbol of man's finitude in time; he destroys the meaning of tomorrow and tomorrow, the ironic consequence of his attempt to control the future.

In his attempt to gain control over the future . . . , Macbeth reveals that his experience of time is compounded of memory and anticipation. In order to gain control of the future, to o'erleap the steps which lie in his way, he must create memories. Memories, the past haunting the present as guilt, reduce Lady Macbeth to her pitiful end. Her "What's done is done" of Act III [III. ii. 12] later becomes, "What's done cannot be undone" [V. i. 68]. It is as a bulwark against memories that Macbeth erects his doctrine of the meaninglessness of life.

Much as he would like, Macbeth cannot separate the present from the past and the future. By the act of murder he has made his own history, and the rest of the play is the account of the fulfillment of that history, ultimately self-defeating. His sin (skillfully portrayed by Shakespeare as a combination of will and temptation) blinds him to the meaning of providential time, while it does not remove him from subordination to it, nor does it remove him from his own inner historical experience. He therefore continues . . . to make use of biblical images of history and human finitude, although entirely without the biblical awareness of grace. The petty pace creeps in "To the last syllable of recorded time" [V. v. 21], a phrase which not only recalls Macbeth's earlier vision of the line which stretches out "to the crack of doom," but which also reflects biblical eschatology. This picture of the mortality of time is followed by that of man's mortality, sketched in four images: the brief candle, the walking shadow, the strutting and fretting upon the stage, and the tale which is told, each of which has biblical parallels. Even in his final despair, therefore, Macbeth is made to speak of an order of time which he has not been able to destroy, although that had been his hope when he and his Lady stood in what proved to be a completely decisive moment upon the "bank and shoal of time" [I. vii. 6].

In *Macbeth* it is possible to speak of three kinds of time—chronological, providential, and that of Macbeth; in the *Oedipus Tyrannus* there are only two, and perhaps even these two are one. There is, to begin with, chronological time, the time of the play's action: roughly, all the incidents from Laius' hearing of the oracle to Oedipus' exile from Thebes, including the narration of events which happened, as we say, before the play began. In addition, time also appears in the *Oedipus Tyrannus* as a deliberate, schematic arrangement of past and present. (pp. 153-55)

In both works, time appears as "fact" and as "meaning." In *Macbeth*, chronological time is simply time on the level of positive fact, but providential time and the time of Macbeth refer to time as it has taken on a meaning and therefore is capable of being used metaphorically. In the *Oedipus Tyrannus* there is also the presentation of chronological time, or time as "fact," but the structural arrangement of past and present is Sophocles' expression of the meaning of time.

The manner in which chronological time is imitated is very different in the two plays. The primary difference comes from the fact that, as we have seen, Sophocles begins his play at the end of the narrative, whereas Shakespeare begins at the beginning. In the *Oedipus Tyrannus* we are, for the most part, told what *did* happen. In using this method Sophocles has followed conventional Greek practice. The Chorus tells us about the plague which has come; Oedipus tells us about having sent Creon to consult the oracle; Jocasta tells about how Laius was killed and about exposing her infant son; Oedipus tells how he left Corinth; the Messenger tells how the infant Oedipus came to Corinth; the Herdsman tells about what he did with the infant who was given him and from whence he got it; the Second Messenger tells what Jocasta and Oedipus have done, etc. There is, of course, also present action, but it is never seen apart from an ironic relation to time past.

In *Macbeth,* on the other hand, we are presented directly with what *is* happening, the scene shifting from place to place and hour to hour as each new event occurs with the result that we are made to *feel* time as it unfolds. Shakespeare has the keenest sense of time as a mode of experience, and he is able to carry the audience along over a progression of time in such a way that when the spectator eventually stops to look back he is surprised at the varied terrain over which he has passed.

> I am in blood
> Stepp'd in so far, that, should I wade no more,
> Returning were as tedious as go o'er.
>
> [III. iv. 135-37]

This ability to present the *feel* of time passing is made possible by the "romantic" form in which Shakespeare wrote. The "classical" form of the Greek theater, which by and large strove to confine itself to one place and one time, could not present the sensation of passing time so well; and therefore it had to deal with time as concept if it was to do much with it at all. In a play such as *Macbeth*, where he is thinking consciously about time, Shakespeare presents us with a stream of metaphors. . . . It is all the more interesting that these metaphors exist on so many different levels. "To beguile the time / Look like the time" is on the colloquial level, time meaning simply "present society." "The seeds of time" is Shakespeare's own poetic creation.

Sophocles has very few metaphors of time. On the contrary, he personifies time as the all-powerful, the all-seeing. The difference between metaphor and personification here is precisely the difference between a reality experienced in process and a reality conceptualized.

Shakespeare and Sophocles would not imitate time so differently, however, if the meanings which they saw in time were not also different, for in both cases form and content are exceedingly well paired. It has already been mentioned that the Sophoclean view of time is ironical. That is to say, it is intimately connected with the question of knowledge. When the past and the present, which at first are disconnected in the *Oedipus Tyrannus,* come together, Oedipus' "amnesia" (his ignorance of his own past and therefore of his own moral offense) is lifted, and the full irony of the situation is seen. Oedipus then understands that he has pronounced a curse upon his own head, and that there is no escape from a punishment already self-directed. It is time as the infinite discloser which thus brings together those two fragmented orders of time, the past and the present, and reveals the irony implicit in the situation of man, whose time, because of his limited knowledge, is broken and finite.

Shakespeare's view of time is not ironical. The irony in *Macbeth*, of which there is much, does not arise from an inherent discontinuity in the nature of time, but from the fact that Macbeth, as goaded by Lady Macbeth, vainly imagines that he can remake time into something which it cannot be. His struggle to establish a barrier between what is and what has been, his attempt to control the future, and his desire to put a stop to a time which cannot be controlled, all form part of the illusion which envelops him ever more completely as the play progresses. The equivocating irony is that he who starts out to "mock the time with fairest show" comes in the end to face the prospect of living "to be the show and gaze o' th' time" [I. vii. 81, V. viii. 24]. This is not an irony in the understanding of time itself, but in Macbeth's opposition to the fundamental time scheme of the universe.

Shakespeare's view of time is inseparable from his view of freedom. It involves the possibility of the new, the possibility of decision. In *Macbeth* we witness two courses of action from their beginning. In the first act we see a Macbeth of noble character and high repute who has been rewarded by the king for his valour and loyalty, and who becomes tempted and falls. We watch him plot a course of action which will, as he thinks, put matters into his own hands. In the fourth act we see the planning of Macbeth's opposers. We watch them initiate the course of war which will dislodge him from his throne. In both cases, there is the situation, the individual's response to the situation, and the ensuing action taken as a result. In this sense, always in *Macbeth* "the time is free" [V. ix. 21].

Not only do Sophocles and Shakespeare imitate chronological time differently, and not only do they see different meanings in time, but they also present differently the relation between time as "fact" and time as "meaning". Sophocles deals with "lumps" of time. We must imagine the time he presents to us spatially or quantitatively: time past, time present, time as infinite duration (all-seeing). Shakespeare deals with several interconnected levels of meaning of time. He does not describe providential time as something apart from chronological time, or as something which is perceived when chronological time is divided up according to various tenses, rearranged, conceptualized. On the contrary, his meaning rises from the interplay of two understandings of the same kind of time. Chronological time is the basis upon which providential time is raised—or, providential time depends upon chronological time for its expression.

The close correspondence between providential and chronological time may be observed best in that remarkable scene (I. vii) in which Macbeth and Lady Macbeth prepare themselves for the murder of Duncan. Here Macbeth's time, providential time, and chronological time are in the closest juxtaposition, the scene depending for its effect on the interplay between time in its most specific and literal sense and time as an avenue of human understanding. The stage directions set a definite time (supper) and place (outside the dining hall):

> Hautboys and torches. Enter, and pass over the
> stage, a Sewer, and divers Servants with dishes
> and service. Then enter Macbeth.

When he enters, however, he begins to speak of time in a general and metaphorical way:

> If it were done when 'tis done, then 'twere well
> It were done quickly. If the assassination
> Could trammel up the consequence, and catch
> With his surcease success; that but this blow
> Might be the be-all and the end-all here,

> But here, upon this bank and shoal of time,
> We'd jump the life to come.
>
> [I. vii. 1-7]

The first sentence grows directly out of the immediate situation, communicating the swiftness and the finality of the act. But in the next line Macbeth is aware that no act is so final it does not have consequences (whatever Lady Macbeth may suppose), and this thought leads into the metaphorical idea of time as an island. On the one hand there is the "bank and shoal of time," "the be-all and the end-all here"; on the other hand there is "the life to come." The image, as Samuel Johnson said, is of a "narrow bank in the ocean of eternity." Time is at once an image of finitude and of infinity.

Macbeth's thought now turns again to the specific instance, and he reviews the history of the situation in which he stands: the present reality is that Duncan is in his house as guest, kinsman, and subject; the past fact is that Duncan "Hath borne his faculties" meekly and has been "clear in his great office" [I. vii. 17-18]; while the future consequence will be that

> his virtues
> Will plead like angels, trumpet-tongu'd, against
> The deep damnation of his taking-off;
> And pity, like a naked new-born babe . . .
> Shall blow the horrid deed in every eye. . . .
>
> [I. vii. 18-24]

Here, when Macbeth's awareness of future consequences is about to dissuade him, Lady Macbeth enters; and suddenly time is cemented to the specific, to the chronology of the deed:

MACB.	How now! what news?
LADY M.	He has almost supp'd. Why have you left the chamber?
MACB.	Hath he ask'd for me?
LADY M.	Know you not he has?

> [I. vii. 28-30]

Macbeth, however, turns back into another review of the situation. He has been honour'd "of late"; it is "so soon" to cast aside the "golden opinions" he has purchased. Lady Macbeth wonders if his former hope was drunk, or whether it has slept and now awakes, looking on its former action "so green and pale" [I. vii. 37]. If so, she will in the same way account his love, "from this time" [I. vii. 38]. When he had courage, then he was a man, and that was when time and place did not agree with the event, very unlike their "fitness now." When he mentions the possibility of failure, her famous reply utilizes an image of temporal readiness:

> But screw your courage to the sticking-place,
> And we'll not fail. . . .
>
> [I. vii. 60-1]

[The] idea is of tension building up to the breaking-point, the moment of release: "One, two," as her mind recalls it later, "why then, 'tis time to do't" [V. i. 35-6].

Her lines now turn again to the specific chronology of the deed. She describes what she will do "when Duncan is asleep," and "when in swinish sleep" his chamberlains lie [I. vii. 1, 67]. Macbeth speaks of how it will be receiv'd "When we have mark'd with blood these sleepy two" [I. vii. 75], and as the plotting is now finished in the most careful detail (that is, as careful as these excited two can make it), the thought turns again to the tension before the moment ("I . . . bend up / Each corporal agent to this terrible feat'' [I. vii. 79-80]) and finally the scene is concluded, as it began, on a metaphorical reference to time:

> Away, and mock the time with fairest show:
> False face must hide what the false heart doth know.
>
> [I. vii. 81-2]

The next scene begins sharply with a specific reference to chronological time:

> BAN. How goest the night, boy?
> FLE. The moon is down; I have not heard the clock.
>
> [II. i. 1-2]

The remarkable impression this scene makes depends upon the numerous levels upon which Shakespeare's understanding of time is operating simultaneously. We move back and forth, with great fluidity, between time as fact and time as meaning. Here we have time as the striking of the clock, the setting of the moon, the rhythm of eating and sleeping. Here we have time as that which is bent up or screwed tight toward the opportune moment, as that which "adheres" for the doing of the deed, as that which Macbeth would make it, the present be-all and end-all. And here we have time as that which it must ultimately be, the present moment standing like an island in an eternal sea. But the scene gives us none of these things in isolation from the others. Now one is emphasized, and now another; but there is no sharp line of demarcation; and we perceive that the striking of the clock is not something different from the island in the eternal sea, but is, in fact, one manifestation of it.

The interplay, and interdependence, of time as fact and time as meaning provides an example of that tension which persists in Judaeo-Christian thought between the event and the interpretation of the event. The facts of time, of this murderous pair's plotting of when and where, are specific, concrete, and irreducible. On the other hand, they cannot be separated from what they mean. If we tried to eliminate the specific, to subsume all under the category of meaning, we would do violence to the writing. This is a play for a theater in which there are hautboys and torches, and servants with dishes, and clocks that strike. In Shakespeare's theater it is sometimes midnight; but that is a matter which has not only prosaic reality, it is a part of the fact that evil appears in the form of "secret, black, and midnight hags!'' [IV. i. 48].

Finally, the difference between *Macbeth* and the *Oedipus Tyrannus* must be seen in the light of Shakespeare's "time future." . . . Shakespeare's view of freedom involves the possibility of the new. Essentially, therefore, the future is open. That does not mean that it is completely uncharted or that it holds an unlimited number of possibilities. It simply means that the anticipation of a not-completely-fixed future is one element which goes to make up the unique moment of the present. This is entirely in line with what has been said . . . [in an unexcerpted chapter] regarding the Judaeo-Christian understanding of the present as being compounded of memory and anticipation.

The future is felt in Macbeth at almost every moment that time is felt. The weird sisters open the play with lines which cause anticipation of the time "When the hurly-burly's done, / When the battle's lost and won" [I. i. 3-4], and Malcolm closes it speaking of what he shall do "in measure, time, and place" [V. ix. 39], and of his approaching coronation. Between these two scenes, the technique Shakespeare follows of moving from moment to moment gives at every point the occasion not only

for memory of former things, but for anticipation of those yet to be. It is true that Macbeth's future does not turn out as he had hoped, that in a sense, his future is cut off; but the future of Scotland is saved by that very fact. Malcolm's prosaic way of putting it is, "I hope the days are near at hand / That chambers will be safe" [V. iv. 1-2]. In *Macbeth* everyone lives acutely in the present, and therefore the future is open.

In the *Oedipus Tyrannus* the future is closed. One might almost say that it does not exist. The time significance of the play must be understood entirely in terms of the relation between present and past. The past is dominant. It contains the facts which explain the present, which control the present; and the play, as it moves forward in time through the events of the terrible day, actually moves backward into the completely decisive past. Teiresias' prophecies look no further ahead than the end of the day, and what they reveal is the blackness of the grave or of blindness: "This day shall be thy birth-day, and thy grave". . . . Oedipus has the freedom, therefore, only to discover the past, and as the past is that in which freedom is not even conceivable ("What's done cannot be undone," as Lady Macbeth discovers—[V. i. 68]), he has only the ironical freedom to discover his lack of it. In the end, his blindness is symbolic of our ability to see nothing further than the conclusion of the play. The imagination does not extend into the future, as it does in *Macbeth*, where a line stretches out to the crack of doom [IV. i. 117]; on the contrary, it turns into the past, where the chain of cause and effect, and the intricate weavings of destiny, stretch backward into the shadow.

The beauty of dramatic structure which *Macbeth* and the *Oedipus Tyrannus* both exhibit would account for their popularity with the critics, but hardly would do so for their popularity with the public through many centuries. To account for the latter it is necessary to realize how the structures of these plays echoed supremely well the fundamental presuppositions of their culture regarding man's place in the cosmos. Time is not a subject on which the ordinary man spends much thought, but it is a basic category of his thinking and a given reality in his existence. When an artist is able to form a work which embodies the culture's unspoken understanding of time, he strikes chords of response in every observer. It was given to Sophocles and Shakespeare to do just that in the *Oedipus Tyrannus* and *Macbeth*. Therefore the two tragedies will excite admiration as long as the cultures of the Greeks and the Christians are known and understood. (pp. 159-67)

> Tom F. Driver, "The Uses of Time: The 'Oedipus Tyrannus' and 'Macbeth'," in his The Sense of History in Greek and Shakespearean Drama, *Columbia University Press, 1960, pp. 143-67.*

JOHN B. HARCOURT (essay date 1961)

[In the following excerpt, Harcourt, like Kenneth Muir (1962), examines the particular appropriateness of the Porter scene in Macbeth. *He argues that the scene is not a spurious interpolation, as Samuel Taylor Coleridge believed (1813-34), but that it is both relevant and authentic, giving "every evidence of careful planning." The Porter's low-comedy, states Harcourt, presents "an intentional deglamorization of Macbeth" by desentimentalizing him and destroying "the pseudo-heroic illusion." Harcourt also notes several situational parallels between the Porter's soliloquy and the larger action of the play, focusing on the Porter's "little morality-scene." He examines the Porter's role as the attendant of hell's gate with reference to Christian mystery plays and the story of Christ's harrowing of hell. Harcourt proposes that Macduff's knocking at the gate of Inverness Castle suggests Christ's*

entrance at the gate of hell and concludes that Macduff "shares something of the symbolic function of a still remembered Harrower of Hell." For another consideration of the significance of the knocking at the gate in Macbeth, *see the excerpt above by Thomas De Quincey (1823).]*

Few scenes in Shakespeare have seen so complete a reversal in critical evaluation as *Macbeth* II. iii. Twentieth-century authorities are virtually unanimous in accepting it as authentically Shakespeare's and as thematically relevant to the larger meanings of the play. We can therefore only note with incredulity that Pope and Hanmer relegated the Porter's lines to the margins of their editions, that Harry Rowe could justify his drastic abridgment of the passage by observing darkly that "too many meretricious weeds grow upon the banks of Avon", that even Coleridge was certain that except for a single sentence (the "everlasting bonfire"), "not one syllable has the ever-present being of Shakespeare" [see excerpt above, 1813-34]. Today, even college Freshmen have been already taught to justify the scene in terms of "comic relief", and, once they have been persuaded to relinquish that thought-paralyzing concept, can be directed to what amounts to an embarrassment of critical riches in contemporary notes and commentaries. . . .

Structurally, the scene gives every evidence of careful planning. At the end of II. ii, Macbeth, momentarily alone with his terror, hears the knocking and instinctively glances down at his blood-stained hands. The noise becomes more insistent with the return of Lady Macbeth, and even her practical suggestions do not succeed in reassuring her husband; he looks fearfully and almost pleadingly towards the direction of the intrusive sound: "Wake Duncan with thy knocking! I would thou couldst!" [II. ii. 71]. The two leave the stage, the Porter enters, and we are now just inside the south entry to the castle. None too steadily, the Porter approaches the gate, impatiently imitating the sound that had disturbed his slumbers. Quite self-consciously, he begins a bit of play-acting: this *might* be Hellgate; he *might* be the infernal porter. Warming to his fancied role, he "admits" three representative figures—one would guess, with appropriate pantomiming—the farmer, the equivocator, the tailor. Then, the cold of a Scottish dawn recalling him to reality, he abandons his part, becomes a simple porter who has been too much in his cups the night before, but who, as he admits Macduff and Lennox, is still capable of another threefold organizational pattern followed by a burst of balanced paradoxes and involved puns, the new material tidily related, through the repetition of the equivocation theme, to the earlier soliloquy. (p. 393)

[Let] us examine the three professions treading their way to the everlasting bonfire. The farmer has, through his hoarding, acted detrimentally to the well-being of society: private gain has prevailed over the public interest. The equivocator has committed treason; the tailor has stolen from clothing that properly belongs to another. If we consider that Macbeth, driven by a ruthless personal ambition, has committed the ultimate in treason, regicide, and has seized the crown and royal robes that were not his by right, it becomes evident that the Porter's three examples were chosen, not at random, but precisely because of their relevance to the dramatic situation. And we must always bear in mind the moment in the play at which the Porter makes his appearance: we have just seen the murderer with his hands still wet with Duncan's blood; he is at this very instant changing his clothing and attempting to wash away the evidence of guilt; in a matter of minutes, Macduff will discover the body and proclaim the horror to the world. With Macbeth necessarily offstage for a few brief moments in the ghastly progress of his

crime, Shakespeare chooses to give us a series of reference points, by which the action unfolding before us may be placed in a universe of ordered moral values.

First of all, Shakespeare achieves, through the Porter, an intentional deglamorization of Macbeth. Audience sympathy, created by the repeated praises of the warrior-thane in the opening scenes, reinforced, even more effectively, by his painful wrestlings with conscience, and perhaps continuing, covertly, through the deed of violence against authority itself, must now be brought up short, in order that the play may continue in a reasoned ethical perspective. The very appearance of the Porter, of a low comedy figure, does not, I think, so much enhance through contrast the figure of the protagonist as scale it down, desentimentalize it, destroy the pseudo-heroic illusion. This process continues through the association of Macbeth with a petty speculator, with a known traitor, currently the object of popular execration (though not unmixed with some admiration and pity, as with Macbeth), and with a tailor. We need not review the extended footnote-skirmishes as to whether French hose were full and baggy (and so an invitation to theft) or tight-fitting (so that to steal from the material would represent a triumph of English ingenuity). The important thing is the link with the pervasive clothing imagery of the play.

> New honors come upon him,
> Like our strange garments, cleave not to their mold
> But with the aid of use.
>
> [I. iii. 144-46]

A petty tailor steals from a gentleman's hose, a subject appropriates his monarch's robes—a significant ratio of disproportion is established here. In all three cases, we find, through the intentional distortions of a comic scene, Macbeth's deed placed unsentimentally in a moral scale where it may be seen in its intrinsic tawdry ugliness.

Secondly, the three examples extend their commentary by suggesting the subsequent course of the action, the consequences of Macbeth's crime. The farmer hanged himself "in th'expectation of plenty", in sheer frustration, that is, at nature's bounty; the green world, advancing upon Dunsinane, fills Macbeth with despair. The equivocator (and we recall that one of Father Garnet's aliases had been Farmer) had been led to the gallows on May 3, 1606. The tailor, if caught out in his thieving, can hardly have come to any happier end; in any event, he, with the other two, stands condemned by a justice greater than that of any human tribunal—none could "equivocate to Heaven".

Apart from these more immediately situational parallels, certain recurrent themes of the tragedy are likewise to be found in the Porter's little morality-scene. That appearances and reality do not stand in any one-to-one correspondence is a major insight of the play; indeed, they would seem, at critical moments, to coexist in some perversely ironic opposition. The almanac had prognosticated a crop failure and the farmer concurred in that reading of the signs, yet all the while the corn was moving resistlessly toward a plentiful harvest. The equivocator, having no Fifth Amendment to invoke and prevented by conscience from outright lying, gave answers that were intentionally ambiguous, with the apparent signification of the words, as intended to be grasped by the listeners, negated by another possible signification known only to the speaker. The tailor produced a garment which seemed to fulfill the specifications of the buyer, but which was actually short of material. The farmer, in the struggle with appearances, is largely self-deluded; the equivocator consciously and conscientiously sets out to manipulate appearances so as to mislead responsible authority by ambiguous answers to judicial questioning; the tailor, without any attempt at theological rationalization ("treason enough for God's sake" [II. iii. 10]), involves himself in an overtly criminal deception. Macbeth too will learn

> To doubt the equivocation of the fiend
> That lies like truth.
>
> [V. v. 42-3]

And, preliminary to this insight, he will have been taken in by deluding signs, have resorted to equivocations of his own to conceal his crime (as at [II. iii. 50, 52, 58]), and then have proceeded to further enormities without even the show of righteous intent. Indeed, the ambiguity of appearances is so essential to the play that Muir can observe . . . that "the equivocator would have earned his place in the Porter scene if Father Garnet had never lived" [see excerpt below, 1962]. (pp. 394-96)

As attendant of Hell-gate, the Porter establishes the disgusting quality of evil—whether in the farmer, the tailor, or, *a fortiori,* in Macbeth himself—by means of the pathology of disease. When he abandons his play-acting and becomes merely the porter of Inverness Castle, his idiom becomes simple bawdry, without references to physical infection. Yet even here the joking is not merely irrelevant banter. The Porter treats of drinking, not in a Falstaffian tribute to its pleasures, but in a mood of rueful, morning-after regret. His paradoxes on the relation between drunkenness and lechery disclose an additional adumbration of the major themes of the play. For the Porter is saying that alcoholically induced desire follows exactly the pattern of intent that cannot be translated into act, promise without fulfillment, will that cannot command performance. And just as the world of Macbeth becomes progressively a world of nightmare fantasy, so the drunken lecher achieves erotic success only in a dream ("equivocates him in a sleep" [II. iii. 35]).

But for all his assumed role, the Porter is not consciously an instrument of the castle's evil. As representative of ordinary humanity, he looks not only backward to the excesses of the night before, but forward to some hope of recovery. His references to equivocation lead—naturally and equivocally— through *lie* into a wrestling context that has its ultimate basis in the religious imagery of Ephesians 6:12; the passage ends in his victory over the powers of darkness. Indeed, the Porter's final line is a veritable symphony of double-entendres: the basic figure of throwing one's opponent combines with the idea of micturition ("took up my legs"; "cast him" in the sense of uroscopy, as in [V. iii. 50-1]) and with the idea of a purge or vomit. All of these restate, in their own inimitable crudeness, the oft repeated Shakespearian theme of evil being violently expelled from the body of the state [V. ii. 28; V. iii. 52, 55]. And we must not forget, in our appraisal of these hints of deliverance, that the action of this scene is illumined by the first faint rays of dawn.

I should like now to consider the larger implications of the Porter's vision of the gates of Inverness Castle as the Gate of Hell. The background for this idea is well established. The apocryphal New Testament provided, in the Gospel of Nicodemus, a version of the Harrowing of Hell that became the foundation for most later developments of the theme: the pertinent pageants in the mystery cycles in the main dramatize Nicodemus, with some filling out of the inherited material with details of contemporary realism. And that one of the devils should have been transformed into a comically imagined porter,

to balance St. Peter at the other gate, was all but inevitable. (p. 399)

The Porter's identification of Macbeth's castle is not only apt; it likewise expresses the complex patterns of irony that we have seen to be related to Shakespeare's probing of the problem of what really is and what only seems to be. A realistic porter bids us imagine the gates of a real castle, Inverness. The porter then pretends, quite unaware of what has really happened within, that he is the porter of Hell-gate; after amusing himself with this conceit, more meaningful to the audience than to him, he abandons the idea and proceeds, *in propria persona,* to unbar the gate and admit the two impatient courtiers. As he continues his garrulous discourse on the more genial vices, the principle of contrast operates to intensify our growing awareness of the Castle as the dwelling place of evil—too cold for hell, yet cold in precisely the way the lowest reaches of hell and of human evil are cold. . . . The symbolic Castle has been invaded by treachery, by moral and social anarchy:

> Confusion now hath made his masterpiece.
> Most sacrilegious murder hath broke ope
> The Lord's anointed temple, and stole thence
> The life o'the building.
>
> [II. iii. 66-9]

these words can refer to more than Duncan alone. In brief, a character who knows nothing of what has happened—and who, unlike Spenser's Ignaro, does not know that he does not know— links the profaned Castle with Hell itself; he then repudiates the linkage for a reason which, to the audience, can only strengthen the parallel. Every reference in these lines has one meaning for the Porter and another for the audience. The Porter's commentary is thus the more devastatingly effective for being almost entirely an unconscious one.

But it is not, I think, the identification of the south entry of Inverness with Hell-gate that is of exclusive importance, although interpretations of the traditional associations of this scene have given that matter most of their attention. A fearsome knocking just before or at the break of dawn, a comic porter calling forth in the name of Beelzebub and the other devil, the opening of the gate, the entrance of the militant Macduff— these details suggest, not so much a place as an event, not Hell-mouth only but the Harrowing of Hell by the triumphant Christ-figure of early Christian and medieval legend.

"He descended into hell", the creeds stated, to deliver the souls of the just, fast imprisoned until, in the fulness of time, their ransom should have been paid on Calvary hill. In the book of Nicodemus (and we must always remember that medieval piety, art, and literature relied far more heavily upon the apocryphal legends than on the canonical New Testament), the fettered saints see a great light approaching which they greet with songs of joy and rehearsals of the familiar strains of prophecy. The King of Hell, Beelzebub, begs Satan that this formidable figure be kept from his borders; yet with echoing thunder and rushing winds, the words are heard:

> ATTOLLITE PORTAS, PRINCIPES, VES-
> TRAS, ET ELEVAMINI, PORTAE AETER-
> NALES; ET INTROIBIT REX GLORIAE!
>
> [Psalm 24]
>
> [Lift up your heads, O ye gates, and be lift up,
> ye everlasting doors, and the King of Glory
> shall come in!]

Twice the formula is repeated; then, all efforts at defense proving fruitless, the King of Glory enters, "in form of man", routs the opposition, and leads the elect to their eternal bliss.

The mystery plays, especially the Chester, York, and Towneley cycles, keep this essential pattern, with increasing vigor of language and individuation of cast. The pageant of the Chester cooks and innkeepers has Secundus Demon, Tercius Demon, etc.; yet in the York and especially in the Towneley plays, the porter-demon has become Rybald, with his endless hallooing ("out, harrow, out!"); Satan organizes a strenuous resistance "to dyng that dastard down", first by calling for his armor, then by engaging Jesus in a lengthy debate in which equivocal meanings play an important part; and he is not so much defeated as placated by the promise of the custody of all truly wicked souls (in an epilogue to the Chester play, a garrulous alewife arrives as his first customer). But while we are likely to stress the vividly realistic touches of the anonymous medieval dramatists, these plays are, in total impact, liturgically solemn— the vernacular realism is shattered into silence by the thundering intonations of the ATTOLLITE; a *Te Deum* climaxes the Chester play; in both a Christ more like the epic Christ of the Anglo-Saxon bards than the later gentle-Jesus stereotypes effectively challenges and overcomes, at least in principle, death and evil.

These are, I would maintain, the dramatic associations that Shakespeare is drawing upon for the working out of his scene. We must attend, not merely to the Porter, to the knocking with all the implications suggested by J. W. Spargo [see Additional Bibliography], to the imagined locale, but also, and even more significantly, to the person who is being admitted—Macduff. This is not to say that Macduff is reducible to one of those Christ-archetypes so familiar in a certain variety of twentieth-century writing; the problem of his leaving his own castle unprotected would of itself tend to limit any rashly allegorizing fantasies. Yet *Macbeth* is a play about good and evil, about the triumph of good over evil, even, perhaps, of the victory of grace over sin; it would be possible to agree with G. R. Elliott [see excerpt above, 1958] that this work is saturated with theological conceptions without joining the camp of those who would read Shakespeare as the dramatic propagandist of Christian orthodoxy. Macduff is, in any interpretation, a figure to reckon with. He enters the castle in obedience to Duncan's command—the last act of obedience to rightful authority; he immediately proclaims the crime for what it is, most sacrilegious murder; he sharply questions Macbeth when the latter admits to killing the grooms; he gives a grim seconding to Banquo's pledge to fight against the undivulged pretense of treasonous malice; he refuses to proceed to Scone for the usurper's coronation; he lives in disgrace by III. vi. The slaughter of Lady Macduff and the children and the revelation of that atrocity to the self-exiled father serve, among other things, to focus our attention upon the importance of Macduff; his colloquy with Malcolm reveals him as the elder statesman if not the king-maker, as the embodiment of what is left of order in the civil life of Scotland. Lady Macbeth's pathetic jingle, "The thane of Fife had a wife" [V. i. 42], reinforces the image of Macduff as the major threat to guilt-ridden consciences. And then, in the final scenes, Macduff appears in apocalyptic power and glory, his role emphasized by his own nativity-legend, by the supernatural portent of Birnam wood. His combat with the adversary climaxes the play. And if we find it disturbing that Shakespeare, who usually finds someone to speak well of even his most flawed tragic heroes, dismisses Macbeth and his Lady as "this dead butcher and his fiend-like Queen" [V. ix. 35],

this apparent anomaly can be in part resolved if we remember the Porter and the implications of his scene. For Macduff, holding the severed head of the murderer, restoring order to the commonwealth in his virtual crowning, with the other hand, as it were, of the young Malcolm, shares something of the symbolic function of a still remembered Harrower of Hell. (pp. 400-02)

> *John B. Harcourt, "'I Pray You, Remember the Porter'," in* Shakespeare Quarterly, *Vol. XII, No. 4, Autumn, 1961, pp. 393-402.*

KENNETH MUIR   (essay date 1962)

[*In addition to his editions of* Richard II, King Lear, *and* Macbeth, *Muir also published numerous volumes of Shakespearean criticism and served as the editor of* Shakespeare Survey. *In the following excerpt, drawn from the introduction to his edition of* Macbeth, *Muir discusses the controversial Porter scene. He challenges the position held by earlier critics, particularly Samuel Taylor Coleridge (1813-34), that the scene is an un-Shakespearean interpolation extraneous to* Macbeth. *Muir argues instead that it is "an integral part of the play" in both style and content. He notes the "antithetical characteristics" in the Porter's speech, an observation also made by Brents Stirling (1953), and relates the issue of equivocation in the Porter's lines to the rest of the play. He further observes that the play's thematic concern with the "contrast between* desire and act" *is also present in the Porter scene and concludes that it is "impossible to regard it as a barbarous interpolation." Unlike Thomas De Quincey (1823), Muir contends that the knocking at the gate heightens the terror rather than relieves it, a reading also suggested by H. N. Hudson (1872). For another explication of the Porter scene, see the excerpt by John B. Harcourt (1961). Muir's introduction was originally published in 1951, but was revised in later editions.*]

Few critics would now agree with Coleridge that the soliloquy with which the [Porter] scene begins was, apart from one obviously Shakespearian phrase, interpolated by the players. The scene is theatrically necessary, because the actor who plays Macbeth has to change his costume and wash his hands, and (as [Edward] Capell suggested [in his *Notes and Various Readings to Shakespeare*]) it was necessary "to give a rational space for the discharge of these actions'. Shakespeare himself was fully conversant with theatrical necessities; but if these were the sole reason for the scene's existence it might have been added by another hand.

Some scene there had to be between the exit of Macbeth and the entrance of Macduff. But this does not explain why Shakespeare should choose or permit a drunken Porter, when a sober Porter, singing an aubade, as in one of the German versions, might seem to do as well. Comic relief is a convenient, but question-begging, term; for Shakespeare, we might suppose, could have used lyrical relief, if relief were needed. As Coleridge pointed out, Shakespeare never introduced the comic 'but when it may react on the tragedy by harmonious contrast'. A great dramatist does not laboriously create feelings of tension and intensity to dissipate them in laughter. Sometimes he may use humour as a laughter-conductor, so as to prevent the audience from laughing in the wrong place, and at the wrong things, thereby endangering the sublimity of the hero. In the present case, too, it is impossible to agree with those critics who think the function of the Porter is to take the present horror from the scene. On the contrary, the effect of the Porter's scene is almost the opposite of this. It is there—I do not say for the groundlings, but for the more judicious—in order to increase the horror of the situation. We are never allowed to forget, throughout the scene, the crime that has been committed and is about to be discovered. If we laugh, it is not the laughter of oblivion.

It is, perhaps, in accordance with the Scottish national character that a Porter in his cups should talk in true Calvinistic fashion of damnation. In his opening words he identifies himself with the traditional figure of the miracle plays, the porter of hell-gate, who was expected to make jests, but who was something more than a jester. The purpose of linking the Porter with this traditional character was two-fold: first, because it transports us from Inverness to the gate of Hell, without violating the unity of place, for Shakespeare has only to tell us the name of the place we were in before. It is the gate of hell because Lady Macbeth has called on the murthering ministers, because Macbeth has called on the stars to hide their fires, and because hell is a state, and not a place, and the murderers might say with Mephostophilis—

where we are is hell,
And where hell is, there must we ever be.

Shakespeare's second reason for recalling the miracle plays was that it enabled him to cut the cable that moored his tragedy to a particular spot in space and time, so that it could become universalized on the one hand, or become contemporary on the other. Macbeth's tragedy might therefore appear as a second Fall, with Lady Macbeth as a second Eve; or it could appear as terrifyingly contemporary. (pp. xxiii-xv)

The reference to treason in the Porter's speech looks back to the executed Thane of Cawdor, the gentleman on whom Duncan had built an absolute trust; and it looks forward to the dialogue between Lady Macduff and her son, and to the long testing of Macduff by Malcolm—which shows the distrust and suspicion which grow from equivocation and hypocrisy. Later in the play, Macbeth complains of

————th' equivocation of the fiend,
That lies like truth:

[V. v. 43]

and of those juggling fiends

That palter with us in a double sense;
That keep the word of promise to our ear,
And break it to our hope.

[V. viii. 20-2]

Indeed, as Dowden pointed out, Macbeth on his next appearance is compelled to equivocate. Later in the same scene there is an even more striking equivocation:

Had I but died an hour before this chance,
I had liv'd a blessed time; for, from this instant,
There's nothing serious in mortality;
All is but toys: renown, and grace, is dead;
The wine of life is drawn, and the mere lees
Is left this vault to brag of.

[II. iii. 91-6]

The audience knows, as Macbeth himself was to know—though he here intended to deceive—that the words are a precise description of the truth about himself. Macbeth's own equivocation, by an ironical twist, becomes merely an aspect of truth. It is a brilliant counterpart to the equivocation of the fiend that lies like truth: it is the equivocation of the murderer who utters truth like lies. Equivocation therefore links up with one of the main themes of the play. . . . (pp. xxv-xxvi)

Nor is the style of the scene un-Shakespearian. Bradley pointed out resemblances between Pompey's soliloquy on the inhabitants of the prison in *Measure for Measure* and the Porter's soliloquy and between the dialogue of Pompey with Abhorson [IV. ii. 22ff.] and the dialogue that follows the Porter's soliloquy. We may go further and suggest that one of the Porter's speeches, often bowdlerized out of existence, provides a valuable clue to one theme of the play. He is speaking of the effects of liquor, in answer to Macduff's question: 'What three things does drink especially provoke?'

Marry, Sir, nose-painting, sleep, and urine. Lechery, Sir, it provokes, and unprovokes: it provokes the desire, but it takes away the performance. Therefore, much drink may be said to be an equivocator with lechery: it makes him, and it mars him; it sets him on, and it takes him off; it persuades him, and disheartens him; makes him stand to, and not stand to: in conclusion, equivocates him in a sleep, and, giving him the lie, leaves him.

[II. iii. 27-36]

Drink 'provokes the desire, but it takes away the performance'; and this contrast between *desire* and *act* is repeated several times in the course of the play. Lady Macbeth, in invoking the evil spirits, begs them not to allow compunctious visitings of nature to shake her fell purpose,

————nor keep peace between
Th' effect and it!

[I. v. 46-7]

That is, intervene between her purpose and its fulfilment. Two scenes later she asks her husband:

Art thou afeard
To be the same in thine own act and valour,
As thou art in desire?

[I. vii. 39-41]

In the last scene in which the weird sisters appear (IV. i), Macbeth gives some variations on the same theme:

The flighty purpose never is o'ertook,
Unless the deed go with it. From this moment,
The very firstlings of my heart shall be
The firstlings of my hand. And even now,
To crown my thoughts with acts, be it thought
and done . . .
This deed I'll do, before this purpose cool.

[IV. i. 145-54]

This passage is linked with one at the end of the Banquet scene, where Macbeth tells his wife:

Strange things I have in head, that will to hand,
Which must be acted, ere they may be scann'd.

[III. iv. 138-39]

The opposition between the hand and the other organs and senses recurs again and again. Macbeth observes the functioning of his own organs with a strange objectivity: in particular, he speaks of his hand almost as though it had an independent existence of its own. He exhorts his eye to wink at the hand; when he sees the imaginary dagger, he decides that his eyes have been made the fools of the other senses, or else worth all the rest; later in the same speech his very footsteps seem, as it were, to be divorced from himself:

> Hear not my steps, which way they walk, for fear
> Thy very stones prate of my where-about,
>
> [II. i. 57-8]

and, after the murder of Duncan, both criminals are obsessed by the thought of their bloody hands. Macbeth speaks of them as 'a sorry sight' and as 'hangman's hands'—the hangman had to draw and quarter his victim; Lady Macbeth urges him to wash the 'filthy witness' from his hand; and in the great speech that follows her exit, Macbeth asks:

> What hands are here? Ha! they pluck out mine eyes.
> Will all great Neptune's ocean wash this blood
> Clean from my hand? No, this my hand will rather
> The multitudinous seas incarnadine,
> Making the green one red.
>
> [II. ii. 56-60]

In the first line of this quotation the hand-eye opposition appears in its most striking, most hallucinated, form. Lady Macbeth persists in her illusion that a little water clears them of the deed—an illusion she has to expiate in the Sleep-walking scene. Just before the murder of Banquo, Macbeth invokes Night:

> Scarf up the tender eye of pitiful Day,
> And, with thy bloody and invisible hand,
> Cancel, and tear to pieces, that great bond
> Which keeps me pale!
>
> [III. ii. 47-50]

The bloody hand has now been completely detached from Macbeth and become a part of Night. Later in the play we are reminded of the same series of images when Angus declares that Macbeth feels

> His secret murthers sticking on his hands. [V. ii. 17]

The Porter's words on lechery have yet another significance. They are written in an antithetical form: *provokes—unprovokes; provokes—takes away; desire—performance; makes—mars; sets on—takes off; persuades—disheartens; stand to—not stand to.* Here concentrated in half a dozen lines we find one of the predominant characteristics of the general style of the play—it consists of multitudinous antitheses. The reader has only to glance at any page of the play. . . . It may even be suggested that the iterative image of ill-fitting garments is a kind of pictorial antithesis, a contrast between the man and his clothes, as in the lines—

> now does he feel his title
> Hang loose about him, like a giant's robe
> Upon a dwarfish thief.
>
> [V. ii. 20-2]

Another recurrent image—not mentioned by Miss Spurgeon—may be regarded as a contrast between the picture and the thing depicted:

> The sleeping, and the dead,
> Are but as pictures; 'tis the eye of childhood
> That fears a painted devil.
>
> [I. vii. 50-2]

This is the very painting of your fear.

> [III. iv. 60]

> Shake off this downy sleep, death's counterfeit,
> And look on death itself!—up, up, and see
> The great doom's image!
>
> [II. iii. 76-8]

These images are linked with the equivocation, deceit, and treachery which have been noted by more than one critic as constituting one of the main themes of the play. These too are a contrast between appearance and reality.

The style of the Porter's speech is not alien to that of the rest of the play. It possesses the antithetical characteristics of the verse, suitably 'transprosed' for semi-comic purposes. The whole scene is linked so closely with the rest of the play, in content as well as in style, that it is impossible to regard it as a barbarous interpolation of the actors. The antithetical style is a powerful means of suggesting the paradox and enigma of the nature of man,

> The glory, jest, and riddle of the world,
> [Alexander Pope in his *An Essay on Man*]

the conflict within him between sin and grace, between reason and emotion, and the shadow which falls

> Between the potency
> And the existence
> Between the essence
> And the descent.
> [T. S. Eliot in his *The Hollow Men*]

This discussion of the authenticity of the scene has led us imperceptibly into a consideration of the play as a whole; and this in itself may serve to show that the Porter is an integral part of the play. (pp. xxvi-xxix)

> *Kenneth Muir, in an introduction to* Macbeth *by William Shakespeare, edited by Kenneth Muir, ninth edition, 1962. Reprint by Methuen, 1983, pp. xi-lxv.*

J. P. DYSON   (essay date 1963)

[*In the excerpt below, Dyson presents a detailed analysis of the banquet scene in* Macbeth, *arguing that it is structurally the most important scene in the play. Dyson proposes that an opposition exists in* Macbeth *between the dark, disruptive "raven" elements—represented by Macbeth—and the lighter, harmonious "martlet" elements embodied in characters like Malcolm and Macduff. This conflict, he contends, is evident in the banquet scene in Act III, Scene iv, during which Macbeth's pretense to a kingship that is the "cornerstone" of degree and order begins to crumble. Throughout this scene, states Dyson, Macbeth is shown to be a raven "attempting to pass himself off as an inhabitant of the 'martlet' world." Dyson also maintains that the appearance of Banquo's ghost marks the turning point in the play, for Macbeth begins to realize that he is not in "control of things," and concludes that the banquet scene reveals to Macbeth the "nothingness" of his kingship.*]

It is by now a commonplace of Shakespearian criticism that Shakespeare, in his major works at least, usually focuses the meaning of each particular play in one or more key scenes. The implication is not that the total meaning of the play is to be found in these single scenes (indeed the great tragedies are so packed with meaning that it is difficult to see how anything could be left out of them), but that a firm grasp of the structure and meaning of such scenes is frequently the key which unlocks the structure and the meaning of the play as a whole. Another way of putting it is to say that exploration of these particular scenes usually leads one into exploration of the issues most relevant to an intelligent interpretation of the play. *Macbeth* has several scenes of great significance. Of these, the banquet scene (III. iv) is, in a number of ways, the most important structurally.

Before we examine the scene itself, perhaps a preliminary word is in order regarding the approach to *Macbeth* as a whole presupposed in this paper. To begin with an obvious point, *Macbeth* is a play about evil and damnation. The evil forces are embodied principally in the Weird Sisters and the Macbeths and in images (dramatic and verbal) of blood, disorder, mutilation, hallucinatory states of mind, vicious animals, etc.; the good is presented partly in terms of characters such as Duncan, Malcolm, and Macduff, but more "by means of imagery, symbolism and iteration" [Kenneth Muir in his introduction to the Arden Edition of *Macbeth*]. The nature of the good and evil in the play is brought out powerfully in the contrasted passages beginning, "The raven himself is hoarse . . ." [I. v. 38] and "This guest of summer / The temple-haunting martlet . . ." [I. vi. 3-4]. The former is a prayer, an invocation to the evil forces at work in the play; the latter is a lyric, a symbol constructed to express many of the positive experiences in the play. The raven passage draws together most of the themes of the *Macbeth* evil: the bird of prey; the constricted, closed-in atmosphere ("battlements", "thick night", "blanket of the dark" [I. v. 40, 50, 53]; mutilation and sterility ("unsex"); hell; hospitality violated; hate—all expressed in verse full of stop consonants, heavy in movement. The latter passage clusters the positive *Macbeth* values around the martlet: values such as the medieval notion of hospitality ("guest"); religion ("temple-haunting"); heaven; procreation, family, and fertility; sleep and security ("pendant bed and procreant cradle" [I. vi. 8]); the lightness and delicacy of the atmosphere, free-playing breezes, and airy heights—all caught in verse as light and delicate as the air it describes. It is out of the experiences formulated in each of these passages that the contrasted values of the play develop. . . . [In] the martlet passage we have a particularized and concentrated expression of order, fulfillment, and harmony; in the raven passage an equally particularized and concentrated expression of the complete perversion of order, fulfillment, and harmony. The concreteness of the two passages grows directly out of the contrasted experiences explored in the play.

It is impossible therefore to dissociate the banquet scene from the rest of the play. Any complete account of *Macbeth* must give full value to the opening scene, a dramatic and verbal image of the demonic "truth" that "Fair is foul and foul is fair" [I. i. 11]; to the raven-martlet contrast just described; to the kingship of Duncan expressed in terms of fertility and grace; to the murder scene—that tense excursion into the demonic and hostile universe; to the banquet scene which we will come to in a moment; to the witches' "banquet"; to the sleepwalking scene, in which the "sleep" theme and the unnatural forms of consciousness found in the play reach the climactic stage of their metamorphosis; and to Macbeth's final soliloquies, the last stages of damnation.

The importance of the banquet scene rests on two facts: First, in this scene, "speech, action and symbolism combine" [L. C. Knights in his *How Many Children Had Lady Macbeth?*] to present analogously the whole movement of the play, the movement, both internal (to Macbeth) and external, from order to chaos; and second, it is in this scene that the whole play

turns over, so to speak. Macbeth begins the scene still hoping to take his place as king; he ends it knowing that he has passed the crisis in his journey toward damnation. It is in this scene that Macbeth achieves the moment of tragic insight: the realization that he is living in an ambiguous world, a world over which he has no control, a world in which dead men return to "push us from our stools" [III. iv. 81].

The scene falls naturally into five sections or "moments", each with its particular significance. The first is from the opening of the scene to the entrance of the First Murderer; it is here that the basic symbolism of the scene is established, the intended direction indicated. The second section is the conversation of Macbeth with the Murderer, an ironic interlude in terms of what precedes and what follows. The third is the central part of the scene, the apparitions of Banquo's ghost; it is here that the play shifts its direction. The fourth section is the chaotic disorder in which the feast ends. The fifth is the aftermath in which it is clearly indicated that Macbeth is not what he was when the scene began; in a sense, the initiative has passed out of his hands. He knows now that he has moved out into the wasteland, the wasteland which can only end in "Tomorrow and tomorrow and tomorrow . . ." [V. iv. 19].

So much notice has been given by Wilson Knight [see excerpt above, 1931] and others to the meaning of banquets in Shakespeare that it is scarcely necessary to demonstrate why a banquet rather than, say, an audience chamber or a field is the setting for this scene. Banquets and feasting are traditional symbols of harmony, fellowship, and union. They are dramatic symbols of life-forces, a fulfillment of nature in a way that parallels the procreation and fertility of the martlet passage.

This emphasis is brought out in the language and gesture of the scene. Macbeth is the "host", Lady Macbeth the "hostess", surrounded by "all our friends" [III. iv. 7]. "Welcome" is the key word of the opening—it is used three times in the first seven lines of the scene.

Related to the notion of banquet as symbol of union is the notion of banquet as symbol of order and hierarchy. The opening line, as has been frequently noted, establishes this immediately: "You know your own degrees, sit down." The scene, in the context of the Elizabethan platform stage, obviously opens with a procession in which the lords are ranged according to "degree". The contrast between this and the later "Stand not upon the order of your going" [III. iv. 118], is a leading motif of the scene. (pp. 369-71)

The "sit down" of the opening line is also a pregnant phrase, because this scene is, symbolically, all about "sitting down". The throne is onstage and Macbeth attempts to occupy it; that is to say, he attempts to take his place in society, to act the part of king, and he simply does not get away with it. The murder of Duncan secured possession of the throne; the banquet scene is what we might call the formal or gestural attempt to enthrone himself, to become the *true* king. We have here a ceremonial, a social ritual at which all sit about under the aegis of "the good king". "The good king" here tries (with almost Scriptural overtones) to play the "humble host" and mingle with his people. (We are reminded perhaps of Henry V, "the good king" *par excellence,* mingling with his soldiers the night before Agincourt.) In this ordered hierarchy of "first and last"— a grouping according to rank or place, but all, nevertheless, within the unity of a family or state—Macbeth is determined to take his place ("Here I'll sit in the midst" [III. iv. 10]). He will join his family and as a further symbol of their unity they will "drink a measure / The table round" [III. iv. 11-12]. The symbolism of the scene here both depends on and helps define for the audience an understanding of the nature of human society and its cornerstone, the king.

There are echoes of an earlier feast, that which preceded Duncan's murder:

> The king's abed.
> He hath been in unusual pleasure, and
> Sent forth great largess to your offices.
> This diamond he greets your wife withal,
> By the name of most kind hostess, and shut up
> In measureless content.
>
> [II. i. 12-17]

This is what Macbeth aspires to be, but his crime has been one against degree. As kinsman, host, and subject, he has violated ties of blood, hospitality, and state. He has overturned the whole order of things; it is in this scene that his actions boomerang—the order of things turns on him.

The incident of the conversation with the Murderer is best understood in the context of the lines preceding and following it:

> *Lady M.* Pronounce it for me, sir, to all our friends,
> For my heart speaks they are welcome.
> [*Enter* FIRST MURDERER *to the door.* . . .]
>
>   *Macb.* Be large in mirth, anon we'll drink a measure
> The table round. [*Approaching the door.*] There's blood
> upon thy face. . . .
>
>   *Macb.*   Get thee gone. Tomorrow
> We'll hear ourselves again. [*Exit* MURDERER.]
>   *Lady M.*   My royal lord,
> You do not give the cheer.
>
> [III. iv. 7-32]

The irony, scarcely needing to be commented on, draws our attention to the completely non-naturalistic technique used here by Shakespeare. From a naturalistic viewpoint, the coming of the Murderer (with or without blood upon his face) to whisper at the door of a state banquet is ridiculous. The contention that Macbeth has to find out somehow the results of the ambush before Banquo's ghost appears is, of course, valid, but does not explain why Shakespeare chose this particular way of doing it.

Perhaps a more profound explanation lies in the fact that Macbeth is here attempting to pass himself off as an inhabitant of the "martlet" world, the ordered and harmonious world of the banquet, while his real habitat is the "raven" world, the world of the First Murderer. He moves from the light of the banquet scene to the outer darkness of the conference because that is where he belongs. The Murderer appears because, in the *Macbeth* universe, the raven world must invade that of the martlet. As a result of the Murderer's visitation Macbeth is left "cabined, cribbed, confined, bound in / To saucy doubts and fears" [III. iv. 23-4]. Lady Macbeth's prayer for the descent of "thick night" [I. v. 50] continues to be fulfilled in the soul of her husband. For him indeed, "light thickens" and will continue to do so till in his isolation he will be "the crow" who "makes wing to the rooky wood" [III. ii. 50-1]. This impingement of darkness upon light will be amply reinforced by the full-scale eruption of the demonic world, in the form of Banquo's ghost, into the brightness of the banquet. By the end of the scene, Macbeth will know for a certainty that the martlet world is for

him a lost dream. Here Shakespeare sets side by side symbolically the two levels of reality before one makes chaos of the other. The total effect is sharpened by the irony of Lady Macbeth and of Macbeth himself—he who would be the Holy King is shown trafficking with the devil.

Macbeth is recalled by his wife to his part in the banquet charade. Called upon in his capacity as (would-be) king to fulfill his part in the "ceremony", he grants, God-like, "good digestion", "appetite", and "health". He is twice invited to take his place. There are religious resonances to the second invitation: "Please't your Highness / To grace us with your royal company" [III. iv. 43-4]. This is high courtesy turned unwittingly to sacrilege. Invited to take his place, Macbeth cannot—a major point of the play. Macbeth attempts to take his place and, quite literally, all hell breaks loose. The demonic wish for the presence of Banquo, the devil's attempt to play God, rebounds: Banquo's ghost appears. (pp. 371-72)

We are here at the center of the play, the moment when Macbeth's world turns over, the moment of tragic insight.

>   The time has been
> That when the brains were out the man would die,
> And there an end. But now they rise again,
> With twenty mortal murders on their crowns,
> And push us from our stools. This is more strange
> Than such a murder is.
>
> [III. iv. 77-82]

Appearance becomes reality; evil becomes more than atmosphere. Macbeth goes into nothingness and explores it until the end. (p. 373)

Macbeth had thought that he could achieve the kingship alone; he suddenly realizes that (in a metaphysical sense) there is someone (or something) else in control of things. The rules have suddenly been switched; he has been catapulted into a world of inverted values.

If we wish, we can psychologize this moment of insight and say that Macbeth is mad; or we can moralize it and say that his conscience has caught up with him. The fact remains, however, that it is not presented in either of these ways. It is presented as a fact, a vision of life.

One further point needs comment. D. A. Traversi speaks of "the ghost of Banquo intervening to occupy the place destined for Macbeth as king at head of his table. The apparition breaks in upon the show of loyalty and order which he seeks, by virtue of his usurped dignity, to command" [see excerpt below, 1968]. Wilson Knight [in his *Principles of Shakespearean Production*] suggests that in staging *Macbeth*, the ghost be made to sit, at his first appearance, in Macbeth's place at the table. When it disappears, Macbeth is to take his place at table, then turn to see the ghost, in his second appearance, ensconced on the throne at one side of the stage. Knight's suggestion would undoubtedly be theatrically effective and the point that both he and Traversi are bringing out is a valid one, namely Macbeth's abortive attempt to gesturally assume the kingship. But it goes deeper than that. Macbeth does not say "push us from our *thrones*", but "push us from our *stools*". The line is not political; it is metaphysical. Macbeth, not as king but as man, suffers insight on the level of the universal. It is a perception not of having no throne, but of having no place at all in the world. This is what makes it tragic.

Here Shakespeare draws out what was implicit in the dialogue of the murder scene:

Macb. I have done the deed. Didst thou not hear the
noise?
Lady M. I heard the owl scream and the crickets cry.
Did you not speak?
Macb.   When?
Lady M.   Now.
Macb.   As I descended?
Lady M. Aye.
Macb. Hark!

[II. ii. 14-17]

The rhythm itself conveys the experience of finding oneself
isolated in a universe suddenly turned hostile, a world of perpetual darkness in which "Good things of day begin to droop
and drowse / Whiles night's black agents to their preys do
rouse" [III. ii. 52-3], a world in which the only refuge is the
death wish of

> Better be with the dead,
> Whom we, to gain our peace, have sent to peace,
> Than on the torture of the mind to lie
> In restless ecstasy. Duncan is in his grave,
> After life's fitful fever he sleeps well.

[III. ii. 19-23]

This, it seems to me, is the turning point of the play, not
Fleance's escape as some editors would still have it. A turning
point such as Fleance's escape is based on a mistaken notion
of a reversal in Macbeth's fortune, a notion which takes reversal
at the wrong level. The presupposition is that, if Fleance had
not escaped, Macbeth would have been successful. But it is
clear that in terms of the play as it exists there is no possibility
of success for Macbeth in the sense of getting away with it. It
is more a question of his perception of the direction in which
he is actually going and has been going since his first appearance. The ghost of Banquo is the catalyst of insight, the message from the underworld which opens Macbeth's eyes to the
new "reality".

The consequence of the ghost's visit is, of course, chaos—
chaos presented verbally in Lady Macbeth's "You have dis-
placed the mirth, broke the good meeting / With most admired
disorder. . . . Stand not upon the order of your going . . ." [III.
iv. 107-08, 118] and dramatically in the scramble of the guests
for the exits, a vivid contrast to the stateliness and order of
the processional entrance. The final twist of the knife is contained in the unwitting irony of the guests' parting remark,
"Good night, and better health attend His Majesty!" [III. iv.
119-20]. "Better health" will never attend His Majesty and
His Majesty now knows it. It is to the clarification of this lack
of "better health" that the remainder of the scene is devoted.
We are witnesses to the aftermath.

"It will have blood. They say blood will have blood" [III. iv.
121], thinks Macbeth. Here by means of an old wives' tale,
Shakespeare crystallizes an experience. Macbeth is in the process of discovering that murdered men are never dead to their
murderers. He has penetrated to a world where nothingness
has come to life; he has seen that which is menacing him.

Macbeth, we have said, is a play about damnation. This final
part of the scene represents the mid-point in Macbeth's progression into hell—not a theological hell strictly speaking, but
a metaphysical one. The murders are not presented just as
crimes, which are against society, though society exacts its
claims on Macbeth; not as sins in a theological sense—the
question of where Macbeth is going after death is certainly not
in the forefront; but as sins or sin in a metaphysical sense, a

sin against the whole order of things. Macbeth's damnation is
not expressed in social or moral terms; his punishment is not
a sanction imposed. It is, rather, a formal consequence of his
actions: by doing *this* you become *that*.

All the significant strands making up the vision of damnation
embodied in the play are here reiterated and clarified. They
grow out of what has gone before and are worked through until
they reach their final modulations in the last act.

Macb.   What is the night?
Lady M. Almost at odds with morning, which is which.

[III. iv. 125-26]

In this brief question and answer we sense again the rocking
ambiguity at the heart of the play. This is a minor analogue
of what seems to me to be the basic structure of the play. (pp.
373-75)

To place the banquet scene structurally in relation to the play
as a whole requires a brief commentary on the over-all structure
of the play itself. *Macbeth* is built on imaginative contrast
governed by progression in the directions already indicated.
Its structure produces and, in a sense, is the tension resulting
from the exploration of opposed areas of experience, those
which we earlier called for convenience the martlet world and
the raven world. The contrast is not merely verbal or logical;
it is not point for point. It is, rather, the exposure of the
paradoxical facets of human experience, the one demonic, the
other paradisal.

The tension grows out of two contradictory progressions in the
good-evil of the play. Macbeth himself moves from the martlet
world (to which he never entirely belonged perhaps) into that
of the raven while the play as a whole moves in the opposite
direction from the world of the raven to that of the martlet.
Macbeth attempts to mask as a good king only to be finally
unmasked; Malcolm seems evil in his flight and attempts to
mask as an evil king (IV. iii), only to be revealed as a good
king. Macbeth becomes quickly identified with the "fog and
filthy air" [I. i. 12] of the opening scene; the praise heaped
on him rapidly vanishes; he wishes to "look like the innocent
flower" while being "the serpent under't" [I. v. 65-6]; he
moves on into a world where fairness and foulness are truly
inverted until the evil with which he has become fully identified
is unmasked: "I begin / To doubt the equivocation of the fiend /
That lies like truth" [V. v. 41-3]. "Be these juggling fiends
no more believed / That palter with us in a double sense" [V.
viii. 19-20]. On the other hand, the play as a whole moves
from the reversed values of the opening scene through the
murder of "the gracious Duncan", past the king of England
whose "sundry blessings hang about his throne / That speak
him full of grace" [IV. iii. 158-59] to the last act with Malcolm's "Your leavy screens throw down / And show like those
you are" [V. vi. 1-2]. The climactic lines of the play's final
speech cap the progression with their vision of order (reinforced
by the religious resonances):

> . . . and what needful else
> That calls upon us, by the grace of Grace
> We will perform in measure, time, and place.

[V. ix. 37-9]

The raven-martlet tension underlies the play structurally on all
levels. It is the keynote to Macbeth himself. In his speech
beginning, "Two truths are told . . .", the raven-martlet struggle can be seen not only in the contrasted ideas that flit in and
out of his mind but in the very rhythm itself with its lurching

and rocking: "... cannot be ill, cannot be good. If ill ... If good ... and nothing is / But what is not" [I. iii. 127ff.]. It is this sort of imaginative contrast built into the character itself which provides an understanding of Macbeth, not realistic psychology.

The pattern of alternation is expressed graphically in the dramaturgy of the last act. The scenes shift back and forth between the forces of good and the forces of evil, between the forces marching under the aegis of "the powers above" and those under the command of the "hellhound". It is only in the final scene that the forces join battle overtly (although for Macbeth the battle is already over; since his "Tomorrow ..." he is merely a corpse waiting for someone to put him out of sight) and reach their ultimate dramatic resolution in the ascension of a new king "of Grace" to the throne.

In the light of all this, the structural function of the banquet scene should be sufficiently clear. It is the great watershed through which the action must pass; it marks the decisive change. It is the great dramatic symbol of order disrupted—the martlet setting (transposed by the tonality of State added to domestic) of harmony and union into which the raven world erupts in the form of the demonic visitation. It is the climactic moment in which the universe of the play turns over, the moment of insight for Macbeth. He has been moving further and further out of the martlet world into that of the raven, but it is only here that he perceives the nature of that which he has embraced. He has chosen nothingness; in the banquet scene nothingness reveals itself to him. (pp. 377-78)

> J. P. Dyson, "The Structural Function of the Banquet Scene in 'Macbeth'," in Shakespeare Quarterly, Vol. XIV, No. 4, Autumn, 1963, pp. 369-78.

WAYNE BOOTH   (essay date 1963)

[*In the following excerpt, Booth discusses the dramatic technique Shakespeare used in portraying Macbeth as a sympathetic tragic hero, a matter also considered by Arthur Quiller-Couch (1918), Robert B. Heilman (1966), and Bertrand Evans (1979). Booth argues that the testimony of other characters and Macbeth's own moral vacillations presented early in the play suggest that Macbeth "is not a naturally evil man, but a man who has every potentiality for goodness." Booth also points out the effect that Macbeth's limited role in the on-stage murders has on his sympathetic portrayal. Duncan's death, he observes, is neither represented nor narrated, and the murders of Banquo and Macduff's family are committed by others so that "Macbeth is never shown in any act of wicked violence." Macbeth's poetic language, argues Booth, is another element in Shakespeare's successful presentation of the tragic hero, an issue also treated by Bertrand Evans (1979). Booth concludes that the spectator "can feel great pity that a man with so much potentiality for greatness should have fallen so low."*]

Considered even in its simplest terms, the problem Shakespeare gave himself in *Macbeth* was immense: take a 'noble' man, full of 'conscience' and 'the milk of human kindness' [I. v. 17], and make of him a 'dead butcher' [V. ix. 35], yet maintain him as a tragic hero with full stature commanding our sympathy to the end. To portray a credible path of moral degeneration is difficult enough in itself; to do so in a form requiring undiminished pity is next to impossible. The attempt would be brash even in fiction, or epic, with all of their additional resources for portraying subtle changes and for building sym-

pathy. But to attempt a moral transformation of such scope in a short play, without muddling the audience's responses, is to court disaster.

One need only consider how rarely authors have achieved tragedy with their sympathetic villains to realize the difficulties involved. In place of the tragic experience offered by *Macbeth*, one usually finds one or another of the following transformations: (1) The protagonist is never really made very wicked, after all: he only *seems* wicked by conventional, unsound standards and is really a highly admirable reform-candidate. (2) The abhorrence for the protagonist becomes so strong that all sympathy is lost, and the work becomes 'punitive', as in *Richard III*. (3) The protagonist reforms in the end, before ever really doing anything very bad (innumerable motion pictures and tragi-comedies). (4) The wickedness is mitigated by comedy, so that the serious conflict between sympathy and moral judgement is diminished (*Lolita, The Ginger Man*). (5) The book or play itself becomes a 'wicked' work; that is, either deliberately or unconsciously the artist makes us take the side of his degenerated hero against morality (The Marquis de Sade). (6) The spectacle of decay is no longer exploited, as in *Macbeth*, for its greatest human effects, but these are subordinated to other, 'purer' ends, as Flaubert, in *Madame Bovary*, often deliberately undercuts the pathos of Emma's gradual corruption in order, as he puts it, 'to make the reader dream' rather than weep. (pp. 180-81)

The first requirement, if we are to believe that Macbeth's fall is a genuinely tragic event, is to convince us that he is an admirable man, a man who matters. One way would be to show him, as Fitzgerald shows Dick Diver, in admirable action. But such a leisurely representation is not possible when great moral distance must be travelled quickly by the protagonist, and Shakespeare quite rightly begins with the first temptation to the fall, using testimony of the liveliest possible kind to establish Macbeth's prior goodness. From the beginning, we are given sign after sign that his greatest nobility was reached at a point just before the play opens. But he has already coveted the crown, as is shown by his extreme response to the witches' prophecy. It is indeed likely that he has already thought of murder. In spite of this, we have ample reason to think Macbeth worthy of our admiration. He is 'brave' and 'valiant', a 'worthy gentleman'; Duncan calls him 'noble Macbeth'. These epithets seem ironic only in retrospect; when they are first applied, one has no reason to doubt them. Indeed, they are accurate, or they would have been accurate if applied, say, a few days or months earlier.

This testimony to his prior virtue would carry little force, however, if it were not supported in several other forms. We have the word of Lady Macbeth (the unimpeachable testimony of a wicked character deploring goodness):

> Yet do I fear thy nature:
> It is too full o' the milk of human kindness
> To catch the nearest way. Thou wouldst be great,
> Art not without ambition, but without
> The illness should attend it. What thou wouldst highly,
> That wouldst thou holily, wouldst not play false,
> And yet wouldst wrongly win.
>
> [I. v. 16-22]

No testimony would be enough, however, if we did not see specific signs of its validity, since we already know of his temptations. Thus the best evidence of his essential goodness

Act I. Scene iii. Macbeth, Banquo, and the Three Witches. By H. Fuseli (n.d.).

is his vacillation before the murder. Just as Raskolnikov is tormented and just as we ourselves—virtuous theatre viewers—would be tormented, so Macbeth is tormented before the prospect of his own crime. Much as he wants the kingship, he decides in Scene 3 against the murder:

> If chance will have me King, why chance may crown me
> Without my stir. . . .
>
> [I. iii. 143-44]

And when he first meets Lady Macbeth he is resolved to resist temptation. Powerful as her rhetoric is, it is barely sufficient to pull him back on the course of murder.

More important is the ensuing soliloquy, since stage conventions give absolute authority to any character's secret thoughts. It shows him weighing not only the bad political consequences of his act but also the moral values involved:

> He's here in double trust:
> First, as I am his kinsman and his subject,
> Strong both against the deed; then, as his host,
> Who should against his murderer shut the door,
> Not bear the knife myself.
>
> [I. vii. 12-16]

We see here again Shakespeare's economy: the very speech which shows just how bad the contemplated act is builds sympathy for the planner.

Macbeth announces once again that he will not go on ('We will proceed no further in this business' [I. vii. 31]), but again Lady Macbeth's eloquence is too much for him. Under her jibes at his 'unmanliness' he progresses from a kind of petulant, but still honourable, boasting ('I dare do all that may become a man; Who dares do more is none' [I. vii. 46-7]), through a state of amoral consideration of mere expediency ('If we should fail?' [I. vii. 59]), to complete resolution, but still with a full understanding of the wickedness of his act ('. . . this terrible feat' [I. vii. 80]). There is never any doubt, first, that he is bludgeoned into the deed by Lady Macbeth and by the pressure of unfamiliar circumstances and, second, that even in his final decision he is tormented by a guilty conscience ('False face must hide what the false heart doth know' [I. vii. 82]). In the dagger soliloquy he is clearly suffering from the horror of the 'bloody business' ahead. He sees fully and painfully the wickedness of the course he has chosen, but not until after the deed, when the knocking has commenced, do we realize how terrifyingly alive his conscience is: 'To know my deed, 'twere best not know myself. Wake Duncan with thy knocking! I would thou couldst' [II. ii. 70-1]. This is the wish of a 'good' man who, though he has become a 'bad' man, still thinks and feels as a good man would.

Finally, we have the testimony to Macbeth's character offered by Hecate:

And, which is worse, all you have done
Hath been but for a wayward son,
Spiteful and wrathful, who, as others do,
Loves for his own ends, not for you.

[III. v. 10-14]

This reaffirmation that Macbeth is not a true son of evil comes, interestingly enough, immediately after the murder of Banquo, at a time when the audience needs a reminder that Macbeth is not fundamentally evil.

His crimes are thus built upon our knowledge that he is not a naturally evil man but a man who has every potentiality for goodness. Indeed, this potentiality and its destruction are the chief ingredients of the tragedy. Macbeth is a man whose progressive external misfortunes seem to produce, and at the same time seem to be produced by, the parallel progression from great goodness to great wickedness.

Our response to his destruction is compounded of three kinds of regret, only one of them known in pre-Shakespearian tragedy. We of course lament the fall of a great man from happiness to misery, as in classical tragedy. To this is added what to most spectators is much more poignant: the pity one feels in observing the *moral* decline of a great man who has once known goodness. Perhaps most influential in the later history of drama and fiction, there is the even greater poignancy of observing the destruction of a highly individualized person, a person one knows and cares for. Later writers have tended to rely more and more on the third of these and to play down the first two; one difference between Macbeth going to destruction and the fall of a typical modern hero (Willy Loman say, or Hemingway's Jake) is that in Macbeth there is some going.

But perhaps the most remarkable achievement is Shakespeare's choice of how to represent the moral decline. He has the task of trying to keep two contradictory streams moving simultaneously: the events showing Macbeth's growing wickedness and the tide of our mounting sympathy. In effect, each succeeding atrocity, marking another step towards depravity, must be so surrounded by contradictory circumstances or technical blandishments as to make us feel that, in spite of the evidence before our eyes, Macbeth is still somehow sympathetic.

Our first sure sign that Shakespeare's attention is on the need for such manipulation is his care in avoiding any representation of the murder of Duncan. It is, in fact, not even narrated. We hear only the details of how the guards reacted and how Macbeth reacted to their cries. We *see* nothing. There is nothing about the actual dagger strokes; there is no report of the dying cries of the good old king. We have only Macbeth's conscience-stricken lament. What would be an intolerable act if depicted with any vividness becomes relatively forgivable when seen only afterward in the light of Macbeth's remorse. This treatment may seem ordinary enough; it is always convenient to have murders take place offstage. But if one compares the handling of this scene with that of the blinding of Gloucester, where the perpetrators must be hated, one can see how important such a detail can be. The blinding of Gloucester is not so wicked an act, in itself, as Duncan's murder: imagine a properly motivated Goneril wringing her hands and crying, 'Methought I heard a voice cry, "Sleep no more." ' Goneril does put out the eyes of sleep . . . I am afraid to think what I have done', and on thus for nearly a full scene.

A second precaution is the highly general portrayal of Duncan before his murder. It is necessary only that he be known as a 'good king', the murder of whom will be a wicked act. He must be clearly the best type of benevolent monarch. But more particular characteristics are carefully kept from us. There is little for us to love or attach our imaginations to. We hear of his goodness; we never see it. We know almost no details about him, and we have little personal interest in him at the time of his death. All of the personal interest is reserved for Macbeth and Lady Macbeth. Thus again the wickedness is played up in the narration but played down in the representation. We must identify Macbeth with the murder of a blameless king, but only intellectually; emotionally we should be attending only to the effects on Macbeth. We know that he has done the deed, but we feel primarily his own suffering.

Banquo is considerably more individualized than Duncan. Not only is he a good man, but we have seen him in action as a good man, and we know a good deal about him. We saw his reaction to the witches, and we know that he has resisted temptations similar to those Macbeth is yielding to. We have heard him in soliloquy, that infallible guide to inner quality. He thus has our lively sympathy; his death is more nearly a personal loss than was Duncan's. Perhaps more important, his murder is shown on the stage. His dying words are spoken in our presence, and they are unselfishly directed to saving his son. We are led to the proper, though illogical, inference: it is more wicked to kill Banquo than to have killed Duncan.

But we must still not lose our sympathy for the criminal. It is helpful, of course, that Macbeth is acting on the basis of a real threat to himself. But the important thing is again the choice of what is represented. The murder is done by accomplices, so that Macbeth is never shown in any act of wicked violence. When we do see him, he is suffering the torments of the banquet scene. Our unconscious inference: the self-torture has already expiated his crime.

The same devices work in the murder of Lady Macduff and her children, the third and last atrocity explicitly shown in the play (the killing of young Seyward, being military, is hardly an atrocity in this sense). Lady Macduff is more vividly portrayed even than Banquo, although she appears on the stage for a much briefer time. Her complaints against the absence of her husband, her loving banter with her son, and her stand against the murderers make her as admirable as the little boy himself, who dies in defence of his father's name. The murder of women and children of such quality is wicked indeed, we feel, and when we move to England and see the effect of the atrocity on Macduff, our active pity for Macbeth's victims—as distinct from our abstract awareness that they are victimized—is at its highest point. For the first time, pity for Macbeth's victims really wars with pity for him, and our desire for his downfall threatens to turn the play into what some critics have claimed it to be: a punitive tragedy like *Richard III*.

Yet even here Macbeth is kept as little to blame as possible. He does not do the deed himself, and we can believe that he would have been unable to, if he had seen the victims as we have. . . . He is much further removed from them than from his other victims; as far as we know, he has never seen them. They are as remote and impersonal to him as they are immediate and personal to the audience, and while this impersonal brutality may make his crime worse in theory, our personal blame against him is attenuated. More important, immediately after Macduff's tears we shift to Lady Macbeth's scene, one effect of which is to 'prove' once again that the suffering of these criminals is worse than their crimes.

All three murders, then, are followed immediately by scenes of suffering and self-torture. It is almost as if Shakespeare were following a rule that Aristotle never dreamed of because none of the plays he knew presented this kind of problem: by your choice of what to represent from the materials provided in your story, insure that each step in your protagonist's degeneration will be counteracted by mounting pity.

This technical brilliance would be useless, of course, if the hard facts of Macbeth's character did not offer grounds for sympathy. Perhaps the most important of these, except for the initial moral stature, is his poetic gift. In his maturer work Shakespeare does not bestow this gift indiscriminately. We naturally tend to feel with the character who speaks the best poetry of the play, no matter what his deeds (Iago would never be misplayed as protagonist if his poetry did not rival, and sometimes surpass, Othello's). When we add to this poetic gift an extremely rich and concrete set of characteristics, we have a man who is more likely to compel our sympathy than any character portrayed only in moral colours. . . . If Macbeth's initial nobility, the manner of representation of his crimes, and his rich poetic gift are all calculated to sustain our sympathy, the kind of mistake he makes in initiating his own destruction is equally well suited to heighten our willingness to forgive while deploring. It could be said that he errs simply in being over-ambitious and under-scrupulous. But this is only part of the truth. What allows him to sacrifice his moral beliefs to his ambition is a mistake of another kind—a kind which is, at least to modern spectators, more credible than any conventional tragic flaw or any traditional tragic error, such as mistaking the identity of a brother or not knowing that one's wife is one's mother. Macbeth knows what he is doing, yet he does not know. He knows the immorality of the act, but he has no conception of the effects of the act on himself or his surroundings. Accustomed to heroic killing, in battle, and having valorously 'carv'd out his passage' with 'bloody execution' [I. ii. 18-19] many times previously, he misunderstands what will be the effect on his own character if he tries to carve out his passage in civil life. (pp. 181-88)

This ignorance is made more convincing by being extended to a misunderstanding of the forces leading him to the murder. Macbeth does not really understand that he has two spurs, besides his own vaulting ambition, 'to prick the sides' [I. vii. 26] of his intent. The first of these, the witches and their prophecy, might seem in no way to mitigate his responsibility, since he chooses wilfully to misinterpret what they say. But to reason in this way is again to overplay the role of logic in our dramatic experience. Surely the effect on the spectator is complex: while it is true that Macbeth ought to realize that if they are true oracles both parts of their prophecy must be fulfilled, it is also true that almost any man could be thrown off his moral balance by such supernatural confirmations. His misunderstanding is thus obvious and dramatically effective and at the same time quite forgivable.

The second force which Macbeth does not understand works less equivocally for our sympathy. While Lady Macbeth fills several functions in the play, beyond her great inherent interest as a character, her chief task, as the textbook commonplace has it, is to incite and confuse Macbeth—and thus ultimately to excuse him. Her rhetoric is brilliant whether we think of it as designed to sway Macbeth or as designed to convince the spectators that Macbeth is worth bothering about. (pp. 188-89)

His tragic error, then, is at least three-fold: he does not understand the two forces working upon him from outside; he

does not understand the difference between 'bloody execution' in civilian life and in military life; and he does not understand his own character—he does not know what will be the effects of the act on his own future happiness. Only one of these— the misunderstanding of the weird sisters—can be considered similar to, say, Iphigenia's ignorance of her brother's identity. The hero here must be really aware, in advance, of the wickedness of his act. The more aware he can be—and still commit the act convincingly—the greater the regret felt by the spectator.

All of these points are illustrated powerfully in the contrast between the final words of Malcolm concerning Macbeth— 'This dead butcher and his fiend-like queen' [V. ix. 35]—and the spectator's own feelings toward Macbeth at the same point. We judge Macbeth, as Shakespeare intends, not merely for his actions but in the light of the total impression of the play. Malcolm and Macduff do not know Macbeth and the forces that have worked on him; the spectator does know him and can feel great pity that a man with so much potentiality for greatness should have fallen so low and should be so thoroughly misjudged. The pity is that everything was not otherwise, when it so easily could have been otherwise. The conclusion brings a flood of relief that the awful blunder has played itself out, that Macbeth has at last been able to die, still valiant, and is forced no longer to go on enduring the knowledge of what he has become. (pp. 189-90)

Wayne Booth, ''Shakespeare's Tragic Villain,'' in Shakespeare's Tragedies: An Anthology of Modern Criticism, *edited by Laurence Lerner, 1963. Reprint by Penguin Books, 1968, pp. 180-90.*

JAN KOTT (essay date 1964)

[*Kott is a Polish-born critic and professor of English and comparative literature now residing in the United States. In his well-known study* Shakespeare, Our Contemporary, *originally published in Polish as* Szkice o Szekspirze *in 1964, he interprets several of the plays as presenting a tragic vision of history. Kott calls this historical pattern the Grand Mechanism. In the following commentary on* Macbeth, *Kott, like G. Wilson Knight (1930), emphasizes the nightmarish quality of* Macbeth, *stating that the inescapable nightmare functions as the Grand Mechanism does in Shakespeare's history plays. He argues that Macbeth chooses between two visions of himself: ''between Macbeth who is afraid to kill, and Macbeth who has killed.'' But while Macbeth kills Duncan because ''he could not accept a Macbeth who would be afraid to kill a king,'' neither can he accept ''the Macbeth who has killed.'' In an effort to escape the nightmare, adds Kott, Macbeth continues to murder and reaches a threshold beyond which all killing is easy—a reaction that Kott terms the ''Auschwitz experience.'' Kott also suggests a parallel between the negative, ambiguous formulas by which Macbeth defines himself and existentialist thought. He further states that Macbeth finally dies with no belief in ''human dignity,'' dragging with him ''into nothingness as many living beings as possible''; thus, the conclusion offers no catharsis.*]

The plot of *Macbeth* does not differ from those of the Histories. But plot summaries are deceptive. Unlike Shakespeare's historical plays, *Macbeth* does not show history as the Grand Mechanism. It shows it as a nightmare. Mechanism and nightmare are different metaphors to depict the same struggle for power and the crown. But the differing metaphors reflect a difference of approach, and, even more than that, different philosophies. History, shown as a mechanism, fascinates by its very terror and inevitablity. Whereas nightmare paralyses and terrifies. In *Macbeth* history, as well as crime, is shown through personal experience. It is a matter of decision, choice and compulsion. Crime is committed on personal responsibility and has to be executed with one's own hands. Macbeth murders Duncan himself.

History in *Macbeth* is confused the way nightmares are; and, as in a nightmare, everyone is enveloped by it. Once the mechanism has been put in motion, one is apt to be crushed by it. One wades through nightmare, which gradually rises up to one's throat.

Says Macbeth:

> . . . I am in blood
> Stepp'd in so far that, should I wade no more,
> Returning were as tedious as go o'er.
>
> [III. iv. 135-37]

History in *Macbeth* is sticky and thick like a brew or blood. (pp. 85-6)

Blood in *Macbeth* is not just a metaphor; it is real blood flowing out of murdered bodies. It leaves its stains on hands and faces, on daggers and swords.

Says Lady Macbeth:

> A little water clears us of this deed.
> How easy is it then!
>
> [II. ii. 64]

But this blood cannot be washed off hands, faces, or daggers, *Macbeth* begins and ends with slaughter. There is more and more blood, everyone walks in it; it floods the stage. A production of *Macbeth* not evoking a picture of the world flooded with blood, would inevitably be false. There is something abstract about the Grand Mechanism. Richard's cruelties mean death sentences. Most of them are executed off stage. In *Macbeth,* death, crime, murder are concrete. So is history in this play; it is concrete, palpable, physical and suffocating; it means the death-rattle, raising of the sword, thrust of the dagger. *Macbeth* has been called a tragedy of ambition, and a tragedy of terror. This is not true. There is only one theme in *Macbeth:* murder. History has been reduced to its simplest form, to one image and one division: those who kill and those who are killed. (p. 87)

In no other Shakespearean tragedy is there so much talk about sleep. Macbeth has murdered sleep, and cannot sleep any more. In all Scotland no one can sleep. There is no sleep, only nightmares.

> . . . When in swinish sleep
> Their drenched natures lie as in a death. . . .
>
> [I. vii. 67-8]

Not only Macbeth and Lady Macbeth struggle with this uneasy sleep, which does not bring forgetfulness, but daytime thoughts of crime. It is the same sort of nightmare that torments Banquo.

> A heavy summons lies like lead upon me,
> And yet I would not sleep. Merciful powers,
> Restrain in me the cursed thoughts that nature
> Gives way to in repose!
>
> [II. i. 6-9]

Both sleep and food have been poisoned. In Macbeth's world—the most obsessive of all worlds created by Shakespeare—murder, thoughts of murder and fear of murder pervade everything. In this tragedy there are only two great parts, but the third *dramatis persona* is the world. We remember the faces of Macbeth and Lady Macbeth more readily, because we see more of them than of the others. But all faces have the same grimace, expressing the same kind of fear. All bodies are just as tormented. Macbeth's world is tight, and there is no escape. (pp. 88-9)

There is no tragedy without awareness. Richard III is aware of the Grand Mechanism. Macbeth is aware of the nightmare. In the world upon which murder is being imposed as fate, compulsion and inner necessity, there is only one dream: of a murder that will break the murder cycle, will be the way out of nightmare, and will mean liberation. For the thought of murder that has to be committed, murder one cannot escape from, is even worse than murder itself.

Says Macbeth:

> If it were done when 'tis done, then 'twere well
> It were done quickly. If th' assassination
> Could trammel up the consequence, . . .
>   . . . that but this blow
> Might be the be-all and the end-all here,
> But here, upon this bank and shoal of time,
> We'ld jump the life to come.
>
> [I. vii. 1-7]

The terrorist Chen in Malraux's *Condition humaine* utters one of the most terrifying sentences written in the mid-twentieth century: "A man who has never killed is a virgin." This sentence means that killing is cognition, just as, according to the Old Testament, the sexual act is cognition; it also means that the experiences of killing cannot be communicated, just as the experience of the sexual act cannot be conveyed. But this sentence means also that the act of killing changes the person who has performed it; from then on he is a different man living in a different world.

Says Macbeth after his first murder:

> . . . from this instant
> There's nothing serious in mortality;
> All is but toys; renown and grace is dead;
> The wine of life is drawn. . . .
>
> [II. iii. 92-5]

Macbeth has killed in order to put himself on a level with the world in which murder potentially and actually exists. Macbeth has killed not only to become king, but to reassert himself. He has chosen between Macbeth who is afraid to kill, and Macbeth who has killed. But Macbeth who has killed is a new Macbeth. He not only knows that one can kill, but that one must kill.

EDMUND

> . . . Know thou this, that men
> Are as the time is. To be tender-minded
> Does not become a sword. . . .

CAPTAIN

> I cannot draw a cart, nor eat dried oats;
> If it be man's work, I'll do't.
>
> [*King Lear*, V. iii. 30-9]

The above fragment is taken from *King Lear*. Edmund orders assassins to hang Cordelia in prison. Murder is man's work. What can a man do? This Nietzschean question has been put for the first time in *Macbeth*.

LADY MACBETH

    . . . Art thou afeard
To be the same in thine own act and valour
As thou art in desire? . . .

MACBETH

    Prithee, peace!
I dare do all that may become a man.
Who dares do more is none.

LADY MACBETH

That made you break this enterprise to me?

                [I. vii. 39-48]

This dialogue takes place before the murder of Duncan. After the murder Macbeth will know the answer. Not only can a man kill; a man is he who kills, and only he. Just as the animal which barks and fawns is a dog. Macbeth calls the assassins and orders them to kill Banquo and his son.

FIRST MURDERER

    We are men, my liege.

MACBETH

Ay, in the catalogue ye go for men,
As hounds and greyhounds, mongrels, spaniels, curs,
Shoughs, water-rugs, and demi-wolves are clipt
All by the name of dogs. . . .

SECOND MURDERER

    We shall, my lord,
Perform what you command us.

                [III. i. 90-126]

This for Macbeth is one end of experience. It can be called the "Auschwitz experience". A threshold has been reached past which everything is easy: "All is but toys; . . ." [II. iii. 94] But this is only part of the truth about Macbeth. Macbeth has killed the king, because he could not accept a Macbeth who would be afraid to kill a king. But Macbeth who has killed cannot accept the Macbeth who has killed. Macbeth has killed in order to get rid of a nightmare. But it is the necessity of murder that makes the nightmare. A nightmare is terrifying just because it has no end. "The night is long that never finds the day" [IV. iii. 240]. The night enveloping Macbeth is deeper and deeper. Macbeth has murdered for fear, and goes on murdering for fear. This is another part of the truth about Macbeth, but it is still not the whole truth.

In its psychology, *Macbeth* is, perhaps, the deepest of Shakespeare's tragedies. But Macbeth himself is not a character, at least not in the sense of what was meant by a character in the nineteenth century. (pp. 90-3)

From the first scenes onwards Macbeth defines himself by negation. To himself he is not the one who is, but rather the one who is not. He is immersed in the world as if in nothingness; he exists only potentially. Macbeth chooses himself, but after every act of choice he finds himself more terrifying, and more of a stranger. ". . . all that is within him does condemn / Itself for being there" [V. ii. 24-5]. The formulas by which Macbeth tries to define himself are amazingly similar to the language of the existentialists. "To be" has for Macbeth an ambiguous, or at least, double, meaning; it is a constant exasperating contradiction between existence and essence, between being "for itself" and being 'in itself".

He says:

    . . . and nothing is
But what is not.

                [I. iii. 141-42]

In a bad dream we are, and are not, ourselves, at the same time. We cannot accept ourselves, for to accept oneself would mean accepting nightmare for reality, to admit that there is nothing but nightmare, that night is not followed by day.

Says Macbeth after the murder of Duncan: "To know my deed, 'twere best not know myself" [II. ii. 70]. Macbeth recognizes that his existence is apparent rather than real, because he does not want to admit that the world he lives in is irrevocable. This world is to him a nightmare. For Richard "to be" means to capture the crown and murder all pretenders. For Macbeth "to be" means to escape, to live in another world where:

Rebellion's head rise never . . .
    . . . and our high-plac'd Macbeth
Shall live the lease of nature, pay his breath
To time and mortal custom.

                [IV. i. 97-100]

The plot and the order of history in Shakespeare's Histories and in *Macbeth* do not differ from each other. But Richard accepts the order of history and his part in it. Macbeth dreams about a world where there will be no more murders, and all murders will have been forgotten; where the dead will have been buried in the ground once and for all, and everything will begin anew. Macbeth dreams of the end of nightmare, while sinking in it more and more. He dreams of a world without crime, while becoming enmeshed in crime more and more deeply. Macbeth's last hope is that the dead will not rise:

LADY MACBETH

But in them Nature's copy's not eterne.

MACBETH

There's comfort yet! They are assailable.
Then be thou jocund.

                [III. ii. 38-40]

But the dead do rise. The appearance at the banquet of murdered Banquo's ghost is one of the most remarkable scenes in *Macbeth*. Banquo's ghost is visible to Macbeth alone. Commentators see in this scene an embodiment of Macbeth's fear and terror. There is no ghost; he is a delusion. But Shakespeare's *Macbeth* is not a psychological drama of the second half of the nineteenth century. Macbeth has dreamed of a final murder to end all murders. Now he knows: there is no such murder. (pp. 93-5)

Macbeth, the multiple murderer, steeped in blood, could not accept the world in which murder existed. In this, perhaps, consists the gloomy greatness of this character and the true tragedy of Macbeth's history. For a long time Macbeth did not want to accept the reality and irrevocability of nightmare, and could not reconcile himself to his part, as if it were somebody else's. Now he knows everything. He knows that there is no escape from nightmare, which is the human fate and condition, or—in a more modern language—the human situation. There is no other.

They have tied me to a stake. I cannot fly,
But bear-like I must fight the course.

                [V. vii. 1-2]

Before his first crime, which was the murder of Duncan, Macbeth had believed that death could come too early, or too late. "Had I but died an hour before this chance, / I had liv'd a blessed time . . ." [II. iii. 91-2]. Now Macbeth knows that death does not change anything, that it cannot change anything, that it is just as absurd as life. No more, no less. For the first time Macbeth is not afraid. "I have almost forgot the taste of fears" [V. v. 9].

There is nothing to be afraid of any more. He can accept himself at last, because he has realized that every choice is absurd, or rather, that there is no choice.

> . . . Out, out, brief candle!
> Life's but a walking shadow, a poor player,
> That struts and frets his hour upon the stage
> And then is heard no more. It is a tale
> Told by an idiot, full of sound and fury,
> Signifying nothing.
>
> [V. v. 23-8]

In the opening scenes of the tragedy there is talk about the Thane of Cawdor, who had betrayed Duncan and become an ally of the King of Norway. After the suppression of rebellion he was captured and condemned to death.

> . . . Nothing in his life
> Became him like the leaving it. He died
> As one that had been studied in his death
> To throw away the dearest thing he ow'd
> As 'twere a careless trifle.
>
> [I. iv. 7-11]

The Thane of Cawdor does not appear in *Macbeth*. All we know of him is that he has been guilty of treason and executed. Why is his death described so emphatically and in such detail? Why did Shakespeare find it necessary? After all, his expositions are never wrong. Cawdor's death, which opens the play, is necessary. It will be compared to Macbeth's death. There is something Senecan and stoic about Cawdor's cold indifference to death. Faced with utter defeat Cawdor saves what can still be saved: a noble attitude and dignity. For Macbeth attitudes are of no importance; he does not believe in human dignity any more. Macbeth has reached the limits of human experience. All he has left is contempt. The very concept of man has crumbled to pieces, and there is nothing left. The end of *Macbeth*, like the end of *Troilus and Cressida*, or *King Lear*, produces no catharsis. Suicide is either a protest, or an admission of guilt. Macbeth does not feel guilty, and there is nothing for him to protest about. All he can do before he dies is to drag with him into nothingness as many living beings as possible. This is the last consequence of the world's absurdity. Macbeth is still unable to blow the world up. But he can go on murdering till the end. (pp. 95-7)

> Jan Kott, "'Macbeth' or Death-Infected," in his Shakespeare, Our Contemporary, *translated by Boleslaw Taborski, 1964. Reprint by W. W. Norton & Company, 1974, pp. 85-97.*

ROBERT B. HEILMAN (essay date 1964)

[*In the following excerpt, Heilman discusses Shakespeare's concern with anagnorisis, or "self-discovery," in* Macbeth *and other tragedies. He notes that while Othello and Lear experience an increasing awareness of themselves, Macbeth avoids self-knowledge. Heilman states that Macbeth's imaginings are the result of his troubled psyche's efforts to "break into open consciousness."*

Lady Macbeth, he continues, encourages Macbeth's denial of anagnorisis, but also illustrates "the eventual psychic bankruptcy" of one who avoids "a saving self-knowledge." Heilman concludes that Macbeth finally uses courageous violence as a barrier against knowing himself. For Heilman's additional comments on Macbeth, *see the excerpt below, 1966.*]

In the three dramas that, written in a relatively short time, bring the period of tragedies to a climax, Shakespeare makes increasingly extensive use of anagnorisis. His interest grows in intensity, and his point of view changes. At no time does he cherish illusions about man's capacity for self-knowledge, but in *Macbeth* we find his most hardbitten view of man's resistance to knowing. The resistance is less compulsory and obsessive in *Othello* and *Lear*. But the slightly earlier dramas differ from each other too. In *Othello* Shakespeare is equally absorbed by the external agency that tortures the hero until he does evil; the dual focus extends the preparation for the main act of violence; and hence the period of illumination and retrospection has to be shorter. We might say that writing Act V, Scene ii of *Othello* really set Shakespeare's imagination off on the dramatic possibilities of anagnorisis, and that in *Lear* he explored these extensively: Lear explodes into injustice in the first scene, so that more than four acts are left for the drama of self-understanding. Macbeth, in turn, knows from the very beginning what is what, and his utterly different problem is to escape what he knows. (p. 91)

[If] Lear yields to knowledge more and more, Macbeth yields to knowledge less and less, and Lady Macbeth seems impregnable to its attacks. Only in retrospect can we measure the pauperizing cost of her apparent invulnerability. When a protagonist "knows" that his course is morally intolerable, but strains frantically against that knowledge lest it impair his obsessive pursuit of the course, the tension between knowing and willing may itself destroy him. In Lady Macbeth Shakespeare catches the eventual psychic bankruptcy of the assured, plunging personality that can fight off, with a façade of nonchalance, all assaults of a saving self-knowledge, not only for herself but for her husband as well. There is a cumulative, but secret, drain of resources; the prodigal expenditure of will exhausts the soul. Lady Macbeth is the spiritual counterpart of the splendidly robust person who seems immune to all ailment and then, in a crisis apparently well within his powers, is suddenly, even mysteriously, overborne. Understandably, Shakespeare dealt with the type only once: it affords a hard, flaring brilliance during the high arc of its career, but then drops down and leaves the writer of tragedy nothing to go on with. Consciousness itself crumbles under the blows of the reality it will not admit, so that it can never reorient itself to the rejected truth; indeed it cannot even carry on with the programmatic action to which it has committed itself solely. The very arena for the climactic tragic action, the drama of seeing, is gone.

In Macbeth there is nothing of his lady's seemingly passionless closure against irruptive truth. From the beginning the troubles in the psyche break into open consciousness. They are pushed down, and then there they are again, up, pressing, twisting Macbeth into doubt or anguish or horror; and then gone, as if banished. The contrast between King and Queen invites us to suppose that a little knowledge is a saving thing: a touch of neurosis forestalls psychosis; a passing illness acknowledges symbolically a truth that, fought off unyieldingly, must in the end assert itself by blasting utterly the one who would exclude it utterly. Faustus and Macbeth both "see things"; yet this temporary ailing is a therapy for or preventive of a worse one, such as Lady Macbeth's; having survived it, each is able to go on in a chosen course, as if feverless, unweakened, safely beyond the challenges of knowledge. Lady Macbeth is a utopian of a sort; Faustus and Macbeth are politic men, freed from inner chains against action in the world; and to name their "success" is to acknowledge the subtle moral diminishment that is in the price.

With Macbeth, moments of acknowledgment bring guilt; yet his guilt can suddenly metamorphose into a sense of consequences, or a fear of them, or even a deflecting gesture. It is tempting to say that he is caught in a dilemma of truth or consequences: which shall he attend to? He might save himself by admitting what he knows instead of pushing it down below consciousness: "Our designs are evil; we cannot go on with them". Yet instead of asking "Is this course morally tenable?" he asks, "Can we get away with it?" "If the assassination / Could trammel up the consequence, and catch / With his surcease success; . . ." [I. vii. 2-4]. "Bloody instructions . . . return / To plague th'inventor" [I. vii. 9-10]. Duncan's "virtues / Will plead like angels, trumpet-tongu'd, against / The deep damnation of his taking-off" [I. vii. 18-20]. Yet the soliloquy as a whole is fascinating because it reveals a sense of truth competing with a sense of consequences. The Macbeth who can cite Duncan's merits and his own obligations, who can speak of the "murderer", of "deep damnation", and of his own "vaulting ambition", has not yet won his quasi-victory against knowledge. Indeed his words to Lady Macbeth, "We will proceed no further in this business" [I. vii. 31], might imply the opposite: a surrender to knowledge. It is not that, however; it is a medley of moral acumen and practical misgiving, of "This may not be undertaken", and "This cannnot be carried through". As soon as Lady Macbeth taxes him with a failure in manly resolution, he pushes knowledge away again, and asks only, "If we should fail?" [I. vii. 59]. She can answer this, and he drifts into resolution. The play implicitly defines resolution: a denial of consequences and a narcotizing of what one knows. If narcosis were not needed or were totally effective, all we would have left would be bloody intrigue, the overt, visible mechanics of triumph or failure in the campaign. This is the kind of drama that Macbeth longs to find himself in; Shakespeare grasps this human lust for pure, insentient action, and tailors his drama to the long shrinking and hardening that must be undergone before one can get down to the tranquillity of bare life-and-death struggle. Resolution is not strong enough to enable Macbeth to use the dagger without first apostrophizing it, sighting "gouts of blood" upon it, and soliloquizing on the nocturnal moves of Witchcraft and Murder [II. i. 33ff.]. After he has done "it", he is almost beaten down by the resurgent knowledge that he has been fencing with and dancing away from; in a close parallel to Faustus' difficulty in sealing his blood-bond with the devil, Macbeth is physically unable to say "Amen" [II. ii. 26]. Nurturing such thoughts, says Lady Macbeth, "will make us mad" [II. ii. 31]; she knows more than she knows she knows. As she pulls Macbeth away from the dangerous abyss of insight, all her key terms show her tack to be the denial that his knowledge is knowledge. It is all an error, a "foolish thought" [II. ii. 19]. "Consider it not so deeply"; don't be "brainsickly"; "Be not lost / So poorly in your thoughts" [II. ii. 27, 43, 68-9]. So he does not stay lost in the realm of truth, but finds himself in action—in snatching the crown and averting consequences. In his next soliloquy the principal theme is success—"to be safely thus" [III. i. 48]; then he coolly coaches the murderers. Still there are "terrible dreams" and "torture of the mind" [III. ii. 18, 21]—"scorpions", of truth, perhaps, but more likely of consequences. The fear of what one may do to others has turned

into the fear of what others may do to one in return. The last flare-up of knowledge—knowledge forced away and then slipping back deviously as illness—is in Macbeth's hallucinations at the banquet: the Faustian brainsickliness, the moral malaise as nervous crisis. That surmounted, there is a kind of freedom for action, a release of all energies into program: for Faustus, traversing the world in quest and jest; for Macbeth, trying to insure his world with killings that can never quite stop. He is all caught up in fierce staff work. He finds the witches' heath less a Delphi, revealing a larger truth to man's dim consciousness, than a dopester's corner, with tips on how the different thoroughbreds will be running in the royal handicap. So Macbeth becomes more "resolute" than ever before, dynamically thrusting ahead in the tactics of surviving the field. Only in the few "I am sick at heart" lines [V. iii. 19ff], reminiscent of Faustus' occasional moments of distress among popes and emperors, does Macbeth suffer, for a moment or two, the pangs of knowledge. For this corrosive, fighting is the required antidote.

Faustus ends in despair, somehow yielding to the horror of his fate through inability to repent: despair as passivity. Macbeth comes to despair too, the profound despair of activity. For both, the comparable and yet divergent movements of the soul are brilliantly done. In the end Faustus knows, only too well: "I know evil so great that I cannot escape it". Macbeth will not know: "I fight fiercely, and thus escape knowledge". The customary way of describing such a struggle as Macbeth's final one is to say that the protagonist "fought desperately": the very familiarity of the phrase reveals the representativeness of the situation, or at least the human mind's representative way of giving it moral form. "Desperately" implies a noble frenzy against excessive odds, an unconditional non-surrender. Yet the well worn adverb, which in popular usage carries a note of moral achievement, is exactly the word to expose a different inner truth. What on some occasions or to some eyes may appear a victory of spirit, a triumph of heart against destined victors, is at Dunsinane the kind of failure signified by the word *despair*: a failure to imagine any other course of action, a rejection of perceiving. Acting violently is not only a surrogate for knowing, but a barrier against knowing. Yet this acting is made obligatory, forced on one. "They have tied me to a stake" [V. vii. I]—*they:* others have put this upon me, and I will be brave, and claim the pity vouchsafed to the doomed. It is one more fold of insulation against the harsh air of truth. Courage to face others becomes equivalent to, perhaps finer than, the courage to face oneself.

Thus Shakespeare finishes off, very profoundly, his analysis of a basic kind of personality—of the man who can look at himself, who at first has to fight off the inclination to do so, who succeeds for practical purposes in not doing so, and eventually fights instead of doing so. Macbeth has got far away from anagnorisis; now he easily substitutes other modes of conduct that, in appropriate contexts, make a claim upon respect: philosophic reflections and heroic actions. He discourses on the absurdity of existence ("a tale / Told by an idiot" [V. v. 26-7]) and vows a fight to the death ("I will not yield" [V. viii. 27]). Early in the play he had to admit, "Look on [what I have done] again I dare not" [II. ii. 49]; to cry, "Stars, hide your fires; / Let not light see my black and deep desires" ([I. iv. 50-1]; cf. Lady Macbeth's "Come, thick night, . . . That my keen knife see not . . . " [I. v. 50-2]); and again to pray, "Come, seeling night" [III. ii. 46]. The extensive imagery of seeing and night work together in constant reminders of the knowledge that continually breaks out into painful view, and of the perpetual need to shut it off. Twice Macbeth states his problem literally, explicitly: "False face must hide what the false heart doth know" [I. vii. 82] and "To know my deed, 'twere best not know myself" [II. ii. 70]. Conceal knowledge, then eliminate it: it is a major theme of the play in which Shakespeare explores, for the last time in full scale, the complex subject of man's mingled openness to and resistance to self-knowledge. (pp. 94-7)

Robert B. Heilman, "'Twere Best Not Know Myself: Othello, Lear, Macbeth," in Shakespeare 400: Essays by American Scholars on the Anniversary of the Poet's Birth, edited by James G. McManaway, Holt, Rinehart and Winston, Inc., 1964, pp. 89-98.

ROBERT B. HEILMAN (essay date 1966)

[*In the following commentary on* Macbeth, *Heilman, like Arthur Quiller-Couch (1918), Wayne Booth (1963), and Bertrand Evans (1979), explores Shakespeare's attempts to evoke sympathy for Macbeth, despite his increasing villainy. Heilman asserts that Shakespeare "so manages the situation that we become Macbeth, or at least assent to complicity with him" and "accept ourselves as murderers." He then comments that Macbeth "agonizes more than he antagonizes" and that we empathize with his fears and anxieties. According to Heilman, even after the murder of Macduff's family, the point at which "we are most likely to be divorced from Macbeth," Macbeth is shown to be meditative, lonely, and "sick at heart," and, thus, not completely reproachable. Heilman concludes that while there may be some value in allowing a reader to "experience empathy with a murderer and thus come into a more complete 'feeling knowledge' of what human beings are like," he also points out Macbeth's moral deficiency and states that "the reader ends his life with and in Macbeth in a way that demands too little of him."*]

The critical uneasiness with the character of Macbeth is different from the usual feelings—uncertainty, attentiveness, curiosity, passion to examine, and so on—stirred by an obscure or elusive character, because it springs from a disturbing sense of discrepancy not evoked, for instance, by Shakespeare's other tragic heroes. We expect the tragic protagonist to be an expanding character, one who grows in awareness and spiritual largeness; yet Macbeth is to all intents a contracting character, who seems to discard large areas of consciousness as he goes, to shrink from multilateral to unilateral being (we try to say it isn't so by deflating the Macbeth of Acts I and II and inflating the Macbeth of Acts IV and V). The diminishing personality is of course not an anomaly in literature, whether in him we follow a gradual decrease of moral possibility or discover an essential parvanimity, but this we expect in satire . . . , not tragedy. This source of uneasiness with Macbeth, however, is secondary; the primary source is a technical matter, Shakespeare's remarkable choice of point of view—that of this ambitious man who, in [Kenneth] Muir's words that sum up the contracting process, 'becomes a villain'. We have to see through his eyes, be in his skin; for us, this is a great breach of custom, and in the effort at accommodation we do considerable scrambling. When we share the point of view of Hamlet, we experience the fear of evil action and of evil inaction; when we share the point of Othello and Lear, we experience passionate, irrational action whose evil is not apprehended or foreseen; but when we share the point of view of Macbeth, we have to experience the deliberate choice of evil. Hence a disquiet altogether distinguishable from the irresoluteness of mind before, let us say, some apparent contradictions in Othello.

The problem is like that which usually comes up when readers must adopt the point of view of a character in whom there are ambiguities. Unless structure is based on contrasts, point of view ordinarily confers authority; but discomforts, which invariably lead to disagreements, arise when authority apparently extends to matters which, on aesthetic, rational, psychological, or moral grounds, the reader finds it difficult to countenance. 'Disagreements', of course, implies studious recollection in tranquillity, or rather, untranquillity; what we are concerned with in this discussion is the immediate, unanalysed imaginative experience which precedes the effort to clarify or define. We are assuming that the person experiencing *Macbeth* is naturally carried into an identification with Macbeth which, if incomplete, is still more far-reaching than that with anyone else in the play. (p. 13)

Behind our condemnation of trivial literature, whether we call it 'sentimental', 'meretricious', or something else, lies the sense that the characters whom for the moment we become give us an inadequate or false sense of reality, call into action too few of our human potentialities. Hence 'tragedy' tends not simply to designate a genre, in which there may be widely separated levels of excellence, but to become an honorific term: it names a noble enterprise, the action of a literary structure which compels us to get at human truth by knowing more fully what we are capable of—'knowing', not by formal acts of cognition but by passing imaginatively through revelatory experiences. In a morality we see a demonstration of what happens; in tragedy we act out what happens, undergoing a kind of kinaesthetic initiation into conduct we would not ordinarily acknowledge as belonging to us. The problem is how far this process of illuminating induction can go without running into resistance that impedes or derails the tragic experience, without exciting self-protective counter-measures such as retreating from tragic co-existence with the hero to censorious observation of him from a distant knoll. *Macbeth* at least permits this way out by its increasingly extensive portrayal, in Acts IV and V, of the counterforces whom we see only as high-principled seekers of justice. Do we, so to speak, defect to them because Macbeth, unlike Lear and Othello, moves into a greater darkness in which we can no longer discern our own lineaments? Do we, then, turn tragedy into melodrama or morality?

That, of course, is a later question. The prior question is the mode of our relationship with Macbeth when he kills Duncan; here we have to consent to participation in a planned murder, or at least tacitly accept our capability of committing it. The act of moral imagination is far greater, as we have seen, than that called for by the germinal misdeeds of Lear or the murder by Othello, since these come out of emotional frenzies where our tolerance, or even forgiveness, is so spontaneous that we need not disguise our kinship with those who realize in action what we act in fantasy. Yet technically Shakespeare so manages the situation that we become Macbeth, or at least assent to complicity with him, instead of shifting to that simple hostility evoked by the melodramatic treatment of crime. We accept ourselves as murderers, so to speak, because we also feel the strength of our resistance to murder. The initial Macbeth has a fullness of human range that makes him hard to deny; though a kind of laziness makes us naturally vulnerable to the solicitation of some narrow-gauge characters, we learn by experience and discipline to reject these (heroes of cape and sword, easy masters of the world, pure devils, simple victims); and correspondingly we are the more drawn in by those with a large store of human possibilities, good and evil. Macbeth can act as courageous patriot [I. ii. 35], discover that he has dreamed of the throne ('. . . why do you start . . . ?' [I. iii. 51]), entertain the 'horrid image' of murdering Duncan [I. iii. 135], be publicly rewarded by the king (I, iv), be an affectionate husband (I, v), survey, with anguished clarity, the motives and consequences of the imagined deed; reject it; feel the strength of his wife's persuasion, return to 'this terrible feat' [I. vii. 80]; undergo real horrors of anticipation [II. i. 31ff.] and of realization that he has actually killed Duncan [II. ii. 14ff.]. Here is not a petty scoundrel but an extraordinary man, so capacious in feeling and motive as to have a compelling representativeness; we cannot adopt him selectively, feel a oneness with some parts of him and reject others; we become the murderer as well as the man who can hardly tolerate, in prospect or retrospect, the idea of murder. (pp. 13-14)

If it be a function of tragedy, as we have suggested, to amplify man's knowledge of himself by making him discover, through imaginative action, the moral capabilities to which he may ordinarily be blind, then Shakespeare, in the first two acts of *Macbeth,* has so managed his tools that the function is carried out superlatively well. He leads the reader on to accept himself in a role that he would hardly dream of as his. If it be too blunt to say that he becomes a murderer, at least he feels murderousness to be as powerful as a host of motives more familiar to consciousness. Whether he knows it or not, he knows something more about himself. It may be that 'knows' takes us too far into the realm of the impalpable, but to use it is at least to say metaphorically that the reader remains 'with' Macbeth instead of drifting away into non-participation and censure. Shakespeare's dramaturgic feat should not be unappreciated.

That behind him, Shakespeare moves ahead and takes on a still greater difficulty: the maintaining of identity, his and ours, with a character who, after a savage initial act, goes on into other monstrosities, gradually loses more of his human range, contracts, goes down hill. Surely this is the most demanding technical task among the tragedies. Othello and Lear both grow in knowledge; however reluctantly and incompletely, they come into a sense of what they have done, and advance in powers of self-placement. With them we have a sense of recovery, which paradoxically accompanies the making of even destructive discoveries. Renouncing blindness is growth. Macbeth does not attract us into kinship in this way; his own powers of self-recognition seem to have been squandered on the night of the first murder and indirectly in the dread before Banquo's ghost. Nevertheless there are passages in which he has been felt to be placing and judging himself. There may indeed be something of tragic selfknowlege in the man who says that he has 'the gracious Duncan . . . murder'd' and

> mine eternal jewel
> Given to the common enemy of man;
>
> [III. i. 65-8]

yet he is not saying 'I have acted evilly', much less 'I repent of my evil conduct', but rather, 'I have paid a high price— and for what? To make Banquo the father of kings.' Macbeth is not so simple and crude as not to know that the price is high, but his point is that for a high price he ought to be guaranteed the best goods; and in prompt search of the best goods he elaborates the remorselessly calculating rhetoric by which he inspirits the murderers to ambush Banquo and Fleance. Again, he can acknowledge his and Lady Macbeth's nightmares and declare buried Duncan better off than they, but have no thought at all of the available means of mitigating this wretchedness; the much stronger motives appear in his pre-

ceding statement 'We have scorch'd the snake, not kill'd it' and his following one, 'O, full of scorpions is my mind . . . that Banquo, and his Fleance, lives' [III. ii. 13, 36-7]. The serpents of enmity and envy clearly have much more bite than the worm of conscience.

> I am in blood
> Stepp'd in so far
>
> [III. iv. 135-36]

encourages some students to speak as if Macbeth were actuated by a sense of guilt, but since no expectable response to felt guilt inhibits his arranging, very shortly, the Macduff murders, it seems more prudent to see in these words only a technical summary of his political method. In 'the sere, the yellow leaf' lines Macbeth's index of the deprivations likely to afflict him in later years [V. iii. 23 ff.] suggests to some readers an acute moral awareness; it seems rather a regretful notice of social behaviour, such as would little trouble the consciousness of a man profoundly concerned about the quality of his deeds and the state of his soul. Finally, in Macbeth's battlefield words to Macduff—

> my soul is too much charg'd
> With blood of thine already—
>
> [V. viii. 5-6]

some critics have detected remorse. It may be so, but in the general context of actions of a man increasingly apt in the sanguinary and freed from refinement of scruple, there is much to be said for the suggestion that he is 'rationalizing his fear' [Kenneth Muir]; possibly, too, he is unconsciously placating the man who has most to avenge and of whom the First Apparition has specifically warned him [IV. i. 72].

Since different Shakespearians have been able to find in such passages a continuance of genuine moral sensitivity in Macbeth, it is possible that for the non-professional reader they do indeed belong to the means by which a oneness with Macbeth is maintained. If so, then we have that irony by which neutral details in an ugly man's portrait have enough ambiguity to help win a difficult assent to him. However, a true change of heart is incompatible with a retention of the profits secured by even the temporarily hardened heart, and the fact is that once Macbeth has become king, all of his efforts are directed to hanging on to the spoils of a peculiarly obnoxious murder. Shakespeare has chosen to deal not only with an impenitent, though in many ways regretful, man, but with one whose crime has been committed only to secure substantial worldly advantages (in contrast with the wrongs done by Lear and Othello). Perhaps what the play 'says' is that such a crime has inevitable consequences, that worldly profit—goods, honour, power—is so corrupting that, once committed to it, the hero can never really abjure it, can never really repent and seeks ways of spirtual alteration, though he may cry out against the thorns and ugliness of the road he cannot leave. However far such a theory can be carried, it is plain that Macbeth, once he has taken the excruciatingly difficult first step on the new route, discovers in himself the talents for an unsurrenderable athleticism in evil.

The artist's problem is that for a reader to accompany such a character and to share in his intensifying depravity might become intolerable; the reader might simply flee to the salvation of condemning the character. This does not happen. For, having chosen a very difficult man to establish our position—to give us shoes and skin and eyes and feeling—Shakespeare so manages the perspective that we do not escape into another position. As with all his tragic heroes, Shakespeare explores the point of view of self, the self-defending and self-justifying motions of mind and heart; alert as we are to self-protectiveness in others, we still do not overtly repudiate that of Macbeth. That is, Macbeth finds ways of thinking about himself and his dilemmas that we find congenial, and, even more than that, ways of feeling which we easily share. . . . [Our] murderer is a man who suffers too much, as it were, really to be a murderer; he agonizes more than he antagonizes. After the murder, we next see him in a painfully taxing and challenging position—the utter necessity of so acting in public, at a moment of frightful public calamity, that neither his guilt will be revealed nor his ambition threatened. The pressure on him shifts to us, who ought to want him caught right there. Can he bring it off? Can we bring it off? In some way we become the terribly threatened individual, the outnumbered solitary antagonist; further, our own secret self is at stake, all our evil, long so precariously covered over, in danger of being exposed, and we of ruin. (pp. 15-17)

Macbeth is in danger of degenerating from Everyman into monster, that is, of pushing us from unspoken collusion to spoken judgment, when he coolly plots against Banquo. But Shakespeare moves Macbeth quickly into a recital of motives and distresses that invite an assent of feeling. Macbeth's important 25-line soliloquy [III. i. 47-71] is in no sense a formal apologia, but it has the effect of case-making by the revelation of emotional urgencies whose force easily comes home to us. There are three of these urgencies. The first is fear, that especial kind of fear that derives from insecurity: ' . . . to be safely thus' [III. i. 48] is a cry so close to human needs that it can make us forget that the threat to safety is made by justice. The fear is of Banquo, a man of 'dauntless temper', of 'wisdom' [III. i. 51-2]; we can credit ourselves with Macbeth's ability and willingness to discriminate at the same time that, unless we make an improbable identification with Banquo, we can enter into the lesser man's sense of injury and his inclination to purge himself of second-class moral citizenship. The second great appeal is that to the horror of being in a cul de sac, of feeling no continuity into something beyond the present: all that we have earned will be nothing if we have but a 'fruitless crown', 'a barren sceptre', 'No son' [III. i. 60-3]. It is the Sisters that did this; 'they' are treating us unfairly, inflicting a causeless deprivation. Our Everyman's share of paranoia is at work. Yet the price has been a high one ('vessel of my peace', loss of 'mine eternal jewel' [III. i. 66-7]); it is as if a bargain had been unfulfilled, and we find ourselves sharing the third emotional pressure—resentment at a chicanery of events which need not be borne.

The anxiety in the face of constant threats, the pain at being cut off from the future, the bitterness of the wretched bargain—these emotions, since they may belong to the most upright life, tend to inhibit our making a conscious estimate of the uprightness of the man who experiences them. This may be a sufficient hedge against our splitting away from Macbeth when he is whipping up the Murderers against Banquo. But since Macbeth can trick us into the desire to 'get away with it', or into discovering that we can have this desire, it may be that even the subornation of murder evokes a distant, unidentified, and unacknowledgeable compliance. (pp. 17-18)

At the banquet scene the courtesy and breeding of the host and hostess hardly seem that of vulgar criminals, from whom we would quickly spring away into our better selves. But before the Ghost appears, Macbeth learns of the escape of Fleance,

and he speaks words that appeal secretly to two modes of responsiveness. He introduces the snake image from [III. ii. 14]: as for Banquo, 'There the grown serpent lies', but then there's Fleance:

> the worm that's fled
> Hath nature that in time will venom breed.
> [III. iv. 28-9]

It is not that we rationally accept Macbeth's definition of father and son, but that we share his desperateness as destined victim; and his image for the victimizing forces, as long as it is not opposed openly in the context, is one to evoke the fellowship of an immemorial human fear. This, however, tops off a subtler evocation of sympathy, Macbeth's

> I am cabin'd, cribb'd, confin'd, bound in
> To saucy doubts and fears.
> [III. iv. 23-4]

The new image for fear, which we have already been compelled to feel, is peculiarly apt and constraining: it brings into play the claustrophobic distress that can even become panic. We do not pause for analysis, stand off, and say, 'It is the claustrophobia of crime'; rather the known phobia maintains our link with the criminal. Then, of course, the moral responsiveness implied by the appearance of the Ghost and by Macbeth's terror make a more obvious appeal, for here the traditional 'good man' is evident. Not only does he again become something of a victim, but the royal pair draw us into their efforts to save a situation as dangerous as it is embarrassing and humiliating. They are in such straits that we cannot now accuse them, much less triumph over them. Macbeth's demoralizing fear, finally, works in a paradoxical way: fear humanizes the warrior and thus brings us closer to him, while his inevitable reaction from it into almost hyperbolic courage, with its conscious virility ('Russian bear', 'Hyrcan tiger', etc. [III. iv, 99 ff.]), strikes a different chord of consent. From now on until the end, indeed, Macbeth is committed to a bravery, not unspontaneous but at once compensating and desperate—a bravura of bravery—that it is natural for us to be allied with.

The danger point is that at which the admired bravery and its admired accompaniment, resolution (such as appears in the visit to the Witches, IV, i), are distorted into the ruthlessness of the Macduff murders. Here we are most likely to be divorced from Macbeth, to cease being actors of a role and become critics of it. At any rate, Shakespeare takes clear steps to 'protect' Macbeth's position. That 'make assurance double sure' [IV. i. 83] has become a cliché is confirmatory evidence that the motive is well-nigh universal; getting rid of Macduff becomes almost an impersonal safety measure, additionally understandable because of the natural wish to 'sleep in spite of thunder' [IV. i. 86]. We come close to pitying his failure to grasp the ambiguity of the oracles, for we can sense our own naiveté and wishful thinking at work; and his disillusionment and emptiness on learning that Banquo's line will inherit the throne, are not so alien to us that Macbeth's retaliatory passion is unthinkable. Shakespeare goes ahead with the risk: we see one of the cruel murders, and the next time Macbeth appears, he is hardly attractive either in his almost obsessive denying of fear [V. iii. 1-10] or in his letting his tension explode in pointless abuse of his servant, partly for fearfulness [V. iii. 11-17]. Still, the impulses are ones we can feel. Now, after Macbeth has been on the verge of breaking out into the savage whom we could only repudiate, things take a different turn, and Macbeth comes back toward us as more than a loathsome criminal. He is 'sick at heart' [V. iii. 19]—words that both speak to a kindred feeling and deny that the speaker is a brute. He meditates on approaching age [V. iii. 22ff.], with universality of theme and dignity of style teasing us into a fellowship perhaps strengthened by respect for the intellectual candour with which he lists the blessings he has forfeited. Above all he has a desperately sick wife: pressed from without, still he must confer with the doctor and in grief seek remedies for a 'mind diseas'd', 'a rooted sorrow', 'that perilous stuff / Which weighs upon the heart' [V. iii. 40-5]. Shakespeare makes him even extend this humane concern, either literally or with a wry irony that is still not unattractive, to the health of Scotland:

find her disease,
And purge it to a sound and pristine health.
[V. iii. 51-2]

Along with all of the troubles that he meets, more often than not with sad equanimity, he must also face crucial desertions: 'the thanes fly from me' [V. iii. 49]. Like us all, he tells his troubles to the doctor. He has become an underdog, quite another figure from the cornered thug, supported by a gang of sinister loyalty, that he might be. This athlete in evil, as we called him earlier, has had to learn endurance and endure, if we may be forgiven, the loneliness of the long-distance runner. Against such solitude we hardly turn with reproof.

Macbeth opened the scene crying down fear; he goes on with three more denials of fear, one at the end [V. iii. 32, 36, 59]; now we are able to see in the repetition an effort to talk down deep misgivings, and the hero again approximates Everyman, ourselves. When Macbeth next appears, just before the battle, it is the same: he opens and closes the scene literally or implicitly denying fear, even though the prophecy of his end seems miraculously fulfilled [V. v. 1-15, 50-1]. Meanwhile the queen's death is reported, and the warrior, moved but finely controlled, turns grief into contemplation, with the seductiveness of common thought in uncommon language. The closing battle scene is a series of denials of fear, appealing to both pity and admiration. Some details are instinctively ingratiating. 'They have tied me to a stake; I cannot fly' [V. viii. 1]—oneself as the victim of others bent on cruel sport. 'Why should I play the Roman fool . . . ?' [V. viii. 1]—no moral retreat, no opting out of adversity. 'I will not yield' [V. viii. 27]—the athlete's last span of endurance, fight against all odds. (pp. 18-20)

To be convinced of Macbeth's retention of our sympathy may seem to imply a denial of our sympathy to Malcolm, Macduff, and the conquering party. By no means: obviously we share their passions whenever these control the action, and we may even cheer them on. Yet we do not remain fixedly and *only* with them, as we do with Richmond and his party in *Richard III*, and with such forces in all dramas with a clearly melodramatic structure. When the anti-Macbeth leaders occupy the stage, we are unable not to be at one with them; but the significant thing is that when his point of view is resumed, Macbeth again draws us back, by the rather rich means that we have examined, into our old collusion. After III, vi, when we first see committed opposition to Macbeth (' . . . this our suffering country, / Under a hand accurs'd!' [III. vi, 48-9]), the two sides alternate on the stage until they come together in battle. In one scene we have the rather easy, and certainly reassuring, identification with the restorers of order; in the next, the strange, disturbing emotional return to the camp of the

outnumbered tyrant. We move back and forth between two worlds and are members of both. As a contemporary novelist says of a character who is watching fox and hounds, 'She wanted it to get away, yet when she saw the hounds she also wanted them to catch it' [Veronica Henriques, *The Face I Had*].

Macbeth, in other words, has a complexity of form which goes beyond that normally available to melodrama and morality play, where the issue prevents ambiguity of feeling and makes us clear-headed partisans. Whether *Macbeth* goes on beyond this surmounting of melodramatic limitations to high achievement as tragedy is the final problem. It turns, I believe, on Shakespeare's treatment of Macbeth, that is, on whether this retains the complexity that cannot quite be replaced by the kind of complexities that *Macbeth* does embrace. Here, of course, we are in the area of our mode of response to character, where all is elusive and insecure, and we can only be speculative. What I have proposed, in general, is that, because of the manifold claims that Macbeth makes upon our sympathy, we are drawn into identification with him in his whole being; one might say that he tricks us into accepting more than we expect or realize. If it is true that we are led to experience empathy with a murderer and thus to come into a more complete 'feeling knowledge' of what human beings are like (tragic experience as the catharsis of self-ignorance), then Shakespeare has had a success which is not trivial. (pp. 21-2)

Shakespeare first chooses a protagonist who in action is worse than the other main tragic heroes, and then tends to make him better than other tragic heroes, in effect to make him now one, and now the other. Shakespeare had to protect Macbeth against the unmixed hostility that the mere villain would evoke; perhaps he over-protected him, letting him do all his villainies indeed, but providing him with an excess of devices for exciting the pity, warmth, and approval which prompt forgetfulness of the villainies. If critics have, as Knights protested [see excerpt above, 1933], sentimentalized Macbeth, it may be that the text gives them more ground than has been supposed, that Shakespeare's own sympathy with Macbeth went beyond that which every artist owes to the evil man whom he wants to realize. We may be driven to concluding that Shakespeare has kept us at one with Macbeth, in whom the good man is all but annihilated by the tragic flaw, by making him the flawed man who is all but annihilated by the tragic goodness—that is, the singular appeal of the man trapped, disappointed, deserted, deprived of a wife, finished, but unwhimpering, contemplative, unyielding. If that is so, Shakespeare has kept us at one with a murderer by making him less than, or other than, a murderer.

This may seem a perverse conclusion after we have been pointing to the 'risks' Shakespeare took by showing Macbeth lengthily arranging the murder of Banquo and by having the murder of Lady Macduff and her children done partly on stage. The risk there, however, was of our separation from Macbeth as in melodrama; the risk here is of an empathic union on too easy grounds. For what is finally and extraordinarily spared Macbeth is the ultimate rigour of self-confrontation, the act of knowing directly what he has been and done. We see the world judging Macbeth, but not Macbeth judging himself. That consciousness of the nature of the deed which he has at the murder of Duncan gives way to other disturbances, and whatever sense of guilt, if any, may be inferred from his later distresses (we surveyed, early in section iii, the passages sometimes supposed to reveal a confessional or penitent strain), is far from an open facing and defining of the evil done—the murders, of course, the attendant lying, and, as is less often noted, the repeated bearing of false witness. . . . Of Cawdor, whose structural relationship to Macbeth is often mentioned, we are told that

> very frankly he confess'd his treasons,
> Implor'd your Highness' pardon, and set forth
> A deep repentance
>
> [I. iv. 5-7]

Macduff, with rather less on his conscience than Macbeth, could say,

> sinful Macduff,
> They were all struck for thee—nought that I am;
> Not for their own demerits, but for mine,
> Fell slaughter on their souls.
>
> [IV. iii. 224-27]

Cawdor and Macduff set the example which Macbeth never follows; or, to go outside the play, Othello and Lear set examples that Macbeth never follows. Part of Hamlet's agonizing is centred in his passion to avoid having to set such an example. Macbeth simply does not face the moral record. Instead he is the saddened and later bereaved husband, the man deprived of friends and future, the thinker, the pathetic believer in immunity, the fighter. These roles are a way of pushing the past aside—the past which cries out for a new sense, in him, of what it has been. If, then, our hypothesis about the nature of tragic participation is valid, the reader ends his life with and in Macbeth in a way that demands too little of him. He experiences forlornness and desolation, and even a kind of substitute triumph—anything but the soul's reckoning which is a severer trial than the world's judgment. He is not initiated into a true spaciousness of character, but follows, in Macbeth, the movement of what I have called a contracting personality. This is not the best that tragedy can offer. (pp. 22-3)

> *Robert B. Heilman, "The Criminal As Tragic Hero: Dramatic Methods," in Shakespeare Survey: An Annual Survey of Shakespearian Study and Production, Vol. 19, 1966, pp. 12-24.*

HERBERT R. COURSEN, JR.   (essay date 1967)

[*In the excerpt below, Coursen argues that one source of* Macbeth's *power is its presentation of an "original myth"—the fall from a state of grace. Like Roy W. Battenhouse (1952) and Robert Pack (1956), Coursen notes the parallels between the action of* Macbeth *and the biblical myth of Lucifer and Adam, tracing them through Macbeth's "moral decision, feminine persuasion, and cosmic retribution." He asserts that Macbeth's rebellion is ironically suggested even in the earlier speeches that praise his valor, an observation later developed by Harry Berger, Jr. (1980). Coursen also compares Lady Macbeth with Eve, stating that each temptress "ignites the ambition latent within her husband's breast." He maintains that Macbeth's final retribution is damnation in hell and further proposes that the name of Macbeth's armor-bearer, Seyton, suggests Satan and thus resembles a satanic agent. Coursen concludes that Seyton-Satan's presence "reinforces the rhythm of damnation with which Macbeth's soul has been merging from the first."*]

The myth vibrating beneath the surface of *Macbeth* is one of the original myths—that of the fall from a state of grace. That it is a source of the play's power suggests its continuing relevance to the human situation, its truth. The manner in which the myth is manifested in *Macbeth* is perhaps best suggested by Lady Macbeth:

> . . . look like the innocent flower,
> But be the serpent under't.
>
> [I. v. 65-6]

The flower suggests Creation and links itself with the play's many images of growing things. The serpent suggests the deception which slithered into Eden to tempt Eve—as the Geneva Bible calls it in the gloss to Revelation xii:9, "That olde serpent called the devill and Satan" which was hurled from Heaven by Michael and "which deceiveth all the worlde." Lady Macbeth here *is* the tempting serpent and, of course, is also the deceived. In that Macbeth is a man in a fallen world, the play concerns the further fall of man—the loss of his soul. But in that Macbeth stands closest to royal favor (with the exception of Malcolm) in a potentially redeemable world, his fall parallels that of Lucifer, who stood closest to God (with the exception of the Son). The fall of Macbeth draws for its precedent on both Genesis and Revelation, the first and the last books of the Bible, a fact which suggests the fundamental implications of his crime. "Christian philosophy", says Walter C. Curry, "recognizes two tragedies of cosmic importance: (1) the fall of Lucifer and a third part of the angelic hosts, who rebelled against God and were cast out, and (2) the fall of Adam, who was originally endowed with perfection and freedom but who set his will against God's will and so brought sin and limited freedom upon mankind." . . . The fall of Macbeth draws on the combined power of those of Lucifer and Adam—and on more, of course, since it is also his own. (pp. 375-76)

The power beneath the surface, then, is the myth of the fall from a state of grace, whether the fall from the beneficent light of God or the expulsion from paradise on Earth. The myth has three basic manifestations in *Macbeth*: moral decision, feminine persuasion, and cosmic retribution.

The auditor of *Macbeth* is projected into a fallen world, one which seems to have eaten of the fruit of the tree of good and evil and which cannot tell the two apart. There are the obvious ambiguities—"Fair is foul, and foul is fair" [I. i. 11], "fair and foul" [I. iii. 38]—which resound so ominously through the early portions of the play. . . . The words of the opening scenes are like those two spent swimmers of whom the wounded Captain speaks—they "cling together / And choke their art" [I. ii. 8-9]. Often the lines say two things about Macbeth—they praise him as a hero and, prophet-like, predict his coming treason:

> Norway himself
> With terrible numbers,
> Assisted by that most disloyal traitor,
> The Thane of Cawdor, began a dismal conflict,
> Till that Bellona's bridegroom, lapp'd in proof,
> Confronted him with self-comparisons,
> Point against point, rebellious arm 'gainst arm. . . .
>
> [I. ii. 51-6]

The lines are constructed to suggest that Macbeth confronted Cawdor as well as Sweno—a self-comparison which becomes an ominous mirror reflecting treason present and future. The hint is reinforced by the adjective "rebellious", which points across the sentence to modify the second arm—Macbeth's. This subversion of a line's primary meaning recurs in Ross's greeting to Macbeth:

> The King hath happily receiv'd, Macbeth,
> The news of thy success; and when he reads
> Thy personal venture in the rebel's fight,

His wonders and his praises do contend,
Which should be thine or his.

> [I. iii. 89-93]

"Personal venture in the rebel's fight"—his heroic effort against rebellion *and* his personal role in the ultimate treason. The contradictory lines continue, the poetry itself committing treason against its ostensible meaning:

He finds thee in the stout Norweyan ranks,
Nothing afeard of what thyself didst make,
Strange images of death.

> [I. iii. 95-7]

As the lines predict, Macbeth will soon be among the enemies of the King, making a stranger image of death, the "great doom's image" [II. iii. 78]. It is that "horrid image" [I. iii. 135] which has already frightened him.

The actions of Duncan during the opening scenes share the predominant ambiguous quality; he attempts to engender Eden on earth yet helps to promote his murder. As Macbeth returns from battle, Duncan assumes the role of Creator, his rightful role within the Kingdom of Scotland:

I have begun to plant thee, and will labour
To make thee full of growing.

> [I. iv. 28-9]

Macbeth is in a state of grace. The choice of remaining in Eden under this beneficent aegis is his. If he does so, he is told that "signs of nobleness, like stars, shall shine / On all deservers" [I. iv. 41-2]. But while attempting to encourage Eden, Duncan unconsciously promotes treason. In language which through an ominous rhyme reverberates again with Delphic tones, the King invests Macbeth with the traitor's title, thus prompting Macbeth to assume the traitor's reality:

No more that Thane of Cawdor shall deceive
Our bosom interest. Go pronounce his present death
And with his former title greet Macbeth.

> [I. ii. 63-5]

No more shall *that* Thane of Cawdor deceive us—but what of the new one? The "careless trifle" [I. iv. 11] which Cawdor discards becomes an "honest trifle" [I. iii. 125] which wins Macbeth. The pervasive confusion of the opening scenes is perhaps suggested best when the gracious Duncan echoes the Weird Sisters [I. i. 4]—as Macbeth had done earlier: "What he hath lost noble Macbeth hath won" [I. ii. 67]. Duncan incites treason further by establishing his estate on Malcolm, just as Milton's God exalts his Son and activates Satan's dormant disobedience. Macbeth adjures the stars to hide their fires [I. iv. 50]; he instructs his own signs of nobleness to extinguish themselves and so facilitate the attainment of his "black and deep desires" [I. iv. 51].

The language of the opening scenes intermingles the possibilities of good and of evil, suggesting the terms of Macbeth's decision. Ironically, as he comes closer to killing Duncan, his awareness of the heinousness of the crime becomes clearer. Like Adam, Macbeth knows clearly what God's word is and what the general results of Duncan's murder must be:

. . . his virtues
Will plead like angels, trumpet-tongu'd, against
The deep damnation of his taking-off.

> [I. vii. 18-20]

An act which would outrage angels, involve the perpetrator in damnation—the dimensions of the fall are suggested by the drop from "angels trumpet tongu'd" to "deep damnation" which the voice must make as the line is read. The attainment of "black and deep desires" will have the "deepest consequence" [I. iii. 126]. (pp. 377-79)

Any discussion of Adam's temptation or of Macbeth's must involve Eve—or Lady Macbeth—the element of feminine persuasion, the spur of which Macbeth speaks at the end of his soliloquy. (p. 379)

While Lady Macbeth is linked unmistakably with the Weird Sisters, the temptation scene rings with echoes of Eden:

> *Macbeth.* Hath he ask'd for me?
> *Lady M.* Know you not he has?
>
> > [I. vii. 30]

God walked through Eden calling, "Where art thou?" to Adam. The Geneva gloss on God's search gives context to Macbeth's departure from the banquet and to the subsequent guilty soliloquy: "The sinnefull conscience fleeth God's presense." To avoid the deed and at the same time placate Lady Macbeth, Macbeth reduces the abstractions of his soliloquy to material terms:

I have bought
Golden opinions from all sorts of people.
Which would be worn now in their newest gloss,
Not cast aside so soon.

> [I. vii. 32-5]

His argument is conditioned by her inability at this point in the play to see beyond the tangible. Macbeth cannot speak of "double trust" or of Duncan's clarity in office; his wife would not understand ("What do you mean?" she asks later, as Macbeth waxes hyperbolic about the sleep which he will never know again [II. ii. 37]). But to employ a materialistic excuse for not pursuing a materialistic course is to open oneself up for counterattack. Lady Macbeth retorts, implying with a sneer that cowardice lurks beneath the thane's new clothes: "When you durst do it, then you were a man" [I. vii. 49]. As Dr. Johnson says, with the certainty of an eighteenth-century critic, "Courage is the distinguishing virtue of a soldier, and the reproach of cowardice cannot be borne by any man without great impatience" [see excerpt above, 1745]. Her skillful blend of scorn and sex—the primordial feminine weapons—upsets the precarious balance within Macbeth. The words in the Geneva margin about Adam's submission become relevant: "Not so much to please his wife, as mooved by ambition at her persuasion." The roles of the sixteenth-century Eve and Lady Macbeth coincide—each ignites the ambition latent within her husband's breast. (pp. 380-81)

Duncan represents God, the creative principle; he is the architect of Scotland's garden. The theme of Eden is perhaps best articulated as Banquo and the King approach Dunsinane:

> *Duncan.* This castle hath a pleasant seat. The air
> Nimbly and sweetly recommends itself
> Unto our gentle senses.
> *Banquo.*   This guest of
> summer,
> The temple-haunting martlet, does approve,
> By his lov'd masonry, that the heaven's
> breath
> Smells wooingly here. No jutty, frieze,
> Buttress, nor coign of vantage, but this bird

Hath made his pendant bed and procreant
    cradle.
Where they most breed and haunt, I have
    observ'd
The air is delicate.

[I. vi. 1-10]

The world which they see, like Eden, exists in harmony with
Heaven; it is a creative world in which nests find the constructions of man hospitable, in which the delicate air of Heaven
at once encourages new life into being and is recreated by that
new life. . . . With the murder of Duncan, procreation vanishes.
The "temple-haunting martlet" is forced to flee when "the
Lord's anointed temple" is desecrated by "most sacrilegious
murther" [II. iii. 67-8]. When Macbeth memorizes "another
Golgotha" [I. ii. 40], the principle of anti-Creation becomes
dominant. The first verses of Genesis, of course, suggest order—the distinction between light ("that it was good") and
darkness, heaven and earth, sea and land, day and night, seasons, years, sun and moon. The opening verses of Genesis
emphasize growing things:

> Then God said, let the earth budde forth the
> fruit of the herbe, that seedeth seed, the fruitfull
> tree, which bareth fruit according to his kinde,
> which hath his seed in itselfe upon the earth. . . .

With the murder, distinctions merely blurred in the opening
scenes become obliterated. An owl, which normally preys on
field mice, rises up to down a towering falcon [II. iv. 12-13].
Horses, "Contending 'gainst obedience", turn wild, eat each
other and seem "as they would make / War with mankind"
[II. iv. 14-18]. Night and morning "at odds" lose their distinctive identities [III. iv. 126]. The well-planned garden of
God and Duncan is destroyed; Scotland becomes a kingdom
of "weeds" [V. ii. 30]. . . . Having suspended the rules of
nature, Macbeth finds that they cannot be reinstated; Banquo
comes to the banquet despite the "twenty mortal murthers"
[III. iv. 80] inflicted upon him. He pushes Macbeth from his
stool [III. iv. 81]—a hint that Banquo's line is destined to
occupy the throne—and breaks up the royal feast "With most
admir'd disorder" [III. iv. 109]. Macbeth's promotion of an
anti-Creation leads inevitably to his despairing demand for his
own annihilation ("Out, out, brief candle!" [V. v. 23]). Lady
Macbeth's command for light [V. i. 23] is pitifully inadequate
before the immensity of her inner darkness.

More permanent than sterility in this life, however, and more
terrifying than annihilation, is damnation in the life-to-come.
We have seen Lady Macbeth groping already in the dun smoke
of her hell, and we have seen Macbeth's life devolve into a
choice between insomnia [II. ii. 35-40] and nightmare [III. ii.
18-19]. His ultimate damnation is implied in an eerie little
scene which goes almost unnoticed between his somber soliloquies and the sweep of the final action. Having dismissed a
pale messenger, Macbeth begins a soliloquy:

> Seyton!—I am sick at heart,
> When I behold—Seyton, I say!
>
> [V. iii. 19-20]

What was to be the object of "behold"? Since the rest of the
soliloquy concerns what Macbeth has lost, it may be that he
was about to mention the soul he has lost. But, perhaps unwilling to confront that loss, he interrupts himself with another
shout to his armor-bearer. But does his call check the thoughts
which may be flowing towards damnation? Perhaps it echoes
the same theme—the eventuality which must be ever lurking

on the borders of Macbeth's consciousness. "Seyton", after
all, sounds almost like "Satan." Macbeth continues:

> I have liv'd long enough. My way of life
> Is fallen into the sere, the yellow leaf.
>
> [V. iii. 22-3]

Macbeth's fall is linked to images of a faded Eden. . . . He
continues, with a barren parade of all that he cannot look to
have: " . . . honour, love, obedience, troops of friends . . . "
[V. iii. 25]. "Deep damnation" becomes "Curses, not loud
but deep" [V. iii. 27]. The soliloquy closes with another shout
of "Seyton!" The cry has been repeated three times, linking
Seyton appropriately with the Weird Sisters. Perhaps each cry
mingles Macbeth's growing awareness of damnation with the
world-weariness suggested by the soliloquy; perhaps he wants
to get on with the inevitable.

As if conjured up by the repeated shouts, Seyton enters, and
with what would seem to be Mephistophelian irony asks, "What's
your gracious pleasure?" [V. iii. 30]. Few words could be
more inappropriate to Macbeth than "gracious pleasure". It
was Duncan who was "gracious", as Lennox says [III. vi. 3],
as Macbeth implies after the murder ("Renown and grace is
dead" [II. iii. 94]), and as he reiterates in a speech which
resembles the one on which Seyton enters:

> For them the gracious Duncan have I murther'd;
> Put rancours in the vessel of my peace
> Only for them, and mine eternal jewell
> Given to the common enemy of man. . . .
>
> [III. i. 65-8]

This speech mentions the loss of his soul—the jewel he has
tossed away like a careless trifle—a loss further suggested by
the image of a defiled communion cup. And Macbeth can know
no pleasure; his speeches list the joys of life which he has
forsaken, the joys which Duncan had in abundance and offered
to Macbeth, which Duncan retains ("he sleeps well" [III. ii.
23]) and which Macbeth will never know again. At the moment
in which Seyton uses it, "pleasure" is doubly ironic; a King's
pleasure is translated immediately into reality. Royal pleasure
means control, and this Macbeth is losing also:

> 1. Witch. [to Macbeth about the First Apparition]
>   He will not be commanded.
>
> [IV. i. 75]

> He cannot buckle his distemper'd cause
> Within the belt of rule.
>
> [V. ii. 15-16]

> Now minutely revolts upbraid his faith-breach.
>
> [V. ii. 18]

The richness of Seyton's irony suggests that he may be more
than a mere armor-bearer.

Macbeth demands more news of him. Seyton tells him that
"All is confirm'd, my lord, which was reported" [V. iii. 31].
All?—perhaps all that the Sisters reported to Macbeth on his
second encounter with them. The line suggests more than a
mere military report; it suggests a strange and encompassing
knowledge of the movement of Birnam Wood and the approach
of the untimely-born Macduff. Macbeth demands his armor.
Seyton tells him that "'Tis not needed yet" [V. iii. 33], implying again a knowledge of the future appropriate to a play
in which prophecies echo through the air. In Act Five, of all
those who appear in Dunsinane before invading forces break
in—the Doctor and the Gentlewoman, Macbeth and Lady Mac-

beth, the two messengers—Seyton alone displays no sign of fear. His attitude is almost complacent.

Later, as the enemy pushes closer, Macbeth hears a shriek and demands, "What is that noise?" [V. v. 7]. Seyton replies, "It is the cry of women, my good lord" [V. v. 8]. Again, irony rings in the terms of address. Seyton leaves and returns with word that "The Queen, my lord, is dead" [V. v. 16]. Within the message of death, Seyton places yet another term of preeminent position. Macbeth's final hope for an heir is snuffed, his last link with this world is snapped. Such crushing news is appropriately delivered by a Seyton-Satan, representative of absolute loss. Seyton, the ironic armor-bearer, exists between two barren soliloquies; he enters and departs to words which define Macbeth's meaninglessness. Seyton's presence implies that death is not all that awaits Macbeth—he reinforces the rhythm of damnation with which Macbeth's soul has been merging from the first. We see Lady Macbeth in Hell; we see Macbeth on the way. (pp. 383-87)

> *Herbert R. Coursen, Jr., "In Deepest Consequence:* *'Macbeth',"* *in* Shakespeare Quarterly, *Vol. XVIII,* *No. 4, Autumn, 1967, pp. 375-88.*

TERENCE EAGLETON   (essay date 1967)

[*Eagleton, an English Marxist critic, is best known for his works on critical theory, including* Marxism and Literary Criticism *(1976) and* Literary Theory: An Introduction *(1983). In his* Shakespeare and Society *(1967), Eagleton examines the tension that exists between individual spontaneous action and social responsibility in Shakespeare's plays. In the following treatment of* Macbeth, *Eagleton describes Macbeth's murder of Duncan as "self-defeating." In Duncan's service, he argues, Macbeth finds self-expression and personal joy, so that in destroying Duncan he essentially destroys himself. Eagleton further states that Macbeth is never allowed to enjoy his "inauthentic" role as king, because he is too busy "pursuing his own act," a point previously noted by J. P. Dyson (1963). Eagleton concludes that Macbeth's regicide, which is an attempt to go beyond the limits of humanity, is a rejection of social responsibility and, finally, devoid of value and meaning.*]

Macbeth centres around a single action—the murder of Duncan—which, like the action of Coriolanus and Antony, is seen as self-defeating. The whole structure of the play makes this clear: Scotland moves from health to sickness and back into health, Macbeth replaces Duncan, and the wheel comes full circle without Macbeth having made any permanent achievement. The energy he expends in trying to secure his position contrasts ironically with this lack of attainment: his actions are cancelled out by the circular movement of the play, and he becomes a momentary aberration in Scotland's history, an aberration without lasting consequence: the history rights itself and continues. Macbeth's action in killing Duncan is marred by a literal sterility: he will have no sons to make his achievement permanently fruitful. But the action is inherently sterile, too, and it is this paradox which the play builds on: an action intended as creative, self-definitive, is in fact destructive, self-undoing.

Act III. Scene i. Two Murderers and Macbeth. By George Cattermole (n.d.).

Macbeth becomes king of Scotland between the end of Act II and the beginning of Act III, but in achieving the status which he saw previously as ultimate, he finds that his troubles have in fact only just begun: he spends the rest of the play fighting to secure his role. He fights to *become* what, objectively, he is: to clear up and tidy the straggling consequences of his action and settle down in the achieved and perfected definition of kingship:

> To be thus is nothing,
> But to be safely thus.
>
> [III. i. 47-8]

The idea of a perfected, completely achieved act is insistent in the play: Macbeth upbraids the witches as 'imperfect speakers', and his reaction to the news of Fleance's escape focusses his frustration as continually falling short of full achievement:

> I had else been perfect,
> Whole as the marble, founded as the rock,
> As broad and general as the casing air,
> But now I am cabin'd, cribb'd, confin'd, bound in
> To saucy doubts and fears.
>
> [III. iii. 20-4]

Every action done to attain security mars itself: every act has a built-in flaw, a consequence which escapes, like Fleance, from the control of the actor and returns to plague him. Macbeth cannot achieve a pure act, a wholeness: his actions unravel themselves, and he longs for a pure act as he longs for the sleep which 'knits up the ravell'd sleave of care' [II. ii. 34]:

> If it were done, when 'tis done, then 'twere well
> It were done quickly. If th'assassination
> Could trammel up the consequence, and catch,
> With his surcease, success; that but this blow
> Might be the be-all and the end-all here—
> But here upon this bank and shoal of time—
> We'd jump the life to come. But in these cases
> We still have judgment here, that we but teach
> Bloody instructions, which being taught return
> To plague th'inventor.
>
> [I. vii. 1-10]

Macbeth wants the action without the consequences, without the uncontrollable, multiplying effects; he dreams of an action which contains and controls all its results within itself. He also wants achievement without the process of reaching it, as Lady Macbeth sees:

> Thou wouldst be great;
> Art not without ambition, but without
> The illness should attend it. What thou wouldst highly,
> That wouldst thou holily; wouldst not play false,
> And yet wouldst wrongly win.
>
> [I. v. 18-22]

But the irony implicit in all action is precisely that any achievement involves a process of reaching and a process of results, and both processes can destroy what it attained. Macbeth wants the static, permanent status of kingship without the fluid, temporal process of actions necessary to win and secure it; he finds that kingship is for him only a process, not the complete definition it was for Duncan. Having become king officially by killing Duncan, he finds that he has achieved nothing: there is always another step to be taken before he is *really* king, secure in his role, and each step taken undoes what he has won because each step breeds more destructive consequences. He is not allowed to become what he is, to be, authentically, king; he spends all his time and energy in consolidating his position and is therefore unable to enjoy kingship at all. He is a man pursuing his own act, chasing himself; his action in killing Duncan both makes and mars him, as drink, according to the Porter, makes and mars a man.

Macbeth's condition is imaged especially in the recurrent metaphor of ill-fitting robes. When Ross and Angus greet him with the title of Cawdor he asks why they dress him in borrowed robes, and Banquo's aside when Macbeth is 'rapt' after the witches' promise captures the significance of this:

> New honours come upon him,
> Like our strange garments, cleave not to their mould
> But with the aid of use.
>
> [I. iii. 144-46]

A role or title can be laid externally on a man, but he must then make it his own, moulding it like new clothes to his own shape so that it is authentic, not external any longer. . . . The importance of names and titles is stressed in the play: Macbeth is given, ceremonially, the former title of Cawdor; Macduff, discovering the murder of Duncan, says it is a deed which tongue and heart 'cannot conceive nor name' [II. iii. 64-5]; the witches perform 'a deed without a name' [IV. i. 49]; Macbeth is a 'tyrant, whose sole name blisters our tongues' [IV. iii. 12], as Malcolm says. In all these cases, names have a peculiarly creative power: things without names are beyond the reach of human meanings, part of the nothingness of the evil lying at the edges of the human community. To receive a name is to be something positive, to have a sanctioned place within the community.

Macbeth's murder of Duncan is a falling from such a place within the community to the pure negativity of evil, the area of nameless deeds. Before the murder, Macbeth's authentic life consists in serving Duncan, and the service is not an external, mechanical obedience but a living self-expression: he wants no reward for his allegiance because

> The service and the loyalty I owe,
> In doing it, pays itself.
>
> [I. iv. 22-3]

He needs no external payment, but is paid by the deed itself; the circularity here is that of the fusion of authentic and responsible action, not the self-destroying circularity which is Macbeth's later condition. It is in Duncan's service that Macbeth finds personal joy: 'The rest is labour, which is not us'd for you' [I. iv. 44]. In destroying Duncan, Macbeth is destroying himself: his own life and peace is in Duncan's possession, and the murder is thus an act of self-violence. It is a self-destroying act, one done to achieve a happiness lost in the very moment of trying to attain it; his action, like his ambition, 'o'er-leaps itself, And falls on the other' [I. vii. 27-8]. In destroying Duncan he is being inauthentic, less than himself: he overreaches himself, falling away from his own positive life into negativity:

> I dare do all that may become a man;
> Who dares do more is none.
>
> [I. vii. 46-7]

To overreach one's limits is to be less than oneself, to undo oneself; authentic living consists in staying freely within these limits of nature, recognising them as creative. To try to be more than human is to be an animal: evil is a kind of failure, a meaninglessness. This is what Lady Macbeth cannot see: to her a man can create his own limits, pushing them out to suit his ambition:

> When you durst do it, then you were a man;
> And to be more than what you were, you would
> Be so much more the man.
>
> [I. vii. 49-51]

Macbeth takes her advice and goes beyond the limits of humanity in an attempt to be more fully human; in trying to achieve a title he goes beyond all names, all definitions, into the negation of evil and chaos. Lady Macbeth cannot see that limits are not what restrict humanity but what make it what it is, as a name creates in defining, in limiting. (pp. 130-35)

Macbeth's attempts to create meaning from a world which Duncan's death drained of value degenerate finally into the peace of embracing chaos, accepting meaninglessness: life is a succession of tomorrows, a tale told by an idiot, and having recognised this he can fight till the flesh is hacked from his bones, trying to the last. He will at least die in harness, enjoying action for its own sake, spending himself freely in his final moments. He can find comfort in absurdity, as he finds constancy in inconstancy:

> Come what come may,
> Time and the hour runs through the roughest day.
>
> [I. iii. 146-47]

There is no final answer in this for Shakespeare, any more than there is in *Antony and Cleopatra*; Macbeth, like Antony, undoes himself in rejecting social responsibility, and whatever value can be forcibly created from the rejection must be inevitably marginal. (pp. 137-38)

Terence Eagleton, " 'Macbeth'," *in his* Shakespeare and Society: Critical Studies in Shakespearean Drama, *Chatto & Windus, 1967, pp. 130-38.*

D. A. TRAVERSI   (essay date 1968)

[*Traversi, an English scholar, has written a number of books on Shakespeare's plays, including* An Approach to Shakespeare *(1938) and* Shakespeare: The Last Phase *(1954). In the introduction to the first of these studies, Traversi proposed to focus his interpretation of the plays on "the word," stating that the experience which forms the impetus to each of Shakespeare's dramas "will find its most immediate expression in the language and verse." In the following excerpt, drawn from the second revision of his* An Approach to Shakespeare *(1968), Traversi emphasizes the symbolic significance of the diction of the two kings in* Macbeth. *Duncan's speeches, he argues, reflect the grace, fertility, and natural and harmonious social order that he represents. Opposed to this, he posits, are Macbeth's abrupt and disjointed speeches, which suggest "a continual jolting of the sensibility into disorder and anarchy." Traversi states that because Macbeth's murder of Duncan is in conflict with the natural order, it must end in "unnatural chaos and inevitable death." He further asserts that even prior to the murder of Macduff's family Shakespeare suggests that the natural order will defeat Macbeth and, like G. R. Elliott (1958), notes the curative powers of Malcolm's "army of deliverance." Traversi concludes that Macbeth, in attempting to destroy harmonious life, freely chooses "his own particular and appropriate hell."*]

Macbeth is, in the first place and above all, a play about the murder of a king; and there is a very real sense in which the center, the focal point of the conception is to be found neither in the criminal usurper nor in the wife who initially urges him

to crime, but in the figure, too easily neglected in its central, normative function, of Duncan. (p. 423)

Duncan's function in the play emerges . . . from the images of light and fertility which surround his person and confer substance and consistency upon the "symbolic" value of his rule. The universal implications of this value . . . are only fully appreciated after due weight has been given to the short initial appearance of the Witches, which establishes the climate, moral as much as merely physical, within which the action is to be conducted. The Witches, as a prelude to the human tragedy, introduce us to a situation in which "Fair is foul, and foul is fair" [I. i. 11]; through the calculated ambiguity of their utterance and through the elemental commotion which surrounds them, they prepare the way for the entry of evil and disintegration into a state which has been, under Duncan, positive, natural, and orderly. When the evil obscurely present in Macbeth's mind is stirred to conceive and execute the murder of Duncan, he introduces both into the Scottish realm and into his own nature a disrupting evil which must work itself out through the process it has initiated. The play, thus conceived as a harmonious dramatic construction, deals with the overthrow of the balance of royalty by Macbeth's crime, with the full development of the malignity which that overthrow implies, and, finally, with the restoration of natural order under the gracious successor of the murdered king.

Macbeth's murder of Duncan is, accordingly, in the first place a crime against the natural foundations of social and moral harmony; it is at the same time an attack by the destructive elements contemplated in Shakespeare's experience upon those which make for unity and untrammeled maturity. As we have already suggested, the positive values of the tragedy are concentrated on the "symbolic" function of Duncan's royalty and upon the poetry in which it finds expression. As king, Duncan is the head of a "single state of man" [I. iii. 140] (we shall see later the full implications of this phrase of Macbeth's), whose members are bound into unity by the accepted ties of loyalty. By virtue of this position he is the source of all the benefits which flow from his person to those who surround him; receiving the free homage of his subjects, he dispenses to them all the riches and graces which are the mark of true kingship, so that the equality of his poetry is above all lifegiving, fertile. The early, light-drenched scenes of the tragedy are dominated by this rich, vital relationship between service spontaneously given and abundant royal bounty. Macbeth himself, still speaking as the loyal general who has saved his country from the consequences of internal rebellion and foreign invasion, describes the subject's duty in repeated protestations of devotion that only in the light of his own later behavior become ironic; in his expression of them his poetry attains, though fugitively and imperfectly, a breadth, a completeness of emotional content, that it will never recover. Duncan, in turn, replies to these professions of loyalty with an overflowing bounty expressed in terms of harvest fullness:

> I have begun to plant thee, and will labour
> To make thee full of growing.
>
> [I. iv. 28-9]

to which the devoted Banquo replies by taking up the same image—

> There if I grow,
> The harvest is your own—
>
> [I. iv. 32-3]

and receives from his king a final expression of abounding joy:

> My plenteous joys,
> Wanton in fullness, seek to hide themselves
> In drops of sorrow.
>
> [I. iv. 33-5]

Duncan and his subjects, in short, vie with one another in the celebration of a relationship that is not one of mastery or subjection, but essentially free, expansive, life-giving. It is in accordance with the spirit of his kingship that Duncan's brief appearances before his murder are invariably invested with images of light and fertility to which are joined, at his moments of deepest feeling, the religious associations of worship in a magnificent, comprehensive impression of overflowing *grace*. (pp. 423-25)

[There] is between Duncan and the loyal Macbeth of these early scenes a relationship rich in honor and fertile in royal bounty. As Duncan's instrument in war, Macbeth wins two arduous battles and becomes Thane of Cawdor. No sooner has he heard the prophecy of the Witches, however, than a new quality enters his meditations, expressing itself in verse of a very different kind. The verse of *Macbeth*, apart from that associated with the loyal personages of the play, is often, at a first reading, so abrupt and disjointed that some critics have felt themselves driven to look for gaps in the text. Yet the difficult passages do not look in the least like the result of omission; they are demonstrably necessary to the feeling of the tragedy. In practically every one of Macbeth's speeches there is a keen sense of discontinuity, a continual jolting of the sensibility into disorder and anarchy. Macbeth, from the time when the thought of murder first forces its way into his consciousness, moves almost continuously in a remarkable state of nervous tension, a state in which a very palpable obscurity is suddenly and unexpectedly shot through by strange revelations and terrifying illuminations of feeling. This state is fully significant only as an inversion of the rich, ordered poetry of Duncan; it is the natural consequence of his murder, a reflection of the entry of evil both into the individual and the state. The quality of this disturbance, which changes with the various stages of Macbeth's own situation, should be carefully considered.

Immediately after his first meeting with the Witches, when the thought of his crime first claims his attention, Macbeth, standing for a moment aside from his companions, speaks with typical disjointed intensity:

> This supernatural soliciting
> Cannot be ill; cannot be good: if ill,
> Why hath it given me earnest of success,
> Commencing in a truth? I am thane of Cawdor;
> If good, why do I yield to that suggestion
> Whose horrid image doth unfix my hair
> And make my seated heart knock at my ribs,
> Against the use of nature? Present fears
> Are less than horrible imaginings:
> My thought, whose murder yet is but fantastical,
> Shakes so my single state of man that function
> Is smothered in surmise, and nothing is
> But what is not.
>
> [I. iii. 130-42]

Nothing quite like this following of thought in the very process of conscious formulation can be found in Shakespeare's early work; it is [a] . . . development new to *Macbeth*. There is nothing accidental about the telescoping of the syntax in the

last few lines; the strange juxtapostion of "thought" and "murder" conveys perfectly the actual birth of the unnatural project in the tangled chaos of ideas. Taken with the rest of the speech it conveys even more. It anticipates the whole disturbance of natural "function," of the "single state of man," which the very thought of such a crime implies; it expresses with unsurpassed nervous directness the shaking to its foundations of what has been a harmonious personality. The speech, indeed, is much more than a mere statement of the ambiguity and tension present in Macbeth's mind. It is a *physical* apprehension of ambiguity, a disordered experience expressing itself in terms of a dislocated functioning. (pp. 426-27)

The fertile poetry of Duncan, based upon so delicate and so complete an organization of the "gentle" senses, depends upon a right ordering of the "single state of man." Harmony in the individual is balanced by harmony in the Scottish *state* under its lawful king. Macbeth's poetry, however, reflects the growth into consciousness within his mind of a willful determination to break down this "single state"; and, by means of it, Shakespeare identifies the evil of his play with the disrupting of a most harmonious experience. The result in psychological terms is presented with rare immediacy in Macbeth's early meditations upon his future course of action. It produces in him a discontinuity between the senses and the mind, between the mind and the conscience (note how the speech already quoted opens with a vain fumbling at the meaning of "good" and "ill"), and between these gaps nothing but an intense awareness of their existence. Considered in this way, *Macbeth* can be related to the whole line of development traced in the earlier plays. Its subject is still the "degree" theme of *Troilus and Cressida*, but now immeasurably enriched by a firmer grasp of personality and by a new, more mature organization of feeling. By the side of this contrast between Duncan and Macbeth, the conception behind Ulysses' discourse on "degree" must strike us as sluggish and, dramatically speaking, unrealized. Here, unlike the earlier play, there is no gap between the statement of the argument and its apprehension in terms of immediate experience. Ulysses, on the whole, *tells us* about the breakdown of "degree" in abstract terms, whereas here we *feel* the personality in dissolution, striving vainly to attain, on the basis of its own illusory desires, an impression of coherence. To the gain in poetic immediacy corresponds an advance in dramatic presentation. The "single state of man," a state which depends for both the individual and the social organism on the due observance of ordered loyalty, is here replaced by a cleavage in the innermost fabric of the mind, an uncertain groping in the bottomless pit of psychological and spiritual darkness, in the first obscure glimpses of a state where fundamental values are inverted, and where "nothing is But what is not." (pp. 428-29)

The connection between *Macbeth* and Shakespeare's previous work becomes still clearer once it is seen that the murder of Duncan is the result of a movement of the "blood," of the deeper sources of passion exercising their potent influence upon the will. The nature of the relationship that unites husband and wife is worth careful consideration. It is implied in the words in which Lady Macbeth, having read her husband's letter, greets him upon his arrival:

> Thy letters have transported me beyond
> This ignorant present, and I feel now
> The future in the instant,
>
> [I. v. 56-8]

and in the ecstatic quality of his response: "My dearest love!" It is precisely this intensity of passion which, diverted from its natural channels, is turned onto a craving for power and issues in murder. To follow the common line of interpretation and call this craving "ambition" is not enough, for ambition is an abstraction and this is something that comes, as we have seen, from the "blood," from the hidden instinctive foundations of the personality. Lady Macbeth's attitude, indeed, logical though it be once its premises are granted, involves a passionate distortion of normal humanity which balances that which she herself helps to produce in her husband. Born of a reversal of nature, its expression is consistently unnatural. Her first prayer, as her purpose takes shape, is *"Unsex* me here!" [I. v. 41]. Her second—prefaced by the significant apostrophe, "Come, thick night!" [I. v. 50]—is an appeal to the darkness that makes possible the exclusion of reason and pity. From this to the expressions of forced, unnatural determination which follow—the declared willingness to kill her own child rather than fail in the course of action which her "blood"-impelled craving for power has dictated, the final conquest of her feeling that the sleeping Duncan resembled her own father—the passage is as easy as it is monstrous, inhuman. The whole crime is, in the words of Ross, from the moment of its conception to that of its final execution, "against nature still" [II. iv. 27]. The overthrow of the royal symbol of order and fruitful unity is the result of a preceding disturbance of the balance between impulse and conscience, instinctive "blood" and reasonable will; and this, in turn, naturally produces a dissociation of bodily function, an anarchy in which animal feeling works in an isolation divorced from all control, and so void of continuity and significance.

After this, the actual murder of Duncan comes as the grotesque climax of a process that has involved from the first an inversion of every natural bond and feeling. (pp. 430-31)

By the time the murder of Duncan has taken place it is abundantly clear that Macbeth's crime is, as we have argued, a rift in the harmony and richness of the unity "symbolized" in the royal rule and realized in the poetry associated with the dead king. Such a rift, once it has appeared, has to exhaust its destructive consequences before coherence can be restored; and in the central part of the play Macbeth's kingship, contrasted with that of Duncan as "evil" with "good," is shown as simply the working out of the negation upon which it was founded. The usurper, as he comes to realize that the crime he has committed to gain, in his wife's overweening words, "solely sovereign sway and masterdom" [I. v. 70], has in fact failed to achieve this goal, progressively loses the illusion of freedom and plunges into a further series of unnatural actions. At the lowest point in his downward progress, he consults the Witches once more in a determination to know "by the worst means the worst" [III. iv. 134]; and the Witches respond (IV. i) both by offering further false "certainties"—in the form of the various apparitions set before his eyes—and by confirming finally, through the vision of Banquo's succession, the sterility of his own line. With this revelation, and the last, useless killing of Macduff's wife and children which immediately follows (IV. ii), the central part of the action, exhausting the possibilities of evil and uniting Macbeth and the realm he has usurped in a common degradation, is logically complete. Its third and last stage will show a process of recovery in which the forces of "good," of life and ordered harmony, drawing their strength originally from the holy ruler of England, flow back like a returning tide over Scotland to sweep away Macbeth's shadow of power and to restore, in the person of Dun-

can's rightful heir, Malcolm, the kingship of "grace." The complete effect, as will be seen, is that of a balanced construction, each successive stage of which, linked to the preceding action by threads of imagery and the logic of events, also prepares the ground for the final resolution.

From the moment of Duncan's murder until the final overthrow of Macbeth the action turns upon a contrast between two royalties: that of the dead king, founded upon natural allegiance and rich in generous bounty, and that of his murderer, which, inititated in a reversal of "nature," can only have as its end unnatural chaos and inevitable death. The terms of the contrast are already established at the moment in which Duncan's dead body is discovered. Macduff, bursting in with the news of the discovery, stresses those aspects of it which imply the reversal of natural order and the commission of sacrilege:

> *Confusion* now hath made his masterpiece!
> Most *sacrilegious* murder hath broke ope
> *The Lord's anointed temple,* and stole thence
> *The life o' the building.*   [II. iii. 66-9]

On his own re-entry, a moment later, Macbeth once more expresses, in the typically heightened and unnatural spirit which reflects his distraught condition, the positive values which he has deliberately chosen to attack. Royalty truly established and freely accepted is, indeed, "the life o' the building," the foundation upon which all natural relationships in society depend; and Macbeth, in his effort to simulate a sorrow which he alone cannot feel, speaks more truly than he knows when he says:

> from this instant,
> There's nothing serious in mortality:
> All is but toys; renown and grace is dead;
> The wine of life is drawn, and the mere lees
> Is left this vault to brag of.
>
> [II. iii. 92-6]

When the murderer thus surrounds the dead majesty of Duncan with images of life and "grace," he both stresses the sacramental quality, so to call it, of the victim's office (even the implications of "the wine of life" may hold a subsidiary meaning in this respect) and reveals how his own deed has left him nothing but the dregs and "toys" which will from now on dominate his utterances to the end of the tragedy. The sense that the future is, for Macbeth, as obscure as the manifestations of darkness and chaos which now surround him leads finally to the complete reversal of the "gracious" imagery of life and light which surrounded the figure of Duncan. "Dark night *strangles* the travelling lamp," the king's horses "contend against obedience," and, most powerfully of all,

> darkness does the face of earth *entomb,*
> When *living* light should *kiss* it.
>
> [II. iv. 7, 17, 9-10]

The point of balance between the happy past and the forebodings of the future is finally expressed in Macduff's remarks to Ross:

Ross:	Will you to Scone?
Macduff:	No, cousin, I'll to Fife.
Ross:	Well, I will thither.
Macduff:	Well, may you see things well done there.—adieu,
	Lest our old robes sit easier than our new.
	[II. iv. 35-8]

Exchanges of this kind repeatedly mark what are in effect turning points in the spiritual not less than in the surface development of the action; their use, indeed, is a typical feature of this most carefully and deliberately constructed of plays. (pp. 434-36)

To Macbeth, indeed, who has murdered not only a man and his kinsman, but, in the person of his king, order, unity itself, sleep can offer no refuge and no restoration. At best he can connect it, not with the renewal of vital energy, but with death, the only release from the continuation of a life the content and significance of which he has killed. In this spirit, when first alone with his wife after their crowning, he opposes his own insomnia nostalgically to the peace which his victim has found in death:

> better be with the dead,
> Whom we, to gain our peace, have sent to peace,
> Than on the torture of the mind to lie
> In restless ecstasy. Duncan is in his grave;
> After life's fitful fever he sleeps well.
>
> [III. ii. 19-23]

To suggest as Santayana once suggested [see Additional Bibliography], that this phrase sums up Shakespeare's attitude toward life (in so far as one can be discovered) is remarkably misleading. Macbeth's state of mind can in no way be identified with the complete conception of this tragedy. Opposed to it there stands, as we have noted and shall see again in the concluding scenes, the norm and plenitude, the splendid ordering of experience achieved in the poetry of Duncan and finally confirmed in the "symbolic" function of Malcolm. Macbeth's attitude toward death cannot be identified with that of Shakespeare in this play (something like it is perhaps the most unambiguous feeling in *Hamlet*), though the dramatist no doubt felt it keenly and persistently as an element in his experience. It is rather the product of Macbeth's original crime against loyalty and order, against the harmony and continuity which makes experience valuable. In murdering Duncan, his usurper murdered the coherence of his own life, so that henceforth we expect of him (as, in reality, he expects of himself) nothing but death.

The turning point of the entire action (if a turning point can properly be spoken of in a series of events so closely and continuously related to their point of departure) is finally reached in the two scenes in which Macbeth, after returning to consult the Witches, proceeds in full disillusionment to the murder of the family of Macduff. The new approach to the Witches involves a fully conscious acceptance of anarchy; he will know the future, he says, even though the result be universal chaos, even though

> the treasure
> Of nature's germins tumble all together,
> Even till destruction sicken.
>
> [IV. i. 58-60]

The reply he receives, ambiguous to the last in accordance with the nature of evil as it presents itself to its servants in this play, at once offers an illusory certainty and, in the succeeding apparitions offered to his eyes, foreshadows the future development of the action. Each of the apparitions, indeed, insinuates a double meaning, offers a fallacious confirmation to Macbeth's evil instincts at the same time that it symbolizes a stage in the birth, through tragedy and retribution, of a new positive order. . . . Seen in this way, the scene turns upon a contrast between the false certainties offered to Macbeth and

the anticipated rebirth of innocence in ordered loyalty; the only unambiguous glimpse into the future conceded to the usurper is that which his insistence wrings from the Witches and which shows him the sterility of his line in contrast to the fruitful succession derived from the loyal Banquo. From this moment the murderer, now aware that his crime has been in vain, knows also that there is no retreat from its consequences, that what remains of his life is inexorably caught in the determined chain of circumstances which his own act has initiated.

The disillusionment produced in Macbeth by the revelation of the Witches henceforth dominates his whole being. The crown placed on his head has proved "fruitless," the scepter grasped by his usurping hands "barren" (the continuation, implied in its opposite, of the imagery of fertility so closely connected with Duncan is most significant), and the supernatural fears of the early scenes have hardened into the conviction that he has indeed, and vainly, surrendered "the eternal jewel" of his soul "to the common enemy of man" [III. i. 67-8]. The decision to murder Macduff and his family (IV. ii) marks his final enslavement to the determined course of events. (pp. 438-41)

The two scenes which thus mark the final disillusionment of Macbeth also convey the lowest point in the misery of Scotland, whose state is now so clearly contrasted with the happiness formerly enjoyed under Duncan. Her sorrows, in Macduff's phrase, "strike heaven in the face" [IV. iii. 6], the loyal remnants have fled, and Macduff himself, with a carelessness that he admits to be unpardonable, has left his family to die at the hands of their butcher. Yet, at the very moment when this particularly gratuitous crime is carried out, Shakespeare confirms through a single speech of Ross that a further decisive stage in the action has been reached. Ross is one of those minor personages to whom Shakespeare, more especially in his later plays, gives some of the functions of a chorus; he comments upon the events which take place before him, and his speeches are often statements of fact so made that their imagery unites them to the poetic construction of the play. Ross now addresses Lady Macduff in these words:

> cruel are the times, when we are traitors
> And do not know ourselves; when we hold rumour
> From what we fear, yet know not what we fear,
> But float upon a wild and violent sea
> *Each way and move.* I take my leave of you;
> Shall not be long but I'll be here again:
> *Things at the worst will cease, or else climb upward*
> *To what they were before.*
>
> [IV. ii. 18-24]

The conclusion clearly anticipates the course of events to follow: Macbeth's overthrow with the recovery of loyalty and the "single state of man" in the triumph of Malcolm. This scene, in fact, in spite of the horrors enacted in it, marks a point of balance in the entire development (that is, the effect so finely conveyed in the suspense of "Each way and move"), with a first suggestion of the recovery. (pp. 441-42)

The last act of *Macbeth*, the logical rounding off of a process conceived from its first moment as a unity, deals with the return of the kingship of "grace." The word, which we shall meet again in the last plays (notably in *The Winter's Tale*), is used by Shakespeare to express the harmony associated with the "single state of man." It is noteworthy that in the very scene between Malcolm and Macduff which we have just considered, the loyal elements scattered by Macbeth's tyranny anticipate the access of new strength to their cause from the action of yet another holy king—Edward the Confessor of England. The Lord who converses with Lennox just before Macbeth's return to the Witches first indicates the coming reaction when he speaks of the sanctity of "the most pious Edward" [III. vi. 27] and associates it openly with the restoration of natural harmony to a wounded society. . . . (p. 443)

As Malcom returns with [the] army of deliverance, the divisions implicit in evil come to the surface in his foes. In contrast to Edward's healing power, the Doctor at Dunsinane cannot cure the disharmony beneath Lady Macbeth's sleepwalking. "More needs she the divine than the physician" [V. i. 74]; the words reveal the absence of the "healing benediction" which Malcolm has triumphantly invoked. From the first, as we have seen, the sleep of the murderers has been wrapped in a darkness shot through with "cursed thoughts," pregnant with subconscious images of retribution. As such, it fails to bring relief to either Macbeth or to his wife. As one sin against "grace," conscience, and human obligation follows another, the chaotic intensity originally present in Macbeth's mind is replaced by a mere weary lack of feeling; even revulsion gives way to dead insensibility. . . . The murderer continues to the last to go through the motions of action, but his deeds are divorced from all desire or feeling, however inhuman. His end, when it comes, is no more than the logical conclusion of a process which aimed at the destruction of harmonious life to replace it by anarchy and death.

In the light of these considerations, we may understand better the final scenes of the tragedy, reading into them something more than a monotonous series of battle episodes leading to a foregone conclusion. To this end, we need to avoid above all the temptation to sentimentalize Macbeth in the hour of his downfall, regarding him primarily as a brave warrior making his last stand against hopeless odds. He is indeed that, in part and up to a point; but it is more important to see him above all as a man who has freely chosen his own particular and appropriate hell and who is now faced with the undisguised consequences of his choice. (pp. 445-46)

> D. A. Traversi, "The Mature Tragedies," in his An Approach to Shakespeare, *revised edition, 1968. Reprint by Doubleday & Company, Inc., 1969, pp. 399-490.*

PAUL A. JORGENSEN   (essay date 1971)

[*In the following excerpt from his* Our Naked Frailties: Sensational Art and Meaning in "Macbeth" *(1971), Jorgensen examines the theme of innocence in* Macbeth, *a theme previously noted by G. Wilson Knight (1931) and L. C. Knights (1933). Laying heavy emphasis on Shakespeare's use of "that most universally appealing symbol of Innocence, babies," Jorgensen discusses Macbeth's violation of innocence and the subsequent triumph of innocence over Macbeth. He also associates the images of milk and nakedness with innocence and states that even Macbeth and Lady Macbeth reflect "a limited but moving degree" of innocence.*]

If Shakespeare achieves terror for [*Macbeth*] through the fact and symbolism of blood, he achieves pity by giving poignant emphasis to the innocence of the victims, and even of the protagonists themselves. Duncan, for example, becomes not the contemptibly weak king of Holinshed but a much older man, a "sainted" sovereign who is meek and clear in his great office, who trusts everyone, who weeps out of goodness of heart—who is hardly, indeed, little more than Innocence personified. The idea of Innocence as victim is so insistent in Shakespeare's concept of the action that it gets into the most

intuitive part of the play, the imagery. And the imagery, as well as the action, is full of that most universally appealing symbol of Innocence, babies.

Perhaps the most deeply felt part of Macbeth's vision of retributive justice is the lines expressing his reaction to destroying so meek and clear a king:

> And Pity, like a naked new-born babe,
> Striding the blast, or heaven's Cherubins, hors'd
> Upon the sightless couriers of the air,
> Shall blow the horrid deed in every eye,
> That tears shall drown the wind.
>
> [I. vii. 21-5]

Pity here takes the form of a babe who is seemingly helpless and yet powerful to blow the horrid deed in every eye. (pp. 94-5)

Shakespeare, even in his earliest plays, conceived of the supreme form of violence as that against Innocence and, at the same time, showed that Innocence is anything but helpless in the working out of providence. Macbeth knew this part of his fate in the "If it were done" soliloquy [I. vii. 1-28], but like other parts of his fate, he did not know its frightful power.

In this soliloquy Macbeth pictures Pity as "a naked new-born babe." He could image nothing more vulnerable, more sensitive. The "naked" adds what "new-born" really does not need, the essence of exposure. But feeling in this play takes the form of nakedness. When, for instance, all the thanes are gathered after Duncan's murder is known and Lady Macbeth has just fainted, Banquo suggests:

> And when we have our naked frailties hid,
> That suffer in exposure, let us meet,
> And question this most bloody piece of work,
> To know it further.
>
> [II. iii. 126-29]

On a literal level Banquo may mean only, since those present are hastily clad, that they should meet after getting dressed. But the "naked frailties" well expresses the exposed feelings of all present, even of Lady Macbeth; and we shall see that in a play unparalleled in sensation, the naked frailties of almost all the actors are of major importance—those who clearly represent Pity and those who, like Macbeth and his Lady, have the horrid deed blown in their eye. And we should look ahead here by noting a feature of the soliloquy which will occupy our attention later: the eye, of all parts of the body, is the most helpless, the most sensitive; and a major part of Macbeth's punishment from Pity will be through the eye.

There are other emphatic examples of helpless babies in the play. Lady Macbeth requires an allusion to a baby in order to give the utmost force to her resolution:

> I have given suck, and know
> How tender 'tis to love the babe that milks me:
> I would, while it was smiling in my face,
> Have pluck'd my nipple from his boneless gums,
> And dash'd the brains out, had I so sworn
> As you have done to this.
>
> [I. vii. 54-9]

It would be difficult to exceed this speech in the combination of innocence and violence. There are words of great softness of feeling; *tender, love, milks, smiling, nipple,* and *boneless gums.* Against these are matched the ferocity of *pluck'd* and *dash'd the brains out.* No speech better illustrates the basis on which sensationalism is built in much of the play: naked frailties violated by brutal evil. And we should not fail to note that the naked frailties exposed here are those of Lady Macbeth. She knows "How tender 'tis to love the babe that milks me"; she has seen the infant smiling in her face. If she were without nakedness, we should not feel the full horror of her demonic resolution ar commitment. That she is here attuning herself to the Witches is suggested by the lines of one of them:

> Finger of birth-strangled babe,
> Ditch-deliver'd by a drab. . . .

> [IV. i. 30-1]

The Witches, too, sacrifice a babe for their brew, and this particular brew differs from Lady Macbeth's sacrifice only in being deliberately prepared for Macbeth's ruin. It will be, like the naked feelings Lady Macbeth sacrifices in the imagined form of a baby, an agent of retribution.

Except for the Apparitions, the other babe figures are less symbolic. The suffering of Scotland under Macbeth as tyrant is expressed by the crying of orphans [IV. iii. 5]. Macduff's penalty for helping to save his country is to have his "babes, / Savagely slaughter'd" [IV. iii. 204-05]. The scenes of the slaughter and the reception of it by Macduff are made much of, doubtless to enhance the strong strain of Pity suffering under tyranny and the necessary, but temporal, sacrifice of Innocence in the ultimate triumph. This purpose is found in another form in the scene of Macduff's grief—Malcolm's testing of Macduff. This scene is often criticized as a lengthy distraction, but we should remember that it contains, besides the report of Macduff's children slaughtered, another theme of Innocence: that of the innocent Malcolm who will soon be victorious. Shakespeare takes great pains to point out not simply the virture of Malcolm but also his almost babelike innocence. He protests to Macduff:

>   I am young; but something
> You may deserve of him through me, and wisdom
> To offer up a weak, poor, innocent lamb,
> T'appease an angry god.

> [IV. iii. 14-17]

In the earnestness of his dramatic message, Shakespeare almost overstates the theme of Innocence violated. We have not just "lamb"—adequate in itself—but "weak, poor, innocent lamb." Malcolm further protests that he is unknown to women, has never told a lie or broken faith [IV. iii. 125-31]. At the risk of making his savior of Scotland Innocence personified rather than a real character, Shakespeare lays on the childlike qualities relentlessly.

The ultimate triumph of babes, including young Malcolm, is figured forth in the Apparitions shown to Macbeth as his destiny. The First Apparition is an armed head, representing probably not Macduff, as some critics think, nor Macbeth's own head, but the armed head of the rebellion that will unseat the tyrant. The Second Apparition, "a bloody child," is almost certainly the baby who was untimely ripped from his mother's womb—Macduff. Significantly, a Witch describes him as "more potent than the first" [IV. i. 76]. The symbolism is perfect for the theme of Innocence ultimately triumphant, for the babe is shown to be more awful to Macbeth than the armed head. It is, moreover, this Apparition who by his message helps to lead Macbeth, through willful blindness, to destruction. The Third Apparition is another babe figure: "a child crowned with a tree in his own hand," obviously Malcolm. He too is of terrible

consequence, for he "wears upon his baby brow the round / And top of sovereignty" [IV. i. 88-9].

Allied to the babe motif in suggestion of Innocence is that of milk. Malcolm, to express the worst possible horror that he would allegedly perpetrate as King, puts it in terms of desecrated milk:

>   Nay, had I power, I should
> Pour the sweet milk of concord into Hell,
> Uproar the universal peace, confound
> All unity on earth.

> [IV. iii. 97-100]

Milk is the ideal substance to betoken concord, that which brings men together in fundamental compassion. Such meaning is hinted at by Lady Macbeth in the first reference to milk in the play. She describes her absent husband as "too full o' the milk of human kindness, / To catch the nearest way" [I. v. 17-18]. Her misgiving is justified, for it is an important part of his tragedy that he can feel for humankind. Without this quality in him the sensationalism of the play would be expended purely from without, upon the observers and victims. Macbeth, as his beautiful description of Duncan shows, has within himself the innocence, the nakedness of feeling, that makes him at first the principal sufferer from the horrid deed. So, to a lesser extent, does Lady Macbeth herself. The most appropriate symbol of the innocence that she is trying to give up is her milk, which she offers in exchange for gall to the murdering ministers [I. v. 47-9]. Indeed, one of the most shocking instances of Innocence violated is her prayer for unsexing.

To exactly what degree she succeeds in destroying her own milk of human kindness, we shall never know. She does faint. She must secretly, nightly, relive the murder until her desperate death. She remains innocent of murder after the first horrible crime. Unlike her husband, she never hardens into further brutality. There is even a pathetic solicitude, a desire to keep his wife innocent, in Macbeth's affectionate concern for her as he plans the murder of Banquo. Her frightened, hopeless "What's to be done?" draws his reassurance, "Be innocent of the knowledge, dearest chuck, / Till thou applaud the deed" [III. ii. 44-6]. And there is a pathetic quality even in the bloody Macbeth after Banquo's murder when he sees his hallucination as "the initiate fear, that wants hard use: / We are yet but young in deed" [III. iv. 142-43]. One never completely loses sight of the pity, in both of them, that is being hardened. But tears do not, for either of them, really drown the wind. The Pity that defeats them is that babelike Innocence that rises triumphant, not within themselves, but in others.

However, one aspect of violated Innocence does arise, within Macbeth himself, to torment him. This is sleep. Macbeth's first reference to sleep as victim shows that he is aware of its vulnerability:

>   Now o'er the one half-world
> Nature seems dead, and wicked dreams abuse
> The curtain'd sleep.

> [II. i. 49-51]

The image is a very good one. It may mean that wicked dreams attack, or deceive, the helpless sleep beneath the closed eyelids, the vulnerable place. Or it may suggest the picture of a bed of state, curtained like Duncan's, behind which protection the insidious intruder may slip in. Lady Macbeth has a skeptical, perhaps resolutely skeptical, idea of both the sleeping and the dead [II. ii. 42-54]. But Macbeth receives horror from the act of murdering the sleeping Duncan. This act enlarges for him the voice which cries:

> "Sleep no more!
> Macbeth does murder Sleep,"—the innocent Sleep. . . .
>
> [II. ii. 32-3]

He will be able to sleep no more, perhaps unto eternity. And it is worth noting that once again Shakespeare makes the victim specifically innocent, and yet potentially terrible.

Innocence may rise victorious in many instances, but its victory is made the more important by the pervasiveness with which it is buffeted and outraged in scattered images throughout the play. Darkness *entombs* the face of the earth when living light should kiss it [II. iv. 9-10]. *Entomb* is a particularly strong verb to apply to *face*, and it achieves strength by contrast with a word of love, *kiss*, singularly rare in *Macbeth*. Dark night also *strangles* the symbol of goodness, the *travelling lamp* [II. iv. 6]. While the face of earth is entombed, "new sorrows / Strike heaven on the face" so that it yells out in dolor [IV. iii. 5-8]. Heaven struck on the face is certainly the supreme symbol of Innocence violated. And we may note that Heaven "felt with Scotland" [IV. iii. 7]. Innocence is not quiescent. Another disturbing instance of darkness as a threat to Innocence comes from Macbeth's observation before the murder of Banquo:

> Good things of Day begin to droop and drowse,
> Whiles Night's black agents to their preys do rouse.
>
> [III. ii. 52-3]

Under Macbeth's tyranny, the good things of day generally suffer. Macduff cries out at the apparent powerlessness of good:

> Bleed, bleed, poor country!
> Great tyranny, lay thou thy basis sure,
> For goodness dare not check thee!
>
> [IV. iii. 31-3]

And of his wife and children he asks, "The tyrant has not batter'd at their peace?" [IV. iii. 178]. But Macbeth, ironically, has more than battered at the innocent peace of others. He has "Put rancours in the vessel" of his own "peace" [III. i. 66]. And not only for others but for himself and his Lady, he violated one of those great symbols of humankindness, human fellowship, when he "broke the good meeting / With most admir'd disorder" [III. iv. 108-09].

Unlike his contemporaries, therefore, Shakespeare extends the horror and pity of outraged Innocence to more than the fact of murder, and to more than babies. He includes the innocence of the mild Duncan, of the good people of daylight, of Heaven, and even—to a limited but moving degree—of Macbeth and Lady Macbeth, who are, in a terrible manner neither of them fully knows, still very young in deed. (pp. 103-09)

> *Paul A. Jorgensen, in his* Our Naked Frailties: Sensational Art and Meaning in "Macbeth," *University of California Press, 1971, 234 p.*

BERNARD Mc ELROY   (essay date 1973)

[*Mc Elroy argues that the tragedy of* Macbeth *lies in the discrepancy between Macbeth's evil actions and his abhorrence of evil. He notes that* Macbeth *is the most internal of Shakespeare's tragedies and that the protagonist is "his own most formidable adversary." Like Jan Kott (1964), Mc Elroy asserts that Macbeth is revolted by the act of killing Duncan, but tantalized by the daring of it. And unlike Robert B. Heilman (1964), Mc Elroy*

maintains that Macbeth is "fully aware of the enormity of his transgressions"; because of this, the critic calls the play a tragedy of self-loathing and self-horror, "the tragedy of a man who comes to condemn all that is in him for being there." Mc Elroy contends, against such critics as Robert Pack (1956), that Macbeth retains his humanity throughout the play because he retains an awareness of the magnitude of his crimes. He concludes that the play offers a pyrrhic victory that is "retributive but not redemptive."]

In *Macbeth*, Shakespeare focuses his attention fully upon a problem he had dealt with peripherally in *Hamlet* and *Measure for Measure*: that of the criminal who is deeply aware of his own criminality, is repulsed by it, but is driven by internal and external pressures ever further into crime. What differentiates such villains as Claudius, Angelo, and Macbeth from Richard III, Iago, and Edmund is that the former fully admit the validity and worth of the moral laws they violate, while the latter dismiss the ethical standards of the world as so much folly and delusion. The latter three relish their superiority over their victims, while the former judge themselves from the same ethical perspectives as their victims. The descendants of the Vice believe in what they do, while the conscience-stricken criminals are in the agonizing position of being committed by their actions to one set of values while committed by their beliefs to quite another. *Macbeth* dramatizes this predicament as experienced by a man who possesses the fundamental qualities of the Shakespearean tragic hero.

For all its emphasis upon blood and violence, *Macbeth* is the most completely internal of all Shakespeare's tragedies. It presents us with a man who has a clear conception of the universe and his own proper place in it. But, when confronted with the possibility of committing a daring though criminal act, he wilfully deceives himself for a short time and embraces an opposite view of the world. In the aftermath of an irrevocable act, he finds himself irrevocably committed to a world-view in which he does not believe. The key to his savagery, and, even more, to the soul-sickness that elevates him to tragedy, is that he must proceed as if the self-delusion were true, when in his mind and heart he knows that it is not. This constant lying to himself, and the discrepancy between his beliefs and the world that he has chosen for himself, produce the self-loathing and the numbing sense of loss that are the essence of his tragedy. (pp. 206-07)

The world Macbeth sees corresponds in striking detail to the world that the play presents us. Indeed, when the Thane describes his microcosm on the eve of the murder, he presents us with a most haunting delineation of the macrocosm, the world of the play:

> Now o'er the one half-world
> Nature seems dead, and wicked dreams abuse
> The curtained sleep. Witchcraft celebrates
> Pale Hecate's offerings; and withered murder,
> Alarumed by his sentinel, the wolf,
> Whose howl's his watch, thus with his stealthy pace,
> With Tarquin's ravishing strides, towards his design
> Moves like a ghost.
>
> [II. i. 49-56]

Because of this coalescence between the macrocosm and the microcosm, Macbeth's own words provide us with the most useful index to the salient qualities of the *Macbeth*-world. (pp. 207-08)

Perhaps the most extraordinary thing about the *Macbeth*-world is that it contains a strong, effective principle of retributive justice in operation throughout the play. This is not something which our experience with the worlds of Shakespeare's trag-edies would lead us to expect. In *Hamlet,* to be sure, there is a heavenly inclination toward justice, but, like all things in the *Hamlet*-world, it works in obscure and devious ways. In *Othel-lo,* there is only that justice which the characters can make for themselves—too late. In *King Lear,* tragedy occurs finally be-cause there is no justice, no way to make ethics and experience congruent. But in *Macbeth,* the title character describes a ver-ifiable phenomenon when he observes:

> But in these cases
> We still have judgment here, that we but teach
> Bloody instructions, which, being taught, return
> To plague th' inventor. This even-handed justice
> Commends th' ingredience of our poisoned chalice
> To our own lips.
>
> [I. vii. 7-12]

Paradoxically, it is the presence rather than the absence of justice in the *Macbeth*-world that gives the tragedy its partic-ularly grim and futile outlook. The forces of conventional good triumph completely, but their triumph is strangely hollow, al-most devoid of any power to mitigate the reality of evil or reconcile humanity to its condition. Justice in the *Macbeth*-world gives the impression of being less real and significant than the problems it successfully confronts. That evil exists is the essential fact in the world of the play; that, in the face of its existence, there is nothing to do but punish it is the essential futility. It is at the moment of justice's complete triumph that the most famous statement of futility echoes sepulchrally from the depths of Macbeth's world and from the *Macbeth*-world itself. It will not do to say that "tomorrow and tomorrow" are the embittered words of a man who has lost his humanity, for they carry far more weight within the context of the play than does anything spoken by the lackluster defenders of right. Jus-tice is necessary, and we greet its reestablishment with a sigh of relief; but to say that justice is necessary is not the same as to say it is meaningful. When Macbeth commits his crime, he seems to embody a dimension of mankind left quite untouched by Macduff's and Malcolm's vengeance upon the individual man. It is almost as if Shakespeare were taking the most op-timistic theological explanation of the operation of divine jus-tice and demonstrating that it, too, contains the seeds of trag-edy.

No other Shakespearean hero faces so pallid an array of an-tagonists. (pp. 214-15)

By pitting Macbeth against a combination of forces whose sum total is so much less compelling than himself, Shakespeare emphasizes that in this play, the protagonist is his own most formidable adversary. As I say, *Macbeth* is the most private and internal of Shakespeare's tragedies, and the tragic suffering that occurs is the torture of the mind that goes on within the hero and heroine. But, further, the comparatively pallid nature of the hero's opponents is essential to the complementary ten-sion of the play, a tension that accounts for the deep ambiv-alence of feeling which the tragedy prompts toward its title character. The central question to which almost all critics have addressed themselves is, "How can anyone who does what Macbeth does command not only our interest but our awe and empathy throughout the play? How can a man who violates his humanity tell us so much about what humanity is?" There is no doubt that Macbeth is wrong, but in his mammoth wrong-ness he completely overshadows the pint-size rightness of Mal-colm and is much closer to realizing the outer limits of human potential than the even-handed characters who remain cau-

tiously in the center. Like many tragic protagonists from Oed-ipus and Orestes to Kurtz and Raskolnikov, he is a lone voyager into the forbidden, who severs his ties with the comfort and security of the community. Such mythic figures do not merely circumvent conventional moral judgment; they pass through and beyond it. Throughout the play, Macbeth is surrounded by men who accept the limitations imposed upon them by the world, and he, too, initially considers his extraordinary powers to be "children and servants" to his king. He transgresses all the bounds that others accept, and in doing so he becomes evil and must be destroyed. But at the same time, in transgressing, fully aware of the enormity of his transgression, he assumes awe-inspiring dimensions quite beyond Duncan, Malcolm, Banquo, and Macduff. Humanity as Macbeth is terrible, but humanity as Malcolm is merely insipid. (pp. 216-17)

No other Shakespearean hero has so firm and correct a sense of self-knowledge, nor so fully developed a concept of the universe and his place in it. Macbeth has a unique ability to foresee both the practical and the ethical outcome of his actions. Lear, in contrast, starts off with a completely mistaken notion of who he is and what the world is like; he blindly pulls down tragedy upon his own head and is shocked and outraged when disaster strikes. Othello, because of his predisposition, con-vinces himself of a falsehood upon virtually no evidence. Ham-let, for all his mercurial brilliance, is hopelessly inept at fore-seeing the logical outcome of his actions. But Macbeth suffers from none of these perceptual shortcomings. The most terrible thing about his tragedy is that he goes to it with his eyes wide open, his vision unclouded, his moral judgment still in perfect working order. He wilfully disregards his own best perceptions and intuitions, but he is never rid of them. More than any other Shakespearean hero, he has a perfectly clear concept of who he is and where he stands—and it is exactly this perception that torments and spiritually destroys him.

In the opening scenes, Macbeth's mind is already under that kind of tension which we have seen to be so characteristic of mature Shakespearean tragedy, the tension that precedes the collapse of the personal world. The opposites are basic and the opposition is total. Macbeth is the most honored peer in the realm, but his honor is based upon incongruous and irrecon-cilable qualities; on the one hand, he is able and willing to dare anything and fear nothing, but, on the other, he accepts limits and boundaries which cannot under any circumstances be transgressed. Gory descriptions of his individual fearless deeds alternate with praise of him as a loyal subject who curbs the lavish spirits of those who dare to rise against their king. The tension of Macbeth's position in the macrocosm is reflected by a corresponding tension in the microcosm, the tension be-tween a deeply moral intellect and an utterly amoral will. (pp. 218-19)

In many respects, Macbeth is, right from the beginning, a poor candidate for the job of political assassin. For one thing, he is not really ambitious in the usual sense of the word. In the scenes leading up to the murder, he scarcely mentions the crown; he has none of his wife's sanguine anticipation of a golden round or nights and days of solely sovereign sway and masterdom. Unlike Tamburlane, he does not find kingship a sort of apotheosis of the human condition, and unlike Richard of Gloucester, he is not driven by a compulsive need to com-mand, to check, and to o'erbear such as are of better person than himself. In conventionally ambitious men, anticipation of the fruits of crime blunts the sensibilities to the crime itself. But Macbeth is just the opposite of this; he scarcely gives a thought to the spoils that will proceed from the act and keeps his attention unwaveringly upon the act itself; and his attitude toward the object of his fixation is mixed attraction and repulsion. His repulsion springs from the deeply moral side of his nature. No other character is so acutely aware of himself as living in the eye of heaven. When he looks into himself and finds there inclinations that are anything but celestial, he is frightened and revolted, and he extends his abhorrence of his own instinct to heaven nature:

> Stars, hide your fires;
> Let not light see my black and deep desires.
> The eye wink at the hand.
>
> [I. iv. 50-2]

Yet on the heels of this can come a reassertion of the impulse to terrible and forbidden action: "yet let that be / Which the eye fears, when it is done, to see" [I. iv. 52-3]. It is the very fearfulness of the deed that seems to exert the strongest attraction for him, since it calls for a degree of resolution and daring quite beyond the slaying of rebels. For Macbeth, action is self-definition; he is revolted by the act, but tantalized by the possibility of doing exactly that which is most expressly forbidden by all laws, sacred and humane. He dares to kill his king not so much to become king himself as to become the man who dared to do it. (pp. 219-20)

Macbeth and his lady have the makings of one murderer between them. She is capable of contemplating the crime with something that borders upon exaltation, but is not, it turns out, capable of dealing the fatal stroke herself. He is quite capable of doing that, but cannot even think of the moral quality of the act without horror and aversion. He would, no doubt, be capable of resisting the temptation to strike were it not for the devastating attack she launches against the foundation of his world-view, his concept of what it means to be a man. Thus, the great confrontation between them in Act 1, scene vii, presents the disconcerting picture of *two* people inciting each other to crime, for the presence of each makes crime possible for the other.

Macbeth's soliloquy at the opening of the scene gives us our first full view of the hero's subjective world; it is a world in which action is a continuum, an ongoing process of cause and effect, act and consequence, a world in which retributive justice is not merely possible but certain. It is also a world of relatedness, a world in which duties and obligations are well defined and divinely sanctioned. In such a world, vaulting ambition, far from being heroic self-assertion, is unconscionable overreaching, a violation of the sacrosanct bonds that define one's humanity. By the end of the soliloquy, Macbeth has decided to abandon all thoughts of regicide, for in such a world, to proceed would be not only appalling, but positively suicidal. When he announces his decision to his wife, the reason he gives, the "golden opinions" his valor has just won from all sorts of people, is an evasion. He cannot explain his real reasons—retribution from heaven, the sacred bonds of obligation—because she simply would not comprehend them, would, in fact, heap scorn upon them. But his stated reason is a significant and characteristic evasion; the golden opinions epitomize his position as a valorous subject who is content to accept the status of subject and live as an honored member of the community.

Lady Macbeth is able to undermine his resolution so quickly not simply because she calls his virility into question, and not simply because she exerts enormous personal power over their

relationship; Macbeth is quite capable of withstanding such pressures. She finally achieves her purposes by suggesting to him that his whole apprehension of reality is mistaken, that action is not an open-ended continuum, but is final and conclusive, and that the essence of humanity is not living within the limits of an assigned place, but daring to do anything. Her attack on Macbeth is the same as Goneril's attack upon Albany; because he is moral, he is a coward and a fool who deceives himself about the way the world really operates. But her arguments are far more effective than Goneril's because she is not telling her husband anything new, but reiterating things he had already told himself. Like Hamlet and Othello, Macbeth has a divided mind about some of the most fundamental issues of existence; Lady Macbeth is the voice of one side of it. (pp. 221-23)

She undermines his confidence in the vision of the soliloquy by pointing out that he does not fully believe in it himself. At one time he had been more than willing to kill the king if only the opportunity would present itself. "If we should fail?" [I. vii. 59]. This, Macbeth's last attempt at resistance, has been widely misunderstood. As the soliloquy showed, he is not in the least worried about the practical possibility of executing the murder: if that were all there were to it, he would proceed at once. But the failure Macbeth fears is the long-range failure in a world of relatedness, where action is a continuum and justice is certain—to be cut off forever from the rest of humanity, to be hated and cursed by all men, and finally to be hounded down by inexorable retribution. It is the long-range failure he had pictured in harrowing detail, and it is, in fact, exactly what happens.... Macbeth accepts the notion that action is final and conclusive, that accomplishment of the deed is tantamount to success, that the consequences of an action may be circumvented:

> Will it not be received,
> When we have marked with blood those sleepy two
> Of his own chamber and used their very daggers,
> That they have done't?
>
> [I. vii. 74-7]

Like Othello's "And yet, how nature erring from itself—" [*Othello*, III. iii. 227], it is the point of no return, for it signals not simply a change of mind, but a movement from one world-view to another. The seeds of Macbeth's tragedy are planted here, not only because he dedicates himself to the first of many brutal crimes, but even more because he does not really *believe* in a world in which a man may dare anything, in which action is final and conclusive. He *wants* to believe in it, for such a world poses no impediments to action. His ruthless will scores a temporary victory over his own best perceptions. But the shallowness and patent self-deception of this speech contrast sharply with the intense and passionate conviction of the soliloquy. From this point on, Macbeth is in the position of having to insist with all the vigor of his will upon the truth of something which, in his own mind, he does not really believe. His method of insistence will be action, and the result will be tragedy. (pp. 224-26)

For the remainder of the play, Macbeth sees himself as being in fundamental conflict with the world itself, with his indomitable will pitted against its moral order, its communal obligations, its immutable and inescapable ethical laws. Like all the Shakespearean tragic heroes, he sees his own actions in cosmic terms; but after the dreadful finality of "I am resolved," he is positively obsessed by the notion of being at the center of a universe which is fundamentally opposed to what he is doing. Like Hamlet, he declares total, all-out war upon the world of the play, but his attack is not against duplicity and corruption, but against humane feeling and divine justice. (p. 226)

The self-delusion that action is final and conclusive crumbles before the realization that the consequences of his deed will last as long as his life: ''Macbeth shall sleep no more'' [II. ii. 50]. He is fully aware that he can never by any means get back to the bank and shoal of time from which he has so precipitously leaped; nothing can change or mitigate the consequences of his act:

> Will all great Neptune's ocean wash this blood
> Clean from my hand? No, this my hand will rather
> The multitudinous seas incarnadine,
> Making the green one red.
>
> [II. ii. 57-60]

But most of all, his crime destroys his capacity to respect or even to tolerate himself. For the remainder of the play, the vantage point from which he judges himself is the world-view from which he is hopelessly estranged. His own hands are unrecognizable to him, savage, hangman's hands that would pluck out his eyes. But, in fact, they do not obliterate his vision; he must continue staring at them and at the self they epitomize. The primary purpose of his act had been to define his manhood. Ironically, it does, but the definition is one he cannot contemplate without horror and revulsion: ''To know my deed, 'twere best not know myself'' [II. ii. 70]. This line sets the tone for the remainder of the tragedy. He *is* his deed in his own eyes, and in his own eyes his deed is appalling. Hence, he faces the characteristic problem of the Shakespearean tragic hero, how to endure what is, for him, simply unendurable. I do not read *Macbeth* as a tragedy of ambition, nor as a tragedy of fear. It is above all a tragedy of self-loathing, of self-horror that leads to spiritual paralysis, the tragedy of a man who comes to condemn all that is in him for being there. Macbeth is indeed terror-stricken in this scene, but what strikes him full of terror is not the deed itself, and still less the fear of being caught, but rather a full realization of what his action has done to him. He has cut himself off from the world he believes in and has committed himself to its antithesis, a world in which man is a predatory animal. The commitment is irrevocable, and all he can do is follow it remorselessly to its conclusion. It is as if by insisting vehemently enough on such a world-view, Macbeth believes he can validate it, can establish its reality by sheer force of will. It is the desperate need to validate the world-view to which he is committed, his determination to win a battle of wills with the macrocosm itself, that plunges him into steadily deepening cruelty in Acts III and IV. (pp. 227-29)

In assuming that the murder of Banquo and Fleance would set his mind at rest, Macbeth was once again wilfully deluding himself, pretending that, if he insisted vehemently enough upon something, and put that insistence into act, then the thing would be true. But even if Fleance had shared his father's fate, it would be difficult to imagine a Macbeth who was not cabined, cribbed, and confined; his prison, his torture chamber, is not the macrocosm but the microcosm, and the death of one man or of thousands is incapable of setting things to rights there. But the escape of Fleance once again makes him see that the murder of Duncan was not a final or definitive act. It will go on through a continuum of cause and effect to produce consequences completely beyond his control. When he confronts the shade of Banquo (or the evil spirit sent by the witches in Banquo's shape, or the product of his own haunted imagina-

tion—there is no way of telling which, and no need to tell), he gives voice, even in his hysteria, to the basic rift in his own subjective world. On the one hand there is the world of infinite daring, but on the other there is the world of swift and terrible justice, in which dead victims rise again to push murderers from their stools. (pp. 232-33)

In the aftermath of his great feast, Macbeth is more convinced than ever that he is living in a macrocosm which implacably requires his destruction:

> It will have blood, they say: blood will have blood.
> Stones have been known to move and trees to speak;
> Augures and understood relations have
> By maggot-pies and choughs and rooks brought forth
> The secret'st man of blood.
>
> [III. iv. 121-25]

Yet, far from impeding him from further action, his conviction only impels him to ever more ruthless action; his insistence upon the world to which he is committed is now fired by desperation. In the face of his implacable will, all causes shall give way. His image of himself is not simply of a man with bloody, hangman's hands, but of a man inundated in blood, bathed in it from head to foot, literally into it over his head. But the total estrangement from all his previous values confers upon Macbeth, as it has upon other Shakespearean heroes, a terrible, lonely freedom. The man who has lost positively everything he cherishes is the freest of all possible men; he has nothing further to lose and nothing to worry about salvaging.

By the time he reaches the witches' abode, the naked force of his will has reached apocalyptic proportions reminiscent of the third act of *King Lear*. Macbeth thinks he has come to learn by the worst means the worst, for to know the worst is to lose a large part of fear of the worst. But the witches *want* Macbeth to struggle and hope, for they know that struggle is futile and hope groundless, and therefore torture. Thus, they tell him what appears to be better news than he had expected to hear. (pp. 233-34)

By far the most usual interpretation of the last act is that Macbeth has completely lost his humanity, has become the monster he set out to be, and though we continue to have grudging admiration for his animal courage, we rejoice with the followers of Malcolm when the tyrant and his fiend-like queen are overthrown. Rather, it seems to me that we are so absorbed in Macbeth's private conflict that his death and the triumph of unimpressive right is almost incidental to the tragedy. Moreover, Macbeth does not lose his humanity because he *cannot* lose his humanity no matter how hard he tries; that is exactly what makes him a tragic hero. His case is in one way analogous to Othello's: the Moor repeatedly resolves to cast away all love for Desdemona, but he simply cannot do it. His love remains, coexistent with his belief she has betrayed him, and the result is excruciating inner torture. Macbeth's humanity is vested in that world-view he unfolded in his first major soliloquy, and, though his most vigorous efforts throughout the play have been to rid himself of that vision, he has never even come close to doing so. It remains as a vantage point from which he must assess all that he has done, all that he has lost, all that he has become: ''I am sick at heart, / When I behold—'' [V. iii. 19-20]. The thought is left uncompleted, but clearly what Macbeth beholds all through these scenes is himself:

> I have lived long enough. My way of life
> Is fall'n into the sear, the yellow leaf,

And that which should accompany old age,
As honor, love, obedience, troops of friends,
I must not look to have.

[V. iii. 22-6]

Honor, love, obedience, and troops of friends are the values of the limited, structured world he had abandoned; in the predatory world he embraced, they should have no importance whatsoever. "To be tender-minded / Does not become a sword," Edmund had observed [*King Lear*, V. iii. 31-2]. But those values are terribly important to Macbeth, and only his loss of them has made him realize how important they are. Alfred Harbage has observed that "no voice in literature has sounded with greater sadness" than Macbeth's in the above speech [see Additional Bibliography]. To have a passionately held, demonstrably valid vision of the world, and yet to be cut off from it by one's own actions, to be hated and cursed by all humanity, to have to struggle against one's own most deeply felt emotions, and to be *aware* of all this with perfect, unblinking clarity, is surely the most harrowing vision of human isolation that has ever been realized in drama. It is perhaps the degree of his self-awareness that most differentiates him from other Shakespearean malefactors: he sees his own situation unflinchingly and refuses either to soften it or to be sentimental about himself. He drains the ingredients of his poisoned chalice to the last bitter dregs. Self-awareness is one of the hallmarks of the Shakespearean tragic hero, and in Macbeth's case, it is the very essence of his tragedy. Also, like the other three, he has a desperate need to have his actions in consonance with a broader scheme of reality, including the rest of humanity and the metaphysical order. But, as Macbeth fully realizes, such consonance is impossible for him because he is so utterly cut off from the only world he believes in or values. In self-recognition and self-horror he realizes he has lost even the capacity to feel fear, and a moment later he cannot feel normal human grief at the death of his wife. Above all, he realizes he has committed himself to action and yet he believes action to be futile, full of sound and fury, but signifying nothing.

That the vision of life offered in Macbeth's final soliloquy is not Shakespeare's ultimate or only significant pronouncement upon the human condition we need only our experience with the canon, including the other tragedies, to attest. Besides, *Macbeth* does not "make a statement" any more than *Lear* did. What Shakespeare was dramatizing was a potentiality of the human condition, in this case a most grim potentiality, but as true in its context as any other embodied in his dramas. It is realized with exceptional conviction and power, and to shrug it off as the observation of a man who has lost his humanity may make the play easier to live with, but undermines its imaginative vigor and ruthless integrity. Macbeth's pronouncement is the only pronouncement on life in the *Macbeth*-world; nothing of comparable weight is there to counterbalance it, and it draws its power not only from the greatness of the verse but also from its dramatic context. And here, I think, is the center of the problem, for is not its context a world which finally is moral, surely the most thoroughly just world Shakespeare created for a tragedy? The *Macbeth*-world is a moral world founded upon a moral incongruity, for while evil seems to issue spontaneously and irrepressibly from its very core, its most basic law is that evil *is* evil and must be destroyed. The same incongruity is repeated in the microcosm; Macbeth is strongly impelled to evil, but he is no less strongly impelled to abhor evil. Hence, he comes to abhor himself. If the world is basically inclined to evil, as the *Macbeth*-world is, then justice becomes

little more than a tragic necessity. Its pyrrhic victory is retributive but not redemptive.

The play, then, explores dialectically the complementary tension between proneness to evil and abhorrence of evil in both the macrocosm and the microcosm. Macbeth is not a tragic hero *in spite* of his criminality but *because* of his criminality. Had he been able to resist his own inclinations and the promptings of his wife, he would be of no more interest than any other successful general. Had he been able to kill without compunction, he would be simply one of our rarer monsters. But he is caught in the tension between his action and his reaction, the primary tension of the *Macbeth*-world, and in his struggle and his failure to reconcile irreconcilable conflicts, he assumes tragic dimensions. (pp. 235-37)

Bernard Mc Elroy, "'Macbeth': The Torture of the Mind," in his Shakespeare's Mature Tragedies, Princeton University Press, 1973, pp. 206-37.

MARILYN FRENCH   (essay date 1975)

[*In the following excerpt, French presents a feminist reading of* Macbeth, *focusing on what she views as a triumph of masculine, "heroic" principles over feminine ones. In* Macbeth's *Scotland, she argues, the perversion and collapse of femininity leads to chaos and an unbridled masculine course of "purposeless slaughter." French contends that this valorization of heroic slaughter extends both before and after Macbeth's career of crime, that at the outset he is rewarded for being a "butcher" in a battle and that at the conclusion "the ability to kill" remains a praiseworthy quality. Like Eugene M. Waith (1950), French considers the definition of manhood presented in* Macbeth, *noting that Macduff's ability to feel implies a more balanced sense of manliness than Macbeth's courage. In the end, she concludes, the feminine principle is still subjugated to the heroic masculine principle.*]

[The] witches who open *Macbeth* symbolize some perversion, signify that something is wrong with the feminine principle in Scotland. Their chant, "Fair is foul and foul is fair" [I. i. 11] is a legend of ambiguity in moral categories, but the ambiguity is more profound than that. It is also an ambiguity of gender: the witches are female but they have beards; they are aggressive and authoritative. The opening scene of *Macbeth* thereby links moral ambiguity to ambiguity about gender.

The first human words in the play place us in the "heroic" world: "What bloody man is that?" [I. ii. 1] Duncan inquires, and the answer describes the hero, Macbeth:

Disdaining Fortune, with his brandish'd steel,
Which smoked with bloody execution,
Like valour's minion carved out his passage
Till he faced the slave;
Which ne'er shook hands, nor bade farewell to him,
Till he unseam'd him from the nave to the chops,
And fix'd his head upon our battlements.

[I. ii. 17-23]

Such a description might shock and appall an audience, might imply that the hero is not totally admirable, but we hear only praise for Macbeth. He is "brave Macbeth," "valour's minion," "valiant cousin," "worthy gentlemen." And the praise comes from Duncan, the king, the authority figure. The sergeant's hideous description of the fighter's motivation—"Except they meant to bathe in reeking wounds, / Or memorize another Golgotha, / I cannot tell" [I. ii. 39-41]—reaps only more praise and rewards.

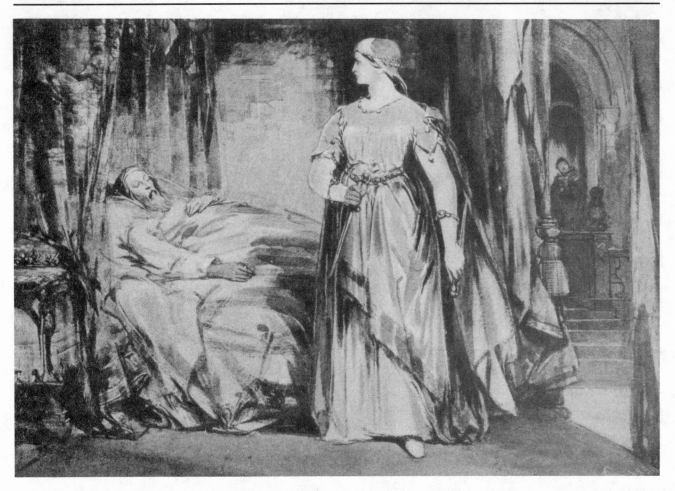

Act II. Scene ii. Duncan and Lady Macbeth. By George Cattermole (n.d.).

At the end of this play we accept without demur the judgment that Macbeth is a butcher. In fact, however, he is no more a butcher then than he is at the opening. His crime is not in being a murderer; he is praised and rewarded for being a murderer. His crime is a failure to make the distinctions his culture accepts among the objects of his slaughter.

A world that maintains itself by violence must, for the sake of sanity, fence off some segment—family, neighborhood, nation—within which violence is not the accepted mode of action. In this "civilized" section of the world, law and custom are supposed to supersede the right of might. Although there seems no reason to find this inner circle more "natural" than the outer one, it too, like feminine and masculine principles, is described as bound in accordance with a principle of nature or of divine law. This smaller world is actually an exemplar of the feminine principle, since it involves acceptance of subordination, a relinquishment of worldly power in favor of an agreed-upon ordering based on principles other than might. Such relinquishment is necessary to felicities such as friendship, ceremony, laws of succession and hospitality, and the essential condition of this inviolable segment of the world is that the laws bind by themselves. They are not enforceable because enforcement is part of the large outer circle. If they must be enforced, the inner circle becomes identical with the outer: they therefore exist only insofar as the members of the group abide by them. Macbeth chooses to break the rules.

The factor responsible for Macbeth's violation of the rules is Lady Macbeth. Although there is a suggestion that Macbeth has previously considered taking the kingdom by force, it is clear from his vacillation that he could rather easily be dissuaded from killing Duncan. And within the masculine/feminine polarity of this play it is Lady Macbeth's function so to dissuade him. But Lady Macbeth, a powerful person, is drawn to the role in which worldly power resides. She seems to be an exemplary wife: she encourages and supports her husband, in true wifely fashion, rather than undermining him; she sees, knows, understands the terms of the world she lives in, and she does not shrink from approving the savage means this culture uses to maintain itself. Yet at the end of the play, when her husband is declared a "butcher," she is called "fiend-like." It is clear that, in Shakespeare's eyes, Macbeth violates moral law: Lady Macbeth violates natural law. MacDonwald is called traitor and slave, but she is seen as supernaturally evil; yet their thinking is the same. Lady Macbeth's crime is so heinous because it violates a social contract that has been erected into a principle of nature: she fails to uphold the feminine principle. If the male must be a butcher, the female must temper and contain aggressiveness; the masculine principle, like Spenser's Talus, is concerned with power and may fail to make delicate moral distinctions. It is up to the feminine principle to draw parameters on aggression. If the masculine principle surrenders (as in *Antony and Cleopatra*) or is, like Troy, totally vanquished, the culture is destroyed or assimilated. If the feminine principle collapses or is vanquished, the result is miserable disharmony or insanity. This is what happens in *Macbeth:* the whole world of Scotland goes insane.

The imagery in the play is also divided into masculine and feminine categories. Blood and royal robes, symbolic of male prowess and authority, are opposed to procreative and nourishing images—babies, children, the female breast, milk. Lady Macbeth informs us of her values at her first appearance: Macbeth is flawed, she says, by being "too full o' the milk of human kindness" [I. v. 17]. This is an astonishing perception when laid against the view of Macbeth that we have previously had, and it is important in delineating the Lady's character. She who, in Shakespeare's view, should properly encourage this milky side of him resolves instead to align herself with the male principle in a passage explicitly connecting gender to role:

> Come, you spirits
> That tend on mortal thoughts, unsex me here,
> And fill me from the crown to the toe top-full
> Of direct cruelty! . . . Come too my woman's breasts
> And take my milk for gall
>
> [I. v. 40-8]

In her conversation with Macbeth (I, vii) she uses what would now be called a typically *macho* argument. Macbeth answers with knowledge he should have held to: "I dare do all that may become a man: / Who dares do more is none," but she insists that "When you durst do it, then you were a man; / And to be more that what you were, you would / Be so much more the man" [I. vii. 46-51]. Her definition of masculinity clearly excludes the compassionate and nurturing side of experience:

> I have given suck, and know
> How tender 'tis to love the babe that milks me:
> I would, while it was smiling in my face
> Have pluck'd my nipple from his boneless gums,
> And dash'd the brains out, had I so sworn as you
> Have done to this.
>
> [I. vii. 53-8]

Both agree that manliness is the highest standard: what they are arguing about is a definition of manliness. At the end, Macbeth accepts his wife's: it is not, after all, different from that of his culture as a whole:

> Bring forth men-children only:
> For thy undaunted mettle should compose
> Nothing but males.
>
> [I. vii. 72-4]

Macbeth, however, continues to vacillate, and Lady Macbeth is shown to perceive that there is something unpleasant about murdering a father. Their trepidations heighten our sense that the inner circle, the place where murder is illegitimate, is indeed sacred. And once the deed is done, Shakespeare suggests that the entire character of the world is changed: when the rules of the inner circle are identical to those of the outer one, the connection between means and ends is broken and life becomes hell. The porter announces the change in scene; the place, he says, is too cold for hell. Lady Macbeth's renunciation of her role leads to the murder of Duncan; both acts create a new ambience, a world in which the feminine principle has been eradicated. That this is a natural calamity is suggested by the "unnatural" events that follow the murder (II, iv): an attack upon a female falcon by a "mousing owl"; Duncan's

horses "contending 'gainst obedience" [II. iv. 17], and eating each other. Malcolm and Donalbain flee a kingdom where "there's no mercy left" [II. iii. 146]. Duncan's murder is called a "breach in nature" [II. iii. 113].

The victory of the masculine principle over the feminine is a victory of purposeless slaughter, as later events in the play demonstrate. The severing of connection between means and ends has consequences even for the "victors." With the eradication of the feminine principle, the felicities that make life worthwhile are also destroyed. When home becomes part of the war zone, life is merely battle. Macbeth's hypocritical lament over the dead Duncan is ironically prophetic:

> Had I but died an hour before this chance
> I had lived a blessed time; for from this instant,
> There's nothing serious in mortality:
> All is but toys: renown and grace is dead;
> The wine of life is drawn, and the mere lees
> Is left this vault to brag of.
>
> [II. iii. 91-6]

There is another level of irony, however. Duncan is always described as being almost saintly: the epithet "gracious" is continually applied to him. He is said to combine authority (masculine) with meekness (feminine) [I. vii. 17]. He is nutritive: he tells Macbeth, "I have begun to plant thee, and will labour / To make thee full of growing" [I. iv. 28-9]. In other words, he combines perfectly masculine and feminine principles: he is the incarnation of harmonious unity. When Macbeth considers the violation the murder of such a man would be, he conflates masculine and feminine images:

> And pity, like a new-born babe,
> Striding the blast, or heaven's cherubim, horsed
> Upon the sightless couriers of the air,
> Shall blow the horrid deed in every eye,
> That tears shall drown the wind.
>
> [I. vii. 21-5]

Nevertheless, Duncan's character is of a piece with the value structure of the play. For Duncan as well as the other characters, the masculine principle has greater value than the feminine principle. His grateful approval of the hideous slaughter performed in the battle, a slaughter designed after all to insure *his* continued supremacy, bathes him as well as Macbeth and the other warriors in the blood of "reeking wounds." It is ironic that he should be destroyed by the principle to which he grants priority.

The scenes following the murder swiftly and sharply delineate a world gone insane from lack of a balancing principle. Murder follows murder until the entire country is a death camp. And the terms used by the characters remain sickeningly the same. Macbeth eggs on the hired murderers with the same challenge used on him by his wife:

> First Mur: We are men, my liege.
> Macbeth: Ay, in the catalogue ye go for men
>
> [III. i. 90-1]

During the scene in which Macbeth is frightened by Banquo's ghost, Lady Macbeth continually turns on her husband with the same contemptuous charge: "Are you a man?" [III. iv. 57]. She says he is "quite unmann'd in folly" [III. iv. 72] and scornfully describes his terror as more suitable to "a woman's story at a winter's fire / Authorized by her grandam" [III. iv. 64-5]. Macbeth insists "What man dare I dare," and argues that only if he were to tremble facing a real enemy might he properly be called "the baby of a girl" [III. iv. 98-105]. When the ghost vanishes, he sighs, "I am a man again" [III. iv. 107].

In such a world, the feminine principle represents either weakness or threat. Although logically Fleance is not presently much of a threat to the childless Macbeth, it is Fleance, the child, whom he fears. The importance of the succession is symbolic of the importance of ends: thus it is two babies who appear in the witches' evocations as redemption figures. The first is bloody, symbolizing Macduff, who, born "unnaturally," will perform the ritual act of killing the tyrant. The second baby is clean, born naturally, able to restore the natural balance of principles to Scotland. He is crowned and bears a tree, which implies the coming of Birnam Wood to Dunsinane, but also a line of succession achieved in accord with a code rather than by sheer physical power.

The play reaches its climax in IV, ii, with the attack on Lady Macduff and the murder of a child onstage. This horrifying scene is emblematic of the character of a world in which ends have been devalued. It depicts the insanity and emptiness of a world given over to the masculine principle which can no longer distinguish the ends it was designed to protect. Victory of males over other males has little meaning if in the process the childbearers and children have been wiped out. But the climax of the play is also its turning point. The scene which follows shows some reassertion of the feminine principle.

It opens with Macduff, ignorant of the awful act, describing the scene in Scotland: "each new morn / New widows howl, new orphans cry" [V. iii. 4-5]. Ross also alludes to depredation of the feminine principle: Scotland "cannot / Be called our mother, but our grave" [V. iii. 165-66]; Malcolm's presence in the country "would create new soldiers, make our women fight" [IV. iii. 187]. The news about his family leaves Macduff aghast. "Dispute it like a man" [IV. iii. 220] Malcolm urges, using the same language we have heard before. But what does that mean?

Macduff adds a new element to the definition of manliness: "But I must also feel it as a man" [IV. iii. 221]. His answer recalls the comment of the blind Gloucester in *Lear* that even without eyes he sees how the world goes, sees it "feelingly." Malcolm continues to urge Macduff to turn grief into anger. Macduff refuses to falsify his state: "O I could play the woman with mine eyes / And braggart with my tongue" [IV. iii. 330-31]. He agrees finally to curtail his mourning, to Malcolm's satisfaction: "This tune goes manly" [IV. iii. 235].

When the feminine principle is required to be subordinate to the masculine, and is denied access to any power greater than patient steadfastness, it cannot survive unless representatives of the masculine principle allow themselves to feel compassion, mercy, grief. Hermione and Hero must wait patiently for the illumination of the male; Cordelia and Desdemona can only pray. Macduff and, at the end of this play, Malcolm, recognize the necessity of feeling. Even Macbeth, cut off from any regeneration, recognizes the cost of his actions: he has jumped not only the life to come but all felicity in his present life, things like "honour, love, obedience, troops of friends" [V. iii. 25]. By repudiating his feminine side, he has cut himself off from feeling (if not from passion): thus the "cry of women" that startles him connotes only fear to him, not sorrow. His wife's death barely touches him. Given the affection between them shown in the early scenes, this may seem strange, but Macbeth can no longer feel, and Lady Macbeth, in renouncing

her participation in the feminine principle, has renounced also her claim on his feeling. For she ceases to be his partner and becomes merely his weaker twin. It is the feminine principle that arises in her to destroy her with remorse. But for her husband she had lost her identity: she forfeits it with her rejection of her "natural" role.

When the feminine principle, however, is reasserted near the end of the play, it emerges as a necessary part of masculinity rather than as a complementary quality. Thus it appears as one among many qualities that go to make up a complete man, and among them it remains in subordinate status. This play ends as it begins, in a masculine world. Courage, the ability to kill, and compassion are not three equal qualities kept in uneasy balance; priority is still given to the first two; the third is a coda, a reminder, an afterthought. Siward's son, for instance, who "only lived but till he was a man" [V. ix. 6] is killed in his first battle. Ross tells old Siward "like a man he died" [V. ix. 9]. The old man should be played by John Wayne: he has only one question: "Had he his hurts before?" [V. ix. 12]. Here it is Malcolm, recalling perhaps his own father's murder, or Macduff's losses, or the slaughter that is a battle, who raises the minority voice: "He's worth more sorrow, / And that I'll spend for him" [V. ix. 16-17]. The implication of this remark, plus the saddened tone of the dialogue after this battle when compared to that after the opening battle of the play, is that balance will be restored to the governance of Scotland.

But it is still an unequal balance. In the dialogue with Malcolm it is old Siward who has the last word: "He's worth no more" [V. ix. 17]. Macduff's announcement to Macbeth that he was not born of woman makes Macbeth as "effeminate" as Juliet makes Romeo: he tells Macduff the statement has "*cow'd* my better part of man" [V. viii. 18] [Italics mine]. And the play ends with Macduff's entrance with the bloody severed head of the butcher in his hands, and his triumphal "Hail, King!"

So, although some balance is restored to the governance of Scotland, there is no change in its value structures. What is really restored is the sacred inner circle, in which men are expected to refrain from applying the standards of the outer one: moral schizophrenia is reasserted. Such values are implicit in "heroic" worlds. As long as we continue to return uncritically to them in search of standards, these standards will be perpetuated. Their perpetuation guarantees that we shall continue to end up in worlds as insane as Scotland. Or My Lai. (pp. 58-65)

Marilyn French, "Macbeth at My Lai: A Study of the Value Structure of Shakespeare's 'Macbeth'," in Soundings, *Vol. LVIII, No. 1, Spring, 1975, pp. 54-68.*

KARL F. ZENDER (essay date 1975)

[*In the excerpt below, Zender discusses the implications of Young Siward's death at the conclusion of* Macbeth. *He asserts that Siward's optimistic response to his son's death is also an ironic comment on the limits of providential order, an interpretation also suggested by Bernard Mc Elroy (1973). Further, argues Zender, Young Siward's death presents a shift in the play's action from "an ameliorative to a pessimistic conception of the significance of human struggle" and allows Macbeth's "nihilistic vision" a temporary victory. He concludes that while Shakespeare does convey a sense of providential order, he also shows its limitations; according to Zender: "tragic error can only be defeated. It cannot be abolished."*]

Among Shakespeare's major tragedies, *Macbeth* most clearly exhibits an ameliorative conclusion. A tyrant dies, and a young man who has been tested and found worthy succeeds him. We do not have any sense here, as we do in *Hamlet,* that the tyrant's death is an accident of the moment, or that the new king is chosen more by elimination and afterthought than by design. Nor do we see here that surfeit of pain which seems to transfix the survivors in *King Lear.* Edgar obeys "The weight of this sad time" [*King Lear,* V. iii. 324], but Malcolm addresses his attention to newly bestowed earldoms, to his own oncoming coronation, and to "what needful else" is to be accomplished "in measure, time, and place" [V. ix. 37-9]. At the end of *Macbeth,* as Macduff says, "the time is free" [V. ix. 21]. Yet even in this relatively untroubled conclusion, Shakespeare includes an ironically contrastive element: the death of Young Siward. He dies in V. vii., and his father and the other warriors must pause in their march toward triumph to vent their grief. They surmount their sorrow more easily than we do. For us, this death stands in counterpoint to the dominant tone of the play's conclusion. Its implications echo throughout the remainder of the act, and serve to remind us of the troubling and ambiguous aspects of the play's treatment of the relationship between tragic loss and providential order. It is the purpose of this article to examine this death and its implications.

The significance of Young Siward's death is more apparent in the ironies which surround his father's discovery of it than in the death scene itself. But even in the brief exchange between Young Siward and Macbeth there are overtones which serve to complicate our perception of the play's movement toward the restoration of order. At first glance, the exchange may appear to be nothing more than the conventional "bravery" in which opponents engage prior to battle. But in a play dominated by ideas and images of damnation and demoniacal possession, we should take quite seriously Young Siward's association of Macbeth's "name" and "title" with the devil and hell. The situation here resembles Ephesians 6:10-17, where we are told that the Christian warrior should "wrestle . . . against the worldly governors, *the princes* of the darkenesse of this world." As Young Siward's associations imply, Macbeth is now one of those "worldly governors," and is in league with "*the princes* of the darkenesse.*" And if we recall that part of the "whole armour" mentioned in Ephesians is the "sword of the Spirit, which is the word of God," then Young Siward's "with my sword / I'll prove the lie thou speak'st" [V. vii. 10-11] is particularly pertinent. Macbeth, in league with the prince of lies, is to be tested by the sword which is truth. But of course the analogy is incomplete. The "worldly governour" defeats the Christian warrior, and denies the analogy by saying "swords I smile at, weapons laugh to scorn, / Brandish'd by man that's of a woman born [V. vii. 12-13]. (pp. 415-16)

What we have in this episode, then, is a dramatic action involving a shift from an ameliorative to a pessimistic conception of the significance of human struggle. While the encounter in this episode is literally between Young Siward and Macbeth, it is also between their two conceptions of its meaning. For Young Siward, the encounter is a type of the Christian struggle against evil, and he expects the victory which Paul promises in Ephesians. For Macbeth, by contrast, it serves only to confirm his sense of power, and the image which he evokes stresses its spiritual insignificance, and the meaninglessness of the life which has been lost. And here, in contrast to the rest of the conclusion of the play, it is Macbeth's nihilistic vision which emerges temporarily triumphant.

This action is available to us if we happen to notice it, but it is not forced on our attention. By itself, it could hardly affect the ameliorative tone of the play's conclusion in significant ways. But it does not stand alone. It is supported by the ironies which attend upon Siward's discovery of his son's death. After we see the confrontation and Young Siward's defeat, we watch Siward, unaware of his son's death, enter with Malcolm, and we hear him say, "the castle's gently render'd," and "The day almost itself professes yours, / And little is to do" [V. vii. 24, 27-8]. Slightly later, he reenters, and scarcely says, "So great a day as this is cheaply bought," when Rosse informs him of his son's death [V. ix. 3-5]. The ironies in these passages serve to complicate our perceptions by commenting on the nature of Siward's assumptions concerning the providential pattern of time in which he moves. When Siward enters the second time, he uses a theatrical metaphor. "Some must go off" [V. ix. 2] he says, and in his statement he implicitly compares life to a play and the battle just completed to a scene within it. For the battle, the action, the scene to progress to its conclusion, "Some must go off" the stage at their appointed time. This metaphor drawn from the stage resembles two of Macbeth's usages, when he speaks of the "deep damnation" of Duncan's "taking-off" [I. vii. 20], and when he informs Banquo's murderers of "that business . . ./ Whose execution takes your enemy off" [III. i. 103-04]. Yet in the difference between "taking-off" and "go off" we see something of the easy optimism Siward entertains, an optimism the dramatic irony of this passage is designed to correct. Macbeth is engaged in murder, and he knows it; he holds no illusion that those who leave the stage of life at his behest do so willingly. Siward, by contrast, is engaged in a virtuous action. In his "Some must go off" we see not only an acknowledgment of a factual expectation with regard to the battle, but a tacit approval of the order of things implied by this expectation. The battle is benignly patterned, and its success is "cheaply bought" by the deaths of so few among the many who willingly ran this risk. The news of his son's death serves, momentarily at least, to undercut Siward's assurance. Rosse conveys the news in a monetary metaphor. "Your son, my Lord, has paid a soldier's debt" [V. ix. 5], he says, and the metaphor reflects back savagely on Siward's "cheaply bought." From the realm of theoretical considerations of how many men might have been expected to die, Siward is brought suddenly and forcefully into the realm of those who actually did. In the slow and unwilling recognition conveyed by his "Then he is dead?" [V. ix. 9] (completing as it does Rosse's half-line "But like a man he died"), we can see his momentary agony.

But the primary significance of the dramatic irony of this scene does not lie in its relation to Siward's character. He recovers his composure, and even though Malcolm says that Young Siward is "worth more sorrow," Siward returns to his monetary metaphor with: "He's worth no more; / They say he parted well and paid his score: / And so, God be with him!" [V. ix. 16-19]. His vision is limited by his military stoicism and his untroubled belief in the beneficence of providential order. His grief is real enough, but once he has been assured that his son had "his hurts before" [V. ix. 12] he can turn his attention to the "newer comfort" which he sees in Macduff's entry. Secure within his faith in the providence which he serves, Siward can overcome his sorrow over his son's death. Our responses, though, are more complex, for the tragic nexus of *Macbeth* requires that we honor the flesh as well as the spirit, tragic loss as well as providential order. Order has been restored, but not without cost. The cost is certainly less than it would have been if the disorder had continued, but it is nonetheless real. And it forces us to contemplate the nature and limits of a providential order whose restoration evidently can only be accomplished by such expensive means. Siward has simplified his conception of the order he serves in a way consistent with his optimism and his warrior's code: he has left out the pain. But the ironies attendant upon his discovery of his son's death, and the death itself, work to ensure that we will not do the same. (pp. 417-19)

Of course, natural and providential order is beneficial and triumphant. It would be an abuse to Shakespeare's text to claim otherwise. As Macduff says at the end of the play, "the time is free" [V. ix. 21]. Yet it is necessary that we have in mind the limits Shakespeare places on this new-won freedom as well as its potencies. This triumph does not mean that paradise has been regained. The right reign of nature and providence does not abolish pain, nor eliminate mystery. Macbeth has been defeated, and the time is free; but the world is still fallen, and nature and providence will still operate by the tension and reconciliation of opposites. There will still be good born of evil, and evil born of good. It is in the service of this vision of victories such as the fallen world affords that Shakespeare includes in *Macbeth* the death of Young Siward, and his father's responses to this death. (p. 422)

[Young Siward's] death reminds us, in the midst of the triumph of natural and providential order, of its limitations. This death is, of course, Macbeth's responsibility, not providence's. Macbeth has enslaved the time, and all who live in it must suffer as a consequence. But this fact offers no final comfort. We cannot say that in terms of dramatic economy Macbeth's character needs the final blackening of this deed; we can say that the triumph of order needs a leaven of salt to give it the taste of reality. We are reminded that even though the time is free, a young man has died before his time. And it is for this reason, perhaps, that Siward's acceptance of his son's death is allowed to ring a little hollow beside the iterated emphasis on the human pain of such deaths. "He only liv'd but till he was a man." "He's worth more sorrow" [V. ix. 6, 16]. At the end of *Macbeth* we have muted triumph. The tyrant is dead, and there will be new things "planted newly with the time" [V. ix. 31]. Under the freed reign of nature and providence, these new things may grow to their fullness before death. They may; but it is not certain. In such a world tragic error can only be defeated. It cannot be abolished. (p. 425)

Karl F. Zender, "The Death of Young Siward: Providential Order and Tragic Loss in 'Macbeth'," in Texas Studies in Literature and Language, *Vol. XVII, No. 2, Summer, 1975, pp. 415-25.*

BERTRAND EVANS   (essay date 1979)

[*In two studies of Shakespearean drama,* Shakespeare's Comedies *(1960) and* Shakespeare's Tragic Practice *(1979), Evans examines what he calls Shakespeare's use of "discrepant awarenesses." He claims that Shakespeare's dramatic technique makes extensive use of "gaps" between the different levels of awareness the characters and audience possess concerning the circumstances of the plot. In the following excerpt, Evans challenges what he considers a pervasive critical tendency to view Macbeth as an essentially good man. Evans contends that Macbeth has no moral conscience, but merely a fear of retribution and a poetic speech which is "everywhere deceptive, its very sound making the speaker seem better than he is." He further states that it is through "the witchcraft of poetry" that Shakespeare manages to present "a cheat and a fraud" as a tragic hero, a fact also noted by Arthur Quiller-Couch (1918), Wayne Booth (1963), and Robert B. Heilman (1966).*]

Evans concludes that while Shakespeare never allows Macbeth "a single pang of conscience," he may have intended the audience to see behind Macbeth's "poetic mask" and, at the same time, retain some degree of sympathy for a "moral idiot." For other considerations of Macbeth's use of language, see the excerpts by John Arthos (1947), Arnold Stein (1951), and D. A. Traversi (1968).]

As the end [of *Macbeth*] nears, Shakespeare uses Macbeth increasingly in the capacity of the moralist, whose example serves as a warning: 'Look at what has happened to me because of my wicked acts,' he seems to say, 'and judge whether you would choose to do as I have done.' Other persons, too, are used to point up his warning function: 'Now does he feel/His secret murders sticking on his hand,' remarks Lennox, and continues,

> Those he commands move only in command,
> Nothing in love. Now does he feel his title
> Hang loose about him, like a giant's robe
> Upon a dwarfish thief.
>
> [V. ii. 16-22]

Pointedly, Macbeth advises that one like him must not look to have honour, love, obedience, troops of friends, but must expect to end his days joylessly. He laments his loss of normal feelings; because he has 'supp'd full with horrors' [V. iv. 13] his senses are dulled. 'Look at me,' he seems to say again: 'to such a one as I have become, life is only a tale told by an idiot, signifying nothing.' And, finally, learning that Macduff was from his mother's womb 'Untimely ripp'd', he figuratively shakes a finger at us in direct warning:

> And be these juggling fiends no more believ'd
> That palter with us in a double sense,
> That keep the word of promise to our ear,
> And break it to our hope.
>
> [V. viii. 19-22]

These and other palpably didactic speeches express the sum of what he has learned from his experience. Were he to speak the Epilogue, he would tell us not to kill a good man, especially one who is our king, kinsman, and guest, because if we do so we shall certainly be caught and punished, first on earth and afterwards eternally. 'Crime', he would admonish us, 'does not pay.'

Macbeth is the tragedy of one whose experience taught him nothing better to teach us than this shallow admonition. But it is only his admonition, not Shakespeare's; to confuse Macbeth's 'lesson' with Shakespeare's would be to cheapen both the tragedy and ourselves, for it would mean setting our own moral level, and Shakespeare's, at Macbeth's level. To imagine that Shakespeare, like Macbeth, made no distinction between moral sense and the mere expedient arguments that Macbeth's limited capability was able to bring against murder is of course absurd, for consciousness of conscience is everywhere in the plays, from first to last. (pp. 216-17)

Macbeth's tragedy is that of one who, because his imagination can supply only shoddy arguments against wrong, succumbs to temptation and never comes to recognize the true error of his ways. After killing Duncan he is denied even such leavening anguish as that which Claudius, for example, suffers; instead, he endures only the meaner torment of one who has stolen what he sought and fears losing it. Our hardest question, at last, is how it can be that *Macbeth* has so regularly been characterized as the tragedy of an 'essentially good man' whose principles give way to overmastering ambition and who thereafter undergoes moral deterioration, experiencing all the while those agonies of conscience that, indeed, only an essentially good man can experience. This pervasive view, which acknowledges no gap between Macbeth's moral awareness and our own, and which does not distinguish between the prick of conscience and mere fear of losing what murder has won, is contradicted . . . by all the evidence of Shakespeare's text.

Two explanations suggest themselves. The first has to do with the quality of the poetry that Shakespeare gives Macbeth to speak; the second concerns our possibly unconscious zeal to prove Macbeth's right to the high title of 'tragic hero'.

It is needless to cite here a wide representation of passages that evince Macbeth's extraordinary poetic gift, which has long been acknowledged and much admired. Macbeth's language is everywhere richly imaginative, vivid in the extreme. It teems with figures of every sort and with ideas that erupt, stage pyrotechnical displays, then yield to new eruptions—all with such rapidity that the effects dazzle eye, ear, and mind alike. Though indeed Macbeth grows in poetic power as his experience of life continues, yet he is prodigiously endowed at the very start. Nor is his habit of poeticizing everything confined to major, extended passages; it is indulged as startlingly in quick, passing phrases and half-line darts as well. He sees, feels, thinks, and speaks habitually as a poet—not, indeed, like one who self-consciously coins clever phrases and devises extravagant conceits, or like one who, as Richard II does, narcissistically exploits his precious lyric voice for the beauty of its sound, but like one who is literally possessed by a poetic demon, who could never speak dully if he tried. His is relentlessly, from start to finish, the imagination of that very *sauvage ivre* ["drunken savage"] that Voltaire improperly charged Shakespeare with being; but of course this drunken savage is not Shakespeare himself, but his creation, whose perfervid imagination is integral to the creation. Only once does Macbeth deliberately call on his imagination to produce what he thinks he needs at the moment—in the flashy, glittery, false-sounding 'Here lay Duncan' speech [II. iii. 108-18]; elsewhere his utterances wildly spill from his intoxicated brain because it is filled to overflowing. His imagination is not under his control; he is its creature. It drives him not only to pour out striking images and splendid sounds in profusion but to see visions, hear voices, conceive bizarre and inexplicable ideas: 'Had I three ears I'd hear thee' [IV. i. 78]. Had not Banquo also seen the Witches, we might be tempted to assume that they and their prophecies were merely bodied forth by Macbeth's fantastically active imagination.

But for all its charm, Macbeth's poetic power does not fool Macduff, who is not even 'in' on his secret, as we are; and perhaps it should never have deceived students of the play. Yet there can be no question but that Macbeth's spellbinding power of language has contributed much to the deception of generations of critics who have found him better than he is— to be, indeed, possessed of moral sense and inner goodness that in plain fact he lacks. Totally self-centred, judging all that lies in past, present, and future in terms of consequence to himself only, he has thrust his sensations upon us in such dazzling images that we have been hoodwinked; so finely are some of his most reprehensible utterances dressed that they have passed for moral sentiments that proclaim the speaker to be nothing if not 'essentially good'. For many generations young students were required to memorize such passages as 'If it were done when 'tis done', 'Is this a dagger', and 'To-morrow, and to-morrow, and to-morrow' [I. vii. 1ff., II. i.

33ff., V. v. 19ff.] and to intone them solemnly as though they were moral profundities. College students, asked to paraphrase the first of these passages in plain prose, often get all the words right, but then, being asked to state on what grounds Macbeth argues himself out of killing Duncan, reply in chorus: 'On moral grounds; he cannot bring himself to kill a good old man who is his king, guest, and kinsman.' So awesome is the tone of the soliloquy that it has bewitched the ablest readers: nothing that sounds so nobly reasoned can be anything but noble. But of course what the dramatist made his villain-hero actually say here is neither noble nor moral: 'I dare not kill this good old king, for if I do I shall have to pay for it.'

And so it is throughout the tragedy. When Macbeth delivers his brief apostrophe to sleep 'that knits up the ravell'd sleeve of care' [II. ii. 34], his images are so golden that he seems a good man merely by uttering them. Much later, complaining of being denied the usual joys and comforts of age, he whines so becomingly that his sentiments seem nothing if not moral. Yet these ingratiating words do not say 'Do not kill, for it is wrong to do so.' They say only, 'Do not kill, for you will be unable to sleep and will be deprived of benefits that should be yours.' When he sums up his experience of life in the magnificent 'To-morrow, and to-morrow, and to-morrow', he does so with such grace that the passage is regularly cited among Shakespeare's noblest sentiments; and yet in fact Macbeth here ignobly blames life itself as a cheat when it is only he who has cheated. Finally, when he confronts Macduff and refuses to fight because 'My soul is too much charg'd/With blood of thine already' [V. viii. 5-6], his wording makes the thought seem no less than magnanimous; but in fact the thought is not at all noble: 'It will be all the rougher with me in the hereafter if I kill you in addition to your wife and children.'

The poetry that Macbeth speaks, thus, is everywhere deceptive, its very sound making the speaker seem better than he is; poetry is his mask, like Iago's mask of honesty. But Macbeth wears his mask with a difference, and it is the only such mask in Shakespeare. Claudius and Iago, to take the immediate contrasts, use their masks to deceive other participants: the 'smiling, damned villain' deceives all Denmark, and 'honest Iago' deceives all Venice and Cyprus. But their masks do not hide Claudius and Iago from *us;* while other participants see only the masks, Shakespeare unfailingly exhibits their naked countenances to us. But Macbeth constantly holds his glittering mask of poetry between his true character and us—and the history of *Macbeth* criticism leaves no doubt that he has done a better job of deceiving the most discriminating among us than of deceiving his peers in the tragedy.

Macbeth himself, of course, can have no possible interest in deceiving us. Hence all the deception must be a practice devised by the dramatist; and if we now ask why Shakespeare should have wished to deceive us by equipping his protagonist with such a blinding gift of words that we should mistake his character utterly, we come to the edge of our second reason why critics, in spite of the text's unequivocal evidence, have, almost universally, pronounced Macbeth an 'essentially good' man whose morality suffers corrosion. By means of the witchcraft of poetry, Shakespeare has managed to foist upon us a protagonist who, as 'tragic hero', is a cheat and a fraud; and, conscious of the dignity that attends the high title of 'tragic hero', critics have been more than willing, actually eager, to be seduced. Whatever, in recent years, we have found to balk at in Aristotle's definition of the tragic hero, we have not balked at one self-evident point: if his action and his disaster are to move us with the effects of true tragedy, the tragic hero must not be beyond the pale of sympathy—so bad that our sympathy is denied him utterly. And precisely there is the rub: how can we sympathize with one who is incapable of moral reasoning, immune to moral feeling, unacquainted with conscience, remorse, repentance, even as empty words?

Yet to deny *Macbeth* the name of tragedy and Macbeth the title of tragic hero is obviously unthinkable: the work has to stand as an absolute masterpiece even in Shakespearian competition. Confronted with a critical dilemma, we have eagerly taken the way that the dramatist, perpetrating for once his own monumental practice upon us, has seductively invited; we have harkened to the sounds of spellbinding poetry and have bestowed on Macbeth the requisite moral sense and agony of conscience that any proper tragic hero must have. Though Shakespeare assiduously denied his villain-hero a single moral impulse, a single thread of moral restraint, a single pang of conscience, a single sigh of repentance, we have done our best to upgrade him with substitutes, citing the Sergeant's stirring account of his bravery in battle, noting that his hair rose at the first thought of murder, repeating Duncan's glowing (and quite mistaken) early praise, citing his 'desolation' at his wife's death; we have even slandered Lady Macbeth, making *her* the one who knows no moral restraint.

With a single stroke like Claudius's 'How smart a lash that speech doth give my conscience!' [*Hamlet,* III. i. 49] Shakespeare could have opened the way to a view of Macbeth as capable of moral feeling. But he made no such stroke, and this hero never deviates into a moral thought. Since the dramatist evidently proceeded deliberately to prevent even a momentary lapse, we do violence to the play by asserting that its tragic hero is moral and therefore worthy of the title. The main problem here is with sympathy as the due of a tragic hero. If we do manage to sympathize with Macbeth, it may be either because we have been misled about his true character or because we recognize him for what he is, a moral cripple, and pity him for his lack of the one attribute that could save him.

Perhaps Shakespeare wagered with himself that he could create a brute with no moral sense and no virtue but the physical, exhibit him in a succession of murders, and yet bless him with such a gift of poetry that we would be moved to sympathy for 'a great soul in torment'. The alternative is to suppose that, though perpetrating a practice on us, Shakespeare meant us to see through it, see his villain-hero for what he is behind his poetic mask—*and, even so, extend some measure of sympathy.* Perhaps what we should hear, above all, in Macbeth's poetry, is the reminder of his tragic lack, for this poetry is the dramatist's primary means of exploiting the gap between our secure moral sense and Macbeth's moral obliviousness. In this way, then, the poetry does indeed serve to move our sympathy, not by masking the moral void, but by magnifying it. Once we have become aware of Macbeth's fatal deficiency, the very brilliance of his language continues to illuminate it, for his imagination supplies his tongue with everything to say except the one right thing, which he dies without ever learning.

In the end he has learned no more than that the only consequences he knew to fear at the beginning are indeed to be feared and that evil spirits are bad counsellors because in following them one comes to disaster. To extend him, on these terms, a measure of the pity due a tragic hero is doubtless harder than to extend it on the usual terms; hence Macbeth is likely to gain far less of our sympathy if we take him for what he is, a moral idiot, than if we take him for what his poetry

has so long deceived us into thinking him, a moral man gone wrong. Sympathy for the latter is easy because it is given to one more or less like ourselves, who might also, under certain conditions, succumb, act wrongfully, and suffer the special torments that afflict moral beings who have done wrong. But to sympathize with Macbeth as a moral idiot is to sympathize with one unlike ourselves, powerless to become like us, doomed by lacking what we take for granted. Surely it entails no diminution of the tragedy if we see Macbeth so. Shakespeare created no other tragic hero who so much tests our capacity for compassion; he does not even, at the last gasp, make it easier for us by expending a kind word or two on his villain-hero's behalf. The deaths of other tragic heroes are accompanied, or immediately followed, by showers of gracious praise—'Goodnight, sweet prince,/And flights of angels sing thee to thy rest!'[*Hamlet,* V. iii. 359-60]—calculated to stimulate a fresh, final surge of emotion in our breasts; Macbeth's death, quite deservedly, is celebrated only with Macduff's jubilant shout: 'Behold where stands/Th' usurper's cursed head' [V. ix. 20-1]. To see him only so, and yet to extend a measure of compassion: this is the true burden the tragedy imposes. (pp. 217-22)

Bertrand Evans, "The Dramatist as Practiser: 'Macbeth'," in his Shakespeare's Tragic Practice, *Oxford at the Clarendon Press, Oxford, 1979, pp. 181-222.*

HARRY BERGER, JR.   (essay date 1980)

[*Berger challenges the position held by a number of critics that the opening scenes of* Macbeth *demonstrate Macbeth's loyalty to Duncan and the natural unity of the Scottish state. Instead, argues Berger, "there is something rotten in Scotland." He offers a detailed analysis of reports of the Sergeant and Rosse in Act I, Scene ii that relate Macbeth's victory over the rebels. Observing that their speeches present a sense of uncertainty and apprehensiveness towards Macbeth's actions, Berger states that "their armored rhetoric is haunted, as their society is shaken, by unknown fears and scruples." He further suggests that Duncan's gratitude toward Macbeth is a response to the threat that Macbeth's violent actions pose to the kingship. Berger also examines the courtly exchanges between Duncan and the Macbeths, noting that they reveal a tension, contention, and a sense that Duncan is in a race with Macbeth and is "lagging behind." He concludes that the Scotland of* Macbeth *illustrates a society in which the more a king does for his subjects, "the less secure can he be of his mastery."*]

Until fairly recently, interpretations of *Macbeth* have moved around a common basic reading in which *restoration*—both natural and supernatural—is the key idea. Duncan's kingship is described as "lawful and beneficent," Scotland has been peaceful, "natural and orderly" under his rule, and it is Macbeth who disrupts the "harmony in the Scottish state." "The play deals with the overthrow of the balance of royalty, with the development of all the evil implicit in that overthrow, and with the restoration of natural order under Duncan's rightful successors" [D. A. Traversi]. The "fertility of the land and the health of the body natural or body politic are dependent alike on the recurrent rhythm of times and seasons. Macbeth suffers in his single state of man all the disorder he has brought upon the greater organism of the state" [M. M. Mahood]. The play shows how evil naturally destroys itself—or else, in a slightly different version, it shows how divine providence again and again offers Macbeth chances to reject temptation, to repent, to regain what one writer calls his "Christian self-esteem."

Critics who espouse this view generally emphasize the traditional, tribal, or medieval character of the society depicted in the play. Commenting on Duncan's address to his subjects as "Sons, kinsmen, thanes," G. Wilson Knight states that "Scotland is a family, Duncan its head. A natural law binds all degrees in proper place and allegiance." The individual's sense of self, status, and role in this society, his sense of the world, his sense of others—these are deeply structured by his position in the order; they are, as anthropologists say, *ascribed,* that is, they are functions of the way community values are embedded in social and political institutions, which in turn are embedded in nature, understood as given, unalterable, and holy. The murder of Duncan and tyranny of Macbeth upset all these relationships. As a result, Scots are assaulted by instant *anomie.* They neither know nor trust each other. Behavior is hard to assess; actions are ambiguous. And the single state of this world is so tightly integrated that ethical and physical disorders converge, as in ancient legend or primitive belief: Macbeth's unholy act of murder seems to trigger off unnatural phenomena. (pp. 1-2)

I think Shakespeare is centrally interested—in this play as in others—in dramatizing failures or evasions of responsibility correlated with problematic structural tendencies that *seem* benign because it is in the interest of self-deceiving characters to view them that way. I would say, for example, that the view of the play I just summarized is the view entertained and articulated by all the "good" characters in *Macbeth;* that they justify themselves and their society by appealing to it; and that it is the view Shakespeare subtly but persistently criticizes. (p. 3)

Macbeth has sometimes been read as a kind of revision of *Richard III,* the last play in the first tetralogy—infinitely deeper and more complex, but essentially similar in its message. What [Sigurd] Burckhardt [in his *Shakespearean Meanings*] wrote about *Richard III* would then apply to *Macbeth:*

> In the end, a frightful disturbance has run its course, a curse has been lifted. 'The bloody dog is dead' and . . . at the end of *Richard III* we are meant to feel, and do feel, that [through God's grace] things have finally come 'round': they are back to where they always should have been.

I would argue that this view of *Richard III,* which Burckhardt in effect ascribes to Shakespeare, cannot be applied to *Macbeth* in the same manner—that is, it cannot be ascribed to Shakespeare as *his* view of the play—but that it *can* be applied. As I suggested earlier, it is the view Shakespeare ascribes to the good Scots, Macbeth's enemies, and it is a view he presents critically as self-justifying, scapegoating, and simplistic. Those who embrace it refuse, by so doing, to acknowledge their own complicity in the events of the play. Thus we are asked to see their pietistic restoration view as contributing to the subtler evil that obscures the Scottish air and envelops the loyal thanes as well as the bloody dog and his wife. In developing this thesis I shall be carrying further some readings of the play which in recent years have begun to challenge the orthodox view. (pp. 3-4)

Symptoms of [the deeper structural tendencies affecting Scottish society] appear in the first Scottish scene, 1. 2, a scene which anyone who thinks there is unity and harmony in the state of Scotland had better look at again: Macdonwald rebels against Duncan assisted by Irish "Kernes and Gallowglasses,"

and after Macbeth defeats him and fixes his head on the battlements, Sweno the Norwegian king attacks the Scots. After hearing that Macbeth and Banquo beat him back we learn that he was helped by "that most disloyal traitor,/ The Thane of Cawdor" [I. ii. 52-3]. By the middle of 1.4 the Scottish king has run into two rebels, a foreign foe, and a budding regicide. These facts have to be set against the persistent praise of Duncan as an ideal king, the head of a harmonious state "whose members are bound into unity by the accepted ties of loyalty" [D. A. Traversi]. But we need not jump immediately to the conclusion that this disorder reflects on Duncan; that possibility will be explored later. On the other hand, it may throw an interesting light on the events of the final act. Macduff's killing Macbeth recalls Macbeth's victory over Macdonwald: Macbeth also has Kernes fighting for him, and his head, Macduff threatens, will end up on a pole, if not on battlements. This may be viewed as poetic justice, the wheel come full circle. But it may also be simple recurrence, more of the same. In killing Macbeth, Macduff steps into his role. Will he become Malcolm's Macbeth? And in killing Macbeth he has killed not merely a tyrant but a properly appointed king, "nam'd" and "invested" at Scone [II. iv. 31]; Malcolm's final reference to being "crown'd at Scone" [V. ix. 41] may remind us that while Macbeth was a regicide he was not a usurper (which Macduff, at [V. ix. 21], wrongly calls him), and this means that Macduff is also a regicide. If Macbeth feels his title "hang loose about him," as Angus puts it [V. ii. 20-1] "like a giant's robe / Upon a dwarfish thief," it is still rightly his title; having killed the king he did not have to steal or usurp the throne because the flight of the king's sons, and their suspicious behavior, left him the next in line. Thus in purely political terms, Malcolm's leading the English army to Dunsinane is no less disloyal to the Scottish throne than Cawdor's treacherous assistance to Norway. Finally, it appears in Act 5 that everyone revolts from Macbeth because of his cruel tyranny; yet there is only a difference of degree between this and the difficulties which the good king Duncan faced. I conclude from these observations that there is something rotten in Scotland—that something intrinsic to the structure of Scottish society, something deeper than the melodramatic wickedness of one or two individuals, generates these tendencies toward instability, conflict, sedition, and murder. If this is so, it is not something the characters of the play—especially the good characters, that is, everyone except the Macbeths—seem aware of. Is it, however, something which goes on in spite of them or is it something to which they lend tacit support? Before dealing with so complex a question, it might be helpful to offer clues as to what this "something" is.

Duncan's first words in the play—the words opening 1. 2, the first Scottish scene—are "What bloody man is that?"; and we assume that the officer to whom he refers is bloodied both by his own wounds and those of his enemies and victims. The two bloods mixing together become a single badge, his medal of honor and pain. And he talks blood as well as dripping it. (pp. 4-5)

Twice interrupted by Duncan, the officer attacks each of the three segments of his speech with a well-wrought simile which reveals more than a touch of epideictic self-consciousness. He is no mere messenger—Malcolm introduces him as "a good and hardy soldier" who "fought / 'Gainst my captivity" [I. ii. 4-5]—and this suggests that Shakespeare wants to give him some claim to the attention due a valiant warrior. On the other hand, he is less than a named character whose motives and contributions to the plot concern us. He appears only to report the news, and vanishes after duly conveying the information requested, to be replaced by the Thane of Rosse, who brings the account up to date. (pp. 5-6)

What, then, is the officer's function in the play? Why is he at once so conspicuous and so marginal? What does he contribute to our image of Scottish society, to our search for the "something [rotten] in Scotland" that *precedes*, rather than *follows from*, the horrors perpetrated by the Macbeths? These questions will inform my decelerated journey through the officer's words.

Duncan infers from the bloody officer's appearance that "he can report . . . of the revolt / The newest state" [I. ii. 1-3] as if—to twist the words a little—the revolt (like Hemingway's war) was always there and this is merely its latest phase. The officer responds to Malcolm's request for an up-to-date report "of the broil" with the first of his odd similes:

> Doubtful it stood;
> As two spent swimmers, that do cling
>   together
> And choke their art. The merciless
>   Macdonwald
> . . . from the western isles
> Of Kernes and Gallowglasses is supplied;
> And Fortune, on his damned quarrel smiling,
> Show'd like a rebel's whore: but all's too
>   weak;
> For brave Macbeth (well he deserves that
>   name),
> Disdaining Fortune, with his brandish'd steel,
> Which smok'd with bloody execution,
> Like Valor's minion, carv'd out his passage,
> Till he fac'd the slave;
> Which ne'er shook hands, nor bade farewell
>   to him,
> Till he unseam'd him from the nave to th'
>   chops,
> And fix'd his head upon our battlements.
>
> Dun: O valiant cousin! worthy gentleman!
>
>   [I. ii. 7-24]
>   (pp. 6-7)

The two swimmers of the opening simile must represent the two opposing forces (or warriors epitomizing them) in the conflict. This dividing and doubling generates ambiguity: are these two fighters (or armies) trying to destroy each other or two swimmers trying to save each other? Or is each swimmer trying (like a fighter) to save himself by using the other as a buoy? In any case, clinging together produces a dysfunctional solidarity: warriors who in their exhaustion choke their warcraft rather than each other fail to destroy each other and begin to rely on each other to preserve themselves; swimmers who choke their swimcraft end up choking rather than saving each other, and they jeopardize themselves because they destroy their means of flotation in the very act of creating it (seizing the other swimmer). The bond joining enemies is no less symbiotic and no more destructive than that joining comrades. The simile projects a situation in which enemies cling together as friends, and friends as enemies. (p. 7)

[The] finality of Macbeth's triumph rubs against the uncertainty expressed in the opening simile. Simile and episode seem unrelated to each other, though one would normally expect the episode to illustrate or elucidate the simile. But what is thereby excluded is not irrelevant; if the two are tacitly connected, this generates the idea that Macbeth in some manner relies on Mac-

donwald, that both together, hero and rebel, are "spent swimmers," perhaps equally victims of a common social weather. Having killed Macdonwald he will eventually, as I suggested earlier, find himself in a similar predicament and meet a similar death. . . . It is Macbeth's "bloody execution" that evokes Duncan's "O valiant cousin! worthy gentleman!" But it isn't only that, for Macbeth is not alone in being carried away by this impulse. The speaker contributes to the overkill. He approves the violence. His salty phrases, his flamboyant verbal gestures, relish in the hero's carnage and add force to his brandished steel. Diminishing the rebel and enhancing the hero, he stands before the king as Macbeth's ally. Yet the alliance is not a comfortable one, as we shall see in the next passage.

After Duncan interrupts to praise his valiant cousin, the officer draws attention back to himself with an even more laborious simile:

> As whence the sun 'gins his reflection,
> Shipwracking storms and direful thunders break,
> So from that spring, whence comfort seem'd to
>   come,
> Discomfort swells. Mark, King of Scotland, mark:
> No sooner justice had, with valor arm'd,
> Compell'd these skipping Kernes to trust their
>   heels,
> But the Norweyan Lord, surveying vantage,
> With furbish'd arms, and new supplies of men,
> Began a fresh assault.
>
>   [I. ii. 25-33]

The simile is a roundabout way of saying that first Macbeth and then Norway attacked from the east. The officer increases suspense by using the historical present ("swells") but also by distinguishing between the comfort that "*seem'd* to come" from Macbeth and the swelling discomfort that follows his first triumph. Macbeth, defending from the west, is now in Macdonwald's position. The image of "shipwracking storms" and the theme of ambivalence both revive the uncertainty of the "spent swimmers" simile. (pp. 8-9)

[The] speech which utters itself through the officer is equivocal. It seconds the officer's countrymen, adding its strength to theirs and so contributing to the harmony of Duncan's realm. At the same time it betrays an uneasiness, an apprehensiveness, about the heroes, and some of its admonitory force seems diffusely aimed at them as well as at foreign foes. It competes defensively against the threat obscurely felt in their power, but it also competes in a simpler more direct manner: its florid and theatrical excess, reducing the heroes to emblematic caricatures, lays claim to the king's attention in its own right. Its twists and turns, its epideictic contentiousness, reflect a move to block, or at least share in, the praises that flow from the king to heroes.

When the Thane of Rosse rushes in to bring the battle report up to date, his language is terser, more abrupt and nervous, but it retains the same self-dramatizing edge and the same equivocal relation to its subject. The pace is quickened by an interlace of alliteration, assonance, homoioteleuton, and repetition, and by the substitution of metaphors for similes. The speech conforms to Lenox' introductory description:

> Len: What a haste looks through his eyes! So
>   should he look
>   That seems to speak things strange.
> Rosse: God save the King!
> Dun: Whence cam'st thou, worthy Thane?

Rosse: From Fife, great
            King!
    Where the Norweyan banners flout the sky,
    And fan our people cold. Norway himself,
    With terrible numbers,
    Assisted by that most disloyal traitor,
    The Thane of Cawdor, began a dismal
            conflict;
    Till that Bellona's bridegroom, lapp'd in
            proof,
    Confronted him with self-comparisons,
    Point against point, rebellious arm 'gainst
            arm,
    Curbing his lavish spirit: and, to conclude,
    The victory fell on us. . . .

                                    [I. ii. 46-58]

Again the speaker begins by exaggerating the threat, and his misleading use of the historical present confuses because, after the officer's account of Banquo and Macbeth, one wonders whether their being overcharged led to a Norwegian victory. But the danger is moved into the past tense and quickly dissipated by Macbeth's victory over Cawdor. This report differs from the officer's in singling out Macbeth and ignoring Banquo. The sudden Norwegian collapse, like that of Macdonwald, is ascribed solely to Macbeth. Since the victory has been won, why the haste, the look of one "that seems to speak things strange," the "God save the King!" (which, however formulaic, resonates here with urgency of Rosse's entrance)? The more ominous overtones of this moment tend to gather around the haunting image of "Bellona's bridegroom, lapp'd in proof," a nightmare amplification of "Valor's minion." "Bellona's bridegroom" is paradoxical because the archaic goddess of war was a fierce unyielding virgin the opposite of Mars's Venus; "lapp'd" means wrapped, swathed (like a baby?), clothed, as in a soft blanket or robe, or as in waves, but the proof is gore. (pp. 11-13)

As Rosse proceeds, the distinction between the two Cawdors fades, and this owes partly to the fact that the clauses are not in parallel structure—Macbeth is the subject of "confronted" but not, presumably, of "rebellious arm"—so that either warrior may be the antecedent, of "his *lavish* spirit." Macbeth has his own spirit to contend with, to curb or pacify, and Rosse's preposition in the next line is ironic in a way he doubtless does not intend—"the victory fell *on* us" (like a rock). The "self-comparisons" fusing Cawdor and Macbeth can certainly have the proleptic function of dramatic irony noted by Roy Walker and others: "Macbeth is to match the Thane of Cawdor in treachery as well as in valor". . . . But there is also a structural irony, and this comes out a little more clearly in Walker's comment on Duncan's "with his former title greet Macbeth" [I. i. 65]: "the last title applied to the Thane of Cawdor was 'that most disloyal traitor'". . . . What Cawdor has lost and "noble Macbeth hath won" [I. ii. 67] is a set of possibilities—for treachery as well as valor—built into the very role of Thane, or into the promotion from a less to a more eminent thaneship which brings one politically closer to the king. As Macbeth outfought Cawdor so perhaps his own lavish spirit will make the thaneship more powerful, and therefore more dangerous. The proleptic dimension of these ironies should not be overstressed: what troubles Scotland is a settled instability and not merely a future harm; it is the instability which makes the harm probable, given the right circumstances. Macbeth is not the only threat: in the final segment of his speech the officer's uneasiness was coequally inspired by Banquo and

Macbeth. In a society which sanctions violence, which relies on the contentiousness of its members no less than on their solidarity, and in which ferocity and praise mutually inspire, intensify, each other, the success of outstanding warriors must always be greeted with muffled concern as well as "great happiness." (pp. 13-14)

Of the two news-bearers in this scene, Rosse is the most important of the minor characters—those with names or titles whose immediate interest (unlike Malcolm or Macduff) is not affected, who contribute little to the action, and therefore speak with a kind of choric authority—while the officer is nameless. The latter has more than twice as many lines as Rosse, yet we do not feel compelled to probe his speech for insight into his personal motives. The cumulative effect of their speeches directs us toward something that transcends the particularities of character, and this is presumably why Shakespeare entrusted such complex responses to anonymous or choric speakers. Theirs is a group response, the refraction of needs, values, and apprehensions common to Duncan's sons, kinsmen, thanes, and their subordinates. Their armored rhetoric is haunted, as their society is shaken, by unknown fears and scruples. The fundamental image projected by 1. 2 is of men *hors de combat*, standing by in relative helplessness, waiting for the latest report from the front. They seem to have reached the limit of their own resources (including Malcolm who had to be saved from capture) and they compose into a group of worried observers who, beneath their nervous and confused movements, appear passive to the point of resignation. They are forced to look beyond themselves toward the exceptional hero, the god-figure, to whom they have psychologically—not merely militarily—committed their fate. And this commitment goes further toward unmanning them, as if the apparition of their avenger, their terrible savior, has sapped all their strength and added it to his own. The paralysis which besets the tyrant's subjects in the fourth act had its origins well before Duncan's murder. (pp. 15-16)

In an odd way, the Scots' treatment of Duncan is no different from their treatment of Macbeth. To sublime a man to a saint is not much better, from a certain standpoint, than reducing him to a monster. A striking fact about the play is that hardly anyone speaks at all about Duncan after he is dead. With the exception of the Macbeths, no one speaks of him as a human being, a loved and loving father, a man as well as a king—who should be an object of pity as well as reverence or terror. They speak of him in terms of kingship or terror only—as a thing, a symbol, the source of their former good and present fear. They evince great respect but little fellow feeling; great horror but little pity. He is memorialized but not remembered; sanctified as a gracious king but hardly mourned for as a man. Both Duncan and Macbeth are reduced from humanity to something more or something less (and more *is* less)—to symbols of good and evil. Both are drained of blood, the wine of life; both are beyond the pale of the milk of human kindness. But like Macbeth Duncan exists in the play as a man and not only as a symbol. His role in the play, his predicament, the peculiarity of his character and speech, the uneasiness of his relations with his subjects—these have generally been glossed over by interpreters. . . . (pp. 16-17)

Duncan has need of warriors eager "to bathe in reeking wounds" [I. ii. 39], and he has reason to be grateful to them. His kingdom is no less shaky than his control of the facts or of his subjects' loyalty. It is not surprising, therefore, that his expressions of gratitude seem unrestrained and spontaneous, and that his generosity superficially displays an easy-come easy-go quality, as in his precipitate transfer of Cawdor's title to Macbeth. It was this, after all, that led Macbeth to take the witches seriously. Did Duncan confer it too quickly—too generously? (p. 17)

There is a certain urgency in his dispatching Rosse to tell Macbeth the news—as if not a moment can be lost. The instant and easy transfer of Cawdor's title—"what he hath lost, noble Macbeth hath won"—may be motivated by something more than Duncan's gratitude and natural "graciousness." When Rosse brings this good news to Macbeth in 1.3, his words betray tensions in the king as well as in himself:

> The King hath happily receiv'd, Macbeth,
> The news of thy success; and when he reads
> Thy personal venture in the rebels' fight,
> His wonders and his praises do contend,
> Which should be thine, or his: silenc'd with that,
> In viewing o'er the rest o' th' selfsame day,
> He finds thee in the stout Norweyan ranks,
> Nothing afeard of what thyself didst make,
> Strange images of death. . . .
>
> 　　　　　　　　　　　　　　　　[I. iii. 89-97]

The prowess by which the hero preserves Duncan's kingdom is at the same time a claim to praise and admiration worthy of a king, and this claim to primacy is a threat against which Duncan feels it necessary to contend.

The remainder of Rosse's speech conveys his own uneasiness more than Duncan's. Wonders and praises contend with an underswell of "discomfort" in his reference to "strange images of death," which recalls Bellona's bridegroom, and also Lenox' "So should he look / That seems to speak things strange." There is further discomfort in his odd image of a hailstorm of praises, which is swelled by previous references to bad weather and by Rosse's earlier "fan our people cold." If Macbeth is "nothing afeard of what thyself didst make," perhaps other people are, and perhaps their apprehension is deepened by his temerity. (pp. 18-19)

Tension and contention, guardedness, distrust, and irritability, shake the basis of Duncan's regime; and beneath that basis are supernatural solicitings and terrible shapes of fantasy. Macbeth is not the only Scot haunted by demonic or apocalyptic images, by unknown fears and desires reaching for definition.

When Duncan and Macbeth first meet, the pressure on both constrains their freedom of address:

> Dun:　　　　　　　　　　　　O worthiest cousin!
> The sin of my ingratitude even now
> Was heavy on me. Thou art so far before,
> That swiftest wing of recompense is slow
> To overtake thee: would thou hadst less
> 　　deserv'd,
> That the proportion both of thanks and
> payment
> Might have been mine! only I have left to
> 　　say
> More is thy due than more than all can pay.
> 　　　　　　　　　　　　　　　[I. iv. 14]

Macbeth has put him under an obligation that challenges his generosity to the limit. The tone is courtly and effusive, but the language is that of competition, debt, and payment. Mac-

beth, who has already heard the witches, answers in a restrained and even terse fashion:

> The service and the loyalty I owe,
> In doing it, pays itself. Your Highness' part
> Is to receive our duties: and our duties
> Are to your throne and state, children and servants;
> Which do but what they should, by doing
> 　　everything
> Safe toward your love and honour.
>
> 　　　　　　　　　　　　　　　　[I. iv. 22]

He defines the bond between ruler and subject precisely, and even understates it, hammering in clipped phrases at the essential words of relationship (your—our—our—your, throne—state—children—servants, service—loyalty—love—honour); and picking away at Duncan's use of the word *due* ("More is thy due") in doing—duties—duties—do—doing. Macbeth seems to be contending rhetorically against Duncan's hyperboles, but also against the more ominous suggestions he might read into Duncan's words, "More is thy due than more than all can pay." (pp. 20-1)

When Duncan greets Lady Macbeth at Inverness, he continues in the same pattern—proclaiming his love and struggling to outdo his hostess in the duel of compliments:

> 　　　　　　　　　　　　See, see! our honor'd
> 　　　　hostess.—
> The love that follows us sometime is our
> 　　trouble,
> Which still we thank as love. Herein I teach
> 　　you,
> How you shall bid God 'ild us for your pains,
> And thank us for your trouble.
> Lady M:　　　　　　　　All our service,
> In every point twice done, and then done
> 　　double,
> Were poor and single business, to contend
> Against those honors deep and broad,
> 　　wherewith
> Your majesty loads our house; for those of
> 　　old,
> And the late dignities heap'd up to them,
> We rest your hermits.
> Dun:　　　　　　　　　　Where's the Thane of
> 　　　　Cawdor?
> We cours'd him at the heels, and had a
> 　　purpose
> To be his purveyor: but he rides well;
> And his great love, sharp as his spur, hath
> 　　holp him
> To his home before us. Fair and noble hostess,
> We are your guest to-night.
>
> 　　　　　　　　　　　　　　　[I. vi. 10-25]
> 　　　　　　　　　　　　　　　(pp. 22-3)

Duncan's courtly phrases are difficult because they are strained, and they are strained because he feels himself to be in a contest, a race, with Macbeth. Macbeth has "gone before," Duncan is lagging behind, and his only means of overtaking is to "purvey"—that is, to impress on his subjects the superior power of royal generosity, but in tones and images of arch humility. His first speech is an effort to catch up by confessing his debt but reinterpreting it as *their* love and *his* trouble, a trouble he magnanimously discounts. By his method of thanking the Macbeths, he will teach them how to discount their pains and give thanks for their trouble. We should note that he does not say "how you shall bid us reward you for your pains," a more likely and therefore conspicuously excluded alternative. His phrasing is more circumspect but his sentiment more aggressive: the initiative will be his, and their gratitude will follow, expressed in prayers because only God can adequately reward or thank a king. Hence although Macbeth has ridden ahead, his love remains behind and "follows us." (p. 23)

"We are your guest to-night" has, I think, the air of an appeal for truce, a reminder that she as hostess ought to respect her bond and leave off sparring. But she persists. By playing against the image of the purveyor she out-humbles him once again and diminishes the power of royal generosity: "Strictly speaking, your Highness is neither our servant nor our guest because this is your house. We and ours belong to you. Our gratitude can best be that of caretakers, not of recipients of outright gifts, since you can't alienate your property to your humble custodians." To this Duncan can only renew his gesture of truce—like Sweno craving composition—and repeat his former sentiments in limp and prosy phrases which contrast sharply to the ambitious syntax of his opening remarks: "we love him highly" weakly parries "your Highness's pleasure" and gives way to the weary reiteration of "and shall continue our graces towards him" [I. vi. 27-30]. . . . (p. 24)

These, sadly, are Duncan's last words in the play. They reflect the plight of the king in this society: the more his subjects do for him, the more he must do for them; the more he does for them, feeding their ambition and their power, the less secure can he be of his mastery. It is as if, in the delicate balance of a zero-sum relation, the stronger he makes them, the weaker he makes himself. (pp. 24-5)

The scenes with Duncan remind me of Marcel Mauss's classic discussion of the primitive economic institutions of exchange, in *The Gift:* "To give is to show one's superiority, to show that one is . . . *magister*. To accept without returning or repaying more is to face subordination,. . . to become *minister*." Duncan's "life-giving, fertile poetry" and his habit of informally bestowing honors like battlefield commissions reflect the pressure of this imperative and show that the spirit of competition is not restricted to overt acts of bloodshed or hostility. It diffuses itself throughout all the expressions and relationships in the play—love, friendship, hospitality, homage, bounty, conversation, even the delivery of news and messages. The Scotland of *Macbeth* dynamically illustrates the working of the principle which [Thomas] Hobbes called *war,* the "war of every man against every man." (pp. 25-6)

Fear and guilt together invade Scotland after the murder, afflicting the Scots with paralysis and self-avoidance. They are emasculated, traumatized, and their control of tone as they speak to each other from 2.3 on is precarious. They waver between sarcasm and defensive hypocrisy; between resignation and fitful resolution; between despairing laments and pious avowals. For they can continue to be manly only so long as they can, so to speak, load all their gentler good on the king. His reliance on them for protection legitimizes their bloody-mindedness, therefore they rely on him to rely on them for protection, but his milkiness and their bloodiness dooms him to jeopardy and them to suspiciousness. He is the good scapegoat, as later Macbeth will become the evil scapegoat, of Scotland. His murder is in one respect a ritual killing of the gold and silver—male and female, solar and lunar—king; and though they have not murdered him, they may be responsible for his

death. Shakespeare shows him increasingly helpless, increasingly encircled first by overt enemies, then by traitors to his state, finally by traitors to his person. (p. 28)

Harry Berger, Jr., "The Early Scenes of 'Macbeth': Preface to a New Interpretation," in ELH, *Vol. 47, No. 1, Spring, 1980, pp. 1-31.*

BRIAN MORRIS (essay date 1982)

[*In the excerpt below, Morris examines the possible motives for Macbeth's actions. He states that, unlike Richard III, Macbeth never shows any concern for "the terrible judgment of God," and that he "does not so much oppose God as ignore him." Morris argues that Macbeth is not interested in Duncan's kingdom because of land, glory, or power. He maintains that for Macbeth Scotland has no value in itself; it is "an eggshell." Morris also notes that the common Shakespearean concern with the glory of kingship is absent from* Macbeth, *as it is from all of the major tragedies, and that Macbeth "seems not even conscious that there are 'glories'." The power involved with kingship, continues Morris, "is what Macbeth seeks least of all." He observes that though Macbeth "inadvertently achieves" a position of power, he does not understand or skillfully employ it, but uses it only to preserve his position. Morris finally proposes that Macbeth is ambitious for social and professional status only, and he points out in support of this claim Macbeth's frequent references to "greatness." He concludes by remarking on the conflict between Macbeth's role as soldier and his imaginative guilt.*]

'We cannot imagine him on his knees', says Kenneth Muir of Macbeth, contrasting him with that other murderer, tyrant and usurper Claudius in *Hamlet*. It is a shrewd contrast, since *Macbeth* has little to offer about prayer, repentance, or contrition, though it has much to say about guilt. Indeed, the play is hardly concerned with religion at all. There is no Church, there are no priests, God impinges but slightly on the affairs of humankind. The play is deeply involved with the supernatural, with prophecies and portents, with 'Augures, and understood relations' [III. iv. 123], above all with a piercing analysis of evil, but the other side of the religious coin—sin, repentance, forgiveness, salvation and grace—is no more seen than the dark side of the moon. Macbeth's perspective is from 'this bank and shoal' to 'the last syllable of recorded time' [I. vii. 6, V. v. 21] but not beyond. In this respect the play is more like Marlowe's *Tamburlaine* than his *Faustus,* though the relationship between the three plays is more complex and rewarding to study than such a simple statement allows. Yet the glance at *Faustus* may help to enforce the truth that *Macbeth* is not sharply and continuously aware of the religious dimension in human experience; life, here, is frankly seen from man's point of view and not *sub specie aeternitatis* ["under the aspect of eternity"].

Macbeth himself makes this quite clear in I. vii when he specifically dismisses eschatological considerations from his planning:

> If it were done when 'tis done, then 'twere well
> If it were done quickly. If th'assassination
> Could trammel up the consequence, and catch
> With his surcease, success; that but this blow
> Might be the be-all and the end-all here—
> But here upon this bank and shoal of time—
> We'd jump the life to come.
>
> [I. vii. 1-7]

Despite (or perhaps because of) the complex syntactical structure of this passage, with its succession of hypothetical clauses, its repetitions and interpolations, the progress of the thought is analytic, cool and clear. . . . Macbeth is content to dismiss death, heaven, hell and judgment from his calculation, and concentrates on the fact that 'We still have judgment here'; this 'even-handed Justice' is the stumbling-block, and his problem is how to circumvent it. He is unconcerned about the *dies irae* [''Judgment Day''] and the terrible judgment of God. The point is enforced in the deadly irony of what follows. Duncan's virtues

> Will plead like angels, trumpet-tongu'd, against
> The deep damnation of his taking-off.

Pity, like heaven's cherubim,

> Shall blow the horrid deed in every eye.
>
> [I. vii. 19-21]

The 'virtues' will arouse the 'pity' in Macbeth's contemporaries, and that would be a nuisance. The angels and the cherubim, God's ministers and messengers, are no more than similes and illustrations of the immediate political problem. This is perfectly in line with Macbeth's previous attitude to the spiritual world. (pp. 30-1)

The tyrant is eventually overthrown by human powers, in hand-to-hand combat, where the presence of God is neither invoked nor declared, though it may be assumed. It is nothing like the end of *Richard III*, where Richmond is identified as God's retributive agent. To that extent, and while not wishing to minimise the imagery of grace and goodness in any way, I would argue that the play focuses on the rise and fall of a temporal tyrant, whose religious experience is presented as minimal. Macbeth does not so much oppose God as ignore him. (p. 33)

Macbeth seeks not the kingdom of God but the kingdom of Duncan. Yet he is supremely uninterested in the land itself. Scotland is not a presence in *Macbeth* as England is in Shakespeare's Histories. This is evident from the very faint frame of geographical reference, and Shakespeare's obvious dramatic intention not to evoke strongly any sense of place. When the play opens the witches, who have come from nowhere, resolve to meet again 'Upon the heath' [I. i. 6], and the following scene is likewise given no specific location. . . . Places are important in political planning; there is a sense of the necessity for urgent movement to the outposts of empire if rebellion is to be constrained. *Macbeth* knows nothing of this. There is no consideration of what Ulysses in *Troilus and Cressida* calls 'the specialty of rule' [*Troilus and Cressida*, I. iii. 78]; indeed, there is no real political dimension to Macbeth's thinking. Above all, there is no sense that for him the nation, the kingdom, has any value in itself. Of its inhabitants we see only the upper class, and many of them are flat and shadowy presences—Lennox, Ross, 'another Lord'. There is no counterpart in the play to Burgundy's speech in Act V, scene ii of *Henry V*, describing at full length the lovely visage of 'Our fertile France' [*Henry V*, V. ii. 37], and making it a prize worth fighting for. Macbeth has no map, as Tamburlaine has and King Lear has, to chart his movements or his boundaries, and for the central scenes of the play the kingdom of Scotland seems a barren tract, ungoverned and unpeopled. As indeed it is, for its inhabitants have, we are told, fled to England to escape the tyranny, and it is in England that we glimpse the only vision the play permits of an ordered and governed state. Act IV, scene iii shows the Scottish nobles in the English court, and it is there that Malcolm learns the arts of government. The theme of the ruler educated in exile is one which recurs reg-

ularly in Shakespeare's later plays. Timon has to leave Athens in order to find himelf; both Antony and Octavius learn their lessons in Egypt; Florizel and Perdita are educated abroad, in the pastoral world of the shepherds, and Prospero has to be exiled by his usurping brother before he can gain the political wisdom necessary to govern his Dukedom. In *Macbeth* the kingdom of Scotland is born again in King Edward's England. The Scotland which Macbeth rules is bereft of people, an eggshell, containing only his enemies or his victims. It is a kingdom in which he has no interest.

If the kingdom, the control and governance of land and people, means little to Macbeth, glory means even less. The word occurs only once in the play, and then in a scene which is almost certainly not by Shakespeare, the Hecate scene, I, II. v. . . . This sense of the *display* of power or honour was not unfamiliar to Shakespeare, as any concordance will witness. He was especially concerned with it in the Histories. . . . *Macbeth* knows nothing of the glory of kingship, and, indeed, it is remarkably absent from the whole group of Shakespeare's major tragedies. It is as if he has explored and exhausted the vision by the time he had written *Henry V*, and perhaps the turning-point occurs in Act IV of *2 Henry IV*, where the Prince anticipates his wearing of the crown, this 'polish'd perturbation! golden care!' [*2 Henry IV*, IV. v. 23], and learns from his father

> How troublesome it sat upon my head.
>
> [IV. v. 186]

The tragedies seem to expand this insight, and there is no glorious king in *Macbeth*, or *Hamlet*, or *King Lear*, and no king at all in *Othello*. It is significant that, after the discovery of Duncan's death, there is but one brief scene before Macbeth's appearance as King in III. i. There is no royal funeral (cf. *1 Henry VI*, I. i), there are no councils to decide the succession, no offering of the crown (cf. *Richard III*, III. vii), and no coronation. The interim is occupied with the related story of flights and portents and auguries of ill. Act III opens with Banquo's foreboding soliloquy, and then follows the stage-direction:

> Sennet sounded. Enter Macbeth as King, Lady
> [Macbeth as Queen] Lenox, Ross, Lords, and
> Attendants.
>
> [III. i. s.d.]

Some sort of processional entry seems to be suggested by this direction, but it is not mandatory, and this moment marks Macbeth's nearest approach to any kind of regal glory. His language is uncertain:

> To-night we hold a solemn supper, Sir,
> And I'll request your presence.
>
> [III. i. 14-15]

Banquo's reply, 'Let your Highness / Command upon me' [III. i. 15-16] indicates that Macbeth has instantly failed to meet the needs of the new decorum, and as the scene develops he moves uneasily between the royal 'We' and 'I'. His speech enforces our sense of his lack of command. It is full of questions: 'Ride you this afternoon?', 'Is't far you ride?', 'Goes Fleance with you?', 'Attend those men our pleasure?', 'Have you consider'd of my speeches?' [III. i. 19, 23, 35, 45, 75]. This is the usurper's interrogative mode, not the imperative of a king. The scene is full of rumour and uncertainty ('We hear, our bloody cousins are bestow'd / In England and in Ireland' [III. i. 29-30]), stratagems rather than orders are the instru-

Act III. Scene iv. Lady Macbeth, Macbeth, Banquo's Ghost, Lennox, and Rosse. By Max Adamo (n.d.).

ments of state, and Macbeth's overwhelming need is not to display glory but to obtain security. . . . Macbeth seems not even conscious that there are 'glories'. A sense of insecurity haunts the following scene (III. ii). There are phrases like 'Unsafe the while', 'restless ecstasy' [III. ii. 32, 22], and they are summed up in Lady Macbeth's epigrammatic couplet before Macbeth's entry:

> 'Tis safer to be that which we destroy,
> Than by destruction dwell in doubtful joy.
>
> [III. ii. 6-7]

From this scene on, there are no moments of glory. Macbeth is totally subdued to the need for securing his position. The only processions are those of the revengers of their country's wrongs, who mass in England and march towards Dunsinane. Macbeth is increasingly isolated and dishonoured, reduced to the iron core of his nature as an heroic warrior. After the banquet scene we may call his name Ichabod, for 'the glory is departed' [1 Samuel, 4:21].

Power is what Macbeth seeks least of all, if by power we mean the possession of control or command over others, or anything to do with influence or authority. He is, at all the significant points of the play, more acted upon than acting. In the opening scenes his active military exploits take place off-stage and are reported by others. When he appears his new title, Thane of

Cawdor, is placed upon him; he does not have to act to achieve it. . . . When he is King, Macbeth never exercises his regal power to do anything except preserve his own position. A glance at *Hamlet* enforces this point, since almost the first thing that Claudius, the usurper does, is dispatch ambassadors, exercise diplomacy in court affairs, issue orders and give permissions about matters of state. This dimension is wholly lacking in Shakespeare's presentation of Macbeth. He himself seldom uses the word 'power', and it is left to Lady Macbeth, once, late in the play, to refer to the sway and domination he has achieved:

> What need we fear who knows it, when none
> can call our power to accompt?
>
> [V. i. 37-8]

Even this insight is achieved only in the extremity of nightmare.

Power is, however, what Macbeth inadvertently achieves, and because he did not particularly seek it and does not understand it, he wields it unskilfully. He lacks both Tamburlaine's rage for dominion and Claudius' delight in manipulating it. It was a false move on his part to kill Duncan's grooms himself; the murder of Banquo and Fleance is botched, the killing of Macduff's wife and children is politically unnecessary, gratuitous and counterproductive. Above all, it was a careless exercise of power to allow Malcolm to escape to England. Macbeth's failure to understand the 'Realpolitik' of his position, his casual and ineffective acts of violence, his lack of planning, all stem from his inability to comprehend the nature of the power which inevitably fell upon him as a result of the act of regicide. He does not understand it because he did not particularly seek it.

Yet the play is, partially, a study of power. In this respect it moves from the edges, not from the centre. Apart from any supernatural energies they may command the witches exercise the power of influence by the quality of their prophecy and suggestion. Duncan, before and after death, displays a power of goodness, the force of which Macbeth recognises and takes into his calculation:

> Duncan
> Hath borne his faculties so meek, hath been
> So clear in his great office, that his virtues
> Will plead like angels, trumpet-tongu'd.
>
> [I. vii. 16-19]

This prophecy is taken up in the later scenes of the play as the 'powers' (the word nearly always occurs in the plural) gather head in England and advance inexorably to cleanse the infected Scotland of the tyrant's stain. But, in terms of initiating action, the most decisive power in the play belongs to Lady Macbeth. Her influence over her husband is total, and she, almost alone in the play, is quite clear about what she wants:

> Glamis thou art, and Cawdor; and shalt be
> What thou art promis'd
>
> [I. v. 15-16]

She assumes full responsibility for the conduct of events:

> and you shall put
> This night's great business into my dispatch;
> Which shall to all our nights and days to come
> Give solely sovereign sway and masterdom.
>
> [I. v. 67-70]

It is significant that Macbeth does not take up this seductive hint of future royal power; he says only 'We will speak further' [I. v. 71]. At and after the murder she, like her husband, is utterly subdued by the event, and there is no 'sovereign sway' for her in the later acts of the play. Her role becomes supportive, reassuring and creating confidence for Macbeth. Power, once gained, provides no pleasures for her; it generates only remorse and regret. At the centre of the play's exploration of the nature of power lies the insistence that what is 'high' must be 'holy'. This is not the central thrust of the narrative, nor is it the main course of the dramatic action, but it is the underlying moral truth, and to this extent it is a moral, though not a religious, play. (pp. 34-41)

[Macbeth's] ambition is not for power, but for status. As we have seen, his desire is not for command over others or for some position from which he can decisively influence the onward course of events, but for personal distinction, recognised and conceded by his society and epitomised by a particular social rank: kingship. This is perhaps the simplest, purest and most naked form of ambition. He does not specifically hunger and thirst after the title and the accoutrements of a king; he simply recognises (instinctively) that a king stands at the top of the ladder, the first link in the great chain, and towards this position of eminence, with the minimum of reflection or meditation, he aims. To use the play's own word, what Macbeth seeks is 'greatness'.

The words 'great', 'greatness', ring like a bell through those early scenes of the play in which Macbeth is concerned. He himself sees the witches' prophecy in these terms:

> Glamis, and Thane of Cawdor!
> The greatest is behind.
>
> [I. iii. 116-17]

This is picked up and reiterated by Lady Macbeth in I. v, when she associates greatness with winning, with success, with 'height', as she reads her husband's letter and glosses it:

> They met me in the day of success . . . my
> dearest partner of greatness . . . by being ig-
> norant of what greatness is promis'd thee. . . .
> Thou wouldst be great; / Art not without am-
> bition . . . what thou wouldst highly . . . wouldst
> wrongly win . . . great Glamis.
>
> [I. v. 1-22]

The word deepens into prophetic irony immediately afterwards, when the messenger enters with tidings of Duncan's arrival:

> Give him tending:
> He brings great news.
>
> [I. v. 37-8]

When Macbeth himself appears the word turns yet again, by its ambiguous association with 'worthiness' in a kind of ironic adjectival sandwich:

> Great Glamis! Worthy Cawdor!
> Greater than both, by the all-hail hereafter!
>
> [I. v. 54-5]

And a coda recapitulates theme and development when Lady Macbeth tells him to 'put / This night's great business into my dispatch' [I. v. 67-8]. (pp. 42-3)

Seen only in terms of its ideals and aspirations, *Macbeth* might seem a shallow, even a shabby, play. Its hero is ambitious for nothing more than social and professional status, he lacks any sense of the glory of kingship, he fails to comprehend the uses of power, and his kingdom is of no interest to him. To see the play so, and only so, would be to chart its physical and social structure and to ignore its ethical, imaginative dimension. But it is necessary to emphasise the social structure to enforce the point: *Macbeth* is not the tragedy of ambition, it is the tragedy of guilt.

There are significant studies of guilt in *Julius Caesar, Hamlet, Measure for Measure,* and elsewhere, but only in *Macbeth* does Shakespeare present such an excruciatingly particular case-study. Macbeth is a soldier, professionally trained to kill his king's enemies and notably successful in doing so. In his moment of triumph he is supernaturally incited to advance his career and secure the ultimate preferment by killing his king. Means and opportunity present themselves, and the precise method is provided by his totally supportive wife. . . . He never claims that he has any right to the throne, nor does he assert that Duncan is a usurper, weak, or in any way inadequate. His clear and undeceived moral intelligence labels the act as utterly evil, and he feels pervasive, dislocating guilt at even the idea of it:

> My thought, whose murder yet is but fantastical,
> Shakes so my single state of man
> That function is smother'd in surmise,
> And nothing is but what is not.
>
> [I. iii. 139-42]

As long ago as 1930 G. Wilson Knight [see excerpt above] noted that this last line is 'the text of the play. Reality and unreality change places.' The intensity of Macbeth's sense of guilt finds release only in the creation of a phantasmagoric world of visions and images which, through the central acts of the play, overwhelms the simpler, more restricted, soldierly world in which his ambitions are pursued. Just as the king has 'two bodies' [as proposed by Ernest Kantorowicz in his *The King's Two Bodies*] so Macbeth has two minds: the prosaic, unpolitical military intelligence, and the powerful, creative visionary imagination, fuelled by guilt. In the one, he acts; in the other, he is tortured. In the end, the haunted vision brings about the self-destruction of the military man. (pp. 47-8)

In the Christian context, as we know from Bunyan's *Grace Abounding to the Chief of Sinners,* and a host of similar testimonies, the sense of guilt leads to conviction of Sin, and the burden of Sin brings about contrition and repentance, and repentance sues for Grace and forgiveness. There is nothing of this in *Macbeth.* The play remains firmly in the realm of morality and never ventures into the territory where Grace can be the sinner's salve. Macbeth has no such utterance as:

> O, my offence is rank, it smells to heaven.
> [*Hamlet,* III. iii. 36]

In his own mind and imagination he has offended mightily against his fellow man, but he never envisages that by Sin he has grieved God's heart of love. (pp. 50-1)

> Brian Morris, "The Kingdom, the Power and the Glory in 'Macbeth'," in Focus on "Macbeth," edited by John Russell Brown, Routledge & Kegan Paul, 1982, pp. 30-53.

STEPHEN BOOTH (essay date 1983)

[*In the excerpt below, Booth discusses the problem of beginnings, middles, and endings in* Macbeth. *He argues that the speech in Act I, Scene iv, in which Duncan rewards his loyal thanes, parallels the final speech by Malcolm and states that other such correspondences between the opening and ending of the play suggest a "vague, free-floating sense that the old cycle is starting over again in the new." Booth also asserts that finality "is regularly unattainable throughout* Macbeth," *while beginnings are similarly surrounded by ambiguity and uncertainty. Thus, continues Booth,* Macbeth *provides "insistent testimony to the artificiality, frailty, and ultimate impossibility of limits," for there are no closed categories, or clear definitions, in the play. Yet, Booth states,* Macbeth is "*ordered, unified, and coherent," for Shakespeare has presented both a tragic sense of limitlessness and the "comforting limitation of artistic pattern."*]

It is easy enough to see that in the tragedies we value, the *imitation* (the play) is complete, has a beginning, a middle, and an end. That is not often true of the actions imitated; it is notably untrue in *Macbeth.*

It is true that *Macbeth* very definitely begins—more definitely than *King Lear* or *Othello* or *Hamlet,* which open on continuing situations. In *Macbeth* the witches come out and plan future action ("When shall we three meet again?"[I. i. 1]) and promise an immediate relationship to the title character ("There to meet with Macbeth" [I. i. 7]). *Macbeth* also ends. Macduff enters with the head of Macbeth; everyone hails Malcolm king,

and, in the last speech of the play, Malcolm ties off all the loose threads of Scottish politics:

> We shall not spend a large expense of time
> Before we reckon with your several loves
> And make us even with you. My Thanes and kinsmen,
> Henceforth be Earls, the first that ever Scotland
> In such an honor named. What's more to do
> Which would be planted newly with the time—
> As calling home our exiled friends abroad
> That fled the snares of watchful tyranny,
> Producing forth the cruel ministers
> Of this dead butcher and his fiend-like queen,
> Who (as 'tis thought) by self and violent hands
> Took off her life—this, and what needful else
> That calls upon us, by the grace of Grace
> We will perform in measure, time, and place.
> So thanks to all at once and to each one,
> Whom we invite to see us crowned at Scone
> [V. ix. 26-41]

On the other hand, it would also be true to say that *Macbeth* is all middle. For instance, this eminently final speech of Malcolm's is curiously reminiscent of Duncan's speeches when the earlier hurlyburly was done, when the earlier battle was lost and won. In Act I—with Macdonwald's head newly fixed upon the battlements in the midst of a battle that seems done and then picks up again—Duncan promised rewards and distributed titles. Specifically, Malcolm's distribution of earldoms and his general invitation to ceremonial journeying echo Duncan's gestures in [I. iv. 35-43]:

> Sons, kinsmen, thanes,
> And you whose places are the nearest, know
> We will establish our estate upon
> Our eldest, Malcom, whom we name hereafter
> The Prince of Cumberland; which honor must
> Not unaccompanied invest him only,
> But signs of nobleness, like stars, shall shine
> On all deservers. From hence to Inverness,
> And bind us further to you.

Malcolm's "What's more to do / Which would be planted newly with the time" echoes Duncan's metaphor when he addresses Macbeth at their first (and only) onstage meeting: "I have begun to plant thee and will labor / To make thee full of growing" [I. iv. 28-9]. A vague, free-floating sense that the old cycle is starting over again in the new can also be evoked by the deluge of *Hail*'s that greets Malcolm's reign, as the witches hailed Macbeth's. Moreover, Malcolm's speech also denies its finality by introducing an audience that is six lines from the end of the play to new and doubtful information about Lady Macbeth, who has, for the last three scenes, been dead and done with in the audience's understanding. (pp. 90-2)

Finality is regularly unattainable throughout *Macbeth:* Macbeth and Lady Macbeth cannot get the murder of Duncan finished: Lady Macbeth has to go back with the knives. They cannot get done with Duncan himself: his blood will not wash off. Banquo refuses death in two ways: he comes back as a ghost, and (supposedly) he lives on in the line of Stuart kings into the actual present of the audience. The desirability and impossibility of conclusion is a regular concern of the characters, both in large matters ("The time has been / That, when the brains were out, the man would die, / And there an end" [III. iv. 77-9]) and in such smaller ones as Macbeth's inability to achieve the temporary finality of sleep and Lady Macbeth's inability to cease her activity even in sleep itself. The concern for finality is incidentally present even in details like Macbeth's incapacity to pronounce "Amen" [II. ii. 28].

What is true of endings is also true of beginnings. Lady Macbeth's mysteriously missing children present an ominous, unknown, but undeniable time before the beginning. Doubtful beginnings are also incidentally inherent in such details of the play as Macduff's non-birth. Indeed, the beginnings, sources, causes, of almost everything in the play are at best nebulous.

Cause and effect do not work in *Macbeth*. The play keeps giving the impression that Lady Macbeth is the source of ideas and the instigator of actions that are already underway. For example, in III. ii the audience may have an impression that Lady Macbeth has some responsibility for the coming attack on Banquo and Fleance, but Macbeth has already commissioned the murderers. People have also tried to show that Lady Macbeth is as much the source of the idea of murdering Duncan as she seems to be. In fact, it is almost impossible to find the source of any idea in *Macbeth;* every new idea seems already there when it is presented to us. The idea of regicide really originates in the mind of the audience, which comes into a world that presents only the positive action of treason or the negative action of opposing it.

The play, as play, has definition—a beginning, a middle, and an end—but its materials, even those that are used to designate its limits, provide insistent testimony to the artificiality, frailty, and ultimate impossibility of limits. A sense of limitlessness infuses every element of the play. (pp. 93-4)

In *Macbeth* no kind of closed category will stay closed around any object. The validity of that general assertion can be demonstrated in the details of almost any scene in the play. I will, however, concentrate on the second scene, the scene that gives an audience its first solid information about the situation from which the play will unfold, and a scene in which characters perform similar but more limited services for other characters. In scene ii, the categories *good* and *bad* fail: Macbeth and Banquo are lumped together, and are in turn hard to distinguish from the traitors. The Captain's first speech provides a good example both of the behavior of the scene and of the play; its first line describes the phenomenon I am talking about: "Doubtful it stood" [I. ii. 7]. (p. 96)

Not only does the speech describe the forces of good and evil so intertwined as to be indistinguishable, it goes on to describe the fight between the evil Macdonwald and the good Macbeth in such a way as to make Macbeth deserving of the epithet applied to Macdonwald—"merciless." Macdonwald is called evil, and Macbeth good, but they are described in a pair of roughly parallel sentences in which they are to some extent equated by echoes—"merciless Macdonwald / (Worthy to be a rebel. . .)" [I. ii. 9-10] is balanced by "brave Macbeth (well he deserves that name)" [I. ii. 16]. Moreover—partly because Macdonwald is described only in passive constructions and partly because Macbeth is so impersonal, ruthless, and violent—Macbeth, the defender of right, sounds more a monster of cruelty than Macdonwald does. (p. 97)

As the play progresses, Macbeth and Lady Macbeth are often hard to distinguish, and they are like several other characters who are regularly in doubt about their own and other people's sexes. Categories will not define. Words, notably the word *man*, whose meaning characters periodically worry over, will not define. The most obvious examples of the insufficiency of limits are the equivocations that are one of the play's recurrent topics. In an equivocation—as in a pun—one is presented with a situation in which sentences and words, things that exist only to define, do not define, do not set limits. One could say, in fact, that *Macbeth* is itself, as a whole, a kind of equivocation between the fact of limitlessness—indefinition, tragedy—and the duty of art to limit and define. (pp. 97-8)

The greatness of *Macbeth,* I think, derives from Shakespeare's ability to minimize neither our sense of limitlessness nor our sense of the constant and comforting limitation of artistic pattern, order, and coherence. Macbeth's soliloquy at the beginning of I. vii provides a microcosm of the whole—a microcosm in which Shakespeare's double action is well demonstrated and which contains examples of most of the qualities I have described.

The soliloquy is the first event of the night of the murder of Duncan—a night that is made to seem endless on the stage, and one that will not end in the play: it is replayed in the sleepwalking scene. The speech is concerned in a variety of ways with conclusion—with being done. The speech itself does not conclude, but is broken off by the entrance of Lady Macbeth, who comes to say that Duncan has almost finished dinner and to inform Macbeth that the event he has been deliberating is already under way. . . . (pp. 102-03)

Nothing here will stay fixed. We would stand here *and* jump there. Time and place will not stay fixed. Even the meaning of the word *but* . . . will not stay fixed. And notice . . . how the two of "double trust" turns out to be three: "I am his kinsman and his subject . . . [and] his host" [I. vii. 13, 14]. The process by which pairs turn into trios in this baby-ridden play is at its largest in III. iii, when the third murderer inexplicably presents himself to the other two. In the last sentence of the soliloquy the sequence of images is peculiarly appropriate both to this play—in which beginning, end, first, and last are nearly meaningless concepts—and to the sentence itself—which describes failure and fails to conclude: the metaphor of spurring (done in the saddle), *precedes* the metaphor of mounting. The speech destroys the idea that any action can be finished; it makes the very idea of limits ridiculous. The word *success* in "catch with his surcease, success" [I. vii. 3-4] is emblematic of the speech and the play. *Success* suggests both triumphant final achievement and, as its Latin root indicates, "that which follows," "succession."

The speech is terrifyingly limitless, but at the same time it is, like the play, ordered, unified, and coherent. Like the coherences by which the whole play is given order, identity, and thus definition, the elements that order the speech are simultaneously those that evoke our sense of its intellectually unmanageable vastness. (p. 104)

The double action of dramatic tragedy in general, of *Macbeth,* and of this speech in particular is summed up in the phrase "pity, like a naked new-born babe / Striding the blast" [I. vii. 21-2]. The phrase is vivid, particular, and intensely visual; *and*—if only because our memories of newborn babies cannot adapt to our mental picture of a striding human figure—cannot be visualized (if you doubt me, just try in your mind's eye to *see* the personified "pity" the phrase assures you it has empowered you to imagine). The phrase is wonderful in all that word's pertinent senses: it is superb; it is amazing; and it is a container filled by a marvel unlimited and undiminished by encapsulation. The phrase presents something limitless—beyond human comprehension—presents it in limited, comprehensible terms and leaves it still the limitless, incomprehensible, unimaginable thing it is. (p. 105)

> *Stephen Booth, "'Macbeth,' Aristotle, Definition, and Tragedy," in his "King Lear," "Macbeth," Indefinition, and Tragedy, Yale University Press, 1983, pp. 79-118.*

ADDITIONAL BIBLIOGRAPHY

Amneus, Daniel. "Macbeth's 'Greater Honor'." *Shakespeare Studies* VI (1970): 223-30.
 Argues that in an earlier version of Shakespeare's play Macbeth was named Prince of Cumberland by Duncan and was the legitimate heir to the throne. Amneus proposes that Shakespeare altered these circumstances to avoid the displeasure of King James, who would have disapproved of both the usurpation of Macbeth's legitimate title and the nonlineal order of descent by which he gained that title.

Asp, Caroline. "'Be bloody, bold and resolute': Tragic Action and Sexual Stereotyping in *Macbeth*." *Studies in Philology* LXXVIII, No. 2 (Spring 1981): 153-69.
 Discusses the effect that the stereotyping of sexual roles has on the major characters in *Macbeth*. Manliness in the play, states Asp, is associated with "violence made socially and ethically acceptable through the ritual of warfare," while womanhood is equated with weakness and is linked to "humane virtues."

Bartholomeusz, Dennis. *Macbeth and the Players.* Cambridge: Cambridge at the University Press, 1969, 302 p.
 Presents a survey of stage productions of *Macbeth* from Shakespeare's time to the present with the intention of illustrating that "players achieve special insights into a text." Bartholomeusz includes discussions of the dramatic interpretations of famous English actors, including Thomas Betterton, David Garrick, Sarah Siddons, John Philip Kemble, William Macready, and others.

Bernard, Miquel A. "The Five Tragedies in *Macbeth*." *Shakespeare Quarterly* XIII, No. 1 (Winter 1962): 49-61.
 Identifies "five distinct tragedies" in *Macbeth*—the physical, the psychological, the moral, the social, and the theological—and states that the play is paradoxically "complex despite an extremely simple plot."

Biggins, Dennis. "Sexuality, Witchcraft, and Violence in *Macbeth*." *Shakespeare Studies* VIII (1975): 255-77.
 Contends that there are "structural and thematic links between sexuality and the various manifestations of violence in *Macbeth*" and that these are also associated with Shakespeare's representation of witchcraft in the play. Biggins cites a number of Jacobean accounts of witchcraft as background for his thesis.

Boyer, Clarence Valentine. "Macbeth." In his *The Villain as Hero in Elizabethan Tragedy*, pp. 187-219. 1914. Reprint. New York: Russell & Russell, 1964.
 Presents a detailed examination of the character of Macbeth, tracing the development of his thought throughout the play's action. Boyer refers frequently to the interpretations of Richard G. Moulton (see entry below) and A. C. Bradley (see excerpt above, 1904).

Brandes, George. "*Macbeth*—*Macbeth* and *Hamlet*—Difficulties Arising from the State of the Text." In his *William Shakespeare*, translated by William Archer and Mary Morrison, pp. 420-32. London: William Heinemann, 1898.
 Compares *Hamlet* to *Macbeth*, contending that the latter play was written soon after the other. Brandes also opines that *Macbeth* is one of Shakespeare's "less interesting efforts; not from the artistic, but from the purely human point of view." He attributes his "coolness" to the play in part to the "shamefully mutilated form in which it has been handed down to us."

Brooke, Stopford A. "*Macbeth*." In his *On Ten Plays of Shakespeare*, pp. 180-220. London: Constable and Co., 1925.
 Discusses the witches, Macbeth's imagination, the conflict between his honor and conscience, Lady Macbeth's lack of imagination and passion, and Banquo's innocence and his role as a foil to Macbeth.

Brown, John Russell. *Shakespeare: The Tragedy of Macbeth.* London: Edward Arnold, 1963, 63 p.
 Offers a general introduction to *Macbeth*, examining the text, historical "actuality," "presentation," and plot.

——, ed. *Focus on "Macbeth".* London: Routledge & Kegan Paul, 1982, 258 p.
 Contains eleven essays on *Macbeth* by various critics, including R. A. Foakes, Brian Morris (see excerpt above, 1982), D. J. Palmer, Marvin Rosenberg, Peter Hall, and others. The subjects of these essays vary from the play's thematic concerns and its language to interdisciplinary interpretations and theatrical considerations.

Bullough, Geoffrey, ed. "*Macbeth*." In his *Narrative and Dramatic Sources of Shakespeare, Vol. VII*, pp. 423-527. London: Routledge and Kegan Paul, 1973.
 Introduction in which the probable sources for Shakespeare's *Macbeth* are discussed, followed by excerpts from Holinshed's account of Macbeth as well as from the histories of Scotland by George Buchanan, John Leslie, and other possible sources. Bullough comments that in adapting his material Shakespeare "departed somewhat from the chronicle and invented much new detail."

Burrell, Margaret D. "*Macbeth*: A Study in Paradox." *Shakespeare Jahrbuch* 90 (1954): 167-90.
 Presents a scene-by-scene analysis of *Macbeth* in support of the thesis that the linguistic anomalies that occur in the play—"antithesis, equivocation, paradox, riddling, oxymoron, chiamus, hysteron proteron, epanalepsis, and irony"—are not accidental or ornamental, but are an organic part of Shakespeare's design.

Campbell, Lily B. "*Macbeth*: A Study in Fear." In her *Shakespeare's Tragic Heroes*, pp. 208-39. 1930. Reprint. New York: Barnes & Noble, 1968.
 Examines the opposition of fear and rash courage in *Macbeth* and considers the background of Renaissance notions of fear and cowardice. Campbell argues that Macbeth never really possesses true courage.

——. "Political Ideas in *Macbeth* IV. iii." *Shakespeare Quarterly* II (1951): 281-86.
 Discusses the political import of Act IV, Scene iii, in which Malcolm tests the loyalty of Macduff. Campbell concludes that this episode, which emphasizes the obedience due to even a bad king and stresses the importance of preserving the rightful order of kingship against all usurpers, was written especially for the pleasure of King James I and expounds his "pet political ideas."

Chambers, E. K. "*Macbeth*." In his *Shakespeare: A Survey*, pp. 226-39. New York: Hill and Wang, 1958.
 Considers *Macbeth* and *King Lear* "cosmic tragedies," in the sense that they transcend psychological interests and "the purely human" and are largely philosophical. Thus, Chambers argues, in both plays "human personalities do but struggle helplessly in the net of the superhuman" and, in the case of *Macbeth*, the hero is driven to sinful action by "resistless forces beyond his own control." Yet, he admits that the psychological interest is not completely excluded and proposes that there is an antithesis between Macbeth and Lady Macbeth, the former being bound by the practical life, the latter by the intellectual.

Charlton, H. B. "*Macbeth*." In his *Shakespearian Tragedy*, pp. 141-88. Cambridge: Cambridge at the University Press, 1948.
 Offers a lengthy and general commentary on *Macbeth*, often making use of character analysis and stressing Macbeth's disruption of social mechanisms.

Clark, Cumberland. *A Study of Macbeth*. Stratford-Upon-Avon: Shake-speare Head Press, 1926, 151 p.

Presents a general discussion of *Macbeth*, considering such issues as date, sources, stage history, and Shakespeare's knowledge of Scotland. Clark also examines, in a general manner, the play's characters and Shakespeare's use of supernatural elements.

Coles, Blache. *Shakespeare Studies: "Macbeth."* 1938. Reprint. New York: AMS Press, 1969, 289 p.

Juxtaposes a close analysis of the scene-by-scene action of *Macbeth* with excerpted comments by Shakespearean scholars on par-ticularly problematic passages. The intention of the book, states Coles, is to provide "a supplementary manual to be used with Shakespeare's text," with an emphasis on character study.

Craig, Hardin. "These Juggling Fiends: On the Meaning of *Macbeth*." In his *The Written Word and Other Essays,* pp. 49-61. Chapel Hill: University of North Carolina Press, 1953.

Proposes that Macbeth "was essentially a good man" but that he was "tempted by the thin delusions of the Devil." Craig concludes that the "original meaning" of *Macbeth* is that the "Devil is a liar."

Crane, R. S. "Toward a More Adequate Criticism of Poetic Struc-ture." In his *The Language of Criticism and the Structure of Poetry*, pp. 140-94. Toronto: University of Toronto Press, 1953.

Uses *Macbeth* to define critical hypotheses about dramatic struc-ture. Although Crane is more concerned with proposing a critical approach than with *Macbeth*, his analysis does include some com-mentary on the dramatic structure of the play.

Cunningham, Dolora G. "*Macbeth*: The Tragedy of the Hardening of the Heart." *Shakespeare Quarterly* XIV, No. 1 (Winter 1963): 39-47.

Asserts that Macbeth, in order to kill Duncan, must "harden his heart and cease to feel as a man." Cunningham compares Mac-beth's nonrepentance and unwillingness to turn away from further evil to Claudius's actions in *Hamlet* and states that the "hardening of the heart against itself that covers Macbeth with irrevocable loss, is, I should judge, a formative element in Shakespearian tragedy generally."

Davidson, Clifford. *The Primrose Way: A Study of Shakespeare's "Macbeth."* Conesville, Iowa: John Westburg & Associates, 1970, 105 p.

Presents a detailed discussion of the action of *Macbeth*, often within the context of Jacobean thought. Davidson, while tracing the course of Macbeth's career, emphasizes the conflict between good and evil and notes that the "pattern of Macbeth's life is directly opposed to the pattern of sainthood."

Diehl, Huston. "Horrid Image, Sorry Sight, Fatal Vision: The Visual Rhetoric of *Macbeth*." *Shakespeare Studies* XVI (1983): 191-203.

Maintains that *Macbeth* is "centrally concerned with the prob-lematics of vision," particularly the interpretation of the visual and the epistemological problems it involves. Diehl examines the references to visual images throughout the play, noting that char-acters often misinterpret these images and impose "their own willful desires onto the visual world." He concludes that in *Mac-beth* Shakespeare "reveals that the internal, ethical, and spiritual cannot be rejected for the merely physical."

Draper, John W. "Political Themes in Shakespeare's Later Plays." *Journal of English and Germanic Philology* XXXV, No. 1 (January 1936): 61-93.

Discusses the status of the monarch in Elizabethan and Jacobean England, particularly as reflected in a number of Shakespearean plays. Draper states that *Macbeth* illustrates the dangerous effects that regicide and usurpation were supposed to have on the whole society.

Duthie, G. I. "Antithesis in *Macbeth*." *Shakespeare Survey* 19 (1966): 25-33.

Argues that evil in *Macbeth* is manifest in the inversion of terms which occurs throughout the play and that it is "symptomatized by the co-existence of opposites in the same thing." The evil and

confusion in Scotland, states Duthie, involve this conception of inversion, but when order is finally restored "the word 'grace' is firmly and unequivocally associated with itself and itself alone."

Empson, William. "Dover Wilson on *Macbeth*." *The Kenyon Review* XIV, No. 1 (Winter 1952): 84-102.

Responds to John Dover Wilson's argument that Shakespeare revised and shortened *Macbeth* (see entry below), contending that these observations are "valuable but untrue." Rejecting Dover Wilson's argument that Shakespeare deleted three scenes, Empson maintains that the action of *Macbeth* presents a "consistent story" that has no "need for three extra scenes that would destroy the pace." Yet, he adds that Dover Wilson's analysis is "valuable," for in arguing that the play has been abridged he reveals that no abridgement was necessary.

Fairchild, Arthur H. R. "The Transformation of Macbeth." In his *Shakespeare and the Tragic Theme*, pp. 58-72. Columbia: University of Missouri, 1944.

Proposes that Macbeth is transformed early in the play from a man of action to a man of thought, noting that his "practical imaginings" result in a "series of bungling practical actions." Fairchild also comments on the gradual separation of Macbeth and Lady Macbeth.

Farnham, Willard. "*Macbeth*." In his *Shakespeare's Tragic Frontier*, pp. 79-137. Berkeley and Los Angeles: University of California Press, 1950.

Treats a number of general issues in *Macbeth*. Farnham classifies the play as a "morality written in terms of Jacobean tragedy" and discusses it within the context of other Jacobean works.

Fergusson, Sir James. "The Man Behind Macbeth." In his *The Man Behind Macbeth and Other Studies*, pp. 22-87. London: Faber and Faber, 1969.

Develops a lengthy and detailed argument to support the thesis that the character of Macbeth may have been suggested by the story of a contemporary figure, Captain James Stewart. Fergusson maintains that Stewart, an ambitious soldier in the Scottish court of King James, resembles Macbeth in "his winning tongue, his tyranny, and his fearful temper." The critic also draws parallels between the wife of Stewart and Lady Macbeth and concludes that *Macbeth* presents "the worldly glory for which the soldier and his wife, like James and Elizabeth Stewart, barter their honour and their souls."

Ferrucci, Franco. "*Macbeth* and the Imitation of Evil." In his *The Poetics of Disguise*, pp. 125-58. Ithaca, N.Y.: Cornell University Press, 1980.

Proposes that *Macbeth* is rife with Shakespeare's reflections on the transference of the English throne from Elizabeth to James, stating: "Almost every phrase is an allusion, every verse an epi-graph." Ferrucci examines the rather subtle, double-edged im-plications of passages in *Macbeth*, often comparing the play's content to Holinshed's account and focusing on the exchange between Malcolm and Macduff. Their restoration to power, he states, "is the restoration of a 'correct' imitation of natural pro-cesses in which an apparent order cloaks the chaos of violence."

Fletcher, George. "Characters in *Macbeth*." In his *Studies of Shake-speare*, pp. 109-23. London: Longman, Brown, Green, and Long-mans, 1847.

Asserts that Lady Macbeth is ambitious for her husband's sake and that Macbeth is the initial mover in the plot to murder Duncan.

Furness, Horace Howard, ed. *Macbeth*, by William Shakespeare. A New Variorum Edition. Philadelphia: J. B. Lippincott, 1873, 491 p.

Contains excerpted essays by major nineteenth-century Shake-spearean scholars on the date, text, and sources of *Macbeth*. The appendix also includes reprints of commentary on the characters of Macbeth and Lady Macbeth and various other issues.

Granville-Barker, Harley. "Preface to *Macbeth*." In his *More Pref-aces to Shakespeare*, edited by Edward M. Moore, pp. 60-93. Prince-ton, N.J.: Princeton University Press, 1974.

Consists largely of directions for stage productions of *Macbeth*, although these in themselves are somewhat interpretive.

Harbage, Alfred. Introduction to *Macbeth*. In *William Shakespeare: The Complete Works*, by William Shakespeare, edited by Alfred Harbage, pp. 1107-09. Baltimore: Penguin Books, 1969.
Offers general commentary on the play and a brief discussion of its date and sources. Harbage remarks that "whatever intrudes upon the stark simplicity of this work of art is an offense."

Harrison, G. B. "*Macbeth.*" In his *Shakespeare's Tragedies*, pp. 184-202. London: Routledge & Kegan Paul, 1951.
Contends that "*Macbeth* has been extravagantly overpraised" and that it is "the weakest of Shakespeare's great tragedies and so full of blemishes that it is hard to believe that one man wrote it." Harrison conjectures on the circumstances surrounding the play's composition, suggesting that, in this instance, Shakespeare did not apply the same careful finish that he did in his other tragedies. Harrison concludes that *Macbeth* is "a play of magnificent moments, and patches of incomparable poetry, but of incomplete design."

Holloway, John. "*Macbeth.*" In his *The Story of the Night*, pp. 51-74. London: Routledge & Kegan Paul, 1961.
Proposes that Macbeth is from the start portrayed as "the bloody man, the image of death." Holloway also examines the horse imagery in the play.

Horwich, Richard. "Integrity in *Macbeth*: The Search for the 'Single State of Man'." *Shakespeare Quarterly* 29, No. 3 (Spring 1978): 365-78.
Discusses the political significance of the characters of Macbeth, Malcolm, and Macduff, stating that Macbeth and Malcolm are similar in their absolute and inflexible personalities. But Macduff, Horwich argues, embodies the flexibility that both Macbeth and Malcolm lack and is thus the more sympathetic character.

Hunter, G. K. "*Macbeth* in the Twentieth Century." *Shakespeare Survey* 19 (1966): 1-11.
Presents a survey of twentieth-century critical commentary on *Macbeth*, outlining such specific issues as sources, topical references, and the role of the witches as well as more general interpretive concerns. This issue of *Shakespeare Survey* is devoted almost entirely to *Macbeth*.

Kemble, Frances Anne. "Notes on *Macbeth*, No. 1" and "Notes on *Macbeth*, No. 2." In her *Notes upon Some of Shakespeare's Plays*, pp. 19-45, pp. 49-79. London: Richard Bently & Son, 1882.
States that *Macbeth* is "pre-eminently the Drama of Conscience" and discusses the characters of Macbeth, Lady Macbeth, and Banquo.

Kermode, Frank. Introduction to *Macbeth*. In *The Riverside Shakespeare*, by William Shakespeare, edited by G. Blakemore Evans, pp. 1307-11. Boston: Houghton Mifflin, 1974.
Offers a general discussion of the play and its date, sources, and text. Kermode calls *Macbeth* the "darkest" of Shakespeare's major tragedies.

Kittredge, George Lyman. Introduction to *Macbeth*, by William Shakespeare, edited by George Lyman Kittredge, pp. vii-xx. Boston: Ginn and Co., 1939.
Comments on the date, text, and sources of *Macbeth*, stating that while it is probable that the play was revised and shortened, "nothing essential has been lost."

Knight, G. Wilson. "Brutus and Macbeth." In his *The Wheel of Fire*, pp. 132-53. London: Oxford University Press, 1930.
Compares Brutus and Macbeth, stating that they undergo a similar "soul-experience" and that they both "suffer a state of division, due to conflicting impulses, for and against murder." Knight emphasizes the imagery of disorder and destruction in both *Julius Caesar* and *Macbeth*.

———. "*Macbeth* and *Antony and Cleopatra.*" In his *The Imperial Theme*, pp. 327-42. London: Oxford University Press, 1931.

Argues that *Macbeth* and *Antony and Cleopatra* "have a certain powerful similarity of exact opposition." Knight notes a number of correspondences in the two plays, such as the dominant woman, the alternately strong and weak protagonist, and the frequent references to air and feasting. Yet, he also observes that while the imagery of *Macbeth* suggests unnatural chaos, the atmospheric essence of *Antony and Cleopatra* is natural and harmonious.

Knights, L. C. "On the Background of Shakespeare's Use of Nature in *Macbeth.*" *Sewanee Review* LXIV, No. 2 (Spring 1956): 207-17.
Examines Shakespeare's perception of nature, especially as it appears in *King Lear*, which, Knights argues, is concerned with the peculiar and intimate relation between man and nature. Knights concludes that this view "lies behind and validates the elaborate and imaginatively powerful analogy between the human order and the order of nature in *Macbeth.*"

Lawlor, John. "Natural and Supernatural." In his *The Tragic Sense in Shakespeare*, pp. 107-46. London: Chatto & Windus, 1966.
Presents a general discussion of *Macbeth*, touching on the subjects of free will, Shakespeare's wordplay, and the imagery in the play.

Leary, William G. "The World of *Macbeth.*" In *How to Read Shakespearean Tragedy*, edited by Edward Quinn, pp. 234-49. New York: Harper & Row, 1978.
Analyzes the "world" of *Macbeth*, dividing it into four parts: the physical, the psychological, the political, and the moral. Leary considers each of these aspects of the "four-dimensional world of *Macbeth*" separately, but maintains that they are "all parts of a unified whole."

Leech, Clifford. "The Dark Side of Macbeth." *The Literary Half-Yearly* 8, Nos. 1 & 2 (January and July 1967): 27-34.
Asserts that the full darkness of *Macbeth* lies in the fact that the "hero was able to achieve a profounder mode of being only through guilt" and a "full consciousness of evil." Leech concludes that commentators have "tried too hard to find a silver lining to this play" and have thus failed to seriously consider this "dark side" of the play.

McGee, Arthur R. "*Macbeth* and the Furies." *Shakespeare Survey* 19 (1966): 55-67.
Discusses the classical background of the witches in *Macbeth*, noting in particular their affinity with the furies of Greek mythology. McGee states that the witches are responsible for tempting Macbeth and ensuring his damnation, and are the cause of the natural disturbances in the play.

Moulton, Richard G. "How Nemesis and Destiny are Interwoven in *Macbeth*" and "Macbeth, Lord and Lady." In his *Shakespeare as a Dramatic Artist*, pp. 125-43, pp. 144-67. Oxford: Oxford at the Clarendon Press, 1888.
Examines in separate chapters the function of nemesis and destiny in *Macbeth*, with frequent references to classical drama, and discusses the characters of Macbeth and Lady Macbeth. The hero, states Moulton, is "essentially the practical man, the man of action," while Lady Macbeth represents "the antithesis of her husband," with her "genius and energy" turned inward.

Muir, Kenneth. "Images and Symbol in *Macbeth.*" *Shakespeare Survey* 19 (1966): 45-54.
Surveys the various studies of *Macbeth* concerned with imagery and symbolism. Muir warns that we must not imagine that *Macbeth* is "merely an elaborate pattern of imagery" or be overly concerned with counting these particular images, but that we should "absorb them unconsciously by means of our imaginative response to the poetry."

———. "*Macbeth.*" In his *Shakespeare's Tragic Sequence*, pp. 142-55. New York: Barnes & Noble, 1979.
Offers a general discussion of *Macbeth*, commenting on the Porter scene, the witches, the political implications of the play, and some earlier critical observations.

Paris, Bernard J. "Bargains with Fate: The Case of *Macbeth.*" *The American Journal of Psychoanalysis* XLII, No. 1 (Spring 1982): 7-20.

> Presents an account of the action of *Macbeth* in psychological terms. Paris describes Macbeth as "a perfectionist person" who believes that his "own rectitude will insure fair treatment from others," but who also violates this "bargain with fate" by murdering Duncan. The critic concludes that the violation of this bargain results in Macbeth's self-hate, despair, and ultimate destruction.

Parker, Barbara L. "*Macbeth*: The Great Illusion." *The Sewanee Review* LXXVIII (1970): 476-87.

> Argues that illusion is "the bedrock on which the thematic structure" of *Macbeth* rests. Parker also treats the elements of duality and paradox in the play.

Paul, Henry N. *The Royal Play of "Macbeth."* New York: Macmillan, 1950, 438 p.

> Attempts to explain *Macbeth* as a reflection of the topical concerns of Jacobean England. Paul asserts that *Macbeth* was written specifically for a performance before King James on August 7, 1606, and posits that the play is compressed because of James's impatience with longer works. Paul comments on a number of other topical events, in a conjectural manner, "to find the meaning of the play."

Petronella, Vincent F. "The Role of Macduff in *Macbeth.*" *Études Anglaises* XXXII, No. 1 (January-March 1979): 11-19

> Proposes that Macduff functions as a parallel figure to a number of other characters, that Macduff's responses to death are significant, and that he also serves as "a perceiver of central truths." Petronella concludes that Macduff "acts aesthetically as the unifying force in the play" and that he is "the moral center."

Rackin, Phyllis. "*Macbeth.*" In her *Shakespeare's Tragedies*, pp. 107-22. New York: Frederick Ungar Publishing Co., 1978.

> Offers a general discussion of *Macbeth*. Rackin's book, which she states is "written for amateurs," includes photographs from numerous productions of the tragedies.

Rauber, D. F. "Macbeth, Macbeth, Macbeth." *Criticism* II (Winter 1969): 59-67.

> Examines the pattern of threes in *Macbeth*, stating that there is "a carefully worked-out tiradic patterning" and that this is opposed, "somewhat fancifully," by a diadic counterforce. Rauber cites examples of these patterns in the play, but concludes that the difficulty of such an analysis "is that one starts in a playful mood but ends in some confusion."

Rogers, H. L. "'Double Profit' in *Macbeth.*" Melbourne: Melbourne University Press, 1964, 65 p.

> Presents a close, etymological analysis of Shakespeare's use of the word "double" in *Macbeth*. Rogers's monograph contains information on the political and historical background of *Macbeth* as well as on some of the sources that Shakespeare may have used. He focuses much of his analysis on the witches' cauldron scene, suggesting that the references to "double" further the thematic concern with equivocation.

Rosenberg, Marvin. *The Masks of Macbeth.* Berkeley and Los Angeles: University of California Press, 1978, 802 p.

> Offers a detailed, scene-by-scene analysis of *Macbeth* from a theatrical perspective. Rosenberg incorporates commentary from both Shakespearean critics and actors along with his own observations in an effort to "know" the play "from the inside, as actors do, as Shakespeare made it for them to know."

Rossiter, A. P. "*Macbeth.*" In his *Angel with Horns*, pp. 209-34. London: Longmans, Green and Co., 1961.

> Notes the contradiction of forces in *Macbeth*, commenting that the theme of the play is "the equivocal nature of Nature: Nature in which all things exist, whether we call them good or evil; which builds and destroys."

Santayana, George. "Tragic Philosophy." In his *Essays in Literary Criticism of George Santayana*, edited by Irving Singer, pp. 266-77. New York: Charles Scribner's Sons, 1956.

> Discusses the philosophy suggested by passages in *Macbeth* and Dante's *Paradiso*, contending that Macbeth's "Tomorrow, and tomorrow, and tomorrow" speech (V. v. 19-28) is not evidence of a Senecan pessimism in Shakespeare's personal philosophy, but rather the likely words of a character in Macbeth's position.

Spargo, John Webster. "The Knocking at the Gate in *Macbeth*: An Essay in Interpretation." In *Joseph Quincy Adams Memorial Studies*, edited by James G. McManaway, Giles E. Dawson, and Edwin E. Willoughby, pp. 269-77. Washington: The Folger Shakespeare Library, 1948.

> Argues against Thomas De Quincey's assertion that the knocking at the gate in *Macbeth* has the dramatic effect of releasing the tension surrounding Duncan's murder (see excerpt above, 1823). Rather, Spargo argues, the knocking increases the tension and is associated with the knocking of Death in both Horace and popular Elizabethan belief. He further suggests that the knocking represents the "crescendo of three ominous portents of death," the other two being the wolf's howl and the owl's screech.

Speaight, Robert. "Nature and Grace in *Macbeth.*" In *Essays by Divers Hands*, edited by Sir George Rostrevor Hamilton, pp. 89-108. London: Oxford University Press, 1955.

> Traces Shakespeare's concern with grace and Macbeth's transgression against nature throughout the action of *Macbeth*, concluding that "no ending in Shakespeare is more profoundly theological than this one."

Stauffer, Donald A. "The Dark Tower: *Macbeth.*" In his *Shakespeare's World of Images*, pp. 209-20. New York: W. W. Norton & Co., 1949.

> States that the central idea of *Macbeth* is that "moral order exists in the microcosm, that there is no escape from conscience, [and] that man is at once criminal and his own executioner." Stauffer further suggests that there is no motive for the murder of Duncan.

Stoll, Elmer Edgar. "The Ghost: *Macbeth.*" In his *Shakespeare Studies*, pp. 190-227. New York: The Macmillan Co., 1927.

> Disputes the argument that Banquo's ghost is insubstantial. Stoll, referring to a number of other Shakespearean plays that feature ghosts, argues that the ghost of Banquo is objective and should therefore be represented on the stage.

Tillyard, E. M. W. "*Macbeth.*" In his *Shakespeare's History Plays*, pp. 315-18. New York: The MacMillan Co., 1946.

> Refers to *Macbeth* as "the epilogue of the Histories" and compares it to *Richard III*, "where likewise the body politic asserts itself against the monstrous individual." Tillyard also states that Malcolm and Macduff are "the instruments of God's all-inclusive order" and that the former represents Shakespeare's conception of the "ideal ruler."

Tomlinson, T. B. "Action and Soliloquy in *Macbeth.*" *Essays in Criticism* VIII, No. 2 (January 1958): 147-55.

> Argues that Shakespeare involved Macbeth in too much introspective thought at the cost of establishing a consistant action in his play. Tomlinson concludes that *Macbeth* "remains a tragedy manqué and a clear example of the danger of an introspective approach to play writing."

Walton, J. K. "*Macbeth.*" In *Shakespeare in a Changing World*, edited by Arnold Kettle, pp. 102-22. London: Lawrence & Wisehart, 1964.

> Discusses Macbeth's individualism and associates this quality with the play's imagery of isolation and sterility. Walton also notes that opposed to this individualism is an integration of forces that challenge Macbeth, stating that the play's optimism is partly suggested by "the fact that a united people overcome the tyrant."

West, Robert H. "Night's Black Agents in *Macbeth.*" *Renaissance Papers* (1956): 17-24.

> Contends that the witches in *Macbeth* are the agents of supernatural evil, suggesting that such an interpretation is necessary to

apprehend the ''wholeness of the dramatic effect.'' West cites a number of critics who have discussed this issue.

Wilson, John Dover. Introduction to *Macbeth*, by William Shakespeare, edited by John Dover Wilson, pp. vii-lxviii. Cambridge: Cambridge at the University Press, 1960.

Presents a lengthy general discussion of *Macbeth*, considering such issues as date, text, and sources and offering commentary on the characters of Macbeth and Lady Macbeth. Of particular interest is Dover Wilson's hypothesis that there were three versions of *Macbeth*: the original, composed by Shakespeare, of ''unknown length and date''; a revised and shortened version intended for a court performance in 1606; and a ''rehandling'' of this version by a ''restorer,'' probably Thomas Middleton, who added the Hecate scenes.

Willson, Robert F., Jr. ''Fearful Punning: The Name Game in *Macbeth*.'' *Cahiers Élisabethains* No. 15 (April 1979): 29-34.

Discusses the wordplay in *Macbeth*, noting particularly the importance of names and titles. Willson observes that titles are "the lures the Witches use to hook their unsuspecting victim," Macbeth, and that the ''name game'' is won by those ''for whom present titles mean nothing.''

Winstanley, Lilian. *"Macbeth," "King Lear" and Contemporary History*. Cambridge: Cambridge at the University Press, 1922, 228 p.

Examines *Macbeth* and *King Lear* within the context of certain historical events, such as the Gunpowder Plot, the massacre of St. Bartholomew, and the Scottish witch trials. Winstanley states that the ''Catholic conspiracy against the Protestant succession is the leading motive in *Macbeth*'' and that Shakespeare creates a sense of terror in these two plays because he himself was terrified at the events of his day, particularly the Gunpowder Plot.

Zandvoort, R. W. ''Dramatic Motivation in *Macbeth*.'' In his *Collected Papers*, pp. 63-75. Groningen, Djakarta: J. B. Wolters, 1954.

Presents a very close reading of Act I of *Macbeth*, arguing that Macbeth is at the beginning a good man, but that he is corrupted by the witches and his wife.

A Midsummer Night's Dream

DATE: Scholars generally agree that *A Midsummer Night's Dream* was written and first performed sometime between 1594 and 1596. The earliest known reference to the play is in Francis Mere's *Palladis Tamia* (1598), although this does not indicate a date of composition, it does demonstrate that the drama was in public performance by this time. Scholars attempting to establish the composition date of *A Midsummer Night's Dream* have frequently focused on its possible topical allusions. For example, it is known that 1594 was a year of abnormally high rainfall and unseasonable weather in England, and some commentators have seen a reference to this fact in Titania's speech (Act II, Scene i) describing the violent climatic conditions resulting from her quarrel with Oberon. If true, this would establish an earliest possible date of late 1594 or early 1595 for the play's composition. In August of 1594 there was a feast at the Scottish court of King James that was to have featured a chariot drawn by a lion, but the plan was altered when it was feared that the audience would be frightened by the animal. Some critics have argued that Shakespeare parodied this incident in *A Midsummer Night's Dream* in the scene where Bottom and his fellow players debate how to represent the lion in their production of *Pyramus and Thisbe*.

Although there is critical agreement that *A Midsummer Night's Dream* was first performed as part of the festivities for a marriage celebration, opinion is divided on the identity of the principals in this wedding. One leading hypothesis is that the play was written to serve as an accompaniment to the wedding of William Stanley, Earl of Derby, to Elizabeth Vere, daughter of the Earl of Oxford, on January 26, 1595. Since Elizabeth I is known to have attended this ceremony, many critics assume that Oberon's allusion to a "fair vestal throned by the west" (II. i. 158) was actually Shakespeare's flattering reference to her. Another possible occasion is the wedding of Elizabeth Carey and Thomas Berkeley on February 19, 1596. Shakespeare had close connections with all of these families, and it is therefore not unlikely that he would have been selected to provide the entertainment for either of these marriage feasts.

A final means of determining the date of composition rests on considerations of the play's poetic style. Many critics have noted that the lyricism of *A Midsummer Night's Dream* is similar to that of *Romeo and Juliet*, also believed to have been written in the mid-1590s. In the estimation of Harold F. Brooks, editor of the New Arden edition of *A Midsummer Night's Dream,* the play's diversity of style seems to link it with Shakespeare's other works of this period, each of which displays not one but a variety of poetic styles. However, these diversities in verse form and language have led some scholars to question Shakespeare's authorship of the play. Walter de la Mare regarded the stylistic differences as evidence that Shakespeare used the work of another dramatist as the basis for *A Midsummer Night's Dream*. John Dover Wilson concurred in this judgment, and he and Arthur Quiller-Couch posited that Shakespeare first, in their words, "handled" the text in 1592 and subsequently revised it twice—in 1594-95 and again in 1598. Thomas Marc Parrott contended that Shakespeare wrote the play as an epithalamion in 1594 or 1595, but later altered it before it was performed on the public stage. However, these arguments represent minority viewpoints, and most scholars agree that *A*

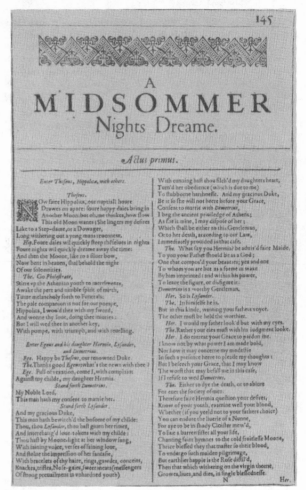

Midsummer Night's Dream is completely Shakespeare's composition.

TEXT: Before its inclusions in the FIRST FOLIO of 1623, *A Midsummer Night's Dream* was twice published in QUARTO form. The First Quarto (Q1) was printed in 1600 by Thomas Fisher and is generally considered to have been typeset from Shakespeare's FOUL PAPERS. The Second Quarto (Q2) was printed in 1619; although the title page of Q2 indicates that it was published by James Roberts in 1600, Walter Greg and others have demonstrated that William Jaggard was actually the printer and that the date is fraudulent. Editors of *A Midsummer Night's Dream* usually regard Q1 as the most reliable of the three texts, primarily because it bears evidence of having been composited from an autograph draft in the playwright's own hand. Q2 is essentially a page-by-page reprint of Q1 with additional stage directions, which suggests to most textual scholars that it was prepared in conjunction with a PROMPT-BOOK. Similarly, the Folio edition is to a large extent a reprint of Q2, but with the inclusion of still more stage directions. There are no scene divisions in either of the quarto versions and only the Folio editors divided the play into separate acts.

SOURCES: Most scholars agree that Shakespeare employed no existing narrative or dramatic source for the plot of *A Midsummer Night's Dream*. However, where most critics have credited Shakespeare with originality in this regard, others, such as Nevill Coghill and Harold C. Brooks, suggested that he may have borrowed his pattern of structural design from Anthony Mundy's *John a Kent and John a Cumber*. Similarly, Robert Adger Law maintained that Shakespeare adapted the plotting of *A Midsummer Night's Dream* from the romantic comedies of John Lyly and Robert Greene.

The tale of Pyramus and Thisbe enacted by the rustic players or "mechanicals" in Shakespeare's play originally appeared in the *Metamorphoses* of OVID. Critics argue that Shakespeare could have adapted the story from any of its numerous retellings in the sixteenth century, for those that survive from this period are written in a style very similar to that of the interlude in Act V. It is also likely that he had read the legend of Theseus in North's translation of PLUTARCH's *Lives of the Noble Grecians and Romans* (1579). Several critics have demonstrated Shakespeare's debt to Chaucer's *The Knight's Tale,* which relates a story of Theseus, Hippolyta, and three young lovers. It is thought that Lucius Apuleius's *The Golden Ass* (perhaps in William Adlington's translation of 1566) served as a basis for Shakespeare's depiction of Bottom's transformation into an ass.

Many scholars have focused on the literary as well as the folkloric origins of the fairies in *A Midsummer Night's Dream*. It is generally believed that John Bourchier Berners's translation of *Huon of Bordeaux* (1534) provided Shakespeare with a model for Oberon, and that Reginald Scot's *Discoverie of Witchcraft* (1584) may have been a source for his representation of Puck, or Robin Goodfellow. Most commentators maintain that, although there was a tradition of fairy folklore surviving up to Shakespeare's time, the dramatist departed from conventional treatments by presenting these creatures as diminutive and benevolent rather than of human size and evil nature. Further studies have demonstrated Shakespeare's use of elements from traditional country festivals associated with May Day celebrations and from rituals connected with the summer solstice.

CRITICAL HISTORY: Critical commentary on *A Midsummer Night's Dream* has been concerned primarily with four issues: Shakespeare's views on the nature of love, the meaning and purpose of art and imagination, the unification or reconciliation of discordant dramatic elements, and the role of perception, illusion, and ambiguity in the play. These issues have rarely been treated separately, but are often discussed as interrelated themes in Shakespeare's overall design. As such, those critics discussing the role of imagination and art have also noted the inherent ability of each to overcome the apparent contradictions in life represented in the play; and those focusing on the nature of love, in an effort to explicate that subject, have also explored the fantasies and illusions of the various characters. Other concerns in the criticism of *A Midsummer Night's Dream* include discussion of the play's dramatic qualities, the debate over the apparent discrepancies in Shakespeare's plot, the characterization of Bottom and the significance of his awakening speech in Act IV, Scene i, Shakespeare's language and imagery, the influence of classical and Christian sources, and the self-conscious or reflexive quality of the play.

According to available evidence, *A Midsummer Night's Dream* enjoyed little critical recognition during the seventeenth and eighteenth centuries. Samuel Pepys dismissed the play as "the

most ridiculous thing I ever saw," and most eighteenth-century commentators disparaged the drama for its shallow plot, lack of characterization, and disunity. Charles Gildon noted that Shakespeare violated the Aristotelian rule of time by representing more than a twenty-four hour period in his play. He also claimed that Shakespeare was familiar with the classics— a much debated issue at that time—because of his use of Ovid's *Metamorphoses* in *A Midsummer Night's Dream*. Francis Gentleman praised the play for its "great poetical and dramatic merit," but maintained that it suffers nonetheless from "a puerile plot, an odd mixture of incidents, and a forced connexion of stiles." Edmond Malone also found the narrative thin and uninteresting, stating that Theseus displays little stature or influence and that the characterization of the young lovers is indistinct and shadowy. Many later commentators also held that the characters of the young Athenians were poorly individualized, but some regarded this shallow characterization as necessary to Shakespeare's allegorical plan. Present-day scholars note that the lack of enthusiasm for *A Midsummer Night's Dream* during the eighteenth century is possibly related to the fact that it was seldom offered in its entirety throughout the period; instead, only the portions featuring the fairies and the sections representing the rude mechanicals were performed.

In the nineteenth century, critics began to reevaluate the unity and structure of *A Midsummer Night's Dream*. August Wilhelm Schlegel became the first to argue that the individual parts of the play are carefully woven together into a highly unified work. He also contended that the relationship of Theseus and Hippolyta provides a framework for the dramatic action—an idea endorsed by many later critics—and asserted that the Pyramus and Thisbe interlude is crucial to the conceptual design. Hermann Ulrici claimed that the highly disparate elements in *A Midsummer Night's Dream* are unified through Shakespeare's comic perspective. To illustrate this point, Ulrici focused on the numerous self-parodies of the different characters and most particularly on the Pyramus-Thisbe interlude that satirizes the main plot. Ulrici maintained that the comic view of life as a dream or illusion is at the heart of Shakespeare's play and compared this with the Platonic philosophy that holds this world to be but a shadow of an ideal reality. Denton J. Snider postulated that the structure of *A Midsummer Night's Dream* is based on three distinct movements corresponding to the three worlds of the play: the Real World of Athens, the imaginary one of the woods, and the world of art as represented by the rehearsal and presentation of the Pyramus and Thisbe story. He proposed that the conflict between the young lovers and Athenian law is mirrored in Titania's rebellion against the authority of Oberon and in the antagonism between Imagination and Understanding inherent in the Pyramus-Thisbe interlude. Snider also regarded the play-within-the-play as Shakespeare's commentary on his own work as well as a point of contrast between the mechanicals' perception of art and the dramatist's.

The role of art and imagination in *A Midsummer Night's Dream* was a leading topic of discussion throughout the nineteenth century. William Maginn was the first commentator to analyze the exchange between Theseus and Hippolyta in Act V, Scene i on the importance of the audience's imagination in comprehending a dramatic work—a passage which many critics continue to regard as central to an understanding of *A Midsummer Night's Dream*. Maginn declared that Shakespeare was demonstrating the limiting conditions of the theater and acknowledging that the playwright, to be effective, requires the audience's willing belief and creative assistance. Theseus's comments on the importance of imagination in art were also addressed by several other critics during the period. Like Maginn, Charles Knight interpreted these lines as an admission by Shakespeare that there can be no successful drama without the audience's imaginative participation. Edward Dowden interpreted Theseus's "the best in this kind are but shadows" comment not as Shakespeare's own judgment on the matter, but as a revelation of the duke's lack of aesthetic discrimination between inferior and superior art. Dowden also asserted that Theseus demonstrates this same limited perception in his speech on the lunatic, lover, and poet. Snider compared the differing responses of Theseus and Hippolyta to the power of poetry and the imagination and concluded that they represent contrasting reactions to the creative process. Frederick S. Boas challenged the opinion that Theseus's comments on both art and artists are ironic, and he maintained that the Pyramus-Thisbe interlude was Shakespeare's means of confronting "the immemorial question of realism in art and on the stage."

Closely related to the question of the role of imagination and art in the play is the role of imagination and love. The only critic of the nineteenth century to seriously examine the theme of love in *A Midsummer Night's Dream* was G. G. Gervinus. Gervinus contended that the play is an allegorical comparison of sensuous love with the errors and misperceptions of a "dream-life." He claimed that Shakespeare chastises, in particular, the type of capricious love embodied in the young Athenians. Gervinus also considered the fairies' role in the intellectual and moral confusion of the play—their delineation as both Cupid's agents and "personified dream-gods"—"the true poetic embodiment of Shakespeare's design." Although a minor concern for Gervinus's contemporaries, the theme of love in *A Midsummer Night's Dream* was to become a dominant issue in twentieth-century readings of the play.

A few nineteenth-century critics were concerned with whether *A Midsummer Night's Dream* succeeds onstage, primarily because its highly poetic and imaginative nature was thought to inhibit the play's dramatic merits. William Hazlitt, the first to comment on this issue, concluded that the drama is too ethereal to be presented in the theater. Maginn, as noted above, maintained that the imaginative response demanded by *A Midsummer Night's Dream* transcended the limits of the stage, and he pointed to the transformation of Bottom's head into that of an ass as a good example of the play's theatrical difficulties. Knight and Gervinus both contended that the play is impossible to stage effectively, and Henry N. Hudson echoed Maginn's assessment, stating that Bottom's transformation works when read but cannot be successfully presented in the theater. Similarly, Snider maintained that the fairy world of *A Midsummer Night's Dream*, as well as its inhabitants, can only be apprehended by the imagination and cannot be represented within the limitations of the theater.

Another critical issue, raised in the nineteenth century and more fully developed in the twentieth, concerned the characterization of Bottom. Maginn offered the first extended examination of the weaver, admiring his poise and imperturbability and declaring that his egotism is the result of the constant flattery of the other mechanicals. Charles Cowden Clarke stressed Bottom's amiability and self-possession and was the first commentator to credit him with a robust imagination, which Clarke detected in his presentation of Pyramus and in his encounter with Titania and her attendants. Hudson considered Bottom the exemplar of "common experience" and the "most accessible" of all the characters in *A Midsummer Night's Dream*. And Boas called him "the protean actor and critic" who, even

after his transformation, "retains his versatile faculty of adapting himself to any part."

The first half of the twentieth century saw a variety of innovative interpretations of *A Midsummer Night's Dream*, perhaps the most significant being the discovery and examination of dark, even nightmarish elements in the play. G. K. Chesterton, writing at the turn of the century, was among the first critics to identify "cruel and ignominous" undercurrents in *A Midsummer Night's Dream*, noting that the events in the woods are indeed threatening to the young lovers. G. Wilson Knight, in an examination of Shakespeare's poetic imagery, asserted that the symbolic language of the play is ambiguous and juxtaposes images of storms and harmony, darkness and light, and the evil as well as the romantic associations of the moonlit forest. He further maintained that the ambivalent language underscores the "*Macbeth*-like quality" of the drama, to the extent that the imaginative atmosphere is imbued with the terror of a nightmare. A number of more recent critics have also stressed the dark and violent aspects of *A Midsummer Night's Dream*. Jan Kott suggested that the nature of the play is brutally erotic, perceiving in the woods outside Athens an environment where the repressed sexual desires of the characters are allowed free expression. Charles R. Lyons concluded that a sense of death and disease is present throughout Shakespeare's play, and that the traditional comic ending, with its triumph of love, is clearly shown to be spurious. Hugh M. Richmond argued that the young lovers are prone to a sadomasochistic form of passion, foolishly seeking out obstacles and conflicts that bar the fulfillment of their love. David Bevington shared Lyons's assessment of the pervasiveness of death beneath the comic structure of *A Midsummer Night's Dream*, pointing out the way in which Shakespeare developed the tension between dark and comic aspects through the presentation of a number of dichotomies. Most recently, Mordecai Marcus disputed the negative view of death in the play, claiming that its presence provides a tension which heightens the emotional and spiritual significance of love.

Twentieth-century commentary on the theme of love in *A Midsummer Night's Dream* has generally been divided between those critics who maintain that Shakespeare was parodying the imaginative, unrealistic passion of the young Athenians and praising the ideal union of Theseus and Hippolyta, and those who claim that he regarded Theseus's philosophy of reason as limiting and that he promoted instead a healthy, responsible imagination as necessary for love's fulfillment. E. K. Chambers noted the capriciousness and inconstancy of the young lovers and identified the folly of love—"as interpreted by the comic spirit"—as the central thematic issue in the play. He also asserted that the fairy influence on the young lovers is symbolic rather than real, since their passion for each other is lawless and inconstant even before the application of the love juice. Samuel B. Hemingway argued that in *A Midsummer Night's Dream* Shakespeare was reacting against the excessive romantic idealism of his earlier drama, *Romeo and Juliet*, and he claimed that the Pyramus-Thisbe interlude parodies not only the love plot and romantic tragedies in general, but in particular his own early tragedy. H. B. Charlton described *A Midsummer Night's Dream* as Shakespeare's dramatization of the foolishness and perilous nature of romantic love; according to the critic, Shakespeare derided lawless love and promoted instead the institution of marriage as a means of stabilizing human relations and strengthening society. Charlton regarded Theseus as the representative of society's institutions and maintained that the lunatic, lover, and poet speech represents Shakespeare's own unromantic, worldly view of love and art. Echoing Charlton, E. C. Pettet concluded that *A Midsummer Night's Dream,* specifically the Pyramus-Thisbe interlude, underscores the mutability of romantic love, depicting it as fallacious and imperfect. However, Ernest Schanzer disputed the conclusions of both Charlton and Pettet, maintaining instead that the object of Shakespeare's satire is an over-imaginative form of love that deceives reason and the senses, and not romantic love in general. He stated that Theseus's lunatic, lover, and poet speech recapitulates the theme of ''inflamed'' imagination and expresses Shakespeare's view that madmen, lovers, and artists ''all live among phantoms of their own creation which are unrelated to society.'' In a slightly different reading of *A Midsummer Night's Dream,* John Vyvyan divided his focus between the issues of love and harmony in the play, claiming that the confusion and discord in the woods ensues from the lovers' pursuit of mistaken ideals, and that when they begin to apprehend a more elevated form of love the situation resolves into harmony. George A. Bonnard declared that Theseus is not an enemy of imagination, but an individual who recognizes imagination's importance to love and life as long as it does not usurp the place of reason and sanity—a conclusion similar to that reached by Schanzer. Bonnard also maintained that the marriage of Theseus and Hippolyta represents an honest love devoid of the follies of romanticism and, as such, endorsed by Shakespeare as a model to be emulated. Similar to Bonnard, R. W. Dent asserted that Shakespeare was not condemning the role of imagination in love or strictly endorsing a philosophy of sexuality grounded in reason, but that the dramatist was criticizing love that is based on idolatry, whose objects are unworthy. Focusing on the Platonic elements in *A Midsummer Night's Dream,* Peter G. Phialas described the union of Theseus and Hippolyta as the ''middle ground,'' endorsed by Shakespeare, between the capricious love of the fairies and the young lovers and the matter-of-fact, mundane attitude expressed by Bottom.

The focus in the twentieth century on the relationship of love and imagination in *A Midsummer Night's Dream* is echoed in the concern over the play's depiction of imagination in art. Howard Nemerov disputed earlier commentators on the implications of Theseus's speeches on poetry and imagination in Act V, Scene i, denying that these passages reflect Shakespeare's own point of view. Instead, he judged that although the dramatist allowed the duke some measure of wisdom in his understanding, he generally portrayed him as possessing an ''aristocratic or courtly disdain for art.'' Nemerov compared this contempt with Hippolyta's more acute apprehension of art as mystery and fantasy. Elizabeth Sewell focused on the play-within-the-play in *A Midsummer Night's Dream*—as have many critics investigating the role of art and imagination in the drama—arguing that the erroneous substitution and garbled exchanges in the mechanicals' speeches during the interlude emphasize Shakespeare's alliance of his art with the characters' imaginative attempts, since these passages direct the audience's attention to the nature of poetic language. For Sewell, the mechanicals represent ''the newly thinking mind'' trying to develop new forms of discourse by which to explain natural phenomena. Also examining the Pyramus-Thisbe interlude, R. W. Dent argued that the play-within-the-play serves not merely to parody the main plot, but shifts the audience's attention from the role of imagination in love to its function in the realm of art by showing the absurdities of ''abused imagination'' in the theater.

Another prominent issue in twentieth-century criticism of *A Midsummer Night's Dream* was the nature of the play's struc-

tural and thematic design, particularly Shakespeare's synthesis of contradictory elements into a unified work. Harold C. Goddard was among the first critics to note how Shakespeare's combination of diverse elements in the overall scheme of *A Midsummer Night's Dream* is echoed in the resolution of discordancies into harmony in the play's conclusion. In addition, Goddard asserted that the exchange between Theseus and Hippolyta in Act IV, Scene i, dealing with the harmonious music of Theseus's hunting dogs, is a metaphysical embodiment of the theme of *discordia concors* presented throughout the play. Paul A. Olson described the dramatic movement of the play as a pattern of order falling into disorder and then being restored as Oberon regains his proper relationship with Titania. As noted earlier, John Vyvyan claimed that the confusion and discord in the woods is resolved into harmony once the young lovers achieve a more spiritualized sense of love's purpose. Stephen Fender argued that in *A Midsummer Night's Dream* rational and Christian values are inadequate in dealing with the mounting discord in the woods. Like Olson, Fender determined that Oberon resolves the play's discordancies, and he further contended that Shakespeare closed Act V with the reappearance of the fairies to emphasize their providential power and control in contrast to the ineffectuality of the mortals. R. A. Zimbardo maintained that *A Midsummer Night's Dream* is based on the principles of *discordia concors* and ''permanence in mutability,'' and that Shakespeare dramatized these concepts in order to enhance the theme of reconciliation that is central to the play. David Bevington noted Shakespeare's ambivalent presentation of dark and comic elements in his plot, such as the contrasting natures of the benevolent Oberon and the malevolent Puck, the tension between the young lovers' potential for sexual licentiousness and their exercise of restraint, and the opposing aspects of the forest itself, which is both a sanctuary and a place of violence and possible tragedy. In an anthropological approach to *A Midsummer Night's Dream,* Florence Falk examined the movement of the dramatic action from Athens to the woods and back to Athens, claiming that this movement recalls a tribal ''rite of passage'' in which a community is symbolically renewed by releasing and reintegrating its disorderly elements. Falk's assessment of the play's dramatic structure echoes that of C. L. Barber, who also stated that the action is based on a movement from societal restraint, to release, and finally to clarification.

Several twentieth-century commentators have evaluated Shakespeare's use of poetic language in *A Midsummer Night's Dream.* As noted above, G. Wilson Knight isolated and discussed the contrasting images of storms and harmony, darkness and light, and evil and love in the play. Thomas Marc Parrott examined the various poetic styles of the different characters and correlated changes in language with new developments in the plot. B. Ifor Evans compared the style of *A Midsummer Night's Dream* with the poetic language of Shakespeare's earlier dramas, concluding that the language here is less self-conscious and more fully integrated than in his preceding works. Like Parrott, David P. Young focused on Shakespeare's use of different verse forms and meters for purposes of individual characterization. He also analyzed the way in which the frequent use of panoramic descriptions of scenes and activities outside the dramatic action contrast with the claustrophobic atmosphere of the woods.

Related to the studies of language and imagery in *A Midsummer Night's Dream* have been the psychoanalytic interpretations of the play's action and the investigation of various literary and cultural influences on Shakespeare's design. Gerald F. Jacobson was among the first critics to examine the "psycho-sexual development" of the characters—in his case, the women—of the play. Jacobson discerned in Hermia's early preference for Lysander instead of Demetrius evidence of an unresolved Oedipal conflict, contending that by the close of Act IV, Scene i she has overcome her ambivalent feelings and achieved a post-Oedipal understanding of her proper relationships with the other characters. In another application of psychoanalytic criticism, M. D. Faber focused on Hermia's dream in Act II, Scene i, maintaining that it demonstrates the conflict between her fears of and desires for a sexual consummation of her love for Lysander. Discussing the possible literary and cultural influences on the structure of *A Midsummer Night's Dream*, Enid Welsford, writing in the 1920s, compared the play to the traditions of the Elizabethan revels and the seventeenth-century court masque. She claimed that the various characters move through the dramatic action in a "figured ballet" or dance common to masques and noted the similarities between the play-within-the-play and the anti-masque which serves as a comic foil to the main movement of the masque. David Ormerod and Mary Ellen Lamb both analyzed *A Midsummer Night's Dream* in relation to the classical legend of Theseus and the Cretan minotaur, comparing the wood outside Athens to the mythical labyrinthine maze. Ormerod asserted that the forest in the play represents a "labyrinthine moral confusion" where the lovers and Titania are motivated by blind, passionate love, and where the figure of the ass's head symbolizes moral mischoice. Lamb argued that Bottom's characterization is ambiguous, for he is both the comic minotaur and the agency by which the lovers are led to safety. She also commented on the differences between the mythical Theseus and the duke in this play, demonstrating that whereas the former is depicted as responsible for the death of his own son, the latter is portrayed as a "reformed heartbreaker" who receives the fairies' blessings on the issue of his marriage bed. In another essay evaluating Shakespeare's adaptation of source material, R. Chris Hassel, Jr., examined the play's allusions to St. Paul's Epistles and Erasmus's *The Praise of Folie* to demonstrate the correlation between Christian doctrine and Shakespeare's comic perspective. He contended that there are close parallels between the speeches of the young lovers as they awaken at the end of Act IV, Scene i and *The Praise of Folie,* concluding that, like the holy fool of Erasmus, the lovers must accept love as an unmerited blessing, since its mysteries cannot be apprehended by reason or the senses. Similarly, Hassel argued that Theseus's contention in the lunatic, lover, and poet speech regarding the limitations of human perception is supported by Pauline theology, which teaches that our willingness to believe in the imaginative world surpasses our capacities to understand it.

A number of twentieth-century commentators focused their attention on the characterization of Bottom and, specifically, his awakening speech at the close of Act IV, Scene i. At the beginning of the century, G. K. Chesterton offered the first substantial assessment of Bottom as an imaginative, resourceful personality, emphasizing his sensitivity to dramatic language as evidence of his creative insight. H. B. Charlton argued that Bottom was the most significant figure in the play for Shakespeare, since he is the only one of the principal characters in close touch with the realities of life. John Palmer contended that the weaver is neither a burlesque nor a foolish figure, but instead represents Shakespeare's own imaginative point of view, for both he and the dramatist are equally at ease with all the diverse characters in the play. Palmer also claimed that Bottom is depicted as superior to all the other mortals with regard to

courtesy, good nature, and ability to understand the process of imaginative art.

Harold C. Goddard, writing near the middle of the twentieth century, was among the first critics to fully examine Bottom's awakening soliloquy at the close of Act IV, Scene i. Goddard discerned in this passage Shakespeare's dramatization of the moment when an individual first perceives—through the agency of his imagination—the possibility of a spiritual life beyond mundane reality. Following up on this point, Peter G. Phialas interpreted Bottom's remark that man is "but an ass, if he go about to expound [his] dream" (IV. i. 206-07) as the most meaningful comment in the play and claimed that it shows the inexplicable and inexpressible nature of the mysteries of love. John A. Allen asserted that Bottom's inability to adequately express the mysteries of his experience with Titania and the fairies reflects the inexplicability of love in general; he also maintained that Bottom's heightened perception following his dream contributes to the quality and sincerity of his performance as Pyramus in the Pyramus-Thisbe interlude. Similar to R. Chris Hassel, Jr., Ronald F. Miller analyzed the implications of the allusions to Pauline theology in Bottom's awakening soliloquy. He commented that, in his lack of discernment between what is explicable and what is not, Bottom approaches the stature of God's holy fool, and he interpreted the weaver's speech as representing the visionary's attempt to explain a momentary glimpse of the unfathomable, nonphysical world. Most recently, J. Dennis Huston contended that Bottom's soliloquy is Shakespeare's commentary on the powers of his art. Noting that the passage occurs directly after the reconciliation of the young lovers with Theseus and Egeus, Huston argued that it "interrupts the audience's emotional involvement in the play" and provokes an intellectual assessment of the significance of the dramatic action.

One of the most dominant issues in the commentary on *A Midsummer Night's Dream* over the past thirty years has been the investigation of the significance of perception, illusion, and ambiguity in Shakespeare's play. Writing in the 1950s, John Russell Brown examined the varying levels of perception afforded each of the characters in *A Midsummer Night's Dream* and concluded that the play demonstrates that just as the audience's imagination is required to correct the mechanicals' performance of the Pyramus and Thisbe story, so a generous sympathy is needed if a lover's awareness of his experience is to be shared by others who have not perceived his vision of love's truth. Differing degrees of perception and awareness in the drama were also analyzed by Bertrand Evans, who pointed to the discrepancies in knowledge of the events between individual characters and asserted that this is the only one of Shakespeare's comedies to conclude without permitting the principal figures to share the audience's perception of the dramatic circumstances. C. L. Barber maintained that the "clarification" that ensues by the end of *A Midsummer Night's Dream* results from an increased awareness on the part of the characters of the relation between humanity and nature. He also asserted that the comic theme of the play centers on the participants' follies of misinterpreting the function of fantasy in life. Similarly, T. Walter Herbert considered the humorous misperceptions of reality held by Lysander and Bottom's Pyramus, noting the irony in the fact that Lysander attributes his actions to "reason," when they are actually governed by external forces, and Bottom, in the role of Pyramus, discerns supernatural intelligence in every inanimate object, when in truth his world is influenced only by human will. Stephen Fender examined the different angles of vision in *A Midsummer*

Night's Dream, claiming that the contrasting apprehensions of the supernatural world by the young lovers, Theseus, and Bottom represent alternative answers to the question of whether there can be any valid response to art. He determined that Shakespeare attributed some degree of verity to each of these responses, so that the audience is left with the question unresolved. In a work recalling Hermann Ulrici's contention more than a century before that the play represents the physical world as merely a shadow or reflection of a larger, ideal world, Sydney R. Homan maintained that the respective spheres of Theseus and Oberon are microcosms within a larger reality, which cannot be understood through reason but can only be apprehended by imagination. As noted earlier, Charles R. Lyons regarded Shakespeare's presentation of love as ambiguous and the play's traditional comic ending as illusory, since the element of death in the drama is never entirely suppressed. Extending the focus on perception in the play, James L. Calderwood asserted that dramatic illusion is, in fact, the central concern of *A Midsummer Night's Dream,* for in his representation of the essential aspects of dramatic art Shakespeare shifted and blurred "the borders between dream, drama, and waking reality" to emphasize that each realm may overlap the others.

Many of the same critics concerned with the importance of perception and illusion in *A Midsummer Night's Dream* have also noted the reflexive, self-conscious quality of the play. Barber discerned this element primarily in the Pyramus-Thisbe interlude, which he claimed parodies the "mimetic impulse to become something by acting it." Calderwood compared the exchange of roles and identities by the young lovers in the forest, as well as the rude mechanicals' failed attempt to submerge their identities in their assumed theatrical roles, with the fundamental process of dramatic production in which real individuals transform themselves into imaginary personae. Most recently, David Marshall argued that *A Midsummer Night's Dream* both explores the relations between the theater and its audience and raises significant questions concerning the traditional view of marriage as enacted in the play. Marshall observed that the women's forced submission to the point of view and domination of the men throughout the drama parallels an audience's exchange of its vision and imagination for those of the playwright and actors.

A review of the critical history of *A Midsummer Night's Dream* reveals that it was not until the twentieth century that scholars began to comprehend the philosophical depth and dramatic complexity of Shakespeare's creation. What was once considered a light, insubstantial play or fairy tale is now regarded as one of Shakespeare's most satisfying works and a keen dramatic investigation into concerns he would treat more seriously in his later comedies and tragedies: the nature of love, the influence of the spiritual world on the mortal, the conflict between appearance and reality, and questions pertaining to his own craft as a dramatist. In *A Midsummer Night's Dream,* as many critics have noted, Shakespeare was nearing the height of his powers as a comic playwright. In fact, numerous commentators place *A Midsummer Night's Dream* with the finest of Shakespeare's mature comedies. As J. Dennis Huston concluded: "[In] spite of their obvious greatness—in offering fuller characterization, greater poetic sophistication, and more complex dramatic worlds—none of the mature comedies manages the dramatic medium as spectacularly as *A Midsummer Night's Dream.*"

FRANCIS KIRKMAN AND HENRY MARSH   (essay date 1661)

[*The following excerpt is from a stationers' advertisement for* The Merry conceited Humours of Bottom the Weaver, *an adaptation of Shakespeare's* A Midsummer Night's Dream *featuring the character of Bottom as the principal figure. The note indicates that the comedy was successfully presented as private entertainment during the period when public plays and playhouses had been suppressed by Parliament.*]

Gentlemen, the entreaty of several Persons, our friends, hath enduced us to the publishing of this Piece, [*The Merry conceited Humours of Bottom the Weaver*], which (when the life of action was added to it) pleased generally well. It hath been the desire of several (who know we have many pieces of this nature in our hands) that we should publish them, and we considering the general mirth that is likely, very suddainly to happen about the Kings Coronation; and supposing that things of this Nature, will be acceptable, have therefore begun with this which we know may be easily acted, and may be now as fit for a private recreation as formerly it hath been for a publike. If you please to encourage us with Your acceptance of this, you will enduce us to bring you forth our store, and we will assure you that we are plentifully furnished with things of this Nature; Receive this then with good will as we intend it, and other shall not only succeed it but you shall continue us

——*Your Servants,*
FRANCIS KIRKMAN,
HENRY MARSH.

Francis Kirkman and Henry Marsh, in an extract from The Shakspere Allusion-Book: A Collection of Allusions to Shakspere from 1591 to 1700, Vol. II, *edited by John Munro, revised edition, 1932. Reprint by Books for Libraries Press, 1970; distributed by Arno Press, Inc., p. 105.*

SAMUEL PEPYS   (diary date 1662)

[*A diversified background of travel, intellectual pursuits, and public office gave Pepys the opportunity to be a close observer of his society. His unique* Diary *is an unreserved study of the affairs and customs of his time and his personal revelations create a document of unusual psychological interest as well as providing a history of the Restoration theater. Pepys's dismissal of* A Midsummer Night's Dream *as "the most insipid ridiculous play that ever I saw in my life" is the earliest known commentary on the drama.*]

[Went] to the King's Theatre, where we saw *Midsummers nights dreame,* which I have never seen before, nor shall ever again, for it is the most insipid ridiculous play that ever I saw in my life. I saw, I confess, some good dancing and some handsome women, which was all my pleasure. (p. 208)

Samuel Pepys, in a diary entry of September 29, 1662, in his The Diary of Samuel Pepys: 1662, Vol. III, *edited by Robert Latham and William Matthews, University of California Press, 1970, pp. 207-08.*

JOHN DRYDEN   (essay date 1677)

[*Dryden, the leading poet and playwright of Restoration England, helped formulate the Neoclassical view of Shakespeare as an irregular genius whose native talent overcame his ignorance of the proper "rules" and language for serious drama. He was also instrumental in establishing Shakespeare's reputation as the foremost dramatist of English literature. In the following excerpt, from the preface to his opera* The State of Innocence, *and the*

Fall of Man *(1677), Dryden defends a poet's presentation of imaginary figures or phenomena ''if they are founded on popular belief.'' He includes in this list ''Fairies, Pigmies, and the extraordinary effects of Magic.'' In the twentieth century, such critics as Frank Sidgwick, Minor White Latham, Roger Lancelyn Green, and K. M. Briggs (see Additional Bibliography) also discussed the extent to which the fairies in* A Midsummer Night's Dream *are ''founded on popular belief.'']*

And Poets may be allow'd the like liberty, for describing things which really exist not, if they are founded on popular belief: of this nature are Fairies, Pigmies, and the extraordinary effects of Magick; and thus are *Shakespeare's Tempest,* his *Midsummers nights Dream,* and *Ben. Johnsons Masque of Witches* to be defended.

> John Dryden, in an extract from The Shakspere Allusion-Book: A Collection of Allusions to Shakspere from 1591 to 1700, Vol. II, edited by John Munro, revised edition, 1932. Reprint by Books for Libraries Press, 1970; distributed by Arno Press, Inc., p. 177.

[CHARLES GILDON]   (essay date 1710)

[Gildon was the first critic to write an extended commentary on Shakespeare's plays. Like many other Neoclassicists, he regarded Shakespeare as an imaginative playwright who nevertheless lacked knowledge of the dramatic ''rules'' necessary for correct writing. In the excerpt below, taken from his ''Remarks on the Plays of Shakespear'' (1710), Gildon states that A Midsummer Night's Dream *''can never bear the Test of the Rules'' because the play violates the order of time established in the first act. The issue of the duration of time in the play was later addressed by Henry A. Clapp (1885), Horace Howard Furness (1895), and Anne Paolucci (1977). Gildon also maintains that Hermia's speech at I. i. 168-78 and other passages in the play demonstrate that Shakespeare was well acquainted with the ancient fables of Ovid and Virgil.]*

[*A Midsummer Night's Dream*] can never bear the Test of the Rules. The time is by *Theseus* in the first Scenes of the Play fixt to at least four Days in these Words

> Now fair *Hippolita,* our Nuptial Hour
> Draws on apace, four happy Days begin
> Another Moon, &c.
>
>   [I. i. 1-3]

The new Moon being the time for their Marriage. But it does not appear that there is any more time spent in the Action than one Day and one Night, and a piece of a Day, and part of one Night.

Tho' this cannot be call'd either Tragedy or Comedy as wanting the Fable requir'd to either; yet it contains abundance of beautiful Reflections, Descriptions, Similes, and Topics. Much of it is in Rhime, in which the Author is generally very smooth and flowing. The first Scene of the Complaint of *Egeus* to *Theseus* is very pretty, the Obstinacy of a peevish old Father, who will dispose of his Daughter without Regard to oher Inclinations, is well express'd, and the Manner of his representing how *Lysander* had rob'd her of her Affections is extreamly agreeable to that Character. . . . (pp. 315-16)

But I cannot omit *Hermias* Oath to meet her Lover that Night and fly with him from *Athens.*

> —*Her.* My good *Lysander;*
> I swear to thee by *Cupid's* strongest Bow;
> By this blest Arrow with the golden Head;
> By the Simplicity of *Venus* Doves;

> By that which knitteth Souls and prospers Love;
> And by that Fire, that burn'd the *Carthage* Queen
> When the false *Trojan* under Sail was seen;
> By all the Vows, that ever Men have broke,
> In Number more, than ever Woman spoke;
> In that same place, thou hast appointed me
> To morrow truly will I meet with thee.
>
>   [I. i. 168-78]

Tho' we cannot perhaps trace the Ancients in the Thoughts of *Shakespear,* yet it is plain from these Verses, and several others about his Plays that *Shakespear* was acquainted with the Fables of Antiquity very well: That some of the Arrows of *Cupid* are pointed with Lead, and the others with Gold, he found in *Ovid:* And that which speaks of *Dido* he has from *Virgil* himself, nor do I know of any Translation of those Poets so ancient as *Shakespear's* Time. (pp. 316-17)

> [Charles Gildon], ''Remarks on the Plays of Shakespear,'' in The Works of Mr. William Shakespear, Vol. 7 by William Shakespeare, 1710. Reprint by AMS Press, Inc., 1967, pp. 257-444.

WILLIAM DUFF   (essay date 1770)

[Duff was a Scottish minister and scholar whose Shakespearean criticism, typical of its age, focused on the evidence of ''taste'' and ''genius'' in Shakespeare's works. In the following excerpt, taken from his Critical Observations on the Writings of the Most Celebrated Original Geniuses in Poetry *(1770), Duff extols the liveliness and exuberance of the dramatist's depiction of the fairies in* A Midsummer Night's Dream, *stating that Shakespeare's genius ''never appears with so much strength and advantage'' as when he portrayed supernatural or imaginary beings. For additional discussion of Shakespeare's inventiveness in his representation of the fairies, see the excerpts by G. G. Gervinus (1849-50), H. N. Hudson (1872), E. K. Chambers (1905), and George A. Bonnard (1956).]*

[The] Genius of Shakespeare delighted in the most uncommonn and astonishing combinations of ideas, and it never appears with so much strength and advantage as when he bursts into the ideal world, and presents to our view the characters and offices of supernatural beings, in which highest exertion of Genius he hath in most instances indeed never been equalled. (p. 368)

[One] sort of ideal characters to be considered by us is the fairy species, in the description of which Shakespeare hath given full scope to the exuberance of his creative Genius.

> [*Fairy.*—Over hill, over dale,
> Thorough bush, thorough brier,
> Over park, over pale,
> Thorough flood, thorough fire,
> I do wander every where,
> Swifter than the moon's sphere;
> And I serve the Fairy Queen,
> To dew her orbs upon the green.
> The cowslips tall her pensioners be,
> In their gold coats spots you see:
> Those be rubies, fairy favors,
> In those freckles live their savors.]
>
>   [II. i. 2-13]

Every reader must observe that the above description which the fairy gives of his employment is distinguished by its vivacity and wildness. The lightness and volatility of these visionary beings seems to be imitated in the quick returns, and (if we may use the expression) brisk boundings of the verse.

How strangely picturesque and original is the description of the employments enjoined by Titania to her fairies, in the third scene of the third act!

> [*Tita.* Be kind and courteous to this gentleman,
> Hop in his walks and gambol in his eyes;
> Feed him with apricocks and dewberries,
> With purple grapes, green figs, and mulberries;
> The honey-bags steal from the humble-bees,
> And from night-tapers crop their waxen thighs,
> And light them at the fiery glow-worm's eyes,
> To have my love to bed and to arise;
> And pluck the wings from painted butterflies,
> To fan the moonbeams from his sleeping eyes.
> Nod to him, elves, and do him courtesies.] ...
> [III. i. 164-74]

In the above passage the imagination of Shakespeare seems to wanton and sport in exuberance. Who but this author ever thought of such fairy courtesies as stealing honey bags from the bees, cropping their waxen thighs to make tapers, lighting them at the glow-worm's eyes, and plucking the wings of butterflies to fan the moon beams from the eyes of one asleep? These employments, so fanciful and so wild, are however at the same time perfectly apposite to the imagined nature and qualities of the fairy species. (pp. 368-69)

> *William Duff, in an extract from* Shakespeare, the Critical Heritage: 1765-1774, Vol. 5, *edited by Brian Vickers, Routledge & Kegan Paul, 1979, pp. 367-72.*

[FRANCIS GENTLEMAN] (essay date 1774)

[*Gentleman was an actor as well as a playwright, and he was especially concerned with how Shakespeare's plays should be performed in the theater. In the following excerpt, originally published in* Bell's Edition of Shakespeare's Plays *in 1774, he argues that in writing* A Midsummer Night's Dream *Shakespeare had two "material points in view": Novelty and Originality. Gentleman maintains that although the play possesses "great poetical and dramatic merit," it also suffers from "a puerile plot, an odd mixture of incidents, and a forced connexion of various stiles." Internal inconsistencies in the dramatic style of* A Midsummer Night's Dream *have led some critics, including Walter de la Mare and, jointly, Arthur Quiller-Couch and John Dover Wilson (see Additional Bibliography), to conclude that the play is Shakespeare's heavily revised version of an earlier work by another dramatist. Also, for further discussion of the originality of Shakespeare's genius in* A Midsummer Night's Dream, *see the excerpt by August Wilhelm Schlegel (1808).*]

In [*A Midsummer Night's Dream*] Shakespeare had evidently two great and very material points in view; Novelty and Originality, the sure road, if attained, to permanency and fame: to these favourite objects, he paid such attention as sometimes to forget probability, though he always preserved character. The following piece has great poetical and dramatic merit, considered in general; but a puerile plot, an odd mixture of incidents, and a forced connexion of various stiles, throw a kind of shade over that blaze of merit many passages would otherwise have possessed. There is no character strongly marked, yet the whole shews a very great master dallying with his own genius and imagination in a wonderful and delightful manner.

> [*Francis Gentleman*], *in an introduction to "A Midsummer Night's Dream" in* Bell's Edition of Shakespeare's Plays, Vol. VIII *by William Shakespeare, 1774. Reprint by Cornmarket Press, 1969, p. 137.*

EDMOND MALONE (essay date 1778)

[*An eighteenth-century Irish literary scholar and editor, Malone was the first critic to establish a chronology of Shakespeare's plays. He was also the first scholar to prepare a critical edition of Shakespeare's sonnets and the first to write a comprehensive history of the English stage based on extensive research into original sources. As the major Shakespearean editor of the eighteenth century, Malone collaborated with George Steevens on Steevens's second and third editions of Shakespeare's plays and issued his own edition in 1790. His importance resides not so much in textual emendation as in his unrivaled knowledge of primary sources. In the following excerpt from his preface to the 1778 edition of Shakespeare's plays, Malone disparages* A Midsummer Night's Dream *for its "meagre and uninteresting" story and a lack of strong characterization in its principal figures, especially Theseus, and he regards the play as one of Shakespeare's "earliest attempts in comedy." Malone's view of Theseus as a poorly delineated character who offers little to the action of* A Midsummer Night's Dream *is contradicted by Edward Dowden (1881) and Denton J. Snider (1890), both of whom view Theseus as an ideal Renaissance figure of authority and order. In a similar vein, H. B. Charlton (1933) argues that the Duke's unromantic worldly realism reflects Shakespeare's own attitude toward human conduct, and such later critics as George A. Bonnard (1956), and Paul A. Olson (see Additional Bibliography) describe Theseus as a figure of sanity and reason and as Shakespeare's corrective to the irrational, amoral behavior of the lovers. Other critics, including M. E. Lamb (1979) and D'Orsay W. Pearson (see Additional Bibliography) maintain that the Elizabethan view of Theseus combined criticism of his personal conduct with praise for his heroic feats.*]

The poetry of [*A Midsummer Night's Dream*], glowing with all the warmth of a youthful and lively imagination, the many scenes which it contains of almost continual rhyme, the poverty of the fable, and want of discrimination among the higher personages, dispose me to believe that it was one of our author's earliest attempts in comedy.

It seems to have been written, while the ridiculous competitions prevalent among the histrionick tribe were strongly impressed by novelty on his mind. He would naturally copy those manners first, with which he was first acquainted. The ambition of a theatrical candidate for applause he has happily ridiculed in Bottom the weaver. But among the more dignified persons of the drama we look in vain for any traits of character. The manners of Hippolita, the Amazon, are undistinguished from those of other females. Theseus, the associate of Hercules, is not engaged in any adventure worthy of his rank or reputation, nor is he in reality an agent throughout the play. Like King Henry VIII. he goes out a Maying. He meets the lovers in perplexity, and makes no effort to promote their happiness; but when supernatural accidents have reconciled them, he joins their company, and concludes his day's entertainment by uttering some miserable puns at an interlude represented by a troop of clowns. Over the fairy part of the drama he cannot be supposed to have any influence. This part of the fable, indeed (at least as much of it as relates to the quarrels of Oberon and Titania), was not of our author's invention.—Through the whole piece, the more exalted characters are subservient to the interests of those beneath them. We laugh with Bottom and his fellows; but is a single passion agitated by the faint and childish solicitudes of Hermia and Demetrius, of Helena and Lysander, those shadows of each other?—That a drama, of which the principal personages are thus insignificant, and the fable thus meagre and uninteresting, was one of our author's earliest compositions, does not, therefore, seem a very improbable conjecture; nor are the beauties with which it is embellished, inconsistent with this supposition; for the genius of Shakspeare, even in its minority, could embroider the coarsest materials with the brightest and most lasting colours. (pp. 333-37)

> *Edmond Malone, "An Attempt to Ascertain the Order in Which the Plays of Shakspeare Were Written," in* The Plays and Poems of William Shakspeare, Vol. II *by William Shakespeare, edited by J. Boswell, 1821. Reprint by AMS Press, Inc., 1966, pp. 288-468.*

AUGUST WILHELM SCHLEGEL   (lecture date 1808)

[Schlegel holds a key place in the history of Shakespeare's reputation in European criticism. His translations of thirteen of the plays are still considered the best German editions of Shakespeare. Schlegel was also a leading spokesman for the Romantic movement which permanently overthrew the Neoclassical contention that Shakespeare was a child of nature whose plays lacked artistic form. In the excerpt below, taken from a lecture delivered in Vienna in 1808, Schlegel maintains that the separate parts of A Midsummer Night's Dream *are "so lightly and happily interwoven that they seem necessary to each other for the formation of the whole." He especially notes the Theseus-Hippolyta framework to the dramatic action and the Pyramus-Thisbe play-within-the-play as evidence of Shakespeare's unifying design, a point expanded upon by Hermann Ulrici (1839) and Denton J. Snider (1890), but countered by G. K. Hunter and Robert Adger Law (see Additional Bibliography)—these last of whom assert that the diverse elements of the plot are not organically related. Schlegel's interpretation of the Pyramus and Thisbe interlude as a parody of the young lovers in the main acion—the first such assessment of this episode—is also held by E. K. Chambers (1905), Paul N. Siegel (1953), C. L. Barber (1959), and Mordecai Marcus (1981).]*

[In *The Midsummer Night's Dream*] there flows a luxuriant vein of the boldest and most fantastical invention; the most extraordinary combination of the most dissimilar ingredients seems to have been brought about without effort by some ingenious and lucky accident, and the colours are of such clear transparency that we think the whole of the variegated fabric may be blown away with a breath. The fairy world here described resembles those elegant pieces of arabesque, where little genii with butterfly wings rise, half embodied, above the flower-cups. Twilight, moonshine, dew, and spring perfumes, are the element of these tender spirits; they assist nature in embroidering her carpet with green leaves, many-coloured flowers, and glittering insects; in the human world they do but make sport childishly and waywardly with their beneficent or noxious influences. Their most violent rage dissolves in good-natured raillery; their passions, stripped of all earthly matter, are merely an ideal dream. To correspond with this, the loves of mortals are painted as a poetical enchantment, which, by a contrary enchantment, may be immediately suspended, and then renewed again. The different parts of the plot; the wedding of Theseus and Hippolyta, Oberon and Titania's quarrel, the flight of the two pair of lovers, and the theatrical manoeuvres of the mechanics, are so lightly and happily interwoven that they seem necessary to each other for the formation of a whole. Oberon is desirous of relieving the lovers from their perplexities, but greatly adds to them through the mistakes of his minister, till he at last comes really to the aid of their fruitless amorous pain, their inconstancy and jealousy, and restores fidelity to its old rights. The extremes of fanciful and vulgar

are united when the enchanted Titania awakes and falls in love with a coarse mechanic with an ass's head, who represents, or rather disfigures, the part of a tragical lover. The droll wonder of Bottom's transformation is merely the translation of a metaphor in its literal sense; but in his behaviour during the tender homage of the Fairy Queen we have an amusing proof how much the consciousness of such a head-dress heightens the effect of his usual folly. Theseus and Hippolyta are, as it were, a splendid frame for the picture; they take no part in the action, but surround it with a stately pomp. The discourse of the hero and his Amazon, as they course through the forest with their noisy hunting-train, works upon the imagination like the fresh breath of morning, before which the shapes of night disappear. Pyramus and Thisbe is not unmeaningly chosen as the grotesque play within the play; it is exactly like the pathetic part of the piece, a secret meeting of two lovers in the forest, and their separation by an unfortunate accident, and closes the whole with the most amusing parody. (pp. 393-94)

> *August Wilhelm Schlegel, "Criticisms on Shakspeare's Comedies," in his* A Course of Lectures on Dramatic Art and Literature, *edited by Rev. A.J.W. Morrison, translated by John Black, revised edition, 1846. Reprint by AMS Press, Inc., 1965, pp. 379-99.*

WILLIAM HAZLITT   (essay date 1817)

[Hazlitt is considered a leading Shakespearean critic of the English Romantic movement. A prolific essayist and critic on a wide range of subjects, Hazlitt remarked in the preface to his Characters of Shakespear's Plays, *first published in 1817, that he was inspired by the German critic August Wilhelm Schlegel and was determined to supplant what he considered the pernicious influence of Samuel Johnson's Shakespearean criticism. Hazlitt's criticism is typically Romantic in its emphasis on character studies. His experience as a drama critic was an important factor in shaping his descriptive, as opposed to analytical, interpretations of Shakespeare. Although we do not know who is signified by the reference to "us" in the second paragraph of the excerpt below, Hazlitt's description of an actual performance of* A Midsummer Night's Dream, *with which he was somehow involved, concludes with the observation that the play is too ethereal to be presented on the stage. This view of the play as a work to be read rather than performed was held by many later nineteenth-century critics, including William Maginn (1837), Charles Knight (1849), G. G. Gervinus (1849-50), and Denton J. Snider (1890).]*

It is astonishing that Shakespear should be considered, not only by foreigners, but by many of our own critics, as a gloomy and heavy writer. . . . His subtlety exceeds that of all other dramatic writers, insomuch that a celebrated person of the present day said that he regarded him rather as a metaphysician than a poet. His delicacy and sportive gaiety are infinite. In the *Midsummer Night's Dream* alone, we should imagine, there is more sweetness and beauty of description than in the whole range of French poetry put together. What we mean is this, that we will produce out of that single play ten passages, to which we do not think any ten passages in the works of the French poets can be opposed, displaying equal fancy and imagery. Shall we mention the remonstrance of Helena to Hermia, or Titania's description of her fairy train, or her disputes with Oberon about the Indian boy, or Puck's account of himself and his employments, or the Fairy Queen's exhortation to the elves to pay due attendance upon her favourite, Bottom; or Hippolita's description of a chace, or Theseus's answer? The two last are as heroical and spirited as the others are full of luscious tenderness. The reading of this play is like wandering in a grove by moonlight: the descriptions breathe a sweetness like odours thrown from bed of flowers. (p. 80)

It had been suggested to us, that the *Midsummer Night's Dream* would do admirably to get up as a Christmas after-piece; and our prompter proposed that Mr. [Edmund] Kean should play the part of Bottom, as worthy of his great talents. He might, in the discharge of his duty, offer to play the lady like any of our actresses that he pleased, the lover or the tyrant like any of our actors that he pleased, and the lion like "the most fearful wild-fowl living." The carpenter, the tailor, and joiner, it was thought, would hit the galleries. The young ladies in love would interest the side-boxes; and Robin Goodfellow and his companions excite a lively fellow-feeling in the children from school. There would be two courts, an empire within an empire, the Athenian and the Fairy King and Queen, with their attendants, and with all their finery. What an opportunity for processions, for the sound of trumpets and glittering of spears! What a fluttering of urchins' painted wings; what a delightful profusion of gauze clouds and airy spirits floating on them!

Alas the experiment has been tried, and has failed; not through the fault of Mr. Kean, who did not play the part of Bottom, nor of Mr. [John] Liston, who did, and who played it well, but from the nature of things. The *Midsummer Night's Dream*, when acted, is converted from a delightful fiction into a dull pantomime. All that is finest in the play is lost in the representation. The spectacle was grand; but the spirit was evaporated, the genius was fled.—Poetry and the stage do not agree well together. The attempt to reconcile them in this instance fails not only of effect, but of decorum. The *ideal* can have no place upon the stage, which is a picture without perspective: every thing there is in the fore-ground. That which was merely an airy shape, a dream, a passing thought, immediately becomes an unmanageable reality. Where all is left to the imagination (as is the case in reading) every circumstance, near or remote, has an equal chance of being kept in mind, and tells accordingly to the mixed impression of all that has been suggested. But the imagination cannot sufficiently qualify the actual impressions of the senses. Any offence given to the eye is not to be got rid of by explanation. Thus Bottom's head in the play is a fantastic illusion, produced by magic spells: on the stage it is an ass's head, and nothing more; certainly a very strange costume for a gentleman to appear in. Fancy cannot be embodied any more than a simile can be painted; and it is as idle to attempt it as to personate *Wall* or *Moonshine*. Fairies are not incredible, but fairies six feet high are so. Monsters are not shocking, if they are seen at a proper distance. When ghosts appear at mid-day, when apparitions stalk along Cheapside, then may the *Midsummer Night's Dream* be represented without injury at Covent-garden or at Drury-lane. The boards of a theatre and the regions of fancy are not the same thing. (pp. 81-3)

> William Hazlitt, "'The Midsummer Night's Dream'," in his Characters of Shakespear's Plays & Lectures on the English Poets, *Macmillan and Co. Limited, 1903, pp. 78-83.*

SAMUEL TAYLOR COLERIDGE   (essay date 1834?)

[*Coleridge's lectures and writings on Shakespeare form a major chapter in the history of English Shakespearean criticism. As the channel for the critical ideas of the German Romantics and as an original interpreter of Shakespeare in the new spirit of Romanticism, Coleridge played a strategic role in overthrowing the last remains of the Neoclassical approach to Shakespeare and in*

establishing the modern view of the dramatist as a conscious artist and masterful portrayer of human character. Coleridge's remarks on Shakespeare come down to posterity largely as fragmentary notes, marginalia, and reports by auditors on the lectures, rather than in polished essays. The excerpt below was reproduced by the Coleridge editor T. A. Raysor from Coleridge's undated notes to the comedies. In it, Coleridge decries Helena's betrayal to Demetrius of Hermia and Lysander's elopement plans. He claims that acting on "passion and inclination" rather than on principle is natural to women, but that its depiction here is "not poetical." In his words: "[W]e shrink from it and cannot harmonize it with the ideal." For further discussions of the relations between Hermia and Helena, see the excerpts by Stephen Fender (1968), Hugh M. Richmond (1971), and David Marshall (1982). Also, Coleridge's initial comment here that Shakespeare viewed A Midsummer Night's Dream as "a dream throughout" has been echoed by H. N. Hudson (1872), George Brandes (1895-96), and Frederick S. Boas (1896).]

I am convinced that Shakespeare availed himself of the title of [*A Midsummer Night's Dream*] in his own mind [as] a *dream* throughout, but especially (and perhaps unpleasingly) in [the] broad determination of ungrateful treachery in Helena, so undisguisedly avowed to herself. . . . [Her betrayal of Hermia in Act I, Scene i] is very natural; the resolve so to act is, I fear, likewise too true a picture of the lax holds that principles have on the female heart, when opposed to, or even separated from, passion and inclination. For women are less hypocrites to their own minds than men, because they feel less abhorrence of moral evil in itself and more for its outward consequences, as detection, loss of character, etc., their natures being almost wholly extroitive [*O.E.D.*: "directed to external objects"]. But still, however just, the representation is not poetical; we shrink from it and cannot harmonize it with the ideal.

> Samuel Taylor Coleridge, "Notes on the Comedies of Shakespeare: 'Midsummer Night's Dream'," in his Shakespearean Criticism, Vol. 1, *edited by Thomas Middleton Raysor, second edition, Dutton, 1960, pp. 90-2.*

WILLIAM MAGINN   (essay date 1837)

[*Born and educated in Ireland, Maginn later lived in London where he developed his career as an essayist, poet, and short story writer. In the following excerpt from an essay originally published in 1837, he provides the earliest analysis of the exchange between Theseus and Hippolyta in Act V, Scene i on the role of the audience's imagination at the performance of a play. Maginn argues that Shakespeare is here presenting "the common calamity of dramatists," namely, that all playwrights, including himself, work under conditions that are less than ideal and that an audience's willing imagination is therefore necessary to the best as well as the worst writer for the success of any play. The exact meaning and significance of Theseus's comments in this exchange have been variously interpreted since Maginn's essay appeared. Some commentators, like Charles Knight (1849) and Frederick S. Boas (1896), claim that the duke is here voicing Shakespeare's own view of art and imagination, whereas others, such as Edward Dowden (1881), Howard Nemerov (1956), and R. W. Dent (1964), believe that Shakespeare was diminishing Theseus's stature as a spokesman in the play, primarily by emphasizing his "administrative" view of art as nothing more than entertainment or diversion. Maginn also offers the first detailed character study of Bottom. He admires the weaver's equanimity and self-possession and attributes his self-conceit to the unrelenting flattery of those around him. For further discussions of the character of Bottom, see the excerpts by Charles Cowden Clarke (1863), G. K. Chesterton (1904), E. K. Chambers (1905), H. B. Charlton (1933), John Palmer (1944), Elizabeth Sewell*]

(1960), John A. Allen (1967), Hugh M. Richmond (1971), and Ronald F. Miller (1975). Also, like William Hazlitt (1817) and H. N. Hudson (1872), Maginn argues that the full impact of Bottom's transformation into an ass is theatrically inexpressible.]

It has often been remarked that it is impossible to play the enchanted scenes of Bottom with any effect. In reading the poem we idealize the ass-head; we can conceive that it represents in some grotesque sort the various passions and emotions of its wearer; that it assumes a character of dull jocosity, or duller sapience, in his conversations with Titania and the fairies; and when calling for the assistance of Messrs. Peasblossom and Mustard-seed to scratch his head, or of the Queen to procure him a peck of provender or a bottle of hay, it expresses some puzzled wonder of the new sensations its wearer must experience in tinglings never felt before, and cravings for food until then unsuited to his appetite. But on the stage this is impossible. As the mangager can not procure for his fairies representatives of such tiny dimensions as to be in danger of being overflown by the bursting of the honey-bag of an humble-bee, so it is impossible that the art of the propertyman can furnish Bottom with an ass-head capable of expressing the mixed feelings of humanity and asinity which actuate the metamorphosed weaver. It is but a paste-board head, and that is all. The jest is over the first moment after his appearance; and, having laughed at it once, we can not laugh at it any more. (pp. 85-6)

Shakespeare in many parts of his plays drops hints, "vocal to the intelligent," that he feels the difficulty of bringing his ideas adequately before the minds of theatrical spectators. In the opening address of the Chorus of *Henry V*. he asks pardon for having dared

> On this unworthy scaffold to bring forth
> So great an object. Can this cockpit hold
> The vasty fields of France? or, may we cram
> Within this wooden O, the very casques
> That did affright the air at Agincourt?
>
> [*Henry V*, prologue, 10-14]

and requests his audience to piece out the imperfections of the theatre with their thoughts. This is an apology for the ordinary and physcial defects of any stage—especially an ill-furnished one; and it requires no great straining of our imaginary forces to submit to them. (pp. 86-7)

We can dispense with the assistance of such downright matter-of-fact interpreters as those who volunteer their services to assure us that the lion in Pyramus and Thisbe is not a lion in good earnest, but merely Snug, the Joiner. But there are difficulties of a more subtle and metaphyscial kind to be got over, and to these, too, Shakespeare not unfrequently alludes. In the play before us—*Midsummer Night's Dream*—for example, when Hippolita speaks scornfully of the tragedy in which Bottom holds so conspicuous a part, Theseus answers, that the best of this kind (scenic performances) are but shadows, and the worst no worse if imagination amend them. She answers that it must be *your* imagination then, not *theirs*. He retorts with a joke on the vanity of actors, and the conversation is immediately changed. The meaning of the Duke is, that however we may laugh at the silliness of Bottom and his companions in their ridiculous play, the author labors under no more than the common calamity of dramatists. They are all but dealers in shadowy representations of life; and if the worst among them can set the mind of the spectator at work, he is equal to the best. The answer to Theseus is, that none but the best, or, at all events,

those who approach to excellence, can call with success upon imagination to invest their shadows with substance. Such playwrights as Quince, the Carpenter—and they abound in every literature and every theatre—draw our attention so much to the absurdity of the performance actually going on before us, that we have no inclination to trouble ourselves with considering what substance in the background their shadows should have represented. Shakespeare intended the remark as a compliment or a consolation to less successful wooers of the comic or the tragic Muse, and touches briefly on the matter; but it was also intended as an excuse for the want of effect upon the stage of some of the finer touches of such dramatists as himself, and an appeal to all true judges of poetry to bring it before the tribunal of their own imagination; making but a matter of secondary inquiry how it appears in a theatre, as delivered by those who, whatever others may think of them, would, if taken at their own estimation, "pass for excellent men" [V. i. 216]. His own magnificent creation of fairy land in the Athenian wood must have been in his mind, and he asks an indulgent play of fancy not more of Oberon and Titania, the glittering rulers of the elements, who meet

> ——on hill, in dale, forest, or mead,
> By paved fountain, or by rushy brook,
> Or on the beached margent of the sea,
> To dance their ringlets to the whistling wind,
>
> [II. i. 83-6]

than for the shrewd and knavish Robin Goodfellow, the lord of practical jokes, or the dull and conceited Bottom, "the shallowest thickskin of the barren sort" [III. ii. 13] rapt so wondrously from his loom and shuttle, his threads and thrums, to be the favored lover of the Queen of Faëry, fresh from the spiced Indian air, and lulled with dances and delight amid the fragance of the sweetest flowers, filling with their luscious perfume a moon-lighted forest.

One part of Bottom's character is easily understood, and is often well acted. Amid his own companions he is the cock of the walk. His genius is admitted without hesitation. When he is lost in the wood, Quince gives up the play as marred. There is no man in Athens able to take the first part in tragedy but himself. Flute declares that he has the best wit of any handicraftman in the city. This does not satisfy the still warmer admirer, who insists on the goodliness of his person, and the fineness of his voice. When it seems hopeless that he should appear, the cause of the stage is given up as utterly lost. When he returns, it is hailed as the "courageous day," and the "happy hour" [IV. ii. 27, 28], which is to restore the legitimate drama. It is no wonder that this perpetual flattery fills him with a most inordinate opinion of his own powers. There is not a part in the play which he can not perform. As a lover, he promises to make the audience weep; but his talent is still more shining in the Herculean vein of tyrant. The manliness of his countenance, he admits, incapacitates him from acting the part of a heroine; but, give him a mask, and he is sure to captivate by the soft melody of his voice. But, lest it should be thought this melodious softness was alone his characteristic, he claims the part of the lion, which he is to discharge with so terrific a roar as to call forth the marked approbation of the warlike Duke; and yet, when the danger is suggested of frightening the ladies, who all, Amazons as they were, must be daunted by sounds so fear-inspiring, he professes himself gifted with a power of compass capable of imitating, even in the character of a roaring lion, the gentleness of the sucking dove, or the sweetness of the nightingale. He is equally fit for all parts calculated to outshine the rest. This is allowed; but, as it is impossible that he can perform them all, he is restricted to the principal. It is with the softest compliments that he is induced to abandon the parts of Thisbe and the lion for that of Pyramus. Quince assures him that he can play none other, because ''Pyramus is a sweet-faced man; a proper man as one shall see in a summer's day; a most lovely, gentlemanlike man; *therefore* YOU must undertake it''[I. ii. 86-9]. What man of woman born, could resist flattery so unsparingly administered? the well-puffed performer consents, and though he knows nothing of the play, and is unable to tell whether the part for which he is cast is that of a lover or a tyrant, undertakes to discharge it with a calm and heroic indifference as the the color of the beard he is to wear, being confident, under any circumstances, of success, whether that most important part of the costume be straw-colored or orange-tawny, French crown or purple in grain. With equal confidence he gets through his performance. The wit of the courtiers, or the presence of the Duke, has no effect upon his nerves. He alone speaks to the audience in his own character, not for a moment sinking the personal consequence of Bottom in the assumed part of Pyramus. He sets Theseus right on a point of the play with cool importance; and replies to the jest of Demetrius (which he does not understand) with the self-command of ignorant indifference. We may be sure that he was abundantly contented with his appearance, retired to drink in, with ear well deserving of the promotion it had attained under the patronage of Robin Goodfellow, the applause of his companions. It is true that Oberon designates him as a ''hateful fool;'' that Puck stigmatizes him as the greatest blockhead of the set; that the audience of wits and courtiers before whom he has performed vote him to be an ass: but what matter is that? He mixes not with them; he hears not their sarcasms; he could not understand their criticisms; and, in the congenial company of the crew of patches and base mechanicals who admire him, lives happy in the fame of being *the* Nicholas Bottom, who, by consent, to him universal and world-encompassing, is voted to be *the* Pyramus—*the* prop of the stage—*the* sole support of the drama. (pp. 88-92)

[Bottom] never long remains out of his own domain, and the jokes and jests upon the unlucky company who undertook to perform

> A tedious brief scene of young Pyramus
> And his love Thisbe, very tragical mirth,
>
> [V. i. 56-7]

are but intrusive matter amid the romantic loves, all chivalrous and a little classical, of Theseus and Hippolita, and the jealousies unearthly, and yet so earthly, of Fairy Land. The romance of early Greece was somtimes strangely confused by the romance of the Middle Ages. It would take a long essay on the mixture of legends derived from all ages and countries to account for the production of such a personage as the ''Duke ycleped Theseus'' and his following; and the fairy mythology of the most authentic superstitions would be ransacked in vain to discover exact authorities for the Shakespearian Oberon and Titania. But, no matter whence derived, the author knew well that in his hands the chivalrous and classical, the airy and the imaginative, were safe. It was necessary for his drama to introduce among his fairy party a creature of earth's mould, and he has so done it as in the midst of his mirth to convey a picturesque satire on the fortune which governs the world, and upon those passions which elsewhere he had with agitating pathos to depict. As Romeo, the gentleman, is *the* unlucky man of Shakespeare, so here does he exhibit Bottom, the block-

head, as *the* lucky man, as him on whom Fortune showers her favors beyond measure.

This is the part of the character which can not be performed. It is here that the greatest talent of the actor must fail in answering the demand made by the author upon our imagination. The utmost lavish of poetry, not only of high conception, but of the most elaborate working in the musical construction of the verse, and a somewhat recondite searching after all the topics favorable to the display of poetic eloquence in the ornamental style, is employed in the decription of the fairy scenes and those who dwell therein. Language more brilliantly bejewelled with whatever tropes and figures rhetoricians catalogue in their books is not to be found than what is scattered forth with copious hand in *Midsummer Night's Dream*.

The compliment to Queen Elizabeth,

> In maiden meditation fancy-free,
>
> [II. i. 164]

was of necessity sugared with all the sweets that the *bon-bon* box of the poet could supply; but it is not more ornamented than the passages all around. The pastoral images of Corin

> Playing on pipes of corn, and versing love
> To amorous Phillida;
>
> [II. i. 67-8]

the homely consequence resulting from the fairy quarrel,

> The ox hath therefore stretched his yoke in vain,
> The ploughman lost his sweat, and the green corn
> Hath rotted ere his youth attained a beard;
> The fold stands empty in the drownéd field,
> And crows are fatted with the murrain flock;
>
> [II. i. 93-7]

and so on, are ostentatiously contrasted with misfortunes more metaphorically related:—

> We see
> The seasons alter; hoary-headed frosts
> Fall on the fresh lap of the crimson rose;
> And on old Hyems' chin and icy crown
> An odorous chaplet of sweet summer buds
> Is, as in mockery, set.   [II. i. 106-11]

The mermaid chanting on the back of her dolphin; the fair vestal throned in the west; the bank blowing with wild thyme, and decked with oxlip and nodding violet; the roundelay of the fairies singing their queen to sleep; and a hundred images besides of aërial grace and mythic beauty, are showered upon us; and in the midst of these splendors is tumbled in Bottom, the Weaver, blockhead by original formation, and rendered doubly ridiculous by his partial change into a literal jackass. He, the most unfitted for the scene of all conceivable personages, makes his appearance, not as one to be expelled with loathing and derision, but to be instantly accepted as the chosen lover of the Queen of the Fairies. The gallant train of Theseus traverse the forest, but they are not the objects of such fortune. The lady, under the oppression of the glamour cast upon her eyes by the juice of love-in-idleness, reserves her raptures for an absurd clown. Such are the tricks of Fortune.

Oberon himself, angry as he is with the caprices of his queen, does not anticipate any such object for her charmed affections.

He is determined that she is to be captivated by "some vile thing" [II. ii. 34], but he thinks only of

> Ounce, or cat, or bear,
> Pard, or boar with bristled hair,"
>
> [II. ii. 30-1]

animals suggesting ideas of spite or terror; but he does not dream that, under the superintendence of Puck, spirit of mischief, she is to be enamored of the head of an ass surmounting the body of a weaver. It is so nevertheless; and the love of the lady is as desperate as the deformity of her choice. He is an angel that wakes her from her flowery bed; a gentle mortal, whose enchanting note wins her ear, while his beauteous shape enthralls her eye; one who is as wise as he is beautiful; one for whom all the magic treasures of the fairy kingdom are to be with surpassing profusion dispensed. For him she gathers whatever wealth and delicacies the Land of Faëry can boast. Her most airy spirits are ordered to be kind and courteous to this *gentleman*—for into that impossible character has the blindness of her love transmuted the clumsy and conceited clown. Apricocks and dewberries, purple grapes, green figs, and mulberries, are to feed his coarse palate; the thighs of bees, kindled at the eyes of fiery glow-worms, are to light him to his flower-decked bed; wings plucked from painted butterflies are to fan the moonbeams from him as he sleeps; and in the very desperation of her intoxicating passion she feels that there is nothing which should not be yielded to the strange idol of her soul. She mourns over the restraints which separate her from the object of her burning affection, and thinks that the moon and the flowers participate in her sorrow.

> The moon, methinks, looks with a watery eye,
> And when she weeps, weeps every little flower,
> *Lamenting some enforced chastity.*
>
> [III. i. 198-200]
> (pp. 96-100)

Ill-mated loves are generally but of short duration on the side of the nobler party, and she awakes to lament her folly. The fate of those who suffer like Titania is the hardest. The man who is deprived of external graces of appearance may have the power of captivating by those of the mind: wit, polish, fame, may compensate for the want of youth or personal attractions. . . . But woe unto the unhappy lady who, like Titania, is obliged to confess, when the enchantment has passed by, that she was "enamored of an *ass!*" [IV. i. 77] She must indeed "loathe his visage" [IV. i. 79], and the memory of all connected with him is destined ever to be attended by a strong sensation of disgust.

But the ass himself of whom she was enamored has not been the less a favorite of Fortune, less happy and self-complacent, because of her late repentance. He proceeds onward as luckily as ever. Bottom, during the time that he attracts the attentions of Titania, never for a moment thinks there is any thing extraordinary in the matter. He takes the love of the Queen of the Fairies as a thing of course, orders about her tiny attendants as if they were so many apprentices at his loom, and dwells in Fairy Land unobservant of its wonders, as quietly as if he were still in his workshop. Great is the courage and self-possession of an ass-head. Theseus would have bent in reverent awe before Titania. Bottom treats her as carelessly as if she were the wench of the next-door tapster. (pp. 101-02)

[Bottom is] dismissed to his ordinary course of life, unaffected by what has passed. He admits at first that it is wonderful, but soon thinks it is nothing more than a fit subject for a ballad in

honor of his own name. He falls at once to his old habit of dictating, boasting, and swaggering, and makes no reference to what has happened to him in the forest. It was no more than an ordinary passage in his daily life. Fortune knew where to bestow her favors. (p. 104)

> *William Maginn, "Characters in the Plays—Bottom, the Weaver," in his* The Shakespeare Papers of the Late William Maginn, LL. D., *edited by Shelton Mackenzie, Redfield, 1856, pp. 85-104.*

HERMANN ULRICI (essay date 1839)

[*A German scholar, Ulrici was a professor of philosophy and the author of works on Greek poetry and Shakespeare. The following excerpt is from an English translation of his* Über Shakespeares dramatische Kunst, und sein Verhältniss zu Calderon und Göthe, *a work first published in 1839. This study exemplifies the "philosophical criticism" developed in Germany during the nineteenth century. The immediate sources for Ulrici's critical approach appear to be August Wilhelm Schlegel's conception of the play as an organic, interconnected whole and Georg Wilhelm Friedrich Hegel's view of drama as an embodiment of the conflict of historical forces and ideas. Unlike his fellow German Shakespearean critic G. G. Gervinus, Ulrici sought to develop a specifically Christian aesthetics, but one which, as he carefully points out in the introduction to the work mentioned above, in no way intrudes on "that unity of idea, which preeminently constitutes a work of art a living creation in the world of beauty." In the following excerpt, Ulrici argues that although we initially may view* A Midsummer Night's Dream *as an unsuccessful or irrational combination of disparate elements, the play is actually unified by its fundamental comic vision of life. For Ulrici, this comic perspective is reflected in the numerous self-parodies of the different characters and, in "its utmost limit," in the Pyramus and Thisbe play-within-the-play. The critic adds that this "ironical parodying of all the domains of life" gives expression to the "special ground-idea" of Shakespeare's play, namely, that life itself is but a dream or illusion. Ulrici maintains that this vision of human existence as a dream can only be represented within "the limits of the comic view"—a mode of expression subject to a "dialectic irony" which modifies it and, ultimately "destroys the one-sided error of its own representation." He compares this process in Shakespeare's* A Midsummer Night's Dream *to that in life itself, where, according to Platonic thought, this world is regarded as but a shadow of an ideal world to come, and in this respect seems no more than a dream; but it is also unlike a dream and very "real" in the sense that it contains within itself the birth of that ideal. Ulrici was the first critic to note the presence of Platonic/idealist philosophy in* A Midsummer Night's Dream *and the first to examine this ideology as a basis of the play's "organic unity." Other critics who have discussed the Platonic element in the play include John Vyvyan (1961), Peter G. Phialas (1966), and David Ormerod (1978). Also, see the excerpts by Sidney R. Homan (1969), Charles R. Lyons (1971), and James L. Calderwood (1971) for further assessments of the significance of illusion in* A Midsummer Night's Dream.]

At the first glance we are no doubt puzzled what to make, in an artistic and aesthetical point of view, of the strange aerial beings which revel before us in the "Midsummer-Night's Dream." Throughout there is such a wanton play of fancy and frolic; such cameleon-like succession of tricks and complicated cross-purpose, that at first sight we are disposed to deny that it can possess any rational meaning. Theseus and Hippolyta, the Queen of the Amazons, are about to celebrate their nuptials; but with the proper action of the piece they have nothing to do. Then we have the loves of two noble Athenian youths and maidens, whose happy union is hindered by the whim of a cross old father and their own caprice. In the midst of all,

Oberon and Titania, in ill-humour and jealous bickering, pursue their own designs, or cross with their wanton tricks the wise plans of poor mortals; and, lastly, a company of amateur players are pressed into the service with their burlesque follies and silliness, who exhibit a play within the play, having as much connexion with the rest as the several parts have with each other. Such are the rare and heterogeneous elements of the piece, which at once give rise to the question whether it really satisfies the first requirement of art that the several parts should round themselves into an organic whole, and if so, what is the centre around which they all adjust themselves?

Now it is the comic view of things itself that forms the basis of the whole piece. Its presence may be traced clearly and distinctly. Not merely in particular cases do the maddest tricks of accident, as well of human caprice, perversity, and folly, destroy each other in turn, but generally the principal pursuits and provinces of life are made to parody and paralyze each other. It is this last particular that distinguishes the "Midsummer-Night's Dream" from all other comedies soever. Theseus and Hippolyta represent the grand heroic and historically important aspect of human life. But instead of maintaining the high dignity and exalted grandeur of history, they come down to a level with the common, every-day sort of folk; while, by seeming to exist for no other purpose than to marry with suitable pomp and splendour, they form with agreeable irony a merry parody on their own heroic importance. The Carpenter, Joiner, Weaver, Bellows-mender, and Tinker, present a merry contrast to the highest ranks in the lowest and vulgarest region, the very prose of every-day life. But they, too, instead of remaining in their own true station, wherein they at once command respect, worm themselves into the higher domain of tragedy and poetry, and render it as well as themselves ridiculous. Between the two extremes stand the lovers, who belong to the middle ranks of life. But instead of behaving agreeably to their station, and regarding life in its plain and sober aspect, they lose themselves in the fantastic humours of a capricious passion, and thereby parody themselves and the class to which they belong. Lastly, the fairy prince, with his interposition in the action, represents that higher power which guides human life with an invisible thread. But even this superintending power is not depicted in its true god-like grandeur and elevation, but, like all the other parties of the piece, is carried away by the same torrent of irony, and either appears as the nimble, frolicsome play of the personified powers of nature, or parodies itself, so far as it is subject to the universal caprice of chance and to its own waywardness; as is distinctly indicated by Titania's passion for the ass-headed Weaver.

It is on this basis of reciprocal parody that the different and heterogeneous groups first coalesce into unity. From it they all derive the same characteristic tendency. The play of the mechanics, which, at its close, so gaily ridicules the dramatic art, and thereby also the very piece, which pursues every thing with its unsparing irony, carries the parodical tendency to its utmost limit, and gives to the whole its point. But even an external bond is not wanting to combine the several parts, which, although but slight and loose, is nevertheless dexterously woven into all the parts. The marriage festival of Theseus and Hippolyta surrounds the whole picture as with a splendid frame of gold. Within it the sports and gambols of the elves and fairies, crossing and recrossing the story of the lovers, and the labours of the theatrical artizans, connect together these two different groups, while the blessings which at the end of the piece they bestow by their presence at the nuptial festival upon the house and lineage of Theseus, give reason and dignity to the part which they have been playing throughout.

The particular modification of the general comic view which results from this ironical parodying of all the domains of life, at once determines and gives expression to the special ground-idea, which first reduces the whole into organic unity. Life is throughout regarded in the light of a *"Midsummer Night's Dream."* With the rapidity of wit the merry piece passes like a dream over our minds; the most rare and motley elements, and the most fantastic shapes, are blended together as in a vision of the night, and form a whole, highly wonderful, both in form and composition. Dream-like does the play within the play hold up its distorting mirror, while a shadow of reason comments upon its own visionary creations, and half-doubting, half-believing their reality, at one moment opposes, and at the next is hurried along by the light gambol which frolics before it in a magic light and darkness.

To look upon life as a dream is no new idea in poetry. In the ideal and poetical philosophy of Plato, it is represented in this light, where he supposes the soul of man to possess an obscure memory of an earlier and truer sphere existence, out of which it spin in this *life* a motley web of truth and falsehood. . . . [But], in sober truth, human life is no dream, nor was it in truth regarded as such by Plato. It is only in a one-sided mode of view (which even as such required to be dialectically refuted) that it appears so; it is merely as one moment in the whole, as one of many aspects of life, that there is truth in its dreaminess. . . . So far, then, as this life subsists only to terminate in a higher existence, and as, consequently, it possesses no true substance and reality in this world, where it cannot fulfill its destination *completely* and independently, and cannot attain to its proper end except in a future state, the present life does appear, in comparison with the latter, as unsubstantial, unreal, and transitory as a *dream*. But, on the other hand, it is no dream when considered as the beginning of a future state of existence, which is to issue from it like the moth from the chrysalis; for, as a transition to the future, it must already possess within itself, and to a certain extent be fulfilling, its vocation; as the reality and substance of the future perfection are already contained in a state of development within the existing germ, the future ceases in consequence to be such absolutely. If, however, the poet would, notwithstanding, represent life as a dream, he cannot do so, legitimately, except within the limits of the *comic* view, which even as such dialectically destroys the one-sided error of its own representation, and thereby brings to light the perfect truth.

Because, then, Shakespeare has regarded human life in this play as a dream, he is right in denying to it both reason and order. In conformity with such a view, the mind seems to have lost its self-consciousness, while all the other faculties, such as *feeling and fancy*, wit and humour, are allowed the fullest scope and license. With the withdrawal of mental order and reason, the intrinsic connection of the outer world, and consequently its truth and reality also, are overthrown. Life appears in travestie; the most ill-assorted elements, the oddest shapes and events which mock reality, dance and whirl about in the strangest confusion. The whole appears a cheat and delusion, which flits before us without form or substance. At last, however, the dialectic or irony which reigns within the comic view assorts the heterogeneous elements; the strange and wonderful creations vanish and dissolve into the ordinary forms of reality: order is finally restored, and out of the entangled web, right and reason result. (pp. 270-74)

Hermann Ulrici, "Criticism of Shakspeare's Dramas: 'Midsummer Night's Dream'—'The Tempest'," in his Shakspeare's Dramatic Art: And His Relations to Calderon and Goethe, *translated by A.J.W. Morrison, Chapman, Brothers, 1846, pp. 270-79.*

JAMES ORCHARD HALLIWELL[-PHILLIPPS] (essay date 1841)

[*A nineteenth-century English bibliophile and scholar, Halliwell-Phillipps originally concentrated on textual criticism in his study of Shakespeare's works. However, later in his career he shifted his interest from textual and critical problems to those of historical background. In so doing, he became the first scholar to make extensive use of town records from Stratford in the study of Shakespeare's life. In the following excerpt from his* An Introduction to Shakespeare's "Midsummer Night's Dream" *(1841), Halliwell-Phillipps comments on the inconsistencies in dramatic time and the historical anachronisms in the play, but concludes that these only demonstrate that Shakespeare was an untutored, natural genius who was ignorant of the "classical rules" he supposedly violated. The confusion in the play between its title and references to the rituals associated with the first day of May have also been addressed by C. L. Barber (1959). For further discussions of the duration of time in* A Midsummer Night's Dream, *see the excerpts by Charles Gildon (1710), Henry A. Clapp (1885), Horace Howard Furness (1895), and Anne Paolucci (1977).*]

The very name of *A Midsummer Night's Dream* has furnished a subjeect for discussion. The time of action is on the night preceding May-day. Theseus goes out a maying, and when he finds the lovers, he observes:—

> No doubt they rose up early, to observe
> The rite of May.
>
> [IV. i. 132-33]

"I am convinced," says Coleridge, "that Shakespeare availed himself of the title of this play in his own mind, and worked upon it as a dream throughout"[see excerpt above, 1834]. Such was no doubt the case, and may we not conclude, that the first idea of the play was conceived on Midsummer Night? [John] Aubrey, in a passage, which refers perhaps to the character of Bottom the weaver, implies that its original was a constable at Grendon, in Buckinghamshire, and adds, "I thinke it was Midsummer Night, that he, [i.e. Shakespeare,] happened to lye there." The title doubtlessly refers to the whole piece, and not to any particular part of it. The poet himself says:—

> If we shadows have offended,
> Think but this, and all is mended;
> That you have but slumbered here,
> While these visions did appear.
> And this weak and idle theme,
> *No more yielding but a dream,*
> Gentles, do not reprehend.
>
> [V. i. 423-29]

In *Twelfth Night,* Olivia observes of Malvolio's seeming frenzy, that it "is a very Midsummer madness" [*Twelfth Night,* III. iv. 56]; and [George] Steevens thinks that as "this time was anciently thought productive of mental vagaries, to that circumstance it might have owed its title." [Thomas] Heywood seems to allude to a similar belief, when he says—

> As mad as a March hare; where madness compares,
> Are not Midsummer hares as mad as March hares?

[Edmond] Malone thinks that the title of the play was suggested by the season in which it was introduced on the stage. The misnomer, however, if it is one, does not imply a greater anachronism than several which the play itself presents. For instance, Theseus marries Hippolita on the night of the new moon; but how does this agree with the discourse of the clowns at the rehearsal?

> *Snug.* Doth the moon shine that night we play our play?
>
> *Bot.* A calendar, a calendar! look in the almanack; find out moonshine, find out moonshine.
>
> *Quin.* Yes, it doth shine that night.
>
> *Bot.* Why, then you may leave a casement of the great chamber window, where we play, open; and the moon may shine in at the casement.
>
> [III. i. 51-8]

Again, the period of action is four days, concluding with the night of the new moon. But Hermia and Lysander receive the edict of Theseus four days before the new moon; they fly from Athens "to-morrow night;" they become the sport of the fairies, along with Helena and Demetrius, *during one night only,* for, Oberon accomplishes all in one night, before "the first cock crows" [II. i. 267]; and the lovers are discovered by Theseus the morning before that which would have rendered this portion of the plot chronologically consistent. For, although Oberon, addressing his queen, says,

> Now thou and I are new in amity;
> And will, *to-morrow midnight,* solemnly,
> Dance in Duke Theseus' house triumphantly.
>
> [IV. i. 87-9]

yet Theseus, when he discovers the lovers, asks Egeus,

>   is not this the day
> That Hermia should give answer of her choice?
>
> [IV. i. 135-36]

and the answer of Egeus, "It is, my Lord" [IV. i. 137] couples with what Theseus says to hermia in the first Act—

> Take time to pause; and by the next new moon
> (The sealing-day betwixt my love and me,
> For everlasting bond of fellowship),
> Upon that day either prepare to die,
> For disobedience to your father's will;
> Or else to wed Demetrius, as he would;
> Or on Diana's altar to protest,
> For aye, austerity and single life.   [I. i. 83-90]

proves that the action of the remaining part of the play is not intended to consist of two days.

The preparation and rehearsal of the interlude present similar inconsistencies. In Act i., Sc. 2, Quince is the only one who has any knowledge of the "most lamentable comedy, and most cruel death of Pyramus and Thisbe" [I. ii. 11-12], and he selects actors for Thisby's mother, Pyramus's father, and Thisby's father, none of whom appear in the interlude itself. In Act iii., Sc. 1, we have the commencement of the play in rehearsal, none of which appears in the piece itself. Again, the play could have been but partially rehearsed once; for Bottom only returns in time to advise "every man look o'er his part"[IV. ii. 37-8]; and immediately before his companions were lamenting the failure of their "sport." How then could the "merry tears" of Philostrate be shed at its rehearsal?

But all these merely tend to prove that Shakespeare wrote with no classical rules before him, and do not in the least detract from the most beautiful poetical drama in this or any other language. Shakespeare was truly the child of nature, and when we find Hermia, contemporary with Theseus, swearing

> by that fire which burn'd the Carthage queen,
> When the false Trojan under sail was seen.
> [I. i. 73-4]

the anachronism is so palpable to any one of the classical acquirements, that the evident conclusion is, that we must receive his works as the production of a genius unfettered by the knowledge of more philosophical canons, and of a power which enabled the bard to create, assisted only by the then barren field of his country's literature, that which "was not of an age, but for all time" [Ben Jonson]. This, we are convinced, must be the conclusion of all who read the works of Shakespeare in a proper spirit, unbiassed by the prejudices of a prosaic age; and it is only then that they can really hear him, as

> Fancy's child,
> Warble his native wood-notes wild.
> [John Milton]
> (pp. 2-5)

James Orchard Halliwell[-Phillipps], "Introduction—Title—Anachronisms," in his An Introduction to Shakespeare's "Midsummer Night's Dream," William Pickering, 1841, pp. 1-5.

CHARLES KNIGHT (essay date 1849)

[*Knight, an English author and publisher, dedicated his career to providing education and knowledge to the Victorian working class. In his essay on* A Midsummer Night's Dream *excerpted below, he comments on Edmond Malone's assessment of the play as the product of an immature but "lively imagination" (see excerpt above, 1778), claiming that those same qualities of the work that Malone cited to support his argument actually evidence a maturity and mastery not found in a beginning writer. Knight proceeds to discuss the role of the reader's or spectator's imagination in the dramatic process with reference to Theseus's speech in Act V, Scene i (in which the Duke asserts that "the best in this kind are but shadows, and / the worst are no worse, if imagination amend them"). Knight argues that Shakespeare is here humbly admitting that without the audience's imaginative faculty there can be no successful dramatic art. For other interpretations of Theseus's speech on imagination and art, see the excerpts by William Maginn (1837), Edward Dowden (1881), Denton J. Snider (1890), Frederick S. Boas (1896), Howard Nemerov (1956), and R. W. Dent (1964). Knight also supports the conviction—first suggested by William Hazlitt (1817)—that* A Midsummer Night's Dream *is better appreciated when read "in the closet" than when it is performed on stage. This assessment reflects an opinion held by many critics in the nineteenth century, most notably, Maginn, G. G. Gervinus (1849-50), H. N. Hudson (1872), and Denton J. Snider (1890).*]

[Edmond] Malone has assigned the composition of 'A Midsummer Night's Dream' to the year 1594. We are not disposed to object to this,—indeed we are inclined to believe that he has pretty exactly indicated the precise year, as far as it can be proved by one or two allusions which the play contains. But we entirely object to the reasons upon which Malone attempts to show that it was one of our author's "*earliest* attempts

in comedy" [see excerpt above, 1778]. He derives the proof of this from "the poetry of this piece, glowing with all the warmth of a youthful and lively imagination, the many scenes which it contains of almost continual rhyme, the poverty of the fable, and want of discrimination among the higher personages." . . . We can understand these terms to apply to the unpruned luxuriance of the 'Venus and Adonis;' but the poetry of this piece, the almost continual rhyme, and even the poverty of the fable, are to us evidences of the very highest art having obtained a perfect mastery of its materials after years of patient study. Of all the dramas of Shakspere there is none more entirely harmonious than 'A Midsummer-Night's Dream.' All the incidents, all the characters, are in perfect subordination to the will of the poet. "Throughout the whole piece," says Malone, "the mere exalted characters are subservient to the interests of those beneath them." Precisely so. An unpractised author—one who had not "a youthful and lively imagination" under perfect control,—when he had got hold of the Theseus and Hippolyta of the heroic ages, would have made them ultraheroical. They would have commanded events, instead of moving with the supernatural influence around them in harmony and proportion. "Theseus, the associate of Hercules, is not engaged in any adventure worthy of his rank or reputation, nor is he in reality an agent throughout the play." Precisely so. An immature poet, again, if the marvellous creation of Oberon and Titania, and Puck, could have entered into such a mind, would have laboured to make the power of the fairies produce some strange and striking events. But the exquisite beauty of Shakspere's conception is, that, under the supernatural influence, "the human mortals" move precisely according to their respective natures and habits. Demetrius and Lysander are impatient and revengeful;—Helena is dignified and affectionate, with a spice of female error;—Hermia is somewhat vain and shrewish. And then Bottom! Who but the most skilful artist could have given us such a character? . . . Bottom the weaver is the representative of the whole human race. His confidence in his own power is equally profound, whether he exclaims, "Let me play the lion too" [I. ii. 70]; or whether he sings alone, "that they shall hear I am not afraid" [III. i. 123-24]; or whether, conscious that he is surrounded with spirits, he cries out, with his voice of authority, "Where's Peasblossom?" [IV. i. 5]. In every situation Bottom is the same,—the same personification of that self-love which the simple cannot conceal, and the wise can with difficulty suppress. . . . The beauties with which ['Midsummer Night's Dream'] is embellished include, of course, the whole rhythmical structure of the versification. The poet has here put forth all his strength. We venture to offer an opinion that, if any single composition were required to exhibit the power of the English language for purposes of poetry, that composition would be the "Midsummer-Night's Dream.' (pp. 208-09)

"This is the silliest stuff that e'er I heard" [V. i. 21] says Hippolyta, when Wall has "discharged" his part. The answer of Theseus is full of instruction:—"The best in this kind are but shadows; and the worst are no worse, if imagination amend them" [V. i. 211-12]. It was in this humble spirit that the great poet judged of his own matchless performances. He felt the utter inadequacy of his art, and indeed of any art, to produce its due effect upon the mind, unless the imagination, to which it addressed itself, was ready to convert the shadows which it presented into living forms of truth and beauty. "I am convinced," says Coleridge, "that Shakspeare availed himself of the title of this play in his own mind, and worked upon it as a dream throughout'' [see excerpt above, 1834]. The poet says so, in express words:—

> If we shadows have offended,
> Think but this, (and all is mended),
> That you have but slumber'd here,
> While these visions did appear.
> And this weak and idle theme,
> No more yielding but a dream,
> Gentles, do not reprehend.
>
> [V. i. 423-29]

But to understand this dream—to have all its gay, and soft, and harmonious colours impressed upon the vision—to hear all the golden cadences of its poesy—to feel the perfect congruity of all its parts, and thus to receive it as a truth—we must not suppose that it will enter the mind amidst the lethargic slumbers of the imagination. We must receive it—

> As youthful poets dream
> On summer eves by haunted stream.
>
> [John Milton's *L'Allegro*]

Let no one expect that the beautiful influences of this drama can be truly felt when he is under the subjection of the literal and prosaic parts of our nature: or, if he habitually refuses to believe that there are higher and purer regions of thought than are supplied by the physical realities of the world. In these cases he will have a false standard by which to judge of this, and of all other high poetry. . . . (p. 210)

Mr. [Henry] Hallam accounts 'A Midsummer-Night's Dream' poetical, more than dramatic; ''yet rather so, because the indescribable profusion of imaginative poetry in this play overpowers our senses, till we can hardly observe anything else, than from any deficiency of dramatic excellence. For, in reality, the structure of the fable, consisting as it does of three, if not four actions, very distinct in their subjects and personages, yet wrought into each other without effort or confusion, displays the skill, or rather instinctive felicity, of Shakspeare, as much as in any play he has written.'' Yet, certainly, with all its harmony of dramatic arrangement, this play is not for the stage—at least not for the modern stage. It may reasonably be doubted whether it was ever eminently successful in performance. The tone of the epilogue is decidedly apologetic, and ''the best of this kind are but shadows'' is in the same spirit. Hazlitt [see excerpt above, 1817] has admirably described its failure as an acting drama in his own day:—

''The 'Midsummer-Night's Dream,' when acted, is converted from a delightful fiction into a dull pantomime. All that is finest in the play is lost in the representation.'' (p. 211)

And yet, just and philosophical as are these remarks, they offer no objection to the opinion of Mr. Hallam, that in this play there is no deficiency of dramatic excellence. We can conceive that, with scarcely what can be called a model before him, Shakspere's early dramatic attempts must have been a series of experiments to establish a standard by which he should regulate what he addressed to a mixed audience. The plays of his middle and mature life, with scarcely an exception, are acting plays; and they are so, not from the absence of the higher poetry, but from the predominance of character and passion in association with it. But even in those plays which call for a considerable exercise of the unassisted imaginative faculty in an audience, such as 'The Tempest,' and 'A Midsummer-Night's Dream,' where the passions are not powerfully roused, and the senses are not held enchained by the interests of plot, he is

still essentially dramatic. . . . ['Midsummer Night's Dream'] exhibits all that congruity of parts, that natural progression of scenes, that subordination of action and character to one leading design, that ultimate harmony evolved out of seeming confusion, which constitute the dramatic spirit. With ''audience fit, though few,'' with a stage not encumbered with decorations, with actors approaching (if it were so possible) to the idea of grace and archness which belong to the fairy troop,—the subtle and evanescent beauties of this drama might not be wholly lost in the representation. But under the most favourable circumstances much would be sacrificed. It is in the closet that we must not only suffer our senses to be overpowered by its ''indescribable profusion of imaginative poetry,'' but trace the instinctive felicity of Shakspere in the ''structure of the fable.'' If the 'Midsummer-Night's Dream' *could* be acted, there can be no doubt how well it would act. Our imagination must amend what is wanting. It is no real objection to this belief that it *has* been acted with surpassing success since these observations were originally written. It was revived at Covent-Garden Theatre as a pantomimic opera, with exquisite scenery, and abundant music, and Oberon and Titania moving in golden chariots amongst silver clouds, and fairies floating in ether, held up by very invisible strings. And so the poetry was borne for the sake of the sight-seeing and the songs. But, for a just comprehension of Shakspere's surpassing beauties in this divine poem, we would rather hear the second scene of Act II. *read* as we have heard it read by a poet, than see the play, accompanied with every scenic propriety and pomp, to show, after all, that ''the best *in this kind* are but shadows.'' (pp. 211-12)

To offer an analysis of this subtle and ethereal drama would, we believe, be as unsatisfactory as the attempts to associate it with the realities of the stage. With scarcely an exception, the proper understanding of the other plays of Shakspere may be assisted by connecting the apparently separate parts of the action, and by developing and reconciling what seems obscure and anomalous in the features of the characters. But to follow out the caprices and illusions of the loves of Demetrius and Lysander, of Helena and Hermia;—to reduce to prosaic description the consequence of the jealousies of Oberon and Titania;—to trace the Fairy Queen under the most fantastic of deceptions, where grace and vulgarity blend together like the Cupids and Chimeras of Raffaelle's Arabesques;—and, finally, to go along with the scene till the illusions disappear—till the lovers are happy, and ''sweet bully Bottom'' is reduced to an ass of human dimensions;—such an attempt as this would be worse even than unreverential criticism. No,—the 'Midsummer-Night's Dream' must be left to its own influences. (p. 213)

> *Charles Knight, '' 'A Midsummer Night's Dream','' in his* Studies of Shakspere: Forming a Companion Volume to Every Edition of the Text, *Charles Knight, 1849, pp. 207-13.*

G. G. GERVINUS (essay date 1849-50)

[*One of the most widely read Shakespearean critics of the latter half of the nineteenth century, the German critic Gervinus was praised by such eminent contemporaries as Edward Dowden, F. J. Furnivall, and James Russell Lowell; however, he is little known in the English-speaking world today. Like his predecessor Hermann Ulrici, Gervinus wrote in the tradition of the ''philosophical criticism'' developed in Germany in the mid-nineteenth century. Under the influence of August Wilhelm Schlegel's literary theory and Georg Wilhelm Friedrich Hegel's philosophy, German critics like Gervinus focused their analyses on a search for the literary work's organic unity and ethical import. Gervinus believed that*

*Shakespeare's works contained a rational ethical system inde-
pendent of any religion—in contrast to Ulrici, for whom Shakespeare's morality was basically Christian. In the following excerpt, Gervinus contends that* A Midsummer Night's Dream *is
not intended to be taken as the reenactment of a mere dream, as
suggested by Samuel Taylor Coleridge (1834), but is meant to
"compare allegorically the sensuous life of love with a dream-
life." Gervinus thus regards the errors and unmotivated caprices
of the lovers in the play as "an allegorical picture of the errors
of a life of dreams." He also considers the fairies' role in this
mental and moral confusion—their delineation as both Cupid's
agents and "personified dream-gods"—"the true poetic embodiment" of Shakespeare's design. This assessment of Shakespeare's moral purpose in* A Midsummer Night's Dream *was
directly disputed by Frederick S. Boas (1896), who claimed that
there is no ethical motive apparent in the play, and indirectly by
H. N. Hudson (1872), who asserted that Shakespeare's work could
be evaluated only as the artistic re-creation of a dream. Other
critics who have similarly argued that the drama exposes the
follies of sensual or romantic love include E. K. Chambers (1905),
H. B. Charlton (1933), E. C. Pettet (1949), George A. Bonnard
(1956), and Peter G. Phialas (1966). Gervinus further comments
on Shakespeare's contrasting characterization of the fairies and
the mortals—the former he describes as imaginative, sensuous,
and non-feeling, the latter as rational, unimaginative, and materialistic—and maintains that the fairies have no spiritual influence on the minds of the mortals, a point also stressed by Chambers. Gervinus concludes his essay with a discussion of his own
country's failure to stage a successful performance of* A Midsummer Night's Dream, *suggesting that such attempts be "utterly
renounced" and that the play remain unstaged. Other nineteenth-
century critics who share this point of view include William Hazlitt
(1817), William Maginn (1837), Charles Knight (1842), H. N.
Hudson (1872), and Denton J. Snider (1890).]*

Upon the most superficial reading we perceive that the actions in the *Midsummer-Night's Dream*, still more than the characters themselves, are treated quite differently to those in other plays of Shakespeare. The presence of an underlying motive—the great art and true magic wand of the poet—has here been completely disregarded. Instead of reasonable inducements, instead of natural impulses arising from character and circumstance, caprice is master here. We meet with a double pair, who are entangled in strange mistakes, the motives to which we, however, seek for in vain in the nature of the actors themselves. Demetrius, like Proteus in the *Two Gentlemen of Verona*, has left a bride, and, like Proteus, wooes the bride of his friend Lysander. This Lysander has fled with Hermia to seek a spot where the law of Athens cannot pursue them. Secretly, we are told, they both steal away into the wood; Demetrius in fury follows them, and, impelled by love, Helena fastens herself like a burr upon the heels of the latter. Alike devoid of conscience, Hermia errs at first through want of due obedience to her father, and Demetrius through faithlessness to his betrothed Helena, Helena through treachery to her friend Hermia, and Lysander through mockery of his father-in-law. The strife in the first act, in which we cannot trace any distinct moral motives, is in the third act changed into a perfect confusion owing to influences of an entirely external character. In the fairy world a similar disorder exists between Oberon and Titania. The play of Pyramus and Thisbe, enacted by the honest citizens, forms a comic-tragic counterpart to the tragic-comic point of the plot, depicting two lovers, who behind their parents' backs 'think no scorn to woo by moonlight,' and through a mere accident come to a tragic end.

The human beings in the main plot of the piece are apparently impelled by mere amorous caprice; Demetrius is betrothed, then Helena pleases him no longer, he trifles with Hermia, and

at the close he remembers this breach of faith only as the trifling of youth. External powers and not inward impulses and feelings appear as the cause of these amorous caprices. In the first place, the brain is heated by the warm season, the first night in May, the ghost-hour of the mystic powers; for even elsewhere Shakespeare occasionally calls a piece of folly the madness of a midsummer-day, or a dog-day's fever; and in the 98th sonnet he speaks of April as the time which puts 'the spirit of youth in everything,' making even the 'heavy Saturn laugh and leap with him.' Then Cupid, who appears in the background of the piece as a real character, misleading the judgment and blinding the eyes, takes delight in causing a frivolous breach of faith. And last of all we see the lovers completely in the hand of the fairies, who ensnare their senses and bring them into that tumult of confusion, the unravelling of which, like the entanglement itself, is to come from without. These delusions of blind passion, this jugglery of the senses during the sleep of reason, these changes of mind and errors of 'seething brains,' these actions without any higher centre of a mental and moral bearing, are compared, as it were, to a dream which unrolls before us with its fearful complications, and from which there is no deliverance but in awaking and in the recovery of consciousness.

The piece is called a *Midsummer-Night's Dream;* the Epilogue expresses satisfaction, if the spectator will regard the piece as a dream; for in a dream time and locality are obliterated; a certain twilight and dusk is spread over the whole; Oberon desires that all shall regard the matter as a dream, and so it is. Titania speaks of her adventure as a vision, Bottom of his metamorphosis as a dream; all the rest awake at last out of a sleep of weariness, and the events leave upon them the impression of a dream. The sober Theseus esteems their stories as nothing else than dreams and fantasies. Indeed these allusions in the play must have suggested to Coleridge [see excerpt above, 1834] and others the idea that the poet had intentionally aimed at letting the piece glide by as a dream. We only wonder that, with this opinion, they have not reached the inner kernel in which this intention of the poet really lies enshrined—an intention which has not only given a name to the piece, but has called forth as by magic a free poetic creation of the greatest value. For it is indeed to be expected from our poet, that such an intention on his side were not to be sought for in the mere shell. If this intention were only shown in those poetical externals, in that fragrant charm of rhythm and verse, in that harassing suspense, and in that dusky twilight, then this were but a shallow work of superficial grace, by the sole use of which a poet like Shakespeare would never have dreamt of accomplishing anything worth the while. (pp. 188-90)

We have before said that the piece appears designed to be treated as a dream; not merely in outer form and colouring, but also in inner signification. The errors of that blind intoxication of the senses, which form the main point of the play, appear to us to be an allegorical picture of the errors of a life of dreams. Reason and consciousness are cast aside in that intoxicating passion as in a dream; Cupid's delight in breach of faith and Jove's merriment at the perjury of the lovers cause the actions of those who are in the power of the God of Love to appear almost as unaccountable as the sins which we commit in a dream. We find moreover that the actions and occupations of Cupid and of the fairies throughout the piece are interwoven or alternate. And this appears to us to confirm most forcibly the intention of the poet to compare allegorically the sensuous life of love with a dream-life; the exchange of functions between Cupid and the fairies is therefore the true poetic embodiment of this comparison. For the realm of dreams is assigned to Shakespeare's fairies; they are essentially nothing else than personified dream-gods, children of the fantasy, which, as Mercutio [*Romeo and Juliet*] says, is not only the idle producer of dreams, but also of the caprices of superficial love.

Vaguely, as in a dream, this significance of the fairies rests in the ancient popular belief of the Teutonic races, and Shakespeare, with the instinctive touch of genius, has fashioned this idea into exquisite form. . . . But that which Shakespeare . . . received in the rough form of fragmentary popular belief he developed in his playful creation into a beautiful and regulated world. He here in a measure deserves the merit which Herodotus ascribes to Homer; as the Greek poet has created the great abode of the gods and its Olympic inhabitants, so Shakespeare has given form and place to the fairy kingdom, and with the natural creative power of genius he has breathed a soul into his merry little citizens, thus imparting a living centre to their nature and their office, their behaviour and their doings. He has given embodied form to the invisible and life to the dead, and has thus striven for the poet's greatest glory; and it seems as if it was not without consciousness of this his work that he wrote in a strain of self-reliance that passage in this very play:—

> The poet's eye, in a fine frenzy rolling,
> Doth glance from heaven to earth, from earth to
>   heaven;
> And as imagination bodies forth
> The forms of things unknown, the poet's pen
> Turns them to shapes, and gives to airy nothing
> A local habitations and a name.
> Such tricks hath strong imagination;
> That, if it would but apprehend some joy,
> It comprehends some bringer of that joy.
>
> [V. i. 12-20]

This he has here effected; he has clothed in bodily form those intangible phantoms, the bringers of dreams of provoking jugglery, of sweet soothing, and of tormenting raillery; and the task he has thus accomplished we shall only rightly estimate, when we have taken into account the severe design and inner congruity of this little world.

If it were Shakespeare's object expressly to remove from the fairies that dark ghost-like character (Act III. sc. 2), in which they appeared in Scandinavian and Scottish fable; if it were his desire to portray them as kindly beings in a merry and harmless relation to mortals; if he wished, in their essential office as bringers of dreams, to fashion them in their nature as personified dreams, he carried out this object in wonderful harmony both as regards their actions and their condition. The kingdom of the fairy beings is placed in the aromatic flower-scented Indies, in the land where mortals live in a half-dreamy state. From hence they come, 'following darkness,' as Puck says, 'like a dream' [V. i. 386]. Airy and swift, like the moon, they circle the earth; they avoid the sunlight without fearing it, and seek the darkness; they love the moon and dance in her beams; and above all they delight in the dusk and twilight, the very season for dreams, whether waking or asleep. They send and bring dreams to mortals; and we need only recall to mind the description of the fairies' midwife, Queen Mab, in *Romeo and Juliet*, a piece nearly of the same date with the *Midsummer-Night's Dream*, to discover that this is the charge essentially assigned to them, and the very means by which they influence mortals. The manner in which Shakespeare has fashioned their inner character in harmony with this outer function is full of profound thought. He depicts them as beings without delicate

feeling and without morality, just as in dreams we meet with no check to our tender sensations and are without moral impulse and responsibility. Careless and unscrupulous, they tempt mortals to infidelity; the effects of the mistakes which they have contrived make no impression on their minds; they feel no sympathy for the deep affliction of the lovers, but only delight and marvel over their mistakes which they have contrived make no impression on their minds; they feel no sympathy for the deep affliction of the lovers, but only delight and marvel over their mistakes and their foolish demeanour. The poet farther depicts his fairies as beings of no high intellectual development. Whoever attentively reads their parts will find that nowhere is reflection imparted to them. Only in one exception does Puck make a sententious remark upon the infidelity of man, and whoever has penetrated into the nature of these beings will immediately feel that it is out of harmony. They can make no direct inward impression upon mortals; their influence over the mind is not spiritual, but throughout material; it is effected by means of vision, metamorphosis, and imitation. Titania has no spiritual association with her friend, but mere delight in her beauty, her 'swimming gait,' and her powers of imitation. When she awakes from her vision there is no reflection: 'Methought I was enamoured of an ass,' she says. 'Oh how mine eyes do hate this visage now!' [IV. i. 77, 79]. She is only affected by the idea of the actual and the visible. There is no scene of reconciliation with her husband; her resentment consists in separation, her reconciliation in a dance; there is no trace of reflection, no indication of feeling. Thus, to remind Puck of a past event no abstract date sufficed, but an accompanying indication, perceptible to the senses, was required. They are represented, these little gods, as natural souls, without the higher human capacities of minds, lords of a kingdom, not of reason and morality, but of imagination and ideas conveyed by the senses; and thus they are uniformly the vehicle of the fancy which produces the delusions of love and dreams. Their will, therefore, only extends to the corporeal. They lead a luxurious, merry life, given up to the pleasure of the senses; the secrets of nature and the powers of flowers and herbs are confided to them. To sleep in flowers, lulled with dances and songs, with the wings of painted butterflies to fan the moonbeams from their eyes, this is their pleasure; the gorgeous apparel of flowers and dewdrops is their joy. When Titania wishes to allure her beloved, she offers him honey, apricots, purple grapes, and dancing. This life of sense and nature is seasoned by the power of fancy and by desire after all that is most choice, most beautiful, and agreeable. They harmonise with nightingales and butterflies; they wage war with all ugly creatures, with hedgehogs, spiders, and bats; dancing, play, and song are their greatest pleasures; they steal lovely children, and substitute changelings; they torment decrepit old age, toothless gossips, aunts, and the awkward company of the players of Pyramus and Thisbe, but they love and recompense all that is pure and pretty. Thus was it of old in the popular traditions; their characteristic trait of favouring honesty among mortals and persecuting crime was certainly borrowed by Shakespeare from these traditions in the *Merry Wives of Windsor,* though not in this play. The sense of the beautiful is the one thing which elevates the fairies not only above the beasts but also above the ordinary mortal, when he is devoid of all fancy and uninfluenced by beauty. Thus, in the spirit of the fairies, in which this sense of the beautiful is so refined, it is intensely ludicrous that the elegant Titania should fall in love with an ass's head. The only pain which agitates these beings is jealousy, the desire of possessing the beautiful sooner than others; they shun the distorting quarrel; their steadfast aim and longing is for undisturbed enjoyment. But in this sweet jugglery they neither appear constant to mortals nor do they carry on intercourse among themselves in monotonous harmony. They are full also of wanton tricks and railleries, playing upon themselves and upon mortals, pranks which never hurt, but which often torment. This is especially the property of Puck, who 'jests to Oberon,' who is the 'lob' at this court, a coarser goblin, represented with broom or threshing-flail, in a leathern dress, and with a dark countenance, a roguish but awkward fellow, skilful at all transformations, practised in wilful tricks, but also clumsy enough to make mistakes and blunders contrary to his intention. (pp. 193-98)

We can now readily perceive why, in this work, the 'rude mechanicals' and clowns, and the company of actors with their burlesque comedy, are placed in such rude contrast to the tender and delicate play of the fairies. Prominence is given to both by the contrast afforded between the material and the aërial, between the awkward and the beautiful, between the utterly unimaginative and that which, ifself fancy, is entirely woven out of fancy. The play acted by the clowns is, as it were, the reverse of the poet's own work, which demands all the spectator's reflective and imitative fancy to open to him this aërial world, whilst in the other nothing at all is left to the imagination of the spectator. The homely mechanics, who compose and act merely for gain, and for the sake of so many pence a day, the ignorant players, with hard hands and thick heads, whose unskilful art consists in learning their parts by heart, these men believe themselves obliged to represent Moon and Moonshine by name in order to render them evident; they supply the lack of side-scenes by persons, and all that should take place behind the scenes they explain by digressions. These rude doings are disturbed by the fairy chiefs with their utmost raillery, and the fantastical company of lovers mock at the performance. Theseus, however, draws quiet and thoughtful contemplation from these contrasts. He shrinks incredulously from the too-strange fables of love and its witchcraft; he enjoins that imagination should amend the play of the clowns, devoid as it is of all fancy. The real, that in this world of art has become 'nothing,' and the 'airy nothing,' which in the poet's hand has assumed this graceful form, are contrasted in the two extremes; in the centre is the intellectual man, who participates in both, who regards the one, namely, the stories of the lovers, the poets by nature, as art and poetry, and who receives the other, presented as art, only as a thanksworthy readiness to serve and as a simple offering.

It is the combination of these skilfully obtained contrasts into a whole which we especially admire in this work. The age subsequent to Shakespeare could not tolerate it, and divided it in twain. Thus sundered, this aesthetic fairy poetry and the burlesque, caricature of the poet have made their own way. (pp. 198-99)

We have frequently referred to the necessity of seeing Shakespeare's plays performed, in order to be able to estimate them fully, based as they are upon the joint effect of poetic and dramatic art. It will, therefore, be just to mention the representation which this most difficult of all theatrical tasks of a modern age has met with in all the great stages of Germany. And, that we may not be misunderstood, we will premise that, however strongly we insist upon this principle, we yet, in the present state of things, warn most decidely against all overbold attempts at Shakespearian representation. If we would perform dramas in which such an independent position is assigned to the dramatic art as it is in these, we must before everything

Title page of the First Quarto of A Midsummer Night's Dream *(1600).*

possess a histrionic art independent and complete in itself. But this art has with us declined with poetic art, and amid the widely distracting concerns of the present time it is scarcely likely soon to revive. . . . This fairy play was produced upon the English stage when they had boys early trained for the characters; without this proviso it is ridiculous to desire the representation of the most difficult parts, with powers utterly inappropriate. When a girl's high treble utters the part of Oberon, a character justly represented by painters with abundant beard, and possessing all the dignity of the calm ruler of this hovering world; when the rude goblin Puck is performed by an affected actress, when Titania and her suite appear in ballcostume, without beauty or dignity, for ever moving about in the hopping motion of the dancing chorus, in the most offensive ballet-fashion that modern unnaturalness has created—what then becomes of the sweet charm of these scenes and figures which should appear in pure aërial drapery, which in their sport should retain a certain elevated simplicity, and which in the affair between Titania and Bottom, far from unnecessarily pushing the awkward fellow forward as the principal figure, should understand how to place the ludicrous character at a modest distance, and to give the whole scene the quiet charm of a picture? If it be impossible to act these fairy forms at the present day, it is equally so with the clowns. The common nature of the mechanics when they are themselves is perhaps intelligible to our actors; but when they perform their work of art few actors of the present day possess the self-denial that would lead them to represent this most foolish of all follies with solemn importance, as if in thorough earnestness, instead of overdoing its exaggeration, self-complacently working by laughter and smiling at themselves. Unless this self-denial be observed,, the first and greatest object of these scenes, that of exciting laughter, is inevitably lost. Lastly, the middle class of mortals introduced between the fairies and the clowns, the lovers driven about by bewildering delusions, what sensation do they excite, when we see them in the frenzy of passion wandering through the wood in kid-gloves, in knightly dress, conversing after the manner of the refined world, devoid of all warmth, and without a breath of this charming poetry?. . . Elements thus contradictory and thus injudiciously united, tasks thus beautiful and thus imperfectly discharged, must always make the friend of Shakespearian performances desire that, under existing circumstances, they were rather utterly renounced. (pp. 201-03)

> G. G. Gervinus, "Second Period of Shakespeare's Dramatic Poetry: 'Midsummer-Night's Dream'," in his Shakespeare Commentaries, translated by F. E. Bunnètt, revised edition, 1877. Reprint by AMS Press Inc., 1971, pp. 187-203.

CHARLES COWDEN CLARKE (essay date 1863)

[Clarke was a scholar, critic, and public lecturer on the arts and drama. His Shakespeare lectures, which he began in 1834, proved to be one of the major factors in the renewed interest in Shakespeare's works during the Victorian era. Clarke also edited with his wife The Shakespearean Key (1879), a kind of topical concordance, and a multivolumed edition of Shakespeare's plays. The excerpt below is taken from his Shakespeare-Characters: Chiefly Those Subordinate (1863). In his discussion of A Midsummer Night's Dream, Clarke focuses on the rude mechanicals—whose depiction he admires for its "fine dramatic nature and verisimilitude"—and especially on the figure of Bottom. Clarke emphasizes Bottom's amiability, good-naturedness, and self-possession, as have such other critics as William Maginn (1837) and E. K. Chambers (1905). Clarke was also one of the first commentators to claim that Bottom possessed "no inconsiderable store of imagination," evidence of which he notes in the Pyramus and Thisbe interlude and in the encounter with Titania and her attendants. Such later critics as G. K. Chesterton (1904), H. B. Charlton (1933), and John Palmer (1944) have also stressed Bottom's creative though somewhat primitive imagination.]

In [A Midsummer Night's Dream], the "subordinate" agents pre-occupy the mind, by reason of their great potency and surpassingly beautiful creation; or by the engrossing demand that others make on our attention, on account of their fine dramatic nature and verisimilitude, with side-shaking broad humour. Really and truly, Demetrius and Lysander, Hermia and Helena, with their love-crosses and perplexities, constitute the chief agents in the drama. Their way of life is the "plot"—disturbed, it is true, by the madcap sprite Puck, whose mischievous agency is so admirably employed to distort the course of their true love; and, with a two-handed scheme to befool poor little Titania, becomes not only the important movement in the machinery, but, in fact, we scarcely think of any other in conjunction with him; he and his fellow-minims of the moon's watery beams are the great (though little) people of the drama. Bottom and his companions are the cap and bells; and the classic stateliness of Theseus and Hypolita, with their sedate and lofty nuptialities, form—as Schlegel happily observes—"a splendid frame to picture" [see excerpt above, 1808]. (p. 96)

It was a happy thought of the poet, in introducing the play within the play, got up by the "Athenian mechanicals," in honour of Duke Theseus's marriage, to make a travesty of the old tragic legend of "Pyramus and Thisbe," and thereby turning it, as it were, into a farce upon the serious and pathetic scenes that occur between the lovers in the piece—Demetrius and Helena, and Lysander and Hermia.

But what a rich set of fellows those "mechanicals" are! and how individual are their several characteristics! Bully Bottom, the epitome of all the conceited donkeys that ever strutted and straddled on this stage of the world. In his own imagination equal to the performance of anything separately, and of all things collectively; the meddler, the director, the dictator. He is for dictating every movement, and directing everybody—when he is not helping himself. He is a choice arabesque impersonation of that colouring of conceit which, by the half-malice of the world, has been said to tinge the disposition of actors, as invariably as the rouge does their cheeks. (p. 97)

The character of Bottom is well worthy of a close analysis, to notice in how extraordinary a manner Shakespeare has carried out all the concurring qualities to compound a thoroughly conceited man. Conceited people, moreover, being upon such amiable terms with themselves, they are ordinarily good-natured, if not good-tempered. And so with Bottom; whether he carry an amendment, or not, with his companions he is always placable; and if foiled, away he starts for some other point—nothing disturbs his equanimity. When Puck has transformed him into the ass, and his companions all scour away from him, exclaiming, "Bless thee, Bottom! thou art translated!" [III. i. 118-19] Snout comes in, and, in amazement, exclaims:—

> "Oh, Bottom, thou art changed! What do I see on thee?
>
> "Bot. What do you see? You see an ass's head of your own, do you?"
>
> [III. i. 114-17]

His temper and self-possession never desert him: "I see their knavery. This is to make an ass of me, and fright me if they could: but I will not stir from this place, do what they can. I will walk up and down here, and I will sing, that they shall hear I am not afraid" [III. i. 120-24].

Combined with his amusing and harmless quality of conceit, the worthy Bottom displays no inconsiderable store of imagination in his intercourse with the little people of the fairy world. How pleasantly he falls in with their several natures and qualities; dismissing them one by one with a gracious speech, like a prince at his levee: "I shall desire of you more acquaintance, good master Cobweb. If I cut my finger I shall make bold with you" [III. i. 182-84]. (pp. 100-01)

[But we] never lose the cock-a-whoop vein in Bottom's character. He patronises his brother-mechanics; he patronises the fairies: he even patronises himself: "If I had wit enough to get out of this wood, I have enough to serve mine own turn" [III. i. 149-51].

Then, there is Snug, the joiner, who can board and lodge only one idea at a time, and that tardily. He begs to have "the lion's part written out, because he is slow of study;" and is amazingly comforted by the intelligence, that he "may do it extempore; for it is nothing but roaring" [I. ii. 68-9].

To him succeeds Starveling, the tailor, a melancholy man, and who questions the feasibility and the propriety of everything proposed. Being timid, he thinks the lion's part had better be omitted altogether: "Will not the ladies be afeard of the lion? *I* fear it, I promise you" [III. i. 27-8].

If, as some writers have asserted, Shakespeare was a profound practical metaphysician, it is scarcely too much to conclude that all this dove-tailing of contingencies, requisite to perfectionate these several characters, was all foreseen and provided in his mind, and not the result of mere accident. By an intuitive power, that always confounds us when we examine its effects, I believe that whenever Shakespeare adopted any distinctive class of character, his "mind's eye" took in at a glance all the concomitant minutiae of features requisite to complete its characteristic identity. "As from a watch-tower," he comprehended the whole course of human action,—its springs, its motives, its consequences; and he has laid down for us a trigonometrical chart of it. I believe that he did nothing without anxious premeditation; and that they who really study—not simply read him, must come to the same conclusion. (pp. 102-03)

> *Charles Cowden Clarke, "'Midsummer Night's Dream',' in his* Shakespeare-Characters: Chiefly Those Subordinate, *1863. Reprint by AMS Press Inc., 1974, pp. 93-110.*

REV. H[ENRY] N. HUDSON   (essay date 1872)

[*Hudson was a nineteenth-century American clergyman and literary scholar whose Harvard edition of Shakespeare's works, published in twenty volumes between 1880 and 1881, contributed substantially to the growth of Shakespeare's popularity in America. Hudson also published two critical works on Shakespeare, one a collection of lectures, the other—and the more successful—a biographical and critical study entitled* Shakespeare: His Life, Art, and Characters *(1872). The following excerpt is from this last-named work. Like Samuel Taylor Coleridge (1834), Hudson adopts the opinion that* A Midsummer Night's Dream *is essentially "an ideal dream" and that on "no other ground can its merits be duly estimated." Its mixture of high and low characters, the beautiful and grotesque, fact and fancy he regards as the exact quality of dreams, and its characterization, he points out, is consistently subordinated to this design. Also, in language closely following that of G. G. Gervinus (1849-50), Hudson comments on Shakespeare's subtle delineation of the fairies to complement this fantastic world, noting their amoral playfulness, imagination, love of beauty, and lack of sympathy for the difficulties which the mortals encounter. He examines the "dream-like grace" that permeates the union of Titania and Bottom and asserts that such an extreme juxtaposition could only happen in a dream. For a contradictory interpretation of the Titania-Bottom relationship, see the excerpt by Jan Kott (1964). Last, Hudson concludes with a brief comment on Bottom, noting how his transformation into an ass works so effectively on our imagination when read, but can never succeed when presented on the stage. A similar assessment of this and other aspects of* A Midsummer Night's Dream *can be found in the essays by William Hazlitt (1817), William Maginn (1837), Charles Knight (1849), G. G. Gervinus (1849-50), and Denton J. Snider (1890).*]

Coleridge says he is "convinced that Shakespeare availed himself of the title of this play in his own mind, and worked upon it as a dream throughout" [see excerpt above, 1834]. This remark no doubt rightly hits the true genius of [*A Midsummer Night's Dream*]; and no other ground can its merits be duly estimated. The whole play is indeed a sort of ideal dream; and it is from the fairy personages that its character as such mainly proceeds. All the materials of the piece are ordered and assimilated to that central and governing idea. This it is that explains

and justifies the distinctive features of the work, such as the constant preponderance of the lyrical over the dramatic, and the free playing of the action unchecked by the conditions of outward fact and reality. Accordingly a sort of lawlessness is, as it ought to be, the very law of the performance. King Oberon is the sovereign who presides over the world of dreams; Puck is his prime minister; and all the other denizens of Fairydom are his subjects and the agents of his will in this capacity. Titania's nature and functions are precisely the same which Mercutio assigns to Queen Mab, whom he aptly describes as having for her office to deliver sleeping men's fancies of their dreams, those "children of an idle brain" [*Romeo and Juliet*, I. iv. 97]. In keeping with this central dream-idea, the actual order of things everywhere gives place to the spontaneous issues and capricious turnings of the dreaming mind; the lofty and the low, the beautiful and the grotesque, the world of fancy and of fact, all the strange diversities that enter into "such stuff as dreams are made of" [*The Tempest*, IV. i. 156-57], running and frisking together, and interchanging their functions and properties; so that the whole seems confused, flitting, shadowy, and indistinct, as fading away in the remoteness and fascination of moonlight. The very scene is laid in a veritable dream-land, called Athens indeed, but only because Athens was the greatest beehive of beautiful visions then known; or rather it is laid in an ideal forest near an ideal Athens,—a forest peopled with sportive elves and sprites and fairies feeding on moonlight and music and fragrance; a place where Nature herself is preternatural; where everything is idealized, even to the sunbeams and the soil; where the vegetation proceeds by enchantment, and there is magic in the germination of the seed and secretion of the sap.

The characteristic attributes of the fairy people are, perhaps, most availably represented in Puck; who is apt to remind one of Ariel, though the two have little in common, save that both are preternatural, and therefore live no longer in the faith of reason. Puck is no such sweet-mannered, tender-hearted, music-breathing spirit, as Prospero's delicate prime-minister; there are no such fine interweavings of a sensitive moral soul in his nature, he has no such soft touches of compassion and pious awe of goodness, as link the dainty Ariel in so smoothly with our best sympathies. Though Goodfellow by name, his powers and aptitudes for mischief are quite unchecked by any gentle relentings of fellow-feeling: in whatever distresses he finds or occasions he sees much to laugh at, nothing to pity: to tease and vex poor human sufferers, and then to think "what fools the mortals be" [III. ii. 115], is pure fun to him. Yet, notwithstanding his mad pranks, we cannot choose but love the little sinner, and let our fancy frolic with him, his sense of the ludicrous is so exquisite, he is so fond of sport, and so quaint and merry in his mischief; while at the same time such is the strange web of his nature as to keep him morally innocent. In all which I think he answers perfectly to the best idea we can frame of what a little dream-god should be.

In further explication of this peculiar people, it is to be noted that there is nothing of reflection or conscience or even of a spiritualized intelligence in their proper life: they have all the attributes of the merely natural and sensitive soul, but no attributes of the properly rational and moral soul. They worship the clean, the neat, the pretty, and the pleasant, whatever goes to make up the idea of purely sensuous beauty: this is a sort of religion with them; whatever of conscience they have adheres to this: so that herein they not unfitly represent the wholesome old notion which places cleanliness next to godliness. Every thing that is trim, dainty, elegant, graceful, agreeable, and sweet to the senses, they delight in: flowers, fragrances, dewdrops, and moonbeams, honey-bees, butterflies, and nightingales, dancing, play, and song,—these are their joy. . . . On the other hand, they have an instinctive repugnance to whatever is foul, ugly, sluttish, awkward, ungainly, or misshapen. . . . (pp. 263-65)

Thus these beings embody the ideal of the mere natural soul, or rather the purely sensuous fancy which shapes and governs the pleasing or the vexing delusions of sleep. They lead a merry, luxurious life, given up entirely to the pleasures of happy sensation,—a happiness that has no moral element, nothing of reason or conscience in it. They are indeed a sort of personified dreams; and so the Poet places them in a kindly or at least harmless relation to mortals as the bringers of dreams. (p. 265)

Any very firm or strong delineation of character, any deep passion, earnest purpose, or working of powerful motives, would clearly go at odds with the spirit of [*A Midsummer Night's Dream*]. . . . It has room but for love and beauty and delight, for whatever is most poetical in nature and fancy, and for such tranquil stirrings of thought and feeling as may flow out in musical expression. Any such tuggings of mind or heart as would ruffle and discompose the smoothness of lyrical division would be quite out of keeping in a course of dream-life. The characters here, accordingly, are drawn with light, delicate, vanishing touches; some of them being dreamy and sentimental, some gay and frolicsome, and others replete with amusing absurdities, while all are alike dipped in fancy or sprinkled with humour. And for the same reason the tender distresses of unrequited or forsaken love here touch not our moral sense at all, but only at the most our human sympathies; love itself being represented as but the effect of some visual enchantment, which the King of Fairydom can inspire, suspend, or reverse at pleasure. Even the heroic personages are fitly shown in an unheroic aspect: we see them but in their unbendings, when they have daffed their martial robes aside, to lead the train of day-dreamers, and have a nuptial jubilee. In their case, great care and art were required, to make the play what it has been blamed for being; that is, to keep the dramatic sufficiently under, and lest the law of a part should override the law of the whole.

So, likewise, in the transformation of Bottom and the dotage of Titania, all the resources of fancy were needed, to prevent the unpoetical from getting the upper hand, and thus swamping the genius of the piece. As it is, what words can fitly express the effect with which the extremes of the grotesque and the beautiful are here brought together? What an inward quiet laughter springs up and lubricates the fancy at Bottom's droll confusion of his two natures, when he talks, now as an ass, now as a man, and anon as a mixture of both; his thoughts running at the same time on honey-bags and thistles, the charms of music and of good dry oats! Who but Shakespeare or Nature could have so interfused the lyrical spirit, not only with, but into and through a series or cluster of the most irregular and fantastic drolleries? But indeed this embracing and kissing of the most ludicrous and the most poetical, the enchantment under which they meet, and the airy, dream-like grace that hovers over their union, are altogether inimitable and indescribable. In this singular wedlock, the very diversity of the elements seems to link them the closer, while this linking in turn heightens that diversity; Titania being thereby drawn on to finer issues of soul, and Bottom to larger expressions of stomach. The union is so very improbable as to seem quite natural: we cannot conceive

how any thing but a dream could possibly have married things so contrary; and that they could not have come together save in dream, is a sort of proof that they *were* dreamed together.

And so, throughout, the execution is in strict accordance with the plan. The play, from beginning to end, is a perfect festival of whatever dainties and delicacies poetry may command,—a continued revelry and jollification of soul, where the understanding is lulled asleep, that the fancy may run riot in unrestrained enjoyment. The bringing together of four parts so dissimilar as those of the Duke and his warrior Bride, of the Athenian ladies and their lovers, of the amateur players and their woodland rehearsal, and of the fairy bickerings and overreaching; and the carrying of them severally to a point where they all meet and blend in lyrical respondence; all this is done in the same freedom from the laws that govern the drama of character and life. Each group of persons is made to parody itself into concert with the others; while the frequent intershootings of fairy influence life the whole into the softest regions of fancy. At last the Interlude comes in as an amusing burlesque on all that has gone before; as in our troubled dreams we sometimes end with a dream that we have been dreaming, and our perturbations sink to rest in the sweet assurance that they were but the phantoms and unrealities of a busy sleep.

Though, as I have already implied, the characterization is here quite secondary and subordinate, yet the play probably has as much of character as were compatible with so much of poetry. (pp. 269-72)

In the two pairs of lovers there are hardly any lines deep and firm enough to be rightly called characteristic. Their doings, even more than those of the other human persons, are marked by the dream-like freakishness and whimsicality which distinguish the piece. Perhaps the two ladies are slightly discriminated as individuals, in that Hermia, besides her brevity of person, is the more tart in temper, and the more pert and shrewish of speech, while Helena is of a rather milder and softer disposition, with less of confidence in herself. So too in the case of Demetrius and Lysander the lines of individuality are exceedingly faint; the former being perhaps a shade the more caustic and spiteful, and the latter somewhat the more open and candid. But there is really nothing of heart or soul in what any of them do: as we see them, they are not actuated by principle at all, or even by any thing striking so deep as motive: their conduct issues from the more superficial springs of capricious impulse and fancy, the "jugglery of the senses during the sleep of reason" [see excerpt above by G. G. Gervinus, 1849-50], the higher forces of a mental and moral bearing having no hand in shaping their action. For the fairy influences do not reach so far as to the proper seat of motive and principle: they have but the skin-depth of amorous caprice; all the elements of character and all the vital springs of faith and loyalty and honour lying quite beyond their sphere. Even here the judgement or the genius of the Poet is very perceptible; the lovers being represented from the start as acting from no forces or inspirations too deep or strong for the powers of Fairydom to overcome. Thus the pre-condition of the two pairs in their whim-bewilderment is duly attempered to the purposed dream-lay of the general action. Nor is the seeming stanchness of Hermia and Demetrius in the outset any exception to this view; for nothing is more wilful and obstinate than amorous caprice or skin-deep love during its brief tenure of the fancy.

Of all the characters in this play, Bottom descends by far the most into the realities of common experience, and is therefore much the most accessible to the grasp of prosaic and critical fingers. It has been thought that the Poet meant him as a satire on the envies and jealousies of the greenroom, as they had fallen under his keen yet kindly eye. But, surely, the qualities uppermost in Bottom the Weaver had forced themselves on his notice long before he entered the greenroom. It is indeed curious to observe the solicitude of this protean actor and critic, that all the parts of the forthcoming play may have the benefit of his execution; how great is his concern lest, if he be tied to one, the others may be "overdone or come tardy off"; and how he would fain engross them all to himself, to the end of course that all may succeed, to the honour of the stage and the pleasure of the spectators. But Bottom's metamorphosis is the most potent drawer-out of his genius. The sense of his new head-dress stirs up all the manhood within him, and lifts his character into ludicrous greatness at once. Hitherto the seeming to be a man has made him content to be little better than an ass; but no sooner is he conscious of seeming an ass than he tries his best to be a man; while all his efforts that way only go to approve the fitness of his present seeming to his former being.

Schlegel happily remarks, that "the droll wonder of Bottom's metamorphosis is merely the translation of a metaphor in its literal sense" [see excerpt above, 1808]. The turning of a figure of speech thus into visible form is a thing only to be thought of or imagined; so that probably no attempt to paint or represent it to the senses can ever succeed. We can bear—at least we often have to bear—that a man should seem an ass to the mind's eye; but that he should seem such to the eye of the body is rather too much, save as it is done in those fable-pictures which have long been among the playthings of the nursery. So a child, for instance, takes great pleasure in fancying the stick he is riding to be a horse, when he would be frightened out of his wits, were the stick to quicken and expand into an actual horse. In like manner we often delight in indulging fancies and giving names, when we should be shocked were our fancies to harden into facts: we enjoy visions in our sleep, that would only disgust or terrify us, should we awake and find them solidified into things. The effect of Bottom's transformation can hardly be much otherwise, if set forth in visible, animated shape. Delightful to think of, it is scarce tolerable to look upon: exquisitely true in idea, it has no truth, or even versimilitude, when reduced to fact; so that, however gladly imagination receives it, sense and understanding revolt at it.

Partly for reasons already stated, and partly for others that I scarce know how to state, A Midsummer Night's Dream is a most effectual poser to criticism. Besides that its very essence is irregularity, so that it cannot be fairly brought to the test of rules, the play forms properly a class by itself: literature has nothing else really like it; nothing therefore with which it may be compared, and its merits adjusted. For so the Poet has here exercised powers apparently differing even in kind, not only from those of any other writer, but from those displayed in any other of his own writings. Elsewhere, if his characters are penetrated with the ideal, their whereabout lies in the actual, and the work may in some measure be judged by that life which it claims to represent: here the whereabout is as ideal as the characters; all is in the land of dreams,—a place for dreamers, not for critics. For who can tell what a dream ought or ought not to be, or when the natural conditions of dream-life are or are not rightly observed? How can the laws of time and space, as involved in the transpiration of human character,—how can these be applied in a place where the mind is thus absolved from their proper jurisdiction? Besides, the whole thing swarms with enchantment: all the sweet witchery of Shakespeare's sweet

genius is concentrated in it, yet disposed with so subtle and cunning a hand, that we can as little grasp it as get away from it: its charms, like those of a summer evening, are such as we may see and feel, but cannot locate or define; cannot say they are here, or they are there: the moment we yield ourselves up to them, they seem to be everywhere; the moment we go to master them, they seem to be nowhere. (pp. 272-75)

Rev. H. N. Hudson, "Shakespeare's Characters: 'A Midsummer Night's Dream'," in his Shakespeare: His Life, Art, and Characters, Vol. I., *revised edition, Ginn & Company, 1872, pp. 259-75.*

EDWARD DOWDEN   (essay date 1881)

[*Dowden was an Irish critic and biographer whose* Shakspere: A Critical Study of His Mind and Art *(rev. ed. 1881) was the leading example of the biographical criticism popular in the English-speaking world near the end of the nineteenth century. In the following excerpt, Dowden provides the earliest extended examination of the character of Theseus in* A Midsummer Night's Dream. *He sees the duke as a "grand ideal figure," the personification of the "heroic man of action." But Dowden argues that Shakespeare does not wholeheartedly endorse the views that Theseus expresses about art, and he considers his linking of the lover, the lunatic, and the poet (Act V, Scene i) an example of the duke's limited perception of aesthetic matters. Dowden interprets Theseus's reaction to the mechanicals' performance in Act V, Scene i—that "the best in this kind are but shadows"—as revealing a lack of discrimination between superior and inferior art and not meant to reflect Shakespeare's own assessment of the matter, as suggested by William Maginn (1837) and Charles Knight (1849). Other critics who have discussed Theseus's comments on art and imagination include Denton J. Snider (1890), Frederick S. Boas (1896), Howard Nemerov (1956), and R. W. Dent (1964).*]

The central figure of [*A Midsummer Night's Dream*] is that of Theseus. There is no figure in the early drama of Shakspere so magnificent. His are the large hands that have helped to shape the world. His utterance is the rich-toned speech of one who is master of events—who has never known a shrill or eager feeling. His nuptial day is at hand; and while the other lovers are agitated, bewildered, incensed, Theseus, who does not think of himself as a lover, but rather as a beneficent conqueror, remains in calm possession of his joy. Theseus, a grand ideal figure, is to be studied as Shakspere's conception of the heroic man of action in his hour of enjoyment and of leisure. With a splendid capacity for enjoyment, gracious to all, ennobled by the glory, implied rather than explicit, of great foregone achievement, he stands as centre of the poem, giving their true proportions to the fairy tribe, upon the one hand, and, upon the other, to the "human mortals." The heroic men of action—Theseus, Henry V., Hector [in *Troilus and Cressida*]—are supremely admired by Shakspere. Yet it is observable that as the total Shakspere is superior to Romeo, the man given over to passion, and to Hamlet, the man given over to thought, so the Hamlet and the Romeo within him give Shakspere an infinite advantage over even the most heroic men of action. He admires these men of action supremely, but he admires them from an outside point of view. "These fellows of infinite tongue," says Henry, wooing the French princess, "that can rhyme themselves into ladies' favors, they do always reason themselves out again. What! a speaker is but a prater, a rhyme is but a ballad." [*Henry V*, V. ii. 155-59]. It is into Theseus's mouth that Shakspere puts the words which class together "the lunatic, the lover, and the poet" [V. i. 7] as of imagination all compact. That is the touch which shows how Shakspere stood off from Theseus, did not identify himself with this grand ideal (which he admired so truly), and admitted to himself a secret superiority of his own soul over that of this noble master of the world.

Comments by Shakspere upon his own art are not so numerous that we can afford to overlook them. It must here be noted that Shakspere makes the "palpable gross" interlude of the Athenian mechanicals serve as an indirect apology for his own necessarily imperfect attempt to represent fairy-land and the majestic world of heroic life. [William] Maginn writes, "When Hippolyta speaks scornfully of the tragedy in which Bottom holds so conspicuous a part, Theseus answers that the best of this kind [scenic performances] are but shadows, and the worst no worse, if imagination amend them. She answers [for Hippolyta has none of Theseus's indulgence towards inefficiency, but rather a woman's intolerance of the absurd] that it must be *your* imagination then, not *theirs*. He retorts with a joke on the vanity of actors, and the conversation is immediately changed. The meaning of the Duke is that, however we may laugh at the silliness of Bottom and his companions in their ridiculous play, the author labors under no more than the common calamity of dramatists. They are all but dealers in shadowy representations of life; and if the worst among them can set the mind of the spectator at work, he is equal to the best" [see excerpt above, 1837].

Maginn has missed the more important significance of the passage. Its dramatic appropriateness is the essential point to observe. To Theseus, the great man of action, the worst and the best of these shadowy representations are all one. He graciously lends himself to be amused, and will not give unmannerly rebuff to the painstaking craftsmen who have so laboriously done their best to please him. But Shakspere's mind by no means goes along with the utterance of Theseus in this instance any more than when he places in a single group the lover, the lunatic, and the poet. With one principle enounced by the Duke, however, Shakspere evidently does agree—namely, that it is the business of the dramatist to set the spectator's imagination to work; that the dramatist must rather appeal to the mind's eye than to the eye of sense; and that the co-operation of the spectator with the poet is necessary. For the method of Bottom and his company is precisely the reverse, as Gervinus has observed, of Shakspere's own method. They are determined to leave nothing to be supplied by the imagination. Wall must be plastered; Moonshine must carry lantern and bush. And when Hippolyta, again becoming impatient of absurdity, exlaims, "I am aweary of this moon! would he would change!" [V. i. 251-52] Shakspere further insists on his piece of dramatic criticism by urging, through the Duke's mouth, the absolute necessity of the man in the moon being *within* his lantern. Shakspere as much as says, "If you do not approve my dramatic method of presenting fairy-land and the heroic world, here is a specimen of the rival method. You think my fairy-world might be amended. Well, amend it with your own imagination. I can do no more unless I adopt the artistic ideas of these Athenian handicraftsmen."

It is a delightful example of Shakspere's impartiality that he can represent Theseus with so much genuine enthusiasm. Mr. Matthew Arnold has named our aristocrats, with their hardy, efficient manners, their addiction to field sports, and their hatred of ideas, "the Barbarians." Theseus is a splendid and gracious aristocrat, perhaps not without a touch of the Barbarian in him. He would have found Hamlet a wholly unintelligible person, who, in possession of his own thoughts, could be contented in a nutshell. When Shakspere wrote *The Two*

Gentlemen of Verona, in which, with little dramatic propriety, the Duke of Milan celebrates "the force of heaven-bred poesy" [*Two Gentlemen of Verona*, III. ii. 71], we may reasonably suppose that the poet might not have been quite just to one who was indifferent to art. But now his self-mastery has increased, and therefore with unfeigned satisfaction he presents Theseus, the master of the world, who, having beauty and heroic strength in actual possession, does not need to summon them to occupy his imagination—the great chieftain to whom art is a very small concern of life, fit for a leisure hour between battle and battle. Theseus, who has nothing antique or Grecian about him, is an idealized study from the life. Perhaps he is idealized Essex, perhaps idealized Southampton. Perhaps some night a dramatic company was ordered to perform in presence of a great Elizabethan noble—we know not whom—who needed to entertain his guests, and there, in a moment of fine imaginative vision, the poet discovered Theseus. (pp. 60-3)

        Edward Dowden, "The Growth of Shakspere's Mind and Art," in his Shakspere: A Critical Study of His Mind and Art, *third edition, Harper & Brothers Publishers, 1881, pp. 37-83.*

HENRY A. CLAPP   (essay date 1885)

[*Beginning with the opening speeches of Theseus and Hippolyta that refer to the four days that will elapse before their wedding takes place, Clapp traces the passage of time in* A Midsummer Night's Dream *through three successive days and concludes that between Act I, Scene i and Act IV, Scene i, "a whole day has somehow dropped out." He explains the discrepancy in time as but another example of the unrealistic nature of the play as a whole. For further discussion of the duration of time in* A Midsummer Night's Dream, *see the excerpts by Charles Gildon (1710), James O. Halliwell-Phillipps (1841), Horace Howard Furness (1895), and Anne Paolucci (1977).*]

[*A Midsummer Night's Dream* is] the only one of Shakespeare's plays in which I have discovered an inexplicable variance between the different parts of his scheme of time. In the very first lines of this comedy the Duke of Athens, Theseus,—a gentleman as protean in his political relations as in his love affairs,—laments to Hippolyta, the buskined Queen of Amazons, whom he has won with his sword, that their wedding must be delayed until "*four* happy days bring in another moon"[I. i. 2-3]; to which his betrothed soothingly and gracefully replies,—

> Four days will quickly steep themselves in
>   nights;
> Four nights will quickly dream away the time;
> And then the moon, like to a silver bow
> New bent in heaven, shall behold the night
> Of our solemnities.
>
>   [I. i. 7-11]

The date of their wedding having been thus fixed by the high contracting parties, old Egeus enters, "full of vexation" [I. i. 22], to complain that his daughter Hermia will not respect his choice of Demetrius as her husband, but persists in clinging to Lysander, a youth after her own heart; and Hermia is then and there warned by the Duke that "by the next new moon," "the sealing day betwixt" his love and him [I. i. 83-84], she must be prepared to elect whether she will obey her father, surrender her life to "chanting faint hymns to the cold, fruitless moon" [I. i. 73] as a votaress of Diana, or die the death of a disobedient child. The important date for which everything is thus fixed must have been, even by the ancient process of princely arithmetic, with all its cheerful counting at both ends, at least three days distant, as we should reckon it. But the play proceeds to cut the time down by a full twenty-four hours. Fixing our *punctum temporis* ["moment of time"] in the first scene of Act I., we find that Lysander and Hermia then arrange to elope "to-morrow night," their trysting-place being a certain wood a league without the town. Near the end of the scene they disclose their purpose to the woe-begone Helena, who has just entered, full of her own heart-grief, and she at once resolves to curry a little miserable favor with her unkind Demetrius by revealing their scheme to him. Scene 2, which succeeds, is plainly contemporaneous with Scene 1, or follows it closely. Here the hard-handed craftsmen of Athens make the original cast of parts in the "lamentable comedy" of Pyramus and Thisbe, and the last word of Quince, their stage manager and prompter, is an appointment to meet "to-morrow night" in the palace wood for a moonlight rehearsal. It is this same "to-morrow night" which teems with wonders for all the chief persons of the piece; the whole of Acts II. and III. is included within it, and in Scene 1 of Act IV. day breaks upon the following morn. This is the night of midsummer dreams and fancies and fairies, of whose enchantment, heightened sometimes by melodies of great musicians, the world has drunk without satiety for more than two centuries. Within this night Puck works all his delicious unmalicious mischief, and makes "all well again"; Oberon and Titania renew their dainty quarrels and their love; and Bottom tastes the doubtful joys of empire in fairyland and in a fairy queen's heart. It is a single night, as is said over and over again by the text in divers ways. But scarcely has the sequent morning dawned in Act IV. when Theseus, out a-hunting, discovers the pairs of lovers asleep upon the ground, awakens them with his horns, and judicially informs Hermia that the day of his marriage and her fateful choice has arrived; and nobody contradicts him, or asks his grace to count up the time once more on his ducal fingers. Scene 2 of Act IV. is in the afternoon of the same day,—all the couples having been married, and "the Duke having dined,"—and shows Bottom's return from dreamland, and the preparation of the humble actors for immediate departure to the palace; and Act V. devotes the "long age of three hours between after supper and bedtime" [V. i. 33-4] to the "tragical mirth" of Pyramus and Thisbe, followed, when the palace is hushed, by the appearance of the fairies and their blessing of the bride-beds. Parts of three successive days have therefore been occupied in the action, and a whole day has somehow dropped out. Nice customs courtesied to great kings in Henry V.'s time, and perhaps in the imperial age of Theseus the calendars made similar obeisance. But on the whole, I think we must believe that the explanation lies in the nature of the play, whose characters, even when clothed with human flesh and blood, have little solidity or reality. I fancy that Shakespeare would smilingly plead guilty as an accessory after the fact to the blunder, and charge the principal fault upon Puck and his crew, who would doubtless rejoice in the annihilation of a mortal's day. If this will not suffice, the problem must remain unsolved in these pages, and may be laid aside in company with the vexing questions, what became of the fathers and fathers-in-law, whose parts were carefully assigned at the first meeting of the troupe, and how Mr. N. Bottom, the leading man of the Quince "combination," could have achieved triumphant success in the exacting character of Pyramus without a single full rehearsal. (pp. 391-92)

Henry A. Clapp, "Time in Shakespeare's Comedies," in The Atlantic Monthly, *Vol. LV, No. CCCXXIX, March, 1885, pp. 386-403.*

DENTON J. SNIDER   (essay date 1890?)

[*Snider was an American scholar, philosopher, and poet who followed closely the precepts of the German philosopher Georg Wilhelm Friedrich Hegel and contributed greatly to the dissemination of his dialectical philosophy in America. Snider's critical writings include studies on Homer, Dante, and Goethe, as well as Shakespeare. Like Hermann Ulrici and G. G. Gervinus, Snider sought for the dramatic unity and ethical import in Shakespeare's plays, but he presented a more rigorous Hegelian interpretation than those two German philosophical critics. In the introduction to his three-volume work* The Shakespearian Drama: A Commentary (1887-90), *Snider states that Shakespeare's plays present various ethical principles which, in their differences, come into "Dramatic Collision," but are ultimately resolved and brought into harmony. He claims that these collisions can be traced in the plays' various "Dramatic Threads" of action and thought, which together form a "Dramatic Movement," and that the analysis of these threads and movements—"the structural elements of the drama"—reveal the organic unity of Shakespeare's art. Snider observes two basic movements in the tragedies—guilt and retribution—and three in the comedies—separation, mediation, and return. In the excerpt below, Snider identifies three movements in* A Midsummer Night's Dream, *which he terms as the Real World of Athens, the imaginary, Ideal World in the woods outside the city, and the world of art represented by the rehearsal and presentation of the Pyramus and Thisbe interlude. The "threads" or elements of the action in the first two worlds, he argues, mirror each other: just as Titania precipitates the conflict in the Fairy World by leaving her husband, the confrontation between the young lovers and the institutions of Law and Family disrupts the Real World. Snider maintains that the third movement, in which the Pyramus and Thisbe tragedy is reduced to burlesque at the hands of the rude mechanicals, unifies the drama in its emphasis on the conflict between Understanding and Imagination, Prose and Poetry—a conflict apparent in the previous two movements. He also asserts that the interlude serves as Shakespeare's commentary on his own play and, as Edward Dowden (1881) noted, establishes a contrast between the mechanicals' concept of art and his own perception. Other critics who have claimed that the Pyramus and Thisbe interlude serves as a contrast to Shakespeare's own art include G. G. Gervinus (1849-50) and George Brandes (1895-96). Snider also argues that Theseus and Hippolyta frame the action of the play because they represent the order that regulates society through its institutions—an order that commences the dramatic action and reestablishes itself at the close; additionally, in their different responses to the power of poetry and the imagination, the duke and queen embody "opposite phases of critical opinion" of the artistic process. Among other critics who have discussed this opposition, Howard Nemerov (1956) views the royal pair as depicting the rational and magical responses to poetry, Paul A. Olson (see Additional Bibliography) sees in them the complementary principles of reason and passion, and John Vyvyan (1961) holds that they frame the dramatic action by virtue of their ability to restore order from chaos.*]

On the stage it is doubtful whether [*A Midsummer Night's Dream*] can be truly successful; it transcends the limits of the theater; Puck, the Fairies, and the whole action of Fairy-land can appear before the Imagination alone, which is, in the present case, its own spectator. Like *The Tempest*, it leaps the bounds of the visible drama, and enters the world of wonders, which are beheld only with the inner eye. Its theatrical history is curious; it has been trimmed up and even cut up into farce, opera, spectacle; but it will not let itself be played in its native form without avenging the wrong. It manifestly does not hold its last allegiance to the stage; in this case, as in many others, the dramatist vanishes in the poet; the professional limit is pushed beyond itself into the unbounded realm of Imagination. Consciously or unconsciously the author is appealing from that confined theater of spectators to his future constituency, the untold millions of readers.

And to his readers, *Midsummer Night's Dream* is, perhaps, the most popular of Shakespeare's comedies. Its weird, ethereal scenery captivates the purely poetical nature; its striking sensuous effects impress the most ordinary mind; while its faint rainbow-like outlines of the profoundest truths entice the thinker with an irresistible charm to explore the hidden meaning of the Poet. There is no work of our author that is so universal—that appeals so strongly to high and low, to old and young, to man and woman. Its shadowy forms appear, disappear, and reappear in the wildest sport, and the critic may sometimes doubt his ability to track them through all their mazy hues. Nor can it be denied that there is a capricious play of fancy over and around the underlying elements of the drama. Still, like all of Shakespeare's pieces, it is based on thought and must look to the same for its justification. (pp. 379-81)

We are well aware that not a few people will regard any attempt to make out a consistent unity in the present play as wanton and absurd refinement. Moreover, the great interpreters of Shakespeare will be pointed to, who call it a caprice—a dream without any necessary connection of its various parts. That is, the work is a chaos. But every person who reads this play with admiration must grant that there is a profound harmony pervading it throughout; that he feels all its essential parts to be in perfect unison with one another; that the effect of the whole is not that of a discordant and ill-assorted poem. Thus, however, the notion of caprice, or of a dream, must be abandoned as the fundamental idea of the work. Both these elements undoubtedly are present; there is a capricious ingredient in certain parts, and the Fairy World is likened to the dream-world; but they are only subordinate members in the organization of the whole. If, then, it must be granted that there is a deep, underlying harmony throughout the entire piece, it must be granted that the attempt to ascertain and state the law of such harmony is not only reasonable, but necessary.

The procedure of this essay . . . will be twofold. First, it will attempt to state the phases or movements of the entire action, and their transition into one another; second, it will seek to trace the various threads which run through each movement of the play. The former divides the total action of the drama into a certain number of parts; the latter unites the characters together into groups. This will give a complete view of the structure of the work, which must be the foundation for all future conclusions. (pp. 381-82)

Following the principles above laid down, we are now ready for the statement of the various phases or movements, which, however, must finally be grasped together into the one complete movement of the play. These are three: First, the Real World, which is embraced in the First Act, and which is called real because its mediations and its collisions are those of common experience, and are based upon the institutions of human Reason; second, the Fairy World, the Ideal Realm, which terminates in the course of the Fourth Act, so named because its mediations and collisions are brought about through the agency of supernatural beings—the creatures of the Imagination; third, the representation in Art, which, together with the return from Fairy-land to the world of reality, takes up the rest of the drama, except the final scene. In this last part, then, the first two parts mirror themselves—the action reflects itself, the play plays itself playing; it is its own spectator, including its audience and itself in one and the same movement. Thus there is reached a totality of Representation, which represents, not only something else besides itself, but represents itself in the act of Representation. The very limits of Dramatic Art are touched here; it can go no further. In this reflection of the play by itself—the play playing itself in the play—is to be found the thought which binds together its multifarious, and seemingly irreconcilable, elements. (pp. 383-84)

The first movement, accordingly, unfolds a picture of the Real World in a special phase of both harmony and conflict. The scene is carried back to the ancient Athens, a realm of order, law and beauty, and is portrayed upon a mystical, heroic background. But this antique setting seems to vanish under our glance, as we catch the inner life of the work; love, romantic love, wells out of the heart everywhere, and we see that the Poet, full of the soul of the Renascence, simply fills the classic form with the modern spirit. Three different strands of the Real World he weaves together into his drama, which has thus three threads. These we shall separately consider.

The first thread is the part of Theseus and Hippolyta, whose mutual love and concord hover over the play from beginning to end—the beautiful arch which spans the entire action. In them is no jar, no collision; the unity is perfect from the start and remains undisturbed to the last; the longing of both for the nuptial hour is the key-note struck in the first lines of the drama. They are thus the types as well as the producers of that harmony in which all the difficulties of the lovers must terminate, and in which all the complications of the play must be solved. (pp. 385-86)

[Theseus's] essential function is that he is the head of the State. He therefore represents the highest rational institutions of man— he is both judge and ruler; through him the Real World is seen to be controlled by an organized system of law and justice— such is the atmosphere which surrounds him everywhere. Hence he stands above the rest and commands them, but does not himself become involved in their collisions. At first he sides with Egeus and asserts absolute submission to parental authority, but in the end he alters his mind and commands the daughter to be united to her chosen lover. The ground for this change of judgment are carefully elaborated by the Poet, and, indeed, the movement from strife to harmony lies just between the two decisions of Theseus.

Next comes the second thread—Egeus and the group of lovers. Here, now, the negative element, discord, is introduced, and the contrast to the preceding pair is manifest. Egeus comes before the Duke Theseus with his refractory daughter, who insists on marrying the one whom she loves, without regarding the selection of her father. Thus it is the old collision, involving the right of choice on the part of the child against the will of the parent. It is a theme which Shakespeare has often handled, and for which he seems to have a particular delight. But this is not the only difficulty which arises. There begins also a complicated love-collision, by which is meant the struggle which takes place when individuals of either sex find out that their love is unrequited by its object. Here two such cases are portrayed—Helena loves and is repelled by Demetrius, Demetrius loves and is repelled by Hermia—the reciprocal love being between Lysander and Hermia, which, however, has to endure the conflict with the will of the parent. Yet even this sole harmony will hereafter be destroyed for a time in Fairy-land. Such are the collisions from which the action starts, and which must be solved by the play.

The law at Athens demands the most implicit submission to parental authority, under the severest penalties, and the Duke will abate none of its rigors. The harshness of Egeus, the father, and the decision of Theseus, the ruler, force the lovers to flee from their home and their city—from Family and State. But whither are they to go? It is just at this point that we must seek for the basis of their transition to a new order of things. We hope the reader will observe carefully the nature and necessity of this transition, for here lies the distinctive characteristic of the play. It must be borne in mind that the lovers do not run away from the world of organized wrong; on the contrary, it is the authority of the parent and of the law—certainly a valid authority—from which they are fleeing. Hence they abandon the world of institutions, in which alone man can enjoy a free and rational existence, and they go to the opposite, for it is just these institutions and the law which have become insupportable to them. They cannot enter another State, for it is the State as such with which they have fallen out, and hence, the same collision must arise. Thus the nature of their place of refuge must be determined by what they reject. The next locality in which we find them is a new and strange world, called by the Poet a "Wood near Athens." (pp. 386-89)

On their entrance into the wood the lovers must, therefore, leave behind them the realized world of Reason—the State, the Family, and the other institutions of society. Now, the object of all these institutions is to secure freedom to man, and to shield him from external accident. By them he is protected against incursions of enemies from abroad, against injustice at home, against every species of rude violence; through civil institutions brute force is shut out, as it were, by mountainbulwarks. Man is only in this way secure of his freedom, and can enjoy his existence as a self-determined being. For in the State all action is determined ultimately through Reason, in the form of laws and institutions—in other words is determined through man himself; thus it is his true abode, in which he sees everywhere the work of his own Intelligence, and whose operations are, therefore, perfectly clear to his mind, and seem not the work of some dark, extraneous power. It is Theseus who represents such a world in the drama before us.

Still it must be granted that the Athenian law is not perfect, it is harsh and harshly administered. Nay, it is at bottom selfcontradictory, it crushes the internal basis of the Family, which it ought to protect; the law enforced to the last letter becomes wrong. Love and institutions thus collide—a collision which must be gotten rid of; love flees to a place where it has no restraint, and loses its rational or institutional element; thus is is mere caprice or passion. This is bad for the lovers, but it is also bad for the State, which must be corrected; it should not drive off love by its fierce legality, but give it a true validity, by recognizing it as the emotional element of the Family—which may be called the Right of Love. So the law and Theseus must change, just as the ancient world with its legal severity toward the Family changes into the modern world which recognizes this Right of Love. Theseus, between his two decisions, steps out of hoar antiquity into the recent centuries, and becomes one of the Poet's fellow-lovers. Still this Athenian world is the established World of Right, in which man lives free, in the edifice built of his own spirit.

The fleeing lovers, accordingly, enter a place where all these spiritual mediations of Intelligence no longer exist, but they are brought into direct contact with the forces of Nature, which determine them from without. Such a place is, hence, represented by the Poet as a wood, dark and wild, a pure product of Nature, inhabited by a race of beings foreign to man and unknown in the world of Reason. The lovers are, therefore, at once exposed to all sorts of external influences. They have now no State above them whose action is their own highest rational principle—hence clear to their minds; but the world which is at work is beyond them, outside of their Intelligence—the world of Nature, of Accident, of Externality. (pp. 389-91)

It is a world of external determination, and is pictured in a Mythology, which is a product of the Imagination, and thus such a world resembles dream-land, where all rushes in without cause, a fact which doubtless gives name to the play. It is also the realm of inner caprice, as the individual has no longer any institutional fixity; moreover it is an imaginative, poetic realm, as distinguished from the prosaic life in society. This brings us to the contrast between poetry and prose, which is now to be treated.

This is the third thread which shows the learning and representation of the theatrical piece by the clowns. The motive thereto is given on the first page of the play, in an external manner, by Theseus calling upon his Master of Revels to stir up the Athenian youth to merriments—to produce something for the entertainment of the court—that is, a demand for Art has arisen. For man's highest want is, after all, to know himself; he desires to behold his own countenance, as it were, in a mirror, which Art holds up before him. Moreover, there is an official attached to the court, and generally to all courts, whose duty it is to provide for the above-mentioned want.

The theme will, therefore, be that which gives a picture of the court—of its chief thought and business at this time, which is love. The content of the drama of *Pyramus and Thisbe* is thus a love-collision. Moreover it is a myth, and can only be learned by going to the mythical world, which is here Fairy-land. Now to compose and exhibit such a work adequately demands the highest skill, both in poet and actor. They must be gifted by nature with true artistic conception; they must polish nature by culture; Art must be their life and living; they must be professional. Such at least is the general rule; dilettanteism beyond the private circle is intolerable, and never was it more happily ridiculed than just in these clowns. Shakespeare has, therefore, chosen to give not a poetic, ideal picture in this part, but a prosaic one; and necessarily so, for what would the second picture otherwise have been but a repetition of the first? In fact, this play of the clowns is the contrast to his own true play; he has exhibited thus in the one and the same totality the negative—that it, humorous—side of his own work.

The idea of the third thread now before us may, therefore, be given in the statement—Prose is trying to be Poetry. The result is a burlesque of the legitimate kind, for it is not Poetry, or any other high and holy thing, which is wantonly caricatured, but the prosaic conception of Poetry. The contradiction is real—inherent; the Prosaic attempts to be what it is not and can never be—the Poetic; its efforts to put on such ethereal robes are simply ludicrous; but we have also the True alongside of the Burlesque; genuine Poetry is to be found just here in the same piece. Thus the Poet does not leave us with a negative result; after his wit has ceased to sparkle there is not left merely a handful of ashes, but the positive side is present also. (pp. 394-96)

Such are the three threads of the First Act. Their unity lies in the common theme love, in three of its manifestations; the love-harmony in Theseus and Hippolyta, the love-conflict in Egeus and the lovers, the burlesque of the love-conflict in the rude mechanicals. Taken together, they show the Real World, which now suddenly is left behind, and we are ushered into the Ideal Realm.

Here begins the second grand movement of the play, which is marked in the most emphatic manner by the appearance of the Marvelous. The inner thought of this transition has been already given; the lovers flee from the institutional world, which is the work of man's reason, and whose object is to secure his freedom, and they enter a Wood, whose characteristic was defined to be external determination. That is, man acts there more or less through influences from without, and not through the works of his own intelligence, not through institutions. Three phases are portrayed, which constitute the three distinct threads of this movement. First, the rational or institutional element being taken out of the Real World, we have the Fairy-land, the domain of external Accident. Secondly, the rational or institutional element being taken out of the individual man, and specially out of the love of man and woman, we have the realm of internal caprice, and specially the caprice of love. Thirdly, this same rational element being taken out of the poetry, the ideal Fairy-land with its art, drops of itself into a burlesque. (pp. 397-98)

Let us now consider the organization of [the] Fairy World, for it is a regular hierarchy. First comes the common fairy, with a description of her functions. She is the servant—she dews the orbs upon the green, spots the cowslips, hangs dew-drops in the flower's ear—that is, she performs the operations usually ascribed to Nature, which is thus mediated in its activity by the fairies. Next are told the doings of Puck, a servant of a higher order, having also a sphere of independent activity, in which he is the embodiment of mischief, and causes what are usually called accidents. . . . But the central principle of the fairy organization, and its chief figures, are the pair Oberon and Titania, to whom all the rest are subordinate.

The main fact here to be observed is that the highest fairies are king and queen; hence are not only sexed, but coupled, or, if the term is applicable to these beings, are married. Such is not the case with the other fairies. This hint will furnish the key to what follows, for the sexual diremption is the deepest contradiction of Nature, and the sexual unity is the profoundest harmony of Nature. The pair, therefore, are monarchs, and are placed on the apex of the physical world, whose highest effort is self-production. At present, however, their unity has been disturbed; the two sexes are in opposition; Titania and Oberon have quarreled. What is the result? All Nature is out of joint— in strife with itself; the seasons do not come in their regular order—winter is in summer and summer in winter; the waters have taken possession of the land and destroyed the labors of man—all of which evils are produced by the quarrel of the royal pair. The cause is explicitly stated by the Poet in the speech of Titania:

> And this same progeny of evil comes
> From our debate—from our dissension;
> We are their parents and original.
>
> [II. i. 115-17]

For, when the central and controlling principle of Nature is thus deranged and in contradiction with itself, the effects must be transmitted to all the subordinate parts. Such is the poetical conception of this hierarchy governing Nature. (pp. 400-01)

Confusion and strife must now reign in the kingdom of Nature. Leaving out of account the mutual charges of infidelity, as equally false or equally true, the fault of the separation would seem to lie with Titania. She is capricious, she breaks the law

of the Family and leaves the husband because he will not "patiently dance in our round" [II. i. 140]. Thus the scission between Law and Caprice is also imaged in Fairy-land. Oberon, however, resolves to assert the husband's right to be head of the family, and is determined to subordinate his refractory wife. His aim is unity and peace—not only in his own domestic relations, but in the entire realm, of which he is the supreme ruler. Oberon loves Titania, he wishes to get her back again; his method is to serve up her own deed to her, as she seems to have the habit of doting on changelings and quitting her husband.

Thus the action sets in towards the reconciliation of the conflict in Fairy-land. Accordingly, he prepares the means for his purpose. It is by dropping the juice of a certain flower upon the eye-lids of Titania when she is asleep, in order to make her fall in love with some ugly monster, the opposite of her nature. The retributive character of this punishment is obvious—if you cannot live in peace with me, one of your own kind, then try the contrary, a horrid brute. Titania, therefore, becomes infatuated with Bottom, the ass. It is the Poetic under the yoke of Prose—the natural result of her separation from her husband, since she has abandoned for the time the beautiful world of the fairies, and its monarch. In this service she undergoes the deepest indignity; in vain she lavishes her choicest love; her ideal perfections are soiled and unappreciated by the gross clown. The cause of the quarrel is at last removed by the repentance of the wife, "she in mild terms begged my patience" [IV. i. 58]. Oberon takes pity on her like a dutiful husband, releases her from her thralldom, and restores her to his bosom. She has had the discipline of caprice, and freed herself of it; but her return is her vanishing along with Fairy-land. Oberon, in these scenes, is the constant one; he is, indeed, a kind of Providence, who employs chance and mistake as his instrument—Puck—to bring her about his ends.

Thus the conflict which harassed Fairy-land has been harmonized, and peace reigns. But mark! now occurs one of those transitions upon which so much stress was laid in the first part of this essay. Night flies away; the darkness of the Wood is driven off by the light of the day; the Fairy World disappears with its own reconciliation; the Real World dawns. But this is not all. Theseus, the monarch, is on hand, ready to judge; Egeus is here, with his former collision; all transpires in the clear sunlight of consciousness; external mediation has ceased. Is it not evident that we have returned to the realm of institutions which we left some time ago?

Having thus brought the first thread to its termination, we are now ready to take up the second thread—the lovers. They arrive from Athens, and enter the Wood in the height of the strife between Oberon and Titania. They also bring along collisions among themselves, for two of them have an unreciprocated love. Fairy-land, therefore, is a picture of the condition of the lovers, for both have collisions, and indeed similar collisions, namely, those of the Family. Hermia has left her father; Titania has left her husband; and also the conflicts of the rejected suitors may be reckoned under this head. Here is the point where the relation between the real and ideal worlds may be seen—the one reflects the other. The internal state of the lovers is thus pictured in the world of the Imagination, which was before said to be this Fairy-land—the poetic abode of such forms.

It was also shown that the flight from society must be a flight to a world of external determination; here it now is in full operation. The lovers are wholly influenced by powers outside of themselves; the chief means, for example, is a flower wounded by Cupid's bolt. But these external forms, like the Fairy World itself, are poetic—are symbolical of the inner spirit of man—and, hence, must be interpreted. The common and most natural view is that this flower represents the effects of what the Poet calls "Fancy," a combination of caprice and love, which chooses and changes with wanton whim the objects of affection. The part of the lovers in the "Wood near Atheens" may thus be interpreted to be a play of fanciful, capricious love. The wood is seen to have two elements—outer accident in Puck and the Fairies, and inner caprice in the lovers. Both belong together, both show man in his unfree condition. But standing above both, and controlling both, is Oberon, the providential director of this world, who is guiding it rapidly to dissolution.

On account of the externality of the means, a mistake is possible—the process of love here is not in the heart and emotions. Puck anoints the wrong person. . . . The mistake destroys the only remaining reciprocal tie; the collisions are now completed; each individual hates his lover and loves his hater. There ensues a love-chase through the woods, which furnishes sport for all Fairy-land, till the parties, weary with fatigue, lie down on the ground and go to sleep. The possible conflicts between the two pairs of lovers are wrought out with a complete, even schematic regularity. Each one loves the one who does not requite the love—the other wants the other—till man and woman are torn asunder, woman and woman quarrel and separate, and a man and man not only quarrel, but seek each other's lives. The result is absolute discord; there can be no unity in the non-institutional world. Individualism, anatgonism reigns; all are drawn apart by caprice and thrown into conflict; even the two women who do not change their love, but are constant, are drawn into the struggle. Such is the comic outcome of the "Wood near Athens," it destroys itself. (pp. 401-06)

The solution of the collision [between the pairs of lovers] seems external—"crush this herb into Lysander's eye" [III. ii. 366], and all will be right. But really it is internal, and is brought about by command of Oberon, the central power, whose highest object all along has been the unity of the Family in his own case; and, hence, to be true to his character, he must manifest the same traits to the lovers who have wandered into his realm. He sympathizes with true love; the separation in his domain cannot continue, for, as before stated, the highest point and goal of Nature is the oneness of the two sexes, whereby the two individuals are made into the ethical unit above both. Such has been the aim of Oberon, or, if you please, the aim of Nature, from the beginning. Love is Nature's attempt to remove the separation between man and woman. We may also say that the lovers have run the course of caprice, and found out what lies in their flight from institutions; they awake out of their delusion and are ready to experience the permanent affection upon which the Family reposes. (pp. 406-07)

The lovers thus find themselves again in the world of institutions—before Theseus the ruler, and Egeus the parent. But, now, the two pairs are in perfect harmony—their love is reciprocal; hence the rational basis of union is present in both couples. Theseus, therefore, reverses his former sentence; he decides in favor of the right of choice on the part of the daughter against the will of the parent—a solution which Shakespeare uniformly gives in all similar collisions. Nor can Theseus consistently act otherwise; for what is he himself doing but celebrating his union with Hippolyta? The return of the lovers from the ideal to the Real World is thus accomplished. (pp. 407-08)

As legislator, judge and executor of the law in one, [Theseus] decrees and enforces the new law, which brings to harmony the Real World. The Right of Love is now realized, that is, it is made institutional; previously it was but subjective, existed merely in feeling and thought. The lovers, also. . . , have had their discipline as well as the State; the one side gets free of caprice, the other of injustice.

The third thread must now be resumed—the clowns in Fairy-land. Why are they, too, here? The question forces itself upon the mind, for this would seem to be a place most uncongenial to them. And so it is; the poetic world is certainly not their natural abode. But in the present instance they have left their prosaic occupation; they are transcending their own sphere, and are trying to represent a play—a work of Art—which lies far out of their comprehension. The attempt, however, brings them into the Fairy-land of Poetry, which is soon found full of strange beings, and they are compelled by terror to leave it with precipitation. A man cannot make, nor indeed act, a drama without entering the mystic Wood—the world of the Imagination. To be sure, the clowns themselves, for going there, can give only a common-place reason—"lest our devices be known;" since, if the plot should be revealed, then there would be no "surprise." But the principle thing to be noticed is how they reduce everything to the dead level of Prose. Their solicitude for the audience is touching; it must be perpetually reminded that these characters are not real, but that they are merely assumed—that I am not Pyramus, but Bottom, the weaver; that I am not a lion—be not afraid!—but Snug, the joiner. The clowns, therefore, have not the primary notion of the drama; they do not comprehend that it is a representation and not a reality. The imaginative form must be at once destroyed, and the illusion of art is always extinguished by their prosaic explanations. This trait is common to all these "mechanicals," and lies deep in their nature; it forms the essence of their comic characterization. They are, verily, mechanical; they reduce all poetic form to Prose. Thus their end is a nullity; they are simply destroying the object which they are seeking to produce—are annihilating their own end—which principle is the essence of Comedy. (pp. 408-10)

We have just seen with what effect the prosaic clowns woo Poetry; what, now, if Poetry should become the lover and servant of Prose? Such is the scene where Titania falls in love with Bottom—the queen of Fairy-land with an ass. The contrast in all its ludcrousness is here portrayed—the two elements are brought fact to face. The motive for her strange conduct has already been stated to lie in her separation from Oberon. The Ethereal is thus subjected to the Gross and Sensual; Imagination and her handmaids, separated from beings of their own spiritual nature, must obey the behests of Prose—nay, be swallowed in its voracious appetite. Her rapt poetic utterances are reduced to groveling common-places; her ambrosial food seems to excite no desire; her soft caresses are turned into grossness; she has at last to tie up her sweetheart's tongue. When she returns to her first love, how she hates the brute. The result, therefore, of the clowns' visit to Fairy-land—the realm of Art—is that they have produced and also beheld a picture, but a picture of their own asininity, and that they have been rudely driven off from the mystic Wood by its inhabitants. Thus they also have returned to the Real World. (pp. 411-12)

Hence we must now pass to the third movement of the work, which has not yet been developed—the Representation. The court has demanded Art in which to see itself, or at least by which to amuse itself. The two actions which have hitherto run alongside of each other are now to be brought up before Theseus and his company, who henceforth assume the part of audience and critics. The poem, therefore, after beholding and reflecting itself, is to criticise itself. But these criticisms will only illustrate the points of view of the different speakers.

The first thread of this movement is the story of the lovers, which has been told to the company, as we see by the words of Hippolyta at the begining of the Fifth Act:

> 'Tis strange, my Theseus, that these lovers speak of.
> [V. i. 1]

Shakespeare, however, could not well repeat the same story in the same play, and, hence, it is here omitted. The main point dwelt upon by the Poet is the criticism of Theseus. How will he treat the Poetic as it was shown in the strange tale of Fairy-land? His conception is purely prosaic; hence in him Prose again appears, but it is now altogether different from the groveling, sensuous form which was manifested in the "rude mechanicals." Here we see education, refinement, abstract culture. Theseus, therefore, represents in this connection the Prose of the cultivated Understanding, whose skepticism assails all poetic conception and tears its forms to pieces. He derides the "antic fables;" he scoffs at "the lunatic, the lover, and the poet" [V. i. 7], placing them in the same category; the Imagination itself is made the subject of his sneers—it is full of "tricks," and is placed in striking contrast with "cool reason." The poet's function is to "give to airy nothing a local habitation and a name" [V. i. 16-17]—that is, the Poet's work is without any actual or rational content. Old Theseus was a downright Philistine, as the Germans would say. It is the prosaic Understanding attempting to criticise Poetry, whose essence is totally outside of its horizon. Theseus will not acknowledge that under this fabulous form may be found the deepest and truest meaning; it is not his form, and, hence, worthless. (pp. 412-14)

Hippolyta, is of quite a different character; she, with all the appreciation inherent in the female nature, is inclined to gently dissent from the negative judgments of her husband. She mildly suggests that there may be some content in these wild, poetic forms of Fairy-land; that the story of the night—

> More witnesseth than fancy's images,
> And grows to something of great constancy;
> But, howsoever, strange and admirable.
> [V. i. 25-7]

With this quiet remark she ceases; she does not pursue the discussion further, for she is a woman, and possesses, perhaps, the immediate feeling and appreciation of Poetry, rather than the ability to give the grounds of her judgment. Such is the contrast: Theseus has at his side the opposite form of consciousness—the husband and wife exhibit opposite phases of critical opinion. It may be added that the Poet does not here represent, and cannot represent, the highest critical comprehension of his work, for that involves the statement of the entire content in an abstract form, while he must necessarily employ for the same content a poetical form.

But the second thread—the play of the clowns—now comes up for representation. It must also be subjected to the criticism of the audience, mainly composed of these two mental principles—Theseus and Hippolyta. The Duke wants to be amused; he rejects the old plays; he must see something new; he, therefore, chooses *Pyramus and Thisbe,* both on account of its novelty and its absurd title, though against the strong protests

of his art critic. The clowns appear and go through with their play. We again observe in them the same elements which were before characterized—the destruction of all artistic form; the introduction of nature in its immediateness, simply for its own sake, and not as the bearer of any spiritual meaning; rant, which lays equal emphasis on what is important and unimportant, without any relief; ignorance of all technical requirements of acting, with a strong infusion of general stupidity and self-importance. Indeed, it may be said that the separation of the lovers in *Pyramus and Thisbe* rests, not upon a moral obstacle, but a natural object; the basis of the collision in the play is a wall. It exhibits the realistic style reduced to absurdity. The critical judgment of the audience serves to bring out more strongly the contradictions of the piece beneath whose sneers it perishes, Theseus pronouncing upon it final sentence. It will be observed that the clowns have fared hard in their artistic efforts. After a very uncomplimentary picture of Bottom—and, in fact of themselves—they are frightened out of Fairy-land, and thus excluded from the world of Poetry; and now their work is torn piecemeal by the critical understanding. Neither Gods nor Men, Poetry nor Prose, can endure mediocrity in Art, much less stupidity. It will also not escape the attention of the reader that the Poet has portrayed, in the drama before us, the two essential phases of the prosaic Understanding in its attempts to attain the beatiful realm of Poetry. Theseus and the clowns have thus a common element.

The three pairs of lovers retire to rest in perfect happiness and peace, and the Poet again allows the Fairy World to flit for a moment across the stage, as if to give one more hint of its meaning. This world is now, too, in harmony; Oberon and Titania, the ideal couple, besides the three real ones, enter with their train and sing an *epithalamium,* whose content is the prosperity and concord of the Family. Thus Fairy-land has done its last duty—it has reflected the peaceful solution of the struggle, whereas previously it had imaged the strife. (pp. 414-17)

> *Denton J. Snider, "'Midsummer Night's Dream',"*
> *in his* The Shakespearian Drama, a Commentary: The
> Comedies, *Sigma Publishing Co., 1890?, pp. 378-427.*

HORACE HOWARD FURNESS   (essay date 1895)

[*Furness was an American lawyer who abandoned law to devote his life to Shakespearean studies. In 1871 he became the first editor of the New Variorum edition of Shakespeare's works with the publication of* Romeo and Juliet. *Eighteen volumes appeared under his editorship, all of which draw heavily on the First Folio of 1623. The value of Furness's work rests on his collection of extensive textual, critical, and annotative notes derived from the best authorities of the time. In the following excerpt from his preface to the New Variorum edition of* A Midsummer Nights Dreame *(1895), Furness offers an ironical response to earlier critics who found inconsistencies or irregularities in the duration of time in the play. He maintains that no discrepancies exist in the time frame of* A Midsummer Night's Dream, *citing several allusions to dawn which indicate that the sun rises three times between the lovers' flight to the woods and the moment when they are awakened by Theseus's hunting party. Anne Paolucci (1977) has also argued that there are no "lost" days in the play. Other commentators who have addressed the question of the duration of time in* A Midsummer Night's Dream *include Charles Gildon (1710), James O. Halliwell-Phillipps (1841), and Henry A. Clapp (1885).*]

[Various critics of *A Midsummer Night's Dream* have expressed views] concerning the DURATION OF THE ACTION. This Duration is apparently set forth by SHAKESPEARE himself with emphatic clearness in the opening lines of the play. Theseus there says that 'four happy days bring in another moon,' and Hippolyta replies that 'four nights will quickly dream away the time' [I. i. 2-3, 8]. When, however, it is sought to compute this number of days and nights in the course of the action, difficulties have sprung up of a character so insurmountable that a majority of the critics have not hesitated to say that SHAKESPEARE failed to fulfill this opening promise, and that he actually miscalculated, in such humble figures, moreover, as three and four, and mistook the one for the other. Nay, to such straits is one critic, FLEAY, driven in his loyalty to SHAKESPEARE that, rather than acknowledge an error, he very properly prefers to suppose that some of the characters sleep for twenty-four consecutive hours—an enviable slumber, it must be confessed when induced by SHAKESPEARE's hand and furnished by that hand with dreams.

That SHAKESPEARE knew 'small Latin and less Greek' is sad enough. It is indeed depressing if to these deficiencies we must add Arithmetic. Is there no evasion of this shocking charge? Is there not a more excellent way of solving the problem?

The great event of the play, the end and aim of all its action, is the wedding of Theseus and Hippolyta. Why did SHAKESPEARE begin the play four days before that event? If the incidents were to occur in a dream, one night is surely enough for the longest of dreams; the play might have opened on the last day of April, and as far as the demands of a dream were concerned the *dramatis personae* have all waked up, after one night's slumber, bright and fresh on May-day morning Why then, was the wedding deferred four days? It is not for us to 'ha'e the presoomption' to say what was in SHAKESPEARE's mind, or what he thought, or what he intended. We can, in a case like this, but humbly suggest that as a most momentous issue was presented to Hermia, either of being put to death, or else to wed Demetrius, or to abjure for ever the society of men, SHAKESPEARE may have thought that in such most grave questions the tender Athenian maid was entitled to at least as much grace as is accorded to common criminals; to give her less would have savoured of needless harshness and tyranny on the part of Theseus, and would have been unbecoming to his joyous marriage mood. Therefore to Hermia is given three full days to pause, and on the fourth, the sealing day 'twixt Theseus and Hippolyta, her choice must be announced. Three days are surely enough wherein a young girl can make up her mind; our sense of justice is satisfied; a dramatic reason intimated for opening the play so long before the main action; and the 'four happy days' of Theseus are justified.

The problem before us, then, is to discover any semblance of probability in the structure of a drama where to four days there is only one night. Of one thing we are sure: it is a midsummer night, and therefore full of enchantment. Ah, if enchantment once ensnares us, and SHAKESPEARE enchantment at that, day and night will be alike a dream after we are broad awake. To the victims of fairies, time is nought, divisions of day and night pass unperceived. It is not those inside the magic circle, but those outside—the spectators or the audience—for whom the hours must be counted. It is we, after all, not the characters on the stage, about whom SHAKESPEARE weaves his spells. It is our eyes that are latched with magic juice. The lovers on the stage pass but a single night in the enchanted wood, and one dawn awakens them on May day. We, the onlookers, are bound in deeper charms, and must see dawn after dawn arise until the tale is told, and, looking back, be conscious of the lapse of days as well as of a night.

If 'four happy days,' as Theseus says, 'bring in another moon' on the evening of the first of May, the play must open on the twenty-seventh of April, and as, I think, it is never the custom when counting the days before an event to include the day that is passing, the four days are: the twenty-eighth, the twenty-ninth, the thirtieth of April, and the first of May. Hippolyta's four nights are: the night which is approaching—namely, the twenty-seventh, the twenty-eighth, the twenty-ninth, and the thirtieth of April. The evening of the first of May she could not count; on that evening she was married. (pp. xxvii-xxviii)

The play has begun, and SHAKESPEARE's two clocks are wound up; on the face of one we count the hurrying time, and when the other strikes we hear how slowly time passes. But before we really begin to listen, SHAKESPEARE presents to us 'one fair enchanted cup,' which we must all quaff. It is but four days before the moon like to a silver bow will be new bent in heaven, and yet when Lysander and Hermia elope on the morrow night, we find, instead of the moonless darkness which should enshroud the earth, that 'Phoebe' is actually beholding 'her silver visage in the watery glass,' and 'decking with liquid pearl the bladed grass' [I. i. 210-11]. It is folly to suppose that this can be our satellite—our sedate Phoebe hides her every ray before a new moon is born. On Oberon, too, is shed the light of this strange moon. He meets Titania 'by moonlight,' and Titania invites him to join her 'moonlight revels.' Even almanacs play us false. Bottom's calendar assures us that the moon will shine on the 'night of the play.' Our new moon sets almost with the sun. In a world where the moon shines bright in the last nights of her last quarter, of what avail are all our Ephemerides, computed by purblind, star-gazing astronomers? And yet in the agonising struggle to discover the year in which SHAKESPEARE wrote this play this monstrous moon has been overlooked, and dusty Ephemerides have been exhumed and bade to divulge the Date of Composition, which will be unquestionably divulged can we but find a year among the nineties of the sixteenth century when a new moon falls on the first of May. But even here, I am happy to say, Puck rules the hour and again misleads night-wanderers. There is a whole week's difference between the new moons in Germany and in England in May, 1590, and our ears are so dinned with Robin Goodfellow's 'Ho! ho! ho!' over the discrepancy that we cannot determine whether Bottom's almanac was in German or in English. (I privately think that, as befits Athens and the investigators, it was in Greek, with the Kalends red-lettered.) Into such dilemmas are we led in our vain attempts to turn a stage moon into a real one, and to discover the Date of Composition from internal evidence.

In *Othello* many days are compressed into thirty-six hours; in *The Merchant of Venice* three hours are made equivalent to three months. In the present play four days are to have but one night, and I venture to think that, thanks to the limitations of SHAKESPEARE's stage, this was a task scarcely more difficult than those in the two plays just mentioned.

Grant that the play opens on Monday, Hippolyta's four nights are then, Monday night, Tuesday night, Wednesday night, and Thursday night. Why does Lysander propose to elope with Hermia '*to-morrow* night,' and Hermia agree to meet him '*morrow* deep midnight' [I. i. 164, 223]? One would think that not only a lover's haste but a wise prudence would counsel flight that very night. Why need we be told with so much emphasis that the Clowns' rehearsal was to be held '*to-morrow* night'? Is it not that both by the specified time of the elopement and by the specified time of the rehearsal we are to be made conscious that Monday night is to be eliminated? If so, there will then remain but three nights to be accounted for before the wedding day, and these three nights are to be made to seem as only one. If while this long night is brooding over the lovers we can be made to see two separate dawns, the third dawn will be May day and the task will be done. We must see Wednesday's dawn, Thursday's dawn, and on Friday morning early Theseus's horns must wake the sleepers.

It is not to be expected that these dawns and the days following them will be proclaimed in set terms. That would mar the impression of one continuous night. They will not be obtruded on us. They will be intimated by swift, fleeting allusions which induce the belief almost insensibly that a new dawn has arisen. To be thoroughly receptive of these impressions we must look at the scene through the eyes of SHAKESPEARE's audience, which beholds, in the full light of an afternoon, a stage with no footlights or side-lights to be darkened to represent night, but where daylight is the rule; night, be it remembered, is to be assumed only when we are told to assume it.

The Second Act opens in the wood where Lysander and Hermia were to meet at 'deep midnight'; they have started on their journey to Lysander's aunt, and have already wandered so long and so far that Demetrius and Helena cannot find them, and they decide to 'tarry for the comfort of the day' [II. ii. 38]. This prepares us for a dawn near at hand. They must have wandered many a weary mile and hour since midnight. Oberon sends for the magic flower, and is strict in his commands to Puck after anointing Demetrius's eyes to meet him 'ere the first cock crow' [II. i. 267]. Again an allusion to dawn, which must be close at hand or the command would be superflous. Puck wanders 'through the forest' in a vain search for the lovers. This must have taken some time, and the dawn is coming closer. Puck finds the lovers at last, chants his charm as he anoints, by mistake, Lysander's eyes, and then hurries off with 'I must now to Oberon' [II. ii. 83]. We feel the necessity for his haste, the dawn is upon him and the cock about to crow. To say that these allusions are purposeless is to believe that SHAKESPEARE wrote haphazard, which he may believe who lists. This dawn, then, whose streaks we see lacing the severing clouds, is that of Wednesday morning. We need but one more dawn, that of Thursday, before we hear the horns of Theseus. Lest, however, this impression of a new day be too emphatic, SHAKESPEARE artfully closes the Act with the undertone of night by showing us Hermia waking up after her desertion by Lysander. Be it never forgotten that while we are looking at the fast clock we must hear the slow clock strike.

The Third Act begins with the crew of rude mechanicals at their rehearsal. If we were to stop to think while the play is going on before us, we should remember that rightfully this rehearsal is on Tuesday night; but we have watched the events of that night which occurred long after midnight; we have seen a new day dawn; and this is a new Act. Our consciousness tells us that it is Wednesday. Moreover, who of us ever imagines that this rehearsal is at night? As though for the very purpose of dispelling such a thought, Snout asks if the moon shines the night of the play, which is only two or three nights off. Would such a question have occurred to him if they had then been acting by moonlight? Remember, on SHAKESPEARE's open-air stage we must assume daylight unless we are told that it is night. Though we assume daylight here at the rehearsal, we are again gently reminded toward the close of the scene, as though at the end of the day, that the moon looks with a watery eye upon Titania and her horrid love.

The next scene is night, Wednesday night, and all four lovers are still in the fierce vexation of the dream through which we have followed them continuously, and yet we are conscious, we scarcely know how, that outside in the world a day has slipped by. Did we not see Bottom and all of them in broad daylight? Lysander and Demetrius *exeunt* to fight their duel; Hermia and Helena depart, and again a dawn is so near that darkness can be prolonged, and the starry welkin covered, only by Oberon's magic 'fog as black as Acheron' [III. ii. 357]. and over the brows of the rivals death-counterfeiting sleep can creep only by Puck's art. So near is day at hand that this art must be plied with haste, 'for night's swift dragons cut the clouds full fast, And yonder shines Aurora's harbinger' [III. ii. 379-80]. Here we have a second dawn, the dawn of Thursday morning. All four lovers are in the deepest slumber—a slumber 'more dead than common sleep' [IV. i. 81-2]. induced by magic. And the First Folio tells us explicitly before the Fourth Act opens that *'They Sleepe all the Act.'*

Wednesday night has passed, and this Act, the Fourth, through which they sleep, befalls on Thursday, after the dawn announced by Aurora's harbinger has broadened into day. Surely it is only on a midsummer noon that we can picture Titania on a bed of flowers, coying Bottom's amiable cheeks and kissing his fair large ears. Never could Bottom even, with or without the ass's nowl, have thought of sending Cavalery Cobweb to kill a red-hipt humble-bee on the top of a thistle at night, when not a bee is abroad. It must be high noon. But Bottom takes his nap with Titania's arms wound round him; the after noon wanes; Titania is awakened and disenchanted; she and Oberon take hands and rock the ground whereon the lovers still are lying, and then, as though to settle every doubt, and to stamp, at the close, every impression ineffaceably that we have reached Thursday night, Oberon tells his Queen that they will dance in Duke Theseus's house *'to-morrow* midnight.' But before the Fairy King and Queen trip away, Puck hears the morning lark, the herald of Friday's dawn, and almost mingling with the song we catch the notes of hunting horns. So the scene closes, with the mindful stage-direction that the *Sleepers Lye Still.* It was not a mere pretty conceit that led SHAKESPEARE to lull these sleepers with fairy music and to rock the ground; this sleep was thus charmed and made 'more dead than common sleep' to reconcile us to the long night of Thursday, until early on Friday morning the horns of Theseus's foresters could be heard. The horns are heard; the sleepers 'all start up'; it is Friday, the first of May, and the day when Hermia is to give answer of her choice.

The wheel has come full circle. We have watched three days dawn since the lovers stole forth into the wood *last night*, and four days since we first saw Theseus and Hippolyta *yesterday*. The lovers have quarrelled, and slept not through one night, but three nights, and these three nights have been one night. Theseus's four days are all right, we have seen them all; Hippolyta's four nights are all right, we have seen them all.

There are allusions in the Second Act, undeniably, to the near approach of a dawn, and again there are allusions in the Third Act undeniably to the near approach of a dawn; wherefore, since divisions into Acts indicate progress in the action or they are meaningless, I think we are justified in considering these allusions, in different Acts, as referring to two separate dawns; that of Wednesday and that of Thursday, the only ones we need before the May-day horns are heard on Friday.

For those who refuse to be spellbound it is, of course, possible to assert that these different allusions refer to one and the same dawn, and that the duration of the action is a hopeless muddle. If such an attitude toward the play imparts any pleasure, so be it; one of the objects of all works of art is thereby attained, and the general sum of happiness of mankind is increased. For my part, I prefer to submit myself an unresisting victim to any charms which SHAKESPEARE may mutter; should I catch him at his tricks, I shall lift no finger to break the spell; and that the spell is there, no one can deny who ever saw this play performed or read it with his imagination on the wing.

Thus far we have been made by SHAKESPEARE to condense time; we are equally powerless when he bids us expand it. Have these days after all really passed so swiftly? Oberon has just come from the farthest steep of India on purpose to be present at this wedding of Hippolyta. We infer that he takes Titania by surprise by the suddenness of his appearance, and yet before the first conference of these Fairies is half through we seem to have been watching them ever since the middle summer's spring, and we are shivering at the remembrance of the effect of their quarrel on the seasons. Oberon knows, too, Titania's haunts, the very bank of wild thyme where she sometimes sleeps at night. He cannot have just arrived from India. He must have watched Titania for days to have found out her haunts. Then, too, how long ago it seems since he sat upon a promontory and marked where the bolt of Cupid fell on a little Western flower!—the flower has had time to change its hue, and for maidens to give it a familiar name. It is not urged that these allusions have any connection with Theseus's four days; it is merely suggested that they help to carry our imaginations into the past, and make us forget the present, to which, when our thoughts are again recalled, we are ready to credit any intimation of a swift advance, be it by a chance allusion or by the sharp division of an Act.

These faint scattered hints are all near the beginning of the Play: it is toward the close, after we have seen the time glide swiftly past, that the deepest impressions of prolonged time must be made on us. Accordingly, although every minute of the dramatic lives of Oberon and Titania has been apparently passed in our sight since we first saw them, yet Oberon speaks of Titania's infatuation for Bottom as a passion of so long standing that at last he began to pity her, and that, meeting her *of late* behind the wood where she was seeking sweet favours for the hateful fool, he obtained the little changeling child. Again, when Bottom's fellows meet to condole over his having been transported, and have in vain sent to his house, Bottom appears with the news that their play has been placed on the list of entertainments for the Duke's wedding. We do not stop to wonder when and where this could have been done, but at once accept a conference and a discussion with the Master of the Revels. Finally, it is in the last Act that the weightiest impression is made of time's slow passage and that many a day has elapsed. When Theseus decides that he will hear the tragical mirth of 'Pyramus and Thisbe,' Egeus attempts to dissuade him, and says that the play made his eyes water *when he saw it rehearsed.* When and where could he have seen it rehearsed? We witnessed the first and only rehearsal, and no one else was present but ourselves and Puck; immediately after the rehearsal Bottom became the god of Titania's idolatry, and fell asleep in her arms; when he awoke and returned to Athens his comrades were still bewailing his fate; he enters and tells them to prepare for an immediate performance before the Duke. Yet Egeus saw a rehearsal of the whole play with all the characters, and laughed till he cried over it.

Enthralled by SHAKESPEARE's art, and submissive to it, we accept without question every stroke of time's thievish prog-

Act II. Scene i. Oberon, Titania, and Fairies. Frontispiece to the Rowe edition (1709). By permission of the Folger Shakespeare Library.

ress, be it fast or slow; and, at the close, acknowledge that the promise of the opening lines has been redeemed. But if, in spite of all our best endeavours, our feeble wits refuse to follow him, SHAKESPEARE smiles gently and benignantly as the curtain falls, and begging us to take no offence at shadows, bids us think it all as no more yielding than a dream. (pp. xxix-xxxiv)

> *Horace Howard Furness, in a preface to* A New Variorum Edition of Shakespeare: "A Midsummer Nights Dreame," *Vol. 10 by William Shakespeare, edited by Horace Howard Furness, J. B. Lippincott Company, 1895, pp. v-xxxiv.*

GEORGE BRANDES   (essay date 1895-96)

[*Brandes was the most influential literary critic of late nineteenth-century Denmark. A scholar with a broad knowledge of literature, his work on Shakespeare, originally published in 1895-96, was translated and widely read in his day. In the following excerpt, Brandes apparently combines the opinions of both Samuel Taylor Coleridge (1834) and G. G. Gervinus (1849-50), calling* A Midsummer Night's Dream *"a lightly flowing, sportive, lyrical fantasy" that nonetheless deals with a concept of philosophical importance, namely, the belief that human beings are irrational and motivated more by their unconcious desires than by reason, especially in matters of love. Brandes also emphasizes autobio-*

graphical elements in A Midsummer Night's Dream, *noting evidence of Shakespeare's "love of nature" in the many references to botanical species and the abundance of folklore material. For further examinations of Shakespeare's use of popular folklore in his portrayal of the fairies, see the excerpt by C. L. Barber (1959) and the entries listed in the Additional Bibliography by K. M. Briggs, Roger Lancelyn Green, Minor White Latham, and Frank Sidgwick. Last, Brandes's reference to the irony with which Shakespeare "treats his own art" in the Pyramus and Thisbe interlude echoes the remarks of Edward Dowden (1881) and Denton J. Snider (1890).*]

How is one to speak adequately of *A Midsummer Night's Dream?* It is idle to dwell upon the slightness of the character-drawing, for the poet's effort is not after characterisation; and, whatever its weak points, the poem as a whole is one of the tenderest, most original, and most perfect Shakespeare ever produced.

It is Spenser's fairy-poetry developed and condensed; it is Shelley's spirit-poetry anticipated by more than two centuries. And the airy dream is shot with whimsical parody. The frontiers of Elf-land and Clown-land meet and mingle.

We have here an element of aristocratic distinction in the princely couple, Theseus and Hippolyta, and their court. We have here an element of sprightly burlesque in the artisans' performance of Pyramus and Thisbe, treated with genial irony and divinely felicitous humour. And here, finally, we have the element of supernatural poetry, which soon after flashes forth again in *Romeo and Juliet*, where Mercutio describes the doings of Queen Mab. Puck and Pease-blossom, Cobweb and Mustard-seed—pigmies who hunt the worms in a rosebud, tease bats, chase spiders, and lord it over nightingales—are the leading actors in an elfin play, a fairy carnival of inimitable mirth and melody, steeped in a midsummer atmosphere of mist-wreaths and flowerscents, under the afterglow that lingers through the sultry night. This miracle of happy inspiration contains the germs of innumerable romantic achievements in England, Germany, and Denmark, more than two centuries later. (pp. 63-4)

We have here no pathos. The hurricane of passion does not as yet sweep through Shakespeare's work. No; it is only the romantic and imaginative side of love that is here displayed, the magic whereby longing transmutes and idealises its object, the element of folly, infatuation, and illusion in desire, with its consequent variability and transitoriness. Man is by nature a being with no inward compass, led astray by his instinct and dreams, and for ever deceived either by himself or by others. This Shakespeare realises, but does not, as yet, take the matter very tragically. Thus the characters whom he here presents, even, or rather especially, in their love-affairs, appear as anything but reasonable beings. The lovers seek and avoid each other by turns, they love and are not loved again; the couples attract each other at cross-purposes; the youth runs after the maiden who shrinks from him, the maiden flees from the man who adores her; and the poet's delicate irony makes the confusion reach its height and find its symbolic expression when the Queen of the Fairies, in the intoxication of a love-dream, recognises her ideal in a journeyman weaver with an ass's head. (p. 64)

A Midsummer Night's Dream is the first consummate and immortal masterpiece which Shakespeare produced.

The fact that the pairs of lovers are very slightly individualised, and do not in themselves awaken any particular sympathy, is a fault that we easily overlook, amid the countless beauties of the play. The fact that the changes in the lovers' feelings are entirely unmotived is no fault at all, for Oberon's magic is simply a great symbol, typifying the sorcery of the erotic imagination. There is deep significance as well as drollery in the presentation of Titania as desperately enamoured of Bottom with his ass's head. Nay, more; in the lovers' ever-changing attractions and repulsions we may find a whole sportive love-philosophy.

The rustic and popular element in Shakespeare's genious here appears more prominently than ever before. The country-bred youth's whole feeling for and knowledge of nature comes to the surface, permeated with the spirit of poetry. The play swarms with allusions to plants and insects, and all that is said of them is closely observed and intimately felt. In none of Shakespeare's plays are so many species of flowers, fruits, and trees mentioned and characterised. (pp. 67-8)

The popular element in Shakespeare is closely interwoven with his love of nature. He has here plunged deep into folklore, seized upon the figments of peasant superstition as they survive in the old ballads, and mingled brownies and pixies with the delicate creations of artificial poetry. . . . (p. 68)

The fairy element introduced into the comedy brings in its train not only the many love-illusions, but other and external forms of thaumaturgy as well. People are beguiled by wandering voices, led astray in the midnight wood, and victimised in many innocent ways. The fairies retain from first to last their grace and sportiveness, but the individual physiognomies, in this stage of Shakespeare's development, are as yet somewhat lacking in expression. Puck, for instance, is a mere shadow in comparison with a creation of twenty years later, the immortal Ariel of *The Tempest*.

Brilliant as is the picture of the fairy world in *A Midsummer Night's Dream*, the mastery to which Shakespeare had attained is most clearly displayed in the burlesque scenes, dealing with the little band of worthy artisans who are moved to represent the history of Pyramus and Thisbe at the marriage of Theseus and Hippolyta. Never before has Shakespeare risen to the sparkling and genial humour with which these excellent simpletons are portrayed. He doubtless drew upon childish memories of the plays he had seen performed in the market-place at Coventry and elsewhere. He also introduced some whimsical strokes of satire upon the older English drama. For instance, when Quince says. . . , "Marry, our play is—The most lamentable comedy, and most cruel death of Pyramus and Thisby" [I. i. 11-12], there is an obvious reference to the long and quaint title of the old play of *Cambyses:* "A lamentable tragedy mixed full of pleasant mirth," &c.

Shakespeare's elevation of mind, however, is most clearly apparent in the playful irony with which he treats his own art, the art of acting, and the theatre of the day, with its scanty and imperfect appliances for the production of illusion. The artisan who plays Wall, his fellow who enacts Moonshine, and the excellent amateur who represents the Lion are deliciously whimsical types. (pp. 69-70)

It is true that *A Midsummer Night's Dream* is rather to be described as a dramatic lyric than a drama in the strict sense of the word. It is a lightly-flowing, sportive, lyrical fantasy, dealing with love as a dream, a fever, an illusion, an infatuation, and making merry, in especial, with the irrational nature of the instinct. That is why Lysander, turning, under the influence of the magic flower, from Hermia, whom he loves, to Helena, who is nothing to him, but whom he now imagines that he adores, is made to exclaim . . . :

> The will of man is by his reason sway'd,
> And reason says you are the worthier maid.
>
> [II. ii. 115-16]

Here, more than anywhere else, he is the mouthpiece of the poet's irony. Shakespeare is far from regarding love as an expression of human reason; throughout his works, indeed, it is only by way of exception that he makes reason the determining factor in human conduct. He early felt and divined how much wider is the domain of the unconscious than of the conscious life, and saw that our moods and passions have their root in the unconscious. The germs of a whole philosophy of life are latent in the wayward love-scenes of *A Midsummer Night's Dream*. (p. 71)

> *George Brandes, "'A Midsummer Night's Dream'— Its Historical Circumstances—Its Aristocratic, Popular, Comic, and Supernatural Elements," translated by William Archer, in his* William Shakespeare, *William Heinemann, 1920, pp. 63-71.*

FREDERICK S. BOAS (essay date 1896)

[*Boas was a nineteenth- and early twentieth-century scholar who specialized in Elizabethan and Tudor drama. Many commentators today regard his work as occupying a transitional period in Shakespearean criticism between the biographical and historical approaches to the plays. In the following excerpt from his* Shakespeare and His Predecessors (1896), *Boas disputes the contention of G. G. Gervinus (1849-50) that there is evidence in* A Midsummer Night's Dream *of an ethical intention on the part of the playwright, arguing instead that the play shows little indication of thoughtful or serious reflection. As such, Boas, like such earlier critics as Samuel Taylor Coleridge (1834) and H. N. Hudson (1872), considers* A Midsummer Night's Dream *a fanciful attempt to emulate the quality of dreams rather than a dramatization of a particular issue. He also disagrees with those critics who interpret Theseus's comments on art and artists as ironic, and he regards the* Pyramus *and* Thisbe *interlude as Shakespeare's means of confronting, in an obvious way, "the immemorial question of realism in art and on the stage"; however, Boas draws no further correlation between the interlude and the play, such as its structural and thematic importance to Shakespeare's design, as proposed by August Wilhelm Schlegel (1808), Hermann Ulrici (1839), Edward Dowden (1881), and Denton J. Snider (1890), but merely regards the play-within-the-play as an example of contemporary artistic issues that occupied Shakespeare during his career as a dramatist. For further discussions of the play-within-the-play in* A Midsummer Night's Dream, *see the excerpts by G. G. Gervinus (1849-50), George Brandes (1895-96), Samuel B. Hemingway (1911), Paul N. Siegel (1953), and Elizabeth Sewell (1960). Also important to note is Boas's description of Theseus as "a great Tudor noble," which may be compared with Edward Dowden's view of him as the "heroic man of action," Denton J. Snider's conception of him as the ideal Renaissance man, and G. K. Chesterton's description of him as a typical "English country squire" (see excerpts above, 1881 and 1890, and below, 1904).*]

In its main plot [*A Midsummer Night's Dream*] is akin to *The Comedy of Errors*, for in both cases a humorous entanglement is created out of mistakes. Already, however, Shakespere shows his extraordinary skill in devising variations upon a given theme, for here the mistakes are those of a night and not of a day, and instead of being external to the mind are internal. . . . As in *The Comedy of Errors*, also, the scene is nominally laid amid classical surroundings, but the whole atmosphere of the play is essentially English and Elizabethan.

Thus Theseus, whose marriage with Hippolyta forms the setting of the story, is no Athenian 'duke,' but a great Tudor noble. He is a brave soldier, who has wooed his bride with his sword, and, strenuous even in his pleasures, he is up with the dawn on May-morning, and out in the woods, that his love may hear the music of his hounds, 'matched in mouth like bells' [IV. i.

123], as they are uncoupled for the hunt. He is a true Tudor lord also in his taste for the drama, as shown in his request for masques and dances wherewith to celebrate his marriage. He exhibits the gracious spirit common to all Shakespeare's leaders of men in choosing, against the advice of his Master of the Revels, the entertainment prepared by Bottom and his fellows:

> I will hear that play
> For never anything can be amiss
> When simpleness and duty tender it;
> [V. i. 81-3]

and though tickled by the absurdities of the performance, he checks more than once the petulant criticisms of Hippolyta, and assures the actors at the close, with a courteous *double-entendre*, that their play has been 'very notably discharged' [V. I. 360-61]. But it has been urged that Theseus shows the limitations of nature which are found in Shakespere's men of action. Though dramatic performances serve to while away the time, even at their best they are to him 'but shadows,' and it is he who dismisses the tale of what the lovers have experienced in the wood as 'fairy toys,' and is thus led on to the famous declaration that

> The lunatic, the lover, and the poet
> Are of imagination all compact.
> [V. i. 7-8]

Only the practical common-sense Theseus, it has been said, would think of comparing the poet or lover to the lunatic, and Shakespere, by putting such words into his mouth, shows by a side-stroke that the man of action fails to appreciate the idealist nature. But such an inference from the passage is hazardous: there is a sense in which Theseus' statement is true, for the artist and the lover do collide, like the madman, with what 'cool reason' chooses to term the realities of life. The eloquent ring of the words is scarcely suggestive of dramatic irony, while the description of the poet's pen as giving to 'airy nothing a local habitation and a name' [V. i. 16-17], applies with curious exactness to Shakespere's own method in *A Midsummer Night's Dream*.

Contrasted with the serene fortunes of Theseus and Hippolyta is the troubled lot of humbler lovers, due, in its orgin, to purely human failings. The fickle Demetrius has shifted his affections from Helena to Hermia, whose father Egeus favours the match, but Hermia is constant to Lysander, while Helena still 'dotes in idolatry' [I. i. 109] upon her inconstant wooer. The Athenian law as expounded by Theseus . . . enforces upon Hermia obedience to her father's wishes on pain of death or perpetual maidenhood. But Lysander suggests escape to a classical 'Gretna Green,' seven leagues from the town, where the sharp Athenian law does not run, and fixes a trysting-place for the following night within the neighbouring wood. That Hermia should reveal the secret to Helena, and that she in her turn should put Demetrius on the fugitive's track, merely to 'have his sight thither and back again' [I. i. 251], is a transparently clumsy device for concentrating the four lovers on a single spot, which betrays the hand of the immature playwright. Within the wood the power of human motive is suspended for that of enchantment, and at a touch of Puck's magic herb, Lysander and Demetrius are 'translated,' and ready to cross swords for the love of the erewhile flouted Helena. Thus all things befall preposterously, and reason holds as little sway over action as in a dream, though it is surely overstrained to find, with Gervinus [see excerpt above, 1849-50], a definitely allegorical significance in the comic entanglement, the more so that the dramatic execution is at this point somewhat crude. Lysander and Demetrius are little more than lay figures, and the only difference between Helena and Hermia is that the latter is shorter of stature, and has a vixenish temper, of which she gives a violent display in the unseemly quarrel scene. But at last, by Oberon's command Dian's bud undoes on the eyes of Lysander the work of Cupid's flower, and the close of the period of enchantment is broadly and effectively marked by the inrush at dawn of exuberant, palpable life in the shape of Theseus' hunting party, whose horns and 'halloes' reawaken the sleepers to everyday realities. But, as in *The Errors,* out of the confusions of the moment is born an abiding result. Demetrius is henceforward true to Helena: the caprice of magic has redressed the caprice of passion, and the lovers return to Athens 'with league whose date till death shall never end' [III. ii. 373].

Deep reflective power and subtle insight into character came slowly to Shakespere, as to lesser men, but fancy has its flowering season in youth, and never has it shimmered with a more delicate and iridescent bloom than the fairy-world of *A Midsummer Night's Dream.* Through woodland vistas, where the Maymoon struggles with the dusk, elfland opens into sight, ethereal, impalpable, spun out of gossamer and dew, and yet strangely consistent and credible. For this kingdom of shadows reproduces in miniature the structure of human society. Here, as on earth, there are royal rulers, with courts, ministers, warriors, jesters, and, in fine, all the pomp and circumstance of mortal sovereignty. And what plausibility there is in every detail, worked out with an unfaltering instinct for just and delicate gradation! In this realm of the microscopic an acorn-cup is a place of shelter, and a cast snake-skin, or the leathern wing of a rear-mouse, an ample coat: the night tapers are honey-bags of humble-bees lit at the glow-worm's eyes, and the fairy chorus, to whom the third part of a moment is a measurable portion of time, charm from the side of their sleeping mistress such terrible monsters as blindworms, spiders, and beetles black. Over these tiny creatures morality has no sway: theirs is a delicious sense life, a revel of epicurean joy in nature's sweets and beauties. To dance 'by paved fountain or by rushy brook' [II. i. 84], to rest on banks canopied with flowers, to feed on apricoks and grapes, and mulberries, to tread the groves till the 'eastern gate all firey red' [III. ii. 391] turns the green sea into gold—such are the delights which make up their round of existence. In Puck, 'the lob of spirits,' this merry temper takes a more roguish form, a gusto in the topsy-turvy, in the things that befall preposterously, and an elfin glee in gulling mortals according to their folly. With his zest for knavish pranks, for mocking practical jokes upon 'gossips' and 'wisest aunts,' this merry wanderer of the night is indeed a spirit different in sort from the ethereal dream fairies, and it is natural that Oberon's vision of Cupid all armed should be hid from his gross sight. Moonlight and woodland have for him no spell of beauty, but they form a congenial sphere in which to play the game of mystification and cross-purposes. Thus his very unlikeness to the other shadows marks him out as the ally and henchman of Oberon in his quarrel with the fairy queen and her court. For the love troubles of mortals have their miniature counterpart in the jealousy of the elfin royal pair, springing in the main, as befits their nature, from an aesthetic rivalry for the possession of a lovely Indian boy, though by an ingenious touch, which unites the natural and supernatural realms, a further incitement is the undue favour with which Oberon regards the 'bouncing Amazon' Hippolyta, balanced by Titania's attachment to Theseus. And as the human wooers are beguiled by the power of Cupid's magic herb, the fairy queen is in like manner victim-

ized. But with correct instinct Shakespere makes her deception far the more extravagant. Fairyland is the world of perennial surprise, and it must be a glaringly fantastic incongruity that arrests attention there. But the most exciting canons of improbability are satisfied when Titania, whose very being is spun out of light and air and dew, fastens her affections upon the unpurged 'mortal grossness' of Bottom, upon humanity with its asinine attributes focussed and gathered to a head. To attack his queen in her essential nature, to make her whose only food is beauty lavish her endearments upon a misshapen monster, is a masterpiece of revenge on Oberon's part. And so persuasive is the art of the dramatist that our pity is challenged for Titania's infatuation, with its pathetically reckless squandering of pearls before swine, and thus we hail with joy her release from her dotage, her reconciliation with Oberon, and the end of jars in fairyland, celebrated with elfin ritual of dance and song.

In designedly aggressive contrast to the dwellers in the shadow world is the crew of hempen homespuns headed by sweet bully Bottom. Among the many forms of genius there is to be reckoned the asinine variety, which wins for a man the cordial recognition of his supremacy among fools, and of this Bottom is a choice type. In the preparation of the Interlude in honour of the Duke's marriage, though Quince is nominally the manager, Bottom, through the force of his commanding personality, is throughout the directing spirit. His brother craftsmen have some doubts about their qualifications for heroic rôles, but this protean actor and critic is ready for any and every part, from lion to lady, and is by universal consent selected as *jeune premier* of the company in the character of Pyramus, 'a most lovely gentleman-like man.' Bereft of his services, the comedy, it is admitted on all hands, cannot go forward: 'it is not possible: you have not a man in all Athens able to discharge Pyramus but he' [IV. ii. 7-8]. Fostered by such hero-worship, Bottom's egregious self-complacency develops to the point where his metamorphosis at the hands of Puck seems merely an exquisitely fitting climax to a natural process of evolution. And even when thus 'translated,' he retains his versatile faculty of adapting himself to any part; the amorous advances of Titania in no wise disturb his equanimity, and he is quite at ease with Peaseblossom and Cobweb. A sublime self-satisfaction may triumph in situations where the most delicate tact or the most sympathetic intelligence would be nonplussed.

But Shakespere, in introducing his crew of patches into his fairy drama, had an aim beyond satirizing fussy egotism or securing an effect of broad comic relief. It is a peculiarity of his dramatic method to produce variations upon a single theme in the different portions of a play. *Love's Labour's Lost* is an instance of this, and *A Midsummer Night's Dream* is further illustration, though of a less obvious kind. For in the rehearsal and setting forth of their comedy, Bottom and his friends enter a debateable domain, which, like that of the fairies, hovers round the solid work-a-day world, and yet is not of it. There is a point of view from which life may be regarded as the reality of which art, and in especial dramatic art, is the 'shadow,' the very word used by Theseus in relation to the workmen's play. Thus in their grotesque devices and makeshifts these rude mechanicals are really facing the question of the relation of shadow to substance, the immemorial question of realism in art and on the stage. The classical maxim that 'Medea shall not kill her children in sight of the audience' lest the feelings of the spectators should be harrowed beyond endurance, finds a burlesque echo in Bottom's solicitude lest the ladies should be terrified by the drawing of Pyramus' sword, or the entrance of so fearful a wild-fowl as your lion. Hence the necessity for a prologue to say tht Pyramus is not killed indeed, and for the apparition of half Snug the joiner's face through the lion's neck, and his announcement that he is not come hither as a lion, but is 'a man as other men are' [III. i. 44]. Scenery presents further difficulties, but here, as there is no risk of wounding delicate susceptibilities, realism is given full rein. The moon herself is pressed into the service, but owing to her capricious nature, she is given an understudy in the person of Starveling carrying a bush of thorns and a lanthorn. It is only the hypercriticism of the Philistine Theseus that finds fault with this arrangement on the score that the man should be put into the lanthorn. 'How is it else the man in the moon?' [V. i. 247-48].

The 'tedious belief scene of young Pyramus and his love Thisbe' [V. i. 56-7], is more elaborated specimen of those plays within plays, of which Shakespere had already given a sketch in *Love's Labour's Lost,* and for which he retained a fondness in all stages of his career. It is a burlesque upon the dramas of the day, in which classical subjects were handled with utter want of dignity, and with incongruous extravagance of style. The jingling metres, the mania for alliteration, the far-fetched and fantastic epithets, the meaningless invocations, the wearisome repetition of emphatic words, are all ridiculed with a boisterous glee, which was an implicit warrant that, when the young dramatist should hereafter turn to tragic or classical themes, his own work would be free from such disfiguring affectations, or, at worst, would take from them only a superficial taint. And, indeed, what potency of future triumphs on the very summits of dramatic art lay already revealed in the genius which out of an incidental entertainment could frame the complex and gorgeous pagentry of *A Midsummer Night's Dream;* and which, when denied, by the necessities of the occasion, an ethical motive, could fall back for inspiration on an enchanting metaphysic, not of the schools but of the stage, whose contrasts of shadow and reality are shot, now in threads of gossamer lightness, now in homelier and coarser fibre, into the web and woof of this unique hymeneal masque. (pp. 184-90)

> *Frederick S. Boas, ''Shakespere's Poems: The Early Period of Comedy,'' in his* Shakespere and His Predecessors, *Charles Scribner's Sons, 1896, pp. 158-96.*

G. K. CHESTERTON (essay date 1904)

[*Chiefly remembered today for his detective stories, Chesterton was also an eminent biographer, essayist, novelist, poet, journalist, dramatist, and critic during the early twentieth century. His essays are characterized by their humor, frequent use of paradox, and rambling style. Chesterton's essay on* A Midsummer Night's Dream *originally appeared as a two-part article in 1904. In the following excerpt from that essay, Chesterton comments on the accuracy with which Shakespeare has reproduced the fantastic and illogical qualities of a dream. He argues that the dreamlike atmosphere softens the impact of the "events in the wandering wood," which are "not merely melancholy but bitterly cruel and ignominious," and transforms them from tragedy into comedy. Although his comment on the dark side of the play is a brief one, Chesterton is one of the first critics to view the dramatic action as equivocal. For further discussion of the tragic and dark undercurrents in* A Midsummer Night's Dream, *see the excerpts by Cumberland Clark (1931), G. Wilson Knight (1932), Jan Kott (1964), Charles R. Lyons (1971), Hugh M. Richmond (1971), David Bevington (1975), and Mordecai Marcus (1981). Chesterton also maintains that although the setting is purportedly classical, Shakespeare has actually presented a portrait of "Merrie England," with Theseus ("only an English squire"), the me-*

chanicals, and the fairies exhibiting qualities that were typical of the inhabitants of the English countryside many centuries ago. Other critics who have treated the bucolic aspects of the play include George Brandes (1895-96) and C. L. Barber (1959). Chesterton's assessment of Bottom as neither vulgar nor unimaginative but sensitive to literature and the sounds of words is echoed by such later critics as H. B. Charlton (1933), John Palmer (1944), and Elizabeth Sewell (1960).]

The greatest of Shakespeare's comedies is also, from a certain point of view, the greatest of his plays. No one would maintain that it occupied this position in the matter of psychological study if by psychological study we mean the study of individual characters in a play. No one would maintain that Puck was a character in the sense that Falstaff is a character, or that the critic stood awed before the psychology of Peaseblossom. But there is a sense in which the play is perhaps a greater triumph of psychology than *Hamlet* itself. It may well be questioned whether in any other literary work in the world is so vividly rendered a social and spiritual atmosphere. There is an atmosphere in *Hamlet,* for instance, a somewhat murky and even melodramatic one, but it is subordinate to the great character, and morally inferior to him; the darkness is only a background for the isolated star of intellect. But *A Midsummer Night's Dream* is a psychological study, not of a solitary man, but of a spirit that unites mankind. (p. 10)

A study of the play from a literary or philosophical point of view must therefore be founded upon some serious realisation of what this atmosphere is. In a lecture upon *As You Like It,* Mr. Bernard Shaw made a suggestion which is an admirable example of his amazing ingenuity and of his one most interesting limitation. In maintaining that the light sentiment and optimism of the comedy were regarded by Shakespeare merely as the characteristics of a more or less cynical pot-boiler, he actually suggested that the title "As You Like It" was a taunting address to the public in disparagement of their taste and the dramatist's own work. If Mr. Bernard Shaw had conceived of Shakesepare as insisting that Ben Jonson should wear Jaeger underclothing or join the Blue Ribbon Army, or distribute little pamphlets for the non-payment of rates, he could scarcely have conceived anything more violently opposed to the whole spirit of Elizabethan comedy than the spiteful and priggish modernism of such a taunt. Shakespeare might make the fastidious and cultivated Hamlet, moving in his own melancholy and purely mental world, warn players against an over-indulgence towards the rabble. But the very soul and meaning of the great comedies is that of an uproarious communion between the public and the play, a communion so chaotic that whole scenes of silliness and violence lead us almost to think that some of the "rowdies" from the pit have climbed over the footlights. (pp. 10-11)

Now in the reason for [Shaw's] modern and pedantic error lies the whole secret and difficulty of such plays as *A Midsummer Night's Dream.* The sentiment of such play, so far as it can be summed up at all, can be summed up in one sentence. It is the mysticism of happiness. That is to say, it is the conception that as man lives upon a borderland he may find himself in the spiritual or supernatural atmosphere, not only through being profoundly sad or meditative, but by being extravagantly happy. The soul might be rapt out of the body in an agony of sorrow, or a trance of ecstasy; but it might also be rapt out of the body in a paroxysm of laughter. Sorrow we know can go beyond itself; so, according to Shakespeare, can pleasure go beyond itself and become something dangerous and unknown. And the reason that the logical and destructive modern school, of which

Mr. Bernard Shaw is an example, does not grasp this purely exuberant nature of the comedies is simply that their logical and destructive attitude have rendered impossible the very experience of this preternatural exuberance. We cannot realise *As You Like It* if we are always considering it as we understand it. We cannot have *A Midsummer's Night Dream* if our one object in life is to keep ourselves awake with the black coffee of criticism. The whole question which is balanced, and balanced nobly and fairly, in *A Midsummer Night's Dream,* is whether the life of waking, or the life of the vision, is the real life, the *sine quâ non* of man. (p. 12)

In pure poetry and the intoxication of words, Shakespeare never rose higher than he rises in this play. But in spite of this fact, the supreme literary merit of *A Midsummer Night's Dream* is a merit of design. The amazing symmetry, the amazing artistic and moral beauty of that design, can be stated very briefly. The story opens in the sane and common world with the pleasant seriousness of very young lovers and very young friends. Then, as the figures advance into the tangled wood of young troubles and stolen happiness, a change and bewilderment begins to fall on them. They lose their way and their wits for they are in the heart of fairyland. Their words, their hungers, their very figures grow more and more dim and fantastic, like dreams within dreams, in the supernatural mist of Puck. Then the dream-fumes begin to clear, and characters and spectators begin to awaken together to the noise of horns and dogs and the clean and bracing morning. Theseus, the incarnation of a happy and generous rationalism, expounds in hackneyed and superb lines the same view of such psychic experiences, pointing out with a reverent and sympathetic scepticism that all these fairies and spells are themselves but the emanations, the unconscious masterpieces, of man himself. The whole company falls back into a splendid human laughter. There is a rush for banqueting and private theatricals, and over all these things ripple one of those frivolous and inspired conversations in which every good saying seems to die in giving birth to another. If ever the son of a man in his wanderings was at home and drinking by the fireside, he is at home in the house of Theseus. All the dreams have been forgotten, as a melancholy dream remembered throughout the morning might be forgotten in the human certainty of any other triumphant evening party; and so the play seems naturally ended. It began on the earth and it ends on the earth. Thus to round off the whole midsummer night's dream in an eclipse of daylight is an effect of genius. But of this comedy, as I have said, the mark is that genius goes beyond itself; and one touch is added which makes the play colossal. Theseus and his train retire with a crashing finale, full of humour and wisdom and things set right, and silence falls on the house. Then there comes a faint sound of little feet, and for a moment, as it were, the elves look into the house, asking which is the reality. "Suppose we are the realities and they the shadows." If that ending were acted properly any modern man would feel shaken to his marrow if he had to walk home from the theatre through a country lane.

It is a trite matter, of course, though in a general criticism a more or less indispensable one to comment upon another point of artistic perfection, the extraordinarily human and accurate manner in which the play catches the atmosphere of a dream. The chase and tangle and frustration of the incidents and personalities are well known to every one who has dreamt of perpetually falling over precipices or perpetually missing trains. While following out clearly and legally the necessary narrative of the drama, the author contrives to include every one of the main peculiarities of the exasperating dream. Here is the pursuit of the man we cannot catch, the flight from the man we cannot see; here is the perpetual returning to the same place, here is the crazy alteration in the very objects of our desire, the substitution of one face for another face, the putting of the wrong souls in the wrong bodies, the fantastic disloyalties of the night, all this is as obvious as it is important. It is perhaps somewhat more worth remarking that there is about this confusion of comedy yet another essential characteristic of dreams. A dream can commonly be described as possessing an utter discordance of incident combined with a curious unity of mood; everything changes but the dreamer. It may begin with anything and end with anything, but if the dreamer is sad at the end he will be sad as if by prescience at the beginning; if he is cheerful at the beginning he will be cheerful if the stars fall. *A Midsummer Night's Dream* has in a most singular degree effected this difficult, this almost desperate subtlety. The events in the wandering wood are in themselves, and regarded as in broad daylight, not merely melancholy but bitterly cruel and ignominious. But yet by the spreading of an atmosphere as magic as the fog of Puck, Shakespeare contrives to make the whole matter mysteriously hilarious while it is palpably tragic, and mysteriously charitable, while it is in itself cynical. He contrives somehow to rob tragedy and treachery of their full sharpness, just as a toothache or a deadly danger from a tiger, or a precipice, is robbed of its sharpness in a pleasant dream. The creation of a brooding sentiment like this, a sentiment not merely independent of but actually opposed to the events, is a much greater triumph of art than the creation of the character of Othello.

It is difficult to approach critically so great a figure as that of Bottom the Weaver. He is greater and more mysterious than Hamlet, because the interest of such men as Bottom consists of a rich subconsciousness, and that of Hamlet in the comparatively superficial matter of a rich consciousness. . . . Greatness is a certain indescribable but perfectly familiar and palpable quality of size in the personality, of steadfastness, of strong flavour, of easy and natural self-expression. Such a man is as firm as a tree and as unique as a rhinoceros, and he might quite easily be as stupid as either of them. Fully as much as the great poet towers above the small poet the great fool towers above the small fool. . . . And this creature so hard to describe, so easy to remember, the august and memorable fool, has never been so sumptuously painted as in the Bottom of *A Midsummer Night's Dream.*

Bottom has the supreme mark of this real greatness in that like the true saint or the true hero he only differs from humanity in being as it were more human than humanity. It is not true, as the idle materialists of today suggest, that compared to the majority of men the hero appears cold and dehumanised; it is the majority who appear cold and dehumanised in the presence of greatness. Bottom, like Don Quixote and Uncle Toby [in Laurence Sterne's *Tristram Shandy*] and Mr. Richard Swiveller [in Charles Dicken's *The Old Curiosity Shop*] and the rest of the Titans, has a huge and unfathomable weakness, his silliness is on a great scale, and when he blows his own trumpet it is like the trumpet of the Resurrection. . . . Bottom's sensibility to literature is perfectly fiery and genuine, a great deal more genuine than that of a great deal many cultivated critics of literature—"the raging rocks, and shivering shocks shall break the locks of prison gates, and Phibbus' car shall shine from far, and make and mar the foolish fates" [I. ii. 31-8] is exceedingly good poetical diction with a real throb and swell in it, and if it is slightly and almost imperceptibly deficient in the matter of sense, it is certainly every bit as sensible as a good many other rhetorical speeches in Shakespeare put into the mouths of kings and lovers and even the spirits of the dead. If Bottom liked cant for its own sake the fact only constitutes another point of sympathy between him and his literary creator. But the style of the thing, though deliberately bombastic and ludicrous, is quite literary, the alliteration falls like wave upon wave, and the whole verse, like a billow mounts higher and higher before it crashes. There is nothing mean about this folly; nor is there in the whole realm of literature a figure so free from vulgarity. . . . It is worth remarking as an extremely fine touch in the picture of Bottom that his literary taste is almost everywhere concerned with sound rather than sense. He begins the rehearsal with a boisterous readiness, ''Thisby, the flowers of odious savours sweete'' [III. i. 82.]. ''Odours, odours,'' says Quince, in remonstrance, and the word is accepted in accordance with the cold and heavy rules which require an element of meaning in a poetical passage. But ''Thisby, the flowers of odious savours sweete'', Bottom's version, is an immeasurably finer and more resonant line. The ''i'' which he inserts is an inspiration of metricism.

There is another aspect of this great play which ought to be kept familiarly in the mind. Extravagant as is the masquerade of the story, it is a very perfect aesthetic harmony down to such *coup-de-maître* [''a master-stroke''] as the name of Bottom, or the flower called Love in Idleness. In the whole manner it may be said that there is one accidental discord; that is in the name of Theseus, and the whole city of Athens in which events take place. Shakespeare's description of Athens in *A Midsummer Night's Dream* is the best description of England that he or any one else ever wrote. Theseus is quite obviously only an English squire, fond of hunting, kindly to his tenants, hospitable with a certain flamboyant vanity. The mechanics are English mechanics, talking to each other with the queer formality of the poor. Above all, the fairies are English; to compare them with the beautiful patrician spirits of Irish legend, for instance, is suddenly to discover that we have, after all, a folk-lore and a mythology, or had it at least in Shakespeare's day. Robin Goodfellow, upsetting the old women's ale, or pulling the stool from under them, has nothing of the poignant Celtic beauty; his is the horse-play of the invisible world. Perhaps it is some debased inheritance of English life which makes American ghosts so fond of quite undignified practical jokes. But this union of mystery with farce is a note of the medieval English. The play is the last glimpse of Merrie England, that distant but shining and quite indubitable country. It would be difficult indeed to define wherein lay the peculiar truth of the phrase ''merrie England'', though some conception of it is quite necessary to the comprehension of *A Midsummer Night's Dream*. (pp. 13-20)

> G. K. Chesterton, '' 'A Midsummer Night's Dream','' in his *The Common Man, Sheed and Ward, 1950, pp. 10-21.*

E. K. CHAMBERS   (essay date 1905)

[*Chambers occupies a transitional position in Shakespearean criticism, one which connects the biographical sketches and character analyses of the nineteenth century with the historical, technical, and textual criticism of the twentieth century. While a member of the education department at Oxford University, Chambers earned his reputation as a scholar with his multivolume works,* The Medieval Stage (1903) *and* The Elizabethan Stage (1923), *while he also edited* The Red Letter Shakespeare. *Chambers both investigated the purpose and limitations of each dramatic genre as Shakespeare presented it and speculated on how the dramatist's work was influenced by contemporary historical issues and his own frame of mind. In the following excerpt, taken from his introduction to* The Red Letter *edition of* A Midsummer Night's Dream (1905), *Chambers maintains that love ''as interpreted by the comic spirit'' is the play's central thematic interest. He argues that the comic view of love emphasizes its capriciousness, lawlessness, and inconstancy and notes that the fairy influence on the young lovers is symbolic rather than actual, since it ''does not bring about anything which would have been impossible or improbable without it.'' Other critics who have discussed the issue of the capriciousness and inconstancy of the young lovers in* A Midsummer Night's Dream *included G. G. Gervinus (1849-50), H. B. Charlton (1933), E. C. Pettet (1949), Ernest Schanzer (1951), George A. Bonnard (1956), John Vyvyan (1961), and Peter G. Phialas (1966). Chambers also remarks on Bottom's complete self-possession in every circumstance and calls him the first of Shakespeare's great comic creations. For additional analyses of Bottom's nature and significance, see the excerpts by William Maginn (1837), Charles Cowden Clarke (1863), G. K. Chesterton (1904), H. B. Charlton (1933), and John Palmer (1944).*]

[*A Midsummer Night's Dream*] is primarily a court revel. It was doubtless written for a wedding, and possibly for a wedding at which Elizabeth was present. It has the profusion of dance and song, the picturesque staging and pretty costumes, the sprinkling of courtly compliment, the piquant contrast of poetry and clowning, which were the delight of the nobles and maids of honour who assembled at Gloriana's palace of Greenwich. But at the same time it is a true comedy, a deliberate picture of life as life reveals itself to the shrewd insight of the comic spirit. The theme is love—an obvious theme for a wedding play, even if it were not the one about which Shakespeare's imagination was principally exercised at the moment. He had written *The Two Gentlemen of Verona*, and had either written or was on the point of writing *Romeo and Juliet*, with its tragic burden of two lives ruined and at the same time ennobled by love. Even in *Romeo and Juliet* the comic as well as the tragic view of love is present. It is incarnate in the critical wit of Mercutio. But in *A Midsummer Night's Dream* it has undisputed sway. . . . Love, as interpreted by the comic spirit, is a certain fine lunacy in the brain of youth; not an integral part of life, but a disturbing element in it. The lover is a being of strange caprices and strange infidelities, beyond the control of reason, and swayed with every gust of passion. He is at odds for the time with all the established order of things, a rebel against the authority of parents, a rebel against friendship, a rebel against his own vows. This is love as it figures in comedy, and in the presentation and analysis of this lies the point of the play.

Bearing then in mind this central idea of the lawlessness and the laughableness of love, one may observe how carefully, for all the apparent whimsicality of structure, it is kept to the front in the working out of the plot. As is generally the case in Shakespeare's comedies, this is composed of several stories, which are woven together with remarkable ingenuity. You have the story of Theseus' wedding, the story of the Athenian lovers, the story of the quarrel of Oberon and Titania, the story of the handicraftsmen's play, and finally the story or interlude of Pyramus and Thisbe. It is the first of these which serves as the link that holds all the rest together; for it is at Theseus' wedding that Hermia's fate is to be decided; it is to celebrate this that the fairies have come from the farthest steppe of India, and it is for this that Bottom and his fellows are painfully conning their interlude. But the most important story from the point of view of the comic idea, and the one to which most space is devoted, is that of the Athenian lovers. (pp. 79-81)

Shakespeare does not, on this occasion, look to psychology to body forth his meaning. In *Romeo and Juliet,* he shows us the difference which love makes, in the actual characters of the lovers as they blossom out before us. But it is a commonplace that the lovers of *A Midsummer Night's Dream* are faintly sketched and barely differentiated. Helena is tall and fair and timid; Hermia is little and dark and shrewish. Demetrius is crabbed and Lysander is languid. It is difficult to say much more. They are but the abstract Hes and Shes of the conventional love-story. But this want of characterization is of little importance, because symbolism comes in to take the place of psychology. The transferences of affection which form the principal revolutions of the story are represented as due to supernatural agency, to the somewhat randomly exercised power of the fairies. Moreover, taking perhaps a hint from Lyly, Shakespeare invites us to consider the whole thing as a dream. Here is the significance of the title. It is life seen through a glass darkly; such a vision of life as a man might have on Midsummer Night, the one season of year around which Elizabethan superstition gathered most closely, when herbs were believed to have their especial virtues, and strange beings to be abroad. And yet it is not all a dream, or, if a dream, it is one which passes very easily into actuality. For these inconstancies, of which Oberon's love in idleness is the cause, are after all not really different in kind from the initial inconstancy of Demetrius to Helena, for which no such reason is proposed. And again, when Demetrius is by magic restored to his first love, the effects of this continue on into the waking life as a quite natural thing which provokes no amazement. So that in fact, as far as the story of the lovers is concerned, the introduction of the supernatural element does not bring about anything which would have been impossible or improbable without it. The magical love in idleness really does nothing more than represent symbolically the familiar workings of actual love in idleness in the human heart. Boys in love change their minds just so, or almost just so, without any whisper of the fairies to guide them. Romeo left his Rosaline quite as suddenly as Lysander left his Hermia. Here, then, is the function of the supernatural in *A Midsummer Night's Dream.* The mystery, so to call it, the inexplicability which is bound up with the central idea of the play, is the existence of that freakish irresponsible element of human nature out of which, to the eye of the comic spirit, the ethical and emotional vagaries of lovers take their rise. And that this element does exist is recognized and emphasized by Shakespeare in his usual way, when he takes the workings of it in the story and explains them symbolically as due to the interference of fairy agency. (pp. 82-4)

When we turn to the fairies, we find that what enters into human life only as a transitory disturbing element, is in them the normal law of their being. They are irresponsible creatures throughout, eternal children. They belong to the winds and the clouds and the flowers, to all in nature that is beautiful and gracious and fleeting; but of the characteristics by which man differs from these, the sense of law and the instinct of self-control, they show no trace. Puck, the fairy jester, is a buffoon of spirits, whose sport it is to bring perplexity upon hapless mortals. Oberon and Titania will be jealous and be reconciled to each other a dozen times a day, while for culmination of their story you have the absurd spectacle of a fairy in love with an ass. So that in them is represented, as it were *in vacuo* ["'in a vacuum"], the very quality of which it is the object of the play to discern the partial and occasional workings in the heart of humanity.

In the story of the handicraftsmen, the central idea does not find any direct illustration. The story is required, partly to

introduce the interlude, but still more to provide that comic contrast which was always an essential feature of a mask, or a play written on the lines of a mask. It is ingeniously interwoven into the fairy story by making Bottom the instrument of Oberon's revenge upon Titania. And it is in the person of Bottom that the whole humour of the thing consists. He is, with the possible exception of the Nurse in *Romeo and Juliet,* the first of Shakespeare's supreme comic creations, greater than the Costard of *Love's Labour's Lost* or the Launce of *The Two Gentlemen of Verona,* as the masterpiece is greater than the imperfect sketch. From beginning to end of the play his absolute self-possession never for a moment fails him. He lords it over his fellow actors, as though he, and not Quince, were poet and stage-manager in one; he accepts the amorous attentions of a queen with calm serenity as no more than might naturally have been expected; nor does he ever, either before or after his transformation, betray the slightest suspicion of the fact that he is after all only an ass. It has often been thought that in the rehearsal scenes Shakespeare was drawing upon the humours of such rustic actors as might have ventured a Whitsun pastoral at Stratford-upon-Avon; yet one fears that the foibles of the green-room are much the same in the humblest and the loftiest walks of the profession, and who shall say that the poet is not poking good-humoured fun at some of his fellows of the Lord Chamberlain's company?

Finally, with the interlude, we come back to the central idea once more. For in the ill-starred loves of Pyramus and Thisbe, their assignation, their elopement, and their terrible end, we have but a burlesque presentment of the same theme which has occupied us throughout. It is all a matter of how the poet chooses to put it. Precisely the same situation that in *Romeo and Juliet* will ask our tears, shall here move unextinguishable laughter. And so the serious interest of the play dissolves in mirth, and while the musicians break into the exquisite poetry of the epithalamium, the playwright stands and watches us with the smile of wise tolerance on his lips. (pp. 85-7)

> *E. K. Chambers, "'A Midsummer Night's Dream'," in his* Shakespeare: A Survey, *1925. Reprint by Hill and Wang, 1959?, pp. 77-87.*

SAMUEL B. HEMINGWAY   (essay date 1911)

[*Adopting a biographical approach, Hemingway argues that* A Midsummer Night's Dream *is Shakespeare's personal reaction against the excessive romantic idealism of his earlier play,* Romeo and Juliet. *He also believes that the Pyramus and Thisbe interlude is "unquestionably a burlesque not only of the romantic tragedy of love in general, but of* Romeo and Juliet *in particular." Among other critics who have similarly interpreted the play-within-the-play, Hugh M. Richmond (1971) has contended that Shakespeare's treatment of sex in* A Midsummer Night's Dream *is an explicit condemnation of Romeo's limited view of love, and Mark Van Doren (see Additional Bibliography) shared Hemingway's estimation of the interlude as Shakespeare's parody of* Romeo and Juliet. *For further commentary on the play-within-the-play in* A Midsummer Night's Dream, *see the excerpts by G. G. Gervinus (1849-50), Edward Dowden (1881), Denton J. Snider (1890), George Brandes (1895-96), Frederick S. Boas (1896), Paul N. Siegel (1953), and Elizabeth Sewell (1960).*]

Various parallels in *Romeo and Juliet* and *A Midsummer Night's Dream* tend to support the theory of Mr. Sidney Lee, Mr. Stopford Brooke, and others that the traditional chronology which puts the *Dream* first is untenable. It is the purpose of this paper to show that wherever parallels exist, the debt is probably from the *Dream* to *Romeo and Juliet,* and that a consideration of the spirit of the two plays, of the different attitudes towards love and life which they present, leads us to the conclusion that there is a close connection between the two, and that the *Dream* is the natural reaction of Shakespeare's mind from *Romeo and Juliet*. (pp. 78-9)

Assuming . . . that the *Dream* was written soon, perhaps immediately, after *Romeo and Juliet*, let us see if a comparative study of the two plays will not support our hypothesis.

> Awake the pert and nimble spirit of mirth,
> Turn melancholy forth to funerals
>
> [I. i. 13-14]

says Theseus in the first scene of the *Dream*, and later in the first scene of Act V:

> Lovers and madmen have such seething brains,
> Such shaping fantasies, that apprehend
> More than cool reason ever comprehends.
> The lunatic, the lover, and the poet
> Are of imagination all compact.
>
> [V. i. 4-8]

These two speeches of Theseus, to whom Shakespeare has given much of his own clear-eyed serenity and benignity, are, it seems to me, significant manifestations of the poet's own mental attitude when he created the *Dream*. He has just finished a passionate, romantic tragedy of love; in this tragedy he has been led into somewhat excessive emotionalism—certainly more so than in any other play—his hero-lover *has* at times been "unseemly woman in a seeming man, and ill-beseeming beast in seeming both" [*Romeo and Juliet*, III. iii. 112-13]; "cool reason," serenity and poise have had no effect upon the "seething brain" of the lover. Now Shakespeare's own brain is not normally a seething one, his "blood and judgment are well commingled"; true, he is not a Friar Laurence nor even a Theseus, but neither is he a Romeo. And now as he looks at his tragedy of love, what impression does it make upon him? Be it remembered that we are now dealing with the young man, Shakespeare, not with the man who, out of the storm and stress of his soul, evolved a Hamlet, an Othello, a Lear, or a Macbeth, but with the joyous, exuberant, deep-souled, clear-eyed poet of the early comedies. Is it not natural that to him, far more than to any one else, the emotionalism and sentimentalism of his tragedy should seem a trifle exaggerated and ridiculous, and the tragic fate of the lovers morbidly gloomy? And so, shaking himself free of romantic ideals of love, he somewhat quizzically allies lovers, lunatics, and poets; shows us in Theseus and Hippolyta the calm and serene love of middle age; represents the young, romantic lovers (the men, at least) as taking themselves very seriously, but in reality being ruled entirely by the fairies, one minute suffering agonies of love for one woman, the next for another; love a mere madness, entirely under the control of the fairies (be it noted that the magic juice has permanent effect upon Demetrius); and at the beginning of the play strikes the keynote of it all:

> Awake the pert and nimble spirit of mirth,
> Turn melancholy forth.
>
> [I. i. 13-14]

The similiarities between the situation at the beginning of the *Dream* and the main situation in *Romeo and Juliet* are obvious, and it seems far more probable that Shakespeare borrowed and condensed material from *Romeo and Juliet*, for mere mechanical purposes here, than that he developed a great tragic plot

from this simple situation in which he does not seem to have been particularly interested. (p. 79)

The only thing in *Romeo and Juliet* which seems to me clearly to be borrowed from the *Dream* is Mercutio's description of Queen Mab. It has the exquisite delicacy and daintiness of the descriptive passages of the *Dream*, but it is not an integral part of *Romeo and Juliet*, and there is no particular reason why, in this play, Shakespeare should be thinking of fairies or fairyland. Moreover, if he had already conceived and created Queen Mab when he wrote the *Dream*, would he not probably have made some reference to her in the fairy scenes of the latter? This is by no means, however, an unsurmountable difficulty in the establishment of our main thesis, for the first edition of *Romeo and Juliet* was published after the composition of *A Midsummer Night's Dream*, and the very episodic nature of the Queen Mab speech makes it quite possible that it was a late addition.

"The tedious, brief scene of Pyramus and Thisbe" [V. i. 56-7] is, I think, unquestionably a burlesque not only of the romantic tragedy of love in general, but of *Romeo and Juliet* in partiuclar. The two catastrophes are almost identical, and it seems hardly probable that any dramatist would write his burlesque first and his serious play afterward. (p. 80)

Samuel B. Hemingway, "The Relation of 'A Midsummer Night's Dream' to 'Romeo and Juliet'," in Modern Language Notes, Vol. XXVI, No. 3, March, 1911, pp. 78-80.

ENID WELSFORD (essay date 1927)

[*In unexcerpted sections of her* The Court Masque: A Study in the Relationship between Poetry & the Revels *(1927), Welsford describes the correlation between Elizabethan revels and the development of the seventeenth-century Court masque. Masques featured "scenic splendour," tableaux, music, and dancing and were commonly part of the entertainment at aristocratic weddings and formal dances. Welsford assesses* A Midsummer Night's Dream *as a "masque-like" play and compares it with John Milton's* Comus. *In the excerpt below, she maintains that the scenic element in Shakespeare's play is similar in importance to that in the masque, but she is principally concerned with the way in which the various characters of* A Midsummer Night's Dream *move through the dramatic action as if they were participating in a "figured ballet." This movement, she notes, lends the play a dance-like structure, an effect heightened by the rhythm of the poetry. She also compares the portions of the play depicting Bottom and the rude mechanicals to the anti-masque, which served as a comic foil to the main movement of the Court masque. Alan Brissenden (1981) has contended that dance is used as a commentary on the patterns of order and disorder in* A Midsummer Night's Dream, *and Richard David (see Additional Bibliography) has attributed the domination of formal poetry in the play to the tradition of the masque. For further discussion of other cultural and literary influences on Shakespeare's play, see the excerpts by David Ormerod (1978), M. E. Lamb (1979), and R. Chris Hassel, Jr. (1980).*]

The scenic element is almost as important in *A Midsummer Night's Dream* as in the masque, but it is treated in a very different way. The wood near Athens is not dependent upon, rather it is antagonistic to, the art of the scene painter. Even if *A Midsummer Night's Dream* was well-staged at Court, still Oberon's description of his surroundings could hardly be translated into terms of paint and canvas, for what scene painter would be quite equal to the 'bank where the wild thyme blows,' or, indeed, what human actor could obey Titania's stage direction:

> Come, now a roundel and a fairy song;
> Then, for the third part of a minute, hence
>   [II. ii. 1-2]

The feeling of the countryside, the romantic fairy-haunted earth has affected the very details of language.

> Your eyes are lode-stars; and your tongue's sweet air
> More tuneable than lark to shepherd's ear,
> When wheat is green, when hawthorn buds appear.
>   [I. i. 183-85]
>   (p. 325)

When Duke Theseus has left the lovers to themselves, Demetrius, still dazed and only half awake, murmurs:

> These thing seem small and undistingushable,
> Like far off mountains turned into clouds.
>   [IV. i. 186-87]

It is a fine image, giving just that suggestion of awe and uncertainty which was needed to soften the transition from dream to waking life. The magic of the phrase lies in the words 'small' and 'undistinguishable.' A lesser poet would probably have given the abstract idea in the first line and in the second its concrete illustration. But the word 'small' (instead of 'strange,' 'vague' or some other word of that kind) at once sets the imagination to work and suggests the picture which the next line expands, and the sound of the word 'undistinguishable,' with its accumulated syllables trailing off into silence, does for the ear what the word 'small' does for the eye, suggests the shimmering atmosphere, the blurred outline and the gradual vanishing of the distant mountains on the horizon.

Shakespeare has absorbed the scenic splendour of the masque, not only in description and picturesque language, but also in a blending of tones, a harmony of colours, which the poet has attained by a most delicate and subtle handling of the laws of resemblance and contrast. The play opens in the daylight, first in the Court, then in the cottage, and brings us into the presence of the two sets of characters who most emphatically belong to daylight and the solid earth, the genial cultivated rulers, the simple-minded artisans, the former serving as a framework, the latter as a foil to the poetry and moonshine of the dream. The excellence of the workmanship lies in the fact that the framework is organically connected with the picture, for Theseus and Hippolyta are accompanied by Philostrate the Master of the Revels. We are in the world of men, but men are in holiday mood. Ordinary workaday business is set aside, pomp, triumph, and revelling are in the air. Anything may happen. The moon is at once made the topic of conversation:

> Four days will quickly steep themselves in night;
> Four nights will quickly dream away the time;
> And then the moon, like to a silver bow
> New-bent in heaven, shall behold the night
> Of our solemnities.
>   [I. i. 7-11]

By the end of the first act our minds are full of the wood where Helena and Hermia used to lie 'upon faint primrose beds' [I. i. 215], where the young people used to meet 'to do observance to a morn of May' [I. i. 167], and where very shortly lovers and workmen are to assemble by moonlight for diverse purposes. Moonshine is almost as real a personage in Shakespeare's as in Bottom's play. Her presence permeates the ac-

tion, a delicate compliment to the maiden Queen, and Titania is merely a glancing beam of her light. Even the workmen help to make her presence felt:

> QUIN. Well, it shall be so. But there is two hard things, that is, to bring the moonlight into a chamber; for, you know, Pyramus and Thisby meet by moonlight.
>
> SNOUT. Doth the moon shine that night we play our play?
>
> BOT. A calendar, a calendar! look in the almanac; find out moonshine, find out moonshine.
>
> QUIN. Yes, it doth shine that night.
>
> BOT. Why, then may you leave a casement of the great chamberwindow, where we lay, open; and the moon may shine in at the casement.
>
> QUIN. Ay; or else one must come in with a bush of thorns and a lanthorne and say he comes to disfigure, or to present, the person of Moonshine.
>   [III. i. 47-61]

But if the transition from daylight to moonlight is delicately wrought, it is far surpassed by the gradual oncoming of the dawn in acts III and IV.

The first hint comes when Oberon commands Puck to cover the starry welkin with fog, the better to mislead the angry lovers. The latter replies:

> My fairy Lord, this must be done with haste,
> For night's swift dragons cut the cloud full fast,
> And yonder shines Aurora's harbinger.
>   [III. ii. 388-90]

Then in comes Lysander vainly hunting for Demetrius. Thwarted by the darkness he lies down to rest. . . . The lovers are all asleep on the flowery bank, when they are joined by Titania, Bottom and the fairies. Bottom has 'an exposition of sleep' [IV. i. 39] come upon him and, as he and the Fairy Queen rest together, Oberon and Puck arrive and conquer Cupid's flower by Dian's bud. Titania wakes, freed from the spell, takes hands with Oberon, and the day dawns.

> PUCK.   Fairy king, attend, and mark:
>   I do hear the morning lark.
> OBE.   Then, my queen, in silence sad,
>   Trip we after the night's shade;
>   We the globe can compass soon,
>   Swifter than the wandering moon.
>   [IV. i. 93-8]

The fairies vanish, a horn winds, Theseus, Hippolyta, and the rest break in with a clatter of horses and hounds, the day breaks and the shadows flee away. But the broad sunlight is not suited to the Midsummer Night's Dream, the day soon passes and gives place to torchlight. It would have been a simple plan to leave the fairy part in the centre of the play as a dream interval in the waking workaday world, but Shakespeare knew better than that. There is nothing more disappointing to a child than to find that the fairy tale was only a dream after all, and children know best how a fairy tale should be conducted.

> The iron tongue of midnight hath tolled twelve;
> Lovers, to bed; 'tis almost fairy time.
>   [V. i. 363-64]

Once more the colouring changes. The mortals are gone, the bright festal lights are dimmed, 'now the wasted brands do glow' [V. i. 375], now the fire is dead and drowsy and very quietly, very lightly, the fairies come in; dreamland has invaded reality, and who shall say which is which, for Puck left behind with his broom and his parting word swept the whole thing away, like the leaves of yester-year.

To compare a very great with a very small thing, the imaginative effect of this kind of plot-weaving is like that of the transformation scenes in ballet or pantomime, where groups of dancers come in like waves of colour, melting one into another. The effect is attractive even when crudely and unbeautifully designed. Transmuted into poetry it is of surpassing charm. (pp. 325-29).

The real soul of the masque . . . was [this] rhythmic movement of living bodies. It is owing to this fact that *A Midsummer Night's Dream* is more nearly related to the genuine masque than is *Comus*. In *Comus* . . . , though dances occur, they are merely incidental, and the play would be scarcely altered by their omission. In *A Midsummer Night's Dream* most—not all—of the dances are vitally connected with the plot. For instance, Titania's awakening in act IV, sc. I. is an important point in the play, for it is the point where the ravel begins to be untangled, and the occasion is celebrated by a dance of reunion between Fairy King and Fairy Queen:

> OBE. Sound, music! Come, my queen,
>   take hands with me,
>   And rock the ground whereon these sleepers be.
>   Now thou and I are new in amity,
>   And will to-morrow midnight solemnly
>   Dance in Duke Theseus' house triumphantly,
>   And bless it to all fair prosperity.
>   There shall the pairs of faithful lovers be
>   Wedded, with Theseus, all in jollity.
>   [IV. i. 85-92]

The rhythm of the poetry is a dance rhythm, the lines rock and sway with the movement of the fairies. Even more closely in the last scene does the verse echo the light pattering steps of the elves. There is nothing like this in *Comus*. The lyrics there are exquisite, melodious, but they are not dance-songs. Even the entry of Comus is poetry of the *Il Penseroso* order, imaginative, intellectual, reminiscent, while Shakespeare's lines are alive with movement, and suggest the repeat and turn and rhythmic beat of dancing. In a word, in *Comus* we have thought turned to poetry, while in *A Midsummer Night's Dream* we have sound and movement turned to poetry.

The influence of the dance has affected not merely isolated songs and speeches, but the whole strucutre of *A Midsummer Night's Dream*. Again a comparison with *Comus* is helpful. The difference in style between *Comus* and *A Midsummer Night's Dream* depends upon a difference of spirit. *Comus* is a criticism of life, it springs from an abstract idea: *A Midsummer Night's Dream* is a dance, a movement of bodies. The plot is a pattern, a figure, rather than a series of events occasioned by human character and passion, and this pattern, especially in the moonlight parts of the play, is the pattern of a dance.

> Enter a Fairie at one doore, and Robin Good-
> fellow at another. . . . Enter the King of Fairies,
> at one doore, with his traine; and the Queene,
> at another with hers.
>   [s.d., II. i. 1, 60]

The appearance and disappaerance and reappearance of the various lovers, the will-o'-the-wisp movement of the elusive Puck, form a kind of figured ballet. The lovers quarrel in a dance pattern: first, there are two men to one woman and the other woman alone, then for a brief space a circular movement, each one pursuing and pursued, then a return to the first figure with the position of the women reversed, then a cross-movement, man quarrelling with man and woman with woman, and then, as finale, a general setting to partners, including not only lovers but fairies and royal personages as well.

This dance-like structure makes it inevitable that the lovers should be almost as devoid of character as masquers or masque-presenters. The harmony and grace of the action would have been spoilt by convincing passion.

The only character study in *A Midsummer Night's Dream* is to be found in the portrayal of Bottom, Theseus, and perhaps Hippolyta. Even in drawing these characters Shakespeare was evidently influenced by the memory of pageants, complimentary speeches and entertainments addressed by townspeople and humble folk to the Queen or to the nobility. . . . One Sunday afternoon, at Kenilworth Castle, Elizabeth and her Court whiled away the time by watching the country-people at a Brideale and Morris Dance. Their amused kindly tolerance is just that of Theseus and the lovers towards the Athenian workmen. So that even in the most solid and dramatic parts of his play Shakespeare is only giving an idealised version of courtly and country revels and of the people that played a part in them.

In *A Midsummer Night's Dream* Bottom and his companions serve the same purpose as the antimasque in the courtly revels. It is true that Shakespeare's play was written before Ben Jonson had elaborated and defined the antimasque, but from the first grotesque dances were popular, and the principle of contrast was always latent in the masque. There is, however, a great difference between Jonson's and Shakespeare's management of foil and relief. In the antimasque the transition is sudden and the contrast complete, a method of composition effective enough in spectacle and ballet. But in a play, as Shakespeare well knew, the greatest beauty is gained through contrast when the difference is obvious and striking, but rises out of a deep though unobtrusive resemblance. This could not be better illustrated than by the picture of Titania winding the ass-headed Bottom in her arms. Why is it that this is a pleasing picture, why is it that the rude mechanicals do not, as a matter of fact, disturb or sully Titania's 'close and consecrated bower' [III. ii. 7]? Malvolio in Bottom's place would be repellent, yet Malvolio, regarded superficially, is less violently contrasted to the Fairy Queen than is Nick Bottom. Bottom with his ass's head is grotesquely hideous, and in ordinary life he is crude, raw, and very stupid. . . . [He] and his fellows did perhaps lack humour (though the interview with the fairies suggests that Bottom had a smack of it), but in its place they possessed unreason. Imagination they did have, of the most simple, primal, childlike kind. It is their artistic ambition that lifts them out of the humdrum world and turns them into Midsummer Dreamers, and we have seen how cunningly Shakespeare extracts from their very stupidity romance and moonshine. But, indeed, grotesqueness and stupidity (of a certain kind) have a kinship with beauty. For these qualities usually imply a measure of spiritual freedom, they lead to at least a temporary relief from the tyranny of reason and from the pressure of the external world. In *A Midsummer Night's Dream* the dominance of the Lord of Misrule is not marked by coarse parody, but by the partial repeal of the laws of cause and effect. By delicate beauty, gentle mockery, and simple romantic foolishness our freedom is gained. (pp. 330-34)

Enid Welsford, "The Masque Transmuted," in her The Court Masque: A Study in the Relationship between Poetry & the Revels, 1927. Reprint by Russell & Russell, Inc., 1962, pp. 324-49.

CUMBERLAND CLARK (essay date 1931)

[*Clark observes that the fairies in* A Midsummer Night's Dream *represent Shakespeare's first dramatic use of the supernatural. He regards them as mischievous rather than malicious, with no "special dramatic purpose beyond the desire to entertain" and having no influence or control over the mortal characters in the play. In earlier essays, G. G. Gervinus (1849-50) contended that the fairies exert a significant influence over the dramatic action, while E. K. Chambers (1905), like Clark, maintained that their effect is mainly symbolic. Clark's view of Shakespeare's originality in depicting the fairies is shared by K. M. Briggs, Roger Lancelyn Green, Minor White Latham, and Frank Sidgwick (see Additional Bibliography). Clark also emphasizes the manner in which the music in the play enhances the fairy atmosphere; for further discussion of music in* A Midsummer Night's Dream, *see the excerpt by John H. Long (1955) and the entry by Richmond Noble listed in the Additional Bibliography. Last, Clark notes an element of "darker, gloomier thought" in Puck's speech at III. ii. 380-87. Other critics who have written about the dark or tragic aspects in* A Midsummer Night's Dream *include G. K. Chesterton (1904), G. Wilson Knight (1932), Jan Kott (1964), Charles R. Lyons (1971), Hugh M. Richmond (1971), David Bevington (1975), and Mordecai Marcus (1981).*]

Shakespeare's use of the Fairies [in *A Midsummer Night's Dream*] is original and clever. He avoids anything heavy. He deserts the unattractive fancies of folk-lore for delightful beings of his own creation. He does not employ the Supernatural in this early play with any special dramatic purpose beyond the desire to entertain. He does not attach any particular meaning or significance to his Little People, nor does he endow them with any great powers or control over mortals. Undoubtedly he shows considerable ingenuity in his dramatic construction by deftly interweaving the three themes—the quarrels of the lovers, the fooling of Bottom and the clowns, and the meddling interference of the Fairies. As a whole, though, he writes in happy, carefree vein, drawing prodigally on his imagination, and adopting the attitude of one who has made startling discoveries of the truth about fairies and has decided to pass his knowledge on to his fellows.

There is the spontaneity of effortless creation in Shakespeare's handling of the Fairies of the *Dream*. He does not keep his light and aery beings separate from his mortal characters, as the Weird Sisters are kept separate in *Macbeth*. The Fairies mix freely with the very worldly men and women of the Court of Theseus; and, be it noted, in these scenes it is the human element that is dominant, whereas the enchanted forest is the kingdom where the Fairies have their own way without effective opposition. The Poet, however, does not in this early incursion into the realm of the Supernatural endow his immortals with any real influence over the human soul. Certainly they are guilty of much mischievous interference, which causes a good deal of temporary annoyance, but there is no evidence of any power to tempt, to deceive with malice, or to destroy. (pp. 47-8)

In *Midsummer Night's Dream* music materially assists Shakespeare in creating that fairy atmosphere which is so enchanting, visionary, and idealistic.

Titania . . . early reveals herself as a music-lover by her protest to Oberon that his brawls have disturbed the fairy dances to the piping winds [II. i. 86-7]. In the following scene she calls to her attendants, "Come, now a roundel and a fairy song" [II. ii. 1], and later says, "Sing me now to sleep . . . and let me rest" [II. ii. 7-8]. She dozes off as the first Fairy sings the dainty song, "You spotted snakes" [II. ii. 9], and all the other little voices join in the soothing lullaby chorus. When releasing Titania from his charm, Oberon bids her "music call"; and Titania responds with "Music, ho! music such as charmeth sleep" [IV. i. 83]. The king and queen then dance together to a lilting strain while the effect of the magic spell passes from the entangled lovers, Lysander, Demetrius, Hermia, and Helena. At the end of the play, when the happily married couples have retired, Oberon, Titania, and their fairy train, led by Puck, creep in by the "glimmering light" of the "drowsy fire," and skipping through the sleeping house, with song and dance pour out a blessing on the newly wed. Though not marked in the Stage Directions, the final passage [V. i. 401.ff.] is usually sung, the lines commencing "Now, until the break of day" being one of the few Shakespearean dance-songs. Similarly, the Fairy's speech, "Over hill, over dale" [II. i. 2-13], is treated as a song; while "I know a bank where the wild thyme blows" [II. i. 249ff.] is frequently made into a solo for Oberon. Apart from Bottom's outburst into a frankly rural ditty, the music of *Midsummer Night's Dream* is in keeping with the immortal and fantastic theme, and gives that airy, gossamer-like effect, which was wonderfully recaptured by the genius of Mendelssohn. (pp. 55-7)

Shakespeare's first dramatic use of the Supernatural is happy, gay, and sprightly. The only hint in this play of the darker, gloomier thought that was soon to supplant his youthful optimism is found in those cold, clammy lines about ghosts:

> . . . Yonder shines Aurora's harbinger;
> At whose approach, ghosts, wandering here and there,
> Troop home to churchyards: damned spirits all,
> That in crossways and floods have burial,
> Already to their wormy beds are gone;
> For fear lest day should look their shames upon,
> They wilfully themselves exile from light,
> And must for aye consort with black-brow'd night.
>
> [III. ii. 380-87]

Here, it would seem, Shakespeare's thought wandered back to the malicious, inimical fairies of folk-lore, who were held by some to be the departed spirits of men and women, and for this reason were often confused with ghosts. We shall find a great deal in this strain in *Hamlet*, and still more in *Macbeth*, but it is not allowed to intrude into *Midsummer Night's Dream*. Oberon immediately dismisses this shadow on their careless joy with, "But we are spirits of another sort" [III. ii. 388].

While the Fairies intermingle with the humans in this first supernatural play, Shakespeare never allows us to forget the gulf beween them—that they live in different worlds governed by different laws. This point is strongly emphasized in his later handling of the Supernatural, when his object has ceased to be light diversion and easy laughter, and has become the portrayal of tragedy in its most awe-inspiring and terrifying mood. (pp. 61-2)

Cumberland Clark, "'Midsummer Night's Dream'," in his Shakespeare and the Supernatural, *Williams & Norgate Ltd., 1931, pp. 44-62.*

G. WILSON KNIGHT (essay date 1932)

[*Knight is one of the most influential Shakespearean critics of the twentieth century; he helped shape a new interpretive approach to Shakespeare's work and promoted a greater appreciation of many of the plays. In his studies* The Wheel of Fire (1930) *and* The Shakespearian Tempest (1932), *Knight rejected criticism which emphasizes sources, character analysis, psychology, and ethics and outlined his principles of interpretation which, he claimed, would "replace that chaos by drawing attention to the true Shakespearian unity." Knight argued that this unity lay in Shakespeare's poetic use of images and symbols, particularly in the opposition of "tempests" and "music." He also maintained that a play's spatial aspects, or "atmosphere," should be as closely considered as the temporal elements of the plot if one is "to see the whole play in space as well as time." In the following excerpt from* The Shakespearian Tempest, *Knight analyzes the interplay of imagery in* A Midsummer Night's Dream, *arguing that Shakespeare's symbolic language is ambiguous since it juxtaposes images of storms and harmony, darkness and light, and presents both the "satanic and romantic attributes of a moonlit woodland." Other critics who have discussed the language and imagery in* A Midsummer Night's Dream *include Thomas Marc Parrott (1949), B. Ifor Evans (1952), David P. Young (1966), and Stephen Fender (1968). Knight further contends that the ambiguity in language enhances the "Macbeth-like quality" of the play's atmosphere, and he maintains that the dream evoked here by Shakespeare contains elements designed to produce the terror of a nightmare. Other critics who share, to one degree or another, Knight's contention regarding the "dark" or nightmarish atmosphere of* A Midsummer Night's Dream *include G. K. Chesterton (1904), Jan Kott (1964), Charles R. Lyons (1971), Hugh M. Richmond (1971), David Bevington (1975), and Mordecai Marcus (1981).*]

In *A Midsummer Night's Dream* all the best of Shakespeare's earlier poetry is woven into so comprehensive and exquisite a design that it is hard not to feel that this play alone is worth all the other romances. . . . In this play fairyland interpenetrates the world of human action. And that world is varied, ranging from the rough simplicity of the clowns, through the solid common sense and kind worldly wisdom of Theseus, to the frenzied fantasies of the lovers: which in their turn shade into fairyland itself. The play thus encloses remarkably a whole scale of intuitions. Nor in any other early romance is the interplay of imagery more exquisitely varied. The night is a-glimmer with moon and star, yet it is dark and fearsome; there are gentle birds and gruesome beasts. There is a gnomish, fearsome, *Macbeth*-like quality about the atmosphere, just touching nightmare. . . . The total result resembles those dreams, of substance unhappy to the memorizing intellect, which yet, on waking, we find ourselves strangely regretting, loath to part from that magic even when it leaves nothing to the memory but incidents which should be painful. Such are the fairies here. They are neither good nor bad. They are wayward spirits which cause trouble to men, yet also woo human love and favour: as when Oberon and Titania quarrel for their Indian boy or wrangle in jealousy of Theseus or Hippolyta. The whole vision sums and expresses, as does no other work, the magic and the mystery of sleep, the dewy sweetness of a midsummer dream, dawn-memoried with sparkling grass and wreathing mists; a morning slope falling from a glade where late the moonbeams glimmered their fairy light on shadowed mossy boles and fearsome dells, and the vast woodland silence.

The action depends largely on Oberon's quarrel with Titania. Dissension has entered fairyland itself, due to these spirits'

desire for human love, just as later human beings are caused trouble by their contact with the fairies:

> Why art thou here,
> Come from the farthest steppe of India?
> But that, forsooth, the bouncing Amazon,
> Your buskin'd mistress and your warrior love,
> To Theseus must be wedded, and you come
> To give their bed joy and prosperity.
>
> [II. i. 68-73]

Oberon parries Titania's speech with reciprocal jealousy. Now this dissension makes 'tempests' in nature, untuning the melodic procession of the seasons:

> *Titania.* These are the forgeries of jealousy:
> And never, since the middle summer's spring,
> Met we on hill, in dale, forest, or mead,
> By paved fountain, or by rushy brook,
> Or in the beached margent of the sea,
> To dance our ringlets to the whistling wind,
> But with thy brawls thou hast disturb'd our sport.
> Therefore the winds, piping to us in vain,
> As in revenge, have suck'd up from the sea
> Contagious fogs; which, falling in the land,
> Have every pelting river made so proud
> That they have overborne their continents:
> The ox hath therefore stretch'd his yoke in vain,
> The ploughman lost his seat; and the green corn
> Hath rotted ere his youth attain'd a beard. . . .
> And thorough this distemperature we see
> The seasons alter: hoary-headed frosts
> Fall in the fresh lap of the crimson rose,
> And on old Hiems' thin and icy crown
> An odorous chaplet of sweet summer buds
> Is, as in mockery, set: the spring, the summer,
> The childing autumn, angry winter, change
> Their wonted liveries: and the 'mazed world,
> By their increase, now knows not which is which:
> And this same progeny of evil comes
> From our debate, from our dissension;
> We are their parents and original.
>
> [II. i. 81-117]

Unruly floods, disorder in the seasons, storm and mud and all natural confusion result from this dissension in fairyland. And this tempest is at the heart of the play, sending ripples outward through the plot, vitalizing the whole middle action. (pp. 142-44)

The play continually suggests a nightmare terror. It is dark and fearsome. The nights here are 'grim-look'd' [V. i. 170]. And yet this atmosphere of gloom and dread is the playground for the purest comedy. Romance and fun interthread our tragedies here. So, too, a pale light falls from moon and star into the darkened glades, carving the trees into deeper darkness, black voiceless giants; yet silvering the mossy slopes; lighting the grass with misty sparkles of flame; setting green fire to the glimmering eyes of prowling beasts; dissolving Oberon and Puck invisible in their magic beams. (p. 146)

When all is still and 'fairy time' . . . possesses the darkness, we have Puck's

> Now the hungry lion roars,
> And the wolf behowls the moon.
>
> [V. i. 371-72]

We may remember the wolf in Macbeth's Tarquin speech that howls at night when 'o'er the one half world nature seems dead' [*Macbeth*, II. i. 49-50]. There are many sombre *Macbeth* effects in *A Midsummer Might's Dream*. The 'moon' here does, in fact, have wide suggestions: moonlight is usually romantic. . . . But the moon also is clearly to be associated directly with darkness, too. It occurs in the 'Hecate' scenes of *Macbeth*. And in this play the satanic and romantic attributes of a moonlit woodland are blended.

The play has stars, too. The nights here are 'glimmering'. 'Didst thou not lead him through the glimmering night?' asks Oberon [II. i. 77], and again:

> Through the house give glimmering light . . .
> > [V. i. 391]

Titania has a fine love-speech continuing this 'glimmer' effect:

> The honey bags steal from the humble-bees,
> And for night tapers crop their waxen thighs
> And light them at the fiery glow-worm's eyes,
> To have my love to bed and to arise.
> > [III. i. 168-71]

Throughout the middle scenes we have thus a glimmering world; and the poor distraught lovers long for daylight to break on their troubled dreams.

All these glimmering lights shine on a world which yet endures fears, mistakes, darkness. Once they are grimly blanketed as by a *Macbeth* murk:

> Thou see'st these lovers seek a place to fight:
> Hie therefore, Robin, overcast the night:
> The starry welkin cover thou anon
> With drooping fog as black as Acheron. . . .
> > [III. ii. 354-57]

In this pitch darkness the 'testy rivals' are to be led 'astray',

> Till o'er their brows death-counterfeiting sleep
> With leaden legs and batty wings doth creep.
> > [III. ii. 364-65]

Notice the sombre suggestion there, again recalling *Macbeth*, where the guests at Inverness are told to 'shake off' the 'downy sleep, death's counterfeit' and to look on 'death itself'. 'Batty', too, enforces a *Macbeth* impression. Sleep, as in *Macbeth*, may here be nightmare. Hermia wakes with a start:

> Help me, Lysander, help me! do thy best
> To pluck this crawling serpent from my breast!
> > [II. ii. 145-46]

Many of the persons sleep: all the lovers, once at least, some twice. Titania is enchanted in her sleep so that she endures a nightmare madness in love. Our world is one of dim fears and sleep-consciousness; gnomish, fearsome, haunted:

> What night-rule now about this haunted grove?
> > [III. ii. 5]

The vast night-poetry of *Hamlet* and *Macbeth* is struck here with a similar grandeur:

> The iron tongue of midnight hath told twelve.
> > [V. i. 363]

Darkness and fear permeate this play. It is a darkness spangled, or shot, with light. So Lysander outlines the tragedies in store for true love:

> Or, if there were a sympathy in choice,
> War, death, or sickness did lay siege to it,
> Making it momentany as a sound,

Act III. Scene i. Snug, Bottom, Starveling, Quince, and Flute. Frontispiece to the Hanmer edition by H. Gravelot (1744). By permission of the Folger Shakespeare Library.

> Swift as a shadow, short as any dream,
> Brief as the lightning in the collied night,
> That, in a spleen, unfolds both heaven and earth,
> And ere a man hath power to say, 'Behold!'
> The jaws of darkness do devour it up:
> So quick bright things come to confusion.
> > [I. i. 141-49]

'Confusion': a pure *Macbeth* idea. And we may observe how a tempest effect, 'lightning', here suggests a positive essence for once, as in the almost exactly similar speech in *Romeo and Juliet* [II. ii. 116-20]; but, indeed, wherever we have lightning emphasized, there is a certain vivid, electric suggestion corresponding to the concept 'spirit'. Continually this play suggests *Macbeth;* elves and gnomes take the place of witches and ghosts, and here our dark strands are inwoven with brighter ones, and the total effect is, as I have observed, that of a dream whose fairyland is sweet even though it be troubled. (pp. 148-51)

> *G. Wilson Knight, "The Romantic Comedies," in his* The Shakespearian Tempest, *1932. Reprint by Methuen & Co. Ltd., 1953, pp. 75-168.*

H. B. CHARLTON　(essay date 1933)

[*An English scholar, Charlton is best known for his* Shakespearian Tragedy *(1948) and* Shakespearian Comedy *(1938)—two important studies in which he argues that the proponents of New Crit-*

[A] *Midsummer Night's Dream,* with all its appearance of fairy, with its apparent revelry in the stuff of which dreams are made, with its alluring unreality, and its evident riot of fantasy, is yet the first play in which Shakespeare reveals his promise as the world's comic dramatist, the first exhibiton of his power to use comedy for its proper function, to show real man encountering the real problem of the world in which he was really living—in other words, for Shakespeare's day, the first play in which he showed contemporary man buffeted by the power felt then to be the primary factor of his existence, his response to the quality and the might of love. *A Midsummer Night's Dream* is admittedly Shakespeare's first masterpiece. But the attributes of it often put forward as the features determining its excellence are rather the results than the cause of its supremacy. Critics note the wonderful dexterity with which three evidently alien kinds of matter are woven into a single composite picture, three distinct and unrelated worlds shaped into one consistent universe. The anachronistic court of a pre-Homeric Athens, the realistic population of a contemporary English countryside, and the realm of a fairy land in which ancient, mediaeval, and modern have broken through the limits of time to exist together in one and the same timeless moment—here are seemingly indissoluble incongruities, apt only to the unintelligible confusions of a nightmare. Yet Shakespeare welds them into the form of a credible society; and all, one is asked to believe, by his technical expertness in plotting, and in particular, by his marvellous employment of the pansy's philtre.

But in fact, this skilful workmanship in plotcraft, in forging links to bind the incidents of three different stories into one, is but the outward execution giving visible unity to a body of matter of which the real harmony has been shaped by imaginative insight. These three separate worlds are moulded into one by a controlling point of view, by an idea, not by a philtre. The unity of the comic idea, not the joinery of episodes, is what makes the greatness of *A Midsummer Night's Dream.* *A Midsummer Night's Dream* is not Shakespeare's first masterpiece because in it he is technically more expert than hitherto in such qualities as deftness in structure; it is because in it he has seized more securely on the vital temper of his generation and embodied with it more of the essential spirit of his time. (pp. 102-03)

To [the Elizabethans], for better or for worse, to live was to love, and to love was to love romantically. That was for them a fact of existence. Whether, of course, it was a fact ultimately giving man cause for joy, or whether it constituted a danger to humanity was a further question. It was precisely one of those questions pertinent to the comic dramatist. For comedy, necessarily leading to a happy denouement, showing its heroes attaining their joy by a successful management of circumstance, must equip its heroes with the qualities apt to triumph over the hindrances and troubles which are part of such life as is reflected in comedy. "What is love?" or rather, "What is the place of love in life?" is the question underlying *A Midsummer Night's Dream;* and as the play is a comedy, life in it will necessarily be life as men are finding it, life which is the thing men such as author and audience find themselves destined to live. And in their direct and daily experience of it, the power of love was an undeniable fact. (p. 108)

A Midsummer Night's Dream is a play of love and of lovers, but it opens only when the nuptial hour is drawing on apace, and Theseus' courtship is already past. Even the Athenian lovers have but a brief four days' nightmare of wooing before they too pass into a maturer life. Theseus has had his wilder gallivantings; echoes of a Perigenia, a fair Aegle, an Ariadne, and an Antiope sound faintly through the glimmering night of years gone by. But the fever has worked itself out of his blood. He stands now as the normal member of the society of men, still conscious of the natural pulsings in the veins, and choosing the earthlier-happy state of wedlock in preference to mortifying the flesh in thrice-blessed but inhuman tasks to master blood and chant faint hymns to the cold fruitless moon. Theseus stamps his mind on the play. He admits love because it is natural; but he circumscribes its scope to lead to marriage, because that has become second nature and so is natural too. (pp. 112-13)

But though Theseus strikes the temper of the play at the outset, and summarises the trend of it at the close, the main incidents in the play present the fashion of romantic love and the ways of romantic lovers. . . . [These lovers] are themselves on trial, and their scheme of values is submitted to correction at the hands of Theseus. They are in the dock, not on the bench. And though to the unhuman eye of Puck their crime is flagrant folly, to the normal human Theseus it is a kind of foolishness to which all human flesh is heir, and which all mortal eyes will see with sympathy. Hermia and Lysander, Helena and Demetrius as devoutly dote, and with as much romantic idolatry as did ever lovers of whom tale and history tell. They interchange their rhymes and their love-tokens as the manner is. They serenade by moonlight, and employ each coin of the hallowed currency—"bracelets of hair, rings, gawds, conceits, knacks, trifles, nosegays, and sweatmeats" [I. i. 33-4]. Their love makes heaven of hell, and hell of heaven. Crosses and hellish spight render its course unsmooth. They spend their passion on misprised moods. Their faith is ardent.

> I'll believe as soon
> The whole earth may be bored and that the moon
> May through the centre creep, and so displease
> Her brother's noontide with the Antipodes.
>
> [III. ii. 52-5]

says Hermia. This is faith indeed, absolute—and absolutely misplaced. So with the other lovers. Their passions and their preferences are entirely inexplicable. Things base and vile to common view, their love has transposed for them to form and dignity. They sway from deepest loathing to intensest rapture, merely as the blood within them burns or freezes—"hot ice, and wondrous strange snow" [V. i. 59], very tragical mirth.

Yet despite it all, these lovers do not leave the common earth so entirely as do their earlier romantic counterparts. [In *The Comedy of Errors*] Antipholus reclines on wisps of Luciana's golden hair spread floating on the sea. Hermia has a firmer couch on yellow primrose beds. Hermia's invocation is not by all the protestations of true lovers in the past, but "by all the vows that ever men have broke, in number more than ever women spoke" [I. i. 175-76], an infinitely more substantial body of experience. Indeed, the love of these Athenians is much more a natural mood than a prescribed attitude. It shows itself in jealousie and wranglings as frequently as in devoted protestations. It has its Billingsgate as well as its liturgy: cat, burr, vile serpent, tawny Tartar, dwarf and minimus are as current as goddess, nymph divine and dear, precious, celestial. The lovers themselves know what a frail and fleeting thing true love has been:

> if ever there were sympathy in choice,
> War, death, or sickness did lay siege to it,
> Making it momentary as a sound,
> Swift as a shadow, short as any dream;
> Brief as the lightning in the collied night,
> That, in a spleen, unfolds both Heaven and earth,
> And, e'er a man hath power to say "Behold,"
> The jaws of darkness do devour it up:
> So quick bright things come to confusion.
>
> [I. i. 141-49]
> (pp. 113-15)

But when the lovers have played out the fond pageant of youth, their human nature will be the power which brings them to health and natural taste.

> The country proverb known
> That every man shall take his own, . . .
> Jack shall have Jill,
> Nought shall go ill,
> The man shall have his mare again and all shall
> go well.
>
> [III. ii. 458-63]

At all events, so much are we bidden to take on trust. As an article of faith, it is made easier of acceptance when Titania and Oberon have revealed the disadvantages of houseless, undomesticated fairyland. Their term of courtship is ended. But, inhabiting the air from pole to pole, they are exempt from the constraints of housekeeping. Acorn-cups impose no fellowship. There is nothing to compound mere whim and vagary. In a house on earth, presumably it little matters whether the Indian

boy be known as master's or as mistress's servant. But in fairyland such problems do not settle themselves. Mere personal preference and mood are left in entire control of fairy life. Affection follows fancy, and the consequent state of sentimental anarchy is never ordered by obligation to the world. Titania and Oberon are, of course, the better fairies for their lack of human principles in their behaviour. But the more fairy, the less fitted for the rsponsibilities of the settled human institution of marriage.

The exposure of Oberon and Titania's conjugal relationship is comedy fulfilling its natural function, glorifying those settled institutions of man's social existence which owe their persistence to mankind's experience that such as these make for his welfare in the substantial problem of living life in the world as the world is. Marriage is to the comic dramatist the beneficent arrangement through which mankind achieves a maximum of human joy and a minimum of social disability. . . . [In] *A Midsummer Night's Dream*, wedlock and housekeeping are imposed on man for his advantage; and the advantage as a social being he gains thereby is made patent by setting beside him the undomesticated irresponsible beings of fairyland. Fairy whim was not even to be trusted to prefer its own authentic king to the monstrous, gross Bottom with the ass's head. And even so, its precious Bottom would have soon revolted against a fairy wife, who, when he pined for bread, offered him a stone—emerald, pearl, or diamond, though it should be.

Hence it comes that Bottom and his fellows are as much a part of the play as are Titania and Oberon, or the Athenian lovers. The spirit of the earth which stirs men's sentiments for nature, producing thence the fairies of its folk-lore, and the springtides which turn men's thoughts to love, has brought forth also, as its most material children, these rustics of the countryside. Like Costard [in *Love's Labour's Lost*] they are straight from the bosom of Mother Earth, and though, for the nonce, they have left the plough for mechanic labours on Athenian stalls, they are still but countrymen and villagers.

And Bottom is sufficient assurance that, though nature makes men liable to love, it gives them also so much mortal grossness that man can never distil himself to a mere airy spirit. Sublimation has its visible limits. Bottom, transported to the lap of an adoring queen of faery, has enough of earth about him to preserve his native self. He is at home anywhere, and turns fairyland to his own needs as Shakespeare has now learnt to turn romance to his. Nothing finally perturbs Bottom. The strangest and most perplexing experiences have no power to alter his essential nature, but merely serve to give additional strength to it. The fairy queen may stick musk-roses in his sleek, smooth head, but he will only take advantage of the scene to call up Peaseblossom, and Cobweb, and Mustardseed to ease him of an itching. No dulcet sound of fairy song will lure him from his preference for tongs and bones. And although he will regale himself on fairy dishes of apricocks and dewberries, he will not fail to order the complementary course, the pecks of the provender on which he naturally subsists. He is, of course, a clown. But it is clownage sufficient for its day. It completes the guarantee for the world's security which Theseus has offered.

From the earliest days, Bottom has been accepted as the best piece of characterisation in *A Midsummer Night's Dream;* the Restoration, in fact, cut the play to the pranks of bully Bottom. But he is the most substanital character because Shakespeare's apprehension has laid more certain hold of him than of the other figures in the play. That is another way of saying that, as a man, he means more to Shakespeare than do the others. He is, to the dramatist, the tangible person who provides in the flesh and in life what the mind of Theseus was to provide in theory and in conjecture about life.

Sanity, cool reason, common sense, is the pledge of Theseus against the undue ravages of fancy and of sentiment in human nature. But in Bottom the place of this intellectual temper is supplied by the crude native matter of human instinct. Bottom is a bigger part of the world than is a Lysander or a Demetrius, and always will be, for he has, above all, the instinct which makes for the preservation of his species. He will take command in any the most unexpected situation, and will impose his will on his fellows or on his superiors. Even when he has been killed upon the stage he will rise again with his "No, I assure you" [V. i. 351], and set the world to rights. He has supreme confidence in himself, and in his ability to play any part in life or in theatricals. And this is no mere overweening conceit, for schemes collapse when he withdraws. The world is safe so long as it produces men like Bottom, for its inhabitants will never be permitted to get completely out of touch with earth, will never be allowed to forget the conditions which real life imposes on actual livers of it. Earth and the world take visible human form in his huge bulk before men's eyes, and in such way that it sharpens their sense of humour, of the difference between what man is, and what he vainly pretends himself to be.

Hence the substance in the seemngly unsubstantial cloudworld of *A Midsummer Night's Dream*. At first glance it appears but as a light excursion into the realms of pure romance, where fairies dance and lovers woo, and magic philtres are the dispensers of fate. Yet the intellectual foundations of it all are embodied in the unromantic worldly realism of Theseus. But it is the realism of an English and an Elizabethan mind, not one of classical Roman comedy. It is the temper of a landed gentry, rather than the outlook of a man about town. It is more humane, more representative, and more sympathetic. Roman comedy bolstered a limited society; it was a defence of the customs and conventions of a narrow social group—the citizens, who even so, were only a minority of the inhabitants of their city. But the comedy in *A Midsummer Night's Dream* looks to the preservation of the whole human race as human beings rather than to the maintenance of a particular social caste. It comprehends the court, the city, and the country. It seeks for what contributes to this larger fellowship of man, rather than for what is discordant with the conventions of a class. It values the normal in mankind at large much more than mere propriety in a particular clique. It lifts comedy from concern with the merely unconventional in manners to envisage the more vital incongruities in personality itself.

> Lovers and madmen have such seething brains,
> Such shaping fantasies, that apprehend
> More than cool reason ever comprehends.
> The lunatic, the lover and the poet
> Are of imagination all compact:
> One sees more devils than vast hell can hold,
> That is the madman: the lover, all as frantic,
> Sees Helen's beauty in a brow of Egypt:
> The poet's eye, in a fine frenzy rolling,
> Doth glance from heaven to earth, from earth to
>   heaven;
> And as imagination bodies forth
> The forms of things unknown, the poet's pen
> Turns them to shapes, and gives to airy nothings
> A local habitation and a name.

> Such tricks hath strong imagination,
> That, if it would but apprehend some joy,
> It comprehends some bringer of that joy,
> Or, in the night, imagining some fear,
> How easy is a bush supposed a bear.

[V. i. 4-22]

In this speech, Shakespeare formulates in set terms his first conscious notion of the comic idea, and adds tersely a summary illustration of its value by recalling one of the homeliest, most familiar and most general of common experiences. Grown man, as the play has shown us, is liable to be distracted by vagaries whose source is his fancy or his emotion. For these are apt to subdue his cool reason and his intuitive common sense. They distort his view of things as things are; like a lover, he sees Helen's fair classic beauty in a gypsy's coarse brown visage; or like a lunatic, he not only sees real things awry, but imagines he sees things which are not; or like a poet, subject to the ills of both, he gives substantial reality to mere figments of his uncontrolling brain. But even the most commonplace of mortals, one neither born to be a great lover nor destined to utter a line of verse, may from his own life realise the harm of poets' and lovers' qualities. He will recall the evening in his childhood when at dusk he had the last half mile of a country lane to traverse in the gloom; he will remember the starts and the shocks endured when the shade of a tree took the shape of lurking footpad, when the rustle of the leaves seemed like pursuing footsteps—and all the myriad other perturbations he suffered through the false creations of his own fancy and of his own fears.

> Or in the night imagining some fear
> How easy is a bush supposed a bear—

These, his common sense will clearly tell him, are features arising from his inability at the moment to control his fancy and his feeling by his cool reason: they are disturbances likely to prevent his competent dealing with circumstance, whether that circumstance be a walk along a coutnry lane at dusk, or whether it be a major episode in a bigger life. Indeed, he may go beyond Shakespeare's illustration. He may recognise that the erratic vision which makes a bush a bear, is just as likely to fail in the converse situation, and mistake a bear for a bush. It needs no imagination at all to grasp at once, not how perturbing, but how fatal such an error is likely to be. At once, he sees that mere survival in the world depends upon man's ability to differentiate rapidly and certainly between bears and bushes, and thus perceives that the attribute of supreme value in the world is the "cool reason" which comprehends things as things are: that men without cool reason, who are the sport of seething brains and of the tumultuous frenzies of fancy and of sentiment, are the victims of the world, and the butts of its comedy. Comedy, leading its action to a happy ending, leaving its characters at the end in harmony with the world, is bound to put its highest values on qualities which make for worldly happiness and success. With Theseus, the philosophy of comedy is finding its voice, and his "cool reason" is its prevailing spirit.

A Midsummer Night's Dream is Shakespeare's first comic masterpiece. In its technical aspect, it is the work of a master of language and of plot: but its greatest attainment is that embodied in it, the controlling power shaping its form and texture, there is this first considerable apprehension of the enduring attitude of comedy, the spirit which gives to comedy its vital significance for man and endows it with the permanence of a fine art. (pp. 116-22)

H. B. Charlton, "'A Midsummer Night's Dream'," in his Shakespearian Comedy, Methuen & Co. Ltd., 1938, pp. 100-22.

JOHN PALMER   (essay date 1944)

[*Whereas such earlier critics as Hermann Ulrici (1839), G. G. Gervinus (1849-50), Denton J. Snider (1890), and H. B. Charlton (1933) all discerned the unity of* A Midsummer Night's Dream *in Shakespeare's thematic concerns, Palmer maintains that the character of Bottom unifies the separate parts of the play. In so doing, he rejects the earlier view of Bottom, expressed by such critics as William Maginn (1837), Gervinus, and Charles Cowden Clarke (1863), as a foolish and egotistical figure; indeed, he argues that Bottom is "the projection of Shakespeare's own imagination" into the dramatic world of the play, for both he and the dramatist are equally at ease with the fairies, the nobles, and the other rustics. Palmer contends that Bottom is shown to be superior to Theseus and the other nobles in terms of courtesy, good nature, and ability to apprehend the function of imaginative art. Other critics who have regarded Bottom as more significant than a burlesque figure in the play include G. K. Chesterton (1904), Charlton, and Elizabeth Sewell (1960). Commentators who have focused on Bottom's awakening speech at the conclusion of Act IV, Scene i include Harold C. Goddard (1951), Peter G. Phialas (1966), John A. Allen (1967), Ronald F. Miller (1975), J. Dennis Huston (1981), and Garrett Stewart (see Additional Bibliography). The following excerpt is taken from Palmer's* Comic Characters in Shakespeare, *a study left unfinished at the time of his death in 1944.*]

It is Bully Bottom who, by reason of his special quality, holds firmly together the gossamer structure of that most aery fabric of a vision which is Shakespeare's 'A Midsummer Night's Dream'. It is not a quality to be easily defined. The French have a word for it. Bottom is *débrouillard*—equal to all occasions and at home wherever he may be. Nothing can disconcert or put him down or prevent him from being entirely and happily himself. He wears an ass's head as imperturbably as he bestows advice upon his rustic companions or corrects Duke Theseus for suggesting that Wall should speak out of his cue. He has been rated for conceit and pushing himself forward overmuch. But that is unjust. He engrosses the play not because he is obtrusive, but because he is ingenuously eager to meet all occasions and to throw himself into any part in life that offers. Nor does his love of life exceed his ability to cope with it. He does not unduly press either himself or his suggestions on the company but yields with good grace to the common voice.

He is, in fact, just the man for Shakespeare's purpose. There has to be someone who can be equally at home in each of the three compartments of this trinity of fantastic worlds—classical antiquity, rural Britain and the kingdom of the fairies. Duke Theseus brings home to Athens a mythological bride won with his sword, exercises patriarchal authority over men and maidens, and hunts with hounds bred out of the Spartan kind. Hippolyta, the bride aforesaid, consorted in her maiden days with Hercules and Cadmus. We are here immersed in the legends of ancient Greece—except that round the corner is a convent in which disobedient daughters may be consigned to wither on the virgin thorn. From legendary Athens we are suddenly transported to a village obviously in the heart of Tudor England, where a carpenter, a weaver, a bellows-maker, a tinker, a tailor and a joiner are met together to devise a pastime for the local squire. Finally we pass, without warning given, to a world to whose inhabitants the cowslips are tall and where elves creep

into acorncups to hide themselves in fear from the chiding of Oberon and Titania.

How does Shakespeare contrive to pass so easily from one of these three compartments of his play to another without disturbing our sense of their mutually destructive realities? Duke Theseus is more than life size; the fairies are minute. In between, like Gulliver alternatively with the Brobdingnagians and the Lilliputians, is the company of Peter Quince. Each group has its own standards of size, quality, sentiment and behaviour. Yet we easily believe in all three at once. Each part confirms the illusion of the whole.

To effect this miracle Shakespeare needs a magician who is none other than Bully Bottom. For Bottom impersonates the quality which puts the poet at the centre of his creation. To Bottom, as to Shakespeare, all these beings, fairy, heroic or human, are equally congenial. Bottom has a welcome ready for all that may betide. He takes everything in his stride of simple, indomitable assurance. His readiness to play the tyrant, the lover, the lady or the lion in the most lamentable comedy and most cruel death of Pyramus and Thisbe enables him, in a wood near Athens, to hold his court as to the manner born among the 'little people', accepting without question the cosseting of Titania and ingenuously confessing to a great desire for a bottle of hay. (pp. 92-3)

Let us now come closer to this most lovely, gentlemanlike man and consider in some detail his part in the comedy.

We meet him first at the house of Peter Quince and, be it noted at once, Peter Quince is master of the company. It is Quince who has chosen the play, called the players together and assigned them their parts. Bottom accepts his authority and never questions his decisions. For Bottom, though prolific in advice, fancying himself in all parts, is neither envious nor pushful, but just immensely eager to get things done. Quince is obviously no leader of men. He needs counsel and support:

> First, good Peter Quince, say what the play
> treats on: then read the names of the actors:
> and so grow to a point. . . . Now, good Peter
> Quince, call forth your actors by the scroll. . . .
> Masters, spread yourselves.
>
> [I. ii. 8-10, 14-15]

And so grow to a point. But Bottom, nudging forward his less ardent companions, is betrayed into holding up the proceedings by the very qualities which make him so helpful and necessary—sheer enthusiasm, good-fellowship, and unfailing readiness to meet all occasions and to identify himself with all sorts and conditions of men. He is set down for Pyramus, a lover that kills himself, most gallant, for love. Bottom sees himself at once in the part. It will ask some tears in the true performing of it and let the audience look at their eyes. He will move storms. He will condole in some measure. But his chief humour is for a tyrant. He could play Ercles rarely or a part to tear a cat in, to make all split. Note, however, that in full flight after his crowding fancies Bottom pulls himself up, not once but repeatedly. 'To the rest' [I. ii. 28], he interjects, motioning Quince to proceed. 'Now name the rest of the players' [I. ii. 39], he urges a moment later. But presently he is off again. He would play Thisbe, too, and speak in a monstrous little voice. Quince checks him in midcareer. Bottom must play Pyramus, and Flute Thisbe. 'Proceed', says Bottom. But the lion is too much for his self-control. Lover, lady or lion—he sees himself equally well in all three. (pp. 98-9)

Bottom's imagination, now focused upon Pyramus, prompts him to raise the question of make-up—a matter of passionate interest to all who engage in amateur theatricals:

> BOTTOM: What beard were I best to play it in?
>
> QUINCE: Why, what you will.
>
> BOTTOM: I will discharge it in either your straw-colour beard, your orange-tawny beard, your purple-in-grain beard, or your French-crown-colour beard, your perfect yellow.
>
> [I. ii. 90-6]

Dr. Johnson, who is very severe on Bottom, regards this passage as a deliberate satire upon the 'prejudices and competition' of players. 'Bottom, who seems bred in a tiring-room, is for engrossing every part and would exclude his inferiors from all possibility of distinction. . . . Here, again, he discovers a true genius for the stage by his solicitude for propriety of dress and his deliberation which beard to choose among many beards, all natural' [see Additional Bibliography]. But where is the evidence that Bottom would exclude his inferiors? And is he for engrossing every part? He certainly enjoys *the idea of himself* in any part that life or the stage may offer, but that is not at all the same thing. Shakespeare has much more in hand than a satire upon the prejudices and competition of players. He is establishing a character who is shortly to play such a part as has not yet entered into the tongue of man to conceive nor his heart to report. Bottom's interest in beards is shared by any villager who undertakes to figure in a local pageant and it is expressed in terms such as would be used quite naturally by a weaver with a professional interest in the dyes of his craft. (pp. 99-100)

Bottom is neither to be flustered nor flattered. He has an unerring sense of the fitness of things which never deserts him—a quality which no self-centred, conceited person—as he is so unfairly charged with being—could possibly have exhibited [upon being transformed into an ass]. Here is a fairy queen protesting that she loves him, voice, shape, virute, intelligence and all. It is a little staggering, disconcerting alike to his modesty and good sense; but Bottom does not lose his presence of mind:

> BOTTOM: Methinks, mistress, you should have little reason for that. And yet, to say the truth, reason and love keep little company together now-a-days. The more the pity, that some honest neighbours will not make them friends. Nay, I can gleek upon occasion.
>
> TITANIA. Thou art as wise as thou art beautiful.
>
> BOTTOM: Not so, neither: but if I had wit enough to get out of this wood, I have enough to serve my own turn.
>
> [III. i. 142-51]

Titania declares that he shall stay with her whether he will or not. She is a spirit of no common rate and promises him fairies to do his pleasure. Bottom is silent but his silence is gracious. Who would interrupt such fairy talk as falls from the lips of Titania?

> Be kind and courteous to this gentleman,
> Hop in his walks and gambol in his eyes,
> Feed him with apricocks and dewberries,
> With purple grapes, green figs, and mulberries.

> The honey-bags steal from the humble-bees,
> And for night-tapers crop their waxen thighs,
> And light them at the fiery glow-worm's eyes,
> To have my love to bed and to arise,
> And pluck the wings from painted butterflies,
> To fan the moonbeams from his sleeping eyes.
> Nod to him, elves, and do him courtesies.
>
> [III. i. 164-74]

But these fairies who come to wait upon him must be answered. Bully Bottom, who, like his author, takes all things in nature as they come, is put upon his mettle. And how featly he rises to the occasion, with nothing but his native good-fellowship and genial acceptance of things as they are to carry him through. For each of them he has an appropriate word. He holds his court with an exquisite, royal courtesy that stoops, without pride, to claim equality with his lieges. . . . (pp. 102-03)

Bottom, playing before Theseus, is the victim of a bad tradition. Professional actors in presenting the lamentable comedy of Pyramus and Thisbe, conscientiously underline every point of the farce, embroider every absurdity and miss no opportunity for comic business. Burlesque is only tolerable in so far as it exposes intelligently the emptiness of a received convention, and it is effective only if played with solemnity. Its exponents must never seem to be aware of their absurdity:

> PYRAMUS: Approach, ye Furies fell!
>   O Fates, come, come,
>   Cut thread and thrum,
>   Quail, crush, conclude and quell!
>
> [V. i. 284-87]

Shakespeare abundantly supplies the nonsense. Pyramus has nothing to do but speak with good accent and good discretion. There must never be any doubt of the sincerity of his *passion* (Theseus' own word). Does not Hippolyta herself declare: 'Beshrew my heart, but I pity the man' [V. i. 290]? Bottom's famous protest to the Duke is no mere impertinence but the forthright gesture of an artist anxious to be well understood. Theseus, with his interruption, is spoiling the game. He must be called to order and put right

> PYRAMUS: O wicked wall, through whom I see no bliss,
>   Cursed be thy stones for thus deceiving me!
> THESEUS: The wall, methinks, being sensible, should curse again.
> PYRAMUS: No, in truth, sir, he should not. 'Deceiving me' is Thisby's cue: she is to enter now, and I am to spy her through the wall. You shall see, it will fall pat as I told you. . . . Yonder she comes.
>
> [V. i. 180-87]

This is not self-centred insolence but the disinterested enthusiasm of an interpreter. Bottom's 'She is to enter now, and I am to spy her through the wall. You shall see, it will fall pat as I told you', recalls Hamlet's more famous interpolation: 'He poisons him i' the garden for's estate; the story is extant and writ in very choice Italian. You shall see anon how the murderer gets the love of Gonzago's wife' [*Hamlet,* III. ii. 261-64].

It may be argued, if satire be intended in this scene, the laugh is at the expense, not of Bottom enacting the woes of Pyramus, but of the lords and ladies who condescend to find it amusing. Theseus is kindly magnanimous:

> For never anything can be amiss,
> When simpleness and duty tender it.

> Our sport shall be to take what they mistake:
> And what poor duty cannot do, noble respect
> Takes it in might, not merit.
>
> [V. i. 82-92]

But condescension, however amiable, is still condescension, and some will prefer the royal good-fellowship of Bottom's 'Give me your neaf, Monsieur Mustardseed' [IV. i. 19], or his friendly concern that Monsieur Cobweb shall not be overflown with a honey-bag. . . . The Duke's comments on the play as delivered fall noticeably short of Bottom's observations on the play in preparation. These gentle auditors cannot hold a candle to Bottom for courtesy or apprehension and their treatment of Moonshine is downright impertinent. Demetrius interupts him with the stale inevitable jest about the horns he should be wearing. Theseus pointlessly objects that the man in the moon should be inside and not outside the lantern and, when they have put the poor fellow out of his part, Demetrius with a clumsy deference caps his Grace's witticism—not only the man but his thornbush and his dog should also be in the lantern.

The laugh, then, is not all on one side where it is commonly assumed to lie. Who is Demetrius to deride the antics of Pyramus, a lover in moonshine? Was he not himself but a few hours since cutting a pretty poor figure in a wood near Athens, actor in the 'fond pageant' which Puck found so delectable. Lord! what fools these mortals be! But Demetrius must be excused where generations of English actors have so sadly mistaken Pyramus and his peers. Nothing is stranger or less creditable to the English theatre than the stage history of 'A Midsummer Night's Dream'. Shakespeare was barely cold in his grave when, to set on some quantity of barren spectators to laugh, Bottom and his company had sunk to the level of the grimacing officious clowns with whom we are only too familiar. (pp. 105-07)

The stiff-necked generations which mistranslated Bottom saw so little coherence or unity in the play that they used it for two hundred years as a quarry for fairy pantomime, burlesque, operatic miscellanies, masques and ballets. Bottom is so much the projection of Shakespeare's own imagination into this mimic world that, if we fail to identify ourselves with his immortal weaver, the comedy falls to pieces. No-one but he can sustain the triple illusion. He takes us along with him by virtue of the very quality which made it possible for Shakespeare himself to creep into the small soul of a fairy as easily as into the noble heart that cracked in the passing of Hamlet—a genius for accommodation with all things within the limits of his imaginable world. From first to last this is Bottom's dream and, if he come not, the play is marred. (pp. 108-09)

> *John Palmer, "Bottom," in his* Comic Characters of Shakespeare, *Macmillan and Co., Limited, 1946, pp. 92-109.*

E. C. PETTET (essay date 1949)

[*In an unexcerpted portion of his* Shakespeare and the Romance Tradition, *Pettet examines the romantic comedy form and the reasons for its popularity in late sixteenth-century England. In the following excerpt, he argues that in* A Midsummer Night's

Dream *Shakespeare was attempting to amend the romantic conception of love as a constant force in human relationships. Pettet points to the numerous instances in the first scene where the mutability of love is repeatedly stressed and to the Pyramus and Thisbe interlude as evidence that although Shakespeare accepted romantic love as part of human nature, he yet considered it "inadequate." Other critics who have discussed the play's depiction of romantic or over-imaginative love include G. G. Gervinus (1849-50), E. K. Chambers (1905), H. B. Charlton (1933), Ernest Schanzer (1951), George A. Bonnard (1956), John Vyvyan (1961), R. W. Dent (1964), and Peter G. Phialas (1966). In related interpretations of* A Midsummer Night's Dream, *Samuel B. Hemingway (1911) and Hugh M. Richmond (1971) have argued that the play represents Shakespeare's reaction against the excessive romanticism of his own* Romeo and Juliet.]

No one can miss the romantic elements in *A Midsummer Night's Dream*—its courtly love adventures in the enchanted wood near Athens, its tissue of romantic love-sentiment, its idealisation of marriage, its fairies, hunting-scene and delicate evocation of the dewy May morning, so rich with old romantic associations. . . . For all this, it contains a strong note of criticism and interrogation, which is announced insistently, even monotonously, in the very first scene.

This note is struck when Lysander openly accuses Demetrius, a 'spotted and inconstant man' [I. i. 110], of having broken his plighted troth to Helena. We might expect to hear no more of it, for a few moments later the true lovers, Lysander and Hermia, whose passionate and unquenchable devotion to each other we have witnessed in the first part of the scene, draw together. But hardly are they in each others' arms before Lysander, so confident and courageous before, is lamenting the precarious mortality of love:

> Or, if there were a sympathy in choice,
> War, death, or sickness did lay siege to it,
> Making it momentany as a sound,
> Swift as a shadow, short as any dream;
> Brief as the lightning in the collied night,
> That, in a spleen, unfolds both heaven and earth,
> And ere a man hath power to say 'Behold!'
> The jaws of darkness do devour it up:
> So quick bright things come to confusion.
>
> [I. i. 141-49]

—a mere straightforward response to the dramatic situation from a lover who is threatened with the loss of his mistress? Perhaps. But why does Hermia, when she is trying to convince Lysander that she will keep her promise to elope with him, serve so curiously from Cupid's strongest bow and Venus' doves to inconstancy and broken vows?—

> And by that fire which burn'd the Carthage queen,
> When the false Troyan under sail was seen,
> By all the vows that ever men have broke,
> In number more than ever women spoke,
> In that same place thou hast appointed me,
> To-morrow truly will I meet with thee.
>
> [I. i. 173-78]

This theme is developed by the soliloquy of Helena on Demetrius, which concludes the scene, for one of the main reasons for this precariousness of love and fickleness of lovers is, so Helen maintains, the complete irrationality of our passion:

> And as he errs, doting on Hermia's eyes,
> So I, admiring of his qualities:
> Things base and vile, holding no quality,
> Love can transpose to form and dignity:

Love looks not with the eyes, but with the mind;
And therefore is wing'd Cupid painted blind:
Nor hath Love's mind of any judgement taste;
Wings and no eyes figure unheedy haste:
And therefore is Love said to be a child,
Because in choice he is so oft beguiled.
As waggish boys in game themselves forswear,
So the boy Love is perjured everywhere.

Analysed then, the opening of *A Midsummer Night's Dream* reveals two distinct and contrasting subjects, both of which are woven into the substance of the sentimental main plot—first, the passionate loyalty and devotion of romantic love which will fight against all obstacles, and secondly, the changefulness, frenzied irrationality and brevity of love. What Shakespeare is surely, if delicately, hinting is that unswerving constancy is a rare and more fragile quality than romance commonly admits. (pp. 109-11)

This second, counter theme, which is perhaps more accurately described as a correction than a criticism of romantic love, is elaborated in two directions. In the first place, the elopement of Lysander and Hermia is complicated by the mistakes of Puck, who, by misusing the magic juice that Oberon has given him, causes Lysander to desert Hermia and, with Demetrius, to transfer his affections to Helena. Admittedly these two examples of fickleness are produced by a purely mechanical means. All the same there is good reason to believe that Shakespeare intended the episode to be more than a piece of pantomimic business. We remember that one of the inconstant lovers, Demetrius, 'the spotted and inconstant man', has already once before—and without any supernatural compulsion—changed the object of his affection. We notice that Shakespeare does not treat the episode in a spirit of near-tragedy, as one who held seriously to the doctrines of romantic love would probably have done; on the contrary, the transformation of Lysander and Demetrius, though they are characters in the main and (on the whole) serious romantic plot, is to be regarded comically. Above all, we must be struck by Shakespeare's mischievous sense of fun in keeping for Demetrius and Lysander the same 'votary's' attitude to love before and afer the enchantment. Lysander in particular is outrageously brazen in wooing Helena with the same terms of frantic and rhetorical devotion as he had previously employed towards Hermia. Only, it appears, has the physical form of the 'goddess' and 'mistress' changed. Small wonder that Puck excuses his carelesness on the grounds that it has, after all, merely produced a situation that Fate normally ordains:

Then fate o'er-rules, that, one man holding troth,
A million fail, confounding oath on oath.

[III. ii. 92-3]

There is, of course, no way of proving conclusively that the entanglement caused by the magic juice has a significance and meaning of the kind we have just indicated, or indeed of proving conclusively that it has any meaning and significance at all. But the story of the Athenian lovers must not be viewed in isolation; it must be linked with the quarrel between Oberon and Titania, which contains a fairy-world, but unmistakable variation of the same theme of fickleness and inconstancy. It is not merely that Titania deserts her husband and comes, under the influence of the magic juice, to dote upon an ass. The whole fairy atmosphere—in the first part of the play at least—is thick with rumours of infidelities: Oberon, disguised as Corin, has been wooing Phillidia and is now casting an amorous eye on Hippolyta; Titania, so Oberon alleges, is in love with The-

seus. Even Theseus, who might otherwise have passed as the one solid, constant and commonsense lover of the play, is degraded by the wrangle between the Fairy King and Queen, since, in his anxiety to prove Titania's fondness for Theseus, Oberon drags up Theseus' unsavoury past of treachery and broken vows:

Didst thou not lead him through the glimmering night
From Perigenia, whom he ravished?
And make him with fair Aegle break his faith,
With Ariadne, and Antiopa?

[II. i. 77-80]

However, the Theseus who is exhibited to us in these lines is a momentary and soon-forgotten figure. The Theseus that we remember is the mature, rational, self-possessed husband (or husband-to-be) who, in a speech that repeats the theme of Helena's earlier soliloquy, brackets the lover with the lunatic, and so, indirectly, utters the play's own comment on the fantastic adventures of its heroes and heroines:

Lovers and madmen have such seething brains,
Such shaping fantasies, that apprehend
More than cool reason ever comprehends.
The lunatic, the lover and the poet
Are of imagination all compact:
One sees more devils than vast hell can hold,
That is, the madman; the lover, all as frantic,
Sees Helen's beauty in a brow of Egypt . . .

[V. i. 4-11]

Such, too, appears to be the attitude of Bottom who, recovering from his surprise at hearing Titania's declaration of love for him, balances himself with the reflection—'to say the truth, reason and love keep little company together now-a-days' [III. i. 143-44].

However, Bottom has more significance for our present inquiry than this one passing remark. It is likely . . . that Shakespeare intended Bottom, like Speed and Launce [in *The Two Gentlemen of Verona*], to embody a mundane, broadly comic antithesis to the romance world. Perhaps that is not his significance in the middle scenes of the play, for if his affair with Titania reduces love to the level of farce and furnishes a ludicrous contrast with the romantic love-making of Lysander, Demetrius, Hermia and Helena, it is love in general rather than love in the romantic form that, directly and by implication, he renders comic. Where Bottom does surely emerge as a distinctive antithesis to romance is in the *Pyramus and Thisbe* Interlude, of which he is the central figure. It is, of course, possible that Shakespeare's choice of the Pyramus and Thisbe story for the play of the mechanicals was entirely fortuitous. But when we think of the scores of suitable tales at hand for Shakespeare's purpose it is somewhat remarkable that he should have utilised one of the most famous of all love romance. And even if his choice of the story was unpremeditated, it is in effect a murderous burlesque of a romance, so murderous indeed that it is impossible to believe that its author could ever regard romantic love with a serious, uncritical, undivided attitude.

Bringing together these various themes that we have traced, we may attempt to state the 'meaning' of the play, which in so delicate a piece of work is not a 'moral' but the shaping attitude behind it. Young love, as Shakespeare here presents it, is passionate, intense, permeated with lyrical wonder and indefinable magic; but it is transient, irrational, full of frenzy and fantasy. The absurdities and extravagances of such love are often ludicrous, and it does no one any harm, least of all the lovers themselves, that we should occasionally laugh at it. But love of this kind is real and true to human nature, and its reality, which we should tolerate, is the truth of the romantic attitude. On the other hand, the romantic conception of love is an inadequate one: first, because it ignores or too lightly dismisses the changefulness, selfishness and unfaithfulness of human beings in their sexual relations; and secondly, because it is essentially a reflection of youthful and pre-marital love. The loves and fancies of Lysander, Demetrius, Hermia and Helena are natural enough, but they represent only a phase, the phase of courtship. The love of marriage, which is the consummation of courtship, should be something cooler, more substantial and rational—an 'everlasting bond of fellowship' as Theseus calls it [I. i. 85].

There is also, by implication at least, a third criticism of the romantic attitude: if love is so irrational, then the romantic claims for its moral and spiritual elevation . . . are grossly exaggerated. (pp. 111-14)

> E. C. Pettet, "Shakespeare's Detachment from Romance," in his Shakespeare and the Romance Tradition, Staples Press, 1949, pp. 101-35.

THOMAS MARC PARROTT (essay date 1949)

[In the following excerpt, Parrott focuses on the romantic lyricism of A Midsummer Night's Dream. He also points to Shakespeare's use of varied poetic styles, including prose, for the speeches of the different characters, noting the change in language with alterations in dramatic circumstances. Brian Vickers (see Additional Bibliography) has also argued that differences between the three groups of characters are enhanced by stylistic variations in their speeches. For additional commentary on the poetic style of A Midsummer Night's Dream, see the excerpts by B. Ifor Ivans (1952), who maintains that the language of the play is successfully integrated with other dramatic elements, and David P. Young (1966), who contends that variations in meter and rhyme, together with shifts in style throughout the drama, help to broaden the perspective of the play. Parrott briefly asserts that there is "nothing satirical or malicious" in A Midsummer Night's Dream and that the "shadow of death or danger" is nowhere apparent. In contrast to this attitude, G. K. Chesterton (1904), Cumberland Clark (1931), G. Wilson Knight (1932), Jan Kott (1964), Charles R. Lyons (1971), Hugh M. Richmond (1971), David Bevington (1975), and Mordecai Marcus (1981) have all discovered malevolent or dark elements in the play.]

A Midsummer Night's Dream has never enjoyed great success upon the stage, but it is one of the most delightful of Shakespeare's plays for the closet. The diction of this play, less marred by fanciful conceits than that of earlier comedies, less obscured by involved passages where thought seems to wrestle with expression as in later and greater plays, offers a constant source of enjoyment to the reader. Through the simple medium of language without the charm of theatrical illusion, Shakespeare tells an interesting story of human lovers and opens to the imaginative reader the magic gates of fairyland. It is in his use of language, as in so much else in this play, that Shakespeare shows himself the master. There is a fair proportion of prose, strictly, reserved for the realistic talk of Bottom and his fellows. Bottom's lines, in particular, have been most carefully written; Shakespeare seems determined to prevent his clown in this play from speaking more than was set down for him. (p. 131)

Over half the verse lines of the Dream are in rhyme. The 'jigging vein' of the Pyramus play is Shakespeare's mockery of the 'mother wits' who wrote plays before the new group of

playwrights, Peele, Marlowe, and Greene, established blank verse and rhymed iambic couplets on the stage. The lovers, for the most part, speak in rhyme, which is as it should be, but Shakespeare restrains here the exuberance that had flourished so freely in Love's Labour's Lost; there are no sonnets embodied in the dialogue of the Dream. The extravagant language of Lysander and Demetrius, awaking after their eyes had been touched by the love juice, is purposely designed to show the power of that spell; they do not rant in this vein either before or after.

The blank verse of the Dream is distinguished at once by ease and beauty; there is little or no rhetorical declamation in this play. Shakespeare has gained full control over the meter he had learned to use from Marlowe, and has put something new into it, a lyric quality of tone. The fairy scenes seem to have been written to music: Shakespeare, it is clear, was able to command for the first performance a group of singing boys whose fresh voices ring out in solo, recitative, and chorus. Their songs, naturally and rightly, are in rhyme, but even in the regular blank verse speeches of Oberon and Titania the lyric note is heard. Take, for example, two passages of many that might be culled from this fair garden, Oberon's words to Puck:

> But I might see young Cupid's fiery shaft
> Quench'd in the chaste beams of the wat'ry moon,
> And the imperial votaress passed on,
> In maiden meditation, fancy-free.
> Yet mark'd I where the bolt of Cupid fell:
> It fell upon a little western flower,
> Before milk-white, now purple with love's wound,
> And maidens call it, Love-in-idleness
>
> [II. i. 161-68]

or Titania's order to her attendant elves:

> Come, now a roundel and a fairy song;
> Then, for the third part of a minute, hence;
> Some to kill cankers in the musk-rose buds,
> Some war with rere-mice for their leathern wings
> To make my small elves coats, and some keep back
> The clamorous owl, that nightly hoots, and wonders
> At our quaint spirits . . .
>
> [II. ii. 1-7]

The distinguishing characteristic of the Dream, in fact, is that it attains what The Two Gentlemen had aimed at and failed to achieve: lyric romantic comedy. Shakespeare was to do still better work than this; he had not yet mastered all the stops of his organ, but there is a gay and youthful freshness in the music of this play that makes it a joy forever. It was surely of the Dream that Milton was thinking when he spoke of Shakespeare warbling 'his native wood-notes wild' [L'Allegro].

There is something more, of course, in A Midsummer Night's Dream than Shakespeare's wood-notes. The central action is concerned with that phase of human love which the Elizabethans called 'fancy': the irrational emotional impulse that draws man to maid and maid to man. Love as 'fancy,' 'love-in-idleness,' is a conception of love proper to comedy, and this early comedy plays with it and exhibits its most fantastic form in Titania's infatuation. Shakespeare's mastery of his art permits him here to sport with his theme in easy good humor. Like Puck he is vastly entertained by human follies. 'What fools these mortals be' [III. ii. 115] might serve as a second title for the play, but there is nothing satirical or malicious in the playwright's laughter. The shadow of death or danger that hangs over his earlier comedies, and was to reappear in still darker shades hereafter has vanished in the enchanted moonlight that floods the wood near Athens. Nowhere in all Shakespeare's work do we hear him singing in so carefree a strain as in *A Midsummer Night's Dream*. (pp. 132-33)

Thomas Marc Parrott, "Apprentice Work," in his Shakespearean Comedy, *Oxford University Press, 1949, pp. 100-33.*

ERNEST SCHANZER (essay date 1951)

[*Schanzer disputes the conclusions of H. B. Charlton (1933) and E. C. Pettet (1949) that in* A Midsummer Night's Dream *Shakespeare is ridiculing romantic love in general. Instead, he argues, the object of Shakespeare's parody is that deviant form of love which is bred "in the imagination and blinds both reason and the senses" and which results in the love-madness typified by Demetrius at the opening of the play. Such other critics as G. G. Gervinus (1849-50), E. K. Chambers (1905), George A. Bonnard (1956), John Vyvyan (1961), R. W. Dent (1964), and Peter G. Phialas (1966), as well as Frank Kermode and Paul A. Olson (see Additional Bibliography), also maintain that the play presents the follies of blind love. Schanzer contends that Theseus's lunatic, lover, and poet speech (Act V, Scene i) recapitulates the theme of "inflamed" imagination and expresses Shakespeare's view that madmen, lovers, and artists "all live among phantoms of their own creation which are unrelated to reality." Other commentators who have discussed Theseus's relation to the themes of love and art in the play include William Maginn (1837), Charles Knight (1849), Edward Dowden (1881), Denton J. Snider (1890), Frederick S. Boas (1896), H. B. Charlton (1933), E. C. Pettet (1949), Howard Nemerov (1956), George A. Bonnard (1956), John Vyvyan (1961), and R. W. Dent (1964). Schanzer further disputes Pettet's conclusion that the Pyramus and Thisbe interlude is yet another example of Shakespeare's condemnation of romantic love; instead, he terms it "a kind of anti-masque to the main masque provided by the fairies and the Athenian lovers"—a point suggested earlier by Enid Welsford (1927).*]

The ridiculing of a certain kind of madness, of love-madness, forms . . . the main theme of [*A Midsummer Night's Dream*] and provides the connecting link between the various episodes and groups of characters. But the butt of Shakespeare's ridicule is not romantic love in general, as Charlton [see excerpt above, 1933] and Pettet [see excerpt above, 1949] seem to believe. For though Shakespeare may smile occasionally at the extravagances of romantic lovers, he always treats them with the utmost indulgence as long as their love conforms to the Shakespearean norm. This norm of love has been well defined by Herford: "Love is a passion, kindling heart, brain, and senses alike in natural and happy proportions; ardent but not sensual, tender but not sentimental, pure but not ascetic, moral but not puritanic, joyous but not frivolous, mirthful and witty but not cynical." It is, then, a love in which reason, senses, and feelings all work together in harmony and keep perfect balance. But the love which Shakespeare ridicules in *A Midsummer Night's Dream* is engendered in the imagination and blinds both reason and the senses. This form of love has cut itself off from reality, from the evidence of the senses, it is a creature of "seething brains," a kind of madness. (p. 234)

Professor Parrott declares that the central action of the play "is concerned with that phase of human love which the Elizabethans called 'fancy,' the irrational impulse that draws man to maid and maid to man" [see excerpt above, 1949]. But the Elizabethans seem to have used the word "fancy" very loosely, applying it to every kind of love. Shakespeare uses the word often vaguely for love in general. . . . In the one place where

he gives to the word a more precise connotation he makes it apply to a deviation from the norm of love very different from that which is ridiculed in *A Midsummer Night's Dream*. I am, of course, referring to the song in *The Merchant of Venice:*

Tell me where is fancy bred,
Or in the heart or in the head?
How begot, how nourished?
  Reply, reply.
It is engender'd in the eyes,
With gazing fed; and fancy dies
In the cradle where it lies.
          [*The Merchant of Venice*, III. ii. 63-9]

The kind of love described here is one in which reason and the feelings are subordinate to the senses. "It is engender'd in the eyes." But in the aberration from true love which Shakespeare criticizes in *A Midsummer Night's Dream* the eyes play no part.

Love looks not with the eyes, but with the mind.
And therefore is wing'd Cupid painted blind.
          [I. i. 234-35]

It is engendered in the imagination, a form of madness which can make Demetrius' love for Helena change to sudden detestation and make him dote on Hermia who is no fairer than Helena, and certainly not as sweet-tempered. It is a love which is entirely divorced from both reason and the evidence of the senses.

The method used by Shakespeare to ridicule this form of love is his favourite one of parody. The whole phantasmagoria which follows upon the infusion of the love-juice into the eyes of Lysander and Demetrius stands in a parody-relationship to Demetrius' love-madness as described at the beginning of the play. There is the same sudden transference of love from one woman to another accompanied by hatred for the object of one's previous affection; there is the same disregard of reason and the evidence of the senses. The little western flower is thus the concrete embodiment of the love-madness which Shakespeare is out to ridicule. Its juice is infused into the eyes, robbing them of their power of unbiased vision, inflaming the imagination, and putting reason to flight. Ironically, its victim is under the illusion that he is following reason in making his new choice. Thus Lysander exclaims upon his transference of his love from Hermia to Helena:

The will of man is by his reason sway'd;
And reason says you are the worthier maid.
Things growing are not ripe until their season;
So I, being young, till now ripe not to reason;
And touching now the point of human skill,
Reason becomes the marshal to my will
And leads me to your eyes; where I o'erlook
Love's stories, written in Love's richest book.
          [II. ii. 115-22]

But the parody of Demetrius' love-madness is carried to its ludicrous extreme in the Titania-Bottom love-scenes. Here, in the infatuation of the Queen of Fairies for a weaver metamorphosed into an ass, we have displayed for our delight, as well as for our more serious reflection, the full absurdity of the kind of love which is engendered in the imagination only, uncorrected by reason and the senses. Bottom, who will not allow himself to be deprived of his mother wit nor depart one jot from his comon-sense view of the world, no matter what the condition in which he finds himself, points the moral of the situation. To Titania's impassioned declaration of love,

> I pray thee, gentle mortal, sing again.
> Mine ear is much enamoured of thy note;
> So is mine eye enthrallèd to thy shape;
> And thy fair virtue's force (perforce) doth move me,
> On the first view, to say, to swear, I love thee,
>
> [III. i. 137-41]

he replies:

> Methinks, mistress, you should have little rea-
> son for that. And yet, to say the truth, reason
> and love keep little company together now-a-
> days. The more the pity that some honest neigh-
> bours will not make them friends. Nay, I can
> gleek, upon occasion.
>
> [III. i. 142-47]

In the mutual relationship of Theseus and Hippolyta reason and love have been made friends and keep company together. For this, as well as for other reasons (for Theseus is to some extent a chorus-character), it is fitting that the final summing up of the theme which is treated throughout the play should be entrusted to Theseus:

> Lovers and madmen have such seething brains,
> Such shaping fantasies, that aprehend
> More than cool reason ever comprehends.
> The lunatic, the lover, and the poet
> Are of imagination all compact.
> One sees more devils than hell can hold:
> That is the madman. The lover, all as frantic,
> Sees Helen's beauty in a brow of Egypt.
> The poet's eye, in a fine frenzy rolling,
> Doth glance from heaven to earth, from earth to
>   heaven;
> And as imagination bodies forth
> The forms of things unknown, the poet's pen
> Turns them to shape, and gives to airy nothing
> A local habitation and a name.
>
> [V. i. 4-17]

The kind of love which Theseus makes fun of in this speech is precisely the one which is ridiculed throughout the play. It is the offspring of an inflamed imagination which makes the lover see "Helen's beauty in a brow of Egypt." Lover, lunatic, and poet all live among phantoms of their own creation which are unrelated to reality. Shakespeare could not have expressed his theme more clearly or forcefully.

We have seen, then, how this central theme ties together apparently unrelated portions of the play: the Demetrius-Helena relationship of the first part, the Bottom-Titania interlude, and the scenes dealing with the lovers' transference of their affection from Hermia to Helena. The Oberton-Titania quarrel is another matter. Here we are not dealing with any particular deviation from Shakespeare's norm of love but rather with the absurdity and irrationality of lovers' quarrels in general. I cannot therefore follow Mr. Pettet when he writes: "The story of the Athenian lovers must not be viewed in isolation; it must be linked with the quarrel between Oberon and Titania, which contains a fairy-world, but unmistakable variation of the same theme of fickleness and inconstancy. It is not merely that Titania deserts her husband and comes, under the influence of the magic juice, to dote upon an ass. The whole fairy atmosphere—in the first part of the play at least—is thick with

rumours of infidelities." But the main theme of the play is not fickleness and inconstancy in general, it is a particular deviation from the norm of love which often *leads* to fickleness and inconstancy. Nor is there any close relation between the main theme and the "very tragical mirth" of Pyramus and Thisbe. There is nothing inherently ridiculous about the Pyramus and Thisbe love-relationship. It is much like that of Romeo and Juliet, and does not offend against the Shakepearean norm. It becomes ridiculous only as interpreted by Bottom and his companions. As such it constitutes a riotous burlesque of romantic love in general, and may thus be said to stand broadly in a parody-relationship to both the Bottom-Titania love-scenes, and to those enacted by the Athenian lovers. Looking at it in another way, we may think of the Pyramus and Thisbe play, as well as its rehearsal in the wood, as a kind of anti-masque to the main masque provided by the fairies and the Athenian lovers. But with what I regard as the central theme of the play it appears to have no connection.

Nevertheless, we see that the play is much less disjointed than has generally been believed. It is unified by a single theme which is emphasized repeatedly, from the opening scene until Theseus' summary of it at the beginning of Act V, and upon which Puck provides a fit comment: "Lord, what fools these mortals be!" [III. ii. 115]. (pp. 235-38)

Ernest Schanzer, "The Central Theme of 'A Mid-
summer Night's Dream'," in *University of Toronto*
Quarterly, Vol. XX, No. 3, April, 1951, pp. 233-38.

HAROLD C. GODDARD (essay date 1951)

[*Goddard notes two passages in* A Midsummer Night's Dream *that he believes "embody" the play's central theme: the first is Theseus's speech on lovers, lunatics, and poets at the beginning of Act V; the other, and that which he closely examines, is the dialogue between Theseus and Hippolyta in Act IV, Scene i. Goddard describes this passage—the conversation on the harmonious music of Theseus's hunting dogs—"as nearly perfect a metaphor as could be conceived for* A Midsummer-Night's Dream *itself." He bases this conclusion on the manner in which both Theseus and Hippolyta, through their language, transform the "confusions and discords" of the present setting into "a single musical effect"—a transformation that echoes the manner in which Shakespeare takes the "incongruities, anachronisms, contradictions, and impossible juxtapositions of* A Midsummer-Night's Dream" *and combines them harmoniously. Other critics who have argued that the reconciliation of conflicting principles into a harmonious conclusion is a central theme of* A Midsummer Night's Dream *include John Vyvyan (1961), Stephen Fender (1968), R. A. Zimbardo (1970), David Bevington (1975), Florence Falk (1980), and Paul A. Olson (see Additional Bibliography). Goddard also analyzes Shakespeare's view of the importance of imagination as expressed in the speeches of Theseus and Hippolyta before and during the performance of the interlude in Act V, Scene i. He contends that Theseus is shown to be judicious about the role of imagination in art, but that Hippolyta is more perceptive about love. For additional discussion of the complementary natures of the royal couple, see the excerpt by Howard Nemerov (1956) and the essay by Paul A. Olson listed in the Additional Bibliography. Other critics who have examined Theseus's comments on art and imagination include William Maginn (1837), Charles Knight (1849), Edward Dowden (1881), Denton J. Snider (1890), Frederick S. Boas (1896), Howard Nemerov (1956) and R. W. Dent (1964). Last, Goddard claims that Bottom's awakening at the close of Act IV, Scene i dramatizes "the original miracle of the Imagination," the moment when spiritual life is first kindled in "the animal man." Goddard's is one of the earliest treatments of this episode as a significant moment in the play. Other critics who*

A Midsummer-Night's Dream is one of the lightest and in many respects the most purely playful of Shakespeare's plays. Yet it is surpassed by few if any of his early works in its importance for an understanding of the unfolding of his genius. It is characteristic of its author that he should have chosen this fanciful dream-play through which to announce for the first time in overt and unmistakable fashion the conviction that underlies every one of his supreme Tragedies: that this world of sense in which we live is but the surface of a vaster unseen world by which the actions of men are affected or overruled. He had already in The Comedy of Errors hinted at a witchraft at work behind events. But that at the moment seemed little more than the author's apology for the amount of coincidence in his plot. Now he begins to explore the causes of coincidence. Not until the end of his career, in The Tempest, was he to treat this theme with such directness, not even in Macbeth. It may be objected that this is taking a mere dream or fantasy quite too seriously. It is of course possible to hold that in A Midsummer-Night's Dream Shakespeare is not so much giving utterance to convictions of his own as recording a folklore which itself carries certain metaphysical implications. There is doubtless some truth in this view—but how much it is hard to tell. But it makes little difference. For the implications, in the latter case, were the seeds of the convictions, and our mistake, if any, is merely that of finding the oak in the acorn. The congruity, in spite of their differences, of A Midsummer-Night's Dream with The Tempest is one of the most striking demonstrations of the continuity and integrity of Shakespeare's genius that his works afford.

There are two passages, as distinct from incidents, in A Midsummer-Night's Dream that perhaps above all others embody its central theme. Each enhances the other. One of them, Theseus' well-known speech on the imagination at the beginning of Act V, has always been accorded due importance. The other, oddly, though almost as universally praised, has generally been looked on as a kind of digression, a purple patch that justifies itself by its own beauty rather than through any particular pertinence to the rest of the play. The lines have been widely and deservedly acclaimed for their sound. But their euphony is only one aspect of their miraculous quality. The passage is the one in the first scene of Act IV where Theseus and Hippolyta, just as the dogs are about to be released for the hunt, speak of the music of the hounds in words that by some magic catch and echo that very music itself:

THE.:   My love shall hear the music of my hounds.
          Uncouple in the western valley; let them go:
          Dispatch, I say, and find the forester.
          We will, fair queen, up to the mountain's top,
          And mark the musical confusion
          Of hounds and echo in conjunction.
HIP.:   I was with Hercules and Cadmus once,
          When in a wood of Crete they bay'd the bear
          With hounds of Sparta: never did I hear
          Such gallant chiding; for, besides the groves,
          The skies, the fountains, every region near
          Seem'd all one mutual cry. I never heard
          So musical a discord, such sweet thunder.

THE.:   My hounds are bred out of the Spartan kind,
          So flew'd, so sanded; and their heads are hung
          With ears that sweep away the morning dew;
          Crook-knee'd, and dew-lapp'd like Thessalian
            bulls;
          Slow in pursuit, but march'd in mouth like
            bells,
          Each under each. A cry more tuneable
          Was never holla'd to, nor cheer'd with horn,
          In Crete, in Sparta, nor in Thessaly:
          Judge, when you hear.
                                                    [IV. i. 106-27]

This a digression! On the contrary it is as nearly perfect a metaphor as could be conceived for A Midsummer-Night's Dream itself and for the incomparable counterpoint with which its own confusions and discords are melted into the "sweet thunder" of a single musical effect. How can British fairies and Athenian nobility be mingled with decency in the same play? As easily as the "confusion" of hounds and echoes can make "conjunction." How can the crossings and bewilderments of the four lovers lead to their happy reunion at the end? As easily as discord can contribute to harmony in music. How can the foolish and awkward pranks of the rustics adorn the wedding celebration of a great duke? As easily, to turn things the other way around, as a fairy dream can enter the head of an ass or as animals who are like bulls can emit sounds that are like bells—as easily as thunder can be sweet.

The very incongruities, anachronisms, contradictions, and impossible juxapositions of A Midsummer-Night's Dream, and the triumphant manner in which the poet reduces them to a harmony, are what more than anything else make this play a masterpiece. The hounds are symbols of the hunt, and so of death. But their voices are transmuted by distance, in the ear of the listener, to symbols of harmony and life. The hunt is called off; the will of the cruel father is overborne; a triple wedding is substituted for it:

          Our purpos'd hunting shall be set aside.
          Away with us to Athens: three and three,
          We'll hold a feast in great solemnity.
                                                    [IV. i. 183-85]

We might discover the whole history of humanity, past and future, in those lines.

It is right here that the passage about the hounds links with Theseus' speech on the imagination. The Duke, in words too well known to need quotation, tells of the power of this faculty, whether in the lunatic, the lover, or the poet, to create something out of nothing. The poet alone, however, has power to capture this "airy nothing" and anchor it, as it were, to reality, even as Shakespeare gives actuality to fairies in this very play. Yet Theseus is suspicious of the "tricks" of imagination, conscious of its illusory quality. He hints that it must be brought to the test of "cool reason." Strictly, what Theseus is talking about is not imagination at all in its proper sense, but fantasy. Hippolyta catches just this distinction and for once seems wiser than her lover. She holds that the miracles of love are even greater than those of fancy, and because the same miracle takes place at the same time in more than one mind she believes that they testify to something solid and lasting that emerges from this "airy nothing." Theseus had called this faculty more strange than true. Hippolyta holds it both strange and true:

          But all the story of the night told over,
          And all their minds transfigur'd so together,

More witnesseth than fancy's images,
And grows to something of great constancy,
But, howsoever, strange and admirable.

[IV. i. 23-7]

In practice Theseus agrees with this exactly, as is shown later in the same scene when he insists on hearing the play that the craftsmen have prepared. The master of revels, Philostrate, protests against its selection:

PHIL.:   in all the play
        There is not one word apt, one player fitted.
        . . . No, my noble lord,
        It is not for you. I have heard it over,
        And it is nothing, nothing in the world. . . .
THE.:   I will hear that play;
        For never anything can be amiss,
        When simpleness and duty tender it. . . .
HIP.:   He says they can do nothing in this kind.
THE.:   The kinder we, to give them thanks for
        nothing.

[V. i. 64-89]

That four-times reiterated ''nothing'' is Shakespeare's way of sending our minds back to the ''airy nothing'' of Theseus' earlier speech which, he then said and now proves, imagination has power to turn into something actual. It is Hippolyta this time who fails.

        This is the silliest stuff that ever I heard,

she protests as the play proceeds. Appropriately, now that it is a question of art, Theseus turns out to be wiser than she, as she was wiser than he when it was a question of love. ''The best in this kind are but shadows,'' he reminds her, ''and the worst are no worse, if imagination amend them'' [V. i. 211-12]. At last, Theseus is using ''imagination'' in its proper sense, and in his words we seem to catch the very accent and secret of the poet's own tolerance and sympathy. (pp. 74-7)

A Midsummer-Night's Dream is a kind of fugue with four voices

        match'd in mouth like bells,
    Each under each.

There are the fairies. There are the lovers. There are the rustics. There is the court. What metaphysical as well as social gulfs divide them! But Imagination bridges them all. Imagination makes them all one.

And the play has four voices in another and profounder sense.

A Midsummer-Night's Dream is itself, as its title says, a dream. Its action occurs mostly at night. Its atmosphere is that of moonlight and shadows. Its characters are forever falling asleep and dreaming. And at the end Puck invites the audience to believe that as they have been sitting there they have nodded and slumbered and that all that has passed before them has been a vision.

But as the other part of its title suggests, *A Midsummer-Night's Dream* is not only a dream, it is ''play'' in the quite literal sense of that term, a piece pervaded with the atmosphere of innocent idleness and joy befitting a midsummer night. It is not merely a play; it is the spirit of play in its essence. From the pranks of Puck and the frolics of the fairies, through the hide-and-seek of the lovers in the wood and the rehearsals of the rustics, on to the wedding festivities of the court and the final presentation of the masque of Pyramus and Thisbe, the tone of the piece is that of love-in-idleness, of activity for the sheer fun of it and for its own sake.

And because *A Midsummer-Night's Dream* is permeated with this spirit of doing things just for the love of doing them or for the love of the one for whom they are done, because the drama opens and closes on the wedding note and what comes between is just an interweaving of love stories, the piece may be said to be not only *dream* from end to end, and *play* from end to end, but also *love* from end to end.

And finally *A Midsummer-Night's Dream* is *art* from end to end—not just a work of art itself, which of course it is, but dedicated in good measure to the theme of art and made up of many little works of art of varying degrees of merit: its innumerable songs, its perpetual references to music, its rehearsal and presentation of the story of Pyramus and Thisbe, to say nothing of its many quotable passages, which, like the one about the hounds, the one about the superiority of silence to eloquence, the one about true love, the one about the mermaid on the dolphin's back, when lifted from their context seem like poems or pictures complete in themselves, whatever subtler values they may have in relation to the whole.

Dream, play, love, art. Surely it is no coincidence that these four ''subjects'' which are here interwoven with such consummate polyphony represent the four main aspects under which Imagination reveals itself in human life. Dream: what is that but a name for the world out of which man emerges into conscious life, the world of the unconscious as we have a habit of calling it today? Play: the instrument by which the child instinctively repeats the experience of the race and so by rehearsal prepares himself for the drama of life. Love: a revelation to each of the sexes that it is but a fragment of Another, which, by combined truth and illusion, seems at first concentrated in a person of the opposite sex. Art: the dream become conscious of itself, play grown to an adult estate, love freed of its illusion and transferred to wider and higher than personal ends. Dream, play, love, art: these four. Is there a fifth?

The fifth perhaps is what we finally have in this play, a union of the other four, Imagination in its quintessence—not just a dream, nor play, nor love, nor art, but something above and beyond them all. With the attainment of it, the first becomes last, dream comes full circle as Vision, an immediate conscious apprehension of an invisible world, or, if you will, transubstantiation of the world of sense into something beyond itself.

The example of Bottom and his transformation will serve to bring these un-Shakespearean abstractions back to the concrete. To the average reader, Puck and Bottom are probably the most memorable characters in the play, Bottom especially. This instinct is right. . . . Bottom symbolizes the earthy, the ponderous, the slow, in contrast with Puck, who is all that is quick, light, and aerial. Bottom is substance, the real in the common acceptation of that term. If Puck is the apex, Bottom is the base without whose four-square foundation the pyramid of life would topple over. He is the antithesis of the thesis of the play, the ballast that keeps the elfin bark of it from capsizing. He is literally what goes to the bottom. Like all heavy things he is content with his place in life, but his egotism is the unconscious selfishness of a child, both a sense and a consequence of his own individuality, not greed but pride in the good significance of that word. His realistic conception of stagecraft is in character. To Puck, Bottom is an ass. Yet Titania falls in love with him, ass's head and all.

        And I will purge thy mortal grossness so
        That thou shalt like an airy spirit go,

[III. i. 160-61]

she promises. And she keeps her promise by sending him Bottom's dream.

The moment when Bottom awakens from this dream is the supreme moment of the play. There is nothing more wonderful in the poet's early works and few things more wonderful in any of them. For what Shakespeare has caught here in perfection is the original miracle of the Imagination, the awakening of spiritual life in the animal man. Bottom is an ass. If Botton can be redeemed, matter itself and man in all his materiality can be redeemed also. Democracy becomes possible. Nothing less than this is what this incident implies. Yet when it is acted, so far as my experience in the theater goes, this divine insight is reduced to nothing but an occasion for roars of laughter. Laughter of course there should be, but laughter shot through with a beauty and pathos close to tears. Only an actor of genius could do justice to it. Bottom himself best indicates its quality when he declares that the dream deserve to be *sung* at the conclusion of a play and that it should be called Bottom's dream "because it hath no bottom" [IV. i. 216]. For a moment in this scene, however far over the horizon, we sense the Shakespeare who was to describe the death of Falstaff, compose *King Lear,* and create Caliban.

Indeed, *A Midsummer-Night's Dream* as a whole is prophetic, in one respect at least, as is no other of the earlier plays, of the course the poet's genius was to take. There are few more fruitful ways of regarding his works than to think of them as

an account of the warfare between Imagination and Chaos— or, if you will, between Imagination and the World—the story of the multifarious attempts of the divine faculty in man to ignore, to escape, to outwit, to surmount, to combat, to subdue, to forgive, to convert, to redeem, to transmute into its own substance, as the case may be, the powers of disorder that possess the world. Taken retrospectively, *A Midsummer-Night's Dream* seems like the argument of this story, like an overture to the vast musical composition which the poet's later masterpieces make up, like a seed from which the Shakespearean flower developed and unfolded. (pp. 77-80)

> Harold C. Goddard, "'A Midsummer-Night's Dream'," in his The Meaning of Shakespeare, *The University of Chicago Press, 1951, pp. 74-80.*

B. IFOR EVANS   (essay date 1952)

[*Evans evaluates the poetic language of* A Midsummer Night's Dream, *particularly in comparison with the style of Shakespeare's earlier plays. He argues that the language is "far less self-conscious" in this work and asserts that it is also much more fully integrated with the other dramatic elements. Other critics who have discussed the poetic style of* A Midsummer Night's Dream *include G. Wilson Knight (1932), Thomas Marc Parrott (1949), David P. Young (1966), and Stephen Fender (1968). Evans additionally comments on the effectiveness of the language in depicting the play's rural setting and maintains that* A Midsummer

Act II. Scene i. Helena, Demetrius, and Oberon with Fairies. By G. F. Sargent (1841). The Department of Rare Books and Special Collections, The University of Michigan Library.

Night's Dream *is the last work by Shakespeare in which the rustic theme is so important. George Brandes (1895-96) and C. L. Barber (1959) have also examined the importance of the bucolic elements in this play.*]

No element in Shakespeare's language has been given so little emphasis as his power of using simple and direct language. The splendours of his imagery have drawn attention away from the effectiveness of these strong, dramatic effects made out of the most unpretentious elements. It is a power that increases with his maturity. In [*A Midsummer Night's Dream*] the direct passages are often thin and slow-moving compared with those in the great tragedies, nor are they given a large place. Further it may be recalled that in exploiting the resounding and elaborate elements in language he was answering the spirit of his age and the practice of his contemporaries, but the quiet language was a dramatic opportunity and necessity that he had to discover for himself, against the fashion of his time, and indeed in opposition to much that was dominant in his own temperament.

The mood in the *Dream* is lyrical and the scenes of the lovers invite a happy play of verbal conceits. In these scenes Shakespeare is not breaking new ground in language but is often doing something again, but with an added grace, because he has done it successfully before.

While using this serviceable if *flat* language in order to move the action, he reserves for the lovers an imagery similiar to that which occupied his mind in the sonnets. So Theseus says to Hermia:

> Thrice-blessed they that master so their blood,
> To undergo such maiden pilgrimage;
> But earthlier happy is the rose distill'd,
> Than that which withering on the virgin thorn
> Grows, lives and dies in single blessedness.
>
> [I. i. 74-8]

This was the very comparison he had explored with singular beauty in the Fifth Sonnet:

> Then, were not summer's distillation left,
> A liquid prisoner pent in walls of glass,
> Beauty's effect with beauty were bereft,
> Nor it nor no remembrance what it was:
>   But flowers distill'd, though they with winter meet,
>   Leese but their show; their substance still lives sweet.

Much of the warm effusiveness of the language which Hermia and Lysander exchange belongs to the sonnet tradition, and the same is true of Helena and Demetrius. Hermia will swear 'by Cupid's strongest bow' [I. i. 169], by 'the simplicity of Venus' doves' [I. i. 171], and by a whole catalogue of such comparisons. Helena in speaking to Hermia uses the very idiom of the sonnet writers, with their play on words, the balance in the line, and the easy and ample imagery:

> Call you me fair? that fair again unsay.
> Demetrius loves your fair: O happy fair!
> Your eyes are lode-stars; and your tongue's sweet air
> More tuneable than lark to shepherd's ear,
> When what is green, when hawthorn buds appear.
>
> [I. i. 181-85]

Hermia and Lysander play upon words, in the manner of the sonnets, until at length Hermia pleads that 'Lysander riddles very prettily' [II. ii. 53].

As a contrast to the sonneteering moods of the lovers there come the happy interludes of rustic prose of Bottom and his friends. The aim here is usually direct and dramatic with a natural realism, and no involved trick in the language as in *Love's Labour's Lost,* though Quince, it is true, cannot avoid the rule of triplicity in giving their parts to his fellow actors: 'I am to *entreat* you, *request* you and *desire* you, to con them by tomorrow night' [I. ii. 99-101].

Apart from Theseus's speech on poetic imagination there is very little direct reference to language. In *Hamlet* the coming of the players is used for the most detailed and elaborate discussion of diction. The rehearsals of Bottom and his fellows give similar opportunities but they have not been taken up and the atmosphere is left uncritical and carefree in this comedy. The only exception is that Bottom is permitted to describe the ranting language which it would give him pleasure to employ: 'That will ask some tears in the true performing of it: if I do it, let the audience look to their eyes; I will move storms, I will condole in some measure. To the rest: yet my chief humour is for a tyrant: I could play Ercles rarely, or a part to tear a cat in, to make all split' [I. ii. 25-30]. (pp. 48-9)

The difference between all this and *Love's Labour's Lost* is that in the earlier play the employment of a witty and decorative language was the major occupation upon which plot and characters depended, while here, in one of the most original and balanced plays in all Shakespeare's work, plot, characters, atmosphere, mood and language are brought into a single dramatic purpose. It may be that this very unity of creative intention makes the use of language far less self-conscious than in *Love's Labour's Lost.* Much of it is simple, as if no mental entanglement stood between Shakespeare and the presentation of the theme, as it did, much later, in the opening scenes of *The Winter's Tale.*

Despite its many affectations of language, *Love's Labour's Lost* did retain an interest in the English countryside and in rustic scenes, and the background of Athens in *A Midsummer-Night's Dream* is also this same England, where Bottom and his companion players can meet and where Puck is the 'merry wanderer of the night' [II. i. 43]. But now, England is given a magic of faery, and that vision is in turn kept in touch with the rustic. Both are united in a lyrical, and mainly rhyming verse, while the moon imagery and atmosphere make the borderlands of faery and reality deliberately difficult to define. Thus, for instance, in the passages where Puck is questioned by the Fairy on his identity:

>   are not you he
> That frights the maidens of the villagery;
> Skim milk, and sometimes labour in the quern
> And bootless make the breathless housewife churn;
> And sometimes make the drink to bear no barm;
> Mislead night-wanderers, laughing at their harm?
> Those that Hobgoblin call you and sweet Puck,
> You do their work, and they shall have good luck:
> Are not you he?
>
> [II. i. 34-42]

It is in such descriptions that one is aware of the genuine rustic England out of which the more visionary elements have been constructed. So Titania describes to Oberon the ways in which he has disturbed her 'sport' in a moving passage realistic in all its elements, though in the passage immediately preceding we have been on 'the farthest steppe of India' and 'through the glimmering night from Perigenia':

> Contagious fogs; which falling in the land
> Have every pelting river made so proud
> That they have overborne their continents:
> The ox hath therefore stretch'd his yoke in vain,
> The ploughman lost his sweat, and the green corn
> Hath rotted ere his youth attain'd a beard;
> The fold stands empty in the drowned field,
> And crows are fatted with the murrion flock;
> The nine men's morris is fill'd up with mud,
> And the quaint mazes in the wanton green
> For lack of tread are undistinguishable.
>
> [II. i. 90-100]

This passage, a part only of which is quoted, belongs to genuine observation of the rural scene. It is followed by the most deliberately magical passage in the play:

> That very time I saw, but thou couldst not,
> Flying between the cold moon and the earth,
> Cupid all arm'd: a certain aim he took
> At a fair vestal throned by the west,
> And loosed his love-shaft smartly from his bow,
> As it should pierce a hundred thousand hearts;
> But I might see young Cupid's fiery shaft
> Quench'd in the chaste beams of the watery moon,
> And the imperial votaress passed on,
> In maiden meditation, fancy-free.
>
> [II. i. 155-64]

There is no return to the language of *A Midsummer-Night's Dream.* Later Shakespeare's poetic speech becomes stronger and more complex, and shakes the imagination more profoundly, but here it is gathered up into the dominant mood of the *Dream,* where myth and romance and the gentle Enlgish scene are at one, and where all is easily intelligible, lyrical in mood and gentle. Sometimes in the lovers' exchanges, following the pattern of the sonnets, the language ranges over human experience for the comparisons. So Lysander says:

> For as a surfeit of the sweetest things
> The deepest loathing to the stomach brings,
> Or as the heresies that men do leave
> Are hated most of those they did deceive,
> So thou, my surfeit and my heresy,
> Of all be hated, but the most of me!
>
> [II. ii. 137-42]

But normally the concentration is on the country scene, either with its real or its faery aspects, and it is in the sudden transfer from one to the other that the play gains some of its most brilliant effects. So in a striking passage Puck describes the effect of the transformation of Bottom on his companions:

> When they him spy,
> As wild geese that the creeping fowler eye,
> Or russet-pated choughs, many in sort,
> Rising and cawing at the gun's report,
> Sever themselves and madly sweep the sky,
> So, at his sight, away his fellows fly.
>
> [III. ii. 19-24]

As often in the early plays, here is the memory of a rustic scene arising directly out of Shakespeare's personal experience.

In other passages he recalls a memory of a nature scene, already half-idealised:

> I know a bank where the wild thyme blows,
> Where oxlips and the nodding violet grows,
> Quite over-canopied with luscious woodbine,
> With sweet musk-roses and with eglantine:
> There sleeps Titania sometime of the night,
> Lull'd in these flowers with dances and delight.
>
> [II.   249-54]

The rural theme will, of course, be found later in the plays, for it is a memory which never dies out, but the primary emphasis on this motive disappears here in *A Midsummer-Night's Dream* after its dominance in the early comedies and the histories. When it returns, actively, as in Falstaff's visit to Justice Shallow [*2 Henry IV,* III. ii. 194-219], the mood is that of the townsman, recalling half-regretfully something which he knows he has outlived. It is present in the last plays in a new and sophisticated way, yet intermingled with simpler passages, and all strangely moving, though some theorists have discovered too much in it. This I would record rather than attempt to explain. It would be easy to press the biographical motive and to say that in the plays that follow the town interests had replaced the native background. At times, certainly, as in *Romeo and Juliet* a conscious art gathers up the language so appropriately to the mood that there is no room for this rustic material. Whatever be the conclusion, *A Midsummer-Night's Dream* seems to mark the end of a period, the exhaustion of the first impulse, and the stretching out of genius towards fresh attainment. (pp. 49-52)

> *B. Ifor Evans, "'A Midsummer-Night's Dream',"* in his The Language of Shakespeare's Plays, *Methuen & Co. Ltd., 1952, pp. 45-52.*

PAUL N. SIEGEL   (essay date 1953)

[*In an unexcerpted portion of his essay on* A Midsummer Night's Dream, *Siegel recommends that the reader imagine himself a member of the aristocratic audience which attended the first performance of the play. He notes that the wedding guests would have perceived the relevance of the play's dramatic action to the couple for whose marriage celebration it was written and would have realized that when the play concluded with the consummation of the stage marriages it would signal the time for the consummation of the actual marriage. In the excerpt below, Siegel contends that the Pyramus and Thisbe interlude in Act V is an illustration of and commentary on the perils experienced by the young Athenian lovers in the main plot. He also regards the interlude as containing Shakespeare's subtle request that his sophisticated audience "aid him with its imagination" and amend any defects in his drama, an interpretation similar to that proposed by Frederick S. Boas (1896) and Elizabeth Sewell (1960). For further discussion of the play-within-the-play in* A Midsummer Night's Dream, *see the excerpts by August Wilhelm Schlegel (1808), G. G. Gervinus (1849), Edward Dowden (1881), Denton J. Snider (1890), George Brandes (1895-96), E. K. Chambers (1905), E. C. Pettet (1949), C. L. Barber (1959), T. Walter Herbert (1964), James L. Calderwood (1971), and Mordecai Marcus (1981); also, see the essays by Alvin B. Kernan and J. W. Robinson listed in the Additional Bibliography.*]

The play put on by the rude country artisans for the Duke . . . is a kind of comment on *A Midsummer Night's Dream* itself which gives added significance to the manner in which it completes it. The story of Pyramus and Thisbe of the play-within-the-play is, like that of *A Midsummer Night's Dream,* an illustration that "true lovers have been ever crossed" [I. i. 150] and that "the course of true love never did run smooth" [I. i. 134]. Like Lysander and Hermia, Pyramus and Thisbe are forbidden by their parents to love. And with them, there is unfortunate misunderstanding and confusion, and Pyramus believes Thisbe to be dead, as for a time Hermia thought Lysander to have been slain by Demetrius. Indeed, if we are to define categories as Polonius did [in *Hamlet*], the story of Lysander and Hermia might more properly than that of Pyramus and Thisbe have been called "very tragical mirth" [V. i. 57], while the story of Pyramus and Thisbe might have been better called "very mirthful tragedy." The play-within-the-play might be said to be a presentation in little of *A Midsummer Night's Dream* as it would be seen through a distorting medium. "This is the silliest stuff that ever I heard" [V. i. 210], says Hippolyta of it. The same might have been said of *A Midsummer Night's Dream* by a hardheaded businesslike man of affairs who would have no truck with fairie and such. In fact, it was said. "It is the most insipid ridiculous play that ever I saw in my life," wrote Mr. Samuel Pepys in his diary after having seen a Restoration performance of Shakespeare's airily fanciful comedy [see excerpt above, 1662]. Through the Pyramus-Thisbe play Shakespeare was subtly asking his aristocratic audience to regard his play with imaginative understanding and sympathy. "The best in this kind are but shadows," replies Theseus to Hippolyta, "and the worst are no worse, if imagination amend them" [V. i. 211-12]. This is lordly graciousness, to which Shakespeare was appealing and which he was at the same time flattering: the aristocratic spectator would remedy in his own mind the defects of the piece being presented before him. "Our sport shall be to take what they mistake; And what poor duty cannot do, noble respect Takes it in might, not merit" [V. i. 90-2].

While asking his audience, however, to aid him with its imagination, Shakespeare was, with the assurance of genius, displaying his mastery of his art. Although the imaginative coöperation of an audience is necessary for the success of a play, the Pyramus-Thisbe scene shows that, despite the Duke's words of gracious condescension, not all of an audience's good will and tolerant receptivity can make rant moving. "This passion, and the death of a dear friend, would go near to make a man sad" [V. i. 288-89]. The contrast between the crude literalism of a man with a lantern representing moonshine of the Pyramus-Thisbe scene and the poetic magic of the moon-drenched imagery of *A Midsummer Night's Dream* itself, between the inept explanatory comments that the play is but a play and not real life ("When lion rough in wildest rage doth roar, Then know that I, as Snug the joiner, am a lion fell," [V. i. 222-24]), and the delicate suggestion that the play, while only reflecting life, may be a kind of enchanted mirror displaying unseen truths—this contrast is a daring virtuosity calling attention to itself at the close of its performance. (pp. 142-43)

Paul N. Siegel, " 'A Midsummer Night's Dream' and the Wedding Guests," in Shakespeare Quarterly, *Vol. IV, No. 2, April, 1953, pp. 139-44.*

JOHN H. LONG (essay date 1955)

[*Long demonstrates that in* A Midsummer Night's Dream *music is principally associated with the fairies and serves to intensify the sense of their unreality. One important use of music, Long argues, occurs at the turning point of the play—when Titania and the young lovers are released from the spell of the love potion and awake from their dreams. He contends that the music and dance at this moment in the drama signal the reestablishment of*

concord and harmony between Titania and Oberon and the restoration of order in the relationships of the young lovers. Among other critics who have examined music and dance in A Midsummer Night's Dream, *Alan Brissenden (1981) maintains that Shakespeare's use of dance is intended to symbolize the end of chaos and a return to order in the play, and Cumberland Clark (1931) indicates the way that music enhances the fairy-like atmosphere. For further discussion of the resolution of discord into harmony depicted in the play, see the excerpts by Harold C. Goddard (1951), John Vyvyan (1961), Stephen Fender (1968), and R. A. Zimbardo (1970); also, see the essay by Paul A. Olson listed in the Additional Bibliography.*]

A Midsummer Night's Dream is a delicate comedy of earthy humor and fantastic conceits, of fairy pranks and noble sentiments. From beginning to end, as its title suggests, it is pervaded by a dreamlike quality, a mixture of sheer fantasy and solid reality, sparkling with some of the most beautiful poetry written by Shakespeare. For all the evanescence of the play, however, its construction reveals a solidity and sureness of technique far above the comedies which preceded it. The artistry of the work is highly complex, composed as it is of a blend of low comedy and high comedy, of the supernatural and the natural, the masque form and the dramatic form, of prose, poetry, and music. Yet these diverse elements, so interfused as to defy complete analysis, achieve a firm dramatic unity. (p. 82)

One of the important problems to be solved by Shakespeare [in *A Midsummer Night's Dream*] was the effective presentation of the fairies; they had to be clearly distingushed from the mortals in the play. Language and costume contributed to the solution of the problem, as did the use of children in suggesting the diminutive size of the fairies. The essential nature of the fairies—their airiness—required a more subtle depiction, however, such as music could most appropriately supply. The first instance of Shakespeare's use of music for this purpose occurs in [II. ii. 1-26], where Titania's fairy attendants sing her to sleep just before she is enchanted by Oberon: "*Enter Queene of Fairies, with her traine. Queene.* Come, now a Roundell, and a Fairy song; / . . . Sing me now asleepe, / Then to your offices, and let me rest."

> *Fairies Sing.*
> You spotted Snakes with double tongue,
> Thorny Hedgehogges be not seene,
> Newts and blinde wormes do no wrong,
> Come not neere our Fairy Queene.
> Philomele with melodie,
> Sing in your sweet Lullaby
> Lulla, lulla, lullaby, lulla, lulla, lullaby,
> Neuer harme, nor spell, nor charme,
> Come our louely Lady nye,
> So good night with Lullaby.
>   2. Fairy. Weaning Spiders come not heere,
> Hence you long leg'd Spinners, hence:
> Beetles blacke approach not neere;
> Worme nor Snayle doe no offence.
> Philomele with melody, &c.
>   1. Fairy. Hence away, now all is well;
> One aloofe, stand Centinell.   *Shee sleepes.*
>   *Enter Oberon.*
>
>   [II. ii. 1-26]

It is not difficult to determine the actions taken by the performers of the song. Titania calls for a roundel, which is a circular dance. The fairy attendants, probably about six in number, apparently join hands and dance around Titania as they sing the song. The song itself is an ayre in the form of a lullaby, a type of song quite popular during the period. The language, the subject matter, and the eleven-line structure of the roundel all suggest an art song, as opposed to a folk form. In structure, the song consists of two quatrains to which is joined a seven-line refrain. (pp. 84-5)

There are several reasons why Shakespeare placed a fairy dance and song at this point of the play. It is necesary for Titania to fall asleep in order that Oberon may cast his spell over her. The song, as the text shows, was composed for the purpose of lulling Titania to sleep.

But why should Titania be so honored when the lovers fell asleep without music? . . . [Music] and the portrayal of the supernatural were closely allied in the Elizabethan drama. On a stage with limited mechanical devices, music often served to achieve the sense of unreality demanded by scenes containing ghostly characters and actions. The fairies with which Shakespeare peopled this play are airy sprites defying time and space, constantly in motion. Even a lullaby is sung to dancing feet. Shakespeare joined music with some of his most delicate poetry in order to set his fairie apart from the gross mortals of the play; it is hardly a coincidence that, throughout the play, music is reserved completely for those episodes involving the fairies or the rustics in contrast to the fairies. Even when Titania falls so far from fairy grace as to become enamored of an ass, the depth of her disgrace is suggested by the contrast between the lovely song to which she falls asleep and the earthy song of Bottom to which she awakes.

After Titania's lullaby the next appearance in the play of music— of a sort—is that by Bottom as an ass in his scene with Titania [III. i. 118-38]:

Enter Peter Quince.
  Pet. Blesse thee *Bottome*, blesse thee; thou
art translated.

                                        Exit.

  Bot. I see their knauery; this is to make an
asse of me, to fright me if they could; but I
will not stirre from this place, do what they
can. I will walk vp and downe here, and I will
sing that they shall heare I am not afraid.
    The Woosel cocke, so blacke of hew,
      With Orenge-tawny bill.
    The Throstle, with his note so true,
      The Wren and little quill.

  Tyta. What Angell wakes me from my flowry bed?

  Bot. The Finch, the Sparrow, and the Larke,
    The plainsong Cuckow gray;
  Whose note full many a man doth marke,
    And deares not answere, nay.

  For indeede, who would set his wit to so foolish
    a bird?
  Who would giue a bird the lye, though he cry
    Cuckow, neuer so?

  Tyta. I pray thee gentle mortall, sing againe,
Mine eare is much enamored of thy note; . . .
                                [III. i. 118-38]

There seems little doubt that here Bottom sings two fragments of a song. The completion of the song, to judge from the text, was probably a refrain. The song resembles a folk type such as would be appropriate for Bottom. The performance of the

song was probably as crude as could be sung with any resemblance to music, since the humor of the situation is derived partly from the dainty Titania's delight in what was, no doubt, a far-from-angelic voice. (pp. 88-9)

We have seen music used to depict the ethereal nature of the fairies in Titania's lullaby and music used in Bottom's song to stress the contrast between the fairies and the clowns. We now find [IV. i. 78-84] music used to emphasize the fairy-gentlefolk relationship in the play. Titania, Oberon, and Puck remove their enchantments from Bottom and from the sleeping lovers: "*Tita.* How came these things to passe? / Oh, how mine eyes doth loath this visage now! / *Ob.* Silence a while. *Robin* take off his head: / *Titania,* musick call, and strike more dead / Then common sleepe; of all these, fine the sense. / *Tita.* Musicke, ho musicke, such as charmeth sleepe. / *Musick still. Rob.* When thou wak'st, with thine owne fooles eies peepe" [IV. i. 78-84].

The cue for the musicians to begin playing is given by Titania. The music played is described in the same line—". . . such as charmeth sleepe." It is the function of the music to restore the sleeping mortals to their senses. At the conclusion of the consort piece, Puck describes the future result of the magical music on the mortals: "When thou wak'st, with thine owne fooles eies peepe." (pp. 91-2)

The passage involving the sleep-inducing song contains three interesting aspects of Shakespeare's dramatic art; in it may be perceived his use of music to suggest the magical powers of the fairies, his adaptation of a common Elizabethan belief in the curative powers of music for human ills, both mental and physical, and his use of music . . . to underscore the turning point of the play.

The relationship of the music to the turning point of the play requires some explanation. It will be remembered that the confusions which beset the mortals in the play are results of the quarrel between Titania and Oberon. The inference made by Shakespeare is that when discord occurs in the fairy world human affairs also become out of tune. We would hence expect that the resolution of the quarrel between Oberon and Titania would be quickly followed by a harmonious adjustment in mortal relationships. As we have seen, the music evoked by Titania was for the purpose of resolving the mortal discord. From the sleep disenchantment episode to the end of the play, all difficulties disappear and joy reigns throughout Athens. The end of the fairy strife and the disenchantment of the mortals clearly mark the turning point of the comedy.

Lest the significance of the passage just discussed be possibly overlooked by his audience, Shakespeare apparently restated the point, again with language, action, and music. . . . For Oberon again calls for music, a cue which a mere casual glance . . . would lead us falsely to associate with the preceding passage:

  Rob. When thou wak'st, with thine owne fooles eies
    peepe.
  Ob. Sound musick; come my Queen, take hands with
    me
  And rocke the ground whereon these sleepers be.
  Now thou and I are new in amity,
  And will to morrow midnight, solemnly
  Dance in Duke *Theseus* house triumphantly,
  And blesse it to all faire posterity,
  There shall the pairs of faithfull Louers be
  Wedded, with *Theseus,* all in iollity.
                                [IV. i. 84-92]

Puck's line, however appears to mark the close of the "musicke such as charmeth sleepe"; hence, Oberon's call for music must be the prelude to another episode. After his command for music, Oberon says, ". . . come, my Queen, take hands with me, . . ." which suggests a dance, especially when Oberon adds, ". . . And rocke the ground whereon these sleepers be." Evidently Oberon and Titania here perform a dance to the music of the hidden consort. After the dance is ended, Oberon announces, "Now thou and I are new in amity, . . ." The music and dance symbolizes the concord re-established between Oberon and Titania. But, more than that, it also apparently symbolizes the harmony restored in the relationship of the mortals. This Oberon indicates by anticipating the events of the following act with the lines: "There shall the paires of faithfull Louers be / Wedded, with *Theseus,* all in iollity." The two passages we have just examined, then, should be considered as having one primary dramatic purpose, though they also have several secondary overtones. Titania's music marks the end of all conflict and, hence, the turning point of the play. Oberon's music symbolizes the new amity between the fairy king and queen, and, together with the dialogue, foreshadows the concord to be reached by the mortals. The music throughout the two episodes also aids the illusion of magic and enchantment. (pp. 93-4)

Upon the exit of Oberon, Titania, and Puck, we are brought back to reality by the hoarse clamor of a hunting horn, the herald of a new day. Theseus, Hippolyta, and their attendants, while hunting discover the lovers asleep in the woods. The lovers are awakened, and in a very interesting manner. We would expect the Duke or one of his attendants to awaken the lovers by speaking to them or by shaking them. Such is not the case; the Duke commands [IV. i. 138]: "*The.* Goe bid the hunts-men wake them with their hornes. *Hornes and they wake. Shout within, they all start up. Thes.* Good morrow friends: Saint *Valentine* is past, / Begin these wood birds but to couple now?" [IV. i. 138-40].

Why would Shakespeare have wanted the lovers awakened in such a complicated fashion? One dramatic consequence we may at least observe: the music of the horns is closely related to Titania's "musicke, such as charmeth sleepe." Her music marks the curative spell under which the lovers sleep; it is fairy music. The hunting horns end the spell and return the lovers to a world of reality. Fairy music charms; mortal music awakes. So it is with the lulling and awakening of the lovers, and so it was with the lulling and awakening of Titania.

The remainder of the music is in the festive spirit of the last act. The clowns perform their "tedious brief tragedy" and offer an epilogue at its conclusion. The Duke refuses the epilogue, choosing instead to be entertained by a Bergamask dance performed, probably, by Moon and Lion. . . . "*Bot.* No, I assure you, the wall is downe, that parted their Fathers. Will it please you to see the Epilogue, or to heare a Bergomask dance, betweene two of our company? *Duk.* No Epilogue, I pray you; . . . But come, your Burgomaske; let your Epilogue alone. The iron tongue of midnight hath told twelue. / Louers to bed, 'tis almost Fairy time. / . . ." [V. i. 351-64].

Dover Wilson suggests that the Bergamask dance performs the functions of an antimask, the grotesque and comic part of masque entertainments, and that it is an introduction to the masque of the fairies which follows it. The suggestion is illuminating, but the dance, probably a jig, is also to be considered as what Bottom proclaims it to be—a part of the en-

tertainment planned by the rustics—an alternative afterpiece to their play. (pp. 94-6)

At the end of the Bergamask dance, a bell tolls the hour of midnight. It is the striking of the hour which separates the jig, aesthetically, from the music and dance which follow it. For, as the Duke proclaims, shifting from prose to blank verse, "The iron tongue of midnight hath told twelue. Louers to bed, 'tis almost Fairy time." It is fairy time. The mortals disappear, taking with them the world of reality and leaving in its stead a world peopled by creatures of the air, spirits of good and spirits of evil who, until cock-crow, flit unseen through the mansions of the living, locked often in silent struggles over the destinies of sleeping mortals. Lest the "damned spirits," mentioned earlier by Puck [III. ii. 382], mar the auspicious occasion, Oberon and Titania, who "are spirits of another sort" [III. ii. 388], come with thir attendant fairies to exorcise the evil spirits from the happy household. Puck appears and explains the purpose of the fairy visitation. The stage is suddenly filled with dancing fairies, flickering tapes, music and song. True to form, the fairie cast their beneficent spell to the sound of music:

> *Enter King and Queene of Fairies, with their traine*
> *Ob.* Through the house giue glimmering light,
> By the dead and drowsie fier,
> Euerie Elfe and Fairie spright,
> Hop as light as bird from brier,
> And this Ditty after me, sing and dance it trippinglie.
> 　*Tita.* First rehearse this song by roate,
> To each word a warbling note.
> Hand in hand, with Fairie grace,
> Will we sing and blesse this place.
> 　　　*The Song*
> Now untill the breake of day,
> Through this house each Fairy stray.
> To the best Bride-bed will we,
> Which by us shall blessed be:
> And the issue there create,
> Euer shall be fortunate:
> So shall all the couples three,
> Euer true in louing be:
> And the blots of Natures hand,
> Shall not in their issue stand.
> Neuer mole, harelip, nor scarre,
> Nor marke prodigious, such as are
> Despised in Natiuitie,
> Shall upon their children be.
> With this field dew consecrate,
> Euery Fairy take his gate,
> And each seuerall chamber blesse,
> Through this Pallace with sweet peace,
> Euer shall in Safety rest,
> And the owner of it blest.
> Trip away, make no stay;
> Meet me all by breake of day.

　　　　　　　　　　　　　　　　　　　[V. i. 391-422]
　　　　　　　　　　　　　　　　　　　　(pp. 97-8)

If we begin the song with Oberon's lines, "Through the house . . ." etc., the entire song will consist of five six-line stanzas and a brisk closing couplet. These stanzas perform two functions; the first two contain directions given by Oberon and Titania to their attendants, that is, they explain what is to be done. The fairies are to sing and dance through the house and are to bless it. In the third and fourth stanzas, the fairies describe the nature of their blessing. In the fifth stanza, Oberon repeats his commands and concludes the song. (p. 99)

On the basis of the evidence presented in this study, the following conclusions regarding Shakespeare's use of music in *A Midsummer Night's Dream* seem to be inescapable:

1. Shakespeare used music in the play for the primary purpose of setting the fairies apart from the mortals.

2. A secondary use of music in the play was to stress the contrast between the dainty Titania and the boorish Bottom.

3. Another secondary use of music was to heighten the dramatic effect of the fairy spells and enchantments.

4. Still another secondary use of music was to symbolize the concord arising from the settlement of the fairy quarrel, and to foreshadow the resulting harmony between the mortals—thus emphasizing the turning point of the play. (p. 101)

The over-all impression we gain from our examination of the music in the play is that Shakespeare employed music much more lavishly than he did in his preceding plays, and that the increase in the quantity of the music is equalled by the increased artistry with which the music was employed. We may readily believe that without the music in the play, performed as Shakespeare intended it to be performed, much of the lyrical charm and fantasy of *A Midsummer Night's Dream* would be lost. (p. 102)

> *John H. Long, "'A Midsummer Night's Dream'," in his* Shakespeare's Use of Music: A Study of the Music and Its Performance in the Original Production of Seven Comedies, *University of Florida Press, 1955, pp. 82-104.*

HOWARD NEMEROV (essay date 1956)

[*While such earlier critics as William Maginn (1837), Charles Knight (1849), H. B. Charlton (1933), Ernest Schanzer (1951), Harold C. Goddard (1951), and Paul N. Siegel (1953) all maintained that Theseus's pronouncements on the nature of poetry and imagination represented Shakespeare's own views, Nemerov offers a differing judgment. Analyzing the duke's speeches in Act V, Scene i, Nemerov concludes that Shakespeare permits him some level of wisdom in his understanding, but generally depicts him as revealing an "aristocratic or courtly disdain for art." Nemerov compares Theseus's contemptuous estimation of art as entertainment with Hippolyta's intuitive and more acute apprehension of art as mystery and fantasy. However, Nemerov cautions against accepting Hippolyta's comments during this scene as an expression of Shakespeare's own sentiments; instead, he suggests that Theseus's and Hippolyta's view of poetry—the one rational and "civic-minded," the other "magical" and dramatic—represented, as Shakespeare joined them in marriage, "the history of poetry in the English language."*]

Those who believe that the "real meaning" of Shakespeare's Plays consist in the one instruction, "to thine own self be true" [*Hamlet,* I. iii. 78]—a principle of behavior distinguishing Iago [in *Othello*] and Edmund [in *King Lear*] not less, certainly, than Polonius [in *Hamlet*]—seem to believe also that the poet's thought about the art he practised is completely revealed in a few lines spoken by Theseus toward the end of *A Midsummer-Night's Dream:*

> The poet's eye, in a fine frenzy rolling,
> Doth glance from heaven to earth, from earth to heaven;
> And, as imagination bodies forth
> The forms of things unknown, the poet's pen
> Turns them to shapes, and gives to airy nothng
> A local habitation and a name.
>
> [V. i. 12-17]
> (p. 633)

There are places in the Plays at which Shakespeare speculates about the poetic art to greater effect than in Theseus' speech: Achilles and Ulysses, ostensibly discussing reputation (*Troilus and Cressida,* III, iii), are really talking, and talking well, about art and life, the thing said and the thing done, poetics and heroics; the relation of art to "great creating Nature" is most subtly resolved, in *Winter's Tale,* IV, iii, along the lines of Hopkins' poem about "Pied Beauty"; and Hamlet's precision in coupling "form and pressure" will bear a good deal of interpretation. But I should like to tease out for a little the sense of Theseus' opinion, in part because this is so frequently offered us as all we know or need to know, and in part because it appears to me that his sentiments are beautifully answered by Hippolyta a moment afterward, in a passage not often remarked.

First, then, as to the context. The night in the dark wood is over, and order has been restored; already the things which have happened "seem small and indistinguishable, / Like far-off mountains turned into clouds," and the lovers themselves "see these things with parted eye, / When everything seems double" [IV. i. 187-90]. Still, they have evidently told their experience as best they can, and Theseus' speech responds to Hippolyta's opening, "'Tis strange, my Theseus, that these lovers speak of" [V. i. 1].

"More strange than true," Theseus replies, and develops his comparison, perhaps remotely based on opinions held by Plato . . . and not necessarily complimentary to poets, among "the lunatic, the lover, and the poet" [V. i. 2-22]. The immediate point of his criticism is that the events recounted by the four lovers are simply not true and therefore more or less worthless; beyond this, that the predilection for dignifying one's subjective fantasies as objective reality (the infinite capacity, if not for lying, for being deceived about things) is one which lovers share with madmen and poets. The quality he refers to three times as "imagination" has in his description a febrile, unsober, or merely wilful appearance, and though it is not much like what a Romantic poet would call "fancy" it is about as far removed from Coleridge's idea of imagination, and is so called a few lines later by Hippolyta, who says that the lovers' story "More witnesseth than fancy's images" [V. i. 25]. In fact, for all the mysteriousness of his talk about the poet's eye, Theseus seems to mean something extremely simple, as his gloss on his own words will make appear:

> Such tricks hath strong imagination,
> That, if it would but apprehend some joy,
> It comprehends some bringer of that joy;
> Or in the night, imagining some fear,
> How easy is a bush suppos'd a bear!

The lovers, in other words, were deluded, and so are poets. . . . (pp. 634-35)

Theseus' attitude toward art, as it is brought out by the remainder of this scene, has in it something at least "administrative," probably priggish, and somewhat suggestive of what might be felt by a highly placed civil servant attending a high-school performance of *A Midsummer Night's Dream* in which his son, perhaps, has the part of Theseus. The components of this attitude are these: none of this is real, none of it matters; whether it is well or badly brought off does not matter; the performance of plays, however, is a sign of order in society, it is "done"; what one looks for is not intellectual delight, so much as an assurance of one's own authority in a rationally stabilized commonwealth; not technique, but the appropriately humble intention of giving pleasure.

All these elements are revealed in Theseus' treatment of the coming performance of *Pyramus and Thisbe*—"what masques, what dances shall we have / To war away this long age of three hours / Between our after-supper and bed-time? . . . Is there no play / To ease the anguish of a torturing hour?" [V. i. 32-7]. (It will charitably be remembered that this is his wedding night.) He decides to hear the play, of all the entertainments offered, against the advice of Philostrate:

> It is not for you; I have heard it over,
> And it is nothing, nothing in the world;
> Unless you can find sport in their intents,
> Extremely stretch'd, and conn'd with cruel pain,
> To do you service.
>
> [V. i. 77-81]

To which he makes the ducal reply, "I will hear that play; / For never anything can be amiss, / When simpleness and duty tender it" [V. i. 81-3]. To Hippolyta's emabrrassed remonstration that the base mechanicals "can do nothing in this kind" [V. i. 88] he develops his lofty tolerance to the height of civil power at which the difference between good art and bad quite simply disappears:

> Our sport shall be to take what they mistake:
> And what poor duty cannot do, noble respect
> Takes it in might, not merit.
> Where I have come, great clerks have purposed
> To greet me with premeditated welcomes;
> Where I have seen them shiver and look pale,
> Make periods in the midst of sentences,
> Throttle their practis'd accents in their fears,
> And, in conclusion, dumbly have broke off,
> Not paying me a welcome. Trust me, sweet,
> Out of this silence yet I picked a welcome;
> And in the modesty of fearful duty
> I read as much as from the rattling tongue
> Of saucy and audacious eloquence.
> Love, therefore, and tongue-tied simplicity
> In least speak most, to my capacity.
>
> [V. i. 90-105]

Nevertheless, he is as willing as the others to make fun of the tedious brief scene, of which he presently says, with an eloquence which somewhat disguises a certain emptiness and insolence about his sense, "The best in this kind are but shadows, and the worst are no worse, if imagination amend them" [V. i. 211-12], leaving no doubt of a quiet confidence that his own "imagination" could "amend" either *Pyramus and Thisbe* or *A Midsummer Night's Dream*.

This is of course not all there is to Theseus, who in a certain remote allegory not to be very fully realized in this play is like God (Shakespeare's habit with Dukes) and has a prescriptive right to regard the intention rather than the result ("noble respect / Takes it in might not merit"), being so great in the scheme of things that the greatest human skill not less than the

least finds itself incapable in his presence. At the same time he is the secular ruler, uniting in his person and that of his queen mysterious powers of society and nature; in this sense the poet has for his demeanor a proper reverence not altogether free of ironic suspicions. The speeches we have quoted from Act V show Shakespeare in some doubt about the Duke and his attitude, which shifts between a serious wisdom in the allegory—"the best in this kind are but shadows"—and an aristocratic or courtly disdain for art, not bad art only but all art, seriously expressed in the opening speech, more brutally in the speech about the "great clerks," and carried out in his wit at the players' expense. (One suspects, whatever Castiglione's original feeling [in *Il Cortegiano*] about *"sprezzatura"* ["unaffectedness"], that the attitude must in practice have included a good deal of this rather beefy superiority.) His attitude is not like Hotspur's—"I had rather be a kitten, and cry mew / Than one of these same metre balled-mongers" [*1 Henry IV*, III. i. 127]—but loftier and more indifferent, and, by so much as it is more "tolerant," more contemptuous.

It is, I suppose, perfectly fitting that in a society such as ours these ducal views of the nature of poetry should be vastly admired and identified as coterminous with the views of William Shakespeare. In fact, I can see only two redeeming points about Theseus' opinion: that, being himself a lover, he comes under the aim of his own attack, and that this attack upon poetry is conducted, elegantly enough, in poetry. These two points restore to his character that element of ironic "reduplication" so admired by existentialist philosophers, and in a degree save him from being merely an outsize bore attractively posed with his hunting dogs against a dawn of Tintoretto's blue ("And since we have the vaward of the day, / My love shall hear the music of my hounds" [IV. i. 105-06]).

We have of course no warrant for identifying Hippolyta's reply with the views of William Shakepeare either; her lines, as a matter of fact, do not directly take up Theseus' remarks about poets, nor mention poetry at all, and the reference of the pronoun is to the lovers' minds:

> But all the story of the night told ever,
> And all their minds transfigur'd so together,
> More witnesseth than fancy's images,
> And grows to something of great constancy;
> But howsoever, strange, and admirable.
>
> [V. i. 23-7]

But I feel these words to be one of the poet's fine summarizing moments, at which his action gives him rich rewards. . . . Hippolyta's lines also, for me, have resonance far beyond the play, forming one of these miraculous instances in which poetry can be seen to have for ultimate subject its own self:

> For speculation turns not to itself
> Till it hath travel'd, and is mirror'd there
> Where it may see itself.
>
> [*Troilus and Cressida,* III. iii. 109-11]

This is not a very complicated or abstruse matter once made visible, and does not call for elaborate interpretations; one either sees it this way or else—like Theseus and other reputable persons, some of them poets—one does not. In the form of propositions, then, as a kind of manifesto of, say, the Amazonian school:

1. The province of the poetic art is "all the story of the night told over," "the night" being a conventional summary expression for all that human beings act and suffer in the world;

as Dante calls it near the beginning of his poem, "La note ch'io passai con tanta pieta" [in *La Divina Commedia*]. The story is "told over," that is to say, there is one story only.

2. The minds of the participants are "transfigured," and not only so but "together"—the story may be improbable, but they all tell it; their views are changed, but all changed in the same way; the relations among them are transfigured, but harmoniously. This line further refers to the minds of the audience, which also are "transfigured so together," and ultimately to the minds of all the poets who have told over "the story of the night."

3. The story, therefore, "grows to something of great constancy." It may not at first appear that way, but visibly, while we follow its development, it *grows* to be that way. It is to be judged in the first instance not as true or untrue but simply as composition, placing-together of elements, as approaching the nature of music. It constitutes on its own a world of ordered relation, rhythm and figure. This world *is,* and, as with the larger world in which it is, our views of its *meaning* are our own responsibility, for which it is not cryptically answerable, yielding to interpretation numerous parables which may contradict but paradoxically do not exclude one another.

4. This world, not less than the material elements of which it is composed, is "strange," both alien and familiar to the one in which we generally believe that we live—"strange, and admirable," the second word having the sense which it is given in the *Tempest:* "Admir'd Miranda! / Indeed, the top of admiration" [*The Tempest,* III. i. 37-8], the sense of the girl's name itself.

I have put the accent all on Hippolyta's part at the expense of Theseus' part, out of inclination and to right a very unbalanced view of this matter. (pp. 635-40)

The poetry of Theseus is rational, civic-minded, discursive, and tends constantly to approach prose. The poetry of Hippolyta is magical, fabulous, dramatic, and constantly approaches music. The excess of Theseus is to declare that art is entertainment; the excess of Hippolyta, to declare that art is mystery. It is perhaps ironic that Theseus' views should seem allied with those of the mysterious and fable-minded Plato, while in Hippolyta's "great constancy" we hear some echo of the plain-spoken other side ("an action, one and entire, having a certain magnitude," as well as "integritas, consonantia, claritas"), but my intention stops short of those high matters.

Now these two, the London Athenian Theseus and the Stratford Amazon Hippolyta, were joined in marriage by William Shakespeare. Their wedded life, with its vicious quarrels and long intervals of separation (not extending as yet to final divorce), is the history of poetry in the English language; a course of true love of which we might have been forewarned by the same poet, when at the beginning of the ceremony he makes Theseus say:

> Hippolyta, I woo'd thee with my sword,
> And won thy love doing thee injuries,
>
> [I. i. 16-17]

a piece of analytical and dialectical piety which may fittingly, for the time being, bring these considerations to their close. (p. 641)

Howard Nemerov, "The Marriage of Theseus and Hippolyta," in The Kenyon Review, *Vol. XVIII, No. 4, Autumn, 1956, pp. 633-41.*

GEORGE A. BONNARD   (essay date 1956)

[*Bonnard contends that in the characters of Theseus and Hippolyta Shakespeare is representing "good honest human love shorn of any romantic nonsense," a point similarly proposed by H. B. Charlton (1933), E. C. Pettet (1949), Ernest Schanzer (1951), John Vyvyan (1961), Peter G. Phialas (1966), and Paul A. Olson (see Additional Bibliography). Those critics who believe that* A Midsummer Night's Dream *offers a more equivocal view of Theseus and Hippolyta's marriage include Charles R. Lyons (1971), M. E. Lamb (1979), and David Marshall (1982), the last of whom maintains that Theseus has coerced Hippolyta into marrying him. Like Harold C. Goddard (1951), Bonnard further argues that Theseus is "no enemy to imagination," but regards it as an integral part of human life—as long as it does not usurp the place of sanity and reason, a point also voiced by R. W. Dent (1964). Finally, the critic judges all the inhabitants of the fairy world to be "exquisite, but brainless creatures" who lack any sense of responsibility or morality. In this estimation he generally follows the viewpoint of G. G. Gervinus (1849-50) and E. K. Chambers (1905).*]

Theseus, the Duke of Athens, and his captive Hippolyta whom he marries are no longer young people. As Oberon reminds Titania, Theseus has had a long and varied experience as a lover before conquering the Queen of the Amazons. And the long war Hippolyta has sustained against Theseus compels us to imagine her past her youth. There is something matter of fact about their union. There is no conventional love-making between them, they never even speak of their love. They remind us of Petruchio and Katharina in the latter part of *The Taming of the Shrew.* Not only do they stand for good honest human love shorn of any romantic nonsense, but what does Theseus tell his bride?

> Hippolyta, I wooed thee with my sword,
> And won thy love doing thee injuries.
>
> [I. i. 16-17]

Could not Petruchio have addressed his wife in the same words? But one thing is certain: their deep happiness, the strong quiet joy they find in each other. Every word of Theseus bespeaks his satisfaction at having found a true mate at last, one that he feels sure will be a good wife to him, a helpful companion through life, one also that will know how to keep her place, as her silence proves when he discusses Hermia's marriage with Egeus and the young lovers. Throughout that scene the Duke acts the sovereign judge of course and Hippolyta knows she has no business to interfere, which is not only tactful but highly sensible of her. And how full of common sense they are when they come upon the lovers asleep in the wood, when they watch the play performed in their honour! In fact, whenever they are present, the air we breathe is light, invigorating, and healthy; the atmosphere is clear, and in it all things appear in their true outlines and colours, in their due proportions and just relations; a wholly sane view of life seems to prevail. In their eyes, the fairy world does not exist. The King and Queen of the fairies may have come to Athens to bless their wedding: they are totally unaware of it. When they come to the wood with their hounds and huntsmen, their arrival is enough to restore sober reality to that scene of so many delusions, to chase all supernatural beings away. Neither Oberon, nor Titania, nor the fairies, nor Puck can possibly meet them; they all vanish "into thin air"; and at the clear, shrill sound of the hunting-horns the lovers wake up, all their dreams at once dispelled. With Theseus and Hippolyta reality reasserts itself, and triumphs over a world from which reason had fled. But large-minded as he is, full of gentle forbearance for the limitations and absurdities of other people, the Duke is no enemy to imagination. He has no desire to suppress it or curb its activity, for he knows its value. He merely wishes it not to usurp the place of reality. For him there must be no confusion between its creations and the actualities among which we live. His outlook is as broad as can be, and eminently reasonable. Hippolyta's is just as sensible, but narrower. Together they stand for experience, intelligent use of it, good sense and reason.

In full contrast to them, Shakespeare has placed his fairies, with their kingdom in that vague, dream-like East from which legends and myths and impossible stories seem to be for ever coming, with their motion that takes no account of space and time, their love of the moon and her beams, their delight in the dusk and the twilight, that is in the season for dreams, whether one is awake or asleep. For the fairies are essentially the bringers of dreams to mortals, as Mercutio tells Romeo. And, as Gervinus rightly notes, Shakespeare has given his fairies a character in harmony with their function [see excerpt above, 1849-50]. Just as in our dreams we lost all sense of responsibility, all moral impulse, so Oberon, Titania and all their subjects have no morality, no delicate feelings. Puck feels no compunction at the effects of his mischievousness, no sympathy for the affliction of the lovers:

> Shall we their fond pageant see?
> Lord, what fools these mortals be! . . .
> Then will two at once woo one;
> That must needs be sport alone.
>
> [III. ii. 114-15, 118-19]

And again when Lysander and Demetrius, sword in hand, step aside to fight their quarrel out, and the comedy suddenly takes on a sinister aspect, Puck not only proclaims himself blameless but adds

> And so far am I glad it so did sort,
> As this their jangling I esteem a sport.
>
> [III. ii. 352-53]

Or take Titania: on awaking from her delusion, she feels no regret, no shame; and there is no scene of reconciliation with her husband: her resentment makes her forsake him, and they make it up in a dance; there is no trace of a real feeling in her. And just as our fairies know no moral impulse, so they never think. They are exquisite, but brainless creatures. The means they use to exert their influence on men are strictly material: changing the lovers' eyes, turning Bottom into an ass-headed monster, counterfeiting voices. Where they reign sense impressions, uncontrolled by reason or common sense, develop unchecked and fancy is allowed free play. No wonder that their life should be all given up to the pleasures of the senses. And because their senses must be for ever delighted, their desire is for all that is most choice, finest and pleasantest; singing and dancing best expresses their unchanging mood of thoughtless happiness. Were it not for that sense of beauty, they would form but an ugly little world, what with their heartlessness, their moral insensitiveness, their thorough materialism, their lack of brains. But their instinctive love of whatever pleases their delicate senses, their natural association with flowers and butterflies, nightingales and glow-worms, their hostility towards all repulsive creatures, spiders and bats, snakes and black-beetles, redeem them in our eyes and lend them a power of enchantment from which there is no escape. Still the atmosphere in which they live and move is, to men in their senses, disquieting, even oppressive. All the laws, moral and material, that govern the world of reality, have no existence

in the dream-world of the fairies. In it therefore we no longer know where we are, we have lost our bearings. . . . Helpless in the grip of lawless fancy, we feel driven here and there . . . until Theseus and Hippolyta, models of human dignity, arrive unexpectedly and, by their mere presence, deliver us of the ''nothings'' that were tormenting us, and we can exclaim with Demetrius

> These things seem small and undistinguishable
> Like far-off mountains turned into clouds.
>
> [IV. i. 186-87]

Dreams, says Mercutio,

> 　　　　　are the children of an idle brain,
> Begot of nothing but vain fantasy,
> Which is as thin of substance as the air
> And more inconstant than the wind.
>
> [*Romeo and Juliet*, I. iv. 97-100]

The world of Theseus and Hippolyta and the world of Oberon and Titania are exclusive of each other. At no point do they really meet. But the two pairs of lovers and the simple-minded artisans waver between them and fall under the influence now of the one and now of the other. Sound sense and the delusions born of *vain fantasy* struggle for the possession of their souls, and in this they are alike. But in every other respect how far apart the lovers and the *hardhanded men*, Bottom and his companions, appear to be. (pp. 269-73)

But however different they may be, our young aristocratic lovers and our poor mechanics all suffer from delusions. Imagination or fantasy makes fools of them all. They all enter the dream-world of the wood where the fairies have them at their mercy. But it is not by mere chance that they fall under their baneful influence. They are partly responsible for their misfortunes. For what is our poor uneducated artisans' ambition to act a play, and act it in the presence of the Duke, but clear evidence that, for the time being, they have lost their common sense? What is Bottom making of himself if not an ass when he confidently proposes to take all the main parts in the tragedy? And as to the lovers, is not love and fancy one and the same thing in their eyes?

What the brief examination of the four main elements of which our comedy is composed is perhaps enough to suggest, namely that the poet did not bring them together without some other purpose than merely to please his audience, an analysis of the structure of the play may bring out more plainly. As its title implies, *Midsummer-Night's Dream* is a dream, such a dream as one might dream on the very night when, according to popular superstition, every one was more or less threatened with lunacy. But it is not altogether a dream. It neither begins nor ends as such. It begins in a world in which people are not only wide awake, but quite normal and it ends in the same matter-of-fact atmosphere. (p. 274)

In the first Act, as we have seen, if owing to the Duke and his bride the outlook is generally healthy, normal and sensible, Lysander and Hermia, despite the genuineness of the love that unites them, still preserve romantic notions ultimately derived from the medieval idealisation of love, Demetrius suffers from a worse delusion and the artisans really live already in the dream-world of those who, unaware of their limitations, are guilty of presumptuousness and are likely to make fools of themselves. In the last Act, with Demetrius cured of his sickness—the word is his—and married to Helena, with Lysander and Hermia man and wife, all trace of romantic nonsense has disappeared from the relations of the lovers towards one another. They have become sensible creatures as Theseus and Hippolyta were from the first. Reality has triumphed over unreality, the world of facts over the world of dreams, the right sort of love that leads to its natural consummation in marriage over the delusions of youthful fancy, a clear and firm apprehension of the actualities among which we must live over the vagaries of uncontrolled imagination. But if sense thus celebrates its victory over nonsense, illusions, dreams, fancies of all kinds cannot be suppressed but will sprout again and proliferate on the slightest provocation. Let *cool reason* go to sleep, and there they are again. After our mortals have gone to bed, the Fairies reappear, and in the dark hall of the ducal palace dimly lighted by the glow of the *wasted brands* on the hearth, hold their revels. But they have not come without a definite purpose: they will bless the house and all its inmates. For if illusions and dreams and fancies can be harmful when they stand between men and reality, hindering him from seeing it, they are a blessing too, and Bottom the weaver would be a poor miserable creature if he could never leave his loom and believe himself a wonderful actor, and if they were not a blessing the poet would never have written *Midsummer-Night's Dream* to bring home to us his conviction that they should not be mistaken for reality, to weigh, as it were, the rival claims of imagination and sober vision and decide in favour of the latter while giving the former its due. (pp. 278-79)

George A. Bonnard, "Shakespeare's Purpose in 'Midsummer-Night's Dream'," in Shakespeare Jahrbuch, *Vol. 92, 1956, pp. 268-79.*

JOHN RUSSELL BROWN　(essay date 1957)

[*In an unexcerpted section of his essay on* A Midsummer Night's Dream, *Brown asserts that Shakespeare's comedies express various ideals of the nature of love and that in this play the dramatist is concerned to present the ideal of love's 'truth.' In the excerpt below, Brown maintains that the perceptions of the lovers in* A Midsummer Night's Dream *are intensely personal and private visions which may or may not be accepted as true by anyone who has not shared in those particular experiences of love. We react to these visions, as Hippolyta and Theseus respond to the lovers' account of their experiences in the woods, according to who we are. Brown also contends that the Pyramus and Thisbe interlude offers us a "flesh-and-blood image" of the sympathy we should extend to "the strange and private 'truth' of those who enact the play of love." In other words, as Theseus asks for the spectators' imagination to amend the mechanicals' performance and as we do exactly that with Shakespeare's play, so too a lover's truth requires our "generosity and imagination" to make it real. For other discussions of the relation of the Pyramus and Thisbe interlude to the main plot of* A Midsummer Night's Dream, *see the excerpts by August Wilhelm Schlegel (1808), G. G. Gervinus (1849-50), Edward Dowden (1881), Denton J. Snider (1890), George Brandes (1895-96), E. K. Chambers (1905), Paul N. Siegel (1953), C. L. Barber (1959), and Mordecai Marcus (1981). The significance of such concepts as perception, awareness, and illusion in Shakespeare's play has also been examined by such critics as Bertrand Evans (1960), T. Walter Herbert (1964), Stephen Fender (1968), Sydney R. Homan (1969), Charles R. Lyons (1971), and James L. Calderwood (1971). For a direct refutation of Brown's interpretation of* A Midsummer Night's Dream, *see the essay by Michael Taylor listed in the Additional Bibliography.*]

[In] seeking further knowledge of the ideals which inform [Shakespeare's comedies] it is well to start with an idea which is expressed in action as well as in speech; we may consider, for example, the notion that lovers, in various ways, 'see' each other.

The commonest form in which Shakespeare presents the mutual recognition of two lovers is the realization of each other's beauty. For the young lovers in *A Midsummer Night's Dream,* such realization carries its own conviction of exclusive truth; Hermia will not 'choose love by another's eyes' [I. i. 140], and, when Duke Theseus orders her to marry Demetrius whom her father favours, she answers in a single line:

> I would my father look'd but with my eyes.
>
> [I. i. 56]

Even if a lover is inconstant he will always demand the use of his own eyes, and neither the authority of a father nor the force of general opinion can displace a conviction based on such experience. Some lovers, like Helena, may live by such a 'truth' even though they recognize that it is exclusive and irrational:

> Things base and vile, holding no quantity,
> Love can transpose to form and dignity:
> Love looks not with the eyes, but with a mind;
> And therefore is wing'd Cupid painted blind: . . . .
>
> [I. i. 232-39]

In this comedy the irrationality of love's choice provides sport rather than grief. The action takes place in a wood where moonlight and fairy influence suspend our belief in lasting hardship; sometimes a bush may seem to be a bear, but contrariwise even a bear may seem to have no more awful reality than a shadow and may vanish as easily. Moreover the dialogue of the lovers is light and agile so that we are not allowed to dwell upon frustration or suffering. When the sport natural to blind Cupid is heightened by Oberon's enchantment of the lovers' eyes and when events befall preposterously, we find that, even in the telling of the 'saddest tale', a 'merrier hour was never wasted' [II. i. 51-7].

But our laughter is not thoughtless, for, by bringing Bottom and his fellows to the wood to rehearse a play for the duke's nuptials, Shakespeare has contrived a contrast to the lovers' single-minded pursuit of their own visions of beauty. . . . Shakespeare's comic vision is expressed in contrasts and relationships; Bottom is the sober man by whom we judge the intoxicated. When Lysander's eyes have been touched with the magic herb, he rationalizes his new love for Helena in the loftiest terms:

> Not Hermia but Helena I love:
> Who will not change a raven for a dove?
> The will of man is by his *reason* sway'd;
> And *reason* says you are the worthier maid.
>
> [II. ii. 113-16]

Without the agency of magic but simply because Demetrius scorns her, Helena has come to believe that she is as 'ugly as a bear' [II. ii. 94], and protests, as if it were self-evident:

> . . . I did never, no, nor never can,
> Deserve a sweet look from Demetrius' eye.
>
> [II. ii. 126-27]

Helena rationally judges that Lysander's love is a 'flout' for her own 'insufficiency'. And when, in the next scene, Titania is charmed to love Bottom whom Puck has disfigured with an ass's head, she too declares her love as if she were convinced by the best of reasons:

> I pray thee, gentle mortal, sing again:
> Mine ear is much enamour'd of thy note;
> So is mine eye enthralled to thy shape;
> And thy fair virtue's force perforce doth move me
> On the first view to say, to swear, I love thee.
>
> [III. i. 137-41]

With more modesty in judgement, Bottom answers the other lovers as well as Titania:

> Methinks, mistress, you should have a little
> *reason* for that: and yet, to say the truth, *reason*
> and love keep little company together now-a-days;
> the more the pity that some honest neighbours
> will not make them friends.
>
> [III. i. 142-46]

Bottom's modesty in judgement is well placed, for life makes fewer demands on him—'if I had wit enough to get out of this wood, I have enough to serve mine own turn' [III. i. 49-51]—he is not asked to love and also to be wise; his judgement is not at the mercy of his eyes.

When Oberon's spell is broken, Bottom seems to have had a strange dream, but it does not count for so much as the helpless game the lovers have played; much as he would like to, Bottom dares not tell his dream, but the lovers must tell theirs, even to the sceptical ear of Theseus. As the vagaries of love and enchantment had seemed perfectly reasonable to those who were involved, and unreasonable or ridiculous to those who had only observed, so the whole action in the wood, once the first sight of day has passed, will seem more real or more fantastic.

Such reflections are made explicit at the beginning of Act V, in the dialogue of Theseus and his bride, Hippolyta. And at this point the play is given a new dimension; previously we had watched the action as if we were Olympians laughing at the strutting seriousness of mortals; now we seem to take a step backwards and watch others watching the action:

> —'Tis strange, my Theseus, that these lovers speak of.
> —More strange than *true:* I never may believe
> These antique fables, nor these fairy toys.
> Lovers and madmen have such seething brains,
> Such shaping fantasies, that apprehend
> More than cool reason ever comprehends.
>
> [V. i. 1-6]

And not content with likening a lover's truth to that of a madman, Theseus equates these with the poet's:

> The lunatic, the lover and the poet
> Are of imagination all compact:
> One sees more devils than vast hell can hold,
> That is, the madman: the lover, all as frantic,
> Sees Helen's beauty in a brow of Egypt:
> The poet's eye, in a fine frenzy rolling,
> Doth glance from heaven to earth, from earth to
>   heaven;
> And as imagination bodies forth
> The forms of things unknown, the poet's pen
> Turns them to shapes and gives to airy nothing
> A local habitation and a name. . . .
>
> [V. i. 7-17]

For a moment, the image in the glass of the stage is strangely lightened; has the action we have witnessed the inconsequence of mere contrivance, or has it the constancy of a poet's imagination? Is it 'more strange than true', or is there some 'truth' in the lovers' visions of beauty, in the moonlight and enchantments, in Oberon's jealousy and Puck's mistaking? Our judgement hesitates with Hippolyta's:

> . . . all the story of the night told over,
> And all their minds transfigured so together,
> More witnesseth than fancy's images
> And grows to something of great constancy;
> But, howsoever, strange and admirable.
>
> [V. i. 23-7]

Possibly we know no more than Demetrius, rubbing his eyes in the daylight:

> . . . I wot not by what power,—
> But by some power it is. . . .
>
> [IV. i. 164-65]

Our reactions will vary, depending on whether we are stalwart like Bottom, disengaged like Puck, or fanciful like lovers, madmen, and poets. From telling an idle story of magic and love's entangling eyes, Shakespeare has led us to contemplate the relationship between nature and the 'art' of lovers and poets; he has led us to recognize the absurdity, privacy, and 'truth' of human imagination.

Hard on the heels of this questioning moment, comes talk of a masque or a play to 'beguile The lazy time' [V. i. 40-1]; this, it seems, is 'where we came in'. But for the 'second time round' the perspective will be changed and we shall watch others watching the play. For us this will be the chief interest of the performance, for, having watched rehearsals, we know precisely the kind of play to expect; again it will be about love and again it will take place by moonlight, but this time the plot will end disastrously. Our interest will lie in whether or not the performance will also be disastrous.

The actors are fully confident; they are so sure of their make-believe that, for fear of frightening the ladies, they must take special precautions before they draw a sword or let their lion roar. But we may doubt whether they will get any help from their text:

> . . . for in all the play
> There is not one word apt, one player fitted.
>
> [V. i. 64-5]
> (pp. 83-8)

In the event the actors put their faith, as the lovers had done before them, in the 'truth' of their fiction:

> Gentles, perchance you wonder at this show;
> But wonder on, till *truth* make all things plain.
>
> [V. i. 127-28]

and again:

> This loam, this rough-cast and this stone doth show
> That I am that same wall; the *truth* is so. . . .
>
> [V. i. 161-62]

But the response wavers, and Bottom has to interfere to correct a wrong impression:

> —The wall, methinks, being sensible, should
> curse again.

—No, in *truth*, sir, he should not. 'Deceiving
me' is Thisby's cue: she is to enter now, . . .
You shall see, it will fall pat as I told you.

[V. i. 182-87]

Bottom's faith is invincible, but he cannot ensure success, and
Hippolyta judges frankly that the play is 'the silliest stuff' that
she has ever heard [V. i. 210].

At this point Theseus reminds them all of the nature of their
entertainment:

—The best in this kind are but shadows; and the worst
are no worse, if imagination amend them.
—It must be your imagination then, and not theirs.
—If we imagine no worse of them than they of themselves,
they may pass for excellent men.

[V. i. 211-16]
(pp. 88-9)

If one wished to describe the judgement which informs *A Midsummer Night's Dream,* one might do so very simply: the play
suggests that lovers, like lunatics, poets, and actors, have their
own 'truth' which is established as they see the beauty of their
beloved, and that they are confident in this truth for, although
it seems the 'silliest stuff' to an outsider, to them it is quite
reasonable; it also suggests that lovers, like actors, need, and
sometimes ask for, our belief, and that this belief can only be
given if we have the generosity and imagination to think 'no
worse of them than they of themselves'.

The play's greatest triumph is the manner in which our wavering acceptance of the illusion of drama is used as a kind of
flesh-and-blood image of the acceptance which is appropriate
to the strange and private 'truth' of those who enact the play
of love. By using this living image, Shakespeare has gone
beyond direct statement in words or action and has presented
his judgement in terms of a mode of being, a relationship, in
which we, the audience, are actually involved. And he has
ensured that this image is experienced at first hand, for the
audience of the play-within-the-play does not make the perfect
reaction; one of them describes what this entails but it is left
for us to make that description good. The success of the play
will, finally, depend upon our reaction to its shadows. (p. 90)

> John Russell Brown, "Love's Truth and the Judge-
> ments of 'A Midsummer Night's Dream' and 'Much
> Ado about Nothing'," in his Shakespeare and His
> Comedies, Methuen & Co., Ltd., 1957, pp. 82-123.

C. L. BARBER (essay date 1959)

[*An American scholar, Barber is one of the most important contemporary critics of Shakespearean comedy. In his influential
study,* Shakespeare's Festive Comedy *(1959), Barber examines
the parallels between Elizabethan holiday celebrations and Shakespeare's comedies. In the introduction, Barber states that the
festival customs and the comic plays both contain a saturnalian
pattern involving "a basic movement which can be summarized
in the formula, through release to clarification." Barber defines
release as a revelry, a mirthful liberation, "an accession of wanton vitality" over the restraint imposed by everyday life; the clarification that follows he characterizes as a "heightened awareness
of the relation between man and 'nature'," which in comedy "puts
holiday in perspective with life as a whole." In the following
excerpt, Barber argues that for its initial performance at an actual
wedding celebration Shakespeare integrated into* A Midsummer
Night's Dream *a pageantry of different festival elements. The
"comic subject" of the play, he asserts, is "the folly of fantasy"—
the tendency of the characters to take fantasy literally—and he*
*perceives this theme enacted through the interplay of the lovers,
the fairies, and the clowns. Encompassing this design, Barber
maintains, is the structural movement typical of all Shakespeare's
festive comedies: namely, an action that proceeds from societal
restraint, to release, and finally to clarification. Other critics who
have focused on the theme of misperception or illusion in* A Midsummer Night's Dream *include John Russell Brown (1957), Bertrand Evans (1960), T. Walter Herbert (1964), Stephen Fender
(1968), Sydney R. Homan (1969), Charles R. Lyons (1971), and
James L. Calderwood (1971). Also, for further commentary on
the structural design of* A Midsummer Night's Dream, *see the
excerpt by Florence Falk (1980). Barber next examines Shakespeare's use of Ovidian metamorphosis and poetic metaphor,
which he calls a form of metamorphosis itself, to dramatize love's
influence on human perception. For further examination of metaphor in the play as reflective of the creative process itself, see
the excerpts by Harold C. Goddard (1951), R. A. Zimbardo (1970),
James L. Calderwood (1971), and J. Dennis Huston (1981). Last,
Barber criticizes those Romantic critics like William Hazlitt (1817)
for misreading* A Midsummer Night's Dream *as a drama of real
supernatural events, "excluding all awareness that 'the play' is
a play" and thereby missing "its most important humor"; he
concludes that this element of self-consciousness in Shakespeare's
art achieves its most telling representation in the Pyramus and
Thisbe interlude, where "the clowns provide a broad burlesque
of the mimetic impulse to become something by acting it, the
impulse which in the main action is fulfilled by imagination and
understood by humor."*]

If Shakespeare had called *A Midsummer Night's Dream* by a
title that referred to pageantry and May games, the aspects of
it with which I shall be chiefly concerned would be more often
discussed. To honor a noble wedding, Shakespeare gathered
up in a play the sort of pageantry which was usually presented
piece-meal at artisocratic entertainments, in park and court as
well as in hall. And the May game, everybody's pastime, gave
the pattern for his whole action, which moves "from the town
to the grove" and back again, bringing in summer to the bridal.
These things were familiar and did not need to be stressed by
a title. (p. 119)

The humor of the play relates superstition, magic and passionate delusion as "fancy's images." The actual title emphasizes a sceptical attitude by calling the comedy a "dream."
It seems unlikely that the title's characterization of the dream,
"a midsummer night's dream," implies association with the
specific customs of Midsummer Eve, the shortest night of the
year, except as "midsummer night" would carry suggestions
of a magic time. . . . Shakespeare was not *simply* writing out
folklore which he heard in his youth, as Romantic critics liked
to assume. On the contrary, his fairies are produced by a complex fusion of pageantry and popular game, as well as popular
fancy. Moreover, as we shall see, they are not serious in the
meanacing way in which the people's fairies were serious.
Instead they are serious in a very different way, as embodiments
of the May-game experience of eros in men and women and
trees and flowers, while any superstitious tendency to believe
in their literal reality is mocked. The whole night's action is
presented as a release of shaping fantasy which brings clarification about the tricks of strong imagination. We watch a
dream; but we are awake, thanks to pervasive humor about the
tendency to take fantasy literally, whether in love, in superstition, or in Bottom's mechanical dramatics. As in *Love's
Labour's Lost* the folly of wit becomes the generalized comic
subject in the course of an astonishing release of witty invention, so here in the course of a more inclusive release of imagination, the folly of fantasy becomes the general subject, echoed
back and forth between the strains of the play's imitative counterpoint.

We can best follow first the strain of the lovers; then the fairies, their persuasive and then their humorous aspects; and finally the broadly comic strain of the clowns. We feel what happens to the young lovers in relation to the wedding of the Duke. Theseus and Hippolyta have a quite special sort of role: they are principals without being protagonists; the play happens for them rather than to them. This relation goes with their being stand-ins for the noble couple whose marriage the play originally honored. In expressing the prospect of Theseus' marriage, Shakespeare can fix in ideal form, so that it can be felt later at performance in the theater, the mood that would obtain in a palace as the "nuptial hour / Draws on apace" [I. i. 1-2]. Theseus looks towards the hour with masculine impatience, Hippolyta with a woman's happy willingness to dream away the time. Theseus gives directions for the "four happy days" [I. i. 2] to his "usual manager of mirth" [V. i. 35], his Master of the Revels, Philostrate:

> Go. Philostrate,
> Stir up the Athenian youth to merriments,
> Awake the pert and nimble spirit of mirth,
> Turn melancholy forth to funerals;
> The pale companion is not for our pomp.
>
> [I. i. 11-15]

The whole community is to observe a decorum of the passions, with Philostrate as choreographer of a pageant where Melancholy's float will not appear. After the war in which he won Hippolyta, the Duke announces that he is going to wed her

> in another key,
> With pomp, with triumph, and with revelling.
>
> [I. i. 18-19]

But his large, poised line is interrupted by Egeus, panting out vexation. After the initial invocation of nuptial festivity, we are confronted by the sort of tension from which merriment is a release. Here is Age, standing in the way of Athenian youth; here are the locked conflicts of everyday. By the dwelling here on "the sharp Athenian law," on the fate of nuns "in shady cloister mew'd" [I. i. 162, 171], we are led to feel the outgoing to the woods as an escape from the inhibitions imposed by parents and the organized community. And this sense of release is also prepared by looking for just a moment at the tragic potentialities of passion. Lysander and Hermia, left alone in their predicament, speak a plaintive, symmetrical duet on the theme, learned "from tale or history," that "The course of true lover never did run smooth" [I. i. 133-34]. . . . But Hermia shakes herself free of the tragic vision, and they turn to thoughts of stealing forth tomorrow night to meet in the Maying wood and go on to the dowager aunt, where "the sharp Athenian law / Cannot pursue us" [I. i. 162-63].

If they had reached the wealthy aunt, the play would be a romance. But it is a change of heart, not a change of fortune, which lets love have its way. The merriments Philostrate was to have directed happen inadvertently, the lovers walking into them blind, so to speak. This is characteristic of the way game is transformed into drama in this play, by contrast with the disabling of the fictions in *Love's Labour's Lost*. Here the roles which the young people might play in a wooing game, they carry out in earnest. And nobody is shown setting about to play the parts of Oberon or Titania. Instead the pageant fictions are presented as "actually" happening—at least so it seems at first glance. (pp. 123-27)

The lovers in *A Midsummer Night's Dream* play "as in Whitsun pastorals" [*The Winter's Tale*, IV. iv. 134], but they are entirely without this sort of consciousness of their folly. They are unreservedly *in* the passionate protestations which they rhyme at each other as they change partners:

> *Helena.* Lysander, if you live, good sir, awake.
> *Lysander.* And run through fire I will for thy sweet sake
> Transparent Helena!
>
> [II. ii. 102-04]

The result of this lack of consciousness is that they are often rather dull and undignified, since however energetically they elaborate conceits, there is usually no qualifying irony, nothing withheld. And only accidental differences can be exhibited, Helena tall, Hermia short. Although the men think that "reason says" now Hermia, now Helena, is "the worthier maid," personalities have nothing to do with the case: it is the flowers that bloom in the spring. The life in the lovers' parts is not to be caught in individual speeches, but by regarding the whole movement of the farce, which swings and spins each in turn through a common pattern, an evolution that seems to have an impersonal power of its own. Miss Enid Welsford describes the play's moement as a dance [see excerpt above, 1927]. . . . This is fine and right, except that one must add that the lovers' evolutions have a headlong and helpless quality that depends on their not being *intended* as dance, by contrast with those of the fairies. (One can also contrast the courtly circle's intended though abortive dances in *Love's Labour's Lost*.) The farce is funniest, and most meaningful, in the climactic scene where the lovers are most unwilling, where they try their hardest to use personality to break free, and still are willy-nilly swept along to end in pitch darkness, trying to fight. When both men have arrived at wooing Helena, she assumes it must be voluntary mockery, a "false sport" fashioned "in spite." She appeals to Hermia on the basis of their relation as particular individuals, their "sister's vows." But Hermia is at sea, too; names no longer work: "Am I not Hermia? Are not you Lysander?" [III. ii. 273]. So in the end Hermia too, though she has held off, is swept into the whirl, attacking Helena as a thief of love. She grasps at straws to explain what has happened by something manageably related to their individual identities:

> *Helena.* Fie, fie! You counterfeit, you puppet you.
> *Hermia.* Puppet? Why so! Ay, that way goes the game.
> Now I perceive that she hath made compare
> Between our statures; she hath urg'd her height . . .
> How low am I, thou painted maypole? Speak!
>
> [III. ii. 288-96]

In exhibiting a more drastic helplessness of will and mind than anyone experienced in *Love Labour's Lost*, this farce conveys a sense of people being tossed about by a force which puts them beside themselves to take them beyond themselves. The change that happens is presented simply, with little suggestion that it involves a growth in insight—Demetrius is not led to realize something false in his diverted affection for Hermia. . . . The comedy's irony about love's motives and choices expresses love's power not as an attribute of special personality but as an impersonal force beyond the persons concerned. The tragedies of love, by isolating Romeo and Juliet, Antony and Cleopatra, enlist our concern for love as it enters into unique destinies, and convey its subjective immensity in individual experience. The festive comedies, in presenting love's effect on a group, convey a different sense of its power, less intense but also less precarious. (pp. 128-30)

Shakespeare, in developing a May-game action at length to express the will in nature that is consummated in marriage,

Act II. Scene ii. Oberon and Titania. By Paul Thumann (n.d.). The Department of Rare Books and Special Collections, The University of Michigan Library.

brings out underlying magical meanings of the ritual while keeping always a sense of what it is humanly, as an experience. The way nature is felt is shaped . . . by the things that are done in encountering it. The woods are a region of passionate excitement where, as Berowne said, love "adds a precious seeing to the eye" [*Love's Labour's Lost,* IV. iii. 330]. This precious seeing was talked about but never realized in *Love's Labour's Lost;* instead we got wit. But now it is realized; we get poetry. Poetry conveys the experience of amorous tendency diffused in nature; and poetry, dance, gesture, dramatic fiction, combine to create, in the fairies, creatures who embody the passionate mind's elated sense of its own omnipotence. The woods are established as a region of metamorphosis, where in liquid moonlight or glimmering starlight, things can change, merge and melt into each other. Metamorphosis expresses both what love sees and what it seeks to do.

The opening scene, like an overture, announces this theme of dissolving, in unobtrusive but persuasive imagery. Hippolyta says that the four days until the wedding will "quickly *steep* themselves in night" and the nights "quickly *dream* away the time" [I. i. 7-8]—night will dissolve day in dream. Then an imagery of wax develops as Egeus complains that Lysander has bewitched his daughter Hermia, "stol'n the *impression* of her fantasy" [I. i. 32]. Theseus backs up Egeus by telling Hermia that

> To you your father should be as a god;
> One that compos'd your beauties; yea, and one

To whom you are but as a form in wax,
By him imprinted, and within his power
To leave the figure, or disfigure it.

[I. i. 47-51]

The supposedly moral threat is incongruously communicated in lines that relish the joy of composing beauties and suggests a god-like, almost inhuman freedom to do as one pleases in such creation. The metaphor of sealing as procreation is picked up again when Theseus requires Hermia to decide "by the next new moon, / The sealing day betwixt my love and me" [I. i. 83-4]. The consummation in prospect with marriage is envisaged as a melting into a new form and a new meaning. Helena says to Hermia that she would give the world "to be to you translated" [I. i. 191], and in another image describes meanings that melt from love's transforming power:

> ere Demetrius look'd on Hermia's eyes,
> He hail'd down oaths that he was only mine;
> And when this hail some heat from Hermia felt,
> So he dissolv'd, and show'rs of oaths did melt.

[I. i. 242-45]

The most general statement, and one that perfectly fits what we are to see in the wood when Titania meets Bottom, is

> Things base and vile, holding no quantity,
> Love can transpose to form and dignity.

[I. i. 232-33]

"The glimmering night" [II. i. 77] promotes transpositions by an effect not simply of light, but also of a half-liquid medium in or through which things are seen:

> Tomorrow night, when Phoebe doth behold
> Her silver visage in the wat'ry glass,
> Decking with liquid pearl the bladed grass,
> (A time that lovers' flights doth still conceal) . . .

[I. i. 209-12]

Miss Caroline Spurgeon pointed to the moonlight in this play as one of the earliest sustained effects of "iterative imagery." To realize how the effect is achieved, we have to recognize that the imagery is not used simply to paint an external scene but to convey human attitudes. We do not get simply "the glimmering night," but

> Didst thou not lead him through the glimmering night
> From Perigouna, whom he ravished?

[II. i. 77-8]

The liquid imagery conveys an experience of the skin, as well as the eye's confusion by refraction. The moon "looks with a wat'ry eye" [III. i. 198] and "washes all the air" [II. i. 104]; its sheen, becoming liquid pearl as it mingles with dew, seems to get onto the eyeballs of the lovers, altering them to reshape what they see, like the juice of the flower with which they are "streaked" by Oberon and Puck. The climax of unreason comes when Puck overcasts the night to make it "black as Acheron" [III.ii. 35]; the lovers now experience only sound and touch, running blind over uneven ground, through bog and brake, "bedabbled with the dew and torn with briers" [III. ii. 443]. There is nothing more they can do until the return of light permits a return of control: light is anticipated as "comforts from the East" [III. ii. 342], "the Morning's love" [III. ii. 389]. The sun announces its coming in a triumph of red and gold over salt green, an entire change of key from the moon's "silver visage in her wat'ry glass":

> the eastern gate, all fiery red,
> Opening on Neptune, with fair blessed beams
> Turns into yellow gold his salt green streams.
>
> [III. ii. 391-93]

Finally Theseus comes with his hounds and his horns in the morning, and the lovers are startled awake. They find as they come to themselves that

> These things seem small and undistinguishable,
> Like far-off mountains turned into clouds.
>
> [IV. i. 186-88]

The teeming metamorphoses which we encounter are placed, in this way, in a medium and in a moment where the perceived structure of the outer world breaks down, where the body and its environment interpenetrate in unaccustomed ways, so that the seeming separateness and stability of identity is lost.

The action of metaphor is itself a process of transposing, a kind of metamorphosis. There is less direct description of external nature *in* the play than one would suppose: much of the effect of being in nature comes from imagery which endows it with anthropomorphic love, hanging a wanton pearl in every cowslip's ear. Titania laments that

> the green corn
> Hath rotted ere his youth attain'd a beard;

while

> Hoary-headed frosts
> Fall in the fresh lap of the crimson rose . . .
>
> [II. i. 94-5, 107-08]

By a complementary movement of imagination, human love is treated in terms of growing things. Theseus warns Hermia against becoming a nun, because

> earthlier happy is the rose distill'd
> Than that which, withering on the virgin thorn
> Grows, lives and dies in single blessedness.
>
> [I. i. 76-8]

Titania, embracing Bottom, describes herself in terms that fit her surroundings and uses the association of ivy with women of the songs traditional at Christmas:

> So doth the woodbine the sweet honeysuckle
> Gently entwist; the female ivy so
> Enrings the barky fingers of the elm.
>
> [IV. i. 42-4]

One could go on and on in instancing metamorphic metaphors. But one of the most beautiful bravura speeches can serve as an epitome of the metamorphic action in the play, Titania's astonishing answer when Oberon asks for the changeling boy:

> Set your heart at rest.
> The fairyland buys not the child of me.
> His mother was a vot'ress of my order;
> And in the spiced Indian air, by night,
> Full often hath she gossip'd by my side,
> And sat with me on Neptune's yellow sands,
> Marking th'embarked traders on the flood;
> When we have laugh'd to see the sails conceive
> And grow big-bellied with the wanton wind;
> Which she, with pretty and with swimming gait
> Following (her womb then rich with my young squire)

> Would imitate, and sail upon the land
> To fetch me trifles, and return again,
> As from a voyage, rich with merchandise.
> But she, being mortal, of that boy did die,
> And for her sake do I rear up her boy;
> And for her sake I will not part from him.
>
> [II. i. 121-37]

The memory of a moment seemingly so remote expresses with plastic felicity the present moment when Titania speaks and we watch. It suits Titania's immediate mood, for it is a glimpse of women who gossip alone, apart from men and feeling now no need of them, rejoicing their own special part of life's power. At such moments, the child, not the lover, is their object—as this young squire is still the object for Titania, who "crowns him with flowers, and makes him all her joy" [II. i. 27]. The passage conveys a wanton joy in achieved sexuality, in fertility; and a gay acceptance of the waxing of the body (like joy in the varying moon). At leisure in the spiced night air, when the proximate senses of touch and smell are most alive, this joy finds sport in projecting images of love and growth where they are not. The mother, having laughed to see the ship a woman with child, imitates it so as to go the other way about and herself become a ship. She fetches trifles, but she is also actually "rich with merchandise," for her womb is "rich with my young squire." The secure quality of the play's pleasure is conveyed by having the ships out on the flood while she sails, safely, upon the *land*, with a pretty and swimming gait that is an overflowing of the security of make-believe. The next line brings a poignant glance out beyond this gamesome world:

> But she, being mortal, of that boy did die.

It is when the flower magic leads Titania to find a new object that she gives up the child (who goes now from her bower to the man's world of Oberon). So here is another sort of change of heart that contributes to the expression of what is consummated in marriage, this one a part of the rhythm of adult life, as opposed to the change in the young lovers that goes with growing up. Once Titania has made this transition, their ritual marriage is renewed:

> Now thou and I are new in amity,
> And will to-morrow midnight solemnly
> Dance in Duke Theseus' house triumphantly
> And bless it to all fair prosperity.
>
> [IV. i. 87-90]

The final dancing blessing of the fairies, "Through the house with glimmering light" [V. i. 391], after the lovers are abed, has been given meaning by the symbolic action we have been describing: the fairies have been made into tutelary spirits of fertility, so that they can promise that

> the blots of Nature's hand
> Shall not in their issue stand.
>
> [V. i. 409-10]

When merely read, the text of this episode seems somewhat bare, but its clipped quality differentiates the fairy speakers from the mortals, and anyway richer language would be in the way. Shakespeare has changed from a fully dramatic medium to conclude, in a manner appropriate to festival, with dance and song. (pp. 132-38)

In promoting the mastery of passion by expression, dramatic art can provide a civilized equivalent for exorcism. The exorcism represented as magically accomplished at the conclusion of the comedy is accomplished, in another sense, by the whole dramatic action, as it keeps moving through release to clarification. By embodying in the fairies the mind's proclivity to court its own omnipotence, Shakespeare draws this tendency, this "spirit," out into the open. They have the meaning they do only because we see them in the midst of the metamorphic region we have just considered—removed from this particular wood, most of their significance evaporates, as for example in [Michael Drayton's] *Nymphidia* and other pretty floral miniatures. One might summarize their role by saying that they represent the power of imagination. But to say what they *are* is to short-circuit the life of them and the humor. They present themselves moment by moment as actual persons; the humor keeps *recognizing* that the person is a personification, that the magic is imagination.

The sceptical side of the play has been badly neglected because romantic taste, which first made it popular, wanted to believe in fairies. Romantic criticism usually praised *A Midsummer Night's Dream* on the assumption that its spell should be complete, and that the absolute persuasiveness of the poetry should be taken as the measure of its success. This expectation of unreserved illusion finds a characteristic expression in Hazlitt:

> All that is finest in the play is lost in the representation. The spectacle is grand; but the spirit was evaporated, the genius was fled. Poetry and the stage do not agree well together . . . [see excerpt above, 1817].

Hazlitt's objections were no doubt partly justified by the elaborate methods of nineteenth-century production. A superfluity of "actual impressions of the senses" came into conflict with the poetry by attempting to reduplicate it. But Hazlitt looks for a complete illusion of a kind which Shakespeare's theater did not provide and Shakespeare's play was not designed to exploit; failing to find it on the stage, he retires to his study, where he is free of the discrepancy between imagination and sense which he finds troublesome. The result is the nineteenth-century's characteristic misreading, which regards "the play" as a series of real supernatural events, with a real ass's head and real fairies, and, by excluding all awareness that "the play" is a play, misses its most important humor.

The extravagant subject matter actually led the dramatist to rely more heavily than elsewhere on a flexible attitude toward representation. The circumstances of the original production made this all the more inevitable: Puck stood in a hall familiar to the audience. [In] holiday shows, it was customary to make game with the difference between art and life by witty transitions back and forth between them. The aim was not to make the auditors "forget they are in a theater," but to extend reality into fiction. The general Renaissance tendency frankly to accept and relish the artificiality of art, and the vogue of formal rhetoric and "conceited" love poetry, also made for sophistication about the artistic process. . . . Shakespeare's auditors had not been conditioned by a century and a half of effort to achieve sincerity by denying art. (pp. 139-41)

It is "the act of mind" and "the idea of the poet" which are brought into focus when, at the beginning of the relaxed fifth act, Theseus comments on what the lovers have reported of their night in the woods. I shall quote the passage in full, despite its familiarity, to consider the complex attitude it conveys:

The lunatic, the lover, and the poet
Are of imagination all compact.

One sees more devils than vast hell can hold:
That is the madman. The lover, all as frantic,
Sees Helen's beauty in a brow of Egypt.
The poet's eye, in a fine frenzy rolling,
Doth glance from heaven to earth, from earth to heaven;
And as imagination bodies forth
The forms of things unknown, the poet's pen
Turns them to shapes, and gives to airy nothing
A local habitation and a name.
Such tricks hath strong imagination
That, if it would but apprehend some joy,
It comprehends some bringer of that joy;
Or in the night, imagining some fear,
How easy is a bush suppos'd a bear!

[V. i. 7-22]

The description of the power of poetic creation is so beautiful that these lines are generally taken out of context and instanced simply as glorification of the poet. But the praise of the poet is qualified in conformity with the tone Theseus adopts towards the lover and the madman. In his comment there is wonder, wonderfully expressed, at the power of the mind to create from airy nothing; but also recognition that the creation may be founded, after all, merely on airy nothing. Neither awareness cancels out the other. A sense of the plausible life and energy of fancy goes with the knowledge that often its productions are more strange than true. (p. 142)

The consciousness of the creative or poetic act itself, which pervades the main action, explains the subject-matter of the burlesque accompaniment provided by the clowns. If Shakespeare were chiefly concerned with the nature of love, the clowns would be in love, after their fashion. But instead, they are putting on a play. That some commoners should honor the wedding, in their own way, along with the figures from pageantry, is of course in keeping with the purpose of gathering into a play the several sorts of entertainments usually presented separately. But an organic purpose is served too: the clowns provide a broad burlesque of the mimetic impulse to become something by acting it, the impulse which in the main action is fulfilled by imagination and understood by humor. Bottom feels he can be anything: "What is Pyramus, a lover, or a tyrant? . . . An I may hide my face, let me play Thisby too. . . . Let me play the lion too" [I. ii. 22, 51-2, 70]. His soul would like to fly out into them all; but he is *not* Puck! In dealing with dramatic illusion, he and the other mechanicals are invincibly literal-minded, carrying to absurdity the tendency to treat the imaginary as though it were real. They exhibit just the all-or-nothing attitude towards fancy which would be fatal to the play as a whole. (pp. 148-49)

There is a great deal of incidental amusement in the parody and burlesque with which *Pyramus and Thisby* is loaded. It burlesques the substance of the death scene in *Romeo and Juliet* in a style which combines ineptitudes from Golding's translation of Ovid with locutions from the crudest doggerel drama. What is most remarkable about it, however, is the way it fits hilarious fun into the whole comedy's development of attitude and understanding. After the exigent poise of the humorous fantasy, laughs now explode one after another; and yet they are still on the subject, even though now we are romping reassuringly through easy-to-make distinctions. Theseus can say blandly

> The best in this kind are but shadows; and the worst are no worse, if imagination amend them.

[V. i. 211-12]

Although we need not agree (Hippolyta says "It must be your imagination then, and not theirs." [V. i. 213-14]), Theseus expresses part of our response—a growing detachment towards imagination, moving towards the distance from the dream expressed in Puck's epilogue. (pp. 152-54)

The confident assumption dominant in *A Midsummer Night's Dream,* that substance and shadow can be kept separate, determines the peculiarly unshadowed gaiety of the fun it makes with fancy. Its organization by polarities—everyday-holiday, town-grove, day-night, waking-dreaming—provides a remarkable resource for mastering passionate experience. By a curious paradox, the full dramatization of holiday affirmations permitted "that side" of experience to be boxed off by Theseus. If we take our stand shoulder to shoulder with Theseus, the play can be an agency for distinguishing what is merely "apprehended" from what is "comprehended." Shakespeare's method of structuring is as powerful, in its way, as Descartes' distinction between mind and body, the formidable engine by which the philosopher swept away "secondary qualities" so that mathematical mind might manipulate geometrical extension. If we do not in our age want to rest in Theseus' rationalistic position (any more than in Descartes'), it remains a great achievement to have got there, and wherever we are going in our sense of reality, we have come via that standing place.

Theseus, moreover, does not quite have the last word, even in this play: his position is only one stage in a dialectic. Hippolyta will not be reasoned out of her wonder, and answers her new Lord with

> But all the story of the night told over,
> And all their minds transfigur'd so together,
> More witnesseth than fancy's images
> And grows to something of great constancy;
> But howsoever, strange and admirable.
>
> [V. i. 23-7]

Did it happen, or didn't it happen? The doubt is justified by what Shakespeare has shown us. We are not asked to think that fairies exist. But imagination, by presenting these figments, has reached to something, a creative tendency and process. What is this process? Where is it? What shall we call it? It is what happens in the play. It is what happens in marriage. To name it requries many words, words in motion—the words of *A Midsummer Night's Dream.* (pp. 161-62)

> C. L. Barber, *"May Games and Metamorphoses on a Midsummer Night,"* in his Shakespeare's Festive Comedy: A Study of Dramatic Form and Its Relation to Social Custom, *Princeton University Press, 1959, pp. 119-62.*

ELIZABETH SEWELL (essay date 1960)

[*The excerpt below is from Sewell's* The Orphic Voice: Poetry and Natural History *(1960), in which she analyzes reflections on the myth of Orpheus—whose music granted him power over the natural world—in the works of poets and scholars from the Renaissance to the late nineteenth century. In one chapter of her study, Sewell compares Francis Bacon's inductive method of distinguishing between the forms of things in nature and those in the human mind—as outlined in his* Novum Organum *(1620)—with Shakespeare's dramatization of man and woman's quest for understanding themselves and their world. In the excerpt below, Sewell argues that the rude mechanicals in* A Midsummer Night's Dream, *especially Bottom the Weaver, represent "the newly thinking mind subjected to natural forms and trying to make forms of its own by which to understand them." She examines the way*]

that Shakespeare, by associating their names with natural objects as well as with their respective trades, links the mechanicals with "the whole universe of nature" and suggests, at the same time, the precariousness with which they "hold to their human status and . . . dignity." Sewell also evaluates the garbled substitutions and exchanges in the clowns' rehearsal speeches and in the Pyramus and Thisbe interlude, claiming that these errors draw specific attention to the nature of poetic language and indicate that Shakespeare was uniting "himself and his art with the mechanicals, lending them his own craft of poetic and mythological drama." Last, Sewell comments on the "forms in transformation" in A Midsummer Night's Dream, both those in nature and those in the human mind; she concludes that Shakespeare's presentation provides us with a sense of the movement of the natural world and makes manifest the essence of mythological thinking in general. For further discussions of Bottom and his significance to the action of A Midsummer Night's Dream, see the excerpts by William Maginn (1837), Charles Cowden Clarke (1863), G. K. Chesterton (1904), E. K. Chambers (1905), H. B. Charlton (1933), John Palmer (1944), Harold C. Goddard (1951), Peter G. Phialas (1966), John A. Allen (1967), Ronald F. Miller (1975), R. Chris Hassel, Jr. (1980), and J. Dennis Huston (1981). Also, for similar opinions on Shakespeare's identification of his own art with that of the mechanicals, see the excerpts by Frederick S. Boas (1896) and Paul N. Siegel (1953).]*

The six mechanicals are no mere accident of comic relief in [*A Midsummer Night's Dream*]. They are Shakespeare's equivalent of Bacon's insistence on the need to observe the mechanical arts. Shakespeare does not argue the point: he presents characters. But each writer is making a case for the special status of the arts in the widest sense, human operation upon nature, as part of natural process and the point at which forms—in nature, mind, and language—interact and interpret one another. They are, for Shakespeare as for Bacon, the bridge between the study of natural history and the study of forms as such. Bacon, true to his Orpheus, directs toward philosophy whatever profit may come from the study of these arts: "My meaning plainly is that all mechanical experiments should be as streams flowing from all sides into the sea of philosophy" (*Parasceve,* Aphorism 5). Carefully, however, he keeps his own art, that of interpreting, separate from the mechanical arts; the latter are to be referred, for translation and collating, to the former. Shakespeare, no less true to *his* Orpheus, goes much further. In an astonishing stroke of genial generosity he unites himself and his art with the mechanicals, lending them his own craft of poetic and mythological drama, since if natural process is really all of a piece and includes arts of all kind, such a union is only logical. Where . . . Bacon stops half way, Shakespeare follows through the logic of post-logic. His mechanicals here take on exactly the task he has himself in hand, the production of a play on the occasion of a wedding.

What Shakespeare presents us with, in these clown scenes, is in the best Baconian sense a "mechanical experiment." Philostrate in v.1 makes this plain:

THESEUS:	What are they that do play it?
PHILOSTRATE:	Hard-handed men, that work in Athens here,
	Which never labour'd in their minds till now.

> [V. i. 71-3]

With these simple minds, versed only in mechanical skills and now attempting art of another kind, a mythological and linguistic piece of work, Shakespeare conducts his own experiment. That is why their play is so important, their sole purpose in Shakespeare's play. All four of their communal scenes are devoted to it—to its casting, its rehearsing, its near-abandonment as marred without Bottom, and then his return with the news "our play is preferred" [IV. ii. 39], and lastly its performance. And between the first two and the last two Shakespeare sets the obligato of Bottom's adventure, which is an experiment of a rather different kind, though Bottom calls it "Bottom's dream," so that we are still within the main framework of Shakespeare's method, and we are accompanied by poetry all the way through. We shall begin with poetry in simple and essential form—the actors' marvelous names and trades.

It is clear that their names and callings are not just to be listed under *Dramatis Personae,* a mere program convention. They are built into that first scene of theirs where Peter Quince is calling the roll of his team. They are, you recall, Peter Quince; his trade is not called because he is doing the calling, but the stage directions give him a carpenter; Nick Bottom the weaver; Francis Flute the bellows mender; Robin Starveling the tailor; Tom Snout the tinker; and Snug (who is given no first name) the joiner. Now look at the names. Dover Wilson says of them that they are "technical names":

> Commentators have remarked that *Bottom* takes
> his name from the "bottom" or core of the
> skein upon which the weaver's yarn is wound;
> but they have not noticed that most of the other
> clowns have technical names likewise. Thus
> *Quince* is simply a spelling of "quines" or
> "quoins," i.e. wedge-shaped blocks of wood
> used for building purposes, and therefore appropriately connected with a carpenter; *Snout*
> means nozzle or spout (v. N.E.D. "snout" 4)
> which suggests the tinker's trade in mending
> kettles; *Snug* means "compact, close-fitting,
> tight,"—a good name for a joiner; and *Flute,*
> the bellows-mender, would of course have to
> repair fluted church-organs as well as the domestic bellows. *Starveling,* indeed, is the only
> nontechnical name among them, though it is
> apt enough, referring as it does to the proverbial
> leanness of tailors, of whom it took "nine to
> make a man."

So far so good, but the names are not merely technical terms. They have that quality of association which goes with poetry, and the associations bear with them not merely the mechanical history of "things artificial" which Bacon commends, but also that other history, of "things natural." "Snout" has obvious animal connections, and was used in Shakespeare's time for fish and bird as well as beast. The name "Starveling" by its image of thinness brings in the body and food, and the word was used not only for human beings but also for animals or plants. "Snug" suggests a bodily, almost animal, warmth, as do the words "snuggle" or "nestle." "Quince" is fruit and tree. Flute the bellows-mender suggests by that combination of woodwind and bellows the moving breath which is life itself (lungs and bellows make as obvious a pair as do heart and pump), a life which is also capable of translation into music. His own quality of voice is drawn to our attention in his choice for Thisbe and his remonstrance, "Nay faith, let me not play a woman, I have a beard coming" [I. ii. 47-8], and in Bottom's desire to out-flute Flute, "I'll speak in a monstrous little voice" [I. ii. 52]. Last and best, there is Bottom himself. He calls attention to his own name: "It shall be called Bottom's Dream because it hath no bottom" [IV. i. 215-16]. It carries its obvious bodily reference and also the trade meaning which I shall

come back to before long. But meantime we can take stock of what the names so far have done for us. They imply the great unity of natural history, plants and trees, animals, man as body and mind, the arts. The mechanicals are dove-tailed into the whole universe of nature which is the subject mater of the *Dream;* but they have their own proper distinction in it. They are not bestialized, nor are they oafs or boors. They have struggled up out of the vegetable and animal into the human condition and they hold to their human status and, one might almost say, dignity, as Theseus recognizes, "If we imagine no worse of them than they of themselves, they may pass for excellent men" [V. i. 215-16]. Because they are human, they form a society, depicted here as the play's cast, close-knit and friendly; and they speak.

Speech, the acting and speaking of their play (notice the constant reference throughout the *Dream* to cues) is their whole endeavor here, and to speech everything is referred. "Have you the Lion's part written? pray you if it be, give it me, for I am slow of study" [I. ii. 66-7], says Snug in their first scene. Moon, Wall, Lion, all are somehow assimilated to the human condition and made to talk, not as in fairy tales with their own voices, but with those of Snug and Snout. Nature is acted upon by words, but not tortured into speech. Because of the simplicity of those who act her or act upon her, these virgin minds, Shakespeare comes as near as is possible to lending nature speech in them and their play. He can then observe the results.

In the very first exchanges between Quince and Bottom, something begins to happen. Bottom says, "You were best to call them generally" [I. ii. 2], where he means "severally"; and Peter Quince announces the play as "the most lamentable comedy" [I. ii. 11-12]. Strange juxtapositions, exchanges, substitutions, occur in the mechanicals' use of words. This pattern set up in their conversation is continued and intensified in their play.

> A tedious brief scene of young Pyramus
> And his love Thisby; very tragical mirth
>
> [V. i. 56-7]

their playbill reads, and Theseus comments, "That is, hot ice, and wondrous strange snow" [V. i. 59]. Sun and moon run together in one of Pyramus' speeches, "Sweet Moon, I thank thee for thy sunny Beams" [V. i. 272]. The senses are exchanged for one another—"he goes but to see a noise that he heard and is to come again" [III. i. 91-2]. "I see a voice, now will I to the chink / To spy an I can hear my Thisby's face"; "Tongue, lose thy light" [V. i. 192-93, 304]. The animals undergo a series of verbal substitutions, begun in Bottom's "I will roar you as gently as any sucking dove; I will roar you an 'twere any nightingale" [I. ii. 82-4], and taken up by the verbal quibbling of the court occasioned by the play's performance: "This lion is a very fox for his valour." "True, and a goose for his discretion." "Well moused, Lion" [V. i. 231-32, 269]. These are of course only verbal play, but they shadow something else, as does Quince's Prologue, where grammar and syntax are all upset, i.e. the forms and structures of language are changed, and the sense is contradicted by the form. This occasions the following remarks,

> LYSANDER: He hath rid his Prologue, like a
> rough colt: he knows not the stop. A good moral
> my Lord. It is not enough to speak, but to speak
> true.
> HIPPOLYTA: Indeed he hath played on his Prologue, like a child on a recorder, a sound, but
> not in government.

THESEUS: His speech was like a tangled chain:
nothing impaired but all disordered.

[V. i. 119-26]

They cannot manage their instrument, but their very mistakes
draw attention to the nature of that instrument and show the
language situation for what it is, a dynamic and not a static
one. Mistakes are nearly always dynamic or working situations.
Language is presented as a net of working forms, and even
though the mechanicals cannot manage its poetry (for that is
what its dynamism is) they point toward it, as Shakespeare's
perfected poetry could not do.

It is here that Bottom has his particular significance. If we turn
back a moment to the question of his name, we find that this
technical term in weaving has other connections. The *Oxford
English Dictionary* says: "BOTTOM: A clew or nucleus on which
to wind thread; also a skein or ball of thread." The first example
given is 1490, from Caxton's *Eneydos:* "He must take wyth
hym a bottome of threade." Later among the examples comes
this, from Ralegh's *History of the World*, "He received from
her [Ariadne] a bottome of threde." It is interesting that the
word "bottom" should apparently have a peculiar right of entry
into the story of Theseus and Ariadne and the labyrinth, the
combination of names reappearing in the *Dream* where Theseus
is a character and Ariadne is mentioned. Is Bottom the weaver
the "clew" to this play and what it says about postlogic?

So far we have been looking at natural history, which in Bacon's and Shakespeare's hands gives the range of postlogic
(the natural universe considered as alive throughout) and its
terms of reference (process as a whole, seen as fertility and
generation and as operation of all kinds, through nature and
up to and including man). Man is language; and here Bottom
is to the fore. Others of the mechanicals show a tendency
toward poetry or rhetoric, as in Quince's confusion of "paragon" and "paramour" for instance. Only a noble feeling for
rhetoric would induce so risky an extension of vocabulary; it
is easy for anyone to be correct in Basic English. But it is
Bottom, regarded by his peers as the fine flower of their society, the best wit in all Athens, the *sine qua non* of their play,
who carries this tendency furthest. Their play with its mythological subject from the *Metamorphoses* is a communal effort,
but it is Bottom who is on familiar terms with myths outside
the play, who speaks of Ercles and Phibbus with a breezy and
inacurrate familiarity. They play in verse, but it is Bottom who
quotes verse outside the play, and who when put to it has a
rude vein of poetry in his own imagination. Bottom is the mind
working with language; he is also dynamics, for he alone moves
out of the framework of the litle play into that of the larger
one, by his "dream" which gives him, even if only briefly,
the entry to another universe. With him we shall move on
now . . . to the transformations in the *Dream* itself. (pp. 127-33)

Forms in transformation—forms in nature and in the mind—
are part of the *Midsummer Night's Dream*. Shakespeare as
dramatist cannot discuss his forms; he has to present them. So
the forms of nature become forms indeed, the forms of Titania
and Oberon, spirits visible to the audience admitted to the
mythological situation or the dream, but invisible to the mortals
in the play ("I am invisible," Oberon says to make things
quite clear, when Demetrius and Helena enter [II. i. 186]). In
mortal form but not of mortal kind, as Titania explains when
she says to Bottom:

And I will purge thy mortal grossness so
That thou shalt like an airy spirit go,

[III. i. 160]

these are spirits which can nonetheless partake of mortal shape,
and their motions, of love or jealousy and disharmony, are
joined with the general course of nature, so that disturbance
in the one breeds a like disturbance in the other. These are
shadows of what will happen in the storm scene in *Lear,* where
not spirit-in-human-shape and nature but man and nature are
set in this same relationship of analogy and unity. Again when
Shakespeare comes to forms as the working of the mind he
can only present us with a character, and what we are given
is Bottom. The two meet in Bottom's interlude with Titania:
forms as operative powers in natural phenomena, and forms
as instruments of the thinking mind. Behind these, however,
the whole of nature is seen to be in movement. Everything is
changing. The seasons change; the lovers exchange partners;
myth itself may alter: "Apollo flies, and Daphne holds the
chase" [II. i. 231]. The word "change" comes round over
and over again.

> The spring, the summer,
> The chiding autumn, angry winter change
> Their wonted liveries.
>
> [III. i. 160]

> Run when you will, the story shall be changed.
>
> [II. i. 230]

> O Bottom, thou art chang'd; what do I see on thee?
>
> [III. i. 114-15]

> What change is this, sweet love?
>
> [III. ii. 262]

And there is a marvelous refrain throughout the play of words
for inner and outer changings, of natural and mental forms.
"The rest I'ld give to be to you translated" [I. i. 191] we
begin with, Helena wishing to be Hermia and Demetrius' beloved. This word occurs twice more: "Bless thee Bottom, bless
thee; thou art translated" [III. i. 118-19], says Peter Quince,
a phrase caught up later by Puck, "And left sweet Pyramus
translated there" [III. ii. 32]. But there are others too. "Things
base and vile, holding no quantity, / Love can transpose to
form and dignity" [I. i. 232-33], Helena says. At the end of
Bottom's idyll, Puck is bidden by Oberon to take "This transformed scalp / From off the head of this Athenian swain" [IV.
i. 64-5]. Later it is said of Bottom, "He cannot be heard of.
Out of doubt he is transported" [IV. ii. 3-4]. And lastly Hippolyta says of the lovers and the whole dream they have undergone, "all their minds transfigur'd so together" [V. i. 24].

The forms in this play are in movement . . . , and Bottom's
metamorphosis and translation are part of this (he moves in
his double capacity—as Bottom translated and as "sweet Pyramus translated"). This is the nature of mythological thinking
made manifest, and because Shakespeare is wholly committed
to it he can afford to make it as funny as it is, our animal
affinities somehow drawn up among the powers of nature which
we as yet neither understand nor control, but to which we are
united. Bottom is the human condition, the newly thinking
mind subjected to natural forms and trying to make forms of
its own by which to understand them. (pp. 139-41)

> *Elizabeth Sewell, "Bacon and Shakespeare: Post-
> logical Thinking," in her* The Orphic Voice: Poetry
> and Natural History, *1960. Reprint by Harper &
> Row, Publishers, 1971, pp 53-168.**

BERTRAND EVANS   (essay date 1960)

[*In two studies of Shakespearean drama*, Shakespeare's Comedies
(1960) and Shakespeare's Tragic Practice *(1979), Evans examines*

what he calls Shakespeare's use of "discrepant awarenesses." He claims that Shakespeare's dramatic technique makes extensive use of "gaps" between the different levels of awareness the characters and audience possess concerning the circumstances of the plot. In the excerpt below, Evans maintains that A Midsummer Night's Dream *is Shakespeare's only comedy to conclude without permitting the principal characters to share the audience's perception of the course of the dramatic action. He argues that the young lovers, following their ordeal in the woods, actually move further away from our understanding, since at this point they cannot recall or report clearly what has happened to them. Evans states that, of all the mortals, only Hippolyta comes near to the truth when she remarks that their accounts contain "something of great constancy" (V. i. 26). For additional discussions of the themes of perception, illusion, and awareness in this play, see the excerpts by John Russell Brown (1957), C. L. Barber (1959), T. Walter Herbert (1964), Stephen Fender (1968), Sydney R. Homan (1969), Charles R. Lyons (1971), and James L. Calderwood (1971). Evans also contends that in the figure of Oberon Shakespeare was for the first time using an "outside force" to direct the dramatic events. He views the fairy king as benevolent in the use of his powers, but notes that even he has limited omniscience, for Puck's first application of the juice of the flower is a mistaken one. Other critics who have regarded Oberon as the controlling force in* A Midsummer Night's Dream *include Fender, David Bevington (1978), Florence Falk (1980), George E. Woodberry and Ernest Schanzer (see Additional Bibliography).]*

In *The Comedy of Errors* a wide but single discrepancy in awarenesses resulted when we were given and the participants were denied one all-important fact, that two sets of identical twins are at large on the streets of the same city. The entire comic action of the play is an exploitation of this single discrepancy. In the other early comedies, multiple discrepancies both among participants and between them and us were created by deceptive practices of several sorts—wearing disguise, overhearing, overpeering, feigning ignorance, exchanging identities, secret conspiring, outright lying. In *A Midsummer-Night's Dream* the ultimate creator of the main discrepancy is again single, as in *The Comedy of Errors;* it is, of course, the magical property of a certain flower:

> Yet mark'd I where the bolt of Cupid fell.
> It fell upon a little western flower,
> Before milk-white, now purple with love's wound,
> And maidens call it love-in-idleness.
>
> [II. i. 165-68]

Squeezed upon the eyelids of two mortals and one fairy, the juice of this extraordinary pansy is the ultimate source—subtler than disguise, eavesdropping, or plain falsehood—of discrepancies which make possible the main action and comic effects of the play.

Though it touches the eyes of only three, the magic juice affects directly or indirectly all the principal persons. It is primarily responsible for the fact that at some time in the action each of them stands on a level of awareness below ours, and for the fact that we hold advantage over some person or persons during seven of the nine scenes. Yet although everything starts with it, the magic juice is not the only means by which the dramatist divides the awarenesses of characters. Here, as in the other major comedies, the disposition of awarenesses is elaborate, with many degrees of differentiation represented between Bottom's bottomless oblivion and Oberon's near omniscience. Though the juice is the first cause of the main gap, additional discrepancies are wrought by more ordinary means—even as ordinary as eavesdropping, and, in the case of Puck's initial

error, as common as simple lack of sufficiently precise information, plus a touch of irresponsibility.

In *A Midsummer-Night's Dream,* for the first time, Shakespeare uses an 'outside force' which interferes in and controls the affairs of men. Oberon moves unseen, unheard, and unsuspected to the solution of the sole problem of the play (so far as the mortals are concerned)—that of restoring Demetrius's love to Helena. Although he differs in form and nature from Shakespeare's later notable forces of control as markedly as they differ from one another, the fairy king is like them all both in his essential dramatic function and in the attributes which enable him to perform this function—superior power and superior awareness. (pp. 33-5)

Although he has come on purpose to bless the bed of Theseus and Hippolyta, Oberon's interference in the dilemma of the four Athenian youths comes about by chance. The juice of the flower for which he sends Puck was meant only for Titania's eyes, to compel her to surrender her little changeling boy. It is while he awaits Puck's return that Demetrius and Helena enter, quarrelling. 'I am invisible,' says the fairy king, 'and I will overhear their conference' [II. i. 186-87]. The 'conference' of the angry young man and the hurt and bitter maid runs through fifty-six lines and represents the play's first use of a discrepancy between the participants' vision and ours: the couple are ignorant by what immortal eye they are being watched. When they have gone, Oberon speaks:

> Fare thee well, nymph. Ere he do leave this grove,
> Thou shalt fly him and he shall seek thy love.
>
> [II. i. 245-46]

Neither now nor ever after are Helena and Demetrius—or, indeed, any of the other human participants—to know that a force from outside their mortal circle has looked on their affairs, apprehended their dilemma, and interceded in the cause of true love. From this first point on, a gap divides the human participants' view from ours. This gap is unique in Shakespeare's comedies in that it remains open even at the end of the play. We alone know that an immortal spirit has manipulated human events and solved a mortal problem.

Immortal, yet not quite omniscient: 'Anoint his eyes,' says Oberon to Puck,

> But do it when the next thing he espies
> May be the lady. Thou shalt know the man
> By the Athenian garments he hath on.
>
> [II. i. 261-64)

'Fear not, my lord,' replies Puck, 'your servant shall do so' [II. i. 268]. But even as Oberon gives these directions, we know, since the dramatist has taken care to advise us, that not one but two young men in Athenian garments are in the forest. Having seen only Demetrius, and being preoccupied with Titania, Oberon does not foresee the possibility of error. From this point until well into III.ii our Olympian perch is set not only above mortals but above immortals also. Dutifully seeking out a youth in Athenian weeds, and finding Lysander and Hermia sleeping far apart on the ground, as Hermia's sense of propriety has required, fallible Puck concludes that these are the estranged mortals who must be made to love each other. 'Believe me, king of shadows, I mistook' [III. ii. 347], he asserts later, when he and Oberon discover what abuse their errors have wrought. Puck errs because Oberon erred in directing him, and thus, though the ultimate cause is the magical juice of the little western flower, the immediate cause of the comic action involving the lovers is a blunder made because immortal intelligence has fallen, for once, a little short of omniscience.

The principal business between the time Puck drops the juice on Lysander's eyes and the time the fault is finally rectified, however, is exploitation not of Oberon's unawareness that Puck has blundered but of the lovers' unawareness of what has happened to them. In the truly enchanted forest outside Athens . . . , the effects of error are a chain reaction of surprise, misunderstanding, mystification, and near frenzy. The beginning is Lysander's waking, ignorant of what has happened as he slept, to perceive Helena through enchanted eyes:

> *Hel.* Lysander, if you live, good sir, awake.
> *Lys. (Awaking.)* And run through fire I will
> for thy sweet sake.
> Transparent Helena! Nature shows art,
> That through thy bosom makes me see thy heart. . . .
>   [II. ii. 102-05]

Equally innocent of the truth, Helena mistakes Lysander's protestations for mockery, thus compounding the initial error, and, startled and angry, runs off into the forest pursued by her bewitched lover. Hermia, waking, is removed even further from the truth, being ignorant not only of the cause of Lysander's change but of the fact that he *has* changed; mystified, filled with false imaginings, she, too, runs off, seeking Lysander. Thus in short order the potent magic of the little flower, misapplied by the fallible Puck, has affected three of the four youths, and exploitation of the swiftly multiplying discrepancies is under way. Briefly, moreover, the world of the mortals is in fact, in our own perspective, out of control, for Oberon is still preoccupied with Titania. (pp. 35-7)

Exploitation not of the fairies' brief unawareness . . . , but of the mortals' mystification and confusion is the business of the first great climactic scene. It begins with the entrance of Lysander and Helena immediately after the final act of deception has been performed, the anointing of Demetrius's eyes by Oberon. Says Puck,

> Then will two at once woo one;
> That must needs be sport alone.
>   [III. ii. 118-19]

The next 400 lines show Shakespeare's finest achievement to this date in representing the comic effects of error. Rushing through moonlight and shadow in the enchanted forest, unknowingly observed by immortal spirits, the confused couples act the 'fond pageant' that answers Puck's hopes. The profound oblivion of the young men, neither knowing what has happened to him, each distrusting the other's motives, is the basis of the action. Each accepts unquestioningly the reversal of his affection, as a plausible and natural event—as in dreams one regards fantastic experiences as ordinary. Thus whereas Lysander had confidently attributed his conversion to the force of 'reason', Demetrius now explains his own change as a natural homecoming:

> Lysander, keep thy Hermia; I will none.
> If e'er I lov'd her, all that love is gone.
> My heart to her but as guest-wise sojourn'd,
> And now to Helen is it home return'd,
> There to remain.
>   [III. ii. 169-73]

Eyes open but glassy, accepting without surprise or wonder events that should astonish them, the rival lovers prefigure the

greater heroes of the later comedies. . . . Mystification leads them to try interpretation, and misinterpretation leads to angry quarrel which threatens violence: all this, for the women as for the men, is the effect of the same basic unawareness of the situation. The heroines of *A Midsummer-Night's Dream*, unlike those of the later comedies, hold advantage over the heroes only in realizing that the situation is unnatural, in distrusting and refusing to accept what Lysander and Demetrius view without surprise.

The quarrel scene ends with a threat of actual violence and physical injury, when Lysander and Demetrius withdraw into the forest to fight it out with their swords and Helena of the longer legs flees the sharper nails of Hermia. It is just here that the dramatist gives us reassurance. . . . Oberon has seen all. 'Stand aside', he said to Puck after anointing the eyes of Demetrius, and the pair silently watched what happens when 'two at once woo one'. At the outset, then, we have occupied a vantage-point from which to view the action not merely as a quarrel, but *as a quarrel of mortals overwatched by benevolent omnipotence*. Given a perspective that includes Oberon, knowing that he knows all and means to direct true love to a happy ending, we can maintain during the violent 'jangling' of the rivals a sense that all is really well. Our awareness provides a perfect climate for comic effect. If we forgot the presence of Oberon during the action, and thus narrowed the vision which the dramatist enabled us to use at full advantage, by so much would the force of the scene be diminished for us. But to make sure that our comfortable sense of Oberon's presence does not fail at the crucial moment, Shakespeare prods it immediately after the confused, angry, desperate mortals run off into the forest. For Oberon here reminds us that he has understood all, chides Puck for his error, and orders him to prevent the youths from hurting one another in their ignorance. (pp. 38-40)

In the enchanted forest of *A Midsummer-Night's Dream*, governed by a fairy king, error can be introduced into mortal affairs by the anointment of human eyes with the juice of a flower, and so also it can be removed by the simple expedient of crushing on the eyes another herb. While the couples sleep in exhaustion after their night-long chase in the forest, Puck anoints Lysander's eyes with the 'remedy' and thus corrects the error without which there would have been no misunderstanding, no quarrel, no danger—and no action. But the magic juice is left in Demetrius's eyes, to make the false lover see true, even as it had made the true one see false. So when the lovers wake, enchantment has ended, and, even as Oberon had foretold, none can recall the night's events. Our advantage over them continues, therefore, after the spell is broken, even to the end of the play, and forever. In this way *A Midsummer-Night's Dream* is unique among Shakespeare's comedies, for in others the denouement closes the gap between the participants' awareness and ours. A principle of Shakespeare's dramatic method is reflected in the fact that in his comedies, histories, and tragedies, the denouement never is needed or used to explain matters of which *we* have been ignorant, but to raise the participants' awareness up, at last, to ours. By coincidence or otherwise, it is only in *A Midsummer-Night's Dream* and *Romeo and Juliet*—plays possibly written in the same year—that the participants' level is not raised to equal ours at the end.

Theseus's party of hunters come upon the sleeping lovers even as the Prince, the rival families, and the citizens of Verona come upon the bodies of Romeo and Juliet, lying dead with

Paris in the Capulet tomb. And though the lovers in the comedy wake, whereas those in the tragedy do not, yet they cannot tell their story. 'When they next wake, all this derision / Shall seem a dream and fruitless vision' [III. ii. 370-71], Oberon had predicted; and so it is. . . . [None] of the lovers will be able to report his adventures. For in truth, on waking after the night is over, the youths have fallen still farther below our vantage-point. While the action of the night continued, they were aware of it even though they were ignorant of the cause; but now that it is over, their remembrance has failed, and they know neither the what nor the why of the night or the morrow.

So also Bottom, the state of whose awareness, in its relation to ours, remains to be probed. . . . Bottom is first in a line that includes such notables as Dogberry [in *Much Ado about Nothing*], Malvolio, and Sir Andrew Aguecheek [in *Twelfth Night*]. These are the mortals whom nature has made oblivious both of the facts of the situation which bounds them and of themselves. Their competitors for the lowest level of awareness are the romantic heroes of the comedies; but even these—in situations that do not involve business with heroines—have moments when they see themselves and their surroundings with clear eyes. . . . Their unawareness is rarely attributable to their own natures; usually they appear unaware to us only because the dramatist has given us specific information that is denied them and which they cannot possibly know at the time, however circumspect they are. In short, [those] who on occasion are ignorant of the facts of their situations are typically so because circumstances make their ignorance unavoidable. But for the select few who dwell at Bottom's depth no device of deception is needed. The dramatist creates them as beings with insulated minds, without perspective, oblivious wherever they are. They are congenitally, chronically unaware. If Rosalind [in *As You Like It*] carries an immunity to unawareness, Bottom carries one to awareness. For Rosalind, brightest of heroines, the dark is light enough; for bully Bottom the light is too dark, and the dark no darker.

To this Bottom alone of the mortals it is given to see the fairies—indeed, to converse with them, shake hands with them, be loved by their queen. And yet to him the fairies are no more remarkable than his hard-handed fellows who work in the shop. If Puck mistook in anointing Lysander's eyes when he should have anointed those of Demetrius, he does not err in selecting from among the homespun players—indeed, in selecting from all the world—none but this Bottom, 'the shallowest thickskin of that barren sort' [III. ii. 13], to be the object of Titania's passion. Bottom's oblivion is fixed and immutable; he sees neither himself nor his situation truly at any moment in the action, either before, during, or after his sojourn with immortals. With his first words, without the dramatist's using any device except the words themselves, a chasm opens between his understanding and ours, and it remains so, neither wider nor narrower, through all the action to the end. . . . He is neither more nor less oblivious in the ass's head; this head is the palpable extension of his native condition: it is unawareness concretized. When the new situations rise about him, he is neither less nor more aware of them than of the old. He steers an undeviating course through the ordinary and the marvellous alike. All places, persons, and things are alike to him; his insulated mind makes no distinction between Theseus and Peter Quince, Peaseblossom and Snout. With Oberon's wife who dotes on him—'O how I love thee! how I dote on thee!' [IV. i. 45]—he behaves just as he would with Snug's or Flute's wife: 'I pray you, let none of your people stir me; I have an exposition of sleep comeupon me' [IV. i. 38-9]. Not Titania's

compulsive doting, but Bottom's unruffled oblivion is the exploitable substance of the first fifty lines of Act IV, which brief scene complements and completes that of the mortal lovers' quarrel and frantic chase through the forest, the two scenes standing together at the summit of the play.

From the perfect vantage-point on which Shakespeare seats us throughout *A Midsummer-Night's Dream,* we perceive more, of course, than the activities of any single group of participants. We are set where our sweep of vision takes in all actions at once—high enough to see that the worlds of fairies, lovers, and artisans, quite separate and alone so far as the participants know, are all one world. We have full view alike of the bewitched lovers overwatched by Oberon in the enchanted forest; of Theseus and Hippolyta awaiting the impending wedding for which the fairies have come to this forest; of Peter Quince and his hard-handed crew, in their relations with both mortals and immortals; and, of course, of the fairies themselves. Except briefly, Oberon and Puck sit with us and see all that we see. But the other groups of participants, whose visions are too confined to take in even what is going on in their own circles, are quite cut off from a view of the whole. The lovers, running, quarrelling, sleeping in the forest, are ignorant of the fairies' existence and of Quince's rough crew. The artisans, except for Bottom, who is transformed and bewitched at the time and can tell nothing even to himself in secret afterwards, know nothing of either the lovers or the fairies. . . . Finally, the royal pair, though they are well acquainted with the young couples, neither know nor can learn what happened in the forest: 'No doubt they rose up early to observe / The rite of May, and, hearing our intent, / Came here in grace of our solemnity', says Theseus, finding the lovers asleep after their frantic night [IV. i. 132-34]. Only Hippolyta senses that there is more than 'fancy's images' in the lovers' incoherent and fragmentary account of the night, and in her opinion that

> . . . all the story of the night told over,
> And all their minds transfigur'd so together,
> More witnesseth than fancy's images,
> And grows to something of great constancy;
> But, howsoever, strange and admirable . . .
> [V. i. 23-7]

she nears the truth as does no other mortal; accordingly, the gap between her awareness and ours comes nearest being closed. But Hippolyta is half supernatural herself, and has an appreciation of things strange and admirable, even as, in contrast, she has no patience with gross reality: 'This is the silliest stuff that ever I heard' [V. i. 210], she says of the artisans' dramatic effort. For the rest of the mortals, including the lovers who have run themselves half to death in the woods, and Bottom, whose itches have been scratched by fairy hands, their ignorance of the marvels we have witnessed from an Olympian peak is epitomized in Theseus's casual, magnificently unwitting words spoken an instant before Oberon, Titania, Puck, and all the fairy train take over the royal household: 'Lovers, to bed; 'tis almost fairy time' [V, i. 364]. (pp. 40-6)

> *Bertrand Evans, "All Shall Be Well: The Way Found,"*
> *in his* Shakespeare's Comedies, *Oxford at the Clarendon Press, Oxford, 1960, pp. 33-67.*

JOHN VYVYAN (essay date 1961)

[*In the following excerpt, Vyvyan discerns the thematic unity of* A Midsummer Night's Dream *in its Neoplatonic vision of love and beauty, specifically, Shakespeare's idea—which Vyvyan perceives in many of his plays—that "love on earth is a recognition between companion souls" who apprehend in each other "the beauty of their divine self-nature." The critic further claims that the action of* A Midsummer Night's Dream *traces the tests and impediments which the young lovers must confront before they can attain this superior degree of recognition and understanding of each other. Vyvyan also regards the confusion and discord in the woods as the result of the lovers pursuing the wrong ideal— a situation resolved in harmony, he notes, when the characters achieve the proper relationship to each other. Other critics who have either mentioned or discussed the presence of Platonic thought in* A Midsummer Night's Dream *include Hermann Ulrici (1839), Peter G. Phialas (1966), David Ormerod (1978), and Andrew D. Weiner (see Additional Bibliography). Also, for further discussion of the resolution of discordant elements in the play, see the excerpts by Harold C. Goddard (1951), Stephen Fender (1968), R. A. Zimbardo (1970), David Bevington (1975), and Paul A. Olson (see Additional Bibliography).]*

The figures of Theseus and Hippolyta, firmly enthroned, save *A Midsummer Night's Dream* from dissolving into moonlight. They are never led astray by the fairies, and they give the play substantiality. This is more than a stage impression, the stiffening is also intellectual. When Theseus hears the story of the night's confusions, his comment is, "More strange than true—" [V. i. 2]. But Hippolyta insists that it "—grows to something of great constancy" [V. i. 26]. The play itself does that. But what is the thing of constancy? The brief answer, I think, is beauty. That may sound deceptively simple; for behind it lies a great part of the Neo-Platonist philosophy of the Renaissance.

Why did Shakespeare choose Theseus and Hippolyta to frame his dream-story? This is the kind of question we ought to ask whenever he brings in mythological figures; because they are always more than ornament, they are part of his parable as well. The Theseus-and-Hippolyta theme—as it is presented to us here—is the turning of a war into a wedding, a sword into a ring: out of chaos has come a birth of beauty. It is to this that the regal couple in the background owe their stability. For the symbolic purpose of this play they have attained the thing of constancy towards which the wavering characters are shown to grow.

This miracle—the bringing of order out of confusion—is performed by love. In Theseus and Hippolyta we see it as achieved; while in the bewildered lovers it is gradually taking place. (pp. 7-8)

As soon as the scene has been established by Theseus and Hippolyta, we have a love-test. The union of a pair of lovers, Lysander and Hermia, is opposed by parental and legal authority. If Hermia refuses to give Lysander up, she will either be put to death, or forced to take the veil:

> For aye to be in shady cloister mewed,
> To live a barren sister all your life.
>
> [I. i. 71-2]

What ought the lovers to do? Nowadays, we have been so conditioned to accept the rightness of free choice in love that we may not notice that there is an ethical problem. But this is quite a recent outlook. In Shakespeare's time, even sweethearts would have granted that parents and the law had a certain claim upon their duty, and this consideration is a part of their dilemma. Shakespeare often presents this situation. It is more than a dramatic *cliché:* it is the problem of Juliet and of Desdemona. And the answer he gives to it is always the same— the highest duty is to love. (pp. 9-10)

Shakespeare's decision in favour of love—not in this play only, but in principle—is a reasoned deduction from certain premises. The most general of these, shared by many of his contemporaries, is that love is "the manifestation in man of the great informing power which brought the universe out of chaos and which now maintains it in order and concord" [J. S. Harrison, in his *Platonism in English Poetry*]. This alone would justify his standpoint, since it must follow that every betrayal of love is a movement towards disintegration. But I think there is a fair amount of evidence to suggest that he makes the general proposition personal and dramatic by a further assumption, also widely current in his time, that love on earth is a recognition between companion souls, who may at least perceive in one another, if they have true love-sight, the beauty of their divine self-nature. I believe this hypothesis could shed light on a number of problems in the difficult plays of Shakespeare's maturity, and that it will be worth while to test it carefully in his earlier work. I will not, therefore, embark on a general discussion of *A Midsummer Night's Dream*, but consider mainly those aspects of it that would seem to be related to this idea.

Hermia, then, bravely refuses the unloved Demetrius, whom authority would force upon her as a husband. And she tells the duke that she would prefer "withering on the virgin thorn" [I. i. 77] to marriage—

> Unto his lordship, whose unwished yoke
> My soul consents not to give sovereignty.
>
> [I. i. 81-2]

Her decision is doubly right. Demetrius, in courting her, is being unfaithful to his own early sweetheart, who is perhaps his predestined partner. And with this desertion, Lysander charges him:

> Demetrius, I'll avouch it to his head,
> Made love to Nedar's daughter, Helena,
> And won her soul; and she, sweet lady, dotes,
> Devoutly dotes, dotes in idolatry,
> Upon this spotted and inconstant man.
>
> [I. i. 106-10]

If our hypothesis is correct, therefore, we have two pairs of companion souls . . . who ought "to work each others joy true content" [Edmund Spenser, in his *An Hymne in Honour of Beautie*]; and if they do, they will achieve something more than their own happiness; for through them a part of the "celestiall harmony" will be realized on earth. We may notice that a conception of relatedness, not quite the same but comparable, is also brought into the fairy plot; for the discord between their king and queen is reflected in the elements, as Titania explains:

> And this same progeny of evil comes
> From our debate, from our dissension:
> We are their parents and original.
>
> [II. i. 115-17]

There may be some folklore in this; but what is more to the point is that it fits in with Shakespeare's wider contention— that the soul-state of his characters is objectified in their world, and that love and hate, however personal their expression, are forces that have repercussions on a cosmic scale. (pp. 79-80)

[Immortal] companions do not always recognize each other when they meet on earth. The body is a disguise to the soul. And the elaborate symbolism of masks and disguises in Shakespeare may well have sprung from this primary idea. Since love-sight is supposed to pierce the disguise and reveal true identity, there is a necessary link between self-knowlege and love, and so we may readily understand the Shakespearean proposition that the way to the one is perfect constancy to the other. But this is far from easy; and therefore,

The course of true love never did run smooth.

> [I. i. 134]

In fact, Shakespeare stages an almost regular series of impediments. To begin with, bewilderment—when "love is a blinded god", and the lovers are pursuing the wrong partners. Then, as soon as they partially recognize each other, to the extent of "a sympathy in choice" [I. i. 141], the tests of constancy begin. Sometimes one of them is tested alone by the temporary infidelity of the other; there is opposition of all kinds, and the trial of separation. This is the stage of which Lysander speaks:

> Or, if there were a sympathy in choice,
> War, death, or sickness did lay siege to it,
> Making it momentany as a sound,
> Swift as a shadow, short as any dream,
> Brief as the lightning in the collied night,
> That, in a spleen, unfolds both heaven and earth;
> And ere a man hath power to say, "Behold!"
> The jaws of darkness do devour it up:
> So quick bright things come to confusion.
>
> [I. i. 141-49]
> (pp. 80-1)

It is a period of uncertainty, when true vision is achieved only in glimpses and flashes. At the mildest, it may be called love's springtime, having "the uncertain glory of an April day" [I. iii. 85]. But always there is more than mere romance; it is part of an ascent or pilgrimage, at the culmination of which the uncertain glory is made lasting. And its trials must not be avoided, but faced. By this standard, Hermia's reply to Lysander is exactly right:

> It stands as an edict in destiny:
> Then let us teach our trial patience,
> Because it is a customary cross,
> As due to love as thoughts and dreams and sighs,
> Wishes and tears; poor Fancy's followers.
>
> [I. i. 151-55]
> (p. 82)

In *A Midsummer Night's Dream*, constancy is stressed up to a point. But the fact that love-sight is controlled by charms—

> And ere I take this charm from off her sight,
> As I can take it with another herb—
>
> [II. i. 183-84]

and not as elsewhere by the hard work of the soul, makes its ethic seem comparatively weak. It might be argued that the first charm produces nothing except "hateful fantasies"; but there are equally cogent objections to this point of view. And even when Titania, under its influence, perceives a kind of divinity in Bottom, I fancy that she is nearer, in Shakespeare's judgement, to a true vision of him than when she sees him only as an ass. The juice of love-in-idleness is certainly a cause of confusion; but eyes that have been anointed with it do nevertheless see something real behind the mask of mortality. What they see is something love-awakening. And therefore, if the parallel with Spenser is a true one, it ought to be a glimpse of the "inmost faire".

The first mortal on whom the juice is tried, by Puck's mistake, is Lysander; and the first evidence we have of its effect is his exclamation:

> Transparent Helena! Nature shows an art
> That through thy bosom makes me see thy heart.
>
> [II. ii. 104-05]

And when Demetrius has been likewise anointed, he exclaims:

> O Helen, goddess, nymph, perfect, divine!
>
> [III. ii. 137]

This is meant to make us laugh, of course; but is there anything beyond the joke? If this new insight is nothing but an hallucination, it is curious that the description of it should fit a theory that Shakespeare has taken seriously in other plays. "Transparent" is precisely the word to illustrate it. Lysander has seen through Helena, and what he has seen is something more beautiful than her outward shape: the whole context of Renaissance thought requires the further assumption that what is more beautiful is also more real. So in spite of the confusion the charm makes, it has conferred something on Lysander that is akin to Spenserian love-sight. (pp. 84-6)

If Shakespeare is seeing his lovers as companion souls, so that only one final pattern of relationships can be absolutely right, then the third act illustrates Spenser's idea of what is to be expected when the wrong partners try to unite—

> It is not love, but a discordant warre,
> Whose unlike parts amongst themselves do iarre.

And the same hypothesis might account for the determination with which the spurned Helena hounds Demetrius down. It is undignified, to say the least; but if they are pre-destined for each other, she is right. This is not the only play in which the heroine behaves like the hound of heaven—there is *All's Well that Ends Well*, for instance; and the current theory of pre-existence, of love cradled in "heavenly bowers", that must be found again and realized upon earth, would justify them all. They are surely in need of some justification; for although no one doubts the ability of the female to hunt the male, it is not usually depicted as a virtue. Helena is painfully aware of this, and calls it a scandal on her sex:

> We should be wooded and were not made to woo.
>
> [II. i. 242]

She is none the less determined to follow Demetrius, "and make a heaven of hell" [II. i. 243], or die in the attempt.

Against all likelihood, she succeeds. And at the close of the fourth act, when the lovers wake at sunrise, their vision restored, the harmony between the four of them reminds us of that which was at last achieved in *The Two Gentlemen of Verona*. Here again we have the theme that rivalry exists only in the phase of illusion—symbolized this time by the moonlit wood—when Theseus exclaims to Lysander and Demetrius:

> I know you two are rival enemies.
> How comes this gentle concord in the world—?
>
> [IV. i. 142-43]

In the earlier play, it was between the women that rivalry might have been expected, here it is chiefly between the men; but there is a similar allegory, I suggest, in both: when the true beauty is rightly apprehended, concord comes to the world. I think Shakespeare is quite serious about this, and he returns to it many times; but if we insist that there is no parable in his plays, we see only the surface of his thoughts. (pp. 88-90)

> *John Vyvyan, "Theseus and Hippolyta" and "'A Midsummer Night's Dream'," in his* Shakespeare and Platonic Beauty, *Chatto & Windus, 1961, pp. 7-14, 77-91.*

GERALD F. JACOBSON (essay date 1962)

[*Jacobson's essay is one of the earliest psychoanalytic interpretations of* A Midsummer Night's Dream. *As a critical methodology, psychoanalytic criticism seeks an underlying significance or subconscious intention through an analysis of the symbols and language of the work in question. Jacobson agrees with Weston A. Gui (see Additional Bibliography) that this play may be read as Shakespeare's attempt to resolve some early aggressive and hostile behavior or attitude the dramatist exhibited toward his mother. Additionally, Jacobson contends that the focus of the play is on "the psycho-sexual development of women." He identifies unresolved Oedipal conflicts in Hermia's early expressions of preference for Lysander rather than Demetrius and in the rivalry between Hermia and Helena. Instead of focusing on Egeus's demand that his daughter love the man of his choice, Jacobson argues, Hermia is unconsciously in love with her father's designate (Demetrius) and, therefore, with father himself. "Rather than marry such an incestuous object," Jacobson asserts, "Hermia must remain virginal." Lysander represents the non-incestuous lover to whom father will not give up his daughter. The other Oedipal theme consists of the ambivalent feelings of the child (Hermia) for her mother/sister—in this instance, Helena. Hermia's fantasy thus proceeds: Father loves me and not mother/ sister—a pattern enacted at the surface level of action in Demetrius's love for Hermia and his disfavor of Helena. According to Jacobson, these Oedipal conflicts are resolved only when the proper relationships are reestablished between the characters. The critic also finds an expression of the problem of sexual identification in Titania's refusal to give up the changeling, for here she is represented as the "emasculating, i.e. castrating woman who feminizes the male child." For additional psychoanalytical interpretations of the young lovers in* A Midsummer Night's Dream, *see the essay by M. D. Faber (1972) and the entries by Melvin Goldstein and Norman N. Holland cited in the Additional Bibliography.*]

The only previously published psychoanalytic paper on Shakespeare's "Midsummer Night's Dream" that has come to my attention was written by Weston A.Gui [see Additional Bibliography]. . . . Gui proposes and carefully documents the thesis that the entire play can be read as a symbolic representation of a primal scene night in the life of a child. The following is a brief synopsis of the remainder of Gui's paper: The "Dream" in the title of the play represents Bottom's dream of his transformation into an ass and his subsequent encounter with Titania. The latent content of this dream refers to oral and Oedipal conflicts around mother. According to Gui, the play further reveals failure to find a non-neurotic solution of these conflicts. (p. 21)

Gui [also] states that the play represents restitution for the attack on mother by the orally frustrated and enraged child. . . . [Evidence] for this contention is the action of Bottom when, as Pyramus, in the play within the play, he plunges his sword into his "left pap," i.e. nipple. Here we see the attack on mother's introjected breast. (pp. 21-2)

If this play is a restitutive gesture towards mother, as I believe it is, it is not surprising that we find in it one strand not referred to by Gui. I have reference to the elucidation of the psychosexual development of women. Just as Bottom's dream represents the unsuccessful working through of the psychic conflicts of the boy, so can we see in the Oberon-Titania, but particularly in the Hermia-Lysander-Helena-Demetrius plots the struggles that culminate in the successful resolution of the analogous conflicts in the girl, and eventually permit her marital happiness. It is considered likely, though not definitely proven, that the play was written for an occasion where three actual marriages were celebrated in some great house in the

Queen's presence. The women are to be pleased, and what will please them better than the unravelling of the vicissitudes of their development with a successful outcome.

If we turn first to the Oberon-Titania conflict, we see that the object of the quarrel between this supernatural pair is

> A lovely boy, stolen from an Indian king
> You never saw so sweet a changeling
> And jealous Oberon would have the child
> Knight of his train, to trace the forests wild:
> But she perforce withholds the loved boy,
> Crowns him with flowers, and makes him all her joy.
> [II. i. 22-7]

Gui interprets this part of the play, correctly, if we see it from Bottom's point of view, as referring to Bottom's jealousy of the younger brother, the Indian prince, whom he displaces, according to wish fulfillment, in the arms of Titania, the mother. However, we may also see something else, if we look at the matter from the standpoint of Titania, the woman. The stolen changeling child may also represent the little girl's fantasy of stealing mother's baby, and killing mother, as in this case the stolen child belonged to a woman who died in childbirth. Further, there can be seen here the problem of sexual identification in women. It is expressed by inquiring into the raising of the Indian child. Shall he have a male role ("knight of his train,") or a female one ("crowns him with flowers"). Titania is here the emasculating, i.e. castrating woman who femininizes the male child. That this is so is also seen in Titania's other identity of Diana, the huntress and in the analogy pointed out by Gui between Titania and the queen of the Amazons. Titania must and does give up the male child, and her claims to possess the penis, before she can once again share Oberon's bed.

The most clearcut references to feminine development occur in theHermia-Lysander-Helena-Demetrius plot. (pp. 22-3)

As the play opens, Hermia's father summons the Duke of Athens, Theseus, to reinforce his wishes that she marry Demetrius. Supporting the father's command, Theseus says:

> Therefore, fair Hermia, question your desires,
> Know of your youth, examine well your blood,
> Whether, if you yield not to your father's choice,
> You can endure the livery of a nun,
> For aye to be in shady cloister mew'd,
> To live a barren sister all your life,
> Chanting faint hymns to the cold fruitless moon.
> Thrice-blessed they that master so their blood
> To undergo such maiden pilgrimage;
> But undergo such maiden pilgrimage;
> Than that which withering on the virgin thorn
> Grows, lives, and dies, in single blessedness.
> [I. i. 67-78]

Hermia's dilemma as stated in the opening quotation, is to obey her father, to die, or to remain single and to repress her sexuality. If we analyze the state of affairs, we see why this is so. Correcting the manifest content for projection and displacement, we see that rather than the father demanding that Hermia love the man of his choice, it is she who is in love with father's designate and therefore with father himself. Demetrius can be thought of as representing father. Rather than marry such an incestuous object, Hermia must remain virginal. Lysander, the rival suitor opposed by father, represents the non-incestuous lover to whom father will not surrender her.

The other major Oedipal theme of ambivalence to mother and sister is clearly represented in the rivalry between Hermia and Helena. The play which is written largely from Hermia's point of view begins with both men—Lysander and Demetrius—in love with Hermia. This is true in spite of Hermia's rejection (in the manifest content) of Demetrius whom Helena in turn loves. Thus is represented the fulfillment of the little girl's fantasy: father really loves me; mother (sister) may love him but he does not return her love. That Helena represents sister is made very clear when Hermia says:

> Is all the counsel that we two have shar'd,
> The sister's vows, the hours that we have spent,
> When we have chid the hasty-footed time
> For parting us—O,is all forgot?
> All school days' friendship, childhood innocence?
> [III. ii. 198-202]

But that Helena must also represent mother is indicated by Hermia's pointed reference to Helena's greater physical height.

> Hermia: 'Puppet!' why so? Ay, that way goes the
>   game.
>   Now I perceive that she hath made compare
>   Between our statures; she hath urged her
>   height;
>   And with her personage, her tall personage,
>   Her height, forsooth, she hath prevail'd with
>   him.
>   And are you grown so high in his esteem
>   Because I am so dwarfish and so low?
>   How low am I, thou painted maypole? Speak.
> [III. ii. 289-96]

This is further supported by the reference to Hermia and Helena's exceedingly close relationship of which Helena speaks when she says:

> So we grew together,
> Like a double cherry, seeming parted,
> But yet in union in partition,
> Two lovely berries moulded on one stem . . .
> [III. ii. 208-11]

Helena—mother—then reproves Hermia for turning away from her and from women towards men.

> And will you rent our ancient love asunder,
> To join with men in scorning your poor friend?
> It is not friendly, 'tis not maiden!;
> Our sex, as well as I, may chide you for it,
> Though I alone do feel the injury.
> [III. ii. 215-19]

Hermia's rage breaks through when Helena appears to emerge the more desired women and Helena says:

> O, when she is angry, she is keen and shrewd;
> She was a vixen when she went to school;
> And, though she be but little she is fierce.
> [III. ii. 323-25]

The final resolution of the Oedipal conflict is in the play brought about by intervention of magic. Puck says "Jack shall have Jill, Nought shall be ill." Yet it is likely that Shakespeare's many references to dreams represent a grasp of the relation between dreams and the unconscious. Thus conceived, the dreamed experiences represent an unconscious working through of infantile conflicts. Each lover gives up the Oedipal wishes, and ends up with the post-Oedipal partner. Demetrius (father)

may marry Helena (mother), while Hermia is reunited with the non-incestuous lover, Lysander.

In this connection Demetrius relates that his love to Hermia is

> Melted as snow, seems to me now
> As the remembrance of an idle gaud
> Which in my childhood I did dote upon . . . .
> [IV. i. 166-68]

Thus the infantile (childhood) objects and strivings are surrendered. As Freud said in his famous discussion, the artist uses his "mysterious ability" to "open out to others the way back to . . . their own unconscious. . . ." Thus both our awe of Shakespeare's genius and our appreciation of the ageless unconscious is increased when we see it reflected alike in his characters, in our patients, and in every woman and man. (pp. 23-6)

> *Gerald F. Jacobson, "A Note on Shakespeare's 'Midsummer Night's Dream'," in* American Imago, *Vol. 19, No. 1, Spring, 1962, pp. 21-6.*

R. W. DENT (essay date 1964)

[*In the following excerpt on* A Midsummer Night's Dream, *Dent argues three points. First, he maintains that in the plot of the young lovers Shakespeare is not condemning the "follies of imagination" in love, nor suggesting that relationships between men and women should be based strictly on reason and understanding—as numerous critics have proposed in describing Theseus and Hippolyta as Shakespeare's "ideal" union in the play (see the excerpts by H. B. Charlton, 1933; E. C. Pettet, 1949; Ernest Schanzer, 1951; George A. Bonnard, 1956; John Vyvyan, 1961; Peter G. Phialas, 1966; and Paul A. Olson in the Additional Bibliography). Instead, Dent claims that Shakespeare presents love as "inexplicable," "illogical," and by its very nature dependent for its existence on a "disciplined" and "healthy" imagination. The type of love Shakespeare does criticize in A Midsummer Night's Dream, Dent contends, is that based on idolatry— "the monomaniacal pursuit of unrequited love"—and that "ridiculous bestowal of affection on an obviously unworthy object," exemplified in Titania's infatuation for the transformed Bottom. Second, Dent asserts that the Pyramus and Thisbe interlude is not merely a parody of the main love story, but "a foil to the entire play." The play-within-the-play shifts the spectator's focus from imagination in the realm of love to imagination in the domain of art. Commentators who have considered the interlude a parody of the main plot of the play include August Wilhelm Schlegel (1808), E. K. Chambers (1905), Paul N. Siegel (1953), C. L. Barber (1959), and Mordecai Marcus (1981). Third, Dent claims that the principal purpose of the Pyramus and Thisbe interlude is not to contrast Shakespeare's artistic methods with those of his rude mechanicals, as suggested most notably by G. G. Gervinus (1849-50), Edward Dowden (1881), Denton J. Snider (1890), and George Brandes (1895-96), but to emphasize "the follies of abused imagination in the theatre." It also conveys to the audience Shakespeare's belief in the necessity of poetic art, despite what the critic regards as "the humility" of the play's epilogue. In contrast to Shakespeare's own evaluation of his craft, Dent argues that Theseus demonstrates, despite his seemingly sympathetic remarks, no appreciation for poetic works beyond mere entertainment. This point has also been proposed by Howard Nemerov (1956).*]

For many years editors and critics have customarily praised *A Midsummer Night's Dream* for its artistic fusion of seemingly disparate elements. Sometimes the praise involves little, really, beyond admiring the skill with which Shakespeare interwove the actions of the four lovers, the fairies, and the mechanicals in the first four acts of the play. Usually, quite properly, it moves somewhat beyond this, relating this interwoven action to the thematic treatment of love in the play. But such praise has rarely concerned itself with the play's fifth act; it has tended to treat *A Midsummer Night's Dream* as essentially complete in four acts, but with a fifth act somehow vaguely appropriate in mood and content to serve as a conclusion. *Pyramus and Thisbe,* that rude offering of the mechanicals, has been briefly commended as loosely paralleling in action and theme the problems of the four lovers, and as delightful enough in itself to need no other artistic justification. Despite the consistency with which *A Midsummer Night's Dream* has been admired for its unity, in short, few critics have had much to say about the whole of the play.

The present essay seeks to reexamine the degree and kind of unity achieved by *A Midsummer Night's Dream*. Without pretending to be strikingly original, it approaches the play from a somewhat different angle, suggesting that the heart of the comedy, its most pervasive unifying element, is the partially contrasting role of imagination in love and in art. (p. 115)

Nothing is more common than the observation that *A Midsummer Night's Dream* is a play "about love", about lovers' lunacy, where "reason and love keep little company together nowadays" [III. i. 143-44], where the follies of imagination-dominated Demetrius and Lysander are reduced to their essential absurdity by the passion of Titania for an ass. It is for the sake of this theme, surely, that Demetrius and Lysander are given so little distinctive characterization; they cannot contrast like a Claudius and a Benedick [in *Much Ado About Nothing*], so that a particular pairing of lovers is demanded by the char-

Act II. Scene i. Puck and Oberon. By Robert Smirke (1828). The Department of Rare Books and Special Collections, The University of Michigan Library.

acters of those involved. For the same reason, paradoxically, Hermia and Helena are differentiated, to heighten the puzzle of love's choices (as well as to increase the potentialities for comedy in the play's middle). By all conventional Elizabethan standards, tall fair gentle Helena should be the one pursued, and when Lysander eventually boasts his use of reason in preferring a dove to a raven his argument, by those standards, is indeed rational. Our laughter stems from recognizing that it is so only accidentally, as rationalization.

According to a good many critics, Shakespeare contrasts from the start the irrationality of the lovers with what these critics regard as the admirable rationality of Theseus-Hippolyta. The latter become a kind of ideal which the lovers approach by the end of the play. If so, the role of imagination in love is simple and obvious; it is a disrupting irrational influence which must eventually be purged, and will prove in simple and total contrast to the disciplined use of imagination essential to Shakespeare's art. But I cannot see that any contrast so mechanical as this is intended.

When, thanks to Dian's bud, Lysander returns to Hermia, his "true love", the return marks a release from dotage but no return to reason as such, any more than does Demetrius' return to Helena by the pansy-juice. Love's choices remain inexplicable, and the eventual pairings are determined only by the constancy of Helena and Hermia in their initial inexplicable choices. As so frequently in Shakespearian comedy, the men fluctuate before finally settling down to a constant attachment such as the heroines exhibit from the start. Men's "fancies are more giddy and unfirm, / More longing, wavering, sooner lost and won, / Than women's are" [*Twelfth Night,* II. iv. 33-5]. In the case of true love, once stabilized—even as in the case of mere dotage—imagination cannot "form a shape, / Besides yourself to like of" [*The Tempest,* III. i. 56-7]; it "carries no favour in't" but that of the beloved [*All's Well that Ends Well,* I. i. 83]. Unlike dotage, however, it is in no obvious conflict with reason, either in its object or its vehemence. By the end of the fourth act we are assured that Demetrius and Lysander have come to stability of this kind. But the terminus, I repeat, is not a rationally determined one. Like Theseus at the play's beginning, at the play's ending Demetrius and Lysander are settled. Jill has Jack, nought shall go back, and the prospect of happy marriage is before them all.

Thus in *A Midsummer Night's Dream* the origin of love never lies in reason. Love may be consistent with reason—e.g., Lysander is undeniably "a worthy gentleman"—and a healthy imagination, although influenced by love, will not glaringly rebel against reason. But as Hermia initially indicates, her choice is dictated not by her judgment but by her "eyes", by the vision of Lysander as her love-dictated imagination reports it. As Helena says at the close of this same introductory scene, love sees with that part of the mind that has no taste of judgment. Essentially this is as true for Hermia as for the others, although her choice conflicts with parental authority rather than with sound evaluation of her beloved's merits. Despite Egeus' initial disapproval, nevertheless, her choice is eventually confirmed. She is not compelled to "choose love by another's eyes" [I. i. 140], to see with her father's judgment (as Theseus at first demanded; [I. i. 57]), nor even to convert her love to one directed by her own judgment. Her love at the end is what it was at the beginning, with the obstacles removed.

Not even Egeus accuses her of dotage, although he does think her somehow "witched" in her refusal to accept his choice rather than her own. "Dotage", in this play, appears essentially reserved for two kinds of amorous excess approaching madness: the monomaniacal pursuit of an unrequited love (thus Helena "dotes in idolatry" [I. i. 109], Demetrius "dotes" on Hermia's eyes, and Lysander dotes for Helena in the night's comedy of errors), or the ridiculous bestowal of affection upon an obviously unworthy object (most grotesquely in Titania's passion for Bottom, but also in the gross excesses of Lysander and Demetrius during their "dream").

In the middle of the play, then, when dotage grows most rampant, so too does imagination. The frenzied praises and dispraises of Lysander and Demetrius are exceeded only by Titania's infatuation for Bottom, her hearing beauty in his voice, seeing beauty in his ears, and so on. Were follies so excessive in the cases of the mortal lovers, we could never end as we do in marriage and lasting love. Yet by the end of Act IV, with all obstacles to happily paired marriages removed—no thanks to the behavior of the lovers—the lovers can sound, and behave, rationally enough. Their love, however, is in its essence as inexplicable as ever. (pp. 116-17)

Pyramus and Thisbe is not merely a play about love with a partial resemblance to the love plot of *A Midsummer Night's Dream*. It is, as Shakespeare's original wedding audience would be inevitably aware, a play for a wedding audience. It provides a foil to the entire play of which it is a part, not merely to the portion involving the lovers. And not only Bottom's play, but his audience as well, invites comparison with Shakespeare's.

It is time to turn to the principal member of Bottom's audience, and to his famous speech beginning Act V. Himself a creation from "antique fable" unconsciously involved in "fairy toys", Theseus believes in neither. His speech, without appearing improbable or inconsistent with his character, is obviously one demanded by Shakespeare's thematic development. Just as Theseus has no dramatically probable reason to refer to "fairy toys", so too he has no reason to digress on poetry while discussing the lunacy of love. But by his speech he can provide for Shakespeare a transition from the earlier emphasis of the play upon love to its final emphasis upon art. He can explicitly link the imagination's role in love with its role in dramatic poetry. For him, with his view that "the best in this kind are but shadows" [V. i. 211], pastimes to be tolerantly accepted when offered, the imagination of the poet commands no more respect than that of the lover.

Theseus' speech introduces the words "image", "imagine", "imagination", and "imagining" to the play. But of course it does not introduce the concepts involved. As we have already seen, and as Theseus reminds us, much of the play has thus far concerned the role of imagination in love. A subordinate part has similarly drawn attention to its role in drama, a role manifested by the entirety of *A Midsummer Night's Dream*.

The success of any play ideally demands effective use of the imagination by the author, the producers, and the audience. Perhaps through modesty, Shakespeare gives us little explicit encouragement to compare his own imaginative creation with that initially provided by Quince. We hear nothing, strictly, of Quince's authorial problems prior to rehearsal. The sources of our laughter spring mainly from mutilation of his text in production, by additions and corruptions, rather than from the text with which the mechanicals began. Yet some measure of comparison of *A Midsummer Night's Dream* with their pre-mutilated text is inescapable. *Pyramus and Thisbe*, with nothing demanded beyond the simple dramatization of a familiar story, could at least have been given imaginative development

in action, characterization, theme, and language. It has none. The first three are less than minimal, and the language—in its grotesque combination of muddled syntax, padded lines, mind-offending tropes, ear-offending schemes—does violence even to what would otherwise be woefully inadequate. We have:

> Anon comes Pyramus, sweet youth and tall,
>   And finds his trusty Thisby's mantle slain;
> Whereat, with blade, with bloody blameful blade,
>   He bravely broach'd his boiling bloody breast,
>
> [V. i. 144-47]

or

> O grim-look'd night! O night with hue so black!
>   O night, which ever art when day is not!
> O night, O night! alack, alack, alack,
>   I fear my Thisby's promise is forgot!
> And thou, O wall, O sweet, O lovely wall,
>   That stand'st between her father's ground and mine!
> Thou wall, O wall, O sweet and lovely wall,
>   Show me thy chink, to blink through with mine eyne!
>
> [V. i. 169-77]

Contrasting in every respect we have *A Midsummer Night's Dream,* perhaps the most obviously "imaginative" of all Shakespeare's plays before *The Tempest*: we have the poetic fusion of classical and native, remote and familiar, high and low, possible and "impossible", romance and farce—all controlled by a governing intention and developed in appropriately varied and evocative language. Unlike Bottom, if not unlike the Quince who calls his play a "Lamentable Comedy", Shakespeare knows what is appropriate for his purposes. He will have infinite variety, but not merely variety as an end in itself. Bottom wishes to have a ballad written of his dream, and "to make it the more gracious" [IV. i. 218] he will sing it over the dead body of Thisbe at the tragedy's end. Shakespeare, very literally "to make it the more gracious", will end his comedy with a song bestowing fairy grace. The contrast needs no laboring.

The contrast in authorial imagination, however, is not the principal cause for turning *Pyramus and Thisbe* from tragedy to farce. In the first appearance of the mechanicals, the largely expository casting scene, we get a hint of the aspect that receives subsequent emphasis: author-director Quince warns that if the lion roars "too terribly" it will "fright the Duchess and the ladies" [I. ii. 75], and Bottom proposes as a solution to "roar you as gently as any sucking dove" [I. ii. 82-3] (a remedy almost as sound as the later suggestion to "leave the killing out" [III. i. 14]).What the mechanicals fail to understand, obviously, is the audience's awareness that drama is drama, to be viewed imaginatively but not mistaken, in any realistic sense, for reality. The idea that these clowns could conceivably create a terrifying lion is in itself ridiculous, but the basic folly lies in their supposing that their prospective intelligent audience will have the naiveté of Fielding's Partridge [in *Tom Jones*]. And it is this aspect that receives all the emphasis of the mechanicals' rehearsal scene. Except for a very few lines of actual rehearsal, enough to heighten our expectation of the eventual production as well as to allow Bottom's "translation" to an ass, the whole rehearsal is concerned with how the mechanicals abuse their own imaginations by a failure to understand those of the audience. On the one hand they fear their audience will imagine what it sees is real, mistaking "shadows" for reality; on the other, they think the audience unable to imagine what it cannot see. Paradoxically, although they lack the understanding to think in such terms, they think their audience both over- and under-imaginative, and in both respects irrational. For each error Shakespeare provides two examples. More would render the point tedious rather than delightful; fewer might obscure it. Thus, to avoid the threat of over-imagination, they resolve by various ludicrous means to explain that Pyramus is not Pyramus and that the lion is not a lion; then, to counteract the audience's under-imagination, they will create Moonshine and Wall. In a play where Shakespeare's audience has been imagining moonshine since the beginning, Bottom and Quince can conceive only of real moonshine or a charcter to "disfigure" it. Of course they choose the latter. So too they can think only of bringing in a real wall, weighing tons, or another disfiguring personification.

Significantly, Shakespeare opens the rehearsal scene as follows:

> *Bottom*. Are we all met?
> *Quince*. Pat, pat; and here's a marvail's convenient place for our rehearsal. This green plot shall be our stage, this hawthorn brake our tiring house. . . .
>
> [III. i. 1-4]

The stage is a stage, not a green plot; the tiring house is a tiring house, not a hawthorn brake. The Lord Chamberlain's Men ask us to imagine a green plot and hawthorn brake, just as they ask us to imagine nonexistent fog or, on the other hand, imagine the invisibility of an obviously visible Oberon. The play perpetually makes such demands upon us, and even greater ones. It asks us not only to accept mortal-sized actors as diminutive fairies but even to let them be bi-sized, sleeping in flowers and yet engaging in intimate association with ass-headed Bottom. Most basic of all, it asks us to enter imaginatively into a world dominated by fairies, and to accept them as the ultimate source of disharmony and of harmony, while at the same time not asking us to "believe" in them at all.

When we next see the mechanicals (except for their brief transitional appearance in IV. ii) it will be after Theseus' speech, with its condescending attitude toward poetry, and after the prefatory discussion by the court concerning the "tedious brief . . . tragical mirth" they wish to enact [V. i. 56-7]. The emphases in the actual production—including both the production itself and the asides by the audience—are just what we have been prepared for in the rehearsal: not the follies of love but the follies of abused imagination in the theatre. When, for example, Quince concludes his Argument,

> For all the rest,
> Let Lion, Moonshine, Wall, and lovers twain
> At large discourse while here they do remain,
>
> [V. i. 149-51]

Theseus cannot yet believe that Quince literally means "discourse":

> *Theseus*. I wonder if the lion be to speak.
> *Demetrius*. No wonder, my lord. One lion may, when many asses do.
>
> [V. i. 152-54]

But before ever they hear the talking lion they listen to "the wittiest partition that ever I heard discourse", that "courteous wall" which provides the "chink to blink through" [V. i. 67-8, 78, 77], only to receive the curses of frustrated Pyramus.

> *Theseus*. The wall, methinks, being sensible, should curse again.

> *Pyramus*. No, in truth, sir, he should not. 'Deceiving me' is Thisby's cue. She is to enter now, and I am to spy her through the wall. You shall see it will fall pat as I told you. Yonder she comes.
>
> [V. i. 182-87]

As Theseus says, a few lines later,

> If we imagine no worse of them than they of themselves, they may pass for excellent men.
>
> [V. i. 215-16]

There is no danger of wounding the feelings of a Bottom by letting him overhear an aside. His imagination, devoid of understanding, can as easily create beauty in his own mind as it can create unintended farce on the stage. Titania's folly, if possible, was less than what we are now witnessing.

Wall's eventual exit provokes further satiric asides, followed by the primary thematic dialogue of the play:

> *Hippolyta*. This is the silliest stuff that ever I heard.
> *Theseus*. The best in this kind are but shadows; and the worst are no worse, if imagination amend them.
> *Hippolyta*. It must be your imagination then, and not theirs.
>
> [V. i. 210-14]

While a successful production depends on the imaginative cooperation of playright, producers, and audience, Bottom's group has placed the entire burden on the audience. Theseus' group quite naturally makes no effort to "amend them". The tragedy is too entertaining as farce, too fitting for their nuptial spirits, and, besides, it would take an imagination transcending Shakespeare's own to give "form and dignity" to this *Pyramus and Thisbe*.

What follows demands no further elaboration. The lion proves "a goose for his discretion" [V. i. 232]; the moon, appearing "by his small light of discretion" to be "in the wane" [V. i. 253-54], ridiculously exits on command from Pyramus. And so on, until "Moonshine and Lion are left to bury the dead" "Ay, and Wall too" [V. i. 348-50].

But we may return to Theseus' comment that "The best in this kind are but shadows". In a sense he is obviously right, as Shakespeare never ceases to remind us, but his estimation of such "shadows" is consistently deprecating. A noble governor, quite willing to accept poetry for a wedding-night pastime and to acknowledge it as the well-intended offering of his faithful subjects, he at no time implies any respect for it. Shakespeare's entire play implies a contrary view, despite the humility of its epilogue. (pp. 124-28)

The age's defenders of poetry—whether in extended defenses like Sidney's, or in prefaces like Chapman's or Jonson's, or even in passing (like Hamlet's)—inevitably stressed the high moral function of poetic imagination. One seldom finds so modest a defense as that prefacing [Thomas Dekker's] *The Shoemakers' Holiday*: "Take all in good worth that is well intended, for nothing is purposed but mirth, mirth lengthneth long life." Yet, after all, as Theseus implied, there is a time for "pastime", and only the most vigorous precisian would have denied it. *A Midsummer Night's Dream* could have been defended as indeed a pleasant pastime, especially appropriate for a wedding occasion but fitting for any moment of merriment. It could be further defended, unmistakably, as a delightful exposition of the follies produced by excessive imagination in love and the pleasures produced by controlled imagination in art. Only the most stubborn precisian could have thought poetry the "mother of lies" after witnessing Shakespeare's thematic distinction, however ambiguous in its ultimate implications, between the worlds of imagination and of "reality". Thus in offering a defense for its own existence the play simultaneously offers us Shakespeare's closest approximation to a "Defense of Dramatic Poesy" in general. (pp. 128-29)

R. W. Dent, "Imagination in 'A Midsummer Night's Dream'," in Shakespeare Quarterly, Vol. XV, No. 2, Spring, 1964, pp. 115-29.

JAN KOTT (essay date 1964)

[Kott is a Polish-born critic and professor of English and comparative literature now residing in the United States. His reading of A Midsummer Night's Dream is a radical departure from earlier criticism that focused on the dramatic representation of romantic love, for he argues that brutality and eroticism are at the heart of the play. Kott maintains that sleep frees Titania from her inhibitions, allowing her to express her long-repressed desires for "animal love" by forcing Bottom to have sexual intercourse with her. He also maintains that the young lovers are similarly freed from repression and experience "the dark sphere of animal love-making" during their night in the woods. Other critics who have focused on the brutal eroticism in A Midsummer Night's Dream include Hugh M. Richmond (1971), David Bevington (1975), David Ormerod (1978) and Allan Lewis (see Additional Bibliography), although both Bevington and Lewis maintain that Kott overstates the significance of this element. Also, see the essay by Thomas McFarland cited in the Additional Bibliography for a refutation of Kott's thesis. For further essays examining the dark and violent atmosphere of A Midsummer Night's Dream, see the excerpts by G. K. Chesterton (1904), Cumberland Clark (1931), G. Wilson Knight (1932), Charles R. Lyons (1971), and Mordecai Marcus (1981). Kott's essay was first published in his Szkice o Szekspirze in 1964.]

The Dream is the most erotic of Shakespeare's plays. In no other tragedy, or comedy, of his, except Troilus and Cressida, is the eroticism expressed so brutally. Theatrical tradition is particularly intolerable in the case of the Dream, as much in its classicist version, with tunic-clad lovers and marble stairs in the background, as in its other, operatic variation, with flowing transparent muslin and ropedancers. For a long time theatres have been content to present the Dream as a Brothers Grimm fable, completely obliterating the pungency of the dialogue and the brutality of the situations.

LYSANDER

Hang off, thou cat, thou burr! Vile thing, let loose,
Or I will shake thee from me like a serpent!

HERMIA

Why are you grown so rude? What change is this,
Sweet love?

LYSANDER

Thy love? Out, tawny Tartar, out!
Out, loathed med'cine! O hated potion, hence!

[III. ii. 260-64]

Commentators have long since noticed that the lovers in this love quartet are scarcely distinguishable from one another. The girls differ only in height and in the colour of their hair. Perhaps only Hermia has one or two individual traits, which let one trace in her an earlier version of Rosaline in Love's Labour's Lost, and the later Rosalind in As You Like It. The young men differ only in names. All four lack the distinctness and uniqueness of so many other, even earlier Shakespearean characters.

The lovers are exchangeable. Perhaps that was his purpose? The entire action of this hot night . . . is based on the complete exchangeability of love partners. I always have the impression that Shakespeare leaves nothing to chance. Puck wanders round the garden at night and encounters couples who exchange partners with each other. It is Puck who makes the observation:

This is the woman; but not this the man.

[III. ii. 42]

Helena loves Demetrius, Demetrius loves Hermia, Hermia loves Lysander. Helena runs after Demetrius, Demetrius runs after Hermia. Later Lysander runs after Helena. This mechanical reversal of the objects of desire, and the interchangeability of lovers is not just the basis of the plot. The reduction of characters to love partners seems to me to be the most peculiar characteristic of this cruel dream; and perhaps its most modern quality. The partner is now nameless and faceless. He or she just happens to be the nearest. As in some plays by Genet, there are no unambiguous characters, there are only situations. Everything has become ambivalent.

HERMIA

. . . Wherefore? O me! what news, my love?
Am not I Hermia? Are not you Lysander?
I am as fair now as I was erewhile.

[III. ii. 272-74]

Hermia is wrong. For in truth there is no Hermia, just as there is no Lysander. Or rather there are two different Hermias and two different Lysanders. The Hermia who sleeps with Lysander and the Hermia with whom Lysander does not want to sleep. The Lysander who sleeps with Hermia and the Lysander who is running away from Hermia. (pp. 218-20)

If Love's Labour's Lost, the transparent comedy about young men who determined to do without women, is rightly considered to have been a play with a secret meaning to the initiated, how much more must this be true of the Dream. The stage and auditorium [of its first performance] were full of people who knew one another. Every allusion was deciphered at once. Fair ladies laughed behind their fans, men elbowed each other, homosexuals giggled softly.

Give me that boy, and I will go with thee.

[II. i. 143]

Shakespeare does not show the boy whom Titania to spite Oberon has stolen from the Indian king. But he mentions the boy several times and stresses the point. For the plot the boy is quite unnecessary. One could easily invent a hundred other reasons for the conflict between the royal couple. Apparently the introduction of the boy was essential to Shakespeare for other, non-dramatic purposes. It is not only the Eastern page boy who is disturbing. The behaviour of all the characters, not only the commoners but also the royal and princely personages, is promiscuous:

. . . the bouncing Amazon,
Your buskin'd mistress and your warrior love, . . .

[II. i. 70-1]

The Greek queen of the Amazons has only recently been the mistress of the king of the fairies, while Theseus has just ended his liaison with Titania. These facts have no bearing on the plot, nothing results from them. They even blur a little the virtuous and somewhat pathetic image of the betrothed couple drawn in Acts I and V. But these details undoubtedly represent allusions to contemporary persons and events.

I do not think it is possible to decipher all the allusions in the *Dream*. Nor is it essential. I do not suppose it matters a great deal whether we discover for whose marriage Shakespeare hastily completed and adapted his *Midsummer Night's Dream*. It is only necessary for the actor, designer, and director to be aware of the fact that the *Dream* was a contemporary play about love. Both "contemporary" and "love" are significant words here. The *Dream* is also a most truthful, brutal, and violent play. (pp. 220-22)

The metaphors of love, eroticism, and sex undergo some essential changes in *A Midsummer Night's Dream*. They are completely traditional to start with: sword and wound; rose and rain; Cupid's bow and golden arrow. The clash of two kinds of imagery occurs in Helena's soliloquy which forms a coda to Act I, scene 1. The soliloquy is about her intellectual capacities and for a while singles her out from the action of the play. It is really the author's monologue, a kind of Brechtian "song" in which, for the first time, the philosophical theme of the *Dream* is stated; the subject being Eros and Tanatos.

> Things base and vile, holding no quantity,
> Love can transpose to form and dignity.
> Love looks not with the eyes, but with the mind;
> And therefore is wing'd Cupid painted blind.
>
> [I. i. 232-35]
> (p. 223)

Starting with Helena's soliloquy Shakespeare introduces more and more obtrusively animal erotic symbolism. He does it consistently, stubbornly, almost obsessively. The changes in imagery are in this case only an outward expression of a violent departure from the Petrarchian idealization of love.

It is this passing through animality that seems to us the midsummer night's dream, or at least it is this aspect of the *Dream* that is the most modern and revealing. This is the main theme joining together all three separate plots running parallel in the play. Titania and Bottom will pass through animal eroticism in a quite literal, even visual sense. But even the quartet of lovers enter the dark sphere of animal love-making:

HELENA

> . . . I am your spaniel; and, Demetrius,
> The more you beat me, I will fawn on you.
> Use me but as your spaniel—spurn me, strike me, . . .
>
> [II. i. 203-05]

And again:

> What worser place can I beg in your love . . .
> Than to be used as you use your dog?
>
> [II. i. 208-10]

Pointers, kept on short leashes, eager to chase or fawning upon their masters, appear frequently in Flemish tapestries representing hunting scenes. They were a favourite adornment on the walls of royal and princely palaces. But here a girl calls herself a dog fawning on her master. The metaphors are brutal, almost masochistic.

It is worth having a closer look at the "bestiary" evoked by Shakespeare in the *Dream*. As a result of the romantic tradition, unfortunately preserved in the theatre through Mendelssohn's music, the forest in the *Dream* still seems to be another version of Arcadia. But in the actual fact, it is rather a forest inhabited by devils and lamias, in which witches and sorceresses can easily find everything required for their practices.

> You spotted snakes with double tongue,
> Thorny hedgehogs, be not seen;
> Newts and blindworms, do no wrong,
> Come not near our Fairy Queen.
>
> [II. ii. 9-12]

Titania lies down to sleep on a meadow among wild thyme, ox-lips, musk-roses, violets, and eglantine, but the lullaby sung by the fairies in her train seems somewhat frightening. After the creatures just quoted they go on to mention long-legged poisonous spiders, black beetles, worms, and snails. The lullaby does not forecast pleasant dreams.

The bestiary of the *Dream* is not a haphazard one. Dried skin of a viper, pulverized spiders, bats' gristles appear in every medieval or Renaissance prescription book as drugs to cure impotence and women's afflictions of one kind or another. All these are slimy, hairy, sticky creatures, unpleasant to touch and often arousing violent aversion. It is the sort of aversion that is described by psychoanalytic textbooks as a sexual neurosis. Snakes, snails, bats, and spiders also form a favourite bestiary of Freud's theory of dreams. Oberon orders Puck to make the lovers sleep that kind of sleep when he says:

> . . . lead them thus
> Till o'er their brows death-counterfeiting sleep
> With leaden legs and batty wings doth creep.
>
> [III. ii. 363-65]

Titania's fairies are called: Peaseblossom, Cobweb, Moth, Mustardseed. In the theatre Titania's retinue is almost invariably represented as winged goblins, jumping and soaring in the air, or as a little ballet of German dwarfs. This sort of visual interpretation is so strongly suggestive that even commentators on the text find it difficult to free themselves from it. However, one has only to think on the very selection of these names to realize that they belong to the same love pharmacy of the witches.

I imagine Titania's court as consisting of old men and women, toothless and shaking, their mouths wet with saliva, who sniggering procure a monster for their mistress.

> The next thing then she, waking, looks upon
> (Be it on lion, bear, or wolf, or bull,
> On meddling monkey or on busy ape)
> She shall pursue it with the soul of love.
>
> [II. i. 179-82]

Oberon openly announces that as a punishment Titania will sleep with a beast. Again the selection of these animals is most characteristic, particularly in the next series of Oberon's threats:

> Be it ounce or cat or bear,
> Pard, or boar with bristled hair . . .
>
> [II. ii. 30-1]

All these animals represent abundant sexual potency, and some of them play an important part in sexual demonology. Bottom is eventually transformed into an ass. But in this nightmarish summer night, the ass does not symbolize stupidity. From antiquity up to the Renaissance the ass was credited with the strongest sexual potency and among all quadrupeds was supposed to have the longest and hardest phallus. (pp. 224-27)

The scenes between Titania and Bottom transformed into an ass are often played for laughs in the theatre. But I think that if one can see humour in this scene, it is the English kind of humour, *"humeur noire"* ["black comedy"], cruel and scatological, as it often is in Swift.

The slender, tender, and lyrical Titania longs for animal love. Puck and Oberon call the transformed Bottom a monster. The frail and sweet Titania drags the monster to bed, almost by force. This is the lover she wanted and dreamed of; only she never wanted to admit it, even to herself. The sleep frees her from inhibitions. The monstrous ass is being raped by the poetic Titania, while she still keeps on chattering about flowers:

> TITANIA
>
> The moon, methinks, looks with a wat'ry eye;
> And when she weeps, weeps every little flower,
> Lamenting some enforced chastity.
> Tie up my love's tongue, bring him silently.
>
> [III. i. 198-201]

Of all the characters in the play Titania enters to the fullest extent the dark sphere of sex where there is no more beauty and ugliness; there is only infatuation and liberation. In the coda of the first scene of the *Dream* Helena had already forecast:

> Things base and vile, holding no quantity,
> Love can transpose to form and dignity.
>
> [I. i. 232-33]

The love scenes between Titania and the ass must seem at the same time real and unreal, fascinating and repulsive. They are to rouse rapture and disgust, terror and abhorrence. They should seem at once strange and fearful.

> Come, sit thee down upon this flow'ry bed,
> While I thy amiable cheeks do coy,
> And stick musk-roses in thy sleek smooth head,
> And kiss thy fair large ears, my gentle joy.
>
> [IV. i. 1-4]

Chagall has depicted Titania caressing the ass. In his picture the ass is sad, white, and affectionate. To my mind, Shakespeare's Titania, caressing the monster with the head of an ass, ought to be closer to the fearful visions of Bosch and to the grotesque of the surrealists. (pp. 228-29)

The night is drawing to a close and the dawn is breaking. The lovers have already passed through the dark sphere of animal love. Puck will sing an ironic song at the end of Act III. It is at the same time a coda and a "song" to summarize the night's experiences.

> Jack shall have Jill;
> Naught shall go ill;
> The man shall have his mare again, and all shall be well.
>
> [III. ii. 461-63]

Titania wakes up and sees a boor with an ass's head by her side. She slept with him that night. But now it is daylight. She does not remember ever having desired him. She remembers nothing. She does not want to remember anything.

> TITANIA
>
> My Oberon, what visions have I seen!
> Methought I was enamour'd of an ass.

> OBERON
>
> There lies your love.

> TITANIA
>
> How came these things to pass?
> O, how mine eyes do loathe his visage now!
>
> [IV. i. 76-9]

All are ashamed in the morning: Demetrius and Hermia, Lysander and Helena. Even Bottom. Even he does not want to admit his dream:

> Methought I was—there is no man can tell what.
> Methought I was, and methought I had—But man is but a patch'd fool if he will offer to say what methought I had.
>
> [IV. i. 207-11]

In the violent contrast between the erotic madness liberated by the night and the censorship of day which orders everything to be forgotten, Shakespeare seems most ahead of his time. The notion that "life's a dream" has, in this context, nothing of baroque mysticism. Night is the key to day!

> . . . We are such stuff
> As dreams are made on; . . .
>
> [*The Tempest*, IV. i. 156-57]

Not only is Ariel an abstract Puck with a sad and thoughtful face; the philosophical theme of the *Dream* will be repeated in *The Tempest*, doubtless a more mature play. But the answers given by Shakespeare in *A Midsummer Night's Dream* seem more unambiguous, perhaps one can even say, more materialistic, less bitter.

> The lunatic, the lover, and the poet
> Are of imagination all compact.
>
> [V. i. 7-8]

The madness lasted throughout the June night. The lovers are ashamed of that night and do not want to talk about it, just as one does not want to talk of bad dreams. But that night liberated them from themselves. They were their real selves in their dreams. (pp. 233-35)

> Jan Kott, "Titania and the Ass's Head," in his Shakespeare, Our Contemporary, *translated by Boleslaw Taborski, 1964. Reprint by W. W. Norton & Company, 1974, pp. 213-36.*

T. WALTER HERBERT (essay date 1964)

[*Herbert declares that in* A Midsummer Night's Dream *Shakespeare confronted his educated, intellectually alert audience with a central issue: whether "living intelligence [is] a necessary hypothesis for what lies beyond the phenomena of nature." Herbert asserts that Shakespeare offered two responses to this query—one reflected in the figure of Lysander, the other in the Pyramus and Thisbe play as enacted by the mechanicals—both of which he speculates would have served as a source of humor for Shakespeare's contemporaries. In the first instance, the humor resides in the fact that Lysander lives as an "atheist" in a world governed by external forces, attributing his actions to "reason" when they are actually controlled by the influence of the fairies. In the second case, an opposite absurdity exists in Pyramus's belief that supernatural intelligence resides in every inanimate object he encounters, such as Wall, Lion, and Moonshine, when in fact his world is devoid of any force beyond human will. Herbert maintains that the young intellectuals in Shakespeare's audience who tended to accept Lysander's atheistic view, and thus laugh contemptuously with him at the behavior of Pyramus, ultimately ended laughing at their own "superior, satirical" amusement, since Lysander's disbelief as demonstrated two acts earlier is just as unfounded and comical as Pyramus's "animism." Herbert's emphasis on the theme of misperception in* A Midsummer Night's Dream *is also apparent in the excerpts by John Russell Brown (1957), C. L. Barber (1959), Bertrand Evans (1960), Stephen Fender (1968), Sydney R. Homan (1969), Charles R. Lyons (1971), and James L. Calderwood (1971).]*

[*A Midsummer Night's Dream*] is a tolerantly genial play which explicitly urges us to be lighthearted about its queries. It has given pleasure to millions who have been content with its sparkling moment-by-moment gaiety. Nobody should relinquish his delight in its pretty fairies, his laughter at the vagaries of its lovers, his applause when each Jack has his proper Jill. Nor is it necessary to be grim about producers and choreographers who leave out essential parts of the intellectual design or about critics who are content to accept Puck's puckish assurance that the play has a weak and idle theme.

But to knowledgeable and intellectually alert members of audiences in the 1590's *A Midsummer Night's Dream* provided an invitation to exercise skill in recognizing multiple allusions with joy; it suggested that belligerent attitudes towards the essential nature of the wide world might be bathed in a gentle laughter and come out sweeter. (p. 29)

Let us begin with a moment in the enchanted wood near Athens and watch the comic artistry. Robin Goodfellow has put the juice of a Cupid-wounded flower in the eyes of Lysander and Demetrius. Whereas an hour before both these young men were madly in love with Hermia, now, suddenly rivals for Helena's love, they decide to have it out with swords.

Shakespeare was offering to his first audience, and is now offering us, a bland invitation to recall the duel on the plain before Troy between Menelaus and the man we moderns know as Paris, and recall the tournament in Chaucer's Knight's Tale to decide between Palamon and Arcite who should have the shining Emily to wife. Those who ignore the invitation still have the joy of laughing at the main thing, at two earnest, self-reliant young angry men whose love and quarrel are absurd because not their own reason but the will of benevolent Oberon, executed by fallible Robin Goodfellow, governs both hearts, both swords. Those who ignore this invitation are still welcome in the audience.

But Shakespeare could reasonably expect his early audiences to contain people in whose memory lingered the mighty *Iliad* and the romantic tale that made even twinkling Chaucer sound half wistful over his narrator's praise of ladies dead and lovely knights. And many an educated Elizabethan, by tradition and by rhetorical drill as well as by new modes of thought, was especially trained to be alert for resemblances and for distinctions between things that resemble each other. (p. 30)

The young gentlemen-scholars in Shakespeare's first audience who carried in their minds the momentous passions of classical heroes and the stately woe of medieval knights while they watched the merely life-sized and petty lifelike follies of the two fickle youngsters on the stage of *A Midsummer Night's Dream*, enjoyed the rich comedy of self-assertive persons and hot actions gently reduced to size. This is the rhetorical device called *diminutio*, a comparison to belittle, here accomplished without venom.

But the laughter is directed not only at lovers; it laps at various headlands in the realm of ideas about the basic organization of the universe. When Shakespeare moved in this realm he refrained from demanding a commitment on a fundamental question facing the bright young men of the 1590's, but he brought up the question: is living intelligence a necessary hypothesis for what lies behind the phenomena of nature? The assertion of the episodes in the woods near Athens goes no farther than this: if cosmic intelligences do exist and are influential, those who say *no* look pretty funny. It is a conditional assertion, which even a good-natured disbeliever—at least in the 1590's—could enjoy.

There is no mistaking that in all three belligerent episodes—of epic, tale, and comedy—the gods determine what is to happen to mortals. Event is decidedly not accident or the simple logical outcome of human conflict.

In the old stories [Paris] is the favorite of Aphrodite, and Lygurge and Palamon are preferred by Venus. The goddess of love insures that her men get their women. But the grim corollary moral ascribable to both stories is that if you are not the favorite of a powerful goddess you are in a sad plight: you are cuckolded as Menelaus was, or killed as Arcite was. *A Midsummer Night's Dream* is lighthearted because the deities are kindly disposed towards all visible mortals, including the young lovers that don't even believe in them.

In the theology of the old stories as well as *A Midsummer Night's Dream,* dissension among deities produced troubles among mortals. But whereas in the old stories we never expect to see a serene Olympus with all the gods satisfied, in *A Midsummer Night's Dream* we justifiably expect that after harmony is restored in Oberon's household, all the mortals will find happiness. This, then, is an unrealistically comfortable comic cosmos that can be playfully dealt with. Even as the most determined orthodox theologian could not seriously have blamed the youngsters for being disbelievers in Puck, the most earnest young philosophical nautralist would hardly feel called upon to put on shining armor and defend their specific disbelief.

If atheism is simply not having a belief in the deities whom one may be expected to acknowledge (the word *agnostic* was invented in the nineteenth century) the young lovers Demetrius and Lysander are atheists. In the old stories the mortals when they desire something pray to the god or beg the goddess. In *A Midsummer Night's Dream* Lysander, Demetrius, Helena, and Hermia make no positive refusal to recognize the living deities. The question does not come up: they never heard of Puck, Oberon, or Titania. As unsuperstitious as a physicist, they attribute events to natural, not supernatural, causes. Especially Lysander. Lysander does not even swear by the conventional Olympian gods, but, when he swears, swears by his life and property. The audience knows that he is the helpless victim of divinely compelling love-juice, but in all sincerity he lectures like a rational philosopher: "The will of man is by his reason swayed," he says to reluctant Helena, "And reason says you are the worthier maid" [II. ii. 115-16]. Lysander's doctrine of will, reason, and mature action is of course not in itself an atheistic doctrine. . . . But in context reason is given the authority that belongs to a tiny deity and the appeal to reason here is a diminutive counterpart of the sin of Pride. It is to defend his right to follow what reason dictates, one might say, that Lysander goes headlong to fight Demetrius. If he were not so absolutely confident, no one would laugh, even though in the constructed world of the play Lysander is absolutely wrong.

Shall we say, then, that Shakespeare was on the side of angels, that he issued a playful warning to the scientific brotherhood who were beginning to suspect that there aren't any angels? No, that won't quite do. In the first place, as Shakespeare knew, the hypothesis of a world without angels or any other ruling spirits was, though not currently orthodox, not a novelty. . . . In the second place, in the fact that confusion among the mortal lovers was wrought by Robin Goodfellow's erroneous execution of Oberon's commands it was easy to recognize a comical statement of a nonastrological concept which only the bold thinkers in the 1590's seriously entertained, though the new star in Cassiopeia had had blazed and dimmed years earlier—the proposition that the heavens as well as the earth are subject to change, subject to imperfection. If Shakespeare is saddled with being on the side of the angels, he must be found suggesting that angels are fallible. In the third place, nobody could take Shakespeare's theology sombrely. Measured against the summoned memories of epic and romance, the events in the comedy stood at the end of an anticlimactic progression of dignity: Homeric to Chaucerian to Puckish. Finally, Shakespeare was already practicing a skill conspicuous in his art: the skill of giving persuasive expression to each of two antagonistic positions in a single play. It was not beyond his capabilities to perceive and dramatize the proposition that if one assumes a world in which events occur without intelligent causes, religious mortals look as comical as atheists look when one assumes an intelligent cosmos. The *Pyramus and Thisby* which Bottom and his crew played before Theseus provided Shakespeare an opportunity to construct by deputy a soulless world, and the mortals with whom his Athenian craftsmen peopled that world were too religious or too superstitious in much the same way as were the men of Athens to whom St. Paul preached.

In this matter there is a distinction between the rude mechanicals who staged the *Pyramus and Thisby* and the characters in their play. Bottom and Flute knew that Moonshine, Wall, and Lion were being represented by men simply as a theatrical expedient, not for metaphysical purposes. But both Pyramus and Thisby attribute intelligences to everything, animate and inanimate. They make little distinction between poetic apostrophe ("O night!" [V. i. 171]) and conversation with mineral matter ("Thanks, courteous wall" [V. i. 178]). As if expecting to be heard, they talk more to inanimate objects than to one another. They speak of Jove, the fates, and their own souls with simple trust. And Pyramus addresses Nature ("O wherefore, Nature, didst thou lions frame?" [V. i. 291]) in words that ascribe a personality to creating nature just as firmly as the mystic Blake when he demanded of the Tiger, "What immortal hand or eye / Dare frame thy fearful symmetry?"

In the world which the action of *Pyramus and Thisby* unmistakably implies, the only intelligence is human intelligence, feeble and fallible. The two lovers are forever attributing intention to the world, and their world has no intention. Much good, then, their own intelligences do them! Thisby sees a lion and supposing it is hungry for her, runs away. But the lion has just digested a good meal; it has no appetite for Thisby. It cares nothing for the mantle Thisby lets fall, but without purpose touches it, as cats will do, and thus stains it with the blood of the kill which has rendered Thisby actually safe from its jaws. When Pyramus then comes to the spot, he sees a picture of reality. It is true in literal detail but his inferences are false, so that the picture is false. Every laborer in the sciences, criticism, history, or philosophy can recognize Pyramus's predicament: he is the man who plausibly imposes his expectations upon the evidence. It is a predicament from which the scientific method—God forgive me—frees a man. The bloody

mantle is the very sign of Thisby's safety, but Pyramus commits suicide because he takes the mantle as a sign of her death. The mortal who undertakes to act upon his own plans in a world such as this may be regarded as the epitome of futility under any condition. But when he ascribes intelligence and purpose to this world or any part of it and acts on the assumption, he is ridiculous. (pp. 32-5)

The world of the artisans' interlude . . . is made ironic for human beings by the extreme animism which Shakespeare, alone among tellers of the [Pyramus and Thisby] tale, foists upon his young lovers. Here we have the stuff of the most chilling tragedy, of course. And the fact that animists are represented isolated and dying in a soulless world remains in the mind even while the belly laughs. But the outrageous staging, giving us inanimate objects capable of amiable conversation with the audience even while they are incapable of doing any good for the lovers, produces mirth.

Not only the staging, for the staging simply provides a superficially plausible excuse for the basic mistake which though it may be construed as tragic is made laughable by every device at Shakespeare's command: mortals ascribing heedful, potent spirits to aspects of the world essentially innocent of spirit. If the audience laughed earlier and laughs now, it has achieved laughter above philosophical partisanship, for the fight over Helena was laughable because in a world peopled with influential spirits the mortals explained events without taking celestial causes into account.

If we are not careful we may assume that the artisans who stage the *Pyramus and Thisby* live at a level of sophistication generally characteristic of artisans in Shakespeare's London. The assumption would detach the play from fact and cancel some of the fun. Granted that despite the Athenian citizenship of Bottom and the rest the audience will hardly avoid having in mind the artisans they know. After all, the names are English nouns. Granted also that some London artisans were as credulous as Pyramus.

But Shakespeare knew that though his Bottom would remind the London audience of the London artisan, the picture is far from complete. London artisans in the 1590's wielded economic and political power. Among them were men who contributed to the scientific revolution. A few, though they were not yet incorporated into a guild, had for years made the clock works which when taken as models representing the world were eventually to dominate the scientific view of nature. What they constructed had an influence on their own thinking as well as on the thought of other men. Though they were often sturdily religious, they were partly responsible for nudging the articulate community of thinkers towards the conviction that a fresh and controlled examination of the raw data of nature was in order, for the sake of what men could materially accomplish thereby and for the sake of men's pure understanding.

Advocates of new approaches to knowledge had for at least sixty years recognized that something could be learned from artisans. (pp. 36-7)

Thus when Shakespeare's first audience saw rude mechanicals creating in their play a mechanical world and placing in it characters who were indomitably foolish animists, a good many of them saw an astringent representation of man and nature which they could at least laughingly ascribe to independent-minded craftsmen, and when that audience saw aristocratic Lysander laughing at a play whose view of nature basically harmonized with his own confident, unsuperstitious rationality, they saw what was not only funny but provocative of an interesting question: might not the rationalist thinkers among gentlefolk be wise to recognize that artisan concepts and intellectual purposes were congenial with their own?

Let us try to think of a member of that first audience not as a statistic but as an individual man. (p. 38)

This member of Shakespeare's audience has laughed at Lysander when, like him, Lysander has trusted his own reason, ignorant of Oberon and Robin Goodfellow; and in laughing at Lysander he has laughed, in a way, at himself. He has laughed over Pyramus and Thisby, laughing along with Lysander the laughter of rational people at superstitious people. This laughter is somewhat less gracious, perhaps, but the young gentleman could laugh amiably, because, let us suppose, recalling his own childhood he has a surviving sympathy for credulous Pyramus as Bottom plays him. As one who has put away childish things, however, he may feel companionable with the contemptuous aspect of Lysander's laughter at the naive animists—until he remembers the kind of world inhabited by Lysander. For satirically laughing Lysander still lives in a world influenced by Oberon. If the young gentleman has allowed himself to laugh at what is funny, therefore, he is now laughing at the laughter of a disbeliever. He may possibly be aware that he is laughing at his own superior, satirical laughter. It is hard to imagine any laughter more knowing, sophisticated, and delightful. And when he goes to his bed that night, if he is properly married . . . he may chuckle again and reflect that if Robin is to be trusted, the joy, fruitfulness, and peace of that bed are assured to him by Oberon. By the time he goes to sleep his laughter, we might hope, may be silent, serene, and cosmic. (pp. 38-9)

> T. Walter Herbert, "Invitations to Cosmic Laughter in 'A Midsummer Night's Dream'," in Shakespearean Essays, *edited by Alwin Thaler and Norman Sanders, The University of Tennessee Press, Knoxville, 1964, pp. 29-39.*

PETER G. PHIALAS (essay date 1966)

[*In the following excerpt, Phialas discerns two antithetical expressions of love apparent in* A Midsummer Night's Dream: *the inconstant, capricious love represented by the fairies and the young Athenians during their flight to the woods, and the matter-of-fact, rational mode reflected in the character of Bottom. Phialas contends, however, that Shakespeare adopts a "middle ground" between these antithetical attitudes, which the critic describes as the Platonic concept of love represented in the union of Theseus and Hippolyta. Other critics who have regarded the union of Theseus and Hippolyta as Shakespeare's ideal model of love in* A Midsummer Night's Dream *include G. G. Gervinus (1849-50), E. K. Chambers (1905), H. B. Charlton (1933), E. C. Pettet (1949), Ernest Schanzer (1951), George A. Bonnard (1956), John Vyvyan (1961), and Paul A. Olson (see Additional Bibliography). Phialas also examines other elements that contribute to the organic unity of* A Midsummer Night's Dream, *including Shakespeare's use of "anticipation and retrospect," the repetition of themes within each of the play's three parts, and the presence of a single atmosphere throughout. Last, Phialas discusses Bottom's remarks on the inexplicable nature of his dream, calling it "the most significant comment in the play." For further analysis of Bottom's awakening speech in Act IV, Scene i, see the excerpts by Harold C. Goddard (1951), John A. Allen (1967), Ronald F. Miller (1975), and J. Dennis Huston (1981), as well as the essays by Frank Kermode and Garrett Stewart cited in the Additional Bibliography.*]

A Midsummer Night's Dream differs from both earlier and later romantic comedies in employing an explicitly symbolic action which is repeated most clearly in Shakespeare's romances at the end of his career. From this it follows that the over-all artistic aim is to present an idea, for which characters and action are selected, but the idea controls all. Consequently, character delineation suffers and is indeed inferior to what we have seen in earlier plays. . . . [Here] Shakespeare creates a plot which deals not with *whether* man falls in love but with whom and why. To this he was led by the desire to explore further the theme of inconstancy which he had treated in earlier plays, particularly *The Two Gentlemen of Verona*. But inconstancy could be explored only by delving into its cause, that is to say, the lover's choice or choices, his falling in love and his betrayal of that love in favor of another. The play would thus extend the theme of inconstancy by dramatizing the mysterious attraction between this man and that woman and not another, or first with one and then another, the inexplicable caprice of choice, the very blindness with which Cupid shoots his fateful shafts. This is the central idea of the play but it is not the only important one. Allied with it is yet another theme which in other comedies occupies the central position, both structurally and thematically, and that is the way to love, the ideal attitude towards the experience of being in love. (pp. 113-14)

Shakespeare began work on the play by first selecting the idea he wished to dramatize and then choosing fables and then characters accordingly. But since that idea, the *why* in the lover's choice, could not be dramatized in direct objective terms, Shakespeare chose to express it by means of a fairy-story. But the fairy-plot, particularly its *locus* and atmosphere, serves the other theme of the play as well, that is, the juxtaposition of opposed attitudes toward love. The world which romantic lovers in Shakespeare's earlier comedies had created through their fancy, the spirituality which they had attributed to their loved ones, the otherworldliness which they had seen in the angelic features of their ladies—all these *A Midsummer Night's Dream* presents in the persons of the fairies in the enchanted woodland beyond Athens. Though not the most important characters in the play, the fairies occupy a pivotal position in the multiple relationships of the stories. They have come to Athens to honor the Theseus-Hippolyta wedding; they have to do also with the lovers as well as Bottom and his artisans. They are here to bless the royal wedding; they tangle and then untangle the love affairs; and they meet the artisans in direct and meaningful interaction. Here the world of immediate fact blends with the world of fancy: as the fairies, ethereal spirits though they are, are given human passions—they exhibit love and jealousy as well as inconstancy—so Bottom dreams a dream and with his mechanicals puts on a playlet of love and constancy; and thus his role in the play is as symbolic as that of the fairies. And the golden mean to which the placing together of these extremes points is represented by the love of Theseus and Hippolyta, whose attitude towards romance is the norm, the ideal, to which men may be admitted in this world. It is to this attitude that the extravagance of the four lovers is reduced at the conclusion of the play.

This, then, is the pattern, and these the parts and their relationships in the structure of *A Midsummer Night's Dream*. It seems as if Shakespeare had felt some impatience with his own hitherto partially successful comedies, as if he here chose to make explicit his comic idea. For the play shows an extremely careful joining together of three plots, thus exhibiting a diagrammatic formality which can be easily expressed in intellectual, one could almost say mathematical, terms. And this is precisely the single weakness of the play. The importance given to the symbolic aspects of the plot reduces its comic possibilities by removing immediate human responsibility from the target of the comic spirit. There is consequently no profound development or comic recognition on the part of the lovers at the end. Related to this is the need . . . to keep realistic characterization at a minimum, at least among the four Athenian lovers. At no point in the play, unless it be the final scene, do we laugh either with or at them. Instead the target at which the comic spirit aims its arrows is transferred to another part of the woods where Titania embraces Bottom, both of whom are secondary characters, though of course very important ones. In this sense the comedy fails to achieve the final integration we observe in *As You Like It,* for instance, where character, in a sense, becomes plot, where the thrust and direction of the action proceeds from character, where character, finally, embodies the idea of the play. But we must bear in mind that such minor inferiority of *A Midsummer Night's Dream* is a matter of choice in the kind, not the execution, of its structure. (pp. 114-16)

[The] play combines elements of startling contrast, a contrast made necessary by the dramatist's resolve to compose a play presenting sudden conflict between lovers as well as antithetical attitudes towards love. The choice to write such a play entails grave risks, for the disparity in its stories and especially in the sets of characters tends to make their blending difficult and the achievement of unity, if not impossible, certainly highly improbable. And yet Shakespeare, meeting the challenge head-on, was able to create an extraordinary degree of unity. How did he do it?

The story of Theseus and Hippolyta, though not directly connected with the story of the lovers, is certainly bound up with the fairy plot and the "Pyramus and Thisbe" playlet. Theseus is not the character of classical legend although he retains many of his Plutarchan attributes. Shakespeare's conception of him adds to the classical outline some of the features of Chaucer's "duc Theseus" and, more significantly, traits of the Renaissance Prince. On his legendary side the character of Theseus admits association with the fairies, while his Renaissance features make it easier to accept his connection with native characters of Shakespeare's Warwickshire. In addition, Theseus and Hippolyta are to end their military conflict with marriage. Like that conflict and reconciliation, the king and queen of the fairies have their own quarrel and reunion. The connection between the Athenian lovers and the royal pair is achieved by a similar thematic parallel. All six are lovers, all three men show inconstancy—Theseus, too, had been an inconstant lover— and all are united in a triple wedding. Finally the artisans put on a love tragedy to celebrate the royal wedding, and one of them is transformed by the same agency which transforms the Athenian lovers and Titania. Furthermore, the love tragedy they enact is a comico-tragic version of the Lysander-Hermia story.

These are the broad relationships of the stories making up the plot of *A Midsummer Night's Dream.* But there are other lines of connection in the weaving together not only of the stories but of individual episodes and scenes. These are addressed to both our conscious and subconscious awareness of the detailed process of the play. For instance, Shakespeare creates a special atmosphere, a special and congruent quality in the scene before us. He creates it by placing before our eyes, and by calling upon our own imaginations to evoke, the moonlit woods and

its fairies with their lullabies and utterly unpredictable ways; he evokes a scene suggestive of unreality, a strange place where incredible things can happen to humans. And he intensifies this impression of unreality in the scene by his innumerable allusions to the moon and moonlight, symbols of change and mystery. Furthermore, the feeling that much of what is happening may not be real is created by the ubiquitous allusion to dreams, by the puzzled self-reassurance of certain characters that what they have done or seen or even what they have been during the night in the woods was a dream. In continuing contrast to the dreamlike atmosphere surrounding the events of the night in the woods is the normal world of everyday life, with its natural as well as social processes. With this world the play begins and to this same world it returns its human characters in the end.

In addition Shakespeare employs other less obvious details which contribute to the impression of unity in the play. The strangeness of the events of the night is anticipated by the strangeness of the Athenian law which would put Hermia to death if she married Lysander. The strife of Oberon and Titania anticipates the strife of the four lovers, and all are anticipated by the former strife between the royal pair. Anticipation and retrospect become in this play an indispensable device which Shakespeare will employ for the creation of supremely ironic effects in later plays, particularly his tragedies. The device addresses itself to our subconscious, supplying it with impressions later to be periodically recalled for the purpose of ironic recognition. (pp. 123-25)

[Passages] of anticipation and retrospect contribute to the unity of the play, but of course the passages have other functions as well. The irony they produce is intended to underscore both the nature and extent of the change in the affections of the lovers, and even more important they demonstrate the *idea* of change, of inconstancy, of the unreason and blindness of Love's choice. And thus the devices employed for achieving structural unity are not mechanical and external but rather internal and organic, for they express aspects of the central idea of the play.

And now let us turn in conclusion to that idea, and the meaning of *A Midsummer Night's Dream.* For meaning it possesses although some scholars have, strangely enough, failed to see it. It is, for instance, difficult to follow Peter Alexander's conclusion that "there is no deep significance in the magic juice, no profound interpretation of life in the adventures of the lovers." It is true that the play "conveys a sense of people being tossed about by a force which puts them beside themselves," but it is going too far to say that the change "is presented simply, with little suggestion that it involves a growth in insight—Demetrius is not led to realize something false in his diverted affection for Hermia" [see excerpt above by C. L. Barber, 1959]. Although deeply puzzled by the change he experienced during the strange night in the woods, the one thing Demetrius does realize is that there was something false in his affection for Hermia and his rejection of Helena:

> To her, my lord,
> Was I betroth'd ere I saw Hermia;
> But like a sickness did I loathe this food;
> But, as in health, come to my natural taste,
> Now I do wish it, love it, long for it,
> And will for evermore be true to it.
>
> [IV. i. 171-76]

Demetrius understands the meaning of his brief change, though not its cause. (pp. 128-29)

The ultimate concern of the play is positive, and one scholar has identified that concern in this manner. "'What is Love?' or rather, 'What is the place of love in life?' is the question underlying *A Midsummer Night's Dream*" [see the excerpt above by H. B. Charlton, 1933]. It is quite clear that the play poses the first question in Professor Charlton's definition, and it is equally clear that the answer given is that there is no certain and positive answer. But Professor Charlton's second question, though central in other Shakespearean comedies, is tangential in *A Midsummer Night's Dream*. That Professor Charlton is thinking about other plays in which the question is at the very center of the plot is strongly suggested by the following comment. "At all events," he writes, "in *A Midsummer Night's Dream,* wedlock and housekeeping are imposed on man for his advantage; and the advantage as a social being he gains thereby is made patent by setting beside him the undomesticated irresponsible beings of fairyland." Professor Charlton's comment is an accurate estimate of the theme of such plays as *Love's Labour's Lost, Much Ado About Nothing,* and *Twelfth Night.* In *A Midsummer Night's Dream* alone among these comedies there is no rejection of love: no characters here oppose love as the king and his lords do in *Love's Labour's Lost* or as Benedick and Beatrice do in their play. There is no Phoebe here mocking the love of Silvius, nor Olivia spurning all thoughts of love in favor of a seven-year mourning. The question here is not *whether* to love, but *whom*. How do lovers fall in love, what is the cause and secret of their choice? "What is love?" is indeed the oblique query to which *A Midsummer Night's Dream* offers its oblique answer. It is the question asked directly at the most critical moment in the chief love affair of . . . *The Merchant of Venice;* it is asked by Nerissa in the opening line of her song even as Bassanio makes his choice.

It was not Shakespeare's way to define but rather to suggest, and his favorite device of doing so, whether he was dealing with love or honor or valor, was by means of juxtaposing different—often antithetical—attitudes or points of view. In the comedies he chose to place side by side the romantic and realistic concepts of love and in so doing to point to a middle ground, to a golden mean. In the play before us Shakespeare not only employed this device but he presented it in the strongest possible terms, in symbolic terms. In the world of the fairies he represents the extremes to which the lovers' fancy takes them in the contemplation of their loves. The dream world is the strange country created by the lovers' "seething brains," the imagined land far removed from our own real world. It is the world Mercutio describes as the product of Queen Mab's machinations, and in that sense it is true that his speech belongs to *A Midsummer Night's Dream*. And although we may agree that it "is a play in the spirit of Mercutio," and that the dreaming in it includes the knowledge "that dreamers often lie" [Barber], *A Midsummer Night's Dream* deals with much more than that. Dreamers may "often lie" but not always. And their dreams, though seeming to belie truth, may lead to it. Shakespeare does not, either in *Romeo and Juliet* or *A Midsummer Night's Dream,* share Mercutio's final view of the matter. But Mercutio's attitude defines that other extreme, which in the play before us is represented by the matter-of-fact world of Bottom. But is it not meaningful that Bottom, like the lovers, had "dreamed a dream," and that he should be the one to make the most significant comment in the play? For it is Bottom who says that man "is but an ass, if he go about to expound his dream" [IV. i. 206-07]. It may be true that "cool reason" comprehends things as they are, but among these love is not one. Theseus is convinced that the lovers'

romanticism is but the work of fancy even as the world of the poet is, but Theseus is not given the final comment on the matter. And Hippolyta's reply remains unanswered, and for Shakespeare no doubt unanswerable:

> But all the story of the night told over,
> And all their minds transfigur'd so together,
> More witnesseth than fancy's images,
> And grows to something of great constancy;
> But, howsoever, strange and admirable.
>
> [V. i. 23-7]

The dream is indeed inexplicable. It is so strange, says Bottom, that "the eye of man hath not heard, the ear of man hath not seen . . ." [IV. i. 211-12]. But to say that a dream, the dream of a lover, is inexplicable is not to place a moral judgment on it; nor is it true that one like Bottom, "neither born to be a great lover nor destined to utter a line of verse, may from his own life realize the harm of poets' and lovers' qualities" [Charlton]. This is precisely what Shakespeare's Bottom does not realize. On the contrary, Bottom's drab existence receives its single magic illumination from contact with at once the poet's and lover's world. No doubt Shakespeare saw man's reason as the means of distinguishing bears from bushes, but it is not at all certain that he considered it the single agency of ultimate truth. Nor does he in the comedies laugh at "men without cool reason, who are the sport of seething brains and of the tumultuous frenzies of fancy and of sentiment," and neither does he consider them "the victims of the world, and the butts of its comedy" [Charlton]. Lovers do indeed exaggerate, and their words fly beyond the bounds whereto cool reason may reach; their words, born of fancy, may seem to impeach their own truth through Petrarchan hyperbole. But this is so only to us who see, not to the lovers who feel and imagine. . . . To the lover love has become the agency of salvation, the way to the "high heavens, temples of the gods," as Spenser calls them in his *Epithalamion*. This is the poet as lover speaking, and his speech is the speech of Shakespeare's romantic lovers. Cool reason may object, but the lover, whether Spenser or anybody else, believes that the high heavens for which he longs can be attained only through love. And it is precisely at this point that the Platonic concept of love replaces Petrarchism. In Shakespeare the Petrarchan attitude towards love may be mocked but never the Platonic. Petrarchism has to do with describing the beauty of the beloved, the pains of the lover, the cruelty of the one and the sufferings of the other. The Platonic concept has to do with the meaning of love itself, from the desire to enjoy beauty to the topmost step on the ladder which leads to the bosom of God.

All this is much more directly expressed in *Love's Labour's Lost* and *The Merchant of Venice* than in *A Midsummer Night's Dream*. The Platonic concept of love is implicit in Berowne's *credo* and in Lorenzo's lines on music in the final act of *The Merchant of Venice,* as well as in Portia's appeal to Shylock for mercy. But we have touched upon the subject here in order to show that Shakespeare's attitude towards lovers' dreams is not moral but psychological. What matters most is not whether those dreams are factual, whether they can be accepted and approved by "cool reason," but rather whether lovers dream. Nor is Shakespeare concerned to separate those dreams from what we call actuality. In *A Midsummer Night's Dream* he is especially anxious to eliminate that line of demarcation between them. And the mastery of fusing the disparate elements of the plot contributes to that impression. And thus the structure of the play, this blending of diversity, reflects this most significant idea of oneness. The world of dreams, the world poets and lovers create, is an aspect of our world in that it is a world wherein men long to be. It is for that reason that the world of romance cannot be called false and that it cannot be considered in moral terms. What is of moment is that the poet and the lover create such a world and that in imagination they inhabit it. That is the supreme truth. (pp. 129-32)

Peter G. Phialas, "'A Midsummer Night's Dream'," in his Shakespeare's Romantic Comedies: The Development of Their Form and Meaning, *The University of North Carolina Press, 1966, pp. 102-33*

DAVID P. YOUNG (essay date 1966)

[*In his* Something of Great Constancy: The Art of "A Midsummer Night's Dream" *(1966), Young provides an extensive analysis of the play and a review of critical commentary to the 1960s. In the following excerpt from that work, he examines the manner in which the language of the play contributes to its unity as well as to its variety. He demonstrates how Shakespeare uses different verse forms and meters for purposes of characterization and contrasting styles for different groups of characters to emphasize the dissimilarities between them. Other critics who have focused on Shakespeare's poetic language in* A Midsummer Night's Dream *include G. Wilson Knight (1932), Thomas Marc Parrott (1949), B. Ifor Evans (1952), Stephen Fender (1968), and René Girard (see Additional Bibliography). Young also evaluates the frequent use of panoramic descriptions of scenes and activities outside the dramatic action of the play and the repeated instances of catalogues or enumerations, especially of natural phenomena, in the speeches of various characters. He contends that these serve as a contrast to the claustrophobic atmosphere of the woods and help to achieve "perspective and distance, both in the geographic and aesthetic senses of those words."*]

Perhaps the first thing to be noted about the style of *A Midsummer Night's Dream* is its variety. If we glance through the text, our attention is caught by the number of different verse forms and line lengths. In addition to the prose and blank verse characteristic of any Shakespearean drama, we find iambic pentameter couplets and quatrains, a good deal of trochaic tetrameter, usually in couplets but with occasional quatrains, and even some shorter lines of two and three stresses. The mechanicals' interlude employs, however stiffly, the same rhymed measures but adds its own peculiar stanza, an anisometric form with four dimeter and two trimeter lines. In addition, of course, there are the songs, familiar in any Shakespearean comedy.

There are good reasons for this variation in meters and verse forms. In the first place, it functions as a means of characterization. We associate Theseus, for example, with blank verse. It suits his oratorical manner, and he employs it royally, measuring out full verse paragraphs:

> Therefore, fair Hermia, question your desires,
> Know of your youth, examine well your blood,
> Whether, if you yield not to your father's choice,
> You can endure the livery of a nun,
> For aye to be in shady cloister mew'd,
> To live a barren sister all your life,
> Chaunting faint hymns to the cold fruitless moon.
> Thrice blessed they that master so their blood
> To undergo such maiden pilgrimage;
> But earthlier happy is the rose distill'd
> Than that which, withering on the virgin thorn
> Grows, lives, and dies in single blessedness.
>
> [I. i. 67-78]

The flexibility of blank verse as a means of characterization is demonstrated in Egeus. His use of it is very different—hurried, repetitive, the fretful exclamation of a nervous and irritable old man:

> Enough, enough, my lord! you have enough.
> I beg the law, the law, upon his head.
> They would have stol'n away; they would, Demetrius!
> Thereby to have defeated you and me—
> You of your wife and me of my consent,
> Of my consent that she should be your wife.
>
> [IV. i. 154-59]

Puck, on the other hand, is "of another sort" than these mortals, so that he is often heard from in trochaic tetrameter, a measure that, by its light, skipping quality, expresses his legerity and freedom from "mortal grossness"; in several contexts it takes on a mysterious, incantatory tone:

> Now the hungry lion roars,
>   And the wolf behowls the moon;
> Whilst the heavy ploughman snores,
>   All with weary task fordone.
> Now the wasted brands do glow
>   Whilst the screech owl, screeching loud,
> Puts the wretch that lies in woe
>   In remembrance of a shroud.
>
> [V. i. 371-78]

Oberon and Titania use this measure too, but they also use fuller measures, as if to express the regality they share with Theseus and Hippolyta, of which Puck does not partake. Their blank verse and pentameter couplets match a rich, exotic diction with a lingering, almost somnolent movement:

> I know a bank where the wild thyme blows,
> Where oxlips and the nodding violets grows;
> Quite over-canopied with luscious woodbine,
> With sweet musk-roses, and with eglantine.
> There sleeps Titania sometime of the night
> Lull'd in these flowers with dances and delight.
>
> [II. i. 249-54]

In addition to individual characterizations, the various meters and rhymes serve to define the groupings in *A Midsummer Night's Dream*. Thus, although the usage is by no means strict, we associate blank verse with Theseus, Hippolyta, and the courtly world at Athens; couplets with the lovers, especially as they move into the woods; lyrical measures, including song and dance, with the fairy world; and prose with the mechanicals, despite their attempts at formal verse. As various groups occupy the center of attention, we hear the particular style associated with them. One reason for this is quite practical; it enables us to follow the quickly shifting patterns of the plot, especially during the night of errors in the woods. We are acclimated to each turn of events by a stylistic change.

The stylist shifts serve to point up important themes as well. As they take us from one group of characters to the next, one setting to the next, they begin to make us aware of the play's strong contrasts—day and night, mortal and fairy, city and woods. These lead us in turn to more abstract sets of opposites like illusion and reality or, as in the mechanicals' rehearsal . . . , the natural qualities of the craftsmen and the artificial qualities of their interlude—art versus nature.

The transitions, with their accompanying interplay of contrasts, can be extremely subtle. In the first scene, for example, Hermia and Lysander, left alone by the others, continue to use the blank verse that began the play. They are permitted a brief and charming conversation about the vicissitudes true lovers must endure. The scene ends, however, with the arrival of Helena and some necessary, but rather artificial, plot business: Helena's irrational decision to inform Demetrius of their flight. This is far better rendered in the more formal couplets that are used throughout to accompany the patterned and mechanical behavior of the four lovers. Already then, before Helena's arrival, the conversation has begun to take on more formal qualities [I. i. 135-40]. Just before Helena's entrance, Hermia begins to speak in couplets, so that her arrival and the couplet scene that follows are prepared for gradually and effectively.

Conversely, when the playwright wants strong contrast, he uses it. The first of the mechanicals' scenes is sandwiched between the one just discussed and our introduction to the fairies, so that we move rather abruptly from Helena's decorous couplets to Bottom's exuberant and error-ridden prose, and, at the end of the scene, from Bottom's expectation of rehearsing "obscenely and courageously" [I. ii. 108] to the lyric that opens the second act, the "amphimacers" whose delicacy Coleridge so greatly admired. That lyric, on the other hand, shifts smoothly into the couplet dialogue of the fairy and Puck, moving to pentameter by way of some tetrameter couplets that, in turn, alter from trochaic to iambic. All of this then merges gracefully into the blank verse passages between Oberon and Titania. And so the play goes.

The variety of styles in this play and the frequently alternating use of them, despite their success and the careful control that has obviously been exercised over them, have frequently called forth strictures from commentators and have been used to cast doubt on the play's authenticity. Discussions of the lovers, for instance, almost always produce comments to the effect that they are poorly characterized, difficult to tell apart, puppets who speak in couplets that are artificial to the point of absurdity. This, it is often remarked, is evidence of Shakespeare's dramatic immaturity; later on, he will learn to provide fuller characterizations and less stilted dialogue.

Such criticism does not do justice to the integrity and unity of *A Midsummer Night's Dream,* nor does it accord with the dramatist's skill as exhibited elsewhere in the play. The four lovers, after all, *are* puppets while they are in the woods, the helpless victims of supernatural enchantments. Their state is pointed up and made amusing by the artificiality of their movements and their speech. Were they more fully characterized we would develop an interest in and sympathy for them which the pace of the play does not allow, and the detachment that we need to laugh at their misfortunes would be threatened. Here, for example, is Hermia at a moment very close to despair:

> Never so weary, never so in woe;
>   Bedabbled with the dew, and torn with briers;
> I can no further crawl, no further go;
>   My legs can keep no pace with my desires.
> Here will I rest me till the break of day.
> Heavens shield Lysander, if they mean a fray!
>
> [III. ii. 442-47]

Having said this, she immediately goes to sleep among the other three lovers. Our attention rests not on her despair but on the completion of a formal movement directed by Robin Goodfellow and the comic discrepancy between what Hermia thinks is going on and what we know to be the truth. "Briers" and "desires" both have serious potential, but paired in a rhyme they maintain the formal and comic tone. The playwright

is clearly in control of our response. To demand that the lovers speak and act more naturally is to demand a different plot and a different play. (pp. 64-9)

If Shakespeare created a multitude of styles for purposes of characterization and contrast in *A Midsummer Night's Dream,* he also took pains to combine them in a way that reconciles them. His problem with such an omnium-gatherum of materials and characters, after all, was not the achievement of diversity; it was the need for consolidation, for the attainment of an organic unity "more tuneable than lark to shepherd's ear" [I. i. 184]. For such a task the dramatist called on every stylistic and structural device he could muster.

We may begin with the iterative imagery to which a succession of critics have called attention in the past thirty years—the strong sense of night and darkness that the play engenders; the recurrent attention to stars, moon, moonlight, and water; and the accompanying imagery of dissension and nightmare, beasts and birds, and jewels and music. Such intricate play of imagery is, of course, everywhere characteristic of Shakespeare, but the *Dream* may be counted among the first plays, along with *Richard II* and *Romeo and Juliet,* to use it consistently and with full success. The image patterns in *Love's Labour's Lost,* as Miss Spurgeon points out, appear to be applied to the play as decoration. This is not the case with *A Midsummer Night's Dream.* Its moon is of the very essence and texture of the play; we could no more root it out of the play's language than we could chop down the woods. It grows naturally out of the subject matter of love, lunacy, and midsummer night and becomes the essential setting of the play and the source by which we are made aware of such themes as illusion, disorder, and imagination. As such, it remains a perfect example of Shakespeare's most effective use of the iterative image.

Other unifying features of *A Midsummer Night's Dream* have not received the kind of critical attention lavished on its imagery. To one of these I would give the label "picturization." Again and again, we are given not merely the glimpse afforded by an image, but a fully drawn picture. Often, these are sketches of human activity. Thus, before the play has gone very far, Egeus has given us a picture of Lysander courting; Theseus has sketched for Hermia the life of a nun; Bottom has demonstrated, since he is not capable of describing, the way a tyrant rants; Puck has shown us a gossip drinking from a bowl and an aunt falling from her stool; and Titania has pictured Oberon, disguised as Corin, piping to "amorous Phillida." These pictorial effects slow down the action; but in their evocation of the imagination, their illustrations of its follies, triumphs, and possibilities, they realize the play's basic theme in a new and significant dimension.

The most effective and memorable pictures in the play are not the glimpses of single figures and activities described above. They are the larger representations, full landscapes with a remarkable sense of spaciousness and distance. These we might call "panoramas." While we catch hints of them in Theseus' picture of his wedding with all of Athens reveling and in the poignant conversation between Hermia and Lysander that follows, they do not really begin to dominate the play until the entrance of the fairies in the second act. Then, they appear in profusion. Titania's fairy starts things with an extensive answer to Puck's "Whither wander you?" [II. i. 1]. He counters by summoning up all the places where Oberon and Titania have quarreled over the changeling boy. Titania and Oberon take it up, she with a reference to "the farthest steep of India," he with a glimpse of her leading Theseus "through the glimmering night / From Perigouna, whom he ravished'' [II. i. 69, 77-8]. The queen then begins her long and Bruegelesque summary of the trouble they have caused in the natural world:

> These are the forgeries of jealousy:
> And never, since the middle summer's spring,
> Met we on a hill, in dale, forest, or mead,
> By paved fountain or by rushy brook,
> Or in the beached margent of the sea,
> To dance our ringlets to the whistling wind,
> But with thy brawls thou hast disturb'd our sport . . . .
> The nine men's morris is fill'd up with mud;
> And the quaint mazes in the wanton green
> For lack of tread are undistinguishable.
>
> [II. i. 81-100]

She goes on to include the different seasons and describe their confusion. Above it all, of course, ''the moon, the governess of floods, / Pale in her anger, washes all the air'' [II. i. 103-04]. Then, as if she had not been exhaustive enough in her cross section of geography, weather, and natural life, Titania presents in her next speech a seascape, with herself and her ''votaress'' in the foreground and the ''embarked traders on the flood'' [II. i. 127] in the distance.

Oberon is not to be outdone at this activity. After his wife has presented her sweeping panoramas for us and left the stage, he has his turn; he even gives us a vantage point for the next great view:

> My gentle Puck, come hither. Thou rememb'rest
> Since once I sat upon a promontory
> And heard a mermaid, on a dolphin's back,
> Uttering such dulcet and harmonious breath
> That the rude sea grew civil at her song,
> And certain stars shot madly from their spheres
> To hear the sea-maid's music.
>
> [II. i. 148-54]

''I remember,'' answers Puck, and we pause to regain control of our dizzying imaginations. But Oberon will not let us rest. He moves on to a vision of even greater proportions:

> That very time I saw (but thou couldst not)
> Flying between the cold moon and the earth,
> Cupid, all arm'd. A certain aim he took
> At a fair Vestal, throned by the West,
> And loos'd his love-shaft smartly from his bow,
> As it should pierce a hundred thousand hearts. . . .
> Yet mark'd I where the bolt of Cupid fell.
> It fell upon a little Western flower;
> Before, milk-white, now purple with love's wound,
> And maidens call it, love-in-idleness.
>
> [II. i. 155-68]

We come finally to rest on something small and familiar, the pansy.

Throughout the night in the woods that follows, confined and hectic as it may be, we get echoes and glimpses of these magnificent views and distances. Oberon's description of the bank where Titania sleeps among the flowers is a smaller panorama, but it has its own sweep and detail. Hermia, as if responding to the fairies' talk of girdling the earth [II. i. 175] and compassing the globe [IV. i. 97], imagines the moon creeping through a hole bored in the earth and emerging on the other side to shine on the Antipodes [III. ii. 52-5]. Puck, searching

for distance in his description of the fleeing mechanicals, widens the prospect:

> As wild geese that the creeping fowler eye,
> Or russet-pated choughs, many in sort,
> Rising and cawing at the gun's report,
> Sever themselves and madly sweep the sky;
> So at his sight away his fellows fly.
>
> [III. i. 20-4]

Even Demetrius, in a flight of passion, can transport us to the mountains of Asia and ''That pure congealed white, high Taurus snow, / Fann'd with the eastern wind'' [III. ii. 141-42].

As daylight returns to the play, the panoramas regain full splendor. First there is Puck's warning of the approaching dawn, with its clouds, shining sky, churchyards, crossways, and floods; then Oberon's answer, a brilliant depiction of sunrise over the sea. Theseus' speech, as he enters the play with full daylight, is in the same vein. He is on his way to arrange a panorama of sight and sound:

> And since we have the vaward of the day,
> My love shall hear the music of my hounds.
> Uncouple in the western valley; let them go.
> Dispatch, I say, and find the forester.
> We will, fair Queen, up to the mountain's top
> And mark the musical confusion
> Of hounds and echo in conjunction.
>
> [IV. i. 105-11]

Hippolyta responds with a spacious description of a similar event when Hercules and Cadmus ''bay'd the bear'' in ''a wood of Crete,'' and ''the groves, / The skies, the fountains, every region near / Seem'd all one mutual cry'' [V. i. 113, 115-17]. We are certainly prepared by all these vistas for Demetrius' wondering comment on the night in the woods:

> These things seem small and undistinguishable,
> Like far-off mountains turned into clouds.
>
> [IV. i. 186-87]

The last full panorama in the play comes at Puck's entrance in the fifth act, a night scene with lion, wolf, snoring ploughman, screech-owl, insomniac, gaping graves, and spirits gliding on the churchway paths, the whole coming to rest at the place of performance, ''this hallowed house'' [V. i. 371-88].

The function of these panoramas is not difficult to discern. They provide, as suggested above, a contrast to the confinement of the woods, escorting us in and drawing us out again. They create perspective and distance, both in the geographic and aesthetic senses of those words. Through them, we are made aware of both man's pettiness and his grandeur, simultaneous extremes that are also expressed through the fairies. Only such comprehensive vantage points could give us this sense of surveying all of nature in order to discover man's unique position in it.

In their richness and variety, the panoramas become a kind of metaphor for the play: *A Midsummer Night's Dream* is itself a panorama of smaller scenes and characters, a great landscape with cities, woods, fields, mountains, valleys, rivers, ocean, and a host of figures representative of society and the supernatural. Theseus' ''The best in this kind are but shadows'' and Puck's ''No more yielding but a dream'' [V .i. 211, 428] take on a perspective of their own when we can link them to Demetrius' ''These things seem small and undistinguishable, / Like far-off mountains turned into clouds.'' Even our initial sense of wonder at these flights of description has its function. C. L. Barber [see excerpt above, 1959] touches on this when, defending the "autonomous bravura passages" in the play, he remarks that they are "calculated to make the audience respond with wonder to the effortless reach of imagination which brings the stars madly shooting from their spheres." Like the patterns of imagery, the panoramas contribute significantly to the play's atmosphere of magic, spaciousness, and limitless possibility, all attributes of the power of imagination which it both derives from and celebrates.

Another unifying characteristic of the style of *A Midsummer Night's Dream* is its profusion. Elizabeth Sewell [see excerpt above, 1960], analyzing the play as "natural history," writes:

> Anyone who is interested may try an experiment with this play: Begin at the beginning and note down references to natural phenomena as they occur. The experimenter will almost certainly be exhausted before getting halfway through. The profusion is astonishing.

This profusion is achieved by the simplest and most direct stylistic means available—listing. Again and again, the characters in the play refuse to content themselves with mentioning one or two events, objects, or contingencies; they break into a list, as if to exhaust every possibility. Egeus is not content to say that Lysander has exchanged love tokens with Hermia; he must name them all:

> bracelets of thy hair, rings, gauds, conceits,
> Knacks, trifles, nosegays, sweetmeats. . . .
>
> [I. i. 33-4]

This is not merely the garrulity of an old man. Every character in the play has the same habit. Lysander and Hermia list all the obstacles to love—blood, years, friends, war, death, and sickness [I. i. 135-42]; Puck and the fairy, when they meet, list the places they haunt and then go on to Goodfellow's activities:

> Are you not he
> That frights the maidens of the villagery;
> Skim milk, and sometimes labour in the quern,
> And bootless make the breathless housewife churn;
> And sometime make the drink to bear no barm;
> Mislead night-wanderers, laughing at their harm?
> Those that Hobgoblin call you, and sweet Puck,
> You do their work, and they shall have good luck.
> Are you not he?
>
> [II. i. 34-42]

The answer to this, of course, is not simply yes, but another list to match it. Titania, as we have seen, lists geographical features, meteorological phenomena, and the seasons. Before she goes to sleep, her fairies sing a song naming all the creatures who are not to disturb her. Oberon, on the other hand, is interested in the beasts who *might* disturb her and with whom she thus might fall in love. He lists them—lion, bear, wolf, bull, meddling monkey, busy ape—when he first hatches his plot [II. i. 180-81] and again—ounce, cat, bear, pard, boar with bristled hair—as he squeezes the juice on her eyelids [II. ii. 30-1]. He also enumerates the flowers among which she sleeps [II. i. 249-52]. Theseus lists the activities of the imagination [V. i. 9ff.] and reads a list of proffered entertainments. Even Bottom is a tabulator. He urges Quince to list the actors and the parts [I. ii. 2ff.]; he enumerates the beards he might

wear [I. ii. 93-6]; and his charming third-act song is a roll call of birds:

> The woosel cock so black of hue,
> With orange-tawny bill,
> The throstle with his note so true,
> The wren with little quill—
> The finch, the sparrow, and the lark,
> The plain-song cuckoo gray,
> Whose note full many a man doth mark,
> And dares not answer nay.
>
> [III. i. 125-33]

Perhaps it is easier for Titania to fall in love with Bottom while he is listing these creatures, for she and the other fairies, including Puck, are the best cataloguers in the play. It was with Titania's speech in [III. i. 164] ("Be kind and courteous to this gentleman") that Miss Sewell gave up counting the references to natural phenomena because, as she says, "in six or seven lines the listmaker suddenly and finally disappears from sight under showers of apricocks and figs and dewberries, not to mention honey and butterflies and bees and glow-worms."

What is the meaning of all these tallies and inventories? Part of it can be attributed to the Elizabethan love of rhetorical

Act IV. Scene i. Hippolyta and Theseus, Demetrius, Lysander, Helena, Hermia, and Egeus. By Charles Geoffroy (n.d.). The Department of Rare Books and Special Collections, The University of Michigan Library.

amplitude, the habit of piling up examples and surrounding an idea with an array of illustration. Lyly did it with elegance; Nashe, with pungency. But the abundance achieved by listing is especially striking in *A Midsummer Night's Dream,* and it contributes to the play some of its most memorable moments. We can see that, like the panoramas, the lists work constantly to widen possibility, to suggest further objects, creatures, places, and events. Moreover, like the reiterated images they serve to create a fully realized world. The moon imagery brings the moonlight, but the lists of beasts, birds, flowers, and features of the landscape create a strong sense of encountering nature in all its prolix immediacy. Here is the imagination again, attempting to comprehend everything available to it, pouring forth a cornucopia of sensuous experience that threatens either to drown us in its profusion or widen our horizons. Here variety and unity are simultaneously expressed. (pp. 74-83)

> *David P. Young, in his* Something of Great Con-
> stancy: The Art of ''A Midsummer Night's Dream,''
> *Yale University Press, 1966, 190 p.*

JOHN A. ALLEN   (essay date 1967)

[*Whereas earlier critics generally concentrated on the comical or burlesque aspects of Bottom's characterization, Allen considers him ''a spokesman, however gross and inadequate, for the power of love as it finds expression in dramatic art.'' He contends that Bottom's inability to communicate directly the mysteries of his experience with Titania represents a shortcoming common to all humanity, but that in his portrayal of Pyramus he conveys something of what he has learned about the nature of love. Allen believes that Bottom has altered his earlier, limited perception of dramatic art as a result of the night in the woods and that this is clear from the quality and sincerity of his performance in the interlude. Other critics who have argued for the dramatic significance of Bottom's dream and his subsequent awakening include Harold C. Goddard (1951), Peter G. Phialas (1966), Ronald F. Miller (1975), J. Dennis Huston (1981), Frank Kermode, and Garrett Stewart (see Additional Bibliography). For further general discussion of the character of Bottom, see the excerpts by William Maginn (1837), Charles Cowden Clarke (1863), G. K. Chesterton (1904), E. K. Chambers (1905), H. B. Charlton (1933), John Palmer (1944) and Hugh M. Richmond (1971).*]

As has often been noticed (and sometimes discounted), the soliloquy in which Bottom reflects upon his supposed dream is a parody of I Corinthians, where St. Paul makes the point that merely human faculties—eye, ear, and heart—cannot see, hear, or conceive ''the things which God hath prepared for them that love him.'' To the list of faculties which are transcended by beatitude, Bottom adds the tongue, recognizing that he or any man ''is but an ass if he go about to expound this dream'' [IV. i. 211-12]. The passage parodied by Bottom's speech is immediately followed by the assertion that God's secrets are revealed to mankind through the Spirit, but are hidden from the natural man, to whom they are only foolishness. As the Tyndale Bible (1534) puts it,

> . . . God hath opened them vnto vs by his sprete.
> For the sprete searcheth al thinges, ye the bot-
> tome of Goddes secretes. . . . For the naturall
> man perceaveth not the thinges of the sprete of
> God. For they are but folysshnes vnto him. . . .

To the rich associations evoked by Bottom's name, one may add that of the depth of God's secrets. Bottom's Dream, as he himself declares, is bottomless. Surely it is appropriate as well as comic that Bottom, the epitome of the natural man, should

remember his experience as consort of the Fairy Queen in terms which recall ''the things which God hath prepared for them that love him'' and should at once experience the inability of human wisdom to impart them. When he has happily returned to his companions, he finds that his wit is, after all, inadequate to serve his own turn. Though he may indeed have ''simply the best wit of any handicraft man in Athens'' [IV. ii. 9-10], Flute believes, it is inadequate to the task of expounding his dream:

> Masters, I am to discourse wonders. But ask
> me not what, for if I tell you I am no true
> Athenian. I will tell you everything right as it
> fell out. . . . Not a word of me.
>
> [IV. ii. 29-34]

His only communicable message is that the Duke has dined and their play has been preferred. What cannot be told directly must be figured forth dramatically in *Pyramus and Thisbe.*

Bottom's performance as the hero of *Pyramus and Thisbe* is prepared for by the scene (I.ii) in which Peter Quince assigns the parts for the play, and our first glimpse of Bottom, enthralled by every role, shows us that he has the ''humor'' of an actor. He believes that he can succeed triumphantly in any role whatever: that of tyrant, male or female lover, or lion, either fierce or gentle. Critics differ widely in their estimate of this aberration. One sees it as megalomania, another as the illusion of a narrow realist, and a third as irrepressible vitality of imagination. There is truth in all of these views. We may agree at once that Bottom is a monstrous egotist, although it might be added that his ''megalomania'' differs only in degree from the self-adulation which is endemic in mankind. It is also clear that he is critically deluded with regard to his prowess as an actor—a condition that is encouraged by his admiring friends, in whose eyes he is a paragon. Inasmuch as ''acting'' here, as in so many of Shakespeare's plays, metaphorically suggests the conduct of life, we may surmise that Bottom's evaluation of his capabilities in general is correspondingly inflated almost to the point of madness.

We must now ask whether Bottom's radical self-delusion may properly be considered a product of imagination. A comparison of Bottom with Dogberry [in *Much Ado about Nothing*] and Malvolio [in *Twelfth Night*] may be instructive. It is doubtful that anyone finds Dogberry imaginative, although he believes himself, contrary to fact, to be wise, learned, and handsome. Conrade is much closer to the truth when he tells him bluntly that he is an ass. Similarly, we recognize in Malvolio as Olivia's supposed beloved a humorless and presumptuous fool, prosaic to the core despite his ability to picture himself in loving detail as Count Malvolio. In point of self-deception, Bottom does not differ substantially from these unimaginative comic butts. Like them, he is quite unaware of the discrepancy between his conception of himself and the impression which he makes on less partial observers. Neither he nor any one of his companions has any suspicion that the performance of *Pyramus and Thisbe* will strike its audience as the silliest stuff that ever they heard, and that they themselves will instantly be put down by the sophisticates as a band of simpletons. Bottom's belief in his ability to play Pyramus affectingly is evidence not of imaginative vitality but of illusion nurtured by complacency. And yet, as we shall see, his performance in that role proves, in one sense, to be very imaginative indeed.

In justice, it must be said that Bottom is from the outset redeemed by his enthusiasm and good humor from the kind of judgment that we make on Dogberry of Malvolio. Further than this, if my reading is correct, Bottom develops during the course of the play. The man who enacts Pyramus is not quite identical with the one who had announced that his suicide most gallantly for love would "ask some tears in the true performing of it" [I. ii. 25-6]. In the interim he has learned something about art as a medium of communication, and circumstances have conspired to give meaning to his role—meaning which is apprehensible not to Theseus and his courtiers but to the audience of *A Midsummer Night's Dream*. In the casting scene, acting is for Bottom an opportunity to project the fancied omnipotence of his own mind. As "Ercles", he imagines himself breaking the locks of prison gates and vying with the foolish Fates themselves. But when the play is performed it has become for him a vehicle which permits him to express the substance of his ineffable dream, and his role has become significant for him not because it exalts him as an individual but because he understands its significance in relation to the action of the play as a whole. The play is about the death of lovers, and Bottom has become conversant with the mysteries of love. (pp. 109-10)

Bottom as Pyramus is more than a shallow thickskin of a weaver. He is a spokesman, however gross and inadequate, for the power of love as it finds expression in dramatic art. *Pyramus and Thisbe*, like all good burlesque, deals lovingly with the matter which it parodies. Its details are as full of meaning as are those of any serious romantic tragedy—say *Romeo and Juliet*. All things are subject to change in the sublunary world, but when Romeo dies, says Juliet, she will "take him and cut him in little stars . . ." [*Romeo and Juliet*, III. ii. 22]. And in *Pyramus and Thisbe*: "How chance Moonshine is gone before Thisbe comes back and finds her lover?" asks Hippolyta; and Theseus replies, "She will find him by starlight" [V. i. 312-14]. The point is, of course, lost on the audience of *Pyramus and Thisbe*, including Theseus, who has little more esteem for poets' fancies than for those of lovers or of madmen. Ironically, however, it is he who unconciously sums up the meaning of the play as it draws to a close. Demetrius has punningly remarked that Pyramus, whose last words are "die, die, die, die, die", is properly to be associated with an ace (ass), "for he is but one" [V. i. 306-07]. He is even less than that, says Lysander, "for he is dead, he is nothing" [V. i. 308-09]. And here Theseus anticipates the return to life of Pyramus: "With the help of a surgeon he might yet recover, and prove an ass" [V. i. 310-11]. As C. L. Barber remarks [see excerpt above, 1959], Bottom's revival might well have suggested, in the mind of contemporary audiences, familiar folk plays in which amateurs of Bottom's breed enacted the death of St. George or the Fool and were promptly brought back to life by a doctor—a crude but cheerful reminder of the victory of life over all that is inimical to it.

Certainly some irony is generated at the expense of Theseus as spectator of *Pyramus and Thisbe*, for he is very like the man of the world to whom the Spirit does not communicate; and this just at the time when the Spirit is strong in prosaic Bottom. But Theseus, who has been called a forerunner of King Henry V, has his own kind of sensibility. He insists upon seeing the play because, as he explains, it cannot be amiss when "simpleness and duty tender it" [V. i. 83]. Because he is a Duke and deals professionally in political realities, he is well aware that a ruler's most valuable asset is the loyal affection of his subjects; the gifts of allegiance is not to be scorned because the donors are clownish and ignorant. A further truth, combined with a certain condescension to the arts, resides in Theseus' subsequent remark that even the best of plays are

"but shadows, and the worst are no worse if imagination amend them" [V. i. 211-12]. The same, of course, is true of lovers and of people generally, and Theseus is aware of this too, although he does not apply the observation to himself. He calls attention to the parallel between the mechanics' complacency and illusion as actors and their everyday capacity as fools: "If we imagine no worse of them than they of themselves, they may pass for excellent men" [V. i. 215-16]. The quality of art, like that of men, is to some degree relative to the beholder; and even excellence in both kinds is fully apprehensible only to someone who is himself imaginative—as every practicing dramatist knows, and every lover whose parents disapprove of his choice. But Theseus and his courtiers, preoccupied with ridiculing the performance of *Pyramus and Thisbe*, cannot be expected to amend its crudity and supply reality to its shadows. Only the inspired Bottom sees the play as altogether excellent and rich in truth. This does not make the play a good one any more than the spectators' love makes their beloveds lovable. But they are privileged to enjoy an imaginative truth of their own—that of love, now about to be consummated to everyone's satisfaction. The younger lovers have recovered from their lunacy, and only Oberon and Puck could tell the story of the mad night which they had passed and which had issue in this highly reasonable brace of loving couples. (pp. 111-12)

Bottom's presence in *A Midsummer Night's Dream* has the effect of short-circuiting attempts to draw a moral from the play, based upon a supposed possibility of choosing between the reasonable and the fanciful as the basis for conducting human affairs. But no one would wish to cure Bottom of his irrationality, even if it were possible. All that is crude and dully matter-of-fact in him is transmuted into a parody of religious and artistic vision by the promptings of the Spirit within him. If *A Midsummer Night's Dream* has a message, it is as inarticulate as Bottom's—or as eloquent. Like Theseus and his courtiers, we may dismiss as mere nonsense the marriage in death of Pyramus and Thisbe, but we cannot choose but accept the counterpart of that very tragical mirth: the joyful promise of physical immortality in the nupitals which the mechanics' play is designed to celebrate. Bottom as Pyramus demonstrates to his own satisfaction the triumph of love over death in tragedy, while, in his own person, he tempers these high matters with the bathetic but engaging reminder that every flight of the spirit must take off from the solid ground of mortal grossness. (p. 113)

It is doubly fitting that Bottom, as the prime representative of mortal grossness in *A Midsummer Night's Dream*, should in his role as Pyramus celebrate the lofty ideal of sacrifice for love and, at the same time, offer *Pyramus and Thisbe* in token of allegiance to his sovereign, Theseus. If death is typically the form which sacrifice assumes in tragedy, marriage, the acceptance of one's place in the mortal scheme of things, is its equivalent in comedy. To Romeo, the vault of the Capulets is "a feasting presence full of light" [*Romeo and Juliet*, V. iii. 86]; and the Athenian lovers, perhaps unconciously, commit themselves, at Theseus' "feast in great solemnity" [IV. i. 185], to a world in which the hunt goes on, the hungry lion roars, and Titania will at last assume the form of sinister Hecate. The burlesque *Liebestod* ["love of death"] of Pyramus and Thisbe, no less than the gentle concord which unites the lovers, suggests that the imagination of the artist and the lover, combined with constancy, can reverse the metamorphosis of Bottom and place a human countenance on the shoulders which have borne an ass's head. Allegiance to a sovereign, like allegiance to one's art, one's beloved, or the Spirit, demands a surrender of self to a larger whole, and calls for the humility with which good subjects serve their nation, artists serve the Muse, and faithful husbands and wives serve each other and imperious nature. As actor and loyal subject, Bottom comically points a truth that is implicit in the play as a whole: "These antique fables" and "these fairy toys" [V. i. 3] of which Theseus is so skeptical can, in the words of Hippolyta, grow to "something of great constancy, / But, however, strange and admirable" [V. i. 26-7]. (pp. 116-17)

John A. Allen, "Bottom and Titania," in Shakespeare Quarterly, Vol. XVIII, No. 1, Winter, 1967, pp. 107-17.

STEPHEN FENDER (essay date 1968)

[*In the following excerpt from his book-length study* Shakespeare: "A Midsummer Night's Dream" *(1968), Fender argues that the dramatic action of the play follows a pattern of increasing disorder until harmony is restored by Oberon in Act IV, Scene i. He contends that Shakespeare demonstrates that the traditional rational and Christian values of Athens are inadequate to deal with the mounting discord and that he closes Act V with the fairies to emphasize their providential power and control in contrast to the mortal's ineffectuality. Other critics who have examined Shakespeare's resolution of discordant elements in* A Midsummer Night's Dream *include Denton J. Snider (1890), Harold C. Goddard (1951), John Vyvyan (1961), R. A. Zimbardo (1970), David Bevington (1975), Florence Falk (1980), and Paul A. Olson (see Additional Bibliography). Fender further examines the degrees to which the human characters in the play are aware of the power of the supernatural agencies, noting that the young lovers' visions of the fairy world are quickly forgotten, that Theseus has no comprehension of its existence, and that Bottom is able to recall but not communicate his experience. Fender maintains that these different angles of vision, and others as well, represent contrasting responses to the events of the night. For example, whereas Theseus rejects the lovers' account as untrue, Hippolyta discovers in it a certain consistency and mystery; similarly, Bottom views his dream as enigmatic and full of significance. Fender interprets these reactions as different answers to the larger question of whether there can be any "valid response to art," concluding that Shakespeare imputes some truth to each of these attitudes, leaving us with ambiguities and puzzles the play never resolves. For additional discussion of Shakespeare's view of imagination and art in* A Midsummer Night's Dream, *see the excerpts by William Maginn (1837), Charles Knight (1849), Edward Dowden (1881), Denton J. Snider (1890), Frederick S. Boas (1896), Paul N. Siegel (1953), Howard Nemerov (1956), Elizabeth Sewell (1960), and R. W. Dent (1964). For further commentary on the themes of perception, awareness, and illusion in the play, see the excerpts by John Russell Brown (1957), C. L. Barber (1959), Bertrand Evans (1960), T. Walter Herbert (1964), Sydney R. Homan (1969), Charles R. Lyons (1971), and James L. Calderwood (1971). In a related matter, Fender analyzes the language of the young lovers as they experience the breakdown of order and the influence of the fairy world, arguing that the courtly, formal style they use in the early scenes devolves into a less conventional and more direct form of address during their flight to the woods. Fender regards this latter form of communication as more reflective of the characters' personal experience, but notes that it is not sustained once the lovers return to the courtly world of Athens. Such other critics as G. Wilson Knight (1932), Thomas Marc Parrott (1949), B. Ifor Evans (1952), and David P. Young (1966) have also analyzed the imagery and language in* A Midsummer Night's Dream.]

[*A Midsummer Night's Dream*] begins with a conflict between generations. Theseus has no sooner announced plans for his marriage than Egeus enters to accuse his daughter of disobeying him. She prefers Lysander over Egeus's own choice, Deme-

trius. Two kinds of relationship—between husband and wife and between father and daughter—are thus mentioned within the first twenty-five lines of the play. What do these two relationships have in common? The answer will define the nature of the norms by which Athens lives.

The Christian marriage, as the wedding service in the Book of Common Prayer makes clear, is based on St. Paul's teaching that the relationship between husband and wife should imitate that of Christ and the Church; the husband should love his wife and she should obey him out of a reciprocal love. But other human associations—notably those of father and child, and master and servant, or in political terms, ruler and subject—should also reflect the union of Christ and Church. Paul even extends the analogy to the microcosm of the individual: our bodies should obey our heads (or our reason) just as the Body of the Church obeys its head, Christ.

A Midsummer Night's Dream is hardly a Christian allegory, but it seems likely that Shakespeare depended on his audience's awareness of these Christian associations in order to establish with the greatest possible economy the norm from which most of the characters are soon to deviate. This would explain why the links between husband and wife, father and daughter, and reason and emotion are mentioned in such rapid succession in the first scene. Theseus comes on stage as a ready-made icon to support the Pauline authority of man over woman in marriage; he has defeated the rebellious females, the Amazons, and now prepares to apply this re-established order in his marriage to their former queen. But no sooner is this norm presented than we hear of another, similar relationship being violated: Hermia's filial bond of obedience to Egeus. Egeus accuses Lysander of having 'bewitched' his daughter with 'rhymes' and a 'feigning voice' and of having impressed his image upon her fancy; he is obviously preoccupied with the extent to which Lysander's various poetic tricks have made her imagination rebel against her reason. Theseus seems to support the distinction between fancy and reason, and (naturally enough, as the head of Minerva's city) to prefer the latter:

Hermia: I would my father looked but with my eyes.
Theseus: Rather your eyes must with his judgement look.
[I. i. 56-7]

Hermia can choose one of two men; one of them has the approval of her father, and one has not. Is she not unreasonable to choose the wrong one? Technically, yes, but in case the audience is tempted to disparage Hermia's criteria, Shakespeare gives the other side a voice almost immediately. Lysander answers that he is, by any objective test, as good a choice as Demetrius ('I am . . . as well derived as he, . . . My fortunes every way as fairly ranked . . .' [I. i. 99-101]), and that furthermore Hermia loves him; 'Why should not I then prosecute my right?' [I. i. 105]. Why, indeed? The question is unanswerable. Hermia and Lysander may be operating according to the unpredictable dictates of the 'eye', choosing each other without regard to practical advantage, but are the supposedly rational criteria of Egeus any more explicable?

To put it another way, our main impression of Act I, when we see it acted, is not that one or the other of the opposing sides is in the right, but that things have gone generally wrong and the traditional values of Athens—its civility, its orderly hierarchies—are no longer sufficient to deal with the situation. Clearly what labour relations experts call the 'bargaining machinery' no longer works; nor do threats to implement the law of the city (the options offered Hermia, either to marry Demetrius or to face death or life in a nunnery, drive her further away from the community, not back into it). In fact, if one had to summarize the action of the first four acts of *A Midsummer Night's Dream,* one could describe it as the process by which Athenian civility, now irrelevant to a new situation, is gradually eroded and replaced with something else. Inexorably the characters in the wood are forced to come to terms with forces within themselves which they never knew existed and in the process to disregard old social, verbal and fictional formulae which are no longer adequate to deal with their new insights. (pp. 31-3)

I have suggested that the action in the wood consists of the characters gradually forgetting the civilities of Athens as they meet with new experiences, and that the change in the kind of language they speak both reflects and makes explicit the changes that take place in their awareness of what goes on around them. To summarise baldly for the moment, they enter the wood speaking in a highly organised, witty, complicated manner, and leave it speaking much more simply.

It is worth taking a closer look at their more formal, courtly level of speech. . . . (p. 36)

In *A Midsummer Night's Dream* . . . the courtly style is used both seriously and ironically—seriously, when the complexities of its tone, vocabulary and syntax are fully engaged to define the subtleties of love; ironically, when it is spoken by a character whose behaviour no longer squares with his view of himself. Early in the play, before the characters have left Athens, the high style seems well suited to the use made of it:

> *Lysander:* Ay me! For aught that I could ever read,
>   Could ever hear by tale or history,
>   The course of true love never did run smooth;
>   But either it was different in blood—
> *Hermia:* O cross!—too high to be enthralled to low.
> *Lysander:* Or else misgraffèd in respect of years—
> *Hermia:* O spite!—too old to be engaged to young.
> *Lysander:* Or else it stood upon the choice of friends—
> *Hermia:* O hell!—to choose love by another's eyes.
>
> [I. i. 132-40]

This is a pretty display, a sort of courtly word game. The proposer offers a certain amount of information, divided into points expressed in parallel syntactic units ('but either . . . Or else . . . Or else'); the respondent takes up each of these points and fits them into an even more formal framework, extending the parallelism to include an apostrophe and an antithesis in each of her answers. The artificiality of this passage suits it well to the several formal definitions of romantic love which Act I provides for the audience; the balanced periods support the idea that love imposes a kind of symmetry by pairing off individuals; the antitheses remind us that the match is often unequal. The formality also expresses Lysander's and Hermia's attempt to buttress themselves against the unknown trials of love awaiting tham. By rehearsing an exaggerated and inclusive account of the possible troubles of romantic love, one can prepare for the worst. As for their present 'cross', it is comforting to have it plotted against a general pattern, especially when the pattern is drawn from stereotypes of hearsay and fiction which cannot possibly apply to them personally.

Yet even at this early stage in the play the audience begins to be aware of slight stresses within the formal style. In their little word game, Hermia answers Lysander and appears to agree with him, yet her very agreement interrupts his flow of ideas. There is an early hint here of the tension between concord and discord which will electrify later scenes in the wood. Again, she appears to control the raw materials of her language, in that she makes her responses even more formal than his propositions, yet her apostrophes become more violent as she proceeds ('O cross! . . . O spite! . . . O hell!'). The impression the audience gets is that Hermia has a surging energy which is pulling increasingly against the rules of the verbal game, just as it will strain and eventually break the 'rules' of Athenian civility.

The business of invoking stereotypes is pushed a stage further when Hermia answers Lysander's plea to meet him in the wood.

> My good Lysander,
> I swear to thee by Cupid's strongest bow,
> By his best arrow with the golden head,
> By the simplicity of Venus' doves,
> By that which knitteth souls and prospers loves,
> And by that fire which burned the Carthage queen
> When the false Trojan under sail was seen,
> By all the vows that ever men have broke—
> In number more than ever woman spoke,—
> In that same place thou hast appointed me
> Tommorrow truly will I meet with thee.
>
> [I. i. 168-78]

The burden of this speech is simply 'I'll be there'; the conventions of the complex courtly style and the stereotype are, therefore, less useful to her purpose than they were to Lysander's. Indeed, they even get in the way, diverting the audience's attention from an otherwise direct line of statement and introducing associations, such as the violence of Dido's suicide, which Hermia cannot really intend. She does not seem entirely in control of her rhetoric.

When the lovers enter the wood the courtly style becomes still less suited to its surroundings and to the use to which it is put. We get the feeling that the more strictly the stereotypes of rhetoric and metaphor are observed in this new context, the less they actually communicate. Immediately before Lysander's transformation, he and Hermia, having lost their way, look for a place to spend the night. He wants to join her on a bank;

> One turf shall serve as a pillow for us both;
> One heart, one bed, two bosoms, and one troth.
>
> [II. ii. 41-2]

Hermia is uneasy about the idea and for modesty's sake would rather lie further off. He answers:

> O, take the sense, sweet, of my innocence!
> Love takes the meaning in love's conference—
> I mean that my heart unto yours is knit,
> So that but one heart we can make of it.
> Two bosoms interchained with an oath—
> So then two bosoms and a single troth.
> Then by your side no bed-room me deny.
> For lying so, Hermia, I do not lie.
>
> [II. ii. 45-52]

As Hermia says, 'Lysander riddles very prettily' [II. ii. 53]. Something about his speech suggests the conventions of love poetry—its puns, its figures to suggest the union of two in one, its promise of troth, its tactic by which the persuasion to physical love is wittily disguised as part of a discourse on metaphysical concepts. But the main feature of witty love poetry is that although it appears 'difficult'—presents a complicated line of argument or a far-fetched comparison—it then resolves itself, so that one can say there is a sense after all in which these two things can be compared, or in which this argument does lead to that conclusion. Lysander's speech does not resolve its tensions, possibly because he rather fussily insists on the convention which admits the union of two hearts but refuses to allow 'bosoms' to combine as well. In the context of a discussion on where they will really lie for the night, the mixture of literal and figurative strikes an odd note. 'I do not lie' in the last line means 'I am not untrue', but to what?—to her concept of propriety which entails that they slept apart, or to her? If the former, how does the preceding argument lead to this conclusion (or have any bearing on it whatsoever)? If the latter, how can it reassure Hermia, since being true to her and assaulting her—even rudely and physically—are not inconsistant procedures? The answer is, of course, that Hermia is not reassured and adheres to her original decision to sleep apart. She is probably as uncertain as the audience as to what Lysander means.

The language in this passage is further undercut by the context in which it is placed. Even the use of the courtly style itself is faintly absurd in a setting so remote—in distance and moral status—from the court. Then there is the fact that the episode is introduced by Lysander by admitting he has lost his way. The more learned among the contemporary audience might have heard an echo here of the first book of [Edmund Spenser's] *The Faerie Queene* (or [Dante's] *The Divine Comedy,* for that matter), in which losing one's way in a dark wood means wandering from the path of truth, and they might have appreciated the irony when (three times in the passage) Lysander talks so confidently of 'truth' or 'troth'. The two words could be used interchangeably in Elizabethan English, and could mean either faithfulness or the facts as they are, so that keeping troth was both an intellectual and a moral act. The second line that Lysander speaks after his entrance, therefore, contains a sort of comic contradiction: 'And—to speak truth—I have forgot our way' [II. ii. 36], and the fact that they have lost way (in the intellectual and moral sense provided by the allusion to the wood of Error) continues to negate all the smooth assertions and promises that follow.

In case we miss the point, the comedy is broadened almost immediately. Puck puts the love juice on Lysander's eyes, and Helena comes into his sight just as he wakes. The transformation is sudden and complete:

> Content with Hermia? No, I do repent
> The tedious minutes I with her have spent.
> Not Hermia but Helena I love.
> Who will not change a raven for a dove?
> The will of man is by his reason swayed,
> And reason says you are the worthier maid.
> Things growing are not ripe until their season;
> So I, being young, till now ripe not to reason.
> And touching now the point of human skill,
> Reason becomes the marshall to my will. . . .
>
> [II. ii. 111-20]

The obvious joke—that he thinks he is acting rationally when he is really following impulses started by the love juice—is enriched for us by a view of the formal style at its most pompous. Now the carefully balanced sense units have degenerated into heavy end-stopped lines, and the couplets, instead of exploring further the subtlety of the subject, undermine it by juxtaposing unlikely combinations: 'reason', which we (and Lysander) think of as the faculty for discerning permanent value, goes badly with the suggestion of flux which 'season'

carries, and one does not normally think of the will embodying 'skill'. There is more 'love poetry' too, more stereotyped than ever. Lysander invokes that well-worn rhyme of 'love' and 'dove' with which Mercutio baits Romeo, and the claim to be acting according to the dictates of reason is almost as much of a convention in love poetry as the plea to throw reason to the winds.

The scene ends on a more serious note, however. Hermia wakes, on a stage now deserted, from a frightening dream in which a snake eats at her heart. The Lysander for whose help she calls in no longer the same person, and he is no longer there. His parting remark to the sleeping Hermia ('Of all be hated, but the most of me' [II. ii. 142]) was funny when he said it. Now, when Hermia shares with us her private vision of a rapacious, irrational animal preying on human beings, the dangerous implications of Lysander's comic misdirection becomes more apparent. It is funny that he should act as an animal and talk as a human being—that he should break their 'single troth' at the first sight of another woman; it is also frightening, when we are allowed to share the victim's viewpoint. A rigidly Christian critic might be tempted to connect Hermia's serpent vision with the Fall. Whether or not one wants to go this far, it is difficult to ignore one important similarity: whatever happens in the future, the relationship between Hermia and Lysander can never be quite the same again. Lysander has lost what he called 'my innocence', and Hermia's feeling of loss at his absence is perhaps the first great shock of her life. It is also the first step towards a new understanding of love.

To dramatise the process by which the courtly style degenerates as the lovers proceed through the wood, Shakespeare provides Helena as a point of contrast. Even at the beginning of the play she experiences a kind of 'cross' in love which the audience takes as more serious that that of Lysander and Hermia (they lack parental approval but she lacks a lover). Her behaviour—at least until the point at which all four of the young lovers finally abandon all traces of courtesy—exhibits a certain civilised scepticism when she rejects the impulsive advances of Lysander and Demetrius. This qualifies her to act—temporarily, at least—as authorial voice, as when she defines the nature of romantic love by an elaborate evocation of the emblem of Cupid in which the rhymed couplets exactly reflect the ironies she wants to convey. When she stops acting as chorus and re-enters the action, her use of conventional formulae provides the audience with as much information about her as about the subject she is discussing. Yet her 'message' is still efficiently conveyed:

> Run when you will. The story shall be changed:
> Apollo flies, and Daphne holds the chase;
> The dove pursues the griffin. . . .
>
> [II. i. 230-32]

She has had enough personal experience of the 'crosses' of love to know that the stereotypes can occasionally be inverted, but not enough to banish them from her conciousness altogether. This may represent an intermediate stage in her development, a point half-way between accepting the norms of fiction as the literal truth of her own experience and using the facts of the individual conciousness as the starting point for a fresh view of reality.

In any case, Helena's integrity is maintained until well after the other characters have 'gone mad' in various ways. Even when the four of them meet (after Lysander has abandoned Hermia, and Demetrius too has received the juice of Cupid's flower), she still speaks with the voice of sanity, trying to remind the others—through the medium of the courtly rhetoric which they have come to abuse—of the greater age which they all once shared:

> We, Hermia, like two artificial gods
> Have with our needles created both one flower,
> Both on one sampler, sitting on one cushion,
> Both warbling of one song, both in one key,
> As if our hands, our sides, voices, and minds
> Had been incorporate. So we grew together
> Like to a double cherry, seeming parted
> But yet an union in partition,
> Two lovely berries moulded on one stem,
> So with two seeming bodies but one heart,
> Two of the first, like coats in heraldry,
> Due but to one, and crowned with one crest.
> And will you rent our ancient love asunder,
> To join with men in scorning your poor friend?
>
> [III. ii. 203-16]

It is very important to distinguish between this and Lysander's 'One heart, one bed, two bosoms, and one troth'. Helena's wit does resolve itself; the image of the double cherry makes quite precise the meaning of 'two beseeming bodies but one heart'. They are two people, but common nurture (the stem of the cherry, if one likes) made them as close as two individuals can be. The heraldry image reinforces this notion and places their 'ancient love' within the context of the medieval, hierarchical world of Athens. The speech is a moving cry of puzzlement and grief.

But it has no effect on the others. They continue, for a few more lines, to use the formal style to accompany the most informal actions. The men prepare to fight a duel over Helena:

> *Lysander:* Helen, I love thee. By my life I do.
>   I swear by that which I will lose for thee
>   To prove him false that says I love thee not.
> *Demetrius:* I say I love thee more than he can do.
> *Lysander:* If thou say no, withdraw, and prove it too.
>
> [III. ii. 251-55]

Lysander's 'To prove him false . . .' is a general formulation, but it can apply only to Demetrius. His '. . . prove it too' rhymes with Demetrius's 'do', suggesting concord when he intends discord. The gap between manner and matter is at its widest at this point in the play. The tension is so great that the courtly style finally snaps. Now the microcosmic society of the four lovers no longer adheres through the subtle agreement of rhyme and metre, but turns directly upon itself. Lysander dismisses Hermia, not with the well-mannered hints he has tried before, but in a savage burst of verbal machine-gun fire:

> Away, you Ethiope! . . .
> Hang off, thou cat, thou burr! Vile thing, let loose,
> Or I will shake thee from me like a serpent.
>
> [III. ii. 257-61]

We recall her dream. She, at last, gets the point, and her answer might stand as epigraph for the whole scene:

> Why are you grown so rude? What change is this,
> Sweet love?
>
> [III. ii. 262-63]

The pace quickens as their actions and language become more basic, more 'rude'. Names, like other words, lose their conventional significance:

> Hate me? Wherefore? O me, what news, my love?
> Am not I Hermia? Are not you Lysander?
>
> [III. ii. 272-73]

Suddenly their physical appearance becomes enormously important; Lysander notices Hermia's dark complexion, and Hermia imagines Helena insults her for her small stature. Later both Helena and Lysander warm to her theme and really do taunt her with her size. Saddest of all, perhaps, Helena herself becomes infected with the general malevolence:

> O, when she is angry she is keen and shrewd.
> She was a vixen when she went to school. . . .
>
> [III. ii. 323-24]

So their common childhood was not an unmixed joy, after all; or is she just telling a lie to serve the moment? Here the contrast between courtly and barbaric behavior becomes most pointed: even the patient, peacemaking Helena, who only a short time ago invoked the harmonies of their past friendship in the balanced, complex rhetoric of the court, is willing to abandon both loyalty and manners when she finds them disintegrating in others around her.

Oberon and Puck intervene at this point. The misunderstanding is discovered and will be put right: Lysander's infatuation for Helena will be cancelled, and Demetrius' will not. The men will be made to chase each other around the dark wood, but under controlled conditions and only so that they will exhaust themselves and fall asleep. 'The man shall have his mare again,' as Puck says, 'and all shall be well' [III. ii. 463-64]. (pp. 38-45)

The entrance of Theseus and his court, with its talk of 'musical confusion / Of hounds and echo in conjunction' [IV. i. 110-11] seems to reassert the values of Athenian civility over the chaos of the wood. Discords are made concords. Yet . . . the fact that Oberon has settled the lovers' problems already implies that the wood itself is capable of evolving its own order and that Theseus's role can be at best to ratify Oberon's order in the terms Athens understands. For the moment our interest must be concentrated on what the lovers say when they awake. Their first words fall naturally into the framework of the balanced court rhetoric which they know Theseus expects, but very shortly the pattern is modified:

> *Lysander:* My lord, I shall reply amazedly,
>   Half sleep, half waking. But as yet, I swear,
>   I cannot truly say how I came here.
>   But as I think—for truly would I speak—
>   And now I do bethink me, so it is:
>   I came with Hermia hither. . . .
> *Demetrius:* But, my good lord—I wot not by what power,
>   But by some power it is—my love to Hermia,
>   Melted as the snow, seems to me now
>   As the remembrance of an idle gaud. . . .
>
> [IV. i. 146-67]

The new feature of their language is a congruence of rhythm and meaning, so that (in this case) the burden of their speeches—their uncertainty—is reflected as it would be in real speech, by rhythmic stops and starts, caesurae and enjambments. The lovers have discovered not only themselves and their rightful partners, but a new rhetoric in which manner and matter at last become fused.

What have they learned? It is easier to say what they have unlearned. They have left behind them their theories of love, their certainty that they know exactly what they are doing. Their theme now is 'truly would I speak' (the conditional mode is as important as the words) and 'I wot not'. Their language, once a stylised pattern of words which took little account of what was being conveyed by those words, has been broken down into its consituents and rebuilt:

> *Hermia:* Methinks I see these things with parted eye,
>   When everything seems double.
> *Helena:*   So methinks,
>   And I have found Demetrius, like a jewel,
>   Mine own and not mine own.
>
> [IV. i. 188-92]

Set against the paradoxes of an earlier era in their lives, this has the ring of personal experience. At last they have found their own way of describing the contradictions of romantic love, and at last they fully apprehend its ambivalence. Their greatest wisdom at this stage is to avoid hasty generalisations about their experience, to eschew casting their impressions too quickly in a verbal mould. Whatever questions their adventures may prompt—from Theseus or his court, or even from each other—their safest answer, for the moment, is Bottom's to the mechanicals: 'Not a word of me!' [IV. ii. 34]. (pp. 46-7)

In *A Midsummer Night's Dream* we are less certain how the characters develop, or indeed if they can be called 'characters' at all in the accepted sense of the word. Yet something enormous and frightening happens to them, and they respond by developing a style more fitting their new situation. This achievement is sufficient to make them plausible inheritors of the renewed order in Athens. But one is reminded of providence here too, not only directly through the visable interventions of the fairies, but indirectly through seeing the humans not entirely deserving or understanding the happy ending which they help bring about.

The lovers deserve [their] new world because they have suffered and because they are now convinced of the need to maintain the Pauline hierarchies of Athens. They will obey Theseus, marry, and submit their affections to the control of reason. To demonstrate how completely they have reassumed the values of the city, the Athenians put the world of unreason behind them. Theseus has already forgotten his adventures with Antiopa and Ariadne and averts his eyes from evidence of similar antics on the part of the younger lovers, when he finds them sleeping in the wood and when he dismisses their story at the beginning of Act V. The four lovers, presented with a pageant that should remind them of their misadventures in the wood, satirise it instead. It is quite right that they should do so. If they are to accept the canons of order, they must reject not only the dramatically inappropriate mechanicals' play, but the disorder which that play would represent if it *were* dramatically effective.

But in putting behind all things unreasonable, the Athenians banish not only delusion but also whatever partial glimpse their imagination may have afforded them of [Sir Philip] Sidney's 'golden world'. This limitation in vision may be concious and necessary, but the audience still feels it as a limitation; in being reminded of what the courtiers have forgotton, we come to realise what we have learned. The human's assumption that they have worked out their own solution emphasises—by contrast—the beneficent power of the superhuman. The process by which Shakespeare limits the human characters in order to suggest the providential power of the supernatural is the 'action' of Act V, and it requires detailed examination.

Theseus and the lovers are limited when they—in their different ways—reflect on what happened in the wood. Theseus takes the most sceptical view of the story the lovers tell:

> I never may believe
> These antique fables, nor these fairy toys.
> Lovers and madmen have such seething brains,
> Such shaping fantasies, that apprehend
> More than cool reason ever comprehends.
> The lunatic, the lover, and the poet
> Are of imagination all compact.
> One sees more devils than vast hell can hold.
> That is the madman. The lover, all as frantic,
> Sees Helen's beauty in a brow of Egypt.
> The poet's eye, in a fine frenzy rolling,
> Doth glance from heaven to earth, from earth to
>   heaven.
> And as imagination bodies forth
> The forms of things unknown, the poet's pen
> Turns them to shapes, and gives to airy nothing
> A local habitation and a name.
>
> [V. i. 2-17]

The rhetoric of this speech clearly places lovers, madmen and poets in the same category. Theseus means to satirise all three equally for their over-active imaginations. But to the attentive audience Theseus says more than he intends to. Shakespeare makes him echo unwittingly two remarks spoken earlier in the play: Lysander's description of love as a lightning bolt which 'unfolds both heaven and earth' [I. i. 146] and Helena's observation that 'Things base and vile, holding no quantity, / Love can transpose to form and dignity' [I. i. 232-33]. The tactics are superb. We are invited to balance Theseus's dismissal of imagination as merely delusive against the opposite view of imagination as a vision of a better world. Theseus wants Hippolyta, to whom he is talking here, to take 'fine frenzy' ironically; the audience is free to take it seriously. He wants to place poets and madmen in the same category; we can, if we like, find a real distinction between looking towards hell and towards heaven, especially when the latter vision is made concrete in the 'local' image. For him seeing a gipsy as Helen of Troy is absurd; for us, granted the gipsy's point of view, it is as close as human beings can come to redeeming the ugly world.

Theseus twice distinguishes between apprehension and comprehension—once in the lines quoted above and again later in this same speech. Comprehension is the art of generalising, or relating things to categories; it is one of the tools of reason. (pp. 48-50)

Theseus's distrust of apprehending accords well with his role as ruler of Athens, and it provides an important clue to his view of the world. He is adept at generalising, at 'comprehending'; he looks constantly beyond the specific fact to the category or 'kind' to which it belongs. In Act I, when he tries to convince Hermia that 'Demetrius is a worthy gentleman' and she answers (convincingly), 'So is Lysander', he says:

> In himself he is;
> But in this kind, wanting your fathers voice.
>
> [I. i. 53-4]

The word 'kind' appears again in Act V, in the course of a discussion between Theseus and Hippolyta about whether the mechanicals should be allowed to produce a play which is clearly going to be beyond their capacities:

> *Hippolyta:* He says they can do nothing in this kind.
> *Theseus:* The kinder we, to give them thanks for
>   nothing.
>
> [V. i. 88-9]

But Theseus makes a serious point too:

> For never anything can be amiss
> When simpleness and duty tender it.
>
> [V. i. 82-3]

As a good generaliser he can see beyond the imperfect thing to the perfect devotion which it represents. Later, when Hippolyta finds the mechanicals' play 'the silliest stuff that I ever heard' [V. i. 210], Theseus generalises once again:

> The best in this kind are but shadows; and the
> worst are no worse, if imagination amend them.
>
> [V. i. 211-12].

Theseus is a politician, in the widest sense of the word—a master in the art of living in and governing a society. From a diplomatic point of view, each of these three generalisations—and much more he says besides—exactly suits the occasion which calls for it. Once Egeus has invoked the law against his daughter, Theseus must be seen to uphold it, but he must, if possible, placate the younger generation too by explaining the law in the gentlest possible terms. He assesses the mechanicals' play not on the grounds of its quality as a performance but for its political implications—what it tells him about their attitude to their ruler. His response to Hippolyta ('The best in this kind . . .') is a diplomatic refusal to enter into controversy at a moment when the players are doubtless watching him anxiously to see how he likes their play. The ruler of the rational society is also a little weary of the performance, 'yet in courtesy, in all reason, we must stay the time' [V. i. 254-55].

But we would miss the point if we saw anything more in these statements than a sensitive, practical response to an immediate situation. Take the case of his advice to Hermia. From the standpoint of one who wants to uphold the Athenian hierarchy and mediate between father and daughter, it makes sense to look beyond the 'fact' of Lysander himself to his lack of parental support. But for Hermia, who sees only the man Lysander, the 'kind' to which he belongs—especially such a negative one as this—can only be irrelevant. Theseus responds to the situation as best he can, but the really complete response would have to take account of the particular as well as the general. Again, 'The best on this kind are but shadows . . .' is not a profound statement about art, though it has been taken as such by some critics. In so far as it is true, it is a truism, since it is obvious that all art is a copy. In so far as it is not a truism, it is misleadingly restrictive. Theseus denigrates the artistic copy with the limiting 'but' and the word 'shadows', which recalls the famous Platonic attack on art. We are aware of another side to the argument. And can we accept his implication that one play is more or less as good as another? Because he can generalise, Theseus is an excellent politician, but reactions to art, as to love, require attention to the thing itself, the concrete image before one, as well as to what the thing signifies or the category to which it belongs. One may argue that the situation hardly calls for a considered aesthetic judgement. This is the point exactly. His reaction to the moment is the height of tact, but his remark is somewhat less than the complete statement about art for which it has been taken. (pp. 50-2)

Theseus rejects the lovers' story since it fits no category except a kind of madness. But even as he speaks we know he is wrong. The story may seem mad. The lovers may be uncertain, when they wake, whether they have been dreaming or awake. But we, the audience, know it happened; it was brought alive for us in the ineradicable image of the action on the stage. But the important point is that we do not know what we know until we have seen Theseus, by contrast, arrive at the wrong conclusion. If one considers his first speech in Act V together with his misunderstanding of what the lovers have been doing when he finds them asleep in the wood, one is faced with a deliberate reduction in his range of view. At the beginning of the play he seems in control of everything—setting the date for his wedding (and thus providing a plausible time-scale within which the drama will take place), coolly deliberating between the opposing forces of Egeus and the younger generation. By the end of Act IV the major events of the play seem to have passed him by. For however adequately his scepticism may respond to the immediate moment, it falls short as an account of what happened.

This is not to say, though, that *A Midsummer Night's Dream* is the story of how Theseus comes to miss the point, or a general satire on politicians. By the end of the play Theseus is not really a character at all; he is a dramatic device used by the author to reinforce the play's main action in the memories of the audience. As Theseus's point of view becomes restricted, so ours expands and becomes firm. When Theseus misunderstands the events in the wood, we are reminded not only of human violence and unreason but of a providential process by which this depravity has been redeemed.

How do the lovers themselves function in Act V? If Theseus considers their story untrue (and thus, indirectly, invites the audience to consider ways in which it *is* true), the lovers simply forget about it. When they wake in the wood, they try desperately to explain to Theseus their feeling that a powerful outside force has been guiding their behaviour. Afterwards they confess to each other that they are not sure what really happened, or whether or not they have been dreaming. This is their moment of greatest honesty and insight: they will not accept easy explanations, and they cannot banish the sense of something bigger than themselves.

Their retreat from even this fragmentary vision, in Act V, is a demand of the comic form: they must reassume the values of their society, and Athens, as its spokesman makes clear at the beginning of Act V, has no place for their story. Yet when they turn from acting in their 'fond pageant' to become the audience at *Pyramus and Thisbe,* we feel a sense of loss. Have they assimilated their experience, or forgotten it? Should not this violent drama of crossed lovers—however absurdly produced—stir in them some memories of their own complaints at being crossed and their own violence?

Instead, taking their cue from Theseus and deriving their witticisms from his, they ridicule the mechanicals. Like Theseus, they are obsessed with categories. Starveling arrives, as 'moon', carrying dog, bush and lantern. Theseus comments:

> This is the greatest error of all the rest; the man
> should be put into the lantern. How is it else
> the man i' th' moon?
>
> [V. i. 246-48]

And a few lines later Demetrius takes up the joke: 'Why, all these should be in the lantern; for all these are in the moon' [V. i. 260-61]. This is unfair. The mechanicals may do their best to destroy dramatic illusion (when they go to such lengths to civilise Lion, for instance), but their audience should surely be expected to make the imaginative leap from Starveling's iconography to what it 'presents'. In their concern for categories, the courtiers miss the impact of the concrete image. They also miss its real meaning for them: the moon—even

Starveling's presentation of it—should remind them of their own antics by moonlight. (pp. 53-4)

Theseus and the lovers, then, discount or forget the influence of the supernatural, reinforcing the audience's awareness of it. But Shakespeare provides another comment on what happened in the wood—Bottom's speech when he awakes at the end of Act IV. For all its apparent absurdity we can take it as a direct guide to the significance of the play's action, something which could not be said for even the smoothest of Theseus's assertions. For Bottom is, after all, the very opposite of Theseus. He is the 'bottom' of the hierarchy of which Theseus is the top. Theseus has a prudent regard for categories, whereas Bottom persistently confuses them, as his speech throughout the play makes clear:

> An I may hide my face, let me play Thisbe too.
> I'll speak in a monstrous little voice: 'Thisne, Thisne!'
>
>   [I. ii. 51-3]

(as Pyramus)

> I see a voice. Now will I to the chink
> To spy an I can hear my Thisbe's face. . . .
> Will it please you to see the epilogue, or to
> hear a Bergomask dance between two of our company?
>
>   [V. i. 192-93, 352-54]

In terms of Athenian society he is an ass. In the wood he is an ass of another sort. Yet this ass, this 'bottom', is the one character to be granted a vision of the Fairy Queen:

> I have had a most rare vision. I have had a dream past the wit of man to say what dream it was. Man is but an ass if he go about to expound this dream. Methought I was—there is no man can tell what. Methought I was—and methought I had—but man is but a patched fool if he will offer to say what methought I had. The eye of man hath not heard, the ear of man hath not seen, man's hand is not able to taste, his tongue to conceive, nor his heart to report what my dream was! I will get Peter Quince to write a ballad of this dream. It shall be called 'Bottom's Dream', because it hath no bottom.
>
>   [IV. i. 204-16]

This is as difficult as it could be from Theseus's reactions to the 'dream'. It is linguistically garbled, whereas his is smoothly delivered. It is not part of the patter of social discourse, but is announced alone, to no one. Whereas Theseus, who experienced nothing of the dream, feels qualified to communicate an opinion on it, Bottom, who saw the Fairy Queen, communicates nothing. (pp. 55-6)

Perhaps Bottom's awkwardness is, after all, the best expression of the inexpressible. And even through the indirection of parody, the allusion to St. Paul still works on us. We know who the ruler of this world is, and can imagine how he will receive the story the lovers tell. And the stern warning, 'Man is but an ass if he go about to expound this dream', stays with us throughout the fifth act. Considered as a single line of action, the scenes from the moment Theseus enters the wood to the end of the play serve to distance the audience—in stages—from the action in the wood. There are several 'plays', of course: the 'fond pageant' itself, the mechanicals' production which is a kind of comment on it, the action which begins

when Theseus announces his wedding date and ends when the Athenians leave the stage for bed, and A Midsummer Night's Dream itself. Each has its actors and its audience; indeed the main interest in the scenes following the end of the first play (the 'fond pageant') arises when actors become spectators. It is when they watch 'plays' involving other characters than themselves that the mortals run the risk of commenting too facilely on what they are watching, and become asses. From this point of view, Theseus is the greatest ass of all, since he was an actor long ago in his own pageant of Ariadne and Antiopa, here he remains outside the action of both the wood and the mechanicals' play. The lovers present a kind of truth, however haltingly, about their own experience, but when they watch Pyramus and Thisbe, they join Theseus in the smart comments which so make asses of them all. It is as though whatever the similarities between a work of art and our own perceptions of the world, we can never make the imaginative leap between them, never 'streight [our] own resemblance find' in the created image. Is this general rule a theme of the play? Does A Midsummer Night's Dream ultimately dismiss the possibility of a valid response to art? Is the audience finally banished as impossible?

I believe the play questions this possibility rather than dismisses it. The question can best be developed through examining briefly the last stage in the process by which the audience is distanced from the wood—the point when the Athenians go to bed and the fairies inherit the stage. If Theseus's point of view were all, or Athens the sum of all wisdom, this (plus or minus an epithalamion) would be the end of the play. Instead, Theseus leaves with what I take to be a figurative, not a literal, reference to fairies: 'Lovers to bed; 'tis almost fairy time' [V. i. 364]. It does not occur to him that there really are fairies in his palace.

But they come on stage, as though to demonstrate where the power lies. Puck's first words, 'Now the hungry lion roars' [V. i. 371], remind us that in the real world there are real lions, not the pasteboard creation of the mechanicals. Oberon bestows his blessings by negating (hence reminding us of) the traditional fairy curses:

> Never mole, harelip, nor scar,
> Nor mark prodigious, such as are
> Despisèd in nativity,
> Shall upon their children be.
>
>   [V. i. 411-14]

It is common for the endings of Shakespearean comedies to remind the audience of the everyday world which we are about to re-enter—think of Feste's 'the rain it raineth every day' [Twelfth Night, V. i. 392]. But this is more than a device for letting us down gently. It reminds us, by contrast, that for an hour or two we have been immersed in the ideal world of comedy; like Bottom's allusion to St. Paul, it underpins our awareness of the mysterious providential plan which comedy can imitate but which lies beyond the terms of the real world and its rulers. But comedy, because much of its delight is communicated through our aesthetic apprehension of its structure, is not only a form of art, but raises questions about the nature of art as well. The ending of A Midsummer Night's Dream reminds us not only of the integrity of the providential action which shapes it, but also of the validity of the golden world. When Puck says:

> If we shadows have offended,
> Think but this, and all is mended:

> That you have but slumbered here
> While these visions did appear.
> And this weak and idle theme,
> No more yielding but a dream, . . .
>
> [V. i. 423-28]

we take it at first that he dismisses the audience in two ways—sends them home and discounts the possibility that they can respond any more accurately to the play than Theseus did to the lovers' story. But Puck's use of 'shadows', an ironic reflection of Theseus's 'The best in this kind are but shadows', provides substance to a word used only negatively before, as though to say, 'Theseus thinks all elements outside his rational viewpoint to be shadows, but here we are'. Our attention is drawn not to the similarity, but to a potential difference, between our response and Theseus's.

And this is obvious enough, if we think back on Act V. An audience does not have to respond as Theseus does, and later the lovers do. Hippolyta, for example, is a different kind of audience. She believes the lovers' story and will not be put off her belief even by her fiancé's lenghty and plausible assertion that they have been plagued by fantasies. In their discussion which opens Act V, she is allowed the last word, an intelligent—even conclusive—answer to the 'More strange than true' speech:

> But all the story of the night told over,
> And all their minds transfigured so together,
> More witnesseth than fancy's images,
> And grows to something of great constancy;
> But howsoever, strange and admirable.
>
> [V. i. 23-7]

This means not only that the lovers all, independently, tell the same story, but that something within her—an instinct, perhaps—prompts her to accept it as true. In other words, she apprehends the resemblance between her experience and the fable, though her feeling of wonder stops her from defining the 'something'.

Shakespeare provides the audience, then, with three responses to the action in the wood. Theseus dismisses the story as a wild flight of fancy—untrue. Hippolyta admits that the story is improbable, but sees a certain consistency in it. Bottom sees it as what Macrobius would call an *oneiros*—that is, an enigmatic dream 'that conceals with strange shapes and veils with ambiguity the true meaning of the information being offered' [*Commentary on the Dream of Scipio*]. We are then invited, indirectly, to apply each of these attitudes to the question of whether *A Midsummer Night's Dream,* or any fiction, is anything more than shadows.

Does any one of these three responses become Shakespeare's 'normative' attitude to fiction? Is Hippolyta's balanced view a model for the audience's approach to the action in the wood and to *A Midsummer Night's Dream?* I think not. It is a mark of the play's inconclusiveness that each of these three views has a certain validity, and that each cancels the other out, to an extent. Even Theseus's doubts about the veracity of the imagination and its works cannot be dismissed as simply wrong. Or rather, one can see his doubts as alternatively 'right' and 'wrong' as one moves further away from the immediate action surrounding his statement. His remarks suit the moment because the audience needs an appropriate sign that the lovers are re-entering the world of reason. Plotted against the action in the wood, his dismissal of the lovers' story is simply wrong, because he says the story is not true, and we know it is. Taken

out of context altogether, his statement regains a certain, even profound rightness. Even 'The best in this kind are but shadows', although limited, is undeniable, and Puck's 'If we shadows have offended', can be taken not only as an ironic reflection on Theseus's scepticism, but as acknowledgement of an inescapable fact about characters in a work of fiction.

The puzzle over the validity of 'the play' is the greatest in a play containing many puzzles. The characters and what they stand for are ambivalent: the fairies can be taken as benevolent and malevolent; Theseus as powerful in one sense and limited in another; the lovers and the love they invoke as sometimes blind, sometimes enlightened by a redeeming vision. The dangers of the wood—from both without and within the human beings wandering there—are constantly present, and yet they are usually distanced by the formality of the characters and their dialogue. (The exception, when the lovers discard their courtly style to engage in a slanging match and when the violence is allowed to come periously close to the surface, is by contrast one of the most frightening moments in the play; it is also one of the funniest.)

Is the danger less frightening because it is distanced? or more frightening because so often ignored by the characters and yet so obviously there? (pp. 56-60)

The puzzles thicken at the end of the play as the audience is withdrawn from the central action. Attempt to solve the puzzles, and you become the ass that Bottom said you would become. You also miss the play's real impact, because it should be obvious by now that Shakespeare uses complexity—or the illusion of complexity—as a dramatic device. You are supposed to remain puzzled, until finally the various 'intellectual' responses to the play (and the play within the play, and the play within that) cancel each other out and force you to look elsewhere for comfort. The real meaning of *A Midsummer Night's Dream* is that no one 'meaning' can be extracted from the puzzles with which a fiction presents its audience. We must share what Keats called Shakespeare's *'Negative Capability'*:

> . . . that is when man is capable of being in
> uncertainties, Mysteries, doubts, without any
> irritable reaching after fact and reason.

And then when the clash of dilemmas dies away, we may recall our *experience* of the action in the wood, and of the play itself; we may remember that we apprehended—even if we did not comprehend (or comprehend how we apprehended)—a certain 'local habitation and a name' called *"A Midsummer Night's Dream."* (p. 61)

Stephen Fender, in his Shakespeare: "A Midsummer Night's Dream," *Edward Arnold (Publishers) Ltd., 1968, 64 p.*

SIDNEY R. HOMAN   (essay date 1969)

[*Homan maintains that the worlds of Athens and the wood in* A Midsummer Night's Dream *are not antithetical; instead, he regards Theseus's realm as a smaller and finite part of Oberon's infinite natural world, and that both Theseus's and Oberon's kingdoms are microcosms within a larger reality, which cannot be understood through reason but only apprehended by imagination. The values represented by these worlds, he argues, are not in conflict with each other, although they appear so, but are necessary and complementary elements for understanding the whole range of existence. Homan's thesis that in* A Midsummer Night's Dream *Shakespeare is dramatizing the Renaissance concept that the life we assume to be "reality"—our conscious, rational world—*

is merely a dream, an illusion of the ultimate reality beyond empirical perception, may be compared with Hermann Ulrici's (1839) very similar point of view, although Ulrici's is anchored in Christian metaphysics. For further commentary on the themes of illusion, perception, and awareness in the play, see the excerpts by John Russell Brown (1957), C. L. Barber (1959), Bertrand Evans (1960), T. Walter Herbert (1964), Stephen Fender (1968), Charles R. Lyons (1971), and James L. Calderwood (1971).]

It has been some time now since *A Midsummer Night's Dream* could be dismissed as a harmless and essentially shallow romance, as "only so much gossamer and moonlight" [see the entry by J. B. Priestley in the Additional Bibliography]. More recent readings of the play, however, tend to force it into the fairly rigid mold of a debate. For some critics the issue is reason in conflict with passion, and therefore to "move from the city to the forest is to choose madness" [see the entry by Paul Olson in the Additional Bibliography]. The clear choice is between Theseus, the apostle of reason, and those fickle lovers who can all too easily degenerate to the ass's head, the image "for carnality and stupidity" [Olson]. Jan Kott would reverse this: Theseus' kingdom represents the "censorship of day," the forest "the erotic madness liberated by night" [see excerpt above, 1964]. From one perspective the wild night spent in Oberon's power warns of the demeaning alternative to anyone who, blinded by emotions, would flaunt Theseus' moral code in which reason holds man's passionate nature in check. Civilization, not supernatural excursions, establishes the meaning and dignity of human existence. From the other perspective the return to Athens signals the return of that surface decorum concomitant with society. Still, it was the night which liberated the Athenians; there, Mr. Kott maintains, they "were their real selves in their dreams" [see excerpt above].

I would like to suggest here that the "worlds" of the play, those of Theseus and Oberon, are not so much antithetical as synthetic, that they are merely unequal parts (Oberon's being the larger) of a single world. (pp. 72-3)

Theseus' vision is bounded by Athens, by that world synonymous with his reason and available to tangible measurements. To say this is not to condemn the Duke's approach to life. We may be thankful that he, rather than some irresponsible lover, reigns over Athens. Yet Theseus's reason, the very virtue that makes him such an effective ruler, inhibits him from seeing that larger world of which Athens forms merely the small center, only the beginning. Stretching beyond the palace is Oberon's vast domain; rather than simply alternating between the city and the forest, as the debate structure suggests, our focus enlarges from finite Athens to the infinite dimensions of the natural world. (p. 73)

Far from being antithetical to Athens, the forest at times seems to be more a projection of the mortals' collective unconsciousness. Egeus inadvertently anticipates Puck's magic when he claims that Lysander has "bewitched the bosom of [his] child" and "stol'n the impression of her fantasy" [I. i. 27, 32]. And Helena's impulsive wish that she might have Hermia's power to attract men is fulfilled literally when Puck's misapplied herb brings her both Demetrius and Lysander as lovers, reducing Hermia to the role of unmourned exile. In a sense the characters unconsciously call the supernatural upon themselves, and a psychoanalytic reading might well diagnose the time spent outside Athens as a form of wish-fulfillment.

The structure of the human drama, in which hate gives way to love, tragedy to comedy, single life to marriage, and barrenness to fertility, is not confined to Athens but informs the super-

natural as well, where discord also turns to accord, jealousy to trust, error to the righting of error, and cosmic disorder to cosmic harmony. The lovers' fickleness, the changing of partners, mirrors a larger swapping as Oberon tries to take the changeling from Titania, or as Titania leaves Oberon for Bottom only to return at last the dutiful wife. The anticipated joys of pregnancy, as the pairs of newly married lovers retire to consummate their marriage on a night made auspicious by the mystical number three [IV. i. 184], are shared equally by Titania as she celebrates motherhood in recalling that time when the changeling's mother grew big-bellied with child. Some basic concerns are common to all the inhabitants, whatever their origins. (pp. 74-5)

The play poses, then, an existential problem of sorts. The true reality, that vast natural world in which both fairies and Athenians are residents, must coexist with a fraudulent reality, the world that the individual wishes to perceive. The irony is that it is the lover, only dimly conscious and lost in a dream world, rather than the conscious (or so Theseus thinks) apostle of reason who perceives this truer and larger reality. Even here there are complications. Emerging from the forest the four young Athenians become inarticulate when they try to describe the strange events of the night; no wonder Theseus remains unconvinced in the midst of such vague descriptions: what has happened to them now seems "small and undistinguishable, / Like far-off mountains turned into clouds," or like things seen "with parted eye" [IV. i. 187-89]. Within two scenes the lovers, no doubt urged on by Theseus to dismiss their dreams, have apparently forgotten that larger world in which aristocrats were mere puppets manipulated by Puck. But for us Demetrius' anguished question, though it will soon cease to be important to him, remains vital: "Are you sure, / That we are awake? It seems to me / That yet we sleep, we dream" [IV. i. 192-94]. Is what we see the ultimate reality, the final dimensions of the world, or is it but a fraudulent reality, a fragment of the real thing, a mere point lost in an infinite circle? And if we think that our overview of the players marks our superiority to them, Puck in his epilogue taunts us with the possibility that we too have "but slumb'red here" [V. i. 425]. (p. 76)

If there is just one expanding world in the play, instead of two antithetical worlds, if the play is not essentially a debate between reason and passion, or repression and freedom, we must ask: what is the nature of Shakespeare's single world view—in the present play at least? Few would deny that *A Midsummer Night's Dream* is a happy comedy, a "festive comedy" as C. L. Barber would call it [see excerpt above, 1959]. Humanity is shown as ultimately decent and kind, if a trifle foolish or shortsighted. The final scene in which the Athenians sink once more into unconsciousness is attended by fairies who will "each several chamber bless," spreading "sweet peace" throughout the palace [V. i. 417-18].

Perhaps it is the many references to life as a dream, a sleep, a shadow, or a play which are disturbing, because having read *Hamlet* or *Macbeth* or *The Tempest* we know that one way of expressing doubt as to the validity or the goodness of earthly existence is to brand this life as a sleeper's dream, "a walking shadow, a poor player" [Macbeth, V. i. 24], something "rounded with a little sleep" [*The Tempest*, IV. i. 158]. Oberon dismisses all that happens to the lovers in the forest as mere "derision" which on their regaining consciousness will "seem a dream and fruitless vision" [III. ii. 370-71], nothing more than "the fierce vexation of a dream" [IV. i. 69]. Yet while they are awake in the forest what happens to the lovers seems to them very real *and* a matter of tragic consequence: girlhood friends quarrel and separate; Hermia accuses Demetrius of murder; the men chase each other (or so they think) eager for a fight. Of course they are all confused as to just what happens, but for us the lovers exist both within and without the forest: what they "are" is not just what they are in the palace. Thus Oberon's lines may be taken as an indictment not just of the forest "tricks" but of life generally, of all that transpires outside the forest as well.

As the forest world recedes and Theseus takes over Oberon's role as arbiter of reality, the certainty—or at least Theseus' certainty—of "what is" and "what is not" becomes more substantial. However, Theseus cannot totally convert Hippolyta to his reasoned view of things, and then just as daylight comes it is gone: the final scene is set somewhere between eleven and midnight. Like it or not, dreaming will take over for walking. Yet rather than merely challenging what passes as consciousness and reality, this fellowship between sleep and the imaginative visions which issue from the sleeper's dreams calls instead for a more catholic definition of reality. The visions of the poet or the lover may be no less valid than the deductions of a logician; indeed, the imagination perceives a dimension of the true reality beyond reason. Breaking down the barriers, blurring the distinction between what seems to be represented by Athens and Oberon's forest, leads to confusion, to be sure, but also to a reward of sorts—a reward similar to the profit and pleasure gained by an audience when it gives a momentary credence to what is otherwise a mere stage illusion. Conversely, a too limited definition of reality, a rejection of dreams and the imagination, is both foolish and unwarranted. Theseus is no less a creature of the poet's imagination than Oberon; his barb that the actors are "but shadows" has a double edge since he too is a mere shadow, an actor's part. His "real" world exists only when we choose to abandon the world outside the theater for the fictive world within. Again, if we presume to call ourselves real men, conscious spectators, Puck challenges even this certainty in his epilogue.

Moreover, it is common among Renaissance philosophers to suggest that life itself is a play, man an actor, the mundane world only a dim shadow, an insubstantial microcosm of a divine macrocosm. To view the present world with a certain distrust therefore represents the beginning of wisdom. (pp. 81-2)

Perhaps Shakespeare had not yet begun to question intensely the concept of earthly existence, the nature of tangible things, as Hamlet would do in elevating the actor playing Hecuba to a status equal with his own. The proximity of life and the artist's fictive world, his vision, may more accord here with the theme of our own initiation by means of art into a fuller awareness of what constitutes reality. The equation of this world with a dream, then, may not be a sure sign of Shakespeare's pessimism, but may emphasize instead the reduced position that humanity occupies generally in the play. Ernest Schanzer argues that in *A Midsummer Night's Dream*, "Dream and nightmare are still securely fenced in, and are made to dissolve at the coming of dawn."

Still, we must confront the fact that to understand man, to know his role in the midst of a partially unseen and ever-changing nature, a background of night, *not day*, provides the necessary mirror. Only one scene in the play (IV. ii.) is set in full daylight. The characters may long to be delivered from the "weary night" [III. ii. 431], but as conventional lovers they also welcome darkness. This ambivalence parallels the strange fact that what they are in the light of day represents an unfurnished portrait; only at night, in the dream, is their identity completed, as well as that of the larger nature benevolently ruling them. We think more often of night as the indispensable *modus operandi* of the tragedies: of Hamlet confronting his father at midnight, Othello executing his misguided justice at bedtime, or of Brutus welcoming the conspirators under the cloak of blackness. Night's three-plied escutcheon might well be emblazoned with Darkness, Death, and Tragedy. Yet it is here in a comedy that night offers the perspective by which man is viewed both as a creature worthy of sympathy, because he is a dreamer in a world ultimately beyond reason, and as something small and undistinguished.

The dichotomy in the play, the so-called debate between reason and passion, or freedom and repression, obscures, I think, not only the expanding world that Shakespeare tries to project . . . and his concern with the imagination in exposing this single world. . . , but also the somber and suggestive undertones that play just below the surface of our laughter. . . . In effect, what constitutes our reality here is both enlarged and then challenged under the moon's light. (pp. 83-4)

> *Sidney R. Homan, "The Single World of 'A Midsummer Night's Dream'," in* Bucknell Review, *Vol. XVII, No. 1, March, 1969, pp. 72-84.*

R. A. ZIMBARDO (essay date 1970)

[*Zimbardo contends that in* A Midsummer Night's Dream *Shakespeare was espousing two basic principles: that a "pattern of never-ending change" governs everything in nature, and that seeming opposites are actually elements of an all-encompassing reality—a point also put forth by Sidney R. Homan (1969). The critic further suggests that these principles of "permanence in mutability" and "discordia concors" contribute to the idea of reconciliation that is central to the play. Zimbardo maintains that the act of reconciliation is dramatized differently within the "four planes of being" represented in* A Midsummer Night's Dream *by the four character groups: Theseus-Hippolyta, Oberon-Titania, the young lovers, and the mechanicals. For each of the characters in these groups, according to the critic, imagination is the "reconciling faculty" which leads them to visionary perceptions of their own natures and their rightful relationships with each other. In the marriage of Theseus and Hippolyta, Zimbardo argues, reconciliation is achieved when the previously warring king and queen become a royal couple; that is, the warrior is transformed into a lover and the bellicose virgin, defeated by Theseus, becomes a matron. Similarly, Oberon and Titania—both of whom represent opposing principles in nature—must come together in a union that will reassert the natural pattern of "discordia concors." Zimbardo claims that, in her refusal to surrender the changeling boy to Oberon, Titania is resisting the natural process of "permanence in mutability" and delaying her passage from motherhood to the next stage of her development. Just as Hippolyta the warrior is destroyed by Theseus, so too the rebellious Titania must be conquered by Oberon before order and harmony are restored to the realm of nature. Zimbardo notes that on the level of the play's imagery, these new beginnings for the two couples are mirrored in the phases of the changing moon, which wanes and dies as it simultaneously gives way to a new one. Other critics who have discussed* A Midsummer Night's Dream *in terms of the theme of harmony from discord and the resolution of opposing elements include Harold C. Goddard (1951), John Vyvyan (1961), Stephen Fender (1968), David Bevington (1975), and Paul A. Olson (see Additional Bibliography). With respect to the young lovers, Shakespeare demonstrates the natural principle of stasis and mutability by dramatizing the manner in which the unyielding law of Athens gives way to their desires once they have established a "proper conjunction with their natural opposites" and achieved their own reconciliation. Zimbardo further perceives the resolution of discord into harmony in the Pyramus and Thisbe interlude, in which Shakespeare emphasizes the function of art as synthesizing discordant elements of human existence through the creative imagination. For additional commentary on this self-conscious view of art in the play, see the excerpts by C. L. Barber (1959), James L. Calderwood (1971), J. Dennis Huston (1981), and David Marshall (1982).]*

[The] central thematic design of *A Midsummer Night's Dream* is shaped by the interaction of two themes: that of permanence in mutability (in the usual sense that Renaissance thought conceived it), and that of discordia concors. I would suggest further, that these two shaping themes explore the play's central idea, reconciliation.

The "dream" of Midsummer night is a vision, the moment of "sacred" time in which those capable of visionary perception can see the whole, the full harmony that grows out of endless reconciliation, or the real concord of what, under the aspect of ordinary time, seem to be opposites: winter and summer, male and female, life and death, reality and fantasy. I cannot agree with [C. L.] Barber when he says, "The actual title emphasizes a skeptical attitude by calling the comedy a dream" [see excerpt above, 1959]. Such a vision is not extra-terrestrial; it is not, as [Paul] Olson suggests, the Platonic Abstract available to reason alone [see Additional Bibliography]. Quite the contrary, reason, the analytical, distinguishing faculty, interferes with the perception of this kind of truth. The vision of endless reconciliation is a "midsummer night's dream"; it is effected through the medium of imagination which ignores or blurs the distinguishing limits and dimensions of things. The lunatic, lover and poet are especially qualified for visionary perception because they are "of imagination all compact" [V. i. 8]. In their eyes the lines of demarcation between subject and object, or reality and fantasy, are erased. Emblematic of the play's dream, or vision, is Bottom's dream. Bottom is not, as he is accused of being, the natural who "will not see God's secret at the bottom of things" [Olson]. He is, rather, a visionary, whose very synesthesia suggests a wholeness of perception that denies the partiality of any one sense: "The eye of man hath not heard, the eare of man hath not seen, man's hand is not able to taste, his tongue to conceive, nor his hearte to report what my dreame was" [IV. i. 211-14]. He is aware, moreover, of the futility of trying to define the indefinable, of trying to report in ordinary language a moment that transcends ordinary experience. He knows that what he has perceived can only be expressed in the imitative synthesis of poetry: "I shall get Peter Quince to write a ballet of this dreame, it shall be called Bottome's Dreame, because it hath no bottome" [IV. i. 214-16]. The dream is "Bottome's dreame" because it gives shape to that recurrent pattern that underlies the movement of ordinary life; yet it is bottomless because in every recurrence the pattern reenacts the archetypal sacred moment.

Concordance of seeming opposites by means of the reconciling faculty, imagination, is the dominant motif on each of the play's four planes of being (represented respectively by Titania and Oberon, Theseus and Hippolita, the two pairs of lovers and the mechanicals). Furthermore the four planes of being are drawn into a larger harmony because they are all subject to an enactment of reconciliation through change that is occurring cosmically. Much attention has been given to the predominance of moon imagery in the play as well as to its multiplicity of Ovidian references. On each of the four planes of life the moon exerts a strong, yet ambiguous influence—ambiguous because

the moon is at once the source and the governing symbol of permanence in mutability.

The play opens with an exchange between Theseus and Hippolita that, establishing the moon as the governor and the emblem of the action to follow, is, in effect, a declaration of theme.

Theseus: but oh, me thinkes, how slow
                This old moon wanes; She lingers my desires
                Like to a Step-dame, or a Dowager
                Long withering out a yong man's revennew.
Hip: Foure days wil quickly steep themselves in nights
                Foure nights wil quickly dreame away the time:
                And then the moon, like to a silver bow
                Now bent in heaven, shal behold the night
                Of our solemnities.

                                                [I. i. 3-11].

Midsummer night . . . is the moment of fullness toward which the moon's growth strains and also the moment toward which the moon's changes have brought summer to its fulfillment. However, at the very instant of fulfillment a new phase of the moon, and with it a new season of nature, must begin in order that the permanence which change insures may be preserved. The pivot upon which the change turns—from ultimate attainment to a new beginning, from the end of an old life to the birth of a new—is the sacred moment of reconciliation.

Theseus and Hippolita have been enemies. Their reconciliation will be celebrated and they will in themselves effect a new beginning at the moment when the old moon becomes the new moon, and when Midsummer night brings the year to its ultimate maturity and begins the renewal of yearly time. The marriage of Theseus and Hippolita is representative of the marriage, a reconciliation of the seasons of nature, or the phases of time, or whatever the divisions may be called that seem to ordinary sight to be separate parts, but that are to the visionary dreamer aspects of a whole. Moreover, Shakespeare is concerned not merely to celebrate this union but to uncover the operations that cause it to occur.

We might consider the complexity with which the twin themes of permanence in mutability and discordia concors are presented in the configuration formed by the marriage of Theseus and Hippolita (an action that is too often thought to provide merely an ornamental frame for the play). The bridegroom, Theseus, ought to be emblematically male, yet his sexual identity is curiously ambiguous. As Oberon tells us, he has been the protégé of Titania, and he is distinguished by activities usually associated with female, rather than male, power: conquest by love rather than war, wantoness and fickleness.

Oberon [to Titania]: . . . I know thy love to Theseus.
                Did'st thou not lead him through the glimmering night
                From Peregenia, whom he ravished?
                And make him with fair Eagles break his faith
                With Ariadne and Atropia?

                                                [II. i. 76-80]

When we encounter Theseus in the first act, he is full of a young man's ardor, chafing against the "Step-dame moon" for delaying the gratification of his desire. Yet in the last act of the play he is full of kingly majesty—highly rational, fully in control not only of himself and Hippolita but of everyone in his presence.

Hippolita presents the twin themes of the play even more emphatically. A bride, she is nevertheless identified with Oberon, with warfare and the chase, so that, like Theseus, she constitutes a paradox within herself. Moreover, her marriage to Theseus figures yet a larger *discordia concors*. They have been a warring king and queen who will become a royal couple. Theseus tells Hippolita that though he has won her by fighting her, at the moment of Midsummer he will turn a new aspect toward her, becoming a lover. The union of these opposites depends upon change. Theseus has had to destroy the Amazon in order to prepare for the maiden who will become the bride. Hippolita must die to her virgin identity in order to bring forth a new beginning. Whereas in Act I Hippolita plays the cool counselor to Theseus' rash youth, reminding him of how quickly time passes, the last act finds her transformed into his queenly, but obviously subordinate wife. The moon has not only caused the passage of time that turns this cycle of change, but it also is itself the explanation of the nature of such change. The old moon dies as the virgin moon is born; the virgin dies as the matron is born; the old life dies in a new beginning.

C. L. Barber has said that the festival "battle of summer and winter" was often rationalized in a "superimposing of classical motifs on holiday games." We might use this suggestion as a bridge to describe the connection between the Theseus-Hippolita level of the play and the Oberon-Titania level: Theseus and Hippolita are the classical motif imposed upon the ritual essence of Oberon and Titania. However, Barber's further assertion that the fairies are "embodiments of the May-game experience of eros in men and women, and trees and flowers" must be qualified. The relation of Oberon and Titania enacts at a level of being beyond that of Theseus and Hippolita the same cosmological dance—*discordia concors* and permanence in mutability, twin forces effecting a grand design of reconciliation. In Oberon and Titania the design is more nearly ritual (hence the resemblence to the holiday battle of winter and summer); the principals are therefore more strongly symbolic and their relationship more obviously a primal pattern. (pp. 36-8)

Titania comes near to symbolizing the moon though she is not to be altogether identified with it. (The moon, "governor of floods," is angered by the quarrel of Oberon and Titania and is therefore obviously a pwwer still larger than they.) She is rather the female principle, that corresponds in its triple nature to the triplicity associated with the moon. As female principle, Titania incorporates among other aspects the Amazonian virginity (Diana) of Hippolita. However, Titania herself is arrested in a different phase of the moon's cycle from Hippolita's. The moment of Midsummer that will bring Hippolita from her maidenhood to the wifely nature that promises fertility will bring Titania from her motherly obsession with the changeling boy through a kind of death (through the "Bottom," so to speak) to a new maidenhood, a phase in which she is ready once more to be wooed and won by Oberon.

Titania and Oberon are opposite principles; the former nurtures living things; the latter, who is called the "King of shadowes" [III. ii. 347], hunts them down. Though Titania and Oberon are opposites, they effect in their opposition a *discordia con-*cors. They must meet at points in the cycle of their being in order for the harmony of nature to be upheld. They have not "met" since "middle Summer's spring" [II. i. 82], that is, since May-day which is the birth of that season that reaches its fullest maturity at Midsummer. We assume that their meeting in Spring caused the advent of summer. Titania is the female principle now in its aspect of motherhood. The changeling's mother was a "Votresse of [Titania's] order" [II. i. 123], the life-promoting order of fertility. (p. 39)

However, the Indian queen, "being mortal, of that boy did die" [II. i. 135]. It is the full implication of this truth that Titania will not recognize. Titania has arrested her own progress through the cycle of change at motherhood, the nurturing of life. In that phase the female principle is independent of the male, and life seems independent of death—but only for the length of a season. Titania, the female principle, must not be permitted to see herself as the all. Titania has tried to stop mutability, to arrest her season of fullness. "The Summer still doth tend upon my state" [III. i. 155], she says. However just as the Indian queen being mortal, has had to die, so must Titania die to motherhood.

The moon, who governs floods and protects boundaries, is angered by the quarrel of Oberon and Titania because their refusal to come together at the appointed time in the cycle of time has disturbed *discordia concors* in nature.

> . . . the Windes, piping to us in vaine,
> [*i.e.,* urging the 'dance' of Titania and Oberon]
> As in revenge, have suck'd up from the sea
> Contagious fogges: Which falling on the Land,
> Hath everie petty River made so proud,
> That they have over-borne their Continents.
> . . . the greene Corne
> Hath rotted ere his youth attained a beard:
> The fold stands empty in the drowned field,
> And Crowes are fatted with the murrain flocke.
> The nine mens Morris is fild up with mud,
> And the queint Mazes in the wanton greene,
> For lack of tread are indistinguishable.
> The human mortals want their winter heere. . . .
> The seasons alter; hoared headed frosts
> Fall in the fresh lap of the crimson Rose,
> And on old Hyems chinne and Icie crowne,
> An odorous Chaplet of sweet Sommer buds
> Is as in Mockery set. The Spring, the Summer,
> The chiding Autumn, angry Winter change
> Their wonted liveries, and the mazed world,
> By their increase, now knowes not which is which.
> And this same progeny of evills,
> Comes from our debate, from our dissention.
>
> [II. i. 88-116]

It is interesting that in style this passage resembles canzone, for the antithesis between its content (the discord of nature) and its style (the linking images, balanced lines and repetition of canzone always emphasizing the harmony of nature) underscores the effect of Oberon's and Titania's quarrel. Unbalance in nature results directly from the refusal of these opposing, yet complementary, principles to reach their seasonal reconciliation. The focus in this passage is upon boundaries that have been violated and natural oppositions that, not being maintained, have become chaotic in their operation. Water has flooded the land; death has stricken the corn in its youth rather than waiting upon its maturity. The domestic order falls before disorder: wild birds consume tame beasts; mud washes away

Act II. Scene ii. Puck. By Sir Joshua Reynolds (n.d.).

the imprint of the human game; the paths of civilization are overgrown by wilderness. The seasons have interpenetrated. In order for the harmony of nature to be restored, its paramount law, mutability, must be obeyed. Titania must die and be reborn in a new aspect.

Oberon destroys the Titania of Act II just as Theseus destroyed the Amazonian Hippolita. However, Oberon is not motivated by the lofty Platonism which Olson ascribes to him. He is "passing fell and wrath" and his purpose is to hurt Titania: "Wel, go thy way: thou shalt not from this grove, / 'Til I torment thee for this injury' [II. i. 20, 146-47]. He follows the operation of the principle he embodies the destructive principle, just as Titania follows the operation of hers, the constructive principle. Both operations are necessary to the harmony of the whole.

Oberon uses Cupid's flower, the power of sexual love, to accomplish the destruction of Titania's motherly phase. Titania undergoes much the same transformation as a mother cat, who going into heat, throws the last litter of kittens over whom she had lavished such excruciating care out of the nest. However, the means by which the change occurs—the object of Titania's sexuality being Bottom with an ass's head—indicates the nature of Oberon's power. Titania falls through the bottom of life into a kind of death before she can enter her new phase. Although Bottom with an ass's head is, on the one hand, merely meant to be grotesquely ugly (contributing in this respect to the theme of the relation of subject to object in imaginative perception), he is, on the other hand, richly suggestive of the levels of being through which Titania must fall in the course of her "death." Titania, pure spirit, must fall through nature—human, bestial,

and even the undifferentiated point of convergence—before she can re-emerge as spirit once more in a new aspect. Significantly the moon and nature respond to Titania's obsession with Bottom in the pastoral elegiac style.

> The Moone methinks lookes with a waterie eie,
> And when she weepes, weepes everie little flower
> Lamenting some enforced chastitie.
>
> [III. i. 198-200]

Titania's going off with a lover on whom she dotes does not on the surface suggest "enforced chastitie," but at a deeper level, the moon and nature, in the pathetic mode, lament the enforced (i.e., necessary to the cycle of mutability) "death" of Titania as nurturing principle.

When Oberon has removed the enchantment, enforcing as he does the interrelation and equality of power between "Dian's bud" and "Cupid's flower," the male and female principles are once more "met." "Now thou and I are in new amity," Oberon declares [IV. i. 87]. We might notice that in Oberon's actions we have observed an enactment of Theseus' description of his own behavior toward Hippolita: "I woo'd thee with my sword / And wonne thy love doing thee injuries" [I. i. 16-17]. On the ritual level of being, too, the warring king and queen become the royal couple; they now address each other as "My queen" and "my lord." Shakespeare underlines the parallel reconciliations—Titania with Oberon, the lovers, Theseus and Hippolita—by immediately following the reconciled Titania and Oberon with the appearance of the earthly king and queen. Theseus uses "faire Queene" in addressing Hippolita just five lines after Oberon's address, "My queene" to Titania. Moreover, the Theseus who enters now is a different Theseus from the love-sick boy of Act I. He is leading the hunt while Hippolita follows him. Here, as he closes the circle he began to draw in Act I, Shakespeare once again uses Theseus and Hippolita to state an open declaration of theme—the discordia concors theme we have just seen operating in the actions of Oberon and Titania.

> Theseus: My love shall heare the musicke of my hounds
> Uncouple in the Westerne valley, let them goe . . .
> We will, faire queene, up to the Mountaine's top,
> And marke the musicall confusion
> Of hounds and eccho in conjunction.
> Hippolita: never did I heare
> Such gallant chiding. For besides the groves,
> The skies, the fountaines, every region neere,
> Seem all one mutual cry. I never heard
> So musicall a discord, such sweet thunder.
>
> [IV. i. 106-18]

The relation, in style and imagery, between this passage and the earlier passage, quoted above, that describes the disharmony in nature resulting from the spirits' quarrel, is striking. Too lengthy a separation of the opposing Oberon-Titania principles caused opposition in nature to fail and all elements to interpenetrate. The reconciliation of these principles through change has restored separation, the opposition in nature that, paradoxically, constitutes its harmony. "Musicall discord" once more evokes nature's "mutual cry."

While Theseus and Hippolita figure the principles of permanence in mutability and discordia concors, and Oberon and Titania ritually enact them, the levels of action dominated by the two pairs of lovers and the mechanicals are concerned with how concord grows from opposition, how the reconciling dream of love or dream of art occurs. In them we see the themes of the play not from the outside, as symbolic pattern or ritual, but from the inside experience. Our attention is focused upon modes of imaginative perception; we are concerned with how the lover or the poet sees. The how of the play is introduced at the very beginning, following immediately upon Theseus' declaration that he has wooed with injury and will now wed "with pomp, with triumph, and with reveling" [I. i. 19]. The entrance of Egeus, Hermia, Lysander and Demetrius at precisely this point begins what we might think of as a running gloss upon Theseus' statement. We are led by the experiences of the lovers to discover how hatred and war become love and marriage. Moreover, we are made to consider not only how reconciliation occurs but what the sacred moment means under the aspect of ordinary or profane time.

The conflict between Egeus and Hermia has two dimensions. It is primarily a conflict between law and love, or more precisely, between two kinds of perception inspired respectively by legalism and love. As Theseus puts it in Act V, there is an opposition in understanding between what "coole reason . . . comprehends" and those "shaping phantasies" that the "seething braines" of lovers and poets project [V. i. 6, 54]. Secondarily, the conflict of Egeus and Hermia relates to the permanence in mutability and discordia concors themes and thereby to the central pattern that dominates those planes of the play we have already considered. Egeus brings into the play an order antithetical to the cyclical lunar order that governs nature, the law. He rejects Lysander because Lysander has operated by a mode contrary to his own. He says that Lysander has prevailed upon the softness of Hermia and "stolen the impression of her fantasie" [I. i. 32], in other words that Lysander, a lover, has evoked Hermia's imaginative perception. What Egeus demands of Hermia is "obedience," and he calls upon "the ancient privilege of Athens" [I. i. 41], the full weight of the law, to enforce his formal, static relationship with his daughter. An exchange between Theseus and Hermia renders the essential conflict of perception upon which the experiences of the lovers in the wood will enlarge.

Hermia: I would my father look'd but with my
          eyes. [the reconciling perception of imagination]
Theseus: Rather your eies must with his judgment
          looke [the differentiating perception of reason]
                                              [I. i. 56-7]

The law rests upon the supposition of an inflexible, unchanging order in human relationships. It is the fiction we create either to hide from ourselves, or to attempt to resist, the pattern of never-ending change that governs our natures. The alternatives to obedience that the "Law of Athens" offers Hermia are illuminating. She can be killed at her father's request (this would, of course, defy the natural order's demand that a new generation supersede the old), or she can be "in a shady cloister mew'd . . . Chanting faint hymes to the cold, fruitless Moone" [I. i. 71, 73]. Egeus (and Theseus in part—the administrator rather than the lover) would invoke the law either to deny the natural order of change, which demands that the life of the new follow upon the death of the old, or it would arrest change to make life barren. It would mew Hermia in virginity and freeze the moon into a single, and therefore a "cold," "fruitless" aspect. The Midsummer night's dream of reconciliation is on this plane of being the triumph of nature over law, and fruitful change over frozen stasis.

The lovers, though they would at first glance appear to be solidly on the side of nature in opposition to law, carry the conflict within themselves. They trust in the permanence of

oaths which, like laws, attempt to arrest change: they yearn for endless union in "true love." However, as Lysander in a lucid moment tells Hermia not all the enemies of true love are social, like "high enthrall'd to low . . . old ingag'd to yong" [I. i. 136, 138] and choice by "merit" rather than passion. Some of true love's enemies are natural.

Lysander: Or if there were a sympathie in choise,
          Warre, death, or sicknesse, did lay siege
            to it;
          Making it momentarie, as a sound:
          Swift as a shadow, short as any dreame.
          Briefe as the lightning in the collied night,
          That (in a spleene) unfolds both heaven
            and earth,
          And ere a man hath power to say, behold,
          The iawes of darkness do devour it up:
          So quicke bright things come to confusion.
                                              [I. i. 141-49]

The sacred moment of reconciliation when we see it enacted at the Oberon-Titania plane of being is one movement in an endless dance of meetings and separations that weave themselves into cosmic harmony. However, under the aspect of profane time, that is, from *within* the experience of poor, foolish mortals, synthesis is perceived as the briefest of moments. After they have experienced the Midsummer night's dream and before they are fully awake the lovers are granted a moment of bi-focal vision wherein they glimpse this dualism.

Demetrius: These things *the matter of the vision*
             [critic's phrase] seeme small and
             indistinguishable. Like farre off
             mountaines turned into clouds.
Hermia: Methinks I see these things with parted
               eye.
             When every things seemes double.
Helena: So me-thinkes
                                              [IV. i. 187-90]

They have been made by their experience in the wood to see that each entity is not only itself but participates by its very nature in a circle of being beyond itself. (pp. 40-4)

The rich comedy of the lovers' situation (the comedy of the human situation itself) is that they can never see the incompatibility of the two systems—law and life, or reason and passion—and consequently they keep attempting *to govern* themselves by the former system at the very moment that they *are governed* by the latter. Lysander, acting under the influence of Cupid's flower, loudly swears that his new choice has been motivated by judgment: "The will of man is by his reason sway'd: / And reason says you are the worthier maide" [II. ii. 115-16]. Hermia, desperately fishing for explanations for Lysander's rejection of her, brings to bear criteria that have relevance only within a judgmental system, like identity ("Am I not Hermia? Are you not Lysander?"), size ("Her height forsooth she hath prevail'd with him"), shape and coloring [II. ii. 273, 293].

What really impels the lovers is, of course, the juice of Cupid's flower. Without attempting an allegory that has been wrestled by champions we can say that the power that moves the lovers is natural. It comes from a flower picked at Midsummer, the height of Nature's fertility. We can say that the wielder of this power is a principle essential in nature: Oberon the male principle. Finally we can say that the effect of this power is to make the lover project his natural passion outward upon the object that he sees. His glance confers beauty upon that object,

> Oberon: Flower of this purple die.
>   Hit with Cupid's archery,
>   Sinke in apple of his eye,
>   When his love he doth espie,
>   Let her shine as gloriously
>   As the venus of the sky.
>   When thou wakst if she be by,
>   Beg for her of remedy.
>
> [III. ii. 102-09]

The lovers undergo a whole complicated process of loving, hating, being loved, being hated that is designed to separate them from their likes and put them into proper conjunction with their natural opposites. Helena's charge against Hermia shows that Hermia has separated herself from girlhood love to be truly prepared for sexual love.

> We Hermia . . .
> As if our hands, our sides, our voices and mindes
> Had been incorporate. So we grew together,
> Like a double cherry seeming parted
> But yet a union in partition. . . .
> And will you rent our ancient love asunder,
> To joyne with men in scorning your poore friend?
>
> [III. ii. 203-16]

But girlhood must be rent asunder in order for a new womanly identity to be born, for the same force is at work here as turned Hippolita from an Amazon into Theseus' bride and Titania from a doting mother into Oberon's wife. Love separates an individual from his former self and brings him to an aspect complementary to that of his sexual opposite.

> Jacke shall have Jill, nought shall goe ill
> The man shall have his Mare againe,
> And all shall be well.
>
> [III. ii. 461-63]

The changes of identity that seem to occur are not true changes of identity since identity implies individualism. Rather they are phases of existence, directed not by will or choice but by the great pattern of harmonious change that governs all nature. The force that Nature uses to bring about the moments of concord required by its scheme is man's own desire and his own imaginative perception—forces within himself that defy the partial truth of law and lead him into a harmony beyond himself.

Theseus asks for explanation of what the lovers have experienced:

> I know you two are Rivall enemies.
> How come this gentle concord in the world,
> That hatred is so farre from jealousie,
> To sleep by hate, and feare no enmity.
>
> [IV. i. 142-45]

However he is unwilling to accept the truth of their reply, even though he has himself been transformed from enemy to lover by the same force that has driven the lovers. He rejects the reconciling dream that the lovers have experienced and clings to the partial truth reason provides: "I never may beleeve / These antique fables, nor these Fairy toyes" [V. i. 2-3]. Theseus' cool reason is inadequate to the task of comprehending visionary truth, for, as Bottom says, how can man's "heart report" the dream. Yet, as Hippolita's comment asserts, whether reason believes or not "something of great constancie / But, howsoever, strange and admirable" [V. i. 26-7] has occurred. The reconciliation of every Jack with his proper Jill bears testimony to the truth.

Reason cannot see the whole truth because reason and the whole system of judgmental thought that it embodies in law is contranatural. It is man's attempt to create a permanence not dependent upon change and *within* the confines of his own experience. Counter to reason, as we have seen in the experience of the lovers, is imaginative perception. Imagination too tries to capture permanence but the permanence at which it aims is not that to which reason aspires. Rather the wrought product of imagination, poetry, attempts to imitate the sacred moment of concord, to effect in imitative gesture the ultimate harmony of nature. . . . The analogy that Shakespeare makes between the imagination of lovers and poets is crucial. For both, the perceptual act wherein the subject invests objective reality with subjective fantasy resolves the duality "which we have to live" [Jean-Paul Sartre] and puts us in touch with a concord beyond our own experience. Moreover, art effects the resolution of conflict and presents us with the resolution "to look at." As we noted earlier, Bottom knows that his Midsummer night's vision is beyond the power of reason, or logical structure, to describe. He must get Peter Quince to write a ballad of it because only the synthesis that poetry effects can imitate the synthesizing movement of ultimate harmony.

The rehearsal in the wood shows us art's synthesis in operation. The actors do not distinguish between Lion and a man in a lion skin roaring, or between Moon and a man carrying a bush and lantern. Bottom is Protean in his transformations; he can be a tiny-voiced Thisby, a roaring lion, a tyrant or a lover with rapid ease because he does not distinguish between his subjective self and the numberless others that his seething imagination projects according to the requirements of whatever play, whatever imitative synthesis, the players would present. Bottom's "identity" changes to fit the needs of the play's design in much the same way as Hermia's, Helena's, Titania's or Hippolita's identities change to fit the requirements of the grand design.

Art also imitates the great discordia concors, resolving in itself the conflict of what in experience appear to be opposites.

> [Theseus:] A tedious breefe Scene of yong Piramus
>   And his love Thisby; very tragicall mirth.
>   Merry and tragicall? Tedious and breefe?
>   That is, hot ice, and wondrous strange
>   snow.
>   How shall we find the concord of this
>   discord?
>
> [V. i. 56-60]

Beyond the obvious self-satire of this passage are serious implications about the nature of art. Tragedy does, after all, give us mirth or pleasure. It does so by fitting what in experience is our greatest dread, the destruction of the self, into the pleasing harmony of a work of art. Art gives us the conflict we are obliged to live resolved into a harmony that we can look at. It reconciles us to our experience by fitting experience to the dimensions of a controlled and harmonious vision.

A Midsummer Night's Dream then is the dream of reconciliation, the concordance of discordant parts. It is a vision of the sacred moment objectified and held up for us to look at and to be consoled by. But it is significant, I think, that Shakespeare forces us to descend from those sacred regions. He ends the play on a note that reinforces his initial position. From the vantage point of poor mortals caught in experience, art, like love, provides only a momentary glimpse of eternal harmony, a glimpse as "brief as lightning in the collied night." Puck gives us a final moment more that carefully cuts off the plane of being where the fairies rejoice from our own mortality. After the royal wedding has been celebrated, he reminds us, another season of human experience begins.

> Now the hungry lions rore,
> And the Wolf beholds the Moone:
> Whilst the heavy ploughman snores,
> All with weary taske fordone. . . .
> Whils't the scritch-owle, scritching loud,
> Puts the wretch that lies in woe,
> In remembrance of a shroud,
> Now it is the time of night,
> That the graves, all gaping wide,
> Every one lets forth his spright,
> In the church-way paths to glide.
> And we Fairies, that do runne,
> By the triple Hecates teame,
> From the presence of the Sunne,
> Following darknesse like a dreame,
> Now are frollicke.
>
> [V. i. 371-87]
> (pp. 46-9)

R. A. Zimbardo, "Regeneration and Reconciliation in 'A Midsummer Night's Dream'," in Shakespeare Studies: An Annual Gathering of Research, Criticism, and Reviews, *Vol. VI, 1970, pp. 35-50.*

CHARLES R. LYONS (essay date 1971)

[*In the following excerpt, Lyons argues that although Shakespeare offers "the image of love's triumph" as a means of overcoming the sense of death present throughout* A Midsummer Night's Dream, *thereby satisfying the play's comic structure, the dramatist also considers this triumph an illusion. The critic finds this intention on Shakespeare's part most evident in the obviously grotesque performance of the tragic story of Pyramus and Thisbe and in the stage audience's unsympathetic reactions to the interlude—both of which, Lyons claims, demonstrate the Athenians' refusal to accept the tragic implications of irrational love and the lovers' inability to see their own vision of love's victory as an illusion. Lyons further maintains that Shakespeare underscores this intent in his play by adding Puck's epilogue at the close of Act V. According to the critic, this passage contributes to the idea that "love's triumph" is only illusory and serves, in addition, as Shakespeare's way of shifting "from the artificial world of the play," where death is suppressed and poses no threat, "to the world of the spectator's experience," where death and decay represent a formidable, unavoidable reality. For further discussions of the importance of illusion, misperception, and ambiguity in* A Midsummer Night's Dream, *see the excerpts by John Russell Brown (1957), C. L. Barber (1959), Bertrand Evans (1960), T. Walter Herbert (1964), Stephen Fender (1968), Sydney R. Homan (1969), and James L. Calderwood (1971). Also, see the essays by G. K. Chesterton (1904), Cumberland Clark (1931), G. Wilson Knight (1932), Jan Kott (1964), Hugh M. Richmond (1971), David Bevington (1975), and Mordecai Marcus (1981) for analyses of the purportedly dark or tragic elements in the play.*]

The assumption that *A Midsummer Night's Dream* was written for a court wedding has become a commonplace in critical commentary. Despite the obvious conjecture implicit in this conventional assumption, internal evidence does suggest the relationship of the play to a wedding celebration, and the relationship of the structure of the play to a court masque defines the suggestion even more clearly. However, *A Midsummer Night's Dream* is a curious epithalamion.

The comedy does not function purely as an exaltation of marital love. Certainly on one level love in the comedy is a regenerative, integrating social force in the archetypal pattern of romantic comedy. The symmetrical pattern of young lovers undergoes the confusions and revelations of disturbed affection in the comic dance in the Athenian wood; the dissension of the supernatural couple, reflected in the tempests of the natural world, is healed; the resolution of the comedy unites the several lovers in the noble wedding celebration, and the fairy couple ultimately blesses the respective marriage beds and promises a perfect progeny from the unions. The complex of worlds—aristocratic, rustic, human and supernatural—is integrated in the final *gamos* ["marriage"] of the traditional comedy. Consistant with this conventional triumph of love, the action dissolves the obstacle which the young lovers face—the objection of Egeus, an objection which is so extreme that he is willing to subject his daughter to the threat of death under Athenian law. In the comic resolution, the threat of death is dismissed in the victory of love. However, this conventional victory is qualified by the existing sense of love in the imaginations of the lovers themselves, an energy which is conceived as a mystery.

In the first scene, the motive of romantic love is introduced in a clear celebration of its creative function. When Theseus defines the alternatives which Hermia faces as a result of her defiance of Egeus, he discusses sexual love as a human fulfillment. According to Athenian law, rebellious Hermia can choose either death or a cloistered, celibate life. However, Theseus significantly conceives of the celibate life as a kind of death. Consider, for example, the quality of the following lines:

> You can endure the livery of a nun—
> For aye to be in shady cloister mewed,
> To live a barren sister all your life,
> Chanting faint hymns to the cold fruitless moon.
> Thrice blessed they that master so their blood,
> To undergo such maiden pilgrimage;
> But earthlier happy is the rose distilled,
> Than that which, withering on the virgin thorn,
> Grows, lives, and dies in single blessedness.
>
> [I. i. 70-8]

As Theseus sees it, the promised grace of a religious vocation is an unsatisfying blessing in comparison with the natural fulfillment of sexual love. He uses the metaphoric equation of the sonnets: the person made fruitful in marriage is "the rose distilled." The ascetic retreat of the cloister, defined by Theseus as sterile and dark, devoted to the "cold fruitless moon", is in opposition to natural increase, the distillation of the rose and the regeneration of marriage. The consequence of the ascetic choice is death; the undistilled rose withers "on the virgin thorn, / Grows, lives, and dies in single blessedness". In the conventional association of the sonnets, the process of life is related to the cycle of seasonal growth. Implicit in Theseus' use of the metaphor is the assumption that only "the rose distilled" can accomodate winter and death in the continuing life of its "substance".

In the first scene, the primary affirmation of love's value is made in the action which provides the dramatic content of the situation. The union of Hermia and Lysander is blocked by parental authority and, submitted to Theseus' jurisdiction, by legal authority as well. John Vyvyan discusses the ethical problem which Hermia confronts, the choice between responsibility to parental and legal authority and the responsibility to love itself:

> Nowadays, we have been so conditioned to accept the rightness of free choice in love that we may not notice that there is an ethical problem. But this is quite a recent outlook. In Shakespeare's time, even sweethearts would have granted that parents and the law had a certain claim upon their duty, and this consideration is part of their dilemma. Shakespeare often presents this situation. It is no more than a dramatic cliche: it is the problem of Juliet and Desdemona. And the answer he gives to it is always the same—the highest duty is to love [see excerpt above, 1961].

The "foundation of the ethic" by which Hermia's choice is made provides the motive for Vyvyan's exploration of its Platonic sources in his study of *Shakespeare and Platonic Beauty*. . . . Yet Vyvyan senses further implications of Hermia's choice in a judgment of the significance of her action:

> . . . I think there is a fair amount of evidence to suggest that he [Shakespeare] makes the general proposition personal and dramatic by a further assumption, also widely current in his time, that love on earth is a recognition between companion souls, who may at last perceive in one another, if they have true lovesight, the beauty of their divine self-nature.

Vyvyan's response to the Platonic rationale of Hermia's action is an exaggeration, but the strength of the ethical action and the significance of this typical action as an important motive in the Shakespearean canon are undeniable. Hermia's choice does affirm the reality of love as a primary value. However, Hermia's apprehension of love is not clear. She senses that she is patient to the force of a mysterious power which has given her strength to deny her father's authority; the same energy has moved Lysander to steal "the impression of her fantasy" [I. i. 32]. When the lovers find themselves alone, naturally they discuss the nature of love; but the metaphors they choose define, not the value, but the deliquescence of love in its swift passage:

> . . . if there were a sympathy in choice,
> War, death, or sickness did lay siege to it,
> Making it momentary as a sound,
> Swift as a shadow, short as any dream,
> Brief as the lightning in the collied night,
> That, in a spleen, unfolds both heaven and earth,
> And ere a man hath power to say 'Behold!'
> The jaws of darkness do devour it up.
> So quick bright things come to confusion.
>
> [I. i. 141-49]

In Lysander's imagination, love is the helpless victim of war, death, and sickness. However, most significantly, love is an instant revelation, contained in the image of lightning which, for a single instant, illumines earth and heaven. But this single image of brightness, of clear revelation, is enclosed in two metaphors of death: "the collied night" and the devouring darkness. It is this concept of love which the troubled lovers,

Hermia and Lysander, carry with them into the confusion of their night in the forest. (pp. 22-5)

The image of death is basic to the comic action of *A Midsummer Night's Dream,* as it is to each of the major romantic comedies: and answering the archetypal pattern, the comic action contains the image of death and its expulsion. It is interesting to note that Mark Van Doren does not find the motive of death apprehensible in this comedy. He writes: "There will be no pretense that reason and love keep company, or that because they do not death lurks at the horizon. There is no death in 'A Midsummer Night's Dream', and the smiling horizon is immeasureably remote." Van Doren might be suggesting that the presence of death provides no threat to life in the comic structure and obvious fiction of Shakespeare's play; however, the image of death is related to the basic concern of deliquescent love. Hermia, controlled by a power whose source is unknown to her, defies her father in her choice of Lysander even though the ultimate consequence of that irrational decision is death according to Athenian law. Theseus' answer is direct; as I have previously discussed, the consequence of her decision is posed to be either actual death or the equivalent death of a cloistered life. Certainly Hermia and Lysander realize acutely that even the most vital love is subject to death,

> Making it momentary as a sound,
> Swift as a shadow, short as any dream,
> Brief as the lightning in the collied night,
> That, in a spleen, unfolds both heaven and earth,
> And ere a man hath power to say 'Behold!'
> The jaws of darkness do devour it up.
>
> [I. i. 143-48]

This image seems to respond to Juliet's cry of love's brief course: "Too like the lightning, which doth cease to be / Ere one can say 'It lightens'" [*Romeo and Juliet,* II. ii. 119-20]. In the early tragedy the rebellious choice of love meets the ultimate consequence of death which, in Hermia's case, is arrested in the comic conception of the action which accomodates death and focuses upon life.

The tragic action, generated by irrational love, is parodied in the rustics' performance of Ovid's tale of Pyramus and Thisbe. Certainly the satire inherent in this burlesque has a complexity of levels . . . . However, in the deliberate structure of illusion and reality, the obvious fiction of the grotesque performance seems to provide a comic answering of the motive of death as a consequence of love which demands consideration. . . . The potential tragic issue of Hermia's defiance is clarified at the beginning of the action: the consequence of her rebellion, like Juliet's, could be death. In the rustics' performance such a death is realized in the play which is so ironically inappropriate to the wedding celebration, *"The most lamentable comedy, and the most cruel death of Pyramus and Thisbe".*

The four Athenian lovers stand in relation to the "*most lamentable comedy*" much in the same manner as Shakespeare's spectators stand in relation to the lovers' comedy of the play itself, which both the spectators and Oberon and Puck watch with delight. Shakespeare's use of this ironic relationship clarifies the comic movement away from death; the very unreality of the play-within-a-play divorces the tragic issue from the image of love's triumph. In his study of the comedies, C. L. Barber suggests the possible source of Bottom's comic resurrection in the folk play: "When the St. George, or Fool, or whoever, starts up, alive again, after the miraculous cure, the reversal must have been played as a moment of comical triumph, an upset, more or less grotesque or absurd, no doubt, but still exhilarating—to come back alive is the ultimate turning of the tables on whatever is an enemy of life.'' The crudity of this fiction justifies the Athenian's unwillingness to accept the validity of the tragic lovers' experience. Or, on the other side of the paradox, the very unreality of the tragic performance does not demonstrate to them the illusory nature of their own experience of love. Helena has defined the experience of love as one in which the lover creates the object of love in an act of the imagination:

> Things base and vile, holding no quantity,
> Love can transpose to form and dignity.
> Love looks not with the eyes, but with the mind;
> And therefore is winged cupid painted blind.
> Nor hath Love's mind of any judgment taste;
> Wings, and no eyes, figure unheedy haste.
>
> [I. i. 232-37]

The commitment to the illusion of love's truth is also seen in Theseus' anatomy of fancy in which the process of poetic creation is the transformation of the "forms of things unknown" [V. i. 15]. In his benevolent wit, Theseus speaks of the spectator of the play as an agent in the creation of poetic illusion: "The best in this kind are but shadows, and the worst are no worst if imagination amend them. . . . If we imagine no worse of them than they of themselves, they may pass for excellent men" [V. i. 211-16]. The obvious fiction of the Pyramus and Thisbe play comes from the literal simplicity with which it is performed. In the play itself, the image of the moon, transforming the vision of the world in "liquid pearl", pervades the comedy; in the staging of the "most lamentable comedy", a man with a lantern stands as a graphic representation of the moon, uncomplicated with the kind of poetic ambiguity involved in the lovers' dance in the forest. Consequently, despite Helena's defination of the creative process of love, the young Athenians do not recognize that the reality of their experience in love, like the reality of the grotesque little play, is determined by the imagination. Yet one aspect of the comic paradox of *A Midsummer Night's Dream* exists in the fact that both fictions, the primitive and the sophisticated, involve the shaping of illusory forms upon external reality.

In *A Midsummer Night's Dream*, the poet projects an image of love as a moment of brightness, a sudden illumination of earth and heaven. Love remains "the lightning in the collied night", and the universe revealed in that instant revelation may be the evanescent creation of the imaginative conciousness of the lover himself. In the relationship of illusion and reality, moreover, it is possible to see the very triumph of love itself as an aspect of the illusion, an obvious fiction. (pp. 35-8)

The conventional triumph of love at the conclusion of *A Midsummer Night's Dream*, the victory of bright love over dark confusion, is subject to the effect of the recurrent images of death. Immediately before the young lovers are discovered in the forest comes the poetic "digression" of Theseus' and Hippolyta's discussion of the sound of the hunt. The hunt is the traditional image of death; as [Harold C.] Goddard states, "The hounds are symbols of the hunt, and so of death. But their voices are transmuted by distance, in the ear of the listener, to symbols of harmony and life" [see excerpt above, 1951]. The sound of the dogs, signalling death, is resolved into an integrated and lovely song:

> Never did I hear
> Such gallant chiding; for, besides the groves,

> The skies, the fountains, every region near
> Seem'd all one mutual cry. I never heard
> So musical a discord, such sweet thunder.
>
> [IV. i. 114-18]

The motive of death present in the rustics' performance of Ovid's love story has been discussed above; however, it is important to realize that this image, so strongly related to the action of the comedy, occurs at the wedding celebration. Again the motive of mortality is present and then transposed—here in the basic unreality of the imitation and, more significantly, in Bottom's crude resurrection. The third reminder of the presence of death is made by Puck immediately after Theseus calls for a fortnight of jollity and revels to speed "The heavy gait of night" [V. i. 368]. Puck invokes images of night which associate the darkness not with love but with death:

> Now the hungry lion roars,
>   And the wolf behowls the moon, . . .
> Now the wasted brands do glow,
>   Whilst the screech owl, screeching loud,
> Puts the wretch that lies in woe
>   In remembrance of a shroud.
> Now it is the time of night
>   That the graves, all gaping wide,
> Every one lets forth his sprite,
>   In the churchway paths to glide.
>
> [V. i. 371-82]

Again, however, the reality of the presence of death is transfigured as Oberon blesses the progeny of the three marriages, promising a perfect issue.

In his marginal notations, Coleridge left the comment that Shakespeare conceived of the whole play of *A Midsummer Night's Dream* as a dream [see excerpt above, 1834]. Shakespeare has played with reality and illusion throughout the comedy, and in this final speech he extends the image of the illusive dream to the entire play:

> If we shadows have offended
> Think but this, and all is mended,
> That you have but slumbered here
> While these visions did appear
> And this weak and idle theme,
> No more yielding than a dream,
> Gentles, do not reprehend.
>
> [V. i. 423-29]

In his analogy between the performance of the play and a dream, Puck plays upon Theseus' equation of the poet, madman, and lover [V. i. 2-22]. The play itself, he reminds the spectators, is a phantasm which is to be apprehended not comprehended. In this romantic comedy, the poet and the spectator have enjoyed the illusion of love's triumph over death. The weakness of love in the face of death is defined early in the play in the image of love as a moment of brightness, a brief illumination of earth and heaven. Love is "the lightning in the collied night"; and the universe revealed in that instant revelation may be the creation of the imaginative conciousness of the lover himself. But the action of the comedy has suspended the threat of death, and the poetry of the play has introduced the motive of death and transposed it. Now the deliberate framing of this epilogue establishes the sense that the infinite happiness of this romantic world is an illusion divorced from the real world into which the spectator will soon return.

It is obvious that in *A Midsummer Night's Dream* Shakespeare uses the image of love's triumph for its full comic value: the illusion of an infinite happiness which arrests the natural disintegration of time and death. But the integrity of his vision did not allow him to resolve the play in illusion, and Puck, speaking in the double voice of Robin Goodfellow and actor, accomplishes the transition from an artificial world of the play to the world of the spectator's experience.

Puck's address to the audience is a deliberate transition from the romantic world of comedy in which love triumphed over death to the actual world of the spectator's experience in which death is still a vital reality. The concious artifice of this speech is consistant with the scheme of illusion and reality throughout the comedy. In *A Midsummer Night's Dream*, the movement from the artificial world to the real world of the spectator is more obvious than the comic epilogues to *As You Like It* and *Twelfth Night*, but this less subtle modulation anticipates the others. Within the conventions of romantic comedy, these later plays are closer to the actual world. With this play they share an examination of the nature of human love, but the range of experience which they study is wider and their analysis is more intense. In the fictive world of *A Midsummer Night's Dream*, the lovers themselves are unable to embody the depth and complexity of love, and the supernaturals are used as manifestations of certain irrational, cruel, kind and forgiving aspects of the relationship between men and women. In the more romantic comedies, wisdom and folly, shrewdness and wonder meet in the lovers themselves in a natural ambiguity. These complexities inform *A Midsummer Night's Dream*, but they resound with greater fullness in the poet's later plays. (pp. 40-3)

> Charles R. Lyons, "'A Midsummer Night's Dream': The Paradox of Love's Triumph," in his Shakespeare and the Ambiguity of Love's Triumph, *Mouton, 1971, pp. 21-43.*

JAMES L. CALDERWOOD   (essay date 1971)

[Calderwood has examined what he calls Shakespeare's "metadrama" in two studies, Shakespearean Metadrama *(1971) and* Metadrama in Shakespeare's Henriad *(1979). In the introduction to his earlier book, Calderwood claims that Shakespeare's plays are not only concerned with various moral, social, and political themes, but are also self-reflexively concerned with dramatic art itself—"its materials, its media of language and theater, its generic forms and conversations, its relationship to truth and the social order." In the following excerpt, he contends that the nature of dramatic illusion is a central concern of* A Midsummer Night's Dream. *Calderwood regards Oberon as the "playwright within the play" who creates fictional enmities between the young lovers and then resolves them into harmonious relations, which are then officially endorsed by Theseus. The critic maintains that as part of his representation of the essential aspects of dramatic art, Shakespeare intentionally shifts and blurs "the borders between dream, drama, and waking reality" to indicate the possibility that each realm can overlap the other, thereby altering our perception of each. Indeed, Calderwood argues, the exchange of roles and identities by the young lovers in the forest reflects the heart of the dramatic process, for in an actual theater, as in Shakespeare's play, actors must transform themselves into new personae; similarly, he argues that the play performed by the rude mechanicals fails because these would-be actors are unable to submerge their identities in their assumed theatrical roles. Other critics who regard* A Midsummer Night's Dream *as a commentary on the creative process itself, or on the nature of Shakespeare's craft as a dramatist, include C. L. Barber (1959), J. Dennis Huston (1981), and David Marshall (1982), although aspects of*

this concern can be traced as far back as William Maginn (1837) and others in the nineteenth century. In addition, such commentators as Stephen Fender (1968), Sydney R. Homan (1969), and Charles R. Lyons (1971) have discussed the role of illusion in the play.]

If Oberon and Theseus are both figures of order, they go about their work in different ways, Oberon specializing in the arts of illusion as befits an illusion and Theseus devoting himself to social rituals as befits a prince. Let me work toward their differences by way of their resemblances, especially as regards the notion of order between the sexes, about which they are both much concerned and one of them sorely vexed.

In affairs of love Theseus has a normative role in the play; his marriage to Hippolyta, the preparations for which structurally bracket the trials of the young lovers, operates as the social ideal against which other relationships are measured. The comic tone of the play and its stress on social rituals naturally preclude a Theseus of full heroic stature. The slayer of Sciron, the Crommyonian sow, and the Cretan minotaur must give way to the exemplar of civil order, justice, and moderation. There is, however, an echo of a less temperate past in Oberon's questioning reminder to Titania:

> Didst thou not lead [Theseus] through the glimmering
>   night
> From Perigenia, whom he ravished?
> And make him with fair Ægle break his faith,
> With Ariadne and Antiopa?
>
> [II. i. 77-80]

Theseus has seen his share of the "glimmering light" and revealed an inconstancy of the sort we are to witness in Demetrius and Lysander. But if his infidelities forecast theirs, his courtship of Hippolyta also forecasts the direction their love will take, from apparent hatred and warfare to devotion and peace:

> Hippolyta, I wooed thee with my sword
> And won thy love doing thee injuries.
>
> [I. i. 16-17]

By reminding us of this peculiar courtship and of Hippolyta's past Shakespeare calls on the familiar Renaissance view of Theseus as the man who righted an imbalance in nature, compelling the Amazonian queen to be true to her sex by becoming subordinate to his, thereby reestablishing the proper hierarchical relationship between man and woman.

This theme reappears of course in fairyland where we find Titania rebelling against Oberon's authority. "Am not I thy lord?" he plaintively protests [II. i. 63]; but although she acknowledges herself his lady, still

> she perforce withholds the loved boy,
> Crowns him with flowers and makes him all her joy.
> And now they never meet in grove or green,
> By fountain clear or spangled starlight sheen
> But they do square.
>
> [II. i. 26-30]

The point seems to be that Titania is violating natural order both by making the changeling child "all her joy" at the expense of Oberon and by refusing to let the boy pass from a feminine into a masculine world where he belongs if natural growth is to have its way. Thus in demonstrating his power over Titania by causing her to dote on Bottom and surrender the boy to him, Oberon is doing essentially what Theseus did when he conquered Hippolyta.

Oberon exercises a similar influence on the lovers. In the forest the rejected but dogged Helena tells Demetrius

> Your wrongs do set a scandal on my sex.
> We cannot fight for love, as men may do.
> We should be wooed and were not made to woo.
> [II. i. 240-42]

Observing this inversion of sexual roles, Oberon sets about restoring order:

> Ere he do leave this grove
> Thou shalt fly him and he shall seek thy love.
> [II. i. 245-46]

And so it falls out, though not without "all this derision" [III. ii. 370] caused by Puck's mistaking Lysander for Demetrius—derision involving the breakdown and readjustment of sexual relations pointed out by C. L. Barber. (p. 125)

Under the direction of Oberon then, Titania is brought properly to heel and the lovers are paired off in a manner that proves acceptable to Theseus. The movement is from asymmetry to symmetry, from division to unity, from the forest fantastic to the rationally real. But just how is the transition made? What makes Theseus, the Theseus who in the opening act is absolute for law, blandly dismiss Egeus's demands in the fourth act ("I beg the law, the law, upon his head" [IV. i. 155]) and send Hermia off to the temple to be married instead of to a nunnery to contemplate the cold chaste moon? The imaginative transformations that Oberon has wrought in the forest Theseus confirms in the palace and temple, which would seem to suggest a final union between imagination and reason. But Theseus places his own rational construction on what it is he confirms. There is no room in that construction for dream or drama, let alone fairy kings and their devious doings, and yet it is by the route of dream, drama, and fairy that the lovers make their way into Theseus's good graces and Athen's social order. (pp. 126-27)

Under the influence of ubiquitous moonlight the borders between dream, drama, and waking reality deliquesce and all three circulate together in strange solution. Seeking to translate himself from weaver into Pyramus during the rehearsal of the workmen's play, Bottom finds himself transported right on through the illusions of drama into a fairyland reality which, when he makes his return journey to the cold hillside of perturbed reason, dissolves into dream. The lovers emerge from the nightmare experience of the forest glancing apprehensively back "with parted eye/When everything seems double" [V. i. 189-90], still uncertain whether they wake or sleep. And in the epilogue Puck invites the audience to take the title of the play in full literalness and translate the dramatic experience into mere dream. Beneath the neatly differentiated Apollonian images of literary form in the theater—the rational sharpness of outline that separates not only bears from bushes in Theseus's well-ordered world [V. i. 22] but art's fantasies from life's facts as well-runs the unindividuated flow of Dionysian dream.

This indistinctness of form and outline lends the lovers' experiences in the forest a mythic aspect. For instance, Ernst Cassirer says of the mythopoeic primitive mind: "Its view of life is a synthetic, not an analytic one [as in scientific thought]. Life is not divided into classes and subclasses. It is felt as an unbroken continuous whole which does not admit of any clean-cut and trenchant distinctions. . . . Nothing has a definite, invariable, static shape. By a sudden metamorphosis everything

may be turned into everything. If there is any characteristic and outstanding feature of the mythical world, any law by which it is governed—it is this law of metamorphosis." An excellent description of the fairy-forest world.

This principle of metamorphosis operates also in the dream world, and in this midsummer night's dream it goes by the name "translation." What in the dream drama is metamorphosis or translation is in poetry "metaphor," by which in Cassirer's phrase "everything may be turned into everything" or, as Northrop Frye puts it, "everything is potentially identical with everything else." The "scientific" mind of Theseus would separate asses from Bottoms and at most perhaps apply a simile. "Bottom is like an ass," whereas the poetic imagination not only employs metaphors but may even claim an identity between tenor and vehicle by setting on Bottom's shoulders the genuine apple-munching ear-twitching article. Not just in particulars like this but in its general breakdown of the barriers between dream, art, myth, historical periods, and inner and outer nature (the forest within and without) Shakespeare's play repeatedly asserts the imaginative unity of all disparates that Cassirer associates with the myth-minded.

My present concern, however, is not myth but metadrama, which specializes in its own forms of dissolution and transformation. In the epilogue, for instance, Puck humorously tells the audience that if they like they can reverse the creative movement from dream to art by imagining that their theatrical experience of *A Midsummer Night's Dream* has been merely a midsummer night's dream. Here is the "uncreating word" of Pope's goddess of Dulness wielded with a vengeance. However, Puck's suggestion merely confirms an interchangeability of dream and drama implied elsewhere in the play. For instance, though in retrospect the lovers' forest experience seems to them a nightmarish dream, while it is in process it bears the likeness of drama—so much so that we may claim to have in a sense two plays within the play. One is the actual play in which Bottom and crew act the role of noble lovers, and of a few stage properties as well; the other is a metaphoric play in which the young lovers figure as unwitting actors in a drama produced, directed, and acted in by Oberon and Puck. Regarding Oberon as a kind of interior dramatist is in keeping with Theseus's patronizing remark about the workmen actors, "The best in this kind are but shadows" [V. i. 211], since Oberon according to Puck is "king of shadows" [III. i. 347]—a royal role that can be assigned also to the playwright Shakespeare, whose commands to his subjects take the form of the script that rules his actors. Oberon and Puck are analogous not only to playwright and players but to the audience as well. Thus as Lysander and Helena approach, Puck asks Oberon "Shall we their fond pageant see?" [III. ii. 114], which echoes the statement Puck made on encountering Bottom's company in rehearsal:

> What, a play toward? I'll be an auditor—
> An actor too perhaps if I see cause.
> [III. i. 79-80]

Consummate actor that he is, he sees cause to take a part in both Bottom's play and the lovers' drama. Bottom, who is unalterably Bottom, wants to act all the parts in his play. Puck, who is mercurially Puck and therefore anything he wishes—he can neigh "in likeness of a filly foal," take the "very likeness of a roasted crab," or assume the shape of a "three-foot stool" [II. i. 46,48,52]—does not play all the parts in the lovers' drama, only those of Lysander and Demetrius as Oberon bids him:

> Like to Lysander sometime frame thy tongue,
> Then stir Demetrius up with bitter wrong;
> And sometime rail thou like Demetrius.
>
> [III. ii. 360-62]

If we accept these various cues and regard the story of the night as the "drama" of the night, then the breakdown of sexual relationships noted earlier becomes part of a general dissolving of past identities analogous to the actor's submerging of personal identity in a fictional role (especially when it is a boy actor adopting a feminine role). "Am not I Hermia? Are not you Lysander?" [III. ii. 273]. . . . Helena had earlier wished to give up everything if only she could be "translated" into Hermia [I. i. 191]; and in the forest that is precisely what happens, both men now loving her with the same devotion they had once accorded Hermia, though she believes them to be "counterfeiting" (as indeed they are in one sense). Transfers of roles and identities are general: Hermia becomes translated into Helena and learns how it feels to be scorned; Lysander plays the Demetrius who once loved Helena; and Demetrius ultimately plays his former self by loving Helena again and permanently. From this standpoint the lovers' experience in the forest is more genuinely dramatic than the carefully re-hearsed and formally presented *Pyramus and Thisbe* since the identities of the lovers are indeed lost in their imposed roles whereas the great failure of *Pyramus and Thisbe* is its actors' inability to act, to lose their identities even imaginatively in fictional roles. By remaining obtrusively present and "untranslated" in *Pyramus and Thisbe*, reality destroys the dramatic fiction—the actors devour the characters as it were—whereas the fiction of the forest drama swallows up and digests reality.

What the fiction of the forest digests reality into is comedy, though not quite the "Lamentable Comedy" that that proto-Polonius [*Hamlet*] and theorist of genre Quince labels his play. The comic movement of this forest play is through the disintegration of its fictional society in "all this derision" to a reformation of it in a happy ending as everyone is united in sleep and love under the same greenwood tree—a social union as paradoxically harmonious as the cries of the Spartan hounds Hippolyta refers to just before the sleeping lovers are found: "I never heard/So musical a discord, such sweet thunder" [IV. i. 117-18]. (pp. 128-32)

If Oberon as playwright within the play has created a drama that is merely illusion and delusion, then perhaps it too deserves the damnation with faint praise bestowed by Theseus on the workmen's play: "This palpable-gross play hath well beguiled/The heavy gait of night" [V. i. 367-68]. For indeed, palpable-gross though it is, the workmen's play is insubstantial as any dream, serving only as idle entertainment to ease the hours before its audience returns to (if it ever really left) untheatrical life and its fictions melt into thin air. And Shakespeare's fictions, we are bound to wonder—do they too melt into thin air at the final curtain? So a good many critics would seem to feel, and so Shakespeare would seem to suggest by having Puck offer the audience the option of thinking

> That you have but slumbered here
> While these visions did appear.
> And this weak and idle theme,
> No more yielding but a dream.
>
> [V. i. 425-28]

As a disavowal of the relevance of art to life and a surrender of all claims to dramatic value, this seems almost criminally modest—rather like the utter frailty Shakespeare ascribes to beauty in Sonnet 65:

> How with this rage [of destroying Time] shall
>   beauty hold a plea,
> Whose action is no stronger than a flower?

Aside from the fact that the action of flowers is very strong indeed in *A Midsummer Night's Dream*, we would want to note that through Puck Shakespeare is inviting his audience to do precisely what the lovers did at the end of their forest drama—allow drama to dwindle into dream and hence to deny any meaningful connection between the story of the night and actual life in Athens. This parallel, however, puts a very different light on Shakespeare's modesty since the forest drama not only absorbs reality by transforming the prior identities of the lovers but, more important, carries over into reality in much the same way that Shakespeare's fairy actors pass with their blessings out of Theseus's palace and into each several chamber of the Elizabethan manor house. For the lovers all charms apparently fly at the touch of cold philosophy personified in Theseus. But only apparently. They may admit afterwards that what they experienced while acting in Oberon's and Puck's "play," though vivid and seeming real, was actually no more yielding than a dream ("And by the way let us recount our dreams," [IV. i. 199]); but nonetheless the realignments of love wrought by the dream-drama of the night no more disappear at dawn than, as Oberon assures us, the fairies do [III. ii. 388ff.]. From the standpoint of cool reason and known fact Theseus says "I know you two are rival enemies" [IV. i. 142]; but for reasons beyond reason Demetrius and Lysander no longer hate one another, and by some strange power, Demetrius says,

> my love to Hermia
> Melted as is the snow, seems to me now
> As the remembrance of an idle gaud
> Which in my childhood I did dote upon.
>
> [IV. i. 165-68]

The dramatic illusions of the forest, having created fictional enmities and then dissolved them into general concord, have dissolved the real enmities of the past as well. And in the waking world, through the agency of Theseus's royal command, they even dissolve the hard stuff of law and overbear the will of Egeus, thus enabling the marriage of true minds to be ratified in the temple. In view of the results of the forest drama then, the modesty of Shakespeare's epilogue is transformed by humorous irony into something along these lines: "If it makes you feel more reasonable you can adopt Theseus's attitude and regard the play as no more significant than a dream—at best an amusing way to pass the time. But like the lovers who also converted their experience into dream—an experience in many ways analogous to drama—whether you realize it or not you have experienced something here of enduring value and with a reality of its own." (pp. 133-34)

James L. Calderwood, "'A Midsummer Night's Dream': Art's Illusory Sacrifice," in his Shakespearean Metadrama: The Argument of the Play in "Titus Andronicus," "Love's Labour's Lost," "Romeo and Juliet," "A Midsummer Night's Dream," and "Richard II," *University of Minnesota Press, Minneapolis, 1971, pp. 120-48.*

HUGH M. RICHMOND (essay date 1971)

[In an unexcerpted portion of his Shakespeare's Sexual Comedy: A Mirror for Lovers *(1971), Richmond contends that Shakespeare regarded* A Midsummer Night's Dream *as an opportunity to further instruct his audience on the dangers that may result from the kind of naive sexuality personified in the character of Romeo, whose intense sexual passion leads him to be "largely responsible for six deaths." In the excerpt below, Richmond argues that all the main characters in* A Midsummer Night's Dream, *with the exception of Bottom, display aversion to love that is easily accessible and instead pursue a love that is denied them. He notes that the young lovers are particularly prone to a sadomasochistic form of passion, foolishly seeming to delight in—and even seeking out—obstacles and conflicts which will bar the fulfillment of their love. Richmond attributes this desire to the characters' naiveté and their belief that these obstacles are necessary to heighten the excitement of sexual love. J. Dennis Huston (1981) shares Richmond's view that the lovers search out their own self-destruction and Mordecai Marcus (1981) discerns in the play a sub-theme that parodies the idea that love must run the risk of death to reach its fullest ardor. Also, see the excerpts by G. K. Chesterton (1904), G. Wilson Knight (1932), Jan Kott (1964), Charles R. Lyons (1971), David Bevington (1975), David Ormerod (1978), and Mordecai Marcus (1981) for further examination of the violent, erotic, and potentially tragic elements in* A Midsummer Night's Dream. *As noted above, Richmond views Bottom as the only major figure in the play who does not require tension and tragedy in his life; instead, he maintains that Bottom reacts to the various circumstances in which he finds himself with the "flexibility and responsiveness" that are "the marks of true sophistication." Other commentators who have remarked on Bottom's poise and self-possession include William Maginn (1837), E. K. Chambers (1905), and John Palmer (1944). Also, for further general discussions of the character of Bottom, see the excerpts by Charles Cowden Clarke (1863), G. K. Chesterton (1904), H. B. Charlton (1933), and Elizabeth Sewell (1960).]*

Though his basic flaw is egotism rather than passion, Bottom's transformation into an ass when he becomes Titania's beloved is . . . a proper figure for Shakespeare's vision of naive sexuality. Shakespeare shows us how undisciplined passion can turn humans into beasts whose sexual reflexes are totally irrational and arbitrary. With this kind of perversity in mind, he makes Helena, a willing victim, exclaim to her alienated lover:

> I am your spaniel; and, Demetrius,
> The more you beat me, I will fawn on you:
> Use me but as your spaniel, spurn me, strike me,
> Neglect me, lose me; only give me leave,
> Unworthy as I am, to follow you.
>
> [II. i. 203-07]

Inevitably this servility fails to trigger the acquisitive sexual instinct of the crudely predatory male; but in passing Helena by, Demetrius only confirms her fixation. Indeed, he pushes it beyond neurosis into suicidal extravagance:

> I'll follow thee and make a heaven of hell,
> To die upon the hand I love so well.
>
> [II. i. 242-43]

The grotesque passion of Titania, the fairy queen, for the assified Bottom is scarcely more perverse.

No significant character in the play is wholly exempt from this sadomasochistic type of sexuality—unless indeed it be Bottom, who has the comparative good fortune to be chiefly devoted to himself: soothed by his own fantasies of mastery he thus articulates his desires without much dependence on others' feelings and largely escapes the emotional entanglements which they get into. By contrast, even Theseus must be recognized as a predatory lover. He shows a certain barbarism when he marries the captive queen of the Amazons, whom he has seized by brute force on the field of battle:

> Hippolyta, I woo'd thee with my sword,
> And won thy love, doing thee injuries.
>
> [I. i. 16-17]

The battle of the sexes can go no further. And the supernatural but primitive world of the fairies displays similar examples of this paradoxical reflex: Oberon quarrels with Titania because he wants her favored boy attendant (whom she in turn stole from the human world), and he only becomes anxious to be reconciled to her when he observes her fatuously in love with another male, whose principal claim to her attention must seem his extravagant inappropriateness as a lover (unless we credit the challenge in the emotional inaccessibility of Bottom's supreme egotism).

A detailed analysis of most of these unrefined passionate relationships in the play seems to suggest an almost mathematical basis for the sexual reflex. Not only are negative emotional values automatically bracketed with positive ones, but any factor reversing the emotional value of a single term in a relationship necessarily also exactly reverses the values of any dependent terms. Lysander thus finds the enforced inaccessibility of Hermia irresistible at the start of the play, while Demetrius is revolted by the surrender of Helena to his suit and inflamed to pathological excitement by Hermia's devotion to Lysander. However, scarcely has Lysander succeeded in making Hermia fully available to himself by their nocturnal flight to the forest than he proves susceptible to the inaccessible attractions of Helena, who has servilely devoted herself to a rival male and thus asserted her total indifference to Lysander. And as soon as Lysander attempts to secure Helena, she proves once more irresistible to Demetrius, who discovers the sign of valid prey in her vigorous resistance to Lysander, which she at once provocatively extends to Demetrius. Of course, the juice of the magical flower which supposedly "produces" these effects is the merest figure for the mathematics of naive sexuality, and Puck's arbitrary administration of it illustrates the accidental quality of the intrusion of passion into human relationships. That the flower is only a dramatic convenience appears in Helena's total revulsion from both her suitors once they avow their new devotion [III. ii. 145ff.]. We can see that her rejection of what she has previously so much desired is precipitated only by the change in others' views, not by magical intervention. Thus the play's fairy world is less an objective force in the plot than a satirical reflection of the fanciful sources of spontaneous human instincts and intuitions. It serves chiefly to make the arbitrariness of human motives more picturesquely explicit, though it can also heighten their best aspects to a healthy ritual magic which reinforces the creative cyclic rhythms submerged in men's nature (compare the disorder described by Titania at [II. i. 81ff.], resulting from her quarrel with her husband Oberon, and the play's concluding incantations after marriage has again made sex socially viable).

The human beings initially fail almost entirely to recognize these sublimal elements of experience. Ironically, only Bottom sees the fairies (perhaps as a poet's testimony to the positive powers of supreme egotism). Like *The Comedy of Errors*, the play opens with a lawcourt scene, but one in which legal disciplines confront emotions even more directly than in the earlier play. Initially a sober attempt is made to regulate love by order of the tribunal—the implication of the participants' attempt being that emotion should be subject to reason and systematic analysis. There is an elusive irony in the fact that even the immature lovers victimized by the verdict assume their passion is governed by rational choice. But Lysander nowhere argues more forcefully for this view of passion than after having switched his devotion from Hermia, to secure whom he had faced the magistrate earlier:

> Not Hermia but Helena I love:
> Who will not change a raven for a dove?
> The will of man is by his reason sway'd;
> And reason says you are the worthier maid.
> Things growing are not ripe until their season:
> So I, being young, till now ripe not to reason;
> And touching now the point of human skill,
> Reason becomes the marshall to my will.
>
> [II. ii. 113-20]

The ratiocinative skill he shows is comparable to Biron's [in *Love's Labour's Lost*], but it is clearly not exploited with Biron's skepticism, which had prevented him from mistaking plausibilities for facts. Helena has already firmly established for us the irrelevance of objective endowments to a lover's evaluation when she argues that Demetrius switched his affections from her to Hermia with as little justification as Lysander's later reversal of this choice:

> Through Athens I am thought as fair as she.
> But what of that? Demetrius thinks not so;
> He will not know what all but he do know:
> And as he errs, doting on Hermia's eyes,
> So I, admiring of his qualities:
> Things base and vile, holding no quantity,
> Love can transpose to form and dignity:
> Love looks not with the eyes, but with the mind.
>
> [I. i. 227-34]

There is amusing irony in her discovery that she is no happier when she is the recipient of the approval whose lack had so distressed her. Like Katharina's [in *The Taming of the Shrew*], Helena's wished-for courtship proves a torture, which she feels compelled to blame on pure malice:

> Have you not set Lysander, as in scorn,
> To follow me and praise my eyes and face?
> And made your other love, Demetrius,
> Who even now did spurn me with his foot,
> To call me goddess, nymph, divine and rare,
> Precious, celestial?
>
> [III. ii. 222-27]

It has usually been assumed that all these emotional oscillations are the forced effects in which broad farce usually takes refuge—to be rationalized at best by Theseus in his too familiar and sweeping assertion that

> Lovers and madmen have such seething brains,
> Such shaping fantasies, that apprehend
> More than cool reason ever comprehends.
> The lunatic, the lover and the poet
> Are of imagination all compact:
> One sees more devils than vast hell can hold,
> That is, the madman: the lover, all as frantic,
> Sees Helen's beauty in a brow of Egypt.
>
> [V. i. 4-11]

But we should recognize that Theseus is only one persona among the many vividly animated by the poet in his play. The ruler himself has illustrated the erratic quality which he censures in the other lovers, being attracted to the woman who

tried to kill him in armed combat. Indeed, we must regard with some skepticism the judgment of a warrior who not only marries his foe but also trains his hunting dogs so that they are unfit for tracking: "slow in pursuit, but match'd in mouth like bells" [IV. i. 123]. Hippolyta opposes his easy judgment that love is wholly whimsical, observing that if analyzed closely the lover's gyrations prove coherent, indeed systematic, in their illustration of "something of great constancy" [V. i. 26]—as I have already hinted in my mathematical analysis.

In this fashion Shakespeare's "imagination bodies forth / The forms of things unknown" [V. i. 14-15]. His play as a whole illuminates love's motives better than the supercilious traditional verdict of Theseus on the arbitrariness of lovers. We have already seen that there is a constant in each of the passionate relationships in the play: they all show a resistance to what is available and a desire for what is not. This factor in their choices is unconsciously defined by two of the lovers themselves:

> The course of true love never did run smooth;
> But, either it was different in blood, . . .
> Or, if there were a sympathy in choice,
> War, death, or sickness did lay siege to it,
> Making it momentany as a sound,
> Swift as a shadow, short as any dream;
> Brief as the lightning in the collied night, . . .
> If then true lovers have been ever cross'd,
> It stands as an edict in destiny.
>
> [I. i. 134-35, 141-45, 150-51]

Obviously phrases like "short as any dream" bear on fluctuations of attitude in the play itself, and the total consistency with which obstacles intrude into all the relationships suggests that what is actually involved is not simply the "opposition of the stars" but also the lovers' delight in an emotion heightened by conflict. Passion may indeed be crossed, but the uniformity with which this occurs proves that it is not by chance: the lovers positively solicit difficulty, tension, and separation. Far from resisting the "edicts of destiny," a lover will foster their evil effects with masochistic satisfaction.

Denis de Rougemont has urged the accuracy of such a view of the European amatory tradition in *Love in the Western World;* there he develops his ideas, not in relation to Shakespeare, but by showing the archetypal nature of the endless obstacles which Tristan invents to prevent the serene fulfillment of his passion for Iseult. De Rougemont sees the fear of sustained and disillusioning communion with one's beloved as the motive for the lovers' cult of complications and separation. Divided from the beloved, one is free to indulge in the full sweep of egotistical emotional excitement, uninhibited by the distracting actuality of the beloved's presence. Cressida corroborates this interpretation in her reactions to the counsel of Pandarus after her separation from Troilus:

> Why tell you me of moderation?
> The grief is fine, full, perfect, that I taste.
>
> [*Troilus and Cressida*, IV. iv. 2-3]

If we grant the possibility of such extravagant satisfactions, we see at once that they provide a rationale for the recurring pattern in Shakespeare's portrayal of merely passionate affairs. In his tragedies the lovers' delight in sentimental absolutism proves fatal when untempered by skeptical good sense and the stoic endurance that marks true love. In the comedies the paradoxes of absolutism legitimize the comic reversals and misunderstandings that we have already sampled. The results may be as intense as some of the exchanges between Katharina and Petruchio [in *The Taming of the Shrew*]; or again they may be merely farcical, as in the "tragical mirth" of *Pyramus and Thisbe* which concludes *A Midsummer Night's Dream*. This grotesque interlude is a deft caricature of all the elements that go to make up the character of the naively passionate love affairs in the play.... Like Romeo and Juliet, Pyramus finds passionate love diminishes his awareness to the point where he can scarcely tell day from night: "Sweet Moon, I thank thee for thy sunny beams" [V. i. 272]. Surely Romeo is nearer to Pyramus in such confusions than to the premeditated misjudgments of Petruchio on the same topic. Indeed, the ludicrous behavior of Bottom in the part of Pyramus echoes the antics which the role of even a pretended lover readily imposes on the most opionated and self-sufficient personality.

In his own character Bottom is fully master of the arts of illusion: in soliciting the various roles in the play (I. ii), his intelligence proves as uncompromised by illusion as that of Theseus often seems. But once he is fully committed to playing the part of Thisbe's sentimental lover, Bottom loses almost all the bluff good fellowship which allowed him to hobnob so merrily with a queen and her fairies. He garbles all his sentiments hopelessly, and in his stilted conduct he resembles Romeo's "fishified" behavior over Rosaline, and sometimes over Juliet. Only the greater detachment of the theater audience from the farce's plot allows them to find Bottom-Pyramus ludicrous when he mistakenly thinks his beloved dead and kills himself. Theseus sees little enough difference between the interlude and any famous tragedy: "The best in this kind are but shadows; and the worst are no worse if imagination amend them" [V. i. 211-12]. Later the commentary of Theseus raises even this farcical love affair closer to the level of tragic poetry when he observes of the dead Pyramus that Thisbe "will find him by starlight. Here she comes; and her passion ends the play" [V. i. 314-15]. Closer still to the tragedy is the outcome of the misunderstandings: "the wall is down that parted their fathers" [V. i. 351-52]. The same climactic resolution of divisions occurs between the Montagues and Capulets after the suicides of their children.

That comical wall itself deserves a little more comment than its quaint manifestation suggests. It is an archetypal image for the obstacle which passion unconsciously solicits as a prerequisite for full ardor. Not only does it provide a concrete analogue to the legal and emotional barriers that create the intensity of all the lovers in the play; it is also a wry distortion of the famous balcony which divides Romeo from his beloved. Just as the balcony fosters Romeo's rhetoric as a sublimation of direct sexual contact, so the farce's Prologue tells us of

> that vile Wall which did these lovers sunder;
> And through Wall's chink, poor souls, they are content
> To whisper. At which let no man wonder.
>
> [V. i. 132-34]

They are "content" with words and separation: this literal meaning is not accidental, as the admonition makes clear. Furthermore, once the lovers uncharacteristically attempt to end their separation, they intensify their own subconscious resistance to genuine mutual involvement. Both readily find excuses for suicide, thus avoiding any need to replace sentimental remoteness with comic realism.

Ironically, the farcical interlude provides the best analogue to the serious tragedy of Romeo and Juliet, for in it Shakespeare seems to be reflecting back sardonically on the theme of "a

lover, that kills himself most gallant for love" [I. ii. 23-4]. The farce could have purged excess in the aristocratic Greek lovers who watch it on the stage, but unlike the ultimate audience offstage they fail to recognize in their own roles the grotesqueries which they ridicule in the performance of the lower classes. We know that they have displayed the same love of tension, confusions of perception, and suicidal instincts. However, in the interlude Shakespeare provides even closer echoes for Romeo's and Juliet's behavior and sentiments, implying that the purgative effect which the interlude should have on its stage audience duplicates the cathartic effect *Romeo and Juliet* was intended to have on its actual audiences. Sadly enough, most spectators have also taken at face value the serious play's tragic sentimentality, which Shakespeare's mature comic vision clearly resists and censures. (pp. 105-14)

Because of its more varied and witty exposition of [the nature of true love], *A Midsummer Night's Dream* may claim to be a maturer, if not a richer, play than *Romeo and Juliet*. In it the potential tragedy of ideal love is recognized and overcome by a lifegiving sense of the comedy of sexual relations. Instead of the simple polarizations of the tragedy (young against old, sentimental enthusiasm against practical satisfaction), the comedy has Shakespeare's characteristic range of illustration. This variety results in a subtler kind of characterization. Because there are so many pairs of lovers, the limitations of the purely subjective view of sexuality are comically visible, and we are not overpowered by a single narrow perspective as we may well be in the tragedy. The virtuosity of the structure of the *Dream* has long been noted and praised, but its worth lies, not simply in the skill with which all the plots are interwoven, but in the way that interweaving allows juxtapositions which comment on the conduct of the individuals involved in each sequence. Above all there is one figure, Bottom, who exists on every level of reality in the comedy. Sustained only by his self-assurance, he moves coolly through his ludicrous metamorphoses, from his "realistic" role as an urban craftsman to the more sophisticated one of actor; and then from involuntarily playing the monstrous lover of the Queen of the Fairies to his own choice of tragicomic role as the Romeo of a classical romance.

Theseus behaves with aristocratic propriety throughout the play, but I think that as a model for most moderns the lower-middle-class Bottom is the more relevant figure. He accepts the idiotic roles afforded or thrust on him by the play with a good will and even satisfaction that never run to complete self-deception. When Titania dotes on his ludicrous charms, he accepts her "love," but he also wryly comments: "Methinks, mistress, you should have little reason for that: and yet to say the truth, reason and love keep little company together now-a-days; the more the pity that some honest neighbours will not make them friends" [III. i. 142-46].... (pp. 120-21)

Bottom is important as a model because he is not trapped in any role and accepts each only as long as it seems worthwhile to those around him. Such flexibility and responsiveness are the marks of true sophistication (as we see in Falstaff), and that sophistication is not completely invalidated by its coexistence with all kinds of plebian mannerisms and grotesque quirks of egotism. Most audiences have still to be shown that while we can allow ourselves to sympathize with Romeo and thus learn vicariously from his incompleteness, we might well positively admire Bottom's diverseness and emulate his poise, while laughing at his egotism. (p. 122)

Hugh M. Richmond, "Low Love and High Passion,"
in his Shakespeare's Sexual Comedy: A Mirror for

Lovers, *The Bobbs-Merrill Company, Inc., 1971, pp. 102-76.*

M. D. FABER (essay date 1972)

[*Applying the methods of psychoanalytic criticism to* A Midsummer Night's Dream, *Faber contends that Hermia's dream in Act II, Scene ii is erotic, one in which her fears of and desires for a sexual consummation of her love for Lysander conflict with each other. Faber also locates in Hermia's dream a dissociation of the threatening side of Lysander from his more benign and innocent aspects, a technique which he claims Shakespeare accomplishes in the play as a whole by presenting the irrational behavior of the young lovers as a consequence of the fairies' intervention, rather than as arising from their own natures. For further psychoanalytical interpretations of* A Midsummer Night's Dream, *see the excerpt by Gerald F. Jacobson (1962) and the essays by Melvin Goldstein, Weston A. Gui, and Norman N. Holland cited in the Additional Bibliography. Last, Faber relates Hermia's struggle "to control opposing tendencies in herself" to society's imposition of order on its various elements. He contends that because this order is "severely patriarchal," it will constantly engender ambivalence and tension among those whom it controls and thus produce "a constant straining toward disorder." David Marshall (1982) has also examined the political dominance of males over females in* A Midsummer Night's Dream; *Florence Falk (1980) has studied the eternal impetus toward tension in a highly structured community; and David Bevington (1975) has analyzed the conflict in the play between sexual desire and rational restraint.*]

I intend to get at what we can call the essential meaning, or the total meaning, of *A Midsummer Night's Dream* by concentrating upon the dream Hermia has while she sleeps in the woods near Athens. (p. 179)

[While] a realistic response to a dream in a work of literature is a distinct critical possibility, the realistic responder must remember that anything does *not* go. Because the literary dream appears in the "organic universe" of the literary work and functions as an integral part of that universe, we are obliged to confine our associations to the dream, and finally our interpretation of the dream, to the limited or finite meanings which arise from the text of the work as a whole. The dream, in short, has something to do with the work and if our realistic interpretation of the dream has something to do with the work then we are entitled to say that our realistic interpretation of the dream is a genuine, though not necessarily correct, critical response and may aid us in understanding how the work operates, may aid us, that to say, in grasping the sort of response the text is capable of generating in those who come into contact with it. . . . I want to analyze Hermia's dream in such a way as to illuminate the total meaning of the comedy, and I believe that to illuminate the total meaning of the comedy will be to understand something about Shakespeare's depiction of mental processes. (p. 180)

We know, of course, that dreams are in some measure determined by what Freud calls "day residue": "In every dream it is possible to find a point of contact with the experiences of the previous day." We know also that this day residue often tells us a good deal about a dream's central *wish.* Turning to Shakespeare's play in an effort to pinpoint the dramatic events which immediately precede Hermia's nocturnal fantasy, we learn that Lysander and Hermia have decided to elope in defiance of Egeus' pronouncement that they may not marry.

> Tomorrow night, when Phoebe doth behold
> Her silver visage in the watery glass, . . .
> [I. i. 209-10]

says Lysander,

> Through Athen's gates have we devised to steal.
> [I. i. 213]

A few moments of stage time later the lovers find themselves in "a wood near Athens." It is late at night, both are tired, and Lysander proposes that they lie down and sleep:

> Fair love, you faint with wandering in the wood,
> And to speak troth, I have forgot our way.
> We'll rest us, Hermia, if you think it good. . . .
> [II. ii. 35-7]

To which Hermia replies:

> Be it so, Lysander. Find you out a bed,
> For I upon this bank will rest my head.
> [II. ii. 39-40]

Unwilling to sleep alone, Lysander announces:

> One turf shall serve as pillow for us both—
> One heart, one bed, two bosoms, and one troth.
> [II. ii. 41-2]

Hermia, however, will have none of this:

> Nay, good Lysander, for my sake, my dear,
> Lie further off yet, do not lie so near,
> [II. ii. 43-4]

an attitude which arouses good Lysander's righteous indignation:

> Oh, take the sense, sweet, of my innocence!
> Love takes the meaning of love's conference.
> I mean that my heart unto yours is knit
> So that but one heart we can make of it.
> Two bosoms interchained with an oath,
> So then two bosoms and a single troth.
> Then by your side no bedroom me deny
> For lying so, Hermia, I do not lie.
> [II. ii. 45-52]

Hermia's response to this exhortation is as follows:

> Lysander riddles very prettily.
> How much beshrew my manners and my pride,
> If Hermia meant to say Lysander lied.
> But, gentle friend, for love and courtesy
> Lie further off; in human modesty,
> Such separation as may well be said
> Becomes a virtuous bachelor and a maid
> So far be distant. And good night, sweet friend.
> Thy love ne'er alter till thy sweet life end!
> [II. ii. 53-61]

Desisting, Lysander remarks:

> Amen, amen, to that fair prayer say I,
> And then end life when I end loyalty!
> Here is my bed. Sleep give thee all his rest!
> [II. ii. 62-4]

And Hermia concludes the matter, and the couplet, with:

> With half that wish the wisher's eye be pressed!
> [II. ii. 65]

Act IV. Scene i. Oberon, Puck, Titania, Bottom, and Fairies. By Henry Fuseli (n.d.).

Some eighty lines later Hermia suddenly awakens. As she cries out for Lysander, she describes for us the dream upon which our discussion is based:

> Help me. Lysander, help me! Do thy best
> To pluck this crawling serpent from my
>   breast!
> Aye me, for pity! What a dream was here!
> Lysander look how I do quake with fear.
> Methought a serpent eat my heart away,
> And you sat smiling at his cruel prey.
>
> [II. ii. 145-50]

Specifically with regard to day residue, a number of points oblige us to postulate that Hermia's is ultimately an erotic dream and that the wish it expresses concerns Lysander. First, we should bear in mind that the elopement itself is an action with obviously erotic overtones; the restraining influence of the father has been negated; the walls of an ordered society have been left behind; Hermia is suddenly alone with Lysander; the woods are "primitive," ungoverned, wild; one is vulnerable there to all kinds of "attack." Second, the erotic speeches of young Lysander, and Hermia's replies, make explicit and striking reference to elements that turn up in the dream. Lysander talks of his "heart" being "knit" to Hermia's. Hermia dreams of a serpent eating her "heart." Lysander refers to "one bed" and "two bosoms." Hermia, upon awakening, asks

Lysander to pluck a serpent from her "breast," Lysander says "amen" to Hermia's "fair prayer." Hermia's dream presents Lysander smiling at the serpent's "cruel prey." Hermia, before she sleeps, speaks of the "separation" that becomes a bachelor and a maid. In her dream, Lysander and the snake are *separated*, for Lysander who "should be" attacking the snake sits watching the snake attacking the woman. Hermia "wishes" that Lysander's "eye be pressed" with sleep. She dreams that his eye is conspicuously open. Indeed, it looks on as the "serpent" goes about its business.

But is not all this unpleasurable, and is not Hermia's dream as a whole a dream of unpleasure? How, with this in mind, can we suggest that it involves a wish of any kind, let alone an erotic one? (pp. 181-82)

Hermia disguises her wish in a number of ways, all of them very primitive and very familiar. To begin with, she transforms the forbidden phallus into a serpent. This is perfectly understandable, for not only are serpents and phalluses similar in shape but serpents are apt to be found in the "wood near Athens" where she and Lysander are sleeping close to one another. The part of Hermia's personality that wants to bring forth the wish-fulfilling fantasy is suggesting that there is nothing very strange in dreaming about a snake while sleeping within a wood. . . . Again, Hermia *detaches* the disguised phallus from the individual to whom it belongs, a common procedure in dreams according to the analytic data. The part of Lysander that most economically expressed the *unconscious* or *forbidden* impulse in Hermia is separated from Lysander who is himself in the dream and behaving very curiously. In other words, the fact that Lysander is not helping Hermia in the dream, indeed is smiling while the serpent attacks her, is easily understood when we remember that the serpent is not a serpent but Lysander's phallus, and that Lysander, as Hermia well knows from the day residue, would "smile" at the opportunity to consummate his relationship with his intended. (pp. 182-83)

[One] of the most striking facts about dreams is that the dreamer's ego often appears, in Freud's words, "several times or in several forms." We have already postulated that Lysander's smiling attests to the underlying significance of the preying serpent; we would now suggest, however, that Hermia's ego is also bound up in the figure of Lysander. In other words, the smiling Lysander expresses not only Lysander's desire as implicitly declared in the day residue, it expresses Hermia's desire as well. Indeed, we would maintain that the part of Hermia which wants the sexual encounter to occur is embodied in the smiling face of Lysander with whom she has come to identify.... Thus Hermia, in her own dream, sees herself beholding with approval the sexual assault which is "foreign to her moral consciousness." It is this "sight" that terrifies her.... Although she appreciates Lysander's impulses and touches upon them in her dream, it is really *her own impulses* that she is dreaming about. To borrow an expression of Kierkegaard's, the anxiety Hermia experiences in her dream arises from desiring what she dreads. (pp. 184-85)

In an effort to precipitate the emergence of her unconscious desires Hermia, as we have seen, dissociates the phallus. The irrational, dangerous, and primitive object, the object that expresses most vividly and most economically the irrational, dangerous, and primitive side of the woman, is fantasied as separate from, indeed as distinct from, the human being to whom it would ordinarily belong. It is as if the dark, deceptive, threatening side of man is over here, and the conscious, innocent, pacific side of man is over there. With this firmly in mind, we are able to understand how Hermia's dream captures for us in miniature precisely what Shakespeare attempts to express through his employment of the love-juice as the main vehicle for arousing the primitive, animal side of his central characters, including Titania. Like the serpent-phallus in Hermia's dream, the love-juice, which precipitates the emergence of primitive, irrational, violent, uncontrolled behavior in the lovers, is entirely dissociated from the lovers' minds. In other words, since man's unconscious or archaic mind obviously "has nothing to do with" his conscious or civilized mind, why associate the two? Since man's dark, primitive, animal side "has nothing to do with" his conscious, civilized, rational side, why not make them separate and distinct from one another? This, as I see it, is Shakespeare's basic comic strategy in the play. He suggests that the two sides of man's mind simply have nothing to do with one another and he underscores this suggestion by making them have nothing to do with one another *in actuality*. Since there is no way to explain man's curious behavior from *within man*, let us place the cause of that behavior in the fairy realm which exists *outside of man*. Let us make incongruity as complete and as "factual" as we possibly can. And it goes without saying, of course, that Shakespeare knew what he was doing when he had Hermia dissociate the serpent in her *sleep* and Puck apply the juice to the eyes of the lovers as they *slept*. By asking at the end of Act IV, "Are you sure/ That we are awake?" [IV. i. 192-93], De-

metrius aligns his experience in the wood with Hermia's experience in the dream. Hence we see that Shakespeare's title, *A Midsummer Night's Dream,* is a comic remark upon the mind of man, particularly with regard to *causality*.

But it is not only with regard to dissociation that Hermia's dream captures in miniature the basic design of the larger, metaphorical dream. Remember, for example, that the love-juice itself is derived from a "flower" which has been invaded by a "bolt" of Cupid [II. i. 165], a textual fact that calls immediately to mind the displacement of the genitals which Hermia effects in her nocturnal fantasy. Then too, when the juice has been applied to the eyes of the lovers they have the extraordinary, dream-like experience of finding themselves in love with "the opposite," with Helena who has suddenly replaced Hermia as the object of their erotic longings. Nor can we fail to mention here the unfortunate Titania who, having been anointed with the love-juice in her sleep, awakens quite suddenly to find herself in love not with the noble, civilized Theseus but with his opposite, the primitive ass. It is not necessary, however, to deal solely in specifics, for the whole business of *distortion* as it expresses itself in Hermia's dream is explicitly connected with the metaphorical dream experienced by the principals:

> These things seem small and undistinguishable.
> Like far-off mountains turned into clouds,
>> [IV. i. 197-98]

says Demetrius at the conclusion of the chaotic episode in the wood, to which Hermia responds:

> Methinks I see these things with parted
>> eye,
> When everything seems double,
>> [IV. i. 188-89[
>> (pp. 186-87)

Of even greater significance to the total drama than the problem of distortion is the problem of anxiety. I refer specifically to the anxiety experienced by Hermia as she makes her abortive attempt to bring forth her unconscious desires. What really interests me in this connection is not Freud's assertion that "anxiety dreams" contain "transformed . . . sexual content," an assertion which lends support to our psychoanalytic interpretation of Hermia's dream as a whole, but our growing awareness, originating with Freud, that anxiety, in dreams and elsewhere, places the subject in a position which obliges him to exercise *control*. In the midst of traumatic, anxiety-provoking episodes, episodes in which something breaks through the "protective shield" of the personality, the system becomes flooded with excitation, and there is, as a result, an attempt on the part of the subject to "bind the stimulus." To put it somewhat differently, we witness in psychically traumatic experiences an archaic, pathologic attempt to master what cannot be mastered in the usual way. Thus Hermia in her dream is ultimately struggling to *master*, to *control*, opposing tendencies in herself.

Now *A Midsummer Night's Dream*, let me stress here, is a play that is concerned in its very essence with the problem of mastering, of controlling, those archaic, uncivilized, ungoverned, inexplicable elements which are apt on occasion to break through the "protective shield" of the ordered human personality. Indeed, it is from this perspective, and from this perspective alone, that we can best understand Theseus' role in the play, his inclination to preserve order, to achieve a just society, to discover a modus vivendi between rigid institutions and instinctual human energies, his understanding of passion (he has gained this through experience), his ability to control his "hounds" and to appreciate their harmonious "cry" [IV. i. 124], an ability which expresses on the metaphorical level his ability to effectively control, or hold in check, his own archaic, primitive impulses, and finally, an interest which differentiates him from the frivolous, silly lovers who see nothing but folly in the tragic tale of passion that Bottom and his fellows enact before the court. (p. 187)

[From] one perspective, *A Midsummer Night's Dream* is largely devoted *to the problem of setting boundaries between male and female*, to establishing firmly the social roles of men and women. This becomes immediately apparent when one thinks upon Hippolyta's submission to Theseus, a submission that announces the play's patriarchal order and that serves ultimately as a model for the quarreling lovers. Nor is the problem of boundaries and sexual identity unrelated to the struggle between Oberon and Titania, a struggle which echoes within the fairy realm the pre-play struggle between Theseus and Hippolyta and which, through its concentration upon the problem of the *changeling* boy, a problem with homosexual overtones, explicitly focuses the problem of achieving sexual identity. It is as if the play is suggesting that *social order* can be achieved only when personal order has been achieved, personal order implying the actualization of the male's masculinity and the female's femininity, or, as I would prefer, femaleness. What complicates the whole business, of course, and what is perhaps, from a historical perspective, the final cause of the play's tension, is that the order for which the play strives is a severely patriachal one which, by its very nature, engenders ambivalence and hostility in women and thus produces a constant straining toward disorder. It is precisely the existence of this double-bind which makes the play's resolution "temporary;" that is, both intra and interpersonal tensions are resolved through social institutions which leave characters relatively *unchanged*. Identity conflict within the person is not "worked through" but "bound" by forces external to the person. Which brings us to our next point.

The vital connection between Hermia's dream and the play's thematic core is further underscored by Freud's basic insight that in dreams "we appear not to think but to experience." Although Hermia experiences in the dream, presumably for the first time, the strength of her unconscious, animal longings and the great difficulty of mastering them, and although the lovers during the course of their "dream" in the "wood near Athens" experience, presumably for the first time as well, the ungovernable violence of their own mad passions which come forth in a trice and which conduct them to the very brink of disaster, neither Lysander, nor Demetrius, nor Helena, nor Hermia learns anything whatsoever from his experiential participation in these events. Unlike Titania, who does come to appreciate the loathsomeness of her behavior toward the ass, the lovers remain blind, completely blind, to the end. The point is, the world of *A Midsummer Night's Dream* is a world that needs its Theseus very badly. Rare is the man, let alone the ruler, who can profit from his experience, indeed, who is able in the first place to distinguish the imaginary from the real. True enough, all the characters are at the play's close protected by the ordered bond of marriage which is, on the thematic level, inextricably associated with the figure of Theseus and irrevocably opposed to the kind of union Hermia fantasies in her little dream. Then too, throughout the concluding moments of the comedy, as they dance and sing and bless the darkened house before making their departure into the night, the fairies

appear to be contented, even benign. Everything, one might say, seems pretty much in order, pretty much in tune. But one never knows when these sleeping lovers will "dream" again, when Oberon and Titania will revert once more to their foolish, interminable quarrel, the quarrel which ultimately stands behind the employment of the "magical," transforming love-juice. Hanging in a universe with an intrinsic potential for disorder, or, to put it more realistically, inhabited by individuals with a powerful "archaic heritage," the world of man, or better, the *patriarchal* world of man, is a precarious place, blessed from time to time with a governor of strength and understanding. (pp. 188-89)

> M. D. Faber, "Hermia's Dream: Royal Road to 'A Midsummer Night's Dream'," *in* Literature and Psychology, *Vol. XXII, No. 4, 1972, pp. 179-90.*

RONALD F. MILLER (essay date 1975)

[*Miller contends that in* A Midsummer Night's Dream *Shakespeare provides a pluralistic vision encompassing both credulity and scepticism in order to emphasize the paradoxical, mysterious, and ambivalent quality of the play. He regards the ambiguous responses to the existence of the fairies, and to the nature of art and love with which they are consistently associated, as the "central intellectual issue of the play" and argues that the alterations in the characters' perceptions of events intensifies the audience's awareness of the relationship between the actual and the transcendent experiences in our own lives. The importance of perception and awareness in* A Midsummer Night's Dream *has also been examined by John Russell Brown (1957), C. L. Barber (1959), Bertrand Evans (1960), T. Walter Herbert (1964), and Stephen Fender (1968). In addition, Miller focuses on Bottom's encounter with the fairies and his response to that experience, noting that he is the only character in the play who openly acknowledges their existence. Because Bottom sees no difference between what is explicable and what is not, the critic claims, he "sees the mysterious and accepts it as perfectly ordinary." Miller analyzes the implications of Bottom's Pauline references in his awakening speech (Act IV, Scene i) and argues that, although Bottom is not God's holy fool, his speech represents the visionary's attempt to explain a glimpse of the unfathomable, nonphysical world. For additional discussions of Bottom's awakening speech, see the excerpts by Harold C. Goddard (1951), Peter G. Phialas (1966), John A. Allen (1967), and J. Dennis Huston (1981); also, see the essays by Frank Kermode and Garrett Stewart cited in the Additional Bibliography.*]

The complex and subtle intellectuality of Shakespeare's comic art was never better illustrated than by *A Midsummer Night's Dream* and, in particular, by Shakespeare's employment of the fairies in that play. Not only are they obviously the most striking feature of the comedy; intellectually they are the most provocative, too. By intruding the fictive worlds of Ovid and English folklore into the doings of the nobles and the workmen of Athens, they pose open-ended questions about illusion and reality, existence and art to those willing to press beyond the older interpretation of the play as a charming theatrical fantasy or a comic medley or a burlesque. Such puzzles have occupied so much recent critical attention that this comedy, once rather generally dismissed as a piece of fluff, is now more likely to be read as a study in the epistemology of the imagination.

And this tendency seems justified. The fairies are a continual and unavoidable reminder of a certain indefiniteness in the world of the play—an indefiniteness culminating in the suggestion by the fairy prankster Puck that the play itself may have only been a dream: "If we shadows have offended, / Think but this, and all is mended, / That you have but slumb'red here / While these visions did appear'' [V. i. 423-26]. With that final insinuation, the frame of dramatic illusion is irreparably compromised, and little remains besides a series of tantalizing riddles. Are the fairies real or unreal? Are the spectators no less than the Athenians subject to Puck's and Oberon's magic? How can we assign precedence to the various levels of reality—including our own—under the sway of Shakespeare's art? Such doubts tease us into abstract thoughts as inescapable as their conclusions are elusive and uncertain.

The intellectual implications of the fairies, however, have scarcely been exhausted once the puzzle of their metaphysical status has been explored. No doubt there *is* a certain fugitiveness to these beings. Shakespeare lets us have our fairies and doubt them too. Yet beyond these formal uncertainties lie other uncertainties residing not in the world of the stage but in the world of ordinary human experience to which every dramatic representation, no matter how sophisticated, must ultimately refer. As theatrical immanences—ambulatory metaphors, if you wish—who secretly manipulate affections, cause transformations, and bring good luck, the fairies obliquely hint that our own offstage existence may be touched by mysteries no less genuine than those that disrupt the world of Theseus, Hermia, Bottom, and the rest. I would not, however, go so far as Harold C. Goddard, who speaks of the fairies as unequivocally representing ''a vaster unseen world by which the actions of men are affected and overruled'' [see excerpt above, 1951]. Shakespeare's art is surely not so blatantly allegorical. It is not so much the fairies per se as the *mystery* of the fairies— the very aura of evanescence and ambiguity surrounding their life on stage—that points to a mysteriousness in our own existence, and specifically in such ambivalent earthly matters as love, luck, imagination, and even faith. These are the elements of human experience with which the fairies are again and again associated. As Shakespeare plays his sly games with the insubstantial fairies, we are forced by the ambivalence in their status to ask questions, ultimately unanswerable, about the substance of those mortal experiences with which they are linked. (pp. 254-55)

When the fairies come on stage themselves, their status is immediately called into question. Puck's first extended speech is full of what C. L. Barber calls ''a conscious double vision'': ''The plain implication of the lines, though Puck speaks them, is that Puck does not really exist—that he is a figment of the naive imagination, projected to motivate the little accidents of household life.'' Though finely said, this is incomplete. Theseus in emphasizing the delusions of the imagination might interpret Puck's words in such a way. Puck's words do assure us that his deeds can all be explained away as accident by those who are so inclined. But Hippolyta might as easily observe that the little accidents of household life are here being shown to suggest something of great constancy, though that something may only work for rustic *joie de vivre* [''joy of living'']:

And sometime lurk I in a gossip's bowl,
In very likeness of a roasted crab,
And when she drinks, against her lips I bob
And on her withered dewlap pour the ale.
The wisest aunt, telling the saddest tale,
Sometime for three-foot stool mistaketh me,
Then slip I from her bum, down topples she,
And ''tailor'' cries, and falls into a cough;
And then the whole quire hold their hips and laugh,
And waxen in their mirth, and neeze, and swear
A merrier hour was never wasted there.
[II. i. 47-57]

Such a passage, as Thersites once said of opinion [in *Troilus and Cressida*], a man may wear on both sides, like a leather jerkin. Paradoxically, the fairies are both real *and* imagined; life provides its little accidents which are at one and the same time pure chance and the work of an immanence bent upon fostering good fellowship and laughter.

A similar paradox characterizes the presentation of the other fairies. We are given to understand in most mannered verse that they are vegetation spirits whose quarrel explains the chaotic effects of bad weather. The very artificiality of their language keeps us from ever becoming truly caught up in Titania and Oberon as dramatic characters. They are stage-figures whose artful speech suggests that they are literary ornamentation. Surely Oberon says a lot when he informs Puck that, though they are not damned spirits that love the night, they are spirits who cannot withstand the full light of day [III. ii. 388-95]. From this perspective they are seen as fanciful entities embodying the chance of agricultural misfortune: an actual reference to the year 1594 has been detected by some scholars. Yet there they are. Visible. Audible. On stage. Has anyone ever found a more believable explanation for climatic vicissitudes? And the fairies do make up at the end, promising a return to good harvests. I assume that if the weather had improved the year *A Midsummer Night's Dream* was produced, the existence of the fairies would have seemed to be confirmed.

Thus when these elusive beings begin to interfere with the lovers and their pairings-off, we have been prepared to interpret the comic transformations effected by their magic in two contradictory ways: first, as a natural disorder mythologized and, second, as the working of some immanence behind events. In defiance of all logic, neither alternative is rejected; both coexist in the complex comic vision. The whirligig in the woods is, no doubt, a fine extended image of the irrationality and arbitrariness of young love, in and out of affection with this or that member of the opposite sex according to availability and chance. The startling result of the juice from a magic plant seems as descriptive a metaphor as any for the ordinary inclination of youth to dote and dote utterly upon one out of a set of apparently interchangeable persons of the opposite sex. Our knowledge of the way of the world and our familiarity with Puck's activities work in concert to underscore the irony of Lysander's speech upon waking to discover his affections changed:

The will of man is by his reason sway'd;
And reason says you are the worthier maid.
Things growing are not ripe until their season,
So I, being young, till now ripe not to reason;
And touching now the point of human skill,
Reason becomes the marshal to my will
And leads me to your eyes, where I o'erlook
Love's stories written in Love's richest book.
[III. ii. 115-22]

So much for reason in love, on or off stage.

Nonetheless, the confusions of the night do ultimately work for the good, whatever the intermediate delight Puck takes in the agitations of the mortals. Judging by the results, the events seem to have been governed by an effective albeit inefficient benevolence. Though all seemed chaotic at the time, in the end (as Puck promises) ''Jack shall have Jill; / Nought shall go ill; / The man shall have his mare again, and all shall be well'' [III. ii. 461-63]. There is something profoundly suggestive in the reverent mix of wonder and joy the lovers convey when they wake to find themselves blessed with an end to their tribulations. They are not unlike Milton's Adam, waking to find his dream was real:

> *Demetrius*. These things seem small and undistinguish-able,
> Like far-off mountains turned into clouds.
> *Hermia*. Methinks I see these things with parted eye,
> When every thing seems double.
> *Helena*.   So methinks;
> And I have found Demetrius like a jewel,
> Mine own, and not mine own.
> *Demetrius*.   [But] are you sure
> That we are [now] awake? It seems to me
> That yet we sleep, we dream.
>
> [IV. i. 187-94]

Something approaching religious awe is revealed in this be-wildered recognition of their mysterious good fortune. So moving is this association of the fairies with immanent benevolence that, for a moment, all formal ambiguities—all questions of the reality of the fairies—fade to insignificance before the greater mysteries underlying all mortal existence.

Waking at the same moment is another dreamer, Bottom, who also rises temporarily bewildered by the wonders of the past night. The slightest uncertainty or hesitation on the part of Bottom is truly noteworthy, for he has previously shown himself to be overwhelmingly matter-of-fact about everything. The anomalies of fairy magic have as little immediate appeal to him as they do to Theseus—but with a difference. Theseus is a conscious rationalist; in his famous speech at the beginning of Act V he condescendingly explains away the inexplicable events of the night as "airy nothings," as the psychological deception of the "strong imagination." Theseus consistently embodies this skeptical side of the dialectic of the play, just as our visual and aural experience of the fairies embodies the credulous side. Even when Theseus defends *Pyramus and Thisby* from attack by Hippolyta ("This is the silliest stuff that ever I heard" [V. i. 210]), he does so with an urbane assurance that all works of the imagination are harmless, airy fantasies: "The best in this kind are but shadows; and the worst are no worse, if imagination amend them" [V. i. 211-12]. In his attitude he is no less condescending toward the dramatist than he is toward the lunatic, the lover, or the poet. If (as now seems conventional) we wish to invert Theseus' statement to affirm the genuine creativity of the imaginative response, we may find justification in the play as a whole, but certainly not in Theseus' own intent.

Bottom, on the other hand, does not represent a position so much as a problem, in particular the characteristic problem of men—*all* men—immersed in an ambivalent reality. In his own benighted way he, more than any other figure on stage, must confront the central intellectual issue of the play. He is consistently shown encountering mysteries, the mystery of the mimetic act, the mystery of love, and (above all else) the mystery of the fairies; and his comic struggles with the complexities of experience are Shakespeare's primary means of exploring the dilemma presented by a world characterized by what Norman Rabkin would call "complementarity," a world in which reality is necessarily perceived in terms of opposing and apparently contradictory modes of being. As the "bottom" of mankind, Bottom's solution for the irreducible complementarity of things is really quite simple: ignore the problem. He sees the mysterious and accepts it as perfectly ordinary; he

behaves as though the inexplicable and the explicable were simply no different at all. The central ambiguities of the play are hidden from him because all experiences, irrational or rational, magical or mundane, are of the same order in his sight.

Consider for a moment his attitude toward the drama. The world of the stage bears a significant resemblance to the world of the fairies. Both define a mode of existence separate from but interacting with quotidian existence; both challenge an outsider either to rejection or to a tentative surrendering of his skeptical instincts. An intelligence capable of understanding that fairies may be real on one level and be metaphors on another is also needed to comprehend that a man may be both an actor on the literal level and a lover or a tyrant on stage. Such subtleties are quite beyond Bottom. According to his understanding, either a lion on stage must be accepted by the spectators as a genuine lion or else the audience must remain continuously aware that the beast is in fact an actor—a *specific* actor—impersonating a lion. "That willing suspension of disbelief . . . which constitutes the poetic faith" [Samuel Taylor Coleridge] is for Bottom indistinguishable from mere credulity, so he must assume that a spectator seeing a lion in the world of the stage fear for his safety in his own sphere of existence:

> *Bottom*. Masters, you ought to consider with yourselves. To bring in—God shield us!—a lion among ladies, is a most dreadful thing; for there is not a more fearful wild-fowl than your lion living; and we ought to look to't.
> *Snout*. Therefore another prologue must tell he is not a lion.
> *Bottom*. Nay, you must name his name, and half his face must be seen through the lion's neck; and he himself must speak through, saying thus, or to the same defect, "Ladies," or "Fair ladies, I would wish you," or "I would request you," or "I would entreat you, not to fear, not to tremble: my life for yours. If you think I come hither as a lion, it were pity of my life. No, I am no such thing; I am a man as other men are;" and there indeed let him name his name, and tell them plainly he is Snug the joiner.
>
> [III. i. 29-46]

Theseus denies the validity of the works of the strong imagination; Bottom acts as if the imagination did not exist at all. (pp. 257-61)

Bottom's approach to the drama deserves special notice . . . because it is of a piece with his approach to other works of the imagination; all the mysteries of life, which certainly include the epistemological mysteries of the drama, are as vulnerable to his literalism as they are to Theseus' rationalism. Yet Bottom's stupidity is actually suggestive, whereas Theseus' attitude, for all its wisdom, is ultimately reductionistic. By *not* detecting complexities that are obvious to the audience, Bottom puts these complexities into bold relief and makes us more, not less, conscious of the myriad-mindedness necessary for men to confront experience whole. As has often been remarked, the various aspects of this play are linked together by the common theme of the imagination, but it is Bottom's undiscriminating desire to treat all products of the imagination as quotidian reality which provides this linkage.

This thematic significance is evident if we look at the havoc wrought by Bottom when he turns his brutal literalism upon the fanciful world of the fairies. As the very embodiment of a sensibility that finds nothing mysterious either in art or in life, as the negative image of that pluralistic intellectual vision toward which Shakespeare's comedy moves, Bottom is bound to prove himself inadequate to the encounter. A lesser artist might have made Bottom symbolically blind to the fairies; in a masterstroke Shakespeare chooses the witty opposite. While the court party sees the fairies only indirectly through their effects and through the intimation of patterns seemingly too constant to be explained as mere chance, Bottom, literalist that he is, meets the fairies face-to-face.

The meeting of course does not work solely to Bottom's disadvantage. His equanimity before the airy nothings of Titania's passion lets us appreciate the silliness of the agitations of all the lovers, fairy and mortal alike. Titania infatuated with ass-headed Bottom provides a perfect image of love's irrational frenzy, and Bottom's prosaic skepticism makes him tellingly superior to this general madness, just as his obtuseness had made him immune to the airy nothings of the stage:

> Titania. I pray thee, gentle mortal, sing again.
> Mine ear is much enamour'd of thy note;
> So is mine eye enthralled to thy shape;
> And thy fair virtue's force perforce doth move me
> On the first view to say, to swear, I love thee.
> Bottom. Methinks, mistress, you should have little reason for that; and yet, to say the truth, reason and love keep little company together now-a-days; the more the pity that some honest neighbours will not make them friends. Nay, I can gleek upon occasion.
> Titania. Thou art as wise as thou art beautiful.
> Bottom. Not so, neither; but if I had wit enough to get out of this wood, I have enough to serve mine own turn.
>
> [III. i. 137-51]

His plain good sense surely triumphs here; yet here is a mortal, transported into the lap of the fairy queen—that *sanctum sanctorum* of an imaginative (and imaginary?) world sustaining and informing the world of common reality—and all he can do is think in terms of country proverbs and homespun experience. Offered any blessing from the rich store of a world freed from the limitations of reason and likelihood, he desires nothing more than a scratch on his head and a peck of provender. If, as suggested, Bottom is a comic image of ourselves, Everyman-as-Fool, then his failure to grasp the wonder and opportunity of his predicament reflects our commom failure to prevent worldliness from dimming our vision and blunting our hopes. (pp. 261-62)

Still, for a comic routine, the dissonance between Titania'a passion and Bottom's obliviousness is hilariously deflating. For just a moment Bottom's imaginative fundamentalism asks us to take the fairies literally and to observe how much these airy, symbolic creatures suffer by the touch of the earthy and the actual. That stroke of making love and reason country neighbors is a triumph of the same literal-mindedness that allows Bottom to treat Cobweb, Peaseblossom, and Mustardseed as a physical cobweb, peaseblossom, and mustardseed, thus reducing personification to vulgar fact:

> Bottom. I cry your worships mercy, heartily.
> I beseech your worship's name.
> Cobweb. Cobweb.

> Bottom. I shall desire you of more acquaintance, good Master Cobweb. If I cut my finger, I shall make bold with you.
>
> [III. i. 179-84]

On one level, of course, this is simply the play's most vivid realization of that double vision which has characterized everything having to do with the fairies. In the comic encounter, extremes meet and coexist: imagination and love and magic at their most entrancing in Titania, philistine realism at its most appealingly vulgar in Bottom. But Shakespeare does not exhaust the suggestiveness of this pairing when he sets these two off against each other. Ironically, Bottom's unblinking acceptance of the fairies provides these metaphoric beings with a solidity that nothing else, not even their presence on stage, can provide. As I have indicated, the fairies are almost always presented in a context that suggests that they could be explained away. The fact that not one of the court party sees them is certainly suggestive. Were it not for Bottom, the fairies might be passed off as simply a personification of the providence that governs, or seems to govern, or we would like to have govern, events. But Bottom is of all men the least prone to the delusions of the imagination, and when he confronts transcendence face-to-face, transcendence itself takes on a certain matter-of-factness. If we have become too complacent in viewing the mysteries of the world of the play and the mysteries of our own world in terms of a neatly compartmentalized vision, Bottom's stumbling across the line into the fairy world gives us a jolt. In other words, the weaver's unimaginative literalism gives Shakespeare a perfect opening to expand the intellectual scope of the play to suggest not just the mystery of our experience in this world, but also the mystery of our experience with some other world.

At the level of pure fun, Bottom's acquisition of an ass's noll may simply be a metaphor objectified, perhaps the only natural way for such a thorough-going imaginative fundamentalist to prove himself an ass; but since the other rude mechanicals see what James Calderwood calls "the genuine apple-munching ear-twitching article" [see excerpt above, 1971], the existence of the supernatural is strongly indicated. Though in the widest perspective falling in love may be as magical a metamorphosis as becoming part beast, Theseus would have a harder time explaining the latter away. The interconnection between actuality and transcendence is palpable in all matters touching Bottom. This is dramatically illustrated by the great parallel waking scene at the end of Act IV. When the lovers awake from the night, they can only speak distractedly about the half-glimpsed wonders they have "dreamed"; they find themselves blessed, but they know not how. Bottom knows, though he finds his language inadequate to describe his "vision":

> I have had a most rare vision. I have had a dream, past the wit of man to say what dream it was. Man is but an ass, if he go about to expound this dream. Methought I was—there is no man can tell what. Methought I was,— and methought I had,—but man is but a patch'd fool, if he will offer to say what methought I had.
>
> [IV. i. 204-11]

Shakespeare's art achieves a density and complexity here that even he seldom attained. The passage is of course funny. To find garrulous Bottom at a loss for words is delightful. His apparently unconscious reference to his past condition in "Man is but an ass" is sure to draw a laugh from the groundings.

His waking reverence clashes pointedly with his phlegmatic approach to the events when he was actually experiencing them. This humor, however, does not prevent Shakespeare from touching deeper chords. By speaking so generally of man and human capacities, Bottom reconfirms himself as a comic mirror for the general human condition. Bottom becomes *any* man awaking from a visionary glimpse into orders other than those of his workaday world. What Bottom has seen is of course hardly ineffable—imexpressible by him though it be—yet Shakespeare gives him language that echoes the traditional humble admission of the mystic that the substance of his visions is beyond recounting by the tongues of men. For Bottom after his earthy fashion *is* a mystic of sorts; in his flatfooted way he has truly entered into a transcendent existence which has been closed to the rest of the morals upon whom the transcendence has also impinged.

A suggestive analogy is thus being established: as Bottom is to the world of the fairies, so man in the height of his powers is to—is to what? If Bottom, the least perceptive of men, can glimpse into the shadowy world of the fairies, what do we who master Bottom's confusions glimpse in our own moments of unarticulated wonder? Here Shakespeare brilliantly reverses the age-old comic tactic off correction through diminution; the comic mirror is here being employed not to belittle that which is reflected but to show by association and suggestion the potential latent even in the lowly image of man we see. A theatrical coup, a witty toying with the levels of reality in the world on stage, comes very close to becoming a parody of mankind caught up in a religious vision of worlds beyond the physical. Amid all the laughter there is something touchingly pitiful in watching poor, stammering Bottom admit his inability to seize and hold in language that fleeting moment when he too saw beneath the surface of things. And that pity is not just for Bottom.

To redouble these associations, Shakespearre has Bottom babble on about his vision. He speaks, of course, only of those mysterious fairies, but in his speech he rises to an echo of St. Paul:

> The eye of man hath not heard, the ear of man hath not seen, man's hand is not able to taste, his tongue to conceive, nor his heart to report, what my dream was. I will get Peter Quince to write a ballad of this dream. It shall be called "Bottom's Dream," because it hath no bottom. . . .
>
> [IV. i. 211-16]

The setting for the corresponding Pauline passage needs to be quoted at some length. I cite Tyndale's version:

> That we speake of, is wysdome amonge them that are perfecte: not the wysdome of this worlde nether of the rulars of this worlde (which go to nought) but we speake the wysdome of God, which is in secrete and lieth hyd, which God ordeyned before the worlde vnto oure glory; which wysdome none of the rulars of the worlde knewe. For had they knowen it, they wolde not have crucified the Lorde of glory. But as it is written: The eye hath not sene, and the eare hath not hearde, nether have entred into the herte of man, the things which God hath prepared for them that love him.

> But God hath opened them vnto vs by his sprete. For the sprete searcheth all things, ye the bottome of Goddes secretes. (I Corinthians ii. 6-10)

Here St. Paul, like his comic avatar Bottom, speaks as a visionary in avouching an insight into a transcendent reality which cool reason cannot comprehend. Throughout the early chapters of I Corinthians Paul related again and again his central distinction between the wisdom of the world and the foolishness of God, bearing witness to the mystery that fools for Christ's sake know truths unfathomable to those wise after the flesh. Shakespeare must surely have expected his Bible-reading patrons to recall amid their laughter at least the general drift of the context wherein St. Paul speaks of God's strange and admirable choice of foolish things to confound the certitudes of the material world. In the twinkling of an eye and the turn of a phrase Shakespeare has associated the fairies, however fugitively, with other realities apart from but informing mortal existence. (pp. 263-66)

What seems to me most important about Bottom's echo is not so much the higher meanings of the dream—if there are any—as the nimble play of the mind reflected in the conjunction between Bottom and St. Paul, the fairies and the objects of faith. Whether the topic be fairies or love or drama, throughout the play Shakespeare has given with the right hand and taken away with the left. In Bottom's remarks upon waking he gives us a fleeting glimpse into St. Paul's vision of the foolishness of faith, and then takes it away by jumbling the words and putting them into the mouth of no holy fool but a fool natural. This playfulness is no different in kind from that which Shakespeare has shown toward the uncertain fairies and the ambiguous human experiences with which the fairies are linked. The important thing is the multivalency of the perspective. In Bottom's speech faith itself is subsumed into the catalog of ambiguities with which the fairies are associated—and in fact there is a kind of startling propriety to the association: the play has consistently encouraged a complementary vision in which credulity and skepticism, acceptance and rejection can coexist, and Bottom speaking of his experiences hints at what is surely the most provocative complementary vision of all, St. Paul's paradox that faith is both folly and the highest wisdom. As Reinhold Niebuhr has pointed out, in I Corinthians St. Paul explores the metaphysics of faith by detailing a whole series of dichotomies, balancing that which seems true to the eye of the flesh against that which is true indeed. To draw an analogy to the mortal-fairy dichotomy in *A Midsummer Night's Dream* seems very tempting, to say the least. No one's eye is more fleshly than Bottom's, and yet in spite of his childish intellectual limitations—and perhaps because of them—he catches a glimpse into a genuine extra-physical order. The mysteriousness of the fairies momentarily becomes linked with the highest mystery of all. Bottom and St. Paul: here indeed "The poet's eye, in a fine frenzy rolling, / Doth glance from heaven to earth, from earth to heaven" [V. i. 12-13]—and winks. The sheer breadth of Shakespeare's daring is almost overwhelming.

But Bottom's provocative hint of higher meanings remains no more than a hint, perhaps even a trap for the unwary. His dream "hath no bottom" in it both because the dream has lifted Bottom for once out of his lowly self and because the fairy world is still far from a vision of (as Tyndale phrases it) "the bottome of Goddes secretes." For all the resonances, the world of comedy cannot really assimilate the mysteries of faith, nor is the gift of an acquaintance with the fairy queen quite the same thing as grace; so Bottom must relapse from a dream that "hath no bottom" into his usual Bottom-y self, ready to make *Pyramus and Thisby* an even more lamentable comedy with his stupidity. But for an instant we are given another perspective, one in which Bottom's simple-mindedness seems enviable rather than ludicrous, and literalism and faith seem impossible to tell apart. A play which has consistently encouraged a pluralistic vision for a moment lets us see that even sophistication can have its disadvantages. (pp. 267-68)

Ronald F. Miller, " 'A Midsummer Night's Dream':
The Fairies, Bottom, and the Mystery of Things,"
in Shakespeare Quarterly, Vol. XXVI, No. 3, Summer, 1975, pp. 254-68.

DAVID BEVINGTON   (lecture date 1975)

[*In the following excerpt from a lecture delivered in 1975, Bevington explores the manner in which Shakespeare develops the tension between the dark and comic aspects of* A Midsummer Night's Dream. *He discerns this dichotomy in a number of different relationships of both character and theme, including that between Oberon and Puck (the one benevolent and the other frightening), between the young lovers' potential for sexual licentiousness and their exercise of restraint during the flight to the woods, between the forest itself as both sanctuary and place of violent death, and between the elements of death, rape, seduction and the overriding comic structure of* A Midsummer Night's Dream. *Like Jan Kott (1964), Bevington notes that it is in the woods, not the city, that the lovers confront their true sexual natures; however, he takes issue with Kott's assessment of the abundance of erotic suggestions in the play and with his interpretation of the licentious relationship between Titania and Bottom. Instead, Bevington claims that sexual desire is consistently controlled by the characters' moral restraint and that the time shared by Titania and Bottom is "touchingly innocent and tender." A focus on the tension in* A Midsummer Night's Dream *between sexual desire and restraint can also be found in the essay by M. D. Faber (1972), and Bevington's assessment that the pervasive element of death is consistently suppressed by the play's comic structure is shared by Charles R. Lyons (1971). For further discussions of the dark or tragic element in* A Midsummer Night's Dream, *see the excerpts by G. K. Chesterton (1904), Cumberland Clark (1931), G. Wilson Knight (1932), Hugh M. Richmond (1971), Mordecai Marcus (1981), and Michael Taylor (see Additional Bibliography). Also, see the excerpts by Denton J. Snider (1890), Harold C. Goddard (1951), John Vyvyan (1961), Stephen Fender (1968), R. A. Zimbardo (1970), Florence Falk (1980), and Paul A. Olson (see Additional Bibliography) for discussions of the play's reconciliation of discordant or contradictory elements.*]

When Oberon instructs Puck, in act 3, scene 2 of *A Midsummer Night's Dream*, to overcast the night with "dropping fog as black as Acheron" [III. ii. 357], and to lead the "testy rivals" Demetrius and Lysander astray so that they will not actually harm one another in their rivalry, while Oberon for his part undertakes to obtain the changeling boy from Titania whom he will then release from her infatuated love of Bottom, Puck replies that the two of them will have to work fast. Such fairy doings need to be accomplished by night, insists Puck. With the approaching break of day, and the shining of Aurora's harbinger or morning star, ghosts and damned spirits will have to trip home to churchyards and their "wormy beds" beneath the ground. Puck's implication seems clear: he and Oberon, being spirits of the dark, are bound by its rules to avoid the light of day.

Just as clearly, however, Oberon protests that Puck is wrong in making such an assumption. "But we are spirits of another sort," Oberon insists.

> I with the Morning's love have oft made sport,
> And, like a forester, the groves may tread
> Even till the eastern gate, all fiery red,

> Opening on Neptune, with fair blessèd beams
> Turns into yellow gold his salt green streams.
>
> [III. ii. 388-93]

Oberon may frolic until late in the dawn, though by implication even he may not stay abroad all day. The association of Oberon with sunlight and dawn is thus more symbolic than practical; it disassociates him from spirits of the dark, even though he must finish up this night's work before night is entirely past. He concedes to Puck the need for hurry: "But notwithstanding, haste; make no delay. / We may effect this business yet ere day" [III. ii. 394-95]. The concession implies that Oberon has made his point about sporting with the dawn not to refute Puck's call for swiftness, but to refute Puck's association of the fairies with ghosts and damned spirits.

This debate between Oberon and Puck reflects a fundamental tension in the play between comic reassurance and the suggestion of something dark and threatening. Although the fairies act benignly, Puck continually hints at a good deal more than simple mischief. The forest itself is potentially a place of violent death and rape, even if the lovers experience nothing more than fatigue, anxiety, and being torn by briars. In the forest, moreover, the experience of love invites all lovers to consider, however briefly, the opportunity for sexual reveling freed from the restraints of social custom. (pp. 80-1)

Puck constantly brings before our eyes a more threatening vision of fairydom than is apparent in Oberon's more regal pronouncements. In part, of course, he is the practical joker making Oberon laugh at his ability to mimic a filly foal, or a three-foot stool, or Demetrius and Lysander. Puck is infinitely versatile in changing shapes, just as he can also put a girdle round the earth in forty minutes. On the other hand, Puck also loves to frighten people. He gladly confesses to being the elf who "frights the maidens of the villagery" [II. i. 35]. It is he who conjures up, for the delectation of the audience, a morbid image of nighttime as fearful, and as associated with gaping graves in churchyards, ghosts and damned spirits, screeching owls, and howling wolves:

> Now the hungry lion roars,
> And the wolf behowls the moon;
> Whilst the heavy ploughman snores,
> All with weary task fordone.
> Now the wasted brands do glow,
> Whilst the screech owl, screeching loud,
> Puts the wretch that lies in woe
> In remembrance of a shroud.
> Now it is the time of night
> That the graves, all gaping wide,
> Every one lets forth his sprite,
> In the churchyard paths to glide.
>
> [V. i. 371-82]
(p. 82)

Even in the action of the play, Puck does in fact frighten many of the persons he meets—virtually all of them, in fact, except Bottom. As he chases Quince, Snout, and the rest from their rehearsal spot in a forest clearing, he makes the incantation:

> I'll follow you, I'll lead you about a round,
> Through bog, through bush, through brake, through brier.
> Sometime a horse I'll be, sometime a hound,
> A hog, a headless bear, sometime a fire;
> And neigh, and bark, and grunt, and roar, and burn,
> Like horse, hound, hog, bear, fire, at every turn.
>
> [III. i. 106-11]

And he later reports to his master, with glee, the startling effect upon the rude mechanicals created by Bottom's reemergence from his hawthorne tiring house with an ass's head on his shoulders:

> When they him spy,
> As wild geese that the creeping fowler eye,
> Or russet-pated choughs, many in sort,
> Rising and cawing at the gun's report,
> Sever themselves and madly sweep the sky;
> So at his sight away his fellows fly,
> And at our stamp here o'er and o'er one falls;
> He murder cries and help from Athens calls.
> Their sense thus weak, lost with their fears thus strong,
> Made senseless things begin to do them wrong,
> For briers and thorns at their apparel snatch:
> Some, sleeves—some, hats; from yielders all things
>   catch.
>
> [III. ii. 19-30]

Our own laughter at this comic chase should not obscure the fact that Puck creates truly frightening illusions in the forest. Similarly, our sense of assurance that Demetrius and Lysander will come to no harm must not cause us to forget that Puck's game with them is to lead them astray, like those night-wanderers whom he is known to mislead, "laughing at their harm" [II. i. 39].

In the relationship of Puck and Oberon, it is Puck who tends to stress the irrational and frightening while Oberon's position is that of a ruler insisting on the establishment of proper obedience to his authority. When Puck mistakenly applies the love-juice intended for Demetrius to Lysander's eyes, thereby inducing Lysander to desert his true love for Helena, Oberon's first reaction is one of dismay:

> What hast thou done? Thou hast mistaken quite
> And laid the love-juice on some true-love's sight.
> Of thy misprision must perforce ensue
> Some true-love turned, and not a false turned true.
>
> [III. ii. 88-91]

Whereupon the fairy king immediately orders Puck to find Helena and return with her, so that Demetrius (who now lies asleep at their feet) can be induced to love her. Oberon seeks always to right unhappy love. His insistence that he and his followers are fairies of "another sort" is thus an appropriate and consistent stance for him, even if what he says does not always square with Puck's role as the hobgoblin who skims milk of its cream, prevents milk from turning into butter, or deprives ale of its "barm" or head. Oberon's very presence at the wedding is intended to assure that such things won't happen to Theseus, Hippolyta, and the rest of the happy young people about to marry; Oberon guarantees that their issue "Ever shall be fortunate," free of "mole, harelip, nor scar," or any other "blots of Nature's hand" [V. i. 406, 411, 409].

Together, Oberon and Puck represent contrasting forces within the fairy kingdom. Perhaps their functions can best be reconciled by reflecting that their chief power to do good lies in withholding the mischief of which they are capable. Like Apollo in book 1 of the *Iliad*, whom the Greek warriors venerate as the god of health because he is also terrifyingly capable of sending plagues, Oberon is to be feared because he has the authority both to prevent birth defects and other marks "prodigious, such as are / Despised in nativity" [V. i. 412-13], and to inflict them. Only when placated by men and called by

such names as Hobgoblin or "sweet Puck" will these spirits work for men and bring them good luck.

The forest shares many of these same ambivalent qualities as do the fairies. It is in part a refuge for young lovers fleeing the sharp Athenian law, a convenient and secluded spot for clandestine play rehearsals, and a fragrant bower for the fairy queen decked out "With sweet musk-roses, and with eglantine" [II. i. 252]. For the young lovers, however, as their quest for amorous bliss grows more and more vexed, the forest becomes increasingly a place of darkness, estrangement, and potential violence. Demetrius warns Helena, in an attempt to be rid of her,

> You do impeach your modesty too much
> To leave the city and commit yourself
> Into the hands of one that loves you not,
> To trust the opportunity of night
> And the ill counsel on a desert place
> With the rich worth of your virginity.
>
> [II. i. 214-19]

Demetrius recognizes the opportunity for a loveless rape and briefly recognizes his own potential for such sexual violence, though he is also virtuous enough to reject the temptation. The alternative he offers Helena is scarcely more kind: he will run from her and leave her "to the mercy of wild beasts" [II. i. 228]. (pp. 82-5)

Nighttime in the forest repeatedly conveys the sense of estrangement and misunderstanding with which the lovers are afflicted. When Puck creates a pitchy darkness into which he can lead Lysander and Demetrius, he is not manufacturing mischief out of nothing but is giving expression to their rivalry in love. As a stage manager of his own little play, he allows the men to parody their own tendencies toward petty vengefulness. The fact that the two young men are rather much alike, that their contention can be resolved by a simple solution (since Demetrius did in fact pay court to Helena before the play began, and need only return to his original attachment to her), adds to the sense of comedy by heightening the comic discrepancy between their anger and its lack of objective cause. Puck's manipulation serves the benign effect of showing (to the lovers themselves, in retrospect) the ridiculousness of exaggerated contentiousness. In a similar way Puck uses night and darkness as an emblem to expose the catty jealousies of the two young women and their tendency toward morbid self-pity. The effect of such cleansing exposure is a comic purgation. Puck is a creature of the night, but he uses darkness to produce ultimate illumination. He mocks pretensions, even in himself, even in the play to which he belongs: "If we shadows have offended, / Think but this, and all is mended— / That you have but slumb'red here / While these visions did appear" [V. i. 423-26].

Darkness and the forest, then, offer the lovers a glimpse of their inner selves. Often, this glimpse suggests much about human nature that is not merely perverse and jealous, but libidinous. Here . . . Jan Kott offers helpful insights, though he has surely gone too far. The motif on which the action of the play is based, that of escape into a forest on the eve of Mayday (Walpurgisnacht) or on Midsummer's Eve, is traditionally erotic. The four lovers are discovered the next morning asleep on the ground, in a compromising position certainly, though not in flagrante delicto. "Begin these woodbirds but to couple now?" [IV. i. 140] asks Theseus humorously and continues to remain skeptical toward the lovers' story of their night—a skepticism prompted in part, one imagines, by their insistence that they have slept apart from one another. We know, in fact, that their night has been a continuous series of proposed matings without any actual consummations. "One turf shall serve as pillow for us both," Lysander suggests to Hermia as night comes on. "One heart, one bed, two bosoms, and one troth" [II. ii. 41-2]. She finds his rhetoric pretty but insists on a propriety that is not mere primness. "Such separation as may well be said / Becomes a virtuous bachelor and a maid, / So far be distant," she instructs him [II. ii. 58-60]. She wants her lover to move away just a little, but not too much. Hermia knows, because of the person she is, that freedom to escape the harsh Athenian law does not mean the license to try anything and that she can justify her elopement only by voluntary obedience to a code she holds to be absolutely good and that she never questions. The serpent of which she dreams, crawling on her breast to eat her heart away while Lysander watches smilingly . . . , is not an image of her own licentiousness but of an infidelity in which she is the innocent victim. Demetrius too would never presume to take advantage of Helena's unprotected condition, however much he may perceive an opportunity for rape. Kott seriously distorts the context of the love imagery in this play when he discovers sodomistic overtones in Helena's likening herself to a spaniel; her meaning, as she clearly explains, is that she is like a patient, fawning animal whose master responds to affection with blows and neglect.

Repeatedly in this play, a presumption of man's licentiousness is evoked, only to be answered by the conduct of the lovers themselves. This representation of desire almost but not quite satisfied is to be sure a titillating one, but it looks forward as do the lovers themselves to legitimate consummation in marriage and procreation. At the very end, the lovers do all go to bed while Oberon speaks of the issue that will surely spring from their virtuous coupling. Earlier, Theseus has proposed to await the marriage day for his consummation, even though he captured his wife through military force; why else should he complain of the aged moon that "lingers" his desires "Like to a stepdame or a dowager" [I. i. 5]? (Hippolyta, with a maiden's traditional reluctance, seems more content with the four-day delay than does her amorous bridegroom.) The tradesmen's play serves as one last comic barrier to the achievement of desire, although it is mercifully brief and can be performed without epilogue in the interest of further brevity. Such waiting only makes the moment of final surrender more pleasurable and meaningful.

The conflict between sexual desire and rational restraint is, then, as essential tension throughout the play reflected in the images of dark and light. This same tension exists in the nature of the fairies and of the forest. The ideal course seems to be a middle one, between the sharp Athenian law on the one hand with its threat of death or perpetual chastity, and a licentiousness on the other hand that the forest (and man's inner self) proposes with alacrity, but from which the lovers are saved chiefly by the steadfastness of the women. They, after all, remain constant; it is the men who change affections under the effect of Oberon's love potion. (pp. 86-8)

This tension between licentiousness and self-mastery is closely related also to the way in which the play itself constantly flirts with genuine disaster but controls that threat through comic reassurance. Hermia is threatened with death in act 1, or with something almost worse than death—perpetual maidenhood, and yet we know already from the emphasis on love and marriage that all such threats to happiness are ultimately to prove illusory. Lysander and Hermia speak of "War, death, or sick-

ness" [I. i. 142] and of other external threats to love, but are resolved on a plan of escape that will avoid all these. Repeatedly in the forest the lovers fear catastrophe only to discover that their senses have been deceiving them. "But who is here?" asks Helena as she comes across a sleeping man, Lysander, on the ground: "Dead, or asleep?" [II. ii. 100-01]. When, shortly afterwards, Hermia awakes to find herself deserted, she sets off after her strangely absent lover: "Either death, or you, I'll find immediately" [II. ii. 156]. The choice seems dire, but the comic sense of discrepancy assures us that the need for such a choice is only a chimera. Later, again, when Helena concludes that all her erstwhile friends have turned against her for some inexplicable reason, she determines to leave them: "'Tis partly my own fault, / Which death or absence soon shall remedy" [III. ii. 243-44]. Only in the story of Pyramus and Thisbe, with its hilarious presentation of the very tragedy of misunderstanding that did not occur in A Midsummer Night's Dream, does comic reassurance fail. Instead of Helena's "Dead, or asleep?" the order is reversed. "Asleep, my love?" asks Thisbe as she finds Pyramus on the ground. "What, dead, my dove?" [V. i. 324-25]. (pp. 88-9)

The fairies of A Midsummer Night's Dream do not govern themselves by the conventional sexual mores of the humans. . . . [Many] things are inverted in the mirror-image world of fairydom: it is the woman rather than the man who is inconstant, the obstacles to love are internal rather than external, and so on. Similarly, the quarrel of Oberon and Titania reflects the recently completed struggle for mastery between Theseus and Hippolyta, and yet is conducted according to the peculiar customs of the fairy kingdom. Titania's love for Theseus is apparently the occasion of her current visit to Athens, in order that she may be at Theseus's wedding; yet her love for the Athenian king has taken strange forms. According to Oberon, Titania's love for Theseus prompts her to "lead him through the glimmering night / From Perigenia, whom he ravishèd, / And make him with fair Aegles break his faith, / With Ariadne, and Antiopa" [II. i. 77-80]. Titania to be sure denies the charge. The point is, however, that Oberon considers his queen perfectly capable of expressing her love for Theseus by encouraging him to ravish and then reject in turn a series of human mistresses. This is the sort of mysterious affection that only a god could practice or understand. Oberon's behavior in love is no less puzzling from a human vantage: he punishes Titania for denying him the changeling boy by forcing her to take a gross and foolish lover. These gods make a sort of inconstancy.

The rivalry about the changeling boy is equally bizarre if measured in human terms. Conceivably, as Kott suggests, Oberon desires the boy as his own minion, although (like so much of what Kott claims) the boy's erotic status cannot be proved from a reading of the text. We are told only that he is a "lovely boy" whom "jealous Oberon" desires as a "Knight of his train" to be his "henchman" [II. i. 22, 24, 25, 121]. When Oberon has succeeded in winning the boy from her, he has the youth sent to his "bower in fairyland" [IV. i. 61]. This slender evidence seems deliberately ambiguous. Any attempts to depict Oberon as bisexual surely miss the point that the fairies' ideas concerning love are ultimately unknowable and incomprehensible. We mortals can laugh at our own libidinous tendencies when we see them mirrored in the behavior of the immortals, but we can never fathom how distant those immortals are from the ordinary pangs of human affection. Oberon is not so busy teaching Titania a lesson that he fails to enjoy Puck's "fond pageant" on the theme of human passion: "Lord, what fools these mortals be" [III. ii. 115].

Titania does of course undergo an experience of misdirected love that is analogous to human inconstancy in love and that is prompted by the same love-juice applied to the eyes of Demetrius and Lysander. . . . Her hours spent with Bottom are touchingly innocent and tender. Like the royal creature that she is, she forbids Bottom to leave her presence. Even if he is her slave, however, imprisoned in an animal form, she is no Circean enchantress teaching him enslavement to sensual appetite. Instead, her mission is to "purge thy mortal grossness so / That thou shalt like an airy spirit go" [III. i. 160-61]. It is because she is prompted by such ethereal considerations that she feeds him with apricots and dewberries, fans the moonbeams from his sleeping eyes, and the like. As Oberon reports later to Puck, having kept close watch over Titania, she graces the hairy temples of Bottom's ass's head "With coronet of fresh and fragrant flowers" [IV. i. 52]. Rather than descending into the realm of human passion and perversity, she has attempted to raise Bottom into her own. Bottom, for his part, speaking the part of the wise fool, has noted the irrationality of love but has submitted himself to deliciously innocent pleasures that are, for him, mainly gastronomic. Titania, and Shakespeare too, have indeed purged his mortal grossness, not by making him any less funny, but by showing how the tensions in this play between the dark and the affirmative side of love are reconciled in the image of Titania and the ass's head. (pp. 89-91)

> David Bevington, " 'But We Are Spirits of Another Sort': The Dark Side of Love and Magic in 'A Midsummer Night's Dream'," in Medieval and Renaissance Studies: Proceedings of the Southeastern Institute of Medieval and Renaissance Studies, *Summer, 1975, edited by Siegfried Wenzel, University of North Carolina Press, 1978, pp. 80-92.*

ANNE PAOLUCCI (essay date (1977))

[*Whereas most critics who have discussed the duration of time in* A Midsummer Night's Dream *discover inconsistencies in Shakespeare's representation of the time scheme in the dramatic action, Paolucci argues that the dramatist has provided clues to indicate the passage of five full days. She remarks that although the original time scheme becomes distorted in the darkened woods, by tracing references to intervals of rest and the occasions when one character or another lies down to sleep we can see that Shakespeare has carefully accounted for the passage of four days between the ends of Act I and Act IV. Other critics who have discussed the duration of time in this play include Charles Gildon (1710), J. O. Halliwell-Phillipps (1841), Henry A. Clapp (1885), and Horace Howard Furness (1895). Paolucci also comments that in his use of contrasting images of night and day, Shakespeare replaces the typical association of light with reason and darkness and the moonlit woods as the source of the lovers' comprehension of reality. G. Wilson Knight (1932), Charles R. Lyons (1971), and Madeleine Doran (see Additional Bibliography) also trace the associations of day and night in the play.*]

"Four days will quickly steep themselves in night," says Hippolyta in the opening scene of *A Midsummer Night's Dream* . . . ; "Four nights will quickly dream away the time" [I. i. 7-8]. The trouble here, as [George Lyman] Kittredge briefly defines it, is that "the four days and four nights," which are by Hippolyta's count to precede the wedding day, "are not fully spanned" in the text of the play as we have it. The dramatic action ought to cover five days; actually, only three are ac-

counted for. Critics have ascribed this apparent time discrepancy, in a play compounded of magical discrepancies, to carelessness on Shakespeare's part (forgivable, to be sure), to his working hastily to meet a deadline (possibly for a court performance or a noble wedding), or to his revising the play at some later date (when he did not catch the inconsistencies in the chronology of the action). (p. 317)

In the absence of incontrovertible proof, one is almost tempted to concede it all—*nolo contendere*—not because the arguments are convincing, but because the alternative of being cornered into defending the retort that Genius Can Do No Wrong is bound to be frustrating. Unfortunately, however, the problem persists, forcing itself upon us with every new reading of the play. Could Shakespeare really have included so many references to time without some sort of dramatic design? Genius may be subject to error and carelessness, but would it make such a point of it? Whatever grudging concession one may make to chameleon logic, instinct shies away from the suggestion that Shakespeare failed, in a work very likely scheduled for court performance, to catch such "inconsistencies."

Surely a dramatic purpose suggests itself in the obvious fact that the "frame" scenes of the play contain specific time references which enable us to date events, whereas the magic wood scenes abound in night images which create confusion and suggest one long uninterrupted dream. Time as measured by the movement of the sun disappears in the enchanted wood. But may we not hope to find some clue within that magic night that will help translate dream into reality, moonlight into suntime?

Night is the kingdom of the fairies. They live and work and travel by night, or (more accurately) *in* night—stuck there, to use the language of astronomy, as the planets are stuck in their respective spheres in the Ptolemaic configurations of the heavens. The world of the fairies is the nighttime of the universe, the condition of *absolute* darkness as it moves around the globe opposite the sun.

The human beings caught up in such a condition naturally find themselves disoriented. Confusion prevails as they try to adjust to their strange surroundings. The lovers shift allegiances abruptly. Bottom is "translated" into something rare and wonderful, which not only cannot be expressed properly after the fact, but cannot even be grasped adequately at the time. The entire machinery of apprehension seems to have been thrown out of gear.

We are aware, in a sense, of having been thrust into the sphere of the moon; hence the human attempt to grasp and describe the experience must necessarily prove inadequate. (pp. 317-18)

In the "unnatural" setting of the magic wood, light and day—like familiar logic and emotional certainty—have temporarily been destroyed. Night, as the means for emotional redirection and insight through confusion, is raised in their place. The sun—symbol of reason and clarity—is replaced by the notoriously "inconstant" moon. And yet, when all is said and done, the experience of that long night will have served to illuminate reality much more effectively than the light of reason ever could. In the middle scenes of the play, the moon takes over as the symbol of the paradox which is the heart of the argument.

Having reviewed in this way the day-night motif of the play, perhaps we may more readily accept the notion that time itself never really comes to a standstill. Shakespeare, far from "slipping" in his calculations, has in fact underscored the passage of time in a number of ways. The fairies themselves, for example, are painfully conscious of time's swift movement. Their reappearance at the very close of the play should remind us that between the lovers' awakening and the end of the wedding festivities, the fairies have, in fact, traced the usual full daily cycle: a whole day has passed and they have brought night back again with them.

The enveloping action—the action Theseus dominates—can be traced accurately enough in time. We learn in the opening scene that the royal marriage is to take place in four days. The reference to the new moon is actually part of an eleven-line statement which enables us to date the outermost limits of the action:

> *The*.Now, fair Hippolyta, our nuptial hour
> Draws on apace. Four happy days bring in
> Another moon; but, O, methinks, how slow
> This old moon wanes! She lingers my desires,
> Like to a stepdame or a dowager,
> Long withering out a young man's revenue.
>   *Hip*.Four days will quickly steep themselves in night;
> Four nights will quickly dream away the time;
> And then the moon, like to a silver bow
> New-bent in heaven, shall behold the night
> Of our solemnities.
>
>   [I.i. 1-11]

This passage sets forth the time-span to be covered in the course of the play; but even more important, it alerts us to *awareness* of time and to the psychological effects we can expect in characters subject to such awareness.

On the morning set for the royal wedding, Theseus reminds us that it is the first day of May: "No doubt they [the lovers] rose up early to observe / The rite of May" [IV. i. 132-33]. The four days referred to in the opening scene have obviously elapsed. For Theseus and Hippolyta, whom we have not seen since the opening of the play, there is all the difference between the old moon and the new moon. The enveloping action thus provides two end-points of time between which the intervening events are to be traced and enables us to date the opening scene as taking place on 27 April. Having established the outer limits of the action, we can now go back to the opening scene and fill in the time sequence as it develops.

Left alone after Theseus' ultimatum, Lysander and Hermia make plans to elope. "If thou lovest me," urges Lysander, "steal forth thy father's house tomorrow night" [I. i. 163-64]. Hermia agrees: "In that same place thou hast appointed me / Tomorrow truly will I meet with thee" [I. i. 177-78]. When Helen comes on the scene, Lysander confides their plans to her: "To-morrow night.... / Through Athens gates have we devis'd to steal" [I. i. 209-13]. Helen quickly devises a plan of her own:

> I will go tell [Demetrius] of fair Hermia's flight.
> Then to the wood will he to-morrow night
> Pursue her. . . .
>
>   [I. i. 246-48]

Shakespeare mentions the time planned for the elopement four times and provides us, indirectly, with the precise date: the flight planned on 27 April (as a result of Theseus' ultimatum to Hermia) will be realized on 28 April—that is, the night of 28-29 April.

The time planned for the elopement of the lovers and for Helena's counter-move to frustrate them is apparently also the time planned for the rehearsal of the artisans. Having distrib-

uted the various parts for the play they will present at the wedding of the King, Peter Quince informs the company that they will meet "to-morrow night . . . a mile without the town, by moonlight" [I. ii. 100-02]. Shakespeare seems to have brought these events together in the *planning* to enable us to pinpoint the time of subsequent events, when references to time disappear.

With the opening of Act II, we find ourselves in the magic wood of the fairies. We learn through Robin Goodfellow—"that merry wanderer of the night"—that Oberon "doth keep his revels here to-night" [II. i. 18]. What night? We suspect (although we cannot be absolutely sure yet) that it is the night referred to earlier, the night of 28-29 April. Our suspicion is reinforced with the arrival of Demetrius and Helena—the girl obviously pursuing the man she loves, Demetrius obviously pursuing Hermia, who, with Lysander, is already in the wood. The rehearsal of the artisans at the beginning of Act III further strengthens the initial impression. It is reasonable to suppose, in other words, that the events of Act II—right up to the appearance of the artisans for their rehearsal at the beginning of Act III—take place, as previously scheduled, on the night of 28-29 April. It is at this point that the reader is apt to lose his bearings in dating events. Not until the reappearance of Theseus in Act IV does time fall back into the familiar pattern.

But the familiar pattern cannot possibly be called on to help us in the magic wood, where everything is distorted and human beings find themselves completely disoriented. We should have been very much surprised, in fact, had the original time scheme been retained in the middle scenes of the play. With the entrance into the wood, we have moved not into "another" night but into a "floating" night, an unnaturally "long and tedious night" which cannot be measured in the usual way. Within this new *dimension*, Shakespeare—far from losing sight of his earlier dramatic precision—has in fact provided us with a set of highly original clues, perfectly suited to the new setting, by means of which we can bridge the apparent time gap right up to the morning of 1 May.

The most revealing of these clues have to do with the *intervals of rest* within the magic wood, and, more particularly, with reminders of *sleep*. The first interval comes between the two events already dated for us: the elopement of the lovers and the rehearsal of the artisans. Titania is already asleep when Lysander and Hermia, exhausted by their flight, stumble on the scene and almost immediately fall asleep. We know for certain that this is the first night in the magic wood—the night of 28-29 April—by the appearance, on schedule, of the artisans at the beginning of the next scene, where Titania awakens, sees Bottom, and claims him for her own.

The second interval of sleep comes in Act III, scene ii, where Demetrius—still pursuing Hermia—lies down to rest and falls asleep. The third interval marks the end of the wild chase and the proper regrouping of the lovers. Robin Goodfellow brings the four young people together at this point (although in the confusion of the "overcast" night they do not actually see one another); utterly exhausted by this time, the four at once fall into a profound sleep. These last two intervals are the ones to be dated and, as a result, distinguished from the first interval, which we may assume to occur on the night of 28-29 April.

The confusion which characterizes the third interval is especially significant in helping us to date the action. In the play's opening scene, the dispute concerning Hermia's suitors, Theseus had set a deadline, by which time Hermia was either to give in to her father's wish that she marry Demetrius or else suffer the punishment of death:

> Take time to pause; and by the next new moon—
> The sealing day betwixt my love and me
> For everlasting bond of fellowship—
> Upon that day either prepare to die
> For disobedience to your father's will,
> Or else to wed Demetrius. . . .
>
> [I. i. 83-8]

The time of the new moon—as we have learned in the opening scene—is 1 May (or, rather, the night of 1-2 May).

At least two other passages emphasize the point. At the rehearsal for their play (III. i), the artisans discuss the problem of providing the moonlight for which the text calls. Bottom in his usual enthusiasm cries: "A calendar, a calendar! Look in the almanac. Find out moonshine, find out moonshine!" [III. i. 53-4]. And Quince reassures him, "Yes, it doth shine that night" [III. i. 55]. But Hippolyta has already told us in the opening scene that it will be a *new* moon, a "silver bow / New-bent in heaven." And at the time of the actual performance, Moonshine takes pains to explain—in answer to Theseus' "he is no crescent, and his horns are invisible within the circumference"—that "this lanthorn doth the horned moon present" [V. i. 242-44]. Shakespeare plays on the idea of the new moon for several more lines:

> *Hip.* I am aweary of this moon. Would that he would change!
> *The.* It appears, by his small light of discretion, that he is in the wane; but yet, in courtesy, in all reason, we must stay the time.
>
> [V. i. 251-55]

Now, if the night of the wedding is the night of the new moon, the night before it must be a night of *no* moon, an "overcast" night, a night in which confusion is very likely to arise because of total darkness. The lantern jokes remind us that the appearance of the new moon coincides with the night of 1-2 May. The "overcast . . . night" which precedes it is a night without moon. The confusion of the exhausted lovers in the third interval of sleep may be considered, therefore, a poetic reminder of the total "eclipse" of the moon on the night preceding the royal festivities, the night of no moon. And it enables us to "date" the third period of sleep (from which the lovers will be awakened by the royal party on the morning of the wedding) as the night of 30 April-1 May. Having thus "dated" the first and third intervals of sleep, we may reasonably conclude that the remaining middle interval of the sequence corresponds to the night of 29-30 April.

Sleep is the major clue in distinguishing the passage of time within the magic night. But there is a second set of clues that reinforce the first: each of the sleep intervals coincides with the casting of one of the love spells. In the first interval, the love juice of the magic flower is administered to Lysander (and Titania); in the second, the magic potion is given to Demetrius; in the third, the magic potion restores Lysander to his former condition. Time is thus translated into a poetic dimension in which the three moments of "conversion" are clearly distinguished, the transition from "before" to "after" underscored in each case by means of sleep.

A third set of phenomena adds to the sensation that time as we know it has been foreshortened but not lost: Hermia's prophetic dream, Bottom's "bottomless dream," and Titania's "vi-

sion." Day-night contrasts cannot guide us here, it is true, but some kind of sequence is discernible. There is, one must admit, some kind of order in the apparent confusion.

It is Theseus who marks the return to the normal diurnal cycle. His very appearance in IV. i is a reminder of sun-time. Several important images suggest the reawakening of life, the correction of "error" in the light of day and reason:

> . . . the vaward of the day. . . .
>
> [IV. i. 105]

> . . . ears that sweep away the morning dew. . . .
>
> [IV. i. 121]

> No doubt they rose up early to observe
> The rite of May. . . .
>
> [IV. i. 132-33]

> Is not this the day
> That Hermia should give answer of her choice?
>
> [IV. i. 135-36]

> Good morrow friends. Saint Valentine is past.
> Begin these woodbirds but to couple now?
>
> [IV. i. 139-40]

> . . . the morning now is something worn. . . .
>
> [IV. i. 182]

The fairies have disappeared "in silence sad" following "night's shade" [IV. i. 95-6]. When we meet them again, it is the night of the royal wedding: Titania and Oberon are back to bless the "best bride bed" [V. i. 403]. They have until daybreak to accomplish their task, for they must flee from the crowing of the cock, the lark's song, the pale streaks of dawn—"Aurora's harbinger" [III. ii. 380]—and run "from the presence of the sun, / Following darkness like a dream" [V. i. 385-86]. Here and elsewhere, we are reminded that the fairies live in perpetual night; it is their natural province. The lovers who stumble into their world are out of place, out of *time,* subject to inconstancy (for this is the sphere of the moon). (pp. 319-24)

The fairy world is not for mortals; Theseus cannot begin to grasp the strange phenomena reported to him by the lovers: "I never may believe / These antique fables nor these fairy toys" [V. i. 2-3]. Even to those who have lived through it, the experience appears—once they have been restored to the light of day—to have been an impossible dream, a suspension of time. Back in their familiar surroundings, they once more become sure of themselves (to the point of arrogance in the case of Demetrius). Restored to their own world, they seem to forget what has transpired and fall easily and quickly into old routines and habits. The experience of "inconstancy" remains with them as a flash of insight, an emotional truth that escapes definition.

But Shakespeare has traced the lesson and the experience for *us* very clearly, providing the necessary clues to follow the lovers through the magic maze. The sleep of the lovers, coupled with the gracious anointment of their eyes and their vivid dreams, enables us to translate the seemingly chaotic events of the long night into part of an ordered sequence, beginning and ending with the familiar patterns of sun-time, which frame the enveloping action and define the limits of the magic night. For us, the entire sequence is consistent and forms an organic whole. (p. 325)

Anne Paolucci, "The Lost Days in 'A Midsummer Night's Dream'," in Shakespeare Quarterly, *Vol. 28, No. 3, Summer, 1977, pp. 317-26.*

DAVID ORMEROD   (essay date 1978)

[*Ormerod's is the earliest published essay on* A Midsummer Night's Dream *that deals explicitly with the classical story of Theseus as the slayer of the Minotaur in the labyrinth of Crete. In a later essay, M. E. Lamb (1979) also relates the character of the duke in this play to the myth of the Minotaur. Ormerod argues that a comparison of the two stories—Shakespeare's and the classical one—can help us achieve a fuller understanding of themes apparent in* A Midsummer Night's Dream; *these themes he identifies as the carnality of blind, passionate love, the necessary progress of the lover from blind passion to the Platonic vision of beauty, and "the imperative reconciliation of opposites into a new discordia concors." He maintains that in* A Midsummer Night's Dream *the opposition of the Athenian city-state and the hostile environment of Crete is reflected in the opposition of Theseus's Athens and the fairy world. Ormerod likens the woods to the Cretan maze in that it represents a "labyrinthine moral confusion" where the lovers and Titania are motivated by love based on appearance rather than "inner reality"; it is also where the figure of the ass's head becomes an image of "the dominant motif in Shakespeare's comic world—moral mischoice." Other critics who have maintained that the play represents the delusions, even sinfulness, of passionate or romantic love include G. G. Gervinus (1849-50), E. K. Chambers (1905), Samuel B. Hemingway (1911), H. B. Charlton (1933), E. C. Pettet (1949), and George A. Bonnard (1956). Also, see the excerpts by John Vyvyan (1961) and Peter G. Phialas (1966) for further discussion of the Platonic ideal in the drama. In a related matter, Ormerod agrees with Jan Kott (1964) that* A Midsummer Night's Dream *is brutally erotic and that the incident in Titania's bower depicts the fairy queen in sexual intercourse with Bottom.*]

For over three hundred years the fairy world of *A Midsummer Night's Dream* has caught and held the imagination of spectators, readers and producers, has worked, in fact, so powerfully that the mutilated versions of the play which held the stages of eighteenth and nineteenth century playhouses concentrated almost exclusively on the world of Oberon and Titania, rejecting as otiose the framing world of Theseus and Hippolyta. The purpose of this essay is to reassess *A Midsummer Night's Dream* as a dual-locale comedy, its meaning essentially linked to the dialectical relationship of Theseus' court to the wood outside Athens. Just as a correct assessment of *The Merchant of Venice* demands consideration of both Venice and Belmont and just as the Forest of Arden has meaning only in antithesis to the court of Duke Frederick, so, I would contend, the function of Theseus in opposition to the fairy world of *A Midsummer Night's Dream* has been insufficiently stressed. This critical omission may be rectified if we invoke a traditional myth whose dynamic presence seems to have been hitherto unsuspected—that is, the myth of Theseus, the labyrinth, and the Minotaur. To view the play in this way is to observe it spring into a new and more acute focus and to bring together, holistically, the Athenian locale, the Duke and his Amazon bride-to-be, the Cretan maze transported across the seas for a renewed moral purpose, an updated Athenian tribute of youths and maidens, and, above all, a metamorphosed Minotaur in the half-beast, half-human figure of the transformed Bottom. Such a reading brings together Renaissance attitudes to the revivification of classical mythology in the context of Christian neo-platonic doctrine, reinforces our expectations concerning the Shakespearean love ethic which, in the world of the comedies, ideally "looks not with the eyes but with the mind" [I. i. 234], and attains contemporary pungency via its basis in beliefs concerning the power of witchcraft. To see the play as underpinned by the narrative of Theseus and the Minotaur is not to reject the achievements of recent scholarship but rather to stress those elements in Shakespeare's comic world which

seem paramount to modern criticism—the rejection of the love which is *alatus et caecus;* the moral purgation necessary, in an amorous context, to enable the lover to progress from Blind Cupid to Anteros, and the imperative reconciliation of opposites into a new *discordia concors.*

For an Elizabethan audience, Theseus was a figure with specific overtones and associations. Plutarch describes him as the founder of Athens and allots to him the parallel life of Romulus, founder of Rome. His gravity and dignity and above all, his rationality, thus receive great stress. Similarly, he is an image of a correct sexual hierarchy with reference to his conquest of Hippolyta and his assertion of the dominance of the male principle in amorous relationships, in contrast to those other dramatic sexual situations (e.g., the Hercules-Omphale motif in *Antony and Cleopatra*) where, in a world of moral chaos, the female principle has swamped or emasculated the male, a motif neatly played upon in Helena's "the story shall be changed; / The dove pursues the griffin; the mild hind / Makes speed to catch the tiger . . . my sex . . . cannot fight for love, as men may do; / We would be wooed and were not made to woo" [II. i. 230-42]. But, above all, Theseus' prime claim to fame is as the slayer of the Minotaur.

The Minotaur, with the head of a bull and the body of a man, product of the monstrous passion of Pasiphae for the Cretan bull, is a compressed image of love's passion reduced to bestiality.... The Minotaur association seems doubly important for *A Midsummer Night's Dream:* the wood of confusion in which the lovers wander, enchanted by the eye-potion of Puck-Cupid, suggests the labyrinth which Theseus threaded.... [And in] Shakespeare's wood, located beside the rationalist Athenian culture founded by Theseus, there is also a monster, this time with the head not of a bull but of an ass, and to this quasi-Cretan labyrinth the young Athenian lovers, willing metaphoric counterparts of the tribute Athens paid to Minos, are impelled by their suicidal passion. The love into which Titania flings herself with a suddenness and a violence imaging the celerity of the young lovers is not only degraded bestiality but is also ludicrous and risible. By substituting the ass-headed Bottom for the bull-headed Minotaur, Shakespeare has added a new dimension. But he has not forfeited the old association either. He does not, of course, reproduce the myth in a mechanical or allegorical fashion; rather, its constituent ingredients are reworked and reassembled so that the conflation of their overtones constitutes a new design. (pp. 39-41)

Jan Kott's impressionistic account of *A Midsummer Night's Dream* has been much derided, and many may have found his assertion of the play's sexuality implausible or even grotesque. But Kott is surely correct when he asserts that "in no other tragedy or comedy of his . . . is the eroticism expressed so brutally" . . . , and it may perhaps be pertinent to scrutinize the scene [between Titania and Bottom] more closely. Titania's precipitate love is explicitly sensuous and sensual. "Hit with Cupid's archery" [III. ii. 103], she provides a compressed icon of romantic love: "So is mine eye enthralled to thy shape, / And thy fair virtue's force perforce doth move me, / On the first view to say, to swear, I love thee" [III. i. 139-41]. Bottom's almost too-explicit comment that "reason and love keep little company together nowadays" [III. i. 143-44] reads like the gloss to an emblem. Moon and flowers weep in Titania's impetuous mind, "Lamenting some enforced chastity" [III. i. 200], and Puck can gleefully announce, "My mistress with a monster is in love [III. ii. 6]. Indeed, yes, as she soon proposes the right true end of love:

Sleep thou, and I will wind thee in my arms . . . .
So doth the woodbine, the sweet honeysuckle,
Gently entwist; the female ivy so
Enrings the barky fingers of the elm.
O how I love thee! How I dote on thee! (*They sleep*)

                                        [IV. i. 40-5]

"Titania and Bottom will pass through animal eroticism in a quite literal, even visual sense," remarks Kott. . . . We do not have to subscribe to Kott's more extravagant pronouncements—"I imagine Titania's court as consisting of old men and women, toothless and shaking, their mouths wet with saliva, who sniggeringly produce a monster for their mistress." . . .—to realize the essential accuracy of the arch statement that "the slender, tender and lyrical . . . the frail and sweet Titania drags the monster to bed, almost by force." . . . It seems perfectly reasonable to assume that, within the limits of what may be deemed theatrically tactful in terms of the conventions of this particular stage, the incident depicts an act of coitus between woman and ass, an act where, paradoxically, the element of reason and restraint has been predicated of an animal ("you should have little reason for that . . . ") and where the bestiality of physical desire unenlightened by moral insight is predicated of the woman. (pp. 42-3)

If *A Midsummer Night's Dream* seems, as a result of this inquiry, a grosser play than many of its admirers will find palatable, it must be contended that it also becomes a more elegantly articulated play. Titania in the copulatory embrace of Bottom, impelled by the ocular misjudgement occasioned by Puck's love-juice splashed upon her eyes, becomes a perfect icon for the Shakespearian commonplace—always the same yet endlessly varied—of the degradation which ensues when passionate love, induced by the arrow of morally blind Cupid, judges by appearance and not by inner reality. To judge by appearance is the ultimate absurdity ("How I dote . . . "); it is also the ultimate state of being towards which carnality impels—physical lust devoid of the animating human principle. (p. 44)

If one should require that the image of the ass-headed Minotaur in the labyrinthine Athenian wood should be linked in conclusive intimacy with Shakespeare's perennial love-ethic, the answer may perhaps be found in Renaissance manuals of iconography. Cesare Ripa describes Obstinacy ("Ostinatione") as a female figure dressed in black, her head surrounded by fog, holding an ass's head in both hands. . . .

The ass's head is therefore an image of the dominant motif in Shakespeare's comic world—moral mischoice. Helena wooed Demetrius. Titania wooed the monster. Everything was topsy-turvy. The order and pomp and procession that was Theseus, monster-slayer, and Hippolyta, Amazon who has met her lord, was overturned, and the headlong passionate characters became involved in labyrinthine moral confusion when they trusted their eyes and their lackbrained devotion to appearance. They were led out of the maze and were offered a dramatic representation of their own foolishness. They sniggered, only half comprehending. Plays are played to audiences, and as the lovers were audience to one play, so we are audience to their play and their partial understanding. If they do not understand, we must try to; we must see how, from such discord, can come the sweet thunder of concord. (p. 46)

[The] wanderings of the young lovers through the labyrinthine woods outside Athens [is] an ongoing image of great richness. It is an icon of blinded wrong choice, exemplified by Cupid's

incarnation in the guise of Puck and the volatility and mutability presented by the ubiquitous moonlight, and it is also the process by which this moral confusion is transcended as the spiralling movements of the conventional emblematic labyrinth yield to the harmonious circles of the conventional concluding dance. The irruption of Herculean hounds of Theseus and Hippolyta introduces the play's counter-thesis through the *discordia concors* of their "so musical a discord, such sweet thunder" [IV. i. 118]. Moonlight and Blind Cupid are transposed into sunlight and a greater degree of amorous insight. . . . Oberon, the "king of shadows," presides over the Platonic cave of *The Republic*, the dream world of the play's title, and in this half light the lovers wander, "fallen . . . in dark uneven way" [III. ii. 417]. It is from this opaque world that the young lovers eventually stumble in a dawn which parallels the rising sun which concludes Castiglione's *The Courtier,* emerging to confront a new world which is, however, only the first step upward in the Platonic ladder of enlightenment, a phase where they still "see these things with parted eye, / When everything seems double" [IV. i. 189-90]. (pp. 48-9)

> *David Ormerod, "'A Midsummer Night's Dream':*
> *The Monster in the Labyrinth," in* Shakespeare Stud-
> ies: An Annual Gathering of Research, Criticism,
> and Reviews, *Vol. XI, 1978, pp. 39-52.*

MARY ELLEN LAMB   (essay date 1979)

[*Lamb maintains that a number of aspects of* A Midsummer Night's Dream *may be more fully appreciated by understanding Shakespeare's use of the classical myth of Theseus and the Cretan minotaur. Like David Ormerod (1978), she discovers a similarity between the woods outside Athens and the labyrinthine maze, noting that in sixteenth-century allegorical interpretations of the myth the labyrinth represented vice, especially that of sensual delights, "in which sinners lose themselves until aided by some external power"—a pattern she finds duplicated in Shakespeare's fairy world. Lamb states that, like the young lovers, Theseus has been led through the maze of irrational love and emerges with happy prospects for a successful relationship with Hippolyta. Such other critics as G. G. Gervinus (1849-50), E. K. Chambers (1905), Samuel B. Hemingway (1911), H. B. Charlton (1933), E. C. Pettet (1949), George A. Bonnard (1956), and Ormerod have all analyzed Shakespeare's dramatization of the irrationality of passionate or romantic love in* A Midsummer Night's Dream. *Lamb also comments on the ambivalence of Bottom's characterization, since he is presented as both the comic minotaur and the "thread" (as in the Theseus myth) which leads the lovers to safety. She regards this inversion of the minotaur myth as one signal of the potentiality for tragedy in the play that is consistently repressed by the comic action. Another is the treatment of Theseus, whose murder of his son in the classical tale is not only excluded from the play, but who instead receives the fairies' blessings on the issue of his marriage bed. The critic sees Theseus here as being presented as a "reformed heartbreaker." For further discussion of the presence of tragic or violent elements in* A Midsummer Night's Dream, *see the excerpts by G. K. Chesterton (1904), G. Wilson Knight (1932), Jan Kott (1964), Charles R. Lyons (1971), Hugh M. Richmond (1971), David Bevington (1975), and Mordecai Marcus (1981). Last, Lamb states that the play provides three views of the labyrinth-forest: 1) the inside one of the lovers, 2) the outside one of Puck and the audience, and 3) that of the dramatist, who shares both of the other two viewpoints. As an insider with regard to the maze, Theseus has experienced only its "terror" and does not see its artistry; thus his lunatic, lover, and poet speech reflects Shakespeare's belief that the artist, like the madman and lover, must explore his own irrationality and pass through his own labyrinth in order to create art.*]

Act IV. Scene i. Titania, Bottom, and Fairies. By Henry Fuseli (n.d.).

There are . . . several ways in which recognition of the influence of the myth of Theseus and the minotaur contributes to an increased understanding and appreciation of [*A Midsummer Night's Dream*]. First, it links the lovers' wanderings to an allegorical tradition of the time; it at least partially accounts for the widely varying critical responses towards Bottom; it explains why Theseus, the figure for the "unkinde" lover, can be represented as an ideal husband. Still more important, this study moves beyond an examination of influence to explore a new metaphor, Daedalus's labyrinth, through which to view the theme of art in *A Midsummer-Night's Dream*, and suggests a new interpretation of Theseus's famous speech comparing lunatics, lovers, and poets. Finally, it explores the implications of the myth of Theseus and the minotaur for the dark side of the play, to discover that the world of the irrational has sinister as well as beneficial possibilities, that the materials of tragedy and comedy are inextricably linked within the nature of man.

According to Golding's Ovid and North's Plutarch, two texts often consulted by Shakespeare, this myth includes the following account: the minotaur was a monster half bull and half human, engendered through the intercourse of Pasiphae, queen of Crete, and a bull. Her husband, King Minos, directed Daedalus to construct an intricate labyrinth to contain this creature, which was fed with human flesh. Included among the minotaur's victims were youths, both male and female, offered periodically as tribute to Crete from conquered Athens. These

unfortunates were placed in the labyrinth, where they were doomed to wander until they starved to death, or until they were consumed by the minotaur. One year, King Aegeus's son Theseus asked to be included in this tribute. When he arrived at Crete, King Minos's daughter Ariadne fell in love with him and provided him with a thread to tie at the entrance of the labyrinth so that he could find his way out. Having vowed his love for Ariadne, Theseus killed the minotaur and, as agreed, took her with him when he escaped Crete. However, he broke his vow on the trip homeward and abandoned her as she slept on an island where the ship had docked. Most of the details of this myth appear in one way or another in *A Midsummer-Night's Dream*.

The labyrinth itself, in which Athenian youth are sacrificed to the minotaur, contains broad implications for *A Midsummer-Night's Dream*. Like the youth of the myth, the young lovers of the play enter a kind of labyrinth, a forest where they become hopelessly lost; and at the center of this labyrinth is a creature, half human and half ass. The similarity between the forest of the play and the labyrinth becomes even more striking when the myth is understood according to the allegorical reading of the day: the minotaur's labyrinth represented vice, especially yielding to sensual delights, in which sinners lose themselves until aided by some external power. In fact, Shakespeare elsewhere uses the labyrinth in a slightly different allegorical sense to represent uncontrollable passion: in *The First Part of King*

Henry the Sixth, the Duke of Suffolk muses on his lust for his future Queen: "But Suffolk stay. / Thou mayst not wander in that labyrinth; / There Minotaurs and ugly treasons lurk" [V. iii. 187-89]; in *The History of Troilus and Cressida,* Thersites exclaims to himself: "How now, Thersites? What, lost in the labyrinth of thy fury?" [II. iii. 1-2]. This allegorical understanding of the labyrinth provides a new context for the lovers' progressive "loss" of themselves in their own passions as the play progresses. They enter the forest-labyrinth with a purpose: Hermia and Lysander are fleeing to Lysander's aunt's house, where they will be free to marry; Demetrius is pursuing his beloved Hermia, somehow to prevent her from marrying Lysander; and Helena is pursuing Demetrius "to have his sight thither and back again" [I. i. 251]. By the end of their sojourn in the forest, however, their motives of love have changed to more violent impulses as they circle each other helplessly, Demetrius and Lysander attempting to slay each other for love of Helena, Helena fleeing Hermia's sharp nails. Like the sinners of the allegorical interpretation, they are unable to save themselves; and it is only through the beneficent aid of the fairies that they emerge, alive and evenly paired, back where they began.

The usual response to these mad lovers chasing each other around the forest-labyrinth of *A Midsummer-Night's Dream* is not, however, consistent with the judgment implied by the myth's allegory. In fact, one critic's harsh claim that "Shakespeare shows us how undisciplined passion can turn humans into beasts whose sexual reflexes are totally irrational and arbitrary" [see excerpt above by Hugh M. Richmond, 1971] seems curiously perverse. *A Midsummer-Night's Dream* is a comedy, not a moral tract; and most audiences react to the lovers with laughter, not condemnation. Audiences know that there will be a happy ending. Unlike the doomed Athenians of the myth, unlike the sinners of the allegory, the lovers are safe. They are watched over by the fairies; and the monster of this maze is no threatening minotaur but a low-life craftsman, the "shallowest thickskin of that barren sort" [III. ii. 13]. So the threats of Demetrius and Lysander against each other's lives are amusing because we know that they will never carry them out. We laugh at the incongruity of the diminutive Hermia reaching up to scratch out the eyes of Helena, her taller adversary who runs away in fright, because we know that Helena's eyes are in no real danger.

The presence of Bottom as the minotaur adapts the Theseus myth to the comic spirit of the play. Yet Bottom is also a creature of the Theseus myth, and his identity as a comic minotaur extends beyond the fact that he is half human and half ass. Bottom is a conflation of the minotaur and the bull which sired him, and the relationship between Bottom and Titania is heavily influenced by the relationship between Pasiphae and this father bull. In the whimsical account in Ovid's *Art of Love,* which differs in this respect from most versions of the myth, Pasiphae is not merely lecherous: she is really in love. She "envies the lovely Heifers to the death," when they seem to be favored by her beloved bull; she would crop "fresh boughs, and mow yong grasse" for her love; she meets the bull "in the wild woods" where she "joyfull skips . . . And proudly jetting on the greene grasse lips, / To please his amorous eye." Her concern for her lover's food, her attempts to please him, her meeting him in the woods—all of these resemble Titania's treatment of Bottom. And like Titania, Pasiphae never gains her love's amorous attention; to consummate her love, Pasiphae has to resort to disguising herself in a cow's skin.

Bottom's roots in the Theseus myth go beyond Pasiphae's bull. At the time his name "bottom" was used to refer to "thread" or "a skein of thread," the household item which played a crucial role in delivering Theseus from the labyrinth. In fact, Caxton's translation of the *Aeneid* uses the exact phrase "a botom of threde" in the description of Theseus's adventure with the minotaur. Furthermore, Bottom's vocation as a weaver would bring the association of this meaning of his name to the mind of an Elizabethan audience.

Bottom is both the monster of this labyrinth and the thread leading the way out of it; and the complexity of our response to him is demonstrated by the widely differing attitudes adopted towards him. On the one hand, Bottom is truly an ass; in fact, he is called an ass twice in the course of the play. Surrounded by magic and moonshine, lying in the arms of the fairy queen, yet oblivious to her considerable charms, Bottom asks only to be fed "your good dry oats" and to be scratched about the face, where he is "marvelous hairy" [IV. i. 32, 34]. As Bertrand Evans has pointed out, Bottom is, of all the characters, the most "congenitally, chronically unaware" [see excerpt above, 1960]. On the other hand, into his braying mouth are placed the wisest sentiments about love expressed in the play. He knows that he is not the paragon Titania admires; when she compliments his beauty and wisdom, his reply shows an honest sense of his own limitations: "Not so, neither" [III. i. 149]. Unlike the other characters, he knows that "reason and love keep little company together now-a-days" [III. i. 143-44]. In short, Bottom is an ass because he does not succumb to love; and he is a thread out of this labyrinth because he refuses to abandon his common sense even in Titania's embrace. Chasing a rival through a nettle-filled forest would never be for him. The paradoxical attitude directed towards Bottom by the play is a paradoxical attitude towards the love: not falling in love is both pathologically foolish and eminently sensible.

The myth of Theseus and the minotaur also clarifies our understanding of Theseus. Long considered the embodiment of "the reasonable man and the ideal ruler of both his lower nature and his subjects" [see the entry by Paul A. Olson in the Additional Bibliography], Theseus has now been recognized as having had a sinister character in the Renaissance. He was, in fact, the figure for the "unkinde" lover, a deserter of women. His reputation for infidelity draws its force from his abandonment of Ariadne, whose complaint was movingly presented in Ovid's *Heroides,* and can be found in several sources well known in the Renaissance: Chaucer's *Legend of Good Women,* Golding's *Ovid,* North's *Plutarch,* Eloyt's *The Boke Named the Governor.* Shakespeare does not ignore this tradition. In fact, if anything, he exaggerates it by telescoping Theseus's various infidelities when Oberon accuses Titania of making Theseus break faith with "fair Aegles . . . With Ariadne, and Antiopa" [II. i. 79-80], of leading him "through the glimmering night / From Perigouna, whom he ravished" [II. i. 77-80].

Far from discrediting him by adding "an ironic dimension to the play" [see the entry by D'Orsay Pearson in the Additional Bibliography], Theseus's broken vows forcefully demonstrate the irrationality of love central to this forest-labyrinth. Theseus, too, has been led through the maze, just as Puck leads the lovers in the play. The lovers will, like Theseus, emerge from the forest; and their broken vows, like Theseus's previous infidelities, highlight by contrast the evident happy stability of the marriages at the end of the play. It is to Theseus, the apparently reformed heartbreaker, more than to Theseus the good prince, that the underlying myth of the play directs us, at this point. (pp. 478-82)

The attitude towards the irrational expressed in the love plot of *A Midsummer-Night's Dream* is, finally, ambivalent. On the one hand, falling in love is a form of madness, which causes perfectly normal young people to act with cruelty towards each other, to become lost in a maze of passionate impulses, to break vows uncontrollably. Clearly, this forest-labyrinth is no place for mortals to dwell; and stable marriages must be lived out in Athens. On the other hand, the lovers, watched over by the fairies, will come to no real harm. In fact, they leave the forest evenly paired and ready to reenter a society they fled only a short time before. The attitude towards their abandonment to the impulses of love is mixed. Their experience within this forest-labyrinth cannot be wholly envied or pitied, any more than Bottom, minotaur and thread, can be praised or blamed for his immunity to the charms of Titania.

Lovers are not the only Athenians to enter the forest-labyrinth of *A Midsummer-Night's Dream;* the ''rude mechanicals'' practice their play there, and their hilarious mistakes introduce the subject of art into the play. The development of this theme in *A Midsummer-Night's Dream* also shares several characteristics with the myth of Theseus and the minotaur. The labyrinth constructed for the minotaur was created by Daedalus, an artificer ''renowned in the lande / For fine devise and workmanship in building.'' Daedalus was, in fact, one of the most famous craftsmen of classical legend; and his work for King Minos apparently justified his reputation. The myth's emphasis upon the artisan Daedalus may have influenced the unusual focus on the vocations of the craftsmen in *A Midsummer-Night's Dream.* At first, there seems to be little justification for identifying Quince as a carpenter, Snug as a joiner, Bottom as a weaver, Flute as a bellows-mender, Snout as a tinker, and Starveling as a tailor; Shakespeare does not specify the vocations of low-life characters in other plays with such precision. Glancing at the underlying myth, however, we see that Bottom's vocation as a weaver calls attention to his role as the thread leading out of the labyrinth. Similarly, the vocation of Peter Quince as a carpenter links him with the builder Daedalus. Even Quince's name has architectural meaning: a ''quoin'' was a wedge-shaped piece of stone or wood, also used to describe a cornerstone. And Shakespeare, the playwright of *A Midsummer-Night's Dream,* is even more closely related to Daedalus figure; he, too, has built a structure, marvellous in its complexity, which contains wandering Athenians and a kind of minotaur. Thus, the underlying myth focuses attention on the playwright as a craftsman who must work with other craftsmen to produce a finished work of art. (pp. 482-83)

The myth of Theseus and the minotaur includes three separate viewpoints of the laybrinth: the viewpoint of the victim, the viewpoint of the outsider, and the viewpoint of the artist, who perceives the labyrinth from the perspectives of both victim and outsider. For example, Ovid's narrator admires the art of Daedalus's labyrinth: ''He confounds his worke with sodaine stopes and stayes, / And with the great uncertaintie of sundrie winding wayes, / Leades in and out, and to and fro.'' . . . He compares the laybrinth with the river Meander which ''meeting with himselfe doth looke if all his streame or no / Come after.''. . . Admiration for the labyrinth seems curiously amoral given its sinister purpose, the minotaur's devouring Athenian youth. *A Midsummer-Night's Dream* also contains this double perspective. In its intricate complications, *A Midsummer-Night's Dream* resembles Daedalus's labyrinth, and Ovid's narrator's description applies equally well to the play, with its ''sodaine stopes and stayes,'' and even with its ''meeting with himselfe'' in its examination of its own craft through the play of Pyramus and Thisbe. And Shakespeare's play also contains its victims, the Athenian lovers, tormented in their desperate and seemingly haphazard wanderings through the forest. Yet their circlings are in reality carefully ordered by Puck, who takes great delight in his art: ''Up and down, up and down, / I will lead them up and down'' [III. ii. 396-97]. And he enjoys equally the patterns which lie outside of his making: ''Then will two at once woo one. / That must needs be sport alone; / And those thing do best please me / That befall prepost'rously'' [III. ii. 118-21]. Like the audience, Puck's response to the lovers' misery is laughter at their plight and delight in the patterns, whether his or fate's, which control them. And here lies the second view of the labyrinth: viewed by the outsider rather than by a victim, it is a dazzling work of art. For the lovers, the laybrinth is the setting for a journey in which they encounter unfamiliar and frightening aspects of themselves. As an audience, however, we do not enter the labyrinth. Instead we appreciate its art and marvel in its complexity. (p. 484).

There is another perspective which transcends these two; besides the viewpoint of the victim and the outsider, there is the viewpoint of the artist. For this we must turn to Theseus's famous speech, which unites the themes of art and love. For a long while the beauty of Theseus's description of how the poet's pen ''gives to airy nothing / A local habitation and a name'' [V. i. 16-17] led critics to interpret his speech as praising the power of poetry. More recently, critics have recognized its explicit deprecation of poetry: like lunatics and lovers, poets are deluded and cannot tell bushes from bears. Many readers have refused to accept Theseus's sentiments as expressing a serious position. Shakespeare was a poet, after all; and he knew that poets were not deluded. Consequently, Hippolyta's reply that ''all the story of the night told over . . . grows to something of great constancy'' [V. i. 23, 26] is often read as a satisfactory answer to Theseus; while art does not meet the test of realistic truth, she is saying, it creates beauty from its ''great constancy.'' In describing the order underlying the lovers' tales, Hippolyta evokes the perspective which views Daedalus's labyrinth as a work of art.

While Hippolyta's position is a valid statement about art, it does not allow us wholly to discount Theseus's speech, so powerful in its expression and so prominently placed at the beginning of the last act. In the end, Theseus's speech does not address the nature of art; it addresses instead the experience of the artist. Like the lovers, Theseus has had no chance to experience the art of the labyrinth; he has experienced only its terror. And in this perspective lies the true significance of Theseus's comparison. Before a poet can create a controlled work of art, he must, like the lover and the madman, reach that highly dangerous state of mind in which a bush seems a bear. The poet, like the lover and the madman, is an explorer of the irrational self; like them, he must lose himself in his own labyrinth and, if he meets a minotaur instead of an ass, risk a kind of death. Only after he experiences the labyrinth as a victim can he discover its order and create from it art.

It is ironic that this statement about the poet is spoken by Theseus, who not only deprecates poetry, but also refuses to believe the lovers' story, so like an ''antique fable'' or a ''fairy toy'' [V. i. 3]. He seems to have forgotten even more of his own experience in the forest than the lovers forgot; and he certainly did not, like Bottom, wake with an urge to have a ballad written of his experience. Theseus distrusts irrationality, and perhaps his refusal to believe the lovers' tale reflects something of his experience in the forest-labyrinth. The differences in the experiences of the lovers, dragging their exhausted bodies through a dark forest, and Bottom, coaxed and coddled by the fairy queen, demonstrate the range off experiences possible to a journey into irrationality. And the lovers and Bottom all explore a labyrinth without a minotaur. Perhaps, despite the kind offices of Titania, Theseus's journey aroused his permanent distrust for such explorations. And perhaps he was right. As the Renaissance audience was aware, Theseus's good fortune at the end of the play was only temporary. Later, after his betrayal of Hippolyta, his uncontrollable fury will be aroused by the evil Phaedra, and he will murder his own son Hippolytus. Oberon's blessing on the marriage bed of Theseus and Hippolyta is perhaps the playwright's request of the audience not to recall this terrible event; yet denying it has the paradoxical effect of bringing it forcefully to mind: "To the best bride-bed will we, / Which by us shall blessed be; / And the issue there create / Ever shall be fortunate" [V. i. 403-06]. As everyone in the Renaissance audience no doubt knew, the issue created in that bed will be very unfortunate indeed.

Even as we laugh at *A Midsummer-Night's Dream*, the underlying myth points to the potential for tragedy in the experience of the lovers and of poets: the myth's allegory implies the destructive effects of passion; but the lovers are finally saved, after considerable initial confusion, by the well-wishing fairies. Theseus will commit one of the most horrible crimes imaginable, the murder of his own son; but at the end of the play, he and Hippolyta express all the joyful serenity possible to a happily married couple. In the woods Bottom loses his full humanity to become a monster, even though he is loved by Titania, even though he emerges from the forest none the worse for his experience. Although there is no minotaur to devour the Athenians, the implication of the myth is still there: not all labyrinths contain Bottoms; some contain minotaurs.

The substitution of Bottom for a minotaur represents the transmutation of the elements of tragedy into comedy. And the close relationship between comedy and tragedy was a problem Shakespeare was exploring in, for example, the farcical production of Pyramus and Thisbe, "very tragical mirth" [V. i. 57]. In fact, Pyramus's humorous invocation to the Furies to "cut thread and thrum" [V. i. 286], deflating grand tragic style by reminding his audience that he is really a weaver at heart, glances at the implications of the myth for tragedy: one can become lost and die in a labyrinth without a thread to lead the way out. This is, in a way, what happens to Pyramus and Thisbe; in the force of his passion, Pyramus leaps to a false conclusion about Thisbe's death, and both lovers commit impulsive suicide. This hilarious short play reminds us of a dark truth: under different circumstances the Atenian lovers, who were also escaping a forbidding father by running into the woods, might also have perished. (pp. 484-86)

Of course, *A Midsummer-Night's Dream* remains a very funny comedy, and its dark side should not be overstated. In the end, the play does not develop the myth's implications for tragedy. The destructive potentialities of the abandonment of reason are only implied; the play itself demonstrates that paradoxically within this irrational world, which turns relatively sane Athenians into madmen and asses, lies the very source of civilization. Without the lovers' absurd excesses of passion, there would be no happy marriages, no children, no regeneratin of society; and without Bottom's even more absurd encounter with

the fairy queen, there would be no ballads of our dreams, no impulse to create art. The lovers wake feeling confusion and relief, but Bottom wakes with a feeling of true awe: "The eye of man hath not heard, the ear of man hath not seen, man's hand is not able to taste, his tongue to conceive, nor his heart to report what my dream was" [IV. i. 211-14]. The process of turning an interior journey into art is truly miraculous, and Bottom's sense of wonder has been expressed by poets of all periods. . . . *A Midsummer-Night's Dream*, analyzed in the context of its influence, the myth of Theseus and the minotaur, shows that this experience, like love, can only be attained by the loss of self within the labyrinth of one's own irrationality. (pp. 487-88)

*Mary Ellen Lamb, " 'A Midsummer-Night's Dream':
The Myth of Theseus and the Minotaur," in* Texas
Studies in Literature and Language, *Vol. XXI, No.
4, Winter, 1979, pp. 478-91.*

FLORENCE FALK   (essay date 1980)

[*In an anthropological reading of* A Midsummer Night's Dream, *Falk analyzes the movement of the play's dramatic action from Athens to the woods and back to Athens in relation to the tribal "rite of passage," which, she maintains, serves to renew a community by the release and reintegration of disorderly elements. She regards the Athens of Act I as representing a society that has grown harsh and legalistic, more concerned with following custom and historical tradition than with fostering harmonious relations among its members. In her view, the "disabused lovers have no recourse but to repair to the woods," a setting that is anarchic and asocial and where they will learn the nature of love. Falk maintains that their rite of passage, presided over by Oberon as shaman of the forest, prepares them for a return to the orderly, institutional world of Athens. She notes, however, that society's social and psychic conflicts are never entirely resolved, for even in the Athens of Act V there is evidence of tension and the impulse toward social release of these conflicts. Falk contends that the reappearance of the fairies at the close of the play, who bring with them the reminder of the experience in the forest, suggests that the anarchy of dreams and the unconscious state may be resorted to once more if society again becomes unyielding and its institutions overly formalized. The reintegration of discordant, disorderly elements in* A Midsummer Night's Dream *has also been analyzed by Harold C. Goddard (1951), John Vyvyan (1961), Stephen Fender (1968), R. A. Zimbardo (1970), David Bevington (1975), and Paul A. Olson (see Additional Bibliography), and the movement between Athens and the woods has been traced by Denton J. Snider (1890), C. L. Barber (1959), and Leon Guilhamet (see Additional Bibliography). Also, see the essay by Arca Vlasopolos cited in the Additional Bibliography for a comparison of* A Midsummer Night's Dream *and midsummer fertility rituals which serve to renew and regenerate society and bring it into harmony with nature.*]

[The] three-part structure of *A Midsummer Night's Dream* (expressed by the movement from Athens to the woods and back again) closely parallels the landscape of "rites of passage," which precipitates fundamental patterns of growth and renewal. Victor Turner's anthropological studies on the structural (and semantic) patterns of ritual process reinforce this cultural analogue to the dream-play pattern. Turner studied performance rites of the Ndembu culture of northwestern Zambia and observed that ritual mapping included *both* village (a structured and ordered society) and bush (an unstable, chaotic community)—the geographical (and psychic) distance between them measured and bounded by a symbolic system of landmarks that assured ritual sojourners safe passage and return.

Thus the symbolic realm embraced what Turner calls *structure* and its antipode, *communitas*. *Structure* refers to the relatively abstract and permanent pattern of a social order whose form is grounded in law and custom; *communitas,* to the spontaneous, temporary, and detached aggregate of persons (and environment) beset by provocative acultural and antistructural conditions. Persons in *communitas* are said to be *liminal personae* ("threshold people") because they exist in an ambiguous and transitional state. They are, in effect, faceless, nameless, "invisible" beings who can profit from a temporary (solar) eclipse. "Transformed" by the rite of passage, these persons return again to *structure.*

The third realm in Turner's cognitive mapping is *societas,* which refers to *structure* that has been renewed and leavened by *communitas.* One might say that *societas* is the net expression of the interaction between *structure* and *communitas* as mediated through transformed ritual subjects. It is also the resolution (at any given moment) of the dialectic between *structure* and *communitas.*

The process is cyclical: persons released from *structure* into *communitas* are rejuvenated by the experience. But the neutral cement of *structure* is always subject to erosion. Hence, the process is reactivated when social and psychic conflict once again threaten to destabilize the social order. (p. 264)

The pattern of transformation and the dream anatomy of *A Midsummer Night's Dream* seem clarified by an analysis along Turner's lines and may even represent a primary cognitive structuring of human interaction: *structure* corresponds to the state of Athens at the beginning of the play *(Athens 1)*, *communitas* to the woods, and *societas* to Athens after the dream *(Athens 2)*. Each location is associated with a more or less imaginative response to the social and psychic exigencies of living, and each will be considered separately.

Structure (Athens 1). *Structure* is the initial condition of Athens. It is jural-political in character, the skeletal form of society that is rooted in the past and extends into the future through language, law, and custom. *Structure* and history are intimately connected because a social entity maintains its form over time. We see in *Athens 1* the incrustation of form; *structure,* uninformed by *communitas,* is in a condition of atrophy and requires some transforming medium to catalyze renewal.

Theseus, ruler of Athens and guardian of its law, provides the rationale for the dream world. At the outset of the play, the transformation of Theseus and Hippolyta has already been effected. Their love vows, in comparison with those of the Athenian lovers, are accompanied by fewer signs of ambivalence. Having "wooed" and won Hippolyta with his "sword," Theseus renounces his past warrior activities to "wed" her "in another key / With pomp, with triumph, and with revelling" [I. i. 18-19]. But these properties belong not to myth, nor to the epic for that matter, but to comedy. Erstwhile residents of myth, Theseus and Hippolyta survive in *A Midsummer Night's Dream* to become secular tenants of history. Theseus, his mythic identity trailing behind him like the tails of a greatcoat, has, in effect, been so diminished as to have a comic role. So eager is he to strike its "key," in fact, that he longs impatiently to take part in the celebratory festivities of comic resolution. (p. 265)

Impatience, one of the primary qualities of historical man, asserts itself in Theseus. His first words are over-determined by clock time: "Four happy days bring in / Another moon, but, O, methinks, how slow / This old moon wanes!" [I. i.

2-4]. Theseus abjures the government of the moon altogether and even circumvents its dream topography by stepping into the woods only at dawn when dreams have been extinguished (IV. i.).

Perhaps the most self-indicting testimony of Theseus' impatience, however, is his famous commentary on the imagination [V. i. 2-22], which simultaneously praises and disparages what the rest of the play extols: the transforming powers of the imagination. Theseus, who in mythic times undertook to free chaos from its monstrous minotaur, sees as his function the spreading of (day)light by means of reason, with only a "passing modulation" allowed to the imagination. His clouded vision in *A Midsummer Night's Dream* suggests that Shakespeare appended an ironic coda to his mythic feat. Detached from myth but ordained by history, Theseus becomes myth breaker in *A Midsummer Night's Dream.* The restraints of an historic imagination compel him to interpret his role as governor of Athens with sharp restraint; without the revelation of myth or the insight of *poesis* to guide him, Theseus is unprepared to allow innovation. His governance is strict, harsh, and limiting, servant to custom and historical tradition.

In Shakespeare's plays the psychic condition of the ruler is always reflected in the behavior of his subjects. Hence discord (demonstrated by false oaths, unsubstantial love vows, and parental tyranny) threatens to undermine the social order. Egeus would rather see his daughter perish than marry without his consent. Theseus seemingly mitigates the harshness of his "law-and-order" demands by advising Hermia of her filial (hence social) obligations: "Be advis'd, fair maid. / To you your father should be as a god" [I. i. 46-7]. But his advice acutely demonstrates that Theseus, though statesmanlike in manner, is decisively authoritarian in matter. All possible forms of redress are thwarted by his legalistic approach to Athenian law. Hermia "must" obey, "Or else the law of Athens yields you up / (Which by no means we may extenuate)" [I. i. 119-20]. We know, of course, that the law can be viewed more flexibly, since Theseus later suspends its strict construction [IV. i. 179-81].

Theseus's edict is rigid and inert, his language and argument closed: "Upon that day either prepare to die / For disobedience to your father's will, / Or else to wed Demetrius, as he would, / Or on Diana's altar to protest, / For aye, austerity and single life" [I. i. 86-90]. There are no grace notes in his words and certainly no sense of ludic potential. Moreover, his advice is gratuitous, even hypocritical, since the argument he offers contradicts his own impulsive and unrestrained pursuit of Hippolyta. Having been impressed into history, Theseus has hardened into form. In arguing for that which is premeditated and routine and against that which is spontaneous and creative, he illustrates the perils of reason unrelieved by imagination. No wonder, then, that Theseus's command for pomp and reveling is immediately obstructed, since weddings, feasts, and celebrations are the harvest of harmonious relations and secure domestic order. The disabused lovers have no recourse but to repair to the woods, a magical, placeless, and protected space that exists in and out of time.

Communitas (the Woods). *Communitas* is the spontaneous, immediate, transitory condition which, like dream, occurs in the "now," the continuing present. It is also the temporary aggregate of persons whose asocial desires require some kind of accomodation to preserve the health of the society. The location of *communitas* is wherever a purgative or transformative ritual needs to be enacted; its time is "whenever," or the mythical time of ritual. *Communitas* is the abode of dream, where the problematic, the taboo, that which is liminal and dangerous, can be domesticated in an appropriate rite of passage. In *A Midsummer Night's Dream communitas* corresponds to the dream sequence in the woods. (pp. 266-67)

The unconscious, says Jung, is not simply a mirror reflection of consciousness but possesses its own reality and its own code of laws. In dramatic terms, dream is a kind of psychodrama that makes the invisible palpable by unmasking unconscious psychic life. Moon illuminates the shadow side of man to reveal the unexpected, the mysterious, the devilish, and the perverse. In moon light we see, first of all, how the unconscious is *mis*governed by its own rules. Disorder is rife; it springs, as Titania chides Oberon, "From our debate, from our dissension; / We are their parents and original" [II. i. 116-17]. Their quarrel recalls the original god and goddess of love, Adam and Eve, who also failed as collaborative stage-managers in their natural habitat.

"Creative disorder" describes the dream space, which metaphorically celebrates the irrational and structurally provides for a symbolic return to chaos. But in *A Midsummer Night's Dream* chaos will eventually seed concord. Oberon's rhapsodic account of the intoxicant mermaid assures us that dissonance will resolve into harmonious order and the fall will be depicted as a fall into life: "Thou rememb'rest," Oberon reminds Puck,

> Since once I sat upon a promontory,
> And heard a mermaid on a dolphin's back
> Uttering such dulcet and harmonious breath
> That the rude sea grew civil at her song
> And certain stars shot madly from their spheres
> To hear the sea maid's music?
>
> [II. i. 148-54]

The fall is indeed ecstatic. Impelled by magical sounds, "certain stars" luxuriate in their surrender. Here is an example of euphoric and extravagant disruption—the fixed and harmonious universe itself in a state of upheaval—poised to hear the mermaid's song. Oberon's lunar speech is a paean to the imagination and to the sublime confusion that reigns in the unconscious before the creative impulse imposes order in the form of art.

Oberon is himself celebrant of the intense *feeling* form of the lyric mode. Indeed, the passage quite literally arrests the movement of the play which, in Theodore Weiss's words, is "held or focused to a pure intensity." This is like the "pure intensity" of the dream, since both lyric and dream are forms that arrest the ordinary and stop time. Oberon's lyric is a cameo version of the dream; thematically, it anticipates the "fortunate fall" that will be enacted in the dream; structurally, it partakes of the metaphysical claim that the disorder and confusion of the creative imagination are, in turn, contained by a higher order (just as the lyric *contains* the stars that shoot "madly" from their sphere, the larger play, *A Midsummer Night's Dream, contains* the anarchic activities engendered in the dream).

The modes of lyric and dream share vital correspondences: both incorporate a scale of intensities that ordinary life rarely includes; both have an intrinsic dramatic structure that derives generally from extreme condensation of imagery, reliance on the more universal and fundamental language of mythology, and the metaphorical bonding of seemingly disparate phenomena into new organic unities. Perhaps a more essential correspondence between lyric and dream, however, is that both are pure "poems"; as such, they can be understood or apprehended only by the mood they convey as a whole. Oberon, the play-

wright's surrogate, establishes in his speech the strategy that underlies the dream play he is about to set into motion: like the lyric that precedes it, the dream conmingles sensuous, concrete, and figurative language and expands the meaning of words through sight, sounds, and symbols. Finally, in *A Midsummer Night's Dream* both lyric and dream work shock the dream inhabitants out of the ordinary and force their participation in the extraordinary. (pp. 268-69)

Through Oberon's intercession, the natural order is waylaid, its energies interrupted and redirected. Certainly Oberon and his fairy train, "spirits of another sort" [III. ii. 388], help to spread the light of insight and illumination. Indeed, Oberon might be said to provide efficacious ritual leadership. As adept, or shaman, he initiates and presides over the rite of passage that dispels disorder in both spirit and mortal worlds. Moreover, he knows the "correct medicines" (the flower called "love-in-idleness") to restore the lovers' troths.

To end the state of crisis, Oberon, together with his assistant, Puck, impel the dream inhabitants to pass through certain ordeals that will redirect their misspent creative energies. Creativity in *A Midsummer Night's Dream* is specifically associated with harnessing the anarchic powers of the libido. In Oberon's determination, at least, Titania's wayward spirit must be tempered. As for the lovers, Hermia must come to comprehend loss, Helena, gain. Lysander must understand the vows of fidelity, and Demetrius the rewards of stability. In short, the lovers must learn that their understanding of love is fundamentally superficial. Each member of the love quartet will be required to repudiate Lysander's facile lamentation about love's mercurial energies:

> Or, if there were a sympathy in choice,
> War, death or sickness did lay siege to it,
> Making it momentany as a sound,
> Swift as a shadow, short as any dream. . . .
>
> [I. i. 141-44]

In the woods each will discover that the greatest obstacles to love are not "war, death or sickness," but their own insufficiencies.

It has often been said that the Athenian lovers are almost indistinguishable from one another, which merely means that they possess dream-like properties and potentialities. . . . During the ritual process the lovers become a play of forces; their behavior is absolved through anonymity, and the configurations they assume suggest others. Featureless dream figures, the Athenians are analogous to "threshold people," the name given to ritual subjects in the liminal state.

The coupling of animal with person accentuates man's "animal nature." It marks the dream as an occasion for sanctioned disrespect and immodesty and, through the agency of extravagant and temporarily licensed behavior, it defuses otherwise dangerous drives and emotions. Hence, the dreamscape is also an enclosure or corral within which all creatures are quarry—fair game for the hunt. The moon, symbolized by Diana, goddess of the hunt, supervises the proceedings. Hippolyta likens it "to a silver bow / Newbent in heaven" [I. i. 9-10]. The simile recalls her status as mythic Amazon warrior before the battle in which she was pursued and captured by her hunter-lover, Theseus. The series of chases that follow are mirror images of their archetypal wooing match. In the woods, the hunted become the hunters. The love-hate dialectic that prevails is evident in the concurrent enactment of wooing and warring. Like animals in primitive times, the ritual subjects are simultaneously objects of adoration and hunted quarry. Transitions from love to hate and back again are immediate and total. Witness, for example, the wooing game between Lysander and Hermia. Rapturously "content" with Hermia one moment, Lysander willingly exchanges this "raven for a dove" (Helena) the next [II. ii. 114].

The antics in the woods also provide abundant examples of status reversal, a feature common to both ritual and dream. Rituals of status reversal reaffirm the order of *structure* by re-establishing relations between people who hold positions in that structure. The idea, of course, is that behavior so elasticized is likely to snap back to accustomed limits once the strain of over-reaching grows too great. In a ritual exchange of status Helena confronts Hermia, her erstwhile friend and supposed rival, to cleanse the wounds of jealousy (III. ii.). Nowhere is status reversal better expressed, however, than in the comic-grotesque coupling of Bottom and Titania, whose relationship celebrates the twinship of mystery and absurdity.

At dawn the dream is extinguished. Restored to their proper mates, the errant lovers are ready to consummate the asocial and anarchic rite enacted in the woods with the social rite of marriage. That ritual—marriage—is of secondary order, the symbolic form given to the creative act of love. The wisdom gained in the woods (most of it unconsciously received) has refashioned the very being of the Athenian lovers. Once again they will be able to adhere to laws and customs whose tautness has been sufficiently relaxed to allow a measure of the spontaneity inherent in *communitas*. Through dream, Theseus's promise to modulate to "another key" will be achieved.

Societas (Athens 2). *Societas* describes the condition of Athens after the sojourn in the woods. It is the secular and social collective existing in time and within *structure*. It is also the outcome of learning processes in which teaching proceeds by way of dream rather than reason. More important, *societas* is the resolution of the dialectic between the dualism of *communitas* and *structure*. The relationship is historical and processive, however, rather than terminal, since a crucial aspect of *communitas* is its potential influence upon *societas*. In other words, the regenerating force of *communitas* raises the possibility of modifying law, language, and custom in ways beneficial to *societas*. In *Athens 2* the reconceived stability of the Athenian social order has this preserving power of *potentiality*. (pp. 270-72)

In *Athens 2* the political authority of Theseus parallels, but does not approximate, the ritual authority of Oberon in the woods. The exchange of dominions is marked by Theseus's *ex post facto* commentary on the imagination, which ushers in the regulatory world of reason just as Oberon's paean to the mermaid had introduced the world of dream:

> I never may believe
> These antique fables, nor these fairy toys.
> Lovers and madmen have such seething brains,
> Such shaping fantasies, that apprehend
> More than cool reason ever comprehends.
> The lunatic, the lover, and the poet
> Are of imagination all compact. . . .
> And as imagination bodies forth
> The forms of things unknown, the poet's pen
> Turns them to shapes, and gives to airy nothing
> A local habitation and a name.
>
> [V. i. 2-8, 14-17]

Custodian of reality, Theseus pays wary tribute to the powers of the active imagination. For one brief moment he overleaps the boundaries of reason and stands at the threshold of intuition ("Such shaping fantasies, that apprehend / More than cool reason ever comprehends"), but the "compact" ordering of "lunatic," "lover," and "poet" indicates how quickly "cool reason" locks him in its tight embrace. His intentions are clear enough: "antique fables," "fairy toys," and "airy nothing" are meant to trivialize the creative experience. Wedged between dream and art (that is, the dream sequence and the "play" of Pyramus and Thisby), Theseus's utterance of bemused tolerance for the imagination turns into an unwitting expression of disproportionate endorsement. Theseus, after all, has not stepped foot into the dream world. We, who have observed the dream, can "correct" his observations by our experience of the fortuitous events that have transpired. (pp. 272-73)

If the dream world displays "interiorized" fantasy, the performance by the Athenian rustics reveals fantasy "exteriorized." "Pyramus and Thisby" is liberally intertwined with a series of witticisms that depends not only on *knowing* the correct rules but on asserting them. The simultaneous rendering of playlet and the "play upon" it is an ingenious illustration of the complementary forces of art and play as socially sanctified forms of expression. We, the secondary audience, observe the Athenians, the primary audience, as they watch the playlet in the play. In this way, we see firsthand the redemptive and transformative energies of wit juxtaposed with those of art-making, *poesis*.

The Athenians respond to the playlet with elegant and courtly banter. They engage in wit play to convert anxiety, since they are at least unconsciously mindful that the "lamentable tragedy" before them is a comic-grotesque looking-glass reflection of their own near-tragic destinies; that the "cruel death" of Hermia was averted by the flight to the woods (and to dream); and that Comedy has playfully thumbed its nose at its star-crossed twin, Tragedy.

While it is clear that wit play is a mechanism for syphoning off some of the anxiety-provoking subject matter of "Pyramus and Thisby," the pleasure derived from wit play results—as in dream—from expressing the inadmissible. Specifically, in wit, pleasure is gained from exercising one's mental prowess, usually at the expense of other people or situations. If dream is an *asocial* form of purging inner conflicts and discharging repressed material, wit play is its *social* equivalent. Freud's careful assessment of wit play and dream reveals how the same processes of modification, displacement, substitution, and condensation appear in both forms; moreover, he shows that wit play and dream share many of the same attributes, especially a preference for nonsense, absurdity, confusion, double meanings, and play on words.

In *Athens 2* wit play not only renders the Athenian courtiers invulnerable, it also proclaims that order is regained and intact. Indeed, order is the most fundamental requirement of wit play. To play (and play against), one must first know the rules of grammar, logic, syntax. Moreover, wit play is the aristocratic form of humor that masks in social forms aggressive and defensive attitudes toward licentious and "taboo" behavior. Finally, wit play is also a kind of foreplay—a mode used to preserve expectancy. Theseus indulges in wit play, among other reasons, to "beguile" the time until the moment of nuptial consummation. (pp. 274-75)

In *A Midsummer Night's Dream* we are offered the dream play, the edifice of art, "Pyramus and Thisby," and wit play, the social response to that art form. Each of these forms—dream, art, and wit play—allows us to assimilate reality. All play is symbolic play, a mandate for self-expression. Piaget says that "because the ego dominates the whole universe in play . . . it is freed from conflicts." The newly-restored society of Athens reminds us that play is an indispensable form of compensation in any social order: *Athens 2* will flourish only if there is "play" in its structure to preserve the state of expectancy needed to sustain vitality. (pp. 275-76)

In *Athens 2* two social forms of release—art and wit play—accommodate material from the unconscious that continues to obtrude on consciousness. But because the dialectic between *structure* and *communitas* is never entirely resolved, reintegration is always marked by a certain ambivalence. Ultimately, the disengagement process will have to be resumed; indeed, seeds for flight have already fallen in the return. The centrality of dream is reasserted at the end of the play when the fairy world consecrates the Athenian household. This slight but final shift of emphasis (away from Athens and back to the spirit world) suggests the triumph of dream and the imagination.

We fancy that when Puck takes up his broom to tidy up the house, he and the spirit world assert the last word over reason:

> If we shadows have offended,
> Think but this, and all is mended,
> That you have but slumber'd here,
> While these visions did appear.
> And this weak and idle theme,
> No more yielding than a dream,
> Gentles, do not reprehend:
> If you pardon, we will mend.
>
> [V. i. 423-30]

That touch of deprecation in the epilogue is a sleight-of-hand gesture by a spirit who artfully beguiles us into discounting those "shadows" and "visions" that link us inextricably to the metaphysical realm of the unconscious. We are left with the suggestion of the world as "dreamed reality." Dream is indeed a *visionary* tale—an archaic, indispensable act of the imagination, as central to our existence as art. And what, after all, is art but dreaming of the impossible? (pp. 277-78)

> Florence Falk, "Dream and Ritual Process in 'A Midsummer Night's Dream'," in Comparative Drama, Vol. 14, No. 3, Fall, 1980, pp. 263-79.

R. CHRIS HASSEL, JR.   **(essay date 1980)**

[*In an unexcerpted portion of his essay on* A Midsummer Night's Dream, *Hassel states his intention to analyze the play's allusions to St. Paul's Epistles and Erasmus's* The Praise of Folie *in order to reveal the relationship between Christian doctrine and Shakespeare's "comic perspective." In the excerpt below, he maintains that the play depicts the parallels between romantic and religious love and those between the imaginative process and religious belief. Thus, Hassel compares lovers and poets with religious mystics to the degree that they must all admit that neither reason nor senses are sufficient to penetrate the highest expressions of human imagination or faith. For further commentary on the role of imagination in love and art as depicted in* A Midsummer Night's Dream, *see the excerpts by G. G. Gervinus (1849-50), E. K. Chambers (1905), H. B. Charlton (1933), E. C. Pettet (1949), Ernest Schanzer (1951), Howard Nemerov (1956), George A. Bonnard (1956), Elizabeth Sewell (1960), John Vyvyan (1961), R. W. Dent (1964), Peter G. Phialas (1966), and David Ormerod (1978). Hassel demonstrates the relationship between* The Praise of Folie *and the speeches of the young lovers as they awaken at*

the end of Act IV, Scene i; he declares that the close parallels in language signal that, like the holy fool of Erasmus, the lovers must "accept love on faith as an undeserved blessing," rather than try to comprehend its existence by means of rational inquiry. Similarly, he contends that Theseus's speech on the lunatic, lover, and poet expresses the belief, supported by Pauline theology, that human willingness to believe in the imaginative world is much greater than its power to comprehend it. For further discussion of the presence of Pauline doctrine in A Midsummer Night's Dream, *see the essays by John A. Allen (1967) and Ronald F. Miller (1975).*]

The most obvious Pauline allusion in [*A Midsummer Night's Dream*] is also the most important, for it alerts us to the central position St. Paul occupies in its comic vision. The allusion occurs during Bottom's delightful monologue upon awakening from his dream, a moment that has always struck the audience as perfectly balanced between the ridiculous and the sublime:

> I have had a most rare vision. I have had a dream, past the wit of man to say what dream it was. Man is but an ass if he go about to expound this dream. Methought I was—there is no man can tell what. Methought . . . I had— But man is but a patched fool if he will offer to say what methought I had. The eye of man hath not heard, the ear of man hath not seen, man's hand is not able to taste, his tongue to conceive, nor his heart to report what my dream was.
>
> [IV. i. 204-14]

We are right when we ascribe Bottom's reluctance to expound upon his dream to his grotesque vision of himself as an ass. Surely his hands reach for those Midas ears and that long, hairy nose as he speaks. But this unmistakable parody of one of the most familiar passages from St. Paul certainly encourages us to speculate that Bottom's dream at least flirts with profundity as well as asshood, and that his one silence may bespeak a momentary if inexpressible wisdom. In his confused silence Bottom may even be asking Shakespeare's audience to understand the vital interrelationships between the act of faith and the fact of folly in St. Paul's Christian community and in Shakespeare's romantic, comic one.

His echo of St. Paul is more extensive than first appears. The obvious allusion is to First Corinthians 2:9, which reads: "The eye hath not seene, and the eare hath not heard, neither have entered into the heart of man, the things which God hath prepared for them that love him." But. . . . there is another Pauline allusion in the same passage which encourages us still further to investigate the doctrinal affinities of Bottom's "most rare vision" and his delicious folly. Second Corinthians 12:1-6 reads:

> It is not expedient doubtlesse for me to glorie, I wil come to visions and revelations of the Lord. For I knew a man in Christ, above fourteene yeeres agoe . . . taken up into the thirde heaven: And I knewe the same man (whether in the body, or out of the body, I cannot tell, God knoweth,) How that he was taken up into paradise, and heard unspeakable wordes, which is not lawfull for man to utter. Of such *a man* wil I glory, yet of my selfe will I not glorie, but in mine infirmities. For though I would desire to glory *of them*, I shall not bee a foole, for I will say the trueth, but I now refraine,

lest any man should thinke of me above *that* which hee seeth me *to be,* or *that* he heareth of me.

Notice briefly the close verbal and structural parallels between Bottom's monologue and this second passage. Both begin with references to visions. Both start twice to reveal a vision, only to stop out of prudence. In both cases the vision is believed, but the visionary realizes that its expression would render him a fool, while its repression proves his wisdom. Such close similarities to both passages almost demand that we pursue the doctrinal relevancies of Bottom's transcendental experience, however close that pursuit leads us to [grow] our own ass' ears. For though we have been well warned, "Man is but an ass if he go about to expound this dream," yet it tantalizes us to try. (pp. 53-4)

Bottom confounds our imaginations with his dream. He has been loved by a fairy queen, and we must look on amazed and not a little envious. Moreover, since he has lost none of his "mortal grossness," he embodies simultaneously our lowest potentiality, our utter folly, our asshood, our comically fallen state. If we can acknowledge both sides of that most rare vision, what we cannot have and what we must have—Titania and ass' ears—we will have taken a large step towards attaining *sapientia,* what St. Paul or Erasmus called supernatural foolishness. Bottom's reluctant discovery of the "mystery" of man's fallen nature finds a higher and more positive comic counterpart in the lover's acceptance of the inexpressible, irrational wonder of love and the audience's celebration of the madness of its own imagination. The lunatic, the lover, and the poet are, after all, types of the religious mystic. All of them walk on the edge of absurdity. (p. 57)

In his tantalizing and frustrating monologue, Bottom thus alerts us to the possibilities and the impossibilities of our own knowing, the limits of human reason and human behavior evoked by all profound fools of Christian or comic persuasion. Hamlet is constantly frustrated by similar epistemological limitations. In fact, he sometimes plays the fool and the madman in his frustration. But Shakespeare's comic vision demands the acceptance of these intellectual limits and their celebration, just as it demands the celebration of inevitable and universal behavioral folly once it has been acknowledged. For Shakespeare's tragic characters this lesson is often too hard to learn. For his comic characters its wisdom is a major prerequisite to joyous festivity.

The attitudes of Theseus and the lovers towards reason and unreason, faith and love, are as important to understand as Bottom's dream if we are to grasp the full dimensions of the Pauline and Erasmian allusions operating in this play and in Shakespeare's comic vision. Theseus's comments about lunatics, poets, lovers, and orators in Act V fit comfortably into the Pauline context of Bottom's dream. And the lovers' common, strenuous progress into an acceptance of love's transcendence of the senses and the reason bears close analogic ties to the same biblical context. Theseus may also allude to St. Paul in some of his most important speeches. The lovers echo important words from *The Praise of Folie* as they grope towards an understanding of their wondrous experience in the forest. Through all of these prominent connections Shakespeare seems to be inviting the audience to understand their own imaginative faith and folly and the blessed madness of poets and lovers, through their analogies to the familiar Christian understanding of the wonders of divine love and the mysteries of religious faith. . . . [This] system of analogies is dramatically

fitting without ever being narrowly dogmatic or allegorical. Far from using drama to teach doctrine, Shakespeare, with the ingenuity we expect of him, is using doctrine which his contemporaries would have known very well to elucidate a new and unusual, even an esoteric, comic interest in the imaginative process. To the degree that the process of imagination is analogous to the process of belief—to that degree his audience might better understand and participate in the comic, romantic action he is portraying for them.

Striking parallels can be shown to exist between the lovers' awakening from their dreams and passages about the analogous experiences of romantic and religious love in Erasmus's *The Praise of Folie.* Even the language describing the two experiences is sometimes similar. . . . Since Erasmus also links romantic and religious madness as closely analogous blessings, it is crucial that we perceive and understand Shakespeare's use of Erasmus in depicting the lovers of *A Midsummer Night's Dream.* (pp. 58-9)

Erasmus's *The Praise of Folie,* like Shakespeare's *A Midsummer Night's Dream,* alludes to St. Paul's most famous passage in First Corinthians as the definitive statement of [the] ultimate promise, [the] ultimate reward of faith and love.

What follows this allusion in *The Praise of Folie* is a description of those that "have suche grace." It is so pertinent to the experiences and the words of Bottom and the lovers in *A Midsummer Night's Dream* as to deserve our most careful attention:

> They are subjecte to a certaine passion muche lyke unto maddesse or witravying, when ravisshed so in the sprite, or beyng in a traunce, thei doo speake certaine thynges not hangyng one with an other, nor after any earthly facion, but rather dooe put foorth a voyce they wote neuer what, muche lesse to be understode of others: and sodeinely without any apparent cause why, dooe chaunge the state of theyr countenaunces. For now shall ye see theim . . . wepe, now thei laugh, now they sighe, for briefe, it is certaine that they are wholy distraught and rapte out of theim selves.

The lovers in *A Midsummer Night's Dream* do not speak in tongues, to be sure. They do appear and often feel mad to themselves and others during their forest experience, speak disconnectedly to one another, change and change and change again under the strange influence of Puck's liquor, but "without any apparent cause why." Theseus even links their "seething brains" and "shaping fantasies" with those of lunatics and poets, and finds their testimony "more strange than true" [V. i. 4, 5, 2]. He cannot understand them, at least not with "cool reason." Still, he might know that their experience is analogous to the prophet's as he glances "from heaven to earth, from earth to heaven" at "the forms of things unknown," but not necessarily nonexistent [V. i. 13, 15]. Hippolyta is more literally believing, and finds in their strange narrative "something of great constancy" [V. i. 26], albeit beyond the veil. We are deliciously left in Act V with this suspended judgment, though we know that the lovers were "wholly distraught and rapte out of theim selves" in the woods.

The next [description by Folie] of this ultimate experience of faith and folly is even more pointedly suggestive of Bottom and the lovers in the forest, almost at times anticipating the very words they use: "In sort that whan a little after thei come againe to their former wittes, thei denie plainly thei wote where thei became, or whether thei were than in theyr bodies, or out of theyr bodies, wakyng or slepying: remembring also as little, either what they heard, saw, saied, or did than, savyng as it were through a cloude, or by a dreame.'' . . . Listen again to the lovers as they try to describe the wondrous experience they have just undergone. Lysander ''shall reply amazedly'':

> Half sleep, half waking; but as yet, I swear,
> I cannot truly say how I came here.
>
> [IV. i. 146-48]

Demetrius similarly testifies,

> But, my good lord, I wot not by what power
> (But by some power it is) my love to Hermia,
> Melted as the snow, seems to me now
> As the remembrance of an idle gaud
> Which in my childhood I did dote upon.
>
> [IV. i. 164-68]

These are almost the very words Folie uses to describe the analogous experience of the foolishness of faith. In fact, Demetrius says just after these words,

> And all the faith, the virtue of my heart,
> The object and the pleasure of mine eye,
> Is only Helena.
>
> [IV. i. 169-71]

He has rediscovered the true faith of love. And the language of his discovery is strongly evocative of its Erasmian source.

Many of their succeeding comments evidence a similar relationship to [Folie's] description of such transcendental experiences, even as they gradually find its ephemeral shapes leaving their minds. Demetrius, for example, finds that

> These things seem small and indistinguishable,
> Like far-off mountains turned into clouds.
>
> [IV. i. 187-88]

Then he asks yet again,

> Are you sure
> That we are awake? It seems to me
> That yet we sleep, we dream
>
> [IV. i. 192-94]

But the dream is over, and so is their experience with transcendental foolishness. It was a midsummer night's dream for them, a midsummer madness, during which they wore, briefly, ass-heads of their own. But how richly analogous was their experience, through St. Paul's prism or Erasmus's, to the divine folly of faith.

Such Erasmian responses to their dream in the forest suggest that the four lovers in *A Midsummer Night's Dream* must free their minds from the evidence of their senses and the rules of their reason in order to discover the transcendent truth of love's madness. In fact, their experience in the play (like that of the audience) is a carefully developed liberation from their misconceptions that love (or transcendental knowledge) has secure rational and sensual foundations, or that it can somehow be earned or deserved. A look at their disabusement from these misconceptions will reveal that once the lovers can dismiss their reason and their senses, once they can accept love on faith as an undeserved blessing, their confusion will come to an end in blessed confusion. We have already seen that their joyous if puzzled discovery of this liberating paradox echoes Erasmian passages about the liberation of religious faith. Just as surely as Bottom's dream it leads the audience to a deeper

appreciation of the wisdom and the folly of their own imaginative experience.

The lovers come to their final accord through an almost anarchic process of finding all of their assumptions concerning love's reason and its desert reversed in the forest. Oberon's potion, Puck's (Love's and the Imagination's?) unpredictability, their own misconceptions, and the mysterious, dreamlike, almost subconscious forest environment combine to reorder their realities. The process deserves some detailing because many of us have taken the lovers' pasteboard qualities for granted for so long that we cannot see them otherwise.

Demetrius obviously assumes that love is a matter of legal right and personal desert. He thinks he has earned Hermia's hand by winning her father's voice:

> Relent, sweet Hermia; and, Lysander, yield
> Thy crazèd title to my certain right.
>
> [I. i. 91-2]

The law of Athens seems to support his assumption. But because of the ''certain'' rationality of his position, Demetrius does not appreciate or deserve that ''crazed'' love which is really his, namely, Helena's. Consequently, he can be justly called ''spotted and inconstant'' as the play begins [I. i. 110]. Demetrius will come painfully to understand this evaluation of himself when he learns from Hermia that love has to be freely given. Then he can better cherish the one love he is so fortunate as to possess.

Helena is equally certain of love's logic and deserving at the beginning of the play, when it is most illogical. Her certainty will cause a humiliation as intense as Olivia's in *Twelfth Night*. Helena assumes that Demetrius must love Hermia for tangible reasons. Evidence to the contrary notwithstanding [I. i. 227], she must be more fair, her eyes lovelier, her tongue ''more tunable'' [I. i. 181-93 *passim*]. Evidence of love's paradoxes and Demetrius's irrationality also surround her. He dotes on Hermia's frown, curses, and hatred; he scorns her own smiles, prayers, and love [I. i. 194-99]. Ignoring this evidence, Helena still concludes that love is explainable and deserved. Her misconceptions culminate in her final soliloquy of Scene i. Calling love blind, irrational, and childlike, she seems finally to have penetrated its paradoxical essence:

> Love looks not with the eyes, but with the mind,
> And therefore is winged Cupid painted blind.
> Nor hath Love's mind of any judgment taste;
> Wings, and no eyes, figure unheedy haste.
> And therefore is Love said to be a child,
> Because in choice he is so oft beguiled.
>
> [I. i. 234-39]

But Helena cannot embrace these paradoxes; they offend her as mutations of her sense of ideal love. Consequently she immediately contradicts her thesis by resolving to do Demetrius a good favor, thereby ''winning'' his love. Her resolution is even irrational in its scope—she plans to further her cause by reuniting her lover with her rival. Surely this is but the latest in this early series of revelations of the transcendent illogic of love. That illogic is part of the mystery which she and her fellows will finally accept with wonder and without question.

The experiences of Hermia and Lysander are somewhat simpler because they begin and end in love. Nevertheless, like Demetrius and Helena, both must learn in the forest that they do not deserve and might not retain each others' love, because love is neither predictable nor logical. Their gamelike, dream-like experience teaches them to cherish the love to which they are restored by illustrating how equally they "deserve" scorn and loneliness. From their insipid, predictable, immature sense of suffering [I. i. 128-55] they come in the forest to sense the paradoxical and violent wellsprings of their passion, and then to transcend them. With that new understanding and a healthy fear of rejection, the fact of love becomes an unexpected and unexplainable gift—a transcendental blessing.

Oberon's potion functions as agent and symbol of love's irrationality and undeserving, just as the forest becomes both setting and symbol of the progress of their minds (and ours) into transcendental awareness. When Lysander is given the potion by mistake and awakens to love Helena and forsake Hermia, he is bewitched, but only in a context which confirms the complexity of love. Confusion is love's dramatic medium; mistaken identity its psychological reality. The potion creates sounder persons who will return to amity strengthened by their "most rare visions." Lysander learns at least how absurdly he can behave, how capable all men are of fickleness. Hermia realizes that she can be both unloved and alone; she was not born to happiness. Helena learns that she can be loved, though it is hard for her to accept it readily. Demetrius grasps the miracle of a single act of love. In mysterious yet discernible ways the lovers are directed—figuratively by the fairies and their potions, literally by their own imagination and ours—to understand love's irrationality, its disdain of desert, and its transcendence of reason and the senses. The curses, the disorder, and the threatened violence of Act III, Scene ii is likewise a necessary prelude to the wondrous amity which follows. Only when they have perceived love's unpredictable madness can they accept and appreciate its transcendent sanity.

Paradoxically, the lovers seem most intensely "real" when they are farthest removed from the "normal" reality of Athens and daylight. Although their violence is like a game, it also contains the passion that love requires, its energy and its complexity. In the last forest moment all of the creative and destructive potentiality of love seems briefly poured forth. Of course, no one can continue to live with the intensity they experience in the forest, or within its suspension of normal human behavior. Order and reason must return to audience as well as lovers and with such normality must come diminished, dim visions, stereotypes of character and action, crude playlets. The lovers call for light and sleep in a fashion that suggests this need for order. But for a moment there was a greater order in the forest—lightless, intense, and transcendental—just before dawn.

When the lovers awaken from their dream, we notice immediately that a transcendent humility of faith has supplanted those earlier assumptions of their deserving and of love's reasonableness. The lovers do not and cannot understand this grace, but they do believe in it, no longer in themselves. (pp. 60-6)

This grace, this faith, is what allows the lovers finally to dismiss their senses. Their experience seems to have taught them a new humility, a healthy sense of folly which urges that there are things that are true that can neither be seen nor understood.... Sleep and awakening, vision and insight, momentarily join for the lovers in the forest, and that mysterious joining frees them briefly from the restraints of their senses and reason. Their resultant acceptance of the miracle of concord, personal and social, is a manifestation of that faith in love and rejoicing in a shared, liberating folly which consis-

tently marks Shakespeare's festive conclusion and becomes a prerequisite for it.

The audience of *A Midsummer Night's Dream* seems to share the lovers' gradual edification into this "graceful," joyous folly of romantic faith. We share it in part because we have seen what they have dreamed and know it to be "real." But such sure knowledge would not constitute a common experience at all. For an analogous imaginative faith would require that we also embrace what we cannot understand, the implausible, irrational, inexpressible, and inconceivable wonders of their forest escapade. And so we are also given a Bottom, who with us flirts with the transcendental, even touches it, but remains the same old "bully Bottom" he always was. His blend of sublimity and absurdity is also ours, and we had better not forget it as we go about to expound his dream, or the lovers'. (pp. 67-8)

Erasmus has [his narrator] Folie make one more comment near the end of her sermon that helps us complete our sense of relationship between these comic and Christian themes, and distinguish between them, too.... Folie concludes of these fools: "This thei know certainely, that whiles their mindes so roved and wandred, thei were most happie and blisfull, so that they lament and wepe at theyr retourne unto theyre former senses, as who saieth, nothyng were leefer unto theim than continually to rave and be deteigned with suche a spece of madnesse. And this is but a certaine smacke or thinne taste of theyr blisse to come." ... The audience too is loath to leave the imaginative madness of good theater for the glaring sanity of the world outside. But these Athenian lovers were most unhappy in their wandering, and they are glad to be awake again. The unreason of love or faith is too threatening for most human sensibilities, and they do not knowingly carry it back to Athens with them. Still, when they awake from their dream they are all "new in amity" [IV. i. 87]. And though they willingly follow Theseus back to Athens, they also want to prolong their forest experience a little longer: "And by the way let us recount our dreams" [IV. i. 199]. These lovers are not equipped to remain such fools for very long. Nor would most of us want them to celebrate such profound folly indefinitely. That way madness lies, or perfect faith. That Shakespeare has invited us to glimpse this much of the wisdom of their folly, or Bottom's, or our own through his Erasmian and Pauline allusions is surely significance enough. Theseus and Hippolyta, with Pyramus and Puck, seal these impressions for us in the final act. (pp. 70-1)

Aware now of some of the possible connections between these Pauline and Erasmian passages and the play, let us look at Theseus in Act V. His articulate distrust of some products of the imagination is part of his more general distrust of the sophisticated, of the worldly, the "tongues" of this life. Theseus, in choosing the rustic's performance, perceives with us and for us that learning and eloquence are not necessarily the greatest wisdom. He similarly distrusts the fabulous tale of the lovers, with good reason. But Theseus is no simple advocate of reason against love or imagination in *A Midsummer Night's Dream*. Pauline echoes in Act V make this quite clear.

The most distinctive echo concerns Theseus's and St. Paul's mutual distrust of tongues. Their reasons are as similar as their articulation of them. Theseus states:

> Where I have come, great clerks have purposèd
> To greet me with premeditated welcomes;

Where I have seen them shiver and look pale,
Make periods in the midst of sentences,
Throttle their practiced accent in their fears,
And, in conclusion, dumbly have broke off,
Not paying me a welcome. Trust me, sweet,
Out of this silence yet I picked a welcome,
And in the modesty of fearful duty
I read as much as from the rattling tongue
Of saucy and audacious eloquence.
Love, therefore, and tongue-tied simplicity
In least speak most, to my capacity.

[V. i. 93-105]

Theseus exhibits worldly wisdom here, of course. But he is also articulating a basic Pauline truth about love, as he says, and about faith: the imperceptible is often also the inexpressible. The most eloquent language, without love, is nothing; love, like faith, best expresses itself in simplicity, even in silence. Listen to St. Paul concerning the language of love and faith. . .: "Though I speake with the tongues of men, and of Angels, and have not charitie, I am *as* sounding brasse, or *as* a tinckling Cymbal: And though I have prophecie, and understand all secrets, and all knowledge: yea, if I have all faith, so that I can remoove mountaines, and have not charitie, I am nothing." (pp. 72-3)

Theseus has a far more cogent Pauline comment to make about prophets or frenzied poets. In fact, our Pauline awareness reveals that Theseus's famous speech about the lunatic, the lover, and the poet, hitherto often considered antagonistic to poets, lovers, and dreamers, is neither absolutely uncharitable nor unimaginative. It is rather directly supported by St. Paul's humble distrust of vain show and empty eloquence, and his realization of man's limited powers of perception. Theseus, then, may be reaffirming Bottom's Pauline awareness: "The eye hath not seene, and the eare hath not heard, neither have entred into the heart of man, the things which God hath prepared for them that love him" (I. Cor. 2:9).

What Theseus says is this:

The lunatic, the lover, and the poet
Are of imagination all compact.
One sees more devils than vast hell can hold:
That is the madman. The lover, all as frantic,
Sees Helen's beauty in a brow of Egypt.
The poet's eye, in a fine frenzy rolling,
Doth glance from heaven to earth, from earth to heaven;
And as imagination bodies forth
The forms of things unknown, the poet's pen
Turns them to shapes, and gives to airy nothing
A local habitation and a name.

[V. i. 7-17]

Far from dismissing true imagination, this speech confirms the ability to believe in the imperceivable, but laughs at futile attempts to perceive, categorize, or express it. Man can understand only so much; he must take the rest on faith. With St. Paul, Theseus smiles charitably at the poet, the prophet, or the lover who tries too hard to shape the shapeless. Like Bottom, he knows that man can become an ass if he goes about expounding all dreams. His speech is thus an affirmation of faith in the imagination, freeing the mind as it does from temporal evidence and its own limited wisdom.

Poor Bottom, for all his flirtation with these Erasmian and Pauline commonplaces, remains unedified, however. His play

of Pyramus is thus a fitting final celebration of the differences between his mind, if mind it can be called, and that of the lovers. His play's literal-minded stumbling over punctuation marks, figurative language, properties, lighting effects, and almost every other convention of poetry and the stage suggests his entrapment by the literal world, the world of the senses and the reason that the others have momentarily escaped. . . . [As] in *Love's Labor's Lost* the hilarity of this fond pageant lies partly in our acknowledgment of kinship with it. "Lord, what fools these mortals be" is thus Puck's vital statement of a comic truth we must all embrace to experience the fullest joy at the end of *A Midsummer Night's Dream*. Only then can we celebrate with the lovers our mutual liberation from excessive reasonableness and our entry into imaginative faith.

Typically, Theseus is charitable but not enthusiastic toward their performance: "The best in this kind are but shadows, and the worst no worse, if imagination amend them" [V. i. 211-12]. At the end he thanks them nobly for their noble efforts. But Hippolyta, as she was toward the lovers' analogous story of their great folly, is moved again by the performance to a moment of aesthetic faith despite her better judgment: "Beshrew my heart but I pity the man" [V. i. 290]. Only the actress can tell us whether she pities Bottom or Pyramus or both for this fleeting moment, but each possiblity is present in the line. Theseus and Hippolyta represent in their responses to the lovers and the players an interesting blend of charity and imagination, forgiveness and faith. He charitably forgives vain attempts to express the inexpressible, for to him all such attempts are, like drama, but shadows of truth. The world of ideas must always transcend them. That he is but another of these shadows undercuts his certainty with some irony. . . . But we have seen that Theseus's position here is not necessarily one of absolute skepticism; he merely questions the possibilities of expressing the transcendental. Hippolyta simply believes. She believes the tale of the lovers. And, "beshrew her heart," she even believes, momentarily, in the illusion of the rude mechanicals. St. Paul says at the end of First Corinthians 13, "Nowe abideth faith, hope, and charitie, these three, but the greatest of these is charitie." It is fitting that Theseus, the ranking lord in the play, should exhibit such charity towards the players, the lovers, and even the fairies at the play's conclusion. But Hippolyta, as ranking lady, is not so much laggard in her faith. Their union is a happy note on which the play could end. Still, the fairies must have their last ephemeral words to remind us of their world, still just tantalizingly beyond our own, though our hands can almost join at certain magical moments.

And so we return at last from Theseus's court to Oberon's. Here the fairies, intangible, nighttime creatures, flit about the stage as the final symbols of that elusive truth Bottom, Theseus, Hippolyta, and the lovers all flirt with during the play. Theirs is no truth for the wise or the prudent. St. Paul warns, "for it is written, I will destroy the wisedome of the wise, and will cast away the understanding of the prudent" (I Cor. 1:19). "God hath chosen the foolish things of the world, to confound the wise" (I Cor. 1:27). Most of the characters in the final scene of *A Midsummer Night's Dream* know in their own ways that they are among the foolish things of this world. The fairies symbolize the fleeting shadows of their imaginations and our own, the truths seen through a glass darkly. Puck's intensely human if paradoxical attempt to communicate with us during his epilogue reveals how important it is that the audience also sense, however dimly, its close kinship to all of these foolish shadows, and celebrate that kinship as well. For only then can the play's festive communion in faith and folly be a completely successful celebration of transcendental, theatrical, and human unity. We must give Puck our hands, our hearts, and our belief for the festive experience to be complete. Without such an expression of our epistemological folly, we cannot truly affirm our imaginative faith. (pp. 74-6)

R. Chris Hassel, Jr., "'Most Rare Vision': Faith in 'A Midsummer Night's Dream'," in his Faith and Folly in Shakespeare's Romantic Comedies, The University of Georgia Press, 1980, pp. 52-76.

MORDECAI MARCUS (essay date 1981)

[In the following excerpt, Marcus takes issue with Jan Kott's and Hugh M. Richmond's studies of the theme of "love-and-death" in A Midsummer Night's Dream (see excerpts above, 1964 and 1971), claiming that Kott overemphasizes the violent "erotic animality" of the imagery in Shakespeare's play and that Richmond overstates the characters' attraction to death in their quest for love. Instead, Marcus argues that the love-and-death theme serves both a negative and positive function in A Midsummer Night's Dream, namely, to underscore "the danger that death will preclude love" and to emphasize "the necessity that the risk and finality of death surround love and bring it to fruition." For Marcus, the constant presence of death in the play as well as in our own perceptions offers a kind of resistance or tension which heightens the emotional and spiritual significance of love. The critic traces the relation of this theme to the various groups of characters and to the Pyramus and Thisbe interlude in Act V, Scene i, which he regards as Shakespeare's parody of his own treatment of love-and-death in the main plot. Other critics who have examined the presence of death and other violent elements beneath the comic structure of A Midsummer Night's Dream include G. K. Chesterton (1904), G. Wilson Knight (1932), Charles R. Lyons (1971), David Bevington (1975), and M. E. Lamb (1979). For additional commentary on the play-within-the-play as a parody of Shakespeare's concerns in the main plot, see the excerpts by August Wilhelm Schlegel (1808), E. K. Chambers (1905), Paul N. Siegel (1953), and C. L. Barber (1959).]

Jan Kott declares that the "philosophical theme" of A Midsummer Night's Dream is "Eros and T[h]anatos" [see excerpt above, 1964]. However, his development of the idea is minimal and obscure. He seems to see the blindness of love and an almost violent animal erotic animality as an equivalent for the death-urge as it surrounds and intensifies the sex act. Hugh M. Richmond's approach [see excerpt above, 1971] is explicitly based on Denis de Rougemont's thesis, in his Love in the Western World, that romantic love pursues obstacles and finally death itself to enhance the desireability of the fading love-object and to achieve in death an extinction of self which love desires but cannot realize. In a passage not directly citing de Rougemont, Richmond summarizes the thesis: "Since the most excitingly intense feelings and idealizations are generated by impediments to love, and since the supreme impediment to love is death, unqualified passion solicits the death of both the beloved and the lover." Richmond believes that all the young lovers in the play are motivated by pursuit of barriers based on this psychology, that the Pyramus-Thisby playlet ridicules this orientation, and that Bottom shows distinct scepticism towards it. Thus, Richmond finds in this play, as in Romeo and Juliet, powerful warnings against the celebration of love-and-death.

If one grants Richmond's interpretation of the young lovers' motives, his reading is coherent, but also one-sided and stiffly moralistic. Perhaps, as in Romeo and Juliet, Shakespeare has intuited both a positive and a negative potential in the pursuit of love-and-death; but clearly Richmond does not grant the

positive potential. Kott does not mention de Rougemont, and rather than moralize he seems to be generalizing with a certain relish about how people are driven by sex. Kott's view achieves less coherence than Richmond's because it forces more violence than imagery and interrelations among the characters justify.

I think that the play yields a reading which justifies an alternative and partly complementary view of love-death. In this view, love-and-death becomes a paradigm of fulfillment—a paradigm which overlaps the themes of order, reconciliation, and maturation in the play's plot. This view is based on an approach presented in Norman O. Brown's undisciplined book Life Against Death. Here, death becomes not only acceptable as passionate fulfillment; it is somehow part of such fulfillment—through the lowering of tension and the fusion of two lovers—but it is all, and this is equally important, a paradigm of some ultimate condition of fulfillment into which love projects its chosen ones. In the de Rougemont view, love-and-death creates a negative madness. From the perspective I am expounding, love-and-death is at best a kind of divine madness sometimes seen as the temporal become the permanent or as a satisfactory merger with the cosmos. This view also finds comfort in the face of death from the fact that love creates children who promise the continuation of life.

In A Midsummer Night's Dream, Shakespeare's imagination has caught the interrelations between death, life-fulfillment, generativity, and sexual satisfaction almost from the play's opening. However, the positive love-and-death theme is more sketchy and less rhetorically emphatic in the plot about the young lovers than in the plots about Theseus and Hippolyta, Oberon and Titania, and perhaps no more emphatic than in the plot about the play-producing clowns. One should probably grant that the greatly superior (often supernally lovely) poetry of the Theseus-Hippolyta and Oberon-Titania plots suggests that they engaged Shakespeare's imagination more than did the story of the young lovers. The love-death theme, I believe, is closely interwoven with harmony achieved, discord become musical, which so many readers find central to the play. "Musical discord" [IV. i. 118] is a paradigm for full sexual satisfaction for its own sake and as part of the rhythm of love and generativity in which the threat of death is kept in balance. The play variously illustrates the love-and-death tension in imbalance and in pursuit of balance. (pp. 269-71)

The Theseus-Hippolyta plot provides a framework for the play and for the love-and-death theme. These lovers have converted aggression into sexual love, which under the aegis of marriage will purge Theseus as rapist and Hippolyta as warrior. This ultimate consummation points towards deepened amity and children. In I, i, withering fruitlessness is opposed to passionate generativity, fruitlessness representing death without love and generativity representing the acceptance and overcoming of death. The waning moon and the "dowager / Long withering out a young man's revenue" [I. i. 5-6] represent the denial of sexual fulfillment and its issue. It is, however, a denial that will not last and also part of the ceremony leading towards fulfillment for Theseus and Hippolyta. The moon "like to a silver bow / New-bent in heaven" [I. i. 9-10], which Hippolyta anticipates, symbolizes sexual tension and its outcome—release of tension and creation of children. Hippolyta's reference to the delay before marriage—"Four days will quickly steep themselves in night" [I. i. 7]—is a prototype for the experience of sexual love surrounded by darkness, merging with darkness, and creating an essence which is a model of love-death as ultimate fulfillment.

Theseus says of "melancholy": "The pale companion is not for our pomp" [I. i. 15] and immediately refers to the warlike injuries that he inflicted on Hippolyta and that he will now heal through the harmony of marriage. Blood is absent from sexless melancholy and it was present but out of proportion and lacking right uses in former warlike acts. Turning melancholy forth to funerals is a way of seeing death as an interruption of the life process. When melancholy is later admitted on the stage in the Pyramus and Thisby production, it is permitted only as farce, probably because it comes as part of melodramatic display and satire more than as part of a risk that preludes fulfillment.

Theseus and Hippolyta next appear offstage—in a dialogue between Oberon and Titania [II. i. 60-145]. Both fairy king and queen see the coming wedding as the subduing of Theseus' wild nature, and Titania accuses Oberon of a reluctant approval of this marriage. Oberon's insistence that Titania has helped Theseus in various rape-like acts implies that she also has some regret about the marriage. Oberon's view is unclear, but Titania's distress at the utter confusion of the natural seasons, which she attributes to her dissension with Oberon, suggests that proper marriage will restore the balance of nature—where death is part of the necessary rhythm of recurrence. At this point the Theseus-Hippolyta and Oberon-Titania plots fuse thematically, as Oberon and Titania use their views of Theseus and Hippolyta to resist a reconciliation like the one these mortals achieve.

When Theseus and Hippolyta next appear (IV, i), the "musical discord" of hounds and echoes symbolizes the coming marriages as the restoration of proper balance infused with sexual energy. The Spartan hounds "dewlapped like Thessalian bulls" and "slow in pursuit but matched in mouth like bells" [IV. i. 122, 123] show the death-aspect of the natural process, the sexual fecundity of bulls, and the restoration of energetic balance. Their occurrence is quite proper for this last scene before the marriages take place.

In the single scene of V, the love-and-death theme as it applies to Theseus and Hippolyta is brought into balanced conjunction with the theme from the three other plots. Theseus can say of the Pyramus-Thisby performance: "This palpable gross play hath well beguiled / The heavy gait of night" [V. i. 367-68] because he recognizes that in the playlet the risks run in the pursuit of love have not been well dramatized, have in fact been comic, not tragic; but his amusement seems an appropriate correlative to sexual-generative fulfillment, especially for those like himself who have truly run risks and therefore both deserve and know how to relish fulfillment. The "best bride bed" [V. i. 403] that Oberon will bless is surely Theseus' and Hippolyta's, not only because of their royal stature but also because, having run the greatest risks, they deserve fulfillment and will know how to relish its contribution to the healing of past wounds.

Oberon and Titania stand both outside and within the love-and-death framework for two reasons: They are immortal and they cannot conceive. Their two trains and their dissension are a substitute for the sexual tension—an essential drive for mortal involvement in recurrence. The child represents for each of them a kind of playing at parenthood, and for Titania, it recalls the sweetness of mortality as suggested by the Indian woman's death. In II, i, where Oberon's and Titania's need to play at dissension is demonstrated by their separate trains, they serve as the negative part of a fertility rite that can bear fruit only outside of the fairies' lives. Titania is explicit about having "forsworn his [Oberon's] bed and company" [II. i. 62] and

she launches into an extraordinary description of fertility reduced to utter confusion by a forced mixture of the seasons. Oberon and Titania are ill-met by moonlight because moonlight ought to be the proper sphere for fairy rites. This moonlight may suggest moonlight as the realm of virginity in I, i, in which case it ambiguously points to the natural infertility of fairy queen and king and the fertility rites they are able to perform without benefit to themselves.

Titania's speech on the changeling child's mother is perhaps the most important comment in the play on the love-and-death theme [II. i. 123-37]. Titania and the child's mother observed together the fullness of "th'embarked traders on the flood." The comparison of swelling sails to the votaress's swelling belly echoes the idea of sexual tension in "the moon, like to a silver bow / New-bent in heaven" (I, i), and it connects the womb's fruitfulness with natural processes (the sea and wind) and human enterprises ("rich with merchandise"). The fact that the votaress "being mortal, of that boy did die" suggests terrible risks run by the conjunction of sex and procreation and a concomitant sexual glory in procreation. The struggle for possession of the child may well suggest a sharp ambiguity. Oberon and Titania wish to possess the child as a substitute for the issue they cannot have and they may insist on separate rather than mutual possession because of a desire individually, and hence jealously, to bridge the real and fairy worlds. Oberon may need to have the child as part of separate masculine rites because he recognizes the fruitlessness of his marriage, and Titania seems to take pleasure in the child because it will help her and her followers to make up a world of separate motherhood. But the most important function of the division over the child is to create a dissension to substitute for that normal sexual tension which can exist only under the aegis of an inevitable death.

The relationship between Titania and Bottom contributes only tangentially to the love-and-death theme. Although Titania sees the transformed Bottom as beautiful and wise, she still declares "I will purge thy mortal grossness so / That thou shalt like an airy spirit go" [III. i. 160-61] because she knows that the worlds of spirit and flesh must remain separate. In a world mixing immortals and clumsy mortals, she is unconsciously thinking of both herself and Bottom: he sexually naive and she sexually disappointed. Bottom is led to her bower and Titania notes that the moon laments "some enforced chastity" [III. i. 200]. We have seen in I, i that the moon represents either sterility as unfulfillment or chastity as the prelude to fulfillment. Here, the moon's grief over forced sexuality seems to represent the pathos of Titania's sad unfulfillment and unpromising desire for sexual union with the gross Bottom. When later (IV, i) Oberon describes the sight of Titania after she sees Bottom for what he truly is, the description of dew "Like tears that did their own disgrace bewail" [IV. i. 56] is a transferred epithet for Titania's own shame over her vain attempt to bridge the worlds. Having lost heart for such a project—also symbolized by her possession of the changeling child—she loses heart to struggle for the boy and gives him up to Oberon.

In V, i, we are prepared for the arrival of the fairies by Theseus' admonition "Lovers, to bed, 'tis almost fairy time," [V. i. 364] which suggests both the limited bridging of natural and spiritual in human life and a miraculous quality in human sexuality. Puck's "Now it is the time of night / That the graves, all gaping wide, / Every one lets forth his sprite" [V. i. 379-81] reminds us of death as the background to human love and procreation, and adds to our conviction that the lovers are now safe in their marriage beds.

The love-and-death theme is present in familiar but simplified fashion in the main plot, the story of the young lovers. Here, the risk of death or perpetual virginity is run almost exclusively by Hermia. Theseus contrasts the fulfillment of "blood" passion with the fruitless life of a nun—"chanting faint hymns to the cold fruitless moon" [I. i. 73]—(that faintness contrasting to the full-blooded music of this play) and though he describes nun-like virginity as "thrice blessed" and though later Oberon pays a very pretty compliment to England's Virgin Queen [II. i. 157-64] the praise of virginity is little more than pious ceremony. The threats of death or virginity for Hermia are very real plot problems, so it is no surprise that Lysander and Hermia are stronger and more passionate characters in I, i than in the following parts of the play, where their problems are largely artificial. The intensive exchange between Lysander and Hermia about the difficulties of true love encapsulates much of the love-and-death theme. Love must run the risks of "War, death, or sickness," which make it "swift as a shadow, short as any dream, / Brief as the lightning in the collied night" [I. i. 142-45]. This threat of brevity stands in contrast to love steeped in night, and when Hermia acknowledges that the barriers to love make "a customary cross" she shows herself aware that risks must be run in order to assure fulfillment. When Lysander proposes that they flee to the house of his "widow aunt, a dowager / Of great revenue . . . [who] hath no child" [I. i. 157-58] we are reminded of Theseus' figure of a dowager "withering out a young man's revenue." Here a dowager is seen as generous and childcaring rather than as depriving. The death-equivalent in her life (childlessness) rather than leading her to deny the needs of youth would make her both welcome Lysander as a child-substitute and help his love-match.

Once the young lovers reach the forest, threats to their lives begin to seem unreal. They only appear to run the risks of additional betrayal, of desertion, animal predation, and death by the sword. In Act II both Helena [II. i. 244] and Hermia [II. ii. 156] anticipate that their lovers' betrayal of them may lead to death, and they may even seem a bit too anxious for such a death. But all of these risks are sufficiently under the control of Oberon and Puck so that we really do not worry greatly about the prospect of them perishing or suffering. When Oberon is preparing the final chemical salvation for the young lovers and he declares "And back to Athens shall the lovers wend / With league whose date till death shall never end" [III. ii. 372-73], his speech implies that they will now be fulfilled before they die, though "whose date till death shall never end" doesn't guarantee a long life. But Oberon's final speech in the play [V. i. 401-22] implies that they will live long enough to have children.

In the world of Bottom and his fellows, the danger that death will preclude love, and the necessity that the risk and finality of death surround love and bring it to fruition, are treated farcically. The love of Pyramus and Thisby is brought quickly and ridiculously to the consummation of death. Bottom's desire to make a ballad about his dream and to "sing it at her [presumably Thisby's] death" [IV. i. 219] shows him aware of some kind of miraculous risk and salvation in the human imagination. In contrast, Bottom's sharing of his fellow's fears that their drama—especially its bloody moments—will be taken too seriously by its audience is actually a denial of the reality of death's threat to love and a denial of the beneficence and emotional penetration of love-and-death rituals. Not surprisingly, then, Pyramus and Thisby is a "comical tragedy" to the clowns and the performance truly makes it so, for in this

performance the sexual gestures and puns rob passion of its dignity, and Pyramus' haste to kill himself echoes the preposterous bravado of the prologue's "with bloody blameful blade, / He bravely broached his boiling bloody breast" [V. i. 146-47]. This bravado is reminiscent of Helena's and Hermia's excessive welcome to the prospect of death when they were cavorting through the forest. The performance of the Pyramus and Thisby playlet is total parody of the idea that love must run the risk of death and if overtaken by the risks has nothing left but a poignantly unfulfilled or very slightly fulfilled union in death.

In the last-act framework for the Pyramus and Thisby performance, we see in Theseus the man of experience and self-acceptance who has little need to look down at people with less courage, wisdom, and experience. Hence his merely gentle chiding of the performance. The young lovers are partly basking in the strength of Theseus and enjoying their own superiority to the silliness of the clowns, forgetting the silliness they demonstrated in the dream-cloud of their forest adventure. The fairies have returned to a ritual way of life and take joy in the prospective fecundity they cannot share. For the lovers, the threats of violent death have been overcome and a more natural death now becomes one of the forces that bend the bow of sexual tension towards its release in consummation, childbearing, and acceptance of an eventual death after a fulfilled life.

One can grant Richmond's view that the young lovers and especially the grotesque Pyramus and Thisby illustrate a haste for the all-too-difficult perfection of love by blind rushing towards a union "blessed" by death. But I believe I have shown the strong possibility that in the relations among the young lovers, Shakespeare also intuits the idea that love requires the risk of death and achieves force and direction from the interweaving of the life impulse with the deathward-release of sexual tension and that the healing force of love is connected to the acceptance of death and vice-versa. Titania and Oberon stand in the background to show the paradox of unresolvable restlessness in a world of immortality, to yearn for an approximation of the satisfactions of the world of recurrence, and to bless the love-and-death union which is beyond them. Theseus and Hippolyta stand in the foreground, looking over the heads and shoulders of the young lovers towards the grotesque drama of Pyramus and Thisby. Here, the deeper meanings stem from the level of imagistic juxtapositions more than from dramatic confrontations. The young lovers are thematically Janus-faced. They look back towards the heroic lesson of Theseus and Hippolyta and forward to the comic lesson of Pyramus and Thisby. They have been partly saved by the intervention of Theseus and Hippolyta from the fate of Pyramus and Thisby, and they have grown sufficiently so that their implied rewards are deserved. (pp. 271-78)

Mordecai Marcus, "'A Midsummer Night's Dream': The Dialectic of Eros-Thanatos," in American Imago, *Vol. 38, No. 3, Fall, 1981, pp. 269-78.*

ALAN BRISSENDEN　(essay date 1981)

[*In the following excerpt from his* Shakespeare and the Dance *(1981), Brissenden maintains that dancing is an essential element in the structure of* A Midsummer Night's Dream *and not a mere embellishment, as it had been in Shakespeare's earlier plays. He contends that the quarrels and discordancies in the play are associated with interrupted dances and notes that the restoration of harmony between Oberon and Titania is celebrated by their dance together. Brissenden also claims that the final fairy appearance*

Act IV. Scene i. Oberon, Titania, Puck, and Fairies. By William Blake (n.d.).

in Act V is related to a carole—a medieval song and dance form used in a ceremonial blessing of the inhabitants of a village—and that it serves to enforce the reestablishment of concord at the close of the play. In related essays, Cumberland Clark (1931) has asserted that Shakespeare's use of music in A Midsummer Night's Dream *enhances the fairy-like atmosphere in the woods; Enid Welsford (1927) has demonstrated how the structure of the play is related to the tradition of the Court masque; John H. Long (1955) has argued that Shakespeare used music in this play to contribute to the dreamy atmosphere of the fairy world and to underscore the movement from chaos to harmony; and C. L. Barber (1959) has noted the parallels between the fairies' blessing and the ritual of bridal bed purification. For a further discussion of the function of song in* A Midsummer Night's Dream, *see the essay by Richmond Noble cited in the Additional Bibliography.*]

Shakespeare's flirtation with dance in comedy ended with *A Midsummer Night's Dream*. From avoiding dance altogether (always excepting the possibility of a concluding dance to *Love's Labour's Lost*), in *A Midsummer Night's Dream* he used it more abundantly than he was ever to do again. And he uses it deliberately to comment on and affect the major pattern of order and disorder in the action.

Dancing was a natural part of summer festivals and while it would be an exaggeration to claim that the May-games of the English countryside were the main inspiration of *A Midsummer Night's Dream*, the spirit of the May-game, with its associa-

tions with love, licence and new life, is an essential part of the play's movement. Discordant notes of unruliness and irregularity in the world of men are sounded in the opening scene, Theseus remarking to Hippolyta

> I woo'd thee with my sword,
> And won thy love doing thee injuries,
>
> [I. i. 16-17]

but for these mature lovers the major conflict is over, the battle has been lost and won. Other violence soon breaks into the court, however, with Hermia's defiance of her father and his demand that she give up Lysander and marry Demetrius or be put to death. Happier disharmony appears in the second scene, when the artisans begin to prepare their interlude and Bottom wants to play all the parts. The malapropisms he distributes so freely reinforce the idea of disorder through their dislocation of language. These different kinds of discord are confirmed and matched in the supernatural world of the next scene, where Titania describes the foul disturbances of nature which have resulted from her quarrel with Oberon. She leaves no doubt that his rude interruption of her dancing with her fairies is a highly important aspect of their dispute:

> . . . never, since the middle summer's spring,
> Met we on hill, in dale, forest, or mead,
> By paved fountain, or by rushy brook,
> Or in the beached margent of the sea,

To dance our ringlets to the whistling wind,
But with thy brawls thou hast disturb'd our sport.
Therefore the winds, piping to us in vain,
As in revenge, have suck'd up from the sea
Contagious fogs; which, falling in the land,
Hath every pelting river made so proud
That they have overborne their continents.

[II. i. 82-92]

The first mention of dance in the play comes after all four groups of characters have been introduced—the courtiers, the lovers, the artisans and the fairies—and the theme of disorder has been related to each of them. Titania's speech, one of the great arias of the play, summarises and enlarges the theatre of conflict. More is to come, for Oberon, who has broken the 'ringlets' of the dancing fairies, that is the perfect form of the circle, refuses Titania's conditional offer of peace when she says

If you will patiently dance in our round,
And see our moonlight revels, go with us.

[II. i. 140-41]

He scorns to join then unless he is given the Indian boy.

It is precisely appropriate that this quarrelsome couple and their attendants are the characters in the play most concerned with dancing for dancing was one of the main occupations of the Elizabethan fairies. One seventeenth-century commentator, Robert Kirk, remarks irresistibly on their 'paroxisms of antic corybantic jollity'. It was their principal means of getting from one place to another. Shakespeare's fairies do not walk or run. They 'skip' [II. i. 61], they 'hop' [V. i. 394], they 'gambol' [III. i. 165], they 'trip away' [V. i. 421]. Flying was used for long distance and speed, and in one place seems to be synonymous with 'trip'; in Act IV when Oberon invites Titania, 'Trip we after night's shade' [IV. i. 96], she replies

Come, my lord; and in our flight,
Tell me how it came this night
That I sleeping here was found
With these mortals on the ground.

[IV. i. 99-102]

Such constant lightness of movement is possible because of the fairies' weightlessness; Kirk refers to 'their bodies of congealed air' and Titania wishes to 'purge' Bottom of his 'mortal grossness' so that he shall 'like an airy spirit go' [III. i. 160-61]. It was just this effect of airy delicacy that the nineteenth-century romantic ballet tried to achieve when its dancers began using pointe shoes for the first time.

The dancing in A Midsummer Night's Dream may have been connected with an unknown occasion for which the play was perhaps written, the most popular view being that it was a wedding in some great house, whose singing boys were available to take part (though the earliest statement about its performance, made in 1600 on the title page of the first edition, says it was 'publicly acted'). Given the circumstances of having actors who could dance and sing, Shakespeare made dancing an essential part of the plot, a summarising action and a universal symbol instead of merely leaving it the delectable embellishment it might have been. The roundel and song which lull Titania asleep in II. ii, for instance, are a charm to keep away evil; they are no proof against the powers of Oberon.

The other characters who dance are the artisans, whose connection with the fairies' dancing is obliquely established when Puck leads in the assified Bottom saying, 'I'll follow you; I'll

lead you about a round' [III. i. 106]. 'Round' here implies a country dance, and Puck's meaning is a variation on the phrase 'to lead someone a dance'. The word 'round' has already been used by Titania in her offer of peace to Oberon, and it is picked up again in yet another sense when Oberon tells Puck how Titania has 'rounded / With coronet of fresh and fragrant flowers' the hairy temples of Bottom [IV. i. 51-2]. Again the form of the ring is a focus of Oberon's attention, and here it becomes a reason for upbraiding his queen; this time he is successful, and she gives him the Indian boy he so covets.

Then, Titania awakened and undeceived, Oberon calls for music and says:

Come, my Queen, take hands with me,
And rock the ground whereon these sleepers be.
Now thou and I are new in amity,
And will to-morrow midnight solemnly
Dance in Duke Theseus' house triumphantly,
And bless it to all fair prosperity.

[IV. i. 85-90]

There is no direction given for when they are to dance; it is most likely after the phrase, 'whereon these sleepers be'. A full stop occurs here in all the early editions, and the dance clearly has two purposes. One is to ensure that the lovers and Bottom sleep well and wake refreshed—the dancers will 'rock the ground' as a mother rocks a cradle. The second, wider, meaning is to confirm the reconciliation of Titania and Oberon, and re-establish their domestic harmony. . . . Their dance completed, Oberon can say, with special significance in the first word, 'Now thou and I are new in amity', and they will therefore be able to carry out the rite of blessing Theseus' house on his wedding night.

It is not only Oberon and Titania who are 'new in amity' of course. The lovers are found in 'gentle concord' [IV. i. 143] and Bottom is soon to be reunited with his mates who had earlier fled from him. The jangling quarrels and jars in the play, however serious for the characters, have been for the audience like the baying of Hippolyta's hounds, 'so musical a discord, such sweet thunder' [IV. i. 118]. Of this discord there is now only the verbal and humorous disjointedness of the interlude, Pyramus and Thisbe, to come, a sly comment on the earlier wranglings. Theseus sums up the paradox:

Merry and tragical! tedious and brief!
That is hot ice and wondrous strange snow.
How shall we find the concord of this discord?

[V. i. 58-60]

And to conclude, a bergomask between two of the company, a burlesque of the dance of Titania and Oberon in Act IV.

There is a double strand of humour here. A bergomask was originally a clumsy dance in ridiculous imitation of the movements of the peasants of Bergamo. Shakespeare has his clowns, already inept, performing a dance imitating the inept. It is the same kind of technique he uses in The Winter's Tale when Perdita, a princess in reality but unknown as such to everyone on the stage, dresses up as royalty for the sheep-shearing festival and then is called by Camillo 'the queen of curds and cream' [The Winter's Tale, IV. iv. 161]. Bottom confuses his words as usual and asks if the audience wishes to 'see the Epilogue, or to hear a Bergomask dance' [V. i. 353-54]; but in truth the dance may well have been heard, for it would have been done with stamping of feet, perhaps accompanied by the tongs and the bones that the metamorphosed Bottom had earlier requested from the fairies.

Their rustic dance, acrobatic perhaps, earthbound certainly, is the extreme contrast in the play between the mortal and the fairy worlds. It serves as an antimasque to the singing and dancing of the fairies which ends both the first night of the wedding festivities and the play itself. The words of Oberon again draw attention to the fairies' lightness when he tells them to 'hop as light as bird from brier' [V. i. 394]. Titania's command, 'Hand in hand with fairy grace, / Will we sing, and bless this place' [V. i. 399-400], is a return to one of the oldest forms of dance, the carole, in which the dancers link hands and move to the music of a song, usually sung by themselves. In medieval times the carole was used in religious ritual and in such ceremonies as blessing the bounds of the parish. The bringing of good luck to houses by the entry of singing dancers, hands linked, survives today as part of the May Day festivities at Padstow and Helston in Cornwall. The 'glimmering light' Oberon tells the fairies to give through the house hints at starlight, and the stars are a reminder of the heavenly harmony existing in the greater universe, so that in this way their dance widens out in its implications. Their grace and their ability to bless the palace and those within it bind together religion and fairy lore. 'Field dew' that can 'consecrate' is a striking indication of this fusion. By the time *A Midsummer Night's Dream* was written religious dancing had long been banished by the church in England, although as late as Henry VIII's reign dancing before the Christ Child on the altar may have been included as a part of Christmas ritual. Shakespeare's fairies here take on the function of priests, both Hymeneal and Christian, with power to bless the rooms and their occupants, to sprinkle holy water and to prevent evil in the form of blemishes on mortal beauty. Their carole finished, they dance through the palace, carrying light and blessings. (pp. 41-6)

> Alan Brissenden, ''The Comedies I,'' in his Shakespeare and the Dance, *Humanities Press, 1981, pp. 34-48.*

J. DENNIS HUSTON   (essay date 1981)

[*In the following excerpt from his* Shakespeare's Comedies of Play *(1981), Huston interprets* A Midsummer Night's Dream *as an exuberant celebration of the powers of the dramatic playwright. He focuses on the numerous parodies in the play as evidence that Shakespeare was ''mentally playing with the art of playwriting in this work,'' and he concludes that ''none of the mature comedies manages the dramatic medium as spectacularly as* A Midsummer Night's Dream.'' *Of particular interest to Huston is Bottom's awakening in Act IV, Scene i, which he asserts is the point at which Shakespeare comments most emphatically on the powers of his art. Coming immediately after the depiction of the reunion between the lovers and the authority figures of Athens, Huston claims, Bottom's awakening interrupts ''the audience's emotional involvement in the play'' and leads to an intellectual examination of the significance of the work. According to the critic, Bottom's soliloquy concentrates the dramatic action as it raises questions about illusion and truth in both dreams and art. For further treatments of the significance of Bottom's awakening soliloquy, see the excerpts by Harold C. Goddard (1951), Peter G. Phialas (1966), John A. Allen (1967), and Ronald F. Miller (1975), as well as the essays by Frank Kermode and Garrett Stewart cited in the Additional Bibliography. Also, see the essays by C. L. Barber (1959), Elizabeth Sewell (1960), James L. Calderwood (1971), and David Marshall (1982) for additional commentary on the self-reflexive nature of* A Midsummer Night's Dream.]

As it is almost impossible to talk about *The Taming of the Shrew* without focusing upon the actions of Petruchio, whose playing repeatedly and conspicuously solicits the attention of an audience, so it is just as difficult to discuss *A Midsummer Night's Dream* without concentrating on the achievements of Shakespeare, whose playwriting so dramatically calls attention to itself. No doubt this effect results partly from the fact that there *is* no principal character in *A Midsummer Night's Dream* because of the plot's multi-plex structure: no character or plot line receives enough attention to be called 'principal'—the longest part in the play, Bottom's, is hardly half the length of Petruchio's—but that fact is precisely my point. In a sense everyone in *A Midsummer Night's Dream* is a minor character, whose importance derives from the use to which he is put by the playwright; and although all characters in all plays attain to their importance in this way, we are rarely as conscious, as we are in this drama, of the playwright's part in shaping his creation.

One way to see how the playwright directs attention towards his achievement in playwriting is to look at what he does to the figure of the player in this work. For the character in *A Midsummer Night's Dream* who most resembles Petruchio, the all-conquering hero of *The Taming of the Shrew,* is Bottom, the all-confounding ass. Bottom shares with Petruchio his energy, his self-confidence, his capacity for play—for assimilating what is around him into the world of his ego. Like Petruchio, too, he plays the part of lover and tyrant, and, during the time that he retreats into an insulated world with a spell-bound fairy princess (or queen) he turns temporarily into a monster. Finally, also like Petruchio, Bottom is cast in the role of hero by an audience of his peers, who recognize him as the only one among them capable of an heroic undertaking. Yet here again similarities matter principally because of what they tell us about differences. Bottom is a parody of Petruchio: he is the fairy tale hero of humble origins who never transcends those origins; he is a player with Petruchio's all-consuming appetite for assimilation but without Petruchio's capacity to turn what he assimilates to effect. As a player Bottom is a creature all of appetite. He may greedily assume the roles of tyrant, lover, lion, Thisbe, and Pyramus, but every part he plays he absorbs completely, turning them all to Bottom.

So self-absorbed is Bottom's Pyramus, for instance, that he cannot even make his audience of young lovers see the correspondence between his lamentable comedy with Thisbe at 'Ninny's' tomb and the lovers' own earlier confusion in the woods. To this self-absorption the mechanicals' wonderfully inept production of *Pyramus and Thisbe* gives clear emphasis, for one of the qualities of Quince's play which keeps it from being dramatic is that Pyramus and Thisbe rarely notice each other. They hardly communicate. Instead they speak to themselves in declamation, even when they are nominally speaking to someone else. For this reason, Bottom the player is, as Quince claims, though for other reasons than he knows, perfectly equipped to play Quince's Pyramus; he is the actor as child, still incapable in his infantile egocentricity of differentiating clearly between self and other.

Why, however, should Shakespeare subject the figure of the comic hero to such a deflation? It is the most striking transformation in a play distinguished by its striking transformations, for in the way of metamorphoses, affixing an ass head on one who is already metaphorically an ass is not nearly as surprising as converting Petruchio to Bottom. Admittedly, that conversion is not direct. Bottom is not immediately *recogniz-*

able as Petuchio transformed, for he is a Shakespearean clown, and Petruchio, a comic hero. As a consequence, the range of their worlds, of their talent for play, of their self-awareness, extends to different reaches, as does their capacity to affect these worlds. But calling attention to the obvious differences between Petruchio and Bottom merely begs the nagging question of their strange correspondence: why should Shakespeare, who made the player a hero and world-conqueror in *The Taming of the Shrew*, make him an ass in *A Midsummer Night's Dream?*

The answer, I think, has to do particularly with the art of playwriting as opposed to acting. Shakespeare may have felt a need, after so glorifying the player, to give the playwright his due. On stage the world often seems to submit to the powers of the player, particularly when he is such an actor as Petruchio (or Richard Burbage), striking all before him with wonder at his play, turning everything about him—his body, his voice, his movements, the people he encounters, the dramatic situation, the things at hand—to his advantage. In the process an audience may sometimes forget that it is the playwright's script which makes the actor's triumph possible. The actor, in the root meaning of the word, may be the doer, the performer who draws attention to himself, but the playwright must first create the play if the actor is going to have anything to do. As a demonstration of his powers, then, Shakespeare may turn Petruchio to Bottom—to emphasize that the play world of any drama belongs first to the playwright, who coaxes it into being and who thus always has the option of turning a comic hero to an ass, even if only to remind us of his creative powers. Still, though, what matters most about characters in a play is not what formulas of dramatic convention they violate or parody, but what purpose they serve in the unique dramatic world created by the playwright; and Bottom is more *suited* to Shakespeare's purposes in this play than Petruchio, as we shall soon see. Thus by deflating the figure of the player in *A Midsummer Night's Dream* Shakespeare is not only serving notice that the playwright possesses the powers to reduce the actor to a poor player strutting and fretting upon the stage; he is also using the playwright's powers to give the player—now reduced from a figure of potency to one of parody—meaning.

That meaning derives at least in part from the fact that *A Midsummer Night's Dream* is a play notable almost as much for its parodies as for its other, more obvious metamorphoses. In addition to Bottom's deflation of Petruchio, the play also offers us: a dramatic travesty of the tragic love story of Pyramus and Thisbe, which doubles as a reductive version of the lovers' mistakings in the wood, and may even triple as a comic rendering of Shakespeare's own dramatic presentation of the story of Romeo and Juliet (if composed by then); a parody of the relationship between the surrogate playwright figure of Oberon and his incorrigible servant-actor Puck in the alliance between the inept playwright Quince and his uncontrollable principal player Bottom; a ridiculous reversal of the fairy tale situation of the princess held in bondage by the monster, in the fairy queen's rapturous capture of the ass-headed Bottom; and Bottom's ludicrously garbled version of a part of St Paul's Epistle to the Corinthians, in his soliloquy upon awaking from charmed sleep. What these parodies signal is the extent to which Shakespeare is mentally playing with the art of playwriting in this work, for a parody is a kind of intellectual play, which calls attention to the mastery of a particular constricting form by comically reshaping that form to new purposes. In order to understand how Shakespeare plays with the limitations of dramatic form in *A Midsummer Night's Dream*, it is thus necessary to see how he uses parody in that world. And since Bottom is

the principal instrument of parody—and also an important indicator of meaning—in this play, he can serve as a point of departure for this discussion.

I begin near the end, with the fourth act and Bottom the player alone on a stage, with drama reduced to its elemental two boards and a passion. Only here, for a moment, there is not even any passion, for the player is asleep, transported beyond the boundaries of the waking world by a magical charm. It is a charm of some considerable range and magnitude since Bottom is not the only one to have been affected by it: earlier it has struck 'more dead / Than common sleep' [IV. i. 81-2] the senses of four Athenian lovers, and long before that it has partly enthralled the faculties of the audience. So now, although they do not sleep like Bottom, they have been transported out of the ordinary and into a world elsewhere. In such a world strange and extraordinary effects are played on their senses, without even attracting notice as strange and extraordinary. There a tedious brief play some ten words long wears away the three hours between supper and bedtime; there the moon, new for Theseus' wedding, has already waxed to brightness by the time of the rustics' production that same night; and there Bottom may lie asleep in plain view of the audience without really being seen.

He has not even, like Oberon earlier, had to *ask* for a willing suspension of disbelief by announcing himself invisible. The lovers and Theseus have just played a scene all around him, and their obliviousness to his presence has conditioned the audience not to see him either. Thus when the lovers exit towards the temple, the audience confronts an empty stage. Only when Bottom fills that emptiness by stirring to life does he make the members of the audience similarly awaken from the binding spell Shakespeare has woven over them. In their theater seats many of them, like Bottom on the stage, will stir in surprise at what has just happened to them, as momentarily the playwright makes them aware of his art *as* art.

This particular example of a Shakespearean *Verfremdungseffekt* ["alienating effect"] does not, however, end quite here; instead it edges over into the beginning of Bottom's soliloquy. He begins: 'When my cue comes...' [IV. i. 200] and the audience may briefly share with the actor playing Bottom the very real knowledge that his cue has indeed come. By then, however, Bottom has already regained his footing literally and dramatically; and in his attempt to summon up first a company of lost players and then a remembrance of things past, he again magically carries the audience away from itself and into a 'most rare vision' [IV. i. 204-05].

Here briefly the themes and actions of the play are focused in a moment of dramatic concentration, whose importance is emphasized in a number of different ways. First, the alienation effect which accompanies Bottom's awakening, by temporarily interrupting the audience's emotional involvement in the play, encourages intellectual speculation about the meaning of the work. Second, the very episode itself is a conspicuous reflection of the action which has just preceded it, when the four sleeping lovers are found by Theseus and his party. Like Bottom, they all awake from the spell of Oberon's magic to contemplate a dream vision in which they have experienced a kind of metamorphosis and a disorienting love affair.

This correspondence is further underscored by the fact that Bottom's speech upon awakening comically combines the very different responses of Lysander and Demetrius to their experience. Lysander meets Theseus' questions with confusion and embarrassment; his speech is halting and unself-assured, marked by interruptions and qualifications. Demetrius, on the other hand, speaks like a man hypnotized, as if he were still under a charm which, in fact, he is. As a consequence, his explanation seems poured out, more rote than felt. Unlike Demetrius and Lysander, Bottom remains incorrigible even in confusion. Combining their particularized responses into his own peculiar 'exposition of sleep' [IV. i. 39], he briefly plays both their parts, though, as always when he presents dramatic renditions, he transmutes them into parody. In his speech there is first Lysander-like confusion and then the rote facileness of a man spellbound, like Demetrius:

> Methought I was—there is no man can tell what.
> Methought I was,—and methought I had,—but
> man is but a patched fool, if he will offer to
> say what methought I had. The eye of man hath
> not heard, the ear of man hath not seen, man's
> hand is not able to taste, his tongue to conceive,
> nor his heart to report, what my dream was.
>
> [IV. i. 207-14]

A third way in which Bottom's awakening calls attention to itself as dramatically significant is purely technical, for here Shakespeare offers him a delight surpassing even those earlier proffered by the fairy queen—a stage all his own. By its very nature soliloquy serves as a focus for thematic meaning simply because it concentrates dramatic action into its barest essence as self confronting world. And in this instance the general importance of soliloquy is further intensified by the fact that Bottom has been, since his initial entrance, intent upon seizing the stage for himself.

Yet another characteristic of this interlude which makes it dramatically conspicuous is its language, not only because it comically reflects the different and noticeably limited responses of the two young noblemen to their night in the woods but also because it periodically suggests depths of emotional experience approaching the ecstatic, where dream, vision, and art are dissolved into a union that passes human understanding. There the distinctions of intellect, with its dependence on logic and on finite boundaries, are subsumed by transcendent mysteries that have 'no bottom' [IV. i. 216].

Of course no such wild and whirling vision possesses Bottom at first; his initial response upon awakening is to ignore the episode with Titania altogether. He returns to the instant just before his metamorphosis, as if nothing had happened and he were still attendant upon the 'odious savours sweet' [III. i. 82-3] of Thisbe's breath: 'When my cue comes, call me, and I will answer.' But there is no cue, for all his company has fled—they must have stolen away while he slept—and he is still literally and figuratively in the woods. But then the memory of his strange metamorphosis breaks over him, in two waves. First there is the remembrance of what he has seen— 'I have had a most rare vision.'—and, shortly afterwards, the more shocking thoughts of what he has been: 'man is but an ass, if he go about to expound this dream. Methought I was— there is no man can tell what' [IV. i. 206-08]. The rest of the speech is Bottom's fumblingly comic attempt to find words and form for just what no man—except the playwright, who has already presented us with this scene—can tell.

It is therefore no surprise either that Bottom bungles the task he has set for himself or that in the process he trips over words in a characteristically Bottom-like way. What *is* surprising is the order periodically perceivable beneath the surface chaos of

his malapropisms. Consider, for example, Bottom's marvelously muddled quotation from St. Paul's first Epistle to the Corinthians (2:9). Here there is a hint of vision as well as of foolishness, for Bottom is not satisfied to dismiss his experience merely as a dream. In addition, he must declare it unique and perhaps give it some meaningful form. That is why Bottom turns to St. Paul, in an attempt to find in the language of religious experience the ordering form he seeks. Religion does not, however, offer him what he wants, since it has very little to do with a dramatic world that, as early as scene one,—when Theseus describes the fate that awaits Hermia as a nun—views religious asceticism as hardly more desirable than death. Art is much more to Bottom's—and to Shakespeare's—purpose here, since at this moment the fool's desires draw attention to what the playwright has achieved: Bottom wishes to have his dream transformed into art, immortalized in a ballad that Peter Quince will write for him and that he himself will present in dramatic performance before the Duke.

Here surely Shakespeare is turning his art in upon itself. He began this interlude with a conspicuous demonstration of the playwright's problems and power—by emptying the stage of all apparent life, pausing briefly so that the audience might momentarily feel with the playwright the oppressive challenge of an empty stage, and then filling the void with Bottom's dramatic resurrection from a formless mass to a vitally formed personality. Now, at the end of this scene, he returns again to another alienation effect and calls attention to his own play as well as to Bottom's. For he too as playwright has had a most rare vision, particularized by outrageous metamorphoses and unions, not only of an ass-headed rustic and the fairy queen but also of myth and folklore, midsummer and May, realism and fantasy, love and hate, drama and declamation, comedy and tragedy, to name just a few. And also like Bottom searching for a way to give lasting form to his vision, Shakespeare has turned to drama and offered his own specially titled *Dream* played before a duke at his wedding celebration. Finally, Shakespeare too proffers his audience a dream that 'hath no bottom'—because as the creation of an artist's imagination it is simultaneously baseless, built on airy nothing, and unbounded, transcending the binding limits of reason and logic.

Bottom's statement, 'it shall be called Bottom's Dream, because it hath no bottom' [IV. i. 215-16], thus propounds a deceptively simple-seeming defense of art. At one level it calls art into doubt as illusory foolishness because it is viewed as dream—passing and insubstantial. But at another level the statement transcends the rules of logic and touches upon truth. At this level what Bottom has to say makes perfect sense; his unique experience is to be preserved as dream in its highest form—as art, vision, and perhaps revelation—because it partakes of what is infinite and eternal. Art as dream is simultaneously both illusion and revealed truth. For a moment at the end of his soliloquy Bottom's excitement about his dream presents a model, albeit simplified and parodied, of the playwright's motivations. Fleetingly we glimpse the playwright's shadow behind the fool.

The model, however, is not to be mistaken for the real thing. Bottom may have the instincts of an artist—to joy in the magic of working words, in unexampled flights of the imagination, and in the play of ego-expanding identifications—but these instincts are in no way informed by the education, discipline, and common sense that would put them to any productive use. As a result Bottom is an ass, not an artist. When he attempts to make words wield matter, that matter recalcitrantly signals its resistance to his control in malapropisms. Similarly, when he would speak with the golden tongue of wisdom, Bottom can do no better than 'gleek' upon the occasion. And, of course, he can never, like Shakespeare, find the appropriate words for the formulation of his dream; Bottom promises to 'discourse wonders' [IV. ii. 29] and delivers only an exposition on the necessity of clean linen, long nails, and sweet breath. His failures, though, call attention to Shakespeare's successes: we have already noted how Bottom parodies Shakespeare's earlier success with Petruchio; now we can see how his behavior emphasizes the playwright's achievement in this play. (pp. 94-102)

Another indication of Shakespeare's self-reflexive interest in his own dramatic art is his use of surrogate playwright figures in the play. Admittedly, the presence of such figures may have much to do with the themes of love and tyranny. Lysander and Hermia trying to shape their lives into a tragic work of art, and Egeus staging his own particular play before Theseus in the first scene are hardly to be taken seriously as prototypes of the artist. The same cannot, however, be said of Quince and Oberon, for both of these characters, in different ways and in different worlds, experiment with the artist's power of invention. Quince writes and stages a play; Oberon conceives and directs two very different romantic comedies in the woods. Both, too, experience the artist's magical powers of resolution. Quince writes a prologue to resolve all the thorny problems associated with dramatic representation; Oberon dispels the young lovers' dilemma by removing the charm from Lysander's eyes, and he does the same for Titania. Moreover, in their roles as artists both Quince and Oberon are shadowed by characters who present creative energies in more primitive forms. Puck, delighting in practical jokes and in his own physical and emotional agility, surely represents instincts for play that serve the artist but sometimes run out of control. In a similar way, as we have already noted, Bottom embodies diffusive impulses for imaginative transportation which the artist must finally infuse into a local habitation and a name. (p. 111)

Oberon . . . shares with Shakespeare a number of important characteristics as a play-maker; and these correspondences call attention to Shakespeare's art: his primary focus of dramatic interest is now not the figure of the actor who, like Petruchio, shapes his world by actively playing with it, but rather the figure of the playwright, whose control of his world is less direct, as much a result of intellectual as of physical play. For Oberon, like Shakespeare, remains often physically detached from the results of his magic. Much of that magic, after all, is accomplished indirectly through his agent Puck, and Oberon himself often serves as audience to, rather than as actor in, his play: 'I am invisible; / And I will overhear their conference' [II. i. 186-87]. He is not, of course, always content to be primarily an observer of action. Like Petruchio, he does declare his love to a kind of princess—in fact, a queen—only to be summarily rejected. Then in order to establish the loving union he desires with her, he places her temporarily under his bondage and subjects her to the powers of a monster, until he at last brings her to understand that her previous resistance to him is in error, and they are united in a celebration of marital harmony near the end. But Oberon's means of success are radically different from Petruchio's; he accomplishes by magic what Petruchio achieves by actively playing with the particulars of his world. This is because in A Midsummer Night's Dream Shakespeare embodies his own magical, dramatic powers in a surrogate playwright figure, whose powers within his insulated world resemble—though they do not match—Shakespeare's.

There is at least one other reason, though, why surrogate playwright figures appear with such frequency in A Midsummer Night's Dream—because characters in this world regularly seek to insulate themselves from the unpredictable welter of reality by confining it within oversimplified, 'pat' [III. i. 2] forms; they would reduce the complexity of life to some simplistic formula, for which the play script, since it controls reality—actors, props, stage situations—by letting in only what the actor and his play can use to advantage, is the emblem in this work. In a sense, then, the characters in this play all aspire to the playwright's power—they wish to create a script which perfectly controls reality—without putting on his knowledge—that such a script is the product not so much of simplified exclusion as of complicated inclusion. As characters in this play bumble through the experience of trying to keep contingencies out of the scripts they would compose to order their worlds, Shakespeare himself makes a success of his play by including in its script not only contingencies but also apparent impossibilities, like the union of Bottom with Titania. Everywhere we look in A Midsummer Night's Dream we find characters parroting formulas, murmuring incantations, trying to prepare the perfect play script, or seeking to insulate themselves from outside disruptions, but always life—and Shakespeare's drama—complicates what they seek to simplify. (pp. 114-15)

The tendency for characters to impose an oversimplifying dramatic script upon the complexity of human experience appears in a variety of forms thoughout A Midsummer Night's Dream. Most obviously, the mechanicals work to create a play script that will hold at bay all contingencies from outside the boundaries of their created play world: the lion must not frighten the ladies, moonshine must come in at a chamber window or enter as a character, and wall must present a chink for Pyramus and Thisbe to talk through. But although the rustics are most clearly involved in insulating their play world against unwanted complexity, almost every other character engages at least once in a similar act of simplistic playwriting, by trying to keep the complications of life out of an imaginatively constructed and delineated world. Titania's fairies sing her to sleep with promises of a rest uninterrupted by wicked spells or vile creatures, but their incantatory magic fails to keep either Oberon's love-juice or Bottom's ass head away from the fairy queen. Philostrate tries to insulate Theseus from the ineptness of the mechanicals' play by discouraging him from choosing it, but he fails either to convince Theseus of his opinion or to anticipate how the unintended comedy of this production is suited to Theseus' desires at the moment. Theseus passes simplistic judgments against the poet (lumping him with the lover and the lunatic) and players (judging the best of their kind no more than shadows) without ever recognizing that the poet, like the lunatic and the lover, may attain occasionally to the ecstasy of visionary experience. Nor can he realize, more importantly, that for all his deprecation of players as shadows, he is himself such a shadow, fleshed out to substance by poet and player, and watched with amused detachment by a group of spectators, who, if they are no better an audience then he, may choose to judge him as insignificant as he judges Pyramus and Thisbe. Finally, Oberon, who comes closest to wielding the playwright's powers in this work, since he does eventually shape a multifaceted play to his desires in the woods, cannot always keep the complexity of his insulated fairy kingdom under perfect control: Titania for a time keeps him out of her bed, and Puck lays the magic love juice on the eyes of the wrong Athenian lover. So even when A Midsummer Night's Dream gives us a playmaker as successful as Oberon, we still feel the greater range and amplitude of Shakespeare's success, since he can shape to the structures and purposes of *his* play all the complexity that confounds the other playwright figures. As a shaper of dramatic comedy, then, Shakespeare reaches the height of his powers in *A Midsummer Night's Dream*, for in spite of their obvious greatness—in offering fuller characterization, greater poetic sophistication, and more complex dramatic worlds—none of the mature comedies manages the dramatic medium as spectacularly as *A Midsummer Night's Dream*. None so obviously affirms, demonstrates, and celebrates the dramatist's play-making powers as this, Shakespeare's most exuberantly self-reflexive comedy of play. (pp. 119-21)

> J. Dennis Huston, "Parody and Play in 'A Midsummer Night's Dream'," in his Shakespeare's Comedies of Play, *Columbia University Press, 1981, pp. 94-121.*

DAVID MARSHALL   (essay date 1982)

[*Marshall argues that* A Midsummer Night's Dream *is a play that both explores the relations between the theater and its audience and raises serious questions about the traditional view of marriage. He maintains that just as an audience must exchange its vision and imagination for those of the playwright and actors, so must the women in Shakespeare's play submit to the point of view and domination of the male characters. While Marshall regards this "theft" of one person's perception by another as a repressive, even hostile, process, he claims that the relation between audience and theatrical production functions on a more equitable basis— for while the audience has its imagination imposed on, it is led through this process to a new perception of human nature and experience. Marshall concludes that this "double vision" the play constructs serves as an "alternative" to the "tyranny" of imagination dramatized in the plot. For further commentary on Shakespeare's reflexive examination of his own craft in* A Midsummer Night's Dream, *see the excerpts by C. L. Barber (1959), James L. Calderwood (1971), and J. Dennis Huston (1981). As part of his commentary on the nature of marriage in* A Midsummer Night's Dream, *Marshall also interprets Hippolyta's silence throughout most of Act I, Scene i not as a reflection of her patient acceptance of the bonds of marriage, but as an indication that she has been coerced into marrying Theseus and that she regards the union with melancholy and resignation. Marshall considers the view of marriage in the play more complex than the usual Elizabethan idea of wedlock, that man's intellect and reason must necessarily dominate woman's irrational passion, regarded by many earlier critics as a central thesis in the play. For further discussions of the depiction of marriage in* A Midsummer Night's Dream, *see the excerpts by H. B. Charlton (1933), Ernest Schanzer (1951), George A. Bonnard (1956), John Vyvyan (1961), Peter G. Phialas (1966), M. D. Faber (1972), and David Bevington (1975); also, see the essays by Richard Cody, Paul A. Olson, and Andrew D. Weiner cited in the Additional Bibliography.*]

"Spirits and fairies cannot be represented, they cannot even be painted,—they can only be believed." *A Midsummer Night's Dream* seems designed to engage the issue at stake in this assertion of Charles Lamb's. Lamb makes his claim after drawing the conclusion that "the plays of Shakespeare are less calculated for performance on a stage, than those of almost any other dramatist whatever." Although he is writing about the fitness of Shakespeare's tragedies for stage representation, one often has the sense that he is describing the problems presented by producing Shakespeare's "dream play" [Edward Dowden]. As spectators to stage representations, writes Lamb, "we find to our cost that instead of realizing an idea, we have materialized and brought down a fine vision to the standard of flesh and blood. We have to let go a dream. . . ." Five years after the publication of Lamb's essay, in 1816, William Hazlitt

took Lamb's position; while watching a performance of *A Midsummer Night's Dream*, Hazlitt realized that the play could not be represented on the stage. His review for the *Examiner* begins: "We hope we have not been accessory to murder, in recommending a delightful poem to be converted into a dull pantomine. . . . We have found to our cost, once for all, that the regions of fancy and the boards of Covent Garden are not the same thing. All that was fine in the play, was lost in the representation." Hazlitt's rehearsal of this review in the pages of his *Characters of Shakespeare's Plays* shows that he was responding not to a particular performance but to what he saw in the character of the stage: "Poetry and the stage do not agree well together. . . . The *idea* can have no place upon the stage, which is a picture without perspective; everything there is in the foreground. That which was merely an airy shape, a dream, a passing thought, immediately becomes an unmanageable reality . . ." [see excerpt above, 1817]. As a play of rare visions, airy shapes, and dreams, *A Midsummer Night's Dream* stages the dilemma of how to marry poetry to the stage.

Of course, Lamb and Hazlitt could be accused of reading Shakespeare from the standpoint of English Romanticism—of trying to turn public plays into private poems. Both are also reacting to the conventions of the nineteenth-century stage: what Lamb calls "contemptible machinery" and "the elaborate and anxious provision of scenery." Clearly, these are not the conditions of dramatic illusion that the prologue to *Henry V* figures in its invocation of the audience's powers of imagination. Their responses, however, should not be disregarded. Lamb and Hazlitt have realized that in the theater a vision of a play is expounded and imposed upon them. Each finds to his cost that some impression of his fantasy has been stolen. I will argue that the experiences of these spectators—these points of view—begin to represent a reading of *A Midsummer Night's Dream;* they reflect the play's presentation and dramatization of the conditions of theater. Hazlitt, in particular, asks us to see that the question of the *Dream's* fitness for the stage is posed by the play itself; he frames a double simile: "Fancy cannot be embodied any more than a simile can be painted; and it is as idle to attempt it as to personate *Wall* or *Moonshine*." Hazlitt's allusion to the mistaken enterprise of the play within the play suggests that *A Midsummer Night's Dream* might contain a dangerous acknowledgment: a threat that the representation of the play itself might be undone. By *undone* I mean not only the senses of incomplete, ruined, negated, and expounded, but also the sense in which the scene that Shakespeare refused to represent before the audience of *The Winter's Tale* is said to be undone by its mere narration: Shakespeare withholds from our sight an encounter which, we are told, "lames report to follow it and undoes description to do it" [*The Winter's Tale*, V. ii. 57-8]. Hazlitt asserts that the attempt to present Shakespeare's *Dream* on the stage would be as counterproductive and literal minded as the mechanical's attempt to figure moonshine; and he implies that the play within the play, in reflecting and figuring the problems of representing *A Midsummer Night's Dream*, might undo Shakespeare's impossible enterprise. (pp. 543-45)

Hazlitt's and Lamb's views about the fitness of *A Midsummer Night's Dream* for stage representation may not be persuasive, but they can teach us that one way to see the play is to recognize in this comic moment a figure for the possibility of the play's impossibility. This would allow us to realize the senses in which the play is about problems of representation and figuration: not only whether the play can be staged but also what it means to present a vision or an image to someone else's mind, to ask another person to see with one's eyes, to become a spectator to someone else's vision. Such questions themselves raise questions about the conditions of theater: the power of one imagination over others; the power to enchant and transform vision; the possibility of autonomous minds or imaginations sharing dreams and fantasies; the difference between picturing a text in private reading and attending a public, collective spectacle. *A Midsummer Night's Dream* asks us to take seriously the dilemma of joining poetry and the stage. In adopting this perspective we will find ourselves considering yet another question: the possibility of what Shakespeare elsewhere called "the marriage of true minds" [Sonnet 116]. (pp. 546-47)

A Midsummer Night's Dream, which raises the curtain on a parody of *Romeo and Juliet* after its marriages have been performed, seems to invite speculation about what will go on— and what has gone on—behind its scenes. Is it asking too much of an antique fable and a fairy toy to be skeptical about the "gentle concord" created by the sudden reconciliation and rearrangement of the lovers at the end of the play? How are we to take Demetrius' recovery from the "sickness" of abandoning Helena and loving Hermia since it is just as much the product of enchantment as Lysander's abandonment of Hermia and love for Helena? Are we to be pleased by the success of Helena's subjection of herself to Demetrius or Titania's sudden and manipulated surrender to Oberon? What about Hippolyta's marriage to the soldier who vanquished her? These are questions that are not presented by the traditional view of the play as a "wedding present" and an epithalamium in which there is a "festive confidence that things will go right" [see excerpt above by C. L. Barber, 1959]. They raise the possibility that *A Midsummer Night's Dream* is not "one of Shakespeare's happiest comedies" but rather a "most lamentable comedy" [I. ii. 11-12] and "very tragical mirth" [V. i. 57].

We don't need to imagine another act, however, to doubt the play's status as a happy comedy. Indeed, as the curtain rises on the first scene, despite some elegant poetry, we have no reason to believe that the conflicts unfolding before us will be resolved any more comically than those of, say, *The Winter's Tale* or even *King Lear*. Even before Hermia is threatened with death in order to force her to marry against her will, the stage is set with an exchange between Theseus and Hippolyta that could be played as tense rather than as festive. Hippolyta speaks only once in the first scene—and she doesn't speak again until the fourth act—yet critics have usually acted as if they knew what was going on in her mind. C. L. Barber describes the characters looking toward their wedding in this way: "Theseus looks forward to the hour with masculine impatience, Hippolyta with a woman's willingness to dream away the time." I don't know how Barber manages to assign genders to these feelings, but, more important, I fail to see any sign of either happiness or willingness in Hippolyta's response to Theseus' expression of impatience. Hippolyta speaks with dignity, reason, and diplomacy—as is appropriate for a queenly prisoner-of-war—but her words are restrained and noncommittal:

> Four days will quickly steep themselves in night,
> Four nights will quickly dream away the time;
> And then the moon, like to a silver bow
> New-bent in heaven, shall behold the night
> Of our solemnities.
>
> [I. i. 7-11]

Theseus, in his opening speech, has figured the moon "Like to a stepdame or a dowager, / Long withering out a young man's revenue" [I. i. 5-6], thereby inaugurating the play's pervasive imagery of gain and loss and prefiguring Lysander's plan to "steal" Hermia by fleeing to his "widow aunt, a dowager / Of great revenue" [I. i. 157-58]. Hippolyta's response pictures the moon as a "silver bow / New-bent": under this sign will an Amazon warrior marry the prince who admits to her, "I wooed thee with my sword, / And won thy love doing thee injuries" [I.i. 16-17]. Theseus' "nuptial hour" [I. i. 1] becomes Hippolyta's "solemnities" (a term that will echo throughout the play, conveying a sense of gravity as well as ceremony). But the most telling interpretation of Hippolyta's revision of these figures comes from Theseus himself. He replies by telling Philostrate to "Stir up the Athenian youth to merriments, / Awake the pert and nimble spirit of mirth, / Turn melancholy forth to funerals; / The pale companion is not for our pomp" [I. i. 12-15]. Theseus addresses Philostrate but clearly he is responding to Hippolyta, as if she were playing Hamlet to his Claudius. He has heard and seen a mournful melancholy in his bride-to-be, not a happy willingness, and he reminds her that they are going to a wedding and not a funeral. Then he thinks to acknowledge that he has wooed her with his sword and done her injuries—one critic calls this a "ravishment disguised in [an] oblique courtesy" [see the entry by W. Moelwyn Merchant in the Additional Bibliography]—but he assures her: "I will wed thee in another key, / With pomp, with triumph, and with revelling" [I. i. 18-19]. It has been argued that Theseus "prizes harmony," but how will the key of this wedding be different from the key in which he won Hippolyta's "love" (his word, not hers) in combat? Pomp, revelling, and particularly triumph sound as much like a military celebration as a wedding; and we should note the possibility of a textual pun produced by the orthography which rendered "revelling" as "reuelling"—which on the page "sounds" like "ruling." Characteristically, Hippolyta does not respond to this half-apologetic assertion of will; nor does she break her silence when Theseus turns to her and says, "Come, my Hippolyta. What cheer, my love?" [I. i. 122] after he has faced Hermia with the choices of marrying according to her father's will, "death, or . . . a vow of single life" [I. i. 121]. What cheer, indeed, would Hippolyta express in response to this scene of wooing with a sword? It is hard to imagine her in the first scene as "a tamed and contented bride" [Celeste Turner Wright], particularly since Theseus seems to have trouble picturing her in this way.

Hippolyta stands as more than an ornament for a masque; her silence is an important key to the conflicts of *A Midsummer Night's Dream*. The problem of how to read her silence—and what it means to imagine what is going on behind the scenes, as it were, in the privacy of her mind—is one of the problems the play can teach us about. As readers who must imagine Hippolyta represented on a stage, we must first hear her silence; we must recognize that she does not speak. Traditionally, however, critics seem to have identified with Theseus at the beginning of the play. They have adopted his point of view, and, in imposing his sentiments upon his bride, they have read happiness in her silence, thus reenacting the telling mistake of Peter Quince in scene ii when he speaks of playing before "the Duke and Duchess on *his* wedding day" ([I. ii. 6-7], my emphasis). David P. Young, who dedicates a chapter about order to Theseus, agrees with other critics about the limits of Theseus' vision in Act V, but sees the first scene with Theseus' eyes: "It is appropriate that Theseus, as representative of daylight and right reason, should have subdued his bride-to-be to the rule of his masculine will. That is the natural order of things." This may have been the ruling ideology in the sixteenth century or in 1966—I don't see that it has ever been the natural order of things—but it is not necessarily the ideology of *A Midsummer Night's Dream*. We should be willing to consider Hippolyta's fortunes as the curtain rises, in the same way that she perhaps weeps Hermia's fortunes in the first scene; to do this, we must take her eyes.

Hippolyta is not silent for the reasons that Cordelia decides to "love, and be silent" [*King Lear*, I. i. 62]. Nor is she performing the "perfect ceremony of love's rite" in which one must "learn to read what silent love has writ" [Sonnet 23]. Hippolyta is, I believe, tongue-tied, as if she were the serious reflection of Bottom at the moment when Titania comically ravishes him with the command to her fairies: "Tie up my lover's tongue, bring him silently" [III. i. 201]. Theseus (who has "heard" of Demetrius' inconsistency but "being over-full of self-affairs" [I. i. 111, 113] manages at least twice to forget about it) can therefore hear in Hippolyta's silence what he likes. He describes himself meeting frightened subjects who, unable to speak,

> dumbly have broke off,
> Not paying me a welcome. Trust me, sweet,
> Out of this silence yet I picked a welcome,
> And in the modesty of fearful duty
> I read as much as from the rattling tongue
> Of saucy and audacious eloquence.
> Love, therefore, and tongue-tied simplicity
> In least speak most, to my capacity.
>
> [III. i. 98-105]

These are noble sentiments; but if Hippolyta is tongue-tied (and she is silent after this speech as well), it does not necessarily follow that one should read love in her silence. Part of Theseus' judgment against Hermia's advocacy of her own will cites that she is "wanting [her] father's voice" [I. i. 54]; that is, she lacks her father's consent *and* she wants to speak in her father's voice, to speak with his authority. Theseus tells Hermia that her voice has no standing in his court; her appeal is overruled because her plea must fall on deaf ears. I suggest that both Hermia and Hippolyta are in effect tongue-tied in the same way: their fate is to have others dictate their sentiments while they are silent or silenced.

The dispute over Hermia is after all the real drama of the first act—to which the brief monologues of Theseus and Hippolyta stand as a prologue. This dispute is figured as an economic one: Egeus insists that his daughter is private property ("she is mine, and all my right of her / I do estate unto Demetrius" [I. i. 97-8]) which Lysander is trying to "filch" [I. i. 36]. (We might imagine that Hermia is named after Hermes: the master thief, the god of commerce and the market place, and the god of dreams.) However, the struggle over Hermia is also pictured as a conflict over control of her imagination and vision. Egeus accuses Lysander: "thou hast given her rhymes . . . / Thou hast by moonlight at her window sung / With feigning voice verses of feigning love, / And stol'n the impression of her fantasy . . ." [I. i. 28-32]. This is not the same accusation as when Hermia calls Helena a "thief of love" who has "stol'n my love's heart from him" [III. ii. 283-84]. Egeus is complaining that Lysander with his voice and poems and fictions and trinkets of love has inscribed his own figure upon Hermia: in the paraphrase of one editor, "stealthily imprinted thine image upon her fancy" [Madeleine Doran in her introduction to *A Midsummer Night's Dream*]. This is a kind of theft because the act of imposing or imprinting upon her imagination, as Theseus figures it, belongs to Egeus. *Her* impression is seen as rightfully *his,* which is why Hermia's claim to think and

speak for herself is also a crime against her father. Theseus pictures the situation for Hermia in this manner:

> To you your father should be as a god,
> One that composed your beauties; yea, and one
> To whom you are but as a form in wax,
> By him imprinted, and within his power
> To leave the figure, or disfigure it.
>
> [I. i. 47-51]

Hermia, in Theseus' eyes, first seems her father's creation: a mixture of Eve and Galatea; but then in Theseus' revision of his figure (which makes more ominous his reference to his wedding with Hippolyta as "the sealing day betwixt my love and me" [I. i. 84]), Hermia becomes a character stamped upon blank wax. It is her father's right to impress his own image upon this wax, to imprint a figure or disfigure it, to dictate what she represents and what she represents to herself: how she looks. "I would my father looked but with my eyes" [I. i. 56], complains Hermia. Theseus insists: "Rather your eyes must with his judgment look" [I. i. 57]. Hermia is told to "choose love by another's eyes" [I. i. 140], to see what others have figured for her fantasy—just as Hippolyta is asked (or assumed) to see her wedding from Theseus' point of view.

This struggle over vision and imagination also characterizes the dispute between Oberon and Titania. Oberon's response to Titania's denial of his question, "Am I not thy lord?" [II. i. 63] is to seek control over her sight, to steal the impression of her fantasy. His strategy and revenge is to "streak her eyes / And make her full of hateful fantasies" [II. i. 257-58]. With his magic he dictates how she will look and love, enthralling her eyes to Bottom's deformed shape until the moment he decides to "undo / This hateful imperfection of her eyes" [IV. i. 62-3] and let her "See as thou wast wont to see" [IV. i. 72]. The changeling boy is ostensibly the object of contention between Oberon and Titania, an occasion for both jealousy and disobedience. But it also represents an impression of Titania's fantasy that has been stolen from Oberon; when he says, "I'll make her render up her page to me" [II. i. 185], we can hear a play on words which resonates in the context of the images and figures we have been juxtaposing. Just as Egeus insists on imprinting his own figures upon Hermia, Oberon wants to be the author of Titania's page. Egeus says that Hermia is his to "render" [I. i. 96]; Oberon is determined to make Titania render up the blank page of her imagination, surrender the rival image impressed on her fancy. It is within his power to replace the image of her love with the disfigured head of Bottom, to command her sight and fancy, to "leave the figure, or disfigure it." As a god, by the authority of his magic, Oberon enacts literally what Egeus and Theseus can perform only figuratively (or by coercion) when they tell Hermia to "fit your fancies to your father's will" [I. i. 118].

The cost of fitting one's fancy to someone else's will (or vision or representation) is the issue with which I began this account of *A Midsummer Night's Dream*. This issue returns us to the scene of the playhouse; but in the terms of Lamb and Hazlitt, we are speaking of what was from the outset the price of admission to the theater. As we become spectators to a representation of the play, we must exchange our privately imagined readings for a publicly shared spectacle and allow ourselves to be silenced and impressed by someone else's vision and point of view. It is fitting, then, that the play should raise its curtain on the imposition of a point of view on tongue-tied Hippolyta, the stealing of Hermia's fantasy and the imprinting of a character on her imagination, and the transformation of

Titania into a blank page to be written and figured upon by someone else's fancy. *A Midsummer Night's Dream* presents a political question: whether these women will be authors of their own characters or representations upon which the voices and visions of others will be dictated and imprinted. The dramatization of this situation, however, simultaneously presents us with a figure for the conditions of theater. (pp. 547-53)

I should acknowledge again that the point of view I have been expounding goes against what seems to be the predominant assumption that *A Midsummer Night's Dream* is a play which makes "luminous a traditional understanding of marriage." I quote this phrase from an impressive and scholarly article that I will take to be representative of this assumption, Paul A. Olson's "*A Midsummer Night's Dream* and the Meaning of Court Marriage." Professor Olson sets out to present "a cursory survey of Renaissance thought concerning the function of festival drama and the significance of wedlock," and then reads *A Midsummer Night's Dream* in this context. He commands an array of sources to claim that marriage, for the Elizabethans, "maintained the patterned hierarchy of society" and "fulfilled its part in the concord of things when the male ruled his mate in the same way that reason was ordained to control both will and passions." However, when the article imposes this ideology, and its twentieth century legacy, upon the play, I want to object on two related grounds. First, we should understand both the uses and the limits of entirely circumstantial evidence. Information about historical and intellectual context can help us to locate where the play takes place and what ideologies it must depend upon or resist as it stakes out a position. However, with such an understanding we may discover in the play a scene of struggle—either a reflection of, or an engagement in, struggle—and not necessarily a display of power: a representation of power relations which confirms or reinforces a particular world-view. This leads to my second point: in considering *A Midsummer Night's Dream*, the recognition of traditional views or relations should not be substituted for a reading of the conflicts that are acted out in the play.

To claim, for example, that "the movement toward an orderly subordination of the female and her passions to the more reasonable male" is "epitomized" in the marriage of Theseus and Hippolyta [Olson] is to turn one's eyes from the contrast, as the play begins, between Theseus' impatience for his wedding night and Hippolyta's reasoned patience. It is also to be as forgetful as Theseus is of Demetrius' seemingly unreasonable and (dare·I say) wanton conduct. Simply to assume that Shakespeare adopted conventional models of Theseus as "the reasonable man and the ideal ruler" and Hippolyta as the Amazon who stood for "a false usurpation of the duties of the male reason by the lower female passions" [Olson] is to insure that the conflicts of the first act—Hippolyta's silence and Hermia's desire to speak with her father's (that is, her own) voice—will fall on deaf ears. (pp. 554-55)

My quarrel with those who would see *A Midsummer Night's Dream* as a traditional celebration of marriage is not simply that they refuse to read parts of the play closely; it is that they act as if it were clear what marriage means to the play. I am claiming that the play swerves away from festive comedy as it radically places in question a social institution that embodies relations of power and stages conflicts of imagination, voice, and vision. However, to say that *A Midsummer Night's Dream* is "anti-marriage" also would be to stop short of understanding the different senses of marriage that the play is concerned with. On more than one level it meditates on the terms of marriage

by considering the conditions of being sundered and being joined. From the outset we see lovers who want to be joined but who find themselves sundered: Demetrius has parted from Helena, Hermia and Lysander are threatened with separation and then divided; in addition, Oberon and Titania are divided because Titania will not part with the changeling boy. The situations which separate, divide, part, and mismatch these various pairs provide the comedy of errors of the middle acts. Then, after the supposedly "gentle concord" which occasions Theseus to command that the "couples shall eternally be knit" [IV. i. 181], we become spectators to the comic and tragic sundering of Pyramus and Thisby: questionable entertainment for a questionable wedding feast. (pp. 557-58)

It has often been remarked that the play within the play reflects the comedy of errors that the lovers enacted in the woods, or the tragedy they might have produced; and that the newly married couples do not appear to notice this, although we might read their mixture of joking, interruption, silence, and impatience as an indication if not an acknowledgment of this recognition. However, we need to recognize as well the serious echoes that these terms and images of parting should recall by the fifth act: in particular, the ridiculous image of sundering that is presented and personated by one of the mechanicals. Separating the lovers but also providing a medium of communication, binding them in a union in partition, this wall stands both as a comic, literal-minded device *and* as a literalization of one of the play's key figures. The wall acts as a visual metaphor, a "translation of a metaphor in its literal sense" (to borrow Schlegel's description of Bottom's transmutation) [see excerpt above, 1808]. The tragedy of Pyramus and Thisby . . . is metamorphosed into a farce for the couples who, for better or for worse, have been "knit." However, at the center of this play within a play is a picture of what has been sundered: a partition that should also remind us of our place. Here is what has faced us throughout *A Midsummer Night's Dream*, what will face us still when we wake from the play and find ourselves in the theater.

These reflections should lead us to wonder about what we are laughing at when we find the mechanicals ridiculous. (This is where the play might be laughing at us.) What, after all, is more ridiculous: to personate the wall that stands between us, thereby insisting that we see it, or to act as if the wall is not there? We are told that the mistake of the mechanicals is to leave nothing to the spectators' imaginations, but *can* we be trusted to see the invisible walls that confront us? Are we so much more observant than the spectators to the play within the play? Throughout *A Midsummer Night's Dream* they figure beholders who can hardly see what is before them: each other or themselves. What is more ridiculous: to have someone "signify wall" or to "let him hold his fingers thus" [III. i. 69-70]—as if either partitions or the people standing for them allowed us openings to see through; as if, like Lysander, we could wake from a death-like slumber and exclaim: "Transparent Helena, Nature shows art, / That through thy bosom makes me see thy heart" [II. ii. 104-05]? He is, of course, enchanted: dreaming. The theater presents itself as an imaginary "wooden O" [*Henry V*, I. i. 13] through or in which we may see its spectacles. But the theater must end by teaching us how to see—not only how to see through—the invisible wall that creates its architecture. This is a wall that we have to imagine to see, yet it won't disappear if we won't see it. Theater shows us both partitions and how we personate partitions. It allows us to hear "partitions discourse," to repeat the play on words Demetrius makes as he watches a man simultaneously present a text and a wall [V.

i. 166-67]. This reminds us that texts, too, are walls that keep us asunder, although we might wish to deliver them, deliver ourselves from them, and thus present ourselves. (pp. 564-65)

Spectators are expected to work their imaginations upon a play (this is what the prologue to *Henry V* requests of us), but at the end of *A Midsummer Night's Dream* we are faced with the possibility that we have been worked upon, that we are owed amends because *our* imaginations have been amended: changed, altered, revised. Have we found to our cost that a vision and a dream have been reduced to an unmanageable reality? Or have we found to our cost that a vision has been imposed upon us, that impressions of our fantasies have been stolen? What does it mean that we have slumbered [V. i. 425]? When Puck causes Helena to slumber, she speaks of "sleep" as that which will "steal me awhile from my own company" [III. ii. 436]. What does it mean that the dream we are told we have witnessed is said to have an "idle theme" [V. i. 427]? It is with the flower called "love-in-idleness" [II. i. 168] that Oberon makes Titania render up her page to him by streaking her eyes and filling her with fantasies. Have we lost ourselves or the figures we imagined for ourselves? What are we to think of this dream that for a while has reduced us to silence and filled our minds with airy shapes and fantasies? As spectators—and as readers—we must wonder what happens when we see with someone else's eyes, allow ourselves to become the blank page upon which an author imprints characters, a play representations. The marriage of true minds that is the dream of theater presents the double prospect that it might mar us as it mends us, steal as it restores. What does theater's figuring or disfiguring add up to? Can theater's "transfiguring" mediate between or synthesize figuring and disfiguring? What do we exchange for our visions?

We have seen that *A Midsummer Night's Dream* dramatizes an economy of exchange, as if, like the *Sonnets,* its figures marked various registers with the expenses of loss and possession. The terms and imagery of theft are set down in the first scene, which pictures the "traffic in women" (to use Emma Goldman's phrase) upon which men for so long have founded their societies; and throughout the play, characters are figured as merchandise or stolen goods. (Hermia, Lysander, Helena, Demetrius, Egeus, Oberon, and Titania each "steal" or are stolen from or are stolen in the course of the play.) The figure for these character-commodities is the child who rivals Hermia as the most contested "property" in the play: the changeling boy that Titania is accused of having "stolen" [II. i. 22]. (According to folk tales, fairies stole lovely children and left deformed "changelings" in exchange; this boy is the changeling the fairies took, not left behind.) When Titania insists to Oberon that "the fairyland buys not the child of me" [II. i. 122], she is perpetuating rather than rejecting terms that inscribe people in a system of economic relations. Her monologue pictures the boy as "merchandise" which his mother's womb, like a trader's ship, was "rich with" [II. i. 127-34]. The changeling comes to represent all of the characters in the play who are traded or fought over as property. It also shows us that the other characters are changelings in the sense that the play's plot revolves around their exchanges: their substitutions and their interchangeability. Demetrius, Lysander, Hermia, and Helena all exchange one another (are exchanged for one another) in almost every possible switch and combination. Bottom, too, is "changed" and "translated" [III. i. 114, 119]. In becoming a disfigured substitute for Titania's changeling boy, he becomes both a changeling for himself (a monster left in his own place) and a changeling for the changeling (which

Titania has been tricked into exchanging). The changeling boy is mysteriously absent in *A Midsummer Night's Dream,* but in a sense he is everywhere; the play casts its characters as changelings. (pp. 567-69)

In another sense, changelings are everywhere in the play because they fill its pages and dialogue: they are its figures of speech. The figures that Titania employs to tell the changeling's story enact and figure exchange in various senses. Describing herself on the shore with the woman who is pregnant with the boy, she tropes the ships to see their "sails conceive / And grow big-bellied with the wanton wind" [III. i. 128-29]. Then the metaphor doubles or reverses—it is exchanged—as Titania tropes the woman to see her "rich" with her own human cargo, just as the woman tropes herself to "imitate" the ships and "sail upon the land / To fetch me trifles, and return again, / As from a voyage, rich with merchandise" [II. i. 131, 132-34]. The woman and the ships stand for each other, exchanging properties in a double sense. If we recognize the act of carrying and trading cargo performed by these literal and figurative ships to be *transport* (as in *metaphérein*) then we see that these double metaphors both dramatize and figure *metaphor* as they transfer, transfigure, exchange, and carry across. Born of this mirror of metaphors, destined to be switched, substituted, and exchanged, the changeling is also a trope for tropes. It makes sense, then, that in *The Arte of English Poesie,* published in 1589, Puttenham invents a rhetorical category called "Figures of Exchange" and names one of those figures "the Changeling." Puttenham refers to exactly the sort of constructions the mechanicals make—"a play with . . . wordes, using a wrong construction for a right, and an absurd for a sensible, by manner of exchange"—but we can see that in a sense all tropes act as changelings. The changeling figures figures.

That Puttenham uses "changeling" to mean something ill-formed which appears in the place of something fair reminds us that in *A Midsummer Night's Dream* the changeling is not the disfigured child. Appropriately, the play ends with a blessing by Oberon, who has authored many of the play's exchanges and deformations in pursuit of his page, to insure for the newly married couples that

> the blots of Nature's hand
> Shall not in their issue stand.
> Never mole, harelip, nor scar,
> Nor mark prodigious, such as are
> Despised in nativity,
> Shall upon their children be.
>
> [V. i. 409-14]

Prefacing Puck's appeal for our blessing and his promise of amends, Oberon's reprise of the figure of the changeling might remind us of the questions facing us at the end of the play. We might wonder again if we who have rendered up the pages of our imaginations in exchange for the play leave the theater free (or freed) from blots or disfigurement. This is what worried us as we let the play imprint its figures on us, risking change and amending. Have we been stolen and left as changelings? I asked the question: What do we exchange for our visions? I meant to suggest that we both give up visions in this exchange *and* get visions in return. In this sense the exchange of visions might be seen as an alternative to the theft of visions in the play. What is at stake appears to be our visions of ourselves: we would not be forced to look with someone else's eyes, to submit to the tyranny of someone else's view or imagination of us.

Yet how do we see ourselves? In the theater, we see ourselves as changelings: capable of seeing ourselves on the stage, substituted for by actors whose parts we take in acts of sympathy or identification. We allow actors to stand as changelings for us, whether or not we recognize them as they present or disfigure us, as they act our parts. In this sense we see with "parted eye" and "everything seems double" [IV. i. 189, 190]; we both take their eyes and see for ourselves. The theater is like the "dark night" that, in Hermia's words, "from the eye his function takes"; it may "impair the seeing sense," but it offers other senses "double recompense" [III. ii. 177-80]. It keeps us in the dark, but it offers to show us ourselves—doubled. The double recompense in this play of double visions would be to learn how to see and to learn how to see others. It is this double vision that Theseus, Egeus, and Oberon in their single-mindedness cannot know. Recall that Hermia—whose eyes are "blessed and attractive" [II. ii. 91] "lodestars" [I. i. 83]—is asked by Helena: "O, teach me how you look" [I. i. 192]. To teach one how you look might be the alternative to the tyranny that forces someone to see with another's eyes or to assume a character that someone else figures and impresses. To learn how you look would be to learn what you look like and to learn how you see: both to take your eyes and to let you see yourself. This is the recompense if you let someone take your eyes and see the figure of yourself. If we risk seeing our visions disfigured—if we figure our visions in order to see them, despite the cost—this is only because we cannot be represented; we can only be believed. To learn this exchange of visions would be to release others from the roles we cast them in, to permit them to stop being changelings. Only when these visions are double—each of us learning how to look— will we able to recognize disfiguring and provide it in exchange

Act III. Scene i. Titania, Bottom, and Fairies. By Henry Fuseli (n.d.).

another sense. *A Midsummer Night's Dream* figures these relations as loss, and in a sense it inscribes us in it. The play, however, might teach us how to look. If we will let one of Bottom's lines echo apart from its comic context, we can hear the admonishment, warning, and offer of vision that the play addresses to its spectators: "let the audience look to their eyes" [I. ii. 26]. (pp. 569-71)

David Marshall, "Exchanging Visions: Reading 'A Midsummer Night's Dream'," in ELH, *Vol. 49, No. 3, Fall, 1982, pp. 543-75.*

ADDITIONAL BIBLIOGRAPHY

Baldwin, T. W. *"A Midsummer-Night's Dream."* In his *On the Literary Genetics of Shakespere's Plays: 1592-1594*, pp. 472-92. Urbana: University of Illinois Press, 1959.

Discussion of possible sources for *A Midsummer Night's Dream*, including North's translation of Plutarch's *Life of Theseus*, Ovid's *Metamorphoses*, and Chaucer's *The Knightes Tale*. Baldwin also traces the "mathematical permutations" of the play's five-act structure, describing the progressive regroupings of characters in terms of squares, circles, and triangles.

Bethurum, Dorothy. "Shakespeare's Comment on Mediaeval Romance in *Midsummer-Night's Dream*." *Modern Language Notes* LX, No. 2 (February 1945): 85-94.

Comparison of the young lovers in *A Midsummer Night's Dream* with Palamon, Arcite, and Emily in Chaucer's *The Knightes Tale*. Bethurum argues that Shakespeare intensified the irony "implicit in Chaucer's story" in order to satirize the literary medieval romance form.

Braddy, Haldeen. "Shakespeare's Puck and Froissart's Orthon." *Shakespeare Quarterly*, 7, No. 1 (Winter 1956): 276-80.

Refutes the traditional assumption that Puck's antecedents can only be found in English folklore. Braddy asserts that Shakespeare's character is similar to a "helpful familiar spirit" in Jean Froissart's *Chronicles*, noting that both are mischievous, nocturnal, and able to make themselves invisible. Braddy thus argues that Froissart's work should be considered part of the "literary foundation" of *A Midsummer Night's Dream*.

Briggs, K. M. "Shakespeare's Fairies." In her *The Anatomy of Puck: An Examination of Fairy Beliefs among Shakespeare's Contemporaries and Successors*, pp. 44-55. London: Routledge and Kegan Paul, 1959.

Agrees with Frank Sidgwick that the diminutive size of the fairies in *A Midsummer Night's Dream* was Shakespeare's own literary innovation, but demonstrates that popular folklore frequently presented these figures as being very small. Briggs sees the supernatural beings in the play as fundamentally benevolent.

Brooks, Harold F. Introduction to *A Midsummer Night's Dream*, by William Shakespeare, edited by Harold F. Brooks, pp. xxi-cxliii. The Arden Edition of the Works of William Shakespeare, edited by Harold F. Brooks, Harold Jenkins and Brian Morris. London: Methuen & Co., 1979.

Comprehensive discussion of the Folio and quarto texts of *A Midsummer Night's Dream* and of the play's sources and antecedents. Brooks contends that love and marriage constitute the central thematic interest, but that errors of the imagination and differentiations between appearance and reality are also significant in the play.

Bryant, J. A., Jr. "Hippolyta's View." In his *Hippolyta's View: Some Christian Aspects of Shakespeare's Plays*, pp. 1-18. Lexington: University of Kentucky Press, 1961.

Asserts that Shakespeare's view of poetry in *A Midsummer Night's Dream* is expressed not by Theseus but by Hippolyta, specifically, in her "something of great constancy" speech (V. i. 23-7). Bryant contends that this passage also contains echoes of the playwright's Christian view of life.

Bullough, Geoffrey. Introduction to *A Midsummer Night's Dream*, by William Shakespeare. In *Narrative and Dramatic Sources of Shakespeare*, Vol. I, edited by Geoffrey Bullough, pp. 367-76. London: Routledge and Kegan Paul, 1961.

> Discussion of Shakespeare's sources and his use of them in *A Midsummer Night's Dream*. In addition to Ovid's *Metamorphoses*, Bullough identifies parallels between the Pyramus and Thisbe interlude and George Pettie's *The Petite Pallace of Pettie his Pleasure*, the story of Romeo and Juliet, and Chaucer's *The Legende of Good Women*.

Bush, Douglas. "The Tedious Brief Scene of Pyramus and Thisbe." *Modern Language Notes* XLVI, No. 3 (March 1931): 144-47.

> Disputes Margaret L. Farrand's conclusion that Thomas Moffett's *The Silkwormes and their Flies* was a direct influence on the interlude in Act V of *A Midsummer Night's Dream*. Bush contends that in the Pyramus and Thisbe play-within-the-play Shakespeare was satirizing the drama of an earlier period.

Chambers, E. K. "The Occasion of '*A Midsummer-Night's Dream*.'" In *A Book of Homage to Shakespeare*, edited by Israel Gollancz, pp. 154-60. London: Oxford University Press, 1916.

> Speculates on the first performance of *A Midsummer Night's Dream*. Chambers offers the possibility that the play was written to celebrate the marriage of William Stanley, Earl of Derby, to Lady Elizabeth Vere on January 26, 1595.

Champion Larry S. "The Comedies of Action." In his *The Evolution of Shakespeare's Comedy: A Study in Dramatic Perspective*, pp. 12-59. Cambridge: Harvard University Press, 1970.

> Argues that the characters in *A Midsummer Night's Dream* are "maneuvered from above rather than motivated from within," so that the spectator never becomes emotionally involved with the lovers and their calamities. Champion further maintains that the play's structure and dramatic action closely parallel Chaucer's *The Knightes Tale*. He views Shakespeare's work as a romantic comedy that parodies the themes taken more seriously by Chaucer.

Clemen, Wolfgang. Introduction to *A Midsummer Night's Dream*, by William Shakespeare, edited by Wolfgang Clemen, pp. 524-29. The Complete Signet Classic Shakespeare, edited by Sylvan Barnet. New York: Harcourt Brace Jovanovich, 1963.

> An overview of various dramatic elements in *A Midsummer Night's Dream*. Clemens supports Shakespeare's method of characterization, asserting that the "flat" delineation of dramatic figures contributes to the dream-like quality of the drama. He also discusses the fairies in general and, in particular, Puck's role as spectator and commentator, maintaining that he is the interpreter of the play's dramatic situations.

———. "Shakespeare's Art of Preparation. A Preliminary Sketch: A First Scene as an Example, *A Midsummer Night's Dream*, I, i." In his *Shakespeare's Dramatic Art: Collected Essays*, pp. 1-18. London: Methuen & Co., 1972.

> Examines the dialogue, dramatic action, and imagery in the initial scene of *A Midsummer Night's Dream* to demonstrate how Shakespeare prepares the audience "for the kind of love which is to be enacted in the play."

Cody, Richard. "*A Midsummer Night's Dream*: Bottom Translated." In his *The Landscape of the Mind*, pp. 127-50. Oxford: At the Clarendon Press, 1969.

> Detailed study of the pastoral and Neoplatonic elements in *A Midsummer Night's Dream*. Cody examines the way in which Shakespeare uses the mythological figures of Bacchus, Venus, and Diana to enhance the play's central progress from chastity to pleasure and from "division into union."

Coghill, Nevill. "Unification." In his *Shakespeare's Professional Skills*, pp. 32-60. Cambridge: At the University Press, 1964.

> Examination of Shakespeare's sources and his adaptation of them in *A Midsummer Night's Dream*. Coghill particularly demonstrates the many similarities between this play and Anthony Mun-

day's *John a Kent and John a Cumber*, noting that both depict young lovers thwarted by parental opposition, a flight to the moonlit woods, a mischievous fairy imp, and a group of clowns who stage an interlude.

Craig, Hardin. "The Beginnings: *A Midsummer Night's Dream*." In his *An Interpretation of Shakespeare*, pp. 35-8. Columbia, Mo.: Lucas Brothers, 1948.

> Extols *A Midsummer Night's Dream* as "the best of Shakespeare's early comedies," maintaining that the playwright's management of the multiple plot structure was unequalled by any other Elizabethan dramatist. Craig agrees with other critics who commend Shakespeare's use of the Theseus and Hippolyta plot as a frame for the dramatic action.

Cutts, John P. "'The Fierce Vexation of a [Midsummer Night's] Dreame.'" *Shakespeare Quarterly* 14, No. 2 (Spring 1963): 183-85.

> Contends that although the Pyramus and Thisbe interlude is primarily a satire on the young lovers, it also provides an ironic contrast to the relationships between Theseus and Hippolyta and Oberon and Titania. Cutts further argues that Shakespeare symbolically used the "love in idleness" flower to enhance the dramatic representation of the excesses of romantic passion.

David, Richard. "Poetry and Drama." In his *The Janus of Poets: Being an Essay on the Dramatic Value of Shakspere's Poetry Both Good and Bad*, pp. 1-33. New York: Macmillan Co., 1935.

> Maintains that the dominance of formal poetry in *A Midsummer Night's Dream* links the play to the tradition of the Court masque. David also comments that the poetry here is often self-conscious, even "trite and quite superfluous."

De la Mare, Walter. "The 'Dream.'" In his *Pleasures and Speculations*, pp. 270-305. London: Faber and Faber, 1940.

> Assessment of the poetic style of *A Midsummer Night's Dream*. De la Mare evaluates some of the verse as "dull and characterless" and remarks on the lack of individualized characterization. He concludes that Shakespeare extensively revised an older play by another dramatist, some of whose "bad verse" remained after the revision process. This view of the authorship of *A Midsummer Night's Dream* is shared by John Dover Wilson (see the entry below).

Doran, Madeleine. "Pyramus and Thisbe Once More." In *Essays on Shakespeare and Elizabethan Drama in Honor of Hardin Craig*, edited by Richard Hosley, pp. 149-61. Columbia: University of Missouri Press, 1962.

> Examination of a twelfth- and a sixteenth-century version of the Pyramus and Thisbe story. Doran points out that there were "countless retellings" of Ovid's tale up to the time of Shakespeare and that the story was "especially ripe for parody."

———. "Titania's Wood." *Rice University Studies* 60, No. 2 (Spring 1974): 55-70.

> Argues that for the woodland setting of Acts II through IV of *A Midsummer Night's Dream* Shakespeare combined elements from popular folklore, mythology, and formal literary tradition. Doran examines in detail the emblematic meanings of the moon and the specific flowers described as adorning Titania's bower.

Draper, John W. "The Queen Makes a Match and Shakespeare a Comedy." *Yearbook of English Studies* 2 (1972): 61-7.

> Discussion of the occasion of the first performance of *A Midsummer Night's Dream*. Draper asserts that astronomical allusions in the play, as well as "parallels of character and plot," suggest that Shakespeare wrote it for the wedding of Lady Dorothy, the sister of the Earl of Essex, to the Duke of Northumberland, which took place on April 30, 1595.

Farrand, Margaret L. "An Additional Source for *A Midsummer Night's Dream*." *Studies in Philology* XXVII, No. 2 (April 1930): 233-43.

> Detailed comparison between the Pyramus and Thisbe scenes in *A Midsummer Night's Dream* and Thomas Moffett's *The Silkwormes and their Flies*. Farrand points out the parallels in phrasing and meter between the two works and contends that Shakespeare

likely read a manuscript version of Moffett's work before writing his play.

Franke, Wolfgang. "The Logic of *Double Entendre* in *A Midsummer Night's Dream*." *Philological Quarterly* 58, No. 3 (Summer 1979): 282-97.

Contends that the language of Bottom and the other mechanicals contains bawdy and indelicate references, but maintains that these would not have offended an aristocratic audience for whom "the romantic and the sexual side of love were not mutually exclusive but complementary." Franke argues that the elements of sexual comedy in the play are fundamentally innocent, emphasizing that Shakespeare presents the mechanicals as being unaware of the indecencies of their words.

Garber, Marjorie B. "Spirits of Another Sort: *A Midsummer Night's Dream*." In her *Dream in Shakespeare: From Metaphor to Metamorphosis*, pp. 59-87. New Haven: Yale University Press, 1974.

Argues that the process of transformation is both the central thematic element of *A Midsummer Night's Dream* and the model for the construction of dramatic events. Garber regards the movement from Athens to the woods as analogous to entering the dream state where conventional ideas about perception and understanding are inverted in a process that leads to heightened self-awareness and compares this with the dramatist's transformation and restructuring of his experience through the crucible of the imagination.

Generosa, Sister M. "Apuleius and *A Midsummer Night's Dream*: Analogue or Source, Which?" *Studies in Philology* XLII, No. 2 (April 1945): 198-204.

Comparison of parallel ideas and divergent treatments of material in Apuleius's *Metamorphoses or The Golden Ass* and Shakespeare's *A Midsummer Night's Dream*. Generosa demonstrates that the love scenes involving Lucius the transformed ass and a noble lady are much coarser than the exchanges between the "translated" Bottom and Titania, but she maintains that the playwright must have been familiar with the earlier tale.

Girard, René. "Myth and Ritual in Shakespeare: *A Midsummer Night's Dream*." In *Textual Strategies: Perspectives in Post-Structuralist Criticism*, edited by Josué V. Harari, pp. 189-212. Ithaca, N.Y.: Cornell University Press, 1979.

Distinguishes between the "surface play" of *A Midsummer Night's Dream* (as represented by Theseus) and the one beneath (represented by Hippolyta), which is discoverable by an examination of the ambiguous language of the drama. Emphasizing the animal imagery and the "increasing violence in the nighttime forest," Girard also argues that by choosing to "love by another's eyes" the lovers erect their own obstacles to reconciliation.

Goldstein, Melvin. "Identity Crises in A Midsummer Nightmare: Comedy as Terror in Disguise." *Psychoanalytic Review* 60, No. 2 (Summer 1973): 169-204.

Maintains that each character in *A Midsummer Night's Dream* is struggling to resolve a crisis arising from an incomplete sexual self-definition. Goldstein focuses on Helena's confusions about her sexual identity and notes that she comes to terms with her sexuality through an acceptance of the animality that is a basic part of her nature.

Granville-Barker, Harley. "Preface to *A Midsummer Night's Dream*." In *More Prefaces to Shakespeare*, by Harley Granville-Barker, edited by Edward M. Moore, pp. 94-134. Princeton, N.J.: Princeton University Press, 1974.

Maintains that the poetry of *A Midsummer Night's Dream* is the predominant dramatic element in the play. Granville-Barker comments on the variations in meter and modulations in tone throughout the play and remarks that these are important in conveying the significance of the characters' speeches.

Green, Roger Lancelyn. "Shakespeare and the Fairies." *Folklore*, No. 73 (Summer 1962): 89-103.

Discussions of Shakespeare's combining folklore and mythology in his representation of the fairies in *A Midsummer Night's Dream*. Green maintains, along with Frank Sidgwick, Minor White La-

tham, and K. M. Briggs, that Shakespeare was one of the first authors to depict fairies in a literary work and that his delineation of their diminutive size was not only innovative but widely copied by later dramatists and fiction writers.

Greenfield, Thelma. "*A Midsummer Night's Dream* and *The Praise of Folly*." *Comparative Literature* XX, No. 3 (Summer 1968): 236-44.

Assessment of Shakespeare's use in *A Midsummer Night's Dream* of ideas and attitudes from Erasmus's *The Praise of Folly*. Greenfield traces parallels between the two works and demonstrates that both offer a comic view of human irrationality and folly.

Gui, Weston G. "Bottom's Dream." *American Imago* 9, Nos. 3 & 4 (Fall-Winter 1952): 251-305.

Psychoanalytic interpretation of the significance of Bottom's dream in *A Midsummer Night's Dream*. Gui views the dramatic action of the play as embodying the experience of a child on a summer's evening and concludes that Bottom's dream is "that of an orally regressed adult"—not Bottom, but Shakespeare himself.

Guilhamet, Leon. "*A Midsummer Night's Dream* as the Imitation of an Action." *Studies in English Literature 1500-1900* XV, No. 2 (Spring 1975): 257-71.

Demonstrates that the unity of dramatic action in *A Midsummer Night's Dream* is based on Shakespeare's development of the Neoplatonic idea that harmony can be achieved from "the union of seeming opposites, love and strife." Guilhamet maintains that the conclusion of the play exhibits the resolution of all the discords between the characters and that the deaths of Pyramus and Thisbe exorcise through laughter the spector of the threat to Hermia.

Hamilton. A. C. "The Resolution of the Early Period: *A Midsummer Night's Dream*." In his *The Early Shakespeare*, pp. 216-33. San Marino, Calif.: The Huntington Library, 1967.

Evaluates *A Midsummer Night's Dream* as the culmination of Shakespeare's early development as a dramatist. Hamilton points to similarities in theme, structure, and style between this play and the ones that preceded it and judges that it is "the most satisfying and complete of the early works."

Hawkins, Harriett. "Fabulous Counterfeits: Dramatic Construction and Dramatic Perspectives in *The Spanish Tragedy*, *A Midsummer Night's Dream*, and *The Tempest*." *Shakespeare Studies* VI (1970): 51-65.

Argues that in both *A Midsummer Night's Dream* and *The Tempest* the audience views the dramatic action from the perspective of the playwright more directly than in any other of Shakespeare's dramas. Hawkins maintains that, with the "multiple levels of dramatic action, and the multiple perspectives" it provides, Thomas Kyd's *The Spanish Tragedy* is an interesting precedent—but not a direct source—for the dramatic organization of *A Midsummer Night's Dream*.

Herbert, T. Walter. *Oberon's Mazéd World*. Baton Rouge: Louisiana State University Press, 1977, 200 p.

Interprets *A Midsummer Night's Dream* through the perception of a "well-educated, energetic, philosophically adventurous sixteenth-century English playgoer." Herbert asserts that the play's design includes concepts from many philosophical points of view and from various ages of the history of ideas—all filtered through Shakespeare's comic perspective.

Holland, Norman N. "Hermia's Dream." *Annual of Psychoanalysis* VII (1979): 369-89.

Maintains that Hermia's dream in Act II, Scene ii of *A Midsummer Night's Dream* dramatizes her conflicting desires to be possessed by Lysander and to remain chaste. Holland views the questions of separations and fusions in Hermia's dream as reflective of the ambiguous presentation of love and cruelty that permeates the entire play.

Hunter, G. K. "*A Midsummer Night's Dream*." In his *William Shakespeare: The Later Comedies*, pp. 7-20. London: Longmans, Green & Co., 1962.

Contends that the total structural pattern of *A Midsummer Night's Dream* is more important than any of its individual, constituent elements and that the play "is constructed by contrast rather than interaction." Hunter also believes that Theseus and Hippolyta together represent a single—albeit limited—perception of the dramatic action.

Hutton, Virgil. "*A Midsummer Night's Dream*: Tragedy in Comic Disguise." *Studies in English Literature 1500-1900* 25, No. 2 (Spring 1985): 289-305.

Claims that Shakespeare intended the Pyramus and Thisbe interlude to convey a warning to the newly married couple for whose wedding celebration *A Midsummer Night's Dream* was written. Hutton maintains that Shakespeare wanted to demonstrate in the play-within-the-play that young lovers must be prepared to endure life's vicissitudes and calamities without the protection or aid of any benevolent supernatural agency—an unorthodox view of the world that had to be carefully concealed in the play's dramatic action.

Kermode, Frank. "The Mature Comedies." In *Early Shakespeare*, edited by John Russell Brown and Bernard Harris, pp. 211-27. London: Edward Arnold, 1961.

Asserts that *A Midsummer Night's Dream* is "a play of marked intellectual content" and that its principal themes are fantasy and the disorders of fantasy. Kermode believes that Bottom's dream, which offers an interpretation of blind love as a transcendent passion, contrasts with the young lovers' final opinions that their experiences have been mere dreams or fantasies.

Kernan, Alvin B. "'A Little O'erparted': Actors and Audiences in *The Taming of the Shrew, Love's Labour's Lost, A Midsummer Night's Dream,* and *1 Henry IV*." In his *The Playwright as Magician: Shakespeare's Image of the Poet in the English Public Theater*, pp. 49-84. New Haven: Yale University Press, 1979.

Examination of the interlude in Act V of *A Midsummer Night's Dream* as reflecting the conflicts Shakespeare experienced when his written dramas became subject to "the conditions of theatrical production." Kernan regards the performance of the Pyramus and Thisbe play as a parody of the efforts of amateur players, the mishaps of stage presentation, and the inability of all audiences to fully comprehend the playwright's intentions.

Lang, Andrew. "*A Midsummer Night's Dream*." *Harper's New Monthly Magazine* XCI, No. DXLIII (August 1895): 327-38.

Shares the traditional nineteenth-century view that *A Midsummer Night's Dream* is too ethereal to be represented on the stage. Lang considers the depiction of Helena pursuing Demetrius an unwelcome spectacle and notes that Hermia, "unamiable even when unenchanted," is "too odious" when bewitched.

Latham, Minor White. *The Elizabethan Fairies*. New York: Columbia University Press, 1930, 313 p.

Comprehensive overview of fairy folklore current in England and Europe in the sixteenth and seventeenth centuries. Latham assesses Shakespeare's depiction of the fairies in *A Midsummer Night's Dream* as innovative not only in terms of their diminutive stature—a point also made by Frank Sidgwick, Roger Lancelyn Green, and K. M. Briggs—but because, for the first time, they were presented as "consistently good" rather than as "mischievous and dangerous beings."

Law, Robert Adger. "The 'Pre-Conceived Pattern' of *A Midsummer Night's Dream*." In *Studies in English 1943*, edited by Henry Nash Smith, pp. 5-14. Austin: University of Texas Press, 1943.

Contends that the structure of *A Midsummer Night's Dream* is neither masterful nor original. Law finds no organic unity among the four elements of the plot, arguing that the lack of permanent influence of any one group upon any of the others is reminiscent of the structure of the comedies of John Lyly and Robert Greene, where characters are also treated as members of groups rather than as individuals.

Leggatt, Alexander. "*A Midsummer Night's Dream*." In his *Shakespeare's Comedy of Love*, pp. 89-115. London: Methuen & Co., 1974.

Maintains that when the four groups of characters in *A Midsummer Night's Dream* come into contact with each other there is no fusion but, instead, a series of comic contrasts serving to emphasize the differences between them and provide a comic perspective from which to view the dramatic action. Leggatt notes that the supernatural figures have a "range of vision and the freedom of actions that the other characters lack," and he further observes that their "sophisticated awareness" is denied to the mortals in the play.

Lewis, Allan. "*A Midsummer Night's Dream*—Fairy Fantasy or Erotic Nightmare?" *Educational Theatre Journal* XXI, No. 3 (October 1969): 251-58.

Regards *A Midsummer Night's Dream* as "a comedy of sex that is both light and dark." Although Lewis sees bitter elements in the play, he asserts that Jan Kott's interpretation is an overstatement of the dark aspects of the drama (see excerpt above, 1964).

Makaryk, Irene Rima. "The Mature Comedies." In her *Comic Justice in Shakespeare's Comedies*, Vol. 1, pp. 76-207. Salzburg Studies in English Literature: Jacobean Drama Studies, 91, edited by James Hogg. Salzburg: Institute für Anglistik und Amerikanistik Universität Salzburg, 1980.

Argues that *A Midsummer Night's Dream* begins as it ends, with the reconciliation of opposing forces. Makaryk claims that the harmony and completeness achieved at the close of the drama is emphasized by the inclusion of the bergomask and the fairies' dance, both of which draw attention to the play's "vision of a union of society with nature and the supernatural."

Martz, William J. "Bottom and Paradox Compounded." In his *Shakespeare's Universe of Comedy*, pp. 61-79. New York: David Lewis, 1971.

Views Bottom as the embodiment of the comic point of view in *A Midsummer Night's Dream*. Martz also claims that the imaginative romping of the rude mechanicals transforms the Pyramus and Thisbe interlude into a blend of farce and love and "a triumph of fellowship."

McFarland, Thomas. "And All Things Shall Be Peace: The Happiness of *A Midsummer-Night's Dream*." In his *Shakespeare's Pastoral Comedy*, pp. 78-97. Chapel Hill: University of North Carolina Press, 1972.

Disputes Kott's interpretation of *A Midsummer Night's Dream* (see excerpt above, 1964) by claiming that the eroticism in the play is only a "barely perceptible undercurrent." McFarland further argues that the opening of the drama establishes the idea of harmony and grace, so that none of the apparent threats to the young lovers will be taken seriously by the audience. Indeed, he maintains that even the threat of Hermia's banishment to a convent "asserts its own austere beauty" because of the language in which it is couched.

McPeek, James A. S. "The Psyche Myth and *A Midsummer Night's Dream*." *Shakespeare Quarterly* 23, No. 2 (Winter 1972): 69-79.

Examines the way in which Shakespeare used the story of Psyche in Lucius Apuleius's *Golden Ass* as a source for *A Midsummer Night's Dream*. McPeek sees in Shakespeare's characterization of the young women an adaptation of the figure of Psyche, who embodies "the concept of the devoted woman patient in adversity and unfailingly true to her love."

Mebane, John S. "Structure, Source, and Meaning in *A Midsummer Night's Dream*." *Texas Studies in Literature and Language* 24, No. 3 (Fall 1982): 255-70.

Examines the relationship between Chaucer's *The Knightes Tale* and *A Midsummer Night's Dream*. Mebane asserts that among the many similarities between the two works are the transformation of discord into harmony, the use of Theseus and Hippolyta to frame the action, the elements of the supernatural, and the dramatization of the "problem of reconciling a faith in cosmic order with our experience of life's apparent chaos."

Merchant, W. Moelwyn. "*A Midsummer Night's Dream*: A Visual Re-creation." In *Early Shakespeare*, edited by John Russell Brown and Bernard Harris, pp. 164-85. London: Edward Arnold, 1961.

A discussion of pictorial representations of characters and settings in *A Midsummer Night's Dream* from the Restoration to the present, focusing on paintings, plates for frontispieces to various editions of the play, and scenery for different productions. Merchant comments that it is only rarely that visual treatments of the play take into account its "disturbing moments of irrationality, treachery, and demonic power."

Miller, Donald C. "Titania and the Changeling." *English Studies* XXII (1940): 66-70.
Emphasizes the descriptions of Titania as "rash," "proud," and "wanton" to support the argument that the fairy queen has made the changeling boy her lover.

Miller, Raeburn. "The Persons of Moonshine: *A Midsummer Night's Dream* and the 'Disfigurement' of Realities." In *Explorations of Literature,* edited by Rima Drell Reck, pp. 25-31. Baton Rouge: Louisiana State University Press, 1966.
Argues that the lovers, the clowns, and the fairies in *A Midsummer Night's Dream* respectively depict the varieties of fantasy in the average man, in the realm of art, and in the dream state. Miller contends that the fairies' interaction with the lovers only exaggerates the distortions already existing in their perceptions of each other. He further notes that their return to Athens and the ritual of marriage symbolizes the incorporation of fantasy into the structure of civilized society.

Muir, Kenneth. "Pyramus and Thisbe: A Study in Shakespeare's Method." *Shakespeare Quarterly* 5, No. 2 (Spring 1954): 141-53.
Shares the view of Margaret L. Farrand that Thomas Moffett's *The Silkwormes and their Flies* was a source for *A Midsummer Night's Dream.* Although he notes that Shakespeare probably had read several versions of the Pyramus and Thisbe story, the interlude in his play is "so close to Moffett's version of the story that it must have been an intentional parody of it."

Noble, Richmond. "*A Midsummer Night's Dream.*" In his *Shakespeare's Use of Song,* pp. 49-59. London: Oxford University Press, 1923.
Evaluates the naturalness and ease with which Shakespeare introduces the fairies' lullaby in Act II, Scene ii of *A Midsummer Night's Dream.* Noble compares this with the more awkward and artificial use of song in the dramatist's earlier plays.

Olson, Paul A. "*A Midsummer Night's Dream* and the Meaning of Court Marriage." *ELH* 24, No. 2 (June 1957): 95-119.
Earliest extensive treatment of thematic elements in *A Midsummer Night's Dream.* Olson argues that Shakespeare's presentation of the marriage of Theseus and Hippolyta reflects the Renaissance view of Theseus as the embodiment of the ideal ruler and of Hippolyta as the Amazonian queen whose nation subverts the fixed authority and hierarchy of wedlock. He further discovers a central antithesis in the play between passionate love and reasonable love and concludes that Shakespeare here presents marriage as a relationship in which men must assert their authority to mirror the hierarchical order of society. D'Orsay W. Pearson later disputed Olson's view of Theseus as "an icon of reason."

Parrott, Thomas Marc. Introduction to *A Midsummer Night's Dream.* In *Shakespeare: Twenty-Three Plays and the Sonnets,* by William Shakespeare, edited by Thomas Marc Parrott, pp. 131-34. New York: Charles Scribner's Sons, 1938.
Postulates the likelihood that Shakespeare revised his 1594-95 version of *A Midsummer Night's Dream,* intended for a private performance, at some later date when it was to be presented on the public stage.

Pearson, D'Orsay W. "'Unkinde' Theseus: A Study in Renaissance Mythography." *English Literary Renaissance* 4, No. 2 (Spring 1974): 276-98.
Disputes Paul A. Olson's view of Theseus as "an icon of reason" and Madeleine Doran's assessment of the Duke as the "ideal Renaissance prince." Pearson examines other literary treatments of Theseus from Ovid to the Renaissance and concludes that the Renaissance view of him included praise for his youthful prowess as a warrior as well as criticism for "his lust, his perfidy, and his tyranny" when he grew older. Pearson further comments that in *A Midsummer Night's Dream,* which many critics have seen as celebrating the ritual of marriage, Shakespeare has made the

final blessing of Theseus and Hippolyta's wedding bed an ironical one, for his audience would have been aware that the mythical Theseus was responsible for the death of their son.

Priestley, J. B. "Bully Bottom." In his *The English Comic Characters,* pp. 1-19. New York: Dodd, Mead and Co., 1925.
Maintains that Bottom is the first of Shakespeare's great comic figures. Priestley argues that vanity is only one part of Bottom's character and that his imagination and creativity serve him so well during his transformation into an ass that "he not only rises to the occasion, he improves it."

Quiller-Couch, Arthur. "*A Midsummer-Night's Dream.*" In his *Shakespeare's Workmanship,* pp. 77-95. London: T. Fisher Unwin, 1918.
Speculates on the processes of Shakespeare's imagination as he composed *A Midsummer Night's Dream.* Quiller-Couch asserts that in the play Shakespeare first found the opportunity to give full rein to his natural gifts for poetry and humor.

Quiller-Couch, Arthur, and Wilson, John Dover, eds. *A Midsummer Night's Dream,* by William Shakespeare. Cambridge: Cambridge University Press, 1924, 176 p.
A comprehensive review and comparison of the Folio and quarto versions of *A Midsummer Night's Dream.* Commenting on the stylistic variations in the play, Quiller-Couch and Dover Wilson contend that Shakespeare's first "handling" of the text occurred in 1592 or earlier, that he revised some portions of it in 1594 or 1595, and that additional revisions and interpolations were made by him in 1598.

Ramsey, Clifford Earl. "*A Midsummer Night's Dream.*" In *Homer to Brecht: The European Epic and Dramatic Traditions,* edited by Michael Seidel and Edward Mendelson, pp. 214-37. New Haven: Yale University Press, 1977.
Maintains that the structure of *A Midsummer Night's Dream* is controlled by the movement of the dramatic action into and out of the wood. Ramsey argues that Athens, the mechanicals' rehearsal site, and the wood each offer a different perspective on reality. He also notes that the green world is the scene of misrule as well as "the natural home of love and the imagination," with powers both to transfigure and to reconcile.

Rickert, Edith. "Political Propaganda and Satire in *A Midsummer Night's Dream.*" *Modern Philology* XXI, No. 1 (August 1923): 53-87.
Examines topical allusions in *A Midsummer Night's Dream* for evidence that Shakespeare was propagandizing on behalf of a claimant to the English throne, the Earl of Hertford. Rickert further argues that the gibes at effeminacy in the play are satiric barbs aimed at the weakness and cowardice of James I.

———. "Political Propaganda and Satire in *A Midsummer Night's Dream.* II." *Modern Philology* XXI, No. 2 (November 1923): 133-54.
Continuation of her earlier discussion of the political circumstances reflected in *A Midsummer Night's Dream.* Additionally, Rickert examines the versification in the play and concludes that the first version of the drama—which she states was written in 1592—included only the plot involving the young lovers, that the Theseus and fairy elements were added in 1595, and that Puck's concluding speech at the end of Act V was added still later as an apology for the political allusions in the play.

Robinson, James E. "The Ritual and Rhetoric of *A Midsummer Night's Dream.*" *PMLA* 83, No. 2 (May 1968): 380-91.
Regards *A Midsummer Night's Dream* as representing two levels of action, one in the fairies' world of ritual and nature, the other in the Athenian world of realism and law. Robinson maintains that as the play concludes with the "social celebration of love and marriage" made possible by the fairies, conflicts between love and law have been resolved and society has been renewed.

Robinson, J. W. "Palpable Hot Ice: Dramatic Burlesque in *A Midsummer-Night's Dream.*" *Studies in Philology* LXI, No. 2, Part 1 (April 1964): 192-204.
Asserts that the Pyramus and Thisbe interlude in *A Midsummer Night's Dream* is a parody of hybrid plays written by such dramatists as Thomas Preston, Thomas Dekker, and John Lyly and

is also a burlesque of the irregular acting companies that preceded the professional troupes of Shakespeare's day.

Schanzer, Ernest. "The Moon and the Fairies in *A Midsummer Night's Dream.*" *University of Toronto Quarterly* XXIV, No. 3 (April 1955): 234-46.

Repudiates E. K. Chambers's view that the fairies in *A Midsummer Night's Dream* are childish and irresponsible (see excerpt above, 1905), noting instead that Titania's attendants "are conscientious and very much overworked servants of the queen, with little time for idle gossiping." Schanzer also contends that Titania and Oberon are the fairy-world's counterparts of Hippolyta and Theseus, and he maintains that the quarrel between the fairy king and queen precipitates and reflects the disorder in the natural world.

Sen Gupta, S. C. "Early Comedies." In his *Shakespearian Comedy*, pp. 82-128. London: Oxford University Press, 1950.

Regards *A Midsummer Night's Dream* as superior to Shakespeare's earlier comedies with respect to characterization, the evocation of dramatic atmosphere, and the unification of diverse elements into the structure of the play. Sen Gupta especially analyzes the characterization of Bottom, whom he sees as self-confident, egotistical, and a realist so devoid of romantic imagination that he is unable to comprehend reality.

Sidgwick, Frank. Introduction to *The Sources and Analogues of "A Midsummer Night's Dream,"* edited by Frank Sidgwick, pp. 1-68. London: Chatto and Windus, 1908.

A comprehensive discussion of literary and folkloric sources for *A Midsummer Night's Dream*. Sidgwick was the earliest critic to demonstrate that Shakespeare's conception of the diminutive size of the fairies was an innovation that permanently influenced both popular and literary treatments of these creatures. This issue has also been addressed by Roger Lancelyn Green, Minor White Latham, and K. M. Briggs.

Smith, Stephen L. "*A Midsummer Night's Dream:* Shakespeare, Play and Metaplay." *The Centennial Review* XXI, No. 2 (Spring 1977): 194-209.

Asserts that the conflict between reality and fantasy in *A Midsummer Night's Dream* is underscored by the themes of "conflict, contradiction, agonistic uncertainty and complementarity." This conflict is also personified, Smith argues, in the figures of Theseus and Bottom, who respectively view the supernatural from the vantage ponts of the profane analyzer, who dismisses it as improbable, and the magician, who bends it to his own use.

Staton, Walter F., Jr. "Ovidian Elements in *A Midsummer Night's Dream.*" *The Huntington Library Quarterly* XXVI, No. 2 (February 1963): 165-78.

Contends that the representation of the fairies in *A Midsummer Night's Dream* is similar to Ovid's depiction of the gods in his works, particularly in showing the effects of "divine bickering" on weather and agriculture in the natural world. Staton further maintains that in the interlude of Act V Shakespeare was parodying Ovidian imitators who retold the story of Pyramus and Thisbe in an overly sentimental and romantic fashion.

Stewart, Garrett. "Shakespearean Dreamplay." *English Literary Renaissance* 11, No. 1 (Winter 1981): 44-69.

A discussion of the reflexive nature of the language in *A Midsummer Night's Dream*, especially in Bottom's awakening speech at the end of Act IV, Scene i. Stewart contends that the non sequiturs, the hesitations between exposition and awe, and the "garbled eloquence" of Bottom's speech emphasize the ambiguous nature of both drama and dreams.

Swinden, Patrick. "*A Midsummer Night's Dream.*" In his *An Introduction to Shakespeare's Comedies*, pp. 51-64. London: Macmillan, 1973.

A general treatment of *A Midsummer Night's Dream*, giving particular attention to the way in which structure, discrepancies in the passage of time, and the imagery all enhance the play's central concern with the manipulation of the senses.

Taylor, Marion A. "The Allegorical Roles of Alençon and Queen Elizabeth in *A Midsummer Night's Dream.*" In her *Bottom, Thou Art Translated: Political Allegory in "A Midsummer Night's Dream" and Related Literature*, pp. 131-65. Amsterdam: Rodopi NV, 1973.

An analysis of topical allusions in *A Midsummer Night's Dream* as they reflect Shakespeare's interest in Elizabethan political problems. Taylor asserts that Bottom is a satiric portrait of François de Valois, Duke of Alençon, whose love affair with Queen Elizabeth was strongly opposed by her countrymen.

Taylor, Michael. "The Darker Purpose of *A Midsummer Night's Dream.*" *Studies in English Literature 1500-1900* IX, No. 2 (Spring 1969): 259-73.

Disputes John Russell Brown's view that *A Midsummer Night's Dream* firmly establishes the "truth of love" (see excerpt above, 1957). Taylor argues that the fairies are presented equivocally as purveyors of mischief and malice as well as charm, that Puck's language is at times ominous, and that the play is "at its harshest and most unfestive in the scenes with the lovers," for Demetrius is vicious towards Helena even before the application of the magic potion leads him to act irrationally. Taylor believes that in this drama Shakespeare is presenting the reality of love, with its complementary aspects of "kindliness and pain."

Van Doren, Mark. "*A Midsummer Night's Dream.*" In his *Shakespeare*, pp. 76-83. New York: Henry Holt and Co., 1939.

Discussion of the imagery of *A Midsummer Night's Dream* and the manner in which it extends the boundaries of the world of the play. Van Doren further comments that the Pyramus and Thisbe interlude is Shakespeare's self-parody of his own *Romeo and Juliet*.

Vickers, Brian. "From Clown to Character." In his *The Artistry of Shakespeare's Prose*, pp. 52-88. London: Methuen & Co., 1968.

Examination of the prose speeches of the rustics in *A Midsummer Night's Dream* in terms of the formal rhetorical tradition of the Renaissance. Vickers particularly credits the "simple syntax" and "artless repetition" of Bottom's speeches with enhancing the gentle image of that character.

Vlasopolos, Anca. "The Ritual of Midsummer: A Pattern for *A Midsummer Night's Dream.*" *Renaissance Quarterly* XXXI, No. 1 (Spring 1978): 21-9.

Analysis of the Christian and pagan elements in *A Midsummer Night's Dream* and their relation to the Midsummer ritual known as St. John's Day. Vlasopolos demonstrates that both the play and the ritual incorporate the rite of fertility in a forest setting and the reemergence of the participants into a renewed, regenerated society that is once more in harmony with nature.

Weiner, Andrew D. "'Multiformities Uniforme': *A Midsummer Night's Dream.*" *ELH* 38, No. 3 (September 1971): 329-49.

Regards "the celebration of the mysteries signified by and associated with marriage" as the central thematic interest of *A Midsummer Night's Dream*. Weiner believes that the play stresses the importance of marriage as a civilizing institution and as a reflection of the divine love that God has for man.

Wells, Stanley. "Shakespeare without Sources." In *Shakespearian Comedy*, edited by David Palmer and Malcolm Bradbury, pp. 58-74. London: Edward Arnold, 1972.

Evaluation of *Love's Labour's Lost*, *A Midsummer Night's Dream*, and *The Tempest* as dramas based on Shakespeare's own plot structures, and not on stories from other sources. Wells argues that all three plays show Shakespeare preoccupied with his own dramatic art, and he concludes that the dramatist required the inspiration of outside source material to depersonalize his efforts.

Wilson, John Dover. "Postscript: Variations on the Theme of *A Midsummer Night's Dream.*" In his *Shakespeare's Happy Comedies*, pp. 184-220. London: Faber and Faber, 1962.

Endorses Walter de la Mare's speculations about the existence of an earlier play by another dramatist which Shakespeare used as the basis for *A Midsummer Night's Dream*. As in his essay coauthored with Arthur Quiller-Couch (see entry above), Dover Wilson asserts that Shakespeare probably revised the play for a second private performance in 1596 and for public performances at some later time.

Woodberry, George E. Introduction to *A Midsummer Night's Dream,* by William Shakespeare, edited by Sidney Lee, pp. ix-xxii. The Complete Works of William Shakespeare, edited by Sidney Lee, Vol. VI. New York: George D. Sproul, 1907.

    Contends that the central theme of the play is illusion and that Shakespeare shows this in various forms—illusions of the senses, of the heart, and of art itself.

Zitner, Sheldon P. "The Worlds of *A Midsummer Night's Dream.*" *The South Atlantic Quarterly* LIX, No. 3 (Summer 1960): 397-403.

    Views *A Midsummer Night's Dream* as a comedy of avoidance, that is, one which presents the possibilities of complications but then moves away from these possibilities, establishing no moral implications in its dramatic action. Zitner argues that Theseus is an atypical Shakespearean monarch who has no interest in war or the problem of succession, that the mechanicals are never shown working, that the fairy world contains no sinister or malevolent overtones, and that the Pyramus and Thisbe interlude has no symbolic function, but is "almost wholly entertainment."

Troilus and Cressida

DATE: Most scholars agree that *Troilus and Cressida* was written by Shakespeare sometime between 1598 and 1602, with late 1601 or 1602 as the most frequently suggested date. The play was first entered in the STATIONERS' REGISTER on February 7, 1603, and, it is thought, must have been composed not long before that date. If, as many critics have argued, Shakespeare used George Chapman's translation of Homer as a source for the play, it could have been written no earlier than 1598, the year when Chapman's book was published. *Troilus and Cressida*'s tonal affinities with *Hamlet* have also suggested to scholars that 1602 is a likely date for its composition. Further support for this dating has been offered by those who contend that the work contains references to the War of the Theaters, a personal feud among playwrights which supposedly took place between 1599 and 1602 and was characterized by satirical allusions to the disputants in the plays of the time. An epistle to the reader which prefaced the 1609 QUARTO edition of *Troilus and Cressida* professed that it was "a new play, neuer stal'd with the stage, neuer clapper-clawed with the palmes of the vulger." This claim, and the peculiar intellectual tone of the play, has led many critics to believe that *Troilus and Cressida* was first performed, sometime near the date of composition, before a private audience at one of the INNS OF COURT, possibly for a gathering of lawyers or some other group educated enough to follow the philosophic nature of the speeches. Nevill Coghill, however, has argued that *Troilus and Cressida* was first publicly performed at the GLOBE THEATRE in 1602, but that a later version of the play was presented at an Inn of Court in 1608, with a satiric prologue and epilogue added to "protect" it from the jeers of an audience of cynical sophisticates.

TEXT: Despite the 1603 entry of *Troilus and Cressida* in the Stationers' Register, the play was not published until 1609, after it had been reentered in the Register by another publisher. This 1609 quarto edition of the play has two different title pages. The first refers to "The Histories of Troylus and Cressid" as "acted by the Kings Majesties servants at the Globe." While the quarto was at press, however, a second title page, making no reference to the public performance, was substituted for the first and an epistle to the reader was added which implied the play had never been publicly performed. The quarto is generally believed to be based on Shakespeare's FOUL PAPERS, although such critics as Kenneth Palmer and W. W. Greg have argued that it is based on a corrected manuscript, or FAIR COPY. This edition and the FOLIO edition of 1623 are the only two known texts of the play. The Folio text, although it is thought to be based on the quarto of 1609 as well as an original manuscript, contains numerous variations, including an additional forty-five lines and a prologue. While most editors of the play use the two texts in conjunction, a preference is given to the quarto, which is generally conceded to be a slightly more authoritative edition because of possible COMPOSITOR's errors in the Folio. Modern critical opinion generally concurs that Shakespeare is the sole author of *Troilus and Cressida*, but some earlier scholars argued that portions of the play—particularly the prologue, epilogue, and last few scenes—are quite uncharacteristic of Shakespeare and were probably written by another playwright. George Steevens, for example, attributed Pandarus's epilogue to an earlier version of the play or to an extemporization by an actor. More recent scholarship, how-

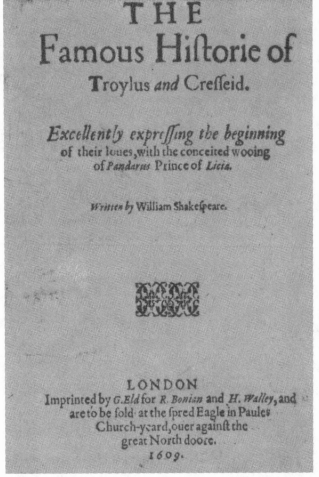

Title page of the quarto of Troilus and Cressida *(1609).*

ever, rejects such hypotheses and, at most, regards the epilogue as Shakespeare's own emendation—an argument most clearly enunciated by Nevill Coghill. The circumstances surrounding the placement of *Troilus and Cressida* in the Folio of 1623 have significant bearing on the question of the play's genre classification. The editors of the Folio originally intended to place *Troilus and Cressida* among the tragedies, but when a copyright problem arose, the play was temporarily deleted from the volume and excluded from the table of contents. Later, when permission to use the play had been granted, the editors placed it in the gap between the histories and the tragedies, thus adding to the subsequent critical confusion regarding its genre.

SOURCES: That Shakespeare was familiar with the legend of Troy and the story of Cressida is evident by the frequent reference made to them throughout his work. He had a wide variety of sources which contained the story available to him and it is therefore somewhat difficult to ascertain exactly which of these he may have used and to what extent he used them in retelling this well-known tale. OVID's *Metamorphosis,* for instance, was almost certainly an influence on Shakespeare's *Troilus and Cressida,* as it was on many of his other writings.

Yet certain elements of *Troilus and Cressida* indicate that Shakespeare probably made use of several specific sources when he wrote the play.

For the war plot, scholars believe that Shakespeare relied most heavily on William Caxton's *The Recuyell of the Historyes of Troye* (1471), an English translation of the story of the Trojan War that had been passed down from the Middle Ages. Caxton's account, like most of the medieval versions, glorified the elements of chivalric honor and was sympathetic towards the Trojans. Another possible source for the war plot of Shakespeare's play is John Lydgate's *Troy Book* (c. 1412-1420), which is quite similar to Caxton's account. A more ancient treatment of the Trojan War is, of course, Homer's *Iliad,* which is more favorable toward the Greek cause. There has been considerable debate over which translation of Homer Shakespeare might have read, for at the time there were only two English versions of the epic, and the rest were either in Latin or French. The most important of these English translations was George Chapman's *Seven Books of the Iliad* (1598), which most critics agree Shakespeare used in writing *Troilus and Cressida.*

The love story in *Troilus and Cressida,* most scholars concur, is derived primarily from Geoffrey Chaucer's poem *Troilus and Criseyde* (c. 1385). Critics have noted, however, that Shakespeare's portrayal of Cressida is less sympathetic than Chaucer's treatment. One explanation for this discrepancy in character is that readers between the time of Chaucer and Shakespeare came to see Cressida as the embodiment of all unfaithful women. Evidence of this transformation of Cressida's reputation can be found in Robert Henryson's *Testament of Cressid* (1532), which focuses on the guilt and retribution of the heroine, and, it is thought, had a great influence on the Elizabethan—and probably the Shakespearean—view of her character.

CRITICAL HISTORY: *Troilus and Cressida* has puzzled and disturbed critics as perhaps no other Shakespearean play. John S. P. Tatlock referred to it as "the chief problem in Shakespearean scholarship," and, indeed, the critical history reveals that scholars have continually sought to resolve the play's difficulties. Critics have offered various explanations for the drama's perplexing characterization, satiric and pessimistic mood, unusual form, philosophical speeches, and generic classification in their efforts to solve this problem. The divergent opinions expressed in three hundred years of criticism, however, suggest that the exact nature of the problems the play presents is itself a puzzle.

The problem of Cressida's character was a frequent concern for some of the play's earliest commentators. The Restoration poet and playwright John Dryden believed *Troilus and Cressida* to be one of Shakespeare's earliest works and saw such confusion in it that he altered the story and produced his own version of the play. Dryden could not understand why Shakespeare allowed the unfaithful Cressida to go unpunished or why the titular figures of the tragedy were left alive, so he changed the play's outcome accordingly. Later, in the eighteenth century, Charlotte Lennox expressed a similar concern for Shakespeare's failure to punish Cressida, whom she described as "a compleat Jilt." Elizabeth Griffith praised Cressida for her prudent hesitance to reveal her love to Troilus, but also found her character to be, overall, "a bad one." Samuel Johnson referred to both Cressida and Pandarus as "vicious characters" who "sometimes disgust, but cannot corrupt," for they are both "detested and contemned."

The moral condemnation of Cressida continued in the Romantic criticism of the nineteenth century, although it became more a subject of peripheral commentary than a central concern. Nonetheless, August Wilhelm Schlegel's indictment of Cressida was no less severe. He regarded her as a "treacherous beauty" who pretended to be chaste only to excite her victims. Schlegel's assessment of Cressida was later supported by G. G. Gervinus in his analysis of the scenes in which Cressida coquettishly manipulates her lovers. William Hazlitt, however, thought Cressida was less scheming than did Schlegel and Gervinus and attributed her actions instead to the fickleness of an "unpractised jilt."

Yet the focal point of the criticism of the Romantics—particularly the German Romantics—was not the moral integrity of Cressida's character, but the problem of satire and irony in the play itself. They thus sought to make sense of *Troilus and Cressida* by considering Shakespeare's satiric intent. Schlegel believed that Shakespeare was parodying not "the venerable Homer," but rather the chivalric romances from which he drew his story. Johann Wolfgang von Goethe, in comparing Homer's *Iliad* with Shakespeare's *Troilus and Cressida,* made an analogy between the lofty eagle and the lowly owl; he maintained that Shakespeare's play compared with Homer's poem suggests neither "parody nor travesty," but merely presents two contrasting subjects from nature. Hermann Ulrici related the problem of satire to Shakespearean ethics and contended that Shakespeare was doing more than simply ridiculing the chivalric heroes derived from ancient legends. *Troilus and Cressida,* said Ulrici, is an "instructive satire" that offers a warning against the elevation of the morally deficient ancient Greek culture above the "true moral perfection" of Christianity. For G. G. Gervinus, the question of satirical intent was more complicated. Gervinus explored whether Shakespeare was indeed parodying Homer or other writers, but concluded that the ambiguity of the play's conclusion prevented any definitive answers. Late in the nineteenth century, Frederick S. Boas suggested that Shakespeare was satirizing George Chapman, the English translator of the *Iliad* and Shakespeare's "rival poet."

Gervinus also asserted that in parodying the events of the Trojan War and subjecting its heroes to derisive mockery, Shakespeare deprived both sides of any moral cause for their struggle. On the other hand, Samuel Taylor Coleridge contended that in *Troilus and Cressida* Shakespeare dramatically opposed the purer morals of the Trojans with the sensual corruptions of the Greeks. Coleridge's emphasis on the contrasting values of the Greeks and Trojans was treated more fully by G. Wilson Knight and later critics and became one of the most important interpretive approaches to the play in the twentieth century.

Toward the end of the nineteenth century, Denton J. Snider discerned in *Troilus and Cressida* the clearest statement of Shakespeare's ethical philosophy found in any of his plays. Snider said that *Troilus and Cressida* was of particular interest because it offered an interfusion of the literature of Homer and Shakespeare. He maintained that it contained the same "ethical germ" as Homer's *Iliad,* especially in Ulysses's speeches on degree and reflection, which, he argued, reveal a strong element of Hegelian thought and assert that the values of the social order should be upheld over individual will. This dichotomy between public and private values was also perceived in the twentieth century by various critics, including H. B. Charlton, who compared *Troilus and Cressida* to *Henry IV* and *Henry V* in its espousal of social order over the will of the individual. Snider also commented that the first three acts of the play present a movement from chaotic disjunction toward harmonious unity, but that the last two acts move from union to disruption and conflict. Snider's interpretation of *Troilus and Cressida* is particularly noteworthy because of the full consideration he gave to the philosophic problems raised by Ulysses's speeches, a critical emphasis common in twentieth-century interpretations of the play.

Also in the latter part of the nineteenth century, several critics sought to explain *Troilus and Cressida* as a reflection of Shakespeare's personal life. Pointing to the play's cynicism, disillusionment, and misogyny, these critics argued that the dark tone of the play paralleled Shakespeare's despairing state of mind at the time of its composition. Edward Dowden referred to *Troilus and Cressida* as "the comedy of disillusion" and said that Shakespeare, while in this mood of "contemptuous depreciation of life," was "spoilt" as a writer of comedies. George Brandes focused on the character of Cressida in his biographical analysis of the play. He noted Cressida's resemblance to other coquettes in Shakespeare's work and postulated that the dramatist's scathing characterization of her indicates a personal disillusion and disgust with feminine inconstancy and a strong tone of misogyny. E. K. Chambers, writing in the first decade of the twentieth century, believed that in *Troilus and Cressida* "a disillusioned Shakespeare" turned his back on his former ideals of heroism and romance. Although many critics have continued to stress the pessimistic nature of *Troilus and Cressida*, the validity of these conjectures concerning the influence of Shakespeare's personal mood on the tenor of the play have often been challenged by twentieth-century critics.

The strongest opponents of the biographical interpretations of *Troilus and Cressida* were those critics who offered new, more deterministic explanations for the cynicism of the play. These commentators examined at length the source materials or dramatic form which Shakespeare followed in composing *Troilus and Cressida* and generally concluded that Shakespeare had little freedom in determining the tone of the play. John S. P. Tatlock, in presenting a detailed analysis of Shakespeare's sources, contended that *Troilus and Cressida* is not as gloomy as the biographical critics believed, for those elements of the play that reflect the greatest bitterness were not invented by Shakespeare, but can be found in his sources. Tatlock further stated that, given these source materials, Shakespeare's treatment of the heroes and lovers is perfectly understandable, if not inevitable. William Witherle Lawrence came to a similar conclusion, remarking that contemporary familiarity with the conclusion of the story demanded that Shakespeare's *Troilus and Cressida* end unhappily.

Oscar James Campbell also rejected the assertions of the biographical critics, but found his explanation for the play's pessimistic tone not in its sources, but in its genre. Campbell argued that in writing *Troilus and Cressida,* Shakespeare was imitating a new dramatic genre, "comicall satyre," which had recently developed in England. He maintained that all forms of satire necessarily suggest disillusionment and cynicism, but that this should not lead critics to making "unjustified inferences" about Shakespeare's mood when he wrote *Troilus and Cressida*. The play's troublesome ending, Campbell explained, is also in accord with the dramatic conventions of satiric comedy. Campbell's study is particularly important to the critical history of *Troilus and Cressida* because it offered a resolution to many of the problems in the drama that had perplexed earlier scholars. Even so, Franklin M. Dickey later charged that Campbell had failed to account for the tragic tone of the play.

By identifying *Troilus and Cressida* as a comical satire, Campbell also claimed to have resolved the difficulty of the play's genre classification—a problem that has existed ever since the first editions, published in Shakespeare's time, referred to it variously as a history and a comedy. As noted above, the compilers of the 1623 Folio of Shakespeare's plays placed *Troilus and Cressida* between the histories and the tragedies, further confusing scholars seeking a definitive categorization. Critics have subsequently argued for the placement of the play in each genre. John Dryden believed it to be a tragedy, but rewrote the story to make it more tragic. Other critics, like Heinrich Heine, contended that while the play is not purely a tragedy, it nonetheless has a pervading tragic tone. Still others, including Denton J. Snider and John S. P. Tatlock, noted *Troilus and Cressida*'s affinity to the history plays, Tatlock remarking that there is "absolutely no essential difference" between it and *Henry IV*. Coleridge, while stating that there is no Shakespearean play which is harder to characterize, placed it between Shakespeare's ancient history plays and his more "legendary plays." Many scholars have called it a comedy, if only because, as S. C. Sen Gupta contended, it lacks the depth and dignity of tragedy. William Witherle Lawrence classified *Troilus and Cressida* as a "problem comedy," because it clearly was not a tragedy and, on the other hand, was too serious and analytic to fit the traditional description of comedy. Northrop Frye discovered strong elements of history, tragedy, and comedy combined in the play. It would seem that despite Campbell's generic classification of *Troilus and Cressida* there has never been a critical consensus on its specific dramatic type.

G. Wilson Knight, in his influential essay on *Troilus and Cressida,* also sought to offer explanations of the play's perplexities, but in a considerably different manner than Campbell. Knight focused on the language and dramatic meaning of the play. Developing the suggestion made earlier by Coleridge that the Greeks and Trojans present an opposition of values, Knight argued that the Greeks reflect a reasoning but cynical intellect, while the Trojans represent romantic faith and emotional intuition. He further stated that Shakespeare intended the Trojans to possess more noble human values than the corrupt Greeks, and that the romantic Troilus champions "the fine values of humanity, fighting against the demon powers of cynicism." Knight's explication of the antithetical nature of the Greeks and Trojans subsequently became a common interpretation of the play, although critics varied the terms of the elements in opposition. Winifred M. T. Nowottny interpreted the dramatic conflict in *Troilus and Cressida* as the struggle between publicly generated Opinion and the Value created by autonomous imagination. She, like Knight and Albert Gérard, argued that Troilus's values indicate his superiority over the Greeks.

A number of other critics, however, while agreeing that there is an opposition between the Greeks and Trojans, rejected the proposition that the Trojans embody higher human values. L. C. Knights argued that the division between the Greek world and the Trojan world is one between objective and subjective perception. But he concluded that the objective social view of the Greeks is as faulty as the subjective perspective of Troilus. Similarly, Terence Eagleton argued that neither the values of the Trojans nor those of the Greeks are sufficient unto themselves, but that they should be merged to form a synthesis. D. A. Traversi, in his examination of the play, contended that the Trojans' idealism is based on sensuality and is therefore false, while the rationalism of the Greeks is incapable of promoting practical action. Thomas G. West contended that the dichotomy between the philosophies of the Trojan and Greek camps represents the division between two opposing views of truth. The introspective Trojans, said West, represent the Oriental perception of truth derived from a fixed faith in the estimations created by will, while the Greeks, who find truth in a knowledge of humanity and nature, represent Hellenic thought. Like other critics who rejected G. Wilson Knight's elevation of Trojan values, West judged that both perspectives are, by themselves, flawed.

Knight discovered another crucial interpretive issue in his analysis of *Troilus and Cressida*. He pointed out the images of time in the play and argued that, at the core of the work's philosophy, time can be seen as "the arch-enemy" and the destroyer of values. Several subsequent critics, including S. C. Sen Gupta, L. C. Knights, Norman Rabkin, and D. A. Traversi, concurred with Knight's interpretation of the role of time. Knights stated that time becomes the "ultimate reality," while Traversi noted the "supremacy of time" in the play. John Bayley saw Shakespeare's concern with time in more formal terms, arguing that while most Shakespearean plays project a sense of time both before and beyond the action of the play, *Troilus and Cressida* seems to be caught in a perpetual present. Thus, said Bayley, the play's characters are trapped in a timeless eternity that denies them both a future and a past. Other critics, however, were not so convinced with this emphasis on time. R. A. Yoder challenged Knight's reading of time in the play, contending that it is not the philosophically unifying theme but rather is merely a means for the characters to evade their present situation. Although many of Knight's conclusions about *Troilus and Cressida* have been rejected by later critics, his basic observations are considered invaluable in promoting new perspectives of the play's significance.

Una Ellis-Fermor's important analysis of *Troilus and Cressida* also offered a fresh interpretation of the play. Unlike most previous critics, Ellis-Fermor did not try to explain away the play's uneasy tone and chaotic form. She argued instead that *Troilus and Cressida* was perhaps one of "the greatest achievements" in expressing a phase of experience beyond the realm of drama. Ellis-Fermor maintained that the disordered form of the play is appropriate to the theme of discordance and disintegration, and she interpreted this as Shakespeare's "unity of intention." In her discussion of *Troilus and Cressida*'s well-known speeches on degree and value, she concluded that these concepts ultimately collapse because of humanity's denial of absolute value. Ellis-Fermor also observed the play's peculiar modernity, noting its affinity with the chaotic experience of modern civilization—a remark also made by a number of later critics.

The problem of order and value in the confused world of *Troilus and Cressida* has been a major focus of the criticism during the last forty years, and most critics, like Ellis-Fermor, have looked to the Trojans' discussion of value and Ulysses's speeches on degree and reflection to resolve this question. Norman Rabkin argued that *Troilus and Cressida* demonstrates that value exists neither in subjective will nor intrinsically in the object, but in time's influence on that object. Terence Eagleton discussed the problem of "mediation" in the play, noting that many of the values in *Troilus and Cressida* are created by others, which thus denies the possibility of any absolute standards. Richard D. Fly viewed the problem of mediation, or "the middleman," as one of Shakespeare's foremost concerns in *Troilus and Cressida*. Richard C. Harrier maintained that the theme of the play is the interrelation of value and honor,

and he proposed that the cynical Thersites and the imaginative Troilus can be seen as antithetical opposites in the struggle to establish value and honor. Harrier also discussed the contradictions in Troilus's logic in determining value, an issue also treated by Albert Gérard. Gérard stated that the contradictions inherent in Troilus's values become increasingly apparent as they gradually disintegrate. J. Hillis Miller treated Troilus's contradictions in a considerably different manner. In Troilus's reaction to Cressida's unfaithfulness, Hillis Miller detected the presence of two contradictory language systems generating a doubling of reason which also reveals itself as madness. Johannes Kleinstück observed that many of the characters' actions ultimately contradict their words, and he particularly noted how Ulysses subverts the very hierarchy of degree that he espouses in his speeches.

The clash between social values and individual will in *Troilus and Cressida*, which Denton J. Snider had discerned in the nineteenth century, has also received considerable critical attention in recent years. Eagleton interpreted the play as presenting a conflict between social responsibility and individual authenticity. Although Eagleton believed that Troilus's willful individualism is necessarily tragic, he nonetheless contended that such a position at least allows Troilus an integrity and authenticity which would otherwise be deprived by a repressive social mechanism. R. A. Yoder took an even dimmer view of the values of the social order in *Troilus and Cressida*, describing that system as an absolute authority which swallows up all individual interests for the sake of the war. Not only is love sacrificed to the absolute state, Yoder claimed, but it becomes sublimated to the demands of duty to the state.

The issue of Cressida's character also resurfaced as a concern in later criticism of the play. Most critics sought not to condemn her, but to defend her or, at least, to declare her not responsible for her actions and to place the blame instead on her environment. Earlier in the century, Tucker Brooke had stated that *Troilus and Cressida* is a study of the effect of environment on character and viewed Cressida as a "flower growing in the Trojan slime." In the 1960s, Barbara Heliodora C. de M. F. de Almeida developed Brooke's suggestion in an analysis of Cressida and her war-torn setting. She concluded that the world of *Troilus and Cressida* is more thoroughly corrupted than that of any other Shakespearean play and that none of its characters—including Cressida—possesses moral responsibility. Jan Kott echoed a similar sentiment, calling Cressida a victim of the long war and a distinctly modern persona, as well as "one of the most amazing [of Shakespeare's] characters."

Troilus and Cressida's affinities with the modern era were also noted by Northrop Frye, who had theorized that Shakepearean comedy usually culminates in the establishment of a new society or a sense of deliverance. *Troilus and Cressida*, said Frye, frustrates this comic movement toward deliverance and suggests instead that reality is partly illusory and that illusion is partly reality—a position which he noted is opposed to the spirit of Shakespeare's romantic comedies. He also stated that the play seems to present a secular version of the fall of man, which results in disillusionment but, nevertheless, serves as a starting point for a "genuine myth of deliverance."

The various interpretive problems posed by *Troilus and Cressida* have not received any lasting solutions. There is very little critical consensus on any of the play's more troubling aspects, and one could perhaps conclude that the only definitive interpretation of the play that can be made is that there is not one. Kenneth Muir has explained that one of the reasons for the wide divergence of critical response to *Troilus and Cressida* lies in the play's constantly shifting point of view and plurality of themes. Muir said that while the fusing of these themes required Shakespeare's extraordinary imaginative power, "the real problem about the play is the failure of most critics to appreciate it."

JOHN DRYDEN   (essay date 1679)

[*Dryden, the leading poet and playwright of Restoration England, helped formulate the Neoclassical view of Shakespeare as an irregular genius whose native talent overcame his ignorance of the proper "rules" and language for serious drama. He was also instrumental in establishing Shakespeare's reputation as the foremost English dramatist, and his assessment of Shakepeare influenced critics well into the following century. In the preface to his adaptation of* Troilus and Cressida *(1679), excerpted below, Dryden asserts that* Troilus and Cressida *is one of Shakespeare's earliest plays and says that although it contains some evidence of "the admirable Genius of the Author; I undertook to remove that heap of Rubbish, under which many excellent thoughts lay wholly bury'd." He also discerns a confusion in the latter part of Shakespeare's play, complaining that Cressida is not punished for her infidelity and that the titular heroes of the tragedy are both left alive. In Dryden's "new model'd" plot, Cressida, while remaining true to Troilus, kills herself, and Troilus is slain by Achilles. He also claims that he has added, deleted, and "improv'd" certain characters in the play and reordered the scenes to provide greater coherence.*]

In the Age of that Poet [Aeschylus], the *Greek* tongue was arriv'd to its full perfection; they had then amongst them an exact Standard of Writing, and of Speaking: The *English* Language is not capable of such a certainty; and we are at present so far from it, that we are wanting in the very Foundation of it, a perfect Grammar. Yet it must be allow'd to the present Age, that the tongue in general is so much refin'd since *Shakespear's* time, that many of his words, and more of his Phrases, are scarce intelligible. And of those which we understand some are ungrammatical, others course; and his whole stile is so pester'd with Figurative expressions, that it is as affected as it is obscure. 'Tis true, that in his later Plays he had worn off somewhat of the rust; but the Tragedy which I have undertaken to correct, was, in all probability, one of his first endeavours on the Stage.

The Original story was Written by one *Lollius* a *Lombard,* in Latin verse, and Translated by *Chaucer* into *English:* intended I suppose a Satyr on the Inconstancy of Women: I find nothing of it among the Ancients; not so much as the name *Cressida* once mention'd. *Shakespear,* (as I hinted) in the Aprenticeship of his Writing, model'd it into that Play, which is now called by the name of *Troilus* and *Cressida;* but so lamely is it left to us, that it is not divided into Acts: which fault I ascribe to the Actors, who Printed it after *Shakespear's* death; and that too, so carelessly, that a more uncorrect Copy I never saw. For the Play it self, the Author sems to have begun it with some fire; the Characters of *Pandarus* and *Thersites,* are promising enough; but as if he grew weary of his task, after an Entrance or two, he lets 'em fall: and the later part of the Tragedy is nothing but a confusion of Drums and Trumpets, Excursions and Alarms. The chief persons, who give name to the Tragedy, are left alive: *Cressida* is false, and is not punish'd. Yet after all, beause the Play was *Shakespear's,* and that

there appear'd in some places of it, the admirable Genius of the Author; I undertook to remove that heap of Rubbish, under which many excellent thoughts lay wholly bury'd. Accordingly, I new model'd the Plot; threw out many unnecessary persons; improv'd those Characters which were begun, and left unfinish'd: as *Hector, Troilus, Pandarus* and *Thersites;* and added that of *Andromache.* After this, I made with no small trouble, an Order and Connection of all the Scenes; removing them from the places where they were inartificially set: and though it was impossible to keep 'em all unbroken, because the Scene must be sometimes in the City, and sometimes in the Camp, yet I have so order'd them that there is a coherence of 'em with one another, and a dependence on the main design: no leaping from *Troy* to the *Grecian* Tents, and thence back again in the same Act; but a due proportion of time allow'd for every motion. I need not say that I have refin'd his Language, which before was obsolete; but I am willing to acknowledge, that as I have often drawn his English nearer to our times, so I have sometimes conform'd my own to his: & consequently, the Language is not altogether so pure, as it is significant. The Scenes of *Pandarus* and *Cressida,* of *Troilus* and *Pandarus,* of *Andromache* with *Hector* and the Trojans, in the second Act, are wholly *New:* together with that of *Nestor* and *Ulysses* with *Thersites;* and that of *Thersites* with *Ajax* and *Achilles.* I will not weary my reader with the Scenes which are added of *Pandarus* and the Lovers, in the Third; and those of *Thersites,* which are wholly alter'd: but I cannot omit the last Scene in it, which is almost half the Act, betwixt *Troilus* and *Hector.* The occasion of raising it was hinted to me by Mr. [Thomas] *Betterton:* the contrivance and working of it was my own. They who think to do me an injury, by saying that it is an imitation of the Scene betwixt *Brutus* and *Cassius* [in *Julius Caesar,* IV. iii], do me an honour, by supposing I could imitate the incomparable *Shakespear:* but let me add, that if *Shakespears* Scene, or that faulty Copy of it in *Amintor* and *Melantius* had never been, yet *Euripides* had furnish'd me with an excellent example in his *Iphigenia,* between *Agamemnon* and *Menelaus:* and from thence indeed, the last turn of it is borrow'd. (pp. 11-13)

> *John Dryden, in a preface to "Troilus & Cressida; or, Truth Found Too Late, a Tragedy," in his* Dryden: The Dramatic Works, Vol. V, *edited by Montague Summers, 1932. Reprint by Gordian Press, 1968, pp. 11-28.*

ALEXANDER POPE   (essay date 1725)

[*Pope, the most eminent poet of the English Augustan period, edited* The Works of William Shakespeare, Collated and Corrected *(1725), an edition that reveals his liberal textual additions and omissions made in an effort to correct and standardize Shakespeare's style according to the editor's interpretations. Pope's freedom with Shakespeare's plays, including his interpolations in* Troilus and Cressida, *was quickly challenged by Lewis Theobald (1726). In the headnote to his edition of* Troilus and Cressida, *excerpted below, Pope disagrees with Dryden's assertion that the play is one of Shakespeare's first efforts (see excerpt above, 1679), contending instead that the political and moral content of the play suggests that it is one of his last.*]

Before this Play of *Troilus and Cressida* printed in 1609 is a Bookseller's preface, showing that first impression to have been before the Play had been acted, and that it was published without *Shakespeare's* knowledge from a copy that had fallen into the Bookseller's hands. Mr. *Dryden* thinks this one of the first of our Author's plays. But on the contrary, it may be judg'd from the foremention'd Preface that it was one of his last; and the great number of observations, both moral and politick (with which this piece is crowded more than any other of his), seems to confirm my opinion. (pp. 417-18)

> Alexander Pope, in an extract from Shakespeare, the Critical Heritage: 1693-1733, Vol. 2, edited by Brian Vickers, Routledge & Kegan Paul, 1974, pp. 417-18.

LEWIS THEOBALD   (essay date 1726)

[Theobald, a dramatist and classical scholar, was one of the most important editors of Shakespeare's plays in the first half of the eighteenth century. Although his reputation as a Shakespearean editor declined after his death and the value of his work remains a question today, he nonetheless contributed significant emendations which have been adopted by modern editors. His adaptations of Shakespeare's plays, revised to adhere to Neoclassical dramatic rules, have been less well received. Theobald's Shakespeare Restored; or, A Specimen of the Many Errors as well committed, as unamended, by Mr. Pope in his late edition of this Poet (1726) was a response to Alexander Pope's interpolations in his edition of Shakespeare's works (see excerpt above, 1725); Pope responded to Theobald's charges by caricaturing him as "the King of Dullness" in The Dunciad. In his comments below, Theobald challenges Pope's editorial integrity by charging him with having "expung'd the Name of ARISTOTLE and substituted in its place graver Sages" to conceal an anachronism in Troilus and Cressida. Theobald contends that Shakespeare's anachronisms are "the Effect of Poetick Licence in him rather than Ignorance." The following excerpt begins with Theobald citing the passage in question from Pope's edition of Troilus and Cressida.]

> Paris and Troilus, you have Both said well:
> And on the Cause and Question now in hand
> Have gloss'd but superficially, not much
> Unlike Young Men, whom GRAVER SAGES think
> Unfit to hear moral Philosophy.

The EDITOR [Pope], I remember, in his Preface, speaking of the Method taken in his Ediiton, tells us that The Various Readings are fairly put in the Margin, so that every one may compare them; and those he has preferr'd into the Text are CONSTANTLY . . . upon Authority. I heartily beg the Pardon of this Gentleman, if, thro' Ignorance, I shall assert a Falsehood here, in being bold to say that This may be call'd an Exception to his Rule, that Graver Sages is preferr'd into the Text without any Authority, and that all the printed Copies read the Passage thus:

> —not much
> Unlike Young Men, whom ARISTOTLE thought
> Unfit to hear moral Philosophy.
>
> [II. ii. 165-67]

'Tis certain indeed that Aristotle was at least 800 Years subsequent in Time to Hector, and therefore the Poet [Shakespeare] makes a remarkable Innovation upon Chronology. But Mr. POPE will have this to be One of those palpable Blunders which the Illiteracy of the first Publishers of his Works has father'd upon the Poet's Memory, and is of Opinion that it could not be of our Author's penning, it not being at all credible, that these could be the Errors of any Man who had the least Tincture of a School, or the least Conversation with such as had. 'Tis for this Reason, and to shelter our Author from such an Absurdity, that the Editor has expung'd the Name of ARISTOTLE and substituted in its place graver Sages. But, with Submission, even herein he has made at best but half a Cure. If the Poet must be fetter'd down strictly to the Chronology of Things it

is every whit as absurd for Hector to talk of PHILOSOPHY as for him to talk of Aristotle. We have sufficient Proofs that Pythagoras was the first who invented the Word Philosophy and call'd himself Philosopher: and he was near 600 Years after the Date of Hector, even from his beginning to flourish. 'Tis true, the Thing which we now understand by Philosophy was then known, but it was only till then call'd knowledge and Wisdom. But to dismiss this Point, I believe this Anachronism of our Poet (and perhaps all the Others that he is guilty of), was the Effect of Poetick Licence in him rather than Ignorance.

It has been very familiar with the Poets, of the Stage especially, upon a Supposition that their Audience were not so exactly inform'd in Chronology to anticipate the Mention of Persons and Things before either the first were born or the latter thought of. SHAKESPEARE, again, in the same Play compares the Nerves of AJAX with those of bull-bearing MILO of Crotona [II. iii. 247], who was not in Being till 600 Years afer that Greek, and was a Disciple of Pythagoras. Again, Pandarus, at the Conclusion of the Play talks of a Winchester-Goose: indeed, it is in an Address to the Audience, and then there may be an Allowance and greater Latitude for going out of Character. (pp. 433-34)

> Lewis Theobald, in an extract from Shakepeare, the Critical Heritage: 1693-1733, Vol. 2, edited by Brian Vickers, Routledge & Kegan Paul, 1974, pp. 426-42.

[CHARLOTTE LENNOX]   (essay date 1754)

[Lennox was an American-born novelist and Shakespearean scholar who compiled Shakespear Illustrated (1754), a three-volume edition of translated texts of the sources used by Shakespeare in twenty-two of his plays, including some analyses of the ways in which he used these sources. In her consideration of Troilus and Cressida, Lennox compares Shakespeare's characters with those of Geoffrey Chaucer's Troylus and Crysede, stating that Shakespeare's Cressida is "a compleat Jilt" who does not receive "due Reward of her Crimes." She perceives this failure to punish Cressida as "an unpardonable Fault" in Shakespeare's judgment, a point also noted by John Dryden (1679). Lennox's condemnation of Cressida is representative of many eighteenth- and nineteenth-century Shakespearean commentators, including Samuel Johnson (1765), August Wilhelm Schlegel (1808), William Hazlitt (1817), and G. G. Gervinus (1849-50). However, such harsh appraisals of Cressida have been questioned by E. K. Chambers (1907), who interprets her as more weak than wanton, and by Tucker Brooke (1928), Barbara Heliodora C. de M. F. de Almeida (1964), Jan Kott (1964), and D. A. Traversi (1968), who explained her as a victim of her environment.]

The Loves of Troilus and Cressida are, in all the Circumstances, exactly copied from Chaucer; but these Circumstances are intirely detached from the rest of the Play, and produce no event worthy our Attention.

Troilus and Cressida give Name to the Tragedy, and, by Consequence, are the most considerable Persons in it; yet Troilus is left alive, and Cressida, too scandalous a Character to draw our Pity, does not satisfy that Detestation her Crimes raise in us by her Death, but escaping Punishment, leaves the play without a Moral, and absolutely deficient in poetical Justice.

The Manners of these two Persons, however, ought to escape the general Charge of Inequality.

Troilus, who is darawn exactly after Chaucer, is every where consistent with his Character of a brave Soldier, and a passionate and faithful Lover.

From *Cressida*'s first and second Appearance we may easily guess what her future Conduct will be; the deep Art with which she conceals her passion for *Troilus*, her loose Conversation with her Uncle, her free Coquettry with the Prince, and her easy yielding to his Addresses, prepare us for her Falshood in the succeeding Part of the Play, and all together make up the Character of a compleat Jilt: Her not being punished is indeed an unpardonable Fault, and brings the greatest Imputation imaginable upon *Shakespear*'s Judgment, who could introduce so vicious a Person in a Tragedy, and leave her without the due Reward of her Crimes.

The Character of *Cressida* is much more consistent in *Shakespear* than *Chaucer*; the latter represents her wise, humble, and modest, nicely sensible of Fame, fond of her Country, not easily susceptible of Love, hard to be won, and rather betrayed than yielding to the Desires of her Lover.

With all these amiable Qualities to engage our Esteem and those alleviating Circumstances that attended her Fall with *Troilus*, we cannot, without Surprize, see her so soon changing her Love, violating her Vows, and basely prostituting her Honour to *Diomede*. The inequality of Manners here is very observable; but *Shakespear* in drawing her Character has avoided falling into the same Fault by copying *Chaucer* too closely, and *Cressida*, throughout the Play, is always equal and consistent with herself. (pp. 92-4)

> [Charlotte Lennox], "The Fable of 'Troilus and Cressida'," in her Shakespear Illustrated; or, The Novels and Histories, on Which the Plays of Shakespear Are Founded, Vol. III, 1754. Reprint by AMS Press Inc., 1973, pp. 89-100.

SAMUEL JOHNSON   (essay date 1765)

[*Johnson has long held an important place in the history of Shakespearean criticism. He is considered the foremost representative of moderate English Neoclassicism and is credited by some literary historians with freeing Shakespeare from the strictures of the three unities valued by strict Neoclassicists: that dramas should have a single setting, take place in less than twenty-four hours, and have a causally connected plot. More recent scholars portray him as a critic who was able to synthesize existing critical theory rather than as an innovative theoretician. Johnson was a master of Augustan prose style and a personality who dominated the literary world of his epoch. In the following excerpt, taken from his 1765 edition of* The Plays of William Shakespeare, *Johnson states that* Troilus and Cressida *is "more correctly written" than most of Shakespeare's other plays and that, while there is "little invention" in the story, the characters are diversified and exact, and the comic figures are "powerfully impressed." Johnson also refers to Cressida and Pandarus as "vicious characters" who are detested and condemned.*]

[*Troilus and Cressida*] is more correctly written than most of Shakespeare's compositions, but it is not one of those in which either the extent of his views or elevation of his fancy is fully displayed. As the story abounded with materials, he has exerted little invention; but he has diversified his characters with great variety, and preserved them with great exactness. His vicious characters sometimes disgust, but cannot corrupt, for both Cressida and Pandarus are detested and contemned. The comick characters seem to have been the favourites of the writer, they are of the superficial kind, and exhibit more of manners than nature, but they are copiously filled and powerfully impressed. (p. 938)

> Samuel Johnson, "Notes on Shakespeare's Plays: 'Troilus and Cressida'," in his The Yale Edition of the Works of Samuel Johnson: Johnson on Shakespeare, Vol. VIII, edited by Arthur Sherbo, Yale University Press, 1968, pp. 909-38.

[FRANCIS GENTLEMAN]   (essay date 1774)

[*Gentleman, an Irish actor and playwright, contributed the introduction to John Bell's 1774 edition of Shakespeare's plays. In the excerpt below, taken from that work, Gentleman states that the purpose of drama is to offer "instruction relished by amusement" and judges* Troilus and Cressida *"void of the essential requisites." He also detects various dramatic difficulties in the play, including the profusion of scenes, the strange blending of characters, and the ill-resolved conclusion.*]

The great end of every drama is, or should be, instruction relished by amusement; so far as any production fails of this, it fails in value. Judging similarly of *Troilus and Cressida*, it is a very censurable effusion of dramatic fancy; for except some very fine sentiments scattered up and down, it is void of the essential requisites; besides, characters are so oddly blended, the scenes are so multiplied, and the plot so very strangely wound up, that we think it stands but a poor chance of giving either public or private satisfaction.

> [Francis Gentleman], in an introduction to "Troilus and Cressida," in Bell's Edition of Shakespeare's Plays, Vol. VI by William Shakespeare, 1774. Reprint by Cornmarket Press, 1969, p. 155.

MRS. [ELIZABETH] GRIFFITH   (essay date 1775)

[*Griffith exemplifies the seventeenth- and eighteenth-century preoccupation with searching through Shakespeare's plays for set speeches and passages that could be read out of dramatic context for their own sake. Griffith, however, avoided the more usual practice of collecting and commenting on poetic "beauties" and concentrated instead on the "moral" subjects treated in the text. In the following excerpt, Griffith comments on the moral propriety of Cressida's concealment of her love for Troilus, but suggests that such sentiment might be inconsistent with her character, which is "unluckily a bad one."*]

Cressida's speech here [I. ii. 282-95], in reference to her wooer Troilus, contains very just reflections and prudent maxims for the conduct of women, in the dangerous circumstance of love. What she says, would become the utterance of the most virtuous matron, though her own character in this piece is unluckily a bad one. But our Author's genius teemed so fertile in document, that he was unable to restrain its impulse, and coolly wait for a fit opportunity of adapting the speaker to the speech. Shakespeare's faults arise from richness, not from poverty; they exceed, not fall short; his monsters never want a head, but have sometimes two. (p. 487)

> Mrs. [Elizabeth] Griffith, "'Troilus and Cressida'," in her The Morality of Shakespeare's Drama Illustrated, 1775. Reprint by Frank Cass & Co. Ltd., 1971, pp. 485-93.

GEORGE STEEVENS   (essay date 1793)

[*Steevens was an English scholar who collaborated with Samuel Johnson on a ten-volume edition of Shakespeare's works in 1773. The subsequent revision of this collection, along with Steevens's own edition of 1793, formed the textual basis for the first two*

Variorum editions of Shakespeare's plays. In his remarks on Troilus and Cressida, taken from his 1793 edition, Steevens contends that Shakepeare intended the play to conclude with the couplet spoken by Troilus, and that the closing speech by Pandarus is either a restoration from an earlier, non-Shakespearean version of the play, as Steevens suggests in an unexcerpted portion of his commentary, or an extemporization by the actor who played Pandarus.]

[The couplet at V. x. 30-1 in *Troilus and Cressida*] affords a full and natural close to the play; and though I once thought differently, I must now declare my firm belief that Shakespeare designed it should end here, and that what follows is either a subsequent and injudicious restoration from . . . [an] elder drama . . . or the nonsense of some wretched buffoon who represented Pandarus. When the hero of the scene was not only alive, but on the stage, our author would scarce have trusted the conclusion of his piece to a subordinate character whom he had uniformly held up to detestation. It is still less probable that he should have wound up his story with a stupid outrage to decency, and a deliberate insult on his audience.—But in several other parts of his drama I cannot persuade myself that I have been reading Shakespeare. (p. 596)

George Steevens, in an extract from Shakespeare, the Critical Heritage: 1774-1801, Vol. 6, edited by Brian Vickers, Routledge & Kegan Paul, 1981, pp. 595-96.

WILLIAM GODWIN   (essay date 1804)

[Godwin, an English novelist and political thinker, composed a biography of Chaucer and, as a publisher, printed Charles Lamb's Tales from Shakespeare. In the excerpt below, Godwin praises passages in Troilus and Cressida and Shakespeare's ability to rise "beyond all didactic morality" and create living characters.]

The historical play of *Troilus and Cressida* exhibits as full a specimen of the different styles in which this wonderful writer was qualified to excel, as is to be found in any of his works. A more poetical passage, if poetry consists in sublime picturesque and beautiful imagery, neither ancient nor modern times have produced, than the exhortation addressed by Patroclus to Achilles, to persuade him to shake off his passion for Polyxena, the daughter of Priam, and reassume the terrors of his military greatness.

Sweet, rouse yourself; and the weak wanton Cupid
Shall from your neck unloose his amorous fold,
And like a dew-drop from the lion's mane,
Be shook to air.

[III. iii. 222-25]

Never did morality hold a language more profound, persuasive and irresistible, than in Shakespear's Ulysses, who in the same scene, and engaged in the same cause with Patroclus, thus expostulates with the champion of the Grecian forces.

For emulation hath a thousand sons,
That one by one pursue. If you give way,
Or hedge aside from the direct forthright,
Like to an enter'd tide, they all rush by,
And leave you hindmost: there you lie,
Like to a gallant horse fallen in first rank,
For pavement to the abject rear, o'er-run
And trampled on. . . .
Then marvel not, thou great and complete man!

That all the Greeks begin to worship Ajax.
————The cry went once on thee,
And still it might, and yet it may again,
If thou wouldst not entomb thyself alive,
And case they reputation in thy tent.

[III. iii. 156-87]

But the great beauty of this play, as it is of all the genuine writings of Shakespear, beyond all didactic morality, beyond all mere flights of fancy, and beyond all sublime, a beauty entirely his own, and in which no writer ancient or modern can enter into competition with him, is that his men are men; his sentiments are living, and his characters marked with those delicate, evanescent, undefinable touches, which identify them with the great delineations of nature. The speech of Ulysses just quoted, when taken by itself, is purely an exquisite specimen of didactic morality; but when combined with the explanation given by Ulysses, before the entrance of Achilles, of the nature of his design, it becomes the attribute of a real man, and starts into life.—Achilles (says he)

————————stands in the entrance of his tent.
Please it our general to pass strangely by him,
As if he were forgot; and princes all,
Lay negligent and loose regard upon him:
I will come last: 'tis like, he'll question me,
Why such unplausive eyes are bent, why turn'd on him:
If so, I have derision med'cinable,
To use between your strangeness and his pride,
Which his own will shall have desire to drink.

[III. iii. 39-46]

When we compare the plausible and seemingly affectionate manner in which Ulysses addresses himself to Achilles, with the key which he here furnishes to his meaning, and especially with the epithet "derision," we have a perfect elucidation of his character, and must allow that it is impossible to exhibit the crafty and smooth-tongued politician in a more exact or animated style. The advice given by Ulysses is in its nature sound and excellent, and in its form inoffensive and kind; the name therefore of "derision" which he gives to it, marks to a wonderful degree the cold and self-centred subtlety of his character. (pp. 503-07)

William Godwin, "Sequel to 'Troilus and Creseide' by Robert Henryson—Tragedy of Shakespeare on the Subject," in his Life of Geoffrey Chaucer, the Early English Poet, Vol. I, second edition, 1804. Reprint by AMS Press Inc., 1974, pp. 486-515.

AUGUST WILHELM SCHLEGEL   (lecture date 1808)

[A prominent German Romantic critic, Schlegel holds a key place in the history of Shakespeare's reputation in European criticism. His translations of thirteen of the plays are still considered the best German editions of Shakespeare. Schlegel was also a leading spokesman for the Romantic movement, which permanently overthrew the Neoclassical contention that Shakespeare was a child of nature whose plays lacked artistic form. In the excerpt below, drawn from a lecture presented in 1808, Schlegel refers to Cressida as a "treacherous beauty" and says that, with the possible exception of Hector, Shakespeare did not intend the characters of Troilus and Cressida to receive much "esteem or sympathy." Schlegel also states that the play is "one continued irony of that crown of all heroic tales, the tale of Troy," a comment that anticipates later discussion of the drama's satirical nature by Hermann Ulrici (1839), G. G. Gervinus (1849-50), and Oscar James Campbell (1938). Schlegel further suggests that it was the medieval chavalric romances based on the Trojan War and not "the venerable Homer" that Shakespeare intended to satirize in Troilus and Cressida.]

Troilus and Cressida is the only play of Shakspeare which he allowed to be printed without being previously represented. It seems as if he here for once wished, without caring for theatrical effect, to satisfy the nicety of his peculiar wit, and the inclination to a certain guile, if I may say so, in the characterization. The whole is one continued irony of that crown of all heroic tales, the tale of Troy. The contemptible nature of the origin of the Trojan war, the laziness and discord with which it was carried on, so that the siege was made to last ten years, are only placed in clearer light by the noble descriptions, the sage and ingenious maxims with which the work overflows, and the high ideas which the heroes entertain of themselves and each other. Agamemnon's stately behaviour, Menelaus' irritation, Nestor's experience, Ulysses' cunning, are all productive of no effect; when they have at last arranged a single combat between the coarse braggart Ajax and Hector, the latter will not fight in good earnest, as Ajax is his cousin. Achilles is treated worst: after having long stretched himself out in arrogant idleness, and passed his time in the company of Thersites the buffoon, he falls upon Hector at a moment when he is defenceless, and kills him by means of his myrmidons. In all this let no man conceive that any indignity was intended to the venerable Homer. Shakspeare had not the *Iliad* before him, but the chivalrous romances of the Trojan war derived from *Dares Phrygius.* From this source also he took the love-intrigue of *Troilus and Cressida,* a story at one time so popular in England, that the name of Troilus had become proverbial for faithful and ill-requited love, and Cressida for female falsehood. The name of the agent between them, Pandarus, has even been adopted into the English language to signify those personages (*panders*) who dedicate themselves to similar services for inexperienced persons of both sexes. The endless contrivances of the courteous Pandarus to bring the two lovers together, who do not stand in need of him, as Cressida requires no seduction, are comic in the extreme. The manner in which this treacherous beauty excites while she refuses, and converts the virgin modesty which she pretends, into a means of seductive allurement, is portrayed in colours extremely elegant, though certainly somewhat voluptuous. Troilus, the pattern of lovers, looks patiently on, while his mistress enters into an intrigue with Diomed. No doubt, he swears that he will be revenged; but notwithstanding his violence in the fight next day, he does no harm to any one, and ends with only high sounding threats. In a word, in this heroic comedy, where, from traditional fame and the pomp of poetry, every thing seems to lay claim to admiration, Shakspeare did not wish that any room should be left, except, perhaps, in the character of Hector, for esteem and sympathy; but in this double meaning of the picture, he has afforded us the most choice entertainment. (pp. 418-19)

August Wilhelm Schlegel, "Criticisms on Shakspeare's Historical Dramas," in his A Course of Lectures on Dramatic Art and Literature, *edited by Rev. A. J. W. Morrison, translated by John Black, revised edition, 1846. Reprint by AMS Press, Inc., 1965, pp. 414-45.*

WILLIAM HAZLITT (essay date 1817)

[*Hazlitt is considered a leading Shakespearean critic of the English Romantic movement. A prolific essayist and critic on a wide range of subjects, Hazlitt remarked in the preface to his* Characters

of Shakespear's Plays, *first published in 1817, that he was inspired by the German critic August Wilhelm Schlegel and was determined to supplant what he considered the pernicious influence of Samuel Johnson's Shakespearean criticism. Hazlitt's criticism is typically Romantic in its emphasis on character studies. Unlike his fellow Romantic critic Samuel Taylor Coleridge, Hazlitt was a dramatic critic whose experience of Shakespeare in the theater influenced his interpretations. In his discussion of* Troilus and Cressida, *taken from the work mentioned above, Hazlitt praises Shakespeare's characterization of Cressida and Pandarus. He also compares the treatment of the story's characters by Shakespeare and Chaucer, concluding that while Chaucer was "deeply implicated in the affairs of his personages," Shakespeare was at once objective and uncommitted towards them.*]

[*Troilus and Cressida*] is one of the most loose and desultory of our author's plays: it rambles on just as it happens, but it overtakes, together with some indifferent matter, a prodigious number of fine things in its way. Troilus himself is no character: he is merely a common lover: but Cressida and her uncle Pandarus are hit off with proverbial truth. By the speeches given to the leaders of the Grecian host, Nestor, Ulysses, Agamemnon, Achilles, Shakespear seems to have known them as well as if he had been a spy sent by the Trojans into the enemy's camp—to say nothing of their affording very lofty examples of didactic eloquence. (p. 51)

The character of Hector, in a few slight indications which appear of it, is made very amiable. His death is sublime, and shews in a striking light the mixture of barbarity and heroism of the age. The threats of Achilles are fatal; they carry their own means of execution with them.

> Come here about me, you my myrmidons,
> Mark what I say.—Attend me where I wheel:
> Strike not a stroke, but keep yourselves in breath;
> And when I have the bloody Hector found,
> Empale him with your weapons round about,
> In fellest manner execute your arms.
> Follow me, sirs, and my proceeding eye.
>
> [V. vii. 1-7]

He then finds Hector and slays him, as if he had been hunting down a wild beast. There is something revolting as well as terrific in the ferocious coolness with which he singles out his prey: nor does the splendour of the achievement reconcile us to the cruelty of the means.

The characters of Cressida and Pandarus are very amusing and instructive. The disinterested willingness of Pandarus to serve his friend in an affair which lies next his heart is immediately brought forward. "Go thy way, Troilus, go thy way; had I a sister were a grace, or a daughter were a goddess, he should take his choice. O admirable man! Paris, Paris is dirt to him, and I warrant Helen, to change, would give money to boot" [I. ii. 235-39]. This is the language he addresses to his niece: nor is she much behind-hand in coming into the plot. Her head is as light and fluttering as her heart. "It is the prettiest villain, she fetches her breath so short as a new-ta'en sparrow" [III. ii. 33-4]. Both characters are originals, and quite different from what they are in Chaucer. In Chaucer, Cressida is represented as a grave, sober, considerate personage (a widow—he cannot tell her age, nor whether she has children or no) who has an alternate eye to her character, her interest, and her pleasure: Shakespear's Cressida is a giddy girl, an unpractised jilt, who falls in love with Troilus, as she afterwards deserts him, from mere levity and thoughtlessness of temper. She may be wooed and won to any thing and from any thing, at a moment's warning; the other knows very well what she would be at, and sticks to it, and is more governed by substantial reasons than by caprice or vanity. Pandarus again, in Chaucer's story, is a friendly sort of go-between, tolerably busy, officious, and forward in bringing matters to bear: but in Shakespear he has "a stamp exclusive and professional": he wears the badge of his trade; he is a regular knight of the game. The difference of the manner in which the subject is treated arises perhaps less from intention, than from the different genius of the two poets. There is no *double entendre* in the characters of Chaucer: they are either quite serious or quite comic. In Shakespear the ludicrous and ironical are constantly blended with the stately and the impassioned. We see Chaucer's characters as they saw themselves, not as they appeared to others or might have appeared to the poet. He is as deeply implicated in the affairs of his personages as they could be themselves. He had to go a long journey with each of them, and became a kind of necessary confidant. There is little relief, or light and shade in his pictures. The conscious smile is not seen lurking under the brow of grief or impatience. Every thing with him is intense and continuous—a working out of what went before.—Shakespear never committed himself to his characters. He trifled, laughed, or wept with them as he chose. He has no prejudices for or against them; and it seems a matter of perfect indifference whether he shall be in jest or earnest. According to him "the web of our lives is of a mingled yarn, good and ill together" [*All's Well That Ends Well*, IV. iii. 71-2]. His genius was dramatic, as Chaucer's was historical. He saw both sides of a question, the different views taken of it according to the different interests of the parties concerned, and he was at once an actor and spectator in the scene. If any thing, he is too various and flexible: too full of transitions, of glancing lights, of salient points. If Chaucer followed up his subject too doggedly, perhaps Shakespear was too volatile and heedless. The Muse's wing too often lifted him from off his feet. (pp. 54-6)

William Hazlitt, "'Troilus and Cressida'," in his Characters of Shakespear's Plays & Lectures on the English Poets, *Macmillan and Co. Limited, 1903, pp. 51-8.*

JOHANN WOLFGANG von GOETHE   (essay date 1824)

[*A distinguished poet, dramatist, and novelist, Goethe is considered the greatest German literary figure. His reverence for Shakespeare was inspired early in his career by his friendship with the German Romantic writer Johann Gottfried Herder. Many of Goethe's works bear Shakespeare's influence, particularly his first published drama,* Götz von Berlichingen mit der eisernen Hand (1773), *which is written in the manner of Shakespeare's history plays. In his discussion of* Troilus and Cressida, *first published in 1824, Goethe compares Shakespeare's play to Homer's* Iliad. *Using the analogy of the eagle and the owl—calling the former "lofty," the latter "base"—Goethe compares the "grand," unadorned style of Homer's poem and the lesser "romantic" style of* Troilus and Cressida. *He discerns "neither parody nor travesty," but two works of art that present a "parallelism in opposites" and illustrate the differences in "the intellectual fibre of two epochs." Goethe also states that the play's reliance on "secondhand narratives" renders it only "half-poetical," but that it nonetheless reveals sincerity and talent in its characterization.*]

A mighty eagle, of the period of Myron or Lysippus, grasping two serpents in its talons, has just alighted on a crag; its wings are still in motion, it is troubled in mind, because that writhing prey threatens danger to it. The snakes twist round its feet, their darting tongues hint at deadly fangs.

In contrast, an owl has perched on a stone wall, wings folded, its feet and claws strong; it has seized some mice, which curl their little tails weakly about its feet, hardly able to show by their faint squeaks that they are still alive.

Consider these two works of art side by side! Here is neither parody nor travesty, but an example of something that is by nature lofty and of something that is by nature base, both fashioned by the same master in the same noble style; it is a parallelism in opposites, which must necessarily please in the individual parts and astonish in the combination of them; the young sculptor would find here a significant theme.

A comparison of the *Iliad* with *Troilus and Cressida* leads to similar conclusions: here, too, there is neither parody nor travesty, but, as in the case [above], two subjects taken from nature were put in striking contrast with each other, so here are contrasted the intellectual fibre of two epochs. The Greek poem is in the grand style, self-restrained and self-sufficient, using only the essential, and, in description and simile, disdaining all ornament,—basing itself on noble myths and tradition. The English classic, on the other hand, one might consider a happy transposition and translation of the other great work into the romantic-dramatic style.

In this connection we should not forget, however, that this piece, like many another, is based on secondhand narratives, already rendered into prose, and only half-poetical.

Yet it is also quite original, as much so as if the ancient piece had never been at all; for it requires just as profound a sincerity, just as decided a talent, to depict for us similar personalities and characters with so light a touch and so lucid a meaning, and represent them for a later age with all the human traits of that age, which thus sees itself reflected in the guise of the ancient story. (pp. 521-22)

Johann Wolfgang von Goethe, in an excerpt, translated in parts by Harold N. Hillebrand and Randolph S. Bourne, in A New Variorum Edition of Shakespeare: "Troilus and Cressida," *Vol. 26, edited by Harold N. Hillebrand with T. W. Baldwin, J. B. Lippincott Company, 1953, pp. 521-22.*

SAMUEL TAYLOR COLERIDGE   (essay date 1834?)

[*Coleridge's lectures and writings on Shakespeare form a major chapter in the history of English Shakespearean criticism. As the channel for the critical ideas of the German Romantics and as an original interpreter of Shakespeare in the new spirit of Romanticism, Coleridge played a strategic role in overthrowing the last remains of the Neoclassical approach to Shakespeare and in establishing the modern view of the dramatist as a conscious artist and masterful portrayer of human character. Coleridge's remarks on Shakespeare come down to posterity largely as fragmentary notes, marginalia, and reports by auditors on the lectures, rather than in polished essays; consequently, the composition date of the following commentary on* Troilus and Cressida *is uncertain and is based on his death date. Coleridge notes the difficulty in classifying the dramatic genre of the play, but suggests that it bridges Shakespeare's more factual ancient history plays with his more fictitious legendary dramas, an observation later supported by Denton J. Snider (1890). Coleridge says that Shakespeare opposes "the inferior civilization but purer morals of the Trojans to the refinements, deep policy, but duplicity and sensual corruptions of the Greeks," an interpretation that is more fully treated in the twentieth century by G. Wilson Knight (1930), Winifred M. T. Nowottny (1954), Albert Gérard (1959), and Thomas G. West (1981). Coleridge also states that Shakespeare's "ruling impulse" was to shape the pagan heroes of Homer's* Iliad *into the "more featurely warriors of Christian chivalry" and give them substance in a romantic drama.*]

The *Troilus and Cressida* of Shakespeare can scarcely be classed with his Greek and Roman *history* dramas; but it forms an intermediate link between the fictitious Greek and Roman histories, which we may call legendary dramas, and the proper ancient histories; *ex. gr.*, between the *Pericles* or *Titus Andronicus* and the *Coriolanus, Julius Caesar*, etc. . . . But my present subject [is] . . . *Troilus and Cressida;* and I suppose that, scarcely knowing what to say of it, I by a cunning of instinct ran off to subjects on which I should find it difficult not to say too much, tho' certain after all I should still leave the better part unsaid, and the gleaning for others richer than my own harvest. Indeed, there is none of Shakespeare's plays harder to characterize. The name and the remembrances connected with it prepare us for the representation of attachment no less faithful than fervent on the side of the youth, and of sudden and shameless inconstancy on the part of the lady. And this, indeed, is the gold thread on which the scenes are strung, tho' often kept out of sight and out of mind by gems of greater value than itself. But as Shakespeare calls forth nothing from the mausoleum of history or the catacombs of tradition without giving or eliciting some permanent and general interest, brings forward no subject which he does not moralize or intellectualize, so here he has drawn in Cressida the portrait of a vehement *passion* that, having its true origin and proper cause in warmth of temperament, fastens on, rather than fixes to, some one object by liking and temporary preference. . . . (pp. 98-9)

This he has contrasted with the profound affection represented in Troilus, and alone worthy the name of love; affection, passionate indeed—swoln from the confluence of youthful instincts and youthful fancy, glowing in the radiance of hope newly risen, in short enlarged by the collective sympathies of nature—but still having a depth of calmer element in a will stronger than desire, more entire than choice, and which gives permanence to its own act by converting it into faith and duty. Hence with excellent judgement and with an excellence higher than mere judgement can give, at the close of the play, when Cressida has sunk into infamy below retrieval and beneath a hope, the same will, which had been the substance and the basis of his love, while the restless pleasures and passionate longings, like sea-waves, had tossed but on its surface,—the same moral energy snatches him aloof from all neighbourhood with her dishonor, from all lingering fondness and languishing regrets, while it rushes with him into other and nobler duties, and deepens the channel which his heroic brother's death had left empty for its collected flood. Yet another secondary and subordinate purpose he has inwoven with the two characters, that of opposing the inferior civilization but purer morals of the Trojans to the refinements, deep policy, but duplicity and sensual corruptions of the Greeks.

To all this, however, there is so little comparative projection given,—nay, the masterly group of Agamemnon, Nestor, Ulysses, and still more in advance, of Achilles, Ajax, and Thersites, so manifestly occupy the foreground that the subservience and vassalage of strength and animal courage to intellect and policy seem to be the lesson most often in our poet's view, and which he has taken little pains to connect with the former more interesting moral impersonated in the titular hero and heroine of the drama. But I am half inclined to believe that Shakespeare's main object, or shall I rather say, that his ruling impulse, was to translate the poetic heroes of paganism into the not less rude

but more intellectually vigorous, more *featurely* warriors of Christian chivalry, to substantiate the distinct and graceful profiles or outlines of the Homeric epic into the flesh and blood of the romantic drama—in short, to give a grand history-piece in the robust style of Albert Dürer.

The character of Thersites well deserves a more particular attention, as the Caliban [*The Tempest*] of demagogues' life—the admirable portrait of intellectual power deserted by all grace, all moral principle, all not momentary purpose; just wise enough to detect the weak head, and fool enough to provoke the armed fist of his betters; whom malcontent Achilles can inveigle from malcontent Ajax, under the condition that he shall be called on to do nothing but to abuse and slander and that he shall be allowed to abuse as much and as purulently as he likes—that is, as [he] can; in short, a mule, quarrelsome by the original discord of its nature, a slave by tenure of his own baseness, made to bray and be brayed, to despise and be despicable.—Ay, sir, but say what you will, he is a devilish clever fellow, tho' the best friends will fall out; but there was a time when Ajax thought he deserved to have a statue of gold erected to him, and handsome Achilles, at the head of the Myrmidons, gave no little credit to his 'friend, Thersites.' (pp. 99-100)

Samuel Taylor Coleridge, "Notes on the Comedies of Shakespeare: 'Troilus and Cressida'," in his Shakespearean Criticism, Vol. 1, *edited by Thomas Middleton Raysor, second edition, Dutton, 1960, pp. 97-100.*

HEINRICH HEINE   (essay date 1838)

[*Heine is considered one of the outstanding German poets of the nineteenth century. Although he wrote in the Romantic period, he sometimes imbued his work with a satirical tone antithetical to Romanticism. In his discussion of* Troilus and Cressida, *taken from an 1838 book of illustrations of Shakespeare's heroines, to which Heine added critical commentary, the critic contrasts the ancient Greek poets with Shakespeare, noting that while the Greeks sought to "glorify reality," Shakespeare looked "more into the depth of things" to discover "the hidden roots of appearances." He also considers the difficulties of determining the play's genre when using Aristotelian guidelines. Heine concludes that while* Troilus and Cressida *is neither a comedy nor a tragedy in the usual sense, "the muse of tragedy," Melpomene, is "everywhere perceptible in this play."*]

Troilus and Cressida is the only play in which Shakespeare introduces those same heroes chosen by Greek poets as the *dramatis personae* of their plays. Thus, while comparing these with the same characters described by the older poets, we get an insight into Shakespeare's method. Whilst the classic Greek poets seem to glorify reality, rising into idealism, our modern tragic poet peers more into the depths of things; he discovers the hidden roots of appearances by the keen edge of his spirit, laying bare before our eyes the silent soil wherein they repose. The ancient writers of tragedy, like the sculptors of old, strove after beauty and nobility, glorifying the form rather than that which the form contained, but Shakespeare aimed at truth and the underlying matter. He is thus a master in character-painting, which often causes him to verge on awkward caricature, whereby he divests the heroes of their bright armour and brings them before us in absurdly homely gear. Those writers who criticised *Troilus and Cressida* according to the rules drawn by Aristotle from the best Greek plays, must often have been in an awkward position, and apt to make ridiculous blunders. As a tragedy the play did not appear to them sufficiently earnest and pathetic, and all came to pass about as naturally as it does with us. The heroes behaved as foolishly and perhaps as barbarously as they do now, the hero in chief is a lout, and the heroine a common wench, of which we have examples enough among our near acquaintants . . . and even the most honoured names, celebrities of the heroic ages, such as the great Pelius Achilles, brave son of Thetis, what miserable appearances do they present. On the other hand the play could hardly rank as a comedy, for it teems with life, and there is a grand air about the wise speeches, as we perceive in the meditations of Ulysses, where he dwells on the necessity of authority, and which to this day merit close attention. (pp. 42-3)

No, *Troilus and Cressida* is neither a comedy nor a tragedy in the usual sense; this play belongs to no special kind of fiction, and still less can it be judged by any received standard; it is thoroughly Shakespearian. We can only testify to its general excellence; were we to criticise it individually, we should need the help of that new aesthetic science which has yet to be written.

By registering this play as a tragedy, I would show from the commencement of what importance I consider these titles. My old poetry-master in the school at Düsseldorff once wittily remarked: "those plays which breathe forth the melancholy spirit of Melpomene instead of Thalia's happy spirit, belong to the domain of tragedy." Perhaps I was thinking of this when I placed *Troilus and Cressida* among the tragedies. And in truth it is pervaded by a gleeful bitterness, a withering irony such as we never find in the plays of the comic muse. Rather is the muse of tragedy everywhere perceptible in this play, and her merriment and her jokes are a pretence. (pp. 44-5)

> *Heinrich Heine, "Cressida," in his* Heine on Shakespeare, *translated by Ida Benecke, Archibald Constable and Co., 1895, pp. 41-5.*

HERMANN ULRICI   (essay date 1839)

[*A German scholar, Ulrici was a professor of philosophy and the author of works on Greek poetry and Shakespeare. The following excerpt is from an English translation of his* Über Shakespeares dramatische Kunst, und sein Verhältniss zu Calderon und Göthe, *a work first published in 1839. This study exemplifies the "philosophical criticism" developed in Germany during the nineteenth century. The immediate sources for Ulrici's critical approach appear to be August Wilhelm Schlegel's conception of the play as an organic, interconnected whole and Georg Wilhelm Friedrich Hegel's view of drama as an embodiment of the conflict of historical forces and ideas. Unlike his fellow German Shakespearean critic G. G. Gervinus, Ulrici sought to develop a specifically Christian aesthetics, but one which, as he carefully points out in the introduction to the work mentioned above, in no way intrudes on "that unity of idea, which preeminently constitutes a work of art a living creation in the world of beauty." This Christian interpretation of Shakespeare's plays is particularly visible in Ulrici's comments on* Troilus and Cressida. *Ulrici says that the play is an examination of the profound moral differences between the ancient civilization of Greece and "the principles of modern Christendom." He asserts that the drama is an "instructive satire" and that Shakespeare is offering a warning against the "unqualified admiration" of Greek culture that might lead to the degradation of the "true moral perfection which Christianity archetypically sets before man." For other considerations of the use and effect of satire in* Troilus and Cressida, *see the excerpts by August Wilhelm Schlegel (1808), G. G. Gervinus (1849-50), Frederick S. Boas (1896), and Oscar James Campbell (1938).*]

The critics have pretty generally admitted the satirical tendency of ["Troilus and Cressida"], although they have overhastily contented themselves with this discovery, without inquiring further after the deep significance of the whole. It is something more than an amusing satire on the chivalry and heroism of *ancient* times, designed as a pendant to the Falstaffiad, to comfort the noble lords of the sixteenth century with the poor consolation that heroic knighthood fared no better than its modern counterpart. *Merely* to ridicule the great and noble, and throw it in the dirt in order to point the finger of derision at the stains which it has contracted by its fall, is a poor pleasure, such as Shakspeare never indulges in. If the satire were *merely* this, it could not have the excuse to plead in its behalf, that its purpose was to amend the ill manners and degraded spirit of the time, by holding up before it its own distorted image. We have, therefore, thought it necessary to protest at the very outset against what we conceive to be the mistake of others, who see nothing more in the piece than such satirical tendency.

But, in truth, Shakspeare has here employed the satirical element merely for the exhibition of a higher view, and one which is of universal importance. As many of his comedies, the "Merchant of Venice," for instance, "Measure for Measure," "Cymbeline," &c. possess an *historical* bearing, not merely in its general but also in its narrower sense—so far, *i.e.* as they pourtray life under its gravest, civil, and political aspects—so here the historical element is exalted to be the proper poetic centre of the whole work of art, and pervades it like a bright streak of sunshine, illuminating the world's history with a peculiar light and hue. The ground-idea, which, in our opinion, it is the object of Troilus and Cressida to bring under the contemplation of the *comic* view, is the profound and all-pervading difference, especially in its *moral* aspect, between the mental character and habits of Grecian antiquity, and the principles of modern Christendom. (pp. 333-34)

From this point, which is not more important in a moral than in an historical sense, does Shakspeare contemplate the ancient civilization of Greece as contrasted with the life and spirit of Christianity. To exhibit this opposition he takes the very basis of the former—the Trojan war—for the subject of a poem, but, as his particular position unquestionably justified him in doing, he throws altogether into the background its ideal import, and sketches it merely in its actual matter-of-fact details, though, as we must admit, not without some slight modifications. The Homeric hero is stripped bare of his poetic ideality, while, on the other hand, his moral weaknesses, which Homer notices no doubt, but, in the true spirit of a Greek, designates them, for the most part, as virtues, are brought forward in the strongest light. The pre-eminence which Homer's heroes owe to the corporeal advantages of strength and animal courage, appears in Shakspeare the rude and reckless right of the stronger; what, indeed, when not under the rule and guidance of mind, it invariably is. Agamemnon prides himself on his empty title of commander-in-chief, which, however, he does not possess even in Homer, since all the more distinguished of the Grecian heroes do exactly as they please. His dignity is merely in appearance, and to attain the object of his own wishes he is forced to condescend to all manner of artifice and meanness. Menelaus is a good-natured, thoughtless simpleton, who allows his own disgrace to be emblazoned on the banners of war, and wafted over the world. Nestor, the old chronicler, can do nothing but blurt out his stale maxims and old stories, which no one is willing to listen to over and over again. Ulysses is painted in the same colours that Homer represents him; he is the same subtle, shrewd, and ready genius, who imperceptibly wins others to his own will: the only difference is, that his fine-spun devices rarely lead to any result. Ajax likewise is much the same character as in Homer; he is the same powerful giant, in bodily strength and prowess the next hero after Achilles; only his haughty defiance, his self-will, and purely animal nature, are painted in broader colours. But Diomed, Achilles, and Patroclus, fare the worst. Diomed seems to trouble himself little enough with the war, and to have no other office than to procure pretty girls of cheap virtue, and to put their first lovers out of the way. Achilles has retired to his tent, where he amuses himself with Patroclus and Thersites, but not on account of Briseis, but of a traitorous love-affair with one of Priam's daughters, and by a second breach of faith violates his engagement to her by again taking the field upon the death of Patroclus. His heroic virtue is a mere sham; by a treacherous attack, and with the aid of his myrmidons, he succeeds in putting Hector to death while he is resting without his arms. Patroclus, lastly, is but "Achilles' tassel," and nothing more. The advantage of noble knighthood is entirely on the side of Troy, although there also immorality is rife. The explanation of this poetical fact is to be drawn not so much from the prejudice of the middle ages, which sympathized with fallen Troy as the ancestress of Rome, as from the necessity which our poet was under of finding some counterfoil to the heroic life of Greece, in order to throw out the more distinctly the rottenness of its morality, and the worthlessness of its chivalry. For there cannot be a doubt that the chief end the poet had in view by this comic delineation was to furnish a vivid picture of the immorality which is involved in the Homeric poems and their subject-matter. Hence we can at once account for the strong language in which the cowardly, slanderous, but witty Thersites characterises the whole armament, and which, from its frequent repetition, sinks deep. (pp. 335-36)

As the satire has its good ground in the subject-matter itself, so also does it possess a full poetical justification. It rises in significance with the grandeur and importance of its subject; and the height to which, in Shakspeare's days, the admiration of the ancient heroism, with its myths and deities, and to which the love and admiration of them was carried by all classes, is well known, and we have already noticed a few historical instances of it. An intelligent mind like Shakspeare's unquestionably could not fail to see and appreciate the beneficial effects which an acquaintance with the high civilization of antiquity had already exercised, and was calculated to have, on the further improvement of the mind of Christian Europe. But he foresaw at the same time the dark abyss of corruption into which religion and morality must inevitably fall, if the Christian surrendered himself to an exclusive and unquestioning love and admiration of it. The religious and moral character would, he saw, be in danger of sinking, for a time at least, to the low level of antiquity; a degradation which, indeed, we may actually discern in the eighteenth century. In this prophetic spirit, which saw with equal clearness through the darkness of futurity as through the mist of the past, Shakspeare sat down to write his instructive satire on the Homeric hero-life. It was no wish of his to bring down the high, or to make the great little, and still less to attack the poetic dignity of Homer, or of heroic poetry. His object was to warn men against that exclusive and unqualified admiration which they are so likely to fall into, and which, whenever it loses sight of that perfect morality which, as shadowed forth in Christianity, is the god-like, eternal end of humanity, becomes nothing less than sinful, while at the same time he laboured to illustrate the universal truth, that whatever is merely human, however illustrious a poetic halo of ideality and a mythic antiquity may render it,

is really but very insignificant and little, when examined by the bird's-eye view of true *moral* ideality. We may, then, venture to assert, that the "Troilus and Cressida," independently of its satirical tendency, has for its fundamental idea the conviction that all human grandeur and greatness—whatever is most commonly admired and ennobled—is but little and worthless, when contemplated from the lofty position of that true moral perfection which Christianity archetypally sets before man. Thus regarded, the piece no longer appears singular; its import becomes as clear as it is profound. (pp. 337-38)

Hermann Ulrici, "Criticisms of Shakspeare's Dramas: 'Merry Wives of Windsor'—'Troilus and Cressida'," in his Shakspeare's Dramatic Art: And His Relation to Calderon and Goethe, *translated by A.J.W. Morrison, Chapman, Brothers, 1846, pp. 323-41.*

G. G. GERVINUS　(essay date 1849-50)

[*One of the most widely read Shakespearean critics of the latter half of the nineteenth century, the German critic Gervinus was praised by such eminent contemporaries as Edward Dowden, F. J. Furnivall, and James Russell Lowell; however, he is little known in the English-speaking world today. Like his predecessor Hermann Ulrici, Gervinus wrote in the tradition of the "philosophical criticism" developed in Germany in the mid-nineteenth century. Under the influence of August Wilhelm Schlegel's literary theory and Georg Wilhelm Friedrich Hegel's philosophy, Gervinus and other German critics tended to focus their analyses around a search for the literary work's organic unity and ethical import. Gervinus believed that Shakespeare's works contained a rational ethical system independent of any religion—in contrast to Ulrici, for whom Shakespeare's morality was basically Christian. In the excerpt below, drawn from his* Shakespeare (1849-50), *Gervinus considers the satirical tone of* Troilus and Cressida, *an issue also treated by August Wilhelm Schlegel (1808), Hermann Ulrici (1839), Frederick S. Boas (1896), and Oscar James Campbell (1938). Gervinus notes the comical aspects of Troilus's trust, Cressida's deceit, and Pandarus's needless interference, but places a greater emphasis on the satire of the Trojan War, the "second action" of the play. In parodying the war's events and revealing the vanity, envy, and ignobility of its participants, Gervinus contends, Shakespeare deprives both Greeks and Trojans of a "moral cause" for their war and casts a "deep gloom" over the whole action. In a statement typical of his ethical focus, Gervinus states that although there may be some "deeper meaning" for Shakespeare's trivialization of the Trojan myth and inversion of the Homeric perspective, the absence of morality in* Troilus and Cressida *proves that "the noblest poetry without a strong moral principle is not what it is capable of being and what it ought to be." He also questions the appropriateness of the subjects of Shakespeare's satire, stating that the medieval accounts of the Trojan War are "too insignificant" and the* Iliad *is too "unconscious and innocent." Gervinus concludes that although Shakespeare's parody may be misdirected, its target remains uncertain because the play's ambiguity makes it difficult to "acquire a clear conception of the satirical intention."*]

It seems to us not altogether impossible that Shakespeare's consciousness of power actually incited him to place himself immediately by the side of Homer in one of his works, and indeed to contrast himself with him. Homer's 'Iliad' was translated by Chapman about 1598, and was published in separate parts. . . . If it be thought that the translation of Homer incited him to any poetic, perhaps, indeed, any rival work (and this would have been as natural as that our own Goethe should be spurred by Homer to rival him in epic pieces), he would not, like Goethe, have been tempted to follow in his track but rather to take an opposite one. And we may well believe that this was really his intention in *Troilus and Cressida*.

It is not of course possible actually to prove this. It might indeed be disputed whether Shakespeare was acquainted with Chapman's translation at all. We think, however, the sum of our observations will incline to this conjecture, although we shall carefully avoid asserting it otherwise than as a conjecture. (pp. 679-81)

If Shakespeare had wished to handle this subject, as Chaucer did, for its own sake, he had in Troilus the choice of depicting wasted fidelity tragically, or of giving the matter a comic aspect by making his foolish confidence the main point of his character, and by so representing Cressida from the first that he would have no occasion to wonder, like Chaucer, at her sudden faithlessness, or rather at his own inadequate characterisation, establishing the connection between the two upon the shallow and artificial mediation of Pandarus. Shakespeare conceived the subject in his play from this comic view, and in his masterly manner he stamped upon the various circumstances the impress of great psychological knowledge, which they entirely lack in Chaucer. The manager of the contract appears here far more distinctly than in Chaucer to be a practised master in the business. Worthless himself, and therefore willingly occupied for others, polite and cringing, foolish, like a member of Polonius' family, inquisitive, chattering, an adept in double meanings, habituated to lies, bragging, and perjury, he understands thoroughly how to rouse and goad the passions by turns with praise and jealousy, fanning the flame even when already burning clear enough, making the fool more foolish, and the wanton still more wanton. He does too much for the crafty woman; he is too noisily officious for her; for the impatient Troilus he can hardly do enough. This youth of three and twenty, with the first down on his chin, is endowed by Shakespeare with the fanciful first love of boyhood, in which ardent sensuality and the madness of desire are hidden under boldness of spirit and romantic courage. He idealises not only the beauty of his chosen one but her manners also; he will stake his life that there is no spot in her heart, and he finds the alluring coquette 'stubborn chaste against all suit' [I. i. 97]; he even idealises the pressing pander as a 'tetchy' man, who must 'be woo'd to woo' [I. i. 96]. In his choice he makes use of no trial or consideration. The best of tempers, honourable and straightforward, he speaks of himself, as indeed he is,

> as true as truth's simplicity,
> And simpler than the infancy of truth.
>
> [III. ii. 169-70]

Open and free in heart and hand, he gives what he has and shows what he thinks. To persist in his love with an 'eternal and fixed soul,' to be a pattern, a proverbial word for fidelity, this is his ambition; the moral of all his wit is 'plain and true'; that shall be his glory; that is, as he says, taking all together— his 'vice!' To this noble youth Pandarus now leads the artful woman, whom only the crafty Ulysses can see through at a glance. Ulysses observes in a moment what the poor Troilus had never discovered:—

> There's language in her eye, her cheek, her lip,
> Nay, her foot speaks; her wanton spirits look out
> At every joint and motive of her body.
> O these encounterers, so glib of tongue,
> That wide unclasp the tables of their thoughts
> To every reader;
>
> [IV. v. 55-61]

except alone to the good Troilus. The poet has endeavoured at first to deceive the reader as well as honest Troilus as to Cressida's character, or to keep him uncertain. She appears at first in company with her uncle, she displays a lighter but not unequal wit, she is, however, without depth, an adept at double entendre, and indelicate in her expressions. She betrays almost at once that she could say more in praise of Troilus than Pandarus does, that she, however, 'holds off,' in order to attract them more methodically, because she knows 'men prize the thing ungain'd more than it is' [I. ii. 289]. In her intercourse with Troilus she maintains her reserve in practice as before in theory, confessing and yielding, and varying the plan of her coquettish allurements, although she is not to appear so much a coquette by profession as by nature, the prey of the first, as afterwards of the second opportunity, when the pander in consequence has so easy a part to play. She was 'won at the first glance,' she tells Troilus, but confesses that it was 'hard to *seem* won' [III. ii. 117-18]. She had held back, although she wished that 'women had men's privilege of speaking first' [III. ii. 128-30]. She acknowledges that she loves him, 'but not so much but she might master it!' [III. ii. 120-21]. And yet this is a lie, for her

> thoughts were like unbridled children, grown
> Too headstrong for their mother!
>
> [III. ii. 122-23]

Thus she trifles with him, and in every concession she plants a sting; she tempts him by an ambiguous expression to kiss her, and then declares she had not meant it. She plays the same game subsequently with Diomedes, promises, draws back, gives him Troilus' sleeve, takes it away again, and all this to sharpen him like a whetstone; Diomedes, understanding all these arts and jests, declines them, and by this manner also attains his end. With Troilus they are better adapted, although superfluous. She wins him merely by her suspicious anger as to his challenging her truth; the very sign of an evil conscience in her he takes for delicate sensitiveness. She enchants him when she assures him that in simplicity 'she'll war with him' [III. ii. 171]. She swears also to be unceasingly true to him, but she does so with ominous and equivocal expressions; 'Time, force, and death,' she says,

> Do to this body what extremes you can;
> But the strong base and building of my love
> Is as the very centre of the earth,
> *Drawing all things to it!*
>
> [IV. ii. 102-05]

With the same suspicious expression Pandarus praises the innate constancy of all her kindred: 'They are burs, they'll stick where they are thrown' [III. ii. 111-12]; that is, to one as well as to another.

This humorous treatment justifies what we have said; Shakespeare has taken hold of the love story of Troilus and Cressida from its comic side. But he has not, therefore, treated it for its own sake. He has connected it, as Thersites (Act v. sc. 4) remarks in the play itself, with a second action, with the proud withdrawal of Achilles and Ajax; and this second action so far surpasses the story of Troilus in importance, length, and force of handling, that the latter only appears like an episode in comparison. Everyone will perceive that the prologue, which names the scene of the Trojan War as the piece, is far more descriptive of its purport than the epilogue spoken by Pandarus, which from its lesson upon pandering relates only to Troilus and Cressida, and which [George] Steevens therefore considers to be only the idle addition of an actor [see excerpt above, 1793]. But even looking away from this second part of the play, we must perceive with regard to the story of Troilus itself that it is of little worth in itself. It is very remarkable, but every reader will confess that this piece creates throughout no real effect on the mind. No one on reading the play will readily feel any sympathy or love for any character, any preference for any part, any pity for any suffering, any joy at any success; not even in the affair between Troilus and Cressida, which speaks to the heart more than any other incident in the piece. The wanton portions will not charm, the elegiac will not move; the character of Troilus just as he is, were he placed in other society, would attract our interest in no slight degree; and we might almost lament that a character drawn in so masterly a manner is not designed with the intention of making it interesting in and for itself; but in such a connection this is not possible. His farewell to Cressida, sustained in the truest language of emotion, would touch us to the utmost if we could imagine it separated from the circumstances that belong to it; here, however, where throughout a concealed intention lurks in the background, we cannot venture to resign ourselves to psychical impressions. We feel throughout the play a wider bearing, a more remote object, and this alone prevents the immediate effect of the subject represented from appearing. The understanding is required to seek out this further aim of our comedy, and the sympathy of the heart is cooled. Here, as in Aristophanes, the action turns not upon the emotions of the soul, but upon the views of the understanding, and accordingly the personages acting occupy the mind as symbols rather than the heart. The comedy becomes a parody, we doubt if it is not even a satire, and it betrays an intention to rise above the earlier comic plays of the poet, in the same way as the later tragedies rose above the earlier. (pp. 682-85).

The aim of this dramatic farce was a parody of 'the crown of all heroic tales' [see excerpt above by August Wilhelm Schlegel, 1808], the Trojan myth; upon this point everyone seems agreed. The question is, however, to what tradition this parodied representation relates, whether to Homer, or the travesties of the middle ages, which treated the story from the Trojan point of view? (p. 686)

As to clothing and form, it could not have been Shakespeare's intention to travesty Homer; that had been done in the old books on Troy. To wish to oppose him from a party view of the matter would at least have been nothing new. Shakespeare had essentially to do *with the matter* of this great poetic theme, and this led him back first to the origin and foundation of the Trojan story; here was its weak side, that on which he could treat it humorously. For this end all elaborations of the story were, truly speaking, equal; but Shakespeare must have felt that he was most sharply opposed to Homer on account merely of the genuine nature of the source. He therefore surveyed all these different sources from one point of view; he took matter from them all, ever according to his intention; he took the travestied form, which suited his object best, out of the books of Troy; the episodical matter, which he wanted especially for his parody, from Chaucer; but in the main action, and in the limits in which he kept it, his drama adheres to the Homeric epos.

If we pass to the examination of the actions and personages of our comedy, we may be induced at the first glance to believe that Shakespeare gave to the reviler Thersites the part of the chorus, which expresses the actual meaning of the piece most distinctly. His abusive tongue destroys the object, indeed, by

plunging in the deepest mire both the action and the actors. . . . Envy and jealousy fill him with the poison and obscenity with which he besmears everything; he calls upon 'the devil, envy,' to say Amen to the curses which he utters upon all. Anger makes him like the 'porcupine,' which turns its quill against everybody; envy, like the 'unsalted leaven,' which makes all the dough mouldy, which places him on the lowest scale among the envy-divided Greeks. But for this very reason *his* voice is not the decisive one, which could lead us to the poet's true meaning. We *can* only take this view of the action before Troy, when, placing ourselves on a level with Thersites, we give our vote for cowardice which mocks at bravery, for envy which depreciates greatness, for ugliness which robs everything of the splendour of beauty, for flat prose which ridicules every ideal motive, for downright badness which sees everything in its worst aspect. In him we hear the sarcastic spirit, which regards everything as utterly bad, and will neither see nor acknowledge the existence of what is good, noble, or beautiful. But on this bad principle, this principle of absolute meanness, Shakespeare has not designed his merry, humorous play.

The question concerning the origin and object of the Trojan struggle has been brought under discussion by our poet in higher circles and has been treated far more fundamentally and poetically than by Thersites. That this origin was a main point with him is shown by his placing in the foreground the relation of Troilus and Diomedes to the abandoned Cressida, as a corresponding one to the similar and previously well-known relation of Paris and Menelaus to Helen. A stolen wife was the cause of the earliest national war between two quarters of the world. Two owners strive for her, as Diomedes says to Paris, both alike foolishly; the one seeks her,

> Not making any scruple of her soilure,
> With such a hell of pain and world of charge;
>
> [IV. i. 57-8]

the other defends her,

> Not palating the taste of her dishonour,
> With such a costly loss of wealth and friends.
>
> [IV. i. 60-1]

The noble Hector feels the ignominy of the matter, when in such eloquent words he defends the right of marriage, and Ulysses, also, when his gall overflows on the subject of the disgrace, for which 'they lose their heads to gild the horns' [IV. v. 31] of Menelaus. (pp. 689-91)

Viewed in a moral and just sense, the cause of the Greeks is not better than that of the Trojans; on the side of honour it is worse. Shakespeare has allowed the Homeric Achilles, who purchased lasting fame with a short life, to degenerate from a hero into a vain, morbidly proud, and effeminate mocker. Not on account of any dispute with Agamemnon, but for the sake of the promised Polyxena, he withdraws from the fight and from glory; he has no sympathy with the common honour, like Hector; he abandons the glory and honour of Greece to follow this love; he cares for nothing in the world but what affects him personally; he rouses himself, therefore, first after the death of Patroclus (this trait also Shakespeare takes from Homer), and even then only for a victory which brings him more ignominy than honour. The weak Ajax imitates him in haughtiness and inactivity, and withdraws, as Achilles had done, in the decisive moment, after having won a little honour. Ulysses takes all possible pains to arouse in both the public spirit, the ambition, and the thirst for glory which overflowed in Hector and Troilus. The finest speeches in the play, as well as the intrigues which lengthen out the action, have reference to this intention. To this we may trace that eloquent speech on the destroyed disipline and deference to rank (Act I. sc. 3), and on the fever of envy which caused those divisions and weakness in the camp, wherein lay the strength of Troy. There is reference to it in the proposal to appoint Ajax for the single combat with Hector, and thereby to rouse Achilles. There is reference to it in the oft-recurring eulogy of the ascendency of mental over bodily strength. There is reference to it in the shameless flattery with which they bait the stupid Ajax and feed his hungry, envious ambition. There is reference to it in the noble lesson (Act III. sc 3) impressed upon Achilles, and which was the purport of Ulysses' first speech, that steadfastness alone keeps honour bright. All this has little effect; the two strong-armed heroes have too little feeling for honour and glory, Hector and Troilus have too much; these latter mean well and do ill, the former mean ill and do well, or rather they escape harm. On the side of the Greeks, Hector and Ulysses fare the best, because they possess at least public spirit and policy. Yet this also is only ordinary cunning which displays profound wisdom in the mysteries of state policy when the question concerns mere espionage, a wisdom which in consequence attains its ends only in an equivocal manner.

By this absence of a moral cause in both Greeks and Trojans, by this want of public-spirited honour, especially among the Greeks universally, Shakespeare has cast a deep gloom over the whole action and story, and this gloom is rendered only the more striking and apparent by the gleams of noble principles and wise reflections that fall upon it. Even in the description of the characters and in the bearing of the style throughout the intention has been to disfigure.... Shakespeare has only to show us Patroclus imitating old Nestor, coughing and spitting, shaking in and out the rivets of his gorget with a 'palsy-fumbling,' in order to render despicable and ridiculous the venerable picture of the 'faint defects of age' [I. iii. 171], which even Homer does not conceal. The poet himself has correctly described his own mode of procedure in that of those mockers, Patroclus and Achilles; sometimes they act Agamemnon's greatness in an exaggerated manner, sometimes Nestor's infirmities so strikingly, 'as like as Vulcan and his wife'; all the 'abilities, gifts, natures, shapes, achievements, and plots' of the princes serve 'as stuff for these two to make paradoxes' [I. iii. 168-84]. And in this similar treatment our comic poet keeps so strictly within the line of truth, that even there, where he caricatures most, the striking resemblance to the Homeric characters is not to be denied, and the carrying out of these distinctive features corresponds closely to the outlines given by the ancient poet. (pp. 692-94)

If it be doubted whether, in this polemic comedy, more has been accomplished than to give vent to a Virgilian sympathy, or to a humorous freedom with regard to Homer and the other Trojan legends, or whether there may be a deeper meaning in this negation of the Homeric point of view, in this removal of all grandeur from the myth, we can at least gather from the whole performance this proximate truth, that the noblest poetry without a strong moral principle is not what it is capable of being and what it ought to be. The collected works of Shakespeare, as we have now learned to know them, show us that in his aesthetic system such a proposition would have ranked in the first place. And when we remember that even in the Grecian times Plato himself, from his philosophcial and religious point of view, found matter for censure morally with regard to Homer, we shall not wonder if Shakespeare, from his poetic starting point, arrived at similar though different

objections to the Trojan traditions.... As the Trojan history lay before him, formed out of so many component parts, it seemed to him to be wanting in the higher moral, and thus at the same time in the connecting link with which he ever sought to unite his poetry directly with life. And this he showed in an exaggerated manner in his comic play, where he so parodied the same action that, joining throughout the commonest traditions, he heaped together all their darker parts, and deprived the actors of every honourable and virtuous motive. By this means he naturally makes his own drama still more deficient in that connecting moral element. Certainly he would not have wished to reckon this play among those which hold up a mirror to the age, since it is not even calculated to produce the simplest psychical effect. The piece, therefore, by its half-satirical character, loses the common aim of the drama, if this were indeed at all intended; it is, however, not impossible that the comedy was never originally designed with this aim, was not indeed intended for representation. In this case this would be no reproach to the piece, so long as the new and unusual aim of the satirical or humorous drama were more certainly and acutely reached. But we doubt if anyone will allow this to be the case. If a humorous and ironical parody of the Trojan war—that is, of the facts in themselves—were aimed at, we must acknowledge that Cervantes grasped his object more successfully when he directed his humorous romance against knight-errantry, a decaying institution, which yet, out of all time and place, continued in the advancing age; whereas Shakespeare brought forward a long-forgotten state of things, which at that time did not even survive in the minds of the learned. But if the object aimed at were rather to satirise the poetic representations of this war, the defects of the play will become evident by another comparison. Aristophanes raised in this way his comedy into a satire; but then he renounced from the beginning the beaten path of the drama; he avoided all subjects which could give grounds for conjecturing an imitation of the usual circumstances of life; he elevated his actions into bold allegories, and never left the spectator divided between the course of one action which excited the feelings and another parallel action which challenged the intellectual and reflective powers. It is this division which injures the Shakespearian piece, in which we are not, it is true, attracted by the subject represented (the loves of Troilus and Cressida) for its own sake; but still we are not free, on the other side, to acquire a clear conception of the satirical intention. In a similar manner (as may have been aimed at here also) Aristophanes represented also literary personages and events from the same moral point of view; but he has not taken them out of remote ages, he has directed his sallies against the living, against poets as well as statesmen; and this should ever be the object of satire, because we war not against the defenceless and the dead. But it may have been that the revived Homer at that day was considered a living author, and we will suppose that this very revival may have tempted Shakespeare to expose the weakness of the ancient, far-famed poetry. But even then the ground was not fairly won, and the scene of action was not clear and smooth. While he mixed together all the old sources of Trojan story, he threw down his glove before the most different combatants, before all who stood in the most different relation to the one cause which was the object of his attack. If it were, as Schlegel was of opinion, the chivalric books on Troy which he attacked, these were objects too insignificant, and even then too obsolete for Shakespeare's assaults; if it were Homer, then these assaults themselves would necessarily appear to us, in the present day, obsolete. A fiction so unconscious and innocent as the Homeric is must ever remain, like everything childlike, unfit for satire; the morals and opinions of such an age can be judged by no other pre-suppositions and conditions than those of the age itself, and Shakespeare had not the means nor the knowledge required for this. Shakespeare has founded his own poems in part upon a basis which, morally considered, was here and there still worse than the actual basis of the Trojan story (which even Homer has nowhere placed in a brilliant light); and in simplifying, in separating, and ennobling his materials, he has not on the whole done otherwise than is there done; we might, therefore, indeed doubt whether, reviewed even from his own position, his attacks, if they refer to Homer and Homer alone, are just and right. It is, however, doubtful if any serious attack were intended; that is, we hesitate whether a humorous or satirical design lay at the bottom of the play, whether he may have written in jest or mockery, whether in jest or mockery of the facts or of their poetic forms, or whether all or which of these forms was the point aimed at. This uncertain character of the drama and the doubtful connection of the poet with doubtful sources are the causes of our quitting this play with greater dissatisfaction than any other of Shakespeare's. The warmest admirers of Shakespeare are undecided about it, and even Coleridge declared that he scarcely knew what to say of it [see excerpt above, 1834]. (pp. 695-97)

> G. G. Gervinus, "Third Period of Shakespeare's Dramatic Poetry: 'Troilus and Cressida'," in his Shakespeare Commentaries, translated by F. E. Bunnétt, revised edition, 1877. Reprint by AMS Press Inc., 1971, pp. 679-97.

EDWARD DOWDEN   (essay date 1877)

[Dowden was an Irish critic and biographer whose Shakspere: A Critical Study of His Mind and Art, first published in 1875 and revised in 1881, was the leading example of the biographical criticism popular in the English-speaking world near the end of the nineteenth century. Biographical critics sought in the plays and poems a record of Shakespeare's personal development. As that approach gave way in the twentieth century to aesthetic theories with greater emphasis on the constructed, artificial nature of literary works, the biographical analysis of Dowden and other critics came to be regarded as limited and often misleading. The following excerpt on Troilus and Cressida is from a general introduction to Shakespeare's works, and not from the more popular Shakspere: A Critical Study of His Mind and Art. In it, Dowden calls Troilus and Cressida "the comedy of disillusion," and suggests that it reflects "a mood of contemptuous depreciation of life" which Shakespeare was experiencing at the time of its composition, a proposition also put forth by George Brandes (1895-96) and E. K. Chambers (1907), but disputed by John S. P. Tatlock (1915) and Oscar James Campbell (1938). Dowden also proposes that while Shakespeare was experiencing this dark state of mind he was incapable of writing comedies.]

With what intention, and in what spirit did Shakspere write this strange comedy? All the Greek heroes who fought against Troy are pitilessly exposed to ridicule; Helen and Cressida are light, sensual, and heartless, for whose sake it seems infatuated folly to strike a blow; Troilus is an enthusiastic young fool; and even Hector, though valiant and generous, spends his life in a cause which he knows to be unprofitable, if not evil. All this is seen and said by Thersites, whose mind is made up of the scum of the foulness of human life. But can Shakspere's view of things have been the same as that of Thersites?

The central theme, the young love and faith of Troilus given to one who was false and fickle, and his discovery of his error, lends its colour to the whole play. It is the comedy of disil-

lusion. And as Troilus passed through the illusion of his first love for woman, so by middle life the world itself often appears like one that has not kept her promises, and who is a poor deceiver. We come to see the seamy side of life; and from this mood of disillusion it is a deliverance to pass on even to a dark and tragic view of life, to which beauty and virtue reappear, even though human weakness or human vice may do them bitter wrong. Now such a mood of contemptuous depreciation of life may have come over Shakspere, and spoilt him, at that time, for a writer of comedy. But for Isabella we should find the coming on of this mood in *Measure for Measure;* there is perhaps a touch of it in *Hamlet.* At this time *Troilus and Cressida* may have been written, and soon afterwards Shakspere, rousing himself to a deeper inquest into things, may have passed on to his great series of tragedies.

Let us call this, then, the comedy of disillusion, and certainly, wherever we place it, we must notice a striking resemblance in its spirit and structure to *Timon of Athens.* Timon has a lax benevolence and shallow trust in the goodness of men; he is undeceived, and bitterly turns away from the whole human race, in a rage of disappointment. In the same play, Alcibiades is, in like manner, wronged by the world; but he takes his injuries firmly, like a man of action and experience, and sets about the subduing of his base antagonists. Apemantus, again, is the dog-like reviler of men, knowing their baseness and base himself. Here, Troilus, the noble green-goose, goes through his youthful agony of ascertaining the unworthiness of her to whom he had given his faith and hope; but he is made of a stronger and more energetic fibre than Timon, and comes out of his trial a man, no longer a boy; somewhat harder, perhaps, than before, but strung-up for sustained and determined action. He is completely delivered from Cressida and from Pandar, and by Hector's death supplied with a motive for the utmost exertion of his heroic powers. Ulysses, the antithesis of Troilus, is the much-experienced man of the world, possessed of its highest and broadest wisdom, which yet always remains worldly wisdom, and never rises into the spiritual contemplation of a Prospero. He sees all the unworthiness of human life, but will use it for high worldly ends; the spirit of irreverence and insubordination in the camp he would restrain by the politic machinery of what he calls "degree" [I. iii. 75-138]. . . . Cressida he reads at a glance, seeing to the bottom of her sensual shallow nature, and he assists at the disillusioning of the young prince, whose nobleness is apparent to him from the first. Thersites also sees through the illusions of the world, but his very incapacity to have ever been deceived is a sign of the ignoble nature of the wretch. He feeds and grows strong upon garbage; physical nastiness and moral sores are the luxuries of his imagination. The other characters—the brute warrior, Ajax; the insolent self-worshipper, Achilles; Hector, heroic but too careless how and when he expends his heroic strength—are of minor importance. As the blindness of youthful love is shown in Troilus, so old age, in its least venerable form, given up to a gratification of sensuality by proxy, is exposed to derision in Pandar. (pp. 128-30)

> Edward Dowden, "Introductions to the Plays and Poems: 'Troilus and Cressida'," in his Shakspere, Macmillan and Co., 1877, pp. 127-31.

ALGERNON CHARLES SWINBURNE   (essay date 1880)

[Swinburne was an English poet, dramatist, and critic who devoted much of his literary career to the study of Shakespeare and other Elizabethan writers. His three books on Shakespeare—A

Study of Shakespeare *(1880),* Shakespeare *(1909), and* Three Plays of Shakespeare *(1909)—all demonstrate his keen interest in Shakespeare's poetic talents and, especially, his major tragedies. Swinburne remarks that while* Troilus and Cressida *is among Shakespeare's "most admirable" plays, it "will always in all probability be also, and as naturally, the least beloved of all." Swinburne also states that in the play Shakespeare endeavored "to brutalize the type of Achilles and spiritualize the type of Ulysses."*]

This wonderful play [*Troilus and Cressida*], one of the most admirable among all the works of Shakespeare's immeasurable and unfathomable intelligence, as it must always hold its natural high place among the most admired, will always in all probability be also, and as naturally, the least beloved of all. It would be as easy and as profitable a problem to solve the Rabelaisian riddle of the bombinating chimaera with its potential or hypothetical faculty of deriving sustenance from a course of diet on second intentions, as to read the riddle of Shakespeare's design in the procreation of this yet more mysterious and magnificent monster of a play. That on its production in print it was formally announced as "a new play never staled with the stage, never clapper-clawed with the palms of the vulgar," we know; must we infer or may we suppose that therefore it was not originally written for the stage? Not all plays were which even at that date appeared in print: yet it would seem something more than strange that one such play, written simply for the study, should have been the extra-professional work of Shakespeare: and yet again it would seem stranger that he should have designed this prodigious nondescript or portent of supreme genius for the public stage: and strangest of all, if so, that he should have so designed it in vain. Perhaps after all a better than any German or Germanising commentary on the subject would be the simple and summary ejaculation of Celia—"O wonderful, wonderful, and most wonderful wonderful, and yet again wonderful, and after that out of all whooping!" [*As You Like It,* III. ii. 191-93]. The perplexities of the whole matter seem literally to crowd and thicken upon us at every step. What ailed the man or any man to write such a manner of dramatic poem at all? and having written, to keep it beside him or let it out of his hands into stranger and more slippery keeping, unacted and unprinted? A German will rush in with an answer where an Englishman . . . will naturally fear to tread.

Alike in its most palpable perplexities and in its most patent splendours, this political and philosophic and poetic problem, this hybrid and hundred-faced and hydra-headed prodigy, at once defies and derides all definitive comment. This however we may surely and confidently say of it, that of all Shakespeare's offspring it is the one whose best things lose least by extraction and separation from their context. That some cynic had lately bitten him by the brain—and possibly a cynic himself in a nearly rabid stage of anthropophobia—we might conclude as reasonably from consideration of the whole as from examination of the parts more especially and virulently affected: yet how much is here also of hyper-Platonic subtlety and sublimity, of golden and Hyblaean eloquence above the reach and beyond the snap of any cynic's tooth! Shakespeare, as under the guidance at once for good and for evil of his alternately Socratic and Swiftian familiar, has set himself as if prepensely and on purpose to brutalise the type of Achilles and spiritualise the type of Ulysses. . . . The hysterics of the eponymous hero and the harlotries of the eponymous heroine remove both alike beyond the outer pale of all rational and manly sympathy; though Shakespeare's self may never have exceeded or equalled for subtle and accurate and bitter fidelity the study here given

Act V. Scene ii. Ulysses, Troilus, Diomedes, Cressida, and Thersites. Frontispiece to the Rowe edition (1709). By permission of the Folger Shakespeare Library.

of an utterly light woman, shallow and loose and dissolute in the most literal sense, rather than perverse or unkindly or unclean; and though [John] Keats alone in his most perfect mood of lyric passion and burning vision as full of fragrance as of flame could have matched and all but overmatched those passages in which the rapture of Troilus makes pale and humble by comparison the keenest raptures of Romeo. (pp. 198-202)

Algernon Charles Swinburne, "Third Period: Tragic and Romantic," in his A Study of Shakespeare, *1880. Reprint by AMS Press Inc., 1965, pp. 170-227.*

DENTON J. SNIDER   (essay date 1890)

[*Snider was an American scholar, philosopher, and poet who followed closely the precepts of the German philosopher Georg Wilhelm Friedrich Hegel and contributed greatly to the dissemination of his dialectical philosophy in America. Snider's critical writings include studies on Homer, Dante, and Goethe, as well as Shakespeare. Like Hermann Ulrici and G. G. Gervinus, Snider sought for the dramatic unity and ethical import in Shakespeare's plays, but he presented a more rigorous Hegelian interpretation than those two German philosophical critics. In the introduction to his three-volume work* The Shakespearian Drama: A Commentary, *Snider states that Shakespeare's plays present various ethical principles which, in their differences, come into "Dra-*

matic Collision," but are ultimately resolved and brought into harmony. He claims that these collisions can be traced in the plays' various "Dramatic Threads" of action and thought, which together form a "Dramatic Movement," and that the analysis of these threads and movements—"the structural elements of the drama"—reveal the organic unity of Shakespeare's art. Snider observes two basic movements in the tragedies—guilt and retribution—and three in the comedies—separation, mediation, and return. In his commentary on Troilus and Cressida, *Snider's Hegelian orientation is especially prominent, while he also anticipates the full philosophic treatments of the play common in twentieth-century interpretations. He states that* Troilus and Cressida *contains the clearest enunciation of Shakespeare's ethical philosophy as well as interfusing two "Literary Bibles," Shakespeare and Homer. Snider argues that Homer's* Iliad *and Shakespeare's play both contain the same "ethical germ," the substance of which is to be found in the philosophical speeches of Ulysses, which bear a striking resemblance to the dialectical system of Hegel. Snider remarks that Ulysses's speech on degree (I. iii.) and his speech on reflection (III. iii.) both assert that individual will should be subordinate to the institutions of the greater social order, an issue also discussed by G. Wilson Knight (1930), H. B. Charlton (1937), Winifred M. T. Nowottny (1954), Terence Eagleton (1967), and R. A. Yoder (1972). Snider also observes two parallel threads of action and thought running through the play, the "love-thread" and the "war-thread." In the first three acts of the play he perceives a general movement in both the love story and the war story "from strife and separation to unity," which culminates when the love of Troilus and Cressida is consummated and Achilles is reunited with the Greek army. The second movement "portrays the passage from union to disruption and conflict," as the lovers are separated and the war remains unresolved. He compares the conclusion of the play to "a goodly ship going to pieces amid the breakers." Snider states in his introduction—not excerpted here—that* Troilus and Cressida *serves as a link between Shakespeare's purely legendary plays and purely historical plays, an observation made earlier by Samuel Taylor Coleridge (1834); but, because of the "preponderance of the political element," he places the drama with the histories, a categorization later made by John S. P. Tatlock (1915).]*

[*Troilus and Cressida*] is of interest to the Shakespearian student for two main reasons: it contains, first, the poet's most direct and philosophical statement of his Ethical World, that is, of what underlies his poetry; it shows, secondly, the relation between two universal poets—the supreme modern genius looking back at and transforming the supreme ancient genius. It is not fundamentally a parody or travesty, as some writers contend; on the contrary it is a serious work, with humorous, satirical, and even mock-heroic lightning playing around it pretty much everywhere. But the heart of the work speaks in dead earnest. (p. 49)

The famous heroes of the *Iliad* are brought before us, but we can hardly recognize them in their modern shape; the beautiful plastic outline is not lost, but is subordinated to the inner element of character. The statue is transformed to flesh and blood. Shakespeare has taken these antique ideal forms and poured into them the subjective intensity of the modern world. This is the greatest and most enduring ground of interest in the present drama. (pp. 49-50)

In the mouths of these old Homeric personages the Poet has placed the most abstract statement of what may be called his philosophy that is to be found in any of his works. His views of society, of life, of institutions, are here expressed in a language as direct and definite as that employed by the thinker trained to the use of the abstruse terms of the schools. (pp. 50-1)

Ulysses and Hector in their reasonings are purely philosophical, though they decorate their abstractions with many a poetic figure. Moreover, they are quite alike in their philosophy; both argue against "the particular will" as opposed to "the general." Achilles in the Greek camp is "in will peculiar," and is "without observance or respect of any" [II. ii. 165]; through his pride he refuses to "communicate his parts to others" [III. iii. 117]. Troilus in the Trojan camp will not listen to "reason," but is led on "by the conduct of my will" [II. ii. 62], though his brother Hector tells him "value dwells not in particular will," but

> holds his estimate and dignity
> As well wherein 'tis precious of itself
> As in the prizer.
>
> [II. ii. 53-6]

That is, value is not merely a subjective matter, "in the prizer," but also in the thing prized. Ulysses in his argument seizes the *Iliad* in its very core; he shows that the individual must subserve the universal order and purpose, or else be reduced to nothing. This is the fundamental point in the modern drama as well as in the ancient epic; it is here that Homer and Shakespeare become one and reveal a common harmony. The whole course of the *Iliad* is the discipline of the refractory individual; the philosophy of this discipline is put by Shakespeare into the mouth of Ulysses. It may be fairly said, that Ulysses, for this reason, is the hero, the intellectual hero of the present play. The English poet shakes hands with Homer across the ages, and with him enforces the deep ethical purport of the Trojan legend, but dethrones Achilles, the man of brawn, and sets up in his stead Ulysses, the man of brain, who is, however, the ancient hero of the *Odyssey,* Homer's second poem.

The argument of Hector, who is the Trojan counterpart of Ulysses, is likewise ethico-philosophical and favors the restoration of Helen, against the passion of Troilus and Paris. Hector moralizes upon the deed of Paris, then philosophises upon morality. (pp. 51-3)

Thus in the Greek and in the Trojan camps Ulysses and Hector unite in enforcing the moral law against "the particular will," which in the one case shows itself in the pride of Achilles, causing him to withdraw from the national conflict, and which, in the other case, shows itself in the passion of Paris and Troilus, causing them to keep Helen.

But Hector in the end abandons his high moral stand and sides with the opposite party for the sake of glory. That decision is his tragic doom; he fights for what he knows and has declared to be wrong; he violates his deepest conviction. Such is also his character and fate in Homer, from whom Shakespeare doubtless drew the outlines of Hector. Here the Trojan moralist differs from the Greek moralist Ulysses, who does not drop back into the opposite of his own principle, but remains the intellectual hero. We also see that Shakespeare did not favor the Trojans more than Homer did, or perchance than Zeus did. (pp. 53-4)

[But] there is also another set of persons here, whose principle and whose actions are unknown to the *Iliad.* Love is with them the main business—not war. The legend of Troilus, Cressida, and Pandarus is the creation of the later romancers, which was grafted on the old story of Troy. It portrays the struggle of the tender passion in one of its phases—the fidelity of man and the falsity of woman. The burning intensity, the fierce conflicts, the supreme power of love, find their expression in this part of the fable, which is, indeed, a later development of human spirit. Still, the relation between the two groups must be traced; the Trojan war was caused by the faithlessness of a woman whose restoration is demanded by the Nation; the refusal calls out the heroes who are seeking to bring her back by force. Female infidelity is the theme; in the one case it involves the Family merely, but in the other case it involves the State. Helen and Cressida, therefore, resemble each other; both perform the same deed, though in different relations; both deceive faithful men, and are captivated by faithless men. In the Trojan and in the Greek world we find the parallelism of love true and false; Troilus, Cressida, Diomed form a trio corresponding to Menelaus, Helen, Paris—the center of both sets being the woman untrue. This is the shadow which darkens the whole drama.

Such are the two threads running through the play. They may be named, according to their leading tendency, the love-thread and the war-thread; though parallel in action, in thought the first is the source of the second. The movements also are two, the division being manifest, not only by a difference in principle, but also by a difference in merit. The first movement, in general, passes from strife and separation to unity. The parted lovers are brought together by the mediation of Pandarus, and are made happy by mutual vows of devotion. In Troy the division of opinion which previously existed is healed; in the Greek host the angry Achilles is wrought upon by the cunning of Ulysses, and seems to resolve to take part again in the war; thus the hostile armies come to internal harmony preparatory to the external struggle. The second movement portrays the passage from union to disruption and conflict. The lovers, on the one hand, are torn asunder by an unforeseen occurrence; Cressida proves faithless, and thus the bond of emotion is broken. The combat, on the other hand, arises between the two hostile forces; after many fluctuations, Hector, the Trojan hero, is slain, and his countrymen cease from their attack and retire to the city; things are left as they were before. The negative termination of the play is striking; Troilus and Cressida are separated, and the foes still confront each other with warlike preparation.

There is no doubt that the first movement, embracing the first three acts, is the most positive, the most organic and the most poetical part of the play. The study of it, therefore, is the study of the Shakespearian conception in all its depth and fullness. Each thread can easily be followed out in order.

Taking up the love-thread and following it through the first movement, we observe that the divine passion has been already excited in the bosoms of the lovers, and moves on speedily to its fruition in the betrothal. (pp. 55-8)

The man resigns himself to his love; many great interests are pressing him, but they are brushed aside—his sacrifice is complete. But the woman subordinates her love to her understanding—to her planning and schemes; she refuses the absolute surrender to the feeling of Family. She, therefore, must be declared to be untrue to the deepest principle of her sex. Her falsity hereafter is adequately motived by this single trait; love—devotion to the one individual—is not the controlling impulse of her nature. But we must advance to the next stage—the good offices of Pandarus bring about their meeting. . . . Troilus, true to his character, make an immediate and unreserved declaration of the most fervent devotion. But Cressida is also true to her character; she hesitates, suspects, make abstract reflections of various kinds. When she does whisper her love she repents—reproaches herself with having "blabbed," and is forever recalling what she has said. "Where is my wit?" [III. ii. 151]

she asks; for wit is her boast—to it she is always trying to subject her words and actions. There is no full, free resignation, but she is continually catching herself and her utterances, as if her thought had to go back and take a glance at itself. Her mind is her pride; she is really ashamed of her love. Cressida is best designated by calling her the opposite of that which Troilus describes himself to be:—

> I am as true as truth's simplicity,
> And simpler than the infancy of truth.
> [III. ii. 169-70]

For she is full of falsity and stratagem. Both take a vow of eternal fidelity, yet with a wonderful difference of manner, which is prophetic of their future separation. (pp. 62-3)

We now pass to the war-thread, the structure of which is somewhat complex, and, therfore, must be carefully analyzed. In the first place, there are two sides—the Trojan and the Grecian—which are arrayed against each other in war. But, in the second place, each side has two parties or factions, which are opposed to each other mainly, though not wholly, on questions of policy. These internal differences are now to be portrayed; the characters which maintain the conflicting opinions are to be grouped and designated; the means are to be shown whereby each side arrives at a substantial harmony within itself. Such is the first movement—from separation to union.

The siege has lasted seven years, and still the walls of Troy are standing. The Grecian princes have lost hope, and seem ready to abandon the enterprise. Failure has to be acknowledged; there can be no longer any disguise. It is a situation of despair; a great national undertaking must be given up, whose abandonment comes next to the loss of civil freedom. This is the trying political situaiton. What is its cause, and what is its cure? The heroes have to address themselves to the dangerous condition of affairs; their various characters will be manifested according to their conduct in the present emergency; it is a time which tries men's souls. (pp. 65-6)

[Ulysses] is the supreme personage of the drama; the proportions of his intellect are truly colossal. He understands the difficulty at once, and sees the remedy. Above all human beings, he possesses insight and invention; he clearly comprehends the causes of the existing evils and knows their cure. He will not be content to utter innocent platitudes—that fortune is fickle, that men must be patient, that reverses show the true worth of the warrior. Failure has overtaken the expedition; there is some good reason for it, and he intends to go to the bottom of the matter. The disease, however deep-seated, must be discovered, and then the medicine can be applied. Such a discussion will lead Ulysses to examine the whole organization of the Greeks before Troy, and his argument will draw in the general principles of all social institutions, and even of individual conduct. (p. 68)

Agamemnon is the embodiment of all the lofty impulses of the grand national enterprise, and, hence, is truly the leader of the people; but his limitations are his feelings—faith, hope, perseverance, good intention, cannot take the place of knowledge. Nestor rises higher; he has appreciative intelligence united with the golden gift of persuasion. He first repeats the somewhat empty exhortations of Agamemnon, but, when the deeper nature of Ulysses opens its treasures for his judgment, he yields an unhesitating assent. The apex is, of course, occupied by Ulysses, whose crowning gift is, as before said, creative intelligence.

Let us now listen to what such a man has to say about the nature of the existing evils and their remedy, for certainly his words will be worthy of attention. "The specialty of rule hath been neglected" [I. iii. 78]—the individual has not performed the particular function allotted to him; there has been no subordination—and, hence, no organization—in the Grecian army. To illustrate his principle, Ulysses goes through the physical and intellectual universe; the same law of harmony prevails everywhere. The planetary system, with its central power, "Sol, in noble eminence enthroned and sphered" [I. iii. 89-90], is a striking example, which is here elaborated in great detail. But it is the social fabric—the institutions of man—in which the necessity of degree, of subordination, is most plainly manifested. Without it the whole realized world of right would crumble to ruin; there would be no security for the weak, no respect for age or consanguinity; Astraea would again take her flight to the skies:—

> Strength should be lord of imbecility,
> And the rude son should strike his father dead;
> Force should be right; or rather, right and wrong—
> Between whose endless jar justice resides—
> Should lose their names, and so should justice, too.
>
> [I. iii. 114-18]

Ulysses sees plainly that subordination is the primal law of institutional life; each person must fill his place in the community and must freely submit to what is above himself. But why not let institutions perish? Then man perishes. The individual is reduced to the wild beast of nature, with all its voracity; he will at once proceed to devour his own species. This ultimate reduction is also stated in all its force and abstractness by the old Greek thinker, or, rather, by Shakespeare:—

> Then everything includes itself in power,
> Power into will, will into appetite;
> And appetite, an universal wolf,
> So doubly seconded with will and power,
> Must make perforce an universal prey,
> And last eat up itself.
>
> [I. iii. 119-24]

Such is the logical outcome of "this neglection of degree" [I. iii. 127]; it is the destruction of institutions, and the destruction of institutions is the destruction of man. The result springs from the most severe dialectical process: The individual is resolved into appetite, and appetite, being universalized, must consume all, which includes itself. No words could more distinctly prove that the Poet was in the habit of *thinking,* in the true sense of the term—that is, of testing every principle by the form of universality. If this were written by a poet of today, it would be laughed at by many a critic as a specimen of pure German transcendentalism. That the inference before mentioned is not far-fetched, note again the language with care. Man becomes mere appetite, which is an *universal* wolf; this wolf must, of necessity, make an *universal* prey, till it finally comes back to itself, and at last *eats up itself*. With what absolute precision is the negative result drawn; with what remorseless rigor is the whole philosophy of sensualism burnt to ashes in two or three short sentences! And must the confession be made? Be merciful, oh ye gods; the statement has the very manner—or, if you please, the very knack—of the Hegelian Dialectic, the most terrible of all metaphysical goblins. (pp. 69-71)

Why is Shakespeare the greatest of poets? Not because of his language, or of his imagery, or of his constructive ability, or

even of his characterization; these are all very wonderful, indeed, but they have been reached by lesser minds. His supreme greatness lies in his comprehension and embodiment of the ethical—that is, institutional—world; its profoundest collisions he penetrates with his inevitable glance; he knows, too, their mediation and final solution. It has been the object of these essays, as the reader doubtless has perceived, to drop all minor points of view and hold the eye unswervingly upon this one element. It is truly the Shakespearian world, into which a person must be initiated if he would wish to stand face to face with the great bard. If we suffer the mind to lose itself in the externalities of his Art—in the words, in the figures, in the versification, or even in the characters—we can obtain but a very partial and very cloudy reflex of the total man.

A further observation may be added. The importance of this institutional element is not confined to the study of Shakespeare; it is the deepest moving principle of that which is vital and permanent in all literature, from the Homeric Epos to the modern novel. Men will cherish and hold on to what is highest in themselves, and the work of Art must adumbrate something which is of eternal interest; such as the conflicts in the Family, State, Society, and institutions generally. Criticism would do well to pay attention to them if it would rise out of the realm of mere subjective opinion to the dignity of a science, for thus it abandons caprice and fastens itself upon the most objective realities. In this connection one expression here deserves attention: "Right and wrong, between whose endless jar justice resides." Manifestly the collisions of the Ethical World are this endless jar between right and wrong, while justice is the institutional order which harmonizes these collisions by giving validity to the supreme right. The highest function of poetry is to reflect back to the man this order, which is the spiritual essence of the world.

Ulysses has now laid bare the evil under which the Grecian army is suffering; its logical consequence also has been unfolded. But these words are still general. Who are the authors of this present state of affairs? This question brings us to the other party of the Greeks. Achilles, the mightiest warrior of them all, has withdrawn from active participation in the conflict and stays in his tent, mocking their discomfiture. (pp. 73-5)

But now comes the remedy, for intelligence here, too, must assert its supremacy and control in some way these men of muscle; they must be won. Ulysses will be equal to the emergency. . . . (p. 77)

Achilles is passed by without the customary marks of respect from the Greeks; he notices the slight and muses on the fickleness of popular favor. While in this mood Ulysses passes before him, perusing a book with great intentness. A strange book was that for camp-reading in Homeric times. Ulysses cites from it the remarkable statement that man

> Cannot make boast to have that which he hath,
> Nor feels not what he owes, but by reflection.
>
> [III. iii. 98-9]

What can this mean, asks the horrified modern reader, with the metaphysical bugbear rising in his imagination. But Achilles, though rather lean in intellect, clearly understands the passage, for he illustrates it with a striking and appropriate comparison; indeed, to him "this is not strange at all" [III. ii. 111]. Wonderful men were those old heroes! The seed has fallen on good ground, and Ulysses enforces the same doctrine a second time with a much stronger turn of expression:

> —No man is the lord of anything,
> Though in and of him there is much consisting,
> Till he communicate his parts to others;
> Nor doth he of himself know them for aught
> Till he behold them formed in the applause
> Where they are extended.
>
> [III. iii. 115-20]

The metaphysical deluge is again upon us. Is there, then, no plan of salvation? But the matter keeps getting worse. We might have pardoned that former abstruse discussion on institutions, for it was a theme so dear to the Poet; yet now he plunges remorselessly into the deepest psychological question known to philosophy. But what has the devout man to do except to struggle after, with the prayerful hope of soon touching bottom? Ulysses here states the doctrine of reflection, and, what is more strange, he uses for his designation exactly the term employed in modern systems of thought. Man cannot truly possess anything unless his possession is reflected through others; nay, he cannot truly know anything till his knowledge is reflected back to himself through others. Then both possession and knowledge are real—objective; otherwise, they are idle figments of the brain. Man is not through himself alone but through his fellow-man; ideally he must be all in order to be himself.

All this reasoning, however, only prepares the way for a practical application of the doctrine to Achilles, who is thus caught in the web of his own principle. . . . The opposition of Achilles is manifestly broken, though he does not directly say that he will return and take part in the war. But afterwards he is present with the other Greek leaders at the intended combat between Ajax and Hector, and there challenges the Trojan hero.

So harmony seems again to be restored in the Greek army. It is the brain of Ulysses which is everywhere seen in these transactions; the feat is purely intellectual. When the fighting comes he steps into the background, and the interest diminishes. The great error of Grecian discipline—lack of subordination—he exposes; the breach between the leaders he heals by winning Ajax and then Achilles. He is the real hero, the intellectual hero. (pp. 78-81)

The war-thread which has just been developed has, perhaps, the most purely intellectual tinge found in the works of Shakespeare. So much reflection and so little action, so much deliberation and so little passion, cannot be pointed out elsewhere in his dramas. Then there is Ulysses, the supremely intellectual hero in a far higher sense than Hamlet. For Hamlet's mind is defective, if not diseased; it is forever caught in its own cobwebs, and cannot march forward to the deed. But the thought of Ulysses, so profound yet so transparent, never destroys itself, but proceeds by necessity to realization; it must find itself reflected, to use his own term, in the world around him.

But now the character of the whole drama begins to change; the thought becomes more jejune, the structure more fragmentary and confused. The second movement, which commences here (end of the 3rd act), is far inferior to that which has preceded and grows worse till the end. (pp. 83-4)

The termination of this drama resembles a goodly ship going to pieces amid the breakers; gradually it splits asunder, and nothing is seen but the disconnected fragments floating on the surface of the angry waters. The play is literally wrecked. The characters become different, and even inconsistent; the great

preparations of the first movement are inadequately carried out, or entirely dropped; the action and the structure are confused; unnecessary parts are introduced and necessary parts are omitted. To name the work has given great difficulty; it is not comedy, tragedy, history, or mediated drama; the editors of the folio of 1623 seem to have been doubtful about its proper classification. But, inasmuch as the true end is wanting, there can be no complete proof for any designation. As it stands, the war-thread terminates in the death of Hector, which must pass for tragic, though Hector is not the leading character of this thread. But the love-thread ends in mere separation, which is no solution at all, as there is no requital for the deed. (p. 89)

The purport of the whole play has been supposed to be satirical and also humorous. That both these elements are present in it must be at once granted, but they are subordinate. The collision is serious—between nations, and on both sides there is violation and justification—a wrong and a right. The Greeks vindicate the Family, but assail the State; while the Trojans vindicate nationality, but violate the Family. It is a genuine conflict in these institutions, and not a delusion. Moreover, the leading characters on both sides are imbued with deep earnestness. The satirists and merry-makers, in one form and another, are found in all conflicts of society, and hence, they are not absent even from the tragedies of Shakespeare. (p. 91)

The student, it has been already said, finds a leading interest of the drama to lie in the fact that Homer, the first and oldest Literary Bible, is transmuted into Shakespeare, the modern Literary Bible, and that the ancient story of Troy is turned into a drama of the Renascence. The Classic and Romantic worlds are not only placed alongside of each other, but are interfused.

What is there in common between the old and the modern poem? First, the external setting for both is about the same, as already observed; then the internal element, the ethical germ, is the same in both. In the *Iliad* as well as in *Troilus and Cressida*, "the specialty of rule hath been neglected"; the strong individual refuses to subordinate himself to the world-order, and has to be put under severe discipline. The offense of Achilles is the same in Homer and in Shakespeare; and, what is a better test, the ethical breach in the character of Hector is the same in both poets, and has the same outcome. But this ethical element is as yet implicit in Homer, while in Shakespeare it is not only explicit, but is voiced by the chief character of the play, Ulysses.

There are many allusions to Homer's incidents and personages in Shakespeare's works, but he could hardly have known the old Greek poet at first hand. Latin literature must have furnished him with much Homeric information; many think he shows a Trojan bias in accord with Roman poets and mediaeval legend. But a nearer source opened to him. In the year 1598 appeared the translation of the first seven books of the *Iliad* by George Chapman, the poet's fellow-dramatist and friend. Thereby a direct stream began to flow from the Greek to the English bard.

In *Troilus and Cressida* there are plainly two elements, which may be designated as the Greek and Greco-Romantic. The first is immediately derived from Homer, and implies a careful study of Homer's fundamental principle. (pp. 93-4)

Then there is the Greco-Romantic element in which we behold the ancient Hellenic world after it has passed through the Byzantine and Mediaeval time down to Shakespeare, and brought along with it the tinge of chivalry, love and romance of the Middle Ages. Here is to be placed the love story with its main persons, Troilus, Cressida, Pandar, whose names are found in Homer, but not their characters, which are an evolution of thousands of years. (pp. 94-5)

Thus Shakespeare, with a true and universal sympathy, took up into his work the old and the new, the Greek and the Romantic elements. The direct Homeric stream, which had again been tapped at its fountain head by the Renascence, he sets to flowing afresh through his poem. The indirect stream from Homer, which had wound down through the centuries, and had received many new hues in its passage, he also turns into his poetical garden. We have already noticed that Shakespeare, especially in his Comedies, shows a polymythical spirit; he lends a sympathetic ear to every truly mythological utterance of a people, in which he seems to hear the primitive voice of poetry among men. Greek, Gothic, Italian, English legendary treasures he seized upon with equal avidity, and sometimes united them all into one poem, as in *Midsummer Night's Dream.* The present drama is a new shift of his mythical combinations, not to be found in any other work of his, being a union of the Greco-Homeric and Greco-Romantic mythus. (pp. 96-7)

> Denton J. Snider, " 'Troilus and Cressida'," in his The Shakespearian Drama, a Commentary: The Histories, *Sigma Publishing Co., 1890, pp. 49-97.*

GEORGE BRANDES (essay date 1895-96)

[*Brandes was a scholar and the most influential literary critic of late nineteenth-century Denmark. His work on Shakespeare was translated and widely read in his day. A writer with a broad knowledge of literature, Brandes placed Shakespeare in a European context, comparing him with other important dramatists. Brandes also often interpreted the works of Shakespeare as biographical reflections of the poet's life. In his comments on* Troilus and Cressida *in his* William Shakespeare, *first published in Danish in 1895-96, Brandes argues that Cressida's deception of and unfaithfulness towards Troilus, because of its bitter presentation, parallels some experience in Shakespeare's own life. The play, Brandes says, contains a misogynist tone which Shakespeare had not displayed since his "early youth." He also compares Shakespeare's treatment of Cressida to that of Cleopatra and the figure commonly known as the Dark Lady of the Sonnets and points out references to Cressida's unfaithfulness in several of the dramatist's other plays. Although the suggestion that* Troilus and Cressida *reflects the dark state of Shakespeare's mind at the time of its composition has also been posited by Edward Dowden (1877) and E. K. Chambers (1907), other critics, such as John S. P. Tatlock (1915) and Oscar James Campbell (1938), have rejected such hypotheses.*]

[In *Troilus and Cressida*] Shakespeare had no interest in delineating that *bellâtre* ["coxcomb"], Prince Paris; he had felt him as little as he had Menelaus. But he had many a time felt as Troilus did—the honest soul, the honourable fool, who was simple enough to believe in a woman's constancy. And he knew well, too well, that Lady Cressida, with the alluring ways, the nimble wit, the warm blood, speaking lawful passion with (to not too true an ear) the lawful modesty of speech. She would rather be desired than confer, would rather be loved than love, says "yes" with a "no" yet upon her lips, and flames up at the least suspicion of her truth. Not that she is false. Oh, no! why false? We believe in her as her lover believes in her, and as she believes in herself—until she leaves him for the Greek camp. Then she has scarcely turned her back upon him than she loses her heart to the first she meets, and her constancy fails at the first proof to which it is put.

All his life through these two forms had preoccupied his imagination. In *Lucretia,* he coupled Troilus with Hector among Trojan heroes. In the [fifth] act of the *Merchant of Venice,* he made Lorenzo say:

> In such a night
> Troilus, methinks, mounted the Trojan walls,
> And sighed his soul towards the Grecian tents
> Where Cressid lay.
>> [*The Merchant of Venice,* V. i. 3-6]

In *Henry V.,* Pistol included Doll Tearsheet among "Cressid's kind," making Doll doubly ridiculous by classing her with the Trojan maid of far-famed charm. In *Much Ado About Nothing,* [V. ii. 31], Benedict called Troilus "the first employer of Pandars." In *As You Like It* (Act IV), Rosalind jested about him, and yet yielded him a certain recognition. Protesting that no man ever yet died for love, she said, "Troilus had his brains dashed out with a Grecian club, yet did what he could to die before, *and he is one of the patterns of love*" [IV. i. 97-100]. In *Twelfth Night* and in *All's Well that Ends Well,* the Fool and Lafeu both jested about Pandarus and his ill-famed zeal in bringing Troilus and Cressida together.

Slowly, like the Hamlet tradition, this subject had been growing ripe in Shakespeare's mind. It had hitherto lived in his imagination in much the same form in which it had been handled by his compatriots. By Chaucer, first and foremost, who in his *Troilus and Cressida* (about 1360) had translated, elaborated, and enlarged Boccaccio's beautiful poem, *Filostrato.* But neither Chaucer nor any other Englishman who had translated or reproduced the subject . . . had found in it any material for satire. Especially had none of its earlier elaborators found any fault with the character of Cressida. (pp. 503-04)

Chaucer, as little as Boccaccio, found anything in the relations of the lovers to satirise. He intends, to the best of his abilities, to prove their love as innocent and lawful as possible. He paints it with a naïve and enraptured simplicity, whch proves how far he is from mockery. He does not even rave over Cressida's faithlessness to Troilus; she is excused, she trembles and hesitates before she falls. Inconstancy is forced upon her by the overwhelming might of hard circumstance.

There is nothing in these two poets that can compare with the passionate heat and hatred, the boundless bitterness with which Shakespeare delineates and pursues his Cressida. His mood is the more remarkable that he in no wise paints her as unlovable or corrupt; she is merely a shallow, frivolous, sensual, pleasure-loving coquette.

She does little, on the whole, to call for such severity of judgment. She is a mere child and beginner in comparison with Cleopatra, for instance, who, for all that, is not so unmercifully condemned. But Shakespeare has aggravated and pointed every circumstance until Cressida becomes odious, and rouses only aversion. The change from love to treachery, from Troilus to Diomedes, is in no earlier poet effected with such rapidity. Whenever Shakespeare expresses by the mouth of one or another of his characters the estimate in which he intends his audience to hold her, one is astounded by the bitterness of the hatred he discloses. It is especially noticeable in the scene [IV. v] in which Cressida comes to the Greek camp and is greeted by the kings with a kiss.

At this point Cressida has as yet offended in nothing. She has, out of pure, vehement love for him, passed such a night with Troilus as Juliet did with Romeo, persuaded to it by Pandarus, as Juliet was by her nurse. Now she accepts and returns the kiss wherewith the Greek chieftains bid her welcome. (pp. 504-05)

For all that, Ulysses, who sees through her at the first glance, breaks out on occasion of this kiss which Cressida returns:

> Fie, fie upon her,
> There's language in her eye, her cheek, her lips,
> Nay, her foot speaks, her wanton spirit looks out
> At every joint and motive of her body.
>
>   [IV. v. 54-7]
>   (p. 505)

So Shakespeare causes his heroine to be described, and doubtless it is his own last word about her. Immediately before her he had portrayed Cleopatra. When we remember the position occupied in his drama by the Egyptian queen, whom he, for all that, has stamped as the most dangerous of all dangerous coquettes, we can only marvel at the distance his spiritual nature has traversed since then.

There was in Shakespeare's disposition, as we have already remarked, a deep and extraordinary tendency to submissive admiration and worship. Many of his flowing lyrics spring from this source. Recall his humility of attitude before the objects of this admiration, before Henry V., for example, and his adoration for the friend in the Sonnets. We still find this need of giving lyrical and ecstatic expression to his hero-worship in *Antony and Cleopatra*. He by no means undertakes a defence of the desolating temptress, but with what glamour he surrounds her! What eulogies he lavishes upon her! She stands in an aureole of the adulation of all the other characters in the drama. At the time Shakespeare wrote this great tragedy, he had still so much of romantic enthusiasm remaining to him that he found it natural to let her live and die gloriously. Let be that she was a sorceress, still she fascinates.

What a change! Shakespeare, who had hitherto worshipped women, has become a misogamist. This mood, forgotten since his early youth, rises up again in hundredfold strength, and his very soul overflows in scorn for the sex.

What is the cause? Has anything befallen him—anything new? Upon what and whom does he think? Does he speak out of new and recent experience, or is it the old sorrow from the time of the Sonnets, of which he made use in the construction of Cleopatra's character, and is this the same grief which has taken new shape in his mind and is turning sour? is it this which has grown increasingly bitter until it corrodes? (pp. 505-06)

It is quite possible . . . that this last woman's character, instead of being only a variant of the Cleopatra type, was a product of a new, fiery, and scorching impression of feminine inconstancy and worthlessness. We are too entirely ignorant of the circumstances of the poet's life to venture any decided opinion, all we can say is, that incidents and novel experiences are not absolutely necessary as an explanation. There is a remote possibility that the first sketch of the play was already written in 1603, in which case it would be more than likely that the dark lady was once more his prototype. On the other hand, it may be, as already suggested, that in a productive soul one circumstance will take the place of many, and an experience which at first seemed wholly tragic may, in the rapid inner development of genius, come to wholly change its character. He has suffered under it; it has sucked his heart's blood and left him a beaten man on his path through life. He has sought to

embody it in serious and worthy forms, until suddenly it stands before him as a burlesque. His misery no longer seems a cruel destiny, but a well-merited punishment for immoderate stupidity, and this bitter mood has sought relief in such scornful laughter as that whose discord strikes so harshly in *Troilus and Cressida*.

We can imagine that Shakespeare began by worshipping his lady-love, complaining of her coldness and hardness, celebrating her fingers in song, cursing her faithlessness, and feeling himself driven nearly wild with grief at the false position in which she had placed him; this is the standpoint of the Sonnets. In the course of years the fever had stormed itself out, but the memory of the enchantment was still visibly fresh, and his mind pictured the loved one as a marvellous phenomenon, half queen, half gipsy, alluring and repellant, true and false, strong and weak, a siren and a mystery; this is the standpoint of *Antony and Cleopatra*. Then, possibly, when life had sobered him down, when he had cooled, as we all do cool in the hardening ice of experience, he suddenly and sharply realised the insanity of an exotic enthusiasm for so worthless an object. He looks upon this condition, which invariably begins with self-deception and must of necessity end in disillusionment, as a disgraceful and tremendous absurdity; and his wrath over wasted feelings and wasted time and suffering, over the degradation and humiliation of its self-deception, and ultimately the treason itself, seeks final and supreme relief in the outburst, "What a farce!" which is in itself the germ of *Troilus and Cressida*. (p. 507)

George Brandes, "Contempt of Women—'Troilus and Cressida'," translated by Diana White with Mary Morison, in his William Shakespeare, *William Heinemann, 1920, pp. 501-07.*

FREDERICK S. BOAS   (essay date 1896)

[*Boas was a nineteenth- and early twentieth-century scholar specializing in Elizabethan and Tudor drama. In his Shakespearean criticism, he focuses on both the biographical element and the historical influence apparent in Shakespeare's works. For this reason, many scholars today regard him as occupying a transitional position in the history of Shakespearean criticism: that between the biographical methods of Edward Dowden and Frank Harris and the historical approach of E. E. Stoll, Hardin Craig, and E. M. W. Tillyard. In the following excerpt, Boas established himself as the first critic to categorize* Measure for Measure, All's Well That Ends Well, Hamlet, *and* Troilus and Cressida *as Shakespeare's "problem-plays." To Boas, these plays are characterized by corrupt, "highly artificial societies" and depict "intricate cases of conscience" by which "we are excited, fascinated, perplexed, for the issues raised preclude a satisfactory outcome." In* Troilus and Cressida, *remarks Boas, Shakespeare satirizes "the high-flown ideal of love" and medieval chivalry and degrades the traditional representation of Cressida by portraying her as "a cold-blooded profligate," an assessment of her character similar to that of August Wilhelm Schlegel (1808) and G. G. Gervinus (1849-50). Also, like Schlegel, Gervinus, and Hermann Ulrici (1839), Boas discusses the intent of Shakespeare's travesty of medieval legends. He proposes that the target of this satire of the Trojan War is not Homer, but Shakespeare's contemporary and "rival poet," George Chapman, who translated the* Iliad. *Boas compares Thersites's "profanation of all things human" to Jonathan Swift's satiric vision of the Yahoos in* Gulliver's Travels, *and he concludes that Shakespeare's bitter treatment of chivalry is too harsh, for the feudal code of love and honor "deserves better than to be made the butt of savage scorn."*]

The opening of the seventeenth century coincides almost exactly with a sharp turning-point in Shakspere's dramatic career. On one side of the year 1601 lie comedies of matchless charm and radiance, and histories which are half comedies. On the other appear plays, in which historical matter is given a tragic setting, or in which comedy for the most part takes the grim form of dramatic satire. The change has been compared to the passage from a sunny charming landscape to a wild mountain-district whose highest peaks are shrouded in thick mist. The causes of this startling alteration in the poet's mood are, as has been shown, in great measure obscure. . . . [A] cause that has been suggested for the dramatist's change from gaiety to gloom, is the failure of the conspiracy of Essex, followed by the execution of the Earl and the imprisonment of Shakspere's friend Southampton. . . . It can scarcely be a mere coincidence that *Julius Caesar* immediately follows the Earl's tragic end, and it is remarkable that most of the plays which with more or less warrant may be assigned to the last three years of Elizabeth's reign, contain painful studies of the weakness, levity, and unbridled passion of young men. This is especially the case with *All's Well that Ends Well, Measure for Measure, Troilus and Cressida,* and *Hamlet.* The last-named play is, of course, distinguished from the others by its tragic ending, but it is akin to them in its general temper and atmosphere. All these dramas introduce us into highly artificial societies, whose civliization is ripe unto rottenness. Amidst such media abnormal conditions of brain and of emotion are generated, and intricate cases of conscience demand a solution by unprecedented methods. Thus throughout these plays we move along dim untrodden paths, and at the close our feeling is neither of simple joy nor pain; we are excited, fascinated, perplexed, for the issues raised preclude a completely satisfactory outcome, even when, as in *All's Well* and *Measure for Measure,* the complications are outwardly adjusted in the fifth act. In *Troilus and Cressida* and *Hamlet* no such partial settlement of difficulties takes place, and we are left to interpret their engimas as best we may. Dramas so singular in theme and temper cannot be strictly called comedies or tragedies. We may therefore borrow a convenient phrase from the theatre of to-day and class them together as Shakspere's problem-plays. (pp. 344-45)

Shakspere's lyrical period lay far behind him when he was attracted to the story of Troilus and Cressida. He saw in it the materials for a merciless satire of the high-flown ideal of love, fostered by the mediaeval cycle of romance, whence the tale had sprung. The absolute devotion of a gallant to his mistress, which this form of literature had glorified, is transformed into the delirious passion of a youth for a mere wanton. The knightly love which Spenser had sung of in *The Faerie Queene* as a sublime and half-unearthly rapture, the all-powerful stimulus to the practice of every virtue, is here exhibited as an intoxication of the senses, paralyzing the will, blinding the gaze, and sapping manhood at its source. (p. 373)

Shakspere's treatment of the story involves the degradation of Cressida. The charming coquette of Benoit, the voluptuous court-lady of Boccaccio, the tender-hearted widow of Chaucer, becomes in the play a scheming cold-blooded profligate. Such a woman does not need to have Troilus' suit pressed upon her by Pandarus, and if she 'holds off' for a time, it is merely, as she frankly confesses, to gratify her vanity and eagerness for despotic sway over her lover. . . . (p. 375)

It is however when we turn to the secondary plot, introducing the chief heroes of the rival hosts, that we have to face the main difficulty of the play. That the creator of a Prince Henry and a Hotspur should bring on the stage in travestied form the glorious paragons of antiquity, an Achilles and an Ajax, is at first sight one of the most startling phenomena in literature. It looks as if Shakspere, conscious that he was wrestling with Homer for the supreme poetic crown of all time, thought to secure victory by heaping ridicule upon his rival. Or, to put it in a more symbolical manner, the genius of Romantic drama might seem to be taking its revenge upon the classical ideals which had sought to strangle it in its cradle. But for such a view there is not the slightest solid foundation. The sources of the secondary plot, like those of the main story, are not classical but mediaeval. . . . [The] majesty, the severe and sculpturesque beauty of the Greek epos, cannot have been revealed to him. For the only form in which he could have become familiar with the *Iliad* was Chapman's version of the first seven books, published in 1598. This version had great and unique merits, but its use of quaint conceits prevented it from reproducing the massive simplicity of the original. Moreover it should not be forgotten that in all probability Chapman was the rival poet who ousted Shakspere from his patron's favour, and that this translation seems to have been one of the causes of his triumph. It is therefore a highly plausible conclusion that Shakspere in this travesty was attacking not Homer but Chapman. The personages for whom Chapman stood as chief literary sponsor would have, in the dramatist's eyes, nothing of the sacrosanct inviolability with which they are clothed for all who have bowed in the temple of Greek art. (pp. 377-78)

[Whatever] rag of nobility still clings to the chief actors in the drama is pitilessly stripped off by Thersites, who to some of his original Homeric characteristics, now adds those of the Shaksperean fool. The result is a loathsome creation, who has enough of coarse plebeian insight to spy out all that is bestial beneath the fair shows of human life, and enough licence of speech to vent the leprous scum of his brain where he will, with nothing worse to fear than a cudgelling. The war on his lips sinks to the level of a brawl in the vilest of resorts. (p. 382)

Whatever Thersites touches he leaves polluted with slime. Mankind as viewed by him does not belie the description of it in *Gulliver's Travels* as 'the most pernicious race of little odious vermin that Nature ever suffered to crawl upon the face of the earth.' And indeed the spirit in which Shakspere conceived the character of Thersites is akin to that in which Swift drew the appalling picture of the Yahoos. Not that this nauseating figure is to be taken as the 'chorus' of the play. His profanation of all things human is as far removed from the sane, equitable worldly wisdom of Ulysses as are the delirium of Troilus, the self-love of Achilles. They are dazzled to realities by the false glitter of fantastic ideals; Thersites is blinded to them by a congenital disease of moral vision. But only in a mood of bitterest disenchantment with the world could such a character have been conceived. Even were he removed, the atmosphere of the play would still be black with the shadow of a great eclipse. And in this case the flight of time has added to, instead of, as often, taking away from the effect of the work. The reader of to-day mourns the degradation of the mediaeval romance of love and chivalry into a satire, however legitimate in itself, of the mediaeval ideals. It is turning the swords of the offspring against their mother's breast. And even if this be pardoned, we shudder, as an Elizabethan would never have done, at the spectacle of the god-like creations of the Greek Muse being dragged through the dirt. It scarcely soothes our pain, though it rectifies our judgement, when we realize that the Achilles of Shakspere is not 'the great Achilles whom we knew,' that his Ajax is simply a *magni nominis umbra* ["shadow of a great name''']. They are mediaeval figures decked out in borrowed trappings, and the shafts that riddle them glance harmless from the glorious forms under whose titles they masquerade. But even as a satire of chivalry, *Troilus and Cressida* overshoots the mark. The feudal code of love and honour, artificial though it be, deserves better than to be made the butt of savage scorn. Cervantes, within almost the same hour, had discovered a more excellent fashion of smiling it away. (pp. 383-84)

Frederick S. Boas, ''The Problem-Plays,'' in his Shakspere and His Predecessors, *Charles Scribner's Sons*, 1896, pp. 344-408.

E. K. CHAMBERS   (essay date 1907)

[*Chambers occupies a transitional position in Shakespearean criticism, one which connects the biographical sketches and character analyses of the nineteenth century with the historical, technical, and textual criticism of the twentieth century. While a member of the education department at Oxford University, Chambers earned his reputation as a scholar with his multivolume works,* The Medieval Stage *(1903) and* The Elizabethan Stage *(1923), while he also edited* The Red Letter Shakespeare *(1904-08). Chambers both investigated the purpose and limitations of each dramatic genre as Shakespeare presented it and speculated on how the dramatist's work was influenced by contemporary historical issues and his own frame of mind. In his comments on* Troilus and Cressida, *which first appeared in 1907 in* The Red Letter Shakespeare, *Chambers counters the traditional reading of Cressida's character put forth by such critics as Charlotte Lennox (1754) and August Wilhelm Schlegel (1808) as that of a ''professional wanton.'' He contends instead that though she was ''but a light woman,'' her love vows were in earnest. This more favorable view of Cressida is later extended by Tucker Brooke (1928), Barbara Heliodora C. de M. F. de Almeida (1964), Jan Kott (1964), and D. A. Traversi (1968), all of whom regard her as a victim of circumstances. Chambers also suggests elements of Shakespeare's disillusionment in the play, an observation previously made by Edward Dowden (1877) and George Brandes (1895-96), but later challenged by John S. P. Tatlock (1915) and Oscar James Campbell (1938).*]

In *Troilus and Cressida* a disillusioned Shakespeare turns back upon his own former ideals and the world's ancient ideals of heroism and romance, and questions them. Love of woman and honour of man; do they really exist, or are they but the thin veils which poetic sentiment has chosen to throw over the grinning realities of wantonness and egoism? The comedy sets the issues with a grave irony which alone differentiates it from a tragedy. The choice of its theme is determined by the audacity of genius. The idealists are challenged upon their own ground. The tale of Troy had had a unique literary history. In its turn it had served as the supreme expression, first of epic and then of romance. Upon Homer's great narrative of the ten years' struggle between Greece and Ilium and of the chivalric heroisms of Hector and Achilles, Chaucer had raised a superstructure in which the relations of Troilus and Cressida were decked out with the last dying splendours of mediaeval amorous romance. It would be the triumph of disillusion to bring the battering-rams of analysis to bear upon this unassailable story, until Achilles shall be displayed as no better than a poltroon and Cressida as the merest light o' love.

The thing is written as a comedy, and the intention does not at once declare itself. But for the doubtful talk of and about Helen and the significant presence of Pandar the early scenes

in Troy might be the introduction to an ordinary love plot. Troilus is an honest boy enough—

As true as truth's simplicity,
And simpler than the infancy of truth;

[III. ii. 169-70]

and although one could wish that Cressida's resentment at her uncle's intervention were more thorough-going, her oncomings and her shrinkings do not differ much, save perhaps for a touch of hotter blood, from those of Rosalind in *As You Like It*. Nor does Shakespeare, to heighten his contrast, spare an expense of poetry in the delineation of the raptures and the vows of the lovers. The illusion must convince before it is pricked and shown to be a bubble. Troilus finds great words with which to sign away his soul for an eternity—

True swains in love shall in the world to come
Approve their truth by Troilus. When their rhymes,
Full of protest, of oath, and big compare,
Want similes, truth tired with iteration,
'As true as steel, as plantage to the moon,
As sun to day, as turtle to her mate,
As iron to adamant, as earth to the centre,'
Yet after all comparisons of truth,
As truth's authentic author to be cited,
'As true as Troilus' shall crown up the verse
And sanctify the numbers.

[III. ii. 173-83]

And the shallowness of Cressida's little nature is hidden when she lifts her eyes to reply—

If I be false, or swerve a hair from truth,
When time is old and hath forgot itself,
When waterdrops have worn the stones of Troy,
And blind oblivion swallowed cities up,
And mighty states characterless are grated
To dusty nothing; yet let memory,
From false to false, among false maids in love,
Upbraid my falsehood!

[III. ii. 186-91]

It is a delicate love-scene too in the cool dawn before the fateful knocking of Aeneas comes upon the door of Pandar's house; and the lark which gives warning that brief night is past can hardly fail to suggest a deliberate reminiscence of the corresponding episode in *Romeo and Juliet*. Then comes the parting, and a reluctant Cressida must to the Grecian camp. The lyric note is sustained to the end, and the vague doubts that already begin to haunt the soul of Troilus lend pathos to his hurried leavetaking—

Injurious Time now, with a robber's haste,
Crams his rich thievery up, he knows not how.
As many farewells as be stars in heaven,
With distinct breath and consigned kisses to them,
He fumbles up into a loose adieu;
And scants us with a single famished kiss,
Distasted with the salt of broken tears.

[IV. iv. 42-8]

Cressida is beheld only twice again; firstly when the cool self-possession which she shows at her somewhat disconcerting reception in the Grecian camp leads Ulysses, who knows the hearts of men and women, to set her down at first sight as a sluttish spoil of opportunity and daughter of the game; and lastly in the midnight scene before the tent of Calchas, where all her coquetries are bestowed upon Diomede before the revolting eyes of Troilus, and the lad's young edifice of faiths and loyalties comes crumbling about his feet. The disillusionment of Troilus is our disillusionment, and to Pandar, with his insolent leer at the 'brethren and sisters of the hold-door trade' [V. x. 51] whom he professes to find in the audience, is committed the epilogue of the play, Troilus will not have us 'square the general sex by Cressid's rule' [V. ii. 132-33]; but indeed it is to be surmised that Shakespeare meant little else. The soul of Cressida is strange to the loyalties of a Juliet before her or an Imogen after her. Her nearest sister is perhaps the pitiful and frail Ophelia. But she is not a psychological monstrosity like her uncle. To set her down as a professional wanton who deliberately angles for the soul of her lover, were to mistake the play. It is in her humanity that the bitterness of it lies. She was not made of the stuff of heroines, but her vows and protestations were real enough when they were uttered. She was but a light woman. And when Shakespeare wrote her story he was in a mood to say, 'She was but a woman.' (pp. 193-96)

> E. K. Chambers, "'Troilus and Cressida'," in his *Shakespeare: A Survey*, 1925. Reprint by Oxford University Press, 1926, pp. 191-99.

JOHN S. P. TATLOCK   (essay date 1915)

[*In a lengthy examination of the source materials of* Troilus and Cressida, *Tatlock claims that Shakespeare made more use of William Caxton's* Recuyell of the Histories of Troy *than of Homer's* Iliad, *and, pointing out the play's affinity with Thomas Heywood's* Iron Age, *proposes that Shakespeare either borrowed from Heywood or that the two playwrights shared a common source in some other, older play, now lost. In the conclusion of his study, excerpted below, Tatlock challenges the view held by such critics as Edward Dowden (1877), George Brandes (1895-96), and E. K. Chambers (1907) that* Troilus and Cressida *reflects a mood of gloom and despair in Shakespeare's life. Tatlock contends, in an argument somewhat similar to that of Oscar James Campbell (1938), that the apparently pessimistic elements of the play are not Shakespeare's inventions, but can be traced back to the sources. He notes that the foolish Ajax, the railing Thersites, and the unfaithful Cressida each have a precedent in earlier literary accounts of the Trojan War. Thus, concludes Tatlock, Shakespeare's portrayal of the heroes is "perfectly intelligible" and the outcome of the love affair is "inevitable," a position later reiterated by William Witherle Lawrence (1931), but questioned by Paul Kendall (1951). Tatlock places* Troilus and Cressida *among the history plays, saying that there "is absolutely no essential difference" between it and* Henry IV.].

With all the critics who have questioned the Sphynx about it, who have even called it the chief problem in Shakespeare, it is surprising that [*Troilus and Cressida*] and its tone have not been more thoroughly analyzed. Many critics see nothing but bitterness in it; others see mainly humor and wisdom. There is truth in both views, for there is scurrility and there is nobility; *but they are not mixed.* Nothing could be more entirely weighty and stately than the personalities and talk in act I, scene iii, where the Greek princes discuss the need of authority, and Aeneas brings Hector's chivalrous challenge; than those in II, ii, where the Trojan peers debate the return of Helen; in III, iii (till near the end), where Achilles' words are almost as wise as Ulysses'; in IV, v, with its chivalrous cordiality (except for the beginning and for Achilles' talk toward the end); or than the heroism and pathos of V, iii. These scenes seem to be largely Shakespeare's own addition to the story, and only a very prejudiced reader can fail to see that he wrote them with perfect seriousness and sympathy. We are always liable to prejudice because we inevitably come to the play with our

minds full of Homer; but Shakespeare came to it with his mind mostly full of Caxton, and he has here risen far above Caxton in dignity and beauty. So far as he knew Homer, he probably felt towards him quite otherwise than we do. The main point is this,—we must exchange the absolute for the relative conception of literature. The normal human reaction to Homer is not one and the same, as the history of his reputation will prove. A poet's renown sometimes becomes fixed only because people cease to read him. To Shakespeare the *Iliad* was one book among many; read probably, if at all, in a crude translation, it may even have seemed to him thin and unreal. On his part an attitude toward the Greeks like that of such moderns as Keats and Swinburne is unthinkable; the austere and serene background of Greek sculpture and architecture against which we see them was utterly unknown to him. The greatest charm of Homer lies in the fact that *all* his people are noble and godlike, but a drama is bound to be less heroic than an epic. Analysis shows such figures as Agamemnon, Ulysses, Achilles, to be more realistic and therefore less heroic or charming, but not really more debased, than Caxton. Shakespeare had no sense that Achilles must be handled with reverence. But he was no more conscious of debasing, through the necessity of humanizing and dramatizing, than conscious of incongruity through the inevitable introduction of chivalry. An open-minded reading of these scenes, the most original part of the play, should make it forever impossible to regard the Shakespeare of *Troilus and Cressida* as full merely of weary disillusion and angry pain.

When we consider the parts of the play which do seem to show a harsh, unsympathetic spirit, we find the chief vehicles of it to be three. The tone embodied in Ajax, Thersites, and the love-motive does need comment. Ajax generally cuts a thoroughly comic figure; but as such he had already had a long history . . . which accounts for his paradoxical character, and his absurd appearance here is a (if not the) natural conception, especially as a dramatic foil to his opponent, the always noble Hector. Thersites too is entirely explicable. Quite definitely the Fool of the play (II, iii) he is merely filled in from the sketch in the second book of the *Iliad;* in Shakespeare he says at large what Homer says he says; . . . Shakespeare was doubtless not the first to introduce him to the Troilus-drama, and . . . he is not greatly intensified beyond what he is in Heywood. Shocking as it was to Victorian Hellenolatry, hateful as it is to us, to read the epithets he applies to Agamemnon and his peers, and to see him brawling and scuffling with that undignified trio Ajax, Patroclus, and Achilles, when the play is witnessed Thersites and his deformed spite and ugly half-truths recede into the remote littleness where they belong. Those who see and hear the nobler Greek princes will not take his view of them. We have been in their stately presence (I, iii) and they have even prepared us for his venom [I. iii. 73-4, 192 ff.], before we ever see him (II, i). Elsewhere Shakespeare gives us lovers, heroes, doubters, murderers, raised to the *n*th power; here he gives us likewise a railer. Thersites must have vastly pleased the groundlings and brought in many a testern. As to the love-story, no sympathy is aroused, or at any rate maintained by it,—by Troilus' callow enthusiasm, Cressida's weak voluptuousness and bold coquetry, and Pandarus' elderly prurience; yet all this is developed beyond what it is in most other versions. All charm in Troilus' Romeo-like loves is destroyed by their instant publicity (IV, i-iv). The poet's attitude toward this story was the only one possible in his day; Chaucer, though he would fain have excused Criseyde, had left her without excuse, Henryson had degraded and chastised her; by Shakespeare's day her good name was gone forever, and she was merely a by-word for a light woman; and in her descent she had necessarily dragged down her lover and her uncle, whose name had already long become that of his trade. Troilus as a man and fighter stands high in grace; only as a lover is he abased. The loves of Paris and Helen fare little better, though they are less prominent; in IV, i, Shakespeare goes out of his way to apply gross language to them. For this too he had ample precedent; yet the harsh fact remains that *Troilus* is Shakespeare's only play except *Timon* with no likable female character and with love prominent but debased, and that he might have slighted but chooses to emphasize them. A study of the play in the light of its sources makes his attitude toward the Greek and Trojan heroes perfectly intelligible, his attitude toward the lovers even inevitable; if it does not wholly explain the prominence he gives a base love-affair, perhaps even the "gentle Shakespeare" found an interest in portraying this new kind of love, enough interest at least to lead him to keep what he found in an older play. Why not?

Analysis then shows the harshness of the play to be less than is often deemed, and so far as it exists to be explicable without deriving it from the poet's mood when he wrote. The undeniably unpleasant effect some critics and readers are penetrating enough to see is due quite as much to its confusion and want of internal harmony as to anything else. We have chivalrous gallantry, stupid and cowardly savagery, stately dignity, voluptuousness without charm, weighty wisdom, low scurrility. This means a bad play; it does not mean an angry and embittered playwright, but rather a handicapped, careless, and indifferent one. A hastily written thing may give a totally different impression from what the writer intends or is even aware of. With so experienced a dramatist as Shakespeare we should ascribe the discord to the essential incongruity of his two conceptions. He did not wish to lower one part of the play to the level of the other. Some parts he wrote with sympathy and interest, some he took as he found them and intensified to add to their effectiveness, but without liking. He poured new wine into old bottles; he sewed a piece of new cloth into an old garment, and the rent was made worse. But for the very reason that the painfulness is partly due to the confusion and internal discord, matters which especially impress the casual reader, it is hard to convince him of the truth of the present interpretation, hard to do the play justice on a mere reading.

The facts seem to favor such an explanation of *Troilus and Cressida* as this. Shakespeare found it expedient to make over an older play (to write, at least) on this highly popular subject. He did it with no great interest, except in the more masculine and statesmanlike scenes. Homer, read, if at all, probably in a poor translation, took no particular hold on him, he admitted the light of common day to the *sanctum sanctorum,* and the general tone of the play followed that of the late mediaeval works which were the chief authority for the Trojan war even in the 16th century. To relieve the heaviness of the deliberations which form so much of the play he made fun for his popular audience by a comic Ajax and by Homer's ribald Thersites. Sated with, perhaps, reacting from, the ordinary light romantic love, indeed finding it incompatible with the material of this play, yet not wishing to omit the love-motive in a play with a popular appeal, perhaps feeling it desirable to develop it, he produced a masterly study of an alluring wanton and the first passion of a full-blooded very young man. The most valuable pointer for interpreting the work is the probability that he wrote it without the deep interest which he put on the greater plays which were to follow directly, such as probably *Hamlet.* So far as we can retrace the mental processes of an impersonal

dramatist three centuries dead, this conclusion seems reasonable; more reasonable than to attribute the work to a fit of misanthropy, love-disillusion, literary jealousy. It is no longer possible to think of Shakespeare as guided only by his own taste and temper in choosing his material from Chaucer, Homer, and Caxton, or from an earlier play; he did not care greatly to modify the literary tradition, as is clear from the close resemblance of his play to *Iron Age,* from its general parallelism to several other works, and probably to the numerous lost versions. The call for a play on a vulgarly popular subject, the lack of our feeling of traditional veneration for some of its sources, want of deep interest in the popular part of the play, will thoroughly account for its tone and spirit. In their desire to banish all mystery, critics have created much mystery where there is little.

[In a footnote Tatlock adds:]

> One question often raised is whether the play is a comedy or a tragedy. I asked it of Mr. Fry, the only Englishman in three centuries known to have put the play on. He said, "It's neither, it's just *a play*." A better answer is that it's both, it's a historical play. Shakespeare meant to give a mingled impression, and was prevented from unifying plot or feeling by the fact that the material was too well known to be much modified. There is absolutely no essential difference between the *Troilus* and *Henry IV*. The charm of seeing on the stage personages familiar in books and tradition atoned for the undramatic character of their story. . . .

A few words more, on the wider bearings of this conclusion, a large subject on which I can barely touch. One critic after another has felt the interpretation of *Troilus and Cressida* to be the chief problem in Shakespeare-criticism. It has been the main support of the theory that in the first few years of the 17th century Shakespeare was in a thoroughly pessimistic frame of mind. For the prevalence of this idea there have been two main reasons. One is the character of the plays written about this time. But it is unnecessary to argue formally that the writing of tragedies does not imply a pessimistic frame of mind; precedent would rather point to just the contrary. Such other themes as those of *Measure for Measure* and *All's Well That Ends Well,* which *may* date from this period, may well have attracted him by reason of their difficulty, and as a practise-school before coming to the exacting themes of tragedy. The other reason is the desire to understand Shakespeare the man, at his worst as at his best. Humanity is grateful to him, and wishes to know its benefactor. There has been an almost touching desire to draw near him through a sacramental Real Presence in his plays. The pessimism theory has been especially developed by critics who have attempted to trace his full spiritual history, and to relate his plays in detail to his life. But the events in his life which have been brought forward to explain the supposed pessimism are absurdly inadequate. It is the duty of sound criticism, dealing with so impersonal, objective, and practical a writer as Shakespeare, to seek first objective explanations. If we find such, as we certainly may for the plays of this period, we must put such theories in the realm of creative imagination, not of scientifically-minded criticism. Of course Shakespeare expressed himself in his plays; but, so far as we can see, it was the whole self which had resulted from his whole experience of life, not his temporary self in an instantaneous rebound from this or that immediate experience. Criticism is moving farther and farther from the 18th century view of him as a closet theorizer, and the mid-19th century idea of a closet dramatist, to that of a practical dramatist who had professional and theatrical reasons for what he did. (pp. 760-70)

> John S. P. Tatlock, "The Seige of Troy in Elizabethan Literature, Especially in Shakespeare and Heywood," in PMLA, 30 Vol. XXX, No. 4, 1915, pp. 673-770.

TUCKER BROOKE (essay date 1928)

[*Brooke was an American scholar and editor of the Yale Shakespeare series, a collection praised by critics for its sound annotations and careful attention to textual problems and source materials. In his study of the history of Tudor and Elizabethan drama, Brooke paid particular attention to the social and intellectual backgrounds of the era. He also contributed significantly to the knowledge of Elizabethan stage conventions, set designs, and the actual productions of plays. In his comments on* Troilus and Cressida, *first published in* The Yale Review *in 1928, Brooke asserts that the play is a study of the effect of environment on character. Thus, unlike such previous critics as Charlotte Lennox (1754) and August Wilhelm Schlegel (1808), Brooke does not characterize Cressida as a duplicitous whore, but rather as "a flower growing in the Trojan slime," a view which is supported by such later critics as Barbara Heliodora C. de M. F. de Almeida (1964), Jan Kott (1964), and D. A. Traversi (1968). He also proposes that* Troilus and Cressida *reflects the state of English politics and society at the start of the seventeenth century and that it anticipates the cleavage between the Royalists and the Puritans later in the century.*]

That colossal and magnificent failure, *Troilus and Cressida,* I should like to present as one of Shakespeare's subtlest studies of the effect of environment on character and as his most definite realization of the social forces operative in England at the end of Queen Elizabeth's reign. Three strands of source material make up its fabric, and the first of these, in importance as in sequence, is Chaucer.

Had Shakespeare, as many have said, read his predecessor's great poem inattentively, or with prejudice and dislike? If so, the less Shakespeare he. (p. 72)

We must not, I think, if we would interpret Shakespeare's play aright, doubt that it bears the proper title—that it is fundamentally the play of Chaucer's defeated lovers, a frailer Romeo and Juliet, "whose misadventur'd piteous overthrows" [*Romeo and Juliet,* Prologue, 7] could not be romantically glorified as a moral victory, and perhaps for just that reason made special appeal to a dramatist who, by the period of *Hamlet* and *Troilus and Cressida,* had lost his joy in successful people.

I cannot believe that Shakespeare shared the contempt which the Elizabethan public generally and the race of modern critics have felt for Cressida. She is a more helpless being than Chaucer's Criseyde, a flower growing in Trojan slime, a little soiled from the first and shrinkingly conscious of her predestined pollution; yet Shakespeare's attitude to her is much more that of Chaucer than that of Ulysses. . . . In her relations with both her lovers he shows us the pathos of a daintiness reaching vainly after nobility, a wistful sincerity which knows it lacks strength to be the thing it would be. (p. 73)

When Shakespeare came—it was probably in 1602, while the Elizabethan age was sluggishly ebbing into the Jacobean—to realize in a play this Chaucerian story of frosted romance, he had recourse to two further books, which he used to create an

outward world for Troilus and Cressida. Since 1596 he might have known the Elizabethan version of Caxton's Troy book, *The Ancient History of the Destruction of Troy.* . . . Since 1598 he can have known the earliest and only relevant installments of Chapman's Homer. Both these bizarrely opposite reconstructions of life at Troy he certainly did know when he wrote his play; and to understand the nature of that play I think it is not necessary to assume that he knew much else, except of course always Chaucer.

Now the two salient features of the Caxton account (translated from Lefèvre's fifteenth-century French) are: first, that it concentrates attention strongly upon the people within the walls of Troy, the Trojans; and, second, that it narrates the incidents of the siege in exaggeratedly medieval, chivalresque manner after the fashion of Malory or Froissart. Armored knights on horseback fight sanguinary battles that are described like tournaments, and bring their copious wounds to scars during long truces of six months each. It is not true that Caxton (or Lefèvre) shows any moral preference for the Trojan side. On the contrary, he makes it far clearer than Homer does that the Trojans are in the wrong: that their policy is vindictive and treacherous, that Priam is thoroughly dishonest, and Paris a dastardly sensualist and assassin. Hector is a noble warrior fighting against his conscience and better judgment; Aeneas and Antenor are "open traitors unto their city and also to their king and lord."

The striking characteristics in Chapman's Homer, on the other hand, are first, that it fixes the interest upon the Greek camp; and second, that Chapman brutalizes and roughens the simplicity of the Greek original. In Chapman, Homer's naïveté of speech becomes unredeemed billingsgate; Homer's temperamental primitives become arrant cowards, braggarts, and bullies.

Where another writer might have attempted to mediate between these two irreconcilable accounts, Shakespeare has seized the essential spirit of each, poetically intensified it, and hurled both, unmixed and forever unmixable, into the seething vortex of his play. Thus he produces a milieu for Troilus and Cressida, the forlorn and fated lovers, wandering between two worlds: the effete, immoral, over-refined world of Troy, and the brutal, quarrelsome, cynical world of the Greeks. Paris is on the one side, Diomed on the other. Shakespeare makes each of these environments develop its special type figure, emblematic of the worst in itself. (pp. 74-5)

Pandarus and Thersites are the Scylla and Charybdis of the lovers' voyage, and their extremes meet in only one point—in lechery, which they keep shrieking, lisping, and insinuating till the echoes meet and merge like a miasma over the whole play, and all the nobility of life is choked.

Greater scenes and more magnificent lines than some that are found in *Troilus and Cressida* it is agreed that Shakespeare seldom wrote. The question is, what was his purpose? I cannot help imagining that he is, however subconsciously, anatomizing the England of the dying Elizabeth: within the wall, the febrile Essex type of decadent chivalry; without, the strident go-getters of the newer dispensation: Cecil-Ulysses and Ralegh-Diomed. I take it that Shakespeare glimpsed somehow the seriousness of the cleavage between Cavalier and Puritan, sensed in Thersites the lowering shadow of Prynne and the iconoclasts, foresaw in Pandarus the portent of the scandalous Carr, Earl of Somerset. Indeed, when reading the great culminating scene (the second of Act V), in which Troilus, the heartbroken young cavalier, and the shrewd old puritan, Ulysses, are drawn together against a giddy and immoral universe, one may almost feel that the writing is prophetic—that the thing must have happened, not at ancient Troy but forty years after the play was created, on some night when Royalist and Cromwellian met beneath the walls of Oxford.

I do not argue that *Troilus and Cressida* is conscious political allegory, but only that Shakespeare, about 1602, had some vision of the extent to which the Chaucerian delicacy of life was threatened by the two great coarsening influences which in fact were then attacking the nation, and that he conceived upon this theme a very wise, spirited, and subtle play. (pp. 76-7)

> Tucker Brooke, "*Shakespeare's Study in Culture and Anarchy,*" in his Essays on Shakespeare and Other Elizabethans, *Archon Books, Hamden, CT, 1969, pp. 71-7.*

G. WILSON KNIGHT   (essay date 1930)

[*Knight is one of the most influential Shakespearean critics of the twentieth century; he helped shape a new interpretive approach to Shakespeare's work and promoted a greater appreciation of many of the plays. In his studies* The Wheel of Fire (1930) *and* The Shakespearian Tempest (1932), *Knight rejected critics who emphasized sources, character analysis, psychology, and ethics and outlined his principles of interpretation which, he claimed, would "replace that chaos by drawing attention to the true Shakespearian unity." Knight argued that this unity lay in Shakespeare's poetic use of images and symbols—particularly in the opposition of "tempests" and "music." He also maintained that a play's spatial aspects, or "atmosphere," should be as closely considered as the temporal elements of the plot if one is "to see the whole play in space as well as time." In his influential discussion of* Troilus and Cressida, *taken from the first work mentioned above, Knight examines the "peculiarly analytic" language of the play and argues that it presents an opposition between the reasoning intellect of the Greeks and the emotional intuition of the Trojans. For the purpose of his essay, Knight equates intellect with cynicism and intuition with romantic faith, identifying Thersites as "the extreme personification of the view of life developed in the Greek party" and Troilus as the champion of Troy fighting for the "fine values of humanity" against the "demon powers of cynicism." He notes, however, that even Troilus is torn between these two world views, and that though he occasionally gives in to "much-despised 'reason',"* he is ultimately moved by "the fires of human nobility and romance." In asserting that Shakespeare endows the Trojans with more noble human values, Knight is in agreement with Samuel Taylor Coleridge (1834), Winifred M. T. Nowottny (1954), and Albert Gérard (1959). On the other hand, Oscar James Campbell (1938), L. C. Knights (1951), Terence Eagleton (1967), D. A. Traversi (1968), and Thomas G. West (1981), while concurring that the two camps present a philosophical opposition, reject Knight's argument that the Trojans are morally superior to the Greeks. Knight also observes a second opposition at work in the play, that between the social order and the individual will, an issue that has also been considered by Denton J. Snider (1890), H. B. Charlton (1937), Terence Eagleton (1967), and R. A. Yoder (1972). Another critical issue that receives its first comprehensive treatment by Knight is Shakespeare's portrayal of time in* Troilus and Cressida. *Knight interprets time in this play as a destroyer of values, a concept which is later treated by S. C. Sen Gupta (1950), L. C. Knights (1951), Norman Rabkin (1965), D. A. Traversi (1968), and R. A. Yoder (1972).*]

Troilus and Cressida is more peculiarly analytic in language and dramatic meaning than any other work of Shakespeare. Often it has been called difficult, incoherent. It may be superficially difficult, but it is not incoherent. The difficulties,

moreover, being essentially those of intellectual complexity, lend themselves naturally to intellectual interpretation. When once we see clearly the central idea—it is almost a 'thesis'—from which the play's thought and action derive their significance, most of the difficulties vanish.

The theme is this. Human values are strongly contrasted with human failings. In Shakespeare there are two primary values, love and war. These two are vividly present in *Troilus and Cressida*. But they exist in a world which questions their ultimate purpose and beauty. The love of Troilus, the heroism of Hector, the symbolic romance which burns in the figure of Helen—these are placed beside the 'scurril jests' and lazy pride of Achilles, the block-headed stupidity of Ajax, the mockery of Thersites. The Trojan party stands for human beauty and worth, the Greek party for the bestial and stupid elements of man, the barren stagnancy of intellect divorced from action, and the criticism which exposes these things with jeers. The atmospheres of the two opposing camps are thus strongly contrasted, and the handing over of Cressida to the Greeks, which is the pivot incident of the play, has thus a symbolic suggestion. These two primary aspects of humanity can next be provisionally equated with the concepts 'intuition' and 'intellect', or 'emotion' and 'reason'. In the play this distinction sometimes assumes the form of an antinomy between 'individualism' and 'social order'. Now human values rest on an intuitive faith or an intuitive recognition: the denial of them—which may itself be largely emotional—if not directly caused by intellectual reasoning, is very easily related to such reasoning, and often looks to it for its own defence. Cynicism is eminently logical to the modern, post-Renaissance, mind. Therefore, though aware that my terms cannot be ultimately justified as exact labels for the two faculties under discussion, I use them for my immediate purpose to point the peculiar dualism that persists in the thought of this play. Thus 'intellect' is considered here as tending towards 'cynicism', and 'intuition' in association with 'romantic faith'—a phrase chosen to suggest the dual values, love and war. We can then say that the root idea of *Troilus and Cressida* is the dynamic opposition in the mind of these two faculties: intuition and intellect.

The language of the play is throughout pregnant with close reasoning. Many of the persons think hard and deep: the most swift and fleeting of love's glances are subjected to piercing intellectual analysis, and the profoundest questions of human fate discussed, analysed, dissected. The metaphoric phraseology is often rich in philosophic meaning; the primary persons, though not alive with the warm humanity of an Othello, yet enjoy a strangely vivid vitality of burning thought. Those who adhere to the cause of intuition think out their intuitions, try to explicate them in terms of intellect. Intelligence here is a primary quality: fools are jeered at for their blunt wits, wise men display their prolix wisdom, the lover analyses the metaphysical implications of his love. We are in a metaphysical universe. In the usual Shakespearian fashion, the problem of the main theme—the rational untrustworthiness in conflict with the intuitive validity of romantic sight—is reflected throughout the play. We are shown throughout different varieties of human vision and different grades of human intellect, insensibly merging into one another, illustrating the numerous mental reactions of man to the realities of love and war. I shall now consider: first, two subsidiary scenes of importance illustrating different forms of the intuition-intelligence opposition underlying the play's movement; second, the general significance of the Greek Party, with especial notice of Thersites; and, third, the dominant love-theme of Troilus and Cressida.

In Act I, Scene iii, the Greek generals discuss the military situation. No scene in the play more clearly illustrates and more closely defines the peculiar analytic quality here obtaining. Agamemnon chides the generals for their depression. The Greeks, he says, have had ill-luck; their plans have not resulted in the looked-for success. But these are God's trials. Not in human success, but in human failure, is the essential nobility of man made manifest. When fortune smiles all men are alike:

> But, in the wind and tempest of her frown,
> Distinction, with a broad and powerful fan,
> Puffing at all, winnows the light away;
> And what hath mass or matter, by itself
> Lies rich in virtue and unmingled.
>
> [I. iii. 26-30]

Agamemnon urges, not stoically but with warmth and feeling, that men should rejoice, not sorrow, at the storms of adversity: an admirable philosophy—but is its logical result likely to win the war? Next Nestor, from whose age the thought comes more appropriately, expands the same idea. Any frail boat dare sail on a smooth sea; but only a 'strong-ribb'd bark' dare adventure on a stormy one. He continues:

> Even so
> Doth valour's show and valour's worth divide
> In storms of fortune; for in her ray and brightness
> The herd hath more annoyance by the breese
> Than by the tiger; but when the splitting wind
> Makes flexible the knees of knotted oaks,
> And flies fled under shade, why, then the thing of
> courage
> As rous'd with rage with rage doth sympathize,
> And with an accent tun'd in selfsame key
> Retorts to chiding fortune.
>
> [I. iii. 46-54]

The imagery and phraseology in both these speeches inevitably call to mind Shakespeare's view of human tragedy. The 'bark' and the 'tempest' are recurring symbols of tragedy, to be found in numerous passages throughout the plays. Storms are symbolic of tragedy when they occur in stage directions. Its 'tempest' is, in fact, an integral part of the Shakespearian tragedy; and Shakespeare's final mystic play, *The Tempest*, primarily owes its plot and name, not to Sir George Somer's shipwreck (with which it may at the same time bear a certain secondary relation), but to the very fact of this poetic symbol. So Agamemnon and Nestor have expressed quite clearly a significant but baffling truth: the purely mystic grandeur of tragedy. The view of tragedy as essentially a victory—which is at the root of our mystic understanding of the Christian cross—though its validity to our imaginations need not be questioned, is yet very difficult if we seek for a practical application: logically, it would seem to lead to chaos or paralysis of action. Hence Ulysses' prolix reply. He answers, not Agamemnon's speech alone, but its ultimate implications. Agamemnon's words imply a philosophy of life which in turn implies a somewhat impractical mind in his conduct of the campaign. Ulysses answers with an opposing philosophy which insists on 'order' and suggests that Agamemnon has been remiss—that the Greeks fail through lack of discipline and unity. His reply is that of reason directed against the irrational grandeur of tragedy. For the tragic view of human existence, if carried to a logical conclusion and correctly symbolized in action, will, it would appear, lead to chaos. Order is essential. This thought Ulysses expands at great length. Again, Nestor counsels the nobility of tragic passion—a Lear's or a Timon's passion whose accent

is tuned to 'retort' to chiding fortune in language tempestuous as man's tempestuous fate. But if tragic passion be the highest good, if discipline and order be not man's ideal—and the choice ultimately rests between these two—then there is an end of natural harmony and human civilization:

> And, hark, what discord follows! each thing meets
> In mere oppugnancy: the bounded waters
> Should lift their bosoms higher than the shores
> And make a sop of all this solid globe:
> Strength should be lord of imbecility,
> And the rude son should strike his father dead:
> Force should be right; or rather, right and wrong,
> Between whose endless jar justice resides,
> Should lose their names and so should justice too.
>
> [I. iii. 110-18]

So, indeed, 'justice' does in truth 'lose its name' in *King Lear*: and not in *King Lear* only, but in all high tragedy properly understood.

Ulysses' speech forms a perfect statement of the case for the moral order against the high mystic philosophy of tragedy and passion. Nor is this to twist the natural meaning of a dramatic speech; for we must observe that the speeches in *Troilus and Cressida* are primarily analytic rather than dramatic, and, if we are to understand its peculiar meaning we must be ready, as are the persons of the play, to respond to the lightest tones and shades of its philosophy. This reading of the argument as a discussion of tragedy does not conflict with the dramatic situation. Agamemnon has expressed a profound and sympathetic commentary on the progress of the war. He has spoken like a mystic; but mystics seldom make good generals. Agamemnon is thus closely analogous to the Duke in *Measure for Measure*. Both speak wisdom, especially the profound mystic wisdom of the tragic philosophy. Both are, however, impractical in the ordinary sense. From the view-point of Thersites Agamemnon is an honest man enough, but a fool [V. i. 51-3]. Ulysses answers Agamemnon's gentle and noble acceptance of misfortune by suggesting that his actual conduct of the war lacks the co-ordinating and directing quality of regal discipline. This we can well believe from what we see of the Greek army. There are, then, two layers of thought here: the purely dramatic and the profoundly universal and philosophic meanings. They are not properly separate, but rather two aspects of the same thing. We have an illuminating instance of what often happens here: the persons are all obsessed with the desire of analysis, and, in the process of their search for truth, continually raise the particular into the realm of the universal. Here the crucial problem of the play is at issue: since intuition and faith accept the tragic philosophy, reason and intellect reject it. In this instance, the intuition-intellect opposition is obviously one with that of individualism and order. Ulysses, exponent always throughout the play of reason, statecraft, and order, attacks the intuitional and emotional—one might almost say the 'sentimental'—arguments of Agamemnon and Nestor. (pp. 47-51)

The next scene I would notice is Act II, Scene ii. The Trojans discuss the question of restoring Helen to the Greeks and so ending the war. Hector counsels such a course. Helen, he says, is not worth the terrific cost in Trojan lives. But Troilus—always the ardent exponent of absolute faith in a supreme value, and the necessity of translating that faith into action—argues that the King's honour is a thing 'infinite' in comparison with 'reasons'. The 'infinity' of such values as love is in different forms a usual space-metaphor in Shakespeare, suggesting the incommensurability of quality in terms of quantity. This dia-

Act IV. Scene iv. Diomedes, Paris, Cressida, Troilus, and Aeneas. Frontispiece to the Hanmer edition by H. Gravelot (1744). By permission of the Folger Shakespeare Library.

logue—and indeed the whole play—is an interesting antidote to the commentary that observes no original philosophic thought in Shakespeare:

> *Troilus.*   Fie, fie, my brother!
> Weigh you the worth and honour of a king
> So great as our dread father in a scale
> Of common ounces? will you with counters sum
> The past proportion of his infinite?
> And buckle in a waist most fathomless
> With spans and inches so diminutive
> As fear and reasons? fie, for godly shame! . . .
>
> > [II. ii. 25-32]

[The] argument gets into deep waters:

> *Hector.* Brother, she is not worth what she doth cost
>   The holding.
> *Troilus.* What is aught, but as 'tis valued?
> *Hector.* But value dwells not in particular will;
>   It holds his estimate and dignity
>   As well wherein 'tis precious of itself
>   As in the prizer: 'tis mad idolatry
>   To make the service greater than the god;
>   And the will dotes that is attributive
>   To what infectiously itself affects,
>   Without some image of the affected merit.
>
> > [II. ii. 51-60]

Hector takes his stand on the objectivity of pure value: subjective emotion by itself weighs nothing—it is sentimentalism, idolatry. The passion ('will') which infects an object in imagination with those very qualities for which it worships it is clearly absurd: it must have at least some clear-cut and objective image or concept of the quality which it adores. The word 'image' is chosen for its clear suggestion of objectivity.

Troilus' answer is of extreme importance. It is difficult. The first pregnant eight lines are as follows:

> I take to-day a wife and my election
> Is led on in the conduct of my will;
> My will enkindled by mine eyes and ears,
> Two traded pilots 'twixt the dangerous shores
> Of will and judgement; how may I avoid,
> Although my will distaste what it elected,
> The wife I chose? there can be no evasion
> To blench from this and to stand firm by honour.
>
> > [II. ii. 61-8]

This outlines a metaphysic of symbolism—which is suggested by other passages of Shakespeare and especially in the imagery of this play—a philosophy which seems to regard the shapes of materiality as bodies infused into life by the vitality of the regarding mind: matter the symbol of spirit. First, we must see clearly that 'will' stands for instinctive, unconscious passion. Troilus' meaning then is: To-day I take a wife, and my choice of her is directed by the urging power of instinctive 'will', erotic desire; this unconscious instinct having been kindled to self-expression by my senses, which serve as skilled pilots to navigate the dangerous waters between unconscious instinct and conscious judgement. That is, dormant desire in me has been awakened by my discovering a sensuous image or symbol of that desire, which image serves to bridge the gulf between consciousness and unconsciousness, between mind and soul. The suggestion is that the lover sees his own soul reflected in what he loves. He awakes to self-knowledge by seeing. His sensuous perception allows his nameless unconscious desire to reach fulfilment in self-consciousness, or 'judgement'. In this speech we have a careful analysis of love's intuition: and thence, perhaps, we may deduce a corresponding though less vivid process of ordinary sensuous perception. It will be clear that the reasoning and analysis of this play go deep: it will be clear that the mind of Shakespeare is here intensely engaged with purely philosophic issues. So Troilus champions the cause of intuition, of immediate values. But he is not consistent. For, once having made a choice, he says, it must be a point of honour to keep to it. Yet, we might ask, if immediate values are everything, why not let one value succeed another? When the 'will' does 'distaste what it elected', why not find a new sensuous image to satisfy it? To argue otherwise seems to call in the aid of the much-despised 'reason'. This is, indeed, at the root of Troilus' love-tragedy. His nature must be loyal to the dictates of a supreme intuition: but the stream of events takes its logical course in hideous reversal of his faith.

The question of Helen is discussed throughout the scene: throughout the scene the thinking is intricate and subtle, yet voiced with fervour and poetic colour. Paris, like Troilus, takes his stand on points of 'honour'. Hector quotes Aristotle, and sums up the discussion, urging the sanctity of marriage, the moral imperative of Helen's restoration, and then, after a speech of cogent reasoning, curiously concludes by asserting:

> > Hector's opinion
> Is thus in way of truth: yet ne'ertheless,

My spritely brethren, I propend to you
In resolution to keep Helen still,
For 'tis a cause that has no mean dependence
Upon our joint and several dignities.

[II. ii. 188-93]

The balance is just. Troilus' argument of immediate values does not altogether satisfy our practical reason. Hector's is eminently logical—but he himself does not act on it. And just in this indecisive fashion do human acts and judgements interpenetrate and preclude each other. Here, we should note, the adherents of intuition win against the rationalists.

I have noticed these two scenes in order to point the peculiar nature of this play: its analytic and metaphysical quality. In both scenes the argument may be said to concern some form of the intuition-intellect opposition: the opposition from which is struck the spark of the central love-theme of Troilus. But before I pass to this the central theme of the play, I shall indicate briefly certain important strata of the life-view expressed in some other subsidiary scenes and persons on the side of the Greek party. This view is pre-eminently analytic and critical: and where it is critical, criticism is levelled, not as in *Measure for Measure,* against moral failings, but rather against lack of wisdom and intellect. This critical attitude extends from the studied commentary of Ulysses to the violent invectives of Thersites. The figures of Achilles and Ajax are selected for especial satire, and their behaviour shown not so much as immoral as essentially stupid. (pp. 52-5)

Both Achilles and Ajax—the latter conceived as a hopeless blockhead—are butts for the invectives of Thersites. Thersites grows naturally enough from this intellectual satirical atmosphere. He is cynicism incarnate: a demoniac spirit of keen critical apprehension, who sees the stupid and sordid aspects of mankind, fit only for jeers with which he salutes them in full measure. His critical intellect measures man always by intellectual standards. He sees folly everywhere, and finds no wisdom in mankind's activity. He sees one side of the picture only: man's stupidity. He is blind to man's nobility. The choice is between these two. For, if values of beauty, love, goodness, honour, be subtracted from our view of man, what is left is profoundly stupid: a critical intellect can prove almost any endeavour to be meaningless, any end illogical, any passionate hope a delusion. What is left is an animal aping something which he cannot attain, with no inherent reason for his absurd pride. Thersites' satire is thus eminently comparable with Swift's: *Gulliver's Travels* is an illuminating and exquisitely apt commentary on this especial mode of the Shakespearian hate-theme which sets the stage for *Troilus and Cressida.* (pp. 57-8)

Thersites is the extreme personification of the view of life developed in the Greek party of *Troilus and Cressida.* We partly endorse his opinion, without countenancing his manners. Mankind and their loves and wars are successfully satirized. The whole business of this war, indeed, seems particularly pointless. (p. 59)

Though the Greek camp is throughout under the shadow of cynicism—we must remember that Agamemnon and Nestor cannot escape our satiric sense, since there is something strangely ineffectual in their acts and words—the Trojans are presented very differently. Whereas the Greeks represent 'intellect' in our crude division, the Trojans stand for 'intuition'. True, on each side there are verbal conflicts between points of view corresponding to these labels, as I have shown: yet in the Greek discussion the rationalist, and in the Trojan the emotional,

argument gains the ascendency. The contrast between the two camps is marked by the Pandarus and Thersites conceptions. Pandarus' humour is always kindly and sympathetic, Thersites' cynical and mocking. From the start Pandarus' fussy interest in his young friends' love-adventure is truly delightful:

Go to, a bargain made: seal it, seal it; I'll be
the witness. Here I hold your hand, here my
cousin's.

[III. ii. 197-98]

We must not be repelled by Pandarus' lax morality in helping these two to illicit love: since, in so far as we regard their love as illicit, we are clearly missing the whole point of this theme. We must see clearly that no such moral criticism may be levelled against Troilus as he is presented and depicted within the action of this play. Troilus' love is throughout hallowed by his constancy, his fire, his truth:

I am as true as truth's simplicity
And simpler than the infancy of truth.

[III. ii. 169-70]

It is conceived and presented throughout as a thing essentially pure and noble. Pandarus' part in this love-story exactly corresponds, at the start, to that of the Nurse in *Romeo and Juliet.* . . . The conception of Pandarus is one of the most exquisite things in this play. But not only is Pandarus' humour like health-bringing sunshine compared with the sickly eclipsing cynicism of Thersites' jeers: the Trojans are conceived throughout on an heroic and chivalrous plane.

Troilus is a 'prince of chivalry' [I. ii. 229], and Hector 'in the vein of chivalry' [V. iii. 32]; phrases which point a quality ever present among the Trojans. Honour is their creed, they hold beauty as a prize, and behave and speak like men dedicate to high purposes:

Life every man holds dear; but the brave man
Holds honour far more precious dear than life.

[V. iii. 27-8]

This is typical:

Can it be
That so degenerate a strain as this
Should once set footing in your generous bosoms?
There's not the meanest spirit on our party
Without a heart to dare or sword to draw
When Helen is defended, nor none so noble
Whose life were ill-bestow'd, or death unfam'd
Where Helen is the subject.

[II. ii. 153-60]

With them there is room for romance, sacrifice, love. Their world is conceived imaginatively, picturesquely: knights of valour pass one by one returning from battle, praised in turn by Pandarus; Cassandra's prophecies and Andromache's dreams suggest the infinite and the unknown purposes of fate or God; the strains of music herald the entry of Helen, queen of romance. Among them we find love and honour of parents, humour, conviviality, patriotism: all which are lacking among the Greeks. The Trojans remain firm in their mutual support. Their cause is worthy, if only because they believe in it. They speak glittering words of honour, generosity, bravery, love. Here is a strange and happy contrast with the shadowed world of the Greek camp, where all seems stagnant, decadent, paralysed. Troy is a world breathing the air of medieval, storied romance; the Greek camp exists on that of Renaissance satire and disillusion. There is thus a sharp dualism of two world-views: the romantic contrasted with the cynical. Between these two modes of consciousness Troilus' mind is drawn asunder until he finds no 'rule in unity itself' [V. ii. 141]: Cressida passes from Troy and his love over to the Greeks and the loose wantonness of Diomed. So between the glancing lights of romance and the shadows of cynicism is worked out the philosophic love-story of Troilus and Cressida. The larger dualism reflects the central one: and both may be roughly equated with the intuition-intellect opposition.

Troilus is shown to us as an ardent and faithful lover, faithful as he more than once says to 'simplicity'. Cressida is shallow and indirect in her thinking and behaviour, though we need not suppose her love for Troilus, whilst it lasts, to be insincere. Now Troilus' love is from the first unrestful. In *Romeo and Juliet* the adverse forces work from without: here they are implicit within long before the separation of the lovers. This is the primary difference between the early and the later play. When we first meet Troilus he is in agonies of unsatisfied aspiration; and he seems throughout the play aware that his love-aspiration is such that it probably cannot be satisfied. (pp. 60-2)

Next Troilus' suit prospers: hence his vigorous defence of values and heroic action in the cause of Troy which I have already noted. The successful lover sees all life's adventure in terms of romance, and is strong in the glistening armour of vision. But when the time comes for him to encounter Cressid his mind again recoils in dismay from the feared impossibility of actual fruition:

> *Troilus.* I am giddy; expectation whirls me round.
>   The imaginary relish is so sweet
>   That it enchants my sense: what will it be,
>   When that the watery palate tastes indeed
>   Love's thrice-reputed nectar? death, I fear me,
>   Swooning destruction, or some joy too fine,
>   Too subtle-potent, tuned too sharp in sweetness,
>   For the capacity of my ruder powers:
>   I fear it much; and I do fear besides,
>   That I shall lose distinction in my joys:
>   As doth a battle, when they charge on heaps
>   The enemy flying.
>
> [III. ii. 17-29]

Troilus fears that love's reality is a thing essentially beyond the capacity of the individual mind: that the mind must break in the attempt to compass it in all its infinity of delight. Here again we see the difference from the time of Romeo; Romeo had no such fears—he was the instinctive and boyish lover thwarted by fate. Troilus is by way of being a metaphysical lover thwarted inwardly by the fine knowledge of human limitations. For Troilus' mind in love aspires only to the infinite, as he says in his dialogue with Cressid a little further on:

> . . . This is the monstruosity in love, lady, that
> the will is infinite and the execution confined;
> that the desire is boundless, and the act a slave
> to limit.
>
> [III. ii. 81-3]

The prose dialogue of the lovers' first meetings is, indeed, throughout pregnant with meaning. . . . The mystic apprehension of romantic love cannot be perfectly bodied into symbols of sex throughout a lifetime: yet this is Troilus' desire—the desire of all who love passionately, while they love passionately. The immediate experience is all-conquering: an expe-rience of something ineffable and infinite. But no finite symbols can contain it through the stretch of years—and if they could, it would be limited in time by death. And here we are at the core of this play's philosophy.

It is the arch-enemy, Time, that kills values. When we next meet the lovers, they have reached the physical fruition of love. It is early morning, and they part to the notes of the morning lark, like Romeo and Juliet. Romeo was forced to leave Juliet by the laws of Verona: but, before ever Troilus and Cressida are forced to part, Troilus shows us that no physical act can sate his aspiration—and his complaint is levelled against time, the destroyer of love-moments:

> *Troilus.* O Cressida! but that the busy day,
>   Waked by the lark, hath rous'd the ribald crows,
>   And dreaming night will hide our joys no longer,
>   I would not from thee.
> *Cressida.*   Night hath been too brief.
> *Troilus.* Beshrew the witch! with venomous wights she stays
>   As tediously as hell, but flies the grasps of love
>   With wings more momentary swift than thought.
>   You will catch cold, and curse me.
>
> [IV. ii. 8-15]

Notice how, with the last line, we are aware of the cold realism which succeeds the faery consciousness of love; notice, too, the time-thought—the thought of the swift passage of intuitions, the swift passing of love's enjoyment.

Time-imagery is recurrent and magnificent in *Troilus and Cressida* beyond any other of Shakespeare's plays. . . . The time-thinking in this play is inextricably twined with the central love-theme. Troilus is throughout half-conscious of the fact that his love is destined to disaster in the world of flesh: it is a spiritual and delicate thing incapable of continued expression and satisfaction among the rough chaotic and temporal symbols of actuality. Hence his reference to Pandarus—love's medium—as 'our doubtful hope, our convoy, and our bark' [I. i. 104]: in the seas of time the frail bark of the soul's desire is to steer a dangerous course. Hence, too, his analysis of love's intuition, in which the senses are 'the traded pilots twixt the dangerous shores of will and judgement' [II. ii. 64-5]. The most fleeting of love's glances has to put out on the waters of sense-perception, that is of materiality, and so of time—for time and materiality as normally understood must be considered as interfused and intrinsicate. Throughout this play, in compressed metaphor, in self-conscious and detailed analysis, and thence to dialogue and incident, we have a philosophy of love which regards it as essentially un-at-home in time and incapable of continued concrete embodiment in the difficult flux of events. The love-interest turns on this theme: the theme of immediate value, killed, or apparently killed, by time; which is again the purest form of the intuition-intellect opposition, since intellect and the time concept are interdependent, and irrational or super-rational faith of some kind or another can alone open to the mind a consciousness beyond the temporal, knowledge of a timeless reality.

Troilus has to part with Cressid: the course of events now leagues itself with Troilus' metaphysical difficulties against his love-aspiration. Or, to put it more crudely—from the view of Pandarus—he at last has a real and honest reason for complaining against the difficulties and limitations of his love. (pp. 63-8)

And then Troilus watches Cressid's inconstancy. He literally doubts his senses—'the attest of eyes and ears' [V. ii. 122]. He tells Ulysses that it was not Cressida they have been watching. And then he breaks out passionately into a speech which tries in vain to resolve the hopeless dualism in his mind:

> *Troilus*. This she? No, this is Diomed's Cressida;
> If beauty have a soul, this is not she;
> If souls guide vows, if vows be sanctimonies,
> If sanctimony be the gods' delight,
> If there be rule in unity itself,
> This is not she. O madness of discourse,
> That cause sets up with and against itself!
> Bi-fold authority! where reason can revolt
> Without perdition, and loss assume all reason
> Without revolt: this is, and is not, Cressid.
> [V. ii. 137-46]

One has only to compare this speech with similar parts of *Othello* to see the peculiarly analytic and intellectual cast of the play's language. Othello may and does doubt Desdemona's faithlessness: but to question her identity with herself in solemn earnest—he does do so once, purely ironically—would seem an absurdity to him. But it is exactly this questioning of Cressida's identity with herself that we are concerned with here. Must Troilus deny his love-faith, and say, like Hamlet, 'I loved you not' [*Hamlet*, III. i. 118]? Or, if he is to stand by his faith in Cressid, must he deny the evidence of his eyes? He cannot love her faithless, yet he loves her—the Cressida of his imagination—still. He still holds fast to his love-vision: it is so deeply rooted in his soul, he may not, dare not, deny it. 'Never did young man fancy with so eternal and so fixed a soul' [V. ii. 165-66]. Are there two Cressids? One of yesterday, one of to-day? That is, it seems, the nearest to a solution. 'Injurious time' 'calumniator time', 'that old common arbitrator time' [IV. v. 225]—has killed the former Cressid. Herein lies the tragedy of Troilus. He puts his faith in an immediately apprehended irrational—or super-rational—experience, and expects it to stand the test of time and reason. It does not do so. To Troilus, whose nature must keep faith with a supreme romantic value, there is now no 'rule in unity itself'. Cressid, with a butterfly temperament flitting from one faith to another, is consistent. She lives emotionally. Thersites, the creature of satire and cynicism, is consistent:

> . . . Lechery, lechery; still, wars and lechery;
> nothing else holds fashion: a burning devil take
> them!
> [V. ii. 194-96]

He lives critically. But Troilus, who would champion to the uttermost throughout time with all his resources of reason and action his once plighted faith in a timeless experience, who would never 'turn back the silks upon the merchant' [II. ii. 69], is wrenched torturingly by the tug of two diverging principles. There is now only one hope for Troilus if he is to keep his sanity intact. In the play we have seen him recognize two values: love, and the honour of Priam's cause in war; the same two realities which Thersites curses—'wars and lechery'. At the opening of the play we saw Troilus' love drive out his warriorship: now he transfers his allegience back to his other value, and passionately throws himself, body and soul, into the war. In the final scenes he fights like one possessed:

> I do not speak of flight, of fear, of death,
> But dare all imminence that gods and men
> Address their dangers in.
> [V. x. 12-14]

He, compact of simplicity and faith and valour, makes the whole host of decadent and absurd Greeks the symbols of his mortal fury. . . . This dynamic and positive passion of Troilus is not understood in all its power, purpose, and direction, till we have a clear sight of all that is involved here in the opposition of the Greeks and Troy: Troilus champions, not only Troy, but the fine values of humanity, fighting against the demon powers of cynicism.

The universe of this play is one of love and war. The most nauseating person in the play exposes the futility and stupidity of these activities so ardently and irrationally pursued by mankind: but the beautiful and the heroic are bound to the fiery wheel of these tormenting calls on their instinctive allegiance. So curiously in *Troilus and Cressida* are intertwined the profitless and ugly event with the aspiring and noble endeavour: here we see the infinite cruelly made 'slave to limit'; it is a works of incommensurables, a world of gleaming beauties, and ardent, fiery desires, pitted against the cynic snarl of Thersites, the stupidity of Ajax, and the cold reason of Ulysses. Above all, it is a world of value and vision ruled by murderous and senseless time, who, ignorant and inexorable, pursues his endless course of destruction and slavery, cramming up his rich thievery, 'he knows not how'. The less noble and beautiful seem to win. Time slays the love of Cressid. Hector, symbol of knighthood and generosity, is slain by Achilles, lumbering giant of egotism, lasciviousness, and pride: but all the fires of human nobility and romance yet light Troilus to the last. (pp. 68-71)

> G. Wilson Knight, "The Philosophy of 'Troilus and Cressida'," in his The Wheel of Fire: Interpretations of Shakespearian Tragedy, *Methuen & Co. Ltd., 1949, pp. 47-72.*

WILLIAM WITHERLE LAWRENCE   (essay date 1931)

[*In the introduction to his* Shakespeare's Problem Comedies *(1931), Lawrence attempts to redefine the term "problem play," first used by Frederick S. Boas (1896), claiming it should apply to those realistic and distressingly complicated plays which "clearly do not fall into the category of tragedy, and yet are too serious and analytic to fit the commonly accepted conception of comedy." He thus places* All's Well That Ends Well, Measure for Measure, *and* Troilus and Cressida *in this classification. In the excerpt below, Lawrence states that although* Troilus and Cressida "*bears unmistakably the seal and imprint of Shakespeare's greatest creative period," it nonetheless has "ugly features." He says that the vulgar characterization and action "make a singularly disagreeable impression," but notes the importance of Pandarus and Thersites who both function as Chorus and Clown. In offering an explanation for the play's inconclusive ending, Lawrence argues that Shakespeare was merely being faithful to the tradition of a well-known tale; for the love story, "only an unhappy ending was possible," and for the war story, Shakespeare remained "in accord with the sources." John S. P. Tatlock (1915) and Oscar James Campbell (1938) have drawn similar conclusions about the effect of source material and dramatic form on the tone of* Troilus and Cressida, *but such arguments have also been challenged by Paul Kendall (1957). And yet, concludes Lawrence, Shakespeare avoided making the play a tragedy by not following the action to its ultimate end, but instead offered an undramatic and realistic dénouement that is true to "the facts of human experience."*]

[*Troilus and Cressida*], never a general favorite with readers or playgoers, and indeed seldom performed on the stage, nevertheless bears unmistakably the seal and imprint of Shakespeare's greatest creative period. It compels instant attention by the beauty of its verse, by the telling imagery of its great speeches, with their pregnant wisdom and mature philosophy, and by the acid brilliancy of its character-drawing. It reveals, too, despite its reflective quality, something of that irresistible power, that magnificent opulence of creative energy, which we feel in *Antony and Cleopatra* or *King Lear*. . . . But this brilliant play has ugly features. Character and action are portrayed in a curiously disillusioned and unsympathetic fashion; the most careless reader is struck by the pettiness and bickering of the Greek chieftains, the futility of the great struggle about the walls of Troy, the sensuality of Helen and Cressida. As interpreters stand the elderly lecher Pandarus and the foul-mouthed Thersites. The very atmosphere is close and unhealthy; cowardice, rancor, boasting, wantonness, and even obscenity are constantly in the air. Moreover, how strangely the whole ends! All these plottings and schemings, all the rhetoric and philosophy, all these amorous intrigues, all these big words and blaring of trumpets bring at the last no settled issue. (pp. 122-23)

Both characterization and action make a singularly disagreeable impression, which increases as the play progresses. Paris is enjoying the adulterous love of Helen, Menelaus is that shabbiest of Elizabethan butts, a cuckold, Cressida is a shameless wanton, Achilles is a slacker, forsaking his military duties for the love of a girl in the citadel of the enemy, and is accused of immoral fondness for Patroclus. Ajax is a bully and a boaster, swollen with his own conceit, Diomedes is sensual and brutal, Patroclus a weakling. But these characters, unlovely as they are, pale beside Pandarus, with his leering ribaldry, and Thersites, the foulest-spoken of all the people of Shakespeare. Yet both Pandarus and Thersites are important; each fills two functions, those of Chorus and of Clown. As though the audience might miss the sensual and calculating passion of Cressida, and be misled by the eager and youthful ardor of Troilus into setting their love upon too high a plane, Pandarus is constantly made to utter comments which no decent girl, even in Elizabethan days of unbridled speech, could hear without a protest. . . . But Pandarus no doubt afforded the audience constant amusement. Thersites, too, is obviously the Clown in a new guise; compare, for instance, the scene in which he asserts that Agamemnon, Achilles, Patroclus and himself are fools [II. iii. 61], and Achilles challenges him, "Derive this; come," with the badinage between Olivia and Feste in *Twelfth Night*, in which Olivia urges on the Clown, "Make your proof," whereupon he proves logically that she is a fool [*Twelfth Night*, I. v. 61]. The functions of Chorus and of Clown are of course closely allied; the privileged half-wit who can utter home truths enlightens the audience while he amuses them. In the light of the comments of Thersites the Greek leaders lose all their Homeric radiance. Nestor is "a stale old mouse-eaten dry cheese," Ulysses "a dog-fox," Ajax a "mongrel cur," Achilles a dog "of as bad a kind," Diomedes "a dissembling abominable varlet" [V. iv. 2-15], Patroclus a "masculine whore" [V. i. 17], and much more to the same general effect. Thersites adds the final touch of degradation to the love of Cressida and Diomedes, "How the Devil Luxury, with his fat rump and potato-finger, tickles these two together! Fry, lechery, fry!" [V. ii. 55-7]. Of all the major characters, indeed, the only ones not bespattered with mud in one form or another are Troilus, Hector, and Aeneas. Troilus and Hector are especially brilliant, sympathetic and moving figures. They are brave and chivalrous, the chief ornaments of the Trojan camp. Hector's cruel death is deeply pathetic, but Troilus is hardly less an object for the beholder's compassion—an ardent, high-spirited boy who gives all the fervor of his idealistic young love to a false

and shallow woman, and tastes the bitterest dregs in the cup of disillusion. It is noteworthy that while Pandarus gibes at the sensual element in his passion, he has no word of abuse for him, even after Troilus has uttered the most stinging of insults, and that Thersites can find nothing worse to say of Troilus than that he is a "scurvy foolish doting young knave," "the Young Trojan ass, that loves the whore" [V. iv. 5-6]. (pp. 140-42)

One of the strangest features of this strange play is its *dénouement*. Both of its plots terminate inconclusively. No poetic justice is meted out to Cressida, such as [Robert] Henryson thought that she deserved, and such as had become, by Shakespeare's day, her traditional punishment. On the contrary, she is left, despite her faithlessness, in the full tide of her love-affair with Diomedes. In Chaucer's poem [*Troilus and Criseyde*] and Heywood's play [*Iron Age*], the pain and disillusion of Troilus end in death; no such solution is found in Shakespeare. As far as we can see, Troilus is left to meet, with a broken heart, the futile continuance of the great struggle into which he had thrown his best energies. Again, the elaborate plan of the Greek chiefs to shame Achilles into action misses fire completely. Achilles is indeed resentful of the slights which have been put upon him, he is indeed moved by the reproaches of Ulysses and Patroclus, but instead of sending a challenge to Hector he merely dispatches Thersites to ask Ajax to invite the Trojans to his tent after the combat. When they do meet, Hector urges him to come into the field and fight, and Achilles promises to do so, but in the next scene he tells Patroclus that he is "thwarted quite" from his great purpose—he has received a letter from Hecuba and a token from Polyxena, his lady-love, "taxing and gaging" him to keep an oath which he has sworn—obviously not to do battle with Hector, Polyxena's own brother. He is finally roused to action by the killing of Patroclus, and contrives the death of Hector by a base trick. But he is not punished for his arrogance or for his inaction, and he is left in triumph after having compassed the death of the most brilliant and sympathetic hero in the play. Nor does the swollen vanity of Ajax meet any rebuff. The net result of it all is, in the words of Thersites, that "now is the cur Ajax prouder than the cur Achilles," and that all the policy of Ulysses and Nestor is "not prov'd worth a blackberry" [V. iv. 9-15].

These inconclusive solutions are all the more striking when the generally skilful workmanship of the main part of the play is considered. The alternation of interest between the scenes in Troy and those in the Greek camp is deftly managed, and after the return of Cressida to the Greeks, and the visit of Hector to the Greek camp, the two plots are interwoven with much dexterity. Moreover, the play shows the hand of the practiced writer in the balance between character and plot, and in the introduction of new material. The Troilus-Cressida theme is essentially undramatic. . . . Its interest lies mainly in character. In this regard it contrasts strikingly with *All's Well* and *Measure for Measure*, which are good stories, with plenty of action. Shakespeare wisely concentrated his energies, then, on the delineation of the emotions and characteristics of Cressida, Troilus, and Pandarus. Yet this left the play somewhat weak in plot-interest and suspense. Everyone knew the outlines of the love-story, and of the tale of the Trojan War. So Shakespeare (or, possibly, the author of an earlier play upon which he worked) devised the ruse of Ulysses and Nestor, which immediately arrests attention, and provokes dramatic interest. How is it all going to end? Well, it does end very strangely, to be sure. Poetic justice is in no wise satisfied; there are neither the reconciliations of comedy nor the purifying calamities of tragedy to round out the action. (pp. 158-60)

It will be clearest to consider the two parts of the action separately.

For the love-story, only an unhappy ending was possible. The theme was so firmly established for an Elizabethan audience by tradition, as involving the separation of the lovers, the heartbreak of the one and the bad faith of the other, that no conventional happy ending could follow. But the Shakespearean ending is not unhappy enough to suit the critics. . . . Tatlock points out that in the *Iron Age,* and two other plays to which he has called attention, Cressida is punished, and in the *Iron Age* Troilus dies. "It is hard to fancy any skilled dramatist dropping his main threads without tying them up; and harder to fancy Shakespeare writing the end of the play and bringing the Achilles-motive to nothing."

To all this there seems to me a very simple answer. Shakespeare did no violence to tradition, for the reason that he did not carry the action to its ultimate end. He chose to end it, or to let someone else end it, with the beginning of the intrigue with Diomedes, just as Chaucer did. Why was he bound to carry it on to a later time, to the beggary and the leprosy, after the break with Diomedes? Why is it wrenching the familiar story to stop short of this? When we compare Heywood's play with Shakespeare's, we can see . . . that Shakespeare omits material which Heywood introduced at the beginning. Why should he not also have omitted material at the end? Moreover, he had already filled a five-act play; I cannot see how he could have packed the desertion of Cressida by Diomedes and the smiting of Cressida with leprosy into a Fifth Act which had only just, in Scene ii, shown the love-intrigue of Cressida and Diomedes for the first time. Could things be made to move as fast as that? Heywood got it all in, after a fashion, but he had ten acts to do it in. (pp. 162-63)

The ending of the camp-scenes is in full accord with the inconclusive ending of the love-story. The issue is again—failure. The Greek chieftains, with all the right on their side, with the shrewdest policy of their wisest leaders to guide them, are powerless, just like Troilus, before egotism, selfishness and lust. The cowardly bully Ajax triumphs, and Achilles, at a word from his Trojan mistress, neglects his most imperative duties as a warrior and general. Here again the cause which engages our sympathies is defeated, and Achilles, who is as little heroic as Cressida, is left, like her, in a shameful triumph. The harmony between the two actions is complete. The ending of the sub-plot, like that of the main plot, is indeed both unsympathetic and ineffective theatrically. But we cannot blame all its shortcomings upon the unknown author of the spurious scenes in Act V (iv-x). The resolution of Achilles to continue his shameful inaction, for the love of Polyxena, is set forth in the opening scene of Act V, which is conceded to be Shakespeare's own work.

This fashion of ending the two actions affords a striking contrast to *All's Well* and *Measure for Measure.* In both those pieces, Shakespeare introduced a theatrically vivid climax, leading to a conventionally happy ending. Psychologically their fifth acts are weak; dramatically they are effective. This is due in part to the sources; Shakespeare followed essentially the same lines as Boccaccio and Whetstone, though with many elaborations. The last act of *Troilus and Cressida* affords a complete contrast; dramatically it is weak, psychologically it is strong. And here again the ending is in accord with the sources. No happy ending was possible for either part of the plot; everyone knew that the tale ended unhappily. Under these circumstances, what was Shakespeare to do? He could indeed have recast the whole play

as tragedy, and deepened the poignancy of the climax. Why he decided not to do this, I shall not presume to say. But it seems clear that this was never his intention. While there is much in this play, in the relentless analysis of the darker side of human passion, which recalls the great tragedies, there is not the intensity of emotion and violence of action which lead inevitably to a tragic climax. Try the experiment of reading the play, and imagining a Fifth Act in which Troilus is killed in battle, and Cressida left in the horrors of leprosy. Would that make of it a satisfactory tragedy? I do not think so; that is not the end to crown the work as Shakespeare wrought it. Perhaps the explanation lies in this: that the whole is too detached and too observant for tragedy. Shakespeare never quite seems to let himself go, to allow the action to sweep him on to an inevitable climax. (pp. 165-66)

The play ends in realistic and severely logical fashion. No concession is made to theatrical effect of the obvious sort, but a very definite impression is created of the futility and misery which come of loving a worthless woman. With this the earlier part of the play is in complete harmony. The whole background of the story is armed strife over another frail lady, Helen of Troy, strife which has become futile and dreary. Hector, the greatest of the Trojan heroes, is willing to continue it, despite its lack of moral justification, through a mistaken idea that Trojan honor demands it. Achilles, the flower of the Greek chivalry, throws honor to the winds because of an infatuation for a princess in the city of his enemies. The evil influence of love without honor, then, ends in the death of Hector, in the shame and the shameful triumph of Achilles in compassing his death, and in the complete disillusionment of Troilus. "Wars and lechery," says the Chorus Thersites, "nothing else holds fashion" [V. ii. 194-95]. And, in a less quoted passage, "What's become of the wenching rogues? I think they have swallowed one another. I would laugh at that miracle; and yet, in a sort, lechery eats itself" [V. iv. 32-5]. The shadows deepen in the closing scenes. Like many a highly emotional boy, with a strong sexual nature, Troilus suffers deeply in the very revulsion of his feeling. He is too heartsick at the faithlessness of his mistress to find harsh words for her, but he curses roundly the older man who has cynically taken advantage of his infatuation. But Cressida, as Boas has emphasized, is to have her Nemesis, too, in the brutality of Diomedes. "The shallow coquette pays a heavy yet just price for her selfish levity, when she exchanges a chivalrous adorer for a harsh and imperious taskmaster." Dramatic justice lies in the future, not in the cheap and illogical solution of leprosy for Cressida and sudden death for Troilus, but in the realization, for both of them, that character and conduct bring inescapable consequences in life. The ending of the tale is in accord with the facts of human experience; life often settles nothing, it leaves the innocent to suffer, and the guilty to prevail. There is nothing else in Shakepearean comedy just like the spirit of these closing scenes; and their complete analogues cannot be found even in the tragedies. Whether Shakespeare himself or another man planned them, they carry steadily to the end the relentless logic of the play, the searching analysis of a reflective criticism of life. (pp. 167-69)

William Witherle Lawrence, "'Troilus and Cressida'," in his Shakespeare's Problem Comedies, *The Macmillan Company, 1931, pp. 122-73.*

CHARLES WILLIAMS (essay date 1932)

[*Williams, an English novelist and literary critic, discusses the inconclusive atmosphere of* Troilus and Cressida, *noting that many of the strains of action in the play are left unfinished. He observes that the lengthy intellectual argument among the Trojans concerning value proves to be inconsequential because Hector, after arguing that Helen should be returned to the Greeks, readily abandons his position. Finally, says Williams, "The whole play is full of this sense of things being left 'in the air'."*]

Troilus and Cressida has always been a problem. It has the signs of a great play, yet it hardly succeeds in being one; indeed it hardly succeeds in being a play at all. No other of Shakespeare's plays so misses a dramatic, a theatrical, conclusion; it ends indeed with the vague statement, by both armies and individuals, 'Well, we'll all fight again to-morrow.' Its love-concern is left as unconcluded, compared to every other Shakespearian love-affair, as its war, and we know that this was not because Shakespeare minded huddling up his characters in order to end a play. Hortensio and the widow at the beginning of his career, Camillo and Paulina at the end, are examples of this. He might not have been able to deal with Troilus—owing to the tradition—quite as easily, but that he should have desired no rounder ending is inconceivable.

Even the theme of Achilles is left unfinished. The policy of Ulysses, by which Achilles was to be brought from his tent into the field, produces no result: he has only succeeded in making Ajax as proud as Achilles, who himself in spite of Ulysses' medicinal treatment—does not emerge until the death of Patroclus. So, as Thersites says, 'policy grows into an ill opinion' [V. iv. 17].

These three themes of the play then are abandoned just as the fight between Ajax and Hector is abandoned. But the abandonment is not only on the side of action, but of intellect also.

Troilus and Cressida differs positively from the other plays in this—that there are here two full-dress debates which are not paralleled elsewhere. There are discussions elsewhere, some shorter, some longer; there are the King and his lords in *Love's Labour's Lost* who talk of what had better be done about their vows to study; and King Henry V's consultation of the Archbishop about his invasion of France, and so on. But none of these have, to anything like the same extent, the serious intellectual argument of the two *Troilus* debates. The first is the discussion between the Greek generals about the unfortunate position of the war. It is interesting because the first 54 lines are an example of Shakespeare's wonderful capacity for saying nothing particular at great length—and saying it superbly. Agamemnon opens by saying:

1. Every earthly design falls short of what was hoped.
2. Checks occur in everything.
3. Every action fails to carry out the original intention.
4. These things are sent to try us.
5. They show us what men are made of.
6. We find out by these difficulties which men are really capable of perseverance.

This takes him 30 lines. Nestor then adds:

1. When things go smoothly everybody is happy.
2. But in dark hours we discover who has pluck and who has not.

This takes him 24 lines.

The second debate takes place between the princes of Troy on the Greek proposal (of which nobody up to then has heard a word) that, if the Trojans will give up Helen, the war shall be concluded, without any indemnities or annexations. There ensues then—a thing unique in Shakespeare—a two-hundred line

discussion which passes from Helen to an abstract question: What exactly *is* value?

Here, if anywhere, here, with really good arguments being exchanged, with a philosophic basis and a particular topical example to illuminate it, here we might expect the Shakespeare of whom we heard so much in our youth—the teacher, the philosopher, the sage—to solve for us one of our profoundest problems. How are we to value things? What principle of relativity ought to govern our actions? Shakespeare sets the two arguments, each with its full emotional vitality, against each other, and then causes the protagonist of one side to throw up his whole case. Hector has throughout been insisting that Helen ought to be given up; at the end of the scene we find, not only that he does not intend to act on his own belief, but that he never has intended to act upon it. (pp. 53-6)

And we are not meant to blame Hector for this; he is not presented as a blameworthy character. It might be argued that his own desire for personal glory is to be supposed to overcome his intellectual beliefs; but in that case, with a consciousness so developed as is Hector's, so vivid and complex a mind, we might reasonably expect to see something of an interior conflict. He shows no hesitation at all at his inconsistency. But as a result of this inconsistency of course the whole discussion stops—'their unanimity is wonderful'. The intellectual arguments then are abandoned—as intellectual arguments—precisely as the action—as action—is abandoned. The whole play is full of this sense of things being left 'in the air'. (p. 57)

Charles Williams, "The Cycle of Shakespeare," in his The English Poetic Mind, *1932. Reprint by Russell & Russell, 1963, pp. 29-109.*

WILLIAM EMPSON　(essay date 1935)

[*An English poet, critic, and scholar, Empson is considered one of the most influential theorists of modern criticism. In his two important studies,* Seven Types of Ambiguity (1930) *and* The Structure of Complex Words (1951), *Empson adapted the ideas of I. A. Richards, the English critic and forerunner of New Criticism, and argued that the value of poetic discourse resides not in any ultimate critical evaluation, but in the correspondences and contradictions of the created structure itself. In short, Empson has been more interested in the manner in which poetic elements work together in a literary piece than in assessing the final value of a creative work as a whole. As a Shakespearean critic, Empson has focused mainly on the emotive and connotative aspects of Shakespeare's language, as well as on the ambiguity present in much of the playwright's verse. Although many critics have attacked his methods and questioned the practicality of his theories, Empson contributed significantly to the development of New Criticism in the twentieth century. In the following excerpt, Empson examines the double plot structure of* Troilus and Cressida. *He notes several points in the language of the play at which the parallel stories coalesce and claims that Shakespeare's punning on "general" serves as "one of the crucial points of contact between the two themes of the play." For another consideration of the double plot in* Troilus and Cressida, *see the excerpt by Norman Rabkin (1965).*]

The two parts [of *Troilus and Cressida*] make a mutual comparison that illuminates both parties ('love and war are alike') and their large-scale indefinite juxtaposition seems to encourage primitive ways of thought ('Cressida will bring Troy bad luck because she is bad'). This power of suggestion is the strength of the double plot; once you take the two parts to correspond, any character may take on *mana* because he seems to cause what he corresponds to or be Logos of what he symbolises. The political theorising in *Troilus* (chiefly about loyalty whether to a mistress or the state) becomes more interesting if you take it as a conscious development by Shakespeare of the ideas inherent in the double-plot convention.

It is with this machinery that Troilus compares the sexual with the political standards, and shows both in disruption. The breaking of Cressida's vow is symbolical of, the breaking of Helen's vow is cause of, what the play shows (chiefly by the combat between Hector and his first cousin Ajax) to be a civil war; Shakespeare's horror of this theme, which history so soon justified, may in part explain the grimness of his treatment (all large towns in the plays are conceived as London); and it is because of this that the disloyal elements in the Greek camp, Ajax and Achilles, compared to Cressida, disloyal because of Briseis, seem only to carry further the social disruption caused by Helen.... From his name, as its rising hope, and because both are victims of women, Troilus becomes a symbol of Troy; as he is loyal to Cressida, so Troy is not broken up by disloyalties like the Greek camp. Yet its isolation is the product of a disloyalty, against hospitality in the theft of Helen, and this is somehow like the original mistake in his choice of Cressida; there is a pathetic irony and fitness in his support of Paris, cuckold supporting cuckold-maker, in the council scene.

If you say he was no husband, that he should deserve this title, then the only reason he wasn't was to make him more like Paris, the private affair more like the publicly important one. But the point is as obscure here as in Chaucer. Critics talk about the 'troubadour convention,' but in its normal form the woman adored was already married. Certainly the play is not interested in marriage so much as in the prior idea of loyalty, but it was to the interest of these lovers to marry so as to have a claim against being separated. Dryden's quarrel scene in which Troilus heroically gives her up for the sake of Troy makes a much more coherent situation, but Shakespeare wanted to make them wild flowers, almost ignorant of the storm that destroyed them, and only as it were naturally parallel to it. (pp. 34-6)

Critics have said that though noble elements exist in *Troilus* it is not organised round them, they seem swamped and isolated; a rather one-eyed complaint; whether or no this is a moral fault it is the point and theory of the play. Its central and most moving expression is Ulysses'

> let not virtue seek
> Remuneration for the thing it was
>
> [III. iii. 169-70]

said sincerely enough to Achilles, to make him fight though he is undervalued; he becomes a sympathetic figure in his talk about this; fight he does, and kills Hector so unfairly as to excite horror. (His talk has been called out of character; it does not aim at character but at manipulation of our sympathies.) We have seen Hector spare many men under much lesser disadvantages, but he must not expect generosity because he is generous; Troilus has told him that his generosity is weakness, and Achilles himself that it is a form of vanity. This same irony hangs over Troilus and his love affairs; it is the two great speeches about time, this to Achilles and that of Troilus' farewell to Cressida, which force us to compare their situations though in themselves they are so unlike. He has objected in the council scene that value *does* dwell in 'particular will' (the phrase echoes through the play in perpetual puzzles of language); not in the object loved but in the force that takes it for a symbol; in the glory of possessing Helen, not in Helen herself;

in what his love for Cressida *was*, therefore, not in a remuneration from his fidelity, and his disillusion shows not that his statement was wrong but that he must take its consequences. People complain that the play is 'bitter'; it is not to be praised for bitterness but for a far-reaching and exhausting generosity, which is piled up onto the pathos of Cressida.

So that in a way, though he puts so much weight on her faults, Shakespeare despises her less than his commentators have; except indeed in a scene that drives home the parallel. After all her outbursts and protestations, after that last pathetic question turned back on him out of curiosity, 'my lord, will you be true?' [IV. iv. 101] ('It is hard to believe even that people like you are; I know I shall not be, but perhaps you will') Cressida is led from Troy, and we hear the blast of a Greek trumpet marking truce; the truce in which she is exchanged, and in which Hector by chivalric combat defends the glory of the Trojan ladies. The moment before she arrives at the Greek camp the same blast again is now seen, a hooting satire, being blown on its trumpet, and immediately she prances round kissing everybody; she must have covered the ground in two minutes; it forces us with something of the brutality of a pun to see with what extreme and as if mechanical buoyancy she has changed. The incident is nonsense, surely, as character-study; it is not the Cressida who was embarrassed by her own tongue in the love scenes who could achieve this change of front without a brief period of self-torture. Shakespeare indeed is always willing to take the dramatic assumptions wholeheartedly; all his people change their minds on the stage and use heightened language where the rest of us use lapse of time; but the reason we have this fearfully striking joke about it here is that Cressida is somehow parallel to public affairs and this is her one public occasion.

People sometimes complain about *Troilus* that it contains not like so many of Shakespeare's plays one, but two unpleasant characters, as who should say 'I expect a dog to have some fleas, but these are too many.' At least there is only one flea to each story, one mocker each to love and heroism; I do not know whether this reflection is any comfort to the complainers. But when Mr. [J. M.] Robertson, for instance, says that the remarks of Thersites cannot possibly be what the Bard wrote or wanted (so that they must be by Chapman—as far as I remember) one must look for a definite answer; I think that a final answer, obtained by pursuing rather queer points of language, is that the verbal ironies in the comic character's low jokes carry on the thought of both plots of the play. It is one of the strange things, chiefly about Shakespeare, but in some degree about most Elizabethans, that this is not irrelevant; I believe myself what the notes say about the mad talk of Ophelia, that it had most elaborate connections with the story, though I have never heard a modern actress make it seem anything but raving. I propose to look at a pun on *general*, used seven times in this play and seldom elsewhere, for which the superb and well-punctuated first words of Thersites act as a sort of official explanation; and if you call this mere verbal fidgets, I reply that one source of the unity of a Shakespeare play, however brusque its handling of character, is this coherence of its subdued puns.

AJAX. Thersites.
THERSITES. Agamemnon, how if he had Biles (ful) all ouer generally.
AJAX. Thersites.
THERSITES. And those Byles did run, say so; did not the General run, were not that a botchy

core?
AJAX. Dog.
THERSITES. Then would come some matter from
him; I see none now.

[II. i. 1-9]

The irony of the word is that though it connects the hero to
the people it implies a failure of his rule; a general commands
an orderly force such as the people ought to be, but the general
is a mob. The core of the state here is botchy and dissolving
into the primitive matter of chaos, and the comparison to syphilis is an appeal from the plot about heroism to the plot about
love. When Thersites next uses the word its irony has turned
against him. (He is railing at the pride of Ajax when chosen
to fight Hector.)

> I said, good-morrow Ajax; and he replyes,
> thankes Agamemnon. What think you of this
> man, that takes me for the Generall? He's grown
> a very landfish, languageless, a monster.

[III. iii. 260-63]

There is too much rather than too little in his language. Thersites, as the barking dog, the critic, is the general to whom
excellence is caviare; Ajax is the monster, 'not presented in
all love's pageant,' which takes one general for the other. And
the real monster that gibbers behind that lovely phrase of Troilus is Pandarus's bone-ache.

This same pun is put to solemn uses of political theorising.

> The specialty of rule hath been neglected
> And look, how many Grecian tents do stand
> Hollow upon the plain, so many hollow factions.
> While that the general is not like the hive
> To whom the foragers shall all repair,
> What honey is expected? Degree being vizarded,
> The unworthiest shows as fairly in the mask. . . .

[I. iii. 78-84]
(pp. 36-40)

The general is given the personal *whom,* but the state is being
personified; Ulysses is speaking to a general, but it is the
general good which is like a hive. Shakespeare indeed thought
that the hive had a king, but not that he had rational means of
control; the hive is a symbol both of absolute regal power and
of a mysteriously self-regulating social order. The general seems
opposed to, but may repeat, the *specialty of rule* (so too the
opposite key phrase *particular will*); and there is the same doubt
in the pun on *mask.* For *degree* may mean 'persons of quality'
or 'the idea of social hierarchy' (the rulers or the whole state);
the *mask* may be what covers the face of the courtier, or the
symbolic dance of ordered function (or the dance of abandonment) in which the whole of society is engaged. Much of the
language of *Troilus,* I think, is a failure; it makes puzzles which
even if they can be unravelled cannot be felt as poetry; but
even so, what they are trying for is a pun of this sort applying
both to the hero and the tribe.

The word which has acquired all this energy (other uses are in
[I. iii. 322, 342; V. iv. 4]) is brought out again for the central
joke against Cressida. For a second time we hear the one blast
of the trumpet that calls a false truce and a sham fight, and
she flounces into the Greek camp:

> AGAMEMNON. Most dearly [expensively?] wel-
> come to the Greeks, dear lady.
> NESTOR. Our general doth salute you with a
> kiss.

ULYSSES [who made the last speech about gen-
eral]. Yet is the kindness but particular;
Twere better she were kissed in general.

[IV. v. 18-21]

So they all do. It is one of the crucial points of contact between
the two themes of the play. (p. 41)

> William Empson, ''Double Plots,'' in his Some Ver-
> sions of Pastoral, *Chatto & Windus, 1935, pp. 27-88.*

H. B. CHARLTON   (essay date 1937)

[*An English scholar, Charlton is best known for his* Shakespearian
Tragedy *and* Shakespearian Comedy—*two important studies in
which he argues that the proponents of New Criticism, particularly T. S. Eliot and I. A. Richards, were reducing Shakespeare's
drama to its poetic elements and in the process losing sight of his
characters. In his introduction to* Shakespearian Tragedy, *Charlton described himself as a ''devout'' follower of A. C. Bradley,
and like his mentor he adopted a psychological, character-ori-
ented approach to Shakespeare's work. In his commentary on*
Troilus and Cressida, *first published in the Bulletin of the John
Rylands Library in 1937, Charlton, presenting a categorical assessment similar to that of John S. P. Tatlock (1915), notes the
play's affinity with Shakespeare's ''political'' plays,* Henry IV
and Henry V, *particularly in its espousal of the priority of social
values over individual will. The character of Achilles, says Charlton, is degraded because he refuses to perform ''his service to
the well-being of society,'' whereas Hector is shown as noble to
the extent that he argues with a ''voice of humanity's need.'' He
also claims that Shakespeare is exposing the limitations of the
''Falstaffian approach to life,'' exemplified in the contemptible
character of Thersites. Because the play also contains a suggestion that time will ultimately mete out justice, Charlton contends
that it is not as cynical or pessimistic as Edward Dowden (1877),
George Brandes (1895-96), and E. K. Chambers (1907) have
suggested. For other discussions of the dominion of social values
over individual will in* Troilus and Cressida, *see the excerpts by
Denton J. Snider (1890), G. Wilson Knight (1930), Terence Eagleton (1967), and R. A. Yoder (1972).*]

Troilus and Cressida shows a larger awareness of the implications of man's necessarily social life than do any preceding
[Shakespearean plays]. For tragedy, life is the relationship of
the moment and eternity, of the individual and the absolute,
of man and God. For comedy, life is the reality of actual
existence, the solving of the problem as to how man may
ameliorate his condition in his existence here and now amongst
his fellows. Comedy is social rather than metaphysical or theological. It is generally agreed that in no play before *Troilus
and Cressida* does Shakespeare give so just a sense of the
dependence of the individual on the social conditions in which
as an individual he has his existence. The wisdom of Ulysses
may have obvious traits of patent diplomacy, but its foundation
is a sense of the inescapable interaction of society as such on
the individuals who are the elements in its being.

In its most immediate bearing the sense of social organisation
is a political one. . . . [In] *Henry IV,* and in the group of the
English history plays, Shakespeare's imagination has been exercised by the movement of communities as distinct from the
progress of individuals. His sense of its basic forces deprives
them of moral sanctions and of human compunctions; even in
the rhetorically and patriotically glorified *Henry V,* the underlying assumptions, though hidden, are not dissimilar. But in
Troilus and Cressida Shakespeare's apprehension of the power
by which communal life progresses is more humane and more
profound. Whilst human ingenuity, mere politics, will still

constrain those in authority to trick the individual for the good of the community, as Ulysses tricks Ajax and tries to trick Achilles, nevertheless the governors themselves have a subtler apprehension of their function. Social well-being, the matters of the world at large, are the object of political organisation. The value of individuals is their contribution to the general good; "value dwells not in particular will" [II. ii. 53]. There is a specifically Platonic notion in this sense of communal as distinct from individual values—

> a strange fellow here
> Writes me: "That man, how dearly ever parted,
> How much in having, or without or in,
> Cannot make boast to have that which he hath,
> Nor feels not what he owes, but by reflection;
> As when his virtues, shining upon others,
> Heats them and they retort that heat again
> To the first giver."
>
> [III. iii. 95-102]

Well-being is not a state of isolated individual attainment, but an activity of well-doing:—

> no man is the lord of anything
> Though in and of him there be much consisting
> Till he communicates his parts to others.
>
> [III. iii. 115-17]

Those who serve the general good may or may not have their current fame: an instant's giving way or hedging aside from the direct forthright may throw them as alms to oblivion—

> For time is like a fashionable host
> That slightly shakes his parting guest by the hand,
> And with his arms outstretch'd, as he would fly,
> Grasps in the comer.
>
> [III. iii. 165-68]

But despite inequalities and injustices in the reward of the individuals, there emerges a sort of controlling justice between the endless jar of right and wrong. As by a mysterious law through which

> The heavens themselves, the planets and this centre
> Observe degree, priority and place,
> Insisture, course, proportion, season, form,
> Office and custom, in all line of order.
>
> [I. iii. 85-8]

the progressive good of humanity is demonstrably the law of social life. Those who for their own satisfaction stand out from or oppose this general good are stigmatised as evil-doers whether their offence is deliberate as is that of Achilles here, or whether such emotional upheavals as is the love of Troilus make the sufferer for the time being a social menace.

There is a mystery in the soul of state: and nowhere more than in *Troilus and Cressida* does Shakespeare recognise it. Ulysses, though still a schemer, has a subtler sense of society than any English King of Shakespeare's. His speech on degree is an infinitely profounder political philosophy than is elsewhere to be found in the plays; it is also more realistic and more humane. In the last resort, it relies largely on the half-intelligible processes by which time itself works for good: and against the individual facts of human experience wherein evil and loss are man's fate, there is the larger view that goodness comes through evil. Trouble, disappointment, suffering

> are indeed nought else
> But the protractive trials of great Jove
> To find persistive constancy in men;
> The fineness of which metal is not found

> In fortune's love; for then the bold and coward,
> The wise and fool, the artist and unread,
> The hard and soft, seem all affined and kin:
> But, in the wind and tempest of her frown,
> Distinction, with a broad and powerful fan,
> Puffing at all, winnows the light away;
> And what hath mass or matter, by itself
> Lies rich in virtue and unmingled.
>
> [I. iii. 19-30]

Once more, of course, it is necessary to remember that to find the underlying sentiment of a play in the speeches of its actors is a method fraught with many dangers. There are, moreover, passages in the play in which Time is apostrophised as the enemy of human life; for Time obviously brings to individual man, if not sufferings in life, yet certainly his final exit from it. But what one has in mind is not so much that which is explicitly said about time: it is the conviction that for those who have seen most of it, take it on the long view, it is a power making for justice and progress: as indeed, in the mere action of the play, it does. And surely such a faith in time, experience, and circumstance is entirely incompatible with the notion that the author of this play was overwhelmed in pessimism when he wrote it. (pp. 226-29)

[The] blackening of Achilles seems to protrude unpleasantly from Shakespeare's picture. There is the devastating low cunning of his conquest of Hector. Why should Achilles invite such ignominy? On the testimony of the story, his temperamental quarrelsomeness and his pride are mere hearsay, and his homosexualism nothing but the report of a known slanderer. But what is certain is that for personal reasons—and in the last resort, these are represented as promptings or obligations of romantic love or of sexual gratification—his hope to achieve the love of the daughter of the enemy Queen—

> Here is a letter from Queen Hecuba,
> A token from her daughter, my fair love,
> Both taxing me, and gaging me to keep
> An oath that I have sworn
>
> [V. i. 39-42]

—for reasons such as these he has decided to defy what is commonly called duty—that is, his service to the well-being of the society of which he is a part.

> Fall Greeks; fall fame; honour or go or stay;
> My major vow lies here, this I'll obey.
>
> [V. i. 43-4]

Recalling that the whole gist of the intellectual undertone of the play is a recognition of the obligations of society, of the conditions on which alone man can live a rich and ordered life amongst his fellows, it is clear that an individual who, through *hubris* and through an assertion of his claims to a merely personal happiness such as Achilles makes, must cast himself for the villain's *rôle*. The denigration of Achilles, on the scheme of the play, is inevitable, and in no wise a cynical speculation. He is condemned not by the jaundiced outlook of a pessimist, but by an upholder of Ulysses' code of wisdom in the matter of corporate well-being. (pp. 238-39)

When Shakespeare was writing his political plays—*Henry IV, Henry V* (and perhaps *Julius Caesar*) there came to him this realisation of the social implications of human goodness: and the first conscious formulation of it is the chief article in the wisdom of Ulysses in *Troilus and Cressida*, even though in that formulation it is merely the political aspect of the principle which is stressed. It may well be that when Shakespeare's imagination was grappling dramatically with these stories which narrate the destiny, not of this man or of that, but of groups and societies of men, races and nations, he was led to pick up his unfinished love-story of Troilus and Cressida and set it against the background of the wider national scenes in the Greek and Trojan conflict. In these, at least, he finds a worthy place for a broken-hearted Troilus: and more than that, in the trend of their implicit ideas, he is feeling for some sort of a system which makes the fate of Troilus both an intelligible and a tolerable part in a universe which is not hostile to man's effort to secure a larger good.

Throughout the play the situation is perpetually poising the will of the individual against the *volonté generale* ["general will"], "Value dwells not in particular will." The achievements of individuals and their merely personal renown are in a real assessment only "baby figures of the giant mass of things to come at large" [I. iii. 345-46]. The real crime of Achilles is that he

> carries on the stream of his dispose
> Without observance or respect of any,
> In will peculiar and in self-admission.
>
> [II. iii. 164-66]

Because he thinks that honour amongst men is the prize of accident rather than of merit he declines to compete for the prize. But again it is Ulysses who formulates the drift of opinion which the action of the play demonstrates and corroborates:

> No man is the lord of anything
> Though in and of him there be much consisting,
> Till he communicates his parts to others;
> Nor doth he of himself know them for aught
> Till he behold them form'd in the applause
> Where they're extended; who, like an arch, reverberates
> The voice again, or, like a gate of steel
> Fronting the sun, receives and renders back
> His figure and his heat.
>
> [III. iii. 115-23]

One must not read this as a code in which philanthropy is exalted above all other virtues: but it implies a sense of values from which it is an easy step to the realisation that in the service of humanity lies the greatest virtue. And that is an apprehension which is particularly manifest in another of the dark comedies. In the meantime, it is enough to assert that Shakespeare's picture of the degraded Achilles is no proof of Shakespeare's cynicism: and sufficient evidence of that is provided by Shakespeare's apprehension of the elements in Achilles' character through which his degradation came.

The problem which seems to be occupying Shakespeare's imaginative exploration most is the tracking of those impulses and motives in man which lead him and the world about him most securely along paths that prove themselves most worth while. What does man owe to his deliberately rational endeavour to control his and his world's future? What, on the other hand, does he owe to the non-rational impulses which prompt him to this or that action? How, in fact, does man stand most securely between the dangerous shores of will and judgment? (pp. 240-42)

But a simpler issue is apparent in the artist's finest figure in the play: his Hector stands above the rest of his characters in manhood and in obvious worth. And what are the springs of Hector's nobility? Unlike so many Homeric heroes in the play,

he is never written down by Shakespeare. He is not, of course, the idealised pattern of the superman: he is noble, yet still a man. . . . (p. 243)

As far as the action of the play attests his nobility in act, the motives of his deeds spring from two opposing sources, his deliberate schemes of conduct, and his impulsive intuitive response to an irrational perception of the circumstances of the moment. The situation is clearest in the Trojan conference which discusses whether to seek peace or to continue the war. Hector at the outset is for sending Helen back to Greece and so preventing further bloodshed in guarding a "thing not ours nor worth to us" [II. ii. 22]. But the romantic Troilus and the interested Paris are against him. . . . But Hector knows that both Paris and Troilus have but glozed superficially on the cause and question in hand. He gives his own view of the manner in which the situation must be faced. The fundamental problem is to make up a free determination 'twixt right and wrong. Hot passion proceeding from distempered blood does not help; it frustrates a sound solution, for pleasure and revenge (a striking diagnosis of the motives, pleasure, of Paris, and revenge, of Troilus—that is, pleasure is Hector's word for love, and revenge, his description of honour) for pleasure and revenge have ears more deaf than adders to the voice of any true decision. He then proceeds with his own examination of the situation. He sees it in the light of the moral laws of nature and of nations:

> Nature craves
> All dues be render'd to their owners: now,
> What nearer debt in all humanity
> Than wife is to the husband? If this law
> Of nature be corrupted through affection,
> And that great minds, of partial indulgence
> To their benumbed wills, resist the same,
> There is a law in each well-order'd nation
> To curb those raging appetites that are
> Most disobedient and refractory.
> If Helen then be wife to Sparta's king,
> As it is known she is, these moral laws
> Of nature and of nations speak aloud
> To have her back return'd.
>
> [II. ii. 173-86]

The conclusion is absolute in the way of truth—

> thus to persist
> In doing wrong extenuates not wrong,
> But makes it much more heavy.
>
> [II. ii. 186-88]

There is no resisting the reasonableness of Hector's analysis. He has done all he could to persuade his people into reason. But even as he concludes his unanswerable plea for justice and for right, he enlists himself on the other side:

> Yet ne'ertheless,
> My spritely brethren, I propend to you
> In resolution to keep Helen still.
>
> [II. ii. 189-91]

Dramatically the situation is a mere confusion in that the play presents no psychological clue to this sudden and complete change of front. We are thrown back on speculation. Does Hector decline from a wider to a narrower vision, and, for the voice of humanity's need, substitute that of personal opportunity? Is it a rejection of the common good, to secure as much as he can of his family's joint and several dignities? Is it that he perceives that the nicely calculated less or more is a mean intrusion where the theme is one of honour and renown? Is it that the rich advantage of a promised personal glory drives him into obliviousness of the wide world's revenue? Who knows? Who can hope to know from this play? It is a problem-play; it presents the problem. It does not provide the answer.

Yet the hint of a way to an answer emerges from the play. Is not demonstrable reason, because by its nature it is demonstrable, too liable to be over-estimated? Is there not a sort of irrational reason in instinct? Are not the obligations of our blood sanctions as valid as the findings of our conscious deliberations? In the last resort, is not the acquired experience of mankind somehow incorporated in his instincts even as certainly as in the momentary decision of his conscious judgments? Again, another problem. But the mere statement of it implies a willingness to allot a large validity to instinct as against reason: and a mood which is even so far willing to find time and experience a guide to humanity is certainly no cynic's mood.

Perhaps the most striking of the many complex threads of *Troilus and Cressida* is its persistent exposure of the limitations of what may be called the Falstaffian approach to life. There is a growing suspicion that a man like Falstaff wears his wits in his belly and his guts on his head. The assumptions on which he builds his realistic pragmatism are inadequate, for *homo* is palpably not a common name for man, when a Thersites and a Hector both are men. Grant Falstaff his assumption, and Achilles' horse makes many Thetis' sons—in other words, Swiftian Yahooism is a true picture of life: but the work of those that with the fineness of their souls by reason guide the execution of human effort is a plain refutation of this consequence.

In many ways the criteria by which Falstaff measures worldly worth are in the same kind as those of Thersites. The determination to cling to life, to mere existence, at all costs is a Falstaffian ideal which is only set in another angle when Thersites puts it in his own idiom: "To be a dog, a mule, a cat, a fitchew, a toad, a lizard, an owl, a puttock, or a herring without a roe, I would not care.... Ask me not what I would be, if I were not Thersites" [V. i. 60-3]. Remember of course that when he says "I would not care," he means "it would nothing perturb me." Though he is here expressing scorn in a mode of humour entirely his own, his acts fit into a plan of life not markedly dissimilar from this conception of it as mere animal existence. To preserve it, he will assume any indignity—

> I am a rascal; a scurvy railing knave and very filthy rogue.
>
> [V. iv. 28-9]

he pleads with Hector, and so saves his skin. Again he claims the ignominy of bastardy to get out of a conflict with Margareton—

> I am a bastard too; I love bastards: I am a bastard begot, bastard instructed, bastard in mind, bastard in valour, in every thing illegitimate. One bear will not bite another, and wherefore should one bastard? Take heed, the quarrel's most ominous to us: if the son of a whore fight for a whore, he tempts judgment.
>
> [V. vii. 16-22]

It is almost as if there was a deliberate writing down of the trickery by which Falstaff avoided combat with Douglas. Fal-

staff's mimicry of Henry IV lamenting the evil ways of Hal is all for our laughter. Patroclus's slanderous pageantry, imitating the Greek leaders with ridiculous and awkward action, is, in the eyes of Ulysses, a mere scurril jest. It is wit misused, it distorts real and proved values—"our abilities, gifts, nature, shape, severals and generals of grace exact" [I. iii. 179-80] are unscrupulously made to serve as stuff to make paradoxes. The wit by which Falstaff achieves his mastery has become a dubious instrument: and the realistic rationalism, the cold reason, which it assumed in measuring the worth of things is directly challenged:

> Here are your reasons:
> You know an enemy intends you harm;
> You know a sword employ'd is perilous,
> And reason flies the object of all harm:
> Who marvels then, when Helenus beholds
> A Grecian and his sword, if he do set
> The very wings of reason to his heels
> And fly like chidden Mercury from Jove
> Or like a star disorb'd?
>
> [II. ii. 38-46]

And though the challenger has in his own way no more reason on his side than has the challenged, he secures the plaudits of human sympathy. It is hardly an overstatement to assert that, if there is anything positive and constructive in the seeming desolation of *Troilus and Cressida,* it is this drift away from Falstaffianism and the exposure of its contemptible though specious triumphs. (pp. 243-47)

Troilus and Cressida is mainly a presentation of the problem at its worst: there are fellows like Thersites; how far can even such as he write down life within the limits of a specious plausibility? It is, of course, a depressing picture—but not the cynical picture it would be if Shakespeare were Thersites. (pp. 247-48)

> H. B. Charlton, "The Dark Comedies," in his Shakespearian Comedy, *Methuen & Co. Ltd., 1938, pp. 208-65.*

OSCAR JAMES CAMPBELL (essay date 1938)

[*An American scholar and critic, Campbell is best known for his* Comicall Satyre and Shakespeare's "Troilus and Cressida" (1938). *In his following publication,* Shakespeare's Satire *(1943), Campbell continued his emphasis on the satiric elements in Shakespeare's plays and established himself as an innovative interpreter of Elizabethan drama, particularly with his characterization of* Timon of Athens *as a tragic satire, rather than a tragedy. Campbell was also the editor of* The Living Shakespeare, *an edition of twenty-one of Shakespeare's most popular plays, and* The Reader's Encyclopedia of Shakespeare, *an indispensable guide to features of the poet's life and work. In the introduction to his influential study of* Troilus and Cressida, *Campbell asserts that the "comicall satyres" written by Ben Jonson and John Marston between 1599 and 1601 were "designed to convert comedy into a vehicle for the spirit and form" of the prose and poetic satires that had been recently outlawed in England. In the excerpt below, he argues that Shakespeare's first intent in modelling* Troilus and Cressida *after these satiric plays was "to devote the drama to attacks upon social follies and ethical lapses and saturate it with a spirit of derision." Campbell also claims that the difficulties of the play can be explained as characteristic of this satiric comedy. In examining the elements of the "necessarily cheerless" dramatic form, he rejects the assertion of G. Wilson Knight (1930) that the Trojans are more noble and less foolish than the Greeks, a contention later supported by L. C. Knights (1951), Terence Eagleton*

(1967), D. A. Traversi (1968), and Thomas G. West (1981). Campbell also challenges the more biographical approach of such critics as Edward Dowden (1877), George Brandes (1895-96), and E. K. Chambers (1907), all of whom postulated that the tone of Troilus and Cressida *reflects Shakespeare's gloomy personal life. Instead, Campbell maintains that the play's concluding sense of futility is "in harmony with the intellectual and structural conventions of dramatic satire." Although Campbell's approach is important to the critical history of* Troilus and Cressida *for the solutions it offers to the problems of the play, such other critics as Paul Kendall (1951) and Franklin M. Dickey (1957) have questioned his findings.]*

Shakespeare composed *Troilus and Cressida* during the years when the vogue of comical satire was at its height. In constructing the play according to the fully developed principles of the new form, he but furnished another instance of his habit of following the dramatic fashion. His first care was to devote the drama to attacks upon social follies and ethical lapses and to saturate it with a spirit of derision. Then he set himself the task of employing and enriching the conventions which Jonson and Marston had established in their efforts to make their satiric plays effective dramatic equivalents of the forbidden satires. These conventions had more or less fixed the nature of the follies and vices to be satirized, and settled the approved methods of construction. (p. 185)

The editors of the first folio were as much baffled in their effort to classify *Troilus and Cressida* as their successors have been. [Charles] Knight was the first to analyze the evidences of their embarrassment. He points out that on the title-page of the first quarto edition the play is described as "a 'Famous Historie,'" but that in the preface of the same edition it is more than once referred to as a comedy. In the folio edition, however, it is given the title "The Tragedie of Troylus and Cressida," and the editors first planned to place it immediately after *Romeo and Juliet.* But upon reflection they apparently realized that it did not have the conventional form of comedy, tragedy, or history. "They therefore," says Knight, "placed it between the Histories and Tragedies, leaving to the reader to make his own classification." Does not this confusion of the editors arise from the fact that Shakespeare did not design the play as any one of these conventional dramatic forms, but as something different from all three of them—as a comical satire? (p. 187)

If we assume that Shakespeare decided in the year 1601 to try his hand at a type of play which Jonson and Marston were then writing, we may speculate as to his reasons for so doing and for choosing the tale of Troy for his vehicle. The work was almost surely written for a special audience. The long philosophical and meditative speeches are not the sort to hold the attention of an Elizabethan popular audience. They do not bear as close a relationship to the emotions aroused by the action as do the soliloquies in the great tragedies. Besides, the characters who utter these tirades are not taking counsel with their most deeply-felt convictions. They are, rather, arguing about intellectual issues which would have interested only a gathering of persons endowed with well trained and subtle minds. Peter Alexander suggests, plausibly, that Shakespeare may have written *Troilus and Cressida* for some festival occasion at one of the Inns of Court [see Additional Bibliography]. Many features of the play would have been unsuited to the taste of Queen Elizabeth. Its vituperation goes so far that, as Mr. Alexander says, "the audience are at times addressed directly and familiarly by the most scurril character in the most scurril terms." And its impudent epilogue "prevents disapproval by implying that there will be no hissing except from bawds or panders or their

unfortunate customers." But these impertinences were nicely calculated to please a crowd of gay and dissolute benchers. (p. 191)

The action ends in no catastrophe for any individual and with no tragic catharsis for the audience. Instead, it reaches a conclusion appropriate to satire, in that the feeling dominant in the denouement is a sense of the characters' ridiculous futility, rather than sympathy with their sufferings or gay satisfaction over their attainment of happiness. The course of the fable neither purges turbulent emotions nor creates elation. It leaves the audience suffused with cynical amusement. It presents no reform, but by exposing the folly and the sin of the characters who come to this dead end it fulfils the principal aim of satiric derision—moral enlightenment.

How does Shakespeare build up, for his audience, his picture of a social institution in a condition of chaos? Ulysses draws the first sketch in a manner appropriate to the dramatic blood brother of Macilente and Criticus and others fulfilling their office in comical satire. In his great speech on degree he enunciates the ethical and political standards by which the anarchistic folly of the Greek warriors is judged and found ridiculous and socially destructive. A careful perusal of that key speech will result in the conviction that what Shakespeare attacks in *Troilus and Cressida* is not war as an institution but, rather, war as carried on by individuals who, because of their insubordination to rightfully constituted authority, are incapable of joining forces for a coherent social effort. His thesis is:

> . . . O, when degree is shak'd,
> Which is the ladder to all high designs,
> Then enterprize is sick! . . .
> Take but degree away, untune that string,
> And, hark, what discord follows!
>
> [I. iii. 101-10]

The action of the drama, so far as it concerns both groups of warriors, illustrates this text. It shows the complete social and moral confusion that results when socially reasonable action is thwarted by the continual triumph of subversive personal emotion or even of mere whim. Plans formed by reason, and so recognized when the characters are temporarily rational, are totally destroyed because, when they begin to act, these men become the slaves of some passion. Then they forthwith illustrate Thersites' characterization of them as creatures of "too much blood and too little brain" [V. i. 47]. Conduct which has thus completely abjured the guidance of reason inevitably produces a morally topsy-turvy crowd of schismatics. (pp. 196-97)

Attached to the play's subtly varied conventional program for the exposure and reform of the humourous character is Thersites. . . . Many of the critics feel that their duty to Thersites has been fulfilled when they have described him as either a chorus or a fool. They have thus recognized that his functions as commentator are like those of two other figures long traditional in drama. But to suggest that he is identical with either of these figures is misleading. Thersites is neither a chorus nor a clown. A chorus suggests classical drama or English Senecan tragedy—forms utterly unlike that of *Troilus and Cressida.* Moreover, a chorus presents, if not the moral views of the author, at least the values by which he wishes the actions of the dramatis personae to be judged, or else it is the ally of the stage manager, recounting events which cannot be crowded into the two hours' traffic of the stage. Thersites fulfils neither of these offices. His voice is not the voice of Shakespeare. All the other characters in the play realize that his opinions are worthless, and say so. (pp. 201-02)

It is true that Thersites is a court fool in that he seems to be attached to Ajax as a kind of licensed jester. Achilles reminds Patroclus of that fact when the latter threatens to punish Thersites for scoring too palpable a hit: "He is a privileg'd man. Proceed, Thersites" [II. iii. 57]. But the fool in Shakespeare . . . is radically different from Thersites. No matter how great the clown's impudence, he always uses it merely as a cover from which arrows barbed with common sense may be shot at his victims. Hence the wise fool, of whom the Fool in *King Lear* is the most notable example, has a single fixed purpose—to clear the eyes of his master from dangerous illusions. He never resembles Thersites by making opprobrious speech an end in itself.

In any case, why should so far-sought a model for Thersites be suggested, when a more complete one lies much nearer at hand. Thersites is a railer, a detractor, and a buffoon in exactly the same sense as was Carlo Buffone [in Jonson's *Every Man Out of His Humour*], and he makes an identical contribution to the satiric spirit of the drama. In the exercise of his office, Thersites, too, in his comments does not observe fitness of time, place, or language. His envy, which we are given to understand is his ruling passion, serves as the recognized credentials for his satiric office. But, being a "prophane Jester," he reflects the author's point of view only in the import of his outbursts and not in their tone. Like Carlo's his speech is designed to evoke amusement and aversion simultaneously. His penchant for bold, "adulterate similes" is as incorrigible as that of Carlo. (pp. 203-04)

His appetite for detraction, when sated on Agamemnon and Menelaus, seems less justified. Then it becomes a part of his Carlo-like role of "common jester, a violent railer." His comments on the meaning of the events and the individual follies that drive the action to futility run the gamut from intelligent comment to foul billingsgate. When he says of Achilles and Patroclus, "With too much blood and too little brain, these two may run mad" [V. i. 48-9], he is presenting Shakespeare's thesis and providing the audience with a standard by which to judge the conduct of the pair and to understand its utter vanity. But when he sums up the Trojan war in such phrases as "All the argument is a cuckold and a whore" [V. ii. 194-95], and "Lechery, lechery; still wars and lechery; nothing else holds fashion" [II. iii. 72-3], though he may permanently jaundice the eyes of all beholders he must be regarded as playing his role of buffoon, to their delight. When, however, he sinks into spouting long passages of spiteful execration, he becomes no more than a foul-mouthed railer, inviting a completely hostile response from his hearers.

Many critics have applied to Thersites the deserved epithet, "the most un-Shakespearean figure" in all the dramatist's works. But the reason is not that the author, when contriving him, designed him to be the mouthpiece of a deep personal despair. The real explanation is much less subjective. It is merely that he tried to transform the Homeric Thersites into one of the conventional, well-nigh indispensable characters of the new satiric comedy. The figure successfully performs all the various offices of the railer and buffoon. If he is offensive in the discharge of his dramatic duties, that is because Shakespeare's higher emotional intensity and superiority in imagination lend to characters, endurable in the art of lesser men, qualities that are aesthetically unacceptable.

The Trojans in *Troilus and Cressida* fare no better than the Greeks. They are a crowd of individuals who have also forsaken reason, but in order to follow slightly different courses of wayward emotion. . . . In spite of critics, like G. Wilson Knight [see excerpt above, 1930], who believe that the Trojans were intended to represent some sort of ideal values, Shakespeare presents them as predominantly irrational and foolish. They first appear gathered in a council of war corresponding to that held by the Greeks. Their representative of wisdom is Hector. Like Ulysses, he is an intellectual mouthpiece of the author. He argues that Helen is not worth the sacrifice which would be involved in insisting on the protection of Paris in his possession of her. Hector's attitude provokes a wild protest from Troilus:

> . . . Nay, if we talk of reason,
> Let's shut our gates and sleep. Manhood and honour
> Should have hare hearts, would they but fat their
>   thoughts
> With this cramm'd reason. Reason and respect
> Makes livers pale and lustihood deject.
>
> [II. ii. 46-50]

This speech seems to Mr. Knight to be an expression of "absolute faith in a supreme value," but to an audience of Elizabethan lawyers it would more likely seem to be a form of *hybris*. Openly to defy reason would be to summon a devil of passion to seize one's soul. (pp. 205-06)

Many critics find it very difficult to admit that Shakespeare gives the love story an intentionally derisive treatment. Like most other mortals, they love a lover, and so cannot resist regarding the author's depiction of both Troilus and Cressida as sympathetic. They appear romantically admirable. Nevertheless, it seems clear that Shakespeare meant their lives to exemplify a form of lust and so to be bound for inevitable disaster. (pp. 207-08)

Act V. Scene iv. Troilus and Diomed. By A. Coopet (1826). The Department of Rare Books and Special Collections, The University of Michigan Library.

The love affair of a deliberately seductive woman and a sensual man, however inexperienced, is not a natural subject for tragedy. Neither of the two is able to win sympathy at the expense of the other, and so become a natural tragic protagonist. On the other hand, the issues raised by such a tale are too serious for the merriment or happy ending of comedy. But lust had been . . . a favorite subject—perhaps the favorite one—of English satirists throughout the 1590's. Shakespeare thus realized that the story of Troilus and Cressida, regarded as the adventures of two virtuosi in sensuality, would display its characteristic features to the best advantage if given the form of a comical satire. He met the first requirement of the literary type by adding to Pandarus' traditional office of pimp, that of satiric observer and mordant commentator. In this way Shakespeare kept the attitude of his audience toward the lovers continuously critical and derisive.

Troilus, however, clearly reveals the nature of his passion, without help from Pandarus. Shakespeare, as we have seen, early presents him as a warrior who makes a virtue of emancipating his will from the control of his reason. When a man with such a philosophy of conduct falls in love, he inevitably becomes passion's slave. His first speech exhibits him, at least in prospect, as an expert in sensuality:

> I am giddy; expectation whirls me round.
> The imaginary relish is so sweet
> That it enchants my sense; what will it be,
> When that the watery palates taste indeed
> Love's thrice repured nectar? Death, I fear me,
> Swooning destruction, or some joy too fine,
> Too subtle, potent, tun'd too sharp in sweetness
> For the capacity of my ruder powers.
> I fear it much; and I do fear besides
> That I shall lose distinction in my joys.
>
> [III. ii. 18-27]

Wilson Knight finds this speech an expression of unsatisfied aspiration or of dismay at "the feared impossibility of actual fruition." A more realistic observer would pronounce it the "agony of unsatisfied sexual desire." Troilus is beset with the sexual gourmet's anxiety lest the morsel which he is about to devour will be so ravishing that thereafter he will lose his sense of nice distinctions in sexual experience. For Troilus is not meant to suggest Shakespeare's idea of a brutish lover, but the uneducated sensuality of an Italianate English roué. (pp. 211-12)

Cressida plays the temptress part not too subtly to make her intentions perfectly clear. She uses those arts of coquetry which she knows will most successfully tease and intensify her lover's passion. She wishes to enjoy it at its most ardent moment. Troilus responds to her efforts in the key of his first sensuous soliloquy:

> Oh that I thought it could be in a woman—
> As, if it can, I will presume in you—
> To feed for aye her lamp and flames of love.
>
> [III. ii. 158-60]

On the surface, he seems to be merely appealing for fidelity. But that wish . . . is his response to a fear that she will never be able to satisfy the demands of his discriminating, if voracious, sensuality. At the end of the dialogue which is directed by Cressida toward the flaming zenith of Troilus' passion, Pandarus all but puts the couple to bed on the stage. (pp. 212-13)

We next see the pair the following morning. Like Romeo and Juliet, they sing an *aubade*. But their matutinal exchange is accompanied, not by the sweet notes of the lark, but by the cawing of ribald crows. Cressida is petulant. She accuses Troilus of being tired of her. Men never stay long enough. Troilus, now released from the enchantment of his Circe, replies realistically that she had better be prudent—put on more clothes, one infers—or she will take cold and curse him for it. This is not the morning after an experience of love's "thrice repured" rapture. It is the fretful dialogue of two sated sensualists. The scene must have aroused derisive laughter among the worldly-wise young barristers who witnessed it. To point and prolong their enjoyment, Pandarus bustles in with a mouthful of suggestive comments.

The infidelity of a highborn harlot like Cressida would be confidently expected. Shakespeare artfully prepares the audience for the awaited act of perfidy. She is made to answer with another shrill vow of eternal faithfulness the first summons to return to her father and the Greeks. To an audience realizing her frailty, her protestations produce effective dramatic irony. (pp. 213-14)

The ending of *Troilus and Cressida* is congenial to the purposes and methods of satire. Troilus' infatuation is presented in a way to provoke mingled feelings of revulsion and derision. This complicated emotion Shakespeare maintained and accentuated in his finale. Two kinds of denouement had become conventional to satire. The characters derided might undergo purgation and reform, as do most of those in Ben Jonson's comical satires, or they might be scornfully ejected. The latter method was, as we have seen, that of formal satire and was applied by Jonson to vicious characters like Sordido, for example. Social affectation might be appropriately purged by exposure that induced promises of amendment. But moral delinquency was too fundamental to the nature of the culprit to be thus easily corrected. It deserved to be pursued to the last by the scornful laughter of both author and audience. Hence the unusual close of the action should not be taken for proof that Shakespeare, when he conceived it, was bitter and disillusioned. Nor should critics be greatly troubled because Cressida is not punished and Troilus is not slain by Achilles on the stage. If we insist in following him beyond the limits of the play, after hearing his hysterical threat to haunt Achilles "like a wicked conscience still" [V. x. 28], we may surmise his fate. But, as a victim of uncontrolled passion for a wanton, he did not deserve the dignity of a death before the eyes of the spectators. And any similar moment of nobility Cressida deserved still less. Futility, Shakespeare clearly believed, was the proper end of characters presented in harmony with the intellectual and structural conventions of dramatic satire.

Pandarus functions as commentator for the love story, just as does Thersites for the events of the war. Though not exactly a buffoon and a railer, Pandarus maintains as successfully as his fellow a derisive attitude on the part of his audience. No one who attends his speeches is in danger of mistaking for noble emotions the calculating passion of Cressida or the refined sensuality of Troilus. Pandarus' every utterance is designed to keep the hostile laughter awake. Even his tears at the imminent parting of the lovers would seem to be either crocodile drops or tokens of the disappointment of a pander at the loss of the office that gave his senile licentiousness vicarious satisfaction. The last lines of the play are devoted to his mock lament over the wretched rewards of a bawd. They show conclusively that it was his spirit that brooded over the chaos of the love story. (pp. 217-18)

The play belongs to a group of satirical dramas which, by 1601-2, had developed clearly defined methods. Like all satires, whatever their form, *Troilus and Cressida* inevitably suggests disillusionment and cynicism. Its tone is necessarily cheerless unless the spectator is able to derive a measure of mirth from critical and derisive laughter. The principal characters, for the same reason, are ridiculous, contemptible, and often detestable.

Other features of *Troilus and Cressida* which have frequently seemed to be revelations of Shakespeare's personal problems can now be shown to be his adaptations of methods standardized by Jonson and Marston in the comical satires they had already composed. Ulysses and Hector are commentators—representatives of the author. Like Macilente, Felice, and Quadratus, they are philosophers of a sort. The pair expound the political theories which their creator had illustrated in some of the chronicle histories, and the ethical system which he was to embody in many of his tragedies. Thersites and Pandarus are buffoons—original variations of the type which Carlo Buffone represented. They are just as contemptuous as the *raisonneurs* of the follies and sins which the play exposes, but are so abandoned in their methods of reprehension that they break all the rules of artistic decorum. However, they awaken the boisterous laughter which all Elizabethan audiences demanded from some part of every comic drama. They serve as equivalents of the louts and clowns of other kinds of comedy.

The abuses which the characters in *Troilus and Cressida* personify are not social absurdities such as Jonson derided in characters like Fastidious Brisk, Fungoso, Saviolina, or the eight pretenders in *Cynthias Revels*. The revival of the forms of chivalric ceremony which Jonson had presented merely as the personal peccadillos of Puntarvolo, is shown in *Troilus and Cressida* to be a dangerous foe to rational behavior, both private and social. Nor are the figures who are marked for ridicule, there, reflections of disordered economic conditions, as is Sordido. Shakespeare's satire in this play was predominantly ethical. He shows that the moral lapses of the warriors follow hard upon the weakening of their political and social obligations. It must be acknowledged that he fails to treat the licentiousness of the lovers as a symptom of decay in the social organizations to which they belong. Their story does not illustrate, as some recent critics would have us believe, the disastrous effects that war has upon sexual morality. Nevertheless, it cogently teaches the devastating consequences of unrestrained physical passion, and thus attaches itself to the persistent and vicious attacks of the formal satirists upon that sin. . . . Jonson, in his depiction of the careers of Ovid and Julia in *Poetaster,* had converted the relatively brutal luxuriousness reprehended by his poetic predecessors into a refined sensuality more like that of the vehement Troilus and the calculating Cressida.

The fate of the principal characters in Shakespeare's drama is harmonious with that prescribed by both the artistic ends and the moral purposes of all satire. Jonson and Marston, in their comical satires, led the dramatic action up to the exposure of the derided figures both to themselves and to the audience. The attainment of this desirable result was assigned to one of the official commentators, who spun for the purpose a plot of a typical wit-intriguer. The victims then usually admitted their faults, submitted to purgation, and announced their reform. Characters who had been addicted only to some kind of social affectation might persuade an audience to accept their promises as adequate proofs of their amendment. But the authors were not content to deal thus indulgently with downright moral delinquency. They thought best to pursue it, to the very end of the play, with scornful laughter, in which the audience was induced to join. The formal satirists had applied precisely that method. They had ejected their evil men and women from their poems, with exclamations of sharp disdain. Jonson, as we have seen, treated his vicious characters in the same manner. He used his whip of steel on Sordido, and drove Ovid out of *Poetaster* into the exile which the historical records conveniently prescribed. Shakespeare himself had banished Malvolio from the action of *Twelfth Night,* to the accompaniment of jibes and jeers from the enemies who had exposed him. The finale of *Troilus and Cressida* is a variation of such an approved catastrophe for the derided characters in a satire, and it must thus be regarded, not as the expression of personal disillusionment with love and its rituals, but as the intelligent use of an accepted artistic convention. Hence the critics who are troubled because Shakespeare does not punish Cressida, or put on the stage Troilus' death at the hands of Achilles, can be convicted of aesthetic confusion. They demand that the author attach to a comical satire an ending proper only to a tragedy. If they will but realize that the drama must close with the satiric spirit clearly dominant, they need not continue to be perplexed by its unusual denouement. (pp. 231-33)

Critics who stigmatize *Troilus and Cressida* as un-Shakespearean may be right. The half-grim, half-derisive mood demanded of the author of satiric drama was, perhaps, not suited to his genius. His mind was unable to assume the required flippancy in the face of human aberrations capable of producing as serious results as those issuing from the abysmal follies of the Greeks and Trojans. The sustained intensity of his mind, joined to his tendency toward philosophical lyricism, lent the play a depth of tone which makes his satire ring with universal meanings.

This, perhaps, is why *Troilus and Cressida* seems little like the poems and plays in which Shakespeare's contemporaries had recently been attacking and deriding the very sins and follies here ridiculed. Partly because he made the play a vehicle for his political philosophy, it gives an impression of wide social and political disintegration. Though he may have intended only to anatomize the faults and foibles abroad in London during the last years of Queen Elizabeth's reign, he has appeared to many to be making a rendezvous with despair and doom. Such a conception palpably throws the work completely out of artistic focus and provokes unjustified inferences about the parlous state of Shakespeare's mind at the time of writing. (p. 234)

> *Oscar James Campbell, "'Troilus and Cressida',"*
> *in his* Comicall Satyre and Shakespeare's "Troilus
> and Cressida," *Huntington Library Publications,*
> *1938, pp. 185-234.*

UNA ELLIS-FERMOR (essay date 1945)

[*An Irish scholar, critic, and editor, Ellis-Fermor devoted a considerable portion of her literary and academic career to the study of Shakespearean and Jacobean drama, although she also contributed studies on the Irish dramatic movement and on modern drama. She served on the advisory board of* Shakespeare Survey *and from 1946 to 1958 was the general editor of* The New Arden Shakespeare. *At the time of her death, Ellis-Fermor left unfinished her only full-length study of Shakespeare, portions of which were later published by Kenneth Muir in his* Shakespeare the Dramatist and Other Essays *(1961). The following excerpt, taken from her* The Frontiers of Drama *(1945), represents a significant break in the critical appreciation of* Troilus and Cressida. *Unlike many previous commentators, Ellis-Fermor contends that the play is not a failed effort to present a "phase of experience" outside the realm of drama, but that it is rather "a great achievement, perhaps one of the greatest, in the expression of that phase." She argues that because disorder and disintegration are central to the theme of* Troilus and Cressida, *the discordant form of the drama is intentional and appropriate, a point later supported by S. C. Sen Gupta (1950). Ellis-Fermor also considers at length the problem of determining value in the play, a subject also discussed by Norman Rabkin (1965) and Terence Eagleton (1967). She states that "the negative principles of disjunction and chaos" are substituted for order and value, and that they are the result of humanity's "denial of absolute value." That such a critical insight is only now possible, she suggests, is attributable to the affinity between modern civilization's "experience of disintegration and disruption" and the world of* Troilus and Cressida, *an observation corroborated by later critics, including Barbara Heliodora C. de M. F. de Almeida (1964), Jan Kott (1964), and R. A. Yoder (1972). The only absolute value that remains, concludes Ellis-Fermor, is the playwright's imagination, which, "by a supreme act of artistic mastery," gives form to the idea of chaos and disjunction.]*

The great play of *Troilus and Cressida,* one of the most weighty in the Jacobean period, has had a strange fate. Its readers have been variously affected by it, and our reflections, when we have not taken refuge in silence, have ranged from dismissing it as a piece of hasty work to defending it as a failure of a grand scale. Commentators describe, in the one case, the ill-digested scenes mixed with graver, sometimes noble, matter, and in the other point out that, though Shakespeare had undoubtedly something which he wished to say (and to say in specifically dramatic terms), he for once mistook 'what may be digested in a play' [Prologue, 29], and, by sheer pressure of content, broke the mould he tried to use.

By repeated readings of the play, helped greatly by seeing it upon the stage, by trying to relate it to the criticism of life offered by some of Shakespeare's Jacobean contemporaries (to say nothing of the criticism of life implicit in some of our own contemporaries), I am driven to believe that this is not enough; that the play of *Troilus and Cressida* is not a great failure to record a phase of experience beyond the scope of dramatic form, but a great achievement, perhaps one of the greatest, in the expression of that phase, transcending those limitations to produce a living work of art. That the actual experience which is thus expressed is of deep significance to our generation I no more doubt than that it is essential to our understanding of Shakespeare's later tragic and constructive plays; but for the generations between Shakespeare's and our own it has been generally avoidable, and therefore rare. It is no light matter to suggest that something in any way important to our understanding of the play should have escaped a long succession of commentators. Nor would anyone venture upon doing so today, were it not that our actual experience of disintegration and disruption, so unlike that of any age between, has thrown fresh light upon the nature and foundations of what we call civilization; prospects once mercifully rare are now common and familiar, and much that has not, in the interval, been generally forced upon the imagination, now lies upon the common road for every man's necessary consideration. (pp. 56-7)

In *Troilus and Cressida* the aspect we are first aware of is, as in many plays, the material of which it is made. For the artist this has meant the choosing, from the infinite and unselected mass of life, of those groups of characters and events to which his mind turns for the purposes of its as yet undefined interpretation; it is the first step in the substitution of the form of

art for the chaos of life. For the reader it means the subject-matter of the play and his general impression derived from it; the series of characters, the chronological sequence of events, the impinging of character and event upon each other. And in *Troilus and Cressida* this takes the form of a succession of violently contrasted characters, events, and sentiments. Characters as discordant as Thersites and Troilus, Nestor and Pandarus, Hector and Cressida, Agamemnon and Achilles are forced into continual and jarring contrast, with no attempt to resolve the contradictions in an enveloping mood of humour or pity. Instead, the nucleus of the character-grouping, upon which our attention is continually focussed as in a well-composed picture, is that of Troilus and Cressida; a serious man, by nature heroic and an honest if confused idealist, and a light woman, equally by nature a

> sluttish spoil of opportunity
> And daughter of the game.
>
> [IV. v. 62-3]

The same pitiless enforcing of contrasts is seen in the relation of character and event, the incompatibility of men's endeavours and their destinies; the ideal love of Troilus and the betrayal it meets at the height of its glory; the honourable, heroic code of Aeneas and Diomede, Hector and Agamemnon, and the collapse of that code in Achilles' murder of Hector; the clear, sustained thought of the debates upon principles and policy in the Greek and Trojan council chambers, and the relapse into petty feuds and ambushes, which serves to show how far that noble sanity can work upon event. And as we watch these passions, ideas, and achievements annihilate each other with no promise of compensation or solution, we fall more and more into agreement with Thersites, the showman who is ever at hand to point the futility, the progressive cancelling out to negation.

The materials of *Troilus and Cressida* are thus more obviously at war than those of any other play of Shakespeare's, and their discord has been a main factor in persuading its readers of the unevenness of the play, of the inconsistency in quality and treatment of the different parts, attributable, it might be, to indifference or weariness in the writer or to alternating and unreconciled moods of admiration on the one hand and expostulation, disgust, or disillusionment upon the other.

But what if this effect be itself art? What if disharmony be, not the result of a photographic reproduction of materials that the artist's mind has registered without full comprehension, but a deliberate commentary? For, significant and familiar as is the bitterness, the loathing of life which brought together the elements of *Troilus and Cressida,* the apposing of these is even more notable than the choosing. That aspect of a play which its readers think of as its form is itself a mode of interpretation of the material, having been for the artist the next step in the freeing of 'that unbodied figure of the thought, That gave it surmised shape' [I. iii. 16-17]. The elements fall into such positions or relations within the scheme of his play as not only emphasize and disengage the nature and quality of each, but indicate the underlying values by which his interpretation of the material was determined.

This is revealed first and most obviously in the sequence of the scenes, and here the effect is best appreciated in a rapid production which preserves the Elizabethan tempo and forces us to see one scene running as it were into the next; by insisting upon their almost merging in presentation, it makes clear to us that they must be merged also in our interpretation; that they are, in fact, inseparable. Thersites or Pandarus (the explicit or the implicit statement of the mood of disillusionment) breaks in upon every scene in which nobility of conception, passion, or conduct is emphasized, following it up, almost before the echoes of the last words have died away. The induction and the conclusion are in the hands of Pandarus. Pandarus' talk precedes the great council-chamber scene in the Greek camp, where Ulysses builds his lofty image of the state; and Nestor and Ulysses (two of the wisest figures of the play) are hardly off the stage before the scurrilous venom of Thersites is poured upon them in the next scene. Straight upon this comes the corresponding council debate in Troy, with its penetrating analysis of one of the fundamentals of the play, the nature of value; and straight upon that again, Thersites calling up vengeance, 'or, rather, the Neapolitan bone-ache' [II. iii. 18-19] upon both armies. Into this meeting of Thersites and Patroclus come again the Greek leaders, their lofty statesmanship tinged now perforce with politic cunning, and upon that again the scene (III, i) between Pandarus, Paris, and Helen; the feverish frivolity of the background of the war jars bitterly with the scenes of camp and battle and yet is inextricably interwoven with them. Straight upon their urbane and matter-of-fact jesting upon the habit of love, come Troilus's ideal, tremulous anticipations, and into this very scene again, Pandarus, that 'wondrous necessary man'. This handling continues all through the play, but the sifting together of the elements becomes closer and closer as it goes on; Pandarus is nearly always present with Troilus and Cressida in Troy, and Thersites takes his place in the scene of Troilus's disillusionment in the Greek camp. The highest altitudes of chivalry are touched in the scene of Hector's visit to Agamemnon, where a noble code makes possible this courteous friendship between honourable enemies. The scene is set between that which sees Cressida 'wide unclasp the table of her thoughts To every ticklish reader' [IV. v. 60-1] and that in which Thersites denounces Patroclus's relations with Achilles. This does not seem like accident.

There is something, then, in the form of this play which leads us to believe in its unity of intention. Moreover, the belief that it is not inconsequent and contradictory but intent and purposeful, is confirmed by our first experience of the imagery and the prosody. The tough resilience of the verbal music, the explosive illumination of the imagery are the marks of a causal, not a casual, direction. The speeches of Ulysses, Agamemnon, Hector, and Nestor are distinguished by close-woven, intricate, and virile imagery, and the ring of the verse throughout these scenes is superb. When Ulysses persuades the Greek councillors, he gives a noble smoothness and simplicity of line to his doctrine of hierarchical 'degree'. When Nestor is alone with Ulysses, a mind thewed like his own, he speaks with cryptic cogency a language of brief hints weighted with implications that he need not elucidate, so that, by the interlocking of imagery, the work of argument itself is done by the images. (pp. 58-61)

[The opposition] of images that, while leading in the reader's mind to a process equivalent to arguing, do indeed fly off from each other 'with impetuous recoile and jarring sound', plays its own part in furthering that impression of disjunction which the art of the play, in major or in minor form, is ceaselessly at work to enforce upon us. The persistence, in fact, of such verse and imagery, right through to Troilus's last speech on the death of Hector, indicates, in a very different way but no less surely than the ruthless choice and the sure handling of material, that this is no plaything for Shakespeare. Here is a task upon which his whole mind was bent in intense and terrific

concentration. Metre and imagery alike wrestle with their subject-matter. Every faculty works at its full height; the last resources of intellect and imagination are in action.

The conclusion, then, from even this brief consideration of the subject and form of the play, is that they collaborate, not fortuitously, but intentionally, that the form illuminates and interprets the theme, is itself ordered by it, each being in some degree an aspect of the other, precisely as we expect in a play which is a major work of dramatic art. And so there is confirmed the impression that here is no failure, nor even partial success. For, given discord as the central theme, it is hard to imagine how else it should be formally reflected but in a deliberately intended discord of form also. Rare this may be—perhaps unique in dramatic art—but, as I have suggested, the experience which the play exists to communicate is rare also. (pp. 62-3)

With this conviction in mind, then, we can turn to the underlying ideas of the play, no longer expecting to find inconsistency in Shakespeare's treatment of the various parts.

It cannot escape our notice that, in *Troilus and Cressida,* the revelation of the writer's values is not, as in most of Shakespeare's work, implicit only, and so dependent upon our ability to receive the artistic experience of the dramatist; there is also much explicit discussion of the abstract question, 'What is value?' This is both easier to distinguish and a direct road to Shakespeare's implicit comment, and for both reasons it is well to consider it first.

Many of the characters—Troilus, Paris, Achilles, Hector, Ulysses, Thersites—are either involved in a bitter fight to harmonize the conflicting evidence of their universe, or are gradually relaxing their efforts and subsiding into a no less bitter equilibrium of disillusionment or loathing. As they make their different interpretations of the meaning or non-meaning of that universe, it begins to be clear that many of the main issues depend for them upon the question of whether value is absolute or relative; inherent in the object or superimposed upon it; objective or subjective to the valuer.

Troilus, at the begining of the play, represents one extreme; he believes that the object of faith or worship (a woman, an ideal, a code, an institution) is invested with value precisely to the degree to which it is valued. 'What is aught', he exclaims, 'but as 'tis valued' [II. ii. 52] and though it never occurs to him to consider the relation of this belief to his estimate of Cressida, there are signs of underlying misgiving in his constant questioning of her. The course of the play brings him out of his belief, through a process of disintegration in which the operation of reasoning is set against the faculty itself, to a state of equilibrium in which he repudiates the two great ideals of his life, love, and soldiership, betrayed in the one by Cressida's perfidy, in the other by the murder of Hector. In their romantic defence of the war at the beginning, he and Paris behave like book collectors who pay £100 for a rare example containing certain typographical peculiarities, not because of its intrinsic beauty or interest, but because that market price has been fixed by other men's willingness to rise to it. For all its romantic dressing, this is at bottom the most purely commercial aspect of value presented in the play, equating merit with the price that can be got for a thing, Helen with so much warfare. When this is advanced in its turn as a reason for continuing to value her, it involves a bland *petitio principii* ["begging of the question"] that neither of the hot-headed young men has time to observe:

> *Paris.* There's not the meanest spirit on our party
>   Without a heart to dare, or sword to draw,
>   When Helen is defended. . . . Then (I say)
>   Well may we fight for her, whom we know well
>   The world's large spaces cannot parallel.
>
>   [II. ii. 156-62]

If the fallacy of their arguments escapes their own notice, it does not escape that of Hector, the clearest exponent of the other view of value, value as something that must be primarily inherent in the object valued:

> But value dwells not in particular will;
> It holds his estimate and dignity
> As well wherein 'tis precious of itself,
> As in the prizer: 'Tis mad idolatry
> To make the service greater than the God;
> And the will dotes that is inclinable
> To what infectiously itself affects,
> Without some image of th' affected merit.
>
>   [II. ii. 53-60]

It is, as he implies later, for lack of this 'image of the affected merit' that the arguments of Paris and Troilus are 'glozed but superficially' and are indeed no reasons [II. ii. 165]. He dismisses the strongest argument on their side, namely that its effect on its worshipper itself invests the idol with value (indeed, with all the value we need to seek), temperately making it clear that the sense of value depends for its stability upon something outside itself, objective and absolute, inherent in the object—in short, upon the 'image of the affected merit'.

But many other characters in the play are seeking, by different methods and with different incidental experience, for just such an 'image'—an absolute value by which to test the evidence of their experience. And they all either come to the same destructive conclusion or themselves furnish notable confirmation by their fates of the destructive philosophies of the rest. (pp. 63-5)

Is Shakespeare, in *Troilus and Cressida,* himself revealing, through [the characters'] conscious analyses as through their experience, a state in which such questions met just such answers in his own mind? I think he is, and I think this brings us to the root of the matter. The writer of this play is a man to whom values have become suspect.

Were the wisdom of Hector and Ulysses allowed to survive, in contrast with the rest of the play but without further comment, this might be less clearly implied. But actually it suffers defeat in both cases; in Hector's by the implications of his betrayal at the hands of a code in whose stability he had trusted; in Ulysses', first by the course of the action, which denies the truth of his idea by the contradiction of event, and, secondly and more specifically, by a later admission of his own, when, arguing that virtue must not seek 'remuneration for the thing it is' [III. iii. 170], he goes on to dismiss the possibility of intrinsic value having, in practice and in the affairs of men, any effective alliance with assessed value:

> Love, friendship, charity, are subjects all
> To envious and calumniating time:
>
>   [III. iii. 173-74]

so that the indispensable condition, without which intrinsic value cannot be liberated into reality, is never there. The reason for this is at once simple and irremediable, it lies in the nature of man's mind:

> One touch of nature makes the whole world kin:
> That all with one consent praise new born gauds,
> Though they are made and moulded of things past,
> And give to dust, that is a little gilt,
> More laud than gilt o'er-dusted.
>
>   [III. iii. 175-79]

That is, man's judgement (his capacity for valuing) is incapable of its task, and absolute value, whether or not it exists, is never discernible.

Even the acute intelligence of Ulysses then, having done its best upon the problem, has met with implicit and explicit defeat, and it is not surprising that the same fate befalls the other characters.

The last position, in descending order of negation, is that of Thersites. He has long taken for granted the conclusion that Ulysses has implied; mankind in his eyes is as incapable of worthy judgement as of worthy conduct; Ulysses, Nestor, Agamemnon, Hector and Troilus are reduced to their lowest terms, no less than Achilles, Ajax, Patroclus, Paris, Helen and Cressida. But he has travelled further. He does not waste time debating the existence of absolute value, or whether or not man can perceive and live by it; he assumes no criterion beyond that fallible human judgement of which he is so eloquent a satirist. Nor does the obscene casualty of fate and circumstance stagger him; for here the paradoxes of circumstances have long ago taken the wind of satire: 'To what form but that he is, should wit larded with malice, and malice forced with wit turn him to? To an ass were nothing; he is both ass and ox; to an ox, were nothing; he is both ox and ass' [V. i. 56-60]. In the world he offers us there is no stability in character, ideals, institutions, judgement, nor in imagination itself. The whole is a shifting, heaving morass where all is relative and nothing absolute, where pullulating worm and insect forms, seething upon the surface, are seen suddenly, as at the dissipating of some soft, concealing cloud, intent upon their task of disintegration and erosion, reducing all things to their own terms and substance.

And yet Thersites is an integral part of the play's form and matter, and that play is a living organism. It is upon the whole fabric that his mind is at work, driven by the passion of his disgust to break down the forms of things into lifeless elements that can never again be human flesh and blood nor even wholesome earth, but must remain barren and negative like deflowered soil. As we read his comment and relate it with the debates in these other minds, his is seen to be the dominant of their scale. For he, to whom all the argument is a cuckold and a whore, who sees the common curse of mankind, folly and ignorance, as deserving only the dry serpigo and war and lechery to confound them, has arrived at his conclusion by the very road that they are travelling—Ulysses by his own reasoning, Troilus by the conversion wrought in him by event, and the rest by their betrayal of or at the hands of their codes. The starting-point of his interpretation is the conclusion to which they too are proceeding: there is no absolute value inherent in the universe imaged in the loves and wars of Greeks and Trojans. There *is* no 'image of the affected merit'.

Once we have isolated this central question (What is the nature of value and has it or has it not an absolute existence?), once we have traced the series of positions, from positive to negative, of Hector, Troilus, Ulysses, and Thersites and the relation of each of those positions to the general evidence of the play, matter and form alike are seen to derive from this conclusion, which makes of the whole a vast, complex but organic artistic experience. The conflict between conduct, ideals, and event which the choice of material lays so clearly before us and the idea of disjunction inescapably enforced by the structure of the play serve now to drive home the conclusion that in this play disjunction was a fundamental principle, if not the most fundamental, in Shakespeare's view of the universe of event.

But we are uneasily aware, at the same time, that this judgement is not limited to the universe of event. Were that so, we should probably find in this play a mood of partial negation only, as in the balanced conflicts of the tragedies, where the positive element contends on equal terms with the negative and the duality is essential in the artistic experience. But in *Troilus and Cressida* our sense of the artistic unity has derived, as we have realized, not from an impression of balance, but from an impression of evil enveloping apparent good; not from a picture of the accidental prevalence of mischance and injustice over wisdom and rectitude, but from the implication of a causal relation between disjunction in event and the absence of absolute criteria in the universe of thought. To make this clear we may look again at some of the noblest thought in the play and see how it is related to the enveloping and prevailing evil and how its destruction carries the principle of disjunction into the domain of the mind itself.

Let us take again Ulysses' defence of 'degree', the foundation upon which civilization and its achievement rests. The hierarchy of his state stands, in its nobility of conception, linked with the hierarchy of the heavens, a microcosm of the great universe:

> The Heavens themselves, the planets, and this centre,
> Observe degree, priority, and place,
>
>   [I. iii. 85-6]

and 'all in line of order' [I. iii. 88]. The heavens maintain their courses and the world of man reflects their ordered process in 'The unity and married calm of states' [I. iii. 100]. But if the planets 'in evil mixture to disorder wander', then 'Degree is shak'd' [I. iii. 95, 101], both in the cosmos and in society, the image of the cosmos created by man's mind. Then, in the two universes alike, in that of the material cosmos and that of man's creating 'each thing meets in mere oppugnancy' [I. iii. 110-11] and chaos is come again. To this 'mere oppugnancy' the play leads us inescapably, by the matter and texture of the concluding acts. The towering thoughts and ideals topple down before a destiny as implacable as that foreseen by Ulysses for the doomed towers of Troy; and if we look immediately from these ideals to the last phases of the action, the ambush and murder of Hector, we have no choice but to measure the chaos and the discord by the gracious assurance, the magnanimity, and the seeming stability that they destroy. Just as we feel the value of the *Oedipus* or the *Oresteia* to be in one way commensurate with the depth and the power of evil which Sophocles and Aeschylus meet and transmute, so in *Troilus* the nobility of that order which in the end proves perishable gives us the measure of the destructive forces which triumph over it. The existence of the principle of cause and order (in the cosmos and in the affairs of men) is therein questioned; it vanishes, revealing destruction as the principle underlying all life. (pp. 67-70)

Moreover, the downfall of the principles of order and value in the world of man's creation, with the substitution of the neg-

ative principles of disjunction and chaos, is traced directly to that inability in man to imagine absolute value which we have already recognized; in Ulysses's words, to the 'touch of nature' that 'makes the whole world kin' [III. iii. 175]. It *is*, indeed, man's 'nature'. Not only is the objective universe, then, the cosmos and society, found subject to this curse of disjunction; the universe of the imagination also is proved incapable of conceiving a stable value. Disjunction, chaos, discord in the spheres, this is the only irreducible and continuing thing. The denial of absolute value, of any real 'image of the affected merit', is, then, carried beyond the world of event within the play; casualty has replaced causality in the world of the imagination also.

It would seem, then, that this play is an attempt, upon a scale whose vastness is measured by the intensity with which every faculty of the poet's mind is engaged, to find that image (of absolute value) in the evidence of man's achievement, in the sum or parts of his experience or, if nowhere else, in the processes of creative imagination. Troilus's love, Agamemnon's chivalry, Ulysses's vision of the hierarchy of state are all, thus, experimental images, in which are tested the absolute value of man's passion, intellect, and imagination. In face of this test, . . . all fail. There is no absolute quality the evidence for which does not resolve itself into a mere subjective illusion of blood or fancy, a

>   mad idolatry,
> To make the service greater than the God.
>
>   [II. ii. 56-7]

The creations of man's spirit, hitherto exalted, are now seen to have survived only by chance, at the mercy all the time of a stronger, natural law of destruction; what in another mood might have appeared tragic accidents, the counterpoint in a fuller harmony, are now seen, instead, to reveal an underlying law to which all is recurrently and inescapably subject. This is the ultimate, indeed the only surviving absolute in *Troilus and Cressida*. The faculty that could perceive degree and the ordered form of a universe, the imagination itself, has been touched and the images of form no longer rise at its command. 'There is no more to say' [V. x. 22]. The dark night of the soul comes down upon the unilluminated wreckage of the universe of vision. The play of *Troilus and Cressida* remains as one of the few living and unified expressions of this experience. (pp. 71-2)

If we turn from this attempt to understand the nature of the underlying ideas in *Troilus and Cressida* and consider the form through which these ideas are revealed, we see that what has been achieved is in fact what we suggested at the outset. The idea of chaos, of disjunction, of ultimate formlessness and negation, has by a supreme act of artistic mastery been given form. It has not been described in more or less abstract terms; it has been imaged. What seemed to be an absolute limitation of drama has been transcended and shown, in this rare achievement, to be but relative. (p. 72)

The value that we finally attach . . . to Aeschylus, to Sophocles, and to Shakespeare rests upon the extent of their comprehension of evil, and upon the extent to which that vision of evil has been brought under the governance of those artistic laws which are themselves the image of the ultimate law of an ordered universe. Thus, in Shakespeare's *Troilus and Cressida* we meet a paradoxical dualism. The content of his thought is an implacable assertion of chaos as the ultimate fact of being; the presence of artistic form is a deeper, unconscious testimony to an order which is actually ultimate and against which the gates of hell shall not prevail. (p. 73)

Una Ellis-Fermor, " 'Discord in the Spheres': The Universe of 'Troilus and Cressida'," in her The Frontiers of Drama, 1945. Reprint by Methuen & Co. Ltd., 1964, pp. 56-76.

S. C. SEN GUPTA (essay date 1950)

[*Sen Gupta, a prominent Indian Shakespearean scholar, produced several books of criticism on Shakespeare's plays. In his discussion of* Troilus and Cressida *in his* Shakespearian Comedy *(1950), Sen Gupta, like Una Ellis-Fermor (1945), claims that the loose structure and the inconclusive ending are "an appropriate reflex of the unsolved riddle of the moral world." Like G. Wilson Knight (1930), L. C. Knights (1951), and Norman Rabkin (1965), he also emphasizes the role of time in the play, stating that it is the "ultimate arbiter of human affairs"—a view which has been challenged by R. A. Yoder (1972).*]

Troilus and Cressida is a puzzle for classifiers. The Quarto calls it a 'history', but in the prefatory address to the reader the play is spoken of more than once as a 'comedy'. In the Folio, the title of the play is *The Tragedie of Troilus and Cressida*. Its pretension to historicity need not be seriously discussed. As for its claim to being considered a tragedy, the play ends, indeed, with the representation of the death of Hector and of the frustration of Troilus, but Hector, who is one of the important characters and not the protagonist of the drama, is so basely slain that it is not possible to take his death as a tragic catastrophe. Troilus's discomfiture, again, has not the dignity and depth we associate with the conclusion of a tragedy. Although sorely touched by Cressida's treachery, Troilus does not utterly collapse but rather derives from this painful experience new energy with which he proceeds to fight on behalf of his country. We have, therefore, no alternative to calling it a comedy, recognizing, however, that it has certain peculiarities distinguishing it from the norm of its class. It has no happy ending, and the plot, too, has none of the disguises, tricks, intrigues and other devices whch form the stuff of comedy. The story is so loose and contains so many episodes, that we feel that here is matter rather for a novel, which permits greater diversity and amorphousness than the more compact art-form of the drama. (pp. 191-92)

The characters of the play are portrayed in a manner that seems to be different from Shakespeare's usual practice. Achilles, Ajax, Ulysses, Hector, Troilus, Helen and Cressida—all of them have certain prominent characteristics which mark off one from another, but they have not that complex individuality, those subtle and delicate nuances, which add richness to the vitality of dramatic creations. In *Troilus and Cressida,* each principal figure is portrayed as a symbol of some virtue or vice or attitude which is, however, made so conspicuous of its kind and is so deftly brought into contact with the other forces of life that what might have been dry allegory has become living drama. Troilus, Cressida and Pandarus are conscious that each of them will live down the ages as symbols of moral qualities:—

> True swains in love shall in the world to come
> Approve their truths by Troilus: when their rimes,
> Full of protest, of oath, and big compare,
> Want similes, truth tir'd with iteration,
> As true as steel, as plantage to the moon,
> As sun to day, as turtle to her mate,
> As iron to adamant, as earth to the centre,
> Yet, after all comparisons of truth,

> As truth's authentic author to be cited,
> 'As true as Troilus' shall crown up the verse
> And sanctify their numbers.
>
>   [III. ii. 173-83]

So Troilus; Cressida, likewise, at the height of her romantic courtship with Troilus, asserts that if she be false, she will become a symbol of unfaithfulness, a permanent subject for derisive comparison [III. ii. 184-96]. Pandarus, again, is drawn as the prototype of all broker-lackeys, and shame and ignominy will 'live aye with [his] name' [V. x. 33-4]. The symbolical suggestiveness of the characters seems to be a part of the deliberate intention of the dramatist. Achilles and Ajax have distinctive personalities, but they are more important as forming the group which opposes the principle of 'valour' against that of 'policy' which finds its champion in Ulysses and Nestor. Both Achilles and Ajax wear their wit in their bellies and their guts in their heads, and indeed, when Ajax describes Achilles in unflattering terms, the Greek lords are amused at the aptness with which the description may be applied to his own self. Menelaus and Paris, too, are less individuals than personifications of a particular attitude for, whatever their peculiarities in other respects, this play takes note only of their fond attachment to a 'whore' whom they 'merit' 'both alike'. (pp. 193-94)

In one respect *Troilus and Cressida* is different from modern problem dramas in which the dramatists deal with concrete social problems and very often indicate the line of solution. Shakespeare takes up no social question of limited significance and appeal but a moral problem that is universal and eternal. It is the problem of value, which resolves itself in the play into many subordinate branches. Is it worth while for the Greeks and the Trojans to fight for a despicable woman for whom neither party cares? What is the place of love in man's life, and how far does the value of an emotion depend on the person who is the object of it? Should a man sacrifice his personal happiness in furtherance of the general good? Yet another aspect of the problem of value is suggested in course of the debate in Priam's palace on the question of the retention of Helen (II. ii). The problem here is whether value is objective or subjective. When Troilus points out that the worth of a thing depends on the way in which it is subjectively valued, Hector thus draws attention to the other side of the question:—

> But value dwells not in particular will;
> It holds his estimate and dignity
> As well wherein 'tis precious of itself
> As in the prizer.
>
>   [II. ii. 53-6]

These are some of the issues which make up the complex fabric of the drama; they clamour in vain for a solution. Shakespeare is a dramatist for whom the living portrait is more important than the abstract conclusion, and arguments are admitted only in so far as they may be vivified by the breath and finer spirit of life. (pp. 197-98)

Not only does the main theme branch out into many corollaries which interpenetrate one another, but the conclusion, too, has inevitably become vague and indeterminate. In a problem play, the plot which has only a subordinate place cannot reach a satisfactory conclusion independently of the thought-content. In *Troilus and Cressida* the theme is not a social problem of a particular age or country but a moral question which transcends the limitations of time and space. As such a problem cannot admit of a final solution, the conclusion to this play allows the chaos to remain as it was at the beginning. Even if the Greeks had been shown as destroying Troy and taking away Helen (as they do in the legend), how would that have helped to solve the ethical problem whether Helen was worth the sacrifice made for her? Supposing Troilus had succeeded in killing Diomed, how would that have influenced our judgement of the value of his passion for Cressida? The loose structure and the inconclusive denouement are an appropriate reflex of the unsolved riddle of the moral world. . . . What marks *Troilus and Cressida* off from other problem comedies is really the stamp of largeness and complexity which is inseparable from Shakespeare's work. We must also remember that though the problems are the abstract problems of value, Shakespeare's treatment is aesthetic rather than ethical, and any attempt to over-simplify the theme or to find a convenient solution will furnish us with a distorted view of Shakespeare's achievement. Man's multifarious emotional and moral reactions to the realities of life are surveyed from different angles of vision with the picture of Father Time remaining appropriately in the background. References to Time sitting as an ultimate arbiter of human affairs recur more in *Troilus and Cressida* than in any other drama of Shakespeare. This is quite in harmony with the spirit of a play that has as its problem the enduring theme of moral value, and in which the comic is derived from the juxtaposition of different attitudes, each of which, considered by itself, appears to be real but is proved to be unreal when pitted against others. It is Time merging itself in Eternity that is trusted to pass the final verdict on Troilus, Cressida and Pandarus. The most magnificent single speech in the play is the one addressed by Ulysses to Achilles on the all-devouring capacities of Time [III. iii. 145-90]. When Cassandra urges Hector to unarm, he declines to listen to her prognostications, because

> Mine honour keeps the weather of my fate:
> Life every man holds dear; but the dear man
> Holds honour far more precious-dear than life.
>
> [V. iii. 26-8]

But he, too, knows that there is a power more far-reaching in its sway than a soldier's honour or a prophetess's inspiration, and it is to this power that he trusts for final judgement:—

> . . . . the end crowns all,
> And that old common arbitrator, Time,
> Will one day end it.
>
> [IV. v. 224-26]

The verdict will never be forthcoming, because, with supreme irony, Time passes on to timelessness and leaves moral riddles unsolved for ever. (pp. 198-200)

> S. C. Sen Gupta, "Dark Comedies," in his Shakespearian Comedy, *Oxford University Press, Delhi, 1950, pp. 174-200.*

L. C. KNIGHTS (essay date 1951)

[*A renowned English Shakespearean scholar, Knights followed the precepts of I. A. Richards and F. R. Leavis and sought an underlying pattern in all of Shakespeare's work. His* How Many Children Had Lady Macbeth? *(1933)—a milestone study in the twentieth-century reaction to the Shakespearean criticism of the previous century—disparages the traditional emphasis on "character" as an approach which inhibits the reader's total response to Shakespeare's plays. In the excerpt below, Knights examines the dichotomy in* Troilus and Cressida *between the public, objective world view of the Greeks, as personified especially in Ulysses,*

and the personal, subjective perception of the Trojans, as personified in Troilus, an opposition which was first fully discussed by G. Wilson Knight (1930). Unlike Knight, however, Knights declares that Shakespeare exposes the flaws in both Troilus's passionate idealism and the Greek's reason and asserts that "if something vital is missing from the public world of the Greeks, Troilus's subjectivism is equally flawed." He further states that both of these perspectives are subject to the "world of appearance" and that time becomes the "ultimate reality" of such views. Time is seen in a similar manner by G. Wilson Knight (1930), S. C. Sen Gupta (1950), and Norman Rabkin (1965), but its central importance has been questioned by R. A. Yoder (1972). The opposition between Greek and Trojan world views has also been commented on by Winifred M. T. Nowottny (1954), Albert Gérard (1957), Terence Eagleton (1967), D. A. Traversi (1968), and Thomas G. West (1981).]

Great poetry demands a willingness to meet, experience and contemplate all that is most deeply disturbing in our common fate. The sense of life's tragic issues comes to different men in different ways. One of the ways in which it came to Shakespeare is not uncommon; it was simply a heightened awareness of what the mere passage of time does to man and all created things. There are many of the Sonnets that show the impact of time and mutability on a nature endowed with an uncommon capacity for delight. And it is surely no accident that one of the first plays in which we recognize the great Shakespeare— the Second Part of *King Henry IV*—is a play of which the controlling theme is time and change. Put together the 'time' sonnets and this play and you see clearly the beginning of the progress that culminates in *King Lear* and the great tragedies.

At the period when Shakespeare wrote the Second Part of *King Henry IV,* however, his concern with the domination of life by time was not an exclusive preoccupation. It did not prevent him from getting on with the business of living or from writing plays that had nothing to do with time's thievish progress to eternity. Neither was it a philosophical interest in an abstract problem. It was simply a part of his emotional and imaginative apprehension of life; and since its expression coincided with a remarkable development of his dramatic power we might presume—even without the evidence of the Sonnets—that it had for him a special signficance.

Now a deeply ingrained preoccupation with time almost inevitably brings with it two further allied preoccupations—with death and with appearance and reality. With death, because it is the supreme instance of the disturbing and thwarting aspects of time's action. With appearance and reality because the mere passage of time,

> whose million'd accidents
> Creep in 'twixt vows, and change decrees of kings,
>
> [Sonnet 115]

reveals different aspects of things. These new aspects may contradict, or seem to contradict, the impressions to which, assuming them to represent an unchangeable reality, we have committed ourselves; and as a consequence an honest and energetic spirit is forced to ask himself what is solid and enduring in the flux.

There is always the risk of anticipating and imposing where it is our business to discover. But there is no doubt that during the period immediately preceding the great tragedies preoccupations such as these entered deeply into Shakespeare's dramatic poetry. . . . Shakespeare does not deal with his themes in the manner of one embarking on a dispassionate enquiry into the sources of self-deceit and the domination of men by appearances. All we can say is that the way experience came to him was soaked in feelings and shot through with perceptions that *crystallized out* as the themes of appearance, death, and so on. But the condition of the defining that his art *is,* was that it should remain as close as possible to the level of presented experience; for the defining is, simultaneously, an exploring. Our talk of themes, in consequence, is simply a way of pointing to the centres of consciousness that exert a kind of gravitational pull, to the dominant tones and emphases of a living mode of experience. Moreover, to use phrases suggesting that Shakespeare is simply an analyst of experience is to obscure the urgent personal nature of the imaginative effort and its genuinely exploratory nature. Thus we may for convenience speak of Shakespeare's investigation of the world of appearance; but this is not an investigation proceeding from established positions to logical conclusions. Indeed in *Troilus and Cressida,* of which I now wish to speak, there are no conclusions.

I have said that Shakespeare's way of presenting and defining is not 'philosophical'. But *Troilus and Cressida,* though far from abstract, comes nearer than any other of the plays to being a philosophical debate. Greeks and Trojans represent different values, and the things they stand for are the subject of frequent exposition, debate and explicit comment. We shall not do violence to the play or wrench its total meaning if we hinge our analysis on three of the major sequences in which there is a deliberate presentation or development of 'ideas' embodied in the action. On certain conditions: first, that we retain a lively sense of the dramatic context of each formal exposition, with its attendant ironies; secondly that we observe in each instance where the poetry qualifies, and where it enters into and reinforces, whatever may be offered by way of statement. There is a third condition, or qualification, which will be mentioned in due course.

We may begin with Ulysses' famous speech [on degree] in the first meeting of the Greek generals [I. iii. 75-137]. . . . Commentators have been perhaps too much impressed by this piece of rhetoric. One speaks for oneself, but to my mind the only part that by Shakespearean standards is great poetry is the last,—'Then everything includes itself in power . . .' [I. iii. 119-24]. For the rest (in spite of some striking lines), the expansive insistence, the smooth unimpeded rhythms, and the general tone of a public address, denote a formal declamation on one of the great Elizabethan commonplaces. I cannot feel, in short, that Shakespeare is *behind* this speech until his imagination catches fire at the vision of the 'chaos' consequent on the unchecked exercise of 'appetite'. The speech, it is true, is one to keep hold of in reading the play as representing, in its way, a positive. It is at least equally important to observe that none of the Greek generals in any significant sense embodies the order that is talked about; none has the *right* to represent the integration for which Ulysses pleads. (pp. 144-47)

[As Ulysses later asserts at III. iii. 112-23, man] only knows his true worth in society: he needs society because it gives him honour and applause. But worth, he proceeds to suggest, isn't really necessary to obtain the public 'reverberation'. Society can create an appearance of worth even when there is no substantial basis for it.

> I was much rapt in this;
> And apprehended here immediately
> The unknown Ajax.
> Heavens, what a man is there! A very horse;

That has he knows not what. Nature, what things there are,
Most abject in regard, and dear in use!
What things, again most dear in the esteem,
And poor in worth! Now shall we see to-morrow,—
An act that very chance doth throw upon him,—
Ajax renown'd. . . .
To see these Grecian lords! why, even already
They clap the lubber Ajax on the shoulder. . . .

[III. iii. 123-39]

That the Greeks do not in fact esteem the lubber Ajax, that Ulysses despises Achilles' craving for applause, and that the whole speech is part of a deliberate stratagem, these facts do not affect the underlying significance of what is said. Ulysses thinks throughout in terms of a public world, in which men are manipulated and it is the public appearance that counts.

And now occurs one of the most interesting transitions in the play. To Achilles' exclamation, 'What! are my deeds forgot?' Ulysses replies with a vivid and vigorous passage on the inevitable connexion between time and oblivion.

> Time hath, my lord, a wallet at his back.
> Wherein he puts alms for oblivion,
> A great-siz'd monster of ingratitudes:
> Those scraps are good deeds past; which are devour'd
> As fast as they are made, forgot as soon
> As done: perseverance, dear my lord,
> Keeps honour bright: to have done is to hang
> Quite out of fashion, like a rusty mail
> In monumental mockery. . . .

[III. iii. 144-53]

Neither the poetic force of this, nor the fact that it echoes the Sonnets, should lead us to take it, unqualified, as a direct expression of Shakespeare's 'philosophy'. There is an urgency that can only come from feelings deeply stirred; and at one point there is what sounds like a note of personal bitterness,—

> For beauty, wit,
> High birth, vigour of bone, desert in service,
> Love, friendship, charity, are subjects all
> To envious and calumniating time.

[III. iii. 171-74]

But it is still Ulysses who is speaking, and Ulysses is still predominantly concerned not with the effect of time on man's life in general but with the relation between time and reputation. Love, friendship and charity are strange intruders from beyond the public world, where what counts is honour, praise and remuneration. It is all perfectly in keeping. Committed to appearances you are inevitably committed to time. Accept time as the governing reality and you only see 'good deeds' as 'scraps' devoured by oblivion. All that remains is the anxiety-ridden struggle (expressed in the repeated imagery of physical effort, 'keep then the path' [III. iii. 155] and so on) to keep up with the fleeting present. These are the logical consequences of the assumptions that underlie the philosophy of the Greeks. For all their formal dignity they are creatures of time and appearance.

Shakespeare's Greeks stand for public life and an impersonal 'reason', divorced from feeling and intuitive intelligence. The Trojans are their complementary opposite. Corresponding to the meeting of the Greek generals in the first act is the Trojan council in the second. The question is whether or not Helen shall be retained and the war continued. Of the two leading speakers, Hector appeals to reason and morality, the law of nature and the law of nations, all of which decree that Helen shall be sent back to her husband. He is, significantly, over-borne by Troilus, whose idiomatic vigour of speech ('you fur your gloves with reasons' [II. ii. 38]) proclaims an intensely *personal* approach to matters that Hector tries to see as examples of a general law. Troilus's theme, like that of Ulysses to Achilles later, is 'honour',—and honour means standing up for your own valuations, for 'What is aught but as 'tis valued?' [II. ii. 53]. Troilus is an excellent orator. What could be more reasonable than the tone and manner of the lines in which he counters Hector's objections?

> I take to-day a wife, and my election
> Is led on in the conduct of my will;
> My will enkindled by mine eyes and ears,
> Two traded pilots 'twixt the dangerous shores
> Of will and judgment. How may I avoid,
> Although my will distaste what it elected,
> The wife I chose? there can be no evasion
> To blench from this and to stand firm by honour....
>
> [II. ii. 61-8]

Yet what could be more absurd than to speak of the *senses* as mediating between the judgment and the will? It is the *judgment* that is the pilot or mediator between the senses and the will. Since Troilus has in fact abjured reason,—'Nay, if we talk of reason, let's shut our gates and sleep' [II. ii. 46-7]—we need not waste time trying to find a moral or psychological system that will make sense of the 'traded pilots' and the 'dangerous shores'. The talk of 'judgment' is bluff,—though it sounds like unconscious bluff. What matters is 'will', and what the will has once 'elected' 'honour' demands that it shall stand by. The scene has a livelier dramatic interest than can appear from quotation or summary. But what is significant for us in the present connexion is that Troilus embodies a mode of judgment based entirely on the subjective ground of passion and will. (pp. 149-52)

There is the same intense subjectivism in Troilus' love poetry.... It is, we may say, the over-active element of subjective fantasy in Troilus's passion that gives to his love poetry its hurried, fevered note, with a suggestion of trying to realize something essentially unrealizable. The actual separation of the lovers, so far from being a turning-point, is in a sense merely incidental, for it only emphasizes what is *intrinsic* to their relationship. The poetry of parting strikes a note almost identical with the poetry of anticipation.

> Injurious time now with a robber's haste
> Crams his rich thievery up, he knows not how:
> As many farewells as be stars in heaven,
> With distinct breath and consign'd kisses to them,
> He fumbles up into a loose adieu,
> And scants us with a single famish'd kiss,
> Distasted with the salt of broken tears.
>
> [IV. iv. 42-8]

It is here that I find myself most in disagreement with Mr. Wilson Knight [see excerpt above, 1930]. Mr. Knight makes some necessary distinctions (he was, I believe, the first to do so) between Greek intellect and Trojan intuition; but he seems to me to attribute to the latter a more positive value than did Shakespeare. It is not merely that Time slays Troilus's love— 'a spiritual and delicate thing'—the whole basis of that love and of the 'idealism' of which it is a part is subjected to as radical a criticism as is the Greek 'reason'. It is Troilus's

subjectivism that commits him to a world of time, appearance, and [anxiety].... It is, in short, not opposed but complementary to the public realism of the Greeks.

I have spoken of a further condition that must qualify our approach to the play through an analysis of the more direct presentation of its major themes in the crucial passages that we have examined. It is difficult to say exactly how we experience the play, not as a succession of parts, but as a living whole. But when we experience it directly in this way it is plain that what we have to deal with, what we are engaged in, is not simply an objective analysis of the ways in which apparently opposed attitudes lead to the same predicament.... [We]—the spectators—are directly involved; and it is *our* confusion that largely contributes to the ambiguousness intrinsic to the play. The material that Shakespeare chose to work on was public property. His audience, he knew, would have some preconceived notions about Agamemnon, Ulysses, Helen and the rest. And he weaves these preconceptions into the texture of the play by the simple device of now appearing to endorse them, now turning them upside down. We are rarely quite clear about the judgment we are required to make. In the Greek camp we may imagine for a time that we have in fact before us the wise and dignified figures of legend. But it is not only Thersites who undermines *that* notion: the generals are quite capable of doing it for themselves; and quite early in the play we find ourselves echoing the words of Aeneas,—

> How may
> A stranger to those most imperial looks
> Know them from eyes of other mortals? ...
>
> [I. iii. 223-25]

The ambiguity that we are made to feel—and not merely to analyse—springs from the shifting appearances of the characters as well as from the trickiness and dubiety of the formal exposition and argument. We, the spectators, in short, are involved in the play's confusions.

We are thus prepared for the way in which Troilus's speech at the play's climax strikes home.

> This she? no; this is Diomed's Cressida.
> If beauty have a soul, this is not she;
> If souls guide vows, if vows be sanctimonies,
> If sanctimony be the gods' delight,
> If there be rule in unity itself,
> This is not she....
>
> [V. ii. 137-42]

Dispassionately considered, these lines complete the demonstration of the identity in opposition of the Greeks and Trojans. Troilus's love—which focuses the Trojan 'idealism', as Ulysses' policy makes manifest the latent implications of Greek 'reason'—has been finally shown as subject to time and change. (pp. 153-55)

Why, Shakespeare seems to be asking, has time its apparently overwhelming power? The answer towards which the play seems to tend is that time is an ultimate reality to those who live in a world of appearance—whether an 'objective' social world, perceived and controlled by the practical reason, a world from which something essential is missing, or a subjective world like Troilus's from which reason is excluded. (p. 156)

[The play's] most powerful imaginative effect is of bewilderment, ambiguity, of being in the labyrinth. But we have also seen that implicit in the presentation of Troilus . . . is a criticism of the kind of attitude and the modes of evaluation that Troilus embodies. Put simply, if something vital is missing from the public world of the Greeks, Troilus's subjectivism is equally flawed. (p. 157)

L. C. Knights, "'Troilus and Cressida' Again," in *Scrutiny*, *Vol. XVIII, No. 2, Autumn, 1951, pp. 144-57.*

PAUL M. KENDALL　(essay date 1951)

[*In the excerpt below, Kendall challenges the assertion, put forth by such critics as John S. P. Tatlock (1915), William Witherle Lawrence (1931), and Oscar James Campbell (1938), that the tone of* Troilus and Cressida *can be attributed to the play's source material or generic conventions. He posits instead that Shakespeare exploited rather than accepted his sources. Kendall contends that inaction is the play's ordering principle, for Shakespeare did not translate human will into action, but, on the contrary, he consciously emphasized the characters' inaction and the ambivalence of their personalities. This pattern, he concludes, is part of a dramatic design that is less rigid than the conventional forms of comedy and tragedy and approaches "the blurred design of life itself," which thus evokes the participation of the audience.*]

[Certain] purely dramatic values in *Troilus and Cressida*, which in my belief have not received their due, not only reinforce the concept of the play as a deliberate experiment but indicate that this experiment was dictated not by the sources but by the dramatist. The "unpleasantness" and "inconclusiveness" of *Troilus and Cressida* result from the way in which Shakespeare has translated the Troy story and the Troilus-Cressida story to the stage and represent his exploitation rather than acceptance of the source materials.

In the first place, Shakespeare has thwarted the expectation of his audience by a violation of customary dramatic ordering; in the second, he has drawn characters more ambivalent than those which dramatists generally exhibit upon a stage.

Whether tragic or comic, drama customarily translates the promptings of human will into action, successful or ill-fated as it may be. Likewise a state of suffering brought about by preceding action—the tragic agony of Othello, for example, or the comic frustraton of Viola [in *Twelfth Night*]—finds resolution in a further action which relieves and satisfies the emotional involvement of the audience. *Troilus and Cressida* is so ordered, however, that the promptings of human will are not translated into action; and the characters, their striving or suffering unresolved, are held suspended, to the audience's frustration.

Ulysses, for example, profits as a member of the Greek host by the fact that Achilles rouses himself to compass the death of Hector; but his own strategem to bring into action the champion of the Greeks has come to nothing. This stratagem is the principal intrigue of the war plot; on it Shakespeare has lavished some of his most splendid poetry; it is given elaborate development. Yet this important line of action is first paralyzed by a romantic attachment, itself grotesque in the hulking Achilles, and then accidentally accomplished by the irrelevancy of Patroclus' death. To affirm that Shakespeare could have scarcely altered this event in the Troy story is to miss the point that Shakespeare was in no way forced to use it as an example of human will come to nothing. And since this camp intrigue is the invention of Shakespeare himself, the fact that its impressive momentum has no issue and that thus the expectation of the audience is thwarted suggests that Shakespeare, far from

being at the mercy of his material, has deliberately adopted *inaction* as an ordering principle of the play.

The scene of Hector's death is a very bald example of the working of this same principle. There is no action, not even the emotional compensation of a sword flourish. The tension of the basic struggle, Greece against Troy, which Hector and Achilles roughly personify, is unrelieved by physical conflict. Even the single combat between Ajax and Hector is broken off without issue; and whereas in the source material these two events—the combat and the death of Hector—are thematically unrelated, in *Troilus and Cressida* they are linked to each other as stages in a cumulative pattern of inaction.

The scene in which Troilus discovers the treachery of Cressida most vividly reveals the operation of this principle. Here, a stunning revelation produces a state of intolerable suffering that demands and indeed inevitably points towards an issue in action. This scene eats its own children. Precisely because it *is* the most brilliant scene of *Troilus and Cressida* with its meshing of three planes or points of view—the scene perhaps for which Shakespeare wrote the play—it the more deeply frustrates the audience when the human suffering it creates is unrelieved by sequent action. Yet it is this failure of the subsequent scenes to offer the customary fulfillment which provides the denouement, neither tragic nor comic, towards which the play moves from its beginning. (pp. 132-34)

The inaction of the camp intrigue and of the denouement is in harmony with the general texture of the play. When Priam and his sons debate the main issue of the war—whether or not to keep Helen—Hector convincingly refutes the chivalry of Troilus, who insists that Helen is a theme of honor, by an appeal to reason and morality. The audience is clearly meant to approve Hector's stand; his argument progressively demonstrates the emptiness of Troilus' romantic claims. But it all suddenly comes to nothing. Hector yields to the passion of Troilus and the line of action indicated by reason is broken off.

Using the same sources available to Shakespeare, Heywood stages a similar scene, though the context is different, at the opening of *The Iron Age*. But in Heywood's handling of the scene, which illustrates an uncritical dramatizing of a traditional narrative, the emphasis is placed upon what conclusion will be reached, and that conclusion then has its issue in action when Paris secures approval of the rape of Helen. In *Troilus and Cressida*, however, the emphasis is placed squarely upon the curious capitulation of Hector which thwarts a developing line of conduct.

Indeed Shakespeare underlines the fact that the quarrel of Greek and Trojan over Helen is itself a triumph of inaction. Both sides proclaim the worthlessness of the *casus belli*. And Diomed's scorning of Greek and Trojan alike for fighting in behalf of such a "flat, tamed piece" [IV. i. 63]—a central moment in the play—drives home to the audience the fundamental paradox that the avowed "action" of the war plot is actually an inertia. (p. 135)

Finally, it is noteworthy that the informing principle of inaction is introduced, in little, in the opening scene of the play, which ironically weaves the war plot and the love plot together. In a fever of, as yet, unrequited love and exacerbated by his interview with Pandar, Troilus exclaims:

> Fools on both sides! Helen must needs be fair,
> When with your blood you daily paint her thus.
> I cannot fight upon this argument;
> It is too starved a subject for my sword.
>
> [I. i. 90-3]

Troilus looks at the war with a jaundiced but accurate perception, a perception which is certainly not the fruit of this febrile moment only. Yet, when Aeneas enters, on his way to the wars, Troilus docilely joins him. Here, Troilus' physical movement towards the battle front represents, psychologically, an inhibiting of dramatic movement.

The principle of inaction in this scene is closely related to a second important dramatic device: Shakespeare's drawing of ambivalent characters. Though Troilus is from the very opening a sympathetic figure, his immediate failure to adhere to an announced line of conduct cannot fail to dim, however slightly, our estimate of him. This ambivalence continues throughout the play. The very intensity of Troilus' devotion is commented on by the speedy treachery of Cressida, a woman whom Diomed as well as Ulysses at once recognizes as a wanton. Further, just as the sententious intellectuality of Ulysses is at least faintly called in question by the scheme which is its issue and by the discomfortable mockery of Thersites, so Troilus' most lyrical moments of love and most passionate avowals of purity are flawed—to the uneasiness of the audience—by the grossness not only of Pandar's jests but his assumptions. Yet, this uneasiness is stimulated in the first place by a pronounced element of sensuality in Troilus' transports—noted by most contemporary scholars—which often reveals itself when Troilus is being most elevated.

Early in the play the ambivalence of Troilus' character is piquantly developed by ironic contrariety. In act one, scene one, Troilus recognizes, when he is all lover and might be thought most ready to sympathize with Paris' love, that Helen is no theme of honor, even though he rushes into battle. As warrior and prince of the Trojan state, however, he assumes in act two, scene two, the reverse attitude and supports a chivalric position, the emptiness of which is exposed by Hector. (pp. 136-37)

In act four, scene five, it is true, Ulysses highly praises Troilus as man and warrior, calling him "Manly as Hector, yet more dangerous" [IV. v. 104], a commendation which, he reports, he has learned from Aeneas. Yet a moment later Ulysses and the audience have an experience which reveals that this is an incomplete view. Guilessly, almost fecklessly, Troilus exposes to Ulysses his tortured heart and displays an adolescent embarrassment that he has done so:

> O, sir, to such as boasting show their scars
> A mock is due. Will you walk on, my lord?
> She was beloved, she loved; she is, and doth:
> But still sweet love is food for Fortune's tooth.
>
> [IV. v. 290-93]

In the scene of Troilus' bitter discovery, Ulysses assumes, consequently, an almost fatherly role in checking the rash outbursts of the suffering youth. It is perhaps worth noting that the next scene contains Hector's single reference to Troilus as a boy. So does Shakespeare balance characterization with the march of events and thus preserve to the end the ambivalence of Troilus.

May not this ambivalence indeed be read in the sharp divergence in scholarly opinion of Troilus' character? In his *Comicall Satyre* O. J. Campbell rigidly types Troilus as a sensualist, a figure of derision, the object of scornful mirth when his illusions are exposed [see excerpt above, 1938]. Tillyard, on the contrary, insists upon the resoluteness of Troilus' character and considers him the peer of Ulysses [see Additional Bibliography].

Cressida is much less elaborately ambivalent because Shakespeare is less interested in her. She illuminates Troilus and thus serves a secondary purpose. Shakespeare fits her into his design pretty much as he inherited her, i.e., with something of the charm of Chaucer's Cressida but with the uncompromising wantonness she had acquired in the succeeding centuries. These two Cressidas Shakespeare takes little trouble to reconcile, probably because reconciling them is not necessary to his design. It is Chaucer's Cressida whom we recognize— once allowance is made for the hardening of her character required to make credible her association with the debased Pandar—in Cressida of Troy; it is the Elizabethan wanton who suddenly appears in the Greek camp.

This scene of Cressida's arrival is not so reported in Shakespeare's sources and is clearly intended as an economical means of preparing the audience for the inevitable shift in her character as well as of furthering Ulysses' reputation for acumen by his immediate realization that she is a "daughter of the game" [IV. v. 63]. Thenceforth she exists only for the great scene of Troilus' disenchantment. (pp. 138-39)

Thersites contributes poignance to this pervasive ambivalence—not directly in his character of bitter railer and allowed fool, but in the painful division of mind which his words force upon the audience. He is a brutal, coarse and shameless creature—Caliban with a mind—who revolts us by his foulness, who rubs raw our sense of human dignity and value. Yet, we are compelled to recognize that almost everything Thersites says is a truth, or at least a possible aspect of truth. (p. 140)

By thwarting the normal expectation of the audience, both the principle of inaction and the drawing of ambivalent characters develop the frustration and inconclusiveness implicit in the story. Shakespeare forges a dramatic design less rigid than comedy or tragedy, in which the great middle ground between them—the ground on which most human beings play their parts—can be meaningfully transferred to the stage. Assuming a critical and detached point of view, he makes a primary assumption about his materials which generates the play: not only has the debasement of the Troy story and the Troilus-Cressida story removed them from the realm of romance, but in thus removing them this debasement has transformed these stories so that they can offer, when properly dramatized, a grim, ironic, rueful and sometimes mordant commentary upon life.

Troilus and Cressida does not exhibit the tight and "synthetic" structure of most late nineteenth- and twentieth-century problem plays, in which experience is so arranged as to focus the attention of the audience upon a specific social issue. The "problem" in Shakespeare is as broad as life itself, the unsatisfactory and frustrating direction that life *can* take; consequently the characters of *Troilus and Cressida* bulk larger and the movement is freer than in the problem play.

There is one important respect, however, in which *Troilus and Cressida* closely resembles this type of contemporary drama. In departing from the clear patterns of comedy and tragedy and approaching the blurred design of life itself, Shakespeare evokes the participation of the audience. The individual reader, each member of the audience, creates the ultimate meaning of the play by relating what happens upon the stage to his own experience. (p. 144)

Paul M. Kendall, "Inaction and Ambivalence in 'Troilus and Cressida'," in English Studies in Honor of James Southall Wilson, *edited by Fredson Bowers, University of Virginia, 1951, pp. 131-45.*

KENNETH MUIR   (lecture date 1953)

[*In addition to his editions of* Richard II, King Lear, *and* Macbeth, *Muir also published numerous volumes of Shakespearean criticism and served as the editor of* Shakespeare Survey. *In the following commentary, first delivered as a lecture at the Shakespeare Conference at Stratford-upon-Avon in August 1953, Muir discusses the concepts of value and order presented in* Troilus and Cressida. *He observes that, unlike other Shakespearean plays,* Troilus and Cressida *provides continually varying points of view which prevent the identification of any one character as Shakespeare's mouthpiece and make the play "difficult to grasp as a unity," a point echoed by R. J. Kaufmann (1965). Muir also states that Shakespeare, while presenting the dissolution of order and value, does not necessarily suggest that order and value are illusory. He concludes that the fusion of the various themes reveals Shakespeare's "extraordinary imaginative power" and that the "real problem about the play is the failure of most critics to appreciate it." For additional comments by Muir, see his introduction to the 1982 Oxford edition of* Troilus and Cressida *cited in the Additional Bibliography.*]

That [*Troilus and Cressida*] is concerned with the nature of Value is borne out by the imagery relating to distribution and exchange—there is similar imagery in *Cymbeline*—though in fact the presentation of values is done directly as well as by means of imagery, and there are three other groups of images of greater importance. The numerous images related to sickness are concerned partly with sex, and partly with the sickness of anarchy in the Greek camp, so that these images serve to link the two plots together. The group of images connected with movement suggests the continual revolutions of Time and the agitated striving of Emulation's thousand sons. Even larger is the group of animal images, the great majority of which are confined to the Greek scenes. . . . However much we discount Thersites's railings, some of the mud he throws is bound to stick; and after we have heard Ajax compared to a bear, an elephant, a mongrel, an ass, a horse, and a peacock; after we have heard Achilles compared frequently to a cur; after Menelaus has been described as worse than a herring without a roe or than the louse of a lazar—they cannot climb again on to their Homeric pedestals. The greater sympathy we feel for the Trojans is partly due to the fact that they are largely spared Thersites's satire. Yet Wilson Knight exaggerates when he suggests that

> The Trojan party stands for human beauty and worth, the Greek party for the bestial and stupid elements of man, the barren stagnancy of intellect divorced from action, and the criticism which exposes these things with jeers [see excerpt above, 1930].

For the only real intellectual in the Greek camp is Ulysses, and even *his* speeches are no more intellectual than those of Hector. Hector's actions, moreover, have little relation to his considered opinions, while Ulysses does carry out the one plan he proposes, futile as it is. Nor can it be said that the Greeks stand for intellect and the Trojans for emotion; for pride and the pursuit of self-interest are no less emotional than sexual desire and the pursuit of honour. The motives of Achilles are love, both of Polyxena and Patroclus, and excessive pride. Ajax is moved merely by brutish vanity. Diomed is moved by a sexual desire that is uncontaminated by respect or affection for the object of the desire. Wilson Knight in the course of his

essay makes or implies some of these qualifications. But his assumption that Shakespeare's two primary values were Love and War, and that in *Troilus and Cressida* they "exist in a world which questions their ultimate purpose and beauty" seems to make the mistake of replacing the idols Shakespeare was anxious to overturn. Whatever views one may deduce from a study of the whole canon, Hector and Priam, as well as Diomed and Thersites, agree that Helen is an unsatisfactory war-aim; and the one glimpse we have of her only confirms their opinion. Whatever else Shakespeare was doing he was not setting her up as an absolute value. (p.35)

[Ulysses's speech on Order] is dramatically necessary to build up a conception of Order, so that its destruction by Cressida's unfaithfulness may be the more devastating. In several of the books suggested as possible sources of the speech, it is Love, rather than Order or Law, which preserves the universe from chaos. It is so in Chaucer's *Troilus and Criseyde*. Order is more appropriate than Love to the war-plot, but the background of the speech facilitated its application to the love-plot. Ulysses argues that the stars in their courses obey the same ultimate laws as the people and classes in a well-ordered State, and he goes on to state that with the removal of degree civil war and anarchy on earth will be reflected in great natural upheavals. The life of man becomes "nasty, brutish and short" [as Thomas Hobbes contends in his *Leviathan*]. If the order is disturbed at one point, chaos everywhere results. Cornwall blinds Gloucester, and nothing but divine intervention can prevent the return of chaos:

> Humanity must perforce prey on itself,
> Like monsters of the deep.
>   [*King Lear*, IV. ii. 49-50]

"When I love thee not", cries Othello while he still loves Desdemona, "Chaos is come again" [*Othello*, III. iii. 91-2]. So chaos comes again to Troilus:

> If beauty have a soul, this is not she;
> If souls guide vows, if vows be sanctimonies,
> If sanctimony be the gods' delight,
> If there be rule in unity itself,
> This is not she. O madness of discourse,
> That cause sets up with and against itself!
> Bi-fold authority! where reason can revolt
> Without perdition, and loss assume all reason
> Without revolt.
>   [V. ii. 138-44]

Cressida's unfaithfulness upsets order both in the microcosm and in the macrocosm—or so Troilus thinks. But before the end of the play he has apparently forgotten his feud with Diomed; he is concerned only with wreaking vengeance on the great-sized coward, Achilles, for the murder of Hector.

Shakespeare, I believe, was more detached than some critics have allowed, though less detached, I hope, than Oscar J. Campbell believes [see excerpt above, 1938]. . . . Even Una Ellis-Fermor argues that the content of the poet's thought is "an implacable assertion of chaos as the ultimate fact of being", though the "idea of chaos, of disjunction, of ultimate formlessness and negation, has by a supreme act of artistic mastery been given form" [see excerpt above, 1945]. We may agree about the artistic mastery, but not that Shakespeare was asserting that life was meaningless. He was asserting something much more limited, and much less pessimistic. He was saying that men are foolish enough to engage in war in support of unworthy causes; that they are deluded by passion to fix their affections on unworthy objects; that they sometimes act in defiance of their consciences; and that in the pursuit of self-interest they jeopardize the welfare of the State. He was not saying, as far as one can judge, that absolute values are illusions. He was certainly not saying that all women are Cressids; for Troilus himself, at the very moment of disillusionment, dissociates himself from any such position:

> Let it not be believed for womanhood!
> Think, we had mothers; do not give advantage
> To stubborn critics, apt, without a theme,
> For depravation, to square the general sex
> By Cressid's rule.
>
> [V. ii. 129-33]

T. S. Eliot's early critics, confronted with the unflattering picture of modern civilization given in *The Waste Land,* generally assumed that the poet was expressing his own disgust and disillusionment, though we can see now that it should not have been difficult to recognize the religious implications of the poem. In a similar way, the violation of order and the betrayal of values in *Troilus and Cressida* do not mean that the Order does not exist, or that all values are illusions. There is clearly a strong element of satire in the play, though it is tragical rather than comical satire. We sympathize with Troilus and Hector: we do not laugh at them. (pp. 36-7)

One of the reasons why *Troilus and Cressida* has been interpreted in so many different ways is that we are continually made to change our point of view. In nearly all the other plays we look at the action through the eyes of one or two closely related characters. We see *Hamlet* through Hamlet's eyes, never through those of Claudius; *King Lear* through Lear's eyes—or Cordelia's, or Kent's—but never through the eyes of Goneril; *The Tempest* through Prospero's eyes. It is true that another point of view is often given, and a character such as Horatio or Enobarbus may sometimes act as a chorus. But in *Troilus and Cressida* the point of view is continually changing. At one moment we watch events through the eyes of Troilus, and the war seems futile. In a later scene we see the events through the eyes of Hector, and Troilus in advocating the retention of Helen seems to be a romantic young fool. In the Greek camp we see everything from Ulysses's point of view; and then, a little later, however much we despise and dislike Thersites, we become infected with his views on the situation:

> Lechery, lechery; still, wars and lechery; nothing else holds fashion: a burning devil take them!
>
> [V. ii. 194-96]

It is this shifting of emphasis which makes the play so difficult to grasp as a unity; but although Tillyard complains that Shakespeare failed to fuse his heterogeneous materials into a unity [see Additional Bibliography], I believe the unity is there. Yet we distort the play if we make any one character to be Shakespeare's mouthpiece. The worldly standards of Ulysses are not Shakespeare's, though Shakespeare apparently shared, until the end of the sixteenth century, some of his views on Order. In general Ulysses appears more of a Baconian than a Shakespearian in his attitude. Others have argued that Shakespeare speaks mainly through the mouth of Thersites, though Thersites was renowned for his knavish railing in all Shakespeare's sources, including the *Iliad,* and also in Heywood's play about the Trojan war, written afterwards. Shakespeare could enjoy writing his curses, as we can enjoy hearing them, without sharing the bitterness of his creature. Others, again, suppose that Hec-

tor is Shakespeare's real spokesman, though perhaps his attitude to the character was not unlike his attitude to Hotspur.

Tillyard thinks that Shakespeare was "exploiting a range of feelings more critical and sophisticated than elemental and unfeignedly passionate", that he plays "with the fire of tragedy without getting burnt", and that "he meant to leave us guessing". We may agree with him that the play provides "a powerful if astringent delight", but doubt whether it is necessary to make all these qualifications. It is quite possible to be critical and sophisticated at the same time as one is elemental and unfeignedly passionate. This, surely, is what the metaphysical poets accomplish when they are at their best; and if we are to place *Troilus and Cressida* it is not with the banned satirists, or even with the satirical plays of Marston and Jonson, it is rather as Shakespeare's excursion into the metaphysical mode. The most remarkable thing about the play is perhaps the way in which the poet managed to fuse thought and feeling, to unify an extraordinary mass of materials, and to counter the sense of chaos and disruption, not so much by the sense of order implicit in the artistic form, as by his establishment of the values denied or corrupted in the action. Cressida does not stain our mothers. In reading most of [Jean] Anouilh's plays we feel that the sordid compromises of adult life make suicide the only proper solution for an idealist. As we quaff our dose of hemlock we murmur: "But for the grace of God (if there were a God) we might have gone on living." But although *Troilus and Cressida* is a kind of *pièce noire,* we should never be in danger, after seeing it performed, of thinking that it gives Shakespeare's verdict on life, at any rate his permanent verdict. Cressida did not cancel out Rosalind and Viola or make it impossible for him to create Desdemona or Cordelia. He did not "square the general sex by Cressid's rule".

The play, from one point of view, in its exposure of 'idealism', might be regarded as the quintessence of Ibsenism as interpreted by Shaw. From another point of view, as we have seen, it is a dramatic statement of the power of Time. From a third point of view it shows how "we are devils to ourselves" [IV. iv. 95]: the world and the flesh make the best the victims of the worst. We may admit that the fusing of these themes required extraordinary imaginative power—a power which Shakespeare on the threshold of the tragic period amply demonstrated. The real problem about the play is the failure of most critics to appreciate it. (pp. 37-8)

> *Kenneth Muir, "'Troilus and Cressida'," in* Shakespeare Survey: An Annual Survey of Shakespearian Study and Production, *Vol. 8, 1955, pp. 28-39.*

WINIFRED M. T. NOWOTTNY   (essay date 1954)

[*Like G. Wilson Knight (1930) and L. C. Knights (1951), Nowottny asserts that* Troilus and Cressida *presents an opposition between the characters of Troilus and Ulysses. Whereas Ulysses represents a Hobbesian social attitude and Policy, argues Nowottny, Troilus embodies the individual poetic imagination. She further states that the play's dramatic antithesis is formed by Opinion and Value, as expressed by Ulysses and Troilus, respectively. Opinion, Nowottny explains, is changeable and subject to the judgment of the public, but Value, created by the poetic imagination, is stable, individual, and autonomous. She concludes that while all other values in the play are destroyed, the poetic Value of Troilus survives because "it can create in the teeth of fact." While Nowottny's interpretation of Troilus's values as uniquely noble concurs with the readings of G. Wilson Knight (1930) and Albert Gérard (1959), such other critics as L. C. Knights (1951), Terence Eagleton (1967), D. A. Traversi (1968), and Thomas G. West (1981) contend that Troilus holds no such privileged position in the play. For other discussions concerning the conflict between private and social values in* Troilus and Cressida, *see the excerpts by Denton J. Snider (1890), H. B. Charlton (1937), Terence Eagleton (1967), and R. A. Yoder (1972).*]

A reader of Hobbes's *Leviathan* who should close his book and say, 'Man in society may be thus and thus, but what of man's creative imagination?' would be asking the question which Shakespeare has dramatized in *Troilus and Cressida*. The problems of Ulysses, attempting to preserve the stability of a society made up of individuals severally intent upon self-glorification, are the problems Hobbes discusses; in contrast to Ulysses stands Troilus, whose attitude of 'What is aught, but as 'tis valued?' [II. ii. 52] (which Shakespeare in this play characterizes as the attitude of the man of creative imagination) is, from the Hobbesian point of view, one of the 'things that weaken, or tend to the dissolution of a commonwealth'. In his chapter on that subject (Ch. xxix) Hobbes speaks of

> the 'diseases' of a commonwealth, that proceed
> from the poison of seditious doctrines, whereof
> one is, 'That every private man is judge of good
> and evil actions'. This is true in the condition
> of mere nature, where there are no civil laws;
> and also under civil government, in such cases
> as are not determined by the law. But otherwise
> it is manifest, that the measure of good and evil
> actions, is the civil law.

Hector's reply to Troilus, in the debate on Helen, turns on the same issue:

> There is a law in each well-order'd nation
> To curb those raging appetites that are
> Most disobedient and refractory.
> If Helen then be wife to Sparta's king,
> As it is known she is, these moral laws
> Of nature and of nations speak aloud
> To have her back return'd.
>
> [II. ii. 180-86]

This does not really dispose of the argument of Troilus.

> Is she worth keeping? why, she is a pearl,
> Whose price has launch'd above a thousand ships.
>
> [II. ii. 81-2]

Hector's reply is merely a denial of the right of the individual to press his private values against the collective values embodied in the law of a society. Here Shakespeare leaves the issue undecided, for, though Hector declares his allegiance to the theory that law should prevail, in practice he adopts the course of action Troilus has defended by reference to Value:

> Hector's opinion
> Is this in way of truth: yet ne'ertheless
> My spritely brethren, I propend to you
> In resolution to keep Helen still.
>
> [II. ii. 188-91]

The antithesis thus brought out in the debate in Troy, between private criteria of value and 'the law in each well-order'd nation', is in essentials the same antithesis as that between the view of Troilus and the view of Ulysses. Troilus asserts his right to value (whether it be Helen or Cressida) as he himself thinks fit, and to act upon those values; this attitude of his is throughout the play so consistent and so much stressed that it has the status of a philosophy of life. Ulysses's philosophy is expressed in the speech on Degree, where he maintains that 'the unity and married calm of states' [I. iii. 100] depends upon the assent of all to that fixed scale of values asserted by society; such words as 'fixure', 'primogenity', 'due' and 'prerogative', and the image of the 'solid' globe and the 'bounded' waters, make the fixity of social values quite clear. To Ulysses's mind, what prevents a collapse into a savage state where 'force should be right' [I. iii. 116] (or, in the phrase of Hobbes, the life of man would be 'solitary, poor, nasty, brutish and short') is precisely the observance of the fixed values asserted by society and upheld by the assent of the individuals who compose and submit to it.

It is against the background of this great antithesis between two approaches to life, that of the statesman and that of the individual creative imagination, that the action, the intellectual debate, the poetry and the characterization of *Troilus and Cressida* are set. That Ulysses typifies Policy is self-evident enough to need no elaboration, but to say that Troilus is a type of the poetic nature does involve further discussion. It will not do merely to argue that Troilus speaks poetry, for so do all Shakespeare's lovers. The relevant argument lies rather in the fact that Troilus, on his first appearance (I. i) is shown *in the act of composing* his own poetry, and is made to appear as being critically aware of the quality of his own poetic invention. This is what makes him a poet in a sense in which Romeo for instance is not. The first unmistakable evidence of this is in the passage where Troilus draws a picture of himself sitting at Priam's table thinking of Cressida:

> At Priam's royal table do I sit;
> And when fair Cressid comes into my thoughts, . . .
>
> [I. i. 29-30]

This, as a description of his state, he immediately corrects, for it implies, if Cressida comes, that she has been for a time absent; the implication is rejected as soon as seen:

> So, traitor! then she comes! When she is thence!
>
> [I. i. 31]

So Troilus rejects this opening, and (having choked off the interruption of Pandarus), substitutes for the words 'when fair Cressid . . .' another opening, 'when my heart, As wedged with a sigh, would rive in twain' [I. i. 34-5], which he promptly develops by the addition of another simile, a conceit, and a moralizing utterance which presumably, but for the next interruption of Pandarus, would have introduced a further poetic flight. . . . The significance of [the following] dialogue is underlined by the soliloquy of Troilus when Pandarus has gone off in a huff: he asks the typically poetic question, what is the identity of the object he contemplates? And it is of Apollo, the god of poetry, that he asks this question, and he then tries, as the poet does, to penetrate the identity of the object by treating of it in poetry:

> Tell me, Apollo, for thy Daphne's love,
> What Cressid is, what Pandar, and what we?
> her bed is India; there she lies, a pearl:
> Between our Ilium and where she resides,
> Let it be call'd the wild and wandering flood,
> Ourself the merchant, and this sailing Pandar
> Our doubtful hope, our convoy and our bark.
>
> [I. i. 98-104]

This poetic flight is interrupted by the entry of Aeneas, that (like the interruptions of Pandarus) being the only way, it would seem, of checking the inexhaustible fecundity of Troilus's poetic invention.

Thus the text warrants one's taking Troilus as a type of the poetic nature, and in looking at the contrasts between Ulysses and Troilus as contrasts between Policy and the Poetic Imagination. To see how these contrasts are explored, it is necessary first to observe that whereas Troilus's poetic imagination, or sense of value, is a force that can inspire choice and action, Ulysses's philosophy of 'degree' cannot of itself be an animating force. Like Hector's concept of law, Ulysses's concept of degree is restrictive only: by reference to it Ulysses can say what ought not to be done. But for getting things done, he is forced to traffic in what is called in the play 'opinion': prestige, reputation, the evaluation of a man by others, or 'honour' (for it is thus honour is spoken of in the Greek camp). Thus the real antithesis between Ulysses and Troilus is that between Opinion and Value—between social values and private imaginative values. If this is seen as a vital issue in the play, it accounts in large measure for the play's total form. The play is felt as two large masses: on the Greek side Ulysses dominating, arranging and interpreting the action, on the Trojan side the story of Troilus; further, the weightiest speeches are felt to be those of Ulysses and Troilus. If Ulysses and Troilus do not stand in a significant dramatic antithesis, then the play as a whole lacks significant form. It may be observed here that Ulysses's massive speech on degree, precisely because it is a plain statement of orthodox Elizabethan political thought, would seem to imply, since it is in a drama, either that it sums up the import of the action or that it represents one extreme of a polar relationship. Since patently it is *not* a summation of postulates underlying and borne out by the total action of the play (compare with it, for instance, the fable of the bees in *Henry V* [I. ii. 183-213], which defines the relationships of the whole community to the King in a way which is borne out by the action) then it must have the alternative function—that of thesis requiring antithesis. Troilus is the antithesis; this, I think, is corroborated by the way in which the persons, episodes and speeches connected with Ulysses himself have visibly antithetical relationships to the persons, episodes and speeches connected with Troilus. The effect, on character and action, of living by reference to Opinion is contrasted with the effect, on character and action, of living by reference to Value. Thus the pride and overweening to which Opinion gives rise (shown in Achilles and Ajax) is in contrast to the humility of Troilus before Cressida; the craft of Ulysses and the complexity of his manipulation of Ajax and Achilles is in contrast to Troilus's much-stressed 'simplicity'; the dependence of Opinion on what comes to the individual from outside—shown in explicit discussion, and stressed in the many metaphors that present the Greeks as knowing their qualities only in the image reflected back to them from other men—is in contrast to the autonomous nature of Value (stressed by Troilus's phrase in which he calls himself the 'authentic author' of truth). These contrasts are brought to a sharp verbal point, and Shakespeare's deliberation in setting the way of the Greeks against the way of Troilus attested, by the utterance given to Troilus himself (in the scene where Cressida is about to go to the Greek camp):

> Whiles others fish with craft for great opinion,
> I with great truth catch mere simplicity.

> [IV. iv. 103-04]

This opposition of two ways of life is of such importance in the play that it is formative not only of significant episode but also of verbal echoes, contrasts and ironies. Thus, to throw into relief the autonomy of Troilus's Value, Shakespeare shows the attempt of Achilles to assert a value within himself independent of what comes from outside, and shows the failure of

that attempt in a speech in which there are distorted and hollow echoes of speeches given to Troilus. Achilles, scorned by his fellows, discovers that

> . . . not a man, for being simply man,
> Hath any honour, but honour for those honours
> That are without him,

> [III. iii. 80-2]

and, attempting to assert his independence of this circularity, he cries,

> . . . But 'tis not so with me:
> Fortune and I are friends: I do enjoy
> At ample point all that I did possess,
> Save these men's looks; who do, methinks, find out
> Something not worth in me such rich beholding
> As they have often given.

> [III. iii. 87-92]

This assertion of autonomy is feeble in itself—we note the significant condition of it, 'Fortune and I are friends'—but further, it fails to stand up against the arguments of Ulysses, petering out into the admissions, 'My fame is shrewdly gored' [III. iii. 228], and 'My mind is troubled, like a fountain stirr'd' [III. iii. 308]. Troilus's Value, in sharp contrast to this, is conceived of as being independent of the vicissitudes of Fortune, for he himself has already claimed (in the debate in Troy) that Fortune cannot affect Value—he accuses the Trojans of deliberately doing to themselves something that even Fortune is powerless to do:

> why do you now
> The issue of your proper wisdoms rate,
> And *do a deed that fortune never did*,
> Beggar the estimation which you prized
> Richer than sea and land?

> [II. ii. 88-92]

And just as Achilles on Fortune gives back this hollow, distorted echo of Troilus, so he does on the subject of Honour. Whereas Achilles discovers that in the Greek camp a man has honour only for those honours that are without him, Troilus in the debate in Troy speaks of Honour as residing in constancy to the values one has once chosen, oneself, to assert. In that speech [II. ii. 61-96] Troilus deals first with the nature of choice, and describes it as an act of the whole man pitting his discrimination against the admitted hazards of man's condition:

> I take to-day a wife, and my election
> Is led on in the conduct of my will;
> My will enkindled by mine eyes and ears,
> Two traded pilots 'twixt the dangerous shores
> Of will and judgment:

then he asserts the irrevocableness of such a choice, once made:

> how may I avoid,
> Although my will distaste what it elected,
> The wife I chose?

Then he goes on to identify Honour itself with this kind of stability:

> there can be no evasion
> To blench from this and to stand firm by honour.

> [II. ii. 61-8]

This is a concept of Honour which makes Achilles's view (Honour = honours) obviously crude. Even the metaphor Troilus chooses [II. ii. 69-70] to illustrate his argument—'We turn not back the silks upon the merchant, When we have soil'd them'—is connected and contrasted with the metaphor used by Ulysses [III. iii. 151-52] in trying to persuade Achilles that Honour is a thing to be procured from other men in an unremitting succession of strenuous acts:

> to have done is to hang
> Quite out of fashion, like a rusty mail.

Whereas to Ulysses and to Achilles, Honour is that which is conferred (and may be withheld) by the admittedly unstable opinion of others, to Troilus it is that which is a man's own, bound up with the expression of his whole self in his own acts of choice, and depending on his being true to himself, and consequently true to those whom he has once pledged his truth and constancy.

Of all the dramatic contrasts between the nature of Opinion and the nature of Value, the most important is this contrast between the instability of the one and the stability of the other. This is the play's great strength, its great irony: Ulysses, who desires stability in society and conceives of that stability as dependent upon the fixity of social values, moves amid the fleeting mirror-images of Opinion, images so unfixed that he himself sets up as a manipulator of their shadow-play; Troilus on the other hand, demanding 'What is aught, but as 'tis valued?' can yet claim that 'As true as Troilus' is the grand exemplar of all the poet's similes of truth, summing up and outdoing 'As true as steel, as plantage to the moon, As sun to day, as turtle to her mate, As iron to adamant, as earth to the centre' [III. ii. 182, 177-79]. This representation of himself is corroborated, significantly, by Ulysses, who describes Troilus as

> firm of word,
> Speaking in deeds and deedless in his tongue;
> Not soon provoked nor being provoked soon calm'd;
> His heart and hand both open and both free;
> For what he has he gives, what thinks he shows;
> Yet gives he not till judgment guide his bounty,
> Nor dignifies an impair thought with breath.
>
> [IV. v. 97-103]

This subtly-articulated system of contrasts is one main feature of the design of the play. It is the conceptual equivalent of the visible battle-array of Trojan against Greek. Thus the play can be seen to have that kind of form which may be described as the correspondence of two spheres of tensions (the tension in the visible and the tension in the invisible); the dramatic situation embodies the dramatic concept. (pp. 282-90)

[To] interpret the play aright, one must realize that there are two possible ways of looking at the cumulative effect of these disasters. One may argue, 'Shakespeare wrote the play so as to stress this', or one may argue, 'Shakespeare wrote the play so as to discuss the validity of varying conceptions in a world where this happens to be true.' That is to say, one can treat the discrepancy between ideal and fact either as the dramatist's Q.E.D. or as his starting-point. If we treat the discrepancy between ideal and fact as the end in view, the Q.E.D., we must argue (as many have done) that the play is bitter. If we treat it as the starting-point, the *datum*, we may argue that the dramatist, accepting this tragic view of life, is concerned chiefly to explore the question of what way of life will stand against the unsatisfactoriness of fact as compared with hope, of action as compared with the ideal it was meant to embody. I believe that in *Troilus and Cressida* Shakespeare is asking this question, and that the answer he gives is, 'The way of life that stands, is the way of Troilus'—not Troilus's idealization of

Cressida, for that is confuted by Cressida, but his refusal, even in the face of the mis-shapen fact of her treachery, to deny the reality of the values by which he has lived. Though Cressida betrays him, this does not, to Troilus, mean that the Value which Cressida had seemed to embody is thereby proved to have had no real existence. The Cressida betraying him before his eyes *is* Cressida, but is *not* the Value he had taken her to embody, and Troilus in that speech is compelled to distinguish between the Value which was the creation of his poetic imagination, and the mere woman upon whom, as upon a theme, he had poetically created it.

> This she? no, this is Diomed's Cressida:
> If beauty have a soul, this is not she;
> If souls guide vows, if vows be sanctimonies,
> If sanctimony be the gods' delight,
> If there be rule in unity itself,
> This is not she. O madness of discourse,
> That cause sets up with and against itself!
> Bi-fold authority! where reason can revolt
> Without perdition, and loss assume all reason
> Without revolt: this is, and is not, Cressid.
>
> [V. ii. 137-46]

Troilus in this speech is shown as discovering that there is a bi-fold authority in the soul: the reason that deals with facts, and the poetic 'reason' that deals with Value; poetic 'reason' can find against the findings of ordinary reason, and the negation of the findings of ordinary reason can be in the poetic sense so highly reasonable as to be no rebellion against ordinary reason itself. Fact and the creation of the poetic imagination *can* co-exist, despite their seeming, to ordinary reason, to be so diametrically opposed as to be mutually destructive. Troilus's words,

> a thing inseparate
> Divides more wider than the sky and earth,
> And yet the spacious breadth of this division
> Admits no orifex for a point as subtle
> As Ariachne's broken woof to enter
>
> [V. ii. 148-52]

are a tremendous poetic achievement, for in them he wrests out of the seeming chaos of opposed possibilities which should in ordinary reason negate one another, the real existence of both. Thus Troilus finds *real* entities in Chaos itself: his speech is the dramatic counterpart, the astonishing transmutation, of that horrific picture of chaos drawn by Ulysses [I. iii. 109-37]

> Take but degree away, untune that string
> And, hark, what discord follows! each thing meets
> In mere oppugnancy. . . .
>
> [I. iii. 109-11]

Ulysses conceives of Degree as the safeguard against an irretrievable descent into Chaos, where 'right and wrong . . . should lose their names', and every distinct entity sink into that entity lower than itself until at last the lowest, appetite, 'must make perforce an universal prey, And last eat up himself'. Troilus's experience of the disruption of his world is not an irretrievable descent into nothingness; it is Chaos 'without perdition' and 'without revolt', where each entity, instead of sinking into nothing, reveals itself as 'bi-fold' and, so far from opposed entities losing their names in mutual destruction, each is newly given its real name. It was a magnificent dramatic stroke to relate both the philosophy of Ulysses and the philosophy of Troilus to the concept of Chaos; its significance is that whereas Ulysses uses Degree as a protection against Chaos

(Degree, or else . . .), Troilus wrests out of the actual experience of Chaos the new perception of the oppugnancy of real and indestructible entities (Chaos, and therefrom . . .). Troilus finds that poetic value may be contradicted by reason and fact, but its existence is not thereby cancelled or negated. Poetic value survives, because it can create in the teeth of fact. It is the only conception in the play which *can* survive, since in the world of the play every conception is challenged by fact. Every conception is tested by difficulties: as Agamemnon says, 'Distinction, with a broad and powerful fan, Puffing at all, winnows the light away' [I. iii. 27-8], and of all the conceptions dealt with in the play, it is only that of Troilus which in the storm of Fortune stands revealed as 'the thing of courage' which (in Nestor's words)

> As roused with rage with rage doth sympathize,
> And with an accent tuned in self-same key
> Retorts to chiding fortune.
>
> [I. iii. 51-4]

There is no other play of Shakespeare's in which there is so much explicit intellectual debating of the relative validity of the conceptions by which action may be animated. No other play of his states and shows so clearly that all action deforms the conception it seeks to embody. The play, by asserting the nullity of action, forces attention towards the degree of validity of the conceptions by which action is inspired. It shows that Opinion, derivative from factual achievements, and Policy, directed towards the realization in fact of what is willed, must inevitably be confounded, but Value (or the poetic imagination) . . . , when confronted by fact, can admit the fact and re-assert itself. Shakespeare in *Troilus and Cressida* has explored the antithesis between the values of the imagination and the values of organized society, and has shown that a society intent upon the preservation of its traditional form defeats itself, firstly because of the very nature of the self-regarding activities which that form sanctions, and secondly because it cuts itself off from that Protean power of imagination which can (in Milton's phrase) 'create a soul under the ribs of death'. In contrast, the play shows that the Value created and enjoyed by the poetic imagination has integrity and autonomy, and also, in its power to re-create itself, by an extension and enriching of its own being, when confronted by the apparently unassimilable fact, has that ultimate stability and life which can 'lie immortal in the arms of fire'. Troilus's final word on his own way of life brings to a fine verbal point the paradox of the inherence, within the apparent licence of the poetic mind, of constancy, permanence and truth:

> never did young man fancy
> With so eternal and so fix'd a soul.
>
> [V. ii. 165-66]
> (pp. 291-94)

Winifred M. T. Nowottny, "'Opinion' and 'Value' in 'Troilus and Cressida'," in Essays in Criticism, Vol. IV, No. 3, July, 1954, pp. 282-96.

FRANKLIN M. DICKEY (essay date 1957)

[In the following excerpt, taken from a study of Shakespeare's love tragedies that focuses primarily on Romeo and Juliet *and* Antony and Cleopatra, *Dickey discusses the similarly tragic nature of* Troilus and Cressida. *Like Paul M. Kendall (1951), Dickey finds Oscar James Campbell's classification of* Troilus and Cressida *as a comical satire (see excerpt above, 1938) insufficient because, he says, it does not account for the tragedy in the final scene. Dickey posits that in* Troilus and Cressida *Shakespeare reveals the "degenerative and ignoble side" of Troilus's love and demonstrates that action motivated by lust leads to a tragic end. He further maintains that a condemnatory view of unbridled sexual desire is found throughout Shakespeare's works. Troilus's tragedy, he concludes, is the result of confusing sexual intimacy with true love, and, at the play's dénouement, Troilus has "paid the price of those who lust."]*

Professor Campbell finds that both in form and tone *Troilus and Cressida* agrees with the practice of "comicall satyre" as it is exemplified in the works of Jonson and Marston. He shows envious Thersites to be similar in nature and function to Jonson's railing Carlo Buffone, and in Pandarus he finds the "satiric observer and mordant commentator" [see excerpt above, 1938] proper to the newly developed genre. The ending of *Troilus and Cressida* is also like that of "comicall satyre," for instead of gratifying the audience with a happy resolution in the manner of comedy or arousing pity and terror in the manner of tragedy, it leaves the characters open to scorn.

He observes further that much of the satire in *Troilus and Cressida* is directed against lust and inconstancy, two ethical lapses particularly dear to Elizabethan satirists. The cynical tone of the play has its counterpart in the savage indignation of Elizabethan imitators of Juvenal, who seems to have been especially attracted by his themes of sexual abnormality and excess.

Yet persuasive as this explanation for the peculiarities of *Troilus and Cressida* is, it does not account for the fact that Shakespeare's "comicall satyre" includes real tragedy in Act V. In no other "comicall satyre" does death darken the comic plot. In this play Achilles' brutal murder of Hector occurs on stage. Such an incident is quite beyond the scope of the genre as Professor Campbell describes it. Even though the Introduction to the Quarto speaks of the play as comedy, the Folio editors call it a tragedy in both the head title and the running title and planned originally to put it after *Romeo and Juliet* among the tragedies. (p. 120)

Whether one looks at it as tragedy, comedy, or "comicall satyre," *Troilus and Cressida* is unconventional. Nor can this unconventionality be explained by reference to medieval or Renaissance attitudes toward Greece and Troy. If Cressida and Helen had suffered a loss of reputation by the sixteenth century, their stories were no more comic than the fall of Troy. Yet throughout the action Shakespeare treats both stories mockingly. The Grecian and Trojan leaders speak in the magnificent rhetoric of high tragedy, but before the play is done, all the major characters except Ulysses and Hector are dragged down from their tragic eminence by ridicule. And the epilogue, granted it is Shakespeare's, is Pandarus's absurdly comic testament to the brethren and sisters of the "hold-door" trade.

Despite the comic epilogue, the spectator does not leave feeling sure that he has seen a comedy. The play has been moving rapidly toward a catastrophe until its mood is so dark that Thersites's cowardly jeering and Pandarus's futile clowning serve if anything to increase the pathos with which the action ends. The play cannot even properly be labeled tragicomedy, for tragicomedy ends in hope, and if a major character dies violently, it is to satisfy the artificial demands of poetic justice that dominate this melodramatic genre. In *Troilus and Cressida* the noblest of the Trojans meets his death in full view of the audience at the hands of a villain, for that is what Shakespeare has made of his lecherous and bullying Achilles. Troilus, hero of the love story, is left seeking his death on the battlefield.

The tragic tone which pervades the last scenes of *Troilus and Cressida* does not certainly invalidate Professor Campbell's hypothesis; the play is closer to "comicall satyre" than it is to any other genre. Nevertheless, by choosing his plot from the tragic history of the Trojan War, Shakespeare has altered that genre, moving it closer to tragedy. The question remains, why did Shakespeare choose a tragic story for comedy and satire? And why is there so much tragedy in this comedy?

The answers are suggested in the cast of his mind as it manifests itself in the erotic poems and the other plays. Sexual desire, and even cuckoldry, may appear as comic themes in Shakespeare's verbal humor, and love is the mainstay of comedy; but whenever lust, which is not to be confused with legitimate physical desire in marriage, appears in *action,* it is violent. Throughout Shakespeare's plays lust produces misery when it occurs in the action. In *Titus Andronicus, Two Gentlemen of Verona, Lucrece, Measure for Measure, King Lear, Antony and Cleopatra, Pericles,* and *Cymbeline,* Shakespeare presents us with characters whose lusts bring about suffering or death. Proteus, Angelo, and Iachimo are saved from violent death only by timely repentance; the Tarquins are driven from Rome; all the others who lust pay for their passion with death. Lust and bloodshed are inseparable in Shakespeare's dramatic practice. Consequently *Troilus and Cressida,* despite its satirical humor and amusing bawdry, is often nearer to Shakespeare's love tragedies than it is to comedy. Like Shakespeare's tragedies the play defines and establishes a moral base from which its great enigmas reveal their meanings, and Shakespeare presents us an action motivated by human passions which work to their unhappy end. As in the tragedies, even the good, like Hector and Cassandra, must suffer. (pp. 121-23)

Certainly there is pathos and even nobility in Troilus's steadfastness in love, but from the beginning of the play to the end Shakespeare shows us the degenerative and ignoble side of that passion. For a play that is to show us the superiority of passion to reason, the action opens oddly on the theme of effeminacy caused by heroic love. As the curtain rises Troilus calls for his page to disarm him. Stricken with love and self-pity, he has no stomach for the war. "The Greeks are strong," he laments,

> But I am weaker than a woman's tear,
> Tamer than sleep, fonder than ignorance,
> Less valiant than the virgin in the night. . . .
>
> [I. i. 7, 9-11]

While pretending to counsel patience, Pandarus, whose loquacity and salacious interest in the lovers' affairs remind us of Juliet's Nurse, whets Troilus's appetite until Troilus cries, "I am mad / In Cressid's love" [I. i. 51-2] and launches into hyperbolical praise of her beauty. When Aeneas enters to ask why Troilus has not been in the field, he answers cynically,

> Because not there. This woman's answer sorts,
> For womanish it is to be from thence.
>
> [I. i. 106-07]

This theme, touched upon in *Venus and Adonis* and in *Romeo and Juliet* and developed further in *Antony and Cleopatra,* is one of the important psychological motivations in *Troilus and Cressida.* Achilles' dalliance with Patroclus, his spiritless affair with Polyxena, and Paris's uxorious life with Helen all show us the result of the kind of love with which Troilus languishes. (p. 124)

In direct contrast to Troilus Shakespeare shows us Cressida teasing Pandarus as he tries to convince her of Troilus's merit.

Whatever Cressida is, she is not lovesick, and the double-entendre with which she answers Pandarus shows a sense of humor which her lover lacks. After Pandarus has left, Cressida turns to the audience to explain frankly what her behavior means. She is coy merely because

> Things won are done, joy's soul lies in the doing.
> That she belov'd knows nought that knows not this:
> Men prize the thing ungain'd more than it is.
> That she was never yet that ever knew
> Love got so sweet as when desire did sue.
>
> [I. ii. 287-91]

Cressida like Cleopatra is a sensual artist who knows how to manage a love affair. There is no innocence here, amusing as her confession is. (p. 125)

Pandarus's loquacious prurience and Troilus's declarations underline the sexual basis of the love affair. Bustling about as he brings in Cressida and urging the lovers to bed with animal imagery, Pandarus offers the ironic commentary which shows Troilus's rapture for what it is, an attempt to build an enduring faith upon lust. When Cressida rightly fears that there are "More dregs than water" [III. ii. 67] in the fountain of their love, Troilus tells her that the only "monstruosity" in love is that the will—i.e., the sexual appetite—

> is infinite and the execution confin'd, that the desire
> is boundless and the act a slave to limit.
>
> [III. ii. 82-3]

This Quixotic ambition to achieve permanent bliss by satisfying sexual desire would have amused the sophisticated in the audience if it did not sadden them. (p. 126)

[Troilus] has this in common with Romeo: he is young and passion has blinded him. Thus when Troilus discovers Cressida's perfidy, he mourns broken vows which in his blindness he had thought holy and eternal. But the vows Troilus swears to entice Cressida to bed, true as his faith may be, could not be "holy." As Cassandra has warned Hector, "The gods are deaf to hot and peevish vows" [V. iii. 16]. Troilus has mistaken his lust for true love. Honest as his mistake is, he pays for it with rage and pain before the action is over.

Cressida does not suffer as much as Troilus does, although one might argue that the audience would have known of her ultimate fate after Diomed rejects her. It might also be argued that she suffers from a divided heart, tormented by her own desires, but Shakespeare does not make much of her twinges of conscience, if indeed her waverings can be so dignified. (p. 130)

Shakespeare's Cressida is an all but shameless wanton. That her kind of love can lead only to misery is one of the central themes of the play. The nature of that love is defined not by Pandarus or Thersites but by Cressida herself. Her final words,

> Minds sway'd by eyes are full of turpitude . . .
>
> [V. ii. 112]

sum up the attitudes toward beauty of the Christian Platonists. True love might, as it does to Romeo and Juliet, begin through the eyes. In fact it usually did enter through the "eye-beams." But love which subsisted upon outward beauty alone was bound for disaster. True love could be based only on virtue.

In Renaissance doctrine love of the eyes alone was false. Physical beauty caused love through the eyes. Physical beauty might

Prologue. The Castle of Tenedos. By G. F. Sargent (1841). The Department of Rare Books and Special Collections, The University of Michigan Library.

cause a man to languish, like Troilus, with love melancholy. But physical beauty without virtue could not preserve a long love, and Cressida's affections, based only on externals, cannot stand firm. While she is with Troilus, she loves him. But since her love is based solely on sight, the old proverb "out of sight, out of mind" applies, and Troilus's fears that she will not be true are well-grounded. Troilus, no less than she, has been deluded by "beauties outward." Mistaking sexual intimacy for true and lasting love, he demands truth where no one else would seek it. This is his tragedy.

Thus Shakespeare's treatment of love in the story of Troilus and Cressida is of a piece with the philosophy which governs the outcome of love in the comedies and in the two tragedies of love. Doting love in the comedies is amusing folly, usually rewarded by marriage. Doting love might, as in *Romeo and Juliet,* produce tragedy, for excessive passion was always potentially dangerous. Lust, however, has no happy conclusion unless paid for with repentance.

The love of Troilus and Cressida does not end in death but in unhappiness. The futile rage and pain of Troilus and the indignities he suffers come close to the sufferings of tragic heroes. Not only is he punished by an unquiet mind but by the terrible humiliation of witnessing Cressida's betrayal of his love and the humiliaton of losing his horse to Diomed, who brings the animal back as a trophy for Cressida. At the end of the play Troilus too has paid the price of those who lust. (pp. 131-32)

Franklin M. Dickey, "'Troilus and Cressida'," in his Not Wisely But Too Well: Shakespeare's Love Tragedies, *The Huntington Library, 1957, pp. 118-43.*

ALBERT GÉRARD   (essay date 1959)

[*In examining the mercantile metaphors used by Troilus in* Troilus and Cressida, *Gérard states that while such images suggest that the Trojans possess strong values, they also reveal the contradictions between Troilus as lover and Troilus as warrior. Gérard asserts that Shakespeare intended to place Troilus in an ironic light and that the contradictions in his values become apparent as they pass through a process of disintegration during the course of the play. This process culminates in Troilus's rejection of Cressida, where hate replaces love as the power that motivates him, and he is eventually depicted only as a warrior. However, Gérard is in agreement with G. Wilson Knight (1930) and Winifred M. T. Nowottny (1954) in perceiving generally higher values in the Trojans than in the Greeks, although this view has been challenged by Oscar James Campbell (1938), L. C. Knights (1951), Terence Eagleton (1967), D. A. Traversi (1968), and Thomas G. West (1981). The contradictions in Troilus are also given brief mention by Knight, but are more fully treated by Richard C. Harrier (1959) and J. Hillis Miller (1977); also, the mercantile language in the play is further discussed by Raymond Southall (1964).*]

Contemporary interest in imagery has brought to light a peculiar stylistic feature of *Troilus and Cressida:* the large number of metaphors and comparisons borrowed from commercial language. Already in the first scene, what we shall call for the sake of brevity the mercantile image, appears prominently at the end of the monologue in which Troilus proclaims his passion for Cressida:

> Her bed is India; there she lies, a pearl:
> Between our Ilium and where she resides,
> Let it be call'd the wild and wandering flood,
> Ourself the merchant, and this sailing Pandar
> Our doubtful hope, our convoy and our bark.
>
> [I. i. 100-04]

It is not only in connection with the love theme that Shakespeare has recourse to mercantile imagery. In the great debate of the Trojans over the continuation of the war, we find it applied over and over to Helen:

> *Hect.* Brother, she is not worth what she doth cost
>   The keeping.
> *Tro.*   What's aught, but as 'tis valued?
> *Hect.* But value dwells not in particular will;
>   It holds his estimate and dignity
>   As well wherein 'tis precious of itself
>   As in the prizer.
>
> [II. ii. 52-6]

And Troilus makes skilful use of Marlowe's well-known phrase when he says:

> Is she worth keeping?—why, she is a pearl,
> Whose price hath launched above a thousand ships,
> And turned crowned kings to merchants.
> If you'll avouch 'twas wisdom Paris went—
> As you must needs, for you all cried 'Go, go';
> If you'll confess he brought home noble prize—
> As you must needs, for you all clapped your hands,
> And cried 'Inestimable!'; why do you now
> The issue of your proper wisdoms rate,
> And do a deed that Fortune never did,
> Beggar the estimation which you prized
> Richer than sea and land?
>
> [II. ii. 81-92]

At first sight, it may seem rather arbitrary to avail oneself of the use which Shakespeare makes of such terms as *worth* and *value* in order to embark on an analysis of the *moral* values which the play is assumed to dramatize. But after all, the word 'value' itself, in its philosophical sense, is a dead metaphor. In Shakespeare, it is still alive. And although the writer, no doubt, uses it without any abstract or allegorical intention in mind, it stands to reason that these commercial terms particularly suited his purpose because they suggest something precious, something to which men aspire, for which they are ready to fight, to make sacrifices, to kill one another.

Starting from this hypothesis, it may be useful to give first a somewhat static definition of the values introduced in the protasis, in connexion with both love and war.

Troilus, it will be noticed, applies the mercantile metaphor to two women. He has two 'pearls': one is Helen, the other Cressida, and each of them embodies one of the two themes of the play. But these two themes are tied together by more than a metaphor: they merge in the personality of Troilus, who is a Trojan warrior and the lover of Cressida. The whole dramatic structure of the play is hinged upon this much-disputed character. . . . Now, it is characteristic of Shakespeare's genius and of his secret intention, that the imaginative unity achieved with such economy of means, should be placed at the same time

under the sign of intellectual confusion: though Troilus unites in himself the theme of war and the theme of love, one cannot help observing from the first that there is in him an inner cleavage, a contradiction, between the lover and the warrior.

In the first scene, Troilus appears as a romantic lover in the courtly tradition. Not only does he list the charms of Cressida in a rhapsodic tone which leaves us in no doubt as to the intensity of his infatuation, but he also makes it clear that nothing counts for him except Cressida. His 'pearl' is the supreme value, the unique value, at least (as we are soon invited to realize), for the time being. When he thinks of her, the din of battle is only 'ungracious clamours' and 'rude sounds' [I. i. 89]; the soldiers, whether Greek or Trojan, are 'fools on both sides' [I. i. 90]; as for Helen, the cause of all this tumult, she

>   must needs be fair,
> When with your blood you daily paint her thus.
>
> [I. i. 90-1]

And he immediately adds:

> I cannot fight upon this argument;
> It is too starved a subject for my sword.
>
> [I. i. 92-3]

But the *warrior* Troilus utters startlingly different opinions during the sitting of the family council which is to decide whether Helen will be returned to the Greeks or not: the 'pearl', now, is the ex-wife of Menelaus.

It is not by chance that Shakespeare places the same image on the lips of Troilus to refer both to Cressida and Helen. This helps us spell out the unstable character of the young man, who, according to circumstances, considers Helen as a pearl or as a doll rouged with blood. And, in the second place, the use of the same metaphor for both Helen and Cressida is perfectly appropriate, and in a most engagingly ironic way, for between the two women, after all, there is not much to choose.

But this is only one of the inner contradictions with which Troilus' character is beset. There is also a glaring and ominous contrast between the picture of Cressida he carries in his heart and Cressida as she really is. Her first appearance is distinctly anticlimatic: Shakespeare makes it obvious that she little deserves the sublime passion which Troilus lavishes upon her. A connoisseur of lust, well acquainted with the niceties of the game of love, she is the worthy niece of the go-between Pandar, with whom she exchanges jokes in somewhat questionable taste.

The second scene ends with a brief monologue by Cressida which neatly balances Troilus' soliloquy in the preceding scene; and it is significant that the mercantile image should occur on the lips of the young woman when she says:

> That she beloved knows nought that knows not this:
> Men prize the thing ungained more than it is.
>
> [I. ii. 288-89]

There is in this a new irony, which also hides a profound truth, namely that Troilus prizes Cressida more than she is worth. The combined effect of these first two scenes is to place the love theme in a rather sarcastic perspective. The value which Troilus pursues is love; in his eyes, Cressida is the embodiment of love. But Troilus is ignorant of the fact that Cressida is an imaginary value, a false pearl, and that his great love is only an illusion. And the play is a diptych, one panel of which shows how the young man is gradually made aware of these depressing truths. The subject of the other panel is war.

Cressida is nothing but a frail bodily vessel, unworthy of the apparently lofty passion which Troilus has conceived for her. Likewise, the second 'pearl', Helen, is simply the unworthy visible symbol of something nobler, which is honour.

In the great debate between Troilus and Hector (II, ii), it is the word 'honour' which comes to the mouth of the former whenever he speaks. . . . (pp. 144-47)

This debate takes place on the highest moral level, dealing as it does with the values which should command the behaviour of man. Troilus wants the Trojans to keep Helen because she is the emblem of glory and honour. On the contrary, Hector would like to turn her over, in the name of both common sense and moral sense. . . . Two ethical systems stand here face to face. The question is, of course, whether Shakespeare has given us any cue as to their comparative merits.

G. Wilson Knight has suggested that this scene marks the triumph of intuition and faith, represented by Troilus, over the prosaic rationalism of Hector [see excerpt above, 1930]. But he fails to mention that here too Troilus is presented in a rather unfavourable light. In addition to the contradictions already pointed out, it is clear that some of his arguments are remarkably inadequate, not to say inept. Knight makes much of Troilus' assertion that the sense of honour and duty which, in his opinion, should lead Troy to keep Helen, is similar to that which obliges a husband to keep his legitimate wife. The audience, one presumes, recalls immediately that Helen is the legitimate wife of Menelaus, as Hector quickly reminds his brother with a great deal of pertinence.

From the contradictions of Troilus and his awkward choice of arguments, we may conclude that Shakespeare meant to place this character in an ironic light, both in the sphere of war and in the sphere of love. If there is one character among the Trojans with whom Shakespeare must have felt in agreement, that character is Hector. It is remarkable that in this play, in which every one speaks badly of every one else, no one utters any words of abuse against him. Furthermore, Hector formulates a conception of the Trojan war similar to that which Shakespeare had expressed in *The Rape of Lucrece:* a traditional conception, to be sure, but nonetheless one which Shakespeare accepts and supports by means of arguments which are undoubtedly valid within the framework of the play. (pp. 147-48)

[The] values which Hector advocates (though he betrays them) are objective: they are based upon the intrinsic merit of the object which embodies them; they are rational and they are essentially moral. Those which Troilus upholds and which Hector rallies to have nothing to do with ethical or logical sense: they are irrational, emotional, subjective.

In Hector's and Troilus' attitudes, there is however a common feature: both brothers are idealists. Whether their ideal be called reason or honour, it is equally elevated, noble and selfless. It is something which is higher than themselves. Their ideal is not their egoism in disguise. If Hector is in favour of peace, it is not because he is afraid of battle. And if Troilus wants the Trojans to go on fighting, it is not for his personal glory, but for the honour of his family and of his city. Especially noticeable, moreover, in Shakespeare's picture of Troy, is the urbanity, the harmony, the solidarity of the Priamides, even in the midst of the tightest discussion. The Greek camp is depicted with quite different colours.

One of the most unexpected things in the first two scenes which take place in the Greek camp is that the mercantile image is completely absent from them. This is all the more surprising as such a manner of speaking could pass as natural in Greek mouths. (p. 148)

It seems to me that the import of this image ought to be interpreted . . . in ethical terms. It points out the presence of values in which men believe and for which they fight. If it is absent from the discourse of the Greeks, that is because the Greeks have no ideal value in view. The Achean heroes as Shakespeare sees them are monsters of egoism, vanity and jealousy, and their anarchy contrasts with the unity of the Trojan family group. In conformity with the medieval tradition, Shakespeare has no respect for the Greeks and he expresses his contempt through a Greek mouthpiece, Ulysses himself, whose speech on degree is a counterpart to the debate between Hector and Troilus.

The three key concepts of this debate are law, reason and honour. In the same way, Ulysses' speech centers on order, intellect and brute strength. Ulysses first points out that the reason why Troy has not yet been destroyed is that

> The specialty of rule hath been neglected.
>
> [I. iii. 78]

And he then gives himself over to a long exposé, since become classic, on the necessity of political order and hierarchy, comparing the internal organization of states to the cosmic order of the solar system. His view of law is not moral, as it is for Hector, but purely political and pragmatic. (p. 149)

It appears, then, that this play is built on an intricate network of values which can be clearly distinguished from each other, the higher values being generally represented by the Trojans, and the lower value by the Greeks: there is an overall contrast between the idealism and the organic harmony of the Trojans on the one hand, and the general pragmatism and anarchical individualism of the Greeks on the other. And by means of purely dramatic devices, Shakespeare has shed on those values and their fate in the world of man a light which is sarcastic to the point of nihilism.

Hector, who stands for moral and rational idealism, might be considered as a heroic figure if there were not that flaw in his character, that weakness of the will which prevents him from acting in accordance with his belief, and thus announces the final catastrophe.

Troilus represents emotional idealism, both in the sphere of love and in the sphere of war. He is the central character, on whom the two main themes are hinged. But his inconsistency signals him as a high-minded young fool. Besides, there remains to be seen whether his infatuation with Cressida is really what Coleridge thought it was: 'the profound affection . . . alone worthy the name of love' [see excerpt above, 1834].

Among the Greeks, Ulysses represents the pragmatism of intellectual cleverness in the service of state policy. But although such critics as Spencer and Craig have been impressed by his statesmanship and his wisdom, a careful reading of his degree speech in its context shows that it too basks in the deadly glare of Shakespeare's irony: we cannot help noticing that the 'Sun' of the Greek camp is Agamemnon, a most insignificant figure endowed with a querulous stoicism which finds its proper expression in obscure generalese; Agamemnon's speeches are ludicrously echoed in Nestor's garrulous redundant and senile oratory; and Ulysses himself takes an unmistakably perverse pleasure in imitating Patroclus imitating Agamemnon and Nestor: the parody is quite to the point and certainly invalidates any application of Ulysses' theories on degree to the Grecian army.

At the bottom of the scale, Achilles and in a grosser way, Ajax, represent the materialism of physical strength and ruthlessness in the service of individual vanity and lust for fame, while the lust of the flesh is exemplified in Cressida, the Trojan woman who goes to live among the Greeks, and in Helen, the Greek woman, whose presence among the Trojans started the conflagration.

This hierarchy of values invites to some reflection. In choosing to devote a play to the Trojan war as seen from the traditional medieval angle, Shakespeare took on the task, so to speak, of putting on the stage the victory of Greek materialism over Trojan idealism. And since Helen had not been returned, he was bound as well to show the emotional idealism of Troilus triumphing over the moral idealism of Hector. We may conjecture that it was probably this particular feature in his material that attracted Shakespeare. As we now go on to study the development of the play itself, we cannot help feeling that the central idea which is the basis of its structure and the principle of its unity is the disintegration of the values thus built up in the course of the first part.

The second part of the play, which comprises Act III and the beginning of Act IV, is mainly focused on the theme of love, which is treated in such a way as to confirm the essential weakness of Cressida and to reveal gradually the emptiness of Troilus' passion. (pp. 150-51)

About the sincerity and loyalty of Troilus there is not the slightest doubt. But his simplicity borders upon stupidity. It is this which led him to contradict himself when he was glorifying war a few moments after cursing it. It is this too which gives him his illusions both over the true essence of his own feelings and over the true nature of Cressida. For Shakespeare has provided a dramatic analysis of the young woman which is perfectly clear. No matter how nobly Cressida gives the cue to Troilus in the great scene of Act III, the audience has been informed that there is little left of the ingénue about her; the spicy joviality of her uncle Pandar establishes with precision the plane on which she is located: it is noticeably lower than that on which Troilus places her. Cressida's love for Troilus is genuine, to be sure, but it is chiefly, or perhaps merely, sensual, and given over to the inclination of the moment. This is what Troilus is at first blind to, and the light comes to him in two stages.

In a recent analysis of *Othello,* Robert Speaight suggested that the deepest source of the Moor's jealousy might be found in the revelations of the wedding night. The fact is that after this experience, Othello shows himself astonishingly receptive to Iago's innuendoes. The probability that there is some truth in this interpretation increases as we notice the curious similarity between the behaviour of Othello and that of Troilus. It seems as if the consummation which was the result of Pandar's tireless good will had taught Troilus something disturbing about Cressida. At the moment when Diomedes comes to take the young woman to the Greek camp, Troilus wavers in a significant way between shrill assurance and querulous [indifference]. 'Be thou but true of heart . . .', he says to Cressida [IV. iv. 58]; then he masochistically lists the athletic and amorous attractions of young Greek heroes: this he perhaps does because he now

knows in Cressida a sensuality which he fears will not remain indifferent to them.

Such is the first chapter in the *éducation sentimentale* of Troilus. The second develops in the Greek camp, where Cressida has considerable success. (pp. 151-52)

[The] shock which overcomes Troilus is the impact of experience on innocence, the shattering of appearances under the revelation of truth, the disintegration of the ideal when brought in contact with hard fact. The pure and vast love, the faithful and total passion of which he had dreamed are only a figment of his imagination. Nothing corresponds to this in real life, where there is only faithlessness and lechery. All the elements which are connected with the love theme converge in order to express from various angles this disenchanted vision. The common unworthiness of Helen and Cressida recalls Hamlet's cruel apostrophe on woman's frailty. Troilus, Diomedes and Thersites have no resemblance whatever to one another; but the poetic anger of Troilus, the worldly cynicism of Diomedes and the filthy sarcasm of Thersites all express the same conviction that there is no greatness, no faith, no selflessness, no purity in love.

But so far as the play itself is concerned, the main interest lies of course in Troilus' response to this painful experience. That the young man is, as F. S. Boas has said, 'startled out of his callow optimism' is certainly true and was inevitable. But does this mean that he has changed for the better? Dowden thinks so, who asserts that after this 'comedy of disillusion' Troilus is 'strung up for sustained and determined action' [see excerpt above, 1877]. But a closer examination of what happens in Troilus' personality invalidates any such conclusion. His speech about Woman is an irresponsible piece of hasty and unwarranted generalization, and this is made manifest through Ulysses' commonsensical remarks. Not without good reason does Thersites call Troilus a 'doting foolish young knave' and a 'young Trojan ass' [V. iv. 3-6]: Troilus' understanding of woman and of life has certainly not become more mature.

On the contrary. For if it is true that he is now strung up for action, it is also true that he is actuated by the basest motive. Little is left of the idealistic warrior who wanted his city to keep on fighting in the name of honour and glory. The source of Troilus' renewed pugnaciousness is entirely egotistic. It is inspired by the spirit of revenge. It springs out of his hatred of the man who has made him a cuckold. Troilus is a new Menelaus.

This is the nadir in a process of disintegration that has developed through four stages. First, the illusoriness of Troilus' image of Cressida is exposed to the audience; then, the true, lustful, nature of Troilus' own feelings is made manifest; after this, Troilus' illusions are shattered to pieces as he is made aware of what Cressida really is; finally, love is replaced by hate as the driving power in Troilus, who will henceforth appear only in his capacity as a warrior. (pp. 153-54)

> *Albert Gérard, "Meaning and Structure in 'Troilus and Cressida'," in* English Studies, *Vol. XL, No. 2, 1959, pp. 144-57.*

JOHANNES KLEINSTÜCK (essay date 1959)

[*Kleinstück examines the relation between words and action in* Troilus and Cressida, *analyzing in particular the implications of Ulysses's speech on degree. Ulysses, he asserts, argues for a system of order that is proven false by the events of the play: the societal hierarchy he outlines is undermined by the inefficiency of the ruler, Agamemnon, as well as by the unpredictable nature of the other characters. In fact, as the play progresses Ulysses inverts the hierarchy of degree himself. That many of the play's other characters also act in direct opposition to their speeches, continues Kleinstück, prohibits any infallible judgments and permits only uncertain opinion of these characters. He concludes that because the world of* Troilus and Cressida *is based on opinion and uncertainty, a stabilized and hierarchically ordered society based on degree is a dream.*]

The critic who believes to have found a spokesman who represents the author's point of view in a Shakespearean play mostly shows that he has failed to react to the play as a whole. For the meaning of the play, if there is any, cannot be found by isolating one voice of the complex unity, in which each voice contributes to the total impression. Ulysses's speech on degree in *Troilus and Cressida* is a case in point. Although it contains, as Dr. Tillyard has pointed out, the main tenets of the *Elizabethan World Picture*, we are by no means compelled nor indeed permitted to assume that Shakespeare used Ulysses for a mouthpiece. If we examine that part in its relation to the whole we shall arrive at different conclusions. (p. 58)

The gist of the speech, which may be given as *unity and subordination guarantee success,* seems valid. We must ask, however, where the lack of unity and the absence of subordination have their cause. Who bears the guilt of the Greek army's disintegration? As Ulysses singles out Achilles for censure it seems that he, together with Patroclus, is the villain of the piece; but must we not go further and ask why Achilles does not co-operate in the common cause? We find an answer by examining the comparison which Ulysses draws between *king* and *sun,* and *body politic* and *the heavens.* In the heavens, it is *the glorious planet Sol* who preserves order and degree, in the body politic it is the king. Now it sometimes happens, as Ulysses insinuates, that *the planets in evil mixture to disorder wander,* yet, interestingly enough, he gives no reason for the disorder. Is it merely the planets' self-will? Or should we not assume the sun sometimes neglects his duty? For how can the planets become self-willed unless the sun grows weak? The same question applied to the state leads to the inevitable conclusion that it is only through Agamemnon's inefficiency as a ruler that Achilles can desert the Greek cause.

Ulysses never states the fact openly, he only hints at it by mentioning that

> the general's disdain'd
> By him one step below. . . .
>
> [I. iii. 129-30]

Shakespeare, however, does his best to make it evident. First of all he gives Agamemnon a speech which, although it contains some good thoughts, is of no use in the present situation where Agamemnon ought to say what is to be done. The situation cries for a remedy, but even Ulysses, who has just given a diagnosis, cannot answer Agamemnon's question:

> The nature of the sickness found, Ulysses,
> What is the remedy?
>
> [I. iii. 140-41]

—in fact he shirks the question by exposing Achilles to public contempt; his description of Achilles *lolling* on his bed, and Patroclus imitating the Greek leaders, does not make things any better. The only remedy would be to depose Agamemnon and find an abler man, but that in turn would be a violation of degree. This second point is perhaps rather subtle; the third,

however, is as plain as can be. A short time after Ulysses's speech on degree Aeneas enters to deliver Hector's challenge; he looks about for Agamemnon whom he in fact sees and speaks with: but he does not recognize him as the king of kings. Obviously Agamemnon cuts a very poor figure on the stage; he does not, like the sun, *make beholders wink.* Perhaps we may conclude with Thersites that *Agamemnon is a fool. . . .*

We may even draw another conclusion. If the preservation of degree depends on the king, who should be powerful and efficient, an inefficient king like Agamemnon makes degree impossible. Thus the gist of Ulysses' speech may be summed up in the rather simple statement that *everything would be right if things were as they should be.*

Even so the speech need not be wholly valueless. A philosophical thought, or a theory of what a state should be like, may remain valuable even if not applicable to an actual need. Ulysses might be taken as someone who points at eternal truths. It seems odd, however, that eternal truths should be pointed at by a man who is mainly concerned with success, and odder still that this man does not make the slightest effort to live up to his own ideal. For Ulysses, in the further course of the play, becomes guilty of the very sin he castigates: he inverts degree. By openly preferring Ajax to Achilles he inverts what must seem to him the natural order of things, for there is no doubt that Achilles is supposed to be the better man of the two. As a consequence Ulysses breeds emulation which, according to his own words, springs from a neglect of degree. He does all this, of course, with the purpose to win Achilles back.

That, however, sheds a new light on his philosophy of degree. We have just seen that Ulysses does not act in accordance with his own ideal, but the attempt to secure Achilles' aid betrays even more: that Ulysses obviously believes more in the value of the fighting-machine Achilles than in the establishment of order and degree. For his chief aims, the fall of Hector and the destruction of Troy, Achilles is of primary importance.

I need not describe the intrigue which Ulysses weaves in order to rouse Achilles to action. He makes the Greek generals slight him and after that scene of humiliation lectures him on two points: first, that a man's value does not lie in himself alone, he must be reflected by the persons around him; second, that a man will be forgotten if he does not keep pace with time. Both points he aptly applies to the present situation: Achilles, having isolated himself, is no longer esteemed by the Greeks; and as he has so long refrained from fighting the Greeks are no longer interested in him: they prefer the *lubber Ajax.* Now we should notice that what Ulysses says may be true in general (a hero may be forgotten on account of his inactivity), but certainly it is not true in the present situation. Actually Achilles is still highly appreciated and his help is desparately desired; by their pretended snub the Greeks do their best to stir him up. Their behaviour, and Ulysses' lectures, show the opposite of what they seem to show. Achilles is appreciated and remembered because he has been inactive.

We here hit upon a fundamental feature of the play. A statement may be true in general, yet the generalization may not hold good in an actual emergency. It may be true that unity is strength, but in the present case it is Achilles, and not unity, which would guarantee a Greek victory; it may be true that an inactive hero will be forgotten, but not Achilles; and it may even be true, what Agamemnon says in his first great speech, that by the Greeks' lack of success *the protractive trials of great Jove* are shown, but he, as a general, should rather instruct his army what steps to take instead of indulging in philosophical commonplaces. Shakespeare emphasizes the hollowness of all these speeches by their style. . . . All these speakers, Agamemnon, Ulysses, and above all garrulous Nestor, who does nothing but expatiate upon a theme which Agamemnon has brought forward, use the most high-sounding terms in order to say what could be said rather simply and need not be said at all. The orotund speeches have bewitched many a critic, but they are off the present mark; one might as well lecture a starving man on the advantage of having one's vital desires under control.

This characteristic feature, that the speeches are not to the point, is closely connected with another one. In our play a man's words are constantly belied by what he either thinks or does. The note is struck in the very first scene in which Pandarus declares that he will no longer act as a go-between for Troilus, only in order to find Cressida and woo her for him; in which Troilus, immediately after having declared that he will not fight for Helen, leaves the stage in order to draw his sword for her. It is repeated by Hector's adducing reasons against continuation of the war which are all anulled by the *roisting challenge* which he had previously sent to the Greeks. Cressida swears eternal fidelity to her lover but breaks her promise after a very short time; Ulysses preaches a philosophy of degree for which he does not show the slightest regard. It is interesting to see that thus Ulysses and Cressida are comparable to each other. They may mean what they say, but they do not act accordingly; perhaps Ulysses is forced through circumstances to desert his ideal; and perhaps we may assume that Cressida, who did intend to be faithful when she left Troilus, was overpowered by her emotions, so in a way she was forced too. Human beings, in *Troilus and Cressida,* are unreasonable and illogical creatures—not very different from the people we meet in actual life.

It therefore becomes quite impossible to judge a person on the ground of his words or his apparent behaviour and, what is more, characters tend to be quite unpredictable. This is shown most clearly in the case of Achilles. The snub and Ulysses' lecture seem to work, Achilles makes up his mind to fight again; yet a letter from Queen Hecuba which he receives some time later makes him relapse into inactivity. Again a little later he does arm, stirred not by Ulysses' policy but by the death of Patroclus, yet here again he does what nobody could possibly have foreseen: instead of killing Hector in single fight he avoids him and later has him treacherously slaughtered by his Myrmidons. We expect to see Achilles as a fighting animal, instead we get a coward, a coward, however, who is successful where Ulysses fails: he kills Hector and thereby ensures the fall of Troy. His method of winning success completely belies Ulysses' description of his character. According to Ulysses, he is a man who esteems *no act but that of hand,* and who has little regard for

> the still and mental parts,
> That do contrive how many hands shall strike,
> When fitness calls them on. . . .
>
> 　　　　　　　　　　　　[I. iii. 200-02]

As a matter of fact, in murdering Hector, Achilles does not stir a finger but he succeeds in contriving *how many hands shall strike, the fitness which calls them on* being the moment when Hector is unarmed. Achilles, instead of living up to his reputation as a mere fighter, proves to be a crafty schemer not very different from Ulysses himself, excepting, however, his

being successful; for although Ulysses knows how to start an intrigue his policy comes to nothing in the end.

It goes without saying, then, that we must not overrate the value of the other character-descriptions given by Ulysses. What he says about Cressida is of course not wholly mistaken, but he does not allow her to be capable of serious emotions, which she certainly is; similarly, his description of Troilus gives only one side of the picture; he does not mention that Troilus under certain circumstances can be a weakling. True, he cannot know everything about him, but there is no reason why we should assume him to speak the full truth especially as we know better. Nobody in this play can pass reliable judgement on anybody.

This leads us back to our first problem, i.e. the value of Ulysses' speech on degree. That Ulysses cannot be Shakespeare's spokesman, we have seen; yet we might retain some belief in his political philosophy. Although it cannot be, nor indeed is, applied to the actual situation, it still might remain an ideal. Let us therefore examine the foundations on which it rests. The idea of degree has its image in the heavens; there, if we make allowance for an outdated cosmic system, it is quite plain that the sun, being the most conspicuous and most powerful planet, should rule over the rest. The heavenly hierarchy is based on facts. A similar state of affairs may seem desirable on earth, but in order to be possible it should be based on facts too. We know that Agamemnon is not like the sun, he does not shine, thus the others do not revolve around him. Another king might cut a better figure; but his power and efficiency would have to be as unmistakeable as the sun's. Similarly, in order to attribute each person his place on the social ladder, one must be unmistakeably sure as to his essence, character, and value. The idea of a hierarchically governed society rests on the pretence, or presupposition, that this is possible; the play of *Troilus and Cressida,* however, shows this pretence to be futile. We have just seen that nobody can really be judged, that a person may do what nobody expected and what, perhaps, not even he himself would have surmised. Thus we have no infallible judgements, we have only opinions. The fact is emphasized by the frequent occurrence of the word itself.

We do not hear that Achilles *is* the best fighter of the Greek army; Ulysses states, much more cautiously

> The great Achilles, whom *opinion* crowns
> The sinew and the forehand of our host. . . .
>
> 　　　　　　　　　　　　[I. iii. 142-43]

As *opinion, reputation,* and related terms are of such a high importance in the play (as anybody who takes the trouble to count will find out) it is not for nothing that Ulysses lectures Achilles on the necessity of making his virtues *shine on others:* it is not enough that a man is virtuous, he must be supposed to be so; in the Trojan camp, likewise, we have a lengthy discussion as to whether value resides in *particular will* or in the thing itself. Thus a general uncertainty as to what is valuable pervades the play; people do not know a man's essence, they can only suppose what he is like. If we are allowed to cast a glance on actual life for a moment, we will see that Shakespeare mirrors it very justly, for in life, as well as in *Troilus and Cressida,* we are never sure of what a man really is. If this is true, however, that we cannot pass safe judgement on anybody's character, a hierarchically ordered society becomes impossible. It presupposes the possibility of infallible judgement, and as we can only have opinions, the idea of a hierarchically ordered society becomes wishful thinking: an utopia.

Having got so far we have only one question to answer. Did Shakespeare believe that such a well ordered society was desirable, if not possible? About this question everybody may indulge in private speculations; a critic, however, should know that he will never find a conclusive answer. And why, after all, should we worry about Shakespeare's private beliefs? *The play's the thing:* and the play of *Troilus and Cressida* shows quite clearly that the idea of a stabilized society, which is based on degree, is a mere dream, a dream, moreover, in which not even the man who preaches it actually believes. (There is no guessing, of course, what Ulysses' private convictions were.) The conclusion may appear discouragingly pessimistic, but here at last we have found something which may be called the meaning of *Troilus and Cressida.* (pp. 59-63)

> *Johannes Kleinstück, "Ulysses' Speech on Degree as Related to the Play of 'Troilus and Cressida'," in* Neophilologus, *Vol. XLIII, 1959, pp. 58-63.*

RICHARD C. HARRIER (essay date 1959)

[*In the excerpt below, Harrier states that the theme of* Troilus and Cressida *is the interrelation of value and honor, claiming that Troilus creates both of these elements by means of will and imagination. Harrier argues that Thersites, with his cynical destruction of value and honor, is the antithesis of Troilus, and that, in the end, the value created by Troilus's imagination cannot triumph over the "naturalistic nihilism" of Thersites. He also contends that Troilus evokes as much admiration as disapproval and notes, like Albert Gérard (1959), that the character is divided by the logic of his reason—an observation treated in a different manner by J. Hillis Miller (1977).*]

One of the most striking departures Shakespeare made in his version of the Troilus and Cressida story was allowing his hero to walk off the stage alive and vengeful. Whether we think of Shakespeare as suspending the plot of the story or giving it an abrupt conclusion, the dramatic effect on the character of Troilus is much the same. Troilus finds no release in violent death. Nor is a future end at the hands of Achilles foreshadowed in the poetry, however well known it may have been to the audience. The closing note is that "Hope of revenge shall hide our inward woe" [V. x. 31]. If many in Shakespeare's audience were familiar with the story as told in Caxton's *Recuyell* or Lydgate's *Troy Book,* they knew, as the play suggests, that Troilus was to fight a long time after Hector's death. But no matter what their knowledge may have been, they saw on the stage a bitterly vibrant Troilus projected into an active future. The dramatic logic of such a close becomes clear if the character of Troilus is correctly viewed from the beginning of the play, and to explain and document Shakespeare's logic is the present task.

That Troilus is dominated by passion is generally agreed. However, since passion may have several manifestations in action, it is still an open question as to what focus the passionate nature of Troilus has. I suggest that the parallel development of Troilus in two roles, as the firebrand of the Trojans in council and afield and as the nearly insane lover of Cressida, indicates that Shakespeare was presenting no mere sensualist. Rather, the point of Troilus is in the inseparability of his passion for a woman and the honor of his city. He conceives of both as creations of the wills and imaginations of dedicated persons. The value of Helen as a symbol of honor and of Cressida as an object of love Troilus can conceive only in the words he throws at Hector: "What is aught, but as 'tis valu'd?" [II. ii. 52]. Therefore the play is not simply the story of a young man

who fell madly in love with an unworthy woman, nor one that teaches the lesson of moderation in using appetites. The theme of the play is the interrelation of value and honor. Shakespeare chose to give the classical tale a chivalric mode because the figure of a knight risking his life and his nation's on a principle of honor developed from an argument about the nature of value was the best way to dramatize the theme.

I should also like to propose that Troilus is intended to evoke as much admiration as disapproval, as much sympathy as pity. He is, like Hamlet or Antony, a flaw'd hero. True, he is wrong in the debate about the return of Helen, and Hector is right (II, ii). Troilus is in error, one must say, by the very nature of his being, and he passes from our view at the end of the play a terribly distorted man. He never realizes the force of his own words in the first scene of the play, when, disorganized by his unsatisfied passion for Cressida, he remarks:

> Peace, you ungracious clamours! Peace, rude sounds!
> Fools on both sides! Helen must needs be fair,
> When with your blood you daily paint her thus.
>
> [I. i. 89-91]

Exactly that kind of thinking about Helen and Cressida is what leads him through a hell of his own making. By the end of the play he has committed himself to painting a Cressida fair whom everyone else knows to be a whore. That is the essence of his tragedy, and it is not mitigated by a moment of realization. It is a bitter projection without resolution. Troilus manages one moment of grace and a semblance of organization before the action is interrupted by Pandarus, who closes the play much as the prologue opened it, "not in confidence / Of author's pen or actor's voice" [Prologue, 23-4].

In what sense, then, is Troilus a hero worthy of something other than our scorn? The answer, I think, is in the partial rightness of his self-destructive nature, a point which must be discussed at some length, and in the evident ways Shakespeare has taken to enhance his figure at the same time it is suffering distortion. To some degree this double process is the same as that applied to Lear, without, of course, the magnitude or complexity. Like other heroes of Shakespeare deeply flawed by passionate error, Troilus has some claim to our sympathy, if only by contrast with those who surround him. (pp. 142-44)

In contrast to Othello, who is destroyed and destroys through passion, or Brutus, who asserts a will peculiar against the law of degree, Troilus has received little imaginative sympathy. It is a commonplace that Troilus violates the natural order the Elizabethans revered and that he willfully triumphs over reason. But such violation is the subject of most of the great tragedies, as [A. C.] Bradley so convincingly demonstrated, and Lear, as much as Troilus, puts his nation in jeopardy. Why, then, has Troilus received such simple condemnation, as if he were a Vice out of an old play? I believe it is in part because the chivalric lover is somewhat out of poetic fashion. Antony rather than Romeo seems to be more to the present taste. In Troilus we have the medieval servant of love combined with the man of affairs, and when he seems ridiculous in one role, the other is affected. However, there is another reason, central to the construction of the whole play, which must be faced. The play is about the interrelation of value and honor, and Troilus, more than any other violator of a reasonable equation between value and honor, represents an appeal against which the rational spectator must keep a conscious guard. There is at least a dramatic validity to the argument of Troilus in the Trojan council scene (II, ii) that challenges the faith of the lawful man in a world where time and war are "natural." To see this let us reconstruct the circumstances *in the play* on which Troilus based his argument that Helen ought not be returned as the price of peace.

Shakespeare's Trojan War was caused by circumstances growing out of the rape of Priam's sister, Hesione, by Telamon, father of Ajax. On that event the Trojans held a council, and with Hector's approval sent Paris to bring back a superior prize. Honor demanded such a gesture. Paris returned with Helen, and Helen was judged a symbol that redeemed the Trojan honor. Hector again concurred. But the rape of Helen brought the princes orgillous to Troy, and as the play opens, seven years of siege have placed a large question on the value of both symbols for which men are daily dying. The arguments of Hector for the return of Helen are too familiar to need repetition here. They parallel those of Ulysses on Degree, and their conclusion is formidable:

> Thus to persist
> In doing wrong extenuates not wrong,
> But makes it much more heavy.
> [II. ii. 186-88]

Then Hector surprisingly capitulates and joins Troilus in the war party, to the destruction of the nation. He surrenders to Troilus with:

> I propend to you
> In resolution to keep Helen still,
> For 'tis a cause that hath no mean dependence
> Upon our joint and several dignities.
> [II. ii. 190-93]

To what kind of reasoning has Hector bowed? It is this: If reason can redefine honor and value according to occasion, honor and value cannot exist at all. Did not Hector once commit himself in council to stake Trojan honor on the rape of a Helen? When Helen was fresh from Greece and Troy safe, did not Hector believe that honor was in Helen and in her possession? If so, where does honor now reside, that Helen is soiled and Troy in great danger? To put it simply: Troilus is asserting that value and honor are but the reflections of human action, the aura given symbols by human reverence demonstrated in action. Value and honor are created by will and imagination translated into action. The sign of their creation is the solemn oath mutually sworn and kept thereafter to the death. Troilus attempts to give this argument force through the symbolism of marriage, an ironic light on his private marriage to Cressida:

> I take to-day a wife, and my election
> Is led on in the conduct of my will,
> My will enkindled by mine eyes and ears,
> Two traded pilots 'twixt the dangerous shores
> Of will and judgement: how may I avoid,
> Although my will distaste what it elected,
> The wife I chose? There can be no evasion
> To blench from this and to stand firm by honour.
> [II. ii. 61-7]

Thus Troilus develops his query "What is aught, but as 'tis valu'd?" with an argument about the nature of choice itself. Nor is his argument cynical. Troilus, thoroughly medieval, sees no escape from the oath that originally defined value and honor. When you argue a change in value, how do you distinguish reason from rationalization? In the psychology of Troilus, the senses, "mine eyes and ears," operate enigmatically, "Two traded pilots," between will and judgment or reason.

Whenever we choose to affirm the value of an object, how can we be sure that we are not confused between will and reason by the instrumentality of the senses? The shadow of appetite lurks in this metaphor and fills the play, but the relationship Troilus is constructing between will as imagination and appetite must be clearly conceived. Troilus is not exalting appetite, or sensuality compounded by will; he is demonstrating the inseparability of the processes by which one chooses honorably and dishonorably. His is the voice of a sincere man who distrusts an appeal to reason framed to redefine the values on which his world has been constructed. His vision is purely national, one might even say tribal, while Hector's is international in scope and therefore has unusual appeal at present. But there is some validity in Troilus' position for any society, even an international one, since oaths of some sort will always be necessary and values cannot be changed daily nor oaths reversed on light occasion. . . . Hector is right because his larger vision into the nature of things argues the survival of value from its accurate perception. The fact that undermines Troilus' case is that he is persevering in a losing cause. When Time unveils Truth (Cressida goes about veiled) Troilus will not perceive. In the council he refuses to admit defeat lest admission create defeat. There he has other wills to build with his own. But in his love he is alone, and it is there that the extremity of his position is most evident. The reason in Hector's argument becomes apparent: that

> value dwells not in particular will;
> It holds his estimate and dignity
> As well wherein 'tis precious of itself
> As in the prizer. 'Tis mad idolatry
> To make the service greater than the god;
> And the will dotes that is inclineable
> To what infectiously itself affects,
> Without some image of th' affected merit.
> [II. ii. 53-60]

For Troilus all value is in the imaginative will of the prizer. He cannot resign that position without resigning the very basis of his life.

The crisis occurs when Troilus is forced to acknowledge "the attest of eyes and ears" that Cressida has delivered herself to Diomed [V. ii. 122]. Unlike Ulysses and Thersites, the other observers of the scene, Troilus cannot separate Cressida from the other values of existence. He cannot say simply: "Cressida's falsehood does not relate to any being but Cressida and my private grief may be mitigated in that knowledge." His reaction is rather like Hamlet's to the over-hasty marriage of his mother:

> Let it not be believ'd for womanhood!
> Think, we had mothers; do not give advantage
> To stubborn critics, apt, without a theme
> For depravation, to square the general sex
> By Cressid's rule. Rather think this is not Cressid.
> [V. ii. 129-33]

And to Ulysses' question: "What hath she done, Prince, that can soil our mothers?" "Nothing at all, unless that this were she" [V. ii. 134-35]. He is driven to conclude that "this is, and is not, Cressid" [V. ii. 146]. (pp. 147-52)

Troilus is trapped by the logic of his argument in the council, which is the logic of his very being. Since the value of Cressida is as she is valued by Troilus, he cannot resign that value, though all the world laugh, without re-creating his own nature. He therefore divides Cressida in two, and he creates two beings within himself. One Troilus still loves a faithful Cressida. One Troilus acknowledges a faithless Cressida and damns her. The two Troiluses function as one, bitterly confused, at the end of the play; for the death of Hector has placed Troilus at the head of the defenses, and the pursuit of Achilles and Diomed combine motives of defense and revenge. By disguising his private motive in a public one he manages to recover a semblance of unity:

> Hector is dead, there is no more to say.
> Stay yet. You vile abominable tents,
> Thus proudly pight upon our Phrygian plains,
> Let Titan rise as early as he dare.
> I'll through and through you! and, thou great-siz'd
>   coward,
> No space of earth shall sunder our two hates.
> I'll haunt thee like a wicked conscience still,
> That mouldeth goblins swift as frenzy's thoughts.
> Strike a free march to Troy. With comfort go;
> Hope of revenge shall hide our inward woe.
>
>   [V. x. 22-31]

Here he is speaking both publicly and privately. The great-sized coward is both Achilles and Diomed. But in his private world Troilus is committed to a parody of the chivalric test. Though he slay Diomed and paint his blood everywhere, he cannot prove Cressida fair. And the half of Troilus who still believes in Cressida must function silently, or he will appear as mad as Don Quixote. The only Cressida Troilus can paint fair with his own blood is imaginary.

Within the play, however, Troilus, in the projection of his irrational powers, is balanced by the cynicism of Thersites. Remarkably, it seems to me, Thersites has sometimes been taken for the chorus of the play, that is, the mind of Shakespeare himself. Yet Thersites is rational without seeing reason. His view of man is that since he is half beast he is all beast. He views all action as lechery and all humanity as diseased. When Troilus makes his final effort to hold an imaginary Cressida:

>   Never did young man fancy
> With so eternal and so fix'd a soul.
> Hark, Greek: as much as I do Cressid love,
> So much by weight hate I her Diomed.
>
>   [V. ii. 165-68]

Thersites can only interpret the effort with: "He'll tickle it for his concupy" [V. ii. 177]. If Troilus represents the inflexible compulsion to create value by will, Thersites represents an equal compulsion to destroy it. Shakespeare unmasks Thersites in the chivalric test. In the battle, first Hector allows him to live because he is not fit for the sword, then the bastard Margarelon confronts him only long enough to let him admit:

> I am a bastard too; I love bastards. I am a
> bastard begot, bastard instructed, bastard in
> mind, bastard in valour, in everything illegitimate.
>
>   [V. vii. 16-18]

Here Thersites, without the charm of Falstaff, declares himself out of the chivalric world he hates. He cannot hide, however, that he hates that world because he has no virtue in it, no place, no self, no meaning. Thersites has imposed his individual worthlessness on the world, and he goes about asserting that everyone reflects the negative qualities he feels. He has one virtue, intelligence, but because he has found no other use for it, he occupies himself with selecting and announcing the evidence of human bestiality. Thersites we may all be, easily

enough. Troilus we may be only by summoning the human capacity for civilization. Troilus is tragically distorted not by lust, not by the mechanization of his sensual instruments, but by the very spiritual power that made the Middle Ages a triumph of the human imagination. When the last Troilus has played his part and the voice of Thersites dominates the stage, the day of naturalistic nihilism is at hand. (pp. 152-54)

Richard C. Harrier, "Troilus Divided," in Studies in the English Renaissance Drama in Memory of Karl Julius Holzknecht, *Josephine W. Bennett, Oscar Cargill, Vernon Hall, Jr., eds., New York University Press, 1959, pp. 142-56.*

BARBARA HELIODORA C. de M. F. de ALMEIDA (essay date 1964)

[*De Almeida develops the thesis of Tucker Brooke (1928) that* Troilus and Cressida *examines the "relation between environment and character" and argues that a link between the morality of the state and individual conduct is present in all of Shakespeare's work. Unlike most early critics, who viewed Cressida as a coquettish deceiver, or like E. K. Chambers (1907), who saw her as shallow and weak, de Almeida believes that "Cressida is the inevitable result of a war started because of the face of Helen," a point made by Jan Kott (1964) as well as by Tucker Brooke. She also discusses the play's modernity in terms of the politically conscious plays of Bertolt Brecht and attributes this modern element to Shakespeare's portrayal of characters as products of their environment and to the effect that this environment has on the lovers' fate. In comparing the play to* Romeo and Juliet *and other Shakespearean tragedies, de Almeida finds that the world of* Troilus and Cressida *is more thoroughly corrupted, that it destroys love and honor, and that none of its characters possesses moral responsibility. She concludes that generic classification is difficult because the play's decadence "is never fully comic" and its complete lack of morality prevents it from reaching tragic stature.*]

Even though Shakespeare is never a particularly didactic author, *Troilus and Cressida* may be, as was suggested [by Tucker Brooke], a particularly striking instance of a study of the relation between environment and character, but it is essential, I believe, to accept such a relationship as a recurrent underlying element in the poet's work rather than as an atypical instance. Because of the unusual emphasis laid on that relationship in *Troilus and Cressida,* however, one may find that it is perhaps the most "modern" of Shakespeare's plays, for in this sense it is nearest one of the most significant dramatic phenomena of the twentieth century, the epic dramaturgy of Bertolt Brecht, which is basically a revival of Shakespearian dramaturgy and very particularly of that of the histories, that is, of the politically-conscious plays. . . . Largely avoiding the pitfalls of poetic justice, Shakespeare's plays seem to carry within them an organic link between the morality of rule and that of individual conduct, that link being expressed in dramatic action: an assessment of the canon will show that romantic love cannot survive materially, or even be successful morally, in a corrupt society; the connection between the disordered state and the moral corruption of the individual is inextricable.

Between *Romeo and Juliet* and *Troilus and Cressida* nearly a decade elapsed, a period not only during which the author matured and deepened his vision, but also in which politics and society decayed under the rule of the aging queen. . . . The obvious intention of *Troilus and Cressida* is to depict decadence, misgovernment, and corruption, and local conditions may have determined his choice of theme; but Shakespeare's mind was ever too penetrating to be limited by merely local significance. *Troilus and Cressida* became, like *Romeo and Juliet*, an exemplum, this time related to all human behaviour in corrupt circumstances. The parallel between these two plays would be, consequently, both closer and more significant than was suggested by Tucker Brooke, and one might consider the two plays as roughly two different versions of the same problem. (pp. 327-28)

The problem of *Troilus and Cressida* seems on occasion to be darkened by the need for hair-splitting reasoning; Prof. O. J. Campbell expands on the idea that government is bad in the play because men have lost their moral sense and the notion of responsibility [see excerpt above, 1938], whereas it seems to me not only important but indeed essential that the characters in *Troilus and Cressida* should be accepted as being corrupt individually because government is, in itself, corrupt. Undoubtedly government cannot become corrupt of itself, but the idea that seems to me to be implied in Shakespeare's plays is that the strength of corruption—even when it exists in a very small number of people—once endowed with the power of government will inevitably cause the downfall of the whole of society. Unlike *Hamlet*, in which Claudius has ruled only for two months when the action starts; unlike *Macbeth*, in which we actually witness the early stages of corruption; unlike *King Lear*, in which neither the rash irresponsibility of Lear in the division of his kingdom nor the chance for the truly evil elements to take active part in the government had manifested themselves until the early stages of the action, *Troilus and Cressida* is not the story of the beginning or of the causes of corruption: when the play starts, corruption had been, for some time, the dominant environment. An irresponsible war had been ravaging the country and, with ever-growing intensity, spreading corruption throughout the population. (pp. 328-29)

Being interested in human conduct, Shakespeare would naturally feel the need to deal with that of his own time; being a dramatic poet he could not but transmute the corruption which surrounded and preoccupied him into a vision that would be valid not for an age but for all time: his vision of corruption, to hit its mark, needed a focal point, a microcosm to reflect the macrocosm, and after nearly a decade he may have smiled at the thought of having once written a story of romantic love in which two lovers achieved a moral victory over a conflicting social body, buying peace with their lives. Older and less trusting, he turned to romantic love again and wrote *Troilus and Cressida*, the story of Romeo and Juliet with a morally unhappy ending. Romantic love cannot survive—or even come to pass—in a society such as he depicted in the new play; the fundamental morality of his work substantiates this fact. Even in *Romeo and Juliet* a private civic crime—the struggle between two houses—is enough to kill the lovers, and if they are not corrupt we must remember that a responsible ruler staunchly defends the peace and order of the city against this private irresponsibility.There are many points of similarity between the two plays: lovers who belong to opposing factions, a willing go-between to arrange their meetings, a forced separation after a first night spent together, even a new love to be accepted (or not) after that separation. Except for a degree of sophistication there is no great difference between Pandarus and the Nurse: her form of expression is vulgar, gross, and her natural temperament that of a go-between; she acts the part without any qualms, and her actions only retain dignity because Romeo and Juliet are in themselves honorable. Her advice to Juliet in regard to the marriage with Paris is in no way superior to that of Pandarus in regard to Troilus.

In *Romeo and Juliet* there is a sense of tragic waste compensated by the achievement of peace between Montagues and Capulets, and the atmosphere is free from actual corruption: it is rather a question of pride and blindness. But *Troilus and Cressida* was written soon after *Hamlet*, in which tragic waste reaches perhaps its maximum degree in the author's work: evil is destroyed at the expense of the life of the man who both the court of Elsinore and the audience could believe "was likely, had he been put on, to have proved most royally" [*Hamlet*, V. ii. 397-98], a high price indeed. And yet even in *Hamlet* all was not lost because, even after his death, there were left men like Horatio, Fortinbras, Marcellus, and Bernardo who, if they were not exceptional, at least represented an honorable and responsible position regarding problems of state. In *Hamlet* indeed we have a case of the beginning of corruption, and we can see for ourselves how fast it breeds; but after the dignity and order of a state had been reconstituted at such high a price, it is not unlikely that Shakespeare may have posed himself a different problem: after a short period of corruption the integrity of a state could be bought by a Hamlet at the cost of his own life, but after a long period, with the state corrupt to the core, would there be anything left worth saving, and would there be any man left strong enough to save it? The answer in *Troilus and Cressida* seems to be painfully negative.

Only two characters in *Troilus and Cressida* seem to have any notion of responsibility or to be aware of the need for a moral revaluation: Ulysses and Hector. And yet neither of these two men lives up to his proclaimed principles in his actions. When Ulysses makes his famous speech on degree in a council of war no one listens to him, and when the time comes to make Achilles fight Ulysses resorts to the cheapest means, unworthy of his earlier position, means which appeal exclusively to personal glory and vanity, ignoring all valid arguments connected with the welfare of his nation. . . . Hector also, at one point, thinks of the state, but his actions are as unfaithful to his words as those of his Greek counterpart. The code of honor which theoretically regulates the lives of these supposed heroes remains so many hollow words; it is not that they do not mean to respect the code, it is just that they do not really know what they are talking about, since only the outer form, the ceremonial appearances, have been preserved, long after the inner meaning has been lost. Hector is the embodiment of this fallacy, since he has the lucidity of knowing that Helen is not worth fighting a war for (*Troi*. II. ii) but nonetheless ends up by agreeing to go on fighting, since not returning Helen to Menelaus has become a "point of honour".

How can romantic love survive in these surroundings? What dignity can human beings have when corruption is so widespread that we can indeed accept Thersites as the symbol of the Greeks and Pandarus as that of the Trojans (cf. Tucker Brooke)? Shakespeare does not seem to despair at the sight of this world, however; his attitude is rather one of disgust. It is not that he has ceased to believe in ultimate values, but that it disgusts him to see these values wilfully ignored in his own or in any decadent age. In no aspect is the play so modern, so un-Renaissance-like, as in this subjection of the fate of the lovers to that of the society which surrounds them, and whatever feelings we may have towards them we must face the fact that, first and foremost, they are the product of their environment. Troilus may be rather romantic and touching, but if we come to ultimate values he is not much better than his fellow-heroes: at length and romantically he defends the idea of not sending Helen back to Menelaus again (*Troi*. II. ii), because keeping her had become a "point of honour"; and yet he makes no effort whatever to keep by his side Cressida, who has no husband to go back to. His passionate, romantic love surely never had marriage as its object, and Cressida somehow was not, to him, a "point of honour". It has been suggested [by John F. Danby in his *Shakespeare's Doctrine of Nature*] that Troilus achieves a victory over the falling-off of Cressida, but I fail to find anything but hate and personal vengeance in his final attitude. Like Achilles, Troilus goes back to fighting without achieving any sense of real responsibility towards the interests of his country: both are willing to go out and kill more men after they live through certain personal crises, but that is all. On the other hand, I can find no great grounds of moral conviction in the scorn that Troilus shows to Pandarus in the last scene of the play [V. x. 33-4]; his attitude seems to be a purely emotional one, issuing from the fact that he has just been betrayed by Cressida and has decided to make up for it by killing some of the people who are so conveniently called the enemy (for surely he shows no signs of knowing why he should be fighting them). Troilus is appropriately haughty and moralizing but, morally speaking, how far above Pandarus is the man who uses Pandarus' services? "Still wars and lechery!" [V. ii. 194-95]; Shakespeare hardly suggests that Troilus' new attitude will change the general state of affairs: neither his warlike gestures nor his protestations of love have the integrity or the strength to triumph over the general corruption; they are not even channeled in that direction. The character of Troilus may be somewhat more romantic and less unattractive than that of Cressida, but he is morally ineffective, and lacking in the perspective that might bring significance to his actions.

Cressida is no better than Troilus, but it is difficult to determine exactly how much worse in a society in which Cassandra is considered insane, since her behavior differs very little from the sane behavior of Helen. Though presented as a wanton she is also presented as a victim of circumstances: her husband was dead, her father had fled to the Greeks, and her position in Troy was therefore highly insecure. In a world in which the adulteress Helen was not only the center of social life but also the point of honor over which a war was being fought it can hardly come as a surprise that Cressida should receive from her utterly corrupt uncle the suggestion that her best chances in Troy lay in establishing a liaison with a Trojan of high standing. She is, throughout the first stages of the play, completely passive, and it is Pandarus who leads every step of the way into the bed-chamber: she is prepared for accepting a lover as carefully as is Juliet for accepting a husband. In fact, Ophelia acted no better than Cressida when she agreed to serve as bait for Hamlet, and if we accept obedience to her elders as extenuation for Ophelia we must also accept it for Cressida; both betrayed the cause of their love, even though Ophelia does not do so through sexual infidelity, this difference being mainly due to the people who advise them. As it happens, Polonius draws a line between sexual and moral dishonesty, while Pandarus draws no line at all. Cressida had been carefully trained to be pleasing to the opposite sex, and the sane thing to do in Troy was to take on Troilus as a lover: arriving at the Greek camp, after leaving Troy without a single attempt on Troilus' part to keep her there, she repeats the "sane" behavior that was supposed to help her to a secure position, only with greater ease, since it is not the first time. Her behavior is, of course, immoral, and even managed to shock Greeks and Trojans alike; but in view of the dominant corruption of her world it was also, and pitifully, logical: Cressida's behavior may have been in conflict with the code of honor these people claimed to live by, but it certainly did not conflict with the way they actually lived. We cannot even exclude the possibility that Cressida

considered returning to Troilus later on, since the Trojans found nothing amiss in the idea of sending Helen back to Menelaus after her episode with Paris. Shakespeare's intention seems to be to remind us that we cannot romanticize Helen because hers was the face that launched a thousand ships: she and Cressida are no different, and indeed Cressida is the inevitable result of a war started because of the face of a Helen.

A decade was enough to change to that extent Shakespeare's view on romantic love, and the destiny that awaited Troy and the Greek Empire was sufficiently known to complete the picture that his epic play presented. *Troilus and Cressida* suffers badly from the universal wish to see it safely classified as either a comedy or a tragedy; and as the all-encompassing vision of decadence that it is, the play cannot be easily defined. Decadence is never fully comic, and yet it cannot reach tragic stature because the people who live in it know nothing of moral responsibility. Bitterness and disgust are the only feelings that can guide a stage production of this vision of evil so triumphant that it is not even recognized as such any longer by those who live within its grip. If the play ends in a rather weak and undecisive note, it may well be that Shakespeare knew that what he had shown in five acts could lead to a further wallowing in corruption, and end in total destruction and final expiation. When Romeo and Juliet are advised by Pandarus rather than by Frair Laurence, romantic love cannot survive: in Verona it was possible to triumph over a restricted form of civil irresponsibility, but *Troilus and Cressida* shows the inevitable fate of all love and honor in a corrupt society governed by men who are oblivious of their duty to their nation and its people. (pp. 329-32)

Barbara Heliodora C. de M. F. de Almeida, "'Troilus and Cressida': Romantic Love Revisited," in Shakespeare Quarterly, *Vol. XV, No. 4, Autumn, 1964, pp. 327-32.*

RAYMOND SOUTHALL　(essay date 1964)

[Troilus and Cressida, *argues Southall, reflects Shakespeare's concern with the weakening of such feudal values as romance and chivalry by the emergence of capitalism and bourgeois ethics in the late sixteenth century. He states that the mercantile imagery in the play, also noted by Albert Gérard (1959), illustrates an emphatic "coarsening of sensibility" towards war and love, especially in the so-called love poetry of Troilus which, he says, reveals his "mercenary-mindedness and appetitiveness." Southall also examines the references to food and eating in* Troilus and Cressida, *associating the images of gluttony and lechery with the spirit of capitalism that Shakespeare observed in Elizabethan England.*]

The undermining of the old feudal relations and the emergence of a potent bourgeois ethic . . . is pertinent to any truly sociological consideration of Elizabethan literature, but it is particularly so, as I hope to show, in the case of Shakespeare's *Troilus and Cressida.*

The Trojan story came to Shakespeare already imbued with feudal notions of chivalry and courtly love. This is obvious in several passages of the play: in the procession of knights returning from the field, watched by Lady Cressida, and including as the main item of interest, 'Brave Troilus! the prince of chivalry' [I. ii. 228-29]; in the argument of the Trojan council scene (II. 2.); in Hector's challenge to the Greeks [I. iii.] and in his preparation to meet Ajax, when:

> The glory of our Troy doth this day lie
> On his fair worth and single chivalry
> [IV. iv. 147-48]

as also in his dismissal of attempts to dissuade him from the day's fighting with the bland assurance:

> I am today i' th' vein of chivalry;
> [V. iii. 32]

in Diomed's decision to wear Cressida's favour and in his order:

> Go, go, my servant, take thou Troilus' horse;
> Present the fair steed to my Lady Cressid.
> Fellow, commend my service to her beauty;
> Tell her I have chastis'd the amorous Troyan,
> And am her Knight by proof.
> [V. v. 1-5]

The Trojan story also had a kind of contemporary, local relevance arising out of the fact that London was, at the time, commonly and proudly eulogized as Troynovant, the New Troy.

Leaving aside the inherent character of the story, the distinctively Shakespearian activity in the play is to be found in the emphatic coarsening of that kind of life represented by romance and chivalry. This is most remarkable in the so-called love poetry of the play. Critics have reached such a unanimity of opinion concerning what J. C. Maxwell has called [in *The Age of Shakespeare*] 'the genuine intensity of the love poetry' that Mr. Maxwell himself did not feel it necessary to consider the matter:

> because it has never gone unrecognised, whereas the degree to which Shakespeare qualifies our response to it has often been underestimated. That the love of Troilus, for all the youthful ardour which sometimes tempts us to think of Shakespeare as entirely carried away by it, essentially belongs to the shallow and corrupt world of Troy, is shown also by the arrangement of the scenes.

But after this slight heresy Mr. Maxwell is quick to return to received opinion and to point out that 'In its intensity Troilus's love is very different' from that of Paris and Helen, 'who must surely represent the norm of sophisticated love-intrigue at Troy'. Apart from the logical oddness of this assertion (the only Trojan love-intrigues are those of Paris and Helen and Troilus and Cressida) it is to be noted that Mr. Maxwell, along with many other critics, implicitly accepts the love ethic of Troilus and all that it entails. Bearing in mind how easy it is for all of us to accept current ethical attitudes without appreciating their actual social implications, this is not perhaps surprising; nonetheless, a certain obtuseness on the part of Shakespearian critics is significant in that it serves as a forcible reminder that we are still in and of a world in which it is natural to view love as a commercial transaction.

In the play itself instances of the coarsening of sensibility which such a view of love involves are so numerous that . . . it is extremely difficult to understand why they should not have been generally recognized. In the first scene of the play Troilus

defines his evaluation of the love relationship for us in the oft-quoted lines:

> Tell me, Apollo, for thy Daphne's love,
> What Cressid is, what Pandar, and what we?
> Her bed is India; there she lies, a pearl;
> Between our Ilium and where she resides
> Let it be call'd the wild and wand'ring flood;
> Ourself the merchant, and this sailing Pandar
> Our doubtful hope, our convoy and our bank.
> [I. i. 98-104]

Thus Troilus remarks his transformation into a merchant for whom Cressida is a desirable commodity and Pandar a trading vessel—elsewhere he describes Pandar as a broker. Later he refers to the more general transformation that has been effected when he seeks to justify the retention of Helen by arguing that she too is a pearl, but one:

> Whose price hath launch'd above a thousand ships,
> And turn'd crown'd kings to merchants.
> [II. ii. 82-3]

Talk about the manumission of feudal relations, therefore, is not an impertinence foisted upon the play, but something to which the text itself draws attention. (pp. 220-22)

Troilus is a 'prince of chivalry', a feudal prince, who has been spiritually transformed and who, when eventually he must part with Cressida, is reduced to the commercially-minded lament:

> We two, that with so many thousand sighs
> Did buy each other, must poorly sell ourselves
> [IV. iv. 39-40]

But the corrupted judgment that weighs men and women in the scales of the market place is not monopolised by Troilus. When Hector has issued his chivalrous challenge to the Greeks, for instance, Ulysses takes Nestor aside and suggests:

> Let us, like merchants, show our foulest wares
> And think perchance they'll sell.
> [I. iii. 358-59]

their 'foulest wares' being Ajax, who is, according to the much maligned Thersites, 'bought and sold among those of any wit, like a barbarian slave' [II. i. 46-7]. After the brief encounter with Ajax, Hector is entertained by the Greeks and Achilles desires the opportunity to look him over, 'As I would buy thee' [IV. v. 238]. In the meantime, Calchas, Cressida's father, pleads with the Greeks that Cressida be procured from Troy as ransom for the captive Trojan Antenor, 'he shall buy my daughter' [III. iii. 28]. Agreeing to the exchange the Greeks dispatch Diomed to effect it. It is whilst this Grecian broker is waiting in Troy for Cressida that Paris asks him who really deserves Helen and Diomed proceeds to strip the war of its chivalrous trappings:

> He merits well to have her that doth seek her,
> Not making any scruple of her soilure,
> With such a hell of pain and world of charge;
> And you as well to keep her that defend her,
> Not palating the taste of her dishonour,
> With such a costly loss of wealth and friends,
> He, like a puling cuckold would drink up
> The lees and dregs of a flat tamed piece;

You, like a lecher, out of whorish loins
Are pleas'd to breed out your inheritors.
Both merits pois'd, each weighs nor less nor more;
But he as he, the heavier for a whore.

[IV. i. 56-67]

Paris, however, is inspired by the same mercenary spirit as Troilus and waves Diomed's biting comments aside with a glib:

Fair Diomed, you do as chapmen do,
Dispraise the thing that you desire to buy;
But we in silence hold this virtue well:
We'll but commend what we intend to sell.

[IV. i. 76-9]

Plainly, and to avoid labouring the obvious, summarily, such expressions of the nature of love and war reveal a spirit that is neither ancient (Greek or Trojan) nor medieval (romantic or chivalrous) but Elizabethan-Jacobean . . . , in short, the spirit of capitalism.

The coarsening of life associated with this spirit is made explicit by Shakespeare, then, in the use of the language of commerce to define, amongst other things, the nature and dignity of love. That this is what Shakespeare is doing in the play requires no external evidence. The coarseness that finds its natural expression in the vocabulary of trade is evident in the character of the 'love' poetry. (pp. 222-24)

[In] the opening scene of the play, Troilus and Pandar discuss the wooing of Cressida in terms of the preparation of a cake and when, towards the end of the play, she passes to Diomed, Troilus remarks that only:

The fractions of her faith, orts of her love,
The fragments, scraps, the bits and greasy relics
Of her o'er-eaten faith, are bound to Diomed.

[V. ii. 158-60]

He almost invariably thinks of Cressida with his belly; beginning as a tasty titbit yet to be enjoyed she ends as piece of left-over meat. The sentiment of these last lines is inherent in the characterization of Troilus. Already in the council scene (II. 2.) he has found it apposite to liken Helen to left-over meat; he argues there that she should not be returned to the Greeks because:

the remainder viands
We do not throw in unrespective sieve,
Because we now are full.

[II. ii. 70-2]

In the reply of Diomed to Paris, which has already been quoted, we are offered an appraisal of Helen remarkably similar to those of Helen and Cressida made by Troilus. According to Diomed, Agamemnon is prepared to 'drink up The lees and dregs of a flat tamed piece', Helen, whom Diomed later describes as 'carrion'. The point of this observation is that the spirit which emerges in the characterization of Troilus is not simply a piece of characterization. The figure of Troilus, as has been seen in his use of the vocabulary of trade, expresses the central preoccupations of the play. The Greeks in the figure of Achilles share the debility of Troilus:

Imagin'd worth
Holds in his blood such swol'n and hot discourse
That 'twixt his mental and his active parts
Kingdom'd Achilles in commotion rages,
And batters down himself.

[II. iii. 172-76]

However, where the disjunction of imagination and action in Troilus arises from the fact that he looks on Cressida to lust after her, in Achilles it arises from self-love, or pride. And as Troilus's passion is defined as the grossest of belly-appetites, so too is the pride of the Greeks, Achilles and Ajax; Ulysses remarks of them:

How one man eats into another's pride,
While pride is fasting in his wantonness!

[III. iii. 136-37]

But the whole of the play is busily reducing life to the demands of the belly:

He that is proud eats up himself.   [II. iii. 154]

. . . lechery eats itself.   [V. iv. 35]

. . . the Troyans taste our dear'st repute
With their fin'st palate   [I. iii. 337-38]

Now . . . I begin to relish thy advice;
And I will give a taste thereof forthwith
To Agamemnon.   [I. iii. 386-88]

The grief is fine, full, perfect, that I taste, . . .
If I could temporize with my affections
Or brew it to a weak and colder palate,
The like allayment could I give my grief.

[IV. iv. 3-8]

He eats nothing but doves, love; and that breeds
hot blood, and hot blood begets hot thoughts,
and hot thoughts beget hot deeds, and hot deeds
is love.

[III. i. 128-30]

And Diomed, it will be remembered, scorns Paris for 'Not palating the taste' of Helen's dishonour. Space forbids exhaustive quotation, but these few examples serve to make the point that Ulysses's contention that 'appetite' is 'a universal wolf' [I. iii. 121] touches the very quick of Shakespeare's conception of the spirit of capitalism as a force which reduces life to the mere satisfaction of the appetites. (pp. 225-27)

The extent of this concern can be seen when Troilus, chaffing against the natural limitations of his appetites, his senses, touches upon the subject of Time. Critics have made it abundantly clear that Time has a special significance in the play; that this is superficial is apparent when Troilus, on parting with Cressida, expands upon the theme of *tempus fugit:*

Injurious time now with a robber's haste
Crams his rich thievery up, he knows not how.
As many farewells as be stars in heaven,
With distinct breath and consign'd kisses to them,
He fumbles up into a loose adieu,
And scants us with a single famish'd kiss,
Distasted with the salt of broken tears.

[IV. iv. 42-8]

The thematic function of Time here is simply to define the sensibility of Troilus and, consequently, that of the play: Time is appetitive, sensual and limiting—Time with 'haste Crams his rich thievery up. . . . And scants us with a single famish'd kiss, Distasted . . .'; more especially, Time is lecherous—'He fumbles up into a loose adieu'; there can be little doubt as to the dominant sense of the ambiguous word 'loose' (cf. 'loose woman'). (p. 227)

Troilus is in contact with the remnants of a chivalrous world, but he is in contact with them as an agent of corruption. It is as such, and certainly not as a chivalrous lover, that Troilus desires access to Cressida, as must be obvious to the most biased reader when Troilus begs Pandar:

> O, be thou my Charon,
> And give me swift transportance to these fields
> *Where I may wallow in the lily beds*
> Propos'd for the deserver!
>
> [III. ii. 10-13]

The real nature of the disjunction between action and imagination in Troilus is, in the lines just quoted, made explicit in his conception of the love relationship. Love to Troilus is the relationship between his own inherent capacity for pig-like (to 'wallow') defilement . . . and what he imagines to be the delicate purity ('the lily beds') of Cressida. . . . And Troilus, with his mercenary-mindedness and appetitiveness, is but an abstract of the corruptive spirit which the play as a whole is 'about'. (p. 228)

The distinctively Shakespearian activity in the play, then, assesses the weakening of feudal relations that had taken place during the sixteenth century by bringing to bear upon a world of romance and chivalry (the world of the Trojan War as traditionally presented by medieval and Elizabethan writers) the powers of personal and social corruption inherent in the appetitive spirit of capitalism. Shakespeare's definition of this spirit in terms of the appetites is a traditional one and belongs to that medieval conception of social life which viewed the appetitive forces as necessary but subservient to what was distinctively human in life, expressing as they did man's animal as opposed to his human nature. Shakespeare, therefore, implicitly condemns the reduction of life to the pursuit of appetitive satisfaction because it is a reduction; it is life depressed to a level at which gluttony and lechery become its dominant qualities and man is devoted to the pursuit of the demands of his appetites and the means to satisfy them, as Troilus is devoted to Cressida. . . . (p. 231)

In the play, the body politic of medieval social theory has become a creature of appetite, 'a universal wolf' to use Ulysses's phrase, and has become afflicted with the incurable diseases that follow in the wake of over-indulgence, it is, therefore, doomed to eventual death. The integriy of this use of medieval social theory can be appreciated if it is borne in mind that the theory reflects medieval social life, feudalism; that form of living had been corrupted and was doomed. The limitation, on the other hand, is that such a view of society, being rigidly feudal, does not allow of any perception of new forms of social growth. Today we can see that out of a coarse and vulgar appetitiveness arose a new respect for man's material well-being and out of sensual curiosity arose modern science. But such an awareness of the limitations within which *Troilus and Cressida* operates is very largely rendered irrelevant by the direction of Shakespeare's interest. Shakespeare concentrates our attention upon an area of life, and that the most intimately human, in which the spirit of capitalism works without hope of redemption. (p. 232)

> Raymond Southall, " 'Troilus and Cressida' and the Spirit of Capitalism," in Shakespeare in a Changing World, *edited by Arnold Kettle, Lawrence & Wishart, 1964, pp. 217-32.*

JAN KOTT   (essay date 1964)

[*Kott is a Polish-born critic and professor of English and comparative literature now residing in the United States. In his well-*

Act V. Scene iii. Cassandra, Hector, and Andromache. By T. Kirk (n.d.).

known study Shakespeare, Our Contemporary, *originally published in Polish as* Szkice o Szekspirze *in 1964, he interprets several of the plays as presenting a tragic vision of history. Kott calls this historical pattern the Grand Mechanism. In his discussion of* Troilus and Cressida, *Kott notes the absurdity of the prolonged and pointless war which is nonetheless rationalized by Ulysses's ideology of hierarchy and supported by the Trojan's anachronistic code of honor. Like Tucker Brooke (1928) and Barbara Heliodora C. de M. F. de Almeida (1964), Kott lays heavy emphasis on the war's effect on Cressida's character. He remarks that she is "one of the most amazing Shakespearean characters" and notes her affinity with a "teenage-girl of the mid-twentieth century" because of her defensive irony and the distrust, reserve, and analysis she imposes on herself. Kott concludes that the play, unlike tragedy, fails to reestablish a moral order or offer catharsis and says, "Grotesque is more cruel than tragedy." Kott's suggestion that the Trojan war is perpetuated by ideology is given a fuller treatment by R. A. Yoder (1972), who also uses Kott's notion of the Grand Mechanism.*]

The great dispute about the sense and cost of war, about the existence and cost of love, goes on from the opening to the final scene of *Troilus and Cressida*. It is a dispute constantly punctuated by buffoonery. One can call it something else: it is a dispute about the existence of a moral order in a cruel and irrational world. Hamlet, the Prince of Denmark, has faced the same trial.

The war goes on. Trojans and Greeks kill each other. If war is just butchery, the world in which war exists is absurd. But the world goes on, and one has to give it a purpose in order to preserve the sense of the world's existence and a scale of values. Helen is a whore, but Helen has been abducted with Priam's permission and that of the Trojan leaders. Helen's cause has become Troy's cause. Helen has become the symbol of love and beauty. Helen will become a whore only when the Trojans return her to Menelaus and admit themselves that she is a whore, not worth dying for. How much is a jewel worth? A trader weighs it on the scales. But a jewel can be worth something else; worth the price of passion it has aroused; the price it has in the eyes of the person who wears it; the price given to it.

Hector knows all about Helen, and almost all about war. He knows that according to the law of nature and the law of the land Helen ought to be returned to the Greeks; that it would be common sense to give her back. But he knows also that to give Helen back would mean a loss of face, an admission that a jewel is weighed on scales and worth only as much as tradesmen give for it in gold; that traders and *nouveau-riche* shipowners are right in thinking that everything, including love, loyalty and even honour, can be bought. The war has lasted seven years. People have died for Helen. To give Helen back would be to deprive those deaths of any meaning. Hector makes a deliberate choice. He is not a young enthusiast, like Troilus; or a crazy lover, like Paris. He knows that the Greeks are stronger and that Troy can be destroyed. He chooses against reason, and against himself. To him reason seems a tradesman's affair. Hector knows he must choose between the physical and moral destruction of Troy. Hector cannot give Helen back.

This dispute is not carried on in a void. *Troilus and Cressida* is from the outset a modern play, a sneering political pamphlet. The Trojan war was in fact a contemporary one. The war went on for a long time after the defeat of the Invincible Armada, and the end was not in sight. The Greeks are down-to-earth, heavy and brutal. They know that the war is being fought over a cuckold and a hussy, and they do not have to make themselves believe that they die for the sake of loyalty and honour. They are part of another, a new world. They are tradesmen. They know how to count. To them the war really makes no sense. The Trojans insist on their ridiculous absolutes and a medieval code of combat. They are anachronistic. But from this it does not follow that they do not know how to defend themselves; or that they must surrender. The war is pointless, but a pointless war, too, has to be won. This is a proof of Shakespeare's realism. Ulysses is a realist, a practician, a rationalist. He even knows mathematics. In his great speech he refers to Euclid's axiom: "That's done, as near as the extremest ends / Of parallels" [I. iii. 167-68].

Ulysses the rationalist is also an ideologist, who constructs a system to suit his practice. He invokes the entire medieval cosmogony and theology. He speaks about the hierarchic principle which rules the universe, the sun and the planets, the stars and the earth. This heavenly hierarchy is paralleled on earth by a hierarchy of class and rank. Hierarchy is a law of nature; its violation is equal to the victory of force over law, anarchy over order. Not only feudal mystics try to find a purpose for this war, fought over a cuckold and a tart. Rationalists also defend the war. Here lies the bitter wisdom and the deep irony of *Troilus and Cressida*.

Hector has been idealized into a knight of the medieval crusades. Having noticed that Achilles's "arms are out of use" [V. vi. 16], he gives up the duel. Achilles has no such feudal scruples. He avails himself of the moment when Hector has laid aside his sword and taken off his helmet, and murders him helped by his Myrmidons. Troy shall fall, as Hector has fallen. She is anachronistic with her illusions about honour and loyalty, in the new Renaissance world where force and money win. Hector is killed by the stupid, base and cowardly Achilles. No one and nothing can save the sense of this war.

War has been ridiculed. Love will be ridiculed too. Helen is a tart, Cressida will be sent to the Greek camp and will become a tart. The transfer of Cressida to the Greek camp is not only part of the action of the play; it is also a great metaphor.

Cressida is one of the most amazing Shakespearean characters, perhaps equally amazing as Hamlet. And, like Hamlet, she has many aspects and cannot be defined by a single formula.

This girl could have been eight, ten, or twelve years old when the war started. Maybe that is why war seems so normal and ordinary to her that she almost does not notice it and never talks about it. Cressida has not yet been touched, but she knows all about love, and about sleeping with men; or at any rate she thinks she knows. She is inwardly free, conscious and daring. She belongs to the Renaissance, but she is also a Stendhal type akin to Lamiel, and she is a teen-age girl of the mid-twentieth century. She is cynical, or rather would be cynical. She has seen too much. She is bitter and ironic. She is passionate, afraid of her passion and ashamed to admit it. She is even more afraid of feelings. She distrusts herself. She is our contemporary because of this self-distrust, reserve, and a need of self-analysis. She defends herself by irony.

In Shakespeare a character never exists without a situation. Cressida is seventeen. Her own uncle procures her for Troilus and brings a lover to her bed. Cynical Cressida wants to be more cynical than her uncle; bitter Cressida scoffs at confidences; passionate Cressida is the first to provoke a kiss. And it is at this point that she loses all her self-confidence, becomes affectionate, blushing and shy; she is now her age again.

> . . . I would be gone.
> Where is my wit? I know not what I speak.
> [III. ii. 150-51]

This is one of Shakespeare's most profound love scenes. The balcony scene in *Romeo and Juliet,* set all in one key, is just a bird's love song. Here we have everything. There is conscious cruelty in this meeting of Troilus and Cressida. They have been brought together by a procurer. His chuckle accompanies them on the first night of their love.

There is no place for love in this world. Love is poisoned from the outset. These wartime lovers have been given just one night. And even that night has been spoilt. It has been deprived of all its poetry. It has been defiled. Cressida had not noticed the war. The war reached her at the break of dawn, after her first night with Troilus.

> Prithee, tarry.
> You men will never tarry.
> O foolish Cressid! I might have still held off,
> And then you would have tarried.
> [IV. ii. 15-18]

Pandarus had procured Cressida like some goods. Now, like goods, she will be exchanged with the Greeks for a captured Trojan general. She has to leave at once, the very morning after her first night. Cressida is seventeen. An experience like this is enough. Cressida will go to the Greeks. But it will be a different Cressida. Until now she has known love only in imagination. Now she has come to know it in reality. During one night. She is violently awakened. She realizes that the world is too vile and cruel for anything to be worth defending. Even on her way to the Greek camp Diomedes makes brutal advances to her. Then she is kissed in turn by the generals and princes, old, great and famous men: Nestor, Agamemnon, Ulysses. She has realized that beauty arouses desire. She can still mock. But she already knows she will become a tart. Only before that happens, she has to destroy everything, so that not even memory remains. She is consistent.

Before her departure for the Greek camp she exchanges with Troilus a glove for a sleeve. Never mind these medieval props. She could equally well have exchanged rings with Troilus. Details are not important. What matters is the pledge of faith itself. That very evening Diomedes will ask Cressida for Troilus's sleeve. And Cressida will give it to him. She did not have to give it. She could have become Diomedes's mistress without doing so. And yet she could not. First she had to kill everything in herself. Cressida went to bed with Diomedes, as Lady Anne went to bed with Richard who had killed her husband and father [in *Richard III*].

In this tragicomedy there are two great parts for clowns. The sweet clown Pandarus in Troy, and the bitter clown Thersites in the Greek camp. Pandarus is a kind-hearted fool who wants to do his best for everybody, and make the bed for every couple. He lives as if the world were one great farce. But cruelty will reach him as well. The old procurer will weep. But his cry will evoke neither pity nor compassion.

Only the bitter fool Thersites is free from all illusions. This born misanthrope regards the world as a grim grotesque:

> Would I could meet that rogue Diomed! I would croak like a raven; I would bode, I would bode. Patroclus will give me anything for the intelligence of this whore. The parrot will not do more for an almond than he for a commodious drab. Lechery, lechery! still wars and lechery! Nothing else holds fashion. A burning devil take them!
>
> [V. ii. 190-96]

Let us imagine a different ending for *Othello*. He does not murder Desdemona. He knows she could have been unfaithful; he also knows he could murder her. He agrees with Iago: If Desdemona could be unfaithful, if he could believe in her infidelity, and if he could murder her, then the world is base and vile. Murder becomes unnecessary. It is enough to leave.

In tragedy the protagonists die, but the moral order is preserved. Their death confirms the existence of the absolute. In this amazing play Troilus neither dies himself, nor does he kill the unfaithful Cressida. There is no catharsis. Even the death of Hector is not fully tragic. Hero that he is, he pays for a noble gesture and dies surrounded by Myrmidons, stabbed by a boastful coward. There is irony in his death, too.

Grotesque is more cruel than tragedy. Thersites is right. But what of it? Thersites is vile himself. (pp. 77-83)

Jan Kott, "'Troilus and Cressida'—Amazing and Modern," in his Shakespeare, Our Contemporary, *translated by Boleslaw Taborski, 1964. Reprint by W. W. Norton & Company, 1974, pp. 75-83.*

R. J. KAUFMANN (essay date 1965)

[*In the following excerpt, Kaufmann argues that* Troilus and Cressida *represents a crucial stage in Shakespeare's development as a tragedian. He states that unlike Shakespeare's earlier plays, in this play Shakespeare allows characters a measure of psychological complexity and "prepares specimens for tragic scrutiny." But, continues Kaufmann, while elements of the characters of Troilus, Thersites, and Ulysses are later synthesized in Hamlet's tragically complex character,* Troilus and Cressida *itself lacks a "psychologically comprehensive protagonist." He maintains that by offering a pluralistic perspective, it also inverts the "diagnostic confidence" with which tragedy usually ends. Like Kenneth Muir (1953), Kaufmann asserts that* Troilus and Cressida *"provides no secure point of vantage from which to evaluate the action." He concludes that the play is a "brilliant dramatic mutation" which resembles a Rorschach ink blot, evoking a different response in each reader.*]

[*Troilus and Cressida*] is a pre-tragic dramatization of human need for ceremonial participation appropriately stressing the imagery and practice of self-consumption, and technically devised to permit complex scrutiny of suspension in multiplicity. The crucial characters each possess a number of potential selves, and they decide to keep one of these alive, while avoiding the kind of conscious choice which will negate all other possibilities. Such desire for trammeling up the negative consequences of choice is expensive to tragic dignity. Such uncertainties in editing the structure of values extend from the individual characters to the play's general strategies. Tragedy does not readily grow from the assumption that the precise location of the sickness ailing a dramatic world is already known, but tragedy does end with diagnostic confidence. *Troilus and Cressida* reverses this familiar tragic sequence. The diagnostic hybris of its opening scenes wilts before experience, so that at the end, we have no firm criteria for assuming Thersites' or Pandarus's limited comprehension of love is any more "realistic" than Hector's, or Troilus's. The final view is pluralistic. In this play about competing modes of knowing, Troilus "knows" love the only way one can know it, by experiencing it. It is real for him, and he "knows" a profound reality in "knowing" it however briefly that "knowledge" may remain intact. There is an ideological permissiveness about the play which differentiates it from poised tragedy or comedy. We should accept this and seek critical means to accommodate this property of suspension. The play is about the disordering power of too many formalized schemes of "knowledge" not of disordering passion merely. The favorite scholarly polarity, Reason and Passion, accounts for Dryden's simplified revision of the play; in Shakespeare the facts of the play far outrun this. Hector is not passionate, but he is destroyed more completely than the rest. (pp. 140-41)

Troilus stands barring the way to Shakespeare's tragic world. It is an unpieced tragic design, too analytically divided, too systematically total. Hamlet, a tragically complex character, includes a Thersites, a Troilus and a Ulysses within himself, even though Horatio contains some of the qualities of Ulysses, Laertes some of those of Troilus, and despite the fact that Hamlet and Hector are, at one level, nearly equatable. As he mastered the tragic style, Shakespeare showed how clearly literary wholes are greater than the sum of their parts, because they are tense with contradictions—each quality is there in itself and is made something more by its resistance to its assertive opposite. Hamlet is spasmodically cynical, because he cares and refuses to cease caring. He cares and is persistent, because he sees with cynic clarity that no one else has imaginative power enough to care. In *Troilus and Cressida*, the tragic potential of such inner antinomies is recognized but too externally handled.

Shakespeare was the most restlessly experimental of dramatists. He had a curiosity about form, about ideas, about the validity of received assumptions which without his craftsman's dedication might have made him defencelessly eclectic like Marston, whose plays often read like a thematic programme for Shakespeare but without his psychological perception and his stern sense of proportion. Nowhere is this complex of assertions more interestingly tested than in *Troilus and Cressida*. In it Shakespeare, in one of his periodic violent wrenchings of his perspective on truth, confronts a whole parade of possibilities. He strikes a variety of critical attitudes towards what he has done thus far as an artist, and through this he attaches himself to a new and deeper vision of the truth. The deep organizing theme of *Troilus and Cressida* is the *self-consuming* nature of all negotiable forms of vice and virtue. As soon as one turns too sharply back on what one is, the self dissolves, or, conversely, if one too ardently equates one's self with any available codified description the act itself falsifies and kills. This is, of course, the uttermost extreme of romanticism; it can be argued, with the example of Marlowe before us, that the high plains of tragedy are usually reached via the psychologically vertiginous cliffs of extreme self-absorption, of something quite close to solipsism. The artist studies those who care too intensely for self, when learning the tragic tone. *Troilus and Cressida* is a competition for protagonal status. It has no fully realized hero, but an abnormal number of candidates.

Troilus and Cressida is, thus, helpfully seen as a necessary overture to high tragic statement, because it clears away a whole family of inadequte tragic formulae. The greatest tragedy requires something more than loyal adherence to some received or public code. You can make a Hotspur from an enthusiastic equation of a man's self with the imperatives of the honor code; you cannot make a Hamlet. Hamlet feels the relevance of the honor code to a final determination of his problem, but he is equally aware of its isolated insufficiency and its psychological sterility. You can transform a Prince Hal into a Henry V by tracing an intelligent and dutiful acceptance of the obligation to perform as an adequate public symbol for others. But, in the process, anything like tragic complexity is lost. . . . In the major late plays of the 1590's, the deeper psychological problems are acknowledged formally by Shakespeare, but the requisite artistic freedom to explore the tragic uncertainties of the protagonist's innermost self is forbidden by the equation of each of them to some obligatory public posture. *Troilus and Cressida* is a brilliant critique of this insufficiently tragic theory of personality which defines a protagonist's essential self as in any way stably equivalent to his chosen mode of self representation. What "happens" to the great tragic heroes is what they disclose to themselves, when they are forced to define themselves. What these enforced definitions leave out is all that is most relevantly human in their natures. That is the reason their experience is felt as tragic.

High tragedy begins when the artist turns his attention from the mechanisms of self-definition to the precise emotional cost of such demanded disciplines. In seeking to be true to what they mistakenly suppose to be their essential selves, Shakespeare's greatest heroes, as in *Othello* and *Macbeth*, blind themselves to a larger human essence shared with those they seek to love, own, save, dominate or reach. *Troilus and Cressida* acts as a critical prolegomena to this exploration. It formally exposes a repertoire of possibilities for crucial psycho-

logical error. It does not explore these choices very patiently, for it is too strongly animated by the intellectual excitement of detection and diagnosis. *Troilus and Cressida* prepares specimens for tragic scrutiny. (pp. 142-44)

For those who love man for his spiritual awkwardness *Troilus and Cressida* was written. The play invents uncomfortable dramatic terms for the truth spoken by Cressida in the central love scene

> . . . for to be wise and love
> Exceeds man's might: that dwells with gods above.
> [III. ii. 156-57]

Both loving and being wise are ultimate human desiderata—tragic art requires them to be, and they are not opposites. *King Lear* is about wise loving.

In confronting this radical dilemma with no present means to resolve it, the play makes few concessions to our illusions about human worth and dignity. Specifically, it affords us no secure vantage point for judgment within the play. The sanctity of this convention of evaluative privilege is itself an illusion; the dramatist is not obliged to provide such orientation, as Brecht's exploitation of his alienation-effects richly proves. Deprived of it, however, we are critically restive. In *Hamlet*, we see the action alternately through the eyes of Hamlet and the eyes of Claudius. It is a power struggle and the viewpoints are different. But we are never in doubt that Shakespeare prefers Hamlet to the scheming and murderous King. The titles of most plays help us to this vantage point; they supply the hero's name or that of the comic butt. Genre classification tells us enough usually about the tonal limit of a play to make us confident in the distribution of our sympathies. Now and then a play leaves fundamental doubts. Then critics, contemplating the strained fantasies others present as rational opinion, nominate another private perspective as the truth, until the play languishes to one side. So it is with Shakespeare's *Troilus and Cressida*. (pp. 144-45)

We have, then, a play of uncertain tone, indeterminate genre, perhaps intended for a special audience. This play, written at the height of Shakespeare's mature powers, is deliberately weighty, essaying philosophical enquiry in a language more Latinate, formal and technical than he had been heretofore capable of or was hereafter to need. This language and manner of thinking is *forensic*, a special fusion of rhetoric and logical argument developed in the forums where opinion is officially fabricated on great public questions. In the forum, the state undertakes continuing self-definition. Pure logic seldom prevails in forensic situation. Nor does it in this forensic play. In tonally determinate early scenes, logical edifices are reared high to crash more resoundingly before resurgent caprice and unreason. Questions of formal choice and, consequently, of relative value are dramatized, as is conventional in Shakespeare tragedy. But, *Troilus and Cressida* provides as well a pyrrhic commentary on its own situations. It is a play of self-subverting interrogation, creating thereby disequilibria which are ceremonially rather than thoughtfully or personally redressed. What questions are raised? Shakespeare questions most drivingly the existential sufficiency of reason as an ordering force. (p. 146)

Troilus and Cressida provides no secure point of vantage from which to evaluate the action. There is no single, reliable choral observer within the play who can orient our responses. The overall strategy of *Troilus and Cressida* not only refuses us this positive convenience, it repeatedly builds up moments or issues tempting us to make such an identification only to violate it in some way. Furthermore, the play provides a number of arguments as to comparative values more detailed and precise than is usual in the theater without furnishing us an established referee. This suggests a deliberate multiple-perspective. This suspension in multiplicity assumes diagrammatic form in the excruciating scene in which Troilus's dream is destroyed. Shakespeare has so manipulated the action that Ulysses and Troilus are plausibly inherently improbable. Along with these two, we observe Cressida succumbing to the crude solicitations of Diomedes. Furthermore, Thersites is watching Ulysses who is watching Troilus watch them. We are placed to watch all at once, from a perspective in which each of the three sets of observers is more deeply recessed from us. Thus we are provoked to a progressively greater detachment, through their respective commentaries, and to take a more and more intellectual view of the main proceeding. After the tense anguish of Troilus, "O withered truth!" [V. ii. 46] no more potent feeling can be adduced; so we watch sequentially what the mind can do in its appalling task of reassembling broken illusions. First, Troilus's spasms of resistance to the corrosive power of the actual: "Let it not be believed," "This is, and is not, Cressid," "Was Cressid here?" "If beauty have a soul, this is not she" [V. ii. 129, 146, 125, 138]. His heart is filled with a hopefulness (an "esperance") "so obstinately strong, That doth invert th' attest of eyes and ears" [V. ii. 121-22]. Until, in nauseated recurrence to the imagery of food and appetite, he sees Cressida for what she *now* is, a pawed over public thing, left-over and staled.

> The fractions of her faith, orts of her love,
> The fragments, scraps, the bits, and greasy relics
> Of her o'ereaten faith, are given to Diomed.
>
> [V. ii. 158-60]

The disillusioned will rejects its chosen food. A new perspective is imposed on reality. What happens to Troilus thereafter is anticlimactic in keeping with the habitual strategy of the play. He ardently pursues the culmination of death, but life is not artistic enough to provide it for him. Further from Cressida's violation of faith and closer to us as spectators, Ulysses stands exercising an almost fatherly sympathy for the distraught and agonized Troilus. But he sees Troilus' loss of Cressida in the elongated perspective of Time which can finally consign to oblivion even the crucifixion of youth's best dream. His counsel is "patience" which sees this loss *sub specie aeternitatis* ["within the perspective of eternity"] and makes it *seem* manageably small. Wise advice but cold. Still more detached stands Thersites to whose abstract judgment this event of searing particularity is only a confirming instance of the properties of man, "Lechery, lechery, still wars and lechery, nothing else holds fashion" [V. ii. 194-95]. The defect of the cynic's view is not general inaccuracy but its excessive focal length. The tragic vision rehabilitates reason in nearly spatial terms. The embracing vision on which tragic response is dependent includes all these carefully balanced elements, never substituting one part for the whole. The audience of tragic drama must be placed imaginatively at the right distance from human feeling. Not so close as to be emotionally immersed with a consequent blurring of focus, not so far as to see human behavior as a wearying repetition of pre-categorized gestures in the cynic manner of Thersites. Within the differential range bracketed by these extremes the tragic area is found. Both the unthinking animal participation in experience of a Cressida and the habits of reductive abstraction of a Thersites are sub-tragic, and they have in common an incapacity to think and feel simultaneously in direct response to events.

The physical staging of Troilus's disillusionment constructs a visual paradigm of the play's inventory of the prerequisites of tragic attitude. The play is crypto-tragic, rather than tragic for one major reason. In *Hamlet*, with which this play imaginatively over-laps in thematic and linguistic terms, the protagonist includes within himself a Troilus, a Thersites and a Ulysses, but these components are not analytically but temporally arranged, the trauma of disillusionment in *Hamlet* inaugurates the action, it does not culminate it as here. The Thersitian component of Hamlet's nature is comprehended in, as it is a defensive expression of, his incapacity to feel with current precision after the shock of his mother's betrayal. Gertrude and Cressida are, morally, sisters, neither is intrinsically vicious, neither in any way transcends the linear progression of forces to which they are successively subjected. Through intelligent suffering, Hamlet achieves a Ulyssian patience in relation to himself as well as to the world around him. The crucial fact for tragedy is that these various codes of response to the harshness of events should produce and condition each other, not merely compete in a world of schematized alternatives. The hunger for truth and the disturbing factor of raw libido; the contradictory wishes for experience and serenity; derision *and* assent are the dynamics of tragedy. They must, however, be composed into a mutually qualifying whole not merely isolated and diagnosed. *Troilus and Cressida* is the taxonomical prelude to Shakespeare's mature tragedies. It lacks the coordinating agent, a psychologically comprehensive protagonist.

As it is, *Troilus and Cressida* is a brilliant dramatic mutation. In its analytical brilliance we follow it as if we were writing the play with Shakespeare. It provides a spectrum of life-visions, or value systems within the action itself. The play provides the dramatic equivalent of a colossal Rorschach inkblot test, each reader confronted by separate alternatives, identifies where he must, and thereby pragmatically indicates his own sympathetic stance within the heteronomy of its suspended judgments. (pp. 156-59)

R. J. Kaufmann, "Ceremonies for Chaos: The Status of 'Troilus and Cressida'," in ELH, *Vol. 32, No. 2, June, 1965, pp. 139-59.*

NORMAN RABKIN (essay date 1965)

[*In the following excerpt, Rabkin presents a detailed examination of the double-plot structure in* Troilus and Cressida, *an issue previously discussed by William Empson (1935), and he contends that through such analysis the play's thematic unity is revealed. Rabkin observes a continually developing concern in both the love plot and the war plot with the metaphysical problem of value and its relation to time. He argues that each plot presents a female character (in the love plot, Cressida; in the war plot, Helen) whose worth is questioned, as well as a male character (in the love plot, Troilus; in the war plot, Achilles) whose values are exaggerated through a subjective willfulness. Rabkin also notes the parallel function of time in both plots, which, he explains, is an organic process that undermines notions of objective value. He concludes that Shakespeare finally asserts that "value exists not in the subjective will of the valuer or in the object he sees, but only in that object as time disposes of it." Thus time is related to value in both plots of the play. The problem of determining value in* Troilus and Cressida *has also been considered by Una Ellis-Fermor (1945) and Terence Eagleton (1967), while the role of time in the play has been discussed by G. Wilson Knight (1930), S. C. Sen Gupta (1950), L. C. Knights (1951), D. A. Traversi (1968), and R. A. Yoder (1972).*]

Ideas have a life in [*Troilus and Cressida*] that they rarely have on the stage. What gives them that life is the way in which, built into a double-plot structure, they are made dramatic. *Troilus and Cressida* is perhaps the most brilliant of all instances of the double plot, that convention which gives a play the power to convey a complex theme implicitly through action and ironic language. Through the use of the double plot, as in other ways through other conventions, Shakespeare and his contemporaries turned ideas into theater so that the two could scarcely be separated. Our understanding of the significance of the double plot has long since enriched our understanding of a number of Shakespeare's plays. I should like to argue, by an analysis of the structure of *Troilus and Cressida,* that "the primary reason for [the play's] baffling, ambivalent final effect lies" not, as Professor Kimbrough claims, "with Shakespeare" [see Additional Bibliography], but with our failure to recognize in Shakespeare's use of a dominant convention of his theater the key to the meaning of one of his greatest plays.

Despite the smoothness of the bond between them, *Troilus and Cressida* presents two distinct plots, as independent of one another as any in Shakespeare: the affair between Troilus and Cressida on the one hand, and the Greek ruse to bring Achilles back into the war and thus end it on the other. Each plot, or action, has its own beginning, middle, and end, and would in itself constitute a strong enough line for a play of its own; neither plot depends for its outcome on the course of the other. Even in such scenes as the Trojan council meeting, where Troilus irrelevantly speaks of the taking of a wife, or the exchange of the prisoners, which deeply concerns the progress of each action, the two plot lines remain separate. With its discrete plots which paradoxically seem to comprise a unified action, *Troilus and Cressida* resembles other plays in which Shakespeare modifies the convention of the double plot—*A Midsummer Night's Dream* and *King Lear,* for example, where we begin with a strong sense of separate plot lines only to learn that they are inextricably intertwined. Whether the illusion Shakespeare creates in a given play is that the actions are independent of one another or that they are, as in *Troilus and Cressida,* part of a complex and integrated whole, the result is always a structural sophistication so purely Shakespearean that perhaps we should not be surprised at the reluctance of centuries to recognize a shared convention in the double plots of Shakespeare and his contemporaries.

In *Troilus and Cressida* the double-plot structure makes possible a thematic exposition, aesthetic rather than conceptual despite the philosophizing for which the play is so remarkable, that makes one realize most poignantly the inadequacy of rational analysis. Only by observing particulars in the order in which they appear, by considering each moment of the play in the contexts of both the whole play and the point at which it occurs, and by recognizing the effects achieved by the parallels between the autonomous plots can we stay clear of the traps into which the critic tempted to make *a priori* statements may fall. My concern is thematic, to be sure. I am not, however, interested in formulating a "one- or two-word subject about which the [play] makes an ineffable statement" [as stated by Sheldon Sacks in his *Fiction and the Shape of Belief*], but rather with determining by an inductive reading of the whole play the principle which unifies and gives meaning to its discrete elements. The analysis of a work whose genius is primarily structural must itself be structural.

Like a glittering and intricate spiderweb, the totality of the play seems implicated in its every node. Almost any point will

do for a start. Let us take the end of the second scene, for example. Watching the heroes return from battle, Cressida and Pandarus have been fencing with each other, Pandarus maladroitly attempting to arouse his niece's interest in a young man toward whom she shows every evidence of indifference. As her uncle leaves, however, Cressida tells us that she actually prizes Troilus more than Pandarus can praise him:

> Yet hold I off. Women are angels, wooing:
> Things won are done; joy's soul lies in the doing.
> That she belov'd knows naught that knows not this:
> Men prize the thing ungain'd more than it is.
>
> [I. ii. 286-89]

Conveyed in the first sententious speech of the play, Cressida's pessimism comes as a greater shock than the more conventional cynicism she has been demonstrating to her uncle, and is an important touch in a character study which will attempt to explain a notoriously inexplicable infidelity. But, like many such speeches in Shakespeare, Cressida's scene-ending soliloquy does not merely characterize: it raises a question. Is she right? Has a moment no value beyond its duration? Is expectation more satisfying than fulfillment? Is there no survival value in achievement?

As might be expected, Shakespeare is not overtly setting out the thematic conclusion of the play, but he is preparing us for the exposition, sounding his theme in the minor so that we will think back, often and crucially, to Cressida's statement as new facets of the theme are revealed. Already we may be called back by the odd similarity of Cressida's self-justification to a remark that Troilus has just made, with savage irony, in the only other soliloquy so far in the play:

> Peace, you ungracious clamours! peace, rude sounds!
> Fools on both sides, Helen must needs be fair
> When with your blood you daily paint her thus!
>
> [I. i. 89-91]

Helen's value, that is, lies in the doing: if so many men fight for her, she must be worth fighting for. Like Cressida's soliloquy, Troilus' sardonic jibe merely foreshadows the arguments to come as to the subjectivity of value; but like hers it has a dramatic significance that no one can miss who knows the old story, for, finding the fickle Helen "too starved a subject" [I. i. 93] for his sword, Troilus immediately and ironically turns to the praise of Cressida.

His theme adumbrated in the love plot, Shakespeare now begins to develop it in the war plot. Listening to the elaborate argumentation of the first Greek council scene (I. iii.), the audience may be rather surprised to recognize in a discussion of matters that seem far removed from the love life of the Trojans a concern with the same questions that have already been raised within the walls of Ilium. (pp. 265-67)

Again a metaphysical question underlies the speeches: what is the value of a man? When can one be sure of that value? The answer suggested by Agamemnon and Nestor is that, as the medium in which fortune distributes adversity, time will ultimately distinguish true value. As the play develops, the idea of time as a process which defines and identifies value will grow increasingly complex and important as its role in both actions becomes clear; here it is being suggested for the first time, and as yet it may not seem particularly relevant.

What follows immediately has all too often been taken as a formulation of the play's theme. Ulysses' great sermon on "the specialty of rule" delights the ear and lingers in the memory;

it is a gorgeously imagined setting of an Elizabethan commonplace. Moreover, it is crucial in the play. Seldom if ever, however, does such a set piece explicitly enunciate the theme of a play by Shakespeare, and we should not simply assume that it does here. Brief reflection, in fact, should be sufficient for the realization that Ulysses' remarks do not hit dead center. (p. 268)

The idea which most looks forward to vigorous development in the play is that of time, whose winnowing function has been described by Agamemnon and Nestor. Already in this scene Ulysses, who is to make the play's most famous speech about time, speaks of it in an odd fashion as he proposes his trick to Nestor:

> I have a young conception in my brain;
> Be you my time to bring it to some shape.
>
> [I. iii. 312-13]

Time is thus a midwife, attendant at an organic process. (pp. 268-69)

[By] the end of the first council scene our attention has been drawn to a question of value and to a notion of time. How these matters are to be related to the play's theme is a larger question that in characteristically Shakespearean fashion withholds its question until later. But after the scurrilous interlude in which we first see Achilles, Ajax, and Thersites, the play takes up these matters again. Once again the scene is a council meeting, this time within Troy. And once again, as if to underline the symmetry between I. iii. and II. ii., rational men make a mockery of reason: as Ulysses in the Greek camp both praised and exemplified the reason that stands in opposition to the universal wolf of appetite, yet found no better use for his reason than to trick Achilles, so Hector in Troy sees and rationally understands what action is necessary, yet impulsively acts against his own decision. Like the scene before Agamemnon's tent, the scene in Priam's palace concerns the war plot, but at a crucial moment in the argument Troilus reveals that his own attitude toward the return of Helen is based on his attitude toward Cressida; and at this moment the developing theme of the play begins to coalesce.

Like the Greeks, the Trojans are reassessing their situation: and like them they discover almost immediately that the attempt to justify what is happening to them leads to a discussion of value.

> *Hect.* Brother, she is not worth what she doth cost
>   The holding.
> *Tro.*   What's aught but as 'tis valu'd?
>
> [II. ii. 51-2]

During the course of the argument, Troilus lets us understand what he meant, in the play's first soliloquy, by his jibe at Helen. To Hector, Helen's value is an objective quantity which, measured against the manhood lost in her defense, makes her surrender a moral necessity: "What merit's in that reason which denies / The yielding of her up?" [II. ii. 24-5]. Reason is the key word here, for objective evaluation is a rational process. (pp. 269-70)

Is Hector right in arguing that reason perceives value, or is Troilus in proposing that will projects value upon the object? Shakespeare insists that we be at least aware of the consequences of Troilus' belief, for the hero's most persuasive argument [II. ii. 61-96] is ended by the unanswerable screams of Cassandra:

> Our firebrand brother Paris burns us all.
> Cry Trojans, cry! a Helen and a woe!
> Cry, cry! Troy burns, or else let Helen go.
>
> [II. ii. 110-12]

The compressed argumentation of II. ii., then, has spelled out a dialectic that we have already seen developed in the first council scene; even more interestingly, it has translated that dialectic from its first adumbration in the initial soliloquies of the hero and heroine of the love plot to parallel arguments about will by Ulysses and Hector in the political world of the war plot. Most interestingly of all, through a bold device Shakespeare calls attention to the symmetrically matched investigations of a single metaphysical question in the two plots. At the climax of Troilus' argument, the moment at which he must most convincingly advocate his proto-existentialist ethic, the willful hero makes an analogy between the two actions in which he is concerned:

> I take to-day a wife, and my election
> Is led on in the conduct of my will,
> My will enkindled by mine eyes and ears....
>
> [II. ii. 61-3]

Immediately one sees the similarity between Helen and Cressida as foci of action who by one standard are worthless, and by another infinitely valuable.

In the main plot Cressida is going to remain the focus of the question of value. In the subplot, however, the same question is going to be asked most insistently not about Helen but about Achilles. Thus, avoiding the symmetry another dramatist might have attempted, Shakespeare creates the illusion of a universe that is not only coherent but also multitudinously rich. The kaleidoscopic fashion in which the dramatist begins to formulate the theme in his subplot in terms of one character only to complete it in terms of another is one of the marks of his genius in the play.

The next scene begins as another depressing interlude in which Achilles, Ajax, Thersites, and company revile each other—note how little of the Troilus and Cressida plot has been generated so far—but the scene grows more significant as Troilus' question, "What's aught but as 'tis valu'd?" becomes Achilles' question. The warrior has "much attribute," Agamemnon concedes to Patroclus; yet, because Achilles does not regard his own virtues virtuously, because he is "in self-assumption greater / Than in the note of judgment" [II. iii. 124-25], because he overvalues himself, Achilles is losing the respect of his colleagues. There is a fatal disparity between the actual, inherent value of the hero, and the opinion of that value which Achilles holds. (pp. 271-72)

In terms of both plot and theme, the exposition of the play is now over in both actions and the development section about to begin. Each plot has presented a woman who, because of the attitudes of those about her, raises the metaphysical question of value; and each has introduced as central male character a man whose patently exaggerated evaluation—of Cressida in Troilus' case, of himself in Achilles'—has been attacked as willful, a matter of blood by a character notably concerned with reason and its relation to social order. As the third act opens, Shakespeare leads us back to the love plot. (pp. 272-73)

As the scene in which Troilus and Cressida finally get together, III. ii. stands at the center of the play. Not surprisingly, it picks up and develops the still emerging theme of the piece, once again simultaneously exposing a number of that theme's facets, but this time fully revealing it. In the first place, as everyone has noticed, the sensuality of Troilus' language gives away the quality of his love; more interestingly, if affirms the accuracy of Hector's unanswered charge that Troilus is moved by will, or blood, rather than by reason:

> I am giddy; expectation whirls me round.
> Th' imaginary relish is so sweet
> That it enchants my sense. What will it be
> When that the wat'ry palates taste indeed
> Love's thrice-repured nectar?
>
> [III. ii. 18-22]

But this is not all. In his fear that expectation must exceed fulfillment . . . the lover shows himself in precise agreement with Cressida's initial reason for withholding herself from love: "Men prize the thing ungain'd more than it is."

Again: what is the relation between the thing and the value men place on it? Such repeated asking of the question—in relation to Achilles, his reputation, and his opinion of himself; to Helen, her intrinsic worthlessness, and the value that has already produced seven years of war; and now to the love of Troilus and Cressida—makes us recognize the justice of the epithet "problem play." As Troilus suggests a position new for him, the crucial scene hints at the play's answer to its basic question:

> Praise us as we are tasted; allow us as we prove.
> Our head shall go bare till merit crown it. No
> perfection in reversion shall have a praise in
> present. We will not name desert before his
> birth, and, being born, his addition shall be
> humble.
>
> [III. ii. 90-5]

With its suggestion that time will tell, Troilus' speech recalls the words of Agamemnon and Nestor at the Greek council meeting; moreover, it picks up the organic metaphors in which first Agamemnon, then Ulysses, and finally Nestor couched their discussion of time. (pp. 273-74)

The incessant personification of time in *Troilus and Cressida* is astonishing. Time is a monster, a witch, an arbitrator, a robber, a fashionable host; it is envious and calumniating, grows old and forgets itself, and walks hand in hand with Nestor. To recognize such a treatment of time, one need not agree with Professor G. Wilson Knight that time is the "arch-enemy," the issue on which the "love-interest turns"[see excerpt above, 1930]; but one must note the play's peculiar emphasis on the organic, almost personal nature of metaphysical process. The answer to Troilus' optimistic faith in the world's ability to meet his expectations of it is roundly answered by what the end of III. ii. tells us: Cressida, like Troilus and Pandarus, is defined not by wishful thinking but by what each will become in time, and action which is not guided by that realization is going to come a cropper.

At the center of the play, then, the theme which has been taking shape from the beginning has become full and clear. As if by design, Shakespeare chooses this moment to stage the turning point in the action of the main plot, the making of the bargain which will send Cressida to the Greeks. The trade of prisoners naturally involves the war as well as the private affairs of Troilus and so we are back in the war subplot almost immediately. Again, if the play's structure is not a matter of

conscious design, one must marvel at the intuitive genius which arranges that, immediately after the climactic exposition of the theme of the relation of time to value in the main plot, that theme should be dramatized with equal emphasis and clarity in the subplot. Thematically, III. ii. and III. iii., one in the main, the other in the subplot, are the crucial scenes of the entire play.

Ulysses' trick has worked, and the neglected Achilles is driven to investigate the cause of the derision he sees aimed at him. Merit, he sees, has little to do with reputation. . . . Having noticed that his deeds do seem to have been forgotten, Achilles cannot deny what Ulysses has been saying, and he is ready to hear his shrewd opponent's explanation of the shortness of reputation:

> Time hath, my lord, a wallet at his back,
> Wherein he puts alms for oblivion,
> A great-siz'd monster of ingratitudes.
> Those scraps are good deeds past, which are devour'd
> As fast as they are made, forgot as soon
> As done. Perseverance, dear my lord,
> Keeps honour bright. To have done is to hang
> Quite out of fashion, like a rusty mail
> In monumental mock'ry.
>
> [III. iii. 145-53]

How many moments of the play crystallize here: not only what Agamemnon and Nestor have already told us about time's determination of value, but also all that we have learned in the last scene. . . . (pp. 276-77)

Ulysses' speech is profoundly pessimistic. For if the love plot has been telling us that value resides not in the valuer (Troilus, Achilles), but in the true nature of the object (Cressida, Achilles), the war plot makes explicit what the ritual at the end of III. ii. dramatized: even the value in the object itself will be defined—and generally that definition is by a process of erosion—by time. By the kind of irony that the double plot in the hands of a master makes possible, the point is dramatically reinforced. As Achilles laments the course his career has taken in time, arrangements are in the making to take Cressida away from Troilus while simultaneously the lovers are enjoying what they take to be the sealing of their love's compact. When we next see Troilus he will be innocent of his impending loss, and the irony will recur. And when Troilus discovers the grim irony of his happiness, he will respond to it in a terse remark that Achilles might as well have made to Ulysses: "How my achievements mock me" [IV. ii. 69]. (pp. 277-78)

The last two acts consist primarily in the working out of the ironic prophecies in both plots. In the war plot the decision to keep Helen eventuates not in the glory that Troilus predicted, but in her continuing degradation (recall Diomedes' opinion) and in the utterly ignoble death of Hector himself, presaging the final catastrophe Cassandra has announced. Like a vengeful deity time has decided the debate in the Trojan camp. And in the love plot we have watched Cressida, in a ritualistic prefiguration of her future, passing lightly from the kisses of one Greek to the next. With Troilus we look on at her final act of betrayal. . . . Troilus' last words reveal that he has learned at last the harsh reality that a man is what time proves he is, not what the optimist wishes him to be:

> Hence, broker, lackey; ignomy and shame
> Pursue thy life, and live aye with thy name.
>
> [V. x. 33-4]

Perhaps it is a signal of the difference between *Troilus and Cressida* and most of Shakespeare's plays that the idealistic hero, with whom for all our awareness of his error we have been led consistently to sympathize, should utter as a last speech words that so clearly reveal the diminution of his stature. Similar reduction affects us in the last appearance of other leading characters whose careers we have followed with concern: Cressida feebly chastizing herself for a disposition to follow Diomedes that she is scarcely capable of recognizing as contemptible, Achilles wretchedly crying the triumph won in fact by his roughneck vassals, Pandarus suddenly aged and bequeathing to the audience his venereal disease. Pandarus, whose coarse and heartless grumbling ends the play, is a paradigm of all the play's characters. In the magical conclusion of III. ii. we have virtually seen etymology staged as Pandarus ironically prophesies the way in which he will become his name, and at the end we see the process complete. Regardless of their own intentions and the best potentialities within them, the major characters of the two plots have been transformed by a process over which none of them has control. That process is time, a time presented so consistently in organic terms that one comes finally to understand its inevitability: it grows according to its own will, not according to the desires of any individual. And that process is the play's answer to the question of value: value exists not in the subjective will of the valuer or in the object he sees, but only in that object as time disposes of it. If this is not a satisfactory answer to a legitimate philosophical question, one must admit that very few readers have suspected that it was Shakespeare's intention in *Troilus and Cressida* to satisfy their skepticism or dispel their pessimism. But the play provides another kind of satisfaction which one seeks more legitimately perhaps in the theater, the aesthetic satisfaction of recognizing a structure brilliantly animated and made coherent by its complex relation to a thematic center. (pp. 279-80)

> *Norman Rabkin, "'Troilus and Cressida': The Uses of the Double Plot," in* Shakespeare Studies: An Annual Gathering of Research, Criticism, and Reviews, *Vol. I, 1965, pp. 265-82.*

TERENCE EAGLETON   **(essay date 1967)**

[*Eagleton, an English Marxist critic, is best known for his works on critical theory, including* Marxism and Literary Criticism *(1976) and* Literary Theory: An Introduction *(1983). In his* Shakespeare and Society *(1967), excerpted below, Eagleton examines the tension that exists between individual spontaneous action and social responsibility in Shakespeare's plays. Eagleton notes that in* Troilus and Cressida *reality is a public process and a common creation and that individual identities and values are created through the mediation or reflection of other individuals. Such a process, he says, is not entirely satisfactory because it leads to the circularity of conferred value and "a loss of authenticity." Opposed to this method of establishing reality and identity, he perceives the authenticity and spontaneity of Troilus, who achieves self-definition only outside a hostile society. Eagleton argues that even though Troilus's view is socially irresponsible and, therefore, "inherently tragic," it nonetheless allows Troilus a genuine "integrity of self." He concludes that although socially responsible values should fuse with values that are authentic and spontaneous, "the play can find no way of making this fusion." The problem of the social order versus the private will in* Troilus and Cressida *has also been considered by Denton J. Snider (1890), G. Wilson Knight (1930), H. B. Charlton (1937), Winifred M. T. Nowottny (1954), and R. A. Yoder (1972).*]

In Act III Scene 3 of *Troilus and Cressida,* Ulysses tries to jolt Achilles into action by pointing out that there is no such thing as private experience:

> . . . no man is the lord of anything,
> Though in and of him there be much consisting,
> Till he communicate his parts to others;
> Nor doth he of himself know them for aught
> Till he behold them formed in th'applause
> Where th'are extended . . . .
>
>   [III. iii. 115-20]

Ulysses is not merely arguing that uncommunicated qualities are inferior or useless; the first three lines of the quotation could be taken as meaning this, and then the argument would be no more than the familiar point that man is a 'sociable' being, at his best when in relationship with others. But the real force of that 'lord of anything' comes through in the next lines, where Ulysses is saying that uncommunicated qualities don't have any real existence at all; a man is not simply known to others through communication, he can only know his own experience by putting it in a communicable form. He does not know his own reality as an individual and then communicate it: the reality forms in the communication. The kind of separation between himself and society which Achilles is trying to force is therefore serious: a man who contracts out of public life is contracting out of reality; he is dead. Individual identity is a public creation: a man is what his society makes of him; he has no meaning outside its response. It is, in fact, impossible to stand completely outside society, to disengage totally; the disengagement itself will usually be just another symptom of the society, part of its whole reality, as the cynicism of Achilles and Thersites is part of the general sickness they analyse and attack.

Troilus and Cressida suggests again and again that reality is a public process, a common creation, and that the play seems to confirm Ulysses's view in its own techniques. This is evident particularly in the way that individuals come to be known through the descriptions of others: in the first scene of the play Pandarus describes Cressida's qualities to Troilus, and Troilus exclaims:

> . . . I tell thee I am mad
> In Cressid's love. Thou answer'st 'She is fair'—
> Pourest in the open ulcer of my heart—
> Her eyes, her hair, her cheek, her gait, her voice,
> *Handlest* in thy discourse . . . .
>
>   [I. i. 51-5]

The physical effect of 'handlest' is significant: it begins the suggestion, expanded throughout the play, that describing someone to someone else is more than a second-hand process, it is a way of actually mediating and conveying their reality to another, re-creating them as individuals. Cressida's reality, for Troilus, is at first totally in the possession of Pandarus: 'I cannot come to Cressid but by Pandar' [I. i. 95]. In the next scene, Pandarus reverses the process by describing Troilus to Cressida. Achilles re-creates the other Greeks by enacting them to Patroclus; Ulysses speaks of Aeneas 'translating' Troilus to him [IV. v. 112]; Agamemnon refuses to be answered 'in second voice' when confronting Achilles [II. iii. 140]. The image of the merchant, the mediator, the go-between dominates the play, most obviously in Pandarus, but also in the plotting of Ulysses to set Ajax on to duel with Hector: two individuals are brought together through and in terms of a third. Ulysses's remark to Nestor when he first conceives the idea of choosing Ajax to face Hector is significant of this process:

> I have a young conception in my brain;
> Be you my time to bring it to some shape.
>
> [I. iii. 312-13]

Nestor will mediate Ulysses's own idea to him, he will be the element through which the idea becomes real. Two people can create, reciprocally, a reality: in the relationships of Troilus and Cressida, Nestor and Ulysses, Achilles and Patroclus, a whole version of experience is created and sustained, and objective experience can come, somehow, to exist in terms of this relationship. Achilles and Patroclus create their own versions of the other Greeks in a way which shapes the Greeks' actual behaviour:

> And in the imitation of these twain—
> Who, as Ulysses says, opinion crowns
> With an imperial voice—many are infect.
>
> [I. iii. 185-87]

Objective reality is moulded to the distortions of the personal version: Achilles imitates the Greeks, who in turn imitate his imitations. In a similar way the reality of Troy as an unconquered city takes its being, not from itself, but from the inactivity of the Greeks:

> . . . To end a tale of length,
> Troy in our weakness stands, not in her strength.
>
> [I. iii. 136-37]

People, things, events can have their being 'in' other realities, other contexts, existing only in terms of these.

Reality, according to Ulysses, is a common creation, and because of this it is relative: it is the shared possession of a group of men, and can change as they change. It is relative, too, because a number of different versions of reality may co-exist, each thinking itself the centre. This is most evident in Troilus and Cressida themselves. . . . They see themselves, now, in terms of each other: they find their real, authentic selves in the new reality of the love-relationship:

> I have a kind of self resides with you;
> But an unkind self, that it self will leave
> To be another's fool . . . .
>
> [III. ii. 148-50]

Love makes a new self by fusing the two individuals, and so to leave each other is to leave themselves, to desert their authenticity. This is why Troilus, confronted with Cressida's unfaithfulness, reacts by seeing her as two people: 'This is, and is not, Cressid' [V. ii. 146]. Cressida to him is the Cressida of their relationship; she has no meaning or existence for him outside this context, as Achilles, according to Ulysses, has no existence outside the defining judgements of his society. People and things seem to draw their meanings from their contexts, but because there are many different contexts, all liable to change, there can be continual confusion about 'real' meanings and values. Cressida, before her defection, thinks of her love for Troilus as standing at the centre of reality:

> . . . the strong base and building of my love
> Is as the very centre of the earth,
> Drawing all things to it.
>
> [IV. ii. 103-05]

and Achilles also sees himself as a center: he

> . . . never suffers matter of the world
> Enter his thoughts, save such as doth revolve
> And ruminate himself . . . .
>
> [II. iii. 186-88]

Ajax, also, is a center, although a created one. Personal reality, according to Ulysses, is the property of the whole community, but reciprocally the whole common reality can become focused in one individual, who then exists in terms of it, as its pivot. Ajax is selected by the Greeks to represent them to the Trojans:

> It is suppos'd
> He that meets Hector issues from our choice;
> And choice, being mutual act of all our souls,
> Makes merit her election, and doth boil,
> As 'twere from forth us all, a man distill'd
> Out of our virtues; who miscarrying,
> What heart receives from hence a conquering part,
> To steel a strong opinion to themselves?
>
> [I. iii. 346-53]

Ajax, as the Greeks' representative, is supposed to be created out of their shared decision, 'distilled' from their pooled ideas and opinions; their cause will be entirely in his keeping, and will stand or fall by his personal action. The reflexive movement is clear again, as it was with the imitations of Achilles: Ajax is a created agent whose actions will in turn mould the fortunes of his creators. He will be the element to mediate them, as a community, to the Trojans: they will 'dress him up in voices' [I. iii. 381], make him the living embodiment of their cause, defined and controlled by them. (pp. 13-18)

Helen, for the Trojans, is also a commonly created reality, the centre of a whole world-view. She exists for them only in terms of this: their discussion of her in Act II Scene 2 is in fact a discussion of the war she symbolises. She is the pivot of a quarrel in which the individual honours of the Trojans are tied up, and in talking about her they are talking about themselves. They define themselves, individually, in terms of the self-expressive action which the war she symbolises affords them, and their self-definition, their sense of personal meaning and identity, is thus in and through her. She represents a quarrel

> Which hath our several honours all engag'd
> To make it gracious.
>
> [II. ii. 124-25]

as Troilus says, and Hector declares that keeping Helen is

> . . . a cause that hath no mean dependence
> Upon our joint and several dignities.
>
> [II. ii. 192-93]

Helen thus serves the same purpose for the Trojans as Ajax serves for the Greeks: she mediates their own sense of themselves to them, she is their living reflection, the arch which Ulysses describes to Achilles as reverberating back the human voice, or the gate of steel which 'receives and renders back' the sun's heat [III. iii. 122]. She ceases to exist for the Trojans as a person and becomes merely a point of reference for their individual self-expression, lending them a tenuous unity. The evident difference between the idealised Helen of Troilus's speeches and the flirt we see on stage is intended to underline the danger involved in this kind of seeing. It is not only the danger involved in the damage done to Helen as a person, the fact that she, like Ajax, is reduced to a pawn while being idealised as a pivot, implicitly compared, by Troilus, to merchandise; it is the danger involved in the fact that a created meaning may be quite different from an actual meaning—the process of reality-making may be completely at odds with things as they really are.

The same problem is there with the Greeks. If it is true, as Ulysses says, that we know ourselves only in terms of each other, then intrinsic meanings and values seem to be cancelled; a man is the sum-total of his relationships, and his reality as a person is flexible, it may alter as the whole pattern of relationships alters. The fact that personal identity is involved with the whole process of communication which is society can be seen as positive: it leaves no room for the individualism of Troilus, affirming the need for personal action to be responsible, responsive to the estimates of a whole society. But it can lead, also, to bewildering relativism, as Thersites's baiting of Achilles and Patroclus makes clear:

> ACHILLES . . . Come, what's Agamemnon?
> THERSITES Thy commander, Achilles. Then tell me,
>   Patroclus, what's Achilles?
> PATROCLUS Thy Lord, Thersites. Then tell me, I pray
>   thee, what's Thersites?
> THERSITES Thy knower, Patroclus. Then tell me,
>   Patroclus, what art thou?
> PATROCLUS Thou must tell that knowest.
>
> [II. iii. 42-50]

Men, as individuals, are defined and known in terms of their relationships with each other, in constant reciprocity: they possess each other's realities, and Patroclus must ask Thersites about his own identity. Thersites brings the process of reciprocal definition artificially to an end by defining himself in relation to Patroclus rather than to someone else, thus making Patroclus knowable in terms of himself. But in fact the process could go on indefinitely, since Thersites's conception of Patroclus includes his conception of how other people see Patroclus, and how Patroclus sees himself (which again depends on how other people see him). What this brief tracing of the process indicates is that the reality of any one member of the Greek camp can only be described in terms of the realities of all the others, and since all the realities include one another, the process is circular, as Patroclus's clinching remark suggests. The system is enclosed, but it can be traced round indefinitely. Patroclus can only know himself in terms of Thersites ('Thou must tell me that knowest'), but Thersites's own sense of himself is part of a process which includes Patroclus: the answer to the question 'what are you?' for Thersites would have to describe the whole nexus of relationships which includes Patroclus. In fact, Thersites tries to set himself outside the system, to detach himself by defining himself in terms of knowing someone else rather than being known: by doing this he can seem to take an absolute stand. But the dominant feeling of the interchange is the feeling of circularity, the circularity of Ulysses's reverberating arch; society is a continuous and changing inter-definition, and no self, no meaning or value or action, is fixed. (pp. 18-21)

The Greeks create each other's identities, the Trojans create their own values, and in both cases the process is circular and self-sustaining: there is no appeal outside the existential context of human action to an absolute norm, the process can appeal only to itself for justification. The rhythm of circularity dominates the play: activity is seen constantly as self-consuming.

Ulysses sees uncontrolled appetite like this in his famous speech on degree:

> Then everything includes itself in power,
> Power into will, will into appetite;
> And appetite, an universal wolf,
> So doubly seconded with will and power,
> Must make perforce an universal prey,
> And last eat up himself.
>
> [I. iii. 119-24]

Appetite consumes power and will (which have consumed everything else), and strengthened by these can more quickly consume everything and itself: the process is circular, but it is also a continual telescoping, a continual increase of bulk and power which drives the circle on at a faster rate. As with Hamlet's mother, increase of appetite grows from what it feeds on.

Self-praise without reference to the judgements of others is another example of circularity: Aeneas reminds himself that

> The worthiness of praise distains his worth,
> If that the prais'd himself bring the praise forth . . . .
>
> [I. iii. 241-42]

and Agamemnon's description of pride to Achilles makes this clearer:

> He that is proud eats up himself. Pride is his
> own glass, his own trumpet, his own chronicle;
> and whatever praises itself but in the deed devours the deed in the praise.
>
> [II. iii. 154-57]

Praise without deed is self-devouring because it is an evaluation closed to the judgement of others: only through action, public self-disclosure, can self-judgement be verified and sealed. Achilles's pride is self-conferred value, without regard either to intrinsic merit or the conferred merit of others: in this condition, objective values and proportions are lost as surely as they are in Troilus's private conferment of value. . . . (pp. 26-7)

Circularity comes from conferred value: self-conferred value as with Achilles, individually conferred value as with Troilus, mutually conferred value as with the Greeks. In all three cases, the permanent, intrinsic values which Ulysses can advance as a theoretical framework for action (I.3) are cancelled.

But intrinsic values seem no more helpful as a guide to action. The dissension in the Greek camp shows the failure of rational weighing and evaluating as a motive to action: the Greeks' rationality devours itself as surely as does the Trojans' activity. Reason obstructs itself: the very closeness and complexity of its functioning becomes a barrier to the action it is meant to motivate. The obstruction is felt as a radical flaw in the nature of action itself:

> The ample proposition that hope makes
> In all designs begun on earth below
> Fails in the promis'd largeness; checks and disasters
> Grow in the veins of actions highest rear'd,
> As knots, by the conflux of meeting sap,
> Infects the sound pine, and diverts his grain
> Tortive and errant from his course of growth.
>
> [I. iii. 2-9]

Reason is necessary for action to be responsible, but it strangles spontaneity: Agamemnon's image does not juxtapose two different kinds of action, rational and spontaneous, but suggests that an action which is somehow in itself spontaneous, organically developing, is meeting with obstruction when it actually emerges into the realm of human, practical activity. But seeing action in this way is part of the trouble: Agamemnon has unconsciously revealed the flaw in the very imagery he uses to talk about it. Agamemnon's conception of action is essentialist: he sees a project, a whole harmonious design, as somehow existing in itself, apart from the human beings involved in executing it; human action, according to this view, is merely an implementation of what is already wholly formed, somewhere below the surface of actuality. The project has to be 'embodied', as Ajax is seen as giving 'our project's life' a 'shape of sense'[I. iii. 384], and breakdown between conception and embodiment is always possible. The Trojans see action as existential, and thus avoid the 'checks and disasters' of the Greeks, while running into others: for them, there is no gap between conception and execution, since the conception is only fully formed in the process of execution—Helen becomes meaningful in the process of fighting over her. Action for the Trojans is therefore spontaneous, conception and execution are united. But the elimination of the gap between conception and action can be the elimination of reason, of social responsibility: it is difficult to apply rational controls to pure spontaneity.

Spontaneity, too, is primarily personal, the expression of the individual's authentic impulses without obstruction. The Greeks think in terms of a project which involves them all, as a body: it is 'our works' which Agamemnon discusses. Action is social, and historical as well: the action of the present can be seen in logical continuity with actions of the past, and a comparison of past and present may clarify the situation: Agamemnon sees that the past projects of the Greeks, 'whereof we have record' [I. iii. 14], have shown similar tendencies to the present. For the Trojans, action is individual and eternally present: the war is a personal exercise for them, a means to personal honour, and the past is 'strewn with husks' [IV. v. 166], dead achievements. The Greeks, camped outside the city, see the war as a permanent condition: the Trojans sally out to the field and return to carry on their private lives in the city. Helen unites them, but it is their 'several honours', their 'joint and several dignities' which are engaged: they remain, essentially, individuals, seeing action as personal self-definition, brought temporarily together in the same quarrel. They are associated in the war, rather than bound, like the Greeks, into a single, interdependent community. (pp. 28-31)

Troilus and Achilles both deny the rational, and thus the socially responsible, aspects of action; as a result, they gain in different ways a kind of authenticity, a truth-to-self and refusal to falsify, which in itself is valuable. The idea of intrinsic values, of rational weighing, can remain intact as long as it stays theoretical, inactive; as soon as it is put into operation it becomes a situation-ethics as relative and shifting as the fluid values of the Trojans. This is most evident in the actual political manoeuvring of Ulysses and Nestor, in trying to induce Achilles to fight. The manoeuvring is indeed governed by rational principle, by a careful weighing of the intrinsic merits of Achilles, Ajax, Hector, and their interrelations; but in practice it leads to a merely tactical attitude to life, stifling authenticity. (pp. 31-2)

[Troilus] can achieve authenticity only outside the network of weighed causes and consequences which is society. He creates, within society, an area of personal freedom where he can find himself fully: this area is his relationship with Cressida. The love-relationship with Cressida contains his authentic self, it

is the way he defines himself; when Cressida is snatched away, he is alienated from himself. And it is society which snatches her away: his real self is destroyed by the pressures of a society which is seen as external, hostile to self-expression, which removes Cressida from him for rational, social reasons he sees as worthless.

The antagonism between 'reason' and 'intuition', between action based on rational weighing and action based on spontaneous impulse, is an antagonism between the 'social' and the 'authentic' self: between the way a man conceives of himself, and the way society tries to force him to see himself. Troilus is not merely an impetuous Romantic, although this is a possible level of reading: more deeply, he is committed, consciously, to expressing spontaneously his true self in action in a way which puts him outside the control of society. . . . (pp. 32-3)

For Troilus, society is a hostile, repressive mechanism, threatening authentic fulfilment, crippling spontaneity: it is deadening, confining, as action itself is confining. And yet a man cannot totally escape from society, as an impulse cannot escape from hardening into act, sooner or later. Existence as pure potential, pure subjectivity, is ultimately impossible: the self becomes objectified in an action or a social role. Troilus's situation is therefore inherently tragic: he tries to act, in society, without ever seeing himself objectified in an action or a social role.

Social responsibility, then, seems to involve a distortion of spontaneity, a loss of authenticity: it demands reason and tactical skill, a willingness to accept others' definitions of oneself, an ability to see personal self-definition in terms of others and of a whole design. But the problem is that the man who rejects this, although irresponsible, will be, in a false sociey, the most genuine man: in refusing the definitions of society he will be asserting his real self, his authentic passion. . . . Troilus's actions may be done without reflection, but he has in his spontaneity a wholeness which is lacking in the Greeks: he is capable of an integrity of self which contrasts favourably with the fragmented self of an Ajax, composed of other men's scraps.

But ultimately Shakespeare sides with reason, with social responsibility. Social responsibility may entail a damaging loss of authenticity, but it is the only way men can live together, for the moment. It is Diomed's opinion of Helen, not Troilus's, which he accepts:

> For every false drop in her bawdy veins
> A Grecian's life has sunk; for every scruple
> Of her contaminated carrion weight
> A Troyan hath been slain.
>
> [IV. i. 70-3]

The weighing and balancing of drops and scruples is a vital process: this, finally, is the only way responsible human decisions can be reached. What is needed is a fusion of the passionate wholeness of Troilus and the rational responsibility of Ulysses; the search is for a way to make authentic energies socially responsible, to make social responsibility authentic and spontaneous. Ulysses's description of Troilus to Agamemnon is hopelessly wrong, but it points to the ideal requirement:

> . . . For what he has he gives, what thinks he shows,
> Yet gives he not till judgment guide his bounty . . . .
>
> [IV. v. 99-100]

It is 'bounty' which is admired, free and open self-giving which is authentic (he gives what he has and shows what he thinks, without distortion) and yet controlled by judgement.

Another way of seeing this necessary fusion is in Hector's terms, as an amalgam of intrinsic and conferred value. Value must draw its 'estimate and dignity' *both* from its intrinsic worth *and* from the judgement of the prizer: things must somehow be seen simultaneously as they are in themselves, and as they gain meaning in particular human contexts. Human creation and conferment of value is not rejected, but held in fusion with a recognition of inherent meanings. Reason examines these meanings and makes responsible decisions; spontaneity is a matter of human creation, human transfiguration of reality, as love transfigures the world.

This is easy to assert: but the play can find no way of making this fusion. Troilus, in trying to forge a permanent reality out of his love for Cressida, explores one possible fusion and finds it unsuccessful: he tries to make out of the humanly created value of love a reality as fixed and unchanging as a rational principle. (pp. 34-7)

The Greeks, too, try to fuse both kinds of value, by applying fixed, rational principles to existential situations. But all that happens is that the existential situations absorb the principles until they are fixed only in abstraction: the difference between Ulysses's theoretical statement of value and his actual practice makes this plain. The play ends with nothing decided: to be wise is to know things as they are through reason and thus act responsibly; to love is to create human meaning and act spontaneously. The two seem impossible to unite:

> . . . for to be wise and love
> Exceeds man's might; that dwells with gods above.
> [III. ii. 156-57]
> (pp. 37-8)

Terence Eagleton, " 'Troilus and Cressida'," in his Shakespeare and Society: Critical Studies in Shakespearean Drama, *Chatto & Windus, 1967, pp. 13-38.*

D. A. TRAVERSI (essay date 1968)

[*Traversi, an English scholar, has written a number of books on Shakespeare's plays, including* An Approach to Shakespeare *(1938) and* Shakespeare: The Last Phase *(1954). In the introduction to the first of these studies, Traversi proposed to focus his interpretation of the plays on "the word," stating that a critical understanding of Shakespeare's canon "will find its most immediate expression in the language and verse." In the excerpt below, drawn from his second revision of* An Approach to Shakespeare *(1968), Traversi asserts that the weak and helpless nature of the characters in* Troilus and Cressida *reflects the ambiguity which surrounds the value of personal experience in the play. This weakness, says Traversi, makes* Troilus and Cressida *a tragedy not of character, but of situation, and "consists less in the personal suffering of the lovers than in the overriding influence exercised by time upon all human relationship and feelings." His emphasis on "the supremacy of time" concurs with the comments of G. Wilson Knight (1930), S. C. Sen Gupta (1950), L. C. Knights (1951), and Norman Rabkin (1965); but such assessments of the role of time have also been questioned by R. A. Yoder (1972). Traversi also finds Trojan idealism as deficient as Greek reason, a point that runs counter to Knight's interpretation of the play, but one supported by Oscar James Campbell (1938), L. C. Knights (1951), and Terence Eagleton (1967). He contends that the idealism of the Trojans is actually based on sensuality and that Greek rationalism leads only to inaction, and that Shakespeare thus*

intended to underscore the play's uncertain attitude toward experience.]

The close relationship between the values of love and war—one of the most marked features of *Troilus and Cressida*—corresponds to a conception of dramatic unity which, although its antecedents can be traced respectively to the sonnets and the historical plays, was, at the time of writing, new in [Shakespeare's] work. The novelty consists in uniting, in a manner mutually illuminating, a personal theme and its public, "social" extension. Instead of a political conflict objectively observed and commented on by a character (such as Falstaff) who stands, in a sense, outside it, we are presented with a personal issue—the story of two lovers of opposed parties—set in the context of the Trojan War. The situation of the lovers is variously connected with the cleavage between the warring parties to which they respectively belong; and the connection thus dramatically established is further strengthened by the pervasive presence of imagery that suggests disruptive tendencies barely contained within a common way of feeling. The result, in terms of poetic drama, is less a finished and coherent creation than a statement of emotional ambiguity, the reflection of an experience deprived of order and seeking clarification through its own expression.

This ambiguity, in so far as it affects the personal action, is connected with themes that found expression, perhaps in some cases almost simultaneously, in the sonnets. Taking as his point of departure the conventional subject of so many Renaissance sonneteers—the union with his mistress desired by the poet—many of Shakespeare's most individual sonnets convert this theme, which is applied to a variety of human relationships, into an apprehension of the parallel fulfillment and destruction of human values by time. Time, which brings passion to its consummation, implies equally its decline; for the union of love, the very desire for which is inconceivable apart from its temporal setting, demands as a necessary condition an unattainable eternity. The desire for unity is inevitably preceded by a state of separation, and to this tragic separateness it equally inevitably, in the flesh, returns:

> Let me confess that we two must be twain,
> Although our undivided loves are one.
> [Sonnet 36]

The action of time, which is at the same time creative and destructive, which both makes love possible and destroys it, is the unavoidable flaw at the heart of passion. (pp. 324-25)

Troilus and Cressida, then, in so far as it deals with the central pair of lovers, projects a metaphysical situation into the evocation of a personal relationship. The play is, in this as in other respects, the product of a profound uncertainty about the value of experience. The consequence of this uncertainty, as it affects more particularly the love poetry of Troilus, is the corruption of romantic sentiment. Once again, we are taken back to the sonnets. The sensation conveyed by some of the most individual of these poems turns upon a combination of conventional Petrarchan devices with an intense and normally disturbing sensual quality; the familiar image of the lily, to take an obvious example, with its associations of beauty and purity, is transformed by a magnificent juxtaposition of convention and immediacy into the potent corruption of "Lilies that *fester* smell far worse than weeds" [Sonnet 94]. A somewhat similar effect, dramatically presented, is apparent in Troilus' first account of Cressida:

> I tell thee I am mad
> In Cressid's love; thou answer'st "she is fair";
> Pour'st in the open ulcer of my heart
> Her eyes, her hair, her cheek, her gait, her voice,
> Handlest in thy discourse, O that her hand,
> In whose comparison all whites are ink
> Writing their own reproach, to whose soft seizure
> The cygnet's down is harsh, and spirit of sense
> Hard as the palm of ploughman.
>
> [I. i. 51-9]

The underlying convention here is clearly Petrarchan, romantically abstracted from common reality. It makes itself felt in the assertion that Troilus is "mad" for love, in the strained use of "pour'st" and "handlest" to describe Pandarus' speech, in the comparison of Cressida's hand to the "cygnet's down," and in the introduction of "ink" to bring out by contrast its superlative whiteness. But the conventional imagery is transformed, as it were, from within in a manner so closely bound up with the convention that it acts as a corrupting agent, intimately related to the surface sentiment. By giving deep sensuous value to the Petrarchan images, it conveys simultaneously an impression of intense feeling and an underlying lack of content. "Handlest in thy discourse" is a farfetched literary image; but it brings with it a notable keenness of touch which is developed in the contrast between harshness and the "soft seizure" of the cygnet's down, between the hardness of the ploughman's hand and the almost unnatural immediacy of "spirit of sense." Yet the conventional note remains, and with it the feeling that Troilus' passion, for all its surface intensity, has an inadequate foundation, is vitiated by the strained self-pity which allows him to refer to "the open ulcer of my heart," and by the weakness to which he confesses in the course of the same scene: "I am weaker than a woman's tear" [I. i. 9].

It is important to realize why this weakness, which Cressida after her own fashion shares with her lover, does not produce a tragedy of character, but of situation. The tragedy indeed consists less in the personal suffering of the lovers than in the overriding influence exercised by time upon all human relationships and feelings. In *Antony and Cleopatra*, at least while the lovers are united by their feeling for one another, personal emotion has become strong enough to overcome mutability; in *Troilus*, the supremacy of time is never really questioned, and so a consistent status as persons inevitably eludes the lovers. Their weakness reflects the uncertainty of mood in which the play was conceived and to which they owe the peculiar poignancy, more than sentimental and less than tragic, with which they meet their personal fortunes. Antony and Cleopatra, as lovers, are fully drawn human beings because their love, while it lasts and within its own clearly defined limitations, is valid and confers upon their emotions a full personal value. Conversely, the complete realization in evil of Regan and Goneril in *King Lear*, with the sensual ferocity that characterizes their behavior, proves that when he wrote that play, Shakespeare felt himself able to distinguish between the various elements in his moral experience without falling into ambiguity and confusion. Antony and Cleopatra, Regan and Goneril have full reality as characters precisely because they proceed from a clear understanding in their creator of the value of human emotion as distinct from the evil possibilities implied in it. *Troilus and Cressida*, however, with its intuition of passion as vain and transitory, is compatible with no such individuality of presen-

tation; for time, as it is understood in this play, destroys personal values and makes them invalid.

This limiting observation can be applied with equal force to the behavior of both lovers, and through the entire action. Cressida's falseness does not spring from a deep-seated perversity or even from a strong positive attraction for Diomed, but from the mere process of events, from a flaw inherent in the human situation. Her tragedy, such as it is, derives from awareness of her helplessness. We feel it in her pathetic appeal when Troilus prepares to leave her after the night they have spent together:

> Prithee, tarry;
> You men will never tarry,
>
> [IV. ii. 15-16]

and in the moment of self-knowledge in which she tells him:

> I have a kind of self resides with you,
> But an unkind self that itself will leave
> To be another's fool.
>
> [III. ii. 148-50]

There is something in the expression of this uncertainty, half punning and conventional, that makes it difficult to conceive of Cressida as a fully realized being. At most, she lives for us only in the mood of the moment, with barely a sign of that responsibility and consistency which is involved in the very conception of character. Any attempt to subject her inconsistency to a moral judgment, of the kind that the medieval elaborators of this legend had in mind when they denounced her "faithlessness," is out of place because the spirit in which Shakespeare created her made it impossible for her to be shown as really responsible for her actions; and without responsibility there can be no moral evaluation. When she comments in the early part of the play on her refusal to reveal her feelings for Troilus:

> Yet hold I off. Women are angels, wooing;
> Things won are done; joy's soul lies in the doing,
>
> [I. ii. 286-87]

her aphoristic lines are not a revelation of wantonness, but simply an impression of the sense, which constitutes the only true tragedy of this play, of the impossibility, the meaninglessness of constancy in a world where time dominates human relationships and where attraction and separation seem necessary and connected aspects of a single situation.

This impossibility also dominates the poetry of Troilus himself and is there further developed from its original basis in romantic sentiment. Troilus' passion, even before it is faced with the necessity for separation, is strong only in anticipation. The intensity of its sensations is conveyed in a refinement of physical feeling, in an attempt to embody in terms of the senses an insubstantial and incorporeal emotion:

> I am giddy; expectation whirls me round.
> The imaginary relish is so sweet
> That it enchants my sense; what will it be,
> When that the watery palates taste indeed
> Love's thrice-repured nectar? death, I fear me,
> Swounding destruction, or some joy too fine,
> Too subtle-potent, turned too sharp in sweetness,
> For the capacity of my ruder powers:
> I fear it much, and I do fear besides
> That I shall lose distinction in my joys . . . .
>
> [III. ii. 18-27]

The sensations of this passage are intense enough, but only through the palate and the senses; like the corresponding emotions of Cressida, they scarcely involve any full personality in the speaker. Troilus' emotions are concentrated on "expectation," on the "*imaginary* relish," and he feels that the "watery palates" will be too weak to sustain the actual consummation. The whole speech turns upon this contrast between the refined intensity of feeling which he seeks, self-consciously and with a touch of indulgence, in "Love's *thrice-repured* nectar," and the giddiness, the "swounding destruction," which would follow its impossible consummation. The experience of love, it is suggested, is so fine, so "subtle-potent," that it surpasses the "ruder powers" of the body and remains an incorporeal aspiration which the senses strive vainly to attain. (pp. 327-31)

This special use of the contrasted implications of sensual experience is extended in the course of the play from the personal to the public action, and contributes thus to the unity of its conception. The refined imagery of taste given to the Trojans, and especially to Troilus, reflects a bodiless ideal which becomes, in the mouths of the scurrilous Thersites and the Greek cynics, a series of clogged, heavy references to the digestive processes. Thersites has "mastic jaws," and Achilles calls him "my cheese, my digestion" [I. iii. 73, II. iii. 41], whilst Agamemnon tells Patroclus that Achilles' virtues

> like fair fruit in an unwholesome dish
> Are like to rot untasted.
>
> [II. iii. 120-21]

In fact, the very sense that expresses the related intensity and lightness of Trojan passion becomes, in the Greeks, a symbol of inaction and distemper out of which issue the boils, "the botchy core" [II. i. 6], of Thersites' disgust.

In this way we pass from the individual to the public action, from the love of Troilus and Cressida to the war between the Greeks and Troy. This connection between the private and the public theme is indeed the most original feature of the play. The two parties, like the two lovers, are divergent within a common type of feeling. The Trojans share the fragile intensity of Troilus. They are deeply concerned with the value of "honour" and with a view of love that aspires to be idealistic, while Hector shows the virtues of war which are so noticeably absent from the bulky Ajax and the graceless Achilles. (pp. 331-32)

The true nature of this Trojan weakness is perhaps most explicitly stated by Troilus when he sets forth, in an attempt at reasoned expression, his argument for the continuation of the war:

> I take to-day a wife, and my election
> Is led on in the conduct of my will;
> My will enkindled by mine eyes and ears,
> Two traded pilots 'twixt the dangerous shores
> Of will and judgement: how may I avoid,
> Although my will distaste what it elected,
> The wife I chose? There can be no evasion
> To blench from this, and to stand firm by honour.
>
> [II. ii. 61-8]

Troilus' terminology is indefinite and the expression of his argument, like so much of what passes for discussion in this play, far more complicated than its content. There seems at one point to be an opposition of "will," which we may associate here with sensual impulse, and "judgement," by which this impulse should normally be restrained and directed; the

opposition, in short, of sensuality and moral control, which becomes a little later the central theme of *Measure for Measure*. In that play, however, the moral conflict is explicitly stated, and—what is more important—takes shape in a dramatic clash of clearly defined personalities; in *Troilus and Cressida* there is only an uncertainty, a sense of uneasiness, which the notable incoherence of the expression reflects. The conclusion reached by "judgement" is that affirmed by Hector—that purposeful action must follow from a dispassionate weighing of alternatives in the light of the principles of reason—but the whole trend of Troilus' reply is to annihilate, or at least willfully to confuse, the distinction between "will" and "judgement" themselves, to show that "judgement" is powerless and irrelevant once the sensual will has impelled man toward action. In other words, the basis of Troilus' "honour" is simply sensual impulse, and its weakness lies largely in his unwillingness to recognize this fact, and in the abstraction and lack of content that follow in the train of this evasion. (pp. 333-34)

The Trojan devotion to honor, Shakespeare would seem to infer, is devotion to an abstraction that has no sufficient basis in reason, that is, in fact, no more than an empty justification of impulse: but—it is equally important to realize—to abandon honor for its lack of rational foundation is to expose oneself to the danger of lethargy, to a rooted disinclination to act at all. Once more we are faced with the split between motive and impulse, moral *value* and sensual substitutes, which dominates this play without a real glimpse of resolution. (p. 335)

Where the Trojans reject reason in favor of ill-considered action, the Greeks accept it and are reduced to inaction. Agamemnon's very first speech, as the head and cornerstone of Greek unity, shows how inconclusive are the intellectual processes so painfully followed by the leaders who accompany him and how closely related they are to the views expressed by Troilus on "crammed reason." . . . (p. 336)

On both sides in this presentation of the Trojan War, indeed, it would seem that the balance between emotion and reason is profoundly disturbed. The "cunning" of the Greek leaders is manifestly out of touch with practical considerations and expends itself in an activity completely disproportionate to the desired end. . . . On the Trojan side the infidelity of Cressida finally undermines Troilus' faith in "honour" as a basis for action and leaves him dimly aware of the incompatible and contrary elements which underlie what he had assumed to be the indivisible simplicity of passion. . . . [The] ambiguous attitude toward experience which so deeply exercised Shakespeare in many of his sonnets is the determining factor in his presentation of both parties. Proceeding from his sense of the disharmony introduced by their subjection to the temporal process into the love of Troilus and Cressida, it extends to embrace the two parties in their fantastic and unreasonable conflict. The Trojans follow a false idealism, which deceives itself with talk of "honour," but is really based on "blood" and ends in a pathetic and helpless realization of its own insufficiency; the Greeks elaborate endlessly a "judgement" that is out of touch with the instinctive sources of action, until Agamemnon's chaotic reasoning finds its proper counterpart in the distorted bitterness of Thersites' diseased sensibility.

Read in this way, *Troilus and Cressida* emerges as an attempt to give expression to a fundamental flaw felt to exist at the heart of human experience, and not readily to be described. The final difficulty is the lack of that *degree,* proper and natural order in distinction, which Ulysses abstractly perceives in the longest and most famous of his speeches:

> Take but degree away, untune that string,
> And, hark, what discord follows! each thing meets
> In mere oppugnancy: the bounded waters
> Should lift their bosoms higher than the shores,
> And make a sop of all this solid globe:
> Strength should be lord of imbecility,
> And the rude son should strike his father dead.
>
> [I. iii. 109-15]

From this general proposition he goes on to paint, in words of universal resonance, his culminating picture of a world in anarchy. . . . In this speech, which represents so much more than a mere reflection of political orthodoxy, we find supremely expressed, in terms of the disorder introduced by passion or "appetite" into the human organism, the nightmare of mere "chaos" which, present on both sides in the conflict between Greeks and Trojans, is the real theme of this fascinating and disturbing play. (pp. 338-40)

> D. A. Traversi, "The Problem Plays," in his An Approach to Shakespeare, *revised edition, 1968. Reprint by Doubleday & Company, Inc., 1969, pp. 323-98.*

T. McALINDON (essay date 1969)

[*In the following excerpt, McAlindon examines the language of* Troilus and Cressida *and the characters' improper use of words. The "discordant juxtaposition" of different language styles, argues McAlindon, reveals a social disunity in the play, best exemplified by the contrast between the low, prosaic speeches of Pandarus and Cressida and the poetry of Troilus. McAlindon concludes that, as in* Love's Labour's Lost *and* Hamlet, *Shakespeare is here concerned with proper decorum in language.*]

For those who regard *Troilus and Cressida* as a play marred by incongruous elements and an uncertain purpose, Act IV, Scene v, will always constitute an obvious source of dissatisfaction. Here, a long-awaited and loudly heralded climax—the duel between Ajax and Hector—rapidly subsides into anticlimax: before Ajax is even warm with action, Hector calls an end to the combat on the ground that he and his opponent are cousins. . . . To Ajax's rueful observation that he came to slay and not to embrace his cousin, Hector responds:

> Not Neoptolemus so *mirable,*
> On whose bright crest Fame with her loud'st oyez
> Cries "This is he," could promise to himself
> A thought of added honour torn from Hector.
>
> [IV. v. 142-45]

Although an element of bombast is traditionally considered decorous in a soldier's "brag," the circumstances in which this brag is delivered are such as to present it as *mere* bombast: loud words which no seen or foreseeable acts can justify. But the jarring effect of Hector's lines stems principally from the Latinized vocabulary and the coinages, more noticeable here than in any other speech in the play. None of the theories commonly advanced to explain the peculiarly Latinate diction of *Troilus and Cressida*—that Shakespeare was adjusting his style to an academic audience and to a philosophical treatment of his subject, that he was energetically exploring all the semantic resources of language—can justify the jingling and outlandish collection of words given at this point of the drama to a character such as Hector. On the available theories, one can

only account for such words by invoking the notion of undisciplined experimentalism and placing them among what one critic has called "the grotesque excesses" in the vocabulary of *Troilus and Cressida.*

The trouble with this explanation is that it credits Shakespeare, at a point in his career when he had already written *Much Ado, Julius Caesar, As You Like It, Twelfth Night,* and, perhaps, *Hamlet,* with having unwittingly added linguistic to dramatic discord; it allows the mature Shakespeare practically no artistic sense at all. An alternative explanation must, then, be found. I would suggest (putting a corollary first) that the anticlimax was part of Shakespeare's whole conception of the play, and that he employed Latinate diction and neologism in order to intensify its dissonant effect. As most readers will have observed, the conceited, antithetical expression in the speech quoted above is almost as effective as the diction in debasing Hector's inherently respectable motive for withdrawal; the strained use of latinized diction is, in fact, only one of several kinds of stylistic dissonance in the play, all of which, I propose, are calculated. The heroic and romantic characters of *Troilus and Cressida* are continually losing their hold on the style which is appropriate to their traditional reputations or to the fine qualities which are intermittently realized for them in the course of the play. They sin against what was for a contemporary audience the first principle of good speech: decorum, the law that word and style should suit the speaker, the person addressed, the subject, and the situation. These errors of speech have a dramatic purpose, being used by Shakespeare to focus attention on the graver maladies which afflict the Greeks and Trojans. (pp. 29-30)

The evaluative comments which the characters of the play make upon one another are often expressed in terms of the relationship between theme ("matter," "argument") and style. It is apparent from these remarks that finding the right style for a given subject (person) is not easy: individuals differ, or, in the process of time, change their minds on whether the subject is noble or base. One is liable, therefore, to treat a noble subject basely, or a base subject nobly. And there are other problems. One may be accused of speaking when one has no "matter" at all; or of having neither speech nor style in which to communicate a true evaluation of a subject. Hence the most inadequate character in the play is the illiterate Ajax. According to Ulysses, Ajax is lord of nothing because he is unable to "communicate his parts to others" [III. iii. 117]; according to Thersites, he is "languageless, a monster" who "raves in saying nothing" [III. iii. 263, 249] and can only express his pseudo-subject (his own greatness) by stalking up and down like a peacock [III. iii. 251]—that is, by ridiculous gestures.

Soldiers and lovers traditionally take a solemn view of their own utterances: their characteristic words are oaths and vows; they are quick to swear. "Word," "oath," "vow," and "swear," a set of terms which occurs frequently in *Troilus and Cressida,* are therefore virtually synonymous in it. Their contexts indicate that there are certain desiderata for the right use of words; and it is clear that these are of the greatest relevance in understanding and assessing character. (pp. 30-1)

The vaunt of Hector which has been quoted at the beginning of this essay is inappropriate partly because he has just withdrawn from the situation which justifies it, partly because the total context—one of verbosity and frustration—suggests that time will treat his words as mere wind. Yet Hector does understand the necessity of establishing a proper relation between words and deeds, even though his greatest failures are in this area. When driven to threatening oaths by the insolence of Achilles, he apologizes to his Greek hosts for the folly which has been drawn from his lips, and adds: "But I'll endeavour deeds to match these words" [IV. v. 259]. Oddly (a typical Shakespearian surprise?), it is Ajax who enunciates the decorum by which the many brags in this play must stand condemned: "let these threats alone / Till accident or purpose bring you to't" [IV. v. 261-62]; only in the context of action itself, and not before or after, have menacing words any justification. (p. 31)

Like Hector, Troilus can fall into heroic oaths which he will never fulfil [IV. iv. 126-27, V. ii. 170-76], and so, like Hector, can disregard his own fleeting awareness of the distinction between "needful talk" and a mere brag [IV. iv. 139]. In Troilus' case, however, the psychological and ethical confusions connected with the faulty use of words stem almost entirely from the nature of lovers' oaths and vows. From the beginning, his use of the language of love reveals more than anything else a distinct lack of judgment and experience. In the first scene he is found attaching a value to Cressida which an Elizabethan would have found comically excessive and at the same time groping self-consciously for apt figures in which to describe his emotional drama ("Let it be called the wild and wandering flood," etc. [I. i. 102]). The whole style and tone of the scene suggest that in the use of language, as in love, he is "skilless as unpractised infancy" [I. i. 12]. This conception of his character has a grim relevance in the two most important scenes in which he subsequently appears, the assignation and the betrayal. In both, the difficulty of thinking (or judging) and acting correctly when passion sways reason is dramatized in the mind's largely abortive effort to strike a just relation between words and meanings, words and deeds. (pp. 31-2)

The juxtaposition of widely different styles is a common form of stylistic discord in *Troilus and Cressida*. An important immediate effect of this technique is that excesses and deficiencies of style which might go unnoticed in a dramatic context are easily perceived. But, like the refusal of one person to speak to another, like evasive answers, rude tapinosis [verbal deflation], and misunderstanding (to which it often gives rise), discordant juxtaposition also has the general effect of exhibiting social disunity. There are in the play too many self-absorbed characters who exaggerate their own idiom, adhere to it inflexibly, and are unable or unwilling to make those sensitive modifications and transitions in style which are essential for harmonious social intercourse and the proper functioning of a hierarchical society.

The chief source of discordant juxtaposition is Troilus' relationship with Pandarus and Cressida; the most poetic character in the play is continually engaged in a doomed attempt to communicate with the two most prosaic. Pandarus speaks almost entirely in prose. Troilus does so only once (though beautifully), and that when Cressida, as he says, has deprived him of all words [III. ii. 54 ff.]. The features of style which mark the profound differences in sensibility between the two lovers are strongly exaggerated in the opening scenes, where they make their debuts independently in conversation with characters whose style is antithetical to their own, and as extreme. In the first scene the distance between the strained poeticizing of Troilus and the kitchen prose of Pandarus (with its sequence of culinary images for courtship) is such that, as we have noted, the attempt at dialogue breaks down abruptly: "Pray you, speak no more to me: I will leave all as I found it, and there an end" [I. i. 87-8]. Like her uncle, Cressida makes her first appearance

as a debunker of courtly style; and although her debunking has the merit of being intentional, it renders her an unattractive personality, since it is devoid of the light finesse to which she obviously aspires. Her flat tone, her factual questioning, and her mocking literalness [I. ii. 11-18] quickly reduce Alexander from blank verse, pastoral prosopopoeia, and metaphor to prose; but only to euphuistic prose [I. ii. 19-30], and not to the characterless stuff in which she herself converses throughout this scene.

That Alexander is Cressida's servant is a point of some dramatic significance. Shakespeare stresses the inadequacy of both niece and uncle by juxtaposing them with social inferiors whose speech is noticeably more cultivated than their own. Pandarus on one occasion reprimands a quibbling servant who has avoided answering his questions correctly: "Friend, we understand not one another: I am too courtly and thou art too cunning" [III. i. 27-8]. The anonymous servant, however, with his adroit playing on words, his lyrical (or mock-lyrical?) description of Helen [III. i. 32-3], and his disgust at Pandarus' crude choice of phrase ("There's a stewed phrase indeed!" [III. i. 41]), proves himself to be much more courtly than the self-styled "Lord Pandarus" [III. i. 11-12]. When, in his ensuing encounter with Paris and Helen, Pandarus does attempt to be courtly, he is grotesque rather than amusing, for he is not then aiming at the style of his betters but simply trying, unsuccessfully, to speak as he ought. The most outstanding characteristic of his prose style, the vice of homiologia (inane repetition), becomes more apparent than ever when he addresses himself to courtly compliment: "What says my sweet queen, my very very sweet queen?" [III. i. 79-80].

Interrupting the musical entertainment of Paris and Helen, Pandarus is accused of having broken the "good broken music" which he politely applauds [III. i. 49]. But he is told that he can make amends with a song, since, says Paris, "he is full of harmony" [III. i. 52-3]. When he protests modestly that he is, "in good sooth, very rude" [III. i. 56], Helen jests: "You shall not bob us out of our melody. If you do, our melancholy upon your head!" [III. i. 68-9]. The harmony-discord theme has immediate metaphoric significance, since the glorious Helen described by the servant a few moments earlier has turned out to be jolly "Nell" [III. i. 53]. But it is only in the love scenes involving Troilus and Cressida that the full import of Pandarus' "broken music" is perceived. Whatever slight chance the dialogues of the lovers might have had of developing into lyrical duets is completely eliminated by him. He is always present at some point, interrupting and commenting, turning poetry into prose and passion into lust.

Before Cressida makes her appearance in the assignation scene, Pandarus is unintentionally at work reminding the audience that she is not at all what Troilus thinks her to be and pointing to the wild loss of judgment already implicit in the lover's erotic verse. Troilus invites him . . . to pluck the wings from Cupid's shoulders and fly with him to Cressida in Elysium [III. ii. 13-15]; Pandarus' short and flat reply almost visibly brings the "giddy" [III. ii. 18] speaker down to earth: "Walk here i' th' orchard; I'll bring her straight" [III. ii. 16-17]. Alone and waiting, Troilus compares his agitation to that of a vassal rendered speechless when encountering the eye of majesty unawares [III. ii. 35-9]. The unfitness of the simile might escape notice were it not that Pandarus has just described this particular queen as "the prettiest villain" who, in anticipation of her lover, "fetches her breath as short as a new-ta'en sparrow" [III. ii. 33-4].

In the waking and parting of the lovers next morning, a specific and exquisite lyric form, the aubade, is evoked only to be degraded; the scene is conceived as one continuous discord. The "busy day" has been "Waked by the lark" but the lark "hath roused the ribald crows" [IV. ii. 8-10]. The lover concludes his expected denunciation of night's brevity with the most unexpected anticlimax in the play: "You will catch cold," he remarks to his lady, "and curse me" [IV. ii. 14]. The lady protests that she will "crack" her "clear voice" and "break" her heart with "sounding" her lover's name [IV. ii. 108-09]. Worst of all, the prompt arrival of the pandar, with his obscene jests and cawing, repetitious prose ("To do what? to do what? let her say what! What have I brought you to do?" [IV. iii. 27-8]), lets a ribald crow into the bedroom of love.

In the scene of final farewell, Pandarus plays the part of an aged, semiliterate spectator at a drama of high passion. He is moved, but only at the crudest level of feeling; and he insists on voicing his thoughts and becoming a participant. As the tearful lovers embrace, he puns farcically and comes between them for his embrace: "What a pair of spectacles is here! Let me embrace too" [IV. iv. 14]. He quotes a quatrain of jingling verse, applauding its aptness to the occasion [IV. iv. 16-22]; and caps the most moving lines in the play with a ludicrously mismanaged, conventional hyperbole [IV. iv. 53-4]. He even intervenes in the dialogue of the lovers, answering a question which one puts to the other [IV. iv. 28-9]: it is remarkable how Shakespeare contrives by every means to present the phenomenon of fractured speech, "broken music."

Except in the opening scene, the intensity of Troilus' feelings is always such that the violent incongruities of style to which he is exposed result in dissonance rather than in bathos. It may be possible to laugh at him, but only at the risk of showing some of that bad taste, that "rudeness" with which the play is so intimately concerned; for he is a lost and confused, not a ridiculous, figure. (pp. 39-41)

An indecorous compliment occasionally paid to *Troilus and Cressida* is that although confused in itself it throws light on other plays in the canon. How much light has not perhaps been fully appreciated; for the extent to which we understand one of Shakespeare's plays must surely affect the manner in which it illuminates another. My final concern here is to substantiate the general interpretation of *Troilus and Cressida* given above by reference to *Love's Labour's Lost* and *Hamlet;* but it is possible that in the process I may, incidentally, be able to add a little to present understanding of Shakespeare's intentions in these two plays as well. Their relevance in an interpretation of *Troilus and Cressida* is, simply, that the design which is implicit throughout this play is disclosed in them with comparative overtness: in *Love's Labour's Lost,* because (perhaps) of the immaturity of the author and the slightness of the material; in *Hamlet,* because of the reflective character of the hero.

It is brought to our notice with almost wearisome emphasis in *Love's Labour's Lost* that the plot turns upon the making and breaking of rash vows. Here is an immediate general connection with *Troilus and Cressida;* but the parallel is much more comprehensive and exact. The errors and follies attendant upon rash vows are dramatised not only as ridiculous but, specifically, as indecorous conduct: "gravity's revolt to wantonness," "foolery in the wise," "misbecom'd . . . gravities" [*Love's Labour's Lost*, V. ii. 74, 76, 768]. And, of course, as indecorous speech. The vices of style which are so extensively exhibited throughout the play are symptoms of the same weakness or imbalance of judgment which gives rise to the abuse of vows and oaths. (p. 41)

Hamlet's concern for fitness is most evident . . . in his references to speech and gesture, acting and plays. These must not be taken simply as signs of a scholarly temperament which renders him unsuited for revenge. Nor must it be thought that the primary function of the observations on methods of acting is satirical and so extraneous to the main issues of the tragedy. All Hamlet's comments on style and drama are, rather, indirect expressions of the problem which most engages his mind: the need for judgment, truth, and balance in word and deed. (p. 42)

So *Hamlet, Love's Labour's Lost,* and *Troilus and Cressida* are concerned with men who lose their proper style. Shakespeare's investigation of the special problems of Berowne, Hamlet, and Troilus brought into play and was enriched by his consciousness of the requirements and pitfalls of his art; the Renaissance conviction that the laws of life and of art coincide in certain fundamentals allowed him to put a great deal of himself into these characters without sacrificing dramatic objectivity. In *Troilus and Cressida,* therefore, one occasionally has the strong impression that Shakespeare is simultaneously scrutinizing characters in action and his own play in the making; that in exposing to censure the contemptuous treatment of the Greek and Trojan heroes by Patroclus, Thersites, and "envious and calumniating Time" [III. iii. 174] he is ruefully contemplating the discourteous truthfulness of his own art and wondering whether it is he, not they, who is guilty of a failure to treat the subject with a proper decorum. (pp. 42-3)

T. McAlindon, "Language, Style, and Meaning in 'Troilus and Cressida'," in PMLA, 84, Vol. 84, No. 1, January, 1969, pp. 29-43.

R. A. YODER (essay date 1972)

[*Yoder considers* Troilus and Cressida *a uniquely contemporary play, particularly in its analysis of a protracted war fought for dubious causes, an observation similar to that of Jan Kott (1964). While most critics, such as G. Wilson Knight (1930), S. C. Sen Gupta (1950), L. C. Knights (1951), and Norman Rabkin (1965), have stressed the central significance of time in the play, Yoder contends that time is not a unifying philosophical theme. Instead, he claims that the characters' conception of time is a way of evading their present situation, for while time confers value for them, it also destroys it—"the end is all, but the end is also empty, nothing." The real focus of the play, says Yoder, is neither time nor value, but consistency, unity, and order; all of the play's philosophic theories support "a collective, public order which is absolute in its authority." He notes that all personal interests in* Troilus and Cressida *are subjugated to the order of this absolute state, or "Grand Mechanism"—a term he borrows from Kott. Consequently, argues Yoder, not only is the love of Troilus and Cressida sacrificed to the demands of the war effort, but Eros itself becomes sublimated for the sake of duty to the absolute state. The importance of the influence of social structure on individual action in* Troilus and Cressida *has also been discussed by Denton J. Snider (1890), G. Wilson Knight (1930), H. B. Charlton (1937), and Terence Eagleton (1967).*]

Of all Shakespeare, *Troilus and Cressida* is our play. It could be rediscovered only by a sensibility tuned to artistic discontinuity and preoccupied with the realities of love and war; and so it had to wait for cubism and atonality, for fascism and Freud. So given over to 'philosophy' and debate, it had to wait for Shaw to rescue this dramatic mode, and probably for the kind of painstaking analysis of texts apart from performance that modern criticism has indulged. In a narrower sense, it is our play because it makes sense to Americans in the 1970s. We know, albeit still in a remote and most vicarious way, the meaning of a protracted seven years' war. We know how the designs of war fail in their promised largeness and how the Greeks must have felt tented in a foreign land, so many hollow factions, with their great engine Achilles useless in seeming mockery of their very designs. Like the Trojans, too, we have heard endlessly the arguments for carrying on a war of doubtful justification, and we know what it really means to settle only for an 'honorable peace'. We have seen good men who spoke truth in council, even in public, suddenly capitulate to save the corporate image. Within the walls of our capital cities—or more accurately, in their gilded suburbs—we may observe an elegant and seething triviality to match the palace society of Troy. Last and worst, we know what this society and its war has done to our best youth—those not literally destroyed have suffered a degradation of spirit, and of those whose ideals are not fully corrupted, many have chosen a life of irreconcilable alienation. There is no doubt, *Troilus and Cressida* gives back our own world.

Not surprisingly, then, some of the most acute Shakespearian criticism of the past decade concerns this play, and these interpretations have been generally pessimistic: the play in some way ridicules or diminishes every character, and ultimately the human character, man himself; no one any longer seems to accept Ulysses's 'degree' speech as the established value of the play, yet for all the times I have read that Thersites is right about this or that incident, no one comfortably or categorically asserts that he speaks for Shakespeare. Instead, there is a tendency to philosophize about this philosophical drama, to gather it all up into one large design and stress the symmetry of parallels and contrasts between settings, persons, and arguments. Then 'multiplicity' rather than any one character's ideas governs the viewpoint of the play. And most of the traditional dichotomies—like Trojan/Greek, love/war, passion/reason, extrinsic/intrinsic theories of value, tragic/comic—are seen as 'complementary' and resolved in more encompassing generalizations. (p. 11)

This larger, philosophical view of *Troilus and Cressida* provides some relief from taxing ideological quarrels and from any lingering sense of aesthetic chaos. Yet its great virtue, I think, is to startle us with still another profound question, as all good philosophy does: Why in a play that so richly evokes an atmosphere, a sense of the here and now, are we asked to look so far beyond it, into the dim abstract, for answers? Why, in short, should we desert the world that is for 'the world to come'? A look at the actual world of Troy, and we may learn why its inhabitants—and following them, the audience—might refuge in a time outside of time and in a space that relieves them of an identity apart from public role.

What is going on at Troy is no secret. Some time ago the 'princes orgulous' came from Greece to meet the courteous Trojans in honorable battle, all over a point of honor in love. Now, 'after seven years' siege' [I. iii. 12]—'after so many hours, lives, speeches spent', and 'honour, loss of time, travail, expense, / Wounds, friends, and what else is dear that is consumed / In hot digestion of this cormorant war' [II. ii. 1, 4-6]—they are still at it. Trojans and Greeks are still playing the game according to the rules of knightly combat and the courtly lover's code. Yet nowhere in Shakespeare is the official standard of conduct more at odds with the action and language of

the play. Even Troilus, at the beginning, dissociates himself as a lover from this absurd war:

> Fools on both sides! Helen must needs be fair,
> When with your blood you daily paint her thus.
> I cannot fight upon this argument

> [I. i. 90-2]

But he finds it easier to brush off this truth than to escape the war. Troilus, youngest son of Priam, a prince raised in the Trojan court, has inherited its code, though, to be sure, his courtly stance is still a bit awkward: he wallows—to use his own egregious verb—in a morass of conceits that invariably betray a less idealistic basis for love than Troilus realizes. Not only do sensuous and financial images undercut his romantic protestations, but the strained pitch of his language leads him to absurd exaggerations—in the parting speeches, for example:

> Nay, we must use expostulation kindly,
> For it is parting from us.
> I speak not 'be thou true', as fearing thee,
> For I will throw my glove to Death himself
> That there's no maculation in thy heart;
> But 'be thou true' say I, to fashion in
> My sequent protestation: be thou true,
> And I will see thee.

> [IV. iv. 60-7]

The challenge to death fits a code that joins love with honor in the field—that is why Troilus cannot escape the war. (pp. 12-13)

The plots of love and war are obviously parallel: Hector's death carries us to the same conclusion as the disillusionment of Troilus, namely, that the ugly realities of this world are at cross-purposes with the codes of courtly love and honor that seem to govern it. Shakespeare's panorama of the Trojan war is an elaboration of his own famous epigram, 'Something is rotten in the state of Denmark' [*Hamlet,* I. iv. 90]—or of the germ in a contemporary analyst's report of the Elizabethan scene: 'I do here grossly fashion our commonweal, sick or diseased' [Armigail Waad]. What is worse, as the disease progresses, cross-purposes do become complementary purposes. The sick world Shakespeare fashions is like the world of *Julius Caesar* or of *Hamlet:* its ceremonies and formal rhetoric disguise the actual condition of life; the truth, told in images of disease and devouring appetite and by the successive, unveiling actions of the play, is an unpleasant truth, and so to avoid seeing their world for what it is, Trojans and Greeks cling desperately to the superstructures they have erected to deny it.

Time itself serves this mechanism of evasion. Time is a complex notion, regarded with both fear and reverence. Everyone in the play holds a proper Elizabethan distrust for time conceived as mere process or in process; the process is too clearly one of decay. What they reverence is time considered teleologically—the process completed, somehow ended so that durable judgments can be made. Such a completed Time is allegorized in Hector's remark to Ulysses:

> *Hector.*   The end crowns all;
>   And that old common arbitrator, Time,
>   Will one day end it.
> *Ulysses.*   So to him we leave it.

> [IV. v. 224-26]

There is an odor of empty circularity or tautology in the exchange, because time in this sense confers value upon objects and renders them meaningless—the end is all, but the end is also empty, nothing. It is like the 'formless oblivion' that comprises past and future for Agamemnon [IV. v. 167-68], whose prescription is to lift the 'extant moment' out of the process, elevating it with chivalry. Thus the code is called into service to combat decay. (pp. 14-15)

Time and timelessness are equally the concern of lovers. Both Troilus and Cressida observe, in the early scenes, that love is a process working gradually toward its goal (Pandarus to Troilus, [I. i. 14-26], Cressida in [I. ii. 286-94]), and in the maxim tossed off by Pandarus—'Well, the gods are above; time must friend or end' [I. ii. 77-8]—lies the same sense of tautology and impotence in the face of time that is found later in the play. Impotence of this sort runs through the love plot: when Cressida says, 'Things won are done—joy's soul lies in the doing' [I. ii. 287], she means that from a woman's viewpoint the stage of courtly wooing is more satisfactory than the consummation; and at the very point of union Troilus seems obsessed with the failure of achieved love to live up to its promise [III. ii. 18-29, 77-83]. Like the generals they fear the ruinous process of decay, and so they too would look beyond to the end, or very nearly the end of time, when with assurance in their judgment 'True swains in love shall in the world to come / Approve their truths by Troilus' [III. ii. 173-74]. Then as myths and metaphors they will have no need to fear, and they will outrival all the hardened similes—steel, iron, the stones of Troy, the sun, and the very earth itself [III. ii. 177 ff.]—as figures of constancy.

Time, then, is not a philosophical theme above the play, containing and unifying the dramatic action; nor are the speeches about time analytical rather than dramatic. The characters of *Troilus and Cressida* share a special and heightened awareness of time, which is appropriate to the world they live in: who would not, after seven years of destruction, fear the procession of time passing before them? Their appeal to ultimate Time, the process ended, is a means of escape from the present.

If Time as the arbitrator of all value is tautological, at once all and nothing, and if the dramatic function of time is to serve as a means of evading the present, then what becomes of the debate over values in the play? The most common exposition of this problem has been to contrast the extrinsic theory proposed by Troilus, in which value is conferred by the evaluator, by the price he offers, with the intrinsic theory set out by Hector, which assigns value according to the inherent worth of the object. . . . Valuable as this analysis is, it does disguise something of what happens. In the first place, this contrast has only limited importance in the debate over values because both parties in the Trojan camp shift their grounds, Hector most obviously and Troilus more subtly. Thus, although a rhetorical question like 'What's aught, but as 'tis valued?' [II. ii. 52] suggests that value is determined by 'particular will' (and Hector would gladly fix on Troilus this appearance of serving appetite), Troilus's argument is actually quite different. . . . What is relevant is one's word, one's honor, and more, the fact that 'our several honours' are all engaged [II. ii. 124] in this enterprise. Hector, it seems to me, misrepresents Troilus and Paris when he contrasts their 'raging appetites' with the 'moral laws / Of nature and of nations' [II. ii. 181-86] and perhaps because they are not so merely willful as he makes out, Hector finds it easier to go over to their side in the end.

> Yet, ne'ertheless,
> My sprightly brethren, I propend to you
> In resolution to keep Helen still;
> For 'tis a cause that hath no mean dependence
> Upon our joint and several dignities.
>
> [II. ii. 189-93]

Those are precisely Troilus's terms—'our several honours'—and behind Hector's reversal may be a feeling he shares with his opponents: what they really want to keep is the 'well-ordered nation' Hector admires, and this state, they know, depends more on the consistency with which its honor is defended than on moral laws or abstract questions of value. (pp. 15-17)

Consistency, unity—in a word, 'order' in the nation is the underlying desideratum in the Trojan council, and the code of honor, as the concluding agreement indicates, is the means to that end. These assumptions about honor, shared implicitly by Troilus and Hector, are explicitly set forth by Ulysses among the Greeks. When his extraordinary portrait of cosmic order, the famous degree speech, finally boils down to the specific complaint, Ulysses attributes the failure of the campaign to social impropriety—the Greek soldiers haven't proper respect for their superiors. . . . (p. 17)

Ulysses's speech on the providence of the state, more sharply than any other, discovers the centripetal pull of all the philosophy and rhetoric in *Troilus and Cressida*. Beneath an apparent disparity, all the theories converge in a way that is more obvious if we consider the total action of the play: they all support, at the expense of privacy, a collective, public order which is absolute in its authority and which is geared to continuing the long, absurd war that stretches across the stage, infecting if not devouring the entire cast. Call it the state, or call it the system, it is a subtle network that both 'reason' and 'honor' serve: it is what supposedly justifies the parleys and games between opposing generals in the midst of slaughter; it is the apology for awful sacrifices on the part of men forever hoping that Time will somehow redeem them; it is a part of the 'necessary form' of history, a Grand Mechanism rising above men, directing them to roles they are hardly conscious of—and not just the mechanism of political struggle, but the superior machinery of war that unifies society while squeezing out its very life. In *Julius Caesar,* and to an extent in the earlier history plays, the acts of successive political figures in their struggles for power begin to mirror each other as the mechanism gathers momentum. In *Troilus and Cressida* the mechanism is superbly efficient: not only acts, but thoughts converge—as the action is all part of the game of war, so the arguments are all ceremonies of rededication to the code that maintains the war and dissolves all forms of personal expression. What needs to be contrasted is not subtle variations among Greek and Trojan leaders, but rather the single dimension in all their reasoning set over against the prophetic cries of Cassandra and Thersites.

> Cry, Trojans, cry! lend me ten thousand eyes,
> And I will fill them with prophetic tears . . . .
>
> [II. ii. 101-02]

> Farewell—yet soft! Hector, I take my leave;
> Thou dost thyself and all our Troy deceive.
>
> [V. iii. 89-90]

Weigh reason against prophecy in this play, and to borrow Thersites's incisive complaint, 'all the argument is a whore and a cuckold' [II. iii. 72-3]—to the appetite of war.

The debate over value, like the descant on time, sustains the illusion fabricated by reason and honor. Bound by their heroic code, Greeks and Trojans march into oblivion; they are caught up in the machinery of a state at war; the only hope they know is that of a timeless, collective memory where reputation—what Cassio, another purveyor of the code, calls the 'immortal part' of man [*Othello,* II. iii. 263]—will be sealed up long after their bodies have turned to dust. In such a world it is natural for Eros to be postponed or channelled to serve the state. And the story of the young lovers, the central characters from whom the play takes its name, reveals the full effect of the grand mechanism at work.

Love and war are traditionally parallel or complementary themes, and in the play the codes of the warrior and the lover are clearly made out to be symbiotic. . . . War thrives on a kind of love—when knights defend their mistresses whose tokens they bear, and mistresses arm and disarm their knights. But privacy in love, as we have seen with Achilles, is dangerous to the field; it must be rooted out. So, in the moment of love's consummation, Shakespeare contrives that 'the time' should undermine the lovers. And this is not personified Time, but the actual moment, war-time, the here and now: Calchas is prompted by 'Th' advantage of the time' [III. iii. 2] to demand an exchange of Antenor for his daughter, and Paris sums up the plight of the lovers—'There is no help; / The bitter disposition of the time / Will have it so' [IV. i. 49-50]. In one of Shakespeare's characteristic dramatic actions, the public world comes knocking early at the private chamber. Troilus and Cressida have awakened, and in lines that recall a similar scene from *Romeo and Juliet* [III. v. 1-42] they lament night's brevity:

> *Troilus.*
> O Cressida! but that the busy day,
> Waked by the lark, hath roused the ribald crows,
> And dreaming night will hide our joys no longer,
> I would not from thee.
> *Cressida.*   Night hath been too brief.
> *Troilus.*
> Beshrew the witch! with venemous wights she stays
> As tediously as hell, but flies the grasps of love
> With wings more momentary-swift than thought.
> You will catch cold, and curse me.
> *Cressida.*   Prithee, tarry.
> You men will never tarry.
> O foolish Cressid! I might have still held off,
> And then you would have tarried.
> [IV. ii. 8-18]

The young nobleman, who naively accepts the courtly code he has inherited, is frightened that the demands of sexual love will conflict with honor; he is afraid of being discovered and would flee with the night. Cressida pleads with him to 'tarry'—the essential of Pandar's recipe for love [I. i. 15]—for she realizes now in a fuller sense that love grows slowly, that it must struggle against the demands of the world, that men fear when it 'swells past hiding' in a sense more profound than her earlier witticism [I. ii. 269] entailed. This kind of love challenges the order, the mechanism.

But here love loses. Consider the response of Troilus, who was 'mad in Cressid's love' [I. i. 51], to the encroachment of the official world:

> *Aeneas.*
> My lord, I scarce have leisure to salute you,
> My matter is so rash . . .
> . . . within this hour,
> We must give up to Diomedes' hand
> The Lady Cressida.
> *Troilus.*   Is it so concluded?
> *Aeneas.*
> By Priam and the general state of Troy.
> They are at hand and ready to effect it.

> *Troilus.*
> How my achievements mock me!
> I will go meet them; and, my Lord Aeneas,
> We met by chance: you did not find me here.
> [IV. ii. 59-71]

This is far from madness—an off-hand question, a wistful comment, and Troilus departs with Aeneas to join the very council that has dealt the blow. . . . Thus there is, in this central incident of the play and moment of high passion, an obvious flattening in the character supposedly most susceptible to feeling. It is not an undramatic slip; surprisingly, perhaps, but with psychological precision, Shakespeare shows that Troilus is calmed, even relieved in returning to his public role—he belongs to 'the general state of Troy' [IV. ii. 67].

The bargain that sends Cressida to the Greek camp is just another of the acts of shame war brings. It must therefore be disguised and treated as an elaborate public ceremony, like the ritualized assassination of Caesar or the murder of Desdemona. Like Othello, Troilus borrows imaginary priestly robes for his task:

> I'll bring her to the Grecian presently;
> And to his hand when I deliver her,
> Think it an altar, and thy brother Troilus
> A priest, there offering to it his own heart.
> [IV. iii. 6-9]

Cressida will be a sacrifice to the gods. Troilus invites religious sanction, and like Agamemnon who saw adversity as the trials of Jove, he explains this calamity as decreed by the gods:

> Cressid, I love thee in so strained a purity,
> That the blest gods, as angry with my fancy,
> More bright in zeal than the devotion which
> Cold lips blow to their deities, take thee from me.
> [IV. iv. 24-7]

Strained indeed, this purity and zeal that sloughs off responsibility on the authority of a world beyond: for we have seen such divine operations before, when the watchful state unveiled, 'almost like the gods', the privacy of lovers. Strained, too, are the phrases of his 'loose adieu', betrayed by the ubiquitous imagery of the market-place [IV. iv. 40] and by that other metaphysical scapegoat, 'injurious Time' [IV. iv. 42], whom Troilus blames for what clearly *the* time and *this* world have done . . . and for what *he* is doing, almost in numbed default. Imagine Romeo or Hamlet in his place—would they be tamed to this hollow, passionless performance? But Troilus never sees beyond his part in the ceremony. (pp. 18-21)

The betrayal of Troilus is an extraordinary scene which, together with the closing action of the play, points toward a number of motifs in *Othello*. At the center is ocular proof of Cressid's infidelity. Troilus, whom Ulysses observes to be, like the noble Moor, 'both open and both free' [IV. v. 100], is shocked almost to silence. . . . Disillusionment paralyzes Troilus only for a moment, and then he begins to swell with hate; he steadies himself with what is most natural and accessible to him, the role of a faithful knight whose 'so eternal and so fixed a soul' [V. ii. 166] swears to avenge its honor. . . . 'Hector is dead; there is no more to say'—but Troilus is never at a loss for words—

> Stay yet. You vile abominable tents,
> Thus proudly pight upon our Phrygian plains,
> Let Titan rise as early as he dare,
> I'll through and through you! And thou great-sized
>   coward,

No space of earth shall sunder our two hates;
I'll haunt thee like a wicked conscience still,
That mouldeth goblins swift as frenzy's thoughts.
Strike a free march to Troy! with comfort go:
Hope of revenge shall hide our inward woe.

[V. x. 22-31]

'Words, words, mere words', Troilus said of Cressida [V. iii. 108], but he cannot say it of himself. This speech is little more than a continuation of his spiteful threats in the betrayal scene and can hardly be construed as tragic recognition. Always what matters is what Troilus does not recognize: that 'after so many hours, lives, speeches spent' [II. ii. 1], another oath of revenge is a terrible folly; that his late heroism and frenzied hatred for the enemy is one more instance of Eros harnessed to the purposes of the state, sublimated into the honorable outlet of duty—and Troilus is, in his own image, 'Mars his heart / Inflamed with Venus' [V. ii. 164-65]; that his world is not governed by the splendid systems and codes rehearsed throughout the play but is pretty much what Ulysses feared it might become:

Then everything includes itself in power,
Power into will, will into appetite;
And appetite, an universal wolf,
So doubly seconded with will and power,
Must make perforce an universal prey,
And last eat up himself.

[I. iii. 119-24]

For the state at war 'everything includes itself in power'—all ceremonies, all speeches and all love, all secrets and all hope are drawn into the mechanism that must finally devour itself. The Troiluses, the Hectors, the Achilles and Ulysses of this world and ours, more or less unwittingly, are sons of the game. Thersites has told them the way things are: but will they ever learn? (pp. 24-5)

> R. A. Yoder, "'Sons and Daughters of the Game':
> An Essay on Shakespeare's 'Troilus and Cressida',"
> in Shakespeare Survey: An Annual Survey of Shake-
> spearean Study and Production, Vol. 25, 1972, pp.
> 11-25.

RICHARD D. FLY (essay date 1973)

[In the excerpt below, Fly contends that the dark tone of Troilus and Cressida reflects Shakespeare's recognition of the frustrations and limitations imposed by the necessity of mediation in drama and language. Mediation, he explains, is that which lies between will and execution, between "the apprehension of a whole harmonious design and the actual realization of it." Like Terence Eagleton (1967), Fly observes the importance of mediation, "the middleman," in determining the relations of characters in Troilus and Cressida, noting in particular Pandarus's position between Troilus and Cressida. He also relates the play's mercantile imagery mentioned by other critics, with its notion of the middleman, to his central concept. A similar concern with mediation, he continues, can be found in the form of the play, which emphasizes the imperfect nature of language as a medium for communication. Finally, concludes Fly, the play is not, as Oscar James Campbell (1938) has argued, a bitter, comical satire in the style of Jonson, but "a tragic confrontation with the aesthetic and ontological problems raised by mediation." For further comments by Fly on Troilus and Cressida, see his essay cited in the Additional Bibliography.]

The essential problem for the creative artist is to bring desired form out of his chosen medium—to achieve articulation and design in opposition to the undifferentiated contingency of his primary material. His conception of the creative enterprise, of the malleability of his medium, and of what constitutes successfully achieved form may, of course, vary greatly. Many artists struggle painfully with their unruly materials and eventually compromise, whereas others, more blessed, seem to conceive of their work as a relatively effortless and fully satisfying activity. Michelangelo's creative sovereignty over his medium results from his ability to conceive of his figures as lying hidden in the blocks of marble on which he chooses to work, so that his task as a sculptor is merely one of removing the stone which covers them. (p. 145)

But even a Michelangelo could not sustain such a god-like supremacy over his material, and in several provocative works he appears to acknowledge that the invincibility of inert matter can almost neutralize even his creative powers. His statue of the "Dying Slave," for instance, suggests that moment when life capitulates before the relentless force of dead matter. But a more extreme instance of artistic impotence is suggested in his haunting statue of Saint Matthew. Michelangelo represents the saint as struggling in tortuous agony as if he were trying desperately to free himself from the imprisoning block of marble that contains him. The artist, that is, seems aware here that his medium is itself capable of successfully resisting his efforts to master it with fully achieved form. And there is perhaps even a suggestion of something demonic and negating in the medium's ability to distort, frustrate, and debilitate the artist's effort at creation—a suggestion of encroaching chaos. At any rate, Michelangelo as creator has made himself very much a part of the statue's total statement, a statement that seriously qualifies the creative optimism informing his other works.

A radical difference, of course, exists between the medium available to the sculptor and painter and the medium available to the dramatist. Yet the dramatist's response to the basic need to confront and master his materials may reveal attitudes toward creation similar to those already mentioned. Like Michelangelo, Shakespeare often conceives of artistic creation as an optimistic and relatively effortless activity. . . . The confrontation between artist and medium assumes a bleaker and more pressing character as Shakespeare matures as a playwright. Troilus and Cressida becomes less of an aberration and more of an instance of great significance for Shakespeare's development when seen against this darkening background, for perhaps no other play raises the issue of the artist's struggle to master his materials quite so intensely as Troilus does. This deeply troubling play seems to be the work of a dramatist no longer in serene control of his craft and, indeed, perilously close to capitulating before a medium that appears to have grown hostile and intransigent to his creative efforts. (pp. 147-48)

The omnipresent sense of frustration and stalemate in Troilus can . . . be traced, I believe, to a shared consciousness in the play-world of the intransigence of medium. Medium in this irreducible sense transcends the recognizable differences between sculptor and dramatist in that it stands for whatever exists and functions between will and execution, whatever power, psychic or material, intervenes between inspiration and consequence. Thus understood, medium should suggest basic concepts of transmission such as means, agency, and instrumentality; medium, that is, is whatever is felt to lie between the apprehension of a whole harmonious design and the actual realization of it. In Troilus these terms do not remain abstract and theoretical but rather tend to assume a palpable dramatic life of their own, a corporeality that allows them to function in the play's unfolding action as active antagonists: "Checks and disasters / Grow[ing] in the veins of actions highest reared'' [I. iii. 5-6].

By examining the dynamics of *Troilus'* plot, for instance, it becomes immediately apparent that an inordinate amount of the actual business of the play is given over to the mediating and conveying of persons, objects, or information from one party to another. It also becomes clear that crucial metaphysical and ontological questions of value and identity are being made to hinge on the nature and outcome of these various transactions. The Greeks intend to fight the Trojans until they ''Deliver Helen,'' and the significance of the possible return of Helen is debated at length in the Trojan council scene. The shadowy figure of Hesione, Ajax's mother and Priam's sister, is recalled as a woman whom ''the Greeks held captive'' [II. ii. 77]. The Trojan seer Calchas has defected to the Greeks and in exchange for safety has ''Incurred a traitor's name'' [III. iii. 6]. And as a result of Calchas' intercession, the captive Antenor is conveyed back to Troy in exchange for his daughter Cressida, who is then conveyed by Diomedes to the Greeks—and the play gives lavish attention to all the details of this exchange. Aeneas suddenly appears as a herald in the middle of the Greek war council to deliver Hector's challenge to duel with a Greek champion ''Midway between'' the Greek tents and the walls of Troy. When the play opens Thersites belongs to Ajax, but we learn in Act II that ''Achilles hath inveigled his fool from him'' [II. iii. 91]. Thersites is made to bear letters from Achilles to Ajax, and presumably from Hecuba and Polyxena to Achilles. Agamemnon's grand sentiments often find themselves rechanneled to his officers through the verbose and slightly comical expression of Nestor: ''Nestor shall apply / Thy latest words'' [I. iii. 32-3]. And Aeneas ''translates'' Troilus' identity to Ulysses who in turn passes it on to Agamemnon [IV. v. 95-112]. Ulysses has ''derision med'cinable / To use between'' the pretended ''strangeness'' of the Greek leaders and Achilles' ''pride'' [III. iii. 44-5]. Our first view of the Trojan warriors is mediated through the running commentary of Pandarus [I. ii. 177-246], and Ajax's strange identity (''half Troyan, and half Greek'') is conveyed to Cressida by Alexander [I. ii. 12-29]. Troilus' ''words, vows, gifts, tears, and love's full sacrifice'' [I. ii. 282] are conveyed to Cressida by Pandarus, and Cressida's beauty and reticence must in turn be relayed back to Troilus by Pandarus. Between the stalemated armies, between the static passivity of the lovers, exists an area of rather hectic mediations. What is particularly noteworthy in all these exchanges is that the desired transaction is most often marred or frustrated by the unpredictable processes of mediation.

The mention of Pandarus suggests the degree to which *Troilus* has incarnated dramatically the concept of the mediator as go-between. The image of the ''middleman'' informs Ulysses' plot to make Ajax Hector's opponent in the duel and it lies at the base of the whole framing story of Paris' rape of Helen, but nowhere is it more obviously operative than in the words and actions of Pandarus. As his name signifies, he is agency incarnate, and he tends to function almost allegorically in the play's action as ''medium'' and the problems it creates, both for character and creator. . . . Pandarus refers to himself as a ''broker,'' a ''trader,'' a ''go-between,'' a ''broker-between,'' an ''agent,'' and he is referred to by others as a ''bawd,'' a ''convoy,'' and a ''broker lackey.'' To Troilus he is ''Charon'' in his ferry at one instant and ''Cupid'' with his wings the next [III. ii. 9-14], but in all cases he is essentially a conveyance, an active mediator. Moreover, he knows the nature of his role in the play and never attempts to disguise it: ''I have had my labor for my travail,'' he tells Troilus petulantly at the

beginning of the play, ''gone between and between, but small thanks for my labor'' [I. i. 71-2]. Halfway through the play he tells the lovers that ''If ever you prove false one to another, since I have taken such pains to bring you together, let all pitiful goers-between be called to the world's end after my name'' [III. ii. 199-202]. And he begins his last speech with the lament, ''O world, world! thus is the poor agent despised'' [V. x. 36-7]. Indeed, at the play's unusual conclusion he actually serves as intermediary between the play-world and the contemporary audience, thereby extending the issue of mediation from the internal workings of the play to the actual theatrical experience. Like the ''prologue armed'' who introduced the play, Pandarus in the ''epilogue'' presents himself as ''suited / In like conditions as our argument'' [Prologue, 24-5]. For in an inclusive and radical sense Pandarus bodies forth the pervasive themes in *Troilus* of betweenness, agency, process—in short, medium. When his role is understood in this manner perhaps the most revealing and despairing words in the play are Troilus' plaintive ''O gods, how do you plague me! / I cannot come to Cressid but by Pandar'' [I. i. 94-5].

How are we then to understand Troilus' cry that he ''cannot come to Cressid but by Pandar''? Is Troilus passively indulging an irresponsible penchant for delegating action to inferiors who can conveniently bear the blame for possible failure; or does that ''cannot'' signify the imposition of an inescapable limitation on the freedom of choice and action granted Troilus within the play-world? The strong emphasis on mediation traced above would seem to suggest the latter: that is, *if* Troilus is to activate his love for Cressida at all it can *only* be through the agency of Pandarus. By constructing the play in this manner Shakespeare calls attention to the inherent ''between-ness'' of all human relationships, to the potentially tragic fact that all communication between selves is a contact based on *mediacy*, not *immediacy*. Shakespeare presents Troilus/Pandarus/Cressida, then, as what they traditionally were in his medieval sources: three inextricably-bound components of a fascinating and tragic configuration representing love-in-action. The indissoluble nature of the trio is underscored by Shakespeare at the climax of the assignation scene when the three principals take hands to form an eternal contract: ''Go to, a bargain made; seal it, seal it,'' Pandarus chants: ''I'll be the witness. Here I hold your hand, here my cousin's'' [III. ii. 197-98]. (pp. 151-54)

The ''contractual'' language Pandarus continually uses in this scene directs us to the particularly modern touch Shakespeare brings to the venerable configuration. As ''agent,'' ''broker,'' and ''trader,'' Pandarus provides dramatic focus for a metaphoric web of references that has as its organizing principle imagery and diction associated with merchandising. *Troilus* is loaded with ''terms and concepts . . . relating to exchange, commerce, estimation, worth, price, buying and selling, trading, and so on'' [see W. R. Elton in the Additional Bibliography], and this language is significant since it helps reinforce the mediated nature of human relationships in the play. For instance, as Troilus glosses his predicament (''I cannot come to Cressid but by Pandar''), he too uses commercial terminology to erect a metaphoric framework that will structure the various interactions of character in the rest of the play:

> Tell me, Apollo, for thy Daphne's love,
> What Cressid is, what Pandar, and what we.
> Her bed is Inida; there she lies, a pearl.
> Between our Ilium and where she resides
> Let it be called the wild and wand'ring flood,
> Ourself the merchant, and this sailing Pandar
> Our doubtful hope, our convoy and our bark.
>
> 　　　　　　　　　　　　　　　　[I. i. 98-104]

These lines are crucial for a proper understanding of the dynamics of character interaction in *Troilus*. Inspired perhaps by Apollo, Troilus imagines himself as a "merchant" and Cressida as the desired merchandise, the "pearl"; he conceives of Pandarus as the all-important middleman, his agent in this transaction. That Troilus assigns to himself and Cressida purely static roles may be seen as a severely self-imposed liability. (pp. 154-55)

To take a moralistic line of argumentation at this point and criticize Troilus, and Cressida too, for exacerbating their impotence by fatuously relying on Pandarus to bring them together may be an appealing alternative for some critical sensibilites. But if Pandarus epitomizes "medium" in the irreducible sense outlined above, it becomes difficult to perceive what other options are open to the lovers in the play. Shakespeare's real interest, it seems, is less in analysis of character than in a tragically-conceived pattern of desire, endeavor, and achievement in which individual choices affect the outcome only indirectly.

The commercial scheme Troilus describes above, for example, is not peculiar to his existential situation. We are reminded in the Trojan council scene that another agent of equally "doubtful" sailing credentials, Paris, was dispatched on a similarly precarious voyage for exactly the same kind of merchandise. As Troilus reminds his fellows of this already completed action, the same three-part metaphoric pattern is again used, with only the names changed. The Trojan Princes replace Troilus as the merchant, Paris replaces Pandarus as the venturesome agent, and Helen replaces Cressida as the sought-after "pearl":

> It was thought meet
> Paris should do some vengeance on the Greeks.
> Your breath with full consent bellied his sails;
> The seas and winds, old wranglers, took a truce
> And did him service; he touched the ports desired,
> And for an old aunt whom the Greeks held captive
> He brought a Grecian queen, whose youth and freshness
> Wrinkles Apollo's and makes stale the morning.
> Why keep we her? The Grecians keep our aunt.
> Is she worth keeping? Why, she is a pearl
> Whose price hath launched above a thousand ships
> And turned crowned kings to merchants.
>
> [II. ii. 72-83]

The close similarity between the language and thought of this passage and Troilus' earlier comments on the mercantile nature of his pursuit of Cressida reveals the strength of the underlying metaphoric conception informing the unfolding action in the various plot strands. There is more to observe here, however, than just interesting double-plot parallelism. This subtle metaphoric cross-reference between the two actions creates a rather dazzling multi-perspective in which the dismal outcome of Troilus' anticipated attainment of the "pearl" Cressida is actually suggested *in advance* by its metaphoric association with the already completed Princes/Paris/Helen action. Why dispatch Pandarus, the juxtaposition subtly implies to us but not to Troilus, when his counterpart Paris brought home such unanticipated consequences? If Helen too was formerly a "pearl," perhaps Cressida had better be left on her "bed in India." (pp. 155-56)

The imagery of buying and selling and the various strategies of salesmanship and merchandising are not simply characteristics of Troilus' speech, but rather, they color the expression of many quite different characters. Like the two plot strands

observed above, for instance, the Ulysses/Ajax/Achilles plot is also conceived in largely the same controlling framework of merchant imagery. If Pandarus and Paris were the agents in their respective actions, Ajax becomes the middleman in this affair. "Ajax employed," Ulysses says succinctly, "plucks down Achilles' plumes" [I. iii. 385]. And as he broaches his scheme to Nestor, Ulysses turns naturally to the familiar "merchant" metaphor:

> Let us, like merchants,
> First show foul wares, and think perchance they'll sell;
> If not the lustre of the better shall exceed
> By showing the worse first.
>
> [I. iii. 358-61]

The reactivation of Achilles (motionless "upon a lazy bed" [I. iii. 147] in his tent rather than upon a "bed in India") is the particular "pearl" Ulysses is seeking, and Ajax seems to him the proper agency through which to effect the acquisition. But again this enterprise is no more successful than the other two ventures, ending in equally total frustration. . . . (pp. 156-57)

By surveying the similarities and differences between the several "merchant" figures in *Troilus,* we can see that character analysis of a moralistic nature will not be entirely responsive to the play's vital concerns. If we accuse Troilus of a self-justifying passivity in his reliance on Pandarus, are we then willing to level the same charge at Priam's Princes for their reliance on Paris, or at Ulysses and Nestor for their use of Ajax? Ulysses is not passive; indeed, he works as hard as he can to make his plan work—and yet his failure is no less complete than the others. Shakespeare seems to be going to some trouble to convince his audience that *all* human plots, reasonable or emotional, are doomed to failure—that, as Sonnet 94 concludes, "sweetest things turn sourest by their deeds." To illustrate the origins of this gloomy and fatalistic attitude, Shakespeare shows us how Pandarus, Paris, and Ajax, in their actions as agents, unintentionally cheapen and pervert the aspirations that have been subjected to their instrumentation. But we are not encouraged to criticize these characters because of their inability to fulfill their assignments; our attention is directed instead to a more radical inadequacy felt in the mediated nature of human action itself. Most importantly, the characters are forced by the requirements of the play to act within the context of an indissoluble trinity of desire, endeavor, and achievement which, by focusing on the debilitating nature of medium, gives deep cogency to Agamemnon's assertion that "In all designs begun on earth below" hope "Fails in the promised largeness' [I. iii. 4-5].

One design "begun on earth below," and therefore presumably destined also to fall short of its "promised largeness," was Shakespeare's play *Troilus and Cressida.* In what manner, then, does the specific *form* of the play reflect Shakespeare's interest in the problems of mediation previously discussed? Structure and substance, of course, are united and indissoluble in reading and performance, and one should not expect to keep a consideration of theme separate from form. (pp. 157-58)

Several commentators have complained that the shaping impulse in the structure of *Troilus'* plot is constantly being clogged, frustrated, or misdirected as it tries to move towards coherent completion. It often seems that the final distorted shape which a scene or episode takes has "not answer[ed] the aim / And that unbodied figure of the thought / That gave't surmisèd shape" [I. iii. 15-17]. . . . Several scenes seem to wander badly from their main concerns (such as II. iii), and others get bogged down in tedious verbiage and rhetoric. Moreover, there is a rather confused sense of continuity in the jerky progression of the scenes, and the temporal synchronization of the love plot and the war plot becomes almost incomprehensible if examined too closely. . . . In *Troilus'* structure as well as in its theme "checks and disasters / Grow in the veins of actions highest reared" [I. iii. 5-6].

But the most troublesome impediment to the realization of highest actions in the play is language. Not only the characters in the play but the rising form of the play itself must struggle with the frustrating resistance that the medium of words can exercise. *Troilus* repeatedly brings two people together ostensibly to exchange information. And in almost all cases the outcome is a tremendous explosion of words, either in the form of pointless punning or of magnificent rant and rhetoric, resulting in either a very trivial exchange of information or total misunderstanding. It takes Ulysses sixteen tortuous lines to ask Agamemnon for permission to address the Greek council [I. iii. 54-69]; Aeneas and Agamemnon struggle for no fewer than forty-two lines simply to make initial contact with each other [I. iii. 215-56]; Pandarus leaves Troilus in a pique after completely misunderstanding Troilus' febrile attempts to praise Cressida [I. i. 70-88]; it takes Pandarus forty-eight lines to tell Cressida his silly and pointless little anecdote about the fifty-two hairs on Troilus' chin [I. ii. 110-67]; Ajax beats Thersites for a full scene trying to get him to "learn me the tenor of the proclamation" and never does learn it [II. i. 1-120]; Pandarus and a servant talk at cross purposes for forty lines without exchanging a dram of information [III. i. 1-40]; communication at one point so completely breaks down that Ajax actually mistakes Thersites for Agamemnon [III. iii. 251-63]; Aeneas and Diomedes exchange pointless oxymoronic talk for thirty-five lines before getting on with the business of exchanging the prisoners [IV. i. 1-35]; Nestor greets Hector with a lengthy encomium that threatens to continue indefinitely before Ulysses mercifully interrupts and changes the subject [IV. v. 183-210]; Aeneas, in particular, is so addicted to high-sounding language that, like his more humorous counterpart Gratiano, he constantly "speaks an infinite deal of nothing" [*Merchant of Venice*, I. i. 114]. A considerable disproportion obviously exists in the play between the verbal energy expended in conversation and the achieved results, a disproportion aptly expressed metaphorically in Thersites' observation that the Greeks "will not in circumvention deliver a fly from a spider, without drawing their massy irons and cutting the web" [II. iii. 15-17]. The Trojans also have verbal "massy irons" which they brandish with equal superfluity.

The sheer bulk of words contained in the above examples makes it clear that a large part of the texture of *Troilus* is made up of various kinds of linguistic mismanagement. . . . In all the above examples . . . it can be seen that Shakespeare is quite aware of what is happening to language and to the attempt at communication. He sees clearly that what should be a transparent and flexible medium for communication and artistic creation has become opaque and resistant, clotted with high-flown rhetoric and uncontrolled verbosity. The man who wrote *Love's Labour's Lost* is not likely to forget how characters can abuse language by becoming fatalistic or arrogantly self-aggrandizing in their efforts to control it. (pp. 158-60)

But despite such clear evidence that the dramatist is exercising some control and perspective on his characters' abuse of language, I don't think we should conclude that Shakespeare's concern with problems of communication is primarily satiric.

Aeneas makes a fool of himself whenever he opens his mouth; but then how *should* Aeneas talk in a late Renaissance play, or Hector? What linguistic decorums apply to the dramatic re-creation of an Agamemnon, Nestor, or Troilus? The problem cannot be resolved by thumbing through some Renaissance handbooks on style, since Agamemnon is not Essex, Nestor is not Lord Burghley, and Troilus is not the Earl of Southampton. Nor is Shakespeare willing to follow the lead of Ben Jonson and endow his characters with a classically proper but anti-quated and anachronistic style. Shakespeare's historical con-sciousness was sufficiently developed for him to realize that he was attempting to mediate between a complex and venerable literary tradition and his modern audience. He must have been sensitive to the contradictory nature of the several linguistic and behavioral models available to him from Homer through Chaucer, Lydgate, and Caxton to his contemporary Chapman. And it is patronizing pseudo-historicism simply to assume that Shakespeare felt compelled to debase Cressida and to ridicule the participants in the war because Henryson and some con-temporary hacks chose to do so. The aesthetic dilemma Shake-speare faced was less cynical: he had to be responsive to the dictates of the received materials while at the same time at-tempting to create a new language for these legendary figures which would give them authentic dramatic existence for his immediate audience. The danger (and the temptation) was that he would inadvertently caricature his subjects, that he would "slander" them with "terms unsquared" . . . and "ridiculous and silly action" [I. iii. 159, 149]—such as another more cynical dramatist within the play, Patroclus, uses when he "pageants" the Greek high command for Achilles' amuse-ment. Shakespeare's dilemma, then, arises from his dual role as maker and mediator, from his integrity as a creator and his allegiance to the dignity of the literary tradition which he passes on.

I suggest, therefore, that the strong satiric element which critics like O. J. Campbell [see excerpt above, 1938] have discerned in *Troilus* should not be attributed to Shakespeare's slavish desire to ape Jonson and Marston, for this is to confuse Shake-speare's intentions with Patroclus' intentions. Instead, the play's bitterness should be traced to Shakespeare's tragic recognition that the dramatist's inevitable problem with language is similar to the inevitable human problem: that man *is* language and mediation is the ground, the Pandar, of being. For instance, Shakespeare knows that his language actually shapes the iden-tity of his characters, sculptures them, makes them emerge as fully articulated beings. And the disheartening implications of this knowledge appear in Patroclus' vulgar dramatization of Agamemnon and Nestor and in Achilles' enthusiastic response: "'Excellent!' 'tis Agamemnon right," he cries, "'Tis Nestor right" [I. iii. 164-70]. Shakespeare makes us aware here that dramatic acts have an ontological dimension, that in mediating the reality of these literary figures to his audience he (like Patroclus) is unavoidably re-creating them in the present mo-ment. We may finally feel that only a very thin line separates the Agamemnon and Nestor Shakespeare represents from Pa-troclus' brutal mimicry of them, but that margin is the differ-ence between a cynical retreat into the satiric mode and a tragic confrontation with the aesthetic and ontological problems raised by mediation. (pp. 161-63)

Richard D. Fly, "'I Cannot Come to Cressid but by Pandar': Mediation in the Theme and Structure of 'Troilus and Cressida'," in English Literary Renaissance, *Vol. 3, No. 1, Winter, 1973, pp. 145-65.*

JOHN BAYLEY   (essay date 1975)

[Bayley contends that while most Shakespearean plays project a "novel time," i.e., a sense of time which extends the possibilities of character and situation both before and after the actual time of the play, in Troilus and Cressida Shakespeare denies the past and the future and places the play in a "perpetual present." In confining the play to the present moment, says Bayley, Shakespeare deprives his characters of historical and personal significance; they become, in Bayley's words, "voices imprisoned in role and argument, figures condemned to tread the mill of time without ever being made free of it."]

Shakespeare's masterpieces wax and wane beween what must be termed novel and play, between Henry James's 'relations that stop nowhere' and the circle of performance in which they must be arbitrarily resolved. But there is one play in which this creation by separation seems to have no part. *Troilus and Cressida* has no novel in it to fill our minds between performances and, conversely, no 'novel moments' to startle us when we have formed our impression of it as a play. It remains purely and simply a play, confined to the time it takes to act. The other plays possess the dimension it lacks, but it has an atmosphere and spirit unique to itself and lacking in them. An enquiry into its two-dimensional unity may reveal something about the ways in which division works in the being of the other plays, and in our response to them.

Troilus exhibits a time element that produces persons and situations not elsewhere found in the plays. It has often been pointed out how frequently it invokes time and its powers. Time is of course one of the most frequent topics of the commonplace not only in Shakespeare but in all Elizabethan literature; the most notorious and by its very familiarity the most reassuring of *topoi* ["motifs"]. It is merciless, devouring, all-conquering. Or it can conquer everything except love, everything except art. Or it is both judge and redeemer, serving 'to unmask falsehood and bring truth to life' [*The Rape of Lucrece*, 940]. We are lulled by these commonplaces, which seem not only familiar to us but doubly familiar from their frequent and regular recurrence in the miniatures of lyric and in the discursive poetry of high sentence.... It is evidently not the emphasis on time that counts here but the dramatic use made of it. In all Shakespeare's other plays we feel that the present time as enacted on the stage, not only depends upon the past but is in the service of the future. Lear has made his plans: the action will reveal their consequences; the unseen future will underwrite a return to normality of a kind, be guarantor, as Edgar says, of 'we that are young' [*King Lear*, V. iii. 326]. But in the formal impact of *Troilus* there is neither past nor future: everything takes place in and ends in, the present.

We need not look far for the formal justification for the device. We all know (even today) how the matter of Troy began, and how it ended. Our action, as the Prologue tells us, will take place in 'the middle'. What follows from this? That the playwright can abolish past and future if he wants to, and see what the consequences are if he does. Novelist's time—and in general Shakespearean time—accumulates character and perspective, and almost any playwright borrows enough of the novelist's time to produce the appearance of these two things. His actors are in the midst of their lives, and his action will admit—if only tacitly—that it cannot tell the whole of their tale, and that other things are in progress outside it. But what if the playwright turns the other way and instead of borrowing time from the novelist deliberately renounces it, and all the space and coherence it assumes? Suppose he implies that if novelist's time does not exist for him he is left with the headless and

senseless trunk of an action, devoid of the reality which can only come from knowledge of what went before and must come after? This is where such a playwright as Beckett begins, starting from the metaphysical premise that life can have no sequential sense or meaning, that all is an ever-repeated mumble of the present. Shakespeare could begin from a more formalized hypothesis: you know the beginning and end of this business, so they need have no meaning in terms of what I am about to show you of the middle. The only surprise here must be a perpetual present.

A characteristic paradox is made of this. It is *because* we know how the siege began and ended that Agamemnon can say,

> What's past and what's to come is strewn with husks
> And formless ruin of oblivion.
>
> [IV. v. 166-67]

Agamemnon, like all the other figures in the play, cares nothing for the logic of past and future, and if neither exists the present itself can have no coherent meaning—he himself no coherent personality. That is the logic in the dramatic world of *Troilus and Cressida,* the more terrible for being implicit and uninsistent. And it is a world that makes us, by contrast, sharply aware of how the sense of character in a Shakespeare play normally comes into being, between an accumulation of impressions that depends on novel time, and quick, often contradictory, response to the dramatic moment.

Let us consider the first scene of Act III, in which Pandarus, Paris and Helen chatter together and sing a song about love. It is like a glimpse in a nightclub, but whereas in real life the spectator might be sufficiently intrigued—enough of a novelist as it were—to wonder about their relationship and about the rest of their lives, Shakespeare inhibits even so small an attempt at coherence, by depriving the characters of the slightest historical and personal significance. The scene makes us feel as confused and unresponsive as if we ourselves were in the same state as the other guests in that nightclub, immersed in the same experience of the contingent and the banal. No novelist can do this, because in drawing our attention to the contingent and the banal he puts us on the outside of it, and manipulates it so that it is fully under our control. This difference is crucial. In novel time the absurdity of the contingent becomes a positive pleasure to be entertained by; but in *Troilus* we are too benightmared by the world of the moment to contemplate it with this enjoyment. Like the actors themselves, we are borne passively on the moment by moment tide of the drama, and we find when it is over that we still cannot get it into shape.

The sense in which Shakespeare here denies and dissolves history might be compared with the drinking scene on board Pompey's galley in *Antony and Cleopatra,* where he deftly and dynamically confirms it. In *Troilus* the game seems to be to deny that the famous and the legendary ever existed as time has reported them, or that we would ever find anything at any moment in history beyond scraps of idiotic dialogue and meaningless event.

And this because the convention of play time is reduced virtually to an *ad absurdum.* The realisation makes clear the play's unique status in the Shakespearean canon and explains things about it which on any other interpretation seem wilful and puzzling at the best and at the worst downright unsatisfactory. The point to recognize is that we are puzzled because there is nothing to be puzzled about, because behind the glitter and coruscation of the language and the rapid charade of the language there is nothing that adds up. We do not know what the characters are like because there is neither time nor occasion to find out, and for the same reason they have no idea of themselves. Neither we, nor they, can be aware here of the other world, of the novelist's world, in which time stretches into past and future, supplying the reality of persons, creating space and leisure, value and meaning. Ulysses is concerned to impress upon Achilles that such a world can only be maintained by constant action and endeavour. The irony of his advice is that it is intended merely for the moment, and that Achilles is in fact spurred to action by the random eruption of another moment—the death of Patroclus. Ulysses is a charade of policy as Nestor is one of age, Troilus of fidelity, Cressida of faithlessness. 'He must, he is, he cannot but be wise' [II. iii. 252] is the ironic comment on Nestor. But all of them must, are, and cannot but be voices imprisoned in role and argument, figures condemned to tread the mill of time without ever being made free of it. Compared to their undifferentiated and claustrophobic world the predicament of Macbeth seems like freedom itself—'as bread and general as the casing air' [*Macbeth*, III. iv. 22]. For it is in Macbeth's own consciousness that coherency and purpose have become extinguished, have become a tale told by an idiot. In the world outside him the logic of time proceeds with its serene, restorative, but for him terrible assurance. He cannot but contemplate the shape and consequence of his action stretching before and after, and thus becomes himself, the real Macbeth, situated in the real and unforgiving dimension of history.

Everywhere in his work, not just in the history plays, Shakespeare's sense of the past is of 'time's jewel', giving meaning to human destiny. It is so assured, so comprehensive and so inevitable that we take it for granted. (pp. 56-60)

Whatever the contrast between them Lady Macbeth is united at last with her husband—an ironic second marriage—when she admits the law of responsibility and causality. Very different is Cressida's comment on her relation with Troilus: 'Well, well 'tis done, 'tis past, and yet it is not' [V. ii. 97]. She has no sense of, and does not want to know, what has taken place: pleasure, boredom and infidelity are alike unsorted phenomena of the moment for her, and she is denied past and future awareness to the point where she is no more than a voice speaking lines in the theatre. Someone said of Marilyn Monroe that she was 'discontinuous with any idea of personality'. It is the same with Cressida. She becomes her words; our 'present eye praises the present object' as Ulysses says [III. iii. 180], and looks no further.

Shakespeare's technique here deliberately abandons his usual sure mode of creating a complete human being, complete not only in terms of history but in relation to a family and a social situation. Such creation may be only a hint or a touch—as in the personality of a Paulina in *The Winter's Tale*, or an Aumerle in *Richard II*—but the sense of character as logically and soundly related to environment is something of the greatest importance to his art that we can usually take for granted. In the Troilus legend all is arbitrary, and again we may feel that the playwright sardonically emphasises this aspect of legend into a corner stone of theatrical technique. We know nothing about these people but this is the story of how they behaved: it is thus as accurate as it is paradoxical to see the legend as a moment in life, left hanging on a note of mockery that is very far from being the 'monumental mockery' which Ulysses sees as the fate of bygone reputation, and action left behind in the past. (p. 61)

If Hamlet does not always speak like a man of this world it is because he lives in different worlds, as both playgoer and victim of its plot: his drama is that of a young man acting who becomes a young man acted upon. Troilus's self-absorption is not so unlike Hamlet's, but it is concerned entirely with the sensations of the moment. The attitude to time is again the key.

> You that look pale and tremble at this chance,
> That are but mutes or audience to this act,
> Had I but time—
>
> [*Hamlet*, V. ii. 334-36]

Hamlet invokes novel time, the spacious dimension which the play will not let him have. For him it is a matter of infinite concern that his wounded name shall be restored, to live behind him in the love and knowledge of his friend Horatio, who will speak

> to the yet unknowing world
> How these things came about.
>
> [*Hamlet*, V. ii. 379-80]

But absence of novel time, and what goes with it, seems the very point of *Troilus*. 'Hector is dead, there is no more to say' [V. x. 22]. To live in reputation and in friendship can have no place in *Troilus*, where all such things are dissolved in the expediency of the moment. We must contrast with this not only *Hamlet* but the powerful ties and dignities of friendship which triumph over politics in *Julius Caesar*. But these things are nothing in *Troilus*, as the tone even of the Prologue makes quite clear.

> our play
> Leaps o'er the vaunt and firstlings of these broils,
> Beginning in the middle; starting thence away
> To what may be digested in a play.
>
> [Prologue, 26-9]
> (p. 63)

John Bayley, "Time and the Trojans," in Essays in Criticism, *Vol. XXV, No. 1, January, 1975, pp. 55-73.*

J. HILLIS MILLER   (essay date 1977)

[*Hillis Miller is a representative of deconstructionist criticism, a school of literary theory which seeks to reveal, on a small scale, how a work of literature undermines its own apparent meaning, and, on a large scale, how all of "logocentric" Western thought inherently betrays its own systems of logic. In analyzing Troilus's reaction to Cressida's unfaithfulness, Hillis Miller asserts that Troilus responds not with a single, unified, monological speech, but with a dialogical speech which admits two contradictory language systems and divides the mind against itself. Troilus's bifold line of argument, says Hillis Miller, is a doubling of reason which, at the same time, presents itself as madness and can ultimately be seen as a subversion of traditional metaphysical logic. He focuses his discussion on the reference to "Ariachne" in Troilus's speech and contends that the word is a conflation of two heroines from Greek mythology: Ariadne, whose clew of thread guided Theseus out of the Cretan labyrinth, and Arachne, who, after having her weaving destroyed by the gods, hanged herself and was later turned into a spider. Like Troilus's speech, Hillis Miller argues, "Ariachne" is dialogical, for while it tells two different stories, it is nonetheless no word at all and its meaning "can never be stilled in a single monological line." He concludes that the reader of* Troilus and Cressida *is reduced to "the same state of exasperated madness of discourse that tears Troilus in two." A similar division in the personality of Troilus has also been noted by Albert Gérard (1959) and Richard C. Harrier (1959).*]

A passage in Shakespeare's *Troilus and Cressida* brilliantly works out the implications of the division of the mind into two when the single narrative line of monologue becomes the doubled line of dialogue. When one *logos* becomes two, the circle an ellipse, all the gatherings or bindings of Western logocentricism are untied or cut. *Logos*, the reader will remember, comes from *legein*, to gather, as wheat is gathered into sheaves or as bits of string are gathered into hanks. In the passage in question Troilus has been watching Cressida dallying with Diomedes. I give the Variorum text, since the question is in part what Shakespeare wrote, and it is necessary to get back as close to that as possible:

> *Troy.* This she? no, this is *Diomids Cressida:*
> If beautie have a soule, this is not she:
> If soules guide vowes; if vowes are sanctimonie;
> If sanctimonie be the gods delight:
> If there be rule in unitie it selfe.
> This is not she: O madnesse of discourse!
> That cause sets up, with, and against they selfe
> By foule authoritie: where reason can revolt
> Without perdition, and losse assume all reason,
> Without revolt. This is, and is not *Cressid:*
> Within my soule, there doth conduce a fight
> Of this strange nature, that a thing inseperate,
> Divides more wider then the skie and earth:
> And yet the spacious bredth of this division,
> Admits no Orifex for a point as subtle,
> As *Ariachnes* broken woofe to enter:
> Instance, O instance! strong as *Plutoes* gates:
> *Cressid* is mine, tied with the bonds of heaven;
> Instance, O instance, strong as heaven it selfe:
> The bonds of heaven are slipt, dissolv'd and loos'd,
> And with another knot five finger tied,
> The fractions of her faith, orts of her love:
> The fragments, scraps, the bits, and greazie reliques,
> Of her ore-eaten faith, are bound to *Diomed*.
>   [V. ii. 137-60]

The word "Ariachnes" leaps to the eye of the reader of this passage or to the ear of its hearer. Slip of the tongue or of the pen? Ignorance on Shakespeare's part? Error of the scribe or of the typesetter who has put in one letter too many? An alteration for the meter's sake? The extra i makes nonsense of the word. The letter too many, "prosthesis" in one possible meaning of the word, calls attention to itself almost as much as a gap, an ellipsis, a syncope, a letter too few, would do. The one letter too many or the one too few come strangely to the same thing. Both produce a gap in the meaning and call attention to the material base of signs, marks on the page which the eye interprets or acoustic disturbances perceptible to the ear. The little i in "Ariachnes" has the effect of a bit of sand in a salad or of a random sound in a symphony, the flautist dropping his flute, the snap of a breaking violin string. The harmony is broken, the string untuned.

The notes in the Variorum *Troilus and Cressida* give amusing evidence of the efforts by editors, emenders, and critics down through the centuries to remove the grain of sand, to root out the i and to return the dialogical "Ariachnes" to the monological "Arachne" or, alternatively, to "Ariadnes." (pp. 44-5)

The force of the monological assumption, one can see, is so great that each of these learned gentlemen can entertain only the hypothesis of an either/or: *either* Ariadne, *or* Arachne, not both; or, on the other hand, the hypothesis of some meaningless error on the part of Shakespeare, a copyist, or the printer, the

absurd sound in the symphony of reason, mere "noise" in the chain of communication. It remained to I. A. Richards [see Additional Bibliography], as far as I know, to have the honor of breaking through the ponderous weight of metaphysical prejudice by observing that "Ariachne" functions perfectly as a "portmanteau" bringing two words together in one receptacle. The conflation in "Ariachne" of two myths which are and are not congruent is precisely in agreement with what happens in Troilus's speech, namely, an anguished confrontation with the subversive possibility of dialogue, reason divided hopelessly against itself by submission to a "bifold authority." (Most editors have preferred the "By-fould" of the quarto to the reading of "By foule" of the folio, which I have given above.) "Portmanteau word" is not quite correct as a name here either, since *slithy* (combining *slimy* and *lithe*) or *chortle* (combining *chuckle* and *snort*) harmoniously combine in one suitcase two compatible or more or less compatible qualities or acts, whereas "Ariachne" brings together two stories which in fact do not fit. (pp. 46-7)

Threading through this speech, however, in its admirable play on various key words and key figures of logocentric metaphysics (the words "unity," "discourse," "cause," "authority," "reason," "instance," the images of threading, folding, or tying), is a recognition that dialogue, in the sense of a division of one mind against itself, is ultimately a matter of language or manifests itself as a subversive possibility of language. This is not to say that Troilus has not seen with his own eyes, "theoretically," as it were, the faithlessness of Cressida. The consequence of that seeing, however, in its contradiction of what he had seen, said, and heard said before, is the possibility of two simultaneous contradictory sign systems centered on Cressida but ultimately organizing everything in the cosmos around this Cressida or, alternatively, around that Cressida. Since these two language systems are enclosed within Troilus's single mind, they double that mind against itself. They make what should be a single-centered circle into an ellipse. Either one of these language systems alone is perfectly sane, but both together in a single mind are madness:

> *Troilus:* But if I tell how these two did coact,
> Shall I not lie in publishing a truth?
> Sith yet there is a credence in my heart,
> An esperance so obstinately strong
> That doth invert th' attest of eyes and ears,
> As if those organs had deceptious functions,
> Created only to calumniate.
> Was Cressid here?
> *Ulysses:*   I cannot conjure, Troyan.
> *Troilus:* She was not, sure.
> *Ulysses:*   Most sure she was.
> *Troilus:* Why, my negation hath no taste of madness.
> *Ulysses:* Nor mine, my lord. Cressid was here but now.
>   [V. ii. 118-28]

Madness is here defined as the impossibility of speaking either truly or falsely. This is precisely the possibility demonstrated in Gödel's theorem, the possibility of a proposition derived logically from other propositions within a system but which can neither be proved false nor proved true. In Troilus's case, he can neither speak truly nor lie, or rather he must inevitably do both at once. Truth is here defined as both truth of internal agreement and truth of external correspondence. Whatever Troilus says is true in relation to one Cressida and to one language system deriving from that Cressida, but false in relation to the other Cressida and to *her* language system. This situation is madness. Cressida's faithlessness, the possibility that her original vows to Troilus were not grounded on her substantial self in its ties to the rest of the ethical, political, and cosmic order all the way up to God, puts in question that whole order. Cressida's lying makes it possible to conceive that the story of that order, as it is told by the reasonable discourse of Western metaphysics, is itself a lie in the sense that it is like that dangerous *mimesis* Plato deplores—fatherless language, language without a head, without a base, without a *logos*. Troilus's speech is an exploration, under the pressure of his anguish, of the metaphysical implications of the possibility of dialogue, taking dialogue as a capacity intrinsic to language, an effect of language. Rather than being, as the word seems to suggest, the juxtaposing of two different minds as sources of language, dialogue is the possibility of lie, the possibility that language may be cut off from any source in a mind, human or divine. It would then generate its own coercive machine making things happen in the human world. The possibility that language may be sourceless, baseless, not modelled on any mind divine or human, but rather coercively modelling them, appears when two different coherent languages struggle for domination within a single mind. (pp. 47-9)

The notion of dialogue is a benign enough principle when it describes two persons conversing, however antagonistically. When it is seen as the possibility of the dividing of a single mind against itself, it is more subversive. Ultimately it puts in question the notions of the mind and of the self and sees them as linguistic fictions, as functions in a system of words without base in the *logos* of any substantial mind. When the monological becomes dialogical, the dialogical loses its *logoi* and becomes alogical. There is no Cressida in the sense of an unalterable self but only the phantasmal appearance of a self created by the baseless performatives of the vows she happens to make, vows sanctified by no divine correspondences. If she makes new vows, she becomes a different person. In the same way, the Troilus who experiences Cressida's faithlessness is himself disintegrated. He becomes not two persons but no person, out of his mind.

If Troilus's speech is taken as a model of narrative discourse, it demonstrates the possibility of a story which is simultaneously two different incompatible stories. These can never be reduced to one by any rule of unity. They can never be simultaneously contained within any one sane mind, sane in the sense of single and orderly, and yet are enclosed within the bounds of one text, one word or set of words. This makes possible the "madness of discourse, / That cause sets up, with and against itself" [V. ii. 142-43], that is, the madness of a running train of language, a line of argument, which is doubled. It is and is not itself. (pp. 51-2)

The rest of Troilus's speech works out the consequences of this self-division. The subjection of Troilus's soul to a bifold authority means that he is like a country at civil war or like the political state of *Troilus and Cressida* itself, divided between Greeks and Trojans engaged in mutual destruction. As each side in the war can "fur its gloves with reason" [II. ii. 38], so each part of Troilus's mind can develop its own entirely stable chain of reasoning based on its central assumption. (This is, or, on the other side, this is not, Cressid.) "Reason can," therefore, "revolt / Without perdition" [V. ii. 144-45]. Reason can be divided against itself like a country at civil war without the loss (perdition) of reason in outright madness, and, on the other hand, "loss" "can assume all reason, / Without revolt" [V. ii. 145-46]. The loss of reason in its doubling, or the loss

of Cressida in her doubling, can express itself in entirely reasonable terms without the perdition of reason in madness. If this is, and is not, Cressid, the mind which sees and reasons about this contradiction of the law of identity is and is not mad. Troilus goes on reasoning sanely but in a way simultaneously subject to two different reasons or centers of reasoning. Troilus himself is simultaneously one and two, his soul at civil war, inseparably one mind, and yet at the same time cleft by an unbridgeable gap which is yet no gap at all, not even the tiniest hole or "orifex." (pp. 52-3)

What is the role of "Ariachne" in this powerful sequence of reasoning about the possible dissolution of reasoning? The conflation of the two myths, that of Ariadne, that of Arachne, in a single word, Ariachne, mimes the mode of relationship between two different myths which exist side by side in a culture and are similar without being identical. The word, moreover, fits perfectly in the context of Troilus's speech. It is a small-scale or microscopic version of that madness of discourse which submits simultaneously to two "causes," is subject to a bifold authority, and so tells two stories at once, absurdly, the dialogical becoming alogical, like a word which is no word but made of bits of two words stuck together, as, for example, Sancho's coinage, *baciyelmo,* in *Don Quixote,* to name the Helmet of Mambrino, which is also a washbasin. Ariachne fits as well the larger context of Shakespeare's play, which has sometimes been accused of being an incoherent string of episodes. It also fits the wider context of Occidental discourse as a whole, in which the coherence of the monological has all along been undermined by the presence within it, inextricably intertwined in any of its expressions, of that other non-system, the "instance" of fragmentation and the absence of unifying authority. The form of relationship between these ever smaller or larger contexts, each repeating the structure of the others on a different scale, is that *mise en abyme* ["made from nothing"] present, for example, in the way a rope is made of braided or intertwined smaller cords, each of which in turn is made of smaller threads enwound, and so on down to the smallest filaments twisted to form the smallest thread.

In the case of "Ariachne" the structure in question is that of anacoluthon. "Ariachne" is an anacoluthon in miniature. It starts off on one path of letters toward Ariadne and switches direction in the middle to complete itself, illogically, as Arachne, in a clash of incompatibles which grates, twists, or bifurcates the mind, precisely as does Troilus's confrontation of a Cressida who is and is not Cressida. The word "anacoluthon" means, etymologically, "not following the same path or track." It describes a syntactical pattern in which there is a shift in tense, number, or person in the midst of a sentence, so that the words do not hang together grammatically. An anacoluthon is not governed by a single *logos*, in the sense of a unified meaning.

If the word "Ariachne" is an anacoluthon in miniature, a similar structure is repeated in the syntactical and figurative incoherence of Troilus's speech, for example in the mixture of the image of bonds and the image of eating, or in the simultaneously active and passive meanings of the word "divides," or in the simultaneous reference of "thing" to Cressida and to Troilus's soul. These double syntactical possibilities have divided critics over the centuries in the hopeless attempt to reduce the sentence containing "divides" and "thing" to a single path of meaning: "Within my soul there doth conduce a fight / Of this strange nature that a thing inseparate / Divides more wider than the sky and earth" [V. ii. 147-49]. The effort of the mind to keep this rope of words from vibrating until it disappears and no longer functions as the tightrope supporting a single line of thought is like the effort to make sense of "Ariachne." The grammatical anacoluthon parallels, in the other direction, the anacoluthon of Troilus's divided mind, the narrative discontinuity of the entire play, and so on up to the immense anacoluthon of Western literature, philosophy, and history as a "whole."

The appropriateness or keeping of "Ariachne" in its non-keeping, however, goes beyond its being one more example of two words which do not fit into the same suitcase. Why Ariadne? Why Arachne? The attempt to follow out the relation between the two myths and their joint relation to Troilus's situation repeats again the mind-twisting or mind-disintegrating experience of anacoluthon. "And yet the spacious breadth of this division [the division of Troilus's mind, the division between the two Cressidas who are yet one Cressida] / Admits no orifex for a point as subtle / As Ariachne's broken woof to enter" [V. ii. 150-52]. The passage is odd, when one thinks of it, odd in the mixture or crisscrossing of the attributes of the two sexes. This is, to be sure, congruent with the superimposition of the two sexes in that "thing inseparate" which is subdivided, Troilus's soul, Cressida's self, but there are further peculiarities. This bifold surface is wide open and yet has no aperture large enough even for that minuscule phallus made of the torn filament of a spider's web or of a broken bit of Ariadne's labyrinth-retracing thread to penetrate. The web, the thread, or the woof, feminine images par excellence, images of veiling or weaving, are transformed into the instruments of a male forced entry. Ariachne's broken woof, figure of a torn or deflowered virginity, becomes, in a mind-twisting reversal of the sexes, itself a "point" which might tear, though it can find in this case no orifex to penetrate, even with its refined subtlety. Tearer and torn here change places, as Ariachne's broken woof both is and is not male, and is and is not female, as the stories of Ariadne and Arachne are both alike and different, and both alike and different from the story of Troilus and Cressida. The motifs of vows and of faithlessness, of the ambiguous relations of the sexes, of weaving or threading which does not hold, of the penetration or non-penetration of a labyrinthine interior which is both male and female, of despair at broken vows, even the motif of hanging—all these return in each of the three stories but in a different order or structure which makes them clash, and leaves them impossible to resolve into versions of a single archetype.

Woof: "the threads that run crosswise in a woven fabric, at right angles to the warp threads. . . . [Variant (influenced by WARP) of Middle English *oof*, Old English *owef: o-*, from *on*, ON + *wefan*, to weave; Root: *Webb-*]." The woof is added to the vertical warp lines already there when the weaving begins. The woof was what was torn by Athene when in her envious rage she cut Arachne's web from top to bottom. The torn web of Arachne becomes the broken thread of Ariadne, woven through the warp of the labyrinth. Ariadne is, according to one version of her story, supposed to have hanged herself with her own thread in despair after Theseus abandoned her, just as Arachne hanged herself after her humiliation by Athene, and was then turned into a spider, as Ariadne was turned into a constellation of stars in a ring. The broken woof of Arachne, the perjured thread of Ariadne become the broken bonds of those vows between Troilus and Cressida, with a crisscross chiasmus changing the sex of betrayer and betrayed from the implicit mother-daughter relation in Arachne's story to the faithless seducer in Theseus and the betrayed lover in Troilus.

Act I. Scene ii. Pandarus and Cressida. By T. Kirk (n.d.).

The meaning of Ariachne in its context lies in the labyrinth of branching incongruous relations it sets up, vibrating resonances which can never be stilled in a single monological narrative line. These resonances reduce the reader to the same state of exasperated dialogical madness of discourse that tears Troilus in two, makes him both be and not be himself. (pp. 55-8)

J. Hillis Miller, "Ariachne's Broken Woof," in The Georgia Review, *Vol. XXXI, No. 1, Spring, 1977, pp. 44-60.*

THOMAS G. WEST (essay date 1981)

[*West presents a reformulation of the dichotomy between the worldviews of the Greeks and Trojans that has been observed in* Troilus and Cressida *by many earlier critics. For West, the two opposing camps express two different views of truth, the Oriental and the Hellenic. He states that the introspective Trojans, representing Oriental principles, derive their truth from a fixed faith in the estimations created by will, while the outward-looking Greeks find truth in a knowledge of humanity and nature. Like D. A. Traversi (1968), West proposes that Trojan truth is undermined by sensuality, but he also notes that the Greeks are susceptible to pride and that, while the Trojans are concerned only with the ends of actions, the Greeks consider only the means. He concludes that* Troilus and Cressida *is out of favor because of its truthfulness, for "truth, when fully exposed, is unpopular."*]

Troilus and Cressida portrays the war between Greece and Troy as the earliest instance of an enduring rivalry between

Act V. Scene ii. Thersites, Ulysses, Troilus, Diomed, and Cressida. By Angelica Kauffman (n.d.).

two understandings of truth. What may be called the Eastern and Western views of truth find their expression in the public and private conduct of the play's characters, in the parallel plots of the Trojan War and the love story. The drama allows us to see how the distinctive casts of human souls answer to their formation by or espousal of one or the other of these contestant alternatives.

Embattled Troy is the most ancient of Shakespeare's settings, and because it is also the setting for the first epic poem of the West, Shakespeare adopts it as an appropriate starting point for his own epic of Western Civilization; *Troilus and Cressida* announces a program that will be executed over the entire range of the dramas. The tension between the Oriental and Hellenic principles runs like a bright thread through the succession of political regimes, whether Roman, Italian, French, or English, that follow the Greek and Trojan beginnings.

The Greeks discover truth in the knowledge of the natures of things, and especially of the nature of man. Keen discernment of the arrangement of the cosmos and a grasp of the human passions through self-knowledge offer a steady foundation for the conduct of life. The Trojans generally identify truth with faith in something whose value is established by an act of the will. This duality surfaces in *Troilus and Cressida* through the juxtaposition of Ulysses and Troilus; it is worked out in the main love plot, which tells the story of Troilus' love for Cres-

sida, its consummation, its dissolution, and Troilus' subsequent destructive fury, and in the war plot depicting Ulysses' scheme to draw Achilles back into the battle by appealing to his pride. (p. 127)

[Troilus] believes that human deficiency mars perfect love, but he attributes the defect to the body's limited strength, not to the satiation that gluts the senses: "This is the monstrosity in love, lady, that the will is infinite and the execution confined" [III. ii. 81-2]. He believes, however, that the lover's pledge of truth to his beloved can transfigure and eternalize the merely sensual appetites that first aroused his passion. Thus he hopes to exempt their love from worldly decay. Troilus affirms that his truthful simplicity, his faithfulness to Cressida, will become a standard for future ages. His very person will become the sacred, eternal principle of truth:

> True swains in love shall in the world to come
> Approve their truth by Troilus. When their rhymes,
> Full of protest, of oath, and big compare,
> Wants similes, . . .
> As truth's authentic author to be cited,
> "As true as Troilus" shall crown up the verse
> And sanctify the numbers.
>
> [III. ii. 173-83]

Caught up in Troilus' enthusiasm, Cressida imitates her lover by calling eternal infamy down upon herself if she should ever

Act II. Scene ii. Cassandra. By G. Romney (n.d.).

prove false to him. (p. 129)

As soon as Cressida arrives at the Greek camp, she is wooed by Diomedes, an intelligent but blunt soldier free of illusions. At the conclusion of the day's combat, Hector and Troilus are invited to dine with the Greek captains, and the visit provides Troilus with a lucky opportunity to spy on Diomedes' courtship of Cressida. With astonishment and despair, Troilus watches Cressida's abrupt repudiation of her earlier promised fidelity as she now consents to become Diomedes' mistress. Confronted with the contradiction between the "true" (faithful) Cressida to whom he is bound by sacred vows "strong as heaven itself" and the "true" (real) Cressida whose "mind is now turned whore" (Thersites' comment), Troilus nearly goes mad [V. ii. 155, 114]. Her truth has proved false, yet if truth is true, as it must be, it cannot be false: "This is, and is not, Cressid" [V. ii. 146]. His speech expresses the shattering of his world:

> Within my soul there doth conduce a fight
> Of this strange nature, that a thing inseparate [namely
>   Cressida]
> Divides more wider than the sky and earth;
> And yet the spacious breadth of this division
> Admits no orifice. . . .
>
>   [V. ii. 147-51]

What has happened, of course, is that the truth supposedly secured by the lovers' oaths has not overcome the previously hidden but now unconcealed truth of the changeable human affections. (pp. 130-31)

For his part, Troilus cannot grasp the truth he has seen because he will not give up the truth certified by his will's commitment:

> Never did young man fancy
> With so eternal and so fixed a soul.
>
>   [V. ii. 165-66]

Incapable of intentionally duplicitous conduct himself (cf. Ulysses' account of him in [IV. v. 97-8]), he cannot understand such waywardness in his sanctified beloved. His first recourse is to seek revenge on Diomedes, Cressida's corrupter. But as the final chaotic battle of the play unfolds in the last act, Troilus' anger becomes increasingly generalized, and when Hector is slain, Achilles replaces Diomedes as the prime object of his wrath. (p. 131)

What has happened to Troilus? The corruption of Cressida has deprived him of his truth, and instead of learning from her example that faith in flesh is no way to eternity, he curses life altogether and is finally content to see Troy fall in order to avenge himself on life. Honorable fidelity to the will's sworn purpose, having been shown to be absurd, is succeeded by irrational fury, for once the world is exposed as false, its annihilation is the only course for one whose will still craves consistency. Nietzsche's claim [in *The Genealogy of Morals*] that "man would rather will nothingness than not will" aptly glosses Troilus' rage at the play's end.

Troilus' principle of truth may be seen at work in a martial setting in the deliberations of the Trojan war council (II. ii.). Offered the opportunity by the Greeks to end the war by returning Helen, the Trojans meet to deliberate. In their discussion Hector argues in favor of giving her back, setting forth reasons of rational fear as well as of justice in accord with the law of nature and nations. He is supported by the priest Helenus, whom Troilus denounces in terms that resemble a Nietzschean attack on reason and priestly morality:

> Nay, if we talk of reason,
> Let's shut our gates and sleep. . . .
> [R]eason and respect
> Make livers pale and lustihood deject.
>
>   [II. ii. 46-50]

Reason is a fit standard for cowardly priests because it reckons nothing more than means to security: its aim is rest and escape from life's sufferings. Against reason Troilus poses the standard of will:

> I take today a wife, and my election
> Is led on in the conduct of my will . . .
>   How may I avoid,
> Although my will distaste what it elected,
> The wife I chose? There can be no evasion
> To blench from this and to stand firm by honor.
>
>   [II. ii. 61-8]

This "mad idolatry," which "makes the service greater than the god" (as Hector quite reasonably calls it [II. ii. 56-7]), excludes all considerations of the goodness or usefulness of an action or purpose. Once a choice is made, honor requires a commitment to its execution even to death. This dedication yields immortality. Whatever Helen's intrinsic worth may be, says Troilus,

> She is a theme of honor and renown,
> A spur to valiant and magnanimous deeds,
> Whose present courage may beat down our foes
> And fame in time to come canonize us.
>
>   [II. ii. 199-202]

Even if the outcome of the war should prove disastrous, it "hath our several honors all engaged / To make it gracious" [II. ii. 124-25]. The grace that flows from faith redeems earthly suffering. Hector seals the decision by explicitly abandoning his reasonable opinion "in way of truth" for the sake of a willful "resolution to keep Helen still" [II. ii. 189-91].

Troilus explains in this scene the principle of his conduct in love as well as war, and Hector shows by his resolution against his own reasonable words that he accepts that principle. Here we see that, on the Trojan side, the unity of the love plot and war plot springs from Troilus' and Troy's fidelity to the will's election, whether it be Cressida or Helen, love or war.

The Greeks exemplify a different approach to truth which depends more upon knowledge than will, and more upon the discovery of analogies than the recitation of oaths. As the play opens, the war against Troy has been dragging on for years without result, and Achilles, reputedly the Greeks' most skillful warrior, is refusing to fight, puffing himself up by consuming the abject supplications that the generals from time to time vainly address to him. A war council is called to discuss the present predicament (I. iii.). Agamemnon, the head of the Greek expedition, and old Nestor open the discussion with platitudinous speeches excusing the absence of results, blaming the war's failure on the vagaries of chance and asserting moreover that a protracted conflict elicits virtue by testing men's mettle with worthy obstacles. Ulysses responds with his famous speech on degree, in which he subtly corrects the elder statesmen by alluding to dangerous omissions in their rule of the Greek camp. The orderly movement of the heavenly bodies around the sun provides men with a fit model of political rule; human life, Ulysses implies, should imitate that eternal and necessary order, as far as it lies within the capacity of human freedom acting upon mortal beings subject to the depredations of temporality. (pp. 132-33)

Ulysses follows his speech on degree with an apparent denunciation of the factious Achilles. In fact, however, the burden of his speech describes how Achilles amuses himself by staging in his tent satirical mimes mocking Agamemnon's pretentious pomposity and Nestor's aged foibles. Ulysses seems to inflame the very infection he has diagnosed, for he further discredits the elders' authority by broadcasting these all-too-plausible portraits. But he has a sensible purpose. Agamemnon's loss is Ulysses', and the Greeks', gain. Ulysses lays the foundation for his own quiet assumption of political power for himself, so that he can administer the remedy that the titular leaders are unable to provide. They are soon ready to follow Ulysses' advice. (p. 134)

Ulysses understands that a public fiction of beauty and "degree" is a necessary part of the political imitation of nature. Just as nature enlists our admiration by its manifest ordered beauty and not by the hidden mechanisms and principles that sustain that beauty, so too man's political regime cannot dispense with its outward look of *kosmos*, although the ugly designs of prudence may uphold the fabric.

This difficulty blemishes Ulysses's solution: he offers no account of the ends of human life. Indeed, conspicuously absent from all the Greek martial deliberations is any consideration of what the war is being fought for and whether it should be continued. All participants in the argument assume the desirability of victory, but no one explains why. The omission obtrudes particularly because in the parallel Trojan war council in II. ii. the only subject of discussion is the purpose of the war and whether it is worth fighting to keep Helen. The Greeks talk of nothing but means, the Trojans of nothing but ends. It appears that although knowledge of natural necessity, especially of the operation of the human passions, can be profitably enlisted in the execution of goals once chosen, it affords no knowledge of the worth of those goals.

Are the Greek ends, then, merely arbitrary, posited by random fiat, passionate intensity, or fraud? Surely Ulysses' cosmic analogy provides nothing like a detailed ethical code of conduct. But in a broader sense the solar system can indeed be a guide for the formation and preservation of political community. Taken as a similitude for political life, it suggests that the citizens be formed into a hierarchy of rulers and ruled according to manifest principles of distinction, whether of birth or accomplishments, by means of laws applicable to all. With the quarrelsome tumult of domestic faction checked by habits and institutions preserving due degree, the most gifted citizens would be in a position to undertake those "high designs" of which Ulysses speaks [I. iii. 102], which the chaos of uncontrolled strife wrecks. A space is cleared for the exercise of the rational faculty, otherwise thwarted by the predominance of rude body and passion. (pp. 135-36)

Thersites believes that reason ought to rule, but all around him he sees weaknesses of mind and body, stupidity and disease. His angry railing against these favorite evils of his betrays his imprudent attachment to the thoughtless opinion that thought should be able to overcome necessity. He calls himself a "knower" who is "a fool to serve such a fool" as Agamemnon and the others who rule him [II. iii. 48-64]. Thersites' truth, then, is the mirror opposite of Troilus': while Troilus believes the will's attachment enables man to hold fast to a truth that escapes necessity, Thersites sees everywhere the repellent sway of necessity. Neither Troilus nor Thersites comprehends that blending of attention to the passions and willful teaching of goals that enables Ulysses to imitate the heavens while trafficking in low motives. (pp. 136-37)

All the Greeks share some knowledge of the difference between the deceptive outward show of things and their concealed inner truth, although not all discern with the same penetration. This knowledge enables Agamemnon to cover his failure in the war with noble words, as it guides Ulysses in his subtle assumption of political authority, allows Diomedes to envy Paris his bed-partner without being blinded to Helen's faults by her enchanting beauty (IV. i), and provides matter for merriment in Achilles' staged mockeries of the generals. The Greek capacity for rational argument, exhibited in the deliberations of their war council, and particularly in Ulysses' calculated machinations and Thersites' biting wit, may be contrasted with the Trojan celebration of irrationality in their own war council, in Troilus' love for Cressida as in Paris' for Helen (Paris says: "Sweet, *above thought* I love thee" [III. i. 159]), in the Trojan regard for dreams and inspired prophecies (II. ii. and V. iii.), and in Hector's stubborn attachment to the chivalric code without consideration of circumstance.

The typical Trojan deviation from truth is sensuality. We have mentioned the imaginative effort Troilus must expend to make himself see Cressida as more than a lily bed to wallow in [III. ii. 12] and abandon once his appetite is sated. The joylessly lascivious scene preceding the lovers' union, which depicts Helen and Paris, whetted by Pandarus, idly indulging the erotic fancies of the moment (III. i.), presages the stale bawdry into which Troilus and Cressida's purer love might easily decline. And Hector's murder is provoked by his greedy pursuit of some nameless Greek soldier's glittering armor [V. vi. 27-31, V. viii. 1-4]. The cloying facilitations of Pandarus minister to the pleasures of his favorites: the inane, obscene ditty he sings at Helen's behest [III. i. 115-26] is no different, in his mind, from his service as go-between for the lovers. Sensuality's debauch threatens to dissipate the honorable firmness to which both Troilus and Hector subscribe.

Similarly, the typical excess in the Greek camp is pride, living for the sake of praise and good opinion. The proud and the prudent man both look to a standard outside themselves, but opinion confuses nature, the eternal order, with convention, what holds fashion here and now. Taking one's bearings from the social order, with its ranks of greater and lesser luminaries, dimly mirrors Ulysses' self-guidance by the knowledge of the natural order. Ajax suffers from a woefully self-ignorant pride that foolishly mistakes transparent flattery for confirmation of his worth. In Achilles' more complicated case the warrior knowingly feeds on praise, whether merited or not, like Helen and Paris on their sensual delights.

These contrasts are more properly described as tendencies than as sharp distinctions, for we see Greek lovers in Achilles and Diomedes, and Trojan concern for present opinion in Paris' speech in the war council [II. ii. 130-31]. As for the two women who leave their countrymen, sensuous Helen and calculating Cressida, they find their ultimate repose where the soul of each is most at home. The Greek-Trojan difference, then, is only in part a consequence of the manner of life in each society; natural differences in individual character incline human beings toward the alternative ways of life embodied in the two warring regimes.

While the Greeks tend to look outside themselves for guidance, the Trojans look within, for the positings of will are as internally provoked as the promptings of sensual desire. This gives to the Trojans an aspect of self-preoccupation; they pay more regard to their poetic fancies, chivalric manners, and prospects of future glory than to the tumultuous present in which they are embroiled. Both sides speak of honor, but for the Greeks that term refers to present praise, whereas the Trojans conceive honor as fidelity to one's sworn purpose or the canonization of future ages. Although the Greeks sometimes swear oaths, they keep them only as long as calculation or passion inclines. Both sensuality and mere reputation are exposed to the oblivion of calumniating time, and honorable faith and knowledgeable conduct are the respective Trojan and Greek redemptive paths. They alone lift men out of the flood and ebb of the bodily desires and fickle opinion.

The Greek way suffers from doubts as to its possibility and from the obscurity of the status of human ends, not to mention the unpredictable dispositions of passion and dispensations of chance. Besides, even if such knowledge is attainable, its elusiveness bars access to all but a very few. Others will necessarily disparage it or despair of gaining it. And the ambiguous issue of Ulysses' scheme shows how circumstance resists government by prudence. Trojan truth, on the other hand, although more generally accessible, cannot satisfy. Its delusion is to forget that the earthly objects dignified by honorable fidelity (Helen or Cressida) must inevitably reveal themselves as corruptible and hence unworthy of that fidelity. By cutting themselves off from rational calculations of relative worth, they find themselves attributing infinite value to things of finite merit. In his fleeting mood of rationality, Hector tells Troilus: "'Tis *mad* idolatry / To make the service greater than the god." . . . When the truth of the body and the truth of faith collide,

madness threatens, for the simplicity of faith is revealed to be untrue to the duplicity of human nature. "Rule in unity" [V. ii. 141] is not a metaphysical truth, as Troilus would like, but, in human affairs at least, a useful fiction, as Ulysses shows through his speeches and deeds. (pp. 139-41)

What about the truth of Shakespeare? In this play at least, it is Greek, and could even be called Thersitean, were it not for the poet's dispassionate, accepting stance toward the low truths he unveils: he is free from Thersites' *ira et studium* ["wrath and zeal"]. By adopting the debunking posture of Thersites, Shakespeare reveals the truth of Ulysses without practicing it. . . . In the case of *Troilus and Cressida* ugliness is a concomitant of truthfulness. We are granted a glimpse into the uncouth engine room of Western civilization. What is revealed here in all frankness is concealed again, for instance, in *A Midsummer Night's Dream,* whose plot shows poetic semblance covering over the harshness of political and erotic passions. There Shakespeare practices the truth of Ulysses without revealing it. Self-knowledge calls for clear-headed insight into the heart of things, but the good life also relies on a public order whose appearance belies its inner truth. Shakespeare points to this duplex truth by allowing us only a single look, in this play about the origins, into the inward motions within the souls of Western men; elsewhere he devotes his art to the making and maintaining of beautiful surfaces, which he permits to remain comparatively undisturbed.

Troilus and Cressida might seem to be peculiarly modern in its ruthless debunking of martial nobility and romantic love. But it would be more accurate to call it philosophic than modern, for its intention is not so much to dethrone the high as to show its inner workings. The overtly philosophical language and manner of many of the play's speeches have been noticed by critics. They have generally not noticed the connection between its philosophicality and its deliberate repulsiveness. Until fairly recently, the play has seldom been produced on the stage, and with but mixed success when it has. It is unpopular because truth, when fully exposed, is unpopular. The letter to the reader preceding the play in the Quarto edition boasts of the distance between the play and the common understanding: "you have here a new play, never staled with the stage, never clapper-clawed with the palms of the vulgar." It also boasts of the play's "wit"—its intelligence. These two features go together. The play is Shakespeare's wittiest comedy, as the letter promises, because it is his most truthful, and being so, it must be remote from the crowd. Here poetry is strained as far as it can go in the direction of philosophy without bursting its self-prescribed limits. If Shakespeare's poetic immortality had depended on this play alone, he might well have been long since forgotten—with some justice, for such is the truth taught by *Troilus and Cressida.* (pp. 141-43)

Thomas G. West, "The Two Truths of 'Troilus and Cressida'," in Shakespeare as Political Thinker, *edited by John Alvis and Thomas G. West, Carolina Academic Press, 1981, pp. 127-43.*

NORTHROP FRYE (essay date 1983)

[*Frye has been called one of the most important critics of the twentieth century and a leader of the anthropological or mythic approach to literature which gained prominence during the 1950s. As outlined in his seminal work* An Anatomy of Criticism (1957), *Frye views all literature as ultimately derived from certain myths or archetypes present in the human psyche, and he therefore sees literary criticism as a peculiar type of science in which the literary critic seeks only to decode the mythic structure inherent in a work of art. Frye's effort was to produce a method of literary interpretation more universal and exact than that suggested in other critical approaches, such as New Criticism, biographical criticism, historical criticism, and so on—all of which he finds valuable but also extremely limited in application. As a Shakespearean critic, Frye made perhaps his greatest contribution in the area of the comedies and romances, especially with his definition of the three main phases of Shakespearean comic and romantic structure, which he defines as the initial phase of "the anticomic society," "the phase of temporarily lost identity," and the establishment of a "new society," or "deliverance," through either marriage or self-knowledge. In the following commentary, which is based on a lecture delivered in March 1981 at the University of Western Ontario, Frye states that the action of* Troilus and Cressida *"does not illustrate the myth of deliverance in comedy," but, instead, seems to show a secular version of the fall of man, containing strong elements of both tragedy and history. He maintains that the nature of this fallen world is revealed in Ulysses's teleological speeches, which, while they seem to present objective "sources of external reality," also suggest "a sense of unreality." Frye thus finds a reversal of reality in Ulysses's speeches and in Shakespeare's theater itself, for both convey "a quality of illusion in what we think of as objective reality, and a quality of reality in what we think of as subjective illusion." He concludes that such a reversal, which is in opposition to Shakespeare's romantic comedies, results in a disillusionment, but adds that such a disillusionment is "the starting point of any genuine myth of deliverance."*]

[Comedy] is a mixture of the festive and the ironic, of a drive toward a renewed society along with a strong emphasis on the arbitrary whims and absurdities that block its emergence. There is a much larger infusion of irony in *Measure for Measure* and *All's Well* than in, say, *As You Like It* or *Twelfth Night,* and of course there are many comedies, especially in modern times, where the ironic emphasis is too strong for the drive toward deliverance, and where the play ends in frustration and blocked movement. In Shakespeare's canon the play that comes nearest to this is *Troilus and Cressida,* a play that, whatever else it may do, does not illustrate the myth of deliverance in comedy. It seems to be designed rather to show us human beings getting into the kind of mess that requires deliverance, a secular counterpart of what Christianity calls the fall of man.

Shakespeare's plays are classified by the Folio as comedies, tragedies, and histories, to which modern critics generally add romance as a fourth genre. *Troilus and Cressida* is hard to 'fit into' these categories (I use quotation marks because 'fitting' is not the point of generic criticism) because it has so many elements of all four. It is a kind of history play, for the Trojan War was the normal beginning of secular history in Shakespeare's day, and the characters in it sometimes seem to realize that they are establishing the patterns and types of the future. The most obvious example is the scene (III. ii.) in which Troilus, Cressida, and Pandarus successively speak as it were to the future, a posterity who will take Troilus to be the pattern of truth and fidelity, Cressida the pattern of falseness, if she proves false, Pandarus to be the patron saint of all panders. (pp. 61-2)

The play also seems to be a tragedy, what with the death of Hector, the destruction of Troilus' trust by Cressida, and the bitter final scene, with Troy approaching its final catastrophe. Yet the author of the curious epistle to the reader which prefaces the reprinted Quarto regards it as a comedy, though he realizes that it is a very black comedy, and unlikely to find a warm response in the public theatre. He suggests that it was not acted in Shakespeare's lifetime: there is other evidence that it was,

but it could hardly have been a popular play then. It is generally recognized, however, that it is a uniquely 'modern' play, with its ambiguous irony, its learned language, and the prominence it gives to the anti-heroic. For the same reason the twentieth century has less difficulty in placing it within the comic context.

The play seems to revolve around the relation of reality and illusion. In the conference of Trojan leaders (II. ii.) the association of fame and glory and the like with the rape of Helen, and the attempt to make that rape seem more glamorous by persisting in fighting for it, is recognized by Hector to be pure illusion, and even Troilus, though he asks 'What's aught but as 'tis valued?' [II. ii. 52], understands this too. The Trojans, then, choose the illusion of fame and glory, knowing it to be an illusion, and knowing that Helen herself is not the real motive for fighting. In Euripides' play on Helen [*Helena*], a version of the legend is adopted in which the Helen who was in Troy during the war was a wraith or illusion, the real Helen being in Egypt the whole time. The very commonplace and minor Helen of Shakespeare's play is not a ghost, but the fact that she is as little worth all that bloodshed as though she were seems to be patent to everyone. Later, when Troilus is forced to watch as Cressida takes up with the Greek Diomed, a similar problem arises in his mind. Which is the real Cressida, the one deserting to the Greeks or the faithful one who was an essential part of his own identity?

The Greeks, though caught up in the same fantasy, are, by comparison, realists. Ulysses makes an impressive speech on the chain of being and the fact that society depends on hierarchical order, in order to suggest that Achilles, who is a 'better' warrior than anyone present, should be brought back into the conflict. The appeal to the chain of being undercuts the personal application, but there is also some expert needling of Agamemnon and Nestor in Ulysses' description of the way in which Achilles ridicules them to Patroclus. The proposal modulates into a scheme of replacing Achilles with Ajax as the number one Greek hero, which should provoke Achilles to re-enter the combat. This scheme is a kind of controlled experiment within a tragic framework: if we disturb the hierarchy of nature by placing Ajax above Achilles, the disturbance is bound to right itself by the return of Achilles. (pp. 62-4)

If Ulysses believed his own speech about hierarchy and degree, then, he would advise the Greek army to go away and leave Troy in peace. Without degree, he says, everything meets in 'mere oppugnancy,' but what else is the Trojan war? In a state of war, authority must come to terms with the fact that the great majority of fighters are motivated by hatred, and that hatred sooner or later makes use of weapons that, in Thersites' phrase, 'proclaim barbarism' and bring about the chaos that Ulysses pretends to dread.

Thersites, though he has not heard the speech, knows that Ulysses' counsel accomplishes very little as such: 'now is the cur Ajax prouder than the cur Achilles, and will not arm today' [V. iv. 14-15]. It is particularly in the relations of Ajax and Achilles that we see how heroism is, in Heidegger's term, 'ecstatic,' outside itself, thrown into situations in which the personality recreates itself to meet each one differently. We first see Ajax as a sullen brute whom the Greek leaders manipulate with contemptuous ease, in contrast to Achilles, who is far more intelligent, and, for all his self-indulgence, not ill-natured. But the manipulation does change the personality, and by IV, v, the scene of Hector's visit to the Greek tents, it is Achilles who has become the brute and Ajax who is speaking with moderation and point. The manipulation is too efficient, in other words, to accomplish its own real aim. (pp. 64-5)

Every history play of Shakespeare makes it clear that, in the art of ruling, Plato's philosopher-king would be an impossible schizophrenic. If a king ever stopped to philosophize, he would lose the rhythm of action on which his effectiveness as a ruler depends. Similarly, in this play it is the primacy of the will which is constantly stressed: the will is there to act, and knowledge and reason have very little function beyond a purely tactical one. Continuity of action is therefore not necessarily consistency of action: one responds to the situation that is there, however different it may be from the previous one. There is no reason to doubt the genuineness of Cressida's affection for Troilus as long as Troilus is present; but when Diomed is present she rationalizes her desertion of Troilus by speaking of the way in which sense perception of the immediate takes control over the shadows of memory.

The great Hindu scripture, the *Bhagavadgita,* is an episode from a heroic epic, the *Mahabharata,* in which two bands of warrior nobles face one another in battle, and a warrior on one side, Arjuna, wonders why he should be fighting an army which contains so many of his own relatives. Similarly, the Greeks and Trojans are more closely related than one might at first expect: the Helen known throughout history as Helen of Troy is the wife of a Greek warrior; her abduction is said to be retaliation for the previous abduction of the Trojan Hesione, who was given to a Greek; Cressida follows her deserting father into the Greek camp; Hector will not risk killing Ajax because Ajax is half Trojan; Achilles' professed reason for abandoning the battle is that he is secretly in love with a daughter of Priam. Arjuna is told by his charioteer, the god Krishna in disguise, to stay and fight because he is a warrior and should fight, and Hector, we saw, agrees in the Trojan council to go on fighting although he knows there is no real reason for doing so. Arjuna is finally rewarded by a vision of the universe within the body of the god Krishna, but in *Troilus and Cressida* we get no such vision, only Ulysses' speeches about the necessity of degree and the oblivion connected with time.

These speeches are partly sepia clouds concealing much more practical aims, but they have a dramatic function far beyond that. They are, in fact, speeches about the two bases of what we think of as reality: about our perception of time and space, space being presented as the hierarchical structure familiar to Shakespeare's audience and time as the devouring monster equally familiar from the sonnets and elsewhere. Ulysses' function in the play is not that of a warrior but of a counsellor, and his speeches represent the detachment of intelligence from the rest of consciousness (rather like Falstaff's speech on honour, in a less farcical context), leaving the warriors to fight with a ferocity untroubled by the calls of the intellect.

When we look at these speeches in the context of the play, the presiding geniuses of space and time appear to be Tantalus and Sisyphus. The imagery of the opening lines of the play speaks of 'tarrying,' waiting endlessly for something not yet to be grasped, and before long Cressida is telling us that this is in fact part of her own strategy to 'hold off.' Men, she says, concentrate on women only as long as they are out of reach: once the women are possessed, the men revert to their former interests. As she says bitterly after her first night with Troilus:

> You men will never tarry.
> O foolish Cressid! I might have still held off,
> And then you would have tarried.

[IV. ii. 16-18]

However, she is soon moved to a Greek context, where what is appropriate is not to hold off but to hold on. The theme of tantalizing also appears in the emphasis on voyeurism of various kinds, in Pandarus' leering stage-management of the union of the lovers, in Thersites' sardonic comments while watching the seduction of Cressida and Troilus' duel with Diomed, and, on a much more pathetic level, Troilus' involuntary spying on Cressida's unfaithfulness. (pp. 66-8)

The speeches of Ulysses define the nature of what Christianity calls a fallen world. We guide ourselves in that world by our perception of time and space, which we perceive in such a way as to make them sources of external authority as well. The cosmos is a world of 'degree'; time is an inexorable wheel of fortune. They are what we have of reality, and produce in us a sense of ineluctable fatality. But no sooner have they done this than they begin to suggest a sense of unreality as well. We noted earlier that Hector and Troilus deliberately choose the illusions of fame and love and glory, knowing them to be illusions. This is of course particularly true of Hector, who talks less about the chain of degree than Ulysses but clearly knows at least as much about it. Yet their decision arouses a response in us that is not only sympathy but a faint perception of a reality that all our metaphysical chains of bondage cannot quite hold in. The inference is that no serious view of life can get established until we have recognized a quality of illusion in what we think of as objective reality, and a quality of reality in what we think of as subjective illusion.

In ordinary experience, what we call real tends to be associated with the objective, with what other people see more or less as we see. What we call illusion is correspondingly associated with the subjective, the world of dream and of the emotions, ranging from love to hatred, that distort our 'real' perspective. It is here, perhaps, that a man of the theatre might have something to say. For Shakespeare was a man of the theatre who concentrated intensely on the theatrical experience: we may even say that in every play he wrote the central character is the theatre itself. When we are in a theatre, the play we see and hear on the stage is, we say, an illusion. But we could search the wings and dressing-rooms forever without finding any reality 'behind' it: it seems clear that in a theatre the illusion *is* the reality. Furthermore, it is as objective a datum as anything else that we see and hear. Whatever is not the play in the theatre is the shared experience of the audience watching it, an experience that will differ with each member of the audience, and yet represents a consensus as well. In a theatre, then, the illusion is objective and the reality subjective. That does not, by itself, completely reverse the nature of reality and illusion, but it suggests that there are other aspects of both to which the drama is relevant. (pp. 69-70)

Troilus and Cressida, the earliest in its chronological setting of any Shakespeare play, is a play about the beginning of history, and shows us how man acquires the sense of illusory reality that the playwright tries to reverse into real illusion. It represents one extreme of Shakespeare's dramatic spectrum, as the more romantic comedies, including the four romances, represent the other. The Trojan war has set up its version of reality, which is a machinery of causation, a pseudo-fatality in which the Trojans must go on fighting to keep Helen. Troilus must therefore agree to Cressida's going to her father in the Greek camp (we note in passing the reversal of the normal comic movement of the heroine from father to lover) in order to maintain the fiction about Helen that he had defended himself. Cressida may be 'faithless,' but fidelity would be impossibly quixotic in the world she is in, a world where heroism degenerates into brutality and love itself is reduced to another kind of mechanical stimulus, as Thersites points out with so much relish. When at the end of the play Pandarus shrivels into a contemporary London pimp, professionally concerned with the spreading of syphilis, there is very little sense of shock or incongruity: we have already realized that this play is about us, if not about the aspect of us that we want to put on exhibition.

It is by a final irony of language that we call the portrayal of such a world 'disillusioned,' and associate the term pejoratively with a weary pessimism. Being disillusioned with a world like that is the starting point of any genuine myth of deliverance. We take our first step towards such disillusionment when we realize that the basis of consciousness in such a world is the perception of time and space as Ulysses expounds them. (pp. 85-6)

> Northrop Frye, "The Reversal of Reality," in his The Myth of Deliverance: Reflections on Shakespeare's Problem Comedies, *University of Toronto Press, 1983, pp. 61-90.*

ADDITIONAL BIBLIOGRAPHY

Acheson, Arthur. "Shakespeare's Satire upon Chapman in 'Troilus and Cressida' in 1598" and "Shakespeare's Satire upon Chapman in 'Troilus and Cressida' in 1609." In his *Shakespeare and the Rival Poet*, pp. 167-88, pp. 189-206. London: John Lane, The Bodley Head, 1903.
> Argues that *Troilus and Cressida* was first written in 1598 and later revised in 1609. Acheson also offers evidence that the play contains satiric references to George Chapman, particularly in the character of Achilles.

Alexander, Peter. "Troilus and Cressida, 1609." *Library* IX, No. 3 (December 1928): 267-86.
> Speculates that *Troilus and Cressida* may have been written "for some festivity at one of the Inns of Court" and examines some of the play's textual difficulties.

Asp, Carolyn. "In Defense of Cressida." *Studies in Philology* LXXIV, No. 4 (October 1977): 406-17.
> Contends that Cressida cannot maintain a true and consistent identity because she subjects herself to "the expectations of the men who value her only insofar as she makes herself pliable to their standards and desires."

Berger, Harry, Jr. "*Troilus and Cressida:* The Observer as Basilisk." *Comparative Drama* II, No. 2 (Summer 1968): 122-36.
> Examines the problem of perspective in *Troilus and Cressida*, concluding that while Shakespeare intends the audience to move toward agreement with Thersites, this is "not the only possible perspective, merely the one to which we seem—a little reluctantly—to find ourselves disposed."

Bethell, S. L. "The Treatment of Character (II)." In his *Shakespeare and the Popular Dramatic Tradition*, pp. 99-131. Durham, N.C.: Duke University Press, 1944.
> Refers to *Troilus and Cressida* as "a consciously philosophical play" in which the dialogue is "frequently developed almost independently of the situation to which it refers." Bethell also notes that the play presents both allegorical and representative character types.

Birney, Alice Latvin. "Thersites and Infectious Satire." In her *Satiric Catharsis in Shakespeare: A Theory of Dramatic Structure*, pp. 99-121. Berkeley and Los Angeles: University of California Press, 1973.
> Discusses the role of Thersites as a satirist whose curses become realized as the play progresses. Birney also observes that Thersites's bitterness is "infectious" and spreads to other characters in the play and that, finally, there is no catharsis in the play's satire.

Bowden, William R. "The Human Shakespeare and *Troilus and Cressida*." *Shakespeare Quarterly* VIII, No. 2 (Spring 1957): 167-77.
> Contends that in *Troilus and Cressida* Shakespeare rejects rationalism as the supreme good and favors the nonrational idealism of Troilus and Hector.

Bradbrook, M.C. "What Shakespeare Did to Chaucer's *Troilus and Criseyde*." *Shakespeare Quarterly* IX, No. 3 (Summer 1958): 311-19.
> Compares Chaucer's poem with Shakespeare's play, stating that Shakespeare presents a "lacerative destruction of Chaucer's whole vision" in which "the sensitive Creseyde, and the recklessly devoted, mockingly sympathetic Pandare" are replaced by "a combine of amateur drab and professional agent."

Bullough, Geoffrey. "*Troilus and Cressida*." In *Narrative and Dramatic Sources of Shakespeare, Vol. VI*, edited by Geoffrey Bullough, pp. 83-221. London: Routledge and Kegan Paul, 1966.
> Contains a discussion of possible sources for *Troilus and Cressida* and excerpts from some of these texts, including George Chapman's translation of the *Iliad*, Robert Henryson's *The Testament of Cresseid*, and the accounts of the Trojan War by John Lydgate and William Caxton.

Burns, M. M. "*Troilus and Cressida:* The Worst of Both Worlds." *Shakespeare Studies* XIII (1980): 105-29.
> Argues that *Troilus and Cressida* is a dramatization of misdirected aggression that is particularly evident in the ill treatment of women in the play. Burns charges that the traditional critical perception of Cressida as either a weak or wanton woman is an extension of this "infectious" aggression and offers instead a more positive view of her character.

Coghill, Nevill. "A Prologue and an 'Epilogue'" and "Morte Hector: A Map of Honour." In his *Shakespeare's Professional Skills*, pp. 78-97, pp. 98-127. Cambridge: Cambridge University Press, 1964.
> Speculates that the prologue and epilogue of *Troilus and Cressida* were added in 1608 for a private performance of the play, possibly for the Christmas Revels at one of the Inns of Court. These sardonic emendations were made, proposes Coghill, to "protect" the play from the derision of a rowdy audience of sophisticates. In his second essay, Coghill examines the conflict between material realism and idealism in both the play and the Elizabethan world, concluding that Shakespeare favors the idealistic values of the Trojans. The defeat of these values, states Coghill, proves the play to be a "straight tragedy" in spite of the added satiric prologue and epilogue.

Cole, Douglas. "Myth and Anti-Myth: The Case of *Troilus and Cressida*." *Shakespeare Quarterly* 31, No. 1 (Spring 1980): 76-84.
> Asserts that by exposing the self-deluding nature of myth through its dramatic portrayal of heroes whose actions contradict their heroic codes, *Troilus and Cressida* challenges the habit of myth-making.

Daniels, F. Quinland. "Order and Confusion in Troilus and Confusion in *Troilus and Cressida* I. iii." *Shakespeare Quarterly* XII, No. 3 (Summer 1961): 285-91.
> Analyzes closely the Greek generals' conference and concludes that while Ulysses's thinking is clear, Agamemnon's is uncertain and confused.

Dusinberre, Juliet. "*Troilus and Cressida* and the Definition of Beauty." *Shakespeare Survey* 36 (1983): 85-95.
> Discusses the problem of defining beauty in *Troilus and Cressida*, with a heavy emphasis on the background of the classical assessment of beauty. Dusinberre concludes that the play lacks a commitment "to the power of beauty to re-create itself."

Duthie, George Ian. "Imaginative Interpretation and *Troilus and Cressida*." In his *Shakespeare*, pp. 89-114. London: Hutchinson's University Library, 1951.

> Challenges the assertion of G. Wilson Knight (see excerpt above, 1930) that the Trojans' values are superior to those of the Greeks. Duthie contends that Hector and Troilus are portrayed as "disordered personalities," as are all of the other characters with the exception of Ulysses and Priam, who serve as "order-figures."

Edwards, Philip. "The Problem Plays (i)." In his *Shakespeare and the Confines of Art*, pp. 95-108. London: Methuen, 1968.

> Describes *Troilus and Cressida* as "astonishingly contemporary," noting its lack of a hero and its tendency towards "anti-art." Edwards explains that one reason for the play's uniqueness in the Shakespearean canon is "the absolute lack of any sense of non-human guidance."

Elton, William. "Shakespeare's Portrait of Ajax in *Troilus and Cressida*." *PMLA* 63 (1948): 744-48.

> Offers additional evidence to support F. G. Fleay's hypothesis (see entry below) that in *Troilus and Cressida* Shakespeare satirizes Ben Jonson in the character of Ajax.

————. "Shakespeare's Ulysses and the Problem of Value." *Shakespeare Studies* II (1966): 95-111.

> Discusses at length the mercantile imagery and the problem of market value in *Troilus and Cressida*. Elton concludes that the relativistic values advocated by Ulysses are consistent with those of Thomas Hobbes.

Evans, Bertrand. "When Degree is Shak'd: *All's Well* and *Troilus and Cressida*." In his *Shakespeare's Comedies*, pp. 144-85. Oxford: Oxford at the Clarendon Press, 1960.

> Concludes that *Troilus and Cressida* represents the "chief deviate" from Shakespeare's normal practice of creating discrepant awarenesses in the characters and audience for dramatic effect, and that it is the "best proof" of his need to "exploit dramatically created discrepancies" as he did in his earlier plays. Evans also argues that the "corruptive disease of the world of *Troilus and Cressida* is a contagious one, catching even to the bones of dramatic structure, leaving them too infirm to support the action."

Farnham, Willard. "Troilus in Shapes of Infinite Desire." *Shakespeare Quarterly* XV, No. 2 (Spring 1964): 257-64.

> Examines Troilus's character as both a lover and a warrior, noting that his aspiration in honor is "infinite," as is his aspiration in love. Troilus the lover, Farnham concludes, "falls tragically," while Troilus the warrior rises to battle.

Fleay, F. G. "The Public Career of Shakespeare." In his *A Chronicle History of the Life and Work of William Shakespeare*, pp. 7-72. London: John C. Nimmo, 1886.

> Hypothesizes on the War of the Theaters and the quarrels between Shakespeare and other playwrights. Fleay states that *Troilus and Cressida* is the play "in which Shakespeare put down all the University men, and purges Ben Jonson's pride." The character of Ajax, asserts Fleay, "hits off Jonson exactly," an assessment supported by such later critics as William Elton (see entry above) and Roscoe Addison Small (see entry below).

Fly, Richard D. "'Suited in Like Conditions as Our Argument': Imitative Form in Shakespeare's *Troilus and Cressida*." *Studies in English Literature* XV, No. 2 (Spring 1975): 273-92.

> Discusses the disjunctive nature of *Troilus and Cressida*, pointing out the failure of language and the frequent procession of characters across the stage "which seems to move inexorably toward something resembling a demonic epiphany." Fly argues that this dramatic experience moves "us and the play inexorably toward a cataclysmic termination."

Foakes, R. A. "*Troilus and Cressida* Reconsidered." *University of Toronto Quarterly* XXXII, No. 2 (January 1963): 142-54.

> Maintains that the tone of the play's closing speeches by Troilus and Pandarus are "not opposed, but complementary, and together establish an 'open' ending." Foakes concludes that the ending is appropriate and that the play is neither tragedy nor comedy, but "an heroic farce, in which the comedy and satire finally reinforce those noble values envisaged in the action."

Gagen, Jean. "Hector's Honor." *Shakespeare Quarterly* XIX, No. 2 (Spring 1968): 129-37.

> Discusses at length the Renaissance notion of honor and suggests that Hector decides to continue fighting the Trojan War, in spite of his reasons to the contrary, because his honor is challenged. Shakespeare's audience, states Gagen, would have been familiar with this compulsion to maintain honor.

Green, Gayle. "Language and Value in Shakespeare's *Troilus and Cressida*." *Studies in English Literature* 21 No. 2 (Spring 1981): 271-85.

> Explains the dissolution of language and value in *Troilus and Cressida* as a reflection of the changing view of order in Elizabethan England. Green argues that the play dramatizes the "division of word from reality which follows from the loss of absolute sanctions of value."

Greg, W. W. "Editorial Problems: *Troilus and Cressida*." In his *The Shakespeare First Folio*, pp. 338-50. Oxford: Oxford at the Clarendon Press, 1955.

> Discusses the textual problems concerning the 1609 quarto of *Troilus and Cressida* and the Folio of 1623.

Helton, Tinsley. "Paradox and Hypothesis in *Troilus and Cressida*." *Shakespeare Studies* X (1977): 115-31.

> Discusses the paradoxes and hypotheses that occur throughout *Troilus and Cressida*, noting especially the contradictions in the characters. Helton attributes the play's "non-committal and detached" tone to its profuse paradoxes and states that Shakespeare's "audience of young intellectuals" would have appreciated them.

Hillebrand, Harold N., ed. *Troilus and Cressida*, by William Shakespeare. A New Variorum Edition of Shakespeare, edited by James G. McManaway. Philadelphia: J. B. Lippincott, 1953, 613 p.

> Contains excerpted essays by major Shakespeare scholars that examine the issue of the date, text, and sources of *Troilus and Cressida*. The appendix also includes reprints of criticism that discuss the play's characters, Ulysses's speech on degree, the stage history, and the contemporary events that may be reflected in the play.

Jago, David M. "The Uniqueness of *Troilus and Cressida*." *Shakespeare Quarterly* 29, No. 1 (Winter 1978): 20-7.

> Compares *Troilus and Cressida* to *Romeo and Juliet*, concluding that love in the world of *Troilus and Cressida* "cannot but be debased." Jago notes that despite its sense of realism, the play is uncharacteristically Shakespearean and a "dramatic failure."

Kaula, David. "Will and Reason in *Troilus and Cressida*." *Shakespeare Quarterly* XXI, No. 3 (Summer 1961): 271-83.

> Compares Troilus and Hamlet, arguing that there is more ambivalence and complexity in Troilus than is generally granted. Kaula discusses at length Troilus's "subversion of reason by passion" and also considers Ulysses's rationalism, concluding that both are "equally ineffectual."

Kermode, Frank. "Opinion, Truth and Value." *Essays in Criticism* V, No. 2 (April 1955): 181-87.

> Challenges Winifred M. T. Nowottny's assertion that Opinion and Value are antithetical opposites in *Troilus and Cressida* (see excerpt above, 1954), proposing instead an opposition between Opinion and Truth. Kermode also states that Thersites is "vital to the balance of the philosophical forces in the play."

Kimbrough, Robert. "The Problem of Thersites." *Modern Language Review* LIX, No. 2 (April 1964): 173-76.

> Argues that Thersites is a "known liar" and that his reference to Patroclus as a "male whore" is not a "revelation of truth." Kimbrough also presents a case for the "sexual normality of Patroclus and Achilles."

————. *Shakespeare's "Troilus and Cressida" and Its Setting.* Cambridge, Mass.: Harvard University Press, 1964, 208 p.

Presents a detailed analysis of *Troilus and Cressida* with a heavy emphasis on its historical setting. Kimbrough offers chapters on the play's theatrical background and literary origins, as well as several chapters on the action of the play itself, in which he combines a historical study of Elizabethan theater with aesthetic criticism. Kimbrough concludes that *Troilus and Cressida* is "not a good drama" because, in writing it, "Shakespeare attempted to meet the current demands of 'box-office' by presenting 'new tricks' along with 'that old *Decorum*'."

Knowland, A. S. "*Troilus and Cressida*." *Shakespeare Quarterly* X, No. 3 (Summer 1959): 353-65.
Challenges two of G. Wilson Knight's assertions about *Troilus and Cressida* (see excerpt above, 1930). Knowland contends that values are destroyed by the characters themselves, not by time, and maintains that the critical tendency to characterize the Greeks and Trojans as opposing camps of thought is an oversimplification.

Lawrence, William Witherle. "The Love Story in 'Troilus and Cressida'." In *Shakespeare Studies*, edited by Brander Matthews and Ashly Horace Thorndike, pp. 187-211. 1916. Reprint. New York: Russell & Russell, 1962.
Traces the sources of the love story of *Troilus and Cressida*, noting that Chaucer and earlier writers were more sympathetic to Pandarus and Cressida, but that changes in the conventions of love in literature during the fifteenth century caused a "degradation of the story."

————. "Troilus, Cressida and Thersites." *Modern Language Review* XXXVII, No. 4 (October 1942): 422-37.
Cautions against regarding *Troilus and Cressida* as a "philosophical poem" instead of a play, contending that it does not present a "carefully considered philosophical system." Lawrence's interpretation relies primarily on character analysis.

March, Derrick R. C. "Interpretation and Misinterpretation: The Problem of *Troilus and Cressida*." *Shakespeare Studies* I (1965): 182-98.
Responds to criticism of *Troilus and Cressida*, claiming that "misinterpretations have frequently arisen from attempts either to make the play accord with some preconceived theory of *genre*, or from the operation of an over-nice sensibility, resulting in a reluctance to allow the play to read as disturbingly as it actually does."

Meyer, George Wilbur. "Order Out of Chaos in Shakespeare's *Troilus and Cressida*." *Tulane Studies in English* IV (1954): 45-56.
Argues that the play's inconclusive ending is consistent with Shakespeare's intentions elsewhere in the play to present "a picture of confusion, of political, social, and moral chaos."

Morris, Brian. "The Tragic Structure of *Troilus and Cressida*." *Shakespeare Quarterly* X, No. 4 (Winter 1959): 482-91.
Comments on *Troilus and Cressida*'s generic status, stating that Shakespearean tragedy should not be judged by Aristotelian standards, but also noting that the play "presents many features alien to the basic tragic effect."

Muir, Kenneth. Introduction to *Troilus and Cressida*, by William Shakespeare, edited by Kenneth Muir, pp. 1-40. Oxford: Clarendon Press, 1982.
Contains information on the date, text, and sources of *Troilus and Cressida* as well as a general discussion of the play and its critical history.

Muller, Herbert J. "Elizabethan Tragedy." In his *The Spirit of Tragedy*, pp. 165-94. New York: Alfred A. Knopf, 1956.
Asserts that *Troilus and Cressida*, while being "more tragic than *Hamlet*," ends in cynicism, which is "fatal to the tragic spirit."

Oates, J. C. "The Ambiguity of *Troilus and Cressida*." *Shakespeare Quarterly* XVII, No. 2 (Spring 1966): 141-50.
Contends that the tragic status of *Troilus and Cressida* is undermined by a mocking of ritualistic and tragic elements and by the "incongruity of a tragic hero in an anti-tragic environment."

Ornstein, Robert. "Shakespeare." In his *The Moral Vision of Jacobean Tragedy*, pp. 222-76. Madison: University of Wisconsin Press, 1960.
Includes a section on *Troilus and Cressida*. Ornstein states that it is a "depressing play, not because it establishes the futility of man's search for ideal values but because it is a sociological and psychological analysis of decadent values."

Palmer, Kenneth. Introduction to *Troilus and Cressida*, by William Shakespeare, edited by Kenneth Palmer, pp. 1-93. The Arden Edition of the Works of William Shakespeare, edited by Harold F. Brooks, Harold Jenkins, and Brian Morris. London: Methuen, 1982.
Includes a discussion of *Troilus and Cressida*'s date, text, and sources and a lengthy critical treatment of the play in general, considering such issues as time, identity, and pride.

Powell, Neil. "Hero and Human: The Problems of Achilles." *Critical Quarterly* 21, No. 2 (Summer 1979): 17-28.
Defends Achilles as the only character of any consistency and integrity, suggesting that his myrmidons kill Hector because he "cannot bring himself to be personally responsible for Hector's death."

Presson, Robert K. *Shakespeare's "Troilus and Cressida" and the Legends of Troy*. Madison: University of Wisconsin Press, 1953, 165 p.
Examines the sources of Shakespeare's play, comparing it scene by scene with parallel passages from Homer, Chaucer, Chapman, Caxton, and others.

Richards, I. A. "*Troilus and Cressida* and Plato." *The Hudson Review* I, No. 3 (Autumn 1948): 362-76.
Discusses the speeches on degree and value in relation to Plato's philosophy, noting the extent to which the play's "central thought seems to accord with Plato's."

Rockas, Leo. "'Lechery eats itself': *Troilus and Cressida*." *ARIEL* 8, No. 1 (January 1977): 17-32.
Examines the parallels between characters in *Troilus and Cressida*, particularly the relationship between Menelaus and Troilus, and Helen and Cressida.

Rossiter, A. P. "*Troilus and Cressida*." In his *Angel with Horns*, pp. 129-51. London: Longmans, Green and Co., 1961.
Presents a general discussion of *Troilus and Cressida* and notes the inconspicuous character of Antenor, who, observes Rossiter, is the only character who is left unscathed by the play's bitterness.

Selincourt, Ernest de. "*Troilus and Cressida*." In his *Oxford Lectures on Poetry*, pp. 78-105. Oxford: Oxford at the Clarendon Press, 1934.
Characterizes Cressida as a "calculating, heartless coquette," whose "predominating instinct is simply to seduce and enthrall." Selincourt also states that the play reflects Shakespeare's mood of "bitter disillusionment."

Shalvi, Alice. "'Honor' in *Troilus and Cressida*." *Studies in English Literature, 1500-1900* V, No. 2 (Spring 1965): 283-302.
Discusses the nature and value of honor in *Troilus and Cressida* and concludes that it is this presentation of honor that marks the play as "definitely Shakespearean."

Small, Roscoe Addison. "William Shakespeare." In his *The Stage-Quarrel between Ben Jonson and the So-Called Poetasters*. Breslau, Germany: Verlag von M. & A. Marcus, 1899, 204 p.
Considers *Troilus and Cressida* in the general context of the personal feud among Elizabethan playwrights known as the War of the Theaters. Small argues that the play is a "free working over" of Chaucer's poem and that "the character of Ajax is a hit at Jonson," a point also made by F. G. Fleay and William Elton (see entries above).

Smith, J. Oates. "Essence and Existence in Shakespeare's *Troilus and Cressida*." *Philological Quarterly* XLVI, No. 2 (April 1967): 167-85.
Identifies *Troilus and Cressida* as "one of the earliest expressions of what is now called the 'existential' vision." Smith also states that infidelity is "the play's great theme."

Spencer, Theodore. "*Hamlet* and *Troilus and Cressida*." In his *Shakespeare and the Nature of Man*, pp. 93-121. New York: Macmillan, 1942.

　　Argues that Shakespeare sets up a standard of conduct in *Troilus and Cressida* that is violated by the action. Spencer concludes that the play "describes in a new way the difference between man as he ought to be and man as he is."

Spurgeon, Caroline F. E. "Leading Motives in the Tragedies." In her *Shakespeare's Imagery and What It Tells Us*, pp. 309-55. 1935. Reprint. Cambridge: Cambridge University Press, 1971.

　　Notes the "closely connected" imagery in *Hamlet* and *Troilus and Cressida* of disease and food, commenting on specific food and cooking images in the latter play.

Tatlock, John S. P. "The Chief Problem in Shakespeare." *The Sewanee Review* XXIV, No. 2 (April 1916): 129-47.

　　Examines the background of *Troilus and Cressida* in an effort to explain its bitter tone and inconclusive ending. Tatlock hypothesizes that Shakespeare may have had little interest in writing a play on "a vulgarly popular subject," except in "the more masculine and statesmanlike scenes." Tatlock also rejects the notion that *Troilus and Cressida* necessarily reflects the pessimism of Shakespeare's mood.

Taylor, George C. "Shakespeare's Attitude Towards Love and Honor in *Troilus and Cressida*." *PMLA* 45 (September 1930): 781-86.

　　Discusses love and honor in several of Shakespeare's plays, concluding that while these concepts are "stripped to the naked hide" in *Troilus and Cressida*, they are similarly treated in almost every Shakespearean play.

Thomson, Patricia. "Rant and Cant in *Troilus and Cressida*." *Essays and Studies* 22 (1969): 33-56.

　　Considers the tragical speeches made by characters in *Troilus and Cressida* and other Shakespearean plays. Thomson suggests that their hyberbole is intended to be comically deflating.

Tillyard, E. M. W. "*Troilus and Cressida*." In his *Shakespeare's Problem Plays*, pp. 36-93. Toronto: University of Toronto Press, 1949.

　　Offers a lengthy discussion of the plot and some of the characters in *Troilus and Cressida*, observing the parallels between Troilus and Ulysses and describing Hector as ineffective and weak-willed. Tillyard also examines some of Shakespeare's sources and influences.

Voth, Grant L., and Evans, Oliver H. "Cressida and the World of the Play." *Shakespeare Studies* VIII (1975): 231-39.

　　Analyzes the character of Cressida, stating that she moves from a state of awareness to self-deception and again to awareness within the course of the play. Voth and Evans also contend that her behavior is determined by her environment and that she is therefore not responsible for her actions.

Walker, Alice. "*Troilus and Cressida*." In her *Textual Problems of the First Folio*, pp. 68-93. Cambridge: Cambridge at the University Press, 1953.

　　Examines the textual difficulties surrounding *Troilus and Cressida*, attributing the variations between the 1609 quarto and the 1623 Folio to "the haste in which the Folio text was printed," and asserting that the Folio was printed from the quarto text. Walker states that editorially *Troilus and Cressida* presents "more problems than any other play."

Appendix

The following is a listing of all sources used in Volume 3 of *Shakespearean Criticism*. Included in this list are all copyright and reprint rights and acknowledgments for those essays for which permission was obtained. Every effort has been made to trace copyright, but if omissions have been made, please let us know.

THE EXCERPTS IN SC, VOLUME 3, WERE REPRINTED FROM THE FOLLOWING PERIODICALS:

American Imago, v. 19, Spring, 1962 for ''A Note on Shakespeare's 'Midsummer Night's Dream''' by Gerald F. Jacobson; v. 38, Fall, 1981 for '''A Midsummer Night's Dream': The Dialectic of Eros-Thanatos'' by Mordecai Marcus. Copyright 1962, 1981 by The Association for Applied Psychoanalysis, Inc. Both reprinted by permission of Wayne State University Press and the respective authors.

Anglia, v. LXXI, 1952-53.

The Atlantic Monthly, v. LV, March, 1885.

Bentley's Miscellany, v. II, 1837.

The British Magazine, v. VIII, October, 1767.

Bucknell Review, v. XVII, March, 1969. Reprinted by permission.

Bulletin of the John Rylands Library, v. 17, January, 1933; v. 21, April, 1937.

Comparative Drama, v. 12, Spring, 1978; v. 14, Fall, 1980. © copyright 1978, 1980, by the Editors of *Comparative Drama*. Both reprinted by permission.

The Dramatic Censor; or, Critical Companion, v. I and II, 1770.

ELH, v. 14, June, 1947; v. 17, December, 1950./ v. 32, June, 1965; v. 47, Spring, 1980; v. 49, Fall, 1982. All reprinted by permission.

English Institute Essays, 1951. Copyright 1952, Columbia University Press. Renewed 1980 by English Institute. Reprinted by permission.

English Literary Renaissance, v. 3, Winter, 1973. Copyright © 1973 by *English Literary Renaissance*. Reprinted by permission.

English Studies, v. XL, 1959; v. XLVIII, December, 1967. © 1959, 1967 by Swets & Zeitlinger B.V. Both reprinted by permission.

The Entertainer, n. 11, November 12, 1754.

Essays in Criticism, v. IV, July, 1954./ v. XXV, January, 1975 for "Time and the Trojans" by John Bayley. Reprinted by permission of the Editor of *Essays in Criticism* and the author./ v. VII, January. Reprinted by permission of the Editor of *Essays in Criticism*.

The European Magazine and London Review, v. VI, April, 1787.

The Georgia Review, v. XXXI, Spring, 1977 for "Ariachne's Broken Woof" by J. Hillis Miller. Copyright, 1977, by J. Hillis Miller. Reprinted by permission of the author.

Good Words, September-October, 1904.

The Kenyon Review, v. XVIII, Autumn, 1956 for "The Marriage of Theseus and Hippolyta" by Howard Nemerov. Copyright 1956, renewed 1984, by Kenyon College. All rights reserved. Reprinted by permission of the publisher and the author.

Literature and Psychology, v. XXII, 1972. © Morton Kaplan 1972. Reprinted by permission.

The London Magazine, v. VIII, October, 1823.

Modern Language Notes, v. XXVI, March, 1911.

Neophilologus, v. XLIII, 1959 for "Ulysses' Speech on Degree as Related to the Play of 'Troilus and Cressida'" by Johannes Kleinstück. © 1959 by H. D. Tjeenk Willink. Reprinted by permission of the publisher and the author.

The New Shakspere Society's Transactions, n. 4, 1875-76.

The Penguin New Writing, n. 3, February, 1941.

PMLA, 15, v. XV, 1900; 30, v. XXX, 1915./ 84, v. 84, January, 1969. Copyright © 1969 by the Modern Language Association of America. Reprinted by permission of the Modern Language Association of America.

Proceedings of the British Academy, v. XXXVI, 1950.

The Psychoanalytic Review, v. XXX, October, 1943. Copyright © 1943, renewed 1971, by the National Psychological Association for Psychoanalysis. Reprinted by permission.

Scrutiny, v. XVIII, Autumn, 1951. Reprinted by permission of Cambridge University Press.

The Sewanee Review, v. LIX, Spring, 1951. © 1951, renewed 1979, by The University of the South. Reprinted by permission of the editor of the *Sewanee Review*.

Shakespeare Jahrbuch, v. 92, 1956.

Shakespeare Quarterly, v. IV, April, 1953; v. IV, October, 1953./ v. X, Spring, 1959; v. XII, Autumn, 1961; v. XIII, Autumn, 1962; v. XIV, Autumn, 1963; v. XV, Spring, 1964; v. XV, Autumn, 1964; v. XVIII, Winter, 1967; v. XVIII, Autumn, 1967; v. XXVI, Summer, 1975; v. 28, Summer, 1977. © The Folger Shakespeare Library 1959, 1961, 1962, 1963, 1964, 1967, 1975, 1977. All reprinted by permission.

Shakespeare Studies: An Annual Gathering of Research, Criticism, and Reviews, v. I, 1965; v. II, 1966; v. VI, 1970; v. XI, 1978. Copyright © 1965, 1966, 1970, 1978, The Council for Research in the Renaissance. All reprinted by permission.

Shakespeare Survey: An Annual Survey of Shakespearian Study and Production, v. 8, 1955./ v. 19, 1966; v. 25, 1972. © Cambridge University Press 1966, 1972. Both reprinted by permission.

Soundings, v. LVIII, Spring, 1975. Copyright © 1975 by The Society for Religion in Higher Education. Reprinted by permission.

Studies in the Literary Imagination, v. V, April, 1972. Copyright 1972 Department of English, Georgia State University. Reprinted by permission.

Studies in Philology, v. XXX, July, 1933; v. LI, July, 1954./ v. LXXVI, Summer, 1979. © 1979 by The University of North Carolina Press. Reprinted by permission.

Tennessee Studies in Literature, v. XXII, 1977. Copyright © 1977, by The University of Tennessee Press. Reprinted by permission of The University of Tennessee Press.

Barber, C. L. From *Shakespeare's Festive Comedy: A Study of Dramatic Form and Its Relation to Social Custom*. Princeton University Press, 1959. Copyright © 1959 by Princeton University Press. All rights reserved. Excerpts reprinted by permission of Princeton University Press.

Bevington, David. From "'But We Are Spirits of Another Sort': The Dark Side of Love and Magic in 'A Midsummer Night's Dream'," in *Medieval and Renaissance Studies: Proceedings of the Southeastern Institute of Medieval and Renaissance Studies, Summer, 1975*. Edited by Siegfried Wenzel. University of North Carolina Press, 1978. Copyright © 1978 The University of North Carolina Press. Reprinted by permission.

Boas, Frederick S. From *Shakspere and His Predecessors*. Charles Scribner's Sons, 1896.

Booth, Stephen. From *"King Lear," "Macbeth," Indefinition, and Tragedy*. Yale University Press, 1983. Copyright © 1983 by Yale University. All rights reserved. Reprinted by permission.

Booth, Wayne. From "Shakespeare's Tragic Villain," in *Shakespeare's Tragedies: An Anthology of Modern Criticism*. Edited by Laurence Lerner. Penguin Books, 1963. Copyright © Penguin Books Ltd., 1968. All rights reserved. Reprinted by permission of Penguin Books Ltd.

Bradbrook, M. C. From *Shakespeare and Elizabethan Poetry: A Study of His Earlier Work in Relation to the Poetry of the Time*. Chatto and Windus, 1951.

Bradley, A. C. From *Shakespearean Tragedy: Lectures on "Hamlet," "Othello," "King Lear," "Macbeth."* Macmillan and Co., Limited, 1904.

Brandes, George. From "'A Midsummer Night's Dream': Its Historical Circumstances—Its Aristocratic, Popular, Comic, and Supernatural Elements," translated by William Archer, in *William Shakespeare: A Critical Study*. By George Brandes. William Heinemann, 1898.

Brandes, George. From "Contempt of Women—'Troilus and Cressida'," translated by Diana White with Mary Morison, in *William Shakespeare: A Critical Study, Vol. II*. By George Brandes. William Heinemann, 1898.

Brissenden, Alan. From *Shakespeare and the Dance*. Humanities Press, 1981. © Alan Brissenden 1981. All rights reserved. Reprinted by permission of Humanities Press International, Inc., Atlantic Highlands, NJ 07716.

Brooks, Cleanth. From *The Well Wrought Urn: Studies in the Structure of Poetry*. Reynal & Hitchcock, 1947. Copyright 1947, 1975, by Cleanth Brooks. All rights reserved. Reprinted by permission of Harcourt Brace Jovanovich, Inc.

Brown, John Russell. From *Shakespeare and His Comedies*. Methuen, 1957. Reprinted by permission of Methuen & Co. Ltd.

Calderwood, James L. From *Shakespearean Metadrama: The Argument of the Play in "Titus Andronicus," "Love's Labour's Lost," "Romeo and Juliet," "A Midsummer Night's Dream," and "Richard II."* University of Minnesota Press, Minneapolis, 1971. © copyright 1971 by the University of Minnesota. All rights reserved. Reprinted by permission.

Campbell, Oscar James. From *Comicall Satyre and Shakespeare's "Troilus and Cressida."* Huntington Library Publications, 1938.

Capell, Edward. From an introduction to *Mr. William Shakespeare, His Comedies, Histories, and Tragedies, Vol. I*. Edited by Edward Capell. J. & R. Tonson, 1768.

Chambers, E. K. From *Shakespeare: A Survey*. Sidgwick & Jackson, 1925.

Clark, Cumberland. From *Shakespeare and the Supernatural*. Williams & Norgate Ltd., 1931.

Clarke, Charles Cowden. From *Shakespeare-Characters: Chiefly Those Subordinate*. Smith, Elder, & Co., 1863.

Clemen, Wolfgang H. From *The Development of Shakespeare's Imagery*. Cambridge, Mass.: Harvard University Press, 1951.

Coleridge, Samuel Taylor. From *Shakespearean Criticism, Vol. I*. Edited by Thomas Middleton Raysor. Cambridge, Mass.: Harvard University Press, 1930.

Coriat, Isador H. From *The Hysteria of Lady Macbeth*. Moffat, Yard and Company, 1912.

Crowne, John. From a dedicatory note to *Henry the Sixth, the First Part, with the Murder of Humphrey, Duke of Glocester.* R. Bentley and M. Magnes, 1681.

Davies, Thomas. From *Dramatic Miscellanies: Consisting of Critical Observations on Several Plays of Shakespeare.* N.p., 1784.

Dickey, Franklin M. From *Not Wisely but Too Well: Shakespeare's Love Tragedies.* The Huntington Library, 1957. Copyright 1957 by Henry E. Huntington Library & Art Gallery. Reprinted by permission.

Dowden, Edward. From *Shakspere.* Macmillan and Co., 1877.

Dowden, Edward. From *Shakspere: A Critical Study of His Mind and Art.* Third edition. Harper & Brothers Publishers, 1881.

Driver, Tom F. From *The Sense of History in Greek and Shakespearean Drama.* Columbia University Press, 1960. © 1960, Columbia University Press. Reprinted by permission.

Dryden, John. From *Troilus and Cressida; or, Truth Found Too Late.* Abel Swall, Jacob Tonson, 1679.

Dryden, John. From "A Defence of the Epilogue; or, An Essay on the Dramatique Poetry of the Last Age," in *The Conquest of Granada by the Spaniards.* By John Dryden. H. Herringman, 1672.

Dryden, John. From a preface to *The State of Innocence, and Fall of Man: An Opera.* By John Dryden. H. Herringman, 1677.

Duff, William. From *Critical Observations on the Writings of the Most Celebrated Original Geniuses in Poetry.* N.p., 1770.

Eagleton, Terence. From *Shakespeare and Society: Critical Studies in Shakespearean Drama.* Chatto & Windus, 1967. © Terence Eagleton, 1967. Reprinted by permission of the author and Chatto & Windus.

Elliott, G. R. From *Dramatic Providence in "Macbeth": A Study of Shakespeare's Tragic Theme of Humanity and Grace.* Princeton University Press, 1958. Copyright © 1958 by Princeton University Press. All rights reserved. Excerpts reprinted by permission of Princeton University Press.

Ellis-Fermor, Una. From *The Frontiers of Drama.* Methuen & Co. Ltd., 1945.

Empson, William. From *Some Versions of Pastoral.* Chatto & Windus, 1935.

Evans, B. Ifor. From *The Language of Shakespeare's Plays.* Methuen & Co. Ltd., 1952.

Evans, Bertrand. From *Shakespeare's Comedies.* Oxford at the Clarendon Press, Oxford, 1960. © Oxford University Press 1960. Reprinted by permission of Oxford University Press.

Evans, Bertrand. From *Shakespeare's Tragic Practice.* Oxford at the Clarendon Press, Oxford, 1979. All rights reserved. Reprinted by permission of Oxford University Press.

A Farther Defence of Dramatick Poetry. N.p., 1698.

Fender, Stephen. From *Shakespeare: "A Midsummer Night's Dream."* Studies in English Literature, No. 35. Edward Arnold (Publishers) Ltd., 1968. © Stephen Fender, 1968. Reprinted by permission.

Fiedler, Leslie A. From *The Stranger in Shakespeare.* Stein and Day, 1972. Copyright © 1972 by Leslie A. Fiedler. All rights reserved. Reprinted with permission of Stein and Day Publishers.

Flathe, J.L.F. From an extract, translated by Mrs. A. L. Wister, in *A New Variorum Edition of Shakespeare: "Macbeth," Vol. II.* By William Shakespeare, edited by Horace Howard Furness. J. B. Lippincott Company, 1873.

French, Marilyn. From *Shakespeare's Division of Experience.* Summit Books, 1981. Copyright © 1981 by Marilyn French. All rights reserved. Reprinted by permission of Summit Books, a division of Simon & Schuster, Inc.

Freud, Sigmund. From "Some Character-Types Met with in Psycho-Analytic Work," translated by E. Colburn Mayne, in *Collected Papers: Papers on Metapsychology, Papers on Applied Psycho-Analysis, Vol. IV.* By Sigmund Freud, authorized translation under the supervision of Joan Riviere. The Hogarth Press and The Institute of Psychoanalysis, 1925.

Frye, Northrop. From *The Myth of Deliverance: Reflections on Shakespeare's Problem Comedies.* University of Toronto Press, 1983. © University of Toronto Press 1983. Reprinted by permission.

Furness, Horace Howard. From a preface to *A New Variorum Edition of Shakespeare:"A Midsommer Nights Dreame," Vol. 10.* By William Shakespeare, edited by Horace Howard Furness. J. B. Lippincott Company, 1895.

Gentleman, Francis. From an introduction to "Troilus and Cressida," in *Bell's Edition of Shakespeare's Plays, Vol. VI.* By William Shakespeare. John Bell, 1774.

Gentleman, Francis. From an introduction to "King Henry VI, Part III," in *Bell's Edition of Shakespeare's Plays, Vol. VII.* By William Shakespeare. John Bell. 1774.

Gentleman, Francis. From an introduction to "A Midsummer Night's Dream" in *Bell's Edition of Shakespeare's Plays, Vol. VIII.* By William Shakespeare. John Bell, 1774.

Gervinus, G. G. From *Shakespeare Commentaries.* Translated by F. E. Bunnètt. Revised edition. Smith, Elder, & Co., 1877.

Gildon, Charles. From "Remarks on the Plays of Shakespear," in *The Works of Mr. William Shakespear, Vol. 7.* By William Shakespeare. E. Curll and E. Sanger, 1710.

Goddard, Harold C. From *The Meaning of Shakespeare.* University of Chicago Press, 1951. Copyright 1951 by The University of Chicago. Renewed 1979 by the Literary Estate of Harold C. Goddard. All rights reserved. Reprinted by permission of The University of Chicago Press.

Godwin, William. From *Life of Geoffrey Chaucer, the Early English Poet, Vol. I.* Second edition. Richard Phillips, 1804.

Goethe, Johann Wolfgang von. From "'Troilus and Cressida'," translated by Randolph S. Bourne, in *Goethe's Literary Essays.* Edited by J. E. Spingarn. Harcourt Brace Jovanovich, 1921.

Goethe, Johann Wolfgang von. From an extract, translated by Harold N. Hillebrand, in *A New Variorum Edition of Shakespeare: "Troilus and Cressida," Vol. 26.* Edited by Harold N. Hillebrand with T. W. Baldwin. J. B. Lippincott Company, 1953.

Greene, Robert. From *Greenes Groats-Worth of Witte, Bought with a Million of Repentance.* William Wright, 1592.

Griffith, Mrs. Elizabeth. From *The Morality of Shakespeare's Drama Illustrated.* T. Cadell, 1775.

Hales, John W. From *Notes and Essays on Shakespeare.* George Bell and Sons, 1884.

Halliwell-Phillipps, James Orchard. From *An Introduction to Shakespeare's "Midsummer Night's Dream."* William Pickering, 1841.

Hamilton, A. C. From *The Early Shakespeare.* Huntington Library, 1967. Copyright 1967 The Henry E. Huntington Library and Art Gallery, San Marino, California. Reprinted by permission.

Harrier, Richard C. From "Troilus Divided," in *Studies in the English Renaissance Drama in Memory of Karl Julius Holzknecht.* Josephine W. Bennett, Oscar Cargill, Vernon Hall, Jr., eds. New York University Press, 1959. Copyright © 1959 by New York University Press. Reprinted by permission of New York University Press.

Hassel, R. Chris, Jr. From *Faith and Folly in Shakespeare's Romantic Comedies.* University of Georgia Press, 1980. Copyright © 1980 by the University of Georgia Press, Athens, 30602. All rights reserved. Reprinted by permission of The University of Georgia Press.

Hazlitt, William. From *Characters of Shakespear's Plays.* R. Hunter, 1817.

Heilman, Robert B. From "'Twere Best Not Know Myself: Othello, Lear, Macbeth," in *Shakespeare 400: Essays by American Scholars on the Anniversary of the Poet's Birth.* Edited by James G. McManaway. Holt, Rinehart and Winston, Inc., 1964. Copyright © 1964 by Holt, Rinehart and Winston. All rights reserved. Reprinted by permission of CBS College Publishing.

Heine, Heinrich. From *Heine on Shakespeare.* Translated by Ida Benecke. Archibald Constable and Co., 1895.

Herbert, T. Walter. From "Invitations to Cosmic Laughter in 'A Midsummer Night's Dream'," in *Shakespearean Essays.* Edited by Alwin Thaler and Norman Sanders. The University of Tennessee Press, Knoxville, 1964. Copyright 1964 by The University of Tennessee Press. Reprinted by permission of the publisher.

Horn, Franz. From an extract, translated by Horace Howard Furness, in *A New Variorum Edition of Shakespeare:"Macbeth," Vol. II.* By William Shakespeare, edited by Horace Howard Furness. J. B. Lippincott Company, 1873.

Hudson, Rev. H. N. From introductions to "King Henry VI," Parts I, II, and III, in *The Works of Shakespeare, Vol. VII.* By William Shakespeare, edited by Rev. H. N. Hudson. J. Munroe and Company, 1851.

Hudson, Rev. H. N. From *Shakespeare: His Life, Art, and Characters, Vols. I and II*. Revised edition. Ginn & Company, 1872.

Huston, J. Dennis. From *Shakespeare's Comedies of Play*. Columbia University Press, 1981. Copyright © 1981 J. Dennis Huston. All rights reserved. Reprinted by permission of the author.

Jameson, Mrs. Anna Brownell. From *Characteristics of Women: Moral, Poetical, and Historical*. Second edition. N.p., 1833.

Johnson, Samuel. From *Miscellaneous Observations on the Tragedy of "Macbeth": With Remarks on Sir T. H.'s Edition of Shakesepear*. E. Cave, 1745.

Johnson, Samuel. From notes to "3 Henry VI," in *The Plays of William Shakespeare, Vol. V*. By William Shakespeare, edited by Samuel Johnson. J. & R. Tonson, 1765.

Johnson, Samuel. From notes on "Macbeth," in *The Plays of William Shakespeare, Vol. VI*. By William Shakespeare, edited by Samuel Johnson. J. & R. Tonson, 1765.

Johnson, Samuel. From notes on "Troilus and Cressida," in *The Plays of William Shakespeare, Vol. VII*. By William Shakespeare, edited by Samuel Johnson. J. & R. Tonson, 1765.

Jorgensen, Paul A. From *Our Naked Frailties: Sensational Art and Meaning in "Macbeth."* University of California Press, 1971. Copyright © 1971 by The Regents of the University of California. Reprinted by permission of the University of California Press.

Kemble, J. P. From *Macbeth, and King Richard the Third: An Essay, in Answer to "Remarks on Some of the Characters of Shakspeare."* John Murray, 1817.

Kendall, Paul M. From "Inaction and Ambivalence in 'Troilus and Cressida'," in *English Studies in Honor of James Southall Wilson*. Edited by Fredson Bowers. University of Virginia, 1951.

Kirkman, Francis, and Henry Marsh. From a stationers' note to *The Merry Conceited Humors of Bottom the Weaver*. F. Kirkman and H. Marsh, 1661.

Kittredge, George Lyman. From *Shakspere: An Address*. Cambridge, Mass.: Harvard University Press, 1916.

Knight, Charles. From *Studies of Shakspere: Forming a Companion Volume to Every Edition of the Text*. Charles Knight, 1849.

Knight, Charles. From "Introductory Notice: 'King Henry VI—Part I'" and "Historical Illustration," in *The Comedies, Histories, Tragedies, and Poems of William Shakspere, Vol. V*. By William Shakespeare, edited by Charles Knight. Second edition. Charles Knight and Co., 1842.

Knight, G. Wilson. From *The Imperial Theme: Further Interpretations of Shakespeare's Tragedies Including the Roman Plays*. Oxford University Press, London, 1931.

Knight, G. Wilson. From *The Shakespearian Tempest*. Oxford University Press, London, 1932.

Knight, G. Wilson. From *The Wheel of Fire: Essays in Interpretation of Shakespeare's Sombre Tragedies*. Oxford University Press, London, 1930.

Knights, L. C. From *How Many Children Had Lady Macbeth? An Essay in the Theory and Practice of Shakespeare Criticism*. The Minority Press, 1933.

Kott, Jan. From *Shakespeare, Our Contemporary*. Translated by Boleslaw Taborski. Doubleday, 1964. Reprinted by permission of Doubleday & Company, Inc. In Canada by Jan Kott. Originally published as *Szkice o Szekspirze*. Panstwowe Wydawnictwo Naukowe, 1964. Copyright © 1964 Panstwowe Wydawnictwo Naukowe. Reprinted by permission.

Lamb, Charles. From *Specimens of English Dramatic Poets Who Lived about the Time of Shakspeare*. Longman, 1808.

Langbaine, Gerard. From *An Account of the English Dramatick Poets*. G. West and H. Clements, 1691.

Lawrence, William Witherle. From *Shakespeare's Problem Comedies*. The Macmillan Company, 1931.

Lennox, Charlotte. From *Shakespear Illustrated; or, The Novels and Histories, on Which the Plays of Shakespear Are Founded, Vols. I and III*. A. Millar, 1753.

Long, John H. From *Shakespeare's Use of Music: A Study of the Music and Its Performance in the Original Production of Seven Comedies*. University of Florida Press, 1955.

Lyons, Charles R. From *Shakespeare and the Ambiguity of Love's Triumph*. Mouton, 1971. © copyright 1971 Mouton & Co., Publishers. Reprinted by permission of Mouton Publishers, a Division of Walter de Gruyter & Co.

Mahood, M. M. From *Shakespeare's Wordplay*. Methuen, 1957. Reprinted by permission of Methuen & Co. Ltd.

Malone, Edmond. From *A Dissertation on the Three Parts of "King Henry VI."* N.p., 1787.

Malone, Edmond. From "An Attempt to Ascertain the Order in Which the Plays Attributed to Shakspeare Were Written," in *The Plays of William Shakspeare, Vol. I.* By William Shakespeare, edited by Samuel Johnson and George Steevens. Revised edition. C. Bathurst, 1778.

Manheim, Michael. From *The Weak King Dilemma in the Shakespearean History Play*. Syracuse University Press, 1973. Copyright © 1973 by Syracuse University Press, Syracuse, New York. All rights reserved. Reprinted by permission.

Marriott, J.A.R. From *English History in Shakspeare*. E. P. Dutton & Company, 1918.

McElroy, Bernard. From *Shakespeare's Mature Tragedies*. Princeton University Press, 1973. Copyright © 1973 by Princeton University Press. All rights reserved. Excerpts reprinted by permission of Princeton University Press.

Mézières, A. From an extract, translated by Horace Howard Furness, in *A New Variorum Edition of Shakespeare: "Macbeth," Vol. II.* By William Shakespeare, edited by Horace Howard Furness. J. B. Lippincott Company, 1873.

Montagu, Elizabeth. From *An Essay on the Writings and Genius of Shakespear*. J. Dodsley, 1769.

Morris, Brian. From "The Kingdom, the Power and the Glory in 'Macbeth'," in *Focus on "Macbeth."* Edited by John Russell Brown. Routledge & Kegan Paul, 1982. © Routledge & Kegan Paul 1982. Reprinted by permission of Routledge & Kegan Paul PLC.

Moulton, Richard G. From *The Moral System of Shakespeare: A Popular Illustration of Fiction as the Experimental Side of Philosophy*. The Macmillan Company, 1903.

Muir, Kenneth. From an introduction to *Macbeth*. By William Shakespeare, edited by Kenneth Muir. Ninth edition. Methuen, 1962. Editorial matter © 1962 Methuen & Co. Ltd. Reprinted by permission of Methuen & Co. Ltd.

Murry, John Middleton. From *Shakespeare*. Jonathan Cape, 1936. Reprinted by permission of The Society of Authors as the literary representative of the Estate of John Middleton Murry.

Nashe, Thomas. From *Pierce Penilesse His Supplication to the Divell*. Richard Ihones, 1592.

Ornstein, Robert. From *A Kingdom for a Stage: The Achievement of Shakespeare's History Plays*. Cambridge, Mass.: Harvard University Press, 1972. Copyright © 1972 by the President and Fellows of Harvard College. All rights reserved. Reprinted by permission of the author.

Palmer, John. From *Comic Characters of Shakespeare*. Macmillan and Co., Limited, 1946.

Parrott, Thomas Marc. From *Shakespearean Comedy*. Oxford University Press, 1949. Copyright 1949 by Thomas Marc Parrott. Renewed 1976 by Frances M. Walters. Reprinted by permission of the Literary Estate of Thomas Marc Parrott.

Pepys, Samuel. From a diary entry of September 29, 1662, in *The Diary of Samuel Pepys: 1662, Vol. III.* By Samuel Pepys, edited by Robert Latham and William Matthews. University of California Press, 1970. Copyright © 1970 by G. Bell & Sons Ltd. Reprinted by permission of the University of California Press.

Pepys, Samuel. From diary entries of January 7, 1667, and April 19, 1667, in *The Diary of Samuel Pepys*. Macmillan & Co., 1905.

Pettet, E. C. From *Shakespeare and the Romance Tradition*. Staples Press, 1949.

Phialas, Peter G. From *Shakespeare's Romantic Comedies: The Development of Their Form and Meaning*. University of North Carolina Press, 1966. Copyright © 1966 by The University of North Carolina Press. Reprinted by permission.

Pierce, Robert B. From *Shakespeare's History Plays: The Family and the State*. Ohio State University Press, 1971. Copyright © 1971 by the Ohio State University Press. All rights reserved. Reprinted by permission.

Pope, Alexander. From a head-note to "Troilus and Cressida," in *The Works of Shakespear, Vol. VI.* By William Shakespeare, edited by Alexander Pope. Jacob Tonson, 1725.

Price, Hereward T. From *Construction in Shakespeare*. The University of Michigan Press, 1951.

Quiller-Couch, Sir Arthur. From *Shakespeare's Workmanship*. T. Fisher Unwin Ltd., 1918.

Reese, M. M. From *The Cease of Majesty: A Study of Shakespeare's History Plays*. Edward Arnold (Publishers) Ltd., 1961. © M. M. Reese 1961. Reprinted by permission of the author.

Reynolds, Sir Joshua. From a note on ''Macbeth,'' in *Supplement to the Edition of Shakspeare's Plays Published in 1778 by S. Johnson and G. Steevens, Vol. I*. Edited by Edmond Malone. C. Bathurst, W. Strahan, 1780.

Ribner, Irving. From *The English History Play in the Age of Shakespeare*. Revised edition. Barnes & Noble, 1965. © 1965 Irving Ribner. By permission of Barnes & Noble Books, a Division of Littlefield, Adams & Co., Inc.

Richmond, H. M. From *Shakespeare's Political Plays*. Random House, 1967. Copyright © 1967 by Random House, Inc. All rights reserved. Reprinted by permission of the author.

Richmond, Hugh M. From *Shakespeare's Sexual Comedy: A Mirror for Lovers*. The Bobbs-Merrill Company, Inc., 1971. Copyright © 1971 Macmillan Publishing Company. Reprinted by permission of the author.

Riggs, David. From *Shakespeare's Heroical Histories: ''Henry VI'' and Its Literary Tradition*. Cambridge, Mass.: Harvard University Press, 1971. Copyright © 1971 by the President and Fellows of Harvard College. All rights reserved. Excerpted by permission.

Rowe, Nicholas. From ''Some Account of the Life, &c. of Mr. William Shakespear,'' in *The Works of Mr. William Shakespear, Vol. I*. By William Shakespeare, edited by Nicholas Rowe. Jacob Tonson, 1709.

Rumelin, Gustav von. From an extract, translated by Horace Howard Furness, in *A New Variorum Edition of Shakespeare: ''Macbeth,'' Vol. II*. By William Shakespeare, edited by Horace Howard Furness. J. B. Lippincott Company, 1873.

Schlegel, August Wilhelm. From *A Course of Lectures on Dramatic Art and Literature*. Edited by Rev. A.J.W. Morrison, translated by John Black. Revised edition. Henry G. Bohn, 1846.

Sen Gupta, S. C. From *Shakespeare's Historical Plays*. Oxford University Press, London, 1964. © Oxford University Press 1964. Reprinted by permission of Oxford University Press.

Sen Gupta, S. C. From *Shakespearian Comedy*. Oxford University Press, Delhi, 1950.

Sewell, Elizabeth. From *The Orphic Voice: Poetry and Natural History*. Yale University Press, 1960. Copyright © 1960 by Elizabeth Sewell. All rights reserved. Reprinted by permission of the author.

Siegel, Paul N. From *Shakespearean Tragedy and the Elizabethan Compromise: A Marxist Study,* 1957. Reprint by University of America Press, 1983. Copyright © 1983 by University of America Press. Reprinted by permission of the author.

Sitwell, Edith. From *A Notebook on William Shakespeare*. Macmillan & Co. Ltd., 1948.

Snider, Denton J. From *The Shakespearian Drama, a Commentary: The Comedies*. Sigma Publishing Co., 1890?.

Snider, Denton J. From *The Shakespearian Drama, a Commentary: The Histories*. Sigma Publishing Co., 1890.

Snider, Denton J. From *The Shakespearian Drama, a Commentary: The Tragedies*. Sigma Publishing Co., 1887.

Southall, Raymond. From '''Troilus and Cressida' and the Spirit of Capitalism,'' in *Shakespeare in a Changing World*. Edited by Arnold Kettle. Lawrence & Wishart, 1964. © Lawrence & Wishart Ltd. 1964. Reprinted by permission.

Spencer, Theodore. From *Shakespeare and the Nature of Man*. Macmillan, 1942. Copyright 1942, 1949, 1977 by Macmillan Publishing Company. Renewed 1970 by Eloise B. Bender and John Spencer. Reprinted with permission of Macmillan Publishing Company.

Spurgeon, Caroline F. E. From *Shakespeare's Imagery and What It Tells Us*. Cambridge at the University Press, 1935.

Steevens, George. From an end-note to ''Troilus and Cressida,'' in *The Plays of William Shakspeare, Vol. XI*. By William Shakespeare, edited by Samuel Johnson and George Steevens. Revised edition. T. Longman, 1793.

Swinburne, Algernon Charles. From *A Study of Shakespeare*. R. Worthington, 1880.

Theobald, Lewis. From *Shakespeare Restored; or, A Specimen of the Many Errors, as Well Committed, as Unamended, by Mr. Pope in His Late Edition of This Poet*. N.p., 1726.

Glossary

APOCRYPHA: A term applied to those plays which have, at one time or another, been ascribed to Shakespeare, but which are outside the canon of the thirty-seven dramas generally accepted as authentic. The second issue of the THIRD FOLIO included seven plays not among the other thirty-six of the FIRST FOLIO: *Pericles, The London Prodigal, Thomas Lord Cromwell, Sir John Oldcastle, The Puritan, A Yorkshire Tragedy,* and *Locrine.* These seven were also included in the FOURTH FOLIO, but of them only *Pericles* is judged to be the work of Shakespeare. Four other plays that were entered in the STATIONERS' REGISTER in the seventeenth century listed Shakespeare as either an author or coauthor: *The Two Noble Kinsmen* (1634), *Cardenio* (1653), *Henry I* and *Henry II* (1653), and *The Birth of Merlin* (1662); only *The Two Noble Kinsmen* is thought to be, at least in part, written by Shakespeare, although *Cardenio*—whose text is lost—may also have been by him. Scholars have judged that there is strong internal evidence indicating Shakespeare's hand in two other works, *Sir Thomas More* and *Edward III*. Among other titles that have been ascribed to Shakespeare but are generally regarded as spurious are: *The Troublesome Reign of King John, Arden of Feversham, Fair Em, The Merry Devil of Edmonton, Mucedorus, The Second Maiden's Tragedy,* and *Edmund Ironside.*

ASSEMBLED TEXTS: The theory of assembled texts, first proposed by Edmond Malone in the eighteenth century and later popularized by John Dover Wilson, maintains that some of the plays in the FIRST FOLIO were reconstructed for the COMPOSITOR by integrating each actor's part with the plot or abstract of the play. According to Dover Wilson, this reconstruction was done only for those plays which had not been previously published in QUARTO editions and which had no company PROMPT-BOOKS in existence, a list he limits to three of Shakespeare's works: *The Two Gentlemen of Verona, The Merry Wives of Windsor,* and *The Winter's Tale.*

BAD QUARTOS: A name attributed to a group of early editions of Shakespeare's plays which, because of irregularities, omissions, misspellings, and interpolations not found in later QUARTO or FOLIO versions of the same plays, are considered unauthorized publications of Shakespeare's work. The term was first used by the twentieth-century bibliographical scholar A. W. Pollard and has been applied to as many as ten plays: The First Quartos of *Romeo and Juliet, Hamlet, Henry V,* and *The Merry Wives of Windsor; The First Part of the Contention betwixt the two famous Houses of Yorke and Lancaster* and *The True Tragedy of Richard Duke of Yorke,* originally thought to have been sources for Shakespeare's *2* and *3 Henry VI,* but now generally regarded as bad quartos of those plays; the so-called "Pied Bull" quarto of *King Lear;* the 1609 edition of *Pericles; The Troublesome Reign of King John,* believed to be a bad quarto of *King John,* and *The Taming of a Shrew,* which some critics contend is a bad quarto of Shakespeare's Shrew drama. The primary distinction of the bad quartos is the high degree of TEXTUAL CORRUPTION apparent in the texts, a fact scholars have attributed to either one of two theories: some have argued that each quarto was composed from a stenographer's report, in which an agent for the printer was employed to surreptitiously transcribe the play during a performance; others have held the more popular explanation that the questionable texts were based on MEMORIAL RECONSTRUCTIONS by one or more actors who had performed in the plays.

BANDELLO, MATTEO: (b. 1480? - d. 1561) Italian novelist and poet who was also a churchman, diplomat, and soldier. His literary reputation is principally based on the *Novelle,* a collection of 214 tragic, romantic, and historical tales derived from a variety of material from antiquity to the Renaissance. Many of the stories in the *Novelle* are coarse and lewd in their presentation of love, reflecting Bandello's secular interests rather than his clerical role. Together with the dedications to friends and patrons that accompany the individual stories, the *Novelle* conveys a vivid sense of historical events and personalities of the Renaissance. Several translations and adaptations appeared in the third quarter of the sixteenth century, most notably in French by François de Belleforest and Pierre Boaistuau and in English by William Painter and Geoffrey Fenton.

BLACKFRIARS THEATRE: The Blackfriars Theatre, so named because it was located in the London precinct of Blackfriars, was originally part of a large monastery leased to Richard Farrant, Master of the Children of Windsor, in 1576 for the purpose of staging children's plays. It was acquired in 1596 by James Burbage, who tried to convert the property into a professional theater, but was thwarted in his attempt by surrounding residents. After Burbage died, the Blackfriars was taken over by his son, Richard, who circumvented the objections of his neighbors and, emulating the tactics of Farrant's children's company, staged both children's and adult plays under the guise of a private house, rather than a public theater. This arrangement lasted for five years until, in 1605, the adult company was suspended by King James I for its performance of the satire *Eastward Ho!* Shortly thereafter, the children's company was also suppressed for performing George Chapman's *Conspiracy and Tragedy of Charles Duke of Byron.* In 1608, Burbage organized a new group of directors consisting of his brother Cuthbert and several leading players of the KING'S MEN, including Shakespeare, John Heminge, Henry Condell, and William Sly. These "housekeepers," as they were called, for they shared no profits accruing to the actors, arranged to have the Blackfriars used by the King's Men alternately with the GLOBE THEATRE, an arrangement that lasted from the autumn of 1609 to 1642. Because it was a private house, and therefore smaller than the public theaters of London at that time, the Blackfriars set a higher price for tickets and, as such, attracted a sophisticated and aristocratic audience. Also, through its years of operation as a children's theater, the Blackfriars developed a certain taste in its patrons—one which appreciated music, dance, and masque in a dramatic piece, as well as elements of suspense, reconciliation, and rebirth. Many critics attribute the nature of Shakespeare's final romances to the possibility that he wrote the plays with this new audience foremost in mind.

BOOKKEEPER: Also considered the bookholder or prompter, the bookkeeper was a member of an Elizabethan acting company who maintained custody of the PROMPT-BOOKS, or texts of the plays. Many scholars believe that the bookkeeper also acted as the prompter during any performances, much as a stage manager would do today; however, other literary historians claim that another official satisfied this function. In addition to the above duties, the bookkeeper obtained a license for each play, deleted from the dramatist's manuscript anything offensive before it was submitted to the government censor, assembled copies of the players' individual parts from the company prompt-book, and drew up the "plot" of each work, that is, an abstract of the action of the play emphasizing stage directions.

COMPOSITOR: The name given to the typesetter in a printing shop. Since the growth of textual criticism in modern Shakespearean scholarship, the habits and idiosyncrasies of the individual compositors of Shakespeare's plays have attracted extensive study, particularly with respect to those works that demonstrate substantial evidence of TEXTUAL CORRUPTION. Elizabethan compositors set their type by hand, one letter at a time, a practice that made it difficult to sustain a sense of the text and which often resulted in a number of meaningless passages in books. Also, the lack of uniform spelling rules prior to the eighteenth century meant that each compositor was free to spell a given word according to his personal predilection. Because of this, scholars have been able to identify an individual compositor's share of a printed text by isolating his spelling habits and idiosyncrasies.

EMENDATION: A term often used in textual criticism, emendation is a conjectural correction of a word or phrase in a Shakespearean text proposed by an editor in an effort to restore a line's original meaning. Because many of Shakespeare's plays were carelessly printed, there exist a large number of errors in the early editions which textual scholars through the centuries have tried to correct. Some of the errors—those based on obvious misprints—have been easily emended, but other more formidable TEXTUAL CORRUPTIONS remain open to dispute and have solicited a variety of corrections. Perhaps the two most famous of these are the lines in *Henry V* (II. iii. 16-17) and *Hamlet* (I. ii. 129).

FAIR COPY: A term often applied by Elizabethan writers and theater professionals to describe the corrected copy of an author's manuscript submitted to an acting company. According to available evidence, a dramatist would presumably produce a rough copy of a play, also known as the author's FOUL PAPERS, which would be corrected and revised either by himself or by a professional scribe at a later date. Eventually, the fair copy of a play would be modified by a BOOKKEEPER or prompter to include notes for properties, stage directions, and so on, and then be transcribed into the company's PROMPT-BOOK.

FIRST FOLIO: The earliest collected edition of Shakespeare's plays, edited by his fellow-actors John Heminge and Henry Condell and published near the end of 1623. The First Folio contains thirty-six plays, exactly half of which had never been previously published. Although this edition is considered authoritative for a number of Shakespeare's plays, recent textual scholarship tends to undermine this authority in calling for a broader consideration of all previous versions of a Shakespearean drama in conjunction with the Folio text.

FOLIO: The name given to a book made up of sheets folded once to form two leaves of equal size, or four pages, typically 11 to 16 inches in height and 8 to 11 inches in width.

FOURTH FOLIO: The fourth collected edition of Shakespeare's plays, published in 1685. This, the last of the FOLIO editions of Shakespeare's dramas, included a notable amount of TEXTUAL CORRUPTION and modernization—751 editorial changes in all, most designed to make the text easier to read.

FOUL PAPERS: The term given to an author's original, uncorrected manuscript, containing the primary text of a play with the author's insertions and deletions. Presumably, the foul papers would be transcribed onto clean sheets for the use of the acting company which had purchased the play; this transcribed and corrected manuscript was called a FAIR COPY. Available evidence indicates that some of Shakespeare's early QUARTOS were printed directly from his foul papers, a circumstance which would, if true, explain the frequent errors and inconsistencies in these texts. Among the quartos alleged to be derived from Shakespeare's foul papers are the First Quartos of *Much Ado about Nothing, A Midsummer Night's Dream, Love's Labour's Lost, Richard II,* and *1* and *2 Henry IV;* among the FIRST FOLIO editions are *The Comedy of Errors, The Taming of the Shrew,* and *Coriolanus.*

GLOBE THEATRE: Constructed in 1599 on Bankside across the Thames from the City of London, the Globe was destroyed by fire in 1613, rebuilt the following year, and finally razed in 1644. Accounts of the fire indicate that it was built of timber with a thatched roof, and sixteenth-century maps of Bankside show it was a polygonal building, but no other evidence exists describing its structure and design. From what is known of similar public theaters of the day, such as the Fortune and the Swan, it is conjectured that the Globe contained a three-tiered gallery along its interior perimeter, that a roof extended over a portion of the three-storied stage and galleries, and that the lowest level of the stage was in the form of an apron extending out among the audience in the yard. Further, there is speculation that the Globe probably included a tiring room or backstage space, that the first two stories contained inner stages that were curtained and recessed, that the third story sometimes served as a musicians' gallery, and that beneath the flat roof, which was also known as ''the heavens,'' machinery was stored for raising and lowering theatrical apparatus. It is generally believed that the interior of the Globe was circular and that it could accommodate an audience of approximately two thousand people, both in its three galleries and the yard. The theater was used solely by the LORD CHAMBERLAIN'S MEN, later known as the KING'S MEN, who performed there throughout the year until 1609, when the company alternated performances at the fully-enclosed BLACKFRIARS THEATRE in months of inclement weather.

HALL (or HALLE), EDWARD: (b. 1498? - d. 1547) English historian whose *The Union of the Noble and Illustre Famelies of Lancastre and York* (1542; enlarged in 1548 and 1550) chronicles the period from the death of Richard II through the reign of Henry VIII. Morally didactic in his approach, Hall shaped his material to demonstrate the disasters that ensue from civil wars and insurrection against monarchs. He traced through the dynastic conflicts during the reigns of Henry VI and Richard III a pattern of cause and effect in which a long chain of crimes and divine retribution was ended by the accession of Henry VII to the English throne. Hall's eye-witness account of the pageantry and festivities of the court of Henry VIII is remarkable for its vivacity and embellished language. His heavy bias on the side of Protestantism and defense of Henry VIII's actions against the Roman Church led to the prohibition of his work by Queen Mary in 1555, but his interpretation of the War of the Roses was adopted by all subsequent Tudor historians. Hall's influence on Shakespeare is most evident in the English history plays.

HOLINSHED, RAPHAEL: (d. 1580?) English writer and editor whose *Chronicles of England, Scotlande, and Irelande* (1577; enlarged in 1587) trace the legends and history of Britain from Noah and the flood to the mid-sixteenth century. The *Chronicles* reveal a Protestant bias and depict the history of the British monarchy in terms of the ''Tudor myth,'' which claimed that Henry IV's usurpation of the crown from Richard II set off a chain of disasters and civil strife which culminated in the reign of Henry VI and continued until the accession to the throne of Henry VII, who, through his marriage to Elizabeth of York, united the two feuding houses of Lancaster and York and brought harmony and peace to England. Holinshed was the principal author of the *Chronicles,* being responsible for the "Historie of England," but he collaborated with William Harrison—who wrote the "Description of England," a vivid account of sixteenth-century customs and daily life—and Richard Stanyhurst and Edward Campion, who together wrote the "Description of Ireland." "The History and Description of Scotland" and the "History of Ireland" were translations or adaptations of the work of earlier historians and writers. The *Chronicles* were immediately successful, in part because of the easily accessible style in which they were composed and because their patriotic celebration of British history was compatible with the rise of nationalistic fervor in Elizabethan England. As in the case of EDWARD HALL, Holinshed's influence on Shakespeare is most evident in the English history plays.

INNS OF COURT: Four colleges of law located in the City of London—Gray's Inn, the Middle Temple, the Inner Temple, and Lincoln's Inn. In the sixteenth and seventeenth centuries, the Inns were not only academic institutions, but were also regarded as finishing schools for gentlemen, providing their students with instruction in music, dance, and other social accomplishments. Interest in the drama ran high in these communities; in addition to producing their own plays, masques, and revels, members would occasionally employ professional acting companies, such as the LORD CHAMBERLAIN'S MEN and the KING'S MEN, for private performances at the Inns. Existing evidence indicates that at least two of Shakespeare's plays were first performed at the Inns: *The Comedy of Errors* and *Twelfth Night.*

KING'S MEN: An acting company formerly known as the LORD CHAMBERLAIN'S MEN. On May 19, 1603, shortly after his accession to the English throne, James I granted the company a royal patent, and its name was altered to reflect the King's direct patronage. At that date, members who shared in the profits of the company included Shakespeare, Richard Burbage, John Heminge, Henry Condell, Augustine Phillips, William Sly, and Robert Armin. Records of the Court indicate that this was the most favored acting company in the Jacobean era, averaging a dozen performances there each year during that period. In addition to public performances at the GLOBE THEATRE in the spring and autumn, the King's Men played at the private BLACKFRIARS THEATRE in winter and for evening performances. Because of the recurring plague in London from 1603 onward, theatrical companies like the King's Men spent the summer months touring and giving performances in the provinces. Besides the work of Shakespeare, the King's Men's repertoire included plays by Ben Jonson, Francis Beaumont and John Fletcher, Thomas Dekker, and Cyril Tourneur. The company continued to flourish until 1642, when by Act of Parliament all dramatic performances were suppressed.

LORD ADMIRAL'S MEN: An acting company formed in 1576-77 under the patronage of Charles Howard, Earl of Nottingham. From its inception to 1585 the company was known as the Lord Howard's Men, from 1585 to 1603 as the Lord Admiral's Men, from 1604 to 1612 as Prince Henry's Men, and from 1613 to 1625 as the Palsgrave's Men. They were the principal rivals of the LORD CHAMBERLAIN'S MEN; occasionally, from 1594 to 1612, these two troupes were the only companies authorized to perform in London. The company's chief player was Edward Alleyn, an actor of comparable distinction with Richard Burbage of the Lord Chamberlain's Men. From 1591 the company performed at the ROSE THEATRE, moving to the Fortune Theatre in 1600. The detailed financial records of Philip Henslowe, who acted as the company's landlord and financier from 1594 until his death in 1616, indicate that an extensive list of dramatists wrote for the troupe throughout its existence, including Christopher Marlowe, Ben Jonson, George Chapman, Anthony Munday, Henry Chettle, Michael Drayton, Thomas Dekker, and William Rowley.

LORD CHAMBERLAIN'S MEN: An acting company formed in 1594 under the patronage of Henry Carey, Lord Hunsdon, who was the Queen's Chamberlain from 1585 until his death in 1596. From

1596 to 1597, the company's benefactor was Lord Hunsdon's son, George Carey, and they were known as Hunsdon's Men until the younger Carey was appointed to his late father's office, when the troupe once again became officially the Lord Chamberlain's Men. The members of the company included Shakespeare, Will Kempe—the famous 'clown' and the most popular actor of his time—, Richard Burbage—the renowned tragedian—, and John Heminge, who served as business manager for the company. In 1594 they began performing at the Theatre and the Cross Key's Inn, moving to the Swan on Bankside in 1596 when the City Corporation banned the public presentation of plays within the limits of the City of London. In 1599 some members of the company financed the building of the GLOBE THEATRE and thus the majority became "sharers," not only in the actors' portion of the profits, but in the theater owners' allotment as well. This economic independence was an important element in the unusual stability of their association. They became the foremost London company, performing at Court on thirty-two occasions between 1594 and 1603, whereas their chief rivals, the LORD ADMIRAL'S MEN, made twenty appearances at Court during that period. No detailed records exist of the plays that were in their repertoire. Ben Jonson wrote several of his dramas for the Lord Chamberlain's Men, but the company's success is largely attributable to the fact that, after joining them in 1594, Shakespeare wrote for no other company.

MEMORIAL RECONSTRUCTION: One hypothesis used to explain the texts of the so-called BAD QUARTOS. Scholars have theorized that one or more actors who had appeared in a Shakespearean play attempted to reconstruct from personal memory the text of that drama. Inevitably, there would be lapses of recall with resultant errors and deviations from the original play. Characteristics of these corrupt "reported texts" include the transposition of phrases or entire speeches, the substitution of new language, omission of dramatically significant material, and abridgements of extended passages. It has been speculated that memorial reconstructions were produced by companies touring the provinces whose PROMPT-BOOKS remained in London, or by actors who sold the pirated versions to printers. W. W. Greg, in his examination of the bad quarto of *The Merry Wives of Windsor,* was the first scholar to employ the term.

MIRROR FOR MAGISTRATES, A: A collection of dramatic monologues in which the ghosts of eminent historical figures lament the sins or fatal flaws that led to their downfalls. Individually and collectively, the stories depict the evils of rebellion against divinely constituted authority, the obligation of rulers to God and their subjects, and the inconstancy of Fortune's favor. William Baldwin edited the first edition (1559) and wrote many of the tales, with the collaboration of George Ferrers and six other authors. Subsequently, six editions appeared by 1610, in which a score of contributors presented the first-person narrative complaints of some one hundred heroic personages, from King Albanact of Scotland to Cardinal Wolsey and Queen Elizabeth. The first edition to include Thomas Sackville's *Induction* (1563) is the most notable; Sackville's description of the poet's descent into hell and his encounters with allegorical figures, such as Remorse, Revenge, Famine, and War, is generally considered the most poetically meritorious work in the collection. With respect to Shakespeare, scholars claim that elements from *A Mirror for Magistrates* are most apparent in the history plays on the two Richards and on Henry IV and Henry VI.

OCTAVO: The term applied to a book made up of sheets of paper folded three times to form eight leaves of equal size, or sixteen pages. The dimensions of a folded octavo page may range from 6 to 11 inches in height and 4 to 7½ inches in width.

OVID [PUBLIUS OVIDIUS NASO]: (b. 43 B.C. - d. 18 A.D.) Roman poet who was extremely popular during his lifetime and who greatly affected the subsequent development of Latin poetry; he also deeply influenced European art and literature. Ovid's erotic poetry is molded in elegiac couplets, a highly artificial form which he reshaped by means of a graceful and fluent style. These erotic poems—*Amores, Heroides, Ars amatoria,* and *Remedia amoris*—are concerned with love and amorous intrigue, depicting these themes in an amoral fashion that some critics have considered licentious. Ovid's *Metamorphoses,* written in rapidly flowing hexameters, presents some 250 stories from Greek and Roman legends that depict various kinds of transformations, from the tale of primeval chaos to the apotheosis of Julius Caesar into a celestial body. *Metamorphoses* is a superbly unified work, demonstrating Ovid's supreme skills in narration and description and his ingenuity in linking a wide variety of sources into a masterly presentation of classical myth. His brilliance of invention, fluency of style, and vivid descriptions were highly praised in the Renaissance, and familiarity with his work was considered an essential part of a formal education. Ovid has been cited as a source for many of Shakespeare's plays, including *The Merry Wives of Windsor, A Midsummer Night's Dream, The Tempest, Titus Andronicus, Troilus and Cressida,* and *The Winter's Tale.*

PLAUTUS, TITUS MACCIUS: (b. 254? - d. 184 B.C.) The most prominent Roman dramatist of the Republic and early Empire. The esteem and unrivaled popularity he earned from his contemporaries have been ratified by scholars and dramatists of the past five hundred years. Many playwrights from the sixteenth to the twentieth century have chosen his works, particularly *Amphitruo, Aulularia, Captivi, Menaechmi, Miles Gloriosus, Mostellaria,* and *Trinummus,* as models for their own. Plautus adapted characters, plots, and settings from Greek drama, combined these with elements from Roman farce and satire, and introduced into his plays incongruous contemporary allusions, plays upon words, and colloquial and newly coined language. His dramatic style is further characterized by extensive use of song and music, alliteration and assonance, and variations in metrical language to emphasize differences in character and mood. His employment of stock character types, the intrigues and confusions of his plots, and the exuberance and vigor of his comic spirit were especially celebrated by his English Renaissance audience. The plays of Shakespeare that are most indebted to Plautus include *The Comedy of Errors, The Taming of the Shrew, The Merry Wives of Windsor, The Two Gentlemen of Verona, Romeo and Juliet,* and *All's Well That Ends Well.* His influence can also be noted in such Shakespearean characters as Don Armado (*Love's Labour's Lost*), Parolles (*All's Well That Ends Well*), and Falstaff (*Henry IV* and *The Merry Wives of Windsor*).

PLUTARCH: (b. 46? - d. 120? A.D.) Greek biographer and essayist whose work constitutes a faithful record of the historical tradition, moral views, and ethical judgments of second century A.D. Graeco-Roman culture. His *Parallel Lives*—translated into English by Sir Thomas North and published in 1579 as *The Lives of the Noble Grecianes and Romans compared together*—was one of the most widely read works of antiquity from the sixteenth to the nineteenth century. In this work, Plutarch was principally concerned with portraying the personal character and individual actions of the statesmen, soldiers, legislators, and orators who were his subjects, and through his warm and lively style with instructing as well as entertaining his readers. His portrayal of these classical figures as exemplars of virtue or vice and his emphasis on the successive turns of Fortune's wheel in the lives of great men were in close harmony with the Elizabethan worldview. His miscellaneous writings on religion, ethics, literature, science, and politics, collected under the general title of *Moralia,* were important models for sixteenth- and seventeenth-century essayists. Plutarch is considered a major source for Shakespeare's *Julius Caesar, Antony and Cleopatra,* and *Coriolanus,* and a minor source for *A Midsummer Night's Dream* and *Timon of Athens.*

PRINTER'S COPY: The manuscript or printed text of a work which the compositor uses to set type pages. The nature of the copy available to the early printers of Shakespeare's plays is important in assessing how closely these editions adhere to the original writings. Bibliographical scholars have identified a number of forms available to printers in Shakespeare's time: the author's FOUL PAPERS; a FAIR COPY prepared either by the author or a scribe; partially annotated foul papers or a fair copy that included prompt notes; private copies, prepared by a scribe for an individual outside the acting company; the company's PROMPT-BOOK; scribal transcripts of a prompt-book; a stenographer's report made by someone who had attended an actual performance; earlier printed editions of the work, with or without additional insertions provided by the author, a scribe, or the preparer of a prompt-book; a transcript of a MEMORIAL RECONSTRUCTION of the work; and an ASSEMBLED TEXT.

PROMPT-BOOK: Acting version of a play, usually transcribed from the playwright's FOUL PAPERS by a scribe or the dramatist himself. This copy, or ''book,'' was then presented to the Master of the Revels, the official censor and authorizer of plays. Upon approving its contents, he would license the play for performance and endorse the text as the ''allowed book'' of the play. A prompt-book represents an alteration or modification of the dramatist's original manuscript. It generally contains detailed stage directions, including cues for music, off-stage noises, and the entries and exits of principal characters, indications of stage properties to be used, and other annotations to assist the prompter during an actual performance. The prompt-book version was frequently shorter than the original manuscript, for cuts would be made in terms of minor characters or dramatic incidents to suit the resources of the acting company. Printed editions of plays were sometimes based on prompt-books.

QUARTO: The term applies to a book made up of sheets of paper folded twice to form four leaves of equal size, or eight pages. A quarto page may range in size from 8½ inches to 12½ inches in height and 6¾ to 10 inches in width.

ROSE THEATRE: Built in 1587 by Philip Henslowe, the Rose was constructed of timber on a brick foundation, with exterior walls of lath and plaster and a roof of thatch. Its location on Bankside—across the Thames River from the City of London—established this area as a new site for public theaters. Its circular design included a yard, galleries, a tiring house, and ''heavens.'' A half-dozen acting companies played there, the most important being the LORD ADMIRAL'S MEN, the chief rival to the LORD CHAMBERLAIN'S MEN, who performed at the Rose from 1594 to 1600, when they moved to the new Fortune Theatre constructed by Henslowe in Finsbury, north of the City of London. Among the dramatists employed by Henslowe at the Rose were Thomas Kyd, Christopher Marlowe, Shakespeare, Robert Greene, Ben Jonson, Michael Drayton, George Chapman, Thomas Dekker, and John Webster. The building was razed in 1606.

SECOND FOLIO: The second collected edition of Shakespeare's plays, published in 1632. While it is essentially a reprint of the FIRST FOLIO, more than fifteen hundred changes were made to modernize spelling and to correct stage directions and proper names.

SENECA, LUCIUS ANNAEUS: (b. 4? B.C. - d. 65 A.D.) Roman philosopher, statesman, dramatist, and orator who was one of the major writers of the first century A.D. and who had a profound influence on Latin and European literature. His philosophical essays castigating vice and teaching Stoic resignation were esteemed by the medieval Latin Church, whose members regarded him as a great moral teacher. His nine tragedies—*Hercules Furens, Thyestes, Phoenissae, Phaedra, Oedipus, Troades, Medea, Agamemnon,* and *Hercules Oetaeus*—were translated into English in 1581 and exerted a strong influence over sixteenth-century English dramatists. Seneca's plays were composed for reading or reciting rather than for performing on the stage, and they evince little attention to character or motive. Written in a declamatory rhetorical style, their function was to instruct on the disastrous consequences of uncontrolled passion and political tyranny. Distinctive features of Senecan tragedy include sensationalism and intense emotionalism, the depiction of wicked acts and retribution, adultery and unnatural sexuality, murder and revenge, and the representation of supernatural beings. Shakespeare's use of Seneca can be discerned most readily in such plays as *King John*, the histories from *Henry VI* to *Richard III*, *Antony and Cleopatra*, *Titus Andronicus*, *Julius Caesar*, *Hamlet*, and *Macbeth*.

STATIONERS' REGISTER: A ledger book in which were entered the titles of works to be printed and published. The Register was maintained by the Stationers' Company, an association of those who manufactured and those who sold books. In Tudor England, the Company had a virtual monopoly—aside from the university presses—on printing works written throughout the country. Having obtained a license authorizing the printing of a work, a member of the Company would pay a fee to enter the book in the Register, thereby securing the sole right to print or sell that book. Many registered texts were acquired by questionable means and many plays were published whose titles were not entered in the records of the Company. However, the Stationers' Register is one of the most important documents for scholars investigating the literature of that period.

TEXTUAL CORRUPTION: A phrase signifying the alterations that may occur as an author's original text is transmitted through the subsequent stages of preparation for performance and printing. In cases where the PRINTER'S COPY was not an author's FAIR COPY, the text may contain unintelligible language, mislineations, omissions, repetitious lines, transposed verse and prose speeches, inaccurate speech headings, and defective rhymes. Through their investigation of the nature of the copy from which a COMPOSITOR set his type, textual scholars attempt to restore the text and construct a version that is closest to the author's original manuscript.

THIRD FOLIO: The third collected edition of Shakespeare's plays, published in 1663. Essentially a reprint of the SECOND FOLIO, it contains some corrections to that text and some errors not found in earlier editions. The Third Folio was reprinted in 1664 and included ''seven Playes, never before Printed in Folio.'' One of these seven—*Pericles*—has been accepted as Shakespeare's work, but the other six are considered apocryphal (see APOCRYPHA).

VARIORUM: An edition of a literary work which includes notes and commentary by previous editors and scholars. The First Variorum of Shakespeare's works was published in 1803. Edited by Isaac Reed, it was based on George Steevens's four eighteenth-century editions and includes extensive material from Samuel Johnson's edition of 1765, together with essays by Edmund Malone, George Chalmers, and Richard Farmer. The Second Variorum is a reprint of the First, and it was published in 1813. The Third Variorum is frequently referred to as the Boswell-Malone edition. Containing prefaces from most of the eighteenth-century editions of Shakespeare's work, as well as the poems and sonnets, which Steevens and Reed omitted, the Third Variorum was published in 1821. Edited by James Boswell the younger and based on the scholarship of Malone, it includes such a wealth of material that it is generally regarded as the most important complete edition of the works of Shakespeare. The Fourth Variorum, known as the ''New Variorum,'' was begun by Horace Howard Furness in 1871. Upon his death, his son, Horace Howard Furness, Jr., assumed the editorship, and subsequently—in 1936—a committee of the Modern Language Association of America took on the editorship. The Fourth Variorum is a vast work, containing annotations, textual notes, and excerpts from eminent commentators throughout the history of Shakespearean criticism.

Cumulative Index to Plays

Cumulative Index to Critics

Abel, Lionel
Hamlet 1:237

Addison, Joseph
Hamlet 1:75
Henry IV, 1 and 2 1:287
King Lear 2:93

Alexander, Peter
Henry VIII 2:43

Allen, John A.
A Midsummer Night's Dream 3:457

Almeida, Barbara Heliodora C. de M. F. de
Troilus and Cressida 3:604

Amhurst, Nicholas
Henry VIII 2:15

Anthony, Earl of Shaftesbury
Hamlet 1:75

Archer, William
Twelfth Night 1:558

Arthos, John
Macbeth 3:250

Auberlen, Eckhard
Henry VIII 2:78

Auden, W. H.
Henry IV, 1 and 2 1:410
Twelfth Night 1:599

Bagehot, Walter
Measure for Measure 2:406

Baker, Harry T.
Henry IV, 1 and 2 1:347

Baldwin, Thomas Whitfield
The Comedy of Errors 1:21

Barber, C. L.
Henry IV, 1 and 2 1:414
Love's Labour's Lost 2:335
A Midsummer Night's Dream 3:427
Pericles 2:582
Twelfth Night 1:620

Barnet, Sylvan
Twelfth Night 1:588

Barton, Anne
The Comedy of Errors 1:61
Twelfth Night 1:656

Battenhouse, Roy W.
Henry IV, 1 and 2 1:434
Macbeth 3:269
Measure for Measure 2:466

Bayley, John
Troilus and Cressida 3:634

Berger, Harry, Jr.
Macbeth 3:340

Bergeron, David M.
Henry VI, 1, 2, and 3 3:149

Berman, Ronald
Henry VI, 1, 2, and 3 3:89
Love's Labour's Lost 2:348

Berry, Ralph
Love's Labour's Lost 2:348

Bertram, Paul
Henry VIII 2:60

Bethell, S. L.
Henry VI, 1, 2, and 3 3:67

Bevington, David M.
Henry VI, 1, 2, and 3 3:103
A Midsummer Night's Dream 3:491

Bickersteth, Geoffrey L.
King Lear 2:179

Black, James
Measure for Measure 2:519

Bliss, Lee
Henry VIII 2:72

Boas, Frederick S.
Measure for Measure 2:416
A Midsummer Night's Dream 3:391
Timon of Athens 1:476
Troilus and Cressida 3:555

Bonazza, Blaze Odell
The Comedy of Errors 1:50

Bonnard, George A.
A Midsummer Night's Dream 3:423

Booth, Stephen
Macbeth 3:349

Booth, Wayne
Macbeth 3:306

Bowers, Fredson Thayer
Hamlet 1:209

Bradbrook, Muriel C.
Henry IV, 1 and 2 1:418
Henry VI, 1, 2, and 3 3:75
Love's Labour's Lost 2:321, 330
Measure for Measure 2:443
Twelfth Night 1:655

Bradley, A. C.
Hamlet 1:120
Henry IV, 1 and 2 1:333
King Lear 2:137
Macbeth 3:213
Twelfth Night 1:566

Brandes, George
Hamlet 1:116
Henry IV, 1 and 2 1:329
King Lear 2:136
Love's Labour's Lost 2:315
Measure for Measure 2:414
A Midsummer Night's Dream 3:389
Pericles 2:551
Timon of Athens 1:474
Troilus and Cressida 3:554

Brigham, A.
King Lear 2:116

Brill, Lesley W.
Timon of Athens 1:526

Brissenden, Alan
A Midsummer Night's Dream 3:513

Brittin, Norman A.
Twelfth Night 1:594

Bronson, Bertrand H.
Love's Labour's Lost 2:326

Brooke, C. F. Tucker
Henry IV, 1 and 2 1:337, 341
Troilus and Cressida 3:560

Brooke, Stopford A.
King Lear 2:149

Brooks, Cleanth
Henry IV, 1 and 2 1:375
Macbeth 3:253

Brooks, Harold
The Comedy of Errors 1:40

Brower, Reuben A.
Hamlet 1:259

Fly, Richard D.
King Lear **2:**271
Timon of Athens **1:**522
Troilus and Cressida **3:**630

Foakes, R. A.
Henry VIII **2:**58
Measure for Measure **2:**516

Forker, Charles S.
Henry VI, 1, 2, and 3 **3:**97

Fortin, René E.
King Lear **2:**286

French, Marilyn
Henry VI, 1, 2, and 3 **3:**157
Macbeth **3:**333

Freud, Sigmund
Hamlet **1:**119
King Lear **2:**147
Macbeth **3:**223

Fripp, Edgar I.
Henry VIII **2:**46

Frost, William
King Lear **2:**216

Frye, Northrop
The Comedy of Errors **1:**32
Henry VIII **2:**65
King Lear **2:**253
Pericles **2:**580
Timon of Athens **1:**512
Troilus and Cressida **3:**642

Fuller, Thomas
Henry IV, 1 and 2 **1:**285

Furness, Horace Howard
A Midsummer Night's Dream **3:**386

Furnivall, F. J.
Twelfth Night **1:**557

Gardner, Helen
Hamlet **1:**224

Gaw, Alison
The Comedy of Errors **1:**19

Gelb, Hal
Measure for Measure **2:**514

Gentleman, Francis
Henry IV, 1 and 2 **1:**295
Henry VI, 1, 2, and 3 **3:**21
Love's Labour's Lost **2:**301
Macbeth **3:**175
A Midsummer Night's Dream **3:**363
Troilus and Cressida **3:**538

Gérard, Albert
Troilus and Cressida **3:**596
Twelfth Night **1:**638

Gerard, Alexander
Measure for Measure **2:**394

Gervinus, G. G.
Hamlet **1:**103
Henry IV, 1 and 2 **1:**317
Henry VI, 1, 2, and 3 **3:**31
Henry VIII **2:**31
King Lear **2:**116
Love's Labour's Lost **2:**305
Macbeth **3:**196
Measure for Measure **2:**402
A Midsummer Night's Dream **3:**372
Pericles **2:**546
Timon of Athens **1:**467

Troilus and Cressida **3:**544
Twelfth Night **1:**551

Gildon, Charles
The Comedy of Errors **1:**13
Hamlet **1:**75, 76
Henry IV, 1 and 2 **1:**286
Henry VI, 1, 2, and 3 **3:**17
King Lear **2:**93
Love's Labour's Lost **2:**299
Macbeth **3:**171
Measure for Measure **2:**387
A Midsummer Night's Dream **3:**362
Timon of Athens **1:**454
Twelfth Night **1:**539

Goddard, Harold C.
Hamlet **1:**194
Henry IV, 1 and 2 **1:**397
Henry VI, 1, 2, and 3 **3:**73
A Midsummer Night's Dream **3:**412

Godwin, William
Troilus and Cressida **3:**539

Goethe, Johann Wolfgang von
Hamlet **1:**91
Henry IV, 1 and 2 **1:**311
Troilus and Cressida **3:**541

Gomme, Andor
Timon of Athens **1:**503

Gorfain, Phyllis
Pericles **2:**588

Gould, Robert
Timon of Athens **1:**453

Granville-Barker, Harley
Hamlet **1:**160
King Lear **2:**154
Love's Labour's Lost **2:**317
Twelfth Night **1:**562

Gray, Henry David
Pericles **2:**558

Green, Andrew J.
Hamlet **1:**207

Greene, Robert
Henry VI, 1, 2, and 3 **3:**16

Greene, Thomas M.
Love's Labour's Lost **2:**351

Greg, W. W.
Hamlet **1:**134

Griffith, Elizabeth
Henry IV, 1 and 2 **1:**296
Henry VIII **2:**19
Troilus and Cressida **3:**538

Guthrie, William
Hamlet **1:**79

Hales, John W.
Macbeth **3:**205

Hallam, Henry
Hamlet **1:**98
King Lear **2:**111

Halliwell-Phillipps, J. O.
Love's Labour's Lost **2:**307
A Midsummer Night's Dream **3:**370

Hamilton, A. C.
Henry VI, 1, 2, and 3 **3:**83

Handelman, Susan
Timon of Athens **1:**529

Hanmer, Thomas
Hamlet **1:**76

Harcourt, John B.
Macbeth **3:**297

Harrier, Richard C.
Troilus and Cressida **3:**602

Harris, Bernard
Henry VIII **2:**67

Harris, Frank
The Comedy of Errors **1:**18
Pericles **2:**555
Timon of Athens **1:**480

Harrison, G. B.
Timon of Athens **1:**499

Hartwig, Joan
Twelfth Night **1:**658

Hassel, R. Chris, Jr.
A Midsummer Night's Dream **3:**506

Hawkes, Terence
Love's Labour's Lost **2:**359

Hazlitt, William
The Comedy of Errors **1:**14
Hamlet **1:**96
Henry IV, 1 and 2 **1:**312
Henry VI, 1, 2, and 3 **3:**25
Henry VIII **2:**23
King Lear **2:**108
Love's Labour's Lost **2:**303
Macbeth **3:**185
Measure for Measure **2:**396
A Midsummer Night's Dream **3:**364
Pericles **2:**544
Timon of Athens **1:**460
Troilus and Cressida **3:**540
Twelfth Night **1:**544

Heilman, Robert Bechtold
Henry IV, 1 and 2 **1:**375
King Lear **2:**191
Macbeth **3:**312, 314

Heine, Heinrich
Troilus and Cressida **3:**542

Hemingway, Samuel B.
Henry IV, 1 and 2 **1:**401
A Midsummer Night's Dream **3:**396

Henneman, John Bell
Henry VI, 1, 2, and 3 **3:**46

Henze, Richard
The Comedy of Errors **1:**57

Herbert, T. Walter
A Midsummer Night's Dream **3:**447

Hic et Ubique
See also **Steevens, George**
Hamlet **1:**87
Twelfth Night **1:**542

Hill, Aaron
Hamlet **1:**76

Hinman, Charlton
Timon of Athens **1:**518

Hoeniger, F. D.
Pericles **2:**576, 578

Hollander, John
Twelfth Night **1:**596, 615

Holloway, John
King Lear **2:**241

Holt, John
The Comedy of Errors **1:**13

Homan, Sidney R.
A Midsummer Night's Dream **3:**466

Honigmann, E.A.J.
Timon of Athens **1:**507

Horn, Franz
Macbeth **3:**190

Hoy, Cyrus
Timon of Athens **1:**523

Hudson, Rev. H. N.
Henry IV, 1 and 2 **1:**323, 324
Henry VI, 1, 2, and 3 **3:**35
Henry VIII **2:**32
King Lear **2:**125
Macbeth **3:**203
Measure for Measure **2:**406
A Midsummer Night's Dream **3:**377
Twelfth Night **1:**555

Hugo, Victor
Henry IV, 1 and 2 **1:**323
King Lear **2:**124

Humphreys, A. R.
Henry IV, 1 and 2 **1:**419

Hunt, Leigh
Timon of Athens **1:**460

Hunter, G. K.
Henry IV, 1 and 2 **1:**402
Twelfth Night **1:**635

Hunter, Joseph
Twelfth Night **1:**549

Huston, J. Dennis
Love's Labour's Lost **2:**375
A Midsummer Night's Dream **3:**516

Hyman, Lawrence W.
Measure for Measure **2:**524

Inchbald, Elizabeth
Henry IV, 1 and 2 **1:**309

Jackson, T. A.
Henry IV, 1 and 2 **1:**361

Jacobson, Gerald F.
A Midsummer Night's Dream **3:**440

Jaffa, Harry V.
King Lear **2:**208

James, D. G.
Hamlet **1:**191
King Lear **2:**201
Pericles **2:**561

Jameson, Anna Brownell
Henry VI, 1, 2, and 3 **3:**26
Henry VIII **2:**24
King Lear **2:**110
Macbeth **3:**191
Measure for Measure **2:**397
Twelfth Night **1:**545

Jekels, Ludwig
Macbeth **3:**226

Jenkins, Harold
Henry IV, 1 and 2 **1:**404
Twelfth Night **1:**610

Critic Index